ProQuest Statistical Abstract of the United States 2016

ProQuest Statistical Abstract of the United States 2016

Issued December 2015

Published by Bernan
An imprint of The Rowman & Littlefield Publishing Group, Inc.
4501 Forbes Boulevard, Suite 200, Lanham, Maryland 20706
www.rowman.com
800-462-6420; info@bernan.com
Unit A, Whitacre Mews, 26-34 Stannary Street, London SE 11 4AB, United Kingdom

ISBN 13: 978-1-59888-793-8

Suggested Citation:
ProQuest LLC. ProQuest Statistical Abstract of the United States, 2016. (4th ed.) Bethesda, MD, 2015

Preface

The *Statistical Abstract of the United States,* published since 1878, is the best-known statistical reference publication in the country. As a comprehensive collection of statistics on the social, political, and economic conditions of the United States, it is a snapshot of America and its people. In the spring of 2011, the Census Bureau announced that the edition published that year would be the last one produced at government expense. Beginning in 2012, ProQuest took on responsibility for updating and releasing this publication, the most used statistical reference tool in U.S. libraries.

The editors at ProQuest have endeavored to continue the tradition established by the Census Bureau Statistical Compendia Branch. Like its predecessors, the *ProQuest Statistical Abstract of the United States* is designed to serve as a convenient volume for statistical reference and as a guide to other statistical publications and sources. The latter function is served by the introductory text to each section, the source note appearing below each table, and Appendix I, which is comprised of the *Guide to Sources of Statistics*, the *Guide to State Statistical Abstracts*, and the *Guide to Foreign Statistical Abstracts*.

This volume includes a selection of data from many statistical sources, both government and private. Publications cited as sources usually contain additional statistical detail and more comprehensive discussions of definitions and concepts. Data not available in publications issued by the contributing agency, but obtained from the Internet or unpublished records are identified in the source notes. More information on the subjects covered in the tables may generally be obtained from the source.

Except as indicated, figures are for the United States as presently constituted. Although emphasis in the *ProQuest Statistical Abstract* is primarily given to national data, many tables present data for regions and individual states and a smaller number for metropolitan areas and cities. "Appendix II, Metropolitan and Micropolitan Statistical Areas: Concepts, Components, and Population," presents explanatory text, a complete current listing, and population data for metropolitan and micropolitan areas defined as of February 2013. Statistics for the Commonwealth of Puerto Rico and for Island Areas of the United States are included in many state tables and are supplemented by information in Section 29.

Statistics in this edition are generally for the most recent year or period available, as of early September 2015. Each year over 1,400 tables are reviewed and evaluated, new tables of current interest are added, continuing series are updated, and less timely data are condensed or eliminated. Text notes and appendices are revised as appropriate.

Changes in this edition—This year ProQuest introduces 39 new tables, presenting new material on a variety of topics, including charter schools; women's earnings as a percent of men's earnings by occupation; terrorism related deaths, injuries, and kidnappings of private U.S. citizens; child immunization by State; and health care spending by medical condition. For a complete list of new tables, see "New Tables," p. xi.

Additionally, within the Health and Nutrition section, tables presenting data on health measures have been arranged into two separate subsections - health measures and health measures for children.

Online edition—*ProQuest Statistical Abstract* is also available in an online edition. This dynamic edition features table-specific capabilities for narrowing results by source, data date, subject, and type of data breakdown. Importantly, the online edition is updated with new statistical content on a monthly basis, enabling users to regularly access new and revised data. The online product functions as a repository for additional back year's data that cannot fit into the print publication. Users will find spreadsheets that correspond to each table in the book. In many cases, these spreadsheets present expanded coverage of the data shown in print. It is available as a stand-alone product or a fully integrated component of *ProQuest Statistical Insight.*

Limitations of the data—The contents of this volume were taken from many sources. All data from censuses, surveys, and administrative records are subject to error arising from a number of factors including the following: sampling variability (for statistics based on samples), reporting errors in the data for individual units, incomplete coverage, nonresponse, and imputation and processing errors (see also Appendix III). ProQuest cannot accept responsibility for the accuracy or limitations of the data presented here. However, selection of the material and its proper presentation is the responsibility of ProQuest.

For additional information on data presented—Please consult the source publications available in local libraries and on the Internet, or contact the agency or organization indicated in the source notes.

Contents

[Numbers following subject are page numbers]

New and Deleted Tables for the 2016 Edition

New Tables for 2016

Tables Deleted Since the 2015 Edition of the Statistical Abstract

[Tables are deleted for several reasons, including: source data has been discontinued, source data was monographic and new data is not expected to be available, data is no longer reliable, and data was previously unpublished and cannot be replicated. Selected tables have been replaced with tables illustrating similar content. Where applicable, please see reference to new table number]

2015 Table	Section and Table Title	Replaced by...
	Section 1: Population	
Table 30........	Geographic Mobility Status of Households by Household Income: 2013	
	Section 2: Births, Deaths, Marriages, and Divorces	
Table 98........	Births by Whether Pregnancy Intended at Conception and Selected Characteristics of Mother: 2006 to 2010	
	Section 4: Education	
Table 300......	Employees in Higher Education Institutions by Sex and Occupation: 1995 to 2011	Table 308
Table 310......	Online Course Enrollment in Degree-Granting Postsecondary Institutions: 2003 to 2012	Table 317
	Section 8: State and Local Government Finances and Employment	
Table 452......	Federal Aid to State and Local Governments by State: 2005 to 2010	
Table 453......	Federal Aid Total and from Dept. of Agriculture and Dept. of Education to State and Local Governments—Selected Programs by State: 2010	
Table 454......	Federal Aid from FEMA, HUD, and Dept. of Labor to State and Local Governments—Selected Programs by State: 2010	
Table 455......	Federal Aid from Dept. of Health and Human Services, Dept. of Transportation, and Other Aid to State and Local Governments—Selected Programs by State: 2010	
	Section 9: Federal Government Employment and Finances	
Table 493......	U.S. Savings Bonds: 1990 to 2011	
Table 508......	Federal Individual Income Tax—Tax Liability and Effective and Marginal Tax Rates for Selected Income Groups: 2000 to 2010	
Table 509......	Federal Individual Income Tax—Current Income Equivalent to 2000 Constant Income for Selected Income Groups: 2000 to 2010	
	Section 10: National Security and Veterans Affairs	
Table 519......	Military Expenditures: 2000 to 2009	
Table 520......	Department of Defense Payroll and Contract Awards by State: 2009	
Table 521......	Expenditures and Personnel for Selected Major Locations: 2009	
Table 522......	Military and Civilian Personnel in Installations: 2009	
Table 527......	Military Reserve Personnel: 1995 to 2010	
Table 528......	Ready Reserve Personnel by Race, Hispanic Origin, and Sex: 1990 to 2010	
Table 529......	National Guard by Sex and Race: 1995 to 2010	
	Section 11: Social Insurance and Human Services	
Table 554......	Selected Benefit Payments to Individuals by Function: 1970 to 2010	
Table 566......	Public Employee Retirement Systems—Participants and Finances: 1980 to 2009	
Table 579......	Persons With Work Disability by Selected Characteristics: 2012	
	Section 12: Labor Force, Employment, and Earnings	
Table 641......	Export-Supported Jobs for Largest Metropolitan Areas: 2010	
	Section 14: Prices	
Table 755......	Producer Price Indexes by Stage of Processing: 1991 to 2013	Table 756
Table 756......	Producer Price Indexes by Stage of Processing and Commodity: 1990 to 2013	Table 757
	Section 16: Science and Technology	
Table 833......	Scientists and Engineers by Selected Demographic Characteristics: 2010	Table 834
	Section 17: Agriculture	
Table 849......	Organic Agriculture—Number of Farms, Acreage, and Value of Sales: 2007	Table 856
	Section 18: Energy and Utilities	
Table 943......	Fossil Fuel Production Prices by Type of Fuel: 1980 to 2011	
Table 956......	Major Petroleum Companies—Financial Summary: 1980 to 2010	
	Section 21: Manufactures	
Table 1045.....	Metalworking Machine Tool Manufacturing—Value of Shipments: 2005 to 2011	
	Section 23: Transportation	
Table 1098.....	Federal Aid to State and Local Governments for Highway Trust Fund by State: 2010	
Table 1130.....	Railroads, Class I—Summary: 1990 to 2010	
Table 1131.....	Railroads, Class-I Line-Haul-Revenue Freight Originated by Commodity Group: 1990 to 2011	
Table 1132.....	Railroads, Class-I Cars of Revenue Freight Loaded, 1990 to 2011, and by Commodity Group, 2010 and 2011	
	Section 24: Information and Communication	
Table 1162.....	Household Internet Usage In and Outside of the Home by Selected Characteristics: 2011	Table 1163
Table 1163.....	Household Internet Usage by State: 2011	Table 1164
Table 1171.....	Public Library Systems Operating Budget Change by Metropolitan Status: 2009 to 2012	
	Section 25: Banking, Finance, and Insurance	
Table 1199.....	Percent of U.S. Households That Use Selected Payment Instruments: 2001 and 2010	
Table 1201.....	Usage of General Purpose Credit Cards by Families: 1995 to 2010	
Table 1215.....	U.S. Purchases and Sales of Foreign Bonds and Stocks, 2000 to 2012, and by Selected Country, 2012	
Table 1217.....	Foreign Purchases and Sales of U.S. Securities by Type of Security, 2000 to 2012, and by Country, 2012	
Table 1221.....	Dow Jones U.S. Index by Industry: 2000 to 2013	
Table 1223.....	Volume of Round Lot Trading on New York Stock Exchange: 2000 to 2012	
	Section 26: Arts, Recreation, and Travel	
Table 1255.....	Retail Sales and Household Participation in Lawn and Garden Activities: 2005 to 2012	
Table 1260.....	College and Professional Football Summary: 1990 to 2013	
Table 1266.....	Sporting Goods Sales by Product Category: 1990 to 2012, and Projection, 2013	
Table 1275.....	North America Cruise Industry in the United States: 2008 to 2011	
	Section 29: Puerto Rico and the Island Areas	
Table 1332.....	Federal Direct Payments: 2010	
	Section 30: International Statistics	
Table 1404.....	Dow Jones Global Index by Country and Industry: 2010 to 2013	
Table 1407.....	U.S. and Foreign Stock Markets—Market Capitalization and Value of Shares Traded: 2000 to 2012	

Guide to Tabular Presentation

Example of Table Structure

Table 1276. Top 20 U.S. Gateway Airports for Nonstop International Air Travel Passengers: 2014

[190,450 represents 190,450,000. International passengers are residents of any country traveling nonstop to and from the United States on U.S. and foreign carriers. The data cover all passengers arriving and departing from U.S. airports on nonstop commercial international flights with 60 seats or more]

Gateway airport	Airport code	2014	Gateway airport	Airport code	2014
Total passengers......................	(X)	**190,450**	Washington (Dulles), DC................	IAD	6,994
Total, top 20...............................	(X)	**171,428**	Dallas-Ft. Worth, TX......................	DFW	6,903
Top 20, percentage of total..............	(X)	90.0	Honolulu, HI.................................	HNL	4,927
			Fort Lauderdale, FL......................	FLL	4,504
New York (JFK), NY.......................	JFK	27,515	Boston, MA..................................	BOS	4,454
Miami, FL.....................................	MIA	20,019	Orlando, FL..................................	MCO	4,269
Los Angeles, CA............................	LAX	18,680	Philadelphia, PA...........................	PHL	3,960
Newark, NJ...................................	EWR	11,493	Seattle-Tacoma, WA......................	SEA	3,678
Chicago (O'Hare), IL.......................	ORD	11,293	Detroit, MI...................................	DTW	3,363
Atlanta, GA..................................	ATL	10,583	Las Vegas, NV..............................	LAS	3,284
San Francisco, CA..........................	SFO	10,066	Charlotte, NC...............................	CLT	3,136
Houston (G. Bush), TX....................	IAH	9,601	Guam Island, GU...........................	GUM	2,707

X Not applicable.

Source: U.S. Department of Transportation, Research and Innovative Technology Administration, Bureau of Transportation Statistics, Office of Airline Information, "T-100 International Segment data," <http://www.transtats.bts.gov/Fields.asp?Table_ID=261>, accessed September 2015.

Headnotes immediately below table titles provide information important for correct interpretation or evaluation of the table as a whole or for a major segment of it.

Footnotes below the bottom rule of tables give information relating to specific items or figures within the table.

Unit indicators show the *specified quantities* in which data items are presented. They are used for two primary reasons. Sometimes data are not available in absolute form and are estimates (as in the case of many surveys). In other cases we round the numbers in order to save space to show more data, as in the case above.

When a table presents data with more than one unit indicator, they are found in the headnotes and column headings (Tables 4 and 28), spanner (Table 35), stub (Table 27), or unit column (Table 195). When the data in a table are shown in the same unit indicator, it is shown as the first part of the headnote (Table 2). If no unit indicator is shown, data presented are in absolute form (Table 1).

Vertical rules are used to separate independent sections of a table (Table 1), or in tables where the stub is continued into one or more additional columns (Table 2).

Averages—An average is a single number or value that is often used to represent the "typical value" of a group of numbers. It is regarded as a measure of "location" or "central tendency" of a group of numbers.

The *arithmetic mean* is the type of average used most frequently. It is derived by summing the individual item values of a particular group and dividing the total by the number of items. The arithmetic mean is often referred to as simply the "mean" or "average."

The *median* of a group of numbers is the middle number or value when each item in the group is arranged according to size (lowest to highest or vice versa); it generally has the same number of items above it as well as below it. If there is an even number

of items in the group, the median is taken to be the average of the two middle numbers.

Per capita (or per person) quantities—a per capita figure represents an average computed for every person in a specified group (or population). It is derived by taking the total for an item (such as income, taxes, or retail sales) and dividing it by the number of persons in the specified population.

Index numbers—An index number is the measure of difference or change, usually expressed as a percent, relating one quantity (the variable) of a specified kind to another quantity of the same kind. Index numbers are widely used to express changes in prices over periods of time, but may also be used to express differences between related subjects for a single point in time.

To compute a price index, a base year or period is selected. The base year price (of the commodity or service) is then designated as the base or reference price to which the prices for other years or periods are related. Many price indexes use the year 1982 as the base year; in tables this is shown as "1982 = 100." A method expressing the price relationship is: The price of a set of one or more items for a related year (e.g. 1990) **divided by** the price of the same set of items for the base year (e.g. 1982). The result multiplied by 100 provides the index number. When 100 is subtracted from the index number, the result equals the percent change in price from the base year.

Average annual percent change—Unless otherwise stated in the *Abstract* (as in Section 1, Population), average annual percent change is computed by use of a *compound interest formula*. This formula assumes that the rate of change is constant throughout a specified compounding period (1 year for average annual rates of change). The formula is similar to that used to compute the balance of a savings account that receives compound interest. According to this formula, at the end of a compounding period the amount of accrued change (e.g., school enrollment or bank interest) is added to the amount that existed at the beginning of the period. As a result, over time (e.g., with each year or quarter), the same rate of change is applied to a larger and larger figure.

The *exponential formula,* which is based on continuous compounding, is often used to measure population change. It is preferred by population experts, because they view population and population-related subjects as changing without interruption, ever ongoing. Both exponential and compound interest formulas assume a constant rate of change. The former, however, applies the amount of change continuously to the base rather than at the end of each compounding period. When the average annual rates are small (e.g., less than 5 percent) both formulas give virtually the same results. For an explanation of these two formulas as they relate to population, see U.S. Census Bureau, *The Methods and Materials of Demography,* Vol. 2, 3d printing (rev.), 1975.

Current and constant dollars—Statistics in some tables in a number of sections are expressed in both current and constant dollars (see, e.g., Table 687 in Section 13, Income, Expenditures, Poverty, and Wealth). Current dollar figures reflect actual prices or costs prevailing during the specified year(s). Constant dollar figures are estimates representing an effort to remove the effects of price changes from statistical series reported in dollar terms. In general, constant dollar series are derived by dividing current dollar estimates by the appropriate price index for the appropriate period (e.g., the Consumer Price Index). The result is a series as it would presumably exist if prices were the same throughout, as in the base year—in other words, as if the dollar had constant purchasing power. Any changes in this constant dollar series would reflect only changes in real volume of output, income, expenditures, or other measure.

Explanation of Symbols

The following symbols, used in the tables throughout this book, are explained in condensed form in footnotes to the tables where they appear:

— Represents zero or rounds to less than half the unit of measurement shown.

B Base figure too small to meet statistical standards for reliability of a derived figure.

D Figure withheld to avoid disclosure pertaining to a specific organization or individual.

NA Data not enumerated, tabulated, or otherwise available separately.

P Data are preliminary.

S Figure does not meet publication standards for reasons other than that covered by symbol B, above.

X Figure not applicable because column heading and stub line make entry impossible, absurd, or meaningless.

Z Entry would amount to less than half the unit of measurement shown.

In many tables, details will not add to the totals shown because of rounding.

Section 1
Population

This section presents statistics on the growth, distribution, and characteristics of the U.S. population. The principal source of these data is the U.S. Census Bureau, which conducts a decennial census of population, a monthly population survey, a program of population estimates and projections, and a number of other periodic surveys.

Decennial censuses—The U.S. Constitution provides for a census of the population every 10 years, primarily to establish a basis for apportionment of members of the House of Representatives among the states. For over a century after the first census in 1790, the census organization was a temporary one, created only for each decennial census. In 1902, the Census Bureau was established as a permanent federal agency, responsible for enumerating the population and also for compiling statistics on other population and housing characteristics.

Historically, the enumeration of the population has been a complete (100 percent) count. That is, an attempt is made to account for every person, for each person's residence, and for other characteristics (sex, age, family relationships, etc.). In the twentieth century, the questions were divided between a "short" and "long" form. Only a subset of the population was required to answer the long-form questions. The most recent census consisted of a short form, which included basic questions about age, sex, race, Hispanic origin, household relationship, and owner/renter status. After the 2000 Census, the long form became the American Community Survey (ACS) and continues to collect long-form-type information. The ACS includes not only the basic short-form questions, but also detailed questions about population and housing characteristics. It is a nationwide, continuous sample survey designed to provide communities with reliable and timely demographic, housing, social, and economic data every year. Since its start, the ACS has been providing a continuous stream of updated information for states and local areas. Sample data may be used with confidence where large numbers are involved and assumed to indicate trends and relationships where small numbers are involved.

Current Population Survey (CPS)—The CPS sample is a probability sample designed primarily to produce national and state estimates of labor force characteristics of the civilian non-institutional population 16 years of age and older. The sample consists of independent samples in each state and the District of Columbia, and each state sample is specifically tailored to the demographic and labor market conditions that prevail in that particular state. About 60,000 housing units are required in order to meet the national and State reliability criteria, drawn from 824 sample areas.

The CPS also serves as a vehicle for inquiries on other subjects. Using CPS data, the Census Bureau issues a series of publications under the general title of *Current Population Reports*.

Estimates of population characteristics based on the CPS will not agree with the counts from the census because the CPS and the census use different procedures for collecting and processing the data for racial groups, the Hispanic population, and other topics. Caution should also be used when comparing estimates for various years because of the periodic introduction of changes into the CPS. Beginning in January 1994, a number of changes were introduced into the CPS that affect all data comparisons with prior years. These changes included the results of a major redesign of the survey questionnaire and collection methodology and the introduction of 1990 census population controls, adjusted for the estimated undercount. Beginning with the 2001 CPS Annual Demographic Supplement, the independent estimates used as control totals for the CPS are based on civilian population benchmarks consistent with Census 2000. In 2003 the name of the March supplement was changed to Annual Social and Economic Supplement (ASEC). Beginning with the 2012 March CPS supplement the estimates are based on Census 2010 population controls. These changes in population controls had relatively little impact on derived measures such as means, medians, and percent distribution, but did have a significant impact on levels.

In 2002, the ASEC incorporated a significant sample expansion. The sample was expanded primarily to improve state estimates of children's health insurance coverage (CHIP). This sample increase of 19,000 households added to the regular sample of 72,500 households and the Hispanic sample of 6,500 gives a total sample size of about 98,000 households. The 2014 CPS ASEC included redesigned questions for income and health insurance coverage. All of the approximately 98,000 addresses were selected to receive the improved set of health insurance coverage items. The improved income questions were implemented using a split panel design. Approximately 68,000 addresses were selected to receive a set of income questions similar to those used in the 2013 CPS ASEC. The remaining 30,000 addresses were selected to receive the redesigned income questions. The source of data for tables in this section is the CPS ASEC sample of 98,000 addresses.

Population estimates and projections—Each year, the United States Census Bureau produces and publishes estimates of the population for the nation, states, counties, state/county equivalents, and Puerto Rico. With each annual release of population estimates, the Population Estimates Program revises and updates the entire time series of estimates from April 1, 2010 to July 1 of the current year, which is referred to as the vintage year. "Vintage" denotes an entire time series created with a consistent population starting point and methodology. The release of a new vintage of estimates supersedes any previous series and incorporates the most up-to-date input data and methodological improvements.

Estimates of the United States population are derived by updating the resident population enumerated in Census 2010 with information on the components of population change: births, deaths, and net international migration. The population estimates base reflects changes to the decennial census population due to the Count Question Resolution program, geographic program revisions, and modifications to the 2010 Census race categories for consistency with the race categories in input data.

Registered births and deaths are estimated from data supplied by the National Center for Health Statistics and the Federal-State Cooperative for Population Estimates (FSCPE). The net international migration component consists of four parts: (1) the net international migration of the foreign born, (2) the net migration of natives to and from the United States, (3) the net migration between the United States and Puerto Rico, and (4) the net overseas movement of the Armed Forces population. Data from the ACS are used to estimate the annual net migration of the foreign-born population. The estimated net migration of the native-born population is produced using the foreign-census method which utilized data from over 80 countries. This work compared estimates of the United States born or United States citizen population living overseas measured by population registers and censuses in other countries at two consecutive time periods. The residual was used to develop estimates of net native migration. Estimates for net migration between Puerto Rico and the U.S. are derived from the ACS and the Puerto Rico Community Survey. Estimates of the net overseas movement of the Armed Forces are derived from data collected by the Defense Manpower Data Center.

Estimates for state and county areas are based on the same components of change data and sources as the national estimates with the addition of net internal migration. Estimates of net internal migration are derived from federal income tax returns from the Internal Revenue Service; group quarters data from the branches of the military, the Department of Veterans Affairs, and the FSCPE; and Medicare data from the Centers for Medicare and Medicaid Services.

Population estimates and projections are available on the Census Bureau Web site, see <http://www.census.gov>. These estimates and projections are consistent with official decennial census figures with no adjustment for estimated net census coverage. For details on methodology, see "Methodology for the United States Population Estimates: Vintage 2014," <http://www.census.gov/popest/methodology/2014-natstcopr-meth.pdf>.

Immigration—Immigration (migration to a country) is one component of international migration; the other component is emigration (migration *from* a country). In its simplest form, international migration is defined as any movement across a national border. In the United States, federal statistics on international migration are produced primarily by the U.S. Census Bureau and the Office of Immigration Statistics of the U.S. Department of Homeland Security (DHS).

The Census Bureau collects data used to estimate international migration through its decennial censuses and numerous surveys of the U.S. population.

The Office of Immigration Statistics publishes immigration data in annual flow reports and the *Yearbook of Immigration Statistics*. Data for these publications are collected from several administrative data sources including the DS-230 *Application for Immigrant Visa and Alien Registration*, the DS-260 *Electronic Application for Immigrant Visa and Alien Registration* of the U.S. Department of State (used by applicants living abroad), and the I-485 *Application to Register Permanent Residence or Adjust Status* of U.S. Citizenship and Immigration Services (USCIS) for applicants living in the United States.

An immigrant, or lawful permanent resident (LPR), is a foreign national who has been granted lawful permanent residence in the United States. New arrivals are foreign nationals living abroad who apply for an immigrant visa at a consular office of the Department of State, while individuals adjusting status are already living in the United States and file an application for adjustment of status to lawful permanent residence with USCIS. Individuals adjusting status include refugees, asylees, and various classes of nonimmigrants. A refugee is an alien outside the United States who is unable or unwilling to return to his or her country of nationality because of persecution or a well-founded fear of persecution. Asylees must meet the same criteria as refugees, but are located in the United States or at a port of entry. Refugees are required to apply for adjustment to legal permanent resident status after one year of residence in the United States. Asylees are eligible to apply one year after they are granted asylum.

Nonimmigrants are foreign nationals granted temporary entry into the United States. The major activities for which nonimmigrant admission is authorized include temporary visits for business or pleasure, academic or vocational study, temporary employment, and to act as a representative of a foreign government or international organization. DHS collects information on the characteristics of a proportion of nonimmigrant admissions, those recorded on the I-94 Arrival/Departure Record.

U.S. immigration law gives preferential immigration status to persons with a close family relationship with a U.S. citizen or legal permanent resident, persons with needed job skills, persons who qualify as refugees or asylees, and persons who are from countries with relatively low levels of immigration to the United States (diversity immigrants). Immigration to the United States can be divided into two general categories: (1) classes of admission subject to the annual worldwide limitation and (2) classes of admission exempt from worldwide limitations. Numerical limits are imposed on visas issued and not on admissions. In 2013, the annual limit for family-sponsored preferences was 226,000 and the limit for employment-based preferences was 158,466.

The Diversity Visa Program is available to nationals of countries with fewer than 50,000 persons granted LPR status during the preceding five years in the employment-based and family-sponsored preferences and immediate relative classes of admission. The annual diversity visa limit has been 50,000 since 1999.

The number of persons who may be admitted to the United States as refugees each year is established by the President in consultation with Congress. The ceiling was 70,000 for 2013. There is no numerical limit on the number of persons who can be granted asylum status in a year.

Classes of admission exempt from the worldwide limitation include immediate relatives of U.S. citizens, refugees and asylees adjusting to permanent residence, and other various classes of special immigrants.

Metropolitan and micropolitan areas—Metropolitan and micropolitan statistical areas (metro and micro areas) are geographic entities delineated by the U.S. Office of Management and Budget (OMB) for use by Federal statistical agencies in collecting, tabulating, and publishing Federal statistics. These areas are the result of the application of published standards to Census Bureau data. Generally, the areas are delineated using the most recent set of standards following each decennial census. Between censuses, the delineations are updated annually to reflect the most recent Census Bureau population estimates. Areas based on the 2010 standards and Census Bureau data were delineated in February of 2013.

The term "Core Based Statistical Area" (CBSA) is a collective term for both metro and micro areas. A metro area contains a core urban area of 50,000 or more population, and a micro area contains an urban core of at least 10,000 (but less than 50,000) population. Each metro or micro area consists of one or more counties and includes the counties containing the core urban area, as well as any adjacent counties that have a high degree of social and economic integration (as measured by commuting to work) with the urban core.

Urban and rural—The Census Bureau's urban-rural classification is fundamentally a delineation of geographical areas, identifying both individual urban areas and the rural areas of the nation. The Census Bureau's urban areas represent densely developed territory, and encompass residential, commercial, and other non-residential urban land uses.

For the 2010 Census, an urban area comprises a densely settled core of census tracts and/or census blocks that meet minimum population density requirements, along with adjacent territory containing non-residential urban land uses as well as territory with low population density included to link outlying densely settled territory with the densely settled core. To qualify as an urban area, the territory identified according to criteria must encompass at least 2,500 people, at least 1,500 of which reside outside institutional group quarters. The Census Bureau identifies two types of urban areas: Urbanized Areas of 50,000 or more people; and Urban Clusters of at least 2,500 and less than 50,000 people. "Rural" encompasses all population, housing, and territory not included within an urban area. For Census 2010, many more geographic entities, including metropolitan areas, counties, and places, contain both urban and rural territory, population, and housing units.

Residence—In determining residence, the Census Bureau counts each person as an inhabitant of a usual place of residence (i.e., the place where one lives and sleeps most of the time). While this place is not necessarily a person's legal residence or voting residence, the use of these different bases of classification would produce the same results in the vast majority of cases.

Race—Census 2000 and 2010 adhere to the federal standards for collecting and presenting data on race and ethnicity as established by the OMB in October 1997. Starting with Census 2000, the OMB requires federal agencies to use a minimum of five race categories: White, Black or African American, American Indian or Alaska Native, Asian, and Native Hawaiian or Other Pacific Islander. Additionally, to collect data on individuals of mixed race parentage, respondents were allowed to select one or more races. For respondents who did not identify with any of these five race categories, the OMB approved and included a sixth category—"Some other race" on the Census 2000 and 2010 questionnaire. The Census 2000 and 2010 question on race included 15 separate response categories and three areas where respondents could

write in a more specific race group. The response categories and write-in answers can be combined to create the five minimum OMB race categories plus "Some other race." People who responded to the question on race by indicating only one race are referred to as the *race alone* population, or the group that reported only one race category. Six categories make up this population: White alone, Black or African American alone, American Indian and Alaska Native alone, Asian alone, Native Hawaiian and Other Pacific Islander alone, and Some other race alone. Individuals who chose more than one of the six race categories are referred to as the *Two or More Races* population, or as the group that reported more than one race. Additionally, respondents who reported one race together with those who reported the same race plus one or more other races are combined to create the race alone or in *combination* categories. For example, the *White alone or in combination group* consists of those respondents who reported only White or who reported White combined with one or more other race groups, such as "White and Black or African American," or "White and Asian and American Indian and Alaska Native." Another way to think of the group who reported White alone or in combination is as the total number of people who identified entirely or partially as White. This group is also described as people who reported White, whether or not they reported any other race.

The *alone or in combination* categories are tallies of *responses* rather than *respondents*. That is, the alone or in combination categories are not mutually exclusive. Individuals who reported two races were counted in two separate and distinct alone or in combination race categories, while those who reported three races were counted in three categories, and so on. Consequently, the sum of all alone or in combination categories equals the number of races reported, which exceeds the total population.

The racial categories included in the census questionnaire generally reflect a social definition of race recognized in this country and not an attempt to define race biologically, anthropologically, or genetically. It is also recognized that the categories of the race item include racial and national origin or sociocultural groups. For example, data are available for the American Indian and Alaska Native tribes. A detailed explanation of race can be found at <http://www.census.gov/prod/cen2010/doc/sf1.pdf>.

Data for the population by race for April 1, 2000 and 2010, (shown in Tables 7, 9, and 10) are modified counts and are not comparable to Census 2000 and 2010 race categories. These numbers were computed using Census 2000 and 2010 data by race and had been modified to be consistent with the 1997 OMB's "Revisions to the Standards for the Classification of Federal Data on Race and Ethnicity," (Federal Register Notice, Vol. 62, No 210, October 1997). A detailed explanation of the race modification procedure appears at <http://www.census.gov/popest/data/historical/files/MRSF-01-US1.pdf>.

In the CPS and other household sample surveys conducted through personal interview, respondents are asked to classify their race as: (1) White; (2) Black, African American, or Negro; (3) American Indian or Alaska Native; (4) Asian; or (5) Native Hawaiian or Other Pacific Islander. Beginning January 2003, respondents were allowed to report more than one race to indicate their mixed racial heritage.

Hispanic population—People who identify with the terms "Hispanic" or "Latino" are those who classify themselves in one of the specific Hispanic or Latino categories listed on the decennial census questionnaire and various Census Bureau survey questionnaires – "Mexican, Mexican American, Chicano" or "Puerto Rican" or "Cuban" – as well as those who indicate that they are "another Hispanic, Latino, or Spanish origin." Origin can be viewed as the heritage, nationality group, lineage, or country of birth of the person or the person's ancestors before their arrival in the United States.

Traditional and current data collection and classification treat race and Hispanic origin as two separate and distinct concepts in accordance with guidelines from the OMB. Race and Hispanic origin are two separate concepts in the federal statistical system. People who are Hispanic may be of any race and people in each race group may be either Hispanic or Not Hispanic. Also, each person has two attributes, their race (or races) and whether or not they are Hispanic. The overlap of race and Hispanic origin is the main comparability issue. For example, Black Hispanics (Hispanic Blacks) are included in both the number of Blacks and in the number of Hispanics. For further information, see <http://www.census.gov/population/www/socdemo/compraceho.html>.

Foreign-born and native populations—The Census Bureau separates the U.S. resident population into two groups based on whether or not a person was a U.S. citizen or U.S. national at the time of birth. Anyone born in the United States, Puerto Rico, or a U.S. Island Area (such as Guam), or born abroad to a U.S. citizen parent is a U.S. citizen at the time of birth and consequently included in the *native population*. The term *foreign-born population* refers to anyone who is not a U.S. citizen or a U.S. national at birth. This includes naturalized U.S. citizens, legal permanent resident aliens (immigrants), temporary migrants (such as foreign students), humanitarian migrants (such as refugees), and people illegally present in the United States. The Census Bureau provides a variety of demographic, social, economic, geographic, and housing information on the foreign-born population in the United States at <http://www.census.gov/topics/population/foreign-born.html>.

Mobility status—The U.S. population is classified according to mobility status on the basis of a comparison between the place of residence of each individual at the time of the survey or census and the place of residence at a specified earlier date. Nonmovers are all persons who were living in the same house or apartment at the end of the period as at the beginning of the period. Movers are all persons who were living in a different house or apartment at the end of the period than at the beginning of the period. Movers are further classified as to whether they were living in the same or different county, state, or region, or were movers from abroad. Movers from abroad include all persons whose place of residence was outside the United States (including Puerto Rico, other U.S. Island Area, or a foreign country) at the beginning of the period.

Living arrangements—Living arrangements refer to residency in households or in group quarters. A "household" comprises all persons who occupy a "housing unit," that is, a house, an apartment or other group of rooms, or a single room that constitutes "separate living quarters." A household includes the related family members and all the unrelated persons, if any, such as lodgers, foster children, or employees who share the housing unit. A person living alone or a group of unrelated persons sharing the same housing unit is also counted as a household. See text, Section 20, Construction and Housing, for definition of housing unit.

All persons not living in housing units are classified as living in group quarters. These individuals may be institutionalized, e.g., under care or custody in juvenile facilities, jails, correctional centers, hospitals, or nursing homes; or they may be residents in noninstitutional group quarters such as college dormitories, group homes, or military barracks.

Householder—The householder is the person, or one of the people, in whose name the home is owned, being bought, or rented. If a home is owned or rented jointly by a married couple, either spouse may be listed first. Two types of householders are distinguished: a family householder and a nonfamily householder. A family householder is a householder living with one or more people related to him or her by birth, marriage, or adoption. The householder and all people in the household related to him or her are family members. A family household may contain people not related to the householder, but those people are not included as part of the householder's family in census tabulations. Thus, the number of family households is equal to the number of families, but family households may include more members than do families.

Nonfamily—A nonfamily householder is a householder living alone or with nonrelatives only.

Subfamily— A subfamily is a married couple with or without children, or a single parent with one or more own never-married children under 18 years old, who does not maintain their own household, but lives in the home of someone else (the householder). Subfamilies are divided into "related" and "unrelated" subfamilies. A related subfamily is related to, but does not include, the householder or the spouse of the householder. Members of a related subfamily are also members of the family with whom they live. The number of related subfamilies, therefore, is not included in the count of families. An unrelated subfamily may include persons such as guests, lodgers, or resident employees and their spouses and/or children; none of whom is related to the householder. The number of unrelated subfamily members is included in the total number of household members, but is not included in the count of family members.

Married couple—A married couple is defined as a husband and wife living together in the same household, with or without children and other relatives.

Statistical reliability—For a discussion of statistical collection and estimation, sampling procedures, and measures of statistical reliability applicable to Census Bureau data, see Appendix III.

Figure 1.1

Percent Change in Population for States: April 1, 2000 to April 1, 2010

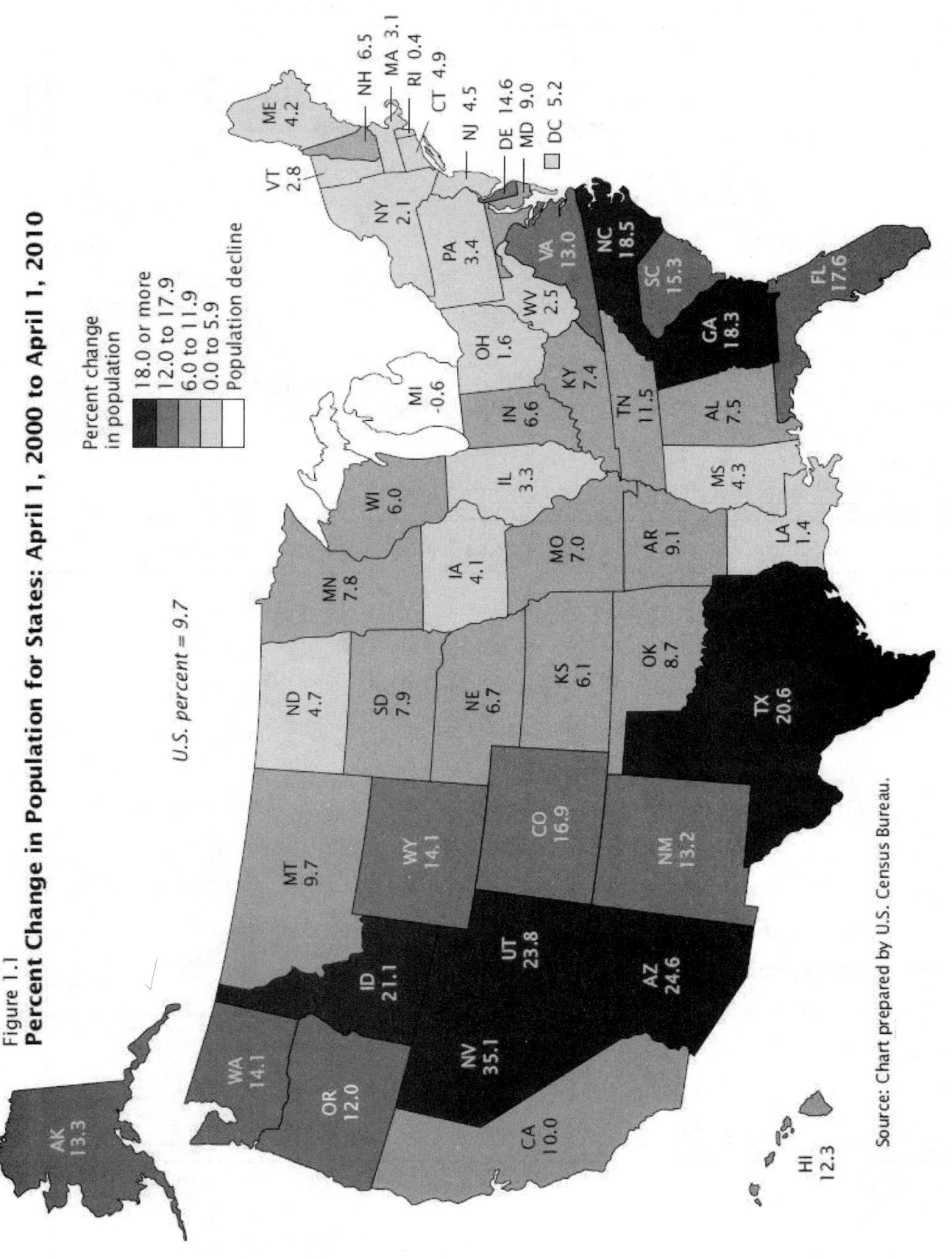

Percent change
in population

- 18.0 or more
- 12.0 to 17.9
- 6.0 to 11.9
- 0.0 to 5.9
- Population decline

U.S. percent = 9.7

AK 13.3

WA 14.1
OR 12.0
CA 10.0
HI 12.3

MT 9.7
ID 21.1
NV 35.1
UT 23.8
AZ 24.6

ND 4.7
SD 7.9
NE 6.7
WY 14.1
CO 16.9
NM 13.2

MN 7.8
IA 4.1
KS 6.1
OK 8.7
TX 20.6

WI 6.0
IL 3.3
MO 7.0
AR 9.1
LA 1.4
MS 4.3

MI -0.6
IN 6.6
OH 1.6
KY 7.4
TN 11.5
AL 7.5

NY 2.1
PA 3.4
WV 2.5
VA 13.0
NC 18.5
SC 15.3
GA 18.3
FL 17.6

VT 2.8
ME 4.2
NH 6.5
MA 3.1
RI 0.4
CT 4.9
NJ 4.5
DE 14.6
MD 9.0
DC 5.2

Source: Chart prepared by U.S. Census Bureau.

Mean Center of Population for the United States: 1790 to 2010

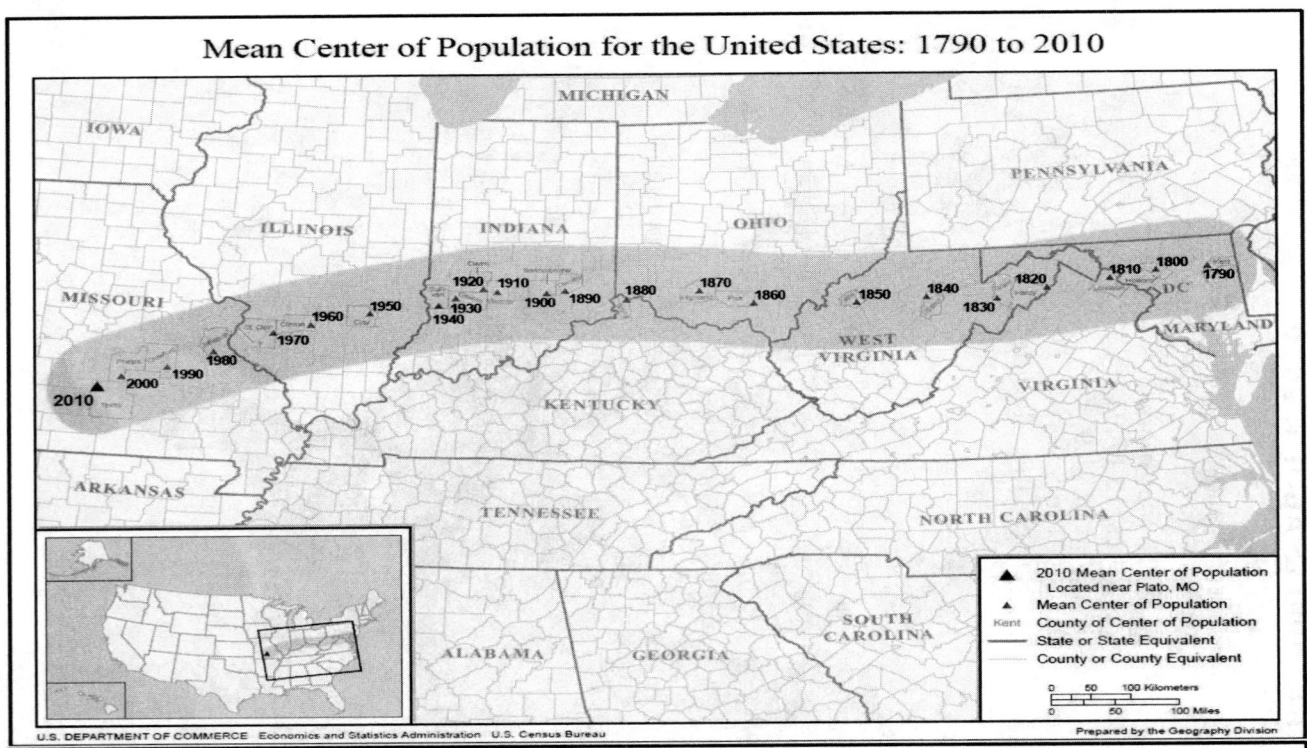

Median Center of Population for the United States: 1880 to 2010

Table 1. Population and Area: 1790 to 2010

[Area figures represent area on indicated date including in some cases considerable areas not then organized or settled, and not covered by the census. Area data include Alaska beginning in 1870 and Hawaii beginning in 1900. Total area figures for 1790 to 1970 have been recalculated on the basis of the remeasurement of states and counties for the 1980 census, but not on the basis of subsequent censuses. The land and water area figures for past censuses have not been adjusted and are not strictly comparable with the total area data for comparable dates because the land areas were derived from different base data, and these values are known to have changed with the construction of reservoirs, draining of lakes, etc. Density figures are based on land area measurements as reported in earlier censuses]

| Census date | Resident population | | | | Area (square miles) | | |
| | Number | Per square mile of land area | Increase over preceding census | | Total | Land | Water [1] |
			Number	Percent			
1790 (Aug. 2).......	3,929,214	4.5	(X)	(X)	891,364	864,746	24,065
1800 (Aug. 4).......	5,308,483	6.1	1,379,269	35.1	891,364	864,746	24,065
1810 (Aug. 6).......	7,239,881	4.3	1,931,398	36.4	1,722,685	1,681,828	34,175
1820 (Aug. 7).......	9,638,453	5.5	2,398,572	33.1	1,792,552	1,749,462	38,544
1830 (June 1)......	12,866,020	7.4	3,227,567	33.5	1,792,552	1,749,462	38,544
1840 (June 1)......	17,069,453	9.8	4,203,433	32.7	1,792,552	1,749,462	38,544
1850 (June 1)......	23,191,876	7.9	6,122,423	35.9	2,991,655	2,940,042	52,705
1860 (June 1)......	31,443,321	10.6	8,251,445	35.6	3,021,295	2,969,640	52,747
1870 (June 1)......	[2] 39,818,449	[2] 11.2	8,375,128	26.6	3,612,299	3,540,705	68,082
1880 (June 1)......	50,189,209	14.2	10,370,760	26.0	3,612,299	3,540,705	68,082
1890 (June 1)......	62,979,766	17.8	12,790,557	25.5	3,612,299	3,540,705	68,082
1900 (June 1)......	76,212,168	21.5	13,232,402	21.0	3,618,770	3,547,314	67,901
1910 (Apr. 15).....	92,228,496	26.0	16,016,328	21.0	3,618,770	3,547,045	68,170
1920 (Jan. 1).......	106,021,537	29.9	13,793,041	15.0	3,618,770	3,546,931	68,284
1930 (Apr. 1).......	123,202,624	34.7	17,181,087	16.2	3,618,770	3,554,608	60,607
1940 (Apr. 1).......	132,164,569	37.2	8,961,945	7.3	3,618,770	3,554,608	60,607
1950 (Apr. 1).......	151,325,798	42.6	19,161,229	14.5	3,618,770	3,552,206	63,005
1960 (Apr. 1).......	179,323,175	50.6	27,997,377	18.5	3,618,770	3,540,911	74,212
1970 (Apr. 1).......	203,302,031	57.5	23,978,856	13.4	3,618,770	3,536,855	78,444
1980 (Apr. 1).......	[3] 226,542,199	64.0	23,240,168	11.4	3,618,770	3,539,289	79,481
1990 (Apr. 1).......	[4] 248,718,302	70.3	22,176,103	9.8	[5] 3,717,796	3,536,278	[5] 181,518
2000 (Apr. 1).......	[6] 281,424,603	79.6	32,706,301	13.1	3,794,083	3,537,438	256,645
2010 (Apr. 1).......	[7] 308,746,065	87.4	27,321,462	9.7	3,796,742	3,531,905	264,837

X Not applicable. [1] Data for 1790 to 1980 cover inland water only. Data for 1990 comprise Great Lakes, inland, and coastal water. Data for 2000 and 2010 comprise Great Lakes, inland, territorial, and coastal water. [2] Revised to include adjustments for underenumeration in southern states; unrevised number is 38,558,371 (10.9 per square mile). [3] Total population count has been revised since the 1980 census publications. Numbers by age, race, Hispanic origin, and sex have not been corrected. [4] The April 1, 1990, census count includes count question resolution corrections processed through December 1997, and does not include adjustments for census coverage errors. [5] Data reflect corrections made after publication of the results. [6] Reflects modifications to the Census 2000 population as documented in the Count Question Resolution program. [7] Reflects modifications to the Census 2010 population as documented in the Count Question Resolution program (updated February 11, 2014).

Source: U.S. Census Bureau, *Notes and Errata, 2010 Census of Population and Housing*, SF/10-1, 2014; 2000 Census of Population and Housing, *Population and Housing Unit Counts, United States Summary*, Series PHC-3-1, and *Notes and Errata*, (2000), SF/01-ER; *Areas of the United States: 1940*; Area data for 1990: unpublished data from TIGER ®; and Davis, Warren, personal correspondence, U.S. Census Bureau, 23 June 2006.

Table 2. Population: 1970 to 2014

[In thousands (205,052 represents 205,052,000). Estimates as of July 1. Civilian population excludes Armed Forces. For basis of estimates, see text, this section]

Year	Resident population, including Armed Forces overseas	Resident population	Civilian population	Year	Resident population, including Armed Forces overseas	Resident population	Civilian population
1970........	205,052	203,984	201,895	1992........	256,894	256,514	254,929
1971........	207,661	206,827	204,866	1993........	260,255	259,919	258,446
1972........	209,896	209,284	207,511	1994........	263,436	263,126	261,714
1973........	211,909	211,357	209,600	1995........	266,557	266,278	264,927
1974........	213,854	213,342	211,636	1996........	269,667	269,394	268,108
1975........	215,973	215,465	213,789	1997........	272,912	272,647	271,394
1976........	218,035	217,563	215,894	1998........	276,115	275,854	274,633
1977........	220,239	219,760	218,106	1999........	279,295	279,040	277,841
1978........	222,585	222,095	220,467	2000........	(NA)	282,162	(NA)
1979........	225,055	224,567	222,969	2001........	(NA)	284,969	(NA)
1980........	227,726	227,225	225,621	2002........	(NA)	287,625	(NA)
1981........	229,966	229,466	227,818	2003........	(NA)	290,108	(NA)
1982........	232,188	231,664	229,995	2004........	(NA)	292,805	(NA)
1983........	234,307	233,792	232,097	2005........	(NA)	295,517	(NA)
1984........	236,348	235,825	234,110	2006........	(NA)	298,380	(NA)
1985........	238,466	237,924	236,219	2007........	(NA)	301,231	(NA)
1986........	240,651	240,133	238,412	2008........	(NA)	304,094	(NA)
1987........	242,804	242,289	240,550	2009........	(NA)	306,772	(NA)
1988........	245,021	244,499	242,817	2010........	309,767	309,347	308,112
1989........	247,342	246,819	245,131	2011........	312,139	311,722	310,504
1990........	250,132	249,623	247,983	2012........	314,449	314,112	312,872
1991........	253,493	252,981	251,370	2013........	316,799	316,498	315,255
				2014........	319,133	318,857	317,631

NA Not available.

Source: U.S. Census Bureau, Population Division, data prior to 2010, <http://www.census.gov/popest/data/historical/index.html>; and 2010 to 2014, "Monthly Population Estimates for the United States: April 1, 2010 to December 1, 2015," <http://www.census.gov/popest/data/national/totals/2014/index.html>, accessed March 2015.

Table 3. Resident Population Projections and Components of Change: 2015 to 2060

[In thousands, except as indicated (321,369 represents 321,369,000). As of July 1. The 2014 National Projections are based on the July 1, 2013 population estimates, which are based on the 2010 Census. The projections were produced using a cohort-component method and are based on assumptions about future births, deaths, and net international migration. More information on methodology and assumptions is available at <http://www.census.gov/population/projections/files/methodology/methodstatement14.pdf>]

Year	Population			Components of Change			
	Total	Numeric change	Percent change [1]	Natural increase	Births	Deaths	Net International migration [2]
2015................	321,369	2,621	0.8	1,380	3,999	2,619	1,241
2016................	323,996	2,627	0.8	1,377	4,027	2,650	1,250
2017................	326,626	2,630	0.8	1,374	4,055	2,681	1,256
2018................	329,256	2,631	0.8	1,369	4,080	2,712	1,262
2019................	331,884	2,628	0.8	1,361	4,104	2,743	1,267
2020................	334,503	2,619	0.8	1,349	4,125	2,777	1,271
2021................	337,109	2,606	0.8	1,331	4,142	2,811	1,275
2022................	339,698	2,589	0.8	1,307	4,155	2,848	1,282
2023................	342,267	2,569	0.8	1,279	4,165	2,887	1,291
2024................	344,814	2,547	0.7	1,246	4,174	2,927	1,301
2025................	347,335	2,521	0.7	1,210	4,181	2,971	1,310
2026................	349,826	2,491	0.7	1,171	4,187	3,016	1,320
2027................	352,281	2,456	0.7	1,127	4,191	3,064	1,329
2028................	354,698	2,417	0.7	1,079	4,194	3,115	1,338
2029................	357,073	2,374	0.7	1,028	4,196	3,168	1,347
2030................	359,402	2,329	0.7	974	4,198	3,224	1,355
2031................	361,685	2,283	0.6	919	4,200	3,281	1,363
2032................	363,920	2,235	0.6	864	4,203	3,339	1,371
2033................	366,106	2,187	0.6	808	4,207	3,399	1,379
2034................	368,246	2,139	0.6	753	4,212	3,459	1,386
2035................	370,338	2,093	0.6	699	4,219	3,520	1,394
2036................	372,390	2,052	0.6	651	4,227	3,576	1,401
2037................	374,401	2,012	0.5	604	4,235	3,631	1,407
2038................	376,375	1,974	0.5	560	4,245	3,685	1,414
2039................	378,313	1,938	0.5	518	4,255	3,737	1,420
2040................	380,219	1,906	0.5	479	4,266	3,787	1,426
2041................	382,096	1,877	0.5	445	4,278	3,833	1,432
2042................	383,949	1,852	0.5	414	4,290	3,876	1,438
2043................	385,779	1,831	0.5	388	4,303	3,916	1,443
2044................	387,593	1,814	0.5	365	4,317	3,952	1,448
2045................	389,394	1,801	0.5	348	4,332	3,984	1,453
2046................	391,187	1,792	0.5	335	4,347	4,012	1,458
2047................	392,973	1,786	0.5	324	4,362	4,038	1,462
2048................	394,756	1,783	0.5	317	4,377	4,060	1,466
2049................	396,540	1,784	0.5	314	4,391	4,077	1,470
2050................	398,328	1,788	0.5	315	4,406	4,091	1,473
2055................	407,412	1,840	0.5	352	4,470	4,117	1,488
2060................	416,795	1,898	0.5	403	4,519	4,116	1,495

[1] Percent change from immediate preceding year. 2015, change from 2014. [2] Net international migration includes the international migration of both native and foreign-born populations. Specifically, it includes: (a) the net international migration of the foreign born, (b) the net international migration of the native born, and (c) the net migration between the United States and Puerto Rico.

Source: U.S. Census Bureau, Population Division, "Table 1. Projections of the Population and Components of Change for the United States: 2015 to 2060 (NP2014-T1)," December 2014, <http://www.census.gov/population/projections/data/national/2014/summarytables.html>, accessed March 2015.

Table 4. Components of Population Change: 2010 to 2014

[In thousands, except as indicated (308,758 represents 308,758,000). Resident population]

Period	Population as of beginning of period	Net increase		Births	Deaths	Net international migration [2]	Population as of end of period
		Total	Percent [1]				
April 1, 2010 to July 1, 2010 [3]....................	308,758	589	0.2	988	599	200	309,347
July 1, 2010 to July 1, 2011......................	309,347	2,375	0.8	3,973	2,512	914	311,722
July 1, 2011 to July 1, 2012......................	311,722	2,390	0.8	3,937	2,502	955	314,112
July 1, 2012 to July 1, 2013......................	314,112	2,385	0.8	3,955	2,569	999	316,498
July 1, 2013 to July 1, 2014......................	316,498	2,360	0.7	3,958	2,594	996	318,857

[1] Percent of population at beginning of period. [2] Net international migration includes the international migration of both native and foreign-born populations. Specifically, it includes: (a) the net international migration of the foreign born, (b) the net migration between the United States and Puerto Rico, (c) the net migration of natives to and from the United States, and (d) the net movement of the Armed Forces population between the United States and overseas. [3] The April 1, 2010 population estimates base reflects changes from the Count Question Resolution program and geographic program revisions.

Source: U.S. Census Bureau, Population Division, "Population, population change, and estimated components of population change: April 1, 2010 to July 1, 2014 (NST-EST2014-alldata)," <http://www.census.gov/popest/data/national/totals/2014/index.html>, accessed March 2015.

Table 5. Components of Population Change by Race and Hispanic Origin: 2010 to 2014

[In thousands (10,099 represents 10,099,000). Resident population. Covers period April 1, 2010 to July 1, 2014. The April 1, 2010 population estimates base reflects changes to the Census 2010 population from the Count Question Resolution program and geographic program revisions. Responses of "Some Other Race" from the 2010 Census are modified. This results in differences between the population for specific race categories shown for the 2010 Census population in this table versus those in the original 2010 Census data. Minus sign (-) indicates decrease]

Race and Hispanic origin	April 1, 2010 to July 1, 2014				
	Net increase	Natural increase	Births	Deaths	Net international migration [1]
Total............	**10,099**	**6,036**	**16,811**	**10,775**	**4,063**
One race..........	9,087	5,118	15,804	10,686	3,969
White..........	4,715	2,970	12,100	9,130	1,745
Black or African American..........	1,904	1,326	2,573	1,247	578
American Indian and Alaska Native..........	221	198	274	76	24
Asian..........	2,179	580	806	226	1,599
Native Hawaiian and Other Pacific Islander..........	67	44	51	7	23
Two or more races..........	1,012	918	1,007	89	94
Race alone or in combination: [2]					
White..........	5,649	3,824	13,026	9,202	1,825
Black or African American..........	2,455	1,840	3,117	1,277	615
American Indian and Alaska Native..........	394	356	478	122	38
Asian..........	2,574	920	1,175	255	1,653
Native Hawaiian and Other Pacific Islander..........	137	107	123	17	30
Hispanic [3]..........	4,909	3,657	4,324	667	1,252
White alone, not Hispanic..........	544	-97	8,424	8,521	642

[1] See footnote 2, Table 4. [2] In combination with one or more other races. The sum of the five race groups adds to more than the total population because individuals may report more than one race. [3] Hispanic origin is considered an ethnicity, not a race. Persons of Hispanic origin may be of any race.

Source: U.S. Census Bureau, Population Division, "Estimates of the Components of Resident Population Change by Race and Hispanic Origin for the United States: April 1, 2010 to July 1, 2014," <http://factfinder.census.gov>, accessed June 2015.

Table 6. Resident Population by Sex and Age: 2000 to 2014

[In thousands, except as indicated (281,425 represents 281,425,000). As of April 1, except 2013 and 2014 as of July 1. Excludes Armed Forces overseas]

Age	2000 [1]			2010 [1]			2013			2014		
	Total	Male	Female	Total	Male	Female	Total	Male	Female	Total	Male	Female
Total...............	281,425	138,056	143,368	308,758	151,790	156,968	316,498	155,741	160,756	318,857	156,936	161,921
Under 5 years........	19,176	9,811	9,365	20,201	10,319	9,882	19,868	10,149	9,718	19,877	10,156	9,721
5 to 9 years..........	20,550	10,523	10,026	20,349	10,390	9,959	20,575	10,508	10,067	20,520	10,478	10,041
10 to 14 years........	20,528	10,520	10,008	20,677	10,580	10,097	20,658	10,549	10,109	20,672	10,551	10,120
15 to 19 years........	20,219	10,391	9,828	22,042	11,305	10,737	21,195	10,859	10,337	21,068	10,784	10,284
20 to 24 years........	18,963	9,688	9,275	21,587	11,015	10,572	22,848	11,696	11,152	22,912	11,739	11,173
25 to 29 years........	19,382	9,799	9,583	21,103	10,637	10,466	21,604	10,952	10,652	21,988	11,161	10,827
30 to 34 years........	20,511	10,322	10,189	19,963	9,997	9,966	21,298	10,685	10,613	21,529	10,809	10,720
35 to 39 years........	22,707	11,319	11,388	20,180	10,043	10,138	19,646	9,796	9,851	19,922	9,940	9,982
40 to 44 years........	22,442	11,130	11,313	20,892	10,395	10,497	20,893	10,375	10,517	20,591	10,219	10,372
45 to 49 years........	20,093	9,890	10,203	22,709	11,210	11,500	21,255	10,519	10,735	20,888	10,347	10,541
50 to 54 years........	17,586	8,608	8,978	22,299	10,934	11,365	22,591	11,085	11,506	22,571	11,078	11,493
55 to 59 years........	13,469	6,509	6,961	19,665	9,524	10,141	21,209	10,288	10,922	21,511	10,444	11,067
60 to 64 years........	10,806	5,137	5,669	16,818	8,078	8,741	18,134	8,677	9,457	18,566	8,878	9,688
65 to 74 years........	18,391	8,303	10,088	21,714	10,097	11,617	25,228	11,797	13,431	26,398	12,349	14,049
75 to 84 years........	12,361	4,879	7,482	13,062	5,477	7,585	13,460	5,765	7,696	13,683	5,893	7,789
85 years and over..................	4,240	1,227	3,013	5,495	1,790	3,705	6,034	2,042	3,992	6,162	2,109	4,053
5 to 13 years..........	37,026	18,964	18,062	36,860	18,834	18,026	37,084	18,936	18,148	36,959	18,865	18,093
14 to 17 years........	16,093	8,285	7,808	17,121	8,792	8,329	16,659	8,519	8,139	16,748	8,562	8,186
18 to 24 years........	27,141	13,873	13,268	30,674	15,663	15,011	31,534	16,156	15,378	31,464	16,125	15,339
18 years and over....	209,130	100,996	108,133	234,576	113,844	120,731	242,887	118,137	124,751	245,273	119,353	125,920
55 years and over....	59,267	26,055	33,212	76,755	34,966	41,789	84,066	38,569	45,498	86,321	39,673	46,648
65 years and over....	34,992	14,410	20,582	40,271	17,364	22,907	44,723	19,604	25,119	46,243	20,351	25,892
75 years and over....	16,601	6,106	10,495	18,557	7,267	11,290	19,495	7,807	11,688	19,845	8,002	11,843

[1] The April 1, 2000 and April 1, 2010 population estimates bases reflect changes to the Census 2000 and Census 2010 population from the Count Question Resolution program and geographic program revisions.

Source: U.S. Census Bureau, "Intercensal Estimates of the United States Population by Age and Sex, 1990-2000: All Months," September 2002, <http://www.census.gov/popest/data/intercensal/national/index.html>; and "Annual estimates of the resident population by single year of age and sex for the United States: April 1, 2010 to July 1, 2014 (NC-EST2014-AGESEX-RES)," <http://www.census.gov/popest/data/datasets.html>, accessed April 2015.

Table 7. Resident Population by Sex, Race, and Hispanic-Origin Status: 2000 to 2014

[281,425 represents 281,425,000. Data shown are modified race counts; see text, this section]

Characteristic	Number (1,000)				Percent change	
	2000 [1] (April)	2010 [1] (April)	2013 (July)	2014 (July)	2000 to 2010	2010 to 2014
BOTH SEXES						
Total	**281,425**	**308,758**	**316,498**	**318,857**	**9.7**	**3.3**
One race	277,527	301,774	308,744	310,861	8.7	3.0
White	228,106	241,945	245,593	246,661	6.1	1.9
Black or African American	35,705	40,255	41,714	42,158	12.7	4.7
American Indian and Alaska Native	2,664	3,740	3,909	3,961	40.4	5.9
Asian	10,589	15,160	16,803	17,339	43.2	14.4
Native Hawaiian and Other Pacific Islander	463	675	725	742	45.9	9.9
Two or more races	3,898	6,984	7,753	7,996	79.2	14.5
Race alone or in combination: [2]						
White	(NA)	248,076	252,433	253,725	(NA)	2.3
Black or African American	(NA)	43,217	45,095	45,672	(NA)	5.7
American Indian and Alaska Native	(NA)	6,139	6,440	6,533	(NA)	6.4
Asian	(NA)	17,677	19,619	20,250	(NA)	14.6
Native Hawaiian and Other Pacific Islander	(NA)	1,333	1,436	1,469	(NA)	10.3
Not Hispanic	246,118	258,279	262,261	263,470	4.9	2.0
One race	242,712	252,675	256,061	257,081	4.1	1.7
White	195,577	197,326	197,777	197,871	0.9	0.3
Black or African American	34,314	37,926	39,156	39,528	10.5	4.2
American Indian and Alaska Native	2,097	2,263	2,330	2,350	7.9	3.8
Asian	10,357	14,662	16,264	16,787	41.6	14.5
Native Hawaiian and Other Pacific Islander	367	497	534	546	35.4	9.8
Two or more races	3,406	5,605	6,200	6,388	64.5	14.0
Race alone or in combination: [2]						
White	(NA)	202,237	203,238	203,507	(NA)	0.6
Black or African American	(NA)	40,287	41,841	42,316	(NA)	5.0
American Indian and Alaska Native	(NA)	4,042	4,182	4,225	(NA)	4.5
Asian	(NA)	16,795	18,649	19,251	(NA)	14.6
Native Hawaiian and Other Pacific Islander	(NA)	1,020	1,096	1,120	(NA)	9.7
Hispanic [3]	35,306	50,479	54,237	55,388	43.0	9.7
One race	34,815	49,099	52,683	53,779	41.0	9.5
White	32,530	44,619	47,816	48,790	37.2	9.3
Black or African American	1,391	2,328	2,558	2,630	67.4	13.0
American Indian and Alaska Native	566	1,476	1,579	1,611	160.6	9.1
Asian	232	498	539	552	114.2	10.9
Native Hawaiian and Other Pacific Islander	95	177	191	196	85.9	10.4
Two or more races	491	1,380	1,554	1,608	180.8	16.5
Race alone or in combination: [2]						
White	(NA)	45,839	49,195	50,218	(NA)	9.6
Black or African American	(NA)	2,930	3,254	3,356	(NA)	14.5
American Indian and Alaska Native	(NA)	2,097	2,258	2,308	(NA)	10.1
Asian	(NA)	881	971	999	(NA)	13.3
Native Hawaiian and Other Pacific Islander	(NA)	312	340	349	(NA)	12.0
MALE						
Total	**138,056**	**151,790**	**155,741**	**156,936**	**9.9**	**3.4**
One race	136,146	148,364	151,924	152,996	9.0	3.1
White	112,478	119,704	121,636	122,195	6.4	2.1
Black or African American	16,972	19,208	19,946	20,170	13.2	5.0
American Indian and Alaska Native	1,333	1,890	1,974	1,999	41.8	5.8
Asian	5,128	7,219	8,000	8,254	40.8	14.3
Native Hawaiian and Other Pacific Islander	235	343	369	377	45.8	10.0
Two or more races	1,910	3,426	3,817	3,941	79.4	15.0
Race alone or in combination: [2]						
White	(NA)	122,721	125,014	125,687	(NA)	2.4
Black or African American	(NA)	20,636	21,587	21,878	(NA)	6.0
American Indian and Alaska Native	(NA)	3,055	3,205	3,251	(NA)	6.4
Asian	(NA)	8,468	9,402	9,704	(NA)	14.6
Native Hawaiian and Other Pacific Islander	(NA)	668	721	738	(NA)	10.5
Not Hispanic	119,894	126,170	128,291	128,919	5.2	2.2
Hispanic [3]	18,162	25,620	27,451	28,018	41.1	9.4
FEMALE						
Total	**143,368**	**156,968**	**160,756**	**161,921**	**9.5**	**3.2**
One race	141,381	153,410	156,820	157,865	8.5	2.9
White	115,628	122,241	123,957	124,465	5.7	1.8
Black or African American	18,733	21,046	21,768	21,988	12.3	4.5
American Indian and Alaska Native	1,331	1,850	1,935	1,962	39.0	6.0
Asian	5,461	7,941	8,804	9,085	45.4	14.4
Native Hawaiian and Other Pacific Islander	227	332	356	364	45.9	9.8
Two or more races	1,987	3,558	3,936	4,056	79.0	14.0
Race alone or in combination: [2]						
White	(NA)	125,355	127,419	128,038	(NA)	2.1
Black or African American	(NA)	22,581	23,508	23,794	(NA)	5.4
American Indian and Alaska Native	(NA)	3,084	3,235	3,281	(NA)	6.4
Asian	(NA)	9,209	10,218	10,546	(NA)	14.5
Native Hawaiian and Other Pacific Islander	(NA)	665	715	732	(NA)	10.0
Not Hispanic	126,224	132,109	133,970	134,551	4.7	1.8
Hispanic [3]	17,144	24,859	26,786	27,370	45.0	10.1

NA Not available. [1] The April 1, 2000 and 2010 population estimates base reflects changes to the Census 2000 and 2010 population from the Count Question Resolution program and geographic program revisions. [2] In combination with one or more other races. The sum of the five race groups adds to more than the total population because individuals may report more than one race. [3] See footnote 3, Table 5.

Source: U.S. Census Bureau, Population Division, "Table 2. (US-EST00INT-02)," September 2011, <http://www.census.gov/popest/data/intercensal/national/nat2010.html>; and "National Population Estimates for the 2010s," <http://www.census.gov/popest/data/national/asrh/2014/2014-nat-res.html>; accessed June 2015.

Table 8. Resident Population Projections by Sex and Age: 2015 to 2060

[In thousands, except as indicated (321,369 represents 321,369,000). As of July 1. The 2014 National Projections are based on the July 1, 2013 population estimates, which are based on the 2010 Census. The projections were produced using a cohort-component method and are based on assumptions about future births, deaths, and net international migration. More information on methodology and assumptions is available at <http://www.census.gov/population/projections/files/methodology/methodstatement14.pdf>]

Age	2015 Total	2015 Male	2015 Female	2020	2025	2030	2035	2040	2050	2060	Percent distribution 2015	2020	2040	2060
Total	321,369	158,345	163,024	334,503	347,335	359,402	370,338	380,219	398,328	416,795	100.0	100.0	100.0	100.0
Under 5 years	19,965	10,211	9,755	20,568	21,010	21,178	21,268	21,471	22,147	22,778	6.2	6.1	5.6	5.5
5 to 9 years	20,463	10,448	10,015	20,274	20,889	21,347	21,529	21,632	22,158	22,894	6.4	6.1	5.7	5.5
10 to 14 years	20,590	10,513	10,076	20,735	20,555	21,182	21,650	21,842	22,171	22,871	6.4	6.2	5.7	5.5
15 to 19 years	21,092	10,796	10,297	21,048	21,219	21,060	21,706	22,190	22,516	23,067	6.6	6.3	5.8	5.5
20 to 24 years	22,740	11,678	11,062	22,059	22,077	22,299	22,183	22,866	23,615	23,999	7.1	6.6	6.0	5.8
25 to 29 years	22,473	11,447	11,026	23,722	23,103	23,179	23,450	23,377	24,646	25,065	7.0	7.1	6.1	6.0
30 to 34 years	21,659	10,906	10,753	23,168	24,450	23,878	23,995	24,302	25,004	25,845	6.7	6.9	6.4	6.2
35 to 39 years	20,346	10,181	10,166	22,060	23,586	24,898	24,360	24,507	24,813	26,151	6.3	6.6	6.4	6.3
40 to 44 years	20,178	10,025	10,153	20,568	22,291	23,840	25,176	24,668	25,190	25,949	6.3	6.1	6.5	6.2
45 to 49 years	20,817	10,324	10,493	20,204	20,613	22,351	23,919	25,274	24,995	25,368	6.5	6.0	6.6	6.1
50 to 54 years	22,312	10,955	11,356	20,638	20,063	20,506	22,257	23,844	24,781	25,395	6.9	6.2	6.3	6.1
55 to 59 years	21,811	10,601	11,210	21,879	20,294	19,777	20,260	22,023	25,023	24,893	6.8	6.5	5.8	6.0
60 to 64 years	19,093	9,131	9,962	21,141	21,265	19,799	19,351	19,880	23,275	24,357	5.9	6.3	5.2	5.8
65 to 69 years	16,094	7,612	8,482	18,194	20,202	20,397	19,071	18,704	21,054	24,112	5.0	5.4	4.9	5.8
70 to 74 years	11,500	5,306	6,193	14,882	16,891	18,830	19,091	17,940	18,294	21,662	3.6	4.4	4.7	5.2
75 to 79 years	8,126	3,615	4,512	10,112	13,154	15,013	16,819	17,143	16,042	18,393	2.5	3.0	4.5	4.4
80 to 84 years	5,806	2,417	3,389	6,527	8,191	10,737	12,343	13,924	13,634	14,274	1.8	2.0	3.7	3.4
85 to 89 years	3,875	1,448	2,427	3,964	4,521	5,747	7,622	8,867	10,492	10,184	1.2	1.2	2.3	2.4
90 to 94 years	1,859	591	1,268	2,024	2,114	2,464	3,192	4,320	5,951	6,184	0.6	0.6	1.1	1.5
95 to 99 years	498	128	370	649	728	782	940	1,254	2,141	2,752	0.2	0.2	0.3	0.7
100 years and over	72	14	58	89	119	138	154	193	387	604	(Z)	(Z)	0.1	0.1
5 to 13 years	36,874	18,827	18,047	36,824	37,316	38,322	38,848	39,087	39,887	41,193	11.5	11.0	10.3	9.9
14 to 17 years	16,796	8,589	8,207	16,737	16,698	16,773	17,303	17,627	17,854	18,338	5.2	5.0	4.6	4.4
18 to 24 years	31,214	16,018	15,196	30,555	30,736	30,794	30,890	31,815	32,717	33,300	9.7	9.1	8.4	8.0
16 years and over	256,107	125,002	131,105	268,750	280,749	291,500	301,559	310,879	327,402	343,677	79.7	80.3	81.8	82.5
18 years and over	247,734	120,718	127,016	260,375	272,319	283,129	292,892	302,034	318,440	334,486	77.1	77.8	79.4	80.3
16 to 64 years	208,277	103,872	104,405	212,309	214,829	217,393	222,326	228,535	239,406	245,513	64.8	63.5	60.1	58.9
55 years and over	88,734	40,863	47,871	99,461	107,479	113,684	118,843	124,248	136,293	147,415	27.6	29.7	32.7	35.4
65 years and over	47,830	21,130	26,700	56,441	65,920	74,107	79,233	82,344	87,996	98,164	14.9	16.9	21.7	23.6
75 years and over	20,236	8,213	12,024	23,365	28,827	34,881	41,070	45,701	48,647	52,391	6.3	7.0	12.0	12.6
85 years and over	6,304	2,181	4,124	6,727	7,482	9,132	11,909	14,634	18,972	19,724	2.0	2.0	3.8	4.7
Median age (years)[1]	37.8	36.5	39.2	38.5	39.3	40.1	41.0	41.6	42.4	43.0	(X)	(X)	(X)	(X)

X Not applicable. Z Less than 0.05 percent. [1] For definition of median, see Guide to Tabular Presentation.

Source: U.S. Census Bureau, "Table 3. Projections of the Population by Sex and Selected Age Groups for the United States: 2015 to 2060 (NP2014-T3)," and "Table 9. Projections of the Population by Sex and Age for the United States: 2015 to 2060 (NP2014-T9)," December 2014, <http://www.census.gov/population/projections/data/national/2014/summarytables.html>; accessed March 2015.

Table 9. Resident Population by Race, Hispanic Origin, and Age: 2010 and 2014

[In thousands, except as indicated (308,758 represents 308,758,000). 2010 as of April 1. 2014 as of July 1]

Age	Total 2010[1]	Total 2014	White alone 2010[1]	White alone 2014	Black or African American alone 2010[1]	Black or African American alone 2014	American Indian, Alaska Native alone 2010[1]	American Indian, Alaska Native alone 2014	Asian alone 2010[1]	Asian alone 2014	Native Hawaiian, Other Pacific Islander alone 2010[1]	Native Hawaiian, Other Pacific Islander alone 2014	Two or more races 2010[1]	Two or more races 2014	Hispanic origin[2] 2010[1]	Hispanic origin[2] 2014	Not Hispanic White alone 2010[1]	Not Hispanic White alone 2014
Total..........	308,758	318,857	241,945	246,661	40,255	42,158	3,740	3,961	15,160	17,339	675	742	6,984	7,996	50,479	55,388	197,326	197,871
Under 5 years........	20,201	19,877	14,691	14,261	3,055	3,027	330	322	948	1,022	59	61	1,119	1,185	5,114	5,131	10,307	9,896
5 to 9 years........	20,349	20,520	15,044	14,897	3,013	3,091	321	332	972	1,038	56	61	944	1,100	4,791	5,181	10,885	10,444
10 to 14 years........	20,677	20,672	15,399	15,233	3,155	3,090	318	322	922	1,039	54	57	829	931	4,525	4,847	11,449	11,020
15 to 19 years........	22,042	21,068	16,347	15,599	3,573	3,231	340	320	999	1,040	60	56	723	821	4,532	4,642	12,387	11,544
20 to 24 years........	21,587	22,912	16,247	16,816	3,240	3,688	319	347	1,149	1,278	66	66	566	718	4,322	4,777	12,468	12,639
25 to 29 years........	21,103	21,988	16,061	16,390	2,912	3,199	300	316	1,279	1,457	64	69	488	556	4,311	4,448	12,268	12,495
30 to 34 years........	19,963	21,529	15,184	16,212	2,744	2,970	275	299	1,284	1,492	56	66	420	489	4,125	4,434	11,534	12,310
35 to 39 years........	20,180	19,922	15,473	15,058	2,707	2,721	261	270	1,334	1,409	49	56	357	409	3,856	4,134	12,018	11,392
40 to 44 years........	20,892	20,591	16,342	15,758	2,752	2,752	251	260	1,188	1,416	45	50	314	356	3,443	3,859	13,250	12,301
45 to 49 years........	22,709	20,888	18,103	16,322	2,902	2,741	255	247	1,105	1,225	43	45	302	308	3,022	3,390	15,387	13,278
50 to 54 years........	22,299	22,571	18,009	17,996	2,754	2,846	228	248	1,004	1,139	37	43	268	298	2,442	2,941	15,813	15,354
55 to 59 years........	19,665	21,511	16,144	17,391	2,246	2,594	177	214	863	1,022	28	35	207	255	1,841	2,324	14,476	15,300
60 to 64 years........	16,818	18,566	14,089	15,255	1,715	2,060	134	163	703	868	21	27	156	193	1,372	1,730	12,839	13,689
65 to 69 years........	12,436	15,325	10,564	12,872	1,181	1,498	89	119	483	675	14	20	105	142	949	1,268	9,694	11,716
70 to 74 years........	9,278	11,073	7,911	9,407	865	1,017	60	77	361	466	9	13	72	94	700	862	7,266	8,616
75 to 79 years........	7,318	7,922	6,341	6,765	625	708	39	50	255	329	6	8	51	62	511	617	5,867	6,197
80 to 84 years........	5,744	5,760	5,079	4,996	430	469	25	30	171	219	4	5	35	40	351	418	4,752	4,608
85 to 89 years........	3,621	3,827	3,244	3,374	248	280	13	17	94	129	2	3	20	24	185	249	3,072	3,142
90 to 94 years........	1,449	1,799	1,300	1,592	101	130	5	7	35	59	1	1	7	11	65	106	1,240	1,493
95 to 99 years........	371	464	328	405	31	38	1	2	9	16	(Z)	(Z)	2	3	18	27	312	381
100 years and over........	53	72	45	59	7	9	(Z)	(Z)	1	3	(Z)	(Z)	(Z)	1	3	5	42	54
5 to 13 years........	36,860	36,959	27,331	27,009	5,530	5,532	576	588	1,707	1,873	99	106	1,617	1,852	8,426	9,063	20,002	19,183
14 to 17 years........	17,121	16,748	12,724	12,391	2,732	2,562	263	257	756	810	45	44	601	684	3,591	3,745	9,582	9,125
18 to 24 years........	30,674	31,464	22,982	23,146	4,719	5,006	459	475	1,579	1,714	92	89	844	1,034	6,154	6,639	17,606	17,340
16 years and over........	243,288	253,625	193,656	199,185	30,362	32,316	2,706	2,921	12,130	14,043	495	552	3,939	4,607	35,154	39,294	162,310	164,241
18 years and over........	234,576	245,273	187,200	193,001	28,938	31,038	2,571	2,794	11,749	13,635	471	530	3,647	4,275	33,348	37,449	157,436	159,667
16 to 64 years........	203,016	207,382	158,843	159,714	26,874	28,167	2,474	2,620	10,720	12,149	459	502	3,646	4,230	32,373	35,743	130,066	128,033
55 years and over........	76,755	86,321	65,045	72,118	7,449	8,803	543	679	2,976	3,784	85	112	656	825	5,996	7,605	59,559	65,197
65 years and over........	40,271	46,243	34,812	39,471	3,488	4,149	232	302	1,410	1,894	36	50	293	376	2,782	3,551	32,244	36,208
75 years and over........	18,557	19,845	16,338	17,193	1,442	1,634	83	106	566	754	13	17	116	141	1,133	1,422	15,285	15,876
85 years and over........	5,495	6,162	4,918	5,431	386	456	19	26	140	206	3	4	30	38	271	387	4,666	5,071
Median age (years)[3].......	37.2	37.7	39.0	39.6	32.0	33.0	29.0	30.4	35.1	36.1	28.3	30.1	19.1	19.8	27.3	28.5	42.0	43.1

Z Less than 500. [1] The April 1, 2010 population estimates base reflects changes to the Census 2010 population from the Count Question Resolution program and geographic program revisions. [2] Hispanic origin is considered an ethnicity, not a race. Hispanics may be of any race. [3] For definition of median, see Guide to Tabular Presentation.

Source: U.S. Census Bureau, Population Division, "National Characteristics: Vintage 2014, Median Age and Age by Sex, Race, and Hispanic Origin," <http://www.census.gov/popest/data/national/asrh/2014/index.html>, and "Annual Estimates of the Resident Population by Sex, Single Year of Age, Race, and Hispanic Origin for the United States: April 1, 2010 to July 1, 2014," <http://factfinder.census.gov>, accessed June 2015.

Table 10. Resident Population by Race, Hispanic Origin, and Single Years of Age: 2014

[In thousands, except as indicated (318,857 represents 318,857,000). As of July 1. For derivation of estimates, see text, this section]

Age	Total	Race						Hispanic origin [1]	Non-Hispanic White alone
		White alone	Black or African American alone	American Indian, Alaska Native alone	Asian alone	Native Hawaiian and Other Pacific Islander alone	Two or more races		
Total.......................	318,857	246,661	42,158	3,961	17,339	742	7,996	55,388	197,871
Under 5 years old.............	19,877	14,261	3,027	322	1,022	61	1,185	5,131	9,896
Under 1 year old.............	3,948	2,826	603	65	202	12	241	1,013	1,968
1 year old...................	3,962	2,829	607	64	211	13	239	1,019	1,965
2 years old..................	3,958	2,838	604	65	204	12	235	1,018	1,975
3 years old..................	4,005	2,886	608	63	201	12	235	1,045	1,992
4 years old..................	4,003	2,882	605	65	204	12	236	1,036	1,997
5 to 9 years old..............	20,520	14,897	3,091	332	1,038	61	1,100	5,181	10,444
5 years old..................	4,005	2,887	610	65	202	12	229	1,023	2,013
6 years old..................	4,134	2,984	630	67	210	12	230	1,056	2,079
7 years old..................	4,154	3,013	630	68	208	12	223	1,057	2,106
8 years old..................	4,120	3,006	615	67	207	12	213	1,034	2,114
9 years old..................	4,107	3,006	606	66	211	12	205	1,011	2,133
10 to 14 years old............	20,672	15,233	3,090	322	1,039	57	931	4,847	11,020
10 years old.................	4,115	3,027	602	65	212	11	198	989	2,170
11 years old.................	4,086	3,011	599	64	211	11	189	971	2,168
12 years old.................	4,069	3,001	609	63	202	11	182	958	2,168
13 years old.................	4,169	3,073	631	64	209	11	182	964	2,233
14 years old.................	4,232	3,122	650	66	205	11	179	964	2,281
15 to 19 years old............	21,068	15,599	3,231	320	1,040	56	821	4,642	11,544
15 years old.................	4,164	3,084	634	64	197	11	174	934	2,270
16 years old.................	4,167	3,084	639	64	201	11	168	924	2,278
17 years old.................	4,185	3,101	639	63	207	11	163	921	2,296
18 years old.................	4,226	3,134	642	63	215	11	160	923	2,326
19 years old.................	4,326	3,196	676	65	221	12	157	938	2,375
20 to 24 years old............	22,912	16,816	3,688	347	1,278	66	718	4,777	12,639
20 years old.................	4,419	3,248	710	67	229	12	153	949	2,417
21 years old.................	4,490	3,293	731	69	236	12	147	954	2,457
22 years old.................	4,612	3,383	747	71	252	13	145	969	2,535
23 years old.................	4,699	3,444	756	71	274	14	140	959	2,608
24 years old.................	4,693	3,447	743	69	286	15	132	946	2,622
25 to 29 years old............	21,988	16,390	3,199	316	1,457	69	556	4,448	12,495
25 years old.................	4,510	3,320	695	66	293	14	122	898	2,537
26 years old.................	4,406	3,273	651	64	289	14	115	891	2,493
27 years old.................	4,333	3,235	626	62	286	14	110	879	2,465
28 years old.................	4,352	3,264	615	62	291	14	106	886	2,487
29 years old.................	4,387	3,298	613	61	298	14	104	894	2,513
30 to 34 years old............	21,529	16,212	2,970	299	1,492	66	489	4,434	12,310
30 years old.................	4,251	3,195	585	60	298	13	100	869	2,431
31 years old.................	4,319	3,251	593	61	301	13	100	887	2,471
32 years old.................	4,320	3,255	592	60	302	13	98	891	2,470
33 years old.................	4,276	3,229	588	59	292	13	96	880	2,454
34 years old.................	4,363	3,283	612	60	299	13	96	907	2,484
35 to 39 years old............	19,922	15,058	2,721	270	1,409	56	409	4,134	11,392
35 years old.................	4,094	3,083	570	55	285	12	88	838	2,344
36 years old.................	4,014	3,036	550	55	277	11	85	835	2,298
37 years old.................	3,974	3,006	543	54	278	11	82	827	2,273
38 years old.................	3,859	2,917	522	52	280	11	78	813	2,194
39 years old.................	3,980	3,016	536	53	289	11	75	821	2,283
40 to 44 years old............	20,591	15,758	2,752	260	1,416	50	356	3,859	12,301
40 years old.................	3,857	2,923	517	51	284	10	71	787	2,219
41 years old.................	3,917	2,967	533	51	286	10	71	776	2,272
42 years old.................	4,096	3,127	551	52	286	10	71	769	2,437
43 years old.................	4,332	3,343	575	53	280	10	72	765	2,657
44 years old.................	4,389	3,399	575	53	281	10	71	762	2,716
45 to 49 years old............	20,888	16,322	2,741	247	1,225	45	308	3,390	13,278
45 years old.................	4,161	3,239	534	50	264	9	65	711	2,601
46 years old.................	4,076	3,168	537	49	252	9	62	693	2,546
47 years old.................	4,082	3,197	535	48	233	9	60	666	2,599
48 years old.................	4,159	3,252	554	49	236	9	60	658	2,661
49 years old.................	4,409	3,466	581	51	239	9	62	663	2,871
50 to 54 years old............	22,571	17,996	2,846	248	1,139	43	298	2,941	15,354
50 years old.................	4,491	3,552	577	51	241	9	61	636	2,981
51 years old.................	4,489	3,561	569	50	240	9	60	606	3,017
52 years old.................	4,480	3,582	562	49	219	9	59	582	3,059
53 years old.................	4,536	3,643	563	49	214	8	58	558	3,141
54 years old.................	4,575	3,658	576	49	225	8	58	558	3,156
55 to 59 years old............	21,511	17,391	2,594	214	1,022	35	255	2,324	15,300
55 years old.................	4,422	3,555	549	46	209	8	55	509	3,098
56 years old.................	4,395	3,550	531	44	209	7	53	481	3,117
57 years old.................	4,347	3,518	525	43	203	7	51	464	3,101
58 years old.................	4,192	3,393	501	41	201	7	49	442	2,995
59 years old.................	4,155	3,376	487	40	199	6	47	427	2,990

See footnotes at end of table.

| Age | Total | Race | | | | | | Hispanic origin [1] | Non-Hispanic White alone |
		White alone	Black or African American alone	American Indian, Alaska Native alone	Asian alone	Native Hawaiian and Other Pacific Islander alone	Two or more races		
60 to 64 years old..............	18,566	15,255	2,060	163	868	27	193	1,730	13,689
60 years old..................	3,985	3,257	456	37	187	6	44	391	2,904
61 years old..................	3,834	3,150	425	34	179	6	41	364	2,820
62 years old..................	3,686	3,040	401	32	169	5	38	337	2,735
63 years old..................	3,572	2,942	395	31	163	5	36	325	2,648
64 years old..................	3,488	2,866	382	30	170	5	35	313	2,582
65 to 69 years old..............	15,325	12,872	1,498	119	675	20	142	1,268	11,716
65 years old..................	3,384	2,810	353	28	157	5	32	288	2,548
66 years old..................	3,348	2,805	333	26	148	4	31	276	2,554
67 years old..................	3,486	2,973	314	26	138	4	31	262	2,734
68 years old..................	2,573	2,156	251	20	118	4	24	227	1,949
69 years old..................	2,535	2,128	247	19	114	3	23	215	1,931
70 to 74 years old..............	11,073	9,407	1,017	77	466	13	94	862	8,616
70 years old..................	2,466	2,089	230	18	105	3	22	197	1,908
71 years old..................	2,520	2,158	224	17	97	3	21	187	1,987
72 years old..................	2,194	1,865	200	15	93	2	18	168	1,711
73 years old..................	2,002	1,697	186	14	86	2	17	157	1,553
74 years old..................	1,890	1,597	178	13	84	2	16	152	1,458
75 to 79 years old..............	7,922	6,765	708	50	329	8	62	617	6,197
75 years old..................	1,775	1,511	160	12	75	2	14	140	1,382
76 years old..................	1,695	1,446	152	11	71	2	13	132	1,325
77 years old..................	1,557	1,329	139	10	65	2	12	121	1,217
78 years old..................	1,482	1,266	133	9	61	1	11	115	1,160
79 years old..................	1,414	1,213	124	8	56	1	11	109	1,112
80 to 84 years old..............	5,760	4,996	469	30	219	5	40	418	4,608
80 years old..................	1,264	1,085	110	7	50	1	9	96	997
81 years old..................	1,216	1,048	103	7	48	1	9	88	967
82 years old..................	1,154	1,003	93	6	43	1	8	83	926
83 years old..................	1,090	954	83	5	40	1	7	78	882
84 years old..................	1,036	906	80	5	38	1	7	74	837
85 to 89 years old..............	3,827	3,374	280	17	129	3	24	249	3,142
85 years old..................	925	813	69	4	32	1	6	63	754
86 years old..................	856	755	62	4	29	1	5	57	702
87 years old..................	771	680	56	3	26	(Z)	5	49	635
88 years old..................	675	596	49	3	22	(Z)	4	43	556
89 years old..................	600	530	43	2	20	(Z)	4	37	496
90 to 94 years old..............	1,799	1,592	130	7	59	1	11	106	1,493
90 years old..................	513	454	36	2	17	(Z)	3	31	426
91 years old..................	427	378	31	2	14	(Z)	3	26	354
92 years old..................	355	314	25	1	11	(Z)	2	21	295
93 years old..................	286	254	20	1	9	(Z)	2	16	239
94 years old..................	219	192	17	1	7	(Z)	1	13	180
95 to 99 years old..............	464	405	38	2	16	(Z)	3	27	381
95 years old..................	157	138	12	1	5	(Z)	1	9	130
96 years old..................	121	106	10	(Z)	4	(Z)	1	7	100
97 years old..................	84	73	7	(Z)	3	(Z)	(Z)	5	69
98 years old..................	60	52	5	(Z)	2	(Z)	(Z)	4	49
99 years old..................	42	36	4	(Z)	2	(Z)	(Z)	3	33
100 years old and over.......	72	59	9	(Z)	3	(Z)	1	5	54
Median age (years) [2]........	37.7	39.6	33.0	30.4	36.1	30.1	19.8	28.5	43.1

Z Less than 500. [1] Persons of Hispanic origin may be of any race. [2] For definition of median, see Guide to Tabular Presentation.

Source: U.S. Census Bureau, Population Division, "Annual Estimates of the Resident Population by Sex, Single Year of Age, Race, and Hispanic Origin for the United States: April 1, 2010 to July 1, 2014," <http://factfinder.census.gov>, accessed July 2015.

Table 11. Resident Population Projections by Race, Hispanic Origin, and Age: 2015

[In thousands (321,369 represents 321,369,000). As of July 1. The 2014 National Projections are based on the July 1, 2013 population estimates, which are based on the 2010 Census. The projections were produced using a cohort-component method and are based on assumptions about future births, deaths, and net international migration. More information on methodology and assumptions is available at <http://www.census.gov/population/projections/files/methodology/methodstatement14.pdf>]

Age group	Total	White alone	Black or African American alone	American Indian /Alaska Native alone	Asian alone	Native Hawaiian /Other Pacific Islander alone	Two or more races	Hispanic origin [1]	Not Hispanic White alone
Total......................	321,369	248,369	42,456	4,005	17,538	746	8,255	56,754	198,354
Under 5 years..............	19,965	14,330	3,000	313	1,035	57	1,230	5,114	9,970
5 to 9 years...............	20,463	14,810	3,087	331	1,044	60	1,130	5,236	10,317
10 to 14 years.............	20,590	15,162	3,042	323	1,050	57	955	4,928	10,882
15 to 19 years.............	21,092	15,627	3,204	321	1,041	56	843	4,741	11,483
20 to 24 years.............	22,740	16,722	3,628	344	1,240	63	743	4,892	12,431
25 to 29 years.............	22,473	16,677	3,336	325	1,479	70	586	4,620	12,627
30 to 34 years.............	21,659	16,318	2,965	302	1,510	66	498	4,495	12,358
35 to 39 years.............	20,346	15,372	2,788	277	1,422	58	429	4,257	11,603
40 to 44 years.............	20,178	15,387	2,701	259	1,421	50	360	3,928	11,868
45 to 49 years.............	20,817	16,228	2,722	248	1,256	46	316	3,482	13,102
50 to 54 years.............	22,312	17,744	2,832	249	1,144	44	299	3,031	15,021
55 to 59 years.............	21,811	17,593	2,658	222	1,037	37	265	2,442	15,397
60 to 64 years.............	19,093	15,661	2,140	171	890	28	204	1,833	14,003
65 to 69 years.............	16,094	13,465	1,608	127	722	21	152	1,353	12,234
70 to 74 years.............	11,500	9,762	1,058	81	486	13	99	912	8,926
75 to 79 years.............	8,126	6,927	733	52	341	9	65	643	6,335
80 to 84 years.............	5,806	5,025	483	32	219	5	42	434	4,623
85 to 89 years.............	3,875	3,414	287	17	129	3	25	264	3,168
90 to 94 years.............	1,859	1,649	135	7	56	1	11	114	1,543
95 to 99 years.............	498	437	41	2	15	(Z)	3	30	410
100 years and over........	72	60	8	(Z)	2	(Z)	(Z)	5	55
5 to 13 years..............	36,874	26,889	5,500	590	1,885	106	1,904	9,192	18,963
14 to 17 years.............	16,796	12,422	2,551	258	819	45	702	3,829	9,080
18 to 24 years.............	31,214	23,010	4,911	472	1,671	85	1,065	6,775	17,070
16 years and over.........	256,107	200,933	32,678	2,972	14,204	560	4,761	40,503	164,901
18 years and over.........	247,734	194,728	31,405	2,844	13,800	537	4,419	38,619	160,341
16 to 64 years.............	208,277	160,195	28,325	2,653	12,234	507	4,364	36,749	127,608
55 years and over.........	88,734	73,992	9,151	711	3,897	118	865	8,029	66,694
65 years and over.........	47,830	40,738	4,353	319	1,970	53	396	3,755	37,293
75 years and over.........	20,236	17,511	1,687	111	763	18	145	1,490	16,133
85 years and over.........	6,304	5,560	472	27	203	4	39	412	5,176

Z Less than 500. [1] Hispanic origin is considered an ethnicity, not a race. Hispanics may be of any race.

Source: U.S. Census Bureau, "Table 1. Projected Population by Single Year of Age, Sex, Race, and Hispanic Origin for the United States: 2014 to 2060," December 2014, <http://www.census.gov/population/projections/data/national/2014/downloadablefiles.html>, accessed March 2015.

Table 12. Resident Population Projections for Native and Foreign-Born Populations by Age Group: 2015 to 2060

[In thousands (321,369 represents 321,369,000), except as indicated. As of July 1. Data shown are modified race counts; see text, this section. Based on 2014 National Projections, see headnote Table 11.]

Nativity and age group	2015	2020	2025	2030	2040	2050	2060
Total population...............	321,369	334,503	347,335	359,402	380,219	398,328	416,795
Under 18 years.................	73,635	74,128	75,015	76,273	78,185	79,888	82,309
Under 5 years.................	19,965	20,568	21,010	21,178	21,471	22,147	22,778
5 to 13 years.................	36,874	36,824	37,316	38,322	39,087	39,887	41,193
14 to 17 years................	16,796	16,737	16,689	16,773	17,627	17,854	18,338
18 to 64 years.................	199,903	203,934	206,400	209,022	219,690	230,444	236,322
18 to 24 years................	31,214	30,555	30,736	30,794	31,815	32,717	33,300
25 to 44 years................	84,657	89,518	93,429	95,795	96,854	99,653	103,010
45 to 64 years................	84,032	83,861	82,235	82,434	91,021	98,074	100,013
65 years and over.............	47,830	56,441	65,920	74,107	82,344	87,996	98,164
Native population.............	278,094	286,611	294,909	302,545	315,103	326,030	338,564
Under 18 years.................	71,156	71,683	72,394	73,486	75,189	76,735	79,055
Under 5 years.................	19,678	20,260	20,687	20,842	21,113	21,773	22,396
5 to 13 years.................	35,700	35,558	35,928	36,868	37,525	38,244	39,497
14 to 17 years................	15,777	15,866	15,779	15,776	16,551	16,718	17,161
18 to 64 years.................	165,514	166,565	166,749	167,447	175,039	183,194	186,633
18 to 24 years................	28,060	27,353	27,678	27,650	28,345	29,049	29,499
25 to 44 years................	67,689	72,016	75,434	77,496	77,708	79,385	81,642
45 to 64 years................	69,765	67,196	63,637	62,302	68,986	74,761	75,493
65 years and over.............	41,424	48,362	55,766	61,612	64,876	66,101	72,876
Foreign-born population.........	43,275	47,892	52,426	56,857	65,116	72,299	78,230
Under 18 years.................	2,480	2,445	2,622	2,787	2,996	3,153	3,254
Under 5 years.................	287	308	323	336	358	374	382
5 to 13 years.................	1,174	1,266	1,388	1,454	1,563	1,644	1,695
14 to 17 years................	1,019	871	911	997	1,075	1,136	1,177
18 to 64 years.................	34,389	37,369	39,651	41,575	44,651	47,250	49,689
18 to 24 years................	3,154	3,202	3,057	3,144	3,471	3,669	3,801
25 to 44 years................	16,968	17,502	17,996	18,299	19,146	20,268	21,368
45 to 64 years................	14,267	16,665	18,598	20,132	22,035	23,313	24,520
65 years and over.............	6,406	8,079	10,154	12,495	17,469	21,895	25,288

Source: U.S. Census Bureau, "2014 National Population Projections: Summary Tables," <http://www.census.gov/population/projections/data/national/2014/summarytables.html>, accessed March 2015.

Table 13. Resident Population Projections by Race/Ethnicity and Hispanic Origin: 2015 to 2060

[In thousands, except as indicated (321,369 represents 321,369,000). As of July 1. Data shown are modified race counts; see text, this section. The 2014 National Projections are based on the July 1, 2013 population estimates, which are based on the 2010 Census. The projections were produced using a cohort-component method and are based on assumptions about future births, deaths, and net international migration. More information on methodology and assumptions is available at <http://www.census.gov/population/projections/files/methodology/methodstatement14.pdf>]

Characteristic	2015	2020	2025	2030	2035	2040	2050	2060
Total................................	**321,369**	**334,503**	**347,335**	**359,402**	**370,338**	**380,219**	**398,328**	**416,795**
One race..............................	313,114	324,865	336,170	346,571	355,706	363,637	377,357	390,772
White................................	248,369	255,357	261,825	267,459	271,981	275,447	280,503	285,314
Black or African American..........	42,456	44,590	46,725	48,768	50,678	52,485	56,007	59,693
American Indian and Alaska Native..	4,005	4,242	4,475	4,694	4,895	5,074	5,370	5,607
Asian................................	17,538	19,869	22,278	24,726	27,175	29,603	34,359	38,965
Native Hawaiian/Other Pacific Islander..........	746	806	866	923	977	1,028	1,118	1,194
Two or more races..................	8,255	9,639	11,165	12,831	14,632	16,582	20,971	26,022
Race alone or in combination: [1]								
White................................	255,682	263,969	271,873	279,081	285,312	290,635	299,896	309,567
Black or African American..........	46,126	49,052	52,081	55,121	58,132	61,158	67,499	74,530
American Indian and Alaska Native..	6,618	7,071	7,526	7,968	8,386	8,777	9,497	10,169
Asian................................	20,534	23,380	26,358	29,426	32,550	35,709	42,099	48,575
Native Hawaiian/Other Pacific Islander..........	1,486	1,631	1,784	1,940	2,098	2,257	2,586	2,929
Not Hispanic..........................	**264,615**	**270,952**	**276,895**	**281,939**	**285,795**	**288,593**	**292,778**	**297,750**
One race..............................	258,022	263,275	268,019	271,761	274,217	275,504	276,293	277,374
White................................	198,354	199,400	199,867	199,403	197,810	195,197	188,419	181,930
Black or African American..........	39,782	41,594	43,404	45,118	46,694	48,162	51,006	54,028
American Indian and Alaska Native..	2,359	2,432	2,499	2,555	2,597	2,623	2,641	2,637
Asian................................	16,978	19,255	21,608	23,999	26,389	28,756	33,391	37,879
Native Hawaiian/Other Pacific Islander.........	549	595	641	685	726	765	836	900
Two or more races..................	6,593	7,678	8,876	10,178	11,578	13,089	16,485	20,376
Race alone or in combination: [1]								
White................................	204,188	206,256	207,854	208,626	208,368	207,201	203,691	200,963
Black or African American..........	42,697	45,140	47,665	50,174	52,623	55,054	60,124	65,773
American Indian and Alaska Native..	4,257	4,449	4,637	4,810	4,960	5,087	5,303	5,507
Asian................................	19,513	22,224	25,053	27,960	30,906	33,872	39,835	45,822
Native Hawaiian/Other Pacific Islander.........	1,132	1,239	1,352	1,466	1,578	1,691	1,920	2,155
Hispanic [2]............................	**56,754**	**63,551**	**70,440**	**77,463**	**84,543**	**91,626**	**105,550**	**119,044**
One race..............................	55,092	61,590	68,150	74,810	81,490	88,133	101,064	113,398
White................................	50,015	55,957	61,959	68,056	74,171	80,250	92,084	103,384
Black or African American..........	2,675	2,997	3,321	3,650	3,984	4,323	5,002	5,665
American Indian and Alaska Native..	1,645	1,810	1,975	2,139	2,298	2,451	2,729	2,970
Asian................................	560	614	670	727	786	847	968	1,086
Native Hawaiian/Other Pacific Islander.........	197	211	225	238	251	262	282	293
Two or more races..................	1,663	1,961	2,289	2,653	3,054	3,493	4,486	5,646
Race alone or in combination: [1]								
White................................	51,494	57,713	64,019	70,455	76,943	83,434	96,205	108,605
Black or African American..........	3,429	3,912	4,416	4,947	5,509	6,103	7,375	8,756
American Indian and Alaska Native..	2,361	2,623	2,889	3,158	3,426	3,690	4,194	4,662
Asian................................	1,021	1,157	1,305	1,467	1,644	1,837	2,264	2,753
Native Hawaiian/Other Pacific Islander.........	354	392	432	475	519	567	666	774
PERCENT DISTRIBUTION								
Total................................	**100.0**	**100.0**	**100.0**	**100.0**	**100.0**	**100.0**	**100.0**	**100.0**
Not Hispanic..........................	**82.3**	**81.0**	**79.7**	**78.4**	**77.2**	**75.9**	**73.5**	**71.4**
One race..............................	80.3	78.7	77.2	75.6	74.0	72.5	69.4	66.5
White................................	61.7	59.6	57.5	55.5	53.4	51.3	47.3	43.6
Black or African American..........	12.4	12.4	12.5	12.6	12.6	12.7	12.8	13.0
American Indian and Alaska Native..	0.7	0.7	0.7	0.7	0.7	0.7	0.7	0.6
Asian................................	5.3	5.8	6.2	6.7	7.1	7.6	8.4	9.1
Native Hawaiian/Other Pacific Islander.........	0.2	0.2	0.2	0.2	0.2	0.2	0.2	0.2
Two or more races..................	2.1	2.3	2.6	2.8	3.1	3.4	4.1	4.9
Hispanic [2]............................	**17.7**	**19.0**	**20.3**	**21.6**	**22.8**	**24.1**	**26.5**	**28.6**
One race..............................	17.1	18.4	19.6	20.8	22.0	23.2	25.4	27.2
White................................	15.6	16.7	17.8	18.9	20.0	21.1	23.1	24.8
Black or African American..........	0.8	0.9	1.0	1.0	1.1	1.1	1.3	1.4
American Indian and Alaska Native..	0.5	0.5	0.6	0.6	0.6	0.6	0.7	0.7
Asian................................	0.2	0.2	0.2	0.2	0.2	0.2	0.2	0.3
Native Hawaiian/Other Pacific Islander.........	0.1	0.1	0.1	0.1	0.1	0.1	0.1	0.1
Two or more races..................	0.5	0.6	0.7	0.7	0.8	0.9	1.1	1.4

[1] In combination with one or more other races. The sum of the five race groups adds to more than the total population because individuals may report more than one race. The original race data from Census 2010 are modified to eliminate the "some other race" category. [2] Persons of Hispanic origin may be of any race.

Source: U.S. Census Bureau, "Table 10. Projections of the Population by Sex, Hispanic Origin, and Race for the United States: 2015 to 2060 (NP2014-T10)," December 2014, <http://www.census.gov/population/projections/data/national/2014/summarytables.html>, accessed March 2015.

Table 14. Resident Population—States: 1990 to 2014

[In thousands (248,791 represents 248,791,000). 1990, 2000, and 2010 data as of April 1, data for other years as of July 1. Insofar as possible, population shown for all years is that of present area of state. See Appendix III]

State	1990, estimates base [1]	2000, estimates base [2]	2005	2009	2010, estimates base [3]	2011	2012	2013	2014
United States	**248,791**	**281,425**	**295,517**	**306,772**	**308,758**	**311,722**	**314,112**	**316,498**	**318,857**
Alabama	4,040	4,447	4,570	4,758	4,780	4,802	4,817	4,834	4,849
Alaska	550	627	667	699	710	723	731	737	737
Arizona	3,665	5,130	5,839	6,343	6,392	6,473	6,556	6,635	6,731
Arkansas	2,351	2,673	2,781	2,897	2,916	2,938	2,949	2,959	2,966
California	29,811	33,872	35,828	36,961	37,255	37,702	38,063	38,431	38,803
Colorado	3,294	4,302	4,632	4,972	5,029	5,120	5,192	5,272	5,356
Connecticut	3,287	3,406	3,507	3,562	3,574	3,591	3,594	3,599	3,597
Delaware	666	784	845	892	898	908	917	925	936
District of Columbia	607	572	567	592	602	620	635	649	659
Florida	12,938	15,983	17,842	18,653	18,805	19,108	19,355	19,600	19,893
Georgia	6,478	8,187	8,926	9,621	9,689	9,813	9,919	9,995	10,097
Hawaii	1,108	1,211	1,293	1,347	1,360	1,378	1,393	1,409	1,420
Idaho	1,007	1,294	1,428	1,554	1,568	1,584	1,596	1,613	1,634
Illinois	11,431	12,420	12,610	12,797	12,832	12,859	12,874	12,891	12,881
Indiana	5,544	6,081	6,279	6,459	6,484	6,517	6,538	6,571	6,597
Iowa	2,777	2,927	2,964	3,033	3,047	3,065	3,076	3,092	3,107
Kansas	2,478	2,689	2,745	2,833	2,853	2,870	2,886	2,896	2,904
Kentucky	3,687	4,042	4,183	4,317	4,339	4,370	4,383	4,400	4,413
Louisiana	4,222	4,469	4,577	4,492	4,533	4,576	4,605	4,629	4,650
Maine	1,228	1,275	1,319	1,330	1,328	1,328	1,329	1,329	1,330
Maryland	4,781	5,297	5,592	5,730	5,774	5,844	5,892	5,939	5,976
Massachusetts	6,016	6,349	6,403	6,518	6,548	6,612	6,656	6,709	6,745
Michigan	9,295	9,939	10,051	9,902	9,884	9,876	9,885	9,898	9,910
Minnesota	4,376	4,920	5,120	5,281	5,304	5,348	5,381	5,422	5,457
Mississippi	2,575	2,845	2,906	2,959	2,968	2,978	2,986	2,992	2,994
Missouri	5,117	5,597	5,790	5,961	5,989	6,011	6,025	6,045	6,064
Montana	799	902	940	984	989	998	1,005	1,015	1,024
Nebraska	1,578	1,711	1,761	1,813	1,826	1,842	1,855	1,869	1,882
Nevada	1,202	1,998	2,432	2,685	2,701	2,719	2,755	2,791	2,839
New Hampshire	1,109	1,236	1,298	1,316	1,316	1,318	1,321	1,323	1,327
New Jersey	7,748	8,415	8,652	8,756	8,792	8,843	8,876	8,912	8,938
New Mexico	1,515	1,819	1,932	2,037	2,059	2,078	2,085	2,087	2,086
New York	17,991	18,977	19,133	19,307	19,378	19,522	19,607	19,696	19,746
North Carolina	6,632	8,046	8,705	9,450	9,536	9,652	9,748	9,849	9,944
North Dakota	639	642	646	665	673	685	702	724	739
Ohio	10,847	11,353	11,463	11,529	11,537	11,545	11,551	11,572	11,594
Oklahoma	3,146	3,450	3,549	3,718	3,752	3,787	3,817	3,853	3,878
Oregon	2,842	3,422	3,613	3,809	3,831	3,868	3,899	3,928	3,970
Pennsylvania	11,883	12,281	12,450	12,667	12,703	12,744	12,770	12,781	12,787
Rhode Island	1,003	1,048	1,068	1,054	1,053	1,052	1,053	1,053	1,055
South Carolina	3,486	4,012	4,270	4,590	4,625	4,673	4,723	4,772	4,832
South Dakota	696	755	775	807	814	824	835	846	853
Tennessee	4,877	5,689	5,991	6,306	6,346	6,398	6,455	6,497	6,549
Texas	16,986	20,851	22,778	24,802	25,146	25,657	26,094	26,506	26,957
Utah	1,723	2,233	2,458	2,723	2,764	2,815	2,855	2,903	2,943
Vermont	563	609	621	625	626	626	626	627	627
Virginia	6,189	7,079	7,577	7,926	8,001	8,110	8,193	8,270	8,326
Washington	4,867	5,894	6,257	6,667	6,725	6,822	6,896	6,974	7,062
West Virginia	1,793	1,808	1,820	1,848	1,853	1,855	1,856	1,854	1,850
Wisconsin	4,892	5,364	5,546	5,669	5,687	5,709	5,725	5,743	5,758
Wyoming	454	494	514	560	564	568	577	583	584

[1] The April 1, 1990 census counts include corrections processed through August 1997, results of special censuses and test censuses, and do not include adjustments for census coverage errors. [2] The April 1, 2000 population estimates base reflects changes to the Census 2000 population from the Count Question Resolution program, legal boundary updates, and other geographic program revisions. [3] The April 1, 2010 population estimates base reflects changes to the Census 2010 population from the Count Question Resolution program and geographic program revisions.

Source: U.S. Census Bureau, "Table CO-EST2001-12-00 - Time Series of Intercensal State Population Estimates: April 1, 1990 to April 1, 2000," April 2002, <http://www.census.gov/popest/data/intercensal/st-co/files/CO-EST2001-12-00.pdf>; "Table 1. Intercensal Estimates of the Resident Population for the United States, Regions, States, and Puerto Rico: April 1, 2000 to July 1, 2010 (ST-EST00INT-01)," September 2011, <http://www.census.gov/popest/data/intercensal/state/state2010.html>; and "Table 1. Annual Estimates of the Population for the United States, Regions, States, and Puerto Rico: April 1, 2010 to July 1, 2014 (NST-EST2014-01)," December 2014, <http://www.census.gov/popest/data/state/totals/2014/index.html>.

Table 15. State Population—Rank, Percent Change, and Population Density: 1990 to 2014

[As of April 1, except 2014 as of July 1. Insofar as possible, population shown for all years is that of present area of state. For land area by State, see Table 387. Minus sign (-) indicates decrease. See Appendix III]

State	Rank				Percent change			Population per square mile of land area [1]		
	1990	2000	2010	2014	1990–2000	2000–2010	2010–2014 [2]	2000	2010	2014
United States	(X)	(X)	(X)	(X)	**13.1**	**9.7**	**3.3**	**79.7**	**87.4**	**90.3**
Alabama	22	23	23	23	10.1	7.5	1.4	87.8	94.4	95.8
Alaska	49	48	47	48	14.0	13.3	3.7	1.1	1.2	1.3
Arizona	24	20	16	15	40.0	24.6	5.3	45.2	56.3	59.3
Arkansas	33	33	32	32	13.7	9.1	1.7	51.4	56.0	57.0
California	1	1	1	1	13.8	10.0	4.2	217.4	239.1	249.1
Colorado	26	24	22	22	30.6	16.9	6.5	41.5	48.5	51.7
Connecticut	27	29	29	29	3.6	4.9	0.6	703.3	738.1	742.8
Delaware	46	45	45	45	17.6	14.6	4.2	402.1	460.8	480.2
District of Columbia	(X)	(X)	(X)	(X)	-5.7	5.2	9.5	9,370.6	9,856.5	10,792.7
Florida	4	4	4	3	23.5	17.6	5.8	298.0	350.6	371.0
Georgia	11	10	9	8	26.4	18.3	4.2	142.3	168.4	175.6
Hawaii	41	42	40	40	9.3	12.3	4.4	188.6	211.8	221.0
Idaho	42	39	39	39	28.5	21.1	4.3	15.7	19.0	19.8
Illinois	6	5	5	5	8.6	3.3	0.4	223.7	231.1	232.0
Indiana	14	14	15	16	9.7	6.6	1.7	169.7	181.0	184.1
Iowa	30	30	30	30	5.4	4.1	2.0	52.4	54.5	55.6
Kansas	32	32	33	34	8.5	6.1	1.8	32.9	34.9	35.5
Kentucky	23	25	26	26	9.6	7.4	1.7	102.4	109.9	111.8
Louisiana	21	22	25	25	5.9	1.4	2.6	103.4	104.9	107.6
Maine	38	40	41	41	3.8	4.2	0.1	41.3	43.1	43.1
Maryland	19	19	19	19	10.8	9.0	3.5	545.6	594.8	615.7
Massachusetts	13	13	14	14	5.5	3.1	3.0	814.0	839.4	864.8
Michigan	8	8	8	10	6.9	-0.6	0.3	175.8	174.8	175.3
Minnesota	20	21	21	21	12.4	7.8	2.9	61.8	66.6	68.5
Mississippi	31	31	31	31	10.5	4.3	0.9	60.6	63.2	63.8
Missouri	15	17	18	18	9.3	7.0	1.2	81.4	87.1	88.2
Montana	44	44	44	44	12.9	9.7	3.5	6.2	6.8	7.0
Nebraska	36	38	38	37	8.4	6.7	3.0	22.3	23.8	24.5
Nevada	39	35	35	35	66.3	35.1	5.1	18.2	24.6	25.9
New Hampshire	40	41	42	42	11.4	6.5	0.8	138.0	147.0	148.2
New Jersey	9	9	11	11	8.9	4.5	1.7	1,144.2	1,195.5	1,215.4
New Mexico	37	36	36	36	20.1	13.2	1.3	15.0	17.0	17.2
New York	2	3	3	4	5.5	2.1	1.9	402.7	411.2	419.0
North Carolina	10	11	10	9	21.4	18.5	4.3	165.6	196.1	204.5
North Dakota	47	47	48	47	0.5	4.7	9.9	9.3	9.7	10.7
Ohio	7	7	7	7	4.7	1.6	0.5	277.8	282.3	283.7
Oklahoma	28	27	28	28	9.7	8.7	3.4	50.3	54.7	56.5
Oregon	29	28	27	27	20.4	12.0	3.6	35.6	39.9	41.4
Pennsylvania	5	6	6	6	3.4	3.4	0.7	274.5	283.9	285.8
Rhode Island	43	43	43	43	4.5	0.4	0.2	1,014.0	1,018.1	1,020.7
South Carolina	25	26	24	24	15.1	15.3	4.5	133.5	153.9	160.8
South Dakota	45	46	46	46	8.5	7.9	4.8	10.0	10.7	11.3
Tennessee	17	16	17	17	16.7	11.5	3.2	138.0	153.9	158.8
Texas	3	2	2	2	22.8	20.6	7.2	79.8	96.3	103.2
Utah	35	34	34	33	29.6	23.8	6.5	27.2	33.6	35.8
Vermont	48	49	49	49	8.2	2.8	0.1	66.1	67.9	68.0
Virginia	12	12	12	12	14.4	13.0	4.1	179.2	202.6	210.8
Washington	18	15	13	13	21.1	14.1	5.0	88.7	101.2	106.3
West Virginia	34	37	37	38	0.8	2.5	-0.1	75.2	77.1	77.0
Wisconsin	16	18	20	20	9.6	6.0	1.2	99.0	105.0	106.3
Wyoming	50	50	50	50	8.9	14.1	3.6	5.1	5.8	6.0

X Not applicable. [1] Persons per square mile were calculated on the basis of land area data from the 2010 census. [2] Based on 2010 population estimates base that reflects changes to the Census 2010 population from the Count Question Resolution program and geographic program revisions.

Source: U.S. Census Bureau, *2000 Census of Population and Housing, PHC-3-1, United States Summary*, 2004, <http://www.census.gov/prod/cen2000/phc3-us-pt1.pdf>; *2010 Census Briefs, Population Distribution and Change: 2000 to 2010*, March 2011, <http://www.census.gov/prod/cen2010/briefs/c2010br-01.pdf>; and "Table 1. Annual Estimates of the Population for the United States, Regions, States, and Puerto Rico: April 1, 2010 to July 1, 2014 (NST-EST2014-01)," December 2014, <http://www.census.gov/popest/data/state/totals/2014/index.html>.

Table 16. State Resident Population—Components of Change: 2010 to 2014

[Covers period April 1, 2010 to July 1, 2014. Minus sign (-) indicates net decrease or net outflow]

State	Numeric population change [1]	Births	Deaths	Natural increase (births minus deaths)	Net migration		
					Total	International [2]	Domestic
United States..........	**10,098,951**	**16,811,002**	**10,775,362**	**6,035,640**	**4,063,311**	**4,063,311**	**(X)**
Alabama.................	69,250	249,818	207,826	41,992	26,687	23,159	3,528
Alaska..................	26,483	47,988	17,081	30,907	-4,700	9,311	-14,011
Arizona.................	339,174	367,725	210,702	157,023	172,848	56,493	116,355
Arkansas................	50,411	162,691	124,578	38,113	13,316	13,118	198
California...............	1,547,997	2,144,767	1,041,844	1,102,923	459,574	648,856	-189,282
Colorado................	326,542	278,842	140,585	138,257	183,324	43,208	140,116
Connecticut.............	22,581	156,554	124,313	32,241	-5,861	69,991	-75,852
Delaware................	37,678	47,400	33,845	13,555	23,974	9,921	14,053
District of Columbia......	57,126	39,983	20,670	19,313	37,229	15,126	22,103
Florida..................	1,088,674	908,600	760,861	147,739	917,135	467,201	449,934
Georgia.................	408,662	556,992	308,766	248,226	151,661	102,677	48,984
Hawaii..................	59,260	80,734	45,388	35,346	24,911	35,968	-11,057
Idaho...................	66,812	96,826	49,597	47,229	18,656	6,766	11,890
Illinois..................	48,993	678,650	433,772	244,878	-190,144	128,843	-318,987
Indiana.................	112,663	353,871	246,674	107,197	8,366	41,995	-33,629
Iowa....................	60,257	163,391	118,503	44,888	16,872	21,447	-4,575
Kansas.................	50,889	170,209	104,162	66,047	-15,299	24,874	-40,173
Kentucky................	74,108	235,345	181,384	53,961	21,472	25,060	-3,588
Louisiana...............	116,197	264,495	176,623	87,872	28,462	31,499	-3,037
Maine..................	1,728	53,972	55,009	-1,037	2,768	5,517	-2,749
Maryland................	202,622	310,306	191,599	118,707	86,740	118,187	-31,447
Massachusetts...........	197,591	309,219	228,008	81,211	122,642	151,731	-29,089
Michigan................	25,744	481,063	381,059	100,004	-72,674	80,485	-153,159
Minnesota..............	153,248	291,521	168,050	123,471	31,088	56,239	-25,151
Mississippi.............	25,976	165,775	123,715	42,060	-16,999	9,779	-26,778
Missouri................	74,666	321,112	236,479	84,633	-8,048	35,491	-43,539
Montana................	34,162	51,465	38,383	13,082	20,502	3,240	17,262
Nebraska...............	55,162	109,785	63,958	45,827	10,030	15,473	-5,443
Nevada.................	138,407	149,568	88,521	61,047	74,737	33,685	41,052
New Hampshire..........	10,347	53,225	45,357	7,868	3,013	8,137	-5,124
New Jersey.............	146,239	444,933	300,194	144,739	6,968	211,165	-204,197
New Mexico.............	26,380	115,471	70,216	45,255	-18,886	10,869	-29,755
New York...............	368,115	1,023,877	638,192	385,685	-1,626	485,224	-486,850
North Carolina...........	408,273	511,558	345,465	166,093	233,880	90,452	143,428
North Dakota............	66,891	42,376	25,140	17,236	48,867	5,521	43,346
Ohio....................	57,438	586,295	471,142	115,153	-50,959	71,072	-122,031
Oklahoma...............	126,435	224,135	157,577	66,558	58,870	23,852	35,018
Oregon.................	139,166	191,586	139,246	52,340	85,464	27,111	58,353
Pennsylvania............	84,325	604,903	539,878	65,025	29,004	118,159	-89,155
Rhode Island............	2,242	46,520	40,353	6,167	-3,441	17,656	-21,097
South Carolina...........	207,081	244,058	182,009	62,049	139,545	27,161	112,384
South Dakota............	38,984	51,014	30,398	20,616	18,038	5,951	12,087
Tennessee..............	203,077	339,088	258,632	80,456	121,745	37,402	84,343
Texas..................	1,810,854	1,626,353	733,219	893,134	905,754	343,093	562,661
Utah....................	179,017	218,387	64,878	153,509	25,597	21,857	3,740
Vermont................	817	25,598	22,735	2,863	-1,653	2,852	-4,505
Virginia.................	325,266	437,406	259,805	177,601	145,072	141,687	3,385
Washington.............	336,987	370,520	214,584	155,936	179,873	95,873	84,000
West Virginia............	-2,707	87,357	92,030	-4,673	3,010	4,756	-1,746
Wisconsin...............	70,275	285,690	203,329	82,361	-11,288	26,088	-37,376
Wyoming................	20,386	31,985	19,028	12,957	7,195	2,033	5,162

X Not applicable. [1] Total population change includes a residual. This residual represents the change in population that cannot be attributed to any specific demographic component. [2] Net international migration includes the international migration of both native and foreign-born populations. Specifically, it includes: (a) the net international migration of the foreign born, (b) the net migration between the United States and Puerto Rico, (c) the net migration of natives to and from the United States, and (d) the net movement of the Armed Forces population between the United States and overseas.

Source: U.S. Census Bureau, Population Division, "Cumulative Estimates of the Components of Resident Population Change for the United States, Regions, States, and Puerto Rico: April 1, 2010 to July 1, 2014 (NST-EST2014-04)," December 2014, <http://www.census.gov/popest/data/state/totals/2014/index.html>, accessed March 2015.

Table 17. Resident Population by Age and State: 2014

[In thousands, except percent (318,857 represents 318,857,000). As of July 1]

State	Total	Under 5 years	5 to 14 years	15 to 24 years	25 to 34 years	35 to 44 years	45 to 54 years	55 to 64 years	65 to 74 years	75 to 84 years	85 years and over	Percent 65 years old and over
U.S......	318,857	19,877	41,191	43,980	43,517	40,513	43,459	40,078	26,398	13,683	6,162	14.5
AL........	4,849	295	622	671	626	606	657	629	435	225	84	15.3
AK........	737	55	102	112	118	90	98	93	47	17	6	9.4
AZ........	6,731	431	919	944	898	837	840	794	622	323	125	15.9
AR........	2,966	192	396	406	387	365	386	370	270	141	55	15.7
CA........	38,803	2,516	5,080	5,552	5,723	5,175	5,244	4,520	2,834	1,470	689	12.9
CO........	5,356	335	709	726	799	723	714	670	410	188	82	12.7
CT........	3,597	189	440	496	441	439	547	487	305	161	90	15.5
DE........	936	56	114	124	124	110	130	124	91	45	18	16.4
DC........	659	43	57	96	150	93	77	69	42	21	11	11.3
FL........	19,893	1,084	2,264	2,488	2,532	2,422	2,737	2,574	2,083	1,187	522	19.1
GA........	10,097	663	1,414	1,438	1,383	1,370	1,399	1,179	769	351	131	12.4
HI........	1,420	91	169	186	211	176	178	180	127	65	37	16.1
ID........	1,634	114	246	227	215	200	199	200	139	67	27	14.3
IL........	12,881	791	1,680	1,770	1,781	1,680	1,772	1,619	1,002	530	256	13.9
IN........	6,597	419	891	941	846	825	891	842	536	279	126	14.3
IA........	3,107	195	408	443	392	363	407	407	260	153	79	15.8
KS........	2,904	201	404	421	388	345	369	362	226	126	64	14.3
KY........	4,413	276	566	601	566	561	611	578	385	193	76	14.8
LA........	4,650	309	621	650	670	566	613	588	371	188	74	13.6
ME........	1,330	65	146	161	153	155	201	206	140	71	32	18.3
MD........	5,976	370	752	791	829	769	878	765	477	234	111	13.8
MA........	6,745	366	774	949	930	838	987	885	563	296	157	15.1
MI........	9,910	570	1,250	1,407	1,201	1,189	1,396	1,366	872	447	211	15.4
MN........	5,457	349	720	721	747	670	758	712	432	232	117	14.3
MS........	2,994	194	415	434	392	369	390	373	249	129	50	14.3
MO........	6,064	374	781	831	803	732	820	791	525	282	125	15.4
MT........	1,024	61	126	139	129	116	131	150	100	49	22	16.7
NE........	1,882	130	262	266	253	225	239	235	145	84	42	14.4
NV........	2,839	176	376	366	407	383	384	346	251	113	38	14.2
NH........	1,327	65	151	180	154	158	210	198	124	59	28	15.9
NJ........	8,938	533	1,125	1,152	1,148	1,174	1,339	1,154	727	391	195	14.7
NM........	2,086	137	282	291	280	243	264	269	187	95	37	15.3
NY........	19,746	1,185	2,314	2,706	2,847	2,508	2,789	2,500	1,602	867	429	14.7
NC........	9,944	607	1,297	1,371	1,292	1,303	1,368	1,243	868	425	170	14.7
ND........	739	51	91	120	108	82	90	92	54	33	18	14.2
OH........	11,594	691	1,484	1,563	1,471	1,407	1,603	1,576	1,006	542	251	15.5
OK........	3,878	265	532	547	533	472	491	475	323	172	68	14.5
OR........	3,970	229	481	512	544	517	512	541	374	176	84	16.0
PA........	12,787	715	1,508	1,705	1,640	1,513	1,805	1,768	1,153	651	331	16.7
RI........	1,055	55	119	156	139	125	153	142	90	48	28	15.7
SC........	4,832	291	613	663	628	596	649	631	466	215	80	15.8
SD........	853	61	116	120	112	96	107	112	69	40	21	15.3
TN........	6,549	400	840	886	858	840	897	842	586	288	111	15.1
TX........	26,957	1,956	4,001	3,906	3,926	3,635	3,472	2,962	1,834	904	362	11.5
UT........	2,943	252	511	474	441	386	307	277	172	88	35	10.0
VT........	627	30	68	90	72	72	92	96	62	30	14	16.9
VA........	8,326	515	1,042	1,142	1,175	1,089	1,176	1,040	679	329	139	13.8
WA........	7,062	447	888	937	1,021	919	946	912	590	274	129	14.1
WV........	1,850	102	212	236	219	230	252	270	191	99	39	17.8
WI........	5,758	341	734	788	730	691	817	780	484	264	128	15.2
WY........	584	38	77	80	83	70	73	81	48	23	10	14.0

Source: U.S. Census Bureau, "Annual Estimates of the Resident Population for Selected Age Groups by Sex for the United States, States, Counties, and Puerto Rico Commonwealth and Municipios: April 1, 2010 to July 1, 2014," <http://factfinder.census.gov>, accessed July 2015.

Table 18. Age Dependency Ratios by State: 2000 to 2014

[As of April, except 2014 as of July]

State	Age dependency ratio [1]			Child dependency ratio [2]			Old-age dependency ratio [3]		
	2000	2010	2014	2000	2010	2014	2000	2010	2014
United States......	**61.6**	**58.9**	**60.2**	**41.5**	**38.2**	**37.0**	**20.1**	**20.7**	**23.2**
Alabama...............	62.1	59.9	61.8	40.9	37.9	36.9	21.1	22.0	24.8
Alaska................	56.5	51.8	53.2	47.6	40.0	38.8	8.9	11.7	14.4
Arizona...............	65.7	64.7	66.6	44.2	42.0	40.1	21.6	22.7	26.5
Arkansas..............	65.1	63.4	65.4	42.0	39.9	39.4	23.1	23.5	26.0
California............	61.1	57.1	57.4	44.0	39.2	37.1	17.1	17.9	20.3
Colorado..............	54.5	54.6	56.2	39.5	37.7	36.3	14.9	16.9	19.8
Connecticut...........	62.7	58.8	58.8	40.2	36.3	34.2	22.5	22.5	24.5
Delaware..............	60.8	59.5	62.0	39.9	36.6	35.4	20.9	23.0	26.7
District of Columbia....	47.8	39.3	40.5	29.7	23.3	24.6	18.1	15.9	15.9
Florida...............	67.7	62.9	65.1	38.3	34.7	33.6	29.5	28.2	31.5
Georgia...............	56.5	57.2	59.0	41.5	40.4	39.2	15.0	16.7	19.7
Hawaii................	60.4	57.9	60.8	39.2	35.3	34.9	21.3	22.7	25.8
Idaho.................	66.1	66.1	68.5	47.4	45.5	44.4	18.7	20.6	24.1
Illinois..............	61.8	58.6	58.9	42.3	38.7	36.9	19.5	19.9	22.1
Indiana...............	62.0	60.7	61.9	41.9	39.9	38.8	20.1	20.9	23.1
Iowa..................	66.6	63.3	64.4	41.8	39.0	38.4	24.8	24.3	26.0
Kansas................	66.0	63.0	64.5	44.0	41.5	40.9	22.0	21.5	23.5
Kentucky..............	59.0	58.5	60.7	39.1	37.4	36.9	19.9	21.1	23.8
Louisiana.............	63.6	58.6	60.2	44.6	39.1	38.4	18.9	19.5	21.8
Maine.................	61.3	57.6	60.7	38.1	32.6	31.3	23.2	25.0	29.4
Maryland..............	58.5	55.5	57.1	40.6	36.4	35.5	17.9	19.1	21.6
Massachusetts.........	59.2	54.9	55.5	37.6	33.6	32.0	21.6	21.4	23.4
Michigan..............	62.3	60.0	61.0	42.4	37.9	36.1	19.9	22.0	24.9
Minnesota.............	61.9	59.0	60.7	42.4	38.5	37.8	19.6	20.5	23.0
Mississippi...........	64.8	62.0	63.2	44.9	41.2	39.9	19.9	20.8	23.4
Missouri..............	64.0	60.8	62.2	41.8	38.3	37.2	22.1	22.5	24.9
Montana...............	63.7	59.8	63.1	41.7	36.1	35.9	21.9	23.7	27.3
Nebraska..............	66.3	63.0	64.5	43.8	41.0	40.8	22.6	22.0	23.7
Nevada................	57.6	57.8	60.0	40.4	38.9	37.4	17.3	19.0	22.7
New Hampshire.........	58.8	54.7	56.4	39.8	33.8	31.5	19.0	20.9	24.9
New Jersey............	61.4	58.7	59.3	40.0	37.3	35.8	21.4	21.4	23.4
New Mexico............	65.6	62.4	64.9	46.3	40.9	39.7	19.3	21.5	25.2
New York..............	60.3	55.8	56.5	39.6	34.8	33.5	20.7	21.1	23.0
North Carolina........	57.3	58.4	60.6	38.4	37.9	36.9	19.0	20.5	23.6
North Dakota..........	66.0	58.2	58.7	41.6	35.2	36.2	24.4	22.9	22.5
Ohio..................	63.2	60.6	62.0	41.5	38.0	36.9	21.7	22.6	25.1
Oklahoma..............	64.1	62.1	64.1	42.4	40.2	40.3	21.7	21.9	23.8
Oregon................	60.1	57.6	60.2	39.6	35.6	34.6	20.5	21.9	25.6
Pennsylvania..........	65.1	59.8	60.8	39.3	35.1	34.0	25.8	24.6	26.8
Rhode Island..........	61.8	55.5	56.1	38.2	33.1	31.5	23.5	22.5	24.6
South Carolina........	59.4	58.8	61.8	40.1	37.1	36.3	19.3	21.7	25.5
South Dakota..........	70.0	64.5	66.5	45.6	41.0	41.1	24.4	23.6	25.4
Tennessee.............	58.6	58.8	61.0	39.0	37.4	36.7	19.6	21.4	24.2
Texas.................	61.7	60.4	61.0	45.7	43.8	42.5	16.1	16.6	18.5
Utah..................	68.6	68.2	68.8	54.3	53.0	51.9	14.4	15.2	16.9
Vermont...............	58.6	54.3	57.1	38.4	31.9	30.5	20.2	22.5	26.6
Virginia..............	55.6	54.7	56.8	38.2	35.9	35.2	17.4	18.9	21.6
Washington............	58.5	55.8	58.1	40.7	36.6	35.9	17.8	19.2	22.2
West Virginia.........	60.2	58.6	62.1	35.6	33.2	33.3	24.5	25.5	28.8
Wisconsin.............	62.9	59.3	60.8	41.6	37.5	36.3	21.3	21.8	24.5
Wyoming...............	60.7	57.4	60.4	41.9	37.8	38.0	18.8	19.6	22.4

[1] The age dependency ratio is derived by dividing the combined under age 18 and age 65-and-over populations by the age 18-to-64 population and multiplying by 100. [2] The child dependency ratio is derived by dividing the population under 18 by the 18-to-64 population and multiplying by 100. [3] The old-age dependency ratio is derived by dividing the population 65 and over by the 18-to-64 population and multiplying by 100.

Source: U.S. Census Bureau, Census 2010 Briefs, "Age and Sex Composition: 2010," May 2011; and "Annual Estimates of the Resident Population for Selected Age Groups by Sex for the United States, States, Counties, and Puerto Rico Commonwealth and Municipios: April 1, 2010 to July 1, 2014," <http://factfinder.census.gov>, accessed July 2015.

Table 19. Resident Population by Hispanic Origin and State: 2014

[In thousands, except as indicated (318,857 represents 318,857,000). As of July 1. Hispanic origin is considered an ethnicity, not a race. Persons of Hispanic origin may be of any race]

State	Number (1,000)				Percent		
	Total population	Hispanic or Latino	Total Non-Hispanic	Non-Hispanic White alone	Hispanic or Latino	Total Non-Hispanic	Non-Hispanic White alone
U.S...........	318,857	55,388	263,470	197,871	17.4	82.6	62.1
AL.............	4,849	201	4,649	3,210	4.1	95.9	66.2
AK.............	737	50	687	456	6.8	93.2	61.9
AZ.............	6,731	2,056	4,675	3,784	30.5	69.5	56.2
AR.............	2,966	209	2,758	2,177	7.0	93.0	73.4
CA.............	38,803	14,989	23,814	14,920	38.6	61.4	38.5
CO.............	5,356	1,135	4,221	3,695	21.2	78.8	69.0
CT.............	3,597	541	3,056	2,475	15.0	85.0	68.8
DE.............	936	83	852	596	8.9	91.1	63.7
DC.............	659	68	591	236	10.4	89.6	35.8
FL.............	19,893	4,789	15,104	11,103	24.1	75.9	55.8
GA.............	10,097	935	9,162	5,487	9.3	90.7	54.3
HI.............	1,420	143	1,276	326	10.1	89.9	23.0
ID.............	1,634	197	1,438	1,353	12.0	88.0	82.8
IL.............	12,881	2,153	10,728	8,023	16.7	83.3	62.3
IN.............	6,597	432	6,165	5,297	6.6	93.4	80.3
IA.............	3,107	174	2,934	2,706	5.6	94.4	87.1
KS.............	2,904	330	2,574	2,229	11.4	88.6	76.8
KY.............	4,413	149	4,264	3,768	3.4	96.6	85.4
LA.............	4,650	225	4,425	2,759	4.8	95.2	59.3
ME.............	1,330	20	1,310	1,247	1.5	98.5	93.8
MD.............	5,976	557	5,419	3,145	9.3	90.7	52.6
MA.............	6,745	731	6,014	5,011	10.8	89.2	74.3
MI.............	9,910	476	9,434	7,513	4.8	95.2	75.8
MN.............	5,457	277	5,180	4,444	5.1	94.9	81.4
MS.............	2,994	89	2,905	1,714	3.0	97.0	57.3
MO.............	6,064	240	5,823	4,858	4.0	96.0	80.1
MT.............	1,024	35	988	888	3.5	96.5	86.7
NE.............	1,882	191	1,690	1,514	10.2	89.8	80.5
NV.............	2,839	790	2,049	1,462	27.8	72.2	51.5
NH.............	1,327	44	1,283	1,211	3.3	96.7	91.3
NJ.............	8,938	1,729	7,209	5,081	19.3	80.7	56.8
NM.............	2,086	994	1,091	811	47.7	52.3	38.9
NY.............	19,746	3,673	16,073	11,163	18.6	81.4	56.5
NC.............	9,944	894	9,050	6,374	9.0	91.0	64.1
ND.............	739	23	716	640	3.2	96.8	86.6
OH.............	11,594	403	11,191	9,288	3.5	96.5	80.1
OK.............	3,878	382	3,497	2,599	9.8	90.2	67.0
OR.............	3,970	497	3,473	3,059	12.5	87.5	77.0
PA.............	12,787	839	11,948	9,958	6.6	93.4	77.9
RI.............	1,055	148	907	787	14.0	86.0	74.5
SC.............	4,832	262	4,571	3,086	5.4	94.6	63.9
SD.............	853	31	823	708	3.6	96.4	83.0
TN.............	6,549	329	6,220	4,888	5.0	95.0	74.6
TX.............	26,957	10,411	16,546	11,735	38.6	61.4	43.5
UT.............	2,943	399	2,544	2,335	13.5	86.5	79.3
VT.............	627	11	615	586	1.8	98.2	93.5
VA.............	8,326	737	7,589	5,257	8.9	91.1	63.1
WA.............	7,062	859	6,203	4,970	12.2	87.8	70.4
WV.............	1,850	27	1,823	1,711	1.5	98.5	92.5
WI.............	5,758	372	5,385	4,733	6.5	93.5	82.2
WY.............	584	57	527	491	9.8	90.2	84.1

Source: U.S. Census Bureau, "Annual Estimates of the Resident Population by Sex, Race, and Hispanic Origin for the United States, States, and Counties: April 1, 2010 to July 1, 2014," <http://factfinder.census.gov>, accessed July 2015.

Table 20. Resident Population by Race and State: 2014

[In thousands, except as indicated (318,857 represents 318,857,000). As of July 1]

| State | Number (1,000) | | | | | | | Percent distribution | | | | | |
	Total population	White [1]	Black [1]	American Indian [1,2]	Asian [1]	Native Hawaiian [1,3]	Two or more races	White [1]	Black [1]	American Indian [1,2]	Asian [1]	Native Hawaiian [1,3]	Two or more races
U.S.	318,857	246,661	42,158	3,961	17,339	742	7,996	77.4	13.2	1.2	5.4	0.2	2.5
AL	4,849	3,378	1,293	34	65	5	75	69.7	26.7	0.7	1.3	0.1	1.5
AK	737	493	29	109	45	9	52	66.9	3.9	14.8	6.1	1.3	7.1
AZ	6,731	5,636	318	358	221	18	180	83.7	4.7	5.3	3.3	0.3	2.7
AR	2,966	2,364	463	29	44	7	57	79.7	15.6	1.0	1.5	0.3	1.9
CA	38,803	28,396	2,541	645	5,586	194	1,440	73.2	6.5	1.7	14.4	0.5	3.7
CO	5,356	4,699	239	85	168	10	154	87.7	4.5	1.6	3.1	0.2	2.9
CT	3,597	2,920	414	18	162	4	79	81.2	11.5	0.5	4.5	0.1	2.2
DE	936	662	208	6	35	1	23	70.8	22.2	0.7	3.8	0.1	2.5
DC	659	287	323	4	26	1	17	43.6	49.0	0.6	4.0	0.2	2.6
FL	19,893	15,486	3,337	99	554	22	395	77.8	16.8	0.5	2.8	0.1	2.0
GA	10,097	6,266	3,184	51	387	12	197	62.1	31.5	0.5	3.8	0.1	2.0
HI	1,420	378	35	6	532	141	326	26.7	2.5	0.4	37.5	10.0	23.0
ID	1,634	1,529	14	28	23	3	38	93.5	0.8	1.7	1.4	0.2	2.3
IL	12,881	9,985	1,892	75	685	8	235	77.5	14.7	0.6	5.3	0.1	1.8
IN	6,597	5,678	631	26	132	4	125	86.1	9.6	0.4	2.0	0.1	1.9
IA	3,107	2,861	106	15	69	3	53	92.1	3.4	0.5	2.2	0.1	1.7
KS	2,904	2,522	182	35	81	3	81	86.8	6.3	1.2	2.8	0.1	2.8
KY	4,413	3,895	363	13	61	4	77	88.3	8.2	0.3	1.4	0.1	1.8
LA	4,650	2,946	1,511	35	83	3	72	63.4	32.5	0.8	1.8	0.1	1.5
ME	1,330	1,264	19	9	16	(Z)	22	95.0	1.4	0.7	1.2	(Z)	1.6
MD	5,976	3,590	1,809	33	380	6	158	60.1	30.3	0.6	6.4	0.1	2.6
MA	6,745	5,574	558	32	425	7	149	82.6	8.3	0.5	6.3	0.1	2.2
MI	9,910	7,916	1,410	71	284	4	225	79.9	14.2	0.7	2.9	(Z)	2.3
MN	5,457	4,678	320	72	257	3	127	85.7	5.9	1.3	4.7	0.1	2.3
MS	2,994	1,786	1,123	18	31	2	35	59.7	37.5	0.6	1.0	0.1	1.2
MO	6,064	5,063	715	33	116	9	128	83.5	11.8	0.5	1.9	0.1	2.1
MT	1,024	915	6	67	8	1	27	89.4	0.6	6.6	0.8	0.1	2.6
NE	1,882	1,682	92	26	41	2	38	89.4	4.9	1.4	2.2	0.1	2.0
NV	2,839	2,163	258	47	236	21	113	76.2	9.1	1.6	8.3	0.7	4.0
NH	1,327	1,248	20	4	34	1	21	94.0	1.5	0.3	2.5	(Z)	1.6
NJ	8,938	6,526	1,321	53	844	9	184	73.0	14.8	0.6	9.4	0.1	2.1
NM	2,086	1,726	53	217	35	3	51	82.8	2.5	10.4	1.7	0.2	2.5
NY	19,746	13,907	3,479	190	1,677	26	467	70.4	17.6	1.0	8.5	0.1	2.4
NC	9,944	7,108	2,196	155	267	12	205	71.5	22.1	1.6	2.7	0.1	2.1
ND	739	659	16	40	9	1	15	89.1	2.1	5.4	1.3	0.1	2.0
OH	11,594	9,618	1,464	32	233	6	241	83.0	12.6	0.3	2.0	0.1	2.1
OK	3,878	2,911	300	351	81	6	229	75.1	7.7	9.0	2.1	0.2	5.9
OR	3,970	3,489	81	71	170	17	143	87.9	2.0	1.8	4.3	0.4	3.6
PA	12,787	10,599	1,485	44	418	9	234	82.9	11.6	0.3	3.3	0.1	1.8
RI	1,055	898	81	10	37	2	27	85.1	7.7	0.9	3.5	0.2	2.6
SC	4,832	3,303	1,342	26	74	5	83	68.3	27.8	0.5	1.5	0.1	1.7
SD	853	731	16	76	11	1	19	85.7	1.9	8.9	1.3	0.1	2.2
TN	6,549	5,169	1,119	29	113	6	113	78.9	17.1	0.4	1.7	0.1	1.7
TX	26,957	21,566	3,364	274	1,224	37	492	80.0	12.5	1.0	4.5	0.1	1.8
UT	2,943	2,690	40	45	69	29	69	91.4	1.3	1.5	2.4	1.0	2.4
VT	627	595	8	2	10	(Z)	11	95.0	1.2	0.4	1.6	(Z)	1.8
VA	8,326	5,872	1,639	46	527	10	233	70.5	19.7	0.5	6.3	0.1	2.8
WA	7,062	5,700	287	133	576	50	316	80.7	4.1	1.9	8.2	0.7	4.5
WV	1,850	1,734	67	7	15	1	29	93.7	3.6	0.2	0.8	(Z)	1.6
WI	5,758	5,058	379	64	153	3	102	87.8	6.6	1.1	2.6	(Z)	1.8
WY	584	542	9	16	6	1	11	92.7	1.6	2.7	1.0	0.1	2.0

Z Less than 500 or 0.05 percent. [1] Data shown for each race alone. [2] Includes Alaska Natives. [3] Includes other Pacific Islanders.

Source: U.S. Census Bureau, "Annual Estimates of the Resident Population by Sex, Race, and Hispanic Origin for the United States, States, and Counties: April 1, 2010 to July 1, 2014," <http://factfinder.census.gov>, accessed August 2015.

Table 21. Large Metropolitan Statistical Areas—Population: 2000 to 2014

[In thousands, except as indicated (695 represents 695,000). As of April 1, except 2014 as of July 1. Covers metropolitan statistical areas with 250,000 and over population in 2014, as delineated by the U.S. Office of Management and Budget as of February 2013. For definitions and components of all metropolitan and micropolitan areas, see Appendix II. Minus sign (-) indicates decrease]

Metropolitan statistical area	2000	2010, estimates base [1]	2014	Change 2000–2010 [2] Number	Change 2000–2010 [2] Percent	Change 2010–2014 Number	Change 2010–2014 Percent	Rank, 2014
Akron, OH	695	703	704	8	1.2	1	0.1	78
Albany-Schenectady-Troy, NY	826	871	880	45	5.4	9	1.1	61
Albuquerque, NM	730	887	905	157	21.6	18	2.0	59
Allentown-Bethlehem-Easton, PA-NJ	740	821	830	81	10.9	9	1.0	69
Amarillo, TX	229	252	260	23	10.2	8	3.2	182
Anchorage, AK	320	381	399	61	19.2	18	4.7	134
Ann Arbor, MI	323	345	357	22	6.8	12	3.4	147
Asheville, NC	369	425	442	56	15.1	17	4.1	117
Atlanta-Sandy Springs-Roswell, GA	4,263	5,287	5,614	1,023	24.0	328	6.2	9
Atlantic City-Hammonton, NJ	253	275	275	22	8.7	1	0.2	170
Augusta-Richmond County, GA-SC	508	565	584	57	11.2	19	3.3	92
Austin-Round Rock, TX	1,250	1,716	1,943	467	37.3	227	13.2	35
Bakersfield, CA	662	840	875	178	26.9	35	4.2	62
Baltimore-Columbia-Towson, MD	2,553	2,711	2,786	157	6.2	75	2.8	20
Baton Rouge, LA	706	803	825	97	13.7	23	2.9	70
Beaumont-Port Arthur, TX	400	403	405	3	0.8	2	0.6	130
Birmingham-Hoover, AL	1,052	1,128	1,144	76	7.2	16	1.4	49
Boise City, ID	465	617	664	152	32.6	48	7.8	81
Boston-Cambridge-Newton, MA-NH	4,391	4,552	4,732	161	3.7	180	3.9	10
Boulder, CO [3]	270	295	313	25	9.2	19	6.4	160
Bremerton-Silverdale, WA	232	251	254	19	8.3	3	1.2	185
Bridgeport-Stamford-Norwalk, CT	883	917	945	34	3.9	29	3.1	57
Brownsville-Harlingen, TX	335	406	420	71	21.2	14	3.5	125
Buffalo-Cheektowaga-Niagara Falls, NY	1,170	1,136	1,136	-35	-3.0	1	0.1	50
Canton-Massillon, OH	407	404	404	-3	-0.6	(-Z)	-0.1	133
Cape Coral-Fort Myers, FL	441	619	680	178	40.3	61	9.8	80
Cedar Rapids, IA	237	258	264	21	8.7	6	2.3	179
Charleston-North Charleston, SC	549	665	728	116	21.1	63	9.5	76
Charlotte-Concord-Gastonia, NC-SC	1,717	2,217	2,380	500	29.1	163	7.4	22
Chattanooga, TN-GA	477	528	545	52	10.8	16	3.1	99
Chicago-Naperville-Elgin, IL-IN-WI	9,098	9,462	9,555	363	4.0	93	1.0	3
Cincinnati, OH-KY-IN	1,995	2,115	2,149	120	6.0	35	1.6	28
Clarksville, TN-KY	220	261	278	41	18.7	18	6.8	168
Cleveland-Elyria, OH	2,148	2,077	2,064	-71	-3.3	-14	-0.7	31
Colorado Springs, CO	537	646	687	108	20.1	41	6.4	79
Columbia, SC	647	767	800	120	18.6	33	4.3	72
Columbus, GA-AL	282	296	314	13	4.6	18	6.3	158
Columbus, OH	1,675	1,902	1,995	227	13.5	93	4.9	32
Corpus Christi, TX	403	428	448	25	6.2	20	4.7	113
Crestview-Fort Walton Beach-Destin, FL	211	236	258	25	11.7	22	9.4	183
Dallas-Fort Worth-Arlington, TX	5,204	6,426	6,954	1,222	23.5	528	8.2	4
Davenport-Moline-Rock Island, IA-IL	376	380	383	4	1.0	3	0.9	137
Dayton, OH	806	799	801	-7	-0.8	2	0.2	71
Deltona-Daytona Beach-Ormond Beach, FL	493	590	610	97	19.7	20	3.3	90
Denver-Aurora-Lakewood, CO [3]	2,179	2,544	2,754	364	16.7	211	8.3	21
Des Moines-West Des Moines, IA	481	570	612	88	18.3	42	7.4	89
Detroit-Warren-Dearborn, MI	4,453	4,296	4,297	-156	-3.5	(Z)	(Z)	14
Duluth, MN-WI	275	280	280	4	1.6	(Z)	(Z)	164
Durham-Chapel Hill, NC	426	507	543	78	18.3	36	7.1	100
El Paso, TX	683	804	837	121	17.7	33	4.1	67
Erie, PA	281	281	278	(-Z)	-0.1	-2	-0.8	167
Eugene, OR	323	352	358	29	8.9	7	1.9	146
Evansville, IN-KY	296	312	315	15	5.2	4	1.2	156
Fayetteville, NC	337	366	378	30	8.8	12	3.2	139
Fayetteville-Springdale-Rogers, AR-MO	347	463	502	116	33.5	38	8.3	105
Flint, MI	436	426	413	-10	-2.4	-13	-3.0	129
Fort Collins, CO	251	300	324	48	19.1	24	8.2	152
Fort Smith, AR-OK	255	281	280	25	9.8	-1	-0.3	165
Fort Wayne, IN	390	416	427	26	6.7	11	2.6	123
Fresno, CA	799	930	966	131	16.4	36	3.8	56
Gainesville, FL	232	264	273	32	13.7	9	3.4	173
Grand Rapids-Wyoming, MI	931	989	1,028	58	6.3	39	3.9	52
Greeley, CO [3]	181	253	278	72	39.7	25	9.8	169
Green Bay, WI	283	306	315	24	8.4	8	2.7	157
Greensboro-High Point, NC	643	724	747	80	12.5	23	3.1	74
Greenville-Anderson-Mauldin, SC	726	824	862	98	13.6	38	4.7	63
Gulfport-Biloxi-Pascagoula, MS	364	371	386	7	1.8	15	4.1	136
Hagerstown-Martinsburg, MD-WV	208	252	260	44	21.1	8	3.4	181
Harrisburg-Carlisle, PA	509	549	561	40	7.9	11	2.1	95
Hartford-West Hartford-East Hartford, CT	1,149	1,212	1,214	64	5.6	2	0.2	47
Hickory-Lenoir-Morganton, NC	342	365	363	24	6.9	-3	-0.7	145
Houston-The Woodlands-Sugar Land, TX	4,693	5,920	6,490	1,227	26.1	570	9.6	5
Huntington-Ashland, WV-KY-OH	362	365	363	3	0.7	-2	-0.4	144
Huntsville, AL	342	418	441	75	22.0	23	5.6	118
Indianapolis-Carmel-Anderson, IN	1,658	1,888	1,971	229	13.8	83	4.4	33
Jackson, MS	525	568	578	42	8.0	10	1.7	93

See footnotes at end of table.

Table 21. Large Metropolitan Statistical Areas—Population: 2000 to 2014-Continued.

See headnote on page 24.

Metropolitan statistical area	2000	2010, estimates base [1]	2014	Change 2000–2010 [2] Number	Change 2000–2010 [2] Percent	Change 2010–2014 Number	Change 2010–2014 Percent	Rank, 2014
Jacksonville, FL	1,123	1,346	1,419	223	19.8	74	5.5	40
Kalamazoo-Portage, MI	315	327	334	12	3.7	7	2.3	151
Kansas City, MO-KS	1,811	2,009	2,071	198	10.9	62	3.1	29
Kennewick-Richland, WA	192	253	274	62	32.1	21	8.3	171
Killeen-Temple, TX	331	405	425	75	22.6	20	4.8	124
Kingsport-Bristol-Bristol, TN-VA	298	310	308	11	3.7	-1	-0.5	161
Knoxville, TN	748	838	858	89	11.9	20	2.4	65
Lafayette, LA	425	467	485	42	9.8	18	3.9	108
Lakeland-Winter Haven, FL	484	602	635	118	24.4	33	5.4	85
Lancaster, PA	471	519	533	49	10.4	14	2.7	102
Lansing-East Lansing, MI	448	464	470	16	3.6	6	1.4	110
Laredo, TX	193	250	267	57	29.6	16	6.5	176
Las Vegas-Henderson-Paradise, NV	1,376	1,951	2,070	576	41.8	118	6.1	30
Lexington-Fayette, KY	408	472	494	64	15.6	22	4.7	107
Lincoln, NE	267	302	319	35	13.3	17	5.6	155
Little Rock-North Little Rock-Conway, AR	611	700	729	89	14.6	29	4.2	75
Los Angeles-Long Beach-Anaheim, CA	12,366	12,829	13,262	463	3.7	433	3.4	2
Louisville/Jefferson County, KY-IN	1,121	1,236	1,270	115	10.2	34	2.8	43
Lubbock, TX	256	291	306	35	13.5	15	5.1	162
Lynchburg, VA	229	253	258	24	10.5	5	2.0	184
Madison, WI	535	605	634	70	13.1	28	4.7	86
Manchester-Nashua, NH	381	401	405	20	5.2	4	1.1	131
McAllen-Edinburg-Mission, TX	569	775	831	205	36.1	56	7.3	68
Memphis, TN-MS-AR	1,213	1,325	1,343	112	9.2	18	1.4	41
Merced, CA	211	256	266	45	21.5	11	4.1	177
Miami-Fort Lauderdale-West Palm Beach, FL	5,008	5,566	5,930	557	11.1	364	6.5	8
Milwaukee-Waukesha-West Allis, WI	1,501	1,556	1,572	55	3.7	16	1.0	39
Minneapolis-St. Paul-Bloomington, MN-WI	3,032	3,349	3,495	317	10.5	146	4.4	16
Mobile, AL	400	413	415	13	3.3	2	0.5	127
Modesto, CA	447	514	532	67	15.1	18	3.4	103
Montgomery, AL	347	375	373	28	8.1	-1	-0.4	141
Myrtle Beach-Conway-North Myrtle Beach, SC-NC	270	377	418	107	39.6	41	10.9	126
Naples-Immokalee-Marco Island, FL	251	322	349	70	27.9	27	8.5	148
Nashville-Davidson-Murfreesboro-Franklin, TN	1,381	1,671	1,793	290	21.0	122	7.3	36
New Haven-Milford, CT	824	862	861	38	4.7	-1	-0.1	64
New Orleans-Metairie, LA	1,338	1,190	1,252	-148	-11.1	62	5.2	45
New York-Newark-Jersey City, NY-NJ-PA	18,945	19,566	20,093	623	3.3	526	2.7	1
North Port-Sarasota-Bradenton, FL	590	702	749	112	19.0	46	6.6	73
Norwich-New London, CT	259	274	274	15	5.8	(-Z)	-0.1	172
Ocala, FL	259	331	339	72	28.0	8	2.4	150
Ogden-Clearfield, UT	485	597	632	112	23.0	35	5.9	87
Oklahoma City, OK	1,095	1,253	1,337	158	14.4	84	6.7	42
Olympia-Tumwater, WA	207	252	266	45	21.7	14	5.4	178
Omaha-Council Bluffs, NE-IA	767	865	904	98	12.8	39	4.5	60
Orlando-Kissimmee-Sanford, FL	1,645	2,134	2,321	490	29.8	187	8.8	26
Oxnard-Thousand Oaks-Ventura, CA	753	823	846	70	9.3	23	2.8	66
Palm Bay-Melbourne-Titusville, FL	476	543	557	67	14.1	14	2.5	97
Pensacola-Ferry Pass-Brent, FL	412	449	474	37	8.9	25	5.6	109
Peoria, IL	367	379	380	12	3.3	1	0.2	138
Philadelphia-Camden-Wilmington, PA-NJ-DE-MD	5,687	5,965	6,051	278	4.9	86	1.4	6
Phoenix-Mesa-Scottsdale, AZ	3,252	4,193	4,489	941	28.9	296	7.1	12
Pittsburgh, PA	2,431	2,356	2,356	-75	-3.1	(-Z)	(-Z)	23
Portland-South Portland, ME	488	514	524	27	5.4	9	1.8	104
Portland-Vancouver-Hillsboro, OR-WA	1,928	2,226	2,348	298	15.5	122	5.5	24
Port St. Lucie, FL	319	424	444	105	32.8	20	4.8	115
Providence-Warwick, RI-MA	1,583	1,601	1,609	18	1.1	8	0.5	38
Provo-Orem, UT	377	527	571	150	39.8	45	8.5	94
Raleigh, NC	797	1,130	1,243	333	41.8	112	10.0	46
Reading, PA	374	412	414	38	10.1	2	0.5	128
Reno, NV	343	425	444	83	24.1	19	4.4	116
Richmond, VA	1,056	1,208	1,260	152	14.4	52	4.3	44
Riverside-San Bernardino-Ontario, CA	3,255	4,225	4,442	970	29.8	217	5.1	13
Roanoke, VA	288	309	313	20	7.1	5	1.5	159
Rochester, NY	1,062	1,080	1,083	17	1.6	4	0.3	51
Rockford, IL	320	349	342	29	9.1	-7	-2.0	149
Sacramento-Roseville-Arden-Arcade, CA	1,797	2,149	2,244	352	19.6	95	4.4	27
St. Louis, MO-IL [4]	2,675	2,788	2,806	112	4.2	18	0.7	19
Salem, OR	347	391	404	44	12.5	13	3.4	132
Salinas, CA	402	415	431	13	3.3	16	3.9	121
Salisbury, MD-DE	313	374	390	61	19.6	16	4.3	135
Salt Lake City, UT	939	1,088	1,153	149	15.8	65	6.0	48
San Antonio-New Braunfels, TX	1,712	2,143	2,329	431	25.2	186	8.7	25
San Diego-Carlsbad, CA	2,814	3,095	3,263	281	10.0	168	5.4	17
San Francisco-Oakland-Hayward, CA	4,124	4,336	4,594	212	5.1	259	6.0	11
San Jose-Sunnyvale-Santa Clara, CA	1,736	1,837	1,953	101	5.8	116	6.3	34

See footnotes at end of table.

Metropolitan statistical area	2000	2010, estimates base [1]	2014	Change 2000–2010 [2] Number	Change 2000–2010 [2] Percent	Change 2010–2014 Number	Change 2010–2014 Percent	Rank, 2014
San Luis Obispo-Paso Robles-Arroyo Grande, CA.	247	270	279	23	9.3	9	3.5	166
Santa Cruz-Watsonville, CA.	256	262	272	7	2.7	9	3.6	175
Santa Maria-Santa Barbara, CA.	399	424	441	25	6.1	17	3.9	120
Santa Rosa, CA.	459	484	500	25	5.5	16	3.4	106
Savannah, GA.	293	348	373	55	18.6	25	7.2	142
Scranton-Wilkes-Barre-Hazleton, PA.	561	564	560	3	0.5	-4	-0.7	96
Seattle-Tacoma-Bellevue, WA.	3,044	3,440	3,671	396	13.0	232	6.7	15
Shreveport-Bossier City, LA.	418	440	445	22	5.3	5	1.2	114
South Bend-Mishawaka, IN-MI.	317	319	319	3	0.8	(Z)	(Z)	154
Spartanburg, SC.	284	313	321	30	10.4	8	2.6	153
Spokane-Spokane Valley, WA.	470	528	541	58	12.4	13	2.5	101
Springfield, MA.	608	622	629	13	2.2	7	1.2	88
Springfield, MO.	368	437	452	68	18.6	16	3.6	112
Stockton-Lodi, CA.	564	685	716	122	21.6	30	4.4	77
Syracuse, NY.	650	663	661	12	1.9	-1	-0.2	82
Tallahassee, FL.	320	369	376	47	14.7	7	1.9	140
Tampa-St. Petersburg-Clearwater, FL.	2,396	2,784	2,916	387	16.2	132	4.7	18
Toledo, OH.	618	610	607	-8	-1.3	-3	-0.4	91
Trenton, NJ.	351	368	372	16	4.5	4	1.1	143
Tucson, AZ.	844	980	1,005	137	16.2	24	2.5	53
Tulsa, OK.	860	938	969	78	9.1	32	3.4	55
Urban Honolulu, HI.	876	953	992	77	8.8	39	4.0	54
Utica-Rome, NY.	300	299	297	(-Z)	-0.2	-3	-0.9	163
Vallejo-Fairfield, CA.	395	413	431	19	4.8	18	4.3	122
Virginia Beach-Norfolk-Newport News, VA-NC.	1,580	1,677	1,717	97	6.1	40	2.4	37
Visalia-Porterville, CA.	368	442	458	74	20.2	16	3.6	111
Waco, TX.	232	253	260	21	8.9	8	3.0	180
Washington-Arlington-Alexandria, DC-VA-MD-WV.	4,837	5,636	6,034	799	16.5	397	7.0	7
Wichita, KS.	580	631	641	51	8.8	10	1.6	84
Wilmington, NC.	201	255	273	53	26.6	18	6.9	174
Winston-Salem, NC.	569	641	655	71	12.5	14	2.3	83
Worcester, MA-CT.	860	917	930	57	6.6	13	1.5	58
York-Hanover, PA.	382	435	441	53	13.9	6	1.3	119
Youngstown-Warren-Boardman, OH-PA.	603	566	553	-37	-6.2	-13	-2.2	98

Z Less than 500 or .05 percent. [1] The April 1, 2010 population estimates base reflects changes to the Census 2010 population from the Count Question Resolution program and geographic program revisions. [2] Based on census data. [3] Broomfield County, CO, was formed from parts of Adams, Boulder, Jefferson, and Weld Counties, CO, on November 15, 2001, and is coextensive with Broomfield city. For purposes of defining and presenting data for metropolitan statistical areas, Broomfield city is treated as if it were a county at the time of the 2000 census. [4] The portion of Sullivan city in Crawford County, Missouri, is legally part of the St. Louis, MO-IL MSA. Data shown here do not include this area.

Source: U.S. Census Bureau, "CPH-T-5. Population Change for Metropolitan and Micropolitan Statistical Areas in the United States and Puerto Rico (February 2013 Delineations): 2000 to 2010," March 2013, <http://www.census.gov/population/www/cen2010/cph-t/cph-t-5.html>; and "Metropolitan and Micropolitan Statistical Areas, Tables, Annual Estimates of the Resident Population: April 1, 2010 to July 1, 2014, and Cumulative Estimates of Resident Population Change and Rankings: April 1, 2010 to July 1, 2014," March 2015, <http://www.census.gov/popest/data/metro/totals/2014/index.html>; accessed March 2015.

Table 22. The 50 Largest Metropolitan Statistical Areas in 2014—Components of Population Change: 2010 to 2014

[328 represents 328,000. Covers period April 1, 2010 to July 1, 2014. Covers metropolitan statistical areas as delineated by the U.S. Office of Management and Budget as of February 2013. For definitions and components of all metropolitan and micropolitan areas, see Appendix II. Minus sign (-) indicates decrease or outmigration]

| Metropolitan statistical area | Number (1,000) | | | | | | | Percent change |
| | Total change [1] | Natural increase | | | Net migration | | | |
		Total	Births	Deaths	Total	Interna-tional	Domes-tic migra-tion	
Atlanta-Sandy Springs-Roswell, GA.	328	168	309	140	155	76	80	6.2
Austin-Round Rock, TX.	227	71	108	37	152	26	126	13.2
Baltimore-Columbia-Towson, MD.	75	44	144	99	32	39	-7	2.8
Birmingham-Hoover, AL.	16	14	62	48	2	5	-3	1.4
Boston-Cambridge-Newton, MA-NH.	180	74	220	147	110	118	-8	3.9
Buffalo-Cheektowaga-Niagara Falls, NY.	1	1	51	50	2	13	-11	0.1
Charlotte-Concord-Gastonia, NC-SC.	163	54	125	71	106	23	83	7.4
Chicago-Naperville-Elgin, IL-IN-WI.	93	227	516	289	-129	108	-238	1.0
Cincinnati, OH-KY-IN.	35	40	117	77	-4	15	-18	1.6
Cleveland-Elyria, OH.	-14	10	99	88	-22	16	-38	-0.7
Columbus, OH.	93	51	113	62	42	22	20	4.9
Dallas-Fort Worth-Arlington, TX.	528	243	410	166	282	98	184	8.2
Denver-Aurora-Lakewood, CO.	211	79	147	68	128	25	104	8.3
Detroit-Warren-Dearborn, MI.	(Z)	46	213	166	-45	45	-90	(Z)
Hartford-West Hartford-East Hartford, CT.	2	8	52	43	-5	23	-27	0.2
Houston-The Woodlands-Sugar Land, TX.	570	247	395	148	322	130	192	9.6
Indianapolis-Carmel-Anderson, IN.	83	49	113	64	34	18	17	4.4
Jacksonville, FL.	74	26	75	49	47	16	31	5.5
Kansas City, MO-KS.	62	50	118	68	13	15	-2	3.1
Las Vegas-Henderson-Paradise, NV.	118	52	112	60	65	29	35	6.1
Los Angeles-Long Beach-Anaheim, CA.	433	389	721	332	56	264	-209	3.4
Louisville/Jefferson County, KY-IN.	34	18	67	49	17	9	8	2.8
Memphis, TN-MS-AR.	18	33	81	47	-15	7	-22	1.4
Miami-Fort Lauderdale-West Palm Beach, FL.	364	81	281	200	279	259	20	6.5
Milwaukee-Waukesha-West Allis, WI.	16	30	85	55	-13	10	-23	1.0
Minneapolis-St. Paul-Bloomington, MN-WI.	146	102	193	91	45	46	-1	4.4
Nashville-Davidson-Murfreesboro-Franklin, TN.	122	41	96	56	80	16	63	7.3
New Orleans-Metairie, LA.	62	21	66	45	40	14	26	5.2
New York-Newark-Jersey City, NY-NJ-PA.	526	470	1,072	601	71	600	-529	2.7
Oklahoma City, OK.	84	34	80	46	49	11	38	6.7
Orlando-Kissimmee-Sanford, FL.	187	49	114	66	136	63	73	8.8
Philadelphia-Camden-Wilmington, PA-NJ-DE-MD.	86	85	310	225	5	80	-75	1.4
Phoenix-Mesa-Scottsdale, AZ.	296	128	252	124	161	42	119	7.1
Pittsburgh, PA.	(-Z)	-14	101	115	17	13	4	(-Z)
Portland-Vancouver-Hillsboro, OR-WA.	122	50	117	68	71	22	49	5.5
Providence-Warwick, RI-MA.	8	9	71	62	(-Z)	21	-21	0.5
Raleigh, NC.	112	38	65	27	73	17	56	10.0
Richmond, VA.	52	21	63	42	31	15	15	4.3
Riverside-San Bernardino-Ontario, CA.	217	143	261	118	72	35	37	5.1
Sacramento-Roseville-Arden-Arcade, CA.	95	49	117	68	45	29	16	4.4
St. Louis, MO-IL [2].	18	40	145	105	-20	18	-38	0.7
Salt Lake City, UT.	65	54	81	26	12	13	-1	6.0
San Antonio-New Braunfels, TX.	186	68	134	65	115	21	94	8.7
San Diego-Carlsbad, CA.	168	103	189	86	65	62	3	5.4
San Francisco-Oakland-Hayward, CA.	259	97	221	124	164	115	49	6.0
San Jose-Sunnyvale-Santa Clara, CA.	116	64	105	42	55	70	-15	6.3
Seattle-Tacoma-Bellevue, WA.	232	95	193	98	137	76	61	6.7
Tampa-St. Petersburg-Clearwater, FL.	132	8	132	124	120	45	75	4.7
Virginia Beach-Norfolk-Newport News, VA-NC.	40	41	97	55	-1	23	-24	2.4
Washington-Arlington-Alexandria, DC-VA-MD-WV.	397	205	343	137	192	176	16	7.0

Z Less than 500 or .05 percent. [1] Total population change includes residual. This residual represents the change in population that cannot be attributed to any specific demographic component of change. [2] The portion of Sullivan city in Crawford County, Missouri, is legally part of the St. Louis, MO-IL MSA. Data shown here do not include this area.

Source: U.S. Census Bureau, "Metropolitan and Micropolitan Statistical Areas, Tables, Estimates of the Components of Resident Population Change: April 1, 2010 to July 1, 2014," March 2015, <http://www.census.gov/popest/data/metro/totals/2014/index.html>, accessed March 2015.

Table 23. Population by Core Based Statistical Area (CBSA) Status and State: 2014

[318,857 represents 318,857,000. As of July 1. Covers core based statistical areas (metropolitan and micropolitan statistical areas) as delineated by the U.S. Office of Management and Budget as of February 2013. For definitions and components of all metropolitan and micropolitan statistical areas, see Appendix II. Minus sign (-) indicates decrease]

State	Total popula-tion, 2014 (1,000)	Inside Core-Based Statistical Area (metropolitan or micropolitan statistical area), 2014				Outside CBSA, 2014		Percent change, 2010–2014		
		Total		Metro-politan (1,000)	Micro-politan (1,000)	Number (1,000)	Percent	Metro-politan	Micro-politan	Outside CBSAs
		Number (1,000)	Percent							
U.S.....	318,857	299,911	94.1	272,668	27,243	18,946	5.9	3.9	0.3	-1.0
AL.......	4,849	4,223	87.1	3,693	530	626	12.9	2.3	-0.3	-2.2
AK.......	737	544	73.9	498	46	192	26.1	4.1	3.2	2.8
AZ........	6,731	6,630	98.5	6,384	246	101	1.5	5.6	0.1	1.0
AR.......	2,966	2,392	80.6	1,821	572	574	19.4	3.9	-0.9	-2.2
CA........	38,803	38,533	99.3	37,972	562	269	0.7	4.3	-1.2	-2.8
CO........	5,356	5,053	94.3	4,666	386	303	5.7	7.5	1.3	-1.0
CT........	3,597	3,597	100.0	3,412	185	0	0.0	0.8	-2.6	0.0
DE........	936	936	100.0	936	0	0	0.0	4.2	0.0	0.0
DC........	659	659	100.0	659	0	0	0.0	9.5	0.0	0.0
FL........	19,893	19,547	98.3	19,189	357	347	1.7	6.0	0.2	-1.0
GA........	10,097	9,310	92.2	8,326	984	787	7.8	5.2	0.2	-0.7
HI........	1,420	1,420	100.0	1,155	265	0	0.0	4.2	5.0	0.0
ID........	1,634	1,497	91.6	1,086	411	137	8.4	6.2	1.5	-1.8
IL........	12,881	12,269	95.3	11,384	886	611	4.7	0.7	-2.1	-2.1
IN........	6,597	6,135	93.0	5,125	1,010	462	7.0	2.4	-0.3	-0.9
IA........	3,107	2,317	74.6	1,821	496	790	25.4	4.3	-0.5	-1.4
KS........	2,904	2,507	86.3	1,954	553	397	13.7	3.0	0.1	-1.8
KY........	4,413	3,422	77.5	2,575	847	992	22.5	3.0	1.4	-1.3
LA........	4,650	4,289	92.2	3,883	405	361	7.8	3.3	-0.7	-1.7
ME.......	1,330	906	68.1	784	121	425	31.9	1.1	-0.9	-1.4
MD.......	5,976	5,894	98.6	5,824	70	82	1.4	3.6	-0.3	-1.6
MA.......	6,745	6,735	99.8	6,646	88	11	0.2	3.0	0.4	6.7
MI........	9,910	9,243	93.3	8,107	1,136	667	6.7	0.5	0.0	-2.0
MN.......	5,457	4,878	89.4	4,219	659	579	10.6	3.9	0.4	-1.2
MS.......	2,994	2,327	77.7	1,367	960	667	22.3	2.9	-0.1	-1.7
MO.......	6,064	5,229	86.2	4,510	719	835	13.8	1.8	0.4	-1.2
MT.......	1,024	666	65.1	362	304	357	34.9	3.5	5.1	2.0
NE.......	1,882	1,540	81.8	1,212	328	342	18.2	5.1	0.3	-1.5
NV.......	2,839	2,806	98.8	2,568	238	33	1.2	5.6	1.0	-0.6
NH.......	1,327	1,279	96.4	831	448	47	3.6	1.5	-0.3	-0.9
NJ........	8,938	8,938	100.0	8,938	0	0	0.0	1.7	0.0	0.0
NM.......	2,086	1,992	95.5	1,390	602	94	4.5	1.4	2.0	-5.2
NY........	19,746	19,348	98.0	18,346	1,002	398	2.0	2.2	-1.3	-2.0
NC........	9,944	9,307	93.6	7,738	1,569	637	6.4	5.5	1.0	-1.2
ND........	739	542	73.3	364	178	198	26.7	9.8	15.9	5.4
OH........	11,594	11,141	96.1	9,223	1,918	453	3.9	0.9	-1.0	-0.9
OK........	3,878	3,334	86.0	2,528	806	544	14.0	4.8	2.0	-0.8
OR........	3,970	3,873	97.5	3,318	554	98	2.5	4.4	-0.1	-0.4
PA........	12,787	12,375	96.8	11,298	1,077	412	3.2	0.9	-1.3	-1.8
RI........	1,055	1,055	100.0	1,055	0	0	0.0	0.2	0.0	0.0
SC........	4,832	4,523	93.6	4,081	442	309	6.4	5.7	-0.4	-3.3
SD.......	853	635	74.5	407	228	218	25.5	7.9	3.0	1.2
TN........	6,549	5,901	90.1	5,054	847	648	9.9	4.0	1.3	-0.5
TX........	26,957	25,549	94.8	23,924	1,625	1,408	5.2	8.1	1.3	0.5
UT........	2,943	2,799	95.1	2,627	172	144	4.9	6.7	7.3	1.9
VT........	627	463	73.8	216	247	164	26.2	2.3	-1.5	-0.2
VA........	8,326	7,543	90.6	7,270	273	783	9.4	4.9	-2.7	-1.0
WA.......	7,062	6,908	97.8	6,348	560	153	2.2	5.5	1.4	0.5
WV.......	1,850	1,443	78.0	1,139	305	407	22.0	0.6	-0.6	-1.7
WI........	5,758	5,034	87.4	4,253	781	724	12.6	1.8	0.2	-0.7
WY.......	584	424	72.5	178	246	160	27.5	6.4	3.3	1.2

Source: U.S. Census Bureau, "Metropolitan and micropolitan statistical area population and estimated components of change: April 1, 2010 to July 1, 2014 (CBSA-EST2014-alldata)," March 2015, <http://www.census.gov/popest/data/metro/totals/2014/index.html>, accessed March 2015.

Table 24. Population of Incorporated Places With 175,000 or More Inhabitants in 2014: 1990 to 2014

[In thousands, except as indicated (223 represents 223,000). As of April 1, except beginning 2013, as of July 1. Data for the 2010 estimates base and July estimates are based on the 2010 Census and reflect changes to the April 1, 2010 population due to the Count Question Resolution program and geographic program revisions. All geographic boundaries for the 2014 population estimates series are defined as of January 1, 2014. For 1990 and 2000, the counts relate to places as defined on January 1, 2010. Minus sign (-) indicates decrease. See Appendix III]

City	Number (1,000)					Percent change		Rank, 2014
	1990	2000	2010, estimates base	2013	2014	2000 to 2010 [1]	2010 to 2014	
Akron, OH.	223	217	199	198	198	-8.3	-0.6	118
Albuquerque, NM.	385	449	546	557	557	21.7	2.0	32
Amarillo, TX.	158	174	191	197	197	9.8	3.5	120
Anaheim, CA.	267	328	336	346	347	2.5	3.1	56
Anchorage, AK.	226	260	292	302	301	12.1	3.1	64
Arlington, TX.	262	333	365	380	383	9.8	4.9	51
Atlanta, GA.	394	416	420	448	456	0.8	8.5	39
Augusta–Richmond County, GA [2].	186	200	196	197	197	-2.0	0.5	121
Aurora, CO.	222	276	325	346	353	17.6	8.8	54
Aurora, IL.	100	143	198	200	200	38.4	1.3	115
Austin, TX.	466	657	811	887	913	20.4	12.5	11
Bakersfield, CA.	175	247	348	364	369	40.6	6.1	52
Baltimore, MD.	736	651	621	623	623	-4.6	0.3	26
Baton Rouge, LA.	223	228	229	229	229	0.7	-0.2	96
Birmingham, AL.	265	243	212	212	212	-12.6	(Z)	101
Boise City, ID.	126	186	206	214	216	10.7	4.9	99
Boston, MA.	575	589	618	650	656	4.8	6.2	24
Brownsville, TX.	114	140	175	182	183	25.3	4.6	130
Buffalo, NY.	328	293	261	260	259	-10.7	-1.0	76
Chandler, AZ.	90	177	236	250	254	33.7	7.7	78
Charlotte, NC.	428	541	736	794	810	35.2	10.1	17
Chesapeake, VA.	152	199	222	230	233	11.6	5.0	92
Chicago, IL.	2,783	2,896	2,696	2,722	2,722	-6.9	1.0	3
Chula Vista, CA.	135	174	244	258	261	40.5	7.0	75
Cincinnati, OH.	364	331	297	298	298	-10.4	0.4	65
Cleveland, OH.	506	478	397	391	390	-17.1	-1.8	48
Colorado Springs, CO.	280	361	417	440	446	15.4	6.8	42
Columbus, GA.	[2] 179	[2] 186	191	204	201	1.9	5.4	111
Columbus, OH.	633	711	789	824	836	10.6	6.0	15
Corpus Christi, TX.	258	277	305	317	320	10.0	5.0	58
Dallas, TX.	1,008	1,189	1,198	1,261	1,281	0.8	7.0	9
Denver, CO.	468	555	600	648	664	8.2	10.6	21
Des Moines, IA.	193	199	204	208	209	2.4	2.5	105
Detroit, MI.	1,028	951	714	687	680	-25.0	-4.7	18
Durham, NC.	137	187	228	246	252	22.1	10.3	81
El Paso, TX.	515	564	649	677	679	15.2	4.6	19
Fayetteville, NC.	76	121	201	204	204	65.7	1.7	109
Fontana, CA.	88	129	196	203	205	52.1	4.5	108
Fort Lauderdale, FL.	149	152	166	173	176	8.6	6.3	135
Fort Wayne, IN.	173	206	254	257	259	23.3	1.9	77
Fort Worth, TX.	448	535	742	794	812	38.6	9.5	16
Fremont, CA.	173	203	214	225	229	5.2	6.9	97
Fresno, CA.	354	428	496	510	516	15.7	4.0	34
Garden Grove, CA.	143	165	171	175	175	3.4	2.4	136
Garland, TX.	181	216	227	235	236	5.1	3.8	91
Gilbert, AZ.	29	110	208	231	239	90.0	14.8	86
Glendale, AZ.	148	219	226	235	238	3.6	4.9	88
Glendale, CA.	180	195	192	197	200	-1.7	4.4	116
Grand Prairie, TX.	100	127	175	184	185	37.6	5.7	127
Grand Rapids, MI.	189	198	188	192	194	-4.9	3.1	123
Greensboro, NC.	184	224	269	280	283	20.4	5.1	67
Henderson, NV.	65	175	257	271	277	47.0	7.8	71
Hialeah, FL.	188	226	225	235	236	-0.8	4.8	90
Houston, TX.	1,631	1,954	2,097	2,204	2,240	7.5	6.8	4
Huntington Beach, CA.	182	190	191	198	201	0.2	5.1	112
Huntsville, AL.	160	158	180	186	188	13.8	4.4	125
Indianapolis, IN [2].	731	792	820	843	849	3.6	3.5	14
Irvine, CA.	110	143	212	237	249	48.4	17.3	82
Irving, TX.	155	192	216	229	232	12.9	7.5	93
Jacksonville, FL.	635	736	822	844	853	11.7	3.8	12
Jersey City, NJ.	229	240	248	259	262	3.1	5.9	74
Kansas City, MO.	435	442	460	467	471	4.1	2.4	37
Knoxville, TN.	165	174	179	183	184	2.9	3.1	129
Laredo, TX.	123	177	236	249	252	33.7	6.9	80
Las Vegas, NV.	258	478	584	604	614	22.0	5.0	29
Lexington–Fayette, KY.	225	261	296	308	311	13.5	5.1	61
Lincoln, NE.	192	226	258	269	273	14.5	5.6	72
Little Rock, AR.	176	183	194	197	198	5.7	2.2	119
Long Beach, CA.	429	462	462	471	474	0.2	2.4	36
Los Angeles, CA.	3,486	3,695	3,793	3,898	3,929	2.6	3.6	2
Louisville/Jefferson County, KY [2].	[3] 270	[3] 256	597	610	613	(X)	2.6	30
Lubbock, TX.	186	200	229	240	244	15.0	6.3	85
Madison, WI.	191	208	233	243	246	12.1	5.4	83
Memphis, TN.	610	650	652	659	657	-0.5	0.8	23
Mesa, AZ.	288	396	440	458	465	10.8	5.6	38
Miami, FL.	359	362	400	421	430	10.2	7.7	44
Milwaukee, WI.	628	597	595	600	600	-0.4	0.8	31
Minneapolis, MN.	368	383	383	401	407	(-Z)	6.4	46
Mobile, AL.	196	199	195	195	195	-1.9	-0.3	122

See footnotes at end of table.

City	Number (1,000)					Percent change		Rank, 2014
	1990	2000	2010, estimates base	2013	2014	2000 to 2010 [1]	2010 to 2014	
Modesto, CA	165	189	203	207	209	6.5	3.0	104
Montgomery, AL	188	202	206	202	200	2.1	-2.5	114
Moreno Valley, CA	119	142	193	201	203	35.8	5.0	110
Nashville–Davidson, TN [2]	488	570	604	635	644	5.5	6.7	25
New Orleans, LA	497	485	344	379	384	-29.1	11.8	50
New York, NY	7,323	8,008	8,175	8,438	8,491	2.1	3.9	1
Newark, NJ	275	274	277	279	281	1.3	1.2	69
Newport News, VA	171	180	181	182	183	0.3	1.1	132
Norfolk, VA	261	234	243	245	245	3.6	1.1	84
North Las Vegas, NV	48	115	217	227	231	87.9	6.5	94
Oakland, CA	372	399	391	408	414	-2.2	5.9	45
Oceanside, CA	128	161	167	173	175	3.8	4.5	137
Oklahoma City, OK	445	506	580	611	621	14.6	7.0	27
Omaha, NE	336	390	423	441	447	4.9	5.5	41
Orlando, FL	165	186	239	255	262	28.2	9.9	73
Overland Park, KS	112	149	173	181	185	16.3	6.5	128
Oxnard, CA	143	170	198	203	205	16.2	3.8	106
Philadelphia, PA	1,586	1,518	1,526	1,556	1,560	0.6	2.2	5
Phoenix, AZ	983	1,321	1,448	1,512	1,537	9.4	6.2	6
Pittsburgh, PA	370	335	306	307	305	-8.6	-0.1	62
Plano, TX	128	222	260	275	278	17.0	7.2	70
Portland, OR	439	529	584	610	619	10.3	6.1	28
Providence, RI	161	174	178	179	179	2.5	0.6	134
Raleigh, NC	212	276	404	432	440	46.3	8.9	43
Reno, NV	134	180	226	233	237	24.8	4.9	89
Richmond, VA	203	198	204	215	218	3.2	6.7	98
Riverside, CA	227	255	304	317	320	19.1	5.1	59
Rochester, NY	230	220	211	211	210	-4.2	-0.3	103
Sacramento, CA	369	407	466	480	485	14.6	4.0	35
Salt Lake City, UT	160	182	186	191	191	2.6	2.4	124
San Antonio, TX	935	1,145	1,328	1,412	1,437	16.0	8.2	7
San Bernardino, CA	165	185	210	214	215	13.2	2.5	100
San Diego, CA	1,111	1,223	1,302	1,360	1,381	6.9	6.1	8
San Francisco, CA	724	777	805	841	852	3.7	5.9	13
San Jose, CA	782	895	953	1,004	1,016	5.7	6.6	10
Santa Ana, CA	294	338	325	335	335	-4.0	3.1	57
Santa Clarita, CA	111	151	176	180	182	16.7	3.0	133
Scottsdale, AZ	130	203	217	226	231	7.2	6.0	95
Seattle, WA	516	563	609	653	668	8.0	9.8	20
Shreveport, LA	199	200	200	200	198	-0.4	-1.1	117
Spokane, WA	177	196	209	211	212	6.8	1.2	102
St. Louis, MO	397	348	319	318	317	-8.3	-0.6	60
St. Paul, MN	272	287	285	295	298	-0.7	4.4	66
St. Petersburg, FL	240	248	245	250	254	-1.4	3.5	79
Stockton, CA	211	244	292	298	302	19.7	3.7	63
Tacoma, WA	177	194	198	203	205	2.5	3.4	107
Tallahassee, FL	125	151	181	186	188	20.4	3.7	126
Tampa, FL	280	303	336	353	359	10.6	6.8	53
Toledo, OH	333	314	287	283	281	-8.4	-2.2	68
Tucson, AZ	405	487	521	527	528	6.9	1.4	33
Tulsa, OK	367	393	392	398	400	-0.3	2.0	47
Urban Honolulu CDP, HI [4]	(NA)	(NA)	337	349	350	(NA)	3.9	55
Virginia Beach, VA	393	425	438	449	451	3.0	3.0	40
Washington, DC	607	572	602	649	659	5.2	9.5	22
Wichita, KS	304	344	382	387	388	11.1	1.6	49
Winston–Salem, NC	143	186	230	237	239	23.6	4.2	87
Worcester, MA	170	173	181	183	183	4.9	1.1	131
Yonkers, NY	188	196	196	200	201	-0.1	2.4	113

NA Not available. X Not applicable. Z Less than .05 percent. [1] Based on census data. [2] Represents the portion of a consolidated city that is not within one or more separately incorporated places. [3] Data are for the incorporated place of Louisville city before consolidation of the city and county governments. [4] CDP=Census Designated Place.

Source: U.S. Census Bureau, 1990, 2000 and 2010 census data: *Census of Population and Housing, 2010, CPH-2. Population and Housing Unit Counts*; and beginning 2010: "Annual Estimates of the Resident Population for Incorporated Places Over 50,000, Ranked by July 1, 2014 Population: April 1, 2010 to July 1, 2014," May 2015, <http://www.census.gov/popest/data/cities/totals/2014/index.html>.

Table 25. Incorporated Places by Population Size: 1990 to 2014

[153.1 represents 153,100,000. See Appendix III]

Population size	Number of incorporated places				Population (mil.)				Percent of total			
	1990	2000	2010	2014	1990	2000	2010	2014	1990	2000	2010	2014
Total.....................	**19,262**	**19,452**	**19,540**	**19,509**	**153.1**	**173.5**	**192.0**	**200.2**	**100.0**	**100.0**	**100.0**	**100.0**
1,000,000 or more.........	8	9	9	10	20.0	22.9	23.6	25.6	13.1	13.2	12.3	12.8
500,000 to 999,999.......	15	20	24	24	10.1	12.9	16.1	16.5	6.6	7.4	8.4	8.3
250,000 to 499,999.......	41	37	40	47	14.2	13.3	14.0	16.2	9.3	7.7	7.3	8.1
100,000 to 249,999.......	131	172	200	214	19.1	25.5	30.2	32.0	12.5	14.7	15.7	16.0
50,000 to 99,999..........	309	363	432	454	21.2	24.9	30.1	31.6	13.8	14.4	15.7	15.8
25,000 to 49,999..........	567	644	723	717	20.0	22.6	25.2	25.0	13.1	13.0	13.1	12.5
10,000 to 24,999..........	1,290	1,435	1,542	1,557	20.3	22.6	24.2	24.6	13.3	13.0	12.6	12.3
Under 10,000...............	16,901	16,772	16,570	16,486	28.2	28.7	28.7	28.7	18.4	16.5	14.9	14.3

Source: U.S. Census Bureau, *1990 Census of Population and Housing, Population and Housing Unit Counts (CPH-2-1)*; Census 2000 *PHC-3, Population and Housing Unit Counts*; 2010 Census Redistricting Data (Public Law 94-171) Summary File; and "Incorporated Places and Minor Civil Divisions Datasets: Subcounty Resident Population Estimates: April 1, 2010 to July 1, 2014," May 2015, <http://www.census.gov/popest/data/cities/totals/2014/SUB-EST2014.html>, accessed June 2015.

Table 26. Urban and Rural Population by State: 2000 and 2010

[222,361 represents 222,361,000. As of April 1. Resident population. Based on current urban definitions, see text, this section]

State	2000		2010			State	2000		2010		
			Urban						Urban		
	Urban (1,000)	Rural (1,000)	Number (1,000)	Percent	Rural (1,000)		Urban (1,000)	Rural (1,000)	Number (1,000)	Percent	Rural (1,000)
U.S......	**222,361**	**59,061**	**249,253**	**80.7**	**59,492**	MO.........	3,883	1,712	4,218	70.4	1,771
AL.........	2,466	1,981	2,822	59.0	1,958	MT.........	488	414	553	55.9	436
AK.........	411	216	469	66.0	241	NE.........	1,194	518	1,336	73.1	491
AZ.........	4,524	607	5,741	89.8	651	NV.........	1,829	170	2,544	94.2	157
AR.........	1,404	1,269	1,638	56.2	1,278	NH.........	732	503	794	60.3	523
CA.........	31,990	1,882	35,374	95.0	1,880	NJ.........	7,939	475	8,324	94.7	468
CO.........	3,633	668	4,333	86.2	696	NM.........	1,364	456	1,594	77.4	465
CT.........	2,988	418	3,145	88.0	429	NY.........	16,603	2,374	17,028	87.9	2,350
DE.........	628	156	748	83.3	150	NC.........	4,849	3,200	6,302	66.1	3,234
DC.........	572	0	602	100.0	0	ND.........	359	283	403	59.9	270
FL.........	14,270	1,712	17,140	91.2	1,661	OH.........	8,782	2,571	8,990	77.9	2,547
GA.........	5,864	2,322	7,272	75.1	2,416	OK.........	2,255	1,196	2,485	66.2	1,266
HI.........	1,108	103	1,250	91.9	110	OR.........	2,694	727	3,104	81.0	727
ID.........	859	434	1,106	70.6	461	PA.........	9,464	2,817	9,991	78.7	2,711
IL.........	10,910	1,510	11,354	88.5	1,477	RI.........	953	95	955	90.7	98
IN.........	4,304	1,776	4,697	72.4	1,787	SC.........	2,427	1,585	3,068	66.3	1,558
IA.........	1,787	1,139	1,950	64.0	1,096	SD.........	391	363	461	56.7	353
KS.........	1,921	768	2,117	74.2	736	TN.........	3,620	2,069	4,213	66.4	2,133
KY.........	2,254	1,788	2,533	58.4	1,806	TX.........	17,204	3,648	21,298	84.7	3,848
LA.........	3,246	1,223	3,318	73.2	1,216	UT.........	1,970	263	2,504	90.6	260
ME.........	513	762	514	38.7	815	VT.........	232	376	243	38.9	382
MD.........	4,559	738	5,034	87.2	739	VA.........	5,170	1,909	6,037	75.5	1,964
MA.........	5,801	548	6,022	92.0	526	WA.........	4,831	1,063	5,652	84.1	1,073
MI.........	7,419	2,519	7,370	74.6	2,514	WV.........	833	976	903	48.7	950
MN.........	3,490	1,429	3,886	73.3	1,418	WI.........	3,664	1,700	3,990	70.2	1,697
MS.........	1,387	1,457	1,464	49.4	1,503	WY.........	321	172	365	64.8	199

Source: U.S. Census Bureau, 2000 Census of Population and Housing, *Population and Housing Unit Counts PHC-3*; 2010 Census of Population and Housing, *Population and Housing Unit Counts, CPH-2-1, United States Summary*; and "Percent Urban and Rural in 2010 by State," <http://www2.census.gov/geo/ua/>, accessed March 2013.

Table 27. Population in Coastal Counties: 1990 to 2014

[1990 to 2010 as of April 1; beginning 2011 as of July 1 (3,537 represents 3,537,000). Data for 1990 and 2000 are based on 675 counties in areas as defined by U.S. National Oceanic and Atmospheric Administration, 1992. Beginning 2010 data cover 678 counties and equivalent areas in a coastal watershed, see headnote, Table 28. See Appendix III]

Year	Total	Counties in coastal regions					Balance of United States
		Total	Atlantic	Gulf of Mexico	Great Lakes	Pacific	
Land area, 2010 (1,000 sq. mi.)......	3,537	888	147	116	115	510	2,649
POPULATION							
1990 (millions).....................	248.7	133.4	59.0	15.2	25.9	33.2	115.3
2000 (millions).....................	281.4	148.3	65.2	18.0	27.3	37.8	133.1
2010 (millions).....................	308.7	159.7	70.2	20.9	27.2	41.4	149.0
2011 (millions).....................	311.7	161.4	71.0	21.2	27.2	42.0	150.4
2012 (millions).....................	314.1	162.6	71.5	21.5	27.2	42.4	151.5
2013 (millions).....................	316.5	163.9	72.1	21.7	27.3	42.8	152.6
2014 (millions).....................	318.9	165.1	72.5	22.1	27.3	43.3	153.7
1990 (percent).....................	100	54	24	6	10	13	46
2000 (percent).....................	100	53	23	6	10	13	47
2010 (percent).....................	100	52	23	7	9	13	48
2011 (percent).....................	100	52	23	7	9	13	48
2012 (percent).....................	100	52	23	7	9	13	48
2013 (percent).....................	100	52	23	7	9	14	48
2014 (percent).....................	100	52	23	7	9	14	48

Source: U.S. Census Bureau, *1990 Census of Population and Housing (CPH1)*; "Annual Estimates of the Resident Population for Counties: April 1, 2000 to July 1, 2009," March 2011, <http://www.census.gov/popest/data/counties/totals/2009/CO-EST2009-01.html>; and "PEPANNRES: Annual Estimates of the Resident Population: April 1, 2010 to July 1, 2014," <http://factfinder.census.gov>, accessed August 2015.

Table 28. States With Coastal Counties—Population and Housing Units, Establishments, and Employees by Coastal Region and State: 2010 to 2014

[308,758 represents 308,758,000. Data for 2010 as of April 1 and reflect population estimates base. Data for 2014 as of July 1. Beginning 2010 data cover 678 counties and equivalent areas in a coastal watershed. A county is considered a coastal watershed county if one of the following criteria is met: (1) at a minimum, 15 percent of the county's total land area is located within a coastal watershed or (2) a portion of, or an entire county accounts for at least 15 percent of a coastal watershed. The 15- percent rule was selected as an appropriate level for capturing counties with a significant impact on coastal and ocean resources. See Appendix III. Minus sign (-) indicates decrease]

Coastal region and state	Population					Housing units			Private nonfarm [2]	
		2014				Number				
	2010 (1,000)	Number (1,000)	Percent of total state population	Percent change, 2010– 2014	Per square mile, 2014 [1]	2010 (1,000)	2014 (1,000)	Percent change, 2010– 2014	Establish- ments, 2013 (1,000)	Employees, 2013 (1,000)
United States, total	**308,758**	**318,857**	**(X)**	**3.3**	**90**	**131,705**	**133,957**	**1.7**	**7,488**	**118,266**
Interior U.S.	149,009	153,720	(X)	3.2	58	64,631	65,882	1.9	3,488	(NA)
Coastal counties, total	**159,749**	**165,137**	**(X)**	**3.4**	**186**	**67,074**	**68,075**	**1.5**	**4,000**	**(NA)**
Atlantic	70,242	72,529	(X)	3.3	492	29,916	30,337	1.4	1,862	27,743
Maine	1,239	1,244	93.5	0.4	62	667	673	0.9	38	460
New Hampshire	1,073	1,086	81.9	1.2	258	485	490	1.0	30	434
Massachusetts	6,318	6,514	96.6	3.1	991	2,712	2,732	0.7	167	2,963
Rhode Island	1,053	1,055	100.0	0.2	1,021	463	463	-0.2	28	406
Connecticut	3,574	3,597	100.0	0.6	743	1,488	1,494	0.4	88	1,456
New York	13,952	14,336	72.6	2.7	1,855	5,601	5,671	1.3	411	5,644
New Jersey	8,683	8,831	98.8	1.7	1,262	3,509	3,546	1.1	227	3,378
Pennsylvania	6,108	6,209	48.6	1.7	905	2,512	2,524	0.5	144	2,558
Delaware	898	936	100.0	4.2	480	406	417	2.8	24	379
Maryland	5,288	5,481	91.7	3.6	729	2,176	2,215	1.8	123	1,977
District of Columbia	602	659	100.0	9.5	10,793	297	306	3.2	22	491
Virginia	5,426	5,683	68.2	4.7	410	2,216	2,272	2.5	133	2,211
North Carolina	2,254	2,301	23.1	2.1	116	1,078	1,107	2.7	46	611
South Carolina	1,932	2,042	42.2	5.7	134	953	979	2.7	45	616
Georgia	945	981	9.7	3.7	83	414	421	1.7	19	268
Florida	10,896	11,576	58.2	6.2	621	4,940	5,028	1.8	316	3,893
Gulf of Mexico	20,888	22,061	(X)	5.6	191	9,294	9,573	3.0	471	7,209
Florida	7,535	7,937	39.9	5.3	246	3,887	3,953	1.7	185	2,309
Georgia	98	98	1.0	(-Z)	61	43	43	0.2	2	25
Alabama	765	781	16.1	2.2	90	363	369	1.8	17	245
Mississippi	629	645	21.6	2.7	95	280	288	3.0	12	179
Louisiana	3,574	3,688	79.3	3.2	141	1,543	1,580	2.4	83	1,346
Texas	8,288	8,913	33.1	7.5	222	3,178	3,340	5.1	172	3,105
Great Lakes	27,191	27,275	(X)	0.3	237	12,128	12,153	0.2	630	10,721
New York	3,635	3,633	18.4	-0.1	170	1,647	1,656	0.5	82	1,362
Pennsylvania	281	278	2.2	-0.8	348	119	120	0.6	6	114
Ohio	4,326	4,296	37.1	-0.7	408	1,967	1,967	(-Z)	100	1,768
Michigan	8,797	8,834	89.1	0.4	173	4,050	4,058	0.2	196	3,129
Indiana	1,433	1,437	21.8	0.3	353	607	611	0.8	31	553
Illinois	5,898	5,952	46.2	0.9	4,285	2,441	2,437	-0.2	150	2,612
Wisconsin	2,569	2,593	45.0	0.9	169	1,165	1,172	0.6	58	1,085
Minnesota	252	252	4.6	0.3	24	132	133	0.4	7	99
Pacific	41,429	43,272	(X)	4.4	85	15,737	16,011	1.7	1,037	(NA)
Washington	5,229	5,514	78.1	5.4	224	2,264	2,326	2.8	142	1,967
Oregon	1,982	2,050	51.6	3.4	98	895	908	1.4	59	776
California	32,259	33,664	86.8	4.4	433	11,803	11,990	1.6	787	11,924
Alaska	598	623	84.6	4.1	2	255	257	0.7	18	(NA)
Hawaii	1,360	1,420	100.0	4.4	221	520	530	2.0	31	484

NA Not available. X Not applicable. Z Less than .05 percent. [1] Calculated on the basis of land area data from the 2010 census. [2] Covers establishments with payroll. Excludes most government employees, railroad employees, and self-employed persons. Employees are for the week including March 12.

Source: U.S. Census Bureau, "PEPANNRES: Annual Estimates of the Resident Population: April 1, 2010 to July 1, 2014"; "PEPANNHU: Annual Estimates of Housing Units for the United States, Regions, Divisions, States, and Counties: April 1, 2010 to July 1, 2014"; and "County Business Patterns"; <http://factfinder.census.gov>, accessed August 2015.

Table 29. Geographic Mobility Status of the Population by Selected Characteristics: 1981 to 2014

[In thousands (221,641 represents 221,641,000). As of March. For persons 1 year old and over, unless otherwise noted. Based on comparison of place of residence in year shown vs. previous year. Excludes members of the Armed Forces except those living off post or with their families on post. Data for 2011 based on population controls from Census 2000. Data for 2014 data based on population controls from Census 2010. Based on Current Population Survey, Annual Social and Economic Supplement. See text, this section and Appendix III. For composition of regions, see map, inside front cover]

Mobility period and characteristic	Total persons (1,000)	Non–movers	Movers (different house in United States)					Movers from abroad
			Total	Same county	Different county			
					Total	Same state	Different state	
1981............................	221,641	82.8	16.6	10.4	6.2	3.4	4.3	0.6
1991............................	244,884	83.0	16.4	10.3	6.1	3.2	4.3	0.6
2001............................	275,611	85.8	13.5	8.0	5.6	2.7	2.8	0.6
2011............................	302,005	88.4	11.3	7.7	3.5	2.0	1.6	0.4
2014, total..................	**309,601**	**88.5**	**11.2**	**7.6**	**3.6**	**2.1**	**1.5**	**0.4**
1 to 4 years old..............	16,065	81.5	18.1	12.9	5.3	3.0	2.3	0.4
5 to 9 years old..............	20,522	86.4	13.2	9.4	3.9	2.3	1.5	0.4
10 to 14 years old............	20,642	89.8	10.0	7.2	2.8	1.7	1.1	0.2
15 to 19 years old............	20,807	89.8	9.8	6.7	3.1	1.8	1.3	0.4
20 to 24 years old............	22,278	75.7	23.5	16.0	7.5	4.4	3.1	0.8
25 to 29 years old............	21,474	76.8	22.3	15.1	7.2	3.9	3.3	0.9
30 to 44 years old............	60,763	86.3	13.2	8.9	4.2	2.4	1.8	0.5
45 to 64 years old............	82,572	93.3	6.5	4.2	2.3	1.4	0.9	0.2
65 to 74 years old............	25,791	96.6	3.3	2.0	1.3	0.7	0.6	0.1
75 to 84 years old............	13,431	96.8	3.0	2.0	1.0	0.6	0.4	0.2
85 years old and over.........	5,255	96.5	3.4	1.9	1.5	1.0	0.6	0.1
Northeast.......................	54,977	91.4	8.2	5.3	2.9	1.7	1.2	0.4
Midwest.........................	66,017	88.5	11.3	7.7	3.6	2.2	1.4	0.2
South...........................	115,632	87.5	12.1	8.1	4.0	2.3	1.7	0.4
West............................	72,974	87.9	11.7	8.3	3.4	1.9	1.5	0.4
Persons 16 years old and over............	**248,243**	**89.0**	**10.7**	**7.1**	**3.5**	**2.0**	**1.5**	**0.4**
Civilian labor force............	155,621	87.6	12.1	8.2	3.9	2.3	1.6	0.3
Employed.....................	144,920	88.0	11.7	8.0	3.7	2.2	1.5	0.3
Unemployed...................	10,701	82.8	16.5	10.6	5.9	3.0	2.9	0.7
Armed Forces...................	985	66.6	29.6	13.3	16.3	4.4	12.0	3.7
Not in labor force.............	91,638	91.4	8.1	5.2	2.8	1.6	1.2	0.5
Employed civilians, 16 years old and over. ..	144,920	88.0	11.7	8.0	3.7	2.2	1.5	0.3
Management, business, and financial..........	22,782	89.6	10.1	6.8	3.3	1.9	1.4	0.2
Professional...................	32,708	88.2	11.5	7.1	4.4	2.5	1.8	0.4
Service........................	25,535	86.0	13.7	10.0	3.7	2.3	1.4	0.3
Sales..........................	16,003	87.0	12.8	8.9	3.9	2.2	1.7	0.1
Office and administrative support...............	17,858	88.9	10.9	7.5	3.4	2.1	1.3	0.1
Farming, fishing, and forestry.................	1,037	87.3	12.0	9.0	3.0	1.4	1.5	0.8
Construction and extraction....................	7,127	86.7	12.9	9.3	3.6	2.3	1.3	0.4
Installation, maintenance, and repair..........	4,699	89.6	10.3	7.5	2.9	1.9	0.9	0.1
Production.....................	8,311	88.3	11.5	7.8	3.6	2.5	1.1	0.2
Transportation and material moving............	8,860	88.7	11.1	7.8	3.4	2.1	1.2	0.2
Tenure:								
Owner occupied units.............	206,295	95.0	4.9	3.2	1.6	1.0	0.6	0.1
Renter occupied units............	99,938	75.2	24.0	16.5	7.5	4.2	3.3	0.8
No cash renter occupied units.................	3,368	83.5	15.9	10.1	5.8	3.1	2.6	0.7

Source: U.S. Census Bureau, "Geographical Mobility: 2013 to 2014," March 2015, and earlier releases, <http://www.census.gov/hhes/migration/data/cps/cps2014.html>, accessed April 2015.

Table 30. Movers by Type of Move and Reason for Moving: 2014

[35,681 represents 35,681,000. As of March. For persons 1 year old and over. Based on comparison of place of residence in 2014 vs. 2013. Excludes members of the Armed Forces except those living off post or with their families on post. Based on Current Population Survey, Annual Social and Economic Supplement. See text, this section and Appendix III]

Reason for move	All movers	Intra-county	Inter-county	From abroad	Reason for move	All movers	Intra-county	Inter-county	From abroad
Total (1,000)..........................	**35,681**	**23,436**	**11,112**	**1,133**	Housing–related reasons.....	47.9	57.1	30.4	30.8
					Wanted to own home/not rent.....................	5.6	6.9	3.2	1.6
PERCENT DISTRIBUTION					New/better house/apartment.....................	15.8	20.6	6.9	2.3
Total................................	100.0	100.0	100.0	100.0	Better neighborhood/less crime.........................	3.0	3.2	2.5	1.1
Family–related reasons..............	29.4	29.4	29.8	26.9	Cheaper housing.............	9.4	11.4	5.9	2.6
Change in marital status............	4.9	4.9	4.7	6.4	Foreclosure/eviction.........	1.3	1.8	0.5	–
To establish own household.........	11.1	12.6	8.7	4.7	Other housing................	12.8	13.1	11.2	23.2
Other family reasons...............	13.4	11.9	16.4	15.9	Other reasons................	2.0	1.4	3.2	2.7
Work–related reasons.................	20.7	12.2	36.6	39.5	Attend/leave college.........	0.5	0.4	0.6	1.6
New job/job transfer...............	9.7	3.3	21.4	27.2	Change of climate...........	0.1	–	0.2	–
To look for work/lost job..........	2.1	1.1	3.9	4.9	Health reasons..............	0.4	0.3	0.5	–
Closer to work/easier commute.....	6.2	6.1	6.8	1.9	Natural disaster.............	–	–	–	–
Retired............................	0.7	0.5	1.1	0.1	Other reason.................	1.0	0.6	1.8	1.1
Other job–related reason...........	1.9	1.1	3.4	5.5					

– Represents or rounds to zero.

Source: U.S. Census Bureau, "Geographical Mobility: 2013 to 2014," March 2015, <http://www.census.gov/hhes/migration/data/cps/cps2014.html>, accessed May 2015.

Table 31. Geographic Mobility Status of Resident Population by State: 2013

[In percent, except as indicated (312,433 represents 312,433,000). Based on comparison of place of residence in 2013 vs. 2012. The American Community Survey universe includes the household population and the population living in institutions, college dormitories, and other group quarters. Based on a sample and subject to sampling variability. See text, this section and Appendix III]

| State | Population 1 year old and over (1,000) | Same house in 2012 | Different house in United States in 2012 | | Different county | | | Abroad in 2012 |
			Total	Same county	Total	Same State	Different State	
United States	**312,433**	**85.0**	**14.4**	**8.9**	**5.5**	**3.2**	**2.3**	0.6
Alabama	4,781	85.1	14.6	9.1	5.5	3.3	2.2	0.3
Alaska	725	80.5	18.5	11.2	7.4	2.6	4.7	1.0
Arizona	6,543	81.3	18.0	12.5	5.5	1.9	3.6	0.7
Arkansas	2,924	84.7	15.0	9.1	5.9	3.5	2.4	0.3
California	37,873	85.0	14.2	10.1	4.1	2.8	1.3	0.8
Colorado	5,206	80.4	18.9	10.1	8.9	4.9	4.0	0.7
Connecticut	3,563	87.8	11.6	7.2	4.4	2.0	2.5	0.6
Delaware	914	86.6	12.9	7.9	5.0	1.0	4.0	0.5
District of Columbia	637	80.1	18.1	10.8	7.3	0.0	7.3	1.7
Florida	19,345	83.7	15.4	9.5	5.8	3.1	2.7	0.9
Georgia	9,870	83.6	15.8	8.7	7.1	4.2	2.8	0.6
Hawaii	1,387	84.9	14.0	9.3	4.7	0.5	4.2	1.1
Idaho	1,593	82.7	16.8	9.4	7.4	3.5	3.9	0.5
Illinois	12,741	86.6	12.8	8.6	4.2	2.5	1.8	0.5
Indiana	6,492	84.7	14.9	9.2	5.7	3.6	2.1	0.4
Iowa	3,054	84.7	14.9	8.8	6.1	3.7	2.5	0.4
Kansas	2,855	83.6	15.9	9.5	6.3	3.2	3.1	0.5
Kentucky	4,345	84.4	15.2	8.9	6.3	4.0	2.4	0.4
Louisiana	4,568	86.3	13.4	7.8	5.5	3.5	2.0	0.4
Maine	1,316	85.8	13.9	8.5	5.5	2.7	2.8	0.3
Maryland	5,857	86.7	12.5	7.2	5.4	2.6	2.8	0.8
Massachusetts	6,620	86.5	12.6	7.7	4.9	2.9	2.0	0.9
Michigan	9,784	84.8	14.7	9.2	5.5	4.0	1.5	0.5
Minnesota	5,353	85.6	13.8	7.3	6.5	4.6	2.0	0.5
Mississippi	2,958	85.6	14.2	8.1	6.1	3.7	2.3	0.2
Missouri	5,973	84.0	15.7	8.7	7.0	4.4	2.7	0.3
Montana	1,003	82.5	17.0	9.4	7.6	3.6	4.0	0.5
Nebraska	1,843	83.9	15.6	9.2	6.4	3.9	2.5	0.5
Nevada	2,757	78.6	20.8	15.2	5.6	1.0	4.6	0.6
New Hampshire	1,311	86.1	13.4	7.7	5.7	2.3	3.4	0.5
New Jersey	8,804	90.2	9.1	5.3	3.8	2.3	1.6	0.7
New Mexico	2,060	85.7	13.7	8.6	5.1	2.3	2.8	0.7
New York	19,432	89.0	10.2	6.3	3.9	2.5	1.4	0.8
North Carolina	9,737	84.6	14.9	8.4	6.5	3.7	2.8	0.5
North Dakota	715	83.1	16.5	7.7	8.8	3.4	5.4	0.5
Ohio	11,440	85.2	14.4	9.4	4.9	3.3	1.6	0.4
Oklahoma	3,802	82.4	17.2	9.9	7.3	4.4	2.9	0.4
Oregon	3,888	81.1	18.4	10.7	7.7	4.0	3.7	0.5
Pennsylvania	12,639	87.9	11.6	7.2	4.3	2.6	1.8	0.5
Rhode Island	1,041	86.9	12.3	7.3	5.0	1.7	3.3	0.7
South Carolina	4,721	84.7	14.9	8.3	6.6	3.1	3.5	0.4
South Dakota	833	83.1	16.7	8.7	8.0	4.4	3.6	0.3
Tennessee	6,419	84.6	15.0	9.2	5.9	3.0	2.9	0.4
Texas	26,087	83.0	16.3	10.0	6.2	4.1	2.1	0.7
Utah	2,855	82.7	16.7	10.2	6.5	3.0	3.4	0.6
Vermont	621	87.2	12.4	6.7	5.7	2.0	3.7	0.4
Virginia	8,164	84.2	15.1	6.7	8.3	5.1	3.3	0.7
Washington	6,889	82.8	16.5	10.6	5.8	2.8	3.0	0.8
West Virginia	1,838	88.2	11.6	6.4	5.3	2.4	2.8	0.2
Wisconsin	5,681	85.8	13.9	8.7	5.2	3.4	1.8	0.3
Wyoming	576	81.5	18.1	9.9	8.3	3.5	4.8	0.3

Source: U.S. Census Bureau, 2013 American Community Survey, B07003, "Residence 1 Year Ago by Sex," <http://factfinder2.census.gov/>, accessed February 2015.

Table 32. Persons 65 Years Old and Over—Characteristics by Sex: 2000 to 2014

[32.6 represents 32,600,000. As of March, except as noted. Covers civilian noninstitutional population. Excludes members of Armed Forces except those living off post or with their families on post. Data for 2000 data based on 1990 Census population controls; data for 2005 and 2010 based on 2000 Census population controls; and data for 2014 based on 2010 Census population controls. Beginning 2005, data based on an expanded sample of households. Based on Current Population Survey. See text, this section and Appendix III]

Characteristic	Total				Male				Female			
	2000	2005	2010	2014	2000	2005	2010	2014	2000	2005	2010	2014
Total (million)............	**32.6**	**35.2**	**38.6**	**44.5**	**13.9**	**15.1**	**16.8**	**19.7**	**18.7**	**20.0**	**21.8**	**24.7**
PERCENT DISTRIBUTION												
Marital status:												
Never married........................	3.9	4.1	4.3	4.4	4.2	4.4	4.1	4.4	3.6	3.9	4.5	4.3
Married.................................	57.2	57.7	57.6	59.6	75.2	74.9	74.5	74.4	43.8	44.7	44.5	47.8
Spouse present.....................	54.6	54.8	55.2	57.4	72.6	71.7	71.7	72.1	41.3	42.0	42.4	45.7
Spouse absent [1]...................	2.6	2.9	2.4	2.2	2.6	3.2	2.8	2.3	2.5	2.7	2.1	2.1
Widowed...............................	32.1	30.3	28.1	24.7	14.4	13.7	12.7	11.4	45.3	42.9	39.9	35.2
Divorced...............................	6.7	7.9	10.0	11.4	6.1	7.0	8.7	9.8	7.2	8.5	11.1	12.6
Educational attainment:												
Less than ninth grade...............	16.7	13.4	10.2	7.9	17.8	13.2	10.2	7.8	15.9	13.5	10.1	8.0
Completed 9th to 12th grade, but no high school diploma...........	13.8	12.7	10.3	8.5	12.7	11.9	9.7	7.8	14.7	13.3	10.8	9.0
High school graduate................	35.9	36.3	36.4	34.5	30.4	31.6	32.0	30.6	39.9	39.9	39.8	37.5
Some college or associate's degree..............................	18.0	18.7	20.6	22.9	17.8	18.4	19.7	21.6	18.2	19.0	21.2	23.9
Bachelor's or advanced degree..............................	15.6	18.9	22.5	26.3	21.4	24.9	28.4	32.2	11.4	14.3	18.0	21.7
Labor force status: [2]												
Employed...............................	12.4	14.5	16.2	17.7	16.9	19.1	20.5	21.9	9.1	11.1	12.9	14.4
Unemployed...........................	0.4	0.5	1.2	0.9	0.6	0.7	1.6	1.1	0.3	0.4	0.9	0.7
Not in labor force.....................	87.2	84.9	82.6	81.4	82.5	80.2	77.9	77.0	90.6	88.5	86.2	84.9

[1] Includes separated. [2] Annual averages of monthly figures. Source: U.S. Bureau of Labor Statistics, "Labor Force Characteristics," <http://www.bls.gov/cps/lfcharacteristics.htm#laborforce>.

Source: Except as noted, U.S. Census Bureau, Current Population Reports, "The Older Population in the United States: March 2000 Detailed Tables," <http://www.census.gov/population/age/data/2000.html>; and "Educational Attainment," <http://www.census.gov/hhes/socdemo/education/> and "Families and Living Arrangements," <http://www.census.gov/hhes/families/data/cps.html>, accessed May 2015.

Table 33. Persons 65 Years and Over—Living Arrangements and Disability Status: 2013

[In thousands (44,664 represents 44,664,000), except as indicated. Based on the American Community Survey (ACS). Disability data limited to civilian noninstitutionalized population. Based on a sample and subject to sampling variability; see text, this section and Appendix III]

Relationship by household type	Number	Percent distribu- tion	Type of disability	Total	65 to 74 years old	75 years old and over
Total.............................	**44,664**	**100.0**	**Persons with any disability**.......	**15,776**	**6,429**	**9,347**
In households........................	43,157	96.6				
In family households................	30,044	67.3	With a hearing difficulty..............	6,572	2,363	4,209
Householder......................	14,783	33.1	With a vision difficulty...............	2,967	1,091	1,876
Spouse............................	10,882	24.4	With a cognitive difficulty............	3,993	1,352	2,641
Parent [1]..........................	3,148	7.0	With an ambulatory difficulty........	10,090	3,943	6,147
Other relatives....................	982	2.2	With a self-care difficulty............	3,688	1,118	2,570
Nonrelatives......................	250	0.6	With an independent living difficulty................................	6,692	1,953	4,739
In nonfamily households............	13,113	29.4				
Householder......................	12,418	27.8				
Living alone....................	11,725	26.3				
Not living alone...................	693	1.6				
Nonrelatives......................	695	1.6				
In group quarters.....................	1,507	3.4				

[1] Includes parent-in-law.

Source: U.S. Census Bureau, 2013 American Community Survey, B09020, "Relationship by Household Type (Including Living Alone) for the Population 65 Years and Over"; B18101, "Sex by Age by Disability Status"; B18102, "Sex by Age by Hearing Difficulty"; B18103, "Sex by Age by Vision Difficulty"; B18104, "Sex by Age by Cognitive Difficulty"; B18105, "Sex by Age by Ambulatory Difficulty"; B18106, "Sex by Age by Self-Care Difficulty"; and B18107, "Sex by Age by Independent Living Difficulty"; <http://factfinder2.census.gov>, accessed February 2015.

Table 34. Selected Characteristics of Racial Groups and Hispanic or Latino Population: 2013

[In thousands (210,911 represents 210,911,000), except as indicated. The American Community Survey universe includes the household population and the population living in institutions, college dormitories, and other group quarters. Based on a sample and subject to sampling variability; see text, this section and Appendix III]

Characteristic	Total population	White alone	Black or African American alone	American Indian, Alaska Native alone	Asian alone	Native Hawaiian and Other Pacific Islander alone	Some other race alone	Two or more races	Hispanic or Latino origin [1]	White alone, not Hispanic or Latino
EDUCATIONAL ATTAINMENT										
Persons 25 years old and over, total	**210,911**	**161,281**	**24,615**	**1,521**	**11,043**	**317**	**8,328**	**3,805**	**29,673**	**141,478**
Less than 9th grade	12,134	7,596	1,164	121	921	17	2,084	231	6,230	3,682
9th to 12th grade, no diploma	16,134	10,806	2,856	192	607	26	1,345	301	4,249	8,097
High school graduate (includes equivalency)	58,659	45,544	7,648	479	1,688	114	2,288	898	8,056	40,169
Some college, no degree	44,510	34,099	6,247	391	1,390	84	1,341	959	5,261	30,547
Associate's degree	17,006	13,386	1,947	127	771	25	414	336	1,727	12,190
Bachelor's degree	38,882	31,109	3,018	140	3,282	37	611	685	2,831	29,057
Graduate degree	23,584	18,741	1,735	71	2,384	13	245	395	1,320	17,737
OCCUPATION										
Employed civilian population, 16 years old and over, total	**145,129**	**110,389**	**16,029**	**928**	**7,881**	**223**	**6,641**	**3,037**	**22,947**	**95,301**
Management, business, science, and arts occupations	52,754	42,000	4,508	234	3,938	56	1,001	1,015	4,506	38,769
Management, business, and financial occupations	21,201	17,352	1,635	89	1,311	23	418	374	1,872	16,003
Computer, engineering, and science occupations	7,783	5,802	487	25	1,177	9	117	166	538	5,411
Education, legal, community service, arts, and media occupations	15,648	12,639	1,548	87	698	17	333	327	1,485	11,587
Healthcare practitioners and technical occupations	8,122	6,208	839	33	752	8	134	149	610	5,767
Service occupations	26,654	18,267	4,131	238	1,343	58	1,947	671	6,081	14,467
Sales and office occupations	35,109	26,986	4,103	213	1,610	56	1,349	792	5,044	23,597
Natural resources, construction, and maintenance occupations	12,924	10,392	831	112	237	19	1,108	225	3,546	8,081
Farming, fishing, and forestry occupations	1,042	792	43	12	13	1	166	15	546	427
Construction and extraction occupations	7,236	5,800	423	67	96	11	712	126	2,204	4,378
Installation, maintenance, and repair occupations	4,647	3,800	365	33	129	7	230	84	790	3,276
Production, transportation, and material moving occupations	17,687	12,744	2,456	132	752	33	1,236	334	3,776	10,388
Production occupations	8,713	6,356	1,010	63	489	12	629	152	1,880	5,191
Transportation occupations	5,230	3,831	826	38	155	11	271	98	908	3,243
Material moving occupations	3,745	2,558	619	31	108	10	336	83	988	1,953
FAMILY INCOME IN THE PAST 12 MONTHS										
Total families	**76,680**	**59,179**	**8,771**	**540**	**3,698**	**98**	**3,041**	**1,354**	**10,918**	**51,840**
Less than $10,000	3,743	2,198	997	62	132	8	244	102	815	1,676
$10,000 to $19,999	5,436	3,460	1,136	61	221	7	417	135	1,350	2,589
$20,000 to $29,999	6,713	4,680	1,101	73	250	8	465	135	1,528	3,690
$30,000 to $39,999	7,013	5,183	984	59	246	10	401	130	1,368	4,276
$40,000 to $49,999	6,656	5,086	815	54	247	10	325	119	1,131	4,335
$50,000 to $59,999	6,226	4,900	684	43	221	9	260	108	914	4,293
$60,000 to $74,999	8,344	6,678	818	53	353	9	295	135	1,082	5,941
$75,000 to $99,999	10,653	8,732	908	58	480	11	293	168	1,137	7,947
$100,000 to $124,999	7,542	6,236	565	34	424	13	156	118	677	5,754
$125,000 to $149,999	4,550	3,783	301	18	292	8	80	70	356	3,528
$150,000 to $199,999	4,794	3,984	277	13	380	6	64	71	314	3,749
$200,000 or more	5,010	4,258	185	9	451	4	40	64	246	4,062
Median family income in the past 12 months (in dollars) [2]	64,030	68,786	41,562	42,421	83,119	54,514	39,796	55,050	42,897	72,421
POVERTY STATUS IN THE PAST 12 MONTHS [3]										
Persons below poverty level	48,811	29,701	10,538	706	2,002	102	3,913	1,848	13,089	21,396
Families below poverty level	8,905	5,353	2,074	128	346	17	755	232	2,430	3,796
HOUSING TENURE										
Total households	**116,291**	**90,262**	**14,120**	**800**	**4,987**	**134**	**3,871**	**2,118**	**14,209**	**80,699**
Owner-occupied	73,844	62,081	5,918	434	2,881	52	1,467	1,010	6,416	57,413
Renter-occupied	42,447	28,180	8,202	366	2,105	81	2,404	1,108	7,793	23,286

[1] Persons of Hispanic origin may be of any race. [2] For definition of median, see Guide to Tabular Presentation. [3] For explanation of poverty level, see text, Section 13.

Source: U.S. Census Bureau, 2013 American Community Survey, Tables B15002, B24010, B19101, B19113, B17001, B17010, and B25003, <http://factfinder2.census.gov/>, accessed March 2015.

Table 35. Social and Economic Characteristics of the Hispanic Population: 2012

[52,358 represents 52,358,000. As of March, except labor force status is annual average. Excludes members of the Armed Forces except those living off post or with their families on post. Based on Current Population Survey, Annual Social and Economic Supplement; see text, this section and Appendix III]

Characteristic	Number (1,000)					Percent distribution				
	Hispanic, total[1]	Mexican	Puerto Rican	Central American[2]	South American[2]	Hispanic, total[1]	Mexican	Puerto Rican	Central American[2]	South American[2]
Total persons	**52,358**	**33,671**	**4,866**	**4,249**	**3,072**	**100.0**	**100.0**	**100.0**	**100.0**	**100.0**
Under 5 years old	5,210	3,613	423	377	224	10.0	10.7	8.7	8.9	7.3
5 to 14 years old	9,648	6,779	884	610	424	18.4	20.1	18.2	14.4	13.8
15 to 44 years old	25,125	16,339	2,136	2,352	1,455	48.0	48.5	43.9	55.4	47.4
45 to 64 years old	9,339	5,422	1,012	740	749	17.8	16.1	20.8	17.4	24.4
65 years old and over	3,036	1,519	412	169	219	5.8	4.5	8.5	4.0	7.1
EDUCATIONAL ATTAINMENT										
Persons 25 years old and over	**28,445**	**17,326**	**2,708**	**2,523**	**1,926**	**100.0**	**100.0**	**100.0**	**100.0**	**100.0**
High school graduate or more	18,489	10,249	2,058	1,408	1,677	65.0	59.2	76.0	55.8	87.1
Bachelor's degree or more	4,133	1,822	473	262	612	14.5	10.5	17.5	10.4	31.8
NATIVITY AND CITIZENSHIP STATUS										
Total	**52,358**	**33,671**	**4,866**	**4,249**	**3,072**	**100.0**	**100.0**	**100.0**	**100.0**	**100.0**
Native	33,661	22,269	4,839	1,577	1,109	64.3	66.1	99.4	37.1	36.1
Foreign born	18,697	11,402	28	2,672	1,964	35.7	33.9	0.6	62.9	63.9
Naturalized citizen	6,041	2,992	14	758	914	11.5	8.9	0.3	17.8	29.7
Not a citizen	12,656	8,411	14	1,914	1,050	24.2	25.0	0.3	45.0	34.2
LABOR FORCE STATUS[3]										
Civilians 16 years old and over	**36,759**	**22,716**	**3,462**	**(NA)**	**(NA)**	**100.0**	**100.0**	**100.0**	**(NA)**	**(NA)**
Civilian labor force	24,391	15,128	2,090	(NA)	(NA)	66.4	66.6	60.4	(NA)	(NA)
Employed	21,878	13,552	1,830	(NA)	(NA)	59.5	59.7	52.9	(NA)	(NA)
Unemployed	2,514	1,577	260	(NA)	(NA)	6.8	6.9	7.5	(NA)	(NA)
Unemployment rate[4]	10.3	10.4	12.4	(NA)	(NA)	(X)	(X)	(X)	(NA)	(NA)
Male	9.9	9.8	13.1	(NA)	(NA)	(X)	(X)	(X)	(NA)	(NA)
Female	10.9	11.3	11.7	(NA)	(NA)	(X)	(X)	(X)	(NA)	(NA)
Not in labor force	12,368	7,588	1,372	(NA)	(NA)	33.6	33.4	39.6	(NA)	(NA)
HOUSEHOLDS[5]										
Total	**14,939**	**8,926**	**1,607**	**1,221**	**993**	**100.0**	**100.0**	**100.0**	**100.0**	**100.0**
Family households	11,585	7,181	1,136	966	752	77.6	80.5	70.7	79.1	75.7
Married-couple families	7,222	4,566	599	584	516	48.3	51.2	37.3	47.8	52.0
Male householder, no spouse present	1,277	827	126	113	74	8.5	9.3	7.8	9.3	7.5
Female householder, no spouse present	3,086	1,789	412	269	161	20.7	20.0	25.6	22.0	16.2
Nonfamily households[6]	3,353	1,745	471	255	242	22.4	19.5	29.3	20.9	24.3
Male householder	1,818	1,016	222	147	127	12.2	11.4	13.8	12.0	12.7
Female householder	1,535	729	249	108	115	10.3	8.2	15.5	8.9	11.6
MONEY INCOME IN 2011										
Total families	**11,585**	**7,181**	**1,136**	**966**	**752**	**100.0**	**100.0**	**100.0**	**100.0**	**100.0**
Less than $5,000	448	281	55	34	18	3.9	3.9	4.9	3.6	2.3
$5,000 to $14,999	994	641	139	65	34	8.6	8.9	12.2	6.7	4.5
$15,000 to $24,999	1,622	1,059	162	143	67	14.0	14.7	14.3	14.8	8.9
$25,000 to $34,999	1,616	1,040	145	166	90	13.9	14.5	12.8	17.2	11.9
$35,000 to $49,999	2,055	1,304	177	188	116	17.7	18.2	15.6	19.5	15.5
$50,000 to $74,999	2,101	1,351	170	179	136	18.1	18.8	15.0	18.5	18.1
$75,000 to $99,999	1,180	671	128	93	113	10.2	9.3	11.2	9.7	15.0
$100,000 and over	1,570	833	160	97	179	13.6	11.6	14.1	10.0	23.8
POVERTY STATUS IN 2011										
Persons below poverty level[7]	**13,244**	**9,115**	**1,416**	**1,051**	**360**	**25.3**	**27.1**	**29.1**	**24.7**	**11.7**

NA Not available. X Not applicable. [1] Includes other Hispanic groups not shown separately. [2] Refers to people whose origin is from Spanish-speaking Central or South American countries. Central American totals exclude Mexican and Cuban. [3] Source: U.S. Bureau of Labor Statistics, "Employment and Earnings Online," January 2014, <http://stats.bls.gov/opub/ee/home.htm>. [4] Total unemployment as percent of civilian labor force. [5] Household type is shown by the Hispanic origin of the householder. [6] A nonfamily household consists of a householder living alone (a one-person household) or where the householder shares the home exclusively with people to whom he/she is not related. [7] Excludes unrelated individuals under 15 years old. For explanation of poverty level; see text, Section 13.

Source: Except as noted, U.S. Census Bureau, "The Hispanic Population in the United States: 2012," December 2013, <http://www.census.gov/population/hispanic/data/2012.html>, accessed April 2014.

Table 36. Native and Foreign-Born Population by State: 2013

[274,781 represents 274,781,000. The American Community Survey universe includes the household population and the population living in institutions, college dormitories, and other group quarters. Based on a sample and subject to sampling variability; see text, this section and Appendix III. See headnote, Table 40]

State	Native population (1,000)	Foreign-born population Number (1,000)	Foreign-born population Percent of total population	Foreign-born population Percent entered 2010 or later	State	Native population (1,000)	Foreign-born population Number (1,000)	Foreign-born population Percent of total population	Foreign-born population Percent entered 2010 or later
U.S........	274,781	41,348	13.1	9.7	MO.........	5,811	233	3.9	15.1
AL..........	4,671	162	3.4	11.9	MT..........	996	19	1.9	15.7
AK..........	684	51	6.9	10.7	NE..........	1,745	123	6.6	14.6
AZ..........	5,730	896	13.5	9.4	NV..........	2,261	529	19.0	5.8
AR..........	2,825	134	4.5	13.6	NH..........	1,248	75	5.7	11.7
CA..........	28,021	10,311	26.9	6.6	NJ..........	6,974	1,926	21.6	9.3
CO..........	4,768	501	9.5	9.4	NM..........	1,874	211	10.1	8.1
CT..........	3,096	500	13.9	10.3	NY..........	15,268	4,383	22.3	9.5
DE..........	849	77	8.3	13.0	NC..........	9,099	749	7.6	11.4
DC..........	554	93	14.4	17.3	ND..........	702	21	2.9	35.5
FL..........	15,755	3,798	19.4	10.1	OH..........	11,093	477	4.1	15.4
GA..........	9,021	971	9.7	10.5	OK..........	3,632	218	5.7	14.4
HI..........	1,158	246	17.6	9.4	OR..........	3,539	391	10.0	9.3
ID..........	1,517	96	5.9	14.6	PA..........	11,978	796	6.2	14.1
IL..........	11,075	1,807	14.0	8.2	RI..........	916	136	12.9	10.2
IN..........	6,256	315	4.8	15.5	SC..........	4,544	231	4.8	8.9
IA..........	2,941	149	4.8	17.6	SD..........	820	24	2.9	20.6
KS..........	2,696	198	6.8	14.2	TN..........	6,191	305	4.7	12.8
KY..........	4,246	149	3.4	17.7	TX..........	22,079	4,369	16.5	9.6
LA..........	4,443	183	3.9	18.0	UT..........	2,664	237	8.2	11.3
ME..........	1,284	45	3.4	13.6	VT..........	600	27	4.3	11.3
MD..........	5,087	842	14.2	10.8	VA..........	7,311	949	11.5	11.3
MA..........	5,647	1,046	15.6	13.2	WA..........	6,028	944	13.5	10.8
MI..........	9,279	617	6.2	15.2	WV..........	1,828	26	1.4	15.9
MN..........	5,017	404	7.4	12.2	WI..........	5,468	275	4.8	11.8
MS..........	2,928	63	2.1	15.9	WY..........	565	18	3.1	13.0

Source: U.S. Census Bureau, 2013 American Community Survey, B05002, "Place of Birth by Nativity and Citizenship Status"; and C05007, "Place of Birth by Year of Entry by Citizenship Status for the Foreign-Born Population"; <http://factfinder2.census.gov>, accessed February 2015.

Table 37. Nativity and Place of Birth of Resident Population—25 Largest Cities: 2013

[In thousands (885 represents 885,000). Largest cities are based on 2014 population; see Table 24. The American Community Survey universe includes the household population and the population living in institutions, college dormitories, and other group quarters. Based on a sample and subject to sampling variability; see text, this section and Appendix III. See headnote, Table 40]

City	Total population (1,000)	Native population Total (1,000)	Native population Born in United States (1,000)	Native population Born outside United States (1,000)	Foreign born Total Number (1,000)	Foreign born Total Percent of total population	Foreign born Entered 2010 or later Number (1,000)	Foreign born Entered 2010 or later Percent of foreign-born population
Austin, TX............................	885	725	711	14	160	18.1	21	13.2
Boston, MA............................	645	466	445	21	179	27.7	31	17.5
Charlotte, NC.........................	793	665	656	9	128	16.1	22	17.0
Chicago, IL...........................	2,719	2,146	2,099	47	573	21.1	52	9.0
Columbus, OH.........................	823	725	716	9	97	11.8	20	20.6
Dallas, TX............................	1,258	951	941	10	306	24.4	29	9.4
Denver, CO............................	649	551	543	9	98	15.2	11	11.2
Detroit, MI...........................	689	654	649	5	35	5.0	4	11.7
El Paso, TX...........................	674	503	485	18	172	25.4	16	9.6
Fort Worth, TX........................	794	656	641	14	139	17.4	12	8.8
Houston, TX...........................	2,197	1,575	1,549	26	623	28.3	74	11.9
Indianapolis, IN [1]..................	838	762	756	6	76	9.1	12	16.0
Jacksonville, FL......................	843	762	742	20	81	9.6	8	10.0
Los Angeles, CA.......................	3,884	2,399	2,359	40	1,486	38.2	89	6.0
Memphis, TN...........................	653	613	607	6	41	6.2	5	13.2
Nashville–Davidson, TN [1]............	634	557	550	7	77	12.2	12	14.8
New York, NY..........................	8,406	5,299	4,995	304	3,107	37.0	292	9.4
Philadelphia, PA......................	1,553	1,356	1,300	56	197	12.7	31	15.7
Phoenix, AZ...........................	1,513	1,214	1,198	16	299	19.7	22	7.4
San Antonio, TX.......................	1,409	1,209	1,182	27	200	14.2	23	11.3
San Diego, CA.........................	1,356	999	971	28	357	26.3	35	9.8
San Francisco, CA.....................	837	546	525	20	292	34.9	33	11.2
San Jose, CA..........................	999	607	593	13	392	39.3	30	7.7
Seattle, WA...........................	652	537	523	14	115	17.7	17	15.2
Washington, DC........................	646	554	542	12	93	14.4	16	17.3

[1] Represents the portion of a consolidated city that is not within one or more separately incorporated places.

Source: U.S. Census Bureau, 2013 American Community Survey, C05002, "Place of Birth by Nativity"; and C05005, "Year of Entry by Nativity in the United States"; <http://factfinder.census.gov>, accessed June 2015.

Table 38. Native and Foreign-Born Populations by Selected Characteristics: 2012

[In thousands (308,827 represents 308,827,000). As of March. The foreign-born population includes anyone who is not a U.S. citizen at birth. This includes legal permanent residents (immigrants), temporary migrants (such as students), humanitarian migrants (such as refugees), and persons illegally present in the United States. Based on Current Population Survey, Annual Social and Economic Supplement, which includes the civilian noninstitutional population plus Armed Forces living off post or with their families on post; see text, this section, and Appendix III]

Characteristic	Total population	Native population	Foreign-born population			
			Total	Natural-ized citizen	Not a U.S. citizen	Year of entry: 2000 or later
Total	**308,827**	**268,851**	**39,976**	**17,934**	**22,042**	**14,960**
Under 5 years old	20,110	19,906	204	68	136	204
5 to 14 years old	41,021	39,444	1,576	368	1,209	1,475
15 to 24 years old	43,117	39,083	4,034	1,060	2,973	2,672
25 to 34 years old	41,219	33,436	7,782	2,184	5,598	4,546
35 to 44 years old	39,927	31,226	8,701	3,402	5,299	3,040
45 to 54 years old	43,955	36,370	7,585	3,899	3,686	1,629
55 to 64 years old	37,971	32,844	5,128	3,328	1,799	823
65 to 74 years old	23,383	20,495	2,889	2,060	829	379
75 to 84 years old	13,117	11,600	1,518	1,123	395	147
85 years old and over	5,006	4,447	559	441	117	46
Median age (years) [1]	37.3	35.9	42.3	49.6	36.9	31.9
Male	151,175	131,557	19,617	8,357	11,260	7,513
Female	157,653	137,294	20,359	9,577	10,782	7,447
MARITAL STATUS						
Persons 15 years old and over	**247,696**	**209,501**	**38,195**	**17,498**	**20,698**	**13,281**
Married	125,691	102,124	23,566	11,436	12,130	7,564
Widowed	14,064	12,282	1,782	1,189	594	261
Divorced	24,923	22,378	2,545	1,478	1,066	475
Separated	5,671	4,495	1,176	514	663	367
Never married	77,347	68,222	9,125	2,881	6,245	4,613
EDUCATIONAL ATTAINMENT						
Persons 25 years old and over	**204,579**	**170,418**	**34,162**	**16,438**	**17,724**	**10,609**
Not high school graduate	25,276	15,592	9,684	2,964	6,720	3,002
High school graduate/some college	116,013	101,479	14,535	7,555	6,980	4,116
Bachelor's degree	40,561	34,444	6,117	3,787	2,330	2,041
Advanced degree	22,730	18,904	3,826	2,132	1,694	1,450
EARNINGS IN 2011 [2]						
Persons 15 years old and over with earnings	**101,676**	**84,929**	**16,746**	**8,049**	**8,698**	**5,431**
Under $15,000 or loss	5,366	3,977	1,389	378	1,011	648
$15,000 to $29,999	22,945	17,557	5,388	1,879	3,509	2,030
$30,000 to $39,999	17,256	14,534	2,722	1,308	1,415	822
$40,000 to $49,999	13,712	11,871	1,841	1,081	760	470
$50,000 to $74,999	21,449	18,906	2,543	1,568	975	693
$75,000 to $99,999	9,123	7,936	1,186	734	452	339
$100,000 and over	11,825	10,148	1,677	1,101	576	429
Median earnings (dollars) [1]	42,086	44,512	35,137	42,113	28,281	30,259
HOUSEHOLD SIZE [3]						
Total households	**121,084**	**103,965**	**17,119**	**8,874**	**8,246**	**4,918**
One person	33,188	30,090	3,098	1,856	1,242	769
Two people	40,983	36,687	4,296	2,533	1,763	1,115
Three people	19,241	16,118	3,123	1,581	1,542	1,036
Four people	16,049	12,696	3,353	1,544	1,809	1,087
Five or more people	11,622	8,373	3,249	1,359	1,890	911
INCOME IN 2011 [3]						
Total family households	**80,506**	**67,285**	**13,220**	**6,733**	**6,487**	**3,779**
Under $15,000 or loss	6,120	4,764	1,355	497	858	536
$15,000 to $29,999	10,675	8,281	2,394	962	1,432	798
$30,000 to $39,999	7,959	6,448	1,511	637	874	460
$40,000 to $49,999	7,148	5,857	1,291	611	680	357
$50,000 to $74,999	15,362	13,049	2,313	1,234	1,079	578
$75,000 to $99,999	11,273	9,814	1,458	872	586	372
$100,000 and over	21,969	19,071	2,898	1,919	979	678
Median income (dollars) [1]	62,273	65,079	50,365	61,672	40,881	42,147
POVERTY STATUS IN 2011 [4]						
Persons below poverty level	46,247	38,661	7,586	2,233	5,353	3,764
Persons at or above poverty level	262,209	229,829	32,380	15,701	16,679	11,186
HOUSEHOLD TENURE [3]						
Total households	**121,084**	**103,964**	**17,119**	**8,874**	**8,245**	**4,918**
Owner occupied unit	79,176	70,387	8,789	5,866	2,923	1,394
Renter occupied unit [5]	41,909	33,578	8,330	3,008	5,323	3,522

[1] For definition of median, see Guide to Tabular Presentation. [2] Covers only year-round, full-time workers. [3] Based on citizenship of householder. [4] Persons for whom poverty status is determined. Excludes unrelated individuals under 15 years old. [5] Includes occupiers who paid no cash rent.

Source: U.S. Census Bureau, "Current Population Survey - March 2012 Detailed Tables, Characteristics of the Foreign-Born Population by Nativity and U.S. Citizenship Status," <http://www.census.gov/population/foreign/data/cps2012.html>, accessed April 2015.

Table 39. Foreign-Born Population—Selected Characteristics by Region of Origin: 2012

[In thousands (39,976 represents 39,976,000). As of March. The term foreign-born refers to anyone who is not a U.S. citizen at birth. This includes naturalized U.S. citizens, legal permanent residents (immigrants), temporary migrants (such as foreign students), humanitarian migrants (such as refugees), and persons illegally present in the United States. Based on Current Population Survey, Annual Social and Economic Supplement; see text, this section and Appendix III]

Characteristic	Total foreign-born	Europe	Asia	Latin America Total	Mexico	Other Latin America	Other areas
Total	**39,976**	**4,546**	**11,587**	**21,034**	**11,621**	**9,413**	**2,809**
Under 5 years old	204	20	85	67	35	32	32
5 to 14 years old	1,576	138	514	756	446	310	169
15 to 24 years old	4,034	311	1,166	2,239	1,258	980	317
25 to 34 years old	7,782	524	2,052	4,717	2,843	1,875	490
35 to 44 years old	8,701	714	2,433	4,941	3,002	1,940	614
45 to 54 years old	7,585	784	2,175	4,056	2,157	1,899	570
55 to 64 years old	5,128	723	1,655	2,382	1,155	1,227	368
65 to 74 years old	2,889	676	927	1,141	457	685	145
75 to 84 years old	1,518	474	457	509	201	308	78
85 years old and over	559	180	126	226	68	158	27
EDUCATIONAL ATTAINMENT							
Persons 25 years old and over	**34,162**	**4,075**	**9,823**	**17,971**	**9,881**	**8,090**	**2,292**
Less than ninth grade	6,260	272	732	5,143	3,767	1,376	113
9th to 12th grade (no diploma)	3,424	128	496	2,710	1,899	811	90
High school graduate	8,973	1,136	2,105	5,187	2,659	2,528	545
Some college or associate's degree	5,562	852	1,551	2,617	963	1,654	542
Bachelor's degree	6,117	973	2,912	1,631	449	1,182	601
Advanced degree	3,826	715	2,027	684	144	540	401
High school graduate or more	24,477	3,675	8,595	10,118	4,215	5,903	2,089
Bachelor's degree or more	9,943	1,688	4,939	2,314	593	1,721	1,002
INCOME IN 2011							
Total family households	**13,220**	**1,527**	**3,807**	**6,968**	**3,931**	**3,037**	**919**
Under $15,000 or loss	1,355	88	268	897	572	325	102
$15,000 to $29,999	2,394	175	456	1,627	1,026	601	136
$30,000 to $39,999	1,511	150	317	965	601	364	79
$40,000 to $49,999	1,291	145	273	815	476	339	58
$50,000 to $74,999	2,313	255	669	1,224	678	546	166
$75,000 to $99,999	1,458	228	480	643	269	374	107
$100,000 and over	2,898	487	1,343	797	309	488	271
Median income (dollars) [1]	50,365	69,107	71,449	39,927	35,790	46,260	61,697
POVERTY STATUS IN 2011 [2]							
Persons below poverty level	7,586	441	1,575	5,061	3,233	1,828	509
Persons at or above poverty level	32,380	4,104	10,007	15,968	8,383	7,585	2,301

[1] For definition of median, see Guide to Tabular Presentation. [2] Persons for whom poverty status is determined. Excludes unrelated individuals under 15 years old.

Source: U.S. Census Bureau, "Current Population Survey - March 2012 Detailed Tables, Characteristics of the Foreign-Born Population by Nativity and U.S. Citizenship Status," <http://www.census.gov/population/foreign/data/cps2012.html>, accessed April 2015.

Table 40. Foreign-Born Population by Citizenship Status and Place of Birth: 2013

[The term foreign-born refers to anyone who is not a U.S. citizen at birth. This includes naturalized U.S. citizens, legal permanent residents (immigrants), temporary migrants (such as foreign students), humanitarian migrants (such as refugees), and persons illegally present in the United States. The American Community Survey universe includes the household population and the population living in institutions, college dormitories, and other group quarters. Based on a sample and subject to sampling variability; see text, this section and Appendix III]

Region and Country	Foreign-born population, total	Naturalized citizens	Not a U.S. citizen Number	Percent of foreign-born
Total [1]	**41,348,066**	**19,294,710**	**22,053,356**	**53.3**
Latin America	21,473,266	7,615,182	13,858,084	64.5
Caribbean	3,953,655	2,280,476	1,673,179	42.3
Cuba	1,144,024	(NA)	(NA)	(NA)
Central America	14,751,230	3,942,195	10,809,035	73.3
Mexico	11,584,977	2,932,523	8,652,454	74.7
Other Central America	3,166,253	1,009,672	2,156,581	68.1
El Salvador	1,252,067	(NA)	(NA)	(NA)
South America	2,768,381	1,392,511	1,375,870	49.7
Asia	12,176,983	7,208,055	4,968,928	40.8
China, excluding Hong Kong and Taiwan	1,804,965	(NA)	(NA)	(NA)
India	2,034,677	(NA)	(NA)	(NA)
Korea	1,070,335	(NA)	(NA)	(NA)
Philippines	1,843,989	(NA)	(NA)	(NA)
Vietnam	1,281,010	(NA)	(NA)	(NA)
Europe	4,803,059	3,070,072	1,732,987	36.1
Africa	1,825,326	(NA)	(NA)	(NA)
Northern America	846,921	(NA)	(NA)	(NA)
Oceania	222,390	(NA)	(NA)	(NA)

NA Not available. [1] Includes persons born at sea.

Source: U.S. Census Bureau, 2013 American Community Survey, B05002, "Place of Birth by Nativity and Citizenship Status"; B05006, "Place of Birth for the Foreign-Born Population in the United States"; B05007, "Place of Birth by Year of Entry by Citizenship Status for the Foreign-Born Population"; <http://factfinder2.census.gov/>, accessed February 2015.

Table 41. American Indian Reservations and Alaska Native Village Statistical Areas With Largest American Indian and Alaska Native Populations: 2010

[As of April. Rankings of the American Indian reservations and Alaska Native village statistical areas are based on the American Indian and Alaska Native alone-or-in-combination population]

Area	Total population	American Indian and Alaska Native			Not American Indian and Alaska Native alone or in combination [1]
		Alone or in combination [1]	Alone	In combin-ation [1]	
AMERICAN INDIAN RESERVATION					
Navajo Nation Reservation and Off-Reservation Trust Land, AZ–NM–UT.	173,667	169,321	166,824	2,497	4,346
Pine Ridge Reservation, SD–NE.	18,834	16,906	16,580	326	1,928
Fort Apache Reservation, AZ.	13,409	13,014	12,870	144	395
Gila River Indian Reservation, AZ.	11,712	11,251	10,845	406	461
Osage Reservation, OK.	47,472	9,920	6,858	3,062	37,552
San Carlos Reservation, AZ.	10,068	9,901	9,835	66	167
Rosebud Indian Reservation and Off-Reservation Trust Land, SD.	10,869	9,809	9,617	192	1,060
Tohono O'odham Nation Reservation and Off-Reservation Trust Land, AZ.	10,201	9,278	9,139	139	923
Blackfeet Indian Reservation and Off-Reservation Trust Land, MT.	10,405	9,149	8,944	205	1,256
Flathead Reservation, MT.	28,359	9,138	7,042	2,096	19,221
ALASKA NATIVE VILLAGE STATISTICAL AREA					
Knik Alaska Native village statistical area.	65,768	6,582	3,529	3,053	59,186
Bethel Alaska Native village statistical area.	6,080	4,334	3,953	381	1,746
Kenaitze Alaska Native village statistical area.	32,902	3,417	2,001	1,416	29,485
Barrow Alaska Native village statistical area.	4,212	2,889	2,577	312	1,323
Ketchikan Alaska Native village statistical area.	12,742	2,605	1,692	913	10,137
Kotzebue Alaska Native village statistical area.	3,201	2,585	2,355	230	616
Nome Alaska Native village statistical area.	3,681	2,396	1,994	402	1,285
Chickaloon Alaska Native village statistical area.	23,087	2,373	1,369	1,004	20,714
Dillingham Alaska Native village statistical area.	2,378	1,583	1,333	250	795
Sitka Alaska Native village statistical area.	4,480	1,240	855	385	3,240

[1] In combination with one or more other race groups.

Source: U.S. Census Bureau, 2010 Census Briefs, *The American Indian and Alaska Native Population: 2010*, January 2012. See also <http://www.census.gov/2010census/data/>.

Table 42. American Indian and Alaska Native Population by Selected Tribal Groupings: 2010

[As of April. Data shown for American Indian and Alaska Native tribes alone or in combination of tribes or races]

Tribal grouping	American Indian and Alaska Native tribal grouping alone or in any combination [1]	Tribal grouping	American Indian and Alaska Native tribal grouping alone or in any combination [1]
Total [2].	**5,220,579**	Navajo.	332,129
AMERICAN INDIAN TRIBES		Osage.	18,576
Apache.	111,810	Ottawa.	13,033
Arapaho.	10,861	Paiute.	13,767
Blackfeet.	105,304	Pima.	26,655
Canadian and French American Indian.	14,822	Potawatomi.	33,771
Central American Indian.	27,844	Pueblo.	62,540
Cherokee.	819,105	Puget Sound Salish.	20,260
Cheyenne.	19,051	Seminole.	31,971
Chickasaw.	52,278	Shoshone.	13,002
Chippewa.	170,742	Sioux.	170,110
Choctaw.	195,764	South American Indian.	47,233
Colville.	10,549	Spanish American Indian.	19,951
Comanche.	23,330	Tohono O'Odham.	23,478
Cree.	7,983	Ute.	11,491
Creek.	88,332	Yakama.	11,527
Crow.	15,203	Yaqui.	32,595
Delaware.	18,264	Yuman.	10,089
Hopi.	18,327	**ALASKA NATIVE TRIBES**	
Houma.	10,768	Alaskan Athabascan.	22,484
Iroquois.	81,002	Aleut.	19,282
Kiowa.	13,787	Inupiat.	33,360
Lumbee.	73,691	Tlingit-Haida.	26,080
Menominee.	11,133	Tsimshian.	3,755
Mexican American Indian.	175,494	Yup'ik.	33,889

[1] The numbers by American Indian and Alaska Native tribal grouping do not add to the total American Indian and Alaska Native population. This is because the American Indian and Alaska Native tribal groupings are tallies of the number of American Indian and Alaska Native responses rather than the number of American Indian or Alaska Native respondents. Respondents reporting several American Indian or Alaska Native groups are counted several times. [2] Includes other tribal groupings not shown separately.

Source: U.S. Census Bureau, 2010 Census Briefs, *The American Indian and Alaska Native Population: 2010*, January 2012. See also <http://www.census.gov/2010census/data/>.

Table 43. Persons Obtaining Legal Permanent Resident Status: 1901 to 2013

[8,795 represents 8,795,000. For fiscal years ending in year shown; see text, Section 8. Rates based on Census Bureau estimates as of July 1 for resident population through 1929 and for total population thereafter (excluding Alaska and Hawaii prior to 1959)]

Period/Year	Number (1,000)	Rate [1]	Period/Year	Number (1,000)	Rate [1]
1901 to 1910	8,795	10.4	1990	1,536	6.1
1911 to 1920	5,736	5.7	1995	720	2.7
1921 to 1930	4,107	3.5	2000	841	3.0
1931 to 1940	528	0.4	2005	1,122	3.8
1941 to 1950	1,035	0.7	2006	1,266	4.2
1951 to 1960	2,515	1.5	2007	1,052	3.5
1961 to 1970	3,322	1.7	2008	1,107	3.6
1971 to 1980	4,399	2.0	2009	1,131	3.7
1981 to 1990	7,256	3.0	2010	1,043	3.4
1991 to 2000	9,081	3.4	2011	1,062	3.4
2001 to 2010	10,501	3.5	2012	1,032	3.3
2011 to 2013	3,084	3.3	2013	991	3.1

[1] Annual rate per 1,000 U.S. population. Rate computed by dividing sum of annual immigration totals by sum of annual U.S. population totals for same number of years.

Source: U.S. Department of Homeland Security, Office of Immigration Statistics, "2013 Yearbook of Immigration Statistics," <http://www.dhs.gov/yearbook-immigration-statistics>, accessed August 2014.

Table 44. Refugee Arrivals and Individuals Granted Asylum by Country of Nationality: 2011 to 2013

[For year ending September 30. Data shown provide information on the number of persons admitted to the U.S. as refugees or granted asylum in the United States in the year shown. In cases with no country of nationality, the applicant's last country of residence is assigned. For definitions of refugee and asylee, see text, this section. Based on data from the Bureau of Population, Refugees, and Migration of the U.S. Department of State and the Executive Office for Immigration Review of the U.S. Department of Justice]

Country of nationality	Refugee arrivals			Country of nationality	Asylees		
	2011	2012	2013		2011	2012	2013
Total	56,384	58,179	69,909	Total	24,904	29,367	25,199
Iraq	9,388	12,163	19,487	China	8,592	10,121	8,604
Burma	16,972	14,160	16,299	Egypt	1,027	2,876	3,407
Bhutan	14,999	15,070	9,134	Ethiopia	1,071	1,121	893
Somalia	3,161	4,911	7,608	Nepal	740	975	854
Cuba	2,920	1,948	4,205	Syria	60	364	811
Iran	2,032	1,758	2,579	Venezuela	1,104	1,090	687
Congo, Democratic Republic	977	1,863	2,563	Iran	474	716	675
Sudan	334	1,077	2,160	Russia	661	718	534
Eritrea	2,032	1,346	1,824	Haiti	872	681	496
Ethiopia	560	620	765	Iraq	379	425	462
Other countries [1]	3,009	3,263	3,285	Other countries [1]	9,924	10,280	7,776

[1] Includes unknown.

Source: U.S. Department of Homeland Security, Office of Immigration Statistics, *Annual Flow Report, Refugees and Asylees: 2013*, August 2014, <http://www.dhs.gov/publication/refugees-and-asylees-2013>. See also <http://www.dhs.gov/yearbook-immigration-statistics>.

Table 45. Estimated Unauthorized Immigrants by Selected Country of Birth and State: 2000 to 2012

[In thousands (8,460 represents 8,460,000). As of January. The unauthorized resident immigrant population is defined as all foreign-born non-citizens who are not legal residents. Most unauthorized residents either entered the United States without inspection or were admitted temporarily and stayed past the date they were required to leave. Unauthorized immigrants applying for adjustment to legal permanent resident status under the Immigration and Nationality Act are unauthorized until they have been granted lawful permanent residence, even though they may have been authorized to work. These estimates were calculated using a "residual method," whereby estimates of the legally resident foreign-born population were subtracted from the total foreign-born population in order to derive the unauthorized immigrant population. All of these component populations were resident in the United States on January 1 and entered during the period from 1980 to the year prior to the year shown. Persons who entered the United States prior to 1980 were assumed to be legally resident. Estimates of the legally resident foreign-born population were based primarily on administrative data of the Department of Homeland Security, while estimates of the total foreign-born population were obtained from the American Community Survey of the U.S. Census Bureau]

Country of birth	2000	2010 [1]	2012	State of residence	2000	2010 [1]	2012
Total	8,460	11,590	11,430	Total	8,460	11,590	11,430
Mexico	4,680	6,830	6,720	California	2,510	2,910	2,820
El Salvador	430	670	690	Texas	1,090	1,780	1,830
Guatemala	290	520	560	Florida	800	730	730
Honduras	160	380	360	New York	540	690	580
Philippines	200	290	310	Illinois	440	550	540
India	120	270	260	New Jersey	350	440	430
Korea	180	220	230	Georgia	220	430	400
China	190	300	210	North Carolina	260	390	360
Ecuador	110	210	170	Arizona	330	350	350
Vietnam	160	190	160	Washington	170	260	270
Other countries	1,940	1,830	1,760	Other states	1,750	3,040	3,110

[1] Revised to be consistent with estimates derived from the 2010 Census.

Source: U.S. Department of Homeland Security, Office of Immigration Statistics, *Estimates of the Unauthorized Immigrant Population Residing in the United States: January 2012*, March 2013. See also <http://www.dhs.gov/immigration-statistics-publications>.

Table 46. Immigrant Orphans Adopted by U.S. Citizens by Sex, Age, Region, and Country of Birth: 2013

[For year ending September 30]

Region and country of birth	Total	Male	Female	Under 1 year old	1 to 4 years old	5 years old and over
REGION						
Total [1]	6,574	2,972	3,599	508	3,738	2,326
Africa	1,872	954	918	313	919	640
Asia	2,986	1,212	1,774	127	2,145	714
Europe	888	436	452	17	375	496
North America [1]	569	257	309	10	221	336
Oceania	34	13	21	20	7	7
South America	225	100	125	21	71	133
COUNTRY						
Total [1,2]	6,574	2,972	3,599	508	3,738	2,326
Brazil	17	9	8	0	4	13
Bulgaria	150	65	85	0	66	84
China	2,268	825	1,443	45	1,751	472
Colombia	142	62	80	18	46	78
Congo, Democratic Republic of the	195	85	110	38	125	32
Congo, Republic of the	77	40	37	12	59	6
Ethiopia	910	486	424	217	401	292
Ghana	157	77	80	(D)	(D)	78
Guatemala	21	8	13	0	0	21
Guyana	36	15	21	3	11	22
Haiti	327	159	168	0	166	161
Hong Kong	17	9	8	0	10	7
Hungary	23	11	12	0	6	17
India	112	36	76	(D)	(D)	34
Jamaica [1]	70	29	38	0	4	64
Japan	21	17	4	(D)	(D)	(D)
Korea, South	176	132	44	8	159	9
Latvia	65	35	30	0	5	60
Marshall Islands	18	8	10	18	0	0
Mexico	20	7	13	0	(D)	(D)
Morocco	21	13	8	8	10	3
Nicaragua	35	9	26	3	14	18
Nigeria	144	62	82	16	76	52
Pakistan	47	29	18	17	13	17
Peru	18	9	9	0	6	12
Philippines	166	79	87	0	51	115
Poland	49	24	25	0	19	30
Russia	248	129	119	5	201	42
Saint Vincent and the Grenadines	18	10	8	6	9	3
Sierra Leone	24	10	14	0	3	21
South Africa	17	10	7	0	11	6
Taiwan	86	48	38	24	39	23
Thailand	34	14	20	0	22	12
Uganda	260	139	121	16	133	111
Ukraine	320	154	166	11	65	244

D Data withheld to limit disclosure. [1] Total column includes children with unknown sex and age. [2] Includes other countries not shown separately.

Source: U.S. Department of Homeland Security, Office of Immigration Statistics, "2013 Yearbook of Immigration Statistics," <http://www.dhs.gov/yearbook-immigration-statistics>, accessed August 2014.

Table 47. Petitions for Naturalization Filed, Persons Naturalized, and Petitions Denied: 1990 to 2013

[For years ending September 30. Naturalizations refer to persons 18 and over who become citizens of the United States]

Year	Petitions filed	Persons naturalized				Petitions denied
		Total	Civilian	Military	Not reported	
1990	233,843	267,586	245,410	1,618	20,558	6,516
1995	959,963	485,720	472,518	3,855	9,347	46,067
1999	765,346	837,418	740,718	711	95,989	379,993
2000	460,916	886,026	812,579	836	72,611	399,670
2001	501,643	606,259	575,030	758	30,471	218,326
2002	700,649	572,646	550,835	1,053	20,758	139,779
2003	523,370	462,435	449,123	3,865	9,447	91,599
2004	662,796	537,151	520,771	4,668	11,712	103,339
2005	602,972	604,280	589,269	4,614	10,397	108,247
2006	730,642	702,589	684,484	6,259	11,846	120,722
2007	1,382,993	660,477	648,005	3,808	8,664	89,683
2008	525,786	1,046,539	1,032,281	4,342	9,916	121,283
2009	570,442	743,715	726,043	7,100	10,572	109,813
2010	710,544	619,913	604,410	9,122	6,381	56,994
2011	756,008	694,193	677,385	8,373	8,435	57,065
2012	899,162	757,434	745,932	7,257	4,245	65,874
2013	772,623	779,929	769,073	6,652	4,204	83,112

Source: U.S. Department of Homeland Security, Office of Immigration Statistics, "2013 Yearbook of Immigration Statistics," <http://www.dhs.gov/yearbook-immigration-statistics>, accessed August 2014.

Table 48. Persons Obtaining Legal Permanent Resident Status by Class of Admission: 2000 to 2013

[For years ending September 30. For definition of immigrants, see text, this section]

Class of admission	2000	2005	2010	2011	2012	2013
Total	841,002	1,122,257	1,042,625	1,062,040	1,031,631	990,553
New arrivals	407,279	383,955	476,049	481,948	484,072	459,751
Adjustments	433,723	738,302	566,576	580,092	547,559	530,802
Family-sponsored preferences	235,092	212,970	214,589	234,931	202,019	210,303
Unmarried sons/daughters of U.S. citizens and their children	27,635	24,729	26,998	27,299	20,660	24,358
Spouses, unmarried sons/daughters of alien residents and their children	124,540	100,139	92,088	108,618	99,709	99,115
Married sons/daughters of U.S. citizens [1]	22,804	22,953	32,817	27,704	21,752	21,294
Brothers or sisters of U.S. citizens age 21 and older [1]	60,113	65,149	62,686	71,310	59,898	65,536
Employment-based preferences	106,642	246,865	148,343	139,339	143,998	161,110
Priority workers [1]	27,566	64,731	41,055	25,251	39,316	38,978
Professionals with advanced degrees or aliens of exceptional ability [1]	20,255	42,597	53,946	66,831	50,959	63,026
Skilled workers, professionals, unskilled workers [1]	49,589	129,070	39,762	37,216	39,229	43,632
Special immigrants [1]	9,014	10,121	11,100	6,701	7,866	6,931
Employment creation (investors) [1]	218	346	2,480	3,340	6,628	8,543
Immediate relatives of U.S. citizens	346,350	436,115	476,414	453,158	478,780	439,460
Spouses	196,405	259,144	271,909	258,320	273,429	248,332
Children [2]	82,638	94,858	88,297	80,311	81,121	71,382
Parents	67,307	82,113	116,208	114,527	124,230	119,746
Refugees	56,091	112,676	92,741	113,045	105,528	77,395
Asylees	6,837	30,286	43,550	55,415	45,086	42,235
Diversity (lottery) [3]	50,920	46,234	49,763	50,103	40,320	45,618
Cancellation of removal	12,154	20,785	8,180	7,430	6,818	5,763
Parolees	3,162	7,715	1,592	1,147	758	556
Children born abroad to alien residents	(NA)	571	716	633	643	643
Nicaraguan Adjustment and Central American Relief Act (NACARA)	20,364	1,155	248	158	183	138
Haitian Refugee Immigration Fairness Act (HRIFA)	435	2,820	386	154	93	62
Other	2,955	4,065	6,103	6,527	7,405	7,270

NA Not available. [1] Includes spouses and children. [2] Includes orphans. [3] The Diversity Visa Program is a lottery available to nationals of countries with fewer than 50,000 persons granted legal permanent residency status during the preceding 5 years in the employment-based and family-sponsored preferences and immediate relative classes of admission. Includes categories of immigrants admitted under three laws intended to diversify immigration: P.L. 99-603, P.L. 100-658, and P.L. 101-649.

Source: U.S. Department of Homeland Security, Office of Immigration Statistics, "2013 Yearbook of Immigration Statistics," <http://www.dhs.gov/yearbook-immigration-statistics>, accessed August 2014.

Table 49. Persons Obtaining Legal Permanent Resident Status by Selected Country of Birth and Selected Characteristics: 2013

[For year ending September 30]

Age, marital status, occupation, class of admission	All countries [1]	Mexico	China	India	Philippines	Dominican Republic	Cuba	Vietnam	Korea, South
Total	990,553	135,028	71,798	68,458	54,446	41,311	32,219	27,101	23,166
AGE									
Under 18 years old	180,247	23,551	10,515	7,336	10,616	13,179	5,801	4,612	3,794
18 to 24 years old	122,587	20,877	7,158	4,430	6,108	5,908	3,869	4,671	2,147
25 to 34 years old	234,690	27,294	16,739	21,216	9,856	7,090	5,743	5,168	4,403
35 to 44 years old	186,102	26,749	15,271	19,624	9,072	5,404	6,395	3,879	6,644
45 to 54 years old	113,819	17,865	9,293	5,410	5,958	4,081	5,191	4,546	4,011
55 to 64 years old	71,724	8,374	6,215	4,766	5,871	2,382	2,675	3,125	1,199
65 years old and over	48,875	6,769	4,940	4,120	3,760	1,404	2,527	1,022	628
Unknown	32,509	3,549	1,667	1,556	3,205	1,863	18	78	340
MARITAL STATUS									
Single	355,199	42,389	20,669	12,495	20,597	23,113	14,001	9,295	6,995
Married	579,295	85,462	47,159	52,924	30,736	16,258	13,798	16,209	15,474
Other	51,671	6,330	3,761	2,847	2,989	1,835	4,269	1,561	614
Unknown	4,388	847	209	192	124	105	151	36	83
OCCUPATION [2]									
Management, professional, and related	117,974	5,136	12,347	19,345	7,094	1,552	690	2,551	4,672
Service	46,841	4,204	4,954	1,473	1,614	3,723	1,258	1,424	495
Sales and office	29,767	(D)	3,099	1,193	1,604	1,792	483	2,084	492
Farming, fishing, and forestry	11,589	2,762	1,277	1,685	941	351	(D)	1,294	21
Construction, extraction, maintenance and repair	6,538	2,308	(D)	42	115	76	234	(D)	40
Production, transportation, and material moving	40,153	12,267	3,702	547	805	1,972	1,987	1,439	318
MAJOR CLASS OF ADMISSION									
Family-sponsored preferences	210,303	35,528	13,109	11,943	15,170	22,147	2,492	13,847	1,795
Employment-based preferences	161,110	8,066	20,245	35,720	10,482	380	12	458	14,300
Immediate relatives of U.S. citizens	439,460	85,476	24,135	19,756	28,653	18,568	3,110	12,528	6,978
Diversity programs	45,618	7	26	39	(D)	26	194	4	16
Refugees and asylees	119,630	597	14,146	754	(D)	90	26,407	214	19
Other	14,432	5,354	137	246	106	100	4	50	58

D Data withheld to avoid disclosure. [1] Includes other countries not shown separately. [2] Those without an occupation and unknown occupation are not shown.

Source: U.S. Department of Homeland Security, Office of Immigration Statistics, "Profiles on Legal Permanent Residents: 2013," <http://www.dhs.gov/profiles-legal-permanent-residents-2013-country>, accessed September 2015.

Table 50. Persons Obtaining Legal Permanent Resident Status by Country of Birth: 1991 to 2013

[In thousands (9,080.5 represents 9,080,500). For years ending Sept. 30. Persons by country prior to 1996 are unrevised]

Region and Country of birth	1991–2000, total	2001–2010, total	2011–2012, total	2013	Region and Country of birth	1991–2000, total	2001–2010, total	2011–2012, total	2013
All countries [1]	**9,080.5**	**10,501.1**	**2,093.7**	**990.6**	Taiwan	106.3	87.9	11.5	5.4
Europe [1]	**1,226.0**	**1,263.9**	**165.5**	**86.6**	Thailand	48.4	68.3	19.4	7.6
Albania	26.2	50.5	7.0	3.2	Turkey	26.3	41.1	8.6	4.1
Bosnia and Herzegovina	[2] 38.8	89.0	1.7	0.7	Vietnam	420.8	306.1	62.5	27.1
Bulgaria	23.1	39.2	5.1	2.8	**Africa** [1]	**382.5**	**860.4**	**207.6**	**98.3**
France	27.4	39.6	7.5	4.4	Egypt	46.7	73.1	16.8	10.3
Germany	67.6	77.7	11.9	6.0	Ethiopia	49.3	109.7	28.3	13.1
Ireland	58.9	15.5	2.9	1.6	Ghana	35.6	65.3	19.4	10.3
Poland	169.5	116.8	13.2	6.4	Kenya	14.0	59.7	14.8	6.1
Romania	57.5	53.6	7.6	3.8	Liberia	16.0	45.2	8.3	3.3
Russia	[2] 127.8	139.7	17.9	9.8	Morocco	20.0	44.4	8.1	3.3
Serbia and Montenegro [3,4]	25.8	46.2	2.2	0.7	Nigeria	67.2	111.2	25.4	13.8
Soviet Union [3]	103.8	37.5	5.0	1.3	Somalia	20.1	64.2	9.7	3.8
Ukraine	[2] 141.0	149.3	15.9	8.2	South Africa	22.6	32.9	5.4	2.6
United Kingdom	135.6	153.5	23.6	13.0	**Oceania** [1]	**47.9**	**58.1**	**9.7**	**5.3**
Asia [1]	**2,973.2**	**3,784.6**	**881.2**	**400.5**	**North America** [1]	**3,910.1**	**3,605.1**	**661.7**	**315.7**
Afghanistan	17.4	24.3	3.3	2.2	Canada	137.2	168.2	25.7	13.2
Bangladesh	66.0	106.7	31.4	12.1	Mexico	2,250.5	1,693.2	289.9	135.0
Burma	11.0	45.0	33.9	12.6	Cuba	178.7	318.4	69.3	32.2
Cambodia	18.5	35.6	5.2	2.6	Dominican Republic	340.8	329.1	87.7	41.3
China	424.4	662.7	168.8	71.8	Haiti	181.7	213.8	44.9	20.4
Hong Kong	74.0	40.8	4.4	2.2	Jamaica	173.4	180.7	40.4	19.4
India	383.0	662.5	135.4	68.5	Trinidad and Tobago	63.2	61.8	10.2	4.7
Iran	112.5	125.9	27.7	12.9	El Salvador	217.3	252.8	34.9	18.3
Iraq	40.7	65.0	41.5	9.6	Guatemala	103.0	160.7	21.4	10.2
Israel	31.9	46.6	8.0	4.0	Honduras	66.7	65.4	13.0	8.9
Japan	61.4	76.1	12.2	5.9	Nicaragua	94.6	60.9	6.4	3.0
Jordan [5]	39.7	38.7	8.0	4.2	**South America** [1]	**539.3**	**906.0**	**165.5**	**80.9**
Korea, South [6]	171.1	221.5	43.7	23.2	Argentina	24.3	50.5	8.8	4.4
Laos	43.5	16.5	1.9	0.9	Brazil	52.2	123.8	23.2	11.0
Lebanon	43.4	39.5	6.2	2.8	Colombia	130.8	251.3	43.6	21.1
Nepal	3.6	33.1	21.5	13.0	Ecuador	76.3	112.5	20.4	10.6
Pakistan	124.5	157.0	30.3	13.3	Guyana	73.8	76.2	12.3	5.9
Philippines	505.3	587.2	114.3	54.4	Peru	105.6	145.7	26.7	12.6
Syria	26.1	25.9	5.8	3.4	Venezuela	29.9	84.4	18.6	9.6

[1] Includes other countries not shown separately. [2] Covers years 1992–2000. [3] Prior to 1992, data include independent republics; beginning in 1992, data are for unknown republic only. [4] Yugoslavia (unknown republic) prior to February 7, 2003. [5] Prior to 2003, includes Palestine; beginning in 2003, Palestine included in Unknown. [6] Prior to 2009, includes a small number of cases from North Korea.

Source: U.S. Department of Homeland Security, Office of Immigration Statistics, "2013 Yearbook of Immigration Statistics," <http://www.dhs.gov/yearbook-immigration-statistics>, accessed August 2014.

Table 51. Refugees and Asylees Obtaining Legal Permanent Resident Status by Country of Birth: 2001 to 2013

[For years ending September 30]

Country of birth	2001–2010, total	2011–2012, total	2013	Country of birth	2001–2010, total	2011–2012, total	2013
Total [1]	**1,325,365**	**319,074**	**119,630**	Thailand	22,405	10,182	3,076
Europe [1]	**296,794**	**8,856**	**4,338**	Uzbekistan	14,047	1,003	337
Albania	10,905	706	227	Vietnam	36,990	2,323	214
Belarus	9,310	656	335	**Africa** [1]	**242,839**	**49,835**	**20,577**
Bosnia and Herzegovina	82,485	418	111	Cameroon	7,564	2,803	1,165
Croatia	9,498	42	23	Congo, Dem. Rep. of the	5,643	3,908	1,190
Moldova	10,813	1,046	579	Egypt	7,987	1,680	2,321
Russia	32,819	1,703	836	Eritrea	4,534	3,166	1,303
Serbia and Montenegro [2]	25,422	400	138	Ethiopia	31,900	8,021	3,858
Ukraine	57,186	1,528	738	Kenya	15,351	4,032	1,307
Asia [1]	**389,469**	**179,711**	**59,649**	Liberia	28,808	3,002	761
Afghanistan	13,533	1,004	**520**	Sierra Leone	10,369	650	204
Armenia	12,408	1,288	387	Somalia	59,069	7,776	2,766
Bhutan	6,762	20,290	8,911	Sudan	23,580	2,371	956
Burma	32,904	30,716	11,110	**Oceania**	**1,453**	**123**	**40**
China	111,632	45,264	14,146	**North America** [1]	**326,846**	**70,986**	**30,854**
India	24,010	2,112	754	Cuba	276,331	61,475	26,407
Indonesia	7,618	843	338	Guatemala	7,399	1,512	734
Iran	45,515	8,816	2,481	Haiti	29,824	4,736	1,997
Iraq	40,789	34,525	6,804	**South America** [1]	**65,912**	**9,178**	**4,101**
Nepal	6,000	11,286	6,137	Colombia	40,321	3,384	1,170
Pakistan	8,339	1,225	696	Peru	7,258	871	328
				Venezuela	10,726	2,876	1,647

[1] Includes other countries and unknown not shown separately. [2] Data are for unknown republic only. Yugoslavia (unknown republic) prior to February 7, 2003.

Source: U.S. Department of Homeland Security, Office of Immigration Statistics, "2013 Yearbook of Immigration Statistics," <http://www.dhs.gov/yearbook-immigration-statistics>, accessed August 2014.

Table 52. Population by Selected Ancestry Group and Region: 2013

[In thousands (316,129 represents 316,129,000), except percent. Covers single and multiple ancestries. Ancestry refers to a person's ethnic origin or descent, "roots," or heritage; or the place of birth of the person, the person's parents, or ancestors before their arrival in the United States. The American Community Survey universe includes the household population and the population living in institutions, college dormitories, and other group quarters. Based on a sample and subject to sampling variability; see text, this section, and Appendix III. For composition of regions of the United States, see map, inside front cover]

Ancestry group	Total, (1,000)	Northeast	Midwest	South	West	Ancestry group	Total, (1,000)	Northeast	Midwest	South	West
Total population [1]	**316,129**	**18**	**21**	**37**	**23**	Irish	33,348	26	24	32	18
						Israeli	131	34	11	26	29
Afghan	95	22	3	25	49	Italian	17,222	44	17	23	17
Albanian	194	58	24	12	5	Latvian	85	29	28	23	20
American	22,218	13	20	54	14	Lithuanian	640	38	27	19	16
Arab [1]	1,823	24	25	29	22	Northern European	259	12	20	21	47
Egyptian	237	38	12	24	26	Norwegian	4,484	5	49	13	33
Iraqi	126	9	40	20	31	Pennsylvania German	294	56	25	13	6
Lebanese	490	23	27	31	19	Polish	9,383	32	37	19	13
Moroccan	91	33	16	38	13	Portuguese	1,374	46	3	13	38
Palestinian	102	16	33	30	21	Romanian	450	24	26	22	28
Syrian	154	33	19	26	22	Russian	2,845	35	17	21	27
Arab	312	16	30	33	22	Scandinavian	585	8	30	20	42
Armenian	464	22	9	9	61	Scotch-Irish	2,977	12	17	51	20
Assyrian/ Chaldean/Syriac	118	2	54	3	41	Scottish	5,310	16	20	38	26
Australian	95	20	17	25	38	Serbian	190	20	44	17	19
Austrian	684	29	24	23	24	Slavic	125	26	28	20	26
Belgian	352	11	53	19	16	Slovak	720	43	33	15	9
Brazilian	368	43	6	36	16	Slovene	171	14	57	14	15
British	1,302	15	17	40	28	Sub-Saharan African [1]	3,077	21	18	45	16
Bulgarian	99	20	26	25	29	Cape Verdean	101	86	1	9	3
Cajun	119	3	4	86	7	Ethiopian	250	9	17	43	31
Canadian	674	26	18	28	29	Ghanaian	120	42	10	39	8
Croatian	401	23	38	16	24	Nigerian	297	23	17	48	13
Czech	1,441	11	44	27	17	Somalian	119	8	52	14	26
Czechoslovakian	298	22	32	26	20	African	1,741	16	17	51	15
Danish	1,311	8	31	15	46	Swedish	3,913	14	38	17	32
Dutch	4,272	15	36	26	23	Swiss	917	15	35	21	29
Eastern European	470	40	13	24	22	Turkish	196	37	13	31	20
English	24,483	16	21	38	25	Ukrainian	969	38	19	18	25
European	3,520	12	19	35	35	Welsh	1,777	19	23	31	28
Finnish	634	12	45	14	29	West Indian [1,2]	2,821	46	4	45	5
French (except Basque)	8,228	25	22	33	20	British West Indian	101	67	3	26	5
French Canadian	2,101	41	20	25	14	Haitian	929	41	2	55	2
German	46,163	16	39	26	19	Jamaican	1,091	49	5	42	5
Greek	1,265	32	23	25	20	Trinidadian and Tobagonian	223	56	3	36	6
Guyanese	228	75	2	20	2	West Indian	271	59	4	31	5
Hungarian	1,438	32	30	21	17	Yugoslavian	291	19	33	21	27
Iranian	459	11	7	27	56						

[1] Includes other groups, not shown separately. [2] Excludes Hispanic-origin groups.

Source: U.S. Census Bureau, 2013 American Community Survey, B04006, "People Reporting Ancestry," <http://factfinder2.census.gov/>, accessed February 2015.

Table 53. Language Spoken at Home and English Speaking Ability: 2013

[See headnote, Table 52]

Language	Number	Percent who speak English less than "very well"	Language	Number	Percent who speak English less than "very well"
Total population 5 years old and over..	**296,358,760**	**(X)**	Urdu	439,129	29.9
Speak only English	234,610,020	(X)	Other Indic languages	886,013	40.4
Spanish or Spanish Creole	38,417,235	42.2	Other Indo-European languages	455,595	36.3
French (including Patois, Cajun)	1,251,815	19.5	Chinese	3,029,042	55.4
French Creole	783,017	42.0	Japanese	454,997	42.5
Italian	641,267	28.2	Korean	1,100,881	53.8
Portuguese or Portuguese Creole	677,329	37.9	Mon-Khmer, Cambodian	220,921	50.4
German	984,669	15.6	Hmong	228,965	45.2
Yiddish	157,165	35.7	Thai	151,061	48.7
Other West Germanic languages	316,377	24.9	Laotian	153,062	48.8
Scandinavian languages	122,111	10.9	Vietnamese	1,428,352	58.4
Greek	294,476	25.4	Other Asian languages	1,016,905	31.3
Russian	895,902	45.6	Tagalog	1,612,465	32.0
Polish	549,661	40.8	Other Pacific Island languages	422,386	37.9
Serbo-Croatian	255,573	38.1	Navajo	160,301	19.1
Other Slavic languages	313,986	38.0	Other Native North American	199,103	13.6
Armenian	236,580	44.8	Hungarian	82,739	29.5
Persian	399,048	37.8	Arabic	1,052,938	36.7
Gujarathi	372,104	33.5	Hebrew	210,908	16.2
Hindi	654,101	19.4	African languages	967,886	31.3
			Other and unspecified languages	152,675	41.1

X Not applicable.

Source: U.S. Census Bureau, 2013 American Community Survey, B16001, "Language Spoken at Home by Ability to Speak English for the Population 5 Years and Over," <http://factfinder2.census.gov/>, accessed February 2015.

Table 54. Language Spoken at Home by State: 2013

[In thousands (296,359 represents 296,359,000), except percent. The American Community Survey universe includes the household population and the population living in institutions, college dormitories, and other group quarters. Based on a sample and subject to sampling variability; see text, this section, and Appendix III]

State	Population 5 years old and over (1,000)	English only (1,000)	Language other than English — Number (1,000)	Language other than English — Percent of population 5 years and over	State	Population 5 years old and over (1,000)	English only (1,000)	Language other than English — Number (1,000)	Language other than English — Percent of population 5 years and over
U.S.........	296,359	234,610	61,749	20.8	MO.........	5,670	5,339	331	5.8
AL............	4,541	4,310	232	5.1	MT.........	954	918	36	3.7
AK............	680	575	105	15.5	NE.........	1,740	1,556	183	10.5
AZ............	6,197	4,536	1,661	26.8	NV.........	2,613	1,821	792	30.3
AR............	2,769	2,579	190	6.9	NH.........	1,258	1,152	105	8.4
CA............	35,832	20,131	15,701	43.8	NJ.........	8,368	5,822	2,546	30.4
CO............	4,935	4,109	826	16.7	NM.........	1,947	1,245	702	36.0
CT............	3,405	2,672	734	21.5	NY.........	18,481	12,911	5,570	30.1
DE............	870	764	105	12.1	NC.........	9,241	8,220	1,021	11.0
DC............	605	497	108	17.9	ND.........	676	640	36	5.3
FL............	18,479	13,412	5,067	27.4	OH.........	10,879	10,159	720	6.6
GA............	9,335	8,068	1,267	13.6	OK.........	3,588	3,234	353	9.8
HI............	1,313	984	330	25.1	OR.........	3,702	3,151	551	14.9
ID............	1,501	1,337	164	10.9	PA.........	12,059	10,786	1,273	10.6
IL............	12,085	9,346	2,739	22.7	RI.........	997	785	213	21.3
IN............	6,147	5,645	502	8.2	SC.........	4,481	4,173	308	6.9
IA............	2,897	2,688	210	7.2	SD.........	786	736	51	6.5
KS............	2,695	2,402	292	10.9	TN.........	6,099	5,704	394	6.5
KY............	4,123	3,918	206	5.0	TX.........	24,522	16,005	8,517	34.7
LA............	4,320	3,963	358	8.3	UT.........	2,647	2,275	373	14.1
ME............	1,264	1,185	79	6.3	VT.........	596	566	30	5.0
MD............	5,562	4,618	944	17.0	VA.........	7,751	6,599	1,152	14.9
MA............	6,329	4,912	1,416	22.4	WA.........	6,529	5,293	1,236	18.9
MI............	9,325	8,487	838	9.0	WV.........	1,751	1,712	40	2.3
MN............	5,074	4,538	536	10.6	WI.........	5,401	4,933	468	8.7
MS............	2,793	2,690	103	3.7	WY.........	544	510	34	6.3

Source: U.S. Census Bureau, 2013 American Community Survey, C16005, "Nativity by Language Spoken at Home by Ability to Speak English for the Population 5 Years and Over," <http://factfinder2.census.gov/>, accessed February 2015.

Table 55. Language Spoken at Home—25 Largest Cities: 2013

[In thousands (825 represents 825,000), except percent. Data shown for population aged 5 and over. Largest cities are based on 2014 population; see Table 24. The American Community Survey universe includes the household population and the population living in institutions, college dormitories, and other group quarters. Based on a sample and subject to sampling variability; see text, this section, and Appendix III]

City	Population 5 years and over (1,000)	English only (1,000)	Language other than English, total [1] — Number (1,000)	Language other than English, total [1] — Percent	Language other than English, total [1] — Speak English less than "very well" (1,000)	Spanish (1,000)	Other Indo-European languages (1,000)	Asian and Pacific Island languages (1,000)
Austin, TX.....................	825	555	270	32.7	101	204	23	34
Boston, MA.....................	610	390	220	36.1	99	103	68	38
Charlotte, NC....................	737	585	151	20.6	71	90	29	23
Chicago, IL.....................	2,539	1,632	907	35.7	400	620	152	100
Columbus, OH.................	761	645	117	15.3	52	35	22	26
Dallas, TX.....................	1,154	665	489	42.4	259	430	22	25
Denver, CO.....................	604	445	159	26.4	67	123	12	14
Detroit, MI.....................	639	572	67	10.5	27	43	11	2
El Paso, TX.....................	620	184	436	70.3	178	422	5	6
Fort Worth, TX..................	728	490	238	32.7	104	196	15	19
Houston, TX.....................	2,025	1,080	945	46.7	459	762	67	85
Indianapolis, IN [2].............	775	674	101	13.1	48	69	15	11
Jacksonville, FL.................	785	680	104	13.3	39	43	29	27
Los Angeles, CA...............	3,634	1,445	2,190	60.2	1,029	1,577	257	306
Memphis, TN.....................	604	550	54	9.0	25	36	5	8
Nashville–Davidson, TN [2]....	589	493	97	16.4	41	53	14	12
New York, NY....................	7,850	4,000	3,850	49.0	1,822	1,939	1,042	671
Philadelphia, PA................	1,445	1,126	318	22.0	144	146	72	78
Phoenix, AZ.....................	1,401	892	509	36.4	190	426	33	26
San Antonio, TX.................	1,308	726	582	44.5	177	531	21	24
San Diego, CA..................	1,265	753	512	40.5	194	286	52	156
San Francisco, CA.............	799	447	352	44.0	168	89	48	208
San Jose, CA..................	932	402	530	56.9	234	225	58	232
Seattle, WA.....................	620	485	135	21.8	50	28	28	62
Washington, DC.................	605	497	108	17.9	33	53	27	14

[1] Includes other language groups, not shown separately. [2] Represents the portion of a consolidated city that is not within one or more separately incorporated places.

Source: U.S. Census Bureau, 2013 American Community Survey, C16005, "Nativity by Language Spoken at Home by Ability to Speak English for the Population 5 Years and Over," <http://factfinder.census.gov/>, accessed June 2015.

Table 56. Marital Status of the Population by Sex, Race, and Hispanic Origin: 2000 to 2014

[In millions, except percent (201.8 represents 201,800,000). As of March. Persons 18 years old and over. Excludes members of Armed Forces except those living off post or with their families on post. Beginning 2005 based on an expanded sample of households. Data for 2005 and 2010 based on population controls from Census 2000. 2014 data based on population controls from Census 2010. Based on Current Population Survey, see text, this section and Appendix III]

Marital status, race and Hispanic origin	Total				Male				Female			
	2000	2005	2010	2014	2000	2005	2010	2014	2000	2005	2010	2014
Total [1]	**201.8**	**217.2**	**229.1**	**239.3**	**96.9**	**104.8**	**111.1**	**115.8**	**104.9**	**112.3**	**118.0**	**123.5**
Never married	48.2	53.9	61.5	67.3	26.1	29.6	33.7	36.3	22.1	24.3	27.8	31.0
Married [2]	120.1	127.4	129.5	132.4	59.6	63.3	64.4	65.7	60.4	64.0	65.1	66.7
Widowed	13.7	13.8	14.3	14.3	2.6	2.7	3.0	3.1	11.1	11.1	11.4	11.2
Divorced	19.8	22.1	23.7	25.3	8.5	9.2	10.0	10.7	11.3	12.9	13.7	14.6
Percent of total	100.0	100.0	100.0	100.0	100.0	100.0	100.0	100.0	100.0	100.0	100.0	100.0
Never married	23.9	24.8	26.9	28.1	27.0	28.2	30.4	31.3	21.1	21.6	23.6	25.1
Married [2]	59.5	58.6	56.4	55.3	61.5	60.4	57.9	56.8	57.6	56.9	55.1	54.0
Widowed	6.8	6.4	6.3	6.0	2.7	2.6	2.7	2.6	10.5	9.9	9.6	9.1
Divorced	9.8	10.2	10.4	10.6	8.8	8.8	9.0	9.3	10.8	11.5	11.7	11.8
White, total [3]	**168.1**	**177.5**	**185.7**	**189.3**	**81.6**	**86.6**	**91.2**	**92.7**	**86.6**	**90.9**	**94.5**	**96.6**
Never married	36.0	39.7	45.1	47.8	20.3	22.6	25.7	26.7	15.7	17.0	19.4	21.2
Married [2]	104.1	108.3	109.4	109.3	51.8	54.0	54.7	54.6	52.2	54.2	54.7	54.7
Widowed	11.5	11.5	11.8	11.6	2.2	2.3	2.5	2.5	9.3	9.2	9.3	9.1
Divorced	16.5	18.1	19.4	20.6	7.2	7.6	8.3	8.9	9.3	10.4	11.1	11.7
Percent of total	100.0	100.0	100.0	100.0	100.0	100.0	100.0	100.0	100.0	100.0	100.0	100.0
Never married	21.4	22.3	24.3	25.3	24.9	26.1	28.2	28.7	18.1	18.7	20.6	21.9
Married [2]	62.0	61.0	58.9	57.8	63.5	62.4	60.0	58.9	60.3	59.7	57.9	56.6
Widowed	6.8	6.5	6.3	6.1	2.7	2.6	2.7	2.7	10.8	10.2	9.8	9.4
Divorced	9.8	10.2	10.4	10.9	8.8	8.8	9.1	9.6	10.7	11.5	11.7	12.1
Black, total [3]	**24.0**	**25.2**	**27.3**	**29.5**	**10.7**	**11.2**	**12.3**	**13.4**	**13.3**	**13.9**	**15.0**	**16.1**
Never married	9.5	10.2	11.7	12.9	4.3	4.7	5.5	6.0	5.1	5.5	6.2	6.9
Married [2]	10.1	10.3	10.6	11.3	5.0	5.0	5.2	5.6	5.1	5.2	5.3	5.7
Widowed	1.7	1.7	1.8	1.8	0.3	0.3	0.4	0.4	1.4	1.4	1.5	1.5
Divorced	2.8	2.9	3.2	3.4	1.1	1.1	1.2	1.3	1.7	1.8	2.0	2.1
Percent of total	100.0	100.0	100.0	100.0	100.0	100.0	100.0	100.0	100.0	100.0	100.0	100.0
Never married	39.4	40.6	42.8	43.9	40.2	42.0	44.5	45.2	38.3	39.5	41.4	42.8
Married [2]	42.1	41.0	38.8	38.4	46.7	45.5	42.7	42.3	38.3	37.4	35.6	35.2
Widowed	7.0	6.6	6.7	6.2	2.8	2.7	2.9	2.8	10.5	10.0	9.8	9.1
Divorced	11.5	11.7	11.7	11.5	10.3	9.8	9.9	9.8	12.8	13.3	13.2	12.9
Asian, total [3]	**(NA)**	**9.4**	**10.7**	**13.4**	**(NA)**	**4.5**	**5.1**	**6.3**	**(NA)**	**4.9**	**5.6**	**7.1**
Never married	(NA)	2.3	2.7	3.6	(NA)	1.3	1.5	2.0	(NA)	1.0	1.2	1.6
Married [2]	(NA)	6.2	7.0	8.6	(NA)	2.9	3.3	4.0	(NA)	3.3	3.7	4.6
Widowed	(NA)	0.4	0.5	0.5	(NA)	0.1	0.1	0.1	(NA)	0.3	0.5	0.4
Divorced	(NA)	0.5	0.5	0.6	(NA)	0.2	0.2	0.2	(NA)	0.3	0.3	0.4
Percent of total	100.0	100.0	100.0	100.0	100.0	100.0	100.0	100.0	100.0	100.0	100.0	100.0
Never married	(NA)	24.8	25.1	26.9	(NA)	29.7	29.8	32.2	(NA)	20.3	20.8	22.2
Married [2]	(NA)	65.6	65.5	64.4	(NA)	64.7	65.5	63.4	(NA)	66.5	65.7	65.3
Widowed	(NA)	4.3	4.9	4.0	(NA)	1.3	1.3	1.4	(NA)	6.7	8.1	6.3
Divorced	(NA)	5.3	4.5	4.7	(NA)	4.1	3.4	3.0	(NA)	6.4	5.4	6.2
Hispanic, total [4]	**21.1**	**27.5**	**31.8**	**36.3**	**10.4**	**14.1**	**16.4**	**18.2**	**10.7**	**13.4**	**15.4**	**18.1**
Never married	5.9	8.6	10.9	13.0	3.4	5.2	6.5	7.4	2.5	3.4	4.4	5.6
Married [2]	12.7	15.6	17.1	18.9	6.2	7.8	8.6	9.2	6.5	7.8	8.5	9.7
Widowed	0.9	1.0	1.2	1.2	0.2	0.2	0.3	0.3	0.7	0.8	0.9	1.0
Divorced	1.6	2.2	2.6	3.1	0.7	0.9	1.1	1.3	1.0	1.3	1.5	1.8
Percent of total	100.0	100.0	100.0	100.0	100.0	100.0	100.0	100.0	100.0	100.0	100.0	100.0
Never married	28.0	31.3	34.2	35.9	32.3	36.7	39.3	40.7	23.4	25.6	28.7	31.0
Married [2]	60.2	57.0	53.8	52.0	59.7	55.6	52.2	50.8	60.7	58.7	55.6	53.4
Widowed	4.2	3.7	3.8	3.4	1.6	1.5	1.8	1.5	6.5	6.1	5.8	5.4
Divorced	7.6	7.9	8.2	8.6	6.4	6.3	6.7	7.1	9.3	9.7	9.9	10.2
Non-Hispanic White, total [3]	**(NA)**	**151.9**	**156.2**	**156.9**	**(NA)**	**73.4**	**75.9**	**76.4**	**(NA)**	**78.5**	**80.3**	**80.5**
Never married	(NA)	31.8	35.2	36.5	(NA)	17.8	19.8	20.2	(NA)	13.9	15.5	16.3
Married [2]	(NA)	93.5	93.3	92.1	(NA)	46.6	46.6	46.2	(NA)	47.0	46.7	46.0
Widowed	(NA)	10.6	10.6	10.5	(NA)	2.1	2.2	2.3	(NA)	8.5	8.4	8.2
Divorced	(NA)	16.0	17.0	17.8	(NA)	6.8	7.3	7.8	(NA)	9.2	9.7	10.0
Percent of total	100.0	100.0	100.0	100.0	100.0	100.0	100.0	100.0	100.0	100.0	100.0	100.0
Never married	(NA)	20.9	22.6	23.3	(NA)	24.3	26.0	26.4	(NA)	17.7	19.3	20.3
Married [2]	(NA)	61.5	59.7	58.8	(NA)	63.5	61.4	60.5	(NA)	59.7	58.1	57.1
Widowed	(NA)	6.9	6.8	6.7	(NA)	2.8	2.9	3.0	(NA)	10.8	10.5	10.2
Divorced	(NA)	10.6	10.9	11.3	(NA)	9.3	9.7	10.2	(NA)	11.7	12.1	12.4

NA Not available. [1] Includes persons of other races not shown separately. [2] Includes persons who are married with spouse present, married with spouse absent, and separated. [3] Beginning 2005, data represent persons who selected this race group only and exclude persons reporting more than one race. The CPS in 2000 only allowed respondents to report one race group. See also comments on race in the text for this section. [4] Hispanic persons may be of any race.

Source: U.S. Census Bureau, Current Population Reports, P20-537, 2001; and "America's Families and Living Arrangements," <http://www.census.gov/hhes/families/data/cps.html>, accessed March 2015.

Table 57. Marital Status of the Population by Sex and Age: 2014

[115,825 represents 115,825,000. As of March. Excludes members of Armed Forces except those living off post or with their families on post. Population controls based on Census 2010. Based on Current Population Survey, see text, this section, and Appendix III]

Sex and age	Number of persons (1,000)					Percent distribution				
	Total	Never married	Married [1]	Widowed	Divorced	Total	Never married	Married [1]	Widowed	Divorced
Male..............	**115,825**	**36,302**	**65,749**	**3,052**	**10,722**	**100.0**	**31.3**	**56.8**	**2.6**	**9.3**
18 to 19 years old......	4,053	3,962	76	–	14	100.0	97.8	1.9	–	0.4
20 to 24 years old......	11,227	10,101	1,063	4	59	100.0	90.0	9.4	–	0.5
25 to 29 years old......	10,816	7,311	3,202	12	291	100.0	67.6	29.6	0.1	2.7
30 to 34 years old......	10,370	4,246	5,545	16	562	100.0	40.9	53.5	0.2	5.4
35 to 39 years old......	9,555	2,497	6,162	27	869	100.0	26.1	64.6	0.3	9.1
40 to 44 years old......	10,035	1,988	6,755	68	1,224	100.0	19.8	67.4	0.7	12.2
45 to 49 years old......	10,145	1,520	7,211	83	1,331	100.0	15.0	71.1	0.8	13.1
50 to 54 years old......	10,906	1,736	7,457	130	1,582	100.0	15.9	68.3	1.2	14.5
55 to 64 years old......	18,996	2,073	13,609	458	2,855	100.0	10.9	71.6	2.4	15.0
65 to 74 years old......	12,069	586	9,301	760	1,421	100.0	4.9	77.1	6.3	11.8
75 to 84 years old......	5,755	221	4,250	867	417	100.0	3.8	73.9	15.1	7.2
85 years old and over...	1,898	59	1,115	627	96	100.0	3.1	58.7	33.1	5.1
Female..............	**123,480**	**31,002**	**66,667**	**11,208**	**14,602**	**100.0**	**25.1**	**54.0**	**9.1**	**11.8**
18 to 19 years old......	3,824	3,649	159	2	14	100.0	95.4	4.1	–	0.4
20 to 24 years old......	11,028	9,162	1,713	17	136	100.0	83.1	15.5	0.2	1.2
25 to 29 years old......	10,629	5,718	4,437	49	423	100.0	53.8	41.8	0.5	4.0
30 to 34 years old......	10,590	3,328	6,443	50	768	100.0	31.4	60.8	0.5	7.3
35 to 39 years old......	9,844	2,078	6,582	91	1,092	100.0	21.1	66.9	0.9	11.1
40 to 44 years old......	10,342	1,552	7,175	149	1,466	100.0	15.0	69.3	1.4	14.2
45 to 49 years old......	10,516	1,311	7,278	205	1,722	100.0	12.5	69.2	1.9	16.4
50 to 54 years old......	11,433	1,280	7,720	447	1,987	100.0	11.2	67.5	3.9	17.4
55 to 64 years old......	20,536	1,853	13,334	1,483	3,866	100.0	9.0	65.0	7.2	18.8
65 to 74 years old......	13,718	646	8,150	2,729	2,193	100.0	4.7	59.4	19.9	16.0
75 to 84 years old......	7,671	292	3,060	3,575	743	100.0	3.8	39.9	46.6	9.7
85 years old and over...	3,348	132	614	2,411	192	100.0	3.9	18.3	72.0	5.7

– Represents or rounds to zero. [1] Includes persons who are married with spouse present, married with spouse absent, and separated.

Source: U.S. Census Bureau, "America's Families and Living Arrangements: 2014: Adults (A table series), Table 1A. Marital Status of People 15 Years and Over, by Age, Sex, Personal Earnings, Race, and Hispanic Origin: 2014," <http://www.census.gov/hhes/families/data/cps2014A.html>, accessed March 2015.

Table 58. Living Arrangements of Persons 15 Years Old and Over by Age and Sex: 2014

[252,224 represents 252,224,000. As of March. See headnote, Table 57]

Living arrangement	Total	15 to 19 years old	20 to 24 years old	25 to 34 years old	35 to 44 years old	45 to 54 years old	55 to 64 years old	65 to 74 years old	75 years old and over
NUMBER (1,000)									
Total.................	**252,224**	**20,797**	**22,255**	**42,406**	**39,776**	**43,000**	**39,532**	**25,787**	**18,673**
Alone........................	34,185	94	1,470	4,211	3,530	5,163	7,171	5,750	6,797
With spouse.................	123,700	152	2,339	18,082	24,610	27,641	25,367	16,842	8,668
With other persons..........	94,339	20,551	18,446	20,113	11,636	10,196	6,994	3,195	3,208
Male........................	122,353	10,581	11,227	21,186	19,590	21,051	18,996	12,069	7,653
Alone........................	15,151	61	684	2,481	2,216	2,683	3,241	2,058	1,728
With spouse.................	61,850	47	859	8,140	11,938	13,743	12,911	9,025	5,186
With other persons..........	45,352	10,473	9,684	10,565	5,436	4,625	2,844	986	739
Female......................	129,871	10,215	11,028	21,219	20,186	21,949	20,536	13,718	11,019
Alone........................	19,034	33	786	1,730	1,314	2,482	3,930	3,692	5,069
With spouse.................	61,850	104	1,481	9,941	12,671	13,898	12,456	7,817	3,482
With other persons..........	48,987	10,078	8,761	9,548	6,201	5,569	4,150	2,209	2,468
PERCENT DISTRIBUTION									
Total........................	100.0	100.0	100.0	100.0	100.0	100.0	100.0	100.0	100.0
Alone........................	13.6	0.5	6.6	9.9	8.9	12.0	18.1	22.3	36.4
With spouse.................	49.0	0.7	10.5	42.6	61.9	64.3	64.2	65.3	46.4
With other persons..........	37.4	98.8	82.9	47.4	29.3	23.7	17.7	12.4	17.2
Male........................	100.0	100.0	100.0	100.0	100.0	100.0	100.0	100.0	100.0
Alone........................	12.4	0.6	6.1	11.7	11.3	12.7	17.1	17.1	22.6
With spouse.................	50.6	0.4	7.7	38.4	60.9	65.3	68.0	74.8	67.8
With other persons..........	37.1	99.0	86.3	49.9	27.7	22.0	15.0	8.2	9.7
Female......................	100.0	100.0	100.0	100.0	100.0	100.0	100.0	100.0	100.0
Alone........................	14.7	0.3	7.1	8.2	6.5	11.3	19.1	26.9	46.0
With spouse.................	47.6	1.0	13.4	46.8	62.8	63.3	60.7	57.0	31.6
With other persons..........	37.7	98.7	79.4	45.0	30.7	25.4	20.2	16.1	22.4

Source: U.S. Census Bureau, "America's Families and Living Arrangements: 2014: Adults (A table series), Table A2. Family Status and Household Relationship of People 15 Years and Over, by Marital Status, Age, and Sex: 2014," <http://www.census.gov/hhes/families/data/cps2014.html>, accessed March 2015.

Table 59. Households, Families, Subfamilies, and Married Couples: 1990 to 2014

[In thousands (93,347 represents 93,347,000), except as indicated. As of March. Excludes members of the Armed Services except those living off post or with their families on post. Beginning 2001 based on an expanded sample of households. Population controls for 2010 based on Census 2000; beginning 2012 population controls based on Census 2010. Based on Current Population Survey (CPS), see text, this section and Appendix III. Minus sign (-) indicates decrease]

Type of Unit	1990	2000	2010	2012	2013	2014	Percent change 1990 to 2000	Percent change 2000 to 2010	Percent change 2010 to 2014
Households	**93,347**	**104,705**	**117,538**	**121,084**	**122,459**	**123,229**	12	12	5
Persons per household	2.63	2.62	2.59	2.55	2.54	2.54	(X)	(X)	(X)
White [1]	80,163	87,671	95,489	96,964	97,705	98,052	9	9	3
Black [1]	10,486	12,849	14,730	15,583	15,872	16,064	23	15	9
Asian [1]	(NA)	(NA)	4,687	5,374	5,560	5,749	(NA)	(NA)	23
Hispanic [2]	5,933	9,319	13,298	14,939	15,589	15,874	57	43	19
Family households	66,090	72,025	78,833	80,506	80,902	81,353	9	9	3
Married couple	52,317	55,311	58,410	58,949	59,204	59,629	6	6	2
Male householder [3]	2,884	4,028	5,580	5,888	6,229	6,304	40	39	13
Female householder [3]	10,890	12,687	14,843	15,669	15,469	15,420	17	17	4
Nonfamily households	27,257	32,680	38,705	40,578	41,558	41,877	20	18	8
Male householder	11,606	14,641	18,263	19,195	19,747	19,658	26	25	8
Female householder	15,651	18,039	20,442	21,383	21,810	22,219	15	13	9
One person	22,999	26,724	31,399	33,188	33,570	34,185	16	17	9
Families	**66,090**	**72,025**	**78,833**	**80,506**	**80,902**	**81,353**	9	9	3
Persons per family	3.17	3.17	3.16	3.13	3.12	3.13	(X)	(X)	(X)
With own children [4]	32,289	34,605	35,218	34,989	35,058	34,955	7	2	-1
Without own children [4]	33,801	37,420	43,615	45,517	45,844	46,398	11	17	6
Married couple	52,317	55,311	58,410	58,949	59,204	59,629	6	6	2
With own children [4]	24,537	25,248	24,575	23,704	23,870	23,933	3	-3	-3
Without own children [4]	27,780	30,062	33,835	35,245	35,333	35,697	8	13	6
Male householder [3]	2,884	4,028	5,580	5,888	6,229	6,304	40	39	13
With own children [4]	1,153	1,786	2,224	2,415	2,560	2,472	55	25	11
Without own children [4]	1,731	2,242	3,356	3,473	3,669	3,832	30	50	14
Female householder [3]	10,890	12,687	14,843	15,669	15,469	15,420	17	17	4
With own children [4]	6,599	7,571	8,419	8,869	8,627	8,550	15	11	2
Without own children [4]	4,290	5,116	6,424	6,799	6,842	6,870	19	26	7
Unrelated subfamilies	534	571	484	604	553	511	7	-15	6
Married couple	68	37	93	108	103	107	(B)	(B)	15
Male reference persons [3]	45	57	44	75	67	52	(B)	(B)	(B)
Female reference persons [3]	421	477	347	421	383	352	13	-27	1
Related subfamilies	2,403	2,984	4,300	4,353	4,253	4,502	24	44	5
Married couple	871	1,149	1,881	1,990	1,988	2,114	32	64	12
Father-child [3]	153	201	313	315	309	337	31	56	8
Mother-child [3]	1,378	1,634	2,106	2,048	1,956	2,051	19	29	-3
Married couples	**53,256**	**56,497**	**60,384**	**61,047**	**61,295**	**61,850**	6	7	2
With own household	52,317	55,311	58,410	58,949	59,204	59,629	6	6	2
Without own household	939	1,186	1,974	2,098	2,091	2,221	26	66	13
Percent without	1.8	2.1	3.2	3.4	3.4	3.6	(X)	(X)	(X)

B Base less than 75,000. NA Not available. X Not applicable. [1] Beginning with the 2003 CPS, respondents could choose more than one race. Beginning in 2003, data represent persons who selected this race group only and exclude persons reporting more than one race. The CPS in prior years only allowed respondents to report one race group. See also comments on race in text for this section. [2] Persons of Hispanic origin may be of any race. [3] No spouse present. [4] Under 18 years old.

Source: U.S. Census Bureau, "America's Families and Living Arrangements," <http://www.census.gov/hhes/families/data/cps.html>, accessed March 2015.

Table 60. Interracially Married Couples by Race and Hispanic Origin of Spouses: 1980 to 2014

[In thousands (49,714 represents 49,714,000). As of March. Persons 15 years old and over. Persons of Hispanic origin may be of any race. Population controls for 2010 based on Census 2000; population controls for 2013 and 2014 based on Census 2010. Based on Current Population Survey; see headnote, Table 59 and Appendix III]

Race and origin of spouses	1980	1990	2000	2010	2013	2014
Married couples, total [1]	**49,714**	**53,256**	**56,497**	**60,384**	**61,295**	**61,850**
Interracial married couples, total	651	964	1,464	2,413	2,731	2,910
White [2] /Black [2]	167	211	363	558	571	602
Black husband/White wife	122	150	268	390	402	400
White husband/Black wife	45	61	95	168	169	202
White [2] /other race [3]	450	720	1,051	1,723	1,994	2,108
Black [2] /other race [3]	34	33	50	132	166	200
HISPANIC ORIGIN						
Hispanic/Hispanic	1,906	3,085	4,739	6,166	6,789	6,898
Hispanic/other origin (not Hispanic)	891	1,193	1,743	2,289	2,714	2,711
All other couples (not of Hispanic origin)	46,917	48,979	50,015	51,928	51,792	52,242

[1] Includes other married couples not shown separately. [2] See footnote 1, Table 59 [3] "Other race," is any race other than White or Black, such as American Indian, Asian, etc. Total excludes combinations of other races by other races.

Source: U.S. Census Bureau, "Families and Living Arrangements, Table MS-3. Interracial Married Couples: 1980 to 2002"; and "America's Families and Living Arrangements, 2014: Family groups (FG table series), Table FG3. Married Couple Family Groups, By Presence Of Own Children Under 18, And Age, Earnings, Education, And Race And Hispanic Origin Of Both Spouses," <http://www.census.gov/hhes/families/data/cps2014FG.html>, accessed March 2015.

Table 61. Households and Persons Per Household by Type of Household: 2000 to 2014

[104,705 represents 104,705,000. As of March. See headnote, Table 59]

Type of household	Households						Persons per household		
	Number (1,000)			Percent distribution			2000	2010	2014
	2000	2010	2014	2000	2010	2014			
Total households.............................	**104,705**	**117,538**	**123,229**	**100**	**100**	**100**	**2.62**	**2.59**	**2.54**
Family households................................	72,025	78,833	81,353	69	67	66	3.24	3.24	3.21
Married couple family......................	55,311	58,410	59,629	53	50	48	3.26	3.24	3.19
Male householder, no spouse present........	4,028	5,580	6,304	4	5	5	3.16	3.24	3.18
Female householder, no spouse present.....	12,687	14,843	15,420	12	13	13	3.17	3.23	3.27
Nonfamily households...........................	32,680	38,705	41,877	31	33	34	1.25	1.26	1.25
Living alone................................	26,724	31,399	34,185	26	27	28	1.00	1.00	1.00
Male householder.............................	14,641	18,263	19,658	14	16	16	1.34	1.35	1.33
Living alone................................	11,181	13,971	15,151	11	12	12	1.00	1.00	1.00
Female householder...........................	18,039	20,442	22,219	17	17	18	1.17	1.18	1.18
Living alone................................	15,543	17,428	19,034	15	15	15	1.00	1.00	1.00

Source: U.S. Census Bureau, Current Population Reports, P20-537, 2001; and "America's Families and Living Arrangements," <http://www.census.gov/hhes/families/data/cps.html>, accessed March 2015.

Table 62. Households by Age of Householder and Size of Household: 1990 to 2014

[In millions (93.3 represents 93,300,000). As of March. Based on Current Population Survey; see headnote, Table 59]

Age of householder and size of household	1990	2000	2005	2010	2011	2012	2013	2014
Total............................	**93.3**	**104.7**	**113.3**	**117.5**	**118.7**	**121.1**	**122.5**	**123.2**
15 to 24 years old...............	5.1	5.9	6.7	6.2	6.1	6.2	6.3	6.4
25 to 29 years old...............	9.4	8.5	9.2	9.4	9.3	9.2	9.3	9.3
30 to 34 years old...............	11.0	10.1	10.1	9.8	10.2	10.6	10.8	10.7
35 to 44 years old...............	20.6	24.0	23.2	21.5	21.3	21.2	21.3	21.1
45 to 54 years old...............	14.5	20.9	23.4	24.9	24.5	24.2	24.1	23.7
55 to 64 years old...............	12.5	13.6	17.5	20.4	21.8	22.8	22.8	23.2
65 to 74 years old...............	11.7	11.3	11.5	13.2	13.3	14.5	15.3	16.0
75 years old and over...........	8.4	10.4	11.6	12.1	12.0	12.3	12.6	12.8
One person......................	23.0	26.7	30.1	31.4	32.7	33.2	33.6	34.2
Male...........................	9.0	11.2	12.8	14.0	14.5	14.8	15.0	15.2
Female.........................	14.0	15.5	17.3	17.4	18.2	18.4	18.6	19.0
Two persons.....................	30.1	34.7	37.4	39.5	39.7	41.0	41.5	41.6
Three persons...................	16.1	17.2	18.3	18.6	18.5	19.2	19.3	19.4
Four persons....................	14.5	15.3	16.4	16.1	15.9	16.0	16.4	16.2
Five persons....................	6.2	7.0	7.2	7.4	7.3	7.3	7.4	7.5
Six persons.....................	2.1	2.4	2.5	2.8	2.8	2.7	2.7	2.8
Seven persons or more...........	1.3	1.4	1.4	1.7	1.7	1.6	1.6	1.6

Source: U.S. Census Bureau, Current Population Reports, P20-537, and earlier reports; and "America's Families and Living Arrangements: 2014: Households (H table series)," <http://www.census.gov/hhes/families/data/cps2014H.html>, accessed March 2015 and earlier releases.

Table 63. Persons Living Alone by Sex and Age: 2000 to 2014

[26,724 represents 26,724,000. As of March. Excludes members of Armed Forces except those living off post or with their families on post. Beginning 2005, based on an expanded sample of households. Data for 2005 and 2010 based on Census 2000 population controls. Data for 2014 based on Census 2010 population controls. Based on Current Population Survey, see text, this section and Appendix III]

Sex and age	Number of persons (1,000)						Percent distribution				
	2000	2005	2010	2014			2000	2010	2014		
				Total	Male	Female			Total	Male	Female
Total.......................	**26,724**	**30,137**	**31,399**	**34,185**	**15,151**	**19,034**	**100**	**100**	**100**	**100**	**100**
15 to 24 years old..........	1,144	1,521	1,367	1,564	745	819	4	4	5	5	4
25 to 34 years old..........	3,848	3,836	3,917	4,211	2,481	1,730	14	12	12	16	9
35 to 44 years old..........	4,109	3,988	3,453	3,530	2,216	1,314	15	11	10	15	7
45 to 64 years old..........	7,842	10,180	11,345	12,334	5,924	6,412	29	36	36	39	34
65 to 74 years old..........	4,091	4,222	4,709	5,750	2,058	3,692	15	15	17	14	19
75 years old and over.......	5,692	6,391	6,608	6,797	1,728	5,069	21	21	20	11	27

Source: U.S. Census Bureau, Current Population Reports, P20-537, 2001; and "America's Families and Living Arrangements: 2014: Adults (A table series), Table A2. Family Status and Household Relationship of People 15 Years and Over, by Marital Status, Age, and Sex," <http://www.census.gov/hhes/families/data/cps2014A.html>, accessed March 2015 and earlier releases.

Table 64. Family Households by Number of Own Children Under 18 Years of Age: 2000 to 2014

[72,025 represents 72,025,000. As of March. Based on Current Population Survey, Annual Social and Economic Supplement; see headnote, Table 67]

Race, Hispanic origin, and year	Number of families (1,000)					Percent distribution				
	Total	No children	One child	Two children	Three or more children	Total	No children	One child	Two children	Three or more children
ALL FAMILIES [1]										
2000	72,025	37,420	14,311	13,215	7,080	100	52	20	18	10
2010	78,833	43,615	15,149	12,947	7,122	100	55	19	16	9
2014, total	**81,353**	**46,398**	**14,910**	**13,044**	**7,001**	**100**	**57**	**18**	**16**	**9**
Married couple	59,629	35,697	9,298	9,536	5,099	100	60	16	16	9
Male householder [2]	6,304	3,832	1,445	731	296	100	61	23	12	5
Female householder [2]	15,420	6,870	4,167	2,778	1,605	100	45	27	18	10
WHITE FAMILIES [3]										
2000	60,251	32,144	11,496	10,918	5,693	100	53	19	18	9
2010	64,120	36,464	11,856	10,275	5,525	100	57	18	16	9
2014, total	**64,904**	**38,108**	**11,248**	**10,158**	**5,389**	**100**	**59**	**17**	**16**	**8**
Married couple	50,284	30,764	7,475	7,834	4,212	100	61	15	16	8
Male householder [2]	4,639	2,760	1,101	563	215	100	59	24	12	5
Female householder [2]	9,981	4,585	2,673	1,761	962	100	46	27	18	10
BLACK FAMILIES [3]										
2000	8,664	3,882	2,101	1,624	1,058	100	45	24	19	12
2010	9,358	4,502	2,142	1,608	1,106	100	48	23	17	12
2014, total	**9,854**	**4,936**	**2,252**	**1,609**	**1,057**	**100**	**50**	**23**	**16**	**11**
Married couple	4,528	2,594	811	680	443	100	57	18	15	10
Male householder [2]	1,064	637	252	111	65	100	60	24	10	6
Female householder [2]	4,262	1,705	1,189	818	551	100	40	28	19	13
ASIAN FAMILIES [3]										
2010	3,592	1,794	777	754	267	100	50	22	21	7
2014, total	**4,320**	**2,241**	**908**	**888**	**284**	**100**	**52**	**21**	**21**	**7**
Married couple	3,469	1,654	761	801	253	100	48	22	23	7
Male householder [2]	339	279	29	27	5	100	82	9	8	1
Female householder [2]	512	308	118	60	25	100	60	23	12	5
HISPANIC FAMILIES [4]										
2000	7,561	2,747	1,791	1,693	1,330	100	36	24	22	18
2010	10,412	4,173	2,344	2,269	1,626	100	40	23	22	16
2014, total	**12,167**	**5,311**	**2,597**	**2,529**	**1,730**	**100**	**44**	**21**	**21**	**14**
Married couple	7,495	3,249	1,464	1,628	1,154	100	43	20	22	15
Male householder [2]	1,380	885	232	183	80	100	64	17	13	6
Female householder [2]	3,292	1,177	901	719	495	100	36	27	22	15
NON-HISPANIC WHITE FAMILIES [3]										
2010	54,445	32,569	9,691	8,173	4,012	100	60	18	15	7
2014, total	**53,992**	**33,288**	**8,952**	**7,927**	**3,826**	**100**	**62**	**17**	**15**	**7**
Married couple	43,422	27,781	6,145	6,341	3,155	100	64	14	15	7
Male householder [2]	3,429	1,975	900	408	146	100	58	26	12	4
Female householder [2]	7,140	3,532	1,906	1,178	524	100	49	27	16	7

[1] Includes other races and non-Hispanic groups, not shown separately. [2] No spouse present. [3] Beginning with the 2003 Current Population Survey (CPS), respondents could choose more than one race. Beginning 2010 data represent persons who selected this race group only and exclude persons reporting more than one race. The CPS prior to 2003 only allowed respondents to report one race group. See also comments on race in the text for this section. [4] Hispanic persons may be of any race.

Source: U.S. Census Bureau, Current Population Reports, P20-537; and "America's Families and Living Arrangements: 2014: Family households (F table series), Table F1. Family Households, By Type, Age Of Own Children, Age Of Family Members, And Age, Race And Hispanic Origin Of Householder," <http://www.census.gov/hhes/families/data/cps2014F.html>, accessed March 2015.

Table 65. Family Households With Own Children Under 18 Years of Age by Type of Family, 2000 to 2014, and by Age of Householder, 2014

[34,605 represents 34,605,000. As of March. See headnote, Table 67]

Age of householder	Family households with children		Married couple households with children		Male householder with children [1]		Female householder with children [1]	
	Number (1,000)	Percent of all family households	Number (1,000)	Percent of all married couple households	Number (1,000)	Percent of all male householder families [1]	Number (1,000)	Percent of all female householder families [1]
2000, total	34,605	48	25,248	46	1,786	44	7,571	60
2010, total	35,218	45	24,575	42	2,224	40	8,419	57
2014, total	**34,955**	**43**	**23,933**	**40**	**2,472**	**39**	**8,550**	**55**
15 to 24 years old	1,533	46	560	54	169	18	802	59
25 to 34 years old	9,702	73	5,937	70	751	51	3,014	89
35 to 44 years old	13,392	81	9,559	81	836	64	2,997	84
45 to 54 years old	8,397	48	6,426	49	546	46	1,425	47
55 to 64 years old	1,589	11	1,211	10	133	16	245	12
65 years old and over	343	2	239	2	38	7	67	3

[1] No spouse present.

Source: U.S. Census Bureau, Current Population Reports, P20-537, 2001; and "America's Families and Living Arrangements: 2014: Family households (F table series), Table F1. Family Households, By Type, Age Of Own Children, Age Of Family Members, And Age, Race And Hispanic Origin Of Householder," <http://www.census.gov/hhes/families/data/cps2014F.html>, accessed March 2015, and earlier releases.

Table 66. Families by Type, Race, and Hispanic Origin: 2014

[In thousands (81,353 represents 81,353,000). As of March. Excludes members of Armed Forces except those living off post or with their families on post. Population controls based on Census 2010 and an expanded sample of households. Based on Current Population Survey, Annual Social and Economic Supplement; see text, this section and Appendix III]

Characteristic	All families	Married couple families						Female family householder[4]						Male family householder[4], all races
		All races[1]	White[2]	Black[2]	Asian[2]	Hispanic[3]	Non-Hispanic White[2]	All races[1]	White[2]	Black[2]	Asian[2]	Hispanic[3]	Non-Hispanic White[2]	
All families	81,353	59,629	50,284	4,528	3,469	7,495	43,422	15,420	9,981	4,262	512	3,292	7,140	6,304
Age of householder:														
Under 25 years old	3,361	1,035	894	86	23	300	622	1,367	824	382	57	378	501	960
25 to 34 years old	13,308	8,457	6,964	631	587	1,595	5,514	3,372	2,009	1,067	102	916	1,237	1,479
35 to 44 years old	16,623	11,767	9,529	945	938	2,028	7,699	3,560	2,240	1,057	120	841	1,515	1,297
45 to 54 years old	17,438	13,215	10,877	1,178	869	1,712	9,301	3,030	2,012	818	91	576	1,506	1,193
55 to 64 years old	15,039	12,261	10,518	950	573	1,061	9,540	1,971	1,350	492	73	323	1,062	807
65 to 74 years old	9,780	8,434	7,492	503	318	519	7,009	1,036	737	237	39	138	607	310
75 years old and over	5,804	4,461	4,011	236	161	280	3,737	1,084	811	210	28	119	711	259
Without own children under 18	46,398	35,697	30,764	2,594	1,654	3,249	27,781	6,870	4,585	1,705	308	1,177	3,532	3,832
With own children under 18	34,955	23,933	19,520	1,934	1,816	4,246	15,641	8,550	5,396	2,557	203	2,115	3,608	2,472
One own child under 18	14,910	9,298	7,475	811	761	1,464	6,145	4,167	2,673	1,189	118	901	1,906	1,445
Two own children under 18	13,044	9,536	7,834	680	801	1,628	6,341	2,778	1,761	818	60	719	1,178	731
Three or more own children under 18	7,001	5,099	4,212	443	253	1,154	3,155	1,605	962	551	25	495	524	296
Age of own children:														
Of any age	48,009	31,267	25,497	2,585	2,324	5,363	20,580	13,056	8,476	3,679	350	2,813	6,059	3,687
Under 25 years old[5]	41,479	28,161	23,001	2,300	2,091	4,901	18,507	10,320	6,532	3,046	271	2,429	4,472	2,998
Under 18 years old	34,955	23,933	19,520	1,934	1,816	4,246	15,641	8,550	5,396	2,557	203	2,115	3,608	2,472
Under 12 years old	25,551	17,605	14,339	1,366	1,408	3,326	11,319	6,139	3,777	1,895	145	1,611	2,424	1,807
Under 6 years old	14,978	10,467	8,542	782	840	2,025	6,715	3,453	2,072	1,108	78	946	1,269	1,058
Under 3 years old	8,423	6,045	4,971	440	448	1,060	4,016	1,746	1,065	546	35	518	620	632
Under 1 year old	2,749	1,937	1,616	129	123	337	1,311	564	374	147	10	168	224	248
Members 65 and older:														
Without members 65 and older	61,486	43,931	36,620	3,529	2,682	6,343	30,840	12,506	7,904	3,662	365	2,840	5,475	5,048
With members 65 and older	19,867	15,698	13,663	999	787	1,153	12,582	2,913	2,077	601	146	452	1,665	1,256
Marital status of householder:														
Married, spouse present	59,629	59,629	50,284	4,528	3,469	7,495	43,422	(X)	(X)	(X)	(X)	(X)	(X)	(X)
Married, spouse absent	900	(X)	(X)	(X)	(X)	(X)	(X)	629	(NA)	(NA)	(NA)	(NA)	(NA)	271
Widowed	2,756	(X)	(X)	(X)	(X)	(X)	(X)	2,261	(NA)	(NA)	(NA)	(NA)	(NA)	495
Divorced	6,733	(X)	(X)	(X)	(X)	(X)	(X)	4,926	(NA)	(NA)	(NA)	(NA)	(NA)	1,807
Separated	1,951	(X)	(X)	(X)	(X)	(X)	(X)	1,528	(NA)	(NA)	(NA)	(NA)	(NA)	423
Never married	9,384	(X)	(X)	(X)	(X)	(X)	(X)	6,076	(NA)	(NA)	(NA)	(NA)	(NA)	3,308

NA Not available. X Not applicable. [1] Includes other races and non-Hispanic groups, not shown separately. [2] Data represent persons who selected this race group only and exclude persons reporting more than one race. See also comments on race in the text for this section. [3] Persons of Hispanic origin may be of any race. [4] No spouse present. [5] Children are included regardless of their marital status.

Source: U.S. Census Bureau, "America's Families and Living Arrangements: 2014," <http://www.census.gov/hhes/families/data/cps2014.html>, accessed March 2015.

Table 67. Family Groups With Children Under 18 Years of Age by Race and Hispanic Origin: 2000 to 2014

[In thousands (37,496 represents 37,496,000). As of March. Family groups are family households, related subfamilies, and unrelated subfamilies; each married couple or parent/child group is counted separately, even if they reside in the same household. Excludes members of Armed Forces except those living off post or with their families on post. Beginning 2005, based on an expanded sample of households. Data for 2005 and 2010 based on Census 2000 population controls. Data for 2014 based on Census 2010 population controls. Based on Current Population Survey, Annual Social and Economic Supplement, see text, this section and Appendix III]

Race and Hispanic origin of householder or reference person	Number (1,000)				Percent distribution			
	2000	2005	2010	2014	2000	2005	2010	2014
All races, total [1]	**37,496**	**39,317**	**39,947**	**39,814**	**100**	**100**	**100**	**100**
Two-parent family groups [2]	25,771	26,482	27,082	26,712	69	67	68	67
One-parent family groups	11,725	12,835	11,686	11,874	31	32	29	30
Maintained by mother	9,681	10,366	9,924	9,929	26	26	25	25
Maintained by father	2,044	2,469	1,762	1,945	5	6	4	5
Grandparent householder with grandchild(ren) under 18	(NA)	(NA)	1,179	1,228	(NA)	(NA)	3	3
White, total [3]	**30,079**	**30,960**	**30,933**	**30,173**	**100**	**100**	**100**	**100**
Two-parent family groups [2]	22,241	22,319	22,457	21,591	74	72	73	72
One-parent family groups	7,838	8,641	7,729	7,779	26	28	25	26
Maintained by mother	6,216	6,747	6,396	6,298	21	22	21	21
Maintained by father	1,622	1,894	1,333	1,481	5	6	4	5
Grandparent householder with grandchild(ren) under 18	(NA)	(NA)	747	803	(NA)	(NA)	2	3
Black, total [3]	**5,530**	**5,495**	**5,903**	**5,953**	**100**	**100**	**100**	**100**
Two-parent family groups [2]	2,135	2,065	2,275	2,300	39	38	39	39
One-parent family groups	3,396	3,430	3,280	3,309	61	62	56	56
Maintained by mother	3,060	3,037	2,977	2,968	55	55	50	50
Maintained by father	335	393	303	341	6	7	5	6
Grandparent householder with grandchild(ren) under 18	(NA)	(NA)	348	344	(NA)	(NA)	6	6
Asian, total [3]	**1,469**	**1,757**	**2,025**	**2,286**	**100**	**100**	**100**	**100**
Two-parent family groups [2]	1,184	1,472	1,694	1,970	81	84	84	86
One-parent family groups	285	285	292	292	19	16	14	13
Maintained by mother	236	222	235	254	16	13	12	11
Maintained by father	49	63	57	38	3	4	3	2
Grandparent householder with grandchild(ren) under 18	(NA)	(NA)	39	24	(NA)	(NA)	2	1
Hispanic, total [4]	**5,503**	**6,752**	**7,572**	**8,237**	**100**	**100**	**100**	**100**
Two-parent family groups [2]	3,625	4,346	4,856	5,230	66	64	64	63
One-parent family groups	1,877	2,406	2,499	2,766	34	36	33	34
Maintained by mother	1,565	1,964	2,186	2,429	28	29	29	29
Maintained by father	313	442	313	337	6	7	4	4
Grandparent householder with grandchild(ren) under 18	(NA)	(NA)	217	241	(NA)	(NA)	3	3
Non-Hispanic White, total [3]	**24,847**	**24,730**	**23,911**	**22,831**	**100**	**100**	**100**	**100**
Two-parent family groups [2]	18,750	18,253	17,911	16,846	75	74	75	74
One-parent family groups	6,096	6,476	5,457	5,399	25	26	23	24
Maintained by mother	4,766	4,984	4,404	4,209	19	20	18	18
Maintained by father	1,331	1,492	1,053	1,190	5	6	4	5
Grandparent householder with grandchild(ren) under 18	(NA)	(NA)	543	586	(NA)	(NA)	2	3

NA Not available. [1] Includes other races and non-Hispanic groups, not shown separately. [2] Beginning 2007, includes children living both with married and unmarried parents. [3] Beginning with the 2003 Current Population Survey (CPS), respondents could choose more than one race. Beginning 2005, data represent persons who selected this race group only and exclude persons reporting more than one race. The CPS prior to 2003 allowed respondents to report only one race group. See also comments on race in the text for this section. [4] Hispanic persons may be of any race.

Source: U.S. Census Bureau, Families and Living Arrangements, Current Population Reports, P20-537, 2001; and "America's Families and Living Arrangements: 2014: Family groups (FG table series), Table FG10. Family Groups: 2014," <http://www.census.gov/hhes/families/data/cps2014FG.html>, accessed March 2015, and earlier releases.

Table 68. Parents and Children in Stay-At-Home Parent Family Groups: 1995 to 2014

[In thousands (22,973 represents 22,973,000). Family groups with children include those families that maintain their own household (family households with own children); those that live in the home of a relative (related subfamilies); and those that live in the home of a nonrelative (unrelated subfamilies). Stay-at-home family groups are married-couple family groups with children under age 15 where one parent is in the labor force all of the previous year and the other parent is out of the labor force for the entire year with the reason 'taking care of home and family.' Only married couples with children under age 15 are included. Based on Current Population Survey; see Appendix III]

Year	Married-couple family groups with children under 15 years old			Children under 15 years old in married-couple family groups		
	Total	With stay-at-home mothers	With stay-at-home fathers	Total	With stay-at-home mothers	With stay-at-home fathers
1995	22,973	4,440	64	41,008	9,106	125
2000	22,953	4,785	93	41,860	10,087	180
2005	23,305	5,584	142	41,111	11,224	247
2010	22,138	5,020	154	41,026	10,833	287
2011 [1]	21,689	4,976	176	40,592	10,763	343
2011 [2]	21,852	5,051	178	39,827	10,465	340
2012	21,334	5,091	189	39,222	10,675	369
2013	21,547	5,215	214	39,448	10,818	434
2014	21,549	5,203	211	39,424	10,791	420

[1] Based on Census 2000 population controls. [2] Begin use of Census 2010 population controls.

Source: U.S. Census Bureau, "Families and Living Arrangements, Table SHP-1. Parents and Children in Stay-At-Home Parent Family Groups: 1994 to Present," <http://www.census.gov/hhes/families/data/families.html>, accessed March 2015.

Table 69. Children Under 18 Years of Age by Presence of Parents: 2000 to 2014

[72,012 represents 72,012,000. As of March. Excludes persons under 18 years old who maintained households or family groups and their spouses. Based on Current Population Survey; see headnote, Table 67]

Race, Hispanic origin, and year	Number (1,000)	Both parents [1]	Percent living with—					Father only	Neither parent
			Mother only						
			Total	Divorced	Married, spouse absent [2]	Never married	Widowed		
ALL RACES [3]									
2000	72,012	69.1	22.4	7.9	4.5	9.2	1.0	4.2	4.2
2005	73,494	67.3	23.4	7.9	4.6	10.1	0.8	4.8	4.5
2010	74,718	69.4	23.1	7.1	5.1	10.1	0.8	3.4	4.1
2013	73,910	68.5	23.7	7.1	4.6	11.4	0.7	4.1	3.7
2014	73,692	68.7	23.6	7.0	4.5	11.3	0.8	3.9	3.8
WHITE [4]									
2000	56,455	75.3	17.3	(NA)	(NA)	(NA)	(NA)	4.3	3.1
2005	56,234	73.5	18.4	7.9	4.0	5.8	0.7	4.7	3.4
2010	56,416	74.9	18.3	6.9	4.5	6.1	0.8	3.5	3.4
2013	54,227	74.3	18.5	7.1	4.1	6.6	0.7	4.0	3.2
2014	53,881	74.1	18.7	7.3	3.9	6.8	0.7	3.9	3.3
BLACK [4]									
2000	11,412	37.6	49.0	(NA)	(NA)	(NA)	(NA)	4.2	9.2
2005	11,293	35.0	50.2	8.7	8.1	32.0	1.3	5.0	9.8
2010	11,272	39.2	49.7	8.6	8.4	31.5	1.2	3.6	7.5
2013	11,086	38.8	50.5	8.4	6.8	34.4	1.0	4.6	6.1
2014	11,080	39.0	50.8	7.6	7.3	34.8	1.0	4.2	6.1
ASIAN [4]									
2005	2,843	83.6	10.2	4.0	2.3	2.7	1.3	3.6	2.5
2010	3,300	85.5	10.1	3.8	3.7	2.1	0.6	2.2	2.1
2013	3,591	84.9	10.7	3.4	4.0	2.8	0.6	2.5	1.9
2014	3,621	86.8	9.6	3.2	3.6	2.2	0.7	1.7	2.0
HISPANIC [5]									
2000	11,613	65.1	25.1	(NA)	(NA)	(NA)	(NA)	4.4	5.4
2005	14,241	64.7	25.4	6.1	7.1	11.4	0.8	4.8	5.2
2010	16,941	67.0	26.3	5.8	8.1	11.7	0.7	2.7	4.0
2013	17,709	65.1	27.9	6.2	7.5	13.5	0.7	3.2	3.9
2014	17,871	64.9	27.5	6.5	7.3	13.1	0.7	3.1	4.4
NON-HISPANIC WHITE [4]									
2005	43,106	75.9	16.4	8.5	3.1	4.2	0.7	4.8	2.9
2010	41,089	77.5	15.5	7.5	3.1	4.2	0.8	3.8	3.1
2013	38,880	77.4	15.3	7.5	2.7	4.4	0.6	4.4	3.0
2014	38,463	77.3	15.5	7.5	2.7	4.6	0.7	4.3	3.0

NA Not available. [1] Beginning in 2007, includes children living both with married and unmarried parents. [2] Includes separated. [3] Includes other races and non-Hispanic groups, not shown separately. [4] Beginning with the 2003 Current Population Survey (CPS), respondents could choose more than one race. Beginning 2005, data represent persons who selected this race group only and exclude persons reporting more than one race. The CPS prior to 2003 allowed respondents to report only one race group. See also comments on race in the text for this section. [5] Hispanic persons may be of any race.

Source: U.S. Census Bureau, "America's Families and Living Arrangements: 2014: Children (C table series), Table C3. Living Arrangements Of Children Under 18 Years And Marital Status Of Parents, By Age, Sex, Race, And Hispanic Origin And Selected Characteristics Of The Child For All Children: 2014," <http://www.census.gov/hhes/families/data/cps2014C.html>, accessed March 2015, and earlier releases.

Table 70. Grandparents Living With Grandchildren by Race, Hispanic Origin, and Sex: 2013

[In thousands (7,189 represents 7,189,000), except percent. Covers both grandparents living in own home with grandchildren present and grandparents living in grandchildren's home. The American Community Survey universe includes the household population and the population living in institutions, college dormitories, and other group quarters. Based on a sample and subject to sampling variability; see text, this section, and Appendix III]

Race, Hispanic origin, and sex	Grandparents living with own grandchildren, total	Grandparents responsible for grandchildren		
		Total	30 to 59 years old	60 years old and over
Grandparents living with own grandchildren under 18 years old (1,000)	**7,189**	**2,682**	**1,685**	**996**
PERCENT DISTRIBUTION				
Total	100.0	100.0	100.0	100.0
White alone	63.1	65.4	64.6	66.9
Black or African American alone	17.6	21.3	21.7	20.6
American Indian and Alaska Native alone	1.3	1.9	1.9	1.8
Asian alone	8.2	3.1	2.4	4.3
Native Hawaiian and Other Pacific Islander alone	0.3	0.3	0.3	0.3
Some other race alone	7.6	6.0	7.2	4.1
Two or more races	1.9	2.0	2.0	2.0
Hispanic origin [1]	25.2	20.2	23.0	15.5
White alone, not Hispanic	46.7	52.4	49.9	56.5
Male	36.0	37.6	34.7	42.6
Female	64.0	62.4	65.3	57.4

[1] Persons of Hispanic origin may be of any race.

Source: U.S. Census Bureau, American Community Survey 2013, S1002, "Grandparents," <http://factfinder2.census.gov/>, accessed February 2015.

Table 71. Nonfamily Households by Sex and Age of Householder: 2014

[In thousands (19,658 represents 19,658,000). As of March. A nonfamily household consists of a householder living alone (a one-person household) or where the householder shares the home exclusively with people to whom he/she is not related. Based on Current Population Survey, Annual Social and Economic Supplement]

Item	Male householder					Female householder				
	Total	15 to 24 yrs. old	25 to 44 yrs. old	45 to 64 yrs. old	65 yrs. old and over	Total	15 to 24 yrs. old	25 to 44 yrs. old	45 to 64 yrs. old	65 yrs. old and over
Total...................	19,658	1,532	6,860	7,142	4,124	22,219	1,512	4,310	7,319	9,078
Living alone................	15,151	745	4,697	5,924	3,786	19,034	819	3,044	6,412	8,761
Living with nonrelatives.......	4,507	787	2,163	1,220	338	3,184	691	1,267	908	319
Never married.................	10,093	1,497	5,128	2,821	647	7,572	1,449	3,286	2,111	727
Married spouse absent........	709	3	275	263	169	496	11	104	233	147
Separated....................	945	14	300	502	130	784	10	209	431	134
Widowed.....................	2,057	0	34	343	1,679	6,967	10	84	979	5,894
Divorced.....................	5,855	18	1,122	3,214	1,502	6,399	31	626	3,565	2,176

Source: U.S. Census Bureau, "America's Families and Living Arrangements: 2014: Adults (A table series), Table A2. Family Status and Household Relationship of People 15 Years and Over, by Marital Status, Age, and Sex," <http://www.census.gov/hhes/families/data/cps2014A.html>, accessed March 2015.

Table 72. Group Quarters Population by Type of Group Quarter and Selected Characteristics: 2013

[In percent, except as indicated (8,030 represents 8,030,000). The American Community Survey universe includes the household population and the population living in institutions, college dormitories, and other group quarters. Based on a sample and subject to sampling variability]

Characteristic	Total group quarters population [1]	Adult correctional facilities	Nursing facilities/ skilled nursing facilities	College/ university housing	Characteristic	Total group quarters population [1]	Adult correctional facilities	Nursing facilities/ skilled nursing facilities	College/ university housing
Total population (1,000).................	8,030	2,234	1,500	2,605	One race (1,000).............	7,750	2,143	1,486	2,498
PERCENT DISTRIBUTION					Two or more races (1,000)...	280	92	14	107
Male.......................	60.7	91.2	33.8	45.5	PERCENT DISTRIBUTION				
Female....................	39.3	8.8	66.2	54.5	One race......................	100.0	100.0	100.0	100.0
					White........................	67.8	50.8	82.4	75.0
Under 15 years old........	0.9	(X)	(X)	(X)	Black........................	23.3	40.1	13.9	13.5
15 to 17 years old..........	1.8	0.2	(X)	1.1	American Indian and				
18 to 24 years old..........	41.6	16.6	0.2	96.8	Alaska Native..............	1.1	2.0	0.5	0.4
25 to 34 years old..........	12.7	33.0	0.7	1.8	Asian.......................	4.2	0.8	1.8	9.0
35 to 44 years old..........	9.4	24.7	1.2	0.2	Native Hawaiian/				
45 to 54 years old..........	8.7	17.2	4.2	0.1	Pacific Islander...........	0.2	0.2	0.1	0.1
55 to 64 years old..........	6.1	6.4	9.8	0.1	Some other race...........	3.5	6.0	1.3	1.9
65 to 74 years old..........	4.5	1.5	16.1	0.0	Hispanic origin [2]..............	12.4	20.6	5.3	8.4
75 to 84 years old..........	5.8	0.2	26.8	(X)	Not Hispanic.................	87.6	79.4	94.7	91.6
85 years old and over.....	8.5	0.0	41.0	(X)	White alone, not Hispanic..	57.9	36.3	77.9	66.4

X Not applicable. [1] Includes other types of group quarters, not shown separately. [2] Persons of Hispanic origin may be of any race.

Source: U.S. Census Bureau, 2013 American Community Survey, S2601A, "Characteristics of the Group Quarters Population"; and S2601B, "Characteristics of the Group Quarters Population by Group Quarters Type"; <http://factfinder2.census.gov/>, accessed February 2015.

Table 73. Population in Group Quarters by State: 2000 to 2014

[In thousands (7,780 represents 7,780,000). As of April, except 2014 as of July. For definition of group quarters, see text, this section]

State	2000 [1]	2010 [2]	2014	State	2000 [1]	2010 [2]	2014	State	2000 [1]	2010 [2]	2014
U.S......	7,780	7,999	8,064	KS........	82	79	79	NC........	254	257	254
AL........	115	116	118	KY........	115	126	130	ND........	24	25	27
AK........	19	26	28	LA........	136	128	129	OH........	299	306	311
AZ........	110	140	151	ME........	35	36	36	OK........	112	112	110
AR........	74	79	82	MD........	134	139	140	OR........	77	87	87
CA........	820	820	817	MA........	221	239	248	PA........	433	427	431
CO........	103	116	117	MI........	250	230	227	RI........	39	43	42
CT........	108	118	118	MN........	136	135	135	SC........	135	139	137
DE........	25	24	26	MS........	95	93	96	SD........	28	34	34
DC........	36	40	40	MO........	164	174	175	TN........	148	154	155
FL........	389	425	431	MT........	25	29	29	TX........	561	582	596
GA........	234	254	262	NE........	51	51	52	UT........	40	46	45
HI........	36	43	44	NV........	34	36	37	VT........	21	25	25
ID........	31	29	30	NH........	36	40	41	VA........	231	240	241
IL........	322	302	300	NJ........	195	187	186	WA........	136	139	141
IN........	178	187	189	NM........	36	43	43	WV........	43	49	49
IA........	104	99	100	NY........	581	586	581	WI........	156	151	149
								WY........	14	14	14

[1] The April 1, 2000, population estimates base reflects changes to the Census 2000 population from the Count Question Resolution program and geographic program revisions. [2] The April 1, 2010 population estimates base reflects changes to the Census 2010 population from the Count Question Resolution program and geographic program revisions.

Source: U.S. Census Bureau, "Annual Resident Population Estimates, Estimated Components of Resident Population Change, and Rates of the Components of Resident Population Change for States and Counties: April 1, 2000 to July 1, 2009," <https://www.census.gov/popest/data/counties/totals/2009/index.html> and "Population, population change and estimated components of population change: April 1, 2010 to July 1, 2014 (CO-EST2014-alldata)," <http://www.census.gov/popest/data/counties/totals/2014/index.html>; accessed May 2015.

Table 74. Same-Sex Couple Households by Sex, Partner Status and Presence of Children—States: 2010

[As of April. These preferred figures revise earlier estimates of same-sex unmarried partners released from the 2010 Census Summary File 1 because Census Bureau staff discovered an inconsistency in the responses in the 2010 Census summary file statistics that artificially inflated the number of same-sex couples. Statistics on same-sex couple households are derived from two questions on the census: relationship to householder and the sex of each person. When data were captured for these two questions on the 2010 Census door-to-door form, the wrong box may have been checked for the sex of a small percentage of opposite-sex spouses and unmarried partners. Because the population of opposite-sex married couples is large and the population of same-sex married couples in particular is small, an error of this type artificially inflates the number of same-sex married partners. After discovering the inconsistency, Census Bureau staff developed another set of estimates to provide a more accurate way to measure same-sex couple households. The revised figures were developed by using an index of names to re-estimate the number of same-sex married and unmarried partners by the sex commonly associated with the person's first name]

State	Same-sex households			Male householder			Female householder		
	Total	With own children under 18 years [1]	Without own children under 18 years	Total	Same-sex unmarried partner	Reported same-sex spouse	Total	Same-sex unmarried partner	Reported same-sex spouse
United States...............	646,464	111,033	535,431	313,577	249,354	64,223	332,887	265,381	67,506
Alabama......................	6,582	1,341	5,241	2,985	2,190	795	3,597	2,688	909
Alaska........................	1,228	284	944	466	331	135	762	619	143
Arizona......................	15,817	2,608	13,209	7,521	6,315	1,206	8,296	7,237	1,059
Arkansas....................	4,226	898	3,328	1,914	1,371	543	2,312	1,815	497
California...................	98,153	15,698	82,455	52,490	38,093	14,397	45,663	31,748	13,915
Colorado....................	12,424	1,975	10,449	5,366	4,567	799	7,058	6,239	819
Connecticut................	7,852	1,338	6,514	3,473	2,329	1,144	4,379	2,819	1,560
Delaware....................	2,646	412	2,234	1,250	1,069	181	1,396	1,197	199
District of Columbia.........	4,822	419	4,403	3,583	3,086	497	1,239	991	248
Florida.......................	48,496	6,453	42,043	26,625	23,040	3,585	21,871	18,672	3,199
Georgia......................	21,318	4,179	17,139	10,703	8,882	1,821	10,615	8,775	1,840
Hawaii.......................	3,239	513	2,726	1,715	1,417	298	1,524	1,242	282
Idaho.........................	2,042	455	1,587	801	592	209	1,241	1,004	237
Illinois.......................	23,049	3,831	19,218	12,068	10,253	1,815	10,981	9,189	1,792
Indiana......................	11,074	2,090	8,984	4,838	4,050	788	6,236	5,421	815
Iowa..........................	4,093	761	3,332	1,730	1,179	551	2,363	1,541	822
Kansas.......................	4,009	873	3,136	1,694	1,272	422	2,315	1,904	411
Kentucky....................	7,195	1,328	5,867	3,230	2,570	660	3,965	3,297	668
Louisiana...................	8,076	1,611	6,465	3,659	2,847	812	4,417	3,498	919
Maine........................	3,958	547	3,411	1,497	1,309	188	2,461	2,242	219
Maryland....................	12,538	2,544	9,994	5,320	4,260	1,060	7,218	5,957	1,261
Massachusetts.............	20,256	3,459	16,797	8,683	5,332	3,351	11,573	6,061	5,512
Michigan....................	14,598	2,650	11,948	6,314	5,262	1,052	8,284	7,134	1,150
Minnesota...................	10,207	1,681	8,526	4,658	4,031	627	5,549	4,846	703
Mississippi..................	3,484	895	2,589	1,459	992	467	2,025	1,442	583
Missouri.....................	10,557	1,828	8,729	4,953	4,127	826	5,604	4,838	766
Montana.....................	1,348	297	1,051	525	373	152	823	689	134
Nebraska....................	2,356	462	1,894	1,040	801	239	1,316	1,045	271
Nevada......................	7,140	1,217	5,923	3,768	3,087	681	3,372	2,801	571
New Hampshire............	3,260	538	2,722	1,186	818	368	2,074	1,426	648
New Jersey.................	16,875	3,323	13,552	8,097	5,962	2,135	8,778	6,466	2,312
New Mexico.................	5,825	1,038	4,787	2,222	1,844	378	3,603	3,123	480
New York....................	48,932	8,025	40,907	26,681	21,572	5,109	22,251	17,235	5,016
North Carolina.............	18,309	3,380	14,929	8,037	6,461	1,576	10,272	8,624	1,648
North Dakota...............	559	121	438	247	169	78	312	244	68
Ohio..........................	19,684	3,480	16,204	8,987	7,643	1,344	10,697	9,380	1,317
Oklahoma...................	6,134	1,280	4,854	2,778	2,092	686	3,356	2,707	649
Oregon......................	11,773	1,920	9,853	4,622	3,746	876	7,151	6,025	1,126
Pennsylvania...............	22,336	3,543	18,793	10,519	8,989	1,530	11,817	10,119	1,698
Rhode Island...............	2,785	432	2,353	1,215	961	254	1,570	1,232	338
South Carolina.............	7,214	1,360	5,854	3,160	2,400	760	4,054	3,218	836
South Dakota...............	714	151	563	313	219	94	401	320	81
Tennessee..................	10,898	1,968	8,930	5,054	4,099	955	5,844	4,840	1,004
Texas........................	46,401	9,191	37,210	22,412	18,137	4,275	23,989	19,867	4,122
Utah..........................	3,909	786	3,123	1,841	1,405	436	2,068	1,695	373
Vermont.....................	2,143	399	1,744	718	463	255	1,425	925	500
Virginia......................	14,243	2,279	11,964	6,990	5,731	1,259	7,253	6,038	1,215
Washington.................	19,003	2,998	16,005	8,636	7,139	1,497	10,367	8,792	1,575
West Virginia...............	2,848	507	2,341	1,330	974	356	1,518	1,194	324
Wisconsin...................	9,179	1,505	7,674	3,936	3,334	602	5,243	4,651	592
Wyoming....................	657	162	495	268	169	99	389	309	80

[1] The "own children" category includes any child under 18 years who is a son or daughter by birth, a stepchild, or an adopted child of the householder.

Source: U.S. Census Bureau, "Same-sex Couple Household Statistics from the 2010 Census, Supplemental Tables," September 2011, <http://www.census.gov/hhes/samesex/data/decennial.html>.

Table 75. Opposite-Sex and Same-Sex Couple Households by Selected Characteristics: 2013

[In percent, except as indicated (55,607 represents 55,607,000). The American Community Survey universe includes the household population and the population living in institutions, college dormitories, and other group quarters. Based on a sample and subject to sampling variability. See text, this section and Appendix III]

| Characteristics | Married opposite-sex couples | Unmarried opposite-sex couples | Married and unmarried same-sex couples | | | Married same-sex couples |
			Total	Male-male couples	Female-female couples	
Total households (1,000)...............	55,607	6,571	727	353	374	252
Age of householder:						
15 to 24 years old............	1.4	12.2	4.1	3.0	5.1	1.6
25 to 34 years old............	13.4	35.2	16.5	15.0	17.9	10.9
35 to 44 years old............	20.2	21.6	19.5	19.3	19.7	16.5
45 to 54 years old............	22.7	16.1	26.8	28.1	25.6	25.1
55 to 64 years old............	21.1	9.6	18.1	19.3	17.0	20.3
65 years old and over.........	21.3	5.3	15.0	15.3	14.8	25.7
Average age of householder (years).........	51.6	38.8	48.5	49.3	47.9	53.9
Average age of spouse/partner (years).........	50.9	37.9	46.7	47.1	46.3	52.7
Race of householder:						
White.........	82.4	76.2	84.1	85.1	83.1	83.0
Black or African American.........	6.9	11.4	7.0	5.4	8.5	7.5
American Indian or Alaska Native.........	0.5	1.1	0.7	0.7	0.6	0.7
Asian.........	5.4	2.4	2.7	3.1	2.3	3.7
Native Hawaiian or Pacific Islander.........	0.1	0.2	0.1	0.1	0.1	0.2
Some other race.........	3.2	6.1	2.5	2.7	2.2	2.7
Two or more races.........	1.5	2.6	2.9	2.8	3.1	2.2
Percent of couples interracial.........	6.7	13.0	14.1	16.5	11.7	9.9
Hispanic origin of householder:						
Hispanic [1].........	12.2	19.0	10.3	10.8	9.8	10.2
White alone, not Hispanic.........	73.9	64.4	77.3	78.0	76.7	76.4
Children in the household:						
Children in the household [2].........	40.0	41.4	16.5	9.7	22.8	23.2
Own children in the household.........	39.9	38.3	15.1	9.2	20.7	22.8
Household income:						
Less than $35,000.........	15.6	28.9	15.4	11.8	18.8	16.4
$35,000 to $49,999.........	12.0	16.0	10.3	9.3	11.3	10.1
$50,000 to $74,999.........	20.0	22.2	17.8	16.9	18.6	17.7
$75,000 to $99,999.........	16.1	13.9	15.4	15.3	15.4	14.8
$100,000 or more.........	36.2	19.0	41.1	46.7	35.9	41.1
Average household income (dollars).........	101,487	69,511	112,576	127,764	98,234	115,135
Housing tenure:						
Owner occupied.........	79.4	41.7	68.1	70.0	66.4	76.8
Renter occupied.........	20.6	58.3	31.9	30.0	33.6	23.2

[1] Persons of Hispanic origin may be of any race. [2]Includes own children and nonrelatives of the householder under 18 years old.

Source: U.S. Census Bureau, 2013 American Community Survey, "Characteristics of Same-Sex Couple Households: 2013," <http://www.census.gov/hhes/samesex/files/ssex-tables-2013.xlsx>, accessed February 2015.

Table 76. Opposite Sex Unmarried Couples, by Presence of Biological Children: 2014

[In thousands (7,913 represents 7,913,000), except percent. As of March. Excludes members of Armed Forces except those living off post or with their families on post. All opposite-sex unmarried couples are included, regardless of householder status. Unmarried couples of the opposite sex with children under 18 years old are included in the estimates if either partner had at least one never-married biological child living with them. Population controls based on Census 2010. Based on Current Population Survey; see text, this section and Appendix III]

| Year and sex and age of partner | Unmarried couples, total | Without children under 18 years old | With children under 18 years old | |
			Number	Percent of total
Total.........	7,913	4,816	3,098	39.2
Age of male partner:				
15 to 24 years old.........	1,083	739	345	31.9
25 to 29 years old.........	1,655	983	672	40.6
30 to 34 years old.........	1,273	612	660	51.8
35 to 39 years old.........	940	377	562	59.8
40 to 44 years old.........	741	337	404	54.5
45 to 49 years old.........	610	380	230	37.7
50 to 54 years old.........	534	404	129	24.2
55 to 64 years old.........	710	633	77	10.8
65 years old and over.........	368	350	18	4.9
Age of female partner:				
15 to 24 years old.........	1,667	1,041	627	37.6
25 to 29 years old.........	1,807	1,049	758	41.9
30 to 34 years old.........	1,092	475	617	56.5
35 to 39 years old.........	784	289	495	63.1
40 to 44 years old.........	657	314	343	52.2
45 to 49 years old.........	547	381	166	30.3
50 to 54 years old.........	459	393	66	14.4
55 to 64 years old.........	619	597	22	3.6
65 years old and over.........	281	276	5	1.8

Source: U.S. Census Bureau, "America's Families and Living Arrangements, 2014: Unmarried Couples (UC table series)," <http://www.census.gov/hhes/families/data/cps2014UC.html>, accessed March 2015.

Table 77. Opposite and Same-Sex Unmarried-Partner Households by Region: 2013

[The American Community Survey universe includes the household population and the population living in institutions, college dormitories, and other group quarters. For composition of regions, see inside front cover. Based on a sample and subject to sampling variability; see text, this section and Appendix III]

Item	Total	Northeast	Midwest	South	West
Total households...........................	**116,291,033**	**20,937,102**	**26,161,479**	**43,399,427**	**25,793,025**
Unmarried-partner households...............	7,046,164	1,279,590	1,625,044	2,376,635	1,764,895
Male householder and male partner............	235,089	43,997	42,298	82,385	66,409
Male householder and female partner............	3,302,287	600,828	768,814	1,108,941	823,704
Female householder and female partner............	239,816	41,288	48,638	83,714	66,176
Female householder and male partner............	3,268,972	593,477	765,294	1,101,595	808,606
All other households...........................	109,244,869	19,657,512	24,536,435	41,022,792	24,028,130

Source: U.S. Census Bureau, 2013 American Community Survey, B11009, "Unmarried-Partner Households by Sex of Partner," <http://factfinder2.census.gov/>, accessed March 2015.

Table 78. Young Adults Living at Home by Sex and Age: 1990 to 2014

[In thousands (12,450 represents 12,450,000), except percent. As of March. Excludes members of Armed Forces except those living off post or with their families on post. Unmarried college students living in dormitories are counted as living in their parent(s) home. Beginning 2005, based on an expanded sample of households. Population controls for 2005 to 2010 based on Census 2000; beginning 2011 population controls based on Census 2010. Based on Current Population Survey; see text, this section and Appendix III]

	Male young adults			Female young adults		
		Child of householder living at home			Child of householder living at home	
Year	Total	Number	Percent of total	Total	Number	Percent of total
18 TO 24 YEARS OLD						
1990...........................	12,450	7,232	58.1	12,860	6,135	47.7
2000...........................	13,291	7,593	57.1	13,242	6,232	47.1
2005...........................	14,060	7,448	53.0	13,933	6,413	46.0
2007...........................	14,409	7,880	54.7	13,976	6,648	47.6
2008...........................	14,378	8,066	56.1	13,983	6,736	48.2
2009...........................	14,498	8,219	56.7	14,161	6,923	48.9
2010...........................	14,824	8,501	57.3	14,469	7,123	49.2
2011...........................	14,979	8,772	58.6	14,820	7,448	50.3
2012...........................	15,154	9,161	60.5	14,971	7,765	51.9
2013...........................	15,137	8,864	58.6	14,867	7,732	52.0
2014...........................	15,280	8,892	58.2	14,852	7,645	51.5
25 TO 34 YEARS OLD						
1990...........................	21,462	3,213	15.0	21,779	1,774	8.1
2000...........................	18,563	2,387	12.9	19,222	1,602	8.3
2005...........................	19,656	2,660	13.5	19,632	1,597	8.1
2007...........................	20,002	2,849	14.2	19,828	1,850	9.3
2008...........................	20,182	3,044	15.1	19,922	2,053	10.3
2009...........................	20,419	3,178	15.6	20,069	1,988	9.9
2010...........................	20,685	3,387	16.4	20,383	2,133	10.5
2011...........................	20,223	3,462	17.1	20,526	1,996	9.7
2012...........................	20,458	3,459	16.9	20,743	2,155	10.4
2013...........................	20,803	3,490	16.8	20,967	2,324	11.1
2014...........................	21,186	3,755	17.7	21,219	2,478	11.7

Source: U.S. Census Bureau, America's Families and Living Arrangements, "Living Arrangements of Adults, Table AD-1. Young Adults Living At Home: 1960 to Present," <http://www.census.gov/hhes/families/data/adults.html>, accessed March 2015.

Table 79. Children of Householders by Age and Whether Biological, Adopted, and Stepchildren: 2010

[88,820 represents 88,820,000. As of April. Includes children of the householder regardless of marital status and excludes persons under age 18 who are not children of the householder. Includes Puerto Rico. Based on 2010 Census of Population; see Appendix III]

Type of relationship	Total	Under 18 years old					18 years old and over		
		Total	Under 6 years old	6 to 11 years old	12 to 14 years old	15 to 17 years old	Total	18 to 24 years old	25 years old and over
NUMBER (1,000)									
Total children of householders..	**88,820**	**64,778**	**20,277**	**21,903**	**11,188**	**11,410**	**24,042**	**13,649**	**10,393**
Adopted children.....................	2,072	1,527	351	569	304	303	545	325	220
Stepchildren.........................	4,166	2,785	284	978	718	806	1,381	889	492
Biological children....................	82,582	60,467	19,643	20,356	10,166	10,301	22,115	12,435	9,681
PERCENT DISTRIBUTION									
Total children of householders.....	100.0	100.0	100.0	100.0	100.0	100.0	100.0	100.0	100.0
Adopted children.....................	2.3	2.4	1.7	2.6	2.7	2.7	2.3	2.4	2.1
Stepchildren.........................	4.7	4.3	1.4	4.5	6.4	7.1	5.7	6.5	4.7
Biological children....................	93.0	93.3	96.9	92.9	90.9	90.3	92.0	91.1	93.1

Source: U.S. Census Bureau, Adopted Children and Stepchildren: 2010, Current Population Reports, P20-572, April 2014. See also <https://www.census.gov/library/publications.html>.

Table 80. Householders' Children Under 18 Years Old by Whether Adopted, Biological, and Stepchildren and Selected Child Characteristics: 2009 to 2011

[In thousands, except as indicated (1,557 represents 1,557,000). Includes children of the householder regardless of marital status and excludes persons under age 18 who are not children of the householder. Based on 2009-2011 American Community Surveys; see Appendix III]

Characteristic of child	Adopted children			Stepchildren			Biological children		
	Total	Male	Female	Total	Male	Female	Total	Male	Female
Total children........................	**1,557**	**725**	**832**	**2,358**	**1,198**	**1,160**	**61,579**	**31,578**	**30,002**
By Age:									
Under 6 years old...............	370	171	199	239	125	115	20,080	10,269	9,811
6 to 11 years old...............	573	263	310	824	414	409	20,682	10,604	10,078
12 to 14 years old...............	313	147	166	618	316	302	10,355	5,323	5,032
15 to 17 years old...............	300	144	157	678	344	334	10,462	5,381	5,081
By Race/Ethnicity:									
White alone........	934	453	481	1,744	884	860	42,970	22,086	20,884
Black or African American alone...............	251	122	129	294	149	144	8,183	4,153	4,031
American Indian and Alaska Native alone........	28	14	14	25	13	12	516	264	252
Asian alone...............	155	44	111	41	21	20	2,756	1,423	1,332
Native Hawaiian and Other Pacific Islander alone........	6	3	3	4	2	2	104	54	51
Some other race alone...............	82	40	42	135	70	64	3,864	1,969	1,895
Two or more races...............	101	50	51	115	58	57	3,186	1,629	1,557
By Hispanic Origin:									
Hispanic or Latino (of any race)...............	293	142	151	495	252	244	13,825	7,065	6,759
White alone, not Hispanic or Latino...............	762	371	391	1,429	725	704	34,171	17,585	16,585
By Nativity:									
Native...............	1,294	623	671	2,239	1,137	1,102	59,579	30,538	29,041
Foreign born...............	263	102	161	119	61	58	2,000	1,039	961
By Disability Status:									
Children 5 to 17 years old with at least one disability...............	148	85	63	133	85	47	2,086	1,333	753
Percent of total children 5 to 17 years old.......	11.6	14.3	9.3	6.0	7.7	4.4	4.6	5.8	3.4

Source: U.S. Census Bureau, *Adopted Children and Stepchildren: 2010*, Current Population Reports, P20-572, April 2014. See also <https://www.census.gov/library/publications.html>.

Table 81. Householders' Children Under 18 Years Old by Whether Adopted, Biological, and Stepchildren and Selected Characteristics of Householder: 2009 to 2011

[In thousands, except as indicated (1,557 represents 1,557,000). Includes children of the householder regardless of marital status and excludes persons under 18 who are not children of the householder. Based on 2009-2011 American Community Surveys; see Appendix III]

Characteristic of householder	Adopted children		Stepchildren		Biological children	
	Number (1,000)	Percent	Number (1,000)	Percent	Number (1,000)	Percent
Total children........................	**1,557**	**100.0**	**2,358**	**100.0**	**61,579**	**100.0**
Child and householder are of different race [1]...............	374	24.0	297	12.6	4,393	7.1
Child and householder are of different Hispanic origin [2]...	157	10.1	226	9.6	2,051	3.3
Living arrangement of householder:						
Married couple households...............	1,136	73.0	1,874	79.4	42,441	68.9
Male householder—no spouse present...............	102	6.5	361	15.3	3,849	6.3
With an unmarried partner...............	36	2.3	292	12.4	1,602	2.6
No unmarried partner present...............	66	4.2	69	2.9	2,247	3.6
Female householder—no spouse present...............	319	20.5	123	5.2	15,290	24.8
With an unmarried partner...............	44	2.8	87	3.7	2,502	4.1
No unmarried partner present...............	275	17.7	37	1.6	12,788	20.8
Average age of householder (years)...............	44.8	(X)	38.5	(X)	38.4	(X)
Household Income (in 2011 dollars):						
Under $25,000 or loss...............	209	13.4	289	12.3	12,551	20.5
$25,000 to $49,999...............	292	18.7	555	23.5	13,555	22.0
$50,000 to $74,999...............	295	19.0	540	22.9	11,030	17.9
$75,000 to $99,999...............	239	15.3	389	16.5	8,230	13.4
$100,000 and over...............	522	33.6	586	24.9	16,214	26.2
Median household income (dollars)...............	73,378	(X)	64,974	(X)	59,905	(X)
Educational attainment of householder:						
Less than high school...............	145	9.3	280	11.9	8,564	13.9
High school graduate...............	309	19.9	713	30.2	14,001	22.7
Some college...............	493	31.7	894	37.9	19,860	32.3
Bachelor's degree...............	339	21.8	327	13.9	11,949	19.4
Graduate or professional school degree...............	270	17.4	144	6.1	7,205	11.7

X Not applicable. [1] Child and householder do not report the same group, where race groups are: White alone, Black alone, American Indian and Alaska Native alone, Asian alone, Native Hawaiian or Pacific Islander alone, some other race alone, or either the child or householder reports multiple race groups. [2] Child is Hispanic and householder is not Hispanic, or vice versa.

Source: U.S. Census Bureau, *Adopted Children and Stepchildren: 2010*, Current Population Reports, P20-572, April 2014. See also <https://www.census.gov/library/publications.html>.

Table 82. Self-Described Religious Identification of Adult Population: 1990, 2001, and 2008

[In thousands (175,440 represents 175,440,000). The methodology of the American Religious Identification Survey (ARIS) 2008 replicated that used in previous surveys. The three surveys are based on random-digit-dialing telephone surveys of residential households in the continental U.S. (48 states): 54,461 interviews in 2008, 50,281 in 2001, and 113,723 in 1990. Respondents were asked to describe themselves in terms of religion with an open-ended question. Interviewers did not prompt or offer a suggested list of potential answers. Moreover, the self-description of respondents was not based on whether established religious bodies, institutions, churches, mosques or synagogues considered them to be members. Instead, the surveys sought to determine whether the respondents regarded themselves as adherents of a religious community. Subjective rather than objective standards of religious identification were tapped by the surveys]

Religious group	1990	2001	2008	Religious group	1990	2001	2008
Adult population, total [1]	**175,440**	**207,983**	**228,182**	Christian Reform	40	79	381
Christian, total [2]	151,225	159,514	173,402	Christian Science	214	194	339
Catholic	46,004	50,873	57,199	Church of the Brethren	206	358	231
Baptist	33,964	33,820	36,148	Mormon/Latter-day Saints	2,487	2,697	3,158
Methodist	14,174	14,039	11,366	Other Christian [4]	105	254	206
Lutheran	9,110	9,580	8,674				
Presbyterian	4,985	5,596	4,723	Other religions, total [2]	5,853	7,740	8,796
Episcopalian/Anglican	3,043	3,451	2,405	Jewish	3,137	2,837	2,680
Orthodox (Eastern)	502	645	824	Buddhist	404	1,082	1,189
United Church of Christ	438	1,378	736	Hindu	227	766	582
Disciples of Christ	144	492	263	Sikh	13	57	78
Reformed/Dutch Reform	161	289	206	Muslim	527	1,104	1,349
Quaker	67	217	130	Unitarian/Universalist	502	629	586
Christian unspecified	8,073	14,190	16,834	Spiritualist	(NA)	116	426
Nondenominational Christian [3]	194	2,489	8,032	Wiccan	8	134	342
Protestant unspecified [3]	17,214	4,647	5,187	Pagan	(NA)	140	340
Evangelical/Born Again [3]	546	1,088	2,154	Native American	47	103	186
Independent Christian Church	25	71	86	Other unclassified [4]	991	774	1,030
Pentecostal unspecified	3,116	4,407	5,416				
Assemblies of God	617	1,105	810	No religion specified, total [2]	14,331	29,481	34,169
Church of God	590	943	663	Agnostic	[5]1,186	991	1,985
Holiness/Holy	610	569	352	Atheist	(5)	902	1,621
Church of the Nazarene	549	544	358	Humanist	29	49	90
Foursquare Gospel	28	70	116	No Religion	13,116	27,486	30,427
Churches of Christ	1,769	2,593	1,921	Other No Religion [4]	(NA)	57	45
Jehovah's Witness	1,381	1,331	1,914				
Apostolic/New Apostolic	117	254	970	Refused to reply to question	4,031	11,246	11,815
Seventh-day Adventist	668	724	938				
Mennonite	235	346	438				

NA Not available. [1] Refers to the total number of adults in all fifty states. All other figures are based on projections from surveys conducted in the continental United States (48 states). [2] Includes other groups, not shown separately. [3] Because of the subjective nature of replies to open-ended questions, these categories are the most unstable as they do not refer to clearly identifiable denominations as much as underlying feelings about religion. Thus they may be the most subject to fluctuation over time. [4] Estimates for subpopulations smaller than 75,000 adults are aggregated to minimize sampling errors. [5] Atheist included in Agnostic.

Source: 1990 data, Barry A. Kosmin and Seymour P. Lachman, "One Nation Under God: Religion in Contemporary American Society, 1993"; 2001 data, Barry A. Kosmin and Ariela Keysar, *Religion in A Free Market: Religious and Non-Religious Americans, Who, What, Why, Where, 2006*; and 2008 data, Barry A. Kosmin & Ariela Keysar, *American Religious Identification Survey (ARIS 2008) Summary Report*, 2009, Institute for the Study of Secularism in Society and Culture, Trinity College, Hartford, CT <http://www.trincoll.edu/Academics/centers/ISSSC/Pages/ARIS-Data-Archive.aspx> and <www.AmericanReligionSurvey-ARIS.org> ©.

Table 83. Religious Adherents and Jewish Population—States: 2010 to 2014

[137,450 represents 137,450,000. Adherents were defined as "all members, including full members, their children and others who regularly attend services." The Jewish population includes Jews who define themselves as Jewish by religion as well as those who define themselves as Jewish in cultural or ethnic terms. Data on Jewish population are based on both scientific studies and informant estimates provided by local Jewish communities]

State	Number (1,000)			Percent of population [3]		
	Christian adherents, [1] 2010	Other religious adherents, [2] 2010	Jewish population, 2014	Christian adherents, [1] 2010	Other religious adherents, [2] 2010	Jewish population, 2014
United States	**137,450**	**10,890**	**6,769**	**44.5**	**3.5**	**2.1**
Alabama	2,948	52	9	61.7	1.1	0.2
Alaska	200	40	6	28.1	5.7	0.8
Arizona	1,894	466	106	29.6	7.3	1.6
Arkansas	1,573	40	2	53.9	1.4	0.1
California	15,021	1,530	1,232	40.3	4.1	3.2
Colorado	1,684	199	103	33.5	4.0	2.0
Connecticut	1,735	48	118	48.6	1.3	3.3
Delaware	349	22	15	38.9	2.5	1.6
District of Columbia	298	16	28	49.6	2.7	4.3
Florida	6,829	400	639	36.3	2.1	3.3
Georgia	4,702	186	127	48.5	1.9	1.3
Hawaii	421	140	7	31.0	10.3	0.5
Idaho	384	417	2	24.5	26.6	0.1
Illinois	6,529	486	298	50.9	3.8	2.3
Indiana	2,793	69	17	43.1	1.1	0.3
Iowa	1,592	46	6	52.3	1.5	0.2
Kansas	1,375	61	17	48.2	2.1	0.6
Kentucky	2,182	49	11	50.3	1.1	0.3
Louisiana	2,688	50	11	59.3	1.1	0.2
Maine	345	19	14	26.0	1.4	1.0
Maryland	2,214	118	238	38.3	2.0	4.0
Massachusetts	3,546	122	275	54.2	1.9	4.1
Michigan	3,910	211	83	39.6	2.1	0.8
Minnesota	2,894	69	46	54.6	1.3	0.8
Mississippi	1,709	33	2	57.6	1.1	0.1
Missouri	2,806	123	59	46.9	2.0	1.0
Montana	326	50	1	33.0	5.0	0.1
Nebraska	974	38	6	53.3	2.1	0.3
Nevada	725	196	76	26.8	7.3	2.7
New Hampshire	444	14	10	33.7	1.1	0.8
New Jersey	4,321	272	516	49.1	3.1	5.8
New Mexico	940	87	13	45.6	4.2	0.6
New York	8,529	611	1,757	44.0	3.2	8.9
North Carolina	4,372	140	32	45.9	1.5	0.3
North Dakota	443	8	(Z)	65.9	1.2	0.1
Ohio	4,861	146	151	42.1	1.3	1.3
Oklahoma	2,148	75	5	57.3	2.0	0.1
Oregon	998	187	41	26.1	4.9	1.0
Pennsylvania	6,530	206	293	51.4	1.6	2.3
Rhode Island	558	10	19	53.1	0.9	1.8
South Carolina	2,337	70	14	50.5	1.5	0.3
South Dakota	464	13	(Z)	57.0	1.6	(Z)
Tennessee	3,425	82	20	54.0	1.3	0.3
Texas	13,062	872	159	51.9	3.5	0.6
Utah	256	1,929	6	9.3	69.8	0.2
Vermont	199	9	6	31.8	1.4	1.0
Virginia	3,206	351	96	40.1	4.4	1.2
Washington	1,945	364	46	28.9	5.4	0.7
West Virginia	635	22	2	34.3	1.2	0.1
Wisconsin	2,973	62	28	52.3	1.1	0.5
Wyoming	158	65	1	28.0	11.5	0.2

Z Fewer than 500 or less than 0.05 percent. [1] Comprises evangelical Protestants, Black Protestants, mainline Protestants, Orthodox and Catholic groups. [2] Includes counts of Jain, Shinto, Sikh, Tao, National Spiritualist Association, Church of Jesus Christ of Latter Day Saints, Unitarian Universalist, Jehovah's Witnesses, Church of Christ Scientist, Bahá'í, three Buddhist groupings, four Hindu groupings, Muslims, and Zoroastrians. Excludes four Judaism groups. [3] Based on U.S. Census Bureau data for resident population enumerated as of April 1, 2010 and estimated as of July 2012.

Source: Religious adherents: Clifford Grammich, Kirk Hadaway, Richard Houseal, Dale E. Jones, Alexei Krindatch, Richie Stanley, and Richard H. Taylor, *2010 U.S. Religion Census: Religious Congregations & Membership Study* ©, 2012, Association of Statisticians of American Religious Bodies. See also <http://www.asarb.org>. Jewish population: Ira M. Sheskin and Arnold Dashefsky, "Jewish Population in the United States, 2014," in Arnold Dashefsky and Ira M. Sheskin (Editors), *The American Jewish Year Book, 2014,* (2014) (Dordrecht: Springer) © in press. See also <http://www.jewishdatabank.org>.

Table 84. Religious Adherents by Metropolitan Area Status and Religious Groups: 2010

[Groups shown have 500,000 adherents or more. Adherents were defined as all members, including full members, their children and the estimated number of other participants who are not considered members. Based on a study of 236 religious bodies sponsored by the Association of Statisticians of American Religious Bodies. Participants included 217 Christian denominations, associations, or communions (including Latter-day Saints, Messianic Jews, and Unitarian/Universalist groups); counts of Jain, Shinto, Sikh, Tao, and National Spiritualist Association congregations, and counts of congregations and individuals for Bahá'í, three Buddhist groupings, four Hindu groupings, four Jewish groupings, Muslims, and Zoroastrians. For definition of metropolitan and micropolitan areas, see Appendix II]

Religious group	Total adherents (1,000)	Percent		
		In metropolitan area	In micropolitan area	Outside metro/micro area
U.S. population, total............................	308,746	83.7	10.0	6.3
Total adherents.................................	**150,686**	**83.5**	**10.0**	**6.5**
Catholic..	58,929	90.5	6.2	3.3
Southern Baptist Convention.....................	19,897	69.3	17.2	13.5
Non-denominational Christian Churches........	12,241	88.7	7.8	3.5
United Methodist Church............................	9,948	73.6	15.3	11.1
Church of Jesus Christ of Latter-day Saints.....	6,145	82.8	11.6	5.6
Evangelical Lutheran Church in America........	4,181	70.4	16.0	13.6
Assemblies of God..................................	2,945	82.7	11.0	6.3
Muslim, estimate.....................................	2,600	97.4	2.0	0.6
Presbyterian Church (U.S.A.)....................	2,452	82.5	11.4	6.1
Lutheran Church—Missouri Synod..............	2,271	72.7	13.7	13.6
Episcopal...	1,952	88.2	8.1	3.7
National Baptist Convention, USA, Inc...........	1,881	90.3	7.0	2.7
Churches of Christ....................................	1,584	69.8	17.1	13.1
American Baptist Churches in the USA..........	1,561	83.8	9.8	6.4
Christian Churches and Churches of Christ.....	1,453	72.6	15.9	11.5
United Church of Christ.............................	1,284	79.3	13.5	7.2
Seventh-day Adventist Church....................	1,195	87.7	8.2	4.1
Church of God (Cleveland, Tennessee)..........	1,110	72.2	17.5	10.3
African Methodist Episcopal Church..............	1,010	77.7	12.3	10.0
Orthodox Judaism....................................	947	99.6	0.0	0.4
Church of the Nazarene.............................	894	76.2	15.6	8.2
Christian Church (Disciples of Christ)............	786	70.3	17.7	12.0
Reform Judaism......................................	766	98.3	1.3	0.4
Mahayana Buddhism................................	733	92.8	6.8	0.4
Church of God in Christ.............................	624	87.8	7.3	4.9
Conservative Judaism..............................	502	99.5	0.4	0.1

Source: Clifford Grammich, Kirk Hadaway, Richard Houseal, Dale E. Jones, Alexei Krindatch, Richie Stanley, and Richard H. Taylor. *2010 U.S. Religion Census: Religious Congregations & Membership Study*, 2012 ©. Association of Statisticians of American Religious Bodies.

Table 85. Religious Bodies—Selected Data: 1988 to 2010

[Includes the self-reported membership of religious bodies with 750,000 or more as reported to the Yearbook of American and Canadian Churches. Groups may be excluded if they do not supply information. The data are not standardized so comparisons between groups are difficult. The definition of "church member" is determined by the religious body]

Religious body	Year reported	Churches reported	Membership
African Methodist Episcopal Church.....................................	2009	4,100	2,500,000
African Methodist Episcopal Zion Church..............................	2010	(NA)	1,400,000
American Baptist Churches in the USA.................................	2010	5,366	1,308,054
Assemblies of God...	2010	12,457	3,030,944
Catholic Church..	2010	18,199	68,202,492
Christian Churches and Churches of Christ............................	1988	5,579	1,071,616
Christian Methodist Episcopal Church..................................	2006	3,500	850,000
Church of God in Christ..	1991	15,300	5,499,875
Church of God (Cleveland, Tennessee)..................................	2010	6,481	1,074,047
Church of Jesus Christ of Latter-day Saints...........................	2010	13,601	6,157,238
Churches of Christ...	2006	13,000	1,639,495
Episcopal Church..	2010	6,794	1,951,907
Evangelical Lutheran Church in America...............................	2010	9,995	4,274,855
Greek Orthodox Archdiocese of America...............................	2006	560	1,500,000
Jehovah's Witnesses...	2010	13,021	1,184,249
Lutheran Church—Missouri Synod.......................................	2010	6,158	2,278,586
National Baptist Convention of America Inc............................	2000	(NA)	3,500,000
National Baptist Convention, U.S.A., Inc...............................	2010	10,358	5,197,512
National Missionary Baptist Convention of America..................	1992	(NA)	2,500,000
Pentecostal Assemblies of the World, Inc..............................	2010	2,550	1,800,000
Presbyterian Church (U.S.A.)..	2010	10,560	2,675,873
Progressive National Baptist Convention, Inc..........................	2009	1,500	1,010,000
Seventh-day Adventist Church...	2010	4,916	1,060,386
Southern Baptist Convention...	2010	45,727	16,136,044
United Church of Christ..	2010	5,227	1,058,423
United Methodist Church..	2009	33,583	7,679,850

NA Not available.

Source: National Council of Churches of Christ in the USA, *2012 Yearbook of American and Canadian Churches* ©. See also <http://nationalcouncilofchurches.us/>.

Section 2
Births, Deaths, Marriages, and Divorces

This section presents vital statistics data on natality, mortality, marriages, and divorces, as well as factors that help explain fertility, such as use of contraception, sexual activity, and prevalence of abortions and fetal deaths. Vital statistics are collected and disseminated for the nation through the National Vital Statistics System by the National Center for Health Statistics (NCHS) and published annually in *Vital Statistics of the United States, National Vital Statistics Reports (NVSR),* and other selected publications. Reports are also issued by various state bureaus participating in the National Vital Statistics System. Factors influencing fertility are collected in NCHS's National Survey of Family Growth and the U.S. Census Bureau's American Community Survey and Current Population Reports (published in *Fertility of American Women*).

Additionally, data on births, deaths, and other public health topics can be accessed via the Center for Disease Control's WONDER Online Databases at <http://wonder.cdc.gov/> and tables and data files available in "VitalStats" at <http://www.cdc.gov/nchs/VitalStats.htm>. Data on abortions are published by the Alan Guttmacher Institute in selected issues of *Perspectives on Sexual and Reproductive Health*.

Registration of vital events—The registration of births, deaths, fetal deaths, and other vital events in the United States is primarily a state and local function. There are 57 vital registration jurisdictions in the United States: the 50 states, five territories (Puerto Rico, etc.), District of Columbia, and New York City. Each of the 57 jurisdictions has a direct statistical reporting relationship with NCHS. Vital events occurring to U.S. residents outside the United States are not included in the data.

Births and deaths—The live-birth, death, and fetal-death statistics prepared by NCHS are based on vital records filed in the registration offices of all states, New York City, and the District of Columbia. The annual collection of death statistics on a national basis began in 1900 with a national death-registration area of ten states and the District of Columbia; a similar annual collection of birth statistics for a national birth-registration area began in 1915, also with ten reporting states and the District of Columbia. Since 1933, the birth- and death-registration areas have comprised the entire United States, including Alaska (beginning 1959) and Hawaii (beginning 1960). National statistics on fetal deaths were first compiled for 1918 and annually since 1922. Prior to 1951, birth statistics came from a complete count of records received in the Public Health Service (now received in NCHS). From 1951 through 1971, they were based on a 50-percent sample of all registered births (except for a complete count in 1955 and a 20- to 50-percent sample in 1967). Since 1972, they have been based on a complete count for states participating in the Vital Statistics Cooperative Program (VSCP) (for details, see the technical appendix in *U.S. Vital Statistics System: Major Activities and Developments, 1950-95*) and on a 50-percent sample of all other areas. Beginning in 1986, all reporting areas participated in the VSCP. Mortality data have been based on a complete count of records for each area (except for a 50-percent sample in 1972). Beginning in 1970, births to and

deaths of nonresident aliens of the United States and U.S. citizens outside the United States have been excluded from the data. Fetal deaths and deaths among Armed Forces abroad are excluded. Data based on samples are subject to sampling error; for details, see annual issues of *National Vital Statistics Reports*.

Mortality statistics by cause of death are compiled in accordance with World Health Organization regulations according to the *International Classification of Diseases* (ICD). The ICD is revised approximately every 10 years. The tenth revision of the ICD was employed beginning in 1999. Deaths for prior years were classified according to the revision of the ICD in use at the time. Each revision of the ICD introduces a number of discontinuities in mortality statistics; for a discussion of those between the ninth and tenth revisions of the ICD, see *National Vital Statistics Reports*, Vol. 63, No. 9. Information on tests of statistical significance, differences between death rates, and standard errors can also be found in the aforementioned report.

Some of the tables present age-adjusted death rates in addition to crude death rates. Age-adjusted death rates shown in this section were prepared using the direct method, in which age-specific death rates for a population of interest are applied to a standard population distributed by age. Age adjustment eliminates the differences in observed rates between points in time or among compared population groups that result from age differences in population composition.

Fertility and life expectancy—The total fertility rate, defined as the number of births that 1,000 women would have in their lifetime if at each year of age they experienced the birth rates occurring in the specified year, is compiled and published by NCHS. See *Births: Final Data for 2013, National Vital Statistics Reports*, Vol. 64, No. 1. Data on life expectancy, the average remaining lifetime in years for persons who attain a given age, are also computed and published by NCHS. See *Deaths: Final Data for 2012, National Vital Statistics Reports*, Vol. 63, No. 9 and <http://www.cdc.gov/nchs/deaths.htm> for details.

Marriage and divorce—In 1957 and 1958 respectively, the National Office of Vital Statistics established marriage- and divorce-registration areas. Originally the marriage-registration area comprised 30 states, plus Alaska, Hawaii, Puerto Rico, and the Virgin Islands; it currently includes 42 states and the District of Columbia. The divorce-registration area, originally 14 states, Alaska, Hawaii, and the Virgin Islands, currently includes a total of 31 states and the Virgin Islands. Procedures for estimating the number of marriages and divorces in the registration states are discussed in *Vital Statistics of the United States, Vol. III—Marriage and Divorce*. Total counts of events for registration and nonregistration states are gathered by collecting already summarized data on marriages and divorces reported by state offices of vital statistics and by county offices of registration. The collection and publication of detailed marriage and divorce statistics was suspended beginning in January 1996. For additional information, contact the National Center for Health Statistics online at <http://www.cdc.gov/nchs/mardiv.htm>.

With the suspension of detailed data collection by the NCHS, data on marriage and divorce can be found in the Census Bureau's American Community Survey data tables. See <https://www.census.gov/programs-surveys/acs/> for information and data access.

Vital statistics rates—Except as noted, vital statistics rates computed by NCHS are based on decennial census population figures as of April 1 for 1960, 1970, 1980, 1990, 2000, and 2010; and on midyear population figures for other years, as estimated by the Census Bureau (see text, Section 1).

Race—Data by race for births, deaths, marriages, and divorces from NCHS are based on information contained in the certificates of registration. The

Census Bureau's Current Population Survey obtains information on race by asking respondents to classify their race as (1) White, (2) Black, (3) American Indian or Alaska Native, (4) Native Hawaiian or Other Pacific Islander, or (5) Asian. Beginning with the 1989 data year, NCHS has tabulated birth data primarily by race of the mother. In 1988 and prior years, births were tabulated by race of the child, which was determined from the race of the parents as entered on the birth certificate. Trend data by race shown in this section are by race of mother beginning with the 1980 data. Hispanic origin of the mother is reported and tabulated independently of race. Thus, persons of Hispanic origin may be of any race. The majority of women of Hispanic origin are reported as White.

Statistical reliability—For a discussion of statistical collection, estimation, and sampling procedures and measures of reliability applicable to data from NCHS and the Census Bureau, see Appendix III.

Table 86. Live Births, Deaths, Marriages, and Divorces: 1960 to 2013

[4,258 represents 4,258,000. Beginning 1970, excludes births to, and deaths of nonresidents of the United States. See Appendix III]

Year	Births (1,000)	Deaths Total (1,000)	Deaths Infant[1] (1,000)	Marriages[2] (1,000)	Divorces[3] (1,000)	Births	Deaths Total	Deaths Infant[1]	Marriages[2]	Divorces[3]
1960	4,258	1,712	111	1,523	393	23.7	9.5	26.0	8.5	2.2
1970	3,731	1,921	75	2,159	708	18.4	9.5	20.0	10.6	3.5
1975	3,144	1,893	51	2,153	1,036	14.6	8.8	16.1	10.0	4.8
1976	3,168	1,909	48	2,155	1,083	14.6	8.8	15.2	9.9	5.0
1977	3,327	1,900	47	2,178	1,091	15.1	8.6	14.1	9.9	5.0
1978	3,333	1,928	46	2,282	1,130	15.0	8.7	13.8	10.3	5.1
1979	3,494	1,914	46	2,331	1,181	15.6	8.5	13.1	10.4	5.3
1980	3,612	1,990	46	2,390	1,189	15.9	8.8	12.6	10.6	5.2
1981	3,629	1,978	43	2,422	1,213	15.8	8.6	11.9	10.6	5.3
1982	3,681	1,975	42	2,456	1,170	15.9	8.5	11.5	10.6	5.1
1983	3,639	2,019	41	2,446	1,158	15.6	8.6	11.2	10.5	5.0
1984	3,669	2,039	40	2,477	1,169	15.6	8.6	10.8	10.5	5.0
1985	3,761	2,086	40	2,413	1,190	15.8	8.8	10.6	10.1	5.0
1986	3,757	2,105	39	2,407	1,178	15.6	8.8	10.4	10.0	4.9
1987	3,809	2,123	38	2,403	1,166	15.7	8.8	10.1	9.9	4.8
1988	3,910	2,168	39	2,396	1,167	16.0	8.9	10.0	9.8	4.8
1989	4,041	2,150	40	2,403	1,157	16.4	8.7	9.8	9.7	4.7
1990	4,158	2,148	38	2,443	1,182	16.7	8.6	9.2	9.8	4.7
1991	4,111	2,170	37	2,371	1,187	16.2	8.6	8.9	9.4	4.7
1992	4,065	2,176	35	2,362	1,215	15.8	8.5	8.5	9.3	4.8
1993	4,000	2,269	33	2,334	1,187	15.4	8.7	8.4	9.0	4.6
1994	3,953	2,279	31	2,362	1,191	15.0	8.7	8.0	9.1	4.6
1995	3,900	2,312	30	2,336	1,169	14.6	8.7	7.6	8.9	4.4
1996	3,891	2,315	28	2,344	1,150	14.4	8.6	7.3	8.8	4.3
1997	3,881	2,314	28	2,384	1,163	14.2	8.5	7.2	8.9	4.3
1998	3,942	2,337	28	2,244	[4] 1,135	14.3	8.5	7.2	8.4	[4] 4.2
1999	3,959	2,391	28	2,358	(NA)	14.2	8.6	7.1	8.6	[4] 4.1
2000	4,059	2,403	28	2,315	[5] 944	14.4	8.5	6.9	8.2	[5] 4.0
2001	4,026	2,416	28	2,326	[5] 940	14.1	8.5	6.9	8.2	[5] 4.0
2002	4,022	2,443	28	2,290	[6] 955	14.0	8.5	7.0	8.0	[6] 3.9
2003	4,090	2,448	28	2,245	[7] 927	14.1	8.4	6.9	7.7	[7] 3.8
2004	4,112	2,398	28	2,279	[8] 879	14.0	8.2	6.8	7.8	[8] 3.7
2005	4,138	2,448	28	2,249	[9] 847	14.0	8.3	6.9	7.6	[9] 3.6
2006	4,266	2,426	29	2,193	[9] 872	14.3	8.1	6.7	[10] 7.5	[9] 3.7
2007	4,316	2,424	29	2,197	[9] 856	14.3	8.0	6.8	7.3	[9] 3.6
2008	4,248	2,472	28	2,157	[9] 844	14.0	8.1	6.6	7.1	[9] 3.5
2009	4,131	2,437	26	2,080	[9] 840	13.5	7.9	6.4	6.8	[9] 3.5
2010	3,999	2,468	25	2,096	[9] 872	13.0	8.0	6.2	6.8	[9] 3.6
2011	3,954	2,515	24	2,118	[9] 877	12.7	8.1	6.1	6.8	[9] 3.6
2012	3,953	2,543	24	2,131	[9] 851	12.6	8.1	6.0	6.8	[9] 3.4
2013	3,932	2,597	23	(NA)	(NA)	12.4	8.2	6.0	(NA)	(NA)

NA Not available. [1] Infant mortality rate; infants under 1 year, excluding fetal deaths. [2] Marriages and marriage rates are by place of occurrence. Beginning 1991, data are provisional. Includes estimates for some States through 1965 and also for 1976 and 1977 and marriage licenses for some states for all years except 1973 and 1975. Beginning 1978, includes nonlicensed marriages in California. [3] Divorces and divorce rates are by place of occurrence. Includes reported annulments and some estimated state figures for all years. Beginning 1991, data are provisional. [4] Excludes data for California, Colorado, Indiana, and Louisiana. [5] Excludes data for California, Indiana, Louisiana, and Oklahoma. [6] Excludes data for California, Indiana, and Oklahoma. [7] Excludes data for California, Hawaii, Indiana, and Oklahoma [8] Excludes data for California, Georgia, Hawaii, Indiana, and Louisiana. [9] Excludes data for California, Georgia, Hawaii, Indiana, Louisiana, and Minnesota. [10] Excludes Louisiana.

Source: U.S. National Center for Health Statistics, *Births: Final Data for 2013*, Vol. 64, No. 1, January 2015; *Deaths: Final Data for 2013*, Vol. 64, No. 2; and "National Marriage and Divorce Rate Trends," <http://www.cdc.gov/nchs/nvss/marriage_divorce_tables.htm>, accessed February 2015.

Table 87. Live Births, Birth Rates, and Fertility Rates by Hispanic Origin: 2010 to 2013

[Births in thousands (3,999 represents 3,999,000). Represents registered births. Excludes births to nonresidents of the United States. Data are based on Hispanic origin and race of mother. Persons of Hispanic origin may be of any race. See Appendix III]

Hispanic-origin status and race of mother	Number of births (1,000) 2010	2011	2012	2013	Birth rate per 1,000 population 2010	2011	2012	2013	Fertility rate[1] 2010	2011	2012	2013
Total [2]	3,999	3,954	3,953	3,932	13.0	12.7	12.6	12.4	64.1	63.2	63.0	62.5
Hispanic	945	918	908	901	18.7	17.6	17.1	16.7	80.2	76.2	74.4	72.9
Mexican	598	567	556	545	18.2	16.9	16.3	(NA)	78.2	73.0	70.7	(NA)
Puerto Rican	66	67	67	68	14.1	13.7	13.5	(NA)	59.7	59.6	58.2	(NA)
Cuban	17	17	17	19	9.0	9.1	8.9	(NA)	46.4	46.1	45.4	(NA)
Central and South American [3]	143	136	132	131	23.4	23.0	22.3	(NA)	97.1	96.3	94.9	(NA)
Other and unknown Hispanic	121	131	135	137	([3])	([3])	([3])	([3])	([3])	([3])	([3])	([3])
Non-Hispanic [4]	3,027	3,008	3,014	3,004	11.8	11.7	11.7	11.6	60.4	60.1	60.3	59.9
White	2,162	2,147	2,134	2,129	10.9	10.8	10.7	10.7	58.7	58.7	58.6	58.7
Black	590	582	583	584	15.1	14.7	14.6	14.4	66.6	65.4	65.0	64.6

NA Not available. [1] Live births per 1,000 women aged 15 to 44 years in specified group. [2] Includes all races and Hispanic origin status not stated. [3] Rates for the Central and South American population include other and unknown Hispanic. [4] Includes other races not shown separately.

Source: U.S. National Center for Health Statistics, National Vital Statistics Reports, *Births: Final Data for 2013*, Vol. 64, No. 1, January 2015. See also <http://www.cdc.gov/nchs/births.htm>.

Table 88. Births, Birth Rates, and Fertility Rates by Sex, and Mother's Race and Age: 1980 to 2013

[Births in thousands (3,612 represents 3,612,000). Excludes births to nonresidents of the United States. For population bases used to derive these data; see text, this section and Appendix III]

Item	1980	1990	2000	2005	2007	2008	2009	2010	2011	2012	2013
Live births [1]	**3,612**	**4,158**	**4,059**	**4,138**	**4,316**	**4,248**	**4,131**	**3,999**	**3,954**	**3,953**	**3,932**
Male	1,853	2,129	2,077	2,119	2,208	2,173	2,114	2,047	2,024	2,021	2,013
Female	1,760	2,029	1,982	2,019	2,108	2,074	2,017	1,952	1,930	1,931	1,919
Males per 100 females (sex ratio)	105	105	105	105	105	105	105	105	105	105	105
Race and age of mother:											
White	2,936	3,290	3,194	3,229	3,337	3,274	3,173	3,069	3,020	3,000	2,986
Black	568	684	623	633	676	671	658	636	633	634	635
American Indian or Alaska Native	29	39	42	45	49	50	49	47	46	46	46
Asian or Pacific Islander	74	142	201	231	254	253	251	247	254	273	266
Under 20 years	562	533	478	421	451	441	415	372	334	309	276
20 to 24 years	1,226	1,094	1,018	1,040	1,082	1,052	1,006	952	925	917	897
25 to 29 years	1,108	1,277	1,088	1,132	1,208	1,196	1,167	1,134	1,128	1,124	1,121
30 to 34 years	550	886	929	951	962	957	955	962	987	1,013	1,037
35 to 39 years	141	318	452	483	500	489	474	465	464	472	484
40 to 44 years	(NA)	(NA)	90	105	105	106	106	107	109	110	109
45 to 54 years	(NA)	(NA)	4	6	7	8	8	8	8	8	8
Mean age of mother at first birth (years)	22.7	24.2	24.9	25.2	25.0	25.1	25.2	25.4	25.6	25.8	26.0
Birth rate per 1,000 population	**15.9**	**16.7**	**14.4**	**14.0**	**14.3**	**14.0**	**13.5**	**13.0**	**12.7**	**12.6**	**12.4**
Race and age of mother:											
White	15.1	15.8	13.9	13.6	13.8	13.5	13.0	12.5	12.2	12.1	12.0
Black	21.3	22.4	17.0	16.1	16.7	16.3	15.8	15.1	14.8	14.7	14.5
American Indian or Alaska Native	20.7	18.9	14.0	12.6	12.9	12.4	11.8	11.0	10.7	10.5	10.3
Asian or Pacific Islander	19.9	19.0	17.1	15.9	16.4	15.7	15.1	14.5	14.5	15.1	14.3
10 to 14 years	1.1	1.4	0.9	0.6	0.6	0.6	0.5	0.4	0.4	0.4	0.3
15 to 19 years	53.0	59.9	47.7	39.7	41.5	40.2	37.9	34.2	31.3	29.4	26.5
20 to 24 years	115.1	116.5	109.7	101.8	105.4	101.8	96.2	90.0	85.3	83.1	80.7
25 to 29 years	112.9	120.2	113.5	116.5	118.1	115.0	111.5	108.3	107.2	106.5	105.5
30 to 34 years	61.9	80.8	91.2	96.7	100.6	99.4	97.5	96.5	96.5	97.3	98.0
35 to 39 years	19.8	31.7	39.7	46.4	47.6	46.8	46.1	45.9	47.2	48.3	49.3
40 to 44 years	3.9	5.5	8.0	9.1	9.6	9.9	10.0	10.2	10.3	10.4	10.4
45 to 54 years [2]	0.2	0.2	0.5	0.6	0.6	0.7	0.7	0.7	0.7	0.7	0.8
Fertility rate per 1,000 women [3]	**68.4**	**70.9**	**65.9**	**66.7**	**69.3**	**68.1**	**66.2**	**64.1**	**63.2**	**63.0**	**62.5**
White [3]	65.6	68.3	65.3	66.8	69.4	68.3	66.4	64.4	63.4	63.0	62.7
Black [3]	84.7	86.8	70.0	68.5	71.7	70.6	68.8	66.3	65.5	65.1	64.7
American Indian or Alaska Native [3]	82.7	76.2	58.7	53.6	55.5	54.0	51.6	48.6	47.7	47.0	46.4
Asian or Pacific Islander [3]	73.2	69.6	65.8	63.0	65.3	63.3	61.3	59.2	59.9	62.2	59.2

NA Not available. [1] Includes other races not shown separately. [2] The number of births shown is the total for women aged 45–54 years. The rate is computed by relating the births to women aged 45–54 years to women aged 45–49 years. [3] Number of live births per 1,000 women, 15 to 44 years old in specified group.

Source: U.S. National Center for Health Statistics, National Vital Statistics Reports, *Births: Final Data for 2013*, Vol. 64, No. 1, January 2015, and earlier reports; and CDC WONDER Online Database, "Natality for 2007-2013," <http://wonder.cdc.gov/natality.html>, accessed February 2015.

Table 89. Births and Multiple Births by Race and Hispanic Origin of Mother: 1990 to 2013

[Represents registered births. Excludes births to nonresidents of the United States. Data are based on Hispanic origin and race of mother. Persons of Hispanic origin may be of any race. See Appendix III]

Birth order	1990 [1]	2000	2010	2011	2012	2013
All births, total number [2]	**4,158,212**	**4,058,814**	**3,999,386**	**3,953,590**	**3,952,841**	**3,932,181**
Twin births	93,865	118,916	132,562	131,269	131,024	132,324
Triplet and higher order multiple births	3,028	7,325	5,503	5,417	4,919	4,700
Multiple birth rate [3]	23.3	31.1	34.5	34.6	34.4	34.8
Twin birth rate [4]	22.6	29.3	33.1	33.2	33.1	33.7
Triplet and higher order multiple birth rate [5]	72.8	180.5	137.6	137.0	124.4	119.5
Non-Hispanic White births, total number	**2,626,500**	**2,362,968**	**2,162,406**	**2,146,566**	**2,134,044**	**2,129,196**
Twin births	60,210	76,018	79,728	78,638	78,449	78,072
Triplet and higher order multiple births	2,358	5,821	3,842	3,670	3,264	3,134
Multiple birth rate [3]	23.8	34.6	38.6	38.3	38.3	38.1
Twin birth rate [4]	22.9	32.2	36.9	36.6	36.8	36.7
Non-Hispanic Black births, total number	**661,701**	**604,346**	**589,808**	**582,345**	**583,489**	**583,834**
Twin births	17,646	20,173	21,804	21,681	21,545	22,346
Triplet and higher order multiple births	306	506	574	634	629	623
Multiple birth rate [3]	27.1	34.2	37.9	38.3	38.0	39.3
Twin birth rate [4]	26.7	33.4	37.0	37.2	36.9	38.3
Hispanic births, total number	**595,073**	**815,868**	**945,180**	**918,129**	**907,677**	**901,033**
Twin births	10,713	16,470	21,359	21,236	20,505	21,511
Triplet and higher order multiple births	235	659	721	723	636	643
Multiple birth rate [3]	18.4	21.0	23.4	23.9	23.3	24.6
Twin birth rate [4]	18.0	20.2	22.6	23.1	22.6	23.9

[1] Data by Hispanic-origin status exclude data for New Hampshire and Oklahoma, which did not report Hispanic origin. [2] Includes other races not shown separately. [3] Number of live births in all multiple deliveries per 1,000 live births. [4] Number of live births in twin deliveries per 1,000 live births. [5] Births in greater than twin deliveries per 100,000 live births.

Source: U.S. National Center for Health Statistics, National Vital Statistics Reports, *Births: Final Data for 2013*, Vol. 64, No. 1, January 2015. See also <http://www.cdc.gov/nchs/births.htm>.

Table 90. Births—Number and Rate by State and Island Area: 2013

[Number of births, except rates. Registered births by place of residence. Excludes births to nonresidents of the United States. Based on race and Hispanic origin of mother. See Appendix III]

State and Island Area	All races [1]	Non-Hispanic White	Non-Hispanic Black	American Indian or Alaska Native	Asian or Pacific Islander	Hispanic [2]	Birth rate [3]	Fertility rate [4]
United States [5]	**3,932,181**	**2,129,196**	**583,834**	**45,991**	**265,673**	**901,033**	**12.4**	**62.5**
Alabama	58,167	35,086	17,906	209	973	4,002	12.0	60.6
Alaska	11,446	6,622	446	2,462	1,053	848	15.6	77.8
Arizona	85,600	38,360	4,437	5,746	3,514	33,885	12.9	66.3
Arkansas	37,832	25,287	7,265	291	1,094	3,834	12.8	65.9
California	494,705	143,531	28,931	3,590	76,424	238,496	12.9	62.0
Colorado	65,007	39,872	3,224	793	2,863	17,821	12.3	61.0
Connecticut	36,085	20,704	4,606	307	2,221	8,208	10.0	52.7
Delaware	10,831	5,942	2,961	25	541	1,348	11.7	60.3
District of Columbia	9,288	2,781	4,798	49	493	1,247	14.4	53.3
Florida	215,407	98,586	49,113	392	7,265	59,206	11.0	59.3
Georgia	128,748	59,379	44,381	325	5,917	16,994	12.9	61.6
Hawaii	18,987	4,940	542	68	12,203	3,003	13.5	71.5
Idaho	22,383	17,951	192	421	491	3,422	13.9	71.8
Illinois	156,931	85,866	26,807	234	9,848	33,454	12.2	60.3
Indiana	83,102	63,820	10,010	127	2,364	6,837	12.6	64.3
Iowa	39,094	32,302	2,116	269	1,353	3,175	12.7	67.1
Kansas	38,839	28,281	2,794	293	1,401	6,143	13.4	69.5
Kentucky	55,686	46,612	5,217	82	1,191	2,693	12.7	65.3
Louisiana	63,201	33,583	24,031	442	1,448	3,899	13.7	67.3
Maine	12,776	11,774	443	118	253	172	9.6	54.4
Maryland	71,953	32,568	23,349	300	5,415	10,515	12.1	60.1
Massachusetts	71,788	45,046	7,100	157	6,460	12,376	10.7	52.8
Michigan	113,489	79,107	22,057	714	4,136	7,318	11.5	60.0
Minnesota	69,159	50,238	7,381	1,458	5,381	4,672	12.8	65.9
Mississippi	38,634	19,730	16,673	292	504	1,496	12.9	64.2
Missouri	75,296	57,361	11,385	402	2,075	3,931	12.5	64.1
Montana	12,377	10,170	86	1,531	132	476	12.2	67.2
Nebraska	26,095	19,237	1,773	592	854	3,895	14.0	72.2
Nevada	35,030	14,951	3,909	425	3,097	12,718	12.6	62.8
New Hampshire	12,396	11,064	215	25	485	513	9.4	50.8
New Jersey	102,575	48,018	15,570	196	11,511	27,251	11.5	59.6
New Mexico	26,354	7,428	432	3,763	597	14,402	12.6	66.1
New York	236,980	115,505	37,613	790	25,394	54,821	12.1	58.8
North Carolina	119,002	66,316	28,952	1,939	5,331	17,508	12.1	60.4
North Dakota	10,599	8,531	335	1,021	263	436	14.7	75.3
Ohio	138,936	104,059	23,772	320	3,915	6,504	12.0	62.7
Oklahoma	53,369	33,978	4,832	6,075	1,583	7,208	13.9	70.6
Oregon	45,155	31,998	1,188	909	2,696	8,448	11.5	58.6
Pennsylvania	140,921	98,751	20,626	423	6,721	14,163	11.0	58.4
Rhode Island	10,809	6,572	936	128	598	2,453	10.3	51.6
South Carolina	56,795	33,085	17,815	201	1,235	4,411	11.9	60.6
South Dakota	12,248	9,127	316	2,100	279	521	14.5	78.1
Tennessee	79,992	54,377	16,810	231	2,097	6,854	12.3	62.1
Texas	387,340	136,608	45,825	1,229	18,861	185,467	14.6	69.9
Utah	50,957	39,401	559	792	1,785	7,706	17.6	80.9
Vermont	5,975	5,597	108	11	153	92	9.5	51.4
Virginia	102,147	59,280	21,919	249	7,835	13,073	12.4	60.9
Washington	86,577	54,779	4,521	2,140	9,820	15,575	12.4	62.6
West Virginia	20,825	19,542	746	19	229	219	11.2	61.5
Wisconsin	66,649	49,357	6,708	1,011	3,197	6,398	11.6	61.3
Wyoming	7,644	6,136	103	305	124	926	13.1	69.3
Puerto Rico	36,486	2,644	276	(NA)	(NA)	33,542	10.1	49.4
Virgin Islands	(NA)	(NA)	(NA)	(NA)	(NA)	(NA)	(NA)	(NA)
Guam	3,285	170	19	5	3,049	50	20.5	95.9
American Samoa	1,077	(NA)	(NA)	–	1,073	(NA)	19.7	83.7
Northern Marianas	686	7	1	1	677	–	13.4	51.7

– Represents zero. NA Not available. [1] Includes persons of other groups, not shown separately. [2] Persons of Hispanic origin may be of any race. [3] Per 1,000 estimated population. [4] Number of births per 1,000 women aged 15 to 44 years. [5] Does not include data for the Island Areas.

Source: U.S. National Center for Health Statistics, National Vital Statistics Reports, *Births: Final Data for 2013*, Vol. 64, No. 1, January 2015. See also <http://www.cdc.gov/nchs/births.htm>.

Table 91. Total Fertility Rate by Race and Hispanic Origin: 1980 to 2013

[Based on race of mother. Excludes births to nonresidents of United States. The *total fertility rate* is the number of births that 1,000 women would have in their lifetime if, at each year of age, they experienced the birth rates occurring in the specified year. A total fertility rate of 2,100 represents "replacement level" fertility for the total population under current mortality conditions (assuming no net immigration). See Appendix III]

Race and Hispanic origin	1980	1990	2000	2005	2010	2011	2012	2013
Total [1]	**1,840**	**2,081**	**2,056**	**2,057**	**1,931**	**1,895**	**1,881**	**1,858**
White	1,773	2,003	2,051	2,079	1,948	1,905	1,886	1,868
Black	2,177	2,480	2,129	2,062	1,957	1,920	1,900	1,883
American Indian or Alaska Native	2,165	2,185	1,773	1,584	1,404	1,374	1,350	1,335
Asian or Pacific Islander	1,954	2,003	1,892	1,785	1,689	1,707	1,770	1,681
Hispanic [2]	(NA)	2,960	2,730	2,792	2,350	2,240	2,190	2,149

NA Not available. [1] For 1980 and 1990, includes births to races not shown separately. Beginning 1992, unknown race of mother is imputed. [2] Persons of Hispanic origin may be of any race.

Source: U.S. National Center for Health Statistics, National Vital Statistics Report, *Births: Final Data for 2013*, Vol. 64, No. 1, January 2015. See also <http://www.cdc.gov/nchs/births.htm>.

Table 92. Teenagers—Births and Birth Rates by Age, Race, and Hispanic Origin: 1990 to 2013

[Birth rates per 1,000 women in specified group. Based on race and Hispanic origin of mother. See text this section]

Item	Number of births					Birth rate				
	1990	2000	2010	2012	2013	1990	2000	2010	2012	2013
All races, 15 to 19 years	[1] **521,826**	**468,990**	**367,678**	**305,388**	**273,105**	**59.9**	**47.7**	**34.2**	**29.4**	**26.5**
15 to 17 years	183,327	157,209	109,173	86,423	74,820	37.5	26.9	17.3	14.1	12.3
18 to 19 years	338,499	311,781	258,505	218,965	198,285	88.6	78.1	58.2	51.4	47.1
White	354,482	333,013	259,058	215,909	194,767	50.8	43.2	31.9	27.4	24.9
Black	151,613	118,954	94,950	77,474	67,537	112.8	77.4	51.1	44.0	39.1
American Indian or Alaska Native	(NA)	8,055	7,408	6,476	5,718	81.1	58.3	38.7	34.9	31.1
Asian or Pacific Islander	(NA)	8,968	6,262	5,529	5,083	26.4	20.5	10.9	9.7	8.7
Hispanic [2]	(NA)	129,469	121,798	102,722	92,960	100.3	87.3	55.7	46.3	41.7
Non-Hispanic White	(NA)	204,056	144,102	119,757	107,886	42.5	32.6	23.5	20.5	18.6
Non-Hispanic Black	(NA)	116,019	88,329	71,286	62,066	116.2	79.2	51.5	43.9	39.0

NA Not available. [1] Includes races other than White and Black, not shown separately. [2] Persons of Hispanic origin may be of any race.

Source: U.S. National Center for Health Statistics, National Vital Statistics Reports, *Births: Final Data for 2013*, Vol. 64, No. 1, January 2015, and earlier reports. See also <http://www.cdc.gov/nchs/births.htm>.

Table 93. Births to Unmarried Women by Race, Hispanic Origin, and Age of Mother: 1990 to 2013

[1,165 represents 1,165,000. Excludes births to nonresidents of the United States. Persons of Hispanic origin may be of any race. Marital status is inferred from a comparison of the child's and parents' surnames on the birth certificate for those states that do not report on marital status. No estimates included for misstatements on birth records or failure to register births. See also Appendix III]

Race/ethnicity and age of mother	Number (1,000)				Percent distribution				Birth rate [1]			
	1990	2000	2010	2013	1990	2000	2010	2013	1990	2000	2010	2013
Total live births [2]	**1,165**	**1,347**	**1,633**	**1,596**	**100.0**	**100.0**	**100.0**	**100.0**	**43.8**	**44.1**	**47.5**	**44.3**
White	670	866	1,102	1,070	57.5	64.3	67.5	67.0	32.9	38.2	44.5	40.8
Black	455	427	459	450	39.1	31.7	28.1	28.2	90.5	70.5	65.3	61.7
American Indian or Alaska Native	(NA)	(NA)	31	31	(NA)	(NA)	1.9	1.9	(NA)	(NA)	(NA)	(NA)
Asian or Pacific Islander	(NA)	(NA)	42	45	(NA)	(NA)	2.6	2.8	(NA)	20.9	22.3	21.8
Hispanic	[3] 219	348	504	480	[3] 18.8	25.8	30.9	30.1	[3] 89.6	87.2	80.6	69.9
Non-Hispanic White	[3] 443	522	628	624	[3] 38.0	38.7	38.4	39.1	[3] 24.4	28.0	32.9	31.7
Non-Hispanic Black	(NA)	415	428	417	(NA)	30.8	26.2	26.1	(NA)	(NA)	(NA)	(NA)
Under 15 years	11	8	4	3	0.9	0.6	0.3	0.2	(NA)	(NA)	(NA)	(NA)
15 to 19 years	350	369	324	242	30.0	27.4	19.8	15.2	42.5	39.0	31.1	24.0
20 to 24 years	404	504	601	587	34.7	37.4	36.8	36.8	65.1	72.2	70.0	63.1
25 to 29 years	230	255	385	402	19.7	18.9	23.6	25.2	56.0	58.5	69.2	66.7
30 to 34 years	118	130	203	232	10.1	9.7	12.5	14.5	37.6	39.3	56.3	56.6
35 to 39 years	44	65	91	102	3.8	4.8	5.6	6.4	17.3	19.7	29.6	31.8
40 years and over [4]	9	16	25	28	0.7	1.2	1.5	1.7	3.6	5.0	8.0	8.3

NA Not available. [1] Rate per 1,000 unmarried women (never-married, widowed, and divorced) estimated as of July 1. Total rate and rates by race cover women 15 to 44 years old. [2] Includes races other than White and Black, not shown separately. [3] Excludes data for New Hampshire and Oklahoma, which did not report Hispanic origin. [4] Beginning in 1997, birth rates computed by relating births to unmarried mothers aged 40 years and over to unmarried women aged 40–44 years.

Source: U.S. National Center for Health Statistics, National Vital Statistics Reports, *Births: Final Data for 2013*, Vol. 64, No. 1, January 2015, and earlier reports. See also <http://www.cdc.gov/nchs/births.htm>.

Table 94. Percent of Births to Teenagers, Unmarried Mothers, and Births With Low Birth Weight by Race and Hispanic Origin of Mother: 1990 to 2013

[Represents registered births. Excludes births to nonresidents of the United States. See Appendix III]

Characteristics of mother	1990	1995	2000	2010	2011	2012	2013
Percent of births to teenage mothers [1]	**12.8**	**13.1**	**11.8**	**9.3**	**8.4**	**7.8**	**7.0**
White	10.9	11.5	10.6	8.5	7.8	7.3	6.6
Black	23.1	23.1	19.7	15.2	13.7	12.4	10.8
American Indian or Alaska Native	19.5	21.4	19.7	16.1	14.9	14.2	12.6
Asian or Pacific Islander	5.7	5.6	4.5	2.6	2.3	2.0	1.9
Hispanic origin [2]	16.8	17.9	16.2	13.1	12.1	11.5	10.5
Mexican	17.7	18.8	17.0	13.8	12.2	12.2	11.1
Puerto Rican	21.7	23.5	20.0	15.3	14.0	13.3	11.8
Cuban	7.7	7.7	7.5	6.2	5.6	5.3	4.6
Central and South American	9.0	10.6	9.9	7.2	6.5	6.1	5.8
Other and unknown Hispanic	(NA)	20.1	18.8	16.3	14.7	13.7	12.4
Non-Hispanic	(NA)	(NA)	10.7	8.1	7.3	6.7	6.0
White	(NA)	(NA)	8.7	6.7	6.1	5.7	5.1
Black	(NA)	(NA)	19.8	15.2	13.7	12.4	10.8
Percent of births to unmarried mothers	**26.6**	**32.2**	**33.2**	**40.8**	**40.7**	**40.7**	**40.6**
White	16.9	25.3	27.1	35.9	35.7	35.9	35.8
Black	66.7	69.9	68.5	72.1	71.8	71.6	71.0
American Indian or Alaska Native	53.6	57.2	58.4	65.6	66.2	66.9	66.4
Asian or Pacific Islander	13.2	16.3	14.8	17.0	17.2	17.0	17.0
Hispanic origin [2]	36.7	40.8	42.7	53.4	53.3	53.5	53.2
Mexican	33.3	38.1	40.7	52.0	52.0	52.1	51.9
Puerto Rican	55.9	60.0	59.6	65.2	65.0	65.1	64.6
Cuban	18.2	23.8	27.3	47.0	48.2	48.8	50.1
Central and South American	41.2	44.1	44.7	51.8	51.2	50.8	50.1
Other and unknown Hispanic	(NA)	44.0	46.2	56.3	55.9	56.4	56.1
Non-Hispanic	(NA)	(NA)	30.8	36.9	36.8	36.9	36.8
White	(NA)	(NA)	22.1	29.0	29.0	29.3	29.3
Black	(NA)	(NA)	68.7	72.5	72.3	72.1	71.5
Percent of births with low birth weight [3]	**7.0**	**7.3**	**7.6**	**8.1**	**8.1**	**8.0**	**8.0**
White	5.7	6.2	6.5	7.1	7.1	7.0	7.0
Black	13.3	13.1	13.0	13.2	13.0	12.8	12.8
American Indian or Alaska Native	6.1	6.6	6.8	7.6	7.5	7.6	7.5
Asian or Pacific Islander	(NA)	6.9	7.3	8.5	8.4	8.2	8.3
Hispanic origin [2]	6.1	6.3	6.4	7.0	7.0	7.0	7.1
Mexican	5.5	5.8	6.0	6.5	6.5	6.5	6.6
Puerto Rican	9.0	9.4	9.3	9.6	9.7	9.4	9.4
Cuban	5.7	6.5	6.5	7.3	7.1	7.4	7.3
Central and South American	5.8	6.2	6.3	6.5	6.7	6.6	6.8
Other and unknown Hispanic	(NA)	7.5	7.8	8.4	8.0	8.0	8.0
Non-Hispanic	(NA)	(NA)	7.9	8.5	8.4	8.3	8.3
White	(NA)	(NA)	6.6	7.1	7.1	7.0	7.0
Black	(NA)	(NA)	13.1	13.5	13.3	13.2	13.1

NA Not available. [1] Mothers under 20 years old. [2] Hispanic persons may be of any race. [3] Births less than 2,500 grams (5 pounds, 8 ounces).

Source: U.S. National Center for Health Statistics, National Vital Statistics Reports, *Births: Final Data for 2013*, Vol. 64, No. 1, January 2015, and earlier reports. See also <http://www.cdc.gov/nchs/births.htm>.

Table 95. Births by Race, Hispanic Origin, and Method of Delivery: 1990 to 2013

[In thousands (4,111 represents 4,111,000), except rate. Persons of Hispanic origin may be of any race. See Appendix III]

Method of delivery	1990 [1]	2000	2010	2012	2013 Total [2]	2013 Hispanic	2013 Non-Hispanic White	2013 Non-Hispanic Black
Births, total	**4,111**	**4,059**	**3,999**	**3,953**	**3,932**	**901**	**2,129**	**584**
Vaginal	3,111	3,108	2,681	2,651	2,643	610	1,446	374
Cesarean	914	924	1,309	1,296	1,284	290	681	209
Not stated	85	27	9	6	5	1	2	1
Cesarean delivery rate [3]	22.7	22.9	32.8	32.8	32.7	32.2	32.0	35.8

[1] 1990 excludes data for Oklahoma, which did not report method of delivery on the birth certificate. [2] Includes other races, not shown separately. [3] Percent of all live births by cesarean delivery.

Source: U.S. National Center for Health Statistics, National Vital Statistics Reports, *Births: Final Data for 2013*, Vol. 64, No. 1, January 2015, and earlier reports. See also <http://www.cdc.gov/nchs/births.htm>.

Table 96. Percent of Births to Teenage Mothers, Unmarried Women, and Births with Low Birth Weight by State: 2012 and 2013

[In percent. By place of residence. Excludes nonresidents of the United States. Data for teenage mothers are not comparable to data in previous editions of this table, as the definition of teenage mothers has changed from women under age 20 to women aged 15-19]

State	Births to teenage mothers [1] 2012	2013	Births to unmarried women 2012	2013	Births with low birth weight [2] 2012	2013	State	Births to teenage mothers [1] 2012	2013	Births to unmarried women 2012	2013	Births with low birth weight [2] 2012	2013
U.S...........	7.7	6.9	40.7	40.6	8.0	8.0	MO.............	8.4	7.7	40.2	40.3	7.7	8.0
AL.............	10.6	9.3	42.6	42.2	10.0	10.0	MT.............	7.4	6.9	36.0	37.4	7.4	7.4
AK.............	7.3	6.2	37.4	34.5	5.7	5.8	NE.............	6.4	5.9	33.3	33.3	6.7	6.4
AZ.............	9.4	8.4	45.5	45.4	6.9	6.9	NV.............	8.2	7.4	45.2	45.3	8.0	8.0
AR.............	11.3	11.0	45.2	45.0	8.7	8.8	NH.............	5.1	4.5	34.5	34.2	7.3	6.8
CA.............	6.9	6.2	40.1	39.7	6.7	6.8	NJ.............	4.6	4.1	36.1	35.6	8.2	8.3
CO.............	6.4	5.9	23.0	23.1	8.8	8.8	NM.............	12.1	11.2	52.1	52.0	8.8	8.9
CT.............	5.2	4.5	37.9	38.2	7.9	7.8	NY.............	5.2	4.7	40.8	40.2	7.9	8.0
DE.............	6.9	6.7	47.4	47.8	8.3	8.3	NC.............	8.4	7.6	41.0	41.4	8.8	8.8
DC.............	8.4	6.9	51.1	50.8	9.6	9.4	ND.............	6.0	5.3	32.4	32.4	6.2	6.4
FL.............	7.5	6.5	47.9	48.0	8.6	8.5	OH.............	8.3	7.5	43.8	43.7	8.6	8.5
GA.............	8.8	8.0	45.2	45.4	9.3	9.5	OK.............	11.1	9.9	42.3	42.2	8.0	8.1
HI.............	5.8	5.1	37.5	37.3	8.1	8.2	OR.............	6.3	5.7	35.4	35.9	6.1	6.3
ID.............	6.8	6.4	27.4	27.1	6.4	6.9	PA.............	7.1	6.1	41.9	41.6	8.1	8.0
IL.............	7.6	6.7	40.4	40.4	8.1	8.2	RI.............	7.0	6.1	46.4	44.6	8.0	6.9
IN.............	8.9	8.1	43.2	43.3	7.9	7.9	SC.............	9.7	8.4	47.9	47.3	9.6	9.7
IA.............	6.5	5.9	34.8	34.4	6.7	6.6	SD.............	7.7	6.6	38.6	38.2	6.2	6.3
KS.............	8.2	7.4	36.7	36.2	7.1	7.0	TN.............	9.8	8.9	44.1	44.0	9.2	9.1
KY.............	10.2	9.7	41.2	41.9	8.7	8.7	TX.............	10.6	9.7	42.1	42.2	8.3	8.3
LA.............	10.3	9.2	53.2	53.0	10.8	10.9	UT.............	4.8	4.4	18.7	18.9	6.8	7.0
ME.............	6.2	5.5	41.5	41.0	6.6	7.1	VT.............	6.0	5.3	40.6	40.2	6.2	6.7
MD.............	5.9	5.1	40.8	40.4	8.8	8.5	VA.............	5.9	5.2	35.2	34.6	8.1	8.0
MA.............	4.4	3.8	34.4	33.5	7.6	7.7	WA.............	5.7	5.1	32.5	32.8	6.1	6.4
MI.............	7.9	6.9	42.3	42.4	8.4	8.2	WV.............	11.6	10.5	44.8	45.2	9.2	9.4
MN.............	4.8	4.3	33.1	32.9	6.6	6.4	WI.............	6.2	5.5	37.3	37.0	7.1	7.0
MS.............	12.4	11.3	54.7	54.5	11.6	11.5	WY.............	8.2	7.1	33.8	32.7	8.5	8.6

NA Not available. [1] Defined as teenage mothers aged 15-19. [2] Less than 2,500 grams (5 pounds, 8 ounces).

Source: U.S. National Center for Health Statistics, National Vital Statistics Reports, *Births: Final Data for 2013, Supplemental Tables*, Vol. 64, No. 1, January 2015, and earlier reports; and "Vital Stats," <http://www.cdc.gov/nchs/vitalstats.htm>, accessed February 2015.

Table 97. Rate of Pregnancy Risk Factors, Obstetric Procedures and Labor or Delivery Characteristics, and Birth Defects by Age of Mother: 2013

[Rates are number of live births with specified risk factor, procedure, or characteristic per 1,000 live births in specified group; birth defects are per 100,000 live births. In 2013, total number of births to residents of areas reporting risk factors, procedure, or defects was 3,932,181]

Factor	Births with factor reported (number)	All ages	Under 20 years	20-24 years	25-29 years	30-34 years	35-39 years	40-54 years
Risk factors in current pregnancy:								
Diabetes.........................	235,484	60.0	20.3	33.9	53.5	72.9	101.3	130.7
Hypertension, pregnancy-associated........	189,441	48.3	51.0	46.6	47.0	46.8	51.5	67.2
Hypertension, chronic.................	60,391	15.4	5.6	8.9	13.3	18.0	26.4	39.7
Obstetric procedures and labor or delivery characteristics:								
Induction of labor.................	903,638	230.1	264.9	249.0	234.1	215.1	203.3	209.0
Breech or malpresentation....................	221,071	57.7	45.7	47.9	54.4	62.1	73.0	92.8
Precipitous labor...........................	119,022	30.4	21.1	26.8	30.5	33.6	34.7	31.8
Birth defects (congenital anomalies):								
Anencephaly..........................	426	10.9	14.9	11.2	10.1	9.8	11.4	(B)
Meningomyelocele or spina bifida............	629	16.1	18.2	17.2	16.5	15.2	13.9	(B)
Omphalocele or gastroschisis................	1,477	37.7	93.8	65.8	30.0	18.7	13.7	31.6
Cleft lip or palate............................	2,831	72.3	75.2	77.6	75.0	63.4	73.0	74.3
Down syndrome........................	1,990	50.8	32.4	26.2	27.9	44.6	103.1	339.0

(B) Base figure too small to meet statistical standards for reliability of a derived figure.

Source: U.S. National Center for Health Statistics, National Vital Statistics Reports, *Births Final Data for 2013: Supplemental Tables*, Vol. 64, No. 1, January 2015. See also <http://www.cdc.gov/nchs/births.htm>.

Table 98. Induction of Labor by Gestational Age: 1990 to 2013

[In percent. Data are for singleton births]

Gestational age	1990 [1]	1995	2000	2005	2007	2008	2009	2010	2011	2012	2013
All gestations...........	9.2	15.9	19.7	22.2	22.7	22.9	23.1	23.3	23.2	22.8	23.0
Under 20 weeks.............	8.2	11.3	13.9	12.0	11.8	10.0	10.2	12.5	11.8	10.9	12.9
20-27 weeks.................	4.1	5.7	6.5	5.5	5.3	5.6	5.7	5.7	5.3	5.6	5.6
28-31 weeks.................	4.6	7.8	9.0	8.7	8.7	8.8	8.8	9.0	8.8	9.0	9.0
32-35 weeks.................	6.4	11.1	13.8	13.9	13.8	13.8	13.8	14.0	13.8	13.7	14.1
36 weeks.....................	7.5	12.8	16.3	17.3	16.9	17.0	16.6	16.7	16.2	16.1	16.3
37-39 weeks.................	7.6	14.2	18.7	21.6	21.8	22.0	21.8	21.9	21.7	21.2	21.2
40 weeks.....................	8.6	16.1	20.6	24.9	26.0	26.1	27.1	27.3	27.2	26.7	26.9
41 weeks.....................	13.0	22.4	26.9	30.7	31.8	32.2	32.9	33.6	33.7	33.4	34.4
42 weeks and over..........	14.4	21.1	24.1	26.0	26.7	27.2	27.8	28.2	28.0	27.5	27.8

[1] Oklahoma did not report induction of labor.

Source: U.S. National Center for Health Statistics, "VitalStats," <http://www.cdc.gov/nchs/vitalstats.htm>, accessed February 2015.

Table 99. Premature Births by Whether Early or Late Preterm and by Age, Race, and Hispanic Origin of Mother: 2013

[Based on race and Hispanic origin of mother. Preterm births are those with less than 37 completed weeks of gestation]

Characteristic	Number Total [1]	Number Early [2]	Number Late [3]	Percent Total	Percent Early [2]	Percent Late [3]
Total [4]............................	**447,361**	**133,503**	**313,858**	**11.4**	**3.4**	**8.0**
Age of mother:						
Under 15 years..............................	652	269	383	21.1	8.7	12.4
15 to 19 years..............................	35,411	11,545	23,866	13.0	4.2	8.8
15 years..................................	1,631	583	1,048	17.4	6.2	11.2
16 years..................................	3,368	1,108	2,260	15.0	4.9	10.0
17 years..................................	5,747	1,921	3,826	13.4	4.5	8.9
18 years..................................	9,839	3,280	6,559	12.9	4.3	8.6
19 years..................................	14,826	4,653	10,173	12.2	3.8	8.3
20 to 24 years..............................	101,254	30,640	70,614	11.3	3.4	7.9
25 to 29 years..............................	117,337	34,118	83,219	10.5	3.1	7.4
30 to 34 years..............................	111,942	32,783	79,159	10.8	3.2	7.6
35 to 39 years..............................	61,379	18,039	43,340	12.7	3.7	9.0
40 to 44 years..............................	17,380	5,457	11,923	15.9	5.0	10.9
45 years and over..........................	2,006	652	1,354	24.6	8.0	16.6
Race and Hispanic origin of mother:						
Non-Hispanic White.........................	216,449	60,976	155,473	10.2	2.9	7.3
Non-Hispanic Black.........................	94,869	34,421	60,448	16.3	5.9	10.4
Hispanic [5]................................	101,839	28,601	73,238	11.3	3.2	8.1

[1] Total includes those unknown, not shown separately. [2] Less than 34 completed weeks of gestation. [3] 34-36 completed weeks of gestation. [4] Includes races other than White and Black, not shown separately. [5] Persons of Hispanic origin may be of any race.

Source: U.S. National Center for Health Statistics, *Births, Final Data for 2013*, Vol. 64, No. 1, January 2015. See also <http://www.cdc.gov/nchs/births.htm>.

Table 100. Women Who Had a Birth in the Past 12 Months by Selected Characteristics: 2013

[For women aged 15 to 50 years old. Based on the 2013 American Community Survey (ACS). The ACS sample includes the household population and the population living in institutions, dormitories, and other group quarters. Based on a sample and subject to sampling variability. See Appendix III for details]

Characteristic	Total women (number)	Women who had a child in the past 12 months — Number	Percent distribution	Rate per 1,000 women	Percent unmarried
Total age 15 to 50 years............................	**76,129,362**	**3,930,417**	**(X)**	**52**	**36.0**
Age:					
15 to 19 years..............................	10,427,332	198,055	5.0	19	86.1
20 to 34 years..............................	32,185,659	2,943,437	74.9	91	37.2
35 to 50 years..............................	33,516,371	788,925	20.1	24	19.1
Race/ethnicity:					
One race..................................	73,948,140	3,812,898	97.0	52	35.7
White......................................	53,688,480	2,689,015	68.4	50	29.8
Black or African American..................	10,729,458	572,070	14.6	53	67.2
American Indian and Alaska Native..........	643,369	41,419	1.1	64	55.5
Asian.....................................	4,633,277	247,937	6.3	54	12.3
Native Hawaiian and Other Pacific Islander....	143,311	8,954	0.2	62	43.4
Some other race...........................	4,110,245	253,503	6.4	62	46.4
Two or more races..........................	2,181,222	117,519	3.0	54	47.5
Hispanic origin:					
Hispanic or Latino origin (of any race)........	14,328,898	884,198	22.5	62	42.5
White alone, not Hispanic or Latino..........	44,328,454	2,111,818	53.7	48	27.1
Nativity:					
Native.....................................	63,522,595	3,148,600	80.1	50	39.2
Foreign born [1]............................	12,606,767	781,817	19.9	62	23.4
Education:					
Less than high school graduate.............	13,534,366	580,393	14.8	43	57.8
High school graduate (includes equivalency)....	16,310,948	909,010	23.1	56	50.0
Some college or associate's degree..........	25,332,363	1,250,510	31.8	49	40.8
Bachelor's degree..........................	14,077,128	751,148	19.1	53	12.2
Graduate or professional degree.............	6,874,557	439,356	11.2	64	5.6
Poverty status in past 12 months:					
Women 15 to 50 years old with poverty status determined......	74,431,908	3,918,982	(X)	53	35.9
Below 100 percent of poverty level.............	14,055,535	1,071,507	27.3	76	65.6
100 to 199 percent of poverty level...........	14,137,931	851,183	21.7	60	39.8
200 percent or more above poverty level.........	46,238,442	1,996,292	50.9	43	18.3
Labor force status:					
In labor force [2]............................	53,009,725	2,417,900	61.7	46	37.2
Public assistance income in past 12 months:					
Received public assistance income..........	1,971,235	243,376	6.2	123	70.4
Did not receive public assistance income........	74,158,127	3,687,041	93.8	50	33.7

X Not applicable. [1] Excludes persons born outside of the United States to a parent who is a U.S. citizen. [2] Data are shown for women aged 16-50 years old.

Source: U.S. Census Bureau, 2013 American Community Survey, S1301, "Fertility," <http://factfinder2.census.gov>, accessed December 2014.

Table 101. Women by Number of Children Ever Born by Age, Marital Status, and Race/Ethnicity: 2014

[75,444 represents 75,444,000. As of June. Data shown are for women aged 15 to 50. Based on the Current Population Survey; for more information, see <http://www.census.gov/cps/methodology>]

Age and marital status	Total women (1,000)	Percent distribution by number of children ever born						
		None	One	Two	Three	Four	Five and six	Seven or more
Total women: [1]	**75,444**	**42.4**	**17.0**	**22.3**	**11.7**	**4.5**	**1.9**	**0.4**
By age:								
15 to 19 years old	10,202	95.9	3.1	0.6	0.3	–	–	–
20 to 24 years old	11,026	75.2	15.8	6.6	1.9	0.5	0.1	–
25 to 29 years old	10,679	49.6	21.2	18.8	7.0	2.3	1.1	–
30 to 34 years old	10,604	28.9	23.5	26.5	13.3	5.7	1.8	0.3
35 to 39 years old	9,873	18.5	17.6	33.8	19.0	7.3	3.4	0.4
40 to 44 years old	10,301	15.3	18.3	34.6	20.2	7.6	3.3	0.8
45 to 50 years old	12,760	16.7	18.7	33.8	19.2	7.6	3.2	0.9
By marital status:								
Women ever married	41,937	16.2	21.3	34.4	18.2	6.9	2.7	0.5
Women never married	33,506	75.2	11.7	7.2	3.5	1.5	0.8	0.2
By race and Hispanic origin:								
White alone	56,490	42.6	16.4	22.9	12.0	4.3	1.6	0.3
White alone, non-Hispanic	43,715	44.1	16.9	22.9	10.8	3.8	1.3	0.2
Black alone	11,000	39.2	20.2	19.5	11.6	6.0	2.8	0.8
Asian alone	4,907	45.5	18.2	23.5	8.2	3.2	1.1	0.4
Hispanic alone [2]	14,456	37.4	14.8	22.7	15.7	6.1	2.8	0.5

– Represents or rounds to zero. [1] Includes women of other races, not shown separately. [2] Persons of Hispanic origin may be of any race.

Source: U.S. Census Bureau, "Fertility of Women in the United States: 2014—Detailed Tables," <http://www.census.gov/hhes/fertility/data/cps/>, accessed April 2015.

Table 102. Women's Relationship Status at First Birth by Selected Characteristics: 2012

[In percent, except total (3,691 represents 3,691,000). As of June. The denominator for each percentage is the total number of women in the given childbearing cohort and age at first birth, race, ethnic origin, or nativity/citizenship category. The numerator is the number of women in that same group who had each relationship status at first birth. Across the line within any given cohort, the percentages will sum to 100 percent, and show how women's relationships at first birth have changed over time. Data are from the Current Population Survey; for more information, see <https://www.census.gov/cps/methodology/>]

Characteristic	Relationship status at first birth for women with less than 5 years since first birth			Relationship status at first birth for women with 20 or more years since first birth		
	Married	Living with unmarried partner	Not married and not living with partner	Married	Living with unmarried partner	Not married and not living with partner
Women aged 15 to 50 (1,000)	**3,691**	**1,822**	**1,636**	**8,091**	**1,640**	**2,146**
Percent	51.6	25.5	22.9	68.1	13.8	18.1
AGE AT FIRST BIRTH						
Younger than 20 years old [1]	13.9	35.3	50.9	51.1	19.7	29.2
20 to 24 years old	31.2	36.9	32.0	71.6	13.1	15.3
25 to 29 years old	70.4	19.2	10.4	86.9	6.5	6.6
30 to 34 years old	79.7	14.2	6.2	92.7	1.9	5.4
35 to 39 years old	81.1	10.4	8.5	(NA)	(NA)	(NA)
40 years old or older [2]	79.9	8.5	11.6	(NA)	(NA)	(NA)
RACE						
White alone	56.4	26.1	17.5	76.0	11.7	12.3
White alone, non-Hispanic	60.7	25.0	14.3	79.4	9.6	10.9
Black alone	21.0	24.9	54.1	34.4	21.3	44.3
Asian alone	86.3	8.9	4.9	81.9	8.2	10.0
All other races, race combinations	30.2	42.6	27.2	49.8	28.7	21.5
HISPANIC ORIGIN						
Hispanic (any race)	40.8	30.6	28.6	64.1	18.9	17.1
Non-Hispanic	54.4	24.2	21.4	69.2	12.5	18.3
NATIVITY AND CITIZENSHIP						
Native born	48.8	26.9	24.3	66.9	13.2	19.9
Foreign born	66.1	18.2	15.6	72.9	16.3	10.8
Naturalized citizen	79.2	12.2	8.7	75.8	13.2	11.0
Not a citizen	60.7	20.8	18.6	70.5	18.8	10.7

NA Not available. [1] Includes women aged 12 to 19 at first birth. [2] Includes women aged 40 to 50 at first birth.

Source: U.S. Census Bureau, *Fertility of Women in the United States: 2012*, P20-575, July 2014. See also <http://www.census.gov/hhes/fertility/>.

Table 103. Women Who Had a Birth in the Past Year Who Are in the Labor Force by Education: 2008 to 2013

[In thousands (2,398 represents 2,398,000), except percent. For women aged 16 to 50 years old. Based on 2008-2013 American Community Surveys (ACS). The ACS universe includes the household population and population living in institutions, college dormitories, and other group quarters. Based on a sample and subject to sampling variability, see Appendix III]

Year	Number of women who had a birth in the past year who are in the labor force					Percent of women who had a birth in the past year who are in the labor force				
	Total	Less than High School diploma	High School diploma or GED	Some college	Bachelor's degree or higher	Total	Less than High School diploma	High School diploma or GED	Some college	Bachelor's degree or higher
2008.........	2,718	307	622	918	871	61.3	39.4	58.4	66.8	71.7
2009.........	2,662	292	614	883	874	61.6	39.2	58.2	66.5	73.0
2010.........	2,562	278	589	859	836	61.6	39.7	57.9	66.4	72.7
2011.........	2,547	275	541	849	882	62.1	41.4	57.5	65.5	73.4
2012.........	2,554	256	536	869	893	62.1	41.0	56.4	65.7	73.4
2013.........	2,418	221	513	805	879	61.7	38.8	56.4	64.4	73.8

Source: U.S. Census Bureau, "Fertility: Historical Time Series Tables," <http://www.census.gov/hhes/fertility/data/cps/historical.html>, accessed April 2015.

Table 104. Women With Births in the Past 12 Months by Citizenship Status, Educational Attainment, and Poverty Status by State: 2013

[In percent, except for total. For women 15 to 50 years old. Based on 2013 American Community Survey (ACS). See headnote, Table 103]

State	Total (number)	Citizenship status		Educational attainment					Below poverty [3]
		Native born	Foreign born [1]	Less than high school graduate	High school graduate [2]	Some college or associate's degree	Bachelor's degree	Graduate or professional degree	
United States......	**3,930,417**	**80.1**	**19.9**	**14.8**	**23.1**	**31.8**	**19.1**	**11.2**	**27.3**
Alabama...............	58,053	94.0	6.0	16.0	27.0	33.7	15.1	8.2	33.1
Alaska.................	10,411	92.2	7.8	11.5	28.6	33.0	21.9	5.0	18.2
Arizona................	83,011	78.5	21.5	17.5	24.3	35.9	15.0	7.3	32.1
Arkansas..............	39,228	89.2	10.8	15.7	28.3	36.0	13.4	6.7	35.1
California.............	477,649	63.9	36.1	17.7	22.0	30.6	18.5	11.2	26.4
Colorado..............	64,982	83.7	16.3	13.9	19.0	31.1	22.9	13.0	22.6
Connecticut...........	35,904	80.3	19.7	9.3	20.0	24.7	23.1	22.9	21.7
Delaware..............	12,589	78.0	22.0	15.1	24.9	25.5	22.4	12.1	24.3
District of Columbia...	9,700	82.1	17.9	14.5	19.2	16.6	18.8	30.9	25.0
Florida................	212,782	73.9	26.1	15.9	23.7	33.5	17.9	8.9	29.8
Georgia...............	126,637	84.2	15.8	16.9	25.2	30.8	17.3	9.7	31.1
Hawaii................	18,332	74.3	25.7	6.2	23.8	39.6	19.5	10.9	10.5
Idaho.................	21,018	92.8	7.2	9.6	27.0	39.1	19.8	4.5	24.4
Illinois................	156,818	79.6	20.4	12.8	22.5	28.8	21.8	14.1	25.7
Indiana...............	83,444	90.5	9.5	15.2	24.3	35.5	16.8	8.2	29.9
Iowa..................	37,894	89.7	10.3	10.9	20.6	38.2	22.3	8.0	22.4
Kansas...............	43,604	87.5	12.5	13.8	21.4	34.3	19.2	11.2	26.6
Kentucky.............	53,643	92.2	7.8	11.5	27.2	36.8	14.3	10.3	33.7
Louisiana.............	64,822	93.2	6.8	17.1	29.4	30.0	17.8	5.6	33.9
Maine................	13,667	95.1	4.9	10.5	22.9	35.3	19.2	12.0	30.5
Maryland..............	76,852	74.6	25.4	11.6	18.7	27.2	23.0	19.5	17.4
Massachusetts........	77,689	74.4	25.6	9.1	19.0	27.2	24.0	20.7	20.9
Michigan..............	121,880	89.2	10.8	12.9	22.7	35.5	18.3	10.6	31.6
Minnesota............	71,629	82.1	17.9	11.1	17.1	34.5	26.1	11.1	21.0
Mississippi...........	38,631	97.1	2.9	15.8	22.8	41.1	12.5	7.8	36.1
Missouri..............	77,139	92.9	7.1	13.1	25.1	34.4	17.7	9.6	28.7
Montana..............	12,242	99.3	0.7	13.5	25.4	38.8	18.1	4.2	24.8
Nebraska.............	26,077	85.9	14.1	11.6	14.9	37.3	25.8	10.4	24.5
Nevada...............	35,476	72.3	27.7	20.0	25.6	33.1	14.4	6.9	24.9
New Hampshire.......	15,795	94.0	6.0	5.7	32.5	30.1	19.0	12.7	18.0
New Jersey...........	100,877	65.7	34.3	11.8	20.5	25.1	26.2	16.2	20.3
New Mexico...........	28,496	83.3	16.7	19.6	22.7	40.3	11.7	5.8	37.7
New York.............	231,584	70.1	29.9	14.4	22.0	25.5	19.3	18.8	25.7
North Carolina........	118,248	82.7	17.3	16.6	20.8	33.5	18.2	10.9	31.4
North Dakota.........	10,066	97.0	3.0	8.4	22.7	34.6	24.5	9.8	18.9
Ohio..................	136,831	92.4	7.6	13.6	23.6	35.8	16.5	10.6	31.7
Oklahoma.............	52,382	90.5	9.5	17.7	27.1	32.3	17.8	5.1	32.2
Oregon...............	45,186	79.6	20.4	15.2	19.6	37.0	18.9	9.4	28.9
Pennsylvania.........	141,870	89.3	10.7	13.3	26.1	26.0	20.7	13.8	27.4
Rhode Island.........	11,650	84.3	15.7	14.8	20.3	28.7	24.1	12.0	27.9
South Carolina.......	58,531	91.7	8.3	15.0	25.9	33.1	17.8	8.3	35.5
South Dakota.........	13,341	93.8	6.2	11.6	23.8	35.0	23.4	6.2	26.0
Tennessee............	83,742	89.6	10.4	14.0	30.2	31.1	16.8	7.9	34.6
Texas................	387,079	75.6	24.4	19.4	25.6	30.7	16.8	7.4	28.1
Utah..................	52,145	89.5	10.5	9.0	18.2	39.1	26.7	6.9	20.2
Vermont..............	5,068	91.3	8.7	4.3	21.8	25.3	29.0	19.5	18.3
Virginia...............	102,576	80.5	19.5	10.2	21.3	31.2	22.4	14.8	18.8
Washington...........	85,373	74.5	25.5	13.1	18.2	34.3	22.1	12.2	21.2
West Virginia.........	16,687	98.8	1.2	19.2	27.9	33.6	11.5	7.9	41.5
Wisconsin.............	63,908	90.8	9.2	9.7	19.5	36.2	22.6	12.1	23.9
Wyoming.............	7,179	95.2	4.8	8.7	22.8	45.2	17.0	6.3	17.6

[1] Foreign born excludes people born outside the U.S. to a parent who is a U.S. citizen. [2] Includes equivalency. [3] The population universe used when determining poverty status excludes people institutionalized, in military group quarters, and in college dormitories, and unrelated individuals under 15 years old.

Source: U.S. Census Bureau, 2013 American Community Survey, Tables "B13008," "B13010," and "B13014," <http://factfinder2.census.gov>, accessed December 2014.

Table 105. Persons Who Have Ever Had Sexual Contact by Selected Characteristics: 2006 to 2008

[In percent except as indicated (62,199 represents 62,199,000). Based on the National Survey of Family Growth conducted from July 2006 through December 2008. See Appendix III]

Characteristic	Number (1,000)	Number of opposite-sex partners in lifetime							Any same-sex sexual contact [3]
		Any [1]	One	Two	3 to 6	7 to 14	15 or more	Median number [2]	
Males, 15 to 44 years old [4]	**62,199**	**88.8**	**15.0**	**7.6**	**26.5**	**18.1**	**21.4**	**5.1**	**5.2**
15 to 19 years old	10,777	58.0	21.2	9.4	17.6	5.4	3.1	1.8	2.5
20 to 24 years old	10,404	85.7	19.1	8.0	26.1	18.1	14.2	4.1	5.6
25 to 44 years old	41,019	97.7	12.3	7.0	28.9	21.5	27.9	6.1	5.8
25 to 29 years old	10,431	96.2	11.8	8.9	29.5	22.9	23.1	5.7	5.2
30 to 34 years old	9,575	96.9	14.2	6.1	26.6	21.7	28.3	6.4	4.0
35 to 39 years old	10,318	98.7	13.3	5.6	29.7	19.6	30.6	6.2	5.7
40 to 44 years old	10,695	98.8	10.3	7.2	29.7	21.6	30.0	6.4	8.1
Hispanic	11,724	92.0	12.5	10.2	32.6	17.8	19.1	4.6	3.8
Non-Hispanic White	37,374	88.5	16.1	7.3	25.7	18.4	20.9	5.1	6.0
Non-Hispanic Black	7,186	90.7	8.3	5.0	25.6	21.6	30.0	6.9	2.4
Currently married	24,763	100.0	19.1	7.5	30.7	20.7	22.1	4.9	3.5
Currently cohabiting	7,301	100.0	10.3	7.6	24.4	25.9	31.8	7.3	3.2
Never married, not cohabiting	27,012	74.2	14.1	8.2	23.6	12.9	14.9	4.1	7.2
Formerly married, not cohabiting	3,123	100.0	1.4	2.2	23.9	25.1	47.4	11.9	6.4
Females, 15 to 44 years old [4]	**61,865**	**89.0**	**22.2**	**10.7**	**31.6**	**16.0**	**8.3**	**3.2**	**12.5**
15 to 19 years old	10,431	53.0	22.7	8.2	15.7	4.1	1.1	1.4	11.0
20 to 24 years old	10,140	87.7	24.5	12.5	31.6	11.7	7.2	2.6	15.8
25 to 44 years old	41,294	98.4	21.4	10.9	35.6	20.1	10.4	3.6	12.0
25 to 29 years old	10,250	96.6	20.0	12.4	31.0	20.4	12.8	3.6	15.0
30 to 34 years old	9,587	98.1	20.9	10.6	31.9	21.3	13.4	4.2	14.2
35 to 39 years old	10,475	99.1	22.2	9.9	38.3	20.8	7.9	3.5	11.5
40 to 44 years old	10,982	99.7	22.4	10.8	40.5	18.0	8.0	3.4	7.9
Hispanic	10,377	89.5	35.0	16.7	26.6	6.6	4.4	1.6	6.3
Non-Hispanic White	37,660	88.4	19.2	9.7	31.4	18.9	8.9	3.7	14.6
Non-Hispanic Black	8,452	90.2	12.3	8.3	40.9	16.7	11.3	4.4	11.3
Currently married	27,006	100.0	32.2	12.3	34.4	15.0	6.1	2.5	8.3
Currently cohabiting	6,821	100.0	12.8	11.6	37.0	24.9	13.7	4.6	20.5
Never married, not cohabiting	22,847	70.1	16.4	9.1	25.2	11.9	6.9	3.2	13.4
Formerly married, not cohabiting	5,190	100.0	6.8	8.7	37.7	28.0	18.8	5.3	19.6

[1] Includes vaginal, oral, or anal sex. [2] Excludes those who have never had sexual intercourse with a person of the opposite sex. For definition of median, see Guide to Tabular Presentation. [3] For females includes oral sex or any sexual experience. For males includes oral or anal sex with male partners. [4] Includes persons of other or multiple race and origin groups, not shown separately.

Source: U.S. National Center for Health Statistics, National Health Statistics Report, No.36, *Sexual Behavior, Sexual Attraction, and Sexual Identity in the United States: Data From the 2006–2008 National Survey of Family Growth*, March 2011. See also <http://www.cdc.gov/nchs/nsfg.htm>.

Table 106. Number and Type of Sexual Partners in the Past 12 Months: 2006 to 2008

[In percent except as indicated (62,199 represents 62,199,000). Based on the National Survey of Family Growth conducted from July 2006 through December 2008. See Appendix III]

Sex and age	Number (1,000)	Sexual partners in last 12 months [1]				
		No partner in last month	Any same-sex partners	One opposite-sex partner, but no same-sex partners	Two or more opposite-sex partners, but no same sex-sex partners	Did not report
Males 15 to 44 years old	**62,199**	**16.0**	**4.3**	**60.2**	**17.6**	**2.0**
15 to 19 years old	10,777	48.9	1.5	25.1	21.2	3.3
20 to 24 years old	10,404	18.3	4.6	48.0	27.2	1.9
25 to 44 years old	41,019	6.8	4.9	72.4	14.2	1.7
25 to 29 years old	10,431	7.6	4.8	65.7	20.3	1.6
30 to 34 years old	9,575	6.6	3.6	75.3	13.0	1.4
35 to 39 years old	10,318	5.1	5.0	73.7	14.2	2.0
40 to 44 years old	10,695	7.7	6.2	75.2	9.3	1.6
Females 15 to 44 years old	**61,865**	**15.9**	**11.7**	**61.3**	**9.4**	**1.7**
15 to 19 years old	10,431	51.3	9.5	24.2	13.5	1.6
20 to 24 years old	10,140	15.8	15.2	49.5	17.7	1.8
25 to 44 years old	41,294	7.0	11.4	73.6	6.3	1.8
25 to 29 years old	10,250	7.6	14.3	65.1	10.6	2.4
30 to 34 years old	9,587	5.2	13.6	73.8	6.0	1.5
35 to 39 years old	10,475	6.8	10.8	76.2	4.2	2.0
40 to 44 years old	10,982	8.3	7.1	79.0	4.5	1.1

[1] Includes vaginal, oral, or anal sex.

Source: U.S. National Center for Health Statistics, National Health Statistics Report, No.36, *Sexual Behavior, Sexual Attraction, and Sexual Identity in the United States: Data From the 2006–2008 National Survey of Family Growth*, March 2011. See also <http://www.cdc.gov/nchs/nsfg.htm>.

Table 107. Sexual Identity Among Men and Women: 2006 to 2008

[In percent except as indicated (55,556 represents 55,556,000). For men and women 18 to 44 years of age. Based on the National Survey of Family Growth conducted from July 2006 through December 2008. See Appendix III]

Characteristic	Number (1,000)	Sexual identity Heterosexual or straight	Homosexual or gay	Bisexual	Something else	Did not report
Males, 18 to 44 years old [1]	**55,556**	**95.7**	**1.7**	**1.1**	**0.2**	**1.3**
18 to 19 years old	4,134	96.6	1.6	1.1	(S)	0.6
20 to 24 years old	10,404	95.1	1.2	2.0	0.4	1.3
25 to 29 years old	10,431	96.3	1.7	0.8	0.5	0.8
30 to 34 years old	9,575	96.2	1.5	0.6	(S)	1.8
35 to 44 years old	21,013	95.2	2.1	1.0	0.2	1.5
Hispanic	10,618	93.4	1.2	0.9	0.6	3.9
Non-Hispanic White	33,573	96.6	1.8	1.1	0.1	0.4
Non-Hispanic Black	6,208	97.8	1.2	(S)	(S)	0.4
Females, 18 to 44 years old [1]	**56,032**	**93.7**	**1.1**	**3.5**	**0.6**	**1.1**
18 to 19 years old	4,598	90.1	1.9	5.8	(S)	(S)
20 to 24 years old	10,140	90.4	1.3	6.3	0.9	1.2
25 to 29 years old	10,250	91.9	1.2	5.4	0.6	0.9
30 to 34 years old	9,587	94.4	1.1	2.9	0.8	1.0
35 to 44 years old	21,457	96.6	0.7	1.1	0.2	1.3
Hispanic	9,272	92.1	0.9	2.2	0.7	4.1
Non-Hispanic White	34,410	94.2	0.9	4.1	0.5	0.4
Non-Hispanic Black	7,520	93.3	1.6	3.0	1.5	0.7

S Figure does not meet publication standards. [1] Includes person of other or multiple race and origin groups, not shown separately.

Source: U.S. National Center for Health Statistics, National Health Statistics Report, No. 36, *Sexual Behavior, Sexual Attraction, and Sexual Identity in the United States: Data From the 2006–2008 National Survey of Family Growth*, March 2011. See also <http://www.cdc.gov/nchs/nsfg.htm>.

Table 108. Current Contraceptive Use by Women by Age, Race, and Hispanic Origin: 2006 to 2010

[61,755 represents 61,755,000. Based on the National Survey of Family Growth conducted from June 2006 to June 2010. Contraceptive use reported by women 15–44 years of age during heterosexual vaginal intercourse. Women using more than one method of contraception are classified by most effective method reported]

Contraceptive status and method	All women [1]	Age 15 to 19 years old	20 to 24 years old	25 to 29 years old	30 to 34 years old	35 to 39 years old	40 to 44 years old	Race/ethnicity White only, Non-Hispanic	Black only, Non-Hispanic	Hispanic [2]
All women (1,000)	**61,755**	**10,478**	**10,365**	**10,535**	**9,188**	**10,538**	**10,652**	**37,384**	**8,451**	**10,474**
PERCENT DISTRIBUTION										
Using contraception (contraceptors) [3]	62.2	30.5	58.3	65.3	69.7	74.6	75.3	65.6	54.2	59.7
Female sterilization	16.5	(S)	1.5	10.7	20.9	27.9	38.1	15.5	20.2	18.9
Male sterilization	6.2	(S)	0.5	2.7	6.6	12.4	15.1	8.7	0.9	3.3
Pill	17.1	16.2	27.4	21.5	17.7	12.7	7.4	21.0	9.9	11.8
Other hormonal methods	4.5	4.9	7.1	7.4	3.9	2.0	1.4	3.5	7.2	5.5
Implant, Lunelle™	0.9	0.7	1.1	1.5	0.9	0.5	(S)	0.5	1.0	1.5
3-month injectable (Depo-Provera™)	2.3	3.5	3.3	3.4	1.7	1.0	0.6	1.6	4.6	2.9
Contraceptive ring	1.3	0.7	2.7	2.4	1.4	0.5	0.4	1.4	1.6	1.0
Intrauterine device (IUD)	3.5	0.8	3.3	4.7	4.9	4.8	2.4	3.6	2.6	4.0
Condom	10.2	6.1	14.9	13.6	10.8	9.0	6.8	9.2	10.5	10.8
Periodic abstinence-calendar rhythm	0.6	(S)	0.2	0.5	0.8	1.0	1.1	0.6	0.2	0.8
Periodic abstinence-natural family planning	0.1	–	–	–	0.4	(S)	(S)	0.1	(S)	(S)
Withdrawal	3.2	2.1	3.3	4.1	3.2	4.1	2.6	3.1	2.4	3.4
Other methods [3]	0.3	0.2	(S)	0.3	0.5	0.6	0.4	0.3	0.1	0.7
Not using contraception	37.8	69.5	41.7	34.7	30.3	25.4	24.7	34.4	45.8	40.3
Surgically sterile-female (noncontraceptive)	0.4	(S)	(S)	0.2	(S)	0.4	1.5	0.3	0.4	0.7
Nonsurgically sterile-female or male	1.7	0.5	1.4	1.4	1.8	2.0	3.1	1.5	2.3	1.6
Pregnant or postpartum	5.0	3.2	8.1	8.4	7.2	2.3	1.4	4.5	6.1	6.7
Seeking pregnancy	4.0	0.6	4.0	6.3	6.0	4.8	2.4	3.6	4.7	4.5
Never had intercourse	11.8	51.4	11.6	3.1	1.9	1.1	0.6	11.3	11.8	12.4
No intercourse in 3 months before interview	7.3	7.1	7.9	7.0	6.6	6.5	8.6	6.4	9.2	7.5
Had intercourse in 3 months before interview	7.7	6.7	8.7	8.4	6.7	8.4	7.1	6.9	11.2	7.0

– Represents zero. S Figure does not meet publication standards. [1] Includes other races not shown separately. [2] Persons of Hispanic origin may be of any race. [3] Includes diaphragm, emergency contraception, female condom or vaginal pouch, foam, cervical cap, Today™ sponge, suppository or insert, jelly or cream, and other methods.

Source: U.S. National Center for Health Statistics, National Survey of Family Growth, *Current Contraceptive Use in the United States, 2006-10, and Changes in Patterns of Use Since 1995*, National Health Statistics Reports, No. 60, October 2012. See also <http://www.cdc.gov/nchs/nsfg.htm>.

Table 109. Abortions—Number and Rate by Race: 1990 to 2010

[In thousands (58,700 represents 58,700,000), except rate. Data for 2000-09 have been revised based on Census Bureau intercensal population estimates, as of October 2012]

Year	All races Women aged 15 to 44	All races Abortions Number (1,000)	All races Abortions Rate per 1,000 women [1]	White Women aged 15 to 44	White Abortions Number (1,000)	White Abortions Rate per 1,000 women [1]	Black Women aged 15 to 44	Black Abortions Number (1,000)	Black Abortions Rate per 1,000 women [1]	Other Women aged 15 to 44	Other Abortions Number (1,000)	Other Abortions Rate per 1,000 women [1]
1990 [2]	58,700	1,609	27.4	48,224	1,039	21.5	7,905	505	63.9	2,571	65	25.1
1991	59,305	1,557	26.2	48,560	982	20.2	8,053	507	62.9	2,692	68	26.2
1992	59,417	1,529	25.7	48,435	943	19.5	8,170	517	63.3	2,812	69	24.4
1993 [2]	59,712	1,495	25.0	48,497	908	18.7	8,282	517	62.4	2,933	70	23.9
1994 [2]	60,020	1,423	23.7	48,592	856	17.6	8,390	492	58.6	3,039	76	23.7
1995	60,368	1,359	22.5	48,719	817	16.8	8,496	462	54.4	3,153	80	25.3
1996	60,704	1,360	22.4	48,837	797	16.3	8,592	483	56.2	3,275	81	24.6
1997 [2]	61,041	1,335	21.9	48,942	777	15.9	8,694	479	55.1	3,405	79	23.1
1998 [2]	61,326	1,319	21.5	49,012	762	15.5	8,785	476	54.2	3,528	81	23.1
1999	61,475	1,315	21.4	48,974	743	15.2	8,851	485	54.8	3,650	87	24.0
2000	61,642	1,313	21.3	48,939	733	15.0	8,911	488	54.8	3,792	92	24.3
2001 [2]	61,795	1,291	20.9	48,877	717	14.7	8,977	476	53.0	3,941	99	25.1
2002 [2]	61,856	1,269	20.5	48,735	706	14.5	9,034	468	51.8	4,088	96	23.4
2003 [2]	61,888	1,250	20.2	48,570	695	14.3	9,092	458	50.4	4,227	97	23.0
2004	61,969	1,222	19.7	48,438	674	13.9	9,168	453	49.4	4,364	95	21.8
2005 [2]	62,071	1,206	19.4	48,321	662	13.7	9,246	452	48.9	4,504	92	20.5
2006 [2]	62,190	1,242	20.0	48,205	681	14.1	9,335	464	49.7	4,649	97	20.8
2007	62,292	1,210	19.4	48,082	668	13.9	9,421	448	47.6	4,789	93	19.5
2008	62,360	1,212	19.4	47,943	664	13.8	9,499	458	48.2	4,918	90	18.4
2009 [2]	62,373	1,152	18.5	47,771	621	13.0	9,562	445	46.6	5,040	86	17.0
2010	62,414	1,103	17.7	47,644	591	12.4	9,613	427	44.4	5,157	85	16.6

[1] Aged 15–44. [2] Total numbers of abortions in 1990, 1993, 1994, 1997, 1998, 2001-2003, 2006, and 2009 have been estimated by interpolation.

Source: R.K. Jones and K. Kooistra, "Abortion Incidence and Access to Services in the United States, 2008," *Perspectives on Sexual and Reproductive Health*, 43.1 (2011) ©; R.K. Jones and J. Jerman, "Abortion Incidence and Service Availability in the United States, 2011," *Perspectives on Sexual and Reproductive Health*, 46.1 (2014) ©; and unpublished data from the Guttmacher Institute ©. See also <http://www.guttmacher.org/>.

Table 110. Abortions by Selected Characteristics: 1990 to 2010

[1,609 represents 1,609,000. Number of abortions from surveys conducted by source; characteristics from the U.S. Centers for Disease Control's (CDC) annual abortion surveillance summaries, with adjustments for changes in states reporting data to the Centers for Disease Control each year. Data for 2000 have been revised based on Census Bureau intercensal population estimates, as of October 2012]

Characteristic	Number (1,000) 1990	Number (1,000) 2000	Number (1,000) 2010	Percent distribution 1990	Percent distribution 2000	Percent distribution 2010	Abortion rate per 1,000 women 1990	Abortion rate per 1,000 women 2000	Abortion rate per 1,000 women 2010
Total abortions	**1,609**	**1,313**	**1,103**	**100.0**	**100.0**	**100.0**	**27.4**	**21.3**	**17.7**
Age of woman:									
Less than 15 years [1]	13	9	5	0.8	0.7	0.5	7.9	4.3	2.5
15 to 19 years	351	235	157	21.8	17.9	14.3	40.6	23.9	14.7
20 to 24 years	532	430	362	33.1	32.7	32.9	56.7	45.9	34.1
25 to 29 years	360	303	272	22.4	23.0	24.7	34.0	31.7	26.0
30 to 34 years	216	190	172	13.4	14.5	15.6	19.7	18.6	17.1
35 to 39 years	108	110	97	6.7	8.4	8.8	10.7	9.7	9.6
40 years and over [2]	29	37	37	1.8	2.8	3.3	3.2	3.2	3.3
Race/ethnicity of woman:									
White	1,039	733	591	64.6	55.8	53.6	21.5	15.0	12.4
Black	505	488	427	31.4	37.2	38.7	63.9	54.8	44.4
Other	65	92	85	4.0	7.0	7.7	25.1	24.3	16.6
Hispanic	195	261	239	12.1	19.8	21.7	35.1	30.3	20.2
Non-Hispanic White	852	479	366	52.9	36.5	33.2	19.7	11.7	9.5
Marital status of woman: [3]									
Married	341	246	164	21.0	19.0	14.8	10.6	7.9	5.8
Unmarried	1,268	1,067	939	79.0	81.0	85.2	47.7	35.0	27.4
Number of prior live births:									
None	780	533	448	49.0	41.0	40.6	32.0	20.2	15.2
One	396	361	296	25.0	28.0	26.8	36.9	32.5	28.0
Two	280	260	208	17.0	20.0	18.9	20.5	18.9	16.3
Three	102	104	95	6.0	8.0	8.6	15.6	14.9	14.5
Four or more	50	56	56	3.0	4.0	5.1	14.7	16.4	17.4
Number of prior induced abortions:									
None	891	699	585	55.0	53.0	53.0	(NA)	(NA)	(NA)
One	443	355	288	28.0	27.0	26.2	(NA)	(NA)	(NA)
Two or more	275	259	229	17.0	20.0	20.8	(NA)	(NA)	(NA)
Weeks of gestation:									
Less than 9 weeks	825	749	696	51.3	57.1	63.1	(NA)	(NA)	(NA)
9 to 10 weeks	416	269	182	25.8	20.5	16.5	(NA)	(NA)	(NA)
11 to 12 weeks	195	138	102	12.1	10.5	9.2	(NA)	(NA)	(NA)
13 weeks or more	173	156	129	10.8	11.9	11.2	(NA)	(NA)	(NA)

NA Not available. [1] Denominator of rate is women aged 14. [2] Denominator of rate is women aged 40–44. [3] Separated women are included with married.

Source: R.K. Jones and K. Kooistra, "Abortion Incidence and Access to Services in the United States, 2008," *Perspectives on Sexual and Reproductive Health*, 43.1 (2011) ©; R.K. Jones and J. Jerman, "Abortion Incidence and Service Availability in the United States, 2011," *Perspectives on Sexual and Reproductive Health*, 46.1 (2014) ©; and unpublished data from the Guttmacher Institute ©. See also <http://www.guttmacher.org/>.

Table 111. Abortions—Number and Rate by State of Occurrence: 2000 to 2010

[Number of abortions by state of occurrence from surveys of hospitals, clinics, and physicians identified as providers of abortion services conducted by the Guttmacher Institute. The Guttmacher Institute reallocates abortions to the woman's state of residence for survey years. Abortion rates are computed per 1,000 women 15 to 44 years of age on July 1 of specified year. Estimates for 2000-08 have been revised based on Census Bureau intercensal population estimates, as of October 2012]

| State | State of occurrence | | | | | | State | State of occurrence | | | | | |
| | Number | | | Rate [1] | | | | Number | | | Rate [1] | | |
	2000	2005	2010	2000	2005	2010		2000	2005	2010	2000	2005	2010
U.S.....	1,312,990	1,206,200	1,102,670	21.3	19.4	17.7	MO......	7,920	8,400	6,160	6.6	7.0	5.2
AL......	13,830	11,340	10,280	14.3	11.9	10.7	MT......	2,510	2,150	2,220	13.5	11.9	12.4
AK......	1,660	1,880	1,930	11.8	13.3	13.4	NE......	4,250	3,220	2,490	11.6	9.0	7.0
AZ......	17,940	19,480	15,180	16.5	16.3	12.0	NV......	13,740	13,530	11,850	32.1	26.8	21.6
AR......	5,540	4,710	4,680	9.8	8.3	8.2	NH......	3,010	3,170	3,040	11.2	11.9	12.2
CA......	236,060	208,430	191,550	31.1	26.8	24.3	NJ......	65,780	61,150	48,840	36.2	34.2	28.1
CO......	15,530	16,120	15,060	15.9	16.3	14.7	NM......	5,760	6,220	5,630	14.7	15.7	14.1
CT......	15,240	16,780	15,430	21.1	23.6	22.3	NY......	164,630	155,960	142,790	39.1	37.9	35.3
DE......	5,440	5,150	6,570	31.3	28.9	36.6	NC......	37,610	34,500	32,700	21.1	18.7	16.8
DC......	9,800	7,230	4,660	68.2	50.2	28.6	ND......	1,340	1,230	1,290	9.9	9.5	10.0
FL......	103,050	92,300	86,180	31.9	26.2	24.2	OH......	40,230	35,060	30,220	16.5	15.0	13.5
GA......	32,140	33,180	35,590	16.9	16.7	17.1	OK......	7,390	6,950	6,290	10.1	9.6	8.5
HI......	5,630	5,350	5,520	22.2	20.7	21.0	OR......	17,010	13,200	11,010	23.5	18.1	14.6
ID......	1,950	1,810	1,740	7.0	6.2	5.7	PA......	36,570	34,150	38,650	14.3	13.7	15.8
IL......	63,690	50,970	44,400	23.2	19.1	16.9	RI......	5,600	5,290	4,290	24.1	23.2	20.0
IN......	12,490	11,150	10,400	9.4	8.6	8.1	SC......	8,210	7,080	6,730	9.3	7.9	7.2
IA......	5,970	6,370	6,000	9.8	10.8	10.4	SD......	870	790	740	5.5	5.1	4.8
KS......	12,270	10,410	7,240	21.4	18.6	13.0	TN......	19,010	18,140	17,850	15.2	14.5	14.0
KY......	4,700	3,870	4,040	5.3	4.5	4.7	TX......	89,160	85,760	79,390	18.7	17.2	14.9
LA......	13,100	11,400	12,710	13.0	11.6	13.7	UT......	3,510	3,630	3,540	6.6	6.5	5.9
ME......	2,650	2,770	2,490	9.9	10.7	10.3	VT......	1,660	1,490	1,370	12.7	11.9	11.6
MD......	34,560	37,590	34,310	29.0	31.1	28.7	VA......	28,780	26,520	27,660	18.1	16.2	16.7
MA......	30,410	27,270	24,360	21.4	19.8	18.0	WA......	26,200	23,260	22,240	20.2	17.7	16.4
MI......	46,470	40,600	30,770	21.6	19.7	16.1	WV......	2,540	2,360	2,540	6.8	6.7	7.4
MN......	14,610	13,910	11,570	13.5	13.0	11.1	WI......	11,130	9,800	8,080	9.6	8.6	7.4
MS......	3,780	3,090	2,300	6.0	5.0	3.8	WY......	100	70	90	1.0	0.7	0.8

[1] Rate per 1,000 women, 15 to 44 years old on July 1 of specified year.

Source: R.K. Jones et al., "Abortion in the United States: Incidence and Access to Services, 2005," *Perspectives on Sexual and Reproductive Health*, 40.1 (2008) ©; R.K. Jones and K. Kooistra, "Abortion Incidence and Access to Services in the United States, 2008," *Perspectives on Sexual and Reproductive Health*, 43.1 (2011) ©; R.K. Jones and J. Jerman, "Abortion Incidence and Service Availability in the United States, 2011," *Perspectives on Sexual and Reproductive Health*, 46.1 (2014) ©; and unpublished data from the Guttmacher Institute ©. See also <http://www.guttmacher.org/>.

Table 112. Percent of Babies Breastfed by Selected Characteristics of Mother: 1972 to 2007

[In percent. Based on the National Survey of Family Growth. Data are from household interviews with a sample of women aged 15-44 years old]

Mother's Characteristics	1972-1974	1986-1988	1989-1991	1992-1994	1995-1998	1999-2001	2002-2004	2005-2007
PERCENT OF BABIES EVER BREASTFED 3 MONTHS OR MORE								
Total.........	62.3	34.6	31.8	33.6	45.8	48.4	50.6	46.6
Age at baby's birth:								
Under 20 years.........	50.0	18.5	(S)	(S)	30.0	30.0	37.6	26.6
20-24 years.........	57.7	26.1	24.1	25.1	36.6	41.8	38.0	38.6
25-29 years.........	68.3	36.9	32.3	35.6	46.3	43.7	50.2	49.0
30-44 years.........	79.4	50.1	46.8	46.7	57.5	62.4	63.9	56.3
Race and Hispanic origin [1]:								
Not Hispanic or Latina:								
White only.........	62.1	37.7	35.2	36.6	47.8	49.7	54.5	49.5
Black or African American only.........	47.8	11.6	11.5	13.3	29.6	33.7	29.2	26.3
Hispanic or Latina.........	64.7	38.2	33.9	35.0	49.7	54.3	55.9	49.4
Education [2]:								
No high school diploma or GED.........	54.4	21.8	17.6	25.2	33.9	37.0	39.9	41.3
High school diploma or GED.........	53.7	28.2	28.0	27.4	36.9	43.1	41.9	36.8
Some college, no bachelor's degree.........	69.5	38.7	33.1	38.7	49.6	52.8	43.2	48.7
Bachelor's degree or higher.........	69.2	55.0	56.1	59.3	64.5	64.1	75.9	65.8
Region:								
Northeast.........	64.6	29.9	37.2	36.4	48.2	48.8	59.9	51.5
Midwest.........	44.4	30.3	31.5	30.1	42.0	42.8	46.8	41.6
South.........	72.6	27.7	20.1	26.2	38.9	44.4	42.7	40.5
West.........	69.0	52.4	42.9	45.3	58.2	59.2	62.6	57.8

S Figure does not meet publication standards. [1] Starting with 1995 data, race-specific estimates are tabulated according to 1997 Revisions to the Standards for the Classification of Federal Data on Race and Ethnicity and are not strictly comparable with estimates for earlier years. Starting with 1995 data, race-specific estimates are for persons who reported only one racial group. Prior to data year 1995, data were tabulated according to the 1977 Standards. Estimates for single-race categories prior to 1995 included persons who reported one race or, if they reported more than one race, identified one race as best representing their race. [2] Educational attainment is presented only for women aged 22-44, as of year of interview.

Source: U.S. National Center for Health Statistics, *Health, United States, 2014*, May 2015. See also <http://www.cdc.gov/nchs/hus.htm>.

Table 113. Women's Use of Infertility Services by Type of Service and Selected Characteristics: 2006 to 2010

[In percent, except total (40,912 represents 40,912,000). For women aged 25 to 44 years old. Based on the 2006-2010 National Survey of Family Growth]

Characteristic	Total women aged 25-44 (1,000)	Any infertility service	Type of medical help to get pregnant							Any medical help to prevent mis-carriage
			Any medical help to get pregnant	Advice	Tests on woman or man	Ovu-lation drugs	Surgery or treat-ment of blocked tubes	Artificial insem-ination	Assisted repro-ductive tech-nology	
Total [1]	40,912	16.8	12.5	9.4	7.3	5.8	1.3	1.7	0.7	6.8
AGE										
25 to 29 years old	10,535	12.5	7.7	6.2	3.3	2.4	0.3	0.3	(B)	6.1
30 to 34 years old	9,188	14.4	11.1	7.8	6.3	5.5	0.5	0.9	0.2	5.7
35 to 39 years old	10,538	20.7	16.4	13.3	10.4	8.6	2.0	2.9	1.5	8.1
40 to 44 years old	10,652	19.3	14.5	9.9	9.0	6.5	2.3	2.8	0.9	7.3
PARITY [2]										
No births	10,340	14.4	13.6	11.4	8.5	5.6	1.8	2.3	0.9	2.7
One or more births	30,572	17.6	12.1	8.7	6.9	5.8	1.1	1.5	0.6	8.2
CURRENT FERTILITY PROBLEM [3]										
Yes	5,791	41.0	36.3	28.9	27.4	19.5	3.2	7.4	3.1	12.8
No	35,121	12.8	8.6	6.1	4.0	3.5	1.0	0.8	0.3	5.8
EDUCATION										
No high school diploma or GED	6,054	9.5	6.4	4.3	3.4	2.4	1.1	0.8	(B)	5.1
High school diploma or GED	9,999	14.7	10.1	7.8	4.9	4.0	1.3	0.7	0.5	6.0
Some college, no bachelor's degree	11,424	17.3	11.9	8.2	6.3	5.2	1.4	1.4	0.3	7.8
Bachelor's degree	9,455	20.8	16.9	13.1	12.1	9.6	1.2	3.7	1.6	7.8
Master's degree or higher	3,980	22.6	19.1	15.7	10.9	8.0	1.5	2.2	1.1	6.5
RACE/ETHNICITY										
White alone, non-Hispanic	25,177	19.1	14.9	11.6	9.3	7.5	1.7	2.4	0.9	7.1
Black alone, non-Hispanic	5,392	11.2	8.0	5.3	4.0	3.4	1.2	0.6	(B)	4.1
Hispanic or Latina	6,836	13.2	7.6	4.9	3.3	2.2	0.1	0.4	0.2	6.9

B Base figure too small to meet statistical standards for reliability of a derived figure. [1] Includes women of other or multiple race/ethnicities, not shown separately. [2] Whether a woman has ever had a live birth. [3] Current fertility problems include impaired fecundity or 12-month infertility at time of interview. Impaired fecundity includes: nonsurgically sterile, subfecund, and long interval without conception. Infertility is defined only for married or cohabiting women and indicates that they have been exposed to the risk of pregnancy with the same husband or partner for at least 12 consecutive months, but have not had a pregnancy.

Source: U.S. National Center for Health Statistics, *Infertility Service Use in the United States: Data from the National Survey of Family Growth, 1982-2010*, January 2014. See also <http://www.cdc.gov/nchs/nsfg.htm>.

Table 114. Assisted Reproductive Technology (ART) Procedures and Outcomes: 2000 to 2013

[In 1996, Centers for Disease Control (CDC) initiated data collection regarding Assisted Reproductive Technology (ART) procedures performed in the United States, as mandated by the Fertility Clinic Success Rate and Certification Act. ARTs include those infertility treatments in which both eggs and sperm are handled in the laboratory for the purpose of establishing a pregnancy (i.e., in vitro fertilization and related procedures)]

Year	Procedures started [1]	Number of pregnancies	Live birth deliveries [2]	Live born infants
2000	99,629	30,557	25,228	35,025
2001	107,587	35,726	29,344	40,687
2002	115,392	40,046	33,141	45,751
2003	122,872	43,503	35,785	48,756
2004	127,977	44,774	36,760	49,458
2005	134,260	47,651	38,910	52,041
2006	138,198	50,571	41,343	54,656
2007	142,435	(NA)	43,412	57,569
2008	148,055	(NA)	46,326	61,426
2009	146,244	56,399	45,870	60,190
2010	147,260	57,773	47,090	61,564
2011	151,923	59,132	47,818	61,610
2012	176,247	(NA)	51,267	65,160
2013 [3]	190,773	(NA)	54,323	67,996

NA Not available. [1] Excludes procedures for which new treatments were being evaluated. [2] A live birth delivery is defined as the delivery of one or more live born infants. [3] Data are preliminary.

Source: U.S. Centers for Disease Control and Prevention, *Assisted Reproductive Technology Surveillance - United States, 2011*, November 2014 and earlier reports; *2012 Assisted Reproductive Technology, National Summary Report*, November 2014 and earlier reports; and "Assisted Reproductive Technology," <http://www.cdc.gov/art/ARTReports.htm>, accessed September 2015.

Table 115. Expectation of Life at Birth, 1940 to 2013, and Projections, 2015 to 2060

[In years. Beginning in 1970, excludes deaths of nonresidents of the United States. See Appendix III]

Year	Total Total	Total Male	Total Female	White Total	White Male	White Female	Black Total	Black Male	Black Female
1940	62.9	60.8	65.2	64.2	62.1	66.6	(NA)	(NA)	(NA)
1950	68.2	65.6	71.1	69.1	66.5	72.2	(NA)	(NA)	(NA)
1960	69.7	66.6	73.1	70.6	67.4	74.1	(NA)	(NA)	(NA)
1970	70.8	67.1	74.7	71.7	68.0	75.6	64.1	60.0	68.3
1980	73.7	70.0	77.4	74.4	70.7	78.1	68.1	63.8	72.5
1990	75.4	71.8	78.8	76.1	72.7	79.4	69.1	64.5	73.6
1991	75.5	72.0	78.9	76.3	72.9	79.6	69.3	64.6	73.8
1992	75.8	72.3	79.1	76.5	73.2	79.8	69.6	65.0	73.9
1993	75.5	72.2	78.8	76.3	73.1	79.5	69.2	64.6	73.7
1994	75.7	72.4	79.0	76.5	73.3	79.6	69.5	64.9	73.9
1995	75.8	72.5	78.9	76.5	73.4	79.6	69.6	65.2	73.9
1996	76.1	73.1	79.1	76.8	73.9	79.7	70.2	66.1	74.2
1997	76.5	73.6	79.4	77.1	74.3	79.9	71.1	67.2	74.7
1998	76.7	73.8	79.5	77.3	74.5	80.0	71.3	67.6	74.8
1999	76.7	73.9	79.4	77.3	74.6	79.9	71.4	67.8	74.7
2000	76.8	74.1	79.3	77.3	74.7	79.9	71.8	68.2	75.1
2001 [1]	77.0	74.3	79.5	77.5	74.9	80.0	72.0	68.5	75.3
2002 [1,2]	77.0	74.4	79.6	77.5	74.9	80.1	72.2	68.7	75.4
2003 [1,2]	77.2	74.5	79.7	77.7	75.1	80.2	72.4	68.9	75.7
2004 [1,2]	77.6	75.0	80.1	78.1	75.5	80.5	72.9	69.4	76.1
2005 [1,2]	77.6	75.0	80.1	78.0	75.5	80.5	73.0	69.5	76.2
2006 [1,2]	77.8	75.2	80.3	78.3	75.8	80.7	73.4	69.9	76.7
2007 [1,2]	78.1	75.5	80.6	78.5	76.0	80.9	73.8	70.3	77.0
2008 [1,2]	78.2	75.6	80.6	78.5	76.1	80.9	74.3	70.9	77.3
2009 [1,2]	78.5	76.0	80.9	78.8	76.4	81.2	74.7	71.4	77.7
2010 [1,2]	78.7	76.2	81.0	78.9	76.5	81.3	75.1	71.8	78.0
2011 [1,2]	78.7	76.3	81.1	79.0	76.6	81.3	75.3	72.2	78.2
2012 [1,2]	78.8	76.4	81.2	79.1	76.7	81.4	75.5	72.3	78.4
2013 [1,2]	78.8	76.4	81.2	79.1	76.7	81.4	75.5	72.3	78.4
Projections: [3]									
2015	79.4	77.1	81.7	80.0	77.7	82.2	76.1	72.9	78.9
2020	80.2	78.0	82.4	80.7	78.6	82.9	77.0	74.0	79.8
2030	81.7	79.6	83.7	82.2	80.2	84.1	78.8	76.1	81.3
2040	83.0	81.2	84.8	83.5	81.7	85.2	80.5	78.0	82.8
2050	84.4	82.7	86.0	84.8	83.2	86.4	82.0	79.8	84.1
2060	85.6	84.0	87.1	86.0	84.5	87.4	83.4	81.4	85.3

NA Not available. [1] Life expectancies for 2001–2013 were calculated using a revised methodology and may differ from those previously published. [2] Multiple-race data were bridged to the single-race categories of the 1977 OMB standards for comparability with other reporting areas. [3] Based on mortality assumptions; for details, see source: U.S. Census Bureau, 2014 National Population Projections, "Table 17: Projected Life Expectancy at Birth by Sex, Race, and Hispanic Origin for the United States: 2015 to 2060 (NP2014-T17)," December 2014, <http://www.census.gov/population/projections/>.

Source: Except as noted. U.S. National Center for Health Statistics, National Vital Statistics Reports (NVSR), *Deaths: Final Data for 2013*, Vol. 64, No. 2. See also <http://www.cdc.gov/nchs/deaths.htm>.

Table 116. Life Expectancy by Sex, Age, and Race: 2013

[Average number of years of life remaining. Excludes deaths of nonresidents of the United States]

Age	Total [1] Total	Total [1] Male	Total [1] Female	White Total	White Male	White Female	Black Total	Black Male	Black Female
0	78.8	76.4	81.2	79.1	76.7	81.4	75.5	72.3	78.4
1	78.3	75.9	80.6	78.5	76.1	80.7	75.4	72.2	78.2
5	74.4	72.0	76.7	74.5	72.2	76.8	71.5	68.3	74.3
10	69.4	67.1	71.7	69.6	67.3	71.8	66.5	63.4	69.4
15	64.5	62.1	66.8	64.6	62.3	66.9	61.6	58.5	64.4
20	59.6	57.3	61.8	59.7	57.5	62.0	56.8	53.7	59.5
25	54.8	52.6	57.0	55.0	52.8	57.1	52.1	49.2	54.7
30	50.1	48.0	52.1	50.2	48.1	52.2	47.4	44.6	49.9
35	45.4	43.3	47.3	45.5	43.5	47.4	42.8	40.1	45.1
40	40.7	38.7	42.6	40.8	38.8	42.6	38.2	35.7	40.4
45	36.1	34.1	37.9	36.2	34.3	37.9	33.7	31.2	35.9
50	31.6	29.7	33.3	31.7	29.9	33.4	29.4	27.0	31.5
55	27.3	25.6	28.9	27.4	25.7	28.9	25.3	23.0	27.3
60	23.2	21.7	24.6	23.3	21.7	24.6	21.6	19.5	23.3
65	19.3	17.9	20.5	19.3	18.0	20.5	18.1	16.3	19.5
70	15.6	14.4	16.6	15.6	14.4	16.5	14.8	13.2	15.9
75	12.2	11.2	12.9	12.1	11.1	12.9	11.8	10.4	12.7
80	9.1	8.3	9.7	9.1	8.3	9.7	9.1	8.0	9.7
85	6.6	5.9	7.0	6.5	5.9	6.9	6.8	6.0	7.2
90	4.6	4.1	4.8	4.5	4.0	4.8	5.1	4.5	5.3
95	3.2	2.8	3.3	3.1	2.8	3.2	3.8	3.4	3.8
100	2.3	2.0	2.3	2.2	2.0	2.3	2.8	2.6	2.8

[1] Includes races other than White and Black.

Source: U.S. National Center for Health Statistics, National Vital Statistics Reports (NVSR), *Deaths: Final Data for 2013*, Vol. 64, No. 2. See also <http://www.cdc.gov/nchs/deaths.htm>.

Table 117. Selected Life Table Values—Life Expectancy and Percent Surviving by Age: 1959 to 2011

[Decennial life tables are based on population data from a decennial census and reported deaths of the 3-year period surrounding the census year; the census year is the middle year. The annual tables are based on deaths in a single year, and except for census years, on postcensal population estimates. Beginning in 1970, data exclude deaths of nonresidents of the United States. See Technical Notes, source]

Age and sex	All races 1959-1961	1969-1971	1979-1981	1989-1991	1999-2001	2011	White 1959-1961	1969-1971	1979-1981	1989-1991	1999-2001	2011	Black [1] 1959-1961	1969-1971	1979-1981	1989-1991	1999-2001	2011
LIFE EXPECTANCY IN YEARS																		
Male by age:																		
At birth	66.8	67.0	70.1	71.8	74.1	76.3	67.6	67.9	70.8	72.7	74.8	76.6	61.5	60.0	64.1	64.5	68.2	72.2
Age 20	49.8	49.5	51.9	53.3	55.2	57.2	50.3	50.2	52.5	54.0	55.7	57.4	45.8	43.5	46.5	46.7	49.9	53.6
Age 30	40.6	40.5	42.8	44.1	45.9	47.9	41.0	41.1	43.3	44.7	46.3	48.1	37.1	35.4	37.8	38.1	41.0	44.6
Age 40	31.4	31.5	33.6	35.1	36.6	38.6	31.7	31.9	34.0	35.6	37.0	38.7	28.7	27.6	29.5	30.1	32.2	35.5
Age 50	23.0	23.1	25.0	26.4	27.8	29.7	23.2	23.3	25.3	26.7	28.1	29.8	21.3	20.7	22.0	22.5	24.1	26.9
Age 60	15.9	16.0	17.5	18.5	19.7	21.6	16.0	16.1	17.6	18.7	19.9	21.7	15.3	14.9	15.9	16.0	17.2	19.4
Age 65	13.0	13.0	14.2	15.1	16.1	17.8	13.0	13.0	14.3	15.2	16.2	17.8	12.8	12.5	13.3	13.3	14.1	16.2
Age 70	10.3	10.4	11.4	12.1	12.8	14.3	10.3	10.4	11.4	12.1	12.9	14.3	10.8	10.4	10.9	10.9	11.4	13.2
Age 80	6.0	6.3	6.8	7.1	7.4	8.2	5.9	6.2	6.8	7.1	7.4	8.2	6.9	7.4	7.0	7.0	7.1	8.0
Female by age:																		
At birth	73.2	74.6	77.6	78.8	79.5	81.1	74.2	75.5	78.2	79.5	80.0	81.3	66.5	68.3	72.9	73.7	75.2	78.2
Age 20	55.6	56.6	59.0	59.9	60.3	61.7	56.3	57.2	59.4	60.4	60.7	61.9	50.1	51.2	54.9	55.5	56.5	59.3
Age 30	46.0	47.0	49.3	50.2	50.6	52.0	46.6	47.6	49.8	50.7	51.0	52.2	40.8	42.0	45.4	46.0	47.0	49.6
Age 40	36.6	37.6	39.8	40.7	41.0	42.4	37.1	38.1	40.2	41.0	41.3	42.6	32.2	33.3	36.3	37.0	37.7	40.3
Age 50	27.7	28.8	30.7	31.4	31.8	33.2	28.1	29.1	31.0	31.7	32.0	33.3	24.3	25.5	27.8	28.4	29.1	31.3
Age 60	19.5	20.6	22.3	22.9	23.1	24.5	19.7	20.8	22.5	23.1	23.3	24.5	17.8	18.7	20.4	20.7	21.2	23.2
Age 65	15.8	16.8	18.4	19.0	19.1	20.4	15.9	16.9	18.6	19.1	19.2	20.4	15.1	15.7	17.1	17.4	17.7	19.4
Age 70	12.4	13.4	14.8	15.4	15.4	16.5	12.4	13.4	14.9	15.5	15.5	16.4	12.5	13.0	14.1	14.3	14.4	15.8
Age 80	6.7	7.7	8.7	9.1	9.1	9.7	6.7	7.6	8.7	9.1	9.0	9.6	7.7	8.9	9.0	9.1	9.0	9.6
PERCENT SURVIVING OUT OF 100,000 BORN ALIVE																		
Male by age:																		
At birth	100.0	100.0	100.0	100.0	100.0	100.0	100.0	100.0	100.0	100.0	100.0	100.0	100.0	100.0	100.0	100.0	100.0	100.0
Age 20	95.5	96.1	97.3	97.9	98.4	98.7	95.9	96.5	97.5	98.1	98.6	98.9	93.1	94.1	96.1	96.3	97.3	97.9
Age 30	93.8	94.1	95.4	96.2	97.1	97.4	94.4	94.7	95.8	96.7	97.4	97.6	90.3	89.6	93.1	93.1	94.9	96.0
Age 40	91.6	91.5	93.3	93.8	95.4	95.9	92.4	92.6	94.0	94.6	95.9	96.1	85.7	83.4	88.5	87.9	91.9	93.7
Age 50	86.2	86.1	89.0	89.9	91.8	92.8	87.4	87.7	90.1	91.1	92.6	93.1	77.2	73.3	80.1	80.0	85.7	89.7
Age 60	73.9	74.0	79.0	81.4	84.6	86.0	75.5	76.0	80.6	83.2	85.8	86.5	61.7	57.5	65.0	66.3	73.6	80.1
Age 65	64.2	64.3	70.6	74.0	78.2	80.7	65.8	66.3	72.4	76.0	79.7	81.4	51.4	47.5	55.1	56.8	65.0	72.6
Age 70	52.2	52.3	59.7	64.1	69.5	73.6	53.8	54.1	61.4	66.2	71.0	74.3	39.9	36.9	44.2	45.7	54.3	63.3
Age 80	25.3	24.9	31.8	36.7	42.8	50.8	26.0	25.9	32.8	38.2	44.1	51.5	20.0	16.6	22.0	22.5	28.5	39.4
Female by age:																		
At birth	100.0	100.0	100.0	100.0	100.0	100.0	100.0	100.0	100.0	100.0	100.0	100.0	100.0	100.0	100.0	100.0	100.0	100.0
Age 20	96.8	97.3	98.2	98.6	98.9	99.1	97.1	97.6	98.4	98.8	99.0	99.2	94.7	95.7	97.2	97.6	98.1	98.5
Age 30	96.0	96.5	97.6	98.0	98.4	98.6	96.5	96.9	97.8	98.3	98.6	98.7	93.1	94.1	96.2	96.5	97.3	97.9
Age 40	94.6	95.1	96.5	97.0	97.5	97.7	95.3	95.8	96.9	97.5	97.8	97.9	89.7	90.8	94.1	94.4	95.6	96.6
Age 50	91.3	91.9	94.1	94.9	95.4	95.8	92.5	92.9	94.7	95.6	96.0	96.0	83.0	84.2	89.6	90.3	91.7	93.7
Age 60	84.4	85.1	88.4	89.7	90.8	91.5	86.3	86.7	89.5	90.8	91.6	91.9	69.9	72.8	80.3	81.9	84.0	87.4
Age 65	78.5	79.7	83.5	85.1	86.4	88.0	80.7	81.6	84.8	86.3	87.4	88.5	60.8	64.7	73.3	75.0	77.9	82.6
Age 70	70.1	72.0	76.7	78.5	80.2	82.8	72.5	74.1	78.1	80.0	81.4	83.4	51.3	54.9	64.7	66.3	69.8	76.0
Age 80	43.1	46.4	54.4	57.0	58.5	64.0	44.7	48.2	55.8	58.5	59.7	64.5	30.3	31.8	41.7	43.6	46.5	55.5

[1] Prior to 1970, data for the black population are not available. Data shown for 1959–1970 are for the non-white population.

Source: U.S. National Center for Health Statistics, National Vital Statistics Reports (NVSR), *United States Life Tables, 2011*, Vol. 64, No. 11, September 2015. See also <http://www.cdc.gov/nchs/products/life_tables.htm>.

Table 118. Life Expectancy at Birth by Sex, Race, and State: 1989 to 2001

[Average number of years of life remaining. Excludes deaths of nonresidents of the United States. Decennial life tables are based on population data from a decennial census and reported deaths of the 3-year period surrounding the census year; the census year is the middle year. The annual tables are based on deaths in a single year, and except for census years, on postcensal population estimates]

State	Total, 1989–1991	1999-2001 Total	Male Total	Male White	Male Black	Female Total	Female White	Female Black
United States...............	**75.37**	**76.83**	**74.10**	**74.74**	**68.08**	**79.45**	**79.97**	**75.12**
Alabama.......................	73.64	74.80	71.32	72.85	66.42	78.34	79.14	74.94
Alaska.........................	74.83	76.63	74.18	75.45	(B)	79.41	80.10	(B)
Arizona........................	76.10	78.15	75.25	75.51	70.95	81.16	81.64	77.70
Arkansas......................	74.33	75.43	72.05	73.17	67.30	78.99	79.59	73.58
California......................	75.86	78.80	76.02	76.11	69.97	81.63	81.36	76.67
Colorado......................	76.96	78.72	76.29	76.23	71.71	81.16	81.31	76.59
Connecticut...................	76.91	78.90	76.13	76.73	71.73	81.63	81.92	77.71
Delaware......................	74.76	77.04	74.24	75.05	70.27	79.78	80.55	75.21
District of Columbia...........	67.99	73.09	68.57	78.94	64.59	77.59	84.31	74.46
Florida........................	75.84	78.10	74.97	75.64	68.98	81.40	82.14	75.53
Georgia.......................	73.61	75.27	72.28	73.88	68.29	78.22	79.53	76.16
Hawaii........................	78.21	80.23	77.17	78.40	(B)	83.65	83.31	(B)
Idaho.........................	76.88	78.29	76.18	76.46	(B)	80.50	80.53	(B)
Illinois........................	74.90	77.06	73.91	75.33	66.81	80.26	80.78	74.20
Indiana.......................	75.39	76.47	73.55	74.24	67.47	79.45	79.69	76.55
Iowa..........................	77.29	78.76	76.11	76.19	70.81	81.39	81.35	75.16
Kansas........................	76.76	77.78	74.84	75.46	68.47	80.88	81.00	75.02
Kentucky......................	74.37	75.20	72.25	72.73	69.01	78.20	78.42	74.46
Louisiana.....................	73.05	74.28	71.12	73.47	66.45	77.44	79.41	75.30
Maine.........................	76.35	77.46	75.23	75.59	(B)	79.63	80.88	(B)
Maryland......................	74.79	76.36	73.55	75.58	68.41	79.08	80.66	75.78
Massachusetts................	76.72	78.76	75.79	76.35	73.14	81.68	81.63	79.33
Michigan......................	75.04	76.90	73.98	75.26	67.38	79.83	80.59	75.95
Minnesota....................	77.76	79.26	76.74	77.03	71.59	81.80	82.61	76.60
Mississippi....................	73.03	73.88	70.30	72.25	66.72	77.62	79.13	73.68
Missouri.......................	75.25	76.52	73.59	74.29	67.22	79.46	79.93	74.50
Montana.......................	76.23	77.74	75.18	75.07	(B)	80.56	81.24	(B)
Nebraska......................	76.92	78.37	76.00	76.17	69.15	80.78	81.14	74.67
Nevada........................	74.18	76.05	73.34	73.49	70.56	79.24	78.97	74.75
New Hampshire...............	76.72	78.79	76.24	76.46	(B)	81.40	81.30	(B)
New Jersey....................	75.42	77.58	74.77	75.82	68.85	80.32	81.32	75.54
New Mexico...................	75.74	77.26	74.52	75.19	71.63	80.06	80.69	74.37
New York......................	74.68	78.20	75.13	75.78	70.13	81.16	81.49	77.84
North Carolina................	74.48	76.27	73.05	74.27	66.33	79.56	80.34	76.68
North Dakota..................	77.62	79.06	75.96	76.65	(B)	82.61	82.67	(B)
Ohio..........................	75.32	76.49	73.94	74.58	68.60	78.95	80.01	74.91
Oklahoma.....................	75.10	75.61	72.75	73.00	68.97	78.59	78.75	74.34
Oregon........................	76.44	78.09	75.82	75.72	70.67	80.37	80.20	78.24
Pennsylvania..................	75.38	77.02	74.09	75.03	67.26	79.90	80.65	75.34
Rhode Island..................	76.54	78.65	75.83	76.06	72.18	81.42	81.60	77.39
South Carolina................	73.51	75.04	71.68	73.76	67.34	78.49	79.77	75.41
South Dakota.................	76.91	78.34	75.19	76.35	(B)	81.79	82.61	(B)
Tennessee....................	74.32	75.29	71.98	73.31	66.86	78.66	79.28	74.16
Texas.........................	75.14	77.04	74.12	74.74	69.18	80.05	80.35	74.76
Utah..........................	77.70	78.89	76.84	76.95	(B)	80.95	80.93	(B)
Vermont.......................	76.54	78.24	76.18	76.30	(B)	80.29	80.90	(B)
Virginia........................	75.22	76.95	74.48	75.62	69.37	79.34	80.69	76.20
Washington....................	76.82	78.64	76.18	76.10	71.90	81.14	80.98	77.11
West Virginia..................	74.26	75.28	72.75	72.75	69.87	77.84	78.36	72.65
Wisconsin.....................	76.87	78.56	75.61	76.12	68.41	81.64	81.87	74.34
Wyoming......................	76.21	76.64	74.83	75.33	(B)	78.55	80.41	(B)

B Base figure too small to meet statistical standards for reliability.

Source: U.S. National Center for Health Statistics, National Vital Statistics Reports (NVSR), *U.S. Decennial Life Tables for 1999-2001: State Life Tables*, Vol. 60, No. 9, September 2012, and earlier reports. See also <http://www.cdc.gov/nchs/products/life_tables.htm>.

Table 119. Deaths and Death Rates by Sex, Race, and Hispanic Origin: 1970 to 2013

[Deaths in thousands (1,921 represents 1,921,000). Rates are per 1,000 population for specified groups. Excludes deaths of nonresidents of the United States and fetal deaths. Rates are based on population enumerated as of April 1 for census years and estimated as of July 1 for all other years. Data for Hispanic origin and specified races other than White and Black should be interpreted with caution because of inconsistent reporting between race and Hispanic Origin on death certificates and censuses and surveys]

Sex and race	1970	1980	1990	2000	2005	2008	2009	2010	2011	2012	2013
Deaths [1]	**1,921**	**1,990**	**2,148**	**2,403**	**2,448**	**2,472**	**2,437**	**2,468**	**2,515**	**2,543**	**2,597**
Male [1]	1,078	1,075	1,113	1,178	1,208	1,226	1,217	1,232	1,255	1,274	1,306
Female [1]	843	915	1,035	1,226	1,240	1,246	1,220	1,236	1,260	1,270	1,291
White	1,682	1,739	1,853	2,071	2,098	2,120	2,086	2,115	2,156	2,175	2,217
Male	942	934	951	1,007	1,028	1,046	1,037	1,052	1,072	1,085	1,111
Female	740	805	902	1,064	1,070	1,074	1,049	1,063	1,084	1,090	1,106
Black	226	233	265	286	293	289	287	287	290	295	303
Male	128	130	145	145	149	147	146	146	147	151	155
Female	98	103	120	141	144	142	140	141	143	145	148
American Indian or Alaska Native	6	7	8	11	14	15	15	16	16	17	17
Male	3	4	5	6	8	8	8	9	9	9	9
Female	2	3	3	5	6	7	7	7	7	7	8
Asian or Pacific Islander	(NA)	11	21	35	43	48	49	51	53	56	60
Male	(NA)	7	12	19	23	25	26	27	27	29	31
Female	(NA)	4	9	16	20	23	24	25	26	28	29
Hispanic origin [2]	(NA)	(NA)	(NA)	107	131	139	142	144	150	156	163
Male	(NA)	(NA)	(NA)	60	74	77	78	80	82	85	89
Female	(NA)	(NA)	(NA)	47	57	62	63	65	68	71	74
Non-Hispanic, White	(NA)	(NA)	(NA)	1,960	1,967	1,981	1,945	1,970	2,006	2,017	2,053
Male	(NA)	(NA)	(NA)	945	954	969	959	972	990	999	1,021
Female	(NA)	(NA)	(NA)	1,015	1,013	1,012	986	998	1,016	1,018	1,032
Death rates [1]	**9.5**	**8.8**	**8.6**	**8.5**	**8.3**	**8.1**	**7.9**	**8.0**	**8.1**	**8.1**	**8.2**
Male [1]	10.9	9.8	9.2	8.5	8.3	8.2	8.1	8.1	8.2	8.2	8.4
Female [1]	8.1	7.9	8.1	8.6	8.3	8.1	7.8	7.9	8.0	8.0	8.0
White	9.5	8.9	8.9	9.0	8.8	8.7	8.5	8.6	8.7	8.8	8.9
Male	10.9	9.8	9.3	8.9	8.7	8.7	8.6	8.7	8.8	8.8	9.0
Female	8.1	8.1	8.5	9.1	8.9	8.7	8.5	8.6	8.7	8.7	8.8
Black	10.0	8.8	8.7	7.8	7.5	7.0	6.9	6.8	6.8	6.8	6.9
Male	11.9	10.3	10.1	8.3	8.0	7.5	7.4	7.3	7.2	7.3	7.4
Female	8.3	7.3	7.5	7.3	7.0	6.6	6.5	6.4	6.4	6.4	6.5
American Indian or Alaska Native	(NA)	4.9	4.0	3.8	3.9	3.7	3.6	3.7	3.7	3.8	3.8
Male	(NA)	6.0	4.8	4.2	4.3	4.1	3.9	4.0	4.0	4.1	4.2
Female	(NA)	3.8	3.3	3.5	3.5	3.3	3.3	3.3	3.4	3.4	3.5
Asian or Pacific Islander	(NA)	3.0	2.8	3.0	3.0	3.0	3.0	3.0	3.1	3.1	3.2
Male	(NA)	3.8	3.3	3.3	3.3	3.2	3.2	3.3	3.3	3.3	3.5
Female	(NA)	2.2	2.3	2.6	2.7	2.8	2.7	2.8	2.8	2.9	3.0
Hispanic origin [2]	(NA)	(NA)	(NA)	3.0	3.0	2.9	2.9	2.9	2.9	3.0	3.0
Male	(NA)	(NA)	(NA)	3.3	3.4	3.2	3.1	3.1	3.1	3.2	3.2
Female	(NA)	(NA)	(NA)	2.7	2.7	2.7	2.6	2.6	2.6	2.7	2.8
Non-Hispanic, White	(NA)	(NA)	(NA)	9.9	9.9	9.9	9.7	9.8	10.0	10.0	10.2
Male	(NA)	(NA)	(NA)	9.8	9.8	9.9	9.8	9.9	10.0	10.1	10.3
Female	(NA)	(NA)	(NA)	10.1	10.0	10.0	9.7	9.8	10.0	10.0	10.1
Age-adjusted death rates [1,3]	**12.2**	**10.4**	**9.4**	**8.7**	**8.2**	**7.7**	**7.5**	**7.5**	**7.4**	**7.3**	**7.3**
Male [1]	15.4	13.5	12.0	10.5	9.7	9.2	8.9	8.9	8.8	8.7	8.6
Female [1]	9.7	8.2	7.5	7.3	6.9	6.6	6.4	6.3	6.3	6.2	6.2
White	11.9	10.1	9.1	8.5	8.0	7.7	7.4	7.4	7.4	7.3	7.3
Male	15.1	13.2	11.7	10.3	9.5	9.1	8.8	8.8	8.7	8.6	8.6
Female	9.4	8.0	7.3	7.2	6.8	6.5	6.3	6.3	6.3	6.2	6.2
Black	15.2	13.1	12.5	11.2	10.4	9.5	9.1	9.0	8.8	8.6	8.6
Male	18.7	17.0	16.4	14.0	12.8	11.7	11.2	11.0	10.7	10.6	10.5
Female	12.3	10.3	9.8	9.3	8.6	7.9	7.6	7.5	7.4	7.2	7.2
American Indian or Alaska Native	(NA)	8.7	7.2	7.1	7.0	6.4	6.2	6.3	6.0	6.0	5.9
Male	(NA)	11.1	9.2	8.4	8.2	7.6	7.1	7.3	6.9	6.9	6.9
Female	(NA)	6.6	5.6	6.0	6.0	5.5	5.4	5.4	5.2	5.1	5.1
Asian or Pacific Islander	(NA)	5.9	5.8	5.1	4.6	4.4	4.2	4.2	4.1	4.1	4.1
Male	(NA)	7.9	7.2	6.2	5.6	5.2	5.1	5.1	4.9	4.8	4.9
Female	(NA)	4.3	4.7	4.2	3.9	3.7	3.6	3.6	3.5	3.5	3.4
Hispanic origin [2]	(NA)	(NA)	(NA)	6.7	6.3	5.8	5.6	5.6	5.4	5.4	5.4
Male	(NA)	(NA)	(NA)	8.2	7.7	7.0	6.8	6.8	6.5	6.4	6.4
Female	(NA)	(NA)	(NA)	5.5	5.1	4.8	4.7	4.6	4.5	4.5	4.5
Non-Hispanic, White	(NA)	(NA)	(NA)	8.6	8.1	7.8	7.6	7.6	7.5	7.5	7.5
Male	(NA)	(NA)	(NA)	10.4	9.6	9.2	8.9	8.9	8.9	8.8	8.8
Female	(NA)	(NA)	(NA)	7.2	6.9	6.7	6.4	6.4	6.4	6.4	6.4

NA Not available. [1] Includes other races not shown separately. [2] Persons of Hispanic origin may be of any race. [3] Age-adjusted death rates are better indicators than crude death rates for showing changes in the risk of death over time when the age distribution of the population is changing, and for comparing the mortality of population subgroups that have different age compositions. All age-adjusted death rates are standardized to the year 2010 population.

Source: U.S. National Center for Health Statistics, National Vital Statistics Reports (NVSR), *Deaths: Final Data for 2013*, Vol. 64, No. 2. See also <http://www.cdc.gov/nchs/deaths.htm>.

Table 120. Death Rates by Age, Sex, and Race: 1960 to 2013

[Rates per 100,000 population]

Characteristic	All ages [1]	Under 1 year	1 to 4 years	5 to 14 years	15 to 24 years	25 to 34 years	35 to 44 years	45 to 54 years	55 to 64 years	65 to 74 years	75 to 84 years	85 years and over
MALE												
1960	1,105	3,059	120	56	152	188	373	992	2,310	4,914	10,178	21,186
1970	1,090	2,410	93	51	189	215	403	959	2,283	4,874	10,010	17,822
1980	977	1,429	73	37	172	196	299	767	1,815	4,105	8,817	18,801
1990	918	1,083	52	29	147	204	310	610	1,553	3,492	7,889	18,057
2000	853	807	36	21	115	139	255	543	1,231	2,980	6,973	17,501
2010	812	680	30	15	98	142	213	506	1,076	2,275	5,694	15,414
2013	839	651	29	15	93	145	214	501	1,088	2,186	5,474	14,912
White:												
1990	931	896	46	26	131	176	268	549	1,467	3,398	7,845	18,268
2000	888	668	33	20	106	124	234	497	1,163	2,906	6,933	17,716
2010	866	584	27	14	92	136	207	492	1,033	2,232	5,704	15,640
2011	876	561	27	15	93	138	209	495	1,033	2,200	5,650	15,336
2012	883	559	27	13	90	139	207	489	1,044	2,151	5,530	15,272
2013	899	566	26	14	87	140	208	492	1,051	2,152	5,507	15,220
Black:												
1990	1,008	2,112	86	41	252	431	700	1,261	2,618	4,946	9,130	16,955
2000	834	1,568	55	28	181	261	453	1,018	2,080	4,254	8,486	16,791
2010	725	1,207	43	20	143	217	308	716	1,662	3,206	6,722	14,715
2011	719	1,150	43	21	140	212	305	706	1,623	3,127	6,359	14,159
2012	728	1,147	42	21	139	213	306	696	1,616	3,078	6,417	13,776
2013	739	1,120	41	20	136	219	312	679	1,628	3,064	6,362	13,657
Asian or Pacific Islander: [2]												
1990	334	605	45	21	76	80	131	287	789	2,041	5,009	12,446
2000	333	529	23	13	55	55	105	250	642	1,661	4,328	12,125
2010	327	434	19	8	43	53	84	214	519	1,226	3,439	10,825
2011	329	410	15	9	43	54	84	217	503	1,167	3,311	10,143
2012	333	431	16	9	42	55	92	217	506	1,109	3,218	10,117
2013	347	409	19	11	42	54	89	220	518	1,126	3,240	10,143
American Indian or Alaska Native: [2]												
1990	476	1,057	77	33	220	256	365	620	1,211	2,462	5,389	11,244
2000	416	700	45	20	136	179	295	520	1,090	2,478	5,351	10,726
2010	398	543	34	18	116	156	258	496	951	1,971	4,452	10,268
2011	395	487	29	13	107	162	251	501	895	1,908	4,241	9,169
2012	410	528	34	17	108	175	249	501	939	1,949	4,190	8,618
2013	417	493	42	12	98	173	244	506	938	1,846	4,225	9,034
FEMALE												
1960	809	2,321	98	37	61	107	229	527	1,196	2,872	7,633	19,008
1970	808	1,864	75	32	68	102	231	517	1,099	2,580	6,678	15,518
1980	785	1,142	55	24	58	76	159	413	934	2,145	5,440	14,747
1990	812	856	41	19	49	74	138	343	879	1,991	4,883	14,274
2000	855	663	29	15	43	64	143	313	772	1,921	4,815	14,719
2010	787	564	23	11	36	64	129	311	644	1,528	4,138	13,219
2013	804	536	22	11	36	66	131	314	647	1,465	4,029	13,022
White:												
1990	847	690	36	18	46	62	117	309	823	1,924	4,839	14,401
2000	912	551	26	14	41	55	126	281	731	1,868	4,785	14,891
2010	857	488	22	11	36	61	123	295	618	1,505	4,165	13,419
2011	869	470	22	11	36	64	125	302	619	1,491	4,158	13,381
2012	870	472	22	10	36	65	124	300	621	1,451	4,111	13,282
2013	879	457	20	11	36	65	127	303	623	1,453	4,072	13,316
Black:												
1990	748	1,736	68	28	69	160	299	639	1,453	2,866	5,688	13,310
2000	733	1,280	45	20	58	122	272	588	1,227	2,690	5,697	13,941
2010	643	994	33	15	43	93	199	481	972	2,021	4,581	12,590
2011	643	962	34	15	44	95	199	468	952	1,969	4,535	12,364
2012	642	944	33	14	44	90	193	462	950	1,919	4,396	12,150
2013	651	981	33	15	41	91	188	454	962	1,909	4,418	11,929
Asian or Pacific Islander: [2]												
1990	234	518	32	13	29	38	70	183	483	1,089	3,128	10,254
2000	262	434	20	12	22	28	66	156	391	996	2,882	9,052
2010	277	342	16	8	17	27	49	128	299	789	2,446	8,590
2011	284	343	12	8	16	25	53	130	304	719	2,446	8,252
2012	292	349	15	7	18	24	50	130	302	732	2,331	8,469
2013	297	329	18	9	18	26	52	128	287	704	2,347	8,240
American Indian or Alaska Native: [2]												
1990	330	689	38	26	69	102	156	381	806	1,679	3,073	8,201
2000	346	492	40	18	59	85	172	285	772	1,900	3,850	9,118
2010	332	366	24	11	44	86	147	326	624	1,482	3,392	9,278
2011	338	412	25	12	45	88	165	337	612	1,376	3,301	8,448
2012	341	426	23	10	48	99	162	330	587	1,390	3,257	7,987
2013	348	306	26	11	43	94	172	335	617	1,315	3,222	8,008

[1] Figures for age not stated are included in "All ages" but not distributed among age groups. [2] The death rates for specified races other than White and Black should be interpreted with caution because of inconsistencies between reporting race on death certificates and censuses and surveys.

Source: U.S. National Center for Health Statistics, *Health, United States*, annual; and CDC WONDER Online database, "Multiple Cause of Death 1999-2013," <http://wonder.cdc.gov/>, accessed January 2015.

Table 121. Age-Adjusted Death Rates by Sex, Race, and Hispanic Origin: 1980 to 2013

[Age-adjusted rates per 100,000 population. Age-adjusted death rates are better indicators than crude death rates for showing changes in the risk of death over time when the age distribution of the population is changing, and for comparing the mortality of population subgroups that have different age compositions. Populations enumerated as of April 1 for census years and estimated as of July 1 for all other years. Excludes fetal deaths and deaths of nonresidents of the United States. Data for Hispanic-origin and specified races other than White and Black should be interpreted with caution because of inconsistencies reporting race on death certificates and on censuses and surveys. See text this section and Appendix III]

Sex, race, and Hispanic origin	1980	1990	2000	2005	2008	2009	2010	2011	2012	2013
ALL RACES [1]										
Total	**1,039**	**939**	**869**	**815**	**775**	**750**	**747**	**741**	**733**	**732**
Male	1,348	1,203	1,054	972	919	891	887	875	865	864
Female	818	751	731	692	660	637	635	632	625	624
WHITE										
Total	**1,013**	**910**	**850**	**801**	**767**	**743**	**742**	**739**	**731**	**731**
Male	1,318	1,166	1,029	953	907	881	879	870	860	859
Female	796	729	715	681	654	631	631	630	624	624
BLACK										
Total	**1,315**	**1,250**	**1,121**	**1,035**	**948**	**913**	**898**	**877**	**865**	**861**
Male	1,698	1,645	1,404	1,281	1,168	1,123	1,104	1,067	1,059	1,053
Female	1,033	975	928	863	792	763	753	740	724	721
AMERICAN INDIAN OR ALASKA NATIVE										
Total	**867**	**716**	**709**	**701**	**644**	**616**	**628**	**601**	**595**	**592**
Male	1,112	916	842	825	757	709	730	692	691	689
Female	662	562	605	602	549	536	542	523	512	508
ASIAN OR PACIFIC ISLANDER										
Total	**590**	**582**	**506**	**460**	**435**	**425**	**424**	**410**	**407**	**405**
Male	787	716	624	561	519	509	512	491	484	488
Female	426	469	417	385	372	361	359	350	349	343
HISPANIC ORIGIN [2]										
Total	**(NA)**	**(NA)**	**666**	**628**	**580**	**560**	**559**	**541**	**539**	**535**
Male	(NA)	(NA)	818	771	695	676	678	647	644	640
Female	(NA)	(NA)	546	514	485	466	463	453	453	449
NON-HISPANIC, WHITE										
Total	**(NA)**	**(NA)**	**856**	**810**	**779**	**755**	**755**	**754**	**746**	**747**
Male	(NA)	(NA)	1,035	962	920	894	893	887	876	877
Female	(NA)	(NA)	722	691	665	643	643	645	638	638
NON-HISPANIC, BLACK										
Total	**(NA)**	**(NA)**	**1,137**	**1,055**	**969**	**934**	**920**	**902**	**887**	**885**
Male	(NA)	(NA)	1,422	1,306	1,195	1,151	1,132	1,098	1,086	1,083
Female	(NA)	(NA)	941	879	810	781	771	760	742	741

NA Not available. [1] For 1980 and 1990 includes deaths among races not shown separately. [2] Persons of Hispanic origin may be of any race.

Source: U.S. National Center for Health Statistics, National Vital Statistics Reports (NVSR), *Deaths: Final Data for 2013*, Vol. 64. No. 2. See also <http://www.cdc.gov/nchs/deaths.htm>.

Table 122. Death Rates by Hispanic-Origin Status, Sex, and Age: 2010 to 2013

[Rates per 100,000 U.S. standard population. Rates are based on populations enumerated as of April 1 for census years and estimated as of July 1 for all other years. Excludes deaths of nonresidents of the United States. Data for Hispanic-origin should be interpreted with caution because of inconsistencies between reporting Hispanic origin and race on death certificates and censuses and surveys]

Age	Hispanic male			Hispanic female			Non-Hispanic White male			Non-Hispanic White female		
	2010	2012	2013	2010	2012	2013	2010	2012	2013	2010	2012	2013
Age adjusted [1]	678	644	640	463	453	449	893	876	877	643	638	638
Crude [2]	311	317	324	261	273	279	988	1,011	1,032	981	999	1,012
Under 1 year	557	509	501	463	429	434	576	558	572	480	469	449
1 to 4 years	25	24	23	20	20	18	28	28	27	22	22	20
5 to 14 years	11	12	12	9	10	10	14	13	14	11	10	11
15 to 24 years	79	76	73	26	26	26	93	92	90	38	38	38
25 to 34 years	101	100	100	39	40	41	144	149	150	67	71	70
35 to 44 years	146	143	143	75	74	78	219	222	223	133	136	139
45 to 54 years	352	343	348	194	192	190	508	508	512	308	315	321
55 to 64 years	815	816	797	450	443	437	1,046	1,058	1,069	632	636	641
65 to 74 years	1,775	1,679	1,710	1,086	1,047	1,040	2,257	2,176	2,174	1,536	1,480	1,484
75 to 84 years	4,462	4,251	4,218	3,067	3,064	3,038	5,770	5,599	5,583	4,233	4,178	4,142
85 years and over	11,780	10,800	10,596	10,237	9,806	9,651	15,817	15,504	15,486	13,544	13,437	13,503

[1] Age-adjusted death rates are better indicators than crude death rates for showing changes in the risk of death over time when the age distribution of the population is changing, and for comparing the mortality of population subgroups that have different age compositions. [2] The total number of deaths in a given time period divided by the total resident population.

Source: U.S. National Center for Health Statistics, *Health, United States*, annual; and CDC WONDER Online database, "Underlying Cause of Death 1999-2013," <http://wonder.cdc.gov/>, accessed January 2015.

Table 123. Deaths and Death Rates by State: 1990 to 2013

[2,148 represents 2,148,000. By state of residence. Excludes deaths of nonresidents of the United States. Caution should be used in comparing death rates by state; rates are affected by the population composition of the area. See also Appendix III]

State	Number of deaths (1,000)						Death rate per 1,000 population [1]						Age-adjusted rate 2013 [1,2]
	1990	2000	2010	2011	2012	2013	1990	2000	2010	2011	2012	2013	
United States........	2,148	2,403	2,468	2,515	2,543	2,597	8.6	8.5	8.0	8.1	8.1	8.2	7.3
Alabama...............	39	45	48	49	49	50	9.7	10.1	10.1	10.1	10.2	10.4	9.3
Alaska.................	2	3	4	4	4	4	4.0	4.6	5.2	5.3	5.3	5.4	7.2
Arizona................	29	41	47	48	50	51	7.9	7.9	7.3	7.5	7.6	7.6	6.7
Arkansas..............	25	28	29	30	30	30	10.5	10.6	9.9	10.1	10.2	10.3	8.9
California..............	214	230	234	240	243	248	7.2	6.8	6.3	6.4	6.4	6.5	6.3
Colorado...............	22	27	31	33	33	34	6.6	6.3	6.3	6.4	6.4	6.4	6.6
Connecticut...........	28	30	29	30	29	30	8.4	8.8	8.0	8.2	8.2	8.2	6.5
Delaware..............	6	7	8	8	8	8	8.7	8.8	8.6	8.6	8.6	8.6	7.3
District of Columbia....	7	6	5	5	5	5	12.0	10.5	7.8	7.4	7.4	7.3	7.5
Florida.................	134	164	174	174	177	181	10.4	10.3	9.2	9.1	9.2	9.3	6.6
Georgia................	52	64	71	71	73	75	8.0	7.8	7.4	7.3	7.3	7.5	8.1
Hawaii.................	7	8	10	10	10	11	6.1	6.8	7.1	7.2	7.4	7.5	5.9
Idaho..................	7	10	11	12	12	12	7.4	7.4	7.3	7.6	7.5	7.7	7.3
Illinois.................	103	107	100	102	102	103	9.0	8.6	7.8	7.9	8.0	8.0	7.2
Indiana................	50	55	57	58	59	61	8.9	9.1	8.8	8.9	9.1	9.2	8.3
Iowa...................	27	28	28	28	28	29	9.7	9.6	9.1	9.2	9.2	9.4	7.2
Kansas................	22	25	25	25	25	25	9.0	9.2	8.6	8.7	8.7	8.8	7.6
Kentucky..............	35	40	42	43	44	44	9.5	9.8	9.7	9.8	10.0	10.0	9.0
Louisiana..............	38	41	41	41	42	43	8.9	9.2	9.0	8.9	9.2	9.4	9.0
Maine..................	11	12	13	13	13	14	9.0	9.7	9.6	9.8	9.7	10.2	7.5
Maryland..............	38	44	43	44	44	46	8.0	8.3	7.5	7.5	7.6	7.7	7.1
Massachusetts........	53	57	53	54	53	55	8.8	8.9	8.0	8.2	8.0	8.2	6.6
Michigan..............	79	87	88	90	90	92	8.5	8.7	8.9	9.1	9.1	9.3	7.8
Minnesota.............	35	38	39	40	40	41	7.9	7.7	7.3	7.5	7.4	7.6	6.5
Mississippi............	25	29	29	29	30	31	9.8	10.1	9.8	9.8	9.9	10.3	9.6
Missouri...............	50	55	55	56	56	57	9.8	9.8	9.2	9.3	9.3	9.5	8.1
Montana...............	7	8	9	9	9	10	8.6	9.0	8.9	9.1	8.9	9.4	7.6
Nebraska..............	15	15	15	15	16	16	9.4	8.8	8.3	8.4	8.4	8.4	7.1
Nevada................	9	15	20	20	21	21	7.8	7.6	7.3	7.5	7.5	7.7	7.7
New Hampshire........	8	10	10	11	11	11	7.7	7.8	7.7	8.2	8.1	8.2	6.8
New Jersey............	70	75	69	71	71	71	9.1	8.9	7.9	8.0	8.0	8.0	6.8
New Mexico............	11	13	16	16	17	17	7.0	7.4	7.7	7.9	8.0	8.1	7.3
New York..............	169	158	146	149	149	151	9.4	8.3	7.6	7.7	7.6	7.7	6.5
North Carolina.........	57	72	79	80	82	83	8.6	8.9	8.3	8.3	8.4	8.5	7.8
North Dakota..........	6	6	6	6	6	6	8.9	9.1	8.8	8.7	8.6	8.6	7.1
Ohio...................	99	108	109	111	112	113	9.1	9.5	9.4	9.7	9.7	9.8	8.1
Oklahoma..............	30	35	37	37	37	38	9.7	10.2	9.7	9.8	9.7	10.0	9.1
Oregon................	25	30	32	33	33	34	8.8	8.6	8.3	8.5	8.4	8.6	7.2
Pennsylvania..........	122	131	125	128	127	129	10.3	10.7	9.8	10.1	9.9	10.1	7.6
Rhode Island..........	10	10	10	10	9	10	9.5	9.6	9.1	9.1	8.9	9.3	7.1
South Carolina.........	30	37	42	42	43	45	8.5	9.2	9.0	9.0	9.1	9.3	8.4
South Dakota..........	6	7	7	7	7	7	9.1	9.3	8.7	8.9	8.8	8.4	6.8
Tennessee.............	46	55	60	61	62	63	9.5	9.7	9.4	9.5	9.6	9.8	8.8
Texas..................	125	150	167	169	174	179	7.4	7.2	6.6	6.6	6.7	6.8	7.5
Utah...................	9	12	15	15	16	16	5.3	5.5	5.3	5.4	5.5	5.6	7.1
Vermont...............	5	5	5	5	5	6	8.2	8.4	8.6	8.7	8.8	9.0	7.1
Virginia................	48	56	59	61	62	63	7.8	8.0	7.4	7.5	7.5	7.6	7.3
Washington............	37	44	48	50	50	51	7.6	7.5	7.2	7.3	7.3	7.4	6.8
West Virginia..........	19	21	21	22	22	22	10.8	11.7	11.5	11.8	11.8	11.8	9.2
Wisconsin..............	43	46	47	48	48	50	8.7	8.7	8.3	8.5	8.4	8.7	7.2
Wyoming...............	3	4	4	4	4	5	7.1	7.9	7.9	7.7	7.8	7.8	7.3

[1] Rates based on enumerated resident population as of April 1 for 1990, 2000, and 2010; estimated resident population as of July 1 for all other years. [2] Age-adjusted death rates are better indicators than crude death rates for showing changes in the risk of death over time when the age distribution of the population is changing, and for comparing the mortality of population subgroups that have different age compositions. See text this section.

Source: U.S. National Center for Health Statistics, CDC WONDER Online Database, "Multiple Cause of Death 1999-2013," <http://wonder.cdc.gov/>; and National Vital Statistics Reports (NVSR), *Deaths: Final Data for 2013*, Vol. 64, No. 2, and earlier reports.

Table 124. Fetal and Infant Deaths: 1990 to 2013

[The term "fetal death," defined on an all inclusive basis to end confusion arising from the use of such terms as stillbirth, spontaneous abortion, and miscarriage, has been adopted by the National Center for Health Statistics (NCHS) as the nationally recommended standard. Fetal deaths do not include induced terminations of pregnancy. See also Appendix III]

Year	Fetal deaths [1]			Infant deaths		Fetal mortality rate [2]			Perinatal mortality rate	
	Total [1]	20 to 27 weeks [3]	28 weeks or more [3]	Less than 7 days	Less than 28 days	Total [1]	20 to 27 weeks [3]	28 weeks or more [3]	Definition I [4]	Definition II [5]
1990.....	31,386	13,427	17,959	19,439	23,591	7.49	3.22	4.30	8.95	13.12
1995.....	27,294	13,043	14,251	15,483	19,186	6.95	3.33	3.64	7.60	11.84
2000.....	27,003	13,497	13,506	14,893	18,733	6.61	3.31	3.32	6.97	11.19
2001.....	26,373	13,122	13,251	14,622	18,275	6.51	3.25	3.28	6.90	11.02
2002.....	25,943	13,072	12,871	15,020	18,791	6.41	3.24	3.19	6.91	11.05
2003.....	26,004	13,348	12,656	15,152	18,935	6.32	3.25	3.08	6.78	10.92
2004.....	26,001	13,068	12,933	14,836	18,602	6.28	3.17	3.14	6.73	10.78
2005.....	25,894	13,326	12,568	15,013	18,782	6.22	3.21	3.03	6.64	10.73
2006.....	25,972	13,269	12,703	15,148	19,041	6.05	3.10	2.97	6.51	10.49
2007.....	26,593	13,822	12,771	15,139	19,094	6.12	3.19	2.95	6.45	10.52
2008.....	26,335	13,347	12,988	14,648	18,238	6.16	3.13	3.05	6.49	10.43
2009.....	24,872	12,813	12,059	13,768	17,261	5.99	3.09	2.91	6.23	10.14
2010.....	24,258	12,388	11,870	12,900	16,193	6.03	3.09	2.96	6.18	10.05
2011.....	24,289	12,432	11,857	12,960	16,065	6.11	3.13	2.99	6.26	10.14
2012.....	24,073	12,334	11,739	12,911	15,887	6.05	3.11	2.96	6.22	10.05
2013.....	23,595	11,874	11,721	12,900	15,893	5.96	3.01	2.97	6.24	9.98

[1] Fetal deaths with stated or presumed gestation of 20 weeks or more. [2] Rate per 1,000 live births and fetal deaths in specified age group. [3] Not stated gestational age proportionally distributed. [4] Infant deaths of less than 7 days and fetal deaths with stated or presumed period of gestation of 28 weeks or more, per 1,000 live births and fetal deaths. [5] Infant deaths of less than 28 days and fetal deaths with stated or presumed period of gestation of 20 weeks or more per 1,000 live births and fetal deaths.

Source: U.S. National Center for Health Statistics, National Vital Statistics Reports (NVSR), *Fetal and Perinatal Mortality, United States, 2013*, Vol. 64. No. 8, July 2015. See also <http://www.cdc.gov/nchs/fetal_death.htm>.

Table 125. Fetal, Infant, Neonatal, and Maternal Mortality Rates by Race: 1980 to 2013

[Deaths per 1,000 live births, except as noted. Data based on death certificates, fetal death records, and birth certificates. Excludes deaths of nonresidents of the United States. See also Appendix III]

Race and year	Infant [1]	Neonatal [1]		Post-neonatal [1]	Fetal mortality rate [2]	Late fetal mortality rate [3]	Perinatal mortality rate [4]	Maternal mortality rate [5]
		Under 28 days	Under 7 days					
ALL RACES								
1980..........	12.6	8.5	7.1	4.1	9.1	6.2	13.2	9.2
1990..........	9.2	5.8	4.8	3.4	7.5	4.3	9.0	8.2
1995..........	7.6	4.9	4.0	2.7	7.0	3.6	7.6	7.1
2000..........	6.9	4.6	3.7	2.3	6.6	3.3	7.0	9.8
2005..........	6.9	4.5	3.6	2.3	6.2	3.0	6.6	[6] 15.1
2010..........	6.1	4.0	3.2	2.1	6.0	3.0	6.2	(NA)
2011..........	6.1	4.1	3.3	2.0	6.1	3.0	6.3	(NA)
2012..........	6.0	4.0	3.3	2.0	6.1	3.0	6.2	(NA)
2013..........	6.0	4.0	3.3	1.9	6.0	3.0	6.2	(NA)
WHITE [7]								
1980..........	10.9	7.4	6.1	3.5	8.1	5.7	11.8	6.7
1990..........	7.6	4.8	3.9	2.8	6.4	3.8	7.7	5.4
1995..........	6.3	4.1	3.3	2.2	5.9	3.3	6.5	4.2
2000..........	5.7	3.8	3.0	1.9	5.6	2.9	5.9	7.5
2005..........	5.7	3.8	3.0	1.9	5.3	2.7	5.7	[6] 11.1
2010..........	5.2	3.5	2.7	1.7	(NA)	(NA)	(NA)	(NA)
2011..........	5.1	3.5	2.8	1.7	(NA)	(NA)	(NA)	(NA)
2012..........	5.1	3.5	2.8	1.6	(NA)	(NA)	(NA)	(NA)
2013..........	5.1	3.5	2.8	1.6	(NA)	(NA)	(NA)	(NA)
BLACK [7]								
1980..........	22.2	14.6	12.3	7.6	14.7	9.1	21.3	22.4
1990..........	18.0	11.6	9.7	6.4	13.3	6.7	16.4	22.4
1995..........	15.1	9.8	8.2	5.3	12.7	5.7	13.8	22.1
2000..........	14.1	9.4	7.6	4.7	12.4	5.4	13.0	22.0
2005..........	13.7	9.1	7.3	4.7	11.4	4.9	12.1	[6] 36.5
2010..........	11.6	7.5	6.0	4.1	(NA)	(NA)	(NA)	(NA)
2011..........	11.5	7.5	6.1	4.0	(NA)	(NA)	(NA)	(NA)
2012..........	11.2	7.3	6.0	3.9	(NA)	(NA)	(NA)	(NA)
2013..........	11.2	7.4	6.1	3.8	(NA)	(NA)	(NA)	(NA)

NA Not available. [1] Infant (under 1 year of age), neonatal (under 28 days), early neonatal (under 7 days), and postneonatal (28 days–11 months). [2] Number of fetal deaths of 20 weeks or more gestation per 1,000 live births plus fetal deaths. [3] Number of fetal deaths of 28 weeks or more gestation (late fetal deaths) per 1,000 live births plus late fetal deaths. [4] Number of late fetal deaths plus infant deaths within 7 days of birth per 1,000 live births plus late fetal deaths. [5] Per 100,000 live births from deliveries and complications of pregnancy, childbirth, and the puerperium. Beginning 2000, deaths are classified according to the tenth revision of the International Classification of Diseases; earlier years classified according to the revision in use at the time; see text, this section. [6] Increase partially reflects the use of a separate item on the death certificate on pregnancy status by an increasing number of states. [7] Infant deaths are tabulated by race of decedent; fetal deaths and live births are tabulated by race of mother.

Source: U.S. National Center for Health Statistics, *Health, United States*, annual; and *Fetal and Perinatal Mortality, United States, 2013*, Vol. 64, No. 8, July 2015. See also <http://www.cdc.gov/nchs/hus.htm>.

Table 126. Infant Mortality Rates by Race, State, and Island Area: 1990 to 2013

[Deaths per 1,000 live births, by place of residence. Represents deaths of infants under 1 year old, exclusive of fetal deaths. Excludes deaths of nonresidents of the United States]

State and Island Area	Total [1]				White				Black			
	1990	2000	2010	2013	1990	2000	2010	2013	1990	2000	2010	2013
United States......	9.2	6.9	6.2	6.0	7.6	5.7	5.2	5.1	18.0	14.1	11.6	11.2
Alabama............	10.8	9.4	8.7	8.6	8.1	6.6	6.6	7.0	16.0	15.4	13.7	12.7
Alaska..............	10.5	6.8	3.8	5.6	7.6	5.8	3.3	4.5	(B)	(B)	(B)	(B)
Arizona.............	8.8	6.7	6.0	5.3	7.8	6.2	5.5	4.6	20.6	17.6	12.1	14.4
Arkansas...........	9.2	8.4	7.3	7.6	8.4	7.0	6.7	6.6	13.9	13.7	10.3	11.3
California...........	7.9	5.4	4.7	4.8	7.0	5.1	4.6	4.6	16.8	12.9	9.8	11.0
Colorado............	8.8	6.2	5.9	5.1	7.8	5.6	5.6	4.9	19.4	19.5	13.1	9.8
Connecticut.........	7.9	6.6	5.3	4.7	6.3	5.6	4.5	4.3	17.6	14.4	11.6	8.6
Delaware...........	10.1	9.2	7.7	6.3	9.7	7.9	6.4	4.6	20.1	14.8	11.9	11.4
District of Columbia...........	20.7	12.0	7.9	6.8	(B)	(B)	(B)	(B)	24.6	16.1	10.5	9.8
Florida..............	9.6	7.0	6.5	6.2	6.7	5.4	5.0	4.8	16.8	12.6	11.3	10.5
Georgia.............	12.4	8.5	6.4	6.9	7.4	5.9	5.1	5.5	18.3	13.9	9.1	9.9
Hawaii..............	6.7	8.1	6.2	6.5	6.1	6.5	3.9	5.5	(B)	(B)	(B)	(B)
Idaho...............	8.7	7.5	4.8	5.6	8.6	7.5	4.8	5.5	(B)	(B)	(B)	(B)
Illinois..............	10.7	8.5	6.8	6.0	7.9	6.6	5.4	4.5	22.4	17.1	13.6	13.1
Indiana.............	9.6	7.8	7.6	7.2	7.9	6.9	6.7	6.0	17.4	15.8	15.0	15.8
Iowa................	8.1	6.5	4.9	4.1	7.9	6.0	4.6	3.7	21.9	21.1	11.2	11.2
Kansas.............	8.4	6.8	6.2	6.4	8.0	6.4	5.7	5.4	17.7	12.2	12.4	18.2
Kentucky...........	8.5	7.2	6.8	6.4	8.2	6.7	6.4	6.0	14.3	12.7	11.1	11.0
Louisiana...........	11.1	9.0	7.6	8.7	8.1	5.9	4.9	5.8	16.7	13.3	11.8	13.3
Maine...............	6.2	4.9	5.4	7.0	6.7	4.8	5.4	7.2	(B)	(B)	(B)	(B)
Maryland............	9.5	7.6	6.8	6.6	6.8	4.8	4.4	5.0	17.1	13.2	11.6	10.2
Massachusetts.......	7.0	4.6	4.4	4.2	6.1	4.0	4.0	3.8	11.9	9.9	7.2	7.7
Michigan............	10.7	8.2	7.1	7.0	7.4	6.0	5.5	5.7	21.6	18.2	14.1	12.8
Minnesota...........	7.3	5.6	4.5	5.1	6.7	4.8	4.2	4.2	23.7	14.6	6.4	10.6
Mississippi..........	12.1	10.7	9.7	9.7	7.4	6.8	6.6	7.5	16.2	15.3	13.8	12.6
Missouri.............	9.4	7.2	6.6	6.5	7.9	5.9	5.8	5.6	18.2	14.7	11.8	11.8
Montana............	9.0	6.1	5.9	5.7	6.0	5.5	5.9	4.6	(B)	(B)	(B)	(B)
Nebraska...........	8.3	7.3	5.3	5.3	6.9	6.4	4.7	5.2	18.9	20.3	13.4	(B)
Nevada.............	8.4	6.5	5.6	5.5	8.2	6.0	4.8	4.8	14.2	12.7	13.8	11.6
New Hampshire.....	7.1	5.7	4.0	5.7	6.0	5.5	3.9	5.7	(B)	(B)	(B)	(B)
New Jersey..........	9.0	6.3	4.8	4.5	6.4	5.0	3.6	3.6	18.4	13.6	10.4	9.3
New Mexico.........	9.0	6.6	5.6	5.5	7.6	6.3	5.5	5.5	(B)	(B)	(B)	(B)
New York............	9.6	6.4	5.1	4.9	7.4	5.4	4.2	4.5	18.1	10.9	9.2	7.6
North Carolina.......	10.6	8.6	7.0	7.0	8.0	6.3	5.4	5.4	16.5	15.7	12.3	11.4
North Dakota.........	8.0	8.1	6.8	6.1	7.2	7.5	5.4	5.4	(B)	(B)	(B)	(B)
Ohio.................	9.8	7.6	7.7	7.3	7.8	6.3	6.3	6.1	19.5	15.4	14.8	13.6
Oklahoma...........	9.2	8.5	7.6	6.8	9.1	7.9	6.3	6.0	14.3	16.9	12.4	15.1
Oregon..............	8.3	5.6	4.9	5.0	7.0	5.5	4.7	4.9	(B)	(B)	(B)	(B)
Pennsylvania........	9.6	7.1	7.3	6.7	7.4	5.8	6.3	5.7	20.5	15.7	12.6	12.0
Rhode Island........	8.1	6.3	7.1	6.5	7.0	5.9	6.7	6.8	(B)	(B)	(B)	(B)
South Carolina.......	11.7	8.7	7.4	6.9	8.1	5.4	5.3	5.3	17.3	14.8	11.3	10.3
South Dakota........	10.1	5.5	6.9	6.5	8.0	4.3	6.0	5.1	(B)	(B)	(B)	(B)
Tennessee..........	10.3	9.1	7.9	6.8	7.3	6.8	6.6	5.6	17.9	18.0	13.3	11.1
Texas...............	8.1	5.7	6.1	5.8	6.7	5.1	5.6	5.2	14.7	11.4	11.2	11.3
Utah................	7.5	5.2	4.9	5.2	6.0	5.1	4.5	4.9	(B)	(B)	(B)	(B)
Vermont.............	6.4	6.0	4.2	4.4	5.9	6.1	4.4	4.2	(B)	(B)	(B)	(B)
Virginia.............	10.2	6.9	6.8	6.2	7.4	5.4	4.8	4.8	19.5	12.4	14.3	11.6
Washington..........	7.8	5.2	4.5	4.5	7.3	4.9	4.0	4.1	20.6	9.4	8.2	9.4
West Virginia........	9.9	7.6	7.3	7.6	8.1	7.4	7.1	7.0	(B)	(B)	(B)	(B)
Wisconsin...........	8.2	6.6	5.8	6.2	7.7	5.5	4.9	4.9	19.0	17.2	14.6	17.0
Wyoming............	8.6	6.7	6.8	4.6	7.5	6.5	6.4	4.7	(B)	(B)	(B)	(B)
Puerto Rico.........	(NA)	9.7	8.1	7.2	(NA)	10.2	8.8	7.9	(NA)	(B)	(B)	(B)
Virgin Islands.......	(NA)	13.4	(B)	(NA)	(NA)	(B)	(B)	(NA)	(B)	(B)	(B)	(NA)
Guam...............	(NA)	5.8	14.1	9.4	(NA)	(B)	(B)	(B)	(B)	(B)	(B)	(B)

B Base figure too small to meet statistical standards for reliability. NA Not available. [1] Includes other races, not shown separately.

Source: U.S. National Center for Health Statistics, National Vital Statistics Reports (NVSR), *Deaths: Final Data for 2013*, Vol. 64, No. 2, and earlier reports. See also <http://www.cdc.gov/nchs/deaths.htm>.

Table 127. Age-Adjusted Death Rates by Major Cause: 1960 to 2013

[Age-adjusted rates per 100,000 population. Age-adjusted death rates were prepared using the direct method, in which age specific death rates for a population of interest are applied to a standard population distributed by age. Age adjustment eliminates the differences in observed rates between points in time or among compared population groups that result from age differences in population composition. Beginning 1999, deaths classified according to tenth revision of International Classification of Diseases; for earlier years, causes of death were classified according to the revisions then in use. Changes in classification of causes of death due to these revisions may result in discontinuities in cause-of-death trends. See Appendix III]

Year	Diseases of the heart	Malignant neoplasms (cancer)	Chronic lower respiratory diseases	Accidents [1]	Cerebrovascular diseases	Alzheimer's disease	Diabetes mellitus	Influenza and pneumonia	Nephritis, nephrotic syndrome and nephrosis	Intentional self-harm (suicide)
1960	559.0	193.9	12.5	63.1	177.9	(NA)	22.5	53.7	10.6	12.5
1961	545.3	193.4	12.6	60.6	173.1	(NA)	22.1	43.4	10.0	12.2
1962	556.9	193.3	14.2	62.9	174.0	(NA)	22.6	47.1	9.6	12.8
1963	563.4	194.7	16.5	64.0	173.9	(NA)	23.1	55.6	9.2	13.0
1964	543.3	193.6	16.3	64.1	167.0	(NA)	22.5	45.4	8.9	12.7
1965	542.5	195.6	18.3	65.8	166.4	(NA)	22.9	46.8	8.3	13.0
1966	541.2	196.5	19.2	67.6	165.8	(NA)	23.6	47.9	7.9	12.7
1967	524.7	197.3	19.2	66.2	159.3	(NA)	23.4	42.2	7.3	12.5
1968	531.0	198.8	20.7	65.5	162.5	(NA)	25.3	52.8	6.1	12.4
1969	516.8	198.5	20.9	64.9	155.4	(NA)	25.1	47.9	6.0	12.7
1970	492.7	198.6	21.3	62.2	147.7	(NA)	24.3	41.7	5.5	13.1
1971	492.9	199.3	21.8	60.3	147.6	(NA)	23.9	38.4	5.2	13.1
1972	490.2	200.3	22.8	60.2	147.3	(NA)	23.7	41.3	5.2	13.3
1973	482.0	200.0	23.6	59.3	145.2	(NA)	23.0	41.2	5.0	13.1
1974	458.8	201.5	23.2	52.7	136.8	(NA)	22.1	35.5	4.7	13.2
1975	431.2	200.1	23.7	50.8	123.5	(NA)	20.3	34.9	4.7	13.6
1976	426.9	202.5	24.9	48.7	117.4	(NA)	19.5	38.8	4.9	13.2
1977	413.7	203.5	24.7	48.8	110.4	(NA)	18.2	31.0	4.8	13.7
1978	409.9	204.9	26.3	48.9	103.7	(NA)	18.3	34.5	4.8	12.9
1979	401.6	204.0	25.5	46.5	97.1	(NA)	17.5	26.1	8.6	12.6
1980	412.1	207.9	28.3	46.4	96.4	(NA)	18.1	31.4	9.1	12.2
1981	397.0	206.4	29.0	43.4	89.5	0.9	17.6	30.0	9.1	12.3
1982	389.0	208.3	29.1	40.1	84.2	1.3	17.2	26.5	9.4	12.5
1983	388.9	209.1	31.6	39.1	81.2	2.2	17.6	29.8	9.6	12.4
1984	378.8	210.8	32.4	38.8	78.7	3.1	17.2	30.6	10.0	12.6
1985	375.0	211.3	34.5	38.5	76.6	4.1	17.4	34.5	10.4	12.5
1986	365.1	211.5	34.8	38.6	73.1	4.6	17.2	34.8	10.4	13.0
1987	355.9	211.7	35.0	38.2	71.6	5.5	17.4	33.8	10.4	12.8
1988	352.5	212.5	36.5	38.9	70.6	5.8	18.0	37.3	10.4	12.5
1989	332.0	214.2	36.6	37.7	66.9	6.1	20.5	35.9	9.6	12.3
1990	321.8	216.0	37.2	36.3	65.3	6.3	20.7	36.8	9.3	12.5
1991	312.5	215.2	37.9	34.7	62.9	6.3	20.7	34.7	9.3	12.3
1992	304.0	213.5	37.7	33.2	61.5	6.3	20.7	32.8	9.4	12.0
1993	308.1	213.5	40.7	34.2	62.7	7.1	21.9	35.0	9.7	12.1
1994	297.5	211.7	40.3	34.2	62.6	7.7	22.6	33.6	9.4	11.9
1995	293.4	209.9	40.1	34.4	63.1	8.4	23.2	33.4	9.5	11.8
1996	285.7	206.7	40.6	34.5	62.5	8.5	23.8	32.9	9.6	11.5
1997	277.7	203.4	41.1	34.2	61.1	8.7	23.7	33.3	9.8	11.2
1998	267.4	202.1	43.8	35.6	62.8	8.6	24.2	24.2	9.8	11.1
1999	266.5	200.8	45.4	35.3	61.6	16.5	25.0	23.5	13.0	10.5
2000	257.6	199.6	44.2	34.9	60.9	18.1	25.0	23.7	13.5	10.4
2001	249.5	196.5	43.9	35.7	58.4	19.3	25.4	22.2	14.1	10.7
2002	244.6	194.3	43.9	37.1	57.2	20.8	25.6	23.2	14.4	10.9
2003	236.3	190.9	43.7	37.6	54.6	22.1	25.5	22.6	14.7	10.8
2004	221.6	186.8	41.6	38.1	51.2	22.6	24.7	20.4	14.5	11.0
2005	216.8	185.1	43.9	39.5	48.0	24.0	24.9	21.0	14.7	10.9
2006	205.5	181.8	41.0	40.2	44.8	23.7	23.6	18.4	14.8	11.0
2007	196.1	179.3	41.4	40.4	43.5	23.8	22.8	16.8	14.9	11.3
2008	192.1	176.4	44.7	39.2	42.1	25.8	22.0	17.6	15.1	11.6
2009	182.8	173.5	42.7	37.5	39.6	24.2	21.0	16.5	15.1	11.8
2010	179.1	172.8	42.2	38.0	39.1	25.1	20.8	15.1	15.3	12.1
2011	173.7	169.0	42.5	39.1	37.9	24.7	21.6	15.7	13.4	12.3
2012	170.5	166.5	41.5	39.1	36.9	23.8	21.2	14.4	13.1	12.6
2013	169.8	163.2	42.1	39.4	36.2	23.5	21.2	15.9	13.2	12.6

NA Not available. [1] Unintentional injuries.

Source: U.S. National Center for Health Statistics, National Vital Statistics Reports, *Health, United States*, annual; and *Deaths: Final Data for 2013*, Vol. 64, No. 2, and earlier reports. See also <http://www.cdc.gov/nchs/products/nvsr.htm>.

Table 128. Deaths by Leading Cause and Race: 2011

[Cause of death based on International Classification of Diseases, Tenth Revision (ICD-10)]

Cause of death	White			Black			American Indian/ Alaskan Native			Asian/ Pacific Islander		
	Rank [1]	Deaths	Per-cent	Rank [1]	Deaths	Per-cent	Rank [1]	Deaths	Per-cent	Rank [1]	Deaths	Per-cent
All causes................	(X)	2,156,077	100.0	(X)	290,100	100.0	(X)	15,945	100.0	(X)	53,336	100.0
Diseases of heart...........	1	513,701	23.8	1	68,372	23.6	1	2,918	18.3	2	11,586	21.7
Malignant neoplasms.......	2	492,348	22.8	2	66,820	23.0	2	2,810	17.6	1	14,713	27.6
Chronic lower respiratory diseases...................	3	131,495	6.1	6	9,086	3.1	6	657	4.1	6	1,705	3.2
Accidents (unintentional injuries).....................	4	109,751	5.1	5	12,531	4.3	3	1,829	11.5	4	2,327	4.4
Cerebrovascular diseases...	5	108,542	5.0	3	15,853	5.5	7	600	3.8	3	3,937	7.4
Alzheimer's disease........	6	78,055	3.6	10	5,482	1.9	13	226	1.4	8	1,211	2.3
Diabetes mellitus [2].........	7	57,974	2.7	4	12,895	4.4	4	927	5.8	5	2,035	3.8
Influenza and pneumonia...	8	46,658	2.2	11	5,167	1.8	9	349	2.2	7	1,652	3.1
Nephritis, nephrotic syn-drome and nephrosis [3]....	9	36,268	1.7	7	8,087	2.8	10	287	1.8	10	949	1.8
Intentional self harm (suicide)...................	10	35,775	1.7	16	2,241	0.8	8	459	2.9	9	1,043	2.0
Chronic liver disease and cirrhosis..................	11	29,507	1.4	15	2,816	1.0	5	821	5.1	13	498	0.9
Septicemia.................	12	28,838	1.3	9	6,028	2.1	11	269	1.7	12	613	1.1
Assault (homicide)..........	18	7,768	0.4	8	7,858	2.7	12	254	1.6	17	358	0.7

X Not applicable. [1] Rank based on number of deaths. [2] Because of coding-rule changes in data year 2011, increases in number of deaths from diabetes mellitus should be interpreted with caution. [3] Because of coding-rule changes in data year 2011, decreases in number of deaths and rank order for Nephritis, nephrotic syndrome and nephrosis should be interpreted with caution.

Source: U.S. National Center for Health Statistics, National Vital Statistics Reports (NVSR), *Deaths: Leading Causes for 2011*, Vol. 64, No. 7, July 2015. See also <http://www.cdc.gov/nchs/deaths.htm>.

Table 129. Deaths by Leading Cause and Hispanic Origin: 2011

[Race and Hispanic origin are reported separately on death certificate. Persons of Hispanic origin may be of any race. Cause of death based on International Classification of Diseases, Tenth Revision (ICD-10). See Appendix III]

Cause of death	Hispanic			Non-Hispanic White			Non-Hispanic Black		
	Rank [1]	Deaths	Per-cent	Rank [1]	Deaths	Per-cent	Rank [1]	Deaths	Per-cent
All causes......................	(X)	149,635	100.0	(X)	2,006,319	100.0	(X)	286,797	100.0
Malignant neoplasms...........................	1	32,381	21.6	2	460,026	22.9	2	66,158	23.1
Diseases of heart................................	2	30,385	20.3	1	482,979	24.1	1	67,595	23.6
Accidents (unintentional injuries)...............	3	11,166	7.5	5	98,605	4.9	5	12,299	4.3
Cerebrovascular diseases.......................	4	7,552	5.0	4	101,043	5.0	3	15,722	5.5
Diabetes mellitus [2].............................	5	7,054	4.7	7	50,964	2.5	4	12,771	4.5
Chronic liver disease and cirrhosis.............	6	4,774	3.2	12	24,752	1.2	15	2,783	1.0
Chronic lower respiratory diseases.............	7	4,355	2.9	3	127,035	6.3	6	8,994	3.1
Alzheimer's disease.............................	8	3,599	2.4	6	74,448	3.7	10	5,446	1.9
Influenza and pneumonia.......................	9	3,256	2.2	8	43,350	2.2	11	5,098	1.8
Nephritis, nephrotic syndrome and nephrosis [3].	10	2,799	1.9	9	33,492	1.7	7	8,044	2.8
Assault (homicide)..............................	11	2,759	1.8	22	5,070	0.3	8	7,764	2.7
Intentional self harm (suicide)..................	12	2,720	1.8	10	33,031	1.6	16	2,194	0.8
Septicemia.....................................	14	2,168	1.4	11	26,669	1.3	9	5,963	2.1

X Not applicable. [1] Rank based on number of deaths. [2] Because of coding-rule changes in data year 2011, increases in number of deaths from Diabetes mellitus should be interpreted with caution. [3] Because of coding-rule changes in data year 2011, decreases in number of deaths and rank order for Nephritis, nephrotic syndrome and nephrosis should be interpreted with caution.

Source: U.S. National Center for Health Statistics, National Vital Statistics Reports (NVSR), *Deaths: Leading Causes for 2011*, Vol. 64, No. 7, July 2015. See also <http://www.cdc.gov/nchs/deaths.htm>.

Table 130. Deaths and Death Rates by Selected Causes: 2012 and 2013

[Rates per 100,000 population. Figures are weighted data rounded to the nearest individual, so categories may not add to total or subtotal. Excludes deaths of nonresidents of the United States. Deaths classified according to tenth revision of International Classification of Diseases (ICD). See also Appendix III]

Cause of death	2012			2013		
	Number	Rate	Age-adjusted rate [1]	Number	Rate	Age-adjusted rate [1]
All causes [2]	2,543,279	810.2	732.8	2,596,993	821.5	731.9
Major cardiovascular diseases [2]	782,985	249.4	223.0	796,494	252.0	221.7
Diseases of heart	599,711	191.0	170.5	611,105	193.3	169.8
Acute rheumatic fever and chronic rheumatic heart disease	3,088	1.0	0.9	3,260	1.0	0.9
Hypertensive heart disease	35,072	11.2	9.9	37,144	11.7	10.3
Hypertensive heart and renal disease	3,924	1.3	1.1	4,028	1.3	1.1
Ischemic heart disease	371,469	118.3	105.4	370,213	117.1	102.6
Acute myocardial infarction	117,944	37.6	33.5	116,793	36.9	32.4
Other heart diseases	186,158	59.3	53.1	196,460	62.1	54.8
Heart failure	60,341	19.2	17.1	65,120	20.6	18.0
Essential (primary) hypertension and hypertensive renal disease	29,115	9.3	8.2	30,770	9.7	8.5
Cerebrovascular diseases	128,546	40.9	36.9	128,978	40.8	36.2
Atherosclerosis	6,946	2.2	2.0	6,685	2.1	1.8
Malignant neoplasms (Cancer) [2]	582,623	185.6	166.5	584,881	185.0	163.2
Malignant neoplasms of lip, oral cavity, and pharynx	8,924	2.8	2.5	8,850	2.8	2.4
Malignant neoplasms of esophagus	14,649	4.7	4.1	14,690	4.6	4.0
Malignant neoplasms of stomach	11,191	3.6	3.2	11,261	3.6	3.2
Malignant neoplasms of colon, rectum and anus	52,028	16.6	14.9	52,252	16.5	14.6
Malignant neoplasms of liver and intrahepatic bile ducts	22,973	7.3	6.4	24,032	7.6	6.5
Malignant neoplasms of pancreas	38,797	12.4	11.0	38,996	12.3	10.8
Malignant neoplasms of trachea, bronchus and lung	157,499	50.2	44.9	156,252	49.4	43.4
Malignant melanoma of skin	9,251	2.9	2.7	9,394	3.0	2.7
Malignant neoplasm of breast	41,557	13.2	11.8	41,325	13.1	11.5
Malignant neoplasm of ovary	14,404	4.6	4.1	14,276	4.5	4.0
Malignant neoplasm of prostate	27,245	8.7	7.9	27,682	8.8	7.8
Malignant neoplasms of kidney and renal pelvis	13,518	4.3	3.8	13,906	4.4	3.9
Malignant neoplasm of bladder	15,246	4.9	4.4	15,757	5.0	4.4
Malignant neoplasms of meninges, brain and other parts of central nervous system	15,276	4.9	4.4	15,345	4.9	4.3
Malignant neoplasms of lymphoid, hematopoietic and related tissue [3]	57,020	18.2	16.6	56,936	18.0	16.2
Non-Hodgkin's lymphoma	20,388	6.5	5.9	20,114	6.4	5.7
Leukemia	23,186	7.4	6.8	23,428	7.4	6.7
Accidents (unintentional injuries)	127,792	40.7	39.1	130,557	41.3	39.4
Transport accidents [2]	39,045	12.4	12.2	37,938	12.0	11.7
Motor vehicle accidents	36,415	11.6	11.4	35,369	11.2	10.9
Nontransport accidents [2]	88,747	28.3	26.9	92,619	29.3	27.7
Falls	28,753	9.2	8.3	30,208	9.6	8.5
Accidental discharge of firearms	548	0.2	0.2	505	0.2	0.2
Accidental drowning and submersion	3,551	1.1	1.1	3,391	1.1	1.1
Accidental exposure to smoke, fire and flames	2,464	0.8	0.7	2,760	0.9	0.8
Accidental poisoning and exposure to noxious substances	36,332	11.6	11.5	38,851	12.3	12.2
Chronic lower respiratory diseases [2]	143,489	45.7	41.5	149,205	47.2	42.1
Bronchitis, chronic and unspecified	616	0.2	0.2	664	0.2	0.2
Emphysema	8,485	2.7	2.4	8,284	2.6	2.3
Asthma	3,531	1.1	1.1	3,630	1.1	1.1
Pneumonitis due to solids and liquids	17,897	5.7	5.1	18,579	5.9	5.2
Influenza and pneumonia [2]	50,636	16.1	14.4	56,979	18.0	15.9
Influenza	1,106	0.4	0.3	3,697	1.2	1.1
Pneumonia	49,530	15.8	14.2	53,282	16.9	14.8
Septicemia (blood poisoning)	35,842	11.4	10.3	38,156	12.1	10.7
Viral hepatitis	8,062	2.6	2.1	8,157	2.6	2.1
Human immunodeficiency virus (HIV) disease	7,216	2.3	2.2	6,955	2.2	2.1
Anemias	5,190	1.7	1.5	4,894	1.5	1.4
Diabetes mellitus	73,932	23.6	21.2	75,578	23.9	21.2
Nutritional deficiencies	3,195	1.0	0.9	3,382	1.1	0.9
Malnutrition	3,014	1.0	0.9	3,224	1.0	0.9
Parkinson's disease	23,818	7.6	7.0	25,196	8.0	7.3
Alzheimer's disease	83,637	26.6	23.8	84,767	26.8	23.5
Chronic liver disease and cirrhosis	34,979	11.1	9.9	36,427	11.5	10.2
Alcoholic liver disease	17,419	5.5	4.9	18,146	5.7	5.1
Nephritis, nephrotic syndrome, and nephrosis [2]	45,622	14.5	13.1	47,112	14.9	13.2
Renal failure	44,988	14.3	12.9	46,425	14.7	13.0
Intentional self-harm (suicide)	40,600	12.9	12.6	41,149	13.0	12.6
Intentional self-harm (suicide) by discharge of firearms	20,666	6.6	6.3	21,175	6.7	6.4
Assault (homicide)	16,688	5.3	5.4	16,121	5.1	5.2
Assault (homicide) by discharge of firearms	11,622	3.7	3.8	11,208	3.5	3.6
Events of undetermined intent	4,737	1.5	1.5	4,587	1.5	1.4
Complications of medical and surgical care	2,603	0.8	0.8	2,768	0.9	0.8
Enterocolitis due to Clostridium difficile [2]	7,739	2.5	2.2	7,665	2.4	2.1
Drug-induced deaths [3]	43,819	14.0	13.8	46,471	14.7	14.6
Alcohol-induced deaths [3]	27,762	8.8	8.0	29,001	9.2	8.2

[1] See text, this section. [2] Includes other causes, not shown separately. [3] Also included in selected other categories.

Source: U.S. National Center for Health Statistics, National Vital Statistics Reports, *Deaths: Final Data for 2013*, Vol. 64, No. 2, and earlier reports; and CDC WONDER Online database, "Multiple Cause of Death 1999-2013," <http://wonder.cdc.gov/>, accessed January 2015. See also <http://www.cdc.gov/nchs/deaths.htm>.

Table 131. Deaths by Age and Selected Cause: 2013

[Deaths are classified according to the tenth revision of the International Classification of Diseases. See Appendix III]

Cause of death	All ages[1]	Under 1 year	1 to 4 years	5 to 14 years	15 to 24 years	25 to 34 years	35 to 44 years	45 to 54 years	55 to 64 years	65 to 74 years	75 to 84 years	85 years and over
All causes[2]	2,596,993	23,440	4,068	5,340	28,486	45,463	69,573	177,724	338,127	454,429	625,013	825,198
Septicemia	38,156	152	53	55	138	333	820	2,445	5,345	7,693	10,274	10,848
Human immunodeficiency virus (HIV) disease	6,955	–	–	2	109	631	1,246	2,378	1,820	587	163	18
Malignant neoplasms (Cancer)[2]	584,881	64	328	895	1,496	3,673	11,349	46,185	113,324	155,552	153,214	98,792
Malignant neoplasm of esophagus	14,690	–	–	3	–	33	228	1,319	3,668	4,441	3,362	1,638
Malignant neoplasms of colon, rectum, and anus	52,252	–	–	3	44	362	1,381	5,052	9,676	12,014	12,921	10,799
Malignant neoplasms of liver and intrahepatic bile ducts	24,032	–	19	14	32	103	349	2,216	7,632	6,211	5,008	2,448
Malignant neoplasm of pancreas	38,996	–	–	2	10	60	454	2,717	7,708	10,951	10,556	6,538
Malignant neoplasms of trachea, bronchus, and lung	156,252	1	–	5	22	124	1,146	10,439	31,433	49,578	44,174	19,328
Malignant neoplasm of breast	41,325	1	–	1	11	350	1,956	5,527	9,053	9,295	8,144	6,987
Malignant neoplasm of ovary	14,276	–	1	1	32	64	300	1,442	2,978	3,883	3,513	2,062
Malignant neoplasm of prostate	27,682	–	1	–	2	3	20	447	2,570	5,984	9,259	9,395
Malignant neoplasms of kidney and renal pelvis	13,906	1	17	22	19	62	238	1,207	2,887	3,826	3,470	2,157
Malignant neoplasm of bladder	15,757	–	–	–	1	13	89	508	1,871	3,426	5,119	4,730
Malignant neoplasms of meninges, brain and other parts of central nervous system	15,345	23	92	322	241	424	818	1,898	3,691	3,854	2,808	1,172
Malignant neoplasms of lymphoid, hematopoietic and related tissue[2]	56,936	21	101	261	469	701	1,129	3,072	7,776	13,863	17,531	12,010
Non-Hodgkins lymphoma	20,114	–	5	24	91	197	361	1,099	2,776	4,749	6,312	4,499
Leukemia	23,428	21	96	233	345	396	587	1,228	2,962	5,460	7,072	5,027
Diabetes mellitus	75,578	8	4	24	193	684	1,952	5,899	13,061	15,279	19,587	16,885
Parkinson's disease	25,196	–	–	–	3	9	7	78	573	3,215	10,549	10,762
Alzheimer's disease	84,767	–	–	–	–	–	8	95	877	4,561	23,073	56,152
Major cardiovascular diseases[2]	796,494	435	210	273	1,170	4,051	12,852	43,230	89,651	125,878	197,484	321,231
Diseases of heart[2]	611,105	309	169	173	941	3,258	10,341	35,167	72,568	98,432	147,255	242,469
Hypertensive heart disease	37,144	–	–	7	44	394	1,473	4,306	6,611	5,743	6,365	12,204
Ischemic heart diseases	370,213	7	7	7	140	1,010	4,991	21,246	47,597	65,089	91,901	138,203
Acute myocardial infarction	116,793	–	2	2	54	387	1,915	8,026	17,666	23,245	29,078	36,419
Heart failure	65,120	19	7	12	31	111	322	1,258	3,481	7,169	16,038	36,672
Essential (primary) hypertension and hypertensive renal disease	30,770	2	1	1	23	120	409	1,513	3,137	4,357	7,216	13,991
Cerebrovascular diseases	128,978	108	38	89	153	508	1,687	5,425	11,364	18,722	36,151	54,729
Influenza and pneumonia	56,979	178	102	128	197	449	881	2,233	4,779	7,441	13,949	26,641
Influenza	3,697	20	32	61	46	77	151	250	374	401	693	1,592
Pneumonia	53,282	158	70	67	151	372	730	1,983	4,405	7,040	13,256	25,049
Chronic lower respiratory diseases[2]	149,205	24	64	155	155	291	760	4,619	15,942	35,603	49,346	42,245
Emphysema	8,284	–	–	1	–	7	34	321	1,073	2,220	2,747	1,880
Pneumonitis due to solids and liquids	18,579	16	4	12	32	85	163	589	1,253	2,274	4,933	9,218
Chronic liver disease and cirrhosis	36,427	1	2	1	1	676	2,491	8,785	11,951	7,087	4,014	1,387
Alcoholic liver disease	18,146	–	–	–	22	546	1,807	5,646	6,458	2,659	846	162
Nephritis, nephrotic syndrome, and nephrosis[2]	47,112	86	5	14	61	266	627	1,982	4,947	8,524	13,317	17,239
Renal failure	46,425	81	4	10	55	256	604	1,982	4,873	8,401	13,150	17,008
Accidents (unintentional injuries)[2]	130,557	1,156	1,316	1,521	11,619	16,209	15,354	20,357	17,057	10,967	14,438	20,537
Transport accidents	37,938	72	442	910	6,968	6,284	4,944	5,879	5,216	3,385	2,514	1,319
Motor vehicle accidents	35,369	68	425	852	6,692	5,955	4,610	5,334	4,696	3,066	2,395	1,270
Nontransport accidents	92,619	1,084	874	611	4,651	9,925	10,410	14,478	11,841	7,582	11,924	19,218
Falls	30,208	15	28	18	205	305	522	1,366	2,283	3,586	7,986	13,892
Accidental poisoning and exposure to noxious substances	38,851	6	29	30	3,293	8,251	8,374	10,651	6,388	1,238	378	208
Intentional self-harm (suicide)	41,149	–	–	395	4,878	6,348	6,551	8,621	7,135	3,794	2,300	1,121
Assault (homicide)	16,121	282	337	277	4,329	4,236	2,581	1,989	1,175	510	279	116
Assault (homicide) by discharge of firearms	11,208	12	39	142	3,704	3,372	1,843	1,158	573	223	103	31
Enterocolitis due to clostridium difficile	7,665	1	–	–	6	18	58	172	520	1,192	2,488	3,208

– Represents zero. [1] Includes persons with age not stated, not shown separately. [2] Includes other causes, not shown separately.

Source: U.S. National Center for Health Statistics, National Vital Statistics Reports (NVSR), *Deaths: Final Data for 2013*, Vol. 64, No. 2. See also <http://www.cdc.gov/nchs/deaths.htm>.

Table 132. Deaths and Death Rates by Leading Cause of Death and Age: 2011

[Rates per 100,000 population in specified group. Data are based on International Classification of Diseases, Tenth Revision (ICD-10). See Appendix III]

Age and cause of death	Number	Rate	Age and cause of death	Number	Rate
ALL AGES [1]			**20 TO 24 YEARS (Cont.)**		
All causes	**2,515,458**	**807.3**	Malignant neoplasms	972	4.4
Diseases of heart	596,577	191.5	Diseases of heart	680	3.1
Malignant neoplasms	576,691	185.1	Congenital malformations, deformations		
Chronic lower respiratory diseases	142,943	45.9	and chromosomal abnormalities	225	1.0
Cerebrovascular diseases	128,932	41.4	Influenza and pneumonia	154	0.7
Accidents (unintentional injuries)	126,438	40.6	Pregnancy, childbirth and		
Alzheimer's disease	84,974	27.3	the puerperium	137	0.6
Diabetes mellitus	73,831	23.7	Diabetes mellitus	118	0.5
Influenza and pneumonia	53,826	17.3	Human immunodeficiency virus (HIV)	117	0.5
Nephritis, nephrotic syndrome and			Cerebrovascular diseases	117	0.5
nephrosis	45,591	14.6			
Intentional self-harm (suicide)	39,518	12.7	**25 TO 34 YEARS**		
			All causes	**43,748**	**104.7**
			Accidents (unintentional injuries)	15,518	37.1
1 TO 4 YEARS			Intentional self-harm (suicide)	6,100	14.6
All causes	**4,246**	**26.3**	Assault (homicide)	4,185	10.0
Accidents (unintentional injuries)	1,377	8.5	Malignant neoplasms	3,499	8.4
Congenital malformations, deformations			Diseases of heart	3,301	7.9
and chromosomal abnormalities	493	3.0	Diabetes mellitus	686	1.6
Assault (homicide)	412	2.5	Human immunodeficiency virus (HIV)	666	1.6
Malignant neoplasms	353	2.2	Cerebrovascular diseases	530	1.3
Diseases of heart	165	1.0	Influenza and pneumonia	515	1.2
Influenza and pneumonia	112	0.7	Chronic liver disease and cirrhosis	505	1.2
Septicemia	61	0.4			
Chronic lower respiratory diseases	53	0.3	**35 TO 44 YEARS**		
In situ neoplasms, benign neoplasms			**All causes**	**69,893**	**172.0**
and neoplasms of uncertain or			Accidents (unintentional injuries)	15,230	37.5
unknown behavior	45	0.3	Malignant neoplasms	11,717	28.8
Cerebrovascular disease	42	0.3	Diseases of heart	10,635	26.2
			Intentional self-harm (suicide)	6,599	16.2
5 TO 9 YEARS			Assault (homicide)	2,519	6.2
All causes	**2,451**	**12.1**	Chronic liver disease and cirrhosis	2,449	6.0
Accidents (unintentional injuries)	761	3.7	Diabetes mellitus	1,842	4.5
Malignant neoplasms	441	2.2	Cerebrovascular diseases	1,718	4.2
Congenital malformations, deformations			Human immunodeficiency virus (HIV)	1,619	4.0
and chromosomal abnormalities	182	0.9	Influenza and pneumonia	859	2.1
Assault (homicide)	129	0.6			
Diseases of heart	92	0.5	**45 TO 54 YEARS**		
Chronic lower respiratory diseases	64	0.3	**All causes**	**183,247**	**409.8**
Influenza and pneumonia	63	0.3	Malignant neoplasms	48,897	109.3
In situ neoplasms, benign neoplasms			Diseases of heart	36,100	80.7
and neoplasms of uncertain or			Accidents (unintentional injuries)	20,749	46.4
unknown behavior	40	0.2	Chronic liver disease and cirrhosis	8,864	19.8
Cerebrovascular disease	40	0.2	Intentional self-harm (suicide)	8,858	19.8
Septicemia	38	0.2	Diabetes mellitus	6,012	13.4
			Cerebrovascular diseases	5,705	12.8
10 TO 14 YEARS			Chronic lower respiratory diseases	4,634	10.4
All causes	**2,950**	**14.2**	Human immunodeficiency virus (HIV)	2,781	6.2
Accidents (unintentional injuries)	874	4.2	Septicemia	2,461	5.5
Malignant neoplasms	419	2.0			
Intentional self-harm (suicide)	282	1.4	**55 TO 64 YEARS**		
Congenital malformations, deformations			**All causes**	**323,315**	**849.4**
and chromosomal abnormalities	176	0.9	Malignant neoplasms	112,572	295.8
Assault (homicide)	154	0.7	Diseases of heart	69,742	183.2
Diseases of heart	111	0.5	Accidents (unintentional injuries)	15,158	39.8
Chronic lower respiratory diseases	72	0.3	Chronic lower respiratory diseases	15,044	39.5
Influenza and pneumonia	55	0.3	Diabetes mellitus	12,688	33.3
Cerebrovascular diseases	47	0.2	Cerebrovascular diseases	11,205	29.4
Septicemia	31	0.1	Chronic liver disease and cirrhosis	10,749	28.2
			Intentional self-harm (suicide)	6,521	17.1
15 TO 19 YEARS			Septicemia	4,953	13.0
All causes	**10,594**	**48.9**	Nephritis, nephrotic syndrome and		
Accidents (unintentional injuries)	4,298	19.9	nephrosis	4,754	12.5
Intentional self-harm (suicide)	1,802	8.3			
Assault (homicide)	1,680	7.8			
Malignant neoplasms	639	3.0			
Diseases of heart	318	1.5	**65 YEARS AND OLDER**		
Congenital malformations, deformations			**All causes**	**1,831,822**	**4,425.3**
and chromosomal abnormalities	207	1.0	Diseases of heart	475,097	1,147.7
Cerebrovascular diseases	69	0.3	Malignant neoplasms	397,106	959.3
Chronic lower respiratory diseases	69	0.3	Chronic lower respiratory diseases	121,869	294.4
Influenza and pneumonia	66	0.3	Cerebrovascular diseases	109,323	264.1
Diabetes mellitus	49	0.2	Alzheimer's disease	84,032	203.0
			Diabetes mellitus	52,402	126.6
20 TO 24 YEARS			Influenza and pneumonia	45,386	109.6
All causes	**19,073**	**86.1**	Accidents (unintentional injuries)	43,258	104.5
Accidents (unintentional injuries)	8,032	36.3	Nephritis, nephrotic syndrome and		
Intentional self-harm (suicide)	3,020	13.6	nephrosis	37,796	91.3
Assault (homicide)	2,874	13.0	Septicemia	26,746	64.6

[1] Includes deaths under 1 year of age.

Source: U.S. National Center for Health Statistics, National Vital Statistics Reports (NVSR), *Deaths: Leading Causes for 2011*, Vol. 64, No. 7, July 2015. See also <http://www.cdc.gov/nchs/deaths.htm>.

Table 133. Age-Adjusted Death Rates for Major Causes of Death by State and Island Area: 2013

[Age-adjusted rates per 100,000 resident population as of July 1. Excludes nonresidents of the United States. Causes of death classified according to the tenth revision of International Classification of Diseases (ICD)]

State and Island Areas	All causes of death	Diseases of heart	Malig-nant neo-plasms	Cerebro-vascular diseases	Chronic lower respira-tory disease	Accidents Total	Accidents Motor vehicle acci-dents	Alz-heimer's disease	Diabetes mellitus	Influ-enza and pneu-monia	Inten-tional self-harm (suicide)
U.S. [1]	731.9	169.8	163.2	36.2	42.1	39.4	10.9	23.5	21.2	15.9	12.6
AL	925.2	228.4	182.2	48.1	54.8	47.2	18.8	26.7	24.3	19.2	14.4
AK	724.4	135.0	171.9	40.7	37.9	52.5	8.6	18.9	20.1	14.1	23.2
AZ	674.2	141.1	147.0	28.6	43.5	48.6	12.7	31.7	23.5	10.4	17.5
AR	893.8	214.1	190.0	47.6	60.1	44.8	18.3	27.2	24.2	23.2	17.3
CA	630.1	151.8	147.0	34.9	35.3	29.2	8.6	30.0	20.6	16.6	10.2
CO	655.4	125.7	139.2	32.0	45.9	46.4	9.5	27.2	15.0	12.0	18.6
CT	646.3	148.9	148.4	28.3	29.7	39.3	8.3	16.2	14.8	12.2	8.7
DE	726.8	168.0	167.6	37.0	43.5	42.9	12.0	17.6	19.4	13.6	12.5
DC	752.0	213.5	178.2	30.1	25.0	33.6	4.7	19.8	17.9	13.2	5.7
FL	663.4	149.8	155.9	30.6	39.9	39.1	12.0	16.9	19.2	9.5	13.8
GA	806.2	178.7	167.6	41.4	45.4	38.3	12.7	25.0	23.0	16.8	12.0
HI	590.8	139.0	135.5	34.8	15.6	30.1	7.8	12.6	15.5	24.1	11.8
ID	730.6	145.4	156.2	35.4	46.7	47.7	16.0	21.0	23.7	15.1	19.2
IL	724.0	170.9	171.9	36.7	39.3	33.6	8.5	19.8	19.7	16.8	9.9
IN	832.2	186.2	179.5	40.7	58.4	43.1	12.4	28.5	26.3	15.3	14.2
IA	723.7	168.8	168.4	33.9	47.8	40.0	10.7	28.2	19.0	17.8	14.4
KS	757.7	156.1	163.1	38.1	50.3	44.4	12.9	20.8	19.8	20.1	14.7
KY	899.9	203.4	199.3	41.7	64.6	55.7	15.3	31.4	24.1	19.1	15.5
LA	897.7	214.1	188.5	44.0	47.3	50.5	16.4	32.9	26.9	18.6	12.4
ME	754.2	152.3	175.2	33.4	49.1	42.6	12.0	21.6	20.4	14.0	17.4
MD	710.4	172.7	162.9	36.1	32.5	27.9	8.7	14.3	19.1	17.2	9.2
MA	663.5	141.5	159.6	27.7	31.7	32.5	5.2	19.4	14.1	18.0	8.2
MI	782.3	199.8	170.5	36.3	46.7	40.1	10.3	26.4	23.8	15.8	12.9
MN	651.0	119.6	155.4	32.0	37.1	40.1	8.3	21.5	18.8	11.6	12.1
MS	959.6	240.0	197.0	47.2	54.3	55.6	22.6	30.0	32.9	24.3	13.0
MO	807.7	194.7	179.4	40.6	52.9	47.0	12.7	27.5	20.5	18.7	15.6
MT	761.3	154.3	154.1	37.6	50.7	57.7	23.3	20.7	19.7	16.4	23.7
NE	714.7	147.9	161.3	36.4	47.7	34.9	12.5	23.6	21.7	14.5	11.6
NV	769.8	195.1	164.7	33.3	54.1	41.9	9.9	18.4	14.8	18.6	18.6
NH	679.1	148.9	158.0	27.6	42.0	42.5	10.0	21.5	18.7	13.9	12.8
NJ	676.4	170.1	156.2	32.4	31.1	31.8	6.1	16.2	19.4	12.6	8.0
NM	731.8	147.1	145.4	30.0	44.7	59.0	15.7	14.9	27.6	14.8	20.3
NY	649.3	184.8	155.8	26.3	30.7	27.7	6.3	10.4	17.8	20.5	8.1
NC	777.6	165.3	167.6	42.4	46.3	42.7	13.5	27.7	21.8	18.3	12.6
ND	709.7	150.7	151.8	32.4	38.2	41.7	17.7	36.6	22.3	14.6	17.3
OH	811.2	187.9	177.6	39.9	49.7	45.0	9.5	26.0	25.4	16.6	12.9
OK	910.1	228.5	185.7	44.5	62.4	62.7	18.7	27.6	29.9	18.0	17.2
OR	717.5	135.1	163.4	37.3	43.0	40.1	8.8	27.2	23.4	10.4	16.8
PA	761.3	179.0	170.6	37.2	39.3	44.9	10.0	17.4	22.6	16.2	13.4
RI	709.6	163.4	174.6	27.7	34.7	45.3	6.7	22.3	18.9	12.9	12.2
SC	837.8	180.0	174.0	47.6	50.8	46.6	16.2	32.4	22.5	14.2	14.0
SD	679.3	150.1	154.5	38.0	39.3	46.7	17.0	34.9	22.7	16.2	18.0
TN	881.1	204.1	185.5	44.4	53.2	52.7	15.5	36.9	24.8	22.1	15.4
TX	751.6	170.7	156.9	40.2	42.4	37.0	13.8	24.3	21.6	14.4	11.7
UT	710.4	149.0	127.6	38.2	32.0	43.4	8.6	19.4	25.3	18.6	21.4
VT	710.6	149.6	163.4	31.7	44.1	49.6	11.4	32.9	17.4	9.3	16.8
VA	724.8	157.2	162.0	38.6	37.3	34.9	9.1	19.7	18.4	17.0	12.5
WA	679.3	138.2	156.1	35.5	39.4	38.7	7.5	43.6	21.3	10.1	14.0
WV	923.8	193.7	190.8	40.7	64.5	71.7	17.5	24.6	34.1	20.2	16.4
WI	720.1	159.3	165.1	36.0	40.3	46.8	10.2	22.7	18.5	15.5	14.4
WY	731.7	152.4	148.2	35.1	63.1	55.2	15.9	21.0	14.2	18.4	21.5
PR	667.8	113.5	116.9	29.9	22.3	25.8	9.4	40.8	70.1	17.0	6.3
VI	(NA)	(NA)	(NA)	(NA)	(NA)	(NA)	(NA)	(NA)	(NA)	(NA)	(NA)
GU	767.6	270.5	141.6	64.5	28.7	28.1	(S)	(S)	29.8	(S)	15.3
AS	1,020.8	123.6	122.6	(S)	(S)	(S)	(S)	(S)	116.5	(S)	(S)
MP	779.0	182.2	144.6	(S)	(S)	(S)	(S)	(S)	(S)	(S)	(S)

NA Not available. S Figure does not meet standards of reliability or precision. [1] Does not include data for Puerto Rico, Virgin Islands, Guam, American Samoa, and Northern Marianas.

Source: U.S. National Center for Health Statistics, National Vital Statistics Reports, (NVSR), *Deaths: Final Data for 2013*, Vol. 64, No. 2. See also <http://www.cdc.gov/nchs/deaths.htm>.

Table 134. Death Rates From Heart Disease by Selected Characteristics: 1980 to 2013

[Rates per 100,000 population. Excludes deaths of nonresidents of the United States. Beginning 1999 deaths classified according to tenth revision of International Classification of Diseases; for earlier years, causes of death were classified according to the revisions then in use. Changes in classification of causes of death due to these revisions may result in discontinuities in cause-of-death trends. See Appendix III]

Characteristics	1980	1990	2000	2005	2009	2010	2011	2012	2013
All ages, age-adjusted [1]	**412.1**	**321.8**	**257.6**	**216.8**	**182.8**	**179.1**	**173.7**	**170.5**	**169.8**
All ages, crude rate	**336.0**	**289.5**	**252.6**	**220.7**	**195.4**	**193.6**	**191.5**	**191.0**	**193.3**
Under 1 year	22.8	20.1	13.0	8.9	9.6	8.3	7.7	8.5	7.8
1 to 4 years	2.6	1.9	1.2	0.9	0.9	1.0	1.0	1.0	1.1
5 to 14 years	0.9	0.9	0.7	0.6	0.5	0.5	0.5	0.4	0.4
15 to 24 years	2.9	2.5	2.6	2.6	2.4	2.4	2.3	2.2	2.1
25 to 34 years	8.3	7.6	7.4	8.3	7.8	7.8	7.9	7.6	7.6
35 to 44 years	44.6	31.4	29.2	29.2	26.7	25.8	26.2	25.9	25.6
45 to 54 years	180.2	120.5	94.2	89.7	82.3	81.6	80.7	79.7	80.3
55 to 64 years	494.1	367.3	261.2	212.8	190.0	186.6	183.2	184.6	184.6
65 to 74 years	1,218.6	894.3	665.6	512.3	422.8	409.2	399.0	388.3	390.3
75 to 84 years	2,993.1	2,295.7	1,780.3	1,458.5	1,210.8	1,172.0	1,134.7	1,103.7	1,095.1
85 years and over	7,777.1	6,739.9	5,926.1	5,188.3	4,316.9	4,285.2	4,111.6	4,046.1	4,013.9
MALE									
All ages, age-adjusted [1]	**538.9**	**412.4**	**320.0**	**268.2**	**229.4**	**225.1**	**218.1**	**214.7**	**214.5**
White	539.6	409.2	316.7	264.8	226.6	222.9	216.9	213.1	213.1
Black	561.4	485.4	392.5	338.8	289.0	280.6	266.1	265.3	262.8
American Indian, Alaska Native	320.5	264.1	222.2	191.7	162.2	158.7	153.4	152.5	152.3
Asian, Pacific Islander	286.9	220.7	185.5	149.4	130.2	127.2	115.1	116.1	118.4
Hispanic origin [2]	(NA)	270.0	238.2	210.5	169.4	165.1	152.2	151.6	151.5
Non-Hispanic, White [2]	(NA)	413.6	319.9	267.9	230.4	226.9	221.6	217.7	217.9
All ages, crude rate	**368.6**	**297.6**	**249.8**	**222.3**	**203.7**	**202.5**	**201.2**	**202.3**	**206.5**
Under 1 year	25.5	21.9	13.3	9.6	10.5	9.8	7.9	9.6	8.7
1 to 4 years	2.8	1.9	1.4	1.0	0.9	1.1	1.0	1.0	1.2
5 to 14 years	1.0	0.9	0.8	0.6	0.5	0.5	0.5	0.5	0.4
15 to 24 years	3.7	3.1	3.2	3.5	3.1	3.2	3.0	2.9	2.8
25 to 34 years	11.4	10.3	9.6	11.2	10.6	10.7	10.5	10.4	10.2
35 to 44 years	68.7	48.1	41.4	41.3	37.5	36.0	36.6	35.8	35.5
45 to 54 years	282.6	183.0	140.2	131.6	119.8	117.8	116.7	114.3	115.1
55 to 64 years	746.8	537.3	371.7	303.9	274.1	269.5	263.6	266.4	267.3
65 to 74 years	1,728.0	1,250.0	898.3	680.1	571.1	553.0	540.4	527.7	530.9
75 to 84 years	3,834.3	2,968.2	2,248.1	1,815.1	1,514.8	1,475.7	1,426.6	1,388.1	1,382.4
85 years and over	8,752.7	7,418.4	6,430.0	5,713.2	4,862.8	4,833.6	4,622.7	4,582.7	4,564.2
FEMALE									
All ages, age-adjusted [1]	**320.8**	**257.0**	**210.9**	**177.5**	**146.6**	**143.3**	**138.7**	**135.5**	**134.3**
White	315.9	250.9	205.6	173.2	143.4	140.4	136.5	133.4	132.0
Black	378.6	327.5	277.6	234.5	191.0	185.3	176.2	172.7	172.1
American Indian, Alaska Native	175.4	153.1	143.6	129.3	104.6	103.5	99.4	92.9	93.9
Asian, Pacific Islander	132.3	149.2	115.7	97.5	83.6	81.2	76.2	74.0	116.1
Hispanic origin [2]	(NA)	177.2	163.7	139.9	109.6	107.8	101.2	98.6	97.0
Non-Hispanic, White [2]	(NA)	252.6	206.8	174.8	145.4	142.5	138.8	135.8	134.6
All ages, crude rate	**305.1**	**281.8**	**255.3**	**219.0**	**187.3**	**184.9**	**182.0**	**180.2**	**180.6**
Under 1 year	20.0	18.3	12.5	8.2	8.8	6.8	7.5	7.3	6.9
1 to 4 years	2.5	1.9	1.0	0.9	1.0	0.9	1.0	0.9	0.9
5 to 14 years	0.9	0.8	0.5	0.6	0.5	0.4	0.5	0.4	0.4
15 to 24 years	2.1	1.8	2.1	1.7	1.6	1.5	1.5	1.5	1.5
25 to 34 years	5.3	5.0	5.2	5.3	5.0	4.9	5.3	4.8	4.9
35 to 44 years	21.4	15.1	17.2	17.2	16.0	15.6	15.9	16.0	15.7
45 to 54 years	84.5	61.0	49.8	49.1	46.0	46.5	45.9	46.0	46.6
55 to 64 years	272.1	215.7	159.3	128.0	111.6	109.3	108.4	108.4	107.5
65 to 74 years	828.6	616.8	474.0	369.5	294.2	284.2	275.7	266.2	266.8
75 to 84 years	2,497.0	1,893.8	1,475.1	1,213.8	993.3	952.7	920.7	893.0	879.8
85 years and over	7,350.5	6,478.1	5,720.9	4,955.1	4,056.0	4,020.3	3,859.7	3,777.5	3,732.9

NA Not available. [1] Age-adjusted death rates were prepared using the direct method, in which age-specific death rates for a population of interest are applied to a standard population distributed by age. Age adjustment eliminates the differences in observed rates between points in time or among compared population groups that result from age differences in population composition. [2] Persons of Hispanic origin may be of any race. Prior to 1997 excludes data from States lacking a Hispanic-origin item on their death certificates. See text, this section.

Source: U.S. National Center for Health Statistics, *Health, United States*, annual; *Deaths: Final Data 2013*, Vol. 64, No. 2; and CDC WONDER Online database, "Multiple Cause of Death, 1999-2013," <http://wonder.cdc.gov/>, accessed January 2015.

Table 135. Death Rates From Cerebrovascular Diseases by Sex and Age: 1990 to 2013

[Rates per 100,000 population. Excludes deaths of nonresidents of the United States. Beginning 1999, deaths classified according to tenth revision of International Classification of Diseases (ICD); for earlier years, causes of death were classified according to the revisions then in use. Changes in classification of causes of death due to these revisions may result in discontinuities in cause-of-death trends. For explanation of age adjustment, see text, this section. See Appendix III]

Characteristics	Total				Male				Female			
	1990	2000	2010	2013	1990	2000	2010	2013	1990	2000	2010	2013
All ages, age-adjusted [1]	65.3	60.9	39.1	36.2	68.5	62.4	39.3	36.7	62.6	59.1	38.3	35.2
All ages, crude rate	57.8	59.6	41.9	40.8	46.7	46.9	34.5	34.5	68.4	71.8	49.1	46.9
Under 1 year	3.8	3.3	3.3	2.7	4.4	3.8	3.2	3.0	3.1	2.7	3.4	2.5
1 to 4 years	0.3	0.3	0.3	0.2	0.3	(B)	0.3	0.3	0.3	0.4	0.3	(B)
5 to 14 years	0.2	0.2	0.2	0.2	0.2	0.2	0.3	0.2	0.2	0.2	0.2	0.2
15 to 24 years	0.6	0.5	0.4	0.3	0.7	0.5	0.5	0.4	0.6	0.5	0.4	0.3
25 to 34 years	2.2	1.5	1.3	1.2	2.1	1.5	1.3	1.3	2.2	1.5	1.2	1.1
35 to 44 years	6.4	5.8	4.6	4.2	6.8	5.8	5.0	4.7	6.1	5.7	4.2	3.7
45 to 54 years	18.7	16.0	13.1	12.4	20.5	17.5	14.9	14.2	17.0	14.5	11.4	10.6
55 to 64 years	47.9	41.0	29.3	28.9	54.3	47.2	34.7	35.1	42.2	35.3	24.3	23.1
65 to 74 years	144.2	128.6	81.7	74.2	166.6	145.0	92.0	85.0	126.7	115.1	72.8	64.8
75 to 84 years	498.0	461.3	288.3	268.9	551.1	490.8	295.2	277.9	466.2	442.1	283.4	262.1
85 years and over	1,628.9	1,589.2	993.8	906.0	1,528.5	1,484.3	892.0	808.4	1,667.6	1,632.0	1,043.0	955.8

B Figure too small to meet statistical standards for reliability. [1] See footnote 1, Table 134.

Source: U.S. National Center for Health Statistics, *Health, United States*, annual; *Deaths: Final Data 2013*, Vol. 64, No. 2; and CDC WONDER Online database, "Multiple Cause of Death, 1999-2013," <http://wonder.cdc.gov/>, accessed January 2015.

Table 136. Death Rates From All and Selected Types of Malignant Neoplasms (Cancer) by Age: 1990 to 2013

[Rates per 100,000 population. Excludes deaths of nonresidents of the United States. Beginning 1999, deaths classified according to tenth revision of International Classification of Diseases (ICD); for earlier years, causes of death were classified according to the revisions then in use. Changes in classification of causes of death due to these revisions may result in discontinuities in cause-of-death trends. For explanation of age adjustment, see text, this section. See Appendix III]

Characteristic	1990	2000	2005	2010	2011	2012	2013
All ages, age-adjusted [1]	216.0	199.6	185.1	172.8	169.0	166.5	163.2
All ages, crude rate	203.2	196.5	189.3	186.2	185.1	185.6	185.0
Under 1 year	2.3	2.4	1.9	1.6	1.8	1.6	1.6
1 to 4 years	3.5	2.7	2.4	2.1	2.2	2.4	2.1
5 to 14 years	3.1	2.5	2.5	2.2	2.1	2.2	2.2
15 to 24 years	4.9	4.4	4.0	3.7	3.7	3.6	3.4
25 to 34 years	12.6	9.8	9.2	8.8	8.4	8.7	8.6
35 to 44 years	43.3	36.6	33.5	28.8	28.8	28.0	28.1
45 to 54 years	158.9	127.5	118.6	111.6	109.3	108.5	105.5
55 to 64 years	449.6	366.7	323.9	300.1	295.8	293.2	288.2
65 to 74 years	872.3	816.3	733.2	666.1	647.6	632.2	616.9
75 to 84 years	1,348.5	1,335.6	1,272.8	1,202.2	1,179.1	1,161.7	1,139.4
85 years old and over	1,752.9	1,819.4	1,778.2	1,729.5	1,676.2	1,658.9	1,635.4
DEATH RATES FOR MALIGNANT NEOPLASM OF BREASTS FOR FEMALES							
All ages, age-adjusted [1]	33.3	26.8	24.2	22.1	21.6	21.3	20.8
All ages, crude rate	34.0	29.2	27.4	26.1	25.9	25.8	25.5
Under 25 years	(B)	(B)	(B)	(B)	(B)	(B)	(B)
25 to 34 years	2.9	2.3	1.8	1.6	1.7	1.7	1.6
35 to 44 years	17.8	12.4	11.4	9.8	9.9	9.7	9.6
45 to 54 years	45.4	33.0	28.7	25.7	25.2	25.2	24.6
55 to 64 years	78.6	59.3	54.0	47.7	46.2	45.4	44.1
65 to 74 years	111.7	88.3	78.5	73.9	72.5	70.0	68.4
75 to 84 years	146.3	128.9	119.6	109.1	108.2	106.9	104.4
85 years old and over	196.8	205.7	191.2	185.8	176.5	177.3	173.0
DEATH RATES FOR MALIGNANT NEOPLASM OF TRACHEA, BRONCHUS, AND LUNG							
All ages, age-adjusted [1]	59.3	56.1	52.7	47.6	46.0	44.9	43.4
All ages, crude rate	56.8	55.3	53.9	51.3	50.4	50.2	49.4
Under 25 years	(Z)	(Z)	(Z)	(Z)	(Z)	(Z)	(Z)
25 to 34 years	0.7	0.5	0.3	0.4	0.3	0.4	0.3
35 to 44 years	6.8	6.1	5.3	3.3	3.1	2.9	2.8
45 to 54 years	46.8	31.6	29.7	26.9	25.7	25.1	23.9
55 to 64 years	160.6	122.4	102.4	85.4	83.5	81.5	79.9
65 to 74 years	288.4	284.2	256.3	223.9	214.3	206.1	196.6
75 to 84 years	333.3	370.8	375.0	357.2	345.9	339.6	328.5
85 years old and over	242.5	302.1	328.2	332.4	323.7	323.7	320.0

B Base figure too small to meet statistical standards for reliability of a derived figure. Z Less than 0.05. [1] Age-adjusted death rates were prepared using the direct method, in which age specific death rates for a population of interest are applied to a standard population distributed by age. Age adjustment eliminates the differences in observed rates between points in time or among compared population groups that result from age differences in population composition.

Source: U.S. National Center for Health Statistics, *Health, United States*, annual; *Deaths: Final Data 2013*, Vol. 64, No. 2; and CDC WONDER Online database, "Multiple Cause of Death, 1999-2013," <http://wonder.cdc.gov/>, accessed January 2015.

Table 137. Death Rates From Suicide by Selected Characteristics: 1990 to 2013

[Rates per 100,000 population. Excludes deaths of nonresidents of the United States. Beginning 2000, deaths classified according to the tenth revision of International Classification of Diseases. See Appendix III]

Characteristic	1990	2000	2005	2010	2011	2012	2013
All ages, age-adjusted [1]	**12.5**	**10.4**	**10.9**	**12.1**	**12.3**	**12.6**	**12.6**
All ages, crude rate	**12.4**	**10.4**	**11.0**	**12.4**	**12.7**	**12.9**	**13.0**
5 to 14 years	0.8	0.7	0.7	0.7	0.7	0.8	1.0
15 to 24 years	13.2	10.2	9.9	10.5	11.0	11.1	11.1
25 to 34 years	15.2	12.0	12.7	14.0	14.6	14.7	14.8
35 to 44 years	15.3	14.5	15.1	16.0	16.2	16.7	16.2
45 to 54 years	14.8	14.4	16.5	19.6	19.8	20.0	19.7
55 to 64 years	16.0	12.1	13.7	17.5	17.1	18.0	18.1
65 to 74 years	17.9	12.5	12.4	13.7	14.1	14.0	15.0
75 to 84 years	24.9	17.6	16.8	15.7	16.5	16.8	17.1
85 years and over	22.2	19.6	18.3	17.6	16.9	17.8	18.6
AGE-ADJUSTED RATES							
Male	21.5	17.7	18.1	19.8	20.0	20.4	20.3
Female	4.8	4.0	4.4	5.0	5.2	5.4	5.5
White male	22.8	19.1	19.8	22.0	22.3	22.6	22.6
Black male	12.8	10.0	9.2	9.1	9.3	9.6	9.3
American Indian, Alaska Native male	20.1	16.1	17.3	15.5	16.4	17.4	18.1
Asian, Pacific Islander male	9.6	8.6	7.3	9.5	8.7	9.4	9.1
Hispanic male [2]	13.7	10.3	9.6	9.9	9.4	9.5	9.3
Non-Hispanic, White male [2]	23.5	20.2	21.4	24.2	24.8	25.2	25.3
White female	5.2	4.3	4.9	5.6	5.9	6.1	6.3
Black female	2.4	1.8	1.8	1.8	1.9	2.0	2.0
American Indian, Alaska Native female	3.6	3.8	4.2	6.1	5.0	4.3	5.3
Asian, Pacific Islander female	4.1	2.8	3.2	3.4	3.4	3.6	3.0
Hispanic female [2]	2.3	1.7	1.8	2.1	2.0	2.2	2.3
Non-Hispanic, White female [2]	5.4	4.7	5.3	6.2	6.7	6.9	7.1

[1] Age-adjusted death rates were prepared using the direct method, in which age-specific death rates for a population of interest are applied to a standard population distributed by age. Age adjustment eliminates the differences in observed rates between points in time or among compared population groups that result from age differences in population composition. [2] Persons of Hispanic origin may be of any race. Excludes data from states lacking a Hispanic-origin item on their death certificates.

Source: U.S. National Center for Health Statistics, *Health, United States*, annual; *Deaths: Final Data for 2013*, Vol. 64, No. 2; and CDC WONDER Online database, "Multiple Cause of Death, 1999-2013," <http://wonder.cdc.gov/>, accessed January 2015.

Table 138. Death Rates From Human Immunodeficiency Virus (HIV/AIDS) Disease by Sex, Age, and Race/Ethnicity: 1990 to 2013

[Rates per 100,000 population. Excludes deaths of nonresidents of the United States. Beginning 2000, deaths classified according to tenth revision of International Classification of Diseases. See Appendix III]

Characteristic	1990	1995	2000	2005	2010	2012	2013
All ages, age-adjusted [1]	**10.2**	**16.2**	**5.2**	**4.2**	**2.6**	**2.2**	**2.1**
All ages, crude	**10.1**	**16.2**	**5.1**	**4.2**	**2.7**	**2.3**	**2.2**
Under 1 year	2.7	1.5	(B)	(B)	(B)	(B)	(B)
1 to 4 years	0.8	1.3	(B)	(B)	(B)	(B)	(B)
5 to 14 years	0.2	0.5	0.1	(B)	(B)	(B)	(B)
15 to 24 years	1.5	1.7	0.5	0.4	0.3	0.3	0.2
25 to 34 years	19.7	28.3	6.1	3.4	1.8	1.5	1.5
35 to 44 years	27.4	44.2	13.1	10.0	4.6	3.3	3.1
45 to 54 years	15.2	26.0	11.0	10.6	6.9	5.8	5.4
55 to 64 years	6.2	10.9	5.1	5.3	5.0	4.6	4.6
65 to 74 years	2.0	3.6	2.2	2.3	2.2	2.3	2.3
75 to 84 years	0.7	0.7	0.7	0.8	0.9	1.0	1.2
85 years and over	(B)	(B)	(B)	(B)	0.4	0.4	(B)
AGE-ADJUSTED RATES							
Male	18.5	27.3	7.9	6.3	3.8	3.2	3.1
Female	2.2	5.3	2.5	2.3	1.4	1.2	1.1
White male	15.7	20.4	4.6	3.7	2.3	2.0	1.9
Black male	46.3	89.0	35.1	27.7	16.5	13.3	12.7
American Indian, Alaska Native male	3.3	10.5	3.5	3.7	2.6	1.5	2.1
Asian, Pacific Islander male	4.3	6.0	1.2	1.0	0.7	0.6	0.7
Hispanic male [2]	28.8	40.8	10.6	7.7	4.6	3.5	3.4
Non-Hispanic, White male [2]	14.1	17.9	3.8	3.0	1.8	1.7	1.6
White female	1.1	2.5	1.0	0.8	0.5	0.4	0.4
Black female	10.1	24.4	13.2	11.9	7.5	6.3	5.7
American Indian, Alaska Native female	(B)	2.5	1.0	1.3	(B)	(B)	(B)
Asian, Pacific Islander female	(B)	0.6	0.2	(B)	(B)	(B)	(B)
Hispanic female [2]	3.8	8.8	2.9	1.9	1.1	1.0	0.9
Non-Hispanic, White female [2]	0.7	1.7	0.7	0.6	0.4	0.3	0.3

B Base figure too small to meet statistical standards. [1] Age-adjusted death rates were prepared using the direct method, in which age-specific death rates for a population of interest are applied to a standard population distributed by age. Age adjustment eliminates the differences in observed rates between points in time or among compared population groups that result from age differences in population composition. [2] Persons of Hispanic origin may be of any race. Excludes data from states lacking a Hispanic-origin item on their death certificates.

Source: U.S. National Center for Health Statistics, *Health, United States*, annual; *Deaths: Final Data 2013*, Vol. 64, No. 2; and CDC WONDER Online database, "Multiple Cause of Death 1999-2013," <http://wonder.cdc.gov/>, accessed January 2015.

Table 139. Suicide Deaths by Age, Sex, and Method: 2009 to 2011

[Data are 2009 to 2011 annual averages. Deaths based on tenth revision of International Classification of Diseases (ICD)]

Method	Total	5-14 years [1]	15-17 years	18-24 years	25-44 years	45-64 years	65-74 years	75-84 years	85+ years
Total [2]	38,264	275	790	3,808	12,334	14,989	3,023	2,096	938
MEN									
Total [2]	30,123	188	594	3,181	9,672	11,394	2,455	1,815	815
Knife or other sharp object	556	0	2	28	163	291	35	20	17
Drowning	245	0	4	27	84	89	19	12	9
Jumping from a high place or other fall	556	2	10	83	212	181	37	17	14
Fire/hot object or substance	107	0	2	12	36	46	7	3	1
Firearm	16,863	68	281	1,578	4,639	6,297	1,865	1,496	637
Poisoning	3,487	4	19	201	1,142	1,765	205	99	50
Hanging, suffocation, strangulation	7,607	113	253	1,148	3,152	2,469	244	147	78
WOMEN									
Total [2]	8,141	88	196	626	2,662	3,595	568	281	123
Knife or other sharp object	111	0	0	4	30	58	12	5	2
Drowning	139	0	1	10	38	60	14	8	7
Jumping from a high place or other fall	202	1	2	20	59	86	15	11	7
Fire/hot object or substance	43	0	0	3	12	23	4	1	0
Firearm	2,509	11	48	165	807	1,125	218	103	31
Poisoning	3,034	6	20	116	951	1,584	213	102	43
Hanging, suffocation, strangulation	1,862	68	117	284	679	556	79	47	32

[1] It is generally accepted that children under 5 years of age cannot commit suicide. [2] May include other methods not shown separately.

Source: U.S. Centers for Disease Control and Prevention, National Center for Health Statistics, "Health Data Interactive," <http://www.cdc.gov/nchs/hdi.htm>, accessed February 2015.

Table 140. Firearm Deaths and Death Rates by Sex and Race/Ethnicity: 2009 to 2013

[Rates are on an annual basis per 100,000 population and are based on populations enumerated as of April 1 for Census years and as of July 1 for all other years. Deaths are those attributable to injury by firearms, see source for details]

Sex and race/ethnicity	Number of deaths					Death rates per 100,000 population				
	2009	2010	2011	2012	2013	2009	2010	2011	2012	2013
Total	31,347	31,672	32,351	33,563	33,636	10.2	10.3	10.4	10.7	10.6
By Sex:										
Male	26,921	27,356	27,738	28,838	28,794	17.9	18.0	18.1	18.7	18.5
Female	4,426	4,316	4,613	4,725	4,842	2.8	2.7	2.9	3.0	3.0
By race/ethnicity:										
White	23,163	23,490	24,092	24,727	25,044	9.5	9.6	9.8	10.0	10.0
Male	19,623	20,014	20,363	20,955	21,116	16.2	16.5	16.6	17.0	17.1
Female	3,540	3,476	3,729	3,772	3,928	2.9	2.8	3.0	3.0	3.1
Black	7,455	7,454	7,525	8,021	7,797	17.9	17.7	17.6	18.6	17.8
Male	6,700	6,721	6,775	7,191	7,016	33.7	33.4	33.2	34.8	33.5
Female	755	733	750	830	781	3.5	3.3	3.4	3.7	3.4
American Indian or Alaska Native	291	317	305	337	326	7.0	7.4	7.0	7.7	7.3
Male	241	267	255	297	281	11.6	12.5	11.7	13.4	12.5
Female	50	50	50	40	45	2.4	2.4	2.3	1.8	2.0
Asian or Pacific Islander	438	411	429	478	469	2.6	2.4	2.5	2.6	2.5
Male	357	354	345	395	381	4.5	4.4	4.1	4.6	4.3
Female	81	57	84	83	88	0.9	0.6	0.9	0.9	0.9
Hispanic [1]	3,202	3,008	2,947	3,061	2,951	6.5	6.0	5.7	5.8	5.5
Male	2,867	2,694	2,608	2,724	2,595	11.4	10.5	9.9	10.1	9.4
Female	335	314	339	337	356	1.4	1.3	1.3	1.3	1.3

[1] Persons of Hispanic origin may be of any race. Data for Hispanic persons are not tabulated separately by race.

Source: U.S. National Center for Health Statistics, National Vital Statistics Reports (NVSR), *Deaths: Final Data for 2010*, Vol. 61, No 4., May 2013; and CDC WONDER Online database, "Multiple Cause of Death 1999-2013," <http://wonder.cdc.gov/>, accessed January 2015. See also <http://www.cdc.gov/nchs/deaths.htm>.

Table 141. Drug Overdoses/Poisoning Deaths Involving Opioid Analgesics and Heroin: 2000 to 2013

[Rates are age-adjusted and per 100,000 population. Deaths are classified using the tenth revision of the International Classification of Diseases (ICD-10)]

Year	Total [1]		Opioid analgesics		Heroin	
	Number	Rate	Number	Rate	Number	Rate
2000	17,415	6.2	4,400	1.5	1,842	0.7
2005	29,813	10.1	10,928	3.7	2,009	0.7
2007	36,010	11.9	14,408	4.8	2,399	0.8
2008	36,450	11.9	14,800	4.8	3,041	1.0
2009	37,004	11.9	15,597	5.0	3,278	1.1
2010	38,329	12.3	16,651	5.4	3,036	1.0
2011	41,340	13.2	16,917	5.4	4,397	1.4
2012	41,502	13.1	16,007	5.1	5,925	1.9
2013	43,982	13.8	16,235	5.1	8,257	2.7

[1] Includes other types of drugs not shown separately.

Source: U.S. National Center for Health Statistics, *Trends in Drug-poisoning Deaths Involving Opioid Analgesics and Heroin: United States, 1999-2012*, December 2014, and *Drug-poisoning Deaths Involving Heroin: United States, 2000-2013*, NCHS Data Brief, No. 190, March 2015. See also <http://www.cdc.gov/nchs/deaths.htm>.

Table 142. People Who Got Married and Divorced in the Past 12 Months by State: 2013

[For 12-month period prior to interview date, which occurred for each month in calendar year. For example, a person interviewed in January 2013 could report they got married between January 2012 and January 2013. Data shown for persons 15 years old and over. Vital event is counted in state in which respondent lived at the time of survey. Based on 2013 American Community Survey (ACS). The ACS universe includes the household population and the group quarters population. Based on a sample and subject to sampling variability. See Appendix III]

State	People who got married in the past 12 months				People who got divorced in the past 12 months			
	Males	Marriage rate per 1,000 men	Females	Marriage rate per 1,000 women	Males	Divorce rate per 1,000 men	Females	Divorce rate per 1,000 women
United States	**2,215,659**	**17.8**	**2,155,669**	**16.5**	**1,071,278**	**8.6**	**1,197,095**	**9.2**
Alabama	36,015	19.3	34,208	16.8	23,479	12.6	24,495	12.0
Alaska	6,905	22.7	5,281	19.4	2,601	8.5	2,551	9.4
Arizona	44,342	17.0	43,760	16.4	22,794	8.7	24,471	9.2
Arkansas	26,560	23.1	25,322	20.9	14,087	12.2	15,805	13.0
California	264,847	17.4	252,574	16.2	109,549	7.2	127,033	8.2
Colorado	46,168	21.9	46,448	22.0	24,563	11.6	22,167	10.5
Connecticut	20,966	14.7	22,101	14.5	10,184	7.1	10,622	6.9
Delaware	7,320	20.3	6,727	17.1	2,876	8.0	2,372	6.0
District of Columbia	6,237	24.2	5,400	18.5	2,712	10.5	2,456	8.4
Florida	122,919	15.6	118,838	14.2	69,845	8.9	83,683	10.0
Georgia	73,141	19.2	70,587	17.2	36,063	9.4	43,504	10.6
Hawaii	12,460	21.6	11,480	20.2	5,216	9.0	3,618	6.4
Idaho	13,325	21.3	12,273	19.5	6,234	9.9	7,531	12.0
Illinois	81,121	16.1	79,330	14.9	34,897	6.9	37,090	7.0
Indiana	49,063	19.2	49,320	18.3	26,618	10.4	29,166	10.8
Iowa	19,917	16.3	21,268	16.7	10,838	8.9	11,239	8.8
Kansas	24,775	21.9	23,211	20.0	11,284	10.0	12,598	10.9
Kentucky	34,218	19.8	34,319	18.9	21,426	12.4	22,783	12.5
Louisiana	30,310	17.0	27,758	14.6	15,672	8.8	21,410	11.2
Maine	8,981	16.6	9,845	17.1	5,845	10.8	5,720	9.9
Maryland	39,592	17.2	38,574	15.4	19,721	8.6	22,436	8.9
Massachusetts	38,079	14.3	40,876	14.1	17,473	6.6	20,733	7.2
Michigan	60,653	15.5	59,540	14.4	34,039	8.7	38,096	9.2
Minnesota	38,368	17.9	38,370	17.4	13,562	6.3	16,101	7.3
Mississippi	22,616	19.8	22,331	18.1	10,274	9.0	14,597	11.8
Missouri	43,129	18.2	43,716	17.4	21,797	9.2	25,392	10.1
Montana	7,620	18.5	7,581	18.2	4,190	10.1	4,247	10.2
Nebraska	15,110	20.7	13,740	18.3	7,406	10.2	7,146	9.5
Nevada	19,913	17.7	20,913	18.7	14,669	13.1	10,890	9.7
New Hampshire	8,371	15.5	8,510	15.1	4,819	8.9	5,685	10.1
New Jersey	51,996	14.9	49,760	13.3	22,932	6.6	25,951	6.9
New Mexico	15,842	19.4	15,111	17.9	6,096	7.5	9,120	10.8
New York	115,691	14.9	113,270	13.5	49,873	6.4	56,386	6.7
North Carolina	74,206	19.4	70,030	17.0	33,929	8.9	38,538	9.4
North Dakota	7,565	25.3	6,961	24.2	1,942	6.5	2,271	7.9
Ohio	72,424	16.0	74,772	15.4	37,661	8.3	43,443	9.0
Oklahoma	34,913	23.3	33,805	21.7	17,856	11.9	20,233	13.0
Oregon	26,694	16.9	26,355	16.1	14,367	9.1	17,952	11.0
Pennsylvania	81,944	16.1	78,619	14.5	37,547	7.4	38,225	7.0
Rhode Island	6,365	15.1	6,135	13.5	3,854	9.1	2,342	5.2
South Carolina	32,491	17.4	32,379	16.1	14,329	7.7	18,963	9.4
South Dakota	7,788	23.4	7,782	23.2	2,743	8.2	2,979	8.9
Tennessee	47,847	18.9	48,203	17.7	27,394	10.8	29,893	11.0
Texas	213,461	21.1	200,003	19.2	99,800	9.9	109,497	10.5
Utah	27,465	25.7	27,153	25.3	11,883	11.1	9,507	8.9
Vermont	4,706	18.3	4,345	16.1	1,767	6.9	1,898	7.0
Virginia	64,523	19.7	59,531	17.3	29,717	9.1	29,696	8.6
Washington	55,996	20.0	55,998	19.7	23,316	8.3	34,027	12.0
West Virginia	12,608	16.7	12,123	15.5	7,406	9.8	9,112	11.6
Wisconsin	33,951	14.8	34,680	14.7	19,593	8.5	18,961	8.0
Wyoming	4,142	17.6	4,449	19.4	2,540	10.8	2,464	10.8

Source: U.S. Census Bureau, 2013 American Community Survey, B12501, "Marriage in the Last Year by Sex by Marital Status for the Population 15 Years and Over," and B12503, "Divorces in the Last Year by Sex by Marital Status for the Population 15 Years and Over;" <http://factfinder2.census.gov>, accessed December 2014.

Table 143. Marriage and Divorce Rates by State: 1990 to 2012

[Rate per 1,000 population residing in area]

State	Marriage rates [1]						Divorce rates [1,2]					
	1990	2000	2005	2010	2011	2012	1990	2000	2005	2010	2011	2012
United States [3].......	**9.8**	**8.2**	**7.6**	**6.8**	**6.8**	**6.8**	**4.7**	**4.0**	**3.6**	**3.6**	**3.6**	**3.4**
Alabama.................	10.6	10.1	9.2	8.2	8.4	8.2	6.1	5.5	4.9	4.4	4.3	3.6
Alaska..................	10.2	8.9	8.2	8.0	7.8	7.2	5.5	3.9	4.3	4.7	4.8	4.5
Arizona.................	10.0	7.5	6.6	5.9	5.7	5.6	6.9	4.6	4.2	3.5	3.9	4.3
Arkansas [4]............	15.3	15.4	12.9	10.8	10.4	10.9	6.9	6.4	6.0	5.7	5.3	5.3
California [4].............	7.9	5.8	6.4	5.8	5.8	6.0	4.3	(NA)	(NA)	(NA)	(NA)	(NA)
Colorado................	9.8	8.3	7.6	6.9	7.0	6.8	5.5	4.7	4.4	4.3	4.4	4.3
Connecticut.............	7.9	5.7	5.8	5.6	5.5	5.2	3.2	3.3	3.0	2.9	3.1	2.7
Delaware................	8.4	6.5	5.9	5.2	5.2	5.8	4.4	3.9	3.8	3.5	3.6	3.5
District of Columbia......	8.2	4.9	4.1	7.6	8.7	8.4	4.5	3.2	2.0	2.8	2.9	2.9
Florida..................	10.9	8.9	8.9	7.3	7.4	7.2	6.3	5.1	4.6	4.4	4.5	4.2
Georgia.................	10.3	6.8	7.0	7.3	6.6	6.5	5.5	3.3	(NA)	(NA)	(NA)	(NA)
Hawaii..................	16.4	20.6	22.6	17.6	17.6	17.5	4.6	3.9	(NA)	(NA)	(NA)	(NA)
Idaho...................	13.9	10.8	10.5	8.8	8.6	8.2	6.5	5.5	5.0	5.2	4.9	4.7
Illinois..................	8.8	6.9	5.9	5.7	5.6	5.8	3.8	3.2	2.6	2.6	2.6	2.4
Indiana.................	9.6	7.9	6.9	6.3	6.8	6.7	(NA)	(NA)	(NA)	(NA)	(NA)	(NA)
Iowa....................	9.0	6.9	6.9	6.9	6.7	6.8	3.9	3.3	2.7	2.4	2.4	2.2
Kansas.................	9.2	8.3	6.8	6.4	6.3	6.3	5.0	3.6	3.1	3.7	3.9	3.4
Kentucky...............	13.5	9.8	8.7	7.4	7.5	7.2	5.8	5.1	4.6	4.5	4.4	4.1
Louisiana...............	9.6	9.1	8.0	6.9	6.4	5.7	(NA)	(NA)	(NA)	(NA)	(NA)	(NA)
Maine...................	9.7	8.8	8.2	7.1	7.2	7.3	4.3	5.0	4.1	4.2	4.2	3.9
Maryland................	9.7	7.5	6.9	5.7	5.8	5.6	3.4	3.3	3.1	2.8	2.9	2.8
Massachusetts...........	7.9	5.8	6.2	5.6	5.5	5.5	2.8	2.5	2.2	2.5	2.7	2.7
Michigan................	8.2	6.7	6.1	5.5	5.7	5.6	4.3	3.9	3.4	3.5	3.4	3.3
Minnesota..............	7.7	6.8	6.0	5.3	5.6	5.6	3.5	3.2	(NA)	(NA)	(NA)	(NA)
Mississippi..............	9.4	6.9	5.8	4.9	4.9	5.8	5.5	5.0	4.4	4.3	4.0	4.0
Missouri................	9.6	7.8	7.0	6.5	6.6	6.5	5.1	4.5	3.6	3.9	3.9	3.7
Montana................	8.6	7.3	7.4	7.4	7.8	7.8	5.1	4.2	4.5	3.9	4.0	3.9
Nebraska...............	8.0	7.6	7.0	6.6	6.6	6.7	4.0	3.7	3.3	3.6	3.5	3.4
Nevada.................	99.0	72.2	57.4	38.3	36.9	35.1	11.4	9.9	7.4	5.9	5.6	5.5
New Hampshire..........	9.5	9.4	7.3	7.3	7.1	6.8	4.7	4.8	3.9	3.8	3.8	3.6
New Jersey.............	7.6	6.0	5.7	5.1	4.8	4.9	3.0	3.0	2.9	3.0	2.9	2.8
New Mexico.............	8.8	8.0	6.6	7.7	8.0	6.9	4.9	5.1	4.6	4.0	3.3	3.0
New York...............	8.6	7.1	6.8	6.5	6.9	7.0	3.2	3.0	2.9	2.9	2.9	2.9
North Carolina...........	7.8	8.2	7.3	6.6	6.7	6.6	5.1	4.5	4.1	3.8	3.7	3.7
North Dakota...........	7.5	7.2	6.8	6.5	6.7	6.6	3.6	3.4	2.9	3.1	2.7	3.1
Ohio....................	9.0	7.8	6.5	5.8	5.9	5.8	4.7	4.2	3.5	3.4	3.4	3.4
Oklahoma...............	10.6	(NA)	7.3	7.2	6.9	6.9	7.7	(NA)	5.6	5.2	5.2	4.8
Oregon.................	8.9	7.6	7.3	6.5	6.6	6.6	5.5	4.8	4.2	4.0	3.8	3.8
Pennsylvania............	7.1	6.0	5.8	5.3	5.3	5.5	3.3	3.1	2.3	2.7	2.8	2.8
Rhode Island............	8.1	7.6	7.0	5.8	6.0	6.1	3.7	2.9	3.0	3.2	3.2	3.2
South Carolina..........	15.9	10.6	8.3	7.4	7.2	7.4	4.5	3.8	2.9	3.1	3.2	3.2
South Dakota...........	11.1	9.4	8.4	7.3	7.5	7.5	3.7	3.5	2.8	3.4	3.3	3.0
Tennessee..............	13.9	15.5	10.9	8.8	9.0	8.8	6.5	5.9	4.6	4.2	4.3	4.2
Texas..................	10.5	9.4	7.8	7.1	7.1	7.3	5.5	4.0	3.3	3.3	3.2	3.0
Utah...................	11.2	10.8	9.8	8.5	8.6	8.4	5.1	4.3	4.1	3.7	3.7	3.3
Vermont................	10.9	10.0	8.9	9.3	8.3	8.2	4.5	4.1	3.6	3.8	3.6	3.5
Virginia.................	11.4	8.8	8.2	6.8	6.8	6.8	4.4	4.3	4.0	3.8	3.8	3.7
Washington.............	9.5	6.9	6.5	6.0	6.1	6.3	5.9	4.6	4.3	4.2	4.1	3.9
West Virginia...........	7.2	8.7	7.4	6.7	7.2	7.0	5.3	5.1	5.1	5.1	5.2	4.7
Wisconsin...............	7.9	6.7	6.1	5.3	5.3	5.4	3.6	3.2	2.9	3.0	2.9	2.9
Wyoming................	10.7	10.0	9.3	7.6	7.8	7.6	6.6	5.8	5.2	5.1	4.8	4.4

NA Not available. [1] Based on provisional counts of marriages or divorces by State of occurrence. [2] Includes annulments. Includes divorce petitions filed or legal separations for some counties or States. [3] Beginning 2000, divorce rates based solely on the combined counts and populations for reporting States and the District of Columbia. [4] Marriage data includes nonlicensed marriages registered.

Source: U.S. National Center for Health Statistics, National Vital Statistics System, "Marriages and Divorces, Detailed State Tables," <http://www.cdc.gov/nchs/mardiv.htm>, accessed February 2015.

Table 144. People Who Got Married or Divorced in the Past 12 Months by Selected Characteristics: 2013

[In thousands (255,017 represents 255,017,000), unless otherwise noted. For 12-month period prior to interview date, which occurred for each month in calendar year. For example, a person interviewed in January 2013 could report they got married between January 2012 and January 2013. Persons 15 years and over. Based on 2013 American Community Survey (ACS). The ACS universe includes the household population and the group quarters population. Based on a sample and subject to sampling variability. See Appendix III]

Characteristic	Total population	Married in the past 12 months		Divorced in the past 12 months	
		Males	Females	Males	Females
Population 15 years old and over...............	**255,017**	**2,216**	**2,156**	**1,071**	**1,197**
AGE					
Median age.........	45.0	31.9	30.0	44.1	42.3
EDUCATIONAL ATTAINMENT					
Population 18 years and over.........	242,542	2,192	2,129	1,069	1,195
Bachelor's degree or higher (percent).........	27.0	30.4	36.1	23.4	26.7
LABOR FORCE PARTICIPATION					
Population 16 years and over.........	250,836	2,202	2,143	1,071	1,197
In labor force (percent).........	63.6	88.4	76.3	80.2	78.2
Not in labor force (percent).........	36.4	11.6	23.7	19.8	21.8
POVERTY STATUS IN PAST 12 MONTHS					
Population for whom poverty status is determined.........	248,162	2,176	2,148	1,038	1,190
Below poverty (percent).........	14.2	9.4	11.3	12.3	22.9
PRESENCE OF OWN CHILD UNDER 18 YEARS					
Population in households.........	247,061	2,173	2,145	1,034	1,188
With an own child under 18 years (percent).........	24.5	32.4	35.2	18.1	40.1
HOUSING TENURE					
Population 15 years and over in occupied housing units.........	247,061	2,173	2,145	1,034	1,188
Owner-occupied housing units (percent).........	66.7	49.4	49.6	54.9	50.4
Renter-occupied housing units (percent).........	33.3	50.6	50.4	45.1	49.6

Source: U.S. Census Bureau, 2013 American Community Survey, S1251, "Characteristics of People with a Marital Event in the Last 12 Months," <http://factfinder2.census.gov>, accessed December 2014.

Table 145. Marital Status of Population and Number of Times Married by Sex and Median Duration of Marriage: 2008 to 2013

[242,953 represents 242,953,000. Data shown are for the population age 15 years and over. Based on the American Community Survey (ACS). The ACS universe includes the household population and the group quarters population. Based on a sample and subject to sampling variability. See Appendix III]

Characteristic	2008	2009	2010	2011	2012	2013
NUMBER (1,000)						
Population aged 15 years and over.........	**242,953**	**245,156**	**248,056**	**250,393**	**252,745**	**255,017**
Male.........	118,573	119,716	120,743	121,988	123,175	124,380
Never married.........	41,012	42,158	42,741	43,675	44,292	45,175
Ever married.........	77,561	77,558	78,001	78,313	78,883	79,205
Once.........	58,466	58,438	58,734	58,865	59,349	59,667
Two times.........	15,079	15,021	15,183	15,332	15,382	15,284
Three or more times.........	4,016	4,098	4,085	4,116	4,152	4,253
Female.........	124,380	125,440	127,313	128,405	129,571	130,637
Never married.........	34,893	35,853	36,899	37,709	38,367	39,145
Ever married.........	89,487	89,587	90,414	90,696	91,203	91,492
Once.........	67,732	67,660	68,330	68,426	68,939	69,185
Two times.........	17,231	17,312	17,449	17,665	17,620	17,533
Three or more times.........	4,524	4,616	4,636	4,605	4,644	4,774
PERCENT DISTRIBUTION						
Male:						
Never married.........	34.6	35.2	35.4	35.8	36.0	36.3
Ever married.........	65.4	64.8	64.6	64.2	64.0	63.7
Once.........	49.3	48.8	48.6	48.3	48.2	48.0
Two times.........	12.7	12.5	12.6	12.6	12.5	12.3
Three or more times.........	3.4	3.4	3.4	3.4	3.4	3.4
Female:						
Never married.........	28.1	28.6	29.0	29.4	29.6	30.0
Ever married.........	71.9	71.4	71.0	70.6	70.4	70.0
Once.........	54.5	53.9	53.7	53.3	53.2	53.0
Two times.........	13.9	13.8	13.7	13.8	13.6	13.4
Three or more times.........	3.6	3.7	3.6	3.6	3.6	3.7
Median duration of marriage (years) [1].........	18.4	18.6	19.0	19.2	19.3	19.5

[1] Data shown for current marriage.

Source: U.S. Census Bureau, American Community Survey, B12504, "Median Duration of Current Marriage in Years By Sex By Marital Status for the Married Population 15 years and Over," and B12505, "Number of Times Married by Sex By Marital Status for the Population 15 Years and Over;" <http://factfinder2.census.gov>, accessed March 2015.

Section 3
Health and Nutrition

This section presents statistics on national and personal health expenditures, health insurance coverage, Medicare and Medicaid, medical personnel, hospitals, nursing homes and other care facilities, injuries, diseases, disability status, substance use (including alcohol, tobacco, and illicit drug use), exercise, nutritional intake of the population, and food consumption. Also includes data on selected conditions among children.

Data on national health expenditures, medical costs, and insurance coverage are compiled by the U.S. Centers for Medicare & Medicaid Services (CMS) and appear on the CMS Web site at <http://www.cms.gov/NationalHealthExpendData/>. Data on Medicare and Medicaid come from the annual *Medicare and Medicaid Statistical Supplement*, and also the annual report to Congress from the Boards of Trustees for Medicare. The Trustees report covers the financial operations and actuarial status of Medicare. Summary statistics showing recent trends in health care and discussions of selected health issues are published annually by the U.S. National Center for Health Statistics (NCHS) in *Health, United States*. Statistics on health insurance are collected by surveys conducted by the Census Bureau. Health insurance and other data are also collected by NCHS's National Health Interview Survey and are published in Series 10 of *Vital and Health Statistics* and in brief reports issued under its Early Release Program. NCHS also tracks food and nutrition, signs of malnutrition, and incidence of health risk indicators such as overweight and obesity, and high blood cholesterol and blood pressure (hypertension). Data are published in Series 10 and 11 of *Vital and Health Statistics*. Statistics on hospitals are published annually by the Health Forum, LLC, an American Hospital Association (AHA) company, in *AHA Hospital Statistics*. Data on nutrition and on annual per capita consumption of food are issued by the U.S. Department of Agriculture, Economic Research Service, and Center for Nutrition Policy and Promotion. Data are available on the Web sites at <http://www.ers.usda.gov/data-products/food-availability-(per-capita)-data-system.aspx> and <http://www.usda.gov/cnpp/>, respectively.

New this year is data from the Health Care Satellite Account (HCSA), developed by the Bureau of Economic Analysis. The HCSA is a new tool that measures health care spending as the cost to treat specific diseases and medical conditions (such as cancer, or diseases of the circulatory system), as opposed to spending on specific types of health care services (physician services, or prescription drugs). The HCSA can help provide answers to questions regarding whether changes in medical expenditures are due to changes in costs of treatments or changes in number of persons receiving care, which medical conditions account for larger portions of spending, and which medical conditions experience the greatest changes in treatment costs. The BEA presents two versions of the HCSA. One version, the "MEPS Account," uses data from the Medical Expenditure Panel Survey; the other version, the "Blended Account," combines data from multiple sources, including large claims databases that cover millions of health insurance enrollees and billions of claims. The table in this section presents data from the Blended Account. See

<http://bea.gov/national/health_care_satellite_account.htm> for detailed information about how the Health Care Satellite Account is constructed.

National health expenditures—CMS compiles estimates of national health expenditures (NHE) to measure spending for health care in the United States. The NHE accounts are structured to show spending by type of expenditure: hospital care, physician and clinical care, dental care, and other professional care; home health care; retail sales of prescription drugs; other medical nondurables; nursing home care and other personal health expenditures; other health expenditures such as public health activities, administration, and the net cost of private health insurance; and medical sector investment, the sum of noncommercial medical research and capital formation in medical sector structures and equipment. The NHE also shows spending by source of funding (e.g., health insurance, out-of-pocket payments, and other third party payers and programs).

Data used to estimate health expenditures come from existing sources, which are tabulated for other purposes. The type of expenditure estimates rely upon statistics produced by such groups as the AHA, the Census Bureau, and the U.S. Department of Health and Human Services (HHS). Source of funding estimates are constructed using administrative and statistical records from the Medicare and Medicaid programs, the U.S. Department of Defense and Veterans Affairs medical programs, the Social Security Administration, Census Bureau's *Governmental Finances*, state and local governments, other HHS agencies, and other nongovernment sources.

Medicare, Medicaid, and Children's Health Insurance Program (CHIP)—The Medicare program has two components. Hospital Insurance (HI), otherwise known as Medicare Part A, helps pay for hospital, home health following hospital stays, skilled nursing facility, and hospice care for the aged and disabled. Supplementary Medical Insurance (SMI) consists of Medicare Part B and Part D. Part B helps pay for physician, outpatient hospital, home health, and other services for the aged and disabled who have voluntarily enrolled. Part D provides subsidized access to drug insurance coverage on a voluntary basis for all beneficiaries and premium and cost-sharing subsidies for low-income enrollees. Medicare also has a Part C, which serves as an alternative to traditional Part A and Part B coverage; Part C is not covered here. Participants in Parts B and D pay monthly premiums. In addition to covering persons age 65 and older, Medicare covers persons under age 65 with a disability and who have been receiving for the past 24 months disability benefits from Social Security or the Railroad Retirement Board; persons of any age with ALS (Amyotrophic Lateral Sclerosis, also known as Lou Gehrig's disease); and persons of any age with end-stage renal disease. Medicare's HI and SMI have separate trust funds, sources of revenue, and categories of expenditures.

Medicaid is a health insurance program for certain low-income people. These include: certain low-income families with children; people on supplemental security income; certain low-income pregnant women and children; and people who have very high medical bills. There are special rules for those who live in nursing homes and for disabled children living at home. Medicaid is funded and administered through a state/federal partnership. Although there are broad federal requirements for Medicaid, states have a wide degree of flexibility to design their program.

The Children's Health Insurance Program Reauthorization Act of 2009 (CHIPRA or Public Law 111-3) reauthorized CHIP, which was originally signed into law in 1997. The program went into effect on April 1, 2009. CHIP replaces the State Children's Health Insurance Program (SCHIP). It preserves coverage for the millions of children who rely on CHIP, and provides the resources for states to reach millions of additional uninsured children. CHIP was designed as a federal/state partnership, similar to Medicaid, with the goal of expanding health insurance to children whose families earn too much money to be eligible for Medicaid, but not enough money to purchase private insurance.

Health resources—Hospital statistics based on data from AHA's yearly survey are published annually in *AHA Hospital Statistics* and cover all hospitals accepted for registration by the Association. To be accepted for registration, a hospital must meet certain requirements relating to number of beds, construction, equipment, medical and nursing staff, patient care, clinical records, surgical and obstetrical facilities, diagnostic and treatment facilities, laboratory services, etc. The NCHS has replaced the National Hospital Discharge Survey (last conducted in 2010) with the National Hospital Care Survey and the National Hospital Ambulatory Medical Care Survey (NHAMCS). Ambulatory care data, including emergency room visits, are presented here from the NHAMCS. Data on physicians generally come from the professional organizations that collect data on medical school graduates and physicians. Statistics on patient visits to health care providers, as reported in health interviews, appear in NCHS Series 10 data from the National Health Interview Survey.

Disability and illness—General health statistics, including morbidity, disability, injuries, preventive care, and findings from physiological testing are collected by NCHS in its National Health Interview Survey and its National Health and Nutrition Examination Surveys and appear in *Vital and Health Statistics*, Series 10 and 11, respectively. Annual incidence data on notifiable diseases are compiled by the Public Health Service (PHS) at its Centers for Disease Control and Prevention in Atlanta, Georgia, and are published as a supplement to its *Morbidity and Mortality Weekly Report* (MMWR). The list of diseases is revised annually and includes those which, by mutual agreement of the states and PHS, are communicable diseases of national importance.

Statistical reliability—For discussion of statistical collection, estimation, and sampling procedures and measures of reliability applicable to data from NCHS and CMS, see Appendix III.

[In billions of dollars (27.4 represents $27,400,000,000). Excludes Puerto Rico and Island Areas. For definitions, methodology, and related information, see <http://www.cms.gov/NationalHealthExpendData/Downloads/dsm-13.pdf>]

Year	Total expenditures [1]	Health consumption expenditures, total [2]	Personal health care expenditures									
			Total [3]	Hospital care	Physician and clinical services	Dental services	Other professional services [4]	Home health care [5]	Nursing care facilities [6]	Prescription drugs	Durable medical equipment [7]	Nondurable medical equipment [8]
1960.....	27.4	24.8	23.4	9.0	5.6	2.0	0.4	0.1	0.8	2.7	0.7	1.6
1961.....	29.2	26.4	24.8	9.8	5.8	2.1	0.4	0.1	0.8	2.7	0.8	1.8
1962.....	31.9	28.4	26.7	10.4	6.3	2.2	0.4	0.1	0.9	3.0	0.9	1.9
1963.....	34.7	30.9	29.1	11.5	7.1	2.4	0.5	0.1	1.0	3.2	0.9	1.9
1964.....	38.5	34.1	32.1	12.5	8.1	2.6	0.5	0.1	1.2	3.3	1.0	2.1
1965.....	42.0	37.2	34.7	13.5	8.6	2.8	0.5	0.1	1.4	3.7	1.1	2.2
1966.....	46.3	41.2	38.4	15.3	9.3	3.0	0.6	0.1	1.7	4.0	1.2	2.4
1967.....	51.8	46.5	43.5	17.8	10.4	3.4	0.6	0.2	2.2	4.2	1.1	2.5
1968.....	58.8	52.8	49.2	20.5	11.3	3.7	0.6	0.2	2.9	4.7	1.3	2.8
1969.....	66.2	59.1	55.5	23.4	12.7	4.2	0.7	0.3	3.4	5.1	1.5	3.0
1970.....	74.9	67.1	63.1	27.2	14.3	4.7	0.7	0.2	4.0	5.5	1.7	3.3
1971.....	83.2	74.4	69.5	30.2	15.9	5.2	0.8	0.2	4.6	5.9	1.8	3.5
1972.....	93.1	83.4	77.2	33.8	17.7	5.6	0.9	0.2	5.2	6.3	2.0	3.7
1973.....	103.4	93.1	86.2	37.9	19.6	6.4	1.0	0.3	6.0	6.8	2.2	4.0
1974.....	117.2	105.9	98.8	44.1	22.2	7.1	1.2	0.4	6.9	7.4	2.5	4.5
1975.....	133.6	121.2	113.3	51.2	25.3	8.0	1.3	0.6	8.0	8.1	2.8	4.9
1976.....	153.0	139.4	129.4	59.4	28.7	9.0	1.6	0.9	9.1	8.7	3.0	5.4
1977.....	174.0	160.0	146.8	67.0	33.1	10.1	2.1	1.1	10.3	9.2	3.2	6.1
1978.....	195.5	180.1	164.3	75.6	35.8	11.0	2.4	1.6	11.8	9.9	3.4	7.1
1979.....	221.7	204.6	187.2	86.2	41.2	12.0	2.8	1.9	13.3	10.7	3.8	8.5
1980.....	255.8	235.7	217.2	100.5	47.7	13.4	3.5	2.4	15.3	12.0	4.1	9.8
1981.....	296.7	273.7	252.0	117.5	55.6	15.8	4.3	2.9	17.3	13.4	4.3	11.3
1982.....	334.7	308.3	283.4	133.6	61.6	17.1	4.9	3.5	19.5	15.0	4.6	12.6
1983.....	369.0	339.7	312.0	144.7	68.6	18.4	5.7	4.2	21.7	17.3	5.3	13.8
1984.....	406.5	375.5	342.1	154.4	77.4	20.0	7.4	5.1	23.8	19.6	6.1	15.0
1985.....	444.6	413.4	376.9	164.6	90.9	21.8	8.1	5.6	26.3	21.8	7.1	16.0
1986.....	476.9	444.4	409.5	175.6	100.7	23.3	9.3	6.4	28.7	24.3	8.1	17.1
1987.....	519.1	483.1	448.5	189.5	112.9	25.5	11.4	6.7	30.7	26.9	9.5	18.3
1988.....	581.7	541.5	499.5	206.5	128.6	27.5	13.8	8.4	34.3	30.6	11.1	19.4
1989.....	647.5	603.5	551.6	226.0	143.3	29.5	14.6	10.2	38.7	34.8	11.9	20.8
1990.....	724.3	675.6	616.8	250.4	158.9	31.7	17.4	12.6	44.9	40.3	13.8	22.4
1991.....	791.5	739.5	677.7	275.8	176.5	33.5	18.7	15.2	49.4	44.4	13.1	23.2
1992.....	857.9	801.0	733.6	298.5	191.3	37.3	21.0	18.7	53.1	47.0	13.5	23.2
1993.....	921.5	860.3	781.2	315.7	202.7	39.2	23.2	22.8	56.0	49.6	14.1	23.7
1994.....	972.7	908.8	823.1	328.4	212.2	41.7	24.2	27.4	58.6	53.1	15.3	24.3
1995.....	1,027.4	961.6	872.9	339.3	222.3	44.8	27.0	32.4	64.5	59.8	15.9	25.1
1996.....	1,081.9	1,014.1	921.8	350.8	231.3	47.1	29.2	35.8	69.6	68.1	17.4	26.0
1997.....	1,142.7	1,070.5	974.6	363.4	242.9	50.5	31.7	37.0	74.4	77.6	19.2	27.6
1998.....	1,209.1	1,129.5	1,029.2	374.9	258.7	53.8	33.8	34.2	79.4	88.4	21.3	28.6
1999.....	1,286.7	1,201.0	1,089.7	393.6	271.9	57.4	35.0	32.9	80.8	104.7	23.0	30.6
2000.....	1,378.0	1,290.0	1,165.7	415.5	290.9	62.3	37.0	32.4	85.1	121.2	25.2	31.6
2001.....	1,494.6	1,402.6	1,265.8	449.4	315.7	67.8	40.6	34.4	90.8	139.1	25.1	32.3
2002.....	1,638.1	1,535.9	1,371.9	486.5	340.9	73.7	43.7	36.6	94.5	158.2	27.1	33.3
2003.....	1,778.3	1,668.1	1,482.1	526.2	368.0	76.3	46.7	39.8	100.3	177.0	28.0	36.2
2004.....	1,905.7	1,788.2	1,592.3	566.0	393.3	82.1	50.3	43.8	105.8	193.0	29.5	38.1
2005.....	2,034.8	1,909.0	1,700.9	609.4	417.2	87.0	52.7	48.7	112.5	205.3	30.9	40.8
2006.....	2,167.2	2,035.6	1,809.3	651.9	438.8	91.4	55.0	52.6	117.4	224.4	32.3	43.7
2007.....	2,303.9	2,158.8	1,921.0	692.5	461.8	97.3	59.5	57.8	126.4	236.0	34.3	47.8
2008.....	2,414.1	2,258.9	2,017.3	728.9	486.5	102.4	64.0	62.3	132.6	242.7	34.9	49.5
2009.....	2,505.8	2,359.5	2,117.9	776.8	503.2	102.5	66.8	67.2	138.5	255.0	35.0	50.3
2010.....	2,604.1	2,454.5	2,196.2	814.9	519.0	105.4	69.8	71.2	143.0	256.2	37.0	51.2
2011.....	2,705.3	2,548.0	2,281.8	849.9	540.8	107.6	73.1	73.8	149.2	263.0	39.1	52.8
2012.....	2,817.3	2,653.6	2,379.3	898.5	565.3	110.0	76.8	77.1	152.2	264.4	41.3	53.7
2013.....	2,919.1	2,754.5	2,468.6	936.9	586.7	111.0	80.2	79.8	155.8	271.1	43.0	55.9

[1] Includes Health Consumption Expenditures plus medical research, and medical structures and equipment. [2] Includes Personal Health Expenditures plus, not shown, government administration, net cost of health insurance, and government public health activities. [3] Includes items shown here, and also other health, residential, and personal services. [4] Includes health practitioners other than physicians and dentists, such as, but not limited to, chiropractors, optometrists, physical, occupational, and speech therapists, podiatrists, and private-duty nurses. [5] Services delivered by freestanding home health care facilities only. [6] Care provided in nursing care facilities (NAICS 6231), continuing care retirement communities (623311), state and local government nursing facilities, and nursing facilities operated by the Department of Veterans Affairs. [7] Retail sales of items such as contact lenses, eyeglasses and other ophthalmic products, surgical and orthopedic products, medical equipment rental, oxygen, and hearing aids. Durable products generally last over 3 years. [8] Non-prescription drugs and sundry medical items.

Source: U.S. Centers for Medicare and Medicaid Services, Office of the Actuary, National Health Statistics Group, "National Health Expenditure Data, Historical," <http://cms.gov/nationalhealthexpenddata>, accessed January 2015.

Table 147. National Health Expenditures by Source of Funds: 1990 to 2013

[In billions of dollars (724.3 represents $724,300,000,000), except percent. Excludes Puerto Rico and Island Areas]

Type of expenditure	1990	2000	2005	2009	2010	2011	2012	2013
National health expenditure, total............	**724.3**	**1,378.0**	**2,034.8**	**2,505.8**	**2,604.1**	**2,705.3**	**2,817.3**	**2,919.1**
Annual percent change [1]......................	11.9	7.1	6.8	3.8	3.9	3.9	4.1	3.6
Percent of gross domestic product.........	12.1	13.4	15.5	17.4	17.4	17.4	17.4	17.4
Out of pocket......................	138.6	201.5	267.2	300.9	306.2	317.3	328.8	339.4
Health insurance.......................	439.5	921.0	1,416.7	1,797.9	1,875.7	1,952.4	2,029.1	2,102.9
Private health insurance.....................	234.2	459.8	703.2	833.1	862.2	899.4	935.7	961.7
Medicare........................	110.2	224.8	339.8	499.7	519.9	544.7	566.6	585.7
Medicaid (Title XIX).................	73.7	200.5	309.5	374.9	397.7	407.5	423.7	449.4
CHIP (Title XIX and Title XXI).................	(X)	3.0	7.6	11.1	11.5	12.0	12.6	13.5
Department of Defense........................	10.4	13.8	26.8	36.7	38.3	40.0	39.8	39.1
Department of Veterans Affairs..........	10.9	19.1	29.8	42.4	46.1	48.9	50.6	53.4
Other third party payers and programs.......	77.5	124.5	167.8	186.7	197.0	204.8	220.9	236.8
Worksite health care......................	2.2	3.5	4.2	4.5	4.6	4.8	5.1	5.3
Other private revenues [2]................	29.6	57.4	70.5	86.1	93.8	97.3	109.6	121.1
Indian health services....................	1.0	2.0	2.5	3.2	3.5	3.6	3.8	3.7
Workers' compensation....................	17.5	26.2	41.3	37.1	37.0	39.8	41.5	44.2
General assistance......................	5.0	3.9	6.2	7.2	7.1	6.7	6.4	6.7
Maternal/Child health....................	1.6	2.7	2.6	2.7	2.6	2.4	2.1	2.0
Vocational rehabilitation..................	0.3	0.4	0.5	0.5	0.6	0.6	0.5	0.5
Other federal programs [3]................	1.6	4.5	6.4	7.3	7.7	9.6	11.7	12.9
Substance Abuse and Mental Health Services Administration......................	1.4	2.6	3.2	3.3	3.4	3.4	3.4	3.3
Other state and local programs [4]..........	16.0	18.8	27.1	30.6	32.4	32.4	32.2	32.6
School health........................	1.3	2.5	3.4	4.2	4.3	4.3	4.4	4.5
Public health activity [5].....................	20.0	43.0	57.2	74.0	75.5	73.5	74.8	75.4
Investment........................	**48.7**	**88.0**	**125.9**	**146.3**	**149.7**	**157.3**	**163.7**	**164.6**
Research [6].....................	12.7	25.5	40.3	45.2	48.7	49.3	48.0	46.7
Structures & equipment [7]......................	36.0	62.5	85.5	101.1	101.0	108.0	115.7	117.9

X Not applicable. [1] Average annual growth from prior year. [2] Most common source of other private funds is philanthropy; support can come from individuals or through philanthropic fund-raising organizations, and also from foundations or corporations. [3] Includes federal general hospital/medical, and pre-existing conditions insurance plans. [4] Includes temporary disability insurance, state and local subsidies to providers, and non-XIX state and local. [5] Governments are involved in providing health services such as epidemiological surveillance, inoculations, immunization/vaccination services, disease prevention programs, and public health laboratories. In the National Health Expenditure Accounts, spending for these activities is reported in government public health activity. [6] Non-profit or government entities. Excludes research and development expenditures by drug and medical supply and equipment manufacturers. [7] Structures are defined as the value of new construction by the medical sector. Includes establishments engaged in providing health care, but does not include retail establishments that sell non-durable or durable medical goods. Construction includes new buildings; additions, alterations, and major replacements; mechanical and electric installations; and site preparation.

Source: U. S. Centers for Medicare and Medicaid Services, Office of the Actuary, National Health Statistics Group, "National Health Expenditure Data, Historical," <http://cms.gov/nationalhealthexpenddata>, accessed January 2015.

Table 148. National Health Expenditure Projections by Source of Funds and Type of Expenditure: 2014 to 2022

[In billions of dollars (3,056.7 represents $3,056,700,000,000). For calendar years. Projections are based on the 2012 version of the National Health Expenditures (NHE) released in January 2014. Projections include effects of the Affordable Care Act, and focus on an outlook for spending in which the scheduled Medicare physician payment rate updates under the Sustainable Growth Rate formula do not occur, including a reduction of approximately 21 percent effective April 1, 2015. Instead, physician fee schedule rates are assumed to grow zero percent in 2015 and 0.6 percent annually for 2016-2023, a method and rate consistent with the projected baseline scenario in the 2014 Medicare Trustees Report. Excludes Puerto Rico and Island areas]

Funding source and expenditure type	2014	2015	2016	2017	2018	2019	2020	2021	2022
Total........................	**3,056.7**	**3,207.3**	**3,386.2**	**3,579.0**	**3,797.5**	**4,042.5**	**4,307.4**	**4,577.8**	**4,861.9**
SOURCE OF FUNDS									
Out-of-pocket........................	338.1	345.7	356.0	372.1	391.2	413.5	437.5	461.1	486.1
Health insurance........................	2,246.1	2,372.5	2,516.2	2,662.2	2,827.8	3,015.2	3,219.1	3,427.5	3,646.7
Private health insurance [1]................	1,012.2	1,082.4	1,136.9	1,191.3	1,252.9	1,330.4	1,410.0	1,489.3	1,569.5
Medicare........................	615.9	632.7	669.2	714.1	769.5	825.3	890.3	958.9	1,033.1
Medicaid........................	507.2	541.1	587.5	626.5	666.7	711.3	760.4	810.3	863.0
Other health insurance programs [2]................	110.8	116.2	122.6	130.2	138.8	148.2	158.4	169.1	181.2
Other third party payers and programs................	472.5	489.2	514.1	544.7	578.4	613.7	650.8	689.2	729.1
TYPE OF EXPENDITURE									
Health consumption expenditures [3]................	2,893.3	3,040.8	3,212.8	3,395.5	3,602.2	3,834.0	4,085.1	4,340.9	4,609.7
Personal health care........................	2,579.3	2,706.0	2,859.9	3,019.8	3,207.4	3,413.1	3,638.1	3,866.7	4,108.9
Hospital care........................	959.9	1,008.5	1,067.9	1,127.6	1,198.7	1,276.1	1,361.3	1,449.0	1,541.9
Physician and clinical services................	618.5	641.9	677.2	713.7	756.8	805.2	857.9	910.8	966.4
Other professional services [4]................	87.6	92.3	98.4	104.5	111.6	119.3	127.5	135.7	144.4
Dental services........................	116.6	122.7	129.3	135.4	143.7	153.0	162.8	172.2	182.0
Other health, residential, and personal care [5]......	153.1	161.5	171.0	182.1	194.2	206.9	220.7	235.3	250.8
Home health care [6]........................	86.2	91.7	98.1	104.8	112.9	121.5	130.7	140.4	151.0
Nursing care facilities and continuing care retirement communities [7]................	162.3	170.2	179.9	190.9	203.0	215.6	228.7	242.2	256.5
Prescription drugs........................	290.7	309.3	325.1	342.2	360.6	381.8	406.1	430.3	456.1
Durable medical equipment................	44.0	45.8	47.3	49.7	52.6	56.0	59.7	63.4	67.3
Other nondurable medical products................	60.5	62.2	65.6	68.9	73.2	77.8	82.6	87.4	92.5
Public health activity [8]................	81.1	84.5	88.4	92.9	97.3	102.1	107.2	112.3	117.6
Research [9]........................	47.2	46.4	47.8	50.1	52.8	55.8	59.0	62.3	65.9
Structures & equipment [10]................	116.2	120.1	125.6	133.5	142.5	152.7	163.4	174.6	186.3

[1] Includes employer sponsored insurance and other private insurance, which includes marketplace plans. [2] Children's Health Insurance Program (Titles XIX and XXI), Department of Defense, and Department of Veterans' Affairs. [3] See footnote 2, Table 146. [4] See footnote 4, Table 146. [5] See footnote 4, Table 149. [6] See footnote 5, Table 146. [7] See footnote 6, Table 146. [8] See footnote 5, Table 147. [9] See footnote 6, Table 147. [10] See footnote 7, Table 147.

Source: U.S. Centers for Medicare and Medicaid Services, Office of the Actuary, National Health Statistics Group, "National Health Expenditure Data, Projected," <http://cms.gov/nationalhealthexpenddata>, accessed January 2015.

Table 149. Health Consumption Expenditures—Per Capita Spending by Type of Expenditure: 2000 to 2013

[In dollars, except percent. Based on U.S. Census Bureau estimates of total U.S. resident population. Health consumption expenditures include all personal health care spending, government administration and the net cost of private health insurance, and public health activities. Excludes research and structures and equipment. Excludes Puerto Rico and Island Areas]

Type of expenditure	2000	2005	2007	2008	2009	2010	2011	2012	2013
Total [1]	**4,570**	**6,461**	**7,170**	**7,433**	**7,698**	**7,943**	**8,192**	**8,473**	**8,733**
Annual percent change [2]	(X)	5.8	5.1	3.7	3.6	3.2	3.1	3.4	3.1
Hospital care	1,472	2,062	2,300	2,399	2,534	2,637	2,733	2,869	2,970
Physician and clinical services	1,030	1,412	1,534	1,601	1,642	1,680	1,739	1,805	1,860
Dental services	221	295	323	337	334	341	346	351	352
Other professional services [3]	131	178	198	211	218	226	235	245	254
Other health, residential, and personal care [4]	229	327	358	374	400	416	426	447	470
Home health care	115	165	192	205	219	230	237	246	253
Nursing care facilities and continuing care retirement communities	302	381	420	436	452	463	480	486	494
Prescription drugs	429	695	784	799	832	829	845	844	859
Durable medical equipment [5]	89	104	114	115	114	120	126	132	136
Other nondurable medical products [6]	112	138	159	163	164	166	170	172	177
Public health activities [7]	152	194	219	235	242	244	236	239	239

X Not applicable. [1] Includes other items, not shown separately. [2] Average annual growth from prior year. [3] See footnote 4, Table 146. [4] Includes expenditures for residential care facilities (NAICS 623210 and 623220), ambulance providers (NAICS 621910), medical care delivered in non-traditional settings (such as community centers, senior citizens centers, schools, and military field stations), and expenditures for Home and Community Waiver programs under Medicaid. [5] See footnote 7, Table 146. [6] See footnote 8, Table 146. [7] See footnote 5, Table 147.

Source: U. S. Centers for Medicare and Medicaid Services, Office of the Actuary, National Health Statistics Group, "National Health Expenditure Data, Historical," <http://cms.gov/nationalhealthexpenddata>, accessed January 2015.

Table 150. Health Consumption Expenditures by Type of Expenditure and Source of Funds: 2013

[In billions of dollars (2,754.5 represents $2,754,500,000,000). Excludes Puerto Rico and Island Areas. Excludes research, structures, and equipment]

Type of expenditure	Total	Out-of-pocket	Health insurance Total	Private health insurance	Medicare	Medicaid	Other health insurance programs [1]	Other third party payers and programs [2]
Total	**2,754.5**	**339.4**	**2,102.9**	**961.7**	**585.7**	**449.4**	**106.1**	**236.8**
Personal health care [3]	2,468.6	339.4	1,907.9	846.0	550.5	410.8	100.6	221.2
Hospital care	936.9	32.7	808.7	348.0	242.7	163.5	54.4	95.6
Physician and clinical services	586.7	55.3	472.2	267.6	130.3	50.1	24.1	59.2
Dental services	111.0	47.1	63.3	52.6	0.5	7.5	2.7	0.5
Other health, residential, and personal care [4]	148.2	7.7	98.7	6.6	5.1	82.6	4.5	41.8
Home health care	79.8	6.4	70.9	6.3	34.4	29.1	1.1	2.4
Nursing care facilities and continuing care retirement communities	155.8	45.8	98.5	12.6	34.6	46.9	4.5	11.5
Prescription drugs	271.1	45.9	222.7	117.9	74.6	21.2	8.9	2.5
Durable medical equipment	43.0	24.7	17.7	5.0	7.7	4.9	0.1	0.6
Government administration [5]	37.0	(X)	33.2	(X)	8.5	20.4	4.3	3.7
Net cost of health insurance [5]	173.6	(X)	161.7	115.7	26.6	18.2	1.1	11.9
Public health activities [6]	75.4	(X)	(X)	(X)	(X)	(X)	(X)	(X)

X Not applicable. [1] Includes Children's Health Insurance Program (CHIP) Titles XIX and XXI, Department of Defense, and Department of Veterans Affairs. [2] Includes worksite health care, other private revenues, Indian Health Service, workers' compensation, general assistance, maternal and child health, vocational rehabilitation, other federal programs, Substance Abuse and Mental Health Services Administration, other state and local programs, and school health. [3] Comprises all medical goods and services that are rendered to treat or prevent a specific disease or condition in a specific person. Includes expenditures for other items, not shown separately. [4] See footnote 4, Table 149. [5] See source for definitions. [6] See footnote 5, Table 147.

Source: U. S. Centers for Medicare and Medicaid Services, Office of the Actuary, National Health Statistics Group, "National Health Expenditure Data, Historical," <http://cms.gov/nationalhealthexpenddata>, accessed January 2015.

Table 151. Personal Health Care Expenditures by Source of Funds: 2000 to 2013

[In billions of dollars (1,165.7 represents $1,165,700,000,000). Excludes Puerto Rico and Island Areas]

Item	2000	2005	2007	2008	2009	2010	2011	2012	2013
Personal health care expenditures	**1,165.7**	**1,700.9**	**1,921.0**	**2,017.3**	**2,117.9**	**2,196.2**	**2,281.8**	**2,379.3**	**2,468.6**
Out-of-pocket	201.5	267.2	293.7	300.9	300.9	306.2	317.3	328.8	339.4
Health insurance	845.5	1,281.3	1,454.6	1,544.5	1,639.2	1,701.4	1,769.9	1,842.0	1,907.9
Private health insurance	407.3	606.5	673.1	706.2	736.1	755.4	788.2	822.9	846.0
Medicare	216.3	326.3	408.8	442.1	471.2	489.2	511.9	532.2	550.5
Medicaid	186.9	287.7	301.6	317.9	346.4	366.2	374.4	389.0	410.8
Other health insurance [1]	34.9	60.8	71.1	78.3	85.6	90.6	95.4	97.8	100.6
Other third party payers and programs [2]	118.7	152.4	172.7	171.9	177.8	188.6	194.6	208.5	221.2

[1] Includes Children's Health Insurance Program (Titles XIX and XXI), Department of Defense, and Department of Veterans Affairs. [2] See footnote 2, Table 153.

Source: U.S. Centers for Medicare and Medicaid Services, Office of the Actuary, National Health Statistics Group, "National Health Expenditure Data, Historical," <http://cms.gov/nationalhealthexpenddata>, accessed January 2015.

Table 152. National Health Expenditures by Sponsor: 2000 to 2013

[In billions of dollars (1,378.0 represents $1,378,000,000,000). Excludes Puerto Rico and Island Areas. Type of sponsor is defined as the entity that is ultimately responsible for financing the health care bill. These sponsors pay health insurance premiums and out-of-pocket costs, or finance health care through dedicated taxes and/or general revenues]

Type of sponsor	2000	2005	2008	2009	2010	2011	2012	2013
Total.	1,378.0	2,034.8	2,414.1	2,505.8	2,604.1	2,705.3	2,817.3	2,919.1
Business, households and other private revenues. . .	888.4	1,231.1	1,416.8	1,415.2	1,446.6	1,508.4	1,592.7	1,652.8
Private business [1]	346.5	486.3	530.5	530.3	533.7	560.4	587.3	610.9
Household [2]	434.0	602.9	713.0	717.3	738.3	764.5	801.5	823.8
Other private revenues.	107.9	141.9	173.3	167.6	174.6	183.5	203.9	218.1
Governments.	489.6	803.7	997.3	1,090.6	1,157.5	1,196.9	1,224.6	1,266.3
Federal government [3]	261.9	452.0	583.6	682.8	733.1	733.1	731.5	757.5
State and local government [4]	227.7	351.7	413.7	407.9	424.5	463.7	493.1	508.8

[1] Excludes Medicare Retiree Drug Subsidy (RDS) payments to private plans as of 2006; and small business tax credits and Early Retirement Reinsurance Program (ERRP) Payments as of 2010. Includes one-half of self employment contribution to Medicare Hospital Insurance (HI) Trust Fund. [2] Excludes government-subsidized COBRA payments as of 2009. Includes one-half self-employment contribution to the Medicare HI Trust Fund, and trust fund revenues from taxation of social security benefits. Beginning in 2010, also includes premiums paid for the Pre-Existing Condition Insurance Plan (PCIP). [3] Includes employer contributions to private health insurance premiums and Medicare HI Trust Fund, adjusted Medicare expenditures, and health program expenditures (excluding Medicare), see source for details. [4] Includes employer contributions to private health insurance premiums and Medicare HI Trust Fund, and expenditures for Medicaid and other programs, see source for details.

Source: U.S. Centers for Medicare and Medicaid Services, Office of the Actuary, National Health Statistics Group, "National Health Expenditure Data, Historical, Sponsor Highlights," <http://cms.gov/nationalhealthexpenddata>, accessed January 2015.

Table 153. Hospital Care, Physician and Clinical Services, Nursing Care Facilities and Continuing Care Retirement Communities, and Prescription Drug Expenditures by Source of Funds: 2000 to 2013

[In billions of dollars (415.5 represents $415,500,000,000). Excludes Puerto Rico and Island Areas]

Source of payment	2000	2005	2008	2009	2010	2011	2012	2013
Hospital care, total.	**415.5**	**609.4**	**728.9**	**776.8**	**814.9**	**849.9**	**898.5**	**936.9**
Out-of-pocket.	13.5	19.5	23.4	25.0	26.6	28.1	30.7	32.7
Health insurance.	358.0	532.6	639.7	680.6	710.9	740.8	780.4	808.7
Private health insurance.	141.6	217.5	265.4	280.7	292.4	311.3	334.5	348.0
Medicare.	123.4	176.4	205.6	215.9	221.2	227.9	236.5	242.7
Medicaid.	71.2	104.8	125.2	137.0	147.0	149.8	156.5	163.5
Other health insurance [1]	21.9	33.8	43.5	47.2	50.2	51.9	52.8	54.4
Other third party payers and programs [2]	44.0	57.3	65.9	71.2	77.4	81.0	87.4	95.6
Physician and clinical services, total.	**290.9**	**417.2**	**486.5**	**503.2**	**519.0**	**540.8**	**565.3**	**586.7**
Out-of-pocket.	32.5	42.7	48.6	47.8	50.9	53.3	54.1	55.4
Health insurance.	222.7	330.2	390.6	409.6	420.2	438.1	456.0	472.2
Private health insurance.	138.0	202.4	232.8	237.8	241.3	249.7	259.7	267.6
Medicare.	58.7	85.6	103.8	111.5	115.1	121.3	127.1	130.3
Medicaid.	19.2	29.8	35.6	39.9	42.6	44.3	45.5	50.1
Other health insurance [1]	6.8	12.5	18.4	20.3	21.2	22.7	23.6	24.1
Other third party payers and programs [2]	35.7	44.3	47.3	45.7	47.9	49.4	55.2	59.2
Nursing care facilities and continuing care retirement communities, total.	**85.1**	**112.5**	**132.6**	**138.5**	**143.0**	**149.2**	**152.2**	**155.8**
Out-of-pocket.	27.2	33.4	39.3	40.0	40.2	41.1	44.3	45.8
Health insurance.	52.0	71.8	84.6	89.3	92.6	97.7	96.6	98.5
Private health insurance.	7.5	7.3	9.6	10.4	10.9	11.4	12.1	12.6
Medicare.	10.8	20.5	27.6	30.0	32.2	35.7	33.8	34.6
Medicaid.	31.9	41.1	43.7	45.0	45.4	46.3	46.3	46.9
Other health insurance [1]	1.9	2.8	3.6	3.9	4.0	4.3	4.4	4.5
Other third party payers and programs [2]	5.9	7.3	8.7	9.2	10.2	10.4	11.2	11.5
Prescription drugs, total.	**121.2**	**205.3**	**242.7**	**255.0**	**256.2**	**263.0**	**264.4**	**271.1**
Out-of-pocket.	33.7	51.5	49.9	49.6	46.1	46.8	46.5	45.9
Health insurance.	85.2	149.9	189.2	201.8	206.6	213.2	215.2	222.7
Private health insurance.	61.2	102.2	111.0	118.3	118.9	120.9	118.6	117.9
Medicare.	2.1	3.9	50.6	54.5	58.9	63.2	67.4	74.6
Medicaid.	19.8	36.4	19.2	20.2	20.0	20.0	20.2	21.2
Other health insurance [1]	2.1	7.4	8.4	8.8	8.7	9.0	9.0	8.9
Other third party payers and programs [2]	2.3	3.9	3.7	3.6	3.5	2.9	2.7	2.5

[1] Includes Children's Health Insurance Program (Titles XIX and XXI), Department of Defense, and Department of Veterans Affairs. [2] Includes worksite health care, other private revenues, Indian Health Service, workers' compensation, general assistance, maternal and child health, vocational rehabilitation, other federal programs, Substance Abuse and Mental Health Services Administration, other state and local programs, and school health.

Source: U.S. Centers for Medicare and Medicaid Services, Office of the Actuary, National Health Statistics Group, "National Health Expenditure Data, Historical," <http://cms.gov/nationalhealthexpenddata>, accessed January 2015.

Table 154. Medical Care Consumer Price Indexes: 1980 to 2014

[Indexes with base of 1982-1984 = 100. Indexes are annual averages of monthly data based on components of consumer price index for all urban consumers; for explanation, see text, Section 14 and Appendix III]

Year	Medical care, total	Medical care services					Medical care commodities		Annual percent change [3]		
		Total [1]	Professional services			Hospital and related services	Total [2]	Pre-scription drugs	Medical care, total	Medical care services	Medical care com-modities
			Total [1]	Physi-cians	Dental						
1980.......	74.9	74.8	77.9	76.5	78.9	69.2	75.4	72.5	11.0	11.3	9.3
1985.......	113.5	113.2	113.5	113.3	114.2	116.1	115.2	120.1	6.3	6.1	7.2
1990.......	162.8	162.7	156.1	160.8	155.8	178.0	163.4	181.7	9.0	9.3	8.4
1995.......	220.5	224.2	201.0	208.8	206.8	257.8	204.5	235.0	4.5	5.1	1.9
2000.......	260.8	266.0	237.7	244.7	258.5	317.3	238.1	285.4	4.1	4.3	3.2
2005.......	323.2	336.7	281.7	287.5	324.0	439.9	276.0	349.0	4.2	4.8	2.5
2009.......	375.6	397.3	319.4	320.8	388.1	567.9	305.1	391.1	3.2	3.2	3.1
2010.......	388.4	411.2	328.2	331.3	398.8	607.7	314.7	407.8	3.4	3.5	3.1
2011.......	400.3	423.8	335.7	340.3	408.0	641.5	324.1	425.0	3.0	3.1	3.0
2012.......	414.9	440.3	342.0	347.3	417.5	672.1	333.6	440.1	3.7	3.9	2.9
2013.......	425.1	454.0	349.5	354.2	431.8	701.3	335.1	442.6	2.5	3.1	0.4
2014.......	435.3	464.8	355.2	359.1	441.0	733.8	343.4	458.3	2.4	2.4	2.5

[1] Includes other services not shown separately. [2] Includes other commodities not shown separately. [3] Percent change from the immediate prior year.

Source: U.S. Bureau of Labor Statistics, Consumer Price Index Databases, <http://www.bls.gov/cpi/data.htm>, accessed January 2015. See also <http://www.bls.gov/cpi/>.

Table 155. Average Annual Expenditures Per Consumer Unit for Health Care: 2013

[In dollars, except percent. Expenditures are direct out-of-pocket expenditures. Consumers units may be all members in a housing unit (families), a person living alone or sharing a household with others and financially independent, or 2 or more unrelated persons living together who share expenses. See also text for Section 13, and source. For composition of regions, see map, inside front cover]

Item	Health care, total		Health insur-ance	Medical services	Drugs and medical sup-plies [1]	Percent distribution		
	Amount	Percent of total expendi-tures				Health insur-ance	Medical services	Drugs and medical sup-plies [1]
Total..........................	**3,631**	**7.1**	**2,229**	**796**	**605**	**61.4**	**21.9**	**16.7**
Age of reference person:								
Under 25 years old.............................	943	3.1	526	272	145	55.8	28.8	15.4
25 to 34 years old..............................	2,189	4.6	1,334	580	274	61.0	26.5	12.5
35 to 44 years old..............................	3,188	5.4	1,944	786	459	61.0	24.6	14.4
45 to 54 years old..............................	3,801	6.3	2,242	918	640	59.0	24.2	16.8
55 to 64 years old..............................	4,378	7.8	2,537	1,053	787	58.0	24.1	18.0
65 years old and older..........................	5,069	12.2	3,347	803	918	66.0	15.8	18.1
Race of reference person:								
White and other [2].............................	3,894	7.4	2,358	883	653	60.6	22.7	16.8
Asian..	3,255	5.4	2,104	650	500	64.7	20.0	15.4
Black..	2,013	5.4	1,421	271	321	70.6	13.5	15.9
Origin of reference person:								
Hispanic.......................................	1,931	4.6	1,188	420	323	61.5	21.8	16.7
Non-Hispanic...................................	3,879	7.4	2,381	851	647	61.4	21.9	16.7
Region of residence:								
Northeast......................................	3,784	6.6	2,466	749	568	65.2	19.8	15.0
Midwest.......................................	4,095	8.1	2,472	994	630	60.4	24.3	15.4
South..	3,295	7.2	2,108	589	597	64.0	17.9	18.1
West..	3,609	6.5	1,999	985	625	55.4	27.3	17.3
Size of consumer unit:								
One person....................................	2,375	7.6	1,423	523	430	59.9	22.0	18.1
Two or more persons...........................	4,169	7.0	2,576	914	678	61.8	21.9	16.3
Two persons.................................	4,532	8.3	2,844	889	799	62.8	19.6	17.6
Three persons...............................	3,919	6.6	2,437	890	593	62.2	22.7	15.1
Four persons................................	3,971	5.8	2,426	955	590	61.1	24.0	14.9
Five persons or more.........................	3,632	5.6	2,119	982	531	58.3	27.0	14.6
Income before taxes, by quintile:								
Lowest 20 percent.............................	1,790	8.0	1,094	352	343	61.2	19.7	19.2
Second 20 percent............................	2,850	8.8	1,831	501	519	64.2	17.6	18.2
Third 20 percent..............................	3,375	7.9	2,154	655	566	63.8	19.4	16.8
Fourth 20 percent.............................	4,386	7.5	2,700	1,010	675	61.6	23.0	15.4
Highest 20 percent............................	5,755	5.8	3,368	1,464	923	58.5	25.4	16.0
Education:								
Less than a high school graduate............	2,009	7.7	1,107	574	328	55.1	28.6	16.3
High school graduate..........................	2,811	8.2	1,839	463	508	65.4	16.5	18.1
High school graduate with some college....	3,122	7.6	1,929	642	551	61.8	20.6	17.6
Associate's degree............................	3,580	7.0	2,254	755	571	63.0	21.1	15.9
Bachelor's degree.............................	4,251	6.7	2,591	1,013	646	61.0	23.8	15.2
Master's, professional, or doctoral degree...	5,336	6.5	3,166	1,269	901	59.3	23.8	16.9

[1] Includes prescription and nonprescription drugs. [2] All other races includes Native Hawaiian or other Pacific Islander, American Indian or Alaska Native, and approximately 1 percent reporting more than one race.

Source: U.S. Bureau of Labor Statistics, "Consumer Expenditure Survey, Annual Calendar Year Tables, 2013," <http://www.bls.gov/cex/tables.htm>, accessed January 2015.

Table 156. Medical Expenditures by Health Condition in Current and Chained (2009) Dollars and Per Capita: 2000 to 2012

[In billions of dollars (1,109.59 represents $1,109,590,000,000), except as noted. Health conditions are classified according to the International Classification of Diseases, 9th revision (ICD-9). Based on Bureau of Economic Analysis' Health Care Satellite Account, Blended Account. The Blended Account blends data from multiple sources, including large claims databases. The BEA also has available health expenditure data based on the Medical Expenditure Panel Survey. See source for details]

Health expense item	Current dollars (billions)			Chained (2009) billion dollars			Per capita (dollars)		
	2000	2010	2012	2000	2010	2012	2000	2010	2012
Total health	**1,109.59**	**2,080.44**	**2,285.73**	**1,676.27**	**2,017.86**	**2,126.44**	**3,932.45**	**6,725.71**	**7,282.32**
Health services	1,052.23	1,979.18	2,174.06	1,615.13	1,916.12	2,015.26	3,729.16	6,398.36	6,926.54
Medical services by disease	900.75	1,722.41	1,903.44	1,394.53	1,665.09	1,761.17	3,192.31	5,568.26	6,064.35
Infectious and parasitic diseases	23.35	58.63	67.59	42.64	54.57	60.98	82.75	189.54	215.34
Neoplasms	61.87	117.25	124.74	102.69	116.00	120.86	219.27	379.05	397.42
Endocrine, nutritional, and metabolic diseases and immunity disorders	54.21	127.72	139.37	80.59	126.47	135.23	192.12	412.90	444.03
Mental illness	39.61	72.35	80.35	55.85	70.75	78.61	140.38	233.90	255.99
Diseases of the nervous system and sense organs	60.39	120.24	134.34	100.46	113.66	119.59	214.03	388.72	428.01
Diseases of the circulatory system	156.34	235.85	243.19	207.74	228.85	234.11	554.08	762.46	774.80
Diseases of the respiratory system	92.32	145.45	158.03	134.95	136.82	141.18	327.19	470.22	503.48
Diseases of the digestive system	56.81	99.17	108.08	88.57	94.74	95.32	201.34	320.60	344.34
Diseases of the genitourinary system	54.33	107.16	113.75	89.92	107.82	113.89	192.55	346.43	362.41
Complications of pregnancy, childbirth, and the puerperium	21.55	33.27	38.92	30.68	31.13	34.14	76.37	107.56	124.00
Diseases of the skin and subcutaneous organs	21.62	39.40	44.66	34.03	38.21	40.32	76.62	127.37	142.29
Diseases of the musculoskeletal system and connective tissue	77.57	170.62	187.65	124.63	162.06	172.96	274.91	551.59	597.85
Injury and poisoning	65.07	109.74	118.84	106.08	105.46	110.38	230.61	354.77	378.62
Symptoms, signs, and ill-defined conditions	83.35	216.27	249.65	136.80	206.56	228.71	295.40	699.16	795.38
Other diseases	32.37	69.28	94.29	59.33	72.13	75.16	114.72	223.97	300.41
Diseases of blood and blood-forming organs	8.84	20.51	37.41	19.02	23.46	23.60	31.33	66.31	119.19
Congenital anomalies	4.95	7.07	7.17	8.29	7.52	7.46	17.54	22.86	22.84
Conditions originating in perinatal period	4.48	5.99	7.68	7.62	6.50	6.77	15.88	19.36	24.47
Residual codes, unclassified, all E codes [1]	14.10	35.71	42.03	24.47	34.63	37.32	49.97	115.44	133.91
Medical services by provider	151.48	256.78	270.62	220.78	251.04	253.98	536.85	830.13	862.19
Dental services	63.57	104.48	109.02	95.42	101.69	101.38	225.30	337.77	347.34
Nursing homes	87.91	152.29	161.60	125.35	149.35	152.62	311.56	492.33	514.86
Proprietary and government nursing homes	56.85	100.22	108.07	81.06	98.28	102.05	201.48	323.99	344.31
Nonprofit nursing homes services to households	31.06	52.07	53.53	44.29	51.08	50.56	110.08	168.33	170.55
Medical products, appliances and equipment	57.36	101.26	111.67	63.43	101.83	111.48	203.29	327.36	355.78
Pharmaceutical and other medical products	25.19	45.64	49.97	27.40	45.86	50.41	89.27	147.55	159.20
Pharmaceutical products (excludes prescription drugs) [2]	23.24	41.66	45.50	25.35	41.79	45.92	82.36	134.68	144.96
Nonprescription drugs	23.24	41.66	45.50	25.35	41.79	45.92	82.36	134.68	144.96
Other medical products	1.95	3.99	4.46	2.06	4.07	4.49	6.91	12.90	14.21
Therapeutic appliances and equipment	32.17	55.61	61.70	36.05	55.97	61.07	114.01	179.78	196.58
Corrective eyeglasses and contact lenses	19.91	29.71	32.87	23.34	29.51	32.07	70.56	96.05	104.72
Therapeutic medical equipment	12.26	25.91	28.84	12.95	26.46	29.01	43.45	83.76	91.88

[1] E codes cover external causes of injury or poisoning. [2] Excludes prescription drugs; prescription drug expenses have been allocated by health condition.

Source: U.S. Bureau of Economic Analysis, Health Care Satellite Account, "Blended Account, 2000-2012," <http://www.bea.gov/national/health_care_satellite_account.htm>, accessed August 2015.

Table 157. Children's Health Insurance Program (CHIP)—Enrollment and Expenditures, by State: 2012 to 2014

[Expenditures in millions of dollars (11,966 represents $11,966,000,000). For fiscal years. CHIP is a federal-state program that provides health benefits coverage to children without health insurance and living in families whose incomes are too high to qualify for Medicaid. States may create CHIP programs as an expansion of Medicaid, a program separate from Medicaid, or a combination of both approaches. Based on analysis of CHIP data from the Centers for Medicare & Medicaid Services; see source for details]

State	FY2012		FY2013		FY2014 Expenditures [2]		
	Total Children enrolled [1]	Total expend-itures	Total Children enrolled [1]	Total expend-itures	Total	Federal	State [3]
United States............	8,143,174	11,966	8,130,793	12,962	12,817	9,033	3,784
Alabama....................	112,972	201	113,490	193	182	141	41
Alaska.....................	13,499	30	16,566	33	30	19	10
Arizona....................	35,679	32	80,238	74	85	66	20
Arkansas..................	114,056	125	109,301	123	97	77	20
California.................	1,784,032	1,918	1,603,283	2,127	2,189	1,423	766
Colorado [4]...............	126,169	194	[5] 126,169	227	197	128	69
Connecticut...............	19,986	25	18,999	28	31	39	-9
Delaware..................	12,850	22	13,180	25	24	17	8
District of Columbia........	7,293	18	9,057	18	21	16	4
Florida....................	415,027	499	473,415	521	647	460	187
Georgia....................	258,425	356	269,906	413	439	335	105
Hawaii.....................	33,764	39	30,979	40	57	38	19
Idaho......................	45,932	44	45,399	61	67	54	13
Illinois....................	347,904	408	337,097	518	454	295	159
Indiana....................	154,262	181	152,415	157	173	133	40
Iowa.......................	80,454	123	83,670	134	146	103	43
Kansas....................	64,229	76	76,164	76	99	69	30
Kentucky..................	85,331	178	84,069	185	178	140	38
Louisiana.................	150,672	227	149,968	203	202	147	55
Maine.....................	36,324	41	29,712	37	31	22	8
Maryland..................	131,898	238	135,454	258	294	191	103
Massachusetts............	145,203	490	148,719	574	519	338	182
Michigan..................	81,429	66	89,670	147	127	97	30
Minnesota.................	4,104	20	3,835	20	17	34	-17
Mississippi................	93,257	208	93,120	208	227	185	43
Missouri...................	92,795	159	92,918	170	181	133	48
Montana [4]................	28,570	75	31,496	92	97	74	23
Nebraska..................	56,266	59	55,783	70	83	57	26
Nevada [4].................	29,854	44	20,277	37	47	35	12
New Hampshire............	11,437	20	19,450	17	16	16	-1
New Jersey................	201,417	947	206,761	958	434	281	152
New Mexico...............	9,582	152	9,368	145	77	60	17
New York [4]..............	547,671	858	490,114	960	1,221	794	427
North Carolina............	259,978	386	283,572	398	423	322	101
North Dakota..............	7,663	24	11,281	27	25	17	9
Ohio.......................	280,650	432	286,817	381	377	280	98
Oklahoma.................	125,889	146	147,911	173	187	140	47
Oregon....................	121,962	187	128,061	209	213	158	55
Pennsylvania..............	271,642	429	267,073	428	449	303	146
Rhode Island..............	26,968	57	26,577	81	58	38	20
South Carolina............	75,281	119	76,191	133	147	116	30
South Dakota..............	17,428	26	17,632	25	23	15	7
Tennessee.................	101,543	252	106,473	260	214	162	52
Texas.....................	999,838	1,201	1,034,613	1,285	1,218	866	352
Utah......................	65,983	75	63,001	69	60	48	13
Vermont...................	7,570	9	7,393	9	9	13	-4
Virginia...................	189,961	276	196,911	301	310	201	108
Washington................	42,614	72	44,073	123	105	105	–
West Virginia..............	37,807	58	37,065	58	57	45	11
Wisconsin.................	169,339	132	167,292	140	241	181	60
Wyoming..................	8,715	16	8,815	16	14	9	5

– Represents or rounds to zero. [1] Enrollment numbers generally include individuals ever enrolled during the year, even if for a single month; in the event individuals were in multiple categories during the year (for example, in Medicaid for the first half of the year but a separate CHIP program for the second half), the individual would only be counted in the most recent category. [2] Components may not add to total due to rounding. [3] Section 2105(g) of the Social Security Act permits 11 qualifying states to use CHIP funds to pay the difference between the regular Medicaid matching rate and the enhanced CHIP matching rate for Medicaid-enrolled, Medicaid-financed children whose family income exceeds 133 percent of the federal poverty level. Although these are CHIP funds, they effectively reduce state spending on children in Medicaid and do not require a state match within the CHIP program. In cases where the sum of 2105(g) federal CHIP spending (for Medicaid enrollees) and regular federal CHIP spending (for CHIP enrollees) exceeds total spending for CHIP enrollees, states are shown in this table as having negative state CHIP spending (Connecticut, Minnesota, New Hampshire, and Vermont). [4] Montana, Nevada, and New York were combination programs in FY2013 but did not report any Medicaid-expansion enrollees in the CHIP Statistical Enrollment Data System (SEDS). Colorado became a combination program in FY2013 but had not yet reported any SEDS data for that year as of March 4, 2014. [5] Enrollment data for Colorado are for FY2012.

Source: Medicaid and CHIP Payment and Access Commission, "MACStats Program Enrollment and Spending: CHIP," <http://www.macpac.gov/macstats>, accessed August 2015.

Table 158. Medicare Enrollees: 1990 to 2012

[In millions (34.2 represents 34,200,000). As of July 1. Includes Puerto Rico and Island Areas and enrollees in foreign countries and unknown place of residence. The Medicare program has two components: Medicare Part A Hospital Insurance (HI); and Supplementary Medical Insurance (SMI), consisting of Part B Medical Insurance, and Part D Prescription Drug Coverage. See text, this section, for details]

Item	1990	1995	2000	2005	2008	2009	2010	2011	2012
Total............................	**34.2**	**37.6**	**39.6**	**42.5**	**45.4**	**46.5**	**47.7**	**48.8**	**50.8**
Aged............................	31.0	33.2	34.3	35.8	37.9	38.8	39.6	40.5	42.2
Disabled.......................	3.3	4.4	5.4	6.7	7.5	7.8	8.0	8.4	8.6
Hospital insurance, Part A.....	33.7	37.2	39.2	42.1	45.1	46.2	47.3	48.5	50.5
Aged............................	30.5	32.7	33.8	35.4	37.6	38.4	39.3	40.1	41.9
Disabled.......................	3.3	4.4	5.4	6.7	7.5	7.8	8.0	8.4	8.6
SMI, Part B.....................	32.6	35.7	37.4	39.7	42.0	43.0	44.0	44.9	46.6
Aged............................	29.7	31.8	32.6	33.8	35.4	36.1	36.8	37.4	38.8
Disabled.......................	2.9	4.0	4.8	6.0	6.7	6.9	7.2	7.5	7.8
SMI, Part D.....................	(X)	(X)	(X)	1.8	25.8	27.0	28.0	29.5	31.9

X Not applicable.

Source: U.S. Centers for Medicare and Medicaid Services, "Medicare & Medicaid Statistical Supplement, 2013 edition," and earlier editions, <http://www.cms.gov/Research-Statistics-Data-and-Systems/Statistics-Trends-and-Reports/MedicareMedicaidStatSupp/index.html>, accessed March 2014.

Table 159. Medicare—Enrollment by State and Other Areas: 2000 to 2012

[In thousands (39,632 represents 39,632,000). Hospital (HI) and/or supplementary medical insurance (SMI) enrollment as of July 1]

State and area	2000	2010	2011	2012	State and area	2000	2010	2011	2012
All areas [1]........	**39,632**	**47,664**	**48,849**	**50,829**	MO.....................	859	1,004	1,022	1,058
U.S................	**38,782**	**46,585**	**47,741**	**49,682**	MT.....................	137	170	174	182
AL.................	686	845	864	896	NE.....................	254	279	283	291
AK.................	42	66	69	73	NV.....................	246	357	372	394
AZ.................	676	930	962	1,009	NH.....................	169	223	229	241
AR.................	434	531	542	559	NJ.....................	1,212	1,327	1,352	1,398
CA.................	3,922	4,757	4,901	5,111	NM.....................	234	313	322	336
CO.................	470	625	650	688	NY.....................	2,695	2,988	3,041	3,138
CT.................	518	568	577	595	NC.....................	1,131	1,490	1,533	1,604
DE.................	115	149	154	161	ND.....................	102	109	110	112
DC.................	75	78	80	82	OH.....................	1,706	1,901	1,934	2,003
FL.................	2,827	3,375	3,472	3,621	OK.....................	507	603	615	636
GA.................	928	1,236	1,281	1,351	OR.....................	496	621	640	672
HI.................	168	206	213	222	PA.....................	2,091	2,283	2,312	2,385
ID.................	167	230	238	250	RI.....................	170	183	186	191
IL.................	1,626	1,839	1,872	1,935	SC.....................	570	774	799	840
IN.................	848	1,006	1,027	1,065	SD.....................	118	137	139	143
IA.................	475	517	523	537	TN.....................	830	1,058	1,086	1,133
KS.................	386	433	439	454	TX.....................	2,268	3,001	3,104	3,256
KY.................	618	760	777	804	UT.....................	209	283	292	307
LA.................	600	687	703	729	VT.....................	89	112	115	120
ME.................	216	265	271	282	VA.....................	896	1,141	1,173	1,227
MD.................	646	785	807	845	WA.....................	736	972	1,005	1,056
MA.................	961	1,061	1,085	1,126	WV.....................	338	382	386	397
MI.................	1,402	1,651	1,689	1,754	WI.....................	776	911	931	966
MN.................	655	786	804	836	WY.....................	66	80	82	86
MS.................	419	497	507	524	Outlying areas [2]......	850	1,079	1,109	1,146

[1] Includes outlying areas. [2] Includes Puerto Rico, Guam, Virgin Islands, residence unknown, and all other outlying areas not shown separately.

Source: U.S. Centers for Medicare and Medicaid Services, "Medicare & Medicaid Statistical Supplement, 2013 edition," and earlier editions, <http://www.cms.gov/Research-Statistics-Data-and-Systems/Statistics-Trends-and-Reports/MedicareMedicaidStatSupp/index.html>, accessed March 2014.

Table 160. Medicaid Enrollment by Race and Ethnicity, Age, and Poverty Status: 2013

[In thousands, except percent (53,786 represents 53,786,000). Based on the 2014 Current Population Survey Annual Social and Economic Supplement (CPS ASEC). Represents number of persons as of March of following year who were enrolled at any time in year shown. Excludes unrelated individuals under age 15. Persons did not have to receive medical care paid for by Medicaid in order to be counted. For explanation of poverty level, see text, Section 13. For methodology, see source report, and also <ftp://ftp2.census.gov/library/publications/2014/demo/p60-249sa.pdf> and <ftp://ftp2.census.gov/programs-surveys/cps/techdocs/cpsmar14.pdf>. Please note that the Census Bureau implemented changes to the CPS ASEC in 2014, including new questions on health insurance; users should exercise caution when comparing 2013 data from the 2014 CPS ASEC to data from previous year surveys]

Poverty status	Total [1]	White alone [2]	Black alone [2]	Asian alone [2]	His- panic [3]	Under 18 years	18–44 years	45–64 years	65 years and over
Persons covered, total......	**53,786**	**35,936**	**12,199**	**2,507**	**15,715**	**27,519**	**15,215**	**8,212**	**2,840**
Below poverty level.............	21,701	13,198	6,514	568	6,887	11,416	6,177	3,271	837
Above poverty level.............	32,085	22,738	5,685	1,938	8,829	16,103	9,038	4,941	2,003
Percent of population covered.......................	**17.2**	**14.8**	**30.0**	**14.7**	**29.0**	**37.4**	**13.5**	**10.0**	**6.4**
Below poverty level.............	47.9	44.1	59.0	31.8	54.0	77.9	35.5	36.2	19.8
Above poverty level.............	12.0	10.7	19.2	12.7	21.3	27.3	9.5	6.7	5.0

[1] Includes other races, not shown separately. [2] Refers to people who reported specified race and did not report any other race category. [3] Persons of Hispanic origin may be of any race.

Source: U.S. Census Bureau, *Health Insurance Coverage in the United States: 2013*, Current Population Reports, P60-250, September 2014; and Detailed Tables "HI02. Health Insurance Coverage Status and Type of Coverage by Selected Characteristics for People in the Poverty Universe: 2013," and "HI03. Health Insurance Coverage Status and Type of Coverage by Selected Characteristics for Poor People in the Poverty Universe: 2013," <http://www.census.gov/hhes/www/hlthins/data/index.html>, accessed January 2015.

Table 161. Medicare Insurance Trust Funds: 1990 to 2014

[In billions of dollars (126.3 represents $126,300,000,000), on cash basis, for calendar years. Medicare has two components: Hospital Insurance (HI), also known as Medicare Part A; and Supplementary Medical Insurance (SMI), consisting of Medicare Part B (medical insurance) and Part D (prescription drug coverage). See text, this section, for details]

Type of trust fund	1990	2000	2005	2009	2010	2011	2012	2013	2014
TOTAL MEDICARE									
Total income	126.3	257.1	357.5	508.3	486.1	530.0	536.9	575.8	599.3
Total expenditures	111.0	221.8	336.4	509.0	522.9	549.1	574.2	582.9	613.3
Assets, end of year	114.4	221.5	309.8	380.8	344.0	324.9	287.6	280.5	266.4
HOSPITAL INSURANCE, PART A									
Net contribution income [1]	71.9	155.5	183.3	208.3	199.5	214.8	228.6	239.3	249.6
Interest and other income [2]	8.5	11.7	16.1	17.1	16.1	14.2	14.5	11.8	11.7
Benefit payments [3]	66.2	128.5	180.0	239.3	244.5	252.9	262.9	261.9	264.9
Trust fund balance, end of year	98.9	177.5	285.8	304.2	271.9	244.2	220.4	205.4	197.3
SMI, PART B									
Premiums from enrollees [4]	11.3	20.6	37.5	56.0	52.0	57.5	58.0	63.1	65.6
Government contributions [5]	33.0	65.9	118.1	162.8	153.5	170.2	163.8	185.8	188.5
Interest and other income [2]	1.6	3.5	1.4	3.1	3.3	5.9	5.2	6.1	5.7
Benefit payments [3]	42.5	88.9	149.9	202.6	209.7	221.7	236.5	243.8	261.9
Trust fund balance, end of year	15.5	44.0	24.0	75.5	71.4	79.7	66.2	74.1	68.1
SMI, PART D									
Premiums from enrollees [6]	(X)	(X)	–	6.3	6.5	7.7	8.3	9.9	11.4
Government contributions [7]	(X)	(X)	1.1	47.1	51.1	52.6	50.1	51.0	58.1
Interest and other income	(X)	(X)	–	–	–	–	–	–	–
Benefit payments [8]	(X)	(X)	1.1	60.5	61.7	66.7	66.5	69.3	77.7
Trust fund balance, end of year	(X)	(X)	–	1.1	0.7	1.0	1.0	1.0	1.1

– Represents or rounds to zero. X Not applicable. [1] Includes income from payroll taxes, taxation of benefits, railroad retirement account transfers, reimbursement for uninsured persons, premiums from voluntary enrollees, and payments for military wage credits. [2] Includes recoveries of amounts reimbursed from the trust fund, receipts from fraud and abuse control program, and other miscellaneous income. [3] Includes monies transferred to the SMI trust fund in 1998-2003 for home health agency costs. In 2008 benefit payments were $223,815 million and include a transfer of $8,484 million to the general fund of the Treasury for HI hospice costs that were misallocated to, and paid from, the Part B account of the SMI trust fund from May 2005 to September 2007. (The general fund, in turn, transferred $8,484 million to the Part B account.) [4] Includes adjustments for benefit checks issued at the end of the year instead of early January. [5] Matching payments from the general fund, plus certain interest-adjustment items. See also footnote 4. [6] Premiums include both amounts withheld from Social Security benefit checks (and other certain Federal benefit payments) and amounts paid directly to Part D plans. [7] Includes, net of transfers from States, all government transfers required to fund benefit payments, administrative expenses, and State expenses for making low-income eligibility determinations. [8] Includes payments to plans, subsidies to employer-sponsored retiree prescription drug plans, payments to States for making low-income eligibility determinations, Part D drug premiums collected from beneficiaries and transferred to Medicare Advantage plans and private drug plans, and premium amounts paid directly by enrollees to plans. (The last item is on an estimated basis; see note 6.) Includes amounts for transitional assistance benefits in 2004-2007.

Source: U.S. Centers for Medicare and Medicaid Services, Trustees Report & Trust Funds, "2015 Expanded and Supplementary Tables," <http://www.cms.gov/Research-Statistics-Data-and-Systems/Statistics-Trends-and-Reports/ReportsTrustFunds/index.html>, accessed July 2015.

Table 162. Medicare Hospital Insurance and Supplementary Medical Insurance—Average Costs per Beneficiary: 1974 to 2015

[In dollars. See headnote, Table 161]

Year	Total	Hospital Insurance	SMI Part B	SMI Part D	Year	Total	Hospital Insurance	SMI Part B	SMI Part D
1974	573	400	173	(X)	1995	5,061	3,130	1,867	(X)
1975	677	472	205	(X)	1996	5,378	3,412	1,954	(X)
1976	788	528	240	(X)	1997	5,635	3,616	2,033	(X)
1977	891	605	273	(X)	1998	5,562	3,468	2,134	(X)
1978	1,010	662	314	(X)	1999	5,614	3,306	2,255	(X)
1979	1,147	753	361	(X)	2000	5,844	3,348	2,496	(X)
1980	1,352	895	423	(X)	2001	6,370	3,610	2,760	(X)
1981	1,583	1,064	490	(X)	2002	6,788	3,813	2,975	(X)
1982	1,819	1,227	570	(X)	2003	7,144	3,924	3,221	(X)
1983	2,025	1,331	658	(X)	2004	7,723	4,163	3,560	(X)
1984	2,236	1,441	724	(X)	2005	8,278	4,440	3,839	(X)
1985	2,373	1,554	795	(X)	2006	10,338	4,603	4,117	1,619
1986	2,504	1,592	907	(X)	2007	10,707	4,762	4,315	1,630
1987	2,661	1,553	1,024	(X)	2008	11,165	4,929	4,574	1,662
1988	2,781	1,620	1,135	(X)	2009	11,635	5,108	4,798	1,730
1989	3,097	1,816	1,237	(X)	2010	11,835	5,120	4,907	1,807
1990	3,334	1,963	1,355	(X)	2011	12,109	5,213	5,038	1,858
1991	3,569	2,076	1,443	(X)	2012	12,143	5,130	5,173	1,840
1992	3,941	2,385	1,530	(X)	2013	12,150	5,090	5,184	1,877
1993	4,259	2,603	1,611	(X)	2014	12,432	4,935	5,417	2,081
1994	4,678	2,825	1,730	(X)	2015	12,560	4,890	5,538	2,132

X Not applicable.

Source: U.S. Centers for Medicare and Medicaid Services, Trustees Report & Trust Funds, "2015 Expanded and Supplementary Tables," <http://www.cms.gov/Research-Statistics-Data-and-Systems/Statistics-Trends-and-Reports/ReportsTrustFunds/index.html>, accessed July 2015.

Table 163. Medicaid—Summary by State: 2010 and 2012

[65,700 represents 65,700,000. For year ending September 30]

State	Beneficiaries [1] (1,000) 2010	[3] 2012	Payments [2] (mil. dol.) 2010	[3] 2012	State	Beneficiaries [1] (1,000) 2010	2012	Payments [2] (mil. dol.) 2010	2012
U.S.........	65,700	53,187	338,994	288,905	MO............	1,141	1,151	6,196	6,594
AL............	931	958	4,042	4,107	MT............	126	140	762	825
AK............	127	137	1,207	1,334	NE............	269	293	1,586	1,693
AZ............	1,805	(NA)	9,511	(NA)	NV............	334	377	1,300	1,377
AR............	773	797	3,799	3,582	NH............	148	163	1,009	1,056
CA............	11,212	10,573	34,686	35,510	NJ............	1,229	1,521	8,558	9,409
CO............	682	(NA)	3,300	(NA)	NM............	557	560	2,771	2,516
CT............	664	750	5,390	5,882	NY............	5,011	5,802	42,724	48,330
DE............	210	239	1,342	1,569	NC............	1,876	2,066	9,591	10,003
DC............	211	(NA)	1,806	(NA)	ND............	83	91	682	776
FL............	3,656	(NA)	16,131	(NA)	OH............	2,319	2,500	14,450	16,188
GA............	1,875	2,168	6,969	9,098	OK............	853	982	3,713	3,885
HI............	288	(NA)	1,353	(NA)	OR............	644	760	3,187	3,756
ID............	430	(NA)	1,235	(NA)	PA............	2,326	2,499	15,894	17,793
IL............	2,758	3,062	11,646	13,447	RI............	214	226	1,574	1,582
IN............	1,177	1,278	5,753	6,550	SC............	953	986	5,090	4,825
IA............	508	559	3,005	3,424	SD............	142	136	777	768
KS............	364	(NA)	2,295	(NA)	TN............	1,532	1,537	9,061	12,294
KY............	959	1,088	5,304	5,664	TX............	4,745	(NA)	20,718	(NA)
LA............	1,237	(NA)	5,491	(NA)	UT............	369	(NA)	1,995	(NA)
ME............	330	(NA)	1,468	(NA)	VT............	181	188	1,000	1,077
MD............	940	1,047	6,838	7,449	VA............	969	1,030	5,861	6,037
MA............	1,637	(NA)	11,069	(NA)	WA............	1,330	1,463	6,312	6,255
MI............	2,219	2,253	11,380	12,302	WV............	397	405	2,690	3,049
MN............	851	1,071	7,136	8,654	WI............	1,230	1,363	5,403	5,811
MS............	801	892	3,364	3,853	WY............	76	76	572	582

NA Not available. [1] Persons who had payments made on their behalf at any time during the fiscal year. [2] Payments are for fiscal year and reflect federal and state contribution payments. Data exclude disproportionate share hospital payments. Disproportionate share hospitals receive higher Medicaid reimbursement than other hospitals because they treat a disproportionate share of Medicaid patients. [3] Fiscal year 2012 data omits Arizona, Colorado, DC, Florida, Hawaii, Idaho, Kansas, Louisiana, Maine, Massachusetts, Texas, and Utah.

Source: U.S. Centers for Medicare and Medicaid Services, "Medicaid Statistical Information System (MSIS) Tables," <https://www.cms.gov/Research-Statistics-Data-and-Systems/Computer-Data-and-Systems/MedicaidDataSourcesGenInfo/MSIS-Tables.html>, accessed June 2015.

Table 164. Medicaid—Beneficiaries and Payments: 2005 to 2012

[57,651 represents 57,651,000. For year ending September 30]

Basis of eligibility and type of service	Beneficiaries (1,000) [1] 2005	2010	[9] 2011	[10] 2012	Payments (mil. dol.) 2005	2010	[9] 2011	[10] 2012
Total....................	57,651	65,700	68,850	53,187	274,851	338,994	365,160	288,905
BASIS OF ELIGIBILITY								
Age 65 and over....................	4,395	4,303	4,300	3,388	63,415	65,769	66,607	53,430
Blind/disabled......................	8,211	9,381	9,695	7,699	119,305	147,238	154,944	125,420
Children........................	26,341	30,775	31,606	24,002	41,863	61,512	65,855	50,356
Adults............................	12,533	15,529	16,266	13,691	32,162	47,561	53,224	45,266
Foster care children.................	874	930	903	675	5,286	5,754	5,607	4,469
BCCA WOMEN [2].................	29	53	52	49	281	668	720	700
Unknown....................	5,268	4,441	5,229	2,786	12,539	10,202	16,770	7,906
SERVICE CATEGORY								
Capitated care [3]....................	33,496	46,493	49,022	37,454	46,421	92,187	108,828	95,909
Clinic services.....................	11,918	13,595	14,399	11,924	8,921	10,754	12,341	10,434
Dental services....................	9,317	12,577	13,443	9,096	3,040	5,436	5,698	3,332
Home health services...............	1,195	1,137	1,094	792	5,362	7,248	7,187	4,094
ICF/IID services [4].................	109	100	94	70	11,709	12,536	13,111	9,858
Inpatient hospital services.........	5,480	4,565	5,136	3,688	35,131	33,535	36,911	30,047
Lab and X-ray services............	15,959	16,922	16,884	12,073	2,917	3,469	3,513	2,092
Mental health facility services [5]...	120	122	123	96	2,301	2,528	2,462	2,120
Nursing facility services...........	1,711	1,547	1,616	1,192	44,790	48,912	48,241	38,360
Other care [6]........................	12,346	12,803	13,384	9,232	26,421	41,353	41,374	32,789
Outpatient hospital services......	16,234	15,905	16,285	11,314	10,011	12,767	13,088	9,408
Other practitioner services........	5,893	6,023	5,727	4,438	1,180	1,145	1,665	1,562
PCCM services [7]...................	8,723	8,715	9,435	7,047	232	423	429	390
Prescribed drugs....................	28,390	29,353	30,284	19,650	42,849	27,187	29,497	17,475
Physician services..................	24,238	24,215	24,006	17,412	11,269	11,921	12,049	8,302
Personal support services [8].......	6,807	7,220	7,117	5,746	20,657	25,940	25,288	22,072
Sterilizations.......................	178	134	131	96	211	137	137	94
Unknown...........................	73	138	132	119	1,428	1,514	3,341	566

[1] Beneficiaries data do not add to total due to number of beneficiaries that are reported in more than one category. [2] Women-Breast and Cervical Cancer Assistance. [3] HMO payments and prepaid health plans. [4] Intermediate care facilities for individuals with intellectual disabilities. [5] Inpatient mental health facilities for individuals under 21 and for individuals 65 years and older. [6] Includes beneficiaries of, and payments for, other care not shown separately. [7] Primary Care Case Management Services. [8] Includes personal care services, rehabilitative services, physical occupational targeted case management services, speech therapies, hospice services, nurse midwife services, nurse practitioner services, private duty nursing services, and religious nonmedical health care institutions. [9] Fiscal year 2011 data omit Maine. [10] Fiscal year 2012 data omit Arizona, Colorado, DC, Florida, Hawaii, Idaho, Kansas, Louisiana, Massachusetts, Maine, Texas, and Utah.

Source: U.S. Centers for Medicare and Medicaid Services, "MSIS (Medicaid Statistical Information System) Tables," <https://www.cms.gov/Research-Statistics-Data-and-Systems/Computer-Data-and-Systems/MedicaidDataSourcesGenInfo/MSIS-Tables.html>, accessed July 2015.

Table 165. Medicaid Managed Care Enrollment by State and Other Areas: 1995 to 2013

[In thousands except as noted (33,373 represents 33,373,000). For year ending June 30. The unduplicated Medicaid enrollment figures include individuals in state health care reform programs that expand eligibility beyond traditional Medicaid eligibility standards. The unduplicated managed care enrollment figures includes enrollees receiving comprehensive and limited benefits]

State and other areas	Total enroll-ment	Managed care enrollment Number	Percent of total	State and other areas	Total enroll-ment	Managed care enrollment Number	Percent of total	State and other areas	Total enroll-ment	Managed care enrollment Number	Percent of total
1995	33,373	9,800	29.4	GA	1,814	1,186	65.4	NM	555	413	74.5
2000	33,690	18,786	55.8	HI	307	303	98.7	NY	5,353	4,039	75.5
2005	45,392	28,576	63.0	ID	255	241	94.6	NC	1,589	1,210	76.1
2008	47,143	33,428	70.1	IL	2,931	2,065	70.5	ND	77	43	55.7
2009	50,472	36,202	71.7	IN	1,126	766	68.0	OH	2,390	1,668	69.8
2010	54,612	39,020	71.5	IA	434	357	82.2	OK	736	540	73.4
2011	57,107	42,385	74.2	KS	399	329	82.5	OR	695	627	90.2
2012	(NA)	(NA)	(NA)	KY	847	717	84.6	PA	3,447	1,861	54.0
2013				LA	1,257	1,101	87.6	RI	197	148	74.9
Total [1]	**62,151**	**44,534**	**71.7**	ME	262	161	61.5	SC	1,002	640	63.8
U.S.	60,512	43,013	71.1	MD	1,089	865	79.4	SD	122	91	74.8
AL	960	571	59.5	MA	1,410	904	64.1	TN	1,216	1,216	100.0
AK	145	–	–	MI	1,816	1,292	71.1	TX	3,879	2,999	77.3
AZ	1,271	1,073	84.4	MN	902	633	70.2	UT	266	262	98.5
AR	614	477	77.7	MS	689	534	77.5	VT	182	103	56.5
CA	8,469	5,711	67.4	MO	868	844	97.2	VA	938	636	67.8
CO	740	705	95.3	MT	119	78	65.5	WA	1,173	790	67.3
CT	622	–	–	NE	244	185	75.7	WV	330	174	52.8
DE	216	182	84.4	NV	329	180	54.9	WI	1,179	741	62.8
DC	253	171	67.7	NH	146	–	–	WY	66	–	(Z)
FL	3,384	2,124	62.8	NJ	1,201	1,056	87.9	PR	1,521	1,521	100.0

– Represents zero. Z Less than 50, or less than .1 percent. NA Not available. [1] Includes enrollment for U.S. territories not shown separately.

Source: U.S. Centers for Medicare and Medicaid Services, Data and System Group, *2013 Medicaid Managed Care Enrollment Report,* and "2013 Enrollment Data by Program and Population." See also <http://www.medicaid.gov/medicaid-chip-program-information/by-topics/data-and-systems/medicaid-managed-care/medicaid-managed-care-enrollment-report.html>.

Table 166. Medicare Hospital Insurance and Supplemental Medical Insurance Expenditures, Total and as a Percent of GDP: 1970 to 2030

[In millions of dollars (1,075,900 represents $1,075,900,000,000), except percent. Incurred amounts relate to expenditures for services performed in a given year, even if payment for those expenditures occurs in a later year. The Medicare program has two components: Medicare Part A Hospital Insurance (HI); and Supplementary Medical Insurance (SMI), consisting of Part B Medical Insurance, and Part D Prescription Drug Coverage. See text in this section for details]

Year	GDP	Medicare expenditures Total	HI Part A	SMI Part B	SMI Part D	Medicare expenditures as percent of GDP Total	HI Part A	SMI Part B	SMI Part D
ACTUAL									
1970	1,075,900	7,638	5,400	2,237	(X)	0.71	0.50	0.21	(X)
1980	2,862,475	36,797	25,249	11,548	(X)	1.29	0.88	0.40	(X)
1990	5,979,550	110,410	66,292	44,118	(X)	1.85	1.11	0.74	(X)
2000	10,284,750	224,013	130,832	93,180	(X)	2.18	1.27	0.91	(X)
2001	10,621,825	246,737	142,778	103,958	(X)	2.32	1.34	0.98	(X)
2002	10,977,525	264,674	151,695	112,979	(X)	2.41	1.38	1.03	(X)
2003	11,510,675	281,917	157,644	124,273	(X)	2.45	1.37	1.08	(X)
2004	12,274,925	309,819	170,093	139,286	440	2.52	1.39	1.13	(X)
2005	13,093,700	339,052	184,417	153,538	1,098	2.59	1.41	1.17	0.01
2006	13,855,900	410,344	195,248	170,446	44,649	2.96	1.41	1.23	0.32
2007	14,477,625	441,329	206,494	183,663	51,173	3.05	1.43	1.27	0.35
2008	14,718,575	460,199	222,535	183,497	54,168	3.13	1.51	1.25	0.37
2009	14,418,725	500,308	236,264	205,851	58,193	3.47	1.64	1.43	0.40
2010	14,964,400	520,713	242,527	215,338	62,849	3.48	1.62	1.44	0.42
2011	15,517,925	545,763	253,097	226,293	66,373	3.52	1.63	1.46	0.43
2012	16,163,150	568,583	259,248	240,429	68,906	3.52	1.60	1.49	0.43
2013	16,768,050	587,318	265,400	248,533	73,385	3.50	1.58	1.48	0.44
2014	17,410,700	615,502	263,992	267,273	84,237	3.54	1.52	1.54	0.48
PROJECTED [1]									
2015	18,163,170	641,641	271,344	281,225	89,073	3.53	1.49	1.55	0.49
2020	23,687,429	909,775	362,311	404,277	143,186	3.84	1.53	1.71	0.60
2025	29,765,273	1,340,606	518,793	606,713	215,099	4.50	1.74	2.04	0.72
2030	37,088,511	1,869,461	704,546	858,495	306,420	5.04	1.90	2.31	0.83

X Not applicable. [1] Projections are a projected baseline, and are based on current law; that is, they assume that laws on the books will be implemented and adhered to with respect to scheduled taxes, premium revenues, and payments to providers and health plans. The one exception is that the projections disregard payment reductions that would result from the projected depletion of the Medicare Hospital Insurance trust fund (Part A). To date, Congress has not allowed the assets of the Medicare Hospital Insurance trust fund to become depleted.

Source: U.S. Centers for Medicare and Medicaid Services, Trustees Report & Trust Funds, "2015 Expanded and Supplementary Tables," <http://www.cms.gov/Research-Statistics-Data-and-Systems/Statistics-Trends-and-Reports/ReportsTrustFunds/index.html>, accessed July 2015.

Table 167. Health Insurance Coverage Status by Selected Characteristics: 2013

[313,395 represents 313,395,000. Persons as of following year for coverage in the year shown. Government health insurance includes Medicare, Medicaid, and military plans. Based on the Current Population Survey Annual Social and Economic Supplement (CPS ASEC); see text, Section 1 and Appendix III. The CPS ASEC in 2014 included new questions on health insurance; users should exercise caution when comparing 2013 data from the 2014 CPS ASEC to data from previous year surveys]

	Number (1,000)							Percent			
		Not covered by health insur-ance	Covered by private or government health insurance					Not covered by health insur-ance	Covered by private or government health insurance		
				Private		Government					
Characteristic	Total persons		Total[1]	Total	Employer based	Medi-care	Medic-aid		Total[1]	Private	Medic-aid
Total..............	313,395	41,953	271,442	201,064	169,015	48,977	54,081	13.4	86.6	64.2	17.3
Age:											
Under 18 years......	74,055	5,441	68,613	44,429	40,556	264	27,814	7.3	92.7	60.0	37.6
Under 6 years......	23,997	1,815	22,182	13,013	12,188	66	10,224	7.6	92.4	54.2	42.6
6 to 11 years.......	24,559	1,650	22,909	14,827	13,755	86	9,487	6.7	93.3	60.4	38.6
12 to 17 years......	25,499	1,977	23,522	16,589	14,613	112	8,103	7.8	92.2	65.1	31.8
18 to 24 years......	30,054	6,208	23,846	19,035	13,793	254	5,193	20.7	79.3	63.3	17.3
25 to 34 years.......	42,466	10,069	32,397	26,647	23,514	615	5,522	23.7	76.3	62.8	13.0
35 to 44 years......	39,789	7,556	32,233	27,661	25,447	948	4,501	19.0	81.0	69.5	11.3
45 to 54 years......	42,898	6,739	36,159	31,250	28,290	1,931	3,943	15.7	84.3	72.8	9.2
55 to 64 years......	39,626	5,247	34,380	28,003	24,400	3,523	4,270	13.2	86.8	70.7	10.8
65 years and over...	44,508	693	43,815	24,039	13,015	41,442	2,840	1.6	98.4	54.0	6.4
Sex:											
Male..................	153,596	22,258	131,339	98,756	84,101	21,779	25,029	14.5	85.5	64.3	16.3
Female..............	159,799	19,696	140,103	102,308	84,914	27,198	29,052	12.3	87.7	64.0	18.2
Race:											
White alone[2]........	243,399	31,053	212,346	162,474	135,230	41,100	36,141	12.8	87.2	66.8	14.8
Black alone[2]........	40,671	6,475	34,196	20,174	17,888	5,113	12,241	15.9	84.1	49.6	30.1
Asian alone[2].......	17,070	2,471	14,599	11,616	10,035	1,811	2,509	14.5	85.5	68.1	14.7
Hispanic origin[3]......	54,253	13,203	41,050	24,725	21,740	3,792	15,791	24.3	75.7	45.6	29.1
Household income:											
Less than $25,000...	55,692	12,052	43,640	14,882	7,664	15,016	21,516	21.6	78.4	26.7	38.6
$25,000–$49,999. ..	70,057	13,125	56,932	35,260	26,639	14,672	16,625	18.7	81.3	50.3	23.7
$50,000–$74,999. ..	57,090	7,480	49,610	39,804	33,808	8,525	7,675	13.1	86.9	69.7	13.4
$75,000 or more.....	130,557	9,297	121,260	111,119	100,904	10,764	8,265	7.1	92.9	85.1	6.3
Persons below poverty.............	45,318	11,276	34,042	10,317	5,749	5,864	21,701	24.9	75.1	22.8	47.9

[1] Includes other private and government insurance, not shown separately. Persons with coverage counted only once in total, even though they may have been covered by more than one type of policy. [2] Refers to people who reported specified race and did not report any other race category. [3] Persons of Hispanic origin may be of any race.

Source: U.S. Census Bureau, *Health Insurance Coverage in the United States: 2013,* Current Population Reports, P60-250, September 2014; and Detailed Tables "HI01. Health Insurance Coverage Status and Type of Coverage by Selected Characteristics: 2013" and "HI03. Health Insurance Coverage Status and Type of Coverage by Selected Characteristics for Poor People in the Poverty Universe: 2013," <http://www.census.gov/hhes/www/cpstables/032014/health/toc.htm>, accessed January 2015. See also <http://www.census.gov/hhes/www/hlthins/>.

Table 168. Persons With and Without Health Insurance Coverage by State: 2013

[265,977 represents 265,977,000. Beginning with 2013, data are from the American Community Survey (ACS) and are not directly comparable to data for prior years. See source for more information]

State	Total persons covered (1,000)	Total persons not covered		Children not covered		State	Total persons covered (1,000)	Total persons not covered		Children not covered	
		Number (1,000)	Percent of total	Number (1,000)	Percent of total			Number (1,000)	Percent of total	Number (1,000)	Percent of total
U.S.........	265,977	45,181	14.5	5,234	7.1	MO..........	5,158	773	13.0	98	7.0
AL...........	4,110	645	13.6	48	4.3	MT..........	835	165	16.5	22	10.1
AK...........	580	132	18.5	22	11.6	NE..........	1,632	209	11.3	25	5.5
AZ...........	5,403	1,118	17.1	192	11.9	NV..........	2,187	570	20.7	99	14.9
AR...........	2,442	465	16.0	39	5.5	NH..........	1,168	140	10.7	10	3.8
CA...........	31,331	6,500	17.2	673	7.4	NJ...........	7,631	1,160	13.2	112	5.6
CO...........	4,444	729	14.1	102	8.2	NM..........	1,669	382	18.6	43	8.5
CT...........	3,209	333	9.4	34	4.3	NY..........	17,331	2,070	10.7	171	4.0
DE...........	828	83	9.1	9	4.5	NC..........	8,136	1,509	15.6	144	6.3
DC...........	594	42	6.7	3	2.4	ND..........	635	73	10.4	13	7.9
FL...........	15,392	3,853	20.0	445	11.1	OH..........	10,141	1,258	11.0	141	5.3
GA...........	7,955	1,846	18.8	238	9.6	OK..........	3,104	666	17.7	95	10.0
HI...........	1,254	91	6.7	9	3.0	OR..........	3,322	571	14.7	50	5.8
ID...........	1,335	257	16.2	38	8.9	PA..........	11,347	1,222	9.7	147	5.4
IL...........	11,086	1,618	12.7	125	4.2	RI...........	916	120	11.6	12	5.4
IN...........	5,569	903	14.0	130	8.2	SC..........	3,939	739	15.8	73	6.7
IA...........	2,798	248	8.1	30	4.1	SD..........	734	93	11.3	13	6.3
KS...........	2,489	348	12.3	44	6.1	TN..........	5,508	887	13.9	85	5.7
KY...........	3,696	616	14.3	60	5.9	TX..........	20,228	5,748	22.1	888	12.6
LA...........	3,772	751	16.6	63	5.7	UT..........	2,472	402	14.0	85	9.5
ME...........	1,167	147	11.2	15	5.9	VT..........	576	45	7.2	4	3.1
MD...........	5,241	593	10.2	59	4.4	VA..........	7,064	991	12.3	101	5.4
MA...........	6,367	247	3.7	21	1.5	WA..........	5,904	960	14.0	95	5.9
MI...........	8,713	1,072	11.0	90	4.0	WV..........	1,570	255	14.0	20	5.3
MN...........	4,923	440	8.2	72	5.6	WI..........	5,151	518	9.1	61	4.7
MS...........	2,425	500	17.1	56	7.6	WY..........	496	77	13.4	8	5.7

Source: U.S. Census Bureau, *Health Insurance Coverage in the United States: 2013,* Current Population Reports, P60-250, September 2014; and Detailed Table "HI05. Health Insurance Coverage Status and Type of Coverage by State and Age for All People: 2013," <http://www.census.gov/hhes/www/hlthins/data/incpovhlth/2013/acs-tables.html>, accessed January 2015. See also <http://www.census.gov/hhes/www/hlthins/index.html>.

Table 169. People Without Health Insurance for the Entire Year by Selected Characteristics: 2012 and 2013

[In thousands, except as noted (311,116 represents 311,116,000). Based on the Current Population Survey (CPS), Annual Social and Economic Supplement (ASEC); see text, Section 1 and Appendix III. The Census Bureau implemented changes to the CPS ASEC in 2014, including new questions on health insurance; users should exercise caution when comparing 2013 data from the 2014 CPS ASEC to data from previous year surveys]

Characteristic	2012			2013		
		Uninsured Persons			Uninsured Persons	
	Total persons	Number	Percent of total persons	Total persons	Number	Percent of total persons
Total [1]	**311,116**	**47,951**	**15.4**	**313,395**	**41,953**	**13.4**
Under 18 years	74,187	6,586	8.9	74,055	5,441	7.3
18 to 24 years	30,030	7,605	25.3	30,054	6,208	20.7
25 to 34 years	41,797	11,435	27.4	42,466	10,069	23.7
35 to 44 years	39,877	8,428	21.1	39,789	7,556	19.0
45 to 54 years	43,446	7,887	18.2	42,898	6,739	15.7
55 to 64 years	38,491	5,370	14.0	39,626	5,247	13.2
65 years and over	43,287	639	1.5	44,508	693	1.6
Male	152,335	25,485	16.7	153,596	22,258	14.5
Female	158,781	22,466	14.1	159,799	19,696	12.3
White alone [2]	242,469	35,625	14.7	243,399	31,053	12.8
Black alone [2]	40,208	7,629	19.0	40,671	6,475	15.9
Asian alone [2]	16,433	2,477	15.1	17,070	2,471	14.5
Hispanic [3]	53,230	15,500	29.1	54,253	13,203	24.3
In families	252,863	35,830	14.2	254,988	31,414	12.3
In married-couple families	188,209	21,561	11.5	189,859	19,020	10.0
In families with male householders, no spouse present	17,570	4,699	26.7	18,121	4,156	22.9
In families with female householders, no spouse present	47,085	9,570	20.3	47,007	8,238	17.5

[1] Includes other races not shown separately. [2] Refers to people who reported specified race and did not report any other race category. [3] Persons of Hispanic origin may be of any race.

Source: U.S. Census Bureau, *Health Insurance Coverage in the United States: 2013*, Current Population Report P60-250, September 2014, and earlier reports; and "Detailed Table HI01," <http://www.census.gov/hhes/www/hlthins/index.html>, accessed January 2015. See also <http://www.census.gov/hhes/www/hlthins/index.html>.

Table 170. Worker Participation in Employer-Sponsored Health Insurance and Benefit Programs, and Participant Contributions: 2014

[Based on the March 2014 National Compensation Survey; survey drew responses from 9,622 private industry establishments of all sizes, representing about 109.1 million workers. Excludes federal government workers, the military, agricultural workers, private household workers, and the self-employed. For more information, see Appendix III, and the Bureau of Labor Statistics (BLS) Handbook of Methods, Chapter 8 online at <http://www.bls.gov/opub/hom/homch8.htm>]

Characteristic	Percent of workers participating—				Single coverage medical plans		Family coverage medical plans	
	Medical care	Dental care	Vision care	Out-patient prescription drug coverage	Percent of employees required to contribute to premiums	Average monthly contribution [1] (dol.)	Percent of employees required to contribute to premiums	Average monthly contribution [1] (dol.)
Total	**50**	**35**	**19**	**49**	**84**	**115.04**	**91**	**448.60**
WORKER CHARACTERISTICS								
Management, professional, and related	66	51	26	64	85	112.93	93	444.65
Management, business, and financial	72	57	29	70	88	112.91	94	452.04
Professional and related	63	47	25	61	83	112.95	92	440.11
Service	23	14	9	23	86	111.32	92	499.04
Sales and office	50	35	17	49	86	118.78	93	459.92
Sales and related	41	29	12	40	92	126.55	95	457.93
Office and administrative support	56	40	20	55	84	114.83	92	460.87
Natural resources, construction, and maintenance	59	34	23	58	74	125.04	82	494.55
Production, transportation, and material moving	57	38	21	56	85	110.97	90	389.73
Production	64	43	22	63	86	111.49	92	380.76
Transportation, and material moving	50	34	21	49	84	110.31	88	401.05
Full-time [2]	63	44	23	62	84	113.56	91	446.12
Part-time [2]	12	8	5	12	88	136.55	92	485.31
Union [3]	78	61	50	77	64	108.43	69	339.60
Nonunion	47	32	16	46	88	115.80	95	461.05
Average hourly wage: [4]								
Less than $11.15	20	11	6	19	88	121.74	95	505.44
Less than $8.65	10	5	3	10	88	128.26	93	496.06
$11.15 to under $16.82	52	34	17	50	87	114.68	94	462.11
$16.82 to under $26.67	66	45	24	65	83	115.45	90	437.41
$26.67 and more	71	57	32	70	82	112.49	89	427.04
$41.46 and more	74	62	35	73	84	111.47	91	431.60

[1] The average is presented for all workers with medical care benefits. Averages are for plans stating a flat monthly cost. [2] Employees are classified as working either a full-time or part-time schedule based on the definition used by each establishment. [3] Union workers are those whose wages are determined through collective bargaining. [4] The National Compensation Survey - Benefits program presents wage data in percentiles rather than dollar amounts; see "Technical Note" in source.

Source: U.S. Bureau of Labor Statistics, Annual Bulletin on Benefit Coverage, *National Compensation Survey: Employee Benefits in the United States, March 2014*, Bulletin 2779, September 2014. See also <http://www.bls.gov/ncs/ebs/benefits/2014/home.htm>.

Table 171. Employer-Sponsored Health Insurance Enrollment by Type of Plan and Employer Size: 2012

[In millions (170.9 represents 170,900,000). Based on the Current Population Survey, Annual and Social Economic Supplement, and Agency for Healthcare Research and Quality's Medical Expenditure Panel Surveys. For persons and their dependents covered by health insurance sponsored by a current or former employer. Abbreviations: HMO = health maintenance organization; PPO = preferred provider organization; POS = point-of-service plan; and HDED = high deductible health plan (including but not limited to IRS-qualified high deductible health plans)]

Employer sector and size	Total					Self-insured plans [1]					Fully insured plans [2]				
	Total	HMO	PPO	POS	HDED	Total	HMO	PPO	POS	HDED	Total	HMO	PPO	POS	HDED
TOTAL															
Total..................	170.9	26.8	102.6	11.4	30.1	93.9	8.5	66.1	3.1	16.2	76.9	18.3	36.4	8.3	13.9
Less than 50 employees.........	27.6	4.2	11.9	4.7	6.8	3.8	0.5	2.2	0.2	1.0	23.9	3.8	9.7	4.5	5.9
50 to 99 employees..............	11.1	1.5	5.0	1.9	2.7	1.8	0.2	1.1	0.1	0.3	9.4	1.3	3.8	1.8	2.4
100 to 499 employees...........	22.7	3.4	13.1	1.6	4.6	8.8	0.3	6.6	0.6	1.3	13.9	3.1	6.5	1.0	3.3
500 to 999 employees...........	11.8	1.6	7.1	0.8	2.3	5.4	0.2	4.1	0.3	0.7	6.4	1.4	3.0	0.4	1.6
1,000 or more employees........	97.7	16.0	65.6	2.4	13.7	74.2	7.4	52.1	1.9	12.9	23.4	8.7	13.5	0.5	0.8
PRIVATE SECTOR [3]															
Total..................	129.2	18.0	76.0	10.2	25.1	78.0	7.2	54.5	2.8	13.5	51.2	10.7	21.5	7.4	11.6
Less than 50 employees.........	26.2	4.1	11.1	4.6	6.5	3.6	0.4	2.1	0.2	0.9	22.6	3.6	9.1	4.4	5.5
50 to 99 employees..............	9.8	1.4	4.4	1.8	2.2	1.6	0.2	1.0	0.1	0.3	8.1	1.2	3.3	1.7	2.0
100 to 499 employees...........	18.9	2.7	11.0	1.4	3.8	7.8	0.3	5.8	0.6	1.2	11.1	2.4	5.2	0.8	2.6
500 to 999 employees...........	9.1	1.2	5.5	0.6	1.8	4.6	0.2	3.4	0.3	0.6	4.6	1.0	2.0	0.3	1.2
1,000 or more employees........	65.2	8.6	44.0	1.9	10.8	60.4	6.1	42.1	1.6	10.5	4.8	2.4	1.8	0.2	0.3

[1] Self-insured plans are those in which the employer directly assumes some or all medical claim and administrative costs. [2] Fully insured plans are those in which the employer contracts with another organization to assume financial responsibility for the enrollees' medical claims and administrative costs. [3] Private sector includes the self-employed.

Source: U.S. Department of Labor, Employee Benefits Security Administration, *Health Insurance Coverage Bulletin: Abstract of Auxiliary Data for the March 2013 Annual Social and Economic Supplement to the Current Population Survey*, August 2014. See also <http://www.dol.gov/ebsa/publications/research.html>.

Table 172. Annual Revenue for Health Care Industries: 2010 to 2013

[In millions of dollars (1,917,183 represents $1,917,183,000,000). For all employer firms, and taxable employer firms. Estimates have been adjusted to the results of the 2007 Economic Census. Based on the Service Annual Survey and administrative data; see Appendix III]

Kind of business	2007 NAICS code [1]	Total, all firms [2]			Taxable employer firms		
		2010	2012	2013	2010	2012	2013
Health care and social assistance [3]......................	**62**	**1,917,183**	**2,095,703**	**2,151,313**	**938,503**	**1,031,257**	**1,051,993**
Ambulatory health care services [3]....................	**621**	**756,477**	**823,252**	**838,556**	**683,658**	**743,754**	**756,654**
Offices of physicians (except mental health specialists)......	621111	368,030	401,409	404,616	368,030	401,409	404,616
Offices of physicians, mental health specialists...............	621112	4,549	4,794	5,163	4,549	4,794	5,163
Offices of dentists..........	6212	101,619	105,587	107,222	101,619	105,587	107,222
Offices of chiropractors............	62131	10,642	11,501	11,839	10,642	11,501	11,839
Offices of optometrists............	62132	11,684	12,633	13,111	11,684	12,633	13,111
Offices of mental health practitioners, (except physicians)...	62133	6,702	8,058	8,871	6,702	8,058	8,871
Offices of PT/OT/speech therapists and audiologists [4]......	62134	22,363	24,459	24,641	22,363	24,459	24,641
Offices of podiatrists............	621391	4,149	4,508	4,516	4,149	4,508	4,516
Family planning centers............	62141	1,864	2,004	2,103	646	731	796
Outpatient mental health and substance abuse centers......	62142	12,985	14,124	15,170	3,594	4,265	4,873
HMO medical centers............	621491	6,200	7,323	7,498	789	771	752
Kidney dialysis centers............	621492	16,447	18,755	19,225	15,030	17,370	17,878
Freestanding ambulatory surgical and emergency centers...	621493	19,616	22,976	24,280	15,888	18,800	19,849
All other outpatient care centers............	621498	31,709	34,672	35,989	9,397	10,273	10,958
Medical laboratories............	621511	27,918	30,147	30,863	27,918	30,147	30,863
Diagnostic imaging centers............	621512	17,400	17,330	16,899	17,400	17,330	16,899
Home health care services............	6216	58,116	64,634	66,919	40,204	44,733	46,439
Ambulance services............	62191	11,982	13,001	13,214	9,281	10,129	10,239
Blood and organ banks............	621991	10,823	11,469	11,804	2,906	3,375	(S)
Hospitals............	**622**	**822,590**	**915,854**	**947,650**	**99,860**	**117,152**	**118,125**
General medical and surgical hospitals, government.........	622118	159,541	177,144	182,415	(X)	(X)	(X)
General medical and surgical hospitals, private...............	622119	608,197	677,721	701,661	79,912	93,055	93,135
Psychiatric and substance abuse hospitals, government.....	622218	10,665	11,434	11,741	(X)	(X)	(X)
Psychiatric and substance abuse hospitals, private..........	622219	8,551	8,813	9,121	4,620	4,766	4,882
Specialty hospitals, government............	622318	6,459	6,939	7,467	(X)	(X)	(X)
Specialty hospitals, private............	622319	29,177	33,803	35,245	15,328	19,331	20,108
Nursing and residential care facilities [3]............	**623**	**192,035**	**205,965**	**210,896**	**118,453**	**129,417**	**133,615**
Nursing care facilities (skilled nursing facilities) [5]............	6231	105,297	112,193	113,926	81,648	88,603	90,297
Residential intellectual/developmental disability facilities [5]...	62321	21,807	23,121	23,550	6,184	6,557	6,627
Residential mental health and substance abuse facilities....	62322	10,141	10,491	11,046	3,701	3,910	4,207
Continuing care retirement communities......................	623311	29,332	31,933	32,614	11,780	12,843	13,599
Homes for the elderly............	623312	17,262	19,699	20,996	13,828	15,990	17,280
Social assistance............	**624**	**146,081**	**150,632**	**154,211**	**36,532**	**40,934**	**43,599**
Child and youth services............	62411	11,725	11,888	12,128	1,125	1,073	1,084
Services for the elderly and persons with disabilities.........	62412	30,466	33,479	35,065	9,592	12,050	13,646
Other individual and family services............	62419	29,656	28,839	29,229	4,115	4,103	4,220
Community food services............	62421	6,720	7,741	8,741	135	151	143
Emergency and other relief services............	62423	9,778	8,695	8,420	58	95	158
Vocational rehabilitation services............	6243	13,220	13,202	13,178	1,980	1,872	1,823
Child day care services............	6244	32,445	34,519	34,956	19,252	21,297	22,224

X Not applicable. S Figure does not meet publication standards. [1] North American Industry Classification System (NAICS), 2007; see text, Section 15. [2] Includes taxable and tax-exempt employer firms. [3] Includes other kinds of business, not shown separately. [4] Offices of physical, occupational, and speech therapists, and audiologists. [5] The industry name and description have been changed to reflect the 2012 NAICS manual in order to be consistent with industry nomenclature.

Source: U.S. Census Bureau, Annual & Quarterly Services, "2013 Annual Services," <http://www.census.gov/services/index.html>, accessed January 2015.

Table 173. Revenue for Selected Health Care Industries by Source of Revenue: 2013

[In millions of dollars (409,779 represents $409,779,000,000). For all employer firms regardless of tax status. Estimates have been adjusted to the results of the 2007 Economic Census, and are shown by industry classification based on the 2007 North American Industry Classification System (NAICS) except as noted. Based on Service Annual Survey and administrative data; see Appendix III]

Source of revenue	Offices of physicians (NAICS 6211)	Offices of dentists (NAICS 6212)	Offices of mental health practitioners (NAICS 62133)	Home health care services (NAICS 6216)	Hospitals (NAICS 622)	Nursing and residential care facilities (NAICS 623)[1]
Total.....................	**409,779**	**107,222**	**8,871**	**66,919**	**947,650**	**210,896**
Government[2]......................	107,857	9,482	3,914	47,734	357,823	126,654
Private insurance...................	182,913	46,508	2,163	10,547	407,608	14,202
Patient out-of-pocket from patients and families........	35,116	42,097	1,474	4,714	40,235	47,642
Patient out-of-pocket from Social Security benefits..........	(S)	359	(S)	14	1,248	(NA)
Other patient care revenue........	57,090	7,769	658	2,263	66,369	7,697
Contributions, gifts, grants.........	2,656	(S)	294	840	17,235	3,408
Investment, property income......	768	(S)	(S)	245	14,296	1,752
All other non-patient revenue............................	21,585	(S)	265	562	42,836	6,369

NA Not available. S Figure does not meet publication standards. [1] The industry description has been changed to reflect the 2012 NAICS manual for consistency with industry nomenclature. Includes NAICS 6231 Nursing care facilities (skilled); NAICS 6232 Residential intellectual and developmental disability, mental health, and substance abuse facilities; NAICS 6233 Community care facilities for the elderly; and NAICS 6239 Other residential care facilities. [2] Includes Medicare, Medicaid, other government, and workers compensation.

Source: U.S. Census Bureau, Annual & Quarterly Services, "2013 Annual Services," <http://www.census.gov/services/index.html>, accessed January 2015.

Table 174. Employment in the Health Service Industries: 1990 to 2014

[In thousands (9,336 represents 9,336,000). See headnote, Table 650. Based on the 2012 North American Industry Classification System (NAICS); see text, Section 15]

Industry	2012 NAICS code	1990	2000	2005	2010	2011	2012	2013	2014
Health care and social assistance[1].........	**62**	**9,336**	**12,857**	**14,794**	**16,734**	**16,979**	**17,357**	**17,743**	**18,057**
Ambulatory health care services[1]................	621	2,842	4,320	5,114	5,975	6,136	6,307	6,477	6,645
Offices of physicians............................	6211	1,278	1,840	2,094	2,313	2,344	2,390	2,429	2,470
Office of mental health physicians.............	621112	26	37	43	46	47	48	49	51
Offices of dentists.............................	6212	513	688	774	828	844	854	870	891
Offices of other health practitioners.............	6213	276	438	549	671	697	727	752	784
Medical and diagnostic laboratories............	6215	129	162	198	228	232	236	243	247
Home health care services......................	6216	288	633	821	1,085	1,140	1,185	1,230	1,262
Hospitals...	622	3,513	3,954	4,345	4,679	4,722	4,779	4,786	4,784
General medical and surgical hospitals........	6221	3,305	3,745	4,096	4,357	4,363	4,416	4,442	4,447
Psychiatric and substance abuse hospitals.......................................	6222	113	86	93	109	120	121	121	121
Other hospitals.................................	6223	95	123	156	213	239	242	223	216
Nursing and residential care facilities[1].........	623	1,856	2,583	2,855	3,124	3,168	3,196	3,229	3,261
Nursing care facilities...........................	6231	1,170	1,514	1,577	1,657	1,670	1,663	1,654	1,652

[1] Includes other industries, not shown separately.

Source: U.S. Bureau of Labor Statistics, Current Employment Statistics, "Employment, Hours, and Earnings—National," <http://www.bls.gov/ces/data.htm>, accessed June 2015.

Table 175. Osteopathic Physicians: 2003 to 2013

[As of May 31. Osteopathic physicians are fully qualified physicians licensed to practice medicine and to perform surgery. Osteopathic medicine has a strong emphasis on the interrelationship of the body's nerves, muscles, bones and organs. Doctors of osteopathic medicine, or D.O.s, apply the philosophy of treating the whole person to the prevention, diagnosis and treatment of illness, disease, and injury]

Characteristics	2003	2008	2013	Characteristics	2003	2008	2013
Total number of DOs..........	**51,684**	**64,000**	**82,146**				
DOs in active practice..........	**(NA)**	**56,978**	**73,074**	Self-identified practice specialty[1].........	35,132	44,366	60,021
Female............................	12,894	19,138	28,390	Family and general practice..............	15,826	18,680	22,176
Male..............................	38,790	44,862	53,722	General internal Medicine................	2,870	4,171	7,817
Age:				Pediatrics/adolescent medicine[2]........	1,056	1,995	3,490
Less than 35 years old..........	11,227	13,251	19,810	Obstetrics and gynecology..............	1,362	1,858	2,771
35 to 44 years old...............	15,226	18,638	23,110	Pediatric specialties[3]...................	338	470	(NA)
45 to 54 years old...............	14,173	15,931	16,161	Osteopathic specialties[4]................	430	656	1,134
55 to 64 years old...............	5,839	9,819	13,805	Other specialties[5]......................	12,634	16,178	22,633
65 years old and over...........	5,165	6,120	8,511	Unknown................................	616	358	13,053
Unknown........................	54	241	749				

NA Not available. [1] DOs are assumed to be in active practice if they are under age 65 and have not informed the AOA that they are retired or inactive. DOs are assumed to be in postdoctoral training (internship, residency or fellowship) if they graduated within the last 3 years or if the AOA received information that they are in a postdoctoral program. [2] "Pediatric and adolescent medicine" includes all specialties where the patient is a child or adolescent and includes both general pediatricians and pediatric specialties. [3] Beginning in 2009, separate data for "Pediatric specialties" are no longer available. [4] Family physicians who stress osteopathic manipulative treatment specialties in their practices, and osteopathic physicians who specialize in osteopathic manipulative medicine. [5] The categories "Family and general practice" and "General internal medicine" do not include family physicians, general practitioners and general internists who also practice secondary specialties. Those osteopathic physicians are counted under "Other Specialties."

Source: American Osteopathic Association, Chicago, IL, AOA Annual Statistics, *2013 Osteopathic Medical Profession Report* ©, and previous reports. See also <http://www.osteopathic.org>.

Table 176. Physicians by Sex and Specialty: 2000 to 2013

[In thousands (813.8 represents 813,800). As of Dec. 31, except 1990 as of Jan. 1, and as noted. Includes Puerto Rico and Island Areas]

Item	2000 Total	2000 Office-based	2010 Total	2010 Office-based	2012 Total	2012 Office-based	2013 Total	2013 Office-based
Doctors of medicine, total...............	**813.8**	**490.4**	**985.4**	**565.0**	**1,026.8**	**585.9**	**1,045.9**	**600.9**
Place of medical education:								
U.S./Canadian medical graduates [1].......	616.8	376.5	731.0	424.8	742.3	(NA)	766.5	(NA)
International medical graduates [2].........	197.0	113.9	254.4	140.2	271.7	147.2	278.5	151.7
Sex:								
Male..........................	618.2	382.3	688.5	399.4	705.0	402.1	712.6	406.9
Female........................	195.5	108.1	296.9	165.6	321.8	183.8	333.3	193.9
Specialty:								
Allergy/immunology.........................	4.0	3.1	4.3	3.4	4.4	3.5	4.6	3.6
Anesthesiology.........................	35.7	27.6	43.4	31.8	44.6	32.6	46.2	33.2
Cardiovascular diseases.................	21.0	16.3	22.9	17.5	28.1	17.5	23.6	17.7
Child/adolescent psychiatry..............	6.2	4.3	7.4	5.4	7.9	5.8	8.3	6.1
Dermatology..........................	9.7	8.0	11.3	9.3	11.8	9.7	12.1	9.9
Diagnostic radiology....................	21.1	14.6	26.1	17.5	26.4	17.9	27.2	18.2
Emergency medicine....................	23.1	14.5	33.3	20.7	35.9	22.2	38.4	23.4
Family practice.......................	71.6	54.2	87.6	69.9	91.4	73.1	93.7	74.7
Gastroenterology......................	10.6	8.5	13.2	10.5	13.8	11.0	14.4	11.3
General practice......................	15.2	13.0	8.6	7.2	7.0	5.9	6.7	5.6
General surgery.......................	36.7	24.5	37.1	24.3	37.7	24.4	39.2	25.0
Internal medicine.....................	134.5	89.7	161.3	110.6	170.7	116.9	177.1	120.4
Neurological surgery...................	5.0	3.7	5.8	4.0	6.0	4.1	6.3	4.2
Neurology............................	12.3	8.6	15.9	10.5	16.8	11.2	17.9	11.8
Obstetrics and gynecology...............	40.2	31.7	42.8	34.1	43.5	34.6	44.3	34.8
Ophthalmology........................	18.1	15.6	18.5	15.7	18.8	16.0	19.4	16.3
Orthopedic surgery....................	22.3	17.4	25.2	19.3	25.7	19.6	26.5	20.0
Otolaryngology.......................	9.4	7.6	10.3	8.0	10.5	8.0	10.8	8.1
Pathology............................	18.8	10.6	19.0	10.7	18.9	10.6	19.2	10.5
Pediatrics............................	63.9	43.2	76.4	53.1	80.8	56.7	84.6	58.2
Physical med./rehab...................	6.5	4.3	9.0	6.5	9.8	7.1	10.5	7.7
Plastic surgery.......................	6.2	5.3	7.4	6.2	7.7	6.3	8.0	6.4
Psychiatry...........................	39.5	25.0	39.7	25.7	39.9	26.2	40.7	26.7
Pulmonary diseases....................	8.7	5.9	11.1	7.8	11.8	8.4	12.6	8.9
Radiology............................	8.7	6.7	9.4	7.0	9.6	7.2	10.2	7.5
Urological surgery....................	10.3	8.5	10.7	8.6	10.8	8.6	11.1	8.6
Unspecified..........................	8.3	3.8	9.5	3.6	12.4	4.1	11.8	4.1
Not classified....................	45.1	(X)	64.2	(X)	57.6	(X)	43.5	(X)
Other categories [3]....................	75.2	(X)	126.4	(X)	143.1	(X)	147.7	(X)

NA Not available. X Not applicable. [1] Includes other categories not shown, including graduates from inactive schools. [2] International medical graduates received their medical education in schools outside the United States and Canada. [3] Includes inactive and address unknown.

Source: American Medical Association, *Physician Characteristics and Distribution in the U.S., 2015 Edition* ©, Chicago, IL, and previous reports. See also <http://www.ama-assn.org/>.

Table 177. Physicians and Nurses by State: 2013

[Rates per 100,000 resident population, based on U.S. Census Bureau estimates as of July 1, 2013. Physicians whose major professional activity is patient care, as of December; registered nurses in health care and social assistance industry sector only, as of May. Excludes doctors of osteopathy]

State	Physicians Total	Physicians Rate	Registered Nurses Total	Registered Nurses Rate	State	Physicians Total	Physicians Rate	Registered Nurses Total	Registered Nurses Rate
United States........	**799,486**	**253**	**2,326,120**	**736**	Missouri................	14,182	235	57,970	959
Alabama................	9,927	205	39,260	812	Montana................	2,096	206	7,770	765
Alaska.................	1,575	214	4,770	649	Nebraska...............	4,392	235	16,310	873
Arizona................	14,126	213	40,250	607	Nevada.................	4,819	173	14,900	534
Arkansas...............	5,820	197	19,680	665	New Hampshire........	3,702	280	10,720	810
California..............	95,986	250	225,630	589	New Jersey............	25,236	284	66,900	752
Colorado...............	13,240	251	36,860	700	New Mexico............	4,638	222	12,000	575
Connecticut............	12,385	344	29,710	826	New York..............	68,929	351	137,870	702
Delaware..............	2,101	227	8,550	924	North Carolina.........	23,412	238	78,540	798
District of Columbia. ..	4,182	647	9,080	1,405	North Dakota...........	1,686	233	6,630	917
Florida................	45,977	235	147,660	755	Ohio...................	29,871	258	110,680	957
Georgia...............	21,098	211	56,820	569	Oklahoma..............	6,460	168	21,460	557
Hawaii................	3,867	275	9,010	642	Oregon.................	10,577	269	24,160	615
Idaho.................	2,651	164	10,660	661	Pennsylvania...........	35,924	281	111,350	872
Illinois................	34,320	266	98,590	765	Rhode Island...........	3,731	355	10,340	983
Indiana................	13,643	208	55,230	841	South Carolina.........	10,435	219	34,840	730
Iowa..................	5,436	176	28,820	933	South Dakota..........	1,853	219	10,180	1,205
Kansas................	6,218	215	24,150	834	Tennessee.............	16,363	252	50,230	773
Kentucky..............	9,746	222	37,110	844	Texas.................	54,241	205	161,870	612
Louisiana..............	11,969	259	35,910	776	Utah...................	5,828	201	16,460	567
Maine.................	3,474	262	11,970	901	Vermont................	2,161	345	5,860	935
Maryland..............	20,893	352	37,700	636	Virginia................	20,816	252	51,300	621
Massachusetts.........	27,981	418	68,710	1,027	Washington............	17,419	250	43,640	626
Michigan..............	24,317	246	82,990	839	West Virginia..........	3,957	213	16,310	880
Minnesota.............	15,322	283	50,770	937	Wisconsin..............	14,290	249	49,780	867
Mississippi............	5,223	175	24,490	819	Wyoming...............	991	170	3,670	630

Source: Physicians: American Medical Association, Chicago, IL, *Physician Characteristics and Distribution in the U.S., 2015 Edition* ©. Nurses: U.S. Bureau of Labor Statistics, Occupational Employment Statistics, "OES Research Estimates by State and Industry, May 2013," <http://www.bls.gov/oes/tables.htm>, accessed April 2015.

Table 178. Medical Record Confidentiality Breaches Reported: Incidents and Persons Affected, by Type and Location of Breach: 2011 to 2014

[Individuals only in thousands (13,126 represents 13,126,000). Data for breaches by date of submission to the Secretary of Health and Human Services (HHS), affecting 500 or more individuals. As required by section 13402(e)(4) of the Health Information Technology for Economic and Clinical Health (HITECH) Act, the Secretary of HHS must post a list of breaches of unsecured protected health information affecting 500 or more individuals. The Privacy Rule of the Health Insurance Portability and Accountability Act of 1996 (HIPAA) provides federal protections for individually identifiable health information held by covered entities and their business associates. Covered entities include health care providers, health plans, and health care clearinghouses]

Item	2011		2012		2013		2014	
	Incidents	Individuals affected	Incidents	Individuals affected	Incidents	Individuals affected	Incidents	Individuals affected
Total..	192	13,126	192	2,750	249	6,869	278	12,503
TYPE OF BREACH [1]								
Theft..	116	4,696	110	897	114	5,368	109	6,941
Hacking/information technology incident.....	16	297	16	901	19	207	31	1,787
Loss/improper disposal.......................	24	6,084	24	110	37	660	37	363
Unauthorized access/disclosure..............	26	118	23	338	51	337	67	2,982
Other/unknown................................	10	1,930	19	505	28	297	34	429
LOCATION OF INFORMATION BREACHED [2]								
Paper/films...................................	45	104	45	197	52	575	60	588
Desktop computer/electronic medical record/network server.........................	57	4,376	47	1,138	77	4,666	86	9,642
Laptop computer..............................	36	382	48	548	61	1,005	39	1,268
E-mail..	2	3	10	294	19	58	36	520
Other/other portable device [3].................	52	8,261	42	573	40	565	57	486

[1] Types of breaches can include a combination of other types of breaches within the categories specified. For example, incidents of improper disposal can also involve loss and/or theft; hacking/IT incidents can also include theft and/or unauthorized access. Incidents are categorized according to the first type of breach as given in the source. [2] Locations of information breached can include a combination of other locations within the categories specified. For example, incidents involving desktop computers can also involve breaches of information via laptop computer, network server, e-mail, paper, and other locations. Incidents are categorized according to the first type as given in the source. [3] Other locations of information breaches can include incidents involving computers, hard drives, computer disks, safes, and other miscellaneous materials. Also includes unknown locations of breaches.

Source: U.S. Department of Health and Human Services, Health Information Privacy: Breach Notification Rule, "Breaches Affecting 500 or More Individuals," <https://ocrportal.hhs.gov/ocr/breach/breach_report.jsf>, accessed July 2015.

Table 179. Nursing Homes, Beds, Residents, and Occupancy Rate by State: 2013

[Based on a census of certified nursing facilities. Annual numbers of nursing homes, beds, and residents are based on the Centers for Medicare & Medicaid Services' reporting cycle. Starting with 2013 data, a new editing rule was used for number of beds. For the U.S., the number of beds decreased by less than 1%. For most states, this caused little or no change in the data. For some states, the number of beds changed by up to 8%. The change in the number of beds also caused a change in some occupancy rates. Because of the methodology change, interpret trends with caution]

State	Nursing homes	Beds	Residents	Occupancy rate [1]	State	Nursing homes	Beds	Residents	Occupancy rate [1]
U.S...........	15,663	1,697,484	1,371,926	80.8	MO.........	513	55,106	37,828	68.7
AL.............	228	26,685	22,764	85.3	MT.........	83	6,713	4,689	69.8
AK.............	17	779	498	63.9	NE.........	217	15,855	12,070	76.1
AZ.............	146	16,607	11,344	68.3	NV.........	51	5,979	4,749	79.4
AR.............	230	24,546	17,774	72.4	NH.........	76	7,510	6,813	90.7
CA.............	1,226	121,381	102,324	84.3	NJ.........	365	52,417	45,450	86.7
CO.............	211	20,371	15,957	78.3	NM.........	71	6,716	5,531	82.4
CT.............	231	27,841	24,610	88.4	NY.........	631	116,448	105,965	91.0
DE.............	46	4,986	4,217	84.6	NC.........	421	44,598	36,908	82.8
DC.............	19	2,766	2,569	92.9	ND.........	81	6,138	5,702	92.9
FL.............	687	83,178	72,679	87.4	OH.........	955	91,563	77,129	84.2
GA.............	358	39,883	33,889	85.0	OK.........	311	29,396	19,376	65.9
HI.............	47	4,215	3,714	88.1	OR.........	138	12,276	7,373	60.1
ID.............	77	5,930	3,909	65.9	PA.........	703	88,284	79,554	90.1
IL.............	769	98,883	72,856	73.7	RI.........	84	8,715	7,986	91.6
IN.............	515	58,764	38,649	65.8	SC.........	189	19,689	16,744	85.0
IA.............	444	32,183	24,980	77.6	SD.........	111	6,909	6,335	91.7
KS.............	345	25,653	18,400	71.7	TN.........	320	37,140	29,990	80.7
KY.............	283	26,170	22,818	87.2	TX.........	1,205	135,350	93,712	69.2
LA.............	280	35,189	25,600	72.8	UT.........	98	8,500	5,383	63.3
ME.............	107	7,020	6,342	90.3	VT.........	38	3,199	2,726	85.2
MD.............	230	28,487	24,360	85.5	VA.........	286	32,638	28,249	86.6
MA.............	421	48,660	41,595	85.5	WA.........	225	21,641	17,199	79.5
MI.............	432	46,970	39,288	83.6	WV.........	126	10,888	9,524	87.5
MN.............	380	30,405	27,201	89.5	WI.........	392	34,730	28,062	80.8
MS.............	205	18,550	16,165	87.1	WY.........	39	2,984	2,377	79.7

[1] Percentage of beds occupied (number of nursing home residents per 100 nursing home beds).

Source: U.S. National Center for Health Statistics, Health, United States, 2014, May 2015. See also <http://www.cdc.gov/nchs/hus.htm>.

Table 180. Long-Term Care Facilities, Staff, and Clients by Provider Type and Selected Characteristics: 2012

[Based on the National Study of Long-Term Care Providers. Long-term care services assist the needs of frail older people and other adults with limited capacity for self-care due to chronic illness, injury, disability, or other health-related conditions. Percentages may not add to 100 because of rounding; percentages are based on unrounded numbers]

Item	Facilities by provider type				
	Adult day services center	Home health agency	Hospice	Nursing home	Residential care community
Number of providers	**4,800**	**12,200**	**3,700**	**15,700**	**22,200**
Number of beds or licensed maximum capacity [1]	276,500	(X)	(X)	1,669,100	851,400
Average capacity [1]	58	(NA)	(NA)	106	38
Average number of people served [2]	39	421	356	88	32
Provider ownership type (percent):					
For profit	40.0	78.7	56.6	68.2	78.4
Not for profit	54.9	15.6	29.7	25.1	20.4
Government and other	5.1	5.7	13.7	6.8	1.2
Services provided (percent):					
Social work	63.5	82.3	100.0	88.9	75.6
Mental health or counseling	47.3	(NA)	97.2	86.6	77.8
Therapy [3]	63.8	96.6	98.4	99.3	88.7
Skilled nursing or nursing	70.1	100.0	100.0	100.0	76.1
Pharmacy or pharmacist	34.9	5.5	(NA)	97.4	92.6
Hospice	24.4	5.6	(X)	78.6	89.4
Total nursing employee FTEs [4]	**20,700**	**143,600**	**57,800**	**952,100**	**278,600**
Percent of total nursing employee FTEs:					
Registered nurse	19.2	54.4	54.7	11.7	7.6
Licensed practical nurse or licensed vocational nurse	11.3	19.0	9.6	22.9	10.2
Aide	69.4	26.6	35.7	65.4	82.1
Clients [2]	**273,200**	**4,742,500**	**1,244,500**	**1,383,700**	**713,300**
By age (percent):					
Under 65	36.5	17.6	5.5	14.9	6.7
65 and over	63.5	82.4	94.5	85.1	93.3
65 to 74	19.4	24.6	16.4	14.9	10.4
75 to 84	27.2	32.2	31.3	27.9	32.4
85 and over	16.9	25.5	46.8	42.3	50.5
By sex (percent):					
Men	40.4	37.3	40.3	32.3	28.0
Women	59.6	62.7	59.7	67.7	72.0
Selected conditions (percent):					
Diagnosed with Alzheimer's or other dementia	31.9	30.1	44.3	48.5	39.6
Diagnosed with depression	23.5	34.7	22.2	48.5	24.8
Need assistance with activities of daily living (percent):					
Bathing	39.6	95.1	(NA)	96.1	61.4
Dressing	37.8	83.8	(NA)	90.9	44.9
Toileting	36.2	64.6	(NA)	86.6	36.8
Eating	25.3	51.2	(NA)	56.0	17.7

NA Not available. X Not applicable. [1] For adult day services, capacity is based on licensed maximum capacity. For nursing homes and residential care communities, capacity is based on number of licensed or certified beds. [2] Participants in adult day services centers and residents in nursing homes and residential care communities are current users on any given day in 2012. Home health patients are patients who received and ended care anytime in 2011. Hospice patients are patients who received care anytime in 2011. [3] Physical, occupational, or speech therapy. [4] FTE is full-time equivalent.

Source: U.S. Centers for Disease Control and Prevention, National Center for Health Statistics, *Long-Term Care Services in the United States: 2013 Overview*, December 2013. See also <http://www.cdc.gov/nchs/nsltcp.htm>.

Table 181. Medicare-Certified Hospices, Utilization, and Costs: 1995 to 2012

[Total persons served and covered days in thousands (309 represents 309,000). Total program payments in millions of dollars (1,873 represents $1,873,000,000)]

Year	Total hospices, number	Persons served (1,000)	Covered days of care		Program payments [1]	
			Number (1,000)	Per person served	Total (mil. dol.)	Per person served (dol.) [2]
1995.................	1,992	309	18,197	59	1,873	6,058
1996.................	2,161	349	18,884	54	1,991	5,704
1997.................	2,344	383	19,166	50	2,058	5,374
1998.................	2,317	421	20,308	48	2,206	5,242
1999.................	2,326	474	21,657	47	2,525	5,324
2000.................	2,267	534	25,958	49	2,926	5,476
2001.................	2,275	595	30,684	52	3,690	6,208
2002.................	2,323	662	36,195	55	4,539	6,863
2003.................	2,434	731	45,512	60	5,630	7,724
2004.................	2,645	800	50,530	64	6,716	8,428
2005.................	2,872	874	57,437	66	7,902	9,118
2006.................	3,071	942	64,997	70	9,236	9,837
2007.................	3,255	1,000	70,552	71	10,343	10,385
2008.................	3,346	1,055	74,017	71	11,196	10,662
2009.................	3,405	1,094	77,410	71	12,084	11,089
2010.................	3,509	1,163	81,655	71	12,950	11,175
2011.................	3,630	1,224	85,449	70	13,828	11,342
2012.................	3,782	1,278	91,723	72	15,111	11,858

[1] Medicare program payments represent fee-for-service only and exclude amounts paid for managed care services. [2] Excludes persons who received covered services, but for whom no program payments were reported during the reporting year.

Source: U.S. Centers for Medicare & Medicaid Services, *Medicare and Medicaid Statistical Supplement, 2013 Edition*, Table 8.1. See also <http://www.cms.gov/Research-Statistics-Data-and-Systems/Statistics-Trends-and-Reports/MedicareMedicaidStatSupp/index.html>.

Table 182. Hospital Outpatient Department Visits by Leading Reason for Visit and Primary Diagnosis: 2011

[125,721 represents 125,721,000. Based on the 2011 National Hospital Ambulatory Medical Care Survey (NHAMCS). NHAMCS is an annual nationally representative sample survey of visits to emergency departments, hospital outpatient departments, ambulatory surgical centers (ASCs) of nonfederal short-stay and general hospitals, and freestanding ASCs. Data are subject to sampling and nonsampling errors]

Leading Reason for Visit	Number of visits (1,000)	Percent distri-bution	Leading Diagnosis for Visit	Number of visits (1,000)	Percent distri-bution
All visits.........................	**125,721**	**100.0**	**All Visits**..............................	**125,721**	**100.0**
Progress visit, not otherwise specified.......	16,695	13.3	Malignant neoplasms..............................	5,196	4.1
General medical examination.................	7,736	6.2	Diabetes mellitus.................................	4,997	4.0
Postoperative visit............................	3,337	2.7	Routine infant or child health check.............	4,307	3.4
Medication, other and unspecified kinds.....	2,711	2.2	Arthropathies and related disorders.............	4,107	3.3
Counseling, not otherwise specified.........	2,698	2.1	Essential hypertension............................	3,743	3.0
Cough..	2,631	2.1	Spinal disorders.................................	3,434	2.7
Prenatal examination, routine.................	2,398	1.9	Acute upper respiratory infections, excluding pharyngitis.............................	3,255	2.6
Diabetes mellitus..............................	2,339	1.9	Normal pregnancy..............................	3,246	2.6
Symptoms referable to throat.................	2,106	1.7	Psychoses, excluding major depressive disorder........................	2,778	2.2
Well-baby examination........................	1,915	1.5	General medical examination....................	2,546	2.0
Preoperative visit for specified and unspecified types of surgery............	1,689	1.3	Heart disease, excluding ischemic..............	1,900	1.5
Earache, or ear infection......................	1,658	1.3	Follow up examination............................	1,830	1.5
Stomach and abdominal pain, cramps and spasms...........................	1,559	1.2	Otitis media and eustachian tube disorders.....	1,815	1.4
Fever...	1,532	1.2	Specific procedures and aftercare..............	1,724	1.4
Psychotherapy.................................	[1] 1,525	[1] 1.2	Rheumatism, excluding back...................	1,710	1.4
Knee symptoms................................	1,508	1.2	Complications of pregnancy, childbirth, and the puerperium..........................	1,705	1.4
Gynecological examination....................	1,489	1.2	Attention deficit disorder.....................	1,439	1.1
Skin rash......................................	1,381	1.1	Major depressive disorder......................	1,417	1.1
Hypertension..................................	1,369	1.1	Gynecological examination.....................	1,297	1.0
Back symptoms................................	1,332	1.1	Potential health hazards related to personal and family history......................	1,245	1.0
All other reasons.............................	66,115	52.6	All other diagnoses..............................	72,031	57.3

[1] Figure does not meet standards of reliability or precision.

Source: U.S. National Center for Health Statistics, *National Hospital Ambulatory Medical Care Survey: 2011 Outpatient Department Summary Tables*. See also <http://www.cdc.gov/nchs/ahcd/web_tables.htm>.

Table 183. Health Care Sources Used Most Often—Percent Distribution of Persons Age 18 and Over by Selected Characteristics: 2012

[In percent, except as noted (234,921 represents 234,921,000). Data are age-adjusted, unless otherwise noted. Based on a survey question that asked, "Is there a place that you usually go to when you are sick or need advice about your health?" If there was at least one such place, a follow-up question was asked: "What kind of place [is it/do you go to most often]—a clinic, a doctor's office, an emergency room, or some other place?" From the National Health Interview Survey, a sample survey of the civilian noninstitutionalized population; see Appendix III]

Characteristic	Adults age 18 and over (1,000)	Without a usual place for health care	With a usual place for health care	Usual place of health care			
				Physician office or Health Maintenance Organization (HMO)	Clinic or health center	Hospital emergency room or outpatient department	Other place
Total [2]............................	234,921	16.9	83.1	74.3	21.7	3.0	1.1
SEX							
Male............................	113,071	21.3	78.7	73.3	21.5	3.7	1.5
Female............................	121,850	12.6	87.4	75.0	21.8	2.3	0.8
AGE [3]							
18 to 44 years old............................	111,034	24.0	76.0	70.1	25.0	3.6	1.3
45 to 64 years old............................	82,038	12.0	88.0	77.0	19.4	2.6	1.0
65 to 74 years old............................	23,760	3.7	96.3	81.4	16.4	1.6	0.6
75 and over............................	18,089	2.8	97.2	83.9	13.9	1.5	0.6
RACE							
Single race [4]............................	230,994	16.9	83.1	74.4	21.6	2.9	1.1
White............................	188,261	16.9	83.1	75.2	21.4	2.3	1.1
Black or African American............................	27,943	16.0	84.0	71.1	21.0	6.9	1.1
American Indian or Alaska Native............	1,916	20.4	79.6	50.3	38.6	[1] 10.5	(B)
Asian............................	12,542	17.5	82.5	73.4	23.0	2.9	[1] 0.8
Native Hawaiian or Other Pacific Islander. ..	332	[1] 23.8	76.2	72.9	(B)	7.7	–
Two or more races [5]............................	3,926	17.0	83.0	67.0	25.6	5.3	[1] 2.1
Black or African American, white.............	778	19.7	80.3	68.3	25.0	[1] 4.2	(B)
American Indian or Alaska Native, white.....	1,611	14.2	85.8	61.9	30.9	[1] 5.5	(B)
HISPANIC ORIGIN AND RACE [6]							
Hispanic or Latino............................	34,946	27.4	72.6	59.4	35.1	4.5	1.1
Mexican or Mexican American...............	21,741	29.3	70.7	55.1	40.4	3.2	1.3
Not Hispanic or Latino............................	199,974	14.7	85.3	76.6	19.6	2.7	1.1
White, single race............................	156,173	14.0	86.0	78.2	18.8	1.9	1.1
Black or African American, single race.........	26,961	15.8	84.2	71.2	20.8	7.0	1.0
EDUCATION [7]							
Less than high school diploma.................	28,311	25.5	74.5	57.3	36.0	6.1	0.7
High school diploma or GED [8].................	52,795	18.1	81.9	74.2	21.6	3.3	0.8
Some college............................	59,577	14.2	85.8	77.0	18.8	2.8	1.4
Bachelor's degree or higher....................	63,036	10.5	89.5	82.4	15.3	1.2	1.0
FAMILY INCOME							
Less than $35,000............................	74,224	24.9	75.1	59.6	32.9	6.2	1.4
$35,000 to $49,999............................	31,186	18.6	81.4	72.1	23.9	2.7	1.3
$50,000 to $74,999............................	39,348	15.6	84.4	77.4	19.3	2.3	1.0
$75,000 to $99,999............................	27,052	11.7	88.3	82.7	15.2	1.4	0.7
$100,000 or more............................	49,001	8.6	91.4	84.3	13.9	0.8	1.0
HEALTH INSURANCE COVERAGE [9]							
Under age 65:							
Private............................	125,065	11.1	88.9	81.2	16.8	1.2	0.9
Medicaid............................	19,101	10.6	89.4	56.5	36.1	6.6	[1] 0.9
Other............................	8,734	12.9	87.1	54.9	31.8	10.4	3.0
Uninsured............................	39,391	51.3	48.7	43.3	44.1	9.8	2.8
Age 65 and over:							
Private............................	21,580	2.6	97.4	86.0	13.0	0.5	0.5
Medicare and Medicaid....................	2,546	3.2	96.8	69.0	27.4	3.2	(B)
Medicare only............................	14,327	3.8	96.2	83.7	14.3	1.7	0.2
Other............................	3,033	[1] 1.1	98.9	66.0	23.9	6.6	3.4
Uninsured............................	286	45.2	54.8	43.7	39.6	[1] 15.2	(B)

– Represents zero. B Figure too small to meet statistical standards for reliability of a derived figure. [1] Figure has a relative standard error greater than 30% and less than or equal to 50%, and does not meet standards of reliability or precision. [2] Includes other races not shown separately and persons with unknown education, family income, and health insurance characteristics. [3] Estimates for age groups are not age adjusted. [4] Persons who indicated only a single race group. [5] Persons who indicated more than one race group. [6] Persons of Hispanic or Latino origin may be of any race or combination of races. [7] Shown only for adults aged 25 and over. [8] GED is General Educational Development high school equivalency diploma. [9] Based on a hierarchy of mutually exclusive categories. Persons with more than one type of health insurance were assigned to the first appropriate category in the hierarchy.

Source: U.S. National Center for Health Statistics, *Summary Health Statistics for U.S. Adults: National Health Interview Survey, 2012*, Vital and Health Statistics, Series 10, Number 260, February 2014. See also <http://www.cdc.gov/nchs/products/series/series10.htm>.

Table 184. Percent Distribution of Visits to Health Care Professionals by Selected Patient Characteristics: 2010 and 2013

[Covers visits to hospital emergency departments, home health care visits, and visits to doctor offices, clinics, or some other place during a 12-month period. Excludes dental visits. Based on the National Health Interview Survey. See source, and Appendix III]

Characteristic	Percent distribution of health care visits							
	None		1–3 visits		4–9 visits		10 or more visits	
	2010	2013	2010	2013	2010	2013	2010	2013
All persons [1,2]	**15.6**	**16.1**	**45.4**	**47.6**	**25.8**	**24.0**	**13.2**	**12.3**
SEX [2]								
Male	20.4	21.0	46.4	47.7	22.7	21.2	10.5	10.1
Female	10.9	11.4	44.4	47.5	28.8	26.7	15.9	14.4
AGE								
Under 18 years	8.1	8.2	55.6	59.7	28.2	25.1	8.2	7.1
Under 6 years	3.7	4.7	48.9	49.6	36.8	37.1	10.6	8.6
6 to 17 years	10.4	9.9	59.1	64.5	23.6	19.3	6.9	6.3
18 to 44 years	24.2	24.8	43.9	45.9	20.6	18.5	11.3	10.7
45 to 64 years	14.8	15.2	42.8	43.0	26.1	26.7	16.4	15.0
65 years and over	5.3	6.4	33.8	35.9	36.7	34.4	24.2	23.2
75 years and over	4.1	4.5	31.0	33.7	38.0	35.4	27.0	26.3
RACE [2,3]								
White	15.3	16.1	44.9	47.3	26.1	24.0	13.7	12.7
Black or African American	15.7	15.2	47.2	47.6	24.7	25.7	12.4	11.5
American Indian or Alaska Native	19.4	16.1	40.3	43.2	28.1	28.3	12.2	12.4
Asian	20.4	18.4	49.9	53.1	22.1	21.3	7.6	7.2
Two or more races	13.9	15.8	42.3	42.6	25.2	24.9	18.6	16.8
HISPANIC ORIGIN AND RACE [2,3,4]								
Hispanic or Latino	23.5	24.0	43.2	45.8	22.6	20.5	10.7	9.7
Mexican	25.2	26.2	43.3	44.6	21.4	20.0	10.1	9.2
Not Hispanic or Latino	14.0	14.4	45.8	47.9	26.5	24.8	13.7	12.9
White, non-Hispanic	13.2	13.9	45.3	47.6	27.1	25.0	14.4	13.5
Black, non-Hispanic	15.6	15.2	47.3	47.7	24.9	25.7	12.2	11.4
HEALTH INSURANCE STATUS [5,6]								
Insured	12.3	12.8	48.5	51.3	26.1	24.1	13.1	11.8
Private	12.4	13.1	51.0	53.8	25.5	23.4	11.1	9.7
Medicaid	10.9	10.8	38.2	41.6	28.0	25.7	23.0	21.9
Uninsured	37.2	39.2	42.2	41.3	15.2	14.2	5.4	5.3
Insured continuously 12 months prior to interview	12.1	12.6	48.6	51.5	26.2	24.2	13.0	11.7
Uninsured for any period up to 12 months prior to interview	18.5	20.0	47.8	46.4	22.0	21.9	11.6	11.7
Uninsured more than 12 months prior to interview	43.8	45.1	39.7	39.9	12.6	11.1	3.9	3.8

[1] Includes other categories not shown separately. [2] Estimates are age adjusted to the year 2000 standard population. [3] Race groups include persons of Hispanic and non-Hispanic origin and are tabulated using the 1997 standards for federal data on race/ethnicity. Race-specific estimates are for persons who reported only once race group; 2 or more races includes persons who reported more than one race. [4] Persons of Hispanic or Latino origin may be of any race. [5] For persons under age 65, at time of interview. Estimates for persons under age 65 are age-adjusted to the year 2000 standard population. [6] Health insurance categories are mutually exclusive. Persons who reported both Medicaid and private coverage are classified as having private coverage. Medicaid coverage includes State-sponsored health plans and the Children's Health Insurance Program (CHIP). The insured category also includes military plans, other government-sponsored health plans, and Medicare, not shown separately. Persons not covered by private insurance, Medicaid, CHIP, state-sponsored or other government-sponsored health plans, Medicare, or military plans are considered to have no health insurance coverage. Persons with only Indian Health Service coverage are considered to have no health insurance coverage.

Source: U.S. National Center for Health Statistics, *Health, United States, 2014*, May 2015. See also <http://www.cdc.gov/nchs/hus.htm>.

Table 185. Emergency Room Visits by Wait Time and Total Time Spent: 2011

[136,296 represents 136,296,000. Based on the 2011 National Hospital Ambulatory Medical Care Survey (NHAMCS). The NHAMCS is an annual nationally representative sample survey of visits to emergency departments, outpatient departments, ambulatory surgical centers (ASCs) of nonfederal short-stay and general hospitals, and freestanding ASCs. Data are subject to sampling and nonsampling errors]

Visit characteristic	Number of visits (1,000)	Percent	Visit characteristic	Number of visits (1,000)	Percent
Total visits [1]	**136,296**	**100.0**	TIME SPENT IN EMERGENCY DEPARTMENT		
TIME SPENT WAITING TO SEE A MEDICAL PROFESSIONAL [2]			Less than 1 hour	16,198	11.9
Fewer than 15 minutes	36,845	27.0	1 hour, but less than 2 hours	33,184	24.3
15-59 minutes	55,477	40.7	2 hours, but less than 4 hours	47,537	34.9
1 hour, but less than 2 hours	18,429	13.5	4 hours, but less than 6 hours	20,420	15.0
2 hours, but less than 3 hours	6,541	4.8	6 hours, but less than 10 hours	10,487	7.7
3 hours, but less than 4 hours	2,142	1.6	10 hours, but less than 14 hours	2,134	1.6
4 hours, but less than 6 hours	1,407	1.0	14 hours, but less than 24 hours	1,340	1.0
6 hours or more	937	0.7	24 hours or more	794	0.6

[1] Totals include nonresponse and nonapplicable categories. [2] Medical professional may be a medical doctor, doctor of osteopathy, physician assistant, or nurse practitioner.

Source: U.S. National Center for Health Statistics, *National Hospital Ambulatory Medical Care Survey: 2011 Emergency Department Summary Tables*. See also <http://www.cdc.gov/nchs/ahcd/web_tables.htm>.

Table 186. Physician Office Visits by Sex and Leading Reason for Visit and Primary Diagnosis: 2012

[928,630 represents 928,630,000. Based on the 2012 National Ambulatory Medical Care Survey (NAMCS). NAMCS is an annual nationally representative sample survey of visits to nonfederal office-based patient care physicians, excluding anesthesiologists, radiologists, and pathologists. The sampling frame for the 2012 NAMCS was composed of all physicians contained in the master files maintained by the American Medical Association and the American Osteopathic Association. Data are subject to sampling and nonsampling errors]

Leading reason for visit	Number of visits (1,000)	Percent distribution Male [1]	Percent distribution Fe-male [2]	Leading diagnosis for visit	Number of visits (1,000)	Percent distribution Male [1]	Percent distribution Fe-male [2]
All visits.	928,630	100.0	100.0	All visits.	928,630	100.0	100.0
Progress visit, not otherwise specified.	74,103	8.3	7.7	Routine infant or child health check.	37,510	4.9	3.4
General medical examination.	70,435	8.9	6.6	Arthropathies and related disorders.	34,169	3.3	4.0
Postoperative visit.	28,829	2.8	3.3	Essential hypertension.	34,016	4.1	3.3
Cough.	25,853	3.0	2.6	Spinal disorders.	33,423	4.0	3.3
Medication, other and unspecified kinds.	18,282	2.2	1.8	General medical examination.	25,948	3.3	2.4
				Acute upper respiratory infections [3].	25,779	3.0	2.6
Prenatal examination, routine.	15,964	(X)	3.0	Diabetes mellitus.	23,556	3.1	2.1
Knee symptoms.	14,608	1.7	1.5	Malignant neoplasms.	20,141	2.4	2.0
Gynecological examination.	14,402	(X)	2.7	Rheumatism, excluding back.	19,012	1.9	2.2
Well baby examination.	13,838	1.8	1.3	Follow up examination.	18,807	1.8	2.2
Low back symptoms.	13,335	1.8	1.2	Specific procedures and aftercare.	17,591	1.7	2.0
Back symptoms.	13,232	1.5	1.4	Normal pregnancy.	16,299	(X)	3.0
Counseling, not otherwise specified.	12,987	1.4	1.4	Gynecological examination.	12,426	(X)	2.3
Symptoms referable to throat.	12,895	1.4	1.4	Heart disease, excluding ischemic.	12,035	1.5	1.1
Skin rash.	12,511	1.6	1.2	Benign neoplasms.	11,449	1.1	1.4
Stomach and abdominal pain, cramps and spasms.	12,284	1.2	1.4	Otitis media and eustachian tube disorders.	11,210	1.5	1.0
For other and unspecified test results.	12,115	1.4	1.2	Disorders of lipoid metabolism.	11,027	1.4	1.0
Diabetes mellitus.	11,706	1.5	1.1	Asthma.	10,529	1.3	1.0
Fever.	10,902	1.4	1.0	Psychoses, excluding major depressive disorder.	10,330	1.3	1.0
Hypertension.	10,546	1.2	1.1				
Earache, or ear infection.	9,701	1.1	1.0	Acute pharyngitis.	9,240	0.9	1.0
All other reasons.	520,102	55.8	56.1	All other diagnoses [4].	534,134	57.3	57.6

X Not applicable. [1] Based on 388,409,000 visits made by males. [2] Based on 540,221,000 visits made by females. [3] Excluding pharyngitis. [4] Includes all other diagnoses not listed above, as well as unknown and blank diagnoses.

Source: U.S. National Center for Health Statistics, *National Ambulatory Medical Care Survey: 2012 State and National Summary Tables.* See also <http://www.cdc.gov/nchs/ahcd/web_tables.htm>.

Table 187. Ambulatory Care Visits to Hospital Outpatient and Emergency Departments: 2011

[125,721 represents 125,721,000. Based on the annual National Ambulatory Medical Care Survey and National Hospital Ambulatory Medical Care Survey, and subject to sampling error; see source for details]

Characteristic	Number of visits (1,000) Outpatient department	Number of visits (1,000) Emergency department	Visits per 100 persons [1] Outpatient department	Visits per 100 persons [1] Emergency department
Total.	125,721	136,296	41.0	44.5
AGE				
Under 15 years old.	24,075	24,823	39.4	40.6
15 to 24 years old.	12,739	22,150	29.8	51.7
25 to 44 years old.	28,394	39,124	35.4	48.7
45 to 64 years old.	37,980	29,828	46.3	36.4
65 to 74 years old.	12,529	8,208	56.3	36.9
75 years old and over.	10,005	12,163	56.1	68.2
SEX				
Male.	49,435	61,676	33.1	41.2
Female.	76,286	74,621	48.6	47.6
EXPECTED PAYMENT SOURCE [2]				
Private insurance.	49,395	47,600	(X)	(X)
Medicare.	24,808	25,060	(X)	(X)
Medicaid/CHIP (Children's Health Insurance Program).	44,005	43,327	(X)	(X)
Worker's compensation.	759	1,503	(X)	(X)
No insurance: [3].	8,544	21,744	(X)	(X)
Self pay.	6,510	19,524	(X)	(X)
No charge/charity.	[4] 2,342	2,767	(X)	(X)

X Not applicable. [1] Rates are based on Census Bureau July 1, 2011 estimates of the civilian noninstitutional population. [2] Estimates include all expected sources of payment reported at the visit. Other and unknown not shown separately. [3] "No insurance" is defined as having only "self-pay" or "no charge/charity" as payment sources. [4] Figure does not meet standards of reliability or precision.

Source: U.S. National Center for Health Statistics, "National Hospital Ambulatory Medical Care Survey: Web Tables, 2011," <http://www.cdc.gov/nchs/ahcd/web_tables.htm#2011>, accessed July 2015.

Table 188. Visits to Hospital Emergency Departments by Diagnosis: 2011

[Number in thousands (61,676 represents 61,676,000). Based on the National Hospital Ambulatory Medical Care Survey]

Leading diagnosis	Number (1,000)	Rate per 1,000 persons [1]	Leading diagnosis	Number (1,000)	Rate per 1,000 persons [1]
MALE			**FEMALE**		
All ages............................	**61,676**	**412**	**All ages**............................	**74,621**	**476**
Under 15 years old [2]...............	**13,439**	**430**	**Under 15 years old [2]**...............	**11,385**	**381**
Acute upper respiratory infections [3].........	1,283	41	Acute upper respiratory infections [3].........	1,003	34
Otitis media (ear infection) and			Pyrexia (fever) of unknown origin.........	646	22
eustachian tube disorders....................	746	24	Otitis media (ear infection) and		
Pyrexia (fever) of unknown origin............	727	23	eustachian tube disorders.................	625	21
Open wound of head.......................	683	22	Contusion with intact skin surface..........	441	15
Contusion with intact skin surface...........	614	20	Open wound of head.......................	383	13
15 to 64 years old [2].....................	**39,897**	**396**	**15 to 64 years old [2]**.....................	**51,204**	**491**
Chest pain.................................	2,139	21	Abdominal pain............................	3,879	37
Open wound, excluding head...............	1,885	19	Chest pain................................	2,067	20
Abdominal pain............................	1,679	17	Spinal disorders..........................	1,965	19
Spinal disorders..........................	1,669	17	Complications of pregnancy, childbirth,		
Contusion with intact skin surface...........	1,320	13	and the puerperium......................	1,790	17
			Contusion with intact skin surface..........	1,569	15
65 years old and over [2]..................	**8,340**	**475**	**65 years old and over [2]**..................	**12,032**	**534**
Chest pain.................................	612	35	Chest pain................................	604	27
Heart disease, excluding ischemic..........	435	25	Abdominal pain............................	528	23
Open wound, excluding head...............	270	15	Heart disease, excluding ischemic..........	485	22
Abdominal pain............................	265	15	Contusion with intact skin surface..........	461	20
Syncope and collapse......................	254	14	Pneumonia................................	401	18

[1] Based on the Census Bureau's July 1, 2011 estimates of the civilian noninstitutional population. [2] Includes other first-listed diagnoses, not shown separately. [3] Excluding pharyngitis.

Source: U.S. National Center for Health Statistics, *National Hospital Ambulatory Medical Care Survey: 2011 Emergency Department Summary Tables*. See also <http://www.cdc.gov/nchs/ahcd/web_tables.htm>.

Table 189. Procedures for Inpatients Discharged From Short-Stay Hospitals: 1990 to 2010

[23,051 represents 23,051,000. Procedure categories are based on the International Classification of Diseases, 9th Revision, Clinical Modification. See headnote, Table 194]

Sex and type of procedure	Number of procedures (1,000)				Rate per 1,000 population [1]			
	1990	2000	2009	2010	1990	2000	2009	2010
Surgical procedures, total [2]....................	**23,051**	**23,244**	**29,215**	**27,804**	**92.4**	**83.6**	**95.5**	**90.3**
Cesarean section...........................	945	855	1,329	1,325	3.8	3.1	4.3	4.3
Repair of current obstetric laceration....................	795	1,136	1,339	1,286	3.2	4.1	4.4	4.2
Cardiac catheterization.....................	995	1,221	1,071	947	4.0	4.4	3.5	3.1
Reduction of fracture [3].....................	609	628	621	651	2.4	2.3	2.0	2.1
Male, total [2]............................	**8,538**	**8,689**	**11,758**	**10,979**	**70.6**	**63.9**	**78.2**	**72.4**
Cardiac catheterization.....................	620	732	622	585	5.1	5.4	4.1	3.9
Coronary artery bypass graft [4]..................	286	371	304	292	2.4	2.7	2.0	1.9
Reduction of fracture [3].....................	300	285	283	272	2.5	2.1	1.9	1.8
Female, total [2]..........................	**14,513**	**14,556**	**17,457**	**16,826**	**113.0**	**102.4**	**112.4**	**107.8**
Cesarean section...........................	945	855	1,329	1,325	7.4	6.0	8.6	8.5
Repair of current obstetric laceration....................	795	1,136	1,339	1,286	6.2	8.0	8.6	8.2
Hysterectomy..............................	591	633	494	497	4.6	4.5	3.2	3.2
Diagnostic and other nonsurgical procedures [5]..........................	**17,455**	**16,737**	**18,748**	**18,530**	**70.0**	**60.2**	**61.3**	**60.2**
Angiocardiography and arteriography [6].................	1,735	2,005	1,919	1,763	7.0	7.2	6.3	5.7
Respiratory therapy........................	1,164	991	1,276	1,264	4.7	3.6	4.2	4.1
Manual assisted delivery....................	750	898	1,246	1,198	3.0	3.2	4.1	3.9
Diagnostic ultrasound......................	1,608	886	902	898	6.4	3.2	2.9	2.9
Fetal electrocardiogram (EKG) and fetal monitoring....	1,377	750	1,038	985	5.6	2.7	3.4	3.2
Male, total [5]............................	**7,378**	**6,965**	**7,439**	**7,437**	**61.0**	**51.2**	**49.5**	**49.0**
Angiocardiography and arteriography [6].................	1,051	1,157	1,061	1,020	8.7	8.5	7.1	6.7
Respiratory therapy........................	586	507	627	639	4.9	3.7	4.2	4.2
Computerized Axial Tomographic scan [7]................	736	345	226	(S)	6.1	2.5	1.5	(S)
Female, total [5]..........................	**10,077**	**9,772**	**11,309**	**11,093**	**78.5**	**68.8**	**72.8**	**71.0**
Manual assisted delivery....................	750	898	1,246	1,198	5.9	6.3	8.0	7.7
Fetal electrocardiogram (EKG) and fetal monitoring....	1,377	750	1,038	985	10.8	5.5	6.7	6.3
Respiratory therapy........................	578	484	649	625	4.5	3.4	4.2	4.0
Diagnostic ultrasound......................	941	501	469	477	7.3	3.5	3.0	3.1

S Figure does not meet publication standards. [1] Based on Census Bureau estimated civilian population as of July 1. Population estimates based on the 1990 census were used to calculate rates for 1990 through 2000. Population estimates based on the 2000 census were used to calculate rates for 2001 through 2010. [2] Includes other types of surgical procedures, not shown separately. [3] Excluding skull, nose, and jaw. [4] It is possible for a discharge to have more than one of these recorded. [5] Includes other nonsurgical procedures, not shown separately. [6] Using contrast material. [7] Also known as CAT scan.

Source: U.S. National Center for Health Statistics, National Hospital Discharge Survey, unpublished data. See also <http://www.cdc.gov/nchs/nhds.htm>.

Table 190. Hospitals—Summary Characteristics: 2000 to 2013

[In units indicated (for beds, 984 represents 984,000). Covers hospitals accepted for registration by the American Hospital Association; see text, this section. Short-term hospitals have an average patient stay of less than 30 days; long-term, an average stay of longer duration. Special hospitals include obstetrics and gynecology; eye, ear, nose, and throat; rehabilitation; orthopedic; chronic; and other special hospitals except psychiatric, tuberculosis, alcoholism, and chemical dependency hospitals]

Item	2000	2005	2007	2008	2009	2010	2011	2012	2013
NUMBER									
All hospitals	5,810	5,756	5,708	5,815	5,795	5,754	5,724	5,723	5,686
With 100 beds or more	3,102	2,942	2,901	2,884	2,861	2,832	2,790	2,772	2,740
Nonfederal [1]	5,565	5,530	5,495	5,602	5,584	5,541	5,516	5,512	5,473
Community hospitals [2]	4,915	4,936	4,897	5,010	5,008	4,985	4,973	4,999	4,974
Nongovernmental nonprofit	3,003	2,958	2,913	2,923	2,918	2,904	2,903	2,894	2,904
For profit	749	868	873	982	998	1,013	1,025	1,068	1,060
State and local government	1,163	1,110	1,111	1,105	1,092	1,068	1,045	1,037	1,010
Long term general and special	131	115	135	128	115	109	110	88	80
Psychiatric	496	456	444	447	444	435	421	413	406
Tuberculosis	4	3	1	1	2	2	2	1	1
Federal	245	226	213	213	211	213	208	211	213
BEDS (1,000) [3]									
All hospitals	984	947	945	951	944	942	924	921	915
Rate per 1,000 population [4]	3.5	3.2	3.1	3.1	3.1	3.0	3.0	2.9	2.9
Beds per hospital	169	165	166	164	163	164	161	161	161
Nonfederal [1]	931	901	899	905	900	897	886	882	876
Community hospitals [2]	824	802	801	808	806	805	797	801	796
Rate per 1,000 population [4]	2.9	2.7	2.7	2.7	2.6	2.6	2.6	2.6	2.5
Nongovernmental nonprofit	583	561	554	557	556	556	548	545	544
For profit	110	114	116	121	122	125	128	135	135
State and local government	131	128	131	131	127	125	121	120	117
Long term general and special	18	15	17	16	16	15	15	11	10
Psychiatric	87	82	79	79	76	76	73	70	69
Tuberculosis	(Z)	(Z)	(Z)	(Z)	(Z)	(Z)	(Z)	(Z)	(Z)
Federal	53	46	46	46	45	45	38	39	39
AVERAGE DAILY CENSUS (1,000) [5]									
All hospitals	650	656	645	649	641	627	615	600	592
Community hospitals [2]	526	540	533	536	528	520	513	507	500
Nongovernmental nonprofit	382	388	380	380	375	368	362	354	351
For profit	61	68	66	70	70	71	73	77	76
State and local government	83	85	87	86	83	80	78	77	74
EXPENSES (bil. dol.) [6]									
All hospitals	395.4	570.5	638.5	690.0	726.7	750.6	773.5	829.7	859.4
Nonfederal [1]	371.5	533.7	599.7	646.1	676.6	698.2	722.3	775.4	801.5
Community hospitals [2]	356.6	515.7	581.0	626.6	656.2	678.0	702.1	756.9	782.0
Nongovernmental nonprofit	267.1	386.0	435.5	468.1	492.9	510.7	528.3	564.0	585.5
For profit	35.0	51.8	55.8	61.8	64.4	67.2	70.3	79.1	81.6
State and local government	54.5	77.9	89.8	96.7	98.9	100.1	103.4	113.8	115.0
Long term general and special	2.8	3.6	3.9	4.5	4.2	4.2	3.9	2.8	3.0
Psychiatric	11.9	13.9	14.5	14.7	15.1	15.8	15.6	15.4	16.1
Tuberculosis	(Z)	(Z)	(Z)	(Z)	(Z)	(Z)	(Z)	(Z)	(Z)
Federal	23.9	36.8	38.8	44.0	50.1	52.4	51.2	54.3	57.9
PERSONNEL (1,000) [7]									
All hospitals	4,454	4,790	5,024	5,116	5,178	5,184	5,196	5,258	5,342
Nonfederal [1]	4,157	4,479	4,699	4,775	4,814	4,825	4,864	4,927	4,984
Community hospitals [2]	3,911	4,260	4,465	4,550	4,585	4,600	4,650	4,731	4,786
Nongovernmental nonprofit	2,919	3,154	3,286	3,340	3,369	3,388	3,427	3,477	3,500
For profit	378	421	432	450	464	474	485	515	553
State and local government	614	681	747	760	751	738	738	739	734
Long term general and special	41	38	44	41	37	39	35	26	25
Psychiatric	200	182	187	182	183	182	175	169	171
Tuberculosis	1	1	1	(Z)	(Z)	(Z)	(Z)	(Z)	(Z)
Federal	297	311	325	341	364	359	331	331	358
OUTPATIENT VISITS (mil.)									
Total	592.7	673.7	693.5	710.0	742.0	750.4	754.5	778.0	787.4
Emergency visits	106.9	118.9	124.7	126.7	131.4	131.5	133.4	137.3	137.5

Z Less than 500 or $50 million. [1] Includes hospital units of institutions. [2] Short-term (average length of stay less than 30 days) general and special (e.g., obstetrics and gynecology; eye, ear, nose and throat; rehabilitation, etc. except psychiatric, tuberculosis, alcoholism, and chemical dependency). Excludes hospital units of institutions. [3] Number of beds at end of reporting period. [4] Based on Census Bureau estimated resident population as of July 1. Data for 2000 and 2010 based on enumerated resident population as of April 1. Other years are estimates, which reflect revisions based on the preceding decennial Census of Population. [5] The average number of people served on an inpatient basis on a single day during the reporting period. [6] Excludes new construction. [7] Includes full-time equivalents of part-time personnel.

Source: Health Forum, An American Hospital Association Company, Chicago, IL, *AHA Hospital Statistics 2015 Edition* ©, and previous editions. See also <http://www.ahadataviewer.com/>.

Table 191. Community Hospital Summary Data by State: 2010 and 2013

[In units indicated (804.9 represents 804,900). Community hospitals are defined as all nonfederal, short-term general, and other special hospitals. Other special hospitals include obstetrics and gynecology; eye, ear, nose, and throat; rehabilitation; orthopedic; and other individually described specialty services. Community hospitals include academic medical centers or other teaching hospitals if they are nonfederal short-term hospitals. Excluded are hospitals not accessible by the general public, such as prison hospitals or college infirmaries]

State	Number of hospitals		Beds (1,000)		Patients admitted (1,000)		Average daily census [1] (1,000)		Outpatient visits (mil.)		Average cost per day (dol.)	
	2010	2013	2010	2013	2010	2013	2010	2013	2010	2013	2010	2013
United States............	4,985	4,974	804.9	795.6	35,149	33,609	519.5	500.2	651.4	678.0	1,910	2,157
Alabama..................	105	97	15.1	15.1	642	641	9.2	9.2	8.8	8.3	1,372	1,486
Alaska...................	22	22	1.5	1.6	57	58	0.9	1.0	1.8	1.4	2,020	2,103
Arizona..................	73	72	13.4	13.3	712	639	8.7	7.9	8.1	8.7	2,173	2,380
Arkansas................	85	84	9.5	9.5	370	352	5.2	5.0	5.0	5.1	1,477	1,645
California...............	343	347	70.4	70.3	3,424	3,255	47.8	45.2	51.7	53.8	2,566	3,128
Colorado................	80	82	10.2	10.3	449	407	6.1	5.9	8.3	8.8	2,190	2,598
Connecticut.............	34	33	8.1	7.8	407	391	6.3	5.9	8.3	9.3	2,154	2,425
Delaware................	7	7	2.2	2.0	102	105	1.6	1.5	1.8	2.1	2,227	2,684
District of Columbia.......	11	11	3.5	3.6	132	133	2.5	2.6	2.3	2.6	2,434	2,555
Florida..................	210	212	53.3	53.2	2,452	2,407	33.4	33.0	24.2	24.0	1,837	2,008
Georgia.................	154	144	25.5	24.7	961	947	16.8	16.5	14.3	16.0	1,338	1,605
Hawaii..................	26	25	3.1	2.8	111	110	2.3	2.1	2.2	2.2	1,755	1,919
Idaho...................	41	40	3.4	3.4	131	126	1.7	1.7	3.2	4.8	1,748	2,398
Illinois..................	189	189	33.3	31.7	1,543	1,427	20.7	18.8	32.6	32.8	1,983	2,274
Indiana.................	125	123	17.8	17.3	718	702	10.3	10.0	18.7	18.4	1,964	2,206
Iowa....................	118	118	10.1	9.8	342	327	5.7	5.5	11.0	10.6	1,288	1,403
Kansas..................	130	130	10.0	10.0	305	290	5.4	5.2	6.7	7.1	1,304	1,383
Kentucky................	106	106	14.2	14.0	609	579	8.6	8.3	10.4	10.5	1,546	1,679
Louisiana...............	126	122	15.4	15.6	625	566	9.2	8.5	12.4	9.7	1,561	1,737
Maine...................	37	35	3.6	3.5	146	140	2.2	2.1	6.0	7.2	2,077	2,238
Maryland................	47	50	11.7	12.4	708	628	8.7	8.7	8.4	9.4	2,383	2,411
Massachusetts...........	79	82	15.7	16.5	823	787	11.4	11.4	21.8	22.1	2,419	2,633
Michigan................	156	151	25.6	25.1	1,208	1,159	17.0	16.2	30.3	32.6	1,959	2,086
Minnesota...............	133	131	15.3	14.8	592	562	9.9	9.4	11.1	11.7	1,731	2,064
Mississippi..............	96	99	12.9	12.8	403	380	7.0	6.8	4.6	5.0	1,154	1,368
Missouri................	122	123	18.7	18.9	821	781	11.5	11.1	19.8	21.8	1,981	2,113
Montana................	48	50	3.7	3.7	97	95	2.3	2.2	3.5	3.8	1,190	1,359
Nebraska................	88	87	7.2	6.8	209	200	4.0	3.7	4.6	4.8	1,516	1,639
Nevada.................	36	38	5.2	5.7	241	254	3.6	3.8	2.7	2.6	1,885	1,913
New Hampshire...........	28	28	2.9	2.8	120	120	1.7	1.7	4.8	5.0	2,164	2,380
New Jersey..............	73	77	21.1	21.3	1,067	1,005	14.9	14.2	16.0	15.6	2,179	2,427
New Mexico.............	36	37	4.0	3.8	186	166	2.3	2.1	4.6	4.5	2,058	2,179
New York...............	185	177	59.5	56.3	2,510	2,332	47.2	43.9	53.7	56.3	1,883	2,194
North Carolina...........	117	117	23.0	22.6	1,038	1,011	16.0	15.7	18.3	19.7	1,633	1,838
North Dakota............	41	40	3.3	2.9	94	95	2.0	1.8	3.1	2.3	1,342	1,806
Ohio....................	183	183	34.3	33.2	1,517	1,456	20.8	19.5	35.8	37.3	2,138	2,490
Oklahoma...............	113	116	11.2	11.4	429	412	6.4	6.1	5.7	6.6	1,499	1,642
Oregon.................	58	59	6.4	6.8	321	337	3.8	4.0	9.2	10.4	2,818	3,106
Pennsylvania............	196	190	39.9	39.0	1,810	1,638	26.8	25.1	38.6	38.0	1,906	2,155
Rhode Island............	11	11	2.5	2.3	123	111	1.7	1.6	2.7	2.0	2,325	2,596
South Carolina...........	67	69	12.5	12.8	523	498	8.2	7.9	6.4	6.7	1,788	1,883
South Dakota............	53	54	4.1	4.2	101	102	2.6	2.6	2.0	2.3	1,113	1,218
Tennessee...............	134	130	20.8	20.3	833	819	12.5	12.4	11.4	11.9	1,462	1,668
Texas...................	426	424	61.4	61.6	2,580	2,522	36.5	36.1	38.3	40.1	1,943	2,242
Utah....................	44	47	5.1	5.2	224	229	2.7	2.7	5.5	6.2	2,233	2,520
Vermont.................	14	14	1.3	1.2	49	48	0.8	0.8	3.4	3.1	1,656	2,156
Virginia.................	89	93	17.7	18.0	777	780	11.8	12.2	13.8	15.8	1,736	1,865
Washington..............	86	90	11.5	12.2	589	601	7.2	7.6	11.8	12.5	2,810	3,154
West Virginia............	56	55	7.3	7.1	278	265	4.4	4.2	6.7	6.9	1,323	1,517
Wisconsin...............	124	129	13.5	12.8	589	566	8.1	7.7	14.6	16.5	1,953	2,064
Wyoming................	24	24	2.0	1.9	50	45	1.1	1.0	1.0	1.3	1,103	1,170

[1] The average number of people served on an inpatient basis on a single day during the reporting period.

Source: Health Forum, An American Hospital Association Company, Chicago, IL, *AHA Hospital Statistics 2015 Edition* ©, and previous editions. See also <http://www.ahadataviewer.com/>.

Table 192. Average Cost to Community Hospitals Per Patient: 1990 to 2013

[In dollars, except percent. Covers non-federal short-term general or specialty hospitals (excluding psychiatric or tuberculosis hospitals and hospital units of institutions). Total cost per patient based on total hospital expenses (payroll, employee benefits, professional fees, supplies, etc.). Data have been adjusted for outpatient visits]

Type of expense and hospital	1990	2000	2005	2007	2008	2009	2010	2011	2012	2013
Average cost per day, total........	**687**	**1,149**	**1,522**	**1,690**	**1,782**	**1,853**	**1,910**	**1,960**	**2,090**	**2,157**
Annual percent change [1]..........	7.8	4.2	5.0	4.8	5.4	4.0	3.1	2.6	6.6	3.2
Nongovernmental nonprofit..........	692	1,182	1,585	1,772	1,876	1,957	2,025	2,088	2,214	2,289
For profit.............................	752	1,057	1,412	1,519	1,556	1,574	1,629	1,628	1,747	1,791
State and local government.........	635	1,064	1,329	1,460	1,552	1,611	1,625	1,667	1,831	1,878
Average cost per stay, total.......	**4,947**	**6,649**	**8,793**	**9,342**	**9,788**	**10,043**	**10,313**	**10,533**	**11,221**	**11,651**
Nongovernmental nonprofit..........	5,001	6,717	8,670	9,574	10,081	10,379	10,652	10,933	11,563	12,000
For profit.............................	4,727	5,642	7,351	7,740	7,985	8,037	8,336	8,263	8,861	9,296
State and local government.........	4,838	7,106	8,793	9,446	9,827	10,068	10,283	10,532	11,668	12,028

[1] Change from immediate prior year.

Source: Health Forum, An American Hospital Association Company, Chicago, IL, *AHA Hospital Statistics 2015 Edition* ©, and previous editions. See also <http://www.ahadataviewer.com/>.

Table 193. Hospital Utilization Rates by Type of Hospital: 1990 to 2013

[In units, as indicated (21.9 represents 21,900,000)]

Type of hospital	1990	2000	2005	2009	2010	2011	2012	2013
COMMUNITY HOSPITALS: [1]								
Admissions per 1,000 population [2]	125	117	119	116	114	112	110	106
Admissions per bed	34	40	44	44	44	44	43	42
Average length of stay (days) [3]	7.2	5.8	5.6	5.4	5.4	5.4	5.4	5.4
Outpatient visits per admission	9.7	15.8	16.6	18.1	18.5	18.8	19.6	20.2
Outpatient visits per 1,000 population [2]	1,207	1,852	1,976	2,091	2,108	2,106	2,150	2,145
Surgical operations (million)	21.9	26.1	27.5	27.5	27.3	26.9	26.8	26.6
Number per admission	0.7	0.8	0.8	0.8	0.8	0.8	0.8	0.8
NONFEDERAL PSYCHIATRIC:								
Admissions per 1,000 population [2]	2.9	2.4	2.5	2.5	2.5	2.4	2.5	2.6
Days in hospital per 1,000 population [2]	190	93	89	80	77	73	69	67

[1] Nonfederal, short-term general, and other specialty hospitals. Other specialty hospitals include obstetrics and gynecology; eye, ear, nose, and throat; rehabilitation; orthopedic; and other individually described specialty services. Includes academic medical centers or other teaching hospitals if they are nonfederal short-term hospitals. Excluded are hospitals not accessible by the general public, such as prison hospitals or college infirmaries. [2] Based on Census Bureau estimated resident population as of July 1. Data for 1990, 2000, and 2010 based on enumerated resident population as of April 1. Other years are estimates, which reflect revisions based on the preceding decennial Census of Population. [3] Number of inpatient days divided by number of admissions.

Source: Health Forum, An American Hospital Association Company, Chicago, IL, *AHA Hospital Statistics 2015 Edition* ©, and previous editions. See also <http://www.ahadataviewer.com/>.

Table 194. Hospital Utilization Rates by Sex: 1990 to 2010

[30,788 represents 30,788,000. Represents estimates of inpatients discharged from noninstitutional, short-stay hospitals, exclusive of federal hospitals. Excludes newborn infants. Based on sample data collected from the National Hospital Discharge Survey, a sample survey of hospital records of patients discharged in year shown; subject to sampling variability]

Item and sex	1990	1995	2000	2005	2006	2007	2008	2009	2010
Patients discharged (1,000)	30,788	30,722	31,706	34,667	34,854	34,369	35,697	36,120	35,079
Patients discharged per 1,000 persons, total [1]	122	116	113	117	117	114	118	118	114
Male	100	94	91	96	95	94	97	98	94
Female	143	136	134	138	138	134	139	138	134
Days of care per 1,000 persons, total [1]	784	620	555	562	558	554	577	575	545
Male	694	551	486	498	495	494	518	518	491
Female	869	686	620	624	619	612	635	630	598
Average stay (days)	6.4	5.4	4.9	4.8	4.8	4.8	4.9	4.9	4.8
Male	6.9	5.8	5.3	5.2	5.2	5.3	5.4	5.3	5.2
Female	6.1	5.0	4.6	4.5	4.5	4.6	4.6	4.6	4.5

[1] Rates are computed using Census Bureau estimates of the civilian population as of July 1. Rates for 1990 and 1995 were based on population estimates adjusted for the net underenumeration in the 1990 census. Rates for 2000 and later were calculated using 2000-based postcensal estimates.

Source: U.S. National Center for Health Statistics, National Hospital Discharge Survey, "Average length of stay and days of care: Number and rate of discharges by sex and age, 2010," <http://www.cdc.gov/nchs/nhds/nhds_products.htm>, accessed March 2013.

Table 195. Hospital Utilization Measures for HIV Patients: 1990 to 2010

[HIV is human immunodeficiency virus. See headnote, Table 194]

Measure of utilization	Unit	1990	1995	2000	2005	2008	2009	2010
Number of patients discharged	1,000	146	249	173	185	215	155	170
Male	1,000	114	183	115	113	133	106	118
Female	1,000	32	66	58	72	81	49	53
Rate of patient discharges [1]	Rate	5.8	9.4	6.2	6.3	7.1	5.1	5.5
Number of days of care	1,000	2,188	2,326	1,257	1,244	1,342	960	1,040
Male	1,000	1,777	1,649	895	751	875	651	732
Female	1,000	411	677	362	493	468	309	308
Rate of days of care [1]	Rate	86.9	87.6	45.2	42.2	44.3	31.4	33.8
Average length of stay	Days	14.9	9.3	7.3	6.7	6.3	6.2	6.1
Male	Days	15.5	9.0	7.8	6.7	6.6	6.2	6.2
Female	Days	12.9	10.3	6.3	6.8	5.7	6.3	5.8

[1] Per 10,000 population. Based on Census Bureau estimated civilian population as of July 1. Rates for 1990 and 1995 were based on population estimates adjusted for the net undernumeration in the 1990 census. Populations for 2000 and later were 2000-based postcensal estimates.

Source: U.S. National Center for Health Statistics, unpublished data. See also <http://www.cdc.gov/nchs/nhds.htm>.

Table 196. Hospital Discharges and Days of Care: 2009 and 2010

[36,120 represents 36,120,000. See headnote, Table 194. For composition of regions, see map, inside front cover]

Age, race, and region	Discharges Number (1,000) 2009	Discharges Number (1,000) 2010	Discharges Per 1,000 persons [1] 2009	Discharges Per 1,000 persons [1] 2010	Days of care per 1,000 persons [1] 2009	Days of care per 1,000 persons [1] 2010	Average stay (days) 2009	Average stay (days) 2010
Total [2].........................	36,120	35,079	118	114	575	545	4.9	4.8
AGE								
Under 1 year old................	661	636	155	153	928	906	6.0	5.9
1 to 4 years old.................	571	593	34	35	104	118	3.1	3.4
5 to 14 years old................	786	744	19	18	85	76	4.4	4.2
15 to 24 years old...............	2,950	2,829	69	66	240	233	3.5	3.5
25 to 34 years old...............	4,104	4,009	100	97	348	320	3.5	3.3
35 to 44 years old...............	3,427	3,193	83	79	343	315	4.1	4.0
45 to 64 years old...............	9,686	9,483	122	118	618	593	5.1	5.0
65 to 74 years old...............	5,312	5,189	255	242	1,389	1,313	5.4	5.4
75 years old and over...........	8,623	8,402	459	440	2,663	2,460	5.8	5.6
RACE								
White...........................	23,109	23,224	95	95	467	459	4.9	4.8
Black...........................	4,954	4,843	126	122	666	609	5.3	5.0
Asian/Pacific Islander..........	657	629	45	42	242	190	5.4	4.5
American Indian/Eskimo/Aleut.......	[3] 148	[3] 159	[3] 47	[3] 50	[3] 305	[3] 472	[3] 6.5	[3] 9.5
REGION								
Northeast.......................	8,085	7,458	146	135	822	737	5.6	5.5
Midwest.........................	8,004	7,973	120	119	526	517	4.4	4.3
South...........................	13,273	13,150	118	116	580	564	4.9	4.9
West............................	6,758	6,497	95	90	420	394	4.4	4.4

[1] Rates were calculated using U.S. Census Bureau 2000-based postcensal estimates of the civilian population as of July 1. [2] Includes other races not shown separately. [3] Figure does not meet standard of reliability or precision.

Source: U.S. National Center for Health Statistics, National Hospital Discharge Survey, unpublished data. See also <http://www.cdc.gov/nchs/nhds.htm>.

Table 197. Hospital Discharges and Days of Care by Selected Diagnosis, by Patient Sex and Age: 2010

[14,200 represents 14,200,000. Represents estimates of inpatients discharged from noninstitutional, short-stay hospitals, exclusive of federal hospitals. Excludes newborn infants. Diagnostic categories are based on the International Classification of Diseases, Ninth Revision, Clinical Modification. See headnote, Table 194]

Sex, age, and selected first-listed diagnosis [1]	Discharges Number (1,000) [2]	Discharges Per 1,000 persons [2]	Average stay (days) [2]	Sex, age, and selected first-listed diagnosis [1]	Discharges Number (1,000) [2]	Discharges Per 1,000 persons [2]	Average stay (days) [2]
MALE				FEMALE			
All ages [3].........................	14,200	93.6	5.2	All ages [3].........................	20,879	133.7	4.5
Under 18 years old [3]................	1,290	33.8	4.7	Under 18 years old [3]................	1,186	32.6	4.1
Injury..........................	131	3.4	4.0	Childbirth......................	107	2.9	2.7
Pneumonia.......................	81	2.1	3.8	Injury..........................	89	2.5	3.2
Asthma..........................	84	2.2	2.2	Schizophrenia, mood disorders, delusional disorders,			
18 to 44 years old [3]................	2,343	41.2	4.5	nonorganic psychoses [5]............	[4] 121	[4] 3.3	[4] 6.6
Injury..........................	342	6.0	4.8	18 to 44 years old [3]................	7,186	129.4	3.3
Schizophrenia, mood disorders, delusional disorders,				Childbirth......................	3,841	69.2	2.7
nonorganic psychoses [5]............	494	8.7	5.5	Schizophrenia, mood disorders, delusional disorders,			
Heart disease...................	135	2.4	3.2	nonorganic psychoses [5]............	412	7.4	5.2
Alcohol and drug [6]................	88	1.5	3.8	Injury..........................	289	5.2	4.2
45 to 64 years old [3]................	4,640	118.4	5.2	Uterine fibroids................	88	1.6	2.1
Heart disease...................	704	18.0	4.1	45 to 64 years old [3]................	4,843	117.6	4.8
Injury..........................	450	11.5	7.1	Heart disease...................	416	10.1	4.8
Cancer, all.....................	230	5.9	6.2	Cancer, all.....................	236	5.7	6.5
65 to 74 years old [3]................	2,511	252.2	5.6	Osteoarthritis..................	272	6.6	3.2
Heart disease...................	481	48.4	4.7	65 to 74 years old [3]................	2,679	233.4	5.3
Cancer, all.....................	164	16.5	6.8	Heart disease...................	351	30.6	4.6
Stroke..........................	123	12.3	4.8	Osteoarthritis..................	204	17.8	3.6
Pneumonia.......................	91	9.1	5.9	Cancer, all.....................	133	11.6	5.2
75 to 84 years old [3]................	2,255	403.5	5.8	Pneumonia.......................	89	7.7	5.8
Heart disease...................	452	80.9	4.8	75 to 84 years old [3]................	2,909	379.9	5.6
Cancer, all.....................	109	19.5	6.6	Heart disease...................	475	62.0	4.9
Pneumonia.......................	104	18.6	4.8	Injury..........................	296	38.7	5.8
Stroke..........................	109	19.6	6.4	Pneumonia.......................	136	17.7	5.7
85 years old and over [3]............	1,161	598.0	5.5	Stroke..........................	152	19.9	6.0
Heart disease...................	220	113.3	5.1	85 years old and over [3]............	2,076	530.2	5.4
Pneumonia.......................	86	44.4	5.0	Heart disease...................	380	97.1	4.8
Injury..........................	115	59.0	5.6	Injury..........................	264	67.4	5.3
				Pneumonia.......................	115	29.3	6.1

[1] The first-listed diagnosis is the one specified as the principal diagnosis or the first diagnosis listed on the face sheet or discharge summary of the medical record. It is usually the main cause of the hospitalization. The number of first-listed diagnoses is the same as the number of discharges. [2] Crude estimates. [3] Includes discharges with first-listed diagnoses not shown in table. [4] Figure does not meet standard of reliability or precision. [5] These estimates are for nonfederal short-stay hospitals only and do not include mental illness discharges from other types of facilities such as Veterans Affairs hospitals. [6] Includes abuse, dependence, and withdrawal. These estimates are for non-federal short-stay hospitals only and do not include alcohol and drug discharges from other types of facilities or programs such as the Department of Veterans Affairs or day treatment programs.

Source: U.S. National Center for Health Statistics, National Hospital Discharge Survey, unpublished data. See also <http://www.cdc.gov/nchs/nhds.htm>.

Table 198. Selected Cosmetic Plastic Surgery and Nonsurgical Procedures: 2005 to 2014

[In thousands (11,428.8 represents 11,428,800). As of December 31. The final data are projected to reflect nationwide statistics and are based on a survey of doctors who have been certified by the American Board of Medical Specialties recognized boards, including but not limited to the American Board of Plastic Surgery. Data for the procedures include but are not limited to those performed by American Society for Aesthetic Plastic Surgery (ASAPS) members. ASAPS members are plastic surgeons certified by the American Board of Plastic Surgery who specialize in cosmetic surgery of the face and the entire body]

Procedure	2005	2009	2010	2011	2012	2013	2014
Total all procedures............	11,428.8	9,964.4	9,183.2	9,194.5	10,105.2	11,248.7	10,663.6
Total surgical procedures [1]............	2,131.0	1,491.9	1,624.3	1,638.5	1,688.7	1,792.7	1,765.0
Liposuction............	455.5	283.7	289.0	325.3	313.0	363.9	342.5
Breast augmentation............	364.6	312.0	318.1	316.8	330.6	313.3	286.7
Blepharoplasty (eyelid surgery)............	231.5	149.9	152.1	147.5	153.2	161.4	165.7
Abdominoplasty (tummy tuck)............	169.3	127.9	144.9	149.4	156.5	160.1	164.0
Rhinoplasty (nose reshaping)............	200.9	138.3	133.5	126.1	143.8	148.0	145.9
Total nonsurgical procedures [1]............	9,297.7	8,472.6	7,558.9	7,556.0	8,416.5	9,456.0	8,898.7
Botox injection [2]............	3,294.8	2,557.1	2,437.2	2,619.7	3,257.9	3,766.1	3,588.2
Hyaluronic acid [3]............	1,194.2	1,313.0	1,315.1	1,206.2	1,423.7	1,872.2	1,696.6
Hair removal [4]............	1,566.9	1,280.0	936.3	919.8	883.9	901.6	828.5
Microdermabrasion [5]............	1,023.9	621.9	450.7	499.4	498.8	479.9	417.0
Photorejuvenation [6]............	(X)	452.2	381.5	439.2	337.5	456.6	370.5
Total female procedures............	10,443.8	9,058.5	8,586.7	8,398.4	9,136.7	10,349.2	9,591.8
Total surgical procedures [1]............	1,918.1	1,310.7	1,479.7	1,493.6	1,528.2	1,694.3	1,593.6
Breast augmentation............	364.6	312.0	318.1	316.8	330.6	313.3	286.7
Liposuction............	402.9	243.2	251.8	283.7	271.4	312.2	302.0
Abdominoplasty (tummy tuck)............	164.1	123.0	137.9	142.7	149.0	151.2	156.4
Breast lift............	121.0	98.3	121.4	127.1	127.8	137.2	132.9
Blepharoplasty (eyelid surgery)............	198.1	124.9	131.4	124.6	129.9	133.2	137.9
Breast reduction............	160.5	113.5	138.2	113.0	112.8	122.8	114.5
Total nonsurgical procedures [1]............	8,525.7	7,747.8	7,107.1	6,904.8	7,608.5	8,654.9	7,998.1
Botox injection [2]............	2,990.7	2,299.3	2,211.9	2,355.5	2,915.9	3,381.5	3,174.9
Hyaluronic acid [3]............	1,149.2	1,221.8	1,245.3	1,127.2	1,318.2	1,739.0	1,561.0
Hair removal [4]............	1,334.7	1,114.0	817.4	812.4	757.5	773.3	721.9
Microdermabrasion [5]............	939.5	565.0	416.3	468.5	454.1	452.4	372.2
Photorejuvenation [6]............	(X)	404.5	345.5	396.9	308.8	413.2	318.8
Chemical peel............	533.0	492.3	469.6	360.3	418.8	412.9	452.9
Sclerotherapy [7]............	548.0	442.0	435.0	348.5	283.2	367.4	305.4
Laser skin resurfacing............	432.6	463.3	518.3	319.8	401.9	334.0	381.9
Total male procedures............	984.9	935.2	750.1	796.1	968.5	1,070.4	1,071.8
Total surgical procedures [1]............	212.9	160.9	142.6	144.9	160.5	188.8	171.3
Liposuction............	52.5	40.5	37.2	41.7	41.6	51.7	40.5
Blepharoplasty (eyelid surgery)............	33.4	25.0	20.7	22.9	23.3	28.2	27.8
Rhinoplasty (nose reshaping)............	45.9	32.7	30.1	24.5	30.0	26.8	32.6
Breast reduction (to treat gynecomastia)........	17.7	16.8	18.3	17.6	22.7	22.6	24.2
Otoplasty (ear surgery)............	11.4	8.3	10.8	9.3	12.1	15.9	11.7
Facelift............	13.0	10.5	10.4	(NA)	11.4	12.3	15.0
Total nonsurgical procedures [1]............	772.0	774.4	607.4	651.2	808.0	881.7	900.5
Botox injection [2]............	304.1	257.8	225.2	264.3	342.0	384.7	413.4
Hyaluronic acid [3]............	45.0	91.2	69.8	79.0	105.5	133.2	135.7
Hair removal [4]............	232.2	166.0	118.9	107.5	126.4	128.3	106.6
Photorejuvenation [6]............	(X)	47.7	35.9	42.3	28.7	43.4	51.7
Chemical peel............	23.2	37.0	24.3	23.9	25.1	31.4	31.2
Microdermabrasion [5]............	84.4	56.9	34.4	31.0	44.8	27.5	44.8

X Not applicable. NA Not available. [1] Totals include procedures not shown separately. [2] As of 2009, includes Dysport. [3] In 2003, the FDA approved hyaluronic acid injections for filling soft tissue defects such as facial wrinkles. [4] Laser or pulsed light hair removal. [5] Procedure for reducing fine lines, "crow's feet," age spots, and acne scars. [6] Intense pulse light for facial rejuvenation. [7] Treatment of varicose and spider veins.

Source: The American Society for Aesthetic Plastic Surgery, *2014 Cosmetic Surgery National Data Bank–Statistics* ©, and earlier reports. See also <http://www.surgery.org/media/statistics>.

Table 199. Organ Transplants: 2000 to 2014

[As of end of year. Based on Organ Procurement and Transplantation Network data; data are from work supported in part by Health Resources and Services Administration contract 234-2005-37011C. The content is the responsibility of the authors alone and does not necessarily reflect the views or policies of the Department of Health and Human Services, nor does mention of trade names, commercial products, or organizations imply endorsement by the U.S. Government]

Procedure	Number of procedures					Number of people waiting				
	2000	2005	2010	2013	2014	2000	2005	2010	2013	2014
Transplant: [1]										
Heart............	2,199	2,125	2,332	2,531	2,655	4,148	2,994	3,189	3,693	3,998
Heart-lung............	48	35	42	23	24	207	141	70	47	45
Lung............	959	1,406	1,769	1,923	1,925	3,636	3,162	1,805	1,608	1,669
Liver............	5,001	6,444	6,291	6,455	6,729	16,832	17,356	16,146	15,825	15,473
Kidney............	13,623	16,485	16,900	16,893	17,106	47,758	64,833	87,757	99,254	101,915
Kidney-pancreas.......	915	903	828	762	709	2,466	2,502	2,224	2,031	2,034
Pancreas............	439	542	349	256	245	1,025	1,686	1,418	1,178	1,133
Intestine............	82	178	151	109	139	150	205	265	256	253
Multi-organ............	222	522	560	674	(NA)	(NA)	(NA)	(NA)	(NA)	(NA)

NA Not available. [1] Kidney-pancreas and heart-lung transplants are each counted as one procedure. All other multiorgan transplants, excluding kidney-pancreas and heart-lung, are included in the multi-organ row.

Source: U.S. Department of Health and Human Services, Health Resources and Services Administration, Organ Procurement and Transplantation Network (OPTN), <http://optn.transplant.hrsa.gov/converge/LatestData/step2.asp>, accessed June 2015; and unpublished data, based on OPTN data as of January 9, 2015.

Table 200. Cancer Survival Rates by Type/Body Site: 1993 to 2011

[For invasive cancer, unless otherwise noted. For top 15 cancers ranked by incidence rates per 100,000 persons for 2008-2012 period. Based on follow-up of patients into 2012. The 5-year relative survival rate, which is derived by adjusting the observed survival rate for expected mortality, represents the proportion of patients alive within 5 years subsequent to their diagnosis of cancer. Data are based on information collected as part of the National Cancer Institute's Surveillance, Epidemiology and End Results (SEER) program, a collection of population-based registries in 9 areas]

Cancer type	5-year relative survival rates by year of diagnosis (percent)									
	White					Black				
	1993 to 1995	1996 to 1998	1999 to 2001	2002 to 2004	2005 to 2011	1993 to 1995	1996 to 1998	1999 to 2001	2002 to 2004	2005 to 2011
All types [1].................	**62.4**	**64.3**	**67.1**	**68.3**	**69.7**	**52.7**	**55.2**	**57.9**	**59.4**	**62.2**
Female breast................	87.6	89.3	90.8	91.4	92.0	72.7	76.1	78.7	77.8	80.5
Prostate......................	95.9	97.8	99.7	99.8	99.7	91.6	94.9	97.3	97.7	97.6
Lung and bronchus............	14.5	14.8	15.5	16.5	18.8	12.8	12.4	12.6	13.2	15.5
Colon and rectum.............	60.4	63.0	66.5	66.7	66.9	51.7	54.0	54.0	56.5	58.7
Melanoma of skin.............	89.5	90.8	92.2	93.1	93.1	[4] 69.5	[4] 73.9	[4] 73.2	[4] 72.0	69.8
Bladder, urinary [2]...........	81.0	79.7	81.0	80.8	79.4	60.5	62.7	67.3	61.3	66.7
Non-Hodgkin's lymphoma [3].....	53.2	59.4	64.9	71.0	73.0	42.1	54.7	55.7	63.5	64.0
Kidney and renal pelvis.........	61.9	62.0	64.9	69.4	74.4	57.5	66.9	63.9	64.9	73.6
Thyroid......................	95.5	95.9	96.8	97.4	98.5	93.2	95.0	92.0	95.9	97.0
Corpus and uterus.............	84.9	85.1	85.9	85.2	85.3	58.6	61.4	60.9	59.9	65.6
Leukemia [3]...................	48.4	49.4	51.6	58.5	62.5	41.2	38.5	43.2	53.0	55.4
Pancreas.....................	3.9	4.1	4.9	5.6	7.8	3.6	3.4	5.6	4.3	7.2
Oral cavity and pharynx.......	60.0	59.8	62.2	65.6	68.1	37.9	35.9	44.6	48.1	44.9
Liver and intrahepatic bile duct............................	5.2	8.4	10.2	14.0	17.6	4.0	4.6	7.6	9.6	13.0
Stomach......................	19.9	20.2	22.2	25.8	29.1	19.3	22.5	23.0	29.3	28.3

[1] Includes other sites, not shown separately. [2] Invasive and in situ. [3] All types combined. [4] The standard error is between 5 and 10 percentage points.

Source: U.S. National Institutes of Health, National Cancer Institute, Surveillance Epidemiology and End Results Program, "SEER Cancer Statistics Review (CSR), 1975-2012," <http://seer.cancer.gov/csr/1975_2012/>, accessed June 2015.

Table 201. Cancer—Estimated New Cases and Deaths by State: 2014

[Excludes basal and squamous cell skin cancers and in situ carcinomas, except urinary bladder. State estimates may not add to U.S. totals due to rounding]

State	New cases [1]			Deaths			State	New cases [1]			Deaths		
	Total [2]	Female breast	Lung & bronchus	Total [2]	Female breast	Lung & bronchus		Total [2]	Female breast	Lung & bronchus	Total [2]	Female breast	Lung & bronchus
U.S........	1,658,370	231,840	221,200	589,430	40,290	158,040	MO......	34,680	4,610	5,380	12,830	900	3,910
AL..........	26,150	3,680	4,150	10,560	680	3,280	MT......	5,950	830	760	2,020	130	540
AK..........	3,700	470	420	1,040	70	290	NE......	9,540	1,230	1,200	3,480	210	890
AZ..........	32,440	4,750	3,740	11,540	770	2,800	NV......	13,640	1,690	1,770	4,880	380	1,410
AR..........	15,830	2,090	2,620	6,760	410	2,180	NH......	8,090	1,120	1,140	2,730	170	770
CA..........	172,090	25,270	18,430	58,180	4,320	12,370	NJ......	51,410	7,310	5,830	16,250	1,290	3,900
CO..........	24,540	3,640	2,560	7,590	540	1,710	NM......	9,970	1,320	990	3,620	270	760
CT..........	21,970	3,190	2,870	6,840	460	1,730	NY......	107,840	14,900	13,180	34,600	2,420	8,740
DE..........	5,280	780	860	2,010	120	600	NC......	50,420	7,820	7,750	19,310	1,340	5,780
DC..........	2,800	430	310	990	80	210	ND......	3,840	510	440	1,280	80	320
FL..........	114,040	15,470	16,810	43,050	2,830	11,920	OH......	65,010	8,950	10,000	25,400	1,740	7,370
GA..........	48,070	7,170	6,460	16,460	1,240	4,640	OK......	19,280	2,770	3,220	8,100	520	2,460
HI..........	6,730	1,140	890	2,470	130	580	OR......	22,410	3,280	2,830	8,040	510	2,070
ID..........	8,080	1,070	910	2,790	190	670	PA......	81,540	9,990	10,540	28,640	1,950	7,520
IL..........	65,460	9,570	8,920	23,940	1,640	6,550	RI......	6,040	730	880	2,120	130	570
IN..........	35,620	4,600	5,510	13,420	870	4,060	SC......	25,550	3,820	4,040	10,130	690	2,970
IA..........	17,140	2,390	2,440	6,440	390	1,770	SD......	4,520	600	570	1,630	110	450
KS..........	14,440	2,130	1,930	5,510	350	1,540	TN......	38,300	4,770	6,200	14,370	890	4,600
KY..........	26,490	3,300	4,680	10,200	590	3,550	TX......	113,630	16,510	13,650	38,520	2,710	9,580
LA..........	24,100	2,900	3,380	9,040	630	2,610	UT......	11,050	1,460	660	2,900	270	460
ME..........	8,810	1,010	1,360	3,300	180	970	VT......	4,020	530	570	1,360	80	400
MD..........	30,050	4,730	3,980	10,470	810	2,700	VA......	41,170	6,090	5,740	14,830	1,090	4,070
MA..........	37,790	5,890	5,150	12,710	770	3,420	WA......	38,180	5,480	4,790	12,700	830	3,220
MI..........	57,420	7,780	8,350	20,920	1,410	6,010	WV......	11,730	1,430	2,080	4,710	270	1,460
MN..........	29,730	3,900	3,250	9,820	620	2,450	WI......	32,700	4,310	4,370	11,550	720	3,050
MS..........	16,260	2,050	2,340	6,360	410	1,950	WY......	2,860	390	320	1,000	70	240

[1] Estimates are offered as a rough guide and should be interpreted with caution. [2] Includes other types of cancer, not shown separately.

Source: American Cancer Society, Inc., *Cancer Facts and Figures 2015* ©, Atlanta, GA, 2015. Reprinted by the permission of the American Cancer Society, Inc., from <www.cancer.org>. All rights reserved.

Table 202. Top 15 Cancers Among Men and Women, by Race/Ethnicity: 2008 to 2012

[Rates per 100,000 population, age-adjusted to the 2000 U.S. standard population. Cancer incidence measures the number of new cancers occurring during a year. Data are for 2008 to 2012 period, based on cancer registries in 18 areas monitored by the Surveillance, Epidemiology, and End Results (SEER) Program, covering about 28 percent of the U.S. population. See source for more information]

Cancer by site, and sex	All race/ethnicities Rank	All race/ethnicities Rate	White Rank	White Rate	Black Rank	Black Rate	Hispanic [1] Rank	Hispanic [1] Rate
TOTAL								
All Sites	(X)	454.8	(X)	463.3	(X)	478.0	(X)	349.9
Breast	1	67.2	1	68.1	2	70.8	2	49.4
Prostate [2]	2	62.7	3	60.0	1	91.2	1	50.7
Lung and bronchus	3	58.7	2	60.2	3	67.0	4	30.4
Colon and rectum	4	42.4	4	41.5	4	52.3	3	35.8
Melanoma of the skin	5	21.6	5	25.6	(X)	(X)	(X)	(X)
Urinary bladder	6	20.3	6	22.2	10	12.6	9	11.2
Non-Hodgkin lymphoma	7	19.7	7	20.6	7	14.6	5	17.8
Kidney and renal pelvis	8	15.6	8	16.1	5	18.1	6	15.4
Thyroid	9	13.5	9	14.3	15	8.0	8	11.5
Corpus and uterus, NOS [2,6]	10	13.4	11	13.6	8	13.6	11	11.0
Leukemia	11	13.3	10	14.0	12	10.6	13	10.5
Pancreas	12	12.4	12	12.3	6	15.7	10	11.1
Oral cavity and pharynx	13	11.0	13	11.5	14	9.3	14	6.8
Liver and IBD [3]	14	8.2	14	7.2	13	9.8	7	12.5
Stomach	15	7.4	(X)	(X)	11	10.9	12	10.9
Brain and ONS [4]	(X)	(X)	15	7.1	(X)	(X)	(X)	(X)
Myeloma	(X)	(X)	(X)	(X)	9	12.8	(X)	(X)
Ovary [2,5]	(X)	(X)	(X)	(X)	(X)	(X)	15	5.9
MEN								
All Sites	(X)	516.6	(X)	519.8	(X)	590.1	(X)	395.0
Prostate	1	137.9	1	130.4	1	214.5	1	114.7
Lung and bronchus	2	70.1	2	70.3	2	90.9	3	37.9
Colon and rectum	3	48.9	3	47.8	3	61.2	2	43.3
Urinary bladder	4	35.8	4	39.0	5	21.4	6	19.6
Melanoma of the skin	5	28.2	5	33.0	(X)	(X)	(X)	(X)
Non-Hodgkin lymphoma	6	23.9	6	24.9	6	17.8	4	20.6
Kidney and renal pelvis	7	21.3	7	21.9	4	25.1	5	20.2
Leukemia	8	17.0	8	17.9	12	13.5	9	12.6
Oral cavity and pharynx	9	16.5	9	17.1	10	14.6	11	10.1
Pancreas	10	14.0	10	14.0	7	17.2	10	11.9
Liver and IBD [3]	11	12.7	11	11.2	8	16.2	7	19.1
Stomach	12	10.1	12	9.2	11	14.6	8	14.2
Myeloma	13	7.9	15	7.5	9	15.1	12	7.3
Brain and ONS [4]	14	7.7	13	8.4	15	4.9	13	5.8
Esophagus	15	7.6	14	8.0	14	7.6	14	5.2
Larynx	(X)	(X)	(X)	(X)	13	8.8	(X)	(X)
Testis	(X)	(X)	(X)	(X)	(X)	(X)	15	4.9
WOMEN								
All Sites	(X)	411.2	(X)	423.9	(X)	401.2	(X)	322.2
Breast	1	124.8	1	127.9	1	124.4	1	92.1
Lung and bronchus	2	50.2	2	52.7	2	50.8	3	25.1
Colon and rectum	3	37.1	3	36.3	3	46.0	2	30.0
Corpus and uterus, NOS [6]	4	25.1	4	25.8	4	24.0	4	20.7
Thyroid	5	20.0	5	21.3	8	11.8	5	18.1
Melanoma of the skin	6	16.8	6	20.2	(X)	(X)	(X)	(X)
Non-Hodgkin lymphoma	7	16.3	7	17.1	7	12.1	6	15.5
Ovary [5]	8	12.1	8	12.8	10	9.8	8	11.0
Pancreas	9	11.0	11	10.8	5	14.4	9	10.3
Kidney and renal pelvis	10	10.8	9	11.1	6	12.8	7	11.6
Leukemia	11	10.4	10	10.9	12	8.5	11	8.9
Urinary bladder	12	8.7	12	9.4	14	6.9	14	5.1
Cervix uteri	13	7.7	13	7.7	11	9.2	10	9.9
Oral cavity and pharynx	14	6.3	14	6.4	15	5.2	(X)	(X)
Brain and ONS [4]	15	5.4	15	5.9	(X)	(X)	(X)	(X)
Myeloma	(X)	(X)	(X)	(X)	9	11.2	15	4.8
Stomach	(X)	(X)	(X)	(X)	13	8.4	12	8.4
Liver and IBD [3]	(X)	(X)	(X)	(X)	(X)	(X)	13	7.0

X Not applicable. [1] Hispanic is not mutually exclusive from other race groups. [2] Rates for sex-specific cancer sites are calculated using the population for both sexes combined. [3] IBD, intrahepatic bile duct. [4] ONS, other nervous system. [5] Ovary excludes borderline cases or histologies 8442, 8451, 8462, 8472, and 8473. [6] NOS, not otherwise specified.

Source: National Institutes of Health, National Cancer Institute, Surveillance, Epidemiology, and End Results Program, "SEER Cancer Statistics Review (CSR), 1975-2012," <http://seer.cancer.gov/csr/1975_2012/>, accessed June 2015.

Table 203. Selected Notifiable Diseases—Cases Reported: 1990 to 2012

[In thousands where indicated (690.2 represents 690,200). As of December 29, 2012. Figures should be interpreted with caution. Although reporting of some of these diseases is incomplete, the figures are of value in indicating trends of disease incidence. Includes cases imported from outside the United States]

Disease	1990	1995	2000	2005	2008	2009	2010	2011	2012
AIDS/HIV [1]	41,595	71,547	40,758	41,120	39,202	36,870	35,741	35,266	35,361
Arboviral diseases: [3]									
West Nile: neuroinvasive	(2)	(2)	(2)	1,309	689	386	629	486	2,872
nonneuroinvasive	(2)	(2)	(2)	1,691	667	334	392	226	2,801
Botulism [4]	92	97	138	135	145	118	112	153	168
Brucellosis (undulant fever)	82	98	87	120	80	115	115	79	114
Coccidoidomycosis	(2)	1,212	2,867	6,542	7,523	12,926	(2)	22,634	17,802
Cryptosporidiosis	(2)	2,970	3,128	5,659	9,113	7,654	8,944	9,250	7,956
Dengue fever and dengue hemorragic fever	(2)	(2)	(2)	(2)	(2)	(2)	700	254	547
Giardiasis	(2)	(2)	(2)	19,733	18,908	19,399	19,811	16,747	15,178
Haemophilus influenza	(2)	1,180	1,398	2,304	2,886	3,022	3,151	3,539	3,418
Hansen disease (Leprosy)	198	144	91	87	80	103	98	82	82
Hepatitis virus, acute: A	31,441	31,582	13,397	4,488	2,585	1,987	1,670	1,398	1,562
Hepatitis virus, acute: B	21,102	10,805	8,036	5,119	4,033	3,405	3,374	2,903	2,895
Hepatitis virus, acute: C	2,553	4,576	3,197	652	877	782	849	1,229	1,782
Invasive pneumococcal disease: [5]	(X)	(X)	(X)	(X)	(X)	(X)	16,569	17,138	15,635
Legionellosis	1,370	1,241	1,127	2,301	3,181	3,522	3,346	4,202	3,688
Listeriosis	(2)	(2)	755	896	759	851	821	870	727
Lyme disease	(2)	11,700	17,730	23,305	35,198	38,468	30,158	33,097	30,831
Malaria	1,292	1,419	1,560	1,494	1,255	1,451	1,773	1,724	1,503
Measles	27,786	309	86	66	140	71	63	220	55
Meningococcal infections	2,451	3,243	2,256	1,245	1,172	980	833	759	551
Mumps	5,292	906	338	314	454	1,991	2,612	404	229
Pertussis (whooping cough)	4,570	5,137	7,867	25,616	13,278	16,858	27,550	18,719	48,277
Rabies, animal	4,826	7,811	6,934	5,915	4,196	5,343	4,331	4,357	4,541
Rubella [6]	1,125	128	176	11	16	3	5	4	9
Salmonellosis [7]	48,603	45,970	39,574	45,322	51,040	49,192	54,424	51,887	53,800
Shiga toxin-producing E. coli (STEC)	(2)	(2)	(2)	(2)	5,309	4,643	5,476	6,047	6,463
Shigellosis [8]	27,077	32,080	22,922	16,168	22,625	15,931	14,786	13,352	15,283
Spotted fever rickettsiosis (including Rocky Mountain Spotted Fever) [9]	(2)	(2)	495	1,936	2,563	1,815	1,985	2,802	4,470
Streptococcal toxic-shock syndrome	(2)	10	83	129	157	161	142	168	194
Tetanus	64	41	35	27	19	18	26	36	37
Toxic-shock syndrome	322	191	135	90	71	74	82	78	65
Tuberculosis [10]	25,701	22,860	16,377	14,097	12,904	11,545	11,182	10,528	9,945
Typhoid fever	552	369	377	324	449	397	467	390	354
Varicella (chickenpox) [11]	173,099	120,624	27,382	32,242	30,386	20,480	15,427	14,513	13,447
Sexually transmitted diseases:									
Chlamydia (1,000)	(2)	477.6	702.1	976.4	1,210.5	1,244.2	1,307.9	1,412.8	1,423.0
Gonorrhea (1,000)	690.2	392.8	359.0	339.6	336.7	301.2	309.3	321.8	334.8
Syphilis (1,000)	134.3	69.0	31.6	33.3	46.3	44.8	45.8	46.0	49.9

[1] Acquired immunodeficiency syndrome/Human immunodeficiency virus. Includes all cases reported to the Division of HIV/AIDS Prevention, National Center for HIV/AIDS, Viral Hepatitis, STD, and TB Prevention. In 2008 CDC published a revised HIV case definition which combined definitions for HIV infection and AIDS into a single case definition for HIV infection that includes AIDS. [2] Disease was not notifiable. [3] Totals reported to the Division of Vector-Borne Diseases (DVBD), National Center for Emerging and Zoonotic Infectious Diseases (NCEZID) (ArboNET Surveillance). [4] Includes foodborne, infant, wound, and unspecified cases. [5] Data for 2010 and 2011 reported as Streptococcus pneumoniae invasive disease. [6] German measles. Excludes congenital syndrome. [7] Excludes typhoid fever. [8] Bacillary dysentery. [9] Data for Rocky Mountain Spotted Fever are now reported under a new category called Spotted Fever Rickettsiosis (including Rocky Mountain Spotted Fever). [10] Totals reported to the Division of Tuberculosis Elimination, NCHHSTP. [11] Varicella (chickenpox) was removed from the nationally notifiable disease list in 1981. Varicella became nationally notifiable again in 2003.

Source: U.S. Centers for Disease Control and Prevention, "Summary of Notifiable Diseases, United States, 2012," *Morbidity and Mortality Weekly Report,* 61:53, September 19, 2014, and earlier reports. See also <http://www.cdc.gov/mmwr/mmwr_nd/index.html>.

Table 204. HIV Diagnoses, Chlamydia, and Lyme Disease Cases Reported by State: 2012

State	HIV diagnoses [1]	Chlamydia [2]	Lyme disease	State	HIV diagnoses [1]	Chlamydia [2]	Lyme disease	State	HIV diagnoses [1]	Chlamydia [2]	Lyme disease
U.S.	35,361	1,422,976	30,831	KS.	147	11,135	19	NC.	1,145	50,596	122
AL.	545	30,621	25	KY.	312	17,273	14	ND.	9	2,908	15
AK.	26	5,462	10	LA.	1,156	27,353	7	OH.	1013	53,141	67
AZ.	590	30,444	13	ME.	38	3,413	1,111	OK.	253	16,843	4
AR.	125	16,611	–	MD.	1,016	26,534	1,651	OR.	205	13,454	48
CA.	4,037	167,695	70	MA.	510	23,550	5,138	PA.	1,273	54,993	5,033
CO.	362	21,631	–	MI.	654	47,566	98	RI.	62	4,313	217
CT.	277	13,065	2,657	MN.	308	18,056	1,515	SC.	716	27,149	44
DE.	136	4,438	669	MS.	441	23,054	1	SD.	27	3,924	4
DC.	509	6,808	(NA)	MO.	496	27,835	2	TN.	822	32,525	30
FL.	4,629	77,644	118	MT.	20	3,827	6	TX.	3,584	127,036	75
GA.	1,236	52,418	31	NE.	58	6,748	15	UT.	65	7,615	5
HI.	43	6,340	(NA)	NV.	326	11,137	10	VT.	4	1,724	522
ID.	24	4,550	5	NH.	44	3,072	1,450	VA.	871	34,963	1,110
IL.	1,388	67,701	204	NJ.	990	27,271	3,576	WA.	498	24,596	15
IN.	472	29,505	74	NM.	109	11,898	1	WV.	69	4,790	97
IA.	116	11,377	165	NY.	3,353	100,546	2,998	WI.	244	23,726	1,766
								WY.	8	2,102	4

– Represents zero. NA Not available. [1] Total number of HIV diagnoses reported to the Division of HIV/AIDS Prevention, National Center for HIV/AIDS, Viral Hepatitis, STD, and TB Prevention, as of December 31, 2012. In 2008, CDC combined separate surveillance case definitions for HIV infection and AIDS into a single case definition for HIV infection that includes AIDS (and incorporates the HIV infection classification system). [2] As of May 29, 2013.

Source: Centers for Disease Control and Prevention, "Summary of Notifiable Diseases, United States, 2012," *Morbidity and Mortality Weekly Report,* 61:53, September 19, 2014. See also <http://www.cdc.gov/mmwr/mmwr_nd/index.html>.

Table 205. Estimated Number of HIV Infection, Stage 3 (AIDS) Diagnoses Among Adults and Adolescents by Sex and Transmission Category: 2008 to 2012

[HIV infection is classified as stage 3 (AIDS) when the immune system of a person infected with the human immunodeficiency virus becomes severely compromised (measured by CD4 cell count) and/or the person becomes ill with an opportunistic infection. Data cover the 50 states, the District of Columbia, and 6 U.S. dependent areas (American Samoa, Guam, Northern Mariana Islands, Puerto Rico, Republic of Palau, and the U.S. Virgin Islands). Estimated data are calculated by applying statistical adjustments to account for reporting delays and missing transmission category, but not for incomplete reporting. Data may not be representative of all persons with HIV; completeness of HIV infection reporting is estimated at more than 80%; see source for more information. As of April 2008, all jurisdictions had implemented confidential name-based HIV infection reporting. Jurisdictions needed to have reported 4 years of name-based surveillance data to CDC before the data could be statistically adjusted to account for reporting delays and missing risk-factor information]

Transmission category	2008	2009	2010	2011	2012	Cumulative through 2012 [1]
Persons 13 years old and over, total [2]	33,178	32,097	29,717	28,302	28,319	1,206,054
Males, total	24,386	23,816	22,177	21,204	21,331	951,050
Male-to-male sexual contact	15,506	15,669	14,925	14,578	15,003	570,485
Injection drug use	3,045	2,696	2,370	2,047	1,949	199,908
Male-to-male sexual contact and injection drug use	1,801	1,602	1,431	1,266	1,206	84,763
Heterosexual contact [3]	3,871	3,722	3,331	3,183	3,056	84,295
Other [4]	162	127	119	131	117	11,600
Females, total	8,755	8,267	7,518	7,081	6,978	245,202
Injection drug use	2,015	1,808	1,576	1,411	1,343	92,258
Heterosexual contact [3]	6,626	6,333	5,799	5,526	5,492	147,045
Other [4]	114	126	144	144	143	5,899

[1] From the beginning of the epidemic through 2012. [2] Because column totals for estimated numbers were calculated independently of the values for the subpopulations, the values in each column may not sum to the column total. [3] Heterosexual contact with a person known to have, or to be at high risk for, HIV infection. [4] Includes hemophilia, blood transfusion, perinatal exposure, and risk factor not reported or not identified.

Source: U.S. Centers for Disease Control and Prevention, *HIV Surveillance Report: Diagnoses of HIV Infection in the United States and Dependent Areas, 2012,* Vol. 24, November 2014. See also <http://www.cdc.gov/hiv/library/reports/surveillance/>.

Table 206. Estimated Number of Persons Living with HIV Infection Ever Classified as Stage 3 (AIDS) Diagnosis by Selected Characteristics: 2008 to 2011

[See headnote, Table 205]

Age and characteristic	2008	2009	2010	2011
Total [1, 2]	462,198	477,424	491,228	505,319
AGE AS OF END OF YEAR				
Less than 13 years	686	532	444	362
13 and 14 years	605	474	326	251
15 to 19 years	2,768	2,700	2,567	2,324
20 to 24 years	6,394	7,093	7,760	8,358
25 to 34 years	43,230	43,920	44,750	45,809
35 to 44 years	141,558	133,449	125,556	118,552
45 to 54 years	177,970	188,169	196,309	201,840
55 to 64 years	71,078	80,491	89,966	100,636
65 years and over	17,908	20,599	23,550	27,186
RACE/ETHNICITY				
American Indian/Alaska Native	1,332	1,389	1,453	1,516
Asian [3]	4,672	4,998	5,325	5,666
Black/African American	187,986	194,712	201,568	208,589
Hispanic/Latino [4]	103,375	107,371	110,767	114,071
Native Hawaiian/Other Pacific Islander	362	397	427	455
White	149,550	153,191	156,095	159,146
Multiple races	14,922	15,367	15,594	15,876
TRANSMISSION CATEGORY				
Males 13 years old and over, total	352,648	364,084	374,486	385,247
Male-to-male sexual contact	217,180	226,689	235,655	244,869
Injection drug use	60,023	59,580	59,092	58,695
Male-to-male sexual contact and injection drug use	32,022	32,211	32,351	32,487
Heterosexual contact [5]	39,128	41,213	42,935	44,680
Other [6]	4,295	4,391	4,453	4,515
Females 13 years old and over, total	108,864	112,808	116,298	119,710
Injection drug use	32,997	33,107	33,146	33,121
Heterosexual contact [5]	72,621	76,320	79,629	82,946
Other [6]	3,246	3,380	3,522	3,643
Children under age 13 at end of year	686	532	444	362
Perinatal	662	512	425	341
Other [6]	24	20	19	21

[1] Total numbers include persons of unknown race/ethnicity. [2] Because column totals were calculated independently of the values for the subpopulations, the values in each column may not sum to the column total. [3] Includes Asian/Pacific Islander legacy cases (see Technical Notes in source). [4] Hispanics/Latinos can be of any race. [5] Heterosexual contact with a person known to have, or to be at high risk for, HIV infection. [6] Includes hemophilia, blood transfusion, perinatal exposure, and risk factor not reported or not identified.

Source: U.S. Centers for Disease Control and Prevention, *HIV Surveillance Report: Diagnoses of HIV Infection in the United States and Dependent Areas, 2012,* Vol. 24, November 2014. See also <http://www.cdc.gov/hiv/library/reports/surveillance/index.html>.

Table 207. Population With a Disability, by Age Group and by State: 2010 and 2013

[In thousands (36,355 represents 36,355,000). Disability data limited to civilian noninstitutionalized population. For children under age 5, covers children with a hearing or vision difficulty. For children age 5 to 17, covers children with a hearing, vision, cognitive, ambulatory, or self-care difficulty. For adults age 18 to 64 and age 65 and over, covers individuals with a hearing, vision, cognitive, ambulatory, self-care, or independent living difficulty. American Community Survey (ACS) disability data should not be compared with disability estimates from Census 2000, and more detailed measures of disability from sources such as the National Health Interview Survey and the Survey of Income and Program Participation. Based on a sample and subject to sampling variability; see text, Section 1 and Appendix III]

State	2010				2013			
	Total [1]	5 to 17 years	18 to 64 years	65 years and over	Total [1]	5 to 17 years	18 to 64 years	65 years and over
United States	**36,355**	**2,799**	**19,048**	**14,352**	**39,138**	**2,880**	**20,322**	**15,776**
Alabama	760	54	423	281	758	46	419	290
Alaska	75	6	48	20	79	6	47	26
Arizona	706	52	364	287	802	50	401	348
Arkansas	468	37	255	173	496	40	269	186
California	3,640	263	1,818	1,539	4,020	283	1,987	1,734
Colorado	499	38	273	185	560	38	304	216
Connecticut	368	28	179	159	378	28	181	167
Delaware	108	8	60	39	115	9	59	46
District of Columbia	66	6	37	23	69	5	40	24
Florida	2,367	148	1,115	1,096	2,584	158	1,196	1,220
Georgia	1,113	96	615	397	1,212	93	673	441
Hawaii	141	11	66	63	151	9	65	77
Idaho	196	17	103	74	209	17	106	86
Illinois	1,291	101	640	544	1,409	97	715	591
Indiana	800	66	435	295	898	74	487	333
Iowa	337	25	172	138	358	26	182	149
Kansas	341	26	178	136	351	28	178	143
Kentucky	711	51	423	233	735	53	422	257
Louisiana	672	58	378	232	679	63	368	245
Maine	198	15	104	78	214	15	118	81
Maryland	581	48	298	231	623	47	321	253
Massachusetts	699	57	354	285	782	64	390	325
Michigan	1,325	109	715	496	1,414	108	772	528
Minnesota	523	45	266	209	563	44	287	230
Mississippi	473	36	267	168	487	33	273	181
Missouri	814	60	440	311	851	60	466	322
Montana	125	8	64	52	140	8	74	57
Nebraska	206	16	104	85	205	15	100	89
Nevada	283	19	152	110	357	26	193	136
New Hampshire	146	14	77	54	166	12	86	68
New Jersey	845	69	398	375	936	71	444	417
New Mexico	269	16	140	112	312	18	165	127
New York	2,020	142	1,012	858	2,172	150	1,081	930
North Carolina	1,235	95	673	460	1,331	102	703	521
North Dakota	69	4	32	32	75	4	38	33
Ohio	1,506	128	804	569	1,555	119	839	592
Oklahoma	577	39	323	212	594	46	319	226
Oregon	525	37	287	198	572	35	308	225
Pennsylvania	1,638	132	824	677	1,689	134	858	690
Rhode Island	140	12	75	53	132	10	66	54
South Carolina	629	37	352	237	680	47	368	263
South Dakota	90	6	43	40	108	8	57	42
Tennessee	947	66	530	348	984	64	547	369
Texas	2,864	273	1,549	1,029	3,047	279	1,602	1,149
Utah	234	22	124	85	274	26	147	100
Vermont	82	7	45	30	86	6	46	34
Virginia	845	59	447	336	908	62	474	366
Washington	792	56	425	307	895	61	482	348
West Virginia	345	21	197	126	369	21	205	141
Wisconsin	606	51	306	246	686	56	355	272
Wyoming	66	5	36	25	68	6	37	26

[1] Total population with a disability includes population under age 5, not shown separately.

Source: U.S. Census Bureau, 2010 and 2013 American Community Survey, S1810, "Disability Characteristics," <http://factfinder2.census.gov>, accessed February 2015.

Table 208. Use of Complementary and Alternative Health Practices Among Adults Age 18 and Over, in the Past 12 Months by Type of Therapy: 2007 and 2012

[3,141 represents 3,141,000. Percentages are age-adjusted. Based on the National Health Interview Survey of civilian noninstitutional population. The denominators for percent calculations exclude persons with unknown complementary health approach use. Estimates are age-adjusted using the projected 2000 U.S. population as the standard population, using age groups 18-24, 25-44, 45-64 and 65/over]

Therapy	2007		2012	
	Number (1,000)	Percent	Number (1,000)	Percent
Acupuncture	3,141	1.4	3,484	1.5
Ayurveda	214	0.1	241	0.1
Biofeedback	362	0.2	281	0.1
Chiropractic or osteopathic manipulation	18,740	8.6	19,369	8.4
Deep-breathing exercises [1]	27,794	12.7	24,218	10.9
Energy healing therapy	1,216	0.5	1,077	0.5
Guided imagery	4,866	2.2	3,846	1.7
Homeopathic treatment [2]	3,909	1.8	5,046	2.2
Hypnosis	561	0.2	347	0.1
Massage therapy	18,068	8.3	15,411	6.9
Meditation [3]	20,541	9.4	17,948	8.0
Naturopathy	729	0.3	957	0.4
Nonvitamin, nonmineral dietary supplements [4]	38,797	17.7	40,579	17.7
Progressive relaxation	6,454	2.9	4,766	2.1
Special diets [5]	6,040	2.8	6,853	3.0
Yoga, tai chi, and qi gong	14,436	6.7	22,281	10.1

[1] In 2012, deep-breathing exercises included deep-breathing exercises as part of hypnosis, biofeedback, Mantra meditation, mindfulness meditation, spiritual meditation, guided imagery, progressive relaxation, yoga, tai chi, or qi gong. In 2007, the use of deep-breathing exercises was asked broadly and not if used as part of other complementary health approaches. [2] No distinction was made between persons who sought treatment from a homeopathic practitioner and those who self-medicated. [3] In 2012, meditation included Mantra, mindfulness, and spiritual meditation; and meditation used as part of other practices. In 2007, the use of meditation was asked broadly and not if practiced as part of other complementary health approaches. [4] While questions were asked about nonvitamin, nonmineral dietary supplements in 2007 and 2012, the data should be interpreted with caution due to question order and the specific nonvitamin, nonmineral dietary supplements covered. [5] Respondents used one or more named special diets for 2 weeks or more in the past 12 months. Special diets included vegetarian (including vegan), macrobiotic, Atkins, Pritikin, and Ornish diets.

Source: U.S. National Center for Health Statistics, *Trends in the Use of Complementary Health Approaches Among Adults: United States, 2002–2012*, National Health Statistics Reports, Number 79, February 10, 2015. See also <https://nccih.nih.gov/research/statistics/NHIS/bibliography> or <http://www.cdc.gov/nchs/products/nhsr.htm>.

Table 209. Respiratory Diseases Among Persons Age 18 and Over by Selected Characteristics: 2012

[In thousands (234,921 represents 234,921,000). Respondents were asked in two separate questions if they had ever been told by a doctor or other health professional that they had emphysema or asthma. Respondents who had been told they had asthma were asked if they still had asthma. Respondents were asked in three separate questions if they had been told by a doctor or other health professional in the past 12 months that they had hay fever, sinusitis, or bronchitis. Based on the National Health Interview Survey, a sample survey of the civilian noninstitutionalized population; see Appendix III]

Selected characteristic	Total persons	Emphy-sema	Asthma Ever	Asthma Still	Hay fever	Sinusitis	Chronic bronchitis	Chronic Obstructive Pulmonary Disease
Total [2]	**234,921**	**4,108**	**29,660**	**18,719**	**17,596**	**28,504**	**8,658**	**6,790**
SEX								
Male	113,071	2,293	12,268	6,770	7,656	10,302	3,199	3,389
Female	121,850	1,815	17,392	11,950	9,940	18,202	5,458	3,400
AGE								
18 to 44 years	111,034	292	14,929	8,943	6,774	10,889	2,721	512
45 to 64 years	82,038	1,853	10,380	6,852	7,965	12,542	3,831	3,074
65 to 74 years	23,760	1,121	2,863	1,837	1,882	3,291	1,165	1,646
75 years and over	18,089	843	1,489	1,088	975	1,783	940	1,558
RACE								
Race alone [3]	230,994	4,074	28,969	18,206	17,268	28,035	8,456	6,668
White	188,261	3,662	23,594	14,562	14,559	23,351	7,151	6,066
Black or African American	27,943	339	4,098	2,855	1,636	3,393	1,038	497
American Indian or Alaska Native	1,916	(B)	262	147	161	221	[4] 112	(B)
Asian	12,542	[4] 36	927	591	903	1,045	156	69
Native Hawaiian or other Pacific Islander	332	–	[4] 88	(B)	(B)	(B)	–	–
Two or more races [5]	3,926	[4] 35	691	513	328	470	201	122
HISPANIC ORIGIN AND RACE [6]								
Hispanic or Latino	34,946	178	3,493	2,145	1,964	2,729	789	288
Mexican or Mexican American	21,741	[4] 96	1,539	869	1,174	1,641	425	160
Not Hispanic or Latino	199,974	3,930	26,167	16,575	15,632	25,775	7,869	6,502
White	156,173	3,494	20,459	12,621	12,763	20,859	6,426	5,804
Black or African American	26,961	329	3,985	2,795	1,584	3,329	1,016	484

– Represents zero. B Figure too small to meet statistical standards for reliability of a derived figure. [1] A person may be represented in more than one column. [2] Total includes other races not shown separately. [3] Refers to persons who indicated only a single race group, including those of Hispanic and Latino origin. [4] Figure does not meet standard of reliability or precision. [5] Refers to all persons who indicated more than one race group. [6] Persons of Hispanic or Latino origin may be of any race or combination of races.

Source: U.S. National Center for Health Statistics, *Summary Health Statistics for U.S. Adults: National Health Interview Survey, 2012*, Vital and Health Statistics, Series 10, Number 260, February 2014. See also <http://www.cdc.gov/nchs/nhis.htm>.

Table 210. Selected Diseases and Conditions Among Persons Age 18 and Over by Selected Characteristics: 2012

[In thousands (234,921 represents 234,921,000). Based on National Health Interview Survey, a sample survey of the civilian noninstitutionalized population; see Appendix III]

Selected characteristic	Total persons	Persons with selected diseases and conditions					
		Diabetes [1, 2]	Ulcers [1]	Kidney disease [3, 4]	Liver disease [3]	Arthritis diagnosis [5]	Chronic joint symptoms [5]
Total [6]	**234,921**	**21,319**	**15,435**	**3,882**	**3,034**	**51,830**	**63,085**
SEX							
Male	113,071	10,357	6,871	1,882	1,350	20,878	28,044
Female	121,850	10,961	8,564	2,000	1,684	30,951	35,041
AGE							
18 to 44 years	111,034	2,673	4,555	633	688	7,582	16,734
45 to 64 years	82,038	10,273	6,452	1,548	1,662	24,223	28,984
65 to 74 years	23,760	4,863	2,393	746	491	11,111	10,076
75 years and over	18,089	3,509	2,035	954	193	8,914	7,291
RACE							
Single race [7]	230,994	20,949	14,997	3,801	2,878	51,110	61,960
White	188,261	16,188	12,809	2,960	2,472	43,586	52,649
Black or African American	27,943	3,463	1,527	629	265	5,777	6,731
American Indian or Alaska Native	1,916	272	114	[8] 59	(B)	323	493
Asian	12,542	1,005	531	150	126	1,377	2,015
Native Hawaiian or other Pacific Islander	332	[8] 21	(B)	(B)	(B)	[8] 46	[8] 73
Two or more races [9]	3,926	369	438	81	156	720	1,125
HISPANIC ORIGIN [10]							
Hispanic or Latino	34,946	3,166	1,679	533	422	4,194	6,382
Mexican or Mexican American	21,741	1,953	975	352	220	2,292	3,879

B Figure too small to meet statistical standards for reliability (relative standard error greater than 50%). [1] Respondents were asked if they had ever been told by a health professional that they had an ulcer or diabetes. A person may be represented in more than one column. [2] Excludes borderline and pregnancy-related diabetes. [3] Respondents who had been told in the last 12 months by a health professional that they had weak or failing kidneys or any kind of liver condition. [4] Excludes kidney stones, bladder infections, or incontinence. [5] Respondents with an arthritis diagnosis had ever been told by a health professional that they had some form of arthritis, rheumatoid arthritis, gout, lupus or fibromyalgia. Respondents with joint symptoms (excluding back and neck) that began more than 3 months prior to interview were classified as having chronic joint symptoms. [6] Total includes other races not shown separately. [7] Refers to persons who indicated only a single race group, including Hispanic or Latino origin. [8] Figure does not meet standard of reliability or precision. [9] Refers to all persons who indicated more than one race group. [10] Persons of Hispanic or Latino origin may be of any race or combination of races.

Source: U.S. National Center for Health Statistics, *Summary Health Statistics for U.S. Adults: National Health Interview Survey, 2012*, Vital and Health Statistics, Series 10, Number 260, February 2014. See also <http://www.cdc.gov/nchs/products/series/series10.htm>.

Table 211. Circulatory Diseases Among Persons Age 18 and Over by Selected Characteristics: 2012

[In thousands (234,921 represents 234,921,000). In separate questions, respondents were asked if they had ever been told by a doctor or other health professional that they had: hypertension (or high blood pressure), coronary heart disease, angina (or angina pectoris), heart attack (or myocardial infarction), any other heart condition or disease not already mentioned, or a stroke. A person may be represented in more than one column. Based on National Health Interview Survey, a sample survey of the civilian noninstitutionalized population; see Appendix III]

Characteristic	Total adults	Selected circulatory diseases			
		Heart disease		Hypertension [3]	Stroke
		All types [1]	Coronary [2]		
Total [4]	**234,921**	**26,561**	**15,281**	**59,830**	**6,370**
SEX					
Male	113,071	13,820	8,752	28,940	2,898
Female	121,850	12,741	6,529	30,890	3,472
AGE					
18 to 44 years	111,034	4,168	980	9,187	635
45 to 64 years	82,038	9,939	5,796	27,578	2,293
65 to 74 years	23,760	5,792	3,848	12,404	1,505
75 years and over	18,089	6,661	4,657	10,661	1,936
RACE					
Race alone [5]	230,994	26,086	15,036	59,039	6,212
White	188,261	22,218	12,715	47,158	4,918
Black or African American	27,943	2,897	1,693	8,964	1,031
American Indian or Alaska Native	1,916	189	109	416	[6] 57
Asian	12,542	743	487	2,391	198
Native Hawaiian or Other Pacific Islander	332	[6] 39	(B)	110	(B)
Two or more races [7]	3,926	474	245	791	158
HISPANIC ORIGIN [8]					
Hispanic or Latino	34,946	2,020	1280	5,588	642
Mexican or Mexican American	21,741	1,180	752	3,110	392

B Figure too small to meet statistical standards for reliability of a derived figure. [1] Heart disease includes coronary heart disease, angina pectoris, heart attack, or any other heart condition or disease. [2] Coronary heart disease includes coronary heart disease, angina pectoris, or heart attack. [3] Persons had to have been told on two or more different visits that they had hypertension, or high blood pressure, to be classified as hypertensive. [4] Includes other races not shown separately. [5] Refers to persons who indicated only a single race group, including Hispanic or Latino origin. [6] Figure does not meet standard of reliability or precision. [7] Refers to all persons who indicated more than one race group. [8] Persons of Hispanic or Latino origin may be of any race or combination of races.

Source: U.S. National Center for Health Statistics, *Summary Health Statistics for U.S. Adults: National Health Interview Survey, 2012*, Vital and Health Statistics, Series 10, Number 260, February 2014. See also <http://www.cdc.gov/nchs/nhis.htm>.

Table 212. Migraine Headaches and Pain in the Neck, Lower Back, Face or Jaw Among Persons Age 18 and Over by Selected Characteristics: 2012

[In thousands (234,921 represents 234,921,000). Based on National Health Interview Survey, a sample survey of the civilian noninstitutionalized population. See Appendix III]

Selected characteristic	Total persons	Migraine and pain [1]			
		Migraine or severe headache [2]	Pain in neck [3]	Pain in lower back [3]	Pain in face or jaw [3]
Total [4]	234,921	32,453	33,515	65,823	11,326
SEX					
Male	113,071	10,156	13,102	29,124	3,677
Female	121,850	22,296	20,414	36,699	7,649
AGE					
18 to 44 years	111,034	18,920	12,528	26,611	5,457
45 to 64 years	82,038	11,136	15,053	26,495	4,296
65 to 74 years	23,760	1,545	3,452	7,104	963
75 years and over	18,089	851	2,482	5,613	611
RACE					
Single race [5]	230,994	31,587	32,720	64,290	11,002
White	188,261	26,040	27,925	54,218	9,483
Black or African American	27,943	3,972	3,003	6,996	985
American Indian or Alaska Native	1,916	338	352	549	154
Asian	12,542	1,162	1,384	2,412	346
Native Hawaiian or other Pacific Islander	332	[6] 76	[6] 56	115	(B)
Two or more races [7]	3,926	865	796	1,533	325
HISPANIC ORIGIN AND RACE [8]					
Hispanic or Latino	34,946	4,689	4,573	8,940	1,490
Mexican or Mexican American	21,741	2,689	2,569	5,143	871
Not Hispanic or Latino	199,974	27,764	28,942	56,884	9,836
White, single race	156,173	21,803	23,763	45,999	8,177
Black or African American, single race	26,961	3,813	2,888	6,786	966

B Base figure too small to meet statistical standards for reliability of a derived figure. [1] A person may be represented in more than one column. [2] Respondents were asked, "During the past 3 months, did you have a severe headache or migraine?" Respondents were instructed to report pain that had lasted a whole day or more and, conversely, not to report fleeting or minor aches or pains. [3] Respondents were asked, "During the past 3 months, did you have a neck pain; or low back pain; or facial ache or pain in the jaw muscles or the joint in front of the ear?" Respondents were instructed to report pain that had lasted a whole day or more and, conversely, not to report fleeting or minor aches or pains. [4] Total includes other races not shown separately. [5] Refers to persons who indicated only a single race group. [6] Figure does not meet standard of reliability or precision. [7] Refers to all persons who indicated more than one race group. [8] Persons of Hispanic or Latino origin may be of any race or combination of races.

Source: National Center for Health Statistics, *Summary Health Statistics for U.S. Adults: National Health Interview Survey, 2012*, Vital and Health Statistics, Series 10, Number 260, February 2014. See also <http://www.cdc.gov/nchs/products/series/series10.htm>.

Table 213. Injury and Poisoning Episodes by Age and Sex: 2012

[In thousands (37,401 represents 37,401,000), except as noted. Covers all medically attended injuries and poisonings occurring during the 5–week period prior to the survey interview. Age adjustment is used to adjust for differences in the age distribution of populations being compared. There may be more than one condition per episode. Based on the National Health Interview Survey, a sample survey of the civilian noninstitutionalized population; see Appendix III]

External cause and nature of injury	Total	Rate, age adjusted [1]	By age					By sex	
			Under 12 years	12 to 17 years	18 to 44 years	45 to 64 years	65 years and over	Male	Female
EPISODES									
Number (1,000) [2]	37,401	(X)	4,976	4,540	11,413	10,621	5,851	18,016	19,385
Annual rate per 1,000 population, total [3]	121.2	120.3	101.9	182.8	102.8	129.5	(NA)	121.2	119.3
BY CAUSE									
Fall	13,402	42.6	2,330	1,292	2,405	3,828	3,546	5,485	7,917
Struck by a person or an object	3,809	12.7	758	845	1,249	571	386	1,989	1,820
Transportation [4]	3,684	11.9	310	[5] 340	1,632	1,157	(B)	1,531	2,153
Overexertion	4,911	15.7	[5] 245	450	2,094	1,453	(NA)	2,619	2,292
Cutting, piercing instruments	3,164	10.2	[5] 127	(B)	1,583	1,157	(B)	1,906	1,258
Poisoning	518	1.7	(B)	(B)	[5] 208	(B)	(B)	[5] 346	[5] 171

B Base figure too small to meet statistical standards for reliability of a derived figure. NA Not available. X Not applicable. [1] Total annual rate per 1,000 population. Age-adjusted using the 2000 standard population. [2] Includes other items not shown separately. [3] Rates by age group are not age adjusted. [4] Includes motor vehicle, bicycle, motorcycle, pedestrian, train, boat, and airplane. [5] Figure does not meet standard of reliability or precision.

Source: National Center for Health Statistics, *Summary Health Statistics for the U.S. Population: National Health Interview Survey, 2012*, Vital and Health Statistics, Series 10, Number 259, December 2013. See also <http://www.cdc.gov/nchs/nhis.htm>.

Table 214. Injuries Associated With Selected Consumer Products: 2013

[Estimates are based on a national probability sample of hospitals in the U.S. and its territories. Patient information is collected from each participating hospital for every emergency visit involving an injury associated with consumer products. From this sample, the total number of product-related injuries treated in hospital emergency rooms nationwide is estimated]

Product type	Number	Product type	Number
Items for infants/children:		Housewares:	
All nursery equipment	102,737	Cans, other containers	286,696
Baby strollers	16,893	Cleaning agents (excludes soaps)	39,876
High chairs	9,299	Drinking glasses	70,557
Playground equipment (excl. swings)	244,722	Knives	335,322
Swings or swings sets	56,808	Tableware and accessories	92,148
Toys	245,935		
		Tools & garden equipment:	
Sports & recreational equipment:		Chain saws	25,848
ATV's, mopeds, minibikes, etc	209,178	Hand garden tools	57,988
Amusement attractions [1]	38,148	Lawn mowers	86,620
Bicycles & accessories	531,340	Power home tools (excl. saws)	29,328
Exercise equipment	472,212	Power home workshop saws	77,187
Fireworks	11,361	Workshop manual tools	131,552
Nonpowder guns, bb's, pellets	19,820		
Skateboards	120,424	Household appliances:	
Toboggans, sleds, snow discs, etc	25,783	Cooking ranges, ovens, etc	52,777
Trampolines	83,665	Heating stoves, space heaters	28,037
Water slides	6,179	Small kitchen appliances	55,913
		Washers, dryers	21,910
Home entertainment equipment:			
Computers (equipment and electronic games)	30,915	Home furnishings & fixtures:	
Television sets & stands	64,739	Bathroom structures & fixtures	461,757
		Bathtubs or showers [3]	318,466
		Beds, mattresses, pillows	739,043
Personal use items:		Carpets, rugs	161,509
Grooming devices	46,289	Chairs, sofas, sofa beds	579,540
Mobility carts, electric [2]	13,085	Hot tubs or home spas	7,574
Razors, shavers, razor blades	54,142	Tables [4]	330,155
		Toilets	112,662

[1] Includes fixed rides in amusement or theme parks; mobile rides; inflatables such as "moon bounces"; rides at shopping malls or restaurants; and waterslides. [2] Motorized vehicles, not elsewhere classified (three or more wheels). [3] Including fixtures or accessories; excluding enclosures, faucets, spigots, and towel racks. [4] Excludes baby-changing tables, billiard or pool tables, and television tables or stands.

Source: U.S. Consumer Product Safety Commission, National Electronic Injury Surveillance System (NEISS), *2013 NEISS Data Highlights;* and "NEISS Estimates Query Builder," <https://www.cpsc.gov/cgibin/NEISSQuery/home.aspx>, accessed June 2015.

Table 215. Food Security Status of Households and Households with Children: 2005 to 2013

[114,437 represents 114,437,000. Food security status of households is measured through a series of questions about experiences and behaviors known to characterize households that are having difficulty meeting basic food needs. All questions refer to the previous 12 months and include a qualifying phrase reminding respondents to report only conditions resulting from inadequate financial resources; restrictions to food intake due to dieting and volunteer fasting are excluded. *Food-secure* households report 0-2 food-insecure conditions. *Food-insecure* households report 3 or more conditions. Low and very low food security differ in the extent and character of the adjustments the household makes to its eating patterns and food intake. Households classified as having *low food security* report multiple indications of food access problems, but typically report few, if any, indications of reduced food intake. Households classified as having *very low food security* report multiple indications of reduced food intake and disrupted eating patterns due to inadequate resources for food. The omission of homeless persons may be a cause of underreporting. Data are from the Food Security Supplement to the Current Population Survey (CPS); for details about the CPS, see text, Section 1 and Appendix III]

Household status	Number (1,000)					Percent distribution				
	2005	2010	2011	2012	2013	2005	2010	2011	2012	2013
Households, total	**114,437**	**118,756**	**119,484**	**121,546**	**122,579**	**100.0**	**100.0**	**100.0**	**100.0**	**100.0**
Food-secure	101,851	101,527	101,631	103,914	105,070	89.0	85.5	85.1	85.5	85.7
Food-insecure	12,586	17,229	17,853	17,632	17,509	11.0	14.5	14.9	14.5	14.3
With low food security [1]	8,158	10,872	11,014	10,679	10,664	7.1	9.1	9.2	8.8	8.7
With very low food security [2]	4,428	6,357	6,839	6,953	6,845	3.9	5.4	5.7	5.7	5.6
Adult members	**217,897**	**229,129**	**231,385**	**234,730**	**237,219**	**100.0**	**100.0**	**100.0**	**100.0**	**100.0**
In food-secure households	195,172	196,505	197,923	201,662	203,913	89.6	85.8	85.5	85.9	86.0
In food-insecure households	22,725	32,624	33,462	33,068	33,306	10.4	14.2	14.5	14.1	14.0
With low food security [1]	15,146	21,357	21,371	20,708	21,115	7.0	9.3	9.2	8.8	8.9
With very low food security [2]	7,579	11,267	12,091	12,359	12,191	3.5	4.9	5.2	5.3	5.1
Child members	**73,604**	**74,905**	**74,508**	**73,631**	**73,634**	**100.0**	**100.0**	**100.0**	**100.0**	**100.0**
In food-secure households	61,201	58,697	57,850	57,733	57,862	83.1	78.4	77.6	78.4	78.6
In food-insecure households	12,403	16,208	16,658	15,898	15,772	16.9	21.6	22.4	21.6	21.4
With very low food security among children [3]	606	976	845	977	765	0.8	1.3	1.1	1.3	1.0

[1] Prior to 2006, USDA described these households as food insecure without hunger. [2] Food intake of one or more members in these households was reduced and normal eating patterns disrupted at some time during the year because of the household's food insecurity. Prior to 2006, USDA described these households as food insecure with hunger. [3] Percentages omit households with no children. The food security survey measures food security status at the household level. Not all children residing in food-insecure households were directly affected by the households' food insecurity. Similarly, not all children in households classified as having very low food security among children were subject to the reductions in food intake and disruptions in eating patterns that characterize this condition. Young children, in particular, are often protected from effects of the households' food insecurity.

Source: U.S. Department of Agriculture, Economic Research Service, *Household Food Security in the United States in 2013*, Economic Research Report Number 173, September 2014. See also <http://www.ers.usda.gov/publications/err-economic-research-report/err173.aspx>.

Table 216. Mammography Use Among Women Age 40 and Over by Patient Characteristics: 1990 to 2013

[Percent of women having a mammogram within the past 2 years. Covers civilian noninstitutional population. Based on National Health Interview Survey; see Appendix III]

Characteristic	1990	2000	2003	2005	2008	2010	2013
Women 40 years old and over, total [1]...........	**51.4**	**70.4**	**69.7**	**66.8**	**67.6**	**67.1**	**66.8**
AGE							
40 to 49 years old..................	55.1	64.3	64.4	63.5	61.5	62.3	59.6
50 years old and over...............	49.7	73.6	72.4	68.4	70.5	69.2	69.5
50 to 64 years old..................	56.0	78.7	76.2	71.8	74.2	72.6	71.4
65 years old and over...............	43.4	67.9	67.7	63.8	65.5	64.4	66.9
RACE AND ETHNICITY							
White, non-Hispanic.................	52.7	72.2	70.5	68.3	68.7	67.8	67.6
Black, non-Hispanic.................	46.0	67.9	70.5	65.2	68.3	67.4	67.2
Hispanic origin [2].................	45.2	61.2	65.0	58.8	61.2	64.2	61.4
HEALTH INSURANCE STATUS [3]							
Insured............................	(NA)	76.0	75.1	72.5	73.4	74.1	72.1
Private insurance...............	(NA)	77.1	76.3	74.5	74.2	75.6	73.4
Medicaid........................	(NA)	61.7	63.5	55.6	64.2	64.4	63.5
Uninsured.......................	(NA)	40.7	41.5	38.1	39.7	36.0	37.3
EDUCATION							
No high school diploma nor GED [4]....	36.4	57.7	58.1	52.8	53.8	53.0	53.6
High school diploma or GED..........	52.7	69.7	67.8	64.9	65.2	64.4	63.4
Some college or more...............	62.8	76.2	75.1	72.7	73.4	72.1	71.6
POVERTY STATUS [5]							
Below 100% poverty.................	30.8	54.8	55.4	48.5	51.4	51.4	49.9
100% to 199% poverty...............	39.1	58.1	60.8	55.3	55.8	53.8	56.7
200% to 399% poverty...............	53.3	68.8	69.9	67.2	64.4	66.2	66.0
400% and over poverty..............	68.7	81.5	77.7	76.6	79.0	78.1	77.2

NA Not available. [1] Includes other races not shown separately and unknown education level and poverty status. [2] Persons of Hispanic origin may be of any race or combination of races. [3] Health insurance status at time of interview, only for women age 40 to 64. [4] GED is General Educational Development high school equivalency diploma. [5] Poverty as percent of Federal poverty level based on family income and family size and composition using U.S. Census Bureau poverty thresholds.

Source: U.S. National Center for Health Statistics, *Health, United States, 2014*, May 2015. See also <http://www.cdc.gov/nchs/hus.htm>.

Table 217. Current Cigarette Smoking Among Adults: 2000 to 2013

[In percent. A current smoker is a person who has smoked at least 100 cigarettes and who now smokes every day or some days. Excludes unknown smoking status. Race groups white and black include persons of Hispanic and non-Hispanic origin. For definition of age adjustment, see text, Section 2. Based on National Health Interview Survey; for details, see Appendix III]

Sex, age, and race	2000	2005	2010	2013	Sex, age, and race	2000	2005	2010	2013
Total smokers, age-adjusted [1]........	**23.1**	**20.8**	**19.3**	**17.9**	Black, total...................	26.2	26.5	24.3	[3] 21.9
Male........................	25.2	23.4	21.2	20.5	18 to 24 years..............	20.9	21.6	18.8	[3] 13.2
Female......................	21.1	18.3	17.5	15.5	25 to 34 years..............	23.2	29.8	25.7	24.8
					35 to 44 years..............	30.7	23.3	22.6	24.0
White male..................	25.4	23.3	21.4	20.5	45 to 64 years..............	32.2	32.4	31.8	25.7
Black male..................	25.7	25.9	23.3	21.8	65 years and over..........	14.2	16.8	10.0	15.5
					Female, total.................	**20.9**	**18.1**	**17.3**	**15.3**
White female................	22.0	19.1	18.3	16.3	18 to 24 years..............	24.9	20.7	17.4	15.4
Black female................	20.7	17.1	16.6	14.9	25 to 34 years..............	22.3	21.5	20.6	17.9
					35 to 44 years..............	26.2	21.3	19.0	16.3
Total smokers [2].............	**23.2**	**20.9**	**19.3**	**17.8**	45 to 64 years..............	21.7	18.8	19.1	18.1
Male, total.................	**25.6**	**23.9**	**21.5**	**20.5**	65 years and over...........	9.3	8.3	9.3	7.5
18 to 24 years..............	28.1	28.0	22.8	21.9	White, total..................	21.4	18.7	17.9	15.9
25 to 34 years..............	28.9	27.7	26.1	24.4	18 to 24 years..............	28.5	22.6	18.4	17.0
35 to 44 years..............	30.2	26.0	22.5	22.1	25 to 34 years..............	24.9	23.1	22.0	19.2
45 to 64 years..............	26.4	25.2	23.2	21.9	35 to 44 years..............	26.6	22.2	20.5	17.0
65 years and over...........	10.2	8.9	9.7	10.6	45 to 64 years..............	21.4	18.9	19.5	18.4
White, total.................	25.7	23.6	21.4	20.3	65 years and over..........	9.1	8.4	9.4	7.9
18 to 24 years..............	30.4	29.7	23.8	23.5	Black, total..................	20.8	17.3	17.0	15.1
25 to 34 years..............	29.7	27.7	26.6	24.6	18 to 24 years..............	14.2	14.2	14.2	11.8
35 to 44 years..............	30.6	26.3	23.1	21.9	25 to 34 years..............	15.5	16.9	19.3	16.4
45 to 64 years..............	25.8	24.5	22.5	21.7	35 to 44 years..............	30.2	19.0	17.2	16.4
65 years and over...........	9.8	7.9	9.6	10.0	45 to 64 years..............	25.6	21.0	19.8	18.8
					65 years and over..........	10.2	10.0	9.4	6.5

[1] Data are age-adjusted to the year 2000 standard population using five age groups: 18–24 years, 25–34 years, 35–44 years, 45–64 years, 65 years and over. [2] Crude, not age-adjusted. [3] Figure does not meet standard of reliability or precision.

Source: U.S. National Center for Health Statistics, *Health, United States, 2014*, May 2015. See also <http://www.cdc.gov/nchs/hus.htm>.

Table 218. Current Cigarette Smoking by Sex and State: 2013

[In percent. Current cigarette smoking is defined as persons age 18 and older who reported having smoked 100 or more cigarettes during their lifetime and who currently smoke every day or some days. Based on the Behavioral Risk Factor Surveillance System, a telephone survey of health behaviors of the civilian, noninstitutionalized U.S. population, age 18 and over. New methods, including surveying cellular telephone-only households, and a new weighting method, were implemented for the 2011 BRFSS; beginning with 2011, data cannot accurately be compared to previous survey results; for details, see source]

State	Total	Male	Female	State	Total	Male	Female	State	Total	Male	Female
U.S.[1]	19.0	21.6	17.2	KS	20.0	22.3	17.8	NC	20.3	23.4	17.3
AL	21.5	25.1	18.2	KY	26.5	28.4	24.6	ND	21.2	22.9	19.5
AK	22.6	22.9	22.2	LA	23.5	27.3	20.0	OH	23.4	24.1	22.6
AZ	16.3	19.3	13.5	ME	20.2	22.4	18.2	OK	23.7	25.8	21.7
AR	25.9	26.7	25.3	MD	16.4	19.4	13.7	OR	17.3	18.7	16.0
CA	12.5	16.2	9.1	MA	16.6	18.7	14.7	PA	21.0	23.5	18.6
CO	17.7	19.0	16.4	MI	21.4	24.7	18.3	RI	17.4	19.1	15.9
CT	15.5	16.8	14.3	MN	18.0	19.4	16.7	SC	22.0	26.2	18.1
DE	19.6	22.0	17.3	MS	24.8	28.0	22.0	SD	19.6	19.7	19.4
DC	18.8	23.4	14.7	MO	22.1	24.3	20.1	TN	24.3	26.8	22.0
FL	16.8	19.5	14.4	MT	19.0	20.7	17.3	TX	15.9	18.8	13.1
GA	18.8	22.6	15.4	NE	18.5	19.8	17.2	UT	10.3	11.9	8.8
HI	13.3	15.7	11.0	NV	19.4	20.6	18.1	VT	16.6	17.9	15.4
ID	17.2	19.4	15.0	NH	16.2	16.7	15.8	VA	19.0	21.6	16.7
IL	18.0	21.2	15.0	NJ	15.7	17.6	13.9	WA	16.1	17.8	14.3
IN	21.9	23.6	20.4	NM	19.1	22.2	16.2	WV	27.3	28.6	26.1
IA	19.5	22.5	16.6	NY	16.6	19.3	14.2	WI	18.7	20.1	17.3
								WY	20.6	22.1	19.2

[1] Represents median value among the states and DC. For definition of median, see Guide to Tabular Presentations.

Source: U.S. Centers for Disease Control and Prevention, Behavioral Risk Factor Surveillance System, "Prevalence Data and Data Analysis Tools: Prevalence and Trends Data," <http://apps.nccd.cdc.gov/brfss/>, accessed February 2015.

Table 219. Substance Abuse Treatment Facilities and Clients: 2010 to 2013

[As of the end of March. Based on the National Survey of Substance Abuse Treatment Services survey, a census of all known public and private facilities that provide substance abuse treatment in the United States and associated jurisdictions. Selected missing data for responding facilities were imputed]

Facility characteristic	Number of facilities			Number of clients		
	2010	2012	2013	2010	2012	2013
Total	**13,339**	**14,311**	**14,148**	**1,175,462**	**1,248,905**	**1,249,629**
FACILITY OPERATIONAL STRUCTURE						
Private non-profit	7,683	8,054	7,820	625,321	653,392	638,858
Private for-profit	3,985	4,450	4,575	372,525	424,871	430,362
Local, county, or community government	751	758	739	70,963	68,903	72,949
State government	380	363	351	47,203	38,226	35,812
Federal government	348	364	370	47,676	41,391	53,695
Dept. of Veterans Affairs	218	215	228	39,157	32,499	44,180
Dept. of Defense	91	89	88	7,035	6,419	6,685
Indian Health Service	36	50	42	1,431	2,271	1,368
Other	3	10	12	53	202	1,462
Tribal government	192	322	293	11,774	22,122	17,953
TYPE OF CARE OFFERED/RECEIVED [1]						
Outpatient	10,753	11,650	11,542	1,056,532	1,120,615	1,127,235
Regular	9,914	10,858	10,771	593,077	629,794	603,315
Intensive	5,990	6,427	6,363	138,188	148,893	147,162
Detoxification	1,227	1,367	1,362	13,216	15,847	13,839
Day treatment/partial hospitalization	1,678	1,762	1,742	22,458	24,530	22,828
Methadone maintenance [2]	1,137	1,316	1,848	289,593	301,551	340,091
Residential (non-hospital)	3,452	3,566	3,450	103,692	110,843	107,727
Detoxification	893	894	861	7,549	10,718	10,244
Short-term treatment (30 days or fewer)	1,691	1,804	1,736	26,014	29,391	27,184
Long-term treatment (more than 30 days)	2,801	2,932	2,858	70,129	70,734	70,299
Hospital inpatient	748	780	753	15,238	17,447	14,667
Detoxification	666	686	660	6,476	6,950	5,768
Treatment	548	578	547	8,762	10,497	8,899
TREATMENT FOR SUBSTANCE ABUSE PROBLEM						
Both alcohol and drug	(X)	(X)	(X)	498,671	543,155	534,078
Drug abuse only	(X)	(X)	(X)	459,069	470,665	491,903
Alcohol abuse only	(X)	(X)	(X)	215,101	223,313	216,856
Both substance abuse and mental health disorders	(X)	(X)	(X)	479,699	537,676	563,071

X Not applicable. [1] Number of facilities can sum to more than the total because a facility could provide more than 1 type of care. [2] Methadone/buprenorphine maintenance or Vivitrol® treatment.

Source: U.S. Substance Abuse and Mental Health Services Administration, *National Survey of Substance Abuse Treatment Services (N-SSATS): 2013 Data on Substance Abuse Treatment Facilities,* September 2014, and earlier reports. See also <http://www.samhsa.gov/data /substance-abuse-facilities-data-nssats>.

Table 220. Drug Use by Type of Drug and Age Group: 2010 to 2013

[In percent. Data comes from the National Survey on Drug Use and Health (NSDUH). Current users are those who used drugs at least once within month prior to this study. Based on a representative sample of the U.S. population 12 years old and over, including persons living in households, noninstitutional group quarters such as dormitories and homeless shelters, and civilians on military bases. Estimates are based on computer-assisted interviews of about 67,500 respondents. Subject to sampling variability; see source]

Age and type of drug	Ever used				Current user			
	2010	2011	2012	2013	2010	2011	2012	2013
12 YEARS OLD AND OVER								
Any illicit drug [1]	47.3	47.0	48.0	48.6	8.9	8.7	9.2	9.4
Marijuana and hashish	42.0	41.9	42.8	43.7	6.9	7.0	7.3	7.5
Cocaine	14.7	14.3	14.5	14.3	0.6	0.5	0.6	0.6
Crack	3.6	3.2	3.5	3.4	0.1	0.1	0.2	0.1
Heroin	1.6	1.6	1.8	1.8	0.1	0.1	0.1	0.1
Hallucinogens	14.8	14.1	14.6	15.1	0.5	0.4	0.4	0.5
LSD	9.2	8.9	9.1	9.4	0.1	0.1	0.1	0.1
Ecstasy	6.3	5.7	6.2	6.8	0.3	0.2	0.2	0.3
Inhalants	8.6	8.0	8.1	8.0	0.3	0.2	0.2	0.2
Any psychotherapeutic [2,3]	20.4	19.9	20.9	20.3	2.7	2.4	2.6	2.5
Pain relievers	13.8	13.3	14.2	13.5	2.0	1.7	1.9	1.7
Tranquilizers	8.7	8.4	9.1	9.0	0.9	0.7	0.8	0.6
Stimulants [3]	8.6	7.9	8.3	8.3	0.4	0.4	0.5	0.5
Methamphetamine [3]	5.1	4.6	4.7	4.7	0.1	0.2	0.2	0.2
Sedatives	3.0	2.9	3.1	2.9	0.1	0.1	0.1	0.1
Cigarettes	64.2	62.8	61.9	61.8	23.0	22.1	22.1	21.3
Smokeless tobacco	17.8	18.0	17.7	17.6	3.5	3.2	3.5	3.4
Cigars	35.0	34.4	34.1	34.0	5.2	5.0	5.2	4.7
Pipe tobacco	13.6	13.4	13.3	13.0	0.8	0.8	1.0	0.9
Alcohol	82.5	82.2	82.3	81.5	51.8	51.8	52.1	52.2
"Binge" alcohol use [4]	(NA)	(NA)	(NA)	(NA)	23.1	22.6	23.0	22.9
12 TO 17 YEARS OLD								
Any illicit drug [1]	25.8	25.5	24.2	23.3	10.1	10.1	9.5	8.8
Marijuana and hashish	17.1	17.5	17.0	16.4	7.4	7.9	7.2	7.1
Cocaine	1.5	1.3	1.1	0.9	0.2	0.3	0.1	0.2
Hallucinogens	4.1	3.7	3.3	2.8	0.9	0.9	0.6	0.6
Inhalants	8.3	7.5	6.5	5.3	1.1	0.9	0.8	0.5
Any psychotherapeutic [2,3]	10.6	10.1	10.0	8.8	3.0	2.8	2.8	2.2
Cigarettes	20.5	19.1	17.4	15.7	8.4	7.8	6.6	5.6
Smokeless tobacco	7.3	6.8	6.4	6.0	2.3	2.1	2.1	2.0
Cigars	11.1	10.7	9.6	8.3	3.2	3.4	2.6	2.3
Alcohol	35.4	34.5	32.4	30.8	13.6	13.3	12.9	11.6
"Binge" alcohol use [4]	(NA)	(NA)	(NA)	(NA)	7.9	7.4	7.2	6.2
18 TO 25 YEARS OLD								
Any illicit drug [1]	57.3	56.9	57.8	57.0	21.6	21.4	21.3	21.5
Marijuana and hashish	51.4	51.9	52.2	51.9	18.5	19.0	18.7	19.1
Cocaine	13.4	12.4	12.3	11.6	1.5	1.4	1.1	1.1
Crack	2.6	2.1	1.9	1.6	0.2	0.1	0.1	0.1
Heroin	1.8	1.7	1.9	1.8	0.3	0.3	0.4	0.3
Hallucinogens	18.5	17.6	17.6	17.6	2.0	1.6	1.7	1.8
Ecstasy	12.4	12.3	12.9	12.8	1.2	0.9	1.0	0.9
Inhalants	10.0	9.1	8.4	7.5	0.4	0.4	0.4	0.3
Any psychotherapeutic [2,3]	28.9	27.3	28.1	26.6	5.9	5.0	5.3	4.8
Pain relievers	23.9	22.2	22.4	20.8	4.4	3.6	3.8	3.3
Illicit drugs except marijuana	36.4	34.6	35.3	34.1	8.0	7.0	7.0	6.7
Cigarettes	62.3	61.0	59.5	57.9	34.3	33.5	31.8	30.6
Smokeless tobacco	21.0	20.4	19.9	20.3	6.4	5.4	5.5	5.8
Cigars	41.1	39.5	39.0	38.5	11.3	10.9	10.7	10.0
Alcohol	85.7	84.3	84.4	83.8	61.4	60.7	60.2	59.6
"Binge" alcohol use [4]	(NA)	(NA)	(NA)	(NA)	40.5	39.8	39.5	37.9
26 YEARS OLD AND OVER								
Any illicit drug [1]	48.2	48.0	49.3	50.2	6.6	6.3	7.0	7.3
Marijuana and hashish	43.5	43.2	44.4	45.7	4.8	4.8	5.3	5.6
Cocaine	16.6	16.3	16.5	16.5	0.5	0.4	0.6	0.5
Crack	4.2	3.7	4.2	4.1	0.2	0.1	0.2	0.2
Heroin	1.8	1.8	1.9	2.0	0.1	0.1	0.1	0.1
Hallucinogens	15.5	14.8	15.4	16.2	0.2	0.1	0.2	0.3
Ecstasy	5.7	4.9	5.6	6.4	0.1	0.1	0.1	0.1
Inhalants	8.4	7.8	8.3	8.4	0.2	0.1	0.1	0.1
Any psychotherapeutic [2,3]	20.2	19.8	21.0	20.6	2.2	1.9	2.1	2.1
Pain relievers	12.6	12.4	13.6	13.0	1.5	1.4	1.5	1.5
Illicit drugs except marijuana	30.7	30.0	31.0	31.1	2.7	2.3	2.8	2.7
Cigarettes	70.0	68.6	67.9	68.1	22.8	21.9	22.4	21.6
Smokeless tobacco	18.5	18.9	18.7	18.5	3.1	3.0	3.3	3.1
Cigars	36.9	36.5	36.3	36.3	4.4	4.2	4.5	4.1
Alcohol	87.8	87.9	88.1	87.3	54.9	55.1	55.6	55.9
"Binge" alcohol use [4]	(NA)	(NA)	(NA)	(NA)	21.9	21.6	22.1	22.4

NA Not available. [1] Illicit drugs include marijuana/hashish, cocaine (including crack), heroin, hallucinogens, inhalants, or prescription-type psychotherapeutics used nonmedically. [2] Nonmedical use of prescription-type psychotherapeutics includes the nonmedical use of pain relievers, tranquilizers, stimulants, or sedatives, and excludes over-the-counter drugs. [3] Includes data from new methamphetamine items added in 2005 and 2006. Previous estimates have been adjusted to be comparable with new data and differ from those in reports prior to the 2007 data year. [4] Binge alcohol use is defined as drinking five or more drinks on the same occasion (i.e., at the same time or within a couple of hours of each other) on at least 1 day in the past 30 days.

Source: U.S. Substance Abuse and Mental Health Services Administration, "Results from the 2013 National Survey on Drug Use and Health: Detailed Tables," September 2014, and earlier reports, <http://www.samhsa.gov/data/population-data-nsduh/reports>, accessed February 2015.

Table 221. Estimated Use of Drugs, Alcohol, and Cigarettes, by State: 2012 to 2013

[24,218 represents 24,218,000. Data in this table are annual averages for 2-year period. Data are based on the National Survey on Drug Use and Health (NSDUH). Current users are those persons 12 years old and over who used drugs at least once within month prior to this study. Based on a representative sample of the U.S. population 12 years old and over, including persons living in households, noninstitutional group quarters such as dormitories and homeless shelters, and civilians on military bases. Data were collected in 2012 and 2013 from 136,147 persons. For methodology information, see "2012-2013 NSDUH Guide to State Tables and Summary of Small Area Estimation Methodology" at <http://www.samhsa.gov/data/population-data-nsduh/reports>]

	Estimated current users (1,000)					Current users as percent of population				
	Any illicit drug [1]	Mari-juana	Any illicit drug other than mari-juana [1]	Binge alcohol [2]	Ciga-rettes	Any illicit drug [1]	Mari-juana	Any illicit drug other than mari-juana [1]	Binge alcohol [2]	Ciga-rettes
U.S........	**24,218**	**19,332**	**8,774**	**59,876**	**56,648**	**9.3**	**7.4**	**3.4**	**22.9**	**21.7**
AL............	304	199	155	860	1,045	7.6	4.9	3.9	21.4	26.0
AK............	75	69	17	128	131	12.9	11.9	3.0	22.1	22.7
AZ............	564	426	210	1,242	1,071	10.4	7.9	3.9	23.0	19.8
AR............	194	138	91	511	651	8.0	5.7	3.8	21.0	26.8
CA............	3,527	2,822	1,226	6,684	5,147	11.2	8.9	3.9	21.2	16.3
CO............	641	547	170	1,097	914	14.9	12.7	3.9	25.5	21.2
CT............	302	272	82	728	545	9.9	9.0	2.7	24.0	17.9
DE............	74	61	26	172	179	9.6	8.0	3.4	22.4	23.2
DC............	83	66	32	185	129	15.2	12.0	5.8	33.7	23.5
FL............	1,423	1,153	504	3,424	3,330	8.6	7.0	3.1	20.8	20.2
GA............	771	624	330	1,598	1,751	9.5	7.7	4.1	19.8	21.7
HI............	117	98	40	261	195	10.3	8.6	3.5	23.0	17.2
ID............	89	72	35	254	275	6.8	5.5	2.7	19.6	21.2
IL............	934	744	303	2,845	2,426	8.7	7.0	2.8	26.6	22.7
IN............	430	340	186	1,206	1,393	7.9	6.3	3.4	22.3	25.7
IA............	188	153	70	672	592	7.3	6.0	2.7	26.3	23.1
KS............	141	103	64	582	537	6.0	4.4	2.8	24.9	23.0
KY............	263	194	115	798	1,098	7.3	5.3	3.2	22.0	30.3
LA............	295	191	152	955	962	7.8	5.1	4.1	25.4	25.6
ME............	130	114	32	247	265	11.3	9.9	2.8	21.6	23.1
MD............	440	342	154	1,138	898	8.9	6.9	3.1	23.1	18.2
MA............	658	563	173	1,470	1,046	11.6	9.9	3.0	25.9	18.4
MI............	954	809	294	2,027	2,107	11.5	9.7	3.5	24.3	25.3
MN............	343	279	111	1,216	964	7.6	6.2	2.5	27.1	21.5
MS............	176	124	88	482	742	7.3	5.1	3.6	19.9	30.6
MO............	443	355	156	1,218	1,410	8.9	7.1	3.1	24.4	28.2
MT............	94	88	24	214	207	11.1	10.3	2.8	25.3	24.5
NE............	103	83	36	361	333	6.8	5.5	2.3	23.7	22.0
NV............	247	183	92	574	554	10.8	8.0	4.0	25.0	24.1
NH............	128	111	40	283	228	11.3	9.8	3.5	24.9	20.0
NJ............	552	389	215	1,608	1,277	7.4	5.2	2.9	21.6	17.1
NM............	182	154	64	417	389	10.6	9.0	3.7	24.4	22.8
NY............	1,645	1,373	513	4,104	3,302	9.9	8.3	3.1	24.8	19.9
NC............	607	497	269	1,614	1,855	7.5	6.2	3.3	20.0	23.0
ND............	38	30	16	178	147	6.5	5.2	2.8	30.4	25.0
OH............	939	734	348	2,396	2,556	9.7	7.6	3.6	24.8	26.5
OK............	240	173	106	725	911	7.7	5.6	3.4	23.3	29.2
OR............	461	395	135	717	699	13.9	11.9	4.1	21.7	21.1
PA............	904	697	339	2,695	2,597	8.4	6.5	3.1	25.0	24.1
RI............	141	126	38	246	184	15.8	14.1	4.3	27.5	20.6
SC............	347	270	145	902	1,023	8.8	6.9	3.7	23.0	26.1
SD............	42	34	17	181	177	6.2	5.0	2.4	26.6	26.0
TN............	386	292	170	911	1,359	7.2	5.4	3.2	16.9	25.2
TX............	1,509	1,117	679	4,710	4,196	7.2	5.3	3.2	22.4	19.9
UT............	156	114	71	364	392	7.0	5.1	3.2	16.3	17.5
VT............	69	64	18	115	116	12.7	11.8	3.4	21.2	21.4
VA............	544	425	196	1,502	1,531	8.0	6.3	2.9	22.2	22.6
WA............	792	708	232	1,200	1,144	13.7	12.3	4.0	20.8	19.8
WV............	100	80	39	306	480	6.3	5.1	2.4	19.4	30.5
WI............	401	311	148	1,439	1,066	8.4	6.5	3.1	30.0	22.2
WY............	32	28	11	116	121	6.6	5.8	2.3	24.4	25.3

[1] Illicit drugs include marijuana/hashish, cocaine (including crack), heroin, hallucinogens, inhalants, or prescription-type psychotherapeutics used nonmedically. [2] Binge alcohol use is defined as drinking five or more drinks on the same occasion (i.e., at the same time or within a couple of hours of each other) on at least 1 day in the past 30 days.

Source: U.S. Substance Abuse and Mental Health Services Administration, "2012-2013 NSDUH State Estimates of Substance Use and Mental Disorders," <http://www.samhsa.gov/data/population-data-nsduh/reports>, accessed February 2015.

Table 222. Prescription Drug Use in Past 30 Days by Selected Characteristics: 2005 to 2012

[Shown as percent of population. Based on the National Health and Nutrition Examination Survey, covering a sample of the civilian noninstitutionalized population]

Sex and Age	Total [1]		White [2]		Black or African American [2]		Mexican origin	
	2005-2008	2009-2012	2005-2008	2009-2012	2005-2008	2009-2012	2005-2008	2009-2012
USING AT LEAST ONE PRESCRIPTION DRUG IN PAST 30 DAYS								
Both sexes, age adjusted [3]	47.2	47.3	52.0	52.4	42.1	43.7	32.2	34.0
Male	41.8	42.7	46.1	47.2	37.2	37.5	28.8	30.7
Female	52.4	51.8	57.9	57.6	46.0	48.8	35.6	37.6
Both sexes, crude	47.9	48.7	55.0	56.5	39.5	42.0	24.5	26.4
Male	41.7	43.4	48.4	50.7	33.9	35.1	21.4	23.5
Female	53.9	53.9	61.5	62.1	44.4	48.0	27.9	29.5
By age:								
Under 18 years	25.3	23.5	29.9	26.7	20.8	22.8	17.0	16.1
18 to 44	37.8	38.1	45.1	46.7	29.4	30.7	17.7	21.2
45 to 64	64.8	67.2	67.7	70.9	62.6	64.6	50.1	49.0
65 and over	90.1	89.8	91.1	90.3	89.1	90.3	76.7	83.9
Male, by age:								
Under age 18	25.3	23.1	29.2	24.8	23.4	23.6	17.3	16.6
18 to 44	27.5	29.6	33.3	37.3	20.9	20.2	14.2	17.1
45 to 64	59.3	63.1	62.3	67.3	54.7	55.6	46.0	43.0
65 and over	89.7	87.7	91.6	88.7	85.1	88.0	67.8	80.0
Female, by age:								
Under age 18	25.2	23.8	30.7	28.7	18.1	21.9	16.7	15.6
18 to 44	47.9	46.4	56.6	56.3	36.6	39.3	22.0	25.9
45 to 64	70.2	71.1	73.0	74.2	69.1	72.2	54.1	55.5
65 and over	90.5	91.4	90.7	91.7	91.7	91.8	83.9	87.5
USING 3 OR MORE PRESCRIPTION DRUGS IN PAST 30 DAYS								
Both sexes, age adjusted [3]	20.8	20.6	22.3	22.0	20.0	21.9	13.8	15.4
Male	18.3	19.1	19.5	20.2	17.5	19.2	11.6	14.0
Female	23.2	22.0	25.1	23.8	21.8	24.0	15.9	16.8
Both sexes, crude	21.4	21.8	25.3	25.9	17.5	20.2	7.8	9.2
Male	17.8	19.4	21.3	23.1	14.4	16.9	6.1	8.3
Female	24.8	24.1	29.1	28.5	20.2	23.1	9.7	10.2
By age:								
Under 18 years	4.4	3.6	5.3	3.3	3.6	5.2	2.7	3.1
18 to 44	9.8	9.6	12.1	12.2	7.3	8.8	2.7	3.5
45 to 64	34.1	34.7	35.6	36.9	34.5	38.2	24.5	24.4
65 and over	65.0	64.8	65.7	64.5	67.0	67.9	52.5	61.7
Male, by age:								
Under age 18	5.0	4.1	5.7	3.2	5.3	6.4	3.5	[4] 3.7
18 to 44	6.2	7.5	8.0	9.4	[4] 4.9	6.6	[4] 1.5	[4] 3.1
45 to 64	28.6	31.4	29.4	34.0	29.0	31.1	19.7	20.7
65 and over	64.6	64.6	66.3	64.5	61.5	64.0	45.0	57.3
Female, by age:								
Under age 18	3.8	3.1	4.8	3.4	[4] 1.9	3.9	1.8	[4] 2.4
18 to 44	13.3	11.8	16.1	15.1	9.4	10.7	4.1	[4] 4.1
45 to 64	39.4	37.8	41.8	39.6	39.1	44.3	29.0	28.3
65 and over	65.3	64.9	65.3	64.5	70.6	70.5	58.6	65.7

[1] Includes persons of all races and Hispanic origins, including those not shown separately. [2] Not Hispanic or Latino. [3] Age-adjusted to the 2000 standard population for age groups under age 18, age 18-44, age 45-64, and age 65 and over. [4] Estimates are considered unreliable. Data have a relative standard error of 20%-30%.

Source: U.S. National Center for Health Statistics, *Health, United States, 2014*, May 2015. See also <http://www.cdc.gov/nchs/hus.htm>.

Table 223. Height in Inches of Population Age 20 and Over by Sex, Age, and Race/Ethnicity: 2007 to 2010

[Data are for the 2007-2010 period. Based on National Health and Nutrition Examination Survey (NHANES), a sample of the civilian noninstitutional population. Data are collected through household interviews and health examinations. Height was measured without shoes. The oversampling of all Hispanic persons is new to the 2007–2010 data collection methodology; see source]

Age and race/ethnicity	Males, height in inches						Females, height in inches					
	Mean	Percentile					Mean	Percentile				
		10th	25th	50th	75th	90th		10th	25th	50th	75th	90th
Total: [1]												
20 years and over......	69.3	65.4	67.3	69.3	71.2	73.0	63.8	60.3	61.9	63.8	65.7	67.3
20-29 years.............	69.4	65.5	67.4	69.4	71.5	73.1	64.2	60.6	62.2	64.1	66.0	67.6
30-39 years.............	69.5	65.4	67.5	69.5	71.6	73.3	64.3	60.9	62.5	64.3	66.1	67.9
40-49 years.............	69.6	66.0	67.6	69.6	71.5	73.5	64.2	60.8	62.4	64.0	66.0	67.6
50-59 years.............	69.5	65.8	67.7	69.7	71.3	72.8	63.9	60.4	62.0	64.0	65.6	67.0
60-69 years.............	68.8	64.8	66.9	69.0	70.7	72.6	63.6	60.2	62.0	63.8	65.3	66.8
70-79 years.............	68.2	64.6	66.3	68.2	70.0	71.9	62.6	59.3	60.7	62.8	64.3	66.1
80 years and over......	67.2	63.7	65.3	67.3	69.2	70.4	61.4	57.9	59.8	61.5	62.9	64.3
Non-Hispanic white:												
20 years and over......	69.8	66.4	68.0	69.8	71.6	73.3	64.2	60.8	62.5	64.2	66.0	67.5
20-39 years.............	70.2	66.9	68.2	70.2	72.1	73.6	64.9	51.7	63.2	64.9	66.5	68.4
40-59 years.............	70.2	67.0	68.5	70.2	71.8	73.6	64.5	61.2	62.8	64.4	66.1	67.6
60 years and over......	68.7	64.9	66.9	68.9	70.6	72.4	63.1	59.8	61.5	63.1	64.8	66.4
Non-Hispanic black:												
20 years and over......	69.5	65.9	67.6	69.4	71.2	73.0	64.2	60.9	62.3	64.1	66.0	67.5
20-39 years.............	69.7	66.2	67.9	69.4	71.4	73.3	64.4	61.2	62.6	64.4	66.2	67.6
40-59 years.............	69.6	66.1	67.7	69.6	71.4	73.2	64.4	61.1	62.5	64.2	66.2	67.6
60 years and over......	68.6	64.9	66.7	68.9	70.3	72.1	63.2	59.9	61.4	63.2	64.9	66.3
Hispanic:												
20 years and over......	67.1	63.5	65.1	67.0	68.9	70.9	61.9	58.6	60.1	61.8	63.6	65.2
20-39 years.............	67.4	63.6	65.2	67.3	69.4	71.6	62.3	58.9	60.5	62.2	63.9	65.6
40-59 years.............	67.1	63.7	65.1	67.0	68.8	70.5	61.9	58.6	60.1	61.7	63.6	64.9
60 years and over......	65.9	62.8	64.2	66.0	67.4	68.8	60.5	57.5	58.8	60.4	62.1	63.6

[1] Total includes persons of other race/ethnicities not shown separately.

Source: U.S. Centers for Disease Control and Prevention, National Health and Nutrition Examination Survey, *Anthropometric Reference Data For Children and Adults: United States, 2007-2010*, Series 11, No. 252, October 2012. See also <http://www.cdc.gov/nchs/nhanes.htm>.

Table 224. Weight of Population Age 20 and Over by Age, Sex, and Race/Ethnicity: 2007 to 2010

[Data are for the 2007-2010 period. Based on National Health and Nutrition Examination Survey (NHANES). Weight was measured without shoes. Pregnant females were excluded from the tabulations on weight. The oversampling of all Hispanic persons is new to the 2007–2010 data collection methodology; see source]

Age and race/ethnicity	Males, weight in pounds						Females, weight in pounds					
	Mean	Percentile					Mean	Percentile				
		10th	25th	50th	75th	90th		10th	25th	50th	75th	90th
Total: [1]												
20 years and over.......	195.5	146.6	165.2	189.8	218.0	252.2	166.2	118.2	134.6	157.2	188.6	225.3
20–29 years.............	183.9	137.9	153.2	176.5	206.6	240.4	161.9	114.8	126.3	149.4	181.2	227.3
30–39 years.............	199.5	149.4	166.2	191.1	222.9	259.7	169.1	118.8	137.2	159.8	194.2	225.4
40–49 years.............	200.6	153.2	173.1	193.7	221.9	256.1	168.0	120.8	134.9	158.4	189.0	228.7
50–59 years.............	201.3	152.2	172.3	195.4	226.9	259.3	170.0	123.3	138.5	161.4	193.8	230.2
60–69 years.............	199.4	149.8	168.5	195.1	223.0	253.8	170.5	126.1	140.4	165.7	192.5	226.3
70–79 years.............	190.6	147.2	165.5	186.8	209.8	241.1	164.9	118.0	136.9	159.4	187.1	218.4
80 years and over.......	174.9	135.5	152.2	171.8	194.4	214.5	143.1	109.8	123.1	140.0	158.5	182.7
Non-Hispanic white:												
20 years and over.......	199.2	151.8	170.3	194.0	221.7	254.9	165.4	118.6	134.9	156.6	187.4	223.7
20–39 years.............	194.7	145.3	162.8	188.1	217.2	250.3	164.7	117.7	132.0	154.0	186.6	225.4
40–59 years.............	204.9	159.0	177.3	198.5	227.4	259.5	167.7	121.3	136.2	158.5	189.7	227.0
60 years and over.......	196.3	152.0	168.8	191.8	217.1	248.1	163.0	117.9	135.2	157.5	185.5	217.1
Non-Hispanic black:												
20 years and over.......	199.4	143.5	163.1	191.3	224.5	264.7	187.9	129.5	151.0	177.5	215.5	255.1
20–39 years.............	198.1	141.6	158.9	188.7	223.5	264.5	186.2	125.6	145.1	176.2	216.6	258.9
40–59 years.............	203.1	146.0	169.5	196.4	227.7	266.3	194.7	133.9	156.4	183.4	221.5	257.3
60 years and over.......	193.6	140.8	158.7	188.0	216.0	256.5	177.8	125.9	149.1	171.4	200.3	233.9
Hispanic:												
20 years and over.......	186.1	143.4	157.5	180.0	205.4	236.4	160.6	117.0	133.4	154.7	181.5	210.7
20–39 years.............	185.1	140.4	154.9	176.1	204.6	241.2	159.4	114.8	129.6	151.4	183.6	212.8
40–59 years.............	189.4	150.3	165.2	184.2	207.7	232.4	164.5	125.6	140.9	158.9	182.3	210.1
60 years and over.......	180.8	138.8	154.7	177.1	200.5	223.7	155.8	114.2	133.5	153.0	174.3	198.8

[1] Total includes persons of other race/ethnicities, not shown separately.

Source: U.S. Centers for Disease Control and Prevention, National Health and Nutrition Examination Survey, *Anthropometric Reference Data For Children and Adults: United States, 2007-2010*, Series 11, No. 252, October 2012. See also <http://www.cdc.gov/nchs/nhanes.htm>.

Table 225. Body Mass Index of Population Age 20 and Over by Age, Sex, and Race/Ethnicity: 2007 to 2010

[Data are for the 2007-2010 period. Body Mass Index (BMI) is a measure that adjusts body weight for height, and is calculated as weight in kilograms divided by height in meters squared. For both men and women, BMI weight categories are: under 18.5 underweight, 18.5-24.9 normal, 25.0-29.9 overweight, and 30.0 and over obese. Data are based on National Health and Nutrition Examination Survey (NHANES), a sample of the civilian noninstitutional population. Data are collected through household interviews and health examinations. Excludes pregnant women. Height and weight were measured without shoes. The oversampling of Hispanic persons is new to the 2007–2010 data collection methodology; see source)]

Age and race/ethnicity	Males, BMI						Females, BMI					
	Mean	Percentile					Mean	Percentile				
		10th	25th	50th	75th	90th		10th	25th	50th	75th	90th
Total: [1]												
20 years and over......	28.6	22.2	24.7	27.8	31.5	35.8	28.7	20.7	23.3	27.3	32.5	38.2
20–29 years............	26.8	20.7	22.9	25.6	29.9	33.8	27.5	19.9	21.7	25.3	31.5	38.0
30–39 years............	29.0	22.4	24.9	28.1	32.0	36.2	28.7	20.6	23.4	27.2	32.8	38.1
40–49 years............	29.0	22.9	25.4	28.2	31.7	36.1	28.6	20.6	23.3	27.3	32.4	38.1
50–59 years............	29.2	22.9	25.5	28.2	32.0	37.1	29.3	21.3	24.0	28.3	33.5	39.3
60–69 years............	29.5	22.7	25.3	28.8	32.5	37.0	29.6	21.6	24.8	28.8	33.5	38.5
70–79 years............	28.8	22.9	25.6	28.3	31.3	35.4	29.5	21.6	24.7	28.6	33.4	38.7
80 years and over......	27.2	21.8	24.4	27.0	29.6	32.7	26.7	20.7	23.1	26.3	29.7	32.5
Non-Hispanic white:												
20 years and over......	28.7	22.4	24.8	27.9	31.5	35.8	28.2	20.5	23.0	26.9	32.0	37.7
20–39 years............	27.7	21.1	23.6	26.8	30.9	34.2	27.5	19.9	22.1	25.6	31.3	37.5
40–59 years............	29.2	23.1	25.5	28.3	31.8	36.8	28.3	20.5	23.2	26.9	32.4	38.0
60 years and over......	29.2	23.2	25.5	28.6	31.9	35.9	28.7	21.4	24.0	27.8	32.2	37.6
Non-Hispanic black:												
20 years and over......	29.0	21.4	23.7	28.0	32.7	38.1	32.0	22.1	25.9	30.8	36.5	42.8
20–39 years............	28.7	21.1	23.1	27.3	32.6	38.1	31.4	21.6	25.0	30.3	35.9	42.1
40–59 years............	29.4	22.1	24.8	28.3	33.1	38.4	33.1	23.0	26.7	31.2	37.7	44.8
60 years and over......	28.8	21.6	24.1	28.2	31.6	36.9	31.1	22.9	26.6	30.3	34.8	40.0
Hispanic:												
20 years and over......	28.9	23.0	25.5	28.1	31.6	35.6	29.5	21.9	24.9	28.5	33.0	38.0
20–39 years............	28.5	21.9	24.8	27.5	31.1	35.5	28.8	21.3	23.6	26.9	32.7	38.2
40–59 years............	29.5	24.2	26.5	28.8	32.1	35.7	30.2	23.0	26.2	29.6	33.2	37.8
60 years and over......	29.2	23.2	25.9	28.3	31.9	35.6	29.9	22.8	25.7	29.4	33.2	37.7

[1] Total includes persons of other race/ethnicities not shown separately.

Source: U.S. Centers for Disease Control and Prevention, National Health and Nutrition Examination Survey, *Anthropometric Reference Data For Children and Adults: United States, 2007-2010*, Series 11, No. 252, October 2012. See also <http://www.cdc.gov/nchs/nhanes.htm>.

Table 226. Leisure-Time Aerobic and Muscle-Strengthening Activity Among Adults Age 18 and Over by Selected Characteristics: 2012

[In percent. Percents are age-adjusted and allow for comparisons to results from earlier surveys and within demographic groups. Covers persons 18 years old and over. Based on the National Health Interview Survey, a sample survey of the civilian noninstitutionalized population. Measures of physical activity reflect the federal 2008 physical activity guidelines for Americans. The guidelines include an aerobic component; the full physical activity guidelines include muscle-strengthening and aerobic activities. For information on the physical activity guidelines, see <http://www.health.gov/paguidelines/guidelines/default.aspx>. NHIS questions ask about frequency and duration of light-to moderate-intensity and vigorous-intensity leisure-time physical activities, and frequency of leisure-time muscle strengthening activities. Questions are phrased in terms of current behavior and lack a specific reference period. For definition of age adjustment, see text, Section 2.]

Characteristic	Inactive/ insufficiently active [1]	Sufficiently active [2]	Met muscle strengthening and aerobic guidelines [3]	Characteristic	Inactive/ insufficiently active [1]	Sufficiently active [2]	Met muscle strengthening and aerobic guidelines [3]
Total...............	**50.0**	**50.1**	**20.7**	Native Hawaiian/ Pacific Islander...............	[8] 30.4	69.6	31.0
SEX				Two or more races............	44.4	55.6	28.7
Male............................	46.1	53.9	24.6				
Female..........................	53.6	46.5	17.1	HISPANIC ORIGIN AND RACE			
				Hispanic or Latino [5]............	57.4	42.5	15.7
AGE [4]				Not Hispanic or Latino			
18 to 44 years of age...........	43.8	56.1	25.7	White, non-Hispanic..........	46.4	53.6	22.9
45 to 64 years of age...........	53.2	46.9	17.2	Black, non-Hispanic...........	59.1	40.9	16.6
65 to 74 years of age...........	55.4	44.6	14.8				
75 years and over...............	71.9	28.1	7.9	EDUCATION [6]			
				Less than high school diploma........................	68.5	31.5	7.6
RACE							
Race alone				High school diploma or GED [7].......................	61.4	38.6	12.3
White............................	48.7	51.4	21.4				
Black or African American.....	58.8	41.1	16.8	Some college................	50.0	49.9	19.8
American Indian/ Alaska Native................	53.9	46.1	18.7	Bachelor's degree or higher....	37.1	62.9	29.5
Asian...........................	51.2	48.8	17.1				

[1] "Inactive" is having no leisure-time aerobic activity that lasted at least 10 minutes. "Insufficiently active" is having aerobic activities for 10 minutes or more but less than 150 minutes per week. [2] "Sufficiently active," which meets the aerobic component of the 2008 federal physical activity guidelines, is participating in moderate-intensity leisure-time physical activity 150 minutes or more per week, or in vigorous-intensity leisure-time physical activity 75 minutes or more per week, or an equivalent combination. [3] Persons who are sufficiently active, and who engage in muscle strengthening activities at least 2 times a week. [4] Age data are not age-adjusted. [5] Persons of Hispanic or Latino origin may be of any race. [6] For persons aged 25 and over. [7] General educational development high school equivalency diploma. [8] Estimates are considered unreliable; estimates have relative standard error greater than 30% and less than or equal to 50%.

Source: U.S. National Center for Health Statistics, *Summary of Health Statistics for U.S. Adults: National Health Interview Survey, 2012*, Series 10, No. 260, February 2014. See also <http://www.cdc.gov/nchs/products/series/series10.htm>.

Table 227. Percent Distribution of Adults Age 18 and Over by Hours of Sleep, by Selected Characteristics: 2008 to 2010

[227,368 represents 227,368,000. Data are crude estimates for civilian noninstitutionalized population aged 18 and older. Based on 76,669 interviews from the Sample Adult component of the 2008-10 National Health Interview Survey. Survey respondents were asked, "On average, how many hours of sleep do you get in a 24 hour period?" Response options were 1-24 hours]

Characteristic	Adults age 18 and over (1,000)	Hours of sleep (percent distribution)		
		6 or less	7 to 8	9 or more
Total [1]	**227,368**	**28.5**	**62.3**	**9.2**
SEX				
Male	109,843	28.4	62.9	8.6
Female	117,525	28.7	61.7	9.7
AGE [2]				
18 to 24 years old	29,130	23.4	62.5	14.0
25 to 44 years old	81,392	30.5	63.2	6.2
45 to 64 years old	78,909	31.3	62.0	6.7
65 to 74 years old	20,585	23.7	63.8	12.5
75 years old and over	17,351	21.0	56.7	22.4
RACE				
Single race [3]				
White	183,907	27.2	63.6	9.2
Black or African American	27,316	36.2	53.6	10.3
American Indian or Alaska Native	1,943	29.7	59.2	11.1
Asian	10,787	29.6	64.5	5.9
Native Hawaiian or Other Pacific Islander	392	39.2	53.2	(S)
Two or more races [4]	3,023	35.3	54.3	10.4
Black or African American, white	532	34.3	52.4	13.3
American Indian or Alaska Native, white	1,411	33.1	53.6	13.3
HISPANIC ORIGIN AND RACE [5]				
Hispanic or Latino	31,330	26.0	64.9	9.1
Mexican or Mexican American	19,496	23.4	66.5	10.1
Not Hispanic or Latino	196,038	28.9	61.9	9.2
White, single race	155,262	27.5	63.3	9.2
Black or African American, single race	26,318	36.3	53.5	10.2
EDUCATION				
Less than high school graduate	33,672	28.2	56.9	14.9
GED diploma [6]	6,405	34.4	53.8	11.8
High school graduate	55,686	28.9	59.8	11.3
Some college, no degree	45,503	31.3	60.3	8.4
Associate of arts degree	23,135	31.5	61.7	6.9
Bachelor of arts, science degree	40,489	25.5	68.7	5.8
Masters, doctorate, medical degree	21,173	23.2	72.2	4.5
POVERTY STATUS [7]				
Below poverty level	28,535	31.0	55.5	13.5
100% to less than 200% poverty level	42,229	30.0	58.0	12.0
200% to less than 400% poverty level	69,616	29.2	61.5	9.3
400% or more of poverty level	86,988	26.5	67.2	6.3
MARITAL STATUS				
Never married	48,209	26.3	62.2	11.6
Married	123,910	27.3	65.0	7.7
Cohabiting	15,650	32.0	59.4	8.7
Divorced or separated	25,654	36.7	55.3	8.0
Widowed	13,586	28.4	54.0	17.6

S Does not meet publication standards. [1] Includes persons of other races and unknown race and ethnicity, unknown education, unknown poverty status, and unknown marital status. [2] Estimates for age groups are not age adjusted. [3] Refers to persons who indicated only a single race group. [4] Refers to all persons who indicated more than one race group. [5] Persons of Hispanic or Latino origin may be of any race or combination of races. [6] General Educational Development high school equivalency diploma. [7] Based on family income and family size using the U.S. Census Bureau poverty thresholds for 2007-2009.

Source: U.S. National Center for Health Statistics, *Health Behaviors of Adults: United States, 2008-10,* Vital and Health Statistics, Series 10, Number 257, May 2013. See also <http://www.cdc.gov/nchs/products/series/series10.htm>.

Table 228. Depression and Receipt of Mental Health Treatment in the Past Year Among Adults Age 18 and Over by Selected Characteristics: 2012 and 2013

[In thousands (16,026 represents 16,026,000), except percent. Based on the National Survey on Drug Use and Health. Covers adults who had a major depressive episode as defined in the 4th edition of the *Diagnostic and Statistical Manual of Mental Disorders* (DSM-IV), which specifies a period of at least 2 weeks when a person experienced a depressed mood or loss of interest or pleasure in daily activities and had a majority of specified depression symptoms. Treatment is defined as seeing or talking to a professional or using prescription medication for depression in the past year; respondents with unknown treatment data were excluded]

Characteristic	Had major depressive episode				Received treatment for depression			
	2012		2013		2012		2013	
	Number (1,000)	Percent of population	Number (1,000)	Percent of population	Number (1,000)	Percent with depression	Number (1,000)	Percent with depression
Total........................	**16,026**	**6.9**	**15,670**	**6.7**	**10,885**	**68.0**	**10,727**	**68.6**
AGE								
18 to 25 years old..................	3,051	8.9	3,007	8.7	1,520	49.8	1,526	50.8
26 to 49 years old..................	7,370	7.6	7,336	7.6	5,071	68.8	4,884	66.7
50 years old and older..............	5,606	5.5	5,327	5.1	4,294	76.8	4,317	81.3
SEX AND AGE								
Male........................	5,811	5.2	5,777	5.1	3,503	60.3	3,464	60.1
18 to 25 years old..................	1,058	6.2	1,018	5.9	437	41.3	445	43.8
26 to 49 years old..................	2,694	5.6	2,902	6.1	1,656	61.5	1,575	54.4
50 years old and older..............	2,059	4.3	1,856	3.8	1,410	68.6	1,444	77.8
Female........................	10,215	8.4	9,893	8.1	7,382	72.4	7,263	73.6
18 to 25 years old..................	1,993	11.6	1,989	11.6	1,084	54.4	1,081	54.4
26 to 49 years old..................	4,675	9.4	4,434	9.0	3,414	73.0	3,309	74.8
50 years old and older..............	3,546	6.5	3,471	6.3	2,884	81.7	2,872	83.2
RACE AND HISPANIC ORIGIN								
Not Hispanic or Latino..............	13,613	6.8	13,617	6.8	9,543	70.2	9,543	70.3
White........................	11,051	7.1	11,375	7.3	7,950	72.0	8,150	71.9
Black or African American..............	1,686	6.3	1,256	4.6	1,047	62.1	811	64.6
American Indian or Alaska Native......	129	10.0	110	8.9	(S)	(S)	(S)	(S)
Native Hawaiian or other Pacific Islander..............	(S)	(S)	12	1.6	(S)	(S)	(S)	(S)
Asian........................	371	3.2	468	4.0	(S)	(S)	(S)	(S)
Two or more races..................	260	7.7	397	11.4	(S)	(S)	(S)	(S)
Hispanic or Latino..................	2,413	7.0	2,053	5.8	1,341	55.6	1,184	57.7

S Figure does not meet publication standards.

Source: U.S. Substance Abuse and Mental Health Services Administration, "Results from the 2013 National Survey on Drug Use and Health: Mental Health Detailed Tables," <http://www.samhsa.gov/data/population-data-nsduh/reports>, accessed February 2015.

Table 229. Autism, Intellectual Disability, Learning Disability, and Other Developmental Delays Among Children by Selected Characteristics: 2011

[In thousands (756 represents 756,000), except percent. Disorder status based on parental report. Based on the National Health Interview Survey]

Characteristic	Autism		Intellectual disability or Down Syndrome		Learning disability		Other developmental delay	
	Number (1,000)	Percent	Number (1,000)	Percent	Number (1,000)	Percent	Number (1,000)	Percent
Total........................	**756**	**1.0**	**846**	**1.1**	**4,660**	**7.5**	**3,340**	**4.5**
AGE								
0 to 4 years old..................	117	0.6	[1] 95	[1] 0.4	[2] 233	[2] 2.6	736	3.5
5 to 11 years old..................	337	1.2	377	1.3	2,029	7.0	1,591	5.5
12 to 17 years old..................	302	1.2	373	1.5	2,398	9.8	1,013	4.1
SEX								
Male........................	625	1.6	535	1.4	2,928	9.2	2,155	5.7
Female........................	131	0.4	311	0.9	1,732	5.7	1,184	3.3
RACE AND HISPANIC ORIGIN								
White, non-Hispanic..................	494	1.2	514	1.2	2,794	8.1	2,086	5.0
Black, non-Hispanic..................	[1] 57	[1] 0.5	151	1.4	803	8.5	577	5.2
Other, non-Hispanic..................	[1] 41	[1] 0.9	[1] 45	[1] 1.0	163	4.5	128	2.9
Hispanic........................	164	0.9	136	0.8	900	6.3	549	3.1
POVERTY STATUS [3]								
Below 100% of Federal poverty level....	135	0.8	223	1.3	1,370	10.1	943	5.6
100% to 199% of Federal poverty level....	160	0.9	274	1.6	1,217	8.4	798	4.6
At or above 200% Federal poverty.......	462	1.1	348	0.9	2,073	6.1	1,599	4.0

[1] Estimate does not meet standards of reliability or precision and has a relative standard error of greater than 30 percent and less than or equal to 50 percent, interpret with caution. [2] Data are estimates for children aged 3 to 4. [3] Estimates are based on a definition of the Federal Poverty Level that incorporates information on family income, size, and composition and is calculated as a percentage of the U.S. Census Bureau's poverty levels.

Source: U.S. Substance Abuse and Mental Health Services Administration, *Behavioral Health, United States, 2012*, 2013. See also <http://samhsa.gov/data/2012BehavioralHealthUS/Index.aspx>.

Table 230. Learning Disability and Attention Deficit Hyperactivity Disorder Among Children Age 3 to 17 Years by Selected Characteristics: 2012

[In thousands, except percent (61,696 represents 61,696,000). Learning disability is based on the question, "Has a representative from a school or a health professional ever told you that (child's name) had a learning disability?" Attention Deficit Hyperactivity Disorder is based on the question, "Has a doctor or health professional ever told you that (child's name) had Attention Hyperactivity Disorder or Attention Deficit Disorder?"]

Selected characteristic	Total	Ever told had—			
		Learning disability		Attention deficit hyperactivity disorder	
		Number [1]	Percent [2]	Number [1]	Percent [2]
Total [3].........	**61,696**	**4,943**	**8.0**	**5,876**	**9.5**
SEX					
Male.........	31,513	3,146	10.0	4,239	13.5
Female.........	30,182	1,796	6.0	1,636	5.4
AGE [4]					
3 to 4 years old.........	8,040	192	2.4	136	1.7
5 to 11 years old.........	28,829	2,338	8.1	2,726	9.5
12 to 17 years old.........	24,827	2,413	9.7	3,014	12.2
RACE					
Race alone [5].........	58,650	4,671	8.0	5,528	9.4
White.........	46,032	3,771	8.2	4,567	9.9
Black or African American.........	8,761	671	7.7	769	8.8
American Indian or Alaska Native.........	852	140	17.4	108	13.5
Asian.........	2,901	[8] 65	2.2	77	2.6
Native Hawaiian or other Pacific Islander.........	104	[8] 24	21.6	(B)	(B)
Two or more races [6].........	3,046	271	9.4	348	12.2
Black or African American and White.........	1,291	112	8.7	151	12.1
American Indian or Alaska Native and White.........	636	43	6.8	[8] 81	12.7
HISPANIC ORIGIN AND RACE [7]					
Hispanic or Latino.........	14,602	1,020	7.1	839	5.8
Mexican or Mexican American.........	9,977	591	6.0	438	4.5
Not Hispanic or Latino.........	47,093	3,923	8.3	5,036	10.6
White, single race.........	32,869	2,888	8.7	3,834	11.5
Black or African American, single race.........	8,353	650	7.8	739	8.9

B Base figure too small to meet statistical standards for reliability of a derived figure. [1] Unknowns for the columns are not included in the frequencies, but they are included in the "Total" column. [2] Unknowns for the column variables are not included in the denominators when calculating percentages. Percents are age adjusted to the 2000 projected U.S. standard population using age groups 3-4 years, 5-11 years, and 12-17 years, except for data shown for each age group. [3] Includes other races not shown separately. [4] Estimates for age groups are not age adjusted. [5] Refers to children of only a single race group. [6] Refers to children of more than once race group. [7] Persons of Hispanic or Latino origin may be of any race. [8] Figures do not meet standard of reliability or precision.

Source: U.S. National Center for Health Statistics, *Summary Health Statistics for U.S. Children: National Health Interview Survey, 2012*, Vital and Health Statistics, Series 10, Number 258, August 2013. See also <http://www.cdc.gov/nchs/products/series/series10.htm>.

Table 231. Children and Youth With Disabilities Served by Type of Disability: 2000 to 2013

[In thousands (5,773.9 represents 5,773,900). As of Fall. For children and youth aged 6 to 21 served under the Individuals with Disabilities Education Act (IDEA) Part B. Includes outlying areas]

Disability	2000	2005	2008	2009	2010	2011	2012	2013
Total.........	**5,773.9**	**6,109.6**	**5,889.8**	**5,882.2**	**5,834.9**	**5,789.9**	**5,823.8**	**5,847.6**
Autism.........	79.6	193.6	292.8	333.2	370.6	407.2	444.0	479.0
Deaf-blind.........	1.3	1.6	1.7	1.4	1.3	1.4	1.3	1.3
Developmental delay [1].........	28.6	79.1	96.9	104.5	109.4	115.6	123.4	133.8
Emotional disturbance.........	474.3	472.4	418.1	405.5	388.2	371.6	361.3	352.3
Hearing impairment.........	70.8	72.4	70.8	70.7	69.9	69.3	68.9	68.2
Intellectual disability.........	613.4	545.5	476.1	461.3	445.8	431.2	424.5	417.6
Multiple disabilities.........	122.9	133.9	124.1	124.5	123.8	125.2	126.3	125.6
Orthopedic impairment.........	73.0	63.1	62.4	58.0	55.8	54.4	52.5	50.3
Other health impairment.........	294.0	561.0	648.4	679.0	706.1	734.3	770.6	809.9
Specific learning disability.........	2,881.6	2,780.2	2,525.9	2,486.4	2,420.0	2,357.5	2,338.3	2,311.1
Speech or language impairment.........	1,093.4	1,157.2	1,122.0	1,107.4	1,093.7	1,071.6	1,061.8	1,047.7
Traumatic brain injury.........	14.9	23.5	24.9	24.4	24.7	24.9	25.1	25.3
Visual impairment.........	26.0	26.0	25.8	25.8	25.7	25.7	25.7	25.5

[1] States had the option of reporting children aged 3 to 9 under developmental delay beginning 1997.

Source: U.S. Department of Education, Office of Special Education Programs, Data & Research, "IDEA Section 618 Data Products: State Level Data Files," <http://www2.ed.gov/programs/osepidea/618-data>, accessed June 2015.

Table 232. Children Under Age 18 Receiving Special Education or Early Intervention Services: 2011 and 2012

[In thousands, except percent (74,517 represents 74,517,000). Receiving special education or early intervention services is based on the question, "Do any of the following (family members under 18 years of age) receive special education or early intervention services?"]

Selected Characteristic	2011			2012		
		Persons under age 18 receiving special education early intervention services			Persons under age 18 receiving special education early intervention services	
	Total	Number [1]	Percent [2]	Total	Number [1]	Percent [2]
Total [3]	74,517	5,153	6.9	73,659	5,408	7.4
SEX						
Male	38,103	3,426	9.0	37,627	3,592	9.6
Female	36,414	1,727	4.8	36,032	1,815	5.1
AGE [4]						
Under 12 years old	50,267	3,135	6.2	48,821	3,363	6.9
12 to 17 years old	24,249	2,018	8.3	24,838	2,045	8.2
RACE						
Race alone [5]	71,430	4,977	7.0	70,134	5,102	7.3
White	55,990	3,981	7.1	55,024	4,068	7.4
Black or African American	10,991	800	7.3	10,617	762	7.2
American Indian or Alaska Native	825	57	6.9	969	135	14.1
Asian	3,454	125	3.7	3,419	123	3.6
Native Hawaiian or other Pacific Islander	171	(B)	(B)	105	(B)	(B)
Two or more races [6]	3,087	176	5.8	3,526	305	9.0
HISPANIC ORIGIN AND RACE [7]						
Hispanic or Latino	17,516	973	5.6	17,662	1,039	6.0
Mexican or Mexican American	11,916	644	5.4	11,893	588	5.0
Not Hispanic or Latino	57,000	4,180	7.3	55,998	4,368	7.8
White, single race	40,451	3,163	7.8	39,146	3,178	8.1
Black or African American, single race	10,252	743	7.2	10,012	728	7.3

B Base figure too small to meet statistical standards for reliability of a derived figure. [1] Unknowns for the columns are not included in the frequencies, but they are included in the "Total" column. [2] Unknowns for the column variables are not included in the denominators when calculating percentages. Percents are age-adjusted to the 2000 projected U.S. standard population using the age groups shown; data for each age group are not age-adjusted. [3] Includes other races not shown separately. [4] Estimates for the age groups are not age adjusted. [5] Refers to persons who indicated only a single race group. [6] Refers to all persons who indicated more than one race group. [7] Persons of Hispanic or Latino origin may be of any race.

Source: National Center for Health Statistics, *Summary Health Statistics for U.S. Children: National Health Interview Survey, 2012*, Vital and Health Statistics, Series 10, Number 258, August 2013, and previous report. See also <http://www.cdc.gov/nchs/products/series/series10.htm>.

Table 233. Depression and Receipt of Mental Health Treatment in the Past Year, Among Youth Age 12-17 by Selected Characteristics: 2005 to 2013

[In percent. Data are from Substance Abuse and Mental Health Services Administration, National Survey on Drug Use and Health. Covers youth age 12 to 17 who had a major depressive episode as defined in the 4th edition of the *Diagnostic and Statistical Manual of Mental Disorders* (DSM-IV), which specifies a period of at least 2 weeks when a person experienced a depressed mood or loss of interest or pleasure in daily activities and had a majority of specified depression symptoms. Treatment is defined as seeing or talking to a medical doctor or other professional, or using prescription medication in the past year for depression. Respondents with unknown incidence of major depressive episode and unknown treatment data were excluded]

Item	Youth with major depressive episode				Youth with depression receiving treatment			
	2005	2010	2012	2013	2005	2010	2012	2013
Total [1]	8.8	8.0	9.1	10.7	37.8	37.8	37.0	38.1
AGE								
12-13 years	5.2	4.3	5.4	6.1	32.9	32.5	30.7	39.1
14-15 years	9.5	9.0	10.2	12.4	41.1	38.4	36.6	37.2
16-17 years	11.5	10.6	11.4	13.2	37.1	39.3	40.0	38.6
SEX								
Male	4.5	4.4	4.7	5.3	34.1	32.0	28.3	29.7
Female	13.3	11.9	13.7	16.2	39.0	40.1	40.1	40.9
RACE ETHNICITY [1]								
White, non-Hispanic	9.1	8.6	9.1	10.9	39.3	41.1	40.7	41.6
Black, non-Hispanic	7.6	6.8	7.9	8.6	39.3	23.0	33.5	28.6
American Indian or Alaska Native	6.1	7.4	5.2	4.5	(NA)	(NA)	(NA)	(NA)
Asian	6.0	5.5	4.2	10.2	(NA)	(NA)	(NA)	(NA)
Two or more races	10.5	9.4	11.3	13.0	(NA)	(NA)	(NA)	(NA)
Hispanic [2]	9.1	7.8	10.5	11.4	31.8	38.4	30.8	36.9
POVERTY STATUS [3]								
Below 100% poverty	8.1	7.2	10.2	10.2	37.3	33.8	35.7	33.6
100-199% poverty	9.6	9.0	9.0	11.3	32.1	39.1	35.9	39.9
200% poverty and above	8.7	7.9	8.7	10.6	40.1	38.4	38.0	39.1

NA Not available. [1] Total includes persons of other races, not shown separately. [2] Persons of Hispanic origin may be of any race. [3] Estimates are based on a definition of poverty level that incorporates information on family income, size, and composition and is calculated as a percentage of the U.S. Census Bureau's poverty thresholds.

Source: Federal Interagency Forum on Child and Family Statistics, "America's Children: Key National Indicators of Well-Being, 2015," <http://www.childstats.gov/americaschildren/index.asp>, accessed July 2015.

Table 234. Immunization of Children Age 19 to 35 Months by Vaccine Type and State: 2013

[In percent. Covers civilian noninstitutionalized children age 19 months to 35 months; born January 2010 to May 2012. Based on estimates from the National Immunization Survey (NIS). The NIS consists of a household survey, and a survey of health care providers of the children to verify and/or complete vaccination information. Abbreviations: DTaP = diphtheria, tetanus toxoids, and acellular pertussis vaccine (includes children who might have been vaccinated with diphtheria and tetanus toxoids vaccine, or diphtheria, tetanus toxoids, and pertussis vaccine); MMR = measles, mumps, and rubella vaccine; HepB = hepatitis B vaccine; HepA = hepatitis A; Hib = Haemophilus influenzae type b vaccine; PCV = pneumococcal conjugate vaccine]

State	DTaP, ≥3 doses	DTaP, ≥4 doses	Polio, ≥3 doses	MMR, 1≥ dose	Hib, primary series[1]	Hib, full series[1]	HepB, ≥3 doses	HepB, birth dose[2]	Vari-cella, ≥1 dose	PCV, ≥3 doses	PCV, ≥4 doses	HepA, ≥2 doses	Rota-virus[3]	Com-bined series[4]
U.S....	**94.1**	**83.1**	**92.7**	**91.9**	**93.7**	**82.0**	**90.8**	**74.2**	**91.2**	**92.4**	**82.0**	**54.7**	**72.6**	**70.4**
AL......	94.3	84.0	93.3	89.7	92.4	85.3	89.8	81.7	92.2	94.3	86.9	59.2	74.8	77.0
AK.....	93.8	75.5	92.0	90.5	93.5	81.4	92.7	59.4	89.6	89.9	78.2	52.5	64.2	63.9
AZ.....	91.8	76.6	91.2	91.4	91.4	79.5	88.4	79.1	89.6	88.4	76.8	55.4	70.9	65.1
AR.....	92.2	74.3	89.4	88.3	92.1	70.3	88.6	79.7	87.2	91.3	69.5	35.8	56.0	57.1
CA.....	91.7	83.1	90.5	90.7	91.8	80.1	91.1	70.3	90.4	89.7	79.1	56.8	76.8	69.3
CO.....	91.7	81.2	90.3	86.0	90.8	82.8	84.1	60.2	84.8	91.0	84.0	47.6	73.8	69.2
CT.....	98.2	88.0	97.6	91.4	97.6	92.6	96.0	75.2	90.8	94.0	91.5	72.1	81.1	78.2
DE.....	98.7	87.9	97.4	94.8	97.5	84.4	93.7	83.6	92.3	96.9	88.0	64.2	83.9	71.8
DC.....	97.2	86.2	96.1	96.2	96.2	87.5	92.5	78.3	95.0	96.6	88.9	66.2	68.4	76.9
FL......	92.6	80.3	91.2	93.4	92.6	79.4	89.0	58.0	92.8	91.1	79.1	48.7	66.0	70.0
GA.....	91.7	83.5	91.5	93.9	94.0	79.7	91.5	76.4	95.0	92.7	81.3	58.0	64.6	69.8
HI......	94.7	83.7	92.6	92.8	95.7	85.3	88.3	77.3	91.4	92.5	82.5	54.2	73.3	66.5
ID......	93.9	84.2	92.6	91.1	94.7	80.0	90.7	72.7	87.9	93.3	87.3	60.7	74.6	70.2
IL.......	93.1	82.7	91.2	91.4	92.0	82.6	89.5	71.4	88.6	91.3	79.7	48.4	72.6	66.8
IN......	93.8	82.1	91.9	92.0	93.8	80.8	92.0	82.8	90.7	92.9	79.2	61.0	65.7	68.5
IA......	97.7	89.6	97.5	94.5	97.5	89.1	96.5	79.5	93.0	96.5	90.7	57.5	74.7	78.3
KS.....	95.0	81.6	93.2	89.4	95.0	80.5	93.8	77.2	89.7	94.1	85.1	60.2	72.6	68.7
KY.....	91.3	84.1	91.0	89.5	92.0	78.6	90.8	88.0	91.5	91.0	81.7	41.4	66.4	72.7
LA.....	91.7	78.5	91.2	88.1	89.8	78.9	93.0	81.6	92.0	88.5	79.7	50.4	69.6	69.1
ME.....	97.3	87.9	94.0	91.0	92.2	80.2	84.5	68.9	90.5	92.6	84.9	57.4	72.0	68.0
MD.....	97.2	87.4	97.0	95.3	95.9	85.8	91.0	75.4	94.2	94.5	85.8	55.6	83.7	75.8
MA.....	98.6	93.3	97.9	95.8	98.3	90.3	92.9	78.0	94.7	96.9	90.6	62.7	84.0	78.5
MI......	91.6	79.6	90.8	89.2	91.4	80.0	87.9	82.5	87.5	91.0	79.1	51.2	70.1	70.0
MN.....	95.9	90.5	94.8	90.8	95.7	89.7	90.3	63.8	89.2	95.6	90.8	54.3	80.3	74.1
MS.....	96.3	87.4	94.9	95.2	96.6	86.0	92.8	79.2	92.9	92.9	96.7	83.4	39.1	63.2	74.6
MO.....	92.2	82.1	91.0	89.8	91.4	80.0	88.4	79.2	88.7	89.5	80.4	45.9	72.4	67.9
MT.....	93.2	79.0	92.7	87.3	91.9	82.3	89.9	73.9	87.1	89.9	76.8	46.4	65.5	65.4
NE.....	96.6	88.3	95.9	92.5	95.7	86.7	94.5	81.3	92.2	96.0	90.7	69.5	76.2	79.0
NV.....	92.7	81.1	92.0	90.4	90.8	76.5	88.8	75.4	88.6	89.7	76.4	61.1	62.1	60.6
NH.....	98.0	91.3	97.2	96.3	95.9	86.7	94.6	74.1	93.0	94.9	89.2	53.3	78.2	74.9
NJ.....	97.8	86.4	91.8	95.6	95.8	85.8	93.2	59.8	91.9	96.5	86.6	51.2	69.0	72.9
NM.....	90.2	79.8	87.6	89.1	89.5	80.0	86.0	67.5	86.9	89.7	78.3	49.3	68.7	65.7
NY.....	97.4	86.6	95.8	95.5	95.1	83.2	92.9	63.7	92.9	94.6	86.8	48.4	73.8	72.2
NC.....	96.0	87.5	95.9	96.0	96.3	87.0	94.3	82.1	94.6	95.7	86.5	51.6	75.4	72.0
ND.....	94.1	78.6	91.5	91.4	94.3	76.4	91.8	82.0	89.8	92.0	81.8	59.5	78.4	72.0
OH.....	91.9	75.8	90.4	86.0	91.8	74.0	87.4	78.1	85.3	88.3	71.6	49.2	66.5	61.7
OK.....	93.0	79.2	92.1	89.8	93.5	77.8	90.9	76.7	88.6	91.1	72.6	51.8	58.8	62.7
OR.....	93.4	83.8	91.0	89.4	91.1	78.3	88.7	66.8	87.1	88.6	79.8	55.9	64.3	66.6
PA.....	95.9	88.7	95.0	93.3	95.3	86.7	92.3	83.3	93.1	94.0	85.4	58.3	77.2	75.5
RI......	98.3	91.6	96.9	95.6	99.0	89.6	96.7	72.7	97.3	98.3	93.0	60.9	84.4	82.1
SC.....	96.8	77.3	95.6	89.2	94.4	80.7	95.0	76.1	89.1	94.8	79.4	52.5	69.9	66.5
SD.....	95.0	86.5	93.4	93.1	92.5	84.7	92.1	70.9	92.5	92.5	83.6	55.4	68.7	73.8
TN.....	95.1	81.1	94.9	92.3	96.0	80.9	92.2	76.6	92.8	95.3	84.2	52.6	73.3	68.5
TX.....	94.8	81.5	91.3	92.7	94.4	82.1	89.5	81.8	93.6	93.1	82.8	64.2	73.8	72.5
UT.....	96.2	90.3	95.1	92.6	94.7	84.9	89.7	81.2	93.6	94.6	89.6	67.6	78.3	75.2
VT.....	96.7	85.8	95.1	91.2	92.7	83.5	92.0	44.8	85.8	92.2	82.4	48.5	73.4	66.9
VA.....	94.4	78.8	95.2	88.6	94.5	82.7	90.8	72.3	91.1	92.4	80.3	48.0	76.2	69.2
WA.....	95.1	79.8	93.1	93.5	94.3	85.5	89.0	75.0	91.7	92.9	81.9	55.7	76.3	70.8
WV.....	91.4	83.4	90.0	86.0	90.8	80.5	85.8	73.9	86.1	89.6	76.4	57.5	68.4	65.5
WI......	96.1	84.0	93.8	93.2	95.6	82.0	94.4	80.5	91.9	92.9	82.6	63.2	73.6	72.8
WY.....	93.1	80.9	90.9	91.6	91.6	79.9	88.9	67.0	90.9	93.2	81.0	33.6	62.5	70.0

[1] Hib primary series: receipt of ≥2 or ≥3 doses, depending on product type received. Full series: receipt of ≥3 or ≥4 doses, depending on product type received (primary series and booster dose). [2] HepB administered from birth through age 3 days. [3] ≥2 or ≥3 doses of Rotavirus vaccine, depending on product type received. [4] The combined (4:3:1:3*:3:1:4) vaccine series includes ≥4 doses of DTaP, ≥3 doses of poliovirus vaccine, ≥1 dose of measles-containing vaccine, full series of Hib vaccine (≥3 or ≥4 doses, depending on product type), ≥3 doses of HepB, ≥1 dose of varicella vaccine, and ≥4 doses of PCV.

Source: U.S. Centers for Disease Control and Prevention, Immunization Managers, "National Immunization Survey (NIS) – Children (19-35 months)," <http://www.cdc.gov/vaccines/imz-managers/coverage/nis/child/data/tables-2013.html>, accessed February 2015.

Table 235. Child Immunization Rates by Vaccine, Race/Ethnicity, and Poverty Status: 2010 and 2013

[In percent. Covers civilian noninstitutionalized children age 19 months to 35 months. Based on estimates from the National Immunization Survey (NIS). The survey also contacts the health care providers of the children to verify and/or complete vaccination information. Results are based on race/ethnic status of the child as reported by parent or guardian. DTaP = diphtheria, tetanus toxoids, and acellular pertussis vaccine (includes children who might have been vaccinated with diphtheria and tetanus toxoids vaccine, or diphtheria, tetanus toxoids, and pertussis vaccine); MMR = measles, mumps, and rubella vaccine; Hib = Haemophilus influenzae type b vaccine; HepB = hepatitis B vaccine; PCV = pneumococcal conjugate vaccine; HepA = hepatitis A vaccine]

| Vaccination | 2010, total | 2013 [1] | | | | | | | |
		Total	White [2]	Black [2]	His-panic [3]	American Indian/ Alaska Native only [2]	Asian [2]	At or above poverty	Below poverty
DTaP, ≥3 doses	95.0	94.1	95.1	92.4	93.4	92.4	96.0	95.6	91.2
DTaP, ≥4 doses	84.4	83.1	85.3	74.7	82.3	78.1	89.0	86.0	77.8
Poliovirus, ≥3 doses	93.3	92.7	93.7	91.2	91.6	92.2	95.5	94.4	89.2
MMR, ≥1 dose	91.5	91.9	91.5	90.9	92.1	96.3	96.7	92.5	90.5
Hib, Primary series [4]	92.2	93.7	94.6	91.4	93.3	94.3	93.8	95.1	91.0
Hib, Full series [4]	66.8	82.0	84.2	74.9	80.9	82.9	82.0	85.3	75.8
HepB, ≥ 3 doses	91.8	90.8	91.0	91.1	89.7	96.1	92.0	92.0	88.3
HepB, 1 dose within 3 days of birth	64.1	74.2	71.9	76.7	77.8	(NA)	73.7	72.1	78.3
Varicella (chickenpox), ≥1 dose [5]	90.4	91.2	90.0	92.1	92.0	95.4	96.0	91.6	90.3
PCV, ≥3 doses	92.6	92.4	93.1	90.8	92.2	92.3	92.0	94.2	88.8
HepA, ≥1 dose	78.3	83.1	80.3	82.4	86.0	89.8	90.9	82.7	84.0
HepA, ≥2 doses	49.7	54.7	53.4	49.1	56.6	(NA)	67.3	56.1	53.5
Rotavirus [6]	59.2	72.6	74.8	62.1	73.7	(NA)	74.9	76.9	64.3
Combined series [7]	56.6	70.4	72.1	65.0	69.3	70.1	72.7	73.8	64.4

NA Not available. [1] 2013 NIS covers children born January 2010 to May 2012. [2] Non-Hispanic. [3] Children of Hispanic origin may be of any race. [4] Hib primary series: receipt of ≥2 or ≥3 doses, depending on product type received. Full series: receipt of ≥3 or ≥4 doses, depending on product type received (primary series and booster dose). [5] At or after child's first birthday, unadjusted for history of varicella illness. [6] Rotavirus vaccine includes ≥2 or ≥3 doses, depending on the product type received (≥2 doses for Rotarix [RV1] or ≥3 doses for RotaTeq [RV5]). [7] The combined (4:3:1:3*:3:1:4) vaccine series includes ≥4 doses of DTaP, ≥3 doses of poliovirus vaccine, ≥1 dose of measles-containing vaccine, full series of Hib vaccine (≥3 or ≥4 doses, depending on product type), ≥3 doses of HepB, ≥1 dose of varicella vaccine, and ≥4 doses of PCV.

Source: U.S. Centers for Disease Control and Prevention, Immunization Managers, "National Immunization Survey – Children (19-35 months)," <http://www.cdc.gov/vaccines/imz-managers/coverage/nis/child/index.html>, accessed February 2015; and Elam-Evans, Laurie et al, "National, State, and Selected Local Area Vaccination Coverage Among Children Aged 19-35 Months—United States, 2013," *Morbidity and Mortality Weekly Report,* 63:34 (2014), <http://www.cdc.gov/mmwr/preview/mmwrhtml/mm6334a1.htm>.

Table 236. Asthma Incidence Among Children Under Age 18 by Selected Characteristics: 2012

[In thousands, except percent (73,661 represents 73,661,000). Based on the National Health Interview Survey, a sample survey of the civilian noninstitutionalized population; see Appendix III]

| Characteristic | Total | Ever told had asthma | | Still have asthma | |
		Number (1,000) [1]	Percent [2]	Number (1,000) [1]	Percent [2]
Total [3]	73,661	10,322	14.0	6,834	9.3
SEX					
Male	37,628	5,988	15.9	3,748	10.0
Female	36,033	4,333	12.1	3,085	8.6
AGE [4]					
0 to 4 years old	20,006	1,406	7.0	1,080	5.4
5 to 11 years old	28,829	4,483	15.6	3,162	11.0
12 to 17 years old	24,827	4,433	17.9	2,591	10.5
RACE					
Single race [5]	70,037	9,714	13.9	6,398	9.2
White	54,943	6,911	12.6	4,395	8.0
Black or African American	10,591	2,265	21.6	1,675	16.0
American Indian or Alaska Native	990	212	21.6	143	14.5
Asian	3,403	310	9.0	173	4.9
Native Hawaiian or Other Pacific Islander	110	(B)	10.9	(B)	7.9
Two or more races [6]	3,625	608	17.5	435	12.3
HISPANIC ORIGIN AND RACE [7]					
Hispanic or Latino	17,663	2,344	13.5	1,552	8.9
Mexican or Mexican American	11,986	1,392	11.8	908	7.7
Not Hispanic or Latino	55,999	7,978	14.2	5,282	9.4
White, single race	39,057	4,881	12.4	3,079	7.9
Black or African American, single race	10,045	2,178	21.8	1,609	16.1

B Figure too small to meet statistical standards for reliability of a derived figure. [1] Unknowns for the columns are not included in the frequencies, but they are included in the "Total" column. [2] Unknowns for the column variables are not included in the denominators when calculating percentages. Percents are age-adjusted to the 2000 projected U.S. standard population using age groups 0-4 years, 5-11 years, and 12-17 years. [3] Includes other races, not shown separately. [4] Estimates for the age groups are not age adjusted. [5] Refers to persons who indicated only a single race group. [6] Refers to all persons who indicated more than one race group. [7] Persons of Hispanic or Latino origin may be of any race or combination of races.

Source: National Center for Health Statistics, *Summary Health Statistics for U.S. Children: National Health Interview Survey, 2012,* Vital and Health Statistics, Series 10, Number 258, August 2013. See also <http://www.cdc.gov/nchs/products/series/series10.htm>.

Table 237. Children Who Are Obese by Age, Sex, Race, and Hispanic Origin: 1988 to 2012

[In percent. For children age 6-17. Data are from U.S. National Center for Health Statistics, National Health and Nutrition Examination Surveys, a program of studies that combines interviews and physical examinations to assess the health and nutritional status of adults and children. Children classified as obese have a body mass index (BMI) at or above the 95th percentile of the sex-specific BMI growth charts]

Selected characteristic	1988–1994	1999–2000	2001–2002	2003–2004	2005–2006	2007–2008	2009–2010	2011-2012
Total [1]	**11.2**	**15.0**	**16.5**	**18.0**	**16.5**	**19.2**	**18.0**	**19.5**
RACE AND HISPANIC ORIGIN								
White, non-Hispanic	10.5	11.3	14.6	17.3	13.8	17.4	14.6	17.0
Black, non-Hispanic	14.0	21.1	20.4	21.7	21.3	22.4	25.7	22.7
Hispanic origin [2,3]	(NA)	(NA)	(NA)	(NA)	(NA)	24.4	23.1	25.1
Mexican-American [2,3]	15.4	24.1	21.5	19.6	25.6	24.2	23.4	26.6
SEX AND AGE								
Male	11.8	15.7	18.0	19.1	17.2	21.0	19.7	18.4
Female	10.6	14.3	15.1	16.8	15.9	17.3	16.2	20.6
Ages 6-11	11.3	15.1	16.3	18.8	15.1	19.6	18.0	17.7
Male	11.6	15.7	17.5	19.9	16.2	21.2	20.1	16.4
Female	11.0	14.3	14.9	17.6	14.1	18.0	15.7	19.1
Ages 12-17	11.1	14.9	16.8	17.2	17.8	18.8	18.0	21.1
Male	12.0	15.6	18.4	18.3	18.1	20.8	19.4	20.3
Female	10.2	14.2	15.2	16.0	17.5	16.7	16.5	21.9

NA Not available. [1] Includes other races not shown separately. [2] Persons of Hispanic and Mexican origin may be of any race. [3] From 1976 to 2006, the survey sample was designed to provide estimates specifically for persons of Mexican origin. Beginning in 2007, the survey allows for reporting of both total Hispanics and Mexican Americans.

Source: Federal Interagency Forum on Child and Family Statistics, "America's Children: Key National Indicators of Well-Being, 2015," <http://www.childstats.gov/americaschildren/index.asp>, accessed July 2015.

Table 238. High School Students Engaged in Physical Activity by Sex: 2013

[In percent. For students in grades 9 to 12. Based on the Youth Risk Behavior Survey, a school-based survey and subject to sampling error; for details, see source]

Characteristic	Participated in 60+ min. of physical activity on 5 of last 7 days [1]	Participated in 60+ min. of physical activity on all 7 days [2]	Did not participate in 60+ min. of physical activity on any day [3]	Attended physical education class Total [4]	Attended daily [5]	Played on at least one sports team [6]	Used computers 3 or more hours/day [7]	Watched TV 3 or more hours/day [8]
All students	**47.3**	**27.1**	**15.2**	**48.0**	**29.4**	**54.0**	**41.3**	**32.5**
Male	**57.3**	**36.6**	**11.2**	**53.3**	**34.9**	**59.6**	**42.3**	**32.8**
Grade 9	60.5	40.5	9.2	67.8	47.8	61.6	43.0	34.6
Grade 10	57.2	34.6	11.2	55.3	35.6	61.3	44.9	32.4
Grade 11	56.8	37.0	11.7	46.9	29.6	59.5	42.4	32.3
Grade 12	53.9	33.5	13.0	40.6	24.4	55.5	38.4	31.9
Female	**37.3**	**17.7**	**19.2**	**42.8**	**24.0**	**48.5**	**40.4**	**32.2**
Grade 9	40.7	20.1	15.5	60.8	36.5	51.2	46.5	35.3
Grade 10	40.7	20.5	17.6	45.5	26.5	55.4	41.0	32.2
Grade 11	33.1	14.4	21.4	32.6	15.4	44.7	37.6	30.4
Grade 12	34.1	15.3	22.6	29.9	16.1	41.7	35.4	30.6

[1] Were physically active doing any kind of physical activity that increased their heart rate and made them breathe hard some of the time for a total of at least 60 minutes/day for at least 5 or more days out of the 7 days preceding the survey. [2] Participated in 60 or more minutes of any kind of physical activity that increased their heart rate and made them breathe hard some of the time on all 7 days before the survey. [3] Did not participate in 60 or more minutes of any kind of physical activity that increased their heart rate and made them breathe hard some of the time on at least 1 day during the 7 days before the survey. [4] On one or more days in an average week when they were in school. [5] Five days in an average week when they were in school. [6] Run by their school or community groups during the 12 months before the survey. [7] Played video or computer games or used computer for something that was not school work on an average school day. [8] On an average school day.

Source: U.S. Centers for Disease Control and Prevention, *Morbidity and Mortality Weekly Report, Surveillance Summaries*, 63:4, June 13, 2014, "Youth Risk Behavior Surveillance—United States, 2013." See also <http://www.cdc.gov/HealthyYouth/yrbs/index.htm>.

Table 239. Prevalence of Allergies Among Children by Allergy Type and Age, Race/Ethnicity, and Poverty Status: 2002 to 2013

[In percent; three-year annual averages. Data shown for children age 17 years and under. Based on the Sample Child component of the National Health Interview Survey of the civilian noninstitutionalized population. A parent or responsible adult for the sample child answered questions to estimate the prevalence of allergic conditions. See source for more information]

Age, race/ethnicity, and poverty status	Hay fever/respiratory allergy				Food allergy				Skin allergy			
	2002-2004	2005-2007	2008-2010	2011-2013	2002-2004	2005-2007	2008-2010	2011-2013	2002-2004	2005-2007	2008-2010	2011-2013
BY AGE												
Total 17 years and under [1]	**16.8**	**16.1**	**17.0**	**16.5**	**3.8**	**3.9**	**4.8**	**5.6**	**9.9**	**8.9**	**12.0**	**12.2**
Age 4 and under	10.8	9.3	10.6	10.6	4.1	4.7	5.2	5.6	11.7	10.9	13.4	14.1
Age 5 to 17	19.1	18.7	19.6	18.8	3.7	3.7	4.6	5.6	9.2	8.1	11.4	11.5
5 to 9 years old	17.3	16.0	17.8	16.6	3.8	3.7	4.7	6.0	9.9	9.1	13.0	12.5
10 to 17 years old	20.1	20.3	20.7	20.2	3.7	3.6	4.6	5.3	8.8	7.6	10.4	10.8
BY RACE/ETHNICITY AND AGE												
White:												
Age 17 and under	17.3	17.1	17.5	16.8	3.8	3.7	4.6	5.3	9.1	8.4	10.9	10.9
4 years and under	10.8	9.6	10.7	10.3	4.1	4.4	4.9	5.4	10.5	9.7	11.7	12.4
5 to 17 years	19.8	19.9	20.1	19.2	3.7	3.5	4.4	5.3	8.6	8.0	10.5	10.3
Black:												
Age 17 and under	15.7	12.1	15.2	15.4	3.6	3.9	5.2	6.6	13.8	10.9	16.5	17.5
4 years and under	11.7	8.5	10.4	12.7	2.6	4.9	4.9	6.3	14.9	17.1	20.2	20.9
5 to 17 years	17.1	13.5	17.1	16.5	4.0	3.5	5.3	6.7	13.4	8.6	15.0	16.2
American Indian/Alaska Native:												
Age 17 and under	16.6	(S)	15.4	14.9	(S)	(S)	6.2	5.1	(S)	(S)	9.4	11.6
4 years and under	(S)	(S)	(S)	(S)	(S)	(S)	(S)	(S)	(S)	(S)	(S)	(S)
5 to 17 years	16.9	(S)	18.4	15.1	(S)	(S)	6.0	6.5	(S)	(S)	10.2	10.5
Asian:												
Age 17 and under	8.1	13.1	13.1	14.1	3.9	4.3	5.2	6.2	9.2	7.0	11.6	11.9
4 years and under	(S)	11.7	8.6	6.5	(S)	(S)	6.1	6.3	17.4	8.8	11.7	12.1
5 to 17 years	9.1	13.6	14.7	16.8	(S)	4.1	4.9	6.1	6.8	6.3	11.5	11.9
Multiracial (more than one race):												
Age 17 and under	21.3	19.8	20.4	18.8	4.7	6.5	5.9	6.5	13.2	13.2	16.6	16.5
4 years and under	11.7	(S)	12.4	11.0	(S)	(S)	5.6	6.3	19.9	12.1	17.0	19.1
5 to 17 years	26.4	26.9	24.5	22.4	(S)	(S)	6.0	6.6	9.6	13.7	16.3	15.3
Hispanic:												
Age 17 and under	12.4	11.9	12.1	13.2	2.9	3.1	3.6	4.4	7.7	7.4	9.4	10.1
4 years and under	9.4	7.7	9.3	8.8	2.9	3.1	3.5	4.2	8.5	7.6	9.8	11.2
5 to 17 years	13.7	13.8	13.4	15.1	2.8	3.2	3.7	4.4	7.3	7.3	9.2	9.6
Non-Hispanic:												
Age 17 and under	17.9	17.2	18.4	17.6	4.1	4.2	5.1	6.0	10.5	9.3	12.7	12.9
4 years and under	11.2	9.8	11.0	11.2	4.4	5.1	5.7	6.1	12.6	11.9	14.6	15.1
5 to 17 years	20.3	19.9	21.2	19.9	3.9	3.8	4.9	5.9	9.7	8.3	12.0	12.1
BY POVERTY STATUS AND AGE												
Poor: [2]												
Age 17 and under	12.9	12.6	13.9	14.3	3.2	3.2	3.8	5.8	9.8	8.6	12.5	12.9
4 years and under	10.5	8.7	10.8	10.5	3.3	4.5	4.2	5.8	8.9	10.2	12.1	14.2
5 to 17 years	14.1	14.6	15.5	16.2	3.1	2.5	3.7	5.8	10.3	7.8	12.7	12.2
Near poor: [3]												
Age 17 and under	16.5	14.2	15.3	15.0	4.3	4.0	4.6	5.5	9.3	9.2	11.3	12.6
4 years and under	11.0	8.1	9.6	10.0	4.7	3.9	3.8	4.9	10.7	11.7	12.6	14.3
5 to 17 years	18.6	17.0	17.6	16.8	4.1	4.0	4.9	5.7	8.7	8.0	10.7	12.0
Not poor: [4]												
Age 17 and under	18.1	17.9	18.9	18.1	3.8	4.2	5.2	5.6	10.2	8.9	12.1	11.8
4 years and under	10.9	10.2	10.9	10.8	4.1	5.2	6.3	5.8	13.2	10.7	14.3	14.0
5 to 17 years	20.6	20.4	21.7	20.6	3.7	3.9	4.9	5.5	9.1	8.3	11.3	11.0

S Prevalence rates with standard error over 30% or based on fewer than 25 interviews. [1] Total includes children of all racial/ethnic groups, including those not shown separately. [2] Data from families below 100% of Federal poverty level. [3] Data from families at 100% to less than 200% of Federal poverty level. [4] Data from families at and over 200% of Federal poverty level.

Source: U.S. National Center for Health Statistics, National Health Interview Surveys, "Health Data Interactive," <http://www.cdc.gov/nchs/hdi.htm>, accessed February 2015.

Table 240. Beverage Availability for Consumption Per Capita by Commodity: 1980 to 2012

[In gallons. See headnote, Table 242. Per capita consumption uses U.S. resident population, July 1, for all beverages except coffee, tea, and fruit juices which use U.S. total population (resident plus Armed Forces overseas), as of July 1]

Beverages	1980	1990	1995	2000	2005	2009	2010	2011	2012
Nonalcoholic	104.0	112.6	107.6	114.8	(NA)	(NA)	(NA)	(NA)	(NA)
Milk (plain and flavored)	27.5	25.6	23.9	22.5	21.0	20.6	20.3	19.8	19.6
Whole	17.0	10.5	8.6	8.0	6.9	5.9	5.6	5.5	5.4
Other [1]	10.5	15.2	15.3	14.4	14.0	14.7	14.7	14.3	14.1
Tea	7.3	6.9	7.9	7.8	8.0	9.0	9.2	9.3	8.9
Coffee	26.7	26.8	20.2	26.3	24.2	23.3	23.5	24.7	24.7
Carbonated soft drinks [2]	35.1	46.2	47.4	49.3	(NA)	(NA)	(NA)	(NA)	(NA)
Diet	5.1	10.7	10.9	11.6	(NA)	(NA)	(NA)	(NA)	(NA)
Regular	29.9	35.6	36.5	37.7	(NA)	(NA)	(NA)	(NA)	(NA)
Fruit juices	7.4	7.0	8.1	8.9	8.1	7.4	7.2	7.0	6.0

NA Not available. [1] Includes buttermilk. [2] Data for carbonated soft drinks through 2003 are from the Census of Manufactures.

Source: U.S. Department of Agriculture, Economic Research Service, "Food Availability (Per Capita) Data System," <http://www.ers.usda.gov/data-products/food-availability-(per-capita)-data-system.aspx>, accessed February 2015.

Table 241. Fruit and Vegetable Availability for Consumption Per Capita by Commodity: 1980 to 2012

[In pounds, farm weight. Available supply of fresh fruits and vegetables at the farm level or early stage of processing for domestic consumption after subtracting measurable uses, such as farm inputs (feed and seed), exports, ending stocks, and industrial uses. Food availability is a popular proxy for actual food consumption. Based on Census Bureau estimated resident population plus Armed Forces overseas for most commodities]

Commodity	1980	1990	1995	2000	2005	2009	2010	2011	2012
Fruits and vegetables, total [1]	**603.7**	**649.1**	**688.3**	**711.1**	**684.5**	**645.9**	**653.5**	**637.6**	**639.6**
Fruits, total	**265.8**	**257.9**	**274.7**	**286.8**	**270.5**	**253.9**	**256.6**	**253.9**	**244.7**
Fresh fruits	106.5	117.0	123.4	128.8	125.3	124.4	128.8	129.8	131.0
Noncitrus [2]	80.5	95.6	99.6	105.3	103.7	103.7	107.4	107.3	107.6
Apples	19.4	19.8	18.9	17.6	16.8	16.4	15.4	15.5	16.1
Avocados	2.1	1.4	1.6	2.2	3.5	4.3	4.1	5.1	5.3
Bananas	20.8	24.3	27.1	28.4	25.2	22.0	25.6	25.5	25.4
Blueberries	0.2	0.1	0.3	0.3	0.4	1.0	1.1	1.3	1.3
Cantaloupes	5.8	9.2	9.0	11.1	9.6	9.1	8.5	8.7	7.6
Cherries	0.7	0.4	0.3	0.6	0.9	1.6	1.3	1.3	1.5
Grapes	4.0	7.9	7.5	7.5	8.7	8.0	8.2	7.7	7.9
Honeydew melons	1.4	2.1	1.9	2.3	1.9	1.6	1.6	1.6	1.5
Mangoes	0.2	0.5	1.1	1.8	1.9	2.0	2.2	2.5	2.5
Papayas	0.2	0.2	0.4	0.7	0.9	1.2	1.2	1.0	1.0
Peaches and nectarines	7.1	5.5	5.3	5.3	4.8	4.4	4.7	4.5	3.9
Pears	2.6	3.3	3.4	3.4	2.9	3.2	2.9	3.2	2.8
Pineapples	1.5	2.0	1.9	3.2	4.9	5.1	5.7	5.7	6.4
Plums and prunes	1.5	1.5	0.9	1.2	1.1	0.7	0.8	0.9	0.6
Strawberries	2.0	3.3	4.1	4.9	5.9	7.2	7.3	7.4	7.8
Watermelons	10.7	13.3	15.2	13.8	13.5	14.9	15.7	14.2	14.8
Fresh citrus	26.1	21.4	23.8	23.5	21.6	20.7	21.4	22.5	23.4
Oranges and temples	14.3	12.4	11.8	11.7	11.4	9.1	9.7	10.0	10.7
Tangerines and tangelos	2.2	1.3	2.0	2.9	2.5	3.2	3.8	4.0	4.0
Lemons	1.9	2.6	2.8	2.4	2.9	3.1	2.7	3.3	3.8
Limes	0.4	0.7	1.2	1.4	2.1	2.5	2.6	2.5	2.6
Grapefruit	7.3	4.4	6.0	5.1	2.6	2.8	2.8	2.7	2.4
Processed fruit	159.3	141.0	151.3	158.0	145.2	129.5	127.7	124.1	113.7
Canned fruit [3]	24.6	21.0	17.3	17.6	16.7	15.5	15.0	14.3	13.8
Fruit juice [4]	119.3	103.1	116.5	124.9	112.6	99.4	97.7	95.0	85.2
Frozen fruit [5]	3.4	4.3	4.3	4.6	5.2	4.9	5.0	4.9	4.9
Dried fruit [6]	11.3	12.2	12.8	10.5	10.1	9.0	9.4	9.3	9.3
Vegetables, total [7]	**337.9**	**391.2**	**413.6**	**424.3**	**414.1**	**392.1**	**396.9**	**383.7**	**394.8**
Fresh vegetables [7]	151.8	176.4	188.1	200.8	196.6	185.9	190.5	187.3	191.7
Asparagus	0.3	0.6	0.6	1.0	1.1	1.3	1.4	1.4	1.4
Bell peppers (all uses)	2.9	5.9	7.0	8.2	9.2	9.8	10.3	10.6	11.7
Broccoli	1.4	3.4	4.3	5.9	5.3	6.2	5.6	5.9	6.3
Cabbage	8.0	8.3	8.1	8.9	7.8	7.3	7.5	6.9	6.7
Carrots	6.2	8.3	11.2	9.2	8.7	7.4	7.8	7.5	7.8
Cauliflower	1.1	2.2	1.6	1.7	1.8	1.7	1.3	1.2	1.2
Celery (all uses)	7.4	7.2	6.9	6.3	5.9	6.2	6.1	6.0	6.0
Corn (sweet)	6.5	6.7	7.8	9.0	8.7	9.2	9.2	8.9	9.8
Cucumbers	3.9	4.7	5.6	6.4	6.2	6.8	6.7	6.4	7.7
Garlic (all uses)	0.9	1.3	1.8	2.2	2.4	2.4	2.3	2.3	2.3
Lettuce, head	25.6	27.7	22.2	23.5	20.9	16.1	15.9	15.8	14.2
Lettuce, Romaine and leaf	(NA)	3.8	5.9	8.4	9.7	10.0	12.0	11.7	11.5
Mushrooms	1.2	2.0	2.0	2.6	2.6	2.4	2.6	2.8	2.8
Onions	11.4	15.1	17.8	18.9	20.9	19.6	19.6	19.1	19.8
Potatoes	51.1	46.7	49.2	47.1	41.3	36.6	36.8	34.1	35.5
Pumpkin (all uses)	(NA)	4.5	6.0	4.7	4.9	4.1	4.5	4.5	5.3
Snap beans	1.3	1.1	1.6	2.0	1.8	1.7	1.9	2.0	2.0
Spinach	0.4	0.8	0.7	1.4	2.3	2.1	1.7	1.8	1.5
Squash (all uses)	2.3	3.5	3.8	4.5	4.4	4.4	4.3	4.5	4.7
Sweet potatoes (all uses)	4.4	4.4	4.2	4.2	4.5	5.3	6.3	7.1	6.9
Tomatoes	12.8	15.5	16.8	19.0	20.2	19.6	20.6	20.4	20.4
Processed vegetables	186.2	214.8	225.4	223.5	217.5	206.2	206.4	196.4	203.2
Vegetables for canning [8]	102.5	110.3	108.2	103.2	104.9	100.7	99.4	91.5	93.0
Vegetables for freezing [9]	51.6	66.7	78.8	79.7	76.4	71.7	71.5	70.2	72.2
Vegetables for dehydrating [10]	10.5	14.7	14.5	17.3	13.9	13.7	12.5	11.9	14.5
Potatoes for chips	16.5	16.3	16.1	15.6	16.0	13.7	15.0	16.8	16.8
Legumes [11]	5.1	6.8	7.7	7.8	6.2	6.4	8.0	6.0	6.7

NA Not available. [1] Excludes wine grapes. [2] Includes other fruits not shown separately. [3] Canned fruit include apples, apricots, cherries, olives, peaches, pears, pineapples, plums, and prunes. [4] Fruit juice includes apple, cranberry, grape, grapefruit, lemon, lime, orange, pineapple, and prune juice. [5] Frozen fruit include apples, apricots, blackberries, blueberries, boysenberries, cherries, loganberries, peaches, plums, prunes, raspberries, strawberries, and other miscellaneous fruit and berries. [6] Dried fruit include apples, apricots, dates, figs, peaches, pears, prunes, and raisins. [7] Includes other vegetables not shown separately. [8] Vegetables for canning include asparagus, lima beans, snap beans, beets, cabbage, carrots, sweet corn, cucumbers, mushrooms, green peas, chile peppers, potatoes, spinach, tomatoes, and other miscellaneous vegetables. [9] Vegetables for freezing include asparagus, lima beans, snap beans, broccoli, carrots, cauliflower, sweet corn, green peas, potatoes, spinach and other miscellaneous vegetables. [10] Onions and potatoes. [11] Dry peas, lentils, and dry edible beans.

Source: U.S. Department of Agriculture, Economic Research Service, "Food Availability (Per Capita) Data System," <http://www.ers.usda.gov/data-products/food-availability-(per-capita)-data-system.aspx>, accessed February 2015.

Table 242. Food Availability for Consumption Per Capita, by Major Food Commodity: 1980 to 2012

[In pounds, retail weight, except as indicated. Available supply for domestic consumption after subtracting measurable uses, such as farm inputs (feed and seed), exports, ending stocks, and industrial uses. Food availability is a proxy for actual food consumption. Based on Census Bureau estimated resident population plus Armed Forces overseas for most commodities. For commodities not shipped overseas in substantial amounts, such as fluid milk and cream, the resident population is used]

Commodity	Unit	1980	1990	2000	2005	2010	2011	2012
Red meat, total (boneless, trimmed weight) [1]..	Pounds	126.4	112.2	113.7	110.2	102.1	97.7	98.0
Beef..	Pounds	72.1	63.9	64.5	62.5	56.7	54.4	54.5
Veal..	Pounds	1.3	0.9	0.5	0.4	0.3	0.3	0.3
Lamb and mutton..............................	Pounds	1.0	1.0	0.8	0.8	0.7	0.6	0.6
Pork...	Pounds	52.1	46.4	47.8	46.6	44.4	42.4	42.6
Poultry (boneless, trimmed weight)............	Pounds	40.8	56.2	67.9	73.7	70.9	71.0	69.2
Chicken..	Pounds	32.7	42.4	54.2	60.5	58.0	58.4	56.6
Turkey..	Pounds	8.1	13.8	13.7	13.2	12.9	12.6	12.6
Fish and shellfish (boneless, trimmed weight)..	Pounds	12.4	14.9	15.2	16.2	15.8	14.9	14.2
Eggs...	Number	271.1	234.1	251.1	255.9	246.5	246.0	249.5
Shell..	Number	236.2	186.2	177.9	176.8	171.0	171.2	173.8
Processed...	Number	34.9	47.9	73.2	79.1	75.5	74.8	75.7
Dairy products, total [2]...........................	Pounds	543.1	568.0	591.9	603.4	603.2	603.1	611.0
Fluid milk products [3]...........................	Gallons	27.8	26.1	23.2	22.2	21.9	21.3	21.2
Beverage milks................................	Gallons	27.5	25.6	22.5	21.0	20.3	19.8	19.6
Plain whole milk............................	Gallons	16.4	10.2	7.7	6.6	5.4	5.3	5.2
Plain reduced-fat milk (2%)...............	Gallons	6.3	9.1	7.1	6.9	7.3	6.7	6.4
Plain reduced-fat milk (1%)...............	Gallons	1.8	2.3	2.6	2.5	2.7	3.0	3.1
Plain skim milk.............................	Gallons	1.3	2.6	3.5	3.1	3.0	2.9	2.9
Flavored whole milk........................	Gallons	0.5	0.3	0.4	0.3	0.2	0.2	0.2
Flavored milk, low-fat and skim...........	Gallons	0.6	0.8	1.0	1.4	1.6	1.5	1.5
Buttermilk....................................	Gallons	0.5	0.4	0.3	0.2	0.2	0.3	0.3
Yogurt (excl. frozen).........................	1/2 pints	4.6	7.8	12.0	19.1	24.9	25.3	26.0
Fluid cream products [4]......................	1/2 pints	10.5	14.3	18.3	24.0	24.0	23.6	21.6
Cream [5]..	1/2 pints	6.3	8.7	11.6	14.9	15.3	15.0	13.2
Sour cream and dips.........................	1/2 pints	3.4	4.7	6.1	8.3	7.9	7.8	7.6
Condensed and evaporated milks............	Pounds	7.0	7.9	5.8	5.9	7.0	7.0	7.4
Whole milk....................................	Pounds	3.8	3.1	2.0	2.2	1.8	1.8	2.1
Skim milk.....................................	Pounds	3.3	4.8	3.8	3.7	5.2	5.2	5.3
Cheese [6]......................................	Pounds	17.5	24.6	29.8	32.5	32.9	33.0	33.5
American [7]..................................	Pounds	9.6	11.1	12.7	13.5	13.3	13.0	13.2
Cheddar......................................	Pounds	6.8	9.1	9.8	11.0	10.0	9.6	9.4
Italian [7]......................................	Pounds	4.4	9.0	12.0	13.2	14.4	14.9	14.9
Mozzarella....................................	Pounds	3.0	6.9	9.3	10.2	11.2	11.5	11.5
Other [7].....................................	Pounds	3.4	4.5	5.2	5.9	5.2	5.3	5.4
Swiss..	Pounds	1.3	1.4	1.0	1.2	1.2	1.2	1.1
Cream and Neufchatel......................	Pounds	1.0	1.7	2.4	2.4	2.4	2.3	2.6
Cottage cheese, total........................	Pounds	4.4	3.3	2.6	2.6	2.3	2.3	2.6
low-fat......................................	Pounds	0.8	1.2	1.3	1.4	1.3	1.2	1.2
Frozen dairy products........................	Pounds	23.9	26.1	28.1	24.8	23.7	23.0	23.9
Ice cream....................................	Pounds	16.4	14.8	15.6	14.6	13.5	12.8	12.9
Low-fat ice cream..........................	Pounds	5.8	6.3	6.4	5.8	6.5	6.2	6.9
Sherbet......................................	Pounds	1.2	1.2	1.1	1.1	1.0	0.9	0.9
Frozen yogurt...............................	Pounds	(NA)	2.8	2.0	1.3	1.0	1.2	1.4
Fats and oils:								
Total, fat content only........................	Pounds	55.6	60.6	81.7	85.5	82.2	(NA)	(NA)
Butter (product weight)......................	Pounds	4.5	4.4	4.5	4.6	5.0	5.4	5.6
Margarine (product weight).................	Pounds	11.3	10.9	8.2	4.0	3.5	(NA)	(NA)
Lard (direct use).............................	Pounds	2.3	0.9	0.8	1.6	1.5	(NA)	(NA)
Edible beef tallow (direct use)..............	Pounds	1.1	0.6	4.0	3.8	3.3	(NA)	(NA)
Shortening...................................	Pounds	16.9	20.6	31.5	29.0	15.3	(NA)	(NA)
Salad and cooking oils......................	Pounds	21.2	25.1	33.7	42.7	53.6	(NA)	(NA)
Other edible fats and oils...................	Pounds	1.5	1.2	1.5	1.6	1.7	(NA)	(NA)
Flour and cereal products [8]...................	Pounds	146.4	181.1	199.5	190.9	194.7	[11] 173.1	[11] 174.7
Wheat flour....................................	Pounds	116.9	135.6	146.3	134.4	134.8	132.5	134.4
Rice, milled....................................	Pounds	11.0	16.2	19.2	19.4	20.4	(NA)	(NA)
Corn products.................................	Pounds	12.9	21.4	28.4	31.4	33.1	34.1	33.9
Oat products...................................	Pounds	3.9	6.5	4.4	4.6	5.2	5.3	5.2
Caloric sweeteners, total [9]...................	Pounds	120.2	132.3	148.7	141.9	131.4	130.3	129.5
Sugar, refined cane and beet...............	Pounds	83.6	64.4	65.5	63.0	65.9	66.8	66.3
Corn sweeteners [10].........................	Pounds	35.3	66.8	81.4	77.2	63.8	61.7	61.4
High-fructose corn syrup....................	Pounds	19.0	49.6	62.3	58.7	48.3	46.6	46.2
Honey...	Pounds	0.8	0.7	1.1	1.1	1.0	1.1	1.1
Other:								
Cocoa, bean equivalent......................	Pounds	3.4	5.4	5.9	6.5	5.5	5.5	5.2
Coffee, green bean equivalent..............	Pounds	10.3	10.3	10.3	9.5	9.2	9.6	9.7
Tea, dry leaf equivalent......................	Pounds	0.8	0.7	0.8	0.8	1.0	1.0	0.9
Peanuts, total.................................	Pounds	5.1	6.1	5.9	6.7	7.0	7.0	6.7
Tree nuts, total................................	Pounds	1.8	2.5	2.6	2.7	3.9	3.8	4.2

NA Not available. [1] Excludes edible offal. [2] Milk-equivalent. Includes fluid milk and cream, butter, cheese, frozen and dry dairy products, and evaporated and condensed milk. [3] Fluid milk figures are aggregates of commercial sales and milk produced and consumed on farms. [4] Includes eggnog, not shown separately. [5] Heavy cream, light cream, and half-and-half. [6] Excludes full-skim American, cottage, pot, and baker's cheese. [7] Includes other cheeses, not shown separately. [8] Includes rye flour and barley products, not shown separately. Excludes quantities used in alcoholic beverages. [9] Dry weight. Includes edible syrups (maple, molasses, etc.), not shown separately. [10] Includes glucose and dextrose, not shown separately. [11] Does not include rice.

Source: U.S. Department of Agriculture, Economic Research Service, "Food Availability (Per Capita) Data System," <http://www.ers.usda. gov/data-products/food-availability-(per-capita)-data-system.aspx>, accessed February 2015.

Table 243. Nutrition—Nutrients in Foods Available for Civilian Consumption Per Capita Per Day: 1970 to 2010

[Computed by the Center for Nutrition Policy and Promotion (CNPP), using food availability data from the Economic Research Service, and nutrient composition of foods data from the Agricultural Research Service. Data represent nutrients in foods available for consumption, not actual nutrient intake, and do not account for nutrient losses from trimming, cooking, plate waste, and spoilage. Includes nutrients added to certain commodities commercially through fortification and enrichment]

Nutrient	Unit	1970	1980	1990	2000	2010
Food energy..........................	Kilocalories	3,300	3,500	3,800	4,200	4,000
Carbohydrate......................	Grams	401	408	468	505	474
Protein...............................	Grams	98	111	118	124	120
Total fat [1]...........................	Grams	147	162	167	191	190
Saturated..........................	Grams	52	56	56	62	59
Monounsaturated...............	Grams	58	65	68	83	77
Polyunsaturated.................	Grams	25	29	32	37	44
Cholesterol........................	Milligrams	470	490	460	470	460
Fiber................................	Grams	19	20	24	25	25
Vitamin A...........................	Micrograms RAE [2]	1,040	1,060	1,080	1,100	920
Carotene...........................	Micrograms	480	580	640	670	630
Vitamin E...........................	Milligrams a-TE [3]	13.3	14.4	16.5	20.3	21.9
Vitamin C...........................	Milligrams	104	115	114	125	105
Thiamin.............................	Milligrams	2.0	2.6	2.9	3.1	2.9
Riboflavin..........................	Milligrams	2.4	2.9	3.2	3.2	3
Niacin...............................	Milligrams	22	30	33	35	34
Vitamin B6.........................	Milligrams	2.0	2.4	2.5	2.6	2.5
Folate [4]............................	Micrograms DFE [5]	301	375	407	916	889
Vitamin B12........................	Micrograms	9.6	10.6	10.1	10	9.3
Calcium.............................	Milligrams	990	950	1,020	1,030	1,030
Phosphorus.......................	Milligrams	1,580	1,690	1,820	1,860	1,810
Magnesium........................	Milligrams	340	350	400	410	410
Iron..................................	Milligrams	15.7	18.4	23.8	25.1	24.6
Zinc..................................	Milligrams	12.8	16.8	17.9	18.2	17.6
Copper..............................	Milligrams	1.7	1.9	2.1	2.2	2.1
Potassium.........................	Milligrams	3,610	3,740	3,910	4,030	3,760
Selenium...........................	Micrograms	129	150	162	191	187
Sodium [6]...........................	Milligrams	1,230	1,260	1,310	1,300	1,210

[1] Includes other types of fat not shown separately. [2] Retinol activity equivalents. [3] Alpha-Tocopherol equivalents. [4] Reflects new terminology from Institute of Medicine's Dietary Reference Intakes reports. [5] Dietary Folate Equivalents (DFE). [6] Does not include amount from processed foods; underestimates actual availability.

Source: U.S. Department of Agriculture, Economic Research Service, "Food Availability (Per Capita) Data System, Nutrient Availability," <http://www.ers.usda.gov/data-products/food-availability-(per-capita)-data-system.aspx>, accessed September 2015.

Education

This section presents data primarily concerning formal education as a whole, at various levels, and for public and private schools. Data shown relate to the school-age population and school enrollment, educational attainment, education personnel, and financial aspects of education. In addition, data are shown for charter schools, homeschooling, post-secondary education, security measures used in schools, and academic libraries. The chief sources are the decennial census of population and the Current Population Survey (CPS), both conducted by the U.S. Census Bureau (see text, Section 1, Population); annual, biennial, and other periodic surveys conducted by the National Center for Education Statistics (NCES), a part of the U.S. Department of Education; and surveys conducted by the National Education Association.

The censuses of population have included data on school enrollment since 1840 and on educational attainment since 1940. The CPS has reported on school enrollment annually and on educational attainment periodically since 1947.

The NCES is continuing the pattern of statistical studies and surveys conducted by the U.S. Office of Education since 1870. The annual *Digest of Education Statistics* provides summary data on pupils, staff, finances, including government expenditures, and organization at the elementary, secondary, and higher education levels. It is also a primary source for detailed information on federal funds for education, projections of enrollment, graduates, and teachers. The *Condition of Education*, issued annually, presents a summary of information on education of particular interest to policymakers. NCES also conducts special studies periodically.

The census of governments, conducted by the Census Bureau every 5 years (for the years ending in "2" and "7"), provides data on school district finances and state and local government expenditures for education. Reports published by the Bureau of Labor Statistics contain data relating civilian labor force experience to educational attainment (see also Tables 611, 639, and 646 in Section 12, Labor Force, Employment, and Earnings).

Types and sources of data—The statistics in this section are of two general types. One type, exemplified by data from the Census Bureau, is based on direct interviews with individuals to obtain information about their own and their family members' education. Data of this type relate to school enrollment and level of education attained, classified by age, sex, and other characteristics of the population. The school enrollment statistics reflect attendance or enrollment in any regular school within a given period; educational attainment statistics reflect the highest grade completed by an individual, or beginning 1992, the highest diploma or degree received.

Beginning in 2012, CPS estimates reflect population controls based on Census 2010. From 2000–2011, the CPS used Census 2000 population controls. From 1994 to 2000, the CPS used 1990 census population controls plus adjustment for undercount. Also

beginning 1994, the survey is conducted through computer-assisted technology rather than by paper forms. For years 1981 through 1993, 1980 census population controls were used; 1971 through 1980, 1970 census population controls had been used. These changes had little impact on summary measures (e.g., medians) and proportional measures (e.g., enrollment rates); however, use of the controls may have significant impact on absolute numbers.

The second type of data, generally exemplified by data from the NCES and the National Education Association, is based on reports from administrators of educational institutions and of state and local agencies having jurisdiction over education. Data of this type relate to enrollment, attendance, staff, and finances for the nation, individual states, and local areas.

Unlike the NCES, the Census Bureau does not regularly include specialized vocational, trade, business, or correspondence schools in its surveys. The NCES includes nursery schools and kindergartens that are part of regular grade schools in their enrollment figures. The Census Bureau includes all nursery schools and kindergartens. At the higher education level, the statistics of both agencies are concerned with institutions granting degrees or offering work acceptable for degree-credit, such as junior colleges.

School attendance—All states require that children attend school. While state laws vary as to the ages and circumstances of compulsory attendance, generally they require that formal schooling begin by age 6 and continue to age 16.

Schools—The NCES defines a school as "a division of the school system consisting of students composing one or more grade groups or other identifiable groups, organized as one unit with one or more teachers to give instruction of a defined type, and housed in a school plant of one or more buildings. More than one school may be housed in one school plant, as is the case when the elementary and secondary programs are housed in the same school plant."

Regular schools are those which advance a person toward a diploma or degree. They include public and private nursery schools, kindergartens, graded schools, colleges, universities, and professional schools.

Public schools are schools controlled and supported by local, state, or federal governmental agencies. *Private* schools are those controlled and supported mainly by religious organizations or by private persons or organizations.

The Census Bureau defines *elementary* schools as including grades 1 through 8; *high* schools as including grades 9 through 12; and *colleges* as including junior or community colleges, regular 4-year colleges, and universities and graduate or professional schools. Statistics reported by the NCES and the National Education Association by type of organization, such as elementary level and secondary level, may not be strictly comparable with those from the Census Bureau because the grades included at the two levels vary, depending on the level assigned to the middle or junior high school by the local school systems.

School year—Except as otherwise indicated in the tables, data refer to the school year which, for elementary and secondary schools, generally begins in September of the preceding year and ends in June of the year stated. For the most part, statistics concerning school finances are for a 12-month period, usually July 1 to June 30. Enrollment data generally refer to a specific point in time, such as Fall, as indicated in the tables.

Statistical reliability—For a discussion of statistical collection, estimation, and sampling procedures and measures of statistical reliability applicable to the Census Bureau and the NCES data, see Appendix III.

Table 244. Federal Funds for Education and Related Programs: 2010 to 2014

[In millions of dollars (183,199,700,000), except percent. For fiscal years ending in September. Figures represent on-budget funds]

Level, agency, and program	2010	2013 [1]	2014 [1]
Total, all programs	**183,199.7**	**183,367.5**	**179,342.4**
Percent of federal budget outlays	5.3	5.3	5.1
Elementary/secondary education programs	**86,681.8**	**79,131.2**	**80,072.3**
Department of Education [2]	49,621.5	38,705.9	37,772.0
Grants for the disadvantaged	15,864.7	15,590.7	15,552.7
School improvement programs	16,999.9	6,543.6	5,883.4
Indian education	127.3	131.6	123.9
Special education	12,587.0	12,661.3	12,497.3
Vocational and adult education	2,016.4	1,742.9	1,702.7
Education reform—Goals 2000	(X)	(X)	(X)
Department of Agriculture [2]	17,875.6	21,781.4	21,895.2
Child nutrition programs	16,383.4	20,487.2	20,487.3
Agricultural Marketing Service—commodities [3]	1,100.0	903.0	1,032.0
Department of Defense [2]	1,981.3	2,220.6	2,262.1
Overseas dependents schools	1,186.6	1,262.5	1,235.3
Section VI schools [4]	435.1	550.7	576.5
Department of Health and Human Services	8,547.0	9,428.3	10,900.5
Head Start	7,234.0	8,107.0	9,621.0
Social security student benefits	1,313.0	1,321.3	1,279.5
Department of Homeland Security	0.5	0.4	0.5
Department of the Interior [2]	781.1	760.8	765.7
Mineral Leasing Act and other funds	73.0	78.7	75.7
Indian Education	707.1	681.1	689.0
Department of Justice	137.5	160.7	151.6
Inmate programs	(X)	(X)	(X)
Department of Labor	6,826.0	5,347.0	5,564.1
Job Corps	1,850.0	1,650.0	1,691.1
Department of Veterans Affairs	760.5	534.8	574.0
Vocational rehab for disabled veterans	760.5	534.8	574.0
Other agencies and programs	150.8	191.4	186.6
Higher education programs	**50,197.8**	**62,784.2**	**56,953.7**
Department of Education [2]	36,539.7	46,131.4	38,981.6
Student financial assistance	25,959.5	37,319.3	31,092.5
Federal Family Education Loans	3,933.0	2,787.8	2,269.3
Department of Agriculture	80.7	79.1	84.4
Department of Commerce	(NA)	(NA)	(NA)
Department of Defense	2,550.7	2,421.0	2,435.3
Tuition assistance for military personnel	669.9	564.6	524.7
Service academies [5]	402.6	372.7	372.7
Senior ROTC	885.5	843.0	885.7
Professional development education	592.6	640.6	652.1
Department of Health and Human Services [2]	1,278.9	1,295.6	1,339.5
Health professions training programs	406.0	438.0	469.2
National Health Service Corps scholarships	41.0	39.9	42.6
National Institutes of Health training grants [6]	775.2	766.0	776.0
Department of Homeland Security	45.8	43.5	36.5
Department of the Interior	174.1	107.5	109.5
Shared revenues, Mineral Leasing Act and other receipts—estimated education share	16.3	20.3	19.5
Indian programs	157.8	87.2	90.0
Department of State	657.7	605.6	584.1
Department of Transportation	95.0	130.0	98.4
Department of Veterans Affairs [2]	8,042.4	11,162.8	12,231.7
Post-Vietnam veterans	0.9	0.8	0.8
All-volunteer-force educational assistance	1,854.9	885.7	746.9
Other agencies and programs [2]	732.9	807.8	1,052.5
National Endowment for the Humanities	47.9	39.4	39.8
National Science Foundation	646.0	709.7	950.3
Other education programs [2]	**9,326.7**	**9,727.8**	**9,454.9**
Department of Education [2]	5,073.1	5,696.2	5,420.1
Administration	1,531.2	2,048.1	1,972.0
Rehabilitative services and handicapped research	3,506.9	3,622.9	3,422.7
Department of Agriculture	567.4	550.0	535.9
Department of Health and Human Services	340.0	339.7	382.3
Department of Homeland Security	341.1	258.0	259.0
Department of Justice	33.6	30.2	31.0
Department of State	120.5	219.2	217.4
Other agencies and programs [2]	2,850.9	2,634.5	2,609.1
Agency for International Development	542.7	602.4	562.7
Library of Congress	516.0	470.2	485.8
National Endowment for the Arts	2.9	3.5	4.5
National Endowment for the Humanities	94.6	74.4	77.5
Research programs at universities and related institutions [2]	**36,993.3**	**31,724.3**	**32,861.6**
Department of Agriculture	737.2	843.9	804.8
Department of Defense	3,154.3	2,440.5	2,574.1
Department of Energy	3,402.6	2,704.2	3,159.5
Department of Health and Human Services	21,796.2	17,744.0	17,891.1
National Aeronautics and Space Administration	1,585.5	2,189.8	2,159.9
National Science Foundation	4,914.7	4,627.7	5,038.8

NA Not available. X Not applicable. [1] Data for research programs at universities and related institutions are estimated. [2] Includes other programs and agencies, not shown separately. [3] Purchased under Section 32 of the Act of August 1935 for use in child nutrition programs. [4] Program provides for the education of dependents of federal employees residing on federal property where free public education is unavailable in the nearby community. [5] Instructional costs only including academics, audiovisual, academic computer center, faculty training, military training, physical education, and libraries. [6] Includes alcohol, drug abuse, and mental health training programs.

Source: U.S. National Center for Education Statistics, *Digest of Education Statistics*, "Advance Release of Selected 2014 Digest Tables," <http://www.nces.ed.gov/programs/digest/>, accessed September 2015.

Table 245. School Expenditures by Type of Control and Level of Instruction in Current and Constant (2013 to 2014) Dollars: 1980 to 2014

[In millions of dollars (160,075 represents $160,075,000,000). For school years ending in year shown. Data shown reflect historical revisions. Total expenditures for public elementary and secondary schools include current expenditures, interest on school debt, and capital outlay. Based on survey of state education agencies; see source for details]

Year	Current dollars			Constant 2013-14 dollars [1]			
		Elementary and secondary schools	Colleges and universities [2]		Elementary and secondary schools		Colleges and universities [2]
	Total			Total	Total	Public	
1980................	160,075	103,162	56,914	484,487	312,231	290,440	172,256
1985................	239,351	149,400	89,951	531,729	331,899	304,351	199,831
1990................	365,825	231,170	134,656	676,956	427,777	393,728	249,179
1995................	485,169	302,200	182,969	757,926	472,095	435,852	285,832
1998................	570,471	361,615	[3] 208,856	828,735	525,326	485,666	[3] 303,410
1999................	603,847	384,638	219,209	862,293	549,263	508,136	313,030
2000................	649,322	412,538	236,784	901,216	572,575	529,966	328,641
2001................	705,017	444,811	260,206	946,103	596,918	551,291	349,185
2002................	752,780	472,064	280,715	992,624	622,469	574,076	370,154
2003................	795,691	492,807	302,884	1,026,646	635,847	586,947	390,798
2004................	830,293	513,542	316,751	1,048,355	648,415	598,793	399,940
2005................	875,988	540,969	335,019	1,073,740	663,091	612,345	410,649
2006................	925,246	571,669	353,577	1,092,513	675,016	623,770	417,497
2007................	984,034	608,495	375,539	1,132,638	700,387	647,095	432,251
2008................	1,054,904	646,414	408,490	1,170,827	717,448	662,953	453,379
2009................	1,089,670	658,926	430,744	1,192,760	721,265	668,067	471,495
2010................	1,100,902	654,418	446,484	1,193,506	709,466	658,079	484,040
2011................	1,123,565	652,356	471,209	1,194,098	693,308	642,295	500,790
2012................	1,137,011	648,567	488,444	1,173,990	669,660	621,338	504,330
2013 [4]............	1,165,000	666,000	498,939	1,183,000	676,000	629,000	507,000
2014 [3]............	1,194,000	682,000	512,000	1,194,000	682,000	635,000	512,000

[1] Constant dollars based on the Consumer Price Index, prepared by the Bureau of Labor Statistics, U.S. Department of Labor, adjusted to a school-year basis. [2] Postsecondary data through 1996 are for institutions of higher education; thereafter, data are for degree-granting institutions. See source for details. [3] Estimated. [4] Data for elementary and secondary education are estimated; data for degree-granting institutions are actual.

Source: U.S. National Center for Education Statistics, *Digest of Education Statistics*, "Advance Release of Selected 2014 Digest Tables," <http://www.nces.ed.gov/programs/digest/>, accessed September 2015.

Table 246. School Enrollment: 1980 to 2023

[In thousands (58,305 represents 58,305,000). As of Fall]

Year	All levels			Pre-kindergarten through grade 8		Grades 9 through 12		College [3]	
	Total	Public	Private	Public	Private [1,2]	Public	Private [1]	Public	Private
1980........................	58,305	50,335	7,971	27,647	3,992	13,231	1,339	9,457	2,640
1985........................	57,226	48,901	8,325	27,034	4,195	12,388	1,362	9,479	2,768
1990........................	60,683	52,061	8,622	29,876	4,512	11,341	1,136	10,845	2,974
1995........................	65,020	55,933	9,087	32,338	4,756	12,502	1,163	11,092	3,169
1996........................	65,911	56,732	9,180	32,762	4,755	12,849	1,178	11,120	3,247
1997........................	66,574	57,323	9,251	33,071	4,759	13,056	1,185	11,196	3,306
1998........................	67,033	57,676	9,357	33,344	4,776	13,195	1,212	11,138	3,369
1999........................	67,725	58,233	9,492	33,486	4,789	13,371	1,229	11,376	3,474
2000........................	68,685	58,956	9,729	33,686	4,906	13,517	1,264	11,753	3,560
2001........................	69,920	59,905	10,014	33,936	5,023	13,736	1,296	12,233	3,695
2002........................	71,015	60,935	10,080	34,114	4,915	14,069	1,306	12,752	3,860
2003........................	71,551	61,399	10,152	34,201	4,788	14,339	1,311	12,859	4,053
2004........................	72,154	61,776	10,379	34,178	4,756	14,618	1,331	12,980	4,292
2005........................	72,674	62,135	10,539	34,204	4,724	14,909	1,349	13,022	4,466
2006........................	73,066	62,496	10,570	34,235	4,631	15,081	1,360	13,180	4,579
2007........................	73,451	62,783	10,668	34,205	4,546	15,087	1,364	13,491	4,757
2008........................	74,076	63,238	10,838	34,286	4,365	14,980	1,342	13,972	5,131
2009........................	75,277	64,172	11,106	34,409	4,179	14,952	1,309	14,811	5,617
2010........................	75,883	64,627	11,256	34,625	4,084	14,860	1,299	15,143	5,873
2011........................	75,784	64,632	11,152	34,773	3,977	14,749	1,291	15,110	5,884
2012, proj [4].............	75,476	64,532	10,944	34,968	3,906	14,684	1,275	14,880	5,762
2013, proj................	75,439	64,607	10,831	35,111	3,856	14,639	1,235	14,857	5,740
2014, proj................	75,736	64,892	10,844	35,062	3,776	14,689	1,197	15,140	5,871
2015, proj................	75,997	65,159	10,838	35,069	3,741	14,770	1,150	15,319	5,947
2016, proj................	76,376	65,497	10,879	35,142	3,725	14,810	1,114	15,545	6,041
2017, proj................	77,078	66,082	10,996	35,412	3,765	14,868	1,087	15,802	6,144
2018, proj................	77,607	66,547	11,060	35,642	3,782	14,901	1,054	16,004	6,223
2019, proj................	78,183	67,042	11,140	35,878	3,809	14,957	1,027	16,208	6,304
2020, proj................	78,807	67,575	11,232	36,115	3,835	15,050	1,009	16,410	6,388
2021, proj................	79,484	68,138	11,346	36,335	3,859	15,151	998	16,652	6,489
2022, proj................	80,182	68,709	11,473	36,585	3,885	15,219	994	16,905	6,594
2023, proj................	80,857	69,256	11,601	36,967	3,920	15,146	990	17,143	6,691

[1] Since the biennial Private School Universe Survey (PSS) is collected in the fall of odd numbered years, even numbered years are estimated based on data from the PSS. [2] Includes private nursery and pre-kindergarten enrollment in schools that offer kindergarten or higher grades. [3] Data beginning 1996 based on new classification system. See footnote 1, Table 290. [4] Pre-K through 12 are projections; college data are actual.

Source: U.S. National Center for Education Statistics, *Digest of Education Statistics*, "Advance Release of Selected 2013 Digest Tables," <http://www.nces.ed.gov/programs/digest/>, accessed February 2015.

Table 247. School Enrollment, Faculty, Graduates, and Finances—Projections: 2014 to 2020

[55,053 represents 55,053,000. As of Fall, except as indicated]

Item	Unit	2014	2015	2016	2017	2018	2019	2020
ELEMENTARY AND SECONDARY SCHOOLS								
School enrollment, total	1,000	55,053	55,307	55,600	55,930	56,257	56,635	57,066
Pre-kindergarten through grade 8	1,000	39,166	39,386	39,675	39,972	40,298	40,646	40,998
Grades 9 through 12	1,000	15,887	15,922	15,926	15,958	15,959	15,989	16,068
Public	1,000	50,018	50,328	50,654	50,999	51,336	51,707	52,124
Pre-kindergarten through grade 8	1,000	35,328	35,557	35,843	36,129	36,432	36,747	37,067
Grades 9 through 12	1,000	14,689	14,771	14,811	14,870	14,903	14,960	15,057
Private	1,000	5,035	4,980	4,947	4,931	4,921	4,928	4,943
Pre-kindergarten through grade 8	1,000	3,838	3,829	3,832	3,843	3,866	3,899	3,931
Grades 9 through 12	1,000	1,197	1,151	1,114	1,088	1,056	1,029	1,011
Classroom teachers, total FTE [1]	1,000	3,524	3,577	3,625	3,676	3,724	3,773	3,830
Public	1,000	3,124	3,177	3,225	3,273	3,319	3,365	3,418
Private	1,000	400	400	401	403	405	408	412
High school graduates, total [2]	1,000	3,323	3,323	3,329	3,366	3,349	3,327	3,353
Public	1,000	3,031	3,048	3,066	3,106	3,101	3,086	3,115
Public schools: [2]								
Average daily attendance (ADA)	1,000	46,751	47,040	47,345	47,668	47,983	48,330	48,719
Current dollars: [3]								
Current school expenditure	Bil. dol.	607	634	(NA)	(NA)	(NA)	(NA)	(NA)
Per pupil in fall enrollment	Dollar	12,138	12,605	(NA)	(NA)	(NA)	(NA)	(NA)
Constant (2010–2011) dollars: [3, 4]								
Current school expenditure	Bil. dol.	579	595	610	625	640	655	670
Per pupil in fall enrollment	Dollar	11,568	11,820	12,052	12,265	12,460	12,662	12,853
HIGHER EDUCATION								
Enrollment, total	1,000	21,575	21,805	22,076	22,376	22,698	23,025	23,309
Male	1,000	9,142	9,163	9,216	9,297	9,389	9,493	9,588
Full-time	1,000	5,862	5,875	5,913	5,970	6,034	6,108	6,177
Part-time	1,000	3,281	3,288	3,303	3,326	3,355	3,385	3,411
Female	1,000	12,433	12,642	12,860	13,079	13,309	13,533	13,721
Full-time	1,000	7,436	7,524	7,619	7,718	7,833	7,960	8,070
Part-time	1,000	4,997	5,117	5,241	5,361	5,476	5,572	5,651
Public	1,000	15,509	15,671	15,863	16,077	16,308	16,545	16,751
Four-year institutions	1,000	8,264	8,345	8,443	8,551	8,668	8,790	8,896
Two-year institutions	1,000	7,245	7,326	7,420	7,526	7,640	7,755	7,855
Private	1,000	6,066	6,134	6,213	6,299	6,390	6,481	6,558
Four-year institutions	1,000	5,620	5,684	5,757	5,836	5,920	6,003	6,073
Two-year institutions	1,000	446	450	456	462	470	477	484
Undergraduate	1,000	18,467	18,639	18,848	19,086	19,349	19,634	19,887
Postbaccalaureate	1,000	3,108	3,166	3,228	3,290	3,349	3,392	3,422
Full-time equivalent	1,000	16,287	16,436	16,619	16,827	17,058	17,305	17,521
Public	1,000	11,206	11,306	11,429	11,572	11,731	11,903	12,054
2-year	1,000	4,310	4,352	4,404	4,464	4,531	4,603	4,666
4-year	1,000	6,896	6,953	7,025	7,108	7,199	7,300	7,389
Private	1,000	5,081	5,130	5,190	5,255	5,327	5,402	5,467
2-year	1,000	413	417	422	428	434	442	448
4-year	1,000	4,668	4,713	4,768	4,828	4,893	4,961	5,019
Degrees conferred, total [2]	1,000	3,936	4,009	4,095	4,172	4,257	4,344	4,434
Associate's	1,000	1,074	1,111	1,151	1,190	1,231	1,275	1,319
Bachelor's	1,000	1,851	1,861	1,882	1,895	1,913	1,934	1,958
Master's	1,000	830	852	873	895	918	938	957
Doctoral	1,000	181	185	189	192	195	197	200

NA Not available. [1] Full-time equivalent. [2] For school year ending in June the following year. [3] Limited financial projections are shown due to the uncertain behavior of inflation over the long term. [4] Based on the Consumer Price Index (CPI) for all urban consumers, U.S. Bureau of Labor Statistics. CPI adjusted to a school year basis by NCES.

Source: U.S. National Center for Education Statistics, *Projections of Education Statistics to 2022*, February 2014. See also <http://www.nces.ed.gov/>.

Table 248. School Enrollment by Control and Level: 1980 to 2014

[In thousands (58,305 represents 58,305,000). As of Fall. Data below college level are for regular day schools and exclude subcollegiate departments of colleges, federal schools, and home-schooled children. College data include degree-credit and nondegree-credit enrollment. Based on survey of state education agencies; see source for details. For more projections, see Table 246 and Table 247]

Control of school and level	1980	1990	1995	2000	2005	2010	2011	2012, proj.	2013, proj.	2014, proj.
Total	58,305	60,683	65,020	68,685	72,674	75,883	75,784	75,476	75,439	75,736
Public	50,335	52,061	55,933	58,956	62,135	64,627	64,632	64,532	64,607	64,892
Private	7,971	8,622	9,087	9,729	10,539	11,256	11,152	10,944	10,831	10,844
Pre-kindergarten through 8	31,639	34,388	37,094	38,592	38,928	38,708	38,750	38,874	38,967	38,839
Public	27,647	29,876	32,338	33,686	34,204	34,625	34,773	34,968	35,111	35,062
Private	3,992	[1] 4,512	4,756	[1] 4,906	4,724	[1] 4,084	3,977	3,906	3,856	3,776
Grades 9 through 12	14,570	12,476	13,665	14,781	16,258	16,159	16,040	15,959	15,874	15,886
Public	13,231	11,341	12,502	13,517	14,909	14,860	14,749	14,684	14,639	14,689
Private	1,339	[1] 1,136	1,163	[1] 1,264	1,349	[1] 1,299	1,291	1,275	1,235	1,197
College [2, 3]	12,097	13,819	14,262	15,312	17,487	21,016	20,994	20,643	20,597	21,011
Public	9,457	10,845	11,092	11,753	13,022	15,143	15,110	14,880	14,857	15,140
Private	2,640	2,974	3,169	3,560	4,466	5,873	5,884	5,762	5,740	5,871
Not-for-profit	2,528	2,760	2,929	3,109	3,455	3,855	3,927	3,954	(NA)	(NA)
For profit	112	214	240	450	1,011	2,018	1,957	1,809	(NA)	(NA)

NA Not available. [1] Estimated. [2] Beginning 2000, reflects new classification system. See footnote 1, Table 290. [3] Data for 2012 are actual.

Source: U.S. National Center for Education Statistics, *Digest of Education Statistics*, "Advance Release of Selected 2013 Digest Tables," <http://www.nces.ed.gov/programs/digest/>, accessed February 2015.

Table 249. School Enrollment by Age: 1970 to 2013

[Enrollment in thousands (60,357 represents 60,357,000); rate as percent of total population. As of October. Covers civilian noninstitutional population enrolled in nursery school and above. Based on Current Population Survey; see text, Section 1 and Appendix III]

Age	1970	1980	1990	1995	2000	2005	2010	2011	2012	2013
ENROLLMENT (1,000)										
Total, 3 to 34 years old	**60,357**	**57,348**	**60,588**	**66,939**	**69,560**	**72,768**	**75,148**	**75,903**	**75,387**	**74,729**
3 and 4 years old	1,461	2,280	3,292	4,042	4,097	4,383	4,706	4,597	4,289	4,449
5 and 6 years old	7,000	5,853	7,207	7,901	7,648	7,486	7,955	8,009	7,728	7,780
7 to 13 years old	28,943	23,751	25,016	27,003	28,296	27,936	27,984	28,260	28,147	28,202
14 and 15 years old	7,869	7,282	6,555	7,651	7,885	8,375	7,736	7,825	8,085	8,150
16 and 17 years old	6,927	7,129	6,098	6,997	7,341	8,472	7,963	7,906	8,070	7,731
18 and 19 years old	3,322	3,788	4,044	4,274	4,926	5,109	5,904	6,017	5,855	5,687
20 and 21 years old	1,949	2,515	2,852	3,025	3,314	4,069	4,552	4,618	4,789	4,532
22 to 24 years old	1,410	1,931	2,231	2,545	2,731	3,254	3,602	3,961	4,004	4,007
25 to 29 years old	1,011	1,714	2,013	2,216	2,030	2,340	3,088	3,139	2,888	2,790
30 to 34 years old	466	1,105	1,281	1,284	1,292	1,344	1,658	1,571	1,532	1,401
35 years old and over	(NA)	1,290	2,439	2,830	2,653	3,013	3,372	3,138	3,038	3,042
ENROLLMENT RATE										
Total, 3 to 34 years old	**56.4**	**49.7**	**50.2**	**53.7**	**55.9**	**56.5**	**56.5**	**56.8**	**56.6**	**55.8**
3 and 4 years old	20.5	36.7	44.4	48.7	52.1	53.6	53.2	52.4	53.5	54.9
5 and 6 years old	89.5	95.7	96.5	96.0	95.6	95.4	94.5	95.1	93.2	93.8
7 to 13 years old	99.2	99.3	99.6	98.9	98.2	98.6	98.0	98.3	98.0	98.1
14 and 15 years old	98.1	98.2	99.0	98.9	98.7	98.0	98.1	98.6	98.2	98.4
16 and 17 years old	90.0	89.0	92.5	93.6	92.8	95.1	96.1	95.7	95.8	93.7
18 and 19 years old	47.7	46.4	57.3	59.4	61.2	67.6	69.2	71.1	69.0	67.1
20 and 21 years old	31.9	31.0	39.7	44.9	44.1	48.7	52.4	52.7	54.0	52.8
22 to 24 years old	14.9	16.3	21.0	23.2	24.6	27.3	28.9	31.1	30.7	29.7
25 to 29 years old	7.5	9.3	9.7	11.6	11.4	11.9	14.6	14.8	14.0	13.3
30 to 34 years old	4.2	6.5	5.8	6.0	6.7	6.9	8.3	7.7	7.5	6.7
35 years old and over	(NA)	1.6	2.1	2.2	1.9	2.0	2.1	2.0	1.9	1.8

NA Not available.

Source: U.S. Census Bureau, Current Population Reports, PPL-148, P-20, and earlier reports; and "School Enrollment," <http://www.census.gov/hhes/school/index.html>, accessed November 2014.

Table 250. School Enrollment by Race, Hispanic Origin, and Age: 2000 to 2013

[Enrollment in thousands (54,257 represents 54,257,000); rate as percent of total population in each age group. As of October. See headnote, Table 249]

Age	White [1]			Black [1]			Hispanic [2]		
	2000	2005	2013	2000	2005	2013	2000	2005	2013
ENROLLMENT (1,000)									
Total, 3 to 34 years old	**54,257**	**55,715**	**54,712**	**11,115**	**10,885**	**11,247**	**9,928**	**12,502**	**16,563**
3 and 4 years old	3,091	3,380	3,103	725	655	723	518	773	975
5 and 6 years old	5,959	5,707	5,607	1,219	1,144	1,209	1,390	1,532	2,015
7 to 13 years old	22,061	21,310	20,804	4,675	4,317	4,143	4,373	5,394	6,726
14 and 15 years old	6,176	6,429	6,052	1,260	1,321	1,239	1,093	1,431	1,815
16 and 17 years old	5,845	6,520	5,762	1,106	1,281	1,148	959	1,357	1,665
18 and 19 years old	3,924	4,006	4,252	716	707	837	617	681	1,120
20 and 21 years old	2,688	3,262	3,292	416	430	689	311	447	833
22 to 24 years old	2,101	2,411	2,903	393	475	540	309	419	721
25 to 29 years old	1,473	1,740	1,930	353	307	481	198	310	449
30 to 34 years old	939	950	1,007	252	248	238	160	158	244
35 years old and over	2,087	2,299	2,201	387	499	578	235	307	408
ENROLLMENT RATE									
Total, 3 to 34 years old	**55.1**	**55.9**	**55.0**	**59.0**	**58.4**	**57.2**	**51.3**	**50.9**	**55.5**
3 and 4 years old	50.2	54.2	54.0	52.1	52.2	57.2	35.9	43.0	45.4
5 and 6 years old	95.3	95.3	93.9	94.2	95.9	94.4	94.3	93.8	93.9
7 to 13 years old	98.2	98.6	98.1	97.9	98.6	97.3	97.5	97.6	98.0
14 and 15 years old	98.4	98.3	98.4	98.0	95.8	98.7	96.2	97.3	98.3
16 and 17 years old	92.8	95.4	93.6	96.2	93.1	92.8	87.0	92.6	93.9
18 and 19 years old	61.3	68.0	67.6	70.0	62.8	64.2	49.5	54.3	59.3
20 and 21 years old	44.9	49.3	52.2	51.6	37.6	47.9	26.1	30.0	43.9
22 to 24 years old	23.7	26.0	28.9	28.1	28.0	27.0	18.2	19.5	26.7
25 to 29 years old	10.4	11.3	12.2	13.9	11.7	16.7	7.4	7.8	10.4
30 to 34 years old	6.0	6.2	6.4	7.8	10.0	8.6	5.6	4.2	5.7
35 years old and over	1.8	1.8	1.6	2.6	3.1	3.1	2.0	2.0	2.0

[1] Starting 2005, data are for persons who selected this race group only. See footnote 4, Table 253. [2] Persons of Hispanic origin may be of any race.

Source: U.S. Census Bureau, Current Population Reports, PPL-148, P-20, and earlier reports; and "School Enrollment," <http://www.census.gov/hhes/school/index.html>, accessed November 2014.

Table 251. Enrollment in Public and Private Schools: 1970 to 2013

[In millions (52.2 represents 52,200,000), except percent. As of October. For civilian noninstitutional population. Prior to 1995, total enrolled does not include the population age 35 and over. Based on Current Population Survey. For enrollment of population age 35 and over, see Table 249]

Year	Public						Private					
	Total	Nursery	Kinder-garten	Elemen-tary	High school	College	Total	Nursery	Kinder-garten	Elemen-tary	High school	College
1970...........	52.2	0.3	2.6	30.0	13.5	5.7	8.1	0.8	0.5	3.9	1.2	1.7
1975...........	52.8	0.6	2.9	27.2	14.5	7.7	8.2	1.2	0.5	3.3	1.2	2.0
1980...........	(NA)	0.6	2.7	24.4	(NA)	(NA)	(NA)	1.4	0.5	3.1	(NA)	(NA)
1985...........	49.0	0.9	3.2	23.8	12.8	8.4	9.0	1.6	0.6	3.1	1.2	2.5
1990 [1]........	53.8	1.2	3.3	26.6	11.9	10.7	9.2	2.2	0.6	2.7	0.9	2.9
1995...........	58.7	2.0	3.2	28.4	13.7	11.4	11.1	2.4	0.7	3.4	1.2	3.3
1997...........	61.6	2.3	3.3	29.3	14.6	12.1	10.5	2.2	0.7	3.1	1.2	3.3
1998...........	60.8	2.3	3.1	29.1	14.3	12.0	11.3	2.3	0.7	3.4	1.2	3.6
1999...........	60.8	2.3	3.2	29.2	14.4	11.7	11.4	2.3	0.7	3.6	1.3	3.5
2000...........	61.2	2.2	3.2	29.4	14.4	12.0	11.0	2.2	0.7	3.5	1.3	3.3
2001...........	62.4	2.2	3.1	29.8	14.8	12.4	10.8	2.1	0.6	3.4	1.2	3.5
2002...........	62.8	2.2	3.0	29.7	15.1	12.8	11.3	2.2	0.6	3.5	1.3	3.7
2003...........	63.8	2.6	3.1	29.2	15.8	13.1	11.1	2.4	0.6	3.4	1.3	3.5
2004...........	64.3	2.5	3.4	29.2	15.5	13.7	11.3	2.3	0.6	3.4	1.3	3.7
2005...........	64.2	2.5	3.3	29.0	15.8	13.4	11.5	2.1	0.6	3.4	1.4	4.0
2006...........	64.1	2.5	3.6	29.0	15.6	13.5	11.1	2.2	0.5	3.1	1.5	3.8
2007...........	65.1	2.6	3.7	29.1	15.8	14.1	10.8	2.1	0.5	3.1	1.3	3.9
2008...........	65.5	2.6	3.6	29.2	15.4	14.7	10.8	2.0	0.5	3.2	1.3	4.0
2009...........	66.9	2.7	3.8	29.4	15.3	15.7	10.4	2.0	0.4	2.9	1.2	4.0
2010...........	67.9	2.8	3.8	29.8	15.3	16.2	10.6	2.1	0.4	2.8	1.2	4.1
2011...........	68.2	2.9	3.7	30.0	15.4	16.1	10.9	2.0	0.5	2.9	1.2	4.3
2012...........	67.8	2.7	3.7	29.9	15.7	15.8	10.7	1.9	0.5	2.8	1.3	4.2
2013...........	67.4	2.6	3.7	30.2	15.5	15.5	10.3	2.1	0.4	2.7	1.1	4.0
Percent White:												
1970...........	84.5	59.5	84.4	83.1	85.6	90.7	93.4	91.1	88.2	94.1	96.1	92.8
1980...........	(NA)	68.2	80.7	80.9	(NA)	(NA)	(NA)	89.0	87.0	90.7	(NA)	(NA)
1990...........	79.8	71.7	78.3	78.9	79.2	84.1	87.4	89.6	83.2	88.2	89.4	85.0
2000...........	77.0	69.4	77.3	76.7	78.0	78.0	83.5	84.9	82.8	85.9	84.6	79.8
2005 [2]........	75.7	71.3	78.0	75.2	76.0	76.7	81.4	83.6	79.0	83.0	83.6	78.4
2010 [2]........	74.9	71.8	72.9	75.0	75.1	75.4	78.9	81.0	79.4	80.9	84.5	74.7
2011 [2]........	74.7	68.8	75.2	74.8	74.8	75.4	80.2	79.7	81.5	84.1	84.8	76.3
2012 [2]........	73.0	70.5	70.1	73.4	73.2	73.1	77.3	77.4	78.2	80.2	78.9	74.6
2013 [2]........	72.8	68.0	69.5	73.2	72.9	73.3	75.9	75.6	81.2	79.5	78.3	72.4

NA Not available. [1] Beginning 1990, based on a revised edit and tabulation package. [2] Beginning 2005, for persons who selected this race group only. See footnote 4, Table 253.

Source: U.S. Census Bureau, "School Enrollment, Historical Time Series Tables," <http://www.census.gov/hhes/school/data/cps/historical/index.html>, accessed November 2014.

Table 252. School Enrollment by Sex and Level: 1970 to 2013

[In millions (60.4 represents 60,400,000). As of October. For the civilian noninstitutional population. Prior to 1980, persons 3 to 34 years old; beginning 1980, 3 years old and over. Elementary includes kindergarten and grades 1–8; high school, grades 9–12; and college, 2-year and 4-year colleges, universities, and graduate and professional schools. Data for college represent degree-credit enrollment. See headnote, Table 249]

Year	All levels [1]			Elementary			High school			College		
	Total	Male	Female	Total	Male	Female	Total	Male	Female	Total	Male	Female
1970...........	60.4	31.4	28.9	37.1	19.0	18.1	14.7	7.4	7.3	7.4	4.4	3.0
1980...........	58.6	29.6	29.1	30.6	15.8	14.9	14.6	7.3	7.3	11.4	5.4	6.0
1990 [2]........	63.0	31.5	31.5	33.2	17.1	16.0	12.8	6.5	6.4	13.6	6.2	7.4
1996...........	70.3	35.1	35.2	35.5	18.3	17.3	15.3	7.9	7.4	15.2	6.8	8.4
1997...........	72.0	35.9	36.2	36.3	18.7	17.6	15.8	8.0	7.7	15.4	6.8	8.6
1998...........	72.1	36.0	36.1	36.4	18.7	17.7	15.6	7.9	7.6	15.5	6.9	8.6
1999...........	72.4	36.3	36.1	36.7	18.8	17.9	15.9	8.2	7.7	15.2	7.0	8.2
2000...........	72.2	35.8	36.4	36.7	18.9	17.9	15.8	8.1	7.7	15.3	6.7	8.6
2001...........	73.1	36.3	36.9	36.9	19.0	17.9	16.1	8.2	7.8	15.9	6.9	9.0
2002...........	74.0	36.8	37.3	36.7	18.9	17.8	16.4	8.3	8.0	16.5	7.2	9.3
2003...........	74.9	37.3	37.6	36.3	18.7	17.6	17.1	8.6	8.4	16.6	7.3	9.3
2004...........	75.5	37.4	38.0	36.5	19.0	17.6	16.8	8.4	8.4	17.4	7.6	9.8
2005...........	75.8	37.4	38.4	36.4	18.6	17.7	17.4	8.9	8.5	17.5	7.5	9.9
2006...........	75.2	37.2	38.0	36.1	18.5	17.6	17.1	8.8	8.4	17.2	7.5	9.7
2007...........	76.0	37.6	38.4	36.3	18.6	17.7	17.1	8.8	8.3	18.0	7.8	10.1
2008...........	76.4	37.8	38.6	36.4	18.7	17.7	16.7	8.5	8.2	18.6	8.3	10.3
2009...........	77.3	38.0	39.3	36.4	18.6	17.7	16.4	8.4	8.1	19.8	8.6	11.1
2010...........	78.5	38.7	39.8	36.8	18.8	18.1	16.6	8.5	8.0	20.3	9.0	11.3
2011...........	79.0	39.2	39.8	37.1	19.0	18.1	16.6	8.6	8.1	20.4	9.1	11.3
2012...........	78.4	38.5	39.9	36.8	19.0	17.9	17.0	8.6	8.5	19.9	8.6	11.3
2013...........	77.8	38.3	39.5	37.0	19.0	18.0	16.6	8.4	8.2	19.5	8.5	10.9

[1] Includes nursery schools, not shown separately. [2] For data beginning 1990, based on a revised edit and tabulation package.

Source: U.S. Census Bureau, Current Population Reports, PPL-148, P20, and earlier reports; and "School Enrollment," <http://www.census.gov/hhes/school/data/cps/index.html>, accessed November 2014.

Table 253. Educational Attainment by Race and Hispanic Origin: 1970 to 2014

[In percent. For persons 25 years old and over. 1970 and 1980 data as of April 1 and based on sample data from the censuses of population. Other years as of March and based on the Current Population Survey; see text, Section 1 and Appendix III. See Table 254 for data by sex]

Year	High school graduate or more [1]					College graduate or more [2]				
	Total [3]	White [4]	Black [4]	Asian and Pacific Islander [4,5]	Hispanic [6]	Total [3]	White [4]	Black [4]	Asian and Pacific Islander [4,5]	Hispanic [6]
1970	52.3	54.5	31.4	62.2	32.1	10.7	11.3	4.4	20.4	4.5
1975	62.5	64.5	42.5	(NA)	37.9	13.9	14.5	6.4	(NA)	6.3
1980	66.5	68.8	51.2	74.8	44.0	16.2	17.1	8.4	32.9	7.6
1985	73.9	75.5	59.8	(NA)	47.9	19.4	20.0	11.1	(NA)	8.5
1990	77.6	79.1	66.2	80.4	50.8	21.3	22.0	11.3	39.9	9.2
1995	81.7	83.0	73.8	(NA)	53.4	23.0	24.0	13.2	(NA)	9.3
2000	84.1	84.9	78.5	85.7	57.0	25.6	26.1	16.5	43.9	10.6
2001	84.1	84.8	78.8	87.6	56.8	26.2	26.6	15.7	47.5	11.1
2002	84.1	84.8	78.7	87.4	57.0	26.7	27.2	17.0	47.2	11.1
2003	84.6	85.1	80.0	87.6	57.0	27.2	27.6	17.3	49.8	11.4
2004	85.2	85.8	80.6	86.8	58.4	27.7	28.2	17.6	49.4	12.1
2005	85.2	85.8	81.1	87.6	58.5	27.7	28.1	17.6	50.2	12.0
2006	85.5	86.1	80.7	87.4	59.3	28.0	28.4	18.5	49.7	12.4
2007	85.7	86.2	82.3	87.8	60.3	28.7	29.1	18.5	52.1	12.7
2008	86.6	87.1	83.0	88.7	62.3	29.4	29.8	19.6	52.6	13.3
2009	86.7	87.1	84.1	88.2	61.9	29.5	29.9	19.3	52.3	13.2
2010	87.1	87.6	84.2	88.9	62.9	29.9	30.3	19.8	52.4	13.9
2011	87.6	88.1	84.5	88.6	64.3	30.4	31.0	19.9	50.3	14.1
2012	87.6	88.1	85.0	88.9	65.0	30.9	31.3	21.2	51.0	14.5
2013	88.2	88.6	85.1	90.1	66.2	31.7	32.0	21.8	53.2	15.1
2014	88.3	88.8	85.8	89.5	66.5	32.0	32.3	22.2	52.3	15.2

NA Not available. [1] Through 1991, completed 4 years of high school or more. [2] Through 1991, completed 4 years of college or more. [3] Includes other races not shown separately. [4] The 2003 Current Population Survey (CPS) allowed respondents to choose more than one race. Beginning 2003, data represent persons who selected this race group only and exclude persons reporting more than one race. The CPS in prior years only allowed respondents to report one race group. See also comments on race in the text for Section 1, Population. [5] Starting in 2003, data are for Asians only, excludes Pacific Islanders. [6] Persons of Hispanic origin may be of any race.

Source: U.S. Census Bureau, U.S. Census of Population, 1970 and 1980, Vol. 1; Current Population Reports, P20-550, and earlier reports; and "Educational Attainment: CPS Historical Time Series Tables," <http://www.census.gov/hhes/socdemo/education/>, accessed January 2015.

Table 254. Educational Attainment by Race, Hispanic Origin, and Sex: 1970 to 2014

[In percent. See Table 253 for headnote and totals for both sexes]

Year	All races [1]		White [2]		Black [2]		Asian and Pacific Islander [2,5]		Hispanic [3]	
	Male	Female	Male	Female	Male	Female	Male	Female	Male	Female
HIGH SCHOOL GRADUATE OR MORE [4]										
1970	51.9	52.8	54.0	55.0	30.1	32.5	61.3	63.1	37.9	34.2
1980	67.3	65.8	69.6	68.1	50.8	51.5	78.8	71.4	45.4	42.7
1990	77.7	77.5	79.1	79.0	65.8	66.5	84.0	77.2	50.3	51.3
2000	84.2	84.0	84.8	85.0	78.7	78.3	88.2	83.4	56.6	57.5
2005	84.9	85.5	85.2	86.2	81.0	81.2	90.4	85.2	57.9	59.1
2010	86.6	87.6	86.9	88.2	83.6	84.6	91.2	87.0	61.4	64.4
2011	87.1	88.0	87.4	88.6	83.8	85.0	90.4	87.1	63.6	65.1
2012	87.3	88.0	87.6	88.5	84.3	85.5	90.4	87.6	64.0	66.0
2013	87.6	88.6	88.0	89.2	84.1	86.0	91.5	89.0	64.6	67.9
2014	87.7	88.9	88.0	89.6	85.3	86.2	91.9	87.4	65.1	67.9
COLLEGE GRADUATE OR MORE [4]										
1970	13.5	8.1	14.4	8.4	4.2	4.6	23.5	17.3	7.8	4.3
1980	20.1	12.8	21.3	13.3	8.4	8.3	39.8	27.0	9.4	6.0
1990	24.4	18.4	25.3	19.0	11.9	10.8	44.9	35.4	9.8	8.7
2000	27.8	23.6	28.5	23.9	16.3	16.7	47.6	40.7	10.7	10.6
2005	28.9	26.5	29.4	26.8	16.0	18.8	54.0	46.8	11.8	12.1
2010	30.3	29.6	30.8	29.9	17.7	21.4	55.6	49.5	12.9	14.9
2011	30.8	30.1	31.5	30.5	18.0	21.4	53.4	47.7	13.1	15.2
2012	31.4	30.6	31.9	30.8	19.2	22.9	53.7	48.8	13.3	15.8
2013	32.0	31.4	32.4	31.6	19.8	23.3	56.1	50.8	13.9	16.2
2014	31.9	32.0	32.3	32.3	20.4	23.7	54.7	50.3	14.2	16.1

[1] Includes other races not shown separately. [2] Beginning 2005, for persons who selected this race group only. See footnote 4, Table 253. [3] Persons of Hispanic origin may be of any race. [4] Through 1990, completed 4 years of high school or more and 4 years of college or more. [5] Starting in 2003, data are for Asians only, excludes Pacific Islanders.

Source: U.S. Census Bureau, U.S. Census of Population, 1970 and 1980, Vol. 1; Current Population Reports, P20-550, and earlier reports; and "Educational Attainment: CPS Historical Time Series Tables," <http://www.census.gov/hhes/socdemo/education/index.html>, accessed February 2015.

Table 255. Educational Attainment by Selected Characteristics: 2014

[209,287 represents 209,287,000. For persons 25 years old and over. As of March. Based on the Current Population Survey; see text, Section 1 and Appendix III]

Characteristic	Population (1,000)	Percent of population—					
		Not a high school graduate	High school graduate	Some college, but no degree	Associate's degree [1]	Bachelor's degree	Advanced degree
Total persons..........................	**209,287**	**11.7**	**29.7**	**16.7**	**9.9**	**20.2**	**11.8**
Age:							
25 to 34 years old.......................	42,466	10.0	26.0	18.3	10.3	24.9	10.5
35 to 44 years old.......................	39,790	11.0	25.7	16.1	11.3	22.5	13.4
45 to 54 years old.......................	42,898	10.6	30.3	16.1	10.9	20.8	11.3
55 to 64 years old.......................	39,626	10.1	31.9	17.0	10.5	18.1	12.4
65 to 74 years old.......................	25,742	12.7	32.9	17.6	7.3	16.1	13.3
75 years old or over....................	18,766	21.3	36.6	13.7	6.3	13.2	8.9
Sex:							
Male...	100,592	12.3	30.5	16.4	8.9	20.0	11.9
Female.....................................	108,695	11.1	29.0	17.0	10.9	20.4	11.6
Race:							
White [2].....................................	166,962	11.2	29.8	16.6	10.1	20.4	11.9
Black [2].....................................	24,864	14.2	33.4	19.9	10.3	14.6	7.6
Asian [2].....................................	11,801	10.5	20.5	9.8	6.9	31.2	21.1
Hispanic origin:							
Hispanic...................................	29,919	33.5	29.9	13.8	7.6	10.6	4.6
Non-Hispanic white....................	140,124	6.9	29.7	17.2	10.6	22.3	13.3
Marital status:							
Never married............................	40,296	12.4	29.7	18.2	9.1	21.6	9.1
Married, spouse present..............	121,369	9.9	28.3	15.6	10.1	21.9	14.2
Married, spouse absent [3].............	3,303	22.7	28.3	13.5	6.9	17.5	11.0
Separated.................................	5,064	20.2	32.8	17.2	9.8	14.1	5.9
Widowed...................................	14,167	21.8	38.5	14.6	7.5	11.1	6.5
Divorced...................................	25,088	10.2	31.6	21.0	12.2	16.6	8.3
Civilian labor force status:							
Employed..................................	126,655	7.9	26.5	16.4	11.1	23.9	14.2
Unemployed..............................	7,687	14.9	33.8	19.7	9.2	16.1	6.2
Not in the labor force..................	74,946	17.7	34.8	16.8	8.1	14.4	8.3

[1] Includes vocational degrees. [2] For persons who selected this race group only. See footnote 4, Table 253. [3] Excludes those separated.

Source: U.S. Census Bureau, "Educational Attainment in the United States: 2014 - Detailed Tables," <http://www.census.gov/hhes/socdemo/education/>, accessed February 2015.

Table 256. Mean Earnings by Highest Level of Education or Degree and Selected Characteristics: 2013

[In dollars. Persons as of March 2014. For persons 18 years old and over with earnings. Based on Current Population Survey, 2014 Annual Social and Economic Supplement; see text, Section 1 and Appendix III. For definition of mean, see Guide to Tabular Presentation]

Characteristic	Total persons [1]	Mean earnings by highest level of education or degree (dollars)							
		Ninth to twelfth grade, non-graduate	High school graduate only	Some college, no degree	Associate's	Bachelor's	Master's	Professional	Doctorate
All persons [2]....................	**46,187**	**23,727**	**32,881**	**33,759**	**41,404**	**59,661**	**76,112**	**139,599**	**113,293**
Age:									
25 to 34 years old...............	39,586	22,630	29,558	33,283	36,321	49,121	59,027	82,471	69,704
35 to 44 years old...............	53,099	26,346	36,317	41,189	43,879	66,566	80,381	148,685	126,863
45 to 54 years old...............	56,315	29,554	38,537	45,315	49,426	72,631	91,211	155,850	127,097
55 to 64 years old...............	55,407	37,535	39,050	45,193	45,623	65,933	82,926	165,679	124,933
65 years old and over..........	43,896	23,712	27,718	35,688	30,534	52,180	54,316	138,519	102,377
Sex:									
Male...............................	54,658	27,735	37,763	40,802	50,059	72,124	97,365	169,135	131,969
Female...........................	36,664	17,118	26,322	26,487	33,946	47,209	58,253	98,454	80,501
White [3].............................	47,452	24,259	34,192	34,813	42,408	60,962	76,578	144,556	112,886
Male...............................	56,215	28,452	39,191	42,209	51,820	74,018	99,486	176,012	130,235
Female...........................	37,222	16,638	27,097	26,783	34,203	47,565	57,592	97,480	82,229
Black [3].............................	35,817	21,607	26,670	30,196	36,504	49,904	65,199	107,933	93,380
Male...............................	40,785	26,982	29,893	36,094	42,845	57,304	80,111	97,578	122,733
Female...........................	31,531	15,635	23,349	25,612	31,849	44,139	56,579	(B)	59,017
Asian [3].............................	54,752	28,577	30,996	32,333	38,793	57,841	82,516	120,448	125,910
Male...............................	64,019	24,472	35,882	36,185	40,465	66,653	94,834	149,428	145,736
Female...........................	43,995	33,066	25,129	28,054	36,860	48,505	66,038	93,842	82,261
Hispanic [4].........................	32,368	22,803	28,415	29,589	37,689	50,673	66,937	122,783	82,017
Male...............................	35,990	25,824	32,070	33,737	45,678	59,368	78,865	(B)	89,079
Female...........................	27,504	17,350	22,999	25,264	30,929	42,216	56,173	(B)	(B)

B Base figure too small to meet statistical standards for reliability of a derived figure. [1] Includes those with less than ninth grade education not shown separately. [2] Includes other races not shown separately. [3] For persons who selected this race group only. See footnote 4, Table 253. [4] Persons of Hispanic origin may be of any race.

Source: U.S. Census Bureau, *Income and Poverty in the United States: 2013*, Current Population Reports, P60-249, and "Detailed Table, PINC-04," <http://www.census.gov/hhes/www/income/data/index.html>, accessed November 2014.

Table 257. Educational Attainment by State: 2000 to 2013

[In percent. 2000 as of April; 2010 and 2013 represents annual averages for calendar year. For persons 25 years old and over. Based on the 2000 Census of Population, and the American Community Survey, which includes the household population and the population living in institutions, college dormitories, and other group quarters. See text, Section 1 and Appendix III. For margin of error data, see source]

State	2000			2010			2013		
	High school graduate or more	Bachelor's degree or more	Advanced degree or more	High school graduate or more	Bachelor's degree or more	Advanced degree or more	High school graduate or more	Bachelor's degree or more	Advanced degree or more
United States	**80.4**	**24.4**	**8.9**	**85.6**	**28.2**	**10.4**	**86.6**	**29.6**	**11.2**
Alabama	75.3	19.0	6.9	82.1	21.9	8.0	84.5	23.5	8.7
Alaska	88.3	24.7	8.6	91.0	27.9	9.4	91.6	28.0	9.8
Arizona	81.0	23.5	8.4	85.6	25.9	9.2	85.9	27.4	10.3
Arkansas	75.3	16.7	5.7	82.9	19.5	6.3	84.4	20.6	7.2
California	76.8	26.6	9.5	80.7	30.1	11.0	81.7	31.0	11.5
Colorado	86.9	32.7	11.1	89.7	36.4	13.0	90.5	37.8	14.0
Connecticut	84.0	31.4	13.3	88.6	35.5	15.3	89.7	37.2	16.6
Delaware	82.6	25.0	9.4	87.7	27.8	11.3	88.3	29.8	12.6
District of Columbia	77.8	39.1	21.0	87.4	50.1	26.9	90.1	55.1	32.4
Florida	79.9	22.3	8.1	85.5	25.8	9.2	86.8	27.2	9.7
Georgia	78.6	24.3	8.3	84.3	27.3	9.8	85.5	28.3	10.6
Hawaii	84.6	26.2	8.4	89.9	29.5	9.6	91.0	31.2	10.4
Idaho	84.7	21.7	6.8	88.3	24.4	7.7	89.4	26.2	8.2
Illinois	81.4	26.1	9.5	86.9	30.8	11.5	87.8	32.1	12.4
Indiana	82.1	19.4	7.2	87.0	22.7	8.1	87.6	23.8	8.6
Iowa	86.1	21.2	6.5	90.6	24.9	7.9	91.6	26.4	8.4
Kansas	86.0	25.8	8.7	89.2	29.8	10.5	90.1	31.1	11.1
Kentucky	74.1	17.1	6.9	81.9	20.5	8.1	84.1	22.6	9.3
Louisiana	74.8	18.7	6.5	81.9	21.4	7.0	83.1	22.5	7.6
Maine	85.4	22.9	7.9	90.3	26.8	9.5	91.8	28.2	10.1
Maryland	83.8	31.4	13.4	88.1	36.1	16.4	89.1	37.4	17.1
Massachusetts	84.8	33.2	13.7	89.1	39.0	16.7	89.9	40.3	17.8
Michigan	83.4	21.8	8.1	88.7	25.2	9.6	89.4	26.9	10.5
Minnesota	87.9	27.4	8.3	91.8	31.8	10.3	92.4	33.5	11.1
Mississippi	72.9	16.9	5.8	81.0	19.5	7.1	82.4	20.4	7.5
Missouri	81.3	21.6	7.6	86.9	25.6	9.5	88.7	27.0	10.0
Montana	87.2	24.4	7.2	91.7	28.8	9.0	92.7	29.0	9.3
Nebraska	86.6	23.7	7.3	90.4	28.6	9.0	90.2	29.4	9.8
Nevada	80.7	18.2	6.1	84.7	21.7	7.4	85.2	22.5	7.5
New Hampshire	87.4	28.7	10.0	91.5	32.8	12.4	92.8	34.6	12.6
New Jersey	82.1	29.8	11.0	88.0	35.4	13.3	88.5	36.6	14.0
New Mexico	78.9	23.5	9.8	83.3	25.0	10.8	84.3	26.4	11.4
New York	79.1	27.4	11.8	84.9	32.5	14.0	85.6	34.1	14.8
North Carolina	78.1	22.5	7.2	84.7	26.5	8.7	85.7	28.4	9.9
North Dakota	83.9	22.0	5.5	90.3	27.6	7.9	91.5	27.1	7.2
Ohio	83.0	21.1	7.4	88.1	24.6	8.9	89.0	26.1	9.7
Oklahoma	80.6	20.3	6.8	86.2	22.9	7.5	86.7	23.8	7.7
Oregon	85.1	25.1	8.7	88.8	28.8	10.5	89.7	30.7	11.5
Pennsylvania	81.9	22.4	8.4	88.4	27.1	10.4	89.2	28.7	11.2
Rhode Island	78.0	25.6	9.7	83.5	30.2	12.2	85.9	32.4	12.6
South Carolina	76.3	20.4	6.9	84.1	24.5	8.8	85.6	26.1	9.5
South Dakota	84.6	21.5	6.0	89.6	26.3	7.7	91.6	26.6	7.6
Tennessee	75.9	19.6	6.8	83.6	23.1	8.5	85.6	24.8	9.2
Texas	75.7	23.2	7.6	80.7	25.9	8.6	81.9	27.5	9.3
Utah	87.7	26.1	8.3	90.6	29.3	9.4	91.5	31.3	10.5
Vermont	86.4	29.4	11.1	91.0	33.6	13.3	91.5	35.7	14.3
Virginia	81.5	29.5	11.6	86.5	34.2	14.2	88.4	36.1	15.1
Washington	87.1	27.7	9.3	89.8	31.1	11.1	90.1	32.7	11.8
West Virginia	75.2	14.8	5.9	83.2	17.5	6.6	84.6	18.9	7.6
Wisconsin	85.1	22.4	7.2	90.1	24.1	9.0	90.9	27.7	9.4
Wyoming	87.9	21.9	7.0	92.3	22.3	8.4	93.5	26.6	8.8

Source: U.S. Census Bureau, 2000 Census of Population, P37, "Sex by Educational Attainment for the Population 25 Years and Over"; and American Community Survey, GCT1501, "Percent of People 25 Years and Over Who Have Completed High School (Includes Equivalency)," GCT1502, "Percent of People 25 Years and Over Who Have Completed a Bachelor's Degree," and GCT1503, "Percent of People 25 Years and Over Who Have Completed an Advanced Degree," <http://factfinder2.census.gov>, accessed November 2014.

Table 258. Children Who Speak a Language Other Than English at Home by Region: 2013

[In thousands (11,742 represents 11,742,000), except percent. For children 5 to 17 years old. For more on languages spoken at home, see Table 54 and Table 55. Based on the American Community Survey; see text Section 1, and Appendix III. For composition of regions, see map inside front cover]

Characteristic	U.S.	Northeast	Midwest	South	West
Children who speak another language at home	**11,742**	**1,968**	**1,445**	**3,958**	**4,371**
Percent of children 5 to 17 years old	21.8	22.3	12.5	19.4	33.7
Speak Spanish	8,458	1,086	869	3,149	3,354
Speak English "very well"	6,717	883	689	2,431	2,714
Speak English less than "very well"	1,742	203	180	718	640
Speak other Indo-European languages	1,485	524	274	382	304
Speak English "very well"	1,205	412	215	317	261
Speak English less than "very well"	280	112	58	66	43
Speak Asian and Pacific Island languages	1,285	243	172	304	567
Speak English "very well"	956	176	124	231	426
Speak English less than "very well"	329	67	48	73	142
Speak other languages	514	115	130	123	145
Speak English "very well"	421	96	106	102	118
Speak English less than "very well"	92	20	24	21	28
Have difficulty speaking English [1]	2,443	403	310	878	853
Language spoken at home in linguistically isolated households [2]	2,788	480	336	987	985
Speak only English	197	48	25	61	63
Speak Spanish	1,985	263	205	785	732
Speak other Indo-European languages	196	76	36	50	33
Speak Asian and Pacific Island languages	319	73	43	70	131
Speak other languages	91	19	26	20	27

[1] Children aged 5 to 17 who speak English less than "very well." [2] A household in which no person aged 14 or over speaks English at least "very well."

Source: U.S. Census Bureau, 2013 American Community Survey, B16003, "Age by Language Spoken at Home for the Population 5 Years and Over" and B16004, "Age by Language Spoken at Home by Ability to Speak English for the Population 5 Years and Over," <http://factfinder2.census.gov>, accessed November 2014.

Table 259. Preprimary School Enrollment—Summary: 1970 to 2013

[10,949 represents 10,949,000. As of October. Civilian noninstitutional population. Includes public and nonpublic nursery school and kindergarten programs. Excludes 5-year-olds enrolled in elementary school. Based on Current Population Survey. See text, Section 1 and Appendix III]

Item	1970	1980	1990	2000	2005	2010	2011	2012	2013
NUMBER OF CHILDREN (1,000)									
Population, 3 to 5 years old	**10,949**	**9,284**	**11,207**	**11,858**	**12,134**	**12,949**	**12,966**	**12,259**	**12,165**
Total enrolled [1]	**4,104**	**4,878**	**6,659**	**7,592**	**7,801**	**8,493**	**8,260**	**7,883**	**7,879**
Nursery	1,094	1,981	3,378	4,326	4,529	4,797	4,911	4,602	4,624
Public	332	628	1,202	2,146	2,409	2,749	2,876	2,712	2,522
Private	762	1,353	2,177	2,180	2,120	2,048	2,035	1,890	2,103
Kindergarten	3,010	2,897	3,281	3,266	3,272	3,449	3,349	3,281	3,254
Public	2,498	2,438	2,767	2,701	2,804	3,079	2,947	2,926	2,927
Private	511	459	513	565	468	369	403	355	327
White [2]	3,443	3,994	5,389	5,861	6,025	6,160	6,128	5,708	5,593
Black [2]	586	725	964	1,265	1,148	1,301	1,230	1,205	1,248
Hispanic [3]	(NA)	370	642	1,155	1,494	1,874	1,878	1,829	1,836
3 years old	454	857	1,205	1,540	1,715	1,718	1,651	1,614	1,674
4 years old	1,007	1,423	2,086	2,556	2,668	2,988	2,946	2,675	2,776
5 years old	2,643	2,598	3,367	3,496	3,418	3,787	3,663	3,594	3,429
ENROLLMENT RATE									
Total enrolled [1]	**37.5**	**52.5**	**59.4**	**64.0**	**64.3**	**63.7**	**63.7**	**64.3**	**64.8**
White [2]	37.8	52.7	59.7	63.2	65.1	63.4	63.6	64.6	64.2
Black [2]	34.9	51.8	57.8	68.5	62.0	64.1	62.8	63.6	66.7
Hispanic [3]	(NA)	43.3	49.0	52.6	56.1	56.0	55.8	57.6	57.4
3 years old	12.9	27.3	32.6	39.2	41.3	38.2	38.5	40.2	41.9
4 years old	27.8	46.3	56.0	64.9	66.2	68.6	65.9	67.4	67.7
5 years old	69.3	84.7	88.8	87.6	86.4	88.1	87.2	84.7	84.4

NA Not available. [1] Includes races not shown separately. [2] Beginning 2005, for persons who selected this race group only. See footnote 4, Table 253. [3] Persons of Hispanic origin may be of any race. The method of identifying Hispanic children was changed in 1980 from allocation based on status of mother to status reported for each child. The number of Hispanic children using the new method is larger.

Source: U.S. Census Bureau, Current Population Reports, PPL-148; earlier PPL and P-20 reports and unpublished data; and "School Enrollment," <http://www.census.gov/hhes/school/index.html>, accessed November 2014.

Table 260. Public Elementary and Secondary School Finances by Enrollment-Size Group: 2013

[In millions of dollars (597,930 represents $597,930,000,000), except per pupil. School fiscal year ending in 2013. Enrollment as of Fall 2012. Data are based on the Annual Government Finance Survey. For details, see source. See also Appendix III]

Item	All school systems	School systems with enrollment of—						
		50,000 or more	25,000 to 49,999	15,000 to 24,999	7,500 to 14,999	5,000 to 7,499	3,000 to 4,999	Under 3,000
TOTAL								
General revenue	**597,930**	**126,889**	**73,204**	**54,059**	**84,172**	**53,910**	**71,529**	**134,168**
From federal sources	54,367	13,298	7,481	5,034	7,207	4,017	5,120	12,210
Through state [1]	49,870	12,353	7,012	4,788	6,429	3,767	4,771	10,750
Child nutrition programs	13,757	3,447	2,034	1,471	1,908	1,080	1,353	2,465
Direct	4,498	945	470	246	777	250	349	1,460
From state sources [1]	272,917	53,928	35,347	28,010	40,178	23,116	30,496	61,842
General formula assistance	184,362	34,117	25,025	19,527	28,087	15,903	20,244	41,458
Compensatory programs	5,550	1,289	903	725	946	393	489	805
Special education	18,169	4,438	1,968	1,470	2,194	1,443	2,238	4,418
From local sources	270,645	59,663	30,376	21,015	36,787	26,776	35,913	60,115
Taxes	184,495	29,775	21,392	15,080	27,119	19,895	26,740	44,494
Contributions from parent government	48,304	22,525	4,464	2,669	4,708	3,700	4,882	5,356
From other local governments	8,192	900	1,208	738	1,058	710	1,024	2,555
Current charges [1]	14,314	2,388	1,663	1,273	1,986	1,259	1,728	4,018
School lunch	6,009	893	701	569	951	616	810	1,469
Other	15,340	4,074	1,648	1,256	1,916	1,213	1,539	3,694
General expenditure	**596,291**	**129,418**	**73,682**	**53,976**	**83,591**	**53,140**	**69,806**	**132,676**
Current spending	530,553	114,312	64,530	47,724	74,396	47,839	62,778	118,973
By function:								
Instruction	321,311	72,782	38,831	28,547	44,949	29,126	38,075	69,001
Support services	181,717	35,556	22,105	16,466	25,546	16,428	21,686	43,930
Other current spending	27,525	5,974	3,594	2,711	3,901	2,285	3,017	6,042
By object:								
Total salaries and wages	307,334	64,870	38,641	28,633	43,996	27,853	36,453	66,888
Total employee benefits	116,266	24,643	13,367	10,367	16,620	10,937	14,212	26,121
Capital outlay	46,989	10,653	6,565	4,486	6,575	3,651	5,028	10,030
Interest on debt	17,017	4,170	2,534	1,732	2,387	1,482	1,832	2,880
Payments to other governments	1,732	284	53	34	233	168	168	793
Debt outstanding	415,239	99,483	59,939	42,280	58,687	36,142	45,300	73,408
Long-term	408,570	98,493	59,192	41,880	57,863	35,394	44,405	71,343
Short-term	6,669	990	747	399	824	748	895	2,064
Long-term debt issued	53,445	10,280	8,118	5,811	8,083	5,070	5,505	10,578
Long-term debt retired	47,154	8,749	6,969	4,730	7,163	4,402	5,619	9,524
PER PUPIL								
Fall enrollment (1,000)	48,300	10,428	6,703	4,931	7,166	4,208	5,440	9,424
General revenue	12,380	12,169	10,920	10,964	11,746	12,812	13,149	14,236
From federal sources	1,126	1,275	1,116	1,021	1,006	955	941	1,296
From state sources [1]	5,650	5,172	5,273	5,681	5,607	5,494	5,606	6,562
General formula assistance	3,817	3,272	3,733	3,960	3,920	3,779	3,721	4,399
Special education	376	426	294	298	306	343	411	469
From local sources [1]	5,603	5,722	4,531	4,262	5,134	6,364	6,602	6,379
Taxes	3,820	2,855	3,191	3,058	3,784	4,728	4,916	4,721
Contributions from parent government	1,000	2,160	666	541	657	879	898	568
Current charges	296	229	248	258	277	299	318	426
School lunch	124	86	105	115	133	146	149	156
General expenditure [1]	12,061	12,013	10,735	10,744	11,436	12,338	12,538	13,824
Current spending	10,700	10,564	9,369	9,476	10,153	11,078	11,246	12,370
By function:								
Instruction	6,480	6,704	5,637	5,697	6,148	6,732	6,819	7,186
Support services	3,762	3,410	3,298	3,339	3,565	3,904	3,987	4,661
By object:								
Total salaries and wages	6,363	6,221	5,764	5,807	6,140	6,620	6,701	7,097
Total employee benefits	2,407	2,363	1,994	2,102	2,319	2,599	2,613	2,772
Capital outlay	973	1,022	979	910	918	868	924	1,064
Interest on debt	352	400	378	351	333	352	337	306
Debt outstanding	8,597	9,540	8,942	8,575	8,190	8,589	8,327	7,789
Long-term	8,459	9,445	8,830	8,494	8,075	8,412	8,163	7,570

[1] Includes other sources not shown separately.

Source: U.S. Census Bureau, *Public Education Finances, 2013*, June 2015. See also <http://www.census.gov/govs/school>.

Table 261. Public Elementary and Secondary School Estimated Finances by State: 2013

[In millions of dollars (597,930 represents $597,930,000,000), except as noted. For the school fiscal year. Includes finances of charter schools whose charters are held directly by a government or government agency]

State	Revenue receipts				Expenditures		Current expenditures [3]		
		Source				Per capita [2] (dol.)	Elementary and secondary schools	Average per pupil [4]	
	Total	Federal	State	Local	Total [1]			Amount (dol.) [5]	Rank
Total........................	597,930	54,367	272,917	270,645	596,291	1,898	530,553	10,700	(X)
Alabama........................	7,153	812	3,898	2,443	7,479	1,552	6,642	8,755	39
Alaska........................	2,545	321	1,707	517	2,666	3,647	2,394	18,175	2
Arizona........................	8,098	1,178	2,934	3,985	7,595	1,158	6,837	7,208	49
Arkansas........................	5,051	572	3,847	632	5,189	1,759	4,522	9,394	34
California........................	66,446	7,836	35,141	23,468	66,823	1,756	58,252	9,220	36
Colorado........................	8,782	696	3,694	4,392	8,652	1,667	7,432	8,647	40
Connecticut........................	10,107	435	3,870	5,802	9,506	2,645	8,889	16,631	5
Delaware........................	1,880	151	1,124	604	1,870	2,039	1,690	13,833	11
District of Columbia..........	1,300	130	(X)	1,170	1,259	1,982	883	17,953	3
Florida........................	24,674	3,027	9,456	12,192	25,245	1,304	23,145	8,433	42
Georgia........................	17,449	1,806	7,578	8,066	17,305	1,745	15,444	9,099	37
Hawaii........................	2,332	311	1,963	58	2,346	1,684	2,199	11,823	17
Idaho........................	2,016	239	1,278	499	1,968	1,233	1,852	6,791	50
Illinois........................	29,392	2,311	10,392	16,688	28,619	2,223	25,785	12,288	14
Indiana........................	11,989	980	7,503	3,505	10,975	1,679	9,659	9,566	31
Iowa........................	6,030	459	3,118	2,452	6,082	1,977	5,178	10,313	27
Kansas........................	5,666	421	3,194	2,051	5,617	1,946	4,808	9,828	28
Kentucky........................	7,215	868	3,961	2,386	7,412	1,691	6,445	9,316	35
Louisiana........................	8,084	1,229	3,370	3,485	7,816	1,697	7,057	10,490	26
Maine........................	2,604	196	1,047	1,361	2,459	1,851	2,336	12,147	15
Maryland........................	13,810	828	6,094	6,888	13,028	2,211	11,905	13,829	12
Massachusetts..............	15,980	818	6,429	8,733	15,833	2,379	14,325	14,515	8
Michigan........................	17,380	1,637	9,882	5,861	17,223	1,742	15,409	10,948	24
Minnesota........................	10,705	648	6,792	3,264	10,777	2,003	9,330	11,089	21
Mississippi........................	4,433	708	2,214	1,512	4,368	1,463	4,024	8,130	47
Missouri........................	10,030	894	4,236	4,901	9,912	1,645	8,789	9,597	30
Montana........................	1,652	211	788	653	1,658	1,650	1,527	10,625	25
Nebraska........................	3,795	366	1,217	2,211	3,895	2,099	3,513	11,579	18
Nevada........................	4,130	392	2,556	1,182	4,055	1,472	3,622	8,339	44
New Hampshire..............	2,876	164	1,020	1,692	2,709	2,051	2,599	13,721	13
New Jersey........................	27,028	1,121	10,458	15,449	26,272	2,960	24,972	17,572	4
New Mexico........................	3,519	519	2,402	597	3,531	1,694	2,952	9,012	38
New York........................	59,399	3,336	23,633	32,430	60,228	3,072	55,066	19,818	1
North Carolina..............	12,729	1,580	7,892	3,258	13,036	1,337	12,383	8,390	43
North Dakota........................	1,362	146	685	530	1,460	2,080	1,215	11,980	16
Ohio........................	21,731	1,721	8,991	11,019	21,941	1,900	19,172	11,197	19
Oklahoma........................	5,876	716	2,890	2,270	5,777	1,514	5,176	7,672	48
Oregon........................	6,022	472	3,042	2,508	6,256	1,605	5,558	9,543	32
Pennsylvania..............	27,024	2,049	9,765	15,211	26,927	2,109	24,372	13,864	10
Rhode Island........................	2,262	193	842	1,226	2,208	2,098	2,128	14,415	9
South Carolina..............	8,242	814	3,819	3,609	8,208	1,738	6,982	9,514	33
South Dakota........................	1,314	195	408	712	1,330	1,594	1,119	8,470	41
Tennessee........................	8,885	1,166	4,098	3,622	8,943	1,385	8,221	8,208	46
Texas........................	49,909	5,696	19,238	24,975	50,509	1,936	40,962	8,299	45
Utah........................	4,302	410	2,236	1,656	4,581	1,604	3,768	6,555	51
Vermont........................	1,619	115	1,432	73	1,599	2,553	1,531	16,377	6
Virginia........................	14,984	1,109	5,874	8,001	15,393	1,879	13,946	10,960	23
Washington........................	12,150	1,042	7,160	3,948	12,058	1,748	10,226	9,672	29
West Virginia........................	3,475	383	2,027	1,064	3,487	1,878	3,183	11,132	20
Wisconsin........................	10,802	827	4,840	5,135	10,545	1,842	9,685	11,071	22
Wyoming........................	1,693	114	881	699	1,661	2,880	1,445	15,700	7

X Not applicable. [1] Includes interest on school debt and payments to state and local governments, not shown separately. [2] Based on U.S. Census Bureau estimated resident population, as of July 1, 2012. [3] Includes expenditures for adult education, community services, and other nonelementary-secondary programs. [4] Based on Fall 2012 enrollment, National Center for Education Statistics, Common Core of Data. [5] Excludes expenditures for payments to other school systems, adult education, community services, and other nonelementary-secondary programs.

Source: U.S. Census Bureau, *Public Education Finances: 2013,* June 2015. See also <http://www.census.gov/govs/school/>.

Table 262. Students Who Are Homeschooled by Selected Characteristics: 2007 and 2012

[51,135 represents 51,135,000. As of Spring. For students age 5 to 17 with a grade equivalent of K–12. Homeschoolers are students whose parents reported them to be schooled at home instead of a public or private school. Excludes students who were enrolled in school for more than 25 hours a week or were homeschooled due to a temporary illness. Based on the Parent and Family Involvement in Education Survey of the National Household Education Surveys Program; see source and Appendix III for details]

Characteristic	2007			2012		
	Total (1,000)	Home-schooled (1,000)	Percent home-schooled	Total (1,000)	Home-schooled (1,000) [1]	Percent home-schooled
Total............................	**51,135**	**1,520**	**3.0**	**51,657**	**1,773**	**3.4**
Grade equivalent: [2]						
K–5............................	23,529	717	3.0	25,842	423	1.6
Kindergarten....................	3,669	(S)	(S)	5,295	(S)	(S)
Grades 1 to 3..................	11,965	406	3.4	12,101	203	1.7
Grades 4 to 5..................	7,895	197	2.5	8,446	142	1.7
Grades 6 to 8..................	12,435	371	3.0	12,006	317	2.6
Grades 9 to 12.................	15,161	422	2.8	13,808	341	2.5
Sex:						
Male...........................	26,286	639	2.4	26,620	499	1.9
Female.........................	24,849	881	3.5	25,037	583	2.3
Race/ethnicity:						
White, non-Hispanic............	29,815	1,171	3.9	26,978	893	3.3
Black, non-Hispanic............	7,523	(S)	(S)	7,191	(S)	(S)
Hispanic [3]....................	9,589	147	1.5	11,814	72	0.6
Asian/Pacific Islander.........	1,580	(S)	(S)	2,849	(S)	(S)
Other..........................	2,629	(S)	(S)	2,825	(S)	(S)
Number of children in the household:						
One child......................	8,463	197	2.3	10,899	179	1.6
Two children...................	20,694	414	2.0	20,337	314	1.5
Three or more children.........	21,979	909	4.1	20,421	589	2.9
Number of parents in the household:						
Two parents....................	37,219	1,357	3.6	34,252	908	2.7
One parent.....................	11,777	118	1.0	15,436	137	0.9
Nonparental guardians..........	2,139	(S)	(S)	1,968	(S)	(S)
Parents' participation in the labor force:						
Two parents—both in labor force.	26,055	518	2.0	22,884	295	1.3
Two parents—one in labor force.	10,754	808	7.5	11,581	618	5.3
One parent in labor force......	10,020	127	1.3	13,083	96	0.7
No parent in labor force.......	4,308	(S)	(S)	4,108	74	1.8
Household income:						
$20,000 or less................	8,488	186	2.2	7,593	59	0.8
$20,001 to 50,000..............	13,648	420	3.1	13,973	321	2.3
$50,001 to 75,000..............	10,289	414	4.0	9,406	278	3.0
$75,001 to 100,000.............	6,899	264	3.8	6,916	211	3.0
$100,000 or more...............	11,811	236	2.0	13,769	214	1.6
Parents' highest educational attainment:						
High school diploma or less....	14,306	208	1.5	16,762	270	1.6
Voc/tech degree or some college.	14,581	559	3.8	15,621	344	2.2
Bachelor's degree..............	11,448	444	3.9	11,675	275	2.4
Graduate/professional school...	10,800	309	2.9	7,599	192	2.5

S Figure does not meet publication standards. [1] The National Center for Education Statistics uses a statistical adjustment for estimates of total homeschoolers in 2012; therefore, data will not add to total. All other estimates about homeschoolers do not use a statistical adjustment. [2] Excludes those ungraded. [3] Persons of Hispanic origin may be of any race.

Source: U.S. National Center for Education Statistics, *Digest of Education Statistics 2013*, May 2015. See also <http://www.nces.ed.gov/programs/digest/>.

Table 263. Public Elementary and Secondary Schools by Type and Size of School: 2013

[Enrollment in thousands (49,474 represents 49,474,000), except for average enrollment. For school year ending in 2013. Data reported by schools, rather than school districts. Based on the Common Core of Data Survey; see source for details]

Enrollment size of school	Number of schools					Enrollment [1]				
	Total	Elemen-tary [2]	Second-ary [3]	Com-bined [4]	Other [5]	Total	Elemen-tary [2]	Second-ary [3]	Com-bined [4]	Other [5]
Total...................	**98,454**	**66,718**	**24,280**	**6,371**	**1,085**	**49,474**	**31,893**	**15,644**	**1,935**	**2**
PERCENT										
Total........................	100.00	100.00	100.00	100.00	100.00	100.00	100.00	100.00	100.00	100.00
Under 100 students........	10.14	5.34	17.35	36.73	86.21	0.88	0.56	1.08	4.42	57.73
100 to 199 students........	9.20	7.74	11.66	16.30	6.90	2.63	2.44	2.48	6.94	12.64
200 to 299 students.......	10.90	11.50	9.30	10.23	6.90	5.28	6.08	3.36	7.52	29.63
300 to 399 students.......	13.62	16.05	7.95	8.11	–	9.15	11.71	4.02	8.37	–
400 to 499 students.......	13.86	16.93	6.87	6.07	–	11.91	15.80	4.46	8.06	–
500 to 599 students.......	11.72	14.24	5.85	5.93	–	12.28	16.19	4.64	9.63	–
600 to 699 students.......	8.64	10.35	4.91	3.71	–	10.70	13.90	4.62	7.13	–
700 to 799 students.......	6.14	7.06	4.23	3.21	–	8.78	10.94	4.59	7.10	–
800 to 999 students.......	6.70	6.94	6.70	3.87	–	11.36	12.74	8.69	10.13	–
1,000 to 1,499 students. ..	5.47	3.52	11.60	3.68	–	12.53	8.47	20.74	13.08	–
1,500 to 1,999 students. ..	2.04	0.29	7.38	1.17	–	6.77	1.00	18.63	5.88	–
2,000 to 2,999 students. ..	1.30	0.03	5.23	0.49	–	5.86	0.14	17.85	3.29	–
3,000 or more students. ..	0.27	–	0.97	0.51	–	1.87	0.02	4.84	8.44	–
Average enrollment [1]...	(X)	(X)	(X)	(X)	(X)	522	481	689	337	61

– Represents or rounds to zero. X Not applicable. [1] Excludes data for schools not reporting enrollment. [2] Includes schools beginning with grade 6 or below and with no grade higher than 8. [3] Includes schools with no grade lower than 7. [4] Includes schools beginning with grade 6 or below and ending with grade 9 or above. [5] Includes special education, alternative, and other schools not classified by grade span.

Source: U.S. National Center for Education Statistics, *Digest of Education Statistics*, "Advance Release of Selected 2014 Digest Tables," <http://www.nces.ed.gov/programs/digest/>, accessed May 2015.

Table 264. Public Elementary and Secondary Schools—Summary: 1990 to 2014

[In units as indicated (44,949 represents 44,949,000). For school year ending in year shown, except as indicated. Data are estimates]

Item	Unit	1990	2000	2005	2010	2012	2013	2014
School districts, total	**Number**	**15,552**	**15,403**	**15,731**	**15,782**	**15,874**	**15,824**	**15,737**
ENROLLMENT								
Population 5-17 years old [1]	1,000	44,949	53,119	53,606	53,979	53,732	53,742	53,707
Percent of resident population	Percent	18.2	18.9	18.1	17.5	17.1	17.0	16.8
Fall enrollment [2]	**1,000**	**40,527**	**46,577**	**48,414**	**49,128**	**49,227**	**49,422**	**49,568**
Percent of population 5-17 years old	Percent	90.2	87.7	90.3	91.0	91.6	92.0	92.3
Elementary [3]	1,000	26,253	29,243	29,630	30,274	30,415	30,549	30,640
Secondary [4]	1,000	14,274	17,334	18,783	18,855	18,813	18,873	18,928
Average daily attendance	1,000	37,573	43,313	45,088	46,883	47,486	47,682	48,015
High school graduates	1,000	2,327	2,544	2,803	3,113	3,187	3,238	3,273
INSTRUCTIONAL STAFF								
Total [5]	**1,000**	**2,685**	**3,273**	**3,509**	**3,659**	**3,522**	**3,553**	**3,560**
Classroom teachers	1,000	2,362	2,891	3,072	3,188	3,101	3,121	3,122
Average salaries:								
Instructional staff	Dollar	32,638	43,837	49,135	56,954	57,119	57,793	58,486
Classroom teachers	Dollar	31,367	41,807	47,516	55,225	55,522	56,065	56,610
REVENUES								
Revenue receipts	**Mil. dol.**	**208,656**	**369,754**	**477,371**	**570,528**	**587,586**	**597,496**	**612,527**
Federal	Mil. dol.	13,184	26,346	42,908	67,343	60,451	58,692	58,891
State	Mil. dol.	100,787	183,986	225,142	255,158	271,016	277,241	284,151
Local	Mil. dol.	94,685	159,421	209,321	248,028	256,119	261,563	269,485
Percent of total:								
Federal	Percent	6.3	7.1	9.0	11.8	10.3	9.8	9.6
State	Percent	48.3	49.8	47.2	44.7	46.1	46.4	46.4
Local/other	Percent	45.4	43.1	43.8	43.5	43.6	43.8	44.0
EXPENDITURES								
Total	**Mil. dol.**	**209,698**	**374,782**	**496,199**	**590,468**	**603,866**	**615,234**	**640,940**
Current expenditures (day schools)	Mil. dol.	186,583	320,954	422,346	512,864	527,980	539,831	562,840
Other current expenditures [6]	Mil. dol.	3,341	6,618	8,710	9,963	9,863	10,084	10,483
Capital outlay	Mil. dol.	16,012	37,552	48,757	49,361	45,067	44,269	45,621
Interest on school debt	Mil. dol.	3,762	9,659	16,385	18,279	20,956	21,049	21,996
Current expenditures per pupil enrolled	Dollar	4,604	6,891	8,724	10,439	10,725	10,923	11,355

[1] Estimated resident population as of July 1 of the previous year, except 1990, 2000, and 2010 population enumerated as of April 1. Estimates reflect revisions based on the 2010 Census of Population. [2] Fall enrollment of the previous year. [3] Kindergarten through grade 6. [4] Grades 7 through 12. [5] Full-time equivalent. [6] Current expenses for summer schools, adult education, post-high school vocational education, personnel retraining, etc., when operated by local school districts and not part of regular public elementary and secondary day-school program.

Source: National Education Association, Washington, DC. Data from *Rankings of the States 2014 and Estimates of School Statistics 2015*, used with permission of the National Education Association © 2015. All rights reserved.

Table 265. Public Elementary and Secondary School Enrollment by Grade: 1980 to 2012

[In thousands (40,877 represents 40,877,000). As of Fall of year shown. Based on survey of state education agencies; see source for details]

Grade	1980	1990	1995	2000	2005	2007	2008	2009	2010	2011	2012
Pupils enrolled [1]	**40,877**	**41,217**	**44,840**	**47,204**	**49,113**	**49,293**	**49,266**	**49,361**	**49,484**	**49,522**	**49,771**
Pre-kindergarten to 8 [1]	27,647	29,878	32,341	33,688	34,205	34,205	34,286	34,409	34,625	34,773	35,018
Pre-K and kindergarten	2,689	3,610	4,173	4,158	4,656	4,691	4,819	4,901	4,961	5,037	5,138
First	2,894	3,499	3,671	3,636	3,691	3,750	3,708	3,729	3,754	3,773	3,824
Second	2,800	3,327	3,507	3,634	3,606	3,704	3,699	3,665	3,701	3,713	3,729
Third	2,893	3,297	3,445	3,676	3,586	3,659	3,708	3,707	3,686	3,703	3,719
Fourth	3,107	3,248	3,431	3,711	3,578	3,624	3,647	3,701	3,711	3,672	3,690
Fifth	3,130	3,197	3,438	3,707	3,633	3,600	3,629	3,652	3,718	3,699	3,673
Sixth	3,038	3,110	3,395	3,663	3,670	3,628	3,614	3,644	3,682	3,724	3,723
Seventh	3,085	3,067	3,422	3,629	3,777	3,701	3,653	3,641	3,676	3,696	3,746
Eighth	3,086	2,979	3,356	3,538	3,802	3,709	3,692	3,651	3,659	3,679	3,699
Grades 9 to 12 [1]	13,231	11,338	12,500	13,515	14,909	15,087	14,980	14,952	14,860	14,749	14,753
Ninth	3,377	3,169	3,704	3,963	4,287	4,200	4,123	4,080	4,008	3,957	3,975
Tenth	3,368	2,896	3,237	3,491	3,866	3,863	3,822	3,809	3,800	3,751	3,730
Eleventh	3,195	2,612	2,826	3,083	3,455	3,558	3,548	3,541	3,538	3,546	3,528
Twelfth	2,925	2,381	2,487	2,803	3,180	3,375	3,400	3,432	3,472	3,452	3,477

[1] Includes unclassified students not shown separately.

Source: U.S. National Center for Education Statistics, *Digest of Education Statistics*, "Advance Release of Selected 2014 Digest Tables," <http://www.nces.ed.gov/programs/digest/>, accessed May 2015.

Table 266. Selected Statistics for the Largest Public School Districts: 2012

[For the 50 largest districts by enrollment size. For school year ending in 2012. Data from the Common Core Data Program; see source for details. School district boundaries are not necessarily the same as city or county boundaries]

School district	City	County	Number of students [1]	Number of full-time equivalent (FTE) teachers [2]	Number of schools [3]	Total expenditures per pupil
New York City Public Schools, NY	New York	New York	990,145	67,046	1,565	25,061
Los Angeles Unified, CA	Los Angeles	Los Angeles	659,639	28,769	939	13,490
City of Chicago School District, IL	Chicago	Cook	403,004	22,460	641	14,246
Dade County School District, FL	Miami	Miami-Dade	350,239	21,117	524	9,729
Clark County School District, NV	Las Vegas	Clark	313,398	14,822	364	9,125
Broward County School District, FL	Fort Lauderdale	Broward	258,478	14,533	329	8,968
Houston Independent School District, TX	Houston	Harris	203,066	10,920	279	11,601
Hillsborough County School District, FL	Tampa	Hillsborough	197,041	13,862	308	9,728
Hawaii Department of Education, HI	Honolulu	Honolulu	182,706	11,458	287	12,833
Orange County School District, FL	Orlando	Orange	180,000	11,308	243	9,824
Fairfax County Public Schools, VA	Falls Church	Fairfax	177,606	13,878	209	14,495
Palm Beach County School District, FL	West Palm Beach	Palm Beach	176,901	11,682	252	10,045
Gwinnett County, GA	Lawrenceville	Gwinnett	162,370	10,324	133	9,794
Dallas Independent School District, TX	Dallas	Dallas	157,575	10,277	237	12,061
Philadelphia City School District, PA	Philadelphia	Philadelphia	154,262	9,299	251	18,241
Wake County Schools, NC	Raleigh	Wake	148,154	9,440	165	9,135
Montgomery County Public Schools, MD	Rockville	Montgomery	146,459	9,622	205	18,073
Charlotte-Mecklenburg Schools, NC	Charlotte	Mecklenburg	141,728	8,791	173	8,763
San Diego Unified, CA	San Diego	San Diego	131,044	6,706	223	10,904
Duval County School District, FL	Jacksonville	Duval	125,429	7,589	195	9,024
Prince George's County Public Schools, MD	Upper Marlboro	Prince George's	123,833	7,796	208	14,903
Memphis City School District, TN	Memphis	Shelby	110,952	7,027	216	10,732
Cypress-Fairbanks Independent School District, TX	Houston	Harris	107,960	6,243	83	8,286
Cobb County, GA	Marietta	Cobb	107,291	7,342	116	11,016
Baltimore County Public Schools, MD	Townson	Baltimore	105,153	7,219	173	14,844
Pinellas County School District, FL	Largo	Pinellas	103,776	7,289	169	9,621
Jefferson County, KY	Louisville	Jefferson	99,191	5,904	173	12,683
Northside Independent School District, TX	San Antonio	Bexar	98,110	5,881	111	9,736
DeKalb County, GA	Decatur	Dekalb	98,088	6,650	135	10,751
Polk County School District, FL	Bartow	Polk	96,070	6,771	163	9,624
Albuquerque Public Schools, NM	Albuquerque	Bernalillo	94,318	6,157	162	10,427
Fulton County, GA	Atlanta	Fulton	92,604	6,195	104	10,824
Austin Independent School District, TX	Austin	Travis	86,528	5,758	122	11,588
Jefferson County, CO	Golden	Jefferson	85,793	4,729	163	9,214
Baltimore City Public Schools, MD	Baltimore	Baltimore City	84,212	5,533	195	17,552
Lee County School District, FL	Fort Myers	Lee	83,895	5,207	126	10,160
Long Beach Unified, CA	Long Beach	Los Angeles	83,691	3,135	92	10,478
Fort Worth Independent School District, TX	Fort Worth	Tarrant	83,109	5,126	144	10,407
Prince William County, VA	Manassas	Prince William	81,937	5,160	88	11,910
Denver County, CO	Denver	Denver	80,890	4,588	164	13,015
Davidson County School District, TN	Nashville	Davidson	80,393	5,377	144	10,875
Milwaukee, WI	Milwaukee	Milwaukee	79,130	3,961	177	15,010
Anne Arundel County Public Schools, MD	Annapolis	Anne Arundel	76,303	5,117	121	14,787
Fresno Unified, CA	Fresno	Fresno	74,235	3,053	106	10,449
Guilford County Schools, NC	Greensboro	Guilford	74,086	4,938	121	10,510
Greenville County Schools, SC	Greenville	Greenville	72,153	4,376	95	9,350
Brevard School District, FL	Viera	Brevard	71,792	4,846	123	8,394
Virginia Beach City Public Schools, VA	Virginia Beach	Virginia Beach	70,978	4,398	85	12,044
Alpine School District, UT	American Fork	Utah	69,639	2,821	80	6,265
Fort Bend Independent School District, TX	Sugar Land	Fort Bend	69,449	3,982	73	8,605

[1] Number of students receiving educational services from the school district. [2] Full-time equivalent is the amount of time required to perform an assignment stated as a proportion of a full-time position. [3] Totals for number of schools may differ from published estimates since they exclude closed, inactive, and future schools.

Source: U.S. Department of Education, National Center for Education Statistics, "Elementary/Secondary Information System," <http://nces.ed.gov/ccd/elsi/default.aspx?agree=0>, accessed September 2015.

Table 267. Public Elementary and Secondary School Enrollment by State: 1990 to 2012

[In thousands (29,878 represents 29,878,000). As of Fall. Includes unclassified students. Based on survey of state education agencies; see source for details]

State	Pre-kindergarten through grade 8					Grades 9 through 12				
	1990	2000	2005	2010	2012	1990	2000	2005	2010	2012
United States...............	**29,878**	**33,688**	**34,205**	**34,625**	**35,018**	**11,338**	**13,515**	**14,908**	**14,860**	**14,753**
Alabama..........................	527	539	529	534	527	195	201	212	222	217
Alaska...........................	85	94	91	92	93	29	39	42	40	38
Arizona..........................	479	641	740	752	768	161	237	355	320	322
Arkansas........................	314	318	336	346	348	123	132	138	136	139
California.......................	3,615	4,408	4,466	4,294	4,332	1,336	1,733	1,971	1,996	1,968
Colorado........................	420	517	550	601	618	154	208	230	242	246
Connecticut.....................	347	406	400	387	381	122	156	175	173	170
Delaware........................	73	81	85	90	91	27	34	36	39	38
District of Columbia...........	61	54	56	54	58	19	15	21	18	18
Florida..........................	1,370	1,760	1,873	1,858	1,893	492	675	802	785	800
Georgia.........................	849	1,060	1,145	1,202	1,222	303	385	453	475	481
Hawaii..........................	123	132	127	128	134	49	52	55	52	51
Idaho...........................	160	170	183	194	202	61	75	79	82	83
Illinois..........................	1,310	1,474	1,480	1,455	1,448	512	575	631	637	625
Indiana..........................	676	703	724	729	725	279	286	311	318	316
Iowa............................	345	334	326	348	355	139	161	157	148	145
Kansas..........................	320	323	321	343	350	117	147	147	141	139
Kentucky........................	459	471	487	480	491	177	194	192	193	194
Louisiana.......................	586	547	482	512	525	199	197	172	184	186
Maine...........................	155	146	133	129	128	60	61	62	60	58
Maryland........................	527	609	589	588	603	188	244	271	264	257
Massachusetts..................	604	703	675	666	667	230	273	297	289	288
Michigan........................	1,145	1,222	1,191	1,076	1,062	440	498	551	511	493
Minnesota.......................	546	578	558	570	583	211	277	281	268	262
Mississippi......................	372	364	358	351	356	131	134	137	140	137
Missouri.........................	588	645	635	643	648	228	268	283	276	270
Montana.........................	111	105	98	98	101	42	50	48	43	42
Nebraska........................	198	195	195	210	215	76	91	92	88	88
Nevada..........................	150	251	296	307	314	51	90	116	130	132
New Hampshire.................	126	147	139	132	128	46	61	67	63	61
New Jersey......................	784	968	971	981	956	306	346	425	421	416
New Mexico.....................	208	225	230	239	241	94	95	97	99	97
New York........................	1,828	2,029	1,909	1,869	1,869	770	853	906	866	842
North Carolina..................	783	945	1,003	1,058	1,080	304	348	413	432	438
North Dakota....................	85	72	66	66	71	33	37	33	30	30
Ohio............................	1,258	1,294	1,261	1,223	1,211	514	541	578	531	519
Oklahoma.......................	425	445	457	483	496	154	178	178	176	177
Oregon..........................	340	379	380	393	409	132	167	173	178	178
Pennsylvania....................	1,172	1,258	1,228	1,210	1,205	496	556	603	584	559
Rhode Island....................	102	114	104	98	98	37	44	50	46	45
South Carolina..................	452	493	498	516	527	170	184	204	210	209
South Dakota...................	95	88	84	88	93	34	41	38	38	37
Tennessee.......................	598	668	677	702	712	226	241	277	286	282
Texas...........................	2,511	2,943	3,268	3,587	3,690	872	1,117	1,257	1,349	1,388
Utah............................	325	333	358	425	444	122	148	151	161	169
Vermont.........................	71	70	65	68	62	25	32	32	29	28
Virginia.........................	728	816	841	871	889	270	329	372	380	376
Washington......................	613	694	699	714	725	227	310	333	330	327
West Virginia...................	224	201	197	201	202	98	85	84	81	81
Wisconsin.......................	566	595	584	598	607	232	285	291	274	266
Wyoming........................	71	60	57	63	65	27	30	27	26	26

Source: U.S. National Center for Education Statistics, *Digest of Education Statistics*, "Advance Release of Selected 2014 Digest Tables," <http://www.nces.ed.gov/programs/digest/>, accessed May 2015.

Table 268. Parent Participation in School-Related Activities by Selected School, Student, and Family Characteristics: 2012

[In percent, except as noted (52,215 represents 52,215,000). For school year ending in 2012. Covers parents with children in kindergarten through grade 12. Homeschooled students are excluded]

Characteristic	Number of students in grades K through 12 (1,000)	Participation in school activities by parent or other household member				
		Attended a general school or PTO/PTA meeting [1]	Attended regularly scheduled parent-teacher conference	Attended a school or class event	Volunteered or served on school committee	Participated in school fundraising
Total	**52,215**	**87**	**76**	**74**	**42**	**58**
School type: [2]						
Public, assigned	40,070	86	74	73	38	56
Public, chosen	7,482	89	76	75	44	57
Private, religious	3,276	96	85	88	69	84
Private, nonreligious	782	95	89	91	65	77
Student's sex:						
Male	26,982	87	76	72	40	57
Female	25,233	88	75	77	44	60
Student's race/ethnicity:						
White, non-Hispanic	26,910	89	77	82	50	67
Black, non-Hispanic	7,464	85	76	68	31	52
Hispanic [3]	12,113	86	73	64	32	46
Asian or Pacific Islander, non-Hispanic	2,886	84	72	64	37	46
Other, non-Hispanic [4]	2,842	88	78	77	44	58
Student's grade level: [5]						
K–2nd grade	13,608	93	89	79	56	67
3rd–5th grade	12,257	92	89	82	50	69
6th–8th grade	11,715	87	71	70	32	53
9th–12th grade	14,635	79	57	66	28	47
Parents' highest education level:						
Less than high school	6,335	77	64	48	19	31
High school graduate or equivalent	10,570	82	72	62	28	46
Vocational/technical or some college	15,804	88	77	77	41	61
Bachelor's degree	11,852	92	80	85	55	71
Graduate or professional school	7,654	95	82	89	61	75
Parents' language at home:						
Both/only parent(s) speak(s) English	44,542	88	77	78	45	63
One or two parents speaks English	1,862	88	69	62	29	38
No parent speaks English	5,812	82	65	50	23	32

[1] Parent Teacher Organization (PTO) or Parent Teacher Association (PTA) meeting. [2] School type classifies the school currently attended as either public or private. Public schools are further classified according to whether the school was chosen or assigned. Private schools are classified as being religious or nonreligious. [3] Persons of Hispanic origin may be of any race. [4] Includes children who were multiracial and not of Hispanic ethnicity, were American Indian or Alaska Native, or were not Hispanic, White, Black, Asian, or Pacific Islander. [5] Students whose parents reported the student's grade equivalent as "ungraded" were excluded from the analyses of grade level.

Source: U.S. Department of Education, National Center for Education Statistics, *Parent and Family Involvement in Education, from the National Household Education Surveys Program of 2012*, May 2015. See also <http://nces.ed.gov/nhes/>.

Table 269. School Enrollment Below Postsecondary—Summary by Sex, Race, and Hispanic Origin: 2013

[In thousands (58,306 represents 58,306,000), except percent. As of October. Covers civilian noninstitutional population enrolled in nursery school through high school. Based on Current Population Survey, see text, Section 1 and Appendix III]

Characteristic	Total			Race and Hispanic origin				
	Number [1]	Male	Female	White [2]		Black [2]	Asian [2]	Hispanic [3]
				Total	Non-Hispanic			
All students	**58,306**	**29,745**	**28,560**	**42,674**	**30,676**	**8,967**	**2,800**	**13,752**
Nursery	4,682	2,374	2,308	3,346	2,531	683	242	991
Full day	2,306	(NA)	(NA)	1,516	1,121	469	101	495
Part day	2,376	(NA)	(NA)	1,830	1,410	214	141	495
Public schools	2,558	(NA)	(NA)	1,740	1,089	465	113	781
Full day	1,249	(NA)	(NA)	787	475	312	35	376
Part day	1,309	(NA)	(NA)	953	614	153	77	405
Private schools	2,124	(NA)	(NA)	1,606	1,442	218	129	210
Full day	1,057	(NA)	(NA)	729	646	157	66	119
Part day	1,068	(NA)	(NA)	878	796	61	63	90
Kindergarten	4,150	2,142	2,008	2,933	1,952	736	165	1,090
Elementary	32,873	16,837	16,036	24,238	17,309	4,848	1,576	7,942
High school	16,601	8,392	8,208	12,157	8,869	2,699	817	3,729
Population 18 to 24 years old	30,556	15,379	15,178	22,657	16,963	4,746	1,639	6,489
Percent dropouts [4]	7.3	7.7	6.8	7.1	5.2	8.3	3.7	13.7
Percent high school graduates	86.1	84.9	87.4	86.8	89.2	81.8	91.2	78.9
Percent enrolled in college	39.9	36.6	43.3	39.9	41.6	33.7	61.1	33.8

NA Not available. [1] Includes other races not shown separately. [2] For persons who selected this race group only. See footnote 4, Table 253. [3] Persons of Hispanic origin may be of any race. [4] For persons not in regular school and who have not completed the 12th grade nor received a general equivalency degree.

Source: U.S. Census Bureau, "School Enrollment, Historical Time Series Tables," <http://www.census.gov/hhes/school/data/cps/historical/index.html>, accessed November 2014.

Table 270. Elementary and Secondary Schools—Teachers, Enrollment, and Pupil-Teacher Ratio: 1970 to 2013

[In thousands (2,292 represents 2,292,000), except ratios. As of Fall. Data are for full-time equivalent teachers. Based on surveys of state education agencies and private schools; see source for details]

Year	Teachers			Enrollment			Pupil-teacher ratio		
	Total	Public	Private	Total	Public	Private	Total	Public	Private
1970	2,292	2,059	233	51,257	45,894	5,363	22.4	22.3	23.0
1980	2,485	2,184	301	46,208	40,877	5,331	18.6	18.7	17.7
1990	2,759	2,398	361	46,864	41,217	5,648	17.0	17.2	15.6
1995	2,974	2,598	376	50,759	44,840	5,918	17.1	17.3	15.7
1997	3,138	2,746	391	52,071	46,127	5,944	16.6	16.8	15.2
1998 [1]	3,230	2,830	400	52,526	46,539	5,988	16.3	16.4	15.0
1999	3,319	2,911	408	52,875	46,857	6,018	15.9	16.1	14.7
2000 [1]	3,366	2,941	424	53,373	47,204	6,169	15.9	16.0	14.5
2001	3,440	3,000	441	53,992	47,672	6,320	15.7	15.9	14.3
2002 [1]	3,476	3,034	442	54,403	48,183	6,220	15.7	15.9	14.1
2003	3,490	3,049	441	54,639	48,540	6,099	15.7	15.9	13.8
2004 [1]	3,536	3,091	445	54,882	48,795	6,087	15.5	15.8	13.7
2005	3,593	3,143	450	55,187	49,113	6,073	15.4	15.6	13.5
2006 [1]	3,622	3,166	456	55,307	49,316	5,991	15.3	15.6	13.2
2007	3,656	3,200	456	55,201	49,291	5,910	15.1	15.4	13.0
2008 [1]	3,670	3,222	448	54,973	49,266	5,707	15.0	15.3	12.8
2009	3,647	3,210	437	54,849	49,361	5,488	15.0	15.4	12.5
2010 [1]	3,529	3,099	429	54,867	49,484	5,382	15.5	16.0	12.5
2011	3,524	3,103	421	54,790	49,522	5,268	15.5	16.0	12.5
2012 [1]	3,523	3,109	414	54,952	49,771	5,181	15.6	16.0	12.5
2013, projected	3,527	3,120	407	55,036	49,942	5,094	15.6	16.0	12.5

[1] Private school numbers are estimated based on data from the Private School Universe Survey.

Source: U.S. National Center for Education Statistics, *Digest of Education Statistics*, "Advance Release of Selected 2014 Digest Tables," <http://www.nces.ed.gov/programs/digest/>, accessed May 2015.

Table 271. Private Schools—Number, Students, and Teachers by School Characteristics: 2011 to 2012

[4,495 represents 4,495,000. Based on the Private School Survey, conducted every 2 years; see source for details. For composition of regions, see map inside front cover]

Characteristic	Schools				Students (1,000)				Teachers (1,000) [1]			
	Number	Elementary	Secondary	Combined	Total	Elementary	Secondary	Combined	Total	Elementary	Secondary	Combined
Total	**30,861**	**19,697**	**2,677**	**8,488**	**4,495**	**2,124**	**757**	**1,613**	**421**	**184**	**65**	**172**
School type:												
Catholic	6,873	5,421	1,046	406	1,928	1,232	560	136	138	84	41	12
Parochial	2,910	2,693	139	79	729	640	61	27	49	43	5	2
Diocesan	2,922	2,308	487	127	831	530	260	41	58	36	18	4
Private	1,041	420	421	201	369	62	239	68	31	6	19	7
Other religious	14,214	7,928	759	5,526	1,677	592	107	977	163	57	11	95
Conservative Christian	4,574	1,590	150	2,834	631	145	19	466	60	14	2	44
Affiliated	3,060	1,917	271	872	487	205	45	238	49	20	5	24
Unaffiliated	6,579	4,421	338	1,820	559	243	43	274	54	23	4	27
Nonsectarian	9,775	6,348	871	2,556	890	300	90	499	120	42	13	64
Regular	4,882	3,522	339	1,021	612	180	63	369	75	23	8	43
Special emphasis	3,280	2,584	262	434	174	108	16	49	26	17	3	6
Special education	1,613	242	271	1,101	105	12	12	81	20	2	2	15
Program emphasis:												
Regular elem/secondary	21,486	12,928	2,014	6,543	4,104	1,934	720	1,450	359	154	59	146
Montessori	2,439	2,305	(B)	124	89	78	(B)	10	14	13	(B)	1
Special program emphasis	676	365	82	229	84	32	12	40	10	4	2	5
Special education	1,859	288	304	1,267	117	13	13	91	22	3	3	17
Vocational/technical	(B)	(B)	(B)	(B)	(B)	(B)	(B)	(B)	(B)	(B)	(B)	(B)
Alternative	813	250	263	300	44	11	12	22	7	2	2	3
Early childhood	3,583	3,560	(X)	22	55	55	(X)	1	9	9	(X)	(Z)
Size:												
Less than 50	13,459	9,829	763	2,866	268	183	16	69	46	29	3	13
50 to 149	7,667	4,592	533	2,542	701	429	47	225	81	45	6	29
150 to 299	5,488	3,544	434	1,510	1,165	746	95	324	102	58	10	34
300 to 499	2,447	1,333	381	732	941	512	147	282	78	36	13	28
500 to 749	1,103	340	320	443	665	200	194	270	53	12	15	26
750 or more	698	58	245	395	754	54	257	443	62	3	18	40
Region:												
Northeast	7,447	4,854	857	1,735	1,078	492	244	342	110	44	23	42
Midwest	7,963	5,665	616	1,682	1,100	643	216	240	91	50	17	24
South	9,203	4,959	619	3,625	1,470	541	159	770	145	52	14	79
West	6,249	4,219	585	1,445	847	448	138	261	75	37	12	26
Urban/Rural Status:												
City	10,005	6,583	1,096	2,326	1,901	892	389	620	173	76	31	66
Suburban	10,911	7,470	868	2,572	1,673	875	264	534	156	74	23	58
Town	2,900	1,735	174	991	301	158	27	115	28	14	3	12
Rural	7,045	3,908	538	2,599	621	199	77	345	64	19	9	35

X Not applicable. B Base figure too small to meet statistical standards. Z Less than 500. [1] Full-time equivalents.

Source: U.S. National Center for Education Statistics, Private School Universe Survey, "Data Tables," <http://nces.ed.gov/surveys/pss/>, accessed September 2015.

Table 272. Public Elementary and Secondary Schools—Number and Average Salary of Classroom Teachers: 1990 to 2013, and by State, 2014

[2,362 represents 2,362,000. Estimates for school year ending in June of year shown. Elementary includes kindergarten]

Year and state	Teachers [1] (1,000)			Avg. salary ($1,000)		
	Total	Elementary	Secondary	All teachers	Elementary	Secondary
1990	2,362	1,390	972	31.4	30.8	32.0
1995	2,565	1,517	1,048	36.7	36.1	37.5
2000	2,891	1,696	1,195	41.8	41.3	42.5
2005	3,072	1,799	1,273	47.5	47.1	47.7
2007	3,151	1,826	1,325	51.1	50.8	51.7
2008	3,183	1,848	1,335	53.0	52.5	53.4
2009	3,207	1,876	1,332	54.4	54.0	54.9
2010	3,188	1,863	1,325	55.2	54.9	55.6
2011	3,158	1,856	1,302	55.6	55.2	56.4
2012	3,101	1,860	1,241	55.5	55.2	55.9
2013	3,121	1,865	1,256	56.1	55.8	56.6
2014, U.S.	**3,122**	**1,869**	**1,253**	**56.6**	**56.4**	**56.9**
AL	46	25	22	48.7	48.1	49.4
AK	8	3	5	65.9	65.9	65.9
AZ	59	42	17	45.3	45.3	45.3
AR	31	14	17	47.3	45.8	48.5
CA	293	196	97	71.4	71.4	71.4
CO	57	30	27	49.6	49.6	49.6
CT	42	29	13	70.6	70.6	70.6
DE	9	4	5	59.3	59.3	59.3
DC	6	4	2	73.2	73.2	73.2
FL	170	89	80	47.8	47.8	47.8
GA	109	66	42	52.9	52.5	53.6
HI	11	6	5	56.3	56.3	56.3
ID	15	8	7	44.5	44.5	44.5
IL	129	96	33	60.1	60.1	60.1
IN	60	32	29	50.3	50.3	50.3
IA	35	24	11	52.0	52.2	51.7
KS	35	17	17	48.2	48.2	48.2
KY	41	29	12	50.6	50.4	50.9
LA	45	31	14	49.1	49.1	49.1

State	Teachers [1] (1,000)			Avg. salary ($1,000)		
	Total	Elementary	Secondary	All teachers	Elementary	Secondary
ME	15	11	4	49.2	49.1	48.7
MD	59	36	24	64.5	64.1	65.4
MA	71	47	24	73.2	73.2	73.2
MI	66	36	29	62.2	62.2	62.2
MN	54	28	27	54.8	54.8	54.8
MS	32	19	13	42.2	42.2	42.2
MO	67	34	33	46.8	46.8	46.8
MT	11	7	3	49.9	49.9	49.7
NE	24	16	8	49.5	49.5	49.7
NV	27	16	12	55.8	55.8	55.8
NH	16	11	5	57.1	57.1	57.1
NJ	115	77	38	68.2	67.4	70.0
NM	22	15	7	45.7	45.0	46.4
NY	201	89	111	76.4	76.4	76.4
NC	95	68	28	45.0	45.0	45.0
ND	8	6	2	48.7	48.7	48.7
OH	108	69	39	55.9	57.0	54.9
OK	42	30	12	44.5	44.1	45.5
OR	26	18	9	58.6	58.3	59.3
PA	118	59	59	63.7	63.7	63.7
RI	10	6	4	64.7	64.7	64.7
SC	49	34	15	48.4	46.6	47.2
SD	9	7	3	40.0	39.9	40.3
TN	65	45	19	47.7	47.7	47.7
TX	335	172	163	49.7	49.2	50.2
UT	27	15	12	45.7	45.7	45.7
VT	8	4	4	56.0	56.0	56.0
VA	102	62	40	49.8	49.8	49.8
WA	55	30	24	53.0	52.5	53.5
WV	20	14	5	45.1	44.8	45.9
WI	57	40	17	53.7	53.3	54.6
WY	7	4	3	56.6	56.0	57.3

[1] Full-time equivalent.

Source: National Education Association, Washington, DC. Data from *Rankings of the States 2014 and Estimates of School Statistics 2015*, used with permission of the National Education Association © 2015. All rights reserved.

Table 273. Public School Teachers, Base Salary, and Additional Income by Selected Characteristics: 2012

[3,139.2 represents 3,139,200. For school year ending in 2012. Data shown for regular full-time teachers only; excludes other staff even when they have full-time teaching duties. Based on the 2011-12 Schools and Staffing Survey and subject to sampling error; for details, see <http://nces.ed.gov/surveys/sass/>]

Characteristic	Number of full-time teachers (1,000)	Base teacher salary (dollars)	Total income from school and nonschool sources [1,2] (dollars)	Teachers with additional income					
				Job outside the school system during the school year		Supplemental school system contract during summer [3]		Employed in a non-school job during the summer	
				Percent of teachers	Average income (dollars)	Percent of teachers	Average income (dollars)	Percent of teachers	Average income (dollars)
Total..........................	3,139.2	53,070	56,410	16.1	4,820	17.8	2,510	15.0	3,430
Sex:									
Male...........................	754.6	54,430	60,360	23.3	6,060	21.4	2,880	23.2	4,560
Female.......................	2,384.6	52,640	55,160	13.9	4,150	16.6	2,360	12.4	2,770
Race/ethnicity:									
White........................	2,556.2	53,020	56,400	17.0	4,740	16.7	2,410	16.1	3,310
Black........................	221.0	52,370	55,790	15.5	4,740	26.2	2,920	9.5	4,540
Hispanic....................	252.2	53,620	56,240	9.5	4,600	20.7	2,710	9.4	3,640
Asian........................	57.5	58,850	62,480	7.9	7,000	19.7	3,080	7.0	5,400
Pacific Islander.............	4.4	52,920	57,280	(S)	(S)	(S)	(S)	(S)	(S)
American Indian/Alaska Native.......................	15.4	46,630	53,000	22.4	(S)	19.2	2,640	21.5	4,470
Two or more races...........	31.2	50,230	53,750	16.0	5,690	14.5	2,610	16.1	3,550
Age:									
Less than 30 years old.......	487.4	41,720	45,160	18.7	3,360	21.5	2,430	24.5	2,980
30 to 39 years old............	921.9	50,020	53,120	15.7	4,380	18.4	2,420	14.8	3,320
40 to 49 years old............	783.7	55,420	58,660	16.8	5,070	17.4	2,490	14.6	3,720
50 or more years old.........	946.2	59,940	63,550	14.6	6,000	15.6	2,680	10.6	3,800
Years of full-time teaching experience:									
1 year or less.................	144.2	40,540	44,610	16.9	4,380	18.7	2,980	31.2	4,860
2 to 4 years..................	395.9	41,480	44,490	17.3	3,970	20.2	2,260	20.6	2,800
5 to 9 years..................	784.6	47,300	50,370	16.6	4,250	19.4	2,380	14.7	3,110
10 to 14 years................	652.1	54,860	58,040	15.7	4,830	17.2	2,670	12.2	3,450
15 to 19 years................	426.2	58,880	62,050	15.4	5,940	17.2	2,430	13.0	3,390
20 to 24 years................	295.8	60,930	64,210	15.2	5,730	13.4	2,460	13.8	4,220
25 to 29 years................	217.9	63,780	67,440	15.9	5,000	16.8	2,550	12.8	3,010
30 or more years.............	222.5	64,820	69,790	15.6	5,400	16.5	2,920	11.0	3,700
Highest degree held:									
Less than bachelors'.........	118.9	51,330	55,430	20.1	7,340	16.6	2,360	20.9	3,750
Bachelor's....................	1,278.2	46,340	49,410	14.5	4,600	16.8	2,360	16.2	3,400
Master's.....................	1,479.3	57,830	61,230	16.6	4,570	18.1	2,600	13.8	3,380
Education specialist.........	228.7	59,680	63,420	17.7	5,330	20.4	2,650	12.2	3,620
Doctorate....................	34.2	60,230	66,140	30.8	6,610	26.9	2,810	18.8	3,940
Instructional level: [4]									
Elementary..................	1,572.3	52,620	54,820	12.8	4,350	16.6	2,270	12.6	2,930
Secondary...................	1,566.9	53,520	58,000	19.5	5,130	19.0	2,720	17.4	3,790
School locale:									
City..........................	(S)	(S)	(S)	(S)	(S)	(S)	(S)	(S)	(S)
Suburban....................	1,016.9	58,470	61,610	15.6	4,300	17.4	2,450	13.8	3,350
Town.........................	382.9	47,780	51,050	16.3	4,910	15.6	2,030	16.0	3,520
Rural.........................	853.0	47,130	50,670	16.3	5,340	15.1	2,290	16.9	3,600

S Figure does not meet publication standards. [1] Includes retirement pension funds paid during the school year. [2] Includes types of income not shown separately. [3] Includes teaching summer sessions and other non-teaching jobs at any school. [4] Teachers were classified as elementary or secondary on the basis of the grades they taught, rather than on the level of the school in which they taught. In general, elementary teachers include those teaching pre-kindergarten through grade 5 and those teaching multiple grades, with a preponderance of grades taught being kindergarten through grade 6. In general, secondary teachers include those teaching grades 7 through 12 and those teaching multiple grades, with a preponderance of grades taught being grades 7 through 12 and usually no grade taught being lower than grade 5.

Source: U.S. National Center for Education Statistics, *Digest of Education Statistics*, "Advance Release of Selected 2013 Digest Tables," <http://www.nces.ed.gov/programs/digest/>, accessed March 2014.

Table 274. Private School Teachers, Base Salary, and Additional Income by Selected Characteristics: 2012

[368.4 represents 368,400. For school year ending in 2012. Data shown for regular full-time teachers only; excludes other staff even when they have full-time teaching duties. Based on the 2011-12 Schools and Staffing Survey and subject to sampling error; for details, see <http://nces.ed.gov/surveys/sass/>]

Characteristic	Number of full-time teachers (1,000)	Base teacher Salary (dollars)	Total income from school and nonschool income [1,2] (1,000)	Teachers with additional income					
				Job outside the school system during the school year		Supplemental school system contract during summer [3]		Employed in a non-school job during the summer	
				Percent of teachers	Average income (dollars)	Percent of teachers	Average income (dollars)	Percent of teachers	Average income (dollars)
Total [4]	368.4	40,200	44,130	19.6	5,440	20.8	3,370	17.1	3,780
Sex:									
Male	92.9	44,470	51,150	26.9	6,550	29.3	3,600	23.3	4,650
Female	275.5	38,760	41,760	17.1	4,850	17.9	3,240	15.0	3,320
Race/ethnicity:									
White	326.0	40,450	44,390	19.4	5,350	20.2	3,410	17.5	3,710
Black	13.0	37,080	41,790	(S)	(S)	29.6	3,560	(S)	(S)
Hispanic	19.8	39,530	42,550	15.3	6,090	18.0	2,590	(S)	3,070
Asian	6.3	36,720	40,170	(S)	(S)	(S)	(S)	(S)	(S)
Two or more races	2.8	39,640	46,660	(S)	(S)	(S)	(S)	(S)	(S)
Age:									
Less than 30 years old	63.2	31,010	34,340	23.6	4,170	24.0	2,050	32.7	3,460
30 to 39 years old	94.3	38,420	42,110	19.4	4,950	23.9	4,270	15.4	3,590
40 to 49 years old	87.9	42,860	45,740	18.2	4,980	20.2	3,460	12.3	2,690
50 or more years old	123.0	44,420	49,580	18.5	7,000	17.1	3,280	13.9	5,000
Years of full-time teaching experience:									
1 year or less	30.9	29,940	33,980	24.5	5,100	21.4	2,330	30.9	4,390
2 to 4 years	61.5	33,540	36,760	22.0	4,250	23.9	2,540	23.5	2,820
5 to 9 years	85.0	37,220	40,990	19.3	5,760	24.8	4,170	16.1	4,080
10 to 14 years	58.6	40,440	43,570	19.3	5,310	18.6	3,740	14.2	3,340
15 to 19 years	43.9	44,820	47,190	15.1	5,110	20.5	3,180	10.6	2,400
20 to 24 years	27.7	48,170	52,380	20.3	6,230	16.0	1,790	15.4	3,860
25 to 29 years	24.3	47,070	52,040	17.6	5,340	17.6	3,230	(S)	(S)
30 or more years	36.5	50,390	57,950	18.4	7,420	15.1	4,700	14.8	2,410
Highest degree held:									
Less than bachelors'	27.9	27,690	30,160	15.3	3,820	19.5	2,760	15.5	3,750
Bachelor's	180.9	36,270	39,450	18.2	5,420	19.6	2,880	18.7	4,000
Master's	134.3	46,400	50,670	20.7	5,070	21.8	4,160	16.3	3,470
Education specialist	17.7	47,450	55,230	25.2	7,280	24.6	2,820	(S)	(S)
Doctorate	7.7	52,590	64,890	(S)	(S)	(S)	(S)	(S)	(S)
Instructional level: [5]									
Elementary	196.8	36,260	39,310	16.0	5,190	17.1	2,770	15.8	3,730
Secondary	171.6	44,720	49,640	23.7	5,640	25.0	3,840	18.7	3,820

S Figure does not meet publication standards. [1] Includes retirement pension funds paid during the school year. [2] Includes types of income not shown separately. [3] Includes teaching summer sessions and other non-teaching jobs at any school. [4] Includes race/ethnicities not shown separately. [5] Teachers were classified as elementary or secondary on the basis of the grades they taught, rather than on the level of the school in which they taught. In general, elementary teachers include those teaching pre-kindergarten through grade 5 and those teaching multiple grades, with a preponderance of grades taught being kindergarten through grade 6. In general, secondary teachers include those teaching grades 7 through 12 and those teaching multiple grades, with a preponderance of grades taught being grades 7 through 12 and usually no grade taught being lower than grade 5.

Source: U.S. National Center for Education Statistics, *Digest of Education Statistics*, "Advance Release of Selected 2013 Digest Tables," <http://www.nces.ed.gov/programs/digest/>, accessed March 2014.

Table 275. Teacher Stayers, Movers, and Leavers by Selected Characteristics: 1989 to 2013

[2,386.5 represents 2,386,500. For school year ending in year shown. Data compare the teaching status of teacher between one school year and the prior year. Stayers are teachers who were teaching in the same school in both years. Movers are teachers who were still teaching in the current school year but in a different school. Leavers are teachers who left the teaching profession. Based on the School and Staffing Survey; see source for details]

Characteristic	Number of teachers				Percent of teachers		
	Total [1]	Stayers	Movers	Leavers	Stayers	Movers	Leavers
1989	2,386.5	2,065.8	188.4	132.3	86.5	7.9	5.6
1992	2,553.5	2,237.3	185.7	130.5	87.6	7.2	5.1
1995	2,555.8	2,205.3	182.9	167.6	86.3	7.2	6.6
2001	2,994.7	2,542.2	231.0	221.4	84.9	7.7	7.4
2005	3,214.9	2,684.2	261.1	269.6	83.5	8.1	8.4
2009	3,380.3	2,854.9	255.7	269.8	84.5	7.6	8.0
Total, 2013	**3,377.9**	**2,846.5**	**271.9**	**259.4**	**84.3**	**8.1**	**7.7**
Age:							
Less than 30 years old	515.9	406.8	70.7	38.4	78.8	13.7	7.5
30 to 39 years old	982.2	847.4	83.1	51.7	86.3	8.5	5.3
40 to 49 years old	843.3	759.5	49.9	33.9	90.1	5.9	4.0
50 years old and over	1,036.4	832.8	68.2	135.4	80.4	6.6	13.1
Sex:							
Male	801.2	686.6	63.0	51.6	85.7	7.9	6.4
Female	2,576.6	2,159.9	208.9	207.8	83.8	8.1	8.1
Race/ethnicity:							
White	2,769.7	2,353.4	207.3	209.0	85.0	7.5	7.5
Black	229.4	179.4	[2] 26.9	[2] 23.1	78.2	[2] 11.7	[2] 10.1
Hispanic	261.2	207.4	33.0	[2] 20.8	79.4	12.6	[2] 8.0
Asian	[2] 63.8	[2] 61.2	[2] 1.6	(S)	95.8	(S)	(S)
American Indian/Alaska Native	[2] 22.3	[2] 17.5	(S)	(S)	78.8	(S)	(S)
Two or more races	[2] 31.2	[2] 27.7	[2] 1.8	(S)	88.8	(S)	(S)
Teaching status:							
Full time	3,126.0	2,678.8	234.2	213.0	85.7	7.5	6.8
Part time	251.8	167.7	37.8	46.4	66.6	15.0	18.4
Teaching experience:							
1 year to 3 years	398.5	320.4	49.8	28.2	80.4	12.5	7.1
4 to 9 years	919.5	749.4	107.6	62.5	81.5	11.7	6.8
10 to 19 years	1,205.4	1,066.2	68.0	71.2	88.5	5.6	5.9
20 years or more	854.5	710.6	46.5	97.4	83.2	5.4	11.4
Base salary:							
Less than $30,000	88.5	61.4	13.9	13.1	69.4	15.7	14.8
$30,000 to $39,999	643.7	527.6	74.9	41.2	82.0	11.6	6.4
$40,000 to $49,999	970.3	815.3	77.5	77.5	84.0	8.0	8.0
$50,000 or more	1,675.3	1,442.2	105.6	127.6	86.1	6.3	7.6
School classification:							
Traditional public	3,264.9	2,754.4	260.4	250.1	84.4	8.0	7.7
Public charter	113.0	92.1	[2] 11.6	9.3	81.5	[2] 10.2	8.2
School level:							
Primary	1,658.0	1,391.8	143.5	122.7	83.9	8.7	7.4
Middle	539.6	459.7	42.1	37.9	85.2	7.8	7.0
High	987.8	844.8	66.5	76.6	85.5	6.7	7.8
Combined	192.4	150.3	[2] 19.8	[2] 22.2	78.1	[2] 10.3	[2] 11.6
School enrollment:							
Less than 200 students	156.8	133.6	13.3	9.9	85.2	8.5	6.3
200 to 499 students	1,068.8	899.5	84.8	84.5	84.2	7.9	7.9
500 to 749 students	866.1	718.2	79.9	68.0	82.9	9.2	7.8
750 or more students	1,286.2	1,095.2	94.0	97.1	85.1	7.3	7.5

S Figure does not meet publication standards. [1] Total teachers in base year, which refers to prior school year. [2] Interpret data with caution. The standard error for this estimate is equal to 30 percent or more of the estimate's value.

Source: U.S. National Center for Education Statistics, *Teacher Attrition and Mobility: Results from the 2012-13 Teacher Follow-up Survey*, September 2014. See also <https://nces.ed.gov/pubsearch/pubsinfo.asp?pubid=2014077>.

Table 276. Public Charter and Traditional Schools by Selected Characteristics: 1999 and 2011

[46,689 represents 46,689,000. As of Fall. A public charter school is a public school that, in accordance with an enabling state statute, has been granted a charter exempting it from selected state and local rules and regulations]

Characteristic	1999			2011		
	Total	Traditional	Public charter	Total	Traditional	Public charter
Enrollment (1,000)	**46,689**	**46,350**	**340**	**49,256**	**47,199**	**2,058**
PERCENT DISTRIBUTION OF STUDENTS						
Race/ethnicity:	100.0	100.0	100.0	100.0	100.0	100.0
White, non-Hispanic	61.8	61.9	42.5	51.7	52.4	35.6
Black, non-Hispanic	17.1	16.9	33.5	15.8	15.2	28.7
Hispanic	15.9	15.9	19.6	23.7	23.6	28.0
Asian/Pacific Islander	4.1	4.1	2.8	5.1	5.1	4.0
American Indian/Alaska Native	1.2	1.2	1.5	1.1	1.1	0.9
Two or more races	(NA)	(NA)	(NA)	2.6	2.6	2.8
Number of teachers (1,000)	2,636	2,623	14	3,028	2,920	108
Pupil/teacher ratio	16.6	16.6	18.8	16.3	16.3	17.6
Total number of schools	**92,012**	**90,488**	**1,524**	**98,328**	**92,632**	**5,696**
PERCENT DISTRIBUTION OF SCHOOLS						
School level:	100.0	100.0	100.0	100.0	100.0	100.0
Elementary [1]	69.7	70.0	54.6	67.8	68.6	54.9
Secondary [2]	24.3	24.3	25.9	24.8	24.8	24.9
Combined [3]	4.4	4.2	18.6	6.4	5.6	19.5
Other	1.6	1.6	0.9	1.0	1.0	0.7
Size of enrollment:	100.0	100.0	100.0	100.0	100.0	100.0
Less than 300 students	31.4	30.7	77.1	30.5	28.9	55.8
300 to 499 students	26.4	26.7	12.0	27.7	28.0	23.1
500 to 999 students	32.6	33.0	8.6	32.8	33.8	17.0
1,000 students or more	9.5	9.7	2.4	9.0	9.3	4.2
Region:	100.0	100.0	100.0	100.0	100.0	100.0
Northeast	16.1	16.3	7.2	15.5	15.9	9.7
Midwest	28.9	29.0	24.9	26.1	26.3	22.3
South	33.1	33.2	28.9	34.9	35.1	30.8
West	21.8	21.6	38.9	23.5	22.7	37.2

NA Not available. [1] Includes schools beginning with grade 6 or below and with no grade higher than 8. [2] Includes schools with no grade lower than 7. [3] Includes schools beginning with grade 6 or below and ending with grade 9 or above.

Source: U.S. National Center for Education Statistics, *Digest of Education Statistics*, "Advance Release of Selected 2013 Digest Tables," <http://www.nces.ed.gov/programs/digest/>, accessed February 2015.

Table 277. Public Charter Schools and Enrollment by State: 2011

[2,057.6 represents 2,057,600. As of Fall]

State	Number of charter schools	Number of students (1,000)	Charter schools as a percent of public schools	Charter school enrollment as a percent of public school enrollment	State	Number of charter schools	Number of students (1,000)	Charter schools as a percent of public schools	Charter school enrollment as a percent of public school enrollment
United States	**5,696**	**2,057.6**	**5.8**	**4.2**	Missouri	61	21.5	2.5	2.3
Alabama	–	–	–	–	Montana	–	–	–	–
Alaska	27	5.9	5.3	4.5	Nebraska	–	–	–	–
Arizona	531	136.3	23.6	12.6	Nevada	39	18.3	6.0	4.2
Arkansas	41	11.4	3.7	2.4	New Hampshire	15	1.2	3.1	0.6
California	985	413.1	9.7	6.7	New Jersey	86	29.0	3.3	2.1
Colorado	178	83.5	9.8	9.8	New Mexico	84	16.9	9.7	5.0
Connecticut	17	6.1	1.5	1.1	New York	183	60.1	3.9	2.2
Delaware	22	10.3	10.0	8.0	North Carolina	100	45.5	3.9	3.0
Dist. of Columbia	100	29.0	43.9	39.3	North Dakota	–	–	–	–
Florida	519	180.9	12.3	6.8	Ohio	355	107.1	9.6	6.2
Georgia	128	80.0	5.4	4.7	Oklahoma	21	9.2	1.2	1.4
Hawaii	31	9.2	10.8	5.0	Oregon	115	24.2	9.1	4.4
Idaho	45	17.3	5.9	6.2	Pennsylvania	162	105.0	5.1	6.0
Illinois	52	49.1	1.2	2.4	Rhode Island	18	4.7	5.8	3.3
Indiana	65	28.3	3.4	2.7	South Carolina	47	17.0	3.8	2.3
Iowa	7	0.4	0.5	0.1	South Dakota	–	–	–	–
Kansas	17	3.1	1.3	0.6	Tennessee	40	9.1	2.2	0.9
Kentucky	–	–	–	–	Texas	581	190	6.7	3.8
Louisiana	99	44.3	6.9	6.3	Utah	81	44.7	7.9	7.5
Maine	–	–	–	–	Vermont	–	–	–	–
Maryland	50	17.3	3.4	2.0	Virginia	4	0.4	0.2	–
Massachusetts	72	30.6	3.9	3.2	Washington	–	–	–	–
Michigan	306	118.2	8.6	7.7	West Virginia	–	–	–	–
Minnesota	174	39.1	7.3	4.7	Wisconsin	234	40.5	10.4	4.7
Mississippi	–	–	–	–	Wyoming	4.0	–	1.1	0.3

– Represents or rounds to zero.

Source: U.S. National Center for Education Statistics, *Digest of Education Statistics*, "Advance Release of Selected 2013 Digest Tables," <http://www.nces.ed.gov/programs/digest/>, accessed February 2015.

Table 278. Average Salary and Wages Paid in Public School Systems: 1985 to 2011

[In dollars. For school year ending in year shown. Data reported by a stratified sample of school systems enrolling 300 or more pupils. Data represent unweighted means of average salaries paid school personnel reported by each school system]

Position	1985	1990	1995	2000	2005	2008	2009	2010	2011
ANNUAL SALARY									
Central-office administrators:									
Superintendent (contract salary)	56,954	75,425	90,198	112,158	128,770	148,387	155,634	159,634	161,992
Deputy/assoc. superintendent	52,877	69,623	81,266	97,251	116,186	134,245	136,832	139,463	138,061
Assistant superintendent	48,003	62,698	75,236	88,913	103,212	116,833	119,755	123,509	122,333
Administrators for—									
Finance and business	40,344	52,354	61,323	73,499	83,678	96,490	98,590	100,306	101,347
Instructional services	43,452	56,359	66,767	79,023	88,950	99,748	102,322	103,974	103,025
Public relations/information	35,287	44,926	53,263	60,655	70,502	80,534	83,235	86,567	84,629
Staff personnel services	44,182	56,344	65,819	76,608	86,966	98,190	100,620	102,269	101,578
Technology	(X)	(X)	(X)	(X)	76,308	86,085	87,898	90,530	90,914
Subject area supervisors	34,422	45,929	54,534	63,103	68,714	78,309	80,290	80,964	80,534
School building administrators:									
Principals:									
Elementary	36,452	48,431	58,589	69,407	76,182	85,907	88,062	89,673	89,591
Junior high/middle	39,650	52,163	62,311	73,877	81,514	91,334	93,478	95,003	95,426
Senior high	42,094	55,722	66,596	79,839	86,938	97,486	99,365	102,387	102,191
Assistant principals:									
Elementary	30,496	40,916	48,491	56,419	63,140	71,192	71,893	73,181	71,764
Junior high/middle	33,793	44,570	52,942	60,842	67,600	76,053	77,476	79,164	78,131
Senior high	35,491	46,486	55,556	64,811	71,401	79,391	81,083	83,074	82,027
Classroom teachers	23,587	31,278	37,264	42,213	45,884	51,329	52,900	54,370	54,220
Auxiliary professional personnel:									
Counselors	27,593	35,979	42,486	48,195	52,500	57,618	58,775	60,142	60,188
Librarians	24,981	33,469	40,418	46,732	50,720	56,933	57,974	59,495	59,093
School nurses	19,944	26,090	31,066	35,540	40,520	46,025	46,476	48,032	48,044
Secretarial/clerical personnel:									
Central office:									
Secretaries	15,343	20,238	23,935	28,405	32,716	36,657	37,785	38,601	38,606
Accounting/payroll clerks	15,421	20,088	24,042	28,498	33,217	37,732	39,031	39,895	39,790
Typists/data entry clerks	12,481	16,125	18,674	22,853	26,214	30,072	31,718	32,555	32,636
School building level:									
Secretaries	12,504	16,184	19,170	22,630	25,381	28,810	29,480	30,474	30,226
Library clerks	9,911	12,152	14,381	16,509	18,443	21,004	21,190	21,639	21,142
HOURLY WAGE RATE									
Other support personnel:									
Teacher aides:									
Instructional	5.89	7.43	8.77	10.00	11.35	12.86	13.23	13.48	13.55
Noninstructional	5.60	7.08	8.29	9.77	11.23	12.70	13.13	13.59	13.58
Custodians	6.90	8.54	10.05	11.35	12.61	14.19	14.59	15.04	14.92
Cafeteria workers	5.42	6.77	7.89	9.02	10.33	11.60	11.94	12.18	12.23
Bus drivers	7.27	9.21	10.69	12.48	14.18	16.56	16.44	16.62	16.61

X Not applicable.

Source: Editorial Projects in Education and Educational Research Service, Bethesda MD, *National Survey of Salaries and Wages in Public Schools*, ©. See also <http://www.edweek.org/ew/marketplace/products/ers/publications.html>.

Table 279. Public School Employment by Occupation, Sex, and Race: 2010 and 2012

[In thousands (4,592 represents 4,592,000). Covers all public elementary-secondary school districts with 100 or more full-time employees]

Occupation	2010					2012				
	Total	Male	Female	White [1]	Black [1]	Total	Male	Female	White [1]	Black [1]
All occupations [2]	**4,592**	**1,155**	**3,437**	**3,420**	**579**	**4,646**	**1,170**	**3,476**	**3,419**	**573**
Officials, administrators	65	31	34	53	7	80	36	43	62	8
Principals and assistant principals	114	52	62	83	20	124	54	70	89	21
Classroom teachers [3]	2,492	594	1,898	2,004	225	2,487	586	1,901	1,987	217
Elementary schools	1,212	154	1,059	966	101	1,163	136	1,028	925	95
Secondary schools	967	375	592	793	85	993	381	612	804	84
Other professional staff	353	62	291	275	46	394	70	324	295	49
Teachers' aides [4]	538	78	459	359	91	537	79	458	356	91
Clerical, secretarial staff	317	19	299	221	37	305	12	293	213	34
Service workers [5]	712	318	393	426	152	720	333	387	417	152

[1] Excludes individuals of Hispanic origin. [2] 2010 data includes other occupations not shown separately. [3] Includes other classroom teachers not shown separately. [4] Includes technicians. [5] Includes craftworkers and laborers.

Source: U.S. Equal Employment Opportunity Commission, "Equal Employment Opportunity, EEO-5 Statistical File–2012, United States Summary," <http://www.eeoc.gov/eeoc/statistics/employment/jobpat-eeo5/index.cfm>, accessed June 2014.

Table 280. SAT Scores and Characteristics of College-Bound Seniors: 1980 to 2014

[For school year ending in year shown. Data are for the SAT I: Reasoning Tests. SAT I: Reasoning Test replaced the SAT in March 1994. Scores between the two tests have been equated to the same 200–800 scale and are thus comparable. Scores for 1995 and prior years have been recentered and revised]

Type of test and characteristic	Unit	1980	1990	2000	2005	2009 [2]	2010	2011	2012	2013	2014
AVERAGE TEST SCORES [1]											
Critical reading, total	Point	502	500	505	508	499	500	497	496	496	497
Male	Point	506	505	507	513	502	502	500	498	499	499
Female	Point	498	496	504	505	497	498	495	493	494	495
Math, total	Point	492	501	514	520	514	515	514	514	514	513
Male	Point	515	521	533	538	533	533	531	532	531	530
Female	Point	473	483	498	504	498	499	500	499	499	499
Writing	Point	(X)	(X)	(X)	(X)	492	491	489	488	488	487
Male	Point	(X)	(X)	(X)	(X)	485	485	482	481	482	481
Female	Point	(X)	(X)	(X)	(X)	498	497	496	494	493	492
PARTICIPANTS											
Total [3]	1,000	991	1,026	1,260	1,476	1,573	1,597	1,647	1,664	1,660	1,672
Male	Percent	48.3	47.8	46.3	46.5	46.7	46.8	46.8	46.7	46.8	46.9
White [4]	Percent	(NA)	73.4	66.4	62.3	57.7	56.3	54.6	53.0	50.3	49.2
Black [4]	Percent	(NA)	10.0	11.1	11.6	13.0	13.3	13.6	13.5	12.7	12.7
Obtaining scores [1] of:											
600 or above:											
Critical reading	Percent	(NA)	20.3	21.0	22.5	20.3	20.3	20.2	19.5	19.7	20.2
Math	Percent	(NA)	20.4	24.2	26.5	25.5	25.2	25.3	25.6	25.1	25.3
Writing	Percent	(X)	(X)	(X)	(X)	18.4	18.2	18.1	17.8	17.9	17.9
Below 400:											
Critical reading	Percent	(NA)	17.3	15.9	15.5	17.8	17.8	18.3	19.0	18.5	19.0
Math	Percent	(NA)	15.8	14.7	13.8	15.5	15.1	15.2	15.5	15.6	15.8
Writing	Percent	(X)	(X)	(X)	(X)	19.8	19.8	20.6	20.9	21.0	21.5

NA Not available. X Not applicable. [1] Minimum score, 200; maximum score, 800. [2] Starting with 2009, data reflect examinees who tested through June of senior year. [3] 991 represents 991,000. [4] Nonresponse excluded from denominator.

Source: The College Board, *2014 College-Bound Seniors: Total Group Profile Report*, © 1975 to 2014. Reproduced with permission. See also <http://www.collegeboard.com>.

Table 281. ACT Program Scores and Characteristics of College-Bound Students: 1970 to 2015

[For academic year ending in year shown. Except as indicated, test scores and characteristics of college-bound students. Through 1980, data based on 10 percent sample; thereafter, based on all ACT tested graduating seniors]

Type of test and characteristic	Unit	1970	1980	1990 [1]	1995 [1]	2000 [1]	2010 [1]	2012 [1]	2013 [1]	2014 [1]	2015 [1]
TEST SCORES [2]											
Composite	**Point**	**19.9**	**18.5**	**20.6**	**20.8**	**21.0**	**21.0**	**21.1**	**20.9**	**21.0**	**21.0**
Male	Point	20.3	19.3	21.0	21.0	21.2	21.2	21.2	20.9	21.1	21.1
Female	Point	19.4	17.9	20.3	20.7	20.9	20.9	21.0	20.9	20.9	21.0
English	Point	18.5	17.9	20.5	20.2	20.5	20.5	20.5	20.2	20.3	20.4
Male	Point	17.6	17.3	20.1	19.8	20.0	20.1	20.2	19.8	20.0	20.0
Female	Point	19.4	18.3	20.9	20.6	20.9	20.8	20.9	20.6	20.7	20.8
Math	Point	20.0	17.4	19.9	20.2	20.7	21.0	21.1	20.9	20.9	20.8
Male	Point	21.1	18.9	20.7	20.9	21.4	21.6	21.7	21.4	21.1	21.3
Female	Point	18.8	16.2	19.3	19.7	20.2	20.5	20.6	20.5	20.5	20.4
Reading [3]	Point	19.7	17.2	(NA)	21.3	21.4	21.3	21.3	21.1	21.3	21.4
Male	Point	20.3	18.2	(NA)	21.1	21.2	21.1	21.2	20.9	21.1	21.2
Female	Point	19.0	16.4	(NA)	21.4	21.5	21.4	21.4	21.4	21.5	21.6
Science reasoning [4]	Point	20.8	21.1	(NA)	21.0	21.0	20.9	20.9	20.7	20.8	20.9
Male	Point	21.6	22.4	(NA)	21.6	21.6	21.4	21.4	21.2	21.2	21.3
Female	Point	20.0	20.0	(NA)	20.5	20.6	20.5	20.5	20.4	20.5	20.6
PARTICIPANTS [5]											
Total [6]	**1,000**	**788**	**822**	**817**	**945**	**1,065**	**1,569**	**1,666**	**1,799**	**1,846**	**1,924**
Male	Percent	52	45	46	44	43	45	46	46	46	47
White	Percent	(NA)	83	73	69	72	62	59	58	56	55
Black	Percent	4	8	9	9	10	14	13	13	13	13
Obtaining composite scores of: [7]											
27 or above	Percent	14	13	12	13	14	16	17	16	17	18
18 or below	Percent	21	33	35	34	32	35	34	36	36	37

NA Not available. [1] Beginning 1990, not comparable with previous years because a new version of the ACT was introduced. Estimated average composite scores for prior years: 1989, 20.6; 1988, 1987, and 1986, 20.8. [2] Minimum score, 1; maximum score, 36. [3] Prior to 1990, social studies; data not comparable with previous years. [4] Prior to 1990, natural sciences; data not comparable with previous years. [5] Beginning 1985, data are for seniors who graduated in year shown and had taken the ACT in their sophomore, junior, or senior years. Data by race are for those responding to the race question. [6] 788 represents 788,000. [7] Prior to 1990, 26 or above and 15 or below.

Source: ACT, Inc., Iowa City, IA, Most recent score reported in the *The ACT® Profile Report - National*, annual ©. Reproduced with permission.

Table 282. Proficiency Levels on Selected NAEP Tests for Students in Public Schools by State: 2013

[Represents percent of public school students scoring at or above basic and proficient levels. Basic denotes mastery of the knowledge and skills that are fundamental for proficient work at a given grade level. Proficient represents solid academic performance. Students reaching this level demonstrated competency over challenging subject matter. For more detail, see <http://nationsreportcard.gov/>. Based on the National Assessment of Educational Progress (NAEP) tests which are administered to a representative sample of students in public schools, private schools, and Department of Defense schools]

State	Grade 4 Math		Grade 8 Math		Grade 4 Reading		Grade 8 Reading	
	At or above Basic	At or above Proficient	At or above Basic	At or above Proficient	At or above Basic	At or above Proficient	At or above Basic	At or above Proficient
U.S. average...............	82	41	73	34	67	34	77	34
Alabama.........................	75	30	60	20	65	31	68	25
Alaska...........................	77	37	72	33	58	27	71	31
Arizona..........................	82	40	69	31	60	28	72	28
Arkansas........................	83	39	69	28	66	32	73	30
California.......................	74	33	65	28	58	27	72	29
Colorado........................	87	50	77	42	74	41	81	40
Connecticut....................	83	45	74	37	76	43	83	45
Delaware........................	86	42	71	33	73	38	77	33
District of Columbia..........	66	28	54	19	50	23	57	17
Florida...........................	84	41	70	31	75	39	77	33
Georgia..........................	81	39	68	29	67	34	75	32
Hawaii...........................	83	46	72	32	62	30	71	28
Idaho.............................	83	40	78	36	68	33	82	38
Illinois...........................	79	39	74	36	64	34	77	36
Indiana..........................	90	52	77	38	73	38	79	35
Iowa..............................	87	48	76	36	72	38	81	37
Kansas...........................	89	48	79	40	71	38	78	36
Kentucky........................	84	41	71	30	71	36	80	38
Louisiana........................	75	26	64	21	56	23	68	24
Maine............................	88	47	78	40	71	37	79	38
Maryland........................	82	47	74	37	77	45	82	42
Massachusetts.................	90	58	86	55	79	47	84	48
Michigan........................	77	37	70	30	64	31	77	33
Minnesota.......................	90	59	83	47	74	41	82	41
Mississippi......................	74	26	61	21	53	21	64	20
Missouri.........................	83	39	74	33	70	35	78	36
Montana.........................	86	45	80	40	70	35	84	40
Nebraska........................	84	45	76	36	71	37	81	37
Nevada...........................	80	34	68	28	61	27	72	30
New Hampshire................	93	59	84	47	80	45	84	44
New Jersey......................	87	49	82	49	75	42	85	46
New Mexico.....................	74	31	63	23	52	21	67	22
New York........................	82	40	72	32	70	37	76	35
North Carolina.................	87	45	75	36	69	35	76	33
North Dakota...................	89	48	82	41	73	34	81	34
Ohio..............................	86	48	79	40	71	37	79	39
Oklahoma.......................	83	36	68	25	65	30	75	29
Oregon...........................	81	40	73	34	66	33	79	37
Pennsylvania...................	85	44	78	42	73	40	81	42
Rhode Island...................	83	42	74	36	70	38	77	36
South Carolina.................	79	35	69	31	60	28	73	29
South Dakota...................	84	40	79	38	66	32	81	36
Tennessee......................	80	40	69	28	67	34	77	33
Texas............................	84	41	80	38	63	28	76	31
Utah..............................	83	44	75	36	71	37	81	39
Vermont.........................	87	52	84	47	75	42	84	45
Virginia..........................	88	47	77	38	74	43	78	36
Washington.....................	86	48	79	42	72	40	81	42
West Virginia...................	81	35	65	24	62	27	70	25
Wisconsin.......................	85	47	78	40	68	35	78	36
Wyoming........................	90	48	81	38	75	37	84	38

Source: U.S. National Center for Education Statistics, "National Assessment of Educational Progress (NAEP), 2013 Mathematics and Reading Assessments," <http://nces.ed.gov/nationsreportcard/naepdata/dataset.aspx>, accessed February 2014.

Table 283. Public High School Graduates by State: 1980 to 2012

[In thousands (2,747.7 represents 2,747,700). For school year ending in year shown. Data include regular diploma recipients, but exclude students receiving a certificate of attendance and persons receiving high school equivalency certificates]

State	1980	1990	2000	2008	2009	2010	2011, proj.	2012, proj.
United States..............	2,747.7	[2] 2,320.3	2,553.8	3,001.3	[2] 3,039.0	3,128.0	3,121.6	3,103.7
Alabama.........................	45.2	40.5	37.8	41.3	42.1	43.2	44.2	44.0
Alaska...........................	5.2	5.4	6.6	7.9	8.0	8.2	7.8	8.0
Arizona..........................	28.6	32.1	38.3	61.7	62.4	61.1	65.0	64.9
Arkansas........................	29.1	26.5	27.3	28.7	28.1	28.3	28.1	28.2
California........................	249.2	236.3	309.9	374.6	372.3	405.0	414.2	415.6
Colorado........................	36.8	33.0	38.9	46.1	47.5	49.3	51.0	51.4
Connecticut....................	37.7	27.9	31.6	38.4	35.0	34.5	36.9	36.3
Delaware........................	7.6	5.6	6.1	7.4	7.8	8.1	8.2	8.3
District of Columbia [1].........	5.0	3.6	2.7	3.4	3.5	3.6	3.3	3.1
Florida...........................	87.3	88.9	106.7	149.0	153.5	156.1	160.6	157.1
Georgia..........................	61.6	56.6	62.6	83.5	88.0	91.6	93.4	91.8
Hawaii...........................	11.5	10.3	10.4	11.6	11.5	11.0	11.1	11.4
Idaho............................	13.2	12.0	16.2	16.6	16.8	17.8	17.4	17.5
Illinois...........................	135.6	108.1	111.8	135.1	131.7	139.0	136.4	134.7
Indiana..........................	73.1	60.0	57.0	61.9	63.7	64.6	65.8	65.1
Iowa.............................	43.4	31.8	33.9	34.6	33.9	34.5	33.4	32.8
Kansas..........................	30.9	25.4	29.1	30.7	30.4	31.6	31.1	30.5
Kentucky........................	41.2	38.0	36.8	39.3	41.9	42.7	41.5	41.8
Louisiana.......................	46.3	36.1	38.4	34.4	35.6	36.6	34.3	34.9
Maine............................	15.4	13.8	12.2	[3] 14.4	[3] 14.1	14.1	14.0	13.7
Maryland........................	54.3	41.6	47.8	59.2	58.3	59.1	58.0	57.8
Massachusetts.................	73.8	55.9	53.0	65.2	65.3	64.5	63.3	63.1
Michigan........................	124.3	93.8	97.7	115.2	112.7	110.7	107.1	105.6
Minnesota......................	64.9	49.1	57.4	60.4	59.7	59.7	58.9	57.2
Mississippi......................	27.6	25.2	24.2	24.8	24.5	25.5	26.2	25.7
Missouri.........................	62.3	49.0	52.8	61.7	63.0	64.0	62.2	60.8
Montana.........................	12.1	9.4	10.9	10.4	10.1	10.1	9.7	9.6
Nebraska........................	22.4	17.7	20.1	20.0	19.5	19.4	19.2	19.3
Nevada..........................	8.5	9.5	14.6	18.8	19.9	21.0	23.5	24.4
New Hampshire................	11.7	10.8	11.8	15.0	14.8	15.0	14.3	14.2
New Jersey......................	94.6	69.8	74.4	95.0	95.1	96.2	94.3	91.1
New Mexico.....................	18.4	14.9	18.0	18.3	17.9	18.6	18.9	19.0
New York........................	204.1	143.3	141.7	176.3	180.9	183.8	185.6	184.9
North Carolina..................	70.9	64.8	62.1	83.3	86.7	88.7	86.6	88.9
North Dakota...................	9.9	7.7	8.6	7.0	7.2	7.2	7.1	6.8
Ohio..............................	144.2	114.5	111.7	120.8	122.2	123.4	110.4	109.4
Oklahoma.......................	39.3	35.6	37.6	37.6	37.2	38.5	37.8	37.7
Oregon..........................	29.9	25.5	30.2	34.9	35.1	34.7	34.7	34.5
Pennsylvania...................	146.5	110.5	114.0	130.3	130.7	131.2	131.0	127.8
Rhode Island...................	10.9	7.8	8.5	10.3	10.0	9.9	9.7	9.8
South Carolina.................	38.7	32.5	31.6	35.3	39.1	40.4	40.1	40.1
South Dakota...................	10.7	7.7	9.3	8.6	8.1	8.2	8.5	8.1
Tennessee......................	49.8	46.1	41.6	57.5	60.4	62.4	62.9	63.1
Texas............................	171.4	172.5	212.9	252.1	264.3	280.9	282.7	283.0
Utah.............................	20.0	21.2	32.5	28.2	30.5	31.5	30.9	31.6
Vermont.........................	6.7	6.1	6.7	7.4	7.2	7.2	6.9	6.7
Virginia..........................	66.6	60.6	65.6	77.4	79.7	81.5	82.1	82.2
Washington.....................	50.4	45.9	57.6	61.6	62.8	66.0	65.8	66.1
West Virginia...................	23.4	21.9	19.4	17.5	17.7	17.7	17.3	17.3
Wisconsin.......................	69.3	52.0	58.5	65.2	65.4	64.7	63.0	61.7
Wyoming........................	6.1	5.8	6.5	5.5	5.5	5.7	5.6	5.6

[1] Beginning in 1990, graduates from adult programs are excluded. [2] U.S. total includes estimates for nonreporting states. [3] Includes 1,161 graduates in 2007-08 and 1,169 graduates in 2008-09 from private high schools that received a majority of their funding from public sources.

Source: U.S. National Center for Education Statistics, *Digest of Education Statistics*, "Advance Release of Selected 2013 Digest Tables," <http://www.nces.ed.gov/programs/digest/>, accessed August 2014.

Table 284. High School Dropouts by Race and Hispanic Origin: 1980 to 2013

[In percent. As of October. Dropouts are persons 18 to 24 years old who have not completed high school and are not enrolled, regardless of when they dropped out]

Item	1980	1985	1990 [1]	1995	2000	2005	2009	2010	2011	2012	2013
Total [2].............................	15.6	13.9	14.4	13.9	12.4	11.3	9.4	8.7	8.3	7.6	7.3
White [3]............................	14.4	13.5	14.1	13.6	12.2	11.3	9.1	8.5	8.2	7.2	7.1
Male.............................	15.7	14.7	15.4	14.3	13.5	13.2	10.5	9.7	9.1	8.1	7.5
Female..........................	13.2	12.3	12.8	13.0	10.9	9.4	7.7	7.3	7.2	6.3	6.7
Black [3]............................	23.5	17.6	16.4	14.4	15.3	12.9	11.6	10.1	8.8	9.9	8.3
Male.............................	26.0	18.8	18.6	14.2	17.4	14.8	13.9	12.1	9.4	11.2	9.6
Female..........................	21.5	16.6	14.5	14.6	13.5	11.2	9.5	8.2	8.3	8.5	7.0
Hispanic [4]........................	40.3	31.5	37.7	34.7	32.3	27.3	20.8	18.5	16.3	15.2	13.7
Male.............................	42.6	35.8	40.3	34.2	36.8	32.1	22.5	21.3	17.5	16.9	14.8
Female..........................	38.1	27.0	35.0	35.4	27.3	21.8	19.1	15.4	14.9	13.2	12.6

[1] Beginning 1990, reflects new editing procedures for cases with missing data on school enrollment. [2] Includes other races, not shown separately. [3] Beginning 2005, for persons who selected this race group only. See footnote 4, Table 253. [4] Persons of Hispanic origin may be of any race.

Source: U.S. Census Bureau, Current Population Reports, PPL-148, P-20, and earlier reports; and "School Enrollment," <http://www.census.gov/hhes/school/index.html>, accessed January 2015.

Table 285. High School Dropouts by Age, Race, and Hispanic Origin: 1980 to 2013

[5,212 represents 5,212,000. As of October. For persons 14 to 24 years old. Dropouts are persons not in regular school and who have not completed the 12th grade nor received a general equivalency degree. Based on Current Population Survey; see text, Section 1 and Appendix III]

Age and race	Number of dropouts (1,000)					Percent of population				
	1980	1990	2000	2010	2013	1980	1990	2000	2010	2013
Total dropouts [1,2]......	**5,212**	**3,854**	**3,883**	**2,952**	**2,754**	**12.0**	**10.1**	**9.1**	**6.4**	**5.8**
16 to 17 years............	709	418	460	227	407	8.8	6.3	5.8	2.7	4.9
18 to 21 years............	2,578	1,921	2,005	1,445	1,157	15.8	13.4	12.9	8.4	6.8
22 to 24 years............	1,798	1,458	1,310	1,144	1,059	15.2	13.8	11.8	9.2	7.8
White [2,3]................	4,169	3,127	3,065	2,232	2,000	11.3	10.1	9.1	6.3	5.7
16 to 17 years............	619	334	366	181	304	9.2	6.4	5.8	2.9	4.9
18 to 21 years............	2,032	1,516	1,558	1,048	825	14.7	13.1	12.6	8.0	6.5
22 to 24 years............	1,416	1,235	1,040	893	774	14.0	14.0	11.7	9.2	7.7
Black [2,3]................	934	611	705	498	486	16.0	10.9	10.9	7.2	6.7
16 to 17 years............	80	73	84	30	77	6.9	6.9	7.0	2.3	6.2
18 to 21 years............	486	345	383	283	221	23.0	16.0	16.0	10.5	8.1
22 to 24 years............	346	185	232	167	172	24.0	13.5	14.3	9.4	8.6
Hispanic [2,4]..............	919	1,122	1,499	1,122	1,000	29.5	26.8	23.5	12.8	9.9
16 to 17 years............	92	89	121	40	80	16.6	12.9	11.0	2.7	4.5
18 to 21 years............	470	502	733	506	444	40.3	32.9	30.0	15.2	11.7
22 to 24 years............	323	523	602	543	445	40.6	42.8	35.5	23.2	16.5

[1] Includes other groups not shown separately. [2] Includes persons 14 to 15 years not shown separately. [3] Beginning 2003, for persons who selected this race only. See footnote 4, Table 253. [4] Persons of Hispanic origin may be of any race.

Source: U.S. Census Bureau, Current Population Reports, series PPL and P-20; and "School Enrollment, Detailed Tables," <http://www.census.gov/hhes/school/data/index.html>, accessed November 2014.

Table 286. School Enrollment Status by Race, Hispanic Origin, and Sex: 2010 and 2013

[17,210 represents 17,210,000. As of October. For persons 18 to 21 years old. For the civilian noninstitutional population. Based on the Current Population Survey; see text, Section 1 and Appendix III]

Characteristic	Total persons 18 to 21 years old (1,000)		Percent distribution							
			Enrolled in high school		High school graduates				Not high school graduates and not enrolled in high school	
					Total		In college			
	2010	2013	2010	2013	2010	2013	2010	2013	2010	2013
Total [1]............	**17,210**	**17,051**	**9.9**	**11.4**	**81.5**	**81.8**	**50.6**	**48.5**	**8.4**	**6.8**
White................	13,176	12,599	9.7	10.7	82.2	82.7	50.8	49.2	8.0	6.5
Black................	2,538	2,744	13.9	16.0	73.0	75.8	41.5	39.5	13.0	8.1
Hispanic [2]............	3,339	3,785	13.5	12.0	71.3	76.3	38.9	39.6	15.2	11.7
Male [1]............	**8,824**	**8,660**	**11.0**	**12.8**	**79.8**	**79.8**	**46.7**	**44.0**	**9.0**	**7.5**
White................	6,867	6,450	10.8	12.5	80.4	80.1	46.6	44.0	8.7	7.4
Black................	1,277	1,320	15.5	16.7	69.1	73.9	36.2	34.4	15.4	9.1
Hispanic [2]............	1,744	1,949	14.0	13.3	70.0	73.1	35.7	33.2	15.8	13.5
Female [1]............	**8,386**	**8,391**	**8.8**	**9.9**	**83.2**	**84.0**	**54.8**	**53.2**	**7.8**	**6.1**
White................	6,308	6,151	8.4	8.8	84.1	85.4	55.5	54.5	7.2	5.7
Black................	1,261	1,424	12.3	15.4	76.9	77.5	46.9	44.2	10.5	7.2
Hispanic [2]............	1,595	1,836	12.9	10.6	72.7	79.7	42.4	46.5	14.4	9.8

[1] Includes other races not shown separately. [2] Persons of Hispanic origin may be of any race.

Source: U.S. Census Bureau, Current Population Reports, PPL-148, P-20, and earlier reports; and "School Enrollment," <http://www.census.gov/hhes/school/index.html>, accessed May 2015.

Table 287. General Educational Development (GED) Credentials Issued: 1980 to 2013

[GEDs issued in thousands (479 represents 479,000). For the 50 states and DC]

Year	GEDs issued	Percent distribution of GED test takers				
		16 to 18 years old [1]	19 to 24 years old [1]	25 to 29 years old	30 to 34 years old	35 years old and over
1980............	479	37	27	13	8	15
1985............	413	32	26	15	10	16
1990............	410	22	39	13	10	15
1995............	504	27	36	13	9	15
2000............	487	33	37	11	7	13
2005............	424	34	37	12	7	11
2006............	398	35	36	12	6	11
2007............	429	35	35	12	7	11
2008............	469	34	35	13	7	11
2009............	448	31	36	13	8	12
2010............	452	27	37	14	9	14
2011............	434	27	37	13	9	14
2012............	401	26	37	14	9	13
2013............	541	22	35	15	11	17

[1] For 1985 and prior years, 19-year-olds are included with the 16- to 18-year-olds instead of the 19- to 24-year-olds.

Source: U.S. National Center for Education Statistics, *Digest of Education Statistics*, "Advance Release of Selected 2014 Digest Tables," <http://www.nces.ed.gov/programs/digest/>, accessed May 2015.

Table 288. College Enrollment of Recent High School Completers: 1970 to 2013

[2,758 represents 2,758,000. For persons 16 to 24 years old who graduated from high school in the preceding 12 months. Includes persons receiving GEDs. Based on surveys and subject to sampling error; data not comparable with that in other tables]

Year	Number of high school completers (1,000)						Percent enrolled in college [5]					
	Total [1]	Male	Female	White [2]	Black [2,3]	His-panic [3,4]	Total [1]	Male	Female	White [2]	Black [2,3]	His-panic [3,4]
1970	2,758	1,343	1,415	2,461	(NA)	(NA)	51.7	55.2	48.5	52.0	(NA)	(NA)
1975	3,185	1,513	1,672	2,701	302	132	50.7	52.6	49.0	51.1	41.7	58.0
1980	3,088	1,498	1,589	2,554	350	130	49.3	46.7	51.8	49.8	42.7	52.3
1985	2,668	1,287	1,381	2,104	332	141	57.7	58.6	56.8	60.1	42.2	51.0
1990	2,362	1,173	1,189	1,819	331	121	60.1	58.0	62.2	63.0	46.8	42.7
1991	2,276	1,140	1,136	1,727	310	154	62.5	57.9	67.1	65.4	46.4	57.2
1992	2,397	1,216	1,180	1,724	354	198	61.9	60.0	63.8	64.3	48.2	55.0
1993	2,342	1,120	1,223	1,719	304	201	62.6	59.9	65.2	62.9	55.6	62.2
1994	2,517	1,244	1,273	1,915	316	178	61.9	60.6	63.2	64.5	50.8	49.1
1995	2,599	1,238	1,361	1,861	349	288	61.9	62.6	61.3	64.3	51.2	53.7
1996	2,660	1,297	1,363	1,875	406	227	65.0	60.1	69.7	67.4	56.0	50.8
1997	2,769	1,354	1,415	1,909	384	336	67.0	63.6	70.3	68.2	58.5	65.6
1998	2,810	1,452	1,358	1,980	386	314	65.6	62.4	69.1	68.5	61.9	47.4
1999	2,897	1,474	1,423	1,978	436	329	62.9	61.4	64.4	66.3	58.9	42.3
2000	2,756	1,251	1,505	1,938	393	300	63.3	59.9	66.2	65.7	54.9	52.9
2001	2,549	1,277	1,273	1,834	381	241	61.8	60.1	63.5	64.3	55.0	51.7
2002	2,796	1,412	1,384	1,903	382	344	65.2	62.1	68.4	69.1	59.4	53.6
2003	2,677	1,306	1,372	1,832	327	314	63.9	61.2	66.5	66.2	57.5	58.6
2004	2,752	1,327	1,425	1,854	398	286	66.7	61.4	71.5	68.8	62.5	61.8
2005	2,675	1,262	1,414	1,799	345	390	68.6	66.5	70.4	73.2	55.7	54.0
2006	2,692	1,328	1,363	1,805	318	382	66.0	65.8	66.1	68.5	55.5	57.9
2007	2,955	1,511	1,444	2,043	416	355	67.2	66.1	68.3	69.5	55.7	64.0
2008	3,151	1,640	1,511	2,091	416	458	68.6	65.9	71.6	71.7	55.7	63.9
2009	2,937	1,407	1,531	1,863	415	459	70.1	66.0	73.8	71.3	69.5	59.3
2010	3,160	1,679	1,482	1,937	461	507	68.1	62.8	74.0	70.5	62.0	59.7
2011	3,079	1,611	1,468	1,747	464	623	68.2	64.7	72.2	68.3	67.1	66.6
2012	3,203	1,622	1,581	(NA)	(NA)	(NA)	66.2	61.3	71.3	65.7	56.4	70.3
2013	2,977	1,524	1,453	(NA)	(NA)	(NA)	65.9	63.5	68.4	68.8	56.7	59.8

NA Not available. [1] Includes other races not shown separately. [2] Beginning 2003, for persons of this race group only. See footnote 4, Table 253. [3] Due to small sample size, data are subject to relatively large sampling errors. [4] Persons of Hispanic origin may be of any race. [5] As of October.

Source: U.S. National Center for Education Statistics, *Digest of Education Statistics*, "Advance Release of Selected 2014 Digest Tables," <http://www.nces.ed.gov/programs/digest/>, accessed April 2015.

Table 289. College Enrollment by Sex and Attendance Status: 2005 to 2013

[In thousands (17,487 represents 17,487,000). As of Fall. Includes enrollment at branch campuses, some additional (primarily 2-year) colleges, and excludes a few institutions that did not award degrees. Includes enrollment at institutions that were eligible to participate in Title IV federal financial aid programs. Includes unclassified students (students taking courses for credit, but are not candidates for degrees)]

Sex and age	2005		2010		2011		2012		2013 proj.	
	Total	Part-time	Total	Part-time	Total	Part-time	Total	Part-time	Total	Part-time
Total	17,487	6,690	21,016	7,934	20,994	7,993	20,643	7,906	20,597	7,855
Male	7,456	2,653	9,045	3,208	9,026	3,233	8,919	3,209	8,985	3,219
14 to 17 years old	68	15	94	23	95	20	109	14	112	22
18 to 19 years old	1,523	184	1,820	245	1,819	287	1,712	239	1,749	292
20 to 21 years old	1,658	260	1,948	362	1,973	382	1,962	406	2,072	488
22 to 24 years old	1,410	428	1,723	508	1,682	510	1,862	609	1,978	665
25 to 29 years old	1,057	551	1,410	695	1,442	706	1,347	641	1,328	624
30 to 34 years old	591	365	731	430	715	419	678	388	643	353
35 years old and over	1,149	850	1,320	944	1,300	908	1,249	912	1,102	774
Female	10,032	4,038	11,971	4,726	11,968	4,760	11,724	4,697	11,613	4,636
14 to 17 years old	119	21	108	9	108	12	107	15	112	19
18 to 19 years old	1,920	233	2,236	316	2,206	325	2,078	315	2,182	411
20 to 21 years old	1,905	327	2,154	377	2,201	400	2,278	442	2,390	521
22 to 24 years old	1,704	564	2,036	666	2,027	694	2,009	677	2,058	711
25 to 29 years old	1,413	745	1,844	953	1,877	985	1,870	1,018	1,777	975
30 to 34 years old	847	526	1,074	630	1,092	629	1,053	609	993	561
35 years old and over	2,123	1,623	2,520	1,775	2,458	1,716	2,328	1,621	2,101	1,438

Source: U.S. National Center for Education Statistics, *2013 Digest of Education Statistics,* May 2015. See also <http://www.nces.ed.gov/programs/digest/>.

Table 290. Higher Education—Institutions and Enrollment: 1980 to 2013

[686 represents 686,000. As of Fall. Covers universities, colleges, professional schools, junior and teachers' colleges, both publicly and privately controlled, regular session. Includes estimates for institutions not reporting. See also Appendix III]

Item	Unit	1980	1990	2000	2005	2010	2011	2012	2013
ALL INSTITUTIONS									
Number of institutions [1]	**Number**	**3,231**	**3,559**	**4,182**	**4,276**	**4,599**	**4,706**	**4,726**	**4,724**
4-year	Number	1,957	2,141	2,450	2,582	2,870	2,968	3,026	3,039
2-year	Number	1,274	1,418	1,732	1,694	1,729	1,738	1,700	1,685
Instructional staff— (lecturer or above) [2]	**1,000**	**686**	**817**	**(NA)**	**1,290**	**(NA)**	**1,524**	**(NA)**	**1,544**
Percent full-time	Percent	66	61	(NA)	52	(NA)	50	(NA)	51
Total enrollment [3,4]	**1,000**	**12,097**	**13,819**	**15,312**	**17,487**	**21,019**	**21,011**	**20,643**	**20,376**
Male	1,000	5,874	6,284	6,722	7,456	9,046	9,034	8,919	8,861
Female	1,000	6,223	7,535	8,591	10,032	11,974	11,976	11,724	11,515
4-year institutions	1,000	7,571	8,579	9,364	10,999	13,335	13,494	13,479	13,407
2-year institutions	1,000	4,526	5,240	5,948	6,488	7,681	7,500	7,164	6,969
Full-time	1,000	7,098	7,821	9,010	10,797	13,087	13,003	12,737	12,597
Part-time	1,000	4,999	5,998	6,303	6,690	7,932	8,008	7,906	7,779
Public	1,000	9,457	10,845	11,753	13,022	15,142	15,116	14,880	14,746
Private	1,000	2,640	2,974	3,560	4,466	5,877	5,894	5,762	5,630
Not-for-profit	1,000	2,528	2,760	3,109	3,455	3,854	3,927	3,954	3,974
For profit	1,000	112	214	450	1,011	2,023	1,967	1,809	1,656
Undergraduate [4]	1,000	10,475	11,959	13,155	14,964	18,079	18,063	17,732	17,475
Men	1,000	5,000	5,380	5,778	6,409	7,835	7,817	7,714	7,660
Women	1,000	5,475	6,579	7,377	8,555	10,244	10,246	10,019	9,815
First-time freshmen	1,000	2,588	2,257	2,428	2,657	3,157	3,091	2,990	2,987
Postbaccalaureate [4]	1,000	1,622	1,860	2,157	2,524	2,937	2,933	2,910	2,901
Men	1,000	874	904	944	1,047	1,209	1,211	1,205	1,201
Women	1,000	748	955	1,213	1,476	1,728	1,722	1,705	1,700
2-YEAR INSTITUTIONS									
Number of institutions [1]	Number	1,274	1,418	1,732	1,694	1,729	1,738	1,700	1,685
Public	Number	945	972	1,076	1,053	978	967	934	934
Private	Number	329	446	656	641	751	771	766	751
Instructional staff— (lecturer or above) [2]	1,000	192	(NA)	(NA)	373	(NA)	409	(NA)	394
Enrollment [3,4]	1,000	4,526	5,240	5,948	6,488	7,681	7,500	7,164	6,969
Public	1,000	4,329	4,996	5,697	6,184	7,218	7,062	6,788	6,625
Private	1,000	198	244	251	304	463	438	376	344
Male	1,000	2,047	2,233	2,559	2,680	3,265	3,172	3,045	2,998
Female	1,000	2,479	3,007	3,390	3,808	4,416	4,328	4,119	3,971
4-YEAR INSTITUTIONS									
Number of institutions [1]	Number	1,957	2,141	2,450	2,582	2,870	2,968	3,026	3,039
Public	Number	552	595	622	640	678	682	689	691
Private	Number	1,405	1,546	1,828	1,942	2,192	2,286	2,337	2,348
Instructional staff— (lecturer or above) [2]	1,000	494	(NA)	(NA)	917	(NA)	1,116	(NA)	1,150
Enrollment [3,4]	1,000	7,571	8,579	9,364	10,999	13,335	13,494	13,479	13,407
Public	1,000	5,129	5,848	6,055	6,838	7,925	8,048	8,093	8,120
Private	1,000	2,442	2,730	3,308	4,162	5,410	5,446	5,386	5,287
Male	1,000	3,827	4,051	4,163	4,776	5,780	5,855	5,874	5,863
Female	1,000	3,743	4,527	5,201	6,224	7,556	7,639	7,604	7,544

NA Not available. [1] Number of institutions includes count of branch campuses. Due to revised survey procedures, data beginning 1990 are not comparable with previous years. Beginning 2000, data reflect a new classification of institutions; this classification includes some additional, primarily 2-year, colleges and excludes a few institutions that did not award degrees. Includes institutions that were eligible to participate in Title IV federal financial aid programs. Includes schools accredited by the National Association of Trade and Technical Schools. [2] Due to revised survey methods, data beginning 1990 not comparable with previous years. [3] Branch campuses counted according to actual status, e.g., 2-year branch in 2-year category. [4] Data include unclassified graduate students. Data through 1995 are for institutions of higher education, while later data are for degree-granting institutions.

Source: U.S. National Center for Education Statistics, *Digest of Education Statistics*, "Advance Release of Selected 2014 Digest Tables," and earlier releases, <http://nces.ed.gov/Programs/digest/>, accessed May 2015.

Table 291. College Enrollment by Selected Characteristics: 1990 to 2013

[In thousands (13,818.6 represents 13,818,600). As of Fall. Nonresident alien students are not distributed among racial/ethnic groups. Beginning in 2000, data reflect a new classification of institutions; this classification includes some additional, primarily 2-year, colleges and excludes a few institutions that did not award degrees. Includes institutions that were eligible to participate in Title IV federal financial aid programs and schools accredited by the National Association of Trade and Technical Schools]

Characteristic	1990	2000	2005	2010	2011	2012	2013
Total	**13,818.6**	**15,312.3**	**17,487.5**	**21,019.4**	**21,010.6**	**20,642.8**	**20,375.8**
Male	6,283.9	6,721.8	7,455.9	9,045.8	9,034.3	8,919.1	8,860.8
Female	7,534.7	8,590.5	10,031.6	11,973.7	11,976.3	11,723.7	11,515.0
Public	10,844.7	11,752.8	13,021.8	15,142.2	15,116.3	14,880.3	14,745.6
Private	2,973.9	3,559.5	4,465.6	5,877.3	5,894.3	5,762.5	5,630.2
2-year	5,240.1	5,948.4	6,488.1	7,683.6	7,511.2	7,164.0	6,968.7
4-year	8,578.6	9,363.9	10,999.4	13,335.8	13,499.4	13,478.8	13,407.1
Undergraduate	11,959.2	13,155.4	14,964.0	18,082.4	18,077.3	17,732.4	17,474.8
Postbaccalaureate	1,859.6	2,156.9	2,523.5	2,937.0	2,933.3	2,910.4	2,901.0
White [1]	**10,722.5**	**10,462.1**	**11,495.4**	**12,720.8**	**12,401.9**	**11,981.1**	**11,590.7**
Male	4,861.0	4,634.6	5,007.2	5,605.8	5,457.2	5,285.0	5,133.1
Female	5,861.5	5,827.5	6,488.2	7,115.0	6,944.6	6,696.1	6,457.6
Public	8,385.4	7,963.4	8,518.2	9,182.1	8,938.2	8,634.3	8,364.1
Private	2,337.0	2,498.7	2,977.3	3,538.7	3,463.6	3,346.9	3,226.6
2-year	3,954.3	3,804.1	3,998.6	4,321.3	4,092.3	3,837.0	3,636.1
4-year	6,768.1	6,658.0	7,496.9	8,399.5	8,309.6	8,144.2	7,954.6
Undergraduate	9,272.6	8,983.5	9,828.6	10,895.9	10,618.6	10,247.4	9,899.2
Postbaccalaureate	1,449.9	1,478.6	1,666.8	1,824.9	1,783.3	1,733.8	1,691.5
Black [1]	**1,247.0**	**1,730.3**	**2,214.6**	**3,039.0**	**3,079.2**	**2,962.1**	**2,872.1**
Male	484.7	635.3	774.1	1,089.0	1,107.8	1,079.4	1,065.0
Female	762.3	1,095.0	1,440.4	1,949.9	1,971.4	1,882.7	1,807.1
Public	976.4	1,319.2	1,580.4	1,988.8	2,014.0	1,937.0	1,886.8
Private	270.6	411.1	634.2	1,050.2	1,065.2	1,025.1	985.3
2-year	524.3	734.9	901.1	1,198.9	1,199.5	1,116.4	1,073.1
4-year	722.8	995.4	1,313.4	1,840.0	1,879.7	1,845.7	1,799.1
Undergraduate	1,147.2	1,548.9	1,955.4	2,677.1	2,708.3	2,592.8	2,504.8
Postbaccalaureate	99.8	181.4	259.2	361.9	370.9	369.3	367.3
Hispanic	**782.4**	**1,461.8**	**1,882.0**	**2,748.8**	**2,893.0**	**2,979.4**	**3,091.1**
Male	353.9	627.1	774.6	1,157.6	1,215.8	1,254.3	1,306.5
Female	428.5	834.7	1,107.3	1,591.2	1,677.2	1,725.1	1,784.6
Public	671.4	1,229.3	1,525.6	2,163.8	2,277.6	2,365.9	2,477.5
Private	111.0	232.5	356.4	585.0	615.4	613.6	613.6
2-year	424.2	843.9	981.5	1,393.0	1,439.5	1,446.1	1,491.2
4-year	358.2	617.9	900.5	1,355.9	1,453.5	1,533.3	1,599.9
Undergraduate	724.6	1,351.0	1,733.6	2,551.0	2,687.9	2,766.1	2,870.2
Postbaccalaureate	57.9	110.8	148.4	197.8	205.1	213.4	221.0
American Indian/ Alaska Native	**102.8**	**151.2**	**176.3**	**196.2**	**186.2**	**172.9**	**162.6**
Male	43.1	61.4	68.4	78.7	73.8	68.6	64.8
Female	59.7	89.7	107.9	117.5	112.5	104.3	97.7
Public	90.4	127.3	143.0	150.8	142.5	131.7	124.6
Private	12.4	23.9	33.3	45.5	43.7	41.2	37.9
2-year	54.9	74.7	80.7	87.2	81.1	74.9	71.0
4-year	47.9	76.5	95.6	109.0	105.1	98.0	91.6
Undergraduate	95.5	138.5	160.4	179.1	170.2	157.5	147.8
Postbaccalaureate	7.3	12.6	15.9	17.1	16.1	15.4	14.8
Asian/Pacific Islander	**572.4**	**978.2**	**1,134.4**	**1,281.6**	**1,277.0**	**1,259.2**	**1,259.6**
Male	294.9	465.9	522.0	600.6	600.7	593.7	594.3
Female	277.5	512.3	612.4	681.0	676.4	665.5	665.3
Public	461.0	770.5	881.9	968.7	958.5	942.5	944.8
Private	111.5	207.7	252.4	312.8	318.6	316.7	314.8
2-year	215.2	401.9	434.4	463.1	445.1	423.7	415.7
4-year	357.2	576.3	700.0	818.5	831.9	835.4	843.9
Undergraduate	500.5	845.5	971.4	1,087.3	1,079.6	1,063.2	1,064.4
Postbaccalaureate	71.9	132.6	163.0	194.3	197.4	196.0	195.2
Nonresident alien	**391.5**	**528.7**	**584.8**	**707.7**	**740.5**	**782.9**	**840.3**
Male	246.3	297.3	309.5	379.6	399.1	424.7	460.1
Female	145.2	231.4	275.3	328.0	341.4	358.2	380.2
Public	260.0	343.1	372.8	453.0	472.0	498.6	534.4
Private	131.4	185.6	212.0	254.7	268.5	284.3	305.9
2-year	67.1	89.0	91.8	99.3	95.9	93.6	92.0
4-year	324.3	439.7	493.1	608.3	644.6	689.2	748.3
Undergraduate	218.7	288.0	314.7	398.4	422.6	450.5	483.4
Postbaccalaureate	172.7	240.7	270.1	309.3	317.9	332.4	356.9

NA Not available. [1] Non-Hispanic.

Source: U.S. National Center for Education Statistics, *Digest of Education Statistics*, "Advance Release of Selected 2014 Digest Tables," and earlier releases, <http://nces.ed.gov/Programs/digest/>, accessed May 2015.

Table 292. Degree-Granting Higher Education Institutions, Number and Enrollment by State and Selected Characteristics: 2013

[20,376 represents 20,376,000. Number of institutions beginning in academic year. Opening Fall enrollment of resident and extension students attending full-time or part-time]

State	Num-ber of institu-tions [1]	Enrollment (1,000)										Non-resi-dent alien
		Total	Male	Female	Public	Private	Full-time	White [2]	Minority			
									Total [3]	Black [2]	His-panic	
United States........	**4,724**	**20,376**	**8,861**	**11,515**	**13,347**	**4,128**	**12,597**	**11,591**	**7,385**	**2,872**	**3,091**	**840**
Alabama...............	77	306	130	176	214	48	207	188	106	90	9	7
Alaska.................	11	35	14	21	29	3	16	22	10	1	3	1
Arizona...............	91	694	269	425	326	254	460	371	286	106	137	19
Arkansas.............	52	172	72	101	138	16	111	119	43	31	8	5
California.............	469	2,637	1,208	1,429	2,043	328	1,442	851	1,565	185	951	111
Colorado.............	92	359	161	198	237	64	207	239	97	27	53	10
Connecticut...........	46	201	86	115	110	56	128	126	62	25	26	9
Delaware.............	12	60	24	35	37	11	37	35	19	13	4	4
District of Columbia....	20	89	37	53	5	42	63	42	37	24	6	9
Florida................	235	1,126	473	652	731	267	655	530	532	222	268	37
Georgia...............	136	533	218	315	374	91	354	270	235	179	30	17
Hawaii................	22	76	33	44	53	15	45	14	39	2	7	5
Idaho.................	19	109	48	61	69	33	63	87	14	1	10	5
Illinois................	185	843	368	475	497	197	485	482	308	124	130	35
Indiana...............	84	444	197	247	298	92	286	328	81	47	22	24
Iowa..................	66	340	135	205	154	140	225	239	84	51	22	11
Kansas................	74	216	97	119	163	27	129	155	42	16	17	13
Kentucky..............	79	273	116	157	195	43	172	222	39	27	7	6
Louisiana.............	70	252	103	149	193	28	171	142	98	79	11	7
Maine.................	31	71	30	41	46	17	45	62	6	2	2	1
Maryland..............	62	364	158	206	258	36	194	180	156	104	26	17
Massachusetts.........	125	514	223	291	201	179	353	320	135	45	51	46
Michigan..............	117	644	286	358	462	96	376	456	142	90	24	30
Minnesota.............	118	441	177	265	242	84	246	308	106	62	20	14
Mississippi............	42	174	69	105	139	14	133	96	73	67	3	2
Missouri..............	136	438	191	247	228	132	272	316	96	63	18	16
Montana...............	22	53	25	28	43	5	38	43	7	(Z)	2	2
Nebraska..............	43	138	61	77	88	25	91	108	23	8	10	5
Nevada................	26	117	52	65	95	11	61	58	50	10	26	2
New Hampshire........	27	92	39	53	39	34	60	75	13	6	4	3
New Jersey............	70	437	199	238	315	59	277	224	187	65	83	18
New Mexico...........	44	153	66	87	131	8	80	54	91	5	69	5
New York..............	304	1,304	568	736	652	414	911	680	506	181	203	95
North Carolina.........	151	575	237	338	415	88	370	345	201	145	32	16
North Dakota..........	21	55	27	28	42	5	38	45	6	2	1	3
Ohio..................	219	698	304	394	459	148	446	521	131	90	22	30
Oklahoma.............	66	221	97	124	166	29	142	137	61	21	15	10
Oregon...............	65	251	114	137	191	29	157	177	51	8	25	12
Pennsylvania..........	263	766	339	427	373	257	549	538	173	89	46	38
Rhode Island..........	13	83	36	47	39	35	62	57	19	6	10	5
South Carolina........	78	258	106	152	188	44	177	161	86	72	9	5
South Dakota..........	25	55	24	31	39	10	34	45	7	2	2	1
Tennessee.............	113	338	142	196	205	86	238	234	89	69	11	8
Texas.................	275	1,541	673	869	1,211	153	827	626	826	209	525	59
Utah..................	41	264	128	136	156	79	178	206	44	9	23	8
Vermont...............	24	44	20	24	24	13	32	37	4	1	2	1
Virginia...............	130	584	252	332	358	129	354	343	206	130	39	17
Washington............	86	363	164	200	287	40	251	230	92	17	37	20
West Virginia..........	44	158	79	79	79	54	81	119	32	20	8	4
Wisconsin.............	88	364	160	204	266	59	233	287	59	24	19	11
Wyoming..............	10	37	18	19	33	2	20	31	4	1	3	1
U.S. military [4]........	5	15	12	3	15	(X)	15	10	4	1	2	(Z)

X Not applicable. Z Fewer than 500. [1] Branch campuses counted as separate institutions. [2] Non-Hispanic. [3] Includes other races not shown separately. [4] Service schools.

Source: U.S. National Center for Education Statistics, *Digest of Education Statistics*, "Advance Release of Selected 2014 Digest Tables," and earlier releases, <http://www.nces.ed.gov/programs/digest/>, accessed May 2015.

Table 293. College Enrollment by Sex, Age, Race, and Hispanic Origin: 1980 to 2013

[In thousands (11,387 represents 11,387,000). As of October for the civilian noninstitutional population, 14 years old and over. Based on the Current Population Survey; see text, Section 1 and Appendix III]

Characteristic	1980	1990 [1]	1995	2000	2005	2008	2009	2010	2011	2012	2013
Total [2]	**11,387**	**13,621**	**14,715**	**15,314**	**17,472**	**18,632**	**19,764**	**20,275**	**20,397**	**19,930**	**19,467**
Male [3]	5,430	6,192	6,703	6,682	7,539	8,311	8,642	9,007	9,132	8,602	8,536
18 to 24 years	3,604	3,922	4,089	4,342	4,972	5,383	5,640	5,698	5,953	5,730	5,629
25 to 34 years	1,325	1,412	1,561	1,361	1,486	1,806	1,843	2,055	1,986	1,770	1,775
35 years old and over	405	772	985	918	1,019	989	1,069	1,161	1,084	970	984
Female [3]	5,957	7,429	8,013	8,631	9,933	10,321	11,123	11,268	11,266	11,327	10,931
18 to 24 years	3,625	4,042	4,452	5,109	5,859	6,083	6,432	6,515	6,618	6,726	6,572
25 to 34 years	1,378	1,749	1,788	1,846	2,115	2,207	2,450	2,569	2,630	2,563	2,291
35 years old and over	802	1,546	1,684	1,589	1,838	1,922	2,124	2,049	1,922	1,899	1,907
White [3, 4]	9,925	11,488	12,021	11,999	13,467	14,405	15,027	15,258	15,412	14,628	14,240
18 to 24 years	6,334	6,635	7,011	7,566	8,499	9,141	9,327	9,324	9,813	9,302	9,050
25 to 34 years	2,328	2,698	2,686	2,339	2,647	2,859	3,163	3,414	3,339	3,050	2,849
35 years old and over	1,051	2,023	2,208	1,978	2,206	2,234	2,377	2,365	2,120	2,072	2,107
Male	4,804	5,235	5,535	5,311	5,844	6,570	6,681	6,883	7,054	6,392	6,241
Female	5,121	6,253	6,486	6,689	7,624	7,834	8,346	8,375	8,358	8,236	7,999
Black [3, 4]	1,163	1,393	1,772	2,164	2,297	2,481	2,889	3,083	3,146	3,038	2,857
18 to 24 years	688	894	988	1,216	1,229	1,349	1,604	1,692	1,639	1,689	1,599
25 to 34 years	289	258	426	567	520	646	663	715	818	769	686
35 years old and over	156	207	334	361	448	451	587	642	651	553	540
Male	476	587	710	815	864	919	1,058	1,185	1,212	1,152	1,116
Female	686	807	1,062	1,349	1,435	1,562	1,831	1,898	1,934	1,886	1,740
Asian [3, 4]	(NA)	(NA)	(NA)	(NA)	1,184	1,219	1,231	1,322	1,204	1,447	1,576
18 to 24 years	(NA)	(NA)	(NA)	(NA)	696	655	768	811	748	914	1,001
25 to 34 years	(NA)	(NA)	(NA)	(NA)	341	381	311	354	288	363	372
35 years old and over	(NA)	(NA)	(NA)	(NA)	130	156	141	125	147	143	173
Male	(NA)	(NA)	(NA)	(NA)	605	567	613	647	567	700	789
Female	(NA)	(NA)	(NA)	(NA)	579	653	619	676	637	747	787
Hispanic origin [3, 5]	443	748	1,207	1,426	1,942	2,227	2,434	2,879	2,953	3,400	3,219
18 to 24 years	315	435	745	899	1,216	1,338	1,465	1,814	2,079	2,403	2,192
25 to 34 years	118	168	250	309	438	500	590	652	582	622	639
35 years old and over	(NA)	130	193	195	257	338	336	372	256	313	345
Male	222	364	568	619	804	1,042	1,080	1,302	1,438	1,510	1,438
Female	221	384	639	807	1,139	1,185	1,354	1,576	1,515	1,890	1,781

NA Not available. [1] Beginning 1990, based on a revised edit and tabulation package. [2] Includes other races not shown separately. [3] Includes persons 14 to 17 years old not shown separately. [4] Beginning 2003, for persons who selected this race group only. See footnote 4, Table 253. [5] Persons of Hispanic origin may be of any race.

Source: U.S. Census Bureau, Current Population Reports, PPL-148, P-20, and earlier reports; and "School Enrollment," <http://www.census.gov/hhes/school/index.html>, accessed November 2014.

Table 294. Foreign (Nonimmigrant) Student Enrollment in U.S. Colleges and Universities by World Region and Selected Country of Origin: 1980 to 2014

[In thousands (286 represents 286,000). For Fall of the previous year]

Region of origin	1980	1990	1995	2000	2004	2005	2006	2007	2008	2009	2010	2011	2012	2013	2014
All regions	**286**	**387**	**453**	**515**	**573**	**565**	**565**	**583**	**624**	**672**	**691**	**723**	**764**	**820**	**886**
Africa [1]	36	25	21	30	38	36	36	36	36	37	37	37	35	36	31
Nigeria	16	4	2	4	6	6	6	6	6	6	7	7	7	7	8
Asia [1, 2, 3]	165	245	292	315	356	356	346	367	405	444	469	504	547	597	569
China	1	33	39	54	62	63	63	68	81	98	128	158	194	236	274
Taiwan	18	31	36	29	26	26	28	29	29	28	27	25	23	22	21
Hong Kong	10	11	13	8	7	7	8	8	8	8	8	8	8	8	8
India	9	26	34	42	80	80	77	84	95	103	105	104	100	97	103
Indonesia	2	9	12	11	9	8	8	7	8	8	7	7	7	8	8
Iran	51	7	3	2	2	2	2	3	3	4	5	6	7	9	10
Japan	12	30	45	47	41	42	39	35	34	29	25	21	20	20	19
Malaysia	4	14	14	9	6	6	6	5	5	6	6	7	7	7	7
Saudi Arabia	10	4	4	5	4	3	3	8	10	13	16	23	34	45	54
South Korea	5	22	34	41	52	53	59	62	69	75	72	73	73	71	68
Thailand	7	7	11	11	9	9	9	9	9	9	9	8	8	7	7
Europe [4]	23	46	65	78	74	72	85	83	84	88	85	84	85	86	87
Latin America [1, 5]	42	48	47	62	66	68	65	65	64	68	66	64	64	67	72
Mexico	6	7	9	11	13	13	14	14	15	15	13	14	14	14	15
Venezuela	10	3	4	5	6	5	5	5	4	5	5	5	6	6	7
North America	16	19	23	24	28	29	29	29	29	30	29	28	27	27	28
Canada	15	18	23	24	27	28	28	28	29	30	28	28	27	27	28
Oceania	4	4	4	5	5	4	5	4	5	5	5	6	6	6	6

[1] Includes countries not shown separately. [2] Includes the Middle East. [3] Beginning 2006, excludes Cyprus and Turkey. [4] Beginning 2006, includes Cyprus and Turkey. [5] Includes Mexico, Central America, Caribbean, and South America.

Source: Institute of International Education, New York, NY, *Open Doors Report on International Educational Exchange* ©, annual (2014). See also <http://www.iie.org/opendoors>.

Table 295. College Enrollment by Type of College, Sex, and Selected Characteristics: 2013

[In thousands (19,467 represents 19,467,000). As of October. Covers civilian noninstitutional population 15 years old and over enrolled in colleges and graduate schools. Based on Current Population Survey. See text, Section 1 and Appendix III]

Characteristic	Total				Male		Female	
	Total enrolled	Two-year college	Four-year college	Graduate school	Total enrolled [1]	Four-year college	Total enrolled [1]	Four-year college
Total enrollment [2].............	**19,467**	**5,270**	**10,468**	**3,729**	**8,536**	**4,707**	**10,931**	**5,759**
Age:								
15 to 19 years old..................	4,259	1,502	2,701	57	1,958	1,192	2,302	1,507
20 to 24 years old..................	8,251	1,991	5,220	1,041	3,820	2,447	4,431	2,773
25 to 34 years old..................	4,066	1,008	1,591	1,468	1,775	731	2,291	860
35 years old and over............	2,891	770	957	1,164	983	338	1,908	619
Race/ethnicity:								
White [3]................................	14,240	3,880	7,702	2,658	6,241	3,480	7,999	4,222
White non-Hispanic [3].............	11,348	2,704	6,319	2,324	4,944	2,888	6,404	3,431
Black [3]................................	2,857	888	1,490	479	1,116	577	1,740	913
Asian [3]..............................	1,576	307	774	495	789	412	787	362
Hispanic [4]..........................	3,219	1,282	1,572	365	1,438	699	1,781	873
Type of school:								
Public.................................	15,514	4,920	8,208	2,386	6,774	3,695	8,741	4,514
Private...............................	3,953	350	2,259	1,344	1,762	1,013	2,190	1,246
Employment status:								
Employed full-time.................	4,778	1,175	1,960	1,642	2,060	853	2,718	1,107
Employed part-time...............	5,353	1,551	3,055	746	2,110	1,193	3,243	1,862
Not employed......................	9,337	2,544	5,452	1,341	4,366	2,661	4,970	2,791
Enrollment status:								
Full time students.................	14,228	3,483	8,631	2,115	6,539	3,988	7,690	4,642
15 to 19 years old.................	3,862	1,254	2,570	38	1,783	1,127	2,079	1,443
20 to 24 years old.................	6,722	1,319	4,557	845	3,157	2,177	3,565	2,381
25 to 34 years old.................	2,474	536	1,073	866	1,173	542	1,301	532
35 years old and over...........	1,171	374	431	366	427	143	744	287
Part time students.................	5,239	1,788	1,837	1,614	1,997	719	3,242	1,117
15 to 19 years old.................	397	249	131	18	175	65	222	64
20 to 24 years old.................	1,529	672	662	196	664	270	866	392
25 to 34 years old.................	1,592	472	517	602	602	189	990	328
35 years old and over...........	1,720	396	526	799	557	194	1,164	332

[1] Includes enrollment in two-year colleges and graduate school not shown separately. [2] Includes other races not shown separately. [3] For persons who selected this race group only. See footnote 4, Table 253. [4] Persons of Hispanic origin may be of any race.

Source: U.S. Census Bureau, "School Enrollment," <http://www.census.gov/hhes/school/index.html>, accessed November 2014.

Table 296. Higher Education Enrollment in Languages Other Than English: 1970 to 2013

[1,153.2 represents 1,153,200. As of Fall. For credit enrollment]

Enrollment	1970	1980	1986	1990	1995	2002	2006	2009	2013
Registrations [1] (1,000)..................	**1,153.2**	**924.3**	**1,003.2**	**1,185.5**	**1,138.8**	**1,395.8**	**1,575.7**	**1,673.5**	**1,562.2**
By selected language (1,000):									
Spanish.......................................	386.6	379.0	411.4	534.1	606.3	745.2	822.1	861.0	790.8
French..	358.5	248.3	275.1	273.1	205.4	202.0	206.0	215.2	197.8
American Sign Language.................	(NA)	(NA)	(NA)	1.6	4.3	60.8	79.7	92.1	109.6
German.......................................	201.8	127.0	120.9	133.6	96.3	91.1	94.1	95.6	86.7
Italian...	34.2	34.8	40.9	49.8	43.8	63.9	78.2	80.3	71.3
Japanese.....................................	6.6	11.5	23.5	45.8	44.7	52.2	65.4	72.4	66.7
Chinese.......................................	6.1	11.4	16.9	19.4	26.5	34.2	51.4	59.9	61.1
Arabic...	1.3	3.5	3.4	3.7	4.4	10.6	24.0	34.9	32.3
Latin...	28.4	25.0	25.0	28.2	25.9	29.8	32.2	32.4	27.2
Russian.......................................	36.4	24.0	33.9	44.5	24.7	23.9	24.8	26.8	22.0
Ancient Greek..............................	16.5	22.1	17.8	16.4	16.3	20.4	22.8	20.0	12.9
Hebrew.......................................	16.6	19.3	15.7	13.0	13.1	22.8	23.8	22.7	19.9
Portuguese..................................	5.1	4.9	5.1	6.1	6.5	8.4	10.3	11.3	12.4
Korean..	0.1	0.4	0.9	2.4	3.3	5.2	7.1	8.4	12.2
Index (1965=100).........................	111.5	89.3	97.0	114.6	110.1	134.9	152.3	161.7	151.0

NA Not available. [1] Includes other languages, not shown separately.

Source: Modern Language Association, David Goldberg, Dennis Looney, and Natalia Lusin. *Enrollments in Languages Other Than English in United States Institutions of Higher Education, Fall 2013*, February 2015 ©. For 1970 to 2009, consult Association of Departments of Foreign Languages (ADFL) Bulletins.

Table 297. College Students Reporting Disability Status by Selected Characteristic: 2011 to 2012

[23,055 represents 23,055,000. Disabled students reported that they had one or more of the following conditions: a specific learning disability, a visual handicap, hard of hearing, deafness, a speech disability, an orthopedic handicap, or a health impairment. Based on the 2011–2012 National Postsecondary Student-Aid Study; see source for details. Includes Puerto Rico. See also Appendix III]

Student characteristic	Undergraduate			Graduate and first-professional		
	All students	Disabled students	Nondisabled students	All students	Disabled students	Nondisabled students
Total students (1,000)...............	23,055	2,563	20,493	3,682	195	3,487
PERCENT DISTRIBUTION						
Total........................	100.0	11.1	88.9	100.0	5.3	94.7
Age:						
15 to 23 years old..................	56.2	45.3	57.6	11.4	8.4	11.5
24 to 29 years old..................	18.4	18.8	18.4	40.3	35.3	40.5
30 years or older..................	25.4	35.8	24.0	48.4	56.3	47.9
Sex:						
Male.............................	43.0	43.7	42.9	39.7	35.7	40.0
Female...........................	57.0	56.3	57.1	60.3	64.3	60.0
Race/ethnicity of student:						
White, non-Hispanic................	57.9	58.0	57.9	63.6	60.4	63.8
Black, non-Hispanic................	16.1	17.6	15.9	11.8	15.5	11.6
Hispanic.........................	16.0	14.9	16.2	8.7	10.5	8.6
Asian............................	5.6	4.0	5.8	12.9	10.4	13.0
Pacific Islander...................	0.5	0.7	0.5	0.6	(S)	0.6
American Indian/Alaska Native......	0.9	1.2	0.9	0.4	(S)	0.4
Two or more races................	3.0	3.6	2.9	2.0	2.5	2.0
Attendance status:						
Full-time, full-year.................	38.4	33.0	39.1	37.8	38.2	37.8
Part-time or part-year..............	61.6	67.0	60.9	62.2	61.8	62.2
Student housing status:						
On-campus.......................	12.1	9.4	12.5	(NA)	(NA)	(NA)
Off-campus.......................	46.1	48.9	45.7	(NA)	(NA)	(NA)
With parents or relatives...........	33.5	34.2	33.5	(NA)	(NA)	(NA)
Attended more than one institution....	8.3	7.4	8.4	(NA)	(NA)	(NA)
Dependency status:						
Dependent.......................	48.7	37.5	50.1	(NA)	(NA)	(NA)
Independent, unmarried............	17.8	22.9	17.2	49.8	53.0	49.6
Independent, married..............	6.0	7.1	5.8	15.4	12.3	15.5
Independent with dependents.......	27.5	32.5	26.9	34.8	34.7	34.8

NA Not available. S Figure does not meet publication standards.

Source: U.S. National Center for Education Statistics, *Digest of Education Statistics*, "Advance Release of Selected 2013 Digest Tables," <http://www.nces.ed.gov/programs/digest/>, accessed July 2014.

Table 298. College Freshmen—Summary Characteristics: 1980 to 2014

[In percent, except family income (24.5 represents $24,500). As of Fall for first-time full-time freshmen in 4-year colleges and universities. Based on sample survey and subject to sampling error; see source]

Characteristic	1980	1990	1995	2000	2005	2010	2012	2013	2014
Sex:									
Male............................	48.8	46.9	45.6	45.2	45.0	44.3	44.1	43.3	43.4
Female..........................	51.2	53.1	54.4	54.8	55.0	55.7	55.9	56.7	56.6
Applied to more than three colleges....................	31.5	42.9	44.4	50.5	55.4	64.1	65.0	69.4	72.5
Average grade in high school:									
A– to A+........................	26.6	29.4	36.1	42.9	46.6	48.4	49.5	52.8	53.1
B– to B+........................	58.2	57.0	54.2	50.5	48.0	47.5	46.4	44.0	43.9
C to C+.........................	14.9	13.4	9.6	6.5	5.4	4.1	4.0	3.2	2.9
D...............................	0.2	0.2	0.1	0.1	0.1	0.1	0.0	0.0	0.0
Political orientation:									
Liberal..........................	21.0	24.6	22.9	24.8	27.1	27.3	26.8	27.7	28.8
Middle of the road...............	57.0	51.7	51.3	51.9	45.0	46.4	47.5	46.3	47.2
Conservative....................	19.0	20.6	21.8	18.9	22.6	21.7	21.1	21.2	19.4
Probable field of study:									
Biological sciences..............	4.5	4.9	8.3	6.6	7.6	10.8	12.9	14.7	13.8
Business........................	21.2	21.1	15.4	16.7	17.4	13.7	14.4	14.5	14.6
Education.......................	8.4	10.3	10.1	11.0	9.9	7.2	5.8	5.2	5.0
Engineering.....................	11.2	9.7	8.1	8.7	8.3	10.3	10.3	11.2	11.7
Physical science.................	3.2	2.8	3.1	2.6	3.1	2.7	2.5	2.4	2.5
Social science...................	8.2	11.0	9.9	10.0	10.7	8.9	11.1	10.1	10.2
Data processing/computer programming.............	1.7	0.7	0.8	1.5	0.5	0.5	(NA)	(NA)	(NA)
Other [1]........................	41.6	39.5	44.3	42.9	42.5	45.9	43.0	42.0	41.5
Communications [2].............	2.4	2.9	1.8	2.7	2.0	1.8	3.0	2.2	2.2
Computer science...............	2.6	1.7	2.2	3.7	1.1	1.0	2.0	2.5	3.5
Personal objectives—very important or essential:									
Being very well off financially.............	62.5	72.3	72.8	73.4	74.5	77.4	81.0	82.0	82.4
Developing a meaningful philosophy of life...........	62.5	45.9	45.4	42.4	45.0	46.9	45.6	44.8	44.6
Keeping up to date with political affairs................	45.2	46.6	32.3	28.1	36.4	33.2	34.5	36.1	35.0
Median family income ($1,000)................	24.5	46.6	54.8	64.4	73.2	76.1	(NA)	(NA)	(NA)

NA Not available. [1] Includes other fields not shown separately. [2] Beginning in 2012, communications majors are reported in combination with journalism majors.

Source: The Higher Education Research Institute, University of California, Los Angeles, CA, *The American Freshman: National Norms Fall 2014* ©, 2014, and earlier editions. See also <http://www.heri.ucla.edu/tfsPublications.php>.

Table 299. Residence and Migration of College Freshmen by State: 2012

[As of Fall. Includes first-time postsecondary students who had graduated from high school in the previous 12 months and were enrolled at public and private not-for-profit 4-year degree-granting institutions that participated in Title IV federal financial aid programs. Excludes respondents for whom state residence and/or migration are unknown. Also excludes U.S. Service Academies (Air Force Academy, Coast Guard Academy, Merchant Marine Academy, Military Academy, and Naval Academy)]

State	Total freshmen enrollment in institutions located in the state	Ratio of in-state students to freshmen enrollment	Ratio of in-state students to residents enrolled in any state [1]	State	Total freshmen enrollment in institutions located in the state	Ratio of in-state students to freshmen enrollment	Ratio of in-state students to residents enrolled in any state [1]
U.S........	1,497,055	0.72	0.74	MO.........	30,848	0.67	0.77
AL..........	23,638	0.62	0.85	MT..........	5,803	0.64	0.79
AK..........	2,847	0.83	0.66	NE..........	10,697	0.74	0.78
AZ..........	23,520	0.61	0.79	NV..........	9,482	0.85	0.75
AR..........	16,875	0.71	0.88	NH..........	8,654	0.36	0.41
CA..........	124,883	0.87	0.77	NJ..........	26,297	0.84	0.42
CO..........	23,789	0.72	0.70	NM..........	7,896	0.80	0.79
CT..........	18,775	0.54	0.42	NY..........	106,726	0.69	0.73
DE..........	6,075	0.45	0.61	NC..........	46,835	0.72	0.84
DC..........	8,284	0.05	0.21	ND..........	6,483	0.45	0.78
FL..........	97,356	0.87	0.88	OH..........	69,385	0.78	0.82
GA..........	50,398	0.83	0.80	OK..........	19,243	0.68	0.87
HI..........	4,274	0.68	0.51	OR..........	14,786	0.58	0.68
ID..........	7,731	0.56	0.67	PA..........	81,632	0.63	0.77
IL..........	48,729	0.75	0.57	RI..........	10,860	0.26	0.53
IN..........	42,880	0.71	0.85	SC..........	23,275	0.62	0.85
IA..........	19,572	0.53	0.78	SD..........	6,111	0.58	0.75
KS..........	14,534	0.72	0.78	TN..........	29,690	0.76	0.78
KY..........	23,498	0.73	0.85	TX..........	93,616	0.91	0.82
LA..........	23,625	0.79	0.89	UT..........	20,482	0.68	0.91
ME..........	6,634	0.61	0.59	VT..........	6,505	0.25	0.45
MD..........	18,385	0.64	0.44	VA..........	42,732	0.67	0.74
MA..........	51,041	0.49	0.59	WA..........	24,698	0.76	0.70
MI..........	49,983	0.82	0.85	WV..........	12,855	0.56	0.88
MN..........	25,729	0.71	0.60	WI..........	36,139	0.72	0.79
MS..........	10,771	0.59	0.81	WY..........	1,499	0.50	0.53

[1] Students residing in a particular state when admitted to an institution anywhere, either in their home state or another state.

Source: U.S. National Center for Education Statistics, *Digest of Education Statistics*, "Advance Release of Selected 2013 Digest Tables," <http://www.nces.ed.gov/programs/digest/>, accessed June 2014.

Table 300. Average Total Price of Attendance of Undergraduate Education: 2012

[In dollars. For school year ending in 2012. Excludes students attending more than one institution. Price of attendance includes tuition and fees, books and supplies, room and board, transportation, and personal and other expenses allowed for federal cost of attendance budgets. Based on the 2011–2012 National Postsecondary Student-Aid Study; see source for details. Includes Puerto Rico. See also Appendix III]

Student characteristic	All institu-tions [1]	Public 2-year	Public 4-year Non-doctorate granting	Public 4-year Doctorate granting	Private not-for-profit 4-year Non-doctorate granting	Private not-for-profit 4-year Doctorate granting	Private for-profit
Total........................	**16,477**	**8,712**	**13,722**	**20,078**	**31,587**	**36,819**	**20,159**
Age: [2]							
18 years or younger..................	20,826	9,680	16,593	23,139	39,029	44,457	23,664
19 to 23 years....................	18,957	8,957	15,252	21,357	36,364	42,352	21,126
24 to 29 years....................	13,540	8,583	11,584	16,626	23,794	24,432	19,972
30 to 39 years....................	13,174	8,574	11,075	14,732	18,746	21,683	19,490
40 years or older..................	11,816	7,790	9,805	13,507	16,029	17,200	19,152
Sex:							
Male...........................	16,533	8,735	13,598	20,363	32,047	37,261	20,326
Female.........................	16,434	8,693	13,817	19,821	31,246	36,470	20,065
Race:							
One race:							
White............................	16,820	8,605	14,238	20,124	31,917	36,529	20,001
Black or African American..................	15,472	8,977	13,018	19,270	26,787	30,585	19,637
Hispanic or Latino [3]........................	14,917	8,424	12,305	19,282	31,762	38,595	21,088
Asian..........................	20,007	9,506	14,167	22,574	40,032	44,623	20,445
American Indian/Alaska Native..............	14,426	8,844	11,095	18,568	(S)	(S)	18,117
Native Hawaiian or other Pacific Islander......................	16,082	9,609	(S)	19,552	(S)	(S)	21,719
More than one race....................	17,815	9,518	15,215	19,786	34,789	36,780	22,090
Attendance pattern:							
Full-time, full-year.....................	26,417	15,031	20,141	24,231	40,087	46,476	29,332
Full-time, part-year.....................	13,522	8,107	11,004	15,040	21,727	24,024	16,555
Part-time, full-year.....................	12,769	9,701	12,279	16,773	22,192	22,873	20,363
Part-time, part-year.....................	6,397	4,868	6,272	8,571	10,638	11,359	11,466

S Data do not meet publication standards. [1] Includes public less-than-2-year and private not-for-profit less-than-4-year. [2] As of December 31, 2011. [3] Persons of Hispanic origin may be of any race.

Source: U.S. Department of Education, National Center for Education Statistics, National Postsecondary Student Aid Study (NPSAS), "Datalab," <http://nces.ed.gov/datalab/>, accessed September 2014.

Table 301. Higher Education Price Indexes: 2005 to 2014 ©

[1983=100. For years ending June 30. The Higher Education Price Index (HEPI), calculated for the July-June academic fiscal year, reflects prices paid by colleges and universities for the following eight cost factors: faculty salaries, administrative salaries, clerical and service employees, fringe benefits, miscellaneous services, supplies and materials, and utilities. Minus sign (-) indicates decrease]

Item and year	Total	Personnel compensation					Contracted services, supplies, and equipment		
		Faculty salaries	Admin-istrative salaries	Clerical salaries	Service employ-ees salaries	Fringe benefits	Miscel-laneous services	Supplies and materials	Utilities
INDEXES									
2005	240.8	240.7	274.0	223.4	201.4	327.2	222.7	145.5	200.2
2006	253.1	248.2	287.7	229.5	205.5	343.7	228.8	158.1	255.7
2007	260.3	257.6	299.2	237.7	213.6	360.8	238.3	165.3	220.6
2008	273.2	268.1	314.0	245.0	220.4	380.7	246.5	180.0	252.0
2009	279.3	277.3	330.9	251.6	226.7	394.4	253.1	181.6	213.8
2010	281.8	280.6	337.6	255.2	230.0	402.8	255.8	179.3	193.6
2011	288.4	284.5	343.2	260.2	233.2	417.6	260.3	193.9	201.5
2012	293.2	289.6	352.3	264.8	235.7	425.3	264.6	203.9	191.7
2013	297.8	294.6	362.4	269.8	239.4	437.5	269.4	180.0	195.6
2014	306.7	301.0	366.4	274.8	242.0	458.3	274.2	200.2	211.4
ANNUAL PERCENT CHANGE [1]									
2005	3.9	2.8	4.1	2.9	1.9	4.6	2.9	7.3	13.5
2006	5.1	3.1	5.0	2.7	2.0	5.0	2.7	8.7	27.7
2007	2.8	3.8	4.0	3.6	4.0	5.0	4.2	4.5	-13.7
2008	5.0	4.1	5.0	3.1	3.2	5.5	3.4	8.9	14.2
2009	2.3	3.4	5.4	2.7	2.9	3.6	2.7	0.9	-15.1
2010	0.9	1.2	2.0	1.4	1.4	2.1	1.1	-1.3	-9.5
2011	2.3	1.4	1.7	2.0	1.4	3.7	1.8	8.2	4.1
2012	1.7	1.8	2.7	1.7	1.1	1.8	1.7	5.2	-4.9
2013	1.6	1.7	2.9	1.9	1.6	2.9	1.8	-11.7	2.0
2014	3.0	2.2	1.1	1.9	1.1	4.8	1.8	11.2	8.1

[1] Percent change from the immediate prior year.

Source: The Commonfund Institute, Wilton, CT ©. See also <http://www.commonfund.org>.

Table 302. Average Out-of-Pocket Net Price of Attendance for Undergraduates: 2012

[In dollars. For school year ending in 2012. Excludes students attending more than one institution. Net price of attendance is the price that students pay to receive postsecondary education after taking financial aid into account. Based on net tuition and net price for all students. Based on the 2011–2012 National Postsecondary Student-Aid Study; see source for details. Includes Puerto Rico. See also Appendix III]

Student characteristic	All institu-tions [1]	Public 2-year	Type of Institution				Private for-profit
			Public 4-year		Private not-for-profit 4-year		
			Non-doctorate granting	Doctorate granting	Non-doctorate granting	Doctorate granting	
Total	**8,657**	**6,013**	**7,725**	**10,585**	**13,155**	**16,640**	**10,350**
Age: [2]							
18 years or younger	10,270	6,912	8,396	11,342	14,225	18,800	12,400
19 to 23 years	10,236	6,482	8,889	11,767	15,236	18,999	11,118
24 to 29 years	6,706	5,660	6,450	7,886	10,407	12,430	10,194
30 to 39 years	6,028	5,421	5,610	6,502	8,446	10,337	9,780
40 years or older	5,937	5,315	5,809	7,225	7,681	8,661	9,758
Sex:							
Male	8,968	6,154	7,800	11,139	13,317	17,453	9,836
Female	8,404	5,901	7,668	10,084	13,036	15,999	10,638
Race:							
One race:							
White	9,221	6,058	8,177	11,342	14,214	17,076	10,302
Black or African American	6,210	5,413	5,866	6,508	7,688	10,769	10,072
Hispanic or Latino [3]	7,370	5,965	7,119	9,071	11,220	13,696	10,733
Asian	12,752	7,367	9,720	14,612	20,138	25,186	11,871
American Indian/Alaska Native	6,292	5,654	5,978	6,275	(S)	(S)	9,105
Native Hawaiian or other Pacific Islander	8,342	6,804	(S)	10,461	(S)	(S)	10,427
More than one race	8,619	6,456	7,564	8,937	11,172	17,020	10,191
Attendance pattern:							
Full-time, full-year	12,834	9,883	10,309	12,274	15,855	20,057	15,023
Full-time, part-year	7,297	5,358	6,706	9,158	10,528	12,536	8,918
Part-time, full-year	7,452	6,716	7,257	8,836	10,781	11,681	9,598
Part-time, part-year	4,195	3,709	4,573	5,646	5,410	7,119	5,485

S Data do not meet publication standards. [1] Includes public less-than-2-year and private not-for-profit less-than-4-year. [2] As of December 2007. [3] Persons of Hispanic origin may be of any race.

Source: U.S. Department of Education, National Center for Education Statistics, National Postsecondary Student Aid Study (NPSAS), "Datalab," <http://nces.ed.gov/datalab/>, accessed September 2014.

Table 303. Federal Student Financial Assistance: 1995 to 2014

[35,477 represents $35,477,000,000. For award years July 1 of year shown to the following June 30. Funds utilized exclude operating costs, etc., and represent funds given to students]

Type of assistance	1995	2000	2005	2010	2012	2013, est.	2014, est.
FUNDS UTILIZED (mil. dol.)							
Total	**35,477**	**44,007**	**72,634**	**144,182**	**137,412**	**136,738**	**135,847**
Federal Pell Grants	5,472	7,956	12,693	35,677	32,061	32,352	32,958
Academic Competitiveness Grants [1]	(X)	(X)	(X)	553	(X)	(X)	(X)
SMART Grants [1]	(X)	(X)	(X)	433	(X)	(X)	(X)
TEACH Grants [2]	(X)	(X)	(X)	121	(NA)	93	96
Federal Supplemental Educational Opportunity Grant	764	907	1,084	1,022	(NA)	926	975
Federal Work-Study	764	939	1,050	1,198	(NA)	1,100	1,159
Federal Perkins Loan	1,029	1,144	1,593	857	(NA)	1,011	1,011
Federal Direct Student Loan (FDSL)	8,296	10,348	12,930	84,704	105,351	101,256	99,647
Federal Family Education Loans (FFEL) [3]	19,152	22,712	43,284	19,618	(X)	(X)	(X)
NUMBER OF AWARDS (1,000)							
Total	**13,667**	**15,043**	**21,317**	**34,895**	**31,140**	**31,834**	**30,802**
Federal Pell Grants	3,612	3,899	5,167	9,308	8,959	8,861	8,711
Academic Competitiveness Grants [1]	(X)	(X)	(X)	729	(X)	(X)	(X)
SMART Grants [1]	(X)	(X)	(X)	140	(X)	(X)	(X)
TEACH Grants [2]	(X)	(X)	(X)	39	(NA)	32	34
Federal Supplemental Educational Opportunity Grant	1,083	1,175	1,419	1,633	(NA)	1,545	1,627
Federal Work-Study	702	713	710	718	(NA)	656	690
Federal Perkins Loan	688	639	727	461	(NA)	500	500
Federal Direct Student Loan (FDSL)	2,339	2,739	2,971	16,647	22,181	20,240	19,240
Federal Family Education Loans (FFEL) [3]	5,243	5,878	10,323	5,220	(X)	(X)	(X)
AVERAGE AWARD (dol.)							
Total	**2,596**	**2,925**	**3,407**	**4,132**	**4,413**	**4,295**	**4,410**
Federal Pell Grants	1,515	2,041	2,456	3,833	3,579	3,651	3,784
Academic Competitiveness Grants [1]	(X)	(X)	(X)	759	(X)	(X)	(X)
SMART Grants [1]	(X)	(X)	(X)	3,095	(X)	(X)	(X)
TEACH Grants [2]	(X)	(X)	(X)	3,137	(NA)	2,873	2,861
Federal Supplemental Educational Opportunity Grant	705	772	764	620	(NA)	599	599
Federal Work-Study	1,088	1,318	1,478	1,668	(NA)	1,678	1,678
Federal Perkins Loan	1,496	1,790	2,190	1,860	(NA)	2,022	2,022
Federal Direct Student Loan (FDSL)	3,547	3,778	4,352	5,088	(NA)	(NA)	(NA)
Federal Family Education Loans (FFEL) [3]	3,653	3,864	4,193	3,758	(X)	(X)	(X)
COHORT DEFAULT RATE [4]							
Federal Perkins Loan	12.6	9.9	8.1	10.5	(NA)	(NA)	(NA)

X Not applicable. NA Not available. [1] National Science and Mathematics Access to Retain Talent (SMART). Funding for Academic Competitiveness Grants and SMART Grants was terminated in 2011. [2] Teacher Education Assistance for College and Higher Education (TEACH) Grant Program. [3] The FFEL Program was terminated effective 2011. [4] As of June 30. Represents the percent of borrowers entering repayment status in year shown who defaulted in the following year.

Source: U.S. Department of Education, Office of Postsecondary Education, unpublished data.

Table 304. Voluntary Financial Support of Higher Education: 1990 to 2014

[9,800 represents $9,800,000,000. For school years ending in years shown. Voluntary support, as defined in Gift Reporting Standards, excludes income from endowment and other invested funds as well as all support received from federal, state, and local governments and their agencies and contract research]

Item	Unit	1990	1995	2000	2005	2010	2012	2013	2014
Estimated support, total	Mil. dol.	**9,800**	**12,750**	**23,200**	**25,600**	**28,000**	**31,000**	**33,800**	**37,450**
Individuals	Mil. dol.	4,770	6,540	12,220	12,100	12,020	13,525	15,200	16,350
Alumni	Mil. dol.	2,540	3,600	6,800	7,100	7,100	7,700	9,000	9,850
Nonalumni individuals	Mil. dol.	2,230	2,940	5,420	5,000	4,920	5,825	6,200	6,500
Organizations total	Mil. dol.	**5,030**	**6,210**	**10,980**	**13,500**	**15,675**	**17,475**	**18,600**	**21,100**
Corporations	Mil. dol.	2,170	2,560	4,150	4,400	4,730	5,250	5,100	5,750
Foundations	Mil. dol.	1,920	2,460	5,080	7,000	8,400	9,150	10,000	11,200
Other organizations	Mil. dol.	940	1,190	1,750	2,100	2,545	3,075	3,500	4,150
Current operations	Mil. dol.	5,440	7,230	11,270	14,200	17,000	18,900	20,200	21,800
Capital purposes	Mil. dol.	4,360	5,520	11,930	11,400	11,000	12,100	13,600	15,650
Institutions reporting support	Number	**1,056**	**1,086**	**945**	**997**	**996**	**1,005**	**1,026**	**1,019**
Total support reported	Mil. dol.	8,214	10,992	19,419	20,953	23,487	25,596	28,667	31,658
Private 4-year institutions	Mil. dol.	5,072	6,500	11,047	11,011	12,189	13,461	13,278	16,927
Public 4-year institutions	Mil. dol.	3,056	4,382	8,254	9,780	11,114	11,933	15,173	14,514
2-year colleges	Mil. dol.	85	110	117	163	185	202	216	217

Source: Council for Aid to Education, New York, NY, *Voluntary Support of Education* ©, annual. See also <www.cae.org>.

Table 305. State and Local Financial Support for Higher Education by State: 2014

[11,137.5 represents 11,137,500. For fiscal year ending in 2014]

State	FTE enrollment [1] (1,000)	Educational appropriations per FTE enrollment [2] (dollars)	State	FTE enrollment [1] (1,000)	Educational appropriations per FTE enrollment [2] (dollars)
Total U.S.	11,137.5	6,552	Missouri	196.8	5,297
Alabama	195.7	5,673	Montana	39.5	4,939
Alaska	20.5	13,978	Nebraska	79.7	7,840
Arizona	269.9	5,171	Nevada	64.5	7,016
Arkansas	119.6	7,653	New Hampshire	37.0	2,360
California	1,511.3	7,509	New Jersey	274.3	5,520
Colorado	184.8	3,022	New Mexico	98.6	8,029
Connecticut	88.7	7,192	New York	565.8	8,454
Delaware	35.7	5,052	North Carolina	402.2	8,562
Florida	608.2	5,798	North Dakota	36.9	7,888
Georgia	347.7	7,297	Ohio	401.9	4,314
Hawaii	40.4	7,618	Oklahoma	145.4	7,080
Idaho	56.2	7,004	Oregon	165.5	4,214
Illinois	326.3	12,293	Pennsylvania	358.8	3,654
Indiana	249.0	5,005	Rhode Island	31.3	4,690
Iowa	127.4	5,335	South Carolina	172.0	4,894
Kansas	138.3	5,648	South Dakota	33.7	4,878
Kentucky	154.8	6,824	Tennessee	190.5	6,959
Louisiana	168.0	5,606	Texas	994.7	8,050
Maine	36.6	6,252	Utah	119.7	5,506
Maryland	232.7	7,512	Vermont	21.0	2,816
Massachusetts	172.6	6,073	Virginia	318.2	4,779
Michigan	400.0	4,765	Washington	245.0	5,700
Minnesota	204.0	5,327	West Virginia	76.2	5,530
Mississippi	131.1	6,514	Wisconsin	223.8	5,786
			Wyoming	25.0	15,561

[1] Full-time equivalent. Includes degree enrollment and enrollment in public postsecondary programs resulting in a certificate or other formal recognition. Includes summer sessions. Excludes medical enrollments. [2] State and local appropriations for general operating expenses of public postsecondary education. Includes state-funded financial aid to students attending in-state public institutions. Excludes appropriations for independent institutions, financial aid for students attending independent institutions, sums for research, and teaching hospitals and medical schools.

Source: State Higher Education Executive Officers, Boulder, CO, *State Higher Education Finance Report* ©, 2015. See also <http://www.sheeo.org/projects/shef-%E2%80%94-state-higher-education-finance>.

Table 306. Institutions of Higher Education—Average Charges: 1985 to 2014

[In current dollars. Estimated. For the entire academic year ending in year shown. Figures are average charges per full-time equivalent student. Room and board are based on full-time students]

Academic control and year	Tuition and required fees [1]			Board rates [2]			Dormitory room charges		
	All institutions	2-yr. colleges	4-yr. institutions	All institutions	2-yr. colleges	4-yr. institutions	All institutions	2-yr. colleges	4-yr. institutions
Public:									
1985	971	584	1,228	1,241	1,302	1,237	1,196	921	1,217
1990	1,356	756	1,780	1,635	1,581	1,638	1,513	962	1,557
1995	2,057	1,192	2,681	1,949	1,712	1,967	1,959	1,232	2,023
2000	2,504	1,348	3,349	2,364	1,834	2,406	2,440	1,549	2,519
2005	3,629	1,849	5,027	2,931	2,353	2,981	3,304	2,174	3,418
2006	3,874	1,935	5,351	3,035	2,306	3,093	3,545	2,251	3,664
2007	4,102	2,018	5,666	3,191	2,390	3,253	3,757	2,407	3,878
2008	4,291	2,061	5,943	3,331	2,409	3,404	3,952	2,506	4,082
2009	4,512	2,136	6,312	3,554	2,769	3,619	4,190	2,664	4,331
2010	4,763	2,283	6,717	3,655	2,571	3,755	4,401	2,854	4,564
2011	5,075	2,441	7,132	3,846	2,683	3,956	4,646	2,955	4,832
2012	5,563	2,651	7,713	3,946	2,866	4,042	4,849	3,100	5,031
2013	5,899	2,792	8,070	4,061	2,889	4,163	5,062	3,247	5,241
2014	6,122	2,882	8,312	4,214	2,953	4,319	5,304	3,447	5,479
Private:									
1985	5,315	3,485	5,556	1,462	1,294	1,469	1,426	1,424	1,426
1990	8,147	5,196	8,396	1,948	1,811	1,953	1,923	1,663	1,935
1995	11,111	6,914	11,481	2,509	2,023	2,520	2,587	2,233	2,601
2000	14,100	8,225	14,616	2,877	2,753	2,879	3,236	3,067	3,242
2005	18,154	12,122	18,604	3,485	3,700	3,483	4,178	4,475	4,173
2006	18,862	12,450	19,292	3,645	4,781	3,637	4,400	4,173	4,404
2007	20,048	12,708	20,517	3,785	3,429	3,788	4,606	4,147	4,613
2008	20,972	13,126	21,427	3,992	4,074	3,991	4,804	4,484	4,808
2009	21,570	13,562	22,036	4,209	4,627	4,206	5,025	4,537	5,032
2010	21,764	14,862	22,269	4,329	4,390	4,329	5,248	5,211	5,248
2011	22,042	13,687	22,677	4,431	4,475	4,431	5,403	4,939	5,410
2012	22,850	13,961	23,464	4,586	4,475	4,586	5,622	5,169	5,627
2013	23,943	14,129	24,525	4,709	3,977	4,712	5,831	5,222	5,837
2014	25,101	14,168	25,696	4,865	4,199	4,867	6,021	5,493	6,026

[1] For public institutions, data are for in-state students. [2] Beginning 1990, rates reflect 20 meals per week, rather than meals served 7 days a week.

Source: U.S. National Center for Education Statistics, *Digest of Education Statistics*, "Advance Release of Selected 2014 Digest Tables," <http://www.nces.ed.gov/programs/digest/>, accessed May 2015.

Table 307. Average Salaries for College Faculty Members: 2013 to 2015

[In thousands of dollars (80.6 represents $80,600). For academic year ending in year shown. Figures are for 9 months teaching for full-time faculty members in 2-year and 4-year institutions with ranks. Fringe benefits averaged in 2015, $25,928 in public institutions and $30,156 in private institutions]

Type of control and academic rank	2013	2014	2015	Type of control and academic rank	2013	2014	2015
Public: All ranks..............	**80.6**	**82.6**	**83.9**	**Private: [1] All ranks**.............	**99.8**	**103.2**	**105.2**
Professor........................	110.1	112.9	115.6	Professor........................	139.6	144.8	148.0
Associate professor...........	78.5	80.4	82.3	Associate professor...........	88.3	91.2	92.5
Assistant professor............	67.1	69.1	70.8	Assistant professor............	74.7	76.9	78.6
Instructor.......................	46.9	48.4	49.2	Instructor.......................	56.5	57.5	59.0

[1] Excludes church-related colleges and universities.

Source: American Association of University Professors, Washington, DC, *AAUP Annual Report on the Economic Status of the Profession* © 2015. See also: <http://www.aaup.org/>.

Table 308. Employees in Higher Education Institutions by Employment Status, Sex, and Occupation: 2013

[In thousands (3,896.1 represents 3,896,100). As of Fall. Based on Integrated Postsecondary Education Data System data]

Primary occupation	Full-time and part-time				Full-time		Part-time	
	Total	Male	Female		Male	Female	Male	Female
			Total	Percent				
All institutions..	**3,896.1**	**1,772.8**	**2,123.4**	**54.5**	**1,113.5**	**1,362.5**	**659.3**	**760.9**
Faculty..	1,544.1	791.3	752.8	48.8	436.5	354.9	354.9	397.8
Instruction..................................	1,436.5	730.4	706.0	49.2	386.5	319.4	343.9	386.7
Research....................................	81.7	48.4	33.3	40.7	41.1	26.9	7.3	6.4
Public service..............................	25.9	12.5	13.5	51.9	8.9	8.7	3.6	4.7
Graduate assistants............................	359.5	189.6	170.0	47.3	(X)	(X)	189.6	170.0
Librarians, curators, and archivists...................	44.7	13.0	31.6	70.8	11.3	26.3	1.7	5.3
Student and academic affairs, and other education services.......................	158.5	52.2	106.3	67.1	30.3	69.7	21.9	36.6
Management.....................................	252.6	113.8	138.7	54.9	110.8	134.0	3.0	4.8
Business and financial operations...................	193.0	52.0	141.0	73.1	48.1	130.4	3.9	10.6
Computer, engineering, and science................	231.8	140.2	91.6	39.5	130.4	79.8	9.8	11.8
Community, social service, legal, arts, design, entertainment, sports, and media..........	167.4	74.7	92.8	55.4	59.4	75.7	15.2	17.1
Healthcare practitioners and technicians.............	121.9	35.4	86.6	71.0	29.3	68.7	6.1	17.8
Service occupations..............................	241.1	140.7	100.5	41.7	118.4	82.0	22.3	18.5
Sales and related occupations......................	15.4	5.4	10.0	65.1	4.6	7.9	0.8	2.1
Office and administrative support....................	471.3	79.3	392.0	83.2	55.0	325.7	24.3	66.3
Natural resources, construction, and maintenance..	75.4	69.2	6.2	8.2	65.8	4.9	3.4	1.3
Production, transportation, and material moving....	19.5	16.1	3.4	17.4	13.6	2.6	2.5	0.8

X Not applicable.

Source: U.S. National Center for Education Statistics, *Digest of Education Statistics*, "Advance Release of Selected 2014 Digest Tables," <http://www.nces.ed.gov/programs/digest/>, accessed May 2015.

Table 309. Faculty in Institutions of Higher Education: 1980 to 2013

[In thousands (686 represents 686,000), except percent. As of Fall. Based on complete census taken every other year; see source]

Year	Total	Employment status		Control		Level		Percent		
		Full-time	Part-time	Public	Private	4-Year	2-Year or less	Part-time	Public	2-Year or less
1980 [1]...............	686	450	236	495	191	494	192	34	72	28
1985 [1]...............	715	459	256	503	212	504	211	36	70	30
1991 [2]...............	826	536	291	581	245	591	235	35	70	28
1995.................	932	551	381	657	275	647	285	41	70	31
2001 [3]...............	1,113	618	495	771	342	764	349	44	69	31
2003 [3]...............	1,174	630	544	792	382	814	359	46	67	31
2005 [3]...............	1,290	676	615	841	449	917	373	48	65	29
2007 [3,4].............	1,371	703	668	877	494	991	381	49	64	28
2009 [3,4].............	1,439	729	710	914	525	1,038	401	49	63	28
2011 [3,4].............	1,524	762	762	954	570	1,116	409	50	63	27
2013 [3,4].............	1,544	791	753	968	576	1,150	394	49	63	26

[1] Estimated on the basis of enrollment. [2] Data beginning 1991 not comparable to prior years. [3] Beginning in 2001, data reflect the new classification of institutions. See footnote 1, Table 290. [4] Beginning in 2007, data include institutions with fewer than 15 full-time employees; these institutions did not report staff data prior to 2007.

Source: U.S. National Center for Education Statistics, *Digest of Education Statistics*, "Advance Release of Selected 2014 Digest Tables," <http://www.nces.ed.gov/programs/digest/>, accessed May 2015.

Table 310. Starting Salaries for New College Graduates by Degree and Field of Study: 2010 to 2014

[In dollars. Data prior to 2012 are average beginning salaries based on offers made by business, industrial, government, nonprofit, and educational employers to graduating students. Beginning in 2014, data are for accepted salary offers only. Data from representative colleges throughout the United States]

Field of study	Bachelor's					Master's [1]				
	2010	2011	2012	2013	2014	2010	2011	2012	2013	2014
Accounting	48,378	49,407	50,400	53,800	49,420	[3] 49,254	46,741	63,800	62,800	(NA)
Business administration/ management [2]	43,991	46,372	52,500	56,300	46,830	[3] 49,875	76,786	64,100	70,000	(NA)
Marketing	41,670	42,923	53,400	52,200	43,123	[3] 40,933	[3] 53,000	(NA)	(NA)	(NA)
Engineering:										
Civil	51,321	52,058	57,500	58,500	54,656	[3] 57,225	[3] 57,812	(NA)	(NA)	(NA)
Chemical	64,889	66,058	66,200	67,500	68,061	[3] 90,333	[3] 72,000	(NA)	(NA)	(NA)
Computer	60,396	62,849	71,800	70,900	68,053	[3] 69,389	[3] 76,822	(NA)	(NA)	(NA)
Electrical	59,512	60,411	60,500	63,000	68,778	[3] 67,844	73,857	73,000	67,100	(NA)
Mechanical	58,110	60,142	61,300	64,500	63,555	67,234	68,065	75,700	68,100	(NA)
Nuclear [4]	[3] 57,417	61,678	(NA)	(NA)	60,164	[3] 69,467	[3] 66,456	(NA)	(NA)	(NA)
Petroleum	77,278	82,740	(NA)	97,000	86,255	[3] 96,000	(NA)	(NA)	(NA)	(NA)
Engineering technology	52,756	55,715	(NA)	61,500	57,090	(NA)	(NA)	(NA)	(NA)	(NA)
Chemistry	39,404	41,001	44,500	45,300	57,900	[3] 58,000	[3] 29,000	(NA)	(NA)	(NA)
Mathematics	48,499	54,333	49,500	50,200	53,604	[3] 53,200	[3] 46,666	48,500	52,800	(NA)
Physics	[3] 52,487	[3] 53,338	33,600	40,700	55,710	[3] 65,500	[3] 45,000	(NA)	(NA)	(NA)
Humanities	[3] 34,982	37,225	37,300	34,700	41,605	[3] 49,250	[3] 43,587	(NA)	(NA)	(NA)
Social sciences [5]	36,433	36,526	38,100	37,800	41,917	[3] 46,030	[3] 49,143	50,000	48,400	(NA)
Computer science	60,473	66,084	62,200	64,700	66,801	[3] 69,753	72,703	80,400	73,500	(NA)

NA Not available. [1] Candidates with 1 year or less of full-time nonmilitary employment. [2] For master's degree, offers are after nontechnical undergraduate degree. [3] Fewer than 50 offers reported. [4] Includes engineering physics. [5] Excludes economics.

Source: National Association of Colleges and Employers, Bethlehem, PA ©. Reprinted with permission from Fall 2010, 2011, 2012, 2013, and 2014 Salary Survey. All rights reserved. See also <http://www.naceweb.org>.

Table 311. Degrees Earned by Level and Sex: 1960 to 2013

[In thousands (477 represents 477,000), except percent. Based on survey; see Appendix III]

Year ending	All degrees		Associate's		Bachelor's		Master's		Doctoral [1]	
	Total	Percent Male	Male	Female	Male	Female	Male	Female	Male	Female
1960	477	65.8	(NA)	(NA)	[2] 254	[2] 138	51	24	9	1
1970	1,271	59.2	117	89	451	341	131	83	54	6
1975	1,666	56.0	191	169	505	418	166	131	71	14
1980	1,732	51.1	184	217	474	456	157	148	70	26
1985	1,828	49.3	203	252	483	497	149	144	66	35
1986	1,830	49.0	196	250	486	502	149	146	65	35
1987	1,823	48.4	191	245	481	510	147	149	63	36
1988	1,835	48.0	190	245	477	518	150	156	63	36
1989	1,873	47.3	186	250	483	535	154	163	63	38
1990	1,940	46.6	191	264	492	560	158	172	64	40
1991	2,025	45.8	199	283	504	590	161	182	64	41
1992	2,108	45.6	207	297	521	616	166	192	67	43
1993	2,167	45.5	212	303	533	632	173	202	67	45
1994	2,206	45.1	215	315	532	637	181	212	67	46
1995	2,218	44.9	218	321	526	634	183	221	67	47
1996	2,248	44.2	220	336	522	642	183	229	67	48
1997	2,288	43.6	224	347	521	652	185	240	68	50
1998	2,298	43.2	218	341	520	664	189	247	67	52
1999	2,330	42.7	221	344	520	682	190	256	65	51
2000	2,385	42.6	225	340	530	708	196	267	65	54
2001	2,416	42.4	232	347	532	712	198	276	64	55
2002	2,494	42.2	238	357	550	742	203	285	63	57
2003	2,623	42.1	253	381	573	776	215	304	63	59
2004	2,755	41.8	260	405	595	804	233	331	64	62
2005	2,850	41.6	268	429	613	826	237	343	67	67
2006	2,936	41.3	270	443	631	855	242	358	69	69
2007	3,007	41.2	275	453	650	875	242	368	71	73
2008	3,093	41.2	283	468	668	895	250	380	73	76
2009	3,205	41.3	298	489	685	916	264	399	76	79
2010	3,351	41.2	323	526	707	943	275	418	77	82
2011	3,554	41.3	361	582	734	982	292	439	80	84
2012	3,740	41.3	393	628	766	1,026	302	453	83	88
2013	3,774	41.4	389	618	787	1,053	302	450	85	90

NA Not available. [1] Includes Ph.D., Ed.D, and comparable degrees at the doctoral level. Includes most degrees formerly classified as first-professional, such as M.D., D.D.S., and law degrees. [2] Includes some degrees classified as master's or doctor's degrees in later years.

Source: U.S. National Center for Education Statistics, *Digest of Education Statistics*, "Advance Release of Selected 2014 Digest Tables," <http://www.nces.ed.gov/programs/digest/>, accessed January 2015.

Table 312. Degrees Earned by Level and Race/Ethnicity: 1990 to 2013

[For school year ending in year shown. Based on Integrated Postsecondary Education Data System surveys; see Appendix III]

Level of degree and race/ethnicity	Total					Percent distribution		
	1990	2000 [1]	2010	2012	2013	2000 [1]	2010	2013
Associate's degrees, total............	455,102	564,933	848,856	1,021,718	1,006,961	100.0	100.0	100.0
White, non-Hispanic..................	376,816	408,772	552,376	635,755	616,990	72.4	65.1	61.3
Black, non-Hispanic..................	34,326	60,221	113,867	142,512	135,777	10.7	13.4	13.5
Hispanic............................	21,504	51,573	112,403	151,807	157,966	9.1	13.2	15.7
Asian or Pacific Islander...........	13,066	27,782	44,026	48,861	49,456	4.9	5.2	4.9
American Indian/Alaska Native......	3,430	6,497	10,101	10,738	10,540	1.2	1.2	1.0
Two or more races..................	(NA)	(NA)	(NA)	14,858	19,402	(NA)	(NA)	1.9
Nonresident alien..................	5,960	10,088	16,083	17,187	16,830	1.8	1.9	1.7
Bachelor's degrees, total.............	1,051,344	1,237,875	1,649,919	1,792,163	1,840,164	100.0	100.0	100.0
White, non-Hispanic..................	887,151	929,106	1,167,322	1,212,417	1,221,576	75.1	70.8	66.4
Black, non-Hispanic..................	61,046	108,013	164,789	185,916	191,180	8.7	10.0	10.4
Hispanic............................	32,829	75,059	140,426	169,736	186,650	6.1	8.5	10.1
Asian or Pacific Islander...........	39,230	77,912	117,391	126,177	130,144	6.3	7.1	7.1
American Indian/Alaska Native......	4,390	8,719	12,405	11,498	11,445	0.7	0.8	0.6
Two or more races..................	(NA)	(NA)	(NA)	27,234	34,338	(NA)	(NA)	1.9
Nonresident alien..................	26,698	39,066	47,586	59,185	64,831	3.2	2.9	3.5
Master's degrees, total [3]	(NA)	463,185	693,313	755,967	751,751	100.0	100.0	100.0
White, non-Hispanic..................	(NA)	324,990	445,158	470,822	455,892	70.2	64.2	60.6
Black, non-Hispanic..................	(NA)	36,606	76,472	86,007	87,988	7.9	11.0	11.7
Hispanic............................	(NA)	19,379	43,603	50,994	52,990	4.2	6.3	7.0
Asian or Pacific Islander...........	(NA)	23,523	42,520	45,379	44,912	5.1	6.1	6.0
American Indian/Alaska Native......	(NA)	2,263	3,965	3,681	3,697	0.5	0.6	0.5
Two or more races..................	(NA)	(NA)	(NA)	9,823	11,839	(NA)	(NA)	1.6
Nonresident alien..................	(NA)	56,424	81,595	89,261	94,433	12.2	11.8	12.6
Doctoral degrees, total [2,3]............	(NA)	118,736	158,590	170,217	175,038	100.0	100.0	100.0
White, non-Hispanic..................	(NA)	82,984	104,419	109,365	110,775	69.9	65.8	63.3
Black, non-Hispanic..................	(NA)	7,078	10,413	11,794	12,084	6.0	6.6	6.9
Hispanic............................	(NA)	5,042	8,085	9,223	10,107	4.2	5.1	5.8
Asian or Pacific Islander...........	(NA)	10,682	16,560	17,896	18,408	9.0	10.4	10.5
American Indian/Alaska Native......	(NA)	708	952	915	900	0.6	0.6	0.5
Two or more races..................	(NA)	(NA)	(NA)	1,571	2,438	(NA)	(NA)	1.4
Nonresident alien..................	(NA)	12,242	18,161	19,453	20,326	10.3	11.5	11.6
First-professional degrees, total.....	70,988	80,057	94,103	98,699	100,356	100.0	100.0	100.0
White, non-Hispanic..................	60,487	59,637	66,172	68,121	68,144	74.5	70.3	67.9
Black, non-Hispanic..................	3,409	5,555	6,850	7,103	7,202	6.9	7.3	7.2
Hispanic............................	2,425	3,865	5,430	6,010	6,595	4.8	5.8	6.6
Asian or Pacific Islander...........	3,362	8,584	12,691	13,449	13,714	10.7	13.5	13.7
American Indian/Alaska Native......	257	564	665	591	538	0.7	0.7	0.5
Two or more races..................	(NA)	(NA)	(NA)	1,038	1,723	(NA)	(NA)	1.7
Nonresident alien..................	1,048	1,852	2,295	2,387	2,440	2.3	2.4	2.4

NA Not available. [1] Beginning 2000, data reflect the new classification of institutions. See footnote 1, Table 290. [2] Includes Ph.D., Ed.D., and comparable degrees at the doctoral level, as well as M.D., D.D.S., and law degrees that were formerly classified as first-professional degrees. [3] Data prior to 2009 have been revised. Revisions for 1990 not available.

Source: U.S. National Center for Education Statistics, *Digest of Education Statistics*, "Advance Release of Selected 2014 Digest Tables," <http://www.nces.ed.gov/programs/digest/>, accessed September 2015.

Table 313. Bachelor's Degrees Earned by Field: 1980 to 2013

[For school year ending in year shown. The new Classification of Instructional Programs was introduced in 2009-2010. Data for previous years has been reclassified where necessary to conform to the new classifications. Based on data from the Integrated Postsecondary Education Data System (IPEDS)]

Field of study	1980	1990	2000	2010	2012	2013
Total [1]..	929,417	1,051,344	1,237,875	1,649,919	1,792,163	1,840,164
Agriculture and natural resources...................	22,802	12,900	24,238	26,343	30,972	33,593
Architecture and related services...................	9,132	9,364	8,462	10,051	9,727	9,757
Area, ethnic, cultural, and gender studies..........	2,840	4,447	6,212	8,620	9,228	8,851
Biological and biomedical sciences.................	46,190	37,204	63,005	86,391	95,850	100,319
Business..	186,264	248,568	256,070	358,119	367,235	360,823
Communication, journalism, and related programs [2]....	28,616	51,572	57,058	86,062	88,754	89,806
Computer and information sciences.................	11,154	27,347	37,788	39,593	47,406	50,962
Education...	118,038	105,112	108,034	101,287	105,656	104,647
Engineering and engineering technologies...........	69,387	82,480	73,419	88,735	98,654	102,984
English language and literature/letters..............	32,187	46,803	50,106	53,229	53,765	52,424
Family and consumer sciences/human sciences......	18,411	13,514	16,321	21,832	23,441	23,934
Foreign languages, literatures, and linguistics......	12,480	13,133	15,886	21,507	21,756	21,673
Health professions and related clinical sciences.....	63,848	58,983	80,863	129,623	163,675	181,144
Homeland security, law enforcement, and firefighting....	15,015	15,354	24,877	43,613	54,091	60,269
Legal professions and studies......................	683	1,632	1,969	3,886	4,595	4,425
Liberal arts and sciences, general studies, and humanities...........	23,196	27,985	36,104	46,963	46,961	46,761
Mathematics and statistics.........................	11,378	14,276	11,418	16,029	18,841	20,453
Multi/interdisciplinary studies......................	11,457	16,557	28,561	37,717	45,717	47,654
Parks, recreation, leisure, and fitness studies.......	5,753	4,582	17,571	33,332	38,998	42,714
Philosophy and religious studies...................	7,069	7,034	8,535	12,503	12,645	12,793
Physical sciences and science technologies.........	23,407	16,056	18,331	23,381	26,664	28,050
Psychology...	42,093	53,952	74,194	97,215	109,099	114,450
Public administration and social services...........	16,644	13,908	20,185	25,421	29,695	31,950
Social sciences and history........................	103,662	118,083	127,101	172,782	178,534	177,778
Theology and religious vocations...................	6,170	5,185	6,789	8,719	9,304	9,385
Transportation and materials moving................	213	2,387	3,395	4,998	4,876	4,526
Visual and performing arts.........................	40,892	39,934	58,791	91,798	95,806	97,796

[1] Includes other fields of study, not shown separately. [2] Includes technologies.

Source: U.S. National Center for Education Statistics, *Digest of Education Statistics*, "Advance Release of Selected 2014 Digest Tables," <http://www.nces.ed.gov/programs/digest/>, accessed February 2015.

Table 314. Associate's Degrees and Certificates Below the Associate's Degree Level by Field: 2013

[For school year ending in 2013. The new Classification of Instructional Programs was introduced in 2013. Covers certificates below the associate's degree level based on postsecondary curriculums of less than 4 years in degree- and nondegree-granting institutions. Based on Integrated Postsecondary Education Data System (IPEDS) survey; see Appendix III]

Field of study	Less than 1-year awards		1- to less than 4-year awards		Associate's degree	
	Total	Female	Total	Female	Total	Female
Total [1]	**452,202**	**256,195**	**513,882**	**334,543**	**1,006,961**	**618,115**
Agriculture and natural resources, total	3,587	1,138	2,470	864	6,827	2,522
Architecture and related services	209	98	135	40	468	163
Area, ethnic, cultural, and gender studies	448	331	101	69	271	170
Biological and biomedical sciences	729	555	124	79	4,185	2,848
Business, management, marketing, and support services	47,248	32,086	24,621	17,909	114,740	73,235
Communications and communications technologies	3,912	1,671	4,825	1,372	9,325	3,870
Computer and information sciences and support services	17,981	5,580	10,495	2,464	38,931	8,293
Construction trades	10,984	537	13,308	555	5,038	236
Education	4,925	4,255	3,288	2,967	18,719	16,516
Engineering technologies and engineering-related fields	17,045	2,450	12,920	1,194	37,501	4,670
English language and literature/letters	2,317	1,516	361	235	2,085	1,410
Family and consumer sciences	14,497	13,078	3,377	3,072	8,994	8,618
Foreign languages, literatures, and linguistics	920	728	631	542	2,130	1,695
Health professions and related programs	171,122	137,975	209,347	179,456	214,004	180,367
Homeland security, law enforcement, and firefighting	26,438	6,618	6,374	2,023	48,425	21,987
Legal professions and studies	1,976	1,627	3,341	2,766	11,826	10,130
Liberal arts and sciences, general studies, and humanities	3,355	2,141	30,821	18,613	344,091	211,516
Library science	212	185	71	66	181	152
Mathematics and statistics	62	10	10	4	1,802	559
Mechanics and repair technologies/technicians	31,741	1,949	52,407	2,026	20,444	1,052
Military technologies and applied sciences	21	5	4	–	1,002	229
Multi/interdisciplinary studies	1,622	819	1,125	586	27,404	16,542
Parks, recreation, leisure, and fitness studies	2,135	1,214	723	327	3,453	1,297
Personal and culinary services	38,160	31,933	105,286	89,064	19,226	11,174
Philosophy and religion	73	35	20	9	326	114
Physical sciences and science technologies	855	247	666	171	6,376	2,586
Precision production trades	17,721	926	13,748	711	3,344	234
Psychology	36	26	70	54	6,119	4,623
Public administration and social service professions	1,139	913	903	747	8,781	7,544
Social sciences and history	874	382	334	153	15,669	9,899
Theology and religious vocations	188	111	1,059	577	881	456
Transportation and material moving	24,529	2,219	987	62	2,087	373
Visual and performing arts	5,141	2,837	9,930	5,766	22,306	13,035

– Represents zero. [1] Includes other fields of study, not shown separately.

Source: U.S. National Center for Education Statistics, *Digest of Education Statistics*, "Advance Release of Selected 2014 Digest Tables," <http://www.nces.ed.gov/programs/digest/>, accessed February 2015.

Table 315. Master's and Doctoral Degrees Earned by Field: 1971 to 2013

[For school years ending in years shown. The new Classification of Instructional Programs was introduced in 2009-2010. Data for previous years has been reclassified where necessary to conform to the new classifications. Based on data from the Integrated Postsecondary Education Data System (IPEDS)]

Field of study	1971	1981	1991	2001	2011	2013
MASTER'S DEGREES						
Total [1]	**235,564**	**302,637**	**342,863**	**473,502**	**730,922**	**751,751**
Agriculture and natural resources	2,457	4,003	3,295	4,272	5,766	6,339
Architecture and related services	1,705	3,153	3,490	4,302	7,788	8,095
Area, ethnic, cultural, gender, and group studies	1,032	802	1,233	1,555	1,913	1,897
Biological and biomedical sciences	5,625	5,766	4,834	7,017	11,324	13,335
Business	26,490	57,888	78,255	115,602	187,178	188,625
Communication, journalism, and related programs	1,770	2,896	4,123	5,218	8,302	8,757
Communications technologies	86	209	204	427	502	577
Computer and information sciences	1,588	4,218	9,324	16,911	19,516	22,777
Education	87,666	96,713	87,352	127,829	185,127	164,624
Engineering	16,813	16,893	24,454	25,174	38,664	40,417
Engineering technologies	134	323	996	2,013	4,515	4,908
English language and literature/letters	10,441	5,742	6,784	6,763	9,475	9,755
Family and consumer sciences/human sciences	1,452	2,570	1,541	1,838	2,918	3,253
Foreign languages, literatures, and linguistics	5,480	2,934	3,049	3,035	3,727	3,708
Health professions and related programs	5,330	16,176	21,354	43,623	75,571	90,931
Homeland security, law enforcement, and firefighting	194	1,538	1,108	2,514	7,433	8,868
Legal professions and studies	955	1,832	2,057	3,829	6,475	7,013
Liberal arts and sciences, general studies, and humanities	885	2,375	2,213	3,193	3,997	3,268
Library science	7,001	4,859	4,763	4,727	7,729	6,983
Mathematics and statistics	5,191	2,567	3,549	3,209	5,866	6,957
Military technologies and applied sciences	2	43	–	–	–	32
Multi/interdisciplinary studies	924	2,356	2,079	3,413	6,762	7,956
Parks, recreation, leisure, and fitness studies	218	643	483	2,354	6,546	7,139
Philosophy and religious studies	1,326	1,231	1,471	1,386	1,839	1,931
Physical sciences and science technologies	6,336	5,246	5,281	5,134	6,386	7,011
Precision production	–	–	–	2	5	9
Psychology	5,717	10,223	11,349	16,539	25,062	27,846
Public administration and social services	7,785	17,803	17,905	25,268	38,614	43,590
Social sciences and history	16,539	11,945	12,233	13,791	21,085	21,585
Theology and religious vocations	7,747	11,061	10,498	9,876	13,170	14,276
Transportation and materials moving	–	–	406	756	1,390	1,420
Visual and performing arts	6,675	8,629	8,657	11,404	16,277	17,869
DOCTORAL DEGREES						
Total [1]	**64,998**	**98,016**	**105,547**	**119,585**	**163,827**	**175,038**
Agriculture and natural resources	1,086	1,067	1,185	1,127	1,246	1,411
Architecture and related services	36	93	135	153	205	247
Area, ethnic, cultural, gender, and group studies	143	161	159	216	278	291
Biological and biomedical sciences	3,603	3,640	4,152	5,225	7,693	7,943
Business	774	808	1,185	1,180	2,286	2,836
Communication, journalism, and related programs	145	171	259	368	577	612
Communications technologies	–	11	13	2	1	–
Computer and information sciences	128	252	676	768	1,588	1,826
Education	6,041	7,279	6,189	6,284	9,642	10,572
Engineering	3,687	2,598	5,316	5,485	8,369	9,356
Engineering technologies	1	10	14	62	56	111
English language and literature/letters	1,554	1,040	1,056	1,330	1,344	1,373
Family and consumer sciences/human sciences	123	247	229	354	320	351
Foreign languages, literatures, and linguistics	1,084	931	889	1,078	1,158	1,304
Health professions and related programs	15,988	29,595	29,842	39,019	60,221	64,195
Homeland security, law enforcement, and firefighting	1	21	28	44	131	147
Legal professions and studies	17,441	36,391	38,035	38,190	44,853	47,246
Liberal arts and sciences, general studies, and humanities	32	121	70	102	95	98
Library science	39	71	56	58	50	50
Mathematics and statistics	1,199	728	978	997	1,586	1,823
Multi/interdisciplinary studies	101	236	306	512	660	730
Parks, recreation, leisure, and fitness studies	2	42	28	177	257	295
Philosophy and religious studies	555	411	464	600	804	796
Physical sciences and science technologies	4,324	3,105	4,248	3,968	5,295	5,514
Psychology	2,144	3,576	3,932	5,091	5,851	6,323
Public administration and social services	174	362	430	574	851	979
Social sciences and history	3,660	3,122	3,012	3,930	4,390	4,619
Theology and religious vocations	312	1,273	1,076	1,461	2,374	2,175
Visual and performing arts	621	654	838	1,167	1,646	1,814

– Represents zero. [1] Includes other fields of study, not shown separately.

Source: U.S. National Center for Education Statistics, *Digest of Education Statistics*, "Advance Release of Selected 2014 Digest Tables," <http://www.nces.ed.gov/programs/digest/>, accessed February 2015.

Table 316. First Professional Degrees Earned in Selected Professions: 1970 to 2013

[First professional degrees include degrees which require at least 6 years of college work for completion (including at least 2 years of preprofessional training). Based on Integrated Postsecondary Education Data System surveys; see Appendix III]

Type of degree and sex of recipient	1970	1980	1985	1990	1995	2000	2005	2010	2012	2013
Medicine (M.D.):										
Institutions conferring degrees..............	86	112	120	124	119	118	120	120	120	122
Degrees conferred, total......................	8,314	14,902	16,041	15,075	15,537	15,286	15,461	16,356	16,927	17,264
Percent to women..........................	8.4	23.4	30.4	34.2	38.8	42.7	47.3	48.2	48.0	48.0
Dentistry (D.D.S. or D.M.D.):										
Institutions conferring degrees..............	48	58	59	57	53	54	53	55	55	55
Degrees conferred, total......................	3,718	5,258	5,339	4,100	3,897	4,250	4,454	5,062	5,109	5,111
Percent to women..........................	0.9	13.3	20.7	30.9	36.4	40.1	43.8	45.8	46.2	48.1
Law (LL.B. or J.D.):										
Institutions conferring degrees..............	145	179	181	182	183	190	198	205	207	209
Degrees conferred, total......................	14,916	35,647	37,491	36,485	39,349	38,152	43,423	44,346	46,445	46,811
Percent to women..........................	5.4	30.2	38.5	42.2	42.6	45.9	48.7	47.3	47.1	46.4
Theological (B.D., M.Div., M.H.L.):										
Institutions conferring degrees..............	(NA)	(NA)	(NA)	(NA)	192	198	(NA)	(NA)	(NA)	(NA)
Degrees conferred, total......................	5,298	7,115	7,221	5,851	5,978	6,129	5,533	5,672	5,931	6,276
Percent to women..........................	2.3	13.8	18.5	24.8	25.7	29.2	35.6	33.8	32.6	31.1

NA Not available.

Source: U.S. National Center for Education Statistics, *Digest of Education Statistics*, "Advance Release of Selected 2014 Digest Tables," <http://www.nces.ed.gov/programs/digest/>, accessed September 2015.

Table 317. Graduate and Undergraduate Students Taking Online Classes and Degree Programs by Selected Characteristics: 2012

[23,055 represents 23,055,000. For school year ending in 2012]

Student characteristics	Undergraduate students					Graduate students				
	Number of students		Percent of students taking—			Number of students		Percent of students taking—		
	Total enroll-ment	Students taking any online classes	Any online classes	Exclus-ively online classes	Entire degree program is online [1]	Total enroll-ment	Students taking any online classes	Any online classes	Exclus-ively online classes	Entire degree program is online [1]
Total......................	**23,055**	**7,368**	**32.0**	**8.4**	**6.5**	**3,682**	**1,326**	**36.0**	**20.1**	**18.2**
Sex:										
Male..........................	9,921	2,831	28.5	6.5	4.9	1,463	461	31.5	17.8	15.9
Female......................	13,135	4,537	34.5	9.8	7.7	2,219	865	39.0	21.7	19.8
Race/ethnicity:										
White......................	13,345	4,472	33.5	9.0	6.8	2,341	864	36.9	20.2	18.2
Black.......................	3,709	1,214	32.7	10.7	9.1	434	212	48.8	33.0	31.4
Hispanic...................	3,696	1,032	27.9	5.5	4.3	321	111	34.6	19.3	17.9
Asian......................	1,292	336	26.0	4.2	2.9	474	92	19.4	7.5	6.0
Pacific Islander.............	119	35	29.9	[2] 3.5	[2] 3.1	20	9	44.2	[2] 20.3	(S)
American Indian or Alaska Native..............	209	68	32.6	9.1	7.0	16	(S)	55.1	[2] 42.5	[2] 43.4
Two or more races..........	686	210	30.6	8.3	5.5	75	30	40.4	20.9	18.4
Age:										
15 to 23 years old..........	12,956	3,429	26.5	4.5	3.2	419	82	19.5	4.5	4.3
24 to 29 years old..........	4,253	1,551	36.5	10.4	8.0	1,483	456	30.8	15.8	14.4
30 years old and over......	5,846	2,388	40.9	15.6	13.0	1,781	788	44.3	27.4	24.9
Attendance status:										
Exclusively full-time........	11,632	3,346	28.8	7.6	6.5	1,713	543	31.7	18.4	17.4
Exclusively part-time.......	7,308	2,583	35.3	10.7	7.4	1,396	572	41.0	22.7	19.5
Mixed full-time and part-time..................	4,116	1,440	35.0	6.4	5.0	573	212	36.9	19.1	17.9
Field of study:										
Business/management....	3,487	1,371	39.3	13.1	11.4	615	246	40.0	26.8	25.1
Education...................	1,175	397	33.8	8.4	6.4	775	379	48.9	26.1	23.7
Engineering.................	1,087	252	23.2	3.8	2.3	(NA)	(NA)	(NA)	(NA)	(NA)
Health......................	4,271	1,420	33.3	8.5	6.7	679	248	36.5	18.9	16.5
Humanities..................	3,817	1,175	30.8	5.8	4.1	290	81	28.1	14.1	12.1
Law........................	(NA)	(NA)	(NA)	(NA)	(NA)	146	15	10.3	2.9	2.5
Social/behavioral sciences..................	1,568	499	31.8	8.9	7.0	223	82	36.6	22.6	21.7
Vocational/technical........	718	160	22.3	4.1	2.8	(NA)	(NA)	(NA)	(NA)	(NA)

S Data do not meet publication standards. NA Not available. [1] Excludes students not in a degree or certificate program. [2] Interpret data with caution. The coefficient of variation (CV) for this estimate is between 30 and 50 percent.

Source: U.S. National Center for Education Statistics, *Digest of Education Statistics*, "Advance Release of Selected 2014 Digest Tables," <http://www.nces.ed.gov/programs/digest/>, accessed June 2015.

Table 318. Mean Student Loan Debt of Households: 1989 to 2010

[In 2011 dollars, unless otherwise noted. Includes education loans that are currently in deferment and loans in scheduled repayment period. Pew Research Center tabulations of Survey of Consumer Finances data. See source for details]

Household Characteristic	1989	1992	1995	1998	2001	2004	2007	2010
All households............................	**9,634**	**11,086**	**11,714**	**17,942**	**17,562**	**20,022**	**23,349**	**26,682**
Age of household head:								
Younger than 35............................	10,304	10,449	11,841	20,682	15,478	19,586	25,795	26,842
35-44..	8,632	12,743	10,056	13,455	26,239	22,651	20,477	27,634
45-54..	11,010	7,659	14,907	17,269	12,717	19,042	22,440	25,152
55-64..	5,488	16,826	11,746	21,203	19,258	17,321	19,778	29,853
65 and older..................................	9,419	10,854	4,794	5,771	2,579	25,145	21,443	17,578
Highest education of household head:								
Less than HS diploma........................	5,156	4,083	5,739	8,104	5,573	9,257	10,260	9,477
HS graduate..................................	6,344	6,280	6,349	7,687	10,745	14,792	13,573	13,227
Some college.................................	8,140	6,716	12,475	16,109	10,756	13,837	14,839	20,509
College graduate.............................	12,373	15,254	14,359	22,310	24,561	25,405	31,470	36,809
Household annual income:								
Lowest fifth...................................	9,126	6,887	9,552	13,444	11,388	18,312	19,018	20,640
Second fifth..................................	5,955	10,328	9,976	16,880	15,861	21,426	17,400	18,659
Middle fifth...................................	12,843	15,474	14,092	19,890	16,610	18,146	20,887	29,953
Fourth fifth...................................	11,083	8,639	9,764	18,157	16,136	19,041	26,283	24,076
80%–89.9%..................................	6,367	10,516	15,804	15,155	19,822	19,678	25,921	31,989
Richest 10%..................................	11,014	17,025	14,756	27,990	33,215	28,855	36,033	44,810
Household wealth:								
Lowest fourth.................................	11,623	13,773	14,842	23,703	18,405	21,352	23,121	35,096
Second fourth................................	6,071	7,598	8,399	11,813	11,923	15,430	20,548	18,071
Third fourth..................................	7,777	8,587	8,319	15,603	14,849	22,800	23,150	21,108
75%–89.9%..................................	15,155	7,797	15,227	9,353	24,981	24,330	27,312	21,564
Wealthiest 10%...............................	6,223	17,883	11,519	19,256	72,373	12,930	37,616	26,145
Percent of student loan debt to household income...................	**1.2**	**1.9**	**2.1**	**2.8**	**2.3**	**3.2**	**3.9**	**6.3**

Source: Pew Research Center, Social and Demographic Trends, *A Record One-in-Five Households Now Owe Student Loan Debt*, September 2012, <http://pewresearch.org/>.

Table 319. Bachelor's Degree Recipients with Loans and Amount Borrowed in Constant (2009) Dollars by Selected Characteristics: 1994 to 2009

[Data shown for first-time Bachelor's degree recipients. Based on Baccalaureate and Beyond Longitudinal Studies]

Characteristic	Percent with loans			Average Cumulative Amount Borrowed for Undergraduate Education (2009 Dollars)		
	1994	2001	2009	1994	2001	2009
Total loans.............................	**49.3**	**63.5**	**65.6**	**14,700**	**21,800**	**24,700**
Sex:						
Male..	50.1	62.5	62.9	15,000	21,300	23,900
Female..	49.4	64.3	67.6	14,400	22,100	25,200
Race/ethnicity: [1]						
White...	47.8	62.2	64.6	14,900	21,700	24,500
Black..	65.5	79.8	80.3	13,800	25,200	28,700
Hispanic......................................	60.5	66.7	67.0	11,400	19,900	22,800
Asian..	43.1	55.5	53.4	16,800	19,100	21,000
Other..	63.4	62.8	68.8	14,900	21,500	25,600
Age at receipt of bachelor's degree:						
18-23..	43.9	60.0	61.0	15,200	20,800	23,700
24-29..	62.9	71.3	76.8	13,800	23,100	24,900
30 and older..................................	55.9	65.7	72.5	13,800	23,000	28,300
Time to complete bachelor's degree:						
48 months or less............................	41.4	59.2	59.5	16,000	21,000	24,100
49-60 months................................	49.5	63.0	64.9	14,900	21,100	23,800
61-72 months................................	51.6	68.5	73.4	14,100	21,500	22,900
73-120 months..............................	63.4	69.3	76.8	13,600	24,500	26,200
Over 120 months............................	56.1	67.0	72.4	13,300	22,100	27,600
Institution type:						
2-Year or less:						
Public 2-year.................................	53.1	67.8	67.5	13,300	21,500	24,500
Other 2-year or less.........................	56.8	64.6	85.0	13,600	24,500	31,600
4-Year:						
Public...	45.7	59.5	62.1	12,900	20,100	21,900
Private nonprofit.............................	53.4	69.0	69.4	18,200	24,100	27,900
For-profit.....................................	63.4	77.3	87.7	(X)	27,400	36,000

X Not applicable. [1] Black includes African American; Hispanic includes Latino; Asian includes Pacific Islander and Native Hawaiian; other includes American Indian, Alaska Native, and graduates having origins in two or more races or a race not listed. Race categories exclude persons of Hispanic ethnicity unless specified. In 1994, graduates of two or more races were asked to choose one category, in subsequent studies graduates could identify as multiracial.

Source: National Center for Education Statistics, *Trends in Debt for Bachelor's Degree Recipients a Year After Graduation: 1994, 2001, and 2009*, December 2012. See also <http://nces.ed.gov/>.

Table 320. Private for Profit Colleges—Summary: 2000 to 2012

[In units as indicated. For school year ending in year shown]

Item	Unit	2000	2005	2008	2009	2010	2011	2012
Private for Profit Colleges, total.............	**Number**	**2,223**	**2,415**	**2,664**	**2,750**	**2,877**	**3,144**	**3,311**
2 YEAR COLLEGES								
Number of colleges.................................	Number	1,267	1,300	1,354	1,365	1,404	1,517	1,595
Total enrolled..	Number	127,818	215,459	196,702	223,278	263,349	271,515	257,434
Average tuition..	Dollars	6,150	9,064	11,401	12,171	12,964	13,632	14,126
Students receiving loans.........................	Percent	43.0	48.3	36.8	43.6	43.2	56.2	55.5
Average loan..	Dollars	2,540	2,805	3,272	3,514	3,424	3,346	3,364
Students receiving Pell Grants...................	Percent	67.1	67.1	59.4	60.5	64.7	67.0	65.4
Average Pell Grant..................................	Dollars	1,717	2,229	2,486	2,822	3,579	3,721	3,385
2-4 YEAR COLLEGES								
Number of colleges.................................	Number	796	773	847	887	951	1,015	1,045
Total enrolled..	Number	200,453	278,920	282,493	321,248	421,911	474,993	432,743
Average tuition..	Dollars	8,043	11,279	12,301	13,053	14,290	13,679	14,044
Students receiving loans.........................	Percent	48.2	52.6	32.2	38.6	39.6	62.7	60.5
Average loan..	Dollars	2,888	3,178	3,550	3,753	3,701	3,613	3,616
Students receiving Pell Grants...................	Percent	63.6	66.6	60.0	60.7	66.3	69.3	66.8
Average Pell Grant..................................	Dollars	1,741	2,327	2,627	2,959	3,876	4,089	3,530
4 YEAR COLLEGES								
Number of colleges.................................	Number	160	342	463	498	522	612	671
Total enrolled..	Number	146,064	375,546	558,579	680,136	763,775	874,559	874,913
Average tuition..	Dollars	8,948	13,058	14,833	15,462	15,673	15,302	15,352
Students receiving loans.........................	Percent	36.0	44.8	25.8	20.1	32.9	63.5	60.1
Average loan..	Dollars	4,118	4,502	4,797	4,954	5,069	5,184	5,100
Students receiving Pell Grants...................	Percent	36.7	46.2	43.0	44.6	50.5	56.1	52.7
Average Pell Grant..................................	Dollars	1,737	2,281	2,498	2,816	3,737	3,990	3,408

Source: Federal Reserve Bank of New York, "Private for-Profit Institutions in Higher Education," <http://www.newyorkfed.org/regional/nonprofit-forprofit-colleges/>, accessed August 2014.

Table 321. Academic Libraries by Selected Characteristics: 2012

[As of Fall of year shown. For information on public libraries, see Table 1174 and Table 1171]

Institution characteristic	Number of libraries	Circulation (1,000)		Expendi-tures (mil. dol.)	Paid staff [1]			
		General collection	Reserve collection		Total [2]	Librar-ians	Other pro-fessional staff	Student assistants
All U.S. academic libraries............	**3,793**	**116,891**	**37,518**	**7,008**	**85,752**	**26,606**	**7,817**	**20,509**
Control:								
Public..	1,560	75,013	24,884	4,078	51,064	15,124	4,477	11,288
Private...	2,233	41,878	12,634	2,930	34,687	11,482	3,339	9,222
Level: [3]								
Total 4-year and above.................	2,489	100,772	30,312	6,395	74,241	22,504	6,821	18,308
Doctor's.....................................	894	75,996	20,820	5,216	55,386	16,243	5,337	12,768
Master's.....................................	842	16,263	6,788	797	12,491	4,066	929	3,688
Bachelor's..................................	753	8,513	2,705	382	6,364	2,195	555	1,852
Less than 4-year...........................	1,304	16,119	7,205	613	11,510	4,102	996	2,202
Size (FTE enrollment): [4]								
Less than 1,000...........................	1,388	6,407	1,197	309	5,579	2,210	572	1,694
1,000 to 2,999.............................	1,108	16,459	6,537	854	12,958	4,390	1,069	3,612
3,000 to 4,999.............................	450	9,385	3,023	527	8,006	2,683	682	2,063
5,000 to 9,999.............................	443	17,084	6,891	1,086	14,232	4,432	1,146	3,457
10,000 to 19,999..........................	268	23,466	9,417	1,646	18,478	5,558	1,619	3,729
20,000 or more............................	136	44,091	10,452	2,587	26,498	7,333	2,729	5,955

[1] Full-time equivalent (FTE) staff is calculated by dividing the total number of hours for all part-time positions by the number of hours the library defines as a full-time position. [2] Includes other staff not shown separately. [3] Level refers to the highest level of any degree offered by the institution. Doctoral, master's, and bachelor's level institutions do not sum to total number of 4-year and above institutions because there are 4-year and above institutions that grant "other" degrees and are thus not included in the breakdown. [4] FTE enrollment is calculated by adding one-third of part-time enrollment to full-time enrollment.

Source: U.S. National Center for Education Statistics, *Academic Libraries: 2012, First Look*, January 2014. See also <http://nces.ed.gov/surveys/libraries/academic.asp>.

Table 322. Public Schools Reporting Incidents of Crime by Incident Type and Selected School Characteristics: 2009 to 2010

[For school year ending in 2010. Includes incidents that happen in school buildings, on school grounds, on school buses, and at places that hold school-sponsored events or activities. Based on sample; see source for details]

School characteristic	Total number of schools	Percent of schools with—				Rate per 1,000 students			
		Violent incidents [1]	Serious violent incidents [2]	Theft [3]	Other incidents [4]	Violent incidents [1]	Serious violent incidents [2]	Theft [3]	Other incidents [4]
All public schools [5]............	**82,800**	**73.8**	**16.4**	**44.1**	**68.1**	**25.0**	**1.1**	**5.5**	**9.2**
Level: [6]									
Primary............................	48,900	64.4	13.0	25.7	57.3	21.3	1.0	1.8	4.5
Middle..............................	15,300	90.5	18.9	65.2	81.9	40.0	1.5	7.4	11.1
High school.......................	12,200	90.9	27.6	82.6	92.2	21.4	1.1	10.1	16.2
Enrollment size:									
Less than 300...................	18,900	62.8	10.4	30.7	55.3	27.2	[7] 1.5	5.2	8.9
300 to 499........................	25,200	71.3	15.7	36.4	63.3	26.5	1.4	3.9	6.9
500 to 999........................	29,800	76.4	15.9	46.7	72.5	25.0	0.8	4.2	6.9
1,000 or more...................	8,900	95.4	32.8	84.9	94.3	23.2	1.2	8.6	14.4
Percent minority enrollment:									
Less than 5 percent............	11,700	69.6	12.6	40.8	59.0	23.3	[7] 1.2	4.9	7.4
5 to 20 percent.................	20,900	67.9	9.9	38.3	61.2	17.2	0.6	4.8	7.1
20 to 50 percent................	20,000	75.9	18.6	46.2	69.7	23.1	1.2	5.8	8.9
50 percent or more.............	30,100	78.2	21.1	48.0	75.5	31.4	1.4	5.8	11.1

[1] Violent incidents include rape, sexual battery other than rape, physical attack or fight with or without a weapon, threat of physical attack with or without a weapon, and robbery with or without a weapon. [2] Serious violent incidents include rape, sexual battery other than rape, physical attack or fight with a weapon, threat of physical attack with a weapon, and robbery with or without a weapon. [3] Theft or larceny (taking things worth over $10 without personal confrontation). Includes pocket picking, stealing purse or backpack (if left unattended or no force was used to take from owner), theft from motor vehicles, etc. [4] Other incidents include possession of a firearm or explosive device, possession of knife or sharp object, distribution of illegal drugs, possession or use of alcohol or illegal drugs, and vandalism. [5] Includes combined schools, not shown separately, which include all other combination of grades, including K–12 schools. [6] Primary schools are defined as schools in which the lowest grade is not higher than grade 3 and the highest grade is not higher than grade 8. Middle schools are defined as schools in which the lowest grade is not lower than grade 4 and the highest grade is not higher than grade 9. High schools are defined as schools in which the lowest grade is not lower than grade 9 and the highest grade is not higher than grade 12. [7] Interpret data with caution.

Source: U.S. National Center for Education Statistics, *Indicators of School Crime and Safety: 2014,* July 2015. See also <http://nces.ed.gov/programs/crimeindicators/crimeindicators2014/>.

Table 323. Percent of Public Schools Reporting Selected Types of Disciplinary Problems Occurring at School by Selected School Characteristics: 2013 to 2014

[In percent. For school year ending in 2014. "At school" includes activities that happen in school buildings, on school grounds, on school buses, and at places that hold school-sponsored events or activities. Based on the "School Safety and Discipline: 2013-14" survey. Respondents to the survey had the option of either completing the survey on paper and mailing it back, or completing the survey online. The online option was not available to respondents in previous years. The change in survey administration may have impacted 2013-14 results. Based on sample; see source for details]

School characteristic	Happens at least once a week					
	Student racial tensions	Student bullying	Student sexual harassment of other students [1]	Student verbal abuse of teachers	Widespread disorder in classrooms	Student acts of disrespect for teachers
All public schools............................	**1.4**	**15.7**	**1.4**	**5.1**	**2.3**	**8.6**
Level: [2]						
Primary..	[3] 1.2	12.2	(S)	4.4	[3] 2.1	6.2
Middle...	[3] 2.5	24.5	3.4	6.1	[3] 2.5	11.1
High school/combined........................	[3] 1.1	17.2	[3] 1.8	6.2	2.8	12.8
Enrollment size:						
Less than 300...................................	(S)	13.5	(S)	(S)	(S)	[3] 5.1
300 to 499..	(S)	14.6	[3] 1.8	6.1	[3] 3.7	7.8
500 to 999..	[3] 2.1	16.1	1.3	5.4	2.4	9.5
1,000 or more...................................	3.7	22.1	[3] 3.8	8.4	[3] 2.6	15.6
Percent minority enrollment:						
Less than 5 percent............................	(S)	[3] 14.6	(S)	[3] (S)	(S)	(S)
5 to 20 percent..................................	(S)	11.9	(S)	[3] 1.6	(S)	4.1
20 to 50 percent................................	[3] 1.5	18.1	[3] 2.2	6.0	[3] 3.6	10.1
50 percent or more.............................	2.5	16.8	1.5	7.8	3.4	11.6

S Figure does not meet publication standards. [1] Sexual harassment was defined as conduct that is unwelcome, sexual in nature, and denies or limits a student's ability to participate in or benefit from a school's education program. The conduct can be carried out by school employees, other students, and non-employee third parties. Both male and female students can be victims of sexual harassment, and the harasser and the victim can be of the same sex. The conduct can be verbal, nonverbal, or physical. [2] Primary schools are defined as schools in which the lowest grade is not higher than grade 3 and the highest grade is not higher than grade 8. Middle schools are defined as schools in which the lowest grade level is not lower than grade 4 and the highest grade is not higher than grade 9. High schools are defined as schools in which the lowest grade is not lower than grade 9 and the highest grade is not higher than grade 12. Combined schools include all other combinations of grades, including K–12 schools. [3] Interpret data with caution.

Source: U.S. National Center for Education Statistics, *Digest of Education Statistics*, "Advance Release of Selected 2014 Digest Tables," <http://www.nces.ed.gov/programs/digest/>, accessed June 2015.

Table 324. Students Who Reported Being Threatened or Injured With a Weapon on School Property by Selected Student Characteristics: 1999 to 2013

[In percent. Based on the Centers for Disease Control and Prevention's Youth Risk Behavior Surveillance System, which surveys students in public and private schools, in grades 9 to 12. Data are for previous 12 months. "On school property" was not defined for survey respondents. "Weapon" was defined as a gun, knife, or club for survey respondents]

Characteristic	1999	2001	2003	2005	2007	2009	2011	2013
Total..........	7.7	8.9	9.2	7.9	7.8	7.7	7.4	6.9
Sex:								
Male..........	9.5	11.5	11.6	9.7	10.2	9.6	9.5	7.7
Female..........	5.8	6.5	6.5	6.1	5.4	5.5	5.2	6.1
Race/ethnicity: [1]								
White..........	6.6	8.5	7.8	7.2	6.9	6.4	6.1	5.8
Black..........	7.6	9.3	10.9	8.1	9.7	9.4	8.9	8.4
Hispanic..........	9.8	8.9	9.4	9.8	8.7	9.1	9.2	8.5
Asian..........	7.7	11.3	11.5	4.6	[2] 7.6	5.5	7.0	5.3
American Indian/Alaska Native..........	[2] 13.2	[2] 15.2	22.1	9.8	5.9	16.5	8.2	18.5
Pacific Islander/Native Hawaiian..........	15.6	24.8	16.3	[2] 14.5	[2] 8.1	12.5	11.3	[2] 8.7
More than one race..........	9.3	10.3	18.7	10.7	13.3	9.2	9.9	7.7
Grade:								
9th..........	10.5	12.7	12.1	10.5	9.2	8.7	8.3	8.5
10th..........	8.2	9.1	9.2	8.8	8.4	8.4	7.7	7.0
11th..........	6.1	6.9	7.3	5.5	6.8	7.9	7.3	6.8
12th..........	5.1	5.3	6.3	5.8	6.3	5.2	5.9	4.9

[1] Race categories exclude persons of Hispanic ethnicity. [2] Interpret data with caution.

Source: U.S. National Center for Education Statistics, *Digest of Education Statistics*, "Advance Release of Selected 2014 Digest Tables," <http://nces.ed.gov/programs/digest/index.asp>, accessed March 2015; and *Indicators of School Crime and Safety*, annual. See also <http://nces.ed.gov/surveys/ssocs/>.

Table 325. Public Schools Using Selected Safety and Security Measures by School Characteristics: 2004 to 2012

[In percent. For school year ending in year shown. Based on the Schools and Staffing Survey responses provided by principals; for details see source]

Measure	Total			Elementary Schools			Secondary Schools		
	2004	2008	2012	2004	2008	2012	2004	2008	2012
Controlled access during school hours:									
Buildings (locked or monitored doors)..........	81.5	88.8	88.2	84.7	92.1	90.4	75.0	82.1	83.9
Grounds (locked or monitored gates)..........	39.4	44.9	44.1	39.0	45.7	45.4	41.4	43.3	39.6
Students required to wear badges or picture IDs..........	6.1	7.5	7.4	3.5	4.1	4.6	14.1	16.8	14.3
Metal detector checks on students:									
Random checks [1]..........	5.7	5.9	5.0	3.4	3.0	2.6	10.2	11.9	7.9
Required to pass through daily..........	2.0	2.3	2.7	0.8	0.3	0.8	3.7	5.2	4.6
Sweeps and technology:									
Random dog sniffs to check for drugs..........	23.6	25.0	24.0	10.8	13.2	10.6	56.5	54.6	57.3
Random sweeps for contraband [1]..........	12.8	14.8	12.1	5.6	7.6	5.0	28.2	30.5	26.1
Security cameras used to monitor school..........	32.5	51.8	64.3	26.3	46.1	57.7	51.1	68.7	81.2
Dress code:									
Required students to wear uniforms..........	13.5	16.5	19.3	14.7	17.5	20.3	8.8	12.1	12.2
Enforced a strict dress code..........	49.3	54.0	49.1	45.2	50.0	44.6	59.7	64.4	58.3
School supplies and equipment:									
Required clear book bags or banned book bags on school grounds..........	6.0	6.8	5.7	3.3	4.7	3.2	11.3	10.5	9.3
Daily presence of police or security personnel:..........	24.8	27.2	28.1	15.5	16.2	17.1	53.9	58.3	57.6

[1] For example, drugs or weapons. Does not include dog sniffs.

Source: U.S. National Center for Education Statistics, *Indicators of School Crime and Safety: 2014*, July 2015. See also <http://nces.ed.gov/programs/crimeindicators/crimeindicators2014/>.

Table 326. Students Who Reported Being Bullied at School or Cyber-Bullied by Student Characteristics: 2013

[In percent. For school year ending in 2013. For students aged 12 through 18. "At school" includes the school building, on school property, on a school bus, or going to and from school. For more information, see Appendix A of source]

Characteristic	Total [1]	Bullied at school					Cyber-bullying anywhere [2]
		Total bullying at school	Made fun of, called names, or insulted	Subject of rumors	Threatened with harm	Pushed, shoved, tripped, spit on	
Total	**23.1**	**21.5**	**13.6**	**13.2**	**3.9**	**6.0**	**6.9**
Sex:							
Male	21.1	19.5	12.6	9.6	4.1	7.4	5.2
Female	25.2	23.7	14.7	17.0	3.7	4.6	8.6
Race/ethnicity: [3]							
White	25.3	23.7	15.6	14.6	4.4	6.1	7.6
Black	21.2	20.3	10.5	12.7	3.2	6.0	4.5
Hispanic	20.5	19.2	12.1	11.5	4.0	6.3	5.8
Asian	11.8	9.2	7.5	3.7	(S)	2.0	5.8
Other	29.7	25.2	16.5	17.3	[4] 4.3	8.5	13.4
Grade:							
6th	29.9	27.8	21.3	16.1	5.9	11.0	5.9
7th	27.3	26.4	17.9	15.5	6.1	11.6	7.0
8th	22.7	21.7	14.5	12.7	3.9	6.5	6.4
9th	24.4	23.0	13.7	13.8	3.6	4.9	6.7
10th	21.4	19.5	12.9	12.9	4.3	3.7	8.6
11th	22.4	20.0	11.2	12.5	3.0	3.4	6.8
12th	15.4	14.1	6.4	9.7	[4] 1.0	3.0	5.9

S Reporting standards not met. [1] Bullying types do not sum to total because students could have experienced more than one type of bullying. Total includes other types of bullying not shown separately. [2] Cyber-bullied students includes students who responded that another student had posted hurtful information about them on the Internet; purposefully shared private information about them on the Internet; harassed them via instant messaging, via Short Message Service (SMS) text messaging, or via email; harassed them while gaming; or excluded them online. [3] Race categories exclude persons of Hispanic ethnicity. Other includes American Indian, Alaska Native, Pacific Islander, and more than one race. [4] Interpret data with caution.

Source: U.S. National Center for Education Statistics, *Digest of Education Statistics*, "Advance Release of Selected 2014 Digest Tables," <http://nces.ed.gov/programs/digest/index.asp>, accessed May 2015; and *Indicators of School Crime and Safety*, annual. See also <http://nces.ed.gov/surveys/ssocs/>.

Table 327. Violent Deaths, Homicides, and Suicides Occurring at Schools, Total and for Youth Aged 5 to 18: 1993 to 2012

[For school year ending in year shown. A school-associated violent death is defined as a homicide, suicide, or legal intervention (involving a law enforcement officer) in which the fatal injury occurred on the campus of a functioning elementary or secondary school in the United States, including while the victim was on the way to or from regular sessions at school or while the victim was attending or traveling to or from an official school-sponsored event. Victims include students, staff members, and others who are not students. Based on data from U.S. Centers for Disease Control and Prevention, and Federal Bureau of Investigation and Bureau of Justice Statistics]

Year	School-associated violent deaths				Homicides of youth aged 5 to 18		Suicides of youth aged 5 to 18	
	Total [1]	Homicides	Suicides [2]	Legal inter-ventions	Total	At school	Total	At school
1993	57	47	10	0	2,721	34	1,680	6
1994	48	38	10	0	2,932	29	1,723	7
1995	48	39	8	0	2,696	28	1,767	7
1996	53	46	6	1	2,545	32	1,725	6
1997	48	45	2	1	2,221	28	1,633	1
1998	57	47	9	1	2,100	34	1,626	6
1999	47	38	6	2	1,777	33	1,597	4
2000 [3]	37	26	11	0	1,567	14	1,415	8
2001 [3]	34	26	7	1	1,509	14	1,493	6
2002 [3]	36	27	8	1	1,498	16	1,400	5
2003 [3]	36	25	11	0	1,553	18	1,331	10
2004 [3]	45	37	7	1	1,474	23	1,285	5
2005 [3]	52	40	10	2	1,554	22	1,471	8
2006 [3]	44	37	6	1	1,697	21	1,408	3
2007 [3]	63	48	13	2	1,801	32	1,296	9
2008 [3]	48	39	7	2	1,744	21	1,231	5
2009 [3]	44	29	15	0	1,605	18	1,344	7
2010 [3]	35	27	5	3	1,410	19	1,467	2
2011 [3]	32	26	6	0	1,339	11	1,456	3
2012 [3]	45	26	14	5	1,199	15	1,568	5

[1] Total includes unintentional firearm-related deaths, not shown separately. [2] Total youth suicides are reported for calendar years 1992 through 2011 (instead of school years 1992-93 through 2011-12). [3] Data from school year 2000 onward are subject to change until interviews with school and law enforcement officials have been completed. The details learned during interviews can occasionally change the classification of a case.

Source: U.S. National Center for Education Statistics, *Digest of Education Statistics*, "Advance Release of Selected 2014 Digest Tables," <http://nces.ed.gov/programs/digest/index.asp>, accessed March 2015; and *Indicators of School Crime and Safety,* annual. See also <http://nces.ed.gov/surveys/ssocs/>.

Table 328. College Campus Crime—Incidents and Rates by Type of Crime and Institution: 2001 to 2012

[For school year ending in year shown. Data are from Department of Education's Campus Safety and Security Reporting System. Data are for degree-granting institutions, which are institutions that grant associate's or higher degrees and participate in Title IV federal financial aid programs. Some institutions that report data as mandated by the Clery Act, specifically, non-degree-granting institutions and institutions outside of the 50 states and the District of Columbia, are excluded from this table. Crimes, arrests, and referrals include incidents involving students, staff, and on-campus guests. Excludes off-campus crimes and arrests even if they involve college students or staff]

Control and level of institution and type of crime	Total, in residence halls and other locations						2012		
	2001	2006	2008	2009	2010	2011	Total	In residence halls	At other locations
NUMBER OF INCIDENTS									
Selected crimes against persons and property	**41,596**	**44,492**	**40,296**	**34,054**	**32,097**	**30,678**	**29,527**	**14,589**	**14,938**
Murder [1]	17	8	12	16	15	16	11	5	6
Negligent manslaughter [2]	2	–	3	–	1	1	1	1	–
Sex offenses, forcible [3]	2,201	2,670	2,639	2,544	2,927	3,387	3,885	2,792	1,093
Sex offenses, nonforcible [4]	461	43	35	65	33	47	44	19	25
Robbery	1,663	1,547	1,576	1,409	1,392	1,304	1,362	232	1,130
Aggravated assault	2,947	2,817	2,495	2,327	2,221	2,270	2,403	803	1,600
Burglary	26,904	31,260	28,737	23,083	21,335	19,610	18,099	10,288	7,811
Motor vehicle theft	6,221	5,231	4,104	3,977	3,441	3,402	3,033	10	3,023
Arson	1,180	916	695	633	732	641	689	439	250
Arrests [5]	**40,348**	**50,187**	**50,639**	**50,066**	**51,519**	**54,439**	**51,387**	**25,762**	**25,625**
Illegal weapons possession	1,073	1,316	1,190	1,077	1,112	1,033	1,031	268	763
Drug law violations	11,854	13,952	15,146	15,871	18,589	20,788	20,842	10,792	10,050
Liquor law violations	27,421	34,919	34,303	33,118	31,818	32,618	29,514	14,702	14,812
Referrals for disciplinary action [5]	**155,201**	**218,040**	**217,526**	**220,987**	**230,269**	**250,079**	**248,882**	**223,334**	**25,548**
Illegal weapons possession	1,277	1,871	1,455	1,275	1,314	1,298	1,405	919	486
Drug law violations	23,900	27,251	32,469	36,344	42,022	51,706	54,009	45,467	8,542
Liquor law violations	130,024	188,918	183,602	183,368	186,933	197,075	193,468	176,948	16,520
INCIDENTS PER 10,000 FTE STUDENTS [6]									
Selected crimes against persons and property	**35.6**	**33.3**	**29.0**	**22.9**	**20.9**	**20.0**	**19.4**	**25.6**	**7.1**
By type of crime:									
Murder [1]	(Z)	(Z)	(Z)	(Z)	(Z)	(Z)	(Z)	(Z)	(Z)
Negligent manslaughter [2]	(Z)	(Z)	(Z)	(Z)	(Z)	(Z)	(Z)	(Z)	(Z)
Sex offenses, forcible [3]	1.9	2.0	1.9	1.7	1.9	2.2	2.6	3.6	0.4
Sex offenses, nonforcible [4]	0.4	(Z)	(Z)	(Z)	(Z)	(Z)	(Z)	(Z)	(Z)
Robbery	1.4	1.2	1.1	0.9	0.9	0.9	0.9	1.0	0.7
Aggravated assault	2.5	2.1	1.8	1.6	1.4	1.5	1.6	1.9	0.9
Burglary	23.0	23.4	20.7	15.5	13.9	12.8	11.9	16.3	3.2
Motor vehicle theft	5.3	3.9	3.0	2.7	2.2	2.2	2.0	2.0	1.9
Arson	1.0	0.7	0.5	0.4	0.5	0.4	0.5	0.6	0.1
By type of institution:									
Public 4-year	36.2	35.5	30.5	24.9	23.4	21.9	21.1	22.5	6.8
Nonprofit 4-year	57.4	57.7	49.3	38.7	35.2	33.1	32.5	34.9	7.0
For-profit 4-year	19.1	9.6	10.3	7.3	6.5	6.3	5.6	10.1	4.4
Public 2-year	19.9	15.4	14.0	11.7	10.2	10.3	9.4	17.3	7.5
Nonprofit 2-year	64.0	81.9	99.3	55.9	48.5	44.9	34.6	61.5	24.9
For profit-2-year	25.4	18.2	14.8	13.1	8.2	7.6	8.0	6.4	8.1
Arrests [5]	**34.6**	**37.6**	**36.4**	**33.7**	**33.5**	**35.5**	**33.8**	**48.9**	**3.7**
Illegal weapons possession	0.9	1.0	0.9	0.7	0.7	0.7	0.7	0.8	0.4
Drug law violations	10.2	10.5	10.9	10.7	12.1	13.6	13.7	19.3	2.5
Liquor law violations	23.5	26.2	24.7	22.3	20.7	21.3	19.4	28.8	0.8
By type of institution:									
Public 4-year	60.1	68.7	66.3	63.6	63.5	67.0	62.5	68.2	4.0
Nonprofit 4-year	24.5	21.0	20.2	18.7	17.1	16.8	16.8	18.2	2.8
For-profit 4-year	0.4	0.8	0.7	0.7	1.9	2.1	1.7	5.6	0.7
Public 2-year	7.8	10.9	9.6	7.9	8.8	9.0	8.7	25.7	4.6
Nonprofit 2-year	27.9	22.0	34.0	22.1	19.8	15.8	16.7	48.2	5.2
For profit-2-year	8.8	1.8	0.9	1.8	1.1	0.6	0.8	11.0	0.4
Referrals for disciplinary action [5]	**132.9**	**163.4**	**156.5**	**148.8**	**149.8**	**163.1**	**163.8**	**244.3**	**3.1**
Illegal weapons possession	1.1	1.4	1.0	0.9	0.9	0.8	0.9	1.3	0.2
Drug law violations	20.5	20.4	23.4	24.5	27.3	33.7	35.6	52.7	1.4
Liquor law violations	111.3	141.6	132.1	123.4	121.6	128.6	127.4	190.4	1.5
By type of institution:									
Public 4-year	153.1	184.6	170.8	169.5	175.5	193.1	192.2	210.9	2.5
Nonprofit 4-year	275.5	354.0	348.7	334.3	329.6	341.0	334.3	364.2	18.8
For-profit 4-year	12.0	7.6	10.2	12.2	8.9	12.1	10.9	52.1	0.6
Public 2-year	10.3	16.0	16.5	17.0	18.6	19.7	18.7	85.0	2.5
Nonprofit 2-year	160.9	176.0	150.8	132.3	152.4	109.2	96.1	360.6	0.4
For profit-2-year	15.4	13.9	9.2	8.6	3.8	4.7	5.4	106.4	1.7

– Represents zero. Z Data rounds to less than .05. [1] Excludes suicides, fetal deaths, traffic fatalities, accidental deaths, and justifiable homicide (such as the killing of a felon by a law enforcement officer in the line of duty). [2] Defined as the killing of another person through gross negligence (excludes traffic fatalities). [3] Any sexual act directed against another person forcibly and/or against that person's will. [4] Includes only statutory rape or incest. [5] If an individual is both arrested and referred to college officials for disciplinary action for a single offense, only the arrest is counted. [6] FTE is full-time equivalent. Although crimes, arrests, and referrals include incidents involving students, staff, and campus guests, they are expressed as a ratio to FTE students because comprehensive FTE counts of all these groups are not available.

Source: U.S. National Center for Education Statistics, *Digest of Education Statistics*, "Advance Release of Selected 2014 Digest Tables," <http://nces.ed.gov/programs/digest/index.asp>, accessed March 2015.

Section 5
Law Enforcement, Courts, and Prisons

This section presents data on crimes committed, victims of crimes, arrests, and data related to criminal violations and the criminal justice system. The major sources of these data are the Bureau of Justice Statistics (BJS), the Federal Bureau of Investigation (FBI), and the Administrative Office of the U.S. Courts. BJS issues many reports—see our Guide to Sources for a complete listing. The Federal Bureau of Investigation's major annual reports are *Crime in the United States, Law Enforcement Officers Killed and Assaulted*, and *Hate Crimes*, which present data on reported crimes as gathered from state and local law enforcement agencies.

Legal jurisdiction and law enforcement—Law enforcement is, for the most part, a function of state and local officers and agencies. The U.S. Constitution reserves general police powers to the states. By act of Congress, federal offenses include only offenses against the U.S. government and against or by its employees while engaged in their official duties, and offenses which involve the crossing of state lines or an interference with interstate commerce. Excluding the military, there are 52 separate criminal law jurisdictions in the United States: one in each of the 50 states, one in the District of Columbia, and the federal jurisdiction. Each of these has its own criminal law and procedure and its own law enforcement agencies. While the systems of law enforcement are quite similar among the states, there are often substantial differences in the penalties for like offenses.

Law enforcement can be divided into three parts: Investigation of crimes and arrests of persons suspected of committing them; prosecution of those charged with crime; and the punishment or treatment of persons convicted of crime.

Crime—The U.S. Department of Justice administers two statistical programs to measure the magnitude, nature, and impact of crime in the nation: the Uniform Crime Reporting (UCR) Program and the National Crime Victimization Survey (NCVS). Each of these programs produces valuable information about aspects of the nation's crime problem. Because the UCR and NCVS programs are conducted for different purposes, use different methods, and focus on somewhat different aspects of crime, the information they produce together provides a more comprehensive panorama of the nation's crime problem than either could produce alone.

Uniform Crime Reports (UCR)—The FBI's UCR Program, which began in 1929, collects information on the following crimes reported to law enforcement authorities: Part 1 offenses, for which detailed data is reported— murder and nonnegligent manslaughter, rape, robbery, aggravated assault, burglary, larceny-theft, motor vehicle theft, and arson; for Part 2 offenses, law enforcement agencies report only arrest data for 20 additional crime categories. UCR definitions of criminal offenses (including those listed) can be found at <https://www.fbi.gov/about-us/cjis/ucr/crime-in-the-u.s/2013/crime-in-the-u.s.-2013/resource-pages/offense-definitions/13-offensedefinitions_final>.

Beginning in 2013, the UCR program implemented a revised definition of rape. Not all state and local agencies have been able to effect the change in their records management systems and some agencies currently can report the offense based on only the legacy definition. Therefore, rape data collected under both definitions are used in the *Crime in the United States* report. Additionally, the ability to show trend data for rape has been impacted. For details, see <https://www.fbi.gov/about-us/cjis/ucr/crime-in-the-u.s/2013/crime-in-the-u.s.-2013/rape-addendum/rape_addendum_final>.

The UCR Program compiles data from monthly law enforcement reports or individual crime incident records transmitted directly to the FBI or to centralized state agencies that then report to the FBI. The Program thoroughly examines each report it receives for reasonableness, accuracy, and deviations that may indicate errors. Large variations in crime levels may indicate modified records procedures, incomplete reporting, or changes in a jurisdiction's boundaries. To identify any unusual fluctuations in an agency's crime counts, the Program compares monthly reports to previous submissions of the agency and with those for similar agencies.

The UCR Program presents crime counts for the nation as a whole, as well as for regions, states, counties, cities, towns, tribal law enforcement, and colleges and universities. This permits studies among neighboring jurisdictions and among those with similar populations and other common characteristics.

The UCR Program annually publishes its findings online in a preliminary release in the spring of the following calendar year, followed by a detailed report, *Crime in the United States*, issued in the fall. In addition to crime counts and trends, this report includes data on crimes cleared, persons arrested (age, sex, and race), law enforcement personnel (including the number of sworn officers killed or assaulted), and the characteristics of homicides (including age, sex, and race of victims and offenders; victim-offender relationships; weapons used; and circumstances surrounding the homicides). Other periodic reports are also available from the UCR Program.

National Crime Victimization Survey (NCVS)—A second perspective on crime is provided by this survey of the Bureau of Justice Statistics (BJS). The NCVS is an annual data collection (interviews of persons aged 12 or older), conducted by the U.S. Census Bureau for the BJS. As an ongoing survey of households, the NCVS measures crimes of violence and property both reported and not reported to police. It produces national rates and levels of personal and property victimization. No attempt is made to validate the information against police records or any other source.

The NCVS measures rape/sexual assault, robbery, assault, pocket-picking, purse snatching, burglary, and motor vehicle theft. The NCVS includes crimes reported to the police, as well as those not reported. Murder and kidnaping are not covered. The so-called victimless crimes, such as drunkenness, drug abuse, and prostitution, also are excluded, as are crimes for which it is difficult to identify knowledgeable respondents or to locate data records.

Crimes of which the victim may not be aware also cannot be measured effectively. Buying stolen property may fall into this category, as may some instances of embezzlement. Attempted crimes of many types probably are under-recorded for this reason. Events in which the victim has shown a willingness to participate in illegal activity also are excluded.

In any encounter involving a personal crime, more than one criminal act can be committed against an individual. For example, a rape may be associated with a robbery, or a household property offense, such as a burglary, can escalate into something more serious in the event of a personal confrontation. In classifying the survey measured crimes, each criminal incident has been counted only once, by the most serious act that took place during the incident, and ranked in accordance with the seriousness classification system used by the FBI. The order of seriousness for crimes against persons is as follows: rape, robbery, assault, and larceny. Personal crimes take precedence over household offenses.

A *victimization*, the basic measure of the occurrence of crime, is a specific criminal act as it affects a single victim. The number of victimizations is determined by the number of victims of such acts. Victimization counts serve as key elements in computing rates of victimization. For crimes against persons, the rates are based on the total number of individuals aged 12 and over or on a portion of that population sharing a particular characteristic or set of traits. As general indicators of the danger of having been victimized during the reference period, the rates are not sufficiently refined to represent true measures of risk for specific individuals or households.

An *incident* is a specific criminal act involving one or more victims; therefore the number of incidents of personal crimes is lower than that of victimizations.

Courts—Statistics on criminal offenses and the outcome of prosecutions are incomplete for the country as a whole, although data are available for many states individually.

From 1986 to 2006, through its National Judicial Reporting Program, the BJS surveyed a nationally representative sample of 300 counties every 2 years and collected detailed information on demographic characteristics of felons, conviction offenses, type of sentences, sentence lengths, and time from arrest to conviction and sentencing.

The bulk of civil and criminal litigation in the country is commenced and determined in the various state courts. Only when the U.S. Constitution and acts of Congress specifically confer jurisdiction upon the federal courts may civil or criminal litigation be heard and decided by them. Generally, the federal courts have jurisdiction over the following types of cases: suits or proceedings by or against the United States;

civil actions between private parties arising under the Constitution, laws, or treaties of the United States; civil actions between private litigants who are citizens of different states; civil cases involving admiralty, maritime, or private jurisdiction; and all matters in bankruptcy.

There are several types of courts with varying degrees of legal jurisdiction. These jurisdictions include original, appellate, general, and limited or special. A court of original jurisdiction is one having the authority initially to try a case and pass judgment on the law and the facts; a court of appellate jurisdiction is one with the legal authority to review cases and hear appeals; a court of general jurisdiction is a trial court of unlimited original jurisdiction in civil and/or criminal cases, also called a "major trial court"; a court of limited or special jurisdiction is a trial court with legal authority over only a particular class of cases, such as probate, juvenile, or traffic cases.

The 94 federal courts of original jurisdiction are known as the U.S. district courts. One or more of these courts is established in every state and one each in the District of Columbia, Puerto Rico, the Virgin Islands, the Northern Mariana Islands, and Guam. Appeals from the district courts are taken to intermediate appellate courts of which there are 13, known as U.S. courts of appeals and the United States Court of Appeals for the Federal Circuit. The Supreme Court of the United States is the final and highest appellate court in the federal system of courts.

Juvenile offenders—For statistical purposes, the FBI and most states classify as juvenile offenders persons under the age of 18 years who have committed a crime or crimes.

Delinquency cases are all cases of youths referred to a juvenile court for violation of a law or ordinance or for seriously "antisocial" conduct. Several types of facilities are available for those adjudicated delinquents, ranging from the short-term physically unrestricted environment to the long-term very restrictive atmosphere.

Prisoners and jail inmates—BJS started to collect annual data in 1979 on prisoners in federal and state prisons and reformatories. Adults convicted of criminal activity may be given a prison or jail sentence. A *prison* is a confinement facility having custodial authority over adults sentenced to confinement of more than 1 year. A *jail* is a facility, usually operated by a local law enforcement agency, holding persons detained pending adjudication and/or persons committed after adjudication to 1 year or less.

Data on inmates in local jails were collected by the BJS for the first time in 1970. Since then, BJS has conducted censuses of facilities and inmates every 5 to 6 years. In 1984, BJS initiated an annual survey of jails conducted in noncensus years.

Statistical reliability—For discussion of statistical collection, estimation and sampling procedures, and measures of statistical reliability pertaining to the National Crime Victimization Survey and Uniform Crime Reporting Program, see Appendix III.

Table 329. Crimes and Crime Rates by Type of Offense: 1980 to 2013

[13,408 represents 13,408,000. Data include offenses reported to law enforcement, and offense estimations for nonreporting and partially reporting agencies within each state. Rates are based on Census Bureau estimated resident population as of July 1, except 1980, 1990, 2000, and 2010, which are enumerated as of April 1. See source for details]

Item and year	All crimes	Violent crime					Property crimes			
		Total	Murder [1]	Forcible rape [2]	Robbery	Aggra-vated assault	Total	Burglary	Larceny/ theft	Motor vehicle theft
Number of offenses (1,000):										
1980	13,408	1,345	23.0	83.0	566	673	12,064	3,795	7,137	1,132
1985	12,430	1,328	19.0	87.7	498	723	11,103	3,073	6,926	1,103
1990	14,476	1,820	23.4	102.6	639	1,055	12,655	3,074	7,946	1,636
1995	13,863	1,799	21.6	97.5	581	1,099	12,064	2,594	7,998	1,472
2000	11,608	1,425	15.6	90.2	408	912	10,183	2,051	6,972	1,160
2002	11,879	1,424	16.2	95.2	421	891	10,455	2,151	7,057	1,247
2003	11,827	1,384	16.5	93.9	414	859	10,443	2,155	7,027	1,261
2004	11,679	1,360	16.1	95.1	401	847	10,319	2,144	6,937	1,238
2005	11,565	1,391	16.7	94.3	417	862	10,175	2,155	6,783	1,236
2006	11,455	1,435	17.3	94.5	449	874	10,020	2,195	6,626	1,198
2007	11,305	1,423	17.1	92.2	447	866	9,882	2,190	6,592	1,100
2008	11,169	1,394	16.5	90.8	444	844	9,774	2,229	6,586	959
2009	10,663	1,326	15.4	89.2	409	813	9,337	2,203	6,338	796
2010	10,364	1,251	14.7	85.6	369	782	9,113	2,168	6,205	740
2011	10,259	1,206	14.7	84.2	355	752	9,053	2,185	6,151	717
2012	10,219	1,217	14.9	85.1	355	762	9,002	2,110	6,169	723
2013	9,796	1,163	14.2	79.8	345	724	8,633	1,928	6,004	700
Rate per 100,000 population:										
1980	5,950	597	10.2	36.8	251	299	5,353	1,684	3,167	502
1985	5,225	558	8.0	36.8	209	304	4,666	1,292	2,911	464
1990	5,803	730	9.4	41.1	256	423	5,073	1,232	3,185	656
1995	5,276	685	8.2	37.1	221	418	4,591	987	3,043	560
2000	4,125	507	5.5	32.0	145	324	3,618	729	2,477	412
2002	4,125	494	5.6	33.1	146	310	3,631	747	2,451	433
2003	4,067	476	5.7	32.3	143	295	3,591	741	2,417	434
2004	3,977	463	5.5	32.4	137	289	3,514	730	2,362	422
2005	3,901	469	5.6	31.8	141	291	3,432	727	2,288	417
2006	3,826	479	5.8	31.6	150	292	3,347	733	2,213	400
2007	3,748	472	5.7	30.6	148	287	3,276	726	2,185	365
2008	3,673	459	5.4	29.8	146	278	3,215	733	2,166	315
2009	3,473	432	5.0	29.1	133	265	3,041	718	2,065	259
2010	3,350	405	4.8	27.7	119	253	2,946	701	2,006	239
2011	3,292	387	4.7	27.0	114	242	2,905	701	1,974	230
2012	3,256	388	4.7	27.1	113	243	2,868	672	1,965	230
2013	3,099	368	4.5	25.2	109	229	2,731	610	1,899	221

[1] Includes nonnegligent manslaughter. [2] As of 2013, the FBI has introduced a revised definition of rape. Data shown here continue to follow the legacy definition of rape. For more information, see <http://www.fbi.gov/about-us/cjis/ucr/crime-in-the-u.s/2013/crime-in-the-u.s.-2013/rape-addendum/rape_addendum_final>.

Source: U.S. Department of Justice, Federal Bureau of Investigation, "Crime in the United States 2013," <http://www.fbi.gov/about-us/cjis/ucr>, accessed December 2014.

Table 330. Crimes and Crime Rates by Offense Type and Metropolitan Status: 2013

[In thousands (1,192.0 represents 1,192,000), except rate. Rate per 100,000 population. See headnote, Table 329]

Type of crime	United States		Metropolitan statistical area [1]		Cities outside metropolitan areas		Nonmetropolitan counties	
	Total	Rate	Total	Rate	Total	Rate	Total	Rate
Violent crime	1,192.0	377.1	1,069.8	397.4	71.8	376.7	50.4	180.8
Murder [2]	14.2	4.5	12.5	4.7	714.0	3.7	934.0	3.4
Forcible rape [3]	108.6	34.4	90.7	33.7	9.7	51	8.1	29.2
Robbery	345.0	109.1	332.2	123.4	9.6	50.3	3.3	11.8
Aggravated assault	724.1	229.1	634.3	235.6	51.8	271.6	38.0	136.4
Property crime	8,632.5	2,730.7	7,579.6	2,815.7	651.4	3,417.2	401.5	1,440.4
Burglary	1,928.5	610.0	1,650.9	613.3	140.7	737.9	136.9	491.0
Larceny-theft	6,004.5	1,899.4	5,280.8	1,961.7	484.5	2,541.8	239.1	857.8
Motor vehicle theft	699.6	221.3	647.8	240.7	26.2	137.6	25.5	91.6

[1] For definition, see Appendix II. [2] Includes nonnegligent manslaughter. [3] Estimated using the revised FBI Uniform Crime Reporting (UCR) definition of rape. Data are not comparable with those found in previous versions of this table. For more information, see <http://www.fbi.gov/about-us/cjis/ucr/crime-in-the-u.s/2013/crime-in-the-u.s.-2013/rape-addendum/rape_addendum_final>.

Source: U.S. Department of Justice, Federal Bureau of Investigation, "Crime in the United States 2013," <http://www.fbi.gov/about-us/cjis/ucr>, accessed December 2014.

Table 331. Crime Rates by State, 2012 and 2013, and by Type, 2013

[For year ending December 31. Rates per 100,000 population. Offenses reported to law enforcement. Based on Census Bureau estimated resident population as of July 1]

State	Violent crime						Property crime				
	2012 total	2013					2012 total	2013			
		Total	Murder	Rape [1]	Rob-bery	Aggra-vated assault		Total	Burglary	Larceny/ theft	Motor vehicle theft
United States............	387.8	367.9	4.5	34.4	109.1	229.1	2,868.0	2,730.7	610.0	1,899.4	221.3
Alabama...................	450.3	418.1	7.2	42.3	96.2	285.2	3,505.5	3,351.3	877.8	2,254.8	218.7
Alaska..................	604.1	602.6	4.6	125.4	84.9	425.5	2,743.6	2,885.2	396.7	2,258.0	230.6
Arizona [2].............	428.6	405.8	5.4	46.0	101.1	263.9	3,536.8	3,399.1	732.4	2,403.5	263.2
Arkansas.................	469.6	445.7	5.4	48.1	76.3	330.5	3,708.3	3,602.6	1,030.1	2,380.6	191.9
California................	423.5	396.2	4.6	25.3	139.9	232.3	2,761.8	2,658.1	605.4	1,621.5	431.2
Colorado.................	307.4	291.2	3.4	55.7	59.8	189.1	2,685.3	2,658.5	476.1	1,944.5	237.9
Connecticut..............	283.5	254.5	2.4	26.6	98.2	135.4	2,148.5	1,974.1	358.5	1,442.6	173.0
Delaware................	550.5	479.1	4.2	41.0	132.4	313.7	3,348.4	3,065.5	662.3	2,259.4	143.9
District of Columbia [3]......	1,241.8	1,281.9	15.9	61.1	630.8	592.5	4,855.7	4,808.3	513.0	3,795.0	500.3
Florida..................	487.0	460.0	5.0	34.6	118.7	312.3	3,276.2	3,105.3	710.5	2,216.3	178.6
Georgia.................	380.0	359.7	5.6	25.8	125.0	209.3	3,423.6	3,346.6	823.2	2,254.9	268.5
Hawaii...................	243.0	245.3	1.5	27.4	80.6	142.2	3,123.5	3,053.7	536.5	2,254.8	262.4
Idaho....................	209.8	204.7	1.7	40.6	13.6	161.0	1,994.6	1,864.9	411.9	1,357.1	95.3
Illinois..................	416.2	372.5	5.5	33.1	137.6	204.0	2,585.5	2,274.3	452.1	1,659.8	162.5
Indiana..................	344.8	349.9	5.4	32.6	108.2	211.3	3,028.5	2,854.0	653.0	1,984.9	216.2
Iowa....................	265.6	260.9	1.4	35.0	30.4	204.6	2,288.0	2,193.9	513.5	1,543.0	137.4
Kansas..................	356.7	327.5	3.9	41.3	46.6	248.1	3,156.1	2,946.8	600.4	2,117.0	229.5
Kentucky................	224.9	198.8	3.8	36.7	73.9	95.5	2,575.5	2,362.9	596.4	1,629.3	137.2
Louisiana................	496.3	510.4	10.8	35.0	119.9	352.8	3,534.7	3,582.0	890.4	2,493.6	198.0
Maine [2].................	122.4	121.6	1.8	33.7	25.2	68.7	2,514.0	2,292.2	488.1	1,735.3	68.8
Maryland................	477.3	467.8	6.4	25.8	169.5	272.0	2,758.1	2,663.5	538.9	1,898.3	226.3
Massachusetts............	407.0	404.0	2.0	40.6	100.2	270.5	2,156.8	2,051.2	459.2	1,455.7	136.3
Michigan................	455.0	429.8	6.4	66.6	102.1	274.8	2,521.1	2,327.6	569.4	1,510.0	248.3
Minnesota...............	230.9	223.2	2.1	37.0	67.8	127.5	2,568.1	2,420.4	419.0	1,854.4	147.0
Mississippi..............	260.1	267.4	6.5	31.1	80.5	156.5	2,810.5	2,724.7	835.6	1,742.3	146.7
Missouri.................	451.3	422.0	6.1	37.8	90.7	298.7	3,316.7	3,137.0	643.0	2,223.9	270.1
Montana [2]..............	278.8	240.7	2.2	40.4	20.1	190.2	2,595.9	2,556.5	400.3	1,974.0	182.2
Nebraska................	258.8	252.2	3.1	42.9	55.7	160.5	2,759.7	2,623.4	476.3	1,908.2	238.9
Nevada..................	608.6	591.2	5.8	50.8	185.8	360.6	2,814.1	2,837.7	826.0	1,653.4	358.3
New Hampshire...........	215.0	199.6	1.7	51.8	49.0	112.7	2,426.9	2,194.3	373.0	1,750.3	71.0
New Jersey..............	290.1	285.6	4.5	12.6	135.8	135.6	2,046.5	1,882.8	403.1	1,325.2	154.5
New Mexico..............	559.6	596.7	6.0	70.3	86.8	449.9	3,604.2	3,704.8	1,029.9	2,391.8	283.2
New York................	406.3	389.8	3.3	17.1	138.6	234.7	1,917.0	1,824.8	287.2	1,458.8	78.8
North Carolina...........	353.5	336.6	4.8	24.1	94.9	218.4	3,370.8	3,128.0	921.0	2,058.7	148.3
North Dakota.............	245.7	256.3	2.2	45.6	22.4	199.9	2,038.5	2,094.0	405.6	1,492.7	195.7
Ohio....................	301.5	275.7	3.9	34.9	124.2	123.2	3,206.4	2,927.5	790.2	1,968.5	168.8
Oklahoma................	474.4	428.1	5.1	56.6	78.7	300.8	3,432.3	3,273.7	866.1	2,116.4	291.2
Oregon..................	247.1	242.9	2.0	48.3	61.0	142.7	3,241.6	3,173.9	528.5	2,394.5	250.9
Pennsylvania [2]..........	355.5	326.6	4.7	29.5	115.6	185.7	2,166.7	2,060.8	407.3	1,545.6	107.8
Rhode Island.............	253.0	244.6	2.9	41.8	65.0	147.4	2,574.4	2,442.0	533.2	1,696.4	212.4
South Carolina...........	560.5	494.8	6.2	45.5	83.2	373.6	3,833.0	3,624.2	857.8	2,502.9	263.5
South Dakota.............	323.8	298.7	2.4	59.1	18.8	236.2	2,077.3	1,914.7	399.1	1,404.6	111.0
Tennessee...............	638.5	579.7	5.0	36.2	112.5	436.9	3,376.1	3,180.9	785.1	2,213.7	182.1
Texas...................	408.6	399.8	4.3	36.9	120.2	246.9	3,363.1	3,258.2	721.8	2,287.8	248.6
Utah....................	208.0	209.2	1.7	49.0	42.8	130.4	3,022.3	2,950.4	459.6	2,233.4	257.3
Vermont.................	142.3	114.9	1.6	20.7	11.6	87.1	2,500.7	2,214.2	528.7	1,632.2	53.3
Virginia.................	191.5	187.9	3.8	27.4	55.3	109.7	2,179.6	2,065.9	322.5	1,640.1	103.3
Washington [2]............	298.1	277.9	2.3	36.9	83.5	166.4	3,689.1	3,710.3	837.0	2,465.9	407.4
West Virginia............	320.1	289.7	3.3	35.2	35.1	226.7	2,396.8	2,103.9	521.7	1,478.9	103.3
Wisconsin [2].............	283.9	271.1	2.8	29.4	84.2	161.6	2,459.2	2,188.7	424.0	1,636.0	128.6
Wyoming................	201.3	197.7	2.9	32.1	12.9	157.2	2,293.0	2,198.4	335.5	1,763.6	99.2

[1] Estimated using the revised FBI Uniform Crime Reporting (UCR) definition of rape. Data are not comparable with those found in previous versions of this table. For more information, see <http://www.fbi.gov/about-us/cjis/ucr/crime-in-the-u.s/2013/crime-in-the-u.s.-2013/rape-addendum/rape_addendum_final>. States may have reported using revised or legacy definitions of rape, see source for details. [2] Because of changes in the state's reporting practices, figures are not comparable to previous years' data. [3] Includes offenses reported by the Zoological Police and the Metro Transit Police.

Source: U.S. Department of Justice, Federal Bureau of Investigation, "Crime in the United States 2013," <http://www.fbi.gov/about-us/cjis/ucr/ucr>, accessed December 2014.

Table 332. Crime Rates by Type—Selected Large Cities: 2013

[For year ending December 31. Rates per 100,000 population. Offenses reported to law enforcement]

Cities ranked by population size, 2013	Violent crime						Property crime			
	Total	Murder	Rape (revised definition) [1]	Forcible rape (legacy definition) [1]	Robbery	Aggravated assault	Total	Burglary	Larceny/ theft	Motor vehicle theft
New York, NY..................	624	4.0	(NA)	13.2	228	378	1,691	198	1,405	89
Los Angeles, CA...............	426	6.5	(NA)	19.7	203	197	2,213	405	1,437	371
Chicago, IL [2]...................	(NA)	15.2	(NA)	(NA)	434	(NA)	3,525	653	2,407	464
Houston, TX....................	963	9.8	(NA)	28.3	454	471	5,087	1,088	3,375	623
Philadelphia, PA..............	1,099	15.9	82.3	(NA)	487	514	3,442	670	2,399	373
Phoenix, AZ....................	632	7.9	(NA)	42.3	215	367	4,000	1,115	2,462	423
Las Vegas, NV.................	758	6.5	(NA)	47.0	271	433	3,197	985	1,769	442
San Antonio, TX...............	631	5.1	(NA)	47.4	157	422	5,715	1,061	4,184	470
San Diego, CA.................	393	2.9	(NA)	23.4	108	259	2,351	471	1,425	455
Dallas, TX.....................	664	11.4	(NA)	43.3	335	274	4,165	1,157	2,420	588
San Jose, CA..................	324	3.8	(NA)	27.2	110	183	2,571	521	1,251	799
Austin, TX.....................	363	3.0	(NA)	25.3	89	246	4,850	762	3,835	252
Indianapolis, IN...............	1,233	15.2	77.2	(NA)	447	693	5,246	1,581	3,076	589
Jacksonville, FL...............	620	11.0	53.4	(NA)	168	387	3,903	836	2,880	186
Charlotte-Mecklenburg, NC...	608	7.0	(NA)	27.5	215	358	3,649	769	2,659	222
San Francisco, CA............	847	5.8	(NA)	19.3	504	318	5,795	711	4,380	703
Fort Worth, TX.................	560	6.1	66.3	(NA)	159	329	4,344	1,054	2,986	304
Detroit, MI.....................	2,072	45.2	88.3	(NA)	682	1,257	5,834	1,679	2,456	1,699
El Paso, TX....................	371	1.5	(NA)	25.9	67	276	2,289	261	1,912	117
Louisville Metro, KY...........	543	7.2	0.0	23.8	213	299	4,288	1,031	2,956	302
Memphis, TN...................	1,656	18.9	66.4	(NA)	476	1,095	6,052	1,798	3,846	408
Denver, CO....................	630	6.2	79.2	(NA)	174	370	3,654	758	2,358	537
Washington, DC................	1,219	15.9	60.8	(NA)	566	576	4,574	513	3,575	487
Boston, MA....................	782	6.1	(NA)	43.3	290	443	2,773	481	2,042	250
Seattle, WA....................	585	3.0	23.8	(NA)	249	309	5,582	1,149	3,763	670
Nashville, TN..................	1,040	5.5	68.7	(NA)	253	712	3,848	883	2,777	188
Baltimore, MD.................	1,401	37.4	(NA)	47.9	600	716	4,945	1,187	3,043	715
Portland, OR..................	483	2.3	(NA)	38.4	151	292	4,865	678	3,647	540
Oklahoma City, OK............	826	10.2	(NA)	74.4	197	545	5,368	1,325	3,370	674
Milwaukee, WI.................	1,364	17.3	66.7	(NA)	547	733	4,496	1,080	2,686	730
Albuquerque, NM..............	775	6.6	(NA)	78.7	187	502	5,470	1,307	3,624	538
Tucson, AZ....................	641	8.9	(NA)	41.1	191	400	6,582	943	5,222	417
Fresno, CA....................	501	7.9	(NA)	10.4	177	306	4,438	1,026	2,614	797
Sacramento, CA...............	656	7.1	(NA)	19.9	242	387	3,760	813	2,349	598
Long Beach, CA...............	500	7.2	(NA)	21.9	238	232	2,768	804	1,462	501
Kansas City, MO...............	1,260	21.3	81.0	(NA)	357	800	5,295	1,377	2,996	921
Mesa, AZ......................	396	4.8	(NA)	44.5	105	242	2,831	517	2,106	209
Atlanta, GA....................	1,223	18.6	(NA)	23.3	524	657	6,103	1,317	3,804	983
Virginia Beach, VA............	162	3.8	31.1	(NA)	67	60	2,491	312	2,080	99
Colorado Springs, CO........	434	6.0	84.8	(NA)	96	247	4,168	854	2,871	442
Raleigh, NC...................	392	2.8	(NA)	18.4	141	230	3,063	736	2,163	164
Omaha, NE....................	576	9.9	(NA)	43.3	169	354	4,495	825	2,945	725
Miami, FL......................	1,182	17.0	22.9	(NA)	530	612	5,002	954	3,590	457
Oakland, CA...................	1,977	22.3	(NA)	44.6	1,219	691	6,233	1,252	3,289	1,692
Minneapolis, MN...............	1,019	9.1	97.2	(NA)	468	444	4,886	1,161	3,327	398
Tulsa, OK.....................	970	15.2	(NA)	94.6	252	608	5,318	1,504	3,208	606
Cleveland, OH.................	1,478	14.1	107.1	(NA)	897	460	5,953	2,122	2,771	1,060
Wichita, KS....................	793	3.9	63.1	(NA)	121	605	5,382	1,018	3,851	513
Arlington, TX..................	485	4.8	(NA)	27.7	148	304	3,960	840	2,872	248
New Orleans, LA..............	786	41.4	(NA)	46.7	302	397	3,853	850	2,435	568
Bakersfield, CA................	513	6.6	(NA)	11.9	196	299	4,647	1,273	2,562	812
Tampa, FL.....................	597	8.0	22.2	(NA)	165	402	2,511	555	1,799	157
Anaheim, CA..................	327	3.2	(NA)	23.7	127	174	2,783	409	1,888	487
Aurora, CO....................	418	6.7	65.2	(NA)	136	210	3,140	577	2,272	291
Santa Ana, CA................	337	3.9	(NA)	15.3	139	178	1,930	241	1,251	438
St. Louis, MO..................	1,594	37.7	104.5	(NA)	457	994	6,619	1,351	4,223	1,045
Riverside, CA..................	420	3.2	(NA)	24.7	156	236	3,352	625	2,184	543
Corpus Christi, TX.............	616	5.7	(NA)	46.7	124	440	4,642	825	3,662	155
Lexington, KY..................	306	5.8	43.4	(NA)	151	106	4,032	834	2,929	269
Pittsburgh, PA.................	734	14.6	25.4	(NA)	311	384	3,266	706	2,359	200
Stockton, CA..................	1,208	10.7	(NA)	30.4	363	804	5,030	1,397	2,918	715
Anchorage, AK................	813	4.7	136.2	(NA)	174	498	4,018	440	3,288	290
Cincinnati, OH.................	953	23.6	67.1	(NA)	543	319	5,812	1,844	3,537	430
St. Paul, MN...................	747	4.8	74.0	(NA)	243	425	3,724	940	2,186	598
Toledo, OH [3].................	1,025	9.9	45.6	(NA)	340	630	(NA)	1,893	(NA)	376
Greensboro, NC...............	519	9.7	(NA)	25.1	178	306	4,130	1,064	2,886	180
Newark, NJ....................	1,264	40.3	(NA)	16.2	874	333	3,222	745	1,436	1,040
Plano, TX......................	141	1.1	30.5	(NA)	38	71	2,150	342	1,715	93
Henderson, NV................	137	3.0	(NA)	16.8	60	57	1,997	524	1,274	200
Lincoln, NE....................	370	1.9	(NA)	53.1	79	236	3,496	532	2,850	114
Buffalo, NY....................	1,255	18.2	(NA)	56.0	511	670	4,827	1,336	3,121	370

NA Not available. [1] Beginning in 2013, the FBI has revised the definition of rape as used in Uniform Crime Reporting (UCR) Program. For more information, see <http://www.fbi.gov/about-us/cjis/ucr/crime-in-the-u.s/2013/crime-in-the-u.s.-2013/rape-addendum/rape_addendum_final>. Cities may have reported data using revised or legacy definitions of rape, see source for details. [2] The data collection methodology for the offense of rape used by Chicago, Illinois does not comply with national UCR Program guidelines. [3] It was determined that the agency did not follow the national UCR program guidelines for reporting an offense. Consequently, selected data are not included in this table.

Source: U.S. Department of Justice, Federal Bureau of Investigation, "Crime in the United States 2013," <http://www.fbi.gov/about-us/cjis/ucr>, accessed December 2014.

Table 333. Murder Victims—Circumstances and Weapons Used or Cause of Death: 2000 to 2013

[For year ending December 31. The FBI's Uniform Crime Reporting (UCR) Program defines murder and nonnegligent manslaughter as the willful (nonnegligent) killing of one human being by another. The classification of this offense is based solely on police investigation as opposed to the determination of a court, medical examiner, coroner, jury, or other judicial body. The UCR Program does not include the following situations in this offense classification: deaths caused by negligence, suicide, or accident; justifiable homicides; and attempts to murder, which are scored as aggravated assaults]

Characteristic	2000	2005	2010	2011	2012	2013
Murders, total [1]	**13,230**	**14,965**	**13,164**	**12,795**	**12,888**	**12,253**
CIRCUMSTANCES						
Felonies, total [1]	2,229	2,189	1,974	1,842	1,842	1,909
Rape [2]	58	45	41	16	16	20
Robbery	1,077	930	803	750	656	686
Burglary	76	91	85	95	91	94
Larceny-theft	23	12	21	12	15	16
Motor vehicle theft	25	32	35	23	22	27
Arson	81	39	35	38	32	37
Prostitution and commercialized vice	6	13	5	3	6	13
Other sex offenses	10	9	14	10	13	9
Narcotic drug laws	589	597	474	397	375	386
Gambling	12	2	7	8	7	7
Suspected felony type	60	45	68	62	137	122
Other than felony type [1]	6,871	7,096	6,485	6,056	6,320	5,782
Romantic triangle	122	118	90	88	98	69
Child killed by babysitter	30	26	36	38	26	30
Brawl due to influence of alcohol	188	123	122	113	84	93
Brawl due to influence of narcotics	99	97	60	121	65	59
Argument over money or property	206	210	187	156	152	133
Other arguments	3,589	3,718	3,280	3,163	3,147	2,889
Gangland killings	65	96	181	149	152	138
Juvenile gang killings	653	756	675	526	722	584
Institutional killings	10	12	17	22	13	15
Unknown	4,070	5,635	4,637	4,835	4,589	4,440
TYPE OF WEAPON OR CAUSE OF DEATH [1]						
Total firearms	8,661	10,158	8,874	8,653	8,897	8,454
Handguns	6,778	7,565	6,115	6,251	6,404	5,782
Rifles	411	445	367	332	298	285
Shotguns	485	522	366	362	310	308
Other guns	53	138	93	97	116	123
Firearms, type not stated	934	1,488	1,933	1,611	1,769	1,956
Knives or cutting instruments	1,782	1,920	1,732	1,716	1,604	1,490
Blunt objects (club, hammer, etc.)	617	608	549	502	522	428
Personal weapons (hands, fists, feet, pushed, etc.)	927	905	769	751	707	687
Fire	134	125	78	76	87	94
Narcotics	20	46	45	33	38	53
Drowning	15	20	10	15	14	4
Strangulation	166	118	122	88	90	85
Asphyxiation	92	96	98	92	106	95

[1] Includes items not shown separately. [2] Rape figures in this table are an aggregate total of data submitted using both the revised and legacy UCR definitions.

Source: U.S. Department of Justice, Federal Bureau of Investigation, "Crime in the United States 2013" and earlier releases, <http://www.fbi.gov/about-us/cjis/ucr>, accessed December 2014.

Table 334. Murder Victims by Age, Sex, and Race/Ethnicity: 2013

[See headnote, Table 333]

Age	Total	Sex [1]		Race [1]			Ethnicity [1,2]	
		Male	Female	White	Black	Other [3]	Hispanic or Latino	Not Hispanic or Latino
Murders, total	**12,253**	**9,523**	**2,707**	**5,537**	**6,261**	**308**	**1,729**	**6,147**
Percent of total [4]	100.0	77.7	22.1	45.2	51.1	2.5	18.1	64.4
Under 18 years old [1]	1,027	715	308	492	482	31	140	519
18 years old and over [1]	11,101	8,728	2,368	4,986	5,738	277	1,577	5,588
Infant (under 1 year old)	162	96	64	110	44	4	19	105
1 to 4 years old	251	148	102	118	113	11	26	131
5 to 8 years old	78	39	39	46	26	4	8	40
9 to 12 years old	68	42	26	35	25	5	5	32
13 to 16 years old	247	194	52	105	134	5	41	113
17 to 19 years old	911	803	107	287	602	13	163	400
20 to 24 years old	2,249	1,923	324	756	1,438	39	371	1,056
25 to 29 years old	1,746	1,468	278	617	1,065	51	230	746
30 to 34 years old	1,497	1,213	283	618	840	32	193	757
35 to 39 years old	1,101	850	251	489	564	36	170	554
40 to 44 years old	826	618	208	413	377	25	216	421
45 to 49 years old	803	570	233	436	340	17	94	433
50 to 54 years old	689	506	183	409	258	20	74	398
55 to 59 years old	543	384	159	335	186	17	53	322
60 to 64 years old	340	233	107	233	89	14	25	207
65 to 69 years old	214	144	70	163	42	5	12	136
70 to 74 years old	140	86	54	102	30	6	7	83
75 years old and over	263	126	136	206	47	4	10	173
Age unknown	125	80	31	59	41	–	12	40

– Represents zero. [1] Does not include unknown victim categories. [2] Not all agencies provide ethnicity data; therefore, data will not sum to total. [3] Includes American Indian or Alaska Native, Asian, and Native Hawaiian or Pacific Islander. [4] Percentages rounded, may not add to 100.

Source: U.S. Department of Justice, Federal Bureau of Investigation, "Crime in the United States 2013," <http://www.fbi.gov/about-us/cjis/ucr>, accessed December 2014.

Table 335. Homicide Trends: 1990 to 2013

[Based on Federal Bureau of Investigation's Uniform Crime Reports Supplementary Homicide Reports. Homicide includes murder and nonnegligent manslaughter, which is the willful killing of one human being by another. Excludes deaths caused by negligence, suicide, or accident; justifiable homicides; and attempts to murder. Justifiable homicides based on the reports of law enforcement agencies are analyzed separately. Deaths from the terrorist attacks of September 11, 2001 are not included. Data based on criminal homicides handled by state and local law enforcement, and as determined solely by police investigation, and not by the determination of a court, medical examiner, coroner, jury, or other non-law enforcement body. Excludes homicides handled by Federal law enforcement]

| Year | Number of victims | | | | | | | Rate [1] | | | | | | |
	Total [2]	Male	Female	White	Black	American Indian/ Alaskan Native	Asian [3]	Total [2]	Male	Female	White	Black	American Indian/ Alaskan Native	Asian [3]
1990...	23,438	18,303	5,115	11,278	11,487	150	250	9.4	15.0	4.0	5.4	37.5	7.3	3.3
1995...	21,606	16,549	5,021	10,374	10,442	160	421	8.1	12.7	3.7	4.7	30.9	6.6	4.4
1996...	19,645	15,149	4,468	9,480	9,473	134	377	7.3	11.5	3.2	4.3	27.5	5.3	3.8
1997...	18,208	14,055	4,124	8,619	8,841	149	375	6.7	10.5	3.0	3.8	25.3	5.7	3.6
1998...	16,974	12,756	4,140	8,391	7,933	141	252	6.2	9.4	2.9	3.7	22.3	5.2	2.3
1999...	15,522	11,704	3,800	7,777	7,139	160	298	5.6	8.6	2.7	3.4	19.7	5.6	2.6
2000...	15,586	11,818	3,733	7,560	7,425	119	280	5.5	8.5	2.6	3.3	20.2	4.0	2.4
2001...	16,037	12,232	3,775	7,884	7,522	105	319	5.6	8.7	2.6	3.4	20.2	3.4	2.6
2002...	16,229	12,429	3,770	7,796	7,770	130	308	5.6	8.8	2.6	3.3	20.6	4.1	2.4
2003...	16,528	12,792	3,707	7,944	7,883	117	351	5.7	9.0	2.5	3.4	20.6	3.5	2.6
2004...	16,148	12,553	3,555	7,939	7,570	134	282	5.5	8.7	2.4	3.4	19.5	3.9	2.0
2005...	16,740	13,149	3,565	8,045	8,016	131	312	5.7	9.1	2.4	3.4	20.4	3.7	2.2
2006...	17,309	13,605	3,661	8,063	8,548	123	343	5.8	9.3	2.4	3.4	21.4	3.3	2.3
2007...	17,128	13,411	3,678	8,017	8,450	104	302	5.7	9.1	2.4	3.3	20.9	2.7	1.9
2008...	16,465	12,844	3,573	7,953	7,860	124	250	5.4	8.6	2.3	3.3	19.1	3.1	1.6
2009...	15,399	11,846	3,535	7,450	7,374	119	290	5.0	7.9	2.3	3.0	17.7	2.9	1.7
2010...	14,722	11,371	3,328	6,851	7,322	117	260	4.8	7.5	2.1	2.8	17.4	2.7	1.5
2011...	14,661	11,354	3,281	6,786	7,277	111	284	4.7	7.4	2.1	2.7	17.0	2.6	1.6
2012...	14,856	11,534	3,302	6,812	7,502	101	285	4.7	7.5	2.1	2.7	17.4	2.3	1.6
2013...	14,196	11,020	3,151	6,463	7,205	103	255	4.5	7.1	2.0	2.6	16.5	2.3	1.4

[1] Rate is per 100,000 inhabitants. [2] Includes unknown sex, race, or ethnicity. [3] Includes Native Hawaiian and Pacific Islanders.

Source: U.S. Department of Justice, Office of Justice Programs, "Easy Access to the FBI's Supplementary Homicide Reports (EZASHR)," <http://www.ojjdp.gov/ojstatbb/ezashr/>; and U.S. Centers for Disease Control and Prevention's WONDER Online Databases, <http://wonder.cdc.gov/>; accessed July 2015.

Table 336. Homicide Victims by Race and Sex: 1990 to 2013

[Excludes deaths to nonresidents of United States. Effective with data for 1999, causes of death are classified by the International Classification of Diseases, Tenth Revision (ICD-10), replacing the Ninth Revision (ICD-9) used for 1979–98 data. In ICD-9, the category Homicide also includes death as a result of legal intervention. ICD-10 differentiates between homicides due to assault and deaths due to legal intervention. Some caution should be used in comparing data. See text, Section 2]

| Year | Homicide victims | | | | | Homicide rate [2] | | | | |
| | Total [1] | White | | Black | | Total [1] | White | | Black | |
		Male	Female	Male	Female		Male	Female	Male	Female
1990............	24,932	9,147	3,006	9,981	2,163	10.0	9.0	2.8	69.2	13.5
1995............	22,895	8,336	3,028	8,847	1,936	8.7	7.8	2.7	56.3	11.1
2000............	16,765	5,925	2,414	6,482	1,385	6.0	5.2	2.1	37.2	7.2
2001............	20,308	8,254	3,074	6,780	1,446	7.1	7.2	2.6	38.2	7.4
2002............	17,638	6,282	2,403	6,896	1,391	6.1	5.4	2.0	38.4	7.0
2003............	17,732	6,337	2,372	7,083	1,309	6.1	5.5	2.0	38.9	6.5
2004............	17,357	6,302	2,341	6,839	1,296	5.9	5.4	2.0	37.0	6.4
2005............	18,124	6,457	2,313	7,412	1,257	6.1	5.5	1.9	39.6	6.1
2006............	18,573	6,514	2,346	7,677	1,355	6.2	5.5	1.9	40.4	6.5
2007............	18,361	6,541	2,373	7,584	1,286	6.1	5.5	1.9	39.3	6.1
2008............	17,826	6,556	2,337	7,148	1,187	5.9	5.5	1.9	36.5	5.5
2009............	16,799	5,983	2,340	6,715	1,159	5.5	4.9	1.9	33.8	5.3
2010............	16,259	5,648	2,215	6,704	1,114	5.3	4.7	1.8	33.4	5.1
2011............	16,238	5,569	2,199	6,739	1,119	5.2	4.6	1.8	33.0	5.0
2012............	16,688	5,639	2,197	7,129	1,112	5.3	4.6	1.8	34.5	4.9
2013............	16,121	5,393	2,130	6,937	1,122	5.1	4.4	1.7	33.1	4.9

[1] Includes races not shown separately. [2] Rates per 100,000 resident population in specified group. Based on enumerated population figures as of April 1 for 1990, 2000, and 2010; estimated resident population as of July 1 for other years.

Source: U.S. National Center for Health Statistics, CDC WONDER Online Database, "Multiple Cause of Death 1999-2013," <http://wonder.cdc.gov/>; and National Vital Statistics Reports (NVSR), *Deaths: Final Data for 2013*, Vol. 64, No. 2, and earlier reports.

Table 337. Criminal Victimizations and Victimization Rates: 2010 to 2013

[20,486 represents 20,486,000. A victimization refers to a single victim or household that experienced a criminal incident. Criminal incidents or crimes are distinguished from victimizations in that one criminal incident may have multiple victims or victimizations. Based on the National Crime Victimization Survey (NCVS). See source for more information]

Type of crime	Number of victimizations (1,000)				Victimization rates [1]			
	2010	2011	2012	2013	2010	2011	2012	2013
Total........	20,486	23,041	26,619	23,041	(X)	(X)	(X)	(X)
Violent victimization [2]........	4,936	5,813	6,843	6,126	19.3	22.6	26.1	23.2
Not Injured........	3,646	4,362	5,269	4,522	14.2	16.9	20.1	17.1
Injured........	1,290	1,451	1,573	1,604	5.0	5.6	6.0	6.1
Serious violent victimization [3]........	1,695	1,855	2,085	1,940	6.6	7.2	8.0	7.3
Rape/sexual assault........	269	244	347	300	1.0	0.9	1.3	1.1
Robbery........	569	557	742	646	2.2	2.2	2.8	2.4
Not Injured........	370	422	459	394	1.4	1.6	1.8	1.5
Injured........	198	135	283	252	0.8	0.5	1.1	1.0
Aggravated assault........	858	1,053	996	994	3.4	4.1	3.8	3.8
Not Injured........	538	625	662	660	2.1	2.4	2.5	2.5
Injured........	320	429	334	335	1.2	1.7	1.3	1.3
Simple assault........	3,241	3,958	4,758	4,186	12.7	15.4	18.2	15.8
Not Injured........	2,619	3,197	3,947	3,322	10.2	12.4	15.1	12.6
Injured........	622	761	811	865	2.4	3.0	3.1	3.3
Personal theft/larceny [4]........	138	166	154	141	0.5	0.6	0.6	0.5
Property crimes........	15,412	17,063	19,623	16,774	125.4	138.7	155.8	131.4
Household burglary........	3,176	3,614	3,765	3,286	25.8	29.4	29.9	25.7
Motor vehicle theft........	607	628	634	661	4.9	5.1	5.0	5.2
Theft [5]........	11,628	12,821	15,225	12,827	94.6	104.2	120.9	100.5

X Not applicable. [1] Per 1,000 persons age 12 or older for "Personal crime"; per 1,000 households for "Property crime." [2] Excludes homicide because the NCVS is based on interviews with victims and therefore cannot measure murder. [3] Includes rape, sexual assault, personal robbery, and aggravated assault, attempted and completed crimes. [4] Includes pocket picking, completed purse snatching, and attempted purse snatching. [5] The taking or attempted unlawful taking of property or cash without personal contact with the victim. Incidents involving theft of property from within a household are classified as theft if the offender has a legal right to be in the house (such as a maid, delivery person, or guest).

Source: U.S. Department of Justice, Bureau of Justice Statistics, "NCVS Victimization Analysis Tool," <http://www.bjs.gov/index.cfm?ty=nvat>, accessed July 2015.

Table 338. Victimization Rates by Type of Crime and Characteristics of the Victim: 2013

[Rate per 1,000 persons age 12 years or older. Based on the National Crime Victimization Survey. See text, this section and Appendix III]

Characteristic of the victim	Violent victimization						Personal theft [1]
	Total	Serious violent victim-ization	Rape/ sexual assault	Robbery	Aggravated assault	Simple assault	
Total........	23.2	7.3	1.1	2.4	3.8	15.8	0.5
Male........	23.7	7.7	0.3	2.7	4.7	16.0	0.5
Female........	22.7	7.0	2.0	2.2	2.9	15.7	0.5
12 to 14 years old........	65.1	12.9	[2] 0.6	[2] 5.5	6.8	52.2	[2] 0.4
15 to 17 years old........	39.2	8.6	[2] 1.5	[2] 3.3	[2] 3.9	30.6	[2] 1.5
18 to 20 years old........	35.9	12.5	3.6	[2] 3.1	5.9	23.4	[2] 1.3
21 to 24 years old........	32.2	9.4	[2] 1.2	4.1	4.0	22.8	[2] 0.8
25 to 34 years old........	29.6	10.2	1.4	3.5	5.2	19.4	[2] 0.6
35 to 49 years old........	20.3	7.1	1.0	2.1	4.1	13.1	[2] 0.4
50 to 64 years old........	18.7	6.9	1.3	2.1	3.6	11.8	[2] 0.2
65 years old and over........	3.1	1.1	[2] 0.1	[2] 0.4	[2] 0.5	2.1	[2] 0.5
White........	22.7	6.9	1.1	2.3	3.5	15.9	0.4
Black........	25.2	9.7	[2] 0.7	2.8	6.2	15.6	[2] 1.3
American Indian/Alaskan Native........	47.6	[2] 31.9	[2] 3.1	[2] 25.0	[2] 3.9	15.7	[2] 1.3
Asian/Native Hawaiian/ Other Pacific Islander........	6.8	[2] 1.5	(Z)	[2] 1.1	[2] 0.4	5.3	[2] 0.5
Two or more races........	74.1	22.4	[2] 7.5	[2] 4.3	10.6	51.7	[2] 0.5
Hispanic........	24.8	7.5	[2] 0.7	3.2	3.7	17.3	[2] 0.7
Non-Hispanic White........	22.2	6.7	1.2	2.0	3.5	15.5	0.4
Non-Hispanic Black........	25.1	9.5	[2] 0.7	2.7	6.0	15.7	[2] 1.4
Household income:							
Less than $7,500........	84.0	28.4	[2] 3.3	10.0	15.2	55.6	[2] 1.0
$7,500 to $14,999........	62.3	19.8	[2] 2.2	7.5	10.1	42.5	[2] 1.7
$15,000 to $24,999........	31.8	12.5	2.3	4.6	5.6	19.3	[2] 0.2
$25,000 to $34,999........	21.6	7.5	[2] 1.3	1.7	4.4	14.1	[2] 0.7
$35,000 to $49,999........	22.8	7.4	[2] 1.9	2.8	2.7	15.3	[2] 0.3
$50,000 to $74,999........	17.8	4.6	[2] 1.5	1.4	1.7	13.3	[2] 0.2
$75,000 or more........	14.4	2.6	[2] 0.1	0.6	1.9	11.8	[2] 0.3
Unknown........	18.2	6.8	0.8	2.3	3.7	11.4	0.8

Z Rounds to less than 0.05 victimizations per 1,000 persons. [1] Includes pocket picking, completed purse snatching, and attempted purse snatching. [2] Based on 10 or fewer sample cases.

Source: U.S. Department of Justice, Bureau of Justice Statistics, "NCVS Victimization Analysis Tool," <http://www.bjs.gov/index.cfm?ty=nvat>, accessed August 2015.

Table 339. Criminal Victimizations by Age of Victim and Selected Characteristics: 2003 to 2013

[In percent, unless otherwise noted. Covers period 2003 to 2013. Data are for violent victimizations that are nonfatal. Based on the National Crime Victimization Survey. For details, see source <http://www.bjs.gov/index.cfm?ty=dcdetail&iid=245>]

Item	Age			
	12–24 years old	25–49 years old	50–64 years old	Aged 65 years or older
VIOLENT VICTIMIZATIONS				
Average annual (number)	2,709,260	2,899,310	834,510	136,720
Rate per 1,000 households	49.9	27.6	15.2	3.6
By type of weapon:				
Total	100.0	100.0	100.0	100.0
No weapon used	72.6	70.2	69.9	69.3
Weapon used	21.5	22.4	21.0	19.5
Firearm	6.2	7.7	7.0	7.6
Knife	6.4	5.9	5.6	4.3
Other	7.2	7.1	6.9	6.2
Type unknown	1.6	1.7	1.5	[5] 1.4
Don't know	5.9	7.5	9.0	11.1
By victim-offender relationship:				
Total	100.0	100.0	100.0	100.0
Known to victim	57.2	50.6	52.1	48.8
Domestic	16.4	26.0	19.9	14.3
Intimate partner [1]	9.9	20.4	9.6	6.1
Immediate family	4.2	3.5	7.3	4.6
Other relative	2.2	2.1	3.0	3.6
Well-known/casual acquaintance	40.8	24.6	32.3	34.5
Stranger	34.0	41.2	39.8	43.4
Unknown [2]	8.8	8.1	8.1	7.8
By location of crime:				
Total	100.0	100.0	100.0	100.0
At or near victim's home	25.4	41.1	43.5	59.3
At or near friend, neighbor, or relative's home	11.3	5.9	5.5	6.0
Other location [3]	63.3	53.1	51.0	34.7
PROPERTY VICTIMIZATIONS [4]				
Average annual (number)	2,031,930	9,924,460	4,307,210	1,796,740
Rate per 1,000 households	262.0	177.1	134.6	72.3

[1] Includes current or former spouses, boyfriends, and girlfriends. [2] Includes unknown victim–offender relationships and unknown number of offenders. [3] Includes commercial places, parking lots or garages, schools, open areas, public transportation, and other locations. [4] Data by age of householder. [5] Interpret with caution.

Source: U.S. Department of Justice, Bureau of Justice Statistics, *Crimes Against the Elderly, 2003–2013*, NCJ 243339, November 2014. See also <http://www.bjs.gov/index.cfm?ty=pbse&sid=21>.

Table 340. Rape and Sexual Assault Rates Among College-Age Females: 1998 to 2013

[Estimated victimization rates per 1,000 females, based on 3-year rolling averages centered on the most recent year. Data from the National Crime Victimization Survey]

Year	Students 18 to 24 years old [1]	Nonstudents 18 to 24 years old [2]	Not college-age females [3]	Year	Students 18 to 24 years old [1]	Nonstudents 18 to 24 years old [2]	Not college-age females [3]
1998	7.8	8.9	3.1	2006	5.4	5.5	1.7
1999	6.0	11.2	3.5	2007	5.5	5.4	1.7
2000	7.1	12.2	2.8	2008	5.2	6.7	1.9
2001	8.8	11.2	3.0	2009	3.7	8.3	1.6
2002	8.9	10.0	2.2	2010	[4] 4.1	8.4	1.6
2003	7.6	8.8	2.2	2011	4.6	7.1	1.4
2004	6.5	7.0	1.8	2012	5.9	4.1	1.3
2005	4.7	5.6	1.6	2013	4.4	4.3	1.4

[1] Includes female victims age 18 to 24 enrolled part time or full time in a post-secondary institution (i.e., college or university, trade school, or vocational school). [2] Includes female victims age 18 to 24 not enrolled in a post-secondary institution. [3] Includes females age 12 to 17 and age 25 or older. [4] Interpret with caution, subject to sampling error.

Source: U.S. Bureau of Justice Statistics, *Rape and Sexual Assault Victimization Among College-Age Females, 1995–2013*, NCJ 248471, December 2014. See also <http://www.bjs.gov/index.cfm?ty=tp&tid=317>.

Table 341. Violent Crime Between Intimate Partners by Sex of Victims: 1994 to 2011

[Intimate partners are defined as current and former spouses, boyfriends, and girlfriends. Estimates based on 2-year rolling averages beginning in 1993. Based on the National Crime Victimization Survey (NCVS); see text this section, and Source]

Year and type of crime	Female victims				Male victims			
	Total intimate partner violence	Rate per 1,000 [1]			Total intimate partner violence	Rate per 1,000 [1]		
		Overall intimate partner violence	Serious violence [3]	Simple assault [4]		Overall intimate partner violence	Serious violence [3]	Simple assault [4]
1994............	1,766,700	16.1	5.9	10.3	303,460	3.0	1.1	1.9
1995............	1,785,590	16.1	4.9	11.3	272,450	2.6	0.8	1.8
1996............	1,676,990	15.0	4.2	10.8	240,280	2.3	0.9	1.4
1997............	1,644,100	14.6	4.8	9.8	185,650	1.8	0.6	1.1
1998............	1,499,130	13.2	4.2	8.9	202,720	1.9	0.6	1.3
1999............	1,250,570	10.9	3.6	7.3	229,510	2.1	0.6	1.6
2000............	974,160	8.4	2.7	5.7	173,190	1.6	0.3	1.3
2001............	882,720	7.5	2.4	5.1	112,450	1.0	0.3	0.7
2002............	889,740	7.5	2.5	5.0	120,350	1.1	0.5	0.6
2003............	852,220	7.0	2.8	4.2	132,810	1.2	0.5	0.7
2004............	861,380	7.0	2.9	4.0	174,620	1.5	0.5	1.0
2005............	718,590	5.8	1.9	3.8	205,270	1.7	0.7	1.0
2006 [2].........	842,410	6.7	2.4	4.3	218,220	1.8	1.0	0.8
2007 [2].........	922,380	7.2	2.6	4.6	183,150	1.5	0.7	0.8
2008............	847,700	6.6	2.3	4.3	156,900	1.3	0.5	0.8
2009............	914,480	7.1	2.0	5.0	157,050	1.3	0.5	0.8
2010............	775,650	5.9	1.6	4.3	130,890	1.1	0.4	0.7
2011............	620,850	4.7	1.6	3.1	191,540	1.5	0.4	1.1

[1] Rates are per 1,000 persons age 12 and older. [2] Due to methodological changes, use caution when comparing 2006 NCVS criminal victimization estimates to other years. [3] Rape or sexual assault, robbery, and aggravated assault. [4] Attack or attempted attack without a weapon that results in no injury, minor injury, or an undetermined injury requiring less than two days of hospitalization.

Source: U.S. Department of Justice, Bureau of Justice Statistics, *Intimate Partner Victimization: Attributes of Victimization, 1993-2011*, NCJ 243300, November 2013. See also <http://bjs.ojp.usdoj.gov/index.cfm?ty=pbdetail&iid=78>.

Table 342. Fraud and Identity Theft—Consumer Complaints by State: 2014

[Rate per 100,000 population. As of December 31. Rates based on U.S. Census Bureau's 2014 population estimates. The Consumer Sentinel Network is a secure online database of consumer complaints available only to law enforcement. Based on unverified complaints reported by consumers. Excludes complaints outside of the U.S. and from the Hawaii Office of Consumer Protection; the Montana, North Carolina and Oregon Departments of Justice; the South Carolina Department of Consumer Affairs; the Tennessee Division of Consumer Affairs; and the Offices of the Attorney General for Alaska, California, Colorado, Idaho, Indiana, Iowa, Louisiana, Maine, Massachusetts, Michigan, Mississippi, Nevada, Ohio, and Washington]

State	Fraud and other complaints		Identity theft victims		State	Fraud and other complaints		Identity theft victims	
	Number	Rate	Number	Rate		Number	Rate	Number	Rate
U.S.......	1,883,553	590.7	296,834	93.1	MO.......	31,304	516.3	7,195	118.7
AL........	27,847	574.2	3,770	77.7	MT.......	4,550	444.5	585	57.2
AK........	3,011	408.7	542	73.6	NE.......	7,807	414.9	914	48.6
AZ........	37,836	562.1	6,460	96.0	NV.......	21,952	773.2	2,846	100.2
AR........	13,800	465.2	2,481	83.6	NH.......	7,464	562.6	726	54.7
CA........	250,138	644.6	38,982	100.5	NJ.......	53,535	598.9	7,144	79.9
CO........	32,060	598.6	4,579	85.5	NM.......	10,556	506.1	1,611	77.2
CT........	18,312	509.1	3,071	85.4	NY.......	101,497	514.0	15,959	80.8
DE........	7,197	769.2	731	78.1	NC.......	50,504	507.9	7,334	73.8
DC........	6,605	1,002.4	941	142.8	ND.......	2,473	334.4	319	43.1
FL........	200,392	1,007.3	37,059	186.3	OH.......	58,704	506.3	9,161	79.0
GA........	78,526	777.7	11,384	112.7	OK.......	16,926	436.5	2,656	68.5
HI........	5,957	419.6	580	40.9	OR.......	20,069	505.5	4,946	124.6
ID........	7,466	456.8	962	58.9	PA.......	69,655	544.7	10,446	81.7
IL........	61,038	473.9	12,317	95.6	RI.......	6,219	589.4	699	66.2
IN........	30,656	464.7	4,498	68.2	SC.......	25,816	534.2	3,540	73.3
IA........	11,354	365.4	1,506	48.5	SD.......	2,974	348.6	310	36.3
KS........	12,569	432.8	1,892	65.2	TN.......	37,347	570.2	4,993	76.2
KY........	19,907	451.1	2,358	53.4	TX.......	174,468	647.2	25,843	95.9
LA........	25,059	538.9	3,430	73.8	UT.......	11,471	389.8	1,586	53.9
ME........	5,909	444.3	693	52.1	VT.......	2,442	389.7	402	64.2
MD........	40,369	675.5	5,734	95.9	VA.......	49,537	594.9	5,921	71.1
MA........	37,422	554.5	5,116	75.8	WA.......	36,127	511.6	10,930	154.8
MI........	74,244	749.2	10,338	104.3	WV.......	8,634	466.6	1,136	61.4
MN........	23,083	423.0	3,229	59.2	WI.......	24,321	422.4	4,283	74.4
MS........	13,276	443.4	2,409	80.5	WY.......	2,968	508.1	287	49.1

Source: U.S. Federal Trade Commission, *Consumer Sentinel Network Data Book for January–December 2014*, February 2015. See also <http://www.ftc.gov/sentinel/reports.shtml>.

Table 343. Stalking and Harassment Victimization in the United States: 2006

[Survey based on a total population 220,995,170, age 18 or older. The survey defines stalking as a course of conduct directed at a specific person that would cause a reasonable person to feel fear. The survey characterizes individuals as victims of harassment who experience the behaviors associated with stalking but neither reported feeling fear as a result of such conduct nor experienced actions that would cause a reasonable person to feel fear]

Characteristic	Total population	Victims as percent of persons age 18 or older		
		All	Stalking	Harassment
Overall..............................	220,995,170	2.4	1.5	0.9
SEX				
Male................................	107,014,170	1.6	0.8	0.9
Female.............................	113,981,000	3.1	2.2	1.0
AGE				
18 to 19 years old................	8,053,370	4.5	2.9	1.6
20 to 24 years old................	20,348,250	4.4	2.8	1.6
25 to 34 years old................	39,760,010	2.9	2.0	0.9
35 to 49 years old................	65,878,490	2.7	1.7	1.0
50 to 64 years old................	51,483,100	1.7	1.0	0.7
65 years old and over............	35,471,950	0.8	0.3	0.4
RACE AND ETHNICITY				
White..............................	181,858,650	2.4	1.5	0.9
Black..............................	25,672,890	2.4	1.4	1.1
American Indian/ Alaska Native.....................	1,483,760	3.8	[1] 2.2	[1] 1.5
Asian/Pacific Islander............	9,837,830	1.3	0.6	0.6
More than one race...............	2,142,040	6.3	4.1	2.3
Hispanic origin				
Hispanic...........................	23,440,950	1.9	1.3	0.6
Non-Hispanic......................	195,655,390	2.5	1.5	0.9
Unknown...........................	1,898,830	2.8	[1] 1.2	[1] 1.6
MARITAL STATUS				
Never married.....................	54,100,740	3.8	2.4	1.4
Married............................	124,145,550	1.4	0.8	0.6
Divorced or separated............	26,704,680	4.8	3.3	1.5
Widowed...........................	14,179,710	1.4	0.7	0.7
Unknown...........................	1,864,500	1.9	[1] 1.5	[1] 0.4
HOUSEHOLD INCOME				
Less than $7,500.................	7,702,700	4.8	3.3	1.5
$7,500 to $14,999................	13,236,960	4.2	2.9	1.3
$15,000 to $24,999..............	20,221,710	3.2	2.2	1.0
$25,000 to $34,999..............	20,373,140	2.9	1.7	1.1
$35,000 to $49,999..............	27,910,030	2.5	1.7	0.8
$50,000 to $74,999..............	34,011,190	2.3	1.4	0.9
$75,000 or more..................	50,709,700	1.8	1.0	0.8
Unknown...........................	46,829,750	1.6	0.9	0.7

[1] Interpret data with caution; estimate based on 10 or fewer sample cases, or the coefficient of variation is greater than 50%.

Source: U.S. Department of Justice, Bureau of Justice Statistics, National Crime Victimization Survey, Supplemental Victimization Survey, *Stalking Victims in the United States—Revised*, NCJ 224527, September 2012. See also <http://bjs.ojp.usdoj.gov/index.cfm?ty=pbdetail&iid=1211>.

Table 344. Property Crime by Selected Household Characteristics: 2013

[127,622 represents 127,622,000. For crimes against households (burglary, theft, and motor vehicle theft), each household affected by a crime is counted as a single victimization. Based on National Crime Victimization Survey (NCVS); see text, this section and Appendix III]

Characteristic	Number of house-holds (1,000)	Property crimes							
		Number of victimizations (1,000)				Victimization rate per 1,000 households			
		Total	Burglary	Motor vehicle theft	Theft	Total	Burglary	Motor vehicle theft	Theft
Total..................	127,622	16,774	3,286	661	12,827	131.4	25.7	5.2	100.5
Race:									
White...................	102,296	12,931	2,462	479	9,991	126.4	24.1	4.7	97.7
Black...................	16,947	2,520	593	124	1,803	148.7	35.0	7.3	106.4
Other...................	6,715	887	153	48	686	132.1	22.9	7.1	102.2
Two or more races.....	1,665	435	78	[1] 10	347	261.5	47.0	[1] 6.1	208.4
Ethnicity:									
Hispanic................	15,953	2,658	544	149	1,965	166.6	34.1	9.4	123.2
Non-Hispanic...........	111,480	14,106	2,743	512	10,851	126.5	24.6	4.6	97.3
Household income:									
Less than $7,500......	4,681	1,081	259	30	791	230.9	55.4	6.4	169.1
$7,500 to $14,999.....	7,630	1,463	352	55	1,055	191.7	46.1	7.3	138.3
$15,000 to $24,999....	10,285	1,518	356	58	1,104	147.6	34.6	5.6	107.3
$25,000 to $34,999....	11,589	1,915	360	107	1,449	165.3	31	9.2	125.0
$35,000 to $49,999....	14,141	1,755	281	43	1,431	124.1	19.8	3.1	101.2
$50,000 to $74,999....	15,345	1,951	369	80	1,501	127.1	24.1	5.2	97.8
$75,000 or more.......	25,827	3,135	415	107	2,613	121.4	16.1	4.1	101.2
Unknown................	38,125	3,957	894	181	2,882	103.8	23.5	4.7	75.6
Number of persons in household:									
1.......................	38,094	3,960	1,124	140	2,696	104.0	29.5	3.7	70.8
2 or 3..................	63,980	7,791	1,368	290	6,132	121.8	21.4	4.5	95.8
4 or 5..................	21,896	4,064	600	180	3,284	185.6	27.4	8.2	150.0
6 or more..............	3,653	959	194	51	714	262.6	53.0	14.0	195.6

[1] Based on 10 or fewer sample cases or the coefficient of variation is greater than 50%.

Source: U.S. Department of Justice, Bureau of Justice Statistics, "NCVS Victimization Analysis Tool," <http://www.bjs.gov/index.cfm?ty=nvat>, accessed September 2015.

Table 345. Robbery and Property Crimes by Type and Average Value Lost: 1990 to 2009

[639 represents 639,000. For year ending December 31]

Characteristic of offense	Number of offenses (1,000)				Rate per 100,000 population				Average value lost (dol.)			
	1990	2000	2005	2009	1990	2000	2005	2009	1990	2000	2005	2009
Robbery, total [1]	**639**	**408**	**417**	**342**	**256.3**	**144.9**	**140.7**	**125.1**	**631**	**1,127**	**1,239**	**1,246**
Type of crime:												
Street or highway	359	188	184	146	144.2	66.7	62.1	53.5	511	858	1,020	865
Commercial house	73	57	60	46	29.5	20.1	20.1	16.9	945	1,685	1,662	1,774
Gas station	18	12	12	8	7.1	4.1	4.0	3.0	423	679	1,104	862
Convenience store	39	26	24	18	15.6	9.3	8.0	6.7	344	566	677	717
Residence	62	50	59	58	25.1	17.7	20.0	21.1	828	1,243	1,332	1,674
Bank	9	9	9	7	3.8	3.1	3.0	2.7	2,885	4,379	4,113	4,202
Weapon used:												
Firearm	234	161	175	131	94.1	57.0	59.0	55.3	(NA)	(NA)	(NA)	(NA)
Knife or cutting instrument	76	36	37	24	30.7	12.8	12.5	9.9	(NA)	(NA)	(NA)	(NA)
Other weapon	61	53	39	27	24.5	18.9	13.2	11.3	(NA)	(NA)	(NA)	(NA)
Strong-arm	268	159	166	126	107.7	56.4	56.0	53.3	(NA)	(NA)	(NA)	(NA)
Burglary, total	**3,074**	**2,050**	**2,154**	**1,955**	**1,232.2**	**728.4**	**726.7**	**715.7**	**1,014**	**1,458**	**1,771**	**2,087**
Forcible entry [2]	2,150	1,297	1,310	1,224	864.5	460.7	440.0	448.1	(NA)	(NA)	(NA)	(NA)
Unlawful entry [2]	678	615	701	655	272.8	218.7	237.5	239.7	(NA)	(NA)	(NA)	(NA)
Attempted forcible entry [2]	245	138	133	129	98.7	49.0	45.2	47.4	(NA)	(NA)	(NA)	(NA)
Residence	2,033	1,335	1,417	1,127	817.4	474.3	477.9	412.9	1,037	1,378	1,813	2,709
Nonresidence	1,041	715	738	407	418.5	254.1	248.8	148.8	967	1,610	1,687	2,521
Occurred during the night [2]	1,135	699	708	625	456.4	248.3	238.9	229.0	(NA)	(NA)	(NA)	(NA)
Occurred during the day [2]	1,151	836	890	910	462.8	297.2	328.8	332.8	(NA)	(NA)	(NA)	(NA)
Larceny-theft, total	**7,946**	**6,972**	**6,783**	**5,560**	**3,185.1**	**2,477.3**	**2,286.3**	**2,035.1**	**426**	**727**	**857**	**865**
Pocket picking	81	36	29	24	32.4	12.7	9.8	8.8	384	437	346	489
Purse snatching	82	37	42	27	32.8	13.2	14.2	9.8	228	387	404	440
Shoplifting	1,291	959	940	1,002	519.1	340.7	317.0	366.9	104	185	184	178
From motor vehicles	1,744	1,754	1,752	1,520	701.3	623.3	590.6	556.5	461	692	704	737
Motor vehicle accessories	1,185	677	693	501	476.3	240.6	233.6	183.2	297	451	482	528
Bicycles	443	312	249	187	178.2	110.9	83.9	67.6	188	273	267	345
From buildings	1,118	914	852	620	449.4	324.6	287.3	226.8	673	1,184	1,738	1,233
From coin-operated machines	63	46	41	22	25.4	16.2	13.8	8.1	144	272	232	348
Other	1,940	2,232	2,184	1,660	780.0	793.0	736.1	607.5	615	957	1,137	1,439
Motor vehicles, total [3]	**1,636**	**1,160**	**1,236**	**731**	**655.8**	**412.2**	**417.4**	**258.6**	**5,117**	**6,581**	**6,204**	**6,495**
Automobiles	1,304	877	907	527	524.3	311.5	304.5	193.0	(NA)	(NA)	(NA)	(NA)
Trucks and buses	238	209	219	205	95.5	74.1	76.2	74.9	(NA)	(NA)	(NA)	(NA)

NA Not available. [1] Includes other crimes, not shown separately. [2] Unknown data not included. [3] Includes other types of motor vehicles, not shown separately.

Source: U.S. Department of Justice, Federal Bureau of Investigation, Uniform Crime Reports, Return A and Supplement to Return A Master Files, unpublished.

Table 346. Hate Crimes—Number of Incidents, Offenses, Victims, and Known Offenders by Bias Motivation: 2000 to 2013

[1,826 law enforcement agencies submitted data on hate crimes. 15,016 law enforcement agencies covering over 295 million people participated in the Hate Crime Statistics Program in 2013. Hate crime offenses cover incidents motivated by race, religion, sexual orientation, ethnicity/national origin, and disability. See source and Appendix III]

Bias motivation	Incidents reported	Offenses	Victims [1]	Known offenders [2]
2000.	8,213	9,619	10,117	7,690
2005.	7,163	8,380	8,804	6,804
2010.	6,628	7,699	8,208	6,008
2013, total.	**5,928**	**6,933**	**7,242**	**5,814**
Race, total.	**2,871**	**3,407**	**3,563**	**2,733**
Anti-White.	653	728	754	680
Anti-Black.	1,856	2,263	2,371	1,747
Anti-American Indian/Alaska native.	129	146	159	108
Anti-Asian.	135	158	164	130
Anti-Native Hawaiian or Other Pacific Islander.	3	3	3	7
Anti-multiracial group.	95	109	112	61
Ethnicity, total.	**655**	**794**	**821**	**743**
Anti-Hispanic.	331	418	432	418
Anti-other ethnicity (not Hispanic).	324	376	389	325
Religion, total.	**1,031**	**1,163**	**1,223**	**682**
Anti-Jewish.	625	689	737	393
Anti-Catholic.	70	74	75	72
Anti-Protestant.	35	42	47	17
Anti-Islamic.	135	165	167	127
Anti-other religious group.	117	135	137	44
Anti-multi-religious group.	42	51	53	25
Anti-atheism/agnosticism/etc.	7	7	7	4
Sexual orientation, total.	**1,233**	**1,402**	**1,461**	**1,514**
Anti-gay (male homosexual).	750	849	890	975
Anti-lesbian (female homosexual).	160	185	191	174
Anti-gay, lesbian, bisexual, transgender.	277	317	329	324
Anti-heterosexual.	21	24	24	20
Anti-bisexual.	25	27	27	21
Disability, total.	**83**	**92**	**99**	**77**
Anti-physical.	22	23	24	23
Anti-mental.	61	69	75	54
Multiple bias [3].	**6**	**12**	**12**	**6**

[1] The term "victim" may refer to a person, business, institution, or a society as a whole. [2] The term "known offender" does not imply that the identity of the suspect is known, but only that an attribute of the suspect has been identified which distinguishes him/her from an unknown offender. [3] A "multiple-bias incident" an incident in which one or more offense types are motivated by two or more biases.

Source: U.S. Department of Justice, Federal Bureau of Investigation, "Hate Crime Statistics 2013," <http://www.fbi.gov/about-us/cjis/ucr/hate-crime/2013>, accessed January 2015.

Table 347. Hate Crimes by Bias Motivation and Location of Incident: 2013

[See headnote, Table 346]

Location	Total incidents	Bias motivation					Multiple-bias incidents [1]
		Race	Religion	Sexual orientation	Ethnicity	Disability	
Total.	**5,928**	**2,871**	**1,031**	**1,233**	**655**	**83**	**6**
Air/bus/train terminal.	63	31	5	21	4	–	–
Bank/savings and loan.	11	4	3	1	2	1	–
Bar/nightclub.	121	53	5	44	16	1	–
Church/synagogue/temple/mosque.	206	13	189	2	2	–	–
Commercial office building.	117	62	17	18	15	3	–
Convenience store.	69	33	10	3	23	–	–
Department/discount store.	59	29	10	8	10	1	–
Drug store/doctor's office/hospital.	48	30	11	3	3	–	–
Field/woods.	53	31	5	14	3	–	–
Government/public building.	107	60	13	15	18	1	–
Grocery/supermarket.	53	32	2	8	10	1	–
Highway/road/alley/street/sidewalk.	1,071	551	92	284	120	15	1
Hotel/motel/etc.	32	13	6	5	7	1	–
Jail/prison/corrections facility.	71	46	5	14	5	–	–
Park/playground.	67	46	7	11	3	–	–
Parking/drop lot/garage.	336	182	28	75	44	–	2
Rental storage facility.	4	1	1	2	–	–	–
Residence/home.	1,865	976	240	397	207	37	1
Restaurant.	126	63	9	30	21	1	–
School/college [2].	234	111	53	45	21	3	–
School—college/university.	100	47	13	23	13	1	1
School—elementary/secondary.	158	92	13	21	27	4	–
Auto service/gas station.	55	30	6	8	10	–	–
Shopping mall.	9	3	2	2	1	1	–
Specialty retail store (TV, fur, etc.).	42	22	6	5	8	1	–
Other/unknown.	782	276	272	164	48	9	1
Multiple locations.	11	8	1	1	–	1	–

– Represents zero. [1] See footnote 3, Table 346. [2] The location designation school/college has been retained for agencies that have not updated their records management systems to include the new location designations of school—college/university and school—elementary/secondary, which allow for more specificity in reporting.

Source: U.S. Department of Justice, Federal Bureau of Investigation, "Hate Crime Statistics 2013," <http://www.fbi.gov/about-us/cjis/ucr/hate-crime/2013>, accessed January 2015.

Table 348. Financial Crimes: 2005 to 2011

[For the year ending September 30. The FBI focuses its financial crimes investigations on such criminal activities as corporate fraud, securities and commodities fraud, health care fraud, financial institution fraud, mortgage fraud, insurance fraud, mass marketing fraud, and money laundering]

Type of financial fraud	Unit indicator	2005	2006	2007	2008	2009	2010	2011
Corporate fraud:								
Cases pending	Number	423	486	529	545	592	661	726
Indictments	Number	178	176	183	160	161	(NA)	242
Convictions	Number	150	134	181	134	162	(NA)	241
Restitution	Bil. dol.	5.6	1.1	12.6	8.2	6.1	(NA)	2.4
Recoveries	1,000 dol.	68.0	41,400.0	27,400.0	6,590.0	16,100.0	(NA)	(NA)
Fines	Mil. dol.	122.4	14.2	38.6	193.7	5.3	(NA)	16.1
Seizures	Mil. dol.	12.6	82.4	70.1	9.3	40.6	(NA)	(NA)
Securities/Commodities fraud:								
Cases pending	Number	1,139	1,165	1,217	1,210	1,510	1,703	1,846
Indictments	Number	327	320	408	359	412	(NA)	520
Convictions	Number	363	279	321	302	309	(NA)	394
Restitution	Bil. dol.	2.3	2.1	1.5	3.0	2.1	(NA)	8.8
Recoveries	Mil. dol.	76.3	20.6	25.4	43.7	47.3	(NA)	36.0
Fines	Mil. dol.	14.8	80.7	202.8	128.5	7.4	(NA)	113.0
Seizures	Mil. dol.	281.9	41.8	83.0	77.5	85.0	(NA)	751.0
Insurance fraud:								
Cases pending	Number	270	233	209	177	152	156	140
Indictments	Number	72	56	39	73	43	(NA)	19
Convictions	Number	79	66	47	60	42	(NA)	21
Restitution	Mil. dol.	171.7	30.4	27.6	553.7	22.9	(NA)	87.6
Recoveries	1,000 dol.	913.0	14.0	21.0	10,400.0	31,400.0	(NA)	(NA)
Fines	1,000 dol.	112.0	212.0	447.0	31.0	138.0	(NA)	(NA)
Seizures	Mil. dol.	10.7	3.5	15.9	25.3	2.2	(NA)	(NA)
Mass marketing fraud:								
Cases pending	Number	161	147	127	100	92	86	96
Indictments	Number	28	15	13	50	9	(NA)	(NA)
Convictions	Number	43	46	11	23	23	(NA)	(NA)
Restitution	Mil. dol.	503.8	273.2	30.6	4.2	4.4	(NA)	(NA)
Recoveries	1,000 dol.	4.0	468.0	542.0	173.0	–	(NA)	(NA)
Fines	1,000 dol.	362.0	86,900.0	121.0	23.0	2.1	(NA)	(NA)
Seizures	Mil. dol.	8.1	12.7	(Z)	–	(Z)	(NA)	(NA)
Health care fraud:								
Cases pending	Number	2,547	2,423	2,493	2,434	2,494	2,573	2,690
Indictments	Number	589	588	847	851	982	(NA)	1,676
Convictions	Number	550	535	642	707	674	(NA)	736
Restitution	Bil. dol.	1.1	0.4	1.1	1.1	1.3	(NA)	1.2
Recoveries	Mil. dol.	115.0	1,600.0	439.8	102.4	517.1	(NA)	(NA)
Fines	Mil. dol.	42.4	172.8	33.7	25.6	68.9	(NA)	1,000.0
Seizures	Mil. dol.	52.7	28.9	86.1	48.3	55.7	(NA)	96.0
Money laundering:								
Cases pending	Number	507	473	443	404	350	323	303
Indictments	Number	126	264	140	114	63	(NA)	37
Convictions	Number	91	112	115	134	96	(NA)	45
Restitution	Mil. dol.	313.0	17.1	69.4	222.4	81.9	(NA)	18.4
Recoveries	Mil. dol.	9.3	3.2	2.7	20.9	0.6	(NA)	0.8
Fines	Mil. dol.	0.3	0.4	11.4	34.1	1.5	(NA)	1.0
Seizures	Mil. dol.	7.8	6.4	10.9	24.2	4.5	(NA)	(NA)
Mortgage fraud:								
Cases pending	Number	721	881	1,211	1,644	2,794	3,129	2,691
Indictments	Number	93	138	328	574	822	(NA)	1,233
Convictions	Number	60	123	283	354	494	(NA)	1,082
Restitution	Mil. dol.	151.2	308.3	600.6	825.2	2,540.0	(NA)	1,380.0
Recoveries	Mil. dol.	(Z)	1.2	21.8	3.3	7.5	(NA)	7.3
Fines	Mil. dol.	44.0	300.8	1.6	3.1	58.4	(NA)	116.3
Seizures	Mil. dol.	(NA)	(NA)	5.1	6.6	5.0	(NA)	15.7
Suspicious Activity Reports (SARs) [1,2]								
Mortgage fraud related—								
Number of violations:								
Mortgage fraud	Number	21,994	35,617	46,717	63,713	67,190	70,533	93,508
Commercial loan	Number	2,126	2,409	3,240	4,189	4,514	3,347	2,947
False statement	Number	11,611	21,023	28,692	37,622	38,159	(NA)	(NA)
Dollars losses reported on:								
Mortgage fraud SARs	Bil. dol.	1.0	0.9	0.8	1.5	2.8	3.2	3.0
Reported on commercial loan SARs	Bil. dol.	0.7	0.5	1.0	1.9	1.7	(NA)	(NA)
False statement SARs	Bil. dol.	1.0	1.4	0.8	2.5	2.1	(NA)	(NA)

– Represents zero. NA Not available. Z represents a value less than 50 thousand. [1] Reports filed by federally-insured financial institutions. [2] SARs are cataloged according to the year in which they are submitted and the information contained within them may describe activity that occurred in previous month or years.

Source: U.S. Department of Justice, Federal Bureau of Investigation, "Financial Crimes Report to the Public" and "2010 Mortgage Fraud Report, Year in Review," <http://www.fbi.gov/stats-services/publications>, accessed May 2012.

Table 349. Firearm Violence, Homicides and Nonfatal Victimizations: 1993 to 2011

[Detail may not sum to total due to rounding. Data are primarily from the Bureau of Justice Statistics' National Crime Victimization Survey and Centers for Disease Control and Prevention's Injury Statistics Query and Reporting System]

Year	Fatal and Nonfatal Firearm Violence				Percent		Rate of nonfatal firearm victimization [3]
	Total	Firearm homicides	Nonfatal firearm victimizations [1]	Nonfatal firearm incidents [2]	All violence involving firearms	All firearm violence that was homicide	
1993.........	1,548,000	18,253	1,529,700	1,222,700	9.2	1.2	7.3
1994.........	1,585,700	17,527	1,568,200	1,287,200	9.3	1.1	7.4
1995.........	1,208,800	15,551	1,193,200	1,028,900	7.9	1.3	5.5
1996.........	1,114,800	14,037	1,100,800	939,500	7.9	1.3	5.1
1997.........	1,037,300	13,252	1,024,100	882,900	7.7	1.3	4.7
1998.........	847,200	11,798	835,400	673,300	7.0	1.4	3.8
1999.........	651,700	10,828	640,900	523,600	6.1	1.7	2.9
2000.........	621,000	10,801	610,200	483,700	7.3	1.7	2.7
2001.........	574,500	11,348	563,100	507,000	7.7	2.0	2.5
2002.........	551,800	11,829	540,000	450,800	7.4	2.1	2.3
2003.........	479,300	11,920	467,300	385,000	6.2	2.5	2.0
2004.........	468,100	11,624	456,500	405,800	6.9	2.5	1.9
2005.........	515,900	12,352	503,500	446,400	7.4	2.4	2.1
2006.........	627,200	12,791	614,400	552,000	7.4	2.0	2.5
2007.........	567,400	12,632	554,800	448,400	8.3	2.2	2.2
2008.........	383,500	12,179	371,300	331,600	6.0	3.2	1.5
2009.........	421,600	11,493	410,100	383,400	7.4	2.7	1.6
2010.........	426,100	11,078	415,000	378,800	8.6	2.6	1.6
2011 [4]......	478,400	11,101	467,300	414,600	8.2	2.3	1.8

[1] A victimization refers to a single victim that experienced a criminal incident. [2] An incident is a specific criminal act involving one or more victims or victimizations. [3] Per 1,000 persons age 12 or older. [4] Preliminary homicide estimates from Centers for Disease Control, *Deaths: Preliminary Data for 2011*, NVSR Vol. 61, No. 6.

Source: Department of Justice, Bureau of Justice Statistics, *Firearm Violence, 1993-2011*, NCJ 241730, May 2013. See also <http://www.bjs.gov/index.cfm?ty=pbdetail&iid=4616>

Table 350. Nonfatal Firearm and Nonfirearm Violence by Victim-Offender Relationship and Location of Crime: 2007 to 2011

[Data are for victimizations. Detail may not sum to total due to rounding. Data from National Crime Victimization Survey]

Characteristic	Total nonfatal violence		Firearm violence		Nonfirearm violence	
	Number	Percent [1]	Number	Percent [1]	Number	Percent [1]
RELATIONSHIP TO VICTIM						
Total..................................	**29,611,300**	(X)	**2,218,500**	7.5	**27,392,800**	92.5
Nonstranger............................	15,715,900	(X)	738,000	4.7	14,977,900	95.3
Intimate [2]............................	4,673,600	(X)	195,700	4.2	4,477,900	95.8
Other relative.........................	2,157,700	(X)	158,100	7.3	1,999,500	92.7
Friend/acquaintance..................	8,884,600	(X)	384,100	4.3	8,500,500	95.7
Stranger................................	10,983,100	(X)	1,177,900	10.7	9,805,200	89.3
Unknown [3]...........................	2,912,300	(X)	302,600	10.4	2,609,600	89.6
LOCATION						
Total..................................	**29,618,300**	100.0	**2,218,500**	100.0	**27,399,800**	100.0
Victim's home or lodging..............	6,491,400	21.9	427,600	19.3	6,063,800	22.1
Near victim's home....................	4,804,700	16.2	504,500	22.7	4,300,200	15.7
In, at, or near a friend, neighbor, or relative's home......	2,175,900	7.3	132,600	6.0	2,043,300	7.5
Commercial place......................	2,878,600	9.7	195,400	8.8	2,683,200	9.8
Parking lot or garage..................	1,688,400	5.7	340,600	15.4	1,347,900	4.9
School [4]..............................	3,931,100	13.3	[5] 12,600	[5] 0.6	3,918,500	14.3
Open area, on street, or public transportation...........	4,636,900	15.7	508,400	22.9	4,128,500	15.1
Other location.........................	3,011,200	10.2	96,800	4.4	2,914,400	10.6

X Not applicable. [1] Percent of total violence is shown for data by relationship to victim. Percent distribution of specified type of violence is shown for data by location. [2] Includes current or former spouses, boyfriends, or girlfriends. [3] Includes relationships unknown and number of offenders unknown. [4] Includes inside a school building or on school property. [5] Interpret with caution. Estimate based on 10 or fewer sample cases, or coefficient of variation is greater than 50%.

Source: Department of Justice, Bureau of Justice Statistics, *Firearm Violence, 1993-2011*, NCJ 241730, May 2013. See also <http://www.bjs.gov/index.cfm?ty=pbdetail&iid=4616>.

Table 351. Victims of Identity Theft by Type of Account and Selected Victim Characteristics: 2012

[16,580.5 represents 16,580,500. Data shown are for persons age 16 or older who experienced at least one identity theft incident during the past 12 months. Estimates are based on the most recent identity theft incident. Includes successful and attempted identity theft in which the victim experienced no loss. Based on the National Crime Victimization Survey's Identity Theft Supplement]

Characteristic	Any Identity theft		Misuse of existing credit card		Misuse of existing bank account		New account or personal information [1]	
	Number of victims	Percent of all persons	Number of victims	Percent of persons with credit card	Number of victims	Percent of persons with bank account	Number of victims	Percent of all persons
Total	**16,580.5**	**6.7**	**7,698.5**	**4.5**	**7,470.7**	**3.5**	**1,864.1**	**0.8**
By Sex:								
Male	7,902.8	6.6	3,932.0	4.8	3,320.1	3.3	851.2	0.7
Female	8,677.7	6.9	3,766.4	4.3	4,150.6	3.8	1,012.9	0.8
By Age:								
16 to 17 years old	[4] 35.2	[4] 0.4	[4] 4.3	[4] 0.7	[4] 16.3	[4] 0.6	[4] 5.8	[4] 0.1
18 to 24 years old	1,466.4	4.8	331.4	2.6	937.4	4.1	182.4	0.6
25 to 34 years old	3,293.5	7.8	1,177.5	4.1	1,718.1	4.7	406.7	1.0
35 to 49 years old	4,914.8	8.0	2,222.1	4.8	2,344.6	4.3	531.9	0.9
50 to 64 years old	4,739.4	7.8	2,590.4	5.4	1,853.3	3.3	501.5	0.8
65 years or older	2,131.1	5.0	1,372.8	4.1	601.1	1.6	235.8	0.6
By Race/Hispanic origin:								
White [2]	12,417.6	7.3	6,258.5	4.9	5,295.0	3.4	1,146.4	0.7
Black [2]	1,494.1	5.0	301.4	2.1	896.3	4.2	361.5	1.2
Hispanic/Latino	1,544.1	5.2	509.1	3.1	834.3	3.8	254.0	0.8
Other race [2,3]	841.4	6.4	523.9	5.4	302.7	2.7	54.0	0.4
Two or more races [2]	270.7	9.0	102.0	5.9	133.4	5.3	48.2	1.6
By Household Income:								
$24,999 or less	1,888.0	4.9	413.2	2.6	1,068.8	3.9	419.4	1.1
$25,000-$49,999	2,809.1	5.4	1,026.1	3.0	1,490.2	3.4	443.5	0.9
$50,000-$74,999	2,598.5	7.7	1,084.6	4.1	1,305.8	4.2	259.0	0.8
$75,000 or more	6,274.8	10.0	3,668.9	6.8	2,389.8	4.0	426.1	0.7
Unknown	3,010.1	5.1	1,505.7	3.7	1,216.2	2.4	316.1	0.5

[1] Includes the misuse of personal information to open a new account or to commit other fraud. [2] Excludes persons of Hispanic or Latino origin. [3] Includes persons identifying as American Indian, Alaska Native, Asian, Hawaiian, or other Pacific Islander. [4] Interpret with caution, estimate is based on 10 or fewer sample cases or coefficient of variation is greater than 50%.

Source: U.S. Department of Justice, Bureau of Justice Statistics, *Victims of Identity Theft, 2012*, NCJ 243779, December 2013. See also <http://www.bjs.gov/index.cfm?ty=pbse&sid=60>.

Table 352. Employment by State and Local Law Enforcement Agencies by Type of Agency and Employee: 2008

[As of September 30. Based on census of all state and local law enforcement agencies operating nationwide, conducted every 4 years]

Type of agency	Number of agencies	Number of employees					
		Full-time			Part-time		
		Total	Sworn	Civilian	Total	Sworn	Civilian
Total [1]	17,985	1,133,905	765,237	368,668	100,340	44,062	56,278
Local police	12,501	593,003	461,054	131,949	58,129	27,810	30,319
Sheriffs' offices	3,063	353,461	182,979	170,482	26,052	11,334	14,718
Primary State	50	93,148	60,772	32,376	947	54	893
Special jurisdiction	1,733	90,262	56,968	33,294	14,681	4,451	10,230
Constable/marshal	638	4,031	3,464	567	531	413	118

[1] Excludes agencies with less than one full-time officer or the equivalent in part-time officers.

Source: U.S. Bureau of Justice Statistics, *Census of State and Local Law Enforcement Agencies, 2008*. See also <http://bjs.ojp.usdoj.gov/index.cfm?ty=dcdetail&iid=249>.

Table 353. Background Checks for Firearm Transfers: 2002 to 2012

[In thousands (7,926 represents 7,926,000), except percent. The Brady Handgun Violence Prevention Act (Brady Act) P.L. 103–159, 1993 requires a background check on an applicant for a firearm purchase from a dealer who is a Federal Firearms Licensee. The period beginning November 30, 1998 is the effective date for the Brady Act. The National Instant Criminal Background Check System (NICS) began operations in 1998. Checks on handgun and long gun transfers are conducted by the FBI, and by state and local agencies. Totals combine Firearm Inquiry Statistics (FIST) estimates for state and local agencies with transactions and denials reported by the FBI]

Inquiries and rejections	Permanent Brady										
	2002	2003	2004	2005	2006	2007	2008	2009	2010	2011	2012
Applications received..............	7,926	7,883	8,133	8,324	8,772	8,836	10,131	11,071	10,643	12,135	15,718
Applications denied.................	136	126	126	132	135	136	147	150	153	160	192
Denied (percent).................	1.7	1.6	1.5	1.6	1.5	1.5	1.5	1.4	1.4	1.3	1.2
Selected reasons for rejection: [1]											
Felony indictment/conviction......	(NA)	(NA)	(NA)	(NA)	(NA)	(NA)	77	67	62	(NA)	82
Other................................	(NA)	(NA)	(NA)	(NA)	(NA)	(NA)	70	83	91	(NA)	110
Felony denials per 1,000 applications.............	(NA)	(NA)	(NA)	(NA)	(NA)	(NA)	7.2	6.2	6.0	(NA)	5.2

NA Not available. [1] Beginning in 2008, the FBI instituted a new classification system; therefore, data prior to 2008 aren't comparable to previously published estimates.

Source: U.S. Department of Justice, Bureau of Justice Statistics, *Background Checks for Firearm Transfers, 2012-Statistical Tables*, NCJ 247815, December 2014. See also <http://bjs.ojp.usdoj.gov/index.cfm?ty=pbse&sid=13>.

Table 354. Federal Drug Incidents and Seizures by Type of Drug: 2000 to 2012

[For fiscal years ending in year shown. Previously, data for amount of drugs seized at the Federal level was obtained from the Federal-wide Drug Seizure System (FDSS). A new system has been created called the National Seizure System (NSS), which broadens the scope of data collected for the amount of drugs seized (in pounds) at the national level. Data for "Seizure in (pounds)" are from NSS. Includes only information that has been reported to El Paso Intelligence Center (EPIC) by Federal, State, Local, Tribal, and International agencies, who reported seizures and may not necessarily reflect total seizures nationwide. There is no mandatory reporting for local and state agencies]

Drug	2000	2005	2007	2008	2009	2010	2011	2012
Number of incidents, total [1]........	**37,201**	**57,127**	**55,064**	**55,593**	**68,541**	**72,612**	**55,046**	**40,271**
Cannabis [2]...............................	21,159	32,735	35,697	36,560	46,362	47,034	31,266	23,708
Methamphetamine......................	5,233	9,310	6,109	5,667	7,014	8,607	8,119	7,207
Cocaine..................................	8,670	11,927	11,061	10,845	12,067	13,543	11,925	6,675
Heroin....................................	2,135	2,941	1,923	2,274	2,803	3,126	3,504	2,532
MDMA [3].................................	4	214	274	247	295	302	232	149
Seizure in (pounds), total...........	**2,447,710**	**3,210,311**	**4,180,386**	**3,665,022**	**4,846,001**	**5,141,789**	**5,359,037**	**4,287,415**
Cannabis [2]...............................	2,339,439	3,062,572	4,025,023	3,539,544	4,705,320	4,990,423	5,173,627	4,133,141
Cocaine..................................	95,231	126,208	133,172	101,364	116,157	115,213	145,078	96,283
Methamphetamine......................	9,966	14,760	14,067	14,042	14,894	24,571	29,436	47,005
Heroin....................................	2,738	4,297	3,764	4,238	5,122	6,619	8,624	9,904
MDMA [3].................................	337	2,474	4,361	5,833	4,509	4,964	2,271	1,081

[1] Seizure of drugs, weapons, currency, etc., which can occur without any arrest taking place. [2] Includes hashish. [3] MDMA methylene dioxymethamphetamine, an amphetamine derivative, used illicitly as a hallucinogen and mood-enhancer.

Source: Drug Enforcement Administration, El Paso Intelligence Center, unpublished data from the National Seizure System.

Table 355. Arrests by Offense, Sex, and Age: 2013

[9,070.0 represents 9,070,000. For year ending December 31. Based on Uniform Crime Reporting Program. Represents arrests reported by 11,951 agencies with a total population of 245,741,701 as estimated by the FBI. Some persons may be arrested more than once during a year; therefore, in some cases, the data in this table could represent multiple arrests of the same person]

Offense charged	Total			Male			Female		
	Total	Under 18 years	18 years and over	Total	Under 18 years	18 years and over	Total	Under 18 years	18 years and over
Total.............................	9,070.0	875.3	8,194.7	6,662.8	622.6	6,040.2	2,407.2	252.6	2,154.5
Violent crime.....................	392.8	43.7	349.1	313.8	35.5	278.3	79.0	8.2	70.9
Murder and nonnegligent manslaughter..	8.4	0.6	7.8	7.4	0.5	6.9	1.0	0.1	0.9
Rape [1]............................	13.6	2.1	11.5	13.4	2.0	11.3	0.3	0.1	0.2
Robbery..........................	78.8	15.9	62.8	68.2	14.4	53.8	10.5	1.5	9.0
Aggravated assault..............	292.0	25.0	267.0	224.7	18.5	206.2	67.3	6.5	60.8
Property crime....................	1,261.1	198.6	1,062.5	785.0	130.8	654.2	476.1	67.8	408.3
Burglary.........................	203.7	34.8	168.9	169.0	30.7	138.3	34.7	4.0	30.7
Larceny-theft....................	996.5	151.4	845.1	567.2	89.8	477.4	429.3	61.6	367.7
Motor vehicle theft..............	52.5	9.5	43.0	42.1	7.8	34.3	10.4	1.6	8.8
Arson...........................	8.4	2.9	5.5	6.8	2.5	4.3	1.7	0.5	1.2
Other assaults...................	885.8	118.3	767.6	639.6	75.2	564.3	246.3	43.1	203.2
Forgery and counterfeiting........	48.8	0.9	48.0	30.6	0.6	30.0	18.3	0.2	18.0
Fraud...........................	113.5	3.5	110.0	68.3	2.4	65.9	45.2	1.2	44.1
Embezzlement...................	12.7	0.3	12.3	6.5	0.2	6.3	6.1	0.1	6.0
Stolen property; buying, receiving, possessing....................	74.8	8.4	66.4	58.7	7.0	51.7	16.1	1.4	14.7
Vandalism........................	162.1	37.7	124.4	129.2	31.7	97.5	32.9	6.0	26.9
Weapons; carrying, possessing, etc........	112.7	16.7	96.0	102.9	14.9	87.9	9.8	1.7	8.1
Prostitution and commercialized vice.....	42.1	0.7	41.5	13.8	0.1	13.7	28.3	0.5	27.8
Sex offenses except rape & prostitution. ...	46.8	8.4	38.4	43.2	7.4	35.8	3.6	1.0	2.7
Drug abuse violations.............	1,209.7	94.2	1,115.5	954.0	77.0	877.0	255.7	17.2	238.5
Gambling........................	5.1	0.6	4.5	4.3	0.6	3.8	0.7	0.0	0.7
Offenses against family and children.......	78.8	2.2	76.6	57.8	1.4	56.4	21.0	0.9	20.1
Driving under the influence.............	918.5	6.0	912.5	689.4	4.5	684.9	229.1	1.5	227.6
Liquor laws......................	280.9	48.1	232.7	199.8	29.3	170.4	81.1	18.8	62.3
Drunkenness.....................	358.0	5.9	352.1	291.2	4.3	286.9	66.8	1.6	65.2
Disorderly conduct...............	375.1	76.3	298.8	270.3	50.0	220.3	104.8	26.3	78.5
Vagrancy........................	21.6	0.7	20.9	17.1	0.6	16.5	4.5	0.2	4.4
All other offenses (except traffic)...........	2,620.3	156.1	2,464.2	1,952.5	114.6	1,837.6	667.9	41.5	626.3
Suspicion........................	0.8	0.2	0.7	0.6	0.1	0.5	0.2	0.1	0.1
Curfew and loitering law violations.........	47.9	47.9	(X)	34.4	34.4	(X)	13.6	13.6	(X)

X Not applicable. [1] The rape figures in this table are an aggregate total of the data submitted using both the revised and legacy Uniform Crime Reporting definitions. For more information, see <http://www.fbi.gov/about-us/cjis/ucr/crime-in-the.u.s/2013/crime-in-the-u.s.-2013/rape-addendum/rape_addendum_final>.

Source: U.S. Department of Justice, Federal Bureau of Investigation, "Crime in the United States 2013," <http://www.fbi.gov/about-us/cjis/ucr>, accessed January 2015.

Table 356. Arrests by Offense and Race/Ethnicity: 2013

[In thousands (9,014.6 represents 9,014,600. See headnote, Table 355]

Offense charged	Total	White	Black	Hispanic or Latino [2]	American Indian/ Alaskan Native	Asian	Native Hawaiian/ other Pacific Islander
Total........................	9,014.6	62,142.0	25,496.6	7,999.3	1,402.9	1,051.1	53.8
Violent crime.................	3,914.7	2,287.8	1,516.3	551.4	51.9	53.5	5.2
Murder and nonnegligent manslaughter....	83.8	38.0	43.8	10.5	1.0	1.0	0.1
Rape [1]........................	135.2	89.5	42.3	20.1	1.6	1.7	0.1
Robbery.......................	785.4	329.5	442.7	84.8	5.8	6.5	0.9
Aggravated assault............	2,910.3	1,830.9	987.5	436.0	43.6	44.2	4.1
Property crime.................	12,547.0	8,552.3	3,639.5	958.5	191.8	156.3	7.0
Burglary.......................	2,030.9	1,369.9	617.1	240.4	19.7	22.0	2.3
Larceny-theft..................	9,909.4	6,771.7	2,843.6	629.5	164.0	126.1	4.0
Motor vehicle theft.............	523.1	348.6	159.6	82.0	6.9	7.3	0.7
Arson.........................	83.6	62.0	19.3	6.6	1.3	1.1	–
Other assaults.................	8,810.9	5,735.5	2,833.6	659.4	140.4	97.2	4.3
Forgery and counterfeiting.....	485.8	312.1	163.8	38.6	2.9	6.8	0.3
Fraud.........................	1,129.2	746.8	359.6	53.2	11.5	10.9	0.4
Embezzlement.................	125.7	78.8	43.9	7.2	0.9	2.1	0.1
Stolen property; buying, receiving, possessing.................	745.4	502.4	226.9	99.9	6.8	8.6	0.7
Vandalism.....................	1,610.8	1,138.4	425.7	151.7	29.5	16.4	0.8
Weapons—carrying, possessing, etc........	1,122.3	653.2	446.7	152.8	8.9	12.5	1.0
Prostitution and commercialized vice........	419.5	226.7	173.8	38.0	3.9	14.9	0.2
Sex offenses except rape & prostitution......	465.5	337.0	114.6	60.7	6.2	7.4	0.3
Drug abuse violations...........	12,041.6	8,151.8	3,657.9	1,188.3	94.1	129.3	8.6
Gambling......................	50.6	14.3	33.6	2.8	0.3	2.3	0.1
Offenses against the family and children.....	784.7	510.2	255.2	25.1	14.1	5.1	–
Driving under the influence......	9,104.7	7,664.4	1,139.3	1,063.8	125.8	168.3	7.0
Liquor laws....................	2,774.4	2,222.0	406.7	186.9	108.6	36.7	0.5
Drunkenness...................	3,564.3	2,881.5	568.9	440.1	74.0	35.5	4.5
Disorderly conduct.............	3,722.0	2,316.0	1,297.8	201.1	79.8	27.8	0.6
Vagrancy......................	213.5	137.3	68.0	17.3	5.8	2.2	0.2
All other offenses (except traffic).............	26,029.4	17,418.6	7,908.5	2,046.5	439.5	250.9	11.9
Suspicion......................	8.3	5.0	3.0	0.1	0.1	0.1	–
Curfew and loitering law violations...........	476.2	250.1	213.5	55.9	6.1	6.3	0.2

– Represents or rounds to zero. [1] See footnote 1, Table 355. [2] Persons of Hispanic origin may be of any race.

Source: U.S. Department of Justice, Federal Bureau of Investigation, "Crime in the United States 2013," <http://www.fbi.gov/about-us/cjis/ucr>, accessed November 2014.

Table 357. Law Enforcement Officers Killed and Assaulted: 1990 to 2013

[The statistics presented in this table are based on information collected by the staff of the FBI's Law Enforcement Officers Killed and Assaulted Program from law enforcement agencies throughout the U.S. and U.S. Territories. It contains statistics on line-of-duty felonious deaths, accidental deaths, and assaults of duly sworn local, state, tribal, and federal law enforcement officers]

Item	1990	1995	2000	2005	2009	2010	2011	2012	2013
OFFICERS KILLED									
Total killed	**132**	**133**	**134**	**122**	**96**	**128**	**125**	**97**	**76**
By region and area:									
Northeast	13	16	13	12	13	11	18	15	7
Midwest	20	19	32	23	14	24	28	9	8
South	68	63	67	58	42	61	56	50	46
West	23	32	19	24	25	29	20	17	15
Puerto Rico	8	2	3	5	2	3	3	5	–
Island Areas	–	1	–	–	–	–	–	1	–
Total feloniously killed	**65**	**74**	**51**	**55**	**48**	**56**	**72**	**49**	**27**
By type of weapon:									
Firearms	56	63	47	50	45	55	63	44	26
Handgun	47	44	33	42	28	38	50	33	18
Rifle	8	14	10	3	15	15	7	7	5
Shotgun	1	5	4	5	2	2	6	3	3
Type of firearm not reported	–	–	–	–	–	–	–	1	–
Knife/cutting instrument	3	1	1	–	–	–	1	1	–
Bomb	–	8	–	–	–	–	–	–	–
Blunt instrument	–	–	–	–	–	–	–	–	–
Personal weapons [1]	2	–	–	–	–	–	2	2	–
Vehicle	1	2	3	5	3	1	6	2	1
Other	3	–	–	–	–	–	–	–	–
Total accidentally killed	**67**	**59**	**83**	**67**	**48**	**72**	**53**	**48**	**49**
OFFICERS ASSAULTED									
Population covered (1,000) [2]	197,426	191,759	204,599	222,874	245,926	248,727	254,535	250,151	247,085
Number of—									
Reporting agencies	9,343	8,503	8,940	10,119	11,691	11,826	12,031	11,794	11,468
Officers employed	410,131	428,379	452,531	489,393	560,387	557,884	539,282	525,217	533,895
Total assaulted	**72,091**	**57,762**	**58,398**	**57,820**	**58,364**	**56,491**	**55,631**	**53,867**	**49,851**
By type of weapon:									
Firearm	3,651	2,354	1,749	2,157	2,007	1,925	2,240	2,276	2,266
Knife/cutting instrument	1,647	1,356	1,015	1,059	886	918	1,003	909	881
Other dangerous weapon	7,423	6,414	8,132	8,379	7,966	7,413	7,856	7,435	6,919
Personal weapons [1]	59,370	47,638	47,502	46,225	47,505	46,235	44,532	43,247	39,785

– Represents zero. [1] Includes hands, fists, feet, etc. [2] Represents the number of persons covered by reporting agencies.

Source: U.S. Department of Justice, Federal Bureau of Investigation, "Law Enforcement Officers Killed and Assaulted, 2013," and previous reports, <http://www.fbi.gov/about-us/cjis/ucr/leoka/2013>, accessed January 2015.

Table 358. Forensic Services Requests and Backlog by Type of Request: 2009

[Numbers are rounded to the nearest hundred. Census of 411 Laboratories, with a 97% return rate. Totals exclude requests outsourced to other laboratories. Request is classified as backlogged if it has been submitted to a crime lab, but has not yet been examined and reported to the submitting agency within 30 days. Estimates based on imputations for labs that did not report backlog data, see source for details]

Type of request	Received Number	Received Percent	Completed Number	Completed Percent	Backlogged requests Number	Backlogged requests Percent
All requests	**4,120,000**	**100**	**3,905,000**	**100**	**1,193,800**	**100**
Forensic biology [1]	1,389,000	34	1,312,000	34	905,200	76
Convicted offender/arrestee samples	1,045,000	25	36,542	26	498,500	42
Casework	343,000	8	295,000	8	406,700	34
Controlled substances	1,356,000	33	1,262,000	32	137,700	12
Latent prints	271,000	7	275,000	7	49,500	4
Firearms/toolmarks	147,000	4	131,000	3	48,700	4
Toxicology	613,000	15	591,000	15	28,600	2
Trace evidence	56,000	1	46,000	1	13,200	(Z)
Impressions	11,000	(Z)	10,000	(Z)	5,700	(Z)
Questioned documents	13,000	(Z)	12,000	(Z)	2,400	(Z)
Digital evidence	31,000	1	31,000	1	1,300	(Z)
Other forensic requests	42,000	1	42,000	1	1,500	(Z)
Crime scene	190,000	5	190,000	5	(NA)	(NA)

Z Less than 0.5%. [1] Includes biology screening and DNA analysis.

Source: U.S. Bureau of Justice Statistics, *Census of Publicly Funded Forensic Crime Laboratories, 2009*, NCJ 238252, August 2012. See also <www.bjs.gov>.

Table 359. State and Local Government Expenditures Per Capita by Criminal Justice Function and State: 2011

[Preliminary data. In dollars. Based on Census Bureau's Annual Government Finance Survey and Annual Survey of Public Employment. Population figures used to calculate per capita rates are from the Bureau of the Census, Current Population Reports, Series P-25, No. 1045, July 2012]

State	Total justice system	Police protec-tion	Judicial and legal	Correc-tions	State	Total justice system	Police protec-tion	Judicial and legal	Correc-tions
Total....................	680	309	138	234	Missouri..................	501	278	79	143
Alabama................	479	237	86	155	Montana................	654	258	154	241
Alaska..................	1,162	452	313	397	Nebraska...............	519	223	97	198
Arizona.................	695	325	144	226	Nevada.................	842	421	165	255
Arkansas...............	439	185	70	184	New Hampshire.........	494	267	87	140
California...............	998	400	236	361	New Jersey.............	780	378	167	234
Colorado................	691	323	132	237	New Mexico.............	760	306	153	300
Connecticut.............	683	299	192	192	New York...............	980	462	217	302
Delaware...............	784	320	170	294	North Carolina..........	531	254	78	199
District of Columbia.....	1,554	955	184	415	North Dakota...........	511	223	111	177
Florida..................	725	385	115	225	Ohio....................	596	277	152	167
Georgia.................	565	232	103	230	Oklahoma...............	497	237	87	173
Hawaii..................	592	280	173	139	Oregon.................	663	279	113	271
Idaho...................	544	241	120	184	Pennsylvania...........	631	246	131	254
Illinois..................	645	360	114	172	Rhode Island...........	643	339	116	188
Indiana.................	427	199	74	154	South Carolina.........	442	227	75	140
Iowa....................	474	210	111	153	South Dakota...........	487	197	95	194
Kansas.................	536	256	105	176	Tennessee..............	522	268	95	159
Kentucky...............	444	161	116	168	Texas..................	590	256	106	228
Louisiana...............	757	329	159	269	Utah....................	532	234	122	175
Maine...................	419	199	73	148	Vermont................	590	276	112	202
Maryland................	801	370	136	295	Virginia.................	591	252	102	237
Massachusetts..........	625	320	145	159	Washington.............	582	230	122	230
Michigan................	580	241	113	227	West Virginia...........	483	192	117	175
Minnesota..............	603	309	131	163	Wisconsin..............	684	310	104	270
Mississippi.............	484	222	76	186	Wyoming................	935	377	204	354

Source: U.S. Department of Justice, Bureau of Justice Statistics, "Justice Expenditure and Employment Extracts, 2011 – Preliminary," NCJ 247020, July 2014, <http://www.bjs.gov/index.cfm?ty=pbse&sid=33>.

Table 360. Denials of Firearm Transfer Applications by Reason and Agency Type: 2009 to 2012

[In percent. Reasons for denials are based on The Brady Handgun Violence Prevention Act, pursuant to 18 U.S.C. 922 and state laws. Denial occurs when an applicant is prohibited from receiving a firearm or a permit that can be used to receive a firearm because a disqualifying factor was found during a background check. Application for firearm transfer is information submitted by a person to a state or local checking agency to purchase a firearm or obtain a permit that can be used for a purchase. Information may be submitted directly to a checking agency or forwarded by a prospective seller. Totals were based on federal and state agencies that reported counts on reasons for denial. Reasons for denial for local agencies were estimated]

Reason for denial	2009			2010			2012		
	FBI [1]	State	Local	FBI [1]	State	Local [2]	FBI [1]	State	Local
Felony indictment/conviction..............	48.5	39.4	21.7	47.4	30.9	(NA)	48.2	29.8	17.8
Felony indictment........................	(NA)	(NA)	(NA)	(NA)	(NA)	(NA)	5.7	1.2	3.7
Felony conviction........................	(NA)	(NA)	(NA)	(NA)	(NA)	(NA)	42.5	28.6	14.1
Felony arrest with no disposition.........	(NA)	(NA)	(NA)	(NA)	(NA)	(NA)	(X)	6.0	2.4
Domestic violence.......................	11.5	13.5	15.8	10.4	10.3	(NA)	10.0	13.6	14.5
Misdemeanor conviction.................	7.2	10.2	13.9	6.2	8.2	(NA)	6.3	5.9	11.0
Restraining order.......................	4.3	3.3	1.9	4.3	2.1	(NA)	3.7	7.7	3.5
Fugitive................................	16.8	7.1	1.0	19.1	6.6	(NA)	18.7	11.6	2.6
Illegal alien............................	1.0	0.3	0.7	0.8	0.3	(NA)	1.2	0.4	0.4
Mental illness or disability................	1.4	6.2	5.3	1.8	5.7	(NA)	2.6	3.4	5.4
Drug user/addict........................	9.3	1.6	15.2	9.6	5.0	(NA)	9.9	3.2	5.6
Local law prohibition.....................	(X)	(NA)	1.5	(X)	(NA)	(NA)	(X)	(NA)	(NA)
State law prohibition.....................	11.2	10.7	6.3	10.6	15.6	(NA)	9.0	20.8	20.0
Other prohibitions [3].....................	0.3	21.2	32.5	0.3	25.5	(NA)	0.3	11.2	31.2

NA Not available. X Not applicable. [1] During 2008 the FBI began a new classification system and reclassified all denials from 1999 to 2008; therefore, data are not comparable with prior years. [2] Data was not available for local law prohibition, see source. [3] Includes juveniles, persons dishonorably discharged from the Armed Services, persons who have renounced their U.S. citizenship, and other unspecified persons.

Source: U.S. Department of Justice, Bureau of Justice Statistics, *Background Checks For Firearm Transfers, 2012 - Statistical Tables*, NCJ 247815, December 2014, and earlier reports. See also <http://bjs.ojp.usdoj.gov/index.cfm?ty=pbse&sid=13>.

Table 361. Suspects Arrested by Drug Enforcement Administration by Type of Drug and Arrestee Characteristics: 2012

[For fiscal year ending in year shown. Data are from Drug Enforcement Administration's (DEA) Defendant Statistical System]

Arrestee characteristic	Total arrested	Percent arrested	Drug type					
			Cocaine powder	Crack cocaine	Marijuana	Metham-phetamine	Opiates	Other or non drug [2]
Total [1]	**31,450**	**100.0**	**7,343**	**2,637**	**6,928**	**5,968**	**3,639**	**4,935**
SEX								
Male	26,066	83.2	6,441	2,274	6,014	4,648	3,058	3,631
Female	5,272	16.8	882	355	878	1,296	574	1,287
RACE								
White	21,410	70.0	4,691	496	5,061	5,411	2,256	3,495
Black/African American	8,274	27.1	2,365	2,062	1,302	209	1,213	1,123
American Indian/Alaska Native	217	0.7	40	25	52	55	14	31
Asian/Pacific Islander	664	2.2	43	20	330	107	19	145
HISPANIC ORIGIN								
Hispanic/Latino	13,649	44.7	4,360	386	2,938	3,119	1,743	1,103
Non-Hispanic/Latino	16,893	55.3	2,811	2,174	3,812	2,712	1,760	3,624
AGE								
18 years old and under	373	1.0	58	34	133	49	51	48
19 to 20 years old	1,301	4.2	210	121	386	226	190	168
21 to 30 years old	11,265	36.0	2,397	1,066	2,538	2,076	1,450	1,738
31 to 40 years old	10,185	32.5	2,726	857	2,070	2,034	1,058	1,440
41 years old and older	8,173	26.1	1,928	549	1,753	1,554	870	1,519

[1] Details may not sum to the total number of arrestees due to missing data. [2] Includes pharmaceutical controlled substances, equipment used to manufacture controlled substances, and drug use paraphernalia.

Source: U.S. Department of Justice, Bureau of Justice Statistics, *Federal Justice Statistics - Statistical Tables 2012*, NCJ 248470, January 2015. See also <http://www.bjs.gov/index.cfm?ty=pbdetail&iid=62>.

Table 362. Missing Person Reports by Selected Characteristics: 2013 and 2014

[As of December 31. Data shown are missing person records entered into the National Crime Information Center's (NCIC) Missing Person File during the year shown and does not include records removed (canceled, cleared, and located). The NCIC contained 84,924 active missing person records remaining in the database as of December 31, 2014; this figure includes entries from earlier years. For more information, see source]

Characteristic	2013			2014		
	All ages	Under 18	18 and older	All ages	Under 18	18 and older
Total missing person entries	**627,911**	**462,567**	**165,344**	**635,155**	**466,949**	**168,206**
By type:						
Juvenile (under age 21) [1]	445,214	440,625	4,589	449,549	445,045	4,504
Endangered [2]	46,057	9,617	36,440	44,029	9,770	34,259
Involuntary [3]	18,841	4,883	13,958	17,631	4,806	12,825
Disability [4]	30,454	4,112	26,342	31,501	4,258	27,243
Catastrophe [5]	285	101	184	269	91	178
Other (over age 21)	87,060	3,229	83,831	92,176	2,979	89,197
By sex:						
Female	316,435	247,931	68,504	320,086	250,418	69,668
Male	311,448	214,617	96,831	315,025	216,500	98,525
Unknown	28	19	9	44	31	13
By race/ethnicity:						
White [6]	370,214	263,403	106,811	377,546	267,273	110,273
Black	218,506	171,801	46,705	217,684	171,865	45,819
Asian	12,595	7,659	4,936	12,547	7,410	5,137
American Indian	9,310	7,507	1,803	9,362	7,346	2,016
Unknown	17,286	12,197	5,089	18,016	13,055	4,961

[1] A person under the age of 21 who is missing and does not meet any of the entry criteria set forth in the other categories. [2] Indicating that physical safety may be in danger. [3] Disappearance may not have been voluntary, i.e. abduction or kidnapping. [4] Proven physical/mental disability or senile and subjecting themselves or others to personal and immediate danger. [5] Person missing after a catastrophe. [6] Includes Hispanic ethnicity or origin.

Source: U.S. Department of Justice, Federal Bureau of Investigation, "NCIC Missing Person and Unidentified Person Statistics for 2014," and earlier releases, <http://www.fbi.gov/about-us/cjis/ncic>, accessed May 2015.

Table 363. U.S. Supreme Court—Cases Filed and Disposition: 1980 to 2013

[Statutory term of court begins first Monday in October. Often the Court grants or denies cases after the Court recesses but before the next statutory term]

Action	1980	1990	1995	2000	2005	2010	2011	2012	2013
Total cases on docket	**5,144**	**6,316**	**7,565**	**8,965**	**9,608**	**9,066**	**8,952**	**8,806**	**8,580**
Appellate cases on docket	2,749	2,351	2,456	2,305	2,025	1,895	1,876	1,806	1,869
From prior term	527	365	361	351	354	337	324	303	301
Docketed during present term	2,222	1,986	2,095	1,954	1,671	1,558	1,552	1,503	1,568
Cases acted upon	2,324	2,042	2,130	2,024	1,703	1,618	(NA)	(NA)	(NA)
Granted review	167	114	92	85	63	76	59	83	68
Denied, dismissed, or withdrawn	1,999	1,802	1,945	1,842	1,554	1,461	(NA)	(NA)	(NA)
Summarily decided	90	81	62	63	46	45	(NA)	(NA)	(NA)
Cases not acted upon	425	309	326	281	322	277	303	303	301
Pauper cases on docket	2,371	3,951	5,098	6,651	7,575	7,167	7,082	6,997	6,706
Cases acted upon [1]	2,027	3,436	4,514	5,736	6,533	6,250	(NA)	(NA)	(NA)
Granted review	17	27	13	14	15	14	7	10	8
Denied, dismissed, or withdrawn	1,968	3,369	4,439	5,658	6,459	6,195	(NA)	(NA)	(NA)
Summarily decided	32	28	55	61	58	37	(NA)	(NA)	(NA)
Cases not acted upon	344	515	584	915	1,042	917	992	898	727
Original cases on docket	24	14	11	9	8	4	3	3	5
Cases disposed of during term	7	3	5	2	4	2	1	0	0
Total cases available for argument	**264**	**201**	**145**	**138**	**122**	**131**	**111**	**123**	**120**
Cases disposed of	162	131	93	89	87	88	80	79	82
Cases argued	154	125	90	86	88	86	79	77	79
Cases disposed of by full opinion	144	121	87	83	82	83	73	76	77
Cases disposed of by *per curiam* opinion	8	4	3	4	5	3	5	1	2
Cases dismissed or remanded without argument	8	6	3	3	1	2	1	2	3
Cases remaining at start of next term	102	70	52	49	31	43	31	45	40
Number of written opinions	123	112	75	77	69	75	64	73	67

NA Not available. [1] Includes cases granted review and carried over to next term, not shown separately.

Source: Office of the Clerk, Supreme Court of the United States, unpublished data. Beginning 2011, *Journal of the Supreme Court of the United States*, July 2014, and earlier reports. See also <http://www.supremecourt.gov/orders/journal.aspx> and <http://www.uscourts.gov/Statistics.aspx>.

Table 364. Judicial Caseloads for the Federal Judiciary: 2000 to 2014

[For 12-month periods ending June 30]

Judicial caseload	2000	2005	2010	2011	2012	2013	2014
U.S. Courts of Appeals [1]:							
Cases filed	54,642	67,999	56,097	55,353	57,699	56,360	55,260
Cases terminated	56,509	59,577	59,343	58,146	57,272	58,534	55,803
Cases pending	40,815	57,349	46,816	44,051	44,529	42,485	41,942
U.S. District Courts Civil:							
Cases filed	263,049	282,758	285,215	289,630	286,232	283,087	298,713
Cases terminated	260,277	280,455	295,908	301,773	286,953	257,057	260,352
Cases pending	247,973	266,938	285,071	275,068	269,671	295,780	334,141
Criminal (includes transfers):							
Cases filed	62,523	69,876	78,213	78,764	73,455	69,642	64,027
Defendants filed	84,147	92,356	100,031	102,605	96,915	91,812	84,017
Cases terminated	57,543	65,239	77,633	78,855	76,589	69,601	67,115
Cases pending	46,796	70,692	80,506	80,415	76,679	77,207	73,829
U.S. Bankruptcy Courts:							
Cases filed	1,276,922	1,637,254	1,572,597	1,529,560	1,311,602	1,137,978	1,000,083
Cases terminated	1,271,300	1,583,959	1,441,419	1,486,950	1,354,274	1,215,118	1,124,534
Cases pending	1,396,916	1,748,038	1,659,399	1,704,548	1,662,461	1,584,972	1,460,753
Post-conviction supervision:							
Persons under supervision	99,577	113,008	126,642	129,319	132,785	132,362	132,597
Pretrial services:							
Total cases activated	86,067	98,946	110,666	113,120	111,557	107,995	103,640
Pretrial services cases activated	84,107	97,045	109,711	112,181	110,593	107,243	102,949
Pretrial diversion cases activated	1,960	1,901	955	939	964	752	691
Total released on supervision	31,607	34,348	29,748	30,265	29,971	28,557	26,197
Pretrial supervision	31,927	32,438	28,440	28,903	28,625	27,472	25,183
Diversion supervision	2,166	1,910	1,308	1,362	1,346	1,085	1,014

[1] Excludes the U.S. Court of Appeals for the Federal Circuit.

Source: Administrative Office of the United States Courts, "Statistical Tables for the Federal Judiciary," <http://www.uscourts.gov/Statistics/StatisticalTablesForTheFederalJudiciary.aspx>, accessed May 2015.

Table 365. U.S. District Courts—Civil Cases Filed: by Basis of Jurisdiction and Nature of Suit: 2008 to 2014

[For 12-month periods ending June 30]

Type of case	Cases filed						
	2008	2009	2010	2011	2012	2013	2014
Cases total [1]	**256,354**	**257,204**	**285,215**	**289,630**	**286,232**	**283,087**	**298,713**
BASIS OF JURISDICTION							
U.S. cases:							
U.S. plaintiff	9,868	9,030	8,427	10,282	9,707	7,863	6,833
U.S. defendant	35,527	33,286	34,306	36,502	37,569	39,778	39,926
Private cases:							
Federal question	134,623	133,697	137,776	141,334	144,387	146,086	149,380
Diversity of citizenship	76,284	81,188	104,703	101,508	94,568	89,359	102,568
NATURE OF SUIT							
Contract actions [1]	34,818	35,229	31,461	32,366	29,771	28,591	28,631
Recovery of overpayments [2]	3,491	3,214	3,079	4,623	4,041	2,499	2,357
Real property actions [1]	5,607	5,413	6,809	10,078	12,609	11,530	8,454
Foreclosure	2,689	2,639	3,836	6,569	8,194	6,832	4,401
Tort actions	59,588	61,936	87,256	79,394	70,204	67,172	81,024
Personal injury	55,777	57,332	82,057	74,921	65,898	62,715	77,443
Personal injury product liability [1]	39,664	43,055	66,958	60,631	51,850	48,754	63,245
Other personal injury [1]	16,113	14,277	15,099	14,290	14,048	13,961	14,198
Medical malpractice	1,242	1,076	1,120	1,089	1,061	1,034	976
Personal property damage	3,811	4,604	5,199	4,473	4,306	4,457	3,581
Actions under statutes [1]	156,277	154,572	159,683	167,791	173,648	175,794	180,604
Bankruptcy suits	2,630	2,334	2,615	2,597	4,073	2,708	2,708
Civil rights [1]	31,632	33,188	34,427	37,000	37,676	35,965	34,829
Employment	13,036	13,778	14,343	15,255	15,207	13,832	12,035
Environmental matters	900	735	826	881	696	1,253	749
Prisoner petitions	55,374	52,237	52,450	53,692	53,606	55,369	62,402
Forfeiture and penalty	2,324	2,322	2,297	2,372	2,297	2,238	1,959
Labor laws	16,685	17,153	18,878	18,025	19,222	17,977	18,702
Immigration	1,110	2,166	1,262	1,097	1,032	1,044	1134
Protected property rights [3]	9,636	8,714	8,519	9,944	10,985	13,232	13,195
Securities commodities and exchanges	1,669	1,720	1,442	1,394	1,422	1,187	1,000
Social security laws	13,329	13,222	13,725	15,697	17,043	19,121	19,530
Tax suits	1,448	1,411	1,171	1,217	1,208	1,103	969
Freedom of information	294	279	315	354	366	367	432
Other actions	64	54	6	1	–	–	–

– Represents zero. [1] Includes other types not shown separately. [2] Includes enforcement of judgments in student loan cases, and overpayments of veterans' benefits. [3] Includes copyright, patent, and trademark rights.

Source: Administrative Office of the United States Courts, "Statistical Tables for the Federal Judiciary," <http://www.uscourts.gov/Statistics/StatisticalTablesForTheFederalJudiciary.aspx>, accessed May 2015.

Table 366. U.S. Courts of Appeals—Nature of Suit or Offense in Cases Arising from the U.S. District Courts: 2000 to 2014

[For 12-month periods ending June 30. Excludes data for the U.S. Court of Appeals for the Federal Circuit. Includes appeals reopened, remanded, and reinstated (after being terminated due to procedural defaults) as well as original appeals]

Nature of suit and offense	2000	2005	2010	2011	2012	2013	2014
Total cases	**46,682**	**48,907**	**43,880**	**43,113**	**44,317**	**42,227**	**41,618**
Criminal cases	10,570	15,831	12,863	12,412	13,580	11,975	11,340
Civil cases	36,112	33,076	31,017	30,701	30,737	30,252	30,278
U.S cases	8,707	9,055	7,772	7,427	7,589	7,513	7,668
U.S. plaintiff	615	356	435	364	360	345	292
U.S. defendant	8,092	8,699	7,337	7,063	7,229	7,168	7,376
Private cases	27,405	24,021	23,245	23,274	23,148	22,739	22,610
Federal question	24,155	21,000	20,599	20,412	20,004	19,647	19,012
Diversity of citizenship	3,239	3,020	2,646	2,860	3,142	3,092	3,598
General local jurisdiction	11	1	–	2	2	–	–
Criminal cases	10,570	15,831	12,863	12,412	13,580	11,975	11,340
Violent offenses	683	768	621	658	610	550	563
Property offenses	1,520	1,974	1,624	1,630	1,749	1,620	1,606
Drug offenses	4,388	5,962	5,066	4,444	5,653	4,547	3,766
Firearms, explosives offenses	1,029	2,488	1,927	1,749	1,749	1,653	1,620
Sex offenses	190	403	651	708	755	732	733
Justice system offenses	179	216	142	147	160	151	138
Immigration offenses	1,109	2,888	1,787	1,736	1,680	1,551	1,473
General offenses	579	553	411	369	346	338	348
Other [1]	893	579	634	971	906	833	1,093

– Represents or rounds to zero. [1] Other includes regulatory, traffic, and unclassified offenses.

Source: Administrative Office of the United States Courts, "Statistical Tables for the Federal Judiciary," <http://www.uscourts.gov/Statistics/StatisticalTablesForTheFederalJudiciary.aspx>, accessed May 2015.

Table 367. Total Incoming Caseloads in State Trial Courts by Case Category: 2010

[Represents total incoming caseloads (i.e., new filings, plus reopened and reactivated cases when provided) as reported to the Court Statistics Project. Some figures may be incomplete and/or overinclusive. Since state court caseload statistics should only be viewed in the context of each state's court structure, comparisons of the data reported here should not be made without additional information]

State	Total	Civil [1]	Domestic relations [2]	Criminal [3]	Juvenile [4]	Traffic/ violations [5]
United States..................	103,461,125	18,966,580	5,862,112	20,437,849	1,854,603	54,564,385
Alabama.........................	2,190,581	215,386	96,275	261,477	50,084	1,567,359
Alaska...........................	162,069	25,783	14,473	38,847	2,737	80,229
Arizona..........................	2,706,028	372,856	137,203	689,712	19,430	1,475,930
Arkansas........................	1,559,910	118,564	54,570	604,553	24,737	757,486
California........................	10,351,728	1,235,421	454,105	1,835,385	127,387	6,699,430
Colorado.........................	1,037,456	378,845	54,294	172,048	19,170	413,099
Connecticut......................	873,508	225,814	39,245	185,140	25,292	398,017
Delaware.........................	534,672	67,523	40,677	179,390	6,832	240,250
District of Columbia.............	109,597	61,556	11,961	30,285	4,183	1,612
Florida...........................	5,118,744	1,471,700	487,096	1,273,280	171,796	1,714,872
Georgia..........................	4,248,308	978,162	177,816	820,694	99,943	441,162
Hawaii...........................	552,330	43,550	14,084	86,311	14,770	393,615
Idaho............................	462,936	83,554	25,709	113,646	14,187	225,840
Illinois...........................	3,828,028	671,908	149,548	428,146	30,896	2,547,530
Indiana..........................	1,927,253	488,379	110,054	299,577	53,813	975,430
Iowa.............................	958,972	162,142	44,515	91,388	12,602	648,325
Kansas..........................	985,992	193,402	40,226	58,409	18,932	675,023
Kentucky........................	971,346	266,465	80,811	236,410	40,649	347,011
Louisiana........................	1,917,154	268,497	59,314	352,225	42,801	1,194,317
Maine............................	285,305	47,225	21,836	61,998	4,364	149,882
Maryland.........................	2,153,056	1,042,848	101,011	292,585	31,964	659,557
Massachusetts...................	1,070,341	405,668	138,461	255,482	33,667	233,482
Michigan.........................	3,929,411	735,548	124,807	930,324	51,053	2,087,679
Minnesota.......................	1,648,579	211,898	49,410	114,757	47,774	1,224,740
Mississippi......................	150,062	83,530	65,518	(NA)	1,014	(NA)
Missouri.........................	2,478,892	317,613	129,845	171,806	14,696	1,844,932
Montana.........................	353,600	66,599	15,038	50,530	2,170	219,263
Nebraska........................	457,759	132,878	23,794	125,429	11,172	159,420
Nevada..........................	1,021,707	166,192	60,455	164,766	15,025	615,269
New Hampshire..................	160,470	53,719	19,443	51,331	1,265	50,325
New Jersey......................	7,502,953	1,023,204	277,256	733,201	62,759	5,406,533
New Mexico......................	449,040	101,231	43,251	116,142	6,837	181,579
New York........................	4,398,340	1,714,862	657,566	750,866	119,315	1,155,731
North Carolina...................	3,273,431	458,803	143,545	1,886,857	36,633	747,593
North Dakota....................	193,953	35,633	12,683	39,437	8,686	97,514
Ohio.............................	3,770,981	786,558	248,240	829,243	133,223	1,773,717
Oklahoma........................	527,648	197,523	43,636	107,400	10,541	168,548
Oregon..........................	566,824	193,458	46,425	89,738	15,229	221,974
Pennsylvania [6].................	3,726,142	549,848	359,253	546,143	51,200	2,219,698
Rhode Island....................	203,992	57,743	13,341	41,012	8,477	83,419
South Carolina...................	1,896,484	355,230	62,338	815,597	15,730	647,589
South Dakota....................	237,337	60,091	16,345	25,967	9,966	124,968
Tennessee.......................	485,140	70,681	87,070	176,463	136,904	(NA)
Texas............................	12,324,024	846,839	389,651	2,377,732	39,842	8,669,960
Utah.............................	854,213	145,423	22,412	121,952	43,670	520,756
Vermont..........................	178,812	22,755	21,316	17,727	1,915	113,078
Virginia..........................	4,051,996	907,267	355,671	1,100,969	82,051	1,606,038
Washington......................	2,698,860	247,572	70,768	338,545	39,997	2,001,978
West Virginia....................	403,932	79,756	54,851	132,166	9,307	127,852
Wisconsin........................	1,014,235	293,153	50,573	121,115	20,212	529,182
Wyoming.........................	198,980	44,152	8,738	29,007	1,498	115,585
Puerto Rico......................	298,014	181,573	35,589	64,639	6,206	10,007

NA Not available. [1] Includes tort, contract, real property, small claims, probate, mental health, and civil appeals cases. [2] Includes divorce/dissolution, paternity, custody, support, visitation, adoption, and civil protection/restraining order cases. [3] Includes felony, misdemeanor, and appeals from limited jurisdiction courts. [4] Includes delinquency, dependency, and status offense petitions. [5] Includes non-criminal traffic violations (infractions), parking violations, and ordinance violations. [6] Data for Pennsylvania are preliminary.

Source: National Center for State Courts, Court Statistics Project, "State Court Caseload Statistics," <http://www.courtstatistics.org/Other-Pages/StateCourtCaseloadStatistics.aspx>, accessed May 2013 ©.

Table 368. U.S. District Courts—National Petit and Grand Juror Service: 2009 to 2014

[For years ending September 30. Includes data on jury selection days only. Data on juror service after the selection day are not included]

Juror service	2009	2010	2011	2012	2013	2014
PETIT JUROR SERVICE						
Jurors present for jury selection or orientation	282,668	262,376	249,266	237,411	237,251	218,203
Percent selected	22.2	22.7	23.0	23.1	22.2	22.4
Percent challenged	37.9	38.5	39.4	39.5	40.3	40.1
Percent not selected or challenged	39.9	38.7	37.7	37.3	37.5	37.4
Voir Dire [1]	24.9	24.9	25.0	24.7	23.5	24.3
Non-Voir Dire [2]	15.0	13.9	12.7	12.7	14.0	13.1
Total juries selected	5,378	5,332	5,565	4,899	4,656	4,278
GRAND JUROR SERVICE						
Juries serving	766	784	799	783	778	763
Sessions convened	9,257	9,277	9,083	8,923	8,531	8,230
Jurors in session	186,194	186,020	182,106	179,076	171,038	164,856
Average per session	20.1	20.1	20.0	20.1	20.0	20.0
Hours in session	44,676	44,845	43,083	41,477	39,565	36,719
Average hours per session	4.8	4.8	4.7	4.6	4.6	4.5
Proceedings filed by indictment:						
Cases	49,144	49,654	49,175	(NA)	(NA)	(NA)
Defendants	69,245	70,433	72,505	66,670	64,015	55,890
Average defendants indicted per session	7.5	7.6	8.0	7.5	7.5	6.8

NA Not available. [1] Jurors who completed pre-screening questionnaires or were in the courtroom during the conducting of voir dire. [2] Other jurors not selected or challenged who were not called to the courtroom or otherwise did not participate in the actual voir dire.

Source: Administrative Office of the United States Courts, "Judicial Business of the United States Courts 2014," <http://www.uscourts.gov/Statistics/JudicialBusiness.aspx>, accessed May 2015.

Table 369. Federal Prosecutions of Public Corruption: 2000 to 2013

[As of December 31. Prosecution of persons who have corrupted public office in violation of Federal Criminal Statutes]

Prosecution status	2000			2010			2012			2013		
	Charged	Con- victed	Await- ing trial	Charged	Con- victed	Await- ing trial	Charged	Con- victed	Await- ing trial	Charged	Con- victed	Await- ing trial
Total [1]	**1,000**	**938**	**327**	**1,184**	**1,036**	**554**	**1,078**	**1,060**	**455**	**1,134**	**1,037**	**499**
Federal officials	441	422	92	422	397	103	381	369	108	337	315	113
State officials	92	91	37	168	108	105	100	78	68	133	119	68
Local officials	211	183	89	296	280	146	319	295	135	334	303	149
Others involved	256	242	109	298	251	200	278	318	144	330	300	169

[1] Includes individuals who are neither public officials nor employees, but were involved with public officials or employees in violating the law, not shown separately.

Source: U.S. Department of Justice, Criminal Division, *Report to Congress on the Activities and Operations of the Public Integrity Section for 2013*, and earlier reports. See also <http://www.justice.gov/criminal/pin/>.

Table 370. Delinquency Cases Disposed by Juvenile Courts by Type of Offense: 1990 to 2013

[In thousands (1,321 represents 1,321,000), except rate. A delinquency offense is an act committed by a juvenile for which an adult could be prosecuted in a criminal court. Disposition of a case involves taking a definite action such as waiving the case to criminal court, dismissing the case, placing the youth on probation, placing the youth in a facility for delinquents, or actions such as fines, restitution, and community service. Data are developed and maintained by the National Center for Juvenile Justice]

Type of offense	1990	1995	2000	2004	2005	2006	2007	2008	2009	2010	2011	2012	2013
All delinquency offenses.......	**1,321**	**1,826**	**1,704**	**1,675**	**1,678**	**1,627**	**1,629**	**1,609**	**1,481**	**1,356**	**1,239**	**1,143**	**1,059**
Case rate [1]............	51.5	63.6	55.4	52.1	52.2	50.6	50.9	50.7	46.9	43.0	39.5	36.6	(NA)
Person offenses [2]..............	258	414	401	419	436	417	412	400	364	344	318	295	278
Criminal homicide................	2	3	2	1	1	1	1	1	1	1	1	1	1
Forcible rape................	5	8	8	9	9	9	8	9	8	8	7	8	8
Robbery................	27	42	22	22	27	30	32	33	29	26	23	21	22
Aggravated assault...............	44	62	49	46	50	47	47	45	39	36	32	29	27
Simple assault................	147	255	278	295	301	284	277	268	247	236	215	198	186
Property offenses [2]..............	773	919	707	634	615	590	602	611	564	500	448	409	367
Burglary................	145	149	117	105	102	104	104	106	97	87	80	74	65
Larceny-theft................	346	442	334	296	280	252	265	283	276	246	220	204	183
Motor vehicle theft................	69	56	38	33	32	29	27	23	19	15	13	12	12
Arson................	6	11	9	9	8	9	8	8	7	6	6	6	5
Drug law violations................	68	164	185	184	183	181	182	176	164	162	154	147	142
Public order offenses [2]..............	223	329	411	437	443	439	434	422	388	350	319	293	272
Obstruction of justice..............	89	136	206	198	196	193	191	190	184	163	150	140	132
Disorderly conduct................	55	88	103	131	133	130	130	125	110	101	91	82	75
Weapons offenses................	30	47	34	39	43	44	40	39	32	30	27	23	22
Liquor law violations................	14	12	16	17	17	19	20	19	17	16	14	12	9
Nonviolent sex offenses...........	10	9	14	14	14	13	12	12	12	11	11	11	11

NA Not available. [1] Number of cases disposed per 1,000 juveniles (ages 10 to upper age of juvenile court jurisdiction). The upper age of juvenile court jurisdiction is defined by statute in each state. [2] Total includes other offenses not shown.

Source: U.S. Department of Justice, Office of Juvenile Justice and Delinquency Prevention, "Delinquency Case Rates by Offense, Sex, and Race (1985-2012)," <http://www.ojjdp.gov/ojstatbb/court/data.html>; and "Easy Access to Juvenile Court Statistics, Detailed Offenses," <http://ojjdp.gov/ojstatbb/ezajcs/>; accessed September 2015.

Table 371. Delinquency Cases Disposed by Juvenile Courts by Type of Offense, Sex, and Race: 2000 to 2013

[See headnote, Table 370. Data are developed and maintained by the National Center for Juvenile Justice]

Sex, race, and offense	Number of cases disposed				Case rate [1]			
	2000	2010	2012	2013	2000	2010	2012	2013
Male, total......................	**1,270,400**	**974,300**	**821,200**	**764,800**	**80.4**	**60.4**	**51.5**	**(NA)**
Person............................	288,500	237,700	200,600	190,800	18.2	14.7	12.5	(NA)
Property..........................	526,100	351,200	291,400	265,600	33.3	21.8	18.3	(NA)
Drugs.............................	154,200	132,900	119,900	114,000	9.8	8.2	7.5	(NA)
Public order......................	301,700	252,500	209,400	194,500	19.1	15.6	13.2	(NA)
Female, total....................	**433,300**	**381,200**	**321,900**	**293,700**	**28.9**	**24.8**	**21.1**	**(NA)**
Person............................	112,400	106,600	94,100	87,500	7.5	6.9	6.2	(NA)
Property..........................	181,200	148,400	117,300	101,100	12.1	9.7	7.7	(NA)
Drugs.............................	30,700	29,100	27,400	27,700	2.0	1.9	1.8	(NA)
Public order......................	109,100	97,000	83,100	77,300	7.3	6.3	5.4	(NA)
White, total.....................	**1,160,800**	**864,700**	**724,600**	**654,200**	**48.0**	**35.9**	**30.4**	**(NA)**
Person............................	251,800	196,900	169,200	154,500	10.4	8.1	7.1	(NA)
Property..........................	497,200	326,000	260,000	224,800	20.6	13.6	10.9	(NA)
Drugs.............................	136,200	123,900	113,600	107,100	5.6	5.1	4.8	(NA)
Public order......................	275,500	217,900	181,800	167,900	11.4	9.0	7.6	(NA)
Black, total.....................	**494,100**	**452,500**	**385,500**	**374,100**	**102.0**	**87.8**	**76.6**	**(NA)**
Person............................	139,000	139,200	118,100	117,200	28.7	27.0	23.5	(NA)
Property..........................	185,400	157,800	135,700	130,200	38.3	30.7	27.0	(NA)
Drugs.............................	44,300	33,400	29,100	30,100	9.2	6.5	5.8	(NA)
Public order......................	125,300	122,000	102,500	96,700	25.9	23.6	20.4	(NA)
American Indian, total..........	**25,700**	**19,900**	**18,100**	**17,000**	**55.8**	**34.5**	**31.8**	**(NA)**
Person............................	5,300	4,500	4,100	3,900	11.5	7.8	7.2	(NA)
Property..........................	12,600	7,600	6,700	6,400	27.3	13.3	11.7	(NA)
Drugs.............................	2,500	2,600	2,600	2,600	5.4	4.6	4.7	(NA)
Public order......................	5,400	5,100	4,600	4,100	11.6	8.9	8.1	(NA)
Asian/Native Hawaiian/ Pacific Islander, total..........	**23,200**	**18,400**	**15,000**	**13,200**	**18.0**	**10.9**	**8.6**	**(NA)**
Person............................	4,700	3,700	3,200	2,800	3.7	2.2	1.9	(NA)
Property..........................	12,000	8,200	6,200	5,300	9.3	4.9	3.6	(NA)
Drugs.............................	1,800	2,000	2,000	1,800	1.4	1.2	1.1	(NA)
Public order......................	4,700	4,500	3,500	3,200	3.6	2.6	2.0	(NA)

NA Not available. [1] Cases per 1,000 juveniles (ages 10 to upper age of juvenile court jurisdiction). The upper age of juvenile court jurisdiction is defined by statute in each state.

Source: U.S. Department of Justice, Office of Juvenile Justice and Delinquency Prevention, "Delinquency Case Rates by Offense, Sex, and Race (1985-2012)," <http://www.ojjdp.gov/ojstatbb/court/data.html>; and "Easy Access to Juvenile Court Statistics, Detailed Offenses," <http://ojjdp.gov/ojstatbb/ezajcs/>; accessed September 2015.

Table 372. Child Victims of Abuse and Neglect, Total and First-Time Victims, by State: 2012 and 2013

[For fiscal years ending in year shown. Data are unique counts, which count a child once, regardless of the number of reports concerning that child. Based on available State submissions to National Child Abuse and Neglect Data System (NCANDS) of alleged child abuse and neglect, see headnote Table 373. States reporting 95 percent or more first-time victims are excluded due to potential issues with data quality. See source for details]

| State | 2012 | | First-time victims | | 2013 | | First-time victims | |
	Total child population	Victims	Number	Rate per 1,000 children	Total child population	Victims	Number	Rate per 1,000 children
Total....................	74,549,919	665,904	489,234	6.8	74,399,940	664,219	486,232	6.8
Alabama.................	1,117,489	9,573	7,965	7.1	1,111,481	8,809	7,232	6.5
Alaska...................	188,162	2,928	1,963	10.4	188,132	2,448	1,634	8.7
Arizona.................	1,617,149	10,039	8,766	5.4	1,616,814	13,171	11,360	7.0
Arkansas...............	710,471	11,133	8,962	12.6	709,866	10,370	8,375	11.8
California..............	9,209,007	76,026	64,057	7.0	9,174,877	75,641	63,698	6.9
Colorado...............	1,232,864	10,482	7,870	6.4	1,237,932	10,161	7,651	6.2
Connecticut............	794,959	8,151	5,660	7.1	785,566	7,287	5,071	6.5
Delaware...............	204,586	2,335	1,823	8.9	203,558	1,915	1,502	7.4
District of Columbia.....	107,642	2,141	1,552	14.4	111,474	2,050	1,457	13.1
Florida.................	4,012,421	53,341	26,506	6.6	4,026,674	48,457	23,785	5.9
Georgia.................	2,487,831	18,752	15,883	6.4	2,489,709	19,062	15,785	6.3
Hawaii..................	305,981	1,398	1,102	3.6	307,266	1,324	1,092	3.6
Idaho...................	427,177	1,428	1,169	2.7	427,781	1,674	1,452	3.4
Illinois.................	3,057,042	27,497	20,348	6.7	3,023,307	29,719	22,074	7.3
Indiana.................	1,589,655	20,223	18,250	11.5	1,586,027	21,755	16,566	10.4
Iowa....................	723,917	10,751	7,382	10.2	724,032	11,345	7,891	10.9
Kansas.................	726,668	1,868	1,707	2.3	724,092	2,063	1,846	2.5
Kentucky...............	1,017,350	17,054	12,068	11.9	1,014,004	20,005	14,200	14.0
Louisiana..............	1,114,620	8,458	6,318	5.7	1,112,957	10,119	7,741	7.0
Maine..................	264,846	3,781	1,699	6.4	261,276	3,820	2,475	9.5
Maryland...............	1,346,235	13,079	10,244	7.6	1,344,522	12,397	9,697	7.2
Massachusetts..........	1,399,417	19,234	10,947	7.8	1,393,946	20,307	11,926	8.6
Michigan...............	2,269,365	33,394	23,027	10.1	2,245,201	33,938	23,112	10.3
Minnesota..............	1,278,050	4,238	3,511	2.7	1,279,111	4,183	3,483	2.7
Mississippi.............	742,941	7,599	6,854	9.2	737,432	7,415	6,616	9.0
Missouri................	1,405,015	4,685	3,971	2.8	1,397,685	1,827	1,535	1.1
Montana................	222,905	1,324	1,031	4.6	223,981	1,414	1,148	5.1
Nebraska...............	462,673	3,888	2,918	6.3	464,348	3,993	2,872	6.2
Nevada.................	659,655	5,437	3,570	5.4	661,605	5,438	3,538	5.3
New Hampshire.........	275,818	901	276	1.0	271,122	822	283	1.0
New Jersey.............	2,035,106	9,031	7,310	3.6	2,022,117	9,490	7,689	3.8
New Mexico............	512,314	5,882	4,372	8.5	507,540	6,530	4,824	9.5
New York...............	4,264,694	68,375	41,997	9.8	4,239,976	64,578	39,463	9.3
North Carolina..........	2,284,122	23,150	18,370	8.0	2,285,605	19,873	15,791	6.9
North Dakota...........	156,765	1,402	1,214	7.7	162,688	1,517	1,264	7.8
Ohio....................	2,668,125	29,250	20,453	7.7	2,649,830	27,562	19,244	7.3
Oklahoma..............	939,911	9,627	7,618	8.1	947,027	11,575	9,050	9.6
Oregon.................	859,910	9,576	6,740	7.8	857,606	10,280	7,119	8.3
Pennsylvania...........	2,737,905	3,417	3,199	1.2	2,715,645	3,260	3,047	1.1
Rhode Island...........	216,591	3,218	2,264	10.5	213,987	3,132	2,135	10.0
South Carolina.........	1,077,455	11,439	8,556	7.9	1,079,798	10,404	7,801	7.2
South Dakota...........	205,298	1,224	933	4.5	207,959	984	749	3.6
Tennessee..............	1,492,689	10,069	8,494	5.7	1,491,577	10,377	8,813	5.9
Texas..................	6,985,807	62,551	50,153	7.2	7,041,986	64,603	51,674	7.3
Utah...................	888,578	9,419	6,845	7.7	896,589	9,306	6,680	7.5
Vermont................	124,555	649	531	4.3	122,701	746	633	5.2
Virginia................	1,861,323	(NA)	(NA)	(NA)	1,864,535	(NA)	(NA)	(NA)
Washington............	1,588,451	6,546	4,694	3.0	1,595,795	7,132	4,856	3.0
West Virginia...........	384,030	4,591	3,540	9.2	381,678	4,695	3,795	9.9
Wisconsin..............	1,316,113	4,645	3,936	3.0	1,307,776	4,526	3,907	3.0
Wyoming...............	136,526	705	616	4.5	137,679	720	601	4.4

NA Not available.

Source: U.S. Department of Health and Human Services, Administration for Children and Families, Statistics and Research, *Child Maltreatment 2013*, January 2015. See also <http://www.acf.hhs.gov/programs/cb/research-data-technology/statistics-research/child-maltreatment>.

Table 373. Child Abuse and Neglect Victims by Type of Maltreatment and Age and Sex of Victim: 2007 to 2013

[For fiscal years ending in year shown. Data are unique counts, which count a child once, regardless of the number of reports concerning that child. Based on available State submissions to National Child Abuse and Neglect Data System (NCANDS) of alleged child abuse and neglect. NCANDS collects case level data on children who received child protective services response in the form of an investigative or alternative response. Each state has its own definition of child abuse and neglect based on standards set by federal law. Child abuse is defined as any recent act or failure to act on the part of a parent or caretaker which results in death, serious physical or emotional harm, sexual abuse or exploitation; or an act or failure to act which presents an imminent risk or serious harm]

Item	2007	2008	2009	2010	2011	2012	2013
Victims, total [1,2]	690,849	704,732	693,507	688,251	676,569	678,810	678,332
TYPES OF MALTREATMENT [3]							
Neglect	489,275	504,717	502,417	499,691	531,413	531,241	539,576
Physical abuse	118,137	121,735	120,510	118,502	118,825	124,544	122,159
Sexual abuse	68,024	68,156	64,358	62,057	61,472	62,936	60,956
Psychological or emotional	49,848	49,947	50,466	53,426	60,839	57,880	59,236
Medical neglect	15,597	16,067	16,373	15,711	15,074	15,705	15,450
Other and unknown	58,035	61,083	64,394	68,590	71,217	73,172	68,266
SEX OF VICTIM							
Male	332,445	340,300	334,404	333,864	329,004	330,620	330,914
Female	356,226	361,787	354,677	352,174	345,587	345,823	345,633
AGE OF VICTIM							
1 year and younger	132,122	138,231	136,502	136,910	133,942	134,024	139,360
2 to 5 years old	171,332	175,573	177,126	180,271	181,140	182,845	179,949
6 to 9 years old	150,593	152,196	147,812	145,354	142,412	145,190	147,888
10 to 13 years old	123,127	123,805	120,577	119,555	117,876	118,021	115,125
14 to 17 years old	108,228	111,493	108,633	103,764	98,607	95,734	93,459
18 years old and over [4]	398	627	638	490	(NA)	(NA)	(NA)
Unknown [5]	4,231	1,938	1,327	979	2,592	2,996	3,151

NA Not available. [1] Total victims is the sum of the states contributing data to the Child File. The number of states not contributing data varies by year. [2] This is a count of the number of distinct victims of the specified types of maltreatment. A child may be a victim of more than one type of maltreatment, so the sum of types is greater than the count of victims. [3] Not all states use this taxonomy, nor do states define the categories in the same way. [4] Beginning in 2011, data included in unknown. [5] Beginning in 2011, includes unborn, unknown, and victims aged 18–21. Unknown age is defined as victims whose ages were unable to be determined or older than 17 years, a few States include victims ages 18–21 as child victims.

Source: U.S. Department of Health and Human Services, Administration for Children and Families, Statistics and Research, *Child Maltreatment 2013*, January 2015, earlier editions, and unpublished data. See also <http://www.acf.hhs.gov/programs/cb/research-data-technology/statistics-research/child-maltreatment>.

Table 374. Prisoners Under Jurisdiction of Federal or State Correctional Authorities—Summary by State: 2000 to 2013

[For years ending December 31. Jurisdiction refers to the legal authority over a prisoner, regardless of where held]

State	2000	2010	2011	2012	2013	State	2000	2010	2011	2012	2013
U.S.	1,394,231	1,613,803	1,598,968	1,570,397	1,575,434	MS	20,241	21,067	21,386	22,319	21,969
Federal [1]	145,416	209,771	216,362	217,815	215,866	MO	27,543	30,623	30,833	31,247	31,537
State	1,248,815	1,404,032	1,382,606	1,352,582	1,359,568	MT	3,105	3,716	3,678	3,609	3,642
AL	26,406	31,764	32,270	32,431	32,381	NE	3,895	4,587	4,616	4,705	5,026
AK [2]	4,173	5,391	5,597	5,633	5,081	NV [7]	10,063	12,653	12,778	12,883	13,056
AZ [3]	26,510	40,209	40,020	40,080	41,104	NH	2,257	2,761	2,614	2,790	3,018
AR	11,915	16,204	16,108	14,654	17,235	NJ	29,784	25,007	23,834	23,225	22,452
CA	163,001	165,062	149,569	134,534	135,981	NM	5,342	6,763	6,998	6,727	6,849
CO	16,833	22,815	21,978	20,462	20,371	NY	70,199	56,656	55,436	54,210	53,550
CT [2]	18,355	19,321	18,324	17,530	17,563	NC	31,266	40,382	39,440	37,136	36,922
DE [2,3]	6,921	6,615	6,739	6,914	7,004	ND	1,076	1,487	1,423	1,512	1,513
DC [4,5]	10,352	(NA)	(NA)	(NA)	(NA)	OH	45,833	51,712	50,964	50,876	51,729
FL	71,319	104,306	103,055	101,930	103,028	OK	23,181	26,252	25,977	25,225	27,547
GA	44,232	56,432	55,944	55,457	54,004	OR	10,580	14,876	14,510	14,840	15,362
HI [2,6]	5,053	5,912	6,037	5,831	5,632	PA	36,847	51,264	51,578	51,125	50,312
ID	5,535	7,431	7,739	7,985	8,242	RI [2,6]	3,286	3,357	3,337	3,318	3,361
IL [7]	45,281	48,418	48,427	49,348	48,653	SC	21,778	23,578	22,914	22,388	22,060
IN	20,125	28,028	28,906	28,831	29,913	SD	2,616	3,434	3,535	3,650	3,651
IA [3]	7,955	9,455	9,116	8,733	8,697	TN	22,166	27,451	28,479	28,411	28,521
KS	8,344	9,051	9,327	9,682	9,763	TX	166,719	173,649	172,224	166,372	168,280
KY	14,919	20,544	21,545	22,110	21,030	UT	5,637	6,807	6,879	6,962	7,075
LA	35,207	39,445	39,710	40,172	39,299	VT [2]	1,697	2,079	2,053	2,034	2,078
ME	1,679	2,154	2,145	2,108	2,173	VA	30,168	37,638	38,130	37,044	36,982
MD	23,538	22,645	22,558	21,522	21,335	WA	14,915	18,235	17,847	17,271	17,984
MA	10,722	11,313	11,623	11,308	10,950	WV	3,856	6,681	6,826	7,070	6,824
MI	47,718	44,165	42,940	43,636	43,759	WI	20,754	22,729	22,657	22,600	22,471
MN	6,238	9,796	9,800	9,938	10,289	WY	1,680	2,112	2,183	2,204	2,310

NA Not available. [1] Includes inmates held in nonsecure privately operated community corrections facilities and juveniles held in contract facilities. [2] Data include both total jail and prison population. Prisons and jails form one integrated system. [3] Numbers are for custody rather than jurisdiction counts. [4] The transfer of responsibility for sentenced felons from the District of Columbia to the federal system was completed by the year end 2001. [5] The District of Columbia inmates sentenced to more than 1 year are now under the responsibility of the Bureau of Prisons. [6] Counts include dual jurisdiction cases where the inmate is currently housed in another jurisdiction's facilities. [7] State did not submit 2012 National Prisoner Statistics (NPS) data; population estimates for 2012 are imputed.

Source: U.S. Department of Justice, Bureau of Justice Statistics, *Prisoners in 2013*, NCJ 247282, September 2014; and "Corrections Statistical Analysis Tool," <http://www.bjs.gov/index.cfm?ty=nps>, accessed May 2015.

Table 375. Jail Inmates by Sex, Race, and Hispanic Origin: 2000 to 2014

[As of the last week day in June. Data for 2000 and 2010-2014 are based on the Annual Survey of Jails; 2005 from Census of Jail Inmates]

Characteristic	2000	2005	2010	[6] 2011	[6] 2012	[6] 2013	[6] 2014
Total inmates [1, 2]	621,149	747,529	748,728	735,601	744,524	731,208	744,592
Incarceration rate per 100,000							
U.S. residents	220	252	242	236	237	231	234
Rated capacity [3]	677,787	786,954	857,918	870,422	877,396	872,943	890,486
Adult	613,534	740,770	741,168	729,700	739,100	726,600	740,400
Male	543,120	646,807	649,284	636,900	640,900	624,700	631,600
Female	70,414	93,963	91,884	92,800	98,100	101,900	108,800
Juveniles [4]	7,615	6,759	7,560	5,900	5,400	4,600	4,200
White, non-Hispanic	260,500	331,000	331,600	329,400	341,100	344,900	352,800
Black, non-Hispanic	256,300	290,500	283,200	276,400	274,600	261,500	263,800
Hispanic/Latino [5]	94,100	111,900	118,100	113,900	112,700	107,900	110,600
American Indian or Alaska Native non-Hispanic	5,500	7,600	9,900	9,400	9,300	10,200	10,400
Asian or Pacific Islander	4,700	5,400	5,100	5,300	5,400	5,100	6,000
Two or more races	(NA)	1,000	800	1,200	1,500	1,600	1,000

NA Not available. [1] Total does not include offenders who were supervised outside of jail facilities. [2] Prior to 2005, race and Hispanic origin data do not include two or more races. [3] Rated capacity is the number of beds or inmates assigned by a rating official to facilities within each jurisdiction. [4] Juveniles are persons held that are age 17 or younger at midyear. Includes juveniles who were tried or awaiting trial as adults. [5] Persons of Hispanic origin may be of any race. [6] Data adjusted for nonresponse and rounded to the nearest 100. See source methodology.

Source: U.S. Department of Justice, Bureau of Justice Statistics, *Jail Inmates at Midyear 2014*, NCJ 248629, June 2015. See also <http://bjs.ojp.usdoj.gov/index.cfm?ty=pbse&sid=38>.

Table 376. Prisoners Under Federal or State Jurisdiction by Sex: 1980 to 2013

[As of December 31. Represents prisoners sentenced to more than one year under jurisdiction of federal or state authorities rather than those in the custody of such authorities. Federal prisoners includes inmates held in nonsecure privately operated community corrections facilities and juveniles held in contract facilities. From the National Prisoner Statistics Program]

Year	Total [1]	Rate [2]	State	Male	Female	Year	Total [1]	Rate [2]	State	Male	Female
1980	315,974	139	295,363	303,643	12,331	2005	1,462,866	492	1,296,693	1,364,178	98,688
1985	480,568	202	447,873	459,223	21,345	2006	1,504,598	501	1,331,065	1,401,261	103,337
1990	739,980	297	689,577	699,416	40,564	2007	1,532,851	506	1,353,647	1,427,088	105,763
1995	1,085,022	411	1,001,359	1,021,059	63,963	2008	1,547,742	506	1,365,409	1,441,384	106,358
2000	1,334,174	470	1,209,130	1,249,130	85,044	2009	1,553,574	504	1,365,688	1,448,239	105,335
2001	1,345,217	470	1,208,708	1,260,033	85,184	2010	1,552,669	500	1,362,028	1,447,766	104,903
2002	1,380,516	477	1,237,476	1,291,450	89,066	2011	1,538,847	492	1,341,797	1,435,141	103,706
2003	1,408,361	483	1,256,442	1,315,790	92,571	2012	1,511,497	480	1,314,923	1,410,208	101,289
2004	1,433,728	487	1,274,591	1,337,730	95,998	2013 [3]	1,515,879	478	1,321,781	1,412,745	104,134

[1] Includes prisoners under the legal authority of state or federal correctional officials. [2] Rate per 100,000 estimated population. Based on U.S. Census Bureau estimated resident population. [3] Total and state estimates include imputed counts for Nevada, In addition, Alaska did not submit sex-specific counts or sentence length data in 2013.

Source: U.S. Department of Justice, Bureau of Justice Statistics, *Prisoners in 2013*, NCJ 247282, September 2014, and earlier reports. See also <http://bjs.ojp.usdoj.gov/index.cfm?ty=pbse&sid=40>.

Table 377. Prisoners Under Death Sentence by Characteristic: 1980 to 2013

[As of December 31. Excludes prisoners under sentence of death who remained within local correctional systems pending exhaustion of appellate process or who had not been committed to prison. Data from the National Prisoner Statistics Program]

Characteristic	1980	1990	2000	2005	2006	2007	2008	2009	2010	2011	2012	2013
Total [1, 2]	692	2,346	3,601	3,245	3,228	3,215	3,210	3,173	3,139	3,065	3,011	2,979
White	418	1,368	1,989	1,802	1,806	1,806	1,795	1,780	1,743	1,721	1,684	1,663
Black and other [3]	270	978	1,612	1,443	1,427	1,409	1,415	1,393	1,396	1,274	1,258	1,248
Under 20 years old	11	8	11	–	–	1	–	–	(NA)	–	–	–
20 to 24 years old	173	168	237	61	51	42	44	39	(NA)	28	26	21
25 to 34 years old	334	1,110	1,103	816	735	680	610	564	(NA)	471	401	374
35 to 54 years old	186	1,006	2,019	2,012	2,043	2,060	2,076	2,062	(NA)	1,982	1,963	1,903
55 years old and over	10	64	223	365	399	437	477	508	(NA)	601	643	681
Years of school completed:												
8 years or less	142	364	447	398	381	372	361	356	(NA)	347	333	318
7 years or less	68	178	214	192	186	183	176	176	(NA)	(NA)	(NA)	(NA)
8 years	74	186	233	206	195	189	185	180	(NA)	(NA)	(NA)	(NA)
9 to 11 years	204	775	1,157	1,030	1,015	989	977	950	(NA)	899	874	847
12 years	162	729	1,184	1,105	1,098	1,089	1,094	1,097	(NA)	1,067	1,063	1,042
More than 12 years	43	209	315	256	248	248	247	238	(NA)	235	232	228
Unknown	163	279	490	465	486	522	528	532	(NA)	534	531	544
Marital status:												
Never married	268	998	1,749	1,586	1,577	1,558	1,552	1,531	(NA)	1,488	1,469	1,450
Married	229	632	739	649	626	635	630	613	(NA)	608	587	569
Divorced/other [4]	217	726	1,105	1,019	1,025	1,027	1,025	1,029	(NA)	986	977	530
Time elapsed since sentencing:												
Less than 12 months	185	231	208	122	105	110	106	103	(NA)	(NA)	(NA)	(NA)
12 to 47 months	389	753	786	399	382	352	339	329	(NA)	(NA)	(NA)	(NA)
48 to 71 months	102	438	507	299	262	262	244	237	(NA)	(NA)	(NA)	(NA)
72 months and over	38	934	2,092	2,434	2,479	2,496	2,518	2,504	(NA)	(NA)	(NA)	(NA)
Legal status at arrest:												
Not under sentence	384	1,345	2,202	1,979	1,952	1,963	1,961	1,931	(NA)	(NA)	(NA)	(NA)
Parole or probation [5]	115	578	921	792	778	760	753	739	(NA)	(NA)	(NA)	(NA)
Prison or escaped	45	128	126	144	142	143	146	156	(NA)	(NA)	(NA)	(NA)
Unknown	170	305	344	339	356	354	347	347	(NA)	(NA)	(NA)	(NA)

– Represents zero. NA Not available. [1] Revisions to the total number of prisoners were not carried to the characteristics except for race. [2] Includes races not shown separately. [3] Beginning 2011, data are shown only for black. [4] Includes persons married but separated, widows, widowers, and unknown. [5] Includes prisoners on mandatory conditional release, work release, other leave, AWOL, or bail. Covers 28 prisoners in 1990; 15 in 2004; 14 in 2005, 2006, 2007, and 2009; and 12 in 2008.

Source: U.S. Department of Justice, Bureau of Justice Statistics, *Capital Punishment, 2013—Statistical Tables*, NCJ 248448, December 2014, and earlier reports. See also <http://www.bjs.gov/index.cfm?ty=pbse&sid=1>.

Table 378. Prisoners Executed Under Civil Authority by Sex and Race: 1930 to 2014

[Excludes executions by military authorities. See source for more information]

Year or period	Total [1]	Male	Female	White [2]	Black [2]	Hispanic	All other races [2,3]
1930 to 1939	1,667	1,656	11	827	816	(NA)	(NA)
1940 to 1949	1,284	1,272	12	490	781	(NA)	(NA)
1950 to 1959	717	709	8	336	376	(NA)	(NA)
1960 to 1967	191	190	1	98	93	(NA)	(NA)
1968 to 1976 [4]	–	–	–	–	–	–	–
1977 to 2013	1,359	1,346	13	770	464	111	14
1985	18	18	–	9	7	2	–
1990	23	23	–	16	7	–	–
1995	56	56	–	31	22	2	1
1996	45	45	–	29	14	2	–
1997	74	74	–	41	26	5	2
1998	68	66	2	40	18	8	2
1999	98	98	–	53	33	9	3
2000	85	83	2	43	35	6	1
2001	66	63	3	45	17	3	1
2002	71	69	2	47	18	6	–
2003	65	65	–	41	20	3	1
2004	59	59	–	36	19	3	1
2005	60	59	1	38	19	3	–
2006	53	53	–	25	20	8	–
2007	42	42	–	22	14	6	–
2008	37	37	–	17	17	3	–
2009	52	52	–	24	21	7	–
2010	46	45	1	28	13	5	–
2011	43	43	–	22	16	5	–
2012	43	43	–	25	11	7	–
2013	39	38	1	23	13	3	–
2014	35	33	2	(NA)	(NA)	(NA)	(NA)

– Represents zero. NA Not available. [1] Prior to 1977, includes races other than White or Black not shown separately. [2] Excludes persons of Hispanic or Latino origin. [3] Includes American Indians, Alaska Natives, Asians, Native Hawaiians, and other Pacific Islanders. [4] In 1972, the US Supreme Court invalidated capital punishment statutes in several states, effecting a moratorium on executions. Executions resumed in 1977 when the Supreme Court found revisions to several state statutes had effectively addressed the issues previously held as unconstitutional.

Source: Through 1978, U.S. Law Enforcement Assistance Administration; thereafter, U.S. Department of Justice, Bureau of Justice Statistics, *Capital Punishment, 2013 —Statistical Tables*, NCJ 248448, December 2014. See also <http://bjs.ojp.usdoj.gov/index.cfm?ty=pbse&sid=1>.

Table 379. Prisoners Executed Under Civil Authority by State: 1977 to 2014

[Alaska, District of Columbia, Hawaii, Illinois, Iowa, Maine, Massachusetts, Michigan, Minnesota, New Jersey, North Dakota, Rhode Island, Vermont, West Virginia, and Wisconsin are jurisdictions without a death penalty. New Mexico abolished the death penalty for offenses committed after July 1, 2009, and Connecticut repealed the death penalty for offenses committed on or after Apr. 25, 2012, and Maryland repealed the death penalty effective Oct. 1, 2013; two men in New Mexico, 10 men in Connecticut, and 5 men in Maryland under previously imposed death sentences are still subject to execution]

State	1977 to 2013	2000	2010	2012	2013	2014	State	1977 to 2013	2000	2010	2012	2013	2014
U.S. [1]	1,359	85	46	43	39	35	Missouri	70	5	–	–	2	10
Alabama	56	4	5	–	1	–	Montana	3	–	–	–	–	–
Arizona	36	3	1	6	2	1	Nebraska	3	–	–	–	–	–
Arkansas	27	2	–	–	–	–	Nevada	12	–	–	–	–	–
California	13	1	–	–	–	–	New Mexico	1	–	–	–	–	–
Colorado	1	–	–	–	–	–	North Carolina	43	1	–	–	–	–
Connecticut	1	–	–	–	–	–	Ohio	52	–	8	3	3	1
Delaware	16	1	–	1	–	–	Oklahoma	108	11	3	6	6	3
Florida	81	6	1	3	7	8	Oregon	2	–	–	–	–	–
Georgia	53	–	2	–	1	2	Pennsylvania	3	–	–	–	–	–
Idaho	3	–	–	1	–	–	South Carolina	43	1	–	–	–	–
Illinois	12	–	–	–	–	–	South Dakota	3	–	–	2	–	–
Indiana	20	–	–	–	–	–	Tennessee	6	1	–	–	–	–
Kentucky	3	–	–	–	–	–	Texas	508	40	17	15	16	10
Louisiana	28	1	1	–	–	–	Utah	7	–	1	–	–	–
Maryland	5	–	–	–	–	–	Virginia	110	8	3	–	1	–
Mississippi	21	–	3	6	–	–	Washington	5	–	1	–	–	–
							Wyoming	1	–	–	–	–	–

– Represents zero. [1] Includes persons executed within the Federal system.

Source: Through 1978, U.S. Law Enforcement Assistance Administration; thereafter, U.S. Department of Justice, Bureau of Justice Statistics, *Capital Punishment, 2013—Statistical Tables*, NCJ 248448, December 2014, and earlier reports. See also <http://bjs.ojp.usdoj.gov/index.cfm?ty=pbse&sid=1>.

Table 380. Adults Under Community Supervision, Probation, and Parole by State: 2013

[As of December 31, 2013, unless otherwise noted. Counts are rounded to nearest hundred. Rates are per 100,000, computed using the estimated U.S. adult resident population in each jurisdiction on January 1, 2014. Counts may not be actual as reporting agencies may provide estimates on some or all detailed data; see source for details. Based on Bureau of Justice Statistics' Annual Survey of Probation and Parole]

Area	Community supervision [1]		Probation		Parole	
	Number	Rate (100,000)	Number	Rate (100,000)	Number	Rate (100,000)
U.S. total	4,751,400	1,950	3,910,647	1,605	853,215	350
Federal	131,900	54	20,676	8	111,226	46
States	4,619,400	1,895	3,889,971	1,596	741,989	304
Alabama [3]	70,800	1,896	61,801	1,655	8,982	241
Alaska	9,500	1,728	7,167	1,308	2,303	420
Arizona	79,200	1,570	71,527	1,418	7,636	151
Arkansas [2,3]	50,200	2,223	29,289	1,298	[2] 21,709	962
California [2,3]	381,600	1,301	294,057	1,003	[2] 87,532	298
Colorado [3]	89,700	2,209	78,843	1,942	10,846	267
Connecticut	45,400	1,608	42,723	1,515	2,640	94
Delaware	16,700	2,299	16,039	2,209	657	90
District of Columbia	12,600	2,326	7,351	1,362	5,623	1,042
Florida [3]	237,800	1,521	233,128	1,491	4,683	30
Georgia [3,4]	536,200	7,117	514,477	6,829	26,611	353
Hawaii	23,300	2,116	21,576	1,958	1,738	158
Idaho	35,200	2,957	31,375	2,634	3,851	323
Illinois	153,400	1,552	123,862	1,253	29,586	299
Indiana	134,000	2,677	123,673	2,471	10,340	207
Iowa	34,700	1,462	29,301	1,233	5,595	235
Kansas	20,500	942	16,446	756	4,065	187
Kentucky [3]	65,900	1,943	51,027	1,505	14,922	440
Louisiana	70,700	2,006	42,046	1,192	28,744	815
Maine	6,700	631	6,719	629	21	2
Maryland	46,300	1,006	40,716	884	5,623	122
Massachusetts	70,000	1,313	67,784	1,273	2,166	41
Michigan [3]	195,200	2,545	176,795	2,305	18,439	240
Minnesota	107,800	2,590	101,762	2,446	5,997	144
Mississippi	38,600	1,707	31,675	1,402	6,901	305
Missouri	70,400	1,511	51,028	1,094	19,401	416
Montana	9,500	1,194	8,472	1,066	1,021	128
Nebraska	14,800	1,048	13,545	960	1,246	88
Nevada	17,600	823	12,102	565	5,522	258
New Hampshire	6,300	593	3,994	379	2,256	214
New Jersey	128,100	1,856	113,231	1,639	14,918	216
New Mexico [3]	18,700	1,184	16,696	1,057	2,010	127
New York	151,400	979	106,409	688	45,039	291
North Carolina	100,600	1,323	94,442	1,242	7,171	94
North Dakota	5,500	959	4,898	860	561	99
Ohio [3]	267,400	2,989	250,630	2,802	16,797	188
Oklahoma	(NA)	(NA)	(NA)	(NA)	2,554	87
Oregon	61,100	1,981	37,891	1,228	23,246	753
Pennsylvania	275,800	2,734	171,970	1,705	103,802	1,029
Rhode Island [3]	23,400	2,791	22,988	2,737	459	55
South Carolina	40,900	1,102	35,825	964	5,556	150
South Dakota	9,500	1,489	6,952	1,084	2,595	405
Tennessee	77,900	1,550	64,216	1,278	13,657	272
Texas	508,000	2,597	399,655	2,043	111,302	569
Utah	14,500	717	11,203	554	3,283	162
Vermont	6,900	1,365	5,791	1,148	1,095	217
Virginia	55,800	869	54,020	841	1,800	28
Washington [3]	111,100	2,056	95,217	1,762	15,908	294
West Virginia [3]	11,000	748	8,465	574	2,553	173
Wisconsin	65,300	1,468	46,758	1,051	20,251	455
Wyoming	6,000	1,338	5,207	1,165	776	174

NA Not known. [1] December 31, 2013 population excludes 12,511 offenders under community supervision who were on both probation and parole. [2] Includes 41,947 parolees in California under post-release community supervision. [3] Includes estimates for nonreporting agencies, see source for explanatory notes. [4] Counts include private agency cases and may overstate the number of persons under supervision.

Source: U.S. Department of Justice, Bureau of Justice Statistics, *Probation and Parole in the United States, 2013*, NCJ 248029, October 2014. See also <http://www.bjs.gov/index.cfm?ty=tp&tid=15>.

Table 381. Rate of Adults Under Community Supervision, Probation, and Parole: 2000 to 2013

[Rate per 100,000 population. Based on Bureau of Justice Statistics' Annual Survey of Probation and Parole. Probation is a court-ordered period of correctional supervision in the community, generally as an alternative to incarceration. In some cases, probation can be a combined sentence of incarceration followed by a period of community supervision. Parole is a period of conditional supervised release in the community following a prison term. It includes parolees released through discretionary or mandatory supervised release from prison, those released through other types of post-custody conditional supervision, and those sentenced to a term of supervised release. The community supervision population includes adults on probation, parole, or any other post-prison supervision]

| Year | Rate | | | U.S. residents on— | | |
	Community supervision [1]	Probation	Parole	Community supervision [1]	Probation	Parole
2000	2,162	1,818	344	1 in 46	1 in 55	1 in 291
2001	2,184	1,842	342	1 in 46	1 in 54	1 in 292
2002	2,198	1,849	349	1 in 45	1 in 54	1 in 287
2003	2,219	1,865	354	1 in 45	1 in 55	1 in 282
2004	2,226	1,875	351	1 in 45	1 in 53	1 in 285
2005	2,215	1,864	351	1 in 45	1 in 54	1 in 285
2006	2,228	1,875	353	1 in 45	1 in 53	1 in 283
2007	2,239	1,878	361	1 in 45	1 in 53	1 in 277
2008 [2, 3]	2,203	1,846	358	1 in 45	1 in 54	1 in 279
2009 [2]	2,147	1,796	353	1 in 47	1 in 56	1 in 284
2010 [2]	2,067	1,715	355	1 in 48	1 in 58	1 in 281
2011 [2]	2,014	1,662	357	1 in 50	1 in 60	1 in 280
2012 [2]	1,980	1,663	353	1 in 50	1 in 61	1 in 284
2013 [2]	1,950	1,605	350	1 in 51	1 in 62	1 in 286

[1] Includes adults on probation and adults on parole. [2] Detail does not sum to total because the community supervision rate was adjusted to exclude parolees who were also on probation. [3] The apparent decrease observed in the community supervision and probation rates between 2007 and 2008 was due to a change in scope for two jurisdictions and does not reflect actual declines in the populations.

Source: U.S. Department of Justice, Bureau of Justice Statistics, *Probation and Parole in the United States, 2013*, NCJ 248029, October 2014, and earlier reports. See also <http://www.bjs.gov/index.cfm?ty=tp&tid=15>.

Table 382. Fire Losses—Total and Per Capita: 1980 to 2013

[5,579 represents $5,579,000,000. Includes allowances for Fair Access to Insurance Requirements Plan and uninsured losses]

Year	Total (mil. dol.)	Per capita [1] (dol.)	Year	Total (mil. dol.)	Per capita [1] (dol.)	Year	Total (mil. dol.)	Per capita [1] (dol.)
1980	5,579	24.56	1998	11,510	45.59	2006	20,340	68.17
1985	7,753	32.70	1999	12,428	45.58	2007	24,399	81.00
1990	9,495	38.07	2000	13,457	47.69	2008	24,734	81.34
1993	11,331	43.96	2001 [2]	17,118	60.07	2009	22,911	74.68
1994	12,778	49.08	2002	17,586	61.14	2010	20,486	66.23
1995	11,887	45.23	2003	21,129	72.83	2011	19,511	62.62
1996	12,544	47.29	2004	17,344	59.23	2012	23,977	76.39
1997	12,940	48.32	2005	20,427	69.12	2013	19,301	61.05

[1] Based on U.S. Census Bureau estimated resident population as of July 1. Enumerated population as of April 1 for 1980, 1990, 2000, and 2010. [2] Does not include insured fire losses related to terrorism.

Source: Insurance Information Institute, New York, NY. *The Insurance Fact Book, 2015* ©, and previous reports. See also <http://www.iii.org>.

Table 383. Fires and Property Loss for Incendiary and Suspicious Fires and Civilian Fire Deaths and Injuries by Selected Property Type: 2007 to 2013

[In thousands (531 represents 531,000), except as indicated. Based on sample survey of fire departments]

Characteristic	2007	2008	2009	2010	2011	2012	2013
NUMBER (1,000)							
Structure fires, total	531	515	481	482	485	481	488
Structure fires that were intentionally set	32	31	27	28	27	26	23
PROPERTY LOSS (mil. dol.) [1]							
Structure fires, total	10,638	12,361	10,842	9,716	9,693	9,776	9,526
Structure fires that were intentionally set	773	866	684	585	601	581	577
CIVILIAN FIRE DEATHS							
Deaths, total [2]	3,430	3,320	3,010	3,120	3,005	2,855	3,240
Residential property	2,895	2,780	2,590	2,665	2,550	2,405	2,785
One- and two-family dwellings	2,350	2,365	2,100	2,200	2,105	2,000	2,430
Apartments	515	390	465	440	415	380	325
Vehicles [3]	385	365	280	310	300	325	320
CIVILIAN FIRE INJURIES							
Injuries, total [2]	17,675	16,705	17,050	17,720	17,500	16,500	15,925
Residential property	14,000	13,560	13,050	13,800	14,360	13,175	12,575
One- and two-family dwellings	9,650	9,185	9,300	9,400	9,485	8,825	8,300
Apartments	3,950	3,975	3,350	3,950	4,425	4,050	3,900
Vehicles [3]	1,675	1,065	1,610	1,590	1,190	975	1,050

[1] Direct property loss only. [2] Includes other not shown separately. [3] Includes highway vehicles, and trains, boats, ships, farm vehicles, and construction vehicles.

Source: National Fire Protection Association, Quincy, MA, *Fire Loss in the United States During 2013* ©, September 2014, and earlier reports. See also <http://www.nfpa.org/research>.

Table 384. The U.S. Fire Service: Departments, Personnel, and Responses by Type: 1990 to 2013

[In thousands (1,025.7 represents 1,025,700), except where noted. A fire department is a public or private organization that provides fire prevention, fire suppression, and associated emergency and non-emergency services to a jurisdiction such as a county, municipality, or organized fire district]

Items	1990	2000	2005	2008	2009	2010	2011	2012	2013
FIRE DEPARTMENTS (NUMBER)									
Total departments	**30,391**	**30,339**	**30,300**	**30,170**	**30,165**	**30,125**	**30,145**	**30,100**	**30,052**
All career	1,949	2,178	2,087	2,315	2,457	2,495	2,550	2,610	2,477
Mostly career	1,338	1,667	1,766	1,790	1,752	1,860	1,865	1,995	1,971
Mostly volunteer	4,000	4,523	4,902	4,830	5,099	5,290	5,530	5,445	5,797
All volunteer	23,104	21,971	21,575	21,235	20,857	20,480	20,200	20,050	19,807
By whether Emergency Medical Service (EMS) provided:									
Provide EMS service only	(NA)	(NA)	12,900	13,352	13,275	13,440	13,555	13,600	13,400
Provide EMS service and advance life support	(NA)	(NA)	4,260	4,418	4,475	4,515	4,590	4,550	5,050
No EMS service	(NA)	(NA)	13,170	12,400	12,415	12,170	12,000	11,950	11,600
FIRE DEPARTMENT PERSONNEL (1,000)									
Total personnel	**1,025.7**	**1,064.2**	**1,136.7**	**1,148.9**	**1,148.1**	**1,103.3**	**1,100.5**	**1,129.3**	**1,140.8**
Career [1]	253.0	286.8	313.3	321.7	336.0	335.2	344.0	346.0	354.6
Volunteer [2]	772.7	777.4	823.7	827.2	812.1	768.2	756.4	783.3	786.2
RESPONSES BY TYPE (1,000)									
Total responses	**13,708**	**20,520**	**23,252**	**25,253**	**26,535**	**28,205**	**30,098**	**31,854**	**31,645**
Fires	2,019	1,708	1,602	1,452	1,349	1,332	1,389	1,375	1,240
Medical aid	7,650	12,251	14,375	15,768	17,104	18,522	19,803	21,706	21,372
False alarms	1,476	2,127	2,134	2,242	2,177	2,187	2,383	2,238	2,343
Malicious mischievous	442	300	241	190	183	163	183	168	165
System malfunctions	593	884	746	765	698	709	748	713	757
Unintentional calls	318	714	838	983	980	992	1,062	1,045	1,080
Other [3]	124	230	310	304	316	324	391	314	341
Mutual aid/assistance	487	864	1,091	1,215	1,296	1,190	1,252	1,327	1,298
Hazardous material	210	319	375	395	397	402	379	360	367
Other hazardous [4]	423	544	667	698	625	660	720	694	678
All other [5]	1,443	2,708	3,009	3,486	3,587	3,913	4,172	4,155	4,347

NA Not available. [1] Includes full-time uniform firefighters regardless of assignment (i.e., suppression, administrative, prevention/inspection, etc.). Does not include firefighters who work for the state or federal government or in private fire brigades. [2] Volunteer firefighters include any active part-time (call or volunteer) firefighters. [3] Bomb scares, etc. [4] Arcing wires, bomb removal, power line down, biological hazard, etc. [5] Smoke scares, lock-outs, animal rescue, unauthorized burning, severe weather, etc.

Source: National Fire Protection Association, Quincy, MA, *U.S. Fire Department Profile 2013* ©; *Fire Loss Activity in the United States 2013* ©, and earlier reports. See also <http://www.nfpa.org/research>.

Table 385. Fires—Number and Loss by Type and Property Use: 2010 to 2013

[Number of fires in thousands (1,331 represents 1,331,000); property loss in millions of dollars (11,593 represents $11,593,000,000). Based on annual sample survey of fire departments. No adjustments were made for unreported fires and losses]

Type and property use	Number (1,000)				Direct property loss (mil. dol.) [1]			
	2010	2011	2012	2013	2010	2011	2012	2013
Fires, total	**1,331**	**1,390**	**1,375**	**1,240**	**11,593**	**11,659**	**12,427**	**11,525**
Structure	482	485	481	488	9,716	9,693	9,776	9,526
Outside of structure [2]	73	79	83	67	413	541	727	520
Brush and rubbish	477	519	529	413	–	–	–	–
Vehicle [3]	216	219	203	188	1,376	1,350	1,838	1,392
Other	85	89	80	85	88	75	86	87
Structure fires by property use:								
Public assembly	12	13	12	13	421	446	281	369
Educational	6	5	5	6	76	44	64	66
Institutional	6	7	6	6	37	52	35	42
Stores and offices	18	19	18	18	730	625	643	611
Residential	384	386	381	387	7,079	7,054	7,199	6,969
1-2 family homes [4]	279	275	268	272	5,895	5,746	5,818	5,626
Apartments	91	96	97	98	1,033	1,168	1,192	1,166
Other residential [5]	15	16	16	18	151	140	189	177
Storage	28	27	29	26	756	721	751	692
Industry, utility, defense [6]	9	10	9	9	515	620	676	637
Special structures	20	19	22	24	102	131	127	140

– Represents zero. [1] Direct property damage figures do not include indirect losses (such as business interruption and temporary shelter costs) and adjustments for inflation. [2] Includes outside storage, crops, timber, etc. [3] In 2013, there were 164,000 highway vehicle fires, and 24,000 fires in other vehicles. Other vehicles include trains, boats, ships, aircraft, farm vehicles, and construction vehicles. [4] Includes manufactured homes. [5] Includes hotels and motels, college dormitories, boarding houses, etc. [6] Data underreported as some incidents were handled by private fire brigades or fixed suppression systems which do not report.

Source: National Fire Protection Association, Quincy, MA, *Fire Loss in the United States During 2013* ©, September 2014, and earlier reports. See also <http://www.nfpa.org/research>.

Table 386. Firefighter On-Duty Fatalities and Injuries: 2005 to 2013

[On-duty refers to involvement in operations at the scene of an emergency, whether it is a fire or nonfire incident; responding to or returning from an incident; performing other officially assigned duties including training; and being on call]

Item	2005	2006	2007	2008	2009	2010	2011	2012	2013
Total fatalities	**115**	**107**	**120**	**122**	**93**	**89**	**84**	**82**	**106**
By incident type									
Wildland related fatalities	19	22	11	26	16	11	10	15	31
Incidents with multiple fatalities	4	6	7	5	6	4	3	4	4
Firefighter classification									
Career	34	29	50	34	36	28	27	28	29
Volunteer [1]	81	77	68	66	47	56	51	42	47
Wildland	10	16	5	18	7	3	5	11	31
Unknown	–	–	–	–	3	2	1	1	–
Cause of fatal injury									
Vehicle collision	25	19	27	28	16	11	5	18	9
Stress/overexertion [2]	62	54	55	52	50	55	50	45	37
Caught/trapped	9	13	7	6	3	5	10	1	29
Fall	5	–	4	6	6	4	6	1	3
Other [3]	14	21	26	28	18	14	13	17	28
Nature of fatal injury									
Trauma	32	24	33	42	26	20	14	24	31
Heart attack	55	50	52	46	39	50	48	39	36
Burns	3	8	7	4	2	–	7	–	23
Asphyxiation	8	12	18	9	5	7	5	5	7
Other [3]	17	13	9	19	21	12	10	14	9
Total nonfatal Injuries	**80,100**	**83,400**	**80,100**	**79,700**	**78,150**	**71,875**	**70,090**	**69,400**	**65,880**
Fireground Injuries	41,950	44,210	38,340	36,595	32,205	32,675	30,505	31,490	29,760
Injuries at nonfire emergencies	12,250	13,090	15,435	15,745	15,455	13,355	14,905	12,760	12,535
Fire department vehicle collisions	15,885	16,020	14,650	14,950	15,100	14,200	14,850	14,300	12,350
Injuries	1,120	1,250	915	670	820	775	970	725	730
Personal vehicle collisions	1,080	1,070	665	1,000	870	1,000	790	750	830
Injuries	125	210	120	70	100	75	190	70	185
Nature of injury									
Burns (fire or chemical)	3,650	3,750	3,255	2,990	2,965	2,585	2,385	2,220	1,975
Smoke or gas inhalation	2,875	2,825	2,675	2,735	2,340	1,500	1,760	1,685	1,895
Other respiratory distress	1,390	1,625	1,005	1,645	915	940	1,060	910	915
Burns and smoke inhalation	1,120	730	1,020	735	565	635	695	320	195
Wound, cut, bleeding, bruise	14,165	14,625	14,390	12,835	11,685	11,110	10,210	9,905	10,530
Dislocation, fracture	2,315	2,160	2,585	1,880	1,950	1,820	1,885	1,695	1,900
Heart attack or stroke	765	1,000	1,000	770	1,140	810	860	780	620
Strain, sprain, muscular pain	39,740	42,895	41,410	42,200	42,585	40,385	39,960	39,535	37,565
Thermal stress (frostbite, heat exhaustion)	3,565	3,100	3,030	2,890	2,530	3,195	2,945	2,465	2,080
Other	10,515	10,690	9,730	11,020	11,475	8,895	8,660	9,885	8,205

– Represents zero. [1] Prior to 2008, includes wildland classification in its total. [2] Stress/overexertion include all firefighter deaths that are cardiac or cerebrovascular in nature such as heart attacks, strokes, and other events such as extreme climatic thermal exposure (heat exhaustion). [3] Includes other categories not shown, such as struck by object, structural collapse, violence, lost/disoriented, and unknown.

Source: Fatalities: U.S. Department of Homeland Security, Federal Emergency Management Agency, *U.S. Fire Administration, Firefighter Fatalities in the United States in 2013*, November 2014, and earlier reports. See also <http://apps.usfa.fema.gov/firefighter-fatalities/fatalityData/statistics>. Nonfatal Injuries: National Fire Protection Association, *Firefighter Injuries in the United States 2013* ©, November 2014, and earlier reports. See also <http://www.nfpa.org/research>.

Section 6
Geography and Environment

This section presents a variety of information on the physical environment of the United States, starting with basic area measurement data and ending with climatic data for selected weather stations around the country. The subjects covered between those points are mostly concerned with environmental trends but include related subjects such as land use, water consumption, air pollutant emissions, toxic releases, oil spills, hazardous waste sites, municipal waste and recycling, threatened and endangered wildlife, and the environmental industry.

The information in this section is selected from a wide range of federal agencies that compile the data for various administrative or regulatory purposes, such as the Environmental Protection Agency (EPA), U.S. Geological Survey (USGS), National Oceanic and Atmospheric Administration (NOAA), Natural Resources Conservation Service (NRCS).

Area—2013 Area measurements are the latest available. These measurements were calculated by computer based on the information contained in a single, consistent geographic database, the Topologically Integrated Geographic Encoding & Referencing system (TIGER®) database, a national geographic and cartographic database prepared by the Census Bureau. The 2013 area measurements may be found in Table 387.

Geography—The USGS conducts investigations, surveys, and research in the fields of geography, geology, topography, geographic information systems, mineralogy, hydrology, and geothermal energy resources as well as natural hazards. The USGS provides United States cartographic data through the Earth Sciences Information Center and water resources data through the *Water Resources of the United States* at <http://water.usgs.gov/pubs/>. In a joint project with the U.S. Census Bureau, during the 1980s, the USGS provided the basic information on geographic features for input into the TIGER® database. Since then, using a variety of sources, the Census Bureau has updated these features and their related attributes (names, descriptions, etc.) and inserted current information on the boundaries, names, and codes of legal and statistical geographic entities. The 2013 area measures, land and water, including their classifications, reflect base feature updates made in the Master Address File (MAF)/TIGER® database through May 2013. The boundaries of the states and equivalent areas are as of January 1, 2013. Maps prepared by the Census Bureau using the TIGER® database show the names and boundaries of entities and are available on a current basis.

An inventory of the nation's land resources by type of use/cover was conducted by the NRCS every 5 years beginning in 1977 through 1997. Since 2000, data have been gathered annually, though major releases of these data continue to be reported at 5-year intervals. The most recent survey results, which were published for the year 2012, covered all nonfederal land for the contiguous 48 states.

Environment—The principal federal agency responsible for pollution abatement and control activities is the EPA. It is responsible for establishing and monitoring national air quality standards, water quality activities, solid and hazardous waste disposal, and control of toxic substances. Many of these series now appear in the "Envirofacts" portion of the EPA Web site at <http://www.epa.gov/enviro/>.

The Clean Air Act, which was last amended in 1990, requires the EPA to set National Ambient Air Quality Standards (NAAQS) (40 CFR part 50) for pollutants considered harmful to public health and the environment. The Clean Air Act established two types of national air quality standards. Primary standards set limits to protect public health, including the health of "sensitive" populations such as asthmatics, children, and the elderly. Secondary standards set limits to protect public welfare, including protection against decreased visibility, damage to animals, crops vegetation, and buildings. See <http://www3.epa.gov/ttn/naaqs/criteria.html> for more information. The EPA Office of Air Quality Planning and Standards (OAQPS) has set National Ambient Air Quality Standards for six principal pollutants, which are called "criteria" pollutants. These pollutants are: carbon monoxide, lead, nitrogen dioxide, particulate matter, ozone, and sulfur dioxide. NAAQS are periodically reviewed and revised to include any additional or new health or welfare data. Table 401 gives some of the health-related standards for the six air pollutants having NAAQS. Data gathered from state networks are periodically submitted to EPA's National Aerometric Information Retrieval System (AIRS) for summarization in annual reports on the nationwide status and trends in air quality. For details, see "Air Trends" on the EPA Web site at <http://www.epa.gov/airtrends/>.

The Toxics Release Inventory (TRI), a database published by the EPA, is a valuable source of information on approximately 689 chemicals that are being used, manufactured, treated, transported, or released into the environment. Sections 313 of the Emergency Planning and Community Right-to-Know Act (EPCRA) and 6607 of the Pollution Prevention Act (PPA), mandate that a publicly-accessible toxic chemical database be developed and maintained by the EPA. The TRI database contains information concerning waste management activities and the release of toxic chemicals by facilities that manufacture, process, or otherwise use said materials. Data on the release of these chemicals are collected from about 21,000 facilities that have the equivalent of 10 or more full time employees and meet the established thresholds for manufacturing, processing, or "other use" of listed chemicals. Facilities must report their releases and other waste management quantities. Since 1994 federal facilities have been required to report their data regardless of industry classification. In May 1997, EPA added seven new industry sectors that reported to the TRI for the first time in July 1999 for the 1998 reporting year. More current information on this program can be found at <http://www2.epa.gov/toxics-release-inventory-tri-program>.

Climate—NOAA, through the National Weather Service and the National Environmental Satellite, Data, and Information Service, is responsible for collecting climate data. NOAA maintains about 8,000 weather stations, of which a portion produce precipitation measurement records, some also take hourly readings of a series of weather elements, and the remainder record data once a day. These data are reported monthly in the *Climatological Data* and *Storm Data*, published monthly and annually in the *Local Climatological Data* (published by location for major cities). Data can be found in tables 416 and 420–424.

Table 387. Land and Water Area of States and Other Entities: 2013

[One square mile = 2.59 square kilometers. The area measurements were derived from the Census Bureau's Master Address File/Topologically Integrated Geographic Encoding and Referencing (MAF/TIGER®) database. The boundaries of the states and equivalent areas are as of January 1, 2013. The land and water areas, including their classifications, reflect base feature updates made in the MAF/TIGER® database through May 2013. For more details, see <http://www.census.gov/geo/maps-data/data/tiger-line.html>]

State and other areas [2]	Total area Sq. mi.	Total area Sq. km.	Land area [1] Sq. mi.	Land area [1] Sq. km.	Water area [1] Total Sq. mi.	Water area [1] Total Sq. km.	Water area [1] Inland (sq. mi.)	Water area [1] Coastal (sq. mi.)	Water area [1] Great Lakes (sq. mi.)	Water area [1] Territorial (sq. mi.)
Total [3]	3,805,972	9,857,423	3,535,952	9,158,072	270,021	699,350	85,747	42,370	60,093	81,811
United States [4]	3,796,787	9,833,634	3,531,925	9,147,643	264,862	685,991	85,631	42,334	60,093	76,804
Alabama	52,420	135,767	50,646	131,172	1,774	4,595	1,057	517	(X)	200
Alaska	665,384	1,723,337	570,601	1,477,849	94,783	245,488	19,346	26,117	(X)	49,320
Arizona	113,990	295,233	113,593	294,205	397	1,028	397	–	(X)	–
Arkansas	53,179	137,732	52,036	134,773	1,142	2,959	1,142	–	(X)	–
California	163,695	423,967	155,786	403,483	7,909	20,484	2,827	245	(X)	4,837
Colorado	104,094	269,603	103,642	268,433	452	1,171	452	–	(X)	–
Connecticut	5,543	14,357	4,842	12,542	701	1,815	171	530	(X)	–
Delaware	2,489	6,446	1,949	5,047	540	1,399	91	355	(X)	94
District of Columbia	68	177	61	158	7	19	7	–	(X)	–
Florida	65,757	170,311	53,629	138,897	12,129	31,414	5,023	1,349	(X)	5,757
Georgia	59,425	153,911	57,515	148,963	1,910	4,948	1,411	46	(X)	454
Hawaii	10,970	28,412	6,423	16,634	4,547	11,778	42	9	(X)	4,496
Idaho	83,569	216,443	82,644	214,046	926	2,398	926	–	(X)	–
Illinois	57,914	149,996	55,519	143,794	2,394	6,202	820	–	1,574	–
Indiana	36,420	94,326	35,826	92,790	593	1,537	361	–	233	–
Iowa	56,273	145,745	55,857	144,669	416	1,076	416	–	(X)	–
Kansas	82,278	213,100	81,758	211,753	520	1,347	520	–	(X)	–
Kentucky	40,408	104,656	39,484	102,262	924	2,393	924	–	(X)	–
Louisiana	52,375	135,651	43,205	111,900	9,170	23,751	4,561	2,876	(X)	1,733
Maine	35,380	91,634	30,843	79,884	4,537	11,750	2,314	591	(X)	1,633
Maryland	12,406	32,131	9,708	25,144	2,698	6,987	768	1,819	(X)	111
Massachusetts	10,554	27,336	7,800	20,203	2,754	7,133	485	1,177	(X)	1,092
Michigan	96,713	250,487	56,547	146,455	40,167	104,031	1,993	–	38,173	–
Minnesota	86,935	225,161	79,628	206,236	7,307	18,924	4,761	–	2,546	–
Mississippi	48,441	125,460	46,924	121,532	1,517	3,928	769	620	(X)	128
Missouri	69,707	180,540	68,741	178,039	966	2,501	966	–	(X)	–
Montana	147,040	380,832	145,546	376,963	1,494	3,868	1,494	–	(X)	–
Nebraska	77,347	200,329	76,824	198,972	524	1,356	524	–	(X)	–
Nevada	110,572	286,380	109,781	284,331	791	2,049	791	–	(X)	–
New Hampshire	9,349	24,214	8,953	23,188	396	1,026	327	–	(X)	69
New Jersey	8,723	22,591	7,355	19,049	1,368	3,543	435	427	(X)	506
New Mexico	121,590	314,917	121,298	314,161	292	756	292	–	(X)	–
New York	54,555	141,297	47,127	122,057	7,428	19,240	1,989	975	3,986	479
North Carolina	53,819	139,391	48,617	125,919	5,202	13,472	4,053	–	(X)	1,149
North Dakota	70,698	183,108	69,000	178,709	1,698	4,399	1,698	–	(X)	–
Ohio	44,826	116,098	40,862	105,831	3,964	10,267	473	–	3,491	–
Oklahoma	69,899	181,037	68,596	177,662	1,303	3,375	1,303	–	(X)	–
Oregon	98,379	254,800	95,988	248,608	2,390	6,191	1,068	72	(X)	1,251
Pennsylvania	46,054	119,280	44,743	115,884	1,311	3,396	563	–	748	–
Rhode Island	1,545	4,001	1,034	2,678	511	1,323	182	64	(X)	266
South Carolina	32,020	82,933	30,061	77,858	1,959	5,075	1,063	110	(X)	786
South Dakota	77,116	199,729	75,811	196,349	1,305	3,380	1,305	–	(X)	–
Tennessee	42,144	109,153	41,236	106,800	908	2,353	908	–	(X)	–
Texas	268,597	695,662	261,236	676,599	7,360	19,063	5,612	401	(X)	1,347
Utah	84,898	219,884	82,194	212,881	2,704	7,003	2,704	–	(X)	–
Vermont	9,616	24,906	9,217	23,872	399	1,034	399	–	(X)	–
Virginia	42,775	110,787	39,491	102,280	3,284	8,506	1,281	1,565	(X)	438
Washington	71,298	184,661	66,456	172,121	4,842	12,540	1,714	2,468	(X)	660
West Virginia	24,230	62,756	24,041	62,267	189	489	189	–	(X)	–
Wisconsin	65,496	169,635	54,158	140,269	11,338	29,366	1,997	–	9,342	–
Wyoming	97,813	253,334	97,094	251,471	719	1,863	719	–	(X)	–
Puerto Rico	5,325	13,791	3,424	8,868	1,901	4,923	76	13	(X)	1,812
Island Areas:	3,860	9,998	603	1,562	3,257	8,436	39	22	(X)	3,196
American Samoa	581	1,505	76	198	505	1,307	8	–	(X)	497
Guam	571	1,478	210	543	361	935	8	1	(X)	352
Northern Mariana Islands	1,976	5,117	182	472	1,793	4,644	6	5	(X)	1,782
U.S. Virgin Islands	733	1,898	134	348	599	1,550	17	16	(X)	565

– Represents or rounds to zero. X Not applicable. [1] Water area calculations in this table include only perennial water. All other water (intermittent, glacier, and marsh/swamp) is included in this table as part of land area calculations. [2] This table does not include area calculations for the U.S. Minor Outlying Islands. [3] Includes all 50 states, the District of Columbia, Puerto Rico, and the Island Areas. [4] Includes all 50 states and the District of Columbia.

Source: U.S. Census Bureau, unpublished data from the MAF/TIGER® database. See <http://www.census.gov/geo/www/tiger/>.

Table 388. Great Lakes Profile

[The Great Lakes contain the largest supply of freshwater in the world, holding about 18% of the world's total freshwater and about 90% of the United States' total freshwater. The Lakes are a series of five interconnecting large lakes, one small lake, four connecting channels, and the St. Lawrence Seaway. Combined, the lakes cover an area of over 94,000 square miles (245,000 square kilometers) and contain over 5,400 cubic miles (23,000 cubic kilometers) of water]

Characteristics	Unit	Lake Superior	Lake Michigan	Lake Huron	Lake Erie	Lake Ontario
Length	Miles	350	307	206	241	193
Breadth	Miles	160	118	183	57	53
Depth:						
Average	Feet	489	279	159	62	283
Maximum	Feet	1,333	923	750	210	802
Volume	Cubic miles	2,935	1,180	849	116	393
Water surface area [1]	Square miles	31,700	22,300	23,000	9,910	7,340
Surface area in U.S	Square miles	20,598	22,300	9,111	4,977	3,560
Retention/replacement time [2]	Years	191	99	22	3	6

[1] Includes surface area in both U.S. and Canada. [2] The amount of time it takes for lakes to get rid of pollutants.

Source: Department of Commerce, National Oceanic and Atmospheric Administration, Great Lakes Environmental Research Laboratory, "About Our Great Lakes, Lake by Lake Profiles," June 2004, <http://www.glerl.noaa.gov/pr/ourlakes/intro.html/>.

Table 389. Great Lakes Length of Shoreline in Separate Basin

[In statute miles]

	Total	Canada	U.S.	MI	MN	WI	IL	IN	OH	PA	NY
Total	10,368	5,127	5,241	3,288	189	820	63	45	312	51	473
Lake Superior	2,980	1,549	1,431	917	189	325	–	–	–	–	–
St. Marys River	297	206	91	91	–	–	–	–	–	–	–
Lake Michigan	1,661	–	1,661	1,058	–	495	63	45	–	–	–
Lake Huron	3,350	2,416	934	934	–	–	–	–	–	–	–
St. Clair River	128	47	81	81	–	–	–	–	–	–	–
Lake St. Clair	160	71	89	89	–	–	–	–	–	–	–
Detroit River	107	43	64	64	–	–	–	–	–	–	–
Lake Erie	860	366	494	54	–	–	–	–	312	51	77
Niagara River	99	34	65	–	–	–	–	–	–	–	65
Lake Ontario	726	395	331	–	–	–	–	–	–	–	331

– Represents zero.

Source: State of Michigan, Department of Environment Quality, "Great Lakes, Shorelines of the Great Lakes," and U.S. Lake Survey, File no. 3-3284 corrected to 1952. <http://www.michigan.gov/deq/0,4561,7-135-3313_3677-15959--,00.html>.

Table 390. Largest Lakes in the United States

[The list of lakes include manmade lakes and those that are only partially within the United States]

Lake	Location	Area in sq. mi.	Lake	Location	Area in sq. mi.
Lake Superior	MI-MN-WI-Ontario	31,700	Lake Pontchartrain	Louisiana	631
Lake Huron	MI-Ontario	23,000	Lake Sakakawea [1]	North Dakota	520
Lake Michigan	IL-IN-MI-WI	22,300	Lake Champlain	NY-VT-Quebec	490
Lake Erie	MI-NY-OH-PA-Ontario	9,910	Becharof Lake	Alaska	453
Lake Ontario	NY-Ontario	7,340	Lake St. Clair	MI-Ontario	430
Great Salt Lake	Utah	2,117	Red Lake	Minnesota	427
Lake of the Woods	MN-Manitoba-Ontario	1,485	Selawik Lake	Alaska	404
Iliamna Lake	Alaska	1,014	Fort Peck Lake [1]	Montana	393
Lake Oahe [1]	ND-SD	685	Salton Sea	California	347
Lake Okeechobee	Florida	662	Rainy Lake	MN-Ontario	345

[1] Manmade lakes.

Source: U.S. Geological Survey, 2003, and National Oceanic and Atmospheric Administration, "Great Lakes, 2002" and The National Atlas of the United States of America, *Lakes*, <http://nationalatlas.gov/articles/mapping/a_general.html>.

Table 391. Coastline Counties Most Frequently Hit by Hurricanes: 1960 to 2008

[Hurricane is a type of tropical cyclone, an intense tropical weather system of strong thunderstorms with a well-defined surface circulation and maximum sustained winds of 74 miles per hour or higher]

County and State	Coastline region	Number of hurricanes	Percent change in population 1960 to 2008	Percent change in population 2000 to 2008	Percent change in housing units 1960 to 2008	Percent change in housing units 2000 to 2008
Monroe County, FL	Gulf of Mexico	15	50.8	-9.2	221.8	4.3
Lafourche Parish, LA	Gulf of Mexico	14	67.2	2.9	151.5	8.9
Carteret County, NC	Atlantic	14	104.3	6.4	366.4	12.4
Dare County, NC	Atlantic	13	465.9	12.1	709.6	22.8
Hyde County, NC	Atlantic	13	-10.1	-11.1	83.7	5.8
Jefferson Parish, LA	Gulf of Mexico	12	108.9	-4.2	201.4	-3.5
Palm Beach County, FL	Atlantic	12	454.7	11.9	616.9	15.2
Miami-Dade County, FL	Atlantic	11	156.5	6.4	180.6	14.9
St. Bernard Parish, LA	Gulf of Mexico	11	17.2	-43.9	-2.6	-67.9
Cameron Parish, LA	Gulf of Mexico	11	4.8	-27.6	87.7	-8.1
Terrebonne Parish, LA	Gulf of Mexico	11	78.7	3.9	179.4	11.0

Source: U.S. National Oceanic and Atmospheric Administration (NOAA), Coastal Services Center, Historical Hurricane Tracks: 1851 to 2008; U.S. Census Bureau, Current Population Reports, P25-1139, Population Estimates and Projections, "Coastline Population Trends in the United States: 1960 to 2008," May 2010. See also <http://www.census.gov/prod/www/abs/p25.html>

Table 392. U.S.–Canada and U.S.–Mexico Border Lengths

[In statute miles. Each statute mile equals one mile. For 2012, there were over 62 million personal vehicle passengers entering the United States from Canada, and over 115 million personal vehicle passengers entering the United States from Mexico]

State	Length of international border	State	Length of international border
United States–Canada total	**5,525**	Ohio	146
Alaska	1,538	Pennsylvania	42
Idaho	45	Vermont	90
Maine	611	Washington	427
Michigan	721		
Minnesota	547	**United States–Mexico total**	**1,933**
Montana	545	Arizona	373
New Hampshire	58	California	140
New York	445	New Mexico	180
North Dakota	310	Texas	1,241

Source: U.S.–Canada lengths: International Boundary Commission, 2003; U.S. Mexico lengths: U.S. Geological Survey; and The National Atlas of the United States, 1976, "Borders," <http://nationalatlas.gov/articles/mapping/a_general.html>.

Table 393. Coastline and Shoreline of the United States by State

[In statute miles. Each statute mile equals one mile. The term coastline is United States coastline measurements were made from small-scale maps, and the coastline was generalized. The coastlines of large sounds and used to describe the general outline of the seacoast. For the table below, bays were included. Measurements were made in 1948. Shoreline is the term used to describe a more detailed measure of the seacoast. The tidal shoreline figures in the table below were obtained in 1939–1940 from the largest-scale charts and maps then available. Shoreline of the outer coast, offshore islands, sounds, and bays was included, as well as the tidal portion of rivers and creeks. Only states with coastline or shoreline are included in the following table]

State	General coastline	Tidal shoreline	State	General coastline	Tidal shoreline
United States	**12,383**	**88,633**	Mississippi	44	359
Alabama	53	607	New Hampshire	13	131
Alaska	6,640	33,904	New Jersey	130	1,792
California	840	3,427	New York	127	1,850
Connecticut	–	618	North Carolina	301	3,375
Delaware	28	381	Oregon	296	1,410
Florida	1,350	8,426	Pennsylvania	–	89
Georgia	100	2,344	Rhode Island	40	384
Hawaii	750	1,052	South Carolina	187	2,876
Louisiana	397	7,721	Texas	367	3,359
Maine	228	3,478	Virginia	112	3,315
Maryland	31	3,190	Washington	157	3,026
Massachusetts	192	1,519			

– Represents zero.

Source: National Oceanic Atmospheric Administration, 1975 and The National Atlas of the United States, "Coastline and Shoreline," <http://nationalatlas.gov/articles/mapping/a_general.html>.

Table 394. Flows of Largest U.S. Rivers—Length, Discharge, and Drainage Area

[A flow of 1,000 cubic ft. per second is equal to 646 million gallons per day, 724,000 acre-feet per year, or 28.3 cubic meters per second. One acre-foot is the volume of water that would cover 1 acre to a depth of 1 foot]

River	Location of mouth	Source stream (name and location)	Length (miles) [1]	Average discharge at mouth (1,000 cubic feet per second)	Drainage area (1,000 sq. miles)
Missouri	Missouri	Red Rock Creek, MT	[2] 2,540	76.2	[3] 529
Mississippi	Louisiana	Mississippi River, MN	2,340	[4] 593	[3,5] 1,150
Yukon	Alaska	McNeil River, Canada	1,980	225	[3] 328
St. Lawrence	Canada	North River, MN	1,900	348	[3] 396
Rio Grande	Mexico-Texas	Rio Grande, CO	1,900	([6])	336
Arkansas	Arkansas	East Fork Arkansas River, CO	1,460	41	161
Colorado	Mexico	Colorado River, CO	1,450	([6])	246
Atchafalaya [7]	Louisiana	Tierra Blanca Creek, NM	1,420	58	95
Ohio	Illinois-Kentucky	Allegheny River, PA	1,310	281	203
Red [7]	Louisiana	Tierra Blanca Creek, NM	1,290	56	93
Brazos	Texas	Blackwater Draw, NM	1,280	([6])	46
Columbia	Oregon-Washington	Columbia River, Canada	1,240	265	[3] 258
Snake	Washington	Snake River, WY	1,040	56.9	108
Platte	Nebraska	Grizzly Creek, CO	990	([6])	85
Pecos	Texas	Pecos River, NM	926	([6])	44
Canadian	Oklahoma	Canadian River, CO	906	([6])	47
Tennessee	Kentucky	Courthouse Creek, NC	886	68	41

[1] From source to mouth. [2] The length from the source of the Missouri River to the Mississippi River and thence to the Gulf of Mexico is about 3,710 miles. [3] Drainage area includes both the United States and Canada. [4] Includes about 167,000 cubic feet per second diverted from the Mississippi into the Atchafalaya River but excludes the flow of the Red River. [5] Excludes the drainage areas of the Red and Atchafalaya Rivers. [6] Less than 15,000 cubic feet per second. [7] In east-central Louisiana, the Red River flows into the Atchafalaya River, a distributary of the Mississippi River. Data on average discharge, length, and drainage area include the Red River, but exclude all water diverted into the Atchafalaya from the Mississippi River.

Source: U.S. Geological Survey, *Largest Rivers in the United States*, September 2005, <http://pubs.usgs.gov/of/1987/ofr87-242/>.

Table 395. Extreme and Mean Elevations by State and Other Areas

[One foot = .305 meter. There are 2,130 square miles of the United States below sea level (Death Valley is the lowest point). There are 20,230 square miles above 10,000 feet (Mount McKinley is the highest point in the United States). Minus sign (-) indicates below sea level]

State and other areas	Highest point Name	Elevation Feet	Elevation Meters	Lowest point Name	Elevation Feet	Elevation Meters	Approximate mean elevation Feet	Approximate mean elevation Meters
U.S.	**Mt. McKinley (AK)**	**20,320**	**6,198**	**Death Valley (CA)**	**-282**	**-86**	**2,500**	**763**
AL.	Cheaha Mountain	2,407	734	Gulf of Mexico	(¹)	(¹)	500	153
AK.	Mount McKinley	20,320	6,198	Pacific Ocean	(¹)	(¹)	1,900	580
AZ.	Humphreys Peak	12,633	3,853	Colorado River	70	21	4,100	1,251
AR.	Magazine Mountain	2,753	840	Ouachita River	55	17	650	198
CA.	Mount Whitney	14,494	4,419	Death Valley	-282	-86	2,900	885
CO.	Mt. Elbert	14,433	4,402	Arikaree River	3,315	1,011	6,800	2,074
CT.	Mt. Frissell on south slope	2,380	726	Long Island Sound	(¹)	(¹)	500	153
DE.	Ebright Road [2]	448	137	Atlantic Ocean	(¹)	(¹)	60	18
DC.	Tenleytown at Reno Reservoir	410	125	Potomac River	1	(Z)	150	46
FL.	Britton Hill	345	105	Atlantic Ocean	(¹)	(¹)	100	31
GA.	Brasstown Bald	4,784	1,459	Atlantic Ocean	(¹)	(¹)	600	183
HI.	Pu'u Wekiu, Mauna Kea	13,796	4,208	Pacific Ocean	(¹)	(¹)	3,030	924
ID.	Borah Peak	12,662	3,862	Snake River	710	217	5,000	1,525
IL.	Charles Mound	1,235	377	Mississippi River	279	85	600	183
IN.	Hoosier Hill	1,257	383	Ohio River	320	98	700	214
IA.	Hawkeye Point	1,670	509	Mississippi River	480	146	1,100	336
KS.	Mount Sunflower	4,039	1,232	Verdigris River	679	207	2,000	610
KY.	Black Mountain	4,145	1,264	Mississippi River	257	78	750	229
LA.	Driskill Mountain	535	163	New Orleans	-8	-2	100	31
ME.	Mount Katahdin	5,268	1,607	Atlantic Ocean	(¹)	(¹)	600	183
MD.	Hoye Crest	3,360	1,025	Atlantic Ocean	(¹)	(¹)	350	107
MA.	Mount Greylock	3,491	1,065	Atlantic Ocean	(¹)	(¹)	500	153
MI.	Mount Arvon	1,979	604	Lake Erie	571	174	900	275
MN.	Eagle Mountain	2,301	702	Lake Superior	601	183	1,200	366
MS.	Woodall Mountain	806	246	Gulf of Mexico	(¹)	(¹)	300	92
MO.	Taum Sauk Mountain	1,772	540	St. Francis River	230	70	800	244
MT.	Granite Peak	12,799	3,904	Kootenai River	1,800	549	3,400	1,037
NE.	Panorama Point	5,424	1,654	Missouri River	840	256	2,600	793
NV.	Boundary Peak	13,140	4,007	Colorado River	479	146	5,500	1,678
NH.	Mount Washington	6,288	1,918	Atlantic Ocean	(¹)	(¹)	1,000	305
NJ.	High Point	1,803	550	Atlantic Ocean	(¹)	(¹)	250	76
NM.	Wheeler Peak	13,161	4,014	Red Bluff Reservoir	2,842	867	5,700	1,739
NY.	Mount Marcy	5,344	1,630	Atlantic Ocean	(¹)	(¹)	1,000	305
NC.	Mount Mitchell	6,684	2,039	Atlantic Ocean	(¹)	(¹)	700	214
ND.	White Butte	3,506	1,069	Red River of the North	750	229	1,900	580
OH.	Campbell Hill	1,550	473	Ohio River	455	139	850	259
OK.	Black Mesa	4,973	1,517	Little River	289	88	1,300	397
OR.	Mount Hood	11,239	3,428	Pacific Ocean	(¹)	(¹)	3,300	1,007
PA.	Mount Davis	3,213	980	Delaware River	(¹)	(¹)	1,100	336
RI.	Jerimoth Hill	812	248	Atlantic Ocean	(¹)	(¹)	200	61
SC.	Sassafras Mountain	3,560	1,086	Atlantic Ocean	(¹)	(¹)	350	107
SD.	Harney Peak	7,242	2,209	Big Stone Lake	966	295	2,200	671
TN.	Clingmans Dome	6,643	2,026	Mississippi River	178	54	900	275
TX.	Guadalupe Peak	8,749	2,668	Gulf of Mexico	(¹)	(¹)	1,700	519
UT.	Kings Peak	13,528	4,126	Beaverdam Wash	2,000	610	6,100	1,861
VT.	Mount Mansfield	4,393	1,340	Lake Champlain	95	29	1,000	305
VA.	Mount Rogers	5,729	1,747	Atlantic Ocean	(¹)	(¹)	950	290
WA.	Mount Rainier	14,411	4,395	Pacific Ocean	(¹)	(¹)	1,700	519
WV.	Spruce Knob	4,863	1,483	Potomac River	240	73	1,500	458
WI.	Timms Hill	1,951	595	Lake Michigan	579	177	1,050	320
WY.	Gannett Peak	13,804	4,210	Belle Fourche River	3,099	945	6,700	2,044
Other areas:								
Puerto Rico	Cerro de Punta	4,390	1,339	Atlantic Ocean	(¹)	(¹)	1,800	549
American Samoa ...	Lata Mountain	3,160	964	Pacific Ocean	(¹)	(¹)	1,300	397
Guam	Mount Lamlam	1,332	406	Pacific Ocean	(¹)	(¹)	330	101
U.S. Virgin Islands ...	Crown Mountain	1,556	475	Atlantic Ocean	(¹)	(¹)	750	229

Z Less than .5 meter. [1] Sea level. [2] At DE–PA state line.

Source: For highest and lowest points, see U.S. Geological Survey, "Elevations and Distances in the United States," <http://egsc.usgs.gov/isb/pubs/booklets/elvadist/elvadist.html>, released April 2005. For mean elevations, see *Elevations and Distances in the United States*, 1983 edition.

Table 396. Acres of Land Cover by Type and Use: 1987 to 2010

[In millions of acres (1,944.1 represents 1,944,100,000), except percent. Excludes Alaska, and District of Columbia. For inventory-specific glossary of key terms, see <http://www.nrcs.usda.gov/wps/portal/nrcs/main/national/technical/nra/nri/>]

| Year | Total surface area | Nonfederal rural land | | | | | | Developed land | Water areas | Federal land |
		Rural land total [1]	Crop-land	Pasture-land	Range-land	Forest land	Other rural land			
Land										
1987	1,944.1	1,416.4	406.1	127.4	414.0	407.3	48.0	77.9	49.9	399.9
1992	1,944.1	1,407.5	381.9	125.5	410.3	407.1	48.5	85.1	49.5	402.0
1997	1,944.1	1,396.1	376.6	120.1	408.9	408.6	49.2	95.9	50.0	402.1
2002	1,944.1	1,386.3	367.9	118.4	409.2	409.4	49.5	104.9	50.5	402.4
2007	1,944.1	1,379.8	359.0	119.6	409.2	408.9	50.7	111.1	50.9	402.4
2010	1,944.1	1,377.4	360.9	120.4	409.1	409.0	51.4	113.3	51.0	402.4
Percent of total land										
1987	100.0	72.9	20.9	6.6	21.3	20.9	2.5	4.0	2.6	20.6
1992	100.0	72.4	19.6	6.5	21.1	20.9	2.5	4.4	2.5	20.7
1997	100.0	71.8	19.4	6.2	21.0	21.0	2.5	4.9	2.6	20.7
2002	100.0	71.3	18.9	6.1	21.0	21.1	2.5	5.4	2.6	20.7
2007	100.0	71.0	18.5	6.2	21.0	21.0	2.6	5.7	2.6	20.7
2010	100.0	70.9	18.6	6.2	21.0	21.0	2.6	5.8	2.6	20.7

[1] Includes Conservation Reserve Program (CRP) land not shown separately. CRP is a federal program established under the Food Security Act of 1985 to assist private landowners to convert highly erodible cropland to vegetative cover for 10 years.

Source: U.S. Department of Agriculture, Natural Resources and Conservation Service, *Summary Report: 2010 National Resources Inventory*, September 2013. See also <http://www.nrcs.usda.gov/technical/NRI>.

Table 397. Wetlands on Nonfederal Land and Water Areas by Land Cover Type and Farm Production Region: 2010

[In thousands of acres (111,399 represents 111,399,000). Covers both palustrine (nontidal) and estuarine (tidal) wetlands; see source]

Farm production region [1]	Total	Crop-land [2]	Forest land	Range-land	Other rural land	Developed land	Water area
Wetlands, total	**111,399**	**16,650**	**66,216**	**8,348**	**15,121**	**1,433**	**3,631**
Lake states	22,644	888	16,589	1,018	3,219	369	562
Southeast	22,286	2,842	15,367	–	3,710	170	198
Delta states	17,938	3,097	11,218	190	2,806	181	446
Northeast	13,764	1,103	10,732	–	1,486	233	210
Northern plains	7,872	3,058	205	3,044	1,119	74	373
Appalachian	7,381	382	6,076	–	531	97	295
Southern plains	5,889	1,035	2,480	985	417	163	809
Mountain	4,960	1,538	242	2,322	718	15	126
Corn belt	4,696	1,336	2,436	–	369	101	455
Pacific	3,850	1,357	823	783	705	30	151

– Represents or rounds to zero. [1] Ten regions established by USDA, Economic Research Service, that group states according to differences in soils, slope of land, climate, distance to market, and storage and marketing facilities. [2] Includes pastureland and Conservation Reserve Program (CRP) lands.

Source: U.S. Department of Agriculture, Natural Resources Conservation Service, *Summary Report: 2010 National Resources Inventory*, September 2013. See also <http://www.nrcs.usda.gov/technical/NRI/>.

Table 398. Acres of Federal and Non-Federal Land Cover by Type and State: 2010

[In thousands of acres (1,944,130 represents 1,944,130,000), except percent. Excludes Alaska, District of Columbia, and Island Areas]

| State | Total surface area [1] | Selected nonfederal rural land, percent of total | | | State | Total surface area [1] | Selected nonfederal rural land, percent of total | | |
		Crop-land	Range-land	Forest land			Crop-land	Range-land	Forest land
United States	**1,944,130**	**18.6**	**21.0**	**21.0**	Montana	94,110	14.9	39.2	5.8
Alabama	33,424	6.7	0.2	65.0	Nebraska	49,510	39.8	46.6	1.6
Arizona	72,964	1.2	44.3	5.6	Nevada	70,763	0.8	11.8	0.4
Arkansas	34,037	21.2	0.1	44.2	New Hampshire	5,941	2.0	–	64.5
California	101,510	9.0	17.6	14.0	New Jersey	5,216	9.5	–	32.2
Colorado	66,625	12.1	37.7	4.9	New Mexico	77,823	1.9	51.9	6.9
Connecticut	3,195	5.5	–	50.4	New York	31,361	16.2	–	55.9
Delaware	1,534	26.9	–	22.3	North Carolina	33,709	15.3	–	46.1
Florida	37,534	7.3	7.1	34.9	North Dakota	45,251	54.3	24.1	1.0
Georgia	37,741	10.9	–	58.0	Ohio	26,445	42.0	–	26.8
Hawaii	4,158	2.8	26.0	39.0	Oklahoma	44,738	19.8	31.2	16.8
Idaho	53,488	9.6	12.3	7.5	Oregon	62,161	5.6	15.0	20.5
Illinois	36,059	66.2	–	11.2	Pennsylvania	28,995	17.1	–	53.9
Indiana	23,158	57.4	–	17.0	Rhode Island	813	2.2	–	44.7
Iowa	36,017	71.6	–	6.6	South Carolina	19,939	11.1	–	56.0
Kansas	52,661	49.0	30.3	3.3	South Dakota	49,358	35.4	44.6	1.1
Kentucky	25,863	20.5	–	41.1	Tennessee	26,974	16.0	–	44.0
Louisiana	31,377	15.9	0.8	42.1	Texas	171,052	14.2	57.0	6.4
Maine	20,966	1.7	–	84.0	Utah	54,339	2.8	20.0	3.4
Maryland	7,870	17.8	–	29.0	Vermont	6,154	8.9	–	66.5
Massachusetts	5,339	4.3	–	47.6	Virginia	27,087	9.9	–	48.2
Michigan	37,349	21.2	–	44.4	Washington	44,035	13.9	13.7	28.5
Minnesota	54,010	39.0	–	30.5	West Virginia	15,508	4.7	–	67.4
Mississippi	30,527	15.4	–	55.5	Wisconsin	35,920	28.4	–	40.9
Missouri	44,614	30.3	0.2	28.0	Wyoming	62,603	3.6	44.2	1.6

– Represents or rounds to zero. [1] Total surface area includes both Federal and non-Federal land.

Source: U.S. Department of Agriculture, Natural Resources and Conservation Service, *Summary Report, 2010 National Resources Inventory*, September 2013. See also <http://www.nrcs.usda.gov/technical/NRI/>.

Table 399. U.S. Wetland Resources and Deepwater Habitats by Type: 2004 and 2009

[In thousands of acres (153,121.4 represents 153,121,400). Wetlands and deepwater habitats are defined separately because the term wetland does not include permanent water bodies. Deepwater habitats are permanently flooded land lying below the deepwater boundary of wetlands. Deepwater habitats include environments where surface water is permanent and often deep, so that water, rather than air, is the principal medium within which the dominant organisms live, whether or not they are attached to the substrate. As in wetlands, the dominant plants are hydrophytes; however, the substrates are considered nonsoil because the water is too deep to support emergent vegetation. In general terms, wetlands are lands where saturation with water is the dominant factor determining the nature of soil development and the types of plant and animal communities living in the soil and on its surface. The single feature that most wetlands share is soil or substrate that is at least periodically saturated with or covered by water. Wetlands are lands transitional between terrestrial and aquatic systems where the water table is usually at or near the surface or the land is covered by shallow water. For more information on wetlands, see the "Classification of Wetlands and Deepwater Habitats of the United States" at <http://www.npwrc.usgs.gov/resource/wetlands/classwet/index.htm>]

Wetland or deepwater category	Estimated area, 2004	Estimated area, 2009	Change, 2004 to 2009
All wetlands and deepwater habitats, total...............	**153,121.4**	**153,206.4**	**85.0**
All deepwater habitats, total......................................	42,999.4	43,146.6	147.2
Lacustrine [1]..	16,786.0	16,859.6	73.6
Riverine [2]..	7,517.9	7,510.5	-7.4
Estuarine Subtidal [3]....................................	18,695.4	18,776.5	81.1
All wetlands, total...	110,122.1	110,059.8	-62.3
Intertidal wetlands [4]...................................	5,869.3	5,785.2	-84.1
Marine intertidal..	219.2	227.8	8.5
Estuarine intertidal nonvegetated.............................	999.4	1,017.7	18.3
Estuarine intertidal vegetated................................	4,650.7	4,539.7	-110.9
Freshwater wetlands...	104,252.7	104,274.6	21.9
Freshwater nonvegetated......................................	6,502.1	6,709.3	207.2
Freshwater vegetated..	97,750.6	97,565.3	-185.3
Freshwater emergent [5].................................	27,162.7	27,430.5	267.8
Freshwater forested [6].................................	52,256.5	51,623.3	-633.1
Freshwater shrub [7]...................................	18,331.4	18,511.5	180.1

[1] The lacustrine system includes deepwater habitats with all of the following characteristics: (1) situated in a topographic depression or a dammed river channel; (2) lacking trees, shrubs, persistent emergents, emergent mosses or lichens with greater than 30 percent coverage; and (3) total area exceeds 20 acres (8 hectares). [2] The riverine system includes deepwater habitats contained within a channel, with the exception of habitats with water containing ocean derived salts in excess of 0.5 parts per thousand. [3] The estuarine system consists of deepwater tidal habitats and adjacent tidal wetlands that are usually semi-enclosed by land but have open, partly obstructed, or sporadic access to the open ocean, and in which ocean water is at least occasionally diluted by freshwater runoff from the land. Subtidal is where the substrate is continuously submerged by marine or estuarine waters. [4] Intertidal is where the substrate is exposed and flooded by tides. Intertidal includes the splash zone of coastal waters. [5] Emergent wetlands are characterized by erect, rooted, herbaceous hydrophytes, excluding mosses and lichens. This vegetation is present for most of the growing season in most years. These wetlands are usually dominated by perennial plants. [6] Forested wetlands are characterized by woody vegetation that is 20 feet tall or taller. [7] Shrub wetlands include areas dominated by woody vegetation less than 20 feet tall. The species include true shrubs, young trees, and trees or shrubs that are small or stunted because of environmental conditions.

Source: U.S. Fish and Wildlife Service, *Status and Trends of Wetlands in the Conterminous United States, 2004 to 2009*, September 2011. See also <http://www.fws.gov/wetlands/Status-And-Trends-2009/index.html>.

Table 400. U.S. Water Withdrawals Per Day by End Use: 1950 to 2010

[In billions (180 represents 180,000,000,000). Includes the District of Columbia, Puerto Rico and U.S. Virgin Islands. Withdrawal signifies water physically withdrawn from a source. Includes fresh and saline water; excludes water used for hydroelectric power. For information on changes in data collection and presentation methods, see 2010 source report]

Year	Total with-drawals	Public supply	Rural domestic and livestock		Irri-gation	Thermo electric power	Other			
			Self supplied domestic	Live-stock			Self supplied industrial	Mining	Com-mercial	Aqua-culture
1950 [1].........	180	14	2.1	1.5	89	40	37	[5]	[5]	[5]
1955 [2].........	240	17	2.1	1.5	110	72	39	[5]	[5]	[5]
1960 [3].........	270	21	2.0	1.6	110	100	38	[5]	[5]	[5]
1965 [4].........	310	24	2.3	1.7	120	130	46	[5]	[5]	[5]
1970 [4].........	370	27	2.6	1.9	130	170	47	[5]	[5]	[5]
1975 [3].........	420	29	2.8	2.1	140	200	45	[5]	[5]	[5]
1980 [3].........	430	33	3.4	2.2	150	210	45	[5]	[5]	[5]
1985 [3].........	397	36.6	3.32	2.23	135	187	25.8	3.44	1.23	2.24
1990 [3].........	404	38.7	3.39	2.25	134	194	22.5	4.93	2.39	2.24
1995 [3].........	398	40.2	3.39	2.28	130	190	21.6	3.59	2.89	3.23
2000 [3].........	413	43.3	3.58	2.39	139	195	19.7	4.16	(NA)	5.78
2005 [3].........	409	44.3	3.71	2.15	127	201	18.1	3.83	(NA)	8.84
2010 [3].........	355	42.0	3.60	2.00	115	161	15.9	5.32	(NA)	9.42

NA Not available. [1] Population covered: 48 states, District of Columbia, and Hawaii. [2] Population covered: 48 states. [3] Population covered: 50 states, District of Columbia, Puerto Rico, and the Virgin Islands. [4] Population covered: 50 states, District of Columbia, and Puerto Rico. [5] Included in "self-supplied industrial."

Source: 1950–1960, U.S. Bureau of Domestic Business Development, based principally on committee prints, *Water Resources Activities in the United States*, for the Senate Committee on National Water Resources, U.S. Senate; thereafter, U.S. Geological Survey, *Estimated Use of Water in the United States in 2010*, circular 1405, November 2014. See also <http://pubs.usgs.gov/circ/1344/>.

Table 401. National Ambient Air Pollutant Concentrations by Type of Pollutant: 2007 to 2013

[Data represent composite averages across monitoring stations meeting minimum data completeness requirements for the trend period. Carbon monoxide is based on the second-highest, nonoverlapping, 8-hour average; ozone, the fourth-highest maximum 8-hour value; particulates (PM-10) on the second highest daily 24-hour average; fine particulates (PM2.5) annual average on the weighted annual mean of daily 24-hour averages; and lead on the 'maximum rolling three-month average. Based on data from the Air Quality System. μmg/m ^{3} = micrograms of pollutant per cubic meter of air; ppm = parts per million; ppb = parts per billion]

Pollutant	Unit	Monitoring stations, number	Air quality standard [1]	2007	2008	2009	2010	2011	2012	2013
Carbon monoxide.............	ppm	205	[2] 9	2.0	1.8	1.7	1.6	1.6	1.5	1.5
Ozone.........................	ppm	874	[3] 0.075	0.078	0.074	0.069	0.072	0.073	0.074	0.067
Sulfur dioxide..................	ppb	235	[4] 75	62	56	48	44	36	35	29
Particulates (PM-10).........	μmg/m ^{3}	449	[5] 150	70.2	69.1	59.4	62.1	66.4	66.2	63.9
Fine particulates (PM2.5) annual average..............	μmg/m ^{3}	537	[6] 12	11.9	10.8	9.8	9.9	9.8	9.1	8.9
Nitrogen dioxide..............	ppb	180	[7] 100	48	47	43	44	43	41	41
Lead...........................	μmg/m ^{3}	43	[8] 0.15	0.20	0.26	0.13	0.12	0.17	0.14	0.12

[1] Refers to the primary National Ambient Air Quality Standard. [2] Based on 8-hour standard of 9 ppm. [3] Based on 8-hour standard of 0.075 ppm. On March 12, 2008, EPA revised the level of the primary and secondary 8-hour ozone standards to 0.075 ppm. [4] Based on annual standard of 0.03 ppm. [5] Based on 24-hour (daily) standard of 150 μg/m ^{3}. The particulates (PM-10) standard replaced the previous standard for total suspended particulates in 1987. In 2006, EPA revoked the annual PM-10 standard. [6] Based on annual standard of 12 μg/m ^{3}. The PM-2.5 national monitoring network was deployed in 1999. National trend data prior to that time is not available. [7] Based on annual standard of 0.053 ppm. [8] Based on 3-month rolling average of 0.15 μmg/m ^{3}.

Source: U.S. Environmental Protection Agency, "Air Trends," <http://www.epa.gov/airtrends/index.html>, accessed September 2015.

Table 402. Selected Air Pollutant Emissions: 1980 to 2014

[In thousands of tons (4,320 represents 4,320,000), except as indicated. The methodology used to estimate emission data for 1970-1984 and for 1985 through the current year is different. Beginning with 1985, the methodology for more recent years is described in the document available at <http://www.epa.gov/ttn/chief/net/2011inventory.html>]

Year	Ammonia	Carbon monoxide	Nitrogen oxide	PM-10 [1]	PM-2.5 [1]	Sulfur dioxide	V.O.C. [2]
1980.............	(NA)	185,408	27,079	7,013	(NA)	25,926	31,107
1990.............	4,320	154,188	25,529	27,753	7,560	23,077	24,108
2000.............	4,907	114,467	22,598	23,747	7,288	16,347	17,512
2005.............	3,929	88,546	20,355	21,302	5,592	14,546	17,753
2010.............	4,271	73,771	14,846	20,823	5,964	7,732	17,835
2011.............	4,232	73,762	14,519	20,723	6,100	6,479	18,154
2012.............	4,227	71,760	13,657	20,687	6,077	5,193	17,813
2013.............	4,221	69,758	13,072	20,651	6,055	5,098	17,471
2014.............	4,216	67,756	12,412	20,616	6,033	4,991	17,130

NA Not available. [1] PM=Particular Matter; PM-10 is equal to or less than ten microns in diameter; PM-2.5 to or less than 2.5 microns effective diameter. [2] Volatile organic compound.

Source: U.S. Environmental Protection Agency, "National Emissions Inventory (NEI) Air Pollutant Emissions Trends Data, 1970-2014," <http://www.epa.gov/ttn/chief/trends/index.html>, accessed July 2015.

Table 403. Selected Air Pollutant Emissions by Pollutant and Source: 2014

[In thousands of tons (4,216 represents 4,216,000). See headnote, Table 402]

Source	Ammonia	Carbon monoxide	Nitrogen oxide	PM-10 [1]	PM-2.5 [1]	Sulfur dioxide	V.O.C. [2]
Total emissions.................	**4,216**	**67,756**	**12,412**	**20,616**	**6,033**	**4,991**	**17,130**
Fuel combustion, stationary sources.................	104	4,598	3,590	979	843	4,089	628
Electric utilities..	25	784	1,776	280	205	3,195	41
Industrial...	13	961	1,258	275	223	676	112
Other fuel combustion................................	66	2,852	555	424	415	219	476
Industrial processes...................................	102	3,083	1,264	1,135	561	605	7,207
Chemical and allied product manufacturing........	23	167	51	22	17	127	83
Metals processing.....................................	1	766	71	63	48	144	34
Petroleum and related industries....................	1	672	685	35	29	119	2,774
Other...	34	337	353	766	277	188	329
Solvent utilization.....................................	1	2	1	4	4	–	2,811
Storage and transport.................................	6	27	20	52	21	9	1,043
Waste disposal and recycling.........................	36	1,111	83	192	165	17	132
Highway vehicles.......................................	108	22,261	4,489	301	167	22	2,159
Off highway [3]...	3	14,037	2,669	186	175	77	1,845
Miscellaneous [4]......................................	3,899	23,777	399	18,015	4,288	198	5,290

– Rounds to zero. [1] See footnote 1, Table 402. [2] Volatile organic compound. [3] Includes emissions from farm tractors and other farm machinery, construction equipment, industrial machinery, recreational marine vessels, and small general utility engines such as lawn mowers. [4] Includes emissions from forest fires and other kinds of burning, various agricultural activities, fugitive dust from paved and unpaved roads, other construction and mining activities, and natural sources.

Source: U.S. Environmental Protection Agency, "National Emissions Inventory (NEI) Air Pollutant Emissions Trends Data, 1970-2014," <http://www.epa.gov/ttn/chief/trends/index.html>, accessed July 2015.

Table 404. Emissions of Greenhouse Gases by Type and Source: 1990 to 2013

[In millions of metric tons of carbon dioxide equivalent (MMT CO2 Eq.). 6,301.1 represents 6,301,100,000 million metric tons. MMT CO2 Eq. weights each gas by its global warming potential (GWP) value. GWP is a quantified measure of the globally averaged relative radiative forcing impacts of a particular greenhouse gas. The reference gas used is CO2; therefore, GWP-weighted emissions are measured in MMT CO2 Eq. See source for details]

Type and source	1990	2005	2010	2011	2012	2013
Total emissions	**6,301.1**	**7,350.2**	**6,898.8**	**6,776.6**	**6,545.1**	**6,673.0**
BY SOURCE						
Energy	5,290.5	6,273.6	5,854.6	5,702.6	5,482.2	5,636.6
Industrial processes and product use [1]	342.1	367.4	353.6	371.0	361.2	359.1
Sulfur hexafluoride (SF6)	31.1	14.0	9.5	10.0	7.7	6.9
Hydrofluorocarbons (HFCs)	46.6	131.4	152.6	157.4	159.2	163.0
Perfluorocarbons (PFCs)	24.3	6.6	4.4	6.9	6.0	5.8
Agriculture	448.7	494.5	524.8	522.1	523.0	515.7
Land use, land-use change, and forestry	13.8	25.5	20.3	36.1	39.8	23.3
Waste	206.0	189.2	145.5	144.9	138.9	138.3
Net CO2 flux from land use, land use change, and forestry	*-767.7*	*-903.0*	*-862.0*	*-872.1*	*-869.6*	*-871.0*
Net emissions (sources and sinks) [2]	5,525.2	6,438.3	6,027.2	5,895.6	5,664.7	5,791.2
BY TYPE						
Carbon dioxide (CO2), total	**5,123.7**	**6,134.0**	**5,704.5**	**5,568.9**	**5,358.3**	**5,505.2**
Energy	4,908.4	5,933.9	5,529.2	5,390.3	5,181.1	5,331.5
Fossil fuel combustion	4,740.7	5,747.7	5,367.1	5,231.3	5,026.0	5,157.7
Electricity	1,820.8	2,400.9	2,258.4	2,157.7	2,022.2	2,039.8
Transportation	1,493.8	1,887.8	1,732.0	1,711.5	1,700.8	1,718.4
Industrial	842.5	827.8	775.7	774.1	784.2	817.3
Residential	338.3	357.8	334.7	327.2	283.1	329.6
Commercial	217.4	223.5	220.2	221.0	197.1	220.7
Biomass (wood) [3]	215.2	206.9	192.5	195.2	194.9	208.6
Industrial	207.2	191.1	165.7	169.7	166.4	163.0
Land Use, land-use change, and forestry (sink)	*-775.8*	*-911.9*	*-871.6*	*-881.0*	*-880.4*	*-881.7*
Methane (CH4), total	**745.5**	**707.8**	**667.2**	**660.9**	**647.6**	**636.3**
Energy	328.5	280.9	279.2	268.2	259.2	263.5
Industrial processes and product use	1.4	1.0	0.7	0.8	0.8	0.8
Agriculture	210.8	234.4	243.4	238.9	239.6	234.5
Land use, land-use change, and forestry	2.5	8.3	4.8	14.6	15.7	5.8
Waste management	202.3	183.2	139.1	138.4	132.4	131.6
Nitrous oxide (N2O), total	**329.9**	**355.9**	**360.1**	**371.9**	**365.6**	**355.2**
Energy	53.6	58.7	46.2	44.1	41.9	41.6
Industrial processes and product use	31.6	22.8	20.1	25.5	20.4	19.1
Agriculture	237.9	260.1	281.4	283.2	283.4	281.1
Land use, land-use change, and forestry	3.1	8.3	6.0	12.6	13.3	6.7
Waste management	3.7	6.0	6.4	6.5	6.6	6.7

[1] Total includes items not shown separately. [2] The net CO2 flux total includes both emissions and sequestration, and constitutes a sink in the United States. Sinks are only included in net emissions total. [3] Emissions from wood biomass and ethanol consumption are not included specifically in summing energy sector totals. Net carbon fluxes from changes in biogenic carbon reservoirs are accounted for in the estimates for land use, land-use change, and forestry.

Source: U.S. Environmental Protection Agency, *Inventory of U.S. Greenhouse Gas Emissions and Sinks, 1990-2013*, April 2015. See also <http://www.epa.gov/climatechange/ghgemissions/usinventoryreport.html>.

Table 405. Carbon Dioxide Emissions from Fossil Fuel Combustion by Fuel Type and Sector: 1990 to 2013

[In millions of metric tons of carbon dioxide equivalent (MMT CO2 Eq.). 4,740.7 MMT represents 4,745,700,000 million metric tons]

Fuel and Sector	1990	2005	2009	2010	2011	2012	2013
Total [1]	**4,740.7**	**5,747.7**	**5,197.1**	**5,367.1**	**5,231.3**	**5,026.0**	**5,157.7**
Coal	**1,718.4**	**2,112.3**	**1,834.2**	**1,927.7**	**1,813.9**	**1,592.8**	**1,658.1**
Residential	3.0	0.8	([2])	([2])	([2])	([2])	([2])
Commercial	12.0	9.3	6.9	6.6	5.8	4.1	3.9
Industrial	155.3	115.3	83.0	90.1	82.0	74.1	75.8
Electricity generation	1,547.6	1,983.8	1,740.9	1,827.6	1,722.7	1,511.2	1,575.0
Natural gas	**1,000.3**	**1,166.7**	**1,216.9**	**1,272.1**	**1,291.5**	**1,352.6**	**1,389.5**
Residential	238.0	262.2	258.8	258.6	254.7	224.8	267.1
Commercial	142.1	162.9	168.9	167.7	170.5	156.9	178.2
Industrial	408.9	388.5	377.6	407.2	417.3	434.8	450.8
Transportation	36.0	33.1	37.9	38.1	38.9	41.3	48.8
Electricity generation	175.3	318.8	372.2	399.0	408.8	492.2	441.9
Petroleum	**2,021.5**	**2,468.4**	**2,145.5**	**2,167.0**	**2,125.5**	**2,080.2**	**2,109.6**
Residential	97.4	94.9	77.6	76.2	72.6	58.3	62.5
Commercial	63.3	51.3	47.7	45.9	44.7	36.1	38.6
Industrial	278.3	324.0	267.0	278.4	274.8	275.4	290.6
Transportation	1,457.7	1,854.7	1,682.4	1,693.9	1,672.7	1,659.5	1,669.6
Electricity generation	97.5	97.9	32.2	31.4	25.8	18.3	22.4

[1] Includes data not shown separately. [2] Does not exceed 0.05 MMT CO2 Eq.

Source: U.S. Environmental Protection Agency, *Inventory of U.S. Greenhouse Gas Emissions and Sinks, 1990-2013*, April 2015. See also <http://www.epa.gov/climatechange/ghgemissions/usinventoryreport.html>.

Table 406. Municipal Solid Waste Generation, Materials Recovery, Combustion With Energy Recovery, and Discards: 1980 to 2013

[In millions of tons (151.6 represents 151,600,000), except as indicated. Covers post-consumer residential, commercial, and institutional solid wastes which comprise the major portion of typical municipal collections. Excludes mining, agricultural and industrial processing, demolition and construction wastes, sewage sludge, junked autos and obsolete equipment wastes. Based on material-flows estimating procedure and wet weight as generated]

Item and material	1980	1990	2000	2010	2011	2012	2013
Waste generated	**151.6**	**208.3**	**243.5**	**250.6**	**250.5**	**251.0**	**254.1**
Per person per day (lb.)	3.7	4.6	4.7	4.4	4.4	4.4	4.4
Total materials recovery	**14.5**	**33.2**	**69.5**	**85.2**	**87.0**	**86.6**	**87.2**
Per person per day (lb.)	0.4	0.7	1.4	1.5	1.5	1.5	1.5
Recovery for recycling	14.5	29.0	53.0	65.1	66.4	65.2	64.7
Per person per day (lb.)	0.4	0.6	1.0	1.2	1.2	1.1	1.1
Recovery for composting [1]	(Z)	4.2	16.5	20.2	20.6	21.3	22.4
Per person per day (lb.)	(Z)	0.1	0.3	0.4	0.4	0.4	0.4
Combustion with energy recovery	2.7	29.7	33.7	29.3	31.8	32.2	32.7
Per person per day (lb.)	0.1	0.7	0.7	0.5	0.6	0.6	0.6
Discards to landfill, other disposal	134.4	145.3	140.3	136.1	131.8	132.3	134.3
Per person per day (lb.)	3.2	3.2	2.7	2.4	2.3	2.3	2.3
PERCENT DISTRIBUTION OF GENERATION							
Percent of total generation	**71.8**	**70.3**	**73.4**	**70.9**	**70.5**	**70.4**	**70.4**
Paper and paperboard	36.4	34.9	36.0	28.5	27.9	27.3	27.0
Glass	10.0	6.3	5.2	4.6	4.6	4.6	4.5
Metals	10.2	7.9	7.8	8.9	8.8	8.9	9.1
Plastics	4.5	8.2	10.5	12.5	12.8	12.7	12.8
Rubber and leather	2.8	2.8	2.7	3.0	3.0	3.0	3.0
Textiles	1.7	2.8	3.9	5.2	5.2	5.7	6.0
Wood	4.6	5.9	5.6	6.3	6.3	6.3	6.2
Other	1.7	1.5	1.6	1.9	1.9	1.8	1.8
Total other waste	**28.2**	**29.7**	**26.6**	**29.1**	**29.5**	**29.6**	**29.6**
Food waste	8.6	11.5	12.6	14.3	14.5	14.5	14.6
Yard trimmings	18.1	16.8	12.5	13.3	13.5	13.5	13.5
Miscellaneous inorganic wastes	1.5	1.4	1.4	1.5	1.5	1.6	1.5

Z Less than 5,000 tons or 0.05 percent. [1] Composting of yard trimmings, food scraps, and other municipal solid waste organic material. Does not include backyard composting.

Source: U.S. Environmental Protection Agency, *Advancing Sustainable Materials Management: Facts and Figures 2013*, June 2015; and "Historical Data Tables," <http://www.epa.gov/osw/conserve/tools/recmeas/msw_improv.htm>, accessed July 2015.

Table 407. Generation and Recovery of Selected Materials in Municipal Solid Waste: 1980 to 2013

[In millions of tons (151.6 represents 151,600,000), except as indicated. Covers post-consumer residential, commercial, and institutional solid wastes which comprise the major portion of typical municipal collections. Excludes mining, agricultural and industrial processing, demolition and construction wastes, sewage sludge, and junked autos and obsolete equipment wastes. Based on material-flows estimating procedure and wet weight as generated]

Item and material	1980	1990	2000	2010	2011	2012	2013
Waste generated, total [1]	**151.6**	**208.3**	**243.5**	**250.6**	**250.5**	**251.0**	**254.1**
Paper and paperboard	55.2	72.7	87.7	71.3	70.0	68.6	68.6
Glass	15.1	13.1	12.8	11.5	11.5	11.6	11.5
Metals: Ferrous	12.6	12.6	14.2	16.8	16.5	16.8	17.6
Aluminum	1.7	2.8	3.2	3.5	3.5	3.5	3.5
Other nonferrous	1.2	1.1	1.6	2.0	2.0	2.0	2.0
Plastics	6.8	17.1	25.6	31.4	32.0	31.9	32.5
Food waste	13.0	23.9	30.7	35.7	36.3	36.4	37.1
Yard trimmings	27.5	35.0	30.5	33.4	33.7	34.0	34.2
Materials recovered, total [1]	**14.5**	**33.2**	**69.5**	**85.2**	**87.0**	**86.6**	**87.2**
Paper and paperboard	11.7	20.2	37.6	44.6	45.9	44.4	43.4
Glass	0.8	2.6	2.9	3.1	3.2	3.2	3.2
Metals: Ferrous	0.4	2.2	4.7	5.8	5.5	5.5	5.8
Aluminum	0.3	1.0	0.9	0.7	0.7	0.7	0.7
Other nonferrous	0.5	0.7	1.1	1.4	1.4	1.4	1.4
Plastics	0.0	0.4	1.5	2.5	2.7	2.8	3.0
Food waste [2]	(Z)	(Z)	0.7	1.0	1.3	1.7	1.8
Yard trimmings	(Z)	4.2	15.8	19.2	19.3	19.6	20.6
Percent of generation recovered, total [1]	**9.6**	**16.0**	**28.5**	**34.0**	**34.7**	**34.5**	**34.3**
Paper and paperboard	21.3	27.8	42.8	62.5	65.6	64.6	63.3
Glass	5.0	20.1	22.6	27.2	27.7	27.7	27.3
Metals: Ferrous	2.9	17.6	33.1	34.2	33.0	32.9	33.0
Aluminum	17.9	35.9	27.0	19.4	20.5	20.2	20.0
Other nonferrous	46.6	66.4	66.3	71.3	70.8	70.2	68.2
Plastics	0.3	2.2	5.8	8.0	8.3	8.8	9.2
Food waste [2]	(Z)	(Z)	2.2	2.7	3.5	4.8	5.0
Yard trimmings	(Z)	12.0	51.7	57.5	57.3	57.7	60.2

Z Less than 5,000 tons or 0.05 percent. [1] Includes products not shown separately. [2] Includes recovery of paper and mixed municipal solid waste for composting.

Source: U.S. Environmental Protection Agency, *Advancing Sustainable Materials Management: Facts and Figures 2013*, June 2015; and "Historical Data Tables," <http://www.epa.gov/osw/conserve/tools/recmeas/msw_improv.htm>, accessed July 2015.

Table 408. Municipal Solid Waste—Generation, Recovery, and Discards by Selected Type of Product: 2013

[68,540 represents 68,540,000. See headnote, Table 407]

Type of product	Generation (1,000 tons)	Recovery Products recovered (1,000 tons)	Recovery Percent of generation	Discards (1,000 tons)
Paper and paperboard products [1]	**68,540**	**43,400**	**63.3**	**25,140**
Nondurable goods	29,980	14,450	48.2	15,530
Newspapers/Mechanical Papers	8,050	5,390	67.0	2,660
Other paper nondurable goods	21,930	9,060	41.3	12,870
Containers and packaging	38,560	28,950	75.1	9,610
Corrugated boxes	30,050	26,590	88.5	3,460
Other paper and paperboard packaging	8,510	2,360	27.7	6,150
Glass products [1]	**11,540**	**3,150**	**27.3**	**8,390**
Containers and packaging	9,260	3,150	34.0	6,110
Beer and soft drink bottles	5,420	2,240	41.3	3,180
Wine and liquor bottles	1,740	600	34.5	1,140
Food and other bottles and jars	2,100	310	14.8	1,790
Metal products [1]	**23,060**	**7,870**	**34.1**	**15,190**
Metals in durable goods	18,670	5,430	29.1	13,240
Ferrous	15,150	4,060	26.8	11,090
Aluminum	1,510	NA	NA	1,510
Other nonferrous	630	(Z)	(Z)	630
Metals in containers and packaging	4,200	2,440	58.1	1,760
Plastics [1]	**32,520**	**3,000**	**9.2**	**29,520**
Plastics in durable goods	12,070	830	6.9	11,240
Plastics in nondurable goods	6,470	130	2.0	6,340
Plastics in containers and packaging	13,980	2,040	14.6	11,940
Rubber and leather [1]	**7,720**	**1,240**	**16.1**	**6,480**
Rubber in tires	3,060	1,240	40.5	1,820

Z Less than 5,000 tons or .05 percent. [1] Includes products not shown separately.

Source: U.S. Environmental Protection Agency, *Advancing Sustainable Materials Management: Facts and Figures 2013,* June 2015. See also <http://www.epa.gov/epawaste/nonhaz/municipal/msw99.htm>

Table 409. Environmental Industry—Revenues and Employment by Industry Segment: 2000 to 2014

[209.7 represents $209,700,000,000. Covers approximately 30,000 private and public companies engaged in revenue-generating environmental activities]

Industry segment	Revenue (billion dollars)				Employment			
	2000	2010	2013	2014	2000	2010	2013	2014
Industry total	**209.7**	**306.8**	**350.7**	**364.6**	**1,299,300**	**1,644,800**	**1,770,400**	**1,773,400**
SERVICES								
Analytical services [1]	1.8	1.9	2.0	2.0	20,200	19,800	19,900	19,500
Wastewater treatment works [2]	28.7	45.5	53.2	55.3	118,800	169,900	187,400	190,900
Solid waste management [3]	39.4	53.4	56.4	58.1	221,400	278,000	289,900	292,300
Hazardous waste management [4]	8.2	9.0	10.2	10.9	45,100	43,600	47,600	49,800
Remediation/industrial services	10.1	12.8	14.1	14.4	100,200	107,900	113,400	111,800
Consulting and engineering	17.4	26.6	29.9	28.6	184,000	255,800	264,500	255,400
EQUIPMENT								
Water equipment and chemicals	19.8	26.9	29.7	30.7	130,500	160,100	169,900	173,100
Instrument manufacturing	3.8	5.4	6.1	6.4	30,200	37,300	40,500	41,400
Air pollution control equipment [5]	19.0	14.9	16.4	16.5	129,600	96,400	103,600	101,500
Waste management equipment [6]	10.0	10.8	11.7	12.1	75,500	73,800	76,000	77,400
Process and prevention technology	1.2	1.9	2.0	2.1	29,000	28,900	29,400	30,400
RESOURCES								
Water utilities [7]	29.9	45.5	52.6	54.3	130,000	180,300	200,700	204,600
Resource recovery [8]	16.0	28.5	32.2	30.2	61,900	102,600	105,200	98,000
Clean energy systems and power [9]	4.5	23.7	34.3	43.0	22,900	90,400	122,400	127,300

[1] Covers environmental laboratory testing and services. [2] Mostly revenues collected by municipal entities for sewage or wastewater plants. [3] Covers such activities as collection, transportation, transfer stations, disposal, landfill ownership and management for solid waste and recyclables. [4] Transportation and disposal of hazardous, medical, and nuclear waste. [5] Includes stationary and mobile sources. [6] Includes vehicles, containers, liners, processing, and remediation equipment. [7] Revenues generated from the sale of water, majority in public sector. [8] Revenues generated from the sale of recovered metals, paper, plastic, etc. [9] Revenues generated from the sale of equipment and systems and electricity.

Source: Environmental Business International, Inc., San Diego, CA, publisher of *Environmental Business Journal;* © 2015 EBI Inc. See also <http://www.ebionline.org>.

Table 410. Toxic Chemical Releases and Transfers by Media: 2009 to 2014

[In millions of pounds (3,397.0 represents 3,397,000,000), except as indicated. Based on reports filed to the Toxic Release Inventory (TRI) Program, as required by Section 313 of the Emergency Planning and Community Right-to-Know Act (EPCRA). The Pollution Prevention Act (PPA) of 1990 mandates collection of data on toxic chemicals that are treated on-site, recycled, and combusted for energy recovery. Owners and operators of facilities within specific North American Industry Classification System industries that have 10 or more full-time employees, and that manufacture, process, or otherwise use any listed toxic chemical in quantities greater than the established threshold in the course of a calendar year are covered and required to report. Includes carcinogens; persistent, bioaccumulative, toxic (PBT) chemicals; and dioxin and dioxin-like compounds. Does not include off-site disposal or other releases transferred to other TRI program facilities that reported the amounts as on-site disposal or other releases]

Media	2009	2010	2011	2012	2013	2014
Total facilities reporting	**21,893**	**21,734**	**21,728**	**21,829**	**21,888**	**21,774**
Total on- and off-site disposal or other releases	**3,397.0**	**3,812.0**	**4,111.2**	**3,599.7**	**4,101.4**	**3,868.2**
On-site releases	3,038.2	3,399.7	3,696.0	3,185.7	3,691.4	3,454.8
Air emissions [1]	925.5	863.0	806.1	744.0	750.1	716.9
Surface water discharges	206.4	231.8	221.7	217.0	212.7	215.0
Underground injection class I	157.3	204.6	196.5	198.0	199.6	197.9
Underground injection class II-V	0.2	0.2	0.2	0.2	2.1	0.3
RCRA subtitle C landfills [2]	83.9	68.1	69.4	94.3	68.1	57.7
Other landfills	240.7	283.9	273.6	267.8	294.4	292.8
Land treatment/application farming	16.2	15.3	15.0	15.9	13.8	13.9
Surface impoundments	793.8	789.1	884.7	724.2	738.0	752.0
Other land disposal	614.3	943.8	1,228.9	924.4	1,412.5	1,208.3
Off-site releases	358.8	412.3	415.2	414.0	410.0	413.4
Total transfers offsite for further waste management	**2,870.7**	**3,279.7**	**3,649.0**	**3,830.5**	**3,488.9**	**3,754.1**
Transfers to recycling	1,655.7	1,920.9	2,298.5	2,403.3	2,095.8	2,329.3
Transfers to energy recovery	367.6	427.9	354.4	388.2	407.3	424.8
Transfers to treatment	230.7	251.3	307.3	344.7	301.3	313.0
Transfers to POTWs (non metals) [3]	218.7	231.7	240.2	246.4	235.3	236.9
Transfers to POTWs metal and metal compounds [3]	0.8	0.8	0.8	0.9	0.7	0.7
Other off-site transfers	(Z)	0.2	0.2	0.1	–	–
Transfers off-site for disposal or other releases	397.3	446.9	447.5	447.8	448.6	449.5
Total production-related waste managed	**20,454.1**	**21,761.3**	**22,806.5**	**22,733.5**	**23,699.5**	**23,994.3**
Recycled on-site	6,146.0	6,150.5	6,522.3	6,854.1	7,148.9	6,888.3
Recycled off-site	1,641.1	1,920.8	2,295.1	2,098.1	2,095.3	2,327.5
Energy recovery on-site	1,864.4	1,983.7	2,108.2	2,308.5	2,307.1	2,829.6
Energy recovery off-site	369.7	428.0	354.7	387.3	406.9	423.7
Treated on-site	6,554.1	6,961.7	6,848.3	6,876.9	7,267.2	7,082.2
Treated off-site	426.3	458.8	522.7	567.2	516.0	523.9
Quantity disposed or otherwise release of on- and off-site	3,452.6	3,858.0	4,155.2	3,641.4	3,958.1	3,919.1
Non-production-related waste managed	10.9	13.3	14.7	14.4	203.8	14.4

– Represents or rounds zero. Z Less than 50,000 pounds. [1] Air emissions include both fugitive and point source. [2] RCRA=Resource Conservation and Recovery Act. [3] POTW (Publicly Owned Treatment Work) is a wastewater treatment facility that is owned by a state or municipality.

Source: Environmental Protection Agency, Toxic Release Inventory (TRI) Program, *2014 TRI National Analysis*. See also <http://www.epa.gov/enviro/facts/tri/index.html>, accessed September 2015.

Table 411. Industrial Pollution—Toxic Chemical Releases by Industry: 2013

[In millions of pounds (4,145.0 represents 4,145,000,000). See headnote, Table 410]

Industry	NAICS [1] code	Total on- and off-site releases	On-site releases Total [2]	On-site releases Air emissions	On-site releases Other surface impoundments	Off-site releases/ transfers to disposal [3]
Total [4]	**(X)**	**4,145.0**	**3,739.5**	**773.0**	**736.3**	**405.4**
Coal mining	2121	10.8	10.8	0.3	0.2	(Z)
Metal mining	2122	1,966.0	1,962.9	2.9	595.8	3.1
Electric utilities	2211	547.9	479.1	197.9	86.3	68.8
Food/beverages/tobacco	311/312	135.7	127.4	43.4	0.2	8.2
Textiles	313/314	3.7	3.1	1.3	0.1	0.6
Apparel	315	(Z)	(Z)	(Z)	–	(Z)
Leather	316	1.3	0.3	0.3	–	1.0
Wood products	321	8.7	8.3	8.1	(Z)	0.4
Paper	322	189.3	181.6	143.6	3.1	7.7
Printing and publishing	323/51	6.4	6.2	6.2	–	0.2
Petroleum	324	78.2	68.1	42.5	(Z)	10.2
Chemicals	325	523.3	453.8	177.9	19.4	69.5
Plastics and rubber	326	39.5	32.4	32.0	(Z)	7.1
Stone/clay/glass	327	25.5	20.0	15.0	0.1	5.4
Cement	32731	6.9	6.9	5.7	(Z)	(Z)
Primary metals	331	357.2	175.3	35.3	28.9	181.9
Fabricated metals	332	41.2	20.1	18.6	(Z)	21.2
Machinery	333	5.8	2.8	2.6	–	3.0
Computers/electronic products	334	4.6	2.9	1.3	–	1.7
Electrical equipment	335	4.2	1.2	1.2	(Z)	2.9
Transportation equipment	336	33.0	25.6	25.5	(Z)	7.4
Furniture	337	4.3	4.2	4.2	–	0.1
Miscellaneous manufacturing	339	2.9	2.1	2.0	–	0.8
Chemical wholesalers	4246	1.4	1.0	1.0	(Z)	0.4
Petroleum bulk terminals	4247	6.4	3.7	1.8	(Z)	2.7
Hazardous waste	562	148.6	111.9	0.5	1.1	36.7
No codes [4]	(X)	31.9	27.9	1.9	1.0	3.9

– Represents zero. X Not applicable. Z less than 50,000 lbs. [1] North American Industry Classification System, see text, Section 12. [2] Includes other on-site releases, not shown separately. [3] Includes off-site disposal to underground injection for Class I wells, Class II to V wells, other surface impoundments, land releases, and other releases, not shown separately. [4] Includes industries with no specific industry identified, and uses a double counting algorithm.

Source: Environmental Protection Agency, Toxic Release Inventory (TRI) Program, *2013 TRI National Analysis*, 2015, and unpublished data. See also <http://www2.epa.gov/toxics-release-inventory-tri-program/tri-data-and-tools>.

Table 412. Pollution—Toxic Chemical Releases by State and Outlying Area: 2013

[In millions of pounds (4,145.0 represents 4,145,000,000). Based on reports filed as required by Section 313 of the EPCRA. See headnote, Table 410]

State and outlying areas	Total on-and off-site releases	On-site releases or other disposal Total [2]	On-site releases or other disposal Total Air emis-sions	On-site releases or other disposal Other surface im-pound-ments	Off-site releases/ trans-fers to disposal	State and outlying areas	Total on-and off-site releases	On-site releases or other disposal Total [2]	On-site releases or other disposal Total Air emis-sions	On-site releases or other disposal Other surface im-pound-ments	Off-site releases/ trans-fers to disposal
Total [1]	4,145.0	3,739.5	773.0	736.3	405.4	MO	72.2	69.1	10.3	42.4	3.1
U.S. total	4,180.4	3,735.7	769.4	736.3	444.7	MT	34.9	34.0	1.9	5.7	0.9
AL	88.5	75.1	32.8	10.9	13.4	NE	26.2	23.6	4.8	0.0	2.6
AK	970.6	970.2	0.5	232.2	0.4	NV	369.8	365.2	1.3	230.9	4.5
AZ	70.6	69.0	2.4	17.6	1.6	NH	0.7	0.6	0.6	–	0.1
AR	35.8	30.8	16.4	1.0	5.0	NJ	11.0	7.7	2.1	(Z)	3.3
CA	49.0	42.9	8.0	0.4	6.1	NM	25.9	22.0	1.1	1.3	3.9
CO	27.3	23.2	2.3	5.0	4.1	NY	16.9	13.2	6.4	0.0	3.7
CT	2.1	1.3	1.1	–	0.8	NC	49.4	42.2	24.7	2.8	7.3
DE	5.5	4.0	1.0	(Z)	1.5	ND	51.7	41.9	25.5	4.6	9.8
DC	0.8	(Z)	(Z)	(Z)	0.8	OH	136.1	105.8	47.2	7.3	30.3
FL	67.3	63.1	25.5	0.2	4.1	OK	30.5	26.7	13.1	0.5	3.8
GA	71.6	68.7	44.7	7.9	2.9	OR	22.9	16.1	6.6	0.0	6.9
HI	3.0	2.4	1.7	–	0.6	PA	98.1	49.2	28.5	1.1	48.9
ID	48.8	47.8	4.4	10.4	1.0	RI	0.3	0.1	0.1	–	0.2
IL	124.1	78.1	28.8	7.4	46.1	SC	49.9	36.4	27.3	0.8	13.5
IN	154.0	102.7	44.4	4.2	51.3	SD	6.7	6.4	1.3	0.0	0.3
IA	39.3	31.7	18.9	0.3	7.6	TN	78.9	66.7	28.9	11.6	12.3
KS	21.4	18.4	11.1	0.2	3.0	TX	226.9	200.3	62.6	4.8	26.6
KY	72.1	63.8	40.3	8.1	8.3	UT	526.7	523.1	6.2	79.2	3.6
LA	142.8	125.7	51.5	4.2	17.1	VT	0.3	0.2	0.0	–	0.1
ME	12.1	9.2	4.4	–	2.9	VA	46.7	39.1	23.3	1.1	7.5
MD	8.3	6.6	4.9	(Z)	1.6	WA	20.5	17.0	9.7	1.4	3.5
MA	3.8	1.3	1.2	(Z)	2.5	WV	38.1	30.0	17.4	1.5	8.2
MI	70.0	40.4	23.3	3.8	29.6	WI	36.1	18.8	12.5	(Z)	17.3
MN	26.4	22.7	9.2	10.3	3.8	WY	20.1	18.1	2.2	3.2	2.0
MS	67.5	63.0	24.9	11.7	4.5	PR	3.6	3.3	3.3	–	0.3

– Represents zero. Z Less than 50,000 lbs. [1] Total includes all states, Puerto Rico, and other outlying areas not shown separately. [2] Includes other types of release, not shown separately.

Source: Environmental Protection Agency, Toxic Release Inventory (TRI) Program, *2013 TRI National Analysis*, 2015, and unpublished data. See also <http://www2.epa.gov/toxics-release-inventory-tri-program/tri-data-and-tools>.

Table 413. Hazardous Waste Sites on the National Priority List by State and Outlying Area: 2014

[As of March 2015. Includes both proposed and final sites listed on the National Priorities List for the Superfund program as authorized by the Comprehensive Environmental Response, Compensation, and Liability Act (CERCLA) of 1980 and the Superfund Amendments and Reauthorization Act (SARA) of 1986. For information on CERCLA and SARA, see <http://www.epa.gov/superfund/policy/cercla.htm>]

State and outlying areas	Total sites	Rank	Per-cent distri-bution	Federal	Non-fed-eral	State and outlying areas	Total sites	Rank	Per-cent distri-bution	Federal	Non-fed-eral
Total [1]	1,371	(X)	(X)	161	1,210	Missouri	33	15	2.4	3	30
United States	1,352	(X)	(X)	159	1,193	Montana	19	22	1.4	–	19
Alabama	16	26	1.2	3	13	Nebraska	15	28	1.1	1	14
Alaska	6	44	0.4	5	1	Nevada	1	50	0.1	–	1
Arizona	9	41	0.7	2	7	New Hampshire	21	20	1.6	1	20
Arkansas	9	41	0.7	–	9	New Jersey	114	1	8.4	6	108
California	98	2	7.2	24	74	New Mexico	15	28	1.1	1	14
Colorado	20	21	1.5	3	17	New York	86	4	6.4	4	82
Connecticut	15	28	1.1	1	14	North Carolina	39	11	2.9	2	37
Delaware	14	32	1.0	1	13	North Dakota	–	51	–	–	–
D.C.	1	50	0.1	1	–	Ohio	43	10	3.2	5	38
Florida	54	6	4.0	6	48	Oklahoma	8	44	0.6	1	7
Georgia	17	25	1.3	2	15	Oregon	14	32	1.0	2	12
Hawaii	3	46	0.2	2	1	Pennsylvania	97	3	7.2	6	91
Idaho	9	41	0.7	2	7	Rhode Island	12	37	0.9	2	10
Illinois	48	9	3.6	5	43	South Carolina	25	18	1.8	2	23
Indiana	38	13	2.8	–	38	South Dakota	2	48	0.1	1	1
Iowa	12	37	0.9	1	11	Tennessee	17	25	1.3	3	14
Kansas	13	35	1.0	1	12	Texas	52	7	3.8	4	48
Kentucky	14	32	1.0	1	13	Utah	18	23	1.3	5	13
Louisiana	14	32	1.0	1	13	Vermont	12	37	0.9	–	12
Maine	13	35	1.0	3	10	Virginia	31	16	2.3	11	20
Maryland	21	20	1.6	10	11	Washington	51	8	3.8	13	38
Massachusetts	33	15	2.4	6	27	West Virginia	9	41	0.7	2	7
Michigan	67	5	5.0	1	66	Wisconsin	38	13	2.8	–	38
Minnesota	25	18	1.8	2	23	Wyoming	2	48	0.1	1	1
Mississippi	9	41	0.7	–	9	Puerto Rico	16	(X)	(X)	1	15

– Represents zero. X Not applicable. [1] Total includes areas not shown separately.

Source: U.S. Environmental Protection Agency, "National Priorities List," <http://www.epa.gov/superfund/sites/npl/>, accessed September 2015.

Table 414. Hazardous Waste Generated, Shipped, and Received by State and Other Areas: 2011

[In thousands of tons (35,334.1 represents 35,334,100). Covers hazardous waste regulated under the Resource Conservation and Recovery Act (RCRA) of 1976 as amended. The data have been revised. See source for exclusions of data from the 2011 National Biennial RCRA Hazardous Waste Report]

State and other areas	Hazardous waste quantity (1,000) tons			State and other areas	Hazardous waste quantity (1,000) tons		
	Generated	Shipped	Received		Generated	Shipped	Received
Total...............	**34,334.1**	**5,951.4**	**6,180.0**	Missouri.....................	251.0	80.9	152.4
				Montana.....................	5.9	6.0	–
United States...............	**34,295.4**	**5,914.8**	**6,178.8**	Nebraska....................	35.4	43.7	37.4
				Nevada......................	9.8	11.9	78.7
Alabama.....................	578.3	193.0	246.2	New Hampshire.............	3.9	3.9	–
Alaska......................	2.5	2.0	–	New Jersey.................	290.5	328.2	242.4
Arizona.....................	202.9	26.5	17.9	New Mexico.................	1,042.4	10.4	4.7
Arkansas....................	922.7	206.6	240.6	New York...................	186.5	165.8	83.4
California..................	534.7	428.7	183.1	North Carolina.............	83.1	91.0	12.3
Colorado....................	31.8	34.6	43.8	North Dakota...............	455.9	1.2	0.3
Connecticut.................	25.0	24.1	8.8	Ohio.......................	1,617.8	565.6	621.1
Delaware....................	43.3	43.0	0.1	Oklahoma...................	44.3	29.9	94.3
District of Columbia........	1.1	1.1	–	Oregon.....................	93.2	77.6	55.2
Florida.....................	198.4	33.5	10.8	Pennsylvania...............	308.7	262.7	428.4
Georgia.....................	211.1	42.3	3.9	Rhode Island...............	8.6	16.2	10.0
Hawaii......................	425.6	1.3	0.2	South Carolina.............	140.5	171.2	154.6
Idaho......................	3.7	6.4	112.2	South Dakota...............	1.3	1.4	0.1
Illinois....................	675.5	205.0	379.9	Tennessee..................	89.4	52.8	28.9
Indiana.....................	888.1	389.4	463.1	Texas......................	15,683.4	607.3	653.6
Iowa........................	51.0	50.7	0.6	Utah.......................	49.7	79.4	145.6
Kansas......................	1,238.3	135.5	262.2	Vermont....................	2.0	2.6	1.5
Kentucky....................	142.2	182.0	106.4	Virginia...................	74.8	71.6	0.5
Louisiana...................	4,399.5	516.5	486.3	Washington.................	334.0	75.7	51.9
Maine.......................	2.4	2.3	0.1	West Virginia..............	62.3	39.5	6.4
Maryland....................	44.3	54.6	56.5	Wisconsin..................	289.4	173.0	52.8
Massachusetts...............	35.6	42.0	8.9	Wyoming....................	4.1	4.1	–
Michigan....................	282.9	177.9	443.7	Guam.......................	0.1	0.1	–
Minnesota...................	357.4	69.2	169.1	Navajo Nation..............	–	–	–
Mississippi.................	1,828.9	73.0	17.9	Puerto Rico................	37.3	35.2	1.2
				Virgin Islands.............	1.3	1.3	–

– Represents or rounds to zero.

Source: U.S. Environmental Protection Agency, *The National Biennial RCRA Hazardous Waste Report (Based on 2011 data)*, 2012. See also <http://www.epa.gov/epawaste/inforesources/data/biennialreport/index.htm>.

Table 415. Oil Spills in U.S. Water—Number and Volume: 2000 to 2011

[These summary statistics are based on reported discharges of oil and petroleum based products into U.S. navigable waters, including territorial waters (extending 3 to 12 miles from the coastline), tributaries, the contiguous zone, onto shoreline, or into other waters that threaten the marine environment]

Spill characteristic	Number of spills				Spill volume (gallons)			
	2000	2005	2010	2011	2000	2005	2010	2011
Total.....................	**8,354**	**3,881**	**3,008**	**3,065**	**1,431,370**	**9,926,581**	**206,712,792**	**210,270**
Size of spill (gallons):								
1 to 100..................	8,058	3,657	2,874	2,924	39,355	31,872	21,846	21,858
101 to 1,000..............	219	167	115	117	78,779	63,123	39,839	41,631
1,001 to 3,000............	37	25	8	12	67,529	43,289	16,645	18,818
3,001 to 5,000............	12	9	2	6	45,512	36,803	7,587	26,085
5,001 to 10,000...........	16	7	4	3	112,415	59,167	32,275	19,790
10,001 to 50,000..........	6	7	1	3	108,400	142,024	18,000	82,088
50,001 to 100,000.........	4	1	–	–	266,380	84,000	–	–
100,001 to 1,000,000......	2	4	3	–	713,000	1,368,236	996,400	–
1,000,000 and over........	–	4	1	–	–	8,098,067	205,580,200	–
Source:								
Tankship..................	111	37	23	26	608,176	2,976	421,583	1,702
Tankbarge.................	229	126	73	67	133,540	2,006,774	965	15,852
All other vessels.........	5,220	1,672	1,412	1,438	291,927	115,058	472,386	90,109
Facilities................	1,054	1,020	869	1,004	311,604	7,633,248	221,642	89,467
Pipelines.................	25	24	34	38	17,021	136,465	4,627	1,687
All other nonvessels......	566	102	105	117	45,136	1,934	206,582,872	3,605
Unknown...................	1,149	900	492	375	23,966	30,126	8,718	7,849

– Represents zero.

Source: U.S. Coast Guard, *Pollution Incidents In and Around U.S. Waters, A Spill/Release Compendium: 1969–2011*, December 2012. See also <http://homeport.uscg.mil>.

Table 416. Tornadoes, Floods, Tropical Storms, and Lightning: 2000 to 2014

Weather type	2000	2005	2007	2008	2009	2010	2011	2012	2013	2014
Tornadoes: [1]										
Number...........................	1,072	1,262	1,102	1,685	1,305	1,543	1,894	1,119	943	1,057
Lives lost...........................	41	38	81	126	21	45	553	70	55	47
Injuries...........................	882	537	659	1,714	351	699	5,483	822	756	641
Property loss (mil. dol.)...............	424	422	1,401	1,846	566	1,107	9,463	1,649	3,642	622
Floods and flash floods:										
Lives lost...........................	38	43	87	82	56	103	113	29	82	38
Injuries...........................	47	38	59	46	27	310	40	25	33	20
Property loss (mil. dol.)...............	1,255	1,538	1,740	3,406	1,050	3,927	7,978	494	2,173	2,626
North Atlantic tropical										
cyclones and hurricanes: [2]...	15	27	17	17	11	21	20	19	15	9
Hurricanes...........................	8	15	6	8	3	12	7	10	2	6
Lives lost...........................	–	1,016	1	12	2	–	9	4	1	12
Property loss (mil. dol.)...............	8	93,064	39	7,619	1	15	344	172	10	3
Lightning:										
Deaths...........................	51	38	45	27	34	29	26	28	23	26
Injuries...........................	364	309	138	216	201	182	187	139	145	154

– Represents zero. [1] Source: U.S. National Weather Service, <http://www.spc.noaa.gov/climo/torn/monthlytornstats.html>. A violent, rotating column of air descending from a cumulonimbus cloud in the form of a tubular- or funnel-shaped cloud, usually characterized by movements along a narrow path and wind speeds from 100 to over 300 miles per hour. Also known as a "twister" or "waterspout." [2] Tropical cyclones include depressions, storms and hurricanes. For data on individual hurricanes, see National Hurricane Center (NHC) at <http://www.nhc.noaa.gov/>.

Source: Except as noted, U.S. National Oceanic and Atmospheric Administration (NOAA), National Weather Service (NWS), Office of Climate, Water, and Weather Services, "Natural Hazard Statistics," <http://www.nws.noaa.gov/om/hazstats.shtml>, accessed August 2015.

Table 417. Number of Earthquakes in the United States: 2000 to 2012

[The United States Geological Survey (USGS) detects but does not generally locate mine blasts (explosions) throughout the United States on any given business day. For more information, see "Routine United States Mining Seismicity" at <http://earthquake.usgs.gov/earthquakes/eqarchives/mineblast/>. For information on "Top Earthquake States," see <http://earthquake.usgs.gov/earthquakes/states/top_states.php>]

Magnitude	2000	2004	2005	2006	2007	2008	2009	2010	2011	2012	Top earthquake states	1974–2003 [1]
Total...............	2,342	3,550	3,685	2,783	2,791	3,618	4,262	8,496	5,237	3,836	Total	21,080
8.0 to 9.9...........	–	–	–	–	–	–	–	–	–	–	AK	[2] 12,053
7.0 to 7.9...........	–	–	1	–	1	–	–	1	1	–	CA	4,895
6.0 to 6.9...........	6	2	4	7	9	9	4	8	3	5	HI	1,533
5.0 to 5.9...........	63	25	47	51	72	85	58	89	51	27	NV	778
4.0 to 4.9...........	281	284	345	346	366	432	288	631	347	271	WA	424
3.0 to 3.9...........	917	1,362	1,475	1,213	1,137	1,486	1,492	3,584	1,838	1,236	ID	404
2.0 to 2.9...........	660	1,336	1,738	1,145	1,173	1,573	2,379	4,132	2,941	2,251	WY	217
1.0 to 1.9...........	–	1	2	7	11	13	26	39	47	43	MT	186
0.1 to 0.9...........	–	–	–	1	–	–	1	–	1	–	UT	139
No magnitude......	415	540	73	13	22	20	14	12	8	3	OR	73

– Represents zero. [1] The total number represents earthquakes of a magnitude range of 3.5 and greater. [2] The number of earthquakes is underreported. Events in the magnitude range of 3.5 to 4.0 in the Aleutian Islands are not recorded on enough seismograph stations to be located.

Source: U.S. Geological Survey, *Earthquake Facts and Statistics*, <http://earthquake.usgs.gov/earthquakes/eqarchives>, accessed September 2013.

Table 418. Wildland Fires, Number, and Acres: 1970 to 2014

[Acres in thousands (3,279 represents 3,279,000), as indicated. As of December 31. There are three distinct types of wildland fires: wildfire, wildland fire use, and prescribed fire. Wildland fire is any nonstructural fire that occurs in the wildland]

Year	Total [1] Fires (number)	Total [1] Acres (1,000)	Year	Total [1] Fires (number)	Total [1] Acres (1,000)	State	Wildland [1] Fires	Wildland [1] Acres	Prescribed [2] Fires	Prescribed [2] Acres
1970.........	121,736	3,279	2003.........	63,629	3,961	Total....	63,312	3,595,613	17,044	2,389,798
1975.........	134,872	1,791	2004 [3]......	65,461	8,098	OR......	3,087	984,629	658	88,887
1980.........	234,892	5,261	2005.........	66,753	8,689	CA......	7,865	555,044	515	36,997
1985.........	82,591	2,896	2006.........	96,385	9,874	WA......	1,480	386,972	98	15,197
1990.........	66,481	4,622	2007.........	85,705	9,328	AK......	384	233,561	7	59,591
1995.........	82,234	1,841	2008.........	78,979	5,292	AZ......	1,543	205,199	133	64,905
1998.........	81,043	1,330	2009.........	78,792	5,922	ID......	1,180	189,430	321	39,050
1999.........	92,487	5,626	2010.........	71,971	3,423	OK......	1,007	157,080	22	4,209
2000.........	92,250	7,393	2011.........	74,126	8,711	TN......	1,249	156,391	35	18,181
2001.........	84,079	3,571	2012.........	67,774	9,326	TX......	9,677	131,138	58	98,247
2002.........	73,457	7,185	2013.........	47,579	4,320	FL......	2,436	101,599	471	360,868

[1] Data are for wildland fires only. The data do not include wildland fire use and prescribed fires. [2] Prescribed fire is any fire which is ignited by management action under certain predetermined conditions to meet specific objectives related to hazardous fuels or habitat improvement. [3] 2004 fires and acres do not include state lands for North Carolina.

Source: National Interagency Coordination Center, *Wildland Fire Summary and Statistics Annual Report, 2014*, and earlier reports. See also <http://www.predictiveservices.nifc.gov/intelligence/intelligence.htm>.

Table 419. Major U.S. Weather and Climate Disasters: 2014

[4 represents $4,000,000,000. Covers only weather and climate related disasters costing $1 billion or more. See source for more information]

Event	Description	Time period	CPI-adjusted estimated cost (billion dollars)	Deaths (number)
Western Drought...............	Historic drought conditions affected the majority of California for all of 2014 making it the worst drought on record for the state. Surrounding states and parts of Texas, Oklahoma and Kansas also experienced continued severe drought conditions. This is a continuation of drought conditions that have persisted for several years.	2014	4	–
Rockies/Plains Severe Weather.........	Severe storms across the Rockies and Plains states (CO, TX, KS). Large hail and high winds created significant damage across eastern Colorado and Texas, particularly in the Dallas metro area.	September 2014	1	–
Michigan and Northeast Flooding........	Heavy rainfall in excess of 5 inches caused significant flooding in cities across Michigan damaging thousands of cars, business, homes and other infrastructure. Flooding also occurred across Maryland and New York's Long Island, as the slow-moving storm system delivered 24-hour rainfall exceeding 6 and 12 inches, respectively, creating more flood damage. Islip, NY received 13.57 inches of rain over a 24-hour period on Aug 12-13 setting a new 24-hour precipitation record for New York.	August 2014	1	2
Rockies/Central Plains Severe Weather..........	Severe storms across the Rockies and Central Plains states (NE, KS, WY, IA, AR). Wind gusts exceeding 90 mph and baseball to softball sized hail caused severe damage to structures and vehicles in central and eastern Nebraska.	June 2014	2	2
Rockies/Midwest/Eastern Severe Weather..........	Severe storms across the Rockies, Midwest and Eastern states (CO, MT, IA, IL, IN, OH, SC, VA, PA, DE, NY) with the most costly damage in Colorado, Illinois and Pennsylvania.	May 2014	4	–
Midwest/Southeast/Northeast Tornadoes and Flooding...........	Tornado outbreak across the Midwest, Southeast and Northeast states (AL, AR, DE, FL, GA, KS, MD, MO, MS, NC, NJ, NY, PA, TN, VA) with 83 confirmed tornadoes. Mississippi had its 3rd greatest number of tornadoes reported for any day since 1950. Torrential rainfall in the Florida panhandle also caused major flooding, as Pensacola set new 1-day and 2-day precipitation records of 15.55 and 20.47 inches, respectively. Flooding rains were also reported in coastal Alabama, as Mobile received 11.24 inches of rain, the third greatest calendar day rainfall total for the city.	April 2014	2	33
Plains Severe Weather.............	Severe storms across the Plains states (IL, KS, MO, TX) causing considerable hail and wind damage in Texas.	April 2014	1	–
Midwest/Southeast/Northeast Winter Storm...............	Winter storm caused widespread damage across numerous Midwest, Southeast and Northeastern states (AL, GA, IL, IN, KY, MD, MI, MO, MS, NC, NJ, NY, OH, PA, SC, TN, VA).	January 2014	2	16

– Represents zero.

Source: U.S. National Oceanic and Atmospheric Administration, National Centers for Environmental Information, "Billion-Dollar Weather and Climate Disasters, 1980-2014," <http://www.ncdc.noaa.gov/billions/events>, accessed August 2015.

Table 420. Highest and Lowest Temperatures by State Through 2014

[Data have been evaluated by the National Oceanic and Atmospheric Administration National Climatic Data Center, and/or by the State Climate Extremes Committee and determined to be valid. The data may come from sources other than official NOAA-supervised weather stations, but are archived, officially recognized observations]

State	Highest temperatures			Lowest temperatures		
	Station	Temperature (°F)	Date	Station	Temperature (°F)	Date
US	**Greenland Ranch**	**134**	**July 10, 1913**	**Prospect Creek Camp**	**-80**	**Jan. 23, 1971**
AL	Centerville	112	Sep. 5, 1925	New Market	-27	Jan. 30, 1966
AK	Fort Yukon	100	June 27, 1915	Prospect Creek Camp	-80	Jan. 23, 1971
AZ	Lake Havasu City	128	June 29, 1994	Hawley Lake	-40	Jan. 7, 1971
AR	Ozark	120	Aug. 10, 1936	Gravette	-29	Feb. 13, 1905
CA	Greenland Ranch	134	July 10, 1913	Boca	-45	Jan. 20, 1937
CO	Sedgwick	114	[1] July 11, 1954	Maybell	-61	Feb. 1, 1985
CT	Danbury	106	[1] July 15, 1995	Coventry	-32	[1] Jan. 22, 1961
DE	Millsboro	110	July 21, 1930	Millsboro	-17	Jan. 17, 1893
FL	Monticello	109	June 29, 1931	Tallahassee	-2	Feb. 13, 1899
GA	Greenville 2 NNW	112	[1] Aug. 20, 1983	CCC Camp F-16	-17	Jan. 27, 1940
HI	Pahala	100	Apr. 27, 1931	Mauna Kea Obs. 111.2	12	May 17, 1979
ID	Orofino	118	July 28, 1934	Island Park Dam	-60	Jan. 18, 1943
IL	East St. Louis	117	July 14, 1954	Congerville	-36	Jan. 5, 1999
IN	Collegeville	116	July 14, 1936	New Whiteland	-36	Jan. 19, 1994
IA	Keokuk	118	July 20, 1934	Elkader	-47	[1] Feb. 3, 1996
KS	Alton	121	July 24, 1936	Lebanon	-40	Feb. 13, 1905
KY	Greensburg	114	July 28, 1930	Shelbyville	-37	Jan. 19, 1994
LA	Plain Dealing	114	Aug. 10, 1936	Minden	-16	Feb. 13, 1899
ME	North Bridgton	105	[1] July 10, 1911	Big Black River	-48	Jan. 16, 2009
MD	Cumberland & Frederick	109	[1] July 10, 1936	Oakland	-40	Jan. 13, 1912
MA	New Bedford & Chester	107	[1] Aug. 2, 1975	Chester	-35	[1] Jan. 12, 1981
MI	Mio Hydro Plant & Stanwood	112	July 13, 1936	Vanderbilt	-51	Feb. 9, 1934
MN	Beardsley	115	July 29, 1917	Tower	-60	Feb. 2, 1996
MS	Holly Springs	115	July 29, 1930	Corinth	-19	Jan. 30, 1966
MO	Warsaw & Union	118	[1] July 14, 1954	Warsaw	-40	Feb. 13, 1905
MT	Medicine Lake	117	[1] July 5, 1937	Rogers Pass	-70	Jan. 20, 1954
NE	Minden	118	[1] July 24, 1936	Oshkosh	-47	[1] Dec. 22, 1989
NV	Laughlin	125	June 29, 1994	San Jacinto	-50	Jan. 8, 1937
NH	Nashua	106	July 4, 1911	Mt. Washington	-47	Jan. 22, 1885
NJ	Runyon	110	July 10, 1936	River Vale	-34	Jan. 5, 1904
NM	Waste Isolat Pilot Plt	122	June 27, 1994	Gavilan	-50	Feb. 1, 1951
NY	Troy	108	July 22, 1926	Old Forge	-52	Feb. 18, 1979
NC	Fayetteville	110	Aug. 21, 1983	Mt. Mitchell	-34	Jan. 21, 1985
ND	Steele	121	July 6, 1936	Parshall	-60	Feb. 15, 1936
OH	Gallipolis (near)	113	July 21, 1934	Milligan	-39	Feb. 10, 1899
OK	Altus Irig Res	120	[1] Aug. 12, 1936	Nowata	-31	[1] Feb. 10, 2011
OR	Pendleton.	119	[1] Aug. 10, 1898	Seneca	-54	[1] Feb. 10, 1933
PA	Phoenixville	111	July 10, 1936	Smethport	-42	Jan. 5, 1904
RI	Providence	104	Aug. 2, 1975	Wood River Junction	-25	Jan. 11, 1942
SC	Columbis Univ. of SC	113	June 29, 2012	Caesars Head	-19	Jan. 21, 1985
SD	Fort Pierre	120	[1] July 15, 2006	McIntosh	-58	Feb. 17, 1936
TN	Perryville	113	Aug. 9, 1930	Mountain City	-32	Dec. 30, 1917
TX	Monahans	120	[1] June 28, 1994	Seminole	-23	Feb. 8, 1933
UT	Saint George	117	July 5, 1985	East Portal	-69	Jan. 5, 1913
VT	Vernon	107	July 7, 1912	Bloomfield	-50	Dec. 30, 1933
VA	Balcony Falls	110	[1] July 15, 1954	Mtn. Lake Bio. Stn.	-30	Jan. 22, 1985
WA	Ice Harbor Dam	118	[1] Aug. 5, 1961	Mazama & Winthrop	-48	[1] Dec. 30, 1968
WV	Martinsburg	112	[1] July 10, 1936	Lewisburg	-37	Dec. 30, 1917
WI	Wisconsin Dells	114	July 13, 1936	Couderay	-55	[1] Feb. 4, 1996
WY	Diversion Dam	115	[1] July 15, 1988	Riverside R.S.	-66	Feb. 9, 1933

[1] Also on earlier dates at the same or other places.

Source: U.S. National Oceanic and Atmospheric Administration, National Climatic Data Center, State Climate Extremes Committee, "Maximum and Minimum Temperature Records," <http://www.ncdc.noaa.gov/extremes/scec/records>, accessed August 2015.

Table 421. Highest Temperature of Record—Selected Cities

[In degrees Fahrenheit. Airport data, except as noted. For period of record through 2012]

State	Station	Length of record (years)	Jan.	Feb.	Mar.	Apr.	May	June	July	Aug.	Sept.	Oct.	Nov.	Dec.	Annual [1]
AL....	Mobile	71	84	82	90	94	100	103	104	105	99	93	87	81	105
AK....	Juneau	68	57	57	61	74	82	86	90	84	73	61	56	54	90
AZ....	Phoenix	75	88	92	100	105	113	122	121	117	118	107	96	88	122
AK....	Little Rock	71	83	85	91	95	98	107	112	114	106	97	86	80	114
CA....	Los Angeles	77	91	92	95	102	97	104	97	98	110	106	101	94	110
CA....	Sacramento	62	74	76	88	95	105	115	114	110	108	104	87	73	115
CA....	San Diego	72	88	90	93	98	96	101	99	98	111	107	100	88	111
CA....	San Francisco	85	72	78	85	92	97	106	105	100	103	99	85	75	106
CO...	Denver	70	73	77	84	90	96	105	105	104	97	89	80	75	105
CT....	Hartford	58	72	73	89	96	99	100	103	102	99	91	81	76	103
DE....	Wilmington	65	75	78	86	94	96	100	103	101	100	91	85	75	103
DC...	Washington	71	79	82	89	95	99	104	105	105	101	94	86	79	105
FL....	Jacksonville	71	85	88	91	95	100	103	105	102	100	96	88	84	105
FL....	Miami	70	88	89	93	96	96	98	98	98	97	95	91	89	98
GA...	Atlanta	64	79	80	89	93	95	106	105	104	98	95	84	79	105
HI....	Honolulu	43	88	88	88	91	93	92	94	93	95	94	93	89	95
ID.....	Boise	73	63	71	81	92	99	109	111	110	102	94	78	65	111
IL.....	Chicago	54	65	72	88	91	97	104	104	101	99	91	78	71	104
IL.....	Peoria	73	70	72	86	92	94	105	104	103	100	93	81	71	105
IN.....	Indianapolis	73	71	76	85	89	93	104	105	102	100	91	81	74	104
IA.....	Des Moines	73	67	73	91	93	98	103	106	108	101	95	81	69	108
KS....	Wichita	60	75	87	89	96	100	110	113	111	108	97	86	83	113
KY....	Louisville	65	77	77	86	91	95	105	106	105	104	93	84	76	106
LA....	New Orleans	66	83	85	89	92	96	101	101	102	101	94	87	84	102
ME...	Portland	72	67	64	88	92	94	98	100	103	95	88	74	71	103
MD...	Baltimore	62	75	79	89	94	98	103	106	105	100	94	83	77	106
MA...	Boston	61	69	70	89	94	95	100	103	102	100	90	79	76	103
MI....	Detroit	54	64	70	86	89	95	104	102	100	98	91	77	69	104
MI....	Sault Ste. Marie	72	45	49	83	85	89	93	97	98	95	81	68	62	98
MN...	Duluth	71	52	55	78	88	90	94	97	97	95	86	71	55	97
MN...	Minneapolis-St. Paul	74	58	61	83	95	97	103	105	102	98	90	77	68	105
MS...	Jackson	49	83	85	89	94	99	105	106	107	104	95	88	84	107
MO...	Kansas City	40	71	78	86	93	95	105	107	109	106	95	82	74	109
MO...	St. Louis	55	76	85	89	93	95	108	108	107	104	94	85	76	107
MT...	Great Falls	75	67	70	78	89	93	101	105	106	98	91	76	69	106
NE....	Omaha	76	69	78	91	97	99	105	114	110	104	96	83	72	114
NV....	Reno	71	71	75	83	90	97	103	108	105	101	93	77	70	108
NH...	Concord	71	69	67	89	95	97	98	102	101	98	90	80	73	102
NJ....	Atlantic City	69	78	75	87	94	99	106	105	103	99	90	84	77	106
NM...	Albuquerque	73	69	76	85	89	98	107	105	101	100	91	77	72	107
NY....	Albany	66	71	68	89	92	94	99	100	99	100	89	82	71	100
NY....	Buffalo	69	72	71	82	94	91	96	97	99	98	87	80	74	99
NY....	New York [2]	144	72	75	86	96	99	101	106	104	102	94	84	75	106
NC...	Charlotte	73	79	82	90	93	100	104	104	104	104	98	85	80	104
NC...	Raleigh	68	80	84	92	95	97	105	105	105	104	98	88	81	105
ND...	Bismarck	73	63	69	81	93	98	111	112	109	105	95	79	65	112
OH...	Cincinnati	51	69	75	84	89	93	102	104	102	100	91	81	75	103
OH...	Cleveland	71	73	74	83	88	92	104	103	102	101	90	82	77	104
OH...	Columbus	73	74	75	85	89	94	102	101	101	100	91	80	76	102
OK...	Oklahoma City	59	80	92	93	100	104	105	110	113	108	96	87	86	110
OR...	Portland	72	66	71	80	90	100	102	107	107	105	92	73	65	107
PA....	Philadelphia	71	74	74	87	95	97	100	104	101	100	96	81	73	104
PA....	Pittsburgh	60	72	76	82	89	91	98	103	100	97	87	82	74	103
RI.....	Providence	59	69	72	85	98	96	97	102	104	100	86	78	77	104
SC...	Columbia	65	84	84	91	94	101	109	107	107	101	101	90	83	107
SD....	Sioux Falls	67	66	70	87	94	100	110	108	108	104	94	81	63	110
TN....	Memphis	71	79	81	86	94	99	104	108	107	103	95	86	81	108
TN....	Nashville	73	78	84	86	91	97	109	107	106	105	94	84	79	107
TX....	Dallas-Fort Worth	59	88	95	96	101	103	113	110	110	111	102	89	89	113
TX....	El Paso	73	80	83	90	98	105	114	112	108	104	96	87	80	114
TX....	Houston	43	84	91	91	95	99	105	104	109	109	96	89	85	109
UT....	Salt Lake City	84	63	69	80	89	99	104	107	106	100	89	75	69	107
VT....	Burlington	69	66	62	84	91	93	100	100	101	98	85	75	67	101
VA....	Norfolk	64	80	82	88	97	100	101	105	104	99	95	86	80	105
VA....	Richmond	83	81	83	93	96	100	104	105	104	103	99	86	81	105
WA...	Seattle-Tacoma	68	64	70	78	85	93	96	103	99	98	89	74	64	103
WA...	Spokane	65	59	63	71	90	96	101	103	108	98	86	67	56	108
WV...	Charleston	65	79	79	89	94	94	103	104	104	102	93	85	80	104
WI....	Milwaukee	72	63	68	84	91	93	101	103	103	98	89	77	68	103
WY...	Cheyenne	77	66	71	74	83	91	100	100	98	95	84	75	69	100
PR....	San Juan	58	92	96	96	97	96	97	95	97	97	98	96	94	98

[1] Represents the highest observed temperature in any month. [2] City office data.

Source: U.S. National Oceanic and Atmospheric Administration, *Comparative Climatic Data*, 2012. See also <http://www.ncdc.noaa.gov/statistical-weather-and-climate-information>.

Table 422. Lowest Temperature of Record—Selected Cities

[In degrees Fahrenheit. Airport data, except as noted. For period of record through 2012]

State	Station	Length of record (years)	Jan.	Feb.	Mar.	Apr.	May	June	July	Aug.	Sept.	Oct.	Nov.	Dec.	An-nual [1]
AL.....	Mobile	71	3	11	21	32	43	49	60	59	42	30	22	8	3
AK....	Juneau	68	-22	-22	-15	6	25	31	36	27	23	11	-5	-21	-22
AZ....	Phoenix	75	17	22	25	32	40	50	61	60	47	34	25	22	17
AR....	Little Rock	71	-4	-5	11	28	40	46	54	52	37	29	17	-1	-5
CA....	Los Angeles	77	23	32	34	39	43	48	49	51	47	41	34	32	23
CA....	Sacramento	62	21	23	26	31	36	41	48	49	42	36	26	18	18
CA....	San Diego	72	29	36	39	41	48	51	55	57	51	43	38	34	29
CA....	San Francisco	85	24	25	30	31	36	41	43	42	38	34	25	20	20
CO....	Denver	70	-25	-30	-11	-2	21	30	43	41	17	3	-8	-25	-30
CT....	Hartford	58	-26	-21	-6	9	28	35	44	36	30	17	1	-14	-26
DE....	Wilmington	65	-14	-6	2	18	30	41	48	43	36	24	14	-7	-14
DC....	Washington	71	-5	4	11	24	34	47	54	49	39	29	16	1	-5
FL.....	Jacksonville	71	7	19	23	31	45	47	61	59	48	33	21	11	7
FL.....	Miami	70	30	32	32	46	53	60	69	68	68	51	39	30	30
GA....	Atlanta	64	-8	5	10	26	37	46	53	55	36	28	3	0	-8
HI.....	Honolulu	43	53	53	55	57	60	65	66	65	66	61	57	54	53
ID.....	Boise	73	-17	-15	6	19	22	31	35	34	23	11	-3	-25	-25
IL......	Chicago	54	-27	-19	-8	7	24	36	40	41	28	17	1	-25	-27
IL......	Peoria	73	-25	-19	-10	14	25	39	47	41	26	19	-2	-23	-25
IN.....	Indianapolis	73	-27	-21	-7	16	28	37	44	41	28	17	-2	-23	-27
IA.....	Des Moines	73	-24	-26	-22	9	30	38	47	40	26	14	-4	-22	-26
KS....	Wichita	60	-12	-21	-2	15	31	43	51	48	31	18	1	-16	-21
KY....	Louisville	65	-22	-19	-1	22	31	42	50	46	33	23	-1	-15	-22
LA.....	New Orleans	66	14	16	25	32	41	50	60	60	42	35	24	11	11
ME....	Portland	72	-26	-39	-21	8	23	33	40	33	23	15	3	-21	-39
MD....	Baltimore	62	-7	-3	6	20	32	40	50	45	35	25	13	0	-7
MA....	Boston	61	-12	-4	5	16	34	45	50	47	38	28	15	-7	-12
MI.....	Detroit	54	-21	-15	-4	10	25	36	41	38	29	17	9	-10	-21
MI.....	Sault Ste. Marie	72	-36	-35	-24	-2	18	26	36	29	25	16	-10	-31	-36
MN....	Duluth	71	-39	-39	-29	-5	17	27	35	32	22	8	-23	-34	-39
MN....	Minneapolis-St. Paul	74	-34	-32	-32	2	18	34	43	39	26	13	-17	-29	-34
MS.....	Jackson	49	2	10	15	27	38	47	51	54	35	26	17	4	2
MO....	Kansas City	40	-17	-19	-10	12	30	42	51	43	31	17	1	-23	-23
MO....	St. Louis	55	-18	-12	-5	22	31	43	51	47	36	23	1	-16	-18
MT....	Great Falls	75	-37	-35	-29	-8	12	31	36	30	16	-11	-25	-43	-43
NE....	Omaha	76	-23	-21	-16	5	27	38	44	43	25	13	-9	-23	-23
NV....	Reno	71	-16	-16	-2	13	18	21	33	24	20	8	1	-16	-16
NH....	Concord	71	-33	-37	-16	8	21	30	35	29	21	10	-5	-22	-37
NJ.....	Atlantic City	69	-10	-11	3	12	25	37	42	40	32	20	10	-7	-11
NM....	Albuquerque	73	-17	-7	8	19	16	40	52	50	37	21	-7	-7	-17
NY....	Albany	66	-28	-21	-21	10	26	36	40	34	24	16	5	-22	-28
NY....	Buffalo	69	-16	-20	-7	12	26	35	43	38	32	20	9	-10	-20
NY....	New York [2]	144	-6	-15	3	12	32	44	52	50	39	28	5	-13	-15
NC....	Charlotte	73	-5	5	4	21	32	45	53	50	39	24	11	2	-5
NC....	Raleigh	68	-9	0	11	23	31	38	48	46	37	19	11	4	-9
ND....	Bismarck	73	-44	-43	-31	-12	15	30	35	33	11	-10	-30	-43	-44
OH....	Cincinnati	51	-25	-11	-11	15	27	39	47	43	31	16	1	-20	-25
OH....	Cleveland	71	-20	-15	-5	10	25	31	41	38	32	19	3	-15	-20
OH....	Columbus	73	-22	-13	-6	14	25	35	43	39	31	20	5	-17	-22
OK....	Oklahoma City	59	-4	-5	3	20	36	47	53	51	36	16	11	-8	-8
OR....	Portland	72	-2	-3	19	29	29	39	43	44	34	26	13	6	-3
PA.....	Philadelphia	71	-7	-4	7	19	28	44	51	44	35	25	15	1	-7
PA.....	Pittsburgh	60	-22	-12	-1	14	26	34	42	39	31	16	-1	-12	-22
RI.....	Providence	59	-13	-7	1	14	29	41	48	40	33	20	6	-10	-13
SC.....	Columbia	65	-1	5	4	26	34	44	54	53	40	23	12	4	-1
SD....	Sioux Falls	67	-36	-31	-23	5	17	33	38	34	22	9	-17	-28	-36
TN....	Memphis	71	-4	-11	12	28	38	48	52	48	36	25	9	-13	-13
TN....	Nashville	73	-17	-13	2	23	34	42	51	47	36	26	-1	-10	-17
TX.....	Dallas-Fort Worth	59	4	7	15	29	41	51	59	56	43	29	20	-1	-1
TX.....	El Paso	73	-8	1	14	23	31	46	57	56	41	25	1	5	-8
TX.....	Houston	43	12	3	22	31	44	52	62	60	48	29	19	7	3
UT....	Salt Lake City	84	-22	-30	2	14	25	35	40	37	27	16	-14	-21	-30
VT.....	Burlington	69	-30	-30	-20	2	24	33	39	35	25	15	-2	-26	-30
VA.....	Norfolk	64	-3	8	18	28	36	45	54	49	45	27	20	7	-3
VA.....	Richmond	83	-12	-10	10	23	31	40	51	46	35	21	10	-1	-12
WA....	Seattle-Tacoma	68	0	1	11	29	28	38	43	44	35	28	6	6	0
WA....	Spokane	65	-22	-24	-7	17	24	33	37	35	22	7	-21	-25	-25
WV....	Charleston	65	-16	-12	0	19	26	33	46	41	34	17	6	-12	-16
WI.....	Milwaukee	72	-26	-26	-10	12	21	33	40	44	28	18	-5	-20	-26
WY....	Cheyenne	77	-29	-34	-21	-8	16	25	38	36	8	-1	-16	-28	-34
PR....	San Juan	58	61	62	60	64	66	69	69	70	69	46	66	59	46

[1] Represents the lowest observed temperature in any month. [2] City office data.

Source: U.S. National Oceanic and Atmospheric Administration, *Comparative Climatic Data*, 2012. See also <http://www.ncdc.noaa.gov/statistical-weather-and-climate-information>.

Table 423. Snow, Hail, Ice Pellets, and Sleet—Selected Cities

[In inches. Airport data, except as noted. For period of record through 2012. T denotes trace. Stations may show snowfall (hail) during the warm months]

State	Station	Length of record (years)	Jan.	Feb.	Mar.	Apr.	May	June	July	Aug.	Sept.	Oct.	Nov.	Dec.	An-nual
AL....	Mobile	70	0.1	0.1	0.1	T	T	–	T	–	–	–	T	0.1	0.4
AK....	Juneau	68	26.7	18.6	15.3	3.5	T	T	–	–	T	1.1	12.8	21.2	99.0
AZ....	Phoenix	62	T	–	T	T	T	–	–	–	–	T	–	T	T
AR....	Little Rock	61	2.5	1.7	0.5	T	T	T	–	–	–	T	0.2	0.8	5.5
CA. ..	Los Angeles	62	T	T	T	–	–	–	–	–	–	–	T	T	T
CA. ..	Sacramento	50	T	T	T	–	T	–	–	–	–	–	–	T	T
CA. ..	San Diego	60	T	–	T	T	–	–	–	–	–	–	T	T	T
CA. ..	San Francisco	69	–	T	T	–	–	–	–	–	–	–	–	–	T
CO....	Denver	68	7.9	7.6	12.1	8.3	1.6	–	T	T	1.6	4.1	8.5	7.9	59.6
CT....	Hartford	55	13.8	12.3	9.7	1.5	T	–	–	–	–	0.3	2.1	11.0	51.0
DE. ..	Wilmington	62	6.7	7.1	3.3	0.2	T	T	T	–	–	0.1	0.9	3.5	22.1
DC. ..	Washington	69	5.1	5.6	2.3	2.3	T	T	T	T	–	–	0.8	3.2	19.5
FL....	Jacksonville	60	T	–	–	T	T	T	T	–	–	–	–	–	T
FL....	Miami	59	–	–	–	–	T	–	–	–	–	–	–	–	T
GA. ..	Atlanta	73	1.0	0.5	0.5	T	–	–	T	–	–	T	T	0.2	2.2
HI. ...	Honolulu	52	–	–	–	–	–	–	–	–	–	–	–	–	–
ID. ...	Boise	73	6.3	3.7	1.7	0.6	0.1	T	T	T	T	0.1	2.4	5.8	20.7
IL.....	Chicago	53	11.4	8.7	6.2	1.6	0.1	T	T	T	T	0.4	2.1	8.7	39.5
IL.....	Peoria	69	6.7	5.6	4.2	0.8	T	T	T	–	T	0.1	2.1	6.5	26.1
IN. ...	Indianapolis	81	7.1	5.8	3.5	0.5	T	T	–	T	–	0.2	1.9	5.7	24.6
IA.....	Des Moines	69	8.5	7.7	5.9	1.9	T	T	T	–	T	0.3	3.1	7.0	34.5
KS....	Wichita	59	4.0	4.3	2.8	0.2	T	T	T	T	T	–	1.4	3.5	16.2
KY....	Louisville	65	5.2	4.3	3.2	0.1	T	T	T	T	–	0.1	1.0	2.6	16.6
LA....	New Orleans	51	T	0.1	T	T	T	–	–	–	–	–	T	0.1	0.2
ME. ..	Portland	72	19.2	16.3	13.0	3.1	0.2	–	T	–	T	0.3	3.3	15.0	70.5
MD. ..	Baltimore	62	6.0	7.5	3.6	0.1	T	T	T	–	–	T	1.0	3.6	22.0
MA. ..	Boston	75	13.1	11.8	7.8	0.9	–	T	T	T	–	–	1.3	8.4	43.7
MI. ...	Detroit	54	11.4	10.1	6.9	2.0	T	–	–	–	T	0.2	2.5	10.1	43.3
MI. ...	Sault Ste. Marie	65	28.9	18.5	14.3	5.9	0.5	T	T	T	0.1	2.5	15.4	30.7	116.7
MN. ..	Duluth	69	17.4	12.1	13.9	6.8	0.8	T	T	T	0.1	1.7	12.4	16.1	81.5
MN. ..	Minneapolis-St. Paul	70	10.3	8.3	10.5	2.8	0.1	T	T	T	T	0.5	7.4	10.3	50.4
MS. ..	Jackson	38	0.5	0.2	0.2	T	–	–	–	T	–	–	T	0.1	1.0
MO. ..	Kansas City	78	5.4	4.8	3.5	0.8	T	T	T	T	T	0.1	1.3	4.5	20.5
MO. ..	St. Louis	76	5.4	4.5	3.8	0.5	T	T	T	T	–	T	1.4	4.2	19.8
MT. ..	Great Falls	75	9.4	8.8	10.4	8.0	1.9	0.4	T	0.1	1.5	3.5	7.7	8.5	60.3
NE. ..	Omaha	77	7.6	7.0	6.1	1.1	0.1	T	T	T	T	0.3	2.6	6.0	30.8
NV. ..	Reno	63	5.7	5.5	4.1	1.2	0.8	–	–	–	–	0.3	2.5	4.8	25.1
NH. ..	Concord	71	18.4	14.4	11.5	2.8	0.1	T	–	–	T	0.4	3.8	14.2	65.9
NJ....	Atlantic City	63	5.2	6.0	2.6	0.3	T	T	T	–	–	T	0.4	2.9	17.5
NM. ..	Albuquerque	73	2.5	2.1	1.8	0.6	T	T	T	T	T	0.1	1.2	3.0	11.3
NY. ..	Albany	66	16.9	13.8	11.2	2.8	0.1	T	–	T	T	0.3	3.8	14.7	64.0
NY. ..	Buffalo	69	24.5	17.9	12.3	3.2	0.2	T	T	T	T	0.7	10.7	24.1	94.2
NY. ..	New York [1]	144	7.9	8.8	5.1	0.9	T	–	T	–	–	–	0.9	5.7	29.4
NC. ..	Charlotte	73	2.2	1.8	1.2	T	T	T	–	–	–	T	0.1	0.5	5.8
NC. ..	Raleigh	68	2.8	2.6	1.3	T	T	T	T	–	–	–	0.1	0.9	7.7
ND. ..	Bismarck	73	7.8	7.0	8.5	4.0	0.9	T	T	T	T	0.2	1.9	6.8	44.9
OH. ..	Cincinnati	65	7.2	5.8	4.2	0.5	–	T	T	T	–	0.3	2.0	4.1	24.2
OH. ..	Cleveland	71	14.9	13.0	10.8	2.9	0.1	T	T	–	T	0.6	4.8	12.4	59.8
OH. ..	Columbus	65	9.0	6.6	4.6	1.0	T	T	T	–	T	0.1	2.2	5.4	28.9
OK. ..	Oklahoma City	73	3.2	2.6	1.5	T	T	T	T	T	T	0.6	2.1	10.0
OR. ..	Portland	55	3.2	1.1	0.4	T	–	T	–	T	T	–	0.4	1.4	6.5
PA....	Philadelphia	70	6.2	7.6	3.5	0.3	T	T	–	–	–	–	0.7	3.8	22.3
PA....	Pittsburgh	60	12.4	10.3	8.0	1.8	0.1	T	T	T	T	0.4	3.4	8.4	44.6
RI. ...	Providence	59	10.0	9.5	7.1	0.7	0.2	–	–	–	–	0.1	1.3	7.6	36.7
SC. ..	Columbia	64	0.6	0.9	0.2	T	T	–	T	T	–	–	T	0.3	2.0
SD. ..	Sioux Falls	67	7.0	8.0	9.0	3.3	T	T	T	T	T	0.9	5.8	7.6	41.6
TN....	Memphis	55	2.3	1.5	0.9	T	T	T	–	–	–	T	0.1	0.6	5.4
TN....	Nashville	66	3.5	3.0	1.5	–	–	T	–	T	–	–	0.4	1.4	9.9
TX....	Dallas-Fort Worth	54	1.1	1.3	0.2	T	T	–	–	–	–	T	0.1	0.3	3.0
TX....	El Paso	63	1.3	0.8	0.4	0.3	T	T	T	–	T	–	1.0	1.7	5.5
TX....	Houston	78	0.2	0.2	T	T	T	–	–	–	–	T	–	T	0.4
UT....	Salt Lake City	84	13.1	9.9	8.9	4.9	0.6	T	T	T	0.1	1.3	7.1	12.2	58.2
VT....	Burlington	69	19.8	17.2	13.7	4.0	0.2	–	T	T	T	0.2	6.5	19.1	80.9
VA....	Norfolk	62	3.1	2.9	1.0	–	T	T	–	T	–	–	–	1.3	8.3
VA....	Richmond	73	5.0	3.8	2.5	0.1	T	–	T	–	–	T	0.4	2.2	14.0
WA. ..	Seattle-Tacoma	56	5.0	1.6	1.3	0.1	T	–	–	–	T	–	1.1	2.4	11.4
WA. ..	Spokane	65	15.1	7.3	4.1	0.8	0.1	T	–	–	T	0.4	6.5	14.7	49.0
WV. ..	Charleston	58	10.8	8.7	5.1	0.9	–	T	T	–	T	0.4	2.4	5.5	33.9
WI. ...	Milwaukee	72	13.9	10.1	8.4	2.0	0.1	T	T	T	T	0.2	3.0	10.9	48.7
WY. ..	Cheyenne	77	6.0	6.7	11.8	9.4	3.5	0.2	T	T	1.1	4.2	7.2	6.9	56.9
PR. ..	San Juan	57	–	–	–	–	–	–	–	–	T	–	–	–	T

– Represents zero. [1] City office data.

Source: U.S. National Oceanic and Atmospheric Administration, *Comparative Climatic Data*, 2012. See also <http://www.ncdc.noaa.gov/statistical-weather-and-climate-information>.

Table 424. Cloudiness, Average Wind Speed, Heating and Cooling Degree Days, and Average Relative Humidity—Selected Cities

[Airport data, except as noted. For period of record through 2012, except Heating and Cooling Degree Days, these are for the 1981-2010 period. M=morning. A=afternoon]

State	Station	Cloudiness-average percentage of days [1] Length of record (yrs.)	An-nual	Average wind speed (miles per hour, m.p.h.) Length of record (yrs.)	An-nual	Jan.	July	Heating degree days	Cooling degree days	Average relative humidity (percent) Length of record (yrs.)	Annual M	Annual A	Jan. M	Jan. A	July M	July A
AL.....	Mobile	47	72.1	64	8.7	10.0	6.9	1,655	2,536	50	81	68	89	69	86	67
AK.....	Juneau	47	87.9	67	8.1	7.9	7.5	8,351	—	46	79	75	79	68	81	71
AZ.....	Phoenix	57	42.3	67	6.2	5.3	7.1	935	4,607	52	62	31	42	20	48	22
AR....	Little Rock	35	67.5	70	7.7	8.4	6.7	3,052	2,206	48	78	67	84	64	81	65
CA....	Los Angeles	60	59.8	64	7.5	6.7	7.9	1,419	551	53	70	60	85	68	79	66
CA....	Sacramento	49	48.5	62	7.7	6.7	8.9	2,619	1,178	26	90	69	77	29	83	46
CA....	San Diego	55	60.0	72	7.0	6.0	7.5	1,225	720	52	71	57	82	67	77	63
CA....	San Francisco	68	56.2	85	10.6	7.2	13.6	2,653	164	53	86	68	86	60	84	63
CO....	Denver	61	68.5	56	8.7	8.7	8.3	6,058	769	44	62	50	66	34	66	41
CT.....	Hartford	41	77.5	58	8.4	8.9	7.3	5,839	805	53	72	56	77	51	76	52
DE....	Wilmington	47	73.4	64	9.0	9.8	7.8	4,819	1,145	65	75	59	78	54	78	55
DC....	Washington	48	73.8	64	9.4	10.0	8.3	4,031	1,549	52	70	55	75	52	74	53
FL.....	Jacksonville	47	74.2	63	7.8	8.1	7.0	1,349	2,665	76	87	56	88	58	88	56
FL.....	Miami	46	79.7	63	9.2	9.4	7.9	128	4,575	48	83	58	81	63	82	61
GA....	Atlanta	61	69.9	74	9.1	10.4	7.7	2,768	1,883	52	78	58	86	58	81	55
HI.....	Honolulu	47	75.3	63	11.2	9.4	13.1	—	4,628	43	79	61	66	51	71	56
ID.....	Boise	56	67.1	73	8.7	7.9	8.4	5,514	942	73	80	70	53	20	68	43
IL.....	Chicago	37	77.0	54	10.3	11.6	8.4	6,340	843	54	77	71	80	63	79	66
IL.....	Peoria	52	73.9	69	9.7	10.7	7.8	5,831	1,039	53	79	72	85	67	82	68
IN.....	Indianapolis	64	76.0	64	9.6	10.9	7.5	5,348	1,058	53	81	70	85	58	83	61
IA.....	Des Moines	46	71.3	63	10.7	11.4	8.9	6,622	777	51	76	71	81	65	79	66
KS.....	Wichita	39	64.9	59	12.2	11.9	11.2	4,626	1,580	59	78	67	77	57	79	62
KY.....	Louisville	47	74.6	65	8.3	9.5	6.8	4,268	1,444	52	77	64	83	56	80	58
LA.....	New Orleans	47	72.3	64	8.2	9.3	6.1	1,280	3,005	64	83	70	89	71	86	68
ME....	Portland	54	72.3	72	8.7	9.0	7.6	7,107	359	72	75	60	79	59	78	59
MD....	Baltimore	45	71.2	62	8.6	9.1	7.5	4,764	1,164	59	72	56	78	52	77	53
MA....	Boston	60	73.2	55	12.3	13.6	11.0	5,681	747	48	68	57	72	56	72	58
MI.....	Detroit	37	79.5	54	10.1	11.6	8.5	6,168	823	54	80	69	80	53	81	59
MI.....	Sault Ste. Marie	54	81.9	71	9.1	9.4	7.8	8,663	196	71	80	73	87	61	84	66
MN....	Duluth	47	79.0	63	11.0	11.5	9.4	9,444	204	51	77	73	84	66	80	69
MN....	Minneapolis- St. Paul	57	74.0	74	10.5	10.5	9.4	7,580	753	53	75	70	78	62	77	65
MS....	Jackson	30	69.6	49	6.8	8.0	5.2	2,218	2,336	49	84	70	91	69	88	67
MO....	Kansas City	23	67.1	40	10.6	11.0	9.1	4,686	1,671	40	76	69	82	68	79	68
MO....	St. Louis	47	72.4	63	9.6	10.6	8.0	4,535	1,646	52	78	69	81	63	80	65
MT....	Great Falls	57	78.4	71	12.5	14.7	10.0	7,726	298	51	66	60	67	30	68	46
NE....	Omaha	49	69.6	76	10.5	10.9	8.8	6,167	1,113	48	78	70	83	67	80	67
NV....	Reno	53	56.7	70	6.6	5.6	7.2	4,924	839	49	78	50	56	17	67	31
NH....	Concord	54	75.3	70	6.7	7.2	5.7	7,235	452	47	76	58	82	51	80	53
NJ.....	Atlantic City	37	74.2	54	9.7	10.6	8.3	4,905	1,055	48	77	57	81	56	80	56
NM....	Albuquerque	56	54.2	73	8.9	8.0	8.9	4,179	1,322	52	66	38	58	27	58	29
NY....	Albany	57	81.1	74	8.9	9.8	7.5	6,680	598	47	77	63	79	55	79	57
NY....	Buffalo	52	85.2	73	11.8	13.8	10.2	6,617	544	52	79	72	77	55	79	62
NY....	New York [2]	42	70.8	74	9.1	10.3	7.5	4,750	1,105	78	67	58	74	55	72	56
NC....	Charlotte	49	70.2	63	7.4	7.8	6.6	3,388	1,518	52	77	54	84	55	81	53
NC....	Raleigh	47	69.7	63	7.5	8.1	6.7	3,247	1,730	48	78	53	86	56	83	53
ND....	Bismarck	56	74.5	73	10.2	10.0	9.2	8,558	520	53	76	72	82	58	80	65
OH....	Cincinnati	44	77.8	65	9.0	10.4	7.2	4,958	1,067	50	80	68	84	57	82	59
OH....	Cleveland	54	81.9	71	10.5	12.2	8.6	5,762	817	52	78	70	80	56	79	62
OH....	Columbus	46	80.3	63	8.3	9.8	6.5	5,250	1,035	53	77	67	82	55	80	58
OK....	Oklahoma City	44	61.9	64	12.2	12.5	10.8	3,365	2,099	47	75	64	77	59	78	63
OR....	Portland	47	81.3	64	7.9	9.8	7.6	4,278	424	72	85	75	81	44	85	59
PA.....	Philadelphia	55	74.5	72	9.5	10.3	8.2	4,613	1,301	53	72	58	77	52	75	54
PA.....	Pittsburgh	43	83.8	60	8.9	10.3	7.3	5,710	736	52	77	65	82	53	79	57
RI.....	Providence	42	73.2	59	10.3	10.8	9.4	5,618	744	49	71	56	75	55	75	55
SC....	Columbia	48	68.5	64	6.8	7.2	6.3	2,552	2,170	46	81	52	86	52	85	50
SD....	Sioux Falls	50	71.2	64	11.0	10.9	9.8	7,706	690	49	78	72	82	64	81	68
TN.....	Memphis	43	67.7	64	8.8	10.0	7.5	2,964	2,258	73	76	65	82	62	79	62
TN.....	Nashville	54	72.0	71	7.9	9.0	6.5	3,688	1,646	47	77	68	85	66	81	65
TX....	Dallas-Fort Worth	42	63.0	59	10.7	11.0	9.7	2,284	2,756	49	76	65	75	57	78	63
TX....	El Paso	53	47.1	70	8.8	8.3	8.3	2,474	2,331	52	63	33	60	29	55	27
TX....	Houston	26	75.3	43	7.6	8.1	6.6	1,291	2,940	43	83	71	90	69	88	70
UT....	Salt Lake City	69	65.8	83	8.8	7.5	9.5	5,607	1,160	52	79	70	50	21	67	44
VT....	Burlington	52	84.1	69	8.9	9.6	8.0	7,434	491	47	73	64	77	53	77	58
VA....	Norfolk	47	71.0	64	10.4	11.3	8.9	3,377	1,629	64	74	58	80	58	78	57
VA....	Richmond	50	72.7	64	7.7	8.1	6.9	3,773	1,549	78	79	56	83	55	82	53
WA....	Seattle-Tacoma	51	84.2	64	8.8	9.5	8.1	4,697	189	53	82	75	81	49	84	62
WA....	Spokane	48	76.4	65	8.9	8.7	8.6	6,593	450	53	86	79	64	26	78	52
WV.....	Charleston	47	82.2	65	5.8	6.9	4.8	4,478	1,097	65	78	62	89	59	83	56
WI.....	Milwaukee	55	75.3	72	11.5	12.6	9.7	6,894	641	52	75	70	80	66	79	68
WY....	Cheyenne	60	71.0	55	12.8	15.0	10.4	7,111	348	53	57	50	68	37	65	45
PR....	San Juan	40	80.0	57	8.3	8.3	9.6	—	5,855	57	81	65	78	67	79	66

— Represents zero. [1] Percent of days that are either partly cloudy or cloudy. [2] Airport data for sunshine.

Source: U.S. National Oceanic and Atmospheric Administration, *Comparative Climatic Data*, 2012. See also <http://www.ncdc.noaa.gov/statistical-weather-and-climate-information>.

Table 425. Drought Conditions—Area and Population Impacted by Level of Drought: 2014

[In percent. For continental United States. Data shown for the last week of each month, as of Tuesday. Drought classifications are measured in four intensity levels—D0: Abnormally dry, D1: Moderate drought, D2: Severe drought, D3: Extreme drought, and D4: Exceptional drought. Data are categorical statistics showing percent of the area or population that is in a certain drought category. See source for details, <http://droughtmonitor.unl.edu/AboutUSDM.aspx>. The U.S. Drought Monitor is jointly produced by the National Drought Mitigation Center at the University of Nebraska-Lincoln, the United States Department of Agriculture, and the National Oceanic and Atmospheric Administration]

Week	Area (Percent of continental U.S. square miles)						Population (Percent of continental U.S. population)					
	None	D0	D1	D2	D3	D4	None	D0	D1	D2	D3	D4
1/28/2014....	43.75	19.76	15.73	13.53	6.40	0.83	55.73	18.10	10.92	6.13	8.44	0.68
2/25/2014....	45.89	18.03	14.54	13.89	5.89	1.76	60.97	12.90	10.07	4.79	8.24	3.03
3/25/2014....	48.02	13.71	15.18	13.39	7.61	2.09	63.21	10.61	8.52	6.10	8.70	2.86
4/29/2014....	51.18	10.39	11.67	13.99	8.89	3.88	66.81	7.44	6.34	6.02	9.64	3.76
5/27/2014....	52.12	9.95	10.20	14.08	10.30	3.35	65.22	9.19	5.21	7.27	9.45	3.65
6/24/2014....	54.67	10.30	10.21	13.59	8.32	2.91	67.17	8.75	4.58	6.51	9.03	3.95
7/29/2014....	52.50	13.45	11.29	12.17	6.69	3.90	64.87	11.91	4.66	5.25	4.24	9.08
8/26/2014....	52.24	13.90	12.31	11.47	6.28	3.80	65.33	10.51	5.67	5.71	3.72	9.07
9/30/2014....	52.22	17.21	11.90	9.25	5.56	3.85	54.34	20.64	7.91	3.80	3.64	9.67
10/28/2014...	56.52	13.87	11.59	8.85	5.18	3.99	57.93	18.84	6.19	3.67	3.64	9.73
11/25/2014...	52.73	18.37	12.10	8.09	5.04	3.68	58.67	19.15	6.10	2.91	3.54	9.63
12/30/2014...	53.20	18.12	11.75	7.96	6.42	2.54	68.16	10.11	5.57	2.97	6.51	6.68

Source: National Drought Mitigation Center, "United States Drought Monitor," <http://droughtmonitor.unl.edu/>, accessed August 2015.

Table 426. Top 20 Significant Flood Event Losses Covered by the National Flood Insurance Program, as of Jan. 31, 2015

[In nominal dollars. Covers period beginning in 1978. A significant event is one with 1,500 or more paid losses, or occasionally one added for other reasons]

Event	Date	Number of paid losses	Amount paid ($)	Average paid loss ($)
Hurricane Katrina.............................	Aug. 2005	167,940	16,311,365,675	97,126
Superstorm Sandy...........................	Oct. 2012	128,830	7,870,157,475	61,089
Hurricane Ike..................................	Sept. 2008	46,555	2,682,521,464	57,620
Hurricane Ivan................................	Sept. 2004	28,282	1,610,532,116	56,945
Hurricane Irene...............................	Aug. 2011	44,207	1,334,948,939	30,198
Tropical Storm Allison........................	June 2001	30,781	1,106,468,668	35,946
Louisiana Flood...............................	May 1995	31,343	585,071,593	18,667
Tropical Storm Isaac.........................	Aug. 2012	11,985	546,761,557	45,620
Hurricane Isabel..............................	Sept. 2003	19,919	498,077,271	25,005
Hurricane Rita.................................	Sept. 2005	9,527	474,492,274	49,805
Hurricane Floyd...............................	Sept. 1999	20,439	462,341,822	22,621
Tropical Storm Lee...........................	Sept. 2011	9,853	457,791,321	46,462
Hurricane Opal................................	Oct. 1995	10,343	405,527,543	39,208
Hurricane Hugo...............................	Sept. 1989	12,840	376,433,739	29,317
Hurricane Wilma..............................	Oct. 2005	9,616	365,464,551	38,006
Nor'Easter.....................................	Dec. 1992	25,142	346,150,356	13,768
Midwest Flood.................................	June 1993	10,472	272,819,515	26,052
Torrential Rain – TN...........................	Apr. 2010	4,110	228,977,068	55,712
PA, NJ, NY Floods............................	June 2006	6,425	228,965,547	35,637
Nor'Easter.....................................	Apr. 2007	8,639	225,903,733	26,149

Source: U.S. Department of Homeland Security, Federal Emergency Management Agency, National Flood Insurance Program Statistics, "Significant Flood Events [since 1978], as of January 31, 2015," <http://www.fema.gov/significant-flood-events>, accessed March 2015.

Table 427. Threatened and Endangered Wildlife and Plant Species: 2015

[As of July 2015. Endangered species: one in danger of becoming extinct throughout all or a significant part of its natural range. Threatened species: one likely to become endangered in the foreseeable future]

Item	Mammals	Birds	Reptiles	Amphibians	Fishes	Snails	Clams	Crustaceans	Insects	Arachnids	Plants
Total listings...............	376	331	126	44	185	47	90	25	76	12	886
Endangered species, total.........................	329	293	83	28	112	35	77	22	65	12	726
United States...............	74	79	14	20	93	34	75	22	61	12	725
Foreign......................	255	214	69	8	19	1	2	–	4	–	1
Threatened species, total.........................	47	38	43	16	73	12	13	3	11	–	160
United States...............	27	21	23	15	70	12	13	3	11	–	158
Foreign......................	20	17	20	1	3	–	–	–	–	–	2

– Represents zero.

Source: U.S. Fish and Wildlife Service, Environmental Conservation Online System, "Summary of Listed Species, Listed Populations, and Recovery Plans," <http://ecos.fws.gov/tess_public/pub/boxScore.jsp>, accessed July 2015.

Section 7
Elections

This section relates primarily to presidential, congressional, and gubernatorial elections. Also presented are summary tables on congressional legislation; state legislatures; minority and female officeholders; population of voting age; voter participation; and campaign finances.

Official statistics on federal elections, collected by the Clerk of the House, are published biennially in *Statistics of the Presidential and Congressional Election* and *Statistics of the Congressional Election*. Federal elections data also appear in the *Congressional Directory* and in official state documents. Data on reported registration and voting for social and economic groups are obtained by the U.S. Census Bureau as part of the Current Population Survey (CPS) and are published in Current Population Reports, Series P20 (see text, Section 1).

Almost all federal, state, and local governmental units in the United States conduct elections for political offices and other purposes. The conduct of elections is regulated by state laws or, in some cities and counties, by local charter. An exception is that the U.S. Constitution prescribes the basis of representation in Congress and the manner of electing the president and grants to Congress the right to regulate the times, places, and manner of electing federal officers. Amendments to the Constitution have prescribed national criteria for voting eligibility. The 15th Amendment, adopted in 1870, gave all citizens the right to vote regardless of race, color, or previous condition of servitude. The 19th Amendment, adopted in 1920, further extended the right to vote to all citizens regardless of sex. The payment of poll taxes as a prerequisite to voting in federal elections was banned by the 24th Amendment in 1964. In 1971, as a result of the 26th Amendment, eligibility to vote in national elections was extended to all citizens, 18 years old and over.

Presidential election—The Constitution specifies how the president and vice president are selected. Each state elects, by popular vote, a group of electors equal in number to its total of members of Congress. The 23rd Amendment, adopted in 1961, grants to the District of Columbia three presidential electors, a number equal to that of the least populous state. Subsequent to the election, the electors meet in their respective states to vote for president and vice president. Usually, each elector votes for the candidate receiving the most popular votes in his or her state. A majority vote of all electors is necessary to elect the president and vice president. If no candidate receives a majority,

the House of Representatives, with each state having one vote, is empowered to elect the president and vice president, again, with a majority of votes required.

The 22nd Amendment to the Constitution, adopted in 1951, limits presidential tenure to two elective terms of 4 years each or to one elective term for any person who, upon succession to the presidency, has held the office or acted as President for more than 2 years.

Congressional election—The Constitution provides that representatives be apportioned among the states according to their population, that a census of population be taken every 10 years as a basis for apportionment, and that each state have at least one representative. At the time of each apportionment, Congress decides what the total number of representatives will be. Since 1912, the total has been 435, except during 1960 to 1962 when it increased to 437, adding one representative each for Alaska and Hawaii. The total reverted to 435 after reapportionment following the 1960 census. Members are elected for 2-year terms, all terms covering the same period. The District of Columbia, American Samoa, Guam, and the Virgin Islands each elect one nonvoting delegate, and Puerto Rico elects a nonvoting resident commissioner.

The Senate is composed of 100 members, two from each state, who are elected to serve for a term of 6 years. One-third of the Senate is elected every 2 years. Senators were originally chosen by the state legislatures. The 17th Amendment to the Constitution, adopted in 1913, prescribed that senators be elected by popular vote.

Voter eligibility and participation—The Census Bureau publishes estimates of the population of voting age and the percent casting votes in each state for presidential and congressional election years. These voting-age estimates include a number of persons who meet the age requirement but are not eligible to vote, (e.g. aliens and some institutionalized persons). In addition, since 1964, voter participation and voter characteristics data have been collected during November of election years as part of the CPS. These survey data include non-citizens in the voting-age population estimates, but exclude members of the Armed Forces and the institutional population.

Statistical reliability—For a discussion of statistical collection and estimation, sampling procedures, and measures of statistical reliability applicable to Census Bureau data, see Appendix III.

Table 428. Participation in Elections for President and U.S. Representatives: 1934 to 2014

[77,997 represents 77,997,000. As of November, except as noted. Estimated resident population 21 years old and over, 1934-70, except as noted, and 18 years old and over thereafter; includes Armed Forces stationed in the U.S. Prior to 1958, excludes Alaska and prior to 1960, excludes Hawaii. District of Columbia is included in votes cast for President beginning 1964]

Year	Resident population (includes aliens) of voting age [1] (1,000)	Votes cast			
		For President (1,000)	Percent of voting-age population	For U.S. Representatives (1,000)	Percent of voting-age population
1934	77,997	(X)	(X)	32,804	42.1
1936	80,174	45,647	56.9	(NA)	(NA)
1938	82,354	(X)	(X)	(NA)	(NA)
1940	84,728	49,815	58.8	(NA)	(NA)
1942	86,465	(X)	(X)	28,074	32.5
1944	85,654	48,026	56.1	45,110	52.7
1946	92,659	(X)	(X)	34,410	37.1
1948	95,573	48,834	51.1	46,220	48.4
1950	98,134	(X)	(X)	40,430	41.2
1952	99,929	61,552	61.6	57,571	57.6
1954	102,075	(X)	(X)	42,583	41.7
1956	104,515	62,027	59.3	58,886	56.3
1958	106,447	(X)	(X)	45,719	43.0
1960	109,672	68,836	62.8	64,124	58.5
1962	112,952	(X)	(X)	51,242	45.4
1964	114,090	70,098	61.4	65,879	57.7
1966	116,638	(X)	(X)	52,902	45.4
1968	120,285	73,027	60.7	66,109	55.0
1970	124,498	(X)	(X)	54,259	43.6
1972	140,777	77,625	55.1	71,188	50.6
1974	146,338	(X)	(X)	52,313	35.7
1976	152,308	81,603	53.6	74,259	48.8
1978	158,369	(X)	(X)	54,584	34.5
1980	163,945	86,497	52.8	77,874	47.5
1982	169,643	(X)	(X)	63,881	37.7
1984	173,995	92,655	53.3	82,422	47.4
1986	177,922	(X)	(X)	59,758	33.6
1988	181,956	91,587	50.3	81,682	44.9
1990	185,812	(X)	(X)	62,355	33.6
1992	189,493	104,600	55.2	97,198	51.3
1994	193,010	(X)	(X)	70,494	36.5
1996	196,789	96,390	49.0	90,233	45.9
1998	201,270	(X)	(X)	66,605	33.1
2000	[2] 209,786	105,594	61.6	98,800	47.1
2002	[2] 214,689	(X)	(X)	74,707	34.8
2004	[2] 219,508	122,349	55.7	113,192	51.6
2006	[2] 224,622	(X)	(X)	80,976	36.0
2008	[2] 229,989	131,407	57.1	122,586	53.3
2010	[2] 235,224	(X)	(X)	86,785	36.9
2012	[2] 240,400	129,140	53.7	122,346	50.9
2014	[2] 245,273	(X)	(X)	78,813	32.1

X Not applicable. NA Not available. [1] Population 18 and over in Georgia, 1944-70, and in Kentucky, 1956–70; and 20 and over in Alaska and Hawaii, 1960–70. Source: Through 1990, U.S. Census Bureau, "Table 4. Participation in Elections for President and U.S. Representatives: 1930 to 1992," May 1994, <http://www.census.gov/population/socdemo/voting/p25-1117/tab03-04.pdf>. For 1992–1998, "Estimates and Projections of the Voting-Age Population, 1992 to 2000, and Percent Casting Votes for President, by State: November 1992 and 1996," July 2000, <http://www.census.gov/population/socdemo/voting/proj00/tab03.txt>. For 2000-2009, "Annual Estimates of the Resident Population for Selected Age Groups by Sex for the United States, States, Counties, and Puerto Rico Commonwealth and Municipios: April 1, 2000 to July 1, 2009," <http://www.census.gov/popest/data/index.html>, accessed June 2015. Starting 2010, "Annual Estimates of the Resident Population for Selected Age Groups by Sex for the United States, States, Counties, and Puerto Rico Commonwealth and Municipios: April 1, 2010 to July 1, 2014," <http://factfinder2.census.gov>, accessed June 2015. [2] As of July 1.

Source: Except as noted, U.S. House of Representatives, Office of the Clerk, *Statistics of the Congressional Election*, March 2015, and earlier reports. See also <http://clerk.house.gov/member_info/election.aspx>.

Table 429. Resident Population of Voting-Age, Total Votes Cast, and Percent Casting Votes—States: 2012 to 2014

[240,186 represents 240,186,000. As of November. Estimated population, 18 years old and over. Includes Armed Forces stationed in each state, aliens, and institutional population]

State	Voting-age population (1,000) [1]		Total votes cast (1,000)			Percent casting votes for–		
			Presidential Electors	U.S. Representative		Presidential Electors	U.S. Representatives	
	2012	2014	2012	2012	2014	2012	2012	2014
U.S.............	240,186	245,273	129,140	122,346	78,813	53.8	50.9	32.1
AL................	3,698	3,742	2,074	1,934	1,081	56.1	52.3	28.9
AK................	544	550	300	290	280	55.2	53.2	50.8
AZ................	4,932	5,110	2,299	2,173	1,468	46.6	44.1	28.7
AR................	2,238	2,259	1,069	1,038	831	47.8	46.4	36.8
CA................	28,801	29,649	13,039	12,204	7,132	45.3	42.4	24.1
CO................	3,956	4,109	2,570	2,450	2,001	64.9	61.9	48.7
CT................	2,797	2,821	1,558	1,467	1,068	55.7	52.4	37.9
DE................	712	731	414	388	232	58.1	54.5	31.7
DC................	523	544	294	(X)	(X)	56.2	(X)	(X)
FL................	15,315	15,840	8,474	7,514	4,999	55.3	49.1	31.6
GA................	7,430	7,604	3,898	3,553	2,306	52.5	47.8	30.3
HI................	1,089	1,111	437	437	370	40.1	40.1	33.3
ID................	1,169	1,203	652	635	435	55.8	54.3	36.2
IL................	9,811	9,892	5,242	5,058	3,568	53.4	51.6	36.1
IN................	4,946	5,015	2,625	2,554	1,342	53.1	51.6	26.8
IA................	2,351	2,381	1,582	1,537	1,120	67.3	65.4	47.0
KS................	2,162	2,181	1,160	1,058	862	53.7	48.9	39.5
KY................	3,362	3,401	1,797	1,745	1,398	53.5	51.9	41.1
LA................	3,484	3,536	1,994	1,706	1,569	57.2	49.0	44.4
ME................	1,063	1,071	725	725	617	68.2	68.2	57.6
MD................	4,541	4,626	2,707	2,586	1,703	59.6	56.9	36.8
MA................	5,245	5,355	3,184	3,184	2,187	60.7	60.7	40.8
MI................	7,616	7,686	4,731	4,575	3,089	62.1	60.1	40.2
MN................	4,103	4,175	2,937	2,813	1,964	71.6	68.6	47.0
MS................	2,240	2,263	1,286	1,208	626	57.4	53.9	27.7
MO................	4,619	4,671	2,757	2,676	1,426	59.7	57.9	30.5
MT................	783	799	484	480	368	61.8	61.3	46.1
NE................	1,392	1,415	794	773	536	57.1	55.5	37.8
NV................	2,095	2,176	1,015	974	543	48.4	46.5	25.0
NH................	1,046	1,060	711	682	481	68.0	65.2	45.4
NJ................	6,838	6,926	3,638	3,282	1,821	53.2	48.0	26.3
NM................	1,571	1,584	784	766	512	49.9	48.8	32.3
NY................	15,307	15,517	7,117	7,116	3,935	46.5	46.5	25.4
NC................	7,466	7,656	4,505	4,384	2,808	60.3	58.7	36.7
ND................	545	571	323	316	249	59.3	58.0	43.6
OH................	8,881	8,956	5,581	5,142	3,000	62.8	57.9	33.5
OK................	2,877	2,925	1,335	1,326	653	46.4	46.1	22.3
OR................	3,039	3,112	1,789	1,708	1,451	58.9	56.2	46.6
PA................	10,024	10,086	5,742	5,556	3,324	57.3	55.4	33.0
RI................	834	842	446	428	316	53.5	51.3	37.5
SC................	3,644	3,748	1,964	1,803	1,156	53.9	49.5	30.8
SD................	629	643	364	361	276	57.8	57.4	43.0
TN................	4,962	5,055	2,459	2,284	1,371	49.5	46.0	27.1
TX................	19,074	19,841	7,994	7,664	4,453	41.9	40.2	22.4
UT................	1,967	2,039	1,017	999	566	51.7	50.8	27.8
VT................	502	505	299	290	192	59.6	57.7	37.9
VA................	6,329	6,457	3,854	3,740	2,135	60.9	59.1	33.1
WA................	5,312	5,459	3,126	3,006	2,030	58.8	56.6	37.2
WV................	1,471	1,470	670	641	439	45.6	43.6	29.9
WI................	4,409	4,457	3,071	2,866	2,356	69.7	65.0	52.8
WY................	441	446	251	251	171	56.9	56.9	38.4

X Not applicable. [1] As of July 1. Source: U.S. Census Bureau, "Annual Estimates of the Resident Population for Selected Age Groups by Sex for the United States, States, Counties, and Puerto Rico Commonwealth and Municipios: April 1, 2010 to July 1, 2014," <http://factfinder2.census.gov>, accessed July 2015.

Source: Except as noted, U.S. House of Representatives, Office of the Clerk, *Statistics of the Congressional Election*, March 2015, and earlier reports. See also <http://history.house.gov/Institution/Election-Statistics/Election-Statistics/>.

Table 430. Voting-Age Population—Reported Registration and Voting by Selected Characteristics: 2000 to 2014

[202.6 represents 202,600,000. As of November. Covers civilian noninstitutional population 18 years old and over. Includes aliens. Figures are based on Current Population Survey (see text, Section 1 and Appendix III) and differ from those in Table 428 based on population estimates and official vote counts]

| Characteristic | Voting-age population (mil.) | | | | | | | Percent reporting they registered | | | | | | | Percent reporting they voted | | | | | | |
| | | | | | | | | Presidential election years | | | | Congressional election years | | | Presidential election years | | | | Congressional election years | | |
	2000	2004	2006	2008	2010	2012	2014	2000	2004	2008	2012	2006	2010	2014	2000	2004	2008	2012	2006	2010	2014
Total [1]	**202.6**	**215.7**	**220.6**	**225.5**	**229.7**	**235.2**	**239.9**	**63.9**	**65.9**	**64.9**	**65.1**	**61.6**	**59.8**	**59.3**	**54.7**	**58.3**	**58.2**	**56.5**	**43.6**	**41.8**	**38.5**
AGE																					
18 to 20 years old	11.9	11.5	11.6	11.7	12.2	12.3	11.9	40.5	50.7	49.3	44.2	37.0	34.4	32.6	28.4	41.0	41.0	35.1	17.1	16.4	14.1
21 to 24 years old	14.9	16.4	16.2	16.6	16.7	17.6	17.8	49.3	52.1	56.2	53.1	44.9	47.2	43.6	35.4	42.5	46.6	40.0	21.9	22.0	17.1
25 to 34 years old	37.3	39.0	39.4	40.2	41.2	41.1	42.3	54.7	55.6	56.5	57.0	50.3	49.8	49.4	43.7	46.9	48.5	46.1	28.3	26.9	24.2
35 to 44 years old	44.5	43.1	42.6	41.5	39.9	39.6	39.6	63.8	64.2	61.4	61.7	59.3	57.3	56.3	55.0	56.9	55.2	52.9	40.1	37.7	32.8
45 to 64 years old	61.4	71.0	75.0	78.1	80.7	82.1	82.8	71.2	72.7	70.4	70.4	69.6	66.3	65.4	64.1	66.6	65.0	63.4	54.3	51.1	46.0
65 years old and over	32.8	34.7	35.8	37.5	39.0	42.5	45.6	76.1	76.9	75.0	76.9	75.4	72.5	73.0	67.6	68.9	68.1	69.7	60.5	58.9	57.5
SEX																					
Male	97.1	103.8	106.5	109.0	111.1	113.2	115.6	62.2	64.0	62.6	63.1	59.5	57.9	57.2	53.1	56.3	55.7	54.4	42.4	40.9	37.2
Female	105.5	111.9	114.1	116.5	118.6	122.0	124.2	65.6	67.6	67.0	67.0	63.5	61.5	61.2	56.2	60.1	60.4	58.5	44.7	42.7	39.6
RACE/ETHNICITY																					
White [2]	168.7	176.6	179.9	183.2	185.8	187.1	189.3	65.6	67.9	66.6	66.7	64.0	61.6	61.3	56.4	60.3	59.6	57.6	45.8	43.4	40.3
Black [2]	24.1	24.9	25.7	26.5	27.4	28.7	29.7	63.6	64.4	65.5	68.5	57.4	58.8	59.7	53.5	56.3	60.8	62.0	38.6	40.7	37.3
Asian [2, 3]	8.0	9.3	9.9	10.5	12.5	12.5	13.5	30.7	34.9	37.3	37.2	32.9	34.1	34.4	25.4	29.8	32.1	31.3	21.8	21.3	19.1
Hispanic [4]	21.6	27.1	29.0	30.9	32.5	35.2	36.8	34.9	34.3	37.6	38.9	32.1	33.8	34.9	27.5	28.0	31.6	31.8	19.3	20.5	18.4
REGION [5]																					
Northeast	38.9	41.0	41.2	41.5	42.3	42.9	43.5	63.7	65.3	63.7	65.2	60.3	59.7	58.3	55.2	58.6	57.4	56.6	42.8	41.6	36.3
Midwest	46.4	48.4	49.1	49.4	50.1	50.6	51.0	70.2	72.8	70.6	71.4	68.3	65.0	65.0	60.9	65.0	63.4	62.3	50.7	45.1	42.3
South	71.8	77.2	80.0	82.4	84.2	87.1	89.2	64.5	65.5	65.5	65.3	62.0	59.4	60.0	53.5	56.4	57.7	55.7	40.3	39.3	38.4
West	45.5	49.1	50.4	52.2	53.2	54.6	56.1	56.9	60.1	59.4	58.9	55.4	55.5	53.7	49.9	54.4	54.6	52.3	42.4	42.7	36.8
EDUCATIONAL ATTAINMENT																					
School years completed:																					
8 years or less	12.9	12.6	12.1	11.1	11.1	10.5	9.9	36.1	32.5	30.1	28.7	29.5	27.0	24.5	26.8	23.6	23.4	21.6	17.1	15.8	13.2
High school: Less than high school graduate	20.1	20.7	20.2	19.1	18.8	18.7	18.6	45.9	45.8	43.2	42.6	39.6	37.8	37.5	33.6	34.6	33.7	32.2	22.8	20.8	18.2
High school graduate or GED [6]	66.3	68.5	70.0	70.4	71.0	70.6	70.6	60.1	61.5	59.5	59.0	57.5	54.0	53.5	49.4	52.4	50.9	48.7	37.6	35.2	31.5
College: Some college or Associate's degree	55.3	58.9	60.2	63.8	65.3	67.7	68.8	70.0	73.7	72.0	71.2	68.3	65.5	64.0	60.3	66.1	65.0	61.5	47.3	44.4	40.0
Bachelor's or advanced degree	48.0	54.9	58.2	61.1	63.5	67.8	72.0	77.3	78.1	76.8	77.2	73.9	72.5	70.8	72.0	74.2	73.3	71.7	59.5	57.1	52.5
EMPLOYMENT STATUS																					
Employed	133.4	138.8	143.8	143.2	138.3	142.6	146.2	64.7	67.1	66.4	67.1	62.7	61.5	60.4	55.5	60.0	60.1	58.6	43.9	42.5	38.2
Unemployed	4.9	7.3	6.2	9.5	13.9	11.1	8.4	46.1	56.3	57.2	56.9	48.5	52.3	50.7	35.1	46.4	48.8	46.1	28.0	31.6	26.9
Not in labor force	64.2	69.6	70.5	72.8	77.5	81.6	85.2	63.8	64.4	62.9	62.8	60.7	58.0	58.2	54.5	56.2	55.5	54.3	44.3	42.3	40.1

[1] Includes other races, not shown separately. [2] Beginning with the 2003 Current Population Survey (CPS), respondents could choose more than one race. As of 2004, data represent persons who selected this race group only and exclude persons reporting more than one race. The CPS in prior years only allowed respondents to report one race group. See also comment on race in the text for Section 1. [3] Prior to 2004, this category was "Asian and Pacific Islanders," therefore rates are not comparable with prior years. [4] Persons of Hispanic origin may be of any race. [5] For composition of regions, see map, inside cover. [6] The General Educational Development (GED) Test measures how well a non-high school graduate has mastered the skills and general knowledge that are acquired in a 4-year high school education. Successfully passing the exam is a credential generally considered to be equivalent to a high school diploma.

Source: U.S. Census Bureau, "Voting and Registration in the Election of November 2014 - Detailed Tables," <http://www.census.gov/hhes/www/socdemo/voting/index.html>, accessed August 2015, and earlier releases.

Table 431. Persons Reporting Voter Registration and Whether Voted by State: 2014

[239,874 represents 239,874,000. As of November. See headnote, Table 430]

State	Voting-age population (1,000)	Percent of voting-age population Registered	Percent of voting-age population Voted	State	Voting-age population (1,000)	Percent of voting-age population Registered	Percent of voting-age population Voted
U.S.	**239,874**	**59.3**	**38.5**	Missouri	4,505	70.9	38.0
Alabama	3,656	64.7	40.9	Montana	788	64.3	49.7
Alaska	521	64.6	49.0	Nebraska	1,400	62.4	41.4
Arizona	4,994	54.8	35.7	Nevada	2,128	51.1	32.6
Arkansas	2,189	59.0	36.5	New Hampshire	1,047	66.3	48.6
California	29,030	48.6	30.8	New Jersey	6,820	57.5	31.5
Colorado	4,009	66.2	55.2	New Mexico	1,536	59.9	42.1
Connecticut	2,783	59.9	43.0	New York	15,274	52.9	30.6
Delaware	712	62.0	42.0	North Carolina	7,412	64.5	42.8
District of Columbia	538	65.6	45.8	North Dakota	567	64.1	49.2
Florida	15,414	56.4	40.4	Ohio	8,772	64.5	38.5
Georgia	7,306	58.9	40.0	Oklahoma	2,851	57.7	32.3
Hawaii	1,035	47.4	38.6	Oregon	3,078	65.2	51.8
Idaho	1,182	56.8	39.1	Pennsylvania	9,924	61.7	38.3
Illinois	9,757	58.8	38.3	Rhode Island	819	59.4	40.4
Indiana	4,913	62.0	33.5	South Carolina	3,667	67.0	41.3
Iowa	2,336	67.8	51.5	South Dakota	625	64.2	43.7
Kansas	2,125	63.7	45.3	Tennessee	4,975	62.1	35.4
Kentucky	3,323	69.2	45.9	Texas	19,354	51.4	30.2
Louisiana	3,450	69.5	48.6	Utah	2,026	54.3	34.7
Maine	1,061	75.4	60.5	Vermont	493	65.7	41.6
Maryland	4,542	65.9	44.7	Virginia	6,221	63.1	39.4
Massachusetts	5,279	61.6	42.8	Washington	5,333	61.5	44.8
Michigan	7,576	68.1	45.1	West Virginia	1,449	61.8	33.4
Minnesota	4,104	68.8	49.9	Wisconsin	4,356	69.0	53.8
Mississippi	2,182	74.6	41.6	Wyoming	441	54.7	39.1

Source: U.S. Census Bureau, "Voting and Registration in the Election of November 2014 - Detailed Tables," <http://www.census.gov/hhes/www/socdemo/voting/index.html>, accessed August 2015.

Table 432. Reported Voting and Registration Among Native and Naturalized Citizens by Race and Hispanic Origin: 2014

[In thousands, except percent, (219,941 represents 219,941,000). As of November]

Nativity status, race, and Hispanic origin	U.S. Citizen Total citizen population (1,000)	Reported registered Number (1,000)	Reported registered Percent	Not registered Number (1,000)	Not registered Percent	Reported voted Number (1,000)	Reported voted Percent	Did not vote Number (1,000)	Did not vote Percent
Total:									
All races [1]	219,941	142,166	64.6	41,101	18.7	92,251	41.9	93,032	42.3
White alone [2]	175,909	115,998	65.9	32,045	18.2	76,366	43.4	73,192	41.6
White alone, non-Hispanic	153,750	104,664	68.1	25,344	16.5	70,351	45.8	60,869	39.6
Black alone [2]	27,908	17,700	63.4	4,730	16.9	11,078	39.7	11,525	41.3
Asian alone [2]	9,504	4,642	48.8	2,534	26.7	2,575	27.1	4,798	50.5
Hispanic [3]	25,092	12,862	51.3	7,556	30.1	6,775	27.0	14,057	56.0
Native citizen:									
All races [1]	200,605	131,359	65.5	36,079	18.0	85,667	42.7	83,569	41.7
White alone [2]	165,058	109,922	66.6	29,237	17.7	72,580	44.0	68,026	41.2
White alone, non-Hispanic	148,766	101,923	68.5	24,173	16.2	68,608	46.1	58,648	39.4
Black alone [2]	25,744	16,362	63.6	4,307	16.7	10,212	39.7	10,605	41.2
Asian alone [2]	3,613	1,498	41.5	839	23.2	818	22.6	1,614	44.7
Hispanic [3]	18,702	9,212	49.3	5,783	30.9	4,528	24.2	10,848	58.0
White alone or in combination [4]	168,136	111,857	66.5	29,959	17.8	73,655	43.8	69,655	41.4
Black alone or in combination [4]	26,981	17,053	63.2	4,630	17.2	10,583	39.2	11,263	41.7
Asian alone or in combination [4]	4,386	1,988	45.3	1,028	23.5	1,099	25.1	2,005	45.7
Naturalized citizen:									
All races [1]	19,336	10,807	55.9	5,022	26.0	6,584	34.1	9,463	48.9
White alone [2]	10,851	6,076	56.0	2,808	25.9	3,786	34.9	5,166	47.6
White alone, non-Hispanic	4,984	2,742	55.0	1,171	23.5	1,743	35.0	2,221	44.6
Black alone [2]	2,164	1,338	61.8	422	19.5	866	40.0	920	42.5
Asian alone [2]	5,890	3,144	53.4	1,695	28.8	1,758	29.8	3,184	54.1
Hispanic [3]	6,390	3,650	57.1	1,773	27.7	2,248	35.2	3,209	50.2
White alone or in combination [4]	10,967	6,121	55.8	2,859	26.1	3,817	34.8	5,231	47.7
Black alone or in combination [4]	2,240	1,369	61.1	456	20.3	886	39.5	965	43.1
Asian alone or in combination [4]	5,946	3,178	53.5	1,705	28.7	1,785	30.0	3,202	53.9

[1] Includes other races, not shown separately. [2] Beginning with the 2003 Current Population Survey (CPS), respondents could choose more than one race. Data shown represent persons who selected this race group only and exclude persons reporting more than one race. [3] Persons of Hispanic origin may be of any race. [4] In combination with one or more races.

Source: U.S. Census Bureau, "Voting and Registration in the Election of November 2014 - Detailed Tables," <http://www.census.gov/hhes/www/socdemo/voting/index.html>, accessed August 2015.

Table 433. Vote Cast for President by Major Political Party: 1948 to 2012

[In thousands (48,834 represents 48,834,000), except percent and electoral vote. Prior to 1960, excludes Alaska and Hawaii; prior to 1964, excludes DC. Vote cast for major party candidates includes the votes of minor parties cast for those candidates]

Year	Candidates for President Democratic	Candidates for President Republican	Vote cast for President Total popular vote [1] (1,000)	Democratic Popular vote Number (1,000)	Democratic Popular vote Percent	Democratic Electoral vote	Republican Popular vote Number (1,000)	Republican Popular vote Percent	Republican Electoral vote
1948..........	Truman	Dewey	48,834	24,106	49.4	303	21,969	45.0	189
1952..........	Stevenson	Eisenhower	61,552	27,315	44.4	89	33,779	54.9	442
1956..........	Stevenson	Eisenhower	62,027	26,739	43.1	73	35,581	57.4	457
1960..........	Kennedy	Nixon	68,836	34,227	49.7	303	34,108	49.5	219
1964..........	Johnson	Goldwater	70,098	42,825	61.1	486	27,147	38.7	52
1968..........	Humphrey	Nixon	73,027	30,989	42.4	191	31,710	43.4	301
1972..........	McGovern	Nixon	77,625	28,902	37.2	17	46,740	60.2	520
1976..........	Carter	Ford	81,603	40,826	50.0	297	39,148	48.0	240
1980..........	Carter	Reagan	86,497	35,481	41.0	49	43,643	50.5	489
1984..........	Mondale	Reagan	92,655	37,450	40.4	13	54,167	58.5	525
1988..........	Dukakis	Bush	91,587	41,717	45.5	111	48,643	53.1	426
1992..........	Clinton	Bush	104,600	44,858	42.9	370	38,799	37.1	168
1996..........	Clinton	Dole	96,390	47,402	49.2	379	39,198	40.7	159
2000..........	Gore	Bush	105,594	50,996	48.3	266	50,465	47.8	271
2004..........	Kerry	Bush	122,349	58,895	48.1	251	61,873	50.6	286
2008..........	Obama	McCain	131,407	69,498	52.9	365	59,948	45.6	173
2012..........	Obama	Romney	129,140	65,752	50.9	332	60,670	47.0	206

[1] Include votes for minor party candidates, independents, unpledged electors, and scattered write-in votes.

Source: U.S. House of Representatives, Office of the Clerk, *Statistics of the Presidential and Congressional Election*, February 2013, and earlier reports. See also <http://clerk.house.gov/member_info/election.html>.

Table 434. Vote Cast for Leading Minority Party Candidates for President: 1948 to 2012

[In thousands (1,169 represents 1,169,000). See headnote, Table 433. Data do not include write-ins, scatterings, or votes for candidates who ran on party tickets not shown, unless otherwise noted]

Year	Candidate	Party	Popular vote (1,000)	Candidate	Party	Popular vote (1,000)
1948..........	Strom Thurmond	States' Rights	1,169	Henry Wallace	Progressive	1,156
1952..........	Vincent Hallinan	Progressive	135	Stuart Hamblen	Prohibition	73
1956 [1]........	T. Coleman Andrews	States' Rights	91	Eric Hass	Socialist Labor	41
1960..........	Eric Hass	Socialist Labor	46	Rutherford Decker	Prohibition	46
1964..........	Eric Hass	Socialist Labor	43	Clifton DeBerry	Socialist Workers	22
1968..........	George Wallace	American Independent	9,446	Henning Blomen	Socialist Labor	52
1972 [1]........	John Schmitz	American	993	Benjamin Spock	People's	9
1976..........	Eugene McCarthy	Independent	680	Roger McBride	Libertarian	172
1980..........	John Anderson	Independent	5,251	Ed Clark	Libertarian	920
1984..........	David Bergland	Libertarian	227	Lyndon H. LaRouche	Independent	79
1988..........	Ron Paul	Libertarian	410	Lenora B. Fulani	New Alliance	129
1992..........	H. Ross Perot	Independent	19,722	Andre Marrou	Libertarian	281
1996..........	H. Ross Perot	Reform	7,137	Ralph Nader	Green	527
2000..........	Ralph Nader	Green	2,530	Pat Buchanan	Reform	324
2004..........	Ralph Nader	Independent	156	Michael Badnarik	Libertarian	369
2008..........	Ralph Nader	Independent	739	Bob Barr	Libertarian	515
2012..........	Gary Johnson	Libertarian	1,216	Jill Stien	Green	401

[1] Data include write-ins, scatterings, and/or votes for candidates who ran on party tickets not shown.

Source: U.S. House of Representatives, Office of the Clerk, *Statistics of the Presidential and Congressional Election*, February 2013, and earlier reports. See also <http://clerk.house.gov/member_info/election.aspx>.

Table 435. Electoral Vote Cast for President by Major Political Party—States: 1972 to 2012

[D = Democratic, R = Republican. For composition of regions, see map, inside front cover]

State	1972[1]	1976[2]	1980	1984	1988[3]	1992	1996	2000[4]	2004[5]	2008[6]	2012
Democratic	**17**	**297**	**49**	**13**	**111**	**370**	**379**	**266**	**251**	**365**	**332**
Republican	**520**	**240**	**489**	**525**	**426**	**168**	**159**	**271**	**286**	**173**	**206**
Northeast:											
Democratic	14	86	4	–	53	106	106	102	101	101	96
Republican	108	36	118	113	60	–	–	4	–	–	–
Midwest:											
Democratic	–	58	10	10	29	100	100	68	57	97	80
Republican	145	87	135	127	108	29	29	61	66	27	38
South:											
Democratic	3	149	31	3	8	68	80	15	16	71	58
Republican	165	20	138	174	168	116	104	168	173	118	138
West:											
Democratic	–	4	4	–	21	96	93	81	77	96	98
Republican	102	97	98	111	90	23	26	38	47	28	30
AL	R-9	D-9	R-9	R-9	R-9	R-9	R-9	R-9	R-9	R-9	R-9
AK	R-3	R-3	R-3	R-3	R-3	R-3	R-3	R-3	R-3	R-3	R-3
AZ	R-6	R-6	R-6	R-7	R-7	R-8	D-8	R-8	R-10	R-10	R-11
AR	R-6	D-6	R-6	R-6	R-6	D-6	D-6	R-6	R-6	R-6	R-6
CA	R-45	R-45	R-45	R-47	R-47	D-54	D-54	D-54	D-55	D-55	D-55
CO	R-7	R-7	R-7	R-8	R-8	D-8	R-8	R-8	R-9	D-9	D-9
CT	R-8	R-8	R-8	R-8	R-8	D-8	D-8	D-8	D-7	D-7	D-7
DE	R-3	D-3	R-3	R-3	R-3	D-3	D-3	D-3	D-3	D-3	D-3
DC	D-3	D-3	D-3	D-3	D-3	D-3	D-3	[4] D-2	D-3	D-3	D-3
FL	R-17	D-17	R-17	R-21	R-21	R-25	D-25	R-25	R-27	D-27	D-29
GA	R-12	D-12	D-12	R-12	R-12	D-13	R-13	R-13	R-15	R-15	R-16
HI	R-4	D-4	D-4	R-4	D-4	D-4	D-4	D-4	D-4	D-4	D-4
ID	R-4	R-4	R-4	R-4	R-4	R-4	R-4	R-4	R-4	R-4	R-4
IL	R-26	R-26	R-26	R-24	R-24	D-22	D-22	D-22	D-21	D-21	D-20
IN	R-13	R-13	R-13	R-12	R-12	R-12	R-12	R-12	R-11	D-11	R-11
IA	R-8	R-8	R-8	R-8	D-8	D-7	D-7	D-7	R-7	D-7	D-6
KS	R-7	R-7	R-7	R-7	R-7	R-6	R-6	R-6	R-6	R-6	R-6
KY	R-9	D-9	R-9	R-9	R-9	D-8	D-8	R-8	R-8	R-8	R-8
LA	R-10	D-10	R-10	R-10	R-10	D-9	D-9	R-9	R-9	R-9	R-8
ME	R-4	R-4	R-4	R-4	R-4	D-4	D-4	D-4	D-4	D-4	D-4
MD	R-10	D-10	D-10	R-10	R-10	D-10	D-10	D-10	D-10	D-10	D-10
MA	D-14	D-14	R-14	R-13	D-13	D-12	D-12	D-12	D-12	D-12	D-11
MI	R-21	R-21	R-21	R-20	R-20	D-18	D-18	D-18	D-17	D-17	D-16
MN	R-10	D-10	D-10	D-10	D-10	D-10	D-10	D-10	[5] D-9	D-10	D-10
MS	R-7	D-7	R-7	R-7	R-7	R-7	R-7	R-7	R-6	R-6	R-6
MO	R-12	D-12	R-12	R-11	R-11	D-11	D-11	R-11	R-11	R-11	R-10
MT	R-4	R-4	R-4	R-4	R-4	D-3	R-3	R-3	R-3	R-3	R-3
NE	R-5	R-5	R-5	R-5	R-5	R-5	R-5	R-5	R-5	[6] R-4	R-5
NV	R-3	R-3	R-3	R-4	R-4	D-4	D-4	R-4	R-5	D-5	D-6
NH	R-4	R-4	R-4	R-4	R-4	D-4	D-4	R-4	D-4	D-4	D-4
NJ	R-17	R-17	R-17	R-16	R-16	D-15	D-15	D-15	D-15	D-15	D-14
NM	R-4	R-4	R-4	R-5	R-5	D-5	D-5	D-5	R-5	D-5	D-5
NY	R-41	D-41	R-41	R-36	D-36	D-33	D-33	D-33	D-31	D-31	D-29
NC	R-13	D-13	R-13	R-13	R-13	R-14	R-14	R-14	R-15	D-15	R-15
ND	R-3	R-3	R-3	R-3	R-3	R-3	R-3	R-3	R-3	R-3	R-3
OH	R-25	D-25	R-25	R-23	R-23	D-21	D-21	R-21	R-20	D-20	D-18
OK	R-8	R-8	R-8	R-8	R-8	R-8	R-8	R-8	R-7	R-7	R-7
OR	R-6	R-6	R-6	R-7	D-7	D-7	D-7	D-7	D-7	D-7	D-7
PA	R-27	D-27	R-27	R-25	R-25	D-23	D-23	D-23	D-21	D-21	D-20
RI	R-4	D-4	D-4	R-4	D-4	D-4	D-4	D-4	D-4	D-4	D-4
SC	R-8	D-8	R-8	R-8	R-8	R-8	R-8	R-8	R-8	R-8	R-9
SD	R-4	R-4	R-4	R-3	R-3	R-3	R-3	R-3	R-3	R-3	R-3
TN	R-10	D-10	R-10	R-11	R-11	D-11	D-11	R-11	R-11	R-11	R-11
TX	R-26	D-26	R-26	R-29	R-29	R-32	R-32	R-32	R-34	R-34	R-38
UT	R-4	R-4	R-4	R-5	R-5	R-5	R-5	R-5	R-5	R-5	R-6
VT	R-3	R-3	R-3	R-3	R-3	D-3	D-3	D-3	D-3	D-3	D-3
VA	[1] R-11	R-12	R-12	R-12	R-12	R-13	R-13	R-13	R-13	D-13	D-13
WA	R-9	[2] R-8	R-9	R-10	D-10	D-11	D-11	D-11	D-11	D-11	D-12
WV	R-6	D-6	D-6	R-6	[3] D-5	D-5	D-5	R-5	R-5	R-5	R-5
WI	R-11	D-11	R-11	R-11	D-11	D-11	D-11	D-11	D-10	D-10	D-10
WY	R-3	R-3	R-3	R-3	R-3	R-3	R-3	R-3	R-3	R-3	R-3

– Represents zero. [1] Excludes one electoral vote cast for Libertarian John Hospers in Virginia. [2] Excludes one electoral vote cast for Ronald Reagan in Washington. [3] Excludes one electoral vote cast for Lloyd Bentsen for President in West Virginia. [4] Excludes one electoral vote left blank by a Democratic elector in the District of Columbia. [5] Excludes one electoral vote cast for Democratic vice presidential nominee John Edwards in Minnesota. [6] Excludes one electoral vote for Barack Obama in Nebraska.

Source: U.S. House of Representatives, Office of the Clerk, *Statistics of the Presidential and Congressional Election*, February 2013. See also <http://clerk.house.gov/member_info/election.html>.

Table 436. Popular Vote Cast for President by Political Party—States: 2008 and 2012

[In thousands (131,407 represents 131,407,000), except percent]

State	2008					2012				
				Percent of total vote					Percent of total vote	
	Total [1]	Demo-cratic party	Republi-can party	Demo-cratic party	Republi-can party	Total [1]	Demo-cratic party	Republi-can party	Demo-cratic party	Republi-can party
United States.........	131,407	69,498	59,948	52.9	45.6	129,140	65,752	60,670	50.9	47.0
Alabama.................	2,100	813	1,267	38.7	60.3	2,074	796	1,256	38.4	60.5
Alaska...................	326	124	194	37.9	59.4	300	123	165	40.8	54.8
Arizona..................	2,293	1,035	1,230	45.1	53.6	2,299	1,025	1,234	44.6	53.7
Arkansas...............	1,087	422	638	38.9	58.7	1,069	394	648	36.9	60.6
California................	13,562	8,274	5,012	61.0	37.0	13,039	7,854	4,840	60.2	37.1
Colorado................	2,401	1,289	1,074	53.7	44.7	2,570	1,323	1,185	51.5	46.1
Connecticut............	1,647	998	629	60.6	38.2	1,558	905	635	58.1	40.7
Delaware...............	412	255	152	61.9	36.9	414	243	165	58.6	40.0
District of Columbia.....	266	246	17	92.5	6.5	294	267	21	90.9	7.3
Florida..................	8,391	4,282	4,046	51.0	48.2	8,474	4,238	4,163	50.0	49.1
Georgia.................	3,924	1,844	2,049	47.0	52.2	3,898	1,774	2,079	45.5	53.3
Hawaii..................	456	326	121	71.5	26.4	437	307	121	70.1	27.7
Idaho...................	655	236	403	36.1	61.5	652	213	421	32.6	64.5
Illinois..................	5,522	3,419	2,031	61.9	36.8	5,242	3,020	2,135	57.6	40.7
Indiana.................	2,751	1,374	1,346	49.9	48.9	2,625	1,153	1,421	43.9	54.1
Iowa....................	1,537	829	682	53.9	44.4	1,582	823	731	52.0	46.2
Kansas.................	1,236	515	700	41.7	56.6	1,160	441	693	38.0	59.7
Kentucky...............	1,827	752	1,048	41.2	57.4	1,797	679	1,087	37.8	60.5
Louisiana..............	1,961	783	1,148	39.9	58.6	1,994	809	1,152	40.6	57.8
Maine...................	731	422	295	57.7	40.4	725	401	292	55.4	40.3
Maryland................	2,632	1,629	960	61.9	36.5	2,707	1,678	972	62.0	35.9
Massachusetts...........	3,103	1,904	1,109	61.4	35.7	3,184	1,921	1,188	60.3	37.3
Michigan................	5,002	2,873	2,049	57.4	41.0	4,731	2,565	2,115	54.2	44.7
Minnesota..............	2,910	1,573	1,275	54.1	43.8	2,937	1,546	1,320	52.7	45.0
Mississippi..............	1,290	555	725	43.0	56.2	1,286	563	711	43.8	55.3
Missouri................	2,925	1,442	1,446	49.3	49.4	2,757	1,224	1,482	44.4	53.8
Montana................	490	232	243	47.3	49.5	484	202	268	41.7	55.4
Nebraska...............	801	333	453	41.6	56.5	794	302	475	38.0	59.8
Nevada.................	968	534	413	55.1	42.7	1,015	531	464	52.4	45.7
New Hampshire..........	711	385	317	54.1	44.5	711	370	330	52.0	46.4
New Jersey.............	3,868	2,215	1,613	57.3	41.7	3,638	2,123	1,478	58.3	40.6
New Mexico.............	830	472	347	56.9	41.8	784	415	336	53.0	42.8
New York...............	7,722	4,805	2,753	62.2	35.6	7,117	4,324	2,223	60.8	31.2
North Carolina...........	4,298	2,143	2,128	49.8	49.5	4,505	2,178	2,270	48.4	50.4
North Dakota............	317	141	169	44.6	53.3	323	125	188	38.7	58.3
Ohio....................	5,708	2,940	2,678	51.5	46.9	5,581	2,828	2,661	50.7	47.7
Oklahoma...............	1,463	502	960	34.4	65.6	1,335	444	891	33.2	66.8
Oregon.................	1,828	1,037	738	56.7	40.4	1,789	970	754	54.2	42.1
Pennsylvania...........	6,013	3,276	2,656	54.5	44.2	5,742	2,990	2,680	52.1	46.7
Rhode Island............	472	297	165	62.9	35.1	446	280	157	62.7	35.2
South Carolina..........	1,921	862	1,035	44.9	53.9	1,964	866	1,072	44.1	54.6
South Dakota...........	382	171	203	44.7	53.2	364	145	211	39.9	57.9
Tennessee..............	2,600	1,087	1,479	41.8	56.9	2,459	961	1,462	39.1	59.5
Texas..................	8,078	3,529	4,479	43.7	55.5	7,994	3,308	4,570	41.4	57.2
Utah....................	952	328	596	34.4	62.6	1,017	252	741	24.7	72.8
Vermont................	325	219	99	67.5	30.4	299	199	93	66.6	31.0
Virginia.................	3,723	1,960	1,725	52.6	46.3	3,854	1,972	1,823	51.2	47.3
Washington.............	3,037	1,751	1,229	57.7	40.5	3,126	1,755	1,291	56.2	41.3
West Virginia............	713	304	397	42.6	55.7	670	238	418	35.5	62.3
Wisconsin...............	2,983	1,677	1,262	56.2	42.3	3,071	1,621	1,411	52.8	45.9
Wyoming................	255	83	165	32.5	64.7	251	69	171	27.6	68.2

[1] Includes other parties.

Source: U.S. House of Representatives, Office of the Clerk, *Statistics of the Presidential and Congressional Election*, February 2013. See also <http://clerk.house.gov/member_info/election.html>.

Table 437. Vote Cast for U.S. Senators, 2012 and 2014, and Incumbent Senators, 2015—States

[2,243 represents 2,243,000. D = Democrat, R = Republican, I = Independent]

State	2012 Total[2] (1,000)	2012 Percent for leading party	2014 Total[2] (1,000)	2014 Percent for leading party	Incumbent senators and year term expires[1] Name, party, and year	Incumbent senators and year term expires[1] Name, party, and year
Alabama	(X)	(X)	818	R-97.3	Jeff Sessions (R) 2021	Richard C. Shelby (R) 2017
Alaska	(X)	(X)	282	R-48.0	Lisa Murkowski (R) 2017	Dan Sullivan (R) 2021
Arizona	2,243	R-49.2	(X)	(X)	Jeff Flake (R) 2019	John McCain (R) 2017
Arkansas	(X)	(X)	848	R-56.5	John Boozman (R) 2017	Tom Cotton (R) 2021
California	12,579	D-62.5	(X)	(X)	Barbara Boxer (D) 2017	Dianne Feinstein (D) 2019
Colorado	(X)	(X)	2,041	R-48.2	Cory Gardner (R) 2021	Michael F. Bennett (D) 2017
Connecticut	1,512	D-52.5	(X)	(X)	Richard Blumenthal (D) 2017	Christopher Murphy (D) 2019
Delaware	400	D-66.4	234	D-55.8	Christopher Coons (D) 2021	Thomas R. Carper (D) 2019
Florida	8,190	D-55.2	(X)	(X)	Marco Rubio (R) 2017	Bill Nelson (D) 2019
Georgia	(X)	(X)	2,568	R-52.9	David A. Perdue (R) 2021	Johnny Isakson (R) 2017
Hawaii	437	D-61.6	370	D-66.8	Brian Schatz (D) 2017	Mazie Hirono (D) 2019
Idaho	(X)	(X)	437	R-65.3	James E. Risch (R) 2021	Mike Crapo (R) 2017
Illinois	(X)	(X)	3,604	D-53.5	Richard J. Durbin (D) 2021	Mark Kirk (R) 2017
Indiana	2,560	D-50.0	(X)	(X)	Daniel Coats (R) 2017	Joe Donnelly (D) 2019
Iowa	(X)	(X)	1,130	R-52.1	Chuck Grassley (R) 2017	Joni Ernst (R) 2021
Kansas	(X)	(X)	866	R-53.1	Jerry Moran (R) 2017	Pat Roberts (R) 2021
Kentucky	(X)	(X)	1,436	R-56.2	Rand Paul (R) 2017	Mitch McConnell (R) 2021
Louisiana[3]	(X)	(X)	1,273	R-55.9	Bill Cassidy (R) 2021	David Vitter (R) 2017
Maine	725	I-52.6	617	R-67.0	Susan M. Collins (R) 2021	Angus King (I) 2019
Maryland	2,633	D-56.0	(X)	(X)	Barbara A. Mikulski (D) 2017	Benjamin L. Cardin (D) 2019
Massachusetts	3,184	D-53.3	2,187	D-59.0	Elizabeth Warren (D) 2019	Ed Markey (D) 2021
Michigan	4,653	D-58.8	3,122	D-54.6	Gary C. Peters (D) 2021	Debbie Stabenow (D) 2019
Minnesota	2,843	D-65.2	1,982	D-53.2	Al Franken (D) 2021	Amy Klobuchar (D) 2019
Mississippi	1,242	R-57.2	632	R-59.9	Thad Cochran (R) 2021	Roger F. Wicker (R) 2019
Missouri	2,726	D-54.8	(X)	(X)	Roy Blunt (R) 2017	Claire McCaskill (D) 2019
Montana	486	D-48.6	370	R-57.8	Steve Daines (R) 2021	John Tester (D) 2019
Nebraska	789	R-57.8	540	R-64.3	Ben Sasse (R) 2021	Deb Fischer (R) 2019
Nevada	998	R-45.9	(X)	(X)	Dean Heller (R) 2019	Harry Reid (D) 2017
New Hampshire	(X)	(X)	488	D-51.5	Kelly Ayotte (R) 2017	Jeanne Shaheen (D) 2021
New Jersey	3,377	D-58.9	1,870	D-55.8	Robert Menendez (D) 2019	Cory A. Booker (D) 2021
New Mexico	776	D-51.0	516	D-55.6	Martin Heinrich (D) 2019	Tom Udall (D) 2021
New York	7,117	D-62.1	(X)	(X)	Kirsten E. Gillibrand (D) 2019	Charles E. Schumer (D) 2017
North Carolina	(X)	(X)	2,915	R-48.8	Richard Burr (R) 2017	Thom Tillis (R) 2021
North Dakota	321	D-50.2	(X)	(X)	Heidi Heitkamp (D) 2019	John Hoeven (R) 2017
Ohio	5,449	D-50.7	(X)	(X)	Sherrod Brown (D) 2019	Rob Portman (R) 2017
Oklahoma	(X)	(X)	821	R-68.0	James Lankford[4] (R) 2017	James M. Inhofe (R) 2021
Oregon	(X)	(X)	1,462	D-55.7	Jeff Merkley (D) 2021	Ron Wyden (D) 2017
Pennsylvania	5,627	D-53.7	(X)	(X)	Robert P. Casey Jr. (D) 2019	Patrick J. Toomey (R) 2017
Rhode Island	418	D-64.8	317	D-70.6	Sheldon Whitehouse (D) 2019	Jack Reed (D) 2021
South Carolina	(X)	(X)	1,240	R-54.3	Tim Scott[5] (R) 2017	Lindsey Graham (R) 2021
South Dakota	(X)	(X)	279	R-50.4	Mike Rounds (R) 2021	John Thune (R) 2017
Tennessee	2,321	R-64.9	1,374	R-61.9	Lamar Alexander (R) 2021	Bob Corker (R) 2019
Texas	7,865	R-56.5	4,648	R-61.6	John Cornyn (R) 2021	Ted Cruz (R) 2019
Utah	1,007	R-65.3	(X)	(X)	Mike Lee (R) 2017	Orrin G. Hatch (R) 2019
Vermont	293	I-71.0	(X)	(X)	Bernard Sanders (I) 2019	Patrick J. Leahy (D) 2017
Virginia	3,802	D-52.9	2,184	D-49.1	Tim Kaine (D) 2019	Mark R. Warner (D) 2021
Washington	3,069	D-60.5	(X)	(X)	Maria Cantwell (D) 2019	Patty Murray (D) 2017
West Virginia	660	D-60.6	454	R-62.1	Joe Manchin III (D) 2019	Shelley Moore Capito (R) 2021
Wisconsin	3,009	D-51.4	(X)	(X)	Ronald H. Johnson (R) 2017	Tammy Baldwin (D) 2019
Wyoming	251	R-73.9	171	R-71.0	Michael B. Enzi (R) 2021	John Barrasso (R) 2019

X Not applicable. [1] As of April 22, 2015, see <http://www.senate.gov/pagelayout/reference/three_column_table/Senators.htm>. [2] Includes vote cast for minor parties. [3] Louisiana holds an open-primary election with candidates from all parties running on the same ballot. Any candidate who receives a majority is elected. No candidate received a majority in the 2014 open-primary and a runoff election was held on Dec. 6, 2014. Data shown are runoff election totals. [4] Elected in a special election on November 4, 2014 to fill the vacancy caused by the resignation of Tom Coburn. [5] Appointed January 2, 2013 to fill the vacancy caused by the resignation of James DeMint, and elected in special election on November 4, 2014 to continue filling the vacancy through the rest of the term.

Source: U.S. House of Representatives, Office of the Clerk, *Statistics of the Congressional Election*, March 2015, and earlier reports; and ProQuest research. See also <http://clerk.house.gov/member_info/election.html>.

Table 438. Apportionment of Membership in House of Representatives by State: 1800 to 2010

[Total membership includes Representatives assigned to newly admitted States after the apportionment acts. Population figures used for apportionment purposes are those determined for States by each decennial census. No reapportionment based on 1920 population census. For method of calculating apportionment and a short history of apportionment, see House Report 91-1314, 91st Congress, 2d session, The Decennial Population Census and Congressional Apportionment]

Membership based on Census of—

State	1800	1820	1830	1840	1850	1860	1870	1880	1890	1900	1910	1920	1930	1940	1950	1960	1970	1980	1990	2000	2010
U.S.	142	213	242	232	237	243	293	332	357	391	435	435	435	435	437	435	435	435	435	435	435
AL	(X)	3	5	7	7	6	8	8	9	9	10	10	9	9	9	8	7	7	7	7	7
AK	(X)	(X)	(X)	(X)	(X)	(X)	(X)	(X)	(X)	(X)	(X)	(X)	(X)	(X)	[1]1	1	1	1	1	1	1
AZ	(X)	(X)	(X)	(X)	(X)	(X)	(X)	(X)	(X)	(X)	[2]1	1	1	2	2	3	4	5	6	8	9
AR	(X)	(X)	[1]1	1	2	3	4	5	6	7	7	7	7	7	6	4	4	4	4	4	4
CA	(X)	(X)	(X)	[1]2	2	3	4	6	7	8	11	11	20	23	30	38	43	45	52	53	53
CO	(X)	(X)	(X)	(X)	(X)	(X)	[1]1	1	2	3	4	4	4	4	4	4	5	6	6	7	7
CT	7	6	6	4	4	4	4	4	4	5	5	5	6	6	6	6	6	6	6	5	5
DE	1	1	1	1	1	1	1	1	1	1	1	1	1	1	1	1	1	1	1	1	1
FL	(X)	(X)	(X)	[1]1	1	1	2	2	2	3	4	4	5	6	8	12	15	19	23	25	27
GA	4	7	9	8	8	7	9	10	11	11	12	12	10	10	10	10	10	10	11	13	14
HI	(X)	(X)	(X)	(X)	(X)	(X)	(X)	(X)	(X)	(X)	(X)	(X)	(X)	(X)	[1]1	2	2	2	2	2	2
ID	(X)	(X)	(X)	(X)	(X)	(X)	(X)	[1]1	1	1	2	2	2	2	2	2	2	2	2	2	2
IL	(X)	1	3	7	9	14	19	20	22	25	27	27	27	26	25	24	24	22	20	19	18
IN	(X)	3	7	10	11	11	13	13	13	13	13	13	12	11	11	11	11	10	10	9	9
IA	(X)	(X)	(X)	[1]2	2	6	9	11	11	11	11	11	9	8	8	7	6	6	5	5	4
KS	(X)	(X)	(X)	(X)	(X)	1	3	7	8	8	8	8	7	6	6	5	5	5	4	4	4
KY	6	12	13	10	10	9	10	11	11	11	11	11	9	9	8	7	7	7	6	6	6
LA	(X)	3	3	4	4	5	6	6	6	7	8	8	8	8	8	8	8	8	7	7	6
ME	(X)	7	8	7	6	5	5	4	4	4	4	4	3	3	3	2	2	2	2	2	2
MD	9	9	8	6	6	5	6	6	6	6	6	6	6	6	7	8	8	8	8	8	8
MA	17	13	12	10	11	10	11	12	13	14	16	16	15	14	14	12	12	11	10	10	9
MI	(X)	(X)	[1]1	3	4	6	9	11	12	12	13	13	17	17	18	19	19	18	16	15	14
MN	(X)	(X)	(X)	(X)	[1]2	2	3	5	7	9	10	10	9	9	9	8	8	8	8	8	8
MS	(X)	1	2	4	5	5	6	7	7	8	8	8	7	7	6	5	5	5	5	4	4
MO	(X)	1	2	5	7	9	13	14	15	16	16	16	13	13	11	10	10	9	9	9	8
MT	(X)	(X)	(X)	(X)	(X)	(X)	(X)	[1]1	1	1	2	2	2	2	2	2	2	2	1	1	1
NE	(X)	(X)	(X)	(X)	(X)	[1]1	1	3	6	6	6	6	6	5	4	4	3	3	3	3	3
NV	(X)	(X)	(X)	(X)	(X)	[1]1	1	1	1	1	1	1	1	1	1	1	1	2	2	3	4
NH	5	6	5	4	3	3	3	2	2	2	2	2	2	2	2	2	2	2	2	2	2
NJ	6	6	6	5	5	5	7	7	8	10	12	12	14	14	14	15	15	14	13	13	12
NM	(X)	(X)	(X)	(X)	(X)	(X)	(X)	(X)	(X)	(X)	[2]1	1	1	2	2	2	2	3	3	3	3
NY	17	34	40	34	33	31	33	34	34	37	43	43	45	45	43	41	39	34	31	29	27
NC	12	13	13	9	8	7	8	9	9	10	10	10	11	12	12	11	11	11	12	13	13
ND	(X)	(X)	(X)	(X)	(X)	(X)	(X)	[1]1	1	2	3	3	2	2	2	2	1	1	1	1	1
OH	[1]1	14	19	21	21	19	20	21	21	21	22	22	24	23	23	24	23	21	19	18	16
OK	(X)	(X)	(X)	(X)	(X)	(X)	(X)	(X)	(X)	[1]5	8	8	9	8	6	6	6	6	6	5	5
OR	(X)	(X)	(X)	(X)	[1]1	1	1	1	2	2	3	3	4	4	4	4	4	5	5	5	5
PA	18	26	28	24	25	24	27	28	30	32	36	36	34	33	30	27	25	23	21	19	18
RI	2	2	2	2	2	2	2	2	2	2	3	3	2	2	2	2	2	2	2	2	2
SC	8	9	9	7	6	4	5	7	7	7	7	7	6	6	6	6	6	6	6	6	7
SD	(X)	(X)	(X)	(X)	(X)	(X)	(X)	[1]2	2	2	3	3	2	2	2	2	2	1	1	1	1
TN	3	9	13	11	10	8	10	10	10	10	10	10	9	10	9	9	8	9	9	9	9
TX	(X)	(X)	(X)	[1]2	2	4	6	11	13	16	18	18	21	21	22	23	24	27	30	32	36
UT	(X)	(X)	(X)	(X)	(X)	(X)	(X)	(X)	[1]1	1	2	2	2	2	2	2	2	3	3	3	4
VT	4	5	5	4	3	3	3	2	2	2	2	2	1	1	1	1	1	1	1	1	1
VA	22	22	21	15	13	11	9	10	10	10	10	10	9	9	10	10	10	10	11	11	11
WA	(X)	(X)	(X)	(X)	(X)	(X)	(X)	[1]1	2	3	5	5	6	6	7	7	7	8	9	9	10
WV	(X)	(X)	(X)	(X)	(X)	(X)	3	4	4	5	6	6	6	6	6	5	4	4	3	3	3
WI	(X)	(X)	(X)	[1]2	3	6	8	9	10	11	11	11	10	10	10	10	9	9	9	8	8
WY	(X)	(X)	(X)	(X)	(X)	(X)	(X)	[1]1	1	1	1	1	1	1	1	1	1	1	1	1	1

X Not applicable. [1] Assigned after apportionment. [2] Included in apportionment in anticipation of statehood.

Source: U.S. Census Bureau, Congressional Apportionment, Census 2010, <http://www.census.gov/population/apportionment/>.

Table 439. Vote Cast for U.S. Representatives by Major Political Party— States: 2010 to 2014

[In thousands (86,785 represents 86,785,000), except percent. R = Republican, D = Democrat, and I = Independent. In each state, totals represent the sum of votes cast in each Congressional District or votes cast for Representative-at-Large in states where only one member is elected. In all years there are numerous districts within the state where either the Republican or Democratic party had no candidate. In some states the Republican and Democratic vote includes votes cast for the party candidate by endorsing parties]

State	2010 Total [1]	2010 Democratic	2010 Republican	2010 Percent for leading party	2012 Total [1]	2012 Democratic	2012 Republican	2012 Percent for leading party	2014 Total [1]	2014 Democratic	2014 Republican	2014 Percent for leading party
U.S......	86,785	38,854	44,594	R-51.4	122,346	59,215	57,623	D-48.4	78,813	35,369	39,927	R-50.7
AL..........	1,368	419	914	R-66.9	1,934	693	1,234	R-63.8	1,081	332	705	R-65.2
AK..........	254	78	175	R-69.0	290	83	185	R-63.9	280	115	143	R-51.0
AZ..........	1,698	712	901	R-53.0	2,173	947	1,132	R-52.1	1,468	578	817	R-55.7
AR..........	774	318	435	R-56.2	1,038	305	638	R-61.4	831	255	510	R-61.4
CA..........	9,648	5,149	4,195	D-53.4	12,204	7,393	4,530	D-60.6	7,132	4,068	2,951	D-57.0
CO..........	1,763	801	884	R-50.1	2,450	1,080	1,144	R-46.7	2,001	936	1,000	R-50.0
CT..........	1,138	635	458	D-55.8	1,467	884	491	D-60.3	1,068	596	410	D-55.8
DE..........	306	174	125	D-56.8	388	250	130	D-64.4	232	137	85	D-59.3
FL [2]........	5,117	1,854	3,004	R-58.7	7,514	3,392	3,827	R-50.9	4,999	2,131	2,713	R-54.3
GA..........	2,469	940	1,528	R-61.9	3,553	1,449	2,104	R-59.2	2,306	956	1,349	R-58.5
HI..........	360	226	129	D-62.9	437	285	138	D-65.2	370	235	120	D-63.7
ID..........	447	151	264	R-59.0	635	208	407	R-64.0	435	160	275	R-63.2
IL..........	3,696	1,876	1,720	D-50.8	5,058	2,744	2,208	D-54.2	3,568	1,823	1,722	D-51.1
IN..........	1,748	679	973	R-55.7	2,554	1,143	1,352	R-52.9	1,342	502	789	R-58.8
IA..........	1,107	480	597	R-54.0	1,537	772	727	D-50.3	1,120	509	596	R-53.2
KS..........	836	275	528	R-63.2	1,058	196	741	R-70.1	862	312	541	R-62.7
KY..........	1,354	506	844	R-62.3	1,745	685	1,028	R-58.9	1,398	508	887	R-63.5
LA [2]........	1,036	311	675	R-65.2	1,706	359	1,143	R-67.0	1,569	406	1,031	R-65.7
ME..........	564	316	248	D-56.0	725	428	266	D-59.0	617	305	228	D-49.5
MD..........	1,825	1,104	674	D-60.5	2,586	1,627	858	D-62.9	1,703	978	704	D-57.4
MA..........	2,224	1,336	808	D-60.1	3,184	2,081	698	D-65.3	2,187	1,475	309	D-67.5
MI..........	3,195	1,415	1,672	R-52.3	4,575	2,328	2,087	D-50.9	3,089	1,519	1,467	D-49.2
MN..........	2,091	1,002	971	D-47.9	2,813	1,561	1,210	D-55.5	1,964	986	914	D-50.2
MS..........	789	351	424	R-53.7	1,208	411	704	R-58.2	626	230	329	R-52.6
MO..........	1,921	708	1,103	R-57.4	2,676	1,120	1,464	R-54.7	1,426	514	838	R-58.8
MT..........	360	122	218	R-60.4	480	205	255	R-53.3	368	149	204	R-55.4
NE..........	486	138	328	R-67.5	773	276	496	R-64.2	536	185	341	R-63.6
NV..........	703	318	357	R-50.9	974	453	457	R-47.0	543	210	305	R-56.1
NH..........	450	201	230	R-51.2	682	341	312	D-50.0	481	247	232	D-51.5
NJ..........	2,122	1,025	1,055	R-49.7	3,282	1,794	1,430	D-54.7	1,821	914	877	D-50.2
NM..........	597	308	289	D-51.6	766	422	343	D-55.1	512	271	241	D-53.0
NY..........	4,744	2,515	1,613	D-53.0	7,116	3,898	1,733	D-54.8	3,935	1,788	1,257	D-45.4
NC..........	2,663	1,205	1,441	R-54.1	4,384	2,218	2,137	D-50.6	2,808	1,234	1,555	R-55.4
ND..........	236	107	130	R-54.9	316	132	174	R-54.9	249	96	138	R-55.5
OH..........	3,825	1,611	2,053	R-53.7	5,142	2,412	2,620	R-51.0	3,000	1,180	1,771	R-59.0
OK [2]........	793	222	520	R-65.5	1,326	410	857	R-64.6	653	174	458	R-70.0
OR..........	1,429	733	657	D-51.3	1,708	853	547	D-49.9	1,451	778	583	D-53.6
PA..........	3,956	1,882	2,034	R-51.4	5,556	2,794	2,710	D-50.3	3,324	1,468	1,833	R-55.2
RI..........	335	186	127	D-55.4	428	233	162	D-54.4	316	193	123	D-61.0
SC..........	1,340	537	754	R-56.3	1,803	714	1,026	R-56.9	1,156	377	734	R-63.5
SD..........	319	147	154	R-48.1	361	154	208	R-57.4	276	92	184	R-66.5
TN..........	1,559	542	955	R-61.3	2,284	797	1,370	R-60.0	1,371	448	849	R-61.9
TX..........	4,746	1,450	3,058	R-64.4	7,664	2,950	4,429	R-57.8	4,453	1,474	2,685	R-60.3
UT..........	640	218	391	R-61.0	999	324	648	R-64.9	566	183	351	R-62.0
VT..........	239	154	76	D-64.6	290	209	68	D-71.9	192	123	59	D-64.4
VA..........	2,190	911	1,186	R-54.2	3,740	1,806	1,877	R-50.2	2,135	846	1,144	R-53.6
WA..........	2,479	1,297	1,135	D-52.3	3,006	1,637	1,370	D-54.4	2,030	1,048	982	D-51.6
WV..........	514	228	283	R-55.0	641	257	384	R-59.9	439	182	243	R-55.3
WI..........	2,140	939	1,166	R-54.5	2,866	1,445	1,402	D-50.4	2,356	1,103	1,233	R-52.4
WY..........	191	46	132	R-69.0	251	58	166	R-66.4	171	38	113	R-66.0

[1] Includes votes cast for minor parties. [2] State law does not require tabulation of votes for unopposed candidates.

Source: U.S. House of Representatives, Office of the Clerk, *Statistics of the Congressional Election*, March 2015, and earlier reports. See also <http://clerk.house.gov/member_info/election.html>.

Table 440. Vote Cast for U.S. Representatives by Major Political Party—Congressional Districts: 2014

[As of March 2015. Does not include special elections or votes received from endorsing parties. If multiple candidates from the same party ran in the general election, only the candidate with the leading number of votes is shown]

State and district	Democratic candidate — Name	Percent of total	Republican candidate — Name	Percent of total
AL......	(X)	(X)	(X)	(X)
1st....	LeFlore	31.7	Byrne	68.2
2d.....	Wright	32.6	Roby	67.3
3d.....	Smith	33.7	Rogers	66.1
4th....	(1)	(1)	Aderholt	98.6
5th....	(1)	(1)	Brooks	74.4
6th....	Lester	23.7	Palmer	76.2
7th....	Sewell	98.4	(1)	(1)
AK.....	Dunbar	41.0	Young	51.0
AZ......	(X)	(X)	(X)	(X)
1st....	Kirkpatrick	52.6	Tobin	47.4
2d.....	Barber	49.9	McSally	50.0
3d.....	Grijalva	55.7	Mercer	44.2
4th....	Weisser	25.8	Gosar	70.0
5th....	Woods	30.4	Salmon	69.6
6th....	Williamson	35.1	Schweikert	64.9
7th....	Gallego	74.9	(1)	(1)
8th....	(1)	(1)	Franks	75.8
9th....	Sinema	54.7	Rogers	41.9
AR.....	(X)	(X)	(X)	(X)
1st....	McPherson	32.4	Crawford	63.3
2d.....	Hays	43.6	Hill	51.9
3d.....	(1)	(1)	Womack	79.4
4th....	Witt	42.6	Westerman	53.7
CA.....	(X)	(X)	(X)	(X)
1st....	Hall	39.0	LaMalfa	61.0
2d.....	Huffman	75.0	Mensing	25.0
3d.....	Garamendi	52.7	Logue	47.3
4th....	(1)	(1)	McClintock	60.0
5th....	Thompson	75.7	(1)	(1)
6th....	Matsui	72.7	McCray	27.3
7th....	Bera	50.4	Ose	49.6
8th....	Conaway	32.4	Cook	67.6
9th....	McNerney	52.4	Amador	47.6
10th...	Eggman	43.9	Denham	56.1
11th...	DeSaulnier	67.3	Phan	32.7
12th...	Pelosi	83.3	Dennis	16.7
13th...	Lee	88.5	Sundeen	11.5
14th...	Speier	76.7	Chew	23.3
15th...	Swalwell	69.8	Bussell	30.2
16th...	Costa	50.7	Tacherra	49.3
17th...	Honda	51.8	(1)	(1)
18th...	Eshoo	67.8	Fox	32.2
19th...	Lofgren	67.2	(1)	(1)
20th...	Farr	75.2	(1)	(1)
21st...	Renteria	42.2	Valadao	57.8
22d..	Aguilera-Marrero	28.0	Nunes	72.0
23d..	Garcia	25.2	McCarthy	74.8
24th...	Capps	51.9	Mitchum	48.1
25th...	(1)	(1)	Knight	53.3
26th...	Brownley	51.3	Gorell	48.7
27th...	Chu	59.4	Orswell	40.6
28th...	Schiff	76.5	(1)	(1)
29th...	Cárdenas	74.6	Leader	25.4
30th...	Sherman	65.6	Reed	34.4
31st...	Aguilar	51.7	Chabot	48.3
32d..	Napolitano	59.7	Alas	40.3
33d..	Lieu	59.2	Carr	40.8
34th...	Becerra	72.5	(1)	(1)
35th...	Torres	63.5	(1)	(1)
36th...	Ruiz	54.2	Nestande	45.8
37th...	Bass	84.3	King	15.7
38th...	Sánchez	59.1	Campos	40.9
39th...	Anderson	31.5	Royce	68.5
40th...	Roybal-Allard	61.2	(1)	(1)
41st...	Takano	56.6	Adams	43.4
42d..	Sheridan	34.3	Calvert	65.7
43d..	Waters	71.0	Wood, Jr.	29.0
44th...	Hahn	86.7	(1)	(1)
45th...	Leavens	34.9	Walters	65.1
46th...	Sanchez	59.7	Nick	40.3
47th...	Lowenthal	56.0	Whallon	44.0
48th...	Savary	35.9	Rohrabacher	64.1
49th...	Peiser	39.8	Issa	60.2
50th...	Kimber	28.8	Hunter	71.2
51st...	Vargas	68.8	Meade	31.2
52d..	Peters	51.6	DeMaio	48.4
53d..	Davis	58.8	Wilske	41.2
CO.....	(X)	(X)	(X)	(X)
1st....	DeGette	65.8	Walsh	29.0
2d.....	Polis	56.7	Leing	43.3
3d.....	Tapia	35.7	Tipton	58.0
4th....	Meyers	29.2	Buck	64.7
5th....	Halter	40.2	Lamborn	59.8
6th....	Romanoff	43.0	Coffman	51.9
7th....	Perlmutter	55.1	Ytterberg	44.9
CT.....	(X)	(X)	(X)	(X)
1st....	Larson	58.5	Corey	36.1
2d.....	Courtney	57.6	Hopkins-Cavanagh	35.5
3d.....	DeLauro	61.9	Brown	33.1
4th....	Himes	51.0	Debicella	44.4
5th....	Esty	49.8	Greenberg	43.3
DC.....	Carney, Jr.	59.3	Izzo	36.8
DE.....	(1)	(1)	(1)	(1)
FL......	(X)	(X)	(X)	(X)
1st....	Bryan	23.4	Miller	70.1
2d.....	Graham	50.5	Southerland II	49.3
3d.....	Wheeler	32.3	Yoho	65.0
4th....	(1)	(1)	Crenshaw	78.3
5th....	Brown	65.5	Smith	34.5
6th....	Cox	37.5	DeSantis	62.5
7th....	Neuman	32.1	Mica	63.6
8th....	Rothblatt	34.1	Posey	65.8
9th....	Grayson	54.0	Platt	43.1
10th...	McKenna	38.5	Webster	61.5
11th...	Koller	33.3	Nugent	66.7
12th...	(1)	(1)	Bilirakis	(2)
13th...	(1)	(1)	Jolly	75.2
14th...	Castor	(2)	(1)	(1)
15th...	Cohn	39.7	Ross	60.3
16th...	Lawrence	38.4	Buchanan	61.5
17th...	Bronson	36.8	Rooney	63.2
18th...	Murphy	59.8	Domino	40.2
19th...	Freeman	32.7	Clawson	64.6
20th...	Hastings	81.6	Bonner	18.4
21st...	Deutch	99.6	(1)	(1)
22d...	Frankel	58.0	Spain	42.0
23d...	Wasserman Schultz	62.7	Kaufman	37.3
24th...	Wilson	86.2	Neree	10.2
25th...	(1)	(1)	Diaz-Balart	(2)
26th...	Garcia	48.5	Curbelo	51.5
27th...	(1)	(1)	Ros-Lehtinen	(2)
GA.....	(X)	(X)	(X)	(X)
1st....	Corwin Reese	39.1	Carter	60.9
2d.....	Bishop, Jr.	59.2	Duke	40.8
3d.....	(1)	(1)	Westmoreland	100.0
4th....	Johnson, Jr.	99.9	(1)	(1)
5th....	Lewis	100.0	(1)	(1)
6th....	Montigel	34.0	Price	66.0
7th....	Wight	34.6	Woodall	65.4
8th....	(1)	(1)	Scott	99.9
9th....	Vogel	19.3	Collins	80.7
10th...	Dious	33.5	Hice	66.5
11th...	(1)	(1)	Loudermilk	100.0
12th...	Barrow	45.2	Allen	54.8
13th...	Scott	100.0	(1)	(1)
14th...	(1)	(1)	Graves	100.0
HI......	(X)	(X)	(X)	(X)
1st....	Takai	51.2	Djou	47.4
2d.....	Gabbard	75.8	Crowley	17.9
ID......	(X)	(X)	(X)	(X)
1st....	Ringo	35.0	Labrador	65.0
2d.....	Stallings	38.6	Simpson	61.4
IL......	(X)	(X)	(X)	(X)
1st....	Rush	73.1	Tillman	26.9
2d.....	Kelly	78.5	Wallace	21.4
3d.....	Lipinski	64.6	Brannigan	35.4
4th....	Gutiérrez	78.1	Concepcion	22.4
5th....	Quigley	63.2	Kolber	30.6
6th....	Mason	32.9	Roskam	67.1
7th....	Davis	85.1	Bumpers	14.9
8th....	Duckworth	55.7	Kaifesh	44.3
9th....	Schakowsky	66.1	Atanus	33.9
10th...	Schneider	48.7	Dold	51.3
11th...	Foster	53.5	Senger	46.5
12th...	Enyart	41.9	Bost	52.5
13th...	Callis	41.3	Davis	58.7
14th...	Anderson	34.6	Hultgren	65.4
15th...	Thorsland	25.1	Shimkus	74.9
16th...	Olsen	29.4	Kinzinger	70.6

See footnotes at end of table.

Table 440. Vote Cast for U.S. Representatives by Major Political Party—Congressional Districts: 2014-Continued.

See headnote on page 282.

State and district	Democratic candidate Name	Democratic Percent of total	Republican candidate Name	Republican Percent of total
17th...	Bustos	55.5	Schilling	44.5
18th...	Miller	25.3	Schock	74.7
IN......	(X)	(X)	(X)	(X)
1st....	Visclosky	60.8	Leyva	35.8
2d.....	Bock	38.3	Walorski	58.9
3d.....	Kuhnle	26.7	Stutzman	65.8
4th....	Dale	33.1	Rokita	66.9
5th....	Denney	30.8	Brooks	65.2
6th....	Heitzman	29.3	Messer	65.9
7th....	Carson	54.7	Ping	41.8
8th....	Spangler	35.8	Bucshon	60.3
9th....	Bailey	33.7	Young	62.2
IA......	(X)	(X)	(X)	(X)
1st....	Murphy	48.8	Blum	51.1
2d.....	Loebsack	52.5	Miller-Meeks	47.4
3d.....	Appel	42.2	Young	52.8
4th....	Mowrer	38.3	King	61.6
KS.....	(X)	(X)	(X)	(X)
1st....	Sherow	32.0	Huelskamp	68.0
2d.....	Wakefield	38.6	Jenkins	57.0
3d.....	Kultala	40.0	Yoder	60.0
4th....	Schuckman	33.3	Pompeo	66.7
KY.....	(X)	(X)	(X)	(X)
1st....	Hatchett	26.9	Whitfield	73.1
2d.....	Leach	30.8	Guthrie	69.2
3d.....	Yarmuth	63.5	Macfarlane	35.6
4th....	Newberry	32.3	Massie	67.7
5th....	Stepp	21.7	Rogers	78.3
6th....	Jensen	40.0	Barr	60.0
LA......	(X)	(X)	(X)	(X)
1st....	Mendoza	10.1	Scalise	77.6
2d.....	Richmond	68.7	(1)	(1)
3d.....	(1)	(1)	Boustany, Jr.	78.7
4th....	(1)	(1)	Fleming	73.4
5th....	Mayo	23.0	Abraham	41.3
6th....	Edwards	25.2	Graves	41.8
ME.....	(X)	(X)	(X)	(X)
1st....	Pingree	58.0	Misiuk	29.4
2d.....	Cain	40.2	Poliquin	45.2
MD.....	(X)	(X)	(X)	(X)
1st....	Tilghman	29.5	Harris	70.4
2d.....	Ruppersberger	61.3	Banach	35.9
3d.....	Sarbanes	59.5	Long	40.3
4th....	Edwards	70.2	Hoyt	28.3
5th....	Hoyer	64.0	Chaffee	35.7
6th....	Delaney	49.7	Bongino	48.2
7th....	Cummings	69.9	Vaughn	27.0
8th....	Van Hollen	60.7	Wallace	39.0
MA.....	(X)	(X)	(X)	(X)
1st....	Neal	73.8	(1)	(1)
2d.....	McGovern	71.9	(1)	(1)
3d.....	Tsongas	60.3	Wofford	35.4
4th....	Kennedy	72.1	(1)	(1)
5th....	Clark	71.0	(1)	(1)
6th....	Moulton	53.6	Tisei	40.2
7th....	Capuano	80.7	(1)	(1)
8th....	Lynch	76.6	(1)	(1)
9th....	Keating	53.1	Chapman	43.5
MI.....	(X)	(X)	(X)	(X)
1st....	Cannon	45.3	Benishek	52.1
2d.....	Vanderstelt	33.3	Huizenga	63.6
3d.....	Goodrich	39.0	Amash	57.9
4th....	Homes	39.1	Moolenaar	56.5
5th....	Kildee	66.7	Hardwick	31.2
6th....	Clements	40.4	Upton	55.9
7th....	Byrnes	41.2	Walberg	53.5
8th....	Schertzing	42.1	Bishop	54.6
9th....	Levin	60.4	Brikho	36.1
10th...	Stadler	29.4	Miller	68.7
11th...	McKenzie	40.5	Trott	55.9
12th...	Dingell	65.0	Bowman	31.3
13th...	Conyers, Jr.	79.5	Gorman	16.3
14th...	Lawrence	77.8	Barr	19.7
MN.....	(X)	(X)	(X)	(X)
1st....	Walz	54.2	Hagedorn	45.7
2d.....	Obermueller	38.9	Kline	56.0
3d.....	Sund	37.8	Paulsen	62.1
4th....	McCollum	61.2	Wahlgren	32.9
5th....	Ellison	70.8	Daggett	24.0
6th....	Perske	38.4	Emmer	56.3
7th....	Peterson	54.2	Westrom	45.7
8th....	Nolan	48.5	Mills	47.1

State and district	Democratic candidate Name	Democratic Percent of total	Republican candidate Name	Republican Percent of total
MS.....	(X)	(X)	(X)	(X)
1st....	Dickey	28.9	Nunnelee	67.9
2d.....	Thompson	67.7	(1)	(1)
3d.....	Magee	27.9	Harper	68.9
4th....	Moore	24.3	Palazzo	69.9
MO.....	(X)	(X)	(X)	(X)
1st....	Clay	73.0	Elder	21.6
2d.....	Lieber	32.6	Wagner	64.1
3d.....	Denton	27.1	Luetkemeyer	68.3
4th....	Irvin	26.4	Hartzler	68.1
5th....	Cleaver	51.6	Turk	45.0
6th....	Hedge	29.5	Graves	66.7
7th....	Evans	28.8	Long	63.5
8th....	Stocker	24.3	Smith	66.7
MT.....	Lewis	40.4	Zinke	55.4
NE.....	(X)	(X)	(X)	(X)
1st....	Crawford	31.2	Fortenberry	68.8
2d.....	Ashford	48.9	Terry	45.6
3d.....	Sullivan	24.6	Smith	75.4
NV.....	(X)	(X)	(X)	(X)
1st....	Titus	56.8	Teijeiro	37.9
2d.....	Spees	27.9	Amodei	65.7
3d.....	Bilbray	36.1	Heck	60.8
4th....	Horsford	45.8	Hardy	48.5
NH.....	(X)	(X)	(X)	(X)
1st....	Shea-Porter	48.1	Guinta	51.7
2d.....	Kuster	54.9	Garcia	44.9
NJ.....	(X)	(X)	(X)	(X)
1st....	Norcross	57.4	Cobb	39.4
2d.....	Hughes, Jr.	37.3	LoBiondo	61.5
3d.....	Belgard	44.4	MacArthur	54.0
4th....	Scolavino	31.1	Smith	68.0
5th....	Cho	43.3	Garrett	55.4
6th....	Pallone, Jr.	59.9	Wilkinson	38.9
7th....	Kovach	38.8	Lance	59.3
8th....	Sires	77.4	Tiscornia	19.0
9th....	Pascrell, Jr.	68.5	Paul	30.1
10th...	Payne, Jr.	85.4	Dentley	12.6
11th...	Dunec	37.4	Frelinghuysen	62.6
12th...	Watson Coleman	61.0	Eck	36.5
NM.....	(X)	(X)	(X)	(X)
1st....	Grisham	58.6	Frese	41.4
2d.....	Lara	35.5	Pearce	64.4
3d.....	Luján	61.5	Byrd	38.4
NY.....	(X)	(X)	(X)	(X)
1st....	Bishop	38.7	Zeldin	43.6
2d.....	Maher	28.5	King	52.3
3d.....	Israel	47.0	Lally	36.9
4th....	Rice	47.8	Blakeman	38.7
5th....	Meeks	80.2	(1)	(1)
6th....	Meng	63.7	(1)	(1)
7th....	Velázquez	68.8	Fernandez	8.3
8th....	Jeffries	74.1	(1)	(1)
9th....	Clarke	69.9	(1)	(1)
10th...	Nadler	65.3	(1)	(1)
11th...	Recchia, Jr.	37.3	Grimm	43.5
12th...	Maloney	66.8	Di Iorio	16.7
13th...	Rangel	69.1	(1)	(1)
14th...	Crowley	67.3	(1)	(1)
15th...	Serrano	86.7	(1)	(1)
16th...	Engel	65.0	(1)	(1)
17th...	Lowey	49.2	Day	35.0
18th...	Maloney	40.8	Hayworth	35.6
19th...	Eldridge	28.8	Gibson	48.5
20th...	Tonko	48.8	Fischer	29.2
21st...	Woolf	29.3	Stefanik	43.9
22d....	(1)	(1)	Hanna	64.8
23d....	Robertson	31.6	Reed	49.5
24th...	Maffei	35.7	Katko	46.2
25th...	Slaughter	44.4	Assini	38.7
26th...	Higgins	57.9	Weppner	22.1
27th...	O'Donnell	23.7	Collins	50.7
NC.....	(X)	(X)	(X)	(X)
1st....	Butterfield	73.4	Rich	26.6
2d.....	Aiken	41.2	Ellmers	58.8
3d.....	Adame	32.2	Jones	67.8
4th....	Price	74.7	Wright	25.3
5th....	Brannon	39.0	Foxx	61.0
6th....	Fjeld	41.3	Walker	58.7
7th....	Barfield, Jr.	37.1	Rouzer	59.4
8th....	Blue	35.1	Hudson	64.9
9th....	(1)	(1)	Pittenger	93.9

See footnotes at end of table.

Table 440. Vote Cast for U.S. Representatives by Major Political Party—Congressional Districts: 2014-Continued.

See headnote on page 282.

State and district	Democratic candidate Name	Percent of total	Republican candidate Name	Percent of total
10th...	MacQueen	39.0	McHenry	51.9
11th...	Hill	37.1	Meadows	62.9
12th...	Adams	75.3	Coakley	24.7
13th...	Cleary	42.7	Holding	57.3
ND.....	Sinner	38.5	Cramer	55.5
OH.....	(X)	(X)	(X)	(X)
1st....	Kundrata	36.8	Chabot	63.2
2d.....	Tyszkiewicz	34.0	Wenstrup	66.0
3d.....	Beatty	64.1	Adams	35.9
4th....	Garrett	32.3	Jordan	67.7
5th....	Fry	28.9	Latta	66.5
6th....	Garrison	38.6	Johnson	58.2
7th....	(1)	(1)	Gibbs	100.0
8th....	Poetter	27.4	Boehner	67.2
9th....	Kaptur	67.7	May	32.2
10th...	Klepinger	31.5	Turner	65.2
11th...	Fudge	79.5	Zetzer	20.5
12th...	Tibbs	27.8	Tiberi	68.1
13th...	Ryan	68.5	Pekarek	31.5
14th...	Wager	33.0	Joyce	63.3
15th...	Wharton	34.0	Stivers	66.0
16th...	Crossland	36.3	Renacci	63.7
OK.....	(X)	(X)	(X)	(X)
1st....	(1)	(1)	Bridenstine	(2)
2d.....	Everett	24.6	Mullin	70.0
3d.....	Robbins	21.4	Lucas	78.6
4th....	Smith	24.7	Cole	70.8
5th....	McAffrey	36.3	Russell	60.1
OR.....	(X)	(X)	(X)	(X)
1st....	Bonamici	57.3	Yates	34.5
2d.....	Christofferson	25.7	Walden	70.4
3d.....	Blumenauer	72.3	Buchal	19.6
4th....	DeFazio	58.6	Robinson	37.6
5th....	Schrader	53.7	Smith	39.3
PA.....	(X)	(X)	(X)	(X)
1st....	Brady	82.8	Rath	17.2
2d.....	Fattah	87.7	James	12.3
3d.....	Lavallee	39.4	Kelly	60.6
4th....	Thompson	25.5	Perry	74.5
5th....	Taylor	36.4	Thompson	63.6
6th....	Trivedi	43.7	Costello	56.3
7th....	Balchunis	38.0	Meehan	62.0
8th....	Strouse	38.1	Fitzpatrick	61.9
9th....	Hartzok	36.5	Shuster	63.5
10th...	Brion	24.8	Marino	62.6
11th...	Ostrowski	33.7	Barletta	66.3
12th...	McClelland	40.7	Rothfus	59.3
13th...	Boyle	67.1	Adcock	32.9
14th...	Doyle	100.0	(1)	(1)
15th...	(1)	(1)	Dent	100.0
16th...	Houghton	42.3	Pitts	57.7
17th...	Cartwright	56.8	Moylan	43.2
18th...	(1)	(1)	Murphy	100.0
RI.....	(X)	(X)	(X)	(X)
1st....	Cicilline	59.5	Lynch	40.2
2d.....	Langevin	62.2	Reis	37.6
SC.....	(X)	(X)	(X)	(X)
1st....	(1)	(1)	Sanford	93.4
2d.....	Black	35.3	Wilson	62.4
3d.....	Mullis	28.8	Duncan	71.2
4th....	(1)	(1)	Gowdy	84.8
5th....	Adams	38.1	Mulvaney	58.9
6th....	Clyburn	72.5	Culler	25.5
7th....	Bromell-Tinbu	40.0	Rice	60.0
SD.....	Robinson	33.5	Noem	66.5
TN.....	(X)	(X)	(X)	(X)
1st....	(1)	(1)	Roe	82.8
2d.....	Scott	22.6	Duncan, Jr.	72.5
3d.....	Headrick	34.6	Fleischmann	62.4
4th....	Sherrell	35.3	DesJarlais	58.3
5th....	Cooper	62.3	Ries	35.7
6th....	Powers	23.0	Black	71.1
7th....	Cramer	26.8	Blackburn	70.0
8th....	Bradley	24.6	Fincher	70.8
9th....	Cohen	75.0	Bergmann	23.3
TX.....	(X)	(X)	(X)	(X)
1st....	McKellar	22.5	Gohmert	77.5
2d.....	Letsos	29.6	Poe	67.9

State and district	Democratic candidate Name	Percent of total	Republican candidate Name	Percent of total
3d.....	(1)	(1)	Johnson	82.0
4th....	(1)	(1)	Ratcliffe	100.0
5th....	(1)	(1)	Hensarling	85.4
6th....	Cozad	36.4	Barton	61.1
7th....	Cargas	34.5	Culberson	63.3
8th....	(1)	(1)	Brady	89.3
9th....	Green	90.8	(1)	(1)
10th...	Walter-Caiden	34.1	McCaul	62.2
11th...	(1)	(1)	Conaway	90.3
12th...	Greene	26.3	Granger	71.3
13th...	Minter	12.8	Thornberry	84.3
14th...	Brown	36.1	Weber, Sr.	61.9
15th...	Hinojosa	54.0	Zamora	43.3
16th...	O'Rourke	67.5	Roen	29.2
17th...	Haynes	32.4	Flores	64.6
18th...	Jackson Lee	71.8	Seibert	24.8
19th...	Marchbanks	18.4	Neugebauer	77.2
20th...	Castro	75.7	(1)	(1)
21st...	(1)	(1)	Smith	71.8
22d....	Briscoe	31.6	Olson	66.5
23d....	Gallego	47.7	Hurd	49.8
24th...	McGehearty	32.3	Marchant	65.0
25th...	Montoya	36.2	Williams	60.2
26th...	(1)	(1)	Burgess	82.7
27th...	Reed	33.7	Farenthold	63.6
28th...	Cuellar	82.1	(1)	(1)
29th...	Green	89.5	(1)	(1)
30th...	Johnson	87.9	(1)	(1)
31st...	Minor	32.0	Carter	64.0
32d....	Perez	35.4	Sessions	61.8
33d....	Veasey	86.5	(1)	(1)
34th...	Vela	59.5	Smith	38.6
35th...	Doggett	62.5	Narvaiz	33.3
36th...	Cole	22.1	Babin	76.0
UT.....	(X)	(X)	(X)	(X)
1st....	McAleer	28.0	Bishop	64.8
2d.....	Robles	32.6	Stewart	60.8
3d.....	Wonnacott	22.5	Chaffetz	72.2
4th....	Owens	45.8	Love	50.9
VT.....	Welch	64.4	Donka	31.0
VA.....	(X)	(X)	(X)	(X)
1st....	Mosher	34.4	Wittman	62.9
2d.....	Patrick	41.1	Rigell	58.7
3d.....	Scott	94.4	(1)	(1)
4th....	Fausz	37.5	Forbes	60.2
5th....	Gaughan	35.9	Hurt	60.9
6th....	(1)	(1)	Goodlatte	74.5
7th....	Trammell	36.9	Brat	60.8
8th....	Beyer, Jr.	63.1	Edmond	31.4
9th....	(1)	(1)	Griffith	72.1
10th...	Foust	40.4	Comstock	56.5
11th...	Connolly	56.9	Scholte	40.4
WA.....	(X)	(X)	(X)	(X)
1st....	DelBene	55.0	Celis	45.0
2d.....	Larsen	60.6	Guillot	39.4
3d.....	Dingethal	38.5	Herrera Beutler	61.5
4th....	(1)	(1)	Newhouse	50.8
5th....	Pakootas	39.3	McMorris Rodgers	60.7
6th....	Kilmer	63.0	McClendon	37.0
7th....	McDermott	81.0	Keller	19.0
8th....	Ritchie	36.7	Reichert	63.3
9th....	Smith	70.8	Basler	29.2
10th...	Heck	54.7	McDonald	45.3
WV.....	(X)	(X)	(X)	(X)
1st....	Gainer III	36.0	McKinley	63.9
2d.....	Casey	43.9	Mooney	47.1
3d.....	Rahall II	44.6	Jenkins	55.4
WI.....	(X)	(X)	(X)	(X)
1st....	Zerban	36.6	Ryan	63.3
2d.....	Pocan	68.4	Theron	31.5
3d.....	Kind	56.5	Kurtz	43.4
4th....	Moore	70.2	Sebring	26.9
5th....	Rockwood	30.4	Sensenbrenner Jr.	69.5
6th....	Harris	40.9	Grothman	56.8
7th....	Westlund	39.4	Duffy	58.9
8th....	Gruett	34.9	Ribble	65.0
WY.....	Grayson	22.1	Lummis	66.0

X Not applicable. [1] No candidate. [2] Unopposed candidate; state law either doesn't require name to appear on the ballot or vote tabulation.

Source: U.S. House of Representatives, Office of the Clerk, *Statistics of the Congressional Election,* March 2015, and earlier reports. See also <http://clerk.house.gov/member_info/election.html>.

Table 441. Composition of Congress by Political Party Affiliation—States: 2009 to 2015

[Figures are for the beginning of the first session, except as noted. Dem. = Democratic; Rep. = Republican]

State	Representatives								Senators							
	111th Cong.,[1] 2009		112th Cong., 2011		113th Cong.,[2] 2013		114th Cong.,[3] 2015		111th Cong.,[4,5] 2009		112th Cong.,[4] 2011		113th Cong.,[6] 2013		114th Cong.,[6] 2015	
	Dem.	Rep.	Dem.	Rep.	Dem.	Rep.	Dem.	Rep.	Dem.	Rep.	Dem.	Rep.	Dem.	Rep.	Dem.	Rep.
U.S.	256	178	193	242	201	232	188	245	55	41	51	47	53	45	44	54
AL	3	4	1	6	1	6	1	6	–	2	–	2	–	2	–	2
AK	–	1	–	1	–	1	–	1	1	1	1	1	1	1	–	2
AZ	5	3	3	5	5	4	4	5	–	2	–	2	–	2	–	2
AR	3	1	1	3	–	4	–	4	2	–	1	1	1	1	–	2
CA	34	19	34	19	38	15	39	14	2	–	2	–	2	–	2	–
CO	5	2	3	4	3	4	3	4	2	–	2	–	2	–	1	1
CT	5	–	5	–	5	–	5	–	1	–	1	–	2	–	2	–
DE	–	1	1	–	1	–	1	–	2	–	2	–	2	–	2	–
FL	10	15	6	19	10	17	10	17	1	1	1	1	1	1	1	1
GA	6	7	5	8	5	9	4	10	–	2	–	2	–	2	–	2
HI	2	–	2	–	2	–	2	–	2	–	2	–	2	–	2	–
ID	1	1	–	2	–	2	–	2	–	2	–	2	–	2	–	2
IL	11	7	8	11	12	6	10	8	1	–	1	1	1	1	1	1
IN	5	4	3	6	2	7	2	7	1	1	–	2	1	1	1	1
IA	3	2	3	2	2	2	1	3	1	1	1	1	1	1	–	2
KS	1	3	–	4	–	4	–	4	–	2	–	2	–	2	–	2
KY	2	4	2	4	1	5	1	5	–	2	–	2	–	2	–	2
LA	1	6	1	6	1	5	1	5	1	1	1	1	1	1	–	2
ME	2	–	2	–	2	–	1	1	–	2	–	2	–	1	–	1
MD	7	1	6	2	7	1	7	1	2	–	2	–	2	–	2	–
MA	10	–	10	–	9	–	9	–	2	–	1	1	2	–	2	–
MI	8	7	6	9	5	9	5	9	2	–	2	–	2	–	2	–
MN	5	3	4	4	5	3	5	3	1	–	2	–	2	–	2	–
MS	3	1	1	3	1	3	1	2	–	2	–	2	–	2	–	2
MO	4	5	3	6	2	5	2	6	1	1	1	1	1	1	1	1
MT	–	1	–	1	–	1	–	1	2	–	2	–	2	–	1	1
NE	–	3	–	3	1	3	1	2	1	1	1	1	–	2	–	2
NV	2	1	1	2	2	2	1	3	1	1	1	1	1	1	1	1
NH	2	–	–	2	2	–	1	1	1	1	1	1	1	1	1	1
NJ	8	5	7	6	6	6	6	6	2	–	2	–	2	–	2	–
NM	3	–	2	1	2	1	2	1	2	–	2	–	2	–	2	–
NY	26	3	21	8	21	6	18	8	2	–	2	–	2	–	2	–
NC	8	5	7	6	4	9	3	10	1	1	1	1	1	1	–	2
ND	1	–	–	1	–	1	–	1	2	–	1	1	1	1	1	1
OH	10	8	5	13	4	12	4	12	1	1	1	1	1	1	1	1
OK	1	4	1	4	–	5	–	5	–	2	–	2	–	2	–	2
OR	4	1	4	1	4	1	4	1	2	–	2	–	2	–	2	–
PA	12	7	7	12	5	13	5	13	1	1	1	1	1	1	1	1
RI	2	–	2	–	2	–	2	–	2	–	2	–	2	–	2	–
SC	2	4	1	5	1	5	1	6	–	2	–	2	–	2	–	2
SD	1	–	–	1	–	1	–	1	1	1	1	1	1	1	–	2
TN	5	4	2	7	2	7	2	7	–	2	–	2	–	2	–	2
TX	12	20	9	23	12	24	11	25	–	2	–	2	–	2	–	2
UT	1	2	1	2	1	3	–	4	–	2	–	2	–	2	–	2
VT	1	–	1	–	1	–	1	–	1	–	1	–	1	–	1	–
VA	6	5	3	8	3	8	3	8	2	–	2	–	2	–	2	–
WA	6	3	5	4	6	4	6	4	2	–	2	–	2	–	2	–
WV	2	1	1	2	1	2	–	3	2	–	2	–	2	–	1	1
WI	5	3	3	5	3	5	3	5	2	–	1	1	1	1	1	1
WY	–	1	–	1	–	1	–	1	–	2	–	2	–	2	–	2

– Represents zero. [1] One vacancy due to the resignation of Rahm Emanuel, January 6, 2009. [2] Two vacancies—one in Missouri due to the resignation of Jo Ann Emerson, January 22, 2013, and one in South Carolina due to the resignation of Tim Scott, January 2, 2013. [3] Two vacancies—one in Mississippi due to the death of Alan Nunnelee, February 6, 2015, and one in New York due to the resignation of Michael G. Grimm, January 5, 2015. [4] Vermont and Connecticut both had one Independent senator. [5] Two vacancies—one in Illinois due to the resignation of Barack Obama, November 16, 2008, and one in Minnesota due to election dispute between Norm Coleman and Al Franken. [6] Vermont and Maine had one Independent senator each.

Source: U.S. House of Representatives, Office of the Clerk, *Official List of Members*, February 2015, and earlier editions. See also <http://clerk.house.gov/member_info/>.

Table 442. Composition of Congress by Political Party: 1977 to 2014

[D = Democratic, R = Republican. As of beginning of first session of each Congress. Data reflect immediate result of elections. Vacancies and third party candidates are noted]

Year	Party and president	Congress	House			Senate		
			Majority party	Minority party	Other	Majority party	Minority party	Other
1977 [1]	D (Carter)	95th	D-292	R-143	–	D-61	R-38	1
1979 [1]	D (Carter)	96th	D-277	R-158	–	D-58	R-41	1
1981 [2]	R (Reagan)	97th	D-242	R-192	1	R-53	D-46	1
1983	R (Reagan)	98th	D-269	R-166	–	R-54	D-46	–
1985	R (Reagan)	99th	D-253	R-182	–	R-53	D-47	–
1987	R (Reagan)	100th	D-258	R-177	–	D-55	R-45	–
1989	R (Bush)	101st	D-260	R-175	–	D-55	R-45	–
1991 [3]	R (Bush)	102d	D-267	R-167	1	D-56	R-44	–
1993 [3]	D (Clinton)	103d	D-258	R-176	1	D-57	R-43	–
1995 [3]	D (Clinton)	104th	R-230	D-204	1	R-52	D-48	–
1997 [4]	D (Clinton)	105th	R-226	D-207	2	R-55	D-45	–
1999 [3]	D (Clinton)	106th	R-223	D-211	1	R-55	D-45	–
2001 [4]	R (Bush)	107th	R-221	D-212	2	D-50	R-50	–
2003 [2, 5]	R (Bush)	108th	R-229	D-204	1	R-51	D-48	1
2005 [2]	R (Bush)	109th	R-232	D-202	1	R-55	D-44	1
2007 [6]	R (Bush)	110th	D-233	R-202	–	D-49	R-49	2
2009 [5, 6, 7]	D (Obama)	111th	D-256	R-178	–	D-55	R-41	2
2011 [6]	D (Obama)	112th	R-242	D-193	–	D-51	R-47	2
2013 [5, 6]	D (Obama)	113th	R-234	D-200	–	D-53	R-45	2
2014 [6]	D (Obama)	114th	R-247	D-188	–	R-54	D-44	2

– Represents zero. [1] Senate had one Independent. [2] House and Senate each had one Independent. [3] House had one Independent-Socialist. [4] House had one Independent-Socialist and one Independent. [5] House had one vacancy. [6] Senate had two Independents. [7] Senate had two vacancies.

Source: U.S. House of Representatives, Office of the Clerk, *Official List of Members, 2015*, annual. See also <http://clerk.house.gov/member_info/>.

Table 443. U.S. Congress—Measures Introduced and Enacted and Time in Session: 1997 to 2014

[Excludes simple and concurrent resolutions]

Item	105th Cong., 1997–98	106th Cong., 1999–00	107th Cong., 2001–02	108th Cong., 2003–04	109th Cong., 2005–06	110th Cong., 2007–08	111th Cong., 2009–10	112th Cong., 2011-12	113th Cong., 2013-14
Measures introduced	7,732	9,158	9,130	8,625	10,703	11,228	10,778	10,612	9,097
Bills	7,532	8,968	8,953	8,468	10,560	11,081	10,629	10,439	8,919
Joint resolutions	200	190	177	157	143	147	149	173	178
Measures enacted	404	604	337	504	590	460	385	239	296
Public [1]	394	580	331	498	589	460	383	238	296
Private [2]	10	24	6	6	1	0	2	1	0
HOUSE OF REPRESENTATIVES									
Number of days	251	272	265	243	241	283	286	327	295
Number of hours	2,001	2,179	1,694	1,894	1,917	2,138	2,126	1,718	1,471
Number of hours per day	8.0	8.0	6.4	7.8	8.0	7.6	7.4	5.3	5.0
SENATE									
Number of days	296	303	322	300	297	374	349	323	292
Number of hours	2,188	2,200	2,279	2,486	2,250	2,364	2,495	2,032	2,003
Number of hours per day	7.4	7.3	7.1	8.3	7.6	6.3	7.1	6.3	6.9

[1] Laws on public matters that apply to all persons. [2] Laws designed to provide legal relief to specified persons or entities adversely affected by laws of general applicability.

Source: U.S. Congress, *Résumé of Congressional Activity*, March 2015, and earlier reports. See also <http://www.senate.gov/pagelayout/reference/two_column_table/Resumes.htm>.

Table 444. Congressional Bills Vetoed: 1961 to 2015

Period	President	Total vetoes	Regular vetoes	Pocket vetoes	Vetoes sustained	Bills passed over veto
1961–1963	John F. Kennedy	21	12	9	21	–
1963–1969	Lyndon B. Johnson	30	16	14	30	–
1969–1974	Richard M. Nixon	43	26	17	36	7
1974–1977	Gerald R. Ford	66	48	18	54	12
1977–1981	Jimmy Carter	31	13	18	29	2
1981–1989	Ronald W. Reagan	78	39	39	69	9
1989–1993	George Bush	44	29	15	43	1
1993–2001	William J. Clinton	37	36	1	35	2
2001–2009	George W. Bush	12	12	–	8	4
2009–2015 [1]	Barack Obama	4	4	–	4	–

– Represents zero. [1] For the period January 20, 2009 through June 1, 2015.

Source: Congressional Research Service, *Regular Vetoes and Pocket Vetoes: An Overview*, April 2013; and U.S. Senate, "Summary of Bills Vetoed," <http://www.senate.gov/reference/Legislation/Vetoes/vetoCounts.htm>, accessed June 2015.

Table 445. Number of Governors by Political Party Affiliation: 1975 to 2015

[Reflects figures after inaugurations for each year. State governors only]

Year	Demo-cratic	Republi-can	Inde-pendent/other	Year	Demo-cratic	Republi-can	Inde-pendent/other	Year	Demo-cratic	Republi-can	Inde-pendent/other
1975............	36	13	1	2004.....	22	28	–	2010.....	26	24	–
1980............	31	19	–	2005.....	22	28	–	2011.....	20	29	1
1985............	34	16	–	2006.....	22	28	–	2012.....	20	29	1
1990............	29	21	–	2007.....	28	22	–	2013.....	20	30	–
1995............	19	30	1	2008.....	28	22	–	2014.....	21	29	–
2000............	18	30	2	2009.....	28	22	–	2015.....	18	31	1

– Represents zero.

Source: ProQuest research.

Table 446. Vote Cast for and Governor Elected by State: 2010 to 2013

[D = Democratic, R = Republican, I = Independent]

State	Current governor [1]	Year of election	Total vote [2]	Republican	Democratic	Percent leading party
Alabama.............	Robert Bentley	2010	1,485,324	860,272	625,052	R-57.9
Alaska.................	Sean Parnell	2010	256,192	151,318	96,519	R-59.1
Arizona...............	Jan Brewer	2010	1,728,081	938,934	733,935	R-54.3
Arkansas.............	Mike Beebe	2010	781,333	262,784	503,336	D-64.4
California............	Jerry Brown	2010	10,095,185	4,127,391	5,428,149	D-53.8
Colorado.............	John Hickenlooper	2010	1,787,730	199,034	912,005	D-51.0
Connecticut.........	Dan Malloy	2010	1,145,799	560,874	567,278	D-49.5
Delaware............	Jack Markell	2012	398,029	113,793	275,993	D-69.3
Florida...............	Rick Scott	2010	5,359,735	2,619,335	2,557,785	R-48.9
Georgia..............	Nathan Deal	2010	2,576,161	1,365,832	1,107,011	R-53.0
Hawaii...............	Neil Abercrombie	2010	382,583	157,311	222,724	D-58.2
Idaho.................	C.L. "Butch" Otter	2010	452,535	267,483	148,680	R-59.1
Illinois...............	Patrick Quinn	2010	3,729,989	1,713,385	1,745,219	D-46.8
Indiana..............	Mike Pence	2012	2,577,329	1,275,424	1,200,016	R-49.5
Iowa..................	Terry Branstad	2010	1,122,013	592,494	484,798	R-52.8
Kansas...............	Sam Brownback	2010	838,790	530,760	270,166	R-63.3
Kentucky............	Steven L. Beshear	2011	833,139	294,034	464,245	D-55.7
Louisiana............	Bobby Jindal	2011	1,023,163	673,239	288,161	R-65.8
Maine................	Paul LePage	2010	572,766	218,065	109,387	R-38.1
Maryland............	Martin O'Malley	2010	1,857,880	776,319	1,044,961	D-56.2
Massachusetts...........	Deval L. Patrick	2010	2,297,039	964,866	1,112,283	D-48.4
Michigan............	Rick Snyder	2010	3,226,088	1,874,834	1,287,320	R-58.1
Minnesota...........	Mark Dayton	2010	2,107,021	910,462	919,232	D-43.6
Mississippi..........	Phil Bryant	2011	893,468	544,851	348,617	R-61.0
Missouri.............	Jay Nixon	2012	2,727,883	1,160,265	1,494,056	D-54.8
Montana.............	Steve Bullock	2012	486,734	158,268	318,670	D-65.5
Nebraska............	Dave Heineman	2010	487,988	360,645	127,343	R-73.9
Nevada..............	Brian Sandoval	2010	716,529	382,350	298,171	R-53.4
New Hampshire.........	Maggie Hassan	2012	693,877	295,026	378,934	D-54.6
New Jersey..........	Chris Christie	2013	2,120,866	1,278,932	809,978	R-60.3
New Mexico.........	Susana Martinez	2010	602,827	321,219	280,614	R-53.3
New York............	Andrew Cuomo	2010	4,654,352	1,548,184	2,911,721	D-62.6
North Carolina.........	Pat McCrory	2012	4,474,892	2,447,988	1,931,750	R-54.7
North Dakota........	Jack Dalrymple	2012	317,814	200,525	109,048	R-63.1
Ohio..................	John Kasich	2010	3,852,469	1,889,186	1,812,059	R-49.0
Oklahoma...........	Mary Fallin	2010	1,034,767	625,506	409,261	R-60.4
Oregon...............	John Kitzhaber	2010	1,453,548	694,287	716,525	D-49.3
Pennsylvania........	Tom Corbett	2010	3,987,551	2,172,763	1,814,788	R-54.5
Rhode Island........	Lincoln Chafee	2010	342,290	114,911	78,896	I-43.4
South Carolina.......	Nikki Haley	2010	1,344,198	690,525	630,534	R-51.4
South Dakota........	Dennis Daugaard	2010	317,083	195,046	122,037	R-61.5
Tennessee...........	Bill Haslam	2010	1,601,549	1,041,545	529,851	R-65.0
Texas................	Rick Perry	2010	4,979,870	2,737,481	2,106,395	R-55.0
Utah.................	Gary Hebert	2012	643,307	412,151	205,246	R-64.1
Vermont.............	Peter Shumlin	2012	295,412	110,940	170,749	D-57.8
Virginia..............	Terry McAuliffe	2013	2,240,314	1,013,354	1,069,789	D-47.8
Washington..............	Jay Inslee	2012	3,002,862	1,404,124	1,598,738	D-53.2
West Virginia........	Earl Ray Tomblin	2012	656,034	299,682	331,116	D-50.5
Wisconsin............	Scott Walker	2010	2,158,974	1,128,941	1,004,303	R-52.3
Wyoming............	Matt Mead	2010	188,463	123,780	43,240	R-65.7

[1] As of January 2014. [2] Includes minor party and scattered votes.

Source: The Council of State Governments, Lexington, KY, *The Book of the States 2014*, and earlier reports ©. See also <http://www.csg.org/>.

Table 447. Political Party Control of State Legislatures by Party: 1990 to 2015

[As of beginning of year. Nebraska has a nonpartisan legislature]

Year	Legislatures under— Democratic control	Split control or tie	Republican control	Year	Legislatures under— Democratic control	Split control or tie	Republican control	Year	Legislatures under— Democratic control	Split control or tie	Republican control
1990	29	11	9	2002	16	15	18	2009	27	8	14
1995	18	12	19	2003	17	15	17	2010	27	8	14
1996	16	15	18	2004	16	12	21	2011	15	8	26
1997	20	11	18	2005	17	11	21	2012	15	8	26
1998	20	12	17	2006	19	10	20	2013	19	4	26
2000	16	15	18	2007	22	12	15	2014	19	3	27
2001	16	15	18	2008	23	14	12	2015	11	8	30

Source: National Conference of State Legislatures, Denver, CO, *State Legislatures* ©. See also <ncsl.org>.

Table 448. Composition of State Legislatures by Political Party Affiliation: 2013 and 2014

[2013 data are as of March; 2014 data are as of February. Figures reflect immediate results of elections, including holdover members in state houses which do not have all of their members running for reelection. Dem. = Democrat, Rep. = Republican, Vac. = Vacancies. In general, Lower House refers to body consisting of state representatives and Upper House of state senators]

State	Lower House 2013 Dem.	Rep.	Other	Vac.	Lower House 2014 Dem.	Rep.	Other	Vac.	Upper House 2013 Dem.	Rep.	Other	Vac.	Upper House 2014 Dem.	Rep.	Other	Vac.
U.S.	2,548	2,825	21	17	2,565	2,794	21	29	884	1,027	6	6	876	1,033	6	8
AL [1]	37	65	1	2	37	64	1	3	11	22	1	1	11	23	1	–
AK [2]	14	26	–	–	14	26	–	–	7	13	–	–	7	13	–	–
AZ [3]	24	36	–	–	23	36	–	1	13	17	–	–	13	17	–	–
AR [2]	49	51	–	–	48	51	1	–	14	21	–	–	13	22	–	–
CA [2]	55	25	–	–	55	25	–	–	26	11	–	3	28	11	–	1
CO [2]	37	28	–	–	37	28	–	–	20	15	–	–	18	17	–	–
CT [3]	99	52	–	–	98	53	–	–	22	14	–	–	22	14	–	–
DE [2]	27	14	–	–	27	14	–	–	13	8	–	–	13	8	–	–
FL [2]	44	76	–	–	45	74	–	1	14	26	–	–	14	26	–	–
GA [3]	60	119	1	–	60	117	1	2	18	38	–	–	18	38	–	–
HI [2]	44	7	–	–	44	7	–	–	24	1	–	–	24	1	–	–
ID [3]	13	57	–	–	13	57	–	–	7	28	–	–	7	28	–	–
IL [4]	71	47	–	–	71	47	–	–	40	19	–	–	40	19	–	–
IN [2]	31	69	–	–	31	69	–	–	13	37	–	–	13	37	–	–
IA [2]	47	53	–	–	47	53	–	–	26	24	–	–	26	24	–	–
KS [2]	33	92	–	–	33	92	–	–	8	32	–	–	8	32	–	–
KY [2]	55	45	–	–	54	46	–	–	14	23	1	–	14	23	1	–
LA [1]	45	58	2	–	44	59	2	–	15	24	–	–	13	26	–	–
ME [3]	58	89	4	–	89	58	4	–	19	15	1	–	19	15	1	–
MD [1]	98	43	–	–	98	43	–	–	35	12	–	–	35	12	–	–
MA [3]	129	29	–	2	125	29	–	4	36	4	–	–	35	4	–	1
MI [2]	51	59	–	–	51	59	–	–	11	26	–	1	12	26	–	–
MN [2]	73	61	–	–	73	61	–	–	39	28	–	–	39	28	–	–
MS [1]	56	65	–	1	57	65	–	–	20	31	–	1	20	32	–	–
MO [2]	52	109	–	2	52	108	–	3	10	24	–	–	9	24	–	1
MT [2]	39	61	–	–	39	61	–	–	21	29	–	–	21	29	–	–
NE [5]	(5)	(5)	(5)	(5)	(5)	(5)	(5)	(5)	(5)	(5)	(5)	(5)	(5)	(5)	(5)	(5)
NV [2]	27	15	–	–	27	15	–	–	11	10	–	–	11	10	–	–
NH [3]	217	178	–	5	216	178	1	5	11	13	–	–	11	13	–	–
NJ [2]	48	31	–	1	48	32	–	–	24	16	–	–	24	16	–	–
NM [2]	38	32	–	–	37	33	–	–	25	17	–	–	25	17	–	–
NY [3]	106	42	1	1	100	40	1	9	33	30	–	–	32	29	–	–
NC [3]	43	77	–	–	43	77	–	–	17	33	–	–	17	33	–	–
ND [1]	23	71	–	–	23	71	–	–	14	33	–	–	14	33	–	–
OH [2]	39	60	–	–	39	60	–	–	10	23	–	–	10	23	–	–
OK [2]	29	72	–	–	29	72	–	–	12	36	–	–	12	36	–	–
OR [2]	34	26	–	–	34	26	–	–	16	14	–	–	16	14	–	–
PA [2]	90	111	–	2	92	110	–	1	23	27	–	–	23	26	–	–
RI [3]	69	6	–	–	69	6	–	–	32	5	1	–	32	5	1	–
SC [2]	46	77	–	1	46	78	–	–	18	28	–	–	18	28	–	–
SD [3]	17	53	–	–	17	53	–	–	7	28	–	–	7	28	–	–
TN [2]	28	70	1	–	27	71	1	–	7	26	–	–	7	26	–	–
TX [2]	56	94	–	–	55	95	–	–	12	19	–	–	12	18	–	–
UT [2]	14	61	–	–	14	61	–	–	5	24	–	–	5	24	–	–
VT [3]	96	45	9	–	96	45	9	–	21	7	2	–	20	7	2	–
VA [2]	32	67	1	–	33	67	–	–	20	20	–	–	20	20	–	–
WA [2]	55	43	–	–	55	43	–	–	26	23	–	–	25	24	–	–
WV [2]	53	47	–	–	53	47	–	–	25	9	–	–	24	10	–	–
WI [2]	39	59	1	–	39	60	–	–	15	18	–	–	15	18	–	–
WY [2]	8	52	–	–	8	52	–	–	4	26	–	–	4	26	–	–

– Represents zero. [1] Members of both houses serve 4-year terms. [2] Upper House members serve 4-year terms and Lower House members serve 2-year terms. [3] Members of both houses serve 2-year terms. [4] Illinois–4- and 2-year term depending on district. [5] Nebraska–4-year term and only state to have a nonpartisan unicameral legislature. For 2014, Nebraska legislature has 49 members.

Source: The Council of State Governments, Lexington, KY, *The Book of the States 2014*, and earlier reports ©. See also <http://www.csg.org/>.

Table 449. Women Holding State Public Offices by Office and State: 2015

[As of January]

State	Total	Statewide elective executive office [1]	State legislature Total	State legislature Percent	State	Total	Statewide elective executive office [1]	State legislature Total	State legislature Percent
U.S.	**1,863**	**77**	**1,786**	**24**	MO.	48	–	48	22
					MT.	51	4	47	27
AL.	22	2	20	14	NE.	10	1	9	20
AK.	17	–	17	28	NV.	21	1	20	29
AZ.	35	3	32	34	NH.	122	–	122	33
AR.	29	2	27	17	NJ.	36	1	35	30
CA.	33	2	31	27	NM.	31	2	29	29
CO.	42	–	42	41	NY.	52	1	51	21
CT.	57	3	54	29	NC.	44	5	39	21
DE.	16	1	15	26	ND.	30	3	27	17
FL.	40	1	39	26	OH.	34	1	33	24
GA.	54	–	54	23	OK.	23	4	19	13
HI.	22	–	22	30	OR.	30	2	28	28
ID.	29	1	28	26	PA.	46	1	45	18
IL.	58	3	55	31	RI.	32	2	30	27
IN.	35	5	30	20	SC.	25	2	23	13
IA.	36	2	34	23	SD.	24	2	22	23
KS.	41	–	41	24	TN.	23	–	23	17
KY.	25	2	23	17	TX.	37	1	36	21
LA.	18	–	18	13	UT.	17	1	16	16
ME.	54	–	54	30	VT.	75	1	74	41
MD.	59	–	59	30	VA.	24	–	24	17
MA.	54	4	50	26	WA.	49	1	48	32
MI.	32	1	31	19	WV.	21	1	20	16
MN.	70	3	67	34	WI.	34	1	33	26
MS.	32	2	30	17	WY.	14	2	12	17

– Represents zero. [1] Excludes women elected to the judiciary, women appointed to state cabinet-level positions, women elected to executive posts by the legislature, and elected members of university Board of Trustees or Board of Education.

Source: Center for the American Woman and Politics, Eagleton Institute of Politics, Rutgers University, New Brunswick, NJ, "Women in Elective Office," <http://www.cawp.rutgers.edu/index.php>, accessed May 2015 ©.

Table 450. Hispanic Public Elected Officials by Office, 2008 to 2015, and by State, 2015

[As of January of year shown. For states not shown, no Hispanic public officials had been identified]

State	Total [1]	State executives and legislators [2]	County and municipal officials	Judicial and law enforcement	Education and school boards	State	Total [1]	State executives and legislators [2]	County and municipal officials	Judicial and law enforcement	Education and school boards
2008	5,240	283	2,266	738	1,952	MA.	40	6	18	0	16
2009	5,695	277	2,264	842	2,037	MI.	22	6	4	5	7
2010	5,763	275	2,270	874	2,072	MN.	12	5	2	4	1
2011	5,876	286	2,282	864	2,173	MO.	2	2	0	0	0
2012	5,954	292	2,293	881	2,225	MT.	3	0	1	1	1
2013	6,042	320	2,285	878	2,287	NE.	2	0	0	0	2
2014	6,115	334	2,313	878	2,322	NV.	18	10	4	3	1
2015	**6,124**	**349**	**2,334**	**860**	**2,342**	NH.	1	1	0	0	0
AK.	2	1	1	0	0	NJ.	134	13	79	1	41
AZ.	350	22	128	46	147	NM.	700	54	330	117	159
AR.	2	0	0	0	2	NY.	172	24	62	47	38
CA.	1,377	34	416	78	727	NC.	2	1	1	0	0
CO.	155	12	84	16	35	OH.	15	2	9	1	3
CT.	55	13	25	0	17	OK.	1	1	0	0	0
DE.	5	2	2	1	0	OR.	22	3	7	6	6
FL.	179	26	93	51	7	PA.	21	2	9	4	6
GA.	8	2	3	2	1	RI.	18	6	11	0	1
HI.	4	4	0	0	0	TN.	5	1	3	1	0
ID.	3	1	0	1	1	TX.	2,536	49	915	449	1,072
IL.	117	15	62	15	17	UT.	9	5	3	0	1
IN.	21	1	10	3	7	VT.	1	1	0	0	0
IA.	5	0	2	0	3	VA.	8	1	4	1	2
KS.	13	6	5	1	1	WA.	41	4	21	0	16
KY.	1	1	0	0	0	WI.	9	2	3	4	0
LA.	5	1	1	2	1	WV.	1	1	0	0	0
MD.	16	6	8	0	2	WY.	11	2	8	0	1

[1] Includes special district officials, not shown separately. [2] Includes U.S. Senators and Representatives, not shown separately.

Source: National Association of Latino Elected and Appointed Officials (NALEO) Educational Fund, Washington, DC, *National Directory of Latino Elected Officials* ©, and earlier reports. See also <http://www.naleo.org/>.

Table 451. Members of Congress—Seniority of Senators and Representatives: 1959 to 2013

[Represents the makeup of Congress on the 1st day of the session]

Congress	Senators					Representatives				
	Number by length of service				Mean years of service	Number by terms served				Mean terms of service
	6 years or less [1]	7-12 years	13-18 years	19 or more years		1-3 terms	4-6 terms	7-9 terms	10+ terms	
86th (1959)	42 (20)	30	14	12	9.4	176	136	64	57	5.2
87th (1961)	42 (7)	25	22	11	9.7	163	131	76	67	5.5
88th (1963)	42 (12)	26	18	14	9.9	182	106	78	68	5.5
89th (1965)	29 (8)	36	16	19	11.1	198	97	73	67	5.1
90th (1967)	28 (7)	34	19	19	11.6	183	108	69	73	5.3
91st (1969)	32 (14)	32	17	19	11.2	171	126	65	73	5.6
92nd (1971)	25 (10)	24	29	22	11.5	162	122	68	83	5.8
93rd (1973)	40 (13)	20	20	20	11.2	162	128	66	76	5.5
94th (1975)	[2] 36 (12)	22	23	19	11.5	196	100	78	61	5.2
95th (1977)	42 (17)	25	13	20	10.6	219	87	70	59	4.9
96th (1979)	48 (20)	24	10	18	9.6	219	95	65	54	4.8
97th (1981)	55 (18)	20	10	15	8.5	209	121	56	49	4.7
98th (1983)	43 (5)	28	16	13	9.6	210	125	45	54	4.7
99th (1985)	32 (7)	38	18	12	10.1	184	138	58	54	5.1
100th (1987)	26 (13)	44	16	14	9.6	163	143	64	65	5.5
101st (1989)	31 (10)	26	29	14	9.8	120	167	86	60	5.8
102nd (1991)	30 (5)	23	28	19	11.1	133	137	91	74	6.1
103rd (1993)	30 (13)	17	32	21	11.3	192	109	69	65	5.2
104th (1995)	29 (11)	26	20	25	12.3	220	78	78	59	4.9
105th (1997)	40 (15)	24	13	23	11.2	243	71	65	56	4.8
106th (1999)	43 (8)	25	12	20	11.0	185	127	58	65	4.8
107th (2001)	45 (11)	18	15	22	11.3	149	155	54	76	5.6
108th (2003)	30 (10)	29	16	25	12.7	149	158	60	68	5.5
109th (2005)	36 (9)	26	15	23	12.4	137	128	97	72	5.9
110th (2007)	36 (10)	23	13	27	12.9	149	116	99	71	6.0
111th (2009)	[3] 32 (11)	19	20	29	14.0	147	102	106	79	6.2
112th (2011)	42 (13)	17	14	27	12.3	170	97	69	97	6.0
113th (2013)	54 (13)	17	11	18	9.9	196	91	72	74	5.7

[1] Numbers in parenthesis are number of freshman senators. Senators who are currently in their first full term are listed under "6 years or less." [2] Total includes John Durkin (D-NH). After a contested election in 1974, the Senate declared the seat vacant as of August 8, 1975. He was then elected by special election, September 16, 1975, to fill the vacancy. [3] Total includes Al Franken (D-MN), who was declared elected after a challenge in court to the vote count by his Republican challenger on June 30, 2009; and Roland Burris (D-IL) who was appointed to fill the seat vacated by Barack Obama on December 31, 2008. Total also includes Joe Biden (D-DE), who resigned his seat on January 15, 2009, but was present on the first day of the session.

Source: The Brookings Institution, *Vital Statistics on Congress*, July 2013 ©. See also <http://www.brookings.edu/research/reports/2013/07/vital-statistics-congress-mann-ornstein>.

Table 452. Women, Black, Asian, and Hispanic Members of Congress by Party Affiliation: 1995 to 2013

[As of beginning of first session of each Congress]

Characteristic	Congress									
	104th (1995)	105th (1997)	106th (1999)	107th (2001)	108th (2003)	109th (2005)	110th (2007)	111th (2009) [1]	112th (2011)	113th (2013) [2]
Women, total	**56**	**60**	**65**	**72**	**73**	**79**	**87**	**91**	**93**	**96**
Representatives	48	51	56	59	59	65	71	74	76	76
Democrat	31	35	40	41	38	42	50	57	52	56
Republican	17	16	16	18	21	23	21	17	24	20
Senators	8	9	9	13	14	14	16	17	17	20
Democrat	5	6	6	10	9	9	11	13	12	16
Republican	3	3	3	3	5	5	5	4	5	4
Black, total	**40**	**38**	**37**	**36**	**37**	**41**	**41**	**39**	**42**	**42**
Representatives	39	37	37	36	37	40	40	39	42	41
Democrat	37	36	36	35	37	40	40	39	40	41
Republican	2	1	1	1	0	0	0	0	2	0
Senators	1	1	0	0	0	1	1	0	0	1
Democrat	1	1	0	0	0	1	1	0	0	0
Republican	0	0	0	0	0	0	0	0	0	1
Asian, total	**7**	**7**	**6**	**7**	**6**	**7**	**8**	**7**	**10**	**11**
Representatives	5	5	4	5	4	5	6	5	8	10
Democrat	4	4	4	5	4	4	5	4	7	10
Republican	1	1	0	0	0	1	1	1	1	0
Senators	2	2	2	2	2	2	2	2	2	1
Democrat	2	2	2	2	2	2	2	2	2	1
Republican	0	0	0	0	0	0	0	0	0	0
Hispanic, total	**17**	**17**	**19**	**19**	**22**	**25**	**26**	**26**	**29**	**31**
Representatives	17	17	19	19	22	23	23	24	27	28
Democrat	14	14	16	16	18	19	20	21	19	23
Republican	3	3	3	3	4	4	3	3	8	5
Senators	0	0	0	0	0	2	3	2	2	3
Democrat	0	0	0	0	0	1	2	1	1	1
Republican	0	0	0	0	0	1	1	1	1	2

[1] Roland Burris was not seated on the first day of the 111th session. [2] Tim Scott, who was appointed on December 17th to replace outgoing Senator Jim DeMint, is included in the Senate totals.

Source: The Brookings Institution, *Vital Statistics on Congress*, April 2014 ©. See also <http://www.brookings.edu/research/reports/2013/07/vital-statistics-congress-mann-ornstein>.

Table 453. Political Action Committees—Number by Committee Type: 1980 to 2014

[As of December 31]

Committee type	1980	1990	2000	2005	2010	2011	2012	2013	2014
Total	2,551	4,172	3,907	4,210	4,859	4,657	6,331	6,849	7,548
Corporate	1,206	1,795	1,545	1,622	1,683	1,652	1,664	1,742	1,804
Labor	297	346	317	290	283	280	290	288	288
Trade/membership/health [1]	576	774	860	925	1,004	985	960	949	967
Nonconnected	374	1,062	1,026	1,233	1,747	1,601	2,193	3,723	4,334
Cooperative	42	59	41	37	39	35	40	40	41
Corporation without stock	56	136	118	103	103	104	107	107	114

[1] As of July 2011, health organizations are no longer an organization type but are included in either the trade or membership categories.

Source: U.S. Federal Election Commission, "Campaign Finance Statistics—Public Action Committee (PAC) Data Summary Tables," <http://www.fec.gov/press/campaign_finance_statistics.shtml>, accessed May 2015.

Table 454. Political Action Committees—Financial Activity Summary by Committee Type: 2009 to 2014

[In millions of dollars (1,305.1 represents $1,305,100,000). Covers financial activity during 2-year calendar period indicated]

Committee type	Receipts			Disbursements [1]			Contributions to candidates		
	2009-10	2011-12	2013-14	2009-10	2011-12	2013-14	2009-10	2011-12	2013-14
Total	1,305.1	2,259.1	2,368.6	1,274.6	2,198.4	2,304.8	431.5	446.3	435.9
Corporate	314.1	361.1	384.8	302.8	343.0	370.7	165.5	181.1	178.1
Labor	261.1	282.6	305.7	256.9	279.4	289.2	64.2	57.5	50.6
Trade	127.7	136.4	146.3	125.6	132.3	140.4	(NA)	79.1	79.2
Membership	145.8	134.0	156.4	143.2	132.2	150.1	(NA)	42.2	40.1
Cooperative	6.3	7.3	7.7	6.3	6.7	7.0	5.0	5.3	4.9
Corporation without stock	16.3	17.3	19.7	15.9	16.2	19.4	7.5	7.5	7.0
Nonconnected	433.8	1,320.4	1,347.9	424.1	1,288.5	1,327.9	74.1	73.5	76.0

NA Not available. [1] Comprises contributions to candidates, independent expenditures, and other disbursements.

Source: U.S. Federal Election Commission, "Campaign Finance Statistics—Public Action Committee (PAC) Data Summary Tables," <http://www.fec.gov/press/campaign_finance_statistics.shtml>, accessed May 2015.

Table 455. Presidential Campaign Finances—Federal Funds for General Election: 2000 to 2012

[In millions of dollars (147.7 represents $147,700,000). Based on FEC certifications, audit reports, and Dept. of Treasury reports]

2000		2004		2008		2012	
Candidate	Amount	Candidate	Amount	Candidate	Amount	Candidate	Amount
Total	147.7	Total	150.1	Total	84.2	Total	1.28
Bush	67.6	Bush	74.6	Obama	–	Obama	–
Gore	67.6	Kerry	74.6	McCain	84.1	Romney	–
Buchanan	12.6	Nader	0.9	Nader	0.1	Johnson	0.6

– Represents zero.

Source: U.S. Federal Election Commission, "Presidential Campaign Receipts," <http://www.fec.gov/press/summaries/2012/ElectionCycle/24m_PresCand.shtml>, accessed September 2013.

Table 456. Presidential Campaign Finances—Primary Campaign Receipts and Disbursements: 2003 to 2012

[In millions of dollars (673.9 represents $673,900,000). Covers campaign finance activity during 2-year calendar period indicated. Covers candidates who received federal matching funds or who had significant financial activity]

Item	Total [1]			Democratic			Republican		
	2003–04	2007–08 [2,3]	2011-12	2003–04	2007–08 [2]	2011-12	2003–04	2007–08 [3]	2011-12
Receipts, total [4]	673.9	1,550.3	1,379.8	401.8	1,073.8	738.5	269.6	472.4	630.4
Individual contributions	611.4	1,325.6	997.0	351.0	932.6	549.6	258.9	390.0	441.0
Federal matching funds	28.0	21.0	1.3	27.2	17.5	–	–	2.6	–
Disbursements	661.1	1,498.0	1,359.8	389.7	1,043.9	737.1	268.9	450.2	633.4

– Represents zero. [1] Includes other parties, not shown separately. [2] Obama activity includes both Primary and General election funds because he used a single committee for both elections. Dodd received $1,961,742 in matching funds; however his committee reported the receipt of $1,447,568. Gravel received an additional $115,966 in matching funds in early 2009. [3] Tancredo received an additional $83,775 in matching funds in early 2009. [4] Includes other types of receipts, not shown separately.

Source: U.S. Federal Election Commission, "Presidential Campaign Finance Summaries," <http://www.fec.gov/press/bkgnd/pres_cf/pres_cf_Even.shtml>, accessed September 2013; and "Presidential Candidate 24-Month Data Summaries", <http://www.fec.gov/press/summaries/2012/ElectionCycle/24m_PresCand.shtml>, accessed September 2013.

Table 457. Congressional Campaign Finances—Receipts and Disbursements: 2005 to 2014

[In millions of dollars (878.7 represents $878,700,000). Covers all campaign finance activity during 2-year calendar period indicated for primary, general, run-off, and special elections. Data have been adjusted to eliminate transfers between all committees within a campaign. For further information on legal limits of contributions, see Federal Election Campaign Act of 1971, as amended]

Item	House of Representatives					Senate				
	2005–06	2007–08	2009–10	2011–12	2013–14	2005–06	2007–08	2009–10	2011–12	2013–14
Total receipts [1]	**878.7**	**983.3**	**1,103.2**	**1,136.5**	**1,033.9**	**565.5**	**433.7**	**757.2**	**742.3**	**635.4**
Individual contributions	479.7	529.5	640.6	637.0	557.0	383.9	268.7	468.0	466.1	439.4
Other committees	295.3	315.0	326.2	351.0	341.9	70.8	78.8	87.6	80.9	98.4
Candidate contributions & loans	71.3	103.1	109.6	108.2	96.4	84.7	30.5	149.6	167.3	51.2
Democrats	416.8	536.8	510.3	486.8	446.4	312.2	237.2	314.7	307.9	299.6
Incumbents	217.3	326.9	393.0	249.1	286.1	176.0	83.8	139.5	172.1	204.1
Challengers	126.7	120.2	64.4	174.8	82.9	91.8	115.5	38.8	71.4	41.3
Open seats [2]	72.8	89.6	52.9	62.9	77.3	44.5	37.9	136.5	64.4	54.1
Republicans	455.0	435.1	587.5	632.7	583.7	245.3	196.0	427.4	416.1	327.9
Incumbents	324.8	246.6	231.7	436.2	355.5	120.4	150.3	109.5	77.8	90.2
Challengers	50.6	103.4	266.0	125.7	119.7	75.5	26.1	148.9	143.1	144.1
Open seats [2]	79.6	85.1	89.8	70.7	108.5	49.4	19.6	169.1	195.3	93.5
Others	6.9	11.4	5.4	17.0	3.9	8.0	0.5	15.0	18.3	8.0
Incumbents	2.5	5.7	1.7	2.2	0.1	(Z)	(Z)	(Z)	6.3	(Z)
Challengers	2.7	3.0	3.2	13.5	1.3	1.7	0.4	0.5	8.7	6.4
Open seats [2]	1.7	2.7	0.5	1.3	2.5	6.3	0.1	14.5	3.3	1.5
Total disbursements	**859.1**	**941.0**	**1,096.3**	**1,099.3**	**960.8**	**563.8**	**442.9**	**737.3**	**747.9**	**654.2**
Democrats	395.0	495.5	534.7	479.1	422.5	307.2	230.6	319.3	315.7	311.5
Republicans	458.0	434.6	556.6	604.3	534.5	248.9	211.9	403.2	417.7	334.8
Others	6.1	10.9	5.1	15.9	3.9	7.8	0.5	14.9	14.5	8.0

Z Less than $50,000. [1] Includes other types of receipts, not shown separately. [2] Elections in which an incumbent did not seek reelection.

Source: U.S. Federal Election Commission, "Campaign Finance Statistics," <http://www.fec.gov/press/campaign_finance_statistics.shtml>, accessed May 2015.

Table 458. Contributions to Congressional Campaigns by Political Action Committees (PAC) by Type of Committee: 2003 to 2014

[In millions of dollars (225.4 represents $225,400,000). Covers amounts given to candidates in primary, general, run-off, and special elections during the 2-year calendar period indicated. For number of political action committees, see Table 453]

Type of committee	Total [1]	Democrats	Republicans	Incumbents	Challengers	Open seats [2]
HOUSE OF REPRESENTATIVES						
2003–04	225.4	98.6	126.6	187.3	15.6	22.5
2005–06	279.2	124.9	154.2	229.3	26.2	23.6
2007–08	308.1	185.6	122.4	253.5	35.8	18.8
2009–10	313.6	184.4	129.2	262.8	30.0	20.7
2011–12	341.3	148.1	192.1	285.4	36.1	19.8
2013–14, total [3]	**341.6**	**149.3**	**192.3**	**298.9**	**17.6**	**25.1**
Corporate	138.9	49.2	89.7	130.7	2.2	6.0
Trade association [4]	64.3	21.3	43.0	59.5	1.4	3.5
Labor	44.5	39.3	5.2	35.3	4.4	4.8
Nonconnected [5]	50.4	19.6	30.8	35.3	7.9	7.3
SENATE						
2003–04	63.7	28.4	35.3	39.3	5.6	18.8
2005–06	66.1	28.6	37.5	47.7	10.0	8.3
2007–08	79.8	33.9	45.9	57.7	13.0	9.1
2009–10	88.8	39.9	49.0	48.9	10.4	29.5
2011–12	103.2	53.5	48.9	70.7	12.8	19.7
2013–14, total [3]	**94.3**	**41.8**	**52.5**	**63.6**	**14.8**	**15.9**
Corporate	39.1	14.9	24.3	28.5	5.3	5.4
Trade association [4]	14.9	5.1	9.8	10.2	2.3	2.4
Labor	6.2	5.8	0.3	4.3	0.5	1.3
Nonconnected [5]	25.6	12.1	13.5	14.9	5.5	5.3

[1] Includes other parties, not shown separately. [2] Elections in which an incumbent did not seek reelection. [3] Includes other types of political action committees, not shown separately. [4] Includes membership organizations and health organizations. [5] Represents "ideological" groups as well as other issue groups not necessarily ideological in nature.

Source: U.S. Federal Election Commission, "Campaign Finance Statistics," <http://www.fec.gov/press/campaign_finance_statistics.shtml>, accessed May 2015.

Section 8
State and Local Government Finances and Employment

This section presents data on revenues, expenditures, debt, and employment of state and local governments. Nationwide statistics relating to state and local governments, their numbers, finances, and employment are compiled primarily by the U.S. Census Bureau through a program of censuses and surveys. Every fifth year (for years ending in "2" and "7"), the Census Bureau conducts a census of governments involving collection of data for all governmental units in the United States. In addition, the Census Bureau conducts annual surveys which cover all the state governments and a sample of local governments.

Annually, the Census Bureau releases information on the Internet which presents financial data for the federal government, nationwide totals for state and local governments, and state-local data by states. Also released annually is a series on state, city, county, and school finances and on state and local public employment. There is also a series of quarterly data releases covering tax revenue and finances of major public employee retirement systems.

Basic information for Census Bureau statistics on governments is obtained by mail canvass from state and local officials; however, financial data for each state government and for many of the large local governments are compiled from their official records and reports by Census Bureau personnel. In over two-thirds of the states, all or part of local government financial data are obtained through central collection arrangements with state governments. Financial data on the federal government are primarily based on the *Budget of the United States Government* published by the Office of Management and Budget.

Governmental units—The governmental structure of the United States includes, in addition to the federal government and the states, thousands of local governments—counties, municipalities, townships, school districts, and many "special districts." In 2012, 90,056 local governments were identified by the census of governments (see table 459 and table 460). As defined by the census, governmental units include all agencies or bodies having an organized existence, governmental character, and substantial autonomy. While most of these governments can impose taxes, many of the special districts—such as independent public housing authorities and numerous local irrigation, power, and other types of districts—are financed from rentals, charges for services, benefit assessments, grants from other governments, and other non-tax sources. The count of governments excludes semi-autonomous agencies through which states, cities, and counties sometimes provide for certain functions—for example, "dependent" school systems, state institutions of higher education, and certain other "authorities" and special agencies which are under the administrative or fiscal control of an established governmental unit.

Finances—The financial statistics relate to government fiscal years ending June 30 or at some date within the 12 previous months. The following governments are exceptions and are included as though they were part of the June 30 group: the state governments of Alabama and Michigan, the District of Columbia, and Alabama school districts, with fiscal years ending September 30; the state government of Texas' ending August 31; and New York State ending its fiscal year on March 31. The federal government ended the fiscal year June 30 until 1976 when its fiscal year, by an act of Congress, was revised to extend from Oct. 1 to Sept. 30. A 3-month quarter (July 1 to Sept. 30, 1976) bridged the transition.

Nationwide government finance statistics have been classified and presented in terms of uniform concepts and categories, rather than according to the highly diverse terminology, organization, and fund structure utilized by individual governments.

Statistics on governmental finances distinguish among general government, utilities, liquor stores, and insurance trusts. *General government* comprises all activities except utilities, liquor stores, and insurance trusts. Utilities include government water supply, electric light and power, gas supply, and transit systems. Liquor stores and dispensaries are operated by 16 states and by local governments in 6 states. Insurance trusts relate to employee retirement, unemployment compensation, and other social insurance systems administered by the federal, state, and local governments.

Data for cities or counties relate only to municipal or county and their dependent agencies and do not include amounts for other local governments in the same geographic location. Therefore, expenditure figures for "education" do not include spending by the separate school districts which administer public schools within most municipal or county areas. Variations in the assignment of governmental responsibility for public assistance, health, hospitals, public housing, and other functions to a lesser degree also have an important effect upon reported amounts of city or county expenditure, revenue, and debt.

Employment and payrolls—These data are based mainly on mail canvassing of state and local governments. Payroll includes all salaries, wages, and individual fee payments for the month specified. Employment relates to all persons on governmental payrolls during a pay period of the month covered, including paid officials, temporary help, and (unless otherwise specified) part-time as well as full-time personnel. Effective with the 1997 Census of Governments, the reference period for measuring government employment was changed from October of the calendar year to March of the calendar year. As a result, there was no annual survey of government employment covering the October 1996 period. The prior reference month of October was used from 1958 to 1995. Figures shown for individual governments cover major dependent agencies such as institutions of higher education, as well as the basic central departments and agencies of the government.

Statistical reliability—For a discussion of statistical collection and estimation, sampling procedures, and measures of statistical reliability applicable to Census Bureau data, see Appendix III.

Table 459. Number of Governmental Units by Type: 1967 to 2012

Type of government	1967	1972	1977	1982	1987	1992	1997	2002	2007	2012
Total units	**81,299**	**78,269**	**79,913**	**81,831**	**83,237**	**85,006**	**87,504**	**87,576**	**89,527**	**90,107**
U.S. government	1	1	1	1	1	1	1	1	1	1
State governments	50	50	50	50	50	50	50	50	50	50
Local governments	81,248	78,218	79,862	81,780	83,186	84,955	87,453	87,525	89,476	90,056
County	3,049	3,044	3,042	3,041	3,042	3,043	3,043	3,034	3,033	3,031
Municipal	18,048	18,517	18,862	19,076	19,200	19,279	19,372	19,429	19,492	19,519
Township and town	17,105	16,991	16,822	16,734	16,691	16,656	16,629	16,504	16,519	16,360
School district	21,782	15,781	15,174	14,851	14,721	14,422	13,726	13,506	13,051	12,880
Special district	21,264	23,885	25,962	28,078	29,532	31,555	34,683	35,052	37,381	38,266

Source: U.S. Census Bureau, Census of Governments, "2012 Census of Governments Organization Tables: Final," <http://www.census.gov/govs/cog/>, accessed November 2013.

Table 460. Number of Local Governments by Type—States: 2012

[Governments in existence in January. Excludes, therefore, a few counties and numerous townships and incorporated places existing as areas for which statistics can be presented as to population and other subjects, but lacking any separate organized county, township, or municipal government. See Appendix III]

State	All govern-mental units [1]	County	Municipal	Township [1]	School district	Special district [2] Total [3]	Natural resources	Fire protection	Housing [4]
United States	**90,056**	**3,031**	**19,519**	**16,360**	**12,880**	**38,266**	**7,335**	**5,865**	**3,438**
Alabama	1,208	67	461	–	132	548	68	12	148
Alaska	177	14	148	–	–	15	–	–	14
Arizona	674	15	91	–	242	326	92	156	–
Arkansas	1,556	75	502	–	239	740	260	73	119
California	4,425	57	482	–	1,025	2,861	479	360	67
Colorado	2,905	62	271	–	180	2,392	168	260	93
Connecticut	643	–	30	149	17	447	1	72	114
Delaware	339	3	57	–	19	260	238	–	4
District of Columbia	2	–	1	–	–	1	–	–	–
Florida	1,650	66	410	–	95	1,079	126	57	95
Georgia	1,378	153	535	–	180	510	37	–	191
Hawaii	21	3	1	–	–	17	16	–	–
Idaho	1,168	44	200	–	118	806	176	158	11
Illinois	6,963	102	1,298	1,431	905	3,227	1,026	837	114
Indiana	2,709	91	569	1,006	291	752	143	2	70
Iowa	1,947	99	947	–	366	535	241	60	28
Kansas	3,826	103	626	1,268	306	1,523	262	1	184
Kentucky	1,338	118	418	–	174	628	126	155	18
Louisiana	529	60	304	–	69	96	10	2	–
Maine	840	16	22	466	99	237	16	–	32
Maryland	347	23	157	–	–	167	130	–	20
Massachusetts	857	5	53	298	84	417	20	12	251
Michigan	2,875	83	533	1,240	576	443	78	24	–
Minnesota	3,672	87	853	1,784	338	610	152	9	157
Mississippi	983	82	298	–	164	439	237	30	55
Missouri	3,768	114	954	312	534	1,854	329	375	125
Montana	1,265	54	129	–	319	763	134	219	13
Nebraska	2,581	93	530	417	272	1,269	84	414	166
Nevada	191	16	19	–	17	139	34	15	3
New Hampshire	541	10	13	221	166	131	11	14	21
New Jersey	1,344	21	324	242	523	234	15	184	–
New Mexico	863	33	103	–	96	631	564	–	4
New York	3,453	57	614	929	679	1,174	3	876	–
North Carolina	973	100	553	–	–	320	138	–	95
North Dakota	2,685	53	357	1,313	183	779	78	279	38
Ohio	3,842	88	937	1,308	668	841	104	100	78
Oklahoma	1,852	77	590	–	550	635	106	27	129
Oregon	1,542	36	241	–	230	1,035	187	271	19
Pennsylvania	4,897	66	1,015	1,546	514	1,756	6	–	90
Rhode Island	133	–	8	31	4	90	4	35	26
South Carolina	678	46	270	–	83	279	45	65	42
South Dakota	1,983	66	311	907	152	547	105	83	46
Tennessee	916	92	345	–	14	465	106	1	96
Texas	5,147	254	1,214	–	1,079	2,600	435	155	387
Utah	622	29	245	–	41	307	81	12	19
Vermont	738	14	43	237	291	153	14	16	9
Virginia	518	95	229	–	1	193	47	–	–
Washington	1,900	39	281	–	295	1,285	179	372	44
West Virginia	659	55	232	–	55	317	14	–	35
Wisconsin	3,128	72	596	1,255	440	765	274	1	168
Wyoming	805	23	99	–	55	628	136	71	–

– Represents zero. [1] Includes town governments in the six New England States and in Minnesota, New York, and Wisconsin. [2] Single function districts. [3] Includes other special districts not shown separately. [4] Includes community development.

Source: U.S. Census Bureau, Census of Governments, "2012 Census of Governments Organization Tables: Final," <http://www.census.gov/govs/cog/>, accessed November 2013.

Table 461. State and Local Government Current Receipts and Expenditures in the National Income and Product Accounts: 1990 to 2014

[In billions of dollars (729.6 represents $729,600,000,000). For explanation of national income, see text, Section 13. Minus sign (-) indicates net loss]

Item	1990	1995	2000	2005	2010	2011	2012	2013	2014
Current receipts	**729.6**	**979.8**	**1,303.1**	**1,708.8**	**1,998.5**	**2,030.5**	**2,057.2**	**2,136.5**	**2,225.0**
Current tax receipts	519.1	672.1	893.2	1,166.5	1,305.6	1,368.3	1,416.1	1,479.8	1,517.5
Personal current taxes	122.6	158.1	236.7	276.4	297.6	324.1	346.7	372.2	383.3
Income taxes	109.6	141.7	217.4	251.5	267.1	292.9	314.3	339.2	349.9
Other	13.0	16.4	19.4	24.9	30.5	31.2	32.4	32.9	33.4
Taxes on production and imports	374.1	482.4	621.3	835.1	960.4	994.0	1,016.9	1,052.2	1,075.9
Sales taxes	184.3	242.7	316.8	402.5	446.0	466.7	482.8	507.2	524.9
Property taxes	161.5	202.6	254.7	351.3	435.0	439.2	442.2	449.5	455.6
Other	28.3	37.0	49.8	81.4	79.4	88.1	92.0	95.4	95.4
Taxes on corporate income	22.5	31.7	35.2	54.9	47.7	50.2	52.5	55.5	58.3
Contributions for government social insurance	10.0	13.6	10.8	24.6	18.1	18.2	18.0	18.6	18.9
Income receipts on assets	68.5	69.1	93.9	88.6	82.6	79.2	75.4	74.3	75.7
Interest receipts	64.1	63.6	86.3	76.8	69.1	64.8	59.8	58.0	58.7
Dividends	0.2	1.0	1.4	2.0	2.3	2.6	3.3	3.7	3.8
Rents and royalties	4.2	4.5	6.3	9.8	11.2	11.7	12.3	12.6	13.2
Current transfer receipts	126.4	214.4	299.7	436.4	612.0	582.1	558.0	571.2	621.5
Federal grants-in-aid	104.4	174.5	233.1	343.4	505.3	472.5	444.0	450.1	494.8
From business (net)	7.1	13.5	28.6	36.5	43.4	44.2	44.0	49.6	48.7
From persons	14.9	26.5	38.0	56.5	63.2	65.4	70.1	71.5	72.8
Current surplus of government enterprises	5.6	10.6	5.4	-7.3	-19.8	-17.4	-10.4	-7.5	-8.6
Current expenditures	**736.0**	**1,011.4**	**1,293.2**	**1,775.4**	**2,235.8**	**2,246.4**	**2,277.9**	**2,323.6**	**2,392.7**
Consumption expenditures	546.2	716.8	969.1	1,256.6	1,518.3	1,524.8	1,536.3	1,560.7	1,601.0
Government social benefit payments to persons	127.7	217.6	271.4	406.6	523.8	530.4	540.0	562.3	609.9
Interest payments	61.8	76.6	52.1	111.8	192.1	190.7	201.2	200.1	181.4
Subsidies	0.4	0.3	0.5	0.4	1.6	0.5	0.5	0.5	0.5
Net state and local government saving	**-6.5**	**-31.5**	**9.9**	**-66.6**	**-237.3**	**-215.9**	**-220.8**	**-187.1**	**-167.7**
Social insurance funds	2.0	4.0	2.0	7.2	3.2	4.4	4.2	4.1	4.2
Other	-8.4	-35.6	7.9	-73.8	-240.5	-220.4	-225.0	-191.2	-171.9

Source: U.S. Bureau of Economic Analysis, National Income and Product Accounts Tables, "Table 3.3 State and Local Government Current Receipts and Expenditures," <http://www.bea.gov/itable/>, accessed July 2015.

Table 462. Federal Grants–in–Aid to State and Local Governments: 1990 to 2015

[135,325 represents $135,325,000,000, except as indicated. For fiscal year ending Sept. 30. Minus sign (-) indicates decrease]

Year	Current dollars							Constant (2009) dollars	
			Grants to individuals		Grants as percent of—				
	Total grants (mil. dol.)	Annual percent change [1]	Grants to individuals, total (mil. dol.)	Percent of total grants	State and local government expenditures from own sources [2]	Federal outlays	Gross domestic product	Total grants (bil. dol.)	Annual percent change [1]
1990	135,325	11.0	77,431	57.2	25.2	10.8	2.3	224.3	6.1
1995	224,991	6.8	145,652	64.7	31.5	14.8	3.0	318.3	4.0
2000	285,874	6.7	186,534	65.3	27.4	16.0	2.8	366.1	3.8
2001	318,542	11.4	208,008	65.3	28.4	17.1	3.0	397.4	8.5
2002	352,895	10.8	231,854	65.7	29.5	17.5	3.2	433.5	9.1
2003	388,542	10.1	251,235	64.7	30.5	18.0	3.4	466.7	7.7
2004	407,512	4.9	267,046	65.5	30.9	17.8	3.4	475.3	1.8
2005	428,018	5.0	278,764	65.1	30.8	17.3	3.3	480.1	1.0
2006	434,099	1.4	277,559	63.9	29.7	16.3	3.2	469.4	-2.2
2007	443,797	2.2	289,460	65.2	28.4	16.3	3.1	464.4	-1.1
2008	461,317	3.9	306,123	66.4	27.4	15.5	3.1	464.1	-0.1
2009	537,991	16.6	362,031	67.3	33.1	15.3	3.7	538.0	15.9
2010	608,390	13.1	391,427	64.3	37.5	17.6	4.1	602.9	12.1
2011	606,766	-0.3	392,713	64.7	(NA)	16.8	3.9	588.8	-2.3
2012	544,569	-10.3	364,095	66.9	(NA)	15.4	3.4	515.1	-12.5
2013	546,171	0.3	379,008	69.4	(NA)	15.8	3.3	508.7	-1.2
2014	576,965	5.6	412,466	71.5	(NA)	16.5	3.3	529.9	4.2
2015, est	628,153	8.9	450,416	71.7	(NA)	16.7	3.5	568.2	11.7

NA Not available. [1] Average annual percent change from previous year. [2] Expenditures from own sources as defined in the national income and product accounts.

Source: U.S. Office of Management and Budget, *Fiscal Year 2016 Budget of the U.S. Government: Historical Tables*, February 2015. See also <http://www.whitehouse.gov/omb/budget>.

Table 463. Total Outlays for Grants to State and Local Governments—Selected Agencies and Programs: 1990 to 2015

[In millions of dollars (135,325 represents $135,325,000,000). For fiscal year ending Sept. 30. Includes trust funds]

Agency and Program	1990	1995	2000	2005	2010	2011	2012	2013	2014	2015 est.
Total outlays for grants	**135,325**	**224,991**	**285,874**	**428,018**	**608,390**	**606,766**	**544,569**	**546,171**	**576,965**	**628,153**
Energy	461	492	433	636	2,656	5,128	4,223	936	759	789
Natural resources and environment	3,745	3,985	4,595	5,858	9,132	8,259	7,777	7,298	6,700	6,737
Environmental Protection Agency[1]	2,874	2,912	3,490	3,734	6,883	5,979	5,572	5,006	4,382	4,170
Agriculture	1,285	780	724	933	843	938	635	670	701	1,017
Transportation	19,174	25,787	32,222	43,370	60,981	60,986	60,749	60,518	62,260	64,499
Grants for airports[1,2]	1,220	1,859	1,624	3,530	3,156	3,095	3,012	3,519	3,100	3,591
Federal-aid highways[1]	13,854	18,945	24,711	30,915	30,385	35,754	39,634	41,388	41,626	42,160
Urban mass transportation[1]	3,728	4,353	5,262	8,114	12,939	11,783	12,098	11,506	12,135	12,622
Community and regional development	4,965	7,230	8,665	20,167	18,908	20,002	20,258	16,781	13,232	16,672
Rural Community Advancement Program	139	333	479	814	–	–	–	–	–	–
Community Development Fund	2,818	4,333	4,955	4,985	7,043	7,037	6,794	5,768	6,369	7,370
Homeland Security	1,184	1,772	2,439	13,541	8,483	9,523	10,206	7,798	4,759	6,853
State and local programs	–	–	–	2,116	3,337	3,319	3,857	4,444	3,510	2,754
Firefighter assistance grants	–	–	–	1,185	–	–	–	–	–	–
Operations, planning, and support	11	79	192	132	–	–	–	–	–	–
Predisaster mitigation grants	–	–	13	39	–	–	–	–	–	–
Disaster relief	1,173	1,693	2,234	10,069	5,141	6,201	6,346	3,281	1,156	3,986
Education, training, employment, social services	21,780	30,881	36,672	57,247	97,586	89,147	68,126	62,690	60,485	65,215
Education for the Disadvantaged[3]	4,437	6,785	8,511	14,539	19,515	19,486	17,047	16,742	15,729	16,476
School improvement programs	1,080	1,288	2,394	6,569	5,184	5,309	4,823	4,637	4,281	4,125
Special education	1,485	2,938	4,696	10,661	17,075	16,832	13,335	12,165	12,410	12,879
Social Services Block Grant	2,749	2,797	1,827	1,822	2,035	1,787	1,715	1,877	1,748	1,954
Children and family services programs	2,618	4,463	5,843	8,490	10,473	10,141	9,492	9,342	9,004	9,923
Training and employment services	3,042	3,620	2,957	3,372	4,592	3,666	3,040	2,891	2,641	2,843
Health	43,890	93,587	124,843	197,848	290,168	292,847	268,277	283,036	320,022	354,031
Substance abuse and mental health services[4]	1,241	2,444	1,931	3,203	2,846	2,964	2,741	2,891	2,713	3,332
Grants to states for Medicaid[4]	41,103	89,070	117,921	181,720	272,771	274,964	250,534	265,392	301,472	333,080
State children's health insurance fund[4]	–	–	1,220	5,129	7,887	8,629	9,065	9,469	9,314	10,558
Income security	36,768	58,366	68,653	90,885	115,156	113,625	102,574	102,190	100,869	105,095
SNAP (formerly Food Stamp Program)[4]	2,130	2,740	3,508	4,385	5,739	5,973	6,832	6,072	5,791	5,753
Child nutrition programs[4]	4,871	7,387	9,060	11,726	16,259	17,112	18,287	19,304	19,468	20,566
Temporary Assistance for Needy Families[4]	–	–	15,464	17,357	17,513	17,116	16,136	17,107	16,266	16,615
Veterans benefits and services[4]	134	253	434	552	836	996	1,081	1,087	1,223	1,271
Administration of justice	574	1,222	5,263	4,784	5,086	4,876	4,690	4,550	4,262	6,336

– Represents zero. [1] Grants include trust funds. [2] Trust funds. [3] Formerly Accelerating Achievement and Ensuring Equity. [4] Includes grants for payments to individuals.

Source: U.S. Office of Management and Budget, *Fiscal Year 2016 Budget of the U.S. Government: Historical Tables*, February 2015. See also <http://www.whitehouse.gov/omb/budget>.

Table 464. State and Local Governments—Summary of Finances: 1990 to 2012

[In millions of dollars (1,032,115 represents $1,032,115,000,000). For fiscal year ending in year shown; see text, this section. Local government amounts are estimates subject to sampling variation; see Appendix III and source. Minus sign (-) indicates deficit]

Item	1990	2000	2005	2010	2011	2012
Revenue [1]	**1,032,115**	**1,942,328**	**2,528,546**	**3,180,023**	**3,440,609**	**3,033,555**
From federal government	136,802	291,950	438,558	623,801	647,606	584,499
Public welfare	59,961	148,549	(NA)	(NA)	(NA)	(NA)
Highways	14,368	24,414	(NA)	(NA)	(NA)	(NA)
Education	23,233	45,873	(NA)	(NA)	(NA)	(NA)
Health and hospitals	5,904	15,611	(NA)	(NA)	(NA)	(NA)
Housing and community development	9,655	17,690	(NA)	(NA)	(NA)	(NA)
Other and unallocable	23,683	39,812	(NA)	(NA)	(NA)	(NA)
From state and local sources	**895,313**	**1,650,379**	**2,089,988**	**2,556,222**	**2,793,003**	**2,449,056**
General, net intergovernmental	712,700	1,249,373	1,587,476	1,887,045	1,970,431	2,013,544
Taxes	501,619	872,351	1,098,513	1,278,847	1,344,170	1,388,155
Property	155,613	249,178	335,779	443,947	445,771	446,099
Sales and gross receipts	177,885	309,290	384,266	435,571	463,979	476,447
Individual income	105,640	211,661	242,273	261,510	285,293	307,335
Corporation net income	23,566	36,059	43,256	44,108	48,422	49,031
Other	38,915	66,164	92,939	93,710	100,704	109,243
Charges and miscellaneous	211,081	377,022	488,963	608,198	626,262	625,389
Utility and liquor stores	58,642	89,546	119,608	154,758	158,029	160,075
Water supply system	17,674	30,515	37,378	49,327	51,554	54,383
Electric power system	29,268	42,436	59,157	76,492	77,201	75,959
Gas supply system	5,216	8,049	6,937	8,219	7,604	6,888
Transit system	3,043	3,954	10,146	13,003	13,737	14,505
Liquor stores	3,441	4,592	5,990	7,716	7,933	8,340
Insurance trust revenue [2]	123,970	311,460	382,904	514,420	664,542	275,437
Employee retirement	94,268	273,881	316,576	416,536	554,286	172,028
Unemployment compensation	18,441	23,366	35,367	75,191	87,578	80,311
Direct expenditure	**972,695**	**1,742,914**	**2,363,696**	**3,110,833**	**3,155,285**	**3,147,545**
By function:						
Direct general expenditure [2]	831,573	1,502,768	2,007,490	2,537,892	2,579,509	2,587,317
Education [2]	288,148	521,612	688,314	860,118	862,271	869,196
Elementary and secondary	202,009	365,181	473,843	573,641	565,284	565,403
Higher education	73,418	134,352	182,003	243,515	252,989	259,736
Highways	61,057	101,336	126,350	155,912	153,895	158,562
Public welfare	107,287	233,350	360,730	456,200	490,645	485,588
Health	24,223	51,366	66,637	81,383	82,392	84,398
Hospitals	50,412	75,976	103,555	145,902	150,626	155,755
Police protection	30,577	56,798	74,131	95,772	96,766	96,972
Fire protection	13,186	23,102	30,830	41,335	41,381	42,405
Natural resources	12,330	20,235	23,519	28,433	28,689	29,009
Sanitation and sewerage	28,453	45,261	57,940	75,620	77,154	75,959
Housing and community development	15,479	26,590	40,014	53,923	56,284	53,141
Parks and recreation	14,326	25,038	31,925	40,247	38,364	37,404
Financial administration	16,217	29,300	36,695	40,241	39,351	38,984
Interest on general debt [3]	49,739	69,814	81,122	105,715	108,478	109,118
Utility and liquor stores [3]	77,801	114,916	160,470	213,914	214,889	213,718
Water supply system	22,101	35,789	45,695	60,655	60,897	61,240
Electric power system	30,997	39,719	58,612	78,478	79,272	76,470
Gas supply system	2,989	3,724	7,075	8,273	7,596	7,041
Transit system	18,788	31,883	44,203	60,149	60,568	62,270
Liquor stores	2,926	3,801	4,885	6,359	6,557	6,697
Insurance trust expenditure [2]	63,321	125,230	195,735	359,027	360,888	346,510
Employee retirement	38,355	95,679	145,796	204,803	220,551	233,227
Unemployment compensation	16,499	18,648	29,849	135,367	121,870	95,554
By character and object:						
Current operation	700,131	1,288,746	1,760,283	2,228,794	2,284,201	2,294,751
Capital outlay	123,102	217,063	278,063	355,437	336,340	330,976
Construction	89,144	161,694	218,691	284,213	269,426	267,681
Equipment, land, and existing structures	33,958	55,369	59,372	71,224	66,914	63,295
Assistance and subsidies	27,227	31,375	37,755	47,636	50,168	50,245
Interest on debt (general and utility)	58,914	80,499	91,859	119,939	123,689	125,063
Insurance benefits and repayments	63,321	125,230	195,735	359,027	360,888	346,510
Expenditure for salaries and wages [4]	340,654	548,796	694,583	844,650	849,094	842,474
Debt outstanding, year end	**858,006**	**1,451,815**	**2,085,026**	**2,844,190**	**2,923,138**	**2,942,295**
Long-term	838,700	1,427,524	2,054,268	2,799,101	2,888,417	2,898,371
Short-term	19,306	24,291	30,758	45,088	34,721	43,925
Long-term debt:						
Issued	108,468	184,831	323,739	398,962	364,591	339,162
Retired	64,831	121,897	224,639	275,810	275,053	335,949

NA Not available. [1] Aggregates exclude duplicative transactions between state and local governments; see source. [2] Includes amounts not shown separately. [3] Interest on utility debt included in "utility and liquor stores expenditure." For total interest on debt, see "Interest on debt (general and utility)." [4] Included in items above.

Source: U.S. Census Bureau, Federal, State, and Local Governments, Government Finance Statistics, "Annual Surveys of State and Local Government Finances," <http://www.census.gov/govs/local/>, accessed March 2015.

Table 465. State and Local Governments—Revenue and Expenditures by Function: 2010 and 2012

[In millions of dollars (3,180,023 represents $3,180,023,000,000). For fiscal year ending in year shown; see text, this section. Local government amounts are estimates subject to sampling variation; see Appendix III and source]

Item	2010 Total	2010 State	2010 Local	2012 Total	2012 State	2012 Local
Revenue [1]	**3,180,023**	**2,039,927**	**1,635,634**	**3,033,555**	**1,907,027**	**1,615,194**
Intergovernmental revenue [1]	623,801	575,372	543,967	584,499	514,139	70,360
Total revenue from own sources [1]	2,556,222	1,464,555	1,091,667	2,449,056	1,392,888	1,544,833
General revenue from own sources	1,887,045	991,835	895,210	2,013,544	1,096,377	917,167
Taxes [2]	1,278,847	705,929	572,917	1,388,155	799,350	588,804
Property	443,947	14,454	429,494	446,099	13,111	432,989
Individual income	261,510	236,987	24,524	307,335	280,693	26,642
Corporation income	44,108	38,006	6,102	49,031	41,821	7,210
Sales and gross receipts	435,571	344,522	91,048	476,447	378,544	97,903
General sales	288,499	224,314	64,185	314,796	245,446	69,350
Selective sales [2]	147,072	120,208	26,864	161,652	133,098	28,553
Motor fuel	37,922	36,632	1,291	41,447	40,139	1,308
Alcoholic beverages	6,021	5,511	511	6,493	5,963	529
Tobacco products	17,303	16,858	444	17,606	17,189	417
Public utilities	28,487	14,653	13,834	28,670	14,564	14,105
Motor vehicle and operators' licenses	22,459	20,861	1,598	24,385	22,631	1,753
Charges and miscellaneous [2]	608,198	285,906	322,293	625,389	297,027	328,362
Current charges [2]	411,200	169,855	241,345	426,780	174,260	252,520
Education [2]	121,138	94,530	26,608	114,895	90,378	24,516
School lunch sales	6,600	34	6,567	6,309	33	6,276
Higher education	105,515	93,081	12,434	99,164	89,228	9,936
Natural resources	4,633	2,788	1,845	4,529	2,626	1,903
Hospitals	113,339	42,938	70,401	123,504	49,791	73,713
Sewerage	43,472	612	42,860	47,276	625	46,650
Solid waste management	15,738	420	15,317	16,589	426	16,164
Parks and recreation	9,329	1,516	7,813	9,662	1,509	8,153
Housing and community development	5,789	622	5,167	6,216	626	5,590
Airports	18,067	1,327	16,740	19,876	1,449	18,427
Sea and inland port facilities	3,881	1,038	2,843	4,408	1,265	3,143
Highways	12,001	6,885	5,116	13,286	7,322	5,964
Interest earnings	59,828	34,523	25,305	50,913	32,750	18,163
Special assessments	7,001	165	6,836	7,402	24	7,377
Sale of property	2,829	692	2,137	3,435	967	2,468
Utility and liquor store revenue	154,758	21,617	133,141	160,075	20,741	139,334
Insurance trust revenue	514,420	451,103	63,316	275,437	256,251	19,186
Expenditures [1]	**3,115,172**	**1,943,523**	**1,666,796**	**3,151,703**	**1,981,511**	**1,663,121**
Intergovernmental expenditure [1]	4,339	485,557	13,929	4,158	481,411	15,677
Direct expenditure [1]	3,110,833	1,457,965	1,652,867	3,147,545	1,500,101	1,647,444
General expenditure [2]	2,537,892	1,108,137	1,429,755	2,587,317	1,167,334	1,419,984
Education [1]	860,118	253,758	606,360	869,196	271,117	598,078
Elementary and secondary education	573,641	7,832	565,809	565,403	6,795	558,609
Higher education	243,515	202,964	40,551	259,736	220,266	39,470
Public welfare	456,200	403,572	52,627	485,588	433,312	52,276
Hospitals	145,902	58,752	87,150	155,755	65,514	90,241
Health	81,383	39,971	41,412	84,398	42,006	42,392
Highways	155,912	93,127	62,786	158,562	97,509	61,053
Police protection	95,772	12,376	83,395	96,972	12,848	84,124
Fire protection	41,335	–	41,335	42,405	–	42,405
Corrections	73,100	46,095	27,005	72,577	46,021	26,556
Natural resources	28,433	19,336	9,097	29,009	18,856	10,153
Sewerage	51,991	1,118	50,873	51,712	773	50,939
Solid waste management	23,629	2,281	21,348	24,247	2,451	21,796
Housing and community development	53,923	11,487	42,437	53,141	10,080	43,061
Governmental administration	126,719	52,147	74,572	123,932	51,010	72,922
Parks and recreation	40,247	4,912	35,335	37,404	4,632	32,773
Interest on general debt	105,715	45,260	60,455	109,118	47,342	61,775
Utility	207,555	23,864	183,691	207,021	23,796	183,224
Liquor store expenditure	6,359	5,244	1,115	6,697	5,608	1,089
Insurance trust expenditure	359,027	320,721	38,306	346,510	303,363	43,147
By character and object:						
Current operation	2,228,794	934,322	1,294,473	2,294,751	987,086	1,307,665
Capital outlay	355,437	118,011	237,426	330,976	119,669	211,307
Construction	284,213	100,962	183,251	267,681	102,757	164,924
Equipment, land, and existing structures	71,224	17,048	54,175	63,295	16,912	46,383
Assistance and subsidies	47,636	37,562	10,074	50,245	40,080	10,166
Interest on debt (general and utility)	119,939	47,351	72,588	125,063	49,903	75,159
Insurance benefits and repayments	359,027	320,721	38,306	346,510	303,363	43,147
Expenditure for salaries and wages [3]	844,650	244,952	599,698	842,474	251,330	591,144

– Represents or rounds to zero. [1] Aggregates exclude duplicative transactions between levels of government; see source. [2] Includes other items, not shown separately. [3] Included in items shown above.

Source: U.S. Census Bureau, Federal, State, and Local Governments, Government Finance Statistics, "Annual Surveys of State and Local Government Finances," <http://www.census.gov/govs/local/>, accessed March 2015.

Table 466. State and Local Governments—Capital Outlays: 1990 to 2012

[In millions of dollars (123,102 represents $123,102,000,000), except percent. For fiscal year ending in year shown; see text, this section. Local government amounts are subject to sampling variation; see Appendix III and source]

Level and function	1990	2000	2005	2008	2009	2010	2011	2012
State & local governments: Total	**123,102**	**217,063**	**278,063**	**349,710**	**362,612**	**355,437**	**336,340**	**330,976**
Percent of direct expenditure	12.7	12.5	11.8	12.3	12.1	11.4	10.7	10.5
By function:								
Education [1]	25,997	60,968	77,780	98,284	101,217	93,562	86,760	84,486
Elementary and secondary	18,057	45,150	54,563	70,285	69,259	60,240	52,989	51,063
Higher education	7,441	15,257	22,735	27,379	31,386	31,644	32,216	32,636
Highways	33,867	56,439	70,689	88,589	86,811	89,895	86,281	90,615
Health and hospitals [2]	3,848	5,502	6,100	9,114	9,424	8,553	8,494	9,089
Natural resources	2,545	4,347	4,541	6,752	6,593	5,214	5,368	5,461
Sewerage	8,356	10,093	14,081	18,902	21,247	21,915	22,921	20,414
Parks and recreation	3,877	6,916	8,136	11,683	11,488	10,711	9,012	8,256
Utilities	16,601	24,847	34,790	41,221	49,536	49,258	47,490	45,824
State governments: Total	**45,524**	**76,233**	**95,155**	**112,695**	**116,990**	**118,011**	**115,571**	**119,669**
Percent of direct expenditure	11.5	10.1	8.9	8.9	8.7	8.1	7.7	8.0
By function:								
Education [1]	7,253	14,077	20,585	25,132	28,358	28,643	29,037	28,649
Elementary and secondary	388	521	447	1,592	1,593	1,066	747	600
Higher education	6,366	12,995	19,656	22,921	26,193	25,899	26,734	27,262
Highways	24,850	41,651	52,607	62,009	61,945	64,755	62,626	67,342
Health and hospitals [2]	1,531	2,228	2,363	3,350	3,048	2,654	2,738	3,298
Natural resources	1,593	2,758	2,667	3,026	3,208	2,337	2,411	2,303
Sewerage	333	403	486	601	516	488	83	188
Parks and recreation	601	1,044	915	1,192	1,076	910	889	732
Utilities	2,605	4,232	4,319	4,809	6,151	5,318	5,351	4,700
Local governments: Total	**77,578**	**140,830**	**182,908**	**237,014**	**245,622**	**237,426**	**220,770**	**211,307**
Percent of direct expenditure	13.5	14.3	14.1	15.0	14.9	14.4	13.4	12.8
By function:								
Education [1]	18,744	46,890	57,195	73,152	72,859	64,919	57,723	55,836
Elementary and secondary	17,669	44,629	54,116	68,694	67,666	59,174	52,242	50,463
Higher education	1,076	2,261	3,079	4,458	5,192	5,745	5,481	5,373
Highways	9,017	14,789	18,083	26,580	24,866	25,140	23,655	23,273
Health and hospitals [2]	2,316	3,274	3,737	5,765	6,376	5,899	5,755	5,790
Natural resources	952	1,589	1,873	3,726	3,385	2,878	2,957	3,158
Sewerage	8,023	9,690	13,595	18,301	20,731	21,426	22,839	20,226
Parks and recreation	3,276	5,872	7,221	10,491	10,412	9,802	8,123	7,524
Utilities	13,996	20,615	30,471	36,413	43,385	43,940	42,139	41,124

[1] Includes other education, not shown separately. [2] After 2003, only includes hospital outlays.

Source: U.S. Census Bureau, Federal, State, and Local Governments, Government Finance Statistics, "Annual Surveys of State and Local Government Finances," <http://www.census.gov/govs/local/>, accessed March 2015.

Table 467. State and Local Governments—Expenditures for Public Works: 2000 to 2012

[In millions of dollars (230,569 represents $230,569,000,000), except percent. Public works include expenditures for current operations and capital outlays on highways, airports, sea and inland port facilities, sewerage, solid waste management, water supply, and mass transit systems. Represents direct expenditures excluding intergovernmental grants]

Item	Total	Highways	Air trans-portation	Sea and inland port facilities	Sewerage	Solid waste manage-ment	Water supply	Mass transit
2000, Total	**230,569**	**101,336**	**13,160**	**3,141**	**28,052**	**17,208**	**35,789**	**31,883**
State	74,974	61,942	1,106	863	955	2,347	354	7,407
Local	155,595	39,394	12,054	2,277	27,098	14,861	35,435	24,476
Capital expenditures (percent)	41.9	55.7	51.0	51.5	36.0	8.9	29.5	30.5
2010, Total	**381,808**	**155,912**	**24,209**	**5,263**	**51,991**	**23,629**	**60,655**	**60,149**
State	111,280	93,127	1,724	1,245	1,118	2,281	378	11,407
Local	270,529	62,786	22,485	4,019	50,873	21,348	60,277	48,742
Capital expenditures (percent)	(NA)	57.7	(NA)	(NA)	42.2	8.9	(NA)	(NA)
2011, Total	**380,266**	**153,895**	**22,685**	**5,067**	**53,538**	**23,616**	**60,897**	**60,568**
State	112,453	92,253	1,794	1,396	698	2,531	349	13,430
Local	267,814	61,642	20,891	3,671	52,840	21,085	60,548	47,137
Capital expenditures (percent)	(NA)	56.1	(NA)	(NA)	42.8	8.1	(NA)	(NA)
2012, Total	**384,864**	**158,562**	**21,533**	**5,300**	**51,712**	**24,247**	**61,240**	**62,270**
State	117,597	97,509	1,892	1,579	773	2,451	420	12,974
Local	267,267	61,053	19,642	3,722	50,939	21,796	60,820	49,296
Capital expenditures (percent)	(NA)	57.1	(NA)	(NA)	39.5	8.0	(NA)	(NA)

NA Not available.

Source: U.S. Census Bureau, Federal, State, and Local Governments, Government Finance Statistics, "Annual Surveys of State and Local Government Finances," <http://www.census.gov/govs/local/>, accessed February 2015, and unpublished data.

Table 468. State and Local Governments—Indebtedness: 1990 to 2012

[In billions of dollars (858.0 represents $858,000,000,000). For fiscal year ending in year shown; see text, this section. Local government amounts are estimates subject to sampling variation; see Appendix III and source]

Item	Debt outstanding Total	Cash and security holdings	Long-term Total	Long-term Public debt for private purposes	All other	Short-term	Net long-term [1]	Debt issued	Debt retired
1990: Total.......	858.0	1,490.8	838.7	294.1	544.6	19.3	474.4	108.5	64.8
State...........	318.3	963.3	315.5	154.4	161.1	2.8	125.5	43.5	22.9
Local...........	539.8	527.5	523.2	139.7	383.5	16.5	348.9	65.0	42.0
1995: Total......	1,115.4	2,058.5	1,088.3	300.6	787.7	27.0	697.3	129.3	95.1
State...........	427.2	1,393.9	421.1	176.8	244.4	6.1	205.3	52.6	37.5
Local...........	688.1	664.6	667.2	123.9	543.3	20.9	491.9	76.8	57.6
2000: Total......	1,451.8	3,503.7	1,427.5	372.6	1,054.9	24.3	959.6	184.8	121.9
State...........	547.9	2,518.9	541.5	227.3	314.2	6.4	266.9	75.0	44.4
Local...........	903.9	984.8	886.0	145.3	740.7	17.9	692.7	109.8	77.5
2001: Total......	1,554.0	3,592.1	1,531.9	395.1	1,136.8	22.1	1,038.6	199.6	130.6
State...........	576.5	2,537.7	572.8	238.2	334.7	3.7	287.4	81.3	50.7
Local...........	977.5	1,054.3	959.1	157.0	802.1	18.5	751.2	118.3	79.9
2002: Total.......	1,681.4	3,650.7	1,638.1	417.7	1,220.5	43.2	1,121.0	262.7	161.9
State...........	636.8	2,555.4	618.2	258.5	359.6	18.6	311.8	104.2	64.9
Local...........	1,044.6	1,095.3	1,020.0	159.2	860.8	24.6	809.2	158.5	97.0
2003: Total.......	1,812.7	3,696.1	1,772.2	431.4	1,340.8	40.5	1,242.7	345.8	215.2
State...........	697.9	2,594.2	681.8	267.3	414.5	16.1	366.2	148.8	85.9
Local...........	1,114.7	1,101.9	1,090.4	164.1	926.3	24.3	876.5	196.9	129.3
2004: Total.......	1,976.6	4,137.8	1,938.3	459.3	1,479.0	38.3	(NA)	359.8	242.1
State...........	779.5	2,944.9	766.0	279.1	486.9	13.6	(NA)	170.8	107.4
Local...........	1,197.0	1,192.9	1,172.3	180.2	992.1	24.7	(NA)	189.0	134.7
2005: Total.......	2,085.0	4,439.2	2,054.3	483.3	1,571.0	30.8	(NA)	323.7	224.6
State...........	810.9	3,153.8	805.3	297.4	507.9	5.6	(NA)	131.6	93.6
Local...........	1,274.2	1,285.4	1,249.0	185.9	1,063.0	25.2	(NA)	192.2	131.1
2006: Total.......	2,204.0	4,818.1	2,170.8	509.6	1,661.3	33.2	(NA)	341.9	229.5
State...........	870.0	3,443.2	859.4	318.0	541.5	10.6	(NA)	148.2	95.9
Local...........	1,334.0	1,374.8	1,311.4	191.6	1,119.8	22.6	(NA)	193.7	133.6
2007: Total.......	2,404.7	5,457.7	2,373.3	553.3	1,820.0	31.4	(NA)	381.8	228.4
State...........	936.0	3,918.8	929.4	353.9	575.6	6.6	(NA)	161.6	93.4
Local...........	1,468.7	1,538.9	1,443.9	199.5	1,244.4	24.8	(NA)	220.3	135.0
2008: Total.......	2,564.4	5,310.8	2,518.7	602.9	1,915.8	45.7	(NA)	373.6	243.5
State...........	1,006.4	3,755.7	992.2	379.0	613.2	14.2	(NA)	151.7	93.4
Local...........	1,558.0	1,555.2	1,526.5	223.9	1,302.6	31.6	(NA)	221.9	150.1
2009: Total.......	2,713.2	4,537.4	2,676.3	627.8	2,048.6	36.9	(NA)	371.3	256.5
State...........	1,048.7	3,082.5	1,041.3	395.1	646.2	7.3	(NA)	154.2	109.0
Local...........	1,664.6	1,454.9	1,635.0	232.7	1,402.3	29.6	(NA)	217.1	147.6
2010: Total.......	2,844.2	4,826.0	2,799.1	625.9	2,173.2	45.1	(NA)	399.0	275.8
State...........	1,115.5	3,323.0	1,100.8	397.1	703.6	14.7	(NA)	183.7	125.1
Local...........	1,728.7	1,503.0	1,698.3	228.8	1,469.6	30.4	(NA)	215.2	150.7
2011: Total.......	2,923.1	5,265.1	2,888.4	616.1	2,272.3	34.7	(NA)	364.6	275.1
State...........	1,139.7	3,681.4	1,134.2	389.1	745.1	5.4	(NA)	138.1	112.4
Local...........	1,783.5	1,583.7	1,754.2	227.0	1,527.2	29.3	(NA)	226.5	162.7
2012: Total.......	2,942.3	5,304.0	2,898.4	596.9	2,301.5	43.9	(NA)	339.2	335.9
State...........	1,145.6	3,699.9	1,130.1	375.6	754.5	15.5	(NA)	136.2	141.0
Local...........	1,796.7	1,604.1	1,768.3	221.2	1,547.0	28.5	(NA)	202.9	195.0

NA Not available. [1] Net long-term debt outstanding is the amount of long-term debt held by a government for which no funds have been set aside for its repayment.

Source: U.S. Census Bureau, Federal, State, and Local Governments, Government Finance Statistics, "Annual Surveys of State and Local Government Finances," <http://www.census.gov/govs/local/>, accessed February 2015.

Table 469. New Security Issues—State and Local Governments: 1990 to 2014

[In billions of dollars (122.9 represents $122,900,000,000)]

Type of issue, issuer, or use	1990	1995	2000	2005	2009	2010	2011	2012	2013	2014
All issues, new and refunding [1]........	**122.9**	**145.7**	**180.4**	**409.6**	**437.1**	**460.8**	**320.2**	**390.4**	**313.9**	**318.5**
By type of issue:										
General obligation...........................	39.5	57.0	64.5	145.8	142.0	137.5	96.0	126.6	116.2	126.4
Revenue.................................	83.3	88.7	115.9	263.8	295.1	323.2	224.2	263.8	197.7	192.1
By type of issuer:										
State.................................	15.0	14.7	19.9	31.6	63.5	55.2	(NA)	(NA)	(NA)	(NA)
Special district or statutory authority [2]....	75.9	93.5	121.2	298.6	270.8	294.9	(NA)	(NA)	(NA)	(NA)
Municipality, county, or township..........	32.0	37.5	39.3	79.4	80.5	86.6	(NA)	(NA)	(NA)	(NA)
Issues for new capital....................	**97.9**	**102.4**	**154.3**	**223.8**	**279.0**	**278.5**	**172.6**	**159.5**	**156.0**	**140.8**
By use of proceeds:										
Education.................................	17.1	24.0	38.7	71.0	60.3	60.4	37.4	34.1	37.1	36.2
Transportation.............................	11.8	11.9	19.7	25.4	23.7	32.3	18.9	20.5	23.3	16.0
Utilities and conservation....................	10.0	9.6	11.9	9.9	14.9	22.3	16.7	11.5	6.4	5.0
Industrial aid.............................	6.6	6.6	7.1	18.6	27.5	35.7	16.5	21.3	11.9	12.6
Other purposes.............................	31.7	30.8	47.3	60.6	105.1	92.4	50.1	48.3	60.1	54.5

NA Not Available [1] Par amounts of long-term issues based on date of sale. [2] Includes school districts.

Source: Board of Governors of the Federal Reserve System, Business Finance, "New Security Issues, State and Local Governments," <http://www.federalreserve.gov/econresdata/statisticsdata.htm>, accessed June 2015.

Table 470. State and Local Governments—Total Revenue and Expenditures by State: 2000 to 2012

[In millions of dollars (1,942,328 represents $1,942,328,000,000). For fiscal year ending in year shown; see text, this section. These data cannot be used to compute the deficit or surplus for any single government, as these are estimates for all state and local governments within a state area. For further information, see the *2006 Government Finance and Employment Classification Manual* at <http://www.census.gov/govs/classification/>]

State	Revenue				Expenditures			
	2000	2005	2010	2012	2000	2005	2010	2012
United States.............	**1,942,328**	**2,528,546**	**3,180,023**	**3,033,555**	**1,746,943**	**2,368,316**	**3,115,172**	**3,151,703**
Alabama...................	25,726	33,377	42,189	43,635	25,319	31,752	**42,255**	**41,809**
Alaska....................	10,525	11,404	15,643	18,250	8,628	10,027	14,450	14,683
Arizona...................	27,778	41,057	54,099	51,803	27,293	39,458	53,432	51,092
Arkansas.................	13,833	18,866	24,539	23,502	12,245	16,682	22,798	24,277
California.................	270,380	381,059	453,354	411,775	236,645	342,546	432,363	448,671
Colorado.................	29,603	38,915	49,260	47,422	26,173	35,063	48,630	49,119
Connecticut.............	25,828	30,490	39,427	39,951	24,011	29,631	39,311	41,502
Delaware.................	6,224	7,637	9,831	9,821	5,153	7,595	9,745	10,499
District of Columbia.......	6,383	10,046	11,644	13,099	6,527	8,947	13,682	13,815
Florida...................	92,402	135,491	166,817	155,390	84,301	130,860	163,536	157,484
Georgia..................	49,310	60,297	76,370	72,604	43,517	60,730	78,158	78,433
Hawaii...................	8,488	11,000	14,666	13,750	8,254	10,534	14,340	14,708
Idaho....................	7,590	10,004	12,490	11,590	6,404	8,915	12,054	11,444
Illinois...................	80,695	99,670	126,384	118,764	74,727	97,723	129,518	129,267
Indiana..................	32,716	44,302	54,803	53,649	31,250	42,164	53,247	52,405
Iowa.....................	17,220	23,204	31,055	31,878	17,275	21,486	29,537	31,795
Kansas..................	16,235	19,990	26,330	26,160	14,419	18,948	26,536	26,561
Kentucky................	25,200	28,069	37,560	35,773	21,473	27,308	38,595	39,616
Louisiana................	27,109	35,858	47,078	42,028	25,018	32,578	48,755	48,079
Maine...................	8,554	11,383	12,557	11,771	7,652	10,207	12,286	12,522
Maryland................	33,949	45,076	57,493	55,661	30,598	41,373	57,485	61,734
Massachusetts...........	46,103	62,019	76,100	73,038	44,362	57,862	76,679	78,612
Michigan................	70,112	81,138	93,819	90,104	61,506	76,063	90,935	88,534
Minnesota...............	38,785	45,465	57,410	56,215	35,424	42,936	55,975	56,749
Mississippi..............	16,672	21,113	28,690	26,779	15,379	20,041	27,216	27,753
Missouri.................	31,635	41,340	51,592	49,141	27,953	37,186	50,040	50,809
Montana.................	5,643	7,438	9,784	10,021	4,983	6,412	9,296	9,378
Nebraska................	11,650	15,905	20,121	20,231	10,831	14,332	19,315	20,080
Nevada..................	11,885	18,953	22,838	22,305	11,230	17,405	23,856	22,817
New Hampshire..........	6,948	8,911	11,581	10,857	6,222	8,679	11,439	11,397
New Jersey..............	62,331	79,126	99,751	91,910	54,590	78,522	102,667	101,849
New Mexico.............	13,073	16,656	21,998	19,734	11,195	15,427	22,372	21,095
New York................	188,907	234,689	313,781	295,510	171,858	226,867	295,467	303,859
North Carolina...........	50,542	64,813	86,699	87,511	46,135	60,080	79,955	83,399
North Dakota............	4,495	5,239	7,890	11,293	4,041	4,794	6,746	7,992
Ohio.....................	80,074	102,498	123,289	108,456	68,418	91,972	113,844	112,765
Oklahoma...............	18,760	24,552	32,939	32,408	15,962	22,044	31,338	31,284
Oregon..................	28,644	32,406	41,031	37,433	24,086	29,084	39,506	39,933
Pennsylvania............	80,546	103,692	124,379	120,127	75,624	101,484	130,085	129,346
Rhode Island............	7,427	9,731	11,726	11,218	6,432	9,226	11,303	11,446
South Carolina..........	23,467	33,278	42,509	40,183	23,436	33,012	42,800	41,543
South Dakota............	4,277	5,857	6,941	6,844	3,760	4,973	6,845	6,931
Tennessee...............	33,625	44,888	54,297	55,198	32,010	42,800	53,554	55,696
Texas...................	120,666	162,806	209,930	221,410	109,634	151,960	218,807	219,215
Utah....................	14,954	19,183	24,149	24,054	13,044	17,247	24,552	25,617
Vermont.................	4,019	5,393	7,016	7,442	3,766	5,172	6,781	6,933
Virginia..................	44,175	56,658	71,093	67,182	38,092	51,529	67,673	71,032
Washington..............	46,372	57,510	71,623	69,231	41,794	55,800	75,167	75,075
West Virginia............	10,760	14,587	16,993	16,582	9,990	12,110	15,685	16,489
Wisconsin...............	43,003	48,235	66,291	53,153	34,559	43,146	55,839	55,814
Wyoming................	7,030	7,269	10,176	9,711	3,743	5,619	8,720	8,744

Source: U.S. Census Bureau, Federal, State, and Local Governments, Government Finance Statistics, "Annual Surveys of State and Local Government Finances," <http://www.census.gov/govs/local/>, accessed March 2015.

Table 471. State and Local Governments—Revenue by State: 2012

[In millions of dollars (3,033,555 represents $3,033,555,000,000). For fiscal year ending in year shown; see text, this section]

State	Total revenue	General revenue Total	Intergovernmental from federal government	General revenue from own sources Total	Select taxes Total	Property	Sales and gross receipt	Individual income	Corporation income	Total	Current charges Total	Education	Hospitals	Sewerage	Miscellaneous revenue Total	Interest earnings	Special assessments	Utility and liquor stores	Insurance trust revenue
U.S.	3,033,555	2,598,043	584,499	2,013,544	1,388,155	446,099	476,447	307,335	49,031	625,389	426,780	114,895	123,504	47,276	198,609	50,913	7,402	160,075	275,437
AL	43,635	33,822	9,192	24,630	14,215	2,553	6,800	3,118	413	10,415	8,346	2,406	4,325	484	2,069	382	9	3,232	6,581
AK	18,250	17,172	3,162	14,010	8,668	1,506	541	—	663	5,342	1,378	210	326	84	3,964	773	14	362	716
AZ	51,803	43,423	11,360	32,063	22,193	6,848	10,762	3,094	648	9,870	6,979	2,193	1,939	860	2,891	566	89	4,598	3,782
AR	23,502	21,166	6,269	14,896	10,394	1,950	5,113	2,402	404	4,503	3,111	1,017	1,140	272	1,392	301	35	1,003	1,333
CA	411,775	332,764	65,268	267,496	183,660	51,566	55,926	55,024	7,949	83,836	60,630	9,382	17,526	6,407	23,206	5,767	1,646	24,854	54,156
CO	47,422	40,825	7,646	33,179	21,187	6,951	7,601	4,876	492	11,992	8,322	2,783	2,026	792	3,670	1,110	141	2,737	3,860
CT	39,951	36,111	6,398	29,713	24,962	9,427	6,695	7,371	629	4,750	2,932	1,255	316	377	1,818	660	39	813	3,028
DE	9,821	8,794	1,890	6,904	4,196	696	505	1,249	267	2,708	1,438	740	9	151	1,270	169	24	436	591
DC	13,099	11,142	3,474	7,668	5,934	1,878	1,539	1,491	466	1,734	652	29	114	262	1,082	91	—	1,041	916
FL	155,390	133,383	27,261	106,123	64,614	24,598	32,726	—	2,003	41,509	28,981	4,223	7,090	3,026	12,528	2,192	1,972	9,628	12,379
GA	72,604	63,378	15,363	48,015	32,308	10,360	12,318	8,142	591	15,707	11,703	3,145	4,000	1,242	4,004	497	42	4,801	4,425
HI	13,750	12,798	2,631	10,167	7,411	1,311	3,975	1,541	80	2,756	2,146	409	562	377	610	39	20	340	612
ID	11,590	10,176	2,666	7,510	4,855	1,393	1,688	1,213	189	2,655	1,911	485	533	199	744	165	53	337	1,077
IL	118,764	104,960	19,086	85,874	66,475	25,531	18,336	15,512	3,495	19,399	12,114	4,297	1,659	1,195	7,285	1,987	573	4,071	9,733
IN	53,649	47,760	11,115	36,646	24,514	6,489	10,098	6,098	795	12,132	8,945	3,680	3,013	1,087	3,186	1,110	23	2,185	3,704
IA	31,878	28,087	6,741	21,345	13,563	4,540	4,557	3,127	426	7,782	5,963	1,759	2,789	496	1,818	346	19	1,312	2,479
KS	26,160	23,600	4,332	19,268	12,508	3,926	4,819	2,894	318	6,760	4,802	1,357	2,162	374	1,958	581	123	1,454	1,105
KY	35,773	30,968	8,606	22,361	15,030	3,130	5,610	4,638	690	7,331	5,149	1,459	1,755	533	2,183	1,002	10	1,674	3,131
LA	42,028	39,130	12,116	27,014	16,954	3,638	9,071	2,475	290	10,059	6,426	1,234	3,374	406	3,633	1,049	58	1,240	1,658
ME	11,771	11,197	3,058	8,139	6,137	2,376	1,755	1,442	232	2,002	1,304	378	155	165	697	230	5	132	442
MD	55,661	51,386	11,499	39,886	30,207	8,058	7,934	11,478	880	9,680	6,399	2,581	179	1,036	3,281	601	25	1,182	3,092
MA	73,038	64,244	14,534	49,710	37,042	13,658	7,619	11,955	2,002	12,668	7,521	2,599	592	1,518	5,147	1,905	26	3,291	5,503
MI	90,104	75,862	19,828	56,035	36,231	13,279	12,925	7,347	804	19,804	14,207	5,415	3,470	1,930	5,597	1,402	208	3,516	10,725
MN	56,215	49,321	10,626	38,695	28,112	7,861	9,443	7,988	1,066	10,584	6,981	2,364	1,591	743	3,603	868	355	2,463	4,431
MS	26,779	24,150	8,265	15,885	9,713	2,594	4,502	1,501	396	6,172	5,124	1,159	3,092	224	1,048	213	10	1,171	1,459
MO	49,141	42,079	11,426	30,653	20,411	5,760	7,608	5,453	378	10,243	6,936	2,404	2,258	723	3,307	1,105	53	2,334	4,728
MT	10,021	7,894	2,470	5,424	3,622	1,379	553	900	132	1,802	1,101	460	97	91	701	242	83	204	1,923
NE	20,231	15,385	3,575	11,810	8,125	2,954	2,484	1,838	234	3,685	2,662	839	845	186	1,023	284	39	4,007	840
NV	22,305	18,065	3,400	14,665	10,620	2,843	6,173	—	—	4,044	2,815	489	617	419	1,229	233	69	995	3,245
NH	10,857	9,421	1,847	7,574	5,271	3,412	875	82	521	2,303	1,306	625	15	129	997	422	1	679	757
NJ	91,910	84,333	14,471	69,862	53,851	25,885	12,170	11,128	1,981	16,011	10,330	3,660	1,252	1,702	5,681	1,319	8	2,098	5,478
NM	19,734	18,074	5,619	12,455	7,553	1,425	3,690	1,150	281	4,902	2,292	874	874	180	2,610	648	13	590	1,071
NY	295,510	254,741	55,301	199,440	151,733	47,577	38,104	47,492	10,523	47,707	27,676	4,363	8,059	2,485	20,031	5,110	127	14,684	26,084
NC	87,511	71,842	17,343	54,498	34,451	8,893	12,064	10,384	1,220	20,047	15,696	3,411	8,380	1,366	4,351	896	25	4,885	10,785
ND	11,293	10,405	1,973	8,432	6,627	792	1,776	433	216	1,805	1,112	430	6	50	693	238	91	163	725
OH	108,456	92,461	23,244	69,216	46,828	13,561	15,159	13,429	351	22,388	15,520	5,824	3,893	2,022	6,868	1,472	245	3,662	12,334
OK	32,408	28,584	7,833	20,750	13,278	2,292	5,798	2,774	446	7,472	4,842	1,972	1,247	352	2,630	486	18	1,814	2,011
OR	37,433	32,670	8,913	23,757	14,777	5,034	1,771	5,826	485	8,980	6,470	1,892	1,724	906	2,510	526	67	1,866	2,897
PA	120,127	103,493	23,463	80,030	57,034	17,069	18,379	14,312	2,144	22,996	16,343	6,206	2,448	2,432	6,653	1,995	91	4,537	12,097
RI	11,218	9,860	2,497	7,362	5,229	2,347	1,503	1,081	123	2,134	1,100	456	5	191	1,034	372	8	220	1,138
SC	40,183	33,758	7,333	26,425	14,265	4,882	4,851	3,097	253	12,160	9,290	2,124	5,313	614	2,871	740	18	3,461	2,963
SD	6,844	6,116	1,817	4,299	2,895	1,008	1,531	—	60	1,403	776	338	53	88	627	265	9	348	380
TN	55,198	42,582	12,107	30,476	19,978	5,134	11,417	182	1,226	10,498	7,113	1,768	2,659	819	3,385	737	96	8,870	3,745
TX	221,410	184,859	41,569	143,290	97,737	40,310	45,368	—	—	45,552	29,943	8,369	9,504	3,496	15,609	4,922	274	12,864	23,687
UT	24,054	20,770	5,155	15,615	9,557	2,679	3,661	2,466	259	6,058	4,476	1,489	1,312	362	1,582	352	73	2,132	1,152

See footnotes at end of table.

Table 471. State and Local Governments—Revenue by State: 2012-Continued.

See headnote on page 302.

State	Total revenue	General revenue																Utility and liquor stores	Insurance trust revenue
		Total	Intergovernmental from federal government	General revenue from own sources	Select taxes					Current charges and miscellaneous revenue									
					Total[1]	Property	Sales and gross receipt	Individual income	Corporation income	Total	Current charges				Miscellaneous revenue				
											Total[1]	Education	Hospitals	Sewerage	Total[1]	Interest earnings	Special assessments		
VT...	7,442	6,328	1,993	4,335	3,215	1,379	986	598	97	1,120	734	494	—	66	386	128	5	280	834
VA...	67,182	61,344	10,781	50,562	33,177	11,339	8,316	10,216	839	17,386	12,004	4,005	3,313	1,245	5,382	1,515	43	2,384	3,455
WA...	69,231	56,535	11,606	44,929	29,434	9,224	17,868	—	—	15,495	11,719	2,717	3,290	2,000	3,776	938	292	6,630	6,066
WV...	16,582	15,371	4,518	10,854	7,062	1,435	2,684	1,756	192	3,792	2,287	824	323	247	1,504	235	31	324	887
WI...	53,153	46,659	9,520	37,139	26,496	10,051	7,436	6,762	934	10,643	7,287	2,336	1,327	801	3,356	1,057	84	1,862	4,632
WY...	9,711	8,797	2,339	6,458	3,846	1,320	1,364	—	—	2,613	1,484	183	949	65	1,129	669	17	309	605

— Represents or rounds to zero. [1] Includes items not shown separately.

Source: U.S. Census Bureau, Federal, State, and Local Governments, Government Finance Statistics, "Annual Surveys of State and Local Government Finances," <http://www.census.gov/govs/local/>, accessed March 2015.

State and Local Government Finances and Employment

Table 472. State and Local Governments—Expenditures and Debt by State: 2012

[In millions of dollars (3,151,703 represents $3,151,703,000,000). For fiscal year ending in year shown; see text, this section]

State	Total expenditures	General expenditures — Total[1]	Direct general expenditures — Total[1]	Education	Public welfare	Health	Hospitals	Highways	Police protection	Corrections	Natural resources	Parks and recreation	Housing and community development	Sewerage	Solid waste	Governmental administration	Interest on general debt	Utility and liquor store expenditures	Insurance trust expenditures	Total debt outstanding
U.S.	3,151,703	2,591,475	2,587,317	869,196	485,588	84,398	155,755	158,562	96,972	72,577	29,009	37,404	53,141	51,712	24,247	123,932	109,118	213,718	346,510	2,942,295
AL	41,809	34,900	34,900	12,645	6,283	932	4,540	2,244	1,156	719	260	386	500	365	263	1,457	936	3,230	3,679	29,468
AK	14,683	12,648	12,648	3,304	1,949	248	383	1,279	321	316	347	120	314	91	99	939	410	707	1,328	9,497
AZ	51,092	41,567	41,567	13,519	8,132	2,160	1,472	2,340	2,072	1,545	510	610	573	939	369	2,179	1,666	4,841	4,683	49,066
AR	24,277	21,321	21,321	8,275	5,186	337	1,092	1,441	587	558	262	202	217	277	218	1,018	502	1,035	1,921	13,961
CA	448,671	351,548	348,787	107,730	60,432	13,175	22,876	16,693	14,882	13,691	5,327	5,365	8,544	6,280	3,956	19,893	16,657	36,561	60,562	419,751
CO	49,119	39,748	39,745	13,213	5,554	1,225	2,399	2,387	1,595	1,244	422	1,181	777	872	107	2,373	2,162	3,379	5,991	51,395
CT	41,502	34,372	34,372	12,255	6,467	802	1,276	1,700	1,118	685	190	284	877	607	367	1,788	1,905	1,519	5,611	42,827
DE	10,499	9,043	9,043	3,339	1,892	446	50	715	304	282	98	64	165	200	76	553	328	532	924	8,234
DC	13,815	10,765	10,765	2,372	2,864	444	230	526	564	241	45	203	547	493	105	440	500	2,543	507	11,604
FL	157,484	134,653	134,653	37,372	22,910	4,928	8,451	7,957	7,318	4,059	3,463	2,845	2,743	3,188	2,385	6,557	4,986	11,160	11,671	146,922
GA	78,433	64,594	64,594	25,277	10,426	1,981	4,991	3,097	2,424	2,283	478	826	1,333	1,310	623	3,354	1,459	6,201	7,638	55,785
HI	14,708	12,315	12,315	3,503	2,022	507	753	601	389	198	95	265	206	244	307	721	535	937	1,456	14,025
ID	11,444	9,975	9,975	3,116	2,056	222	539	880	400	305	255	129	131	194	137	576	255	343	1,126	6,247
IL	129,267	102,728	102,728	35,372	16,155	3,136	2,887	7,197	4,601	2,061	642	2,657	2,175	2,057	515	4,761	6,286	7,055	19,484	146,233
IN	52,405	45,860	45,832	16,913	8,595	893	3,497	2,822	1,150	959	363	700	1,111	1,205	265	1,900	1,950	2,541	4,004	49,563
IA	31,795	27,930	27,930	9,803	5,050	600	3,105	2,370	689	523	588	361	249	689	273	1,024	649	1,386	2,478	18,170
KS	26,561	22,954	22,953	8,427	3,485	652	2,239	1,806	738	481	293	308	274	334	148	1,107	1,057	1,428	2,179	26,685
KY	39,616	32,742	32,742	11,632	7,185	991	1,655	2,490	680	739	358	278	449	773	214	1,460	1,915	2,116	4,759	42,491
LA	48,079	42,526	42,526	12,634	6,278	759	4,496	2,761	1,552	1,326	946	759	1,431	892	356	2,130	1,677	1,435	4,118	35,946
ME	12,522	11,277	11,271	3,353	2,937	537	216	889	246	194	171	131	340	193	117	500	356	166	1,080	8,638
MD	61,734	53,848	53,848	18,751	10,078	1,750	486	5,060	2,140	1,750	520	852	1,393	919	645	2,738	1,837	2,406	5,481	46,107
MA	78,612	63,613	63,393	19,633	14,985	1,233	1,530	2,609	2,136	1,056	315	397	2,937	1,142	413	2,555	3,607	4,904	10,096	96,187
MI	88,534	73,807	73,792	28,695	13,147	4,282	3,723	3,282	2,356	2,232	376	783	1,335	1,988	457	2,854	2,762	4,073	10,654	76,352
MN	56,749	48,666	48,666	15,438	13,139	964	2,150	3,571	1,636	864	703	1,041	922	819	339	2,089	1,991	2,639	5,443	48,446
MS	27,753	24,136	24,136	7,445	5,083	462	3,401	1,737	662	558	302	255	326	405	182	1,003	558	1,159	2,459	14,584
MO	50,809	42,902	42,820	14,534	8,336	1,878	3,284	2,936	1,680	862	399	615	656	840	164	1,501	1,693	2,790	5,117	46,288
MT	9,378	8,200	8,199	2,578	1,379	272	160	1,051	275	238	287	73	113	117	79	536	202	263	916	5,754
NE	20,080	14,911	14,867	5,940	2,325	445	945	1,220	405	362	353	220	194	227	89	577	342	4,161	1,009	15,102
NV	22,817	18,539	18,537	5,406	2,461	363	1,020	1,682	1,099	705	364	609	163	441	30	1,207	969	1,450	2,829	29,050
NH	11,397	10,034	10,034	3,840	1,915	121	45	743	352	183	67	81	212	141	116	511	503	610	753	10,769
NJ	101,849	83,049	83,030	31,483	14,933	1,579	2,469	4,126	3,324	2,075	624	871	1,402	1,483	1,002	3,364	3,499	3,446	15,354	102,886
NM	21,095	18,140	18,140	6,290	4,044	545	1,140	1,035	648	602	282	330	190	175	191	1,070	499	753	2,202	16,506
NY	303,859	238,465	237,735	71,490	50,947	6,683	15,584	10,266	9,284	5,772	719	2,663	5,914	4,313	2,998	10,178	11,511	29,255	36,140	340,093
NC	83,399	70,264	70,264	23,692	12,681	2,800	8,103	3,916	2,852	1,892	766	920	1,449	1,461	787	2,621	2,246	5,352	7,783	50,779
ND	7,992	7,210	7,210	2,353	956	166	53	1,293	172	143	384	184	86	73	53	287	168	269	513	4,744
OH	112,765	91,436	91,423	32,530	19,993	3,777	4,353	5,369	3,224	1,819	435	1,157	2,341	2,039	478	4,989	2,771	3,962	17,367	81,238
OK	31,284	26,646	26,589	9,446	5,783	1,028	1,246	2,314	928	655	250	411	477	335	196	1,148	711	1,911	2,727	18,790
OR	39,933	32,064	32,064	10,339	5,784	1,318	1,881	1,861	1,150	1,071	543	556	637	907	128	1,942	1,216	2,374	5,495	34,573
PA	129,346	107,147	107,002	35,323	24,582	4,978	3,072	8,675	3,245	3,303	755	939	2,083	2,593	856	6,074	4,628	6,181	16,019	129,428
RI	11,446	9,310	9,292	3,133	2,255	175	70	440	354	199	66	72	223	129	91	503	626	345	1,791	11,934
SC	41,543	34,487	34,487	12,134	5,870	1,127	5,157	1,562	1,055	676	217	454	527	581	320	1,417	1,464	3,273	3,783	40,395
SD	6,931	6,101	6,101	2,001	943	203	76	945	169	165	171	157	107	118	47	344	205	366	464	5,857
TN	55,696	42,864	42,863	13,680	10,205	1,277	3,089	2,485	1,664	1,049	369	475	988	746	356	1,975	1,132	9,154	3,678	37,046
TX	219,215	183,968	183,968	70,749	30,798	4,613	13,616	11,326	6,469	5,473	1,735	2,147	2,193	3,422	1,286	7,197	9,645	16,349	18,898	270,737
UT	25,617	21,256	21,256	8,207	3,025	507	1,113	1,962	658	518	202	515	373	437	160	1,333	582	2,663	1,699	19,721

See footnotes at end of table.

Table 472. State and Local Governments—Expenditures and Debt by State: 2012-Continued.

See headnote on page 304.

State	Total expenditures	General expenditures Total[1]	Direct general expenditures Total[1]	Education	Public welfare	Health	Hospitals	Highways	Police protection	Corrections	Natural resources	Parks and recreation	Housing and community development	Sewerage	Solid waste	Governmental administration	Interest on general debt	Utility and liquor store expenditures	Insurance trust expenditures	Total debt outstanding
VT....	6,933	6,237	6,237	2,375	1,500	193	16	671	177	126	89	51	140	88	41	236	152	308	387	4,575
VA....	71,032	62,783	62,781	23,191	10,080	1,650	3,662	4,221	2,083	2,167	289	933	1,015	1,410	638	3,123	2,452	2,710	5,540	65,332
WA....	75,075	58,368	58,364	19,284	8,530	2,556	4,522	4,135	1,627	1,559	996	1,027	1,262	1,889	673	2,550	2,668	8,594	8,113	75,592
WV....	16,489	14,567	14,567	5,507	3,247	361	372	1,294	364	334	200	183	159	277	78	866	351	442	1,480	10,923
WI....	55,814	47,265	47,265	16,989	9,944	1,787	1,301	3,823	1,779	1,545	733	606	351	921	375	1,895	1,857	2,104	6,445	43,602
WY....	8,744	7,727	7,721	2,519	783	329	969	760	220	215	382	155	21	76	79	518	78	340	677	2,397

[1] Includes items not shown separately.

Source: U.S. Census Bureau, Federal, State, and Local Governments, Government Finance Statistics, "Annual Surveys of State and Local Government Finances," <http://www.census.gov/govs/local/>, accessed March 2015.

Table 473. Estimated State and Local Taxes Paid by a Family of Three for Largest City in Selected States: 2013

[Data based on average family of three (two wage earners and one school age child) owning their own home and living in a city where taxes apply. Comprises state and local sales, income, auto, and real estate taxes. For definition of median, see Guide to Tabular Presentation]

City	Total taxes paid by gross family income level (dollars)					Total taxes paid as percent of income				
	$25,000	$50,000	$75,000	$100,000	$150,000	$25,000	$50,000	$75,000	$100,000	$150,000
Albuquerque, NM.......	1,566	3,721	6,543	9,035	13,814	6.3	7.4	8.7	9.0	9.2
Anchorage, AK.........	2,142	2,782	4,385	5,843	8,643	8.6	5.6	5.8	5.8	5.8
Atlanta, GA.............	3,012	4,331	7,381	10,095	15,696	12.0	8.7	9.8	10.1	10.5
Baltimore, MD..........	2,324	6,323	10,470	14,306	21,924	9.3	12.6	14.0	14.3	14.6
Boston, MA.............	3,582	4,429	7,858	11,087	17,222	14.3	8.9	10.5	11.1	11.5
Charlotte, NC..........	2,928	5,005	8,364	11,432	17,100	11.7	10.0	11.2	11.4	11.4
Chicago, IL.............	3,677	5,262	8,335	11,088	16,255	14.7	10.5	11.1	11.1	10.8
Columbus, OH..........	2,546	5,850	9,340	12,742	19,374	10.2	11.7	12.5	12.7	12.9
Denver, CO.............	2,330	3,501	5,726	7,667	11,578	9.3	7.0	7.6	7.7	7.7
Detroit, MI.............	2,477	6,609	11,163	15,051	22,791	9.9	13.2	14.9	15.1	15.2
Honolulu, HI............	4,111	2,931	5,445	7,766	12,032	16.4	5.9	7.3	7.8	8.0
Houston, TX............	2,330	4,149	6,013	7,985	11,316	9.3	8.3	8.0	8.0	7.5
Indianapolis, IN........	2,872	4,852	7,516	10,834	16,440	11.5	9.7	10.0	10.8	11.0
Jacksonville, FL........	2,345	2,725	4,690	6,324	9,365	9.4	5.4	6.3	6.3	6.2
Kansas City, MO........	2,661	4,456	7,660	10,263	16,100	10.6	8.9	10.2	10.3	10.7
Las Vegas, NV..........	2,637	2,976	4,583	5,838	8,437	10.5	6.0	6.1	5.8	5.6
Los Angeles, CA.......	3,904	6,247	9,838	13,357	21,596	15.6	12.5	13.1	13.4	14.4
Memphis, TN...........	2,699	2,689	4,077	4,979	6,849	10.8	5.4	5.4	5.0	4.6
Milwaukee, WI.........	2,127	7,364	12,066	16,124	24,488	8.5	14.7	16.1	16.1	16.3
New Orleans, LA......	2,727	4,140	7,006	9,459	14,490	10.9	8.3	9.3	9.5	9.7
New York City, NY.....	3,336	5,159	8,728	12,142	19,065	13.3	10.3	11.6	12.1	12.7
Oklahoma City, OK.....	2,160	4,370	7,122	9,486	14,103	8.6	8.7	9.5	9.5	9.4
Omaha, NE.............	1,872	4,841	8,156	11,476	18,646	7.5	9.7	10.9	11.5	12.4
Philadelphia, PA.......	4,210	10,433	15,762	20,866	30,659	16.8	20.9	21.0	20.9	20.4
Phoenix, AZ............	2,552	3,974	6,525	8,668	13,337	10.2	7.9	8.7	8.7	8.9
Portland, OR...........	1,573	5,083	8,540	12,050	18,602	6.3	10.2	11.4	12.1	12.4
Seattle, WA............	2,860	3,244	5,001	6,460	8,969	11.4	6.5	6.7	6.5	6.0
Virginia Beach, VA.....	3,069	4,150	6,955	9,432	14,707	12.3	8.3	9.3	9.4	9.8
Washington, DC........	3,112	3,417	6,174	8,617	13,740	12.4	6.8	8.2	8.6	9.2
Wichita, KS............	2,053	4,181	6,998	9,425	14,397	8.2	8.4	9.3	9.4	9.6
Average [1].............	**2,512**	**4,669**	**7,719**	**10,489**	**16,083**	**10.0**	**9.3**	**10.3**	**10.5**	**10.7**
Median [1]...............	**2,552**	**4,331**	**7,298**	**10,095**	**15,520**	**10.2**	**8.7**	**9.7**	**10.1**	**10.3**

[1] Based on selected cities and District of Columbia. For complete list of cities, see Table 474.

Source: Government of the District of Columbia, Office of the Chief Financial Officer, *Tax Rates and Tax Burdens in the District of Columbia – A Nationwide Comparison 2013*, November 2014, and earlier reports. See also <http://cfo.dc.gov/>.

Table 474. Residential Property Tax Rates for Largest City in Each State: 2013

[The real property tax is a function of housing values, real estate tax rates, assessment levels, homeowner exemptions and credits. Effective rate is the amount each jurisdiction considers based upon assessment level used. Assessment level is ratio of assessed value to assumed market value. Nominal rates represent the "announced" rates levied by the jurisdiction]

City	Effective tax rate per $100		Assessment level (percent)	Nominal rate per $100	City	Effective tax rate per $100		Assessment level (percent)	Nominal rate per $100
	Rank	Rate				Rank	Rate		
Detroit, MI.............	1	3.39	50.0	6.78	Louisville, KY.............	28	1.32	100.0	1.32
Philadelphia, PA........	2	3.13	32.0	9.77	Wilmington, DE.........	29	1.32	32.5	4.07
Milwaukee, WI.........	3	3.13	100.0	3.13	Boston, MA.............	30	1.31	100.0	1.31
Bridgeport, CT.........	4	2.93	70.0	4.19	Albuquerque, NM........	31	1.30	33.0	3.91
Indianapolis, IN........	5	2.91	100.0	2.91	Phoenix, AZ............	32	1.29	10.0	12.89
Newark, NJ.............	6	2.62	89.0	2.95	Charlotte, NC...........	33	1.28	100.0	1.28
Houston, TX............	7	2.56	100.0	2.56	Kansas City, MO........	34	1.20	19.0	6.55
Des Moines, IA.........	8	2.55	54.0	4.69	Oklahoma City, OK......	35	1.20	11.0	11.57
Columbus, OH.........	9	2.29	34.0	6.80	Los Angeles, CA........	36	1.14	100.0	1.14
Manchester, NH.......	10	2.22	100.0	2.22	Seattle, WA............	37	0.94	90.9	1.03
Omaha, NE.............	11	2.11	96.0	2.20	Virginia Beach, VA.......	38	0.92	99.0	0.93
Burlington, VT.........	12	2.10	88.2	0.02	Billings, MT.............	39	0.92	1.4	66.75
Baltimore, MD..........	13	2.09	93.0	2.25	Salt Lake City, UT......	40	0.92	55.0	1.67
Columbia, SC..........	14	2.04	4.0	50.90	Washington DC.........	41	0.85	100.0	0.85
Portland, ME..........	15	1.94	100.0	1.94	Memphis, TN...........	42	0.85	25.0	3.40
Providence, RI.........	16	1.93	100.0	1.93	New York City, NY......	43	0.85	4.0	19.13
Jacksonville, FL........	17	1.80	100.0	1.80	Charleston, WV.........	44	0.82	60.0	1.36
Jackson, MS............	18	1.74	10.0	17.39	Denver, CO.............	45	0.69	8.0	8.70
Atlanta, GA............	19	1.59	37.0	4.35	Cheyenne, WY..........	46	0.67	10.0	7.10
Anchorage, AK.........	20	1.56	100.0	1.56	Chicago, IL.............	47	0.55	10.0	5.46
Minneapolis, MN.......	21	1.51	96.0	1.58	Honolulu, HI............	48	0.35	100.0	0.35
Sioux Falls, SD.........	22	1.49	85.0	1.75	Boise, ID...............	49	0.02	93.0	0.02
New Orleans, LA.......	23	1.49	10.0	0.15	Las Vegas, NV..........	50	0.01	35.0	3.12
Wichita, KS............	24	1.42	12.0	12.31	Birmingham, AL.........	51	0.01	10.0	0.07
Little Rock, AR.........	25	1.40	20.0	7.01					
Portland, OR...........	26	1.40	63.7	2.20	**Unweighted average...**	(X)	**1.52**	**62.0**	**6.90**
Fargo, ND.............	27	1.39	4.3	32.57	**Median.................**	(X)	**1.40**	**85.0**	**2.91**

X Not applicable.

Source: Government of the District of Columbia, Office of the Chief Financial Officer, *Tax Rates and Tax Burdens in the District of Columbia—A Nationwide Comparison 2013*, November 2014. See also <http://cfo.dc.gov/>.

Table 475. Gross Revenue From Parimutuel and Amusement Taxes and Lotteries by State: 2011 to 2013

[In millions of dollars (61,552.2 represents $61,552,200,000). For fiscal years; see text, this section]

State	2011, total gross revenue	2012, total gross revenue	2013 Total gross revenue	2013 Amuse-ment taxes [1]	2013 Pari-mutuel taxes	2013 Lottery revenue Total [2]	Apportionment of funds Prizes	Apportionment of funds Adminis-tration	Apportionment of funds Proceeds available from ticket sales
United States.........	**61,552.2**	**66,344.1**	**69,392.9**	**6,879.3**	**129.7**	**62,383.9**	**38,792.9**	**3,209.0**	**20,382.0**
Alabama..................	2.1	1.9	1.7	0.1	1.6	(X)	(X)	(X)	(X)
Alaska....................	8.3	7.7	8.4	8.4	(X)	(X)	(X)	(X)	(X)
Arizona..................	545.1	603.7	646.6	0.5	0.2	645.9	426.1	43.0	176.7
Arkansas................	456.9	478.0	453.8	36.1	3.1	414.6	292.1	34.8	87.7
California................	3,452.1	4,091.5	4,460.0	–	14.1	4,445.9	2,652.1	224.1	1,569.7
Colorado................	575.8	597.5	629.0	104.3	0.6	524.1	345.6	39.6	138.8
Connecticut............	1,376.1	1,408.3	1,449.2	382.4	6.9	1,059.9	699.1	43.3	317.6
Delaware...............	451.3	415.4	453.0	–	0.1	453.0	99.3	44.5	309.2
Florida..................	3,928.5	4,375.0	4,916.5	165.8	9.2	4,741.6	3,162.9	147.6	1,431.1
Georgia.................	3,109.3	3,335.6	3,407.0	–	–	3,407.0	2,332.5	145.6	929.0
Hawaii..................	–	–	0.0	–	–	(X)	(X)	(X)	(X)
Idaho...................	136.2	163.4	183.4	–	1.2	182.2	122.9	11.2	48.2
Illinois..................	2,762.7	3,231.0	3,437.4	598.9	5.9	2,832.6	1,743.7	317.7	771.2
Indiana.................	1,603.0	1,627.8	1,627.3	754.2	2.5	870.5	581.3	63.7	225.5
Iowa....................	552.1	609.8	613.9	270.7	4.0	339.3	200.8	52.6	85.9
Kansas..................	219.0	232.1	230.9	0.4	–	230.5	138.6	19.7	72.2
Kentucky................	676.9	720.7	763.7	0.2	4.8	758.7	494.9	37.8	226.0
Louisiana...............	1,039.2	1,081.9	1,102.5	675.2	4.7	422.6	236.2	26.0	160.5
Maine...................	232.7	244.5	266.1	51.2	2.1	212.9	143.9	14.9	54.1
Maryland...............	1,697.4	1,836.1	2,047.6	25.3	1.2	2,021.1	1,038.5	341.0	641.7
Massachusetts..........	4,172.0	4,467.3	4,569.7	2.7	1.8	4,565.2	3,523.9	94.3	947.0
Michigan................	2,258.5	2,328.2	2,382.7	117.0	4.7	2,260.9	1,493.4	70.8	696.7
Minnesota..............	510.6	531.4	564.8	37.3	0.5	527.0	365.8	25.4	135.8
Mississippi..............	147.0	152.1	139.6	139.6	–	(X)	(X)	(X)	(X)
Missouri................	1,379.4	1,421.7	1,496.8	379.8	–	1,117.0	753.0	50.0	314.0
Montana................	93.2	103.1	117.5	57.3	–	60.2	32.2	8.0	20.0
Nebraska...............	128.9	163.4	175.3	4.2	0.2	170.8	93.1	17.0	60.7
Nevada.................	885.8	910.8	921.9	921.9	–	(X)	(X)	(X)	(X)
New Hampshire.........	217.7	241.0	264.9	0.5	0.7	263.8	173.4	16.0	74.5
New Jersey.............	2,755.7	2,844.6	2,878.4	214.9	–	2,663.5	1,631.7	70.9	883.6
New Mexico............	200.1	185.1	207.6	67.4	0.9	139.3	79.5	18.3	41.4
New York...............	7,008.5	7,425.6	7,721.0	1.0	22.3	7,697.7	4,219.0	388.6	3,090.1
North Carolina..........	1,375.1	1,498.3	1,585.6	14.7	(X)	1,570.9	1,024.3	72.2	474.3
North Dakota...........	30.8	31.9	32.9	5.5	0.7	26.6	14.2	4.1	8.3
Ohio....................	2,447.2	2,593.8	2,762.7	225.4	6.2	2,531.0	1,668.0	99.9	763.1
Oklahoma..............	229.6	233.4	222.2	20.8	1.2	200.2	104.5	23.6	72.1
Oregon.................	839.8	849.9	866.4	–	2.1	864.2	206.8	70.2	587.2
Pennsylvania...........	4,336.2	4,755.1	4,901.6	1,447.2	13.1	3,441.3	2,299.0	72.3	1,070.0
Rhode Island...........	506.9	541.2	540.2	–	1.2	539.0	153.2	6.2	379.6
South Carolina..........	1,010.7	1,094.1	1,153.6	39.2	–	1,114.4	775.5	37.1	301.9
South Dakota...........	150.2	148.4	156.4	9.3	0.5	146.5	32.4	7.8	106.4
Tennessee..............	1,108.9	1,224.7	1,278.3	–	–	1,278.3	720.2	57.1	501.0
Texas...................	3,645.5	4,001.4	4,176.0	29.4	7.2	4,139.5	2,767.4	182.0	1,190.1
Utah....................	–	–	0.0	–	–	(X)	(X)	(X)	(X)
Vermont................	89.9	95.0	96.1	–	–	96.1	64.6	8.6	22.9
Virginia.................	1,398.9	1,525.4	1,594.3	0.1	–	1,594.3	1,025.2	80.7	488.4
Washington.............	480.3	503.5	535.6	–	1.6	534.0	339.4	50.0	144.7
West Virginia...........	817.2	863.6	786.4	70.3	2.3	713.9	116.2	32.9	564.7
Wisconsin...............	502.9	547.9	566.3	0.2	–	566.1	329.2	38.2	198.7
Wyoming................	0.1	0.1	0.1	–	0.1	(X)	(X)	(X)	(X)

– Represents or rounds to zero. X Not applicable. [1] Represents nonlicense taxes. [2] Excludes commissions.

Source: U.S. Census Bureau, "2013 Annual Survey of State Government Finances," <http://factfinder2.census.gov>, accessed June 2015. See also <http://www.census.gov/govs/state>.

Table 476. Lottery Sales—Type of Game and Proceeds: 1990 to 2014

[In millions of dollars (20,137 represents $20,137,000,000). For fiscal years]

Game	1990	1995	2000	2005	2010	2012	2013	2014
Total ticket sales......................	**20,137**	**32,147**	**37,201**	**52,055**	**60,846**	**68,175**	**68,467**	**70,653**
Instant [1]...............................	5,204	11,511	15,387	26,006	30,665	35,281	37,543	38,740
Three-digit [2]...........................	4,572	5,738	5,780	5,858	5,861	5,817	5,776	5,819
Four-digit [2]............................	1,302	1,918	2,273	2,869	3,424	3,553	3,561	3,665
Lotto [3].................................	8,563	10,594	9,339	9,828	10,879	11,905	12,179	12,169
Other [4]................................	497	2,388	4,423	7,493	10,017	11,620	9,408	10,260
State proceeds (net income) [5]..........	7,703	11,100	11,871	15,792	17,957	18,656	19,738	20,084

[1] Player scratches a latex section on ticket which reveals instantly whether ticket is a winner. [2] Players choose and bet on three or four digits, depending on game, with various payoffs for different straight order or mixed combination bets. [3] Players typically select six digits out of a large field of numbers. Varying prizes are offered for matching three through six numbers drawn by lottery. [4] Includes break-open tickets, spiel, keno, video lottery, etc. [5] Sales minus prizes and expenses equal net government income.

Source: TLF Publications, Inc. © 2015. All Rights Reserved.

Table 477. State Financial Resources, Expenditures, and Balances: 2013 and 2014

[In millions of dollars (1,689,542 represents $1,689,542,000,000). For fiscal year ending in year shown; see text; this section. General funds exclude special funds earmarked for particular purposes, such as highway trust funds and federal funds; they support most on-going broad-based state services, and are available for appropriation to support any governmental activity. Minus sign (-) indicates deficit]

| State | Expenditures by fund source | | | | State general fund | | | | | |
| | Total, 2013 actual | 2014 estimated | | | Resources [2,3] | | Expenditures [3] | | Balance [4] | |
		Total [1]	General fund	Federal fund	2013	2014 prelim.	2013	2014 prelim.	2013	2014 prelim.
United States......	**1,689,542**	**1,785,276**	**723,796**	**541,151**	**742,051**	**764,142**	**694,535**	**728,884**	**38,982**	**28,161**
Alabama............	24,520	24,388	7,835	9,288	7,468	7,836	7,164	7,522	304	–
Alaska...............	11,838	11,591	7,053	2,971	6,992	5,339	7,783	7,323	-978	-1,714
Arizona.............	28,297	29,534	8,848	12,837	9,558	9,386	8,463	8,812	896	574
Arkansas..........	21,445	22,743	4,865	6,511	4,728	4,944	4,728	4,944	–	–
California...........	211,432	229,987	100,711	81,059	98,800	104,077	96,562	100,711	2,527	3,903
Colorado...........	29,035	30,287	8,684	7,756	9,351	9,304	7,912	8,742	1,446	557
Connecticut.......	27,852	29,401	17,045	5,501	19,184	17,200	19,026	16,980	177	248
Delaware...........	9,162	9,608	3,794	1,903	4,294	4,209	3,659	3,794	636	414
Florida..............	63,971	74,240	26,690	25,416	27,604	29,475	24,712	27,152	2,892	2,323
Georgia.............	42,444	42,229	19,121	11,834	19,210	20,097	18,310	19,109	900	988
Hawaii..............	11,584	12,585	6,275	2,148	6,510	6,940	5,666	6,275	844	665
Idaho...............	6,691	7,372	2,789	2,814	2,777	2,828	2,697	2,784	80	45
Illinois..............	65,287	72,738	30,740	19,964	36,403	36,922	30,292	30,811	154	74
Indiana.............	28,171	27,260	14,553	9,978	16,593	16,110	14,247	14,553	1,428	1,036
Iowa................	19,531	20,150	6,641	6,122	7,341	7,168	6,413	6,462	928	707
Kansas.............	13,969	15,050	6,026	3,511	6,844	6,696	6,135	5,999	709	697
Kentucky...........	25,673	28,835	9,705	9,614	9,807	10,046	9,527	9,864	123	80
Louisiana..........	27,317	29,147	8,612	11,091	8,530	8,401	8,369	8,401	161	–
Maine..............	7,679	8,089	3,150	2,696	3,206	3,214	3,082	3,200	8	13
Maryland...........	36,255	38,449	15,684	9,859	15,607	15,686	15,105	15,539	502	148
Massachusetts.....	57,541	59,060	29,018	15,135	35,769	37,585	33,894	36,176	1,874	1,409
Michigan...........	47,398	51,472	9,828	20,632	10,038	9,644	8,851	9,207	1,187	437
Minnesota..........	33,074	36,133	19,678	9,492	20,451	21,016	18,739	19,678	1,712	1,338
Mississippi.........	18,512	18,933	4,888	8,197	4,894	5,348	4,744	5,041	54	41
Missouri............	22,943	23,178	8,348	7,208	8,471	8,574	8,024	8,352	447	222
Montana............	6,040	6,188	2,041	2,149	2,533	2,613	1,997	2,188	538	424
Nebraska...........	10,162	10,542	3,792	2,817	4,404	4,465	3,589	3,791	815	674
Nevada.............	8,897	8,745	3,278	2,823	3,636	3,557	3,289	3,280	300	268
New Hampshire......	5,017	5,149	1,253	1,703	1,460	1,405	1,257	1,252	82	29
New Jersey.........	50,811	54,365	32,511	13,566	31,765	33,074	31,455	32,774	310	300
New Mexico.........	14,696	16,226	5,893	6,126	6,497	6,713	5,826	6,027	651	579
New York...........	133,097	137,526	61,243	41,171	60,570	63,478	58,960	61,243	1,610	2,235
North Carolina.......	43,105	44,229	21,082	12,850	20,954	20,504	20,631	20,234	324	269
North Dakota.......	5,712	6,793	3,237	1,590	3,930	4,324	2,353	3,237	1,396	1,087
Ohio................	58,268	61,222	28,902	13,046	30,532	31,872	27,893	30,595	2,639	1,277
Oklahoma..........	21,430	22,301	7,101	7,425	6,411	6,500	6,276	6,500	133	–
Oregon.............	25,803	28,423	7,925	8,090	7,226	7,955	6,739	7,925	487	30
Pennsylvania.......	85,378	87,466	28,492	23,810	28,258	28,476	27,731	28,597	541	81
Rhode Island.......	7,866	7,881	3,289	2,543	3,344	3,441	3,216	3,336	104	68
South Carolina.......	22,208	21,438	6,329	6,993	7,346	7,599	6,200	6,329	1,046	1,163
South Dakota........	4,098	4,110	1,442	1,420	1,316	1,476	1,291	1,442	24	10
Tennessee..........	30,491	32,329	13,465	13,231	12,809	13,148	11,458	12,535	800	273
Texas...............	93,244	101,246	49,394	34,676	46,322	51,325	40,816	47,649	5,506	3,676
Utah................	12,679	13,388	5,317	3,644	5,594	5,636	5,127	5,420	348	216
Vermont............	4,965	5,269	1,389	1,771	1,345	1,396	1,323	1,386	–	–
Virginia.............	45,737	45,599	18,052	9,568	18,016	18,964	17,136	18,959	880	5
Washington.........	33,996	35,956	15,867	9,102	15,647	16,452	15,479	16,089	168	363
West Virginia........	22,320	23,888	4,256	4,412	4,811	4,626	4,271	4,208	512	412
Wisconsin...........	42,769	44,893	14,634	11,006	15,111	15,313	14,333	14,674	759	517
Wyoming............	9,132	7,645	3,031	2,082	1,788	1,787	1,788	1,787	–	–

– Represents zero. [1] Includes bonds and other state funds, not shown separately. [2] Includes funds budgeted, adjustments, and balances from previous year. [3] May or may not include budget stabilization fund transfers, depending on state accounting practices. [4] Resources less expenditures, minus adjustments.

Source: National Association of State Budget Officers, Washington, DC, *State Expenditure Report: Examining Fiscal 2012-2014 State Spending* ©, 2014; and *Fiscal Survey of the States, Fall 2014* ©, 2014. See also <http://www.nasbo.org>.

Table 478. State Governments—Summary of Finances: 2000 to 2013

[In millions of dollars (1,260,829 represents $1,260,829,000,000). For fiscal year ending in year shown; see text, this section]

Item	2000	2005	2010	2011	2012	2013
Total revenue	**1,260,829**	**1,642,468**	**2,039,927**	**2,266,850**	**1,905,807**	**2,216,076**
General revenue	984,783	1,286,899	1,567,207	1,658,378	1,629,268	1,709,786
Intergovernmental revenue	274,382	407,792	575,372	595,029	533,655	551,464
From federal	259,114	386,314	555,592	575,789	514,139	513,479
From local	15,268	21,478	19,779	19,240	19,516	37,985
Total taxes	539,655	650,612	705,929	762,379	798,587	847,077
General sales and gross receipts taxes	174,461	212,921	224,314	237,814	245,239	254,792
Selective sales and gross receipts taxes	77,685	99,663	120,208	131,662	133,895	138,972
License taxes	32,598	42,584	50,429	51,701	54,474	55,461
Individual income taxes	194,573	221,597	236,987	259,613	280,614	309,524
Corporation net income taxes	32,522	38,691	38,006	41,280	41,724	45,016
All other taxes	27,815	35,155	35,985	40,308	42,642	43,312
Current charges	86,467	123,129	169,855	181,092	174,234	183,434
Miscellaneous general revenue	84,279	105,367	116,051	119,878	122,792	127,811
Utility revenue	4,513	14,628	15,122	14,991	13,626	13,575
Liquor stores revenue	3,895	5,118	6,495	6,739	7,114	7,480
Insurance trust revenue [1]	267,639	335,822	451,103	586,742	255,798	485,235
Unemployment compensation systems	23,260	35,243	75,038	(NA)	80,110	74,233
State-administered pension systems	230,166	269,617	353,374	(NA)	152,591	388,425
Workers' compensation systems	11,845	23,353	15,311	(NA)	15,526	15,296
Other insurance trust systems	2,368	7,609	7,381	(NA)	7,572	7,282
Total expenditure	**1,084,097**	**1,472,542**	**1,943,523**	**2,005,948**	**1,981,198**	**2,005,912**
Direct expenditure	757,027	1,066,617	1,457,965	1,509,116	1,499,315	1,517,129
Current operations	523,114	738,886	934,322	984,181	986,063	1,020,377
Capital outlay	76,233	95,155	118,011	115,571	119,668	114,980
Insurance benefits and repayments	105,456	168,200	320,721	320,564	303,670	292,448
Assistance and subsidies	22,136	28,403	37,562	39,762	40,078	40,795
Interest on debt	30,089	35,974	47,351	49,038	49,835	48,529
Exhibit: salaries and wages	154,504	194,907	244,952	252,453	251,329	259,635
General expenditure	964,723	1,278,434	1,593,694	1,654,429	1,648,196	1,683,170
Intergovernmental general expenditure	327,070	405,925	485,557	496,832	481,883	488,783
Direct general expenditure	637,653	872,508	1,108,137	1,157,596	1,166,312	1,194,387
General expenditure, by function:						
Education	346,465	454,348	571,147	592,863	588,340	599,152
Public welfare	238,890	368,765	462,431	494,829	489,162	519,178
Hospitals	32,578	43,623	64,509	65,986	69,266	67,433
Health	42,066	48,634	58,245	60,035	61,356	63,247
Highways	74,415	92,816	111,170	109,398	115,297	112,174
Police protection	9,788	11,395	13,828	14,249	14,276	15,107
Correction	35,129	40,562	48,550	49,167	48,440	48,408
Natural resources	15,967	18,822	21,515	21,990	22,051	21,346
Parks and recreation	4,676	5,334	5,720	5,761	5,721	5,666
Governmental administration	35,527	46,464	53,976	53,224	52,627	52,751
Interest on general debt	29,187	34,242	45,260	46,653	47,274	46,139
Other and unallocable	100,034	113,427	137,344	140,275	134,386	132,569
Utility expenditure	10,723	21,827	23,864	25,549	23,724	24,662
Liquor store expenditure	3,195	4,082	5,244	5,407	5,608	5,632
Insurance trust expenditure [1]	105,456	168,200	320,721	320,564	303,670	292,448
Unemployment compensation systems	18,583	29,776	134,908	(NA)	95,318	71,181
State-administered pension systems	75,971	118,333	166,956	(NA)	190,623	203,455
Workers' compensation systems	8,317	12,740	12,025	(NA)	10,923	10,895
Other insurance trust systems	2,585	7,351	6,831	(NA)	6,806	6,917
Debt outstanding, long term and short term [2]	**547,876**	**810,852**	**1,115,463**	**1,139,664**	**1,148,934**	**1,137,364**
Cash and security holdings	**2,518,936**	**3,153,795**	**3,323,047**	**3,672,783**	**3,667,671**	**3,837,747**

[1] Within insurance trust revenue, net earnings of state-administered pension systems is a calculated statistic, and thus can be positive or negative. Net earnings is the sum of earnings on investments plus gains on investments minus losses on investments. [2] As of fiscal year 2005 the Census Bureau no longer collects government debt information by the character of long-term debt. For further information see the 2006 Government Finance and Employment Classification Manual at http://www.census.gov/govs/pubs/.

Source: U.S. Census Bureau, "State and Local Government Finances," <http://www.census.gov/govs/local/>; and SGF001 and SGF003 "State Government Finances," <http://factfinder.census.gov/>; accessed August 2015.

Table 479. State Government Tax Collections by State: 2014

[In millions of dollars (865,752 represents $865,752,000,000)]

State	All taxes	Total property taxes	Selective sales and gross receipts — Total general sales and gross receipts, Total	Selective sales and gross receipts — receipts	Selective sales tax, Total [1]	Alcoholic beverage sales	Insurance premiums	Motor fuels sales	Public utilities	Tobacco products	Other	License taxes, Total [1]	Corporation	Motor vehicle operators	Occupancy and business n.e.c. [2]	Income taxes, Total	Individual income	Corporation net income	Other taxes, Total [1]	Death and gift	Severance
U.S.	865,752	14,233	411,414	271,287	140,127	6,155	18,095	41,500	14,154	16,913	43,312	51,120	6,195	2,506	13,811	357,105	310,829	46,276	31,880	4,748	17,781
AL	9,294	330	4,813	2,393	2,419	181	304	534	734	117	548	386	78	21	58	3,613	3,207	406	152	–	115
AK	3,393	128	258	(X)	258	39	62	42	4	72	38	142	–	–	43	409	(X)	409	2,456	–	2,456
AZ	13,084	824	7,760	5,994	1,766	71	448	780	22	312	133	437	10	30	131	4,038	3,462	575	26	–	26
AR	8,937	1,077	4,324	3,130	1,194	52	182	455	–	226	279	369	28	18	130	3,001	2,602	398	166	–	109
CA	138,070	2,176	50,002	37,224	12,778	354	2,363	6,063	663	833	2,501	8,923	60	280	4,269	76,854	67,996	8,858	115	–	39
CO	11,755	(X)	4,474	2,616	1,859	41	239	647	11	194	726	660	18	29	45	6,376	5,658	718	246	–	245
CT	15,938	(X)	6,782	3,981	2,801	61	206	503	315	376	1,340	433	28	44	133	8,400	7,773	627	322	148	(X)
DE	3,176	(X)	480	(X)	480	20	86	113	59	115	88	1,302	1,003	6	231	1,319	1,040	279	75	49	(X)
FL	35,384	–	29,047	21,481	7,566	452	702	2,423	2,719	371	898	2,133	299	187	198	2,044	(X)	2,044	2,160	2	(X)
GA	18,629	788	7,310	5,126	2,185	182	372	1,006	–	217	407	610	48	91	84	9,909	8,966	944	11	–	(X)
HI	6,033	(X)	3,848	2,825	1,023	48	142	94	166	108	465	224	2	–	29	1,872	1,745	126	91	15	6
ID	3,672	(X)	1,821	1,374	448	9	75	248	2	48	66	316	10	10	75	1,528	1,338	190	6	–	(X)
IL	39,183	55	15,759	8,515	7,243	280	359	1,294	1,651	860	2,799	2,676	346	116	469	20,343	16,058	4,285	351	294	3
IN	16,847	8	10,395	7,003	3,392	46	223	815	253	448	1,608	590	7	207	46	5,763	4,896	867	90	88	(X)
IA	8,272	(X)	3,772	2,659	1,113	14	106	453	–	225	315	808	35	22	116	3,586	3,198	389	106	91	(X)
KS	7,334	81	3,891	2,984	907	127	198	442	98	249	42	395	64	20	66	2,842	2,512	330	125	–	125
KY	11,104	562	5,354	3,131	2,223	129	142	886	64	130	754	472	101	17	126	4,424	3,749	674	291	46	242
LA	9,695	55	5,116	2,923	2,192	57	429	589	9	136	978	427	188	12	110	3,235	2,754	481	862	–	862
ME	3,847	36	1,911	1,192	720	18	106	241	32	136	186	254	9	10	102	1,597	1,414	183	49	24	(X)
MD	18,929	726	8,023	4,196	3,827	31	475	813	139	402	1,966	854	107	37	213	8,757	7,774	983	570	214	(X)
MA	25,236	3	7,933	5,519	2,414	79	347	732	24	660	573	1,013	26	105	317	15,441	13,246	2,195	846	402	(X)
MI	24,804	1,920	12,310	8,419	3,890	144	362	964	28	942	1,450	1,512	23	55	164	8,756	7,875	881	307	–	91
MN	23,129	837	9,759	5,442	4,317	81	403	893	4	582	2,358	1,314	7	44	440	10,844	9,528	1,316	374	165	–
MS	7,575	25	4,705	3,305	1,400	42	264	410	–	146	534	559	183	40	100	2,194	1,667	526	92	–	91
MO	11,241	30	4,915	3,286	1,630	36	302	696	–	100	496	564	59	16	135	5,720	5,362	358	12	–	7
MT	2,656	269	550	(X)	550	30	88	197	47	85	102	314	3	8	99	1,213	1,063	150	309	–	306
NE	4,877	–	2,304	1,764	540	43	43	335	53	63	16	127	67	27	10	2,431	2,124	307	16	–	–
NV	7,143	259	5,714	3,829	1,885	43	265	297	23	102	1,156	608	51	12	239	(X)	(X)	(X)	562	–	111
NH	2,283	383	877	(X)	877	10	85	146	70	215	352	280	276	53	92	636	93	543	107	–	(X)
NJ	29,679	7	12,752	8,886	3,866	139	599	539	1,012	741	836	1,517	24	–	496	14,342	11,974	2,368	1,062	685	–
NM	5,757	106	2,800	2,099	701	45	100	235	30	81	210	282	63	146	40	1,503	1,297	206	1,066	–	1,066
NY	76,979	(X)	23,545	12,669	10,876	251	1,345	1,630	930	1,446	5,273	1,885	617	111	176	47,826	42,965	4,862	3,723	1,238	2
NC	23,397	(X)	9,978	5,842	4,136	343	476	1,916	403	282	716	1,600	–	5	233	11,751	10,391	1,361	67	20	(X)
ND	6,120	3	1,848	1,320	528	9	51	228	40	31	168	227	1,026	82	87	749	499	250	3,293	23	3,293
OH	27,021	(X)	15,618	10,218	5,400	98	510	1,840	1,125	816	1,011	2,928	...	...	941	8,425	8,425	–	50	39	(X)
OK	9,103	(X)	3,989	2,599	1,390	111	295	451	46	293	195	1,058	35	20	79	3,359	2,962	397	697	1	679
OR	9,684	22	1,445	(X)	1,445	18	85	512	85	258	486	961	29	41	295	7,145	6,649	495	112	85	(X)
PA	34,193	45	17,419	9,498	7,922	346	773	2,231	1,285	1,028	2,258	2,303	230	55	982	13,111	10,810	2,302	1,314	849	(X)
RI	2,966	3	1,566	915	651	17	86	96	105	135	212	132	5	5	47	1,209	1,088	120	57	39	(X)
SC	8,933	22	4,628	3,371	1,258	162	215	530	28	26	297	472	95	9	96	3,750	3,423	328	60	39	(X)
SD	1,608	(X)	1,297	915	382	16	77	138	4	62	85	278	5	4	136	25	(X)	25	9	–	9
TN	11,806	(X)	8,758	6,192	2,566	148	749	845	7	261	555	1,335	676	47	293	1,416	239	1,177	297	107	–
TX	55,261	(X)	45,747	32,336	13,411	1,067	1,886	3,326	768	1,446	4,918	3,500	125	139	669	(X)	(X)	(X)	6,014	(X)	6,014
UT	6,312	(X)	2,682	1,823	859	48	113	373	24	113	187	277	–	16	53	3,198	2,890	308	156	–	156
VT	2,963	985	1,015	355	660	24	60	104	22	72	379	110	3	8	19	781	675	106	71	36	(X)

See footnotes at end of table.

Table 479. State Government Tax Collections by State: 2014-Continued.
See headnote on page 310.

State	All taxes	Total property taxes	Selective sales and gross receipts		Selective sales tax							License taxes	Selected license taxes			Income taxes			Other taxes	Selected other taxes	
			Total general sales and gross receipts Total	Selective sales tax Total [1]	Alcoholic beverage sales	Insurance premiums	Motor fuels sales	Public utilities	Tobacco products	Other	Total [1]	Corporation	Motor vehicle oper-ators	Occupancy and oper- business n.e.c. [2]	Total	Individual income	Corporation net income	Total [1]	Death and gift	Sever-ance
VA........	18,949	36	6,063	3,556	2,507	208	460	695	107	181	857	796	59	40	200	11,618	10,878	741	437	–	2
WA........	19,448	1,974	15,210	11,767	3,443	321	467	1,156	498	443	557	1,415	32	103	294	–	(X)	(X)	848	157	42
WV........	5,380	–	2,561	1,222	1,339	17	155	441	154	102	470	153	5	108	12	1,974	1,770	204	692	–	682
WI........	16,411	159	7,360	4,628	2,731	58	186	1,001	380	641	467	1,041	21	40	367	7,780	6,793	986	72	–	9
WY........	2,263	300	926	766	160	2	25	101	5	24	3	148	13	2	26	–	(X)	(X)	889	–	883

X Not applicable. – Represents zero or rounds to zero. [1] Includes other items not shown separately. [2] n.e.c. means not elsewhere classified.

Source: U.S. Census Bureau, Census of Governments, "2014 Annual Survey of State Government Tax Collections," <http://factfinder2.census.gov>, accessed June 2015. See also <http://www.census.gov/govs/statetax>.

Table 480. State Governments—Expenditures and Debt by State: 2012

[In millions of dollars (1,981,511 represents $1,981,511,000,000) except as indicated. For fiscal year ending in year shown; see text, this section]

State	Total expenditures	Intergovernmental	Total	Direct general expenditures: Total [1]	Education	Public welfare	Health	Hospitals	Highways	Police protection	Corrections	Parks and recreation	Housing and community development	Sewerage	Solid waste management	Governmental administration	Interest on general debt	Other	Utility and liquor store	Insurance trust	Cash and security holdings	Total debt outstanding
U.S...	1,981,511	481,411	1,500,101	1,167,334	271,117	433,312	42,006	65,514	97,509	12,848	46,021	4,632	10,080	773	2,451	51,010	47,342	82,719	29,404	303,363	3,699,871	1,145,577
AL..	27,686	6,563	21,123	17,400	5,387	6,247	577	1,378	1,433	141	515	21	15	–	2	564	342	777	249	3,474	38,263	8,719
AK..	11,729	1,897	9,832	8,365	1,469	1,941	190	51	1,067	97	313	19	163	–	–	634	282	2,140	166	1,300	72,598	5,909
AZ..	31,888	8,024	23,864	19,452	4,291	7,934	1,878	695	1,349	229	888	51	88	–	1	584	673	791	32	4,381	48,452	14,507
AR..	19,618	5,047	14,571	12,691	3,290	5,170	290	923	990	101	413	60	28	1	13	622	149	643	–	1,880	26,848	3,656
CA..	269,055	85,426	183,629	131,720	30,793	44,032	1,387	8,694	8,919	1,529	8,494	389	262	183	1,463	7,809	7,321	10,446	1,632	50,277	519,751	153,529
CO..	28,238	6,105	22,133	16,325	5,100	4,661	895	665	993	134	873	97	109	3	143	847	840	1,107	41	5,767	64,411	16,000
CT..	28,370	4,615	23,755	18,161	3,265	6,359	651	1,276	1,077	220	685	51	207	–	–	1,220	1,531	1,476	608	4,986	41,156	31,966
DE..	8,316	1,161	7,154	6,147	1,500	1,892	412	50	578	119	282	34	75	–	53	411	258	483	136	871	15,056	5,797
FL..	79,482	17,340	62,142	52,179	9,717	21,598	3,767	966	4,844	530	2,238	95	351	–	191	2,080	1,398	4,404	147	9,816	188,200	38,171
GA..	44,751	10,223	34,528	27,459	8,118	10,190	963	947	1,788	307	1,410	188	249	9	37	826	688	1,738	42	7,027	79,160	13,401
HI..	11,566	195	11,371	9,903	3,503	1,988	483	753	405	30	198	92	115	–	–	381	339	1,616	12	1,456	15,991	8,398
ID..	8,301	1,957	6,345	5,123	1,062	2,019	168	168	581	49	226	25	85	–	–	281	166	409	97	1,125	19,099	3,946
IL..	72,622	15,867	56,755	42,201	7,947	15,405	2,285	1,339	4,181	411	1,351	74	332	12	26	1,337	3,344	4,158	–	14,554	125,248	64,302
IN..	35,833	9,297	26,536	22,641	7,100	8,524	517	163	2,219	213	607	50	673	1	6	576	977	1,014	–	3,895	57,965	22,512
IA..	20,408	4,805	15,603	12,962	3,032	4,951	140	1,506	1,297	94	377	23	95	1	2	504	254	687	165	2,475	37,990	6,166
KS..	16,747	3,954	12,794	10,696	2,600	3,446	360	1,414	1,104	92	287	33	100	–	29	425	270	564	–	2,097	19,265	6,860
KY..	29,349	5,029	24,320	19,616	5,315	7,143	557	1,153	2,023	158	494	95	238	–	–	833	709	869	–	4,704	38,823	15,104
LA..	31,686	6,388	25,298	21,372	4,531	6,180	567	1,950	1,835	291	560	298	773	–	–	871	904	2,613	5	3,920	54,757	15,415
ME..	9,128	1,286	7,842	6,758	1,020	2,900	502	129	593	70	121	21	208	–	–	281	243	668	4	1,080	17,069	5,606
MD..	41,139	8,309	32,831	27,350	5,326	9,824	1,299	485	4,042	438	1,392	116	347	106	27	1,311	1,098	1,539	990	4,490	58,040	25,813
MA..	56,479	9,291	47,188	36,364	5,993	14,897	1,100	483	1,818	698	1,056	151	1,220	355	11	1,676	3,086	3,819	2,362	8,462	89,307	79,524
MI..	61,727	19,021	42,706	32,898	10,030	11,989	1,169	2,722	1,249	268	1,607	93	853	–	4	715	1,005	1,194	697	9,111	78,540	30,824
MN..	38,613	10,833	27,779	22,576	5,349	11,600	255	537	1,295	262	427	193	48	–	13	770	799	1,028	7	5,196	61,023	13,230
MS..	20,051	5,138	14,913	12,235	2,374	5,050	357	1,051	1,065	105	305	84	58	–	–	382	299	1,104	219	2,459	25,683	7,194
MO..	31,361	5,878	25,483	20,952	4,144	8,149	1,496	1,653	1,689	242	686	40	194	106	3	477	839	1,342	–	4,531	69,726	20,386
MT..	7,063	1,317	5,746	4,750	919	1,318	154	47	826	49	189	13	62	–	1	341	142	687	81	916	18,400	3,995
NE..	9,526	2,170	7,356	6,618	1,832	2,225	396	255	679	73	246	36	2	2	9	210	89	562	–	738	14,398	2,073
NV..	13,477	4,120	9,357	6,439	1,538	2,119	237	259	891	101	269	19	14	4	7	279	201	505	90	2,829	28,229	3,897
NH..	7,424	1,205	6,219	4,997	1,081	1,703	93	45	493	57	112	22	109	1	17	229	392	642	481	741	12,443	8,030
NJ..	68,122	11,789	56,333	38,671	8,606	13,794	1,201	2,095	2,809	541	1,385	268	368	2	47	1,692	2,177	3,686	2,318	15,344	109,070	64,852
NY..	181,226	57,406	123,820	86,839	12,853	40,075	2,786	6,333	4,699	797	2,806	452	496	–	114	5,556	4,214	5,659	12,524	24,458	320,854	135,884
NC..	53,624	13,515	40,110	32,297	9,029	11,013	1,296	1,693	3,301	459	1,322	155	276	3	11	1,163	639	1,937	60	7,753	93,965	18,292
ND..	6,315	1,643	4,672	4,177	1,044	889	121	53	846	29	102	35	23	–	11	147	101	789	–	495	17,866	2,084
OH..	76,524	17,932	58,592	40,901	9,480	17,503	1,364	2,950	2,975	292	1,363	75	296	–	34	1,665	1,310	1,595	519	17,172	204,735	33,602
OK..	22,599	4,230	18,368	15,045	3,962	5,758	818	282	1,501	208	526	83	175	2	5	573	451	709	667	2,656	38,414	9,979
OR..	26,862	5,658	21,205	15,587	3,364	5,532	634	1,570	999	163	625	68	133	–	5	1,042	448	1,004	256	5,362	69,404	13,782
PA..	87,340	18,526	68,813	52,671	10,026	20,574	1,983	3,062	6,846	871	1,957	269	75	11	36	3,075	1,664	2,222	1,540	14,602	119,211	46,199
RI..	8,326	1,143	7,182	5,434	991	2,246	160	70	322	67	182	29	45	37	45	325	508	407	150	1,598	16,036	9,212
SC..	27,791	5,312	22,479	16,994	4,771	5,822	962	1,514	1,152	153	483	67	160	–	–	536	540	833	1,706	3,779	38,105	14,854
SD..	4,424	754	3,671	3,224	662	927	168	22	617	34	115	44	46	–	–	173	124	293	–	446	12,887	3,608
TN..	31,498	7,181	24,317	21,220	4,752	10,049	882	408	1,710	212	631	86	244	–	5	825	253	1,161	–	3,097	44,861	6,168
TX..	126,128	29,497	96,631	79,443	22,425	30,328	2,406	4,857	6,602	762	3,473	135	113	3	48	1,918	1,720	4,651	–	17,188	300,307	45,626

See footnotes at end of table.

Table 480. State Governments—Expenditures and Debt by State: 2012-Continued.

See headnote on page 312.

State	Total expend-itures	Inter-govern-mental	Direct expenditures Total	Direct general expenditures Total [1]	Educa-tion	Public welfare	Health	Hospi-tals	High-ways	Police protec-tion	Correc-tions	Parks and recre-ation	Housing and com-munity devel-opment	Sewer-age	Solid waste man-age-ment	Gov-ern-men-tal admin-istra-tion	Inter-est on gen-eral debt	Other	Utility and liquor store	Insur-ance trust	Cash and security holdings	Total debt out-stand-ing
UT...	17,109	3,029	14,080	12,190	3,992	2,903	310	1,066	1,449	140	300	41	92	–	–	692	285	920	195	1,695	26,645	7,067
VT...	5,959	1,636	4,323	3,896	898	1,498	183	16	428	82	126	14	83	6	8	135	125	293	51	377	7,227	3,391
VA...	46,760	11,654	35,106	29,991	8,241	8,566	703	3,381	3,313	320	1,191	105	195	29	4	1,112	1,125	1,707	489	4,626	77,334	27,786
WA...	45,501	9,530	35,971	27,580	7,528	8,333	1,368	2,157	2,510	232	967	66	77	–	10	985	1,350	1,995	495	7,896	81,891	29,090
WV...	13,223	2,618	10,605	9,091	2,309	3,242	300	125	1,203	81	283	55	21	–	9	430	250	783	77	1,437	19,707	7,307
WI...	37,753	9,741	28,012	22,053	5,531	8,121	479	1,270	1,688	134	1,035	17	16	–	9	712	1,060	1,981	12	5,947	97,410	22,996
WY...	5,774	1,703	4,071	3,312	624	761	275	7	552	48	147	30	11	–	5	232	56	566	82	677	25,056	1,322

– Represents or rounds to zero. [1] Includes other direct general expenditures not shown separately.

Source : U.S. Census Bureau, LGF001 "State and Local Government Finances by Level of Government and by State: 2012," <http://factfinder2.census.gov/>, accessed December 2014.

Table 481. Local Governments—Revenue by State: 2012

[In millions of dollars (1,615,194 represents $1,615,194,000,000). For fiscal year ending in year shown; see text, this section. Minus sign (−) indicates decrease]

State	Total revenue	General revenue, total	Intergovernmental revenue	Gen. rev. from own sources — Total	Taxes Total	Property	Sales and gross receipt	Individual income	Corporation income	Other taxes	Current charges and misc. general revenue	Cur. charges & misc. — Total¹	Current charges: Education	Hospitals	Sewerage	Misc. Total¹	Interest earnings	Special assessment	Utility revenue	Liquor store revenue	Insurance trust revenue
U.S.	1,615,194	1,456,674	539,507	917,167	588,804	432,989	97,903	26,642	7,210	24,062	328,362	252,520	24,516	73,713	46,650	75,842	18,163	7,377	138,109	1,226	19,186
AL	20,508	17,440	6,808	10,631	5,166	2,232	2,174	101	—	659	5,465	4,558	340	2,892	484	907	124	9	2,965	—	104
AK	4,817	4,465	1,913	2,552	1,619	1,291	293	—	—	35	934	776	26	322	84	158	47	14	341	4	7
AZ	27,076	22,319	8,015	14,305	9,196	6,093	2,696	—	—	407	5,109	3,772	484	776	860	1,337	228	89	4,568	—	188
AR	9,820	8,794	5,112	3,682	2,106	941	1,130	—	—	35	1,576	1,062	152	157	272	514	169	35	1,003	—	23
CA	252,050	224,652	99,088	125,564	68,481	49,486	14,585	—	—	4,411	57,082	43,925	2,246	10,691	6,407	13,157	3,396	1,646	23,811	—	3,587
CO	27,739	24,946	7,255	17,691	10,924	6,951	3,511	—	—	463	6,768	5,312	479	1,542	792	1,456	249	141	2,737	—	56
CT	17,107	16,086	5,083	11,003	9,542	9,427	—	—	—	115	1,461	1,164	127	—	377	297	36	39	776	—	245
DE	3,246	2,817	1,449	1,368	849	696	14	56	5	78	519	369	16	114	151	150	16	24	419	—	10
DC	13,099	11,142	3,474	7,668	5,934	1,878	1,539	1,491	466	560	1,734	652	29	—	262	1,082	91	—	1,041	—	916
FL	91,081	80,231	22,082	58,149	31,617	24,598	5,459	—	—	1,560	26,531	19,972	1,981	6,434	3,026	6,560	1,309	1,972	9,606	—	1,244
GA	42,432	37,471	11,753	25,718	15,592	10,291	4,926	—	—	375	10,126	8,134	539	3,781	1,242	1,992	289	42	4,791	—	170
HI	3,389	3,049	513	2,536	1,895	1,311	393	—	—	191	641	565	—	—	377	76	8	17	340	—	—
ID	5,261	5,051	2,147	2,904	1,481	1,393	24	—	—	64	1,423	1,192	92	478	199	231	29	53	209	—	1
IL	68,011	62,122	21,235	40,887	30,218	25,466	4,040	—	—	711	10,670	7,557	1,310	975	1,195	3,113	538	573	4,071	—	1,818
IN	27,753	25,473	10,613	14,860	8,184	6,482	217	1,332	—	153	6,676	5,414	351	3,013	1,087	1,262	186	23	2,185	—	95
IA	15,724	14,655	5,305	9,350	5,631	4,540	924	97	—	71	3,719	3,147	502	1,465	496	572	97	19	1,066	—	2
KS	13,864	12,380	4,081	8,299	5,089	3,851	1,133	2	—	103	3,210	2,208	430	780	374	1,001	408	123	1,454	—	30
KY	14,764	13,068	5,192	7,876	4,524	2,601	575	1,126	114	109	3,352	2,360	122	647	533	992	709	10	1,674	—	22
LA	22,213	20,910	8,020	12,890	7,960	3,587	4,182	—	—	192	4,930	3,720	71	2,098	406	1,210	502	58	1,233	—	71
ME	4,680	4,547	1,490	3,057	2,360	2,338	7	—	—	16	697	565	45	75	165	131	28	5	132	—	—
MD	27,096	25,664	8,665	16,999	13,112	7,302	760	4,361	—	689	3,887	3,162	710	591	925	725	83	25	781	266	385
MA	32,931	28,281	10,174	18,107	14,221	13,653	306	—	—	262	3,886	3,087	327	—	1,107	799	56	26	2,617	—	2,033
MI	44,316	41,185	19,971	21,214	12,311	11,368	271	426	—	247	8,903	7,147	1,179	862	1,930	1,756	306	208	2,660	—	471
MN	28,422	25,922	11,662	14,260	7,551	7,053	304	—	—	194	6,709	4,797	500	1,452	743	1,912	589	355	2,148	315	38
MS	12,685	11,785	5,126	6,659	2,759	2,570	105	—	—	84	3,900	3,429	408	2,357	224	471	86	10	899	—	—
MO	24,608	22,124	7,144	14,981	9,609	5,730	2,843	321	76	638	5,372	4,318	699	1,590	723	1,054	241	53	2,334	—	150
MT	3,611	3,486	1,507	1,979	1,162	1,122	8	—	—	32	817	579	77	91	91	237	38	83	126	—	—
NE	12,504	8,291	2,468	5,823	3,758	2,954	390	—	—	414	2,065	1,709	238	622	186	355	108	39	4,007	—	206
NV	12,726	11,821	5,120	6,700	3,845	2,609	941	—	—	296	2,855	2,177	44	596	419	678	157	67	905	—	—
NH	5,352	5,230	1,623	3,607	3,063	3,031	—	—	—	32	545	432	53	—	127	113	14	8	121	—	—
NJ	46,976	45,879	13,050	32,829	26,394	25,880	161	—	—	354	6,434	4,950	1,310	330	1,682	1,484	167	8	1,095	—	3
NM	8,390	7,800	4,117	3,684	2,460	1,365	1,037	—	—	58	1,224	915	102	157	180	309	52	13	590	—	—
NY	171,847	162,110	55,167	106,943	80,187	47,577	15,234	8,720	5,956	2,700	26,756	18,774	1,518	4,250	2,485	7,982	1,811	127	6,662	—	3,075
NC	43,693	38,794	14,497	24,297	11,738	8,893	2,525	—	—	321	12,559	10,949	651	7,029	1,366	1,609	212	25	4,272	613	14
ND	3,421	3,238	1,550	1,688	1,007	790	181	—	—	36	681	392	54	—	50	289	22	91	163	—	20
OH	54,533	51,691	20,516	31,174	20,899	13,561	2,035	4,399	234	670	10,275	7,839	1,222	1,342	2,022	2,436	445	245	2,798	—	44
OK	13,247	11,970	4,435	7,535	4,439	2,292	2,074	—	—	73	3,096	2,451	290	979	352	645	79	18	1,230	—	46
OR	18,005	16,602	6,697	9,905	6,077	5,019	372	—	52	634	3,827	3,020	575	282	906	807	191	67	1,401	—	3
PA	62,178	57,220	23,355	33,865	24,084	17,030	1,227	4,210	306	1,311	9,780	7,313	933	35	2,432	2,467	1,045	91	2,879	—	2,079
RI	4,275	4,060	1,156	2,905	2,401	2,344	25	—	—	32	503	377	29	—	112	126	11	8	187	—	28
SC	19,364	17,803	5,293	12,509	6,229	4,874	653	—	—	702	6,281	5,323	245	3,650	614	958	383	18	1,560	—	2
SD	3,258	2,890	925	1,965	1,374	1,008	334	—	—	32	591	456	94	53	88	135	40	9	321	27	20
TN	31,209	22,094	7,653	14,442	7,995	5,134	2,455	—	—	407	6,446	5,163	280	2,639	819	1,283	447	96	8,870	—	244

See footnotes at end of table.

Table 481. Local Governments—Revenue by State: 2012-Continued.

See headnote on page 314.

State	Total revenue	General revenue, total	Inter-govern-mental revenue	General revenue from own sources Total	Taxes Total	Taxes Prop-erty	Taxes Sales and gross receipt	Taxes Indi-vidual income	Taxes Corpo-ration income	Other taxes	Current charges and miscel-laneous general revenue	Current charges Total [1]	Current charges Educa-tion	Current charges Hospi-tals	Current charges Sewer-age	Misc. general revenue Total [1]	Misc. Interest earn-ings	Misc. Special assess-ments	Utility re-venue	Liquor store re-venue	Insur-ance trust re-venue
TX...	120,276	106,319	33,170	73,149	49,141	40,310	7,936	–	–	894	24,009	18,041	2,096	4,880	3,496	5,968	1,958	274	12,864	–	1,093
UT...	11,364	9,504	3,578	5,926	3,747	2,679	939	–	–	129	2,179	1,520	85	44	362	660	101	72	1,862	–	-3
VT...	2,674	2,436	1,666	770	458	430	18	–	–	10	312	213	26	–	66	99	11	5	231	–	8
VA...	34,916	32,777	11,869	20,907	15,032	11,305	2,455	–	–	1,272	5,876	4,399	426	270	1,245	1,477	534	43	1,774	–	366
WA...	39,083	32,978	12,112	20,866	11,809	7,327	3,696	–	–	786	9,057	7,500	354	2,141	2,000	1,557	267	292	6,018	–	87
WV...	5,519	5,261	2,343	2,918	1,776	1,429	125	–	–	222	1,142	881	37	250	244	261	46	31	233	–	25
WI...	27,375	25,351	10,534	14,816	10,501	9,895	428	–	–	178	4,315	3,471	538	889	801	844	177	67	1,862	–	162
WY...	4,705	4,489	1,736	2,753	1,295	1,003	244	–	–	47	1,459	1,309	76	947	65	150	24	17	216	–	–

– Represents or rounds to zero. [1] Includes items not shown separately.

Source: U.S. Census Bureau, Federal, State, and Local Governments, Government Finance Statistics, "Annual Surveys of State and Local Government Finances," <http://www.census.gov/govs/local/>, accessed January 2015.

State and Local Government Finances and Employment

Table 482. Local Governments—Expenditures and Debt by State: 2012

[In millions of dollars (1,663,121 represents $1,663,121,000,000). For fiscal year ending in year shown; see text, this section]

State	Total expenditures [1]	Direct expenditures Total [1]	Direct general expenditures Total	Education	Public welfare	Hospitals	Health	Highways	Police protection	Corrections	Parks and recreation	Housing and community development	Sewerage	Solid Waste Management	Governmental administration	Interest on general debt	Other	Utility expenditures	Insurance trust expenditures	Debt outstanding
U.S.	1,663,121	1,647,444	1,419,984	598,078	52,276	90,241	42,392	61,053	84,124	26,556	32,773	43,061	50,939	21,796	72,922	61,775	123,799	183,224	43,147	1,796,719
AL	20,710	20,687	17,501	7,258	36	3,162	355	811	1,015	204	365	485	365	261	892	594	1,580	2,981	205	20,749
AK	4,851	4,851	4,283	1,834	–	333	58	212	225	4	101	152	91	99	305	128	355	538	27	3,587
AZ	27,423	27,227	22,115	9,228	197	777	282	991	1,843	658	559	485	939	367	1,594	993	1,891	4,810	302	34,558
AR	9,721	9,706	8,630	4,985	16	169	47	452	486	145	142	189	276	205	397	352	786	1,035	41	10,306
CA	262,468	262,281	217,067	76,937	16,400	14,182	11,788	7,774	13,353	5,197	4,976	8,281	6,097	2,493	12,084	9,336	18,890	34,929	10,285	266,223
CO	27,013	26,982	23,420	8,112	893	1,733	330	1,394	1,461	371	1,083	668	869	106	1,526	1,323	1,987	3,338	225	35,395
CT	17,753	17,747	16,211	8,990	108	–	151	623	898	–	233	670	607	224	568	374	1,344	911	625	10,862
DE	3,346	3,344	2,896	1,839	–	1	34	137	185	–	30	90	200	23	142	70	275	396	52	2,437
DC	13,815	13,815	10,765	2,372	2,864	230	444	526	564	241	203	547	493	105	440	500	953	2,543	507	11,604
FL	95,750	95,342	82,473	27,656	1,312	7,485	1,161	3,112	6,788	1,821	2,750	2,392	3,188	2,194	4,477	3,587	6,792	11,014	1,855	108,751
GA	43,943	43,905	37,135	17,159	236	4,043	1,018	1,309	2,117	873	637	1,084	1,301	586	2,528	771	3,366	6,159	611	42,384
HI	3,337	3,337	2,412	–	34	–	24	196	359	79	174	90	244	307	340	197	196	925	–	5,627
ID	5,100	5,100	4,852	2,054	37	488	54	299	351	710	104	45	194	137	295	88	423	246	2	2,301
IL	72,512	72,512	60,527	27,425	750	1,548	851	3,016	4,189	351	2,583	1,842	2,045	489	3,424	2,943	5,182	7,055	4,930	81,932
IN	25,841	25,841	23,191	9,813	70	3,334	376	603	937	–	650	438	1,204	258	1,324	973	2,033	2,541	109	27,052
IA	16,297	16,192	14,968	6,770	99	1,600	461	1,073	595	146	338	154	688	271	520	396	1,311	1,221	3	12,004
KS	13,773	13,766	12,256	5,827	39	825	291	702	646	193	275	173	334	148	683	787	1,092	1,428	82	19,825
KY	15,315	15,296	13,126	6,317	43	502	433	467	521	245	183	212	772	185	627	1,206	1,171	2,116	55	27,387
LA	22,807	22,782	21,154	8,273	97	2,547	192	926	1,261	766	462	658	892	356	1,259	773	1,846	1,430	198	20,531
ME	4,677	4,675	4,513	2,333	37	87	35	296	176	72	110	132	193	117	218	113	392	161	–	3,032
MD	29,009	28,904	26,497	13,425	254	–	451	1,017	1,703	358	736	1,046	812	618	1,426	739	2,258	1,183	991	20,294
MA	32,104	31,205	27,029	13,640	88	1,047	133	790	1,439	–	246	1,717	787	402	878	521	2,542	2,542	1,634	16,663
MI	46,062	45,813	40,894	18,664	1,158	1,001	3,113	2,033	2,088	625	690	482	1,988	453	2,139	1,757	3,619	3,376	1,543	45,528
MN	29,061	28,969	26,090	10,089	1,539	1,613	709	2,276	1,373	437	847	873	819	326	1,319	1,193	2,341	2,336	247	35,216
MS	12,841	12,840	11,901	5,071	33	2,350	105	672	557	253	171	269	405	182	621	259	1,095	939	–	7,390
MO	25,246	25,245	21,868	10,390	187	1,630	382	1,247	1,438	177	575	462	840	162	1,025	853	1,937	2,790	586	25,902
MT	3,632	3,631	3,450	1,659	61	114	118	225	226	48	60	52	116	78	195	60	301	182	–	1,759
NE	12,684	12,682	8,249	4,108	101	690	50	540	332	115	184	192	223	80	367	253	723	4,161	272	13,029
NV	13,472	13,459	12,098	3,867	342	761	126	791	998	436	590	150	441	23	928	768	1,022	1,360	–	25,153
NH	5,262	5,178	5,037	2,759	212	–	28	249	295	70	60	103	139	98	282	111	441	130	12	2,739
NJ	45,923	45,497	44,359	22,877	1,139	375	379	1,317	2,783	690	603	1,033	1,481	955	1,672	1,322	3,663	1,128	10	38,034
NM	8,551	8,527	7,773	3,884	119	194	83	371	533	222	276	129	175	191	524	195	690	753	–	8,956
NY	189,907	179,309	150,896	58,636	10,873	9,251	3,897	5,568	8,487	2,966	2,211	5,418	4,313	2,884	4,623	7,297	12,642	16,731	11,682	204,209
NC	43,450	43,289	37,967	14,663	1,668	6,410	1,504	615	2,394	570	765	1,173	1,458	775	1,457	1,608	3,506	4,759	30	32,488
ND	3,328	3,320	3,033	1,310	67	–	45	447	143	41	149	62	73	53	140	67	260	269	18	2,660
OH	54,683	54,160	50,523	23,050	2,490	1,403	2,413	2,394	2,932	456	1,082	2,045	2,039	444	3,324	1,461	4,553	3,443	195	47,636
OK	12,861	12,859	11,544	5,484	26	965	210	813	720	129	328	302	335	195	576	260	1,034	1,244	71	8,811
OR	18,732	18,729	16,477	6,976	252	311	684	862	987	446	487	505	905	122	900	768	1,421	2,118	134	20,791
PA	60,399	60,388	54,331	25,297	4,008	10	2,995	1,830	2,373	1,346	669	2,008	2,582	820	2,999	2,964	4,990	4,641	1,416	83,229
RI	4,245	4,245	3,857	2,142	8	–	15	117	288	17	43	178	91	46	178	118	324	195	193	2,722
SC	19,083	19,063	17,493	7,364	48	3,643	165	410	902	193	387	366	581	320	881	924	1,618	1,566	4	25,540
SD	3,262	3,261	2,877	1,338	16	54	36	328	136	49	113	61	118	47	171	81	255	342	18	2,250
TN	31,380	31,378	21,643	8,928	156	2,681	395	774	1,451	418	389	744	746	351	1,150	879	1,906	9,154	581	30,878
TX	123,727	122,584	104,526	48,324	470	8,759	2,207	4,724	5,707	2,000	2,011	2,080	3,419	1,238	5,278	7,926	9,414	16,349	1,710	225,110
UT	11,632	11,538	9,066	4,215	122	47	197	513	518	218	475	281	437	160	641	297	812	2,468	3	12,654

See footnotes at end of table.

Table 482. Local Governments—Expenditures and Debt by State: 2012-Continued.

See headnote on page 316.

State	Total expenditures [1]	Direct expenditures Total [1]	Direct general expenditures Total	Education	Public welfare	Hospitals	Health	Highways	Police protection	Corrections	Parks and recreation	Housing and community development	Sewerage	Solid Waste Management	Governmental administration	Interest on general debt	Other	Utility expenditures	Insurance trust expenditures	Debt outstanding
VT...	2,611	2,610	2,341	1,477	2	–	10	243	96	–	37	57	82	32	101	27	216	258	11	1,184
VA....	35,947	35,925	32,790	14,950	1,514	281	948	908	1,763	977	827	820	1,382	634	2,012	1,327	2,834	2,220	914	37,546
WA...	39,186	39,100	30,784	11,755	197	2,365	1,188	1,624	1,395	592	960	1,185	1,889	664	1,565	1,318	2,670	8,098	217	46,502
WV...	5,888	5,884	5,476	3,198	5	247	60	91	283	51	128	137	277	69	437	100	508	365	43	3,616
WI...	27,829	27,802	25,212	11,459	1,823	30	1,308	2,135	1,646	510	589	335	921	365	1,183	797	2,310	2,091	499	20,606
WY...	4,668	4,667	4,409	1,895	22	963	55	208	172	69	125	10	76	74	286	23	398	258	–	1,076

– Represents or rounds to zero. [1] Includes other items not shown separately.

Source: U.S. Census Bureau, Federal, State, and Local Governments, Government Finance Statistics, "Annual Surveys of State and Local Government Finances," <http://www.census.gov/govs/local/>, accessed January 2015.

Table 483. State Governments—Revenue by State: 2012

[In millions of dollars (1,907,027 represents $1,907,027,000,000). For fiscal year ending in year shown. See text, this section. Includes local shares of state imposed taxes]

State	Total revenue [1,2]	General revenue Total	Intergovernmental revenue Total [1]	Intergovernmental revenue From federal government	General revenue from own sources Total	Total taxes	Current charges	Miscellaneous general revenue	Utilities and liquor store revenue	Insurance trust revenue
United States........	1,907,027	1,630,035	533,658	514,139	1,096,377	799,350	174,260	122,766	20,741	256,251
Alabama................	28,970	22,226	8,228	8,113	13,999	9,049	3,788	1,162	267	6,477
Alaska.................	15,050	14,324	2,866	2,861	11,458	7,049	602	3,806	16	710
Arizona................	32,134	28,511	10,753	10,395	17,758	12,996	3,208	1,554	30	3,594
Arkansas..............	18,434	17,124	5,910	5,901	11,215	8,288	2,049	878	–	1,310
California.............	250,971	199,359	57,426	54,145	141,933	115,179	16,705	10,049	1,043	50,569
Colorado..............	25,688	21,884	6,396	6,311	15,488	10,263	3,010	2,214	–	3,804
Connecticut...........	27,328	24,508	5,799	5,782	18,709	15,421	1,768	1,521	37	2,783
Delaware..............	8,015	7,417	1,881	1,814	5,536	3,347	1,069	1,120	17	581
Florida................	82,386	71,230	23,256	22,851	47,974	32,997	9,009	5,968	21	11,134
Georgia...............	40,644	36,379	14,083	13,795	22,296	16,715	3,569	2,012	10	4,255
Hawaii................	10,601	9,989	2,358	2,352	7,631	5,516	1,581	534	–	612
Idaho.................	8,308	7,104	2,498	2,479	4,607	3,374	720	513	128	1,076
Illinois................	68,902	60,986	15,999	15,647	44,987	36,258	4,557	4,172	–	7,915
Indiana................	35,910	32,301	10,515	10,441	21,786	16,330	3,531	1,925	–	3,609
Iowa..................	21,080	18,357	6,362	6,073	11,995	7,932	2,817	1,246	246	2,476
Kansas................	16,144	15,069	4,100	4,061	10,969	7,418	2,594	957	–	1,076
Kentucky..............	25,684	22,574	8,089	8,057	14,485	10,506	2,789	1,191	–	3,109
Louisiana.............	26,931	25,337	11,213	11,136	14,123	8,994	2,706	2,423	7	1,587
Maine.................	8,418	7,976	2,894	2,884	5,082	3,777	739	566	–	442
Maryland..............	36,104	33,262	10,374	10,030	22,887	17,095	3,236	2,556	135	2,707
Massachusetts........	49,001	44,857	13,255	12,920	31,603	22,821	4,434	4,348	673	3,470
Michigan..............	63,986	52,876	18,055	17,850	34,821	23,920	7,060	3,841	857	10,254
Minnesota.............	38,554	34,160	9,725	9,608	24,435	20,561	2,184	1,691	–	4,394
Mississippi............	18,765	17,035	7,809	7,725	9,225	6,953	1,695	578	271	1,459
Missouri...............	31,066	26,487	10,815	10,441	15,673	10,802	2,618	2,253	–	4,578
Montana...............	7,653	5,651	2,207	2,202	3,445	2,459	522	464	78	1,923
Nebraska..............	9,815	9,181	3,194	3,141	5,987	4,367	952	668	–	634
Nevada................	14,318	10,983	3,018	2,798	7,964	6,775	638	551	90	3,245
New Hampshire........	7,153	5,838	1,872	1,693	3,966	2,208	873	885	558	757
New Jersey............	57,582	51,103	14,070	13,413	37,033	27,456	5,380	4,197	1,003	5,476
New Mexico............	15,196	14,125	5,353	5,171	8,771	5,093	1,377	2,301	–	1,071
New York..............	179,605	148,573	56,076	48,699	92,497	71,546	8,902	12,050	8,022	23,009
North Carolina........	56,470	45,700	15,498	15,193	30,202	22,713	4,747	2,741	56	10,770
North Dakota..........	9,246	8,541	1,797	1,750	6,744	5,620	720	404	–	705
Ohio..................	72,471	59,317	21,275	20,688	38,042	25,929	7,681	4,432	864	12,289
Oklahoma..............	23,263	20,715	7,500	7,363	13,215	8,839	2,390	1,985	583	1,965
Oregon................	25,059	21,699	7,846	7,831	13,853	8,700	3,450	1,703	466	2,894
Pennsylvania..........	78,467	66,792	20,627	20,440	46,165	32,950	9,029	4,186	1,657	10,018
Rhode Island..........	7,947	6,803	2,346	2,311	4,458	2,828	722	908	33	1,110
South Carolina........	26,106	21,243	7,327	6,893	13,916	8,036	3,967	1,913	1,901	2,962
South Dakota..........	4,351	3,991	1,658	1,630	2,334	1,521	320	492	–	360
Tennessee.............	30,803	27,303	11,269	11,199	16,034	11,982	1,950	2,102	–	3,500
Texas.................	130,720	108,125	37,985	37,311	70,140	48,597	11,902	9,641	–	22,595
Utah..................	15,601	14,176	4,487	4,481	9,689	5,810	2,956	922	270	1,155
Vermont...............	6,349	5,474	1,908	1,904	3,566	2,757	521	288	49	826
Virginia...............	43,138	39,439	9,784	9,278	29,655	18,145	7,605	3,905	609	3,089
Washington............	40,665	34,074	10,011	9,743	24,063	17,625	4,220	2,219	612	5,979
West Virginia..........	13,247	12,295	4,359	4,267	7,935	5,286	1,406	1,243	91	862
Wisconsin..............	35,881	31,411	9,088	8,855	22,323	15,995	3,816	2,512	–	4,470
Wyoming...............	6,845	6,147	2,442	2,213	3,705	2,551	175	979	93	605

– Represents or rounds to zero. [1] Includes amounts for categories not shown separately. [2] Duplicate intergovernmental transactions are excluded.

Source: U.S. Census Bureau, Federal, State, and Local Governments, Government Finance Statistics, "Annual Surveys of State and Local Government Finances," <http://www.census.gov/govs/local/>, accessed January 2015.

Table 484. Government Employment and Payrolls by Type and Level of Government: 1982 to 2013

[Employees in thousands (15,841 represents 15,841,000); payroll in millions of dollars (23,173 represents $23,173,000,000). Data through 1992 are for the month of October. Beginning with the 1997 survey, data are for the month of March. Covers both full-time and part-time employees. Local government data are estimates subject to sampling variation; see Appendix III and source]

Type of government	1982	1987	1992	1997	2000	2005	2010	2011	2012	2013
EMPLOYEES (1,000)										
Total	**15,841**	**17,212**	**18,745**	**19,540**	**20,876**	**21,725**	**22,607**	**22,267**	**22,040**	**21,831**
Federal (civilian)[1]	2,848	3,091	3,047	2,807	2,899	2,720	3,008	2,854	2,793	2,745
State and local	12,993	14,121	15,698	16,733	17,976	19,004	19,599	19,413	19,247	19,086
Percent of total	82	82	84	86	86	87	87	87	87	87
State	3,744	4,116	4,595	4,733	4,877	5,078	5,326	5,314	5,286	5,282
Local	9,249	10,005	11,103	12,000	13,099	13,926	14,274	14,099	13,961	13,804
PAYROLLS (mil. dol.)										
Total	**23,173**	**32,669**	**43,120**	**49,156**	**58,166**	**71,599**	**86,643**	**86,496**	**87,862**	**87,940**
Federal (civilian)[1]	5,959	7,924	9,937	9,744	11,485	13,475	16,238	16,119	16,867	16,503
State and local	17,214	24,745	33,183	39,412	46,681	58,123	70,404	70,378	70,995	71,437
Percent of total	74	76	77	80	80	81	81	81	81	81
State	5,022	7,263	9,828	11,413	13,279	16,062	19,579	19,972	20,173	20,502
Local	12,192	17,482	23,355	27,999	33,402	42,062	50,825	50,406	50,822	50,936

[1] Includes employees outside the United States.

Source: U.S. Census Bureau, Census of Governments, "2013 Annual Survey of Public Employment and Payroll," <http://factfinder2.census.gov>, accessed June 2015. See also <http://www.census.gov/govs/apes/>.

Table 485. Government Employment and Payroll by Function: 2013

[Employees in thousands (21,831 represents 21,831,000); payroll in millions of dollars (87,940.4 represents $87,940,400,000). See headnote, Table 484]

Function	Employees (1,000) Total	Federal (civilian)[1]	State and local Total	State	Local	Payrolls (mil. dol.) Total	Federal (civilian)[1]	State and local Total	State	Local
Total, 2013	**21,831**	**2,745**	**19,086**	**5,282**	**13,804**	**87,940.4**	**16,503.0**	**71,437.4**	**20,501.6**	**50,935.7**
Financial administration	537	117	420	171	249	2,298.6	519.0	1,779.6	768.0	1,011.7
Other government administration	424	24	400	58	342	1,344.4	160.6	1,183.8	247.8	936.0
Judicial & legal	489	62	427	176	251	2,509.8	460.3	2,049.5	936.6	1,112.9
National defense[2]	776	776	(X)	(X)	(X)	3,385.4	3,385.4	(X)	(X)	(X)
Police protection	1,162	192	970	105	865	6,066.0	1,003.4	5,062.6	583.8	4,478.8
Fire protection	420	(X)	420	(X)	420	2,044.0	(X)	2,044.0	(X)	2,044
Corrections	741	39	702	439	263	3,204.2	226.2	2,978.0	1,859.6	1,118.3
Streets & highways	512	3	509	223	287	2,158.0	19.0	2,139.0	999.0	1,140.0
Air transportation	96	47	49	3	45	591.9	354.2	237.7	17.3	220.4
Water transport/terminals	18	5	14	5	9	89.9	15.1	74.8	25.3	49.5
Public welfare	531	10	521	238	283	2,042.7	81.6	1,961.1	904.7	1,056.5
Health	638	165	473	205	268	3,101.7	1,228.7	1,873.0	849.8	1,023.2
Hospitals	1,260	216	1,045	420	625	6,209.8	1,483.1	4,726.7	1,864.7	2,862.0
Social insurance administration	149	66	83	83	–	751.1	412.5	338.6	336.2	2.4
Housing & community development	129	13	116	–	116	580.3	98.1	482.1	0.3	481.8
Parks & recreation	423	26	397	41	356	1,013.6	136.7	876.9	120.2	756.7
Natural resources	365	178	187	143	44	1,817.0	1,092.0	725.1	568.4	156.7
Solid waste management	113	(X)	113	3	110	422.5	(X)	422.5	14.2	408.3
Sewerage	131	(X)	131	2	129	582.7	(X)	582.7	10.3	572.5
Water supply	183	(X)	183	1	183	812.8	(X)	812.8	4.4	808.4
Electric power	81	(X)	81	4	77	542.2	(X)	542.2	28.4	513.8
Gas supply	11	(X)	11	–	11	51.4	(X)	51.4	–	51.4
Transit	236	(X)	236	32	204	1,272.8	(X)	1,272.8	199.4	1,073.4
Elem. and secondary education	7,627	(X)	7,627	61	7,566	26,161.0	(X)	26,161.0	230	25,930.8
Higher education	3,157	(X)	3,157	2,580	578	10,300.7	(X)	10,300.7	8,678.5	1,622.1
Other education	103	10	93	93	–	450.0	72.9	377.1	377.1	–
Libraries	188	4	184	1	183	455.0	27.4	427.6	1.7	426
Space research and technology	18	18	(X)	(X)	(X)	175.4	175.4	(X)	(X)	(X)
Postal Service	580	580	(X)	(X)	(X)	4,043.6	4,043.6	(X)	(X)	(X)
State liquor stores	11	(X)	11	11	–	27.7	(X)	27.7	27.7	–
Other & unallocable	720	195	526	187	339	3,434.1	1,507.8	1,926.3	848.3	1,078.0

– Represents or rounds to zero. X Not applicable. [1] Includes employees outside the United States. [2] Includes international relations.

Source: U.S. Census Bureau, Census of Governments, "2013 Annual Survey of Public Employment and Payroll," <http://factfinder2.census.gov>, accessed June 2015. See also <http://www.census.gov/govs/apes/>.

Table 486. State and Local Government—Employer Costs Per Hour Worked: 2015

[In dollars. As of March. Based on a sample; see source for details]

Occupation and industry	Total compensation	Wages and salaries	Benefit cost					
			Total	Paid leave	Supplemental pay	Insurance	Retirement and savings	Legally required benefits
Total workers........................	**44.25**	**28.33**	**15.92**	**3.21**	**0.35**	**5.25**	**4.49**	**2.60**
OCCUPATIONAL GROUP								
Management, professional, and related............	53.51	35.67	17.85	3.54	0.26	5.73	5.35	2.97
Professional and related...........................	52.60	35.28	17.33	3.20	0.25	5.72	5.31	2.85
Teachers [1]................................	60.23	41.72	18.51	2.89	0.15	6.16	6.22	3.10
Primary, secondary, and special education school teachers................................	60.30	41.24	19.06	2.60	0.17	6.82	6.57	2.90
Sales and office..................................	30.43	18.13	12.30	2.64	0.20	4.78	2.76	1.91
Office and administrative support................	30.60	18.19	12.41	2.67	0.20	4.84	2.79	1.91
Service...	33.26	19.32	13.94	2.88	0.60	4.44	3.85	2.16
INDUSTRY GROUP								
Education and health services....................	46.17	30.69	15.48	2.88	0.22	5.39	4.47	2.53
Educational services..............................	46.92	31.39	15.53	2.73	0.16	5.46	4.67	2.50
Elementary and secondary schools............	46.02	30.83	15.19	2.35	0.17	5.59	4.71	2.37
Junior colleges, colleges, and universities......	50.18	33.56	16.62	4.01	0.13	4.92	4.64	2.93
Health care and social assistance................	41.43	26.26	15.18	3.80	0.60	4.92	3.16	2.70
Hospitals..	46.25	29.68	16.57	4.34	0.77	5.19	3.44	2.83
Public administration.............................	42.30	25.09	17.21	3.93	0.59	5.16	4.76	2.76

[1] Includes postsecondary teachers; primary, secondary, and special education teachers; and other teachers and instructors.

Source: U.S. Bureau of Labor Statistics, National Compensation Survey, *Employer Costs for Employee Compensation–March 2015*, June 2015. See also <http://www.bls.gov/ncs/ect/>.

Table 487. State and Local Government—Full-Time Employment and Salary by Sex and Race and Ethnic Group: 1980 to 2013

[2,350 represents 2,350,000. As of June 30. Excludes school systems and educational institutions. Based on reports from state governments (42 in 1980; 49 in 1984 through 1987; and 50 in 1989 through 1991) and a sample of county, municipal, township, and special district jurisdictions employing 15 or more nonelected, nonappointed full-time employees. Beginning 1993, only for state and local governments with 100 or more employees. For definition of median, see Guide to Tabular Presentation]

Year and occupation	Employment (1,000)						Median annual salary ($1,000)					
				Minority						Minority		
	Male	Female	White [1]	Total [2]	Black [1]	Hispanic [3]	Male	Female	White [1]	Total [2]	Black [1]	Hispanic [3]
1980........................	2,350	1,637	3,146	842	619	163	15.2	11.4	13.8	11.8	11.5	12.3
1984........................	2,700	1,880	3,458	1,121	799	233	21.4	16.2	19.6	17.4	16.5	18.4
1985........................	2,789	1,952	3,563	1,179	835	248	22.3	17.3	20.6	18.4	17.5	19.2
1986........................	2,797	1,982	3,549	1,230	865	259	23.4	18.1	21.5	19.6	18.7	20.2
1987........................	2,818	2,031	3,600	1,249	872	268	24.2	18.9	22.4	20.9	19.3	21.1
1989........................	3,030	2,227	3,863	1,394	961	308	26.1	20.6	24.1	22.1	20.7	22.7
1990........................	3,071	2,302	3,918	1,456	994	327	27.3	21.8	25.2	23.3	22.0	23.8
1991........................	3,110	2,349	3,965	1,494	1,011	340	28.4	22.7	26.4	23.8	22.7	24.5
1993........................	2,820	2,204	3,588	1,436	948	341	30.6	24.3	28.5	25.9	24.2	26.8
1995........................	2,960	2,355	3,781	1,534	993	379	33.5	27.0	31.4	26.3	26.8	28.6
1997........................	2,898	2,307	3,676	1,529	973	392	34.6	27.9	32.2	30.2	27.4	29.5
1999........................	2,939	2,393	3,723	1,609	1,012	417	37.0	29.9	34.8	31.1	29.6	31.2
2001........................	3,080	2,554	3,888	1,746	1,077	471	39.8	32.1	37.5	34.0	31.5	33.8
2003........................	3,134	2,610	3,919	1,826	1,097	508	42.2	34.7	40.0	35.9	33.6	36.6
2005........................	3,185	2,644	3,973	1,856	1,100	532	44.1	36.4	41.5	37.7	35.3	38.9
2007........................	3,383	2,823	4,156	(NA)	(NA)	(NA)	(NA)	(NA)	(NA)	(NA)	(NA)	(NA)
2009........................	3,239	2,742	3,976	2,004	1,145	601	50.3	41.5	47.6	46.8	40.3	44.8
2011........................	2,924	2,477	3,561	1,839	1,015	570	51.8	43.1	49.1	48.2	41.7	47.0
2013, total.............	**3,055**	**2,568**	**3,671**	**1,952**	**1,057**	**634**	**52.5**	**43.8**	**49.9**	**49.8**	**42.0**	**46.8**
Officials/ administrators.........	217	156	284	88	50	23	72.3	70.7	71.7	72.0	70.9	71.9
Professionals............	637	898	1,044	389	249	131	65.0	55.7	60.0	59.5	52.5	58.3
Technicians..............	250	187	291	146	71	51	51.7	41.9	48.5	47.7	40.8	45.9
Protective service.......	954	236	811	378	204	144	53.7	41.6	52.3	53.5	42.2	57.5
Paraprofessionals.......	107	269	203	173	110	48	38.0	35.2	37.2	36.6	33.0	36.0
Administrative support..	116	680	490	307	156	116	38.8	36.8	36.7	38.7	36.5	37.9
Skilled craft..............	385	21	286	120	62	44	47.4	42.4	36.7	51.0	45.6	47.9
Service/maintenance. ..	389	122	261	249	155	77	39.4	31.3	30.3	39.1	36.3	38.2

NA Not available. [1] Non-Hispanic. [2] Includes other minority groups, not shown separately. [3] Persons of Hispanic origin may be of any race.

Source: U.S. Equal Employment Opportunity Commission, 1980–1991, "Job Patterns for Minorities and Women in State and Local Government," annual; beginning 1993, biennial, <www.eeoc.gov>, accessed March 2015.

Table 488. State and Local Government Full-Time Equivalent Employment by Selected Function and State: 2013

[In thousands (1,769.5 represents 1,769,500). For March. Local government amounts are estimates subject to sampling variation; see Appendix III and <http://www.census.gov/govs/apes/>]

State	Total State	Total Local	Education: Elementary/secondary State	Elementary/secondary Local	Higher education State	Higher education Local	Public welfare State	Public welfare Local	Health State	Health Local	Hospitals State	Hospitals Local	Highways State	Highways Local	Police protection State	Police protection Local	Fire protection State	Fire protection Local	Corrections State	Corrections Local	Parks and recreation State	Parks and recreation Local
U.S.	1,769.5	6,855.9	48.1	6,525.9	1,721.3	330.0	233.3	265.2	196.0	239.2	390.5	569.2	218.1	272.4	103.5	810.7	(X)	340.9	435.5	255.4	35.5	224.7
AL	41.3	99.0	—	99.0	41.3	—	4.0	6.4	5.4	6.4	11.7	25.0	4.2	6.3	1.4	12.6	(X)	6.0	4.9	3.4	0.6	3.8
AK	9.0	17.5	3.1	17.4	5.9	0.1	1.9	0.1	0.7	0.3	0.2	0.7	3.2	0.8	0.7	1.1	(X)	0.9	2.1	0.1	0.1	0.6
AZ	31.6	125.3	—	113.4	31.6	11.9	5.8	1.2	2.4	4.0	0.6	2.8	2.9	4.1	1.9	17.8	(X)	9.0	9.8	5.3	0.3	4.4
AR	26.0	69.4	—	69.3	26.0	0.1	4.0	0.1	4.3	0.6	6.8	1.3	3.4	3.5	1.2	6.9	(X)	2.8	5.5	2.5	1.1	1.3
CA	161.5	673.3	—	610.2	161.5	63.1	3.7	69.6	13.5	44.0	41.9	70.0	20.0	21.8	10.9	89.4	(X)	33.2	51.5	30.9	3.3	30.6
CO	43.1	103.3	—	102.1	43.1	1.1	2.2	6.6	1.3	4.4	5.6	10.6	3.1	5.1	1.2	13.6	(X)	6.0	7.0	3.7	1.0	8.1
CT	18.2	88.7	—	88.7	18.2	—	5.6	1.7	3.9	1.3	6.5	—	3.2	3.3	2.0	7.9	(X)	4.4	6.7	—	0.2	1.9
DE	8.4	17.6	—	17.6	8.4	—	1.6	—	2.1	0.4	1.5	—	1.5	0.4	1.1	1.5	(X)	0.2	2.9	—	0.3	0.2
DC	(X)	8.5	(X)	7.5	(X)	1.0	(X)	2.0	(X)	0.7	(X)	1.4	(X)	0.8	(X)	4.5	(X)	1.3	(X)	1.3	(X)	0.5
FL	62.1	372.1	—	344.1	62.1	28.0	9.0	4.6	19.1	5.3	4.0	48.9	6.4	12.5	4.1	56.7	(X)	27.7	24.6	16.0	1.4	16.9
GA	58.8	236.3	25.2	236.3	58.8	—	8.5	1.5	7.8	8.6	7.8	18.8	4.8	7.6	2.0	24.9	(X)	12.7	17.0	10.1	2.0	2.1
HI	35.9	—	—	—	10.7	—	0.4	0.2	2.0	0.3	4.6	—	0.9	1.0	—	3.8	(X)	1.9	2.3	—	0.2	2.1
ID	8.5	35.0	—	33.1	8.5	1.9	1.6	0.1	1.7	0.9	0.6	3.6	1.5	1.6	0.5	3.6	(X)	1.4	2.0	1.6	0.2	0.8
IL	62.1	301.7	—	278.5	62.1	23.2	9.0	5.4	2.2	5.7	9.8	11.6	7.0	10.8	3.2	50.4	(X)	17.7	10.9	10.6	0.4	19.1
IN	53.9	133.7	—	133.7	53.9	—	4.8	1.0	1.7	3.1	1.9	22.3	3.7	5.4	1.9	13.8	(X)	7.6	6.3	6.2	0.2	3.1
IA	22.5	74.8	—	67.8	22.5	7.0	2.7	1.2	0.4	1.9	6.8	11.3	2.2	5.0	0.9	6.0	(X)	2.0	3.0	1.6	0.1	2.0
KS	21.3	100.4	—	92.6	21.3	7.9	2.2	0.5	1.0	3.1	8.1	8.2	2.9	4.6	1.1	7.6	(X)	3.3	3.4	3.1	0.6	2.3
KY	38.8	102.1	1.4	102.1	38.8	—	7.6	0.4	3.1	5.7	5.7	5.1	4.6	2.6	1.7	7.5	(X)	4.6	4.3	3.9	1.1	1.7
LA	29.2	94.4	—	94.4	27.7	—	5.2	0.7	2.4	1.7	10.4	19.0	2.1	1.8	1.7	15.5	(X)	4.9	5.9	6.6	1.0	3.9
ME	7.4	36.3	—	36.3	7.3	—	2.7	0.1	1.0	0.3	0.5	1.1	2.1	1.5	0.5	2.5	(X)	1.7	1.2	0.8	0.2	0.7
MD	27.3	136.6	2.2	124.0	27.3	12.6	6.6	3.1	6.0	5.0	3.6	—	4.5	4.7	2.5	16.8	(X)	6.7	12.1	3.6	0.9	6.4
MA	33.6	150.8	—	150.7	31.4	0.1	6.8	2.2	7.1	3.0	5.5	2.8	3.1	5.6	7.9	16.5	(X)	12.2	6.9	—	0.2	2.4
MI	73.9	174.3	—	160.8	73.9	13.5	12.2	3.5	5.1	10.3	17.2	7.5	2.7	7.9	2.5	18.4	(X)	7.2	13.3	5.6	0.6	3.6
MN	36.6	117.2	—	117.2	36.6	—	2.8	10.2	3.1	2.9	4.3	5.9	4.5	7.2	0.9	10.9	(X)	2.9	4.1	4.8	0.6	4.9
MS	19.5	81.1	—	74.7	19.5	6.5	3.0	0.5	3.8	0.3	11.7	18.0	3.4	4.4	1.1	8.1	(X)	3.5	3.3	2.2	0.6	1.4
MO	28.5	139.8	—	133.6	28.5	6.2	7.0	3.2	3.6	4.0	10.2	12.7	5.2	6.5	2.5	15.9	(X)	7.5	12.1	3.1	0.6	4.3
MT	7.4	22.0	—	21.5	7.4	0.5	1.7	0.5	0.9	1.1	0.6	0.8	2.1	1.3	0.5	2.1	(X)	0.7	1.3	0.7	0.1	0.5
NE	12.5	51.4	—	48.1	12.5	3.3	2.4	1.6	0.6	0.6	3.8	4.5	2.1	3.0	0.8	4.2	(X)	1.4	2.9	1.5	0.3	1.1
NV	9.3	38.9	—	38.9	9.3	—	1.8	0.9	1.3	0.8	1.3	4.0	1.7	1.1	0.9	7.1	(X)	2.6	3.6	2.3	0.3	3.4
NH	6.8	34.1	—	34.1	6.8	—	1.9	2.5	0.8	0.2	0.6	—	1.7	1.5	0.5	3.2	(X)	1.9	1.1	—	0.3	0.5
NJ	50.7	219.7	15.7	207.8	35.0	11.9	8.9	8.7	4.0	3.7	17.2	2.3	5.9	7.5	3.8	25.7	(X)	7.5	9.0	5.9	1.0	4.8
NM	17.5	49.8	—	46.5	17.5	3.4	1.7	0.9	2.3	0.7	7.5	1.1	2.1	2.0	0.5	5.3	(X)	2.4	3.6	2.4	0.6	1.9
NY	53.7	494.5	—	470.0	53.7	24.5	4.4	45.8	8.0	16.0	42.9	49.5	11.1	24.3	5.8	78.4	(X)	23.8	29.6	23.3	2.6	12.7
NC	60.4	226.6	—	204.2	60.4	22.5	1.1	15.6	2.3	14.4	18.5	48.0	10.8	4.0	3.5	23.9	(X)	9.0	20.7	5.6	0.2	5.9
ND	9.9	16.1	—	16.1	9.9	—	0.5	1.0	1.4	0.6	0.9	—	1.0	1.2	0.2	1.4	(X)	0.4	0.8	0.5	0.2	0.9
OH	72.1	248.6	—	243.7	72.1	5.0	2.7	18.8	3.2	14.4	15.6	10.9	6.3	11.8	2.6	27.2	(X)	16.9	13.2	7.6	0.7	8.4
OK	30.2	88.3	—	88.1	30.2	0.2	5.8	0.1	5.2	1.7	1.8	10.4	2.8	5.2	2.6	9.2	(X)	4.4	4.7	1.9	0.7	1.6
OR	23.7	71.3	—	62.7	23.7	8.6	7.5	1.1	1.6	4.5	7.9	2.1	3.7	3.3	1.3	7.5	(X)	3.9	5.1	3.2	0.4	3.5
PA	55.3	252.3	—	242.0	55.3	10.3	11.2	17.7	1.7	5.7	11.1	—	13.7	10.1	6.6	25.2	(X)	5.2	18.4	12.8	2.6	3.2
RI	6.1	19.5	0.4	19.5	5.7	—	1.2	0.1	0.8	0.1	0.8	—	0.7	0.8	0.3	2.6	(X)	2.1	1.6	—	0.1	3.4
SC	31.2	100.8	—	100.8	31.2	—	4.7	0.4	5.4	2.3	7.0	23.2	4.4	2.6	2.1	11.6	(X)	5.4	8.2	3.4	0.8	3.4
SD	5.6	21.4	—	20.7	5.6	0.7	1.7	0.2	0.6	0.3	0.4	0.4	1.0	1.4	0.3	1.6	(X)	0.5	0.9	0.7	0.3	0.7
TN	35.2	134.9	—	134.9	35.2	—	7.5	2.2	3.8	4.2	3.8	20.9	3.6	6.4	1.7	19.0	(X)	7.9	7.1	5.3	1.1	3.9
TX	135.7	723.6	—	681.3	135.7	42.3	22.5	4.1	31.0	24.9	24.8	52.8	12.8	20.3	6.7	66.3	(X)	26.2	40.2	28.5	1.2	15.8
UT	24.5	53.4	—	53.4	24.5	—	2.8	0.6	1.9	3.4	8.6	0.4	1.6	1.7	0.8	5.2	(X)	2.4	3.0	2.1	0.3	2.1
VT	5.0	19.8	—	19.5	5.0	—	1.4	—	0.5	0.1	0.2	—	1.1	1.0	0.6	1.0	(X)	0.3	1.1	—	0.1	0.2
VA	56.8	196.6	—	195.4	56.8	1.2	2.8	9.0	5.4	5.8	14.2	2.3	7.2	4.2	3.1	18.2	(X)	10.6	13.5	11.0	1.0	7.3
WA	43.6	97.5	—	97.5	43.6	—	9.6	1.3	6.7	3.8	7.4	16.4	6.8	6.5	2.2	11.5	(X)	9.4	8.4	4.8	0.5	4.9
WV	14.3	43.5	—	43.5	14.3	—	3.5	—	0.8	1.1	1.7	2.4	5.3	0.8	0.8	2.9	(X)	1.0	3.6	—	0.6	0.8
WI	38.9	121.4	—	112.0	38.9	9.4	2.1	11.0	1.6	4.3	3.6	1.1	1.4	8.9	0.8	14.5	(X)	5.2	9.7	3.7	0.1	2.9
WY	4.0	20.4	—	18.3	4.0	2.1	0.7	—	0.8	0.5	0.7	6.8	1.8	0.8	0.3	1.7	(X)	0.4	1.3	0.7	0.2	0.8

– Represents or rounds to zero. X Not applicable. [1] Includes other categories, not shown separately.

Source: U.S. Census Bureau, Census of Governments, "2013 Annual Survey of Public Employment and Payroll," <http://factfinder2.census.gov>, accessed June 2015.

Table 489. State and Local Government Employment and Average Monthly Earnings by State: 2000 to 2013

[4,083 represents 4,083,000. As of March. Full-time equivalent is a computed statistic representing the number of full-time employees that could have been employed if the reported number of hours worked by part-time employees had been worked by full-time employees. This statistic is calculated separately for each function of a government by dividing the "part-time hours paid" by the standard number of hours for full-time employees in the particular government and then adding the resulting quotient to the number of full-time employees]

| State | Full-time equivalent employment (1,000) | | | | | | Average monthly earnings [2] (dol.) | | | | | |
| | State | | | Local [1] | | | State | | | Local [1] | | |
	2000	2010	2013	2000	2010	2013	2000	2010	2013	2000	2010	2013
United States...	**4,083**	**4,378**	**4,306**	**10,995**	**12,171**	**11,756**	**3,374**	**4,620**	**4,933**	**3,169**	**4,310**	**4,487**
Alabama...........	80	90	89	182	198	193	2,841	4,099	4,335	2,431	3,240	3,390
Alaska.............	23	27	27	25	28	28	3,842	5,176	5,587	3,818	4,935	5,107
Arizona...........	65	67	71	182	225	213	3,055	4,365	4,551	2,942	4,163	4,149
Arkansas.........	49	63	64	96	106	105	2,842	3,795	3,849	2,175	3,208	3,314
California.........	355	411	397	1,322	1,381	1,313	4,451	5,740	6,603	4,062	5,787	6,070
Colorado..........	66	71	78	164	199	199	3,779	5,033	5,230	3,076	4,230	4,395
Connecticut.......	66	63	63	111	123	123	3,909	5,632	6,244	3,856	5,063	5,486
Delaware..........	24	26	27	21	23	24	3,222	4,113	4,385	3,163	4,484	4,784
District of Columbia.......	(X)	(X)	(X)	45	44	45	(X)	(X)	(X)	3,923	5,900	6,391
Florida............	185	184	179	580	727	683	3,149	3,861	4,091	2,865	3,986	3,972
Georgia...........	120	124	129	334	392	383	2,899	3,795	3,869	2,677	3,439	3,440
Hawaii............	55	58	57	14	15	16	2,926	3,943	4,279	3,352	5,040	4,914
Idaho.............	23	22	23	51	55	57	3,022	4,280	4,486	2,478	3,341	3,409
Illinois............	128	131	127	493	513	518	3,441	5,324	5,698	3,307	4,716	5,128
Indiana............	83	90	85	232	254	234	2,990	4,023	4,380	2,711	3,547	3,700
Iowa..............	55	51	49	121	124	122	3,656	5,326	5,997	2,727	3,831	4,147
Kansas............	43	44	50	128	156	152	3,071	4,178	4,455	2,491	3,361	3,513
Kentucky..........	74	81	82	149	161	154	3,051	3,940	4,098	2,339	3,101	3,398
Louisiana.........	95	89	78	185	187	179	2,807	4,282	4,381	2,278	3,397	3,488
Maine.............	21	21	21	51	51	52	2,983	4,063	4,162	2,609	3,545	3,652
Maryland..........	91	88	86	182	215	213	3,312	4,650	4,914	3,535	5,190	5,205
Massachusetts. ..	96	95	99	232	233	224	3,683	4,973	5,404	3,403	4,800	5,140
Michigan..........	142	146	143	351	329	291	3,934	5,208	5,549	3,518	4,618	4,612
Minnesota.........	73	80	81	206	201	196	3,892	5,338	5,470	3,255	4,447	4,683
Mississippi........	56	57	58	133	136	135	2,752	3,537	3,729	2,121	2,985	3,052
Missouri...........	91	89	86	208	234	231	2,678	3,518	3,611	2,678	3,502	3,588
Montana...........	18	20	21	34	38	36	2,931	4,016	4,323	2,546	3,476	3,803
Nebraska..........	30	33	32	78	88	88	2,514	4,013	4,155	2,779	3,785	4,158
Nevada...........	22	28	27	61	86	75	3,444	4,891	4,770	3,817	5,149	5,243
New Hampshire...	19	19	19	46	53	50	3,079	4,584	4,833	2,830	3,813	4,122
New Jersey.......	133	152	144	316	356	329	4,075	5,767	6,076	3,967	5,449	5,678
New Mexico.......	48	48	45	70	80	79	2,811	3,978	4,524	2,494	3,440	3,525
New York..........	251	251	239	924	975	933	3,859	5,484	5,961	3,961	5,315	5,639
North Carolina....	123	146	146	328	402	403	3,012	3,886	4,404	2,708	3,690	3,725
North Dakota......	16	18	19	23	26	26	2,826	4,103	4,397	2,778	3,550	3,816
Ohio..............	136	140	137	459	466	443	3,369	4,995	5,130	3,118	4,101	4,194
Oklahoma.........	64	71	66	134	146	142	2,821	3,864	3,960	2,280	3,119	3,293
Oregon............	53	65	66	124	133	124	3,269	4,452	4,789	3,332	4,348	4,721
Pennsylvania.....	150	168	159	388	429	409	3,436	4,564	4,733	3,296	4,290	4,603
Rhode Island......	20	19	19	36	31	29	3,772	5,298	5,632	3,550	4,953	5,301
South Carolina....	79	77	79	155	171	178	2,741	3,810	3,949	2,474	3,557	3,609
South Dakota.....	13	14	14	28	31	32	2,777	3,938	4,224	2,359	3,149	3,262
Tennessee........	81	83	81	218	247	247	2,786	3,822	4,291	2,631	3,358	3,480
Texas..............	269	318	317	909	1,134	1,106	3,095	4,280	4,626	2,643	3,604	3,763
Utah..............	49	51	54	73	90	88	2,880	4,409	4,609	2,836	3,706	3,872
Vermont...........	14	14	14	23	26	25	3,153	4,645	4,819	2,534	3,589	3,840
Virginia............	119	125	125	269	319	314	3,229	4,384	4,553	2,928	3,905	4,091
Washington.......	112	123	106	193	226	215	3,551	4,913	4,889	3,835	5,416	5,812
West Virginia......	32	39	41	61	62	64	2,694	3,554	3,708	2,517	3,219	3,252
Wisconsin.........	64	72	72	220	211	202	3,710	4,901	5,000	3,210	4,239	4,546
Wyoming.........	11	14	13	29	37	37	2,589	4,240	4,368	2,660	4,068	4,297

X Not applicable. [1] Estimates subject to sampling variation; see Appendix III and source. [2] For full-time employees.

Source: U.S. Census Bureau, Census of Governments, "2013 Annual Survey of Public Employment and Payroll," <http://factfinder2.census.gov>, accessed June 2015. See also <http://www.census.gov/govs/apes/>.

Table 490. City Government Employment and Payroll—Largest Cities: 2000 to 2013

[In thousands (458.1 represents 458,100), except as noted. As of March. Full-time equivalent is a computed statistic; see headnote, Table 489 for details]

Cities ranked by 2013 population [1]	Total employment (1,000)			Full-time equivalent employment total (1,000)			Payroll (mil. dol.)			Average monthly earnings for full-time employees (dol.)		
	2000	2010	2013	2000	2010	2013	2000	2010	2013	2000	2010	2013
New York, NY	458.1	444.0	420.8	429.3	413.0	406.9	1,708.8	2,407.5	2,406.5	4,150	5,918	6,031
Los Angeles, CA	49.4	55.1	51.9	48.4	51.0	47.5	230.1	385.2	378.6	4,793	7,850	8,312
Chicago, IL	41.3	35.8	45.4	40.7	35.8	45.1	171.3	216.5	290.9	4,239	6,052	6,487
Houston, TX	25.2	22.8	21.4	24.9	22.6	21.1	75.2	99.0	98.8	3,037	4,389	4,693
Philadelphia, PA	31.1	30.8	30.2	30.0	29.9	29.5	109.2	144.7	155.3	3,637	4,867	5,294
Phoenix, AZ	13.0	14.9	13.8	12.7	14.4	13.3	50.3	80.7	70.7	4,024	5,718	5,410
San Antonio, TX	16.9	16.5	16.4	15.7	15.4	15.7	48.0	64.9	78.0	3,160	4,293	5,039
San Diego, CA	12.3	10.8	10.2	11.4	10.2	9.3	46.9	63.0	62.3	4,201	6,288	6,798
Dallas, TX	15.6	15.5	14.7	15.2	15.1	14.3	50.4	72.8	70.5	3,332	4,884	4,966
San Jose, CA	7.6	7.6	6.0	6.9	6.7	5.2	36.3	52.5	38.7	5,569	8,401	7,926
Austin, TX	10.6	12.6	13.2	10.1	12.3	12.7	31.2	59.5	68.4	3,128	4,863	5,458
Indianapolis, IN	12.4	14.2	12.6	12.0	13.7	12.2	36.7	54.8	51.7	3,115	4,050	4,217
Jacksonville, FL	10.1	9.7	9.9	9.7	9.4	9.7	35.6	41.8	44.5	3,815	4,487	4,668
San Francisco, CA	27.7	30.7	31.9	27.7	27.3	30.2	141.6	207.2	238.3	5,112	7,666	8,132
Columbus, OH	9.1	8.2	8.6	8.8	7.9	8.2	30.1	40.6	44.2	3,478	5,210	5,470
Charlotte, NC	5.2	7.4	7.8	5.1	6.9	7.2	17.1	31.2	35.7	3,408	4,570	4,973
Ft Worth, TX	6.1	6.3	6.6	5.7	6.2	6.2	18.9	28.7	32.9	3,394	4,618	5,397
Detroit, MI	40.7	13.1	11.9	36.1	12.9	11.8	132.1	58.4	55.0	3,693	4,570	4,665
El Paso, TX	5.9	5.9	6.5	5.8	5.6	6.4	15.6	21.2	25.5	2,701	3,836	4,051
Memphis, TN	28.2	24.5	25.8	26.9	23.5	24.1	80.3	87.1	83.1	3,024	3,746	3,510
Seattle, WA	11.4	13.9	10.3	10.3	12.5	10.2	48.3	72.4	73.1	4,726	5,948	7,401
Denver, CO	14.5	13.0	13.1	13.7	12.3	12.6	47.3	65.2	67.9	3,534	5,388	5,478
Washington, DC	37.7	35.2	35.0	36.5	34.0	34.2	139.4	197.8	206.7	3,863	5,893	6,321
Boston, MA	23.3	19.9	20.1	22.0	19.3	19.6	80.2	104.0	115.8	3,734	5,452	6,001
Nashville, TN	20.6	23.9	24.0	19.6	21.7	21.7	62.3	91.4	87.5	3,235	4,311	4,136
Baltimore, MD	30.8	27.9	26.9	29.2	26.7	25.6	95.3	121.8	122.7	3,361	4,597	4,922
Oklahoma City, OK	5.1	4.7	4.7	4.8	4.4	4.5	16.0	21.0	24.5	3,457	4,858	5,566
Louisville, KY	4.6	8.9	8.5	4.3	8.6	8.2	11.8	33.9	33.5	2,844	4,028	4,165
Portland, OR	6.2	6.8	7.0	5.4	5.8	6.1	23.4	35.1	36.4	4,416	6,253	6,159
Las Vegas, NV	2.6	3.2	3.0	2.5	2.9	2.6	11.2	19.3	17.8	4,681	7,162	7,352
Milwaukee, WI	7.9	6.9	6.9	7.7	6.7	6.6	28.5	33.3	34.4	3,706	5,020	5,268
Albuquerque, NM	7.1	7.0	6.9	6.6	6.5	6.4	18.3	22.9	33.7	2,868	3,654	5,532
Tucson, AZ	7.1	5.6	5.1	5.8	5.3	4.8	16.0	23.5	22.2	2,787	4,545	4,744
Fresno, CA	3.2	4.1	3.2	3.1	4.0	3.1	12.7	20.2	18.4	4,073	5,260	6,100
Sacramento, CA	4.4	5.7	5.2	4.0	5.0	4.8	17.0	28.1	34.7	4,400	6,061	7,606
Long Beach, CA	6.1	6.6	5.7	5.7	6.1	5.3	25.7	35.0	36.1	4,855	5,982	7,218
Kansas City, MO	6.8	6.4	6.5	6.6	6.3	6.5	21.3	27.3	21.8	3,246	4,324	3,363
Mesa, AZ	3.5	3.6	3.7	3.3	3.5	3.6	13.4	19.2	21.1	4,072	5,532	5,889
Virginia Beach, VA	19.7	19.2	19.9	17.4	17.7	17.6	43.4	61.1	64.5	2,679	3,775	3,852
Atlanta, GA	8.8	8.1	7.7	8.6	8.1	7.7	25.6	31.5	32.5	2,974	3,872	4,232
Colorado Springs, CO	7.4	8.3	7.5	6.9	7.6	7.0	25.3	39.8	37.7	3,747	5,307	5,518
Omaha, NE	3.4	3.1	3.1	2.9	2.9	2.9	10.6	14.8	16.5	3,874	5,491	6,086
Raleigh, NC	3.2	5.1	5.0	2.9	4.2	4.0	8.9	16.3	16.8	3,114	4,166	4,413
Miami, FL	3.8	4.3	4.1	3.6	4.1	3.8	15.1	21.2	19.2	4,276	5,378	5,146
Oakland, CA	4.2	4.1	4.5	4.2	3.6	3.9	24.8	28.4	30.4	5,861	8,702	8,511
Minneapolis, MN	6.3	5.5	5.2	5.8	5.1	4.8	21.3	25.7	25.2	3,866	5,159	5,392
Tulsa, OK	4.5	4.0	4.0	4.5	3.9	4.0	13.7	16.8	17.7	3,126	4,376	4,449
Cleveland, OH	10.1	8.4	7.8	9.4	7.9	7.3	27.8	35.2	34.6	2,989	4,462	4,784
Wichita, KS	3.6	3.1	3.1	3.1	3.1	2.9	9.3	13.0	12.6	3,072	4,198	4,488
Arlington, TX	3.0	2.9	2.9	2.4	2.6	2.6	7.1	12.1	12.6	3,090	4,878	5,076
New Orleans, LA	(NA)	6.9	6.3	(NA)	6.8	6.2	(NA)	25.9	25.6	(NA)	3,815	4,162
Bakersfield, CA	1.3	1.5	1.5	1.2	1.5	1.4	5.3	8.2	8.6	4,469	5,691	6,104
Tampa, FL	4.3	4.5	4.3	4.2	4.4	4.2	14.1	23.2	22.6	3,370	5,376	5,453
Honolulu, HI	9.8	9.5	9.9	9.1	8.8	9.2	30.9	45.8	45.3	3,435	5,266	4,995
Aurora, CO	2.5	2.6	2.6	2.5	2.6	2.6	9.0	13.8	14.6	3,682	5,374	5,569
Anaheim, CA	3.2	3.2	2.7	2.5	2.6	2.2	11.5	17.4	15.9	5,267	7,982	8,583
Santa Ana, CA	2.5	1.7	3.4	2.2	1.5	2.7	10.1	12.1	12.8	5,606	8,623	4,840
St Louis, MO	8.0	6.9	6.2	7.6	6.8	6.2	24.1	26.8	26.8	3,176	3,973	4,373
Riverside, CA	2.1	2.4	2.5	1.9	2.2	2.3	8.0	13.8	14.7	4,625	6,536	6,660
Corpus Christi, TX	3.5	2.8	2.8	3.3	2.8	2.8	8.6	10.5	11.2	2,675	3,848	4,087
Lexington, KY	4.0	4.1	3.9	3.6	3.8	3.6	10.2	16.6	16.3	2,910	4,575	4,616
Pittsburgh, PA	4.4	3.3	3.3	4.3	3.3	3.2	15.3	13.8	17.6	3,593	4,210	5,670
Anchorage, AK	10.1	11.1	10.5	9.0	9.9	9.5	34.6	50.6	50.1	3,973	5,142	5,374
Stockton, CA	2.3	1.8	2.1	1.9	1.6	1.9	7.1	9.4	11.9	4,054	6,160	6,198
Cincinnati, OH	6.5	5.9	5.9	6.4	5.6	5.4	21.3	27.9	25.0	3,504	5,122	4,906
St Paul, MN	4.2	3.2	3.7	3.2	3.0	3.5	13.3	16.4	18.8	4,189	5,751	5,542
Toledo, OH	2.8	2.6	2.1	2.8	2.6	2.1	10.0	11.7	10.2	3,628	4,551	4,900
Greensboro, NC	(NA)	3.4	3.4	(NA)	3.1	3.1	(NA)	11.6	11.9	(NA)	3,837	3,879
Newark, NJ	5.5	4.7	3.8	5.2	4.5	3.7	22.3	26.6	21.1	4,371	6,061	5,825
Plano, TX	2.0	2.5	2.5	1.8	2.2	2.1	6.4	10.2	10.6	3,702	4,927	5,184
Henderson, NV	(NA)	2.7	2.8	(NA)	2.2	2.2	(NA)	13.7	13.9	(NA)	7,007	7,231
Lincoln, NE	2.7	2.9	2.9	2.5	2.6	2.6	8.2	12.4	14.0	3,382	4,982	5,493
Buffalo, NY	11.4	11.3	10.2	10.5	10.0	9.0	43.4	45.9	47.2	4,457	4,569	5,251
Jersey City, NJ	(NA)	3.6	3.2	(NA)	3.4	3.0	(NA)	20.2	19.7	(NA)	6,122	6,955
Chula Vista, CA	(NA)	1.4	1.1	(NA)	1.3	1.0	(NA)	7.9	6.7	(NA)	6,314	7,034
Ft Wayne, IN	(NA)	2.1	2.1	(NA)	2.0	2.0	(NA)	8.6	8.8	(NA)	4,319	4,555

NA Not available. [1] Based on estimated resident population as of July 1.

Source: U.S. Census Bureau, Census of Governments, "2013 Annual Survey of Public Employment and Payroll," <http://factfinder2.census.gov>, accessed June 2015. See also <http://www.census.gov/govs/apes/>.

Table 491. County Government Employment and Payroll—Largest Counties: 2010 to 2013

[In units as indicated (107.5 represents 107,500). As of March. Full-time equivalent employment is a derived statistic that provides an estimate of a government's total full-time employment by converting part-time employees to a full-time amount; see headnote, Table 489 for details]

Counties ranked by 2013 population [1]	Total employment (1,000)			Total full-time equivalent employment (1,000)		Payroll (mil. dol.)			Average monthly earnings for full-time employees (dol.)	
	2010	2012	2013	2010	2013	2010	2012	2013	2010	2013
Los Angeles, CA..........	107.5	104.8	102.9	103.9	100.2	610.3	615.7	601.0	5,925	6,042
Cook, IL..................	22.8	22.5	23.3	22.8	23.3	120.7	127.7	133.3	5,305	5,729
Harris, TX................	27.8	25.5	26.6	26.4	25.7	119.8	113.4	118.2	4,537	4,661
Maricopa, AZ.............	13.7	12.9	13.0	13.1	12.8	54.2	53.5	53.9	4,188	4,224
San Diego, CA............	20.9	19.6	20.5	19.5	19.2	101.1	97.4	100.2	5,201	5,149
Orange, CA...............	17.7	17.8	18.3	16.9	17.8	102.9	105.2	105.9	6,103	6,023
Miami-Dade, FL..........	51.1	45.2	37.8	49.9	36.7	285.0	274.2	215.7	5,794	6,045
Dallas, TX................	18.1	17.9	18.7	16.8	17.3	76.6	79.9	85.1	4,536	4,930
Riverside, CA.............	21.0	21.6	21.3	20.1	20.9	110.8	117.4	121.0	5,517	5,839
San Bernardino, CA......	21.2	20.1	20.2	19.9	19.3	101.7	100.4	100.8	5,269	5,396
King, WA.................	14.1	13.7	13.7	13.4	12.9	82.3	78.8	78.6	6,321	6,173
Clark, NV................	22.4	21.0	20.7	20.3	19.0	121.5	120.2	119.8	6,155	6,498
Tarrant, TX...............	11.0	12.7	12.9	10.7	12.2	46.0	50.4	51.6	4,307	4,215
Santa Clara, CA..........	19.0	18.7	19.0	18.2	18.1	129.6	126.6	130.4	7,297	7,380
Broward, FL..............	12.1	11.6	11.0	11.7	10.6	61.4	54.1	50.3	5,313	4,815
Bexar, TX................	11.0	10.9	11.2	10.6	10.8	41.3	43.0	45.8	3,865	4,190
Wayne, MI................	4.7	4.3	4.3	4.7	4.2	21.5	20.3	20.5	4,645	4,943
Alameda, CA.............	12.1	12.2	12.4	11.5	11.8	77.2	81.9	84.2	6,885	7,199
Suffolk, NY..............	15.0	15.6	15.1	13.2	12.9	74.7	82.3	81.3	5,813	6,365
Sacramento, CA..........	13.1	12.0	12.6	12.7	11.8	72.5	71.4	73.9	5,736	6,329
Palm Beach, FL..........	11.3	11.1	11.1	10.9	10.6	60.7	58.8	59.2	5,634	5,732
Nassau, NY..............	18.0	16.2	15.6	16.0	13.6	88.5	83.4	80.7	5,748	5,973
Hillsborough, FL.........	10.5	9.9	9.8	10.1	9.5	45.7	42.6	42.6	4,583	4,547
Cuyahoga, OH...........	14.6	14.3	14.0	14.2	13.4	62.1	64.2	63.5	4,305	4,642
Allegheny, PA............	7.1	7.6	7.1	7.0	6.9	26.3	26.9	27.0	3,853	3,938
Oakland, MI..............	4.3	4.6	4.6	4.0	4.2	18.8	19.9	20.0	4,764	4,837
Orange, FL...............	11.3	11.1	10.9	10.4	10.2	43.8	44.0	42.0	4,235	4,147
Franklin, OH.............	6.7	6.4	6.3	6.4	6.1	25.3	25.2	25.0	3,957	4,167
Hennepin, MN............	7.7	7.5	7.5	7.6	7.4	40.3	40.3	41.6	5,449	5,805
Fairfax, VA...............	47.6	49.7	48.5	39.2	40.2	200.7	205.6	211.7	5,170	5,314
Travis, TX................	5.3	5.4	5.7	5.2	5.6	22.0	22.7	25.0	4,228	4,482
Contra Costa, CA........	8.6	8.3	8.3	7.9	7.6	49.8	48.5	49.0	6,337	6,467
Salt Lake, UT............	7.1	7.8	7.5	5.4	5.4	20.8	20.3	20.3	4,198	4,162
Montgomery, MD........	43.3	44.7	45.2	36.3	37.9	232.5	231.0	236.1	6,859	6,591
St. Louis, MO............	4.1	4.0	4.0	4.0	3.9	15.9	15.4	15.7	4,042	4,049
Pima, AZ.................	7.7	7.0	7.0	7.2	6.5	28.3	26.6	26.3	4,056	4,086
Mecklenburg, NC........	28.3	26.9	27.1	26.2	25.2	104.4	94.3	93.9	4,040	3,780
Fulton, GA...............	6.0	5.8	5.6	6.0	5.5	23.1	22.6	21.7	3,890	4,126
Wake, NC................	25.5	26.2	27.2	21.9	23.5	88.1	89.4	89.9	4,018	3,841
Westchester, NY..........	11.6	10.6	10.8	10.3	9.5	66.5	64.8	67.0	6,463	7,086
Milwaukee, WI...........	7.3	7.0	6.2	6.8	5.9	30.1	30.0	27.8	4,436	4,773
Fresno, CA...............	9.0	7.9	8.0	8.4	7.6	37.6	32.1	33.0	4,513	4,389
Shelby, TN...............	13.9	14.2	14.2	13.4	13.3	48.5	51.0	53.2	3,641	3,986
Du Page, IL..............	3.0	2.5	2.5	2.9	2.4	12.5	10.5	10.6	4,403	4,382
Pinellas, FL..............	6.2	5.1	5.5	6.1	5.4	26.9	23.3	24.8	4,430	4,620
Bergen, NJ...............	6.0	5.9	5.8	4.9	4.8	26.8	27.2	28.5	5,674	6,328
Erie, NY.................	11.2	7.6	9.4	10.0	8.0	44.2	27.6	42.6	4,583	5,369
Prince Georges, MD......	35.7	29.9	28.5	29.4	25.7	155.6	134.0	133.9	5,489	5,456
Kern, CA.................	11.3	9.9	9.8	10.7	9.4	55.6	55.1	52.0	5,263	5,650
Macomb, MI..............	3.1	3.2	2.8	2.9	2.6	11.7	12.6	11.0	4,241	4,401
Gwinnett, GA.............	5.3	5.2	5.1	4.9	4.9	20.4	20.6	20.1	4,200	4,213
Ventura, CA..............	9.3	9.5	9.5	8.9	8.9	57.0	58.1	57.7	6,584	6,641
Collin, TX................	2.0	1.8	1.8	2.0	1.8	7.6	7.5	7.4	3,875	4,082
El Paso, TX..............	5.1	5.2	5.5	5.0	5.4	20.4	21.4	23.1	4,173	4,404
Middlesex, NJ............	4.6	4.4	4.2	3.7	3.6	19.5	20.1	21.0	5,448	6,135
Baltimore, MD............	30.6	31.3	31.2	26.2	26.4	122.2	122.2	124.0	4,979	5,039
Pierce, WA...............	3.5	3.5	3.5	3.3	3.4	20.2	20.9	20.6	6,108	6,108
Hidalgo, TX..............	2.9	2.8	2.8	2.9	2.8	9.1	9.0	9.1	3,140	3,250
Montgomery, PA..........	3.6	3.6	3.5	3.5	3.4	13.0	13.1	13.2	3,824	4,004
Hamilton, OH.............	5.1	4.8	4.7	5.0	4.6	19.0	18.6	18.1	3,838	3,983
Essex, NJ................	5.2	5.4	5.3	4.6	4.7	24.3	26.6	26.4	5,351	5,751
Multnomah, OR...........	4.9	5.0	5.0	4.6	4.6	22.4	23.6	23.8	4,998	5,295
Oklahoma, OK............	2.4	2.3	2.3	2.2	2.2	6.5	6.7	7.0	2,977	3,319
San Mateo, CA...........	7.3	6.4	6.5	6.9	5.8	41.7	38.3	38.8	7,042	7,071
Monroe, NY..............	7.1	7.0	6.9	6.2	5.9	25.6	25.6	25.5	4,279	4,469
Snohomish, WA..........	2.7	2.7	2.6	2.7	2.6	14.9	16.1	14.8	5,481	5,641
Denton, TX...............	1.9	1.9	1.9	1.9	1.8	7.0	6.9	7.1	3,763	3,841
Cobb, GA................	5.0	5.0	4.7	4.5	4.3	18.7	18.6	17.8	4,235	4,221
Dekalb, GA...............	7.5	6.6	6.5	7.4	6.4	27.9	24.7	24.3	3,827	3,821
San Joaquin, CA.........	8.3	7.3	7.5	7.2	6.6	37.6	36.4	38.0	5,334	5,904
Lake, IL.................	3.3	3.2	3.1	3.0	2.8	14.2	14.6	14.7	4,809	5,536
Will, IL..................	2.4	2.4	2.4	2.3	2.3	9.7	10.6	10.5	4,259	4,637
Jackson, MO..............	2.0	1.9	1.8	2.0	1.7	6.7	6.5	5.8	3,417	3,369

[1] Based on estimated resident population as of July 1.

Source: U.S. Census Bureau, Census of Governments, "2013 Annual Survey of Public Employment and Payroll," <http://factfinder2.census.gov>, accessed June 2015. See also <http://www.census.gov/govs/apes/>.

Section 9
Federal Government Finances and Employment

This section presents statistics relating to the financial structure and the civilian employment of the federal government. The fiscal data cover taxes, other receipts, outlays, and debt. The principal sources of fiscal data are the *Budget of the United States Government* and related documents, published annually by the Office of Management and Budget (OMB), and the U.S. Department of the Treasury's *Combined Statement of Receipts, Outlays, and Balances of the United States Government*. Detailed data on tax returns and collections are published annually by the Internal Revenue Service. The personnel data relate to staffing and payrolls. They are published by the Office of Personnel Management. Data on federally owned land and real property are collected by the General Services Administration and presented in its annual *Federal Real Property Report*.

Budget concept—Under the unified budget concept, all federal monies are included in one comprehensive budget. These monies comprise both federal funds and trust funds. Federal funds are derived mainly from taxes and borrowing and are not restricted by law to any specific government purpose. Trust funds, such as the Unemployment Trust Fund, collect certain taxes and other receipts for use in carrying out specific purposes or programs in accordance with the terms of the trust agreement or statute. Fund balances include both cash balances with the Treasury and investments in U.S. securities. Part of the balance is obligated, part unobligated. Prior to 1985, the budget totals, under provisions of law, excluded some federal activities—including the Federal Financing Bank, the Postal Service, the Synthetic Fuels Corporation, and the lending activities of the Rural Electrification Administration. The Balanced Budget and Emergency Deficit Control Act of 1985 (P.L.99-177) repealed the off-budget status of these entities and placed Social Security (Federal Old-Age and Survivors Insurance and the Federal Disability Insurance Trust Funds) off-budget. Though Social Security is now off-budget and, by law, excluded from coverage of the congressional budget resolutions, it continues to be a federal program.

Receipts arising from the government's sovereign powers are reported as governmental receipts and all other receipts, i.e., from business or market-oriented activities, are offset against outlays. Outlays are reported on a checks-issued (net) basis (i.e., outlays are recorded at the time the checks to pay bills are issued).

Debt concept—For most of U.S. history, the total debt consisted of debt borrowed by the Treasury (i.e., public debt). The present debt series includes both public debt and agency debt. The *gross federal debt* includes money borrowed by the Treasury and by various federal agencies; it is the broadest generally used measure of the federal debt. *Total public debt* is covered by a statutory debt limitation and includes only borrowing by the Treasury.

Treasury receipts and outlays—All receipts of the government, with a few exceptions, are deposited to the credit of the U.S. Treasury regardless of ultimate disposition. Under the Constitution, no money may be withdrawn from the Treasury unless appropriated by the Congress.

The day-to-day cash operations of the federal government clearing through the accounts of the U.S. Treasury are reported in the *Daily Treasury Statement*. Extensive detail on the public debt is published in the *Monthly Statement of the Public Debt of the United States*.

Budget receipts such as taxes, customs duties, and miscellaneous receipts, which are collected by government agencies, and outlays represented by checks issued and cash payments made by disbursing officers as well as government agencies are reported in the *Monthly Treasury Statement of Receipts and Outlays of the United States Government* and in the Treasury's *Combined Statement of Receipts, Outlays, and Balances of the United States Government*. These deposits in and payments from accounts maintained by government agencies are on the same basis as the unified budget.

The quarterly *Treasury Bulletin* contains data on fiscal operations and related Treasury activities, including financial statements of government corporations and other business-type activities.

Income tax returns and tax collections—Tax data are compiled by the Internal Revenue Service of the Treasury Department. The annual *Internal Revenue Service Data Book* gives a detailed account of tax collections by kind of tax. The agency's annual *Statistics of Income* reports present detailed data from individual income tax returns and corporation income tax returns. The quarterly *Statistics of Income Bulletin* presents data on such diverse subjects as tax-exempt organizations, unincorporated businesses, fiduciary income tax and estate tax returns, sales of capital assets by individuals, international income and taxes reported by corporations and individuals, and estate tax wealth.

Employment and payrolls—The Office of Personnel Management collects employment and payroll data from all departments and agencies of the federal government, except the Central Intelligence Agency, the National Security Agency, the National Geospatial-Intelligence Agency, and the Defense Intelligence Agency. Employment figures represent the number of persons who occupied civilian positions at the end of the report month shown and who are paid for services rendered to the federal government, regardless of the nature of appointment or method of payment. Federal payrolls include all payments for personnel services rendered during the report month and payments for accumulated annual leave of employees who separate from the service. Since most federal employees are paid on a biweekly basis, the calendar month earnings are partially estimated on the basis of the number of work days in each month where payroll periods overlap.

Federal employment and payroll figures are published by the Office of Personnel Management in its *Federal Civilian Workforce Statistics—Employment and Trends* and the FedScope database system. It also publishes employment data on minority groups, white- and blue-collar workers, employment by geographic area, and salary and wage distribution of federal employees. General schedule is primarily white-collar; wage system primarily blue-collar. Data on federal employment are also issued by the Bureau of Labor Statistics in its *Monthly Labor Review* and *Employment and Earnings Online* and by the U.S. Census Bureau in its annual report series *Federal, State, and Local Governments: Public Employment and Payroll Data*.

Table 492. Federal Budget—Receipts and Outlays: 1960 to 2015

[92.5 represents $92,500,000,000. For fiscal years ending in year shown; See text, Section 8. See also headnote, Table 494]

Fiscal year	In current dollars (bil. dol.)			In constant (2009) dollars (bil. dol.)			As percentage of GDP [1]		
	Receipts	Outlays	Surplus or deficit (-)	Receipts	Outlays	Surplus or deficit (-)	Receipts	Outlays	Surplus or deficit (-)
1960	92.5	92.2	0.3	655.5	653.4	2.1	17.3	17.2	0.1
1970	192.8	195.6	-2.8	1,015.3	1,030.3	-15.0	18.4	18.6	-0.3
1980	517.1	590.9	-73.8	1,308.2	1,494.9	-186.8	18.5	21.1	-2.6
1990	1,032.0	1,253.0	-221.0	1,654.3	2,008.6	-354.3	17.4	21.2	-3.7
1995	1,351.8	1,515.7	-164.0	1,850.0	2,074.4	-224.4	17.8	20.0	-2.2
1996	1,453.1	1,560.5	-107.4	1,947.8	2,091.8	-144.0	18.2	19.6	-1.3
1997	1,579.2	1,601.1	-21.9	2,074.7	2,103.4	-28.7	18.6	18.9	-0.3
1998	1,721.7	1,652.5	69.3	2,241.5	2,151.4	90.2	19.2	18.5	0.8
1999	1,827.5	1,701.8	125.6	2,349.5	2,188.0	161.5	19.2	17.9	1.3
2000	2,025.2	1,789.0	236.2	2,540.7	2,244.3	296.4	20.0	17.6	2.3
2001	1,991.1	1,862.8	128.2	2,432.9	2,276.2	156.7	18.8	17.6	1.2
2002	1,853.1	2,010.9	-157.8	2,227.3	2,416.9	-189.6	17.0	18.5	-1.5
2003	1,782.3	2,159.9	-377.6	2,083.4	2,524.7	-441.4	15.7	19.1	-3.3
2004	1,880.1	2,292.8	-412.7	2,141.6	2,611.7	-470.1	15.6	19.0	-3.4
2005	2,153.6	2,472.0	-318.3	2,371.0	2,721.5	-350.5	16.7	19.2	-2.5
2006	2,406.9	2,655.0	-248.2	2,561.6	2,825.7	-264.1	17.6	19.4	-1.8
2007	2,568.0	2,728.7	-160.7	2,662.8	2,829.4	-166.6	17.9	19.1	-1.1
2008	2,524.0	2,982.5	-458.6	2,528.8	2,988.2	-459.4	17.1	20.2	-3.1
2009	2,105.0	3,517.7	-1,412.7	2,105.0	3,517.7	-1,412.7	14.6	24.4	-9.8
2010	2,162.7	3,457.1	-1,294.4	2,137.3	3,416.4	-1,279.2	14.6	23.4	-8.7
2011	2,303.5	3,603.1	-1,299.6	2,232.5	3,492.0	-1,259.5	15.0	23.4	-8.5
2012	2,450.0	3,537.0	-1,087.0	2,330.7	3,364.7	-1,034.0	15.3	22.1	-6.8
2013	2,775.1	3,454.6	-679.5	2,603.5	3,241.1	-637.5	16.7	20.8	-4.1
2014	3,021.5	3,506.1	-484.6	2,791.2	3,238.9	-447.7	17.5	20.3	-2.8
2015, est	3,176.1	3,758.6	-582.5	2,895.2	3,426.2	-531.0	17.7	20.9	-3.2

[1] Gross domestic product; see text, Section 13.

Source: U.S. Office of Management and Budget, *Fiscal Year 2016 Budget of the U.S. Government: Historical Tables*, February 2015. See also <http://www.whitehouse.gov/omb/budget>.

Table 493. Federal Budget Debt: 1960 to 2015

[290.5 represents $290,500,000,000. As of the end of the fiscal year. See text, Section 8]

Fiscal year	Total (bil. dol.)					As percentages of GDP [1]				
	Gross federal debt	Federal government accounts	Held by the public			Gross federal debt	Federal government accounts	Held by the public		
			Total	Federal Reserve System	Other			Total	Federal Reserve System	Other
1960	290.5	53.7	236.8	26.5	210.3	54.3	10.0	44.3	5.0	39.3
1970	380.9	97.7	283.2	57.7	225.5	36.3	9.3	27.0	5.5	21.5
1980	909.0	197.1	711.9	120.8	591.1	32.5	7.0	25.5	4.3	21.1
1985	1,817.4	310.2	1,507.3	169.8	1,337.5	42.6	7.3	35.3	4.0	31.3
1990	3,206.3	794.7	2,411.6	234.4	2,177.1	54.2	13.4	40.8	4.0	36.8
1991	3,598.2	909.2	2,689.0	258.6	2,430.4	58.9	14.9	44.0	4.2	39.8
1992	4,001.8	1,002.1	2,999.7	296.4	2,703.3	62.2	15.6	46.6	4.6	42.0
1993	4,351.0	1,102.6	3,248.4	325.7	2,922.7	64.0	16.2	47.8	4.8	43.0
1994	4,643.3	1,210.2	3,433.1	355.2	3,077.9	64.5	16.8	47.7	4.9	42.8
1995	4,920.6	1,316.2	3,604.4	374.1	3,230.3	64.9	17.4	47.5	4.9	42.6
1996	5,181.5	1,447.4	3,734.1	390.9	3,343.1	64.9	18.1	46.8	4.9	41.9
1997	5,369.2	1,596.9	3,772.3	424.5	3,347.8	63.3	18.8	44.5	5.0	39.5
1998	5,478.2	1,757.1	3,721.1	458.2	3,262.9	61.2	19.6	41.6	5.1	36.4
1999	5,605.5	1,973.2	3,632.4	496.6	3,135.7	58.9	20.7	38.2	5.2	33.0
2000	5,628.7	2,218.9	3,409.8	511.4	2,898.4	55.5	21.9	33.6	5.0	28.6
2001	5,769.9	2,450.3	3,319.6	534.1	2,785.5	54.6	23.2	31.4	5.1	26.4
2002	6,198.4	2,658.0	3,540.4	604.2	2,936.2	57.0	24.4	32.5	5.6	27.0
2003	6,760.0	2,846.6	3,913.4	656.1	3,257.3	59.7	25.1	34.5	5.8	28.7
2004	7,354.7	3,059.1	4,295.5	700.3	3,595.2	60.8	25.3	35.5	5.8	29.7
2005	7,905.3	3,313.1	4,592.2	736.4	3,855.9	61.3	25.7	35.6	5.7	29.9
2006	8,451.4	3,622.4	4,829.0	768.9	4,060.0	61.8	26.5	35.3	5.6	29.7
2007	8,950.7	3,915.6	5,035.1	779.6	4,255.5	62.5	27.3	35.2	5.4	29.7
2008	9,986.1	4,183.0	5,803.1	491.1	5,311.9	67.7	28.4	39.3	3.3	36.0
2009	11,875.9	4,331.1	7,544.7	769.2	6,775.5	82.4	30.0	52.3	5.3	47.0
2010	13,528.8	4,509.9	9,018.9	811.7	8,207.2	91.4	30.5	60.9	5.5	55.5
2011	14,764.2	4,636.0	10,128.2	1,664.7	8,463.5	96.0	30.1	65.9	10.8	55.0
2012	16,050.9	4,769.8	11,281.1	1,645.3	9,635.8	100.2	29.8	70.4	10.3	60.1
2013	16,719.4	4,736.7	11,982.7	2,072.3	9,910.4	100.8	28.6	72.3	12.5	59.8
2014	17,794.5	5,014.6	12,779.9	2,451.7	10,328.1	103.2	29.1	74.1	14.2	59.9
2015, est	18,627.6	5,121.2	13,506.3	(NA)	(NA)	103.6	28.5	75.1	(NA)	(NA)

NA Not available. [1] Gross domestic product; see text, Section 13.

Source: U.S. Office of Management and Budget, *Fiscal Year 2016 Budget of the U.S. Government, Historical Tables*, February 2015. See also <http://www.whitehouse.gov/omb/budget>.

Table 494. Federal Budget Outlays by Type: 1990 to 2015

[1,253.0 represents $1,253,000,000,000. For fiscal years ending September 30. Given the inherent imprecision in adjusting outlays for inflation, the data shown in constant dollars present a reasonable perspective, not precision. The deflators and the categories that are deflated are as comparable over time as feasible. Minus sign (-) indicates offset]

Type	Unit	1990	2000	2005	2010	2013	2014	2015, est.
Current dollar outlays	**Bil. dol.**	**1,253.0**	**1,789.0**	**2,472.0**	**3,457.1**	**3,454.6**	**3,506.1**	**3,758.6**
National defense [1]	Bil. dol.	299.3	294.4	495.3	693.5	633.4	603.5	597.5
Nondefense, total	Bil. dol.	953.7	1,494.6	1,976.7	2,763.6	2,821.2	2,902.6	3,161.1
Payments for individuals	Bil. dol.	592.4	1,067.4	1,511.9	2,305.9	2,405.0	2,507.7	2,666.3
Direct payments [2]	Bil. dol.	513.5	876.6	1,229.0	1,906.7	2,023.6	2,090.9	2,212.0
Grants to state and local governments	Bil. dol.	78.9	190.7	282.9	399.2	381.5	416.9	454.3
All other grants	Bil. dol.	56.2	95.1	145.1	209.2	164.7	160.1	173.9
Net interest [2]	Bil. dol.	184.3	222.9	184.0	196.2	220.9	229.0	229.2
All other [2]	Bil. dol.	157.4	151.7	200.9	134.4	123.4	93.9	227.6
Undistributed offsetting receipts [2]	Bil. dol.	-36.6	-42.6	-65.2	-82.1	-92.8	-88.0	-135.8
Constant (2009) dollar outlays	**Bil. dol.**	**2,008.6**	**2,244.3**	**2,721.5**	**3,416.4**	**3,241.1**	**3,238.9**	**3,426.2**
National defense [1]	Bil. dol.	512.2	406.9	552.6	691.3	612.0	574.2	560.9
Nondefense, total	Bil. dol.	1,496.7	1,837.5	2,169.1	2,725.2	2,629.3	2,664.7	2,865.4
Payments for individuals	Bil. dol.	886.6	1,288.6	1,647.0	2,269.1	2,239.9	2,301.1	2,415.3
Direct payments [2]	Bil. dol.	768.3	1,057.6	1,338.3	1,876.1	1,884.7	1,918.6	2,003.8
Grants to state and local governments	Bil. dol.	118.3	231.0	308.7	393.0	355.3	382.5	411.5
All other grants	Bil. dol.	105.0	134.2	171.1	209.8	153.5	147.4	156.8
Net interest [2]	Bil. dol.	278.1	273.7	201.5	194.5	207.5	211.8	209.2
All other [2]	Bil. dol.	303.2	200.9	223.1	133.0	116.9	87.4	210.4
Undistributed offsetting receipts [2]	Bil. dol.	-76.3	-60.0	-73.6	-81.3	-88.7	-82.9	-126.2
Outlays as percent of GDP [3]	**Percent**	**21.2**	**17.6**	**19.2**	**23.4**	**20.8**	**20.3**	**20.9**
National defense [1]	Percent	5.1	2.9	3.8	4.7	3.8	3.5	3.3
Nondefense, total	Percent	16.1	14.7	15.3	18.7	17.0	16.8	17.6
Payments for individuals	Percent	10.0	10.5	11.7	15.6	14.5	14.5	14.8
Direct payments [2]	Percent	8.7	8.6	9.5	12.9	12.2	12.1	12.3
Grants to state and local governments	Percent	1.3	1.9	2.2	2.7	2.3	2.4	2.5
All other grants	Percent	1.0	0.9	1.1	1.4	1.0	0.9	1.0
Net interest [2]	Percent	3.1	2.2	1.4	1.3	1.3	1.3	1.3
All other [2]	Percent	2.7	1.5	1.6	0.9	0.7	0.5	1.3
Undistributed offsetting receipts [2]	Percent	-0.6	-0.4	-0.5	-0.6	-0.6	-0.5	-0.8

[1] Includes a small amount of grants to state and local governments and direct payments for individuals. [2] Includes some off-budget amounts; most of the off-budget amounts are direct payments for individuals (social security benefits). [3] Gross domestic product; see text, Section 13.

Source: U.S. Office of Management and Budget, *Fiscal Year 2016 Budget of the U.S. Government, Historical Tables*, February 2015. See also <http://www.whitehouse.gov/omb/budget>.

Table 495. Federal Budget Outlays by Agency: 1990 to 2015

[In billions of dollars (1,253.0 represents $1,253,000,000,000). For fiscal years ending September 30]

Department or other unit	1990	2000	2005	2010	2013	2014	2015, est.
Outlays, total [1]	**1,253.0**	**1,789.0**	**2,472.0**	**3,457.1**	**3,454.6**	**3,506.1**	**3,758.6**
Legislative branch	2.2	2.9	4.0	5.8	4.3	4.2	4.9
Judicial branch	1.6	4.1	5.5	7.2	7.1	6.9	7.6
Agriculture	45.9	75.1	85.3	129.5	155.9	141.8	147.5
Commerce	3.7	7.8	6.1	13.2	9.1	7.9	10.0
Defense—Military	289.7	281.0	474.4	666.7	607.8	577.9	567.7
Education	23.0	33.5	72.9	93.7	40.9	59.6	103.3
Energy	12.1	15.0	21.3	30.8	24.7	23.6	30.1
Health and Human Services	175.5	382.3	581.4	854.1	886.3	936.0	1,013.0
Homeland Security	7.2	13.2	38.7	44.5	57.2	43.3	45.7
Housing and Urban Development	20.2	30.8	42.5	60.1	56.6	38.5	42.4
Interior	5.8	8.0	9.3	13.2	9.6	11.3	13.0
Justice	5.9	16.8	22.4	29.6	29.7	28.6	36.1
Labor	26.1	31.9	46.9	173.1	80.3	56.8	52.8
State	4.8	6.7	12.7	23.8	26.0	27.5	30.5
Transportation	25.6	41.6	56.6	77.8	76.3	76.2	80.2
Treasury	253.9	390.5	410.2	444.3	399.1	446.9	506.4
Veterans Affairs	29.0	47.0	69.8	108.3	138.5	149.1	160.8
Corps of Engineers—Civil Works	3.3	4.2	4.7	9.9	6.3	6.5	7.5
Other Defense—Civil Programs	21.7	32.8	43.5	54.0	56.8	57.4	59.7
Environmental Protection Agency	5.1	7.2	7.9	11.0	9.5	9.4	8.3
Executive Office of the President	0.2	0.3	7.7	0.6	0.4	0.4	0.4
International Assistance Programs	10.1	12.1	15.0	20.0	19.7	18.7	24.0
National Aeronautics and Space Administration	12.4	13.4	15.6	18.9	17.0	17.1	18.1
National Science Foundation	1.8	3.4	5.4	6.7	7.4	7.1	7.1
Office of Personnel Management	31.9	48.7	59.5	69.9	83.9	87.9	94.7
Social Security Administration (on-budget)	17.3	45.1	54.6	70.8	109.8	81.2	88.6
Social Security Administration (off-budget)	245.0	396.2	506.8	683.4	757.5	824.6	865.2
Undistributed offsetting receipts [2]	-98.9	-173.0	-226.2	-267.9	-249.5	-246.2	-286.7

[1] Includes other agencies, not shown separately. [2] Includes some off-budget amounts; most of the off-budget amounts are direct payments to individuals (social security benefits).

Source: U.S. Office of Management and Budget, *Fiscal Year 2016 Budget of the U.S. Government, Historical Tables*, February 2015. See also <http://www.whitehouse.gov/omb/budget>.

Table 496. Federal Budget Outlays by Detailed Function: 1990 to 2015

[In billions of dollars (1,253.0 represents $1,253,000,000,000). For fiscal years ending September 30. Minus sign (-) indicates decrease]

Superfunction and function	1990	2000	2005	2010	2011	2012	2013	2014	2015, est.
Total outlays	**1,253.0**	**1,789.0**	**2,472.0**	**3,457.1**	**3,603.1**	**3,537.0**	**3,454.6**	**3,506.1**	**3,758.6**
National defense [1]	299.3	294.4	495.3	693.5	705.6	677.9	633.4	603.5	597.5
Department of Defense—Military	289.7	281.0	474.1	666.7	678.1	650.9	607.8	577.9	567.7
Military personnel	75.6	76.0	127.5	155.7	161.6	152.3	150.8	148.9	149.2
Operation and maintenance	88.3	105.8	188.1	276.0	291.0	282.3	259.7	244.5	234.2
Procurement	81.0	51.7	82.3	133.6	128.0	124.7	114.9	107.5	106.2
Research, development, test, and evaluation	37.5	37.6	65.7	77.0	74.9	70.4	66.9	64.9	66.3
Military construction	5.1	5.1	5.3	21.2	19.9	14.6	12.3	9.8	9.8
Atomic energy defense activities	9.0	12.1	18.0	19.3	20.4	19.2	17.6	17.4	21.2
International affairs [1]	13.8	17.2	34.6	45.2	45.7	47.2	46.2	46.7	55.0
International development and humanitarian assistance	5.5	6.5	17.7	19.0	21.3	21.9	22.6	23.5	26.8
International security assistance	8.7	6.4	7.9	11.4	12.0	11.5	10.0	11.4	12.5
Conduct of foreign affairs	3.0	4.7	9.1	13.6	12.5	13.5	13.0	12.9	14.5
General science, space, and technology	14.4	18.6	23.6	30.1	29.5	29.1	28.9	28.6	29.8
General science and basic research	2.8	6.2	8.8	11.7	12.4	12.5	12.5	12.0	12.3
Space flight, research, and supporting activities	11.6	12.4	14.8	18.4	17.0	16.6	16.4	16.6	17.6
Energy [1]	3.3	-0.8	0.4	11.6	12.2	14.9	11.0	5.3	9.9
Energy supply	2.0	-1.8	-0.9	5.8	8.1	9.0	9.0	4.1	7.5
Natural resources and environment [1]	17.1	25.0	28.0	43.7	45.5	41.6	38.1	36.2	41.7
Water resources	4.4	5.1	5.7	11.7	11.6	9.2	7.7	7.9	9.2
Conservation and land management	4.0	6.8	6.2	10.8	12.0	11.1	10.7	9.7	13.2
Recreational resources	1.4	2.5	3.0	3.9	4.2	3.8	3.5	3.4	3.7
Pollution control and abatement	5.2	7.4	8.1	10.8	10.9	10.8	9.6	8.6	8.5
Agriculture	11.6	36.5	26.6	21.4	20.7	17.8	29.7	24.4	21.8
Farm income stabilization	9.6	33.4	22.0	16.5	15.9	13.1	25.2	20.0	16.0
Agricultural research and services	2.1	3.0	4.5	4.9	4.8	4.7	4.5	4.4	5.8
Commerce and housing credit [1]	67.6	3.2	7.6	-82.3	-12.6	40.6	-83.2	-94.9	-28.6
Mortgage credit	3.8	-3.3	-0.9	35.8	14.2	-8.1	-87.9	-84.3	-34.1
Postal service	2.1	2.1	-1.2	-0.7	0.9	2.7	-1.8	-2.5	-0.5
Deposit insurance	57.9	-3.1	-1.4	-32.0	-8.7	6.7	4.3	-13.8	-7.9
Transportation [1]	29.5	46.9	67.9	92.0	93.0	93.0	91.7	91.9	92.9
Ground transportation	19.0	31.7	42.3	60.8	60.9	61.3	60.0	60.8	62.3
Air transportation	7.2	10.6	18.8	21.4	21.4	21.7	21.5	20.9	20.3
Water transportation	3.2	4.4	6.4	9.4	10.4	9.7	9.8	9.8	9.6
Community and regional development [1]	8.5	10.6	26.3	23.9	23.9	25.1	32.3	20.7	27.2
Community development	3.5	5.5	5.9	9.9	9.6	8.8	7.8	7.9	8.9
Disaster relief and insurance	2.1	2.6	17.7	10.7	10.2	11.9	23.0	9.7	14.2
Education, training, employment, and social services [1]	37.2	53.8	97.6	128.6	101.2	90.8	72.8	90.6	136.8
Elementary, secondary, and vocational education	9.9	20.6	38.3	73.3	66.5	47.5	42.4	40.8	43.4
Higher education	11.1	10.1	31.4	20.9	1.1	12.1	-0.5	20.1	60.8
Research and general education aids	1.6	2.5	3.1	3.6	3.7	3.7	3.7	3.6	3.5
Training and employment	5.6	6.8	6.9	9.9	9.1	7.8	7.3	7.0	7.7
Social services	8.1	12.6	16.3	19.2	18.9	17.9	18.1	17.3	19.5
Health	57.7	154.5	250.5	369.1	372.5	346.7	358.3	409.4	481.2
Health care services	47.6	136.2	219.6	330.7	332.2	308.2	321.8	374.6	443.6
Health research and training	8.6	16.0	28.1	34.2	36.2	34.5	32.9	30.9	32.6
Consumer and occupational health and safety	1.5	2.3	2.9	4.1	4.1	4.1	3.6	4.0	5.1
Medicare	98.1	197.1	298.6	451.6	485.7	471.8	497.8	511.7	536.4
Income security [1]	148.8	253.7	345.8	622.2	597.4	541.3	536.5	513.6	522.5
General retirement and disability insurance (excluding social security)	5.1	5.2	7.0	6.6	6.7	7.8	7.0	8.8	7.6
Federal employee retirement and disability	52.0	77.2	93.4	119.9	124.5	122.4	131.7	134.6	139.0
Unemployment compensation	18.9	23.0	35.4	160.1	120.6	93.8	70.7	45.7	42.2
Housing assistance	15.9	28.9	37.9	58.7	55.4	47.9	46.7	47.6	49.5
Food and nutrition assistance	24.1	32.5	50.8	95.1	103.2	106.9	109.7	102.9	107.4
Social security	248.6	409.4	523.3	706.7	730.8	773.3	813.6	850.5	896.3
Veterans' benefits and services [1]	29.0	47.0	70.1	108.4	127.2	124.6	138.9	149.6	161.4
Income security for veterans	15.3	24.9	35.8	49.2	58.7	55.9	65.9	70.9	78.0
Veterans education, training, and rehabilitation	0.2	1.3	2.8	8.1	10.7	10.4	12.9	13.5	14.4
Hospital and medical care for veterans	12.1	19.5	28.8	45.7	50.1	50.6	52.5	56.2	61.0
Veterans housing	0.5	0.4	0.9	0.5	1.3	1.4	1.3	2.1	0.6
Administration of justice	10.2	28.5	40.0	54.4	56.1	56.3	52.6	50.5	58.7
Federal law enforcement activities	4.8	12.1	19.9	28.7	29.8	29.0	27.3	26.1	28.6
Federal litigative and judicial activities	3.6	7.8	10.7	14.5	15.1	16.2	14.8	14.2	17.7
Federal correctional activities	1.3	3.7	4.8	6.3	6.5	6.8	6.8	6.8	6.9
Criminal justice assistance	0.5	4.9	4.6	4.8	4.6	4.3	3.8	3.4	5.5
General government	10.5	13.0	17.0	23.0	27.5	28.0	27.7	26.9	22.8
Net interest [1]	184.3	222.9	184.0	196.2	230.0	220.4	220.9	229.0	229.2
Interest on Treasury debt securities (gross)	264.7	361.9	352.3	413.9	454.0	359.2	415.7	429.5	431.6
Interest received by on-budget trust funds	-46.3	-69.3	-69.2	-67.3	-72.0	-14.8	-51.0	-57.8	-54.9
Interest received by off-budget trust funds	-16.0	-59.8	-91.8	-118.5	-116.0	-112.4	-105.7	-100.3	-96.0
Allowances	–	–	–	–	–	–	–	–	1.9
Undistributed offsetting receipts [2]	-36.6	-42.6	-65.2	-82.1	-88.5	-103.5	-92.8	-88.0	-135.8

– Represents or rounds to zero. [1] Includes functions not shown separately. [2] Includes some off-budget amounts; most of the off-budget amounts are direct payments for individuals (social security benefits).

Source: U.S. Office of Management and Budget, *Fiscal Year 2016 Budget of the U.S. Government: Historical Tables*, February 2015. See also <http://www.whitehouse.gov/omb/budget>.

Table 497. Federal Budget Outlays for Payments for Individuals by Category and Major Program: 1990 to 2015

[In billions of dollars (592.4 represents $592,400,000,000). For fiscal years ending September 30]

Category and program	1990	2000	2005	2010	2011	2012	2013	2014	2015, est.
Total, payments for individuals	**592.4**	**1,067.4**	**1,512.6**	**2,307.0**	**2,368.0**	**2,316.9**	**2,406.3**	**2,508.9**	**2,667.6**
Social security and railroad retirement	253.3	410.7	523.5	706.6	730.7	773.9	814.5	853.2	899.6
Social security:									
Old age and survivors insurance	221.9	351.4	434.0	576.6	595.6	631.4	667.2	702.5	744.8
Disability insurance	24.4	54.4	84.2	123.5	128.6	135.7	140.1	141.9	145.5
Railroad retirement (excl. social security)	7.0	4.8	5.4	6.5	6.5	6.8	7.3	8.8	9.3
Federal employees' retirement and insurance	64.2	100.4	127.0	166.8	181.4	176.0	194.2	202.7	213.0
Military retirement	21.6	32.9	39.0	50.7	55.0	48.9	54.4	55.4	56.3
Civil service retirement	31.0	45.1	54.7	69.5	70.4	74.0	77.2	79.5	82.1
Veterans service-connected compensation	10.7	20.8	30.9	43.5	52.8	50.1	59.4	64.4	71.0
Other	0.8	1.7	2.4	3.2	3.3	3.1	3.2	3.4	3.6
Unemployment assistance	17.5	21.1	33.1	158.3	118.6	92.3	68.3	43.5	38.7
Medical care [1]	167.4	368.6	575.4	876.8	925.0	889.7	935.8	1,006.2	1,090.7
Medicare:									
Hospital insurance	65.9	127.9	181.3	245.6	255.7	254.5	262.4	262.6	268.0
Supplementary medical insurance	41.5	87.2	150.0	264.9	292.7	283.2	305.5	322.4	344.8
State children's health insurance	–	1.2	5.1	7.9	8.6	9.1	9.5	9.3	10.6
Medicaid	41.1	117.9	181.7	272.8	275.0	250.5	265.4	301.5	333.1
Indian health	1.1	2.4	3.1	4.4	4.2	4.5	4.3	4.5	5.0
Hospital and medical care for veterans	12.3	20.1	30.7	48.5	52.7	53.0	55.1	58.9	60.7
Health resources and services	1.4	3.9	5.9	7.1	7.5	7.8	7.3	7.6	7.9
Substance abuse and mental health services	1.2	2.5	3.2	3.3	3.4	3.0	3.2	3.2	3.9
Health care tax credit	–	–	(Z)	(Z)	(NA)	(NA)	(NA)	(NA)	(NA)
Uniformed Services retiree health care fund	–	–	6.3	8.4	8.6	8.7	8.2	9.3	10.6
Other	2.9	5.4	8.2	14.0	13.1	11.9	12.0	12.3	13.1
Assistance to students	11.2	10.9	32.1	55.5	58.6	59.9	58.1	70.1	84.3
Veterans' education benefits	0.8	1.6	3.3	8.8	11.1	10.7	13.2	13.7	14.7
Student assistance, Department of Education and other	10.4	9.2	28.9	46.8	47.5	49.1	44.9	56.3	69.6
Housing assistance	15.9	28.6	37.5	57.6	54.4	46.9	45.6	46.6	48.4
Food and nutrition assistance	24.0	32.4	50.7	95.0	103.1	106.7	109.6	102.8	107.3
SNAP (including Puerto Rico) [2]	15.9	18.3	32.6	70.5	77.6	80.4	82.5	76.2	78.8
Child nutrition and special milk programs	5.0	9.2	11.9	16.4	17.3	18.3	19.3	19.5	20.6
Supplemental feeding programs (WIC and CSFP [3])	2.1	4.0	5.0	6.5	6.8	6.8	6.6	6.3	6.5
Commodity donations and other	1.0	0.9	1.2	1.6	1.3	1.2	1.1	0.8	1.4
Public assistance and related programs [1]	34.9	88.5	123.4	183.2	188.6	163.8	172.5	175.2	177.5
Supplemental security income program	11.5	29.7	35.4	44.0	49.7	44.2	50.3	51.5	52.8
Family support payments to states and TANF [4]	12.2	18.4	21.3	21.9	21.3	20.1	21.2	20.4	20.9
Low income home energy assistance	1.3	1.5	2.1	4.6	4.4	3.8	3.5	3.5	3.0
Earned income tax credit	4.4	26.1	34.6	54.7	55.7	54.9	57.5	60.1	60.1
Payments to states for daycare assistance	–	3.3	4.9	5.9	6.1	5.0	5.0	5.1	5.4
Veterans' non-service-connected pensions	3.6	3.0	3.7	4.4	4.7	4.5	5.2	5.3	5.6
Payments to states for foster care/adoption assistance	1.6	5.5	6.4	7.0	6.9	6.8	6.8	6.9	7.1
Payment where child credit exceeds tax liability	–	0.8	14.6	22.7	22.7	22.1	21.6	21.5	21.5
Other public assistance	0.3	0.3	0.4	17.1	16.7	2.1	1.2	1.0	1.0
All other payments for individuals	4.0	6.2	9.8	7.2	7.7	7.7	7.8	8.6	8.1
Coal miners and black lung benefits	1.5	1.5	1.4	0.5	0.5	0.5	0.4	0.4	0.4
Veterans' insurance and burial benefits	1.4	1.4	1.4	1.3	1.3	1.2	1.2	1.2	1.3
D.C. employee retirement	–	0.4	2.2	–	(NA)	(NA)	(NA)	(NA)	(NA)
Aging services programs	–	0.9	1.4	1.5	1.6	1.5	1.4	1.5	1.7
Energy employees compensation fund	–	–	0.6	1.1	1.2	1.2	1.2	1.1	1.2
September 11th victim compensation	–	–	(Z)	–	–	(Z)	(Z)	(Z)	0.4
Refugee assistance and other	1.1	2.4	5.0	2.8	3.1	3.4	3.4	4.4	3.1

– Represents zero. NA Not available. Z Less than $50,000,000. [1] Includes other items not shown separately. [2] Supplemental Nutrition Assistance Program, formerly known as food stamps. [3] WIC is Women, Infants, and Children. CSFP is Commodity Supplemental Food Program. [4] TANF is Temporary Assistance for Needy Families.

Source: U.S. Office of Management and Budget, *Fiscal Year 2016 Budget of the U.S. Government: Historical Tables*, February 2015. See also <http://www.whitehouse.gov/omb/budget>.

Table 498. Federal Budget Receipts by Source: 1990 to 2015

[In billions of dollars (1,032.0 represents $1,032,000,000,000). For fiscal years ending September 30. Receipts reflect collections. Covers both federal funds and trust funds; see text, this section. Minus sign (-) indicates decrease]

Source	1990	2000	2005	2010	2011	2012	2013	2014	2015, est.
Total federal receipts........................	**1,032.0**	**2,025.2**	**2,153.6**	**2,162.7**	**2,303.5**	**2,450.0**	**2,775.1**	**3,021.5**	**3,176.1**
(On-budget).............................	750.3	1,544.6	1,576.1	1,531.0	1,737.7	1,880.5	2,101.8	2,285.9	2,410.5
(Off-budget)............................	281.7	480.6	577.5	631.7	565.8	569.5	673.3	735.6	765.6
Individual income taxes.....................	466.9	1,004.5	927.2	898.5	1,091.5	1,132.2	1,316.4	1,394.6	1,478.1
Corporation income taxes..................	93.5	207.3	278.3	191.4	181.1	242.3	273.5	320.7	341.7
Social insurance and retirement receipts.......	380.0	652.9	794.1	864.8	818.8	845.3	947.8	1,023.5	1,065.0
Excise taxes.............................	35.3	68.9	73.1	66.9	72.4	79.1	84.0	93.4	95.9
Other....................................	56.2	91.7	80.9	141.0	139.7	151.1	153.4	189.4	195.4
Social insurance and retirement receipts..........................	**380.0**	**652.9**	**794.1**	**864.8**	**818.8**	**845.3**	**947.8**	**1,023.5**	**1,065.0**
Employment and general retirement, total......	353.9	620.5	747.7	815.9	758.5	774.9	887.4	965.0	1,005.0
Old–age and survivors insurance (off–budget)............................	255.0	411.7	493.6	540.0	483.7	486.8	575.6	628.8	654.4
Disability insurance (off–budget).............	26.6	68.9	83.8	91.7	82.1	82.7	97.7	106.8	111.1
Hospital insurance........................	68.6	135.5	166.1	180.1	188.5	201.1	209.3	224.1	233.9
Railroad retirement/pension fund.............	2.3	2.7	2.3	2.3	2.4	2.5	2.8	3.0	3.2
Unemployment insurance funds.................	21.6	27.6	42.0	44.8	56.2	66.6	56.8	55.0	56.4
Other retirement..........................	4.5	4.8	4.5	4.1	4.0	3.7	3.6	3.5	3.7
Federal employees retirement—employee share...............................	4.4	4.7	4.4	4.1	4.0	3.7	3.5	3.4	3.6
Excise taxes, total........................	**35.3**	**68.9**	**73.1**	**66.9**	**72.4**	**79.1**	**84.0**	**93.4**	**95.9**
Federal funds [1]	15.6	22.7	22.5	18.3	18.9	20.4	28.3	34.2	37.8
Alcohol..................................	5.7	8.1	8.1	9.2	9.3	9.8	9.3	9.8	9.6
Tobacco.................................	4.1	7.2	7.9	17.2	16.7	16.4	15.1	15.6	15.3
Telephone...............................	3.0	5.7	6.0	1.0	0.9	0.8	0.7	0.6	0.6
Ozone–depleting chemicals/products........	0.4	0.1	–	–	–	–	–	–	–
Transportation fuels......................	–	0.8	-0.8	-11.0	-8.6	-5.8	-2.7	-3.5	-3.4
Indoor tanning services...................	–	0.0	–	–	0.1	0.1	0.1	0.1	0.1
Trust funds [1]	19.8	46.2	50.5	48.7	53.5	58.7	55.7	59.1	58.1
Highway.................................	13.9	35.0	37.9	35.0	36.9	40.2	36.5	39.0	39.3
Airport and airway........................	3.7	9.7	10.3	10.6	11.5	12.5	12.9	13.5	13.1
Black lung disability.......................	0.7	0.5	0.6	0.6	0.6	0.6	0.5	0.6	0.6
Inland waterway..........................	0.1	0.1	0.1	0.1	0.1	0.1	0.1	0.1	0.1
Hazardous substance superfund.............	0.8	(Z)	–	–	–	–	–	–	–
Oil spill liability...........................	0.1	0.2	–	0.5	0.5	0.5	0.4	0.4	0.5
Aquatic resources........................	0.2	0.3	0.4	0.6	0.6	0.6	0.5	0.6	0.5
Leaking underground storage tank...........	0.1	0.2	0.2	0.2	0.2	0.2	0.2	0.2	0.2
Tobacco assessments.....................	–	–	0.9	0.9	0.9	0.9	0.9	1.1	0.3
Vaccine injury compensation...............	0.2	0.1	0.1	0.2	0.3	0.3	0.2	0.2	0.2

– Represents zero. Z Less than $50,000,000. [1] Includes other funds, not shown separately.

Source: U.S. Office of Management and Budget, *Fiscal Year 2016 Budget of the U.S. Government: Historical Tables*, February 2015. See also <http://www.whitehouse.gov/omb/budget>.

Table 499. Federal Trust Fund Income, Outlays, and Balances: 2014 to 2016

[In billions of dollars (13.8 represents $13,800,000,000). For fiscal years ending September 30. Income reflects receipts deposited. Outlays are on a checks-issued basis less refunds collected. Balances reflect funds that have not been spent. See text, this section, for discussion of the budget concept and trust funds]

Description	Income			Outlays			Balances [1]		
	2014	2015, est.	2016, est.	2014	2015, est.	2016, est.	2014	2015, est.	2016, est.
Airport and airway trust fund....................	13.8	13.5	15.0	12.9	15.4	15.4	14.2	12.2	11.9
Civil service retirement and disability fund......	94.2	95.2	96.4	79.6	82.1	84.5	857.2	870.3	882.2
Federal employees' health benefits fund.......	46.3	48.6	51.9	46.1	48.0	50.7	23.6	24.2	25.3
Foreign military sales trust fund.................	29.3	29.7	27.1	26.6	29.6	27.7	21.7	21.8	21.3
Medicare:									
Hospital insurance (HI) trust fund..............	271.2	282.9	298.4	275.2	281.4	296.4	202.4	203.9	205.9
Supplemental medical insurance trust fund...	332.5	348.1	387.2	331.0	352.6	397.5	71.3	66.7	56.5
Military retirement fund.......................	112.8	113.9	118.6	55.4	56.2	62.0	478.1	535.7	592.3
Railroad retirement trust funds..................	13.4	12.1	12.0	12.3	12.8	12.7	23.2	22.5	21.9
Social security: Old-age, survivors and disability insurance trust funds................	889.0	920.9	958.1	862.1	908.5	957.2	2,782.6	2,795.1	2,796.2
Transportation trust fund........................	61.7	39.6	79.7	53.1	53.7	60.5	14.8	0.8	20.0
Unemployment trust funds.......................	62.1	58.5	58.4	47.2	42.8	45.3	15.2	30.8	44.0
Veterans' life insurance trust funds.............	0.6	0.6	0.4	1.3	1.4	1.2	7.5	6.6	5.9
Other trust funds...............................	18.9	51.9	27.0	14.6	21.6	14.9	91.5	101.4	113.5

[1] Balances available on a cash basis (rather than an authorization basis) at the end of the year. Balances are primarily invested in federal debt securities.

Source: U.S. Office of Management and Budget, *Fiscal Year 2016 Budget of the U.S. Government: Analytical Perspectives*, February 2015. See also <http://www.whitehouse.gov/omb/budget>.

Table 500. Tax Expenditure Estimates Relating to Individual and Corporate Income Taxes by Selected Function: 2014 to 2017

[In millions of dollars (12,960 represents $12,960,000,000). For fiscal years ending September 30. Tax expenditures are defined as revenue losses attributable to provisions of the federal tax laws which allow a special exclusion, exemption, or deduction from gross income or which provide a special credit, a preferential rate of tax, or a deferral of liability. Minus sign (-) indicates decrease]

Function and provision	2014	2015	2016	2017
National defense:				
Exclusion of benefits and allowances to armed forces personnel.	12,960	13,570	14,110	13,060
International affairs:				
Exclusion of income earned abroad by U.S. citizens.	5,700	5,990	6,280	6,600
Exclusion of certain allowances for Federal employees abroad.	1,180	1,240	1,300	1,370
Inventory property sales source rules exception.	3,650	3,960	4,290	4,660
Deferral of income from controlled foreign corporations (normal tax method).	61,710	64,560	67,780	71,170
Deferred taxes for financial firms on certain income earned overseas.	4,250	–	–	–
General science, space, and technology:				
Expensing of research and experimentation expenditures (normal tax method).	7,060	7,110	7,040	7,320
Credit for increasing research activities.	6,020	3,620	3,090	2,630
Energy:				
Alternative fuel production credit.	–	–	–	–
Energy production credit.	2,240	2,570	2,540	2,380
Energy investment credit.	1,870	1,490	1,320	1,040
Commerce and housing:				
Financial institutions and insurance:				
Exclusion of interest on life insurance savings.	13,370	13,100	17,730	22,430
Housing:				
Deductibility of mortgage interest on owner–occupied homes.	66,910	69,480	75,260	83,100
Deductibility of state and local property tax on owner–occupied homes.	31,590	33,120	35,520	38,190
Capital gains exclusion on home sales.	35,540	36,930	39,560	42,380
Exclusion of net imputed rental income.	75,240	78,810	82,420	86,800
Exception from passive loss rules for $25,000 of rental loss.	7,220	8,330	8,820	9,340
Credit for low–income housing investments.	8,120	7,980	7,890	8,190
Commerce:				
Capital gains (except agriculture, timber, iron ore, and coal).	76,140	85,360	93,030	97,560
Step–up basis of capital gains at death.	60,370	63,440	66,670	70,070
Accelerated depreciation of machinery and equipment (normal tax method).	-9,360	-12,260	4,770	17,690
Graduated corporation income tax rate (normal tax method).	3,960	3,890	3,860	3,700
Deduction for U.S. production activities.	13,930	14,500	15,230	15,930
Transportation:				
Exclusion of reimbursed employee parking expenses.	2,690	2,800	2,910	3,040
Education, training, employment, and social services:				
Education:				
Exclusion of scholarship and fellowship income (normal tax method).	2,980	3,090	3,200	3,310
Lifetime Learning tax credit.	2,240	2,430	2,460	2,480
American Opportunity tax credit.	15,710	15,660	15,690	15,760
Exclusion of interest on bonds for private nonprofit educational facilities.	2,300	2,450	2,780	3,130
Parental personal exemption for students age 19 years or over.	4,390	4,460	4,540	4,640
Deductibility of charitable contributions (education).	4,840	5,120	5,480	5,890
Training, employment, and social services:				
Child credit.	23,800	23,900	24,070	24,160
Credit for child and dependent care expenses.	4,420	4,510	4,590	4,690
Deductibility of charitable contributions, other than education and health.	41,910	44,280	47,380	51,170
Health:				
Exclusion of employer contributions for medical insurance premiums and medical care.	195,050	206,430	216,080	226,860
Self–employed medical insurance premiums.	6,380	6,660	6,970	7,270
Deductibility of medical expenses.	6,810	7,080	7,660	7,700
Exclusion of interest on hospital construction bonds.	3,500	3,730	4,230	4,770
Deductibility of charitable contributions (health).	4,740	5,010	5,350	5,780
Income security:				
Exclusion of workers' compensation benefits.	9,890	9,990	10,090	10,190
Net exclusion of pension contributions and earnings:				
Defined benefit employer plans.	42,780	44,640	46,260	48,040
Defined contribution employer plans.	62,530	68,040	73,910	74,670
Individual Retirement Accounts (IRAs).	16,580	17,240	18,270	19,230
Keogh (self–employed) plans.	23,240	25,480	28,020	30,780
Exclusion of other employee benefits:				
Premiums on group term life insurance.	2,200	2,320	2,420	2,520
Earned income tax credit.	3,660	5,030	5,090	4,300
Social security:				
Exclusion of social security benefits:				
Social security benefits for retired workers.	26,200	27,080	28,300	29,850
Social security benefits for disabled.	8,050	8,310	8,580	8,660
Social security benefits for dependents and survivors.	4,330	4,390	4,530	4,710
Veterans' benefits and services:				
Exclusion of veterans' death benefits and disability compensation.	5,720	6,380	6,860	7,200
General purpose fiscal assistance:				
Exclusion of interest on public purpose state and local bonds.	29,090	31,070	35,190	39,690
Deductibility of nonbusiness state and local tax, other than owner-occupied homes.	45,720	47,490	51,180	55,300
Interest:				
Deferral of interest on U.S. savings bonds.	1,030	1,020	1,010	1,000
Addendum: Aid to state and local governments:				
Deductibility of:				
Property taxes on owner–occupied homes.	31,590	33,120	35,520	38,190
Nonbusiness state and local taxes other than on owner–occupied homes.	45,720	47,490	51,180	55,300
Exclusion of interest on state and local bonds for:				
Public purposes.	29,090	31,070	35,190	39,690
Private nonprofit educational facilities.	2,300	2,450	2,780	3,130

– Represents zero.

Source: U.S. Office of Management and Budget, *Fiscal Year 2016 Budget of the U.S. Government: Supplemental Materials*, February 2015. See also <http://www.whitehouse.gov/omb/budget/>.

Table 501. Internal Revenue Gross Collections by Type of Tax: 2005 to 2014

[2,269 represents $2,269,000,000,000, except percent. For fiscal years ending September 30. See text, this section, for information on taxes]

Type of tax	Gross collections (bil. dol.)						Percent of total					
	2005	2010	2011	2012	2013	2014	2005	2010	2011	2012	2013	2014
United States, total............	**2,269**	**2,345**	**2,415**	**2,524**	**2,855**	**3,064**	**100.0**	**100.0**	**100.0**	**100.0**	**100.0**	**100.0**
Individual income taxes............	1,108	1,164	1,331	1,371	1,540	1,614	48.8	49.7	55.1	54.3	53.9	52.7
Withheld by employers...........	787	900	1,010	1,038	1,123	1,170	34.7	38.4	41.8	41.1	39.3	38.2
Tax payments [1]...................	321	264	321	333	416	444	14.1	11.3	13.3	13.2	14.6	14.5
Estate and trust income tax.......	(NA)	12	15	16	25	29	(NA)	0.5	0.6	0.7	0.9	1.0
Employment taxes.................	771	824	768	784	898	976	34.0	35.1	31.8	31.1	31.4	31.9
Old-age and disability insurance......................	760	813	756	772	884	962	33.5	34.7	31.3	30.6	31.0	31.4
Unemployment insurance........	7	7	7	7	8	9	0.3	0.3	0.3	0.3	0.3	0.3
Railroad retirement..............	5	5	5	5	6	6	0.2	0.2	0.2	0.2	0.2	0.2
Business income taxes [2]........	307	278	243	281	312	353	13.5	11.9	10.1	11.1	10.9	11.5
Estate and gift taxes..............	26	20	9	14	20	20	1.1	0.8	0.4	0.6	0.7	0.7
Excise taxes......................	57	47	49	56	61	71	2.5	2.0	2.0	2.2	2.1	2.3

NA Not available. [1] Includes estimated income tax collections and payments made with tax filings. Also includes estate and trust income tax for 2005. [2] Includes corporate income tax and tax-exempt organization unrelated business income tax.

Source: U.S. Internal Revenue Service, *IRS Data Book 2014*, March 2015, and earlier editions. See also <http://www.irs.gov/uac/SOI-Tax-Stats-IRS-Data-Book>.

Table 502. Individual Income Tax Returns Filed—Audits Coverage: 1995 to 2014

[114,683 represents 114,683,000, except percent. See the annual *IRS Data Book* (Publication 55B) for a detailed explanation. An IRS audit is a review/examination of an organization's or individual's tax return]

Year	Returns filed [1] (1,000)	Returns examined		Total recommended additional tax [3] ($1,000)	Average recommended additional tax per return (dol.) [3]
		Total [2] (1,000)	Percent coverage		
1995.........................	114,683	1,919	1.7	7,756,954	4,041
1996.........................	116,060	1,942	1.7	7,600,191	3,915
1997.........................	118,363	1,519	1.3	8,363,918	5,505
1998.........................	120,342	1,193	1.0	6,095,698	5,110
1999.........................	122,547	1,100	0.9	4,458,474	4,052
2000.........................	124,887	618	0.5	3,388,905	5,486
2001.........................	127,097	732	0.6	3,301,860	4,512
2002.........................	129,445	744	0.6	3,636,486	4,889
2003.........................	130,341	849	0.7	4,559,902	5,369
2004.........................	130,134	997	0.8	6,201,693	6,220
2005.........................	130,577	1,199	0.9	13,355,087	11,138
2006.........................	132,276	1,284	1.0	13,045,221	10,160
2007.........................	134,543	1,385	1.0	15,705,155	11,343
2008.........................	137,850	1,392	1.0	12,462,770	8,956
2009 [4]......................	138,950	1,426	1.0	14,940,892	10,478
2010.........................	142,823	1,581	1.1	15,066,486	9,527
2011.........................	140,837	1,565	1.1	14,652,239	9,364
2012.........................	143,400	1,482	1.0	15,310,908	10,331
2013.........................	145,819	1,405	1.0	14,049,657	10,000
2014.........................	145,236	1,242	0.9	11,885,411	9,566

[1] Returns generally filed in previous calendar year. [2] Includes taxpayer examinations by correspondence. [3] For 1995, amount includes associated penalties. [4] Excludes returns filed by individuals only to receive an economic stimulus payment and who had no other reason to file.

Source: U.S. Internal Revenue Service, *IRS Data Book, 2014*, March 2015, and earlier editions. See also <http://www.irs.gov/uac/SOI-Tax-Stats-IRS-Data-Book>.

Table 503. Federal Individual Income Tax Returns—Adjusted Gross Income, Taxable Income, and Total Income Tax: 2010 to 2012

[142,892 represents 142,892,000. For tax years. Based on a sample of returns, see source and Appendix III]

Year	2010		2011		2012		Percent change in amount, 2011-12
	Number of returns (1,000)	Amount (mil. dol.)	Number of returns (1,000)	Amount (mil. dol.)	Number of returns (1,000)	Amount (mil. dol.)	
Adjusted gross income (less deficit).....	**142,892**	**8,089,142**	**145,370**	**8,374,143**	**144,948**	**9,042,369**	**8.0**
Exemptions [1]................................	287,679	1,049,272	289,306	1,069,958	289,036	1,097,471	2.6
Taxable income...............................	107,304	5,502,001	108,649	5,746,218	109,144	6,356,630	10.6
Total income tax..............................	84,476	951,674	91,694	1,045,511	93,149	1,191,570	14.0
Alternative minimum tax.....................	4,020	27,461	4,248	30,479	4,251	29,121	-4.5

[1] The number of returns columns represent the number of exemptions.

Source: U.S. Internal Revenue Service, Statistics of Income Bulletin, "Historical Tables," <http://www.irs.gov/uac/SOI-Tax-Stats-SOI-Bulletin-Historical-Tables-and-Appendix>, accessed March 2015.

Table 504. Federal Individual Income Tax Returns—Adjusted Gross Income (AGI) by Selected Source of Income and Income Class: 2012

[In millions of dollars (9,100,131 represents $9,100,131,000,000), except as indicated. For the tax year. Minus sign (-) indicates net loss was greater than net income. Based on sample; see Appendix III]

Item	Total [1]	Under $10,000 [1]	$10,000 to $19,999	$20,000 to $29,999	$30,000 to $39,999	$40,000 to $49,999	$50,000 to $99,999	$100,000 and over
Number of all returns (1,000)..............	144,928	24,465	24,248	18,903	14,451	10,874	31,089	20,899
Adjusted gross income [2].................	**9,100,131**	**-75,459**	**360,479**	**467,587**	**502,651**	**486,762**	**2,215,014**	**5,143,096**
Salaries and wages........................	6,301,358	113,554	262,185	371,578	408,353	391,350	1,701,108	3,053,231
Interest received..........................	182,856	10,673	5,009	5,001	4,651	5,213	24,343	127,966
Dividends in AGI..........................	464,795	12,355	7,284	9,779	7,775	8,135	46,722	372,745
Business, profession, net profit less loss.......................	304,192	8,934	36,222	18,571	15,331	12,874	53,192	159,066
Sales of property, net gain less loss [3]......................	611,312	-2,008	42	658	795	1,663	12,766	597,396
Pensions and annuities in AGI...........	612,544	12,035	34,842	39,640	41,763	42,779	209,611	231,873
Rents and royalties, net income less loss [4]..................	53,070	-4,335	713	540	-135	-320	3,969	52,638

[1] Includes a small number of returns with no adjusted gross income. [2] Includes other sources, not shown separately. [3] Includes sales of capital assets and other property. [4] Excludes rental passive losses disallowed in the computation of AGI.

Source: U.S. Internal Revenue Service, *Statistics of Income--Individual Income Tax Returns 2012*, Publication 1304, July 2014. See also <http://www.irs.gov/uac/Tax-Stats-2>.

Table 505. Federal Individual Income Tax Returns—Total and Selected Sources of Adjusted Gross Income: 2012 and 2013

[144,928 represents 144,928,000. For tax years. Based on a sample of returns, see source and Appendix III. Minus sign (-) indicates decrease]

Item	2012 Number of returns (1,000)	2012 Amount (mil. dol.)	2013 Number of returns (1,000)	2013 Amount (mil. dol.)	Change in amount, 2012-13 Net change (mil. dol.)	Change in amount, 2012-13 Percent change
Adjusted gross income (less deficit) [1].......................	**144,928**	**9,100,131**	**147,351**	**9,093,629**	**-6,503**	**-0.1**
Salaries and wages..	119,851	6,301,358	122,189	6,475,381	174,023	2.8
Taxable interest..	47,973	111,790	44,921	100,649	-11,141	-10.0
Ordinary dividends...	27,975	260,393	27,688	214,973	-45,421	-17.4
Qualified dividends..	25,491	204,402	25,494	158,069	-46,332	-22.7
Business or profession net income (less loss).....................	23,035	304,192	23,530	302,073	-2,119	-0.7
Net capital gain..	22,721	622,887	23,993	489,621	-133,266	-21.4
Capital gain distributions [2].....................................	10,412	17,829	12,845	44,774	26,945	151.1
Sales of property other than capital assets, net gain (less loss)...	2,039	-9,358	2,139	1,029	10,387	-111.0
Sales of property other than capital assets, net gain.........	908	20,400	982	26,292	5,892	28.9
Taxable social security benefits..................................	17,772	223,597	18,507	243,327	19,730	8.8
Total rental and royalty net income (less net loss) [3].............	11,269	53,070	11,544	57,505	4,435	8.4
Partnership and S corporation net income (less loss)...........	8,306	535,007	8,460	531,614	-3,393	-0.6
Estate and trust net income (less loss)...........................	646	25,182	649	24,423	-759	-3.0
Farm net income (less loss)......................................	1,836	-5,532	1,813	-7,798	-2,267	41.0
Farm net income...	589	18,186	589	17,343	-843	-4.6
Unemployment compensation.....................................	11,342	71,234	9,287	51,923	-19,311	-27.1
Taxable pensions and annuities..................................	27,290	612,544	27,756	638,659	26,115	4.3
Taxable Individual Retirement Account (IRA) distributions......	13,196	230,783	13,331	213,602	-17,181	-7.4
Other net income (less loss) [4]..................................	6,635	37,415	6,810	37,172	-243	-0.6
Gambling earnings...	1,926	29,236	1,918	29,978	743	2.5

[1] Includes other sources of income, not shown separately. [2] Includes both Schedule D and Form 1040 or 1040A capital gain distributions. [3] Includes farm rental net income (less loss). [4] Other net income (less loss) represents data reported on Form 1040, line 21, except net operating losses, foreign-earned income exclusions, cancellation of debt, taxable health savings account distributions, and gambling earnings.

Source: U.S. Internal Revenue Service, Statistics of Income, "SOI Tax Stats - Individual Statistical Tables by Size of Adjusted Gross Income," <http://www.irs.gov/uac/SOI-Tax-Stats---Individual-Statistical-Tables-by-Size-of-Adjusted-Gross-Income>, accessed September 2015.

Table 506. Federal Individual Income Tax Returns—Net Capital Gains and Capital Gain Distributions From Mutual Funds: 1990 to 2013

[14,288 represents 14,288,000. For tax years. Based on a sample of returns, see source and Appendix III. Minus sign (-) indicates decrease]

Tax year	Net capital gain (less loss)				Capital gain distributions [2]			
	Number of returns (1,000)	Current dollars (mil. dol.)	Constant (1982–1984) dollars [1]		Number of returns (1,000)	Current dollars (mil. dol.)	Constant (1982–1984) dollars [1]	
			Amount (mil. dol.)	Percent change			Amount (mil. dol.)	Percent change
1990...................	14,288	114,231	87,400	-25.6	5,069	3,905	2,988	-32.4
1991...................	15,009	102,776	75,460	-13.7	5,796	4,665	3,425	14.6
1992...................	16,491	118,230	84,269	11.7	5,917	7,426	5,293	54.5
1993...................	18,409	144,172	99,773	18.4	9,998	11,995	8,301	56.8
1994...................	18,823	142,288	96,011	-3.8	9,803	11,322	7,640	-8.0
1995...................	19,963	170,415	111,821	16.5	10,744	14,391	9,443	23.6
1996...................	22,065	251,817	160,495	43.5	12,778	24,722	15,757	66.9
1997...................	24,240	356,083	221,859	38.2	14,969	45,132	28,120	78.5
1998...................	25,690	446,084	273,671	23.4	16,070	46,147	28,311	0.7
1999...................	27,701	542,758	325,785	19.0	17,012	59,473	35,698	26.1
2000...................	29,521	630,542	366,169	12.4	17,546	79,079	45,923	28.6
2001...................	25,956	326,527	184,375	-49.6	12,216	13,609	7,685	-83.3
2002...................	24,189	238,789	132,734	-28.0	7,567	5,343	2,970	-61.4
2003...................	22,985	294,354	159,975	20.5	7,265	4,695	2,552	-14.1
2004...................	25,267	473,662	250,747	56.7	10,733	15,336	8,119	218.1
2005...................	26,196	668,015	342,046	36.4	13,393	35,581	18,219	124.4
2006...................	26,668	779,462	386,638	13.0	14,511	59,417	29,473	61.8
2007...................	27,156	907,656	437,758	13.2	15,714	86,397	41,669	41.4
2008...................	23,731	469,273	217,959	-50.2	11,544	21,954	10,197	-75.5
2009...................	20,291	231,548	107,929	-50.5	4,191	2,411	1,124	-89.0
2010...................	21,315	364,410	167,118	54.8	6,567	6,270	2,875	155.9
2011...................	22,154	377,037	167,618	0.3	8,859	14,171	6,300	119.1
2012...................	22,721	622,887	271,299	61.9	10,412	17,829	7,766	23.3
2013...................	23,993	489,621	210,176	-22.5	12,845	44,774	19,220	147.5

[1] Constant dollars were calculated using the U.S. Bureau of Labor Statistics consumer price index for urban consumers (CPI-U, 1982–84 = 100). See Table 745. [2] Capital gain distributions are included in net capital gain (less loss). For 1991–1996, and 1999 and later years, capital gain distributions from mutual funds are the sum of the amounts reported on the Form 1040 and Schedule D. For 1997 and 1998, capital gain distributions were reported entirely on the Schedule D.

Source: U.S. Internal Revenue Service, Statistics of Income, "SOI Tax Stats - Individual Statistical Tables by Size of Adjusted Gross Income," <http://www.irs.gov/uac/SOI-Tax-Stats---Individual-Statistical-Tables-by-Size-of-Adjusted-Gross-Income>, accessed September 2015.

Table 507. Alternative Minimum Tax: 1986 to 2013

[609 represents 609,000. For tax years. Based on a sample of returns, see source and Appendix III]

Tax year	Highest statutory alternative minimum tax rate (percent)	Alternative minimum tax		Tax year	Highest statutory alternative minimum tax rate (percent)	Alternative minimum tax	
		Number of returns (1,000)	Amount (mil. dol.)			Number of returns (1,000)	Amount (mil. dol.)
1986..............	20	609	6,713	2000..............	[1] 28	1,304	9,601
1987..............	21	140	1,675	2001..............	[1] 28	1,120	6,757
1988..............	21	114	1,028	2002..............	[1] 28	1,911	6,854
1989..............	21	117	831	2003..............	[1] 28	2,358	9,470
1990..............	21	132	830	2004..............	[1] 28	3,096	13,029
1991..............	24	244	1,213	2005..............	[1] 28	4,005	17,421
1992..............	24	287	1,357	2006..............	[1] 28	3,967	21,565
1993..............	28	335	2,053	2007..............	[1] 28	4,109	24,110
1994..............	28	369	2,212	2008..............	[1] 28	3,935	25,649
1995..............	28	414	2,291	2009..............	[1] 28	3,828	22,580
1996..............	28	478	2,813	2010..............	[1] 28	4,020	27,461
1997..............	[1] 28	618	4,005	2011..............	[1] 28	4,248	30,479
1998..............	[1] 28	853	5,015	2012..............	[1] 28	4,225	32,770
1999..............	[1] 28	1,018	6,478	2013..............	[1] 28	3,940	27,426

[1] Top rate on most long-term capital gains was 20 percent; beginning 2003, the rate was 15 percent.

Source: U.S. Internal Revenue Service, Statistics of Income, "SOI Tax Stats - Individual Statistical Tables by Size of Adjusted Gross Income," <http://www.irs.gov/uac/SOI-Tax-Stats---Individual-Statistical-Tables-by-Size-of-Adjusted-Gross-Income>, accessed September 2015.

Table 508. Federal Individual Income Tax Returns—Sources of Net Losses Included in Adjusted Gross Income: 2012 and 2013

[27,500 represents 27,500,000. For tax years. Based on a sample of returns, see source and Appendix III]

Item	2012 Number of returns (1,000)	2012 Amount (mil. dol.)	2013 Number of returns (1,000)	2013 Amount (mil. dol.)	Percent change in amount, 2012–13
Total net losses	27,500	489,723	25,930	488,765	-0.2
Business or profession net loss	5,463	52,259	5,561	55,291	5.8
Net capital loss [1]	10,480	24,186	9,009	20,909	-13.6
Net loss, sales of property other than capital assets	1,131	29,758	1,156	25,262	-15.1
Total rental and royalty net loss [2]	4,840	47,800	4,752	46,536	-2.6
Partnership and S corporation net loss	2,708	113,241	2,689	116,349	2.7
Estate and trust net loss	60	2,724	59	4,286	57.3
Farm net loss	1,247	23,717	1,224	25,141	6.0
Net operating loss [3]	1,294	189,073	1,212	189,041	0.0
Other net loss [4]	277	6,963	269	5,949	-14.6

[1] Includes only the portion of capital losses allowable in the calculation of adjusted gross income. Only $3,000 of net capital loss per return ($1,500 for married filing separately) are allowed to be included in negative total income. Any excess is carried forward to future years. [2] Includes farm rental net loss. [3] Net operating loss is a carryover of the loss from a business when taxable income from a prior year was less than zero. [4] Other net loss represents losses reported on Form 1040, line 21, except net operating loss and the foreign-earned income exclusion.

Source: U.S. Internal Revenue Service, Statistics of Income, "SOI Tax Stats - Individual Statistical Tables by Size of Adjusted Gross Income," <http://www.irs.gov/uac/SOI-Tax-Stats---Individual-Statistical-Tables-by-Size-of-Adjusted-Gross-Income>, accessed September 2015.

Table 509. Federal Individual Income Tax Returns—Number, Income Tax, and Average Tax by Size of Adjusted Gross Income: 2011 and 2012

[145,370 represents 145,370,000. Based on sample of returns; see Appendix III. Minus sign (-) indicates net loss was greater than net income]

Size of adjusted gross income	Number of returns (1,000) 2011	Number of returns (1,000) 2012 [2]	Adjusted gross income (AGI) (bil. dol.) 2011	Adjusted gross income (AGI) (bil. dol.) 2012 [2]	Income tax total [1] (bil. dol.) 2011	Income tax total [1] (bil. dol.) 2012 [2]	Taxes as percent of AGI (for taxable returns only) 2011	Taxes as percent of AGI (for taxable returns only) 2012 [2]	Average tax (for taxable returns only) (dol.) 2011	Average tax (for taxable returns only) (dol.) 2012 [2]
Total	145,370	144,948	8,374	9,042	1,046	1,192	13.6	14.2	11,402	12,792
No AGI [3]	2,451	2,013	-196	-173	123	79	(X)	(X)	21,510	13,531
$1 to $999	1,906	1,629	1	1	–	–	0.4	4.5	4	43
$1,000 to $2,999	4,337	4,244	9	9	–	–	3.8	3.4	76	71
$3,000 to $4,999	4,450	4,397	18	18	–	–	6.0	3.9	232	155
$5,000 to $6,999	4,600	4,463	28	27	–	–	1.5	1.4	96	87
$7,000 to $8,999	4,961	4,631	40	37	–	–	3.0	2.8	237	222
$9,000 to $10,999	5,401	5,327	54	53	–	–	2.6	2.6	267	260
$11,000 to $12,999	5,276	4,998	63	60	1	1	2.2	2.2	269	267
$13,000 to $14,999	5,075	5,167	71	72	1	1	3.1	3.1	436	429
$15,000 to $16,999	5,094	4,957	81	79	1	1	3.8	3.7	607	588
$17,000 to $18,999	4,540	4,504	82	81	2	2	4.3	4.2	781	760
$19,000 to $21,999	6,488	6,507	133	133	3	3	4.8	4.8	989	983
$22,000 to $24,999	5,969	5,887	140	138	4	4	5.5	5.3	1,288	1,251
$25,000 to $29,999	8,988	8,736	246	240	9	9	6.1	6.1	1,681	1,676
$30,000 to $39,999	14,520	14,458	505	503	25	24	6.8	6.8	2,381	2,361
$40,000 to $49,999	10,984	10,887	492	487	31	30	7.4	7.4	3,329	3,318
$50,000 to $74,999	18,949	19,015	1,166	1,170	93	94	8.6	8.6	5,281	5,280
$75,000 to $99,999	11,926	12,199	1,032	1,055	96	99	9.5	9.5	8,219	8,225
$100,000 to $199,999	14,756	15,670	1,977	2,104	249	266	12.7	12.7	17,005	17,076
$200,000 to $499,999	3,802	4,179	1,081	1,194	212	234	19.7	19.7	56,092	56,307
$500,000 to $999,999	598	693	404	469	98	114	24.3	24.3	164,175	164,846
$1,000,000 to $1,499,999	135	163	163	198	40	49	24.9	25.0	301,552	302,395
$1,500,000 to $1,999,999	56	73	96	126	24	32	25.2	25.3	432,931	433,864
$2,000,000 to $4,999,999	79	107	236	319	59	80	25.0	25.1	744,620	752,981
$5,000,000 to $9,999,999	19	27	131	188	32	46	24.2	24.6	1,649,391	1,704,267
$10,000,000 or more	11	18	322	455	66	102	20.5	22.5	5,763,301	5,556,810

– Represents or rounds to zero. X Not applicable. [1] Consists of income tax after credits (including alternative minimum tax). [2] Preliminary data. [3] In addition to low-income taxpayers, this size class (and others) includes taxpayers with "tax preferences," not reflected in adjusted gross income or taxable income, which are subject to the "alternative minimum tax" (included in total income tax).

Source: U.S. Internal Revenue Service, "Statistics of Income Bulletin, Historical Tables," <http://www.irs.gov/uac/Tax-Stats-2>, accessed September 2015.

Table 510. Federal Individual Income Tax Returns—Selected Itemized Deductions and the Standard Deduction: 2012 and 2013

[45,582 represents 45,582,000. For tax years. Based on a sample of returns, see source and Appendix III. Minus sign (-) indicates decrease]

Item	2012		2013		Percent change, 2012–13	
	Number of returns [1] (1,000)	Amount (mil. dol.)	Number of returns [1] (1,000)	Amount (mil. dol.)	Number of returns [1] (1,000)	Amount (percent)
Total itemized deductions...........................	**45,582**	**1,238,693**	**44,330**	**1,188,595**	**-2.7**	**-4.0**
Medical and dental expenses after Adjusted Gross Income (AGI) limitation......................	10,216	85,313	8,998	84,507	-11.9	-0.9
Taxes paid [2]..	45,233	483,082	43,977	506,191	-2.8	4.8
State and local income taxes........................	33,424	282,964	32,590	304,274	-2.5	7.5
State and local general sales taxes..............	10,483	16,539	10,077	16,597	-3.9	0.3
Interest paid [3]..	35,416	354,058	33,898	317,317	-4.3	-10.4
Home mortgage interest...........................	34,838	332,611	33,279	296,186	-4.5	-11.0
Charitable contributions............................	37,367	199,270	36,431	194,664	-2.5	-2.3
Other than cash contributions....................	22,183	49,047	22,176	51,591	0.0	5.2
Casualty and theft losses...........................	160	4,945	97	2,463	-39.2	-50.2
Total limited miscellaneous deductions after 2% AGI limitation................................	11,851	90,389	12,302	98,383	3.8	8.8
Total unlimited miscellaneous deductions....................	1,264	21,650	1,205	21,498	-4.7	-0.7
Itemized deductions in excess of limitation...................	2	14	2,517	36,428	101,807.4	266,597.2
Basic Standard deduction............................	**97,209**	**773,693**	**100,899**	**823,063**	**3.8**	**6.4**
Additional Standard deduction........................	**13,702**	**23,709**	**14,287**	**25,583**	**4.3**	**7.9**

[1] Returns with no adjusted gross income are excluded from the deduction counts. For this reason, the sum of the number of returns with total itemized deductions and the number of returns with total standard deduction is less than the total number of returns for all filers. [2] Includes real estate taxes, personal property taxes, and other taxes, not shown separately. [3] Includes investment interest, deductible mortgage "points," and qualified mortgage interest premiums, not shown separately.

Source: U.S. Internal Revenue Service, Statistics of Income, "SOI Tax Stats - Individual Statistical Tables by Size of Adjusted Gross Income," <http://www.irs.gov/uac/SOI-Tax-Stats---Individual-Statistical-Tables-by-Size-of-Adjusted-Gross-Income>, accessed September 2015.

Table 511. Federal Individual Income Tax Returns—Statutory Adjustments: 2012 and 2013

[36,623 represents 36,623,000. For tax years. Based on a sample of returns, see source and Appendix III. Minus sign (-) indicates decrease]

Item	2012		2013		Percent change in amount, 2012–13
	Number of returns (1,000)	Amount (mil. dol.)	Number of returns (1,000)	Amount (mil. dol.)	
Total statutory adjustments............................	**36,623**	**134,028**	**37,666**	**139,882**	**4.4**
Payments to an Individual Retirement Account (IRA).................	2,575	11,795	2,713	12,973	10.0
Educator expenses deduction..........................	3,790	958	3,838	964	0.7
Certain business expenses of reservists, performing artists, etc.....	143	521	157	587	12.7
Moving expenses adjustment...........................	1,137	3,088	1,244	3,561	15.3
Student loan interest deduction........................	10,765	10,694	11,460	11,618	8.6
Tuition and fees deduction............................	2,113	4,687	1,893	4,341	-7.4
Health savings account deduction......................	1,083	3,355	1,195	3,716	10.8
Self-employment tax deduction........................	18,671	27,536	18,875	27,912	1.4
Self-employment health insurance deduction................	3,902	25,678	3,996	27,139	5.7
Payments to a self-employed retirement (Keogh) plan...............	923	20,849	955	22,408	7.5
Forfeited interest penalty.............................	769	456	691	221	-51.5
Alimony paid..	623	11,156	652	11,761	5.4
Domestic production activities deduction..............	659	11,158	717	11,229	0.6
Other adjustments [1].................................	162	2,098	150	1,452	-30.8

[1] Includes foreign housing adjustment, medical savings accounts deduction, and other adjustments.

Source: U.S. Internal Revenue Service, Statistics of Income, "SOI Tax Stats - Individual Statistical Tables by Size of Adjusted Gross Income," <http://www.irs.gov/uac/SOI-Tax-Stats---Individual-Statistical-Tables-by-Size-of-Adjusted-Gross-Income>, accessed September 2015.

Table 512. Federal Individual Income Tax Returns—Itemized Deductions and Statutory Adjustments by Size of Adjusted Gross Income: 2013

[44,330 represents 44,330,000. Based on a sample of returns; see Appendix III]

Item	Unit	Total [1]	Under $10,000 [1]	$10,000 to $19,999	$20,000 to $29,999	$30,000 to $39,999	$40,000 to $49,999	$50,000 to $99,999	$100,000 and over
Returns with itemized deductions:									
Number of returns [2]	1,000	44,330	788	1,645	2,200	2,887	3,293	15,372	18,146
Amount [2, 3]	Mil. dol	1,188,595	12,471	24,502	34,347	45,354	53,069	292,698	726,154
Medical and dental expenses: [4]									
Returns	1,000	8,998	562	1,083	1,064	1,059	924	3,081	1,225
Amount	Mil. dol	84,507	5,202	8,538	8,916	8,574	7,236	29,066	16,975
Taxes paid:									
Returns	1,000	43,977	749	1,595	2,141	2,838	3,243	15,300	18,111
Amount	Mil. dol	506,191	2,715	5,410	7,223	10,486	14,177	96,679	369,500
State and local taxes: [5]									
Returns	1,000	42,667	655	1,439	2,010	2,715	3,118	14,904	17,826
Amount	Mil. dol	320,871	547	1,341	2,205	3,909	6,025	48,391	258,453
Real estate taxes:									
Returns	1,000	37,803	577	1,190	1,511	2,095	2,549	13,172	16,710
Amount	Mil. dol	174,273	2,024	3,838	4,562	6,040	7,516	44,959	105,335
Interest paid:									
Returns	1,000	33,898	444	872	1,238	1,881	2,330	12,010	15,123
Amount	Mil. dol	317,317	3,240	5,912	8,695	12,666	15,941	94,057	176,806
Home mortgage interest:									
Returns	1,000	33,279	423	853	1,214	1,847	2,305	11,872	14,766
Amount	Mil. dol	296,186	3,166	5,664	8,267	11,959	15,047	89,083	163,000
Charitable contributions:									
Returns	1,000	36,431	438	1,123	1,574	2,114	2,464	12,521	16,197
Amount	Mil. dol	194,664	528	2,133	3,718	5,225	6,756	38,709	137,596
Unreimbursed employee business expenses:									
Returns	1,000	14,545	82	315	709	1,062	1,227	5,685	5,464
Amount	Mil. dol	85,605	305	1,685	4,454	7,187	7,705	31,954	32,315
Returns with statutory adjustments:									
Number of returns [1]	1,000	37,666	4,597	5,110	3,601	3,336	2,966	9,650	8,406
Amount of adjustments [3]	Mil. dol	139,882	6,770	6,636	6,184	6,890	6,610	27,758	79,034
Payments to IRAs: [6]									
Returns	1,000	2,713	68	139	201	305	267	988	746
Amount	Mil. dol	12,973	228	380	716	1,117	1,078	4,633	4,821
Deduction for self-employment tax:									
Returns	1,000	18,875	3,548	3,682	1,705	1,309	1,107	3,585	3,939
Amount	Mil. dol	27,912	1,668	2,972	1,807	1,583	1,380	5,456	13,045
Self-employment health insurance:									
Returns	1,000	3,996	386	315	284	260	244	939	1,567
Amount	Mil. dol	27,139	1,590	1,214	1,247	1,270	1,198	5,586	15,033
Payments to Keogh plans:									
Returns	1,000	955	12	13	24	16	19	144	726
Amount	Mil. dol	22,408	87	49	104	86	176	1,635	20,271

[1] For returns with statutory adjustments, includes a small number of taxable returns with no adjusted gross income. [2] After limitations. [3] Includes other deductions and adjustments, not shown separately. [4] Before limitation. [5] State and local taxes include income taxes and sales taxes. [6] Individual Retirement Accounts. .

Source: U.S. Internal Revenue Service, Statistics of Income, "SOI Tax Stats - Individual Statistical Tables by Size of Adjusted Gross Income," <http://www.irs.gov/uac/SOI-Tax-Stats---Individual-Statistical-Tables-by-Size-of-Adjusted-Gross-Income>, accessed September 2015.

Table 513. Federal Individual Income Tax Returns—Selected Tax Credits: 2012 and 2013

[47,359 represents 47,359,000. For tax years. Based on a sample of returns, see source and Appendix III]

Item	2012 Number of returns (1,000)	2012 Amount (mil. dol.)	2013 Number of returns (1,000)	2013 Amount (mil. dol.)	Percent change, 2012-13 Number of returns (1,000)	Percent change, 2012-13 Amount (mil. dol.)
Total tax credits [1]	**47,359**	**72,928**	**48,104**	**74,614**	**1.6**	**2.3**
Child care credit	6,340	3,412	6,316	3,459	-0.4	1.4
Earned income credit [2]	4,152	1,213	4,241	1,294	2.1	6.7
Foreign tax credit	7,096	19,115	7,488	20,238	5.5	5.9
General business credit	466	2,581	462	3,065	-0.9	18.8
Minimum tax credit	262	684	322	1,005	23.0	46.9
Child tax credit [3]	22,890	27,727	22,563	27,233	-1.4	-1.8
Education credits	10,079	10,523	10,197	10,646	1.2	1.2
Retirement savings contribution credit	6,926	1,203	7,412	1,317	7.0	9.5
Residential energy credits [2]	2,225	1,267	3,036	1,614	36.4	27.4

[1] Includes credits not shown separately. [2] Represents portion of credit used to offset income tax before credits. [3] Excludes refundable portion.

Source: U.S. Internal Revenue Service, Statistics of Income, "SOI Tax Stats - Individual Statistical Tables by Size of Adjusted Gross Income," <http://www.irs.gov/uac/SOI-Tax-Stats---Individual-Statistical-Tables-by-Size-of-Adjusted-Gross-Income>, accessed September 2015.

Table 514. Federal Individual Income Tax Returns by State: 2013

[In units as indicated (146,543 represents 146,543,000). For tax year. Data may not agree with data in other tables due to differing survey methodology used to derive state data]

State	Total number of returns (1,000)	Adjusted gross income (mil. dol.)			Itemized deductions (mil. dol.)				Income tax (mil. dol.)
		Total [1]	Salaries and wages	Net capital gain [2]	Total [1]	State and local income tax	Real estate taxes	Home mortgage interest paid	
U.S.	146,543	9,057,169	6,450,671	486,556	1,200,006	305,302	174,136	293,883	1,228,719
Alabama	2,049	103,845	76,139	2,917	11,853	2,153	604	3,061	11,717
Alaska	359	22,931	16,556	691	1,670	28	308	675	3,120
Arizona	2,814	152,738	110,787	6,280	19,314	3,121	1,784	5,900	18,743
Arkansas	1,220	61,473	43,368	1,926	6,715	1,896	420	1,377	6,996
California	17,172	1,181,367	838,735	79,221	205,942	68,217	24,700	53,948	169,422
Colorado	2,503	164,067	116,393	9,646	20,736	4,662	1,930	6,753	22,342
Connecticut	1,750	155,371	104,435	11,977	23,964	8,254	4,857	4,949	26,490
Delaware	440	26,108	18,668	794	3,330	876	327	1,091	3,193
District of Colombia. ..	331	27,260	19,316	1,897	4,371	1,678	353	976	4,534
Florida	9,316	520,166	338,725	38,829	56,036	2,983	8,153	14,280	75,298
Georgia	4,359	235,982	178,326	8,419	35,273	7,877	3,309	8,764	29,060
Hawaii	675	37,478	26,566	1,550	5,130	1,379	306	1,860	4,188
Idaho	692	34,404	24,576	1,650	4,543	1,105	411	1,231	3,772
Illinois	6,101	399,202	283,082	22,258	52,312	13,099	11,516	12,063	55,926
Indiana	3,048	158,757	117,410	4,340	15,294	4,052	1,421	3,779	18,427
Iowa	1,435	81,928	57,678	2,704	9,233	2,611	1,274	1,834	9,485
Kansas	1,326	78,516	54,829	3,352	8,644	2,130	1,080	1,776	9,953
Kentucky	1,886	93,261	68,715	2,797	10,742	3,331	1,000	2,514	10,162
Louisiana	2,004	109,193	78,898	3,825	11,337	2,095	697	2,523	14,167
Maine	636	32,700	23,254	1,275	4,024	1,153	685	1,012	3,545
Maryland	2,942	203,829	150,829	6,647	36,805	11,416	4,550	9,986	26,991
Massachusetts	3,301	262,986	182,912	19,433	35,471	10,805	6,383	8,886	41,172
Michigan	4,657	252,106	178,109	8,022	28,159	6,579	4,325	6,838	31,399
Minnesota	2,653	172,892	125,347	7,269	24,301	7,727	3,033	6,051	22,554
Mississippi	1,246	56,012	41,643	1,338	6,512	1,087	437	1,305	5,827
Missouri	2,743	148,434	106,659	5,525	17,223	4,368	1,904	3,992	18,013
Montana	488	24,976	16,471	1,411	3,143	810	328	784	2,855
Nebraska	880	50,727	36,060	2,197	5,867	1,609	869	1,131	6,106
Nevada	1,308	75,468	50,419	7,853	8,831	502	753	2,433	10,262
New Hampshire	682	44,790	32,762	2,200	5,317	501	1,449	1,529	5,922
New Jersey	4,327	335,600	246,194	13,910	54,134	15,260	14,069	11,995	51,446
New Mexico	906	43,941	30,799	1,597	4,712	891	458	1,384	4,953
New York	9,443	698,576	468,339	65,396	115,747	46,285	19,757	18,039	111,209
North Carolina	4,336	232,422	171,049	7,802	32,215	8,852	3,305	8,202	27,035
North Dakota	362	25,006	15,702	1,282	1,554	320	177	332	3,702
Ohio	5,537	296,428	214,651	8,598	32,889	9,998	5,267	7,562	35,528
Oklahoma	1,631	91,923	63,938	3,834	10,274	2,085	805	1,920	11,451
Oregon	1,794	101,826	70,520	4,646	16,323	5,002	2,191	4,362	11,862
Pennsylvania	6,154	368,060	264,567	14,745	42,825	10,551	7,900	10,436	48,273
Rhode Island	518	30,572	22,162	1,169	4,210	1,082	838	1,109	3,925
South Carolina	2,106	105,954	75,683	3,536	14,482	3,371	1,067	4,491	11,810
South Dakota	413	23,167	14,762	1,390	1,711	75	226	377	2,979
Tennessee	2,908	151,117	111,772	5,627	13,558	518	1,410	3,816	18,703
Texas	11,889	737,453	535,904	42,347	68,583	1,513	12,923	16,046	106,520
Utah	1,196	68,994	51,411	3,351	10,760	2,303	880	2,910	7,684
Vermont	321	17,451	12,220	999	2,107	543	460	506	2,000
Virginia	3,835	264,027	194,710	9,778	38,067	9,683	4,734	12,020	35,434
Washington	3,293	222,349	159,456	12,781	24,627	728	3,979	8,892	30,756
West Virginia	784	37,821	27,770	793	3,398	925	186	734	4,020
Wisconsin	2,798	159,418	114,968	6,138	21,111	6,416	3,941	4,556	19,392
Wyoming	284	20,545	12,379	3,028	1,895	158	136	437	3,011
Other [3]	695	55,553	54,049	5,566	2,732	641	262	455	5,385

[1] Includes other items, not shown separately. [2] Less loss. [3] Includes returns filed from Army Post Office and Fleet Post Office addresses by members of the armed forces stationed overseas; returns by other U.S. citizens abroad; and returns filed by residents of Puerto Rico with income from sources outside of Puerto Rico or with income earned as U.S. government employees.

Source: U.S. Internal Revenue Service, Statistics of Income Bulletin, "Historical Data Tables," <http://www.irs.gov/uac/SOI-Tax-Stats-Historical-Data-Tables>, accessed September 2015.

Table 515. Federal Civilian Employment and Annual Payroll by Branch: 1970 to 2014

[2,997 represents 2,997,000. For fiscal year ending in year shown. See text, Section 8. Includes employees in U.S. territories and foreign countries. Data represent employees in active-duty status, including intermittent employees. Annual employment figures are averages of monthly figures. Excludes Central Intelligence Agency; National Security Agency; as of November 1984, Defense Intelligence Agency; and, as of October 1996, National Geospatial-Intelligence Agency]

| Year | Employment | | | | | | Payroll (mil. dol.) | | | | |
| | Total (1,000) | Percent of U.S. employed [1] | Executive (1,000) | | Legislative (1,000) | Judicial (1,000) | Total | Executive | | Legislative | Judicial |
			Total	Defense				Total	Defense		
1970	[2]2,997	3.81	2,961	1,263	29	7	27,322	26,894	11,264	338	89
1975	2,877	3.35	2,830	1,044	37	10	39,126	38,423	13,418	549	154
1980	[2]2,987	3.01	2,933	971	40	14	58,012	56,841	18,795	883	288
1985	3,001	2.80	2,944	1,080	39	18	80,599	78,992	28,330	1,098	509
1990	[2]3,233	2.72	3,173	1,060	38	23	99,138	97,022	31,990	1,329	787
1995	2,943	2.36	2,880	852	34	28	118,304	115,328	31,753	1,598	1,379
2000	[2]2,879	2.10	2,816	681	31	32	130,832	127,472	29,607	1,619	1,741
2005	2,701	1.91	2,636	671	31	34	152,222	148,275	29,331	2,048	1,900
2006	2,700	1.87	2,637	676	29	34	160,570	156,543	29,580	2,109	1,918
2007	2,699	1.85	2,636	673	30	33	161,394	157,010	29,025	2,119	2,265
2008	2,758	1.90	2,694	694	30	34	167,166	162,675	29,749	2,162	2,328
2009	2,838	2.03	2,774	737	31	34	174,804	170,349	30,995	2,203	2,252
2010	2,841	2.04	2,777	773	31	34	152,321	147,554	32,377	2,515	2,251
2011	2,820	2.02	2,756	774	30	34	166,508	161,897	33,075	2,359	2,255
2012	2,761	1.94	2,697	730	30	34	182,030	177,332	32,670	2,442	2,256
2013	2,731	1.90	2,668	729	29	34	165,697	161,004	32,810	2,438	2,255
2014	2,726	1.86	2,663	723	29	34	154,777	150,172	28,639	2,350	2,256

[1] Civilian employment only. See Table 604, Section 12. [2] Includes temporary census workers.

Source: U.S. Office of Personnel Management, "Federal Civilian Workforce Statistics—Employment and Trends," <http://www.opm.gov/policy-data-oversight/data-analysis-documentation/federal-employment-reports/#url=Employment-Trends>; and unpublished data.

Table 516. Full-Time Federal Civilian Employment—Employees and Average Pay by Pay System: 2010 to 2014

[(1,950 represents 1,950,000). As of September 30. Data are shown for all full-time nonseasonal employees. Includes employees in U.S., U.S. territories, foreign countries, and unspecified locations. Excludes postal employees and other selected agencies, see <http://www.fedscope.opm.gov/datadefn/aboutehri_sdm.asp> for details. See text, this section, for explanation of general schedule and wage system]

| Pay system | Employees (1,000) | | | | Average annual pay (dol.) | | | |
	2010	2012	2013	2014	2010	2012	2013	2014
Total	1,950	1,949	1,918	1,912	75,704	77,742	78,759	79,853
General schedule and equivalently graded	1,410	1,448	1,424	1,418	73,656	76,032	77,012	78,061
Prevailing rate pay plans (blue collar)	195	189	182	183	52,051	52,575	52,934	53,225
Other white collar pay plans	344	312	312	311	97,459	100,940	101,826	103,679

NA Not available.

Source: U.S. Office of Personnel Management, "FedScope," <http://www.fedscope.opm.gov/>, accessed August 2015.

Table 517. Federal Government Civilian Employment by State: 2010 to 2014

[In thousands (2,061.3 represents 2,061,300). As of September 30. For agencies excluded from total, see <http://www.fedscope.opm.gov/datadefn/aboutehri_sdm.asp>]

State	2010	2013	2014	State	2010	2013	2014	State	2010	2013	2014
U.S. [1]	2,061.3	2,018.1	1,998.7	KS	17.8	17.1	16.8	NC	43.7	45.2	45.3
AL	42.3	40.4	39.7	KY	26.5	25.1	24.5	ND	6.7	6.2	6.2
AK	14.1	12.4	12.1	LA	21.1	20.7	20.3	OH	53.0	51.4	51.2
AZ	42.4	41.9	41.4	ME	11.1	10.8	10.9	OK	39.5	38.2	37.9
AR	14.7	14.2	14.1	MD	128.3	134.1	133.1	OR	22.5	21.3	21.4
CA	172.5	167.1	165.4	MA	29.2	28.2	27.7	PA	69.8	65.3	64.6
CO	40.7	40.4	39.9	MI	30.0	30.1	29.6	RI	7.1	7.3	7.3
CT	8.7	8.8	8.9	MN	18.6	18.4	18.2	SC	21.7	22.4	22.2
DE	3.4	3.3	3.2	MS	19.4	18.9	19.1	SD	8.8	8.5	8.5
DC	167.9	161.5	159.1	MO	38.4	36.0	35.6	TN	28.8	28.5	27.9
FL	88.9	90.1	89.5	MT	12.0	11.2	11.2	TX	140.3	139.4	137.4
GA	80.2	76.9	75.8	NE	10.7	11.0	11.1	UT	31.1	28.8	28.5
HI	25.4	24.6	24.4	NV	11.5	12.8	12.7	VT	4.5	5.0	5.0
ID	10.5	10.1	10.1	NH	4.4	4.7	4.7	VA	145.4	146.3	144.4
IL	51.1	48.0	47.5	NJ	30.1	25.9	25.6	WA	57.9	56.9	57.7
IN	24.7	23.7	23.5	NM	27.7	25.2	24.7	WV	16.3	16.4	16.4
IA	9.2	9.1	9.1	NY	68.2	66.0	65.2	WI	15.8	16.2	16.3
								WY	6.6	6.5	6.4

[1] Total includes data that has been suppressed for security purposes, see source for details.

Source: U.S. Office of Personnel Management, "FedScope," <http://www.fedscope.opm.gov/>, accessed July 2015.

Table 518. Federal Civilian Employment by Branch and Agency: 1990 to 2014

[For years ending September 30. Annual averages of monthly figures. Excludes Central Intelligence Agency, National Security Agency, Defense Intelligence Agency, and as of October 1996, National Geospatial-Intelligence Agency]

Agency	1990	2000	2005	2010	2013	2014
Total, all agencies [1]	**3,128,267**	**2,708,101**	**2,700,965**	**2,841,143**	**[6] 2,730,551**	**2,725,590**
Legislative branch	37,495	31,157	30,816	30,643	28,672	28,910
Judicial branch	23,605	32,186	34,064	33,756	[6] 33,776	33,766
Executive branch	3,067,167	2,644,758	2,636,085	2,776,744	2,668,103	2,662,914
Executive Office of the President	1,731	1,658	1,693	1,965	[6] 1,828	[6] 1,823
Executive departments	2,065,542	1,592,200	1,685,211	1,937,291	1,898,443	1,894,472
State	25,288	27,983	33,948	39,016	41,768	[6] 41,768
Treasury	158,655	143,508	107,950	110,099	[6] 112,461	[6] 112,461
Defense	1,034,152	676,268	671,364	772,601	728,823	723,175
Justice	83,932	125,970	105,458	117,916	115,616	114,055
Interior	77,679	73,818	75,973	70,231	71,543	69,807
Agriculture [2]	122,594	104,466	107,852	106,867	95,223	94,083
Commerce [2]	69,920	47,652	39,836	56,856	45,035	43,182
Labor	17,727	16,040	15,383	17,592	17,187	[6] 16,796
Health & Human Services [3]	123,959	62,605	60,736	69,839	72,703	71,862
Housing & Urban Development	13,596	10,319	9,941	9,585	8,136	7,795
Transportation [4]	67,364	63,598	55,559	57,972	55,288	54,790
Energy	17,731	15,692	15,010	16,145	15,213	14,802
Education	4,771	4,734	4,321	4,452	4,166	4,123
Veterans Affairs	248,174	219,547	235,210	304,665	323,208	[6] 339,903
Homeland Security [4]	(X)	(X)	146,670	183,455	192,073	[6] 185,870
Independent agencies [1]	999,894	1,050,900	949,181	837,488	[6] 767,832	766,619
Board of Governors Federal Reserve System	1,525	2,372	1,860	1,873	[6] 1,873	[6] 1,873
Environmental Protection Agency	17,123	18,036	17,824	18,740	17,002	[6] 16,871
Equal Employment Opportunity Commission	2,880	2,780	2,360	2,543	[6] 2,219	[6] 2,219
Federal Communications Commission	1,778	1,965	1,885	1,838	1,759	1,720
Federal Deposit Insurance Corporation	17,641	6,958	4,635	6,436	[6] 7,587	7,094
Federal Trade Commission	988	1,019	1,007	1,131	[6] 1,131	[6] 1,131
General Services Administration	20,277	14,334	12,769	12,820	11,819	11,482
National Archives & Records Administration	3,120	2,702	3,029	3,523	[6] 3,201	3,041
National Aeronautics & Space Administration	24,872	18,819	18,752	18,664	18,001	17,685
National Labor Relations Board	2,263	2,054	1,869	1,715	1,588	1,589
National Science Foundation	1,318	1,247	1,305	1,474	[6] 1,491	1,420
Nuclear Regulatory Commission	3,353	2,858	3,242	4,240	3,863	3,863
Office of Personnel Management	6,636	3,780	4,939	5,892	[6] 5,558	[6] 5,558
Peace Corps	1,178	1,065	1,072	1,082	1,068	[6] 1,069
Securities & Exchange Commission	2,302	2,955	3,907	3,917	4,136	4,136
Small Business Administration	5,128	4,150	4,343	4,037	[6] 4,037	[6] 4,037
Smithsonian Institution	5,092	5,065	4,901	4,984	[6] 4,900	[6] 4,676
Social Security Administration [3]	(X)	64,474	66,144	69,975	62,549	64,689
Tennessee Valley Authority	28,392	13,145	12,703	12,457	12,612	[6] 11,843
Broadcasting Board of Governors [5]	8,555	2,436	2,175	1,953	[6] 1,845	1,728
U.S. Agency for International Development	4,698	2,552	2,493	2,515	[6] 2,515	[6] 2,515
U.S. Postal Service	816,886	860,726	764,165	643,420	584,027	583,400

X Not applicable. [1] Includes agencies not shown separately. [2] Includes enumerators for the 1990 and 2000 censuses. [3] The Social Security Administration was separated from the Department of Health and Human Services to become an independent agency effective April 1995. [4] See text, Section 10, National Security and Veteran Affairs, concerning the development of the Department of Homeland Security. [5] Prior to 1999, data for U.S. Information Agency. [6] Preliminary employment totals were used.

Source: U.S. Office of Personnel Management, "Federal Civilian Workforce Statistics--Employment and Trends," <http://www.opm.gov/policy-data-oversight/data-analysis-documentation/federal-employment-reports/#url=Employment-Trends>, accessed July 2015; and unpublished data.

Table 519. Federal Employees—Summary Characteristics: 1990 to 2013

[In percent, except as indicated. As of September 30. For civilian employees of executive branch agencies participating in Office of Personnel Management's Central Personnel Data File (CPDF)]

Characteristics	1990	1995	2000	2005	2009	2010	2011 [3]	2012	2013
Average age (years) [1]	42.3	44.3	46.3	46.9	46.8	46.8	(NA)	47.0	47.3
Average length of service (years)	13.4	15.5	17.1	16.4	15.1	14.3	(NA)	13.7	13.9
Retirement eligible: [2]									
Civil Service Retirement System	8.0	10.0	17.0	33.0	51.4	57.0	(NA)	67.0	72.0
Bachelor's degree or higher	35.0	39.0	41.0	43.0	45.3	46.0	(NA)	48.1	49.3
Sex: Male	57.0	56.0	55.0	56.0	55.7	55.9	(NA)	56.4	56.5
Female	43.0	44.0	45.0	44.0	44.3	44.1	(NA)	43.6	43.5
Race and national origin:									
Total minorities	27.4	28.9	30.4	31.7	33.0	33.3	(NA)	34.0	34.4
Black	16.7	16.8	17.1	17.0	17.5	17.5	(NA)	17.7	17.9
Hispanic	5.4	5.9	6.6	7.4	7.7	7.7	(NA)	8.0	8.1
Asian/Pacific Islander	3.5	4.2	4.5	5.1	5.6	5.6	(NA)	5.8	6.5
American Indian/Alaska Native	1.8	2.0	2.2	2.1	2.1	2.1	(NA)	2.1	2.0
Disabled	7.0	7.0	7.0	7.0	6.9	7.0	(NA)	7.9	8.7
Veterans preference	30.0	26.0	24.0	22.0	22.7	23.1	(NA)	24.5	24.9
Vietnam era veterans	17.0	17.0	14.0	11.0	7.1	8.0	(NA)	5.0	4.4
Retired military	4.9	4.2	3.9	5.4	6.6	7.0	(NA)	7.7	7.9
Retired officers	0.5	0.5	0.5	1.0	1.4	1.6	(NA)	1.7	1.8
Average base salary (dollar) [1]	32,026	41,557	51,618	64,175	73,994	76,231	(NA)	78,061	79,030

NA Not available. [1] For full-time permanent employees. [2] Represents full-time permanent employees under the Civil Service Retirement System (excluding hires since January 1984), and the Federal Employees Retirement System (since January 1984). [3] Data for 2011 was not made available.

Source: U.S. Office of Personnel Management, Office of Workforce Information, *The Fact Book, Federal Civilian Workforce Statistics*, annual. Beginning 2008, Central Personnel Data File, "Profile of Federal Civilian Non-Seasonal Full-Time Employees," <http://www.opm.gov/policy-data-oversight/data-analysis-documentation/federal-employment-reports/reports-publications/profile-of-federal-civilian-non-postal-employees/>, accessed September 2014.

Table 520. Federal Executive Branch (Non-postal) Employment by Race and Hispanic Origin: 1990 to 2010

[As of September 30. Covers total employment for executive branch agencies]

Pay system	1990	1995	2000	2005	2006	2008	2010
All personnel [1]	**2,150,359**	**1,960,577**	**1,755,689**	**1,856,966**	**1,848,339**	**1,916,726**	**2,108,639**
White, non-Hispanic	1,562,846	1,394,690	1,224,836	1,267,922	1,254,308	1,297,772	1,406,609
General schedule and related	1,218,188	1,101,108	961,261	973,767	948,740	858,050	1,029,711
Grades 1 to 4	132,028	79,195	55,067	46,671	43,450	44,324	50,000
Grades 5 to 8	337,453	288,755	239,128	227,387	219,168	211,004	233,096
Grades 9 to 12	510,261	465,908	404,649	408,111	399,400	351,302	428,980
Grades 13 to 15	238,446	267,250	262,417	291,598	286,722	251,420	317,635
Total executive/senior pay levels	9,337	13,307	14,332	16,409	16,118	21,793	22,947
Wage pay system	244,220	186,184	146,075	135,383	133,942	134,933	136,493
Other pay systems	91,101	94,091	103,168	142,363	155,508	282,996	217,458
Black	356,867	327,302	298,701	315,644	317,697	337,742	368,814
General schedule and related	272,657	258,586	241,135	246,691	246,248	236,525	283,175
Grades 1 to 4	65,077	41,381	26,895	19,774	18,326	18,286	19,238
Grades 5 to 8	114,993	112,962	99,937	94,655	93,717	90,410	98,964
Grades 9 to 12	74,985	79,795	82,809	90,809	91,869	86,054	110,023
Grades 13 to 15	17,602	24,448	31,494	41,453	42,336	41,775	54,950
Total executive/senior pay levels	479	942	1,180	1,270	1,218	1,565	1,857
Wage pay system	72,755	55,637	42,590	37,666	37,378	38,540	37,260
Other pay systems	10,976	12,137	13,796	30,017	32,853	61,973	46,522
Hispanic	115,170	115,964	115,247	138,507	138,596	136,167	163,975
General schedule and related	83,218	86,762	89,911	104,927	105,236	95,016	123,913
Grades 1 to 4	15,738	11,081	8,526	7,768	6,854	5,459	6,890
Grades 5 to 8	28,727	31,152	31,703	33,653	33,834	31,261	35,813
Grades 9 to 12	31,615	34,056	36,813	46,268	46,951	42,542	57,491
Grades 13 to 15	7,138	10,473	12,869	17,238	17,597	15,754	23,719
Total executive/senior pay levels	154	382	547	682	699	1,109	1,191
Wage pay system	26,947	22,128	16,926	15,945	15,822	15,639	15,643
Other pay systems	4,851	6,692	7,863	16,953	16,839	28,646	23,228
American Indian, Alaska Native, Asian, and Pacific Islander	115,476	122,621	116,905	134,893	136,593	145,045	169,241
General schedule and related	81,499	86,768	86,074	97,866	97,870	93,197	119,895
Grades 1 to 4	15,286	11,854	9,340	8,357	7,877	7,608	8,710
Grades 5 to 8	24,960	26,580	25,691	27,417	26,986	26,046	30,794
Grades 9 to 12	31,346	33,810	33,167	38,276	38,492	35,259	47,656
Grades 13 to 15	9,907	14,524	17,876	23,816	24,515	24,284	32,735
Total executive/senior pay levels	148	331	504	804	873	2,851	3,176
Wage pay system	24,927	21,553	17,613	16,938	16,728	17,022	17,753
Other pay systems	8,902	13,969	12,714	19,285	21,122	33,834	28,417

[1] Beginning 2006, includes persons classified as multiracial, not shown separately.

Source: U.S. Office of Personnel Management, *Demographic Profile of the Federal Workforce as of September 2010,* April 2011, and earlier reports. See also <http://www.opm.gov/policy-data-oversight/data-analysis-documentation/federal-employment-reports/demographics/2010-demographic-profile/>.

Table 521. Area of Federally Owned Buildings in the United States by State: 2013

[3,287.1 represents 3,287,100,000. As of September 30. For executive branch departments and agencies subject to the Chief Financial Officers Act of 1990]

State	Total building area (mil. sq. ft.)	Owned building area (mil. sq. ft.) [2]	Leased building area (mil. sq. ft.)	State	Total building area (mil. sq. ft.)	Owned building area (mil. sq. ft.) [2]	Leased building area (mil. sq. ft.)
U.S. [1]	**3,287.1**	**2,739.1**	**548.0**	Missouri	56.5	45.5	11.0
Alabama	55.0	50.1	4.9	Montana	17.1	14.8	2.3
Alaska	44.0	41.5	2.5	Nebraska	15.3	13.7	1.6
Arizona	54.3	50.0	4.3	Nevada	27.2	25.1	2.1
Arkansas	23.0	21.5	1.5	New Hampshire	4.7	4.1	0.6
California	289.6	269.0	20.6	New Jersey	46.1	41.1	5.0
Colorado	59.0	51.6	7.4	New Mexico	57.6	53.8	3.8
Connecticut	13.7	12.8	1.0	New York	91.2	82.1	9.1
Delaware	6.3	5.8	0.4	North Carolina	92.7	87.0	5.7
Dist. of Columbia	95.2	69.1	26.1	North Dakota	22.9	21.8	1.1
Florida	115.0	102.1	12.9	Ohio	67.9	62.3	5.6
Georgia	123.5	112.9	10.6	Oklahoma	54.8	45.5	9.3
Hawaii	47.3	46.3	1.0	Oregon	23.5	20.4	3.1
Idaho	18.2	16.4	1.7	Pennsylvania	81.0	71.8	9.2
Illinois	67.9	62.1	5.9	Rhode Island	14.1	13.5	0.6
Indiana	29.6	26.8	2.8	South Carolina	50.8	48.5	2.3
Iowa	16.7	14.8	1.9	South Dakota	18.0	15.9	2.1
Kansas	33.2	30.2	3.0	Tennessee	57.1	53.8	3.4
Kentucky	48.6	43.8	4.8	Texas	194.9	171.1	23.8
Louisiana	43.3	39.3	4.0	Utah	30.3	27.4	2.9
Maine	11.5	10.6	0.9	Vermont	4.5	3.3	1.2
Maryland	133.1	109.1	24.0	Virginia	179.2	150.0	29.2
Massachusetts	34.7	31.7	3.0	Washington	84.7	78.9	5.7
Michigan	28.3	22.9	5.3	West Virginia	23.7	21.0	2.7
Minnesota	21.9	19.4	2.5	Wisconsin	22.8	20.2	2.5
Mississippi	42.4	39.8	2.6	Wyoming	14.0	13.2	0.8

[1] Includes property in other locations not shown separately. [2] Includes Federal Government owned, foreign government owned, museum trust, and state government owned. Non-federal government entities hold title to the real property asset but rights for use have been granted to the Federal Government in a method other than a leasehold arrangement; in the case of a museum trust, the trust holds title but Federal funds may be received to cover operational and maintenance costs.

Source: U.S. General Services Administration, "Real Property Management Policy—Asset Management, FRPP Summary Report Library," <http://www.gsa.gov/portal/content/102880>, accessed March 2015.

National Security and Veterans Affairs

This section displays data for national security (national defense and homeland security) and benefits for veterans. Data are presented on national defense and its human and financial costs; active and reserve military personnel; federally sponsored programs and benefits for veterans; and funding, budget and selected agencies for homeland security. The principal sources of these data are the *Annual Report of Secretary of Veterans Affairs*, U.S. Department of Veterans Affairs; *Budget in Brief*, U.S. Department of Homeland Security; and *The Budget of the United States Government*, Office of Management and Budget. For data on international expenditures and personnel, see Table 1405, Section 30.

Department of Defense (DoD)—The U.S. Department of Defense is responsible for providing the military forces of the United States. It includes the Office of the Secretary of Defense, the Joint Chiefs of Staff, the Army, the Navy, the Air Force, and the defense agencies. The President serves as Commander-in-Chief of the Armed Forces; from him, the authority flows to the Secretary of Defense and through the Joint Chiefs of Staff to the commanders of unified and specified commands (e.g., U.S. Strategic Command).

Reserve components—The Reserve Components of the Armed Forces consist of the Army National Guard of the United States, Army Reserve, Naval Reserve, Marine Corps Reserve, Air National Guard, Air Force Reserve, and Coast Guard Reserve. They provide trained personnel and units available for active duty in the Armed Forces during times of war or national emergency, and at such other times as national security may require. The National Guard has dual federal/state responsibilities and uses jointly provided equipment, facilities, and budget support. The President is empowered to mobilize the National Guard and to use such of the Armed Forces as he considers necessary to enforce federal authority in any state. There is in each Armed Force a ready reserve, a standby reserve, and a retired reserve. The Ready Reserve includes the Selected Reserve, which provides trained and ready units and individuals to augment the active forces during times of war or national emergency, or at other times when required; and the Individual Ready Reserve, which is a manpower pool that can be called to active duty during times of war or national emergency and would normally be used as individual fillers for active, guard, and reserve units, and as a source of combat replacements. Most of the Ready Reserve serves in an active status.

Department of Veterans Affairs (VA)—A veteran is someone 18 years and older (there are a few 17-year-old veterans) who is not currently on active duty, but who once served on active duty in the United States Army, Navy, Air Force, Marine Corps, or Coast Guard, or who served in the Merchant Marine during World War II. There are many groups whose active service makes them veterans including: those who incurred a service-connected disability during active duty for training in the Reserves or National Guard, even though that service would not otherwise have counted for veteran status and members of a national guard or reserve component who have been ordered to active duty by order of the President or those who have a full-time military job. The latter are called AGRs (Active Guard and Reserve). No one who has received a dishonorable discharge is a veteran.

The VA administers laws authorizing benefits for eligible former and present members of the Armed Forces and for the beneficiaries of deceased members. Veterans' benefits available under various acts of Congress include compensation for service-connected disability or death; pensions for non-service-connected disability or death; vocational rehabilitation, education and training; home loan insurance; life insurance; health care; special housing and automobiles or other conveyances for certain disabled veterans; burial and plot allowances; and educational assistance to families of deceased or totally disabled veterans, servicemen missing in action, or prisoners of war. Since these benefits are legislated by Congress, the dates they were enacted and the dates they apply to veterans may be different from the actual dates the conflicts occurred. VA estimates of veterans cover all persons discharged from active U.S. military service under conditions other than dishonorable.

Department of Homeland Security (DHS)—The creation of DHS, which began operations in March 2003, represents a fusion of 22 federal agencies from different legacy agencies (the Coast Guard and Secret Service remained intact) to coordinate and centralize the leadership of many homeland security activities under a single department. The largest organizations under DHS include: Customs and Border Protection (CBP), Immigration and Customs Enforcement (ICE), Transportation Security Administration (TSA), Federal Emergency Management Agency (FEMA), and the Coast Guard.

Coast Guard—With more than 218 years of service to the Nation, the Coast Guard is a military, multi-mission, maritime organization that promotes safety and safeguards U.S. economic and security interests throughout the maritime environment. As one of the five Armed Services of the United States, it is the only military organization within the DHS. Unlike its sister services in the Department of Defense (DoD), the Coast Guard is also a law enforcement and regulatory agency with broad domestic authorities.

Federal Emergency Management Agency (FEMA)—FEMA manages and coordinates the federal response to and recovery from major domestic disasters and emergencies of all types in accordance with the Robert T. Stafford Disaster Relief and Emergency Assistance Act. The agency ensures the effectiveness of emergency response providers at all levels of government in responding to terrorist attacks, major disasters, and other emergencies. Through the Disaster Relief Fund, FEMA provides individual and public assistance to help families and communities impacted by declared disasters rebuild and recover. FEMA is also the principal component for preparing state and local governments to prevent or respond to threats or incidents of terrorism and other catastrophic events, through their state and local programs.

The Customs and Border Protection (CBP)—CBP is responsible for managing, securing, and controlling U.S. borders. This includes carrying out traditional border-related responsibilities, such as stemming the tide of illegal drugs and illegal aliens; securing and facilitating legitimate global trade and travel; and protecting the food supply and agriculture industry from pests and disease. CBP is composed of the Border Patrol and Inspections (both moved from INS) along with Customs (absorbed from the U.S. Department of Treasury) and Animal and Plant Health Inspections Services (absorbed from the U.S. Department of Agriculture).

The Immigration and Customs Enforcement (ICE)—ICE's mission is to protect America and uphold public safety by targeting the people, money, and materials crossing the nation's borders that support terrorist and criminal activities. ICE is the largest investigation arm of DHS. ICE is composed of five law enforcement divisions: Investigations, Intelligence, Federal Protective Service, International Affairs, and Detention and Removal Operations. ICE investigates a wide range of national security, financial, and smuggling violations including drug smuggling, human trafficking, illegal arms exports, financial crimes, commercial fraud, human smuggling, document fraud, money laundering, child pornography/exploitation, and immigration fraud.

The Transportation Security Administration (TSA)—TSA was created as part of the Aviation and Transportation Security Act on November 19, 2001. TSA was originally part of the U.S. Department of Transportation, but was moved to DHS. TSA's mission is to provide security to our nation's transportation systems with a primary focus on aviation security.

Table 522. National Defense Outlays and Veterans' Benefits: 1960 to 2016

[In billions of dollars (53.6 represents $53,600,000,000), except percent. For fiscal year ending in year shown, see text, Section 8. Includes outlays of Department of Defense, Department of Veterans Affairs, and other agencies for activities primarily related to national defense and veterans programs. For explanation of average annual percent change, see Guide to Tabular Presentation. Minus sign (-) indicates decrease]

Year	National defense and veterans' outlays				Annual percent change [1]			Defense outlays, percent of—	
		Defense outlays							
	Total outlays	Current dollars	Constant (2009) dollars	Veterans' outlays	Total outlays	Defense outlays	Veterans' outlays	Federal outlays	Gross domestic product [2]
1960	53.6	48.1	(NA)	5.4	-1.63	-1.81	-0.04	52.2	9.0
1970	90.4	81.7	468.9	8.7	0.26	-0.98	13.60	41.8	7.8
1980	155.2	134.0	361.3	21.2	13.88	15.17	6.30	22.7	4.8
1990	328.4	299.3	512.2	29.0	-1.56	-1.39	-3.23	23.9	5.1
2000	341.4	294.4	406.9	47.0	7.37	7.13	8.88	16.5	2.9
2001	349.7	304.7	406.6	45.0	2.45	3.52	-4.29	16.4	2.9
2002	399.4	348.5	449.0	50.9	14.21	14.35	13.24	17.3	3.2
2003	461.7	404.7	491.2	57.0	15.61	16.15	11.89	18.7	3.6
2004	515.6	455.8	533.0	59.7	11.66	12.62	4.85	19.9	3.8
2005	565.4	495.3	552.6	70.1	9.67	8.66	17.36	20.0	3.8
2006	591.6	521.8	558.1	69.8	4.64	5.36	-0.44	19.7	3.8
2007	624.1	551.3	571.4	72.8	5.48	5.64	4.31	20.2	3.8
2008	700.7	616.1	614.9	84.7	12.28	11.76	16.25	20.7	4.2
2009	756.4	661.0	661.0	95.4	7.95	7.30	12.73	18.8	4.6
2010	801.9	693.5	691.3	108.4	6.01	4.91	13.58	20.1	4.7
2011	832.7	705.6	692.6	127.2	3.85	1.74	17.35	19.6	4.6
2012	802.4	677.9	659.0	124.6	-3.64	-3.93	-2.04	19.2	4.2
2013	772.4	633.4	611.9	138.9	-3.75	-6.55	11.51	18.3	3.8
2014	753.1	603.5	574.2	149.6	-2.50	-4.73	7.69	17.2	3.5
2015 estimate	758.9	597.5	560.8	161.4	0.78	-0.99	7.89	15.9	3.3
2016 estimate	795.8	615.5	568.7	180.3	4.86	3.01	11.71	15.4	3.3

NA Not available. [1] Change from immediate prior year. [2] Represents fiscal year GDP; for definition, see text, Section 13.

Source: U.S. Office of Management and Budget, *Fiscal Year 2016 Budget of the U.S. Government: Historical Tables*, February 2015. See also <http://www.whitehouse.gov/omb/budget/>.

Table 523. National Defense Budget Authority and Outlays for Defense Functions: 1990 to 2016

[In billions of dollars (303.3 represents $303,300,000,000). For year ending September 30. Data includes defense budget authority and outlays by other departments. Minus sign (-) indicates decrease]

Function	1990	1995	2000	2005	2010	2011	2012	2013	2014	2015 est.	2016 est.
Total budget authority	**303.3**	**266.4**	**304.0**	**505.7**	**721.2**	**717.0**	**681.4**	**610.2**	**622.3**	**596.8**	**620.9**
Department of Defense—Military	292.9	255.7	290.3	483.8	695.6	691.5	655.4	585.2	595.7	569.3	592.3
Military personnel	78.9	71.6	73.8	121.3	157.1	158.4	158.4	153.5	150.2	146.2	147.5
Operation and maintenance	88.4	93.7	108.7	179.2	293.6	305.2	286.8	258.3	262.5	247.5	250.8
Procurement	81.4	43.6	55.0	96.6	135.8	131.9	118.3	97.8	100.4	102.6	115.0
Research, development, test, and evaluation	36.5	34.5	38.7	68.8	80.2	76.7	72.0	63.3	63.5	65.2	70.0
Military construction	5.1	5.4	5.1	7.3	22.6	16.0	11.4	8.1	8.4	5.7	7.0
Family housing	3.1	3.4	3.5	4.1	2.3	1.8	1.7	1.5	1.4	1.1	1.4
Other	-0.4	3.4	5.4	6.6	4.0	1.4	6.9	2.8	9.4	0.9	0.5
Atomic energy defense activities	9.7	10.1	12.4	17.9	18.2	18.5	18.3	17.5	18.4	19.2	20.5
Defense-related activities	0.7	0.6	1.3	4.0	7.3	7.0	7.7	7.4	8.2	8.3	8.1
Total outlays	**299.3**	**272.1**	**294.4**	**495.3**	**693.5**	**705.6**	**677.9**	**633.4**	**603.5**	**597.5**	**615.5**
Department of Defense—Military	289.7	259.4	281.0	474.1	666.7	678.1	650.9	607.8	577.9	567.7	586.5
Military personnel	75.6	70.8	76.0	127.5	155.7	161.6	152.3	150.8	148.9	149.2	148.1
Operation and maintenance	88.3	91.0	105.8	188.1	276.0	291.0	282.3	259.7	244.5	234.2	250.9
Procurement	81.0	55.0	51.7	82.3	133.6	128.0	124.7	114.9	107.5	106.2	102.7
Research, development, test, and evaluation	37.5	34.6	37.6	65.7	77.0	74.9	70.4	66.9	64.9	66.3	70.3
Military construction	5.1	6.8	5.1	5.3	21.2	19.9	14.6	12.3	9.8	9.8	9.2
Family housing	3.5	3.6	3.4	3.7	3.2	3.4	2.3	1.8	1.4	1.5	1.5
Other	-1.2	-2.4	1.4	1.5	0.1	-0.8	4.3	1.4	0.9	0.5	3.7
Atomic energy activities	9.0	11.8	12.1	18.0	19.3	20.4	19.2	17.6	17.4	21.2	20.8
Defense-related activities	0.6	0.9	1.2	3.2	7.5	7.1	7.8	8.0	8.1	8.6	8.3

Source: U.S. Office of Management and Budget, *Fiscal Year 2016 Budget of the U.S. Government: Historical Tables*, February 2015. See also <http://www.whitehouse.gov/omb/budget/>.

Table 524. Military Personnel on Active Duty by Location: 1980 to 2014

[In thousands (2,051 represents 2,051,000). As of September 30. Prior to 2012, data from DOD Statistical Information Analysis Division (SIAD). Beginning 2012, data from Defense Manpower Data Center (DMDC)]

Location	1980	1990	1995	2000	2005	2010	2011	2012	2013	2014
Total	**2,051**	**2,046**	**1,518**	**1,384**	**1,389**	**1,431**	**1,425**	**1,388**	**1,370**	**1,326**
Shore-based [1]	1,840	1,794	1,351	1,237	1,262	1,328	1,325	(NA)	(NA)	(NA)
Afloat [2]	211	252	167	147	127	103	101	(NA)	(NA)	(NA)
United States [3]	1,562	1,437	1,280	1,127	1,098	1,134	1,220	1,214	1,209	1,168
Foreign countries	489	609	238	258	291	297	205	135	125	124

NA Not available. [1] Includes Navy personnel temporarily on shore. [2] Includes Marine Corps. [3] Includes Puerto Rico and Island Areas.

Source: U.S. Department of Defense, DoD Personnel and Procurement Statistics, "Active Duty Military Personnel By Service By Region/Country," January 2014 and earlier reports, <https://www.dmdc.osd.mil/>, accessed December 2014.

Table 525. Department of Defense Personnel by Service Branch and Sex: 1960 to 2014

[In thousands (2,475 represents 2,475,000). As of end of fiscal year; see text, Section 8. Includes National Guard, Reserve, and retired regular personnel on extended or continuous active duty. Excludes Coast Guard. Other officer candidates are included under enlisted personnel]

Year	Total 1,2	Army Total 1	Army Male Officers	Army Male Enlisted	Army Female Officers	Army Female Enlisted	Navy 2 Total 1	Navy Male Officers	Navy Male Enlisted	Navy Female Officers	Navy Female Enlisted	Marine Corps Total 1	MC Male Officers	MC Male Enlisted	MC Female Officers	MC Female Enlisted	Air Force Total 1	AF Male Officers	AF Male Enlisted	AF Female Officers	AF Female Enlisted
1960	2,475	873	97	762	4.3	8.3	617	67	540	2.7	5.4	171	16	153	0.1	1.5	815	126	677	3.7	5.7
1965	2,654	969	108	846	3.8	8.5	670	75	583	2.6	5.3	190	17	172	0.1	1.4	825	128	685	4.1	4.7
1970	3,065	1,323	162	1,142	5.2	11.5	691	78	600	2.9	5.8	260	25	233	0.3	2.1	791	125	648	4.7	9.0
1975	2,128	784	98	640	4.6	37.7	535	62	449	3.7	17.5	196	19	174	0.3	2.8	613	100	478	5.0	25.2
1980	2,051	777	91	612	7.6	61.7	527	58	430	4.9	30.1	189	18	164	0.5	6.2	558	90	404	8.5	51.9
1985	2,151	781	99	599	10.8	68.4	571	64	449	6.9	45.7	198	19	169	0.7	9.0	602	96	431	11.9	58.1
1986	2,169	781	99	597	11.3	69.7	581	65	457	7.3	47.2	200	19	170	0.6	9.2	608	97	434	12.4	61.2
1987	2,174	781	96	596	11.6	71.6	587	65	462	7.2	47.7	200	19	170	0.6	9.1	607	94	432	12.6	63.2
1988	2,138	772	95	588	11.8	72.0	593	65	466	7.3	49.7	197	19	168	0.7	9.0	576	92	405	12.9	61.5
1989	2,130	770	95	584	12.2	74.3	593	65	464	7.5	52.1	197	19	168	0.7	9.0	571	91	399	13.4	63.7
1990	2,044	732	92	553	12.4	71.2	579	64	451	7.8	52.1	197	19	168	0.7	8.7	535	87	370	13.3	60.8
1991	1,986	711	91	535	12.5	67.8	570	63	444	8.0	51.4	194	19	166	0.7	8.3	510	84	350	13.3	59.1
1992	1,807	610	83	449	11.7	61.7	542	61	417	8.3	51.0	185	18	157	0.6	7.9	470	77	320	12.7	56.1
1993	1,705	572	77	420	11.1	60.2	510	58	390	8.3	49.3	178	17	153	0.6	7.2	444	72	302	12.3	54.5
1994	1,610	541	74	394	10.9	59.0	469	54	355	8.0	47.9	174	17	149	0.6	7.0	426	69	287	12.3	54.0
1995	1,518	509	72	365	10.8	57.3	435	51	324	7.9	47.9	175	17	150	0.7	7.4	400	66	266	12.1	52.1
1996	1,472	491	70	347	10.6	59.0	417	50	308	7.8	46.9	175	17	149	0.8	7.8	389	64	256	12.0	52.8
1997	1,439	492	69	346	10.4	62.4	396	48	290	7.8	44.8	174	17	148	0.8	8.5	377	62	246	12.0	53.8
1998	1,407	484	68	340	10.4	61.4	382	47	280	7.8	42.9	173	17	146	0.9	8.9	368	60	237	12.0	54.2
1999	1,386	479	67	337	10.5	61.5	373	46	271	7.7	43.9	173	17	145	0.9	9.3	361	58	232	11.8	54.6
2000	1,384	482	66	339	10.8	62.9	373	46	272	7.8	43.8	173	17	146	0.9	9.5	356	57	227	11.8	55.0
2001	1,385	481	65	337	11.0	63.4	378	46	273	8.0	46.6	173	17	145	1.0	9.6	354	57	224	12.0	55.6
2002	1,414	487	66	341	11.5	63.2	385	47	279	8.2	47.3	174	17	146	1.0	9.5	368	59	233	12.9	58.6
2003	1,434	499	68	352	12.0	63.5	382	47	276	8.2	47.3	178	18	149	1.1	9.6	375	61	237	13.5	60.0
2004	1,427	500	69	358	12.3	61.0	373	46	273	8.1	46.1	178	18	149	1.1	9.7	377	61	242	13.6	60.2
2005	1,389	493	69	353	12.4	57.9	363	45	266	7.8	44.5	180	18	151	1.0	9.8	354	60	225	13.4	55.6
2006	1,385	505	69	365	12.5	58.5	350	44	255	7.6	43.2	180	18	151	1.1	10.0	349	58	223	12.8	55.8
2007	1,380	522	71	379	13.0	58.8	338	44	244	7.6	42.2	186	18	156	1.1	10.5	333	54	214	11.8	53.4
2008	1,402	544	74	392	13.5	59.7	332	44	235	7.7	41.4	199	19	167	1.2	11.1	327	53	207	11.9	51.4
2009	1,419	553	76	399	14.3	59.4	329	44	231	7.9	42.2	203	19	170	1.2	11.7	333	53	211	12.1	52.0
2010	1,431	566	79	407	15.1	60.3	328	44	228	8.2	43.4	202	18	169	3.0	12.2	334	54	212	12.4	50.9
2011	1,425	565	82	403	15.7	60.2	325	44	224	8.5	44.0	201	21	167	1.3	12.4	333	53	213	12.3	50.3
2012	1,400	550	82	390	16.0	57.4	318	44	217	8.6	44.3	198	20	164	1.3	12.6	333	53	214	12.5	49.8
2013	1,383	532	82	373	16.2	55.7	324	45	219	9.0	47.0	196	20	162	1.4	12.8	330	52	213	12.7	49.1
2014	1,338	508	81	353	16.2	53.8	326	45	219	9.2	48.1	188	20	154	1.4	12.8	316	50	203	12.4	46.7

[1] Includes cadets, midshipmen, and others, not shown separately. [2] Beginning 1980, excludes Navy Reserve personnel on active duty for Training and Administration of Reserves (TARS).

Source: U.S. Department of Defense, Statistical Information Analysis Division, *Selected Manpower Statistics*, discontinued; and "Active Duty Military Personnel by Rank/Grade," <https://www.dmdc.osd. mil/appj/dwp/dwp_reports.jsp>, accessed November 2014.

Table 526. Military Personnel on Active Duty by Rank or Grade: 2000 to 2014

[In thousands (1,384.3 represents 1,384,300). As of September 30]

Rank/grade	2000	2005	2010	2011	2012	2013	2014
Total	1,384.3	1,389.4	1,431.0	1,425.1	1,399.6	1,382.7	1,338.5
Total Officers	217.2	226.6	234.0	237.4	238.1	238.5	235.0
General – Admiral	(Z)	(Z)	(Z)	(Z)	(Z)	(Z)	(Z)
Lieutenant General – Vice Admiral	0.1	0.1	0.2	0.2	0.2	0.2	0.1
Major General – Rear Admiral (U)	0.3	0.3	0.3	0.3	0.3	0.3	0.3
Brigadier General – Rear Admiral (L)	0.4	0.4	0.5	0.5	0.4	0.4	0.4
Colonel – Captain	11.3	11.4	12.2	12.1	11.9	12.0	11.6
Lieutenant Colonel – Commander	27.5	28.1	28.8	28.8	28.7	28.9	27.9
Major – LT Commander	43.2	44.4	45.3	46.2	46.5	46.2	45.6
Captain – Lieutenant	68.1	72.5	75.0	76.5	74.8	75.6	76.2
1st Lieutenant – Lieutenant (JG)	24.7	27.5	25.5	27.0	30.8	31.1	29.9
2nd Lieutenant – Ensign	26.4	25.9	27.1	26.1	25.0	24.5	23.6
Chief Warrant Officer W-5	0.5	0.5	0.7	0.8	0.8	0.8	0.8
Chief Warrant Officer W-4	2.0	2.2	3.2	3.3	3.2	3.0	2.9
Chief Warrant Officer W-3	3.8	4.6	4.8	4.7	5.1	5.1	5.3
Chief Warrant Officer W-2	6.7	6.2	7.5	8.1	8.1	8.1	8.0
Warrant Officer W-1	2.1	2.5	2.9	2.6	2.4	2.2	2.2
Total Enlisted	1,154.6	1,149.9	1,183.2	1,174.2	1,148.5	1,131.3	1,090.8
E-9	10.2	10.5	10.2	10.3	10.3	10.5	10.2
E-8	26.0	27.1	27.3	27.3	27.1	27.5	27.3
E-7	97.7	97.8	97.1	96.2	96.6	96.4	94.1
E-6	164.9	172.4	170.9	168.7	165.7	163.9	159.7
E-5	229.5	248.5	250.0	244.0	237.2	234.7	227.4
E-4	251.0	261.7	279.3	290.0	293.1	277.4	268.7
E-3	196.3	201.7	228.2	223.6	206.6	196.2	190.5
E-2	99.0	70.8	75.2	69.7	64.9	70.0	65.9
E-1	80.0	59.5	45.1	44.3	47.1	54.6	47.0
Cadets and Midshipmen	12.5	12.9	13.8	13.5	13.1	12.9	12.7

Z Fewer than 50.

Source: U.S. Department of Defense, Statistical Information Analysis Division, *Military Personnel Statistics*, annual; and "Active Duty Military Personnel by Rank/Grade," <https://www.dmdc.osd.mil/appj/dwp/dwp_reports.jsp>, accessed November 2014.

Table 527. Military Retirement System—Disabled and Non-Disabled Personnel and Payments: 2014

[Payment in thousands of dollars (4,299,193 represents $4,299,193,000). As of September 30. The data published in the source report are produced from files maintained by the Defense Manpower Data Center. This report compiles data primarily from the "Retiree Pay and Survivor Pay" files. Any grouping of members by address reflects mailing, not necessarily residence address. Only those members in plans administered by the Department of Defense (DoD) are included in this table. The data are preliminary because of reporting delays about members who retired or died within one month of the September 30 reporting date. These data were not processed in time to be included in this report. For more information, see Introduction and Overview, source]

State	Retired military personnel [1]			Monthly payment ($1,000)	State	Retired military personnel [1]			Monthly payment ($1,000)
	Total	Disabled [2]	Non-disabled			Total	Disabled [2]	Non-disabled	
Total [3]	2,107,336	224,816	1,882,520	4,299,193	MS	27,539	2,659	24,880	48,795
U.S.	2,065,536	220,485	1,845,051	4,220,728	MO	38,045	4,735	33,310	67,395
AL	59,868	5,643	54,225	120,860	MT	9,204	992	8,212	17,383
AK	10,399	1,010	9,389	21,099	NE	14,551	1,279	13,272	30,410
AZ	55,678	5,422	50,256	116,365	NV	28,588	2,227	26,361	59,247
AR	25,834	2,906	22,928	46,366	NH	9,579	971	8,608	19,516
CA	161,263	17,143	144,120	332,071	NJ	19,688	2,858	16,830	31,886
CO	51,823	5,551	46,272	122,104	NM	21,347	1,966	19,381	45,783
CT	10,339	1,346	8,993	18,463	NY	39,570	6,781	32,789	59,080
DE	8,856	683	8,173	16,560	NC	92,553	9,890	82,663	193,299
DC	2,503	386	2,117	5,807	ND	5,282	444	4,838	9,002
FL	192,784	17,872	174,912	422,186	OH	46,418	6,513	39,905	83,668
GA	94,615	10,289	84,326	188,592	OK	36,161	3,931	32,230	67,121
HI	17,385	1,367	16,018	38,858	OR	21,019	2,893	18,126	38,396
ID	13,713	1,399	12,314	26,425	PA	51,220	6,570	44,650	90,015
IL	36,919	5,065	31,854	69,065	RI	5,453	595	4,858	10,913
IN	25,616	3,857	21,759	41,416	SC	58,552	5,351	53,201	116,635
IA	12,837	1,623	11,214	20,442	SD	8,101	674	7,427	15,178
KS	21,687	2,393	19,294	43,482	TN	54,591	5,997	48,594	103,916
KY	28,462	3,836	24,626	51,954	TX	201,715	23,145	178,570	429,934
LA	26,399	3,407	22,992	49,087	UT	16,625	1,495	15,130	32,318
ME	12,029	1,268	10,761	21,412	VT	3,810	429	3,381	6,357
MD	54,641	4,535	50,106	124,320	VA	154,427	9,622	144,805	424,551
MA	18,814	2,661	16,153	31,372	WA	72,609	6,509	66,100	152,836
MI	29,724	5,009	24,715	46,633	WV	11,137	1,547	9,590	18,484
MN	18,820	2,390	16,430	29,395	WI	21,314	2,856	18,458	33,973
					WY	5,430	495	4,935	10,303

[1] Represents military personnel (officers and enlisted) receiving and not receiving pay from DoD. [2] A disabled military member is entitled to disability retired pay if the disability is not the result of the member's intentional misconduct or willful neglect, was not incurred during a period of unauthorized absence, and either: (1) the member has at least 20 years of service; or (2) at the time of determination, the disability is at least 30 percent (under a standard schedule of rating disabilities by the Veterans Administration) and one of four additional conditions are met. For details on these conditions and additional information, see Overview, source. [3] Includes states, U.S. territories, and retirees living in foreign countries.

Source: U.S. Department of Defense, Office of the Actuary, *Statistical Report on the Military Retirement System, Fiscal Year 2014*, June 2015. See also <http://www.defenselink.mil/actuary/>.

Table 528. U.S. Active Duty Military Deaths by Manner of Death: 1980 to 2012

[As of December 11, 2013]

Manner of death	1980	1990	1995	2000	2004	2005	2006	2007	2008	2009	2010	2011	2012
Deaths, total	**2,392**	**1,507**	**1,040**	**832**	**1,874**	**1,929**	**1,882**	**1,953**	**1,440**	**1,515**	**1,485**	**1,446**	**1,307**
Accident	1,556	880	538	429	605	646	561	561	506	467	424	423	396
Hostile action	–	–	–	–	735	739	769	847	352	346	456	393	239
Homicide	174	74	67	37	46	54	47	52	47	77	39	41	44
Illness	419	277	174	180	256	280	257	237	244	277	238	246	244
Pending	–	–	–	–	–	1	8	22	6	19	22	17	31
Self-inflicted	231	232	250	153	197	182	213	211	259	302	289	292	336
Terrorist attack	1	1	7	17	–	–	–	–	1	–	–	2	–
Undetermined	11	43	4	16	8	27	27	23	25	27	17	32	17
Deaths per 100,000 of personnel strength	**110.8**	**66.7**	**62.6**	**54.4**	**107.9**	**115.9**	**116.8**	**121.4**	**85.6**	**92.3**	**88.1**	**87.4**	**80.4**
Accident	72.0	39.0	32.4	28.0	35.3	38.8	34.8	34.9	30.1	28.5	25.2	25.6	24.4
Hostile action	–	–	–	–	42.9	44.4	47.7	52.7	20.9	21.1	27.1	23.8	14.7
Homicide	8.1	3.3	4.0	2.4	2.7	3.2	2.9	3.2	2.8	4.7	2.3	2.5	2.7
Illness	19.4	12.3	10.5	11.8	15.0	16.8	15.9	14.7	14.5	16.9	14.1	14.9	15.0
Pending	–	–	–	–	–	0.1	0.5	1.4	0.4	1.2	1.3	1.0	1.9
Self-inflicted	10.7	10.3	15.0	10.0	11.5	10.9	13.2	13.1	15.4	18.4	17.1	17.7	20.7
Terrorist attack	–	–	0.4	1.1	–	–	–	–	0.1	–	–	0.1	–
Undetermined	0.5	1.9	0.2	1.0	0.5	1.6	1.7	1.4	1.5	1.6	1.0	1.9	1.0

– Represents zero.

Source: Defense Manpower Data Center, data prior to 2010, "Defense Casualty Analysis System," <https://www.dmdc.osd.mil/dcas/pages/main.xhtml>; and 2010 to 2012, unpublished data obtained via Freedom of Information Act request.

Table 529. U.S. Military Personnel on Active Duty in Selected Foreign Countries: 1995 to 2014

[As of September 30. Prior to 2012, data from Statistical Information Analysis Division (SIAD). Beginning 2012, data from Defense Manpower Data Center (DMDC)]

Country	1995	2000	2005	2010	2011	2012	2013	2014
Total in foreign countries [1]	**238,064**	**257,817**	**290,997**	**297,286**	**205,118**	**173,929**	**161,194**	**158,650**
Ashore	208,836	212,858	268,214	277,151	186,476	(NA)	(NA)	(NA)
Afloat	29,228	44,959	22,783	20,135	18,642	(NA)	(NA)	(NA)
Australia	314	175	196	130	198	346	170	173
Bahrain	618	949	1,641	1,349	2,142	2,713	2,992	3,372
Belgium	1,689	1,554	1,366	1,252	1,205	1,174	1,157	1,211
Bosnia and Herzegovina	1	5,708	263	8	9	9	2	2
Canada	214	156	150	127	130	147	135	131
Colombia	44	224	52	62	63	73	47	47
Cuba (Guantanamo)	5,129	688	950	913	929	996	836	732
Diego Garcia [2]	897	625	683	238	292	529	517	528
Djibouti	7	2	622	1,379	335	168	5	5
Egypt	1,123	499	410	275	251	280	237	283
Germany	73,280	69,203	66,418	53,951	53,766	47,761	41,007	38,826
Greece	489	678	428	338	382	351	353	386
Greenland	131	125	146	133	142	139	140	142
Honduras	193	351	438	403	354	408	367	360
Italy	12,007	11,190	11,841	9,646	10,801	10,922	10,790	11,317
Japan	39,134	40,159	35,571	34,385	39,222	50,937	50,104	49,503
Korea, South	36,016	36,565	30,983	(NA)	(NA)	(NA)	(NA)	(NA)
Kuwait	771	4,602	([3])	([3])	([3])	(NA)	(NA)	(NA)
Netherlands	687	659	583	442	405	374	348	371
Portugal	1,066	1,005	970	703	723	743	702	647
Qatar	2	52	463	555	621	806	611	600
Saudi Arabia	1,077	7,053	258	239	274	284	299	324
Senegal	13	10	42	9	13	15	7	7
Singapore	166	411	169	132	163	154	171	188
Spain	2,799	2,007	1,660	1,240	1,479	1,727	1,475	2,177
Turkey	3,111	2,006	1,780	1,530	1,491	1,505	1,471	1,524
United Kingdom	12,131	11,207	10,752	9,229	9,382	9,317	9,450	9,231
DEPLOYMENTS								
Operation Enduring Freedom (OEF) [4]	(X)	(X)	19,500	105,900	109,200	78,055	66,732	33,427
Operation Iraqi Freedom (OIF) and Operation New Dawn (OND) [5]	(X)	(X)	192,600	96,200	92,200	1,171	342	494

X Not applicable. NA Not available. [1] Includes items not shown separately. [2] British Indian Ocean Territory. [3] Military personnel data for Kuwait are included with the Operation New Dawn (OND) data. [4] Total (in/around Afghanistan as of September 30) includes Reserve/National Guard. [5] Total (in/around Iraq as of September 30) includes Reserve/National Guard. Prior to 2010, operations in/around Iraq were known as Operation Iraqi Freedom (OIF).

Source: U.S. Department of Defense, DoD Personnel and Procurement Statistics, "Active Duty Military Personnel By Service By Region/Country," November 2014 and earlier reports, <https://www.dmdc.osd.mil/>, accessed February 2015.

Table 530. Suicides and Attempted Suicides of Military Personnel by Selected Characteristics: 2009 to 2013

[Data are shown for suicides reported in Department of Defense Suicide Event Report (DoDSER). Covers all service members in active status at time of event, including Reserve component service members in active status. DoDSER standardizes suicide surveillance efforts across the military services to support the DoD's suicide prevention mission. Confirmed suicides are those that have been confirmed by the Armed Forces Medical Examiner System (AFMES)]

Characteristics	Suicides 2009	2010	2011	2012	2013	Suicide Attempts Reported [1] 2009 [2]	2010	2011	2012	2013
TOTAL										
Suicide attempts reported..................	(X)	(X)	(X)	(X)	(X)	502	863	935	869	1,080
Confirmed suicides..........................	299	281	287	259	245	(X)	(X)	(X)	(X)	(X)
Suicides confirmed and pending confirmation......................	309	295	301	319	259	(X)	(X)	(X)	(X)	(X)
DEMOGRAPHICS										
By Sex:										
Male...	300	281	285	295	244	373	653	687	663	796
Female.......................................	9	14	16	24	15	129	210	248	206	284
By Race/ethnicity:										
White..	247	235	231	244	193	319	587	600	589	799
Black or African American...............	33	36	37	44	33	78	133	172	165	171
Asian or Pacific Islander.................	15	16	17	13	8	14	23	36	28	50
American Indian or Alaskan Native......	10	6	6	4	6	(NA)	11	13	11	17
Other/Unknown............................	4	2	10	14	19	65	109	114	76	43
By Hispanic Origin:										
Hispanic or Latino........................	(NA)	(NA)	18	27	21	21	(NA)	99	102	122
Non-Hispanic or Latino...................	(NA)	(NA)	283	287	231	(NA)	(NA)	836	641	953
By Age:										
Under 25...................................	141	140	114	130	109	298	514	535	506	616
25-29......................................	73	76	91	89	74	119	190	220	201	236
30-39......................................	69	63	68	81	58	69	122	141	121	169
30-34...................................	43	30	32	49	32	(NA)	(NA)	(NA)	74	118
35-39...................................	26	33	36	32	26	(NA)	(NA)	(NA)	47	51
40 and older..............................	26	16	28	19	18	16	37	39	40	55
40-44...................................	15	14	22	11	10	(NA)	(NA)	(NA)	30	36
45 and older...........................	11	2	6	8	8	(NA)	(NA)	(NA)	10	19
Unknown..................................	–	–	–	–	–	–	–	–	–	4
By Education:										
Some high school, did not graduate.....	2	2	5	3	1	7	7	2	5	11
GED (general educational development)..............................	44	26	32	27	18	89	63	44	35	70
High school graduate.....................	208	206	194	214	168	171	398	409	411	803
Some college or technical school........	16	15	16	16	18	142	210	273	238	129
Degree/certificate less than four years...	9	18	18	18	16	19	43	55	33	(NA)
Four-year college degree.................	17	18	22	23	22	18	39	31	35	48
Master's degree or greater..............	10	3	6	9	6	3	16	13	9	14
Unknown...................................	3	7	8	9	10	53	87	108	103	5
By Marital Status:										
Never Married.............................	105	125	107	134	108	215	364	390	385	510
Married.....................................	159	147	167	171	125	220	364	406	364	499
Legally Separated.........................	–	1	–	–	2	15	41	28	21	5
Divorced...................................	37	20	23	14	22	41	73	80	59	62
Widowed...................................	1	–	4	–	–	2	1	1	2	1
Unknown...................................	7	2	–	–	2	9	20	30	38	3
SERVICE DETAILS										
By Rank:										
E1-E4......................................	167	161	148	162	126	373	616	664	575	737
E5-E9......................................	112	118	128	124	110	109	209	240	188	299
Officer.....................................	23	15	25	25	22	12	32	25	24	33
Warrant Officer...........................	4	–	–	6	–	1	4	2	4	6
Cadet/Midshipman........................	(NA)	1	–	2	1	2	1	4	2	2
Unknown or Not Applicable...............	3	–	–	–	–	5	(NA)	–	76	3
By Service Component: [3]										
Regular....................................	284	269	267	296	224	458	817	893	829	1,030
Reserve....................................	8	9	12	22	7	16	24	18	32	18
National Guard............................	17	17	22	(NA)	14	25	20	19	(NA)	32
Other......................................	(NA)	(NA)	(NA)	(NA)	(NA)	3	2	5	8	(NA)
By Selected Location: [4]										
United States..............................	234	232	235	275	221	396	707	830	741	937
Iraq..	31	12	10	(NA)	–	43	26	3	(NA)	–
Afghanistan................................	7	17	18	21	7	8	20	20	8	23
Asia [5]....................................	7	11	4	6	5	17	45	36	33	52
Europe [6].................................	8	2	9	5	7	26	50	36	43	37
Canada or Mexico.........................	2	–	–	(NA)	–	3	3	2	(NA)	3
Other [7]..................................	7	7	5	4	4	7	9	4	16	23
Unknown...................................	1	–	6	7	1	2	3	4	28	5

– Represents zero. X Not applicable. NA Not available. [1] Data are for DoDSERS submitted for suicides, which may include more than one report per individual. [2] 2009 attempt data is for Army only. [3] Suicide data for 2009-2012 are based on confirmed and pending suicides. Data for 2013 are for confirmed suicides only. [4] Suicide data for 2009-2011 and 2013 are based on confirmed suicides only. Data for 2012 include pending suicides. [5] May include Korea and/or Japan. [6] May include Germany, United Kingdom, and/or other Europe. [7] May include Central or South America, Kuwait, shipboard or at sea, and/or other.

Source: U.S. Department of Defense, National Center for Telehealth and Technology, *Department of Defense Suicide Event Report, Calendar Year 2013 Annual Report*, July 2014, and earlier reports. See also <http://t2health.dcoe.mil/programs/dodser>.

Table 531. Sexual Assault in the Military—Incident Reports and Victims by Type of Report and Selected Characteristics: 2010 to 2014

[Reports of sexual assault (rape, aggravated sexual assault, sexual assault, aggravated sexual contact, abusive sexual contact, wrongful sexual contact, non-consensual sodomy, and attempts to commit these offenses) by or against Service Members. Restricted Reporting allows victim confidential access to medical care and advocacy services. When a victim makes an Unrestricted Report, the report is also referred to a Military Criminal Investigation Organization for investigation and command is notified]

Item	Unrestricted					Restricted [1]				
	2010	2011	2012	2013	2014	2010	2011	2012	2013	2014
REPORTS [2]										
Total	**2,410**	**2,439**	**2,558**	**3,768**	**4,611**	**882**	**877**	**981**	**1,501**	**1,471**
Service member on Service member	1,358	1,366	1,590	2,310	2,502	352	342	555	560	577
Service member on Non-Service member	691	648	573	806	712	(NA)	(NA)	37	46	33
Non-Service member on Service member	104	139	124	207	206	115	195	195	368	397
Unidentified subject on Service member	257	286	271	445	555	415	340	194	527	226
Unknown	–	–	–	–	636	–	–	–	–	238
VICTIMS IN COMPLETED INVESTIGATIONS [3]										
Total	**1,741**	**1,783**	**2,940**	**3,652**	**4,241**	(X)	(X)	(X)	(X)	(X)
Service member victims	1,303	1,349	2,256	2,886	3,357	(X)	(X)	(X)	(X)	(X)
Non-Service member victims	438	434	684	766	884	(X)	(X)	(X)	(X)	(X)
VICTIMS [4]										
By Sex:										
Male	180	212	345	520	735	114	122	133	227	243
Female	1,561	1,571	2,595	3,132	3,310	739	732	826	1,186	1,224
Unknown	–	–	–	–	196	29	23	22	88	4
By Age:										
0-15 years old	(NA)	(NA)	(NA)	(NA)	19	(NA)	(NA)	(NA)	(NA)	192
16-19 years old	324	312	516	686	851	191	173	202	315	339
20-24 years old	864	916	1,505	1,685	1,820	392	406	434	524	577
25-34 years old	402	404	729	809	770	188	186	214	234	251
35-49 years old	96	102	131	181	195	49	44	48	56	59
50-64 years old	8	13	13	12	18	–	–	3	3	1
65 years and older	–	–	1	–	1	–	–	–	–	–
Unknown	47	36	45	279	567	62	68	80	369	52
SERVICE MEMBER VICTIMS										
By Service Branch:										
Army	681	759	1,122	1,201	1,402	327	342	214	356	400
Navy	302	218	593	813	914	169	176	250	288	287
Marines	134	136	239	436	428	51	52	102	308	354
Air Force	183	236	297	431	611	287	290	359	433	391
Coast Guard	3	–	5	5	1	4	3	1	2	1
Unknown	–	–	–	–	1	44	14	24	68	–
By Service Component:										
Active Duty	1,206	1,202	2,028	2,624	3,155	733	759	829	1,255	1,340
Reserve (activated)	41	60	109	120	138	24	16	25	49	57
National Guard (Activated Title 10)	44	69	78	125	37	49	33	21	31	15
Cadet/Midshipmen	12	18	40	17	24	23	42	48	31	20
Academy Prep School Student	(NA)	(NA)	(NA)	(NA)	3	(NA)	(NA)	(NA)	(NA)	1
Unknown	–	–	1	–	–	47	27	27	88	–

– Represents zero. X Not applicable. NA Not available. [1] For 2010 and 2011 service member victims only. Beginning in 2012, data shown for all victims. [2] Reports of sexual assault during the fiscal year. [3] Victims in investigations completed during the fiscal year. [4] For unrestricted reports, data shown for victims in investigations completed during the fiscal year.

Source: U.S. Department of Defense, *Annual Report on Sexual Assault in the Military, Fiscal Year 2014*, April 2015, and earlier reports. See also <http://www.sapr.mil/index.php/annual-reports>.

Table 532. U.S. Military Sales and Assistance to Foreign Governments: 1995 to 2013

[In millions of dollars (7,989 represents $7,989,000,000). For year ending September 30. Department of Defense (DoD) sales deliveries cover deliveries against sales orders authorized under Arms Export Control Act, as well as earlier and applicable legislation. For details regarding individual programs, see source]

Item	1995	2000	2005	2008	2009	2010	2011	2012	2013
Military sales agreements...............	7,989	10,568	9,847	27,556	29,121	21,404	26,080	62,827	23,606
Military construction sales agreements........................	24	284	301	145	918	894	402	908	347
Military sales deliveries [1]..............	12,912	10,976	11,338	11,991	16,474	13,535	13,909	14,477	17,021
Military construction sales deliveries...	218	183	349	267	204	459	511	488	497
Military financing program.............	3,155	4,333	4,956	4,506	4,580	5,016	5,320	5,929	4,874
Commercial exports licensed under Arms Export Control Act [2]............	3,166	478	30,146	33,510	–	–	–	–	–
Military assistance program delivery [3]............................	24	17	65	7	–	–	13	2	36
IMET program/deliveries [4].............	26	50	86	83	90	108	106	105	99

– Represents zero. [1] Includes military construction sales deliveries. [2] The total dollar value of deliveries made for purchases of munitions-controlled items by foreign governments directly from U.S. manufacturers. [3] Includes Military Assistance Service Funded (MASF) program data and Section 506(a) drawdown authority. [4] International Military Education and Training. Includes military assistance services and emergency drawdowns.

Source: U.S. Department of Defense, Defense Security Cooperation Agency, DSCA Data & Statistics, *DSCA Fiscal Year Series, as of September 30, 2013*. See also <http://dsca.mil/publications>.

Table 533. U.S. Military Sales Deliveries by Selected Country: 2000 to 2013

[In millions of dollars (10,976 represents $10,976,000,000). For year ending September 30. Represents Department of Defense military sales]

Country	2000	2005	2007	2008	2009	2010	2011	2012	2013
Total [1]..................	**10,976**	**11,338**	**12,607**	**11,991**	**16,474**	**13,535**	**13,909**	**14,477**	**17,021**
International Organizations...............	61	62	49	41	4,022	86	147	116	166
Afghanistan....................	–	340	62	22	11	18	17	4	8
Argentina......................	10	4	8	23	10	26	12	14	14
Australia.......................	332	350	751	890	374	914	732	639	637
Bahrain........................	55	63	84	42	101	111	51	98	70
Belgium........................	61	49	49	44	39	26	27	61	46
Brazil..........................	61	11	62	53	46	32	37	133	55
Canada........................	84	150	239	468	518	382	400	288	311
Colombia.......................	14	41	199	125	112	431	149	122	147
Denmark.......................	43	40	62	57	43	43	67	45	94
Ecuador........................	1	4	7	3	1	3	1	1	2
Egypt..........................	1,186	1,454	1,226	886	924	957	942	846	1,583
El Salvador.....................	14	3	2	6	10	6	5	6	4
Finland........................	690	38	28	86	82	127	94	82	106
France.........................	217	69	45	57	58	112	132	125	186
Georgia........................	3	12	25	72	18	10	28	18	36
Germany.......................	136	207	206	173	162	296	160	142	151
Greece........................	389	466	201	197	1,251	278	149	163	62
India..........................	–	100	85	40	15	31	57	167	194
Iraq...........................	–	–	175	685	721	423	767	619	528
Israel..........................	585	1,623	1,357	1,447	780	938	791	926	945
Italy...........................	52	127	153	76	92	179	101	87	70
Japan.........................	433	410	638	609	857	779	437	498	357
Jordan.........................	52	140	204	306	182	173	212	377	339
Kenya.........................	2	7	2	1	6	2	16	29	3
Korea, South....................	1,399	581	728	791	477	594	719	724	611
Kuwait.........................	321	291	455	245	252	242	434	262	313
Malaysia.......................	411	49	19	17	23	45	30	40	42
Mexico.........................	9	4	6	4	4	59	38	8	20
Morocco........................	8	17	8	4	10	28	1,042	503	213
Netherlands.....................	278	178	238	254	249	202	184	177	764
Nigeria.........................	–	7	4	–	3	5	13	8	14
Norway.........................	64	106	163	88	281	127	147	95	170
Pakistan........................	–	61	196	265	117	1,129	549	382	306
Poland.........................	13	84	1,483	705	133	75	190	162	157
Portugal........................	20	84	39	45	94	29	36	47	17
Saudi Arabia....................	1,988	872	1,045	911	1,748	1,679	1,520	1,657	3,661
Singapore......................	131	229	173	177	188	297	251	244	211
Spain..........................	141	126	143	169	176	156	99	67	100
Taiwan.........................	784	1,399	790	688	640	863	768	975	811
Thailand........................	114	92	46	40	47	42	91	62	82
Turkey.........................	216	185	182	306	306	251	876	1,243	761
United Arab Emirates.............	3	149	62	83	119	584	639	1,357	771
United Kingdom.................	347	381	423	297	755	269	346	311	1,296
Venezuela......................	13	8	1	1	–	–	–	–	–

– Represents or rounds to zero. [1] Includes countries not shown.

Source: U.S. Department of Defense, Defense Security Cooperation Agency, DSCA Data & Statistics, *DSCA Fiscal Year Series, as of September 30, 2013*. See also <http://dsca.mil/resources/publications>.

Table 534. Arms Transfer Agreements with Developing Nations by Supplier: 2004 to 2011

[In millions of current U.S. dollars (26,983 is 26,983,000,000). Developing nations category excludes the United States, Europe, Canada, Japan, Australia, and New Zealand. All data are for the calendar year given except for U.S. MAP (Military Assistance Program), IMET (International Military Education and Training), and Excess Defense Article data, which are included for the particular fiscal year. All amounts given include the values of all categories of weapons, spare parts, construction, all associated services, military assistance, excess defense articles, and training programs. Statistics for foreign countries are based upon estimated selling prices. All foreign data are rounded to the nearest $100 million]

Supplier	2004	2005	2006	2007	2008	2009	2010	2011	2004-2011
Total..........................	26,983	30,193	39,035	41,218	52,923	50,582	32,279	71,503	344,716
United States................	6,783	5,493	8,435	11,518	28,023	14,582	14,079	56,303	145,216
Russia..........................	8,500	8,000	15,300	9,600	6,400	13,000	7,600	4,100	72,500
France..........................	1,100	5,400	500	1,400	3,600	9,200	1,800	2,700	25,700
United Kingdom.............	4,100	2,800	4,000	9,500	200	1,100	1,200	300	23,200
China...........................	1,000	2,700	2,000	2,500	2,100	2,300	1,600	2,100	16,300
Germany.......................	200	700	2,400	1,700	4,700	500	0	0	10,200
Italy.............................	300	500	600	1,000	1,600	1,300	1,800	1,100	8,200
All other European..........	2,400	3,600	2,700	2,100	4,400	4,700	2,700	2,400	25,000
All others......................	2,600	1,000	3,100	1,900	1,900	3,900	1,500	2,500	18,400

Source: Congressional Research Service, *Conventional Arms Transfers to Developing Nations, 2004-2011*, R42017, August 2012.

Table 535. Veterans by Selected Period of Service and State: 2014

[In thousands (21,999 represents 21,999,000). As of September 30. The Veteran Population Projection Model 2014 (VetPop2014) is the Department of Veterans Affairs (VA) latest official estimate and projection of the veteran population. It is based on tabulations prepared for the VA Office of the Actuary; recent American Community Survey, Internal Revenue Service, and Social Security Administration data; administrative data and projections of service member separations from active duty provided by the Department of Defense, Defense Manpower Data Center and the Office of the Actuary; and VA data on veterans benefits]

State/Area	Total [1,2]	Gulf War era [3]	Vietnam era [4]	State/Area	Total [1,2]	Gulf War era [3]	Vietnam era [4]
United States............	21,999	7,033	7,247	Montana.......................	100	31	35
Alabama.....................	414	156	134	Nebraska......................	143	50	47
Alaska........................	73	36	21	Nevada........................	228	71	80
Arizona.......................	532	160	186	New Hampshire..............	114	31	38
Arkansas.....................	249	85	83	New Jersey...................	428	101	143
California....................	1,851	552	624	New Mexico..................	172	53	62
Colorado.....................	413	152	141	New York......................	892	223	278
Connecticut.................	213	51	70	North Carolina...............	775	291	249
Delaware.....................	30	10	8	North Dakota.................	57	22	18
District of Columbia.......	78	24	25	Ohio............................	866	238	294
Florida........................	1,584	460	515	Oklahoma.....................	338	117	114
Georgia.......................	753	295	235	Oregon........................	332	86	124
Hawaii........................	121	51	38	Pennsylvania.................	939	236	309
Idaho..........................	132	44	48	Rhode Island.................	72	20	22
Illinois........................	722	207	242	South Carolina...............	418	148	142
Indiana.......................	476	140	149	South Dakota................	72	25	22
Iowa...........................	232	66	78	Tennessee....................	506	167	168
Kansas.......................	221	77	74	Texas..........................	1,680	655	542
Kentucky.....................	331	110	111	Utah...........................	152	57	46
Louisiana....................	330	125	106	Vermont.......................	49	13	16
Maine.........................	127	35	45	Virginia........................	781	382	223
Maryland.....................	438	167	127	Washington...................	604	208	208
Massachusetts.............	380	86	126	West Virginia.................	167	48	60
Michigan.....................	658	156	238	Wisconsin.....................	414	111	140
Minnesota...................	369	98	130	Wyoming......................	50	19	17
Mississippi..................	220	84	68	Puerto Rico...................	93	21	30
Missouri......................	494	147	167	Island Areas & Foreign...	114	35	33

[1] Veterans serving in more than one period of service are counted only once in the total. [2] Current civilians discharged from active duty, other than for training only without service-connected disability. [3] Service from August 2, 1990 to the present. [4] Service from August 5, 1964 to May 7, 1975.

Source: U.S. Department of Veterans Affairs, National Center for Veterans Analysis and Statistics, "The Veteran Population Projection Model 2014 (VetPop2014)," <http://www.va.gov/vetdata/veteran_population.asp>, accessed January 2015.

Table 536. Veterans Benefits—Expenditures by Program and Compensation for Service-Connected Disabilities: 1995 to 2014

[In millions of dollars (37,775 represents $37,775,000,000). For years ending September 30]

Program	1995	2000	2005	2010	2011	2012	2013	2014
Total expenditures.................................	37,775	47,086	69,667	108,635	122,859	120,405	142,822	161,229
Medical programs.................................	16,255	19,637	29,433	42,372	43,085	45,521	55,994	59,424
Construction..	641	466	483	1,618	1,813	1,538	1,330	1,536
General operating expenses...........................	954	1,016	1,294	6,101	6,655	6,445	6,890	7,602
Compensation and pension.......................	17,765	22,012	34,694	47,785	57,596	53,243	63,575	75,265
Vocational rehabilitation and education...............	1,317	1,610	2,937	8,260	10,630	10,425	11,949	13,681
All other [1]...	844	2,345	826	2,499	3,079	3,233	3,085	3,721
Compensation for service-connected disabilities..................................	11,644	15,511	24,515	36,486	39,374	44,359	49,150	(NA)

NA Not available. [1] Includes insurance, indemnities, and miscellaneous funds and expenditures and offsets from public receipts. (Excludes expenditures from personal funds of patients.)

Source: U.S. Department of Veterans Affairs, "Summary of Expenditures By State," <http://www.va.gov/vetdata/Expenditures.asp>, accessed July 2015; and *Annual Benefits Report*, September 2014, and earlier reports. See also <http://www.benefits.va.gov/reports/annual_performance_reports.asp>.

Table 537. Veterans Living by Period of Service, Age, and Sex: 2014

[(21,999 represents 21,999,107). As of September 30. Includes those veterans living outside the United States. Based on an actuarial projection model]

Period of service and age	Total	Male	Female	Period of service and age	Total	Male	Female
Total	**21,999**	**19,979**	**2,020**	30 to 34 years old	1,058	858	200
PERIOD OF SERVICE				35 to 39 years old	1,095	894	201
Wartime vets [1]	16,503	15,010	1,493	40 to 44 years old	1,313	1,110	203
Gulf War Era [2]	7,033	5,881	1,153	45 to 49 years old	1,588	1,367	220
Vietnam Era [3]	7,247	6,987	260	50 to 54 years old	1,878	1,615	263
Korean conflict [4]	1,886	1,831	55	55 to 59 years old	1,989	1,752	238
World War II	1,017	962	55	60 to 64 years old	2,085	1,915	170
Peacetime	5,496	4,969	527	65 to 69 years old	3,196	3,089	106
AGE				70 to 74 years old	2,127	2,062	65
Under 20 years old	6	4	2	75 to 79 years old	1,648	1,602	46
20 to 24 years old	284	227	56	80 to 84 years old	1,486	1,445	41
25 to 29 years old	754	619	135	85 years & over	1,493	1,419	74

[1] Veterans who served in more than one wartime period are counted only once in the total. [2] Service from August 2, 1990 to the present. [3] Service from August 5, 1964 to May 7, 1975. [4] Service during period June 27, 1950 to January 31, 1955.

Source: U.S. Department of Veterans Affairs, National Center for Veterans Analysis and Statistics, "Veteran Population 2014," <http://www1.va.gov/vetdata/Veteran_Population.asp>, accessed September 2015.

Table 538. Veteran Income, Education, Poverty, and Disability Status Compared to Nonveteran Population: 2012 and 2013

[239,179 represents 239,179,000. Data are based on American Community Survey (ACS). The ACS universe includes the civilian household and group quarters population. Based on a sample and subject to sampling variability]

Characteristic	2012			2013		
	Total	Veterans	Non-veterans	Total	Veterans	Non-veterans
Population 18 years old and over (1,000)	**239,179**	**21,231**	**217,948**	**241,557**	**19,589**	**221,968**
INCOME						
Median income in past 12 months (dollars) [1]	26,278	36,264	25,337	26,638	36,381	25,820
By sex:						
Male	(X)	36,672	31,586	(X)	36,740	31,898
Female	(X)	30,929	21,071	(X)	31,365	21,383
EDUCATIONAL ATTAINMENT						
Population 25 years old and over	208,103	20,907	187,197	210,305	19,305	191,000
Less than high school graduate (percent)	13.7	7.1	14.4	13.4	7.3	14.1
High school graduate (includes equivalency) (percent)	28.1	29.2	27.9	27.9	29.1	27.7
Some college or associate's degree (percent)	29.2	36.9	28.3	29.1	36.8	28.3
Bachelor's degree or higher (percent)	29.1	26.7	29.3	29.6	26.8	29.9
POVERTY AND DISABILITY STATUS						
Population for whom poverty status is determined	232,774	20,850	211,924	235,135	19,257	215,878
Below poverty in the past 12 months (percent)	13.9	7.2	14.6	13.9	7.3	14.5
With any disability (percent)	14.8	26.6	13.7	15.3	28.5	14.1

X Not applicable. [1] For population with income.

Source U.S. Census Bureau, American Community Survey, S2101, "Veteran Status," <http://factfinder2.census.gov>, accessed July 2015.

Table 539. Veterans by Sex, Race, and Hispanic Origin: 2012 and 2013

[Data are based on the American Community Survey (ACS). The survey universe includes the household population and the population living in institutions, college dormitories, and other group quarters. Based on a sample and subject to sampling variability]

Characteristic	2012			2013		
	Total number	18 to 64 years	65 years and over	Total number	18 to 64 years	65 years and over
Total	**21,230,865**	**11,659,939**	**9,570,926**	**19,588,586**	**10,320,312**	**9,268,274**
Male	19,617,634	10,304,926	9,312,708	18,036,876	9,043,733	8,993,143
Female	1,613,231	1,355,013	258,218	1,551,710	1,276,579	275,131
White alone	17,775,714	9,090,235	8,685,479	16,371,593	8,003,189	8,368,404
Male	16,614,826	8,157,312	8,457,514	15,258,821	7,132,122	8,126,699
Female	1,160,888	932,923	227,965	1,112,772	871,067	241,705
Black or African American alone	2,404,522	1,807,787	596,735	2,204,812	1,601,582	603,230
Male	2,076,418	1,499,174	577,244	1,893,420	1,311,712	581,708
Female	328,104	308,613	19,491	311,392	289,870	21,522
American Indian/Alaska Native alone	161,686	113,622	48,064	140,716	94,040	46,676
Male	144,100	97,789	46,311	123,932	79,295	44,637
Female	17,586	15,833	1,753	16,784	14,745	2,039
Asian alone	270,630	172,359	98,271	276,867	167,910	108,957
Male	243,178	148,357	94,821	248,535	142,768	105,767
Female	27,452	24,002	3,450	28,332	25,142	3,190
Native Hawaiian and Other Pacific Islander alone	32,303	24,880	7,423	30,021	23,510	6,511
Male	28,518	21,444	7,074	25,467	19,545	5,922
Female	3,785	3,436	349	4,554	3,965	589
Two or more races	351,534	263,839	87,695	333,174	248,227	84,947
Male	302,241	218,459	83,782	282,402	201,775	80,627
Female	49,293	45,380	3,913	50,772	46,452	4,320
Hispanic or Latino origin [1]	1,209,717	894,635	315,082	1,172,074	842,902	329,172
Male	1,083,340	777,784	305,556	1,045,339	726,441	318,898
Female	126,377	116,851	9,526	126,735	116,461	10,274

[1] Persons of Hispanic or Latino origin may be of any race.

Source: U.S. Census Bureau, 2013 American Community Survey, Tables B21001, B21001A, B21001B, B21001C, B21001D, B21001E, B21001F, B21001G, and B21001I, <http://factfinder2.census.gov>, accessed November 2014.

Table 540. Veterans Compensation and Pension Benefits—Number on Rolls by Period of Service and Status: 1990 to 2013

[In thousands (3,584 represents 3,584,000). As of September 30. Living veterans refers to veterans receiving compensation for disability incurred or aggravated while on active duty, and war veterans receiving pension benefits for non-service connected disabilities and/or who are age 65 and older. Survivors include veterans' spouses, dependent children, and (based on need) dependent parents of veterans]

Period of service and veteran status	1990	1995	2000	2005	2009	2010	2011	2012	2013
Total	3,584	3,330	3,236	3,503	3,919	4,070	4,226	4,425	4,639
Living veterans	2,746	2,669	2,672	2,973	3,384	3,524	3,668	3,852	4,051
Compensation [1]	2,184	2,236	2,308	2,637	3,070	3,210	3,355	3,537	3,743
Pension [2]	562	433	364	336	314	314	314	315	308
Survivors of veterans	838	662	564	530	535	546	557	574	587
Compensation [1]	320	307	307	323	341	347	355	366	377
Pension [2]	518	355	257	207	194	199	202	207	210
World War I and earlier	198	89	34	13	7	6	5	5	4
Living veterans	18	3	(Z)	(Z)	(Z)	(Z)	(Z)	(Z)	(Z)
World War II	1,723	1,307	968	718	559	529	498	469	434
Living veterans	1,294	961	676	466	329	298	271	245	215
Korean conflict [3]	390	368	323	295	276	275	275	274	271
Living veterans	305	290	255	231	213	209	207	204	199
Vietnam era [4]	774	868	969	1,218	1,393	1,447	1,524	1,594	1,660
Living veterans	685	766	848	1,068	1,214	1,261	1,326	1,381	1,433
Gulf War era [5]	(X)	138	334	630	1,028	1,140	1,239	1,383	1,561
Living veterans	(X)	134	326	617	1,007	1,117	1,215	1,357	1,523
Peacetime	495	559	607	627	655	673	685	701	709
Living veterans	444	514	567	591	621	638	650	665	683

X Not applicable. Z Fewer than 500. [1] Compensation is based on military service-connected disability and death. [2] Pension is based on need and includes coverage for veterans with disabilities not connected to military service. [3] Service during period June 27, 1950 to January 31, 1955. [4] Service from August 5, 1964 to May 7, 1975. [5] Service from August 2, 1990 to the present.

Source: U.S. Department of Veterans Affairs, 1990 to 1995, *Annual Report of the Secretary of Veterans Affairs*; 1996 to 2010, *Annual Accountability Report* and unpublished data; and beginning 2011, *Annual Benefits Report*, September 2014 and earlier reports. See also <http://www.vba.va.gov/REPORTS/abr/index.asp>.

Table 541. Federal Funding Obligations for Selected Homeless Veterans Programs: 1988 to 2014

[In thousands of dollars (12,932 represents $12,932,000). For fiscal year ending September 30]

Year	Department of Veterans Affairs						Department of Labor
	Health care for homeless veterans [1]	Domiciliary care for homeless veterans	Compensated work therapy/ therapeutic residence	Grant and per diem program	HUD-VA Supported Housing (Supportive Services) [2]	Supportive Services for Veteran Families	Homeless Veterans Reintegration Program
1988	12,932	15,000	(NA)	(NA)	(NA)	(NA)	1,915
1989	13,252	10,367	(NA)	(NA)	(NA)	(NA)	1,877
1990	15,000	15,000	(NA)	(NA)	(NA)	(NA)	1,920
1991	[3] 15,461	15,750	([3])	(NA)	(NA)	(NA)	2,018
1992	[3] 16,500	16,500	([3])	(NA)	2300	(NA)	1,366
1993	22,150	22,300	400	(NA)	2000	(NA)	5,055
1994	24,513	27,140	3,051	8,000	3,235	(NA)	5,055
1995	[4] 38,585	38,948	3,387	([4])	4270	(NA)	[5] 107
1996	[4] 38,433	41,117	3,886	([4])	4829	(NA)	–
1997	[4] 38,063	37,214	3,628	([4])	4958	(NA)	–
1998	36,407	38,489	8,612	5,886	5,084	(NA)	3,000
1999	32,421	39,955	4,092	20,000	5,223	(NA)	3,000
2000	38,381	34,434	8,068	19,640	5,137	(NA)	9,636
2001	58,602	34,576	8,144	31,100	5,219	(NA)	17,500
2002	54,135	45,443	8,028	22,431	4,729	(NA)	18,250
2003	45,188	49,213	8,371	43,388	4,603	(NA)	18,131
2004	42,905	51,829	10,240	62,965	3,375	(NA)	18,888
2005	40,357	57,555	10,004	62,180	3,243	(NA)	20,832
2006	56,998	63,592	19,529	63,621	5,297	(NA)	21,780
2007	71,925	77,633	21,514	81,187	7,487	(NA)	21,809
2008	77,656	96,098	21,497	114,696	4,854	(NA)	23,620
2009	80,219	115,373	22,206	128,073	26,601	218	26,330
2010	109,727	175,979	61,205	175,057	71,137	3,881	36,330
2011	200,808	221,938	73,420	148,097	119,603	60,541	[6] 36,257
2012	118,889	218,962	73,067	208,046	169,873	99,974	[6] 38,185
2013	128,500	245,228	71,687	200,329	288,107	299,921	[7] 36,188
2014 [8]	137,013	183,362	60,565	214,990	326,851	300,000	38,109

– Represents zero. NA Not available. [1] Through 1991 the program was called the Homeless Chronically Ill Veterans program. [2] Covers funding allocated for supportive services, but not the cost of providing housing. [3] For 1991 and 1992, funds from Homeless Chronically Mentally Ill Veterans program and substance abuse treatment funds were used for the program. [4] For 1995 through 1997, funds were obligated with funds for the Health Care for Veterans program. Department of Veterans Affairs budget documents do not provide a separate breakdown for grant and per diem obligations. [5] Congress appropriated $5.011 million for the program in 1995. A subsequent rescission reduced the amount. [6] Reflects rescissions of 0.2% in FY2011 and 0.189% in FY2012 on all discretionary accounts. [7] Reflects deductions for sequestration and an across-the-board rescission of 2%. [8] FY2014 data are estimates.

Source: Congressional Research Service, *Veterans and Homelessness*, RL34024, November 2014.

Table 542. Homeland Security Funding by Agency: Fiscal Years 2010 to 2015

[In millions of dollars (70,009 represents 70,009,000,000). A total of 28 agencies comprise federal homeland security funding. Department of Homeland Security (DHS) is the designated department to coordinate and centralize the leadership of many homeland security activities under a single department. In addition to DHS, the Departments of Defense (DoD), Justice (DoJ), Health and Human Services (HHS), State Department and Energy (DOE) account for 95% of the total government-wide homeland security funding]

Agency	2010	2011	2012	2013	2014 [1]	2015 [1]
Total budget authority [2, 3]	70,009	66,983	68,586	66,037	66,244	70,871
Department of Agriculture	614	580	435	431	509	529
Department of Commerce	284	262	338	613	2,104	5,739
Department of Defense	19,054	16,994	17,780	16,527	11,908	11,965
Department of Education	29	30	31	31	37	36
Department of Energy	2,016	1,994	1,938	1,991	1,910	1,946
Department of Health and Human Services	7,196	4,182	4,118	4,016	4,784	4,825
Department of Homeland Security [4]	32,609	34,901	35,088	33,715	35,763	35,955
Department of Housing and Urban Development	5	3	2	2	3	–
Department of the Interior	52	58	58	57	55	57
Department of Justice	4,094	3,966	4,039	3,685	4,018	4,086
Department of Labor	40	43	46	37	36	32
Department of State	1,793	1,949	2,674	2,929	3,029	3,425
Department of Transportation	228	243	245	249	207	209
Department of the Treasury	125	126	122	119	112	119
Department of Veterans Affairs	427	413	381	368	312	361
Corps of Engineers	36	36	15	16	8	9
Environmental Protection Agency	154	108	102	96	94	90
Executive Office of the President	12	9	10	9	8	9
General Services Administration	214	19	38	36	225	369
National Aeronautics and Space Administration	218	228	225	209	226	223
National Science Foundation	390	386	444	434	443	439
Office of Personnel Management	2	2	1	1	(NA)	(NA)
Social Security Administration	190	213	212	231	207	240
District of Columbia	15	15	15	23	24	13
Federal Communications Commission	1	3	3	1	1	2
Intelligence Community Management Account [5]	14	13	9	(X)	(X)	(X)
National Archives and Records Administration	20	22	23	23	27	24
Nuclear Regulatory Commission	65	73	79	74	76	62
Securities and Exchange Commission	6	6	8	8	8	7
Smithsonian Institution	99	98	97	97	101	102
United States Holocaust Memorial Museum	10	10	11	11	11	11

X Not applicable. NA Not available. – Represents or rounds to zero. [1] In addition, Homeland Security Budget Authority includes $409.0 million in FY2014 supplemental emergency funding, and $257.9 million in FY2015 supplemental funding. [2] The federal spending estimates are for the Executive branch's homeland security activities. These estimates do not include the activities of the Legislative or Judicial branches. [3] The Department of Homeland Security Appropriations Act, 2004, provided $5.6 billion for Project BioShield, to remain available through 2013. Including this uneven funding stream can distort year-over-year comparisons. [4] Not all activities carried out by DHS constitute homeland security funding (e.g. response to natural disasters and Coast Guard search and rescue activities). DHS estimates in this table do not represent the entire DHS budget. See Table 543. [5] Funding for Intelligence Community Management Account was moved under DoD beginning in 2013.

Source: U.S. Office of Management and Budget, *Budget of the U.S. Government, Fiscal Year 2016: Analytical Perspectives*, February 2015, and earlier reports. See also <http://www.whitehouse.gov/omb/budget/>.

Table 543. Department of Homeland Security Total Budget Authority and Personnel by Organization: 2014 and 2015

[In thousands of dollars (60,417,017 represents $60,417,017,000). For the fiscal year ending September 30. Not all activities carried out by the Department of Homeland Security (DHS) constitute homeland security funding (e.g., Coast Guard search and rescue activities)]

Organization or Activity	Budget authority		Full-time employees	
	2014 [1]	2015	2014 [1]	2015
Total	60,417,017	61,125,061	217,617	225,951
Departmental management and operations [2]	728,269	748,024	1,971	1,939
Analysis and operations	300,490	302,268	845	850
Office of the Inspector General	139,437	145,457	681	725
U.S. Customs & Border Protection	12,463,893	12,764,835	60,896	61,707
U.S. Immigration & Customs Enforcement	5,948,161	5,359,065	19,332	19,374
Transportation Security Administration	7,420,517	7,305,098	52,285	52,555
U.S. Coast Guard	10,098,753	9,810,468	48,575	49,547
U.S. Secret Service	1,845,272	1,895,905	6,572	6,572
National Protection and Programs Directorate	2,810,413	2,857,666	1,885	2,092
Office of Health Affairs	126,763	125,767	99	99
Federal Emergency Management Agency (FEMA)	10,869,247	12,179,177	9,559	12,140
FEMA Grants [3]	2,530,000	2,225,469	([4])	([4])
U.S. Citizenship & Immigration Services	3,368,805	3,770,026	13,801	15,311
Federal Law Enforcement Training Center	258,730	259,595	1,058	1,075
Science & Technology Directorate (S&T)	1,220,212	1,071,818	457	467
Domestic Nuclear Detection Office	288,055	304,423	121	127

[1] Revised enacted. [2] Comprised of the Office of the Secretary & Executive Management, the Under Secretary for Management, the Office of the Chief Financial Officer, the Office of the Chief Information Officer, and DHS Headquarters Consolidation. [3] Includes State and Local Programs and Emergency Management Performance Grants, and Assistance to Firefighters Grants. [4] Employee data are included among FEMA full-time employees.

Source: U.S. Department of Homeland Security, *Budget-in-Brief, Fiscal Year 2016*, 2015. See also <http://www.dhs.gov/dhs-budget>.

Table 544. Homeland Security Grants by State and Outlying Area: 2014 and 2015

[In thousands of dollars (1,043,346 represents $1,043,346,000). For years ending September 30. The Homeland Security Grant Program consists of the following: State Homeland Security Program (SHSP), Urban Areas Security Initiative (UASI), and Operation Stonegarden]

State/territory	2014	2015	State/territory	2014	2015	State/territory	2014	2015
Total.........	1,043,346	1,044,000	KY.............	3,978	3,978	OK.............	3,733	3,735
U.S............	1,036,837	1,035,712	LA.............	7,247	4,220	OR.............	4,837	6,837
AL.............	3,833	3,885	ME.............	4,248	4,595	PA.............	31,600	31,670
AK.............	3,733	3,735	MD.............	11,625	11,654	RI.............	3,733	3,735
AZ.............	22,484	21,768	MA.............	23,622	23,645	SC.............	3,733	3,735
AR.............	3,733	3,735	MI.............	12,559	12,918	SD.............	3,733	3,735
CA.............	188,644	192,753	MN.............	9,866	9,995	TN.............	3,978	3,978
CO.............	6,979	6,979	MS.............	3,783	3,805	TX.............	85,072	80,998
CT.............	3,978	3,978	MO.............	7,978	6,978	UT.............	4,733	3,735
DE.............	3,733	3,735	MT.............	4,350	4,670	VT.............	3,933	4,036
DC.............	57,119	58,142	NE.............	3,733	3,735	VA.............	8,414	7,446
FL.............	21,382	20,691	NV.............	4,733	6,735	WA.............	12,903	13,513
GA.............	12,307	12,307	NH.............	3,832	3,865	WV.............	3,733	3,735
HI.............	4,733	6,735	NJ.............	30,154	29,154	WI.............	3,978	3,978
ID.............	3,763	3,766	NM.............	6,380	6,735	WY.............	3,733	3,735
IL.............	85,857	85,909	NY.............	256,952	259,577	AS [1].........	854	854
IN.............	4,978	3,978	NC.............	9,489	8,489	GU [1].........	854	854
IA.............	3,733	3,735	ND.............	4,166	4,356	NM [1]........	854	854
KS.............	3,733	3,735	OH.............	11,121	8,453	PR [1].........	4,543	4,742
						VI [1]..........	854	984

[1] AS—American Samoa, GU—Guam, NM—Northern Mariana Islands, PR—Puerto Rico, VI—Virgin Islands.

Source: U.S. Department of Homeland Security, *FY2015 Homeland Security Grant Program Fact Sheet*, July 2015, and earlier reports. See also <http://www.fema.gov/preparedness-non-disaster-grants>.

Table 545. Urban Areas Security Initiative (UASI) Grant Program: 2015

[In thousands of dollars (587,000 represents $587,000,000). For year ending September 30. The UASI Program provides financial assistance to address the unique multi-disciplinary planning, operations, equipment, training, and exercise needs of high-threat, high-density urban areas. A total of 39 high-threat, high-density urban areas were eligible for funding under the FY2014 UASI program. For a listing of all grant programs and their descriptions, see <http://www.fema.gov/preparedness-non-disaster-grants>]

State	Urban area	Amount	State	Urban area	Amount
Total..........	(X)	587,000	MD.............	Baltimore	5,500
AZ.............	Phoenix	5,500	MA.............	Boston	18,000
CA.............	Anaheim/Santa Ana	5,500	MI.............	Detroit	5,500
CA.............	San Francisco/ Bay	28,400	MN.............	Minneapolis-Saint Paul (Twin Cities)	5,500
CA.............	Los Angeles/Long Beach	69,500	MO.............	St. Louis	3,000
CA.............	Riverside	3,000	NV.............	Las Vegas	3,000
CA.............	San Diego	16,874	NJ.............	Jersey City/Newark	20,800
CO.............	Denver	3,000	NY.............	New York City	180,926
DC.............	National Capital Region	54,000	NC.............	Charlotte	3,000
FL.............	Miami/Fort Lauderdale	5,500	OR.............	Portland	3,000
FL.............	Tampa	3,000	PA.............	Philadelphia	18,500
GA.............	Atlanta	5,500	PA.............	Pittsburgh	3,000
HI.............	Honolulu	3,000	TX.............	Dallas/Fort Worth/Arlington	15,500
IL.............	Chicago	69,500	TX.............	Houston	24,000
			WA.............	Seattle	5,500

X Not applicable.

Source: U.S. Department of Homeland Security, *FY2015 Homeland Security Grant Program Fact Sheet*, July 2015. See also <http://www.fema.gov/homeland-security-grant-program>.

Table 546. Preparedness Grant Programs: 2011 to 2014

[In dollars. For years ending September 30]

Program	2011	2012	2013	2014
Total [1]........................	2,191,248,008	1,381,476,000	1,507,260,327	1,616,346,000
Homeland Security Grant Program [1]................................	1,289,296,132	830,976,000	968,389,689	1,043,346,000
State Homeland Security Program................................	526,874,100	294,000,000	354,644,123	401,346,000
Urban Areas Security Initiative................................	662,622,100	490,376,000	558,745,566	587,000,000
Operation Stonegarden................................	54,890,000	46,600,000	55,000,000	55,000,000
Emergency Management Performance Grants Program........	329,040,400	339,500,000	332,456,012	350,100,000
Transit Security Grant Program [1]................................	200,079,000	87,500,000	83,716,813	90,000,000
Port Security Grant Program................................	235,029,000	97,500,000	93,207,313	100,000,000

[1] Includes programs not listed separately.

Source: U.S. Department of Homeland Security, Federal Emergency Management Agency, Information Bulletin No. 398, *FY2014 DHS Preparedness Grant Programs Allocation Announcement,* July 2014, and earlier reports. See also <http://www.fema.gov/preparedness-non-disaster-grants>.

Table 547. Deportable Aliens Apprehended or Arrested by Program and Border Patrol Sector: 2000 to 2013

[As of the end of September. Deportable aliens located refer to Border Patrol apprehensions and Immigration and Customs Enforcement (ICE) administrative arrests]

Program and sector	2000	2005	2010	2011	2012	2013
Total.	1,814,729	1,291,065	796,587	678,606	671,327	662,483
Investigations.	138,291	102,034	18,290	16,261	15,937	11,996
Enforcement and Removal Operations (ERO) [1].	(X)	–	314,915	322,093	290,622	229,698
Border Patrol (apprehensions).	1,676,438	1,189,031	463,382	340,252	364,768	420,789
All southwest sectors.	1,643,679	1,171,462	447,731	327,577	356,873	414,397
Rio Grande Valley, TX.	133,243	134,161	59,766	59,243	97,762	154,453
Tucson, AZ.	616,346	439,105	212,202	123,285	120,000	120,939
Laredo, TX.	108,973	75,330	35,287	36,053	44,872	50,749
San Diego, CA.	151,681	126,915	68,565	42,447	28,461	27,496
Del Rio, TX.	157,178	68,504	14,694	16,144	21,720	23,510
El Centro, CA.	238,126	55,790	32,562	30,191	23,916	16,306
El Paso, TX.	115,696	122,691	12,251	10,345	9,678	11,154
Yuma, AZ.	108,747	138,430	7,116	5,833	6,500	6,106
Big Bend, TX [2].	13,689	10,536	5,288	4,036	3,964	3,684
All other sectors.	32,759	17,569	15,651	12,675	7,895	6,392
Miami, FL.	6,237	7,243	4,651	4,401	2,509	1,738
Ramey, PR.	1,731	1,619	398	642	702	924
Buffalo, NY.	1,570	406	2,422	2,114	1,143	796
Detroit, MI.	2,057	1,793	1,669	1,531	950	650
Swanton, VT.	1,957	1,936	1,422	815	702	531
New Orleans, LA.	6,478	1,358	3,171	1,509	474	500
Grand Forks, ND.	562	754	543	468	418	469
Blaine, WA.	2,581	1,000	673	591	537	360
Spokane, WA.	1,324	279	356	293	317	299
Havre, MT.	1,568	948	290	270	102	88
Houlton, ME.	489	233	56	41	41	37
Livermore, CA [3].	6,205	(X)	(X)	(X)	(X)	(X)

X Not applicable. – Represents zero. [1] Includes arrests of fugitive and nonfugitive aliens under the Office of Detention and Removal Operations (DRO), National Fugitive Operations Program. Beginning in 2008, includes all administrative arrests conducted by ICE ERO. [2] Formerly known as Marfa, TX. [3] Livermore sector closed August 31, 2004.

Source: U.S. Department of Homeland Security, Office of Immigration Statistics, *2013 Yearbook of Immigration Statistics*, September 2014, and earlier reports. See also <http://www.dhs.gov/yearbook-immigration-statistics>.

Table 548. U.S. Border Patrol Apprehensions by Border, Gender, Age, and Country of Nationality: 2007 to 2010

[As of the end of September]

Characteristic	2007		2008		2009		2010	
	Number	Percent	Number	Percent	Number	Percent	Number	Percent
Border total.	876,803	100.0	723,840	100.0	556,032	100.0	463,382	100.0
Southwest.	858,737	97.9	705,022	97.4	540,851	97.3	447,731	96.6
Coastal.	11,687	1.3	10,895	1.5	8,374	1.5	8,220	1.8
Northern.	6,379	0.7	7,923	1.1	6,807	1.2	7,431	1.6
GENDER								
Male.	730,217	83.3	606,761	83.8	469,994	84.5	397,198	85.7
Female.	146,574	16.7	117,061	16.2	86,023	15.5	66,173	14.3
Unknown.	12	–	18	–	15	–	11	–
AGE								
17 years and under.	77,778	8.9	59,578	8.2	40,461	7.3	31,291	6.8
18 to 24 years.	325,901	37.2	257,409	35.6	182,740	32.9	148,969	32.1
25 to 34 years.	301,002	34.3	255,261	35.3	205,173	36.9	173,763	37.5
35 to 44 years.	127,285	14.5	112,941	15.6	95,922	17.3	82,236	17.7
45 to 54 years.	36,661	4.2	32,003	4.4	26,668	4.8	22,981	5.0
55 years and over.	7,384	0.8	6,235	0.9	5,029	0.9	4,125	0.9
Unknown.	792	0.1	413	0.1	39	–	17	–
COUNTRY OF NATIONALITY								
Mexico.	808,773	92.2	661,773	91.4	503,379	90.5	404,365	87.3
Honduras [1].	22,914	2.6	19,351	2.7	14,630	2.6	13,580	2.9
Guatemala.	17,337	2.0	16,395	2.3	15,575	2.8	18,406	4.0
El Salvador [1].	14,114	1.6	12,684	1.8	11,693	2.1	13,723	3.0
Cuba.	4,295	0.5	3,351	0.5	910	0.2	712	0.2
Ecuador.	958	0.1	1,579	0.2	1,313	0.2	1,777	0.4
Nicaragua.	1,646	0.2	1,467	0.2	975	0.2	909	0.2
Brazil [1].	1,214	0.1	977	0.1	798	0.1	812	0.2
China, People's Republic.	837	0.1	836	0.1	1,499	0.3	1,157	0.2
Dominican Republic.	562	0.1	819	0.1	865	0.2	1,330	0.3
Canada.	554	0.1	610	0.1	490	0.1	690	0.1
Other.	3,599	0.4	3,998	0.6	3,905	0.7	5,921	1.3

– Represents zero. [1] Between 2005 and 2008, the percentage of persons apprehended who were from Honduras, El Salvador, and Brazil declined substantially. These decreases reflect the end of "catch and release," the practice of apprehending illegal aliens from countries other than Mexico and releasing them on their own recognizance pending a removal hearing.

Source: U.S. Department of Homeland Security, Office of Immigration Statistics, *Apprehensions by the U.S. Border Patrol: 2005-2010*, July 2011. See also <http://www.dhs.gov/publications>.

Table 549. Deportable Aliens Apprehended or Arrested: 1925 to 2013

[See headnote, Table 547. Prior to 1952, data refer to Border Patrol Apprehensions. Detention and Removal Operations data are included beginning in FY2006. Beginning in 2008, includes all administrative arrests conducted by the ICE, Office of Enforcement and Removal Operations. Beginning in 2009, data also include administrative arrests conducted under the 287(g) program (Delegation of Immigration Authority)]

Year	Number	Year	Number	Year	Number	Year	Number
1925.	22,199	1975.	766,600	1994.	1,094,719	2004.	1,264,232
1930.	20,880	1980.	910,361	1995.	1,394,554	2005.	1,291,065
1935.	11,016	1985.	1,348,749	1996.	1,649,986	2006.	1,206,417
1940.	10,492	1987.	1,190,488	1997.	1,536,520	2007.	960,772
1945.	69,164	1988.	1,008,145	1998.	1,679,439	2008.	1,043,799
1950.	468,339	1989.	954,243	1999.	1,714,035	2009.	889,203
1955.	254,096	1990.	1,169,939	2000.	1,814,729	2010.	796,587
1960.	70,684	1991.	1,197,875	2001.	1,387,486	2011.	678,606
1965.	110,371	1992.	1,258,481	2002.	1,062,270	2012.	671,327
1970.	345,353	1993.	1,327,261	2003.	1,046,422	2013.	662,483

Source: U.S. Department of Homeland Security, Office of Immigration Statistics, *2013 Yearbook of Immigration Statistics*, September 2014. See also <http://www.dhs.gov/yearbook-immigration-statistics>.

Table 550. Aliens Returned or Removed by Leading Crime Category and Country of Nationality: 2008 to 2013

[For definitions of immigration enforcement terms, see source. "Crime categories" and "Countries of nationality" are ranked by data for most recent year]

Crime category and country of nationality	2008	2009	2010	2011	2012	2013
Total aliens returned or removed:	**1,171,058**	**974,221**	**856,498**	**709,258**	**648,783**	**616,792**
Returns [1]	811,263	582,624	474,233	322,124	230,386	178,371
Removals [2]	359,795	391,597	382,265	387,134	418,397	438,421
Noncriminal.	254,529	259,760	212,609	198,170	218,254	240,027
Criminal [3]	105,266	131,837	169,656	188,964	200,143	198,394
Leading crime category:						
Immigration.	(NA)	20,491	31,828	37,606	47,616	62,194
Dangerous drugs.	(NA)	38,940	42,890	43,378	42,679	30,603
Criminal traffic offenses.	(NA)	20,877	31,062	43,154	46,162	29,844
Assault.	(NA)	9,675	12,175	12,783	13,045	20,181
Burglary.	(NA)	3,893	4,213	3,808	3,569	5,505
Weapon offenses.	(NA)	(NA)	(NA)	2,730	2,513	5,296
Larceny.	(NA)	4,331	5,459	5,728	5,428	5,290
Fraudulent Activities.	(NA)	2,997	3,889	4,232	3,879	5,179
Sexual assault.	(NA)	2,886	3,268	3,576	3,353	3,166
Forgery.	(NA)	(NA)	(NA)	(NA)	2,430	3,032
Robbery.	(NA)	3,359	3,646	3,757	(NA)	(NA)
Family offenses.	(NA)	2,685	(NA)	(NA)	(NA)	(NA)
Public peace (including disorderly conduct).	(NA)	(NA)	2,240	2,493	(NA)	(NA)
Other, including unknown.	(NA)	21,703	28,986	25,719	29,469	28,104
Leading country of nationality of criminals removed:						
Mexico.	77,531	99,616	128,396	145,133	151,444	146,298
Honduras.	5,476	6,998	10,420	10,825	13,815	16,609
Guatemala.	5,138	6,547	9,432	11,718	13,494	15,365
El Salvador.	5,558	6,344	8,368	8,507	8,674	9,440
Dominican Republic.	2,046	2,207	2,241	2,142	2,182	1,805
Jamaica.	1,214	1,246	1,169	1,225	1,150	993
Colombia.	1,081	1,124	1,241	1,048	1,055	956
Nicaragua.	533	620	804	696	731	691
Ecuador.	532	602	692	704	706	580
Haiti.	416	473	126	251	568	448
Canada.	347	418	457	417	383	376
Brazil.	368	388	487	550	424	366

NA Not available. [1] Returns are the confirmed movement of an inadmissible or deportable alien out of the U.S. not based on an order of removal. Most voluntary departures are of Mexican nationals who have been apprehended by the U.S. Border Patrol and are returned to Mexico. [2] Removals are the compulsory and confirmed movement of an inadmissible or deportable alien out of the U.S. based on an order of removal. An alien who is removed has administrative or criminal consequences placed on subsequent reentry. [3] Persons removed based on a criminal charge or those with a criminal conviction.

Source: U.S. Department of Homeland Security, Office of Immigration Statistics, *2013 Yearbook of Immigration Statistics*, October 2014; and *Immigration Enforcement Actions: 2013*, September 2014, and previous editions. See also <http://www.dhs.gov/yearbook-immigration-statistics>.

Table 551. Coast Guard Migrant Interdictions by Nationality of Alien: 2000 to 2014

[For the year ending September 30]

Year	Total	Haiti	Dominican Republic	China	Cuba	Mexico	Ecuador	Other
2000.	4,210	1,113	499	261	1,000	49	1,244	44
2005.	9,455	1,850	3,612	32	2,712	55	1,149	45
2010.	2,088	1,377	140	–	422	61	–	88
2011.	2,474	1,137	222	11	985	68	1	50
2012.	2,955	977	456	23	1,275	79	7	138
2013.	2,094	508	110	5	1,357	31	1	82
2014.	3,587	1,103	293	–	2,111	48	–	32

– Represents zero.

Source: U.S. Department of Homeland Security, United States Coast Guard, "Alien Migrant Interdiction," <http://www.uscg.mil/hq/cg5/cg531/AMIO/amio.asp>, accessed April 2015.

Table 552. Terrorism Related Deaths, Injuries, and Kidnappings of Private U.S. Citizens by Selected Country: 2010 to 2014

[Private U.S. citizen refers to any U.S. citizen overseas not acting in an official capacity on behalf of the U.S. government. This includes U.S. government employees' households and U.S. citizens working for contractors hired by the U.S. government. Figures do not include U.S. military personnel while on active duty or employees of the Department of State and other federal agencies while overseas on U.S. government orders]

Incident type and location	2010	2011	2012	2013	2014
DEATHS					
Total	**15**	**17**	**10**	**16**	**24**
Afghanistan	13	15	10	12	10
Algeria	–	–	–	3	–
Egypt	–	–	–	–	1
Iraq	1	1	–	–	–
Israel, Jerusalem, West Bank, Gaza	–	1	–	–	5
Lebanon	–	–	–	1	–
Somalia	–	–	–	–	3
Syria	–	–	–	–	4
Uganda	1	–	–	–	–
United Arab Emirates	–	–	–	–	1
INJURIES					
Total	**9**	**14**	**2**	**[1]7**	**8**
Afghanistan	–	10	1	1	2
Egypt	–	–	–	–	–
Germany	1	–	–	–	–
Iraq	–	1	1	–	–
Israel, Jerusalem, West Bank, Gaza	–	3	–	–	5
Kenya	–	–	–	6	–
Philippines	1	–	–	–	–
Saudi Arabia	–	–	–	–	1
Uganda	7	–	–	–	–
KIDNAPPINGS					
Total	**–**	**3**	**3**	**13**	**3**
Afghanistan	–	–	–	–	2
Colombia	–	–	–	1	–
Iraq	–	1	–	–	–
Libya	–	–	–	1	–
Nigeria	–	–	1	3	1
Pakistan	–	1	–	–	–
Somalia	–	1	1	–	–
Syria	–	–	–	7	–
Yemen	–	–	1	1	–

– Represents zero. [1] Does not include 2 citizens held hostage in Algeria and 48 citizens present, but not medically injured, at the Westgate Mall attack in Kenya

Source: U.S. State Department, Bureau of Counterterrorism, "Country Reports on Terrorism," <http://www.state.gov/j/ct/rls/crt/index.htm>, accessed July 2015.

Table 553. Value of Counterfeit Goods Seized for Intellectual Property Rights Violations by Commodity and Country of Origin: 2013 and 2014

[In thousands of dollars (1,743,516 represents $1,743,516,000), except as indicated. Customs and Border Protection enforces Intellectual Property Rights (IPR), most visibly by seizing products that infringe IPR such as trademarks, copyrights, and patents. Value of goods seized represent Manufacturer's Suggested Retail Price (MSRP), which is the price at which merchandise is sold at retail to the consumer or what the value of the counterfeit goods would have been at retail had they been genuine]

Commodity	2013	2014	Country of origin	2013	2014
Number of IPR Seizures	**24,361**	**23,140**	China	1,180,919	772,629
			Hong Kong	437,538	310,437
Total MSRP value of IPR seizures	**1,743,516**	**1,226,348**	India	20,684	5,541
Handbags/wallets/backpacks	700,177	342,032	Korea, South	6,308	2,515
Jewelry, watches, and parts	502,836	375,397	Singapore	5,065	2,538
Consumer electronics [1]	145,867	162,209	Vietnam	4,406	2,422
Wearing apparel/accessories	116,150	113,686	Taiwan	3,975	3,082
Pharmaceuticals	79,637	72,939	Great Britain	2,421	(NA)
Footwear	54,886	49,523	Bangladesh	1,914	(NA)
Computers/technology components	47,732	26,652	Pakistan	1,336	(NA)
Labels/tags	41,769	17,675	Canada	(NA)	12,460
Media [2]	26,831	18,781	United Arab Emirates	(NA)	3,791
Toys	8,794	8,178	Kenya	(NA)	2,293
All other commodities	18,837	39,273	All other countries	78,948	108,639

NA Not available. [1] Consumer electronics include cell phones and accessories, radios, power strips, electrical tools and appliances. [2] Includes motion pictures on tape, laser disc, and DVD; interactive and computer software on CD-ROM and floppy discs; and music on CD or tape.

Source: U.S. Department of Homeland Security, Customs and Border Protection, *Intellectual Property Rights FY2014 Seizure Statistics*, April 2015, and earlier reports. See also <http://www.cbp.gov/trade/priority-issues/ipr/statistics>.

Section 11
Social Insurance and Human Services

This section presents data related to government expenditures for social insurance and human services; population receiving government assistance; government programs for Old-Age, Survivors, and Disability Insurance (OASDI), commonly known as Social Security; government employee retirement; private retirement plans; government unemployment and disability insurance; federal supplemental security income payments and aid to the needy; child and other welfare services; and federal food programs. Also included here are selected data on workers' compensation, child support, child care, homelessness, social assistance organizations, charitable contributions, and philanthropic foundations.

The principal source for these data is the Social Security Administration's *Annual Statistical Supplement to the Social Security Bulletin* which presents current data on many of the programs. Additional sources of data include the Census Bureau and the Department of Health and Human Services' Administration for Children and Families.

Social insurance under the Social Security Act—Programs established by the Social Security Act provide protection against wage loss resulting from retirement, prolonged disability, death, or unemployment, and protection against the cost of medical care during old age and disability. The federal OASDI program provides monthly benefits to retired or disabled insured workers and their dependents and to survivors of insured workers. To be eligible, a worker must have had a specified period of employment in which OASDI taxes were paid. The age of eligibility for full retirement benefits had been 65 years old for many years. However, for persons born in 1938 or later that age gradually increases until it reaches age 67 for those born after 1959. Reduced benefits may be obtained as early as age 62. The worker's spouse is under the same limitations. Survivor benefits are payable to dependents of deceased insured workers. Disability benefits are payable to an insured worker under full retirement age with a prolonged disability and to the disabled worker's dependents on the same basis as dependents of retired workers. Disability benefits are provided at age 50 to the disabled widow or widower of a deceased worker who was fully insured at the time of death. Disabled children, aged 18 or older, of retired, disabled, or deceased workers are also eligible for benefits. A lump sum benefit is generally payable on the death of an insured worker to a spouse or minor children. For information on the Medicare program, see Section 3, Health and Nutrition.

Retirement, survivors, and disability insurance benefits are funded by a payroll tax on annual earnings (up to a maximum share of earnings set by law) of workers, employers, and the self-employed. The maximum taxable earnings are adjusted annually to reflect increasing wage levels (see Table 560). Tax receipts and benefit payments are administered through federal trust funds. Special benefits for uninsured persons; hospital benefits for persons aged 65 and over with specified amounts of social security coverage less than that required for cash benefit eligibility; and that part of the cost of supplementary

medical insurance not financed by contributions from participants are all financed from federal general revenues.

Unemployment insurance is presently administered by the U.S. Employment and Training Administration and each state's employment security agency. By agreement with the U.S. Secretary of Labor, state agencies also administer unemployment compensation for eligible ex-military personnel and federal employees. Under state unemployment insurance laws, benefits related to an individual's past earnings are paid to unemployed eligible workers. State laws vary concerning the length of time benefits are paid and their amount. In most states, benefits are payable for 26 weeks and, during periods of high unemployment, extended benefits are payable under a federal-state program to those who have exhausted their regular state benefits. Some states also supplement the basic benefit with allowances for dependents. Unemployment insurance is financed through Federal and state employer payroll taxes. Generally, employers pay both Federal and state unemployment taxes for workers paid $1,500 or more during any quarter of a calendar year, or if they had at least 1 employee during any day of week during 20 weeks in a calendar year (weeks need not be consecutive).

Retirement programs for government employees—The Civil Service Retirement System (CSRS) and the Federal Employees' Retirement System (FERS) are the two major programs providing old-age, disability, and survivor annuities for federal civilian employees. In general, employees hired after December 31, 1983, are covered under FERS and the Social Security program (OASDI), and employees on staff prior to that date are members of CSRS and are covered under Medicare. CSRS employees were offered the option of transferring to FERS during 1987 and 1998. There are separate retirement systems for the uniformed services (supplementing OASDI) and for certain special groups of federal employees. State and local government employees are covered for the most part by state and local retirement systems similar to the federal programs. In many jurisdictions these benefits supplement OASDI coverage.

Workers' compensation—All states provide protection against work-connected injuries and deaths, although some states exclude certain workers (e.g., domestic workers). Federal laws cover federal employees, private employees in the District of Columbia, and longshoremen and harbor workers. In addition, the Department of Labor administers "black lung" benefit programs for coal miners disabled by pneumoconiosis and for specified dependents and survivors. Specified occupational diseases are compensable to some extent. In most states, benefits are related to the worker's salary. The benefits may or may not be augmented by dependents' allowances or automatically adjusted to prevailing wage levels.

Income support—Income support programs are designed to provide benefits for persons with limited income and resources. The Supplemental Security Income (SSI) program and Temporary Assistance for Needy Families (TANF) program are the major programs providing monthly payments. In addition, a number of programs provide money payments or in-kind benefits for special needs or purposes. Several programs offer food and nutritional services. Also, various federal-state programs provide energy assistance, public housing, and subsidized housing to individuals and families with low incomes. General assistance may also be available at the state or local level.

The SSI program, administered by the Social Security Administration, provides income support to persons aged 65 or older and to blind or disabled adults and children. Eligibility requirements and federal payment standards are nationally uniform. Most states supplement the basic SSI payment for all or selected categories of persons.

The Personal Responsibility and Work Opportunity Reconciliation Act of 1996 contained provisions that replaced the Aid to Families With Dependent Children (AFDC), Job Opportunities and Basic Skills (JOBS), and Emergency Assistance programs with the TANF block grant program. This law contains strong work requirements, comprehensive child support enforcement, support for families moving from welfare to work, and other features. The TANF program became effective as soon as each state submitted a complete implementation plan, but no later than July 1, 1997. The older AFDC program provided cash assistance based on need, income, resources, and family size.

Federal food stamp program—Under the Supplemental Nutrition Assistance Program (SNAP), formerly known as the food stamp program, single persons and those living in households meeting nationwide standards for income and assets may receive benefit payments redeemable for food at most retail food stores through electronic benefits transfer. The monthly amount of benefits or allotments a unit receives is determined by household size and income. Households without income receive the determined monthly cost of a nutritionally adequate diet for their household size. This amount is updated to account for food price increases. Households with income receive the difference between the amount of a nutritionally adequate diet and 30 percent of their income, after certain allowable deductions.

For the fiscal year ending 2016, a household qualifying for SNAP may have no more than $2,250 in disposable assets ($3,250 if one member is aged 60 or older), gross income below 130 percent of the official poverty guidelines for the household size, and net income below 100 percent of the poverty guidelines. Households with a person aged 60 or older or a disabled person receiving SSI, social security, state general assistance, or veterans' disability benefits may have gross income exceeding 130 percent of the poverty guidelines. All households in which all members receive TANF or SSI are categorically eligible for SNAP without meeting these income or resource criteria. Households are certified for varying lengths of time, depending on their income sources and individual circumstances.

Health and welfare services—Programs providing health and welfare services are aided through federal grants to states for child welfare services, vocational rehabilitation, activities for the aged, maternal and child health services, maternity and infant care projects, comprehensive health services, and a variety of public health activities. For information about the Medicaid program, see Section 3, Health and Nutrition.

Noncash benefits—The U.S. Census Bureau annually collects data on the characteristics of recipients of noncash (in-kind) benefits to supplement the collection of annual money income data in the Current Population Survey (see text, Section 1, Population, and Section 13, Income, Expenditures, Poverty, and Wealth). Noncash benefits are those benefits received in a form other than money which serve to enhance or improve the economic well-being of the recipient. As for money income, the data for noncash benefits are for the calendar year prior to the date of the interview. The major categories of noncash benefits covered are public transfers (e.g., food stamps, school lunch, public housing, and Medicaid) and employer or union-provided benefits to employees.

Statistical reliability—For discussion of statistical collection, estimation, and sampling procedures and measures of statistical reliability applicable to Social Security Administration and Census Bureau data, see Appendix III.

Table 554. Government Transfer Payments to Individuals—Summary: 1990 to 2013

[In billions of current dollars (566.1 represents $566,100,000,000)]

Year	Transfer payments, total	Retirement and disability insurance benefits	Medical payments	Income main-tenance benefits	Unemploy-ment insurance benefits	Veterans benefits	Education and training assistance payments [1]	Other [2]
1990	566.1	263.9	188.8	63.5	18.2	17.7	12.3	1.7
2000	1,028.1	424.5	427.2	106.3	21.0	25.0	21.9	2.3
2001	1,127.0	449.8	480.8	109.4	32.1	26.6	25.4	3.0
2002	1,230.5	474.5	521.9	120.7	53.7	29.5	27.8	2.4
2003	1,299.8	493.4	556.5	133.2	53.6	31.8	28.3	3.0
2004	1,382.6	517.0	611.4	144.6	37.1	34.0	30.8	7.6
2005	1,468.9	545.5	655.6	161.3	32.3	36.4	33.0	4.8
2006	1,570.5	577.2	720.5	165.2	30.9	38.9	34.8	3.0
2007	1,674.6	608.8	776.8	174.7	33.4	41.7	36.8	2.5
2008	1,828.6	639.0	826.8	219.2	52.0	45.0	42.5	3.9
2009	2,081.2	698.4	891.7	226.7	132.0	51.5	53.5	27.4
2010	2,212.9	724.9	938.7	268.9	139.7	58.0	64.5	18.2
2011	2,236.2	747.7	970.2	278.0	107.9	63.3	64.8	4.4
2012	2,285.3	796.7	1,001.8	265.6	84.4	70.1	63.0	3.6
2013	2,349.4	833.3	1,040.9	267.8	62.8	79.0	62.0	3.6

[1] See footnote 9, Table 555. [2] See footnote 10, Table 555.

Source: U.S. Bureau of Economic Analysis, Interactive Regional Data, GDP & Personal Income, "Personal Current Transfer Receipts (SA35)," <http://www.bea.gov/iTable/index_regional.cfm>, accessed March 2015.

Table 555. Government Transfer Payments to Individuals by Type: 1990 to 2013

[In millions of current dollars (566,100 represents $566,100,000,000)]

Item	1990	2000	2005	2010	2011	2012	2013
Total	566,100	1,028,107	1,468,895	2,212,862	2,236,240	2,285,266	2,349,356
Retirement & disability insurance benefits	263,888	424,461	545,484	724,934	747,736	796,725	833,321
Social security	244,135	401,393	512,728	690,174	713,261	762,139	799,044
Railroad retirement and disability	7,221	8,267	9,194	10,779	10,961	11,410	11,676
Workers' compensation (federal & state)	8,618	10,898	15,863	15,544	15,191	14,915	14,811
Other government disability insurance & retirement [1]	3,914	3,903	7,699	8,437	8,323	8,261	7,790
Medical payments	188,808	427,194	655,613	938,709	970,200	1,001,818	1,040,885
Medicare	107,638	219,117	332,161	513,820	536,007	555,216	572,362
Public assistance medical care [2]	78,176	205,021	315,197	410,834	419,541	431,161	454,427
Military medical insurance [3]	2,994	3,056	8,255	14,055	14,652	15,441	14,096
Income maintenance benefits	63,481	106,285	161,338	268,867	277,971	265,599	267,804
Supplemental Security Income (SSI)	16,670	31,675	38,261	49,159	50,484	53,038	54,870
Earned income tax credit	4,353	26,126	34,603	54,746	55,804	55,044	57,614
Supplemental Nutrition Assistance Program	14,741	14,565	29,492	66,515	72,730	74,861	74,640
Family assistance [4]	19,187	18,440	18,355	22,421	20,795	20,171	20,981
Other, excluding family assistance [5]	8,530	15,479	40,627	76,026	78,158	62,485	59,699
Unemployment insurance compensation	18,208	20,989	32,276	139,712	107,869	84,434	62,769
State unemployment insurance compensation	17,644	20,223	31,001	137,015	105,129	81,851	60,805
Unemployment compensation for federal civilian employees	215	226	224	535	671	480	399
Unemployment compensation for railroad employees	89	81	72	114	85	83	82
Unemployment compensation for veterans	144	181	446	1,155	1,245	1,167	867
Other unemployment compensation [6]	116	278	533	893	739	853	616
Veterans benefits	17,687	25,000	36,382	57,961	63,265	70,113	78,951
Veterans pension and disability	15,550	21,966	32,505	48,455	52,101	58,352	65,684
Veterans readjustment [7]	257	1,322	2,256	7,976	9,652	10,327	11,889
Veterans life insurance benefits	1,868	1,706	1,596	1,442	1,411	1,340	1,280
Other assistance to veterans [8]	12	10	25	88	101	94	98
Federal education & training assistance payments [9]	12,286	21,851	33,017	64,480	64,765	62,951	61,982
Other payments to individuals [10]	1,742	2,323	4,785	18,199	4,434	3,626	3,644

[1] Mostly temporary disability, pension benefit guaranty, black lung, and Panama Canal construction annuity payments. [2] Medicaid and other medical vendor payments. [3] Payments made under TriCare Management Program (formerly called CHAMPUS) for medical care of dependents of active duty and retired military personnel and their dependents at nonmilitary medical facilities. [4] Through 1995, consists of Emergency Assistance and Aid to Families with Dependent Children. Beginning with 1998, consists of benefits from Temporary Assistance for Needy Families. [5] Mostly general assistance; food expenditures under Special Supplemental Nutrition Program for Women, Infants, and Children (WIC); Other Needs Assistance; refugee assistance; foster home care and adoption assistance; 2008 Economic Stimulus Act Rebates; Child Tax Credits; ARRA funded tax credits; other tax credits; and energy assistance. [6] Trade readjustment allowance, Redwood Park benefit, public service employment benefit, and transitional benefit. [7] Mostly veterans' readjustment benefit payments, educational assistance to spouses and children of disabled or deceased veterans, and payments to paraplegics and for autos and conveyances for disabled veterans. [8] Mostly state and local government payments to veterans. [9] Mostly federal fellowship payments (National Science Foundation fellowships and traineeships, subsistence payments to state maritime academy cadets, and other federal fellowships), interest subsidy on higher education loans, Pell Grants, Job Corps payments, education exchange payments, and state education assistance payments. [10] Mostly Bureau of Indian Affairs payments; Alaska Permanent Fund dividend payments; compensation of survivors of public safety officers; compensation of victims of crime; disaster relief payments; compensation for Japanese internment; American Recovery and Reinvestment Act of 2009 funded Federal Additional Compensation for unemployment, COBRA premium reduction, and Economic Recovery lump sum payment; and other special payments to individuals.

Source: U.S. Bureau of Economic Analysis, Interactive Regional Data, GDP & Personal Income, "Personal Current Transfer Receipts (SA35)," <http://www.bea.gov/iTable/index_regional.cfm>, accessed March 2015.

Table 556. Government Transfer Payments to Individuals by State: 2010 to 2013

[In millions of current dollars not adjusted for inflation (2,212,862 represents $2,212,862,000,000)]

State	2010, total	2012, total	2013							
			Total	Retirement and disability insurance benefits	Medical payments	Income maintenance benefits	Unemployment insurance benefits	Veterans benefits	Education and training assistance payments [1]	Other [2]
United States.........	2,212,862	2,285,266	2,349,356	833,321	1,040,885	267,804	62,769	78,951	61,982	3,644
Alabama.................	36,285	37,643	38,511	15,049	15,232	4,761	467	1,868	1,098	34
Alaska..................	5,022	5,207	5,060	1,182	1,929	827	197	287	65	575
Arizona.................	46,192	46,452	47,633	17,274	20,403	4,896	590	1,849	2,444	177
Arkansas...............	22,674	23,648	24,101	9,073	10,045	2,573	471	1,058	862	20
California...............	253,337	261,780	273,243	82,915	128,772	34,646	10,677	7,374	8,526	333
Colorado................	27,619	29,355	30,512	11,474	12,654	2,868	936	1,618	914	49
Connecticut............	27,677	28,647	29,001	10,191	13,826	2,507	1,315	498	631	34
Delaware...............	6,902	7,488	7,849	2,887	3,653	652	170	216	263	8
District of Columbia....	5,248	5,522	5,757	1,052	3,383	874	164	116	161	8
Florida..................	144,471	151,397	156,554	58,876	67,907	17,366	2,071	5,948	4,171	215
Georgia.................	58,577	61,706	63,941	23,083	25,049	9,283	1,325	3,096	2,031	74
Hawaii..................	8,757	9,197	9,551	3,494	3,760	1,316	273	506	188	13
Idaho...................	9,676	10,057	10,411	4,311	4,087	1,074	214	408	301	16
Illinois.................	88,457	85,954	89,913	32,051	38,991	10,850	3,528	1,881	2,507	106
Indiana.................	44,975	47,462	47,885	19,089	19,735	5,196	892	1,315	1,613	45
Iowa....................	20,823	21,529	21,730	8,862	8,990	1,962	527	619	750	21
Kansas.................	18,128	18,719	19,011	7,787	7,634	2,011	449	672	436	22
Kentucky...............	33,894	34,870	35,753	13,215	14,916	4,264	795	1,292	1,241	29
Louisiana..............	32,848	34,485	35,531	11,333	17,218	4,675	307	1,201	764	33
Maine..................	10,820	11,506	12,248	4,270	5,786	1,189	241	539	210	13
Maryland...............	36,979	39,187	40,632	14,045	18,799	4,129	1,252	1,463	887	57
Massachusetts.........	53,658	55,147	55,723	17,430	27,656	5,995	2,406	1,259	923	53
Michigan...............	79,077	79,714	81,503	31,951	34,045	9,362	2,064	1,995	2,014	71
Minnesota.............	36,936	37,830	39,278	14,081	18,102	3,718	1,008	1,196	1,127	46
Mississippi............	23,125	24,074	24,718	8,439	11,214	3,300	329	797	610	29
Missouri................	43,488	45,516	46,505	17,597	20,918	4,378	780	1,666	1,126	41
Montana...............	6,693	6,942	7,136	3,063	2,745	618	171	348	172	17
Nebraska..............	11,175	11,728	11,893	4,824	4,900	1,121	153	584	298	13
Nevada................	15,879	16,484	16,485	6,589	6,339	1,697	765	699	361	35
New Hampshire........	8,600	8,894	9,249	4,100	3,638	825	141	339	196	10
New Jersey............	67,268	67,902	68,606	25,356	29,655	6,686	4,061	1,187	1,550	110
New Mexico............	15,216	15,527	15,712	5,282	6,688	2,078	325	796	437	106
New York...............	175,106	179,210	181,325	53,485	94,448	21,566	4,971	2,725	3,833	295
North Carolina.........	67,321	71,471	72,841	27,009	31,100	8,207	1,534	3,280	1,633	79
North Dakota...........	4,288	4,494	4,617	1,911	1,881	412	101	182	102	27
Ohio....................	86,514	88,656	91,220	33,869	40,869	10,157	1,805	2,264	2,177	80
Oklahoma..............	26,416	27,797	28,386	10,550	11,939	3,054	338	1,764	706	36
Oregon.................	27,900	28,752	29,919	11,601	11,920	3,250	1,106	1,300	700	42
Pennsylvania..........	106,298	108,320	110,292	40,727	50,307	10,422	4,047	2,546	2,147	97
Rhode Island..........	9,143	9,202	9,302	3,226	4,194	1,058	331	243	241	9
South Carolina........	34,822	35,956	37,009	14,593	14,284	4,412	512	1,875	1,296	36
South Dakota..........	5,077	5,275	5,414	2,208	2,177	543	41	254	140	52
Tennessee.............	48,209	50,260	51,944	18,992	22,535	6,449	660	1,993	1,268	46
Texas..................	149,860	156,803	162,701	52,477	73,862	21,145	3,633	7,611	3,797	176
Utah...................	12,746	13,370	13,886	5,341	5,239	1,852	282	461	672	39
Vermont................	5,097	5,362	5,619	1,949	2,701	568	97	147	152	5
Virginia................	46,464	49,714	51,745	20,268	20,617	5,261	756	3,320	1,461	62
Washington............	47,638	48,556	49,550	19,732	18,467	5,761	1,808	2,251	1,453	79
West Virginia..........	16,202	16,909	17,259	6,831	7,206	1,727	354	711	419	13
Wisconsin.............	39,850	40,058	41,035	16,682	17,072	4,006	1,235	1,181	810	49
Wyoming...............	3,430	3,533	3,658	1,646	1,401	260	94	152	97	8

[1] Mostly federal fellowship payments (National Science Foundation fellowships and traineeships, subsistence payments to state maritime academy cadets, and other federal fellowships), interest subsidy on higher education loans, Pell Grants, Job Corps payments, education exchange payments, and state education assistance payments. [2] Mostly Bureau of Indian Affairs payments; Alaska Permanent Fund dividend payments; compensation of survivors of public safety officers; compensation of victims of crime; disaster relief payments; compensation for Japanese internment; the American Recovery and Reinvestment Act of 2009 funded Federal Additional Compensation for unemployment, COBRA premium reduction, and the Economic Recovery lump sum payment; and other special payments to individuals.

Source: U.S. Bureau of Economic Analysis, Interactive Regional Data, GDP & Personal Income, "Personal Current Transfer Receipts (SA35)," <http://www.bea.gov/iTable/index_regional.cfm>, accessed March 2015.

Table 557. Number of Persons With Income by Source of Income: 2013

[In thousands (218,662 represents 218,662,000). Persons 15 years old and over as of March of following year. Based on Current Population Survey (CPS), Annual Social and Economic Supplement; see text, Sections 1 and 13, and Appendix III]

Source of income	Total persons with income	Under 65 years	65 years and over	Men	Women	White[1]	Black[1]	Hispanic origin[2]
Total	**218,662**	**175,729**	**42,933**	**108,706**	**109,956**	**174,936**	**26,017**	**30,518**
Earnings	158,101	148,252	9,848	83,555	74,545	126,389	18,233	24,653
Wages and salary	149,483	141,013	8,471	78,263	71,220	119,083	17,595	23,390
Nonfarm self-employment	11,708	10,349	1,359	7,014	4,694	9,800	989	1,614
Farm self-employment	2,292	1,917	375	1,518	774	1,968	201	166
Unemployment compensation	6,824	6,402	422	4,008	2,816	5,316	1,033	1,108
State or local only	6,508	6,113	395	3,809	2,699	5,071	979	1,037
Combinations	316	289	27	199	117	245	55	72
Workers' compensation	1,551	1,363	189	872	679	1,212	212	221
State payments	461	404	57	249	212	370	48	88
Employment insurance	662	600	62	384	278	522	86	89
Own insurance	43	40	3	32	11	36	7	2
Other	577	493	83	307	270	438	94	60
Social Security	48,377	11,732	36,645	21,454	26,923	40,670	5,175	3,587
SSI (Supplemental Security Income)	6,053	4,786	1,267	2,667	3,386	3,920	1,594	1,064
Public assistance, total	1,997	1,911	86	456	1,541	1,123	694	508
TANF/welfare (AFDC) only [3]	1,281	1,249	32	206	1,075	648	530	335
Other assistance only	677	624	53	245	433	448	154	166
Both	39	38	1	6	33	27	11	7
Veterans' benefits	3,517	1,888	1,630	2,899	619	2,830	476	243
Disability only	2,177	1,259	917	1,995	181	1,768	278	138
Survivors only	274	71	203	11	263	228	34	26
Pension only	669	297	373	577	92	533	96	31
Education only	134	134	1	81	53	88	31	18
Other only	122	41	81	112	10	101	18	12
Combinations	142	86	55	122	20	112	19	19
Means-tested	645	400	245	549	96	537	71	60
Nonmeans-tested	2,873	1,488	1,385	2,350	523	2,293	405	183
Survivors benefits [4]	3,033	957	2,075	645	2,387	2,688	225	140
Company or union	1,226	195	1,031	199	1,027	1,102	87	44
Federal government	289	97	191	26	262	252	17	17
Military retirement	271	69	201	13	257	216	37	7
Disability benefits [4]	1,771	1,543	227	905	866	1,308	320	191
Workers' compensation	253	221	32	141	112	187	45	25
Company or union	341	299	41	178	162	268	58	23
Federal government	167	141	26	68	99	122	29	18
Military retirement	77	50	27	53	24	51	21	10
State or local government	266	235	31	106	160	200	43	41
Pension income [4]	18,118	5,035	13,083	10,413	7,705	15,649	1,739	825
Company or union retirement	11,944	2,948	8,996	6,809	5,134	10,306	1,139	585
Federal government retirement	1,957	700	1,258	1,014	943	1,627	227	103
Military retirement	1,314	689	625	922	393	1,061	186	63
State or local government retirement	4,858	1,661	3,197	2,047	2,811	4,255	423	222
Property income [5]	92,394	70,130	22,264	46,309	46,085	79,403	5,963	6,409
Interest	86,142	65,640	20,502	42,986	43,156	74,120	5,487	5,869
Dividends	29,920	21,678	8,242	16,108	13,812	26,683	1,206	1,152
Rents, royalties, estates or trusts	11,907	7,983	3,925	6,230	5,677	10,421	600	733
Educational assistance [4]	9,087	9,033	53	3,814	5,273	6,634	1,466	1,477
Pell grant only	3,107	3,087	20	1,129	1,978	2,071	716	668
Other government only	1,113	1,109	3	497	615	842	161	201
Scholarships only	2,619	2,610	9	1,152	1,467	2,076	253	294
Child support	4,613	4,580	34	349	4,265	3,536	808	817
Alimony	367	308	59	22	344	328	23	29
Financial assistance from outside the household	2,667	2,440	227	1,099	1,568	1,865	423	336
Other income, not elsewhere classified	1,026	807	219	468	558	838	81	63
Combinations of income types:								
Government transfer payments	69,668	30,997	38,671	32,023	37,645	56,016	9,388	7,110
Public assistance or SSI or both	7,758	6,447	1,312	3,036	4,722	4,874	2,198	1,520

[1] Refers to people who reported specified race only and no other race category. [2] Persons of Hispanic origin may be of any race. [3] TANF is Temporary Assistance for Needy Families Program; AFDC is Aid to Families With Dependent Children Program. [4] Includes other sources not shown separately. [5] Includes estates and trusts reported as survivor benefits.

Source: U.S. Census Bureau, *Income and Poverty in the United States: 2013,* Current Population Reports, P60-249, September 2014; and "Detailed Tables: Person Table PINC-09," <http://www.census.gov/hhes/www/income/data/incpovhlth/2013/index.html>, accessed December 2014. See also <http://www.census.gov/hhes/www/income/index.html>.

Social Insurance and Human Services 365

Table 558. Participation in Means-Tested Government Assistance Programs by Selected Participant Characteristics and Program: 2010 and 2012

[As percent of total population, except as noted (48,304 represents 48,304,000). Data are average monthly participation rates. Means-tested programs, which provide cash and noncash assistance, are those that require the income and/or assets of an individual or family to fall below specific thresholds in order to qualify for benefits. There may be additional eligibility requirements. Based on Census Bureau's Survey of Income and Program Participation (SIPP), 2008 Panel, Waves 2-14]

Characteristic	All programs 2010	All programs 2012	Medicaid[1] 2010	Medicaid[1] 2012	SNAP[1] 2010	SNAP[1] 2012	Housing assistance 2010	Housing assistance 2012	SSI[2] 2010	SSI[2] 2012	TANF or GA[3] 2010	TANF or GA[3] 2012
Total number of recipients (1,000s)	**48,304**	**52,249**	**35,558**	**37,520**	**28,970**	**33,032**	**10,110**	**10,248**	**6,655**	**7,465**	**2,759**	**2,377**
As percent of the population	20.2	21.3	14.9	15.3	12.1	13.4	4.2	4.2	2.8	3.0	1.2	1.0
Age:												
Under 18 years	37.3	39.2	33.3	34.9	21.1	22.9	6.2	6.1	1.6	1.8	3.2	2.6
18 to 64 years	15.1	16.6	9.2	9.7	10.0	11.5	3.3	3.4	2.9	3.2	0.6	0.5
65 years and over	13.3	12.6	8.3	7.8	6.1	6.9	5.1	4.2	4.4	4.3	0.2	0.1
Sex:												
Male	18.3	19.3	13.5	13.9	10.6	11.8	3.3	3.3	2.5	2.9	1.0	0.8
Female	22.1	23.2	16.2	16.6	13.5	15.0	5.2	5.0	3.0	3.2	1.3	1.1
Race and Hispanic origin:[4]												
White	16.7	17.6	12.3	12.6	9.4	10.6	2.5	2.4	2.2	2.3	0.8	0.7
White, non-Hispanic	12.7	13.2	9.3	9.3	7.3	8.1	2.0	1.9	2.0	2.1	0.5	0.4
Black	40.9	41.6	29.1	29.3	29.0	30.1	15.4	14.5	6.4	7.0	3.4	2.5
Asian or Pacific Islander	18.0	17.8	14.5	14.2	7.5	7.9	3.3	3.9	3.5	3.6	0.6	0.3
Hispanic	35.7	36.4	27.1	26.9	20.8	22.0	5.9	5.3	3.2	3.4	2.3	1.9
Non-Hispanic	17.2	18.1	12.5	12.9	10.5	11.7	3.9	3.9	2.7	3.0	0.9	0.8
Family status:												
In families	20.8	21.8	15.7	16.0	12.6	13.8	3.8	3.7	2.2	2.5	1.3	1.1
Married-couple families	13.9	14.7	10.4	10.7	7.1	8.1	1.2	1.3	1.4	1.5	0.5	0.4
Male householder[5]	28.1	29.5	20.6	21.1	17.2	18.8	2.5	2.3	3.4	3.8	1.6	1.2
Female householder[5]	48.5	50.0	37.5	37.3	34.8	36.7	15.2	14.7	5.6	6.1	4.9	3.7
Unrelated individuals	17.5	18.6	10.8	11.4	10.0	11.7	6.6	6.5	5.5	5.8	0.3	0.5
Marital status:[6]												
Married	9.1	9.8	5.1	5.2	5.7	6.6	1.2	1.2	1.4	1.7	0.2	0.2
Separated, divorced, or widowed	21.2	22.0	12.9	13.1	13.4	14.8	6.6	6.1	6.1	6.2	0.5	0.5
Never married	22.5	24.0	14.8	15.3	14.0	15.7	6.7	6.7	4.9	5.0	1.1	0.9
Educational attainment:[6]												
Less than high school graduate	35.9	37.3	22.7	22.7	23.6	26.4	9.4	8.9	10.0	10.1	1.2	1.2
High school graduate, no college	19.4	21.6	11.8	12.8	12.0	14.4	4.6	4.8	3.9	4.4	0.7	0.6
One or more years of college	8.7	9.6	5.2	5.5	5.3	6.1	2.1	2.1	1.5	1.8	0.3	0.3
Employment or labor force status:[6]												
Employed full-time[7]	5.9	6.7	2.6	2.7	3.8	4.5	1.1	1.2	0.2	0.3	0.1	0.1
Employed part-time[7]	16.0	17.6	9.2	9.6	10.1	12.0	3.3	3.5	1.4	1.7	0.4	0.5
Unemployed	29.0	33.5	15.9	16.4	22.3	26.8	6.3	7.7	1.6	1.6	1.5	1.6
Not in labor force	24.4	25.3	16.8	17.2	14.5	16.1	6.8	6.3	8.3	8.4	0.9	0.9
Disability status:[8]												
With a work disability	42.3	44.7	31.7	33.1	25.9	28.7	10.6	10.7	19.1	20.2	1.6	1.5
With no work disability	11.9	13.0	7.0	7.3	7.7	8.8	2.4	2.4	0.5	0.6	0.5	0.5

[1] Supplemental Nutrition Assistance Program. [2] Supplemental Security Income. [3] Temporary Assistance for Needy Families, or General Assistance. [4] Hispanics may be of any race. [5] No spouse present. [6] For persons age 18 and older. [7] Full-time and part-time employment reflect monthly employment status. [8] For persons age 15 to 64.

Source: U.S. Census Bureau, *Dynamics of Economic Well-Being: Participation in Government Programs, 2009–2012: Who Gets Assistance?*, Current Population Report, P70-141, May 2015. See also <http://www.census.gov/sipp/>.

Table 559. Persons Living in Households Receiving Selected Noncash Benefits by Selected Characteristics: 2013

[312,965 represents 312,965,000, except percent. Based on Current Population Survey (CPS), 2014 Annual Social and Economic Supplement; see text of Section 1 and Appendix III. Persons who lived with someone (a nonrelative or a relative) who received aid. Not every person tallied here received the aid themselves. Persons living in households receiving more than one type of aid are counted only once. Excludes members of the Armed Forces except those living off post or with their families on post. Population controls are based on Census 2010. SNAP = Supplemental Nutrition Assistance Program]

Characteristic	Total (1,000)	In household that received means-tested assistance [1] (1,000)	Percent	In household that received means-tested cash assistance (1,000)	Percent	In household that received food stamps (SNAP) (1,000)	Percent	In household in which one or more persons were covered by Medicaid (1,000)	Percent	Lived in public or authorized housing (1,000)	Percent
Total	312,965	104,743	33.5	20,306	6.5	40,661	13.0	83,613	26.7	11,732	3.7
Under 18 years	73,625	36,592	49.7	5,288	7.2	15,407	20.9	30,343	41.2	3,777	5.1
18 to 24 years	30,054	11,268	37.5	2,044	6.8	4,207	14.0	9,163	30.5	1,524	5.1
25 to 34 years	42,466	15,024	35.4	2,451	5.8	6,082	14.3	12,377	29.1	1,536	3.6
35 to 44 years	39,789	13,686	34.4	2,327	5.8	4,585	11.5	10,736	27.0	1,086	2.7
45 to 54 years	42,898	11,238	26.2	2,709	6.3	3,920	9.1	8,715	20.3	1,058	2.5
55 to 59 years	21,156	5,018	23.7	1,630	7.7	1,867	8.8	3,943	18.6	595	2.8
60 to 64 years	18,470	4,097	22.2	1,366	7.4	1,499	8.1	3,270	17.7	503	2.7
65 years and over	44,508	7,818	17.6	2,491	5.6	3,094	7.0	5,066	11.4	1,653	3.7
Male	153,361	49,571	32.3	9,527	6.2	18,303	11.9	39,442	25.7	4,797	3.1
Female	159,605	55,172	34.6	10,779	6.8	22,359	14.0	44,171	27.7	6,935	4.3
White alone [2]	243,085	72,008	29.6	12,816	5.3	25,656	10.6	57,393	23.6	5,806	2.4
Black alone [2]	40,615	21,686	53.4	5,453	13.4	11,348	27.9	17,360	42.7	4,628	11.4
Asian alone [2]	17,063	5,288	31.0	930	5.4	1,047	6.1	4,387	25.7	409	2.4
Hispanic [3]	54,145	30,592	56.5	4,649	8.6	11,725	21.7	24,719	45.7	2,486	4.6
In married couple families	189,859	50,688	26.7	8,188	4.3	13,631	7.2	40,863	21.5	2,393	1.3
In families with male householder, no spouse present	18,121	8,845	48.8	1,632	9.0	3,228	17.8	7,370	40.7	727	4.0
In families with female householder, no spouse present	47,007	30,905	65.7	6,842	14.6	16,879	35.9	25,653	54.6	5,197	11.1

[1] Means-tested assistance includes means-tested cash assistance, food stamps, Medicaid, and public or authorized housing. [2] Refers to people who reported specific race and did not report any other race category. [3] People of Hispanic origin may be of any race.

Source: U.S. Census Bureau, *Income and Poverty in the United States: 2013*, Current Population Reports, P60-249, September 2014, "Detailed Table POV26," <http://www.census.gov/hhes/www/cpstables/032014/pov/toc.htm>, December 2014. See also <http://www.census.gov/hhes/www/poverty/index.html>.

Table 560. Social Security—Covered Employment, Earnings, and Contribution Rates: 1990 to 2014

[164.4 represents 164,400,000. Includes the Island areas of the U.S. Represents all reported employment. Data are estimated. OASDI = Old-age, survivors, and disability insurance; SMI = Supplementary medical insurance. All data are subject to revision by source]

Item	Unit	1990	2000	2005	2009	2010	2011	2012	2013	2014
Workers with insured status [1]	Million	164.4	185.1	194.8	202.9	204.0	205.3	207.3	209.4	211.5
Male	Million	86.8	95.3	99.5	103.0	103.3	103.9	104.8	105.7	106.7
Female	Million	77.6	89.7	95.3	99.9	100.6	101.4	102.5	103.7	104.8
Under 20 years old	Million	4.8	4.9	3.6	3.1	2.5	2.1	2.2	2.4	2.6
Age 20 to 24	Million	16.6	15.9	16.4	16.3	16.0	15.7	15.6	15.4	15.1
Age 25 to 29	Million	20.6	17.5	18.3	19.3	19.3	19.3	19.3	19.4	19.5
Age 30 to 34	Million	21.3	19.2	18.1	18.3	18.7	19.0	19.4	19.6	19.7
Age 35 to 39	Million	19.3	21.2	19.5	18.7	18.3	17.9	17.9	18.1	18.4
Age 40 to 44	Million	17.0	21.4	21.3	19.6	19.6	19.6	19.5	19.2	18.8
Age 45 to 49	Million	12.8	19.1	21.3	21.5	21.2	20.7	20.2	19.8	19.5
Age 50 to 54	Million	10.1	16.5	18.8	20.6	20.9	21.1	21.2	21.2	21.1
Age 55 to 59	Million	8.8	12.2	16.0	17.8	18.3	18.8	19.3	19.7	20.0
Age 60 to 64	Million	8.5	9.3	11.7	14.6	15.4	15.8	16.0	16.5	17.0
Age 65 to 69	Million	8.0	7.8	8.8	10.8	11.1	11.8	12.6	13.1	13.8
Age 70 to 74	Million	6.5	7.0	7.0	7.8	8.0	8.4	8.9	9.4	9.9
Age 75 and older	Million	10.1	12.8	13.8	14.6	14.8	15.1	15.3	15.7	16.0
Workers reported with—										
Taxable earnings [2]	Million	133	155	159	158	157	159	161	163	166
Maximum earnings [2]	Million	8	10	10	9	9	10	10	9	9
Earnings in covered employment [2]	Bil. dol.	2,716	4,841	5,694	6,180	6,312	6,586	6,919	7,118	7,455
Reported taxable [2]	Bil. dol.	2,359	4,008	4,763	5,270	5,307	5,486	5,709	5,937	6,163
Percent of total	Percent	86.8	82.8	83.7	85.3	84.1	83.3	82.5	83.4	82.7
Average per worker:										
Total earnings [2]	Dollars	20,399	31,252	35,768	39,142	40,120	41,432	42,905	43,574	45,017
Taxable earnings [2]	Dollars	17,715	25,875	29,924	33,383	33,732	34,510	35,400	36,342	37,218
Annual maximum taxable earnings [3]	Dollars	51,300	76,200	90,000	106,800	106,800	106,800	110,100	113,700	117,000
Contribution rates for OASDI: [4]										
Each employer and employee	Percent	7.65	7.65	7.65	7.65	7.65	7.65	7.65	7.65	7.65
Self-employed [5]	Percent	15.30	15.30	15.30	15.30	15.30	15.30	15.30	15.30	15.30
SMI, monthly premium (as of Jan. 1)	Dollars	28.60	45.50	78.20	96.40	110.50	115.40	99.90	104.90	104.90

[1] Estimated number fully insured for retirement and/or survivor benefits as of end of year. [2] Includes self-employment. Averages per worker computed with unrounded earnings and worker amounts, and may not agree with rounded table amounts. [3] Beginning in 1994, the upper limit on earnings subject to HI taxes was removed. [4] OASDI tax rates for employees and self-employed workers were reduced by 2 percent for 2011 and 2012. This reduction is being made up by transfers from the General Fund of the Treasury to the OASI and DI trust funds. [5] Half of self-employment tax is deductible for income tax purposes and for computing self-employment income subject to social security tax.

Source: U.S. Social Security Administration, *Annual Statistical Supplement to the Social Security Bulletin,* April 2015, and unpublished data. See also <http://www.ssa.gov/policy/docs/statcomps/supplement/2014/>.

Table 561. Social Security (OASDI)—Benefits by Type of Beneficiary: 1990 to 2014

[39,832 represents 39,832,000. A person eligible to receive more than one type of benefit is generally classified or counted only once as a retired-worker beneficiary. OASDI = Old-age, survivors, and disability insurance. See also headnote, Table 562]

Type of beneficiary	1990	1995	2000	2005	2009	2010	2011	2012	2013	2014
Number of benefits [1] (1,000)	**39,832**	**43,387**	**45,415**	**48,434**	**52,523**	**54,032**	**55,404**	**56,758**	**57,979**	**59,007**
Retired workers [2] (1,000)	24,838	26,673	28,499	30,461	33,514	34,593	35,600	36,720	37,893	39,009
Disabled workers [3] (1,000)	3,011	4,185	5,042	6,519	7,788	8,204	8,576	8,827	8,941	8,955
Wives and husbands [2, 4] (1,000)	3,367	3,290	2,963	2,680	2,502	2,477	2,456	2,443	2,442	2,452
Children (1,000)	3,187	3,734	3,803	4,025	4,231	4,313	4,375	4,419	4,413	4,355
Under age 18	2,497	2,956	2,976	3,130	3,158	3,209	3,245	3,258	3,237	3,166
Disabled children [5]	600	686	729	769	921	949	977	1,007	1,030	1,049
Students [6]	89	92	98	127	152	155	153	154	146	140
Of retired workers	422	442	459	488	561	580	594	612	625	635
Of deceased workers	1,776	1,884	1,878	1,903	1,921	1,913	1,907	1,907	1,899	1,892
Of disabled workers	989	1,409	1,466	1,633	1,748	1,820	1,874	1,900	1,888	1,828
Widowed mothers and fathers [7] (1,000)	304	275	203	178	160	158	158	154	150	143
Widows and widowers [2, 8] (1,000)	5,111	5,226	4,901	4,569	4,327	4,286	4,239	4,193	4,139	4,092
Parents [2] (1,000)	6	4	3	2	2	2	2	1	1	1
Special benefits [9] (1,000)	7	1	(Z)	(Z)	(Z)	(Z)	(Z)	(NA)	(NA)	(NA)
AVERAGE MONTHLY BENEFIT, CURRENT DOLLARS										
Retired workers [2]	603	720	844	1,002	1,164	1,176	1,229	1,262	1,294	1,329
Retired worker and wife [2]	1,027	1,221	1,420	1,660	1,913	1,930	2,019	2,078	2,140	2,209
Disabled workers [3]	587	682	786	938	1,064	1,068	1,111	1,130	1,146	1,165
Wives and husbands [2, 4]	298	354	416	485	556	561	587	605	626	651
Children of retired workers	259	322	395	493	570	577	603	617	632	647
Children of deceased workers	406	469	550	656	747	752	783	799	814	831
Children of disabled workers	164	183	228	279	318	318	330	336	341	349
Widowed mothers and fathers [7]	409	478	595	725	842	849	884	900	918	935
Widows and widowers, nondisabled [2]	556	680	810	967	1,124	1,134	1,185	1,215	1,244	1,276
Parents [2]	482	591	704	851	988	998	1,045	1,073	1,094	1,121
Special benefits [9]	167	192	217	247	276	276	286	(NA)	(NA)	(NA)
AVERAGE MONTHLY BENEFIT, CONSTANT (2014) DOLLARS [10]										
Retired workers [2]	1,058	1,101	1,140	1,196	1,266	1,259	1,278	1,290	1,304	1,329
Retired worker and wife [2]	1,802	1,868	1,916	1,981	2,080	2,068	2,101	2,125	2,157	2,209
Disabled workers [3]	1,030	1,043	1,061	1,119	1,158	1,144	1,155	1,156	1,156	1,165
Wives and husbands [2, 4]	523	542	562	578	605	601	610	619	631	651
Children of deceased workers	713	717	742	783	813	805	815	817	820	831
Widowed mothers and fathers [7]	718	731	803	864	915	909	919	921	925	935
Widows and widowers, nondisabled [2]	976	1,040	1,093	1,153	1,222	1,215	1,233	1,243	1,254	1,276
Number of benefits awarded (1,000)	**3,717**	**3,882**	**4,290**	**4,672**	**5,728**	**5,697**	**5,567**	**5,655**	**5,533**	**5,361**
Retired workers [2]	1,665	1,609	1,961	2,000	2,740	2,634	2,578	2,735	2,794	2,772
Disabled workers [3]	468	646	622	830	971	1,027	999	960	869	779
Wives and husbands [2, 4]	379	322	385	379	429	409	399	420	420	428
Children	695	809	777	908	1,008	1,045	1,017	959	877	810
Widowed mothers and fathers [7]	58	52	40	38	33	32	30	29	27	25
Widows and widowers [2, 8]	452	445	505	517	547	550	545	552	546	547
Parents [2]	(Z)	(Z)	(Z)	(Z)	(Z)	(Z)	(Z)	(Z)	(Z)	(Z)
Special benefits [9]	(Z)	(Z)	(Z)	(Z)	(Z)	(Z)	(Z)	(NA)	(NA)	(NA)
BENEFIT PAYMENTS DURING YEAR (bil. dol.)										
Total [11]	**247.8**	**332.6**	**407.6**	**520.8**	**675.5**	**701.6**	**725.1**	**774.8**	**812.2**	**848.4**
Monthly benefits [12]	247.6	332.4	407.4	520.6	675.3	701.4	724.9	774.6	812.0	848.4
Retired workers [2]	156.8	205.3	253.5	321.7	424.0	443.4	461.2	497.5	528.9	560.1
Disabled workers [3]	22.1	36.6	49.8	78.4	109.5	115.1	119.6	127.2	130.4	132.2
Wives and husbands [2, 4]	14.5	17.9	19.4	20.5	24.2	24.6	24.8	26.0	26.9	28.1
Children	12.0	16.1	19.3	24.5	30.2	30.7	31.2	0.0	32.7	33.0
Under age 18	9.0	11.9	14.1	17.9	21.2	21.4	21.2	22.2	22.2	22.2
Disabled children [5]	2.5	3.6	4.6	5.8	7.8	8.0	8.7	8.9	9.2	9.6
Students [6]	0.5	0.6	0.7	0.8	1.2	1.3	1.3	1.3	1.3	1.3
Of retired workers	1.3	1.7	2.1	2.9	3.9	4.1	4.3	4.6	4.8	5.0
Of deceased workers	8.6	10.7	12.5	15.1	18.1	18.0	18.1	18.8	18.9	19.2
Of disabled workers	2.2	3.7	4.7	6.5	8.2	8.5	8.8	9.1	9.0	8.9
Widowed mothers and fathers [7]	1.4	1.6	1.4	1.5	1.6	1.6	1.6	1.7	1.7	1.6
Widows and widowers [2, 8]	40.7	54.8	63.9	73.4	85.6	86.0	86.5	89.9	91.4	93.2
Parents [2]	(Z)	(Z)	(Z)	(Z)	(Z)	(Z)	(Z)	(Z)	(Z)	(Z)
Special benefits [9]	(Z)	(Z)	(Z)	(Z)	(Z)	(Z)	(Z)	(NA)	(NA)	(NA)
Lump sum	0.2	0.2	0.2	0.2	0.2	0.2	0.2	0.2	0.2	0.2

NA Not available. Z Fewer than 500 or less than $50 million. [1] Number of benefit payments in current-payment status, i.e., actually being made at a specified time with no deductions or with deductions amounting to less than a month's benefit. [2] Age 62 and over. [3] Disabled workers under age 65. [4] Includes wife beneficiaries with entitled children in their care and entitled divorced wives. [5] 18 years old and over. Disability began before age 22. [6] Full-time students aged 18 and 19. [7] Includes surviving divorced mothers with entitled children in their care and widowed fathers with entitled children in their care. [8] Includes widows aged 60–61, surviving divorced wives aged 60 and over, disabled widows and widowers aged 50 and over; and widowers aged 60–61. [9] Benefits for persons aged 72 and over not insured under regular or transitional provisions of Social Security Act. [10] Constant dollar figures are based on the consumer price index (CPI-U) for December as published by the U.S. Bureau of Labor Statistics. [11] Represents total disbursements of benefit checks by the U.S. Department of the Treasury during the years specified. [12] Distribution by type estimated.

Source: U.S. Social Security Administration, *Annual Statistical Supplement to the Social Security Bulletin,* April 2015. See also <http://www.ssa.gov/policy/index.html>.

Table 562. Social Security—Beneficiaries, Annual Payments, and Average Monthly Benefit, 1990 to 2013, and by State and Other Areas, 2014

[39,832 represents 39,832,000. Number of beneficiaries in current-payment status, and annual and average monthly benefit as of December. Data for 1990 to 2005 are based on 10-percent sample of administrative records. All other years are 100 percent data. See also headnote, Table 561]

Year, state, and other area	Number of beneficiaries (1,000)				Annual payments [2] (mil. dol.)				Average monthly benefit (dol.)		
	Total	Retired workers and dependents [1]	Survivors	Disabled workers and dependents	Total	Retired workers and dependents [1]	Survivors	Disabled workers and dependents	Retired workers [3]	Disabled workers	Widows and widowers [4]
1990	39,832	28,369	7,197	4,266	247,796	172,042	50,951	24,803	603	587	557
2000	45,417	31,761	6,981	6,675	407,431	274,645	77,848	54,938	845	787	810
2010	54,032	37,489	6,358	10,184	701,436	471,505	105,740	124,191	1,176	1,068	1,134
2011	55,404	38,486	6,305	10,613	724,943	489,698	106,310	128,935	1,229	1,111	1,185
2012	56,758	39,613	6,256	10,889	774,626	527,402	110,346	136,878	1,262	1,130	1,215
2013	57,979	40,804	6,189	10,988	812,050	559,946	112,032	140,072	1,294	1,146	1,244
Total, 2014 [5, 6]	59,007	41,918	6,790	10,931	848,228	592,616	114,037	141,620	1,329	1,165	1,276
United States	57,510	40,884	6,570	10,681	834,364	584,352	111,296	138,761	(NA)	(NA)	(NA)
Alabama	1,096	677	127	292	15,314	9,402	2,209	3,703	1,304	1,146	1,226
Alaska	89	64	10	15	1,215	851	166	198	1,265	1,148	1,225
Arizona	1,207	906	112	189	17,722	13,049	2,118	2,555	1,356	1,208	1,318
Arkansas	673	425	737	175	9,113	5,743	1,240	2,130	1,262	1,110	1,199
California	5,539	4,151	537	851	78,795	57,114	10,172	11,509	1,307	1,197	1,275
Colorado	795	591	75	128	11,449	8,305	1,447	1,697	1,320	1,182	1,303
Connecticut	655	497	58	99	10,417	7,838	1,232	1,347	1,461	1,212	1,432
Delaware	192	142	18	33	2,973	2,164	351	458	1,424	1,238	1,397
District of Columbia	80	55	8	17	1,058	732	125	201	1,235	1,031	1,103
Florida	4,223	3,170	379	674	60,672	44,652	7,178	8,842	1,321	1,177	1,301
Georgia	1,677	1,145	182	350	23,702	16,003	3,185	4,514	1,311	1,169	1,250
Hawaii	252	202	21	28	3,613	2,838	399	376	1,315	1,193	1,235
Idaho	306	223	29	54	4,285	3,068	544	673	1,294	1,137	1,307
Illinois	2,155	1,570	233	352	32,186	22,880	4,619	4,687	1,361	1,188	1,352
Indiana	1,286	891	139	256	19,337	13,298	2,720	3,319	1,391	1,174	1,375
Iowa	616	458	64	94	8,971	6,546	1,262	1,163	1,329	1,109	1,320
Kansas	522	376	54	92	7,741	5,521	1,057	1,163	1,367	1,140	1,359
Kentucky	954	581	116	257	13,054	7,812	1,999	3,243	1,268	1,138	1,195
Louisiana	854	525	132	198	11,499	6,829	2,244	2,426	1,242	1,126	1,182
Maine	325	223	29	73	4,362	2,954	533	875	1,236	1,085	1,232
Maryland	936	687	93	156	14,133	10,209	1,807	2,117	1,388	1,205	1,327
Massachusetts	1,224	860	109	255	17,908	12,505	2,147	3,256	1,355	1,163	1,330
Michigan	2,122	1,463	222	437	32,591	22,274	4,464	5,853	1,422	1,215	1,390
Minnesota	965	722	88	155	14,317	10,586	1,743	1,988	1,367	1,157	1,334
Mississippi	641	396	79	165	8,583	5,293	1,274	2,016	1,251	1,113	1,163
Missouri	1,246	846	131	270	17,726	11,913	2,399	3,414	1,309	1,136	1,295
Montana	213	158	21	33	2,930	2,122	393	415	1,257	1,102	1,274
Nebraska	326	241	34	51	4,699	3,421	648	630	1,322	1,102	1,308
Nevada	476	358	41	76	6,852	5,019	781	1,052	1,315	1,228	1,313
New Hampshire	284	201	22	61	4,256	3,019	448	789	1,401	1,192	1,384
New Jersey	1,568	1,173	147	249	25,141	18,533	3,067	3,541	1,472	1,280	1,410
New Mexico	400	279	43	79	5,366	3,680	717	969	1,248	1,109	1,186
New York	3,483	2,523	325	635	52,284	37,370	6,416	8,498	1,388	1,200	1,332
North Carolina	1,949	1,364	184	401	27,935	19,441	3,255	5,239	1,327	1,165	1,257
North Dakota	124	92	16	17	1,726	1,231	290	205	1,257	1,080	1,223
Ohio	2,268	1,564	273	431	32,669	22,083	5,231	5,400	1,320	1,126	1,307
Oklahoma	750	506	88	156	10,494	6,985	1,565	1,944	1,290	1,122	1,260
Oregon	798	598	71	129	11,595	8,493	1,405	1,697	1,330	1,164	1,340
Pennsylvania	2,723	1,937	287	499	40,805	28,600	5,708	6,497	1,375	1,168	1,344
Rhode Island	216	152	18	46	3,146	2,222	348	576	1,347	1,135	1,337
South Carolina	1,041	692	104	218	14,961	10,260	1,819	2,882	1,334	1,183	1,247
South Dakota	165	125	18	23	2,265	1,669	315	281	1,252	1,082	1,211
Tennessee	1,372	916	149	307	19,401	12,896	2,619	3,886	1,318	1,137	1,250
Texas	3,842	2,660	466	716	53,527	36,214	8,351	8,962	1,298	1,144	1,235
Utah	366	267	38	60	5,289	3,805	725	759	1,349	1,162	1,368
Vermont	141	101	12	28	2,009	1,438	234	337	1,333	1,097	1,291
Virginia	1,416	1,014	142	259	20,679	14,643	2,653	3,383	1,354	1,173	1,277
Washington	1,230	907	110	214	18,391	13,351	2,206	2,834	1,387	1,180	1,368
West Virginia	465	287	62	115	6,608	3,951	1,134	1,523	1,312	1,182	1,247
Wisconsin	1,153	848	107	198	17,119	12,448	2,137	2,534	1,366	1,159	1,355
Wyoming	101	75	10	16	1,481	1,079	197	205	1,338	1,159	1,332
American Samoa	6	3	1	2	55	24	14	17	875	875	766
Guam	16	11	3	2	156	100	33	23	895	1,025	846
Northern Mariana Islands	3	2	1	(Z)	21	12	6	3	708	776	621
Puerto Rico	846	509	107	229	8,518	4,619	1,303	2,596	888	1,036	782
U.S. Virgin Islands	21	17	2	2	269	210	32	27	1,168	1,180	1,009
Abroad	613	492	106	15	4,845	3,299	1,353	193	694	1,106	1,276

NA Not available. Z Less than 500. [1] Data for 1990-2006 include special benefits for persons aged 72 years and over not insured under regular or transitional provisions of Social Security Act. [2] Unnegotiated checks not deducted. 1990 data include lump-sum payments to survivors of deceased workers. [3] Excludes persons with special benefits. [4] Nondisabled only. [5] Includes those with state or area unknown. [6] 2014 data are preliminary.

Source: U.S. Social Security Administration, *Annual Statistical Supplement to the Social Security Bulletin*, April 2015 and earlier reports. See also <http://www.ssa.gov/policy/index.html>.

Table 563. Social Security Trust Funds: 1995 to 2014

[In billions of dollars (342.8 represents $342,800,000,000)]

Type of trust fund	1995	2000	2005	2009	2010	2011	2012	2013	2014
OLD-AGE AND SURVIVORS INSURANCE (OASI)									
Total income [1]	342.8	490.5	604.3	698.2	677.1	698.8	731.1	743.8	769.4
Net payroll tax contributions	304.7	421.4	506.9	570.4	544.8	482.4	503.9	620.8	646.2
Taxation of benefits	5.5	11.6	13.8	19.9	22.1	22.2	26.7	20.7	28.0
Interest received [2]	32.8	57.5	84.0	107.9	108.2	106.5	102.8	98.1	94.8
Total expenditures [1]	297.8	358.3	441.9	564.3	584.9	603.8	645.5	679.5	714.2
Benefit payments [3]	291.6	352.7	435.4	557.2	577.4	596.2	637.9	672.1	706.8
Assets, end of year	458.5	931.0	1,663.0	2,336.8	2,429.0	2,524.1	2,609.7	2,674.0	2,729.2
DISABILITY INSURANCE (DI)									
Total income [1]	56.7	77.9	97.4	109.3	104.0	106.3	109.1	111.2	114.9
Net payroll tax contributions	54.4	71.1	86.1	96.9	92.5	81.9	85.6	105.4	109.7
Taxation of benefits	0.3	0.7	1.1	2.0	1.9	1.6	0.6	0.4	1.7
Interest received [2]	2.2	6.9	10.3	10.5	9.3	7.9	6.4	4.7	3.4
Total expenditures [1]	42.1	56.8	88.0	121.5	127.7	132.3	140.3	143.5	145.1
Benefit payments [3]	40.9	55.0	85.4	118.3	124.2	128.9	136.9	140.1	141.7
Assets, end of year	37.6	118.5	195.6	203.6	179.9	153.9	122.7	90.4	60.2

[1] Includes other income or expenses not shown separately. [2] Includes relatively small amounts of gifts to the fund. [3] Includes payments for vocational rehabilitation services furnished to disabled persons receiving benefits because of their disabilities. Amounts reflect deductions for unnegotiated benefit checks.

Source: U.S. Social Security Administration, Office of the Chief Actuary, "Statistical Tables," <http://www.ssa.gov/oact/STATS/index.html>, accessed May 2015.

Table 564. Retirement Employee Benefit Participation by Worker Characteristics: 2010 to 2014

[In percent. Based on National Compensation Survey. The March 2014 NCS obtained data from 9,622 private industry establishments, representing over 109 million workers; see Appendix III. Defined benefit plans provide retirement benefits based on employer benefit formulas that may take into account salary, years of service, and age. Defined contribution plans provide benefits based on employer and employee contributions to individual employee accounts and the rate of return on money invested; the retirement benefit depends on the account balance at retirement. See source for more information]

Characteristic	Total [1]				Defined benefit				Defined contribution			
	2010	2012	2013	2014	2010	2012	2013	2014	2010	2012	2013	2014
All workers	**50**	**48**	**49**	**48**	**19**	**17**	**16**	**16**	**41**	**41**	**42**	**42**
Management, professional, and related	68	68	68	67	25	24	23	23	60	61	61	61
Service	23	21	21	21	7	6	6	6	18	16	17	17
Sales and office	53	51	51	49	16	14	14	13	46	45	46	45
Natural resources, construction, and maintenance	51	51	53	53	26	23	23	23	40	42	44	44
Production, transportation, and material moving	51	50	51	53	24	21	20	20	38	38	39	42
Full-time	59	59	59	58	22	20	19	19	50	51	51	52
Part-time	21	19	20	19	8	7	7	6	15	14	15	15
Union	82	85	86	83	67	66	68	66	44	45	44	45
Nonunion	46	45	45	45	13	12	11	11	41	41	42	42

[1] Total is less than the sum of the individual retirement items because many employees participated in both types of plans.

Source: U.S. Bureau of Labor Statistics, *National Compensation Survey: Employee Benefits in the United States, March 2014*, September 2014. See also <http://www.bls.gov/ncs/ebs/benefits>.

Table 565. Percent of U.S. Households Owning Individual Retirement Accounts (IRAs): 2000 to 2014

[Prior to 2014, incidence of individual retirement account (IRA) ownership is based on an annual tracking survey of approximately 4,000 randomly selected, representative U.S. households conducted via landline telephones only. For 2014, the survey was expanded and is based on a dual frame sample of landline and cell phone numbers, for a total of approximately 6,000 U.S. households. See source for details]

Year and characteristic	Any type of IRA [1]	Traditional IRA	Roth IRA	Employer-sponsored IRA [2]	Year and characteristic	Any type of IRA [1]	Traditional IRA	Roth IRA	Employer-sponsored IRA [2]
2000	35.7	28.7	9.2	6.8	2012	40.4	32.5	16.8	7.6
2005	37.9	30.0	12.8	7.4	2013	37.6	29.4	15.6	7.5
2006	38.3	31.7	13.4	7.7	**2014, total** [3, 4]	**33.7**	**25.3**	**15.6**	**6.0**
2007	39.8	32.5	14.9	7.9	Under 35 years	28.0	16.0	16.0	5.0
2008	40.5	32.1	15.9	8.6	35 to 44 years	34.0	22.0	20.0	8.0
2009	39.3	31.2	14.5	8.2	45 to 54 years	36.0	28.0	19.0	6.0
2010	41.4	32.8	16.6	8.0	55 to 64 years	37.0	30.0	16.0	7.0
2011	38.8	31.2	15.7	7.5	65 years and over	34.0	30.0	10.0	5.0

[1] Excludes ownership of Coverdell Education Savings Accounts, which were referred to as Education IRAs before July 2001. [2] Employer-sponsored IRAs include SEP IRAs, SARSEP IRAs, and SIMPLE IRAs. [3] Lower incidence in 2014 likely results in part from a revised sampling methodology. See source for details. [4] Age is based on the age of the sole or co-decision maker for household saving and investing.

Source: Investment Company Institute, Washington, DC, Holden, Sarah, and Daniel Schrass, "Appendix: Additional Data on IRA Ownership in 2014," ICI Research Perspective 21, No. 1A, January 2015 ©. See also <www.ici.org/pdf/per21-01a.pdf>.

Table 566. State and Local Government Retirement Systems—Beneficiaries and Finances: Fiscal Years 1990 to 2013

[In billions of dollars (111.3 represents $111,300,000,000), except as indicated. For fiscal years closed during the 12 months ending June 30. Minus sign (-) indicates negative earnings on investment. Based on the Annual Survey of Public Pensions]

Year and level of government	Number of beneficiaries (1,000)	Receipts					Benefits and withdrawals			Cash and security holdings
		Total [1]	Employee contributions	Government contributions		Earnings on investments	Total [1]	Benefits	Withdrawals	
				State	Local					
1990: All systems	4,026	111.3	13.9	14.0	18.6	64.9	38.4	36.0	2.4	721
State-administered	3,232	89.2	11.6	14.0	11.5	52.0	29.6	27.6	2.0	575
Locally administered	794	22.2	2.2	(Z)	7.0	12.9	8.8	8.4	0.4	145
2000: All systems	6,292	297.0	25.0	17.5	22.6	231.9	95.7	91.3	4.4	2,169
State-administered	4,786	247.4	20.7	17.2	16.7	192.8	76.0	72.2	3.8	1,798
Locally administered	1,506	49.7	4.3	0.4	5.9	39.1	19.8	19.1	0.7	371
2010: All systems	8,271	125.8	39.3	36.2	50.3	347.5	216.5	200.6	4.2	2,671
State-administered	7,020	98.0	33.2	35.6	29.2	291.1	176.5	163.4	3.5	2,218
Locally administered	1,252	27.9	6.1	0.6	21.2	56.5	40.0	37.2	0.7	453
2013: All systems	9,296	153.8	45.1	45.9	62.8	383.3	260.8	242.9	5.5	3,287
State-administered	7,913	119.2	37.5	45.1	36.6	315.7	213.4	199.1	4.5	2,726
Locally administered	1,383	34.6	7.6	0.8	26.1	67.5	47.4	43.7	1.0	561

Z Less than 50 million. [1] May include items not shown separately.

Source: U.S. Census Bureau, through 1995, *Finances of Employee-Retirement Systems of State and Local Governments*, Series GF, No. 2, annual; and beginning 2000, "Federal, State, and Local Governments—Survey of Public Pensions: State & Local Data," <http://www.census.gov/govs/retire/index.html>, accessed March 2015.

Table 567. Defined Benefit Retirement Plan Participation Among Workers by Plan Status: 2014

[In percent. All workers participating in defined benefit plans = 100 percent. Based on the March 2014 National Compensation Survey; survey drew responses from 9,622 private industry establishments of all sizes, representing approximately 109 million workers. Excludes farm and private households, the self-employed, Federal government, and establishments with no workers in the survey scope. For more information, see Appendix III, and source <http://www.bls.gov/ncs/ebs/home.htm>]

Characteristics	Open plans [1]	Frozen plans [2]			Workers in plans frozen over 5 years
		No participants accrue benefits [3]	All participants accrue benefits	Some participants accrue benefits	
All workers	**68**	**9**	**21**	**2**	**58**
OCCUPATION					
Management, professional, and related	62	10	26	1	61
Management, business, and financial	59	13	27	2	58
Professional and related	65	8	26	1	64
Service	86	(S)	10	(S)	51
Protective service	57	(S)	27	(S)	59
Sales and office	63	14	20	2	43
Sales and related	60	16	21	4	56
Office and administrative support	64	14	20	2	39
Natural resources, construction, and maintenance	81	4	13	2	59
Construction, extraction, farming, fishing, and forestry	95	(S)	3	(S)	73
Installation, maintenance, and repair	67	8	22	3	57
Production, transportation, and material moving	71	7	20	2	74
Production	63	(S)	26	(S)	78
Transportation and material moving	78	5	15	1	69
WORK STATUS					
Full time	68	10	21	2	58
Part time	76	(S)	19	(S)	61
UNION STATUS					
Union	84	(S)	14	(S)	56
Nonunion	60	13	25	2	59
AVERAGE WAGE PERCENTILE: [4]					
Lowest 25 percent	73	(S)	18	(S)	(S)
Lowest 10 percent	78	(S)	18	(S)	32
Second 25 percent	70	11	17	2	50
Third 25 percent	70	10	19	2	61
Highest 25 percent	66	8	24	2	61
Highest 10 percent	60	10	29	1	64
INDUSTRY					
Goods-producing industries	68	8	23	2	69
Manufacturing	58	10	29	2	68
Service-providing industries	69	10	20	2	55
Trade, transportation, and utilities	72	(S)	23	(S)	65
Information	38	(S)	40	(S)	57
Financial activities	55	22	20	3	40
Professional and business services	73	(S)	20	(S)	71
Education and health services	77	(S)	15	(S)	51

S No workers in this category or data do not meet publication standards. [1] Plans open to new participants. [2] New employees are not allowed in the plan. Benefit accruals may continue for existing participants. [3] Participants in these plans stop accruing benefits on the date the plan is frozen. The benefit the employee receives is calculated as of the day the plan was frozen. [4] The percentiles were computed using earnings and scheduled hours of work reported for individual workers in sampled establishment jobs. For more information, and values, see "Technical Note" in source.

Source: U.S. Bureau of Labor Statistics, *National Compensation Survey: Employee Benefits in the United States, March 2014*, September 2014, Bulletin 2779. See also <http://www.bls.gov/ncs/ebs/>.

Table 568. Defined Benefit Retirement Plans—Selected Features: 2013

[In percent. All workers participating in defined benefit plans = 100 percent. As of March. Covers full-time employees in private industry. Based on approximately 2,500 private industry establishments participating in the 2013 National Compensation Survey, representing approximately 107.2 million workers; see Appendix III. For definitions of retirement benefit formulas, see source <http://www.bls.gov/ncs/ebs/glossary20132014.htm>. For definition of defined benefit, see headnote, Table 569]

| Characteristics | Tradi-tional | Traditional plan formula | | | | Non-traditional | Non-traditional plan formula | |
		Percent of terminal earnings	Percent of career earnings	Dollar times years [1]	Percent of employer contri-bution		Cash balance	Pension equity
WORKER CHARACTERISTICS								
All workers....................	**68**	**37**	**(S)**	**21**	**(S)**	**32**	**30**	**(S)**
Management, professional, and related........	60	49	(S)	(S)	(S)	40	38	(S)
Service..................	79	37	(S)	(S)	(S)	21	19	(S)
Sales and office.....................	58	28	7	22	(S)	42	42	(S)
Natural resources, construction, and maintenance.....................	88	(S)	(S)	43	23	12	12	(S)
Production, transportation, and material moving...........................	81	35	(S)	41	(S)	19	17	(S)
Full time..............................	67	39	(S)	18	(S)	33	31	(S)
Part time..............................	82	22	(S)	54	(S)	18	17	(S)
Union.................................	91	26	(S)	51	(S)	9	8	(S)
Nonunion.............................	55	44	(S)	3	(S)	45	43	(S)
ESTABLISHMENT CHARACTERISTICS								
Goods producing industries.....................	79	38	(S)	31	(S)	21	20	(S)
Service providing industries.....................	65	37	(S)	18	(S)	35	33	(S)
1 to 99 workers.....................	71	37	(S)	22	(S)	29	29	(S)
100 workers or more...........................	67	37	(S)	21	(S)	33	31	(S)

S No data were reported or data do not meet publication criteria. [1] Benefits are based on a dollar amount per month for each year of service recognized by the plan.

Source: U.S. Bureau of Labor Statistics, *National Compensation Survey: Health and Retirement Plan Provisions in Private Industry in the United States, 2013*, August 2014, Bulletin 2778. See also <http://www.bls.gov/ncs/ebs/detailedprovisions/2013/ownership/private/home.htm>.

Table 569. Private Pension Plans—Summary by Type of Plan: 2000 to 2012

[In units as indicated (735.7 represents 735,700). "Pension plan" is defined by the Employee Retirement Income Security Act (ERISA) as "any plan, fund, or program which was heretofore or is hereafter established or maintained by an employer or an employee organization, or by both, to the extent that such plan (a) provides retirement income to employees, or (b) results in a deferral of income by employees for periods extending to the termination of covered employment or beyond, regardless of the method of calculating the contributions made to the plan, the method of calculating the benefits under the plan, or the method of distributing benefits from the plan." A defined benefit plan provides a definite benefit formula for calculating benefit amounts—such as a flat amount per year of service or a percentage of salary times years of service. A defined contribution plan is a pension plan in which the contributions are made to an individual account for each employee. The retirement benefit is dependent upon the account balance at retirement. The balance depends upon amounts contributed, investment outcomes, and, in the case of profit sharing plans, amounts which may be allocated to the account due to forfeitures by terminating employees. Employee Stock Ownership Plans (ESOP) and 401(k) plans are included among defined contribution plans. Data are based on Form 5500 series reports filed with the U.S. Department of Labor and exclude (1) selected pension plans qualified under sections 403(b), 457(b) and 457(f) of the Internal Revenue Code, (2) most SARSEP, SEP and SIMPLE IRA plans, (3) unfunded excess benefit plans, (4) selected church plans, (5) top hat plans, (6) individual retirement accounts (IRAs), and (7) governmental plans]

| Item | Unit | Total | | | | Defined contribution plan | | | | Defined benefit plan | | | |
		2000	2005	2010	2012	2000	2005	2010	2012	2000	2005	2010	2012
Number of plans [1].........	1,000	735.7	679.1	701.0	676.6	686.9	631.5	654.5	633.0	48.8	47.6	46.5	43.6
Total participants [2]........	Million	103.3	117.4	129.7	130.6	61.7	75.5	88.3	90.8	41.6	41.9	41.4	39.8
Active participants [3].....	Million	73.1	82.7	90.6	91.2	50.9	62.4	73.4	75.4	22.2	20.3	17.2	15.7
Assets [4]...................	Bil. dol	4,203	5,062	6,282	6,966	2,216	2,808	3,833	4,264	1,986	2,254	2,448	2,702
Contributions [5]............	Bil. dol	231.9	341.4	445.3	481.2	198.5	248.8	314.3	352.8	33.4	92.7	131.1	128.4
Benefits [6]..................	Bil. dol	341.0	354.5	456.9	531.5	213.5	218.0	287.3	333.8	127.5	136.6	169.6	197.6

[1] Excludes all plans covering only one participant. [2] Includes active, retired, and separated vested participants not yet in pay status. Also includes double counting of workers in more than one plan. [3] Includes any workers currently in employment covered by a plan and who are earning or retaining credited service under a plan. Also includes any nonvested former employees who have not yet incurred breaks in service. [4] Asset amounts shown exclude funds held by life insurance companies under allocated group insurance contracts for payment of retirement benefits. These excluded funds make up roughly 10 to 15 percent of total private fund assets. [5] Includes both employer and employee contributions. [6] Includes benefits paid directly from trust and premium payments made from plans to insurance carriers. Excludes benefits paid directly by insurance carriers.

Source: U.S. Department of Labor, Employee Benefits Security Administration, "Research Program, Pension Plan Bulletins and Form 5500 Data," <http://www.dol.gov/ebsa/publications/research.html>, accessed March 2015.

Table 570. Characteristics of U.S. Households Owning Individual Retirement Accounts (IRAs): 2014

[Prior to 2014, incidence of individual retirement account (IRA) ownership is based on an annual tracking survey of approximately 4,000 randomly selected, representative U.S. households conducted via landline telephones only. For 2014, the survey was expanded and is based on a dual frame sample of landline and cell phone numbers, for a total of approximately 6,000 U.S. households. See source for details]

| Characteristic | Unit | Households owning IRAs | | | | House-holds not own-ing IRAs |
		Total [1]	Tradi-tional IRA	Roth IRA	Employer-spon-sored [1]	
MEDIAN PER HOUSEHOLD						
Age of household sole or co-decision maker for investing..........	Years	52	54	48	52	50
Household income [2]........	Dollars	80,500	82,000	87,500	87,500	38,000
Household financial assets [3]........	Dollars	200,000	250,000	200,000	200,000	35,000
Household financial assets in all types of IRAs........	Dollars	50,000	72,500	50,000	92,500	(X)
Share of household financial assets in type of IRA indicated.......	Percent	38	32	13	19	(X)
PERCENT OF HOUSEHOLDS						
Household has defined contribution account or defined benefit plan coverage (total) [4]........	Percent	85	85	88	84	43
Defined contribution retirement plan account........	Percent	78	77	83	81	33
Defined benefit plan coverage........	Percent	40	42	37	33	22
Types of IRAs owned: [4]						
Traditional IRA........	Percent	75	100	58	56	(X)
Roth IRA........	Percent	46	36	100	42	(X)
Employer-sponsored IRA [1]........	Percent	18	13	16	100	(X)

X Not applicable. [1] Employer-sponsored IRAs include SEP IRAs, SAR-SEP IRAs, and SIMPLE IRAs. [2] Total reported is household income before taxes in 2013. [3] Household financial assets include assets in employer-sponsored retirement plans but exclude the household's primary residence. [4] Multiple responses are included.

Source: Investment Company Institute, Washington, DC. Holden, Sarah, and Daniel Schrass, "Appendix: Additional Data on IRA Ownership in 2014," ICI Research Perspective 21, No. 1A, January 2015 ©. See also <www.ici.org/pdf/per21-01a.pdf>.

Table 571. Percent Distribution of Assets in Individual Retirement Accounts (IRAs) by Type of IRA: 2013 and 2014

[Prior to 2014, incidence of individual retirement account (IRA) ownership is based on an annual tracking survey of approximately 4,000 randomly selected, representative U.S. households conducted via landline telephones only. For 2014, the survey was expanded and is based on a dual frame sample of landline and cell phone numbers, for a total of approximately 6,000 U.S. households. See source for details]

| Assets by type of IRA | Unit | 2013 | | | 2014 | | |
| | | Total assets in IRAs | Type of IRA owned | | Total assets in IRAs | Type of IRA owned | |
			Traditional IRAs	Roth IRAs		Traditional IRAs	Roth IRAs
PERCENT DISTRIBUTION OF ASSETS IN IRAs							
Less than $10,000........	Percent	18	17	30	20	17	32
$10,000 to $24,999........	Percent	17	18	25	15	16	21
$25,000 to $49,999........	Percent	14	14	16	12	12	15
$50,000 to $99,999........	Percent	18	17	15	17	18	14
$100,000 to $249,999........	Percent	17	18	9	18	18	12
$250,000 or more........	Percent	16	16	5	18	19	6
TOTAL ASSETS IN IRAs							
Mean........	Dollars	135,000	132,600	58,400	153,000	151,600	69,400
Median........	Dollars	50,000	50,000	20,000	50,000	60,000	20,000

Source: Investment Company Institute, Washington, DC. Holden, Sarah, and Daniel Schrass, "Appendix: Additional Data on IRA Ownership in 2014," ICI Research Perspective 21, No. 1A, January 2015 ©. See also <www.ici.org/pdf/per21-01a.pdf>.

Table 572. Defined Contribution 401(k) Plans—Participants, Assets, Contributions, and Benefits by Type of Plan: 2012

[Participants in thousands (74,881 represents 74,881,000); values in millions of dollars (3,530,122 represents $3,530,122,000,000). Based on Form 5500 filings with Department of Labor]

Type of plan [1]	Total plans [2]	Total participants (1,000) [3]	Total assets (mil. dol.)	Total contributions (mil. dol.) [4]	Total benefits (mil. dol.) [5]
Total........	**516,293**	**74,881**	**3,530,122**	**306,092**	**284,677**
Profit sharing and thrift-savings........	513,922	73,681	3,462,705	301,471	278,867
Stock bonus........	191	526	43,983	2,730	4,227
Target benefit........	30	1	31	3	3
Money purchase........	570	280	13,114	905	844
Annuity—403(b)(1)........	682	186	5,839	487	397
Custodial account—403(b)(7)........	340	85	1,481	186	111
Other defined contribution........	558	121	2,968	310	229

[1] About 1 percent of defined contribution plans report more than one plan type. [2] Excludes plans covering only one participant. [3] Includes active, retired, and separated vested participants not yet in pay status. [4] Includes both employer and employee contributions. [5] Amounts shown include benefits paid directly from trust funds and premium payments made by plans to insurance carriers.

Source: U.S. Department of Labor, Employee Benefits Security Administration, *Private Pension Plan Bulletin: Abstract of 2012 Form 5500 Annual Reports,* January 2015. See also <http://www.dol.gov/ebsa/publications/research.html>.

Table 573. State Unemployment Insurance—Summary: 1990 to 2013

[In units as indicated (2,522 represents 2,522,000). Includes unemployment compensation for state and local government employees where covered by state law]

Item	Unit	1990	1995	2000	2005	2009	2010	2011	2012	2013
Insured unemployment, average weekly	1,000	2,522	2,572	2,110	2,661	5,724	4,487	3,681	3,297	2,947
Percent of covered employment [1]	Percent	2.4	2.3	1.7	2.1	4.5	3.6	2.9	2.5	2.2
Percent of civilian unemployed	Percent	35.8	34.7	37.1	35.1	40.1	30.3	26.8	26.4	25.7
Unemployment benefits, average weekly	Dollars	162	187	221	267	309	299	296	303	310
Percent of weekly wage	Percent	36.0	35.5	32.9	34.6	35.8	33.7	32.4	32.4	32.8
Weeks compensated	Million	116.0	118.3	96.0	121.2	266.0	203.1	165.5	147.6	132.2
Beneficiaries, first payments	1,000	8,629	8,035	7,033	7,917	14,173	10,727	9,475	8,662	7,819
Average duration of benefits [2]	Weeks	13.4	14.7	13.7	15.3	18.8	18.9	17.5	17.0	16.9
Claimants exhausting benefits	1,000	2,323	2,662	2,144	2,856	7,530	6,365	4,837	4,228	3,689
Percent of first payment [3]	Percent	29.4	34.3	31.8	35.9	55.3	53.4	48.8	47.2	44.6
Contributions collected [4]	Bil. dol.	15.2	22.0	19.9	34.8	28.2	35.9	44.1	50.5	47.4
Benefits paid	Bil. dol.	17.3	20.1	19.4	29.3	75.9	53.8	43.2	39.8	36.5
Unemployment trust fund reserves [5]	Bil. dol.	38.4	35.4	54.1	29.0	11.1	9.5	11.3	16.7	23.0
Average employer tax rate [6]	Percent	1.95	2.44	1.75	2.86	2.29	3.00	3.40	3.50	3.26

[1] Insured unemployment as percent of average covered employment. [2] Weeks compensated during the year divided by the number of first payments. May include more than one period of continuous unemployment. [3] Based on first payments for 12-month period ending June 30. [4] Contributions collected through unemployment taxes paid by employers and by employees in states that tax workers. [5] Reserves as of December 31 are the funds on deposit in a State's account - as reported by the U.S. Treasury. Trust fund balances are the major portion of reserves. The reserves for all States have been adjusted to contain amounts loaned or advanced from the Federal Unemployment Account. These advances, which can be used only for the payment of unemployment benefits, must be repaid. [6] As percent of taxable wages.

Source: U.S. Department of Labor, Employment and Training Administration, "Unemployment Insurance Financial Data Handbook," <https://ows.doleta.gov/unemploy/hb394.asp>, accessed March 2015.

Table 574. State Unemployment Insurance by State and Island Area: 2013

[In units, as indicated (7,819 represents 7,819,000). See headnote, Table 573. For state data on insured unemployment, see Table 648]

State and Island areas	Beneficiaries, first payments (1,000)	Benefits paid (mil. dol.)	Avg. weekly unemployment benefits (dol.)	Average duration of benefits (weeks)	State and Island areas	Beneficiaries, first payments (1,000)	Benefits paid (mil. dol.)	Avg. weekly unemployment benefits (dol.)	Average duration of benefits (weeks)
Total	7,819	36,454	310	16.9	MT	27	114	290	17.6
AL	87	273	207	15.8	NE	34	105	276	12.6
AK	34	141	250	19.4	NV	83	426	308	17.3
AZ	103	332	221	16.0	NH	25	100	287	15.2
AR	75	259	289	15.0	NJ	333	2,177	398	18.9
CA	1,167	5,725	301	18.3	NM	39	221	303	18.7
CO	108	548	356	14.8	NY	570	2,808	308	18.9
CT	146	731	345	18.1	NC	211	862	290	17.4
DE	21	107	245	20.2	ND	19	100	396	12.0
DC	28	144	299	18.8	OH	232	1,100	318	16.5
FL	226	949	231	19.2	OK	53	246	293	16.6
GA	228	622	267	11.3	OR	114	667	316	18.5
HI	32	199	424	16.6	PA	443	2,482	360	17.7
ID	46	131	264	12.5	RI	37	200	351	16.4
IL	400	2,076	324	17.9	SC	83	249	248	12.7
IN	142	526	243	15.6	SD	7	30	276	14.6
IA	94	401	337	13.7	TN	127	448	235	15.0
KS	66	248	341	16.1	TX	450	2,166	341	16.0
KY	71	408	292	22.0	UT	50	196	345	13.3
LA	62	195	207	15.3	VT	21	77	313	13.8
ME	39	151	285	15.0	VA	124	555	295	16.1
MD	134	696	329	17.3	WA	195	1,067	387	16.2
MA	227	1,467	424	17.3	WV	52	214	275	15.9
MI	297	1,086	293	13.6	WI	214	783	276	15.9
MN	139	742	376	17.2	WY	15	75	359	15.4
MS	58	161	194	15.7	PR	88	211	119	20.4
MO	138	443	242	14.7	VI	3	14	337	19.4

Source: U.S. Department of Labor, Employment and Training Administration, "Unemployment Insurance Financial Data Handbook," <http://www.ows.doleta.gov/unemploy/hb394.asp>, accessed March 2015.

Table 575. Workers' Compensation Payments: 2000 to 2013

[In units as indicated (127.1 represents 127,100,000). See headnote, Table 576]

Item	2000	2005	2006	2007	2008	2009	2010	2011	2012	2013
Workers covered (mil.)................	127.1	128.2	130.3	131.7	130.6	124.9	124.5	125.8	127.9	129.6
Covered wages (bil. dol.)...............	4.5	5.2	5.5	5.9	6.0	5.7	5.8	6.0	6.3	6.5
Employer costs [1] (bil. dol.)............	**60.7**	**89.8**	**87.5**	**86.5**	**80.6**	**73.9**	**72.5**	**77.8**	**83.1**	**88.5**
Private carriers [1]......................	36.0	51.0	51.6	52.3	47.3	43.0	42.3	46.2	50.7	54.9
State funds...........................	8.9	18.2	15.7	13.9	12.2	10.6	9.8	9.9	10.5	11.8
Federal programs [2]..................	3.6	4.1	4.1	4.2	4.3	4.1	4.2	4.4	4.5	4.5
Self-insured employers...............	12.1	16.5	16.0	16.1	16.7	16.3	16.2	17.3	17.5	17.3
Benefits paid [3] (bil. dol.)............	**47.7**	**57.1**	**54.9**	**56.4**	**58.8**	**58.8**	**58.9**	**60.9**	**63.0**	**63.6**
By private carriers....................	26.9	29.0	27.9	29.4	30.7	31.3	31.6	32.7	34.4	35.3
From state funds......................	7.4	11.1	10.6	10.2	10.3	9.9	9.7	9.8	10.0	9.6
Federal programs [2]..................	3.0	3.3	3.3	3.3	3.4	3.5	3.7	3.8	3.8	3.7
Self-insured employers...............	10.5	13.7	13.1	13.5	14.3	14.0	13.9	14.6	14.9	15.0
Type of benefit:										
Medical...............................	20.9	26.4	26.2	27.1	29.0	28.6	29.3	30.5	31.5	31.5
Cash.................................	26.8	30.7	28.7	29.3	29.8	30.2	29.6	30.4	31.5	32.0
Per $100 of covered wages: (dol.)										
Employer costs.......................	1.35	1.72	1.58	1.48	1.35	1.30	1.25	1.29	1.32	1.37
Benefits paid.........................	1.06	1.09	0.99	0.96	0.99	1.04	1.01	1.01	1.00	0.98

[1] Costs are employer expenditures in the calendar year for workers' compensation benefits, administrative costs, and/or insurance premiums; for private carriers, includes benefit payments made under deductible provisions. [2] Federal costs and benefits include costs to the federal government and benefits paid, under the Federal Employees' Compensation Act, and costs associated with and benefits paid via the Federal Black Lung Disability Trust Fund. Data for 1997-2012 also account for the Longshore and Harbor Workers' Compensation Act. [3] Benefits are payments in the calendar year to injured workers and to providers of their medical care, including benefits paid by employers under deductible provisions in their workers' compensation insurance.

Source: National Academy of Social Insurance, Washington, DC, *Workers' Compensation: Benefits, Coverage, and Costs, 2013*, August 2015, and earlier reports ©. See also <http://www.nasi.org>.

Table 576. Workers' Compensation Payments by State: 2000 to 2013

[In millions of dollars (47,699 represents $47,699,000,000). Calendar-year data. Workers' compensation provides medical care, rehabilitation, and cash benefits for workers who are injured on the job or who contract work-related illnesses. It also pays benefits to families of workers who die of work-related causes. Workers' compensation benefits are paid by private insurance carriers, by state or federal workers' compensation funds, or by self-insured employers. See source for data estimation methodology]

State	2000	2005	2010	2012	2013	State	2000	2005	2010	2012	2013
Total....................	47,699	57,067	58,916	63,030	63,574	Montana...................	155	227	266	249	247
Alabama..................	529	620	629	650	639	Nebraska..................	230	306	316	300	305
Alaska....................	139	183	222	248	253	Nevada...................	347	457	430	367	359
Arizona...................	498	571	702	755	752	New Hampshire...........	177	229	252	225	215
Arkansas.................	214	227	214	207	202	New Jersey...............	1,378	1,702	2,067	2,246	2,239
California.................	9,449	10,868	10,102	11,508	12,100	New Mexico..............	144	259	276	306	267
Colorado.................	810	932	800	880	859	New York................	2,761	3,378	4,617	5,371	5,544
Connecticut..............	638	720	795	920	950	North Carolina...........	865	1,382	1,357	1,569	1,569
Delaware.................	118	215	212	217	240	North Dakota.............	70	82	120	151	194
District of Columbia......	78	92	105	91	102	Ohio.....................	2,099	2,447	2,209	2,169	2,070
Florida...................	2,577	3,474	2,777	3,085	3,131	Oklahoma................	485	638	843	923	878
Georgia..................	965	1,409	1,459	1,575	1,566	Oregon..................	425	555	681	663	669
Hawaii...................	231	251	242	248	260	Pennsylvania............	2,379	2,741	2,910	2,910	2,966
Idaho....................	114	243	240	237	252	Rhode Island............	127	137	160	171	162
Illinois...................	1,944	2,419	3,003	2,953	2,923	South Carolina..........	515	925	891	905	878
Indiana..................	545	569	599	653	674	South Dakota...........	63	86	100	87	94
Iowa.....................	343	487	563	659	669	Tennessee..............	774	862	781	838	808
Kansas..................	323	390	405	428	387	Texas...................	2,160	1,597	1,491	1,838	1,768
Kentucky................	584	703	663	686	698	Utah....................	172	257	275	283	282
Louisiana................	547	705	802	854	870	Vermont.................	101	122	137	139	142
Maine...................	245	281	252	246	248	Virginia.................	597	852	786	980	953
Maryland................	641	784	954	971	945	Washington.............	1,527	1,848	2,309	2,311	2,332
Massachusetts...........	801	922	1,016	982	1,062	West Virginia...........	661	765	543	476	436
Michigan................	1,474	1,474	1,272	1,189	1,134	Wisconsin...............	765	1,170	1,072	1,124	1,126
Minnesota...............	798	949	1,035	1,042	1,065	Wyoming................	89	117	154	162	192
Mississippi..............	293	290	338	336	333						
Missouri.................	780	892	801	869	874	Federal, total [1]..........	2,957	3,258	3,672	3,776	3,691

[1] Federal benefits include: those paid under the Federal Employees' Compensation Act for civilian employees; the portion of the black lung benefit program that is financed by employers; and a portion of benefits under the Longshore and Harbor Workers' Compensation Act (LHWCA) that are not reflected in state data, namely, benefits paid by self-insured employers and by special funds under the LHWCA. See Appendix H in source for more information about federal programs.

Source: National Academy of Social Insurance, Washington, DC, *Workers' Compensation: Benefits, Coverage, and Costs, 2013*, August 2015, and earlier reports ©. See also <http://www.nasi.org>.

Table 577. Supplemental Security Income—Recipients and Payments: 1990 to 2013

[Recipients in thousands (4,817 represents 4,817,000); payments in millions of dollars (16,133 represents $16,133,000,000); except as noted. Recipients and monthly payment as of December. Total payments for calendar year. Data cover federal SSI payments and/or state supplementation]

Program	Unit	1990	1995	2000	2005	2009	2010	2011	2012	2013
Recipients, total.............	1,000	4,817	6,514	6,602	7,114	7,677	7,912	8,113	8,263	8,363
Aged.............................	1,000	1,454	1,446	1,289	1,214	1,186	1,184	1,182	1,156	1,157
Blind.............................	1,000	84	84	79	75	69	69	69	68	68
Disabled........................	1,000	3,279	4,984	5,234	5,825	6,421	6,659	6,862	7,039	7,139
Payments, total [1].............	Mil. dol.	16,133	27,037	30,672	37,236	46,592	48,195	49,520	52,075	53,900
Aged.............................	Mil. dol.	3,559	4,239	4,540	4,965	5,569	5,454	5,431	5,486	5,592
Blind.............................	Mil. dol.	329	367	386	414	427	423	422	427	432
Disabled........................	Mil. dol.	12,245	22,431	25,746	31,857	40,597	42,317	43,667	46,162	47,875
Average monthly payment, total...............	Dollars	276	335	379	439	499	501	502	519	529
Aged.............................	Dollars	208	250	300	360	399	400	398	409	417
Blind.............................	Dollars	319	355	413	475	520	522	520	532	542
Disabled........................	Dollars	303	358	398	455	517	518	519	537	547

[1] Totals for Aged, Blind, and Disabled are derived. The derivation creates slight discrepancies between the sum of the group totals and total payments.

Source: U.S. Social Security Administration, *Annual Statistical Supplement to the Social Security Bulletin, 2014,* February 2015. See also <http://www.ssa.gov/policy/index.html>.

Table 578. Supplemental Security Income (SSI)—Recipients and Payments by State and Other Area: 2010 to 2013

[Recipients as of December (7,912 represents 7,912,000); payments for calendar year ($48,195 represents $48,195,000,000). Data cover federal SSI payments and/or federally administered state supplementation]

State and other area	Recipients (1,000)		Payments for the year (mil. dol.)			State and other area	Recipients (1,000)		Payments for the year (mil. dol.)		
	2010	2013	2010	2012	2013		2010	2013	2010	2012	2013
Total [1]..............	7,912	8,363	48,195	52,075	53,900	MO..................	134	142	785	848	886
U.S..................	7,911	8,362	48,189	52,067	53,892	MT..................	18	19	98	108	112
AL....................	172	177	996	1,062	1,091	NE..................	26	27	144	158	165
AK....................	12	13	70	75	77	NV..................	41	48	241	284	305
AZ....................	110	118	644	715	747	NH..................	18	20	103	117	120
AR....................	107	113	603	667	695	NJ..................	169	181	1,001	1,087	1,129
CA....................	1,269	1,306	8,870	9,216	9,440	NM..................	60	64	340	372	388
CO....................	66	72	377	429	450	NY..................	681	700	4,445	4,669	4,774
CT....................	58	62	340	378	393	NC..................	219	234	1,243	1,351	1,423
DE....................	16	17	91	100	104	ND..................	8	8	43	46	48
DC....................	24	27	153	180	185	OH..................	286	311	1,784	1,954	2,031
FL....................	484	548	2,760	3,141	3,340	OK..................	94	98	541	587	613
GA....................	228	253	1,317	1,511	1,594	OR..................	75	83	439	497	528
HI....................	25	25	157	164	168	PA..................	358	379	2,229	2,425	2,502
ID....................	27	30	155	175	186	RI..................	33	33	201	201	208
IL....................	273	279	1,662	1,753	1,796	SC..................	112	118	635	697	722
IN....................	118	127	716	785	815	SD..................	14	15	75	83	86
IA....................	48	51	266	287	302	TN..................	175	184	1,023	1,118	1,147
KS....................	46	49	269	293	305	TX..................	617	666	3,316	3,744	3,908
KY....................	192	191	1,116	1,154	1,174	UT..................	28	31	160	184	193
LA....................	175	182	989	1,081	1,116	VT..................	15	16	87	95	97
ME....................	35	37	196	218	224	VA..................	148	153	832	911	939
MD....................	107	117	658	738	773	WA..................	137	150	881	958	992
MA....................	193	188	1,211	1,174	1,163	WV..................	80	79	472	491	495
MI....................	254	277	1,581	1,747	1,820	WI..................	107	117	625	690	725
MN....................	86	94	516	570	601	WY..................	6	7	35	38	41
MS....................	126	126	699	739	757	N. Marianas......	1	1	6	7	7

[1] Includes Northern Mariana Islands.

Source: U.S. Social Security Administration, *Annual Statistical Supplement to the Social Security Bulletin, 2014*, February 2015. See also <http://www.ssa.gov/policy/>.

Table 579. Temporary Assistance for Needy Families (TANF)—Families and Recipients: 1980 to 2014

[In thousands (3,712 represents 3,712,000). Average monthly families and recipients for calendar year. Prior to TANF, the cash assistance program to families was called Aid to Families with Dependent Children (1980–1996). Under the Personal Responsibility and Work Opportunity Reconciliation Act of 1996, the program became TANF. See text, this section. Includes Puerto Rico, Guam, and Virgin Islands]

Year	Families	Recipients	Year	Families	Recipients	Year	Families	Recipients
1980	3,712	10,774	1999	2,554	6,824	2007	1,674	3,897
1985	3,701	10,855	2000	2,215	5,778	2008	1,633	3,795
1990	4,057	11,695	2001	2,104	5,359	2009	1,769	4,154
1994	5,033	14,161	2002	2,048	5,069	2010	1,858	4,403
1995	4,791	13,418	2003	2,024	4,929	2011	1,846	4,363
1996	4,434	12,321	2004	1,979	4,748	2012	1,723	4,017
1997	3,740	10,376	2005	1,894	4,469	2013	1,612	3,713
1998	3,050	8,347	2006	1,777	4,148	2014	1,502	3,462

Source: U.S. Department of Health and Human Services, Administration for Children and Families, "Temporary Assistance for Needy Families, Caseload Data," <http://www.acf.hhs.gov/programs/ofa/programs/tanf/data-reports>, accessed April 2015.

Table 580. Temporary Assistance for Needy Families (TANF)—Recipients by State and Other Areas: 2000 to 2014

[In thousands (2,215 represents 2,215,000). Average monthly families and recipients for calendar year. See headnote, Table 579]

State or other area	Families 2000	Families 2010	Families 2014	Recipients 2000	Recipients 2010	Recipients 2014	State or other area	Families 2000	Families 2010	Families 2014	Recipients 2000	Recipients 2010	Recipients 2014
Total [1]	2,215	1,858	1,502	5,778	4,403	3,462	MT	5	4	3	13	9	7
U.S.	2,181	1,843	1,489	5,678	4,361	3,425	NE	9	8	5	24	18	11
AL	19	22	17	45	53	40	NV	6	11	12	16	27	32
AK	7	3	4	21	9	10	NH	6	5	3	14	11	6
AZ	33	28	13	84	60	28	NJ	50	34	28	125	81	65
AR	12	8	6	29	19	13	NM	23	20	13	69	54	36
CA	489	584	535	1,262	1,437	1,293	NY	250	122	114	695	272	261
CO	11	11	17	28	29	45	NC	45	24	16	98	46	29
CT	27	17	14	64	34	29	ND	3	2	1	7	5	3
DE	6	5	5	12	15	13	OH	95	104	62	235	238	120
DC	17	8	7	45	19	17	OK	14	9	7	35	21	16
FL	65	58	49	142	105	85	OR	17	28	23	38	72	56
GA	52	20	15	125	38	29	PA	88	54	69	241	130	171
HI	14	9	8	46	26	24	RI	16	7	5	44	17	13
ID	1	2	2	2	3	3	SC	18	19	11	42	44	25
IL	78	23	20	234	66	44	SD	3	3	3	7	7	6
IN	37	35	10	101	86	20	TN	57	61	46	147	157	108
IA	20	18	13	53	46	32	TX	129	51	36	347	117	78
KS	13	15	7	32	38	16	UT	8	6	4	21	18	10
KY	38	30	28	87	62	57	VT	6	3	3	16	6	6
LA	27	11	6	71	24	12	VA	31	35	26	69	79	55
ME	11	11	6	28	26	12	WA	56	67	40	148	162	93
MD	29	25	21	71	60	50	WV	13	10	8	33	23	18
MA	43	50	42	100	97	78	WI	17	23	27	38	53	64
MI	72	68	26	198	179	59	WY	1	–	–	1	1	1
MN	39	23	20	114	50	43	PR	30	14	12	88	37	33
MS	15	12	8	34	25	17	GU	3	1	1	10	3	3
MO	47	36	27	125	86	65	VI	1	1	–	3	2	1

– Represents or rounds to zero. [1] Includes Puerto Rico, Guam, and the Virgin Islands.

Source: U.S. Department of Health and Human Services, Administration for Children and Families, "Temporary Assistance for Needy Families, Caseload Data," <http://www.acf.hhs.gov/programs/ofa/programs/tanf/data-reports>, accessed April 2015.

Table 581. Household Use of Food Pantries and Emergency (Soup) Kitchens: 2013

[In thousands (122,194 represents 122,194,000), except percent. Based on 2013 Current Population Survey Food Security Supplement. Estimates are for households using food pantries or emergency kitchens at least once during the 12-month period ended December 2013. Covers persons occupying housing units; survey excludes homeless persons, and may also miss persons in tenuous housing arrangements (such as temporarily living with another family)]

Category	Food pantries Total households [1]	Food pantries Number of users	Food pantries Percent using	Emergency (soup) kitchens Total households [1]	Emergency (soup) kitchens Number of users	Emergency (soup) kitchens Percent using
All households	**122,194**	**6,194**	**5.1**	**122,216**	**710**	**0.6**
All persons in households	309,655	17,081	5.5	309,774	1,579	0.5
Adults in households	236,482	11,501	4.9	236,529	1,188	0.5
Children in households	73,173	5,580	7.6	73,244	391	0.5
Households by food security status: [2]						
Food-secure households	104,766	1,669	1.6	104,802	143	0.1
Food-insecure households	17,335	4,520	26.1	17,316	562	3.3
Households with low food security	10,590	2,141	20.2	10,585	181	1.7
Households with very low food security	6,745	2,379	35.3	6,731	381	5.7

[1] Totals exclude households that did not answer questions about using food pantries and emergency kitchens, and also households that did not answer questions about food security. [2] Food secure households report zero or 1-2 indications, typically anxiety over food sufficiency or supply, with little or no indication of changes in diets or food intake. Households with low food security report reduced quality, variety, or desirability of diet, with little or no indication of reduced food intake. Households with very low food security report multiple indications of disrupted eating patterns and reduced food intake. See also headnote, Table 215.

Source: U.S. Department of Agriculture, Economic Research Service, *Household Food Security in the United States in 2013: Statistical Supplement*, No. 066, September 2014. See also <http://www.ers.usda.gov/topics/food-nutrition-assistance/food-security-in-the-us.aspx>.

Table 582. Temporary Assistance for Needy Families (TANF)—Expenditures by State: Fiscal Years 2000 to 2013

[In millions of dollars (24,781 represents $24,781,000,000). Represents federal and state funds expended in fiscal year. Negative values occur when contracted obligations are fulfilled or terminated and the actual cost for the service is less than the obligated amount. Expenditures on assistance include benefits directed at basic needs (food, clothing, shelter, utilities, household goods, personal care items, and general incidental expenses) even when conditioned on participation in a work experience or community service activity. It also includes child care, transportation, and supports for families that are not employed]

State	2000, Total	2010, Total	2013 Total [1]	2013 Expenditures on assistance	State	2000, Total	2010, Total	2013 Total [1]	2013 Expenditures on assistance
U.S.	24,781	33,255	29,147	9,880	MO	321	405	374	101
AL	96	191	166	49	MT	44	47	44	18
AK	93	62	74	48	NE	79	98	92	24
AZ	261	350	359	-22	NV	69	108	90	44
AR	139	233	157	13	NH	73	86	68	31
CA	6,481	7,239	6,667	3,644	NJ	321	1,446	1,211	332
CO	205	323	314	74	NM	149	237	189	53
CT	436	500	459	84	NY	3,512	5,347	4,984	1,869
DE	55	75	83	18	NC	440	563	539	60
DC	157	251	250	74	ND	33	37	34	19
FL	781	901	827	190	OH	995	1,331	964	306
GA	386	563	494	56	OK	130	179	155	62
HI	162	378	229	66	OR	169	392	324	163
ID	43	35	37	7	PA	1,327	964	870	279
IL	879	1,255	1,160	86	RI	172	149	166	45
IN	342	344	217	29	SC	245	180	230	37
IA	163	194	175	67	SD	21	31	25	18
KS	151	207	147	55	TN	293	338	308	124
KY	203	281	253	151	TX	727	908	821	131
LA	118	264	205	26	UT	100	132	70	29
ME	108	141	86	63	VT	62	78	79	28
MD	336	564	561	139	VA	418	299	258	101
MA	690	1,022	1,001	339	WA	535	1,494	776	202
MI	1,264	1,703	1,352	207	WV	134	199	134	82
MN	381	475	432	94	WI	382	524	526	134
MS	62	106	80	24	WY	34	29	31	4

[1] Includes other items not shown separately.

Source: U.S. Department of Health and Human Services, Administration for Children and Families, "Temporary Assistance for Needy Families, Expenditure Data," <http://www.acf.hhs.gov/programs/ofa/programs/tanf/data-reports>, accessed April 2015.

Table 583. Federal Food Programs: Fiscal Years 1990 to 2014

[20.0 represents 20,000,000, except as noted. For fiscal years ending September 30. Data for 2014 are preliminary. Program data include Puerto Rico, Virgin Islands, Guam, American Samoa, Northern Marianas, and the former Trust Territory when a federal food program was operated in these areas. Participation data are average monthly figures except as noted. Participants are not reported for The Emergency Assistance Program (TEFAP)]

Program	Unit	1990	2000	2005	2010	2011	2012	2013	2014
Supplemental nutrition assistance program (SNAP): [1]									
Participants	Million	20.0	17.2	25.6	40.3	44.7	46.6	47.6	46.5
Value of benefits	Mil. dol.	14,143	14,983	28,568	64,702	71,811	74,619	76,066	70,000
Average monthly benefit value per recipient	Dollars	58.78	72.62	92.89	133.79	133.85	133.41	133.07	125.35
Nutrition assistance program for Puerto Rico: [2]									
Federal grant	Mil. dol.	937	1,268	1,495	2,001	2,001	2,001	2,001	2,061
National school lunch program (NSLP):									
Children participating [3]	Million	24.1	27.3	29.6	31.8	31.8	31.7	30.7	30.4
Free lunches served	Million	1,662	2,205	2,477	2,948	3,066	3,109	3,168	3,191
Reduced-price lunches served	Million	273	409	479	498	445	449	425	403
Federal cost (cash payments)	Mil. dol.	3,214	5,493	7,055	9,752	10,105	10,414	11,057	11,353
School breakfast (SB):									
Children participating [3]	Million	4.1	7.6	9.4	11.7	12.2	12.9	13.2	13.6
Federal cash payments	Mil. dol.	596	1,393	1,927	2,859	3,034	3,277	3,514	3,686
Special supplemental food program (WIC): [4]									
Participants	Million	4.5	7.2	8.0	9.2	9.0	8.9	8.7	8.3
Federal cost for food	Mil. dol.	1,637	2,853	3,603	4,562	5,020	4,810	4,497	4,326
Child and adult care (CACFP): [5]									
Participants [6]	Million	1.5	2.7	3.1	3.4	3.4	3.5	3.7	3.9
Federal cash payments	Mil. dol.	719	1,500	1,904	2,398	2,472	2,590	2,721	2,851
Federal cost of food commodities for: [7]									
School food programs [8]	Mil. dol.	617	655	975	1,128	1,195	1,164	1,163	1,302
TEFAP [9]	Mil. dol.	282	182	314	566	462	378	629	560

[1] The program name was changed from Food Stamp to Supplemental Nutrition Assistance (SNAP) in October 2008. [2] Puerto Rico receives a grant in lieu of SNAP benefits. [3] Average participation per day are 9-month averages (excludes summer months). Includes children in public and nonprofit private elementary and secondary schools and in residential child care institutions. [4] WIC serves pregnant and postpartum women, infants, and children up to age 5. [5] CACFP provides year-round subsidies to feed preschool children in child care centers and family day care homes. Certain care centers serving disabled or elderly adults also receive meal subsidies. [6] Average quarterly daily attendance at participating institutions. [7] Includes the federal cost of commodity entitlements, cash-in-lieu of commodities, and bonus foods. [8] National school lunch and breakfast programs, and special milk program. [9] The Emergency Food Assistance Program distributes foods through nonprofit local emergency feeding organizations.

Source: U.S. Department of Agriculture, Food and Nutrition Service, "Program Data, Overview," <http://www.fns.usda.gov/pd/Overview.htm>, accessed March 2015.

Table 584. Federal Supplemental Nutrition Assistance Program (SNAP) by State: 2000 to 2014

[17,194 represents 17,194,000. Participation data are average monthly number participating in fiscal year ending September 30]

State	Persons (1,000) 2000	2010	2014	Benefits (mil. dol.) 2000	2010	2014	State	Persons (1,000) 2000	2010	2014	Benefits (mil. dol.) 2000	2010	2014
Total [1]....	17,194	40,302	46,536	14,983	64,702	70,000	MS..........	276	576	657	226	847	913
U.S.........	17,156	40,245	46,461	14,927	64,562	69,836	MO..........	423	901	858	358	1,361	1,236
AL..........	396	805	902	344	1,226	1,318	MT..........	59	114	125	51	177	176
AK..........	38	76	87	46	159	174	NE..........	82	163	174	61	238	239
AZ..........	259	1,018	1,044	240	1,588	1,477	NV..........	61	278	384	57	415	537
AR..........	247	467	492	206	686	664	NH..........	36	104	112	28	152	141
CA..........	1,831	3,239	4,350	1,639	5,692	7,411	NJ..........	345	622	883	304	1,030	1,291
CO..........	156	405	505	127	688	766	NM..........	169	357	431	140	542	630
CT..........	165	336	439	138	570	697	NY..........	1,439	2,758	3,123	1,361	4,985	5,201
DE..........	32	113	150	31	171	220	NC..........	488	1,346	1,576	403	2,072	2,384
DC..........	81	118	143	77	196	223	ND..........	32	60	54	25	95	76
FL..........	882	2,603	3,526	771	4,417	5,473	OH..........	610	1,607	1,752	520	2,734	2,583
GA..........	559	1,591	1,816	489	2,565	2,828	OK..........	253	582	608	208	900	865
HI..........	118	138	194	166	358	525	OR..........	234	705	802	198	1,067	1,162
ID..........	58	194	212	46	300	296	PA..........	777	1,575	1,796	656	2,333	2,574
IL..........	817	1,646	2,015	777	2,784	3,203	RI..........	74	139	179	59	238	280
IN..........	300	813	893	268	1,291	1,311	SC..........	295	797	835	249	1,256	1,236
IA..........	123	340	408	100	526	532	SD..........	43	95	101	37	153	149
KS..........	117	270	293	83	403	395	TN..........	496	1,224	1,313	415	1,966	1,952
KY..........	403	778	828	337	1,186	1,171	TX..........	1,333	3,552	3,853	1,215	5,447	5,331
LA..........	500	826	877	448	1,286	1,288	UT..........	82	247	230	68	367	317
ME..........	102	230	231	81	356	322	VT..........	41	86	93	32	124	130
MD..........	219	561	788	199	878	1,133	VA..........	336	786	919	263	1,213	1,303
MA..........	232	749	863	182	1,166	1,273	WA..........	295	956	1,096	241	1,387	1,548
MI..........	603	1,776	1,679	457	2,809	2,576	WV..........	227	341	363	185	487	476
MN..........	196	430	534	165	625	670	WI..........	193	715	842	129	1,000	1,113
							WY..........	22	35	36	19	52	49

[1] Includes Guam and the Virgin Islands. Several outlying areas receive nutrition assistance grants in lieu of SNAP (Puerto Rico, American Samoa, and the Northern Marianas).

Source: U.S. Department of Agriculture, Food and Nutrition Service, "Program Data, Supplemental Nutrition Assistance Program," <http://www.fns.usda.gov/pd/SNAPmain.htm>, accessed March 2015.

Table 585. Selected Characteristics of Supplemental Nutrition Assistance Program (SNAP) Households and Participants: 1990 to 2013

[7,811 represents 7,811,000. For fiscal years ending September 30. Data for 1990 exclude Guam and the Virgin Islands. Based on a sample of households from the SNAP Quality Control System]

Fiscal Year	Households Total [1] (1,000)	Percent of total With children	With elderly [2]	With disabled [3]	Participants Total (1,000)	Percent of total Children	Elderly [2]
1990..................	7,811	60.3	18.1	8.9	20,440	49.6	7.7
1995..................	10,883	59.7	16.0	18.9	26,955	51.5	7.1
1996..................	10,552	59.5	16.2	20.2	25,926	51.0	7.3
1997..................	9,452	58.3	17.6	22.3	23,117	51.4	7.9
1998..................	8,246	58.3	18.2	24.4	19,969	52.8	8.2
1999..................	7,670	55.7	20.1	26.4	18,149	51.5	9.4
2000..................	7,335	53.9	21.0	27.5	17,091	51.3	10.0
2001..................	7,450	53.6	20.4	27.7	17,297	51.1	9.6
2002..................	8,201	54.1	18.7	27.0	19,041	51.0	8.9
2003..................	8,971	55.1	17.1	22.1	20,764	50.8	8.1
2004..................	10,069	54.3	17.3	22.7	23,279	50.0	8.2
2005..................	10,852	53.7	17.1	23.0	24,794	49.9	8.3
2006..................	11,313	52.0	17.9	23.1	25,472	49.1	8.7
2007..................	11,561	51.0	17.8	23.8	25,775	48.9	8.8
2008..................	12,464	50.6	18.5	22.6	27,607	48.4	9.1
2009..................	14,981	49.9	16.6	21.2	32,889	47.5	8.3
2010..................	18,369	48.7	15.5	19.8	39,759	46.6	7.8
2011..................	20,803	47.1	16.5	20.2	44,148	45.1	8.5
2012..................	22,046	45.3	17.2	20.0	46,022	44.5	9.0
2013..................	22,802	44.8	17.4	20.3	47,098	44.4	9.3

[1] Total does not include those who are ineligible or those receiving disaster benefits. [2] Persons 60 years old and over. [3] The substantial increase in 1995 and decrease in 2003 are due in part to the changes in definition of a disabled household. Prior to 1995, disabled households were defined as households with SSI income but no members over age 59. In 1995, that definition changed to households with at least one member under age 65 who received SSI, or at least one member age 18-61 who received Social Security, veterans' benefits, or other government benefits as a result of a disability. In 2003, the definition of a disabled household changed to households with either SSI income, or a medical expense deduction and without an elderly person, and households containing a nonelderly adult working fewer than 30 hours per week and receiving Social Security, veterans' benefits, or workers' compensation.

Source: U.S. Department of Agriculture, Food and Nutrition Service, *Characteristics of Supplemental Nutrition Assistance Program Households: Fiscal Year 2013*, Report No. SNAP-14-CHAR, December 2014. See also <http://www.fns.usda.gov/ops/supplemental-nutrition-assistance-program-snap-research>.

Table 586. Supplemental Nutrition Assistance Program (SNAP) Households and Participants—Summary: 2013

[22,802 represents 22,802,000. For fiscal year ending September 30. Based on a sample of households from the Supplemental Nutrition Assistance Program Quality Control (QC) System. Figures are lower than official participation counts because they do not include ineligible participants or those receiving disaster food stamp assistance]

Household type and income source	Households Number (1,000)	Percent	Age, sex, race, and ethnicity	Participants Number (1,000)	Percent
Total............................	**22,802**	**100.0**	**Total**............................	**47,098**	**100.0**
With children........................	10,224	44.8	Children............................	20,889	44.4
Single-parent households............	5,822	25.5	Under 5 years old..................	6,714	14.3
Married-couple households..........	1,848	8.1	5 to 17 years old..................	14,175	30.1
Other [1]............................	2,555	11.2	Nonelderly adults..................	21,845	46.4
With elderly........................	3,972	17.4	18 to 35 years old................	11,269	23.9
Living alone........................	3,169	13.9	36 to 59 years old................	10,576	22.5
Not living alone....................	803	3.5	Elderly (60 years old and over).......	4,365	9.3
Disabled nonelderly.................	4,624	20.3			
Living alone........................	2,777	12.2	Male..............................	20,651	43.8
Not living alone....................	1,847	8.1	Female............................	26,447	56.2
With earned income.................	7,112	31.2	White, non-Hispanic................	17,807	37.8
Wages and salaries.................	6,274	27.5	Black, non-Hispanic................	12,172	25.8
			Hispanic...........................	7,571	16.1
Unearned income...................	12,964	56.9	Asian..............................	1,148	2.4
TANF [2]...........................	1,486	6.5	Native American....................	657	1.4
Supplemental security income.......	4,545	19.9	Multiracial, non-Hispanic..............	7,382	15.7
Social security.....................	5,390	23.6	Race unknown......................	360	0.8
No income..........................	4,911	21.5			

[1] Other households with children include other multiple-adult households and children-only households. [2] Temporary Assistance for Needy Families (TANF) program.

Source: U.S. Department of Agriculture, Food and Nutrition Service, *Characteristics of Supplemental Nutrition Assistance Program Households: Fiscal Year 2013*, Report No. SNAP-14-CHAR, December 2014. See also <http://www.fns.usda.gov/ops/supplemental-nutrition-assistance-program-snap-research>.

Table 587. Primary Child Care Arrangements for Children Under Age 5, by Selected Characteristics: Spring 2011

[In percent, except as indicated (10,859 represents 10,859,000). For children with employed mothers. The primary child care arrangement is defined as the arrangement used the most hours per week. The numbers for all arrangements may exceed the total number of children because of ties among arrangements in the greatest number of hours per week. Based on Survey of Income and Program Participation (SIPP), 2008 Panel, Wave 8, January-April 2011. Estimates are based on responses from a sample of the population, and may differ from the actual values because of sampling variability and other factors. Apparent differences between the estimates of two or more groups may not be statistically different]

Characteristic	Children Number (1,000)	Type of arrangement [1] (percent) In relative care	In non-relative care	In day care center	No child care arrange-ment
Total............................	**10,859**	**51.7**	**40.0**	**19.8**	**11.0**
MARITAL STATUS OF MOTHER					
Married............................	7,692	51.0	40.0	19.6	11.7
Widowed, separated, divorced..........	816	47.5	39.0	20.1	11.5
Never married......................	2,352	55.2	40.3	20.6	8.6
RACE AND HISPANIC ORIGIN OF MOTHER					
White alone........................	8,391	51.7	39.8	19.3	11.9
Non-Hispanic......................	6,945	48.9	42.7	21.3	12.5
Black alone........................	1,539	52.2	38.5	21.2	8.6
Asian alone........................	497	52.1	41.4	19.0	9.3
Hispanic (of any race)...............	1,604	65.6	25.6	9.7	8.3
AGE OF MOTHER					
15-24 years........................	1,413	64.5	30.2	18.2	9.4
25-34 years........................	5,830	51.5	41.0	20.7	10.8
35+ years..........................	3,616	47.0	42.1	19.2	12.0
EDUCATION OF MOTHER					
Less than high school................	751	58.1	22.1	6.5	19.3
High school graduate................	2,091	59.7	31.9	16.1	10.8
Some college.......................	3,690	57.3	36.3	17.2	9.3
Bachelor's degree or higher..........	4,327	42.0	50.1	26.3	11.1
WORK STATUS OF MOTHER					
Employed full-time..................	7,264	48.0	45.4	24.1	9.7
Employed part-time.................	2,808	62.2	28.6	12.5	11.6
Self-employed......................	787	48.2	30.4	6.9	20.3
FAMILY INCOME (monthly)					
Less than $1,500....................	1,150	58.4	31.8	12.5	12.2
$1,500 - $2,999....................	1,788	56.4	35.4	19.2	11.0
$3,000 - $4,499....................	1,668	59.8	36.0	17.5	8.7
$4,500 and over....................	6,068	46.7	44.4	22.5	11.2
AGE OF CHILD					
Less than 1 year....................	1,870	58.0	20.3	14.4	13.4
1-2 years..........................	4,682	54.2	23.3	23.4	10.5
3-4 years..........................	4,307	46.3	48.3	18.3	10.5

[1] Columns do not add to 100.0 because some children participated in more than one type of arrangement.

Source: U.S. Census Bureau, Survey of Income and Program Participation (SIPP), 2008 Panel, Wave 8, *Who's Minding the Kids? Child Care Arrangements: Spring 2011*; and "Detailed Tables," <http://www.census.gov/hhes/childcare/index.html>, accessed June 2013.

Table 588. Child Support—Award and Recipient Status of Custodial Parents: 2011

[In thousands except as noted (14,440 represents 14,440,000). Income and support received in 2011 dollars. Based on the Child Support Supplement to the April 2012 Current Population Survey. Custodial parents 15 years and older with own children under 21 years of age living with them, and receiving support from noncustodial parents living elsewhere. Covers civilian noninstitutional population]

Award and recipient status	All custodial parents				Custodial parents below poverty level			
	Total				Total			
	Number	Percent distribution	Mothers	Fathers	Number	Percent distribution	Mothers	Fathers
Total................................	**14,440**	**(X)**	**11,797**	**2,643**	**4,180**	**(X)**	**3,753**	**427**
With child support agreement or award [1].........	7,057	(X)	6,297	760	1,992	(X)	1,878	115
Supposed to receive payments in 2011.........	6,262	100.0	5,588	674	1,707	100.0	1,612	95
Actually received payments in 2011............	4,641	74.1	4,182	459	1,241	72.7	1179	62
Received full amount............................	2,716	43.4	2,438	279	676	39.6	638	38
Received partial payments......................	1,925	30.7	1,745	180	565	33.1	542	23
Did not receive payments in 2011..............	1,621	25.9	1,405	216	466	27.3	433	33
Child support not awarded........................	7,383	(X)	5,499	1,883	2,187	(X)	1,875	312
MEAN INCOME AND CHILD SUPPORT								
Received child support payments in 2011:								
Mean total money income (dol.)................	31,517	(X)	30,363	42,042	8,676	(X)	8,699	(B)
Mean child support received (dol.)..............	5,088	(X)	5,160	4,433	4,503	(X)	4,490	(B)
Received the full amount due:								
Mean total money income (dol.)..............	33,269	(X)	32,487	40,111	9,193	(X)	9,090	(B)
Mean child support received (dol.)............	6,590	(X)	6,738	5,297	6,135	(X)	6,172	(B)
Received partial payments:								
Mean total money income (dol.)..............	29,044	(X)	27,394	45,028	8,058	(X)	8,239	(B)
Mean child support received (dol.)...........	2,969	(X)	2,955	3,096	2,551	(X)	2,510	(B)
Received no payments in 2011:								
Mean total money income (dol.)................	29,631	(X)	26,231	51,791	8,323	(X)	8,209	(B)
Without child support agreement or award:								
Mean total money income (dol.)................	31,691	(X)	25,095	50,950	7,073	(X)	7,014	7,425

X Not applicable. B Base figure too small to meet statistical standards for reliability of a derived figure. [1] As of April of following year (e.g., 2011 data is as of April 2012).

Source: U.S. Census Bureau, *Custodial Mothers and Fathers and Their Child Support: 2011* and *Detailed Tables*, Current Population Report P60-246, October 2013. See also <http://www.census.gov/people/childsupport/>.

Table 589. Child Support Enforcement Program—Caseload and Finances: 2009 to 2013

[In units as indicated (15,798 represents 15,798,000). For fiscal years ending September 30. Includes Puerto Rico, Guam, and the Virgin Islands. The Office of Child Support (OCSE) locates absent parents, establishes paternity of children, and establishes and enforces support orders. The OCSE does not assist families directly but rather helps child support agencies in the states and tribes to develop, manage and operate their programs. Case types include IV-A cases in which children are eligible for Temporary Assistance for Needy Families (TANF); and IV-E cases in which children are entitled to foster care maintenance; case types reflect Social Security Act Titles IV-A and IV-E. Child support collected for families not receiving TANF goes to the family to help it remain self-sufficient. Most child support collected on behalf of TANF and foster care families goes to Federal and State governments to offset program payments. Some States pass-through a portion of their collections to help families become self-sufficient. Based on data reported by state agencies. Minus sign (-) indicates net outlay]

Item	Unit	2009	2010	2011	2012, Prelim.	2013, Prelim.
Total cases.........................	**1,000**	**15,798**	**15,859**	**15,832**	**15,747**	**15,589**
Number of children.......................	1,000	17,414	17,509	17,340	17,157	16,900
Paternities established or acknowledged, total [1].......	1,000	643	620	615	588	526
Support orders established, total.....................	1,000	1,267	1,297	1,248	1,205	1,142
FINANCES						
Total distributed collections........................	**Mil. dol.**	**26,386**	**26,556**	**27,297**	**27,719**	**28,007**
Total payments to families or foster care................	Mil. dol.	24,288	24,471	25,117	25,562	25,950
Total medical support..................................	Mil. dol.	260	305	365	423	464
Total passed through...................................	Mil. dol.	117	135	139	122	123
Total fees withheld by state............................	Mil. dol.	35	37	33	49	51
Total assistance reimbursement [2]......................	Mil. dol.	1,686	1,607	1,642	1,564	1,418
State share..	Mil. dol.	741	704	719	687	627
Federal share..	Mil. dol.	945	903	923	876	791
Current Assistance Collections [3]......................	Mil. dol.	978	1,015	1,010	961	908
Former Assistance Collections [4].......................	Mil. dol.	9,294	8,971	8,930	8,889	8,772
Medicaid Never Assistance Collections [5]...............	Mil. dol.	4,177	4,729	5,535	6,111	6,945
Never Assistance Collections [6]........................	Mil. dol.	11,936	11,840	11,822	11,759	11,381
Total administrative expenditures.......................	Mil. dol.	5,850	5,776	5,661	5,661	5,588
Federal share..	Mil. dol.	3,887	3,811	3,477	3,407	3,344
State share..	Mil. dol.	1,963	1,964	2,184	2,254	2,244
Cost effectiveness ratio................................	Mil. dol.	4.78	4.88	5.12	5.19	5.31

[1] Does not include in-hospital paternities. [2] Total assistance reimbursement equals collections that will be divided between State and Federal governments to reimburse their respective shares of either Title IV-A (TANF) payments or Title IV-E (foster care) maintenance payments. [3] Current Assistance Collections are made on behalf of families currently receiving Title IV-A (TANF) or Title IV-E (foster care) assistance. [4] Former Assistance Collections are made on behalf of families formerly receiving Title IV-A (TANF) or Title IV-E (foster care) assistance. [5] Medicaid Never Assistance Collections are those received and distributed on behalf of children who are receiving Child Support Enforcement services under Title IV-D of the Social Security Act, and who are either currently receiving or who have formerly received Medicaid payments under Title XIX of the Social Security Act, but who were not currently receiving and who have never formerly received assistance under either Title IV-A (TANF or AFDC) or Title IV-E (Foster Care) of the Social Security Act. [6] Never Assistance Collections are those made on behalf of families never receiving public assistance under TANF or Foster Care.

Source: U.S. Department of Health and Human Services, Administration for Children & Families, Office of Child Support Enforcement, *Annual Report to Congress, FY2013 Preliminary Report*, April 2014. See also <http://www.acf.hhs.gov/programs/css/resource/fy2013-preliminary-report>.

Table 590. Selected Characteristics of Support Provided on Behalf of Children Under 21 Years Old Living in Another Household by Gender of Provider: 2010

[Numbers in thousands (4,547 represents 4,547,000), except as noted. Data are for whole year. Based on Survey of Income and Program Participation (SIPP), 2008 Panel, Wave 6, May-August 2010. Estimates are based on responses from a sample of the population, and may differ from the actual values because of sampling variability and other factors. Apparent differences between the estimates of two or more groups may not be statistically different]

| Characteristics | Providers on Behalf of Children Under Age 21 | | | | | | | | |
| | Total | | | Male providers | | | Female providers | | |
	Total providers	Percent of providers	Median support provided (dollars)	Total	Percent of providers	Median support provided (dollars)	Total	Percent of providers	Median support provided (dollars)
Total [1]	4,547	100.0	3,600	3,881	100.0	3,900	666	100.0	2,400
NUMBER OF CHILDREN SUPPORTED									
1 child	2,658	58.5	3,000	2,197	56.6	3,200	461	69.2	2,200
2 children	1,416	31.1	5,460	1,290	33.2	5,700	127	19.1	4,416
3 or more children	473	10.4	5,200	395	10.2	5,200	78	11.7	2,892
BASIS FOR SUPPORT									
Child support agreement or court order	3,375	74.2	3,880	3,056	78.7	4,160	319	47.9	2,400
Voluntary and ratified by the court	747	16.4	4,000	702	18.1	4,300	45	6.8	(B)
Court-ordered agreement	2,377	52.3	3,720	2,125	54.8	4,140	252	37.8	2,400
Other written agreement	68	1.5	(B)	60	1.5	(B)	7	1.1	(B)
Non-written agreement	183	4.0	3,600	168	4.3	3,100	15	2.3	(B)
Not result of agreement or court order	1,173	25.8	3,000	826	21.3	3,500	347	52.1	2,500
PAYMENT METHOD									
Wage withholding	1,075	23.6	4,320	991	25.5	4,680	85	12.8	2,500
Directly to other parent	1,011	22.2	4,800	911	23.5	4,800	100	15.0	3,000
Directly to court	454	10.0	2,496	414	10.7	2,600	39	5.9	(B)
Directly to child support agency	702	15.4	3,120	630	16.2	3,600	72	10.8	(B)
Other method	133	2.9	2,400	110	2.8	2,400	23	3.5	(B)
HEALTH INSURANCE PROVISIONS									
Non-custodial parent provides	1,325	29.1	5,000	1,222	31.5	5,184	103	15.5	2,400
Custodial parent provides	839	18.5	4,200	764	19.7	4,200	75	11.3	2,544
Non-custodial parent pays bills	186	4.1	4,800	169	4.4	4,800	17	2.6	(B)
Included in child support payments	138	3.0	3,000	134	3.5	3,000	3	0.5	(B)
Other provision	280	6.2	3,600	253	6.5	3,600	28	4.2	(B)
No provision	845	18.6	2,712	740	19.1	3,000	104	15.6	1,800
CUSTODY ARRANGEMENTS									
Joint legal and physical custody	660	14.5	3,600	587	15.1	4,200	74	11.1	(B)
Joint legal with mother physical custody	1,053	23.2	5,160	1,031	26.6	5,160	22	3.3	(B)
Joint legal with father physical custody	130	2.9	2,544	17	0.4	(B)	113	17.0	2,400
Mother legal and physical custody	971	21.4	3,120	967	24.9	3,120	3	0.5	(B)
Father legal and physical custody	64	1.4	(B)	19	0.5	(B)	45	6.8	(B)
Split custody	230	5.1	4,613	224	5.8	4,800	6	0.9	(B)
Other custody arrangements	268	5.9	2,400	211	5.4	2,400	57	8.6	(B)

B Base figure too small to meet statistical standards for reliability of a derived figure. [1] Excludes 208,000 providers who also provided support for other adult nonhousehold members.

Source: U.S. Census Bureau, People and Households, Child Support, "Support Providers: 2010," <http://www.census.gov/people/childsupport/>, accessed July 2013.

Table 591. Children in Foster Care and Awaiting Adoption: 2013

[Data cover the period from October 1 of prior year through September 30 of year shown. Data are preliminary; estimates as of July 2014]

Characteristic	In foster care [1]	Entered foster care	Exited foster care	Waiting to be adopted [1]	Adopted from foster care
Total	402,378	254,904	238,280	101,840	50,608
SEX					
Male	210,738	(NA)	(NA)	53,234	25,789
Female	191,608	(NA)	(NA)	48,602	24,812
AGE					
Under 1 year	26,677	43,085	10,384	3,942	1,161
1 to 5 years	130,860	78,480	82,575	41,256	27,752
6 to 10 years	86,551	51,378	51,996	26,858	13,389
11 to 15 years	86,566	54,847	42,641	22,451	6,661
16 to 17 years	53,990	25,582	24,203	7,333	1,436
18 to 20 years	17,348	1,492	24,612	(X)	204
Mean age, years	8.9	7.5	9.1	7.7	6.2
Median age, years	8.2	6.4	8.1	6.8	5.1
RACE/ETHNICITY [2]					
White	168,302	114,666	106,487	42,344	23,594
Black	98,201	54,835	56,053	24,312	10,800
Asian	2,114	1,620	1,692	413	241
American Indian/Alaska Native	8,652	5,465	4,758	1,805	787
Hispanic origin [3]	86,993	53,786	48,661	23,281	10,695
Two or more races	24,935	15,240	13,889	7,335	3,773
TIME IN CARE					
Mean months	21.8	(X)	20.0	33.5	(NA)
Median months	12.8	(X)	13.5	25.2	(NA)

NA Not available. X Not applicable. [1] As of September 30. [2] All races exclude children of Hispanic origin. [3] Children of Hispanic origin may be of any race.

Source: U.S. Department of Health and Human Services, Administration for Children and Families, *The Adoption and Foster Care Analysis and Reporting System Report, Preliminary FY2013 Estimates as of July 2014,* No. 21. See also <http://www.acf.hhs.gov/programs/cb/research-data-technology/statistics-research/afcars>.

Table 592. Child Care Expenditures of Families with Employed Mothers Making Payments by Selected Characteristics: 2011

[In units indicated (6,720 represents 6,720,000). Based on Survey of Income and Program Participation (SIPP), 2008 Panel, Wave 8, January-April 2011. Estimates are based on responses from a sample of the population, and may differ from the actual values because of sampling variability and other factors]

Characteristic	Number (1,000)	Income		Expenditures		
		Average monthly family income (dollars)	Average monthly mother's income (dollars)	Average weekly child care expenditures (dollars)	Percent of family monthly income spent on child care [1]	Ratio of child care expenditures to mother's income [2]
Families with children under age 15.......	**6,720**	**8,673**	**3,729**	**143**	**7.2**	**16.6**
MARITAL STATUS OF MOTHER						
Married..	4,787	10,622	4,017	157	6.4	16.9
Widowed, separated, divorced................	791	4,264	3,701	106	10.8	12.4
Never married................................	1,142	3,556	2,538	112	13.6	19.1
RACE/HISPANIC ORIGIN OF MOTHER						
White alone.....................................	5,287	9,159	3,810	145	6.8	16.4
Non-Hispanic..............................	4,483	9,859	4,044	150	6.6	16.1
Black alone.....................................	883	4,824	2,873	115	10.4	17.4
Asian alone....................................	333	12,361	5,029	207	7.3	17.9
Hispanic (of any race).......................	864	5,152	2,472	113	9.5	19.9
AGE OF MOTHER						
15 to 24 years.................................	382	3,574	1,507	110	13.4	31.7
25 to 34 years.................................	2,742	6,484	3,190	150	10.0	20.4
35 or more years..............................	3,596	10,883	4,376	141	5.6	14.0
EDUCATION OF MOTHER						
Less than high school.........................	310	3,483	1,740	111	13.8	27.7
High school graduate..........................	861	4,666	2,319	112	10.4	21.0
Some college..................................	2,359	5,730	2,711	111	8.4	17.7
Bachelor's degree or higher..................	3,190	12,433	5,054	178	6.2	15.3
WORK STATUS OF MOTHER						
Employed full-time............................	5,192	8,135	4,134	148	7.9	15.5
Employed part-time...........................	1,122	6,791	2,243	120	7.7	23.2
Self-employed.................................	406	20,744	2,653	143	3.0	23.3
MONTHLY FAMILY INCOME						
Less than $1,500..............................	410	1,023	1,002	91	38.7	39.5
$1,500 to $2,999..............................	923	2,194	1,750	95	18.7	23.4
$3,000 to $4,499..............................	945	3,717	2,372	116	13.6	21.3
$4,500 and over...............................	4,440	11,782	4,681	164	6.0	15.1
FAMILY POVERTY LEVEL						
Below poverty level............................	521	1,297	1,046	91	30.3	37.6
At or above poverty level......................	6,199	9,293	3,954	147	6.9	16.2

[1] Percent is a ratio of average monthly child care payments (prorated from weekly averages) to average family monthly income. [2] Ratio is of average monthly child care payments (prorated from weekly averages) to mother's average monthly income, shown as a percentage.

Source: U.S. Census Bureau, "Who's Minding the Kids? Child Care Arrangements: 2011: Detailed Tables," <http://www.census.gov/hhes/childcare/data/sipp/index.html>, accessed July 2013.

Table 593. Head Start—Summary: 2009 to 2014

[Data in thousands (904.2 represents 904,200), except as noted. For fiscal years. Data on cumulative enrollment, staff, and volunteers are submitted by Head Start grantees and delegates, and are as of August 31. Federal funding covers all Head Start programs, including American Indian and Alaska Native and Migrant and Seasonal Programs, and support activities]

Item	2009 [1]	2010	2011	2012	2013	2014
Federal funding (million dollars)........	7,112.8	7,234.8	7,559.6	7,968.5	7,573.1	[4] 8,598.1
Funded enrollment slots [2]..............	904.2	904.1	964.4	956.5	903.7	917.7
Cumulative enrollment [3]............	**1,056.8**	**1,117.7**	**1,141.9**	**1,146.5**	**1,129.8**	**1,076.1**
Children age 2 and under..............	108.1	146.3	174.0	176.4	177.0	173.2
Children age 3...........................	378.5	386.7	389.4	388.2	392.4	375.9
Children age 4...........................	531.9	548.0	542.1	547.1	531.9	497.1
Children age 5 and older................	28.7	23.2	19.8	18.5	12.9	15.3
Hispanic/Latino........................	376.1	405.4	420.3	423.8	419.9	406.6
Non-Hispanic/non-Latino...............	680.7	712.3	721.6	722.0	709.8	669.5
American Indian/Alaska Native.........	42.8	41.7	44.7	44.2	44.1	45.2
Asian......................................	18.1	19.0	19.4	20.2	19.9	19.8
Black/African American.................	314.4	326.5	325.0	331.0	326.5	309.9
Native Hawaiian/Pacific Islander.......	6.5	6.9	7.3	7.2	6.5	7.0
White.....................................	417.7	450.3	468.6	473.5	476.4	458.0
Biracial/multiracial......................	81.6	83.9	90.5	97.9	104.4	102.2
Other/unspecified.......................	175.7	189.4	186.4	172.5	100.7	134.1
Total staff...................................	212.2	228.3	233.4	230.6	236.7	226.0
Total volunteers............................	1,277.7	1,335.9	1,324.0	1,315.7	1,234.6	1,167.1
Parent volunteers......................	852.1	881.1	873.2	867.4	817.8	800.2

[1] The American Recovery and Reinvestment Act (ARRA), enacted in February of 2009, appropriated $2.1 billion in additional funding to the Head Start program and was available for obligation over a two-year period. [2] Funded enrollment is the number of children and pregnant women supported by federal Head Start funds at any one time during the year. Data are derived from the annual Administration for Children and Families budget and congressional documents, and do not reflect changes made during the year. [3] Cumulative enrollment refers to actual number of children and pregnant women served, including enrollees who left during the year and enrollees who filled those empty slots. More children and families may receive Head Start services cumulatively throughout the year than indicated by funded enrollment numbers. [4] Represents funding available after Congress restored funds in the amount of the previous year's fiscal sequestration.

Source: U.S. Department of Health and Human Services, Administration for Children and Families, Early Childhood Learning & Knowledge Center, "Head Start Program Facts Sheets," <http://eclkc.ohs.acf.hhs.gov/hslc/data>; and "Office of Head Start Enterprise System," <https://hses.ohs.acf.hhs.gov/pir/welcome>; accessed June 2015.

Table 594. Social Assistance Services—Nonemployer Establishments and Receipts: 2005 to 2013

[Receipts in millions of dollars (10,265 represents $10,265,000,000). Includes only firms subject to federal income tax. Nonemployers are businesses with no paid employees. Nonemployer firm receipts may include commissions or earnings]

Kind of business	NAICS code [1]	Establishments			Receipts		
		2005	2010	2013	2005	2010	2013
Social assistance, total.....................................	624	807,729	912,247	861,579	10,265	12,753	12,813
Individual and family services...............................	6241	112,909	141,971	154,024	1,920	2,599	3,016
Community/emergency and other relief services..........	6242	5,533	6,080	6,058	81	96	98
Vocational rehabilitation services...........................	6243	11,022	11,984	12,769	245	287	312
Child day care services......................................	6244	678,265	752,212	688,728	8,018	9,772	9,387

[1] North American Industry Classification System; see text, Section 15. Data for 2005 based on NAICS 2002; data for 2010 based on NAICS 2007; and data for 2013 based on NAICS 2012.

Source: U.S. Census Bureau, Nonemployer Statistics, "Geographic Area Series: Nonemployer Statistics by Legal Form of Organization: 2013," <http://factfinder2.census.gov/>, accessed May 2015. See also <http://www.census.gov/econ/nonemployer/index.html>.

Table 595. Social Assistance Services—Revenue for Employer Firms: 2010 and 2013

[In millions of dollars (146,081 represents $146,081,000,000). Estimates have been adjusted to the results of the 2007 Economic Census. Based on the Service Annual Survey and administrative data; see Appendix III]

Kind of business	2007 NAICS code [1]	2010			2013		
		Total	Taxable firms	Tax-exempt firms	Total	Taxable firms	Tax-exempt firms
Social assistance, total..........................	624	146,081	36,532	109,549	154,211	43,599	110,612
Individual and family services.......................	6241	71,847	14,832	57,015	76,422	18,950	57,472
Child and youth services.........................	62411	11,725	1,125	10,600	12,128	1,084	11,044
Services for elderly and disabled persons.......	62412	30,466	9,592	20,874	35,065	13,646	21,419
Other individual and family services..............	62419	29,656	4,115	25,541	29,229	4,220	25,009
Community, emergency and other relief services.............................	6242	28,569	(NA)	28,101	29,655	602	29,053
Community food services.........................	62421	6,720	135	6,585	8,741	143	8,598
Community housing services.....................	62422	12,071	275	11,796	12,494	301	12,193
Emergency and other relief services..............	62423	9,778	(S)	9,720	8,420	158	8,262
Vocational rehabilitation services..................	6243	13,220	1,980	11,240	13,178	1,823	11,355
Child day care services..............................	6244	32,445	19,252	13,193	34,956	22,224	12,732

NA Not available. S Estimate does not meet publication standards. [1] Based on the North American Industry Classification System, 2007; see text, Section 15.

Source: U.S. Census Bureau, Annual & Quarterly Services, "2013 Annual Services," <http://www.census.gov/services/index.html>, accessed January 2015.

Table 596. Number of Emergency and Transitional Beds in Homeless Assistance Systems Nationwide: 2014

[Data include beds located in Puerto Rico, Guam, and the Virgin Islands. Data were reported by Continuums of Care, and were collected for a point-in-time during the last week in January 2014. Data were not independently verified by Department of Housing and Urban Development (HUD)]

Homeless programs	Total year-round beds	Year-round units/beds [1]				Other beds	
		Family units	Family beds	Adult-only beds	Child-only beds	Seasonal beds [2]	Overflow/ voucher [3]
Total.......................................	772,788	120,857	366,580	401,461	4,747	22,399	28,331
Emergency, safe haven, and transitional housing...................	424,880	66,959	217,401	202,938	4,541	22,399	28,331
Emergency shelters.........................	249,497	36,152	123,252	123,173	3,072	22399	28331
Safe haven [4].............................	2,159	(X)	(X)	2,159	(X)	(X)	(X)
Transitional housing.......................	173,224	30,807	94,149	77,606	1,469	(X)	(X)
Permanent housing..........................	347,908	53,898	149,179	198,523	206	(X)	(X)
Permanent supportive housing...........	300,282	42,210	113,487	186,623	172	(X)	(X)
Rapid re-housing............................	37,783	9,657	29,506	8,253	24	(X)	(X)
Other permanent housing.................	9,843	2,031	6,186	3,647	10	(X)	(X)

X Not applicable. [1] Year-round beds are available for use throughout the year and are considered part of the stable inventory of beds for homeless persons. [2] Seasonal beds are typically available during particularly high-demand seasons of the year (e.g. winter months in the North or summer months in the South) to accommodate increased need for emergency shelters to prevent illness or death due to the weather. [3] Overflow beds are typically used during unanticipated emergencies (e.g., precipitous temperature drops or a natural disaster that displaces residents). Voucher beds are made available in a hotel or motel, and often function like overflow beds. [4] Private or semi-private long-term housing for people with severe mental illness.

Source: U.S. Department of Housing and Urban Development, 2014 Continuum of Care Homeless Assistance Programs: Housing Inventory Count Report, October 2014. See also <https://www.hudexchange.info/manage-a-program/coc-housing-inventory-count-reports/>.

Table 597. Homeless Population by Type and Shelter Status: 2008 to 2014

[Data are point-in-time (PIT) counts made on a single night in January by Continuums of Care (CoCs) in all States, DC, Puerto Rico, Guam, and Virgin Islands. Data are not independently verified by the Department of Housing and Urban Development (HUD). CoCs are required to provide an unduplicated count of homeless persons according to HUD standards. See HUD's guide to conducting point-in-time counts of homeless people at <https://www.hudexchange.info/resource/4036/point-in-time-count-methodology-guide/>. Sheltered homeless people may be staying in emergency shelters, transitional housing programs, or safe havens (long-term housing for people with severe mental illness)]

Homeless population by type	2008	2009	2010	2011	2012	2013	2014
Total	**643,668**	**633,616**	**640,466**	**625,217**	**622,982**	**591,768**	**578,424**
Sheltered	386,361	403,308	403,543	392,316	390,155	394,698	401,051
Unsheltered	257,307	230,308	236,923	232,901	232,827	197,070	177,373
Individuals [1]	407,422	395,506	398,515	389,036	383,579	369,571	362,163
Sheltered	204,855	215,995	212,218	205,834	199,159	203,127	209,148
Unsheltered	202,567	179,511	186,297	183,202	184,420	166,444	153,015
Persons in families with children	236,246	238,110	241,951	236,181	239,403	222,197	216,261
Sheltered	181,506	187,313	191,325	186,482	190,996	191,571	191,903
Unsheltered	54,740	50,797	50,626	49,699	48,407	30,626	24,358
Chronically homeless individuals [2]	120,790	108,333	107,183	103,915	96,661	86,455	84,291
Sheltered	45,418	45,592	43,329	38,971	32,647	29,418	31,203
Unsheltered	75,372	62,741	63,854	64,944	64,014	57,037	53,088
Chronically homeless people in families [2]	(NA)	(NA)	(NA)	15,512	15,770	16,539	15,143
Sheltered	(NA)	(NA)	(NA)	7,198	6,913	8,150	9,362
Unsheltered	(NA)	(NA)	(NA)	8,314	8,857	8,389	5,781
Veterans	62,989	74,050	74,770	65,645	60,769	55,779	49,933
Sheltered	38,485	43,409	43,437	40,033	35,143	34,909	32,048
Unsheltered	24,504	30,641	31,333	25,612	25,626	20,870	17,885
Children under age 18, unaccompanied	12,028	9,394	8,153	6,826	6,632	6,197	6,274
Sheltered	8,224	5,712	4,349	2,981	2,746	2,522	2,554
Unsheltered	3,804	3,682	3,804	3,845	3,886	3,675	3,720
Severely mentally ill	119,249	105,037	108,469	112,222	108,851	117,764	117,084
Sheltered	69,264	70,298	71,989	70,884	65,443	69,005	70,253
Unsheltered	49,985	34,739	36,480	41,338	43,408	48,759	46,831
Chronic substance abuse	158,506	141,757	141,152	140,795	127,912	127,275	116,770
Sheltered	96,268	95,858	95,049	87,630	75,581	76,021	70,500
Unsheltered	62,238	45,899	46,103	53,165	52,331	51,254	46,270
Persons with HIV/AIDS	15,875	14,413	14,542	12,979	11,480	11,856	12,247
Sheltered	11,066	10,909	10,590	9,698	8,300	8,847	9,638
Unsheltered	4,809	3,504	3,952	3,281	3,180	3,009	2,609
Domestic violence victims	70,092	68,018	67,146	72,248	73,458	62,134	58,182
Sheltered	49,618	48,896	49,709	53,055	54,142	44,900	42,893
Unsheltered	20,474	19,122	17,437	19,193	19,316	18,789	16,709

NA Not available. [1] People who are not part of a family. Includes homeless single adults, unaccompanied youth, or individuals in multiple-adult or multiple-child households. [2] An individual or household head of a family with a disability, and continuously homeless for a year or more, or with at least four episodes of homelessness in the last 3 years.

Source: U.S. Department of Housing and Urban Development, PIT and HIC Data Since 2007, "2007 - 2014 PIT Counts by State," December 2014, <https://www.hudexchange.info/resource/3031/pit-and-hic-data-since-2007/>, accessed February 2015; and *2014 Continuum of Care (CoC) Homeless Assistance Programs: Populations and Subpopulations,* October 2014 and earlier reports (reissued January 2015). See also <https://www.hudexchange.info/manage-a-program/coc-homeless-populations-and-subpopulations-reports/>.

Table 598. Volunteers by Selected Characteristics: 2014

[In percent, except as noted (62,757 represents 62,757,000). Based on a Current Population Survey supplement. Data on volunteers relate to persons who performed unpaid volunteer activities for an organization at any point from September 2013 through September 2014. Data represent the percent of the population involved in the activity]

Type of main organization [1]	Total, both sexes	Sex		Educational attainment [2]			
		Male	Female	Less than a high school diploma	High school graduate, no college [3]	Less than a bachelor's degree [4]	College graduates
Total volunteers (1,000)	**62,757**	**26,375**	**36,381**	**2,100**	**10,075**	**15,494**	**26,619**
Percent of population	25.3	22.0	28.3	8.8	16.4	27.3	39.4
Median annual hours [5]	50	52	50	50	52	50	52
Civic and political [6]	5.2	6.6	4.2	3.4	4.5	5.1	6.1
Educational or youth service	25.1	23.7	26.2	21.3	20.5	23.7	26.8
Environmental or animal care	2.6	2.6	2.6	1.8	2.5	2.4	2.5
Hospital or other health	7.4	6.1	8.4	3.3	5.4	7.6	7.6
Public safety	1.1	1.8	0.5	1.1	1.7	1.3	0.6
Religious	33.3	32.2	34.1	49.6	41.0	35.7	30.0
Social or community service	14.4	14.8	14.2	11.8	14.5	14.1	14.7
Sport and hobby [7]	3.9	4.7	3.3	2.1	3.1	3.7	4.6

[1] Main organization is defined as the organization for which the volunteer worked the most hours during the year. [2] Data refer to persons age 25 and over. [3] Includes high school diploma or equivalent. [4] Includes the categories "some college, no degree" and "associate degree." [5] At all organizations. For those reporting annual hours. [6] Includes professional and/or international activities. [7] Includes cultural and/or arts activities.

Source: U.S. Bureau of Labor Statistics, *Volunteering in the United States—2014*, News Release USDL-15-0280, February 2015. See also <http://www.bls.gov/news.release/volun.toc.htm>.

Table 599. Charitable Giving by Source and Type of Recipient Organization: 1990 to 2014

[In billions of dollars (98.5 represents $98,500,000,000). Individual giving is estimated using Internal Revenue Service information from individual tax returns, and from a study of approximately 8,000 households participating in the Philanthropy Panel Study conducted by Indiana University Lilly Family School of Philanthropy. Data on foundation giving are provided by the Foundation Center. Corporate giving data are based on itemized contributions claimed on federal tax returns, and also from the Foundation Center. Data on contributions by bequest are primarily based on data from the Council for Aid to Education, with additional calculations performed by Giving USA. Giving to recipient organizations are from various research organizations, including the Evangelical Council for Financial Accountability, and Urban Institute's National Center for Charitable Statistics]

Source and allocation	1990	2000	2005	2006	2007	2008	2009	2010	2011	2012	2013	2014
Total charitable giving	**98.5**	**229.7**	**292.4**	**296.1**	**311.1**	**299.6**	**274.8**	**288.2**	**298.5**	**329.3**	**334.5**	**358.4**
Individuals	79.0	174.1	220.8	224.8	233.1	213.8	200.8	208.0	213.9	241.1	244.6	258.5
Foundations [1]	7.2	24.6	32.4	34.9	40.0	42.2	41.1	41.0	43.8	46.4	49.9	54.0
Corporations	5.5	10.7	15.2	14.5	14.2	12.4	13.8	15.8	15.6	17.2	15.6	17.8
Charitable bequests	6.8	20.3	24.0	21.9	23.8	31.2	19.1	23.4	25.2	24.7	24.4	28.1
Giving by recipient organization:												
Religion	49.8	77.0	90.9	94.6	97.8	98.2	99.6	97.5	101.8	105.8	112.1	114.9
Health	7.8	15.3	20.3	24.2	25.3	24.1	26.1	27.7	26.0	27.2	28.8	30.4
Education	11.8	28.8	35.0	40.1	42.7	35.9	35.0	42.2	44.2	48.3	52.1	54.6
Human services	6.7	20.8	30.4	30.7	31.5	35.4	36.0	36.8	38.0	40.2	40.7	42.1
Arts, culture, and humanities	3.7	10.6	12.4	13.9	14.9	12.3	12.6	13.4	13.6	15.3	15.8	17.2
Public/societal benefit	6.6	15.0	20.8	23.2	20.0	18.0	17.3	19.2	22.2	23.5	25.0	26.3
Environment/wildlife	1.3	4.9	6.5	7.4	8.1	7.7	7.3	7.9	8.6	9.3	9.8	10.5
International affairs	2.1	6.3	12.7	13.5	15.8	20.6	16.4	13.9	15.4	16.8	15.4	15.1
Gifts to foundations [1]	3.8	24.7	24.5	27.1	37.7	30.1	32.4	26.3	30.4	39.8	40.9	41.6
Unallocated [2]	5.0	26.4	36.0	17.5	14.1	13.7	-12.0	-1.4	-7.6	-2.9	-13.2	-0.8

[1] Data are from the Foundation Center. [2] Money deducted as a charitable contribution by donors but not allocated to sources. May include gifts to governmental entities, in-kind giving, or gifts to new charities.

Source: Giving USA Foundation, Chicago, IL, *Giving USA 2015: The Annual Report on Philanthropy for the Year 2014* ©, researched and written at the Indiana University Lilly Family School of Philanthropy. See also <http://www.givingusareports.org/>.

Table 600. Domestic Private Foundations—Financial Information: 1995 to 2011

[Financial data in billions of dollars (195.6 represents $195,600,000,000). Minus sign (-) indicates loss]

Item	1995	2000	2003	2004	2005	2006	2007	2008	2009	2010	2011
Number of tax returns	47,917	66,738	76,348	76,897	79,535	81,850	84,613	90,850	92,624	93,436	92,990
Nonoperating foundations [1]	43,966	61,501	70,004	70,613	72,800	74,364	77,457	83,024	84,660	86,254	85,500
Operating foundations [2]	3,951	5,238	6,344	6,284	6,734	7,486	7,156	7,826	7,964	7,181	7,490
Total assets, book value [3]	195.6	409.5	418.5	455.5	481.8	569.3	591.2	531.4	550.9	584.2	594.3
Total assets, fair market value [3]	242.9	471.6	475.0	509.9	545.9	645.8	652.4	526.5	588.5	641.0	641.3
Investments in securities	190.7	361.4	344.3	361.2	373.1	403.7	400.3	287.6	324.7	353.3	344.8
Total revenue	30.8	72.8	48.4	58.7	76.4	94.1	107.3	49.7	52.2	72.5	79.4
Total expenses	17.2	37.4	35.1	36.6	42.8	48.8	58.8	60.3	56.2	60.1	64.3
Contributions, gifts, and grants paid	12.3	27.6	26.7	27.6	31.9	34.9	42.6	42.8	40.9	44.7	46.9
Excess of revenue over expenses (net)	13.6	35.3	13.3	22.1	33.5	45.3	48.6	-10.6	-4.0	12.3	15.1
Net investment income [4]	20.4	48.8	25.2	34.0	44.3	54.2	62.8	23.1	17.6	29.8	34.2

[1] Generally provide charitable support through grants and other financial means to charitable organizations; the majority of foundations are nonoperating. [2] Generally conduct their own charitable activities, e.g., museums. [3] For Tax Years 2007, 2008, 2009, 2010, and 2011, data shown for book and fair market assets were reduced by $38.7 billion, $29.6 billion, $33.4 billion, $36.7 billion, and $33.8 billion, respectively, to avoid overstating joint assets of Bill and Melinda Gates Foundation and Bill and Melinda Gates Foundation Trust. [4] This equals gross investment income less allowable deductions. Represents income not considered related to a foundation's charitable purpose, e.g., interest, dividends, and capital gains. Foundations could be subject to an excise tax on such income.

Source: Internal Revenue Service, *Statistics of Income Bulletin*, "SOI Tax Stats – Domestic Private Foundation and Charitable Trust Statistics," <http://www.irs.gov/uac/Tax-Stats-2>, accessed May 2015.

Table 601. Foundations—Number and Finances by Foundation Type: 1990 to 2012

[In millions of dollars (142,480 represents $142,480,000,000), except number of foundations. Figures are for fiscal years, and cover foundations that reported giving. Covers nongovernmental nonprofit organizations with funds and programs managed by their own trustees or directors, whose goals were to maintain or aid social, educational, religious, or other activities deemed to serve the common good. Excludes organizations that make general appeals to the public for funds, act as trade associations for industrial or other special groups, or do not currently award grants]

Year	Number	Assets (million dollars)	Gifts received (million dollars)	Total giving [1] (million dollars)
1990	32,401	142,480	5,000	8,680
2000	56,582	486,085	27,614	24,563
2005	71,097	550,553	31,465	36,402
2010	76,610	643,974	37,961	45,858
2011	81,777	662,336	42,159	48,999
Total, 2012	**86,192**	**715,456**	**52,096**	**51,824**
Independent	78,582	584,007	32,224	35,403
Operating	4,218	43,347	7,763	6,025
Corporate	2,629	23,161	4,617	5,458
Community	763	64,940	7,492	4,938
Family [2]	41,754	320,462	23,934	22,373

[1] Includes grants, scholarships, and employee matching gifts; excludes set-asides, loans, program-related investments (PRIs), and program expenses. [2] These funders are included in independent foundation data.

Source: The Foundation Center, New York, NY ©, "Foundation Stats," <http://data.foundationcenter.org/#/foundations/all/nationwide/total/list/2012>, accessed June 2015.

Table 602. Nonprofit Charitable Organizations—Financial Information: 2000 to 2011

[In billions of dollars (1,562.5 represents $1,562,500,000,000), except as indicated. Includes data reported by organizations described in Internal Revenue Code, Section 501(c)(3), excluding private foundations and most religious organizations. Prior to 2010, organizations with receipts under $25,000 were not required to file. Beginning with 2010, organizations with receipts under $50,000 were not required to file]

Year	Number of tax returns (1,000)	Total assets	Net assets	Revenue Total	Revenue Program service revenue [1]	Revenue Contributions, gifts, and grants	Total expenses	Excess of revenue over expenses (net)
2000	230.2	1,562.5	1,023.2	866.2	579.1	199.1	796.4	69.8
2001	240.6	1,631.7	1,020.3	897.0	630.8	212.4	862.7	34.3
2002	251.7	1,733.9	1,040.3	955.3	691.8	214.5	934.7	20.6
2003	263.4	1,899.9	1,164.3	1,072.2	754.6	230.0	1,009.7	62.5
2004	276.2	2,058.6	1,276.1	1,153.0	801.2	248.6	1,058.5	94.5
2005	286.6	2,241.9	1,411.3	1,252.9	852.6	276.3	1,137.9	115.0
2006	301.2	2,549.7	1,617.7	1,370.9	920.2	303.2	1,230.4	140.5
2007	313.1	2,683.4	1,674.4	1,445.9	980.3	324.5	1,317.2	128.7
2008	315.2	2,521.2	1,434.7	1,378.3	1,038.0	320.7	1,396.4	-18.1
2009	320.8	2,697.1	1,564.2	1,481.1	1,085.9	327.4	1,433.9	47.2
2010	269.5	2,946.5	1,772.4	1,593.0	1,147.3	344.9	1,497.2	95.8
2011	274.3	3,030.1	1,781.9	1,647.9	1,194.2	357.4	1,558.4	89.5

[1] Represents fees collected by organizations in support of their tax-exempt purposes, such as tuition and fees at educational institutions, hospital patient charges, and admission and activity fees collected by museums and other nonprofit organizations or institutions.

Source: Internal Revenue Service, Statistics of Income Bulletin "Nonprofit Charitable Organizations, 2011," Spring 2015, and previous reports. See also <http://www.irs.gov/uac/SOI-Tax-Stats-Charities-and-Other-Tax-Exempt-Organizations-Statistics>.

Table 603. Individual Charitable Contributions by State: 2012

[In millions of dollars (198,552 represents $198,552,000,000), except as indicated. Covers returns primarily for 2012 tax year that were filed during 2013, but may also include a limited number of returns for tax years before 2012 that were also received during 2013. Data will not agree with data in other tables due to differing survey methodology used to derive state data]

State	Number of returns (1,000)	Amount (mil. dol.)	State	Number of returns (1,000)	Amount (mil. dol.)	State	Number of returns (1,000)	Amount (mil. dol.)	State	Number of returns (1,000)	Amount (mil. dol.)
U.S. [1,2]	37,491	198,552	ID	167	932	MO	626	3,212	PA	1,518	6,513
AL	502	3,064	IL	1,710	8,104	MT	112	574	RI	149	469
AK	63	328	IN	613	2,981	NE	215	1,214	SC	516	2,717
AZ	713	3,003	IA	358	1,539	NV	280	1,529	SD	60	521
AR	236	1,541	KS	322	1,988	NH	175	548	TN	535	3,761
CA	4,883	25,606	KY	428	1,964	NJ	1,546	5,648	TX	2,198	16,076
CO	710	3,377	LA	376	2,141	NM	170	798	UT	381	3,304
CT	621	3,416	ME	142	425	NY	2,811	16,465	VT	68	269
DE	122	476	MD	1,126	5,271	NC	1,196	5,915	VA	1,217	5,721
DC	108	895	MA	1,035	4,870	ND	52	314	WA	854	4,513
FL	1,833	11,184	MI	1,127	4,983	OH	1,263	5,194	WV	103	485
GA	1,268	7,280	MN	835	3,394	OK	330	2,489	WI	771	2,741
HI	165	626	MS	251	1,574	OR	534	2,262	WY	46	3,765

[1] The sum for the states does not add to the total because other components are not shown in this table. [2] U.S. totals do not agree with Table 510 in Section 9 because this table also includes (1) "substitutes for returns," whereby the IRS constructs returns for certain nonfilers on the basis of available information and imposes an income tax on the resulting estimate of the tax base and (2) returns of nonresident or departing aliens. In addition, in this table, income tax includes the alternative minimum tax, but differs from total income tax in Table 510 in that it is after subtraction of all tax credits except a portion of the earned income credit.

Source: Internal Revenue Service, Statistics of Income, Individual Income Tax Return (Form 1040) Statistics: State Data, "SOI Tax Stats - Historic Table 2," <http://www.irs.gov/uac/SOI-Tax-Stats-Historic-Table-2>, accessed May 2015.

Labor Force, Employment, and Earnings

This section presents statistics on the labor force; its distribution by occupation and industry affiliation; and the supply of, demand for, and conditions of labor. The chief source of these data is the Current Population Survey (CPS) conducted by the U.S. Census Bureau for the Bureau of Labor Statistics (BLS). Comprehensive historical and current data are available from the BLS Internet site at <http://www.bls.gov/cps/>. These data are published on a current basis in the BLS monthly publication *Employment and Earnings Online*. Detailed data on the labor force are also available from the Census Bureau's decennial census of population.

Types of data—Most statistics in this section are obtained by two methods: household interviews or questionnaires and reports of establishment payroll records. Each method provides data that the other cannot suitably supply. Population characteristics, for example, are readily obtainable only from the household survey, while detailed industrial classifications can be readily derived only from establishment records.

CPS data are obtained from a monthly sample survey of the population. The CPS is used to gather data for the calendar week, generally the week including the 12th of the month, and provides current comprehensive data on the labor force (see text, Section 1, Population). The CPS provides information on the work status of the population without duplication since each person is classified as employed, unemployed, or not in the labor force. Employed persons holding more than one job are counted only once, according to the job at which they worked the most hours during the survey week.

Employment and Earnings Online presents data including national totals of the number of persons in the civilian labor force by sex, disability status, race, Hispanic origin, and age; the number employed; hours of work; industry and occupational groups; usual weekly earnings; and the number unemployed, as well as reasons for and duration of unemployment. Annual data shown in this section are averages of monthly figures for each calendar year, unless otherwise specified. Historical national CPS data are available at <http://www.bls.gov/cps/>.

The CPS also produces annual estimates of employment and unemployment for each state, 50 large metropolitan statistical areas, and selected cities. These estimates are published annually in *Geographic Profile of Employment and Unemployment* available at <http://www.bls.gov/gps/>.

Data based on establishment records are compiled by the BLS and cooperating state agencies as part of an ongoing Current Employment Statistics (CES) program. The BLS collects survey data monthly from a probability-based sample of nonfarm, business establishments through internet electronic data interchange, touchtone data entry, and computer-assisted telephone interviews, Internet, other electronic media, fax, transcript, or mail. CES data are adjusted annually to data from government unemployment insurance administrative records, which are supplemented by data from other government agencies. The estimates exclude self-employed persons, private household workers, unpaid family workers, agricultural workers, and members of the Armed Forces.

The establishment survey counts workers each time they appear on a payroll during the reference period (the payroll period that includes the 12th of the month). Thus, unlike the CPS, a person with two jobs is counted twice. The establishment survey is designed to provide estimates of nonfarm wage and salary employment, average weekly hours, and average hourly and weekly earnings by detailed industry for the nation, states, and selected metropolitan areas. Establishment survey data also are published in *Employment and Earnings Online*. Historical national data are available at <http://www.bls.gov/ces/>. Historical data for states and metropolitan areas are available at <http://www.bls.gov/sae/>. CES estimates are currently classified by the 2012 North American Industry Classification System (NAICS). All published series for the nation have a NAICS-based history extending back to at least 1990. Employment series for total nonfarm and other high-level aggregates start in 1939.

For more information on data concepts, sample design, and estimating methods for the CES Survey, see the BLS Handbook of Methods, Chapter 2 <http://www.bls.gov/opub/hom/>.

A sample redesign and the conversion to NAICS for state and metropolitan area establishment survey data were implemented in March 2003 with the release of January 2003 estimates. For information regarding revisions see <http://www.bls.gov/ces/cesrevinfo.htm>.

Labor force—According to the CPS definitions, the civilian labor force comprises all civilians in the noninstitutionalized population 16 years and over classified as "employed" or "unemployed" according to specific criteria. Employed civilians comprise (a) all civilians, who, during the reference week, did any work for pay or profit (minimum of an hour's work) or worked 15 hours or more as unpaid workers in a family enterprise and (b) all civilians who were not working but who had jobs or businesses from which they were temporarily absent for noneconomic reasons (illness, weather conditions, vacation, labor-management dispute, etc.) whether they were paid for the time off or were seeking other jobs. Unemployed persons comprise all civilians who had no employment during the reference week, who made specific efforts to find a job within the previous 4 weeks (such as applying directly to an employer or to a public employment service or checking with friends) and who were available for work during that week, except for temporary illness. Persons on layoff from a job and expecting recall also are classified as unemployed. All other civilian persons, 16 years old and over, are classified as "not in the labor force."

Various breaks in the CPS data series have occurred over time due to the introduction of population adjustments and other changes. For details on these breaks in series and the effect that they had on the

CPS data, see the BLS Web site at <www.bls.gov/cps/documentation.htm#concepts>.

Beginning in January of each year, the CPS data reflect the introduction of revised population controls. For additional information on the effects of revised population controls on estimates from the CPS, see <www.bls.gov/cps/documentation.htm#pop>.

Hours and earnings—Average hourly earnings, based on establishment data, are gross earnings (i.e., earnings before payroll deductions) and include overtime premiums; they exclude irregular bonuses and value of payments in kind. Hours are those for which pay was received. Annual wages and salaries from the CPS consist of total monies received for work performed by an employee during the income year. It includes wages, salaries, commissions, tips, piece-rate payments, and cash bonuses earned before deductions were made for taxes, bonds, union dues, etc. Persons who worked 35 hours or more are classified as working full-time.

Industry and occupational groups—Industry data derived from the CPS for 1983-91 utilize the 1980 census industrial classification developed from the 1972 Standard Industrial Classification (SIC). CPS data from 1971 to 1982 were based on the 1970 census classification system, which was developed from the 1967 SIC. Most of the industry categories were not affected by the change in classification.

The occupational classification system used in the 1980 census and in the CPS for 1983-91, evolved from the 1980 Standard Occupational Classification (SOC) system, first introduced in 1977. Occupational categories used in the 1980 census classification system are so radically different from the 1970 census system used in the CPS through 1982 that their implementation represented a break in historical data series.

Beginning in January 1992, the occupational and industrial classification systems used in the 1990 census were introduced into the CPS. (These systems were largely based on the 1980 SOC and the 1987 SIC systems, respectively.)

Beginning in 2003, the 2002 occupational and industrial classification systems were introduced into the CPS. These systems were derived from the 2000 SOC and the 2002 NAICS. The composition of detailed occupational and industrial classifications in the new classification systems was substantially changed from the previous systems in use, as was the structure for aggregating them into broad groups. Consequently, the use of the new classification systems created breaks in existing data series at all levels of aggregation. CPS data using the new classification systems are available beginning 2000. Additional information on the occupational and industrial classifications systems used in the CPS, including changes over time, appear on the BLS Web site at <www.bls.gov/cps/documentation.htm#oi>. Establishments responding to the establishment survey are classified according to the 2012 NAICS. Previously they were classified according to the SIC manual. See text, Section 15, Business Enterprise, for information about the SIC manual and NAICS.

Productivity—BLS publishes data on output per hour (labor productivity), output per combined unit of labor and capital input (multifactor productivity), and, for industry groups and industries, output per combined unit of capital, labor, energy, materials, and purchased service inputs. Labor productivity and related indexes are published for the business sector as a whole and its major subsectors: nonfarm business, manufacturing, and nonfinancial corporations, and for over 200 detailed industries. Productivity indexes that take into account capital, labor, energy, materials, and service inputs are published for 18 major manufacturing industry groups, 86 detailed manufacturing industries, utility services, and air and railroad transportation. The major sector data are published in the BLS quarterly news release *Productivity and Costs* and in the annual *Multifactor Productivity Trends* release. Industry productivity measures are updated and published annually in the news releases *Productivity and Costs by Industry* and *Multifactor Productivity Trends by Industry*. The latest data are available at the Labor Productivity and Costs Web site at <http://www.bls.gov/lpc/> and the Multifactor Productivity Web site at <http://www.bls.gov/mfp>. Detailed information on methods, limitations, and data sources appears in the BLS *Handbook of Methods*, BLS Bulletin 2490 (1997), Chapters 10 and 11 at <http://www.bls.gov/opub/hom/home.htm> and <http://www.bls.gov/lpc/lpcmethods.htm>

Unions—As defined here, unions include traditional labor unions and employee associations similar to labor unions. Data on union membership status provided by BLS are for employed wage and salary workers and relate to their principal job. Earnings by union membership status are usual weekly earnings of full-time wage and salary workers. The information is collected through the Current Population Survey.

Work stoppages—Work stoppages include all strikes and lockouts known to BLS that last for at least 1 full day or shift and involve 1,000 or more workers. All stoppages, whether or not authorized by a union, legal or illegal, are counted. Excluded are work slowdowns and instances where employees report to work late or leave early to attend meetings or rallies.

Seasonal adjustment—Many economic statistics reflect a regularly recurring seasonal movement that can be estimated on the basis of past experience. By eliminating that part of the change which can be ascribed to usual seasonal variation (e.g., climate or school openings and closings), it is possible to observe the cyclical and other nonseasonal movements in the series. However, in evaluating deviations from the seasonal pattern—that is, changes in a seasonally adjusted series—it is important to note that seasonal adjustment is merely an approximation based on past experience. Seasonally adjusted estimates have a broader margin of possible error than the original data on which they are based, since they are subject not only to sampling and other errors, but also are affected by the uncertainties of the adjustment process itself. Consistent with BLS practices, annual estimates will be published only for not seasonally-adjusted data.

Statistical reliability—For discussion of statistical collection, estimation, sampling procedures, and measures of statistical reliability applicable to Census Bureau and BLS data, see Appendix III.

Table 604. Civilian Population—Employment Status: 1970 to 2014

[In thousands (137,085 represents 137,085,000), except as indicated. Annual averages of monthly figures. Civilian noninstitutionalized population 16 years old and over. Data not strictly comparable with data for earlier years, see BLS Handbook of Methods, <http://www.bls.gov/opub/hom/>. Based on Current Population Survey; see text, Section 1 and Appendix III]

Year	Civilian noninsti-tutional population	Civilian labor force				Unemployed		Not in labor force	
		Total	Percent of population	Employed	Employ-ment/ population ratio [1]	Number	Percent of labor force	Number	Percent of population
1970	137,085	82,771	60.4	78,678	57.4	4,093	4.9	54,315	39.6
1980	167,745	106,940	63.8	99,303	59.2	7,637	7.1	60,806	36.2
1990	189,164	125,840	66.5	118,793	62.8	7,047	5.6	63,324	33.5
1995	198,584	132,304	66.6	124,900	62.9	7,404	5.6	66,280	33.4
2000	212,577	142,583	67.1	136,891	64.4	5,692	4.0	69,994	32.9
2001	215,092	143,734	66.8	136,933	63.7	6,801	4.7	71,359	33.2
2002	217,570	144,863	66.6	136,485	62.7	8,378	5.8	72,707	33.4
2003	221,168	146,510	66.2	137,736	62.3	8,774	6.0	74,658	33.8
2004	223,357	147,401	66.0	139,252	62.3	8,149	5.5	75,956	34.0
2005	226,082	149,320	66.0	141,730	62.7	7,591	5.1	76,762	34.0
2006	228,815	151,428	66.2	144,427	63.1	7,001	4.6	77,387	33.8
2007	231,867	153,124	66.0	146,047	63.0	7,078	4.6	78,743	34.0
2008	233,788	154,287	66.0	145,362	62.2	8,924	5.8	79,501	34.0
2009	235,801	154,142	65.4	139,877	59.3	14,265	9.3	81,659	34.6
2010	237,830	153,889	64.7	139,064	58.5	14,825	9.6	83,941	35.3
2011	239,618	153,617	64.1	139,869	58.4	13,747	8.9	86,001	35.9
2012	243,284	154,975	63.7	142,469	58.6	12,506	8.1	88,310	36.3
2013	245,679	155,389	63.2	143,929	58.6	11,460	7.4	90,290	36.8
2014	247,947	155,922	62.9	146,305	59.0	9,617	6.2	92,025	37.1

[1] Civilian employed as a percent of the civilian noninstitutional population.

Source: U.S. Bureau of Labor Statistics, "Employment and Earnings Online," <www.bls.gov/opub/ee/home.htm>, accessed March 2015.

Table 605. Civilian Labor Force and Participation Rates With Projections: 1990 to 2022

[125.8 represents 125,800,000. Civilian noninstitutionalized population 16 years old and over. Annual averages of monthly figures. Rates are based on annual average civilian noninstitutional population of each specified group and represent proportion of each specified group in the civilian labor force. Based on Current Population Survey; see text, Section 1 and Appendix III]

Race, Hispanic origin, sex, and age	Civilian labor force (mil.)						Participation rate (percent) [1]					
	1990	2000	2005	2010	2012	2022, proj.	1990	2000	2005	2010	2012	2022, proj.
Total [2]	125.8	142.6	149.3	153.9	155.0	163.5	66.5	67.1	66.0	64.7	63.7	61.6
White [3]	107.4	118.5	122.3	125.1	123.7	126.9	66.9	67.3	66.3	65.1	64.0	61.7
Male	59.6	64.5	66.7	67.7	66.9	69.0	77.1	75.5	74.1	72.0	71.0	68.3
Female	47.8	54.1	55.6	57.4	56.8	57.9	57.4	59.5	58.9	58.5	57.4	55.3
Black [3]	13.7	16.4	17.0	17.9	18.4	20.2	64.0	65.8	64.2	62.2	61.5	59.8
Male	6.8	7.7	8.0	8.4	8.6	9.5	71.0	69.2	67.3	65.0	63.6	61.7
Female	6.9	8.7	9.0	9.4	9.8	10.7	58.3	63.1	61.6	59.9	59.8	58.3
Asian [3, 4]	(NA)	6.3	6.5	7.2	8.2	10.1	(NA)	67.2	66.1	64.7	63.9	63.2
Male	(NA)	3.4	3.5	3.9	4.3	5.3	(NA)	76.1	74.8	73.2	72.2	71.4
Female	(NA)	2.9	3.0	3.4	3.9	4.8	(NA)	59.2	58.2	57.0	56.5	56.1
Hispanic [5]	10.7	16.7	19.8	22.7	24.4	31.2	67.4	69.7	68.0	67.5	66.4	65.9
Male	6.5	9.9	12.0	13.5	14.0	17.9	81.4	81.5	80.1	77.8	76.1	74.8
Female	4.2	6.8	7.8	9.2	10.4	13.3	53.1	57.5	55.3	56.5	56.6	56.8
Male	69.0	76.3	80.0	82.0	82.3	86.9	76.4	74.8	73.3	71.2	70.2	67.6
16 to 19 years	4.1	4.3	3.6	3.0	2.9	2.3	55.7	52.8	43.2	34.9	34.0	27.8
20 to 24 years	7.9	7.5	8.1	7.9	8.1	7.3	84.4	82.6	79.1	74.5	74.5	69.9
25 to 34 years	19.9	17.8	17.8	18.4	18.1	20.2	94.1	93.4	91.7	89.7	89.5	88.8
35 to 44 years	17.5	20.1	19.5	18.1	17.6	19.1	94.3	92.7	92.1	91.5	90.7	90.4
45 to 54 years	11.1	16.3	18.1	18.9	18.4	16.5	90.7	88.6	87.7	86.8	86.1	85.1
55 to 64 years	6.6	7.8	10.0	12.1	12.9	14.4	67.8	67.3	69.3	70.0	69.9	71.0
65 years and over	2.0	2.5	3.0	3.7	4.3	7.2	16.3	17.7	19.8	22.1	23.6	27.2
Female	56.8	66.3	69.3	71.9	72.6	76.5	57.5	59.9	59.3	58.6	57.7	56.0
16 to 19 years	3.7	4.0	3.6	2.9	2.9	2.2	51.6	51.2	44.2	35.0	34.6	26.7
20 to 24 years	6.8	6.7	7.1	7.2	7.4	6.7	71.3	73.1	70.1	68.3	67.4	64.7
25 to 34 years	16.1	14.9	14.5	15.3	15.4	16.6	73.5	76.1	73.9	74.7	74.1	73.4
35 to 44 years	14.7	17.5	16.5	15.2	15.1	15.7	76.4	77.2	75.8	75.2	74.8	73.3
45 to 54 years	9.1	14.8	16.3	17.1	16.7	15.1	71.2	76.8	76.0	75.7	74.7	74.9
55 to 64 years	4.9	6.6	8.9	11.2	11.8	13.9	45.2	51.9	57.0	60.2	59.4	64.3
65 years and over	1.5	1.8	2.3	3.0	3.4	6.3	8.6	9.4	11.5	13.8	14.4	19.5

NA Not available. [1] Civilian labor force as a percent of the civilian noninstitutional population. [2] Includes other races, not shown separately. [3] The 2003 Current Population Survey allowed respondents to choose more than one race. Beginning 2005, data represent persons who selected this race group only and exclude persons reporting more than one race. Prior to 2003 the CPS allowed respondents to report one race group only. See also comments on race in the text for Section 1. [4] Prior to 2003, includes Pacific Islanders. [5] Persons of Hispanic origin may be of any race.

Source: U.S. Bureau of Labor Statistics, "Employment and Earnings Online," January 2012; "Monthly Labor Review," November 2011; and "Employment Projections Program," <http://www.bls.gov/emp/ep_data_labor_force.htm>, accessed May 2014.

Table 606. Civilian Population—Employment Status by Sex, Race, and Ethnicity: 1980 to 2014

[In thousands (79,398 represents 79,398,000), except as indicated. Annual averages of monthly figures. Data not strictly comparable with data for earlier years, see BLS Handbook of Methods, <http://www.bls.gov/opub/hom/>; see Table 604 for U.S. totals and coverage]

Year, sex, race, and Hispanic origin	Civilian noninstitutionalized population	Civilian labor force						Not in labor force	
		Total	Percent of population	Employed	Employment/population ratio [1]	Unemployed		Number	Percent of population
						Number	Percent of labor force		
Male:									
1980................	79,398	61,453	77.4	57,186	72.0	4,267	6.9	17,945	22.6
1990................	90,377	69,011	76.4	65,104	72.0	3,906	5.7	21,367	23.6
2000................	101,964	76,280	74.8	73,305	71.9	2,975	3.9	25,684	25.2
2010................	115,174	81,985	71.2	73,359	63.7	8,626	10.5	33,189	28.8
2012................	117,343	82,327	70.2	75,555	64.4	6,771	8.2	35,017	29.8
2013................	118,555	82,667	69.7	76,353	64.4	6,314	7.6	35,889	30.3
2014................	119,748	82,882	69.2	77,692	64.9	5,190	6.3	36,865	30.8
Female:									
1980................	88,348	45,487	51.5	42,117	47.7	3,370	7.4	42,861	48.5
1990................	98,787	56,829	57.5	53,689	54.3	3,140	5.5	41,957	42.5
2000................	110,613	66,303	59.9	63,586	57.5	2,717	4.1	44,310	40.1
2010................	122,656	71,904	58.6	65,705	53.6	6,199	8.6	50,752	41.4
2012................	125,941	72,648	57.7	66,914	53.1	5,734	7.9	53,293	42.3
2013................	127,124	72,722	57.2	67,577	53.2	5,146	7.1	54,401	42.8
2014................	128,199	73,039	57.0	68,613	53.5	4,426	6.1	55,159	43.0
White: [2]									
1980................	146,122	93,600	64.1	87,715	60.0	5,884	6.3	52,523	35.9
1990................	160,625	107,447	66.9	102,261	63.7	5,186	4.8	53,178	33.1
2000................	176,220	118,545	67.3	114,424	64.9	4,121	3.5	57,675	32.7
2005................	184,446	122,299	66.3	116,949	63.4	5,350	4.4	62,148	33.7
2010................	192,075	125,084	65.1	114,168	59.4	10,916	8.7	66,991	34.9
2012................	193,204	123,684	64.0	114,769	59.4	8,915	7.2	69,520	36.0
2013................	194,333	123,412	63.5	115,379	59.4	8,033	6.5	70,920	36.5
2014................	195,498	123,327	63.1	116,788	59.7	6,540	5.3	72,170	36.9
Black: [2]									
1980................	17,824	10,865	61.0	9,313	52.2	1,553	14.3	6,959	39.0
1990................	21,477	13,740	64.0	12,175	56.7	1,565	11.4	7,737	36.0
2000................	24,902	16,397	65.8	15,156	60.9	1,241	7.6	8,505	34.2
2010................	28,708	17,862	62.2	15,010	52.3	2,852	16.0	10,846	37.8
2012................	29,907	18,400	61.5	15,856	53.0	2,544	13.8	11,508	38.5
2013................	30,376	18,580	61.2	16,151	53.2	2,429	13.1	11,797	38.8
2014................	30,843	18,873	61.2	16,732	54.3	2,141	11.3	11,970	38.8
Asian: [2,3]									
2000................	9,330	6,270	67.2	6,043	64.8	227	3.6	3,060	32.8
2010................	11,199	7,248	64.7	6,705	59.9	543	7.5	3,951	35.3
2012................	12,815	8,188	63.9	7,705	60.1	483	5.9	4,627	36.1
2013................	13,296	8,584	64.6	8,136	61.2	448	5.2	4,712	35.4
2014................	13,785	8,760	63.6	8,325	60.4	436	5.0	5,024	36.4
Hispanic: [4]									
1980................	9,598	6,146	64.0	5,527	57.6	620	10.1	3,451	36.0
1990................	15,904	10,720	67.4	9,845	61.9	876	8.2	5,184	32.6
2000................	23,938	16,689	69.7	15,735	65.7	954	5.7	7,249	30.3
2010................	33,713	22,748	67.5	19,906	59.0	2,843	12.5	10,964	32.5
2012................	36,759	24,391	66.4	21,878	59.5	2,514	10.3	12,368	33.6
2013................	37,517	24,771	66.0	22,514	60.0	2,257	9.1	12,746	34.0
2014................	38,400	25,370	66.1	23,492	61.2	1,878	7.4	13,030	33.9
Mexican:									
1990................	9,752	6,707	68.8	6,146	63.0	561	8.4	3,045	31.2
2000................	15,333	10,783	70.3	10,144	66.2	639	5.9	4,550	29.7
2010................	21,267	14,403	67.7	12,622	59.4	1,781	12.4	6,864	32.3
2012................	22,716	15,128	66.6	13,552	59.7	1,577	10.4	7,588	33.4
2013................	23,277	15,366	66.0	13,979	60.1	1,387	9.0	7,911	34.0
2014................	23,829	15,768	66.2	14,629	61.4	1,139	7.2	8,061	33.8
Puerto Rican:									
1990................	1,718	960	55.9	870	50.6	91	9.5	758	44.1
2000................	2,193	1,411	64.3	1,318	60.1	92	6.6	783	35.7
2010................	3,110	1,906	61.3	1,612	51.8	293	15.4	1,204	38.7
2012................	3,462	2,090	60.4	1,830	52.9	260	12.4	1,372	39.6
2013................	3,428	2,066	60.2	1,784	52.0	282	13.6	1,363	39.8
2014................	3,515	2,114	60.1	1,891	53.8	224	10.6	1,401	39.9
Cuban:									
1990................	918	603	65.7	559	60.9	44	7.2	315	34.3
2000................	1,174	740	63.1	707	60.3	33	4.5	434	37.0
2010................	1,549	970	62.6	850	54.9	120	12.4	579	37.4
2012................	1,702	1,102	64.7	994	58.4	108	9.8	601	35.3
2013................	1,700	1,043	61.3	963	56.6	80	7.7	657	38.6
2014................	1,659	1,009	60.8	950	57.3	59	5.8	650	39.2

[1] Civilian employed as a percent of the civilian noninstitutional population. [2] Beginning in 2002, the Current Population Survey (CPS) allowed respondents to choose more than one race. For 2002 and beyond, data represent persons who selected this race group only and exclude persons reporting more than one race. The CPS in prior years only allowed respondents to report one race group. See also comments on race in the text for Section 1. [3] Prior to 2002, includes Pacific Islanders. [4] Persons of Hispanic origin may be of any race. Includes persons of other Hispanic or Latino ethnicity, not shown separately.

Source: U.S. Bureau of Labor Statistics, "Employment & Earnings Online," 2015 and earlier releases, <http://www.bls.gov/opub/ee/home.htm>.

Table 607. Foreign-Born and Native-Born Populations—Employment Status by Selected Characteristics: 2014

[247,947 represents 247,947,000. For civilian noninstitutional population 16 years old and over, except as indicated. The foreign born are persons who reside in the United States but who were born outside the country or in one of its outlying areas to parents who were not U.S. citizens. The foreign born include legally admitted immigrants, refugees, temporary residents such as students and temporary workers and undocumented immigrants. Annual averages of monthly figures. Based on Current Population Survey; see text, Section 1 and Appendix III]

Characteristic	Civilian noninstitutionalized population (1,000)	Civilian labor force					Not in the labor force (1,000)
		Total (1,000)	Participation rate [1]	Employed (1,000)	Unemployed		
					Number (1,000)	Unemployment rate	
Total............................	**247,947**	**155,922**	**62.9**	**146,305**	**9,617**	**6.2**	**92,025**
Male...........................	119,748	82,882	69.2	77,692	5,190	6.3	36,866
Female........................	128,199	73,039	57.0	68,613	4,426	6.1	55,160
FOREIGN BORN							
Total [2].........................	**38,997**	**25,735**	**66.0**	**24,282**	**1,453**	**5.6**	**13,262**
Male...........................	18,997	14,957	78.7	14,204	753	5.0	4,040
Female........................	20,000	10,779	53.9	10,078	700	6.5	9,221
Age:							
16 to 24 years old..........	3,543	1,852	52.3	1,645	207	11.2	1,691
25 to 34 years old..........	7,554	5,647	74.8	5,324	323	5.7	1,907
35 to 44 years old..........	8,897	7,032	79.0	6,697	336	4.8	1,865
45 to 54 years old..........	7,949	6,441	81.0	6,109	332	5.2	1,508
55 to 64 years old..........	5,534	3,715	67.1	3,515	200	5.4	1,819
65 years old and over......	5,520	1,047	19.0	992	55	5.2	4,473
Race and Hispanic ethnicity:							
White non-Hispanic........	7,564	4,500	59.5	4,290	211	4.7	3,064
Black non-Hispanic.........	3,243	2,305	71.1	2,106	199	8.6	938
Asian non-Hispanic........	9,729	6,211	63.8	5,924	287	4.6	3,518
Hispanic [3]...................	18,053	12,431	68.9	11,692	739	5.9	5,622
Educational attainment:							
Total, 25 years old and over........	35,455	23,883	67.4	22,637	1,246	5.2	11,572
Less than a high school diploma...	9,649	5,684	58.9	5,321	363	6.4	3,965
High school graduates, no college [4]......	8,924	5,856	65.6	5,547	309	5.3	3,068
Some college or associate's degree...........	5,816	4,168	71.7	3,932	236	5.7	1,648
Bachelor's degree and higher [5]...............	11,065	8,176	73.9	7,838	338	4.1	2,889
NATIVE BORN							
Total [2].........................	**208,949**	**130,187**	**62.3**	**122,023**	**8,164**	**6.3**	**78,762**
Male...........................	100,751	67,926	67.4	63,488	4,437	6.5	32,825
Female........................	108,199	62,261	57.5	58,535	3,726	6.0	45,938
Age:							
16 to 24 years old..........	35,170	19,443	55.3	16,797	2,646	13.6	15,727
25 to 34 years old..........	34,577	28,551	82.6	26,651	1,901	6.7	6,026
35 to 44 years old..........	30,668	25,473	83.1	24,270	1,203	4.7	5,195
45 to 54 years old..........	34,866	27,621	79.2	26,446	1,175	4.3	7,245
55 to 64 years old..........	34,230	21,787	63.6	20,880	907	4.2	12,443
65 years old and over......	39,439	7,311	18.5	6,979	332	4.5	32,128
Race and Hispanic ethnicity:							
White non-Hispanic........	153,630	96,161	62.6	91,456	4,705	4.9	57,469
Black non-Hispanic.........	25,844	15,437	59.7	13,608	1,829	11.8	10,407
Asian non-Hispanic........	3,738	2,325	62.2	2,195	130	5.6	1,413
Hispanic [3]...................	20,347	12,939	63.6	11,800	1,139	8.8	7,408
Educational attainment:							
Total, 25 years and over.......	173,780	110,744	63.7	105,226	5,518	5.0	63,036
Less than a high school diploma...	14,493	5,144	35.5	4,531	613	11.9	9,349
High school graduates, no college [4]...........	53,136	30,177	56.8	28,319	1,858	6.2	22,959
Some college or associate's degree...........	49,878	33,153	66.5	31,367	1786	5.4	16,725
Bachelor's degree and higher [5]...............	56,272	42,270	75.1	41,010	1,261	3.0	14,002

[1] Civilian labor force as a percent of the civilian noninstitutionalized population. [2] Includes other races, not shown separately. [3] Persons of Hispanic origin may be of any race. [4] Includes persons with a high school diploma or equivalent. [5] Includes persons with bachelor's, master's, professional, and doctoral degrees.

Source: U.S. Bureau of Labor Statistics, *Foreign-Born Workers: Labor Force Characteristics—2014*, News Release, USDL 15-0971, May 2015. See also <http://www.bls.gov/news.release/forbrn.toc.htm>.

Table 608. Employment Status of Veterans by Period of Service and Sex: 2014

[In thousands (239,049 represents 239,049,000). For civilian noninstitutional population 18 years old and over. Veterans are defined as men and women who have previously served on active duty in the U.S. Armed Forces and who were civilians at the time they were surveyed. See text, Section 10. Annual averages of monthly figures. Beginning with 2014, estimates for veterans incorporate updated weighting procedures. The primary impact of the change was an increase in the "Gulf War-era I" veteran population and a decrease in the number of veterans in the "Other service periods" category. For more information, see <http://www.bls.gov/cps/vetsweights2014.pdf>. Based on Current Population Survey; see text, Section 1 and Appendix III]

Veteran status, period of service, and sex	Civilian non-institu-tionalized popula-tion	Civilian labor force		Employed		Unemployed		Not in labor force
		Total	Percent of popula-tion	Total	Percent of popula-tion	Total	Percent of labor force	
Total, 18 years and over....................	239,049	153,951	64.4	144,760	60.6	9,191	6.0	85,098
Veterans................................	**21,229**	**10,744**	**50.6**	**10,171**	**47.9**	**573**	**5.3**	**10,485**
Gulf War era, total............................	6,540	5,302	81.1	5,003	76.5	298	5.6	1,238
Gulf War era II [1].............................	3,185	2,535	79.6	2,353	73.9	182	7.2	649
Gulf War era I [2].............................	3,356	2,766	82.4	2,650	79.0	117	4.2	589
WWII, Korean War, and Vietnam era [3]......	9,372	2,654	28.3	2,522	26.9	132	5.0	6,718
Other service periods [4].....................	5,317	2,788	52.4	2,645	49.7	143	5.1	2,529
Nonveterans [5]...............................	217,820	143,207	65.7	134,589	61.8	8,618	6.0	74,613
Male, 18 years and over.................	115,235	81,924	71.1	76,963	66.8	4,960	6.1	33,311
Veterans................................	**19,023**	**9,358**	**49.2**	**8,868**	**46.6**	**490**	**5.2**	**9,664**
Gulf War era, total............................	5,268	4,393	83.4	4,157	78.9	236	5.4	875
Gulf War era II [1].............................	2,549	2,096	82.2	1,952	76.6	144	6.9	453
Gulf War era I [2].............................	2,719	2,297	84.5	2,205	81.1	92	4.0	421
WWII, Korean War, and Vietnam era [3]......	9,023	2,559	28.4	2,432	27.0	127	5.0	6,464
Other service periods [4].....................	4,732	2,406	50.8	2,279	48.2	127	5.3	2,326
Nonveterans [5]...............................	96,213	72,565	75.4	68,095	70.8	4,470	6.2	23,647
Female, 18 years and over.................	123,814	72,027	58.2	67,796	54.8	4,231	5.9	51,787
Veterans................................	**2,206**	**1,386**	**62.8**	**1,303**	**59.0**	**83**	**6.0**	**821**
Gulf War era, total............................	1,272	909	71.4	847	66.5	62	6.8	364
Gulf War era II [1].............................	635	439	69.2	402	63.3	37	8.5	196
Gulf War era I [2].............................	637	469	73.7	445	69.8	25	5.2	168
WWII, Korean War, and Vietnam era [3]......	349	95	27.2	90	25.7	5	5.4	254
Other service periods [4].....................	585	382	65.3	366	62.6	16	4.2	203
Nonveterans [5]...............................	121,607	70,641	58.1	66,494	54.7	4,148	5.9	50,966

[1] Gulf War era II: September 2001–present. [2] Gulf War era I: August 1990–August 2001. [3] World War II: December 1941–December 1946. Korean War: July 1950–January 1955. Vietnam era: August 1964–April 1975. [4] Other service periods; all other time periods. [5] Nonveterans are men and women who never served on active duty in the U.S. Armed Forces.

Source: U.S. Bureau of Labor Statistics, *Employment Situation of Veterans—2014*, USDL-15-0426, March 2015. See also <http://www.bls.gov/news.release/vet.nr0.htm>.

Table 609. Labor Force Status of Persons With and Without a Disability: 2014

[29,219 represents 29,219,000. For civilian noninstitutionalized population 16 years old and over, except as indicated. Persons with a disability are those who have a physical, mental, or emotional condition that causes serious difficulty with their daily activities. Annual averages of monthly figures. Based on Current Population Survey; see text, Section 1 and Appendix III]

Characteristic	Civilian non-institutional-ized popula-tion (1,000)	Civilian labor force			Unemployed		Not in the labor force (1,000)
		Total (1,000)	Participation rate [1]	Employed (1,000)	Number (1,000)	Unemploy-ment rate	
WITH DISABILITY							
Total [2]...........................	**29,219**	**5,699**	**19.5**	**4,985**	**714**	**12.5**	**23,520**
Sex:							
Male...........................	13,580	3,108	22.9	2,719	389	12.5	10,472
Female...........................	15,639	2,591	16.6	2,266	325	12.5	13,047
Age:							
16 to 64 years...................	15,612	4,717	30.2	4,062	656	13.9	10,895
16 to 19 years...................	585	137	23.5	81	56	41.0	448
20 to 24 years...................	840	368	43.9	274	95	25.7	471
25 to 34 years...................	1,783	757	42.5	622	135	17.9	1,026
35 to 44 years...................	2,127	748	35.2	645	103	13.8	1,379
45 to 54 years...................	4,058	1,196	29.5	1,057	139	11.6	2,863
55 to 64 years...................	6,220	1,511	24.3	1,384	128	8.4	4,709
65 years and over.................	13,606	981	7.2	923	58	5.9	12,625
WITHOUT DISABILITY							
Total [2]...........................	**218,728**	**150,223**	**68.7**	**141,320**	**8,903**	**5.9**	**68,505**
Sex:							
Male...........................	106,168	79,775	75.1	74,974	4,801	6.0	26,393
Female...........................	112,560	70,448	62.6	66,347	4,101	5.8	42,112
Age:							
16 to 64 years...................	187,375	142,847	76.2	134,273	8,574	6.0	44,528
16 to 19 years...................	16,048	5,517	34.4	4,467	1,050	19.0	10,532
20 to 24 years...................	21,240	15,273	71.9	13,620	1,653	10.8	5,967
25 to 34 years...................	40,348	33,442	82.9	31,353	2,088	6.2	6,906
35 to 44 years...................	37,438	31,758	84.8	30,322	1,436	4.5	5,680
45 to 54 years...................	38,756	32,866	84.8	31,499	1,368	4.2	5,890
55 to 64 years...................	33,544	23,991	71.5	23,012	979	4.1	9,553
65 years and over.................	31,353	7,376	23.5	7,048	329	4.5	23,977

[1] Civilian labor force as a percent of the civilian noninstitutional population. [2] Total includes persons of other races not shown separately.

Source: U.S. Bureau of Labor Statistics, Current Population Survey, "Persons with A Disability: Labor Force Characteristics—2014," <http://www.bls.gov/cps/demographics.htm#disability>, accessed July 2015.

Table 610. Civilian Labor Force—Percent Distribution by Sex and Age: 1980 to 2014

[106,940 represents 106,940,000. Civilian noninstitutionalized population 16 years old and over. Annual averages of monthly figures. Data not strictly comparable with data for earlier years, see BLS Handbook of Methods, <http://www.bls.gov/opub/hom/>. Based on Current Population Survey; see text, Section 1 and Appendix III]

Year and sex	Civilian labor force (1,000)	Percent distribution						
		16 to 19 years	20 to 24 years	25 to 34 years	35 to 44 years	45 to 54 years	55 to 64 years	65 years and over
Total:								
1980.............	106,940	8.8	14.9	27.3	19.1	15.8	11.2	2.9
1990.............	125,840	6.2	11.7	28.6	25.5	16.1	9.2	2.7
2000.............	142,583	5.8	10.0	23.0	26.3	21.8	10.1	3.0
2010.............	153,889	3.8	9.8	21.8	21.7	23.4	15.1	4.4
2014.............	155,922	3.6	10.0	21.9	20.8	21.8	16.4	5.4
Male:								
1980.............	61,453	8.1	14.0	27.6	19.3	16.1	11.8	3.1
1990.............	69,011	5.9	11.4	28.8	25.3	16.1	9.6	2.9
2000.............	76,280	5.6	9.9	23.4	26.3	21.3	10.2	3.3
2010.............	81,985	3.6	9.6	22.4	22.1	23.0	14.8	4.5
2014.............	82,882	3.4	9.9	22.3	21.2	21.6	16.1	5.5
Female:								
1980.............	45,487	9.6	16.1	26.9	19.0	15.4	10.4	2.6
1990.............	56,829	6.5	12.0	28.3	25.8	16.1	8.7	2.6
2000.............	66,303	6.0	10.2	22.5	26.4	22.3	9.9	2.7
2010.............	71,904	4.1	10.0	21.2	21.2	23.8	15.6	4.2
2014.............	73,039	3.9	10.2	21.5	20.5	22.1	16.6	5.2

Source: U.S. Bureau of Labor Statistics, Employment & Earnings Online, "Employment status of the civilian noninstitutional population by age, sex, and race," February 2015, and earlier releases, <www.bls.gov/opub/ee/home.htm>.

Table 611. Civilian Labor Force and Participation Rates by Educational Attainment, Sex, Race, and Hispanic Origin: 2000 to 2014

[120,061 represents 120,061,000. Civilian noninstitutional population 25 years old and over. Annual averages of monthly figures. Data not strictly comparable with data for earlier years, see BLS Handbook of Methods, <http://www.bls.gov/opub/hom/>. See Table 646 for unemployment data. Rates are based on annual average civilian noninstitutional population of each specified group and represent proportion of each specified group in the civilian labor force]

Year, sex, and race/ethnicity	Civilian labor force					Participation rate (percent) [1]				
		Percent distribution								
	Total (1,000)	Less than a high school diploma	High school graduate, no college	Less than a bachelor's degree	College graduate	Total	Less than a high school diploma	High school graduate, no college	Less than a bachelor's degree	College graduate
Total: [2]										
2000..............	120,061	10.4	31.4	27.7	30.5	67.3	43.5	64.4	73.9	79.4
2005..............	127,030	10.0	30.1	27.5	32.4	67.1	45.5	63.2	72.5	77.9
2010..............	132,955	8.9	28.8	27.7	34.6	66.5	46.3	61.6	70.5	76.7
2014..............	134,627	8.0	26.8	27.7	37.5	64.3	44.9	58.1	67.0	74.9
Male:										
2000..............	64,490	11.8	31.1	25.9	31.2	76.1	56.0	75.1	80.9	84.4
2005..............	68,389	11.7	30.9	25.4	32.1	75.4	58.6	73.6	79.3	82.9
2010..............	71,129	10.6	30.4	25.6	33.4	74.1	59.1	71.4	76.7	81.3
2014..............	71,873	9.7	28.8	25.9	35.6	71.7	57.8	67.9	73.1	79.4
Female:										
2000..............	55,572	8.8	31.8	29.7	29.7	59.4	32.3	55.5	68.0	74.0
2005..............	58,641	8.0	29.2	30.0	32.8	59.4	32.9	53.8	66.8	72.9
2010..............	61,825	7.0	26.9	30.1	36.0	59.5	33.5	52.4	65.4	72.4
2014..............	62,753	6.2	24.5	29.8	39.6	57.6	31.9	48.6	61.8	70.8
White: [3]										
2000..............	99,964	10.1	31.4	27.5	31.0	67.0	44.1	63.6	73.1	79.0
2005..............	104,240	9.8	29.9	27.6	32.7	66.9	46.4	62.5	72.0	77.5
2010..............	108,274	8.9	28.7	27.5	34.9	66.5	47.7	61.2	70.1	76.5
2014..............	106,924	8.0	26.7	27.6	37.7	64.1	46.2	57.6	66.3	74.3
Black: [3]										
2000..............	13,582	12.4	36.0	31.2	20.5	68.2	39.3	69.9	79.3	84.4
2005..............	14,252	11.2	36.4	30.2	22.2	67.2	39.8	67.9	75.6	82.0
2010..............	15,114	9.4	33.3	32.8	24.5	65.8	38.8	63.8	73.5	79.5
2014..............	15,886	8.2	31.3	33.1	27.3	63.9	37.8	59.4	70.0	78.6
Asian: [3, 4]										
2000..............	5,402	9.1	20.7	20.2	50.1	70.9	46.0	65.6	76.4	79.1
2005..............	5,805	8.0	17.7	17.3	57.0	69.4	45.3	61.8	71.6	77.5
2010..............	6,601	7.3	18.8	17.1	56.7	68.7	44.1	62.8	70.6	75.9
2014..............	7,924	6.2	17.0	16.6	60.1	67.5	40.6	59.2	68.5	75.3
Hispanic: [5]										
2000..............	12,975	36.7	29.3	20.6	13.4	71.5	61.9	75.0	80.8	83.5
2005..............	16,135	35.5	29.4	20.9	14.2	70.8	61.4	74.3	78.8	81.7
2010..............	18,987	31.4	30.8	21.7	16.0	71.4	61.9	73.9	77.8	81.7
2014..............	20,946	27.7	30.3	23.5	18.6	69.6	59.8	69.8	76.0	80.2

[1] Civilian labor force as a percent of the civilian noninstitutional population. [2] Includes other races, not shown separately. [3] Beginning in 2003, data represent persons who selected this race group only and exclude persons reporting more than one race. See footnote 3, Table 605. [4] 2000 data include Pacific Islanders. [5] Persons of Hispanic origin may be of any race.

Source: U.S. Bureau of Labor Statistics, Employment & Earnings Online, "Employment status of the civilian noninstitutional population 25 years and over by educational attainment, sex, race, and Hispanic or Latino ethnicity," February 2015 and earlier releases, <www.bls.gov/opub/ee/home.htm>.

Table 612. Civilian Labor Force by Employment Status and Sex, by State: 2013

[In thousands (155,389 represents 155,389,000), except ratio and rate. Civilian noninstitutionalized population 16 years old and over. Annual averages of monthly figures. Data for states may not sum to national totals due to rounding]

State	Total Number	Total Female	Employed Total	Employed Female	Employ- ment/ population ratio [1]	Unemployed Total Number	Unemployed Total Female	Rate [2] Total	Rate [2] Male	Rate [2] Female	Participation rate [3] Male	Participation rate [3] Female
United States	**155,389**	**72,722**	**143,929**	**67,577**	**58.6**	**11,460**	**5,146**	**7.4**	**7.6**	**7.1**	**69.7**	**57.2**
Alabama	2,185	1,048	2,034	977	54.0	151	71	6.9	7.0	6.8	63.6	52.9
Alaska	364	166	340	157	63.2	24	9	6.6	7.7	5.3	72.3	63.0
Arizona	3,012	1,386	2,770	1,278	54.6	242	109	8.0	8.2	7.8	65.8	53.2
Arkansas	1,306	610	1,204	563	52.9	102	47	7.8	7.9	7.8	63.7	51.6
California	18,657	8,439	17,001	7,711	57.3	1,657	728	8.9	9.1	8.6	70.4	55.6
Colorado	2,765	1,272	2,583	1,193	63.6	183	79	6.6	6.9	6.2	74.5	61.8
Connecticut	1,852	893	1,710	828	59.9	142	64	7.7	8.1	7.2	70.1	60.0
Delaware	440	213	409	198	56.1	31	15	7.0	6.9	7.1	65.8	55.5
District of Columbia	372	190	340	174	63.6	32	16	8.6	8.7	8.5	73.9	65.9
Florida	9,433	4,465	8,763	4,166	55.9	671	299	7.1	7.5	6.7	66.3	54.6
Georgia	4,747	2,226	4,358	2,020	57.6	390	206	8.2	7.3	9.3	70.4	55.9
Hawaii	645	300	614	288	57.4	31	12	4.8	5.5	4.1	66.2	54.7
Idaho	774	351	724	326	59.8	51	26	6.5	5.9	7.3	71.2	57.1
Illinois	6,553	3,102	5,960	2,846	59.5	593	256	9.1	9.8	8.2	71.4	59.8
Indiana	3,192	1,491	2,948	1,374	58.2	244	118	7.7	7.4	7.9	69.4	57.0
Iowa	1,679	801	1,600	767	66.6	78	34	4.7	5.0	4.3	74.3	65.5
Kansas	1,486	709	1,403	671	64.3	83	38	5.6	5.7	5.4	73.0	63.3
Kentucky	2,069	980	1,901	907	55.9	168	73	8.1	8.7	7.4	66.5	55.5
Louisiana	2,096	982	1,949	917	55.3	147	65	7.0	7.3	6.7	66.7	52.9
Maine	711	347	663	325	61.0	48	22	6.8	7.2	6.2	69.3	61.9
Maryland	3,128	1,535	2,919	1,440	62.9	209	95	6.7	7.1	6.2	72.5	62.8
Massachusetts	3,484	1,697	3,239	1,589	60.1	245	108	7.0	7.7	6.3	69.4	60.3
Michigan	4,724	2,218	4,317	2,029	55.3	407	189	8.6	8.7	8.5	66.5	54.9
Minnesota	2,960	1,404	2,815	1,341	66.6	145	63	4.9	5.3	4.5	74.8	65.5
Mississippi	1,259	603	1,149	551	50.8	110	52	8.8	8.9	8.6	61.7	50.3
Missouri	3,015	1,428	2,817	1,331	60.0	198	96	6.6	6.4	6.7	70.4	58.6
Montana	512	241	484	229	60.4	28	11	5.5	6.2	4.7	68.0	59.8
Nebraska	1,030	479	988	460	69.4	42	20	4.1	4.0	4.1	78.7	66.2
Nevada	1,384	626	1,249	566	57.7	136	60	9.8	9.9	9.6	70.5	57.6
New Hampshire	743	353	704	336	65.7	39	17	5.2	5.7	4.8	74.3	64.5
New Jersey	4,521	2,132	4,153	1,972	59.3	369	160	8.2	8.7	7.5	71.1	58.5
New Mexico	918	422	852	393	53.4	66	28	7.2	7.6	6.7	64.2	51.2
New York	9,661	4,626	8,925	4,304	57.0	736	322	7.6	8.2	7.0	67.5	56.4
North Carolina	4,675	2,225	4,305	2,053	56.7	370	172	7.9	8.1	7.7	68.2	55.7
North Dakota	408	188	397	183	70.8	12	4	2.9	3.3	2.3	77.9	67.7
Ohio	5,702	2,744	5,270	2,556	58.2	432	188	7.6	8.3	6.8	68.0	58.3
Oklahoma	1,815	811	1,714	766	58.7	101	45	5.6	5.6	5.5	71.1	53.8
Oregon	1,900	891	1,749	826	55.8	150	65	7.9	8.4	7.3	65.9	55.6
Pennsylvania	6,456	3,056	5,971	2,846	58.6	485	210	7.5	8.1	6.9	69.6	57.7
Rhode Island	554	267	503	244	59.3	51	23	9.2	9.8	8.6	71.0	60.2
South Carolina	2,189	1,052	2,022	970	54.5	167	81	7.6	7.5	7.7	64.9	53.8
South Dakota	446	211	430	204	67.1	16	7	3.6	3.9	3.4	74.1	65.1
Tennessee	3,064	1,406	2,817	1,297	55.6	246	108	8.0	8.3	7.7	68.4	53.2
Texas	12,835	5,750	12,033	5,378	61.2	802	371	6.3	6.1	6.5	74.2	56.9
Utah	1,425	618	1,363	591	65.9	62	27	4.4	4.4	4.4	78.5	59.5
Vermont	350	170	335	163	65.4	15	7	4.3	4.6	4.0	71.9	64.9
Virginia	4,231	2,024	3,993	1,909	62.5	238	115	5.6	5.6	5.7	72.4	60.7
Washington	3,461	1,601	3,221	1,498	59.2	241	103	7.0	7.4	6.4	69.6	57.8
West Virginia	801	370	748	351	50.3	53	19	6.6	7.8	5.1	59.6	48.4
Wisconsin	3,092	1471	2,884	1,387	63.9	208	84	6.7	7.7	5.7	73.3	64.0
Wyoming	307	136	293	129	65.0	14	7	4.6	4.5	4.8	75.2	61.1

[1] Civilian employment as a percent of civilian noninstitutionalized population. [2] Percent unemployed of the civilian labor force. [3] Percent of civilian noninstitutionalized population of each specified group in the civilian labor force.

Source: U.S. Bureau of Labor Statistics, *Geographic Profile of Employment and Unemployment, 2013*, Bulletin 2780, October 2014. See also <http://www.bls.gov/gps/>.

Table 613. Civilian Labor Force Status by Selected Metropolitan Areas: 2014

[155,922 represents 155,922,000. Civilian noninstitutional population 16 years old and over. Annual averages of monthly figures. Data are derived from the Local Area Unemployment Statistics program, a Federal-State cooperative effort in which monthly estimates of total employment and unemployment are prepared for approximately 7,300 areas. For definitions of metropolitan areas, see Appendix II]

Metropolitan area ranked by population, 2010	Civilian labor force (1,000)	Unemployment rate [1]	Metropolitan area ranked by population, 2010	Civilian labor force (1,000)	Unemployment rate [1]
U.S. total, 2014	**155,922**	**6.2**	San Antonio-New Braunfels, TX	1,095	4.6
New York-Newark-Jersey City, NY-NJ-PA	9,939	6.4	Orlando-Kissimmee-Sanford, FL	1,212	5.9
Los Angeles-Long Beach-Anaheim, CA	6,601	7.6	Cincinnati, OH-KY-IN	1,078	5.4
Chicago-Naperville-Elgin, IL-IN-WI	4,904	7.0	Cleveland-Elyria, OH	1,046	6.2
Dallas-Fort Worth-Arlington, TX	3,560	5.0	Kansas City, MO-KS	1,101	5.6
Philadelphia-Camden-Wilmington, PA-NJ-DE-MD	3,024	6.1	Las Vegas-Henderson-Paradise, NV	1,020	7.8
Houston-The Woodlands-Sugar Land, TX	3,258	4.9	Columbus, OH	1,027	4.8
Washington-Arlington-Alexandria, DC-VA-MD-WV	3,262	5.0	Indianapolis-Carmel-Anderson, IN	993	5.7
Miami-Fort Lauderdale-West Palm Beach, FL	3,003	6.3	San Jose-Sunnyvale-Santa Clara, CA	1,024	5.3
Atlanta-Sandy Springs-Roswell, GA	2,808	6.8	Austin-Round Rock, TX	1,051	4.2
Boston-Cambridge-Nashua, MA-NH NECTA [2]	2,610	5.2	Virginia Beach-Norfolk-Newport News, VA-NC	844	5.7
San Francisco-Oakland-Hayward, CA	2,459	5.2	Nashville-Davidson-Murfreesboro-Franklin, TN	904	5.2
Detroit-Warren-Dearborn, MI	2,021	8.5	Providence-Warwick, RI-MA NECTA [2]	680	7.5
Riverside-San Bernardino-Ontario, CA	1,920	8.2	Milwaukee-Waukesha-West Allis, WI	826	6.0
Phoenix-Mesa-Scottsdale, AZ	2,108	6.0	Jacksonville, FL	719	6.2
Seattle-Tacoma-Bellevue, WA	1,938	5.2	Memphis, TN-MS-AR	607	7.6
Minneapolis-St. Paul-Bloomington, MN-WI	1,917	3.9	Oklahoma City, OK	646	4.0
San Diego-Carlsbad, CA	1,546	6.4	Louisville-Jefferson County, KY-IN	630	5.9
St. Louis, MO-IL	1,455	6.3	Hartford-West Hartford-East Hartford, CT NECTA [2]	615	6.6
Tampa-St. Petersburg-Clearwater, FL	1,443	6.1	Richmond, VA	656	5.5
Baltimore-Columbia-Towson, MD	1,455	6.1	New Orleans-Metairie, LA	599	6.4
Denver-Aurora-Lakewood, CO	1,495	4.8	Buffalo-Cheektowaga-Niagara Falls, NY	550	6.2
Pittsburgh, PA	1,210	5.6	Raleigh, NC	631	4.9
Portland-Vancouver-Hillsboro, OR-WA	1,200	6.3	Birmingham-Hoover, AL	534	6.0
Charlotte-Concord-Gastonia, NC-SC	1,192	6.0	Salt Lake City, UT	606	3.7
Sacramento-Roseville-Arden-Arcade, CA	1,049	7.2	Rochester, NY	525	5.8

[1] Percent unemployed of the civilian labor force. [2] New England City and Town Areas. See Appendix II.

Source: U.S. Bureau of Labor Statistics, "Local Area Unemployment Statistics," <http://www.bls.gov/lau/>, accessed August 2015.

Table 614. School Enrollment and Labor Force Status of Teenagers and Young Adults: 2014

[In thousands (38,650 represents 38,650,000), except percent rate. As of October. Covers civilian noninstitutional population age 16 to 24. Based on Current Population Survey; see text, Section 1 and Appendix III]

Characteristic	Population	Civilian labor force	Employed	Unemployed Total	Unemployed Rate [1]	Not in labor force
Total, 16 to 24 years [2]	**38,650**	**21,589**	**18,924**	**2,666**	**12.3**	**17,061**
Enrolled in school [2]	**21,790**	**8,279**	**7,441**	**837**	**10.1**	**13,511**
Enrolled in high school	9,445	2,109	1,722	387	18.4	7,335
Male	4,883	1,027	830	197	19.1	3,856
Female	4,562	1,083	892	191	17.6	3,479
Enrolled in college	12,345	6,169	5,719	450	7.3	6,176
Enrolled in two-year college	3,288	1,936	1,752	184	9.5	1,351
Enrolled in four-year college	9,057	4,233	3,967	266	6.3	4,824
By race/ethnicity:						
White:						
Enrolled in high school	6,974	1,630	1,377	253	15.5	5,343
Enrolled in college	9,212	4,918	4,599	319	6.5	4,295
Black or African American:						
Enrolled in high school	1,459	292	208	84	28.6	1,167
Enrolled in college	1,577	709	608	101	14.3	868
Asian:						
Enrolled in high school	466	43	41	2	([4])	422
Enrolled in college	1,039	337	323	14	4.1	701
Hispanic: [3]						
Enrolled in high school	2,056	358	258	100	27.8	1,698
Enrolled in college	2,331	1,255	1,146	109	8.7	1,076
Not enrolled [2]	**16,861**	**13,311**	**11,482**	**1,828**	**13.7**	**3,550**
White	12,463	10,007	8,868	1,138	11.4	2,457
Black	2,912	2,153	1,642	511	23.7	760
Asian	523	415	362	53	12.8	107
Hispanic [3]	3,958	2,961	2,582	378	12.8	997

[1] Percent unemployed of civilian labor force in each category. [2] Includes other races, not shown separately. [3] Persons of Hispanic origin may be of any race. [4] Data not shown where base is less than 75,000.

Source: U.S. Bureau of Labor Statistics, *College Enrollment and Work Activity of 2014 High School Graduates*, News Release, USDL 15-0608, April 2015. See also <http://www.bls.gov/news.release/hsgec.toc.htm>.

Table 615. Labor Force Participation Rates by Marital Status, Sex, and Age: 1970 to 2014

[In percent. For the civilian noninstitutional population 16 years old and over. Annual averages of monthly figures. Participation rate is the civilian labor force as a percent of the civilian noninstitutional population. Based on Current Population Survey; see text, Section 1 and Appendix III]

Marital status and year	Male participation rate							Female participation rate						
	Total	16–19 years	20–24 years	25–34 years	35–44 years	45–64 years	65 years and over	Total	16–19 years	20–24 years	25–34 years	35–44 years	45–64 years	65 years and over
Single: [1]														
1970	65.5	54.6	73.8	87.9	86.2	75.7	25.2	56.8	44.7	73.0	81.4	78.6	73.0	19.7
1980	72.6	59.9	81.3	89.2	82.2	66.9	16.8	64.4	53.6	75.2	83.3	76.9	65.6	13.9
1990	74.8	55.1	81.6	89.9	84.5	67.3	15.7	66.7	51.7	74.5	80.9	80.8	66.2	12.1
2000	73.6	52.5	80.5	89.4	82.9	69.7	17.3	68.9	51.1	76.1	83.9	80.9	69.9	10.8
2006	70.7	43.4	77.8	87.7	83.5	69.9	19.3	65.7	43.7	71.8	81.4	79.8	70.5	15.0
2007	70.1	40.8	76.9	88.5	84.0	70.3	22.6	65.3	41.4	72.6	82.1	78.0	70.4	18.4
2008	69.9	39.8	77.1	87.9	84.3	69.5	24.7	65.3	40.3	71.9	82.6	79.6	70.4	20.5
2009	68.3	37.1	74.6	86.5	83.7	68.5	26.1	64.2	37.5	71.4	81.6	79.5	69.3	19.7
2010	67.3	34.6	73.1	85.8	83.7	67.6	25.0	63.3	34.9	69.8	81.3	78.2	69.4	20.1
2011	67.0	33.4	73.3	85.4	82.6	67.4	23.8	62.8	34.3	69.1	79.9	77.8	67.8	21.7
2012	66.8	33.7	72.9	85.8	81.7	67.1	23.6	62.8	34.5	68.5	79.8	78.1	68.2	20.5
2013	66.9	34.0	72.5	85.4	82.2	66.9	24.5	63.0	34.5	69.2	79.2	77.5	67.3	22.7
2014	66.7	33.3	72.5	85.1	82.4	64.4	25.9	62.9	34.4	69.1	79.9	77.6	65.5	21.3
Married: [2]														
1970	86.1	92.3	94.7	98.0	98.1	91.2	29.9	40.5	37.8	47.9	38.8	46.8	44.0	7.3
1980	80.9	91.3	96.9	97.5	97.2	84.3	20.5	49.8	49.3	61.4	58.8	61.8	46.9	7.3
1990	78.6	92.1	95.6	96.9	96.7	82.6	17.5	58.4	49.5	66.1	69.6	74.0	56.5	8.5
2000	77.3	79.5	94.1	96.7	95.8	83.0	19.2	61.1	53.2	63.8	70.3	74.8	65.4	10.1
2006	77.1	79.2	93.3	95.5	95.2	83.6	21.8	61.0	39.6	59.8	69.0	73.3	67.8	12.4
2007	76.9	86.9	92.9	95.7	95.3	83.6	21.8	61.0	43.3	61.7	68.6	73.1	67.7	13.6
2008	76.8	83.4	92.0	95.3	95.2	84.0	22.8	61.4	38.0	62.3	69.5	73.8	68.3	14.1
2009	76.3	75.8	91.2	94.7	94.8	83.8	23.3	61.4	44.7	61.8	69.4	73.7	68.6	14.9
2010	75.8	78.2	89.3	94.3	94.5	83.6	23.5	61.0	40.2	60.9	68.8	72.8	68.8	15.2
2011	74.9	75.9	90.2	93.9	94.3	82.8	24.5	60.2	44.7	60.6	68.2	72.5	68.0	15.3
2012	74.6	83.7	91.3	94.2	94.3	83.0	25.6	59.5	42.1	60.5	68.5	72.3	67.3	15.9
2013	74.2	81.7	90.1	94.0	94.1	83.0	25.7	58.9	46.3	58.4	67.8	71.3	67.1	16.5
2014	73.5	76.8	92.0	93.4	94.0	82.9	24.9	58.4	45.1	58.9	67.7	71.3	66.6	16.8
Other: [3]														
1970	60.7	(B)	90.4	93.7	91.1	78.5	19.3	40.3	48.6	60.3	64.6	68.8	61.9	10.0
1980	67.5	(B)	92.6	94.1	91.9	73.3	13.7	43.6	50.0	68.4	76.5	77.1	60.2	8.2
1990	68.9	(B)	93.1	93.0	90.7	74.9	12.0	47.2	53.9	65.4	77.0	82.1	65.0	8.4
2000	66.8	60.5	88.1	93.2	89.9	73.9	12.9	49.0	46.0	74.0	83.1	82.9	69.8	8.7
2006	65.6	47.8	86.0	91.5	88.9	73.8	16.3	49.6	45.3	71.5	78.2	80.9	69.3	10.9
2007	65.6	43.4	82.5	92.1	89.4	73.7	16.1	49.5	44.6	63.8	78.4	81.4	69.3	11.4
2008	65.0	43.2	84.9	90.7	89.4	73.2	16.8	49.2	39.7	64.9	77.4	81.4	69.1	12.1
2009	63.7	42.6	78.6	88.5	88.5	71.8	17.0	49.3	39.0	68.3	78.2	80.5	68.8	12.1
2010	63.0	37.6	78.8	89.0	88.5	71.8	17.2	48.8	35.2	66.3	77.7	80.7	68.8	12.1
2011	62.4	39.7	76.2	88.3	87.2	71.1	17.8	48.8	39.9	65.6	77.1	79.2	68.3	12.3
2012	61.7	35.1	78.3	88.5	87.4	70.9	17.6	48.3	34.9	64.4	77.4	79.8	67.6	12.6
2013	60.2	29.2	74.1	89.4	88.3	69.4	16.8	47.3	36.6	63.8	76.4	79.7	66.6	12.8
2014	59.6	31.2	80.3	88.8	87.1	70.4	16.9	47.3	38.2	66.3	77.2	80.1	66.8	13.0

B Percentage not shown where base is less than 50,000. [1] Never married. [2] Spouse present. [3] Widowed, divorced, and married (spouse absent).

Source: U.S. Bureau of Labor Statistics, unpublished data. See also <http://www.bls.gov/cps/home.htm>.

Table 616. Marital Status of Women in the Civilian Labor Force: 1970 to 2014

[31,543 represents 31,543,000. For civilian noninstitutional population 16 years and over. Annual averages of monthly figures. Based on the Current Population Survey; see text, Section 1 and Appendix III]

Year	Female civilian labor force (1,000)				Female participation rate (percent) [3]			
	Total	Never married	Married [1]	Other [2]	Total	Never married	Married [1]	Other [2]
1970	31,543	7,265	18,475	5,804	43.3	56.8	40.5	40.3
1980	45,487	11,865	24,980	8,643	51.5	64.4	49.8	43.6
1990	56,829	14,612	30,901	11,315	57.5	66.7	58.4	47.2
2000	66,303	17,849	35,146	13,308	59.9	68.9	61.1	49.0
2005	69,288	19,183	35,941	14,163	59.3	66.0	60.7	49.4
2007	70,988	19,745	36,881	14,362	59.3	65.3	61.0	49.5
2008	71,767	20,231	37,194	14,342	59.5	65.3	61.4	49.2
2009	72,019	20,224	37,264	14,531	59.2	64.2	61.4	49.3
2010	71,904	20,592	36,742	14,570	58.6	63.3	61.0	48.8
2011	71,642	20,878	36,141	14,623	58.1	62.8	60.2	48.8
2012	72,648	21,506	36,436	14,706	57.7	62.8	59.5	48.3
2013	72,722	22,070	36,137	14,515	57.2	63.0	58.9	47.3
2014	73,039	22,320	36,082	14,637	57.0	62.9	58.4	47.3

[1] Husband present. [2] Widowed, divorced, or separated. [3] Civilian labor force as a percent of the civilian noninstitutional population.

Source: U.S. Bureau of Labor Statistics, unpublished data. See also <http://www.bls.gov/cps/home.htm>.

Table 617. Employment Status of Women by Marital Status and Presence and Age of Children: 1970 to 2014

[As of March (7.0 represents 7,000,000). Data from Current Population Survey, Annual Social and Economic Supplement (ASEC), which includes civilian noninstitutionalized population, age 16 years old and over. For more information; see text, Section 1 and Appendix III]

Item	Total			With any children under 18								
				Total			Children 6 to 17 years			Children under 6 years		
	Single[1]	Married[2]	Other[3]	Single[1]	Married[2]	Other[3]	Single[1]	Married[2]	Other[3]	Single[1]	Married[2]	Other[3]
IN LABOR FORCE (mil.)												
1970	7.0	18.4	5.9	(NA)	10.2	1.9	(NA)	6.3	1.3	(NA)	3.9	0.6
1980	11.2	24.9	8.8	0.6	13.7	3.6	0.2	8.4	2.6	0.3	5.2	1.0
1990	14.0	31.0	11.2	1.5	16.5	4.2	0.6	9.3	3.0	0.9	7.2	1.2
2000	17.8	35.0	13.2	3.1	18.2	4.5	1.2	10.8	3.4	1.8	7.3	1.1
2010	20.0	37.2	14.7	3.6	17.6	4.5	1.6	10.4	3.3	2.1	7.2	1.2
2013	21.7	36.3	14.7	4.1	16.8	4.2	1.8	10.0	3.1	2.3	6.7	1.1
2014	22.2	36.3	14.9	4.0	16.9	4.3	1.8	10.2	3.2	2.2	6.7	1.1
PARTICIPATION RATE[4]												
1970	53.0	40.8	39.1	(NA)	39.7	60.7	(NA)	49.2	66.9	(NA)	30.3	52.2
1980	61.5	50.1	44.0	52.0	54.1	69.4	67.6	61.7	74.6	44.1	45.1	60.3
1990	66.4	58.2	46.8	55.2	66.3	74.2	69.7	73.6	79.7	48.7	58.9	63.6
2000	68.6	62.0	50.2	73.9	70.6	82.7	79.7	77.2	84.9	70.5	62.8	76.6
2010	62.3	61.7	49.2	70.1	69.7	79.2	77.0	75.9	81.8	65.6	62.5	73.1
2013	62.3	59.2	47.9	71.3	68.1	79.7	75.8	72.8	81.2	68.2	62.0	76.0
2014	62.8	58.6	48.4	71.4	68.4	81.3	76.8	73.8	82.4	67.6	61.5	78.1
EMPLOYMENT (mil.)												
1970	6.5	17.5	5.6	(NA)	9.6	1.8	(NA)	6.0	1.2	(NA)	3.6	0.6
1980	10.1	23.6	8.2	0.4	12.8	3.3	0.2	8.1	2.4	0.2	4.8	0.9
1990	12.9	29.9	10.5	1.2	15.8	3.8	0.5	8.9	2.7	0.7	6.9	1.1
2000	16.4	34.0	12.7	2.7	17.6	4.3	1.1	10.6	3.2	1.6	7.1	1.1
2010	17.5	35.0	13.3	3.0	16.5	4.0	1.3	9.8	2.9	1.6	6.7	1.1
2013	19.3	34.6	13.5	3.4	15.9	3.8	1.5	9.5	2.9	1.9	6.4	1.0
2014	20.0	34.8	13.8	3.4	16.2	3.9	1.6	9.9	3.0	1.8	6.3	1.0
UNEMPLOYMENT RATE[5]												
1970	7.1	4.8	4.8	(NA)	6.0	7.2	(NA)	4.8	5.9	(NA)	7.9	9.8
1980	10.3	5.3	6.4	23.2	5.9	9.2	15.6	4.4	7.9	29.2	8.3	12.8
1990	8.2	3.5	5.7	18.4	4.2	8.5	14.5	3.8	7.7	20.8	4.8	10.2
2000	7.3	2.7	4.3	11.0	2.9	5.1	8.7	2.6	4.8	12.6	3.5	5.9
2010	12.3	6.0	9.7	18.1	6.3	11.1	14.4	6.0	10.3	20.9	6.7	13.4
2013	11.1	4.7	8.1	16.7	5.3	9.8	13.6	5.4	8.1	19.1	5.2	14.6
2014	9.9	4.1	7.2	14.6	4.3	8.2	11.1	3.8	7.7	17.3	5.0	9.8

NA Not available. [1] Never married. [2] Spouse present. [3] Widowed, divorced, or separated (including married, spouse absent). [4] Percent of women in each specific category in the labor force. [5] Unemployed as a percent of civilian labor force in specified group.

Source: U.S. Bureau of Labor Statistics, unpublished data. See also <http://www.bls.gov/cps/home.htm>

Table 618. Labor Force Participation Rates for Wives, Husband Present, by Age of Own Youngest Child: 1990 to 2014

[In percent. As of March. Base on Current Population Survey, Annual Social and Economic Supplement (ASEC), which includes civilian noninstitutionalized population, 16 years old and over, and military personnel who live in households with at least one other civilian adult. Armed Forces includes only those Armed Forces members living on or off post with their families; all other members of the Armed Forces are excluded. Data refer to persons in primary families. For more information; see text, Section 1 and Appendix III]

Presence and age of child	1990	2000	2010	2013	2014				
					Total	White[1]	Black[1]	Asian[1,2]	Hispanic[3]
Wives, total	**58.3**	**62.2**	**61.9**	**59.5**	**58.8**	**58.4**	**64.1**	**57.4**	**54.3**
No children under 18 years	51.1	54.8	56.0	53.5	52.3	51.9	55.5	53.4	52.1
With children under 18 years	66.5	70.9	70.1	68.4	68.5	68.7	75.9	61.2	55.8
Under 6 years, total	59.1	63.1	62.9	62.6	61.8	62.7	67.4	50.6	49.3
Under 3 years	55.9	59.4	59.5	60.3	60.4	62.0	60.3	50.4	47.9
under 1 year	53.9	58.4	59.0	58.2	59.9	62.9	39.0	54.9	44.1
1 year	(NA)	(NA)	57.6	60.5	61.1	61.3	69.6	52.1	48.1
2 years	60.9	61.9	62.4	62.3	60.1	61.7	69.8	44.3	51.2
3 to 5 years	64.1	68.6	67.7	65.7	63.6	63.6	77.0	50.9	50.7
3 years	63.0	66.0	66.4	63.6	62.3	63.1	79.7	48.6	50.3
4 years	65.0	69.6	68.9	65.9	63.0	62.7	74.0	49.7	51.1
5 years	64.4	70.7	68.1	68.1	65.5	65.1	77.4	54.9	50.9
6 to 13 years	73.1	76.0	74.8	71.2	72.4	72.2	80.3	69.1	57.9
14 to 17 years	75.0	80.8	79.0	76.8	76.6	76.1	84.7	74.3	71.2

NA Not available. [1] Persons in this race group only. See footnote 3, Table 605. [2] Excludes Pacific Islanders. [3] Persons of Hispanic origin may be of any race.

Source: U.S. Bureau of Labor Statistics, unpublished data. See also <http://www.bls.gov/cps/home.htm>

Table 619. Married Couples by Labor Force Status of Spouses: 1990 to 2014

[As of March. 52,317 represents 52,317,000. Based on the Annual Social and Economic Supplement (ASEC) to the Current Population Survey, for details see source and Appendix III]

Year	Number (1,000)					Percent distribution				
	All married couples	In labor force			Husband and wife not in labor force	All married couples	In labor force			Husband and wife not in labor force
		Husband and wife	Husband only	Wife only			Husband and wife	Husband only	Wife only	
TOTAL										
1990	52,317	28,056	13,013	2,453	8,794	100.0	53.6	24.9	4.7	16.8
2000	55,311	31,095	11,815	3,301	9,098	100.0	56.2	21.4	6.0	16.4
2007	60,676	33,337	13,351	4,031	9,958	100.0	54.9	22.0	6.6	16.4
2008	60,129	32,988	13,141	4,118	9,882	100.0	54.9	21.9	6.8	16.4
2009	60,844	33,249	13,207	4,314	10,074	100.0	54.6	21.7	7.1	16.6
2010	60,384	32,731	13,074	4,526	10,053	100.0	54.2	21.7	7.5	16.6
2011	60,840	32,231	13,455	4,516	10,636	100.0	53.0	22.1	7.4	17.5
2012	61,047	31,803	13,820	4,595	10,830	100.0	52.1	22.6	7.5	17.7
2013	61,295	31,673	13,901	4,656	11,065	100.0	51.7	22.7	7.6	18.1
2014	61,850	31,666	13,913	4,708	11,563	100.0	51.2	22.5	7.6	18.7
WITH CHILDREN UNDER 18										
1990	24,537	15,768	7,667	558	544	100.0	64.3	31.2	2.3	2.2
2000	25,248	17,116	6,950	795	387	100.0	67.8	27.5	3.1	1.5
2007	26,802	17,670	7,743	920	469	100.0	65.9	28.9	3.4	1.7
2008	25,778	16,977	7,398	932	471	100.0	65.9	28.7	3.6	1.8
2009	25,799	17,054	7,284	963	501	100.0	66.1	28.2	3.7	1.9
2010	25,317	16,710	7,220	962	425	100.0	66.0	28.5	3.8	1.7
2011	24,936	16,189	7,270	1,007	469	100.0	64.9	29.2	4.0	1.9
2012	24,445	15,752	7,226	1,009	457	100.0	64.4	29.6	4.1	1.9
2013	24,677	15,755	7,408	1,051	462	100.0	63.8	30.0	4.3	1.9
2014	24,775	15,945	7,336	949	545	100.0	64.4	29.6	3.8	2.2
WITH CHILDREN UNDER 6										
1990	12,051	6,932	4,692	192	235	100.0	57.5	38.9	1.6	2.0
2000	11,393	6,984	4,077	211	121	100.0	61.3	35.8	1.9	1.1
2007	12,468	7,337	4,633	331	167	100.0	58.8	37.2	2.7	1.3
2008	11,848	6,976	4,382	321	168	100.0	58.9	37.1	2.7	1.4
2009	11,760	6,917	4,330	329	185	100.0	58.8	36.8	2.8	1.6
2010	11,599	6,924	4,181	335	159	100.0	59.7	36.0	2.9	1.4
2011	11,416	6,720	4,152	368	177	100.0	58.9	36.4	3.2	1.6
2012	11,055	6,509	3,986	383	176	100.0	58.9	36.1	3.5	1.6
2013	10,867	6,347	3,951	403	166	100.0	58.4	36.4	3.7	1.5
2014	10,887	6,378	3,965	340	204	100.0	58.6	36.4	3.1	1.9

Source: U.S. Census Bureau, Families and Living Arrangements, Detailed Table MC-1, "Married Couples by Labor Force Status of Spouses: 1986 to Present," January 2015, <http://www.census.gov/hhes/families/mc1.xls>.

Table 620. Employed Civilians and Weekly Hours: 1980 to 2014

[In thousands (99,303 represents 99,303,000), except as indicated. Annual averages of monthly figures. Civilian noninstitutionalized population 16 years old and over. Based on Current Population Survey; see text, Section 1 and Appendix III]

Item	1980	1990	2000	2010	2011	2012	2013	2014
Total employed	**99,303**	**118,793**	**136,891**	**139,064**	**139,869**	**142,469**	**143,929**	**146,305**
Age:								
16 to 19 years old	7,710	6,581	7,189	4,378	4,327	4,426	4,458	4,548
20 to 24 years old	14,087	13,401	13,229	12,699	13,036	13,408	13,599	13,894
25 to 34 years old	27,204	33,935	31,549	30,229	30,537	30,701	31,242	31,975
35 to 44 years old	19,523	30,817	36,433	30,663	30,270	30,576	30,650	30,966
45 to 54 years old	16,234	19,525	30,310	33,191	32,867	32,874	32,523	32,556
55 to 64 years old	11,586	11,189	14,002	21,636	22,186	23,239	23,776	24,395
65 years old and over	2,960	3,346	4,179	6,268	6,647	7,245	7,681	7,971
Class of worker:								
Nonagricultural industries	95,938	115,570	134,427	136,858	137,615	140,283	141,799	139,118
Wage and salary worker [1]	88,525	106,598	125,114	127,914	128,934	131,452	133,111	130,998
Self-employed	7,000	8,719	9,205	8,860	8,603	8,749	8,619	8,055
Unpaid family workers	413	253	108	84	78	81	70	64
Agriculture and related industries	3,364	3,223	2,464	2,206	2,254	2,186	2,130	2,237
Wage and salary worker [1]	1,425	1,740	1,421	1,353	1,380	1,377	1,310	1,459
Self-employed	1,642	1,378	1,010	821	846	780	789	756
Unpaid family workers	297	105	33	33	28	29	31	22
Weekly hours:								
Nonagricultural industries:								
Wage and salary workers [1]	38.1	39.2	39.6	38.3	38.4	38.6	38.7	38.7
Self-employed	41.2	40.8	39.7	35.6	35.6	36.0	35.9	35.9
Unpaid family workers	34.7	34.0	32.5	33.3	33.0	33.2	32.1	33.3
Agriculture and related industries:								
Wage and salary workers [1]	41.6	41.2	43.2	41.6	(NA)	(NA)	(NA)	(NA)
Self-employed	49.3	46.8	45.3	42.0	(NA)	(NA)	(NA)	(NA)
Unpaid family workers	38.6	38.5	38.3	42.1	(NA)	(NA)	(NA)	(NA)

NA Not available. [1] Includes the incorporated self-employed.

Source: U.S. Bureau of Labor Statistics, "Labor Force Statistics from the Current Population Survey," <http://www.bls.gov/cps>, accessed March 2015.

Table 621. Persons at Work by Hours Worked: 2014

[In thousands (141,276 represents 141,276,000), except as indicated. Annual averages of monthly figures. Persons "at work" are a subgroup of employed persons. This subgroup excludes those absent from their jobs during reference period for reasons such as vacation, illness, or industrial dispute. Civilian noninstitutionalized population 16 years old and over. Based on Current Population Survey; see text, Section 1, and Appendix III.]

Hours of work	Persons at work (1,000)			Percent distribution		
	Total	Agriculture and related industries	Non-agricultural industries	Total	Agriculture and related industries	Non-agricultural industries
Total..	**141,276**	**2,158**	**139,118**	**100.0**	**100.0**	**100.0**
1 to 34 hours.................................	34,873	561	34,312	24.7	26.0	24.7
1 to 4 hours...............................	1,433	47	1,386	1.0	2.2	1.0
5 to 14 hours.............................	5,263	128	5,135	3.7	5.9	3.7
15 to 29 hours...........................	17,519	246	17,273	12.4	11.4	12.4
30 to 34 hours...........................	10,658	140	10,518	7.5	6.5	7.6
35 hours and over..........................	106,403	1,597	104,806	75.3	74.0	75.3
35 to 39 hours...........................	9,504	107	9,397	6.7	5.0	6.8
40 hours...................................	61,280	633	60,647	43.4	29.3	43.6
41 hours and over.......................	35,619	857	34,762	25.2	39.7	25.0
41 to 48 hours........................	12,229	150	12,079	8.7	7.0	8.7
49 to 59 hours........................	13,778	260	13,518	9.8	12.1	9.7
60 hours and over....................	9,612	446	9,166	6.8	20.7	6.6
Average weekly hours of:						
Total persons at work.................	38.6	42.3	38.6	(X)	(X)	(X)
Persons usually working full-time [1]...	42.5	48.0	42.5	(X)	(X)	(X)

X Not applicable. [1] Full-time workers are those who usually worked 35 hours or more (at all jobs).

Source: U.S. Bureau of Labor Statistics, CPS Tables, "Persons at Work in Agriculture and Nonagricultural Industries by Hours of Work," <http://www.bls.gov/cps/tables.htm>, accessed March 2015.

Table 622. Persons With a Job, But Not at Work by Reason: 1980 to 2014

[In thousands (5,881 represents 5,881,000), except percent. For civilian noninstitutionalized population 16 years old and over. Annual averages of monthly figures. Based on Current Population Survey; see text, Section 1 and Appendix III]

Reason for not working	1980	1990	2000	2007	2008	2009	2010	2011	2012	2013	2014
All industries, number............	**5,881**	**6,160**	**5,681**	**5,719**	**5,539**	**5,434**	**5,060**	**4,990**	**5,132**	**5,003**	**5,029**
Percent of employed...............	5.9	5.2	4.2	3.9	3.8	3.9	3.6	3.6	3.6	3.5	3.4
Reason for not working:											
Vacation.............................	3,320	3,529	3,109	3,056	2,916	2,806	2,487	2,500	2,633	2,501	2,512
Illness................................	1,426	1,341	1,156	1,064	1,026	993	942	921	906	940	953
Child care problems................	(NA)	(NA)	(NA)	(NA)	(NA)	(NA)	(NA)	23	20	22	28
Other family/personal obligations..	(NA)	(NA)	(NA)	(NA)	(NA)	(NA)	(NA)	229	253	245	258
Labor/industrial dispute............	105	24	14	10	7	6	8	9	6	6	3
Bad weather.........................	155	90	89	140	141	126	172	169	107	112	138
Maternity or paternity leave........	(NA)	(NA)	(NA)	(NA)	(NA)	(NA)	(NA)	254	286	279	288
School/training......................	(NA)	(NA)	(NA)	(NA)	(NA)	(NA)	(NA)	114	119	113	120
Civic/military duty...................	(NA)	(NA)	(NA)	(NA)	(NA)	(NA)	(NA)	6	11	9	7
All other.............................	876	1,177	1,313	1,449	1,449	1,503	1,451	766	792	775	721

NA Not available.

Source: U.S. Bureau of Labor Statistics, Current Population Survey, unpublished data. See also <http://www.bls.gov/cps/>.

Table 623. Class of Worker by Sex and Selected Characteristics: 2014

[In percent, except as indicated (9,358 represents 9,358,000). Civilian noninstitutionalized population 16 years old and over. Annual averages of monthly figures. Based on Current Population Survey; see text, Section 1 and Appendix III]

Characteristic	Unincorporated self-employed			Incorporated self-employed			Wage and salary workers [1]		
	Total	Male	Female	Total	Male	Female	Total	Male	Female
Total (1,000)......................	**9,358**	**5,712**	**3,646**	**5,430**	**3,898**	**1,531**	**131,431**	**68,049**	**63,383**
PERCENT DISTRIBUTION.........	100.0	100.0	100.0	100.0	100.0	100.0	100.0	100.0	100.0
Age:									
16 to 19 years old.................	0.8	0.8	0.9	0.1	0.2	0.1	3.4	3.2	3.6
20 to 24 years old.................	2.7	2.7	2.7	1.2	1.3	1.1	10.3	10.3	10.4
25 to 34 years old.................	13.8	13.3	14.5	9.6	9.2	10.8	22.9	23.8	22.1
35 to 44 years old.................	20.1	20.2	20.0	20.7	20.7	20.5	21.3	21.7	20.8
45 to 54 years old.................	25.6	25.4	25.9	29.5	29.6	29.3	21.7	21.3	22.1
55 to 64 years old.................	23.2	23.2	23.3	26.2	26.1	26.6	15.8	15.3	16.3
65 years old and over.............	13.7	14.4	12.7	12.6	13.0	11.6	4.6	4.5	4.6
Race/ethnicity:									
White [2].............................	85.7	86.3	84.7	86.6	87.4	84.5	79.1	80.4	77.7
Black [2].............................	6.7	6.7	6.8	5.1	5.0	5.3	12.0	10.6	13.5
Asian [2].............................	4.7	4.2	5.6	6.9	6.3	8.3	5.7	5.7	5.7
Hispanic [3].........................	15.7	17.4	13.0	8.5	8.5	8.7	16.4	18.1	14.6
Country of birth:									
U.S. born...........................	80.4	79.1	82.5	83.1	83.4	82.1	83.6	81.9	85.6
Foreign-born.......................	19.6	20.9	17.5	16.9	16.6	17.9	16.4	18.1	14.4

[1] Excludes the incorporated self-employed. [2] For persons in this race group only. [3] Persons of Hispanic origin may be of any race.

Source: U.S. Bureau of Labor Statistics, Current Population Survey, unpublished data. See also <http://www.bls.gov/cps>.

Table 624. Self-Employed Workers by Industry and Occupation: 2000 to 2014

[In thousands (10,214 represents 10,214,000). Civilian noninstitutionalized population 16 years old and over. Annual averages of monthly figures. Data represent the unincorporated self-employed; the incorporated self-employed are considered wage and salary workers. Based on the occupational and industrial classification derived from those used in the 2000 census. See text, this section. Based on the Current Population Survey (CPS); see text, Section 1 and Appendix III]

Item	2000	2010	2011	2012	2013	2014
Total self-employed............................	10,214	9,681	9,449	9,529	9,408	9,358
INDUSTRY						
Agriculture and related industries.............................	1,010	821	846	780	789	756
Mining.......................................	12	20	20	20	16	20
Construction..	1,728	1,699	1,585	1,518	1,530	1,595
Manufacturing..	334	304	273	308	275	278
Wholesale and retail trade........................	1,221	962	949	872	825	851
Transportation and utilities.........................	348	360	352	355	340	368
Information..............................	139	139	131	141	126	132
Financial activities...........................	735	641	615	651	651	628
Professional and business services.........................	1,927	1,999	2,011	2,109	2,057	1,984
Education and health services..........................	1,107	1,100	1,077	1,101	1,072	1,074
Leisure and hospitality............................	660	610	636	659	671	658
Other services.........................	993	1,028	956	1,016	1,055	1,014
OCCUPATION						
Management, professional, and related occupations..........	4,169	3,928	3,857	4,009	3,963	3,878
Service occupations..........................	1,775	1,885	1,872	1,984	2,030	1,969
Sales and office occupations..........................	1,982	1,586	1,520	1,494	1,449	1,438
Natural resources, construction, and maintenance occupations..........................	1,591	1,635	1,572	1,395	1,365	1,462
Production, transportation, and material moving occupations..........................	698	647	628	648	602	610

Source: U.S. Bureau of Labor Statistics, "Labor Force Statistics from the Current Population Survey," <http://www.bls.gov/cps/tables.htm>, accessed August 2015; and unpublished CPS data.

Table 625. Type of Work Flexibility Provided to Employees: 2014

[In percent. The National Study of Employers does not ask employers to report on whether they have "written policies," but rather whether their organization "allows employees to" or "provides the following benefits or programs." The wording is used for two reasons. First, employers may have written policies, but not allow employees to use them. Second, smaller employers are less likely to have written policies than larger ones. For methodology, see source]

Type of work flexibility provided to employees	Organizations allowing flexibility to all or most employees		
	Total employers	Employers with 50 to 99 employees	Employers with 1,000 or more employees
FLEX TIME AND PLACE			
Periodically change starting and quitting times within some range of hours......................	27	33	20
Change starting and quitting times on a daily basis....................................	10	14	5
Compress workweek by working longer hours on fewer days for at least part of the year......	10	14	5
Work some regular paid hours at home occasionally....................................	8	11	4
Work some regular paid hours at home on regular basis................................	3	4	2
CHOICES IN MANAGING TIME			
Have control over when to take breaks................................	61	66	52
Have choices about and control over which shifts to work................................	7	7	14
Have control over paid and unpaid overtime hours................................	25	26	15
REDUCED TIME			
Move from full time to part time and back again while remaining in same position or level...........................	6	6	10
Work part year (work reduced time on annual basis)......................	2	2	2
CAREGIVING LEAVE			
Return to work gradually after childbirth or adoption........................	47	53	37
TIME OFF			
Family or personal time off without loss of pay........................	49	52	36
Do volunteer work during regular work hours........................	21	24	20
FLEX CAREERS			
Phase into retirement by working reduced hours over time prior to full retirement..............	18	19	12
Take sabbaticals (paid or unpaid for six months or more)............................	10	12	8
Take extended career breaks for caregiving or other personal or family reasons................	32	34	26
Receive special consideration when returning to the organization after an extended career break....................	8	9	8

Source: Families and Work Institute, *2014 National Study of Employers* ©. See also <http://www.familiesandwork.org/2014-national-study-of-employers/>.

Table 626. Multiple Jobholders: 2014

[7,146 represents 7,146,000. Annual average of monthly figures. Civilian noninstitutionalized population 16 years old and over. Multiple jobholders are employed persons who either had jobs as wage or salary workers with two employers or more; were self-employed and also held a wage and salary job; or were unpaid family workers and also held a wage and salary job. Based on the Current Population Survey; see text, Section 1 and Appendix III]

Characteristic	Total Number (1,000)	Total Percent of employed	Male Number (1,000)	Male Percent of employed	Female Number (1,000)	Female Percent of employed
Total [1,2]	**7,146**	**4.9**	**3,511**	**4.5**	**3,636**	**5.3**
Age:						
16 to 19 years old	194	4.3	80	3.6	113	4.9
20 to 24 years old	811	5.8	346	4.8	465	6.9
25 to 54 years old	4,712	4.9	2,362	4.6	2,350	5.3
55 to 64 years old	1,146	4.7	557	4.4	588	5.1
65 years old and over	284	3.6	165	3.8	119	3.3
Race and ethnicity:						
White	5,817	5.0	2,877	4.6	2,940	5.5
Black	822	4.9	392	5.0	430	4.8
Asian	278	3.3	133	3.0	145	3.7
Hispanic [3]	779	3.3	426	3.1	353	3.6
Marital status:						
Married, spouse present	3,651	4.6	2,084	4.7	1,567	4.5
Widowed, divorced, or separated	1,218	5.2	389	4.0	829	6.1
Single, never married	2,277	5.2	1,038	4.4	1,239	6.1
Full- or part-time status:						
Primary job full-time, secondary job part-time	3,768	(X)	2,081	(X)	1,686	(X)
Both jobs part-time	1,955	(X)	665	(X)	1,291	(X)
Both jobs full-time	254	(X)	159	(X)	95	(X)
Hours vary on primary or secondary job	1,120	(X)	583	(X)	538	(X)

X Not applicable. [1] Includes a small number of persons who work part-time on their primary job and full-time on their secondary job(s), not shown separately. [2] Includes other races, not shown separately. [3] Persons of Hispanic origin may be of any race.

Source: U.S. Bureau of Labor Statistics, CPS Tables, "Multiple Jobholders by Selected Characteristics," <http://www.bls.gov/cps/tables. htm>, accessed March 2015.

Table 627. Average Number of Jobs Held From Ages 18 to 48 during 1978 to 2012

[For persons ages 47 to 56 in 2012-13 (and who were ages 14 to 22 when first interviewed in 1979). A job is an uninterrupted period of work with a particular employer. Educational attainment as of 2012-13. Based on the National Longitudinal Survey of Youth 1979; see source for details]

Sex, race, ethnicity and educational attainment	Total [1]	18 to 24 years	25 to 29 years	30 to 34 years	35 to 39 years	40 to 46 years
Total [2]	**11.7**	**5.5**	**3.0**	**2.4**	**2.1**	**2.4**
Less than a high school diploma	11.5	5.0	2.9	2.4	2.0	2.1
High school graduates, no college	11.2	5.1	2.8	2.4	2.1	2.3
Some college or associate's degree	12.3	5.8	3.1	2.5	2.1	2.5
Bachelor's degree or more	11.8	6.1	3.0	2.4	2.1	2.3
Male	11.8	5.7	3.1	2.5	2.1	2.4
Less than a high school diploma	12.9	5.7	3.5	2.6	2.1	2.5
High school graduate, no college	11.7	5.5	3.1	2.6	2.1	2.3
Some college or associate's degree	12.4	6.0	3.2	2.7	2.1	2.5
Bachelor's degree or more	11.2	5.8	2.8	2.4	2.2	2.3
Female	11.5	5.3	2.8	2.3	2.1	2.4
Less than a high school diploma	9.6	4.0	2.2	2.1	1.9	1.7
High school graduate, no college	10.7	4.6	2.5	2.2	2.1	2.3
Some college or associate's degree	12.3	5.6	3.0	2.4	2.2	2.6
Bachelor's degree or more	12.5	6.4	3.2	2.3	2.0	2.4
White, non-Hispanic	11.7	5.7	3.0	2.4	2.1	2.3
Less than a high school diploma	12.1	5.4	3.1	2.6	2.1	2.2
High school graduate, no college	11.4	5.3	2.9	2.4	2.1	2.3
Some college or associate's degree	12.3	5.9	3.1	2.5	2.1	2.5
Bachelor's degree or more	11.8	6.2	3.0	2.3	2.0	2.3
Black, non-Hispanic	11.4	4.6	2.9	2.5	2.1	2.5
Less than a high school diploma	10.1	3.7	2.6	2.2	1.7	1.9
High school graduate, no college	10.9	4.4	2.8	2.5	2.2	2.4
Some college or associate's degree	12.6	5.1	3.1	2.6	2.4	2.8
Bachelor's degree or more	11.9	5.6	3.0	2.6	2.1	2.8
Hispanic [3]	11.4	4.9	2.8	2.3	2.1	2.4
Less than a high school diploma	10.9	4.3	2.8	2.1	1.9	2.3
High school graduate, no college	10.9	4.9	2.7	2.3	2.1	2.4
Some college or associate's degree	12.5	5.2	3.1	2.5	2.3	2.8
Bachelor's degree or more	11.6	5.5	2.8	2.5	2.2	2.1

[1] Jobs held in more than one age category were counted in each category, but only once in the total. [2] Includes other races, not shown separately. [3] Persons of Hispanic origin may be of any race.

Source: U.S. Bureau of Labor Statistics, *Number of Jobs Held, Labor Market Activity, and Earnings Growth Among the Youngest Baby Boomers: Results from a Longitudinal Survey,* USDL 15-0528, March 2015. See also <http://www.bls.gov/news.release/nlsoy.nr0.htm>.

Table 628. Distribution of Workers by Tenure With Current Employer by Selected Characteristics: 2014

[129,128 represents 129,128,000. As of January. From the 2014 Displaced Worker Supplement to the Current Population Survey. For employed wage and salary workers 16 years old and over. Data exclude the incorporated and unincorporated self-employed; see source and Appendix III]

Characteristic	Number employed (1,000)	Percent distribution by tenure with current employer								Median years [1]
		12 months or less	13-23 months	2 years	3-4 years	5-9 years	10-14 years	15-19 years	20 years or more	
Total [2]........	**129,128**	**21.3**	**6.4**	**5.3**	**16.5**	**21.5**	**12.0**	**6.5**	**10.6**	**4.6**
AGE AND SEX										
16 to 19 years old........	3,919	72.4	10.8	8.2	8.2	0.4	–	–	–	(NA)
20 years old and over........	125,209	19.7	6.2	5.2	16.8	22.2	12.3	6.7	10.9	(NA)
20 to 24 years old........	13,061	49.2	11.8	11.4	20.3	7.2	0.1	–	–	1.3
25 to 34 years old........	29,683	26.6	8.9	7.2	24.2	25.8	6.6	0.8	–	3.0
35 to 44 years old........	27,970	16.7	5.7	4.6	16.7	27.5	17.1	8.4	3.3	5.2
45 to 54 years old........	28,258	12.0	4.2	3.4	13.2	22.3	16.1	10.4	18.4	7.9
55 to 64 years old........	20,323	8.9	3.2	2.6	10.6	19.4	15.5	10.9	28.8	10.4
65 years old and over........	5,914	7.8	2.9	2.4	11.0	21.0	16.7	9.9	28.4	10.3
Male........	**66,325**	**20.9**	**6.3**	**5.2**	**16.4**	**21.4**	**11.8**	**6.6**	**11.3**	**4.7**
16 to 19 years old........	1,847	71.8	10.9	7.5	9.4	0.5	–	–	–	(NA)
20 years old and over........	64,478	19.5	6.2	5.2	16.6	22.0	12.2	6.8	11.6	(NA)
20 to 24 years old........	6,573	46.6	11.8	12.0	21.7	7.9	–	–	–	1.4
25 to 34 years old........	15,724	26.4	8.5	6.9	23.8	26.3	7.2	0.9	–	3.1
35 to 44 years old........	14,722	15.8	5.9	4.4	16.4	27.2	17.3	9.4	3.6	5.4
45 to 54 years old........	14,268	12.5	4.2	3.2	12.2	21.1	15.7	10.8	20.4	8.2
55 to 64 years old........	10,180	9.3	2.9	2.6	10.5	18.8	14.3	10.2	31.4	10.7
65 years old and over........	3,010	9.0	3.8	2.8	11.2	20.1	15.9	8.9	28.3	10.0
Female........	**62,803**	**21.7**	**6.4**	**5.4**	**16.6**	**21.7**	**12.1**	**6.3**	**9.8**	**4.5**
16 to 19 years old........	2,072	73.0	10.8	8.8	7.1	0.4	–	–	–	(NA)
20 years old and over........	60,732	20.0	6.3	5.2	17.0	22.4	12.5	6.5	10.1	(NA)
20 to 24 years old........	6,488	51.8	11.8	10.7	18.9	6.6	0.1	–	–	1.3
25 to 34 years old........	13,959	26.8	9.4	7.5	24.6	25.2	5.8	0.7	–	2.9
35 to 44 years old........	13,247	17.7	5.5	4.7	17.0	27.9	16.8	7.3	2.9	5.1
45 to 54 years old........	13,990	11.5	4.2	3.6	14.2	23.5	16.6	10.0	16.3	7.6
55 to 64 years old........	10,143	8.6	3.5	2.5	10.8	20.1	16.7	11.6	26.2	10.2
65 years old and over........	2,905	6.5	1.9	1.9	10.9	21.9	17.6	11.0	28.4	10.5
RACE AND HISPANIC ORIGIN										
White [3]........	102,939	20.7	6.5	5.1	16.3	21.3	12.0	6.8	11.4	(NA)
Male........	53,760	20.3	6.4	5.1	16.3	21.0	11.8	6.8	12.2	(NA)
Female........	49,179	21.2	6.6	5.1	16.1	21.6	12.2	6.7	10.4	(NA)
Black [3]........	14,939	24.9	5.5	5.7	17.5	21.5	11.1	5.4	8.4	(NA)
Male........	6,721	25.7	5.4	4.9	16.8	22.0	11.1	5.8	8.2	(NA)
Female........	8,218	24.3	5.6	6.3	18.0	21.0	11.1	5.1	8.6	(NA)
Asian [3]........	7,370	18.5	6.4	6.5	18.6	25.6	13.3	5.5	5.8	(NA)
Male........	3,843	18.0	6.7	6.4	17.7	25.6	14.4	5.7	5.7	(NA)
Female........	3,527	19.0	6.0	6.6	19.6	25.5	12.0	5.3	5.9	(NA)
Hispanic [4]........	20,915	24.4	6.3	7.0	19.1	22.7	11.2	4.1	5.2	(NA)
Male........	11,813	24.1	6.2	7.4	19.4	22.5	11.0	3.9	5.5	(NA)
Female........	9,102	24.8	6.4	6.4	18.8	23.1	11.4	4.4	4.7	(NA)

– Less than .05 percent. NA Not available. [1] For definition of median, see Guide to Tabular Presentation. [2] Includes other races, not shown separately. [3] For persons in this race group only. See footnote 4, Table 605. [4] Persons of Hispanic origin may be of any race.

Source: U.S. Bureau of Labor Statistics, "Employee Tenure in 2014," USDL 14-1714, September 2014, <http://www.bls.gov/news.release/tenure.toc.htm>.

Table 629. Part-Time Workers by Reason: 2014

[In thousands (34,873 represents 34,873,000), except hours. For persons working 1 to 34 hours per week. For civilian noninstitutionalized population 16 years old and over. Annual average of monthly figures. Based on the Current Population Survey; see text, Section 1 and Appendix III]

Reason	All industries			Nonagricultural industries		
	Total	Usually work—		Total	Usually work—	
		Full-time	Part-time		Full-time	Part-time
Total working fewer than 35 hours........	**34,873**	**9,772**	**25,102**	**34,312**	**9,610**	**24,702**
Economic reasons........	7,213	1,600	5,613	7,109	1,555	5,554
Slack work or business conditions........	4,327	1,363	2,964	4,267	1,333	2,934
Could find only part time work........	2,552	(S)	2,552	2,533	(S)	2,533
Seasonal work........	228	131	97	205	118	87
Job started or ended during the week........	106	106	(S)	104	104	(S)
Noneconomic reasons........	27,660	8,171	19,489	27,203	8,055	19,148
Child-care problems........	954	68	886	949	67	882
Other family or personal obligations........	4,733	652	4,081	4,662	643	4,019
Health or medical limitations........	860	(S)	860	846	(S)	846
In school or training........	5,798	75	5,723	5,747	74	5,673
Retired or social security limit on earnings........	2,356	(S)	2,356	2,246	(S)	2,246
Vacation or personal day........	3,450	3,450	(S)	3,410	3,410	(S)
Holiday, legal, or religious........	835	835	(S)	830	830	(S)
Weather-related curtailment........	875	875	(S)	847	847	(S)
Other........	7,799	2,216	5,583	7,666	2,183	5,483
Average hours per week:						
Economic reasons........	22.9	24.0	22.6	23.0	24.0	22.7
Noneconomic reasons........	21.4	25.1	19.9	21.5	25.1	20.0

S No data or data do not meet publication standards.

Source: U.S. Bureau of Labor Statistics, CPS Tables, "Persons at work 1 to 34 hours in all and in nonagricultural industries by reason for working less than 35 hours and usual full- or part-time status," <http://www.bls.gov/cps/tables.htm>, accessed March 2015.

Table 630. Displaced Workers by Selected Characteristics: 2013

[In percent, except total (4,292 represents 4,292,000). As of January 2014. For persons 20 years old and over with job tenure of 3 years or more who lost or left a job between January 2011 and December 2013 because of plant closings or moves, insufficient work for workers to do, or the abolishment of their positions. Based on Current Population Survey; see source and Appendix III]

Characteristic	Total (1,000)	Employment status in January 2014			Reason for job loss, 2011-2013		
		Employed	Unemployed	Not in the labor force	Plant or company closed down or moved	Insufficient work	Position or shift abolished
Total [1]	**4,292**	**61.3**	**20.8**	**17.9**	**35.3**	**32.6**	**32.1**
20 to 24 years old	91	58.7	24.6	16.7	45.6	33.1	21.3
25 to 54 years old	2,897	68.2	20.2	11.6	35.1	34.6	30.3
55 to 64 years old	1,004	53.2	24.3	22.5	34.2	28.8	37.0
65 years old and over	301	22.5	13.7	63.7	37.1	25.8	37.1
Males	2,390	64.1	21.6	14.3	35.0	37.8	27.2
20 to 24 years old	42	([2])	([2])	([2])	([2])	([2])	([2])
25 to 54 years old	1,659	69.8	21.5	8.7	35.4	39.7	24.9
55 to 64 years old	525	57.6	26.2	16.3	34.5	31.0	34.5
65 years old and over	164	23.9	8.5	67.6	32.8	39.0	28.3
Females	1,902	57.7	19.9	22.4	35.5	26.1	38.4
20 to 24 years old	49	([2])	([2])	([2])	([2])	([2])	([2])
25 to 54 years old	1,237	66.0	18.6	15.4	34.7	27.8	37.5
55 to 64 years old	479	48.4	22.3	29.3	33.8	26.4	39.8
65 years old and over	137	20.9	20.0	59.1	42.2	10.1	47.7
White [3]	3,499	62.2	20.1	17.6	35.4	31.1	33.6
Male	1,966	64.4	21.5	14.1	36.0	36.3	27.8
Female	1,533	59.4	18.5	22.1	34.6	24.4	41.0
Black [3]	465	54.6	30.6	14.8	40.1	38.0	21.8
Male	209	63.0	26.7	10.3	41.9	41.7	16.4
Female	256	47.7	33.7	18.5	38.7	35.0	26.3
Asian [3]	192	58.7	15.1	26.2	36.2	28.4	35.4
Male	120	61.9	18.7	19.5	28.0	39.5	32.5
Female	71	([2])	([2])	([2])	([2])	([2])	([2])
Hispanic [4]	685	64.5	20.7	14.8	41.5	40.0	18.4
Male	413	70.8	20.6	8.6	46.8	39.6	13.6
Female	273	54.9	20.9	24.2	33.7	40.6	25.7

[1] Includes other races, not shown separately. [2] Data not shown where base is less than 75,000. [3] For persons in this race group only. [4] Persons of Hispanic origin may be of any race.

Source: U.S. Bureau of Labor Statistics, *Worker Displacement: 2011-2013,* USDL 14-1605, August 2014. See also <http://www.bls.gov/news.release/disp.toc.htm>.

Table 631. Persons Not in the Labor Force By Age, Sex, and Reason: 2014

[In thousands (92,025 represents 92,025,000). For civilian noninstitutional population 16 years old and over. Persons who are neither employed nor unemployed are not in the labor force. This includes retired persons, students, those taking care of children or other family members, and others who are neither working nor seeking work. Annual average of monthly figures. Based on the Current Population Survey; see text, Section 1, and Appendix III]

Status and reason	Total	Age			Sex	
		16 to 24 years old	25 to 54 years old	55 years old and over	Male	Female
Total not in the labor force	**92,025**	**17,418**	**23,744**	**50,863**	**36,865**	**55,159**
Do not want a job now [1]	85,702	15,377	21,075	49,250	33,932	51,770
Want a job now	6,323	2,041	2,669	1,614	2,934	3,389
In the previous year—						
Did not search for a job	3,448	1,072	1,337	1,039	1,524	1,924
Did search for a job, but not in past 4 weeks [2]	2,875	969	1,332	574	1,409	1,465
Not available for work now	667	303	284	81	270	397
Available for work now, but not looking for work [3]	2,207	666	1,048	493	1,139	1,068
Reason for not currently looking for work:						
Discouraged over job prospects [4]	739	184	350	205	443	296
Family responsibilities	239	34	160	45	65	174
In school or training	267	208	54	4	149	118
Ill health or disability	161	16	84	61	82	80
Other [5]	801	224	398	179	400	401

[1] Includes some persons who are not asked if they want a job. [2] Persons who had a job in previous 12 months must have searched since the end of that job. [3] Persons who have searched for work in previous 12 months and are available to work now also are referred to as "marginally attached to the labor force." [4] Includes such things as believes no work available, could not find work, lacks necessary schooling or training, employer thinks too young or old, and other types of discrimination. [5] Includes such things as child care and transportation problems.

Source: U.S. Bureau of Labor Statistics, CPS Tables, "Persons not in the labor force by desire and availability for work, age, and sex," <http://www.bls.gov/cps/tables.htm>, accessed March 2015.

Table 632. Employment Status of Parents by Age of Youngest Child and Family Type: 2011 to 2014

[In thousands (34,269 represents 34,269,000), except percent distribution. Annual average of monthly figures. For families with own children (sons, daughters, step-children, and adopted children). Based on the Current Population Survey, see text, Section 1, and Appendix III]

Characteristic	Number				Percent distribution			
	2011	2012	2013	2014	2011	2012	2013	2014
WITH OWN CHILDREN UNDER 18 YEARS OLD								
Total families	**34,269**	**34,566**	**34,392**	**34,434**	**100.0**	**100.0**	**100.0**	**100.0**
Parent(s) employed	29,891	30,351	30,336	30,545	87.2	87.8	88.2	88.7
No parent employed	4,379	4,215	4,056	3,889	12.8	12.2	11.8	11.3
Married-couple families	23,334	23,297	23,259	23,330	100.0	100.0	100.0	100.0
Parent(s) employed	22,360	22,429	22,408	22,528	95.8	96.3	96.3	96.6
Mother employed	15,267	15,243	15,200	15,347	65.4	65.4	65.4	65.8
Both parents employed	13,649	13,739	13,746	14,033	58.5	59.0	59.1	60.2
Mother employed, not father	1,618	1,503	1,454	1,314	6.9	6.5	6.3	5.6
Father employed, not mother	7,093	7,186	7,208	7,181	30.4	30.8	31.0	30.8
Neither parent employed	974	868	851	801	4.2	3.7	3.7	3.4
Families maintained by women [1]	8,538	8,757	8,575	8,589	100.0	100.0	100.0	100.0
Mother employed	5,622	5,872	5,851	5,958	65.9	67.1	68.2	69.4
Mother not employed	2,916	2,885	2,724	2,632	34.1	32.9	31.8	30.6
Families maintained by men [1]	2,397	2,512	2,558	2,515	100.0	100.0	100.0	100.0
Father employed	1,908	2,050	2,077	2,059	79.6	81.6	81.2	81.9
Father not employed	489	462	481	456	20.4	18.4	18.8	18.1
WITH OWN CHILDREN 6 to 17 YEARS OLD								
Total families	**14,969**	**14,989**	**19,767**	**19,850**	**100.0**	**100.0**	**100.0**	**100.0**
Parent(s) employed	12,864	12,996	17,592	17,768	85.9	86.7	89.0	89.5
No parent employed	2,105	1,992	2,175	2,082	14.1	13.3	11.0	10.5
Married-couple families	10,407	10,315	13,183	13,239	100.0	100.0	100.0	100.0
Parent(s) employed	9,972	9,958	12,676	12,753	95.8	96.5	96.2	96.3
Mother employed	6,149	6,215	9,213	9,321	59.1	60.3	69.9	70.4
Both parents employed	5,512	5,635	8,291	8,453	53.0	54.6	62.9	63.9
Mother employed, not father	636	580	922	868	6.1	5.6	7.0	6.6
Father employed, not mother	3,824	3,744	3,463	3,432	36.7	36.3	26.3	25.9
Neither parent employed	435	357	507	486	4.2	3.5	3.8	3.7
Families maintained by women [1]	3,495	3,609	5,125	5,130	100.0	100.0	100.0	100.0
Mother employed	2,047	2,161	3,727	3,811	58.6	59.9	72.7	74.3
Mother not employed	1,448	1,448	1,398	1,319	41.4	40.1	27.3	25.7
Families maintained by men [1]	1,067	1,065	1,459	1,481	100.0	100.0	100.0	100.0
Father employed	845	877	1,188	1,204	79.2	82.4	81.4	81.3
Father not employed	222	188	271	277	20.8	17.6	18.6	18.7
WITH OWN CHILDREN UNDER 6 YEARS OLD								
Total families	**19,301**	**19,577**	**14,625**	**14,584**	**100.0**	**100.0**	**100.0**	**100.0**
Parent(s) employed	17,027	17,355	12,745	12,777	88.2	88.6	87.1	87.6
No parent employed	2,274	2,222	1,880	1,807	11.8	11.4	12.9	12.4
Married-couple families	12,927	12,982	10,076	10,091	100.0	100.0	100.0	100.0
Parent(s) employed	12,388	12,471	9,732	9,775	95.8	96.1	96.6	96.9
Mother employed	9,118	9,028	5,987	6,027	70.5	69.5	59.4	59.7
Both parents employed	8,136	8,104	5,455	5,580	62.9	62.4	54.1	55.3
Mother employed, not father	982	924	532	447	7.6	7.1	5.3	4.4
Father employed, not mother	3,270	3,443	3,745	3,749	25.3	26.5	37.2	37.1
Neither parent employed	539	511	344	315	4.2	3.9	3.4	3.1
Families maintained by women [1]	5,043	5,149	3,450	3,460	100.0	100.0	100.0	100.0
Mother employed	3,575	3,711	2,124	2,147	70.9	72.1	61.6	62.1
Mother not employed	1,468	1,437	1,326	1,313	29.1	27.9	38.4	37.9
Families maintained by men [1]	1,330	1,447	1,100	1,034	100.0	100.0	100.0	100.0
Father employed	1,063	1,173	889	854	79.9	81.1	80.9	82.7
Father not employed	267	274	210	179	20.1	18.9	19.1	17.3

[1] No spouse present.

Source: U.S. Bureau of Labor Statistics, *Employment Characteristics of Families—2014*, USDL 15-0689, April 2015, and earlier releases. See also <http://www.bls.gov/news.release/famee.toc.htm>.

Table 633. Employed Civilians by Occupation, Sex, Race, and Hispanic Origin: 2014

[146,305 represents 143,305,000. Civilian noninstitutionalized population 16 years old and over. Annual average of monthly figures. Based on Current Population Survey; see text, Section 1 and Appendix III. Occupational classifications are those used in the 2010 Census]

Occupation	Total employed (1,000)	Percent of total			
		Female	Black [1]	Asian [1]	Hispanic [2]
Total, 16 years and over............................	**146,305**	**46.9**	**11.4**	**5.7**	**16.1**
Management, professional and related occupations....................	**56,050**	**51.6**	**8.8**	**7.5**	**8.7**
Management, business, and financial operations occupations..............	23,171	43.7	7.5	6.1	8.9
Management occupations [3].............................	16,199	38.6	6.7	5.4	9.1
Chief executives..................................	1,603	26.3	3.0	4.7	4.7
General and operations managers....................	887	29.5	6.2	3.9	11.5
Marketing and sales managers......................	917	46.1	3.9	5.9	8.3
Administrative services managers....................	134	40.8	8.1	2.7	9.0
Computer and information systems managers........	629	26.7	6.3	11.6	4.9
Financial managers................................	1,194	53.4	7.8	6.9	10.5
Human resources managers........................	236	74.4	11.8	3.3	10.0
Industrial production managers......................	273	17.8	4.2	3.6	8.4
Purchasing managers..............................	193	42.6	7.6	8.9	11.6
Transportation, storage, and distribution managers....	260	21.6	7.0	6.1	12.4
Farmers, ranchers, and other agricultural managers.....	941	23.8	0.9	0.8	4.2
Construction managers.............................	711	7.4	3.7	2.3	10.2
Education administrators...........................	838	63.3	13.3	2.1	9.1
Architectural and engineering managers..............	122	7.6	2.7	9.9	8.4
Food service managers............................	1,113	44.9	9.8	10.0	16.4
Lodging managers.................................	146	54.6	8.1	15.5	7.1
Medical and health services managers...............	593	71.8	11.0	5.5	8.1
Property, real estate, and community association managers..............	674	48.9	7.5	3.1	12.9
Social and community service managers..............	362	65.3	14.6	5.3	7.6
Business and financial operations occupations [3].....	6,972	55.7	9.5	7.6	8.4
Wholesale and retail buyers, except farm products.....	216	53.4	6.1	7.0	8.8
Purchasing agents, except wholesale, retail, and farm products........	271	55.3	10.8	3.5	9.0
Claims adjusters, appraisers, examiners, and investigators..............	311	60.3	15.2	3.3	9.7
Compliance officers...............................	239	46.4	10.4	5.3	9.3
Cost estimators..................................	105	13.7	2.4	3.8	5.6
Human resources workers..........................	615	71.8	13.3	4.0	12.1
Management analysts..............................	850	41.3	7.7	9.6	5.8
Accountants and auditors..........................	1,724	63.0	8.2	10.7	7.8
Appraisers and assessors of real estate.............	95	40.1	5.4	1.6	4.2
Financial analysts................................	261	40.5	4.9	15.8	7.2
Personal financial advisors........................	434	35.5	8.1	5.7	7.1
Insurance underwriters............................	113	60.5	12.3	2.4	7.6
Credit counselors and loan officers.................	288	59.4	10.3	6.3	11.0
Tax preparers....................................	103	67.8	16.5	5.7	13.1
Professional and related occupations...............	32,879	57.2	9.7	8.6	8.6
Computer and mathematical occupations [3].........	4,303	25.6	8.3	19.2	6.6
Computer programmers............................	509	21.4	5.7	19.7	6.4
Software developers, applications and systems software..............	1,235	19.8	5.3	31.9	5.2
Computer support specialists.......................	524	26.6	14.3	8.1	9.4
Database administrators...........................	108	28.0	11.7	13.3	4.6
Network and computer systems administrators........	205	19.1	9.5	8.4	7.9
Operations research analysts......................	138	55.4	11.0	11.9	10.5
Architecture and engineering occupations [3]..........	2,798	15.4	5.2	11.7	8.2
Architects, except naval...........................	178	25.3	4.1	10.0	7.2
Aerospace engineers..............................	147	15.6	6.2	10.7	11.4
Civil engineers...................................	349	16.5	6.1	9.7	8.8
Computer hardware engineers......................	84	15.3	7.4	22.8	9.5
Electrical and electronics engineers.................	271	12.3	3.9	21.4	5.3
Industrial engineers, including health and safety........	194	16.0	5.5	9.7	8.6
Mechanical engineers.............................	303	8.8	3.3	9.9	5.6
Drafters..	138	18.1	5.3	4.3	6.5
Engineering technicians, except drafters..............	369	20.5	8.2	8.7	13.2
Life, physical, and social science occupations [3]......	1,355	45.6	6.4	12.3	7.5
Biological scientists..............................	110	45.9	5.3	10.5	6.0
Medical scientists................................	143	52.5	5.1	33.8	7.9
Chemists and materials scientists..................	102	29.8	8.1	12.7	6.0
Environmental scientists and geoscientists...........	91	24.5	1.3	3.9	6.6
Psychologists....................................	232	71.9	5.7	1.3	8.0
Community and social services occupations [3]........	2,495	64.3	17.5	3.4	11.6
Counselors......................................	737	71.1	18.7	2.8	10.6
Social workers...................................	799	81.9	21.3	2.4	13.2
Miscellaneous community and social service specialists..............	114	69.3	14.6	1.7	17.4
Clergy..	433	18.6	8.3	6.9	7.5
Legal occupations................................	1,814	50.8	7.5	4.5	7.9
Lawyers...	1,132	32.9	5.7	4.4	5.6
Judges, magistrates, and other judicial workers........	53	51.7	10.9	3.2	4.8
Paralegals and legal assistants....................	417	87.3	9.5	4.3	14.2
Miscellaneous legal support workers................	200	75.8	12.8	5.1	8.9
Education, training, and library occupations [3]........	8,686	74.1	10.3	4.4	9.5
Postsecondary teachers...........................	1,259	50.2	6.1	12.2	6.1
Preschool and kindergarten teachers................	664	97.2	15.8	3.4	13.9
Elementary and middle school teachers..............	3,102	80.9	10.2	2.5	8.7
Secondary school teachers........................	1,099	57.0	10.0	2.2	7.6
Special education teachers........................	336	83.7	8.9	1.5	6.8
Other teachers and instructors.....................	836	65.4	11.5	6.0	11.1
Librarians.......................................	198	84.8	3.6	4.0	5.7
Teacher assistants...............................	904	90.3	14.4	3.0	17.1
Arts, design, entertainment, sports, and media occupations [3].............	2,935	47.4	6.3	5.0	9.8

See footnotes at end of table.

Table 633. Employed Civilians by Occupation, Sex, Race, and Hispanic Origin: 2014-Continued.

See headnote on page 407.

Occupation	Total employed (1,000)	Percent of total			
		Female	Black [1]	Asian [1]	Hispanic [2]
Artists and related workers....................	203	48.8	2.1	5.7	9.1
Designers................................	830	56.3	4.1	7.1	11.1
Producers and directors...................	161	36.5	4.6	4.0	11.7
Athletes, coaches, umpires, and related workers..........	294	34.3	6.5	2.5	8.8
Musicians, singers, and related workers........	194	34.0	12.6	3.0	6.1
News analysts, reporters and correspondents.......	80	43.9	7.5	6.3	13.8
Public relations specialists.................	136	60.5	9.0	4.0	9.2
Editors..................................	163	48.2	2.8	5.5	7.1
Writers and authors.......................	221	59.1	6.2	3.2	5.6
Miscellaneous media and communication workers......	78	73.6	4.8	11.6	33.3
Broadcast and sound engineering technicians and radio operators.......	108	13.0	15.2	4.8	10.5
Photographers............................	174	51.0	4.3	3.7	10.1
Healthcare practitioner and technical occupations [3]..........	8,493	74.2	11.2	9.4	7.7
Dentists.................................	192	29.1	5.6	15.5	6.8
Dietitians and nutritionists.................	123	92.4	10.6	10.2	5.1
Pharmacists..............................	293	56.3	8.1	18.9	5.6
Physicians and surgeons...................	1,014	36.7	5.5	21.0	6.3
Physician assistants.......................	84	74.5	6.4	11.3	5.9
Occupational therapists....................	111	92.4	5.7	3.0	5.2
Physical therapists........................	244	69.8	6.7	12.5	4.6
Speech-language pathologists...............	137	98.4	7.2	3.2	8.4
Registered nurses.........................	2,888	90.0	11.8	8.2	6.7
Clinical laboratory technologists and technicians...	293	74.0	18.2	12.8	10.9
Dental hygienists.........................	175	97.1	4.3	5.5	9.9
Diagnostic-related technologists and technicians...	331	73.6	6.5	5.3	8.0
Emergency medical technicians and paramedics...	232	25.8	7.7	1.2	8.4
Health practitioner support technologists and technicians........	583	81.4	13.2	6.8	13.2
Licensed practical and licensed vocational nurses...	641	89.0	27.9	5.0	9.9
Medical records and health information technicians...	138	90.2	19.8	4.4	12.7
Service occupations....................	**25,854**	**56.7**	**16.2**	**5.4**	**23.4**
Healthcare support occupations [3]............	3,461	87.6	25.7	5.2	16.2
Nursing, psychiatric, and home health aides......	1,980	88.5	35.9	4.5	15.4
Massage therapists........................	172	82.7	4.3	10.6	8.4
Dental assistants.........................	273	96.6	5.1	5.4	23.5
Medical assistants........................	508	92.8	14.3	5.0	21.9
Protective service occupations [3]............	3,140	21.8	19.7	2.3	14.4
First-line supervisors of police and detectives...	126	15.9	14.4	0.7	7.0
Firefighters..............................	300	5.7	10.2	0.7	9.6
Bailiffs, correctional officers, and jailers........	395	28.6	20.6	1.7	16.0
Detectives and criminal investigators..........	164	21.0	14.6	1.6	13.2
Police and sheriff's patrol officers............	680	12.4	15.6	1.8	13.2
Private detectives and investigators...........	98	37.7	14.5	3.0	13.5
Security guards and gaming surveillance officers...	899	22.6	30.3	3.7	19.0
Lifeguards and other protective service workers...	141	49.7	12.6	1.8	11.1
Food preparation and serving related occupations...	8,112	55.1	12.6	6.0	24.9
Chefs and head cooks.....................	430	21.4	15.3	16.4	18.3
First-line supervisors of food preparation and serving workers........	545	59.1	13.7	4.7	19.1
Cooks..................................	1,992	40.6	16.5	4.9	34.0
Food-preparation workers...................	885	54.7	13.4	6.9	27.2
Bartenders..............................	416	57.5	6.0	1.9	15.5
Combined food preparation and serving workers, including fast food........	428	61.9	20.5	3.3	18.7
Counter attendants, cafeteria, food concession, and coffee shop..........	254	70.4	13.9	4.3	21.6
Waiters and waitresses.....................	2,054	71.8	7.5	6.6	19.4
Food servers, nonrestaurant................	185	61.9	23.5	6.1	20.8
Dining room and cafeteria attendants and bartender helpers............	375	49.2	7.6	5.5	34.1
Dishwashers.............................	246	21.2	12.3	5.7	40.2
Hosts and hostesses, restaurant, lounge, and coffee shop...............	297	85.2	10.9	6.5	18.2
Building and grounds cleaning and maintenance occupations............	5,803	40.2	14.6	3.4	36.7
First-line supervisors of housekeeping and janitorial workers........	282	42.3	14.7	2.8	24.1
First-line supervisors of landscaping, lawn service, and groundskeeping workers.........	210	4.8	8.3	1.4	22.7
Janitors and building cleaners...............	2,328	33.2	17.5	3.4	31.5
Maids and housekeeping cleaners............	1,514	88.6	16.8	5.5	43.8
Pest control workers.......................	80	3.7	10.9	0.5	17.0
Grounds maintenance workers...............	1,389	6.3	8.3	1.7	43.6
Personal care and service occupations [3].......	5,337	77.4	15.0	8.4	16.6
First-line supervisors of gaming workers........	151	45.2	4.4	6.4	7.3
First-line supervisors of personal service workers...	202	71.3	11.5	18.2	13.7
Nonfarm animal caretakers..................	201	69.9	2.8	0.9	12.2
Gaming services workers...................	99	41.8	8.0	19.4	12.5
Barbers.................................	110	16.8	36.3	5.4	23.7
Hairdressers, hairstylists, and cosmetologists....	760	94.6	12.4	4.8	15.3
Miscellaneous personal appearance workers......	296	88.9	5.9	55.3	10.3
Baggage porters, bellhops, and concierges......	85	20.2	17.2	6.0	24.8
Child care workers........................	1,218	95.5	15.9	3.5	21.6
Personal care aides.......................	1,254	83.9	23.0	7.9	18.2
Recreation and fitness workers..............	404	63.0	9.2	2.9	11.6
Sales and office occupations............	**33,416**	**61.8**	**12.0**	**4.8**	**14.9**
Sales and related occupations [3]............	15,646	49.2	10.7	5.3	14.7
First-line supervisors of retail sales workers......	3,285	44.3	8.8	6.1	12.1

See footnotes at end of table.

Table 633. Employed Civilians by Occupation, Sex, Race, and Hispanic Origin: 2014-Continued.

See headnote on page 407.

Occupation	Total employed (1,000)	Percent of total			
		Female	Black [1]	Asian [1]	Hispanic [2]
First-line supervisors of non retail sales workers.........	1,200	26.0	5.6	4.8	11.2
Cashiers..	3,242	72.2	18.3	6.9	22.0
Counter and rental clerks...........................	113	49.8	11.8	4.5	22.5
Parts salespersons.................................	93	15.3	4.8	0.5	12.2
Retail salespersons................................	3,316	49.8	12.3	4.6	16.2
Advertising sales agents............................	227	48.7	7.9	4.5	12.7
Insurance sales agents..............................	562	47.0	8.3	4.9	13.2
Securities, commodities, and financial services sales agents...............	256	32.5	4.9	4.6	9.5
Travel agents......................................	82	81.4	7.9	13.2	9.9
Sales representatives, services, all other............	480	29.5	6.6	4.3	11.0
Sales representatives, wholesale and manufacturing....	1,309	29.3	5.3	3.8	9.3
Real estate brokers and sales agents................	868	54.9	5.4	4.2	10.5
Telemarketers.....................................	75	67.4	19.6	3.6	18.5
Door-to-door sales workers, news and street vendors, and related workers....	175	64.0	10.6	3.5	21.7
Office and administrative support occupations [3].......	17,771	72.9	13.1	4.4	15.1
First-line supervisors of office and administrative support workers.......	1,351	67.4	11.1	3.6	12.2
Bill and account collectors..........................	165	66.6	20.3	1.5	13.9
Billing and posting clerks...........................	507	91.2	13.3	5.2	12.2
Bookkeeping, accounting, and auditing clerks.........	1,231	90.2	8.0	4.8	10.9
Payroll and timekeeping clerks......................	146	89.4	15.1	3.9	12.1
Tellers..	361	81.6	10.5	7.1	16.8
Court, municipal, and license clerks.................	69	77.4	12.7	0.8	14.1
Customer service representatives...................	2,086	64.6	17.0	4.5	16.5
File clerks...	226	81.6	15.6	3.8	18.3
Hotel, motel, and resort desk clerks.................	120	63.5	12.4	9.3	25.1
Interviewers, except eligibility and loan..............	160	80.5	23.9	4.8	11.3
Library assistants, clerical..........................	98	84.0	7.3	3.2	10.2
Loan interviewers and clerks........................	143	78.1	11.4	3.9	9.6
Order clerks.......................................	104	59.9	9.5	5.8	19.1
Receptionists and information clerks.................	1,301	91.3	10.5	4.1	18.7
Reservation and transportation ticket agents and travel clerks...........	94	57.4	16.0	9.9	18.5
Couriers and messengers..........................	233	16.0	14.4	3.2	20.4
Dispatchers.......................................	267	60.9	14.0	1.8	14.9
Postal service clerks...............................	117	52.3	30.8	8.7	7.9
Postal service mail carriers.........................	311	38.7	19.2	5.3	12.9
Postal service mail sorters, processors, and processing machine operators.........	61	59.1	27.5	5.7	9.5
Production, planning, and expediting clerks...........	244	54.3	11.4	4.5	13.5
Shipping, receiving, and traffic clerks...............	606	32.3	13.3	3.2	23.2
Stock clerks and order fillers.......................	1,483	35.9	16.0	4.2	22.3
Weighers, measurers, checkers, and samplers, recordkeeping...........	75	41.8	14.7	1.5	22.2
Secretaries and administrative assistants............	2,995	94.2	9.8	3.3	12.7
Computer operators................................	87	55.0	12.5	4.3	8.5
Data entry keyers..................................	292	78.7	16.1	8.4	12.9
Word processors and typists........................	101	88.4	18.4	5.3	10.7
Insurance claims and policy processing clerks........	288	82.8	15.2	2.9	10.1
Mail clerks and mail machine operators, except postal service...........	79	53.0	20.0	10.3	13.8
Office clerks, general...............................	1,230	84.6	13.3	6.1	15.5
Natural resources, construction, and maintenance occupations........	**13,537**	**4.4**	**7.3**	**2.1**	**27.6**
Farming, fishing, and forestry occupations [3].........	1,022	22.4	6.0	1.6	43.4
Construction and extraction occupations [3]...........	7,637	2.6	6.9	1.3	32.3
First-line supervisors of construction trades and extraction workers.........	696	2.4	5.7	1.1	18.9
Brickmasons, blockmasons, and stonemasons........	142	0.7	8.1	0.3	43.9
Carpenters..	1,282	1.7	5.0	1.4	31.9
Carpet, floor, and tile installers and finishers.........	170	2.3	4.8	3.6	44.2
Cement masons, concrete finishers, and terrazzo workers............	58	–	9.5	–	48.7
Construction laborers..............................	1,686	2.5	9.4	1.8	42.1
Operating engineers and other construction equipment operators.........	336	1.8	6.8	0.1	16.9
Drywall installers, ceiling tile installers, and tapers....	162	2.1	1.8	0.3	61.5
Electricians.......................................	769	2.4	6.5	1.8	18.2
Painters, construction and maintenance..............	561	6.0	7.3	1.4	48.2
Pipelayers, plumbers, pipefitters, and steamfitters....	564	1.6	6.9	1.6	21.4
Roofers...	206	0.5	4.3	0.5	58.1
Sheet metal workers...............................	110	5.2	5.2	0.8	10.2
Construction and building inspectors................	78	12.2	3.3	2.3	5.3
Highway maintenance workers.......................	123	1.5	9.3	–	17.1
Installation, maintenance, and repair occupations [3]....	4,879	3.5	8.4	3.3	16.8
First-line supervisors of mechanics, installers, and repairers.........	284	4.8	8.4	3.3	11.2
Computer, automated teller, and office machine repairers................	265	13.3	12.2	7.9	12.3
Radio and telecommunications equipment installers and repairers.....	134	7.4	12.5	6.3	8.7
Aircraft mechanics and service technicians...........	127	3.3	9.0	6.9	12.5
Automotive body and related repairers...............	133	1.6	5.9	1.7	18.3
Automotive service technicians and mechanics........	883	1.4	9.0	4.5	24.1
Bus and truck mechanics and diesel engine specialists................	323	0.3	7.8	0.6	15.6
Heavy vehicle and mobile equipment service technicians and mechanics.........	211	0.5	3.8	0.6	15.5
Heating, air conditioning, and refrigeration mechanics and installers.........	378	1.2	8.5	2.4	16.4
Industrial and refractory machinery mechanics........	454	2.8	6.3	1.7	13.3
Maintenance and repair workers, general.............	471	3.2	9.9	3.6	17.2

See footnotes at end of table.

Table 633. Employed Civilians by Occupation, Sex, Race, and Hispanic Origin: 2014-Continued.

See headnote on page 407.

Occupation	Total employed (1,000)	Percent of total			
		Female	Black [1]	Asian [1]	Hispanic [2]
Electrical power-line installers and repairers..................	115	3.0	5.2	0.9	7.8
Telecommunications line installers and repairers..........	184	4.4	12.1	4.7	17.3
Production, transportation, and material moving occupations..........	**17,448**	**21.7**	**15.0**	**4.7**	**22.0**
Production occupations [3].........................	8,438	28.0	12.5	6.2	21.9
First-line supervisors of production and operating workers..............................	789	18.6	11.0	3.4	17.0
Electrical, electronics, and electromechanical assemblers.................	164	46.7	15.3	16.8	22.9
Bakers.....................................	224	62.8	10.1	7.5	22.9
Butchers and other meat, poultry, and fish processing workers...........	331	23.5	20.2	8.0	35.4
Food batchmakers............................	95	61.5	13.1	6.1	25.3
Cutting, punching, and press machine setters, operators, and tenders, metal and plastic.................	85	24.2	14.0	0.9	15.9
Machinists.................................	391	4.5	3.9	4.1	15.4
Welding, soldering, and brazing workers.................	615	4.8	8.8	2.0	22.4
Printing press operators.......................	187	19.6	13.2	5.7	21.7
Laundry and dry-cleaning workers.................	156	59.7	16.1	11.5	38.0
Sewing machine operators.......................	158	81.9	15.0	21.1	34.6
Tailors, dressmakers, and sewers................	92	80.6	9.5	16.7	30.4
Stationary engineers and boiler operators..........	96	2.0	7.0	4.3	15.2
Water and wastewater treatment plant and system operators..............	72	4.5	10.7	2.3	14.7
Crushing, grinding, polishing, mixing, and blending workers..............	69	11.7	14.1	3.5	22.4
Inspectors, testers, sorters, samplers, and weighers..................	752	35.1	12.7	6.8	16.8
Medical, dental, and ophthalmic laboratory technicians....................	85	52.3	3.0	14.3	12.3
Packaging and filling machine operators and tenders..................	259	56.2	19.0	8.9	36.0
Painting workers.............................	156	12.7	8.1	4.3	27.0
Transportation and material-moving occupations [3]..........	9,010	15.7	17.3	3.4	22.1
Supervisors, transportation and material-moving workers............	199	18.3	9.0	2.0	22.1
Aircraft pilots and flight engineers..............	133	7.2	1.9	0.5	2.7
Bus drivers.................................	584	45.0	25.9	2.5	12.8
Driver/sales workers and truck drivers...............	3,406	5.8	15.6	2.5	20.5
Taxi drivers and chauffeurs.......................	383	12.7	28.8	13.9	16.5
Parking lot attendants.......................	78	10.5	26.3	9.9	28.7
Automotive and water craft service attendants........	97	7.5	13.7	15.7	21.9
Industrial truck and tractor operators............	564	7.4	24.4	2.2	29.3
Cleaners of vehicles and equipment................	375	12.4	22.5	1.9	33.4
Laborers and freight, stock, and material movers, hand...................	1,867	18.3	15.6	3.2	23.8
Packers and packagers, hand....................	505	53.8	18.2	5.9	43.3
Refuse and recyclable material collectors.............	84	8.6	19.0	0.8	36.8

– Represents or rounds to zero. [1] The Current Population Survey (CPS) allows respondents to choose more than one race. Data represent persons who selected this race group only and exclude persons reporting more than one race. The CPS in prior years only allowed respondents to report one race group. See also comments on race in the text for Section 1. [2] Persons of Hispanic origin may be of any race. [3] Includes other occupations, not shown separately.

Source: U.S. Bureau of Labor Statistics, CPS Tables, "Employed persons by detailed occupation, sex, race, and Hispanic or Latino ethnicity," <http://www.bls.gov/cps/tables.htm>, accessed March 2015.

Table 634. Green Goods and Services Employment by Industry Sector and Type: 2011

[Covers employment in 325 of the 1,083 detailed industries in the 2012 North American Industry Classification System (NAICS) identified by BLS as potentially providing goods and services that directly benefit the environment or conserve natural resources. Data compiled through the Green Goods and Services (GGS) survey under the Quarterly Census of Employment and Wages (QCEW) program. Data may not add to total or sub-total due to rounding. Industries may not add to total because of unclassified employment in the QCEW, not shown separately]

Industry	2012 NAICS code [1]	Private		Federal government		State government		Local government	
		Number	Per-cent [2]	Number	Per-cent [2]	Number	Per-cent [2]	Number	Per-cent [2]
Total, all industries		**2,515,200**	**2.3**	**213,340**	**7.5**	**248,539**	**5.5**	**424,201**	**3.1**
Natural resources and mining....................	11,21	64,689	3.4	(S)	(S)	1,725	79.2	(S)	(S)
Utilities..................................	22	71,129	12.9	7,218	52	(S)	(S)	93,644	38.9
Construction.............................	23	487,709	8.9	(S)	(S)	(S)	(S)	1242	1.2
Manufacturing............................	31-33	507,168	4.3	(S)	(S)	(S)	(S)	(S)	(S)
Wholesale & Retail Trade...................	42,44-45	223,079	1.1	(S)	(S)	(S)	(S)	(S)	(S)
Transportation and warehousing..............	48-49	238,755	5.9	(S)	(S)	27,583	52.3	209,063	77.9
Information.............................	51	29,412	1.1	(S)	(S)	516	7.4	3,644	2.8
Financial activities.......................	52,53	475	–	(S)	(S)	(S)	(S)	(S)	(S)
Professional, scientific, and technical services......	54	381,981	5	39,714	55.1	(S)	(S)	1131	6.1
Management of companies and enterprises....	55	69,310	3.6	(X)	(X)	(X)	(X)	(X)	(X)
Administrative and waste services.............	56	335,417	4.3	(S)	(S)	(S)	(S)	32,577	46.4
Education and health services.................	61,62	26,123	0.1	(S)	(S)	42,423	1.7	10,020	0.1
Leisure and hospitality.....................	71,72	23,696	0.2	21,489	36.5	9,024	38.8	20,596	5.3
Other services, except public administration. ..	81	56,257	1.3	(S)	(S)	228	7.3	2,873	6.5
Public administration......................	92	(X)	(X)	139,884	8.8	164,952	9	49,229	1.3

S Data does not meet disclosure standards. X Not applicable. – Represents zero [1] North American Industry Classification System, 2012; see text, Section 15. [2] Percent of GGS employment compared to total employment.

Source: U.S. Bureau of Labor Statistics, *Employment in Green Goods and Services, 2011*, March 2013. See also <http://www.bls.gov/ggs/>.

Table 635. Employment and Annual and Hourly Wages by Occupation: 2014

[in dollars, except employment. Data shown for occupations with more than 1,500,000 employees. Data from the Occupational Employment Statistics survey. For definition of mean and median, see Guide to Tabular Presentation]

Occupation	Employment	Annual wages [1]	Mean hourly wage	Median hourly wage
All occupations [3]............................	**135,128,260**	**47,230**	**22.71**	**17.09**
Management occupations............................	6,741,640	112,490	54.08	46.75
Top executives............................	2,351,130	122,060	58.68	48.51
General and operations managers............................	2,049,870	117,200	56.35	46.77
Operations specialties managers............................	1,624,000	117,390	56.44	50.84
Other management occupations............................	2,136,840	93,720	45.06	40.77
Business and financial operations occupations............................	6,828,940	72,410	34.81	31.15
Business operations specialists............................	4,264,370	70,060	33.69	30.71
Financial specialists............................	2,564,560	76,320	36.69	31.83
Computer and mathematical occupations............................	3,834,180	83,970	40.37	38.18
Computer occupations............................	3,692,980	83,840	40.31	38.17
Architecture and engineering occupations............................	2,418,020	81,520	39.19	36.43
Engineers............................	1,574,480	93,630	45.01	42.65
Community and social service occupations............................	1,930,750	45,310	21.79	19.85
Counselors, social workers, and other community and social service specialists............................	1,857,280	45,310	21.78	19.85
Education, training, and library occupations............................	8,435,780	52,210	25.10	22.43
Postsecondary teachers............................	1,522,210	75,780	(2)	(2)
Preschool, primary, secondary, and special education school teachers............................	4,045,100	55,510	(2)	(2)
Elementary and middle school teachers............................	1,997,640	57,080	(2)	(2)
Arts, design, entertainment, sports, and media occupations............................	1,793,700	55,790	26.82	21.72
Healthcare practitioners and technical occupations............................	7,854,380	76,010	36.54	29.67
Health diagnosing and treating practitioners............................	4,833,840	94,880	45.62	36.26
Registered nurses............................	2,687,310	69,790	33.55	32.04
Health technologists and technicians............................	2,876,000	45,060	21.66	19.92
Healthcare support occupations............................	3,940,500	28,820	13.86	12.71
Nursing, psychiatric, and home health aides............................	2,352,100	25,020	12.03	11.33
Protective service occupations............................	3,297,180	43,980	21.14	17.88
Food preparation and serving related occupations............................	12,277,720	21,980	10.57	9.20
Cooks and food preparation workers............................	3,077,690	22,310	10.73	9.93
Cooks............................	2,227,470	22,680	10.91	10.16
Food and beverage serving workers............................	6,883,630	20,480	9.85	8.96
Fast food and counter workers............................	3,607,860	19,210	9.23	8.87
Combined food preparation and serving workers, including fast food............................	3,131,390	19,110	9.19	8.85
Waiters and waitresses............................	2,445,230	21,640	10.40	9.01
Building and grounds cleaning and maintenance occupations............................	4,371,450	26,370	12.68	11.19
Building cleaning and pest control workers............................	3,150,530	24,760	11.91	10.64
Building cleaning workers............................	3,082,890	24,590	11.82	10.57
Janitors and cleaners, except maids and housekeeping cleaners............................	2,137,730	25,460	12.24	10.98
Personal care and service occupations............................	4,154,360	24,980	12.01	10.22
Other personal care and service workers............................	2,556,920	23,890	11.49	10.14
Sales and related occupations............................	14,248,470	38,660	18.59	12.19
Retail sales workers............................	8,648,920	24,020	11.55	9.66
Cashiers............................	3,417,910	20,670	9.94	9.17
Retail salespersons............................	4,562,160	25,760	12.38	10.29
Sales representatives, services............................	1,736,660	68,870	33.11	24.72
Sales representatives, wholesale and manufacturing............................	1,730,180	69,860	33.59	28.07
Office and administrative support occupations............................	21,638,470	35,530	17.08	15.64
Financial clerks............................	3,217,850	35,770	17.20	16.35
Bookkeeping, accounting, and auditing clerks............................	1,575,060	38,070	18.30	17.51
Information and record clerks............................	5,439,370	32,870	15.80	14.64
Customer service representatives............................	2,511,130	33,890	16.29	15.00
Material recording, scheduling, dispatching, and distributing workers............................	3,880,030	33,140	15.93	14.04
Stock clerks and order fillers............................	1,878,860	25,380	12.20	10.99
Secretaries and administrative assistants............................	3,649,920	38,750	18.63	17.30
Secretaries and administrative assistants, except legal, medical, and executive............................	2,207,220	34,500	16.59	15.98
Other office and administrative support workers............................	3,925,760	31,850	15.31	14.28
Office clerks, general............................	2,889,970	30,820	14.82	13.78
Construction and extraction occupations............................	5,290,270	46,600	22.40	19.90
Construction trades workers............................	3,915,350	45,360	21.81	19.30
Installation, maintenance, and repair occupations............................	5,244,670	45,220	21.74	20.25
Vehicle and mobile equipment mechanics, installers, and repairers............................	1,507,680	42,120	20.25	18.97
Other installation, maintenance, and repair occupations............................	2,729,400	42,930	20.64	19.13
Production occupations............................	8,934,050	35,490	17.06	15.25
Assemblers and fabricators............................	1,810,560	31,720	15.25	14.08
Metal workers and plastic workers............................	1,918,310	38,140	18.33	17.37
Other production occupations............................	2,471,030	33,270	16.00	14.56
Transportation and material moving occupations............................	9,249,310	34,460	16.57	14.20
Motor vehicle operators............................	3,741,430	35,970	17.29	16.15
Driver/sales workers and truck drivers............................	2,828,110	37,620	18.09	16.98
Heavy and tractor-trailer truck drivers............................	1,625,290	41,930	20.16	19.00
Material moving workers............................	4,364,160	28,120	13.52	11.92
Laborers and material movers, hand............................	3,519,730	26,120	12.56	11.24
Laborers and freight, stock, and material movers, hand............................	2,400,490	27,180	13.07	11.74

[1] Annual wages have been calculated by multiplying the hourly mean wage by a "year-round, full-time" hours figure of 2,080 hours; for those occupations where there is not an hourly mean wage published, the annual wage has been directly calculated from the reported survey data. [2] Wages for some occupations that do not generally work year-round, full time, are salaries depending on how they are typically paid.

Source: U.S. Bureau of Labor Statistics, Occupational Employment Statistics, *Occupational Employment and Wages—May 2014*, USDL 15-0479, March 2015. See also <http://www.bls.gov/oes/>.

Table 636. Employed Civilians by Occupation—States: 2013

[In thousands (143,929 represents 143,929,000). Excludes persons with no previous work experience. Based on the Current Population Survey see text, Section 1 and Appendix III]

| State | Management, professional, and related occupations | | | Service occupa-tions | Sales and office occupations | | Natural resources, construc-tion, and maintenance occupations | | | Production, transportation, and material-moving occupations | |
	Total	Manage-ment, business, and financial opera-tions	Profes-sional and related occupa-tions		Sales and related occupa-tions	Office and admin-istrative occupa-tions	Farming, fishing, and forestry occupa-tions	Construc-tion and extraction occupa-tions	Instal-lation, mainte-nance, and repair occupa-tions	Produc-tion occupa-tions	Transpor-tation and material-moving occupa-tions
Total.......	143,929	22,794	31,917	25,929	15,444	17,802	964	7,130	4,964	8,275	8,709
AL............	2,034	249	427	320	224	277	(S)	114	81	187	144
AK............	340	55	72	62	31	45	(S)	22	15	(S)	22
AZ............	2,770	435	567	554	312	396	(S)	134	105	108	145
AR............	1,204	166	223	221	138	135	(S)	54	54	106	91
CA............	17,001	2,812	3,840	3,155	1,853	2,006	227	803	499	861	944
CO............	2,583	476	592	442	278	330	(S)	148	81	108	118
CT............	1,710	307	459	293	178	177	(S)	89	49	92	65
DE............	409	67	95	75	41	56	(S)	20	15	15	21
DC............	340	88	121	55	24	32	(S)	6	3	3	8
FL............	8,763	1,355	1,763	1,801	1,144	1,161	30	420	318	289	482
GA............	4,358	727	962	727	498	503	(S)	200	163	245	318
HI............	614	86	124	137	72	78	(S)	35	21	17	40
ID............	724	112	144	122	86	84	21	42	28	39	47
IL............	5,960	971	1,289	1,038	675	764	(S)	234	194	384	394
IN............	2,948	435	596	503	307	334	(S)	153	116	281	206
IA............	1,600	260	332	270	157	192	(S)	67	52	136	116
KS............	1,403	227	326	244	132	162	(S)	73	54	92	83
KY............	1,901	259	380	333	186	275	(S)	83	75	149	147
LA............	1,949	233	395	356	239	279	(S)	128	74	106	122
ME............	663	98	152	119	68	81	12	35	25	38	34
MD............	2,919	550	812	479	280	355	(S)	144	84	79	129
MA............	3,239	585	935	566	285	399	(S)	141	75	121	126
MI............	4,317	621	1,007	745	448	495	(S)	148	161	420	249
MN............	2,815	510	669	471	283	318	(S)	106	78	191	168
MS............	1,149	156	243	174	119	147	16	67	44	103	79
MO............	2,817	473	583	488	297	363	(S)	142	109	163	180
MT............	484	91	94	91	47	59	(S)	31	16	19	30
NE............	988	172	202	149	105	118	(S)	45	31	90	60
NV............	1,249	158	203	333	158	157	(S)	62	51	38	85
NH............	704	124	180	102	83	82	(S)	36	24	38	32
NJ............	4,153	710	956	721	454	553	(S)	184	123	160	284
NM............	852	121	220	174	80	101	(S)	52	27	34	35
NY............	8,925	1,401	2,190	1,807	965	1,072	(S)	388	260	338	486
NC............	4,305	610	963	776	456	535	32	216	171	275	268
ND............	397	73	82	63	41	50	(S)	23	14	20	27
OH............	5,270	774	1,065	1,004	505	663	(S)	231	197	449	359
OK............	1,714	260	336	299	174	232	(S)	118	78	108	101
OR............	1,749	292	393	289	192	215	31	82	52	98	107
PA............	5,971	932	1,337	1,032	615	760	34	263	200	370	428
RI............	503	79	126	96	49	61	(S)	20	13	36	22
SC............	2,022	257	443	316	237	272	(S)	93	88	177	122
SD............	430	76	81	72	41	57	(S)	22	17	31	24
TN............	2,817	401	554	527	289	342	(S)	156	111	219	202
TX............	12,033	1,757	2,424	2,182	1,341	1,520	57	825	460	683	783
UT............	1,363	220	293	205	155	197	(S)	75	51	75	85
VT............	335	55	88	57	30	38	(S)	18	10	20	16
VA............	3,993	766	977	662	372	443	(S)	221	136	171	219
WA............	3,221	545	777	539	317	364	44	152	123	163	197
WV............	748	101	169	130	77	92	(S)	62	24	36	56
WI............	2,884	461	609	501	282	342	23	118	100	272	176
WY............	293	41	52	52	26	35	4	31	14	15	23

S Data are not shown when the labor force base does not meet publication standard of reliability for the particular area, as determined by the sample size.

Source: U.S. Bureau of Labor Statistics, *Geographic Profile of Employment and Unemployment, 2013*, Bulletin 2780, October 2014. See also <http://www.bls.gov/gps/>.

Table 637. Fastest Growing and Largest Occupations Projected with Education Needed and Median Wages: 2012 to 2022

[In thousands (1.6 represents 1,600), except percent and wage. Estimates based on the Current Employment Statistics Program, the Occupational Employment Statistics Survey, and the Current Population Survey. See source for methodological assumptions. Occupations based on the 2010 Standard Occupational Classification system. Additional occupation information in the Occupational Outlook Handbook <http://www.bls.gov/ooh>]

Occupation	Employment (1,000)		Change, 2012–2022		Median annual wage (in dollars), 2012	Typical Education Needed for Entry [1]
	2012	2022	Number (1,000)	Percent		
FASTEST GROWING						
Industrial-organizational psychologists	1.6	2.5	0.9	53.4	83,580	Master's degree
Personal care aides	1,190.6	1,771.4	580.8	48.8	19,910	Less than high school
Home health aides	875.1	1,299.3	424.2	48.5	20,820	Less than high school
Insulation workers, mechanical	28.9	42.4	13.5	46.7	39,170	High school diploma or equivalent
Interpreters and translators	63.6	92.9	29.3	46.1	45,430	Bachelor's degree
Diagnostic medical sonographers	58.8	85.9	27.0	46.0	65,860	Associate's degree
Helpers–brickmasons, blockmasons, stonemasons, and tile and marble setters	24.4	34.9	10.5	43.0	28,220	Less than high school
Occupational therapy assistants	30.3	43.2	12.9	42.6	53,240	Associate's degree
Genetic counselors	2.1	3.0	0.9	41.2	56,800	Master's degree
Physical therapist assistants	71.4	100.7	29.3	41.0	52,160	Associate's degree
Physical therapist aides	50.0	70.1	20.1	40.1	23,880	High school diploma or equivalent
Skincare specialists	44.4	62.0	17.7	39.8	28,640	Postsecondary non-degree award
Physician assistants	86.7	120.0	33.3	38.4	90,930	Master's degree
Segmental pavers	1.8	2.4	0.7	38.1	33,720	High school diploma or equivalent
Helpers–electricians	60.8	83.3	22.4	36.9	27,670	High school diploma or equivalent
Information security analysts	75.1	102.5	27.4	36.5	86,170	Bachelor's degree
Occupational therapy aides	8.4	11.4	3.0	36.2	26,850	High school diploma or equivalent
Health specialties teachers, postsecondary	190.0	258.6	68.6	36.1	81,140	Doctoral or professional degree
Medical secretaries	525.6	714.9	189.2	36.0	31,350	High school diploma or equivalent
Physical therapists	204.2	277.7	73.5	36.0	79,860	Doctoral or professional degree
Orthotists and prosthetists	8.5	11.5	3.0	35.5	62,670	Master's degree
Brickmasons and blockmasons	71.0	96.2	25.2	35.5	46,440	High school diploma or equivalent
Nursing instructors and teachers, postsecondary	67.8	91.8	24.0	35.4	64,850	Master's degree
Nurse practitioners	110.2	147.3	37.1	33.7	89,960	Master's degree
Audiologists	13.0	17.3	4.3	33.6	69,720	Doctoral or professional degree
Dental hygienists	192.8	256.9	64.2	33.3	70,210	Associate's degree
Meeting, convention, and event planners	94.2	125.4	31.3	33.2	45,810	Bachelor's degree
Therapists, all other	28.8	37.9	9.1	31.7	53,210	Bachelor's degree
Market research analysts and marketing specialists	415.7	547.2	131.5	31.6	60,300	Bachelor's degree
Substance abuse and behavioral disorder counselors	89.6	117.7	28.2	31.4	38,520	High school diploma or equivalent
LARGEST JOB GROWTH						
Personal care aides	1,190.6	1,771.4	580.8	48.8	19,910	Less than high school
Registered nurses	2,711.5	3,238.4	526.8	19.4	65,470	Associate's degree
Retail salespersons	4,447.0	4,881.7	434.7	9.8	21,110	Less than high school
Home health aides	875.1	1,299.3	424.2	48.5	20,820	Less than high school
Combined food preparation and serving workers, including fast food	2,969.3	3,391.2	421.9	14.2	18,260	Less than high school
Nursing assistants	1,479.8	1,792.0	312.2	21.1	24,420	Postsecondary non-degree award
Secretaries and administrative assistants, except legal, medical, and executive	2,324.4	2,632.3	307.8	13.2	32,410	High school diploma or equivalent
Customer service representatives	2,362.8	2,661.4	298.7	12.6	30,580	High school diploma or equivalent
Janitors and cleaners, except maids and housekeeping cleaners	2,324.0	2,604.0	280.0	12.1	22,320	Less than high school
Construction laborers	1,071.1	1,331.0	259.8	24.3	29,990	Less than high school
General and operations managers	1,972.7	2,216.8	244.1	12.4	95,440	Bachelor's degree
Laborers and freight, stock, and material movers, hand	2,197.3	2,439.2	241.9	11.0	23,890	Less than high school
Carpenters	901.2	1,119.4	218.2	24.2	39,940	High school diploma or equivalent
Bookkeeping, accounting, and auditing clerks	1,799.8	2,004.5	204.6	11.4	35,170	High school diploma or equivalent
Heavy and tractor-trailer truck drivers	1,701.5	1,894.1	192.6	11.3	38,200	Postsecondary non-degree award
Medical secretaries	525.6	714.9	189.2	36.0	31,350	High school diploma or equivalent
Childcare workers	1,312.7	1,496.8	184.1	14.0	19,510	High school diploma or equivalent
Office clerks, general	2,983.5	3,167.6	184.1	6.2	27,470	High school diploma or equivalent
Maids and housekeeping cleaners	1,434.6	1,618.0	183.4	12.8	19,570	Less than high school
Licensed practical and licensed vocational nurses	738.4	921.3	182.9	24.8	41,540	Postsecondary non-degree award
First-line supervisors of office and administrative support workers	1,418.1	1,589.6	171.5	12.1	49,330	High school diploma or equivalent
Elementary school teachers, except special education	1,361.2	1,529.1	167.9	12.3	53,400	Bachelor's degree
Accountants and auditors	1,275.4	1,442.2	166.7	13.1	63,550	Bachelor's degree
Medical assistants	560.8	723.7	162.9	29.0	29,370	Postsecondary non-degree award
Cooks, restaurant	1,024.1	1,174.2	150.1	14.7	22,030	Less than high school
Software developers, applications	613.0	752.9	139.9	22.8	90,060	Bachelor's degree
Landscaping and groundskeeping workers	1,124.9	1,264.0	139.2	12.4	23,570	Less than high school
Receptionists and information clerks	1,006.7	1,142.6	135.9	13.5	25,990	High school diploma or equivalent
Management analysts	718.7	852.5	133.8	18.6	78,600	Bachelor's degree
Sales representatives, wholesale and manufacturing, except technical and scientific products	1,480.7	1,612.8	132.0	8.9	54,230	High school diploma or equivalent

[1] An occupation is placed into 1 of 8 categories that best describe the typical education needed by most workers to enter that occupation. For more information, see "Measures of Education and Training" at <http://www.bls.gov/emp/ep_education_tech.htm>.

Source: U.S. Bureau of Labor Statistics, "Occupational employment projections to 2022," *Monthly Labor Review*, December 2013. See also <http://www.bls.gov/emp/ep_pub_occ_projections.htm>.

Table 638. Employment Projections by Industry: 2012 to 2022

[5,640.9 represents 5,640,900. Estimates based on the Current Employment Statistics program. See source for methodological assumptions. Minus sign (-) indicates decline]

Industry	2007 NAICS code [1]	Employment 2012 (1,000)	Employment 2022 (1,000)	Change, 2012– 2022 (1,000)	Average annual rate of change 2012– 2022
LARGEST GROWTH					
Construction	23	5,640.9	7,263.0	1,622.1	2.6
Offices of health practitioners	6211, 6212, 6213	3,968.0	5,193.8	1,225.8	2.7
Retail trade	44, 45	14,875.3	15,966.2	1,090.9	0.7
Food services and drinking places	722	9,963.3	10,851.5	888.2	0.9
Hospitals, private	622	4,791.0	5,605.8	814.8	1.6
Employment services	5613	3,147.9	3,929.6	781.7	2.2
Nursing and residential care facilities	623	3,193.5	3,954.2	760.7	2.2
Home health care services	6216	1,198.6	1,914.3	715.7	4.8
Individual and family services	6241	1,311.4	2,022.9	711.5	4.4
Computer systems design and related services	5415	1,620.3	2,229.0	608.7	3.2
Outpatient, laboratory, and other ambulatory care services	6214, 6215, 6219	1,151.4	1,673.7	522.3	3.8
Wholesale trade	42	5,672.8	6,143.2	470.4	0.8
Management, scientific, and technical consulting services	5416	1,121.1	1,577.1	456.0	3.5
General local government educational services compensation	(X)	7,779.3	8,233.7	454.4	0.6
Junior colleges, colleges, universities, and professional schools	6112, 6113	1,763.2	2,196.6	433.4	2.2
Services to buildings and dwellings	5617	1,829.6	2,109.0	279.4	1.4
Architectural, engineering, and related services	5413	1,323.3	1,595.5	272.2	1.9
Child day care services	6244	855.5	1,052.0	196.5	2.1
Securities, commodity contracts, and other financial investments and related activities	523	814.4	1,001.0	186.6	2.1
Accommodation	721	1,817.0	1,998.8	181.8	1.0
FASTEST GROWTH					
Home health care services	6216	1,198.6	1,914.3	715.7	4.8
Individual and family services	6241	1,311.4	2,022.9	711.5	4.4
Outpatient, laboratory, and other ambulatory care services	6214, 6215, 6219	1,151.4	1,673.7	522.3	3.8
Management, scientific, and technical consulting services	5416	1,121.1	1,577.1	456.0	3.5
Computer systems design and related services	5415	1,620.3	2,229.0	608.7	3.2
Cement and concrete product manufacturing	3273	161.6	218.9	57.3	3.1
Office administrative services	5611	426.4	571.3	144.9	3.0
Offices of health practitioners	6211, 6212, 6213	3,968.0	5,193.8	1,225.8	2.7
Veneer, plywood, and engineered wood product manufacturing	3212	63.8	83.5	19.7	2.7
Facilities support services	5612	125.8	164.4	38.6	2.7
Construction	23	5,640.9	7,263.0	1,622.1	2.6
Commercial and industrial machinery and equipment rental and leasing	5324	132.2	167.1	34.9	2.4
Software publishers	5112	286.0	359.1	73.1	2.3
Other professional, scientific, and technical services	5419	609.5	761.0	151.5	2.2
Employment services	5613	3,147.9	3,929.6	781.7	2.2
Junior colleges, colleges, universities, and professional schools	6112, 6113	1,763.2	2,196.6	433.4	2.2
Nursing and residential care facilities	623	3,193.5	3,954.2	760.7	2.2
Other educational services	6114–7	671.5	830.3	158.8	2.1
Funds, trusts, and other financial vehicles	525	86.8	107.3	20.5	2.1
Child day care services	6244	855.5	1,052.0	196.5	2.1
Securities, commodity contracts, and other financial investments and related activities	523	814.4	1,001.0	186.6	2.1
MOST RAPIDLY DECLINING					
Apparel manufacturing	315	148.1	62.3	−85.8	−8.3
Leather and allied product manufacturing	316	29.4	18.5	−10.9	−4.5
Communications equipment manufacturing	3342	109.5	78.6	−30.9	−3.3
Postal Service	491	611.2	442.1	−169.1	−3.2
Computer and peripheral equipment manufacturing	3341	158.6	118.7	−39.9	−2.9
Spring and wire product manufacturing	3326	41.6	31.3	−10.3	−2.8
Newspaper, periodical, book, and directory publishers	5111	451.8	346.8	−105.0	−2.6
Hardware manufacturing	3325	25.0	19.4	−5.6	−2.5
Textile mills and textile product mills	313, 314	234.6	183.1	−51.5	−2.4
Other miscellaneous manufacturing	3399	268.4	211.1	−57.3	−2.4
Glass and glass product manufacturing	3272	80.0	64.0	−16.0	−2.2
Sugar and confectionery product manufacturing	3113	66.8	53.5	−13.3	−2.2
Pulp, paper, and paperboard mills	3221	108.2	86.8	−21.4	−2.2
Pesticide, fertilizer, and other agricultural chemical manufacturing	3253	36.8	29.8	−7.0	−2.1
Manufacturing and reproducing magnetic and optical media	3346	21.0	17.2	−3.8	−2.0
Pipeline transportation	486	43.9	36.1	−7.8	−1.9
Audio and video equipment manufacturing	3343	19.9	16.4	−3.5	−1.9
Natural gas distribution	2212	109.7	92.1	−17.6	−1.7
Other chemical product and preparation manufacturing	3259	80.8	67.9	−12.9	−1.7

X Not applicable. [1] Based on the North American Industry Classification System, 2007; see text, Section 15.

Source: U.S. Bureau of Labor Statistics, "Industry employment and output projections to 2022," *Monthly Labor Review*, December 2013. See also <http://www.bls.gov/opub/mlr/2013/>.

Table 639. Occupations of the Employed by Race/Ethnicity and Educational Attainment: 2014

[In thousands (127,863 represents 127,863,000). Annual averages of monthly figures. Civilian noninstitutional population 25 years old and over. Based on Current Population Survey; see text, Section 1 and Appendix III]

Race and educational attainment	Total employed	Managerial, professional, and related	Service	Sales and office	Natural resources, construction, and maintenance	Production, transpor-tation, and material-moving
Total [1]	**127,863**	**52,674**	**20,013**	**27,778**	**12,097**	**15,301**
Less than a high school diploma	9,852	624	3,173	1,128	2,435	2,492
High school graduate, no college	33,865	5,552	7,353	8,699	5,111	7,150
Some college or associate degree	35,299	11,326	6,408	9,891	6,071	4,122
Bachelor's degree or higher	48,848	35,172	3,079	8,060	3,699	1,537
White [2]	102,245	42,871	14,667	22,498	10,497	11,711
Less than a high school diploma	7,895	523	2,375	902	2,145	1,950
High school graduate, no college	27,132	4,724	5,281	7,165	4,450	5,512
Some college or associate degree	28,112	9,347	4,690	7,938	3,052	3,085
Bachelor's degree or higher	39,106	28,277	2,321	6,493	850	1,164
Black [2]	14,437	4,636	3,408	3,143	920	2,330
Less than a high school diploma	1,084	53	457	141	142	291
High school graduate, no college	4,442	531	1,385	974	420	1,132
Some college or associate degree	4,793	1,300	1,173	1,294	294	732
Bachelor's degree or higher	4,117	2,752	392	734	65	174
Asian [2]	7,589	3,979	1,196	1,377	268	769
Less than a high school diploma	459	27	196	46	39	151
High school graduate, no college	1,289	159	439	310	74	306
Some college or associate degree	1,252	369	289	343	97	155
Bachelor's degree or higher	4,589	3,425	272	679	57	157
Hispanic [3]	19,686	4,442	4,851	3,729	3,324	3,339
Less than a high school diploma	5,365	194	1,830	444	1,579	1,318
High school graduate, no college	5,954	667	1,612	1,307	1,086	1,282
Some college or associate degree	4,626	1,222	1,001	1,326	527	551
Bachelor's degree or higher	3,741	2,360	408	652	132	189

[1] Includes other races, not shown separately. [2] For persons in this race group only. See footnote 3, Table 605. [3] Persons of Hispanic origin may be of any race.

Source: U.S. Bureau of Labor Statistics, Current Population Survey, unpublished data. See also <http://www.bls.gov/cps/>.

Table 640. Employment by Industry, Sex, and Race/Ethnicity: 2000 to 2014

[In thousands (136,891 represents 136,891,000), except percent. Civilian noninstitutional population 16 years old and over. Annual average of monthly figures. Based on Current Population Survey; see text, Section 1, Population, and Appendix III]

Industry	Total				2014, percent			
	2000	2005	2010	2014	Female	Black [1]	Asian [1]	Hispanic [2]
Total employed	**136,891**	**141,730**	**139,064**	**146,305**	**46.9**	**11.4**	**5.7**	**16.1**
Agriculture and related industries	2,464	2,197	2,206	2,237	24.7	2.8	1.0	23.1
Mining	475	624	731	1,088	13.3	5.7	1.6	18.6
Construction	9,931	11,197	9,077	9,813	8.9	5.9	1.8	27.3
Manufacturing	19,644	16,253	14,081	15,100	29.3	9.7	6.6	15.8
Durable goods	12,519	10,333	8,789	9,542	25.2	8.8	6.9	13.9
Nondurable goods	7,125	5,919	5,293	5,559	36.2	11.1	6.1	19.2
Wholesale trade	4,216	4,579	3,805	3,642	30.2	8.6	4.8	15.8
Retail trade	15,763	16,825	15,934	16,609	48.2	11.8	5.6	16.5
Transportation and utilities	7,380	7,360	7,134	7,581	23.0	16.6	4.3	17.2
Transportation and warehousing	6,096	6,184	5,880	6,377	23.0	18.0	4.6	18.2
Utilities	1,284	1,176	1,253	1,204	22.7	8.9	2.9	11.8
Information	4,059	3,402	3,149	3,115	38.8	10.4	7.0	10.5
Financial activities	9,374	10,203	9,350	9,871	53.2	9.1	6.3	11.3
Finance and insurance	6,641	7,035	6,605	6,956	56.2	9.4	7.4	9.8
Real estate and rental and leasing	2,734	3,168	2,745	2,915	46.2	8.2	3.7	15.0
Professional and business services	13,649	14,294	15,253	17,004	41.2	9.5	7.5	16.0
Professional and technical services	8,266	8,584	9,115	10,327	42.6	6.5	10.1	8.2
Management, administrative, and waste services	5,383	5,709	6,138	6,677	39.2	14.0	3.4	28.2
Education and health services	26,188	29,174	32,062	32,830	74.7	14.5	5.6	11.5
Educational services	11,255	12,264	13,155	13,253	68.9	11.2	4.4	10.5
Health care and social assistance	14,933	16,910	18,907	19,577	78.6	16.8	6.4	12.1
Hospitals	5,202	5,719	6,249	6,586	75.6	14.7	8.2	9.4
Health services, except hospitals	7,009	8,332	9,406	9,930	78.6	17.1	5.9	12.6
Social assistance	2,722	2,860	3,252	3,060	84.8	20.5	4.2	16.3
Leisure and hospitality	11,186	12,071	12,530	13,489	51.4	11.6	6.6	22.3
Arts, entertainment, and recreation	2,539	2,765	2,966	3,082	46.7	9.1	4.8	12.6
Accommodation and food services	8,647	9,306	9,564	10,407	52.8	12.4	7.1	25.2
Other services	6,450	7,020	6,769	7,169	52.8	10.2	7.0	19.0
Other services, except private households	5,731	6,208	6,102	6,349	47.7	10.4	7.3	16.7
Private households	718	812	667	820	92.2	8.9	5.1	36.5
Public administration	6,113	6,530	6,983	6,757	45.4	16.8	4.8	11.4

[1] Persons in this race group only. See footnote 3, Table 605. [3] Persons of Hispanic origin may be of any race.

Source: U.S. Bureau of Labor Statistics, CPS Tables, "Employed persons by detailed industry, sex, race, and Hispanic or Latino ethnicity," February 2015, and earlier releases, <http://www.bls.gov/cps/tables.htm>.

Table 641. Unemployed Workers—Summary: 1990 to 2014

[In thousands (7,047 represents 7,047,000), except as indicated. For civilian noninstitutionalized population 16 years old and over. Annual averages of monthly figures. Data not strictly comparable with data for earlier years. Based on the Current Population Survey; see text, Section 1 and Appendix III]

Item	1990	2000	2005	2010	2011	2012	2013	2014
UNEMPLOYED								
Total [1]	**7,047**	**5,692**	**7,591**	**14,825**	**13,747**	**12,506**	**11,460**	**9,617**
16 to 19 years old	1,212	1,081	1,186	1,528	1,400	1,397	1,327	1,106
20 to 24 years old	1,299	1,022	1,335	2,329	2,234	2,054	1,997	1,747
25 to 34 years old	1,995	1,207	1,661	3,386	3,187	2,764	2,504	2,224
35 to 44 years old	1,328	1,133	1,400	2,703	2,389	2,158	1,913	1,539
45 to 54 years old	723	762	1,195	2,769	2,493	2,181	1,945	1,507
55 to 64 years old	386	355	630	1,660	1,579	1,470	1,340	1,107
65 years and over	105	132	184	449	465	482	435	387
Male	3,906	2,975	4,059	8,626	7,684	6,771	6,314	5,190
16 to 19 years old	667	599	667	863	786	787	746	605
20 to 24 years old	715	547	775	1,398	1,275	1,163	1,143	996
25 to 34 years old	1,092	602	844	1,993	1,795	1,476	1,381	1,185
35 to 44 years old	711	557	715	1,534	1,316	1,124	1,015	813
45 to 54 years old	413	398	624	1,614	1,370	1,142	1,039	782
55 to 64 years old	249	189	331	962	882	811	741	600
65 years and over	59	83	102	262	261	268	250	210
Female	3,140	2,717	3,531	6,199	6,063	5,734	5,146	4,426
16 to 19 years old	544	483	519	665	613	609	581	501
20 to 24 years old	584	475	560	931	960	891	854	751
25 to 34 years old	902	604	817	1,392	1,392	1,288	1,123	1,039
35 to 44 years old	617	577	685	1,169	1,073	1,034	898	726
45 to 54 years old	310	364	571	1,156	1,123	1,039	906	725
55 to 64 years old	137	165	299	698	697	659	600	507
65 years and over	46	50	82	187	204	214	185	177
White [2]	5,186	4,121	5,350	10,916	9,889	8,915	8,033	6,540
Black [2,3]	1,565	1,241	1,700	2,852	2,831	2,544	2,429	2,141
Asian [2,3]	(NA)	227	259	543	518	483	448	436
Hispanic [4]	876	954	1,191	2,843	2,629	2,514	2,257	1,878
UNEMPLOYMENT RATE [5] (percent)								
Total [1]	**5.6**	**4.0**	**5.1**	**9.6**	**8.9**	**8.1**	**7.4**	**6.2**
16 to 19 years old	15.5	13.1	16.6	25.9	24.4	24.0	22.9	19.6
20 to 24 years old	8.8	7.2	8.8	15.5	14.6	13.3	12.8	11.2
25 to 34 years old	5.6	3.7	5.1	10.1	9.5	8.3	7.4	6.5
35 to 44 years old	4.1	3.0	3.9	8.1	7.3	6.6	5.9	4.7
45 to 54 years old	3.6	2.5	3.5	7.7	7.1	6.2	5.6	4.4
55 to 64 years old	3.3	2.5	3.3	7.1	6.6	5.9	5.3	4.3
65 years and over	3.0	3.1	3.5	6.7	6.5	6.2	5.4	4.6
Male	5.7	3.9	5.1	10.5	9.4	8.2	7.6	6.3
16 to 19 years old	16.3	14.0	18.6	28.8	27.2	26.8	25.5	21.4
20 to 24 years old	9.1	7.3	9.6	17.8	15.7	14.3	14.0	12.2
25 to 34 years old	5.5	3.4	4.7	10.9	9.7	8.2	7.6	6.4
35 to 44 years old	4.1	2.8	3.7	8.5	7.4	6.4	5.8	4.6
45 to 54 years old	3.7	2.4	3.5	8.6	7.4	6.2	5.7	4.4
55 to 64 years old	3.8	2.4	3.3	8.0	7.1	6.3	5.6	4.5
65 years and over	3.0	3.3	3.4	7.1	6.5	6.2	5.5	4.6
Female	5.5	4.1	5.1	8.6	8.5	7.9	7.1	6.1
16 to 19 years old	14.7	12.1	14.5	22.8	21.7	21.1	20.3	17.7
20 to 24 years old	8.5	7.1	7.9	13.0	13.4	12.1	11.5	10.1
25 to 34 years old	5.6	4.1	5.6	9.1	9.1	8.4	7.3	6.6
35 to 44 years old	4.2	3.3	4.1	7.7	7.2	6.8	6.0	4.9
45 to 54 years old	3.4	2.5	3.5	6.8	6.7	6.2	5.5	4.5
55 to 64 years old	2.8	2.5	3.3	6.2	6.1	5.6	5.0	4.2
65 years and over	3.1	2.7	3.5	6.2	6.5	6.3	5.1	4.7
White [2]	4.8	3.5	4.4	8.7	7.9	7.2	6.5	5.3
Black [2,3]	11.4	7.6	10.0	16.0	15.8	13.8	13.1	11.3
Asian [2,3]	(NA)	3.6	4.0	7.5	7.0	5.9	5.2	5.0
Hispanic [4]	8.2	5.7	6.0	12.5	11.5	10.3	9.1	7.4
PERCENT WITHOUT WORK FOR—								
Fewer than 5 weeks	46.3	44.9	35.1	18.7	19.5	21.1	22.5	25.7
5 to 14 weeks	32.0	31.9	30.4	22.0	21.8	22.9	24.1	25.3
15 weeks and over	21.6	23.2	34.5	59.3	58.8	55.9	53.4	49.0
15 to 26 weeks	11.7	11.8	14.9	16.0	15.0	14.9	15.8	15.6
27 weeks and over	10.0	11.4	19.6	43.3	43.8	41.1	37.6	33.5
Unemployment duration, average (weeks)	12.0	12.6	18.4	33.0	39.3	39.4	36.5	33.7

NA Not available. [1] Includes other races not shown separately. [2] See footnote 3, Table 605. [3] Prior to 2005, includes Pacific Islanders. [4] Persons of Hispanic or Latino origin may be of any race. [5] Unemployed as percent of civilian labor force in specified group.

Source: U.S. Bureau of Labor Statistics, "Labor Force Statistics from the Current Population Survey," <http://www.bls.gov/cps>, accessed March 2015.

Table 642. Unemployed Jobseekers' Job Search Methods: 2014

[9,617 represents 9,617,000. For the civilian noninstitutionalized population 16 years old and over. Annual averages of monthly data. Based on the Current Population Survey; see text, Section 1 and Appendix III]

Characteristic	Population (1,000)		Jobseekers' job search methods (percent)							
	Total unem-ployed	Total jobseek-ers [1]	Contact em-ployer directly	Sent out a resume or filled out applica-tions	Placed or ans-wered ads	Friends or relatives	Public employ-ment agency	Private employ-ment agency	Other activi-ties	Average number of methods used
Total, 16 years and over [2]....	**9,617**	**8,609**	**50.1**	**57.1**	**16.0**	**27.8**	**18.3**	**8.8**	**15.1**	**1.9**
AGE										
16 to 19 years old.............	1,106	1,049	48.0	62.0	11.1	19.2	7.5	3.4	10.0	1.6
20 to 24 years old.............	1,747	1,641	51.7	59.5	14.6	24.7	16.0	6.6	14.1	1.9
25 to 34 years old.............	2,224	2,000	51.7	58.9	16.6	28.2	20.5	9.6	14.0	2.0
35 to 44 years old.............	1,539	1,351	48.9	57.1	16.6	28.9	21.3	9.8	16.1	2.0
45 to 54 years old.............	1,507	1,300	51.1	55.1	18.4	32.5	22.9	12.2	17.1	2.1
55 to 64 years old.............	1,107	954	49.1	51.8	18.9	32.3	20.7	11.1	19.0	2.0
65 years old and over........	387	314	44.1	42.4	14.5	32.5	13.1	7.9	18.5	1.7
SEX										
Male, total........................	5,190	4,572	50.9	54.6	16.1	29.6	18.5	9.0	15.3	1.9
16 to 19 years old.............	605	571	48.1	59.8	11.2	20.7	7.9	3.7	9.6	1.6
20 to 24 years old.............	996	925	50.2	57.9	14.6	26.9	16.4	6.3	13.2	1.9
25 to 34 years old.............	1,185	1,038	53.5	56.0	17.1	31.3	20.9	10.3	14.5	2.0
35 to 44 years old.............	813	692	50.5	53.9	16.9	29.2	21.3	9.5	16.8	2.0
45 to 54 years old.............	782	662	53.4	51.3	18.0	34.5	24.1	12.5	17.7	2.1
55 to 64 years old.............	600	511	50.2	48.9	19.8	33.6	20.8	11.4	20.5	2.1
65 years old and over........	210	172	42.8	42.9	13.5	33.5	12.0	10.1	20.3	1.8
Female, total.....................	4,426	4,037	49.3	60.0	15.9	25.8	18.0	8.5	14.8	1.9
16 to 19 years old.............	501	478	47.8	64.6	11.0	17.3	7.0	3.0	10.5	1.6
20 to 24 years old.............	751	715	53.6	61.5	14.6	21.9	15.4	6.9	15.3	1.9
25 to 34 years old.............	1,039	961	49.7	62.0	16.0	25.0	20.1	8.8	13.6	2.0
35 to 44 years old.............	726	659	47.2	60.4	16.3	28.7	21.2	10.2	15.3	2.0
45 to 54 years old.............	725	638	48.7	59.0	18.8	30.4	21.6	11.8	16.6	2.1
55 to 64 years old.............	507	443	47.9	55.1	17.8	30.7	20.7	10.7	17.3	2.0
65 years old and over........	177	142	45.7	41.7	15.6	31.4	14.5	5.3	16.2	1.7
RACE/ETHNICITY										
White [3]............................	6,540	5,731	50.7	56.5	16.7	28.3	17.4	8.8	15.8	1.9
Male............................	3,572	3,071	51.8	54.2	16.8	30.2	17.7	9.1	16.0	2.0
Female.........................	2,968	2,661	49.4	59.2	16.5	26.1	17.0	8.6	15.5	1.9
Black [3]............................	2,141	2,013	49.0	58.3	14.4	25.8	22.3	8.5	12.6	1.9
Male............................	1,091	1,019	49.8	55.0	14.6	27.4	22.2	8.5	12.5	1.9
Female.........................	1,050	994	48.2	61.6	14.1	24.1	22.5	8.6	12.8	1.9
Asian [3]............................	436	413	48.6	56.4	15.9	34.3	14.0	10.2	18.4	2.0
Male............................	246	236	47.0	53.8	15.1	33.9	15.0	11.3	19.5	2.0
Female.........................	190	177	50.7	59.8	17.0	34.8	12.7	8.8	16.9	2.0
Hispanic [4]........................	1,878	1,673	52.2	51.9	11.8	32.8	19.6	9.8	14.2	1.9
Male............................	996	869	54.3	49.3	12.4	33.4	20.3	9.9	14.3	1.9
Female.........................	882	804	49.9	54.8	11.2	32.0	18.8	9.7	14.1	1.9

[1] Excludes persons on temporary layoff. [2] Includes other races not shown separately. [3] Data for this race group only. See footnote 3, Table 605. [4] Persons of Hispanic or Latino origin may be of any race.

Source: U.S. Bureau of Labor Statistics, CPS Tables, "Unemployed jobseekers by sex, age, race, Hispanic or Latino ethnicity, and active jobsearch methods used," February 2015, <http://www.bls.gov/cps/tables.htm>, accessed March 2015.

Table 643. Unemployed Persons by Sex and Reason: 1990 to 2014

[In thousands (3,906 represents 3,906,000). For civilian noninstitutionalized population 16 years old and over. Annual averages of monthly figures. Data not strictly comparable with data for earlier years. Based on Current Population Survey; see text, Section 1 and Appendix III]

Sex and reason	1990	2000	2005	2006	2007	2008	2009	2010	2011	2012	2013	2014
Male, total..............	**3,906**	**2,975**	**4,059**	**3,753**	**3,882**	**5,033**	**8,453**	**8,626**	**7,684**	**6,771**	**6,314**	**5,190**
Job losers [1]...............	2,257	1,516	2,188	2,021	2,175	3,055	5,967	5,919	4,968	4,103	3,690	2,926
Job leavers................	528	387	445	406	408	458	438	457	494	487	465	416
Reentrants.................	806	854	1,067	1,015	956	1,128	1,504	1,608	1545	1,481	1,491	1,279
New entrants...............	315	217	359	312	343	393	545	641	678	699	668	569
Female, total..........	**3,140**	**2,717**	**3,531**	**3,247**	**3,196**	**3,891**	**5,811**	**6,199**	**6,063**	**5,734**	**5,146**	**4,426**
Job losers [1]...............	1,130	1,001	1,479	1,300	1,340	1,735	3,193	3,331	3,139	2,774	2,383	1,952
Job leavers................	513	393	427	421	385	438	444	432	463	480	467	408
Reentrants.................	1,124	1,107	1,319	1,223	1,186	1,345	1,683	1,858	1,857	1,864	1,716	1,550
New entrants...............	373	217	306	304	285	374	491	579	605	617	579	517

[1] Beginning 2000, persons who completed temporary jobs are identified separately and are included as job losers.

Source: U.S. Bureau of Labor Statistics, CPS Tables, "Unemployed jobseekers by sex, reason for unemployment, and active jobsearch methods used," February 2015, and earlier releases, <http://www.bls.gov/cps/tables.htm>.

Table 644. Unemployment Rates by Industry and by Sex: 2010 to 2014

[In percent. Civilian noninstitutionalized population 16 years old and over. Annual averages of monthly figures. Rate represents unemployment as a percent of labor force in each specified group. Based on Current Population Survey; see text, Section 1 and Appendix III. See also headnote, Table 624, regarding industries]

Industry	Total				Male		Female	
	2010	2012	2013	2014	2013	2014	2013	2014
All employed [1]	**9.6**	**8.1**	**7.4**	**6.2**	**7.6**	**6.3**	**7.1**	**6.1**
Wage and salary workers:								
Agriculture and related industries	13.9	12.4	10.1	9.4	8.5	8.0	15.4	14.1
Mining, quarrying, and oil and gas extraction	9.4	6.0	5.8	4.7	5.8	5.0	5.9	2.5
Construction	20.6	13.9	11.3	8.9	11.6	9.3	8.9	5.5
Manufacturing	10.6	7.3	6.6	4.9	6.3	4.5	7.4	5.8
Wholesale trade	7.3	6.0	5.4	4.4	4.8	4.2	6.9	4.9
Retail trade	10.0	8.6	7.7	6.5	7.4	5.9	8.0	7.1
Transportation and utilities	8.4	6.9	6.6	5.7	6.4	5.3	7.4	7.1
Transportation and warehousing	9.4	7.4	7.1	6.3	6.8	5.9	8.0	7.9
Utilities	3.4	4.3	4.1	2.1	4.1	1.8	4.1	3.2
Information	9.7	7.6	6.2	5.2	5.9	5.0	6.7	5.6
Telecommunications	9.2	7.2	6.1	4.0	4.7	3.6	8.6	4.7
Financial activities	6.9	5.1	4.5	4.0	4.8	3.6	4.3	4.3
Finance and insurance	6.6	4.5	4.0	3.8	4.0	3.2	4.0	4.2
Real estate and rental and leasing	7.6	6.6	6.0	4.5	6.4	4.4	5.5	4.6
Professional and business services	10.8	8.9	8.3	6.9	8.2	6.6	8.4	7.4
Professional and technical services	6.5	5.4	4.9	4.1	4.3	3.5	5.5	4.8
Management, administrative, and waste services	16.8	13.7	13.1	11.2	13.2	10.8	13.0	11.7
Education and health services	5.8	5.5	4.9	4.2	4.8	4.3	5.0	4.1
Educational services	6.4	6.5	6.0	4.9	5.5	5.8	6.3	4.5
Health care and social assistance	5.6	5.3	4.6	4.0	4.5	3.6	4.7	4.0
Leisure and hospitality	12.2	10.4	10.0	8.6	9.9	8.5	10.1	8.7
Arts, entertainment, and recreation	11.6	9.7	9.3	8.4	10.3	9.5	8.2	7.2
Accommodation and food services	12.3	10.6	10.1	8.6	9.8	8.2	10.4	9.1
Other services [2]	8.5	7.2	6.9	5.7	6.5	5.3	7.2	6.0
Government workers	4.4	4.3	4.0	3.2	4.0	3.4	4.0	3.2

[1] Includes the self-employed; unpaid family workers; persons with no previous work experience, not shown separately; and a small amount of persons whose last job was in the Armed Forces. [2] Includes private household workers.

Source: U.S. Bureau of Labor Statistics, CPS Tables, "Unemployed persons by industry, class of worker, and sex," February 2015, and earlier releases, <http://www.bls.gov/cps/tables.htm>.

Table 645. Unemployment by Occupation: 2010 to 2014

[14,825 represents 14,825,000. Civilian noninstitutionalized population 16 years old and over. Annual averages of monthly data. Rate represents unemployment as a percent of the labor force for each specified group. Based on Current Population Survey; see text, Section 1 and Appendix III. See also headnote, Table 624, regarding occupations]

Occupation	Number unemployed (1,000)				Unemployment rate				
							2014		
	2010	2012	2013	2014	2010	2013	Total	Male	Female
Total [1]	**14,825**	**12,506**	**11,460**	**9,617**	**9.6**	**7.4**	**6.2**	**6.3**	**6.1**
Management, professional, and related occupations	2,566	2,318	2,036	1,777	4.7	3.6	3.1	3.0	3.2
Management, business, and financial operations	1,117	935	831	704	5.1	3.5	2.9	2.7	3.3
Management	762	615	547	440	4.8	3.3	2.6	2.4	3.1
Business and financial operations	355	320	284	263	5.6	4.0	3.6	3.7	3.6
Professional and related occupations	1,449	1,383	1,205	1,073	4.5	3.6	3.2	3.2	3.1
Computer and mathematical	195	144	149	120	5.2	3.6	2.7	2.7	2.8
Architecture and engineering	173	123	102	91	6.2	3.5	3.1	3.2	3.1
Life, physical, and social science	69	55	49	54	4.6	3.6	3.8	4.1	3.5
Community and social services	114	113	93	79	4.6	3.8	3.1	2.7	3.3
Legal	48	50	54	44	2.7	2.9	2.4	1.9	2.8
Education, training, and library	379	426	350	306	4.2	3.9	3.4	3.7	3.3
Arts, design, entertainment, sports, and media	269	225	216	193	8.9	7.0	6.2	6.4	6.0
Healthcare practitioner and technical	203	246	193	186	2.5	2.3	2.1	1.7	2.3
Service occupations	2,819	2,540	2,444	2,048	10.3	8.6	7.3	7.5	7.2
Healthcare support	276	276	266	197	7.6	7.0	5.4	5.7	5.4
Protective service	207	205	143	145	5.9	4.4	4.4	4.1	5.7
Food preparation and serving-related	1,079	925	883	758	12.4	9.7	8.5	8.8	8.3
Building and grounds cleaning and maintenance	780	692	678	550	12.8	10.7	8.7	8.5	8.8
Personal care and service	477	443	475	397	8.7	8.1	6.9	7.7	6.7
Sales and office occupations	3,315	2,775	2,575	2,119	9.0	7.2	6.0	5.6	6.2
Sales and related	1,596	1,318	1,212	1,022	9.4	7.3	6.1	5.0	7.3
Office and administrative support	1,719	1,457	1,363	1,096	8.7	7.1	5.8	6.7	5.5
Natural resources, construction, and maintenance	2,504	1,668	1,423	1,171	16.1	9.8	8.0	7.8	11.6
Farming, fishing, and forestry	193	167	124	134	16.3	11.4	11.6	9.5	18.2
Construction and extraction	1,809	1,181	1,016	813	20.1	12.5	9.6	9.6	9.4
Installation, maintenance, and repair	503	320	284	224	9.3	5.4	4.4	4.4	4.1
Production, transportation, and material moving	2,365	1,845	1,690	1,385	12.8	9.1	7.4	6.9	9.1
Production	1,206	865	792	632	13.1	8.7	7.0	6.3	8.6
Transportation and material moving	1,159	980	898	754	12.4	9.4	7.7	7.3	9.9

[1] Includes persons with no previous work experience and a small amount of persons whose last job was in the Armed Forces.

Source: U.S. Bureau of Labor Statistics, CPS Tables, "Unemployed persons by occupation and sex," February 2015, and earlier releases, <http://www.bls.gov/cps/tables.htm>.

Table 646. Unemployed and Unemployment Rates by Educational Attainment, Sex, Race, and Hispanic Origin: 2000 to 2014

[3,589 represents 3,589,000. Annual averages of monthly figures. Civilian noninstitutionalized population 25 years old and over. See Table 611 for civilian labor force and participation rate data. Data not strictly comparable with data for earlier years. Based on Current Population Survey; see text, Section 1 and Appendix III]

Year, sex, and race/ethnicity	Unemployed (1,000)					Unemployment rate [1]				
	Total	Less than a high school diploma	High school graduate, no college	Some college or associate's degree	Bachelor's degree or more	Total	Less than a high school diploma	High school graduate, no college	Some college or associate's degree	Bachelor's degree or more
Total: [2]										
2000	3,589	791	1,298	890	610	3.0	6.3	3.4	2.7	1.7
2010	10,968	1,765	3,943	3,093	2,167	8.2	14.9	10.3	8.4	4.7
2014	6,764	976	2,167	2,022	1,599	5.0	9.0	6.0	5.4	3.2
Male:										
2000	1,829	411	682	427	309	2.8	5.4	3.4	2.6	1.5
2010	6,365	1,137	2,452	1,646	1,130	8.9	15.0	11.3	9.0	4.8
2014	3,589	557	1,280	968	784	5.0	8.0	6.2	5.2	3.1
Female:										
2000	1,760	380	616	463	301	3.2	7.8	3.5	2.8	1.8
2010	4,603	628	1,492	1,447	1,037	7.4	14.6	9.0	7.8	4.7
2014	3,175	419	887	1,054	815	5.1	10.8	5.8	5.6	3.3
White: [3]										
2000	2,644	564	924	667	489	2.6	5.6	2.9	2.4	1.6
2010	8,174	1,337	2,937	2,278	1,622	7.5	13.9	9.5	7.6	4.3
2014	4,680	670	1,467	1,391	1,152	4.4	7.8	5.1	4.7	2.9
Black: [3]										
2000	731	179	315	169	68	5.4	10.7	6.4	4.0	2.5
2010	2,022	321	795	614	292	13.4	22.5	15.8	12.4	7.9
2014	1,451	225	534	468	224	9.1	17.2	10.7	8.9	5.2
Asian: [3, 4]										
2000	146	28	34	35	49	2.7	5.7	3.0	3.2	1.8
2010	446	54	95	92	205	6.8	11.1	7.6	8.1	5.5
2014	335	34	61	64	176	4.2	6.9	4.5	4.9	3.7
Hispanic: [5]										
2000	569	297	150	85	38	4.4	6.2	3.9	3.2	2.2
2010	2,041	787	674	399	182	10.8	13.2	11.5	9.7	6.0
2014	1,260	428	395	286	151	6.0	7.4	6.2	5.8	3.9

[1] Unemployed as percent of the civilian labor force. [2] Includes other races, not shown separately. [3] Data for 2010 and 2014 are for persons in this race group only. See footnote 3, Table 605. [4] 2000 data include Pacific Islanders. [5] Persons of Hispanic origin may be of any race.

Source: U.S. Bureau of Labor Statistics, CPS Tables, "Employment status of the civilian noninstitutional population 25 years and over by educational attainment, sex, race, and Hispanic or Latino ethnicity," February 2015, and earlier releases, <http://www.bls.gov/cps/tables.htm>.

Table 647. Unemployed Persons by Reason for Unemployment and Duration: 2014

[9,617 represents 9,617,000. Annual averages of monthly data. Based on Current Population Survey; see text, Section 1 and Appendix III]

Age, sex, and reason	Total unemployed (1,000)	Percent distribution by duration				
		Less than 5 weeks	5 to 14 weeks	15 weeks and over		
				Total	15 to 26 weeks	27 weeks or longer
Total 16 years old and over	**9,617**	**25.7**	**25.3**	**49.0**	**15.6**	**33.5**
16 to 19 years old	1,106	38.8	30.3	30.9	15.0	15.9
Total 20 years old and over	8,511	(NA)	(NA)	(NA)	(NA)	(NA)
Males, 20 years old and over	**4,585**	**23.9**	**23.9**	**52.2**	**15.8**	**36.4**
Job losers and persons who completed temporary jobs	2,839	26.4	24.9	48.7	16.1	32.5
On temporary layoff	583	50.6	31.7	17.6	12.5	5.1
Not on temporary layoff	2,255	20.1	23.2	56.7	17.1	39.6
Permanent job losers	1,617	18.2	22.4	59.4	17.2	42.2
Persons who completed temporary jobs	638	25.0	25.1	49.9	16.9	33.0
Job leavers	392	27.6	29.2	43.2	15.8	27.4
Reentrants	1,109	18.0	20.5	61.5	15.3	46.2
New entrants	245	15.9	19.1	65.1	13.8	51.3
Females, 20 years old and over	**3,926**	**24.1**	**25.5**	**50.5**	**15.5**	**35.0**
Job losers and persons who completed temporary jobs	1,899	26.6	25.0	48.3	14.8	33.5
On temporary layoff	367	57.0	29.6	13.3	8.1	5.2
Not on temporary layoff	1,533	19.4	23.9	56.7	16.4	40.3
Permanent job losers	1,147	17.3	23.0	59.7	17.0	42.7
Persons who completed temporary jobs	386	25.3	26.7	48.0	14.8	33.2
Job leavers	388	27.0	30.0	42.9	18.0	24.9
Reentrants	1,393	20.9	25.1	54.0	15.4	38.6
New entrants	245	17.9	23.7	58.4	16.7	41.7

NA Not available.

Source: U.S. Bureau of Labor Statistics, CPS Tables, "Unemployed persons by reason for unemployment, sex, age, and duration of unemployment," February 2015, <http://www.bls.gov/cps/tables.htm>.

Table 648. Total Unemployed and Insured Unemployed by State: 2000 to 2013

[5,692 represents 5,692,000. Civilian noninstitutionalized population 16 years old and over. Annual averages of monthly figures. State total unemployment estimates come from the Local Area Unemployment Statistics program, while U.S. totals come from the Current Population Survey; see text, Section 1 and Appendix III. U.S. totals derived by independent population controls; therefore state data may not add to U.S. totals. Unemployment data are based on population controls from Census 2010]

State	Total unemployed								Insured unemployed [2,4]			
	Number (1,000)				Percent [1]				Number (1,000)		Percent [3]	
	2000	2010	2012	2013	2000	2010	2012	2013	2010	2013	2010	2013
United States.........	5,692	14,825	12,506	11,460	4.0	9.6	8.1	7.4	4,486.8	2,947.0	3.6	2.2
Alabama.................	87	200	153	138	4.1	9.2	7.1	6.5	52.9	33.1	3.0	1.8
Alaska...................	20	29	25	24	6.2	8.0	6.9	6.5	13.9	12.0	4.6	3.8
Arizona..................	100	324	252	240	4.0	10.4	8.3	8.0	79.2	40.1	3.5	1.6
Arkansas...............	53	106	101	100	4.2	7.9	7.5	7.5	43.9	28.8	4.0	2.6
California................	833	2,268	1,929	1,663	4.9	12.4	10.4	8.9	655.0	462.9	4.6	3.1
Colorado................	65	245	215	187	2.7	9.0	7.8	6.8	64.0	39.7	3.0	1.7
Connecticut...........	39	178	156	145	2.3	9.3	8.3	7.8	67.1	51.1	4.3	3.1
Delaware................	14	35	31	30	3.3	8.0	7.1	6.7	13.2	9.0	3.4	2.2
District of Columbia.....	18	35	33	31	5.7	10.1	9.1	8.3	5.4	5.4	1.1	1.0
Florida...................	300	1,036	820	683	3.8	11.3	8.8	7.2	224.9	110.7	3.2	1.5
Georgia.................	148	479	430	389	3.5	10.2	9.0	8.2	117.0	62.2	3.2	1.6
Hawaii...................	24	44	37	31	4.0	6.7	5.7	4.8	17.3	11.4	3.1	1.9
Idaho....................	31	66	56	48	4.6	8.7	7.3	6.2	26.5	13.7	4.5	2.2
Illinois..................	291	692	588	600	4.5	10.5	8.9	9.2	220.4	151.8	4.1	2.7
Indiana..................	92	317	257	239	2.9	10.0	8.1	7.5	78.8	46.9	3.0	1.7
Iowa.....................	45	105	86	78	2.8	6.3	5.2	4.6	40.4	26.6	2.9	1.8
Kansas..................	53	106	86	80	3.8	7.1	5.8	5.4	36.6	23.6	2.9	1.8
Kentucky...............	83	211	172	171	4.2	10.2	8.3	8.3	49.8	33.6	3.0	1.9
Louisiana...............	101	153	135	129	5.0	7.4	6.5	6.2	55.3	25.6	3.1	1.4
Maine....................	22	57	51	47	3.3	8.2	7.2	6.7	18.1	13.1	3.2	2.3
Maryland...............	100	241	216	206	3.6	7.9	6.9	6.6	72.7	57.1	3.1	2.4
Massachusetts.........	92	287	235	246	2.7	8.3	6.8	7.1	115.9	86.5	3.7	2.7
Michigan................	190	603	426	413	3.7	12.7	9.1	8.8	160.1	93.1	4.3	2.3
Minnesota..............	87	218	166	150	3.1	7.4	5.6	5.1	80.5	54.9	3.2	2.1
Mississippi.............	74	139	120	111	5.7	10.6	9.2	8.6	36.1	23.4	3.4	2.2
Missouri.................	98	283	209	197	3.3	9.3	7.0	6.5	75.1	47.2	3.0	1.8
Montana................	22	33	31	29	4.8	6.7	6.0	5.6	16.9	10.9	4.2	2.6
Nebraska...............	27	47	41	40	2.8	4.7	4.0	3.9	18.9	10.8	2.1	1.2
Nevada..................	48	192	159	135	4.5	13.8	11.5	9.8	53.6	31.3	4.9	2.7
New Hampshire.........	19	46	41	39	2.7	6.2	5.5	5.3	18.2	8.8	3.1	1.4
New Jersey.............	157	437	425	372	3.7	9.6	9.3	8.2	165.6	133.8	4.5	3.6
New Mexico............	42	74	65	64	5.0	8.0	7.1	6.9	25.2	16.3	3.4	2.1
New York...............	416	827	815	737	4.5	8.6	8.5	7.7	290.3	233.6	3.5	2.7
North Carolina..........	155	503	435	377	3.7	10.8	9.2	8.0	156.1	89.3	4.2	2.3
North Dakota...........	10	14	12	12	2.9	3.8	3.0	2.9	5.2	3.8	1.5	0.9
Ohio.....................	234	586	424	425	4.0	10.0	7.4	7.4	144.3	84.7	3.0	1.7
Oklahoma...............	52	122	96	99	3.1	6.9	5.4	5.4	34.3	20.1	2.4	1.3
Oregon..................	93	212	172	149	5.1	10.8	8.8	7.7	82.8	47.2	5.3	2.9
Pennsylvania...........	255	541	513	478	4.2	8.5	7.9	7.4	264.7	181.9	4.9	3.3
Rhode Island...........	23	67	57	53	4.2	11.7	10.3	9.5	17.8	12.8	4.1	2.9
South Carolina..........	71	241	196	165	3.6	11.1	9.0	7.6	70.8	30.8	4.1	1.7
South Dakota...........	11	22	19	17	2.7	5.1	4.2	3.8	4.4	2.6	1.2	0.7
Tennessee..............	115	304	253	252	4.0	9.9	8.2	8.2	68.3	41.3	2.7	1.6
Texas....................	452	1,007	864	813	4.4	8.2	6.8	6.3	215.7	155.9	2.2	1.4
Utah.....................	38	110	74	63	3.4	8.1	5.4	4.4	27.6	15.1	2.5	1.2
Vermont.................	9	23	17	15	2.7	6.4	4.9	4.4	10.3	6.1	3.6	2.1
Virginia..................	82	294	248	235	2.3	7.1	5.9	5.5	61.6	42.6	1.8	1.2
Washington.............	151	349	281	243	5.0	9.9	8.1	7.0	109.0	1.1	4.0	2.9
West Virginia...........	44	68	58	51	5.5	8.5	7.2	6.5	21.5	67.8	3.2	2.3
Wisconsin...............	101	261	212	207	3.4	8.5	6.9	6.7	121.5	17.2	4.7	2.5
Wyoming................	10	21	17	14	3.8	7.0	5.4	4.6	6.9	76.7	2.6	2.8

[1] Total unemployment as percent of civilian labor force. [2] Number of jobless workers who are receiving state unemployment benefits. Source: U.S. Employment and Training Administration, "Unemployment Insurance, Financial Data Handbook 394," <http://www.oui.doleta.gov/unemploy/hb394.asp>, accessed September 2014. [3] Those currently collecting unemployment insurance as a percent of the total number of eligible workers. [4] U.S. totals include Puerto Rico and the Virgin Islands.

Source: Except as noted, U.S. Bureau of Labor Statistics, Local Area Unemployment Statistics, <http://www.bls.gov/lau/>, accessed September 2014.

Table 649. Nonfarm Establishments—Employees, Hours, and Earnings by Industry: 1990 to 2014

[109,527 represents 109,527,000. Annual averages of monthly data. Based on data from establishment reports. Includes all full- and part-time employees who worked during, or received pay for, any part of the pay period including the 12th of the month. Excludes proprietors, the self-employed, farm workers, unpaid family workers, private household workers, and Armed Forces. Establishment data shown here conform to industry definitions in the 2012 North American Industry Classification System (NAICS) and are adjusted to March employment benchmarks. Based on the Current Employment Statistics Program; see source and Appendix III]

Item and year	Total nonfarm	Private industry																Government
		Total [1]	Construction	Manufacturing	Wholesale trade	Retail trade	Transportation and warehousing	Utilities	Information	Finance and insurance	Real estate and rental and leasing	Professional and technical services	Administrative and waste services	Educational services	Health care and social assistance	Arts entertainment and recreation	Accommodations and food services	
EMPLOYEES (1,000)																		
1990	109,527	91,112	5,263	17,695	5,268	13,182	3,476	740	2,688	4,976	1,637	4,538	4,643	1,688	9,336	1,132	8,156	18,415
2000	132,019	111,230	6,787	17,263	5,933	15,280	4,410	601	3,630	5,773	2,011	6,702	8,168	2,390	12,857	1,788	10,074	20,790
2005	134,005	112,201	7,336	14,227	5,764	15,280	4,361	554	3,061	6,063	2,134	7,025	8,170	2,836	14,794	1,892	10,923	21,804
2009	131,233	108,678	6,016	11,847	5,587	14,522	4,236	560	2,804	5,844	1,994	7,509	7,203	3,090	16,460	1,916	11,162	22,555
2010	130,275	107,785	5,518	11,528	5,452	14,440	4,191	553	2,707	5,761	1,934	7,441	7,414	3,155	16,734	1,913	11,135	22,490
2011	131,842	109,756	5,533	11,726	5,543	14,668	4,302	553	2,674	5,769	1,927	7,666	7,732	3,250	16,979	1,919	11,434	22,086
2012	134,104	112,184	5,646	11,927	5,667	14,841	4,416	553	2,676	5,828	1,955	7,892	8,016	3,341	17,357	1,969	11,800	21,920
2013	136,393	114,541	5,856	12,020	5,733	15,079	4,498	552	2,706	5,886	2,000	8,121	8,291	3,354	17,743	2,030	12,224	21,853
2014	139,042	117,180	6,138	12,188	5,826	15,364	4,640	553	2,740	5,933	2,046	8,348	8,579	3,417	18,057	2,103	12,606	21,863
WEEKLY EARNINGS [2] (dol.)																		
1990	(NA)	349.63	513.43	436.13	444.48	235.56	471.82	670.80	479.50	(NA)	(NA)	504.83	273.60	(NA)	319.27	219.02	147.92	(NA)
2000	(NA)	480.99	685.78	591.01	631.24	333.41	562.56	955.09	700.92	(NA)	(NA)	745.94	387.59	(NA)	447.47	273.79	207.44	(NA)
2005	(NA)	544.05	750.37	673.30	685.00	377.58	618.55	1,095.91	805.11	(NA)	(NA)	862.76	431.92	(NA)	556.40	330.31	226.48	(NA)
2009	(NA)	616.01	851.76	726.12	784.49	388.57	677.56	1,239.34	931.08	(NA)	(NA)	1,036.37	517.27	(NA)	636.50	359.71	261.87	(NA)
2010	(NA)	636.25	891.83	765.15	816.50	400.07	710.85	1,262.89	939.85	(NA)	(NA)	1,073.92	535.79	(NA)	653.75	363.91	266.78	(NA)
2011	(NA)	653.19	921.84	784.29	845.44	412.09	737.00	1,296.92	964.85	(NA)	(NA)	1,091.88	551.61	(NA)	679.58	373.65	269.12	(NA)
2012	(NA)	665.82	942.14	794.63	860.70	422.10	742.23	1,298.23	973.52	(NA)	(NA)	1,108.50	550.84	(NA)	689.59	377.92	276.19	(NA)
2013	(NA)	677.67	958.72	807.37	875.79	423.07	762.06	1,344.70	1,003.65	(NA)	(NA)	1,129.48	557.81	(NA)	696.09	379.58	280.48	(NA)
2014	(NA)	694.89	977.05	822.24	897.74	431.64	789.26	1,389.61	1,029.73	(NA)	(NA)	1,172.92	568.41	(NA)	706.26	388.53	290.06	(NA)
WEEKLY HOURS [2]																		
1990	(NA)	34.3	38.3	40.5	38.4	30.6	37.7	41.6	35.8	(NA)	(NA)	36.1	32.3	(NA)	31.8	26.1	25.9	(NA)
2000	(NA)	34.3	39.2	41.3	38.8	30.7	37.4	42.0	36.8	(NA)	(NA)	36.2	33.1	(NA)	32.1	25.6	26.2	(NA)
2005	(NA)	33.8	38.6	40.7	37.7	30.6	37.0	41.1	36.5	(NA)	(NA)	35.7	32.8	(NA)	32.8	25.7	25.7	(NA)
2009	(NA)	33.1	37.6	39.8	37.6	29.9	36.0	42.0	36.6	(NA)	(NA)	35.7	33.4	(NA)	32.4	23.8	25.0	(NA)
2010	(NA)	33.4	38.4	41.1	37.9	30.2	37.1	42.0	36.3	(NA)	(NA)	35.9	33.9	(NA)	32.3	23.8	25.0	(NA)
2011	(NA)	33.6	39.0	41.4	38.5	30.5	37.8	42.1	36.2	(NA)	(NA)	36.0	34.0	(NA)	32.5	23.8	24.9	(NA)
2012	(NA)	33.7	39.3	41.7	38.7	30.6	38.0	41.1	36.0	(NA)	(NA)	36.0	34.2	(NA)	32.5	23.7	25.2	(NA)
2013	(NA)	33.7	39.6	41.8	38.7	30.2	38.5	41.7	35.9	(NA)	(NA)	36.1	34.3	(NA)	32.2	23.9	25.1	(NA)
2014	(NA)	33.7	39.6	42.0	38.6	30.0	38.4	42.3	35.9	(NA)	(NA)	36.4	34.5	(NA)	32.2	24.1	25.3	(NA)
HOURLY EARNINGS [2] (dol.)																		
1990	(NA)	10.20	13.42	10.78	11.58	7.71	12.50	16.14	13.40	(NA)	(NA)	13.99	8.48	(NA)	10.03	8.41	5.70	(NA)
2000	(NA)	14.02	17.48	14.32	16.28	10.87	15.05	22.75	19.07	(NA)	(NA)	20.61	11.69	(NA)	13.93	10.68	7.92	(NA)
2005	(NA)	16.12	19.46	16.56	18.16	12.36	16.70	26.68	22.06	(NA)	(NA)	24.14	13.16	(NA)	16.95	12.85	8.80	(NA)
2009	(NA)	18.61	22.66	18.24	20.84	13.01	18.81	29.48	25.45	(NA)	(NA)	29.03	15.51	(NA)	19.67	15.08	10.49	(NA)
2010	(NA)	19.05	23.22	18.61	21.54	13.25	19.16	30.04	25.87	(NA)	(NA)	29.94	15.80	(NA)	20.27	15.27	10.68	(NA)
2011	(NA)	19.44	23.65	18.93	21.97	13.51	19.49	30.82	26.62	(NA)	(NA)	30.30	16.21	(NA)	20.94	15.67	10.79	(NA)
2012	(NA)	19.74	23.97	19.08	22.24	13.82	19.54	31.61	27.04	(NA)	(NA)	30.76	16.10	(NA)	21.23	15.96	10.96	(NA)
2013	(NA)	20.13	24.22	19.30	22.62	14.02	19.81	32.27	27.98	(NA)	(NA)	31.32	16.28	(NA)	21.59	15.88	11.16	(NA)
2014	(NA)	20.61	24.67	19.56	23.24	14.39	20.53	32.88	28.66	(NA)	(NA)	32.21	16.49	(NA)	21.96	16.15	11.47	(NA)

NA Not available. [1] Includes other industries not shown separately. [2] Average hours and earnings of production and nonsupervisory employees.

Source: U.S. Bureau of Labor Statistics, Current Employment Statistics, "Employment, Hours, and Earnings—National," <http://www.bls.gov/ces/home.htm>, accessed September 2015.

Table 650. Employees in Nonfarm Establishments—States: 2014

[In thousands (139,231 represents 139,231,000). Includes all full- and part-time employees who worked during, or received pay for, any part of the pay period reported. Excludes proprietors, the self-employed, farm workers, unpaid family workers, private household workers, and Armed Forces. Compiled from data supplied by cooperating state agencies. Based on North American Industry Classification System, 2012; see text, section 15]

State	Total [1]	Construction	Manufacturing	Trade, transportation and utilities	Information	Financial activities [2]	Professional and business services [3]	Education and health services [4]	Leisure and hospitality [5]	Other services [6]	Government
U.S.	139,231	6,128	12,175	26,356	2,741	7,940	19,092	21,551	14,656	5,512	22,198
AL	1,923.2	79.6	252.6	373.1	22.0	94.8	223.0	223.9	184.5	80.2	377.9
AK	337.4	17.3	14.2	64.9	6.2	12.2	29.8	46.8	34.1	11.8	82.2
AZ	2,568.4	125.3	156.5	493.0	43.1	189.0	382.4	381.3	286.2	88.2	410.3
AR	1,188.8	45.9	154.7	244.8	13.7	49.7	133.6	172.2	108.3	43.8	213.4
CA	15,645.1	675.4	1,269.6	2,871.1	457.9	784.3	2,433.4	2,414.4	1,757.1	539.8	2,411.0
CO	2,460.8	142.3	136.6	431.8	69.9	153.3	385.2	298.8	300.7	100.4	408.0
CT	1,666.1	55.5	159.7	301.3	31.8	128.6	211.8	325.0	151.0	63.0	237.9
DE	437.7	20.4	25.7	79.5	4.9	45.1	59.5	72.5	46.8	18.4	64.9
DC	753.8	14.3	1.0	30.7	17.2	30.3	157.8	127.4	69.8	70.4	234.9
FL	7,824.5	397.4	330.5	1,622.6	136.2	522.7	1,164.9	1,160.1	1,085.6	324.1	1,074.7
GA	4,155.6	156.1	367.2	871.8	107.3	232.8	618.7	523.7	430.1	154.3	684.7
HI	625.3	31.6	13.7	117.4	8.5	27.4	82.3	79.0	113.3	26.5	125.6
ID	655.1	36.0	60.0	132.0	9.3	33.0	79.4	94.0	66.2	22.7	118.7
IL	5,872.5	201.3	579.3	1,175.0	99.0	369.3	915.1	886.6	556.2	252.4	828.5
IN	2,980.3	122.6	507.1	575.5	35.6	128.3	320.4	438.2	293.3	125.7	426.6
IA	1,548.2	74.5	216.7	312.7	25.6	104.1	136.1	223.5	137.7	59.0	256.0
KS	1,392.6	59.9	162.2	263.7	27.9	79.8	169.7	189.8	123.2	49.2	256.8
KY	1,857.8	72.4	234.5	376.8	26.3	89.8	210.6	261.0	182.5	63.7	323.6
LA	1,980.7	139.3	147.7	389.2	26.0	91.8	212.1	299.0	221.0	71.8	329.1
ME	604.4	25.8	50.2	119.0	7.5	30.4	63.3	122.4	62.6	20.9	99.8
MD	2,619.0	151.1	103.4	454.9	37.9	144.2	423.8	427.7	260.0	112.2	503.7
MA	3,413.5	127.7	249.7	561.4	86.2	208.0	517.3	736.4	340.9	133.3	451.7
MI	4,179.7	141.3	575.9	757.3	57.0	204.8	619.0	644.4	405.3	171.0	595.4
MN	2,813.4	107.0	312.1	516.7	52.8	178.6	352.8	498.9	254.3	113.4	419.6
MS	1,119.5	49.0	139.3	219.9	13.1	43.5	100.8	135.1	125.9	38.8	245.1
MO	2,734.0	109.8	256.2	522.6	57.2	164.2	353.7	435.0	285.6	113.6	432.0
MT	453.8	24.8	18.9	92.9	6.5	24.9	39.6	70.0	60.3	17.7	89.2
NE	993.3	47.0	97.3	203.8	17.1	72.5	112.8	148.4	87.1	36.9	170.5
NV	1,215.3	62.8	41.6	230.2	13.6	57.2	155.7	116.2	336.7	34.8	152.3
NH	647.8	23.3	66.5	136.7	12.0	35.8	73.4	115.9	66.9	25.9	90.5
NJ	3,962.2	141.9	242.6	837.3	75.1	247.0	634.9	635.1	357.7	168.8	620.5
NM	820.2	42.6	28.1	138.1	12.4	33.4	99.2	127.4	90.7	28.6	191.9
NY	9,083.9	339.6	452.3	1,555.2	264.3	691.7	1,228.2	1,848.5	867.9	394.4	1,436.7
NC	4,141.9	179.5	449.1	775.8	72.4	211.1	571.2	568.7	444.0	150.0	714.7
ND	460.7	34.4	26.0	106.1	6.8	24.0	36.1	59.3	40.7	16.9	80.6
OH	5,330.7	194.1	673.0	993.1	72.6	288.3	708.4	889.8	528.8	209.1	758.7
OK	1,653.7	75.5	138.7	300.8	21.7	79.5	185.8	228.1	155.0	59.3	348.0
OR	1,717.2	79.2	178.9	324.9	32.2	92.1	218.9	248.5	182.2	59.0	293.6
PA	5,790.1	231.0	567.2	1,110.7	85.2	315.2	758.6	1,180.3	537.7	254.9	711.9
RI	477.3	16.5	40.9	74.9	8.9	32.5	60.5	105.0	55.0	22.9	60.1
SC	1,948.6	82.3	230.1	373.1	26.5	96.5	254.1	225.8	228.5	71.7	356.3
SD	423.4	22.2	42.4	85.6	6.1	29.6	30.1	68.4	45.3	15.8	77.9
TN	2,815.4	111.0	325.2	591.6	43.9	141.4	372.4	402.8	296.3	105.9	424.8
TX	11,550.2	650.5	884.7	2,310.2	203.3	700.6	1,542.8	1,525.1	1,188.6	409.5	1,828.0
UT	1,327.9	78.3	120.6	253.3	33.3	75.0	184.9	174.6	128.4	37.5	229.7
VT	309.9	14.7	31.2	55.8	4.8	12.1	26.6	62.5	35.4	10.2	55.9
VA	3,774.0	177.9	231.6	643.3	71.3	193.2	677.6	496.4	371.4	195.6	706.3
WA	3,075.8	159.4	289.1	569.7	109.5	153.7	372.1	453.6	296.5	114.5	551.6
WV	762.4	33.4	47.8	134.8	9.6	30.9	66.7	126.4	73.8	55.4	153.4
WI	2,845.1	103.7	464.8	524.7	47.8	150.6	306.4	429.7	263.8	138.3	411.1
WY	292.5	23.6	9.8	54.9	3.8	11.2	18.4	27.1	35.2	9.9	71.5

[1] Includes mining and logging, not shown separately. [2] Finance and insurance; real estate and rental and leasing. [3] Professional, scientific, and technical services; management of companies and enterprises; and administrative and support and waste management and remediation services. [4] Education services; health care and social assistance. [5] Arts, entertainment, and recreation; accommodations and food services. [6] Includes repair and maintenance; personal and laundry services; and membership associations and organizations.

Source: U.S. Bureau of Labor Statistics, State and Metro Area Employment, Hours, and Earnings, "Employees on nonfarm payrolls in States and selected areas by major industry," <http://www.bls.gov/sae/tables.htm>, accessed April 2015.

Table 651. Nonfarm Industries—Employees and Earnings: 1990 to 2014

[Annual averages of monthly figures (109,527 represents 109,527,000). Covers all full- and part-time employees who worked during, or received pay for, any part of the pay period including the 12th of the month. See also headnote, Table 649]

Industry	2012 NAICS code[1]	All employees (1,000)					Average hourly earnings[2] (dol.)		
		1990	2000	2010	2013	2014	2000	2010	2014
Total nonfarm................................	(X)	**109,527**	**132,019**	**130,275**	**136,393**	**139,042**	**(NA)**	**(NA)**	**(NA)**
Goods-producing [3]............................	(X)	23,723	24,649	17,751	18,738	19,223	15.27	20.28	21.59
Service-providing [4]...........................	(X)	85,804	107,370	112,524	117,655	119,820	(NA)	(NA)	(NA)
Total private................................	(X)	**91,112**	**111,230**	**107,785**	**114,541**	**117,180**	**14.02**	**19.05**	**20.61**
Mining and logging........................	(X)	**765**	**599**	**705**	**863**	**896**	**16.55**	**23.82**	**26.85**
Logging.......................................	1133	85	79	50	52	53	13.70	18.85	20.69
Mining......................................	21	**680**	**520**	**655**	**811**	**844**	**16.94**	**24.24**	**27.22**
Oil and gas extraction....................	211	190	125	159	194	198	19.43	27.36	31.25
Mining, except oil and gas..............	212	302	225	205	210	207	18.07	24.63	26.97
Support activities for mining...........	213	188	171	292	408	439	14.55	22.95	26.20
Construction...............................	23	**5,263**	**6,787**	**5,518**	**5,856**	**6,138**	**17.48**	**23.22**	**24.67**
Construction of buildings................	236	1,413	1,633	1,230	1,286	1,357	16.74	22.73	24.22
Residential building....................	2361	673	823	572	612	661	15.18	19.80	21.50
Nonresidential building................	2362	741	809	658	674	696	18.18	25.13	26.58
Heavy and civil engineering construction [5].....	237	813	937	825	885	915	16.80	23.76	25.68
Highway, street, and bridge construction......	2373	289	340	287	293	295	18.17	23.76	24.99
Specialty trade contractors.............	238	3,037	4,217	3,463	3,684	3,867	17.91	23.22	24.53
Building foundation and exterior contractors...	2381	703	919	680	714	749	16.93	21.20	22.27
Building equipment contractors.........	2382	1,282	1,897	1,634	1,749	1,825	19.52	24.89	26.35
Building finishing contractors..........	2383	665	857	634	668	710	16.44	22.06	23.48
Manufacturing.............................	31-33	**17,695**	**17,263**	**11,528**	**12,020**	**12,188**	**14.32**	**18.61**	**19.56**
Durable goods.............................	(X)	10,737	10,877	7,064	7,548	7,685	14.93	19.80	20.66
Wood products..........................	321	543	615	342	353	372	11.63	14.85	15.58
Nonmetallic mineral products..........	327	528	554	371	373	386	14.53	17.48	19.15
Cement and concrete products.......	3273	195	234	170	168	174	14.64	17.84	20.89
Primary metals.........................	331	689	622	362	395	401	16.64	20.13	22.40
Iron and steel mills and ferroalloy production...	3311	187	135	87	91	91	(NA)	(NA)	(NA)
Foundries.............................	3315	214	217	112	125	127	14.72	18.22	19.34
Fabricated metal products..............	332	1,610	1,753	1,282	1,432	1,455	13.77	17.94	18.68
Architectural and structural metals....	3323	357	428	321	350	362	13.43	17.47	18.19
Machine shops and threaded products.......	3327	309	365	313	368	371	14.53	18.68	19.35
Machinery................................	333	1,410	1,457	996	1,105	1,129	15.21	18.96	21.00
Agricultural, construction, and mining machinery.........	3331	229	222	208	250	255	14.21	18.95	19.99
Heating, ventilation and air conditioning, and commercial refrigeration equipment.........	3334	165	194	125	127	128	13.10	16.16	17.10
Metalworking machinery................	3335	267	274	155	178	182	16.66	20.00	20.95
Computer and electronic products......	334	1,903	1,820	1,095	1,066	1,050	14.73	22.78	23.36
Computer and peripheral equipment....	3341	367	302	158	158	163	(NA)	(NA)	(NA)
Communications equipment...........	3342	223	239	117	101	94	14.39	23.88	24.19
Semiconductors and electronic components...	3344	574	676	369	375	368	13.46	20.35	20.81
Electronic instruments.................	3345	635	488	406	394	388	15.80	24.82	26.76
Electrical equipment and appliances........	335	633	591	360	374	375	13.23	16.87	18.28
Household appliances.................	3352	114	106	60	58	60	(NA)	(NA)	(NA)
Electrical equipment.................	3353	244	210	136	144	144	13.28	16.51	17.81
Transportation equipment..............	336	2,135	2,057	1,333	1,509	1,563	18.89	25.23	24.96
Motor vehicles.......................	3361	271	291	153	182	199	24.45	29.04	27.83
Motor vehicle parts..................	3363	653	840	419	509	537	17.95	20.66	19.91
Aerospace products and parts........	3364	841	517	478	495	488	20.52	33.65	35.73
Ship and boat building...............	3366	174	154	125	132	139	(NA)	(NA)	(NA)
Furniture and related products.........	337	602	680	357	360	373	11.73	15.06	15.67
Household and institutional furniture....	3371	398	441	223	224	235	11.39	14.75	15.54
Miscellaneous manufacturing...........	339	686	728	567	581	583	11.93	16.56	17.31
Medical equipment and supplies.......	3391	283	305	303	307	308	12.70	17.56	17.72
Nondurable goods........................	(X)	6,958	6,386	4,464	4,472	4,503	13.31	16.80	17.74
Food manufacturing....................	311	1,507	1,553	1,451	1,474	1,481	11.77	14.41	15.55
Fruit and vegetable preserving and specialty...	3114	218	197	173	170	169	11.90	14.56	15.83
Dairy products.......................	3115	145	136	130	134	134	14.85	18.92	20.69
Animal slaughtering and processing.......	3116	427	507	489	482	480	10.27	12.69	13.63
Bakeries and tortilla manufacturing......	3118	292	306	277	286	294	11.45	14.44	15.23
Textile mills..........................	313	492	378	119	117	118	11.23	13.56	14.15
Textile product mills..................	314	236	230	119	114	115	10.31	11.79	13.35
Apparel...............................	315	903	484	157	145	140	8.61	11.43	13.51
Cut and sew apparel..................	3152	750	380	124	120	115	(NA)	(NA)	(NA)
Leather and allied products............	316	133	69	28	30	28	(NA)	(NA)	(NA)
Paper and paper products..............	322	647	605	395	378	371	15.91	20.04	20.35
Pulp, paper, and paperboard mills......	3221	238	191	112	107	104	20.62	25.12	25.57
Converted paper products............	3222	409	413	282	271	267	13.58	17.81	18.05
Printing and related support activities....	323	809	807	488	452	453	14.09	16.91	18.01
Petroleum and coal products...........	324	153	123	114	110	111	22.80	31.31	35.36
Chemicals.............................	325	1,036	980	787	793	804	17.09	21.07	21.49
Basic chemicals.....................	3251	249	188	142	143	147	21.06	24.93	26.79
Resin, rubber, and artificial fibers....	3252	158	136	89	92	93	17.09	21.11	21.75
Pharmaceuticals and medicines......	3254	207	274	277	276	280	17.27	21.95	23.12
Plastics and rubber products..........	326	825	951	625	659	675	12.70	15.71	16.51
Plastics products....................	3261	618	737	502	528	542	12.04	15.47	16.27
Rubber products.....................	3262	207	214	123	131	133	14.83	16.64	17.49
Trade, transportation, and utilities...	(X)	**22,666**	**26,225**	**24,636**	**25,862**	**26,384**	**13.31**	**16.82**	**18.27**
Wholesale trade........................	42	**5,268**	**5,933**	**5,452**	**5,733**	**5,826**	**16.28**	**21.54**	**23.24**
Durable goods...........................	423	2,834	3,251	2,714	2,864	2,910	16.71	20.95	22.78

See footnotes at end of table.

Industry	2012 NAICS code [1]	All employees (1,000)					Average hourly earnings [2] (dol.)		
		1990	2000	2010	2013	2014	2000	2010	2014
Motor vehicles and parts............	4231	309	356	309	325	331	14.27	17.61	20.28
Lumber and construction supplies.......	4233	181	227	188	190	201	13.61	18.45	20.44
Commercial equipment.................	4234	597	722	604	619	618	20.29	25.03	26.36
Electric goods......................	4236	357	425	309	317	323	19.43	23.12	24.22
Hardware and plumbing...............	4237	216	247	218	229	235	15.07	19.82	21.50
Machinery and supplies...............	4238	690	725	608	661	675	16.47	21.03	23.68
Nondurable goods...................	424	1,900	2,065	1,928	1,985	2,018	14.33	19.62	20.47
Paper and paper products............	4241	162	177	124	121	124	15.65	22.48	23.51
Druggists' goods....................	4242	136	192	190	190	194	18.98	23.39	27.59
Apparel and piece goods.............	4243	152	163	137	142	146	14.58	21.34	20.90
Grocery and related products.........	4244	623	689	704	727	738	13.57	19.07	18.95
Alcoholic beverages.................	4248	115	128	163	181	185	15.72	20.01	21.66
Electronic markets and agents and brokers. ..	425	535	618	811	884	898	20.79	28.32	31.59
Retail trade......................	**44,45**	**13,182**	**15,280**	**14,440**	**15,079**	**15,364**	**10.87**	**13.25**	**14.39**
Motor vehicle and parts dealers.......	441	1,494	1,847	1,629	1,793	1,861	14.94	17.06	18.69
Automobile dealers................	4411	983	1,217	1,012	1,138	1,185	16.95	18.22	20.30
Auto parts, accessories, and tire stores......	4413	418	499	489	521	537	11.04	14.54	15.33
Furniture and home furnishings stores........	442	432	544	438	446	455	12.33	15.25	16.29
Furniture stores...................	4421	244	289	217	213	216	13.37	16.17	17.49
Home furnishings stores............	4422	188	254	221	233	239	11.06	14.03	14.90
Electronics and appliance stores........	443	451	647	522	497	491	13.16	16.83	21.50
Building material and garden supply stores. ..	444	891	1,142	1,132	1,208	1,235	11.25	14.11	14.85
Building material and supplies dealers.......	4441	753	982	1,005	1,062	1,083	11.30	14.13	14.89
Food and beverage stores............	445	2,779	2,993	2,808	2,930	2,994	9.76	12.03	12.46
Grocery stores....................	4451	2,406	2,582	2,461	2,563	2,621	9.71	12.12	12.52
Specialty food stores..............	4452	232	270	211	221	227	9.97	11.13	12.05
Beer, wine, and liquor stores.......	4453	141	141	136	146	146	10.40	11.89	11.75
Health and personal care stores.........	446	792	928	981	1,016	1,021	11.68	16.99	17.40
Gasoline stations...................	447	910	936	819	866	881	8.05	10.25	10.62
Clothing & clothing accessories stores........	448	1,313	1,322	1,353	1,391	1,379	9.96	11.59	12.55
Clothing stores....................	4481	930	954	1,040	1,059	1,041	9.88	10.91	12.01
Shoe stores......................	4482	216	193	182	194	200	8.96	11.80	12.83
Jewelry, luggage, and leather goods stores..	4483	167	175	131	138	137	11.48	15.56	15.26
Sporting goods, hobby, book, and music stores........	451	464	603	579	603	613	9.38	11.69	12.77
Sporting goods and musical instrument stores........	4511	352	437	459	511	523	9.55	11.82	12.99
Book stores and news dealers..............	4512	111	166	120	92	90	8.91	11.10	11.57
General merchandise stores............	452	2,500	2,820	2,998	3,060	3,114	9.22	10.98	11.51
Department stores.................	4521	1,494	1,755	1,502	1,348	1,350	(NA)	(NA)	(NA)
Miscellaneous store retailers...........	453	738	1,007	762	803	818	10.20	12.50	13.89
Florists.........................	4531	121	130	69	65	64	8.95	11.05	11.58
Office supplies, stationery, and gift stores....	4532	358	471	303	294	293	10.46	13.06	14.91
Used merchandise stores.............	4533	56	107	125	157	164	8.07	10.72	10.85
Nonstore retailers...................	454	419	492	421	467	504	13.22	17.73	20.13
Electronic shopping and mail-order houses..	4541	157	257	247	298	329	13.38	18.22	21.38
Transportation and warehousing.............	**48,49**	**3,476**	**4,410**	**4,191**	**4,498**	**4,640**	**15.05**	**19.16**	**20.53**
Air transportation...................	481	529	614	458	444	442	13.57	24.56	31.86
Scheduled air transportation...........	4811	503	570	417	406	405	(NA)	(NA)	(NA)
Rail transportation..................	482	272	232	216	231	235	(NA)	(NA)	(NA)
Water transportation................	483	57	56	62	65	67	(NA)	(NA)	(NA)
Truck transportation.................	484	1,122	1,406	1,250	1,382	1,416	15.86	18.62	20.60
General freight trucking.............	4841	807	1,013	868	944	968	16.37	18.51	20.74
Specialized freight trucking...........	4842	315	393	383	438	448	14.51	18.88	20.29
Transit and ground passenger transportation......	485	274	372	430	449	465	11.88	14.98	15.57
Urban, interurban, rural, and charter bus transportation........	4851, 2,5	72	97	94	97	99	(NA)	(NA)	(NA)
Taxi and limousine service............	4853	57	72	68	77	79	(NA)	(NA)	(NA)
School and employee bus transportation. ...	4854	114	152	186	184	193	11.42	14.90	16.20
Pipeline transportation...............	486	60	46	42	45	47	19.86	29.54	37.83
Scenic and sightseeing transportation........	487	16	28	27	29	31	(NA)	(NA)	(NA)
Support activities for transportation........	488	364	537	543	598	625	14.57	21.09	21.37
Support activities for air transportation.....	4881	96	141	154	169	176	13.42	17.04	18.61
Support activities for water transportation....	4883	91	97	91	95	99	19.57	35.16	33.99
Support activities for road transportation....	4884	35	66	80	88	93	13.98	15.68	16.37
Freight transportation arrangement..........	4885	111	178	169	190	198	13.46	21.24	21.18
Couriers and messengers..............	492	375	605	528	544	574	13.51	17.67	16.53
Couriers and express delivery services......	4921	340	546	480	488	514	(NA)	(NA)	(NA)
Warehousing and storage..............	493	407	514	633	711	738	14.46	15.50	15.45
Utilities...........................	**22**	**740**	**601**	**553**	**552**	**553**	**22.75**	**30.04**	**32.88**
Power generation and supply..........	2211	550	434	398	394	392	23.13	31.25	34.25
Natural gas distribution............	2212	155	121	108	111	113	23.41	28.36	31.96
Water, sewage and other systems...........	2213	35	46	47	48	48	16.93	23.73	22.80
Information.........................	**51**	**2,688**	**3,630**	**2,707**	**2,706**	**2,740**	**19.07**	**25.87**	**28.66**
Publishing industries, except Internet. ..	511	871	1,035	759	733	725	(NA)	26.78	33.43
Newspaper, book, and directory publishers. ..	5111	773	774	498	433	412	(NA)	20.98	24.07
Software publishers..................	5112	98	261	261	300	313	28.48	36.41	45.10
Motion picture and sound recording industries.....	512	255	383	370	371	376	21.25	22.11	23.39
Broadcasting, except Internet..........	515	284	344	290	284	286	16.74	24.01	27.63
Radio and television broadcasting..............	5151	232	253	210	215	223	(NA)	(NA)	(NA)
Cable and other subscription programming. ..	5152	52	91	80	69	63	(NA)	(NA)	(NA)

See footnotes at end of table.

Table 651. Nonfarm Industries—Employees and Earnings: 1990 to 2014-Continued.

See headnote on page 423.

Industry	2012 NAICS code [1]	All employees (1,000)					Average hourly earnings [2] (dol.)		
		1990	2000	2010	2013	2014	2000	2010	2014
Telecommunications..............................	517	1,009	1,397	903	853	856	18.59	26.24	25.70
Wired telecommunications carriers.........	5171	760	922	603	605	607	18.62	25.99	25.77
Wireless telecommunications carriers (except satellite)................................	5172	36	186	170	155	155	14.40	25.35	26.08
Data processing, hosting and related services....................................	518	211	316	243	270	279	16.97	27.03	29.92
Financial activities................................	**(X)**	**6,614**	**7,783**	**7,695**	**7,886**	**7,979**	**15.04**	**21.55**	**24.71**
Finance and insurance........................	**52**	**4,976**	**5,773**	**5,761**	**5,886**	**5,933**	**(NA)**	**(NA)**	**(NA)**
Monetary authorities—central bank...........	521	24	23	20	18	18	(NA)	(NA)	(NA)
Credit intermediation and related activities....	522	2,425	2,548	2,550	2,614	2,567	13.14	18.25	20.91
Depository credit intermediation [5]...........	5221	1,909	1,681	1,729	1,734	1,708	11.97	17.55	19.40
Commercial banking............................	52211	1,362	1,251	1,306	1,314	1,294	11.83	17.56	19.58
Nondepository credit intermediation..........	5222	398	644	562	591	574	15.30	20.14	25.03
Activities related to credit intermediation.....	5223	119	222	259	290	284	15.39	18.29	20.96
Securities, commodity contracts, investments.......................................	523	489	851	850	865	881	20.04	31.21	40.27
Securities and commodity contracts brokerage and exchanges....................	5231,2	341	569	471	449	448	20.05	31.72	43.19
Other financial investment activities..........	5239	148	282	379	416	434	20.03	30.51	37.06
Insurance carriers and related activities......	524	2,039	2,351	2,341	2,389	2,467	17.47	24.58	27.18
Insurance carriers...............................	5241	1,349	1,544	1,445	1,433	1,459	18.03	25.95	28.64
Insurance agencies, brokerages, and related services...........................	5242	690	807	896	956	1,008	16.32	22.18	24.86
Real estate and rental and leasing...........	**53**	**1,637**	**2,011**	**1,934**	**2,000**	**2,046**	**(NA)**	**(NA)**	**(NA)**
Real estate.......................................	**531**	**1,109**	**1,316**	**1,396**	**1,459**	**1,487**	**12.26**	**17.37**	**19.14**
Lessors of real estate............................	5311	566	610	565	575	575	11.19	16.52	17.62
Offices of real estate agents and brokers....	5312	217	281	286	282	289	12.57	17.10	18.98
Activities related to real estate................	5313	327	424	544	602	624	13.60	18.37	20.58
Rental and leasing services.....................	532	514	667	514	518	535	11.69	15.96	17.89
Automotive equipment rental and leasing....	5321	163	208	161	179	188	(NA)	(NA)	(NA)
Consumer goods rental.........................	5322	220	292	198	163	162	(NA)	(NA)	(NA)
Machinery and equipment rental and leasing...........................	5324	84	103	114	136	146	14.95	19.83	22.77
Lessors of nonfinancial intangible assets......	533	14	28	25	24	24	(NA)	(NA)	(NA)
Professional and business services.........	**(X)**	**10,848**	**16,666**	**16,728**	**18,515**	**19,096**	**15.52**	**22.78**	**24.28**
Professional and technical services [5].......	**54**	**4,538**	**6,702**	**7,441**	**8,121**	**8,348**	**20.61**	**29.94**	**32.21**
Legal services....................................	5411	944	1,066	1,114	1,129	1,120	21.38	31.04	32.26
Accounting and bookkeeping services........	5412	664	866	887	932	958	14.42	21.04	23.53
Architectural and engineering services.......	5413	942	1,238	1,275	1,346	1,380	20.49	30.22	31.35
Specialized design services.....................	5414	82	132	113	123	127	15.32	22.36	25.80
Computer systems design and related.........	5415	410	1,254	1,449	1,702	1,778	27.13	37.16	39.45
Management and technical consulting.........	5416	305	673	999	1,180	1,244	20.83	28.52	31.99
Scientific research and development..........	5417	494	515	621	632	635	21.39	35.67	37.46
Advertising and related services...............	5418	382	497	408	452	476	16.99	24.61	28.12
Management of companies and enterprises..	**55**	**1,667**	**1,796**	**1,872**	**2,103**	**2,169**	**15.28**	**23.79**	**27.01**
Administrative and waste services...........	**56**	**4,643**	**8,168**	**7,414**	**8,291**	**8,579**	**11.69**	**15.80**	**16.49**
Administrative and support services [5]..........	561	4,413	7,855	7,057	7,913	8,194	11.53	15.59	16.25
Office administrative services...................	5611	211	264	407	450	462	14.68	23.56	25.65
Facilities support services.......................	5612	58	97	133	132	131	16.73	20.97	19.77
Employment services [5]...........................	5613	1,512	3,849	2,723	3,269	3,421	11.89	16.19	16.36
Temporary help services.....................	56132	1,156	2,636	2,094	2,617	2,767	11.79	14.23	15.64
Business support services.......................	5614	505	787	809	856	884	11.08	14.49	15.48
Travel arrangement and reservation..........	5615	250	299	186	195	196	12.72	17.10	19.18
Investigation and security services............	5616	507	689	781	834	859	9.78	14.14	14.75
Services to buildings and dwellings...........	5617	1,175	1,571	1,745	1,885	1,940	10.02	12.97	13.89
Waste management and remediation services [5].......................................	562	229	313	357	378	386	15.29	19.32	21.02
Waste collection.................................	5621	82	100	141	154	160	12.97	17.50	18.36
Waste treatment and disposal..................	5622	77	119	96	96	93	15.02	20.29	24.44
Education and health services.................	**(X)**	**11,024**	**15,247**	**19,889**	**21,097**	**21,475**	**13.91**	**19.98**	**21.65**
Educational services............................	**61**	**1,688**	**2,390**	**3,155**	**3,354**	**3,417**	**(NA)**	**(NA)**	**(NA)**
Elementary and secondary schools............	6111	461	716	849	897	929	(NA)	(NA)	(NA)
Junior colleges...................................	6112	44	79	99	75	71	(NA)	(NA)	(NA)
Colleges and universities........................	6113	939	1,196	1,591	1,699	1,706	(NA)	(NA)	(NA)
Business, computer, and management training..	6114	60	86	78	73	84	(NA)	(NA)	(NA)
Technical and trade schools.....................	6115	72	91	126	137	136	(NA)	(NA)	(NA)
Other schools and instruction..................	6116	96	184	309	359	369	(NA)	(NA)	(NA)
Educational support services...................	6117	17	39	103	114	122	(NA)	(NA)	(NA)
Health care and social assistance.............	**62**	**9,336**	**12,857**	**16,734**	**17,743**	**18,057**	**13.93**	**20.27**	**21.96**
Health care.......................................	621,2,3	8,211	10,858	13,777	14,492	14,690	14.63	21.71	23.64
Ambulatory health care services...............	621	2,842	4,320	5,975	6,477	6,645	14.99	21.67	24.01
Offices of physicians...........................	6211	1,278	1,840	2,313	2,429	2,470	15.65	24.03	29.01
Offices of dentists..............................	6212	513	688	828	870	891	15.96	22.65	23.24
Offices of other health practitioners..........	6213	276	438	671	752	784	14.24	20.48	21.85
Outpatient care centers........................	6214	261	386	600	680	711	15.29	22.65	23.60
Medical and diagnostic laboratories..........	6215	129	162	228	243	247	15.74	23.48	22.20
Home health care services.....................	6216	288	633	1,085	1,230	1,262	12.86	16.64	17.12
Hospitals...	622	3,513	3,954	4,679	4,786	4,784	16.71	26.11	28.51
General medical and surgical hospitals......	6221	3,305	3,745	4,357	4,442	4,447	16.75	26.33	28.88
Psychiatric and substance abuse hospitals...	6222	113	86	109	121	121	(NA)	(NA)	(NA)
Nursing and residential care facilities..........	623	1,856	2,583	3,124	3,229	3,261	10.67	14.21	14.62

See footnotes at end of table.

Table 651. Nonfarm Industries—Employees and Earnings: 1990 to 2014-Continued.

See headnote on page 423.

Industry	2012 NAICS code [1]	All employees (1,000)					Average hourly earnings [2] (dol.)		
		1990	2000	2010	2013	2014	2000	2010	2014
Nursing care facilities............	6231	1,170	1,514	1,657	1,654	1,652	11.08	15.26	15.58
Residential mental health facilities............	6232	269	437	565	594	607	9.96	13.06	13.43
Community care facilities for the elderly......	6233	330	478	741	822	843	9.83	12.89	13.52
Social assistance............	624	1,125	1,999	2,957	3,252	3,367	9.72	12.77	13.50
Individual and family services............	6241	429	817	1,578	1,913	2,033	10.31	13.13	13.76
Emergency and other relief services.......	6242	67	117	143	148	151	10.95	14.41	15.96
Vocational rehabilitation services............	6243	242	370	388	348	331	9.57	12.47	13.76
Child day care services............	6244	388	696	848	843	853	8.88	11.99	12.44
Leisure and hospitality............	(X)	**9,288**	**11,862**	**13,049**	**14,254**	**14,710**	**8.32**	**11.31**	**12.09**
Arts, entertainment, and recreation............	**71**	**1,132**	**1,788**	**1,913**	**2,030**	**2,103**	**10.68**	**15.27**	**16.15**
Performing arts and spectator sports..........	711	273	382	406	419	448	13.11	21.01	22.35
Museums, historical sites, zoos, and parks....	712	68	110	128	140	145	12.20	15.60	16.87
Amusements, gambling, and recreation.......	713	791	1,296	1,379	1,470	1,510	9.86	13.38	14.11
Accommodation and food services.........	**72**	**8,156**	**10,074**	**11,135**	**12,224**	**12,606**	**7.92**	**10.68**	**11.47**
Accommodation............	721	1,616	1,884	1,760	1,865	1,889	9.48	13.02	13.26
Traveler accommodation and other longer-term accommodation............	7211	1,582	1,837	1,703	1,807	1,826	9.49	13.07	13.28
Food services and drinking places............	722	6,540	8,189	9,376	10,359	10,717	7.49	10.15	11.11
Full-service restaurants............	7221	3,070	3,845	4,482	4,923	5,058	7.78	10.93	12.11
Limited-service eating places............	7222	2,429	3,042	3,418	3,821	3,966	6.80	8.86	9.32
Special food services............	7223	392	491	543	601	642	9.45	11.83	14.12
Drinking places, alcoholic beverages.........	7224	312	391	341	356	360	7.24	10.15	11.34
Other services............	**81**	**4,261**	**5,168**	**5,331**	**5,483**	**5,573**	**12.73**	**17.06**	**18.52**
Repair and maintenance............	811	1,009	1,242	1,139	1,217	1,240	13.28	16.82	18.24
Automotive repair and maintenance...........	8111	659	888	801	848	869	12.45	15.55	16.95
Electronic equipment repair and maintenance............	8112	100	107	98	102	101	16.31	19.41	21.28
Commercial machinery repair and maintenance............	8113	161	161	172	197	199	15.53	21.03	22.41
Personal and laundry services............	812	1,120	1,243	1,265	1,342	1,369	10.18	13.42	14.22
Personal care services............	8121	430	490	601	642	655	10.18	13.97	15.12
Death care services............	8122	123	136	131	134	133	13.04	17.46	17.91
Dry-cleaning and laundry services............	8123	371	388	302	298	299	9.17	11.80	12.03
Dry-cleaning and laundry services, except coin-operated............	81232	215	211	146	141	140	8.14	10.56	10.91
Other personal services............	8129	196	229	232	268	282	10.52	12.43	13.52
Pet care services, except veterinary..........	81291	23	31	63	80	87	12.12	12.83	14.17
Parking lots and garages............	81293	68	93	111	125	128	8.81	11.18	11.12
Membership associations & organizations......	813	2,132	2,683	2,926	2,925	2,964	13.66	18.76	20.60
Grantmaking and giving services............	8132	113	116	178	169	174	14.65	23.51	28.74
Social advocacy organizations............	8133	126	143	202	212	217	12.08	17.36	19.03
Civic and social organizations............	8134	377	404	392	393	393	9.85	12.16	13.65
Professional and similar organizations.........	8139	379	473	477	466	478	15.98	22.67	25.01
Government............	(X)	**18,415**	**20,790**	**22,490**	**21,853**	**21,863**	**(NA)**	**(NA)**	**(NA)**
Federal............	(X)	3,196	2,865	2,977	2,769	2,729	(NA)	(NA)	(NA)
State............	(X)	4,305	4,786	5,137	5,046	5,060	(NA)	(NA)	(NA)
Local............	(X)	10,914	13,139	14,376	14,037	14,074	(NA)	(NA)	(NA)

NA Not available. X Not applicable. [1] Based on the North American Industry Classification System, 2012. See text, Section 15. [2] Production employees in the goods-producing industries and nonsupervisory employees in service-providing industries. [3] Mining and logging, construction, and manufacturing. [4] Trade, transportation and utilities, information, financial activities, professional and business services, education and health services, leisure and hospitality, other services, and government. [5] Includes other industries, not shown separately.

Source: U.S. Bureau of Labor Statistics, Current Employment Statistics, "Employment, Hours, and Earnings—National," <http://www.bls.gov/ces/data.htm>, accessed September 2015.

Table 652. Women Employees on Nonfarm Payrolls by Major Industry: 1990 to 2014

[51,619 represents 51,619,000. Annual averages of monthly data. For coverage, see headnote, Table 649]

Industry	Women employees (1,000)				Percent of total employees			
	1990	2000	2010	2014	1990	2000	2010	2014
Total nonfarm [1]	**51,619**	**63,396**	**65,016**	**68,633**	**47.1**	**48.0**	**49.9**	**49.4**
Total private	41,764	51,625	52,186	56,148	45.8	46.4	48.4	47.9
Construction	656	846	723	778	12.5	12.5	13.1	12.7
Manufacturing	5,702	5,359	3,268	3,313	32.2	31.0	28.3	27.2
Trade, transportation, and utilities	9,363	10,859	10,007	10,686	41.3	41.4	40.6	40.5
Wholesale trade	1,611	1,827	1,641	1,718	30.6	30.8	30.1	29.5
Retail trade	6,696	7,680	7,226	7,738	50.8	50.3	50.0	50.4
Transportation and warehousing	879	1,202	1,002	1,096	25.3	27.3	23.9	23.6
Utilities	177	151	139	134	24.0	25.1	25.1	24.3
Information	1,324	1,697	1,104	1,099	49.3	46.7	40.8	40.1
Financial activities	4,055	4,697	4,530	4,575	61.3	60.3	58.9	57.3
Professional and business services	5,105	7,680	7,454	8,521	47.1	46.1	44.6	44.6
Professional and technical services	2,209	3,146	3,522	3,882	48.7	46.9	47.3	46.5
Management of companies and enterprises	849	924	939	1,067	50.9	51.4	50.1	49.2
Administrative and waste services	2,048	3,610	2,993	3,572	44.1	44.2	40.4	41.6
Education and health services	8,455	11,700	15,364	16,498	76.7	76.7	77.2	76.8
Educational services	958	1,417	1,929	2,068	56.8	59.3	61.2	60.5
Health care and social assistance	7,496	10,282	13,434	14,430	80.3	80.0	80.3	79.9
Leisure and hospitality	4,829	6,082	6,819	7,643	52.0	51.3	52.3	52.0
Arts, entertainment, and recreation	516	815	886	978	45.6	45.6	46.3	46.5
Accommodation and food services	4,312	5,267	5,933	6,665	52.9	52.3	53.3	52.9
Other services	2,164	2,614	2,820	2,917	50.8	50.6	52.9	52.3
Government	9,855	11,771	12,829	12,486	53.5	56.6	57.0	57.1
Federal	1,378	1,231	1,326	1,207	43.1	43.0	44.5	44.2
State government	2,137	2,464	2,639	2,658	49.6	51.5	51.4	52.5
Local government	6,340	8,076	8,864	8,621	58.1	61.5	61.7	61.3

[1] Includes other industries, not shown separately.

Source: U.S. Bureau of Labor Statistics, Current Employment Statistics, "Employment, Hours, and Earnings–National," <http://www.bls.gov/ces/data.htm>, accessed March 2015.

Table 653. Private Nonfarm Extended Mass Layoff Activity by Industry and Reason for Layoff: 2000 to 2012

[Covers layoffs of at least 31 days duration that involve 50 or more individuals from a single employer. Based on administrative records of unemployment filings and establishment classifications, supplemented with employer confirmation of layoffs, plant closings, and additional employer provided data. See source for more information]

Industry	2012 NAICS code [1]	Extended mass layoff events	Employee separations	Initial unemployment claimants [2]
2000	(X)	4,591	915,962	846,267
2005	(X)	4,881	884,661	834,533
2008	(X)	8,259	1,516,978	1,670,042
2009	(X)	11,824	2,108,202	2,442,000
2010	(X)	7,247	1,257,134	1,415,766
2011	(X)	6,596	1,112,710	1,295,273
Total, 2012	**(X)**	**6,500**	**1,257,212**	**1,336,276**
Mining, quarrying, and gas extraction	21	85	10,717	10,303
Utilities	22	18	3,222	4,060
Construction	23	1,269	167,121	199,811
Manufacturing	31–33	1,050	180,352	186,194
Wholesale trade	42	146	20,759	18,058
Retail trade	44,45	441	107,480	115,213
Transportation and warehousing	48,49	380	77,347	71,038
Information	51	307	128,168	162,701
Finance and Insurance	52	129	25,596	26,002
Real estate and rental and leasing	53	38	8,537	7,488
Professional and technical services	54	318	70,567	75,368
Management of companies and enterprises	55	32	4,753	4,642
Administrative and waste services	56	947	202,435	241,941
Educational services	61	97	12,635	13,300
Health care and social assistance	62	378	55,093	47,348
Arts, entertainment, and recreation	71	242	49,655	36,313
Accommodation and food services	72	484	113,111	97612
Other services	81	124	17,926	17,108
Unclassified	(X)	15	1,738	1,776
Reason for layoff:				
Business demand	(X)	2,345	461,328	583,810
Disaster/safety	(X)	45	7,900	9,484
Financial issues	(X)	418	85,946	77,049
Organizational changes	(X)	313	71,128	51,431
Production specific	(X)	75	14,313	15,179
Seasonal	(X)	2,217	402,445	390,775
Other/miscellaneous	(X)	1,087	214,152	208,548

X Not applicable. [1] Based on North American Industry Classification System, 2012. See text, Section 15. [2] A person who files any notice of unemployment to initiate a request either for a determination of entitlement to and eligibility for compensation, or for a subsequent period of unemployment within a benefit year or period of eligibility.

Source: U.S. Bureau of Labor Statistics, *Extended Mass Layoffs in 2012*, September 2013. See also <http://www.bls.gov/mls/home.htm>.

Table 654. Job Gains and Job Losses of Private Sector Establishments by Industry Sector: 2000 to 2014

[In thousands (16,096 represents 16,096,000). For year ending in March. Based on the Quarterly Census of Employment and Wages (QCEW). Excludes self-employed and certain nonprofit organizations. Minus sign (-) indicates a decrease in employment and comes from either closing establishments or contracting establishments. For more information, see source]

Year and industry	Gross job gains			Gross job losses			Net change [1]
	Total	Expanding establishments	Opening establishments	Total	Contracting establishments	Closing establishments	
2000..................................	16,096	10,618	5,478	13,118	8,284	4,834	2,978
2003..................................	13,191	8,599	4,592	13,923	9,290	4,633	-732
2004..................................	13,307	8,953	4,354	12,428	8,237	4,191	879
2005..................................	13,759	9,403	4,356	11,767	7,672	4,095	1,992
2006..................................	14,019	9,625	4,394	11,438	7,711	3,727	2,581
2007..................................	13,441	9,238	4,203	11,941	8,246	3,695	1,500
2008..................................	12,704	8,714	3,990	12,609	8,772	3,837	95
2009..................................	10,048	6,664	3,384	15,912	11,703	4,209	-5,864
2010..................................	9,985	6,834	3,151	12,683	9,137	3,546	-2,698
2011..................................	11,543	8,288	3,255	9,637	6,618	3,019	1,906
2012..................................	12,085	8,650	3,435	9,492	6,503	2,989	2,593
2013..................................	12,425	8,532	3,893	9,871	6,819	3,052	2,554
2014, Total private.............	**12,281**	**8,697**	**3,584**	**10,002**	**6,936**	**3,066**	**2,279**
Goods producing....................	2,226	1,742	484	1,843	1,358	485	383
Natural resources and mining......	274	205	69	228	164	64	46
Construction.......................	1,123	823	300	890	614	276	233
Manufacturing......................	829	714	115	725	580	145	104
Service providing..................	10,057	6,956	3,101	8,157	5,578	2,579	1,900
Wholesale trade....................	596	448	148	485	320	165	111
Retail trade.......................	1,396	976	420	1,081	765	316	315
Transportation and warehousing....	434	335	99	338	230	108	96
Utilities..........................	28	23	5	29	25	4	-1
Information........................	272	206	66	258	192	66	14
Financial activities..............	741	532	209	693	485	208	48
Professional and business services..	2,537	1,892	645	2,091	1,486	605	446
Education and health services.....	1,642	1,196	446	1,370	942	428	272
Leisure and hospitality...........	1,764	1,024	740	1,367	863	504	397
Other services....................	475	314	161	410	265	145	65

[1] Net change is the difference between total gross job gains and total gross job losses.

Source: U.S. Bureau of Labor Statistics, Business Employment Dynamics, "Annual Business Employment Dynamics Data," <http://www.bls.gov/bdm/bdmann.htm#TOTAL>, accessed February 2015.

Table 655. Private Sector Gross Job Gains and Job Losses by State: 2014

[In thousands (12,288 represents 12,288,000). For year ending in March. Based on the Quarterly Census of Employment and Wages (QCEW). Excludes self-employed and certain nonprofit organizations. Minus sign (-) indicates a decrease in employment and comes from either closing establishments or contracting establishments. For more information, see source]

State	Gross job gains			Gross job losses			Net change [1]	State	Gross job gains			Gross job losses			Net change [1]
	Total	Expanding establishments	Opening establishments	Total	Contracting establishments	Closing establishments			Total	Expanding establishments	Opening establishments	Total	Contracting establishments	Closing establishments	
U.S....	12,288	8,700	3,588	10,012	6,943	3,069	2,276	MO.....	212	153	59	186	132	54	26
AL.......	153	109	45	140	102	38	13	MT.....	37	26	11	34	23	12	3
AK.......	25	19	6	23	17	6	2	NE.....	74	52	22	61	45	16	14
AZ.......	238	171	67	189	131	58	49	NV.....	121	87	35	84	59	25	38
AR.......	92	65	27	87	63	25	5	NH.....	49	36	13	41	29	12	8
CA.......	1,675	1,158	517	1,283	847	436	392	NJ.....	342	231	111	329	223	106	13
CO.......	237	170	67	169	116	53	68	NM.....	68	45	23	64	44	20	4
CT.......	117	88	29	109	83	26	9	NY.....	795	547	248	653	432	220	142
DE.......	37	25	13	29	21	8	8	NC.....	372	268	103	300	209	90	72
DC.......	55	38	18	45	32	12	11	ND.....	47	33	14	34	25	9	13
FL.......	894	566	328	680	404	275	214	OH.....	419	316	103	347	256	92	72
GA.......	417	288	129	311	205	106	106	OK.....	142	93	48	123	86	37	19
HI.......	50	36	14	42	28	13	8	OR.....	156	117	40	115	80	35	42
ID.......	66	42	23	48	32	16	17	PA.....	407	299	108	375	277	99	32
IL.......	478	342	136	410	285	125	68	RI.....	36	26	10	31	22	9	5
IN.......	228	175	54	193	139	54	35	SC.....	175	124	51	126	92	35	48
IA.......	117	85	32	96	71	25	21	SD.....	31	24	8	25	19	6	6
KS.......	120	84	35	97	67	30	23	TN.....	234	175	59	188	136	52	46
KY.......	158	113	46	132	97	34	27	TX.....	1,094	797	298	817	590	227	278
LA.......	194	131	63	161	116	46	33	UT.....	129	94	35	97	71	26	32
ME.......	44	32	12	38	27	11	6	VT.....	23	16	7	21	15	6	2
MD.......	206	144	62	199	141	58	7	VA.....	283	208	75	280	200	80	3
MA.......	257	183	74	215	150	65	42	WA.....	275	198	77	204	147	57	72
MI.......	344	250	93	273	186	87	71	WV.....	56	40	16	61	44	17	-5
MN.......	199	154	46	181	128	53	18	WI.....	193	145	48	164	124	40	29
MS.......	90	63	26	80	58	22	9	WY.....	25	18	7	22	16	5	3

[1] Net change is the difference between total gross job gains and total gross job losses.

Source: U.S. Bureau of Labor Statistics, Business Employment Dynamics, "Annual Business Employment Dynamics Data," <http://www.bls.gov/bdm/bdmann.htm>, accessed August 2015.

Table 656. Hires and Separations Affecting Establishment Payrolls By Industry: 2011 to 2014

[50,283 represents 50,283,000. Hires represent any additions to payrolls, including new and rehired employees, full- and part-time workers, short-term and seasonal workers, etc. Separations represent terminations of employment, including quits, layoffs, and discharges, etc. Based on a monthly survey of private nonfarm establishments and governmental entities]

Industry	Annual hires (1,000)				Annual separations (1,000)			
	2011	2012	2013	2014	2011	2012	2013	2014
Total	**50,283**	**52,367**	**54,241**	**58,657**	**48,227**	**50,047**	**51,783**	**55,524**
Total private industry	47,179	48,916	50,787	55,048	44,757	46,545	48,280	51,992
Mining and logging	339	379	346	407	241	359	330	361
Construction	4,193	3,969	3,844	3,799	3,981	3,855	3,613	3,526
Manufacturing	3,040	2,982	2,895	3,115	2,825	2,808	2,776	2,899
Durable goods	1,771	1,793	1,740	1,838	1,540	1,648	1,649	1,643
Nondurable goods	1,270	1,186	1,151	1,280	1,287	1,158	1,126	1,257
Trade, transportation, and utilities	10,001	10,480	11,153	12,776	9,487	10,067	10,592	12,184
Wholesale trade	1,508	1,558	1,422	1,760	1,386	1,467	1,363	1,654
Retail trade	6,808	6,999	7,810	8,827	6,512	6,832	7,420	8,525
Transportation, warehousing, and utilities	1,683	1,922	1,919	2,187	1,590	1,765	1,809	2,006
Information	742	767	844	926	741	781	802	883
Financial activities	1,882	2,183	2,406	2,322	1,841	2,092	2,320	2,194
Finance and insurance	1,193	1,412	1,580	1,534	1,157	1,351	1,535	1,469
Real estate and rental and leasing	689	771	825	788	684	739	783	728
Professional and business services	10,458	10,604	10,970	12,109	9,871	10,001	10,420	11,412
Education and health services	5,801	6,229	6,463	6,887	5,417	5,750	6,138	6,374
Educational services	947	883	900	992	823	862	863	903
Health care and social assistance	4,856	5,344	5,565	5,896	4,595	4,887	5,274	5,469
Leisure and hospitality	8,510	9,099	9,634	10,469	8,191	8,645	9,131	9,996
Arts, entertainment, and recreation	1,452	1,540	1,569	1,719	1,474	1,451	1,490	1,637
Accommodation and food services	7,057	7,559	8,063	8,749	6,718	7,193	7,641	8,360
Other services	2,216	2,226	2,241	2,238	2,159	2,191	2,158	2,165
Government workers	3,104	3,450	3,453	3,611	3,472	3,501	3,504	3,532
Federal	335	364	368	375	370	384	434	385
State and local	2,769	3,086	3,084	3,237	3,101	3,116	3,068	3,145

Source: U.S. Bureau of Labor Statistics, *Job Openings and Labor Turnover—January 2015*, USDL 15-0385, March 2015. See also <http://www.bls.gov/jlt/news.htm>.

Table 657. Type of Separations Affecting Establishment Payrolls: 2014

[30,522 represents 30,522,000. Covers all private nonfarm establishments. Separations are the total number of terminations of employment occurring at any time during the reference month, and are reported by type of separation—quits, layoffs and discharges, and other separations. Annual rate estimates are computed by dividing annual levels by the Current Employment Statistics (CES) annual average employment level and multiplying that quotient by 100]

Industry	Number (1,000)			Rate (percent) [1]		
	Annual quits level [2]	Annual layoffs and discharge levels [3]	Annual other separations [4]	Annual quits level [2]	Annual layoffs and discharge levels [3]	Annual other separations [4]
Total	**30,522**	**20,418**	**4,584**	**22.0**	**14.7**	**3.3**
Total private industry	28,842	19,347	3,801	24.6	16.5	3.2
Mining and logging	182	144	34	20.3	16.1	3.8
Construction	1,323	2,049	154	21.6	33.4	2.5
Manufacturing	1,450	1,163	288	11.9	9.5	2.4
Durable goods	798	679	164	10.4	8.8	2.1
Nondurable goods	652	483	124	14.5	10.7	2.8
Trade, transportation, and utilities	7,032	3,965	1,187	26.7	15.0	4.5
Wholesale trade	903	616	137	15.5	10.6	2.4
Retail trade	5,153	2,516	854	33.5	16.4	5.6
Transportation, warehousing, and utilities	976	834	196	18.8	16.1	3.8
Information	490	305	89	17.9	11.1	3.2
Financial activities	1,179	650	364	14.8	8.1	4.6
Finance and insurance	758	411	298	12.8	6.9	5.0
Real estate and rental and leasing	421	240	67	20.6	11.7	3.3
Professional and business services	5,614	5,120	676	29.4	26.8	3.5
Education and health services	3,856	2,022	498	18.0	9.4	2.3
Educational services	452	393	60	13.2	11.5	1.8
Health care and social assistance	3,402	1,630	440	18.8	9.0	2.4
Leisure and hospitality	6,468	3,154	375	44.0	21.4	2.5
Arts, entertainment, and recreation	607	989	39	28.8	47.0	1.9
Accommodation and food services	5,861	2,163	332	46.5	17.2	2.6
Other services	1,248	777	141	22.4	13.9	2.5
Government workers	1,679	1,070	783	7.7	4.9	3.6
Federal	125	130	130	4.6	4.8	4.8
State and local	1,555	940	649	8.1	4.9	3.4

[1] As a percent of total employment. [2] Quits are voluntary separations by employees (except for retirements, which are reported as other separations). [3] Layoffs and discharges are involuntary separations initiated by the employer and include layoffs with no intent to rehire; formal layoffs lasting or expected to last more than seven days; discharges resulting from mergers, downsizing, or closings, firings or other discharges for cause; terminations of permanent or short term employees; and terminations of seasonal employees. [4] Other separations include retirements, transfers to other locations, deaths, and separations due to disability.

Source: U.S. Bureau of Labor Statistics, *Job Openings and Labor Turnover—January 2015*, USDL 15-0385, March 2015. See also <http://www.bls.gov/jlt>.

Table 658. Productivity and Related Measures for Selected NAICS Industries: 1987 to 2013 and 2013 to 2014

[For a discussion of productivity measures and methodology, see text, this section and BLS Handbook of Methods, Chapter 11, <http://www.bls.gov/opub/hom/homch11.htm>. Minus sign (-) indicates decrease]

Industry	2012 NAICS code [1]	Average annual percent change [2]							
		1987-2013 [3, 4, 5, 6]				2013-2014			
		Output per hour	Output	Hours	Unit labor costs	Output per hour	Output	Hours	Unit labor costs
Mining........................	21	-0.2	0.7	0.9	4.5	3.9	11.6	7.5	-3.1
Oil and gas extraction..............	211	0.6	0.6	0.1	5.0	11.5	13.4	1.7	-6.1
Mining, except oil and gas...........	212	1.4	0.2	-1.2	1.8	1.2	4.7	3.5	-3.2
Coal mining........................	2121	1.6	-0.6	-2.1	1.3	5.4	6.7	1.2	-8.2
Utilities									
Power generation and supply.........	2211	3.4	2.2	-1.1	0.5	1.5	1.9	0.4	-0.2
Natural gas distribution.............	2212	0.8	-0.5	-1.2	3.8	-1.5	2.8	4.3	3.7
Water, sewage and other systems......	2213	-1.7	0.7	2.5	5.0	0.8	4.5	3.6	-0.6
Manufacturing									
Food...........................	311	1.2	1.5	0.2	1.4	3.0	1.9	-1.0	0.6
Fruit and vegetable preserving and specialty. ...	3114	1.4	1.2	-0.3	1.5	2.4	3.0	0.5	-2.4
Dairy products................	3115	1.8	1.5	-0.4	1.6	5.5	3.0	-2.4	-1.6
Animal slaughtering and processing...........	3116	1.0	1.9	0.9	1.4	-0.8	-1.4	-0.6	3.5
Bakeries and tortilla manufacturing...........	3118	0.4	0.3	-0.1	1.7	4.7	3.3	-1.4	-1.5
Beverages and tobacco products............	312	0.5	0.0	-0.5	1.6	0.1	1.2	1.1	6.4
Textile mills........................	313	3.4	-2.2	-5.5	-0.5	1.6	1.5	0.0	1.2
Apparel........................	315	-0.7	-7.1	-6.4	1.7	1.5	1.2	-0.3	-2.1
Leather and allied products...........	316	1.1	-4.1	-5.1	1.3	18.0	3.5	-12.3	-7.3
Wood products................	321	1.5	-0.1	-1.6	1.5	1.0	4.2	3.1	2.2
Paper and paper products............	322	2.3	0.2	-2.0	1.0	-1.8	-2.5	-0.7	4.1
Converted paper products...........	3222	1.7	0.3	-1.4	1.5	-1.4	-1.6	-0.2	3.3
Printing and related support activities...........	323	1.4	-0.6	-2.0	1.1	-1.2	-0.3	0.9	1.2
Petroleum and coal products...........	324	2.3	1.2	-1.1	2.6	2.7	2.3	-0.4	-0.7
Chemicals........................	325	1.7	1.1	-0.7	1.8	0.9	2.1	1.2	2.2
Pharmaceuticals and medicines..............	3254	-0.3	1.6	1.9	3.7	4.5	1.0	-3.4	5.2
Plastics and rubber products...........	326	2.0	1.4	-0.6	1.1	2.5	6.9	4.3	-3.1
Plastics products................	3261	1.9	1.7	-0.2	1.2	2.7	6.9	4.0	-3.3
Nonmetallic mineral products...........	327	1.3	0.1	-1.2	1.4	1.6	5.7	4.1	-1.5
Primary metals................	331	2.9	0.9	-2.0	0.2	1.4	4.4	3.0	-2.1
Fabricated metal products............	332	1.2	1.0	-0.2	1.5	1.3	4.0	2.6	-0.8
Forging and stamping.............	3321	2.7	1.6	-1.1	0.5	6.8	9.1	2.1	-3.9
Cutlery and hand tools.............	3322	1.2	-1.0	-2.2	1.4	5.0	-4.4	-9.0	7.7
Architectural and structural metals.......	3323	0.6	0.7	0.2	2.2	0.9	3.9	3.0	1.3
Machine shops and threaded products..........	3327	1.9	2.7	0.9	1.2	1.6	4.8	3.1	-1.6
Other fabricated metal products................	3329	0.8	0.2	-0.6	1.7	1.9	4.9	3.0	-4.5
Machinery........................	333	2.4	1.6	-0.7	0.6	3.7	7.0	3.1	-3.5
Agriculture, construction, and mining machinery................	3331	2.5	3.2	0.7	0.4	7.7	9.2	1.3	-6.4
Industrial machinery..............	3332	1.9	0.8	-1.1	0.9	5.6	8.5	2.7	-4.9
Computer and electronic products............	334	10.6	8.0	-2.4	-6.6	4.2	3.8	-0.4	-2.9
Semiconductors and electronic components. ...	3344	15.0	13.1	-1.6	-10.7	9.8	8.0	-1.6	-5.4
Electronic instruments.............	3345	3.6	1.6	-1.9	0.1	8.2	5.9	-2.1	-6.3
Electrical equipment and appliances..............	335	2.2	0.0	-2.2	1.0	3.2	1.6	-1.6	-0.1
Transportation equipment................	336	3.1	1.9	-1.2	-0.5	2.4	5.9	3.4	-1.3
Motor vehicles................	3361	3.8	1.8	-1.9	-0.9	-3.3	8.5	12.3	-0.7
Motor vehicle parts................	3363	3.3	2.7	-0.6	-1.7	1.9	6.1	4.0	0.6
Ship and boat building.............	3366	2.0	0.9	-1.0	1.7	6.7	11.4	4.4	-7.0
Furniture and related products............	337	1.7	-0.2	-1.9	1.4	1.4	7.0	5.5	-2.2
Household and institutional furniture............	3371	1.4	-0.9	-2.2	1.7	2.8	11.4	8.4	-4.9
Miscellaneous manufacturing............	339	2.5	2.1	-0.4	1.4	3.3	4.5	1.1	-0.8
Medical equipment and supplies................	3391	3.1	4.0	0.8	0.9	4.2	6.2	1.9	-1.3
Wholesale trade................	42	3.1	3.4	0.3	0.7	2.6	4.3	1.7	0.5
Durable goods................	423	5.0	4.9	0.0	-1.0	2.4	4.7	2.3	-0.2
Nondurable goods................	424	1.4	1.5	0.1	2.6	3.1	4.1	1.0	1.2
Electronic markets and agents and brokers.......	425	1.4	3.8	2.4	0.9	2.4	3.6	1.2	1.6
Retail trade................	44-45	2.9	3.3	0.4	-0.1	1.9	3.9	2.0	0.8
Motor vehicle and parts dealers................	441	2.1	2.7	0.6	0.6	3.7	7.5	3.7	-1.1
Automobile dealers................	4411	2.2	2.8	0.6	0.5	4.4	8.1	3.6	-0.6
Other motor vehicle dealers.............	4412	2.8	3.3	0.6	0.9	3.8	8.4	4.5	-2.8
Auto parts, accessories, and tire stores..........	4413	1.0	1.7	0.7	1.4	-2.4	1.1	3.6	1.8
Furniture and home furnishings stores...........	442	4.0	3.5	-0.5	-1.1	-0.2	6.1	6.4	1.0
Furniture stores................	4421	3.4	2.8	-0.5	-0.7	1.7	7.5	5.8	-1.0
Home furnishings stores................	4422	4.9	4.4	-0.5	-1.7	-2.4	4.5	7.0	3.3
Electronics and appliance stores................	443	12.4	13.5	0.9	-8.6	5.7	9.3	3.5	-6.5
Building material and garden supply stores.......	444	2.6	3.2	0.6	-0.1	3.6	4.6	0.9	-0.5
Building material and supplies dealers...........	4441	2.3	3.1	0.8	0.2	4.4	4.0	-0.4	-1.1
Lawn and garden equipment and supplies stores...........	4442	4.4	4.1	-0.3	-2.0	-1.1	8.1	9.4	4.0
Food and beverage stores................	445	0.4	0.3	-0.1	2.5	-1.3	1.3	2.7	3.1
Grocery stores................	4451	0.2	0.2	0.0	2.7	-2.0	0.9	2.9	3.5
Specialty food stores................	4452	0.4	-0.2	-0.6	1.6	3.0	6.7	3.5	0.6
Beer, wine and liquor stores................	4453	2.1	1.1	-0.9	0.8	6.7	3.7	-2.9	-3.8
Health and personal care stores................	446	2.0	3.2	1.1	1.4	5.0	3.9	-1.0	-0.8
Gasoline stations................	447	1.6	1.0	-0.6	1.2	-0.4	-0.1	0.3	4.1
Clothing and clothing accessories stores..........	448	4.3	4.0	-0.3	-1.3	1.5	2.3	0.8	0.8
Clothing stores................	4481	4.6	4.4	-0.1	-1.6	4.7	2.0	-2.6	-0.6
Shoe stores................	4482	3.0	2.2	-0.8	-0.5	-7.2	2.9	10.8	2.4
Jewelry, luggage, and leather goods stores.....	4483	3.9	3.2	-0.7	-0.5	-2.9	3.4	6.5	4.4
Sporting goods, hobby, book, and music stores...	451	4.0	3.9	0.0	-0.9	-2.1	1.3	3.4	2.6
Sporting goods and musical instrument stores..	4511	4.6	5.2	0.5	-1.5	-1.0	1.7	2.7	2.8

See footnotes at end of table.

Table 658. Productivity and Related Measures for Selected NAICS Industries: 1987 to 2013 and 2013 to 2014-Continued.

See headnote on page 430.

Industry	2012 NAICS code [1]	Average annual percent change [2]							
		1987-2013 [3,4,5,6]				2013-2014			
		Output per hour	Output	Hours	Unit labor costs	Output per hour	Output	Hours	Unit labor costs
Book, periodical, and music stores...............	4512	2.4	0.5	-1.9	0.6	-8.2	-1.0	7.8	1.0
General merchandise stores.........................	452	3.2	4.6	1.4	-1.1	2.8	2.6	-0.2	0.5
Department stores.................................	4521	0.8	1.1	0.4	0.5	1.2	-0.8	-2.0	2.0
Other general merchandise stores.............	4529	5.6	8.2	2.5	-2.5	2.6	3.8	1.2	0.6
Miscellaneous store retailers.......................	453	3.5	3.4	-0.2	-1.4	0.3	2.6	2.3	2.5
Florists..	4531	2.7	-0.4	-3.0	0.1	-11.7	4.4	18.2	9.2
Office supplies, stationery and gift stores........	4532	5.8	4.8	-0.9	-3.1	3.7	0.9	-2.7	-2.8
Used merchandise stores........................	4533	4.6	6.0	1.4	-2.2	2.8	4.0	1.2	2.8
Other miscellaneous store retailers..............	4539	1.4	2.3	1.0	-0.2	-0.5	3.0	3.4	5.2
Nonstore retailers.....................................	454	8.5	8.9	0.3	-4.6	-1.8	6.3	8.2	4.6
Electronic shopping and mail-order houses.....	4541	10.6	14.6	3.6	-6.1	-1.3	8.5	9.9	6.3
Vending machine operators.....................	4542	0.9	-1.9	-2.8	2.3	-6.8	-1.7	5.5	5.4
Direct selling establishments....................	4543	3.0	1.2	-1.7	-0.2	-8.2	-2.7	6.1	6.9
Transportation and warehousing:									
Air transportation......................................	481	3.3	2.6	-0.8	0.3	-0.2	2.7	2.9	4.0
Line-haul railroads....................................	482111	3.7	2.0	-1.7	-0.5	-1.2	0.3	1.5	7.0
Truck transportation.................................	484	0.6	1.9	1.3	0.8	3.5	7.5	3.9	-1.1
General freight trucking..........................	4841	1.2	2.3	1.1	0.8	3.2	7.2	3.9	-1.7
Used household and office goods moving.......	48421	-1.4	-0.6	0.9	2.8	(NA)	(NA)	(NA)	(NA)
Postal service...	491	0.7	-0.6	-1.3	3.2	-1.6	-2.4	-0.7	4.3
Couriers and messengers..........................	492	-1.7	0.4	2.1	4.1	-6.5	-1.4	5.4	6.3
Warehousing and storage...........................	493	2.9	6.3	3.3	-0.9	0.6	2.0	1.3	3.9
General warehousing and storage...............	49311	4.2	7.7	3.3	-1.7	(NA)	(NA)	(NA)	(NA)
Refrigerated warehousing and storage..........	49312	0.0	2.9	2.9	1.3	(NA)	(NA)	(NA)	(NA)
Information									
Publishing..	511	3.8	3.3	-0.4	1.4	5.7	3.2	-2.3	3.4
Newspaper, book, and directory publishers.....	5111	-0.3	-2.5	-2.2	4.3	(NA)	(NA)	(NA)	(NA)
Software publishers...............................	5112	12.2	18.9	5.9	-6.5	6.7	8.4	1.5	2.7
Motion picture and video exhibition..............	51213	1.6	1.6	0.0	1.8	(NA)	(NA)	(NA)	(NA)
Broadcasting, except Internet......................	515	2.4	2.7	0.3	1.8	8.9	5.6	-3.0	-4.0
Radio and television broadcasting...............	5151	1.7	1.2	-0.4	2.1	9.5	6.1	-3.1	1.3
Cable and other subscription programming.....	5152	3.7	6.9	3.1	2.8	8.3	5.3	-2.8	-15.8
Wired telecommunications carriers...............	5171	3.7	2.8	-0.8	-0.9	-0.1	0.8	0.9	0.5
Wireless telecommunications carriers............	5172	11.1	19.8	7.8	-6.6	4.2	9.7	5.3	-4.9
Finance and Insurance									
Commercial banking.................................	52211	3.5	3.4	-0.1	1.9	(NA)	(NA)	(NA)	(NA)
Real Estate and Rental and Leasing									
Passenger car rental.................................	532111	2.1	2.6	0.5	2.0	(NA)	(NA)	(NA)	(NA)
Truck, trailer and RV rental and leasing..........	53212	2.5	2.2	-0.3	1.0	1.0	8.8	7.7	0.3
Video tape and disc rental..........................	53223	6.3	-0.2	-6.1	-1.8	(NA)	(NA)	(NA)	(NA)
Professional and Technical Services									
Architectural services................................	54131	1.4	2.0	0.6	2.1	(NA)	(NA)	(NA)	(NA)
Engineering services.................................	54133	1.2	2.9	1.7	3.1	-8.3	-6.7	1.8	10.6
Advertising agencies.................................	54181	2.2	2.6	0.4	2.0	(NA)	(NA)	(NA)	(NA)
Photography studios, portrait.......................	541921	0.2	1.0	0.8	2.3	(NA)	(NA)	(NA)	(NA)
Administrative and Waste Services									
Employment placement agencies..................	56131	4.3	5.3	0.9	0.1	(NA)	(NA)	(NA)	(NA)
Travel arrangement and reservation services....	5615	5.7	2.7	-2.8	-1.0	6.2	1.9	-4.1	4.6
Janitorial services....................................	56172	1.9	3.6	1.6	1.5	(NA)	(NA)	(NA)	(NA)
Health Care and Social Assistance									
Medical and diagnostic laboratories...............	6215	2.4	5.7	3.2	0.3	1.3	1.8	0.4	1.6
Arts, Entertainment, and Recreation									
Amusement and theme parks.......................	71311	-1.3	1.7	3.1	4.3	(NA)	(NA)	(NA)	(NA)
Fitness and recreational sports centers...........	71394	4.4	4.0	-0.4	-1.2	(NA)	(NA)	(NA)	(NA)
Bowling centers.......................................	71395	-0.1	-1.4	-1.3	3.0	(NA)	(NA)	(NA)	(NA)
Accommodation and food services.................	72	0.8	2.2	1.4	2.7	(NA)	(NA)	(NA)	(NA)
Accommodation......................................	721	2.2	2.7	0.6	1.7	(NA)	(NA)	(NA)	(NA)
Traveler accommodation.........................	7211	2.2	2.8	0.6	1.7	(NA)	(NA)	(NA)	(NA)
Food services and drinking places.................	722	0.4	2.0	1.6	3.1	0.3	3.7	3.3	1.6
Special food services.............................	7223	1.3	2.3	1.0	1.3	-4.7	4.0	9.0	-1.6
Drinking places, alcoholic beverages............	7224	-0.4	-0.7	-0.4	3.3	0.0	1.3	1.4	2.2
Restaurants and other eating places.............	72251	0.4	2.1	1.7	3.3	0.9	3.8	2.9	2.0
Other Services									
Automotive repair and maintenance...............	8111	0.9	1.2	0.3	2.4	-1.2	0.8	2.0	5.2
Reupholstery and furniture repair..................	81142	-0.6	-3.0	-2.4	3.7	(NA)	(NA)	(NA)	(NA)
Personal care services...............................	8121	2.0	3.3	1.2	1.9	(NA)	(NA)	(NA)	(NA)
Funeral homes and funeral services...............	81221	-0.6	-0.4	0.2	4.3	(NA)	(NA)	(NA)	(NA)
Dry cleaning and laundry services.................	8123	1.7	0.7	-1.0	1.8	7.1	6.3	-0.7	-0.9
Coin-operated laundries and drycleaners.........	81231	2.6	0.3	-2.3	2.1	(NA)	(NA)	(NA)	(NA)
Drycleaning and laundry services..................	81232	0.7	-1.2	-1.8	2.2	(NA)	(NA)	(NA)	(NA)
Photofinishing..	81292	1.9	-4.8	-6.6	2.4	(NA)	(NA)	(NA)	(NA)

[1] North American Industry Classification System, 2012 (NAICS); see text, Section 15. [2] Average annual percent changes based on compound rate formula. Rates of change are calculated using index numbers to three decimal places. [3] For NAICS industries, 484, 4841, 48411, 4931, 49311, and 49312, annual percent changes are for 1992-2013. [4] For NAICS industries 561311 and 6215, average annual percent changes are for 1994-2013. [5] For NAICS industry 5615, average annual percent change is for 1997-2013. [6] For NAICS industry 71394 and 71394 average annual percent change is for 2002-2013.

Source: U.S. Bureau of Labor Statistics. Labor Productivity and Costs, "Productivity and Costs by Industry," <http://www.bls.gov/lpc/data.htm>, accessed September 2015.

Table 659. Productivity and Related Measures: 1970 to 2014

[See text, this section. Minus sign (-) indicates decrease]

Item	1970	1980	1990	2000	2010	2011	2012	2013	2014
INDEXES (2009=100)									
Output per hour, business sector..................	44.6	53.4	64.1	79.9	103.3	103.4	104.1	104.6	105.2
Nonfarm business.......................	46.1	54.8	64.7	80.2	103.3	103.5	104.4	104.4	105.2
Manufacturing.......................	(NA)	(NA)	50.3	75.0	110.6	116.8	117.7	118.5	120.0
Output, [1] business sector......................	29.5	41.9	59.3	87.3	103.2	105.3	108.4	110.6	113.9
Nonfarm business.......................	29.6	42.1	59.4	87.5	103.2	105.5	108.8	110.6	114.0
Manufacturing.......................	(NA)	(NA)	75.6	111.5	110.6	119.2	122.8	124.6	128.3
Hours, [2] business sector......................	66.3	78.4	92.5	109.3	99.9	101.9	104.1	105.7	108.3
Nonfarm business.......................	64.3	76.8	91.8	109.0	99.9	101.9	104.1	105.9	108.4
Manufacturing.......................	(NA)	(NA)	150.4	148.7	100.0	102.1	104.4	105.2	106.9
Compensation per hour, [3] business sector.......	12.9	29.1	49.7	73.9	101.9	104.1	107.0	108.3	111.1
Nonfarm business.......................	13.0	29.4	49.9	74.0	102.0	104.2	107.0	108.2	111.1
Manufacturing.......................	(NA)	(NA)	50.1	73.3	101.2	103.0	104.8	105.0	107.9
Real hourly compensation, [3] business sector....	65.0	72.2	79.1	92.0	100.2	99.3	100.0	99.7	100.7
Nonfarm business.......................	65.7	73.0	79.5	92.3	100.3	99.4	100.0	99.6	100.7
Manufacturing.......................	(NA)	(NA)	79.8	91.3	99.6	98.3	97.9	96.8	97.8
Unit labor costs, [4] business sector..............	28.9	54.5	77.6	92.4	98.6	100.7	102.7	103.6	105.6
Nonfarm business.......................	28.3	53.7	77.2	92.3	98.7	100.7	102.5	103.6	105.7
Manufacturing.......................	(NA)	(NA)	99.7	97.8	91.5	88.2	89.1	88.7	89.9
ANNUAL PERCENT CHANGE [5]									
Output per hour, business sector..................	2.0	-0.1	2.2	3.4	3.3	0.1	0.7	0.4	0.6
Nonfarm business.......................	1.5	-0.1	1.9	3.3	3.3	0.2	0.9	0.0	0.7
Manufacturing.......................	(NA)	(NA)	3.0	7.1	10.6	5.6	0.7	0.7	1.3
Output, [1] business sector......................	-0.1	-0.9	1.6	4.5	3.2	2.1	2.9	2.0	3.0
Nonfarm business.......................	-0.1	-0.9	1.5	4.4	3.2	2.2	3.1	1.7	3.0
Manufacturing.......................	(NA)	(NA)	0.5	5.7	10.6	7.8	3.0	1.5	2.9
Hours, [2] business sector......................	-2.0	-0.9	-0.6	1.0	-0.1	2.0	2.2	1.6	2.4
Nonfarm business.......................	-1.6	-0.8	-0.4	1.0	-0.1	2.0	2.2	1.7	2.3
Manufacturing.......................	(NA)	(NA)	-2.5	-1.3	0.0	2.1	2.3	0.8	1.6
Compensation per hour, [3] business sector.......	7.5	10.7	6.5	7.3	1.9	2.2	2.8	1.2	2.6
Nonfarm business.......................	7.0	10.7	6.2	7.4	2.0	2.2	2.7	1.1	2.7
Manufacturing.......................	(NA)	(NA)	5.0	7.6	1.2	1.7	1.8	0.2	2.7
Real hourly compensation, [3] business sector....	1.7	-0.4	1.5	3.8	0.2	-1.0	0.7	-0.2	1.0
Nonfarm business.......................	1.2	-0.4	1.2	3.9	0.3	-0.9	0.6	-0.4	1.1
Manufacturing.......................	(NA)	(NA)	–	4.0	-0.4	-1.4	-0.3	-1.2	1.0
Unit labor costs, [4] business sector..............	5.4	10.8	4.2	3.8	-1.4	2.1	2.0	0.8	2.0
Nonfarm business.......................	5.4	10.8	4.2	4.0	-1.3	2.1	1.7	1.1	2.0
Manufacturing.......................	(NA)	(NA)	1.9	0.4	-8.5	-3.6	1.0	-0.5	1.4

– Represents or rounds to zero. NA Not available. [1] Refers to gross sectoral product, a chain–type, current–weighted index. [2] Hours at work of all persons engaged in the business and nonfarm business sectors (employees, proprietors, and unpaid family workers), and employees' and proprietors' hours in manufacturing. [3] Wages and salaries of employees plus employers' contributions for social insurance and private benefit plans. Also includes an estimate of same for self-employed. Real compensation deflated by the Consumer Price Index research series; see text, Section 14. [4] Hourly compensation divided by output per hour. [5] All changes are from the immediate prior year.

Source: U.S. Bureau of Labor Statistics, Labor Productivity and Costs, "Major Sector Productivity and Costs," <http://www.bls.gov/lpc/home.htm>, accessed September 2015.

Table 660. Employed Persons and Average Hours Worked Per Day at Workplace and at Home: 2014

[153,681 represents 153,681,000. Civilian noninstitutionalized population 15 years old and over, except as indicated. Includes work at main job and any other jobs. Excludes travel related to work. Based on the American Time Use Survey]

Characteristic	Total employed (1,000)	Employed persons who worked on an average day [1]								
		Total			Worked at workplace			Worked at home [2]		
		Number (1,000)	Percent of employed	Hours of work	Number (1,000)	Percent of those who worked	Hours of work	Number (1,000)	Percent of those who worked	Hours of work
Total.....................	**153,681**	**105,658**	**68.8**	**7.75**	**89,796**	**85.0**	**7.95**	**24,354**	**23.1**	**3.17**
Work status: [3]										
Full-time workers [4]........	120,531	87,562	72.6	8.18	75,443	86.2	8.28	20,395	23.3	3.32
Part-time workers [4].......	33,151	18,096	54.6	5.68	14,353	79.3	6.23	3,959	21.9	2.39
Male [3]......................	82,273	57,877	70.3	8.14	48,945	84.6	8.29	13,765	23.8	3.41
Full-time workers [4]........	69,626	51,309	73.7	8.43	43,787	85.3	8.52	12,233	23.8	3.51
Part-time workers [4].......	12,647	6,568	51.9	5.86	5,157	78.5	6.31	1,533	23.3	2.56
Female [3]......................	71,408	47,782	66.9	7.28	40,851	85.5	7.56	10,589	22.2	2.86
Full-time workers [4]........	50,905	36,254	71.2	7.82	31,656	87.3	7.96	8,162	22.5	3.04
Part-time workers [4].......	20,503	11,528	56.2	5.58	9,195	79.8	6.18	2,427	21.1	2.28
Jobholding status:										
Single jobholders.........	139,983	94,548	67.5	7.71	81,032	85.7	7.94	20,282	21.5	3.09
Multiple jobholders........	13,698	11,110	81.1	8.05	8,764	78.9	8.13	4,072	36.6	3.56
Educational attainment: [5]										
Less than high school....	8,384	6,085	72.6	7.84	5,422	89.1	7.91	701	11.5	3.54
High school diploma [6]....	36,333	24,818	68.3	8.08	22,587	91.0	8.06	3,413	13.8	4.07
Some college..............	34,139	22,462	65.8	8.24	20,266	90.2	8.36	3,939	17.5	3.10
Bachelor's degree or higher....................	52,215	38,638	74.0	7.50	28,676	74.2	7.96	15,098	39.1	3.10

[1] Individuals may have worked at more than one location. [2] "Working at home" includes any time persons did work at home and is not restricted to persons whose usual workplace is their home. [3] Includes workers whose hours vary. [4] Full-time workers usually worked 35 or more hours per week at all jobs combined; part-time workers fewer than 35 hours per week. [5] For those 25 years old and over. [6] Includes persons with a high school diploma or equivalent.

Source: U.S. Bureau of Labor Statistics, American Time Use Survey—2014 Results, USDL 15-1236, June 2015. See also <http://www.bls.gov/tus/home.htm#news>.

Table 661. Annual Total Compensation and Wages and Salary Accruals Per Full-Time Equivalent Employee by Industry: 2000 to 2014

[In dollars. Compensation is equal to the sum of wages and salaries and of supplements to wages and salaries; supplements are made on behalf of employees but are not included in regular wage payments to employees, such as contributions for employee pension and insurance funds, and employer contributions for government social insurance. Wages and salaries consists of cash remuneration of labor, including sick or vacation pay, severance pay, commissions, tips, and bonuses. Based on the 2002 North American Industry Classification System (NAICS); see text, Section 15]

Industry	Total annual compensation				Annual salary and wages			
	2000	2010	2013	2014	2000	2010	2013	2014
Compensation of employees................	**47,619**	**66,472**	**70,361**	**71,161**	**39,238**	**53,247**	**56,628**	**57,534**
Domestic industries.................................	47,520	66,085	69,862	70,653	39,166	52,951	56,240	57,137
Private industries.................................	46,136	62,414	66,392	67,246	38,862	51,906	55,416	56,350
Agriculture, forestry, fishing, and hunting........	25,875	37,525	41,749	44,075	22,146	31,058	34,547	36,190
Mining.................................	70,434	107,698	117,438	135,003	58,134	91,870	99,936	116,022
Utilities.................................	84,821	123,870	133,854	137,055	64,772	89,595	98,720	101,545
Construction.................................	46,190	63,590	67,269	67,491	38,551	52,753	55,996	56,217
Manufacturing.................................	54,167	75,493	79,131	81,347	43,957	60,018	63,575	65,466
Wholesale trade.................................	59,068	78,047	84,199	84,981	50,896	67,163	72,390	73,078
Retail trade.................................	31,224	38,457	40,401	36,650	26,589	32,029	33,518	30,614
Transportation and warehousing.................	48,462	62,399	66,505	73,240	39,055	49,710	53,337	60,180
Information.................................	72,135	98,949	112,901	118,678	62,571	81,295	94,357	98,779
Finance and insurance.................................	76,234	104,096	112,003	118,007	64,574	88,166	95,437	100,734
Real estate and rental and leasing...............	43,235	57,905	63,452	66,113	37,150	49,081	54,638	57,255
Professional, scientific, and technical services..	71,592	95,328	102,746	106,020	62,472	82,524	88,774	92,084
Management of companies and enterprises [1]...	90,766	126,733	139,242	143,809	74,253	103,874	117,196	123,282
Administrative and waste management services.................................	28,921	44,875	46,493	47,627	25,035	37,369	39,238	40,047
Educational services.................................	34,164	50,674	54,254	56,201	29,244	41,324	43,831	44,628
Health care and social assistance...............	42,009	59,635	61,844	62,468	35,249	48,993	50,523	51,373
Arts, entertainment, and recreation...............	37,384	49,764	53,027	54,320	32,482	42,715	45,127	46,229
Accommodation and food services..............	20,819	27,955	29,852	30,839	18,045	24,133	25,629	26,451
Other services, except government...............	30,412	41,703	45,416	46,061	25,990	35,857	38,991	39,737
Government.................................	55,070	83,990	88,469	89,433	40,824	58,045	60,661	61,478
Federal.................................	61,449	105,049	108,795	111,209	46,749	74,665	76,006	77,856
State and local.................................	53,288	78,242	83,008	83,755	39,169	53,509	56,538	57,208

[1] Consists of offices of bank and other holding companies and of corporate, subsidiary, and regional managing offices.

Source: U.S. Bureau of Economic Analysis, National Income and Product Accounts Tables, "Table 6.2D. Compensation of Employees by Industry," "Table 6.5D. Full-Time Equivalent Employees by Industry," and "Table 6.6D. Wage and Salary Accruals Per Full-Time Equivalent Employee by Industry," <http://www.bea.gov/itable/>, accessed August 2015.

Table 662. Average Hourly and Weekly Earnings by Private Industry Group: 2000 to 2014

[In dollars. Average earnings include overtime. Data are for production and nonsupervisory employees. See headnote, Table 649]

Private industry group	Current dollars					Constant (1982–84) dollars [1]				
	2000	2010	2012	2013	2014	2000	2010	2012	2013	2014
AVERAGE HOURLY EARNINGS										
Total private.................................	**14.02**	**19.05**	**19.74**	**20.13**	**20.61**	**8.30**	**8.90**	**8.73**	**8.78**	**8.85**
Mining and logging.........................	16.55	23.82	25.79	26.80	26.85	9.80	11.13	11.40	11.69	11.53
Construction.................................	17.48	23.22	23.97	24.22	24.67	10.35	10.85	10.60	10.56	10.60
Manufacturing.................................	14.32	18.61	19.08	19.30	19.56	8.48	8.70	8.43	8.42	8.40
Trade, transportation, and utilities [2]........	13.31	16.82	17.43	17.74	18.27	7.88	7.86	7.70	7.74	7.85
Information.................................	19.07	25.87	27.04	27.98	28.66	11.29	12.09	11.95	12.20	12.31
Financial activities [2].........................	15.04	21.55	22.82	23.87	24.71	8.90	10.07	10.09	10.41	10.62
Professional and business services [2].....	15.52	22.78	23.29	23.72	24.28	9.19	10.65	10.29	10.34	10.43
Education and health services [2]...........	13.91	19.98	20.94	21.29	21.65	8.24	9.34	9.26	9.28	9.30
Leisure and hospitality [2]....................	8.32	11.31	11.62	11.78	12.09	4.93	5.29	5.14	5.14	5.19
Other services.................................	12.73	17.06	17.59	18.00	18.52	7.54	7.97	7.78	7.85	7.96
AVERAGE WEEKLY EARNINGS										
Total private.................................	**481**	**636**	**666**	**678**	**695**	**285**	**297**	**294**	**296**	**299**
Mining and logging.........................	735	1,063	1,202	1,230	1,271	435	497	531	536	546
Construction.................................	686	892	942	959	977	406	417	416	418	420
Manufacturing.................................	591	765	795	807	822	350	358	351	352	353
Trade, transportation, and utilities.........	450	560	589	597	614	266	262	260	261	264
Information.................................	701	940	974	1,004	1,030	415	439	430	438	442
Financial activities [2].........................	540	780	840	875	908	320	365	371	382	390
Professional and business services [2].....	535	799	823	839	864	317	373	364	366	371
Education and health services [2]...........	448	641	676	683	692	265	299	299	298	297
Leisure and hospitality [2]....................	217	281	291	294	304	129	131	128	128	131
Other services.................................	413	524	539	554	569	245	245	238	241	244

[1] Earnings in current dollars divided by the Consumer Price Index (CPI-W) on a 1982–84 base; see text, Section 14. [2] For composition of industries, see Table 644.

Source: U.S. Bureau of Labor Statistics, Current Employment Statistics, "Employment, Hours, and Earnings—National," <http://www.bls.gov/ces/data.htm>, accessed September 2015.

Table 663. Employment and Wages of Private Sector and Government Employees: 2000 to 2013

[7,879 represents 7,879,000. Based on federal-state cooperative program, The Quarterly Census of Employment and Wages (QCEW), also referenced as ES-202. Includes workers covered by state unemployment insurance laws and for federal civilian workers covered by unemployment compensation for federal employees, approximately 97 percent of employees on nonfarm payrolls in 2013. Excludes most agricultural workers on small farms, all Armed Forces, elected officials in most states, railroad employees, most domestic workers, most student workers at school, value of meals and lodging, and tips and other gratuities]

Employment and wages	Unit	2000	2008	2009	2010	2011	2012	2013
Establishments:								
Total	1,000	7,879	9,082	9,003	8,993	9,073	9,122	9,206
Excluding federal	1,000	7,829	9,018	8,938	8,926	9,006	9,057	9,144
Private	1,000	7,622	8,789	8,709	8,696	8,776	8,826	8,912
State government	1,000	65	68	67	67	66	66	66
Local governments	1,000	141	161	161	164	164	164	165
Federal government	1,000	50	64	66	67	67	65	62
Average annual employment:								
Total	1,000	129,877	134,806	128,608	127,820	129,411	131,696	133,968
Excluding federal	1,000	127,006	132,044	125,781	124,840	126,548	128,876	131,198
Private	1,000	110,015	113,189	106,947	106,201	108,185	110,646	112,958
State government	1,000	4,370	4,643	4,640	4,606	4,554	4,524	4,525
Local governments	1,000	12,620	14,212	14,194	14,032	13,809	13,706	13,714
Federal government	1,000	2,871	2,762	2,827	2,981	2,863	2,821	2,771
Annual wages:								
Total	Bil. dol.	4,588	6,142	5,859	5,976	6,217	6,491	6,673
Excluding federal	Bil. dol.	4,455	5,959	5,668	5,769	6,008	6,284	6,471
Private	Bil. dol.	3,888	5,135	4,829	4,934	5,173	5,444	5,614
State government	Bil. dol.	159	223	226	226	229	232	238
Local governments	Bil. dol.	409	601	612	610	607	608	619
Federal government	Bil. dol.	133	183	192	206	209	207	202
Average annual wage per employee:								
Total	Dol.	35,323	45,563	45,559	46,751	48,043	49,289	49,808
Excluding federal	Dol.	35,077	45,129	45,060	46,215	47,478	48,763	49,320
Private	Dol.	35,337	45,371	45,155	46,455	47,815	49,200	49,701
State government	Dol.	36,296	47,980	48,742	48,960	50,252	51,366	52,544
Local governments	Dol.	32,387	42,274	43,140	43,493	43,926	44,373	45,115
Federal government	Dol.	46,228	66,293	67,756	69,198	73,001	73,340	72,903
Average weekly wage per employee:								
Total	Dol.	679	876	876	899	924	948	958
Excluding federal	Dol.	675	868	867	889	913	938	948
Private	Dol.	680	873	868	893	920	946	956
State government	Dol.	698	923	937	942	966	988	1,010
Local governments	Dol.	623	813	830	836	845	853	868
Federal government	Dol.	889	1,275	1,303	1,331	1,404	1,410	1,402

Source: U.S. Bureau of Labor Statistics, Quarterly Census of Employment and Wages, "Employment and Wages Online Annual Averages, 2013," and earlier releases, <http://www.bls.gov/cew/>, accessed February 2015.

Table 664. Average Annual Wage, by State: 2012 and 2013

[In dollars, except percent change. See headnote, Table 663]

State/area	Average wage per employee 2012	Average wage per employee 2013	Percent change, 2012–2013	State/area	Average wage per employee 2012	Average wage per employee 2013	Percent change, 2012–2013
United States	**49,289**	**49,808**	**1.05**	Montana	37,096	37,575	1.29
Alabama	41,990	42,276	0.68	Nebraska	39,268	39,965	1.77
Alaska	50,614	51,566	1.88	Nevada	43,667	44,119	1.04
Arizona	45,593	45,921	0.72	New Hampshire	48,272	48,963	1.43
Arkansas	38,226	38,941	1.87	New Jersey	58,644	59,467	1.40
California	56,784	57,111	0.58	New Mexico	40,698	40,809	0.27
Colorado	50,563	50,873	0.61	New York	62,669	63,089	0.67
Connecticut	62,085	62,357	0.44	North Carolina	43,110	43,795	1.59
Delaware	51,734	52,040	0.59	North Dakota	45,909	47,779	4.07
District of Columbia	82,783	83,054	0.33	Ohio	44,244	44,671	0.97
Florida	43,211	43,649	1.01	Oklahoma	41,633	42,457	1.98
Georgia	46,267	46,760	1.07	Oregon	44,258	45,019	1.72
Hawaii	43,385	43,845	1.06	Pennsylvania	48,397	49,077	1.41
Idaho	36,152	36,836	1.89	Rhode Island	46,716	47,732	2.17
Illinois	52,194	52,590	0.76	South Carolina	39,286	39,792	1.29
Indiana	41,240	41,660	1.02	South Dakota	36,534	37,225	1.89
Iowa	40,343	41,107	1.89	Tennessee	43,961	44,091	0.30
Kansas	41,118	41,548	1.05	Texas	50,579	51,201	1.23
Kentucky	40,451	40,793	0.85	Utah	41,301	41,792	1.19
Louisiana	43,300	44,008	1.64	Vermont	40,967	42,043	2.63
Maine	38,606	39,279	1.74	Virginia	51,646	51,918	0.53
Maryland	54,035	54,052	0.03	Washington	51,962	53,050	2.09
Massachusetts	60,898	61,790	1.46	West Virginia	39,727	40,201	1.19
Michigan	46,720	47,131	0.88	Wisconsin	41,966	42,777	1.93
Minnesota	49,349	50,116	1.55	Wyoming	44,580	44,972	0.88
Mississippi	35,875	36,455	1.62	Puerto Rico	26,948	26,905	-0.16
Missouri	42,695	43,066	0.87	Virgin Islands	38,862	37,611	-3.22

Source: U.S. Bureau of Labor Statistics, Quarterly Census of Employment and Wages, "Employment and Wages Online Annual Averages, 2013," and earlier editions, <http://www.bls.gov/cew/home.htm>, accessed February 2015.

Table 665. Full-Time Wage and Salary Workers—Number and Earnings: 2010 to 2014

[99,531 represents 99,531,000. Earnings shown in current dollars; data represent annual averages of usual weekly earnings. Full time workers are those who usually worked 35 hours or more at all jobs combined. Based on the Current Population Survey; see text, Section 1 and Appendix III. For definition of median, see Guide to Tabular Presentation]

Characteristic	Number of workers (1,000)			Median weekly earnings (dollars)		
	2010	2013	2014	2010	2013	2014
All workers [1]	**99,531**	**104,262**	**106,526**	**747**	**776**	**791**
Male	55,059	57,994	59,450	824	860	871
Female	44,472	46,268	47,076	669	706	719
White [2]	80,656	82,672	84,177	765	802	816
Black [2]	11,658	12,439	12,910	611	629	639
Asian [2]	4,946	6,073	6,273	855	942	953
Hispanic [3]	14,837	16,859	17,475	535	578	594
OCCUPATION						
Management, professional and related occupations	39,145	41,820	43,016	1,063	1,132	1,137
Management, business, and financial operations	15,648	17,137	17,561	1,155	1,208	1,227
Professional and related occupations	23,497	24,683	25,455	1,008	1,071	1,078
Computer and mathematical occupations	3,202	3,621	3,879	1,289	1,365	1,368
Architecture and engineering occupations	2,366	2,540	2,527	1,255	1,365	1,377
Life, physical, and social science occupations	1,127	1,063	1,124	1,062	1,152	1,168
Community and social services occupations	1,909	1,913	2,005	802	847	858
Legal occupations	1,248	1,305	1,313	1,213	1,253	1,271
Education, training, and library occupations	6,535	6,589	6,595	913	937	953
Arts, design, entertainment, sports, and media	1,431	1,510	1,573	920	988	956
Healthcare practitioner and technical occupations	5,678	6,142	6,438	986	1,048	1,033
Service occupations	14,424	15,052	15,019	479	493	505
Healthcare support occupations	2,219	2,324	2,368	471	491	498
Protective service occupations	2,872	2,685	2,740	747	783	833
Food preparation and serving-related occupations	3,823	4,140	4,017	406	416	439
Building and grounds cleaning and maintenance	3,310	3,421	3,568	446	475	480
Personal care and service occupations	2,199	2,482	2,326	455	481	487
Sales and office occupations	23,060	23,120	23,402	631	659	666
Sales and related occupations	9,121	9,376	9,626	666	708	705
Office and administrative support occupations	13,939	13,744	13,776	619	638	651
Natural resources, construction, and maintenance	9,869	10,341	10,763	719	747	756
Farming, fishing, and forestry occupations	729	720	776	416	448	429
Construction and extraction occupations	5,020	5,353	5,756	709	732	756
Installation, maintenance, and repair occupations	4,120	4,268	4,231	794	821	821
Production, transportation, and material-moving	13,034	13,930	14,326	599	621	642
Production occupations	6,861	7,307	7,481	599	623	646
Transportation and material-moving occupations	6,172	6,623	6,845	599	619	637

[1] Includes other races, not shown separately. [2] For persons in this race group only. See footnote 3, Table 605. [3] Persons of Hispanic origin may be of any race.

Source: U.S. Bureau of Labor Statistics, CPS Tables, "Median weekly earnings of full-time wage and salary workers by selected characteristics" and "Median weekly earnings of full-time wage and salary workers by detailed occupation and sex," February 2015, and earlier releases, <http://www.bls.gov/cps/tables.htm>.

Table 666. Median Usual Weekly Earnings of Full-Time Wage and Salary Workers by Sex and Education: 1980 to 2014

[In current dollars, except as indicated. For wage and salary workers 25 years old and over. Based on Current Population Survey; see text, Section 1 and Appendix III. Wages and salaries are collected before taxes and other deductions and include overtime pay, commissions, or tips usually received at principal job. Earnings reported on basis other than weekly are converted to a weekly equivalent. Excludes all incorporated and unincorporated self employed. Data not strictly comparable to data for earlier years. See text this section and <http://www.bls.gov/cps/eetech_methods.pdf]

Year and sex	Total	Less than a high school diploma	High school, no college [1]	Some college or associate's degree	Bachelor's degree and higher [2]
CURRENT DOLLARS					
Male:					
1980	339	267	327	358	427
1990	512	349	459	542	741
2000	693	406	591	691	1,020
2010	874	486	710	845	1,330
2013	912	500	732	858	1,395
2014	922	517	751	872	1,385
Female:					
1980	213	164	201	231	290
1990	369	240	315	395	535
2000	516	304	420	505	756
2010	704	388	543	638	986
2013	740	400	573	657	1,043
2014	752	409	578	661	1,049
WOMEN'S EARNINGS AS PERCENT OF MEN'S					
1980	62.8	61.4	61.5	64.5	67.9
1990	72.1	68.8	68.6	72.9	72.2
2000	74.5	74.9	71.1	73.1	74.1
2010	80.5	79.8	76.5	75.5	74.1
2013	81.1	80.0	78.3	76.6	74.8
2014	81.6	79.1	77.0	75.8	75.7

[1] Includes persons with a high school diploma or equivalent. [2] Includes persons with a bachelor's, master's, professional, or doctoral degree.

Source: U.S. Bureau of Labor Statistics, "Labor Force Statistics," <http://www.bls.gov/cps/data.htm>, accessed January 2015.

Table 667. Workers With Earnings by Occupation of Longest Held Job and Sex: 2013

[74,545 represents 74,545,000. As of March. For definition of median, see Guide to Tabular Presentation. Beginning with 2009 income data, the Census Bureau expanded the income intervals used to calculate medians to $250,000 or more. Medians falling in the upper open-ended interval are plugged with "$250,000." Before 2009, the upper open-ended interval was $100,000 and a plug of "$100,000" was used. Based on Annual Social and Economic Supplement (ASEC) of Current Population Survey; includes civilian noninstitutional population, 15 years old and over, and military personnel who live in households with at least one other civilian adult. See text, Section 1, and Appendix III]

Major occupation group of longest job held in 2013	All workers				Full-time, year-round			
	Female		Male		Female		Male	
	Number (1,000)	Median earnings (dol.)	Number (1,000)	Median earnings (dol.)	Number (1,000)	Median earnings (dol.)	Number (1,000)	Median earnings (dol.)
Total...........................	74,545	27,736	83,555	39,903	45,068	39,157	60,769	50,033
Management, business, and financial occupations........................	10,698	50,081	13,357	68,817	8,412	55,371	11,323	74,253
Professional and related occupations........................	19,789	41,469	14,583	61,928	12,688	50,422	11,343	71,577
Service occupations........................	16,253	15,916	12,199	21,188	7,330	24,105	7,245	31,394
Sales and office occupations..............	22,929	25,427	14,130	34,163	13,774	35,151	9,928	44,626
Natural resources, construction, and maintenance........................	767	17,036	13,679	34,008	339	30,168	9,681	41,064
Production, transportation, and material-moving occupations..............	4,041	21,512	14,872	31,732	2,462	28,162	10,624	39,373
Armed Forces........................	68	(B)	735	45,371	62	(B)	625	49,336

B Base less than 75,000.

Source: U.S. Census Bureau, *Income and Poverty in the United States: 2013*, September 2014, Current Population Reports, P60-249; and "Detailed Tables: Person Table PINC-06," <http://www.census.gov/hhes/www/income/data/index.html>, accessed November 2014.

Table 668. Employment Cost Index (ECI) for Total Compensation, by Occupation and Industry: 2010 to 2014

[As of December (2005 = 100). The ECI is a measure of the rate of change in compensation (wages, salaries, and employer costs for employee benefits). Data are not seasonally adjusted. Industry classifications based on North American Industry Classification System (NAICS); occupation classifications based on the 2010 Standard Occupational Classification (SOC)]

Occupational group and industry	Indexes (December 2005 = 100)				Percent change for 12 months ending December			
	2010	2012	2013	2014	2010	2012	2013	2014
Civilian workers [1]........................	**113.2**	**117.7**	**120.0**	**122.7**	**2.0**	**1.9**	**2.0**	**2.2**
State and local government........................	**116.2**	**119.9**	**122.2**	**124.7**	**1.8**	**1.9**	**1.9**	**2.0**
Workers, by occupational group:								
Management, professional and related occupations. . .	115.5	119.2	121.2	123.7	1.5	2.0	1.7	2.1
Sales and office occupations........................	116.6	120.9	123.4	126.4	1.9	2.1	2.1	2.4
Service occupations........................	118.0	121.7	124.3	127.1	2.3	1.8	2.1	2.3
Workers, by industry division: [2]								
Service-providing industries: [2]								
Education and health services........................	115.6	119.1	121.1	123.4	1.5	1.8	1.7	1.9
Schools........................	115.3	118.7	120.6	123.0	1.4	1.9	1.6	2.0
Health care and social assistance........................	117.9	122.2	125.0	126.8	2.2	1.7	2.3	1.4
Hospitals........................	117.0	121.2	123.7	125.0	2.4	1.7	2.1	1.1
Public administration [3]........................	116.8	120.7	123.4	126.4	1.9	2.1	2.2	2.4
Private industry workers [4]........................	**112.5**	**117.1**	**119.4**	**122.2**	**2.1**	**1.8**	**2.0**	**2.3**
Workers, by occupational group:								
Management, professional, and related occupations...	113.0	117.7	120.2	123.0	2.1	2.0	2.1	2.3
Sales and office occupations........................	111.6	116.3	119.0	121.9	2.2	1.8	2.3	2.4
Natural resources, construction, and maintenance occupations........................	113.3	117.8	120.1	123.2	1.9	1.7	2.0	2.6
Production, transportation, and material moving occupations........................	111.5	116.0	118.0	120.6	2.4	1.6	1.7	2.2
Service occupations........................	113.5	117.4	119.0	121.1	1.5	1.7	1.4	1.8
Workers, by industry division:								
Goods-producing industries........................	111.1	115.6	117.7	120.3	2.3	1.6	1.8	2.2
Construction........................	112.7	116.3	118.6	120.7	0.9	1.6	2.0	1.8
Manufacturing........................	110.0	114.9	117.0	119.8	2.8	1.6	1.8	2.4
Service-providing industries [2]........................	113.0	117.6	120.0	122.8	2.0	2.0	2.0	2.3
Trade, transportation, and utilities........................	111.4	116.4	119.5	122.6	2.4	2.0	2.7	2.6
Information........................	110.0	116.9	117.8	124.4	1.6	3.9	0.8	5.6
Financial activities........................	111.4	115.9	118.9	121.0	2.6	1.5	2.6	1.8
Professional and business services........................	114.6	119.3	121.2	124.2	2.0	1.9	1.6	2.5
Education and health services........................	114.7	118.9	121.2	123.3	1.7	2.1	1.9	1.7
Leisure and hospitality........................	114.1	116.5	117.6	119.6	1.2	1.1	0.9	1.7
Bargaining status:								
Union........................	114.8	120.5	122.6	126.7	3.3	2.2	1.7	3.3
Nonunion........................	112.1	116.6	119.0	121.5	1.8	1.8	2.1	2.1

[1] Includes private industry and state and local government workers and excludes farm, household, and federal government workers. [2] Includes all other service industries not shown separately. For a description of NAICS industries, see text, this section. [3] Consists of executive, legislative, judicial, administrative, and regulatory activities. [4] Excludes farm and household workers.

Source: U.S. Bureau of Labor Statistics, Employment Cost Trends, "Employment Cost Index," <http://www.bls.gov/ncs/ect/home.htm#data>, accessed August 2015.

Table 669. Federal and State Minimum Wage Rates: 1940 to 2015

[In current dollars. Wage rates are as of January 1, unless otherwise noted. Where an employee is subject to both the state and federal minimum wage laws, the employee is entitled to the higher minimum wage rate]

Year	Federal minimum wage rates per hour	State	2015 minimum wage rates per hour	State	2015 minimum wage rates per hour	State	2015 minimum wage rates per hour
1940	0.30	AL	(X)	KY	7.25	ND	7.25
1945 (as of Oct. 24)	0.40	AK	8.75	LA	(X)	OH	[7] 7.25/8.10
1950 (as of Jan. 25)	0.75	AZ	8.05	ME	7.50	OK	[8] 2.00/7.25
1960	1.00	AR	[2] 7.50	MD	8.00	OR	9.25
1965 (as of Sept. 3)	1.25	CA	9.00	MA	9.00	PA	7.25
1970 (as of Feb. 1)	1.45	CO	8.23	MI	[1] 8.15	RI	9.00
1975	2.10	CT	9.15	MN	[4] 7.25/9.00	SC	(X)
1980	3.10	DE	7.75	MS	(X)	SD	8.5
1985	3.35	DC	10.50	MO	7.65	TN	(X)
1990 (as of Apr. 1)	3.80	FL	8.05	MT	[5] 4.00/8.05	TX	7.25
1995	4.25	GA	[3] 5.15	NE	[2] 8.00	UT	7.25
2000	5.15	HI	7.75	NV	[6] 7.25/8.25	VT	[1] 9.15
2005	5.15	ID	7.25	NH	7.25	VA	[2] 7.25
2007 (as of Jul. 24)	5.85	IL	[2] 8.25	NJ	8.38	WA	9.47
2008 (as of Jul. 24)	6.55	IN	[1] 7.25	NM	7.50	WV	[3] 8.00
2009 (as of Jul. 24)	7.25	IA	7.25	NY	8.75	WI	7.25
2015	7.25	KS	7.25	NC	7.25	WY	5.15

X Not applicable. [1] Employers of 2 or more. [2] Employers of 4 or more. [3] Employers of 6 or more. [4] Large employer (receipts of $500,000 or more) and small employer (with annual receipts of less than $500,000). [5] Except businesses with gross annual sales of $110,000 or less. [6] Nevada: $8.25 with no health insurance benefits provided by employer. $7.25 with health insurance provided by employer and received by employee. [7] Ohio: $7.25 for those employers grossing $297,000 or less. [8] Oklahoma: employers of 10 or more full time employees at any one location, and employers with gross sales over $100,000 regardless of number of full-time employees. All other employers $2.00.

Source: U.S. Department of Labor, Wage and Hour Division, "History of Federal Minimum Wage Rates Under the Fair Labor Standards Act," and "Minimum Wage Laws in the States—January 1, 2015," <http://www.dol.gov/esa/minwage/america.htm>, accessed September 2015.

Table 670. Workers Paid Hourly Rates At or Below Federal Minimum Wage by Selected Characteristics: 2014

[77,207 represents 77,207,000. Data are annual averages. For employed wage and salary workers, excluding the incorporated self-employed. Based on the Current Population Survey; see text, Section 1 and Appendix III]

Characteristic	Number of workers paid hourly rates (1,000)				Percent of workers paid hourly rates		
		At or below federal minimum wage				At or below federal minimum wage	
	Total	Total	At prevailing federal minimum wage	Below prevailing federal minimum wage	Total	At prevailing federal minimum wage	Below prevailing federal minimum wage
Total, 16 years and over [1]	77,207	2,992	1,255	1,737	3.9	1.6	2.2
16 to 24 years	15,324	1,443	705	738	9.4	4.6	4.8
25 years and over	61,883	1,549	550	999	2.5	0.9	1.6
Male, 16 years old and over	38,405	1,114	516	598	2.9	1.3	1.6
16 to 24 years	7,701	572	299	273	7.4	3.9	3.5
25 years and over	30,704	542	217	325	1.8	0.7	1.1
Female, 16 years old and over	38,802	1,878	739	1,139	4.8	1.9	2.9
16 to 24 years	7,623	870	406	464	11.4	5.3	6.1
25 years and over	31,179	1,007	333	674	3.2	1.1	2.2
White [2]	60,245	2,284	891	1,393	3.8	1.5	2.3
Men	30,420	857	377	480	2.8	1.2	1.6
Women	29,825	1,427	514	913	4.8	1.7	3.1
Black [2]	10,669	460	257	203	4.3	2.4	1.9
Men	4,845	168	91	77	3.5	1.9	1.6
Women	5,824	292	166	126	5.0	2.9	2.2
Asian [2]	3,498	109	41	68	3.1	1.2	1.9
Men	1,670	40	17	23	2.4	1.0	1.4
Women	1,828	69	24	45	3.8	1.3	2.5
Hispanic [3]	15,301	519	249	270	3.4	1.6	1.8
Men	8,656	223	104	119	2.6	1.2	1.4
Women	6,645	297	145	152	4.5	2.2	2.3
Full-time workers	56,607	1,031	373	658	1.8	0.7	1.2
Men	31,333	438	178	260	1.4	0.6	0.8
Women	25,273	593	195	398	2.3	0.8	1.6
Part-time workers [4]	20,482	1,954	880	1,074	9.5	4.3	5.2
Men	7,003	672	338	334	9.6	4.8	4.8
Women	13,479	1,283	543	740	9.5	4.0	5.5
Private sector industries	67,956	2,843	1,178	1,665	4.2	1.7	2.5
Public sector industries	9,251	149	77	72	1.6	0.8	0.8

[1] Includes races not shown separately. Also includes a small number of multiple jobholders whose full- or part-time status cannot be determined for their principal job. [2] For persons in this race group only. See footnote 3, Table 605. [3] Persons of Hispanic or Latino origin may be of any race. [4] Working fewer than 35 hours per week.

Source: U.S. Bureau of Labor Statistics, *Characteristics of Minimum Wage Workers: 2014*, April 2015. See also <http://www.bls.gov/cps/publications.htm>.

Table 671. Average Hours Spent Per Day on Primary Activities by Married Mothers and Fathers by Employment Status: 2009 to 2013

[Data are shown for households with own children under 18. Primary activity refers to an individual's main activity. Other activities done simultaneously are not included]

Activity	Both spouses work full time		Mother employed part time and father employed full time		Mother not employed and father employed full time	
	Mothers	Fathers	Mothers	Fathers	Mothers	Fathers
Total, all activities..................	24.00	24.00	24.00	24.00	24.00	24.00
Personal care activities................	8.98	8.61	9.17	8.61	9.56	8.78
Sleeping...........................	8.14	8.00	8.42	8.02	8.92	8.17
Household activities..................	1.91	1.30	2.69	1.20	3.50	1.00
Housework.......................	0.78	0.25	1.13	0.21	1.57	0.20
Food preparation and cleanup...........	0.81	0.39	1.06	0.34	1.47	0.28
Lawn and garden care...............	0.06	0.23	0.12	0.18	0.13	0.17
Purchasing goods and services...........	0.51	0.32	0.64	0.32	0.68	0.37
Grocery shopping....................	0.13	0.07	0.17	0.07	0.20	0.08
Consumer goods purchases, except grocery shopping........	0.31	0.20	0.37	0.20	0.37	0.24
Caring for and helping household members..........	1.36	0.90	1.83	0.92	2.59	0.85
Caring for and helping household children...........	1.35	0.88	1.81	0.91	2.57	0.82
Physical care...................	0.57	0.26	0.70	0.28	0.99	0.26
Education-related activities...........	0.12	0.09	0.17	0.07	0.30	0.05
Reading to/with children...........	0.05	0.03	0.07	0.03	0.08	0.03
Playing/doing hobbies with children...........	0.26	0.26	0.34	0.31	0.64	0.32
Working and work-related activities [1]...........	5.21	6.06	2.69	5.95	0.11	6.19
Working [1].......................	5.18	6.03	2.64	5.91	0.04	6.16
Leisure and sports..................	2.93	3.66	3.41	3.69	4.03	3.56
Socializing and communicating...........	0.60	0.59	0.78	0.61	0.82	0.57
Watching television................	1.50	2.09	1.59	1.99	2.10	2.03
Participating in sports, exercise, and recreation...........	0.20	0.28	0.24	0.34	0.24	0.30
Travel...........................	1.36	1.45	1.43	1.47	1.14	1.39
Travel related to caring for/helping household children........	0.25	0.15	0.30	0.12	0.30	0.10
Other activities, not elsewhere classified...........	1.74	1.70	2.14	1.83	2.39	1.86

[1] Estimates include a small amount of work time done by persons who do not meet the American Time Use Survey definition of employed.

Source: U.S. Bureau of Labor Statistics, "American Time Use Survey," <http://www.bls.gov/tus/#tables>, accessed November 2014.

Table 672. Median Earnings of College Graduates by Degree and Occupation: 2012

[In dollars. Estimated annual earnings of the full-time, year-round civilian employed population aged 25 to 64 with a bachelor's degree or higher level of education. Data are from the 2012 American Community Survey. Based on a sample and subject to sampling variability]

Field of bachelor's degree and occupation	Total	Male	Female	White, not Hispanic [1]	Black or African- American	Asian	Hispanic or Latino [2]
Total..................	**65,150**	**76,365**	**55,281**	**66,789**	**52,993**	**72,553**	**52,979**
FIELD OF BACHELOR'S DEGREE							
Biological, agricultural, and environmental science..........	70,360	78,031	60,962	71,070	60,241	74,753	60,312
Business..................	67,105	76,690	56,685	72,055	53,036	60,717	52,701
Communications..................	56,258	61,849	51,777	58,152	48,804	60,199	50,646
Computers, mathematics, and statistics...........	80,985	84,621	71,196	83,677	62,325	85,211	60,984
Education..................	51,068	58,289	49,361	51,531	50,637	45,600	46,625
Engineering..................	92,883	95,911	80,996	99,514	72,443	92,033	67,954
Liberal arts and history..................	57,694	61,955	50,902	60,625	48,208	50,117	51,454
Literature and languages..................	59,537	67,149	54,584	60,550	52,417	60,890	51,027
Multidisciplinary studies..................	55,186	67,278	51,250	57,710	50,015	60,805	47,475
Physical and related science..................	78,458	89,558	61,907	81,415	61,216	77,566	61,534
Psychology..................	55,478	69,590	50,955	57,174	48,101	62,052	50,603
Science- and engineering-related..................	69,736	77,456	66,065	70,303	61,901	77,212	59,961
Social sciences..................	70,295	80,920	57,119	74,134	52,413	66,678	59,430
Visual and performing arts..................	50,684	54,702	47,002	51,128	46,473	51,412	45,839
OCCUPATION							
Agriculture..................	41,195	41,973	36,320	44,549	28,888	32,242	26,431
Architects..................	75,745	79,512	60,915	76,272	61,902	84,058	69,063
Arts and entertainment..................	55,852	60,761	51,425	56,035	52,439	60,593	52,442
Business and financial..................	70,268	80,273	61,490	71,838	59,269	71,391	61,014
Computer workers..................	86,679	90,354	78,859	87,337	72,092	90,791	74,951
Construction and maintenance..................	51,284	51,317	50,757	52,219	48,560	50,364	41,465
Education..................	51,030	56,255	49,441	51,362	49,314	51,187	49,109
Engineers..................	90,866	92,173	79,101	91,618	77,252	94,528	80,494
Health care..................	75,462	102,306	68,127	75,032	67,408	86,624	70,335
Legal..................	100,958	120,954	76,852	102,386	73,315	92,022	81,798
Life scientists..................	61,858	63,917	60,408	61,406	65,976	66,220	54,565
Managers (non-STEM) [3]..................	85,930	97,449	72,171	89,240	71,312	90,270	72,262
Mathematicians and statisticians..................	85,787	92,917	76,207	88,155	76,674	81,082	80,190
Office support..................	42,116	51,346	40,124	42,708	41,107	43,335	40,049
Physical scientists..................	71,442	77,024	62,159	72,858	62,378	70,446	59,936
Production..................	49,140	51,041	40,393	52,456	42,437	38,194	33,073
Sales..................	64,091	71,975	51,467	70,272	47,341	50,608	50,160
Service..................	41,144	50,776	32,217	44,900	38,618	32,340	32,361
Social scientists..................	70,642	80,461	64,206	70,933	62,297	84,331	64,045
Social services..................	44,983	46,871	43,815	45,926	42,074	45,010	43,602

[1] Persons who are not Hispanic and reported White and no other race. [2] Persons of Hispanic origin may be of any race. [3] STEM is science, technology, engineering and mathematics.

Source: U.S. Census Bureau, Industry and Occupation, Table Packages, "Median Earnings of College Graduates by Field of Bachelor's Degree and Occupation: 2012," <http://www.census.gov/people/io/publications/table_packages.html>, accessed July 2014.

Table 673. Earnings by Sex and Women's Earnings as a Percent of Men's Earnings by Occupation: 2013

[Median earnings in 2013 inflation-adjusted dollars for the full-time, year round civilian employed population age 16 years and over. Estimates subject to sampling variability. Based on the American Community Survey]

Occupation	Median earnings		Women's earnings as a percent of men's earnings
	Female	Male	
Total:..	**38,233**	**48,520**	**78.8**
Management, business, science, and arts................	52,237	72,695	71.9
Management, business, and financial..................	56,417	76,495	73.8
Management..	59,964	79,836	75.1
Business and financial operations...................	52,958	70,670	74.9
Computer, engineering, and science..................	65,160	78,480	83.0
Computer and mathematical...........................	69,795	80,509	86.7
Architecture and engineering........................	64,961	79,244	82.0
Life, physical, and social science..................	57,617	66,913	86.1
Education, legal, community service, arts, and media.	45,482	56,887	80.0
Community and social service........................	41,485	43,927	94.4
Legal...	61,432	116,689	52.6
Education, training, and library....................	44,667	55,349	80.7
Arts, design, entertainment, sports, and media......	47,086	52,617	89.5
Healthcare practitioners and technical..............	56,710	80,723	70.3
Health diagnosing and treating practitioners and other technical..................	65,314	102,250	63.9
Health technologists and technicians................	39,590	45,627	86.8
Service...	23,351	30,950	75.4
Healthcare support..................................	26,743	30,838	86.7
Protective service..................................	40,760	51,159	79.7
Fire fighting and prevention, and other protective service workers including supervisors..........	34,834	41,534	83.9
Law enforcement workers including supervisors........	46,816	59,318	78.9
Food preparation and serving related................	20,049	22,483	89.2
Building and grounds cleaning and maintenance........	20,844	27,873	74.8
Personal care and service...........................	22,294	30,217	73.8
Sales and office....................................	32,972	44,622	73.9
Sales and related...................................	31,747	50,259	63.2
Office and administrative support...................	33,637	38,713	86.9
Natural resources, construction, and maintenance....	30,351	40,696	74.6
Farming, fishing, and forestry......................	18,998	26,271	72.3
Construction and extraction.........................	33,236	40,078	82.9
Installation, maintenance, and repair...............	40,347	43,781	92.2
Production, transportation, and material moving......	26,339	37,377	70.5
Production..	26,544	39,170	67.8
Transportation......................................	30,304	41,222	73.5
Material moving.....................................	23,419	30,415	77.0
SELECTED DETAILED OCCUPATIONS			
Agricultural engineers..............................	39,356	73,207	53.8
Aircraft pilots and flight engineers................	50,770	101,007	50.3
Announcers..	41,437	40,829	101.5
Biological scientists...............................	57,107	57,653	99.1
Buyers and purchasing agents, farm products.........	50,742	51,063	99.4
Counselors..	42,369	42,299	100.2
Counter and rental clerks...........................	27,194	27,449	99.1
Crane and tower operators...........................	51,941	51,448	101.0
Dental assistants...................................	30,399	26,823	113.3
Derrick, rotary drill, and service unit operators, oil, gas, and mining..........	31,710	67,593	46.9
Dishwashers...	17,332	17,302	100.2
Elevator installers and repairers...................	87,403	85,807	101.9
Fabric and apparel patternmakers....................	52,582	53,500	98.3
Fence erectors......................................	16,111	30,669	52.5
Helpers, construction trades........................	34,839	27,431	127.0
Industrial truck and tractor operators..............	30,981	31,002	99.9
Judicial law clerks.................................	55,883	54,778	102.0
Maintenance workers, machinery......................	57,318	45,579	125.8
Massage therapists..................................	29,240	29,272	99.9
Mathematicians......................................	99,362	73,799	134.6
Mining and geological engineers, including mining safety engineers.....................	108,500	86,617	125.3
Models, demonstrators, and product promoters........	27,018	50,929	53.1
Musicians, singers, and related workers.............	42,279	42,988	98.4
Podiatrists...	62,064	126,978	48.9
Railroad conductors and yardmasters.................	65,256	65,462	99.7
Recreational therapists.............................	41,782	42,004	99.5
Ship and boat captains and operators................	37,067	70,159	52.8
Shoe machine operators and tenders..................	21,970	21,536	102.0
Small engine mechanics..............................	31,591	31,369	100.7
Special education teachers..........................	47,378	46,932	101.0
Tellers...	25,222	25,564	98.7

Source: U.S. Census Bureau, 2013 American Community Survey, B24022, "Sex by Occupation and Median Earnings in the Past 12 Months (in 2013 Inflation-Adjusted Dollars) for the Full-time, Year-Round Civilian Employed Population 16 Years and Over," <http://factfinder2.census.gov/>, accessed July 2015.

Table 674. Employer Costs for Employee Compensation Per Hour Worked: 2014

[In dollars. As of December. Based on the National Compensation Survey (NCS). See Appendix III]

Compensation component	Total civilian workers	State and local government workers	Private Industry workers						
			Total	Goods producing[1]	Service providing[2]	Union workers	Non-union workers	1–99 workers	100 workers or more
Total compensation	**33.13**	**43.95**	**31.32**	**37.21**	**30.10**	**46.50**	**29.83**	**26.23**	**37.35**
Wages and salaries	22.65	28.17	21.72	24.61	21.13	27.76	21.13	19.01	24.94
Total benefits	10.49	15.78	9.60	12.60	8.98	18.74	8.70	7.22	12.41
Paid leave	2.31	3.20	2.16	2.44	2.10	3.25	2.05	1.53	2.91
Vacation	1.13	1.19	1.13	1.27	1.09	1.65	1.07	0.78	1.53
Holiday	0.70	0.95	0.66	0.85	0.61	0.95	0.63	0.49	0.85
Sick	0.35	0.84	0.26	0.22	0.27	0.48	0.24	0.18	0.36
Supplemental pay	0.99	0.35	1.10	1.49	1.02	1.44	1.07	0.90	1.33
Overtime[3]	0.25	0.19	0.26	0.57	0.20	0.87	0.20	0.18	0.35
Insurance	2.92	5.22	2.54	3.46	2.34	6.01	2.20	1.78	3.43
Health insurance	2.78	5.09	2.39	3.26	2.21	5.64	2.07	1.69	3.22
Retirement and savings	1.75	4.42	1.30	2.02	1.16	4.38	1.00	0.76	1.95
Defined benefit	1.11	4.04	0.62	1.14	0.51	3.25	0.36	0.32	0.97
Defined contributions	0.64	0.38	0.69	0.88	0.65	1.13	0.64	0.44	0.98
Legally required	2.51	2.59	2.50	3.19	2.35	3.66	2.38	2.25	2.79
Social Security and Medicare	1.82	1.95	1.80	2.09	1.74	2.30	1.75	1.55	2.10
Social Security[4]	1.45	1.50	1.44	1.68	1.39	1.83	1.40	1.24	1.68
Medicare	0.37	0.45	0.36	0.41	0.35	0.47	0.35	0.31	0.42
Federal unemployment	0.03	(5)	0.04	0.04	0.04	0.04	0.04	0.04	0.04
State unemployment	0.20	0.09	0.22	0.28	0.20	0.30	0.21	0.22	0.22
Workers' compensation	0.45	0.54	0.44	0.78	0.37	1.02	0.38	0.44	0.44

[1] Based on the North American Industry Classification System, 2002 (NAICS). See text, this section. Includes mining, construction, and manufacturing. The agriculture, forestry, farming, and hunting sector is excluded. [2] Based on the 2002 NAICS. Includes utilities; wholesale and retail trade; transportation and warehousing; information; finance and insurance; real estate and rental and leasing; professional and technical services; management of companies and enterprises, administrative and waste services; education services; health care and social assistance; arts, entertainment, and recreation; accommodations and food services; and other services, except public administration. [3] Includes premium pay for work in addition to regular work schedule, such as, overtime, weekends, and holidays. [4] Comprises the Old-Age, Survivors, and Disability Insurance Program (OASDI). [5] Cost per hour worked is $0.01 or less.

Source: U.S. Bureau of Labor Statistics, *Employer Costs for Employee Compensation—December 2014*, USDL 15-0386, March 2015. See also <http://www.bls.gov/ncs/ect/home.htm>.

Table 675. Percent of Workers in Private Industry With Access to Retirement and Health Care Benefits by Selected Characteristics: 2013

[In percent (all workers = 100 percent). As of March. Based on National Compensation Survey (NCS). See headnote, Table 676, and Appendix III. See Table 170 for data on health benefit program participation]

Characteristic	Retirement benefits			Healthcare benefits			
	All plans[1]	Defined benefit[2]	Defined contribution[2]	Medical care	Dental care	Vision care	Outpatient prescription drug coverage
Total	**64**	**19**	**59**	**70**	**45**	**24**	**68**
WORKER CHARACTERISTICS							
Management, professional, and related occupations	79	26	76	87	64	35	85
Service occupations	38	7	34	40	22	13	40
Sales and office occupations	69	17	64	71	45	21	70
Natural resources, construction, and maintenance occupations	66	24	59	77	44	30	75
Production, transportation, and material moving occupations	68	23	58	76	47	26	74
Full-time[3]	74	22	69	85	56	30	84
Part-time[3]	37	9	31	24	13	8	23
Union[4]	94	72	55	95	73	58	94
Nonunion[4]	61	13	60	67	42	21	66
AVERAGE HOURLY WAGE[5]							
Lowest 25 percent (under $11.00)	38	6	34	34	16	9	33
Lowest 10 percent (under $8.50)	28	4	24	20	9	6	20
Second 25 percent ($11.00 to $16.58)	65	13	61	74	45	21	73
Third 25 percent ($16.59 to $26.17)	75	24	69	86	55	30	84
Highest 25 percent ($26.18 and over)	85	35	79	93	71	41	91
Highest 10 percent ($40.44 and over)	87	35	84	94	77	43	92
ESTABLISHMENT CHARACTERISTICS							
1 to 99 workers	49	8	46	57	30	16	55
100 or more workers	82	31	75	85	63	34	83
Goods producing[6]	75	25	69	86	57	32	84
Service producing[6]	62	17	57	66	43	23	65

[1] Employees may have access to both defined benefit and defined contribution plans. Total excludes duplication. [2] A defined benefit plan is a retirement plan that uses a specific, predetermined formula to calculate the amount of an employee's guaranteed future benefit. A defined contribution plan is a type of retirement plan in which the employer makes specified contributions to individual employee accounts, but the amount of the retirement benefit is not specified. [3] Employees are classified as working either a full-time or part-time schedule based on the definition used by each establishment. [4] See footnote 6, Table 676. [5] The National Compensation Survey—Benefits program presents wage data in percentiles rather than dollar amounts; for calculation detail, see "Technical Note" in source. [6] See Table 651 for composition of goods- and service-producing industries.

Source: U.S. Bureau of Labor Statistics, *National Compensation Survey: Employee Benefits in the United States, March 2013*, Bulletin 2776, September 2013. See also <http://www.bls.gov/ncs/ebs/home.htm>.

Table 676. Percent of Workers In Private Industry With Access to Selected Employee Benefits: 2013

[As of March. Based on National Compensation Survey (NCS). The NCS benefits survey obtained data from 6,268 private industry establishments of all sizes, representing over 106 million workers. Excludes agricultural establishments, private households, and the self-employed. An employee has access to a benefit plan if the plan is made available by the employer, regardless of whether the employee participates in the plan. See Appendix III]

Characteristic	Leave benefits						Quality of life benefits			Nonproduction bonuses	
	Paid holidays	Paid sick leave	Paid vacation	Paid jury duty leave	Family leave [1] Paid	Family leave [1] Unpaid	Employer assistance for child care [2]	Flexible work- place [3]	Subsidized commuting	All non- production bonuses [4]	End of year bonus
Total	77	61	77	62	12	85	10	6	6	40	10
WORKER CHARACTERISTIC											
Management, professional, and related occupations	89	83	88	81	20	91	18	15	11	51	13
Service occupations	53	40	55	39	6	78	9	1	3	25	6
Sales and office occupations	79	64	79	65	12	88	8	5	6	43	11
Natural resources, construction, and maintenance occupations	84	53	81	53	8	80	5	2	3	38	11
Production, transportation, and material moving occupations	84	54	83	64	7	85	5	2	2	41	9
Full-time [5]	90	74	91	72	14	88	11	7	7	47	12
Part-time [5]	39	24	36	32	5	77	6	1	2	23	4
Union [6]	92	71	91	83	11	91	14	2	5	36	6
Nonunion [6]	76	60	75	60	12	85	9	6	6	41	11
AVERAGE HOURLY WAGE [7]											
Less than $11.00	49	30	49	35	5	78	6	1	2	26	6
Less than $8.50	36	20	39	26	4	76	7	(S)	1	19	5
$11.00 to under $16.59	84	63	83	64	10	85	7	3	4	40	9
$16.59 to under $26.18	90	74	90	74	14	89	10	7	7	46	12
$26.18 and more	92	84	91	83	21	92	18	15	12	54	14
$40.44 and more	92	87	92	87	22	92	19	19	15	57	17
ESTABLISHMENT CHARACTERISTICS											
Goods producing [8]	91	57	89	67	8	86	7	5	3	49	14
Service producing [8]	74	62	74	61	12	85	10	6	6	39	9
1 to 99 workers	68	51	69	49	9	79	4	4	3	35	11
100 or more workers	87	72	86	77	15	93	16	8	9	47	9
GEOGRAPHIC AREA [9]											
New England	77	65	75	73	13	88	14	6	9	33	11
Middle Atlantic	77	65	76	72	11	85	11	6	9	41	11
East North Central	78	56	78	64	10	85	11	6	4	44	12
West North Central	76	59	76	56	12	83	9	4	4	36	10
South Atlantic	80	61	79	62	12	84	10	7	5	43	8
East South Central	80	58	78	66	7	88	7	6	4	40	8
West South Central	80	63	80	67	14	86	8	6	2	48	13
Mountain	73	58	76	52	10	83	8	3	7	44	13
Pacific	73	63	73	49	13	87	9	5	8	31	8

S Indicates no workers in this category or data did not meet publication criteria. [1] Some workers may have access to both types of plans. [2] A workplace program that provides for either the full or partial cost of caring for an employee's children in a nursery, day care center, or a baby sitter in facilities either on or off the employer's premises. [3] Permits employees to work an agreed-upon portion of their work schedule at home or at some other approved location. [4] All nonproduction bonuses include cash profit sharing bonuses, employee recognition bonuses, holiday bonuses, end of year bonuses, payment in lieu of benefits bonuses, referral bonuses, and other bonuses. [5] Employees are classified as working either a full-time or part-time schedule based on the definition used by each establishment. [6] Union workers are those whose wages are determined through collective bargaining. [7] The National Compensation Survey—Benefits program presents wage data in percentiles rather than dollar amounts; see "Technical Note" in source. [8] See Table 651, for composition of goods- and service-producing industries. [9] Composition of divisions: New England = Connecticut, Maine, Massachusetts, New Hampshire, Rhode Island, and Vermont; Middle Atlantic = New Jersey, New York, and Pennsylvania; East North Central = Illinois, Indiana, Michigan, Ohio, and Wisconsin; West North Central = Iowa, Kansas, Minnesota, Nebraska, North Dakota, and Missouri; South Atlantic = Delaware, District of Columbia, Florida, Georgia, Maryland, North Carolina, South Carolina, Virginia, and West Virginia; East South Central = Alabama, Kentucky, Mississippi, and Tennessee; West South Central = Arkansas, Louisiana, Oklahoma, and Texas; Mountain = Arizona, Colorado, Idaho, Montana, Nevada, New Mexico, Utah, and Wyoming; and Pacific = Alaska, California, Hawaii, Oregon, and Washington.

Source: U.S. Bureau of Labor Statistics, *Employee Benefits in the United States, March 2013*, Bulletin 2776, September 2013. See also <http://www.bls.gov/ncs/ebs/home.htm>.

Table 677. Industries With the Highest Total Case Incidence Rates for Nonfatal Injuries and Illnesses: 2013

[Rates per 100 full-time employees. Private industry unless otherwise noted. Incidence rates refer to any Occupational Safety & Health Administration (OSHA)-recordable occupational injury or illness, whether or not it resulted in days away from work, job transfer, or restriction. Incidence rates were calculated as: number of injuries and illnesses divided by total hours worked by all employees during the year multiplied by 200,000 as base for 100 full-time equivalent workers (working 40 hours per week, 50 weeks per year)]

Industry	2007 NAICS code [1]	Inci- dence rate	Industry	2007 NAICS code [1]	Inci- dence rate
All Industries, including State and local government [2]	(X)	3.5	Travel trailer and camper manufacturing	336214	9.3
Nursing and residential care facilities [4]	623	13.7	Manufactured home (mobile home) manufacturing	321991	9.2
Pet and pet supplies stores	45391	11.8	Concrete block and brick manufacturing	327331	8.6
Police protection [3]	92212	11.5	Other concrete product manufacturing	32739	8.4
Fire protection [3]	92216	11.2	Scheduled passenger air transportation	481111	8.3
Veterinary services	54194	11.0	Nursing and residential care facilities [3]	623	8.1
Skiing facilities	71392	10.1	Heavy and civil engineering construction [3]	237	8.0
Truss manufacturing	321214	9.9	Framing contractors	23813	8.0
Iron foundries	331511	9.9	Bottled water manufacturing	312112	8.0
Recreational and vacation camps (except campgrounds)	721214	9.6	Prefabricated wood building manufacturing	321992	8.0
			Steel foundries (except investment)	331513	8.0

X Not applicable [1] Based on the North American Industry Classification System, 2007 (NAICS). See text, this section. [2] Excludes farms with fewer than 11 employees. [3] Local Government. [4] State Government.

Source: U.S. Bureau of Labor Statistics, Industry Injury and Illness Data, "Supplemental News Release Tables," <http://www.bls.gov/iif/oshsum.htm>, accessed July 2015.

Table 678. Nonfatal Occupational Injuries and Illnesses by Industry: 2013

[3,753.3 represents 3,753,300. Rates per 100 full-time employees. Except as noted, data refer to any Occupational Safety and Health Administration (OSHA) recordable occupational injury or illness, whether or not it resulted in days away from work, job transfer, or restriction. Incidence rates were calculated as: number of injuries and illnesses divided by total hours worked by all employees during the year multiplied by 200,000 as base for 100 full-time equivalent workers (working 40 hours, per week, 50 weeks per year)]

Industry	2007 NAICS code [1]	Number of cases (1,000)	Incidence rate of cases
Total	(X)	**3,753.3**	**3.5**
Private industry [2]	(X)	**3,007.3**	**3.3**
Agriculture, forestry, fishing, hunting	11	54.9	5.7
Mining [3]	21	16.9	2.0
Construction	23	203.0	3.8
Manufacturing	31–33	476.7	4.0
Wholesale trade	42	173.8	3.1
Retail trade	44–45	438.3	3.8
Transportation and warehousing [4]	48–49	192.0	4.7
Utilities	22	11.4	2.1
Information	51	38.0	1.5
Finance and insurance	52	38.6	0.7
Real estate and rental and leasing	53	52.4	2.9
Professional, scientific, and technical services	54	74.7	1.0
Management of companies and enterprises	55	22.8	1.2
Administrative and support and waste management and remediation services	56	126.0	2.7
Educational services	61	36.9	2.0
Health care and social assistance	62	629.5	4.7
Arts, entertainment, and recreation	71	61.4	4.8
Accommodation and food services	72	284.9	3.7
Other services, except public administration	81	75.0	2.5
State and local government [2]	(X)	**746.0**	**5.2**
State government	(X)	160.4	3.9
Local government	(X)	585.7	5.7

X Not applicable. [1] North American Industry Classification System, 2007; see text, this section. [2] Excludes farms with fewer than 11 employees. [3] Data for Mining (2007 NAICS Sector 21) include establishments not governed by the Mine Safety and Health Administration rules and reporting, such as those in Oil and Gas Extraction and related support activities. Data for mining operators in coal, metal, and nonmetal mining are provided to BLS by the Mine Safety and Health Administration, U.S. Department of Labor. Independent mining contractors are excluded from the coal, metal, and nonmetal mining industries. These data do not reflect the changes the Occupational Safety and Health Administration made to its recordkeeping requirements effective January 1, 2002; therefore, estimates for these industries are not comparable to estimates in other industries. [4] Data for employers in railroad transportation are provided to BLS by the Federal Railroad Administration, U.S. Department of Transportation.

Source: Bureau of Labor Statistics, News Release, Workplace Injuries and Illnesses—2013. News Release, USDL 14-2183, December 2014. See also <http://www.bls.gov/iif/home.htm>.

Table 679. Fatal Work Injuries by Event or Exposure: 2013

[For the 50 states and the District of Columbia. Based on the Census of Fatal Occupational Injuries. For details, see source]

Event or exposure	Number of fatalities	Percent distribution	Event or exposure	Number of fatalities	Percent distribution
Total.	**4,585**	**100**	Contacts with objects and equipment [1].	721	16
Transportation incidents [1].	1,865	41	Struck by object or equipment [1].	509	11
Highway incident [1].	1,099	24	Struck by falling object or equipment.	245	5
Collision between motor vehicles, mobile equipment.	564	12	Struck by flying object.	29	1
Noncollision incidents.	201	4	Caught in or compressed by equipment or objects.	131	3
Nonhighway incident (farm, industrial premises).	227	5	Caught in or crushed in collapsing materials.	78	2
Aircraft accidents.	136	3			
Pedestrians struck by a vehicle, mobile equipment.	294	6	Falls.	724	16
Water vehicle accidents.	60	1	Exposure to harmful substances or environments [1].	335	7
Railway accidents.	41	1	Contact with electric current.	141	3
Assaults and violent acts [1].	773	17	Exposure to caustic, noxious or allergenic substances.	124	3
Homicides [1].	404	9	Oxygen deficiency.	30	1
Shooting.	322	7			
Stabbing.	38	1			
Self-inflicted injury.	282	6	Fires and explosions.	149	3

[1] Includes other causes, not shown separately.

Source: U.S. Bureau of Labor Statistics, "Census of Fatal Occupational Injuries—Current and Revised Data," <http://www.bls.gov/iif/oshcfoi1.htm>, accessed May 2015.

Table 680. Workers Killed on the Job by Industry and Occupation: 2014

[Excludes homicides and suicides]

Industry group	Deaths Number	Deaths Rate [1]	Occupations with highest fatal work injury rates	Deaths Number	Deaths Rate [1]
Total.	**4,679**	**3.3**	Logging workers.	77	109.5
			Fishers and related fishing workers.	22	80.8
			Aircraft pilots and flight engineers.	81	63.2
Agriculture [2].	568	24.9	Other extraction workers.	22	51.9
Mining [3].	181	14.1	Roofers.	81	46.2
Construction.	874	9.5	Refuse and recyclable material collectors.	27	35.8
Manufacturing.	341	2.2	Farmers, ranchers, and other agricultural managers.	263	26.0
Wholesale trade.	179	4.8	Structural iron and steel workers.	15	25.2
Retail trade.	267	1.8	Driver/sales workers and truck drivers.	835	23.4
Transportation and warehousing.	735	13.5	Electrical power-line installers and repairers.	25	19.2
Utilities.	17	1.7	Miscellaneous agricultural workers.	141	18.2
Information.	32	1.1	First-line supervisors/managers of construction trades and extraction workers.	130	17.9
Financial activities [4].	114	1.2			
Professional & business services [4].	418	2.6	Taxi drivers and chauffeurs.	63	17.2
Educational & health services.	144	0.7	Construction laborers.	206	16.8
Leisure & hospitality [4].	207	1.9	First-line supervisors of landscaping, lawn service, and groundskeeping workers.	32	15.9
Other services [5].	174	2.6			
Government.	428	1.9	Maintenance and repairs workers, general.	67	14.2

[1] The rate represents the number of fatal occupational injuries per 100,000 full-time equivalent workers. [2] Includes forestry, fishing, and hunting. [3] Includes oil and gas extraction. [4] For composition of industry, see Table 651. [5] Excludes public service administration.

Source: U.S. Bureau of Labor Statistics, Census of Fatal Occupational Injuries, "Fatal Injury Rates," <http://stats.bls.gov/iif/oshcfoi1.htm#rates>, accessed September 2015.

Table 681. Nonfatal Occupational Injury and Illness Cases in Private Industry by Type of Injury or Illness and Days Away from Work: 2013

[917.1 represents 917,100. Covers work-related injuries and illnesses involving one or more days of missed work]

Type of work-related injury or illness	Number of injury or illness cases (1,000) All cases	1 day	2 days	3-5 days	6-10 days	11-20 days	21-30 days	31 days or more	Median number of days away from work
Total [1].	**917.1**	**129.8**	**101.6**	**155.7**	**109.7**	**99.1**	**58.3**	**263.0**	**8**
Traumatic injuries and disorders.	881.3	124.9	97.9	150.9	106.1	95.0	55.6	251.1	8
Fractures.	78.0	4.1	4.2	7.4	6.3	8.4	7.1	40.6	34
Sprains, strains, tears.	327.1	35.3	31.9	59.8	42.1	38.2	21.0	98.9	10
Concussions.	10.7	1.6	1.8	1.9	1.4	0.9	0.7	2.3	6
Soreness, pain, hurt-nonspecified injury.	154.0	24.7	17.0	25.3	18.5	16.2	9.7	42.7	7
Hernia.	20.5	1.6	1.6	2.6	2.2	2.7	2.0	7.6	17
Disease and disorders of body systems.	6.4	0.3	0.4	0.5	0.6	0.9	0.6	3.1	30
Carpal tunnel syndrome.	13.5	0.2	0.4	0.8	1.2	3.2	2.1	5.6	25
Disorders of the eye, adnexa, vision.	0.9	0.3	0.2	0.2	0.1	0.1	0.0	0.1	2
Infectious and parasitic diseases.	2.3	0.7	0.5	0.4	0.3	0.2	0.1	0.1	2
Mental disorders or syndromes.	3.9	0.3	0.1	0.2	0.2	0.5	0.3	2.4	37

[1] Total includes unclassified and ill-defined conditions.

Source: U.S. Bureau of Labor Statistics, Survey of Occupational Injuries and Illnesses, 2013 Supplemental Tables, "Detailed nature by number of days away from work," <http://stats.bls.gov/iif/oshcdnew2013.htm>, accessed August 2015.

Table 682. Workplace Violence Rates for Government and Private Sector Employees by Selected Characteristics: 2002 to 2011

[Rates per 1,000 population. Data shown for nonfatal workplace violence, which includes rape or sexual assault, robbery, aggravated assault, and simple assault against employed persons age 16 or older that occurred while at work or on duty. Based on Bureau of Justice Statistics' National Crime Victimization Survey]

Victim characteristic	All employees		Non-law enforcement and security employees	
	Government	Private-sector	Government	Private-sector
Total	**22.3**	**6.2**	**10.8**	**5.6**
SEX				
Male	35.3	6.7	11.2	5.6
Female	12.0	5.6	10.5	5.6
RACE [2]				
White	25.0	6.7	12.0	6.0
Black or African American	10.6	6.4	5.7	5.4
American Indian or Alaska Native	[1] 42.5	19.1	[1] 28.3	18.1
Asian or Pacific Islander	[1] 8.7	4.9	[1] 4.3	5.0
Two or more races	69.7	14.1	[1] 14.5	14.3
Origin/Ethnicity				
Hispanic	18.3	3.1	9.4	2.8
AGE				
16–17	([1])	5.6	([1])	5.6
18–24	18.5	8.6	6.1	7.6
25–34	35.8	8.0	12.1	6.9
35–49	22.8	5.8	11.4	5.3
50–64	16.3	4.4	11.6	4.2
65 or older	3.7	1.0	3.6	0.9
MARITAL STATUS				
Never married	20.7	8.7	9.9	7.7
Married	20.8	4.2	9.8	3.8
Widowed	16.9	7.3	6.2	7.4
Divorced or separated	33.5	9.0	18.2	8.1
ANNUAL HOUSEHOLD INCOME				
Less than $25,000	13.3	7.4	10.3	6.3
$25,000 to $49,999	21.4	6.7	10.2	5.7
$50,000 to $74,999	33.6	7.6	15.5	7.2
$75,000 or more	21.5	5.5	11.2	5.1
Unknown	16.8	4.9	6.1	4.3

[1] Estimate is based on 10 or fewer sample cases or coefficient of variation is greater than 50%. [2] Excludes persons of Hispanic or Latino origin.

Source: Department of Justice, Bureau of Justice Statistics, *Workplace Violence Against Government Employees, 1994-2011*, NCJ 241349, April 2013. See also <http://www.bjs.gov/index.cfm?ty=pbdetail&iid=4615>.

Table 683. Work Stoppages: 1960 to 2014

[896 represents 896,000. Excludes work stoppages involving fewer than 1,000 workers and lasting less than 1 day. The term "major work stoppage" includes both worker-initiated strikes and employer-initiated lockouts that involve 1,000 workers or more. Information is based on reports of labor disputes appearing in daily newspapers, trade journals, and other public sources. The parties to the disputes are contacted by telephone, when necessary, to clarify details of the stoppages]

Year	Number of work stop-pages [1]	Workers involved [2] (1,000)	Days idle total		Year	Number of work stop-pages [1]	Workers involved [2] (1,000)	Days idle total	
			Number [3] (1,000)	Percent estimated working time [4]				Number [3] (1,000)	Percent estimated working time [4]
1960	222	896	13,260	0.09	1996	37	273	4,889	0.02
1970	381	2,468	52,761	0.29	1997	29	339	4,497	0.01
1975	235	965	17,563	0.09	1998	34	387	5,116	0.02
1980	187	795	20,844	0.09	1999	17	73	1,996	0.01
1981	145	729	16,908	0.07	2000	39	394	20,419	0.06
1982	96	656	9,061	0.04	2001	29	99	1,151	(Z)
1983	81	909	17,461	0.08	2002	19	46	660	(Z)
1984	62	376	8,499	0.04	2003	14	129	4,091	0.01
1985	54	324	7,079	0.03	2004	17	171	3,344	0.01
1986	69	533	11,861	0.05	2005	22	100	1,736	0.01
1987	46	174	4,481	0.02	2006	20	70	2,688	0.01
1988	40	118	4,381	0.02	2007	21	189	1,265	(Z)
1989	51	452	16,996	0.07	2008	15	72	1,954	0.01
1990	44	185	5,926	0.02	2009	5	13	124	(Z)
1991	40	392	4,584	0.02	2010	11	45	302	(Z)
1992	35	364	3,989	0.01	2011	19	113	1,020	(Z)
1993	35	182	3,981	0.01	2012	19	148	1,131	(Z)
1994	45	322	5,021	0.02	2013	15	55	290	(Z)
1995	31	192	5,771	0.02	2014	11	34	200	(Z)

Z Less than 0.005 percent. [1] Beginning in year indicated. [2] Workers counted more than once if involved in more than one stoppage during the year. [3] Resulting from all stoppages in effect in a year, including those that began in an earlier year. [4] Agricultural and government employees are included in the total working time; private household and forestry and fishery employees are excluded.

Source: U.S. Bureau of Labor Statistics, *Major Work Stoppages in 2014*, USDL 15-0211, February 2015. See also <http://www.bls.gov/wsp>.

Table 684. Labor Union Membership by Sector: 1990 to 2014

[Annual averages of monthly figures (16,740 represents 16,740,000). For wage and salary workers in agriculture and non-agriculture. Data represent union members by place of residence. Based on the Current Population Survey and subject to sampling error. For methodological details, see source]

Sector	1990	1995	2000	2005	2010	2011	2012	2013	2014
TOTAL (1,000)									
Wage and salary workers:									
Union members..................	16,740	16,360	16,258	15,685	14,715	14,755	14,349	14,516	14,570
Covered by unions..................	19,058	18,346	17,944	17,223	16,290	16,281	15,906	16,016	16,142
Public sector workers:									
Union members..................	6,485	6,927	7,111	7,430	7,623	7,550	7,319	7,203	7,214
Covered by unions..................	7,691	7,987	7,976	8,262	8,406	8,309	8,062	7,894	7,923
Private sector workers:									
Union members..................	10,255	9,432	9,148	8,255	7,092	7,204	7,030	7,313	7,356
Covered by unions..................	11,366	10,360	9,969	8,962	7,884	7,972	7,844	8,122	8,219
PERCENT									
Wage and salary workers:									
Union members..................	16.1	14.9	13.5	12.5	11.9	11.8	11.2	11.2	11.1
Covered by unions..................	18.3	16.7	14.9	13.7	13.1	13.0	12.5	12.4	12.3
Public sector workers:									
Union members..................	36.5	37.7	37.5	36.5	36.2	37.0	35.9	35.3	35.7
Covered by unions..................	43.3	43.5	42.0	40.5	40.0	40.7	39.6	38.7	39.2
Private sector workers:									
Union members..................	11.9	10.3	9.0	7.8	6.9	6.9	6.6	6.7	6.6
Covered by unions..................	13.2	11.3	9.8	8.5	7.7	7.6	7.3	7.5	7.4

Source: Bloomberg BNA, *Union Membership and Earnings Data Book: Compilations from the Current Population Survey* (2015 edition), authored by Barry Hirsch of Georgia State University and David Macpherson of Trinity University. Internet sites: <http://www.bna.com/databook> and <http://unionstats.gsu.edu>. © 2015 by The Bureau of National Affairs, Inc., Research and Customs Solutions (800-372-1033), <http://www.bna.com>.

Table 685. Union Members by Selected Characteristics: 2014

[In units as indicated (131,431 represents 131,431,000). Annual averages of monthly data. Covers employed wage and salary workers 16 years old and over. Excludes self-employed workers whose businesses are incorporated and not incorporated although they technically qualify as wage and salary workers. Based on Current Population Survey, see text, Section 1 and Appendix III]

Characteristic	Employed wage and salary workers			Median usual weekly earnings [3] (dollars)			
		Percent					
	Total (1,000)	Union members [1]	Represented by union [2]	Total	Union members [1]	Represented by union [2]	Not represented by union
Total [4].............................	**131,431**	**11.1**	**12.3**	**791**	**970**	**965**	**763**
SEX							
Men.................................	68,048	11.7	12.8	871	1,015	1,013	840
Women.................................	63,383	10.5	11.7	719	904	899	687
AGE							
16 to 24 years old..................	18,019	4.5	5.3	477	602	605	470
25 to 34 years old..................	30,158	9.5	10.6	726	874	867	705
35 to 44 years old..................	27,948	12.4	13.7	881	1,034	1,029	848
45 to 54 years old..................	28,540	13.8	15.0	899	1,025	1,022	872
55 to 64 years old..................	20,781	14.1	15.5	911	1,014	1,017	885
65 years and over..................	5,985	9.7	10.9	824	908	920	813
RACE/ETHNICITY							
White [5].............................	104,065	10.8	12.0	816	997	992	784
Men.................................	54,747	11.5	12.6	897	1,043	1,041	867
Women.................................	49,318	10.1	11.4	734	929	923	704
Black [5].............................	15,830	13.2	14.6	639	810	807	611
Men.................................	7,243	14.5	15.8	680	835	833	648
Women.................................	8,586	12.2	13.5	611	792	788	590
Asian [5].............................	7,476	10.4	11.6	953	979	998	948
Men.................................	3,921	9.2	10.6	1,080	1,028	1,041	1,087
Women.................................	3,555	11.8	12.6	841	939	950	823
Hispanic [6].............................	21,571	9.2	10.3	594	811	795	573
Men.................................	12,339	9.4	10.4	616	860	838	596
Women.................................	9,232	8.9	10.1	548	757	739	520
INDUSTRY [7]							
Private sector.........................	111,228	6.6	7.4	763	907	900	753
Mining...............................	1,040	4.8	5.9	1,136	1,150	1,176	1,130
Construction..........................	6,968	13.9	14.7	775	1,123	1,108	724
Manufacturing........................	14,471	9.7	10.5	812	861	854	807
Wholesale and retail trade..............	18,372	4.2	4.9	641	669	670	638
Transportation and utilities..............	5,750	20.1	21.2	826	1,011	1,009	785
Information..........................	2,681	8.6	9.5	1,040	1,115	1,090	1,029
Financial activities....................	8,481	2.0	2.4	941	879	884	942
Professional and business services.......	13,300	2.3	2.9	915	805	851	918
Education and health services............	21,147	8.2	9.5	777	926	925	763
Leisure and hospitality..................	11,997	3.2	3.8	505	636	624	500
Other services........................	5,821	2.9	3.3	644	871	843	636
Public sector..........................	20,203	35.7	39.2	927	1,014	1,014	850

[1] Members of a labor union or an employee association similar to a labor union. [2] Members of a labor union or an employee association similar to a union as well as workers who report no union affiliation but whose jobs are covered by a union or an employee association contract. [3] For full-time employed wage and salary workers. [4] Includes races not shown separately. Also includes a small number of multiple jobholders whose full- and part-time status cannot be determined for their principal job. [5] For persons in this race group only. [6] Persons of Hispanic origin may be of any race. [7] For composition of industries, see Table 651.

Source: U.S. Bureau of Labor Statistics, *Union Members—2014*, USDL 15-0072, January 2015. See also <http://www.bls.gov/news.release/union2.toc.htm>.

Table 686. Labor Union Membership by State: 1990 and 2014

[Annual averages of monthly figures (16,739.8 represents 16,739,800). For wage and salary workers in agriculture and non-agriculture. Data represent union members by place of residence. Based on the Current Population Survey and subject to sampling error. For methodological details, see source]

| State | Union members (1,000) | | Workers covered by unions (1,000) | | Percent of workers | | | | | |
| | | | | | Union members | | Covered by unions | | Private sector union members | |
	1990	2014	1990	2014	1990	2014	1990	2014	1990	2014
United States......	**16,739.8**	**14,569.9**	**19,057.8**	**16,142.4**	**16.1**	**11.1**	**18.3**	**12.3**	**11.9**	**6.6**
Alabama [1]............	194.6	203.9	230.0	227.7	12.3	10.8	14.5	12.1	10.4	6.9
Alaska................	46.9	69.9	52.6	74.7	23.1	22.8	25.9	24.3	14.0	10.8
Arizona [1]............	111.6	137.4	135.5	172.5	7.8	5.3	9.5	6.6	4.9	3.1
Arkansas [1]..........	91.4	52.3	107.6	60.4	10.3	4.7	12.2	5.4	8.7	2.9
California.............	2,219.4	2,468.8	2,569.1	2,648.2	18.4	16.3	21.3	17.5	13.0	9.2
Colorado.............	153.6	220.8	176.6	249.7	10.5	9.5	12.0	10.7	7.3	7.4
Connecticut..........	272.0	231.1	303.3	245.1	17.7	14.8	19.8	15.7	11.7	7.1
Delaware.............	46.8	37.9	52.7	43.2	14.9	9.8	16.8	11.2	11.3	4.8
District of Columbia..	41.4	28.0	50.7	34.6	16.1	8.6	19.7	10.7	11.6	5.4
Florida [1]..............	416.9	455.1	545.7	560.4	8.1	5.7	10.5	7.0	4.3	2.5
Georgia [1]............	186.9	169.6	230.7	193.1	6.9	4.3	8.5	4.9	5.7	2.9
Hawaii................	130.8	124.2	141.4	130.8	29.1	21.7	31.5	22.9	21.4	13.7
Idaho [1]..............	37.0	33.8	43.0	42.8	9.4	5.3	11.0	6.7	7.3	2.9
Illinois...............	1,059.1	829.8	1,155.6	879.2	20.8	15.1	22.7	16.0	16.5	9.1
Indiana [3]............	480.0	298.9	516.2	334.9	19.9	10.7	21.4	12.0	18.6	8.7
Iowa [1]...............	183.6	155.9	238.6	184.0	15.5	10.7	20.1	12.6	11.6	6.9
Kansas [1]............	119.0	95.2	154.6	116.0	11.3	7.4	14.7	9.0	9.4	5.0
Kentucky.............	206.4	188.7	223.6	218.8	14.3	11.0	15.5	12.7	12.5	8.7
Louisiana [1]..........	116.1	95.9	141.4	117.7	7.7	5.2	9.4	6.4	5.8	3.8
Maine................	88.5	62.2	107.5	71.0	17.5	11.0	21.2	12.5	9.7	4.4
Maryland.............	319.9	310.6	374.2	347.4	14.5	11.9	17.0	13.3	10.5	5.2
Massachusetts.......	471.7	414.8	505.1	444.2	17.6	13.7	18.8	14.6	10.7	5.7
Michigan [3]...........	974.0	584.6	1,038.8	629.5	25.4	14.5	27.1	15.6	20.2	9.9
Minnesota...........	395.7	360.3	429.7	379.9	20.3	14.2	22.0	14.9	14.0	8.0
Mississippi [1]........	75.7	38.0	92.0	46.1	7.9	3.7	9.6	4.5	7.5	3.9
Missouri.............	299.2	213.1	342.8	248.3	13.7	8.3	15.7	9.7	13.1	6.5
Montana.............	54.5	52.6	61.7	57.1	18.1	12.7	20.5	13.8	12.4	5.7
Nebraska [1]..........	74.7	63.8	104.1	78.7	11.0	7.3	15.3	9.0	7.2	3.8
Nevada [1]............	85.9	169.3	96.9	192.6	16.3	14.4	18.4	16.4	13.2	11.9
New Hampshire......	59.6	62.1	67.4	71.8	11.5	9.9	13.0	11.5	6.6	3.6
New Jersey..........	827.2	637.2	902.8	665.5	24.1	16.5	26.3	17.2	17.3	8.9
New Mexico.........	38.4	43.5	52.2	56.5	7.0	5.7	9.5	7.4	6.7	3.4
New York............	2,083.7	1,980.1	2,270.2	2,080.6	28.2	24.6	30.7	25.8	18.2	14.9
North Carolina [1].....	150.6	76.3	187.2	125.7	5.2	1.9	6.5	3.2	3.8	1.2
North Dakota [1]......	29.6	17.7	37.8	24.4	12.0	5.0	15.3	6.9	7.4	3.3
Ohio.................	968.5	614.6	1,076.7	688.1	21.0	12.4	23.3	13.9	17.6	7.4
Oklahoma [2].........	130.3	88.2	158.7	105.6	10.6	6.0	12.9	7.2	7.1	2.7
Oregon..............	237.3	243.2	273.4	263.7	20.4	15.6	23.4	17.0	13.5	8.2
Pennsylvania........	1,023.0	701.9	1,136.9	753.2	20.4	12.7	22.7	13.6	15.6	7.7
Rhode Island........	78.6	68.3	84.6	71.5	18.2	15.1	19.6	15.8	10.8	6.7
South Carolina [1].....	67.3	40.3	89.5	60.6	4.6	2.1	6.1	3.2	3.7	1.9
South Dakota [1]......	22.3	17.7	30.2	22.2	8.4	4.9	11.3	6.1	4.6	2.5
Tennessee [1].........	235.5	127.2	283.2	141.1	11.7	5.1	14.1	5.6	9.8	2.7
Texas [1]..............	446.9	543.4	589.8	699.7	6.4	4.8	8.4	6.2	4.7	2.8
Utah [1]...............	61.5	45.8	85.3	56.3	9.4	3.7	13.0	4.6	5.3	2.1
Vermont.............	29.9	31.7	35.9	37.5	12.6	11.1	15.2	13.1	6.5	4.2
Virginia [1]...........	230.4	178.7	298.6	228.5	8.4	4.9	10.9	6.2	6.3	2.7
Washington..........	466.4	490.1	531.0	535.4	22.8	16.8	26.0	18.4	16.9	10.9
West Virginia........	121.8	72.7	138.0	79.8	19.3	10.6	21.9	11.6	18.7	7.8
Wisconsin............	451.2	305.6	474.0	327.0	20.6	11.6	21.6	12.5	15.1	8.2
Wyoming [1]..........	26.5	17.1	33.1	19.0	13.5	6.7	16.8	7.5	8.8	5.3

[1] Right to work state. [2] Passed right to work law in 2001. [3] Passed right to work law in 2012.

Source: Bloomberg BNA *Union Membership and Earnings Data Book: Compilations from the Current Population Survey* (2015 edition), authored by Barry Hirsch of Georgia State University and David Macpherson of Trinity University. Internet sites: <http://www.bna.com/databook> and <http://unionstats.gsu.edu>. © 2015 by The Bureau of National Affairs, Inc., Research and Customs Solutions (800-372-1033), <http://www.bna.com>.

Section 13
Income, Expenditures, Poverty, and Wealth

This section presents data on gross domestic product (GDP), gross national product (GNP), national and personal income, savings and investment, money income, poverty, and national and personal wealth. The data on income and expenditures measure two aspects of the U.S. economy. One aspect relates to the National Income and Product Accounts (NIPA), a summation reflecting the entire complex of the nation's economic income and output and the interaction of its major components; the other relates to personal and household income and wealth, and consumer expenditures.

The primary source for data on GDP, GNP, national and personal income, gross saving and investment, and fixed assets and consumer durables is the *Survey of Current Business*, published monthly by the Bureau of Economic Analysis (BEA). These data are also available in tables accessible through an interactive tool on the BEA's Web site, <http://www.bea.gov/itable/index.cfm>. Revisions occur annually, however, the BEA conducts a comprehensive revision approximately every 5 years. The most recent comprehensive revision to the NIPA was released beginning in July 2013. Discussions of the revision are available at the BEA's Web site.

Sources of income distribution data are the decennial censuses of population, the Annual Social and Economic Supplement of the Current Population Survey (CPS), and the American Community Survey, all products of the U.S. Census Bureau (see text, Section 1). Annual data on income of families, individuals, and households are presented in *Current Population Reports, Income and Poverty in the United States,* in print and online. Detailed statistics and historical data are available on the Census Bureau's Web site at <http://www.census.gov/hhes/www/income/>.

Data on the household sector's savings and assets are published by the Board of Governors of the Federal Reserve System in the quarterly statistical release *Financial Accounts of the United States.* The Federal Reserve Board also periodically conducts the *Survey of Consumer Finances,* which presents financial information on family assets and net worth. The most recent survey is available at <http://www.federalreserve.gov/econresdata/scf/scfindex.htm>. Detailed information on personal wealth is published periodically by the Internal Revenue Service (IRS) in *the SOI (Statistics of Income) Bulletin.*

National income and product—GDP is the total output of goods and services produced by labor and property located in the United States, valued at market prices. GDP can be viewed in terms of the expenditure categories that comprise its major components: personal consumption expenditures, gross private domestic investment, net exports of goods and services, and government consumption expenditures and gross investment. The goods and services included are largely those bought for final use (excluding illegal transactions) in the market economy. A number of inclusions, however, represent imputed values, the most important of which is the rental value of owner-occupied housing. GDP, in this broad context, measures the output attributable to the factors of production located in the United States. GDP

by state is the gross market value of the goods and services attributable to labor and property located in a state. It is the state counterpart of the nation's GDP.

The featured measure of real GDP is an index based on chain-type annual weights. Changes in this measure of real output and prices are calculated as the average of changes based on weights for the current and preceding years. (Components of real output are weighted by price, and components of prices are weighted by output.) These annual changes are "chained" (multiplied) together to form a time series that allows for the effects of changes in relative prices and changes in the composition of output over time. Quarterly and monthly changes are based on quarterly and monthly weights, respectively.

The output indexes are expressed as 2005 = 100 or 2009 = 100, and for recent years, in 2005 or 2009 dollars. Price indexes are based to 1982-84 = 100. For more information on chained-dollar indexes, see the article on this subject in the November 2003 issue of the *Survey of Current Business.*

Chained (2009) dollar estimates of most components of GDP are not published for periods prior to 1990, because during periods far from the base period, the levels of the components may provide misleading information about their contributions to an aggregate. Values are published in index form (2009 = 100) for 1929 to the present to allow users to calculate the percent changes for all components, which are accurate for all periods. In addition, BEA publishes estimates of contributions of major components to the percent change in GDP for all periods.

Gross national product measures the output attributable to all labor and property supplied by United States residents, including residents working abroad. The GNP takes into account net income payments to the rest of the world. In brief, the GNP is the result of subtracting net income payments to the rest of the world from GDP.

National income includes all net incomes, net of consumption of fixed capital (CFC), earned in production. National income is the sum of compensation of employees, proprietors' income with inventory valuation adjustment (IVA) and capital consumption adjustment (CCAdj), rental income of persons with CCAdj, corporate profits with IVA and CCAdj, net interest and miscellaneous payments, taxes on production and imports less subsidies, business current transfer payments (net), and current surplus of government enterprises, less subsidies.

Capital consumption adjustment for corporations and for nonfarm sole proprietorships and partnerships is the difference between capital consumption based on income tax returns and capital consumption measured using empirical evidence on prices of used equipment and structures in resale markets, which have shown that depreciation for most types of assets approximates a geometric pattern. The tax return data are valued at historical costs and reflect changes over time in service lives and depreciation patterns as permitted by tax regulations. Inventory valuation adjustment represents the difference between the book value of inventories used up in production and the cost of replacing them.

Personal income is the current income received by persons from all sources minus their personal contributions for government social insurance. Classified as "persons" are individuals (including owners of unincorporated firms), nonprofit institutions that primarily serve individuals, private trust funds, and private noninsured welfare funds. Personal income includes personal current transfer receipts (payments not resulting from current production) from government and business such as social security benefits, public assistance, etc., but excludes transfers among persons. Also included are certain nonmonetary types of income; chiefly, estimated net rental value to owner-occupants of their homes and the value of services furnished without payment by financial intermediaries. Capital gains (and losses) are excluded.

Disposable personal income is personal income less personal current taxes. It is the income available to persons for spending or saving. Personal current taxes are tax payments (net of refunds) by persons (except personal contributions for government social insurance) that are not chargeable to business expense. Personal taxes include income taxes, personal property taxes, motor vehicle licenses, and other miscellaneous taxes.

Gross domestic product by industry—The BEA also prepares estimates of value added by industry. *Value added* is a measure of the contribution of each private industry and of government to the nation's GDP. It is defined as an industry's gross output (which consists of sales or receipts and other operating income, commodity taxes, and inventory change) minus its intermediate inputs (which consist of energy, raw materials, semi-finished goods, and services that are purchased from domestic industries or from foreign sources). These estimates of value added are produced for 61 private industries and for 4 government classifications—federal general government and government enterprises, and state and local general government and government enterprises.

The estimates by industry are available in current dollars and are derived from the estimates of gross domestic income, which consists of three components—the compensation of employees, gross operating surplus, and taxes on production and imports, less subsidies. Real, or inflation-adjusted, estimates are also prepared.

Regional Economic Accounts—These accounts consist of estimates of state and local area personal income and of gross domestic product by state and are consistent with estimates of personal income and gross domestic product in the BEA's national economic accounts. BEA's estimates of state and local area personal income provide a framework for analyzing individual state and local economies, and they show how the economies compare with each other. The *personal income* of a state and/or local area is the income received by, or on behalf of, the residents of that state or area. Estimates of labor and proprietors' earnings by place of work indicate the economic activity of business and government within that area, and estimates of personal income by place of residence indicate the income within the area that is

available for spending. BEA prepares estimates for states, counties, metropolitan areas, and BEA economic areas.

Gross domestic product by state estimates measure the value added to the nation's production by the labor and property in each state. GDP by state is often considered the state counterpart of the nation's GDP. The GDP by state estimates provide the basis for analyzing the regional impacts of national economic trends. GDP by state is measured as the sum of the distributions by industry and state of the components of gross domestic income; that is, the sum of the costs incurred and incomes earned in the production of GDP by state. The GDP estimates are presented in current dollars and in real (chained dollars) for 64 industries.

Consumer Expenditure Survey—The Consumer Expenditure Survey program began in 1980. The principal objective of the survey is to collect current consumer expenditure data, which provide a continuous flow of data on the buying habits of American consumers. The data are necessary for future revisions of the Consumer Price Index.

The survey conducted by the Census Bureau for the Bureau of Labor Statistics consists of two components: (1) an interview panel survey in which the expenditures of consumer units are obtained in five interviews conducted every 3 months, and (2) a diary or recordkeeping survey completed by participating households for two consecutive 1-week periods.

Each component of the survey queries an independent sample of consumer units. Data are collected in 91 areas of the country that are representative of the U.S. civilian noninstitutional population. The survey includes students in student housing. For the diary survey, the Census Bureau selects 12,500 addresses each year for participation; usable diaries are collected from approximately 7,100 households. The placement of diaries is spread out equally over the 52 weeks of the year. The interview survey contacts 15,000 addresses each quarter; usable interviews are obtained from approximately 7,100 households each quarter. Data from the two surveys are combined; integration is necessary to permit analysis of total family expenditures because neither the diary nor quarterly interview survey was designed to collect a complete account of consumer spending.

Money income of households, families, and individuals—Money income statistics are based on data collected in various field surveys of income conducted since 1936. Since 1947, the Census Bureau has collected the data on an annual basis and published them in *Current Population Reports*, P60 Series. In each of the surveys, field representatives interview samples of the population with respect to income received during the previous year. *Money income* as defined by the Census Bureau differs from the BEA concept of "personal income." Data on consumer income collected in the CPS by the Census Bureau cover money income received (exclusive of certain money receipts such as capital gains) before payments for personal income taxes, social security, union dues, Medicare deductions, etc. Money income does not reflect the fact that some families receive part of their income in the form of noncash benefits (see Section 11) such as food stamps, health benefits, and subsidized housing; that some farm families receive noncash benefits in the form of goods produced and consumed on the farm; or that noncash benefits are also received by some nonfarm residents, which often take the form of the use of business transportation and facilities, full or partial payments by business for retirement programs, medical and educational expenses, etc. These elements should be considered when comparing income levels. None of the aggregate income concepts (GDP, national income, or personal income) is exactly comparable with money income, although personal income is the closest. For a definition of families and households, see text, Section 1.

Poverty—Families and unrelated individuals are classified as being above or below poverty following the Office of Management and Budget's Statistical Policy Directive 14. The Census Bureau uses a set of thresholds that vary by family size and composition.

The official poverty thresholds do not vary geographically, but they are updated for inflation using the consumer price index (CPI-U). The official poverty definition uses money income before taxes and does not include capital gains or noncash benefits (such as public housing, Medicaid, and food stamps).

The original thresholds were based on the U.S. Department of Agriculture's 1961 Economy Food Plan and reflected the different consumption requirements of families. The poverty thresholds are updated every year to reflect changes in the Consumer Price Index. The following technical changes to the thresholds were made in 1981: (1) distinctions based on sex of householder were eliminated, (2) separate thresholds for farm families were dropped, and (3) the matrix was expanded to families of nine or more persons from the old cutoff of seven or more persons. These changes were incorporated in the calculation of poverty data beginning with data for 1981. Besides the Census Bureau Web site at <http://www.census.gov/hhes/www/poverty/about/overview/measure.html>, information on poverty guidelines and research may be found at the U.S. Department of Human Services Web site at <http://aspe.hhs.gov/poverty-research>.

In the recent past, the Census Bureau has published a number of technical papers and reports that presented experimental poverty estimates based on income definitions that counted the value of selected government noncash benefits. The Census Bureau has also published reports on after-tax income.

Statistical reliability—For a discussion of statistical collection and estimation, sampling procedures, and measures of statistical reliability pertaining to Census Bureau data, see Appendix III.

Table 687. Gross Domestic Product in Current and Chained (2009) Dollars: 1990 to 2014

[In billions of dollars (5,980 represents $5,980,000,000,000). For explanation of gross domestic product and chained dollars, see text, this section. Minus sign (-) indicates decline in inventories or net imports]

Item	1990	1995	2000	2001	2002	2003	2004	2005	2006	2007	2008	2009	2010	2011	2012	2013	2014
CURRENT DOLLARS																	
Gross domestic product	5,980	7,664	10,285	10,622	10,978	11,511	12,275	13,094	13,856	14,478	14,719	14,419	14,964	15,518	16,155	16,663	17,348
Personal consumption expenditures	3,826	4,984	6,792	7,103	7,384	7,766	8,260	8,794	9,304	9,751	10,014	9,847	10,202	10,689	11,051	11,392	11,866
Durable goods	497	636	913	942	985	1,018	1,080	1,127	1,156	1,185	1,102	1,023	1,071	1,125	1,192	1,238	1,280
Nondurable goods	994	1,180	1,540	1,584	1,613	1,704	1,820	1,953	2,080	2,177	2,273	2,175	2,292	2,471	2,547	2,599	2,668
Services	2,334	3,169	4,340	4,578	4,786	5,044	5,360	5,714	6,068	6,389	6,638	6,649	6,839	7,093	7,312	7,556	7,918
Gross private domestic investment	994	1,318	2,034	1,929	1,925	2,028	2,277	2,527	2,681	2,644	2,425	1,878	2,101	2,240	2,512	2,665	2,860
Fixed investment	979	1,286	1,979	1,967	1,907	2,009	2,213	2,468	2,614	2,609	2,457	2,026	2,039	2,198	2,450	2,593	2,783
Change in private inventories	15	31	55	-38	19	19	64	60	67	35	-32	-148	62	42	62	72	77
Net exports of goods and services	-78	-90	-376	-369	-427	-504	-619	-721	-771	-719	-723	-395	-513	-580	-566	-508	-530
Exports	552	813	1,097	1,027	1,003	1,040	1,182	1,309	1,476	1,665	1,842	1,588	1,852	2,106	2,198	2,263	2,342
Imports	630	903	1,473	1,395	1,429	1,544	1,801	2,030	2,247	2,383	2,565	1,983	2,365	2,686	2,764	2,772	2,872
Government consumption expenditures and gross investment	1,238	1,452	1,834	1,959	2,095	2,221	2,357	2,494	2,642	2,802	3,003	3,089	3,174	3,169	3,159	3,114	3,152
Federal	560	575	632	669	741	825	892	946	1,002	1,050	1,156	1,218	1,304	1,304	1,293	1,231	1,220
National defense	403	376	392	413	457	520	570	608	642	679	754	788	833	837	818	768	748
Nondefense	157	199	241	257	284	305	322	338	360	371	402	429	471	467	475	463	472
State and local	678	877	1,202	1,290	1,354	1,396	1,465	1,547	1,640	1,752	1,848	1,871	1,870	1,865	1,866	1,884	1,932
CHAINED (2009) DOLLARS [1]																	
Gross domestic product	8,955	10,175	12,560	12,682	12,909	13,271	13,774	14,234	14,614	14,874	14,830	14,419	14,784	15,021	15,355	15,583	15,962
Personal consumption expenditures	5,673	6,528	8,171	8,383	8,599	8,868	9,208	9,532	9,822	10,042	10,007	9,847	10,036	10,264	10,413	10,590	10,876
Durable goods	(NA)	(NA)	758	798	857	918	993	1,047	1,092	1,142	1,083	1,023	1,086	1,152	1,236	1,308	1,384
Nondurable goods	(NA)	(NA)	1,864	1,896	1,931	1,999	2,064	2,132	2,202	2,239	2,215	2,175	2,224	2,263	2,278	2,320	2,368
Services	(NA)	(NA)	5,599	5,731	5,838	5,967	6,157	6,353	6,527	6,656	6,709	6,649	6,728	6,851	6,908	6,977	7,145
Gross private domestic investment	1,241	1,551	2,376	2,231	2,218	2,309	2,511	2,673	2,730	2,644	2,396	1,878	2,120	2,230	2,466	2,577	2,718
Fixed investment	(NA)	(NA)	2,316	2,280	2,201	2,290	2,444	2,611	2,663	2,610	2,433	2,026	2,056	2,187	2,400	2,502	2,634
Change in private inventories	(NA)	(NA)	66	-46	-23	23	71	64	72	36	-34	-148	58	38	55	61	68
Net exports of goods and services	(NA)	(NA)	-478	-502	-584	-642	-735	-782	-794	-713	-558	-395	-459	-459	-447	-418	-443
Exports	645	912	1,258	1,185	1,165	1,185	1,301	1,382	1,507	1,646	1,741	1,588	1,777	1,898	1,963	2,018	2,086
Imports	722	1,013	1,736	1,687	1,749	1,827	2,035	2,164	2,301	2,359	2,299	1,983	2,235	2,358	2,410	2,436	2,529
Government consumption expenditures and gross investment	2,224	2,258	2,498	2,592	2,706	2,764	2,808	2,826	2,869	2,914	2,995	3,089	3,091	2,997	2,942	2,855	2,838
Federal	(NA)	(NA)	818	850	911	973	1,017	1,035	1,061	1,079	1,152	1,218	1,271	1,236	1,214	1,144	1,116
National defense	(NA)	(NA)	512	530	567	615	653	666	679	696	748	788	814	795	768	717	689
Nondefense	(NA)	(NA)	305	320	343	358	365	369	382	383	404	429	457	441	445	428	427
State and local	(NA)	(NA)	1,689	1,752	1,802	1,795	1,793	1,792	1,809	1,836	1,842	1,871	1,821	1,761	1,728	1,710	1,721
Residual	-106	-60	-84	-91	-71	-46	-20	-2	-4	-10	-14	(Z)	-1	-11	-20	-24	-35

NA Not available. Z Less than $500 million. [1] Chained (2009) dollar series are calculated as the product of the chain-type quantity index and the 2009 current-dollar value of the corresponding series, divided by 100. Because the formula for the chain-type quantity indexes uses weights of more than one period, the corresponding chained-dollar estimates are usually not additive. The residual line is the difference between the first line and the sum of the most detailed lines.

Source: U.S. Bureau of Economic Analysis, National Income and Product Accounts Tables, "Table 1.1.5. Gross Domestic Product," and "Table 1.1.6. Real Gross Domestic Product, Chained Dollars," <http://www.bea.gov/iTable/>, accessed July 2015.

Table 688. Real Gross Domestic Product, Chained (2009) Dollars—Annual Percent Change: 1990 to 2014

[Percent change from immediate previous year; for example, 1990, change from 1989. Minus sign (-) indicates decrease]

Component	1990	2000	2005	2008	2009	2010	2011	2012	2013	2014
Gross domestic product (GDP)...........	**1.9**	**4.1**	**3.3**	**-0.3**	**-2.8**	**2.5**	**1.6**	**2.2**	**1.5**	**2.4**
Personal consumption expenditures...........	2.1	5.1	3.5	-0.3	-1.6	1.9	2.3	1.5	1.7	2.7
Durable goods....................	-0.4	8.6	5.4	-5.1	-5.5	6.1	6.1	7.4	5.8	5.9
Nondurable goods................	1.2	3.2	3.3	-1.1	-1.8	2.2	1.8	0.6	1.9	2.1
Services.....................	3.0	5.0	3.2	0.8	-0.9	1.2	1.8	0.8	1.0	2.4
Gross private domestic investment............	-2.6	6.5	6.4	-9.4	-21.6	12.9	5.2	10.6	4.5	5.4
Fixed investment......................	-1.4	6.9	6.8	-6.8	-16.7	1.5	6.3	9.8	4.2	5.3
Nonresidential.................	1.1	9.1	7.0	-0.7	-15.6	2.5	7.7	9.0	3.0	6.2
Structures.....................	1.5	7.8	1.7	6.1	-18.9	-16.4	2.3	12.9	1.6	8.1
Equipment......................	-2.1	9.7	9.6	-6.9	-22.9	15.9	13.6	10.8	3.2	5.8
Intellectual property products.........	8.4	8.9	6.5	3.0	-1.4	1.9	3.6	3.9	3.8	5.2
Residential.................	-8.5	0.7	6.6	-24.0	-21.2	-2.5	0.5	13.5	9.5	1.8
Exports........................	8.8	8.6	6.3	5.7	-8.8	11.9	6.9	3.4	2.8	3.4
Goods........................	8.6	10.1	7.3	6.1	-12.1	14.4	6.5	3.6	2.8	4.4
Services.....................	9.5	4.7	3.8	4.8	-1.1	6.8	7.6	3.0	2.7	1.2
Imports........................	3.6	13.0	6.3	-2.6	-13.7	12.7	5.5	2.2	1.1	3.8
Goods........................	2.9	13.1	6.7	-3.7	-15.8	14.9	5.8	2.1	1.0	4.3
Services.....................	6.5	12.6	4.5	3.7	-3.8	3.8	4.0	3.0	1.5	1.6
Government consumption expenditures and gross investment...................	3.2	1.9	0.6	2.8	3.2	0.1	-3.0	-1.9	-2.9	-0.6
Federal....................	2.1	0.3	1.7	6.8	5.7	4.4	-2.7	-1.9	-5.7	-2.4
National defense............	0.3	-0.9	2.0	7.5	5.4	3.2	-2.3	-3.4	-6.7	-3.8
Nondefense................	7.3	2.3	1.3	5.5	6.2	6.4	-3.4	0.9	-4.0	-0.1
State and local................	4.1	2.8	–	0.3	1.6	-2.7	-3.3	-1.9	-1.0	0.6

– Represents or rounds to zero.

Source: U.S. Bureau of Economic Analysis, National Income and Product Accounts Tables, "Table 1.1.1. Percent Change From Preceding Period in Real Gross Domestic Product," <http://www.bea.gov/iTable/index_nipa.cfm>, accessed August 2015.

Table 689. Gross Domestic Product in Current and Chained (2009) Dollars by Type of Product and Sector: 1990 to 2014

[In billions of dollars (5,980 represents $5,980,000,000,000). For explanation of chained dollars, see text, this section]

Type of product and sector	1990	2000	2005	2009	2010	2011	2012	2013	2014
CURRENT DOLLARS									
Gross domestic product.................	**5,980**	**10,285**	**13,094**	**14,419**	**14,964**	**15,518**	**16,155**	**16,663**	**17,348**
Product:									
Goods............................	2,121	3,437	3,889	4,057	4,397	4,636	4,922	5,122	5,313
Durable goods....................	1,176	2,083	2,316	2,216	2,447	2,600	2,761	2,834	2,939
Nondurable goods................	946	1,355	1,574	1,842	1,950	2,036	2,161	2,289	2,373
Services [1]........................	3,309	5,862	7,766	9,220	9,519	9,822	10,070	10,310	10,714
Structures........................	549	986	1,439	1,141	1,048	1,060	1,164	1,231	1,321
Sector:									
Business [2].........................	4,553	7,892	9,920	10,598	11,060	11,536	12,097	12,524	13,078
Nonfarm [3]....................	4,475	7,816	9,815	10,488	10,930	11,370	11,946	12,334	12,901
Farm.........................	78	76	105	110	130	166	152	190	177
Households and institutions..............	643	1,203	1,600	1,914	1,929	1,974	2,029	2,086	2,172
General government [4]..................	785	1,191	1,574	1,908	1,976	2,007	2,029	2,053	2,098
Federal..........................	304	359	488	604	644	664	669	663	670
State and local....................	480	832	1,087	1,304	1,332	1,343	1,360	1,390	1,428
CHAINED (2009) DOLLARS									
Gross domestic product..............	**8,955**	**12,560**	**14,234**	**14,419**	**14,784**	**15,021**	**15,355**	**15,583**	**15,962**
Product:									
Goods............................	2,205	3,431	3,953	4,057	4,410	4,577	4,805	4,992	5,177
Durable goods....................	(NA)	1,903	2,261	2,216	2,468	2,614	2,769	2,844	2,954
Nondurable goods................	(NA)	1,532	1,691	1,842	1,943	1,965	2,040	2,149	2,225
Services [1]........................	5,778	7,675	8,658	9,220	9,323	9,407	9,447	9,467	9,624
Structures........................	1,090	1,457	1,627	1,141	1,052	1,040	1,111	1,139	1,180
Sector:									
Business [2].........................	6,282	9,253	10,612	10,598	10,934	11,164	11,489	11,717	12,068
Nonfarm [3]....................	6,228	9,173	10,513	10,488	10,823	11,061	11,406	11,603	11,952
Farm.........................	56	84	102	110	112	106	94	115	118
Households and institutions..............	1,200	1,634	1,829	1,914	1,931	1,946	1,962	1,977	2,003
General government [4]..................	1,573	1,681	1,794	1,908	1,920	1,912	1,904	1,890	1,892
Federal..........................	576	501	541	604	624	631	630	619	613
State and local....................	993	1,181	1,254	1,304	1,295	1,281	1,274	1,271	1,279

NA Not available. [1] Includes government consumption expenditures, which are for services (such as education and national defense) produced by government. In current dollars, these services are valued at their cost of production. [2] Equals gross domestic product excluding gross value added of households and institutions and of general government. [3] Equals gross domestic business value added excluding gross farm value added. [4] Equals compensation of general government employees plus general government consumption of fixed capital.

Source: U.S. Bureau of Economic Analysis, "National Income and Product Accounts Tables," <http://www.bea.gov/iTable/index_nipa.cfm>, accessed August 2015.

Table 690. Gross Domestic Product in Current and Chained (2009) Dollars by Industry: 2000 to 2014

[In billions of dollars (10,285 represents $10,285,000,000,000). Based on 2007 North American Industry Classification System (NAICS); see text, Section 15. Value added GDP is the contribution of each industry's labor and capital to its gross output and to the overall gross domestic product (GDP) of the United States. Value added is equal to an industry's gross output (sales or receipts and other operating income, commodity taxes, and inventory change) minus its intermediate inputs (consumption of goods and services purchased from other industries or imported). Current-dollar value added is calculated as the sum of distributions by an industry to its labor and capital which are derived from the components of gross domestic income]

Industry	Current dollars				Chained (2009) dollars [1]			
	2000	2010	2013	2014	2000	2010	2013	2014
Gross domestic product	**10,285**	**14,964**	**16,768**	**17,419**	**12,560**	**14,784**	**15,710**	**16,086**
Private industries	8,956	12,827	14,556	15,175	10,826	12,650	13,483	13,830
Agriculture, forestry, fishing, and hunting	99	160	227	210	106	140	145	135
Farms	76	130	192	(NA)	84	112	114	(NA)
Forestry, fishing, and related activities	23	31	35	(NA)	23	29	32	(NA)
Mining	111	332	439	461	211	273	333	357
Oil and gas extraction	68	209	292	(NA)	119	159	204	(NA)
Mining, except oil and gas	29	77	79	(NA)	75	70	68	(NA)
Mining support activities	14	45	69	(NA)	25	46	62	(NA)
Utilities	180	267	277	291	304	274	282	282
Construction	462	542	620	653	769	552	582	578
Manufacturing	1,555	1,831	2,029	2,091	1,603	1,818	1,863	1,924
Durable goods	927	957	1,089	1,136	806	976	1,089	1,117
Wood products	28	22	26	(NA)	25	21	22	(NA)
Nonmetallic mineral products	43	36	40	(NA)	51	37	39	(NA)
Primary metals	47	48	64	(NA)	47	38	57	(NA)
Fabricated metal products	122	120	140	(NA)	162	129	140	(NA)
Machinery	113	122	145	(NA)	130	128	141	(NA)
Computer and electronic products	226	249	255	(NA)	92	256	273	(NA)
Electrical equipment, appliances, and components	46	50	51	(NA)	54	51	49	(NA)
Motor vehicles, bodies & trailers, & parts	138	93	138	(NA)	107	100	150	(NA)
Other transportation equipment	71	112	123	(NA)	92	112	117	(NA)
Furniture and related products	34	22	25	(NA)	41	23	25	(NA)
Miscellaneous manufacturing	59	81	83	(NA)	62	82	80	(NA)
Nondurable goods	628	874	940	955	807	844	786	820
Food & beverage & tobacco	164	230	235	(NA)	210	233	220	(NA)
Textile mills and textile product mills	28	16	17	(NA)	30	16	16	(NA)
Apparel and leather and allied products	22	11	10	(NA)	20	11	10	(NA)
Paper products	62	55	52	(NA)	73	53	48	(NA)
Printing and related support activities	44	39	37	(NA)	41	40	40	(NA)
Petroleum and coal products	53	130	170	(NA)	76	99	90	(NA)
Chemical products	189	331	346	(NA)	263	330	297	(NA)
Plastics and rubber products	66	63	73	(NA)	79	65	68	(NA)
Wholesale trade	625	869	999	1,038	741	848	908	930
Retail trade	696	869	971	1,014	783	862	903	931
Transportation and warehousing	306	425	481	506	380	421	441	447
Air transportation	56	72	80	(NA)	69	70	67	(NA)
Rail transportation	23	35	44	(NA)	35	34	36	(NA)
Water transportation	8	16	16	(NA)	5	14	19	(NA)
Truck transportation	98	113	132	(NA)	121	120	131	(NA)
Transit & ground passenger transport	18	28	31	(NA)	28	27	27	(NA)
Pipeline transportation	9	19	21	(NA)	11	17	17	(NA)
Other transportation & support	66	96	109	(NA)	86	91	89	(NA)
Warehousing and storage	27	46	50	(NA)	31	48	58	(NA)
Information	472	730	779	808	445	735	782	808
Publishing industries (except Internet, includes software)	116	182	207	(NA)	130	185	205	(NA)
Motion picture and sound recording	54	108	115	(NA)	61	107	114	(NA)
Broadcasting and telecommunications	278	371	380	(NA)	230	373	382	(NA)
Data processing, Internet publishing, & related services	24	70	78	(NA)	24	70	81	(NA)
Finance and insurance	750	1,006	1,207	1,261	783	969	1,067	1,085
Real estate and rental and leasing	1,242	1,946	2,175	2,266	1,540	1,957	2,080	2,112
Professional, scientific, and technical services	656	1,022	1,155	1,221	818	1,009	1,088	1,133
Legal services	134	206	225	(NA)	211	198	190	(NA)
Computer systems design, related services	114	190	235	(NA)	107	193	239	(NA)
Miscellaneous services	409	626	696	(NA)	504	619	662	(NA)
Management of companies & enterprises	173	268	323	345	273	266	314	344
Administrative and waste management services	282	440	504	533	328	443	494	512
Educational services	86	169	185	191	125	165	163	164
Health care and social assistance	595	1,079	1,196	1,244	798	1,056	1,118	1,149
Ambulatory health care services	288	518	577	(NA)	361	505	546	(NA)
Hospitals	182	346	383	(NA)	262	339	353	(NA)
Nursing and residential care facilities	73	124	133	(NA)	106	122	126	(NA)
Social assistance	53	92	103	(NA)	70	90	94	(NA)
Arts, entertainment, and recreation	99	144	164	175	129	145	157	164
Performing arts, spectator sports, museums, and related activities	49	79	90	(NA)	68	78	86	(NA)
Amusements, gambling, & recreation	50	66	73	(NA)	61	67	71	(NA)
Accommodation and food services	287	396	458	483	392	396	429	439
Accommodation	93	111	133	(NA)	118	112	125	(NA)
Food services and drinking places	194	286	325	(NA)	273	285	304	(NA)
Other services, except government	280	332	369	385	404	324	331	337
Government	1,329	2,138	2,212	2,244	1,876	2,080	2,049	2,043
Federal	422	701	704	705	587	680	658	650
State and local	907	1,437	1,507	1,539	1,289	1,399	1,391	1,393

NA Not available. [1] Chained (2009) dollar series are calculated as the product of the chain-type quantity index and the 2009 current-dollar value of the corresponding series, divided by 100. Because the formula for the chain-type quantity indexes uses weights of more than one period, the corresponding chained-dollar estimates are usually not additive.

Source: U.S. Bureau of Economic Analysis, Industry Economic Accounts Data, "GDP by Industry," <http://www.bea.gov/industry/index.htm>, accessed August 2015.

Table 691. Gross Domestic Product by State in Current and Chained (2009) Dollars: 2005 to 2014

[In billions of dollars (13,022.5 represents $13,022,500,000,000). Data for 2014 are preliminary and subject to revision. For definition of gross domestic product by state or chained dollars, see text, this section]

State	Current dollars					Chained (2009) dollars				
	2005	2010	2012	2013	2014	2005	2010	2012	2013	2014
United States [1]	13,022.5	14,869.5	16,060.7	16,665.2	17,316.3	14,211.3	14,637.7	15,148.9	15,432.0	15,773.5
Alabama	157.9	176.4	187.0	194.7	199.4	173.0	173.5	176.6	181.1	182.3
Alaska	40.3	52.7	57.9	57.3	57.1	41.3	48.5	51.4	49.4	48.7
Arizona	227.0	248.5	267.5	274.7	284.2	250.6	245.9	255.0	257.2	260.8
Arkansas	90.1	106.0	114.1	118.6	121.4	99.1	104.5	107.8	109.9	110.7
California	1,760.5	1,966.6	2,125.1	2,213.0	2,311.6	1,902.1	1,936.8	2,008.3	2,055.2	2,113.3
Colorado	222.4	258.2	276.8	288.3	306.7	240.2	253.5	261.6	267.2	279.7
Connecticut	208.2	232.5	239.9	246.9	253.0	229.4	230.3	228.9	231.2	232.6
Delaware	52.9	57.5	59.1	60.8	62.8	56.6	56.6	55.6	56.0	56.7
District of Columbia	84.0	104.2	109.9	111.7	115.5	93.0	102.0	104.0	103.4	105.0
Florida	700.2	730.9	766.3	800.7	839.9	773.3	723.5	731.3	749.3	769.7
Georgia	376.6	412.2	438.8	456.5	476.5	413.7	407.8	417.4	425.7	435.5
Hawaii	58.1	67.7	72.7	75.1	77.4	64.3	66.9	69.0	70.0	70.5
Idaho	48.0	55.7	58.4	61.1	64.0	52.1	54.8	54.7	56.1	57.6
Illinois	588.8	655.0	710.3	724.8	745.9	648.6	647.5	670.6	672.1	680.4
Indiana	247.0	283.0	300.3	311.2	317.8	270.9	279.8	281.8	288.1	289.3
Iowa	124.0	142.3	159.7	166.8	170.6	135.6	140.5	148.6	151.9	152.5
Kansas	106.9	127.9	140.4	142.4	147.1	116.9	126.0	131.0	130.5	132.9
Kentucky	144.2	166.2	178.7	183.6	188.6	160.1	163.6	168.2	170.2	171.9
Louisiana	200.4	233.2	250.7	246.7	251.4	215.3	221.0	217.4	211.9	216.0
Maine	46.1	51.7	53.2	54.6	55.8	51.1	51.1	50.6	50.9	51.0
Maryland	264.7	314.4	330.5	339.4	348.6	291.7	311.1	316.4	318.7	321.3
Massachusetts	344.1	398.1	428.4	441.5	459.9	375.1	394.8	410.7	415.4	425.0
Michigan	396.3	386.6	415.1	434.7	451.5	432.7	384.4	398.3	409.6	417.3
Minnesota	244.8	273.0	295.7	307.3	316.2	268.5	269.4	278.4	284.2	288.1
Mississippi	82.3	95.5	103.4	104.1	104.9	90.2	93.8	96.7	95.6	94.5
Missouri	225.3	256.2	266.7	276.7	284.5	249.3	253.4	253.0	257.5	259.8
Montana	30.4	37.3	41.9	43.0	44.3	33.8	36.4	38.4	38.8	39.4
Nebraska	74.4	91.8	102.8	109.4	112.2	82.2	90.3	94.7	98.5	99.2
Nevada	116.8	119.5	124.9	128.0	132.1	131.0	118.3	118.7	119.6	120.8
New Hampshire	56.1	62.9	66.5	68.7	71.6	61.6	62.4	63.9	64.8	66.3
New Jersey	445.0	494.1	523.3	537.4	549.1	493.0	489.4	498.0	502.2	504.2
New Mexico	74.1	84.0	88.2	90.8	93.0	79.5	81.4	81.9	82.7	83.6
New York	1,024.3	1,199.4	1,302.5	1,341.6	1,404.5	1,117.2	1,183.5	1,236.1	1,248.4	1,279.9
North Carolina	357.7	422.1	445.7	467.1	483.1	393.6	418.4	422.6	434.2	440.3
North Dakota	24.7	35.3	49.3	51.0	55.1	26.8	34.3	45.0	45.4	48.2
Ohio	468.2	494.4	542.1	562.8	583.3	513.5	487.9	510.4	521.2	532.0
Oklahoma	125.1	152.1	169.3	176.4	183.5	133.0	146.1	155.2	158.0	162.4
Oregon	147.6	191.5	203.4	204.9	215.7	153.8	190.7	198.8	196.8	203.8
Pennsylvania	505.1	585.7	619.4	640.3	662.9	560.8	579.0	589.3	598.4	609.1
Rhode Island	45.3	49.3	51.3	53.3	55.0	49.9	48.8	49.0	49.9	50.5
South Carolina	144.8	165.4	176.3	182.4	190.3	161.0	164.1	168.5	170.8	174.6
South Dakota	31.6	38.7	43.2	44.7	45.9	33.2	37.7	39.2	39.6	39.8
Tennessee	228.7	253.7	280.2	290.1	300.6	252.2	251.4	266.9	271.3	275.8
Texas	999.6	1,247.6	1,449.3	1,557.2	1,648.0	1,057.9	1,201.1	1,323.2	1,395.4	1,467.3
Utah	94.9	118.5	128.1	135.0	141.4	102.9	116.0	119.9	124.3	128.2
Vermont	23.5	26.5	28.3	28.8	29.6	25.8	26.2	27.1	27.0	27.2
Virginia	358.7	424.2	444.6	455.0	463.6	395.8	420.2	425.4	427.4	427.5
Washington	296.7	362.5	390.6	407.2	427.1	325.5	358.1	370.4	379.0	390.5
West Virginia	53.3	66.2	68.7	70.6	75.3	61.1	64.6	63.9	64.7	68.0
Wisconsin	227.0	254.3	273.1	284.7	292.9	251.0	252.5	260.4	266.0	268.7
Wyoming	27.7	40.2	40.9	41.8	44.2	29.7	37.4	35.6	35.7	37.6

[1] For chained (2009) dollar estimates, states will not add to U.S. total.

Source: U.S. Bureau of Economic Analysis, Regional Economic Accounts, "Gross Domestic Product by State," <http://www.bea.gov/iTable/index_regional.cfm>, accessed June 2015.

Table 692. Gross Domestic Product by Selected Industries and State: 2014

[In billions of dollars (17,316.3 represents $17,316,300,000,000). Data are preliminary. For definition of gross domestic product by state, see text, this section. Industries based on 2007 North American Industry Classification System; see text, Section 15]

State	Total [1]	Manu-facturing	Whole-sale trade	Retail trade	Infor-mation	Finance and insur-ance	Real estate, rental, and leasing	Profes-sional and technical services	Health care and social assist-ance	Govern-ment [2]
United States	**17,316.3**	**2,090.7**	**1,037.7**	**1,014.0**	**808.0**	**1,261.3**	**2,265.8**	**1,220.8**	**1,244.3**	**2,141.0**
Alabama	199.4	35.3	11.0	15.0	4.5	8.9	21.7	11.0	13.8	33.1
Alaska	57.1	1.4	1.2	2.2	1.2	1.1	5.1	2.3	3.4	10.4
Arizona	284.2	23.8	15.9	22.2	7.9	20.8	41.5	15.8	23.3	39.2
Arkansas	121.4	16.8	8.7	8.1	7.8	4.8	12.9	4.0	9.2	15.2
California	2,311.6	255.5	135.9	135.0	185.1	117.7	366.6	199.3	145.0	284.3
Colorado	306.7	21.7	16.8	16.5	22.2	17.3	41.3	27.3	18.4	37.2
Connecticut	253.0	27.0	14.8	13.2	12.6	36.4	38.2	16.2	20.2	26.0
Delaware	62.8	3.8	2.4	2.9	1.8	17.6	8.4	4.9	4.4	6.8
District of Columbia	115.5	0.2	1.1	1.4	6.0	4.3	10.8	23.9	5.2	40.0
Florida	839.9	41.6	58.6	65.1	32.2	50.4	139.5	57.7	72.0	104.2
Georgia	476.5	52.3	38.0	28.4	29.4	37.7	55.3	32.9	30.5	60.4
Hawaii	77.4	1.5	2.5	5.3	1.7	2.3	15.3	3.2	5.0	17.1
Idaho	64.0	8.1	3.8	5.0	1.2	2.9	8.5	3.4	4.9	8.6
Illinois	745.9	99.7	55.2	38.0	24.9	72.0	97.7	60.2	51.5	73.3
Indiana	317.8	93.6	17.1	18.5	6.4	15.2	32.0	12.3	24.7	29.2
Iowa	170.6	31.2	9.8	9.5	4.2	18.0	18.7	5.3	11.3	19.0
Kansas	147.1	19.3	10.0	9.4	6.1	8.3	15.2	7.3	11.0	19.9
Kentucky	188.6	36.2	12.5	11.0	4.8	8.8	18.9	7.2	14.9	27.6
Louisiana	251.4	53.2	12.0	14.7	4.6	7.9	25.4	11.1	15.8	26.1
Maine	55.8	5.1	3.0	4.7	1.1	3.8	8.4	2.8	6.5	7.6
Maryland	348.6	18.8	15.1	18.8	15.0	18.2	58.6	35.2	25.8	72.1
Massachusetts	459.9	45.7	22.9	19.6	23.2	41.7	68.4	52.6	43.2	50.9
Michigan	451.5	90.7	29.7	30.6	12.1	23.6	50.6	32.2	37.2	49.6
Minnesota	316.2	43.9	21.8	17.9	11.3	24.5	39.1	19.4	28.8	31.7
Mississippi	104.9	15.7	5.1	8.4	2.1	4.6	10.9	3.2	7.7	17.9
Missouri	284.5	35.7	18.4	17.4	12.6	22.7	30.9	16.9	24.0	34.4
Montana	44.3	3.3	2.5	2.9	0.9	1.9	5.9	2.0	4.0	6.6
Nebraska	112.2	13.7	6.1	6.1	2.6	9.4	10.9	4.5	7.7	13.6
Nevada	132.1	6.2	5.5	10.1	2.8	6.0	17.9	6.5	7.5	15.5
New Hampshire	71.6	8.1	4.6	5.3	3.0	5.7	10.8	4.8	6.3	8.4
New Jersey	549.1	44.3	45.5	32.8	23.4	40.0	96.4	48.4	41.8	59.7
New Mexico	93.0	5.6	3.0	5.5	2.4	2.7	12.0	6.1	6.4	21.8
New York	1,404.5	69.1	70.2	66.6	109.3	262.2	196.9	116.1	97.3	156.4
North Carolina	483.1	95.8	27.1	25.5	14.7	43.8	54.5	24.8	31.7	65.3
North Dakota	55.1	3.7	4.6	3.1	1.2	2.1	6.1	1.8	3.5	5.3
Ohio	583.3	98.7	36.9	34.9	14.6	49.7	65.5	30.6	50.2	65.7
Oklahoma	183.5	17.5	10.0	11.2	4.0	7.0	18.2	7.2	12.2	27.7
Oregon	215.7	55.8	11.1	10.3	6.5	8.2	27.8	10.0	15.8	24.9
Pennsylvania	662.9	79.6	41.0	35.4	30.4	42.2	86.3	47.9	64.8	68.9
Rhode Island	55.0	4.4	2.8	2.9	2.7	5.1	8.2	3.0	5.6	7.7
South Carolina	190.3	31.0	11.3	14.2	4.8	8.4	24.0	9.5	12.8	30.8
South Dakota	45.9	4.2	3.0	3.2	1.2	7.2	4.5	1.2	3.9	5.2
Tennessee	300.6	48.4	20.1	20.9	8.8	16.2	34.0	16.5	29.2	35.7
Texas	1,648.0	238.4	115.7	93.0	52.0	75.3	150.1	99.9	85.8	159.1
Utah	141.4	17.5	7.2	9.7	5.8	12.2	18.1	8.9	8.0	18.4
Vermont	29.6	2.9	1.3	2.3	0.8	1.5	4.3	1.8	3.0	4.5
Virginia	463.6	42.4	18.9	24.8	17.9	23.1	67.7	58.3	28.2	86.5
Washington	427.1	57.8	23.5	30.0	44.4	16.2	57.2	27.6	27.0	59.9
West Virginia	75.3	7.4	3.3	5.1	1.6	2.2	7.3	2.8	7.0	11.8
Wisconsin	292.9	55.1	17.3	17.3	9.9	20.6	36.6	12.0	25.1	34.1
Wyoming	44.2	2.2	1.6	1.9	0.6	1.0	4.4	1.1	1.6	5.7

[1] Includes industries not shown separately. [2] Includes federal civilian and military, and state and local government.

Source: U.S. Bureau of Economic Analysis, Regional Economic Accounts, "Gross Domestic Product by State," <http://www.bea.gov/iTable/index_regional.cfm>, accessed June 2015.

Table 693. Relation of GDP, GNP, Net National Product, National Income, Personal Income, Disposable Personal Income, and Personal Saving: 2000 to 2014

[In billions of dollars (10,285 represents $10,285,000,000,000). For definitions, see text, this section. Minus sign (-) indicates deficit or net disbursement]

Item	2000	2005	2009	2010	2011	2012	2013	2014
Gross domestic product (GDP)...............	**10,285**	**13,094**	**14,419**	**14,964**	**15,518**	**16,155**	**16,663**	**17,348**
Plus: Income receipts from the rest of the world..	383	576	649	720	793	802	826	854
Less: Income payments to the rest of the world...	346	483	498	514	546	564	576	591
Equals: Gross national product (GNP).........	**10,322**	**13,186**	**14,570**	**15,170**	**15,765**	**16,393**	**16,914**	**17,611**
Less: Consumption of fixed capital.................	1,514	1,982	2,368	2,382	2,451	2,534	2,633	2,747
Equals: Net national product....................	**8,808**	**11,204**	**12,201**	**12,789**	**13,314**	**13,859**	**14,281**	**14,865**
Less: Statistical discrepancy........................	-100	-36	75	49	-38	-203	-178	-212
Equals: National income.........................	**8,907**	**11,240**	**12,126**	**12,740**	**13,352**	**14,062**	**14,458**	**15,077**
Less: Corporate profits [1]..........................	781	1,478	1,397	1,746	1,817	1,998	2,037	2,073
Taxes on production and imports less subsidies..	663	874	968	1,001	1,043	1,074	1,119	1,156
Contributions for government social insurance..	706	873	964	984	918	952	1,107	1,159
Net interest and miscellaneous payments on assets...	565	497	563	489	488	528	514	532
Business current transfer payments (net).......	85	94	125	129	132	105	119	127
Current surplus of government enterprises......	11	-6	-21	-23	-25	-19	-19	-18
Plus: Personal income receipts on assets.........	1,454	1,667	1,818	1,740	1,914	2,124	2,060	2,118
Personal current transfer receipts................	1,087	1,517	2,148	2,325	2,361	2,366	2,427	2,529
Equals: Personal income.........................	**8,637**	**10,614**	**12,095**	**12,477**	**13,255**	**13,915**	**14,068**	**14,694**
Less: Personal current taxes........................	1,237	1,213	1,152	1,239	1,453	1,511	1,673	1,780
Equals: Disposable personal income...........	**7,401**	**9,401**	**10,943**	**11,238**	**11,801**	**12,404**	**12,396**	**12,914**
Less: Personal outlays..............................	7,093	9,158	10,275	10,608	11,091	11,457	11,806	12,294
Equals: Personal saving..........................	**308**	**243**	**667**	**630**	**710**	**947**	**590**	**620**

[1] Corporate profits with inventory valuation and capital consumption adjustments.

Source: U.S. Bureau of Economic Analysis, National Income and Product Accounts Tables, "Table 1.7.5. Relation of Gross Domestic Product, Gross National Product, Net National Product, National Income, and Personal Income," and "Table 2.1. Personal Income and Its Disposition," <http://www.bea.gov/iTable/index_nipa.cfm>, accessed August 2015.

Table 694. Gross Saving and Investment: 2000 to 2014

[In billions of dollars (2,120 represents $2,120,000,000,000), except as noted. Minus (-) sign indicates deficit]

Item	2000	2005	2009	2010	2011	2012	2013	2014
Gross saving......................................	**2,120**	**2,339**	**2,068**	**2,252**	**2,435**	**2,861**	**3,039**	**3,267**
Net saving..	606	357	-301	-130	-16	327	406	520
Net private saving..............................	439	728	1,220	1,436	1,444	1,638	1,234	1,319
Domestic business............................	131	485	553	812	734	691	645	699
Undistributed corporate profits............	97	660	629	906	724	824	769	834
Inventory valuation adjustment, corporate.......	-17	-32	7	-41	-68	-14	3	-3
Capital consumption adjustment, corporate.....	51	-144	-82	-53	78	-119	-128	-132
Households and institutions......................	308	243	667	630	710	947	590	620
Personal saving..............................	308	243	667	630	710	947	590	620
Net government saving............................	166	-371	-1,521	-1,566	-1,460	-1,311	-828	-799
Federal..	157	-305	-1,249	-1,329	-1,244	-1,090	-641	-632
State and local.................................	10	-67	-272	-237	-216	-221	-187	-168
Consumption of fixed capital.....................	1,514	1,982	2,368	2,382	2,451	2,534	2,633	2,747
Private..	1,237	1,635	1,926	1,924	1,971	2,038	2,127	2,230
Domestic business...........................	1,007	1,273	1,522	1,523	1,573	1,633	1,699	1,775
Households and institutions..................	230	362	403	401	398	405	427	455
Government.......................................	278	347	443	458	480	496	506	517
Federal..	162	189	235	245	257	264	268	271
State and local.................................	116	157	208	213	222	232	239	246
Gross domestic investment, capital account transactions, and net lending.......	**2,020**	**2,303**	**2,143**	**2,307**	**2,396**	**2,658**	**2,862**	**3,055**
Gross domestic investment.......................	2,424	3,041	2,525	2,753	2,878	3,126	3,257	3,456
Gross private domestic investment.............	2,034	2,527	1,878	2,101	2,240	2,512	2,665	2,860
Gross government investment....................	390	514	647	652	638	614	592	596
Capital account transactions (net) [1]............	(Z)	-13	1	1	2	-7	1	1
Net lending or net borrowing......................	-404	-725	-383	-447	-483	-462	-397	-402
Statistical discrepancy............................	-100	-36	75	49	-38	-203	-178	-212
Addenda:								
Gross private saving.............................	1,676	2,363	3,146	3,360	3,415	3,676	3,361	3,549
Gross government saving........................	444	-25	-1,078	-1,108	-981	-815	-322	-282
Federal..	318	-115	-1,014	-1,083	-987	-826	-373	-361
State and local.................................	126	91	-64	-25	6	11	51	78
Net domestic investment........................	910	1,059	157	371	427	592	625	709
Gross saving as a percentage of gross national income................................	20.3	17.7	14.3	14.9	15.4	17.2	17.8	18.3
Net saving as a percentage of gross national income................................	5.8	2.7	-2.1	-0.9	-0.1	2.0	2.4	2.9
Disaster losses [2].................................	–	110	–	–	–	46	–	–

– Represents or rounds to zero. Z Less than 500 million. [1] Consists of capital transfers and the acquisition and disposal of nonproduced nonfinancial assets. [2] Consists of damages to fixed assets.

Source: U.S. Bureau of Economic Analysis, National Income and Product Accounts Tables, "Table 5.1 Saving and Investment by Sector," <http://www.bea.gov/iTable/index_nipa.cfm>, accessed August 2015.

Table 695. Financial Accounts of the United States—Composition of Individuals' Savings: 1990 to 2014

[In billions of dollars (646.0 represents $646,000,000,000). Combined statement for households, nonprofit organizations, and nonfinancial noncorporate business. Minus sign (-) indicates decrease]

Composition of savings	1990	2000	2005	2010	2011	2012	2013	2014
Net acquisition of financial assets	**646.0**	**596.9**	**1,352.2**	**775.0**	**1,146.8**	**1,294.1**	**1,076.6**	**1,337.6**
Foreign deposits	1.4	7.6	2.1	4.5	-9.9	-7.7	2.8	0.9
Checkable deposits and currency	-9.2	-95.0	-37.2	36.2	326.1	197.5	142.5	142.8
Time and savings deposits	52.7	354.5	505.0	165.8	375.3	422.0	212.7	423.4
Money market fund shares	39.2	176.5	46.8	-180.5	-12.6	-4.6	27.2	-12.7
Securities	200.7	-644.6	-162.7	-10.6	-180.3	146.2	49.1	24.3
Open market (commercial) paper	5.8	12.4	14.7	-1.5	-1.8	-0.6	-3.8	-0.1
Treasury securities, including U.S. savings bonds	96.6	-210.7	-121.3	318.9	-224.9	217.4	-191.3	-140.6
Agency and GSE-backed securities [1]	35.3	29.4	148.4	-11.7	-4.9	-129.4	-91.3	-101.4
Municipal securities	34.7	6.0	77.9	44.1	-65.4	-143.5	-43.8	-77.9
Corporate and foreign bonds	47.0	76.2	-71.4	-422.0	89.0	-165.9	-200.2	-128.8
Corporate equities [2]	-50.8	-640.3	-412.5	-221.2	-307.7	-240.1	-56.9	-47.2
Mutual fund shares	31.5	79.4	195.5	280.9	334.9	607.7	635.5	518.3
Life insurance reserves	26.5	50.1	15.1	6.2	73.5	-26.6	19.2	36.4
Pension fund reserves	300.3	468.6	598.6	596.4	498.3	497.6	498.7	556.9
Miscellaneous and other assets	34.3	279.1	384.5	167.4	80.3	78.5	130.9	171.5
Gross investment in nonfinancial assets	**825.1**	**1,590.6**	**2,197.1**	**1,694.0**	**1,783.0**	**1,918.0**	**2,078.4**	**2,178.5**
Minus: Consumption of fixed capital	617.8	1,009.9	1,381.1	1,580.8	1,601.5	1,637.0	1,693.4	1,723.5
Equals: Net investment in nonfinancial assets	**207.3**	**580.7**	**816.0**	**113.2**	**181.5**	**281.0**	**384.9**	**455.0**
Net increase in liabilities	**237.5**	**917.1**	**1,702.3**	**-146.1**	**18.4**	**379.8**	**372.4**	**650.7**
Home mortgages	206.9	423.0	1,120.8	-155.0	-86.0	-75.1	-4.3	27.7
Other mortgages	-4.4	106.7	117.8	-31.4	-5.6	2.1	71.4	129.2
Consumer credit	15.1	176.5	100.4	-25.3	108.5	169.7	174.3	218.4
Policy loans	4.1	2.8	0.8	3.4	2.4	1.4	0.9	1.3
Security credit	-3.7	7.2	-31.6	75.2	-39.3	64.9	35.4	30.4
Other liabilities	19.5	200.7	394.1	-12.9	38.4	216.9	94.6	243.7
Personal saving, FOF concept (FOF) [3]	631.5	296.2	431.0	1,005.9	1,310.3	1,185.4	1,108.8	1,152.3
Personal saving, NIPA concept (FOF) [3]	554.7	52.9	184.1	927.2	1,198.1	1,034.1	922.2	905.7
Personal saving, NIPA concept (NIPA) [4]	335.4	307.2	237.9	628.0	711.1	896.2	608.1	631.0

[1] GSE = government-sponsored enterprises. [2] Only directly held and those in closed-end and exchange-traded funds. Other equities are included in mutual funds and life insurance and pension reserves. [3] Flow of Funds measure. [4] National Income and Product Accounts measure.

Source: Board of Governors of the Federal Reserve System, "Financial Accounts of the United States, Z.1: Summary Table F.10 Derivation of Measures of Personal Saving," March 2015, <http://www.federalreserve.gov/datadownload/default.htm>, accessed May 2015.

Table 696. Government Consumption Expenditures and Gross Investment by Level of Government and Type: 2000 to 2014

[In billions of dollars (1,834 represents $1,834,000,000,000). Government consumption expenditures are services (such as education and national defense) produced by government that are valued at their cost of production; excludes government sales to other sectors and government own-account investment (construction, software, and research and development). Gross government investment consists of general government and government enterprise expenditures for fixed assets; inventory investment is included in government consumption expenditures. For explanation of national income and chained dollars, see text, Section 13]

Item	Current dollars				Chained (2009) dollars			
	2000	2010	2013	2014	2000	2010	2013	2014
Government consumption expenditures and gross investment, total	**1,834**	**3,174**	**3,114**	**3,152**	**2,498**	**3,091**	**2,855**	**2,838**
Consumption expenditures	1,444	2,522	2,522	2,556	1,998	2,445	2,300	2,290
Gross investment	390	652	592	596	501	647	554	547
Structures	190	313	269	274	305	312	244	243
Equipment	87	151	135	134	80	151	133	132
Intellectual property products	113	187	188	187	127	183	176	173
Federal	**632**	**1,304**	**1,231**	**1,220**	**818**	**1,271**	**1,144**	**1,116**
Consumption expenditures	475	1,004	961	955	646	975	889	868
Gross investment	157	300	269	265	174	295	255	248
Structures	14	33	18	18	21	33	17	16
Equipment	49	109	95	93	47	109	93	90
Intellectual property products	95	158	156	155	108	154	146	142
National defense	**392**	**833**	**768**	**748**	**512**	**814**	**717**	**689**
Consumption expenditures	308	653	614	600	423	636	571	549
Gross investment	83	180	153	149	91	178	146	140
Structures	5	17	7	5	8	17	6	5
Equipment	38	90	79	75	38	90	77	73
Intellectual property products	40	73	68	68	46	71	63	62
Nondefense	**241**	**471**	**463**	**472**	**305**	**457**	**428**	**427**
Consumption expenditures	167	351	347	356	223	339	318	319
Gross investment	74	120	116	116	82	118	110	108
Structures	8	16	12	12	13	16	11	11
Equipment	11	19	16	17	9	19	16	17
Intellectual property products	55	85	88	87	62	83	83	80
State and local	**1,202**	**1,870**	**1,884**	**1,932**	**1,689**	**1,821**	**1,710**	**1,721**
Consumption expenditures	969	1,518	1,561	1,601	1,356	1,470	1,411	1,421
Gross investment	233	352	323	331	334	351	298	299
Structures	176	281	251	257	285	280	227	227
Equipment	39	42	40	42	33	42	41	42
Intellectual property products	18	30	32	33	19	29	31	31

Source: U.S. Bureau of Economic Analysis, National Income and Product Accounts, "Table 3.9.5. Government Consumption Expenditures and Gross Investment" and "Table 3.9.6. Real Government Consumption Expenditures and Gross Investment, Chained Dollars," <http://www.bea.gov/iTable/index_nipa.cfm>, accessed August 2015.

Table 697. Personal Consumption Expenditures by Function: 2000 to 2014

[In billions of dollars (6,792 represents $6,792,000,000,000). In current and chained (2009) dollars. For definition of chained dollars, see text, this section. Minus sign (-) indicates decrease]

Function	Current dollars				Chained (2009) dollars			
	2000	2010	2013	2014	2000	2010	2013	2014
Personal consumption expenditures [1]	**6,792**	**10,202**	**11,392**	**11,866**	**8,171**	**10,036**	**10,590**	**10,876**
Food and nonalcoholic beverages purchased for off-premises consumption	463	676	742	760	591	674	684	686
Alcoholic beverages purchased for off-premises consumption	77	113	123	126	93	112	119	121
Clothing, footwear, and related services	298	336	379	386	276	338	358	364
Clothing	251	274	307	313	227	277	291	295
Footwear [2]	47	62	72	73	48	61	67	69
Housing [1]	1,011	1,610	1,753	1,825	1,321	1,609	1,652	1,674
Rental of tenant-occupied nonfarm housing [3]	228	373	424	449	306	372	395	406
Imputed rental of owner-occupied nonfarm housing [4]	769	1,215	1,304	1,351	993	1,215	1,236	1,248
Household utilities and fuels	204	326	332	346	311	318	305	305
Water supply and sanitation	50	78	85	87	77	73	69	68
Electricity, gas, and other fuels	154	248	247	260	234	244	236	238
Furnishings, household equipment, and routine household maintenance [1]	343	417	467	482	336	429	490	516
Furniture, furnishings, and floor coverings [5]	115	138	153	157	101	144	169	179
Household appliances [6]	38	46	51	51	40	48	52	55
Tools and equipment for house and garden	17	18	20	21	17	18	20	21
Medical products, appliances, and equipment	191	390	452	493	247	378	411	437
Pharmaceutical and other medical products [7]	159	334	389	428	211	322	350	374
Outpatient services	437	768	845	875	541	751	798	819
Physician services [8]	229	403	437	451	270	393	414	425
Dental services	64	105	110	114	95	102	99	100
Paramedical services [9]	144	261	297	310	178	257	285	294
Hospital and nursing home services	482	923	1,036	1,079	680	898	946	972
Transportation	795	942	1,136	1,168	930	870	933	968
Motor vehicles	321	287	353	375	293	269	317	336
New motor vehicles	211	182	250	266	198	179	232	245
Net purchases of used motor vehicles	111	104	103	109	95	91	88	94
Motor vehicle operation [1]	400	575	689	693	567	525	540	553
Motor vehicle parts and accessories	42	56	64	66	53	54	59	61
Motor vehicle fuels, lubricants, and fluids	169	307	386	373	266	260	256	258
Motor vehicle maintenance and repair	127	152	169	177	175	150	157	162
Public transportation	74	81	95	100	84	77	80	83
Telephone and facsimile equipment	6	13	15	17	3	13	18	21
Postal and delivery services	10	12	10	11	14	11	9	9
Telecommunication services	126	152	157	164	126	153	161	170
Internet access	16	63	89	96	13	63	88	95
Recreation [1]	634	888	1,001	1,041	569	911	1,069	1,122
Video and audio equipment	80	100	103	104	34	115	165	179
Information processing equipment	44	90	101	103	12	97	139	149
Services related to video/audio goods and computers	57	87	97	100	74	86	89	90
Sports and recreational goods and related services	146	174	203	213	130	179	223	241
Magazines, newspapers, books, and stationery	81	90	104	108	91	90	99	101
Pets, pet products, and related services	40	76	88	93	57	76	82	86
Education [1]	134	245	269	277	237	234	226	225
Higher education	77	158	175	179	140	150	145	143
Food services	354	532	608	642	470	525	557	574
Accommodations [10]	55	86	102	109	65	84	95	97
Financial services	360	473	531	565	386	453	439	443
Insurance [1]	206	290	307	318	276	281	275	280
Life insurance	65	88	93	93	85	86	85	83
Net health insurance	94	136	143	151	131	130	128	134
Net motor vehicle and other transportation	43	59	61	64	54	57	54	55
Personal care [11]	132	204	234	248	157	203	226	235
Personal items [12]	64	88	107	107	66	87	100	102
Social services and religious activities [13]	81	139	154	161	104	136	142	146
Professional and other services [1]	113	163	173	180	163	158	155	157
Legal services	65	91	96	98	95	88	85	86
Accounting and other business services	17	27	30	32	25	26	26	27
Funeral and burial services	16	25	27	28	23	24	24	25
Tobacco	69	106	106	104	119	96	88	84
Net foreign travel and expenditures abroad by: U.S. residents [1]	-26	-27	-40	-33	-20	-28	-34	-26
Foreign travel by U.S. residents	72	107	130	141	102	102	115	124
Less: Expenditures in the United States by nonresidents	102	140	176	180	129	135	155	156
Final consumption expenditures of nonprofit institutions serving households (NPISHs) [14]	158	275	304	322	163	278	300	306

[1] Includes other expenditures not shown separately. [2] Also includes repair and hire of footwear. [3] Rent for space (see footnote 4) and rent for appliances, furnishings, and furniture. [4] Rent for space and for heating and plumbing facilities, water heaters, lighting fixtures, kitchen cabinets, linoleum, storm windows and doors, window screens, and screen doors, excludes rent for appliances and furniture and purchases of fuel and electricity. [5] Includes clocks, lamps, lighting fixtures, other household decorative items, and repair of furniture, furnishings, and floor coverings. [6] Major and small electric household appliances, and repair of appliances. [7] Excludes drug preparations and related products dispensed by physicians, hospitals, and other medical services. [8] Offices of physicians, HMO medical centers, and freestanding ambulatory surgical and emergency centers. [9] Includes home health care, medical laboratories, and other health professionals (except physicians) and services. [10] Hotels, motels, other traveler accommodations, clubs, and housing at schools. [11] Cosmetics and toiletries, and personal care appliances and services. [12] Jewelry, watches, luggage, and similar items. [13] Household purchases from business, government, and nonprofit institutions providing social services and religious activities. Purchases from nonprofit establishments exclude unrelated sales, secondary sales, and sales to businesses, government, and the rest of the world, but include membership dues and fees. [14] Net expenses of NPISHs, defined as their gross operating expenses less primary sales to households.

Source: U.S. Bureau of Economic Analysis, National Income and Product Accounts, "Table 2.5.5 Personal Consumption Expenditures by Function," and "Table 2.5.6 Real Personal Consumption Expenditures by Function, Chained Dollars," <http://www.bea.gov/iTable/index_nipa.cfm>, accessed September 2015.

Table 698. Personal Income By Source and Disposition: 2000 to 2014

[In billions of dollars (8,637 represents $8,637,000,000,000), except as indicated. For definition of personal income and chained dollars, see text, this section]

Item	2000	2005	2009	2010	2011	2012	2013	2014
Personal income	**8,637**	**10,614**	**12,095**	**12,477**	**13,255**	**13,915**	**14,068**	**14,694**
Compensation of employees, received	5,857	7,087	7,787	7,961	8,269	8,610	8,840	9,249
Wages and salaries	4,826	5,692	6,251	6,378	6,633	6,930	7,114	7,478
Supplements to wages and salaries	1,031	1,395	1,536	1,584	1,636	1,680	1,725	1,771
Proprietors' income[1]	758	979	973	1,033	1,144	1,241	1,285	1,347
Farm	32	46	36	46	76	62	89	78
Nonfarm	726	933	938	987	1,068	1,180	1,196	1,269
Rental income of persons[2]	188	238	334	403	485	525	563	611
Personal income receipts on assets	1,454	1,667	1,818	1,740	1,914	2,124	2,060	2,118
Personal interest income	1,070	1,088	1,264	1,195	1,232	1,289	1,271	1,302
Personal dividend income	383	578	554	545	682	835	789	816
Personal current transfer receipts	1,087	1,517	2,148	2,325	2,361	2,366	2,427	2,529
Government social benefits to persons[3]	1,045	1,491	2,109	2,282	2,310	2,324	2,386	2,487
Social security[4]	401	513	665	690	713	762	799	835
Unemployment insurance	21	32	131	139	107	84	62	36
Veterans' benefits	25	36	52	58	63	70	79	84
Other current transfer receipts, from business (net)	42	26	39	43	50	43	41	42
Less: Contributions for government social insurance	706	873	964	984	918	952	1,107	1,159
Less: Personal current taxes	1,237	1,213	1,152	1,239	1,453	1,511	1,673	1,780
Equals: Disposable personal income	**7,401**	**9,401**	**10,943**	**11,238**	**11,801**	**12,404**	**12,396**	**12,914**
Less: Personal outlays	7,093	9,158	10,275	10,608	11,091	11,457	11,806	12,294
Personal consumption expenditures	6,792	8,794	9,847	10,202	10,689	11,051	11,392	11,866
Personal interest payments[5]	218	249	274	251	241	241	244	254
Personal current transfer payments	83	115	154	155	161	166	169	174
Equals: Personal saving	**308**	**243**	**667**	**630**	**710**	**947**	**590**	**620**
Personal saving as a percentage of disposable personal income	4.2	2.6	6.1	5.6	6.0	7.6	4.8	4.8
Addenda:								
Disposable personal income:								
Total, billions of chained (2009) dollars[6]	8,902	10,189	10,943	11,055	11,331	11,688	11,523	11,836
Per capita:								
Current dollars	26,206	31,760	35,616	36,274	37,804	39,440	39,123	40,461
Chained (2009) dollars	31,524	34,424	35,616	35,684	36,298	37,165	36,369	37,084

[1] With inventory valuation and capital consumption adjustments. [2] Includes capital consumption adjustment. [3] Includes other benefits not shown separately. [4] Social security benefits include benefits distributed from the Old-Age and Survivors Insurance Trust Fund and the Disability Insurance Trust Fund. [5] Consists of nonmortgage interest paid by households. [6] The current-dollar measure is deflated by the implicit price deflator for personal consumption expenditures.

Source: U.S. Bureau of Economic Analysis, National Income and Product Accounts, "Table 2.1 Personal Income and Its Disposition," <http://www.bea.gov/iTable/index_nipa.cfm>, accessed August 2015.

Table 699. Selected Per Capita Income and Product Measures in Current and Chained (2009) Dollars: 1980 to 2014

[In dollars. Based on U.S. Census Bureau estimated population including Armed Forces abroad, and institutionalized population; based on monthly averages. For explanation of chained dollars, see text, this section]

Year	Current dollars					Chained (2009) dollars				
	Gross domestic product	Gross national product	Personal income	Disposable personal income	Personal consumption expenditures	Gross domestic product	Gross national product	Personal income	Disposable personal income	Personal consumption expenditures
1980	12,570	12,720	10,177	8,861	7,705	28,325	28,707	20,158	—	17,528
1985	18,225	18,331	14,743	12,991	11,416	31,839	32,068	22,960	20,175	—
1990	23,901	24,040	19,611	17,235	15,291	35,794	36,024	25,555	22,674	—
1995	28,749	28,857	23,561	20,753	18,696	38,167	38,326	27,180	24,486	—
1996	30,033	30,150	24,719	21,615	19,532	39,156	39,325	27,719	25,047	—
1997	31,538	31,626	25,941	22,527	20,372	40,427	40,556	28,397	25,681	—
1998	32,913	32,979	27,498	23,759	21,376	41,737	41,836	29,723	26,741	—
1999	34,585	34,682	28,599	24,617	22,579	43,196	43,330	30,350	27,838	—
2000	36,419	36,550	30,585	26,206	24,053	44,475	44,649	31,524	28,933	—
2001	37,240	37,422	31,525	27,179	24,904	44,464	44,694	32,075	29,390	—
2002	38,122	38,291	31,789	28,127	25,643	44,829	45,041	32,754	29,862	—
2003	39,606	39,837	32,657	29,198	26,720	45,664	45,943	33,342	30,512	—
2004	41,857	42,160	34,280	30,697	28,166	46,967	47,321	34,221	31,399	—
2005	44,237	44,549	35,859	31,760	29,711	48,090	48,442	34,424	32,203	—
2006	46,369	46,595	38,130	33,589	31,136	48,905	49,156	35,458	32,868	—
2007	47,987	48,404	39,776	34,826	32,319	49,300	49,738	35,866	33,284	—
2008	48,330	48,895	41,052	36,101	32,881	48,697	49,270	36,078	32,860	—
2009	46,930	47,422	39,366	35,616	32,050	46,930	47,422	35,616	32,050	—
2010	48,302	48,967	40,274	36,274	32,931	47,719	48,323	35,684	32,395	—
2011	49,710	50,500	42,459	37,804	34,242	48,116	48,822	36,298	32,878	—
2012	51,368	52,124	44,245	39,440	35,137	48,822	49,482	37,165	33,111	—
2013	52,592	53,382	44,402	39,123	35,956	49,184	49,865	36,369	33,425	—
2014	54,353	55,178	46,038	40,461	37,177	50,010	50,715	37,084	34,075	—

Source: U.S. Bureau of Economic Analysis, National Income and Product Accounts, "Table 7.1. Selected Per Capita Product and Income Series in Current and Chained Dollars," <http://www.bea.gov/iTable/index_nipa.cfm>, accessed August 2015.

Table 700. Personal Income in Current and Constant (2009) Dollars by State: 2000 to 2014

[In billions of dollars (8,630.6 represents $8,630,600,000,000). Represents a measure of income received from all sources during the calendar year by residents of each state. Data exclude federal employees overseas and U.S. residents employed by private U.S. firms on temporary foreign assignment. Totals may differ from those in Table 693, Table 698, and Table 699]

State	Current dollars					Constant (2009) dollars [1]				
	2000	2005	2010	2013	2014	2000	2005	2010	2013	2014
United States	**8,630.6**	**10,605.6**	**12,417.7**	**14,151.4**	**14,708.6**	**10,381.9**	**11,495.2**	**12,215.7**	**13,184.6**	**13,523.4**
Alabama	109.7	138.0	162.2	176.3	181.8	131.9	149.6	159.6	164.3	167.2
Alaska	19.8	24.9	32.5	36.9	39.0	23.8	27.0	32.0	34.3	35.8
Arizona	136.9	189.3	217.9	245.1	255.1	164.7	205.2	214.3	228.3	234.5
Arkansas	61.0	77.8	93.6	108.6	112.0	73.4	84.4	92.0	101.2	103.0
California	1,134.0	1,396.0	1,578.6	1,856.6	1,944.4	1,364.2	1,513.1	1,552.9	1,729.8	1,787.7
Colorado	148.1	177.8	210.5	247.1	261.0	178.2	192.7	207.0	230.2	240.0
Connecticut	144.0	171.2	197.6	218.1	224.7	173.2	185.6	194.4	203.2	206.6
Delaware	25.2	32.4	36.9	41.5	43.0	30.4	35.1	36.3	38.7	39.5
District of Columbia	24.7	31.6	42.0	48.7	50.4	29.7	34.3	41.3	45.4	46.4
Florida	474.5	646.9	725.2	811.4	848.4	570.8	701.2	713.4	755.9	780.0
Georgia	235.9	294.6	333.6	378.2	394.8	283.8	319.3	328.1	352.3	363.0
Hawaii	35.1	46.1	56.8	63.5	65.9	42.2	50.0	55.9	59.1	60.6
Idaho	32.8	42.8	50.4	58.3	61.3	39.5	46.4	49.6	54.3	56.4
Illinois	409.5	475.4	539.7	605.2	619.8	492.6	515.2	530.9	563.9	569.9
Indiana	171.3	197.6	222.9	253.8	260.1	206.0	214.2	219.3	236.4	239.2
Iowa	80.8	97.9	119.1	138.3	140.2	97.2	106.1	117.1	128.9	128.9
Kansas	77.5	91.8	111.0	128.5	132.3	93.2	99.5	109.2	119.8	121.6
Kentucky	101.0	122.2	143.2	159.2	166.2	121.5	132.4	140.8	148.3	152.8
Louisiana	105.3	134.5	169.1	190.6	196.6	126.7	145.7	166.3	177.6	180.8
Maine	34.6	42.5	49.4	54.4	56.0	41.6	46.1	48.6	50.6	51.4
Maryland	187.6	244.9	289.6	319.1	329.6	225.7	265.5	284.9	297.3	303.0
Massachusetts	244.5	285.7	337.9	383.2	399.2	294.1	309.6	332.4	357.0	367.0
Michigan	298.7	331.2	346.5	386.5	401.9	359.3	359.0	340.8	360.1	369.5
Minnesota	159.5	193.2	226.1	257.5	265.8	191.8	209.5	222.4	239.9	244.4
Mississippi	61.4	78.0	91.6	101.4	102.8	73.9	84.5	90.1	94.5	94.5
Missouri	157.0	189.4	219.5	245.8	252.3	188.9	205.3	215.9	229.0	232.0
Montana	21.3	27.7	34.3	40.0	41.6	25.6	30.0	33.7	37.2	38.2
Nebraska	49.6	61.1	73.1	88.1	88.6	59.7	66.2	71.9	82.1	81.4
Nevada	63.0	93.8	99.1	109.5	113.8	75.8	101.7	97.5	102.0	104.6
New Hampshire	42.5	51.0	59.2	67.5	70.5	51.1	55.3	58.2	62.9	64.8
New Jersey	330.1	387.2	448.4	492.9	507.7	397.1	419.6	441.1	459.2	466.8
New Mexico	42.6	56.2	68.5	75.0	78.4	51.3	61.0	67.4	69.9	72.1
New York	670.9	795.5	961.8	1,070.2	1,110.3	807.0	862.2	946.2	997.1	1,020.9
North Carolina	225.1	281.1	338.7	381.0	394.2	270.8	304.7	333.2	354.9	362.5
North Dakota	16.6	20.4	29.2	38.5	40.6	20.0	22.1	28.7	35.8	37.4
Ohio	325.2	375.5	417.9	475.0	493.6	391.2	407.0	411.1	442.5	453.8
Oklahoma	85.7	110.6	135.0	161.2	167.3	103.1	119.9	132.8	150.2	153.8
Oregon	99.0	117.7	137.7	156.6	165.5	119.1	127.5	135.5	145.9	152.1
Pennsylvania	374.4	447.2	529.2	590.2	610.3	450.4	484.7	520.6	549.9	561.1
Rhode Island	31.7	39.0	45.3	49.4	51.5	38.2	42.3	44.5	46.0	47.4
South Carolina	101.1	125.4	151.5	171.1	178.5	121.6	135.9	149.0	159.4	164.1
South Dakota	20.6	25.9	33.1	38.9	39.5	24.8	28.1	32.6	36.2	36.4
Tennessee	156.8	190.1	225.2	257.0	266.3	188.6	206.1	221.5	239.4	244.8
Texas	593.6	756.3	961.0	1,160.1	1,224.5	714.0	819.7	945.3	1,080.8	1,125.9
Utah	55.6	72.3	90.0	106.3	111.1	66.9	78.4	88.6	99.0	102.2
Vermont	17.4	21.4	25.1	28.5	29.7	20.9	23.2	24.7	26.6	27.3
Virginia	230.6	301.9	359.8	403.4	413.9	277.4	327.2	353.9	375.9	380.5
Washington	194.3	235.5	286.9	332.7	350.1	233.7	255.3	282.2	309.9	321.9
West Virginia	39.9	48.1	59.0	65.9	67.8	48.0	52.1	58.0	61.4	62.3
Wisconsin	157.9	190.6	220.3	248.3	256.7	189.9	206.6	216.7	231.4	236.0
Wyoming	14.3	20.1	25.4	30.8	32.0	17.2	21.8	25.0	28.7	29.4

[1] Constant dollar estimates are computed by ProQuest using the national implicit price deflator for personal consumption expenditures from the Bureau of Economic Analysis' National Income and Product Accounts Tables. Any regional differences in the rate of inflation are not reflected in these constant dollar estimates.

Source: Except as noted, U.S. Bureau of Economic Analysis, Regional Economic Accounts, State Annual Personal Income and Employment, "Table SA1 Personal Income Summary," <http://www.bea.gov/regional/index.htm#data>, accessed June 2015.

Table 701. Personal Income Per Capita in Current and Constant (2009) Dollars by State: 2000 to 2014

[In dollars, except as indicated. Represents a measure of income received from all sources during the calendar year by residents of each state. Data exclude federal employees overseas and U.S. residents employed by private U.S. firms on temporary foreign assignment. Totals may differ from those in Table 693, Table 698, and Table 699]

State	Current dollars				Constant (2009) dollars [1]				Income rank [2]	
	2000	2010	2013	2014	2000	2010	2013	2014	2010	2014
United States..............	30,587	40,144	44,765	46,129	36,794	39,491	41,707	42,412	(X)	(X)
Alabama.........................	24,628	33,894	36,481	37,493	29,626	33,343	33,989	34,472	43	48
Alaska...........................	31,491	45,565	50,150	52,901	37,881	44,824	46,724	48,638	7	10
Arizona.........................	26,538	33,993	36,983	37,895	31,923	33,440	34,456	34,841	42	42
Arkansas.......................	22,782	32,017	36,698	37,751	27,405	31,496	34,191	34,709	49	44
California.......................	33,366	42,282	48,434	50,109	40,137	41,594	45,125	46,071	15	11
Colorado.......................	34,227	41,689	46,897	48,730	41,172	41,011	43,693	44,803	17	15
Connecticut..................	42,198	55,216	60,658	62,467	50,761	54,318	56,514	57,434	2	2
Delaware.......................	32,097	40,969	44,815	45,942	38,610	40,303	41,753	42,240	20	23
District of Columbia...........	43,206	69,431	75,329	76,532	51,973	68,302	70,183	70,365	1	1
Florida..........................	29,570	38,478	41,497	42,645	35,570	37,852	38,662	39,209	27	29
Georgia.........................	28,672	34,341	37,845	39,097	34,490	33,783	35,259	35,947	41	41
Hawaii..........................	28,927	41,668	45,204	46,396	34,797	40,990	42,116	42,657	19	21
Idaho...........................	25,258	32,100	36,146	37,533	30,383	31,578	33,677	34,509	48	47
Illinois..........................	32,934	42,033	46,980	48,120	39,617	41,349	43,770	44,243	16	17
Indiana.........................	28,114	34,344	38,622	39,433	33,819	33,786	35,983	36,256	40	40
Iowa............................	27,583	39,033	44,763	45,115	33,180	38,398	41,705	41,480	24	26
Kansas.........................	28,764	38,811	44,417	45,546	34,601	38,180	41,382	41,876	25	24
Kentucky.......................	24,938	32,929	36,214	37,654	29,998	32,394	33,740	34,620	45	45
Louisiana.......................	23,552	37,199	41,204	42,287	28,331	36,594	38,389	38,880	29	31
Maine...........................	27,108	37,213	40,924	42,071	32,609	36,608	38,128	38,681	30	32
Maryland.......................	35,331	50,035	53,826	55,143	42,500	49,221	50,149	50,700	5	6
Massachusetts................	38,430	51,487	57,248	59,182	46,228	50,650	53,337	54,413	3	3
Michigan........................	30,015	35,082	39,055	40,556	36,106	34,512	36,387	37,288	38	37
Minnesota......................	32,326	42,572	47,500	48,711	38,886	41,880	44,255	44,786	13	16
Mississippi.....................	21,564	30,834	33,913	34,333	25,940	30,333	31,596	31,567	51	51
Missouri........................	28,006	36,606	40,663	41,613	33,689	36,011	37,885	38,260	32	34
Montana........................	23,593	34,612	39,366	40,601	28,381	34,049	36,677	37,329	39	36
Nebraska.......................	28,967	39,926	47,157	47,073	34,845	39,277	43,935	43,280	23	20
Nevada.........................	31,208	36,657	39,235	40,077	37,541	36,061	36,554	36,848	31	38
New Hampshire................	34,280	44,963	51,013	53,149	41,236	44,232	47,528	48,866	9	9
New Jersey.....................	39,156	50,941	55,386	56,807	47,102	50,113	51,602	52,230	4	4
New Mexico....................	23,417	33,175	35,965	37,605	28,169	32,636	33,508	34,575	44	46
New York.......................	35,307	49,582	54,462	56,231	42,472	48,776	50,741	51,700	6	5
North Carolina.................	27,859	35,435	38,683	39,646	33,512	34,859	36,040	36,451	36	39
North Dakota...................	25,872	43,275	53,182	54,951	31,122	42,571	49,549	50,523	11	7
Ohio............................	28,620	36,199	41,049	42,571	34,428	35,610	38,245	39,141	33	30
Oklahoma......................	24,802	35,912	41,861	43,138	29,835	35,328	39,001	39,662	34	28
Oregon.........................	28,867	35,898	39,848	41,681	34,725	35,314	37,126	38,322	35	33
Pennsylvania...................	30,482	41,635	46,202	47,727	36,667	40,958	43,045	43,881	18	18
Rhode Island...................	30,201	43,013	46,989	48,838	36,329	42,314	43,779	44,903	12	14
South Carolina.................	25,124	32,669	35,831	36,934	30,222	32,138	33,383	33,958	46	49
South Dakota..................	27,260	40,613	46,039	46,345	32,792	39,953	42,894	42,611	21	22
Tennessee.....................	27,483	35,426	39,558	40,654	33,060	34,850	36,855	37,378	37	35
Texas...........................	28,341	38,065	43,862	45,426	34,092	37,446	40,865	41,766	28	25
Utah............................	24,770	32,447	36,640	37,766	29,796	31,919	34,137	34,723	47	43
Vermont........................	28,547	40,134	45,483	47,330	34,340	39,481	42,376	43,516	22	19
Virginia.........................	32,453	44,836	48,838	49,710	39,038	44,107	45,501	45,704	10	12
Washington.....................	32,865	42,547	47,717	49,583	39,534	41,855	44,457	45,588	14	13
West Virginia...................	22,096	31,798	35,533	36,644	26,580	31,281	33,105	33,691	50	50
Wisconsin......................	29,384	38,728	43,244	44,585	35,347	38,098	40,290	40,992	26	27
Wyoming........................	28,930	45,025	52,826	54,810	34,800	44,293	49,217	50,394	8	8

X Not applicable. [1] Constant dollar estimates are computed by ProQuest using the national implicit price deflator for personal consumption expenditures from the Bureau of Economic Analysis' National Income and Product Accounts tables. Any regional differences in the rate of inflation are not reflected in these constant dollar estimates. [2] Ranking based on current dollar income.

Source: Except as noted, U.S. Bureau of Economic Analysis, Regional Economic Accounts, State Annual Personal Income & Employment, "Table SA1 Personal Income Summary," <http://www.bea.gov/regional/index.htm>, accessed June 2015.

Table 702. Disposable Personal Income Per Capita in Current and Constant (2009) Dollars by State: 2000 to 2014

[In dollars, except as indicated. Per capita disposable personal income is total disposable personal income divided by total midyear population. Disposable personal income is total personal income minus personal current taxes. It is the portion of personal income that is available for consumption expenditures, interest payments, current transfer payments, or saving. The estimate of personal income in the United States is derived as the sum of the state estimates and the estimate for the District of Columbia; it differs from the estimate of personal income in the national income and product accounts (NIPAs) because of differences in coverage, in the methodologies used to prepare the estimates, and in the timing of the availability of source data. See text, Section 13. For methodology on how personal income is derived, see <http://www.bea.gov/regional/pdf/spi2013.pdf>]

State	Current dollars				Constant (2009) dollars [1]				Index, compared to U.S. average [2]	
	2000	2010	2013	2014	2000	2010	2013	2014	2010	2014
United States...........	26,224	36,296	39,513	40,670	31,545	35,706	36,813	37,393	100.0	100.0
Alabama..................	21,916	31,279	33,150	34,064	26,363	30,770	30,885	31,319	86.2	83.8
Alaska...................	28,064	41,984	45,600	48,132	33,759	41,301	42,485	44,254	116.1	118.3
Arizona..................	23,211	31,413	33,399	34,202	27,921	30,902	31,117	31,446	86.4	84.1
Arkansas.................	20,239	29,496	33,205	34,173	24,346	29,016	30,936	31,419	81.3	84.0
California...............	27,631	37,651	41,866	43,258	33,238	37,039	39,006	39,772	103.7	106.4
Colorado.................	29,106	37,538	41,137	42,684	35,012	36,928	38,327	39,245	103.4	105.0
Connecticut..............	34,115	47,594	50,743	52,250	41,038	46,820	47,276	48,040	131.3	128.5
Delaware.................	27,517	37,047	39,783	40,748	33,101	36,445	37,065	37,465	101.9	100.2
District of Columbia......	36,185	61,900	65,507	66,559	43,528	60,893	61,032	61,196	171.3	163.7
Florida..................	25,883	35,537	37,332	38,250	31,135	34,959	34,781	35,168	97.9	94.0
Georgia..................	24,746	31,288	33,832	34,921	29,767	30,779	31,521	32,107	86.2	85.9
Hawaii...................	25,357	38,315	40,730	41,827	30,502	37,692	37,947	38,457	105.5	102.8
Idaho....................	22,150	29,691	32,746	34,016	26,645	29,208	30,509	31,275	81.7	83.6
Illinois.................	28,174	37,894	40,990	41,889	33,891	37,278	38,190	38,514	104.5	103.0
Indiana..................	24,637	31,327	34,573	35,281	29,636	30,818	32,211	32,438	86.4	86.7
Iowa.....................	24,427	35,802	40,076	40,252	29,384	35,220	37,338	37,009	98.6	99.0
Kansas...................	25,129	35,274	39,660	40,613	30,228	34,700	36,950	37,340	97.1	99.9
Kentucky.................	21,878	30,097	32,579	33,925	26,317	29,608	30,353	31,191	82.9	83.4
Louisiana................	21,057	34,405	37,307	38,213	25,330	33,846	34,758	35,134	94.8	94.0
Maine....................	23,638	34,073	36,790	37,846	28,435	33,519	34,277	34,796	93.7	93.1
Maryland.................	29,883	44,501	46,880	48,083	35,947	43,777	43,677	44,209	122.6	118.2
Massachusetts............	31,003	45,103	48,808	50,394	37,294	44,370	45,473	46,333	124.2	123.9
Michigan.................	25,907	32,072	34,637	35,941	31,164	31,550	32,271	33,045	88.4	88.4
Minnesota................	27,508	38,059	41,215	42,221	33,090	37,440	38,399	38,819	104.9	103.8
Mississippi..............	19,499	28,656	31,164	31,529	23,456	28,190	29,035	28,988	78.9	77.5
Missouri.................	24,451	33,480	36,452	37,267	29,413	32,936	33,962	34,264	92.2	91.6
Montana..................	20,905	31,694	35,045	36,148	25,147	31,179	32,651	33,235	87.2	88.9
Nebraska.................	25,440	36,493	42,244	42,019	30,602	35,900	39,358	38,633	100.5	103.3
Nevada...................	27,105	33,715	35,283	35,946	32,605	33,167	32,872	33,050	92.9	88.4
New Hampshire............	29,464	41,296	46,071	47,894	35,443	40,624	42,923	44,035	113.7	117.8
New Jersey...............	32,823	45,227	48,012	49,267	39,483	44,492	44,732	45,297	124.7	121.1
New Mexico...............	20,867	30,784	32,816	34,360	25,101	30,283	30,574	31,591	84.8	84.5
New York.................	29,302	43,024	46,100	47,522	35,248	42,324	42,950	43,693	118.3	116.8
North Carolina...........	24,199	32,333	34,588	35,437	29,109	31,807	32,225	32,582	89.1	87.1
North Dakota.............	23,373	39,617	46,425	47,621	28,116	38,973	43,253	43,784	109.0	117.1
Ohio.....................	24,683	32,815	36,442	37,800	29,692	32,281	33,952	34,754	90.6	92.9
Oklahoma.................	21,920	33,103	37,736	38,863	26,368	32,565	35,158	35,731	91.2	95.6
Oregon...................	24,683	32,337	35,015	36,652	29,692	31,811	32,623	33,699	89.0	90.1
Pennsylvania.............	26,371	37,606	40,917	42,253	31,722	36,994	38,122	38,848	103.7	103.9
Rhode Island.............	26,055	39,177	41,870	43,534	31,342	38,540	39,009	40,026	107.8	107.0
South Carolina...........	22,209	30,192	32,456	33,440	26,716	29,701	30,239	30,745	83.2	82.2
South Dakota.............	24,715	38,010	42,065	42,133	29,730	37,392	39,191	38,738	104.6	103.6
Tennessee................	24,803	33,222	36,463	37,398	29,836	32,682	33,972	34,385	91.5	92.0
Texas....................	25,003	35,141	39,528	40,798	30,077	34,570	36,827	37,511	96.9	100.3
Utah.....................	21,707	29,765	32,727	33,718	26,112	29,281	30,491	31,001	82.0	82.9
Vermont..................	24,886	36,833	40,894	42,609	29,936	36,234	38,100	39,176	101.4	104.8
Virginia.................	27,594	40,091	42,807	43,605	33,193	39,439	39,882	40,091	110.4	107.2
Washington...............	28,409	39,254	42,937	44,504	34,174	38,616	40,004	40,918	108.0	109.4
West Virginia............	19,737	29,181	32,176	33,237	23,742	28,706	29,978	30,559	80.3	81.7
Wisconsin................	25,322	35,114	38,331	39,543	30,460	34,543	35,712	36,357	96.8	97.2
Wyoming..................	24,982	41,047	46,028	47,595	30,051	40,380	42,883	43,760	113.1	117.0

[1] Constant dollar estimates are computed by ProQuest using the national implicit price deflator for personal consumption expenditures from the Bureau of Economic Analysis' National Income and Product Accounts Tables. Any regional differences in the rate of inflation are not reflected in these constant dollar estimates. [2] Indexes calculated using disposable personal income per capita in current dollars.

Source: Except as noted, U.S. Bureau of Economic Analysis, Regional Economic Accounts, State Annual Personal Income & Employment, "Table SA51 Disposable Personal Income Summary," <http://www.bea.gov/regional/index.htm>, accessed June 2015.

Table 703. Personal Income by Selected Large Metropolitan Area: 2000 to 2013

[7,609,148 represents $7,609,148,000,000. MSA = Metropolitan Statistical Area. The MSAs used by the Bureau of Economic Analysis are county-based areas developed by the Office of Management and Budget (OMB); see OMB Bulletin No. 13-10, February 28, 2013. Per capita personal income was computed using Census Bureau midyear population estimates. Estimates for 2010-2013 reflect county population estimates available as of March 2014]

Metropolitan statistical areas ranked by 2013 population	Personal income			Personal income per capita			
	2000 (mil. dol.)	2010 (mil. dol.)	2013 (mil. dol.)	2000 (dol.)	2010 (dol.)	2013 (dol.)	Index (U.S.= 100), 2013
United States, metro portion	**7,609,148**	**10,932,066**	**12,463,711**	**32,057**	**41,563**	**46,177**	**100.0**
New York-Newark-Jersey City, NY-NJ-PA MSA	758,189	1,063,896	1,181,931	39,947	54,291	59,246	128.3
Los Angeles-Long Beach-Anaheim, CA MSA	392,777	551,832	635,892	31,694	42,964	48,425	104.9
Chicago-Naperville-Elgin, IL-IN-WI MSA	324,115	418,452	468,001	35,565	44,186	49,071	106.3
Dallas-Fort Worth-Arlington, TX MSA	176,507	266,843	320,035	33,714	41,353	46,989	101.8
Houston-The Woodlands-Sugar Land, TX MSA	157,443	263,570	327,841	33,374	44,307	51,930	112.5
Philadelphia-Camden-Wilmington, PA-NJ-DE-MD MSA	198,222	284,957	316,838	34,825	47,720	52,503	113.7
Washington-Arlington-Alexandria, DC-VA-MD-WV MSA	205,171	328,854	365,955	42,187	58,052	61,507	133.2
Miami-Fort Lauderdale-West Palm Beach, FL MSA	161,203	231,910	264,464	32,075	41,550	45,377	98.3
Atlanta-Sandy Springs-Roswell, GA MSA	144,445	198,872	228,135	33,643	37,493	41,307	89.5
Boston-Cambridge-Newton, MA-NH MSA	185,226	253,524	289,276	42,085	55,548	61,754	133.7
San Francisco-Oakland-Hayward, CA MSA	203,681	253,430	312,195	49,247	58,332	69,127	149.7
Phoenix-Mesa-Scottsdale, AZ MSA	95,195	148,819	170,431	29,081	35,359	38,745	83.9
Riverside-San Bernardino-Ontario, CA MSA	77,549	126,497	144,677	23,665	29,805	33,025	71.5
Detroit-Warren-Dearborn, MI MSA	152,603	164,012	184,199	34,251	38,219	42,887	92.9
Seattle-Tacoma-Bellevue, WA MSA	118,377	168,396	199,243	38,784	48,833	55,190	119.5
Minneapolis-St. Paul-Bloomington, MN-WI MSA	111,690	154,391	177,051	36,687	46,016	51,183	110.8
San Diego-Carlsbad, CA MSA	96,358	141,243	165,008	34,081	45,501	51,384	111.3
Tampa-St. Petersburg-Clearwater, FL MSA	71,389	106,713	116,042	29,696	38,263	40,425	87.5
St. Louis, MO-IL MSA	85,733	114,937	128,826	32,004	41,197	45,992	99.6
Baltimore-Columbia-Towson, MD MSA	87,755	134,816	150,886	34,307	49,650	54,457	117.9
Denver-Aurora-Lakewood, CO MSA	83,001	117,616	140,123	38,232	46,055	51,946	112.5
Pittsburgh, PA MSA	75,151	102,496	115,799	30,948	43,492	49,049	106.2
Charlotte-Concord-Gastonia, NC-SC MSA	53,579	82,958	97,256	30,996	37,307	41,645	90.2
Portland-Vancouver-Hillsboro, OR-WA MSA	63,409	87,357	101,210	32,773	39,135	43,728	94.7
San Antonio-New Braunfels, TX MSA	46,765	76,530	90,990	27,189	35,541	39,951	86.5
Orlando-Kissimmee-Sanford, FL MSA	46,236	73,710	83,892	27,905	34,454	36,992	80.1
Sacramento-Roseville-Arden-Arcade, CA MSA	57,103	88,563	103,030	31,584	41,108	46,499	100.7
Cincinnati, OH-KY-IN MSA	61,940	82,797	93,882	30,977	39,104	43,923	95.1
Cleveland-Elyria, OH MSA	68,274	83,263	94,455	31,792	40,114	45,747	99.1
Kansas City, MO-KS MSA	58,955	83,136	93,597	32,430	41,285	45,558	98.7
Las Vegas-Henderson-Paradise, NV MSA	42,160	69,329	75,957	30,246	35,497	37,457	81.1
Columbus, OH MSA	51,871	73,221	86,289	30,838	38,411	43,867	95.0
Indianapolis-Carmel-Anderson, IN MSA	54,245	72,466	83,125	32,599	38,295	42,542	92.1
San Jose-Sunnyvale-Santa Clara, CA MSA	93,840	103,634	132,849	53,970	56,259	69,205	149.9
Austin-Round Rock, TX MSA	41,569	67,402	84,286	32,862	39,010	44,760	96.9
Nashville-Davidson--Murfreesboro--Franklin, TN MSA	44,784	67,995	80,440	32,279	40,571	45,759	99.1
Virginia Beach-Norfolk-Newport News, VA-NC MSA	44,224	69,255	76,414	27,905	41,220	44,756	96.9
Providence-Warwick, RI-MA MSA	47,264	67,698	74,351	29,799	42,264	46,345	100.4
Milwaukee-Waukesha-West Allis, WI MSA	50,236	67,551	74,854	33,437	43,398	47,688	103.3
Jacksonville, FL MSA	34,521	53,291	60,176	30,650	39,502	43,149	93.4
Memphis, TN-MS-AR MSA	36,058	48,992	54,994	29,646	36,931	40,987	88.8
Oklahoma City, OK MSA	29,943	48,128	58,435	27,267	38,261	44,280	95.9
Louisville/Jefferson County, KY-IN MSA	33,810	46,495	52,355	30,078	37,561	41,477	89.8
Richmond, VA MSA	33,792	50,446	57,452	31,911	41,691	46,118	99.9
New Orleans-Metairie, LA MSA	35,678	50,010	55,529	26,639	41,823	44,746	96.9
Hartford-West Hartford-East Hartford, CT MSA	43,568	61,652	67,269	37,856	50,784	55,355	119.9
Raleigh, NC MSA	27,703	45,833	53,374	34,450	40,298	43,947	95.2
Salt Lake City, UT MSA	26,682	40,490	47,384	28,308	37,098	41,547	90.0
Birmingham-Hoover, AL MSA	31,025	43,533	48,542	29,455	38,556	42,570	92.2
Buffalo-Cheektowaga-Niagara Falls, NY MSA	32,639	44,931	50,242	27,919	39,575	44,301	95.9
Rochester, NY MSA	31,852	43,476	49,497	29,867	40,253	45,692	98.9
Grand Rapids-Wyoming, MI MSA	27,087	33,689	38,950	28,996	34,057	38,314	83.0
Tucson, AZ MSA	21,434	33,883	36,935	25,275	34,504	37,063	80.3
Honolulu, HI MSA	27,143	43,220	47,990	30,963	45,202	48,798	105.7
Tulsa, OK MSA	24,402	37,027	45,479	28,333	39,398	47,297	102.4

Source: U.S. Bureau of Economic Analysis, Regional Economic Accounts, Local Areas Personal Income and Employment, "Table CA1. Personal Income, Population, Per Capita Personal Income," <http://www.bea.gov/regional/index.htm>, accessed June 2015.

Table 706. Average Annual Expenditures of All Consumer Units by Major Type of Expenditure: 1990 to 2013

[Consumer units in thousands (96,968 represents 96,968,000); expenditures in dollars. Based on Consumer Expenditure Survey. Data are averages for the noninstitutional population. Expenditures are direct out-of-pocket expenditures. Consumers units may be all members in a housing unit (families), a person living alone or sharing a household with others and financially independent, or 2 or more unrelated persons living together who share expenses]

Type of expenditure	1990	1995	2000	2005	2010	2011	2012	2013
Number of consumer units (1,000)............	96,968	103,123	109,367	117,356	121,107	122,287	124,416	125,670
Expenditures, avg. (dol.) [1]..................	**28,381**	**32,264**	**38,045**	**46,409**	**48,109**	**49,705**	**51,442**	**51,100**
Food..........	4,296	4,505	5,158	5,931	6,129	6,458	6,599	6,602
Food at home [1]............................	2,485	2,803	3,021	3,297	3,624	3,838	3,921	3,977
Cereals and bakery products................	368	441	453	445	502	531	538	544
Meats, poultry, fish, and eggs..............	668	752	795	764	784	832	852	856
Dairy products..........................	295	297	325	378	380	407	419	414
Fruits and vegetables..........................	408	457	521	552	679	715	731	751
Other food at home.......................	746	856	927	1,158	1,278	1,353	1,380	1,412
Food away from home.......................	1,811	1,702	2,137	2,634	2,505	2,620	2,678	2,625
Alcoholic beverages...........................	293	277	372	426	412	456	451	445
Housing [1]..	8,703	10,458	12,319	15,167	16,557	16,803	16,887	17,148
Shelter......................................	4,836	5,928	7,114	8,805	9,812	9,825	9,891	10,080
Utilities, fuels, and public services............	1,890	2,191	2,489	3,183	3,660	3,727	3,648	3,737
Apparel and services...........................	1,618	1,704	1,856	1,886	1,700	1,740	1,736	1,604
Transportation [1]................................	5,120	6,014	7,417	8,344	7,677	8,293	8,998	9,004
Vehicle purchases...........................	2,129	2,638	3,418	3,544	2,588	2,669	3,210	3,271
Gasoline and motor oil.......................	1,047	1,006	1,291	2,013	2,132	2,655	2,756	2,611
Other vehicle expenses.......................	1,642	2,015	2,281	2,339	2,464	2,454	2,490	2,584
Public transportation.........................	302	355	427	448	493	516	542	537
Health care..................................	1,480	1,732	2,066	2,664	3,157	3,313	3,556	3,631
Entertainment................................	1,422	1,612	1,863	2,388	2,504	2,572	2,605	2,482
Personal care products and services...........	364	403	564	541	582	634	628	608
Reading......................................	153	162	146	126	100	115	109	102
Education....................................	406	471	632	940	1,074	1,051	1,207	1,138
Tobacco products, smoking supplies...........	274	269	319	319	362	351	332	330
Personal insurance and pensions..............	2,592	2,964	3,365	5,204	5,373	5,424	5,591	5,528
Life and other personal insurance............	345	373	399	381	318	317	353	319
Pensions and Social Security..................	2,248	2,591	2,966	4,823	5,054	5,106	5,238	5,209

[1] Includes expenditures not shown separately.

Source: U.S. Bureau of Labor Statistics, Consumer Expenditure Survey program, "Annual Calendar Year Tables, 2013," September 2014, <http://www.bls.gov/cex/tables.htm>, accessed April 2015.

Table 707. Average Annual Expenditures of All Consumer Units by Metropolitan Statistical Area: 2012 to 2013

[In dollars. Covers 2-year period, 2012-2013. MSA = Metropolitan Statistical Area. See text, Section 1 and Appendix II. See headnote, Table 706]

Metropolitan statistical area	Total expenditures [1]	Food	Housing Total [1]	Housing Shelter	Housing Utility, fuels [2]	Transportation Total [1]	Transportation Vehicle purchases	Transportation Gasoline and motor oil	Health care
Atlanta, Georgia MSA........................	50,782	6,374	16,975	9,828	3,983	8,682	3,193	3,025	3,147
Baltimore, Maryland MSA....................	62,012	6,807	20,165	12,238	3,930	9,589	2,395	3,045	3,722
Boston, Massachusetts MSA................	65,650	8,705	21,384	12,894	4,143	10,219	3,488	2,775	4,518
Chicago, Illinois MSA.........................	57,919	7,373	20,527	13,054	3,751	9,026	3,176	2,780	3,982
Cleveland, Ohio MSA.........................	49,438	6,346	15,644	9,047	3,663	8,977	3,846	2,292	3,251
Dallas-Fort Worth, Texas MSA..............	56,827	7,177	19,033	10,902	4,278	10,196	3,588	3,060	3,744
Detroit, Michigan MSA.......................	53,835	7,268	16,130	8,900	3,768	10,623	3,629	3,067	3,675
Houston, Texas MSA.........................	59,724	7,155	19,747	11,180	4,151	12,560	5,355	3,404	3,174
Los Angeles, California MSA................	55,852	7,510	21,353	13,902	3,421	8,599	2,267	2,979	2,859
Miami, Florida MSA..........................	40,604	5,695	16,212	10,983	3,219	6,573	[3] 1,089	2,562	2,204
Minneapolis-St. Paul, Minnesota MSA.....	66,678	7,554	21,315	11,918	3,491	12,222	4,961	3,162	4,754
New York City MSA..........................	60,791	7,225	24,187	16,257	4,200	8,235	2,067	2,180	3,585
Philadelphia, Pennsylvania MSA............	55,766	7,662	19,740	11,468	4,388	8,595	2,914	2,282	3,597
Phoenix, Arizona MSA.......................	54,168	7,358	18,864	11,033	4,041	10,240	3,794	2,548	3,312
San Diego, California MSA..................	60,279	6,915	23,009	15,707	3,154	9,502	2,427	3,075	3,781
San Francisco, California MSA..............	70,807	8,401	25,366	17,343	3,522	9,675	2,861	2,521	4,312
Seattle, Washington MSA...................	63,759	8,265	21,294	12,980	4,135	9,975	3,446	2,927	3,964
Washington, DC MSA........................	80,452	8,762	28,416	17,883	4,457	13,450	5,298	2,973	4,450

[1] Includes expenditures not shown separately. [2] Includes public services. [3] Data are likely to have large sampling errors.

Source: U.S. Bureau of Labor Statistics, Consumer Expenditure Survey program, "Metropolitan Statistical Area Tables," <http://www.bls.gov/cex/tables.htm>, accessed April 2015.

Table 708. Average Annual Expenditures of All Consumer Units by Race, Hispanic Origin, and Age of Householder: 2013

[In dollars. See headnote, Table 706. See source for definitions, standard errors, and other information]

Type	All consumer units [1]	White and all other races	Asian	Black or African American	Hispanic [2]	Age of householder Under 25 years	Age of householder 65 years old and over
Expenditures, total	**51,100**	**52,740**	**60,167**	**37,080**	**41,958**	**30,373**	**41,403**
Food	6,602	6,743	8,073	5,168	6,771	4,698	5,191
Food at home	3,977	4,057	4,413	3,290	4,042	2,602	3,327
Cereals and bakery products	544	553	627	453	519	363	457
Cereals and cereal products	185	184	258	169	194	130	139
Bakery products	359	369	369	284	326	233	318
Meats, poultry, fish, and eggs [3]	856	844	981	899	1,009	580	689
Beef	219	223	188	200	286	141	177
Pork	170	169	190	167	190	105	148
Poultry	170	160	185	229	217	126	118
Fish and seafood	122	112	259	150	126	93	101
Eggs	56	56	72	52	70	40	52
Dairy products [3]	414	439	367	263	419	274	351
Fresh milk and cream	152	158	162	105	184	109	122
Fruits and vegetables [3]	751	764	1,020	574	828	448	663
Fresh fruits	270	276	410	185	311	147	249
Fresh vegetables	236	239	382	166	264	137	206
Processed fruits	115	116	113	107	122	79	102
Other food at home [3]	1,412	1,458	1,418	1,101	1,267	936	1,168
Sugar and other sweets	143	150	117	105	110	89	133
Nonalcoholic beverages	384	397	378	298	396	276	308
Food away from home	2,625	2,686	3,660	1,878	2,729	2,096	1,864
Alcoholic beverages	445	486	326	201	365	379	326
Housing	17,148	17,463	20,918	13,748	15,316	10,379	14,204
Shelter	10,080	10,186	14,143	7,992	9,314	6,944	7,755
Owned dwellings	6,108	6,403	8,291	3,406	3,886	1,003	5,284
Mortgage interest and charges	3,078	3,164	4,660	1,969	2,177	449	1,560
Property taxes	1,848	1,952	2,653	883	1,034	403	2,065
Maintenance, repair, insurance, other expenses	1,182	1,287	978	554	675	151	1,659
Rented dwellings	3,324	3,084	5,049	4,325	5,195	5,728	1,808
Other lodging	649	699	803	261	232	213	663
Utilities, fuels, and public services	3,737	3,770	3,481	3,605	3,351	1,842	3,480
Natural gas	393	386	463	413	309	163	411
Electricity	1,422	1,426	1,119	1,499	1,264	728	1,351
Fuel oil and other fuels	142	162	61	42	42	30	214
Telephone	1,271	1,281	1,286	1,203	1,270	737	985
Water and other public services	509	516	551	448	467	184	520
Household operations	1,144	1,180	1,377	826	878	428	1,007
Personal services	368	359	585	355	400	134	146
Other household expenses	776	821	792	471	478	293	861
Housekeeping supplies [3]	645	682	490	441	567	323	682
Laundry and cleaning supplies	154	158	127	138	193	93	148
Postage and stationery	140	150	111	87	85	38	174
Household furnishings and equipment [3]	1,542	1,645	1,427	884	1,206	842	1,280
Household textiles	97	101	80	77	82	56	104
Furniture	382	405	340	249	358	258	261
Major appliances	214	223	270	138	142	95	182
Miscellaneous household equipment	727	785	630	366	541	343	630
Apparel and services [3]	1,604	1,583	2,073	1,595	1,924	1,513	1,022
Men and boys	374	362	590	391	484	316	193
Women and girls	636	640	812	558	688	516	517
Footwear	307	297	334	365	423	333	141
Other apparel products and services	211	214	194	197	232	197	150
Transportation	9,004	9,381	9,165	6,437	7,622	5,672	6,760
Vehicle purchases (net outlay) [3]	3,271	3,470	2,797	2,114	2,484	2,262	2,133
Cars and trucks, new	1,563	1,669	1,922	737	1,038	805	1,335
Cars and trucks, used	1,669	1,756	841	1,378	1,432	1,371	788
Gasoline and motor oil	2,611	2,689	2,557	2,117	2,578	1,717	1,799
Other vehicle expenses	2,584	2,689	2,419	1,940	2,210	1,444	2,302
Vehicle finance charges	204	209	168	180	178	108	101
Maintenance and repair	835	882	759	547	661	491	738
Vehicle insurance	1,013	1,035	867	909	936	616	985
Vehicle rental, leases, licenses, other charges	533	562	625	305	435	229	478
Public transportation	537	534	1,393	266	350	249	527
Health care [4]	3,631	3,894	3,255	2,013	1,931	943	5,069
Entertainment [5]	2,482	2,661	2,321	1,344	1,635	1,243	2,027
Personal care products and services	608	621	666	506	524	342	563
Reading	102	111	89	50	38	46	138
Education	1,138	1,098	3,233	687	497	2,055	319
Tobacco products and smoking supplies	330	357	122	217	154	219	185
Miscellaneous	645	690	462	407	421	207	628
Cash contributions	1,834	1,900	2,148	1,289	884	473	2,574
Personal insurance and pensions	5,528	5,754	7,315	3,417	3,876	2,203	2,396
Life and other personal insurance	319	330	286	255	127	50	421
Pensions and social security	5,209	5,424	7,029	3,162	3,748	2,153	1,975
Personal taxes	**7,432**	**7,948**	**10,204**	**3,054**	**2,480**	**1,355**	**3,271**

[1] Includes other races not shown separately. [2] People of Hispanic origin may be of any race. [3] Includes other types, not shown separately. [4] For additional health care expenditures, see Table 155. [5] For additional recreation expenditures, see Section 26.

Source: U.S. Bureau of Labor Statistics, Consumer Expenditure Survey Program, "Annual Calendar Year Tables, 2013," <http://stats.bls.gov/cex/>, accessed April 2015.

Table 709. Average Annual Expenditures of All Consumer Units by Region and Size of Unit: 2013

[In dollars. For composition of regions, see map, inside front cover. See headnote, Table 706. See source for definitions, standard errors, and other information]

Type	Region				Size of consumer unit				
	North-east	Mid-west	South	West	One person	Two persons	Three persons	Four persons	Five or more
Expenditures, total	**57,027**	**50,527**	**45,956**	**55,460**	**31,248**	**54,568**	**59,029**	**68,299**	**65,129**
Food	7,033	6,592	6,056	7,180	3,654	6,586	7,679	9,588	9,825
Food at home	4,222	4,119	3,607	4,267	2,126	3,862	4,730	5,794	6,309
Cereals and bakery products	604	584	492	544	289	506	643	822	910
Cereals and cereal products	204	200	165	188	93	166	223	281	340
Bakery products	400	384	326	356	196	340	420	541	569
Meats, poultry, fish, and eggs [1]	943	821	835	856	412	834	1,025	1,237	1,495
Beef	221	212	224	213	91	215	268	318	405
Pork	165	172	175	163	78	172	203	247	282
Poultry	203	153	164	169	80	156	209	251	319
Fish and seafood	159	97	109	140	73	121	131	177	187
Dairy products	462	436	352	458	233	402	476	615	630
Fresh milk and cream	164	156	139	159	82	139	177	227	264
Other dairy products	298	280	213	299	151	263	300	387	366
Fruits and vegetables [1]	819	781	634	862	419	746	865	1,066	1,159
Fresh fruits	287	283	215	337	159	261	302	388	424
Fresh vegetables	268	227	198	283	130	248	276	307	355
Processed fruits	127	125	96	127	64	110	131	181	171
Other food at home [1]	1,394	1,497	1,293	1,548	773	1,375	1,721	2,054	2,116
Sugar and other sweets	146	156	127	155	77	145	164	208	212
Nonalcoholic beverages	395	382	380	382	214	379	477	536	557
Food away from home	2,811	2,473	2,449	2,913	1,528	2,725	2,949	3,794	3,516
Alcoholic beverages	527	436	360	528	339	573	428	464	316
Housing	20,341	15,914	15,000	19,376	11,751	17,757	19,039	22,511	21,617
Shelter	12,517	9,055	8,327	12,053	7,530	10,316	10,859	12,871	12,253
Owned dwellings	7,742	5,917	5,141	6,590	3,384	6,588	6,902	8,989	7,869
Mortgage interest and charges	3,155	2,700	2,714	4,001	1,433	2,900	3,816	5,293	4,637
Property taxes	3,127	1,966	1,337	1,547	1,115	2,121	1,989	2,550	2,060
Maintenance, repair, insurance, other expenses	1,460	1,251	1,090	1,041	836	1,567	1,096	1,146	1,172
Rented dwellings	4,012	2,437	2,670	4,739	3,837	2,803	3,233	3,171	3,791
Other lodging	763	701	517	724	308	925	724	711	593
Utilities, fuels, and public services	4,126	3,564	3,772	3,535	2,341	3,822	4,368	4,735	5,451
Natural gas	562	555	225	374	260	400	434	484	591
Electricity	1,331	1,287	1,679	1,199	939	1,454	1,616	1,746	2,070
Fuel oil and other fuels	460	105	61	58	97	159	166	164	161
Telephone services	1,360	1,195	1,287	1,249	735	1,290	1,557	1,707	1,837
Water and other public services	412	422	521	656	310	519	595	634	792
Household operations	1,387	1,068	1,000	1,264	610	1,033	1,486	2,044	1,419
Personal services	554	392	289	325	67	113	685	1,143	606
Other household expenses	832	675	711	940	543	921	801	901	814
Housekeeping supplies [1]	648	665	586	721	368	726	666	906	803
Laundry and cleaning supplies	145	154	149	170	79	165	171	230	211
Postage and stationery	168	137	114	166	102	167	129	189	117
Household furnishings and equipment [1]	1,665	1,563	1,315	1,802	903	1,859	1,660	1,954	1,690
Household textiles	93	95	72	146	64	100	95	171	96
Furniture	415	389	342	417	203	475	429	472	440
Major appliances	207	211	193	259	106	251	262	239	315
Miscellaneous household equipment	815	755	606	832	460	880	743	944	694
Apparel and services [1]	1,816	1,485	1,453	1,801	861	1,522	1,974	2,486	2,362
Men and boys	428	313	347	435	207	334	423	664	554
Women and girls	650	637	592	701	358	649	745	909	891
Footwear	412	253	267	342	138	258	424	513	527
Other apparel products and services	249	198	177	250	141	251	241	245	197
Transportation	9,354	9,102	8,673	9,168	4,952	9,491	11,160	12,529	11,789
Vehicle purchases (net outlay) [1]	3,279	3,494	3,222	3,124	1,592	3,370	4,381	5,023	4,053
Cars and trucks, new	1,867	1,367	1,603	1,446	705	1,757	2,246	2,084	1,810
Cars and trucks, used	1,350	2,078	1,605	1,629	847	1,556	2,125	2,911	2,210
Gasoline and motor oil	2,389	2,616	2,726	2,594	1,373	2,686	3,144	3,670	3,942
Other vehicle expenses	2,889	2,463	2,395	2,768	1,676	2,741	3,083	3,216	3,208
Vehicle finance charges	178	189	225	203	86	210	270	322	283
Maintenance and repair	800	866	760	959	529	916	939	1,090	1,008
Vehicle insurance	1,094	882	1,048	1,013	744	1,043	1,192	1,190	1,192
Vehicle rental, leases, licenses, other charges	816	527	362	594	317	573	681	614	726
Public transportation	797	528	330	682	311	693	553	621	586
Health care [2]	3,784	4,095	3,295	3,609	2,375	4,532	3,919	3,971	3,632
Entertainment [3]	2,615	2,460	2,165	2,928	1,547	2,676	2,604	3,452	3,238
Personal care products and services	626	575	556	714	360	695	650	815	728
Reading	117	113	79	119	74	136	83	101	113
Education	1,870	1,207	728	1,159	643	944	1,733	1,663	1,658
Tobacco products/smoking supplies	343	358	344	267	244	353	391	377	359
Miscellaneous	654	656	587	720	509	697	758	685	659
Cash contributions	1,527	2,081	1,683	2,089	1,382	2,503	1,572	1,754	1,561
Personal insurance and pensions	6,422	5,453	4,975	5,801	2,558	6,103	7,038	7,904	7,274
Life and other personal insurance	376	310	310	295	158	426	352	366	348
Pensions and social security	6,045	5,143	4,665	5,506	2,400	5,676	6,686	7,538	6,926
Personal taxes	**9,674**	**7,870**	**5,944**	**7,663**	**3,838**	**9,539**	**8,872**	**10,049**	**5,866**

[1] Includes other types not shown separately. [2] For additional health care expenditures, see Table 155. [3] For additional recreation expenditures, see Section 26.

Source: U.S. Bureau of Labor Statistics, Consumer Expenditure Survey Program, "Annual Calendar Year Tables, 2013," <http://stats.bls.gov/cex/home.htm>, accessed April 2015.

Table 710. Average Annual Expenditures of All Consumer Units by Income Level: 2013

[In dollars. See headnote, Table 706. See source for definitions, standard errors, and other information]

Income level	Total expenditures [1]	Food	Housing Total [1]	Housing Shelter	Housing Utilities, fuels [2]	Transportation Total [1]	Transportation Vehicle purchases	Transportation Gasoline and motor oil	Health care	Pensions and social security
All consumer units........	51,100	6,602	17,148	10,080	3,737	9,004	3,271	2,611	3,631	5,209
Consumer units with incomes:										
Less than $70,000.............	34,900	5,005	12,595	7,379	3,088	6,256	2,045	2,044	2,866	2,065
$70,000 to $79,999...........	58,978	7,762	18,433	10,520	4,237	10,845	3,981	3,234	4,278	6,400
$80,000 to $99,999...........	66,650	8,347	21,743	12,650	4,689	11,881	4,510	3,498	4,655	7,964
$100,000 and over.............	101,686	11,422	31,515	18,761	5,552	17,310	7,028	4,117	5,800	15,226
$100,000 to $119,999........	79,530	9,775	24,408	14,463	4,875	15,217	6,223	3,968	5,046	10,143
$120,000 to $149,999........	90,450	10,848	27,905	16,502	5,265	15,843	6,506	4,099	5,502	13,240
$150,000 and over............	126,242	13,198	39,348	23,507	6,252	19,901	7,986	4,239	6,573	20,361

[1] Includes expenditures not shown separately. [2] Includes public services.

Source: U.S. Bureau of Labor Statistics, Consumer Expenditure Survey, "Annual Calendar Year Tables, 2013," <http://stats.bls.gov/cex/home.htm>, accessed April 2015.

Table 711. Annual Expenditure Per Child by Husband-Wife Families by Family Income and Expenditure Type: 2013

[In dollars. Excludes expenses for college. Estimates are based on 2005-06 Consumer Expenditure Survey data updated to 2013 dollars by using the Consumer Price Index. Data are for the younger child in a two-child family. Estimates are about the same for the older child, so to calculate expenses for two children, figures should be summed for the appropriate age categories. To estimate expenses for an only child, multiply the total expense for the appropriate age category by 1.25. To estimate expenses for each child in a family with three or more children, multiply the total expense for each appropriate age category by 0.78; for expenses on all children in a family, these totals should be summed. For methodology, see source]

Family income and age of child	Total	Expenditure type Housing	Food	Transportation	Clothing	Health care	Child care and education [1]	Miscellaneous [2]
INCOME: LESS THAN $61,530								
Less than 2 years old.......................	9,480	3,100	1,210	1,200	670	670	2,200	430
3 to 5 years old.............................	9,520	3,100	1,310	1,250	530	630	2,070	630
6 to 8 years old.............................	9,130	3,100	1,780	1,380	600	700	920	650
9 to 11 years old............................	9,950	3,100	2,050	1,390	610	760	1,400	640
12 to 14 years old...........................	10,370	3,100	2,220	1,510	720	1,150	950	720
15 to 17 years old...........................	10,400	3,100	2,210	1,670	760	1,080	980	600
INCOME: $61,530 to $106,540								
Less than 2 years old.......................	12,940	4,070	1,450	1,730	790	900	3,090	910
3 to 5 years old.............................	12,970	4,070	1,550	1,780	640	850	2,960	1,120
6 to 8 years old.............................	12,800	4,070	2,180	1,910	710	990	1,810	1,130
9 to 11 years old............................	13,680	4,070	2,490	1,910	740	1,060	2,280	1,130
12 to 14 years old...........................	14,420	4,070	2,680	2,040	870	1,500	2,060	1,200
15 to 17 years old...........................	14,970	4,070	2,670	2,200	940	1,410	2,600	1,080
INCOME: MORE THAN $106,540								
Less than 2 years old.......................	21,430	7,370	1,980	2,610	1,100	1,040	5,500	1,830
3 to 5 years old.............................	21,440	7,370	2,080	2,670	920	990	5,370	2,040
6 to 8 years old.............................	21,330	7,370	2,740	2,800	1,010	1,140	4,220	2,050
9 to 11 years old............................	22,290	7,370	3,100	2,800	1,050	1,220	4,700	2,050
12 to 14 years old...........................	23,750	7,370	3,320	2,930	1,220	1,710	5,080	2,120
15 to 17 years old...........................	25,700	7,370	3,310	3,090	1,330	1,620	6,980	2,000

[1] Includes only families with child care and education expenses. [2] Expenses include personal care items, entertainment, and reading materials.

Source: U.S. Department of Agriculture, Center for Nutrition Policy and Promotion, *Expenditures on Children by Families, 2013*, August 2014. See also <http://www.cnpp.usda.gov/ExpendituresonChildrenbyFamilies>.

Table 712. Money Income of Households—Percent Distribution by Income Level, Race, and Hispanic Origin, in Constant (2013) Dollars: 2000 to 2013

[In percent except as noted (108,209 represents 108,209,000). Households as of March of following year. Constant dollars based on CPI-U-RS deflator. Based on Current Population Survey, Annual Social and Economic Supplement (ASEC); see text, this section and Section 1, and Appendix III. For definition of median, see Guide to Tabular Presentation. A household consists of all the persons who occupy a house, an apartment, or other group of rooms, or a room, which constitutes a housing unit. Household count excludes persons living in group quarters and institutions. Beginning with the 2003 CPS covering data for 2002, refers to respondents reporting only one race. Two basic ways of defining a race group are possible: a group such as Asian may be defined as 1) those who reported Asian and no other race (the race-alone concept), or 2) those who reported Asian regardless of whether they also reported another race (the race-alone-or-in-combination concept). For 2001 data and earlier, the CPS allowed respondents to report only one race group]

Year	Number of house-holds (1,000)	Percent distribution							Median income (dollars)
		Under $15,000	$15,000 to $24,999	$25,000 to $34,999	$35,000 to $49,999	$50,000 to $74,999	$75,000 to $99,999	$100,000 and over	
ALL HOUSEHOLDS [1]									
2000 [4]	108,209	10.7	10.1	9.9	13.7	18.4	12.9	24.3	56,800
2010 [5]	119,927	12.8	11.5	10.5	13.3	17.6	11.8	22.6	52,646
2012	122,459	12.8	11.6	10.6	13.5	17.4	11.7	22.3	51,759
2013	122,952	12.7	11.3	10.4	13.6	17.6	11.9	22.5	51,939
WHITE [2]									
2000 [4]	90,030	9.5	9.8	9.6	13.7	18.5	13.3	25.7	59,406
2010 [5]	96,306	10.9	11.2	10.3	13.4	17.9	12.3	24.0	55,246
2012	97,705	11.0	11.2	10.6	13.5	17.8	12.3	23.7	54,487
2013	97,774	11.0	10.9	10.1	13.5	18.1	12.7	23.8	55,257
BLACK [2]									
2000 [4]	13,174	19.3	13.1	12.6	14.6	18.0	9.5	12.9	40,131
2010 [5]	15,265	24.4	14.2	12.3	14.4	15.4	8.5	10.8	34,321
2012	15,872	23.8	15.3	11.9	14.3	14.9	8.6	11.1	33,805
2013	16,108	22.9	14.8	12.7	14.7	14.8	8.2	11.9	34,598
ASIAN AND PACIFIC ISLANDER [2]									
2000 [4]	3,963	8.4	6.8	7.3	11.0	16.4	13.9	36.1	75,423
2010 [5]	5,212	10.3	8.8	7.6	9.7	18.1	11.3	34.2	68,654
2012	5,560	10.4	7.3	7.6	10.8	17.1	12.8	34.1	69,633
2013	5,759	11.0	7.8	7.6	11.6	16.9	11.3	33.7	67,065
HISPANIC [3]									
2000 [4]	10,034	12.8	13.4	12.1	16.9	19.9	10.9	13.9	44,867
2010 [5]	14,435	16.4	14.0	13.8	15.0	17.8	9.9	13.0	40,205
2012	15,589	16.6	14.5	13.6	15.6	17.2	9.7	12.7	39,572
2013	15,811	15.9	13.8	13.3	16.2	17.1	10.5	13.1	40,963

[1] Includes other races not shown separately. [2] Beginning with 2002, data represent White alone, Black alone, or Asian alone. [3] People of Hispanic origin may be of any race. [4] Data reflect implementation of Census 2000-based population controls and a 28,000 household sample expansion to 78,000 households. [5] Median income is calculated using $2,500 income intervals. Beginning with 2009 income data, the Census Bureau expanded the upper income intervals used to calculate medians to $250,000 or more. Medians falling in the upper open-ended interval are plugged with "$250,000." Before 2009, the upper open-ended interval was $100,000 and a plug of "$100,000" was used. Implementation of Census 2010-based population controls.

Source: U.S. Census Bureau, *Income and Poverty in the United States: 2013,* Current Population Reports, P60-249, September 2014; and "Historical Income Data: Households, Table H-17," <http://www.census.gov/hhes/www/income/data/historical/household/>, accessed November 2014.

Table 713. Money Income of Households—Median Income by Race and Hispanic Origin, in Current and Constant (2013) Dollars: 1980 to 2013

[In dollars. See headnote, Table 712]

Year	Median income in current dollars					Median income in constant (2013) dollars				
	All house-holds [1]	White [2]	Black [2]	Asian, Pacific Islander [2]	His-panic [3]	All house-holds [1]	White [2]	Black [2]	Asian, Pacific Islander [2]	His-panic [3]
1980	17,710	18,684	10,764	(NA)	13,651	47,668	50,290	28,972	(NA)	36,743
1990	29,943	31,231	18,676	38,450	22,330	51,735	53,960	32,268	66,433	38,581
1995 [4]	34,076	35,766	22,393	40,614	22,860	51,719	54,284	33,987	61,642	34,696
2000 [5, 6]	41,990	43,916	29,667	55,757	33,168	56,800	59,406	40,131	75,423	44,867
2005	46,326	48,554	30,858	61,094	35,967	55,278	57,936	36,821	72,899	42,917
2010 [7]	49,276	51,709	32,124	64,259	37,631	52,646	55,246	34,321	68,654	40,205
2011 [8]	50,054	52,214	32,229	65,129	38,624	51,842	54,079	33,380	67,456	40,004
2012	51,017	53,706	33,321	68,636	39,005	51,758	54,486	33,805	69,633	39,572
2013	51,939	55,257	34,598	67,065	40,963	51,939	55,257	34,598	67,065	40,963

NA Not available. [1] Includes other races, not shown separately. [2] Beginning with 2002, refers to people who reported specified race and did not report any other race category; for "Asian Pacific Islander," refers to people who reported "Asian alone." [3] People of Hispanic origin may be of any race. [4] Data reflect full implementation of the 1990 Census-based sample design and metropolitan definitions, 7,000 household sample reduction, and revised race edits. [5] Implementation of Census 2000-based population controls. [6] Implementation of a 28,000 household sample expansion. [7] Median income is calculated using $2,500 income intervals. Beginning with 2009 income data, the Census Bureau expanded the upper income intervals used to calculate medians to $250,000 or more. Before 2009, the upper open-ended interval was $100,000 and a plug of "$100,000" was used. [8] Implementation of Census 2010-based population controls.

Source: U.S. Census Bureau, *Income and Poverty in the United States: 2013,* Current Population Reports, P60-249, September 2014; and "Historical Income Data: Households, Table H-5," <https://www.census.gov/hhes/www/income/data/historical/household/>, accessed November 2014. See also <https://www.census.gov/hhes/www/income/index.html>.

Table 714. Money Income of Households—Distribution by Income Level and Selected Characteristics: 2013

[122,952 represents 122,952,000. Households as of March of the following year. Based on Current Population Survey, Annual Social and Economic Supplement (ASEC); see text, this section and Section 1, and Appendix III. For definition of median, see Guide to Tabular Presentation. Median income is calculated using $2,500 income intervals. Medians falling in the upper open-ended interval are plugged with "$250,000." For methodological information, see source and <ftp://ftp2.census.gov/programs-surveys/cps/techdocs/cpsmar14.pdf>. See also headnote, Table 712]

Characteristic	Number of households (1,000)								Median house- hold income (dollars)
	Total house- holds	Under $15,000	$15,000 to $24,999	$25,000 to $34,999	$35,000 to $49,999	$50,000 to $74,999	$75,000 to $99,999	$100,000 and over	
Total............	122,952	15,633	13,898	12,756	16,678	21,659	14,687	27,642	51,939
Age of householder:									
15 to 24 years...............	6,323	1,299	1,001	909	1,092	988	471	562	34,311
25 to 34 years...............	20,008	2,268	1,951	2,103	3,001	4,046	2,763	3,876	52,702
35 to 44 years...............	21,046	1,814	1,756	1,782	2,723	3,857	2,923	6,188	64,973
45 to 54 years...............	23,809	2,337	1,732	1,875	2,820	4,227	3,371	7,446	67,141
55 to 64 years...............	23,036	2,951	2,268	2,093	2,779	3,947	2,867	6,125	57,538
65 years and over............	28,729	4,963	5,189	3,994	4,261	4,592	2,292	3,434	35,611
Region: [1]									
Northeast............	22,053	2,749	2,348	2,030	2,672	3,796	2,568	5,891	56,775
Midwest............	27,214	3,296	2,930	2,944	3,861	4,969	3,482	5,731	52,082
South............	46,499	6,419	5,696	5,128	6,634	8,120	5,425	9,076	48,128
West............	27,186	3,169	2,925	2,654	3,511	4,775	3,213	6,940	56,181
Type of household:									
Family household.............	81,192	5,702	6,432	7,483	10,832	15,520	11,599	23,622	65,587
Married-couple............	59,669	2,138	3,400	4,515	7,270	11,677	9,598	21,067	76,509
Male householder, spouse absent............	6,330	574	650	777	1,112	1,260	807	1,149	50,625
Female householder, spouse absent............	15,193	2,991	2,382	2,191	2,451	2,584	1,194	1,406	35,154
Nonfamily household............	41,760	9,929	7,467	5,272	5,845	6,139	3,088	4,018	31,178
Male householder............	19,494	3,766	2,948	2,562	2,923	3,171	1,676	2,444	36,876
Female householder.........	22,266	6,163	4,518	2,710	2,923	2,967	1,412	1,574	26,425
Size of household:									
One person............	33,853	9,336	6,818	4,560	4,662	4,519	1,953	1,998	26,379
Two people............	41,877	3,269	3,918	4,437	6,367	8,512	5,699	9,675	57,441
Three people............	19,372	1,437	1,507	1,627	2,404	3,782	2,826	5,789	66,898
Four people............	16,148	931	896	1,158	1,756	2,759	2,493	6,157	79,605
Five people............	7,366	405	497	615	908	1,252	1,052	2,636	75,117
Six people............	2,719	168	166	220	366	513	416	870	71,786
Seven or more people.........	1,617	89	97	138	215	319	249	510	70,673
Educational attainment of householder: [2]									
Total............	116,628	14,332	12,897	11,846	15,585	20,673	14,216	27,079	53,231
Less than 9th grade............	4,819	1,413	1,055	760	618	547	233	194	24,194
9th to 12th grade (no diploma)............	7,854	2,202	1,639	1,052	1,146	1,049	417	348	25,672
High school graduate............	32,688	5,195	4,829	4,220	5,010	6,183	3,420	3,832	40,701
Some college, no degree........	21,112	2,460	2,377	2,450	3,331	4,143	2,708	3,644	49,683
Associate's degree............	11,978	1,146	1,086	1,306	1,684	2,414	1,736	2,607	56,185
Bachelor's degree or more.....	38,177	1,918	1,912	2,060	3,797	6,333	5,704	16,452	86,411
Bachelor's degree............	23,936	1,365	1,315	1,463	2,666	4,235	3,748	9,144	79,522
Master's degree............	10,178	439	434	440	845	1,639	1,496	4,886	95,948
Professional degree............	1,804	50	63	65	121	196	189	1,120	130,643
Doctoral degree............	2,259	63	100	90	166	264	270	1,305	121,284
Number of earners:									
No earners............	29,097	10,785	6,405	4,003	3,339	2,647	1,010	909	19,996
One earner............	45,623	4,333	6,388	6,507	8,536	9,294	4,504	6,062	43,916
Two earners and more........	48,232	514	1,106	2,245	4,802	9,718	9,174	20,674	89,685
Two earners............	38,934	466	1,030	2,057	4,194	8,311	7,478	15,399	85,049
Three earners............	7,026	49	68	160	535	1,180	1,329	3,702	103,721
Four earners or more........	2,272	–	7	27	72	229	366	1,574	127,128
Work experience of householder:									
Total............	122,952	15,633	13,898	12,756	16,678	21,659	14,687	27,642	51,939
Worked............	80,538	4,071	6,120	7,256	10,951	16,064	11,973	24,102	67,566
Worked at full-time jobs......	66,755	1,847	4,197	5,673	9,022	13,795	10,563	21,657	72,217
50 weeks or more...........	57,467	746	3,131	4,568	7,576	12,109	9,467	19,869	76,024
27 to 49 weeks...........	5,783	333	636	690	920	1,146	728	1,331	55,411
26 weeks or less...........	3,506	768	430	414	527	540	367	458	39,026
Worked at part-time jobs....	13,783	2,224	1,922	1,584	1,927	2,268	1,411	2,446	43,661
50 weeks or more...........	7,645	878	1,091	884	1,112	1,298	849	1,533	47,858
27 to 49 weeks...........	3,028	514	427	362	422	481	282	540	41,067
26 weeks or less...........	3,109	832	404	338	393	490	281	372	34,156
Did not work............	42,414	11,562	7,780	5,499	5,726	5,596	2,714	3,536	27,950
Housing Tenure:									
Owner occupied............	79,520	6,193	6,975	7,243	9,962	14,734	11,207	23,206	65,021
Renter occupied............	41,798	8,963	6,650	5,287	6,519	6,684	3,366	4,330	34,998
Occupier paid no cash rent...	1,634	474	275	226	197	241	115	105	28,210

– Represents zero. [1] For composition of regions, see map, inside front cover. [2] People 25 years old and over.

Source: U.S. Census Bureau, *Income and Poverty in the United States: 2013*, Current Population Reports, P60-249, September 2014; and "Detailed Tables: Household Income Table HINC-01," <http://www.census.gov/hhes/www/cpstables/032014/hhinc/toc.htm>, accessed November 2014. See also <http://www.census.gov/hhes/www/income/data/index.html>.

Table 715. Money Income of Households—Number and Distribution by Race and Hispanic Origin: 2013

[122,952 represents 122,952,000. Households as of March of the following year. Based on Current Population Survey, Annual Social and Economic Supplement (ASEC); see text, this section and Section 1, and Appendix III. As of 2003, CPS respondents were allowed to choose more than one race. Two basic ways of defining a race group are possible. A group such as Asian may be defined as those who reported Asian and no other race (the race-alone or single-race concept), or as those who reported Asian regardless of whether they also reported another race (the race-alone-or-in-combination concept). See also comments on race in the text for Section 1]

Income interval	Number of households (1,000)					Percent distribution				
	All races	White alone	Black alone	Asian alone	His-panic [1]	All races	White alone	Black alone	Asian alone	His-panic [1]
All households.............	**122,952**	**97,774**	**16,108**	**5,759**	**15,811**	**100.0**	**100.0**	**100.0**	**100.0**	**100.0**
Under $10,000.................	8,940	5,860	2,288	432	1,467	7.3	6.0	14.2	7.5	9.3
$10,000 to $14,999...........	6,693	4,880	1,406	200	1,050	5.4	5.0	8.7	3.5	6.6
$15,000 to $19,999...........	7,321	5,583	1,314	203	1,076	6.0	5.7	8.2	3.5	6.8
$20,000 to $24,999...........	6,577	5,057	1,066	246	1,109	5.3	5.2	6.6	4.3	7.0
$25,000 to $29,999...........	6,302	4,885	1,000	213	1,033	5.1	5.0	6.2	3.7	6.5
$30,000 to $34,999...........	6,454	4,992	1,044	223	1,067	5.2	5.1	6.5	3.9	6.7
$35,000 to $39,999...........	5,827	4,566	868	201	901	4.7	4.7	5.4	3.5	5.7
$40,000 to $44,999...........	5,565	4,462	768	224	828	4.5	4.6	4.8	3.9	5.2
$45,000 to $49,999...........	5,286	4,128	726	245	836	4.3	4.2	4.5	4.3	5.3
$50,000 to $59,999...........	9,547	7,741	1,170	378	1,288	7.8	7.9	7.3	6.6	8.1
$60,000 to $74,999...........	12,112	9,990	1,221	596	1,418	9.9	10.2	7.6	10.3	9.0
$75,000 to $84,999...........	7,086	5,946	651	343	788	5.8	6.1	4.0	6.0	5.0
$85,000 to $99,999...........	7,601	6,433	670	311	871	6.2	6.6	4.2	5.4	5.5
$100,000 to $149,999........	15,266	12,751	1,243	946	1,356	12.4	13.0	7.7	16.4	8.6
$150,000 to $199,999........	6,463	5,448	387	513	436	5.3	5.6	2.4	8.9	2.8
$200,000 to $249,999.........	2,600	2,175	145	239	136	2.1	2.2	0.9	4.2	0.9
$250,000 and above...........	3,313	2,878	138	245	151	2.7	2.9	0.9	4.3	1.0

[1] Persons of Hispanic origin may be of any race.

Source: U.S. Census Bureau, *Income and Poverty in the United States: 2013*, Current Population Reports, P60-249, September 2014; and "Detailed Tables: Household Income Table HINC-06," <http://www.census.gov/hhes/www/cpstables/032014/hhinc/toc.htm>, accessed November 2014. See also <http://www.census.gov/hhes/www/income/data/index.html>.

Table 716. Share of Aggregate Income Received by Each Fifth and Top 5 Percent of Households: 1980 to 2013

[In units as indicated (82,368 represents 82,368,000). Households as of March of the following year. Income in constant 2013 CPI-U-RS-adjusted dollars. The shares method ranks households from highest to lowest on the basis of income and then divides them into groups of equal population size, typically quintiles. The aggregate income of each group is then divided by the overall aggregate income to derive shares. Based on the Current Population Survey, Annual Social and Economic Supplement (ASEC); see text, this section and Section 1, and Appendix III. For data collection changes over time, see source]

Year	Number of house-holds (1,000)	Income at selected positions in constant (2013) dollars					Percent distribution of aggregate income					
		Upper limit of each fifth				Top 5 percent, lower limit	Lowest 5th	Second 5th	Third 5th	Fourth 5th	Highest 5th	Top 5 percent
		Lowest	Second	Third	Fourth							
1980..........	82,368	20,128	37,747	57,869	84,731	136,358	4.2	10.2	16.8	24.7	44.1	16.5
1990..........	94,312	21,597	40,883	62,546	95,382	163,703	3.8	9.6	15.9	24.0	46.6	18.5
1995 [1].......	99,627	21,856	40,849	63,748	98,842	171,505	3.7	9.1	15.2	23.3	48.7	21.0
2000 [2, 3].......	108,209	24,241	44,639	70,576	110,606	196,440	3.6	8.9	14.8	23.0	49.8	22.1
2005..........	114,384	22,884	42,956	68,802	109,425	198,077	3.4	8.6	14.6	23.0	50.4	22.2
2006..........	116,011	23,147	43,642	69,321	112,106	201,045	3.4	8.6	14.5	22.9	50.5	22.3
2007..........	116,783	22,797	43,928	69,656	112,348	198,856	3.4	8.7	14.8	23.4	49.7	21.2
2008..........	117,181	22,409	42,194	67,863	108,451	194,744	3.4	8.6	14.7	23.3	50.0	21.5
2009 [4]........	117,538	22,213	41,867	67,118	108,603	195,487	3.4	8.6	14.6	23.2	50.3	21.7
2010 [5]........	119,927	21,368	40,599	65,706	106,870	192,829	3.3	8.5	14.6	23.4	50.3	21.3
2011..........	121,084	20,986	39,896	64,664	105,211	192,645	3.2	8.4	14.3	23.0	51.1	22.3
2012..........	122,459	20,898	40,342	65,520	105,609	193,934	3.2	8.3	14.4	23.0	51.0	22.3
2013..........	122,952	20,900	40,187	65,501	105,910	196,000	3.2	8.4	14.4	23.0	51.0	22.2

[1] Data reflect full implementation of the 1990 Census-based sample design and metropolitan definitions, 7,000 household sample reduction, and revised race edits. [2] Implementation of Census 2000-based population controls. [3] Implementation of a 28,000 household sample expansion. [4] Beginning with 2009 income data, the Census Bureau expanded the upper income interval used to calculate medians and Gini indexes to $250,000 or more. Medians falling in the upper open-ended interval are plugged with "$250,000." [5] Implementation of Census 2010-based population controls.

Source: U.S. Census Bureau, *Income and Poverty in the United States: 2013,* Current Population Reports, P60-249, September 2014; and "Historical Income Tables: Households, Tables H1 and H2," <http://www.census.gov/hhes/www/income/data/historical/household/>, accessed November 2014. See also <http://www.census.gov/hhes/www/income/index.html>.

Table 717. Money Income of Families—Number and Distribution by Race and Hispanic Origin: 2013

[81,217 represents 81,217,000. Families as of March of the following year. Based on Current Population Survey, Annual Social and Economic Supplement (ASEC); see text, this section, Section 1, and Appendix III. A family is a group of persons residing together and related by birth, marriage, or adoption]

Income interval	Number of families (1,000)					Percent distribution				
	All races	White alone	Black alone	Asian alone	His-panic [1]	All races	White alone	Black alone	Asian alone	His-panic [1]
All families............	**81,217**	**64,702**	**9,923**	**4,360**	**12,119**	**100.0**	**100.0**	**100.0**	**100.0**	**100.0**
Under $10,000............	4,010	2,532	1,084	166	977	4.9	3.9	10.9	3.8	8.1
$10,000 to $14,999............	2,486	1,697	564	119	670	3.1	2.6	5.7	2.7	5.5
$15,000 to $19,999............	3,214	2,281	712	115	740	4.0	3.5	7.2	2.6	6.1
$20,000 to $24,999............	3,463	2,582	581	154	860	4.3	4.0	5.9	3.5	7.1
$25,000 to $29,999............	3,732	2,809	651	153	851	4.6	4.3	6.6	3.5	7.0
$30,000 to $34,999............	3,975	3,058	625	171	873	4.9	4.7	6.3	3.9	7.2
$35,000 to $39,999............	3,661	2,841	541	140	714	4.5	4.4	5.5	3.2	5.9
$40,000 to $44,999............	3,617	2,864	528	156	642	4.5	4.4	5.3	3.6	5.3
$45,000 to $49,999............	3,493	2,759	452	179	654	4.3	4.3	4.6	4.1	5.4
$50,000 to $59,999............	6,464	5,264	739	282	973	8.0	8.1	7.4	6.5	8.0
$60,000 to $74,999............	8,686	7,154	818	476	1,116	10.7	11.1	8.2	10.9	9.2
$75,000 to $84,999............	5,237	4,367	468	296	590	6.4	6.7	4.7	6.8	4.9
$85,000 to $99,999............	6,049	5,130	496	273	733	7.4	7.9	5.0	6.3	6.0
$100,000 to $149,999............	12,623	10,501	1,083	801	1,138	15.5	16.2	10.9	18.4	9.4
$150,000 to $199,999............	5,456	4,580	327	456	363	6.7	7.1	3.3	10.5	3.0
$200,000 to $249,999............	2,159	1,800	123	196	114	2.7	2.8	1.2	4.5	0.9
$250,000 and above............	2,889	2,485	128	229	112	3.6	3.8	1.3	5.3	0.9

[1] Persons of Hispanic origin may be of any race.

Source: U.S. Census Bureau, *Income and Poverty in the United States: 2013,* Current Population Reports, P60-249, September 2014; and "Detailed Tables: Family, Table FINC-07," <http://www.census.gov/hhes/www/cpstables/032014/faminc/toc.htm>, accessed November 2014. See also <http://www.census.gov/hhes/www/income/data/incpovhlth/2013/index.html>.

Table 718. Money Income of Families—Percent Distribution by Income Level in Constant (2013) Dollars: 2000 to 2013

[73,778 represents 73,778,000. Families as of March of the following year. Income in 2013 Consumer Price Index Research Series Using Current Methods (CPI-U-RS) adjusted dollars. Based on Current Population Survey, Annual Social and Economic Supplement (ASEC); see text, this section, Section 1, and Appendix III. For data collection changes over time, see <http://www.census.gov/hhes/www/income/data/historical/history.html>. For definition of median, see Guide to Tabular Presentation. Beginning with the 2003 CPS covering data for 2002, respondents were allowed to choose more than one race. Two basic ways of defining a race group are possible: group such as Asian may be defined as 1) those who reported Asian and no other race (the race-alone or single-race concept), or 2) those who reported Asian regardless of whether they also reported another race (the race-alone-or-in-combination concept). For 2001 data and earlier, CPS respondents could report only one race group]

Year	Number of families (1,000)	Percent distribution							Median income (dollars)
		Under $15,000	$15,000 to $24,999	$25,000 to $34,999	$35,000 to $49,999	$50,000 to $74,999	$75,000 to $99,999	$100,000 and over	
ALL FAMILIES [1]									
2000 [4]............	73,778	6.1	7.5	8.6	13.3	19.3	15.0	30.2	68,626
2010 [5]............	79,559	8.3	8.4	9.4	12.9	18.6	13.7	28.6	64,356
2012............	80,944	8.3	8.6	9.6	13.1	18.4	13.7	28.2	63,145
2013............	81,217	8.0	8.2	9.5	13.3	18.7	13.9	28.4	63,815
WHITE [2]									
2000 [4]............	61,330	5.0	6.8	8.1	13.1	19.5	15.6	32.0	71,733
2010 [5]............	63,976	6.8	7.6	9.1	12.9	18.9	14.4	30.4	67,217
2012............	64,735	6.7	7.8	9.5	12.9	18.7	14.3	29.9	66,837
2013............	64,702	6.5	7.5	9.1	13.1	19.2	14.7	29.9	67,255
BLACK [2]									
2000 [4]............	8,731	14.0	12.6	12.3	15.4	18.8	11.1	15.7	45,554
2010 [5]............	9,571	18.2	13.1	12.3	14.9	17.1	10.3	14.1	41,234
2012............	9,823	17.8	14.2	11.4	14.8	16.7	10.4	14.7	41,106
2013............	9,923	16.6	13.0	12.9	15.3	15.7	9.7	16.7	41,588
ASIAN AND PACIFIC ISLANDER [2]									
2000 [4]............	2,982	5.2	5.8	6.3	10.0	16.9	14.6	41.3	84,703
2010 [5]............	3,879	6.3	7.4	6.6	10.0	17.3	12.6	39.8	80,361
2012............	4,122	6.3	6.3	6.7	10.8	16.9	13.3	39.7	78,995
2013............	4,360	6.5	6.1	7.4	10.9	17.4	13.1	38.5	76,402
HISPANIC ORIGIN [3]									
2000 [4]............	8,017	10.9	12.9	12.5	17.6	20.0	11.3	14.8	46,590
2010 [5]............	11,284	14.9	13.8	13.9	15.1	18.6	10.1	13.6	41,988
2012............	11,961	14.2	14.7	13.6	16.2	17.6	9.9	13.7	41,356
2013............	12,119	13.6	13.2	14.2	16.6	17.2	10.9	14.3	42,269

[1] Includes other races not shown separately. [2] Beginning with 2002, data represent White alone, Black alone, or Asian alone. [3] People of Hispanic origin may be of any race. [4] Data reflect implementation of Census 2000-based population controls and a 28,000 household sample expansion to 78,000 households. [5] Median income is calculated using $2,500 income intervals. Beginning with 2009 income data, the Census Bureau expanded the upper income intervals used to calculate medians to $250,000 or more. Medians falling in the upper open-ended interval are plugged with "$250,000." Before 2009, the upper open-ended interval was $100,000 and a plug of "$100,000" was used. Implementation of Census 2010-based population controls.

Source: U.S. Census Bureau, *Income and Poverty in the United States: 2013,* Current Population Reports, P60-249, September 2014; and "Historical Income Data: Families, Table F-23," <http://www.census.gov/hhes/www/income/data/historical/families/>, accessed November 2014.

Table 719. Money Income of Families—Median Income by Race and Hispanic Origin in Current and Constant (2013) Dollars: 1990 to 2013

[In dollars. Beginning with the 2003 CPS covering data for 2002, respondents were allowed to choose more than one race. Two basic ways of defining a race group are possible. A group such as Asian may be defined as those who reported Asian and no other race (the race-alone or single-race concept), or as those who reported Asian regardless of whether they also reported another race (the race-alone-or-in-combination concept). For 2001 data and earlier, the CPS allowed respondents to report only one race group. See also comments on race in the text for Section 1, Population]

Year	Median income in current dollars					Median income in constant (2013) dollars				
	All Races [1]	White [2]	Black [2]	Asian, Pacific Islander [2]	His-panic [3]	All Races [1]	White [2]	Black [2]	Asian, Pacific Islander [2]	His-panic [3]
1990 [4]...........	35,353	36,915	21,423	42,246	23,431	61,082	63,781	37,014	72,992	40,484
1995 [4]..........	40,611	42,646	25,970	46,356	24,570	61,637	64,726	39,416	70,357	37,291
2000 [5, 6].........	50,732	53,029	33,676	62,617	34,442	68,626	71,733	45,554	84,703	46,590
2005.............	56,194	59,317	35,464	68,957	37,867	67,053	70,779	42,317	82,282	45,184
2009 [7]............	60,088	62,545	38,409	75,027	39,730	65,257	67,926	41,713	81,482	43,148
2010 [8]............	60,236	62,914	38,594	75,217	39,300	64,356	67,217	41,234	80,361	41,988
2011.............	60,974	64,081	40,495	72,996	40,061	63,152	66,370	41,942	75,604	41,492
2012.............	62,241	65,880	40,517	77,864	40,764	63,145	66,837	41,106	78,995	41,356
2013.............	63,815	67,255	41,588	76,402	42,269	63,815	67,255	41,588	76,402	42,269

[1] Includes other races not shown separately. [2] Beginning with 2002, data represent White alone, Black alone, or Asian alone. [3] People of Hispanic origin may be of any race. [4] Data reflect full implementation of the 1990 Census-based sample design and metropolitan definitions, 7,000 household sample reduction, and revised race edits. [5] Implementation of Census 2000-based population controls. [6] Implementation of 28,000 household sample expansion. [7] Median income calculated using $2,500 income intervals. Beginning 2009, Census Bureau expanded upper income intervals used to calculate medians to $250,000 or more. Medians falling in the upper open-ended interval are plugged with "$250,000." Before 2009, the upper open-ended interval was $100,000 and a plug of "$100,000" was used. See also comments on race in the text for Section 1. [8] Implementation of Census 2010-based population controls.

Source: U.S. Census Bureau, *Income and Poverty in the United States: 2013*, Current Population Reports, P60-249, September 2014; and "Historical Income Data: Families, Table F-05," <http://www.census.gov/hhes/www/income/data/historical/families/>, accessed December 2014. See also <http://www.census.gov/hhes/www/income/index.html>.

Table 720. Money Income of Families—Distribution by Family Characteristics and Income Level: 2013

[81,217 represents 81,217,000. See headnote, Table 718. Median income is calculated using $2,500 income intervals. Medians falling in the upper open-ended interval are plugged with "$250,000." For composition of regions, see map inside front cover]

Characteristic	Number of families (1,000)								Median income (dollars)
	Total	Under $15,000	$15,000 to $24,999	$25,000 to $34,999	$35,000 to $49,999	$50,000 to $74,999	$75,000 to $99,999	$100,000 and over	
All families.......................	**81,217**	**6,495**	**6,677**	**7,707**	**10,771**	**15,151**	**11,287**	**23,128**	**63,815**
Age of householder:									
15 to 24 years old.................	3,290	736	431	502	534	506	255	322	34,291
25 to 34 years old.................	13,310	1,705	1,327	1,440	1,804	2,418	1,902	2,714	52,804
35 to 44 years old.................	16,434	1,186	1,249	1,351	1,995	2,938	2,398	5,315	70,239
45 to 54 years old.................	17,561	1,081	990	1,209	1,874	3,095	2,729	6,584	79,246
55 to 64 years old.................	15,013	882	1,041	1,054	1,738	2,800	2,196	5,302	74,915
65 years old and over............	15,608	905	1,637	2,152	2,825	3,396	1,807	2,885	51,486
Region:									
Northeast..........................	14,331	1,009	1,070	1,244	1,635	2,519	1,978	4,874	71,365
Midwest...........................	17,489	1,278	1,183	1,579	2,403	3,442	2,675	4,929	65,974
South..............................	30,956	2,689	2,932	3,201	4,421	5,918	4,217	7,578	58,401
West...............................	18,441	1,518	1,491	1,683	2,311	3,272	2,418	5,746	66,016
Type of family:									
Married-couple families...........	59,692	2,152	3,414	4,556	7,298	11,692	9,580	21,000	76,339
Male householder, no spouse present.............................	6,330	717	772	926	1,112	1,131	705	968	44,475
Female householder, no spouse present.............................	15,195	3,627	2,490	2,226	2,361	2,327	1,003	1,163	31,408
Unrelated subfamilies.............	595	230	91	116	85	41	10	26	22,093
Educational attainment of householder:									
Persons 25 years old and over, total.................................	77,927	5,759	6,245	7,205	10,237	14,647	11,032	22,803	65,531
Less than 9th grade................	3,236	566	662	617	541	476	192	180	31,170
9th to 12th grade (no diploma).....	5,056	928	919	836	896	812	372	293	32,494
High school graduate (includes equivalency).......................	21,442	1,970	2,252	2,611	3,562	4,779	2,956	3,313	51,154
Some college, no degree...........	14,038	1,091	1,125	1,398	2,254	2,993	2,068	3,108	59,517
Associate's degree.................	8,212	492	569	793	1,022	1,692	1,396	2,247	67,103
Bachelor's degree or more.........	25,944	712	719	950	1,961	3,893	4,046	13,664	103,256
Bachelor's degree.................	16,075	490	488	661	1,401	2,726	2,733	7,575	95,042
Master's degree...................	7,041	173	166	209	400	948	1,027	4,119	112,201
Professional degree...............	1,280	17	17	42	80	93	128	903	153,683
Doctoral degree...................	1,547	32	47	38	81	127	158	1,063	151,008
Number of earners:									
No earners.........................	13,403	3,593	2,251	2,183	2,131	1,850	713	687	28,695
One earner.........................	27,242	2,547	3,594	3,828	4,872	5,388	2,797	4,219	45,619
Two earners or more...............	40,571	356	832	1,696	3,769	7,917	7,779	18,225	92,480

Source: U.S. Census Bureau, *Income and Poverty in the United States: 2013*, Current Population Reports, P60-249, September 2014; and "Detailed Tables: Family, Table FINC-01," <http://www.census.gov/hhes/www/cpstables/032014/faminc/toc.htm>, accessed November 2014. See also <http://www.census.gov/hhes/www/income/index.html>.

Table 721. Median Income of Families by Type of Family in Current and Constant (2013) Dollars: 1990 to 2013

[In dollars. See headnote, Table 718. For definition of median, see Guide to Tabular Presentation]

| Year | Current dollars | | | | | | Constant (2013) dollars | | | | | |
| | All families | Married-couple families | | | Male house-holder, no spouse present | Female house-holder, no spouse present | All families | Married-couple families | | | Male house-holder, no spouse present | Female house-holder, no spouse present |
		Total	Wife in paid labor force	Wife not in paid labor force				Total	Wife in paid labor force	Wife not in paid labor force		
1990.............	35,353	39,895	46,777	30,265	29,046	16,932	61,082	68,930	80,820	52,291	50,185	29,255
1995 [1].........	40,611	47,062	55,823	32,375	30,358	19,691	61,637	71,428	84,725	49,137	46,076	29,886
2000 [2, 3].........	50,732	59,099	69,235	39,982	37,727	25,716	68,626	79,944	93,655	54,084	51,034	34,786
2005.............	56,194	65,906	78,755	44,457	41,111	27,244	67,053	78,641	93,973	53,048	49,055	32,508
2009 [4].........	60,088	71,627	85,948	47,649	41,501	29,770	65,257	77,789	93,342	51,748	45,071	32,331
2010 [5].........	60,236	72,241	87,397	48,733	43,206	29,155	64,356	77,182	93,374	52,066	46,161	31,149
2011.............	60,974	73,790	89,017	50,414	43,069	30,259	63,152	76,426	92,197	52,215	44,608	31,340
2012.............	62,241	75,535	91,779	50,881	42,358	30,686	63,145	76,633	93,113	51,620	42,974	31,132
2013.............	63,815	76,339	94,299	51,839	44,475	31,408	63,815	76,339	94,299	51,839	44,475	31,408

[1] Data reflect full implementation of the 1990 Census-based sample design and metropolitan definitions, 7,000 household sample reduction, and revised race edits. [2] Implementation of Census 2000-based population controls. [3] Implementation of a 28,000 household sample expansion. [4] Median income is calculated using $2,500 income intervals. Beginning with 2009 income data, the Census Bureau expanded the upper income intervals used to calculate medians to $250,000 or more. Before 2009, the upper open-ended interval was $100,000. [5] Implementation of Census 2010-based population controls.

Source: U.S. Census Bureau, *Income and Poverty in the United States: 2013,* Current Population Reports, P60-249, September 2014; and "Historical Income Data: Families, Table F-7," <http://www.census.gov/hhes/www/income/data/historical/families/>, accessed November 2014. See also <http://www.census.gov/hhes/www/income/index.html>.

Table 722. Married-Couple Families—Number and Median Income by Work Experience of Husbands and Wives and Presence of Related Children: 2013

[59,692 represents 59,692,000. Based on Current Population Survey, Annual Social and Economic Supplement; see text, Sections 1 and 13, and Appendix III. For methodology, see <http://www.census.gov/prod/techdoc/cps/cpsmar13.pdf>. Median income calculated using $2,500 income intervals. Beginning in 2010, data reflect implementation of Census 2010-based population controls. For definition of median, see Guide to Tabular Presentation]

| Work experience of husband or wife | Number (1,000) | | | | | Median income (dollars) | | | | |
| | All married-couple families | With no related children | One or more related children under 18 years old | | | All married-couple families | With no related children | One or more related children under 18 years old | | |
			Total	One child	Two children or more			Total	One child	Two children or more
All married-couple families........	**59,692**	**34,357**	**25,335**	**9,968**	**15,367**	**76,339**	**70,803**	**84,916**	**87,171**	**82,339**
Husband worked.......................	44,824	21,421	23,403	9,057	14,346	89,586	90,512	88,610	91,597	86,424
Wife worked........................	31,688	15,355	16,332	6,873	9,459	100,128	99,262	100,594	100,560	100,620
Wife did not work..................	13,136	6,065	7,071	2,184	4,887	62,150	66,913	58,486	60,549	57,252
Husband worked year-round, full-time................................	36,531	16,500	20,031	7,653	12,379	95,569	96,943	94,107	97,641	91,723
Wife worked........................	26,317	12,260	14,057	5,875	8,182	105,180	105,020	105,290	105,429	105,157
Wife did not work..................	10,214	4,239	5,975	1,778	4,197	68,751	72,679	64,154	68,914	62,109
Husband did not work..............	14,868	12,936	1,932	911	1,022	42,826	43,321	38,984	45,480	33,351
Wife worked........................	4,485	3,420	1,065	483	582	55,536	58,095	47,356	52,878	41,850
Wife did not work..................	10,383	9,515	867	428	440	37,426	38,209	25,751	32,637	19,293

Source: U.S. Census Bureau, *Income and Poverty in the United States: 2013,* Current Population Reports, P60-249, September 2014; and "Detailed Tables: Family, Table FINC-04," <http://www.census.gov/hhes/www/cpstables/032014/faminc/toc.htm>, accessed November 2014. See also <http://www.census.gov/hhes/www/income/index.html>.

Table 723. Median Income of People in Constant (2013) Dollars by Sex, Race, and Hispanic Origin: 2000 to 2013

[In dollars. People as of March of following year. People 15 years old and over. Constant dollars based on CPI-U-RS deflator. Based on the Current Population Survey, Annual Social and Economic Supplement (ASEC); see text, this section and Section 1 and Appendix III. For data collection changes over time, see <http://www.census.gov/hhes/www/income/data/historical/history.html>. Beginning with the 2003 CPS covering data for 2002, respondents were allowed to choose more than one race. Two basic ways of defining a race group are possible. A group such as Asian may be defined as 1) those who reported Asian and no other race (the race-alone or single-race concept), or 2) those who reported Asian regardless of whether they also reported another race (the race-alone-or-in-combination concept). For 2001 data and earlier, the CPS allowed respondents to report only one race group]

| Race and Hispanic origin | Male | | | | | Female | | | | |
	2000 [1]	2005	2010 [2]	2012	2013	2000 [1]	2005	2010 [2]	2012	2013
All races [3]................	**38,340**	**37,318**	**34,408**	**34,397**	**35,228**	**21,729**	**22,166**	**22,196**	**21,833**	**22,063**
White [4]......................	40,307	38,397	36,725	36,207	36,549	21,750	22,276	22,325	22,146	22,421
Black [4]......................	28,871	27,030	24,889	25,285	24,855	21,482	21,038	20,990	20,312	20,044
Asian [4]......................	41,708	40,826	38,273	40,812	40,153	23,478	25,823	25,175	23,674	24,840
Hispanic [5]..................	26,375	26,357	23,953	24,949	25,411	16,568	17,941	17,406	16,968	17,762
White non-Hispanic..........	42,621	42,175	39,695	39,314	40,122	22,543	23,210	23,200	23,235	23,780

[1] Implementation of Census 2000-based population controls and sample expanded by 28,000 households. [2] See footnotes 4 and 5, table 721. [3] Includes other races not shown separately. [4] Data for 2005 and later refer to people reporting White alone, Black alone, or Asian alone ("Asian alone" replaced "Asian and Pacific Islander"). [5] People of Hispanic origin may be of any race.

Source: U.S. Census Bureau, *Income and Poverty in the United States: 2013,* Current Population Reports, P60-249, September 2014; and "Historical Income Data: People, Table P-2," <http://www.census.gov/hhes/www/income/data/historical/people/>, accessed November 2014. See also <http://www.census.gov/hhes/www/income/index.html>.

Table 724. Money Income of People—Selected Characteristics by Income Level: 2013

[122,414 represents 122,414,000. People as of March of following year. Covers people 15 years old and over. For definition of median, see Guide to Tabular Presentation. Median income is calculated using $2,500 income intervals. Medians falling in the upper open-ended interval are plugged with "$250,000." For composition of regions, see map, inside front cover. Based on the Current Population Survey, Annual Social and Economic Supplement (ASEC), see Appendix III]

Characteristic	All persons (1,000)	Total (1,000)	Under $5,000 or loss	$5,000 to $9,999	$10,000 to $14,999	$15,000 to $24,999	$25,000 to $34,999	$35,000 to $49,999	$50,000 to $74,999	$75,000 and over	Median income (current dollars)
MALE											
Total	**122,414**	**108,706**	**7,072**	**7,227**	**7,751**	**17,781**	**14,160**	**16,671**	**17,354**	**20,689**	**35,228**
15 to 24 years old	21,822	13,454	3,866	2,343	1,513	2,693	1,293	913	549	285	11,288
25 to 34 years old	21,217	19,604	947	1,230	1,144	3,388	3,235	3,482	3,524	2,656	34,170
35 to 44 years old	19,593	18,477	450	819	855	2,424	2,203	3,221	3,576	4,929	45,942
45 to 54 years old	20,932	19,835	668	840	944	2,200	2,267	3,195	3,944	5,777	48,300
55 to 64 years old	19,087	18,121	678	991	1,242	2,365	2,261	2,867	3,285	4,433	41,915
65 years old and over	19,763	19,216	465	1,003	2,052	4,711	2,902	2,994	2,477	2,609	29,327
Region:											
Northeast	22,033	19,693	1,315	1,251	1,242	3,019	2,368	2,966	3,296	4,233	37,466
Midwest	26,218	23,928	1,674	1,526	1,554	3,727	3,230	3,976	4,062	4,178	35,626
South	45,070	39,588	2,312	2,753	3,102	6,813	5,284	6,080	6,297	6,950	33,542
West	29,092	25,498	1,771	1,697	1,854	4,221	3,278	3,648	3,700	5,331	34,600
Educational attainment of householder: [1]											
Total	**100,592**	**95,253**	**3,208**	**4,883**	**6,239**	**15,088**	**12,868**	**15,756**	**16,805**	**20,407**	**39,602**
Less than 9th grade	4,945	4,464	181	547	782	1,467	656	438	275	118	19,701
9th to 12th grade [2]	7,403	6,557	313	794	909	1,853	1,002	900	550	234	21,417
High school graduate [3]	30,718	28,677	1,045	1,850	2,387	5,634	5,102	5,401	4,576	2,685	31,288
Some college, no degree	16,457	15,615	633	759	948	2,403	2,372	3,134	3,030	2,336	37,424
Associate's degree	8,973	8,654	259	322	398	1,203	1,194	1,728	1,939	1,612	42,176
Bachelor's degree											
or more	32,095	31,285	777	611	814	2,525	2,542	4,156	6,436	13,423	65,526
Bachelor's degree	20,099	19,513	559	440	605	1,699	1,823	2,997	4,332	7,059	58,170
Master's degree	7,846	7,705	162	130	144	548	508	827	1,498	3,884	75,407
Professional degree	1,821	1,802	26	4	28	113	106	132	274	1,118	101,504
Doctoral degree	2,329	2,265	29	37	36	166	103	201	330	1,359	93,712
Housing tenure:											
Owner-occupied	83,957	75,308	4,558	3,918	4,631	10,888	9,173	11,781	13,226	17,135	40,309
Renter-occupied	36,973	32,118	2,372	3,101	2,995	6,668	4,810	4,753	3,979	3,444	26,396
Occupier paid no cash rent	1,484	1,281	143	209	125	224	177	136	151	116	22,376
FEMALE											
Total	**129,930**	**109,956**	**11,888**	**13,431**	**13,772**	**20,495**	**14,481**	**14,575**	**12,257**	**9,058**	**22,063**
15 to 24 years old	21,235	13,041	3,874	2,562	1,815	2,559	1,231	628	272	102	10,175
25 to 34 years old	21,248	17,946	1,906	1,637	1,594	3,331	2,850	3,181	2,308	1,138	26,375
35 to 44 years old	20,196	17,356	1,681	1,241	1,537	2,805	2,400	2,847	2,802	2,041	30,571
45 to 54 years old	21,966	19,539	1,654	1,544	1,678	3,230	2,752	3,269	2,835	2,578	30,957
55 to 64 years old	20,539	18,357	1,724	1,878	1,996	2,934	2,567	2,593	2,503	2,167	26,889
65 years old and over	24,745	23,717	1,050	4,570	5,151	5,637	2,681	2,057	1,538	1,032	16,301
Region:											
Northeast	23,654	20,446	2,236	2,439	2,384	3,579	2,437	2,782	2,576	2,015	23,325
Midwest	27,632	24,421	2,677	2,888	2,950	4,587	3,516	3,358	2,732	1,714	22,515
South	48,681	40,541	4,177	5,116	5,370	8,031	5,321	5,338	4,182	3,007	21,352
West	29,963	24,548	2,798	2,989	3,069	4,297	3,207	3,097	2,770	2,320	22,188
Educational attainment of householder: [1]											
Total	**108,695**	**96,915**	**8,015**	**10,870**	**11,956**	**17,937**	**13,251**	**13,947**	**11,985**	**8,954**	**24,756**
Less than 9th grade	4,968	3,633	394	1,107	906	814	272	88	41	12	11,395
9th to 12th grade [2]	7,142	5,677	677	1,588	1,215	1,324	508	199	130	36	11,869
High school graduate [3]	31,522	27,482	2,287	3,894	4,796	6,748	4,190	3,256	1,700	609	18,325
Some college, no degree	18,462	16,805	1,448	1,903	2,136	3,514	2,839	2,619	1,588	756	22,814
Associate's degree	11,818	10,887	780	994	1,058	2,053	1,884	2,003	1,447	671	27,340
Bachelor's degree											
or more	34,784	32,432	2,430	1,384	1,844	3,485	3,555	5,783	7,083	6,871	43,115
Bachelor's degree	22,157	20,430	1,689	990	1,334	2,507	2,585	3,803	4,094	3,427	39,201
Master's degree	9,926	9,397	554	326	410	799	815	1,701	2,434	2,358	50,507
Professional degree	1,327	1,294	88	39	50	108	62	117	246	583	68,826
Doctoral degree	1,374	1,310	98	29	50	70	93	161	309	501	64,001
Housing tenure:											
Owner-occupied	87,988	75,817	8,048	8,403	8,772	13,245	9,794	10,562	9,470	7,524	24,419
Renter-occupied	40,572	33,016	3,702	4,845	4,821	6,988	4,526	3,911	2,710	1,513	18,882
Occupier paid no cash rent	1,370	1,123	139	185	178	262	161	102	74	20	17,041

[1] Population age 25 and over. [2] No diploma attained. [3] Includes high school equivalency.

Source: U.S. Census Bureau, *Income and Poverty in the United States: 2013*, Current Population Reports, P60-249, September 2014; and "Detailed Tables: Person, Table PINC-01," <http://www.census.gov/hhes/www/cpstables/032014/perinc/toc.htm>, accessed November 2014. See also <http://www.census.gov/hhes/www/income/index.html>.

Table 725. Average Earnings of Year-Round, Full-Time Workers by Educational Attainment: 2013

[In dollars. For people 18 years old and over, as of March of the following year. Based on the Current Population Survey, Annual Social and Economic Supplement (ASEC); see text, this section and Section 1, and Appendix III]

Sex and age	All workers	Less than 9th grade	9th to 12th grade (no diploma)	High school graduate [1]	Some college, no degree	Associate degree	Bachelor's degree or more
			High school		**College**		
Male, total	**65,958**	**32,385**	**37,839**	**44,803**	**53,917**	**57,454**	**98,188**
18 to 24 years old	31,008	22,366	24,249	29,554	28,530	33,552	43,529
25 to 34 years old	51,566	27,407	32,303	37,300	49,323	50,127	69,056
35 to 44 years old	69,499	29,879	35,404	46,864	55,202	59,467	103,304
45 to 54 years old	75,216	40,392	40,969	49,049	61,707	64,205	112,219
55 to 64 years old	77,330	33,676	54,743	52,498	63,574	63,279	113,607
65 years old and over	75,325	34,091	41,011	47,985	59,478	48,238	106,017
Female, total	**48,150**	**21,644**	**26,983**	**34,951**	**38,568**	**42,136**	**64,778**
18 to 24 years old	26,542	(B)	22,138	23,023	23,585	26,994	35,067
25 to 34 years old	43,666	20,690	23,663	35,555	33,400	35,535	53,642
35 to 44 years old	50,849	20,862	27,340	32,602	38,760	41,200	69,527
45 to 54 years old	51,525	22,458	24,949	37,503	43,336	47,517	70,511
55 to 64 years old	52,909	22,071	37,170	37,674	45,128	48,876	72,888
65 years old and over	49,466	(B)	27,373	34,734	43,757	44,344	72,991

B Base figure too small to meet statistical standards for reliability of derived figure. [1] Includes equivalency.

Source: U.S. Census Bureau, *Income and Poverty in the United States: 2013,* Current Population Reports, P60-249, September 2014; and "Detailed Tables: Person, Table PINC-04," <http://www.census.gov/hhes/www/cpstables/032014/perinc/toc.htm>, accessed November 2014. See also <http://www.census.gov/hhes/www/income/index.html>.

Table 726. Per Capita Money Income in Current and Constant (2013) Dollars by Race and Hispanic Origin: 1990 to 2013

[In dollars. Constant dollars based on 2013 CPI-U-RS deflator. People as of March of following year. Based on the Current Population Survey, Annual Social and Economic Supplement (ASEC); see text, this section, Section 1, and Appendix III. For data collection changes over time, see <http://www.census.gov/hhes/www/income/data/historical/history.html>. See Table 723 for information on race]

Year	All races [1]	White	Black	Asian and Pacific Islander	His-panic [2]	All races [1]	White	Black	Asian and Pacific Islander	His-panic [2]
	Current dollars					**Constant (2013) dollars**				
1990	14,387	15,265	9,017	(NA)	8,424	24,858	26,375	15,579	(NA)	14,555
1995 [3]	17,227	18,304	10,982	16,567	9,300	26,146	27,781	16,668	25,145	14,115
2000 [4]	22,346	23,582	14,796	23,350	12,651	30,228	31,900	20,015	31,586	17,113
2005 [5]	25,036	26,496	16,874	27,331	14,483	29,874	31,616	20,135	32,612	17,282
2010 [6]	26,558	28,356	18,019	28,673	15,044	28,374	30,295	19,251	30,634	16,073
2011	27,554	29,401	18,988	29,235	15,479	28,538	30,451	19,666	30,279	16,032
2012	28,281	30,114	19,267	31,905	16,125	28,692	30,552	19,547	32,369	16,359
2013	28,829	30,723	19,957	31,761	16,677	28,829	30,723	19,957	31,761	16,677

NA Not available. [1] Includes other races, not shown separately. [2] People of Hispanic origin may be of any race. [3] Data reflect full implementation of the 1990 Census-based sample design and metropolitan definitions, 7,000 household sample reduction, and revised race edits. [4] Implementation of Census 2000-based population controls, and of a 28,000 household sample expansion. [5] Data have been revised to reflect a correction to the weights in the 2005 ASEC. [6] As of 2009, upper income interval used to calculate medians expanded to $250,000/more, and medians in upper open-ended interval plugged with $250,000. Implementation of Census 2010-based population controls.

Source: U.S. Census Bureau, *Income and Poverty in the United States: 2013,* Current Population Reports, P60-249, September 2014; and "Historical Income Data: People, Table P-1," <http://www.census.gov/hhes/www/income/data/historical/people/>, accessed November 2014.

Table 727. Money Income of People—Number by Income Level and by Sex, Race, and Hispanic Origin: 2013

[In thousands (122,414 represents 122,414,000). People age 15 years and over as of March of the following year. Based on Current Population Survey, Annual Social and Economic Supplement (ASEC); see text, this section, Section 1, and Appendix III]

Income interval	All races [1]	White alone	Black alone	Asian alone	His-panic [2]	All races [1]	White alone	Black alone	Asian alone	His-panic [2]
	Male					**Female**				
Total	**122,414**	**97,616**	**14,383**	**6,635**	**19,683**	**129,930**	**101,349**	**17,109**	**7,369**	**19,476**
Under $10,000 [3]	28,007	19,892	5,156	1,681	5,800	45,293	33,952	6,375	3,167	9,419
$10,000 to $19,999	16,585	12,806	2,326	852	3,474	24,917	19,639	3,548	968	3,659
$20,000 to $29,999	16,053	12,921	1,926	676	3,436	16,842	13,268	2,260	780	2,458
$30,000 to $39,999	13,082	10,909	1,274	534	2,228	12,467	9,808	1,734	577	1,516
$40,000 to $49,999	10,643	8,853	1,026	504	1,517	9,097	7,269	1,111	494	893
$50,000 to $59,999	8,226	6,928	711	425	895	6,067	4,998	680	288	528
$60,000 to $74,999	9,128	7,664	740	546	893	6,190	5,002	658	373	486
$75,000 to $84,999	4,547	3,806	388	250	423	2,742	2,233	265	182	177
$85,000 to $99,999	4,139	3,529	234	261	347	1,874	1,535	186	124	102
$100,000 to $149,999	7,051	5,960	430	543	457	3,010	2,407	238	302	156
$150,000 to $199,999	2,413	2,135	71	171	110	830	723	42	61	54
$200,000 to $249,999	997	896	39	55	42	278	243	5	17	4
$250,000 and above	1,542	1,320	60	135	62	324	274	9	34	25

[1] Includes races not shown separately. [2] Persons of Hispanic origin may be of any race. [3] Includes persons without income.

Source: U.S. Census Bureau, *Income and Poverty in the United States: 2013,* Current Population Reports, P60-249, September 2014; and "Detailed Tables: Person, Table PINC-11," <http://www.census.gov/hhes/www/cpstables/032014/perinc/toc.htm>, accessed November 2014. See also <http://www.census.gov/hhes/www/income/index.html>.

Table 728. Household, Family, and Per Capita Income, and Individuals and Families Below Poverty Level, by City: 2013

[The American Community Survey universe includes the household population and the population living in institutions, college dormitories, and other group quarters. Based on a sample and subject to sampling variability; see text, Section 1 and Appendix III. For definition of median, see Guide to Tabular Presentation. CDP is Census designated place]

City	Median household income (dol.)	Median family income (dol.)	Per capita income (dol.)	Number below poverty level [1]		Percent below poverty level	
				Individuals [1]	Families	Individuals [1]	Families
Albuquerque, NM	48,357	59,846	26,163	103,788	19,659	18.8	14.8
Anaheim, CA	57,550	62,283	24,105	63,013	11,734	18.5	15.6
Anchorage, AK	79,045	90,480	36,344	19,585	2,250	6.7	3.1
Arlington, TX	51,400	62,391	24,828	60,263	11,367	16.1	12.4
Atlanta, GA	46,485	61,659	36,257	103,943	15,020	24.8	18.8
Aurora, CO	49,142	55,976	22,921	61,557	11,528	18.0	14.3
Austin, TX	56,351	71,511	32,297	154,172	21,885	17.8	12.0
Bakersfield, CA	54,763	61,193	22,343	72,586	14,093	20.1	17.3
Baltimore, MD	42,266	51,303	26,159	139,067	22,749	23.3	18.8
Boston, MA	53,583	59,702	34,139	130,115	21,352	21.6	17.7
Charlotte, NC	51,034	61,516	30,955	132,234	23,329	17.0	13.1
Chicago, IL	47,099	54,423	28,548	611,717	105,926	23.0	18.9
Cincinnati, OH	34,605	42,430	25,046	89,552	15,518	31.3	25.0
Cleveland, OH	26,096	32,374	17,545	139,957	26,474	36.9	31.2
Colorado Springs, CO	53,550	68,373	29,030	55,688	9,434	12.9	8.6
Columbus, OH	44,426	53,636	24,367	182,063	28,549	22.7	16.5
Corpus Christi, TX	49,686	57,817	24,676	54,048	10,711	17.5	13.6
Dallas, TX	41,978	44,852	28,522	302,484	58,722	24.4	21.2
Denver, CO	51,089	65,155	33,995	118,913	18,098	18.7	14.2
Detroit, MI	24,820	30,273	14,721	276,186	51,214	40.7	35.4
El Paso, TX	41,129	46,420	19,687	139,280	28,512	20.9	18.0
Fort Worth, TX	52,430	61,651	24,836	156,667	28,016	20.1	15.4
Fresno, CA	40,179	43,605	18,736	164,711	29,921	32.8	26.5
Greensboro, NC	41,150	54,430	27,202	55,367	10,857	20.6	15.9
Houston, TX	45,353	49,886	27,989	484,614	94,942	22.4	19.1
Indianapolis, IN	41,361	50,308	24,322	176,614	34,277	21.6	18.0
Jacksonville, FL	47,424	58,031	25,521	142,507	25,038	17.3	12.8
Kansas City, MO	45,551	57,686	26,202	86,711	14,568	18.9	14.1
Las Vegas, NV	49,289	55,552	24,457	110,384	18,486	18.6	13.6
Lexington-Fayette, KY	47,535	66,148	28,924	57,572	8,908	19.5	12.2
Long Beach, CA	52,116	59,511	25,993	94,784	16,422	20.5	16.7
Los Angeles, CA	48,466	52,382	27,778	877,062	147,970	23.0	18.5
Louisville/Jefferson County, KY [2]	44,893	59,251	27,240	104,063	18,550	17.4	12.5
Memphis, TN	36,722	42,089	22,393	176,695	33,124	27.7	22.9
Mesa, AZ	47,561	57,113	23,771	75,610	13,686	16.6	12.5
Miami, FL	31,070	34,010	22,692	118,448	21,268	28.9	24.6
Milwaukee, WI	35,186	39,772	19,371	168,883	32,614	29.0	25.4
Minneapolis, MN	50,563	67,125	32,791	81,188	10,594	21.2	14.3
Nashville-Davidson, TN [2]	46,803	57,838	27,306	111,613	17,966	18.2	13.2
New Orleans, LA	36,631	48,552	26,957	97,970	18,280	26.7	22.9
New York, NY	52,223	58,012	32,540	1,731,634	321,135	20.9	17.5
Newark, NJ	32,973	35,856	16,539	81,061	15,288	30.4	26.4
Oakland, CA	54,394	60,412	31,966	78,285	12,073	19.5	14.1
Oklahoma City, OK	46,232	58,947	25,685	104,692	19,223	17.5	13.5
Omaha, NE	47,512	62,601	26,628	76,763	13,108	18.1	12.9
Philadelphia, PA	36,836	44,584	22,361	396,963	60,881	26.3	20.6
Phoenix, AZ	46,601	52,943	23,703	353,303	60,760	23.6	18.6
Pittsburgh, PA	42,004	57,276	28,176	64,109	9,108	22.7	14.8
Portland, OR	55,571	71,933	32,915	108,976	14,464	18.2	11.2
Raleigh, NC	55,170	68,890	31,145	62,104	9,490	15.1	10.4
Riverside, CA	54,300	60,554	21,095	61,306	10,001	20.0	15.3
Sacramento, CA	48,034	55,149	24,531	110,539	20,119	23.4	19.7
San Antonio, TX	45,399	52,808	22,414	271,108	49,775	19.6	15.7
San Diego, CA	63,456	75,992	33,492	209,045	32,156	15.8	11.0
San Francisco, CA	77,485	95,421	51,686	113,517	12,371	13.8	7.8
San Jose, CA	80,977	88,962	34,977	126,423	20,768	12.8	9.1
San Juan, Puerto Rico	21,230	26,254	16,500	150,642	31,712	42.2	37.8
Santa Ana, CA	47,914	44,214	15,687	74,563	12,740	22.8	20.8
Seattle, WA	70,172	102,459	45,029	89,806	11,117	14.2	8.4
St. Louis, MO	34,488	41,990	22,921	81,999	13,854	26.6	22.0
St. Paul, MN	49,469	61,570	26,566	62,950	9,855	22.0	16.3
Stockton, CA	42,114	47,626	18,857	80,674	15,188	27.6	23.0
Tampa, FL	42,649	58,545	29,473	73,061	12,122	21.4	15.8
Toledo, OH	31,907	42,479	18,800	77,682	14,783	28.2	23.7
Tucson, AZ	35,720	44,347	19,669	127,328	20,637	25.3	18.3
Tulsa, OK	41,495	52,119	26,833	76,870	15,052	19.7	15.8
Urban Honolulu CDP, HI	61,559	74,319	32,115	40,466	5,935	12.0	7.9
Virginia Beach, VA	62,855	74,621	31,973	38,245	6,992	8.8	6.1
Washington, DC	67,572	72,337	45,477	115,551	18,901	18.9	15.7
Wichita, KS	43,538	58,318	24,502	68,235	13,180	17.9	14.3

[1] Poverty status was determined for all people except institutionalized people, people in military group quarters, people in college dormitories, and unrelated individuals under 15 years old. [2] Represents metropolitan government (balance) of locality.

Source: U.S. Census Bureau, 2013 American Community Survey, 2013 ACS 1-year estimates: DP03, B01003, B17001, and B17019, <http://factfinder2.census.gov>, accessed January 2014. See also <http://www.census.gov/acs/www/>.

Table 729. Individuals and Families Below Poverty Level—Number and Rate by State: 2003 and 2013

[In thousands (35,846 represents 35,846,000), except as indicated. Represents number and percent below poverty in the past 12 months. Prior to 2006, the American Community Survey universe was limited to the household population and excluded the population living in institutions, college dormitories, and other group quarters. Poverty status was determined for all people except institutionalized people, people in military group quarters, people in college dormitories, and unrelated individuals under 15 years old. These groups were excluded from the numerator and denominator when calculating poverty rates. Based on a sample and subject to sampling variability; see Appendix III]

State	Number below poverty (1,000)				Percent below poverty			
	Individuals		Families		Individuals		Families	
	2003	2013	2003	2013	2003	2013	2003	2013
United States.........	35,846	48,811	7,143	8,905	12.7	15.8	9.8	11.6
Alabama.................	748	883	164	175	17.1	18.7	13.7	14.3
Alaska....................	61	67	13	10	9.7	9.3	8.0	5.9
Arizona..................	839	1,206	166	214	15.4	18.6	11.9	13.6
Arkansas................	421	565	89	109	16.0	19.7	12.1	14.5
California................	4,610	6,329	849	1,093	13.4	16.8	10.5	12.6
Colorado................	433	667	88	112	9.8	13.0	7.3	8.7
Connecticut...........	273	374	58	68	8.1	10.7	6.4	7.6
Delaware...............	69	111	12	19	8.7	12.4	5.8	8.5
District of Columbia.....	105	116	21	19	19.9	18.9	18.5	15.7
Florida...................	2,174	3,253	422	574	13.1	17.0	9.7	12.4
Georgia.................	1,125	1,844	234	347	13.4	19.0	10.8	14.5
Hawaii...................	132	148	21	22	10.9	10.8	7.4	7.1
Idaho....................	183	247	35	43	13.8	15.6	9.8	10.4
Illinois...................	1,389	1,845	265	336	11.3	14.7	8.5	10.8
Indiana..................	633	1,015	119	196	10.6	15.9	7.5	11.9
Iowa.....................	286	379	53	64	10.1	12.7	6.9	8.1
Kansas..................	284	393	51	71	10.8	14.0	7.1	9.6
Kentucky...............	696	801	159	165	17.4	18.8	14.2	14.5
Louisiana..............	882	888	191	173	20.3	19.8	16.6	15.3
Maine...................	133	181	26	32	10.5	14.0	7.6	9.6
Maryland...............	439	586	86	102	8.2	10.1	6.1	7.1
Massachusetts.........	582	771	118	139	9.4	11.9	7.5	8.6
Michigan...............	1,118	1,648	224	305	11.4	17.0	8.6	12.3
Minnesota..............	383	592	75	99	7.8	11.2	5.6	7.2
Mississippi.............	553	696	121	141	19.9	24.0	16.4	19.0
Missouri................	646	931	133	176	11.7	15.9	8.6	11.5
Montana................	126	164	24	29	14.2	16.5	9.9	11.3
Nebraska...............	182	239	36	42	10.8	13.2	8.2	8.8
Nevada.................	252	434	47	74	11.5	15.8	8.7	11.6
New Hampshire.........	96	111	17	18	7.7	8.7	5.1	5.1
New Jersey............	704	999	145	192	8.4	11.4	6.6	8.7
New Mexico...........	340	448	70	79	18.6	21.9	14.8	16.3
New York...............	2,501	3,056	499	556	13.5	16.0	10.7	12.1
North Carolina.........	1,136	1,715	239	323	14.0	17.9	10.7	13.1
North Dakota..........	71	82	13	13	11.7	11.8	8.4	7.0
Ohio.....................	1,343	1,797	280	340	12.1	16.0	9.4	11.6
Oklahoma..............	546	627	112	120	16.1	16.8	12.4	12.5
Oregon..................	481	642	88	109	13.9	16.7	9.7	11.3
Pennsylvania..........	1,296	1,690	260	293	10.9	13.7	8.2	9.3
Rhode Island..........	117	144	22	28	11.3	14.3	8.2	10.7
South Carolina.........	563	860	121	168	14.1	18.6	11.3	14.1
South Dakota..........	81	115	14	20	11.1	14.2	7.2	9.2
Tennessee.............	780	1,127	164	220	13.8	17.8	10.6	13.3
Texas...................	3,508	4,530	712	860	16.3	17.5	13.1	13.6
Utah.....................	244	361	43	63	10.6	12.7	7.6	9.3
Vermont................	57	74	10	12	9.7	12.3	6.4	7.8
Virginia.................	642	939	126	172	9.0	11.7	6.6	8.4
Washington............	654	967	121	163	11.0	14.1	7.9	9.5
West Virginia..........	326	332	76	65	18.5	18.5	15.5	13.5
Wisconsin..............	554	756	101	134	10.5	13.5	7.2	9.2
Wyoming...............	47	62	10	12	9.7	10.9	7.3	8.4

Source: U.S. Census Bureau, 2013 American Community Survey: B17001, "Poverty Status in the Past 12 Months by Sex By Age"; and B17019, "Poverty Status in the Past 12 Months of Families by Household Type by Tenure"; <http://factfinder2.census.gov>, accessed January 2015. See also <http://www.census.gov/acs/www/>.

Table 730. Poverty Thresholds by Size of Family Unit: 1980 to 2013

[In dollars per year. The official poverty definition uses money income before taxes and does not include capital gains and noncash benefits (such as public housing and food stamps). For information on the official poverty thresholds, see text, this section. For more on poverty, see <http://www.census.gov/hhes/www/poverty/about/overview/measure.html>]

Size of family unit	1980	1990	1995	2000 [1]	2005	2010 [3]	2011	2012	2013
One person (unrelated individual) [2]......	4,190	6,652	7,763	8,791	9,973	11,137	11,484	11,720	11,888
Under 65 years old.......................	4,290	6,800	7,929	8,959	10,160	11,344	11,702	11,945	12,119
65 years old and over....................	3,949	6,268	7,309	8,259	9,367	10,458	10,788	11,011	11,173
Two persons................................	5,363	8,509	9,933	11,235	12,755	14,216	14,657	14,937	15,142
Householder under 65 years old........	5,537	8,794	10,259	11,589	13,145	14,676	15,139	15,450	15,679
Householder 65 years old and over.....	4,983	7,905	9,219	10,418	11,815	13,194	13,609	13,892	14,095
Three persons.............................	6,565	10,419	12,158	13,740	15,577	17,373	17,916	18,284	18,552
Four persons..............................	8,414	13,359	15,569	17,604	19,971	22,315	23,021	23,492	23,834
Five persons..............................	9,966	15,792	18,408	20,815	23,613	26,442	27,251	27,827	28,265
Six persons...............................	11,269	17,839	20,804	23,533	26,683	29,904	30,847	31,471	31,925
Seven persons.............................	12,761	20,241	23,552	26,750	30,249	34,019	35,085	35,743	36,384
Eight persons.............................	14,199	22,582	26,237	29,701	33,610	37,953	39,064	39,688	40,484
Nine or more persons......................	16,896	26,848	31,280	35,150	40,288	45,224	46,572	47,297	48,065

[1] Implementation of Census 2000-based population controls and sample expanded by 28,000 households. [2] A person living alone or with non-relatives. [3] Implementation of Census 2010-based population controls.

Source: U.S. Census Bureau, *Income and Poverty in the United States: 2013,* Current Population Reports, P60-249, September 2014; and "Historical Poverty Tables: People, Table 1," <http://www.census.gov/hhes/www/poverty/data/historical/people.html>, accessed November 2014. See also <http://www.census.gov/hhes/www/poverty/data/incpovhlth/2013/index.html>.

Table 731. People Below Poverty Level by Race and Hispanic Origin, and Below 125 Percent of Poverty Level: 1985 to 2013

[33,064 represents 33,064,000. People as of March of the following year. Based on Current Population Survey, Annual Social and Economic Supplement (ASEC); see text, this section, Section 1, and Appendix III. Beginning 2002, data refer to persons of specified race only and who did not report any other race category; for Asian Pacific Islander, data refer to persons who reported Asian alone. For information on measuring poverty, see <http://www.census.gov/hhes/www/poverty/about/overview/measure.html>]

Year	Number of persons below poverty (1,000)					Percent of persons below poverty					Below 125 percent of poverty level [1]	
	All races [2]	White	Black	Asian and Pacific Islander	His-panic [3]	All races [2]	White	Black	Asian and Pacific Islander	His-panic [3]	Number (1,000)	Percent of total pop-ulation
1985.........	33,064	22,860	8,926	(NA)	5,236	14.0	11.4	31.3	(NA)	29.0	44,166	18.7
1990.........	33,585	22,326	9,837	858	6,006	13.5	10.7	31.9	12.2	28.1	44,837	18.0
1991.........	35,708	23,747	10,242	996	6,339	14.2	11.3	32.7	13.8	28.7	47,527	18.9
1992 [4].......	38,014	25,259	10,827	985	7,592	14.8	11.9	33.4	12.7	29.6	50,592	19.7
1993 [5].......	39,265	26,226	10,877	1,134	8,126	15.1	12.2	33.1	15.3	30.6	51,801	20.0
1994.........	38,059	25,379	10,196	974	8,416	14.5	11.7	30.6	14.6	30.7	50,401	19.3
1995.........	36,425	24,423	9,872	1,411	8,574	13.8	11.2	29.3	14.6	30.3	48,761	18.5
1996.........	36,529	24,650	9,694	1,454	8,697	13.7	11.2	28.4	14.5	29.4	49,310	18.5
1997.........	35,574	24,396	9,116	1,468	8,308	13.3	11.0	26.5	14.0	27.1	47,853	17.8
1998.........	34,476	23,454	9,091	1,360	8,070	12.7	10.5	26.1	12.5	25.6	46,036	17.0
1999 [6].......	32,791	22,169	8,441	1,285	7,876	11.9	9.8	23.6	10.7	22.7	45,030	16.3
2000 [7].......	31,581	21,645	7,982	1,258	7,747	11.3	9.5	22.5	9.9	21.5	43,612	15.6
2001.........	32,907	22,739	8,136	1,275	7,997	11.7	9.9	22.7	10.2	21.4	45,320	16.1
2002.........	34,570	23,466	8,602	1,161	8,555	12.1	10.2	24.1	10.1	21.8	47,084	16.5
2003.........	35,861	24,272	8,781	1,401	9,051	12.5	10.5	24.4	11.8	22.5	48,687	16.9
2004 [8].......	37,040	25,327	9,014	1,201	9,122	12.7	10.8	24.7	9.8	21.9	49,693	17.1
2005.........	36,950	24,872	9,168	1,402	9,368	12.6	10.6	24.9	11.1	21.8	49,327	16.8
2006.........	36,460	24,416	9,048	1,353	9,243	12.3	10.3	24.3	10.3	20.6	49,688	16.8
2007.........	37,276	25,120	9,237	1,349	9,890	12.5	10.5	24.5	10.2	21.5	50,876	17.0
2008.........	39,829	26,990	9,379	1,576	10,987	13.2	11.2	24.7	11.8	23.2	53,805	17.9
2009.........	43,569	29,830	9,944	1,746	12,350	14.3	12.3	25.8	12.5	25.3	56,840	18.7
2010 [9].......	46,343	31,083	10,746	1,899	13,522	15.1	13.0	27.4	12.2	26.5	60,669	19.8
2011..........	46,247	30,849	10,929	1,973	13,244	15.0	12.8	27.6	12.3	25.3	60,949	19.8
2012.........	46,496	30,816	10,911	1,921	13,616	15.0	12.7	27.2	11.7	25.6	61,202	19.7
2013.........	45,318	29,936	11,041	1,785	12,744	14.5	12.3	27.2	10.5	23.5	60,215	19.2

NA Not available. [1] Includes those in poverty, plus those who have income above poverty but less than 1.25 times their poverty threshold. [2] Includes other races, not shown separately. [3] People of Hispanic origin may be of any race. [4] Implementation of 1990 Census population controls. [5] The March 1994 income supplement was revised to allow for the coding of different income amounts on selected questionnaire items. Limits either increased or decreased in the following categories: earnings increased to $999,999; Social Security increased to $49,999; Supplemental Security Income and public assistance increased to $24,999; veterans' benefits increased to $99,999; child support and alimony decreased to $49,999. [6] Implementation of Census-2000-based population controls. [7] Implementation of sample expansion by 28,000 households. [8] Data have been revised to reflect a correction to the weights in the 2005 ASEC. [9] Implementation of Census 2010-based population controls.

Source: U.S. Census Bureau, *Income and Poverty in the United States: 2013,* Current Population Reports, P60-249, September 2014; and "Historical Poverty Tables: People, Tables 2 and 6," <http://www.census.gov/hhes/www/poverty/data/historical/people.html>, accessed November 2014. See also <http://www.census.gov/hhes/www/poverty/index.html>.

Table 732. Children Below Poverty Level by Race and Hispanic Origin: 1985 to 2013

[12,483 represents 12,483,000. Persons as of March of the following year. Covers only related children under age 18, in families. Beginning 2002, data refer to persons of specified race only and who did not report any other race category; for Asian Pacific Islander, data refer to persons who reported Asian alone. Based on Current Population Survey, Annual Social and Economic Supplement (ASEC); see text, this section, Section 1, and Appendix III]

Year	Number of children below poverty level (1,000)					Percent of children below poverty level				
	All races [1]	White	Black	Asian and Pacific Islander	His-panic [2]	All races [1]	White	Black	Asian and Pacific Islander	His-panic [2]
1985	12,483	7,838	4,057	(NA)	2,512	20.1	15.6	43.1	(NA)	39.6
1990	12,715	7,696	4,412	356	2,750	19.9	15.1	44.2	17.0	37.7
1991	13,658	8,316	4,637	348	2,977	21.1	16.1	45.6	17.1	39.8
1992 [3]	14,521	8,752	5,015	352	3,440	21.6	16.5	46.3	16.0	39.0
1993 [4]	14,961	9,123	5,030	358	3,666	22.0	17.0	45.9	17.6	39.9
1994	14,610	8,826	4,787	308	3,956	21.2	16.3	43.3	17.9	41.1
1995	13,999	8,474	4,644	532	3,938	20.2	15.5	41.5	18.6	39.3
1996	13,764	8,488	4,411	553	4,090	19.8	15.5	39.5	19.1	39.9
1997	13,422	8,441	4,116	608	3,865	19.2	15.4	36.8	19.9	36.4
1998	12,845	7,935	4,073	542	3,670	18.3	14.4	36.4	17.5	33.6
1999 [5]	11,678	7,194	3,698	367	3,561	16.6	13.1	32.8	11.5	29.9
2000 [6]	11,005	6,834	3,495	407	3,342	15.6	12.4	30.9	12.5	27.6
2001	11,175	7,086	3,423	353	3,433	15.8	12.5	30.0	11.1	27.4
2002	11,646	7,203	3,570	302	3,653	16.3	13.1	32.1	11.4	28.2
2003	12,340	7,624	3,750	331	3,982	17.2	13.9	33.6	12.1	29.5
2004 [7]	12,473	7,876	3,702	265	3,985	17.3	14.3	33.4	9.4	28.6
2005	12,335	7,652	3,743	312	3,977	17.1	13.9	34.2	11.0	27.7
2006	12,299	7,522	3,690	351	3,959	16.9	13.6	33.0	12.0	26.6
2007	12,802	8,002	3,838	345	4,348	17.6	14.4	34.3	11.8	28.3
2008	13,507	8,441	3,781	430	4,888	18.5	15.3	34.4	14.2	30.3
2009	14,774	9,440	3,919	444	5,419	20.1	17.0	35.3	13.6	32.5
2010 [8]	15,598	9,590	4,271	477	5,815	21.5	17.9	39.0	14.0	34.3
2011	15,539	9,643	4,247	466	5,820	21.4	18.1	38.6	13.0	33.7
2012	15,437	9,547	4,097	470	5,773	21.3	17.9	37.5	13.3	33.3
2013	14,142	8,428	4,153	354	5,273	19.5	15.9	38.0	9.8	30.0

NA Not available. [1] Includes other races, not shown separately. [2] People of Hispanic origin may be of any race. [3] Implementation of 1990 Census population controls. [4] See Table 731, footnote 5. [5] Implementation of Census 2000-based population controls. [6] Sample expanded to 28,000 households. [7] Data have been revised to reflect a correction to the weights in the 2005 ASEC. [8] Implementation of Census 2010-based population controls.

Source: U.S. Census Bureau, *Income and Poverty in the United States: 2013,* Current Population Reports, P60-249, September 2014; and "Historical Poverty Tables: People, Table 3," <http://www.census.gov/hhes/www/poverty/data/historical/people.html>, accessed December 2014. See also <http://www.census.gov/hhes/www/poverty/index.html>.

Table 733. People Below Poverty Level by Selected Characteristics: 2013

[45,318 represents 45,318,000. People as of March of the following year. Based on Current Population Survey (CPS), 2014 Annual Social and Economic and Supplement. Data by education are for people age 25 and over. Data by nativity or citizenship are for people age 15 and older]

Sex, age, education, region, nativity	Number below poverty level (1,000)					Percent below poverty level				
	All races [1]	White alone	Black alone	Asian alone	His-panic [2]	All races [1]	White alone	Black alone	Asian alone	His-panic [2]
Total	**45,318**	**29,936**	**11,041**	**1,785**	**12,744**	**14.5**	**12.3**	**27.2**	**10.5**	**23.5**
Male	20,119	13,325	4,824	837	5,957	13.1	11.1	25.4	10.3	21.8
Female	25,199	16,611	6,217	948	6,787	15.8	13.5	28.8	10.6	25.3
Under 18 years old	14,659	8,808	4,244	367	5,415	19.9	16.4	38.3	10.1	30.4
18 to 24 years old	5,819	3,757	1,494	278	1,358	19.4	16.9	32.0	17.2	21.3
25 to 34 years old	6,694	4,463	1,518	352	1,918	15.8	13.9	26.1	12.2	22.0
35 to 44 years old	4,871	3,334	1,093	210	1,548	12.2	10.9	21.2	7.6	20.0
45 to 54 years old	4,533	3,188	979	155	1,076	10.6	9.4	18.5	6.5	17.5
55 to 59 years old	2,476	1,737	604	71	427	11.7	10.1	24.1	7.2	19.6
60 to 64 years old	2,036	1,452	411	96	327	11.0	9.6	19.6	10.7	18.8
65 years old and over	4,231	3,197	698	256	676	9.5	8.4	17.6	13.6	19.8
65 to 74 years old	2,135	1,608	368	117	395	8.3	7.4	15.7	10.1	19.7
75 years old and over	2,095	1,590	330	139	280	11.2	9.8	20.3	19.4	20.1
No high school diploma	10,230	6,956	2,374	328	4,157	24.3	21.8	37.5	16.7	29.0
High school, no college	10,563	7,026	2,776	343	2,140	14.8	12.5	27.7	12.7	19.4
Some college, less than 4-year degree	8,120	5,715	1,786	302	1,293	11.8	10.5	19.0	10.5	14.4
College, 4-year degree or higher	3,789	2,709	460	507	385	5.4	4.8	8.0	7.9	8.0
Northeast	7,046	4,505	1,745	411	1,884	12.7	10.5	24.4	11.1	26.0
Midwest	8,590	5,729	2,189	251	1,009	12.9	10.2	31.6	12.9	21.3
South	18,870	11,604	6,077	401	4,973	16.1	13.5	26.6	9.8	24.7
West	10,812	8,097	1,031	722	4,878	14.7	14.0	27.7	9.9	22.1
Native	37,921	24,988	10,003	611	8,524	13.9	11.4	27.8	9.5	23.9
Foreign born	7,397	4,949	1,039	1,174	4,221	18.0	20.1	22.7	11.0	22.9
Naturalized citizen	2,425	1,452	395	518	995	12.7	14.4	16.7	8.3	16.2
Not a citizen	4,972	3,496	644	656	3,225	22.8	24.1	29.2	14.8	26.2

[1] Includes other races, not shown separately. [2] Persons of Hispanic origin may be of any race.

Source: U.S. Census Bureau, *Income and Poverty in the United States: 2013,* Current Population Reports, P60-249, September 2014; "Detailed Tables POV01, POV29, and POV41," <http://www.census.gov/hhes/www/cpstables/032014/pov/toc.htm>, accessed December 2014. See also <http://www.census.gov/hhes/www/poverty/data/incpovhlth/2013/index.html>.

Table 734. Work Experience of People During Year by Poverty Status, by Sex and Age: 2013

[105,839 represents 105,839,000. Covers only persons 16 years old and over. Based on Current Population Survey, 2014 Annual Social and Economic Supplement (ASEC); see text, this section, Section 1, and Appendix III]

Sex and age	Worked full-time year-round			Did not work full-time year-round			Did not work		
	Number (1,000)	Below poverty level		Number (1,000)	Below poverty level		Number (1,000)	Below poverty level	
		Number (1,000)	Percent		Number (1,000)	Percent		Number (1,000)	Percent
BOTH SEXES									
Total...........	**105,839**	**2,812**	**2.7**	**52,039**	**8,213**	**15.8**	**90,359**	**20,986**	**23.2**
16 to 17 years old.......	106	4	3.6	1,663	113	6.8	7,128	1,234	17.3
18 to 64 years old.......	100,855	2,771	2.7	45,397	7,965	17.5	48,581	15,693	32.3
18 to 24 years old.......	6,989	347	5.0	12,423	2,273	18.3	10,642	3,199	30.1
25 to 34 years old.......	23,736	899	3.8	10,332	2,367	22.9	8,398	3,428	40.8
35 to 54 years old.......	51,112	1,304	2.6	15,389	2,440	15.9	16,187	5,660	35.0
55 to 64 years old.......	19,019	221	1.2	7,253	885	12.2	13,354	3,405	25.5
65 years old and over....	4,878	37	0.8	4,979	135	2.7	34,651	4,059	11.7
MALE									
Total...........	**60,769**	**1,586**	**2.6**	**22,651**	**3,484**	**15.4**	**36,891**	**8,326**	**22.6**
16 to 17 years old.......	54	4	(B)	761	61	8.1	3,617	629	17.4
18 to 64 years old.......	57,735	1,560	2.7	19,437	3,365	17.3	18,946	6,429	33.9
18 to 24 years old.......	4,003	174	4.4	6,024	948	15.7	5,262	1,500	28.5
25 to 34 years old.......	13,779	501	3.6	4,568	966	21.2	2,870	1,244	43.3
35 to 54 years old.......	29,352	772	2.6	5,837	1,061	18.2	5,335	2,221	41.6
55 to 64 years old.......	10,600	112	1.1	3,008	389	12.9	5,479	1,465	26.7
65 years old and over....	2,981	23	0.8	2,454	58	2.3	14,328	1,268	8.9
FEMALE									
Total...........	**45,070**	**1,226**	**2.7**	**29,388**	**4,729**	**16.1**	**53,468**	**12,660**	**23.7**
16 to 17 years old.......	52	–	(X)	902	52	5.8	3,511	606	17.2
18 to 64 years old.......	43,121	1,211	2.8	25,960	4,600	17.7	29,634	9,264	31.3
18 to 24 years old.......	2,986	172	5.8	6,399	1,325	20.7	5,380	1,699	31.6
25 to 34 years old.......	9,957	397	4.0	5,765	1,400	24.3	5,527	2,184	39.5
35 to 54 years old.......	21,759	532	2.4	9,552	1,379	14.4	10,852	3,440	31.7
55 to 64 years old.......	8,419	109	1.3	4,245	496	11.7	7,875	1,941	24.6
65 years old and over....	1,897	15	0.8	2,525	77	3.1	20,323	2,791	13.7

– Represents zero. B Base figure too small to meet statistical standards for reliability of a derived figure. X Not applicable.

Source: U.S. Census Bureau, *Income and Poverty in the United States: 2013*, Current Population Reports, P60-249, September 2014; "Detailed Tables, Table POV22," <http://www.census.gov/hhes/www/cpstables/032014/pov/toc.htm>, accessed December 2014. See also <http://www.census.gov/hhes/www/poverty/data/incpovhlth/2013/index.html>.

Table 735. Families Below Poverty Level and Below 125 Percent of Poverty by Race and Hispanic Origin: 1980 to 2013

[6,217 represents 6,217,000. Families as of March of the following year. Based on Current Population Survey, Annual Social and Economic Supplement (ASEC); see text, this section and Section 1, and Appendix III. For data collection changes over time, see <http://www.census.gov /hhes/www/income/data/historical/history.html>. Beginning with the 2003 CPS covering data for 2002, respondents were allowed to choose more than one race. Two basic ways of defining a race group are possible: a group such as Asian may be defined as those who reported Asian and no other race (the race-alone concept), or as those who reported Asian regardless of whether they also reported another race (the race-alone-or-in-combination concept). For 2001 data and earlier, the CPS allowed respondents to report only one race group. See also comments on race in the text for Section 1, Population]

Year	Number of families below poverty (1,000)					Percent of families below poverty					Below 125 percent of poverty level	
	All races [1]	White [2]	Black [2]	Asian and Pacific Islander [2]	His-panic [3]	All races [1]	White [2]	Black [2]	Asian and Pacific Islander [2]	His-panic [3]	Number (1,000)	Percent
1980........	6,217	4,195	1,826	(NA)	751	10.3	8.0	28.9	(NA)	23.2	8,764	14.5
1985........	7,223	4,983	1,983	(NA)	1,074	11.4	9.1	28.7	(NA)	25.5	9,753	15.3
1990........	7,098	4,622	2,193	169	1,244	10.7	8.1	29.3	11.0	25.0	9,564	14.4
1995........	7,532	4,994	2,127	264	1,695	10.8	8.5	26.4	12.4	27.0	10,223	14.7
2000 [4]......	6,400	4,333	1,686	233	1,540	8.7	7.1	19.3	7.8	19.2	9,032	12.2
2005........	7,657	5,068	1,997	289	1,948	9.9	8.0	22.1	9.0	19.7	10,442	13.5
2006........	7,668	5,118	2,007	260	1,922	9.8	8.0	21.6	7.8	18.9	10,531	13.4
2007........	7,623	5,046	2,045	261	2,045	9.8	7.9	22.1	7.9	19.7	10,551	13.5
2008........	8,147	5,414	2,055	341	2,239	10.3	8.4	22.0	9.8	21.3	11,164	14.2
2009........	8,792	5,994	2,125	337	2,369	11.1	9.3	22.7	9.4	22.7	11,620	14.7
2010 [6]......	9,400	6,305	2,311	362	2,739	11.8	9.9	24.1	9.3	24.3	12,448	15.6
2011........	9,497	6,334	2,334	401	2,651	11.8	9.8	24.2	9.7	22.9	12,500	15.5
2012........	9,520	6,299	2,327	387	2,807	11.8	9.7	23.7	9.4	23.5	12,669	15.7
2013........	9,130	6,032	2,267	379	2,613	11.2	9.3	22.8	8.7	21.6	12,375	15.2

NA Not available. [1] Includes other races, not shown separately. [2] Beginning 2002, data refer to persons who reported specified race only and no other race category; for Asian and Pacific Islander, data refer to persons who reported Asian only. [3] People of Hispanic origin may be of any race. [4] Implementation of Census 2000 based population controls and sample expanded by 28,000 households. [5] Implementation of Census 2010-based population controls.

Source: U.S. Census Bureau, *Income and Poverty in the United States: 2013*, Current Population Reports, P60-249, September 2014; "Historical Poverty Family Table 4," and "Detailed Table POV04," <http://www.census.gov/hhes/www/poverty/data/incpovhlth/2013/index.html>, accessed December 2014.

Table 736. Families Below Poverty Level by Selected Characteristics: 2013

[In thousands (9,130 represents 9,130,000), except as noted. All families as of March of the following year. Based on Current Population Survey (CPS), Annual Social and Economic Supplement (ASEC); see text, this section and Section 1, and Appendix III. Data below represent persons who selected each race group only and exclude persons reporting more than one race. See also comments on race in the text for Section 1. For composition of regions, see map, inside front cover]

Characteristic	Number below poverty level (1,000)					Percent below poverty level				
	All races [1]	White alone	Black alone	Asian alone	His-panic [2]	All races [1]	White alone	Black alone	Asian alone	His-panic [2]
Total families.............	9,130	6,032	2,267	379	2,613	11.2	9.3	22.8	8.7	21.6
Age of householder:										
18 to 24 years old.............	859	517	230	18	264	27.7	23.4	39.7	13.0	29.7
25 to 34 years old.............	2,488	1,593	671	86	820	18.7	15.9	34.7	10.7	28.5
35 to 44 years old.............	2,043	1,322	536	85	675	12.4	10.5	24.2	7.6	21.3
45 to 54 years old.............	1,574	1,075	389	51	433	9.0	7.7	17.4	5.2	17.5
55 to 64 years old.............	1,148	787	263	55	235	7.6	6.4	16.2	7.7	15.5
65 years old and over..........	970	713	164	77	171	6.2	5.3	12.7	13.0	15.3
Region:										
Northeast....................	1,399	892	358	95	399	9.8	7.8	21.3	9.7	24.5
Midwest......................	1,726	1,142	451	42	184	9.9	7.6	27.8	8.9	18.2
South........................	3,840	2,397	1,236	85	1,047	12.4	10.2	21.8	7.8	22.3
West.........................	2,166	1,601	223	157	984	11.7	10.8	23.6	8.6	20.5
Type of family:										
Married couple.................	3,476	2,677	416	254	1,069	5.8	5.3	8.9	7.3	14.2
Male householder, no spouse present...........	1,008	649	255	46	254	15.9	14.0	23.1	13.4	18.0
Female householder, no spouse present.............	4,646	2,706	1,596	80	1,290	30.6	27.4	38.5	14.9	40.4

[1] Includes other races, not shown separately. [2] Hispanic persons may be of any race.

Source: U.S. Census Bureau, *Income and Poverty in the United States: 2013*, Current Population Reports, P60-249, September 2014; and "Detailed Tables POV04 and POV44," <http://www.census.gov/hhes/www/poverty/data/incpovhlth/2013/index.html>, accessed December 2014.

Table 737. Top Wealth Holders With Gross Assets of $2.0 Million or More—Debts, Mortgages, and Net Worth: 2007

[2,290 represents 2,290,000. Net worth is defined as assets minus liabilities. Figures are estimates from the Personal Wealth Study, based on a sample of federal estate tax returns (Form 706). Based on the estate multiplier technique; for more information on this methodology, see source]

Sex and net worth	Total assets		Debts and mortgages		Net worth	
	Number of top wealth holders (1,000)	Amount (mil. dol.)	Number of top wealth holders (1,000)	Amount (mil. dol.)	Number of top wealth holders (1,000)	Amount (mil. dol.)
Both sexes, total......................	2,290	13,221,799	1,792	1,124,478	2,290	12,097,321
Size of net worth:						
Under $2.0 million [1]...............	449	860,731	403	390,799	449	469,932
$2.0 million under $3.5 million..............	1,008	2,810,250	744	196,440	1,008	2,613,810
$3.5 million under $5.0 million..............	364	1,607,665	275	96,621	364	1,511,044
$5.0 million under $10.0 million..............	286	2,091,670	222	141,875	286	1,949,794
$10.0 million under $20.0 million...........	116	1,687,934	95	97,133	116	1,590,801
$20.0 million or more..............	66	4,163,549	54	201,609	66	3,961,939
Males, total.......................	1,320	8,062,977	1,038	872,850	1,320	7,190,127
Size of net worth:						
Under $2.0 million [1]...............	324	613,092	284	325,369	324	287,723
$2.0 million under $3.5 million..............	526	1,502,230	385	134,813	526	1,367,417
$3.5 million under $5.0 million..............	190	846,527	146	62,021	190	784,506
$5.0 million under $10.0 million..............	169	1,257,007	131	107,010	169	1,149,997
$10.0 million under $20.0 million...........	71	1,029,068	58	67,473	71	961,595
$20.0 million or more..............	41	2,815,052	35	176,164	41	2,638,888
Females, total.......................	970	5,158,822	754	251,629	970	4,907,194
Size of net worth:						
Under $2.0 million [1]...............	125	247,639	119	65,430	125	182,209
$2.0 million under $3.5 million..............	482	1,308,020	359	61,627	482	1,246,393
$3.5 million under $5.0 million..............	175	761,139	129	34,600	175	726,538
$5.0 million under $10.0 million..............	117	834,663	91	34,866	117	799,797
$10.0 million under $20.0 million...........	46	658,866	37	29,660	46	629,206
$20.0 million or more..............	26	1,348,496	20	25,445	26	1,323,051

[1] Includes individuals with zero net worth.

Source: U.S. Internal Revenue Service, Statistics of Income Division, "SOI Tax Stats - Personal Wealth Statistics," January 2012. See also <http://www.irs.gov/uac/SOI-Tax-Stats-Personal-Wealth-Statistics>.

Table 738. Top Wealth Holders With Gross Assets of $2.0 Million or More by Type of Property, Sex, and Size of Net Worth: 2007

[2,290 represents 2,290,000. Net worth is defined as assets minus liabilities. Figures are estimates from the Personal Wealth Study, based on a sample of federal estate tax returns (Form 706). Based on the estate multiplier technique; for more information on this methodology, see source]

Sex and net worth	Number of top wealth holders (1,000)	Assets (mil. dol.)				
		Total [1]	Personal residences	Other real estate	Closely held stock	Publicly traded stock
Both sexes, total............................	**2,290**	**13,221,799**	**1,247,026**	**1,659,926**	**1,577,715**	**2,553,437**
Size of net worth:						
Under $2.0 million [2]............................	449	860,731	181,133	208,138	56,760	63,121
$2.0 million under $3.5 million....................	1,008	2,810,250	413,215	435,218	140,964	467,856
$3.5 million under $5.0 million....................	364	1,607,665	193,726	236,360	115,070	311,686
$5.0 million under $10.0 million...................	286	2,091,670	195,830	310,222	242,341	384,644
$10.0 million under $20.0 million..................	116	1,687,934	134,600	195,331	203,913	361,193
$20.0 million or more............................	66	4,163,549	128,522	274,657	818,667	964,936
Males, total..................................	**1,320**	**8,062,977**	**656,699**	**978,024**	**1,142,747**	**1,445,410**
Size of net worth:						
Under $2.0 million [2]............................	324	613,092	117,898	144,801	46,276	42,054
$2.0 million under $3.5 million....................	526	1,502,230	192,820	232,863	95,870	215,697
$3.5 million under $5.0 million....................	190	846,527	91,968	121,207	77,869	143,539
$5.0 million under $10.0 million...................	169	1,257,007	114,668	175,414	193,956	205,132
$10.0 million under $20.0 million..................	71	1,029,068	68,834	119,681	155,875	197,680
$20.0 million or more............................	41	2,815,052	70,510	184,059	572,901	641,308
Females, total................................	**970**	**5,158,822**	**590,327**	**681,902**	**434,968**	**1,108,027**
Size of net worth:						
Under $2.0 million [2]............................	125	247,639	63,235	63,337	10,484	21,068
$2.0 million under $3.5 million....................	482	1,308,020	220,395	202,355	45,094	252,159
$3.5 million under $5.0 million....................	175	761,139	101,757	115,153	37,201	168,148
$5.0 million under $10.0 million...................	117	834,663	81,162	134,808	48,385	179,512
$10.0 million under $20.0 million..................	46	658,866	65,765	75,650	48,038	163,513
$20.0 million or more............................	26	1,348,496	58,012	90,599	245,766	323,628

[1] Includes other types of assets, not shown separately. [2] Includes individuals with zero or negative net worth.

Source: U.S. Internal Revenue Service, Statistics of Income Division, "SOI Tax Stats - Personal Wealth Statistics," January 2012. See also <http://www.irs.gov/uac/SOI-Tax-Stats-Personal-Wealth-Statistics>.

Table 739. Top Wealth Holders With Net Worth of $2.0 Million or More—Number and Net Worth by State: 2007

[1,841 represents 1,841,000. Estimates based on a sample of federal estate tax returns (Form 706). Estimates of wealth by state can be subject to significant year-to-year fluctuations, especially for individuals at the extreme tail of the net worth distribution and for states with relatively small decedent populations. Based on the estate multiplier technique; for more information on this methodology, see source]

State	Number of top wealth holders (1,000)	Net worth (mil. dol.)	State	Number of top wealth holders (1,000)	Net worth (mil. dol.)
Total [1]........................	**1,841**	**11,627,389**	Montana...........................	7	34,794
Alabama..........................	17	94,464	Nebraska..........................	6	36,643
Alaska............................	3	11,579	Nevada............................	16	226,904
Arizona...........................	34	196,438	New Hampshire....................	13	68,492
Arkansas.........................	8	91,058	New Jersey........................	71	332,456
California.........................	329	1,941,513	New Mexico.......................	10	40,482
Colorado..........................	32	243,210	New York..........................	159	1,201,654
Connecticut.......................	36	286,124	North Carolina.....................	45	240,370
Delaware..........................	5	23,788	North Dakota......................	4	13,673
District of Columbia...............	3	30,140	Ohio..............................	50	237,826
Florida............................	155	1,105,649	Oklahoma.........................	17	76,728
Georgia...........................	41	213,487	Oregon............................	24	90,338
Hawaii............................	7	75,601	Pennsylvania......................	57	323,679
Idaho.............................	8	52,888	Rhode Island......................	6	29,640
Illinois............................	83	493,809	South Carolina....................	25	189,396
Indiana...........................	25	115,056	South Dakota......................	7	78,126
Iowa..............................	14	56,740	Tennessee.........................	26	116,288
Kansas............................	11	58,061	Texas.............................	100	662,518
Kentucky..........................	15	76,777	Utah..............................	9	49,879
Louisiana.........................	16	129,584	Vermont...........................	6	23,205
Maine.............................	8	39,673	Virginia...........................	49	269,648
Maryland..........................	43	331,467	Washington........................	41	359,004
Massachusetts....................	51	394,752	West Virginia......................	5	27,085
Michigan..........................	39	217,591	Wisconsin.........................	32	165,770
Minnesota.........................	24	158,224	Wyoming..........................	6	45,258
Mississippi........................	9	37,101			
Missouri...........................	26	145,218	Other areas [1]....................	8	67,541

[1] Includes U.S. territories and possessions.

Source: U.S. Internal Revenue Service, Statistics of Income Division, "SOI Tax Stats - Personal Wealth Statistics," January 2012. See also <http://www.irs.gov/uac/SOI-Tax-Stats-Personal-Wealth-Statistics>.

Table 740. Nonfinancial Assets Held by Families by Type of Asset: 2013

[Value of assets in thousands of constant (2013) dollars (177.9 represents $177,900). Families include one-person units and, as used in this table, are comparable to the U.S. Census Bureau's household concept. Based on internal data from the Survey of Consumer Finances; see Appendix III. For definition of median, see Guide to Tabular Presentation. For data on financial assets, see Table 1184]

Family characteristic	Any financial or non-financial asset	Any non-financial asset	Vehicles	Primary residence	Other residential property	Equity in nonresidential property	Business equity	Other asset
PERCENT OF FAMILIES HOLDING ASSET								
All families, total...................	**97.9**	**91.0**	**86.3**	**65.2**	**13.2**	**7.2**	**11.7**	**7.3**
Age of family head:								
Under 35 years old...................	97.1	84.9	82.7	35.6	4.7	1.8	6.5	5.2
35 to 44 years old....................	97.5	92.8	89.9	61.7	9.2	5.7	15.6	4.7
45 to 54 years old....................	97.9	91.8	87.7	69.1	15.8	7.0	14.6	7.9
55 to 64 years old....................	98.1	92.9	89.2	74.2	18.4	8.9	15.5	8.2
65 to 74 years old....................	98.9	95.9	89.4	85.8	21.3	14.1	11.0	11.3
75 years old and over..............	99.0	89.6	76.0	80.2	12.8	8.9	4.4	7.8
Race or ethnicity of respondent:								
White non-Hispanic.................	99.3	94.9	90.3	73.8	15.9	8.7	13.9	8.5
Non-White or Hispanic..............	95.2	83.2	78.1	47.4	7.8	4.0	7.2	4.8
Tenure:								
Owner occupied.....................	100.0	100.0	93.6	100.0	17.8	10.0	15.4	8.6
Renter occupied or other...........	94.1	74.3	72.6	(B)	4.8	1.8	4.7	4.7
MEDIAN VALUE [1] ($1,000)								
All families, total...................	**177.9**	**148.4**	**15.8**	**170.0**	**123.8**	**60.0**	**67.5**	**13.0**
Age of family head:								
Under 35 years old...................	29.6	22.0	12.5	140.0	102.5	45.0	23.8	5.0
35 to 44 years old....................	163.0	135.8	16.8	170.0	107.0	54.2	50.0	16.0
45 to 54 years old....................	214.9	174.9	19.2	180.0	100.0	37.0	93.2	15.0
55 to 64 years old....................	261.0	189.6	17.1	185.0	150.0	96.0	110.0	19.0
65 to 74 years old....................	304.0	206.8	16.4	175.0	137.0	96.5	100.0	20.0
75 years old and over..............	217.0	158.1	10.5	145.0	120.0	55.0	157.5	10.0
Race or ethnicity of respondent:								
White non-Hispanic.................	236.8	178.7	17.5	180.0	135.0	72.0	90.0	15.0
Non-White or Hispanic..............	57.4	60.6	12.3	143.0	80.0	30.0	30.0	10.0
Tenure:								
Owner occupied.....................	298.9	213.4	19.5	170.0	122.0	65.0	100.0	15.0
Renter occupied or other...........	13.5	10.3	9.3	(B)	132.0	20.0	17.8	6.5

B Base too small to meet statistical standards for reliability of derived figure. [1] Median value of asset for families holding such assets.

Source: Board of Governors of the Federal Reserve System, 2013 Survey of Consumer Finances, *Changes in U.S. Family Finances From 2010 to 2013: Evidence from the Survey of Consumer Finances*, Federal Reserve Bulletin, Vol. 100, No. 4, September 2014. See also <http://www.federalreserve.gov/econresdata/scf/scfindex.htm>.

Table 741. Family Net Worth—Median and Mean Net Worth in Constant (2013) Dollars by Selected Family Characteristics: 2004 to 2013

[Net worth in thousands of constant (2013) dollars (114.8 represents $114,800). Constant dollar figures are based on Consumer Price Index for all urban consumers published by U.S. Bureau of Labor Statistics. Families include one-person units and as used in this table are comparable to the U.S. Census Bureau's household concept. Based on internal data from the Survey of Consumer Finances; see Appendix III. For definition of mean and median, see Guide to Tabular Presentation]

Family characteristic	2004 Median	2004 Mean	2007 Median	2007 Mean	2010 Median	2010 Mean	2013 Median	2013 Mean
All families...........................	**114.8**	**554.2**	**135.4**	**626.3**	**82.8**	**534.5**	**81.2**	**534.6**
Age of family head:								
Under 35 years old.....................	17.5	90.7	13.2	119.0	10.0	70.0	10.4	75.5
35 to 44 years old......................	85.6	369.9	99.1	366.4	45.2	233.0	46.7	347.2
45 to 54 years old......................	179.1	670.7	207.6	743.5	126.3	614.1	105.3	530.1
55 to 64 years old......................	310.8	1,046.4	285.3	1,057.5	192.3	943.6	165.9	798.4
65 to 74 years old......................	234.5	852.1	268.8	1,140.4	221.5	909.2	232.1	1,057.0
75 years old and over................	201.1	651.2	239.7	716.7	232.3	726.5	194.8	645.2
Race or ethnicity of respondent:								
White non-Hispanic...................	173.8	694.7	192.3	779.2	139.9	701.4	142.0	705.9
Non-white or Hispanic.................	30.6	188.9	31.8	257.5	21.9	188.5	18.1	183.9
Tenure:								
Owner occupied.......................	227.8	772.6	263.7	875.9	187.0	764.6	195.4	783.0
Renter occupied or other..............	4.9	66.7	5.8	80.0	5.4	61.3	5.4	70.3

Source: Board of Governors of the Federal Reserve System, 2013 Survey of Consumer Finances, *Changes in U.S. Family Finances From 2010 to 2013: Evidence from the Survey of Consumer Finances*, Federal Reserve Bulletin, Vol. 100, No. 4, September 2014. See also <http://www.federalreserve.gov/econresdata/scf/scfindex.htm>.

Table 742. Household and Nonprofit Organization Sector Balance Sheet: 1990 to 2014

[In billions of dollars (25,685 represents $25,685,000,000,000), unless otherwise noted. As of December 31. Sector includes domestic hedge funds, private equity funds, and personal trusts. For details of financial assets and liabilities, see Table 1183 and Table 1185]

Item	1990	1995	2000	2005	2010	2012	2013	2014
Assets	**25,685**	**34,276**	**51,188**	**74,002**	**76,231**	**83,152**	**92,636**	**97,067**
Nonfinancial assets [1]	9,733	11,498	16,924	28,530	23,347	25,076	27,688	29,074
Real estate	7,591	8,835	13,533	24,136	18,379	19,818	22,315	23,539
Households [2, 3]	6,797	8,055	12,213	22,028	16,404	17,513	19,647	20,633
Consumer durable goods [4]	2,039	2,529	3,202	4,108	4,587	4,840	4,942	5,087
Financial assets [1]	15,952	22,779	34,263	45,472	52,883	58,076	64,947	67,992
Deposits [1]	3,528	3,428	4,462	6,258	8,071	9,275	9,655	10,231
Time and savings deposits	2,674	2,345	3,072	4,965	6,451	7,194	7,400	7,872
Money market fund shares	389	472	937	943	1,129	1,110	1,136	1,120
Credit market instruments [1]	1,749	2,389	2,466	3,461	4,916	4,201	3,875	3,356
Treasury securities	504	837	578	426	1,124	937	954	706
Municipal securities	648	533	532	1,601	1,871	1,662	1,618	1,540
Corporate and foreign bonds	245	617	565	599	1,361	1,245	1,014	949
Corporate equities [2]	1,961	4,434	8,097	8,026	8,665	9,593	12,407	13,365
Mutual fund shares [5]	512	1,253	2,585	3,521	4,636	5,703	7,142	7,804
Security credit	65	145	461	623	725	757	815	868
Life insurance reserves	392	566	819	1,083	1,137	1,186	1,233	1,277
Pension entitlements	4,435	6,718	10,020	13,471	17,036	18,461	19,894	20,814
Equity in noncorporate business [6]	3,057	3,518	4,974	8,420	6,889	8,027	9,001	9,338
Liabilities [1]	**3,690**	**5,042**	**7,349**	**12,162**	**13,783**	**13,643**	**13,791**	**14,154**
Credit market instruments [1]	3,568	4,845	6,960	11,721	13,231	13,060	13,169	13,497
Home mortgages [7]	2,489	3,319	4,814	8,913	9,916	9,495	9,406	9,380
Consumer credit	824	1,168	1,741	2,321	2,647	2,924	3,098	3,316
Net worth	**21,995**	**29,235**	**43,839**	**61,839**	**62,448**	**69,509**	**78,844**	**82,912**
Replacement cost value of structures:								
Residential [1]	4,287	5,595	7,732	12,244	12,730	13,229	14,187	15,084
Households	4,184	5,485	7,596	12,052	12,527	13,020	13,968	14,850
Nonresidential (nonprofits)	469	588	808	1,183	1,421	1,508	1,596	1,641
Disposable personal income	4,312	5,533	7,400	9,401	11,238	12,384	12,505	12,987
Owners' equity in household real estate	4,308	4,736	7,399	13,115	6,489	8,018	10,241	11,253
Owners' equity as percent of household real estate	63.4	58.8	60.6	59.5	39.6	45.8	52.1	54.5

[1] Includes types of assets and/or liabilities not shown separately. [2] At market value. [3] Includes all types of owner-occupied housing including farm houses and mobile homes, second homes that are not rented, vacant homes for sale, and vacant land. [4] At replacement (current) cost. [5] Value based on the market values of equities held and the book value of other assets held by mutual funds. [6] Net worth of nonfinancial noncorporate business and owners' equity in unincorporated security brokers and dealers. [7] Includes loans made under home equity lines of credit and home equity loans secured by junior liens.

Source: Board of Governors of the Federal Reserve System, "Financial Accounts of the United States, Z.1: Balance Sheet Table B.101," March 2015, <http://www.federalreserve.gov/datadownload/default.htm>, accessed March 2015.

Table 743. Net Stock of Fixed Assets and Consumer Durable Goods in Current and Chained (2009) Dollars: 1990 to 2014

[In billions of dollars (18,868 represents $18,868,000,000,000)]

Item	1990	2000	2005	2010	2011	2012	2013	2014
CURRENT DOLLARS								
Net stock, total	**18,868**	**30,897**	**43,403**	**50,446**	**52,037**	**53,655**	**56,072**	**58,260**
Fixed assets	16,829	27,695	39,295	45,860	47,314	48,806	51,134	53,222
Private	12,772	21,398	30,609	34,345	35,178	36,284	38,209	39,984
Nonresidential	7,070	11,588	15,461	18,562	19,287	19,921	20,716	21,464
Equipment	2,424	3,806	4,482	5,268	5,478	5,671	5,871	6,125
Structures	4,055	6,471	9,320	11,189	11,606	11,952	12,424	12,816
Intellectual property products	591	1,311	1,659	2,105	2,202	2,297	2,421	2,523
Residential	5,702	9,810	15,148	15,783	15,891	16,364	17,493	18,520
Government	4,057	6,298	8,686	11,515	12,135	12,522	12,925	13,239
Nonresidential	3,908	6,066	8,350	11,183	11,798	12,174	12,550	12,843
Equipment	514	646	728	926	958	973	981	994
Structures	2,897	4,767	6,818	9,228	9,782	10,115	10,456	10,715
Intellectual property products	496	653	805	1,029	1,059	1,086	1,113	1,133
Residential	149	232	335	332	337	348	375	396
Consumer durable goods	2,039	3,202	4,108	4,587	4,723	4,849	4,938	5,038
Motor vehicles and parts	650	1,051	1,313	1,288	1,319	1,362	1,400	1,454
Furnishings and durable household equipment	649	977	1,259	1,412	1,458	1,495	1,497	1,509
Recreational goods and vehicles	419	724	963	1,084	1,091	1,118	1,149	1,174
Other	322	449	573	802	855	875	893	902
CHAINED (2009) DOLLARS								
Net stock, total	**(NA)**	**40,217**	**46,305**	**50,332**	**50,822**	**51,438**	**52,117**	**52,867**
Fixed assets	(NA)	37,595	42,340	45,622	45,993	46,444	46,948	47,503
Private	(NA)	28,341	32,044	34,302	34,519	34,868	35,295	35,783
Nonresidential	(NA)	15,402	17,062	18,513	18,719	19,026	19,351	19,735
Equipment	(NA)	4,037	4,717	5,205	5,312	5,481	5,656	5,856
Structures	(NA)	10,053	10,624	11,240	11,275	11,346	11,426	11,534
Intellectual property products	(NA)	1,417	1,730	2,067	2,129	2,198	2,271	2,353
Residential	(NA)	12,958	14,976	15,789	15,799	15,838	15,941	16,049
Government	(NA)	9,273	10,301	11,319	11,471	11,574	11,652	11,721
Nonresidential	(NA)	8,967	9,977	10,984	11,132	11,234	11,311	11,381
Equipment	(NA)	698	763	910	927	938	942	944
Structures	(NA)	7,527	8,362	9,090	9,202	9,280	9,345	9,408
Intellectual property products	(NA)	745	855	983	1,003	1,016	1,024	1,028
Residential	(NA)	302	322	336	339	340	340	340
Consumer durable goods	(NA)	2,840	3,977	4,711	4,833	5,005	5,194	5,408

NA Not available.

Source: U.S. Bureau of Economic Analysis, National Data, "Fixed Assets Accounts Tables," <http://www.bea.gov/iTable/index_FA.cfm>, accessed September 2015.

Section 14
Prices

The Prices section contains producer and consumer price indexes and actual prices for selected commodities. The primary sources of the data are monthly publications of the U.S. Department of Labor, Bureau of Labor Statistics (BLS), which include *Consumer Price Index Detailed Report*, *Producer Price Index Detailed Report*, and *U.S. Import and Export Price Indexes*. Additionally, BLS provides comprehensive databases for the respective price indexes at <http://www.bls.gov/data/>. The Bureau of Economic Analysis (BEA) is the source for gross domestic product measures. Cost of living data for many urban and metropolitan areas are provided by The Council for Community and Economic Research (C2ER), a private organization in Arlington, VA. Table 748 on housing price indexes, contains data from the Federal Housing Finance Agency Housing Price Index. Other commodity, housing, and energy prices may be found in the Energy and Utilities; Forestry, Fishing and Mining; and Construction and Housing sections.

Most price data is measured by an index. An index is a tool that simplifies the measurement of movements in a numerical series. An index allows you to properly compare two or more values in different time periods or places by comparing both to a base year. An index of 110, for example, means there has been a 10-percent increase in price since the reference period; similarly, an index of 90 means a 10-percent decrease. Movements of the index from one date to another can be expressed as changes in index points (simply, the difference between index levels), but it is more useful to express the movements as percent changes. This is because index points are affected by the level of the index in relation to its reference period, while percent changes are not.

Consumer price indexes (CPI)—The CPI is a measure of the average change in prices over time in a "market basket" of goods and services purchased either by urban wage earners and clerical workers or by all urban consumers. The all urban consumer group represents approximately 87 percent of the total U.S. population and is based on the expenditures of residents of urban or metropolitan areas, including professionals, the self-employed, the poor, the unemployed, and retired people, as well as urban wage earners and clerical workers. Not included in the CPI are the spending patterns of people living in rural nonmetropolitan areas, farm families, people in the Armed Forces, and those in institutions, such as prisons and mental hospitals. Consumer inflation for all urban consumers is measured by two indexes, the Consumer Price Index for All Urban Consumers (CPI-U) and the Chained Consumer Price Index for All Urban Consumers (C-CPI-U). The broadest and most comprehensive CPI is called the All Items Consumer Price Index for All Urban Consumers (CPI-U) for the U.S. City Average. CPIs in this section generally have a base of 1982–84 = 100.

The CPI is a product of a series of interrelated samples. Data from the 1990 Census of Population determines the urban areas from which data on prices are collected and the housing units within each area that are eligible for use in the shelter component of the CPI. The Census of Population also provides data on the number of consumers represented by each area selected as a CPI price collection area. A sample (of about 14,500 families each year) serves as the basis for a Point-of-Purchase Survey that identified the places where households purchased various types of goods and services. The CPI market basket is developed from detailed expenditure information provided by families and individuals on what they actually bought. In calculating the index, each item is assigned a weight to account for its relative importance in consumers' budgets. Price changes for the various items in each location are then averaged and local data are combined to obtain a U.S. city average. For the current CPI, this information was collected from the Consumer Expenditure Surveys for 2011 and 2012. In each of those years, about 7,000 families from around the country provided information each quarter on their spending habits in the interview survey. To collect information on frequently purchased items, such as food and personal care products, another 7,000 families in each of these years kept diaries listing everything they bought during a 2-week period. Over the 2 year period, expenditure information came from approximately 28,000 weekly diaries and 60,000 quarterly interviews used to determine the importance, or weight, of the more than 200 item categories in the CPI index structure.

The CPI represents all goods and services purchased for consumption by the reference population. BLS has classified all expenditure items into more than 200 categories, arranged into eight major groups which are food and beverages, housing, apparel, transportation, medical care, recreation, education and communication, and other goods and services. The CPI does not include investment items, such as stocks, bonds, real estate, and life insurance, as these items relate to savings and not to day-to-day consumption expenses.

Producer price index (PPI)— Dating from 1890, the PPI is the oldest continuous statistical series published by BLS. The PPI is a family of indexes that measures the average change over time in the selling prices received by domestic producers of goods and services. Imports are excluded. The target set of goods and services included in the PPI is the entire marketed output of U.S. producers. The set includes both goods and services purchased by other producers as inputs to their operations or as capital investment, as well as goods and services purchased by consumers either directly from the service producer or indirectly from a retailer. About 10,000 PPIs for individual products and groups of products are released each month.

PPIs are published for the output of almost all industries in the goods-producing sectors of the U.S. economy, and, while more indexes are gradually being introduced, currently are available for slightly less than three-quarters of the service sector. For any given industry, producers are usually selected for the PPI survey using a systematic sampling from a listing of all firms that file with the Unemployment Insurance System. Establishments are asked to report their prices as of Tuesday of the week containing the 13th of the month. Each month over 100,000 prices are solicited from roughly 25,000 reporters. Currently, some PPIs have an index base set at 1982 = 100, while the remainder have an index base that corresponds with the month prior to the month that the index was introduced. For further detail regarding the PPI, see the *BLS Handbook of Methods*, Chapter 14, <http://www.bls.gov/opub/hom/homch14.htm>.

In January 2014, PPI transitioned from the Stage of Processing (SOP) system to the Final Demand–Intermediate Demand (FD-ID) system as its primary index aggregation structure. The transition to the FD-ID system is the culmination of a long-standing PPI objective to improve the SOP system (domestically produced goods for domestic, nongovernment consumption) by incorporating PPIs for services, construction, government purchases, and exports. The FD portion of the FD-ID system expands coverage relative to the finished goods stage of the SOP system by including indexes that examine inflation from the producer perspective for goods, services, and construction sold as personal consumption, capital investment, government purchase, and export. The ID portion of the system allows data users to examine inflation from the producer perspective for goods, services, and construction sold to businesses as inputs to production, excluding capital investment.

BEA price indexes—BEA chain-weighted price indexes are weighted averages of the detailed price indexes used in the deflation of the goods and services that make up the gross domestic product (GDP) and its major components. Growth rates are constructed for years and quarters using quantity weights for the current and preceding year or quarter; these growth rates are used to move the index for the preceding period forward a year or quarter at a time. All chain-weighted price indexes are expressed in terms of the reference year value 2009 = 100.

Personal consumption expenditures (PCE) price and quantity indexes are based on market transactions for which there are corresponding price measures. The price index provides a measure of the prices paid by persons for domestic purchases of goods and services. PCEs are defined as market value of spending by individuals and not-for-profit institutions on all goods and services. Personal consumption expenditures also include the value of certain imputed goods and services—such as the rental value of owner-occupied homes and compensation paid in kind—such as employer-paid health and life insurance premiums. More information on this index may be found at <http://www.bea.gov/national/index.htm>.

Measures of inflation—Inflation is a period of rising price levels for goods and factors of production. Inflation results in a decline in the purchasing power of the dollar. It is suggested that changes in price

levels be compared from the same month of the prior year and not as a change from the prior month. The BLS offers several indexes that measure different aspects of inflation, three of which are included in this section. The CPI measures inflation as experienced by consumers in their day-to-day living expenses. The PPI measures prices at the producer level only. The International Price Program measures change in the prices of imports and exports of nonmilitary goods between the United States and other countries.

Whereas the CPI and PPI measure a benchmark approach to price levels, the BEA's Personal Consumption Expenditures uses a chain-weight approach which links weighted averages from adjoining years.

Other measures of inflation include the futures price and spot market price indexes from the Commodity Research Bureau and the employment cost, hourly compensation, and unit labor cost indexes from the BLS. Found in Section 12, Labor Force, Employment, and Earnings, these BLS indexes are used as a measure of the change in cost of the labor factor of production and changes in long-term interest rates that are often used to measure changes in the cost of the capital factor of production.

International price indexes—The BLS International Price Program produces Import/Export Price Indexes (MXP) for nonmilitary goods traded between the United States and the rest of the world.

The U.S. Import and U.S. Export Price Indexes measure the change over time in the prices of goods or services purchased from abroad by U.S. residents (imports) or sold to foreign buyers by U.S. residents (exports). The reference period for the indexes is 2000 = 100, unless otherwise indicated. The product universe for both the import and export indexes includes raw materials, agricultural products, semifinished manufactures, and finished manufactures, including both capital and consumer goods. Price data for these items are collected primarily by mail questionnaire. In nearly all cases, the data are collected directly from the exporter or importer.

To the extent possible, the data gathered refer to prices at the U.S. border for exports and at either the foreign border or the U.S. border for imports. For nearly all products, the prices refer to transactions completed during the first week of the month. Survey respondents are asked to indicate all discounts, allowances, and rebates applicable to the reported prices, so that the price used in the calculation of the indexes is the actual price for which the product was bought or sold.

Table 744. Purchasing Power of the Dollar: 1950 to 2014

[Indexes: PPI, 1982 = $1.00; CPI, 1982-84 = $1.00. Producer prices prior to 1961 and consumer prices prior to 1964 exclude Alaska and Hawaii. Producer prices based on finished goods index. Obtained by dividing the average price index for the 1982 = 100, PPI; 1982-84 = 100, CPI base periods (100.0) by the price index for a given period and expressing the result in dollars and cents. Annual figures are based on average of monthly data]

Year	Annual average as measured by—		Year	Annual average as measured by—	
	Producer prices	Consumer prices		Producer prices	Consumer prices
1950	3.546	4.149	1985	0.955	0.929
1955	3.279	3.731	1986	0.969	0.912
1957	3.077	3.559	1987	0.949	0.880
1958	3.012	3.460	1988	0.926	0.845
1959	3.021	3.436	1989	0.880	0.806
1960	2.994	3.378	1990	0.839	0.765
1961	2.994	3.344	1991	0.822	0.734
1962	2.985	3.311	1992	0.812	0.713
1963	2.994	3.268	1993	0.802	0.692
1964	2.985	3.226	1994	0.797	0.675
1965	2.933	3.175	1995	0.782	0.656
1966	2.841	3.086	1996	0.762	0.637
1967	2.809	2.994	1997	0.759	0.623
1968	2.732	2.874	1998	0.765	0.613
1969	2.632	2.725	1999	0.752	0.600
1970	2.545	2.577	2000	0.725	0.581
1971	2.469	2.469	2001	0.711	0.565
1972	2.392	2.392	2002	0.720	0.556
1973	2.193	2.252	2003	0.698	0.543
1974	1.901	2.028	2004	0.673	0.529
1975	1.718	1.859	2005	0.642	0.512
1976	1.645	1.757	2006	0.623	0.496
1977	1.546	1.650	2007	0.600	0.482
1978	1.433	1.534	2008	0.565	0.464
1979	1.289	1.377	2009	0.580	0.466
1980	1.136	1.214	2010	0.556	0.459
1981	1.041	1.100	2011	0.525	0.445
1982	1.000	1.036	2012	0.515	0.436
1983	0.984	1.004	2013	0.509	0.429
1984	0.964	0.962	2014	0.499	0.422

Source: U.S. Bureau of Labor Statistics, "CPI Databases," <http://www.bls.gov/cpi/#data>, and "PPI Databases," <http://www.bls.gov/ppi/#data>; accessed May 2015.

Table 745. Consumer Price Indexes (CPI-U) by Major Group: 1990 to 2014

[1982-84 = 100, except as indicated. Represents annual averages of monthly figures. Reflects buying patterns of all urban consumers. Minus sign (-) indicates decrease. See text, this section]

Year	All items	Com-mod-ities	Ser-vices	Food	Energy	All items less food and energy	Food and bever-ages	Hous-ing	Apparel	Trans-porta-tion	Medical care	Educa-tion and com-munica-tion [1]
1990	130.7	122.8	139.2	132.4	102.1	135.5	132.1	128.5	124.1	120.5	162.8	(NA)
1995	152.4	136.4	168.7	148.4	105.2	161.2	148.9	148.5	132.0	139.1	220.5	92.2
2000	172.2	149.2	195.3	167.8	124.6	181.3	168.4	169.6	129.6	153.3	260.8	102.5
2003	184.0	151.2	216.5	180.0	136.5	193.2	180.5	184.8	120.9	157.6	297.1	109.8
2004	188.9	154.7	222.8	186.2	151.4	196.6	186.6	189.5	120.4	163.1	310.1	111.6
2005	195.3	160.2	230.1	190.7	177.1	200.9	191.2	195.7	119.5	173.9	323.2	113.7
2006	201.6	164.0	238.9	195.2	196.9	205.9	195.7	203.2	119.5	180.9	336.2	116.8
2007	207.3	167.5	246.8	202.9	207.7	210.7	203.3	209.6	119.0	184.7	351.1	119.6
2008	215.3	174.8	255.5	214.1	236.7	215.6	214.2	216.3	118.9	195.5	364.1	123.6
2009	214.5	169.7	259.2	218.0	193.1	219.2	218.2	217.1	120.1	179.3	375.6	127.4
2010	218.1	174.6	261.3	219.6	211.4	221.3	220.0	216.3	119.5	193.4	388.4	129.9
2011	224.9	183.9	265.8	227.8	243.9	225.0	227.9	219.1	122.1	212.4	400.3	131.5
2012	229.6	187.6	271.4	233.8	246.1	229.8	233.7	222.7	126.3	217.3	414.9	133.8
2013	233.0	187.7	277.9	237.0	244.4	233.8	237.0	227.4	127.4	217.4	425.1	135.9
2014	236.7	187.9	285.1	242.7	243.6	237.9	242.4	233.2	127.5	215.9	435.3	137.5
PERCENT CHANGE [2]												
1990	5.4	5.2	5.5	5.8	8.3	5.0	5.8	4.5	4.6	5.6	9.0	(NA)
1995	2.8	1.9	3.4	2.8	0.6	3.0	2.8	2.6	-1.0	3.6	4.5	3.8
2000	3.4	3.3	3.4	2.3	16.9	2.4	2.3	3.5	-1.3	6.2	4.1	1.3
2003	2.3	1.0	3.2	2.2	12.2	1.4	2.1	2.5	-2.5	3.1	4.0	1.8
2004	2.7	2.3	2.9	3.4	10.9	1.8	3.4	2.5	-0.4	3.5	4.4	1.6
2005	3.4	3.6	3.3	2.4	17.0	2.2	2.5	3.3	-0.7	6.6	4.2	1.9
2006	3.2	2.4	3.8	2.4	11.2	2.5	2.4	3.8	–	4.0	4.0	2.7
2007	2.8	2.1	3.3	4.0	5.5	2.3	3.9	3.1	-0.4	2.1	4.4	2.4
2008	3.8	4.3	3.5	5.5	13.9	2.3	5.4	3.2	-0.1	5.9	3.7	3.4
2009	-0.4	-2.9	1.4	1.8	-18.4	1.7	1.9	0.4	1.0	-8.3	3.2	3.0
2010	1.6	2.9	0.8	0.8	9.5	1.0	0.8	-0.4	-0.5	7.9	3.4	2.0
2011	3.2	5.3	1.7	3.7	15.4	1.7	3.6	1.3	2.2	9.8	3.0	1.2
2012	2.1	2.0	2.1	2.6	0.9	2.1	2.5	1.6	3.4	2.3	3.7	1.8
2013	1.5	–	2.4	1.4	-0.7	1.8	1.4	2.1	0.9	0.0	2.5	1.5
2014	1.6	0.1	2.6	2.4	-0.3	1.7	2.3	2.6	0.1	-0.7	2.4	1.2

– Represents or rounds to zero. NA Not available. [1] Dec. 1997 = 100. [2] Change from immediate prior year. 1990 change from 1989.

Source: U.S. Bureau of Labor Statistics, "CPI Databases," <http://www.bls.gov/cpi/#data>, accessed May 2015.

Table 746. Consumer Price Indexes (CPI-U) and Annual Percent Change From Prior Year—Selected Areas: 2014

[Percent changes computed from annual averages of monthly figures published by source. Local area CPI indexes are by-products of the national CPI program. Each local index has a smaller sample size than the national index and is therefore subject to substantially more sampling and other measurement error. As a result, local area indexes show greater volatility than the national index, although their long-term trends are similar. Minus sign (-) indicates decrease. See also text, this section and Appendix III]

Area	Consumer Price Index								Percent change, 2013-2014							
	All items	Food and beverage	Food	Housing	Apparel	Transportation	Medical care	Fuel and other utilities	All items	Food and beverage	Food	Housing	Apparel	Transportation	Medical care	Fuel and other utilities
U.S. city average	236.7	242.4	242.7	233.2	127.5	215.9	435.3	234.6	1.6	2.3	2.4	2.6	0.1	-0.7	2.4	4.2
Anchorage, AK	215.8	206.6	212.2	196.2	158.5	225.7	491.3	277.2	2.2	1.3	1.3	2.7	1.5	-0.6	3.2	6.2
Atlanta, GA	221.0	244.5	255.0	211.5	137.7	210.8	393.4	293.5	2.2	2.6	2.6	3.3	1.5	-0.4	4.1	4.2
Boston-Brockton-Nashua, MA-NH-ME-CT	255.2	250.8	251.1	251.3	144.7	206.2	589.2	261.2	1.6	1.1	1.1	3.2	-0.9	-0.6	0.4	6.3
Chicago-Gary-Kenosha, IL-IN-WI	228.5	236.8	236.0	229.7	94.7	199.3	450.8	209.0	1.7	3.0	3.0	3.3	0.0	-1.9	1.8	16.1
Cincinnati-Hamilton, OH-KY-IN	224.1	218.0	214.8	204.5	139.3	212.6	458.1	224.6	1.9	2.4	2.3	1.9	-1.3	1.0	3.8	3.8
Cleveland-Akron, OH	220.6	246.0	251.1	201.2	132.7	212.7	396.0	200.7	1.5	2.0	2.1	2.6	0.7	-1.4	1.6	4.8
Dallas-Fort Worth, TX	218.4	246.9	241.5	194.5	114.4	220.2	393.3	231.9	1.1	1.9	2.1	2.7	-1.1	-2.3	2.3	4.4
Denver-Boulder-Greeley, CO	237.2	222.0	225.3	220.7	103.7	264.6	507.9	230.0	2.8	2.5	2.6	4.9	-5.1	0.7	3.1	7.7
Detroit-Ann Arbor-Flint, MI	221.8	218.2	218.4	200.2	122.8	247.9	399.9	243.5	1.0	2.6	2.6	2.2	2.3	-1.2	2.3	-0.3
Honolulu, HI	257.6	256.0	256.2	273.5	111.1	236.4	351.8	375.7	1.4	2.0	2.2	1.3	-6.6	1.4	1.9	3.3
Houston-Galveston-Brazoria, TX	213.4	219.3	219.0	197.1	186.4	189.5	433.0	180.8	2.8	2.2	2.3	4.1	9.3	0.2	1.6	7.7
Kansas City, MO-KS	222.7	252.5	257.9	208.3	118.3	208.4	338.1	232.5	0.5	3.0	3.1	1.4	-2.8	-1.7	-0.5	3.1
Los Angeles-Riverside-Orange County, CA	242.4	244.5	244.7	260.1	112.9	209.3	418.0	297.3	1.3	2.3	2.4	2.1	1.3	-1.4	2.1	4.1
Miami-Fort Lauderdale, FL	243.1	251.8	254.2	239.7	144.6	233.1	431.4	177.4	2.1	2.7	2.9	3.1	0.4	-1.2	3.1	4.9
Milwaukee-Racine, WI	227.8	245.0	249.4	211.4	144.0	204.1	479.7	226.2	1.2	1.5	1.6	1.9	3.0	-1.6	2.5	8.5
Minneapolis-St. Paul, MN-WI	232.0	268.4	257.1	205.5	148.7	214.0	480.1	208.3	1.4	0.5	0.5	2.2	4.6	-0.7	3.1	5.5
New York-Northern New Jersey-Long Island, NY-NJ-CT-PA	260.2	251.0	251.0	276.6	125.8	229.4	437.0	204.4	1.3	1.8	1.9	2.2	-0.5	-0.8	2.7	1.3
Philadelphia-Wilmington-Atlantic City, PA-NJ-DE-MD	244.1	228.0	227.8	247.7	112.2	219.4	469.0	216.0	1.3	2.0	2.1	1.6	-0.4	-0.5	2.5	0.1
Phoenix-Mesa, AZ	127.8	137.8	138.7	123.2	136.2	124.1	161.1	163.3	1.6	2.0	2.5	2.6	3.5	-1.1	3.6	1.7
Pittsburgh, PA	239.0	249.8	249.4	237.1	153.5	195.8	455.8	248.2	1.3	1.9	1.9	2.9	-1.0	1.3	-0.8	3.1
Portland-Salem, OR-WA	241.2	228.6	230.6	234.2	125.3	240.0	509.1	258.4	2.4	3.3	3.4	3.5	-3.3	0.0	2.8	5.0
San Diego, CA	265.1	243.3	240.3	293.2	138.6	223.3	(NA)	271.4	1.9	2.3	2.2	2.6	2.8	-1.0	(NA)	9.2
San Francisco-Oakland-San Jose, CA	252.0	252.9	253.0	277.5	116.7	198.2	(NA)	326.6	2.8	2.9	2.9	4.2	-2.1	0.4	(NA)	3.0
Seattle-Tacoma-Bremerton, WA	246.0	252.5	255.3	261.7	130.3	227.9	383.3	211.7	1.8	2.6	2.6	4.2	-2.2	-1.2	1.1	1.7
St. Louis, MO-IL	220.2	244.9	243.7	207.0	153.6	201.0	395.2	211.7	1.9	3.9	4.0	1.7	-1.5	-2.0	3.2	1.2
Tampa-St. Petersburg-Clearwater, FL	210.8	213.8	213.3	196.8	163.2	209.7	356.9	212.3	1.9	3.4	3.5	3.2	0.2	-2.7	5.3	4.5
Washington-Baltimore, DC-MD-VA-WV	154.8	153.7	155.1	164.3	96.7	154.2	171.4	185.5	1.5	2.1	2.0	1.9	1.2	0.1	1.7	2.0

NA Not available.

Source: U.S. Bureau of Labor Statistics, CPI Databases, "All Urban Consumers (Current Series)," <http://www.bls.gov/cpi/data.htm>, accessed May 2015.

Table 747. Consumer Price Indexes for All Urban Consumers (CPI-U) for Selected Items and Groups: 2000 to 2014

[1982-84 = 100, except as noted. Annual averages of monthly figures. See headnote, Table 745]

Item	2000	2005	2009	2010	2011	2012	2013	2014
All items	**172.2**	**195.3**	**214.5**	**218.1**	**224.9**	**229.6**	**233.0**	**236.7**
Food and beverages	**168.4**	**191.2**	**218.2**	**220.0**	**227.9**	**233.7**	**237.0**	**242.4**
Food	167.8	190.7	218.0	219.6	227.8	233.8	237.0	242.7
Food at home	167.9	189.8	215.1	215.8	226.2	231.8	233.9	239.5
Cereals and bakery products	188.3	209.0	252.6	250.4	260.3	267.7	270.4	271.1
Cereals and cereal products	175.9	186.7	221.8	217.6	227.2	232.9	232.7	232.9
Rice, pasta, and cornmeal	150.7	165.3	229.9	224.4	234.1	239.4	239.4	238.1
Rice [1,2]	99.3	108.8	161.0	156.9	163.9	167.3	170.2	170.7
Bakery products	194.1	220.5	268.9	268.0	278.0	286.6	291.5	292.5
Bread [2]	107.4	126.2	162.6	159.8	168.7	173.4	176.8	176.4
Cakes, cupcakes, and cookies	187.9	209.8	250.7	251.7	256.0	266.2	271.0	273.5
Other bakery products	191.5	211.4	245.9	247.1	253.1	260.4	263.5	264.8
Meats, poultry, fish and eggs	154.5	184.7	203.8	207.7	223.2	231.0	236.0	253.0
Meats, poultry, and fish	155.5	186.7	204.6	208.6	223.9	231.9	236.7	253.7
Meats	150.7	187.5	200.5	206.2	224.4	232.0	234.8	256.5
Beef and veal	148.1	200.4	218.3	224.5	247.4	263.1	268.3	300.7
Uncooked ground beef	125.2	175.1	198.5	203.6	226.7	242.7	246.8	276.0
Uncooked beef steaks [2]	109.1	145.1	150.1	153.3	166.5	177.0	179.9	199.9
Pork	156.5	177.7	181.4	190.0	206.1	206.6	208.6	227.6
Poultry	159.8	185.3	204.2	204.0	209.9	221.4	231.7	236.3
Chicken [2]	102.5	120.6	132.6	131.8	134.3	140.8	148.2	151.7
Fish and seafood	190.4	200.1	240.6	243.2	260.5	266.7	273.3	289.0
Eggs	131.9	144.1	190.0	192.8	210.5	217.1	224.2	243.0
Dairy products	160.7	182.4	197.0	199.2	212.7	217.3	217.6	225.3
Milk [2]	107.8	127.0	129.0	133.6	145.8	147.4	149.2	156.6
Cheese and related products	162.8	183.3	203.5	204.8	217.5	222.4	221.9	234.1
Ice cream and related products	164.4	177.6	196.6	195.0	209.1	215.5	215.5	215.4
Fruits and vegetables	204.6	241.4	272.9	273.5	284.7	282.8	290.0	294.4
Fresh fruits and vegetables	238.8	285.3	312.7	314.8	328.9	322.3	332.8	339.2
Fresh fruits	258.3	297.4	324.4	322.3	333.1	336.6	343.2	359.7
Fresh vegetables	219.4	271.7	299.3	305.5	322.5	306.1	320.5	316.3
Processed fruits and vegetables [2]	105.6	119.3	148.6	146.6	150.9	156.7	157.2	157.3
Nonalcoholic beverages and beverage materials	137.8	144.4	163.0	161.6	166.8	168.6	166.9	166.0
Juices and nonalcoholic drinks [2]	105.6	110.6	126.3	124.5	126.7	128.2	127.8	127.1
Carbonated drinks	123.4	131.9	154.1	154.7	158.8	161.0	159.5	158.8
Nonfrozen noncarbonated juices and drinks [2]	104.2	106.5	118.0	114.8	116.0	116.9	117.0	116.2
Beverage materials including coffee and tea [2]	97.9	102.4	113.3	114.0	122.5	123.7	119.8	118.9
Coffee	154.0	161.2	186.3	186.4	213.8	217.4	204.7	201.0
Other food at home	155.6	167.0	191.2	191.1	197.4	204.8	204.8	206.2
Sugar and sweets	154.0	165.2	196.9	201.2	207.8	214.7	211.0	209.3
Candy and chewing gum [2]	103.8	109.5	130.2	132.5	136.0	140.9	139.6	139.7
Fats and oils	147.4	167.7	201.2	200.6	219.2	232.6	229.3	229.7
Other foods	172.2	182.5	205.5	204.6	209.3	216.6	217.7	219.9
Frozen and freeze dried prepared food	148.5	153.2	168.1	165.3	167.8	169.8	167.8	168.7
Snacks	166.3	178.5	213.2	216.6	224.3	238.8	242.8	244.3
Spices, seasonings, condiments, sauces	175.6	188.0	214.7	214.4	219.9	225.9	226.4	229.7
Other miscellaneous food [2]	107.5	111.3	122.4	121.7	124.0	128.3	129.2	130.4
Food away from home	169.0	193.4	223.3	226.1	231.4	238.0	243.1	249.0
Full service meals and snacks [2]	106.8	121.9	139.2	141.1	144.4	148.1	151.5	155.3
Limited service meals and snacks [2]	106.3	122.4	142.6	143.9	147.1	151.7	154.6	158.4
At employee sites and schools [2]	104.4	118.6	137.3	141.0	145.7	150.2	155.3	158.2
From vending machines and mobile vendors [2]	102.4	112.6	129.7	133.1	135.8	140.2	143.3	143.1
Other food away from home [2]	109.0	131.3	155.9	159.3	162.8	166.5	169.6	173.8
Alcoholic beverages	174.7	195.9	220.8	223.3	226.7	230.8	234.6	237.3
Alcoholic beverages at home	158.1	172.3	190.3	191.0	191.8	193.4	195.7	197.0
Beer, ale, and other malt beverages at home	156.8	176.4	197.4	201.0	203.9	207.6	211.1	213.8
Distilled spirits at home	162.3	177.4	189.2	188.8	189.0	188.9	191.0	192.4
Wine at home	151.6	156.2	172.1	169.7	168.5	168.2	169.2	169.0
Alcoholic beverages away from home	207.1	244.5	285.6	291.9	300.9	310.5	317.9	323.8
Housing	**169.6**	**195.7**	**217.1**	**216.3**	**219.1**	**222.7**	**227.4**	**233.2**
Shelter	193.4	224.4	249.4	248.4	251.6	257.1	263.1	270.5
Rent of primary residence	183.9	217.3	248.8	249.4	253.6	260.4	267.7	276.2
Lodging away from home [2]	117.5	130.3	134.2	133.7	137.4	140.5	142.4	148.5
Other lodging away from home including hotels and motels	252.4	274.2	279.2	280.4	287.4	292.6	294.8	307.8
Owners' equivalent rent of primary residence [3]	198.7	230.2	256.6	256.6	259.6	264.8	270.7	277.8
Tenants' and household insurance [2]	103.7	117.6	121.5	125.7	127.4	131.3	135.4	141.9
Fuels and utilities	137.9	179.0	210.7	214.2	220.4	219.0	225.2	234.6
Household energy	122.8	161.6	188.1	189.3	193.6	189.3	193.8	202.2
Fuel oil and other fuels	129.7	208.6	239.8	275.1	337.1	335.9	332.0	338.9
Fuel oil	130.3	216.4	240.2	282.9	367.8	376.1	370.2	365.0
Propane, kerosene and firewood [4]	155.5	240.6	293.1	320.6	348.1	328.4	327.6	358.4
Energy services	128.0	166.5	193.6	192.9	194.4	189.7	194.8	203.4
Electricity	128.5	150.8	192.7	193.1	196.7	196.6	200.8	208.0
Utility (piped) gas service	132.0	215.4	193.7	189.7	184.3	166.6	174.5	186.8
Water and sewer and trash collection services [2]	106.5	130.3	161.1	170.9	179.6	189.3	197.6	204.9
Water and sewerage maintenance	227.5	283.4	354.4	380.7	402.9	428.6	449.7	468.1
Garbage and trash collection [5]	269.8	314.0	376.4	384.4	395.1	404.7	416.2	425.8
Household furnishings and operations	**128.2**	**126.1**	**128.7**	**125.5**	**124.9**	**125.7**	**124.8**	**123.1**
Furniture and bedding	134.4	125.9	124.8	119.7	118.6	120.2	118.7	115.5
Living room, kitchen, and dining room furniture [2]	102.4	92.7	90.7	88.9	88.9	90.8	90.1	87.1
Appliances [2]	96.3	86.9	91.1	86.9	85.9	88.1	86.3	82.5
Other household equipment and furnishings [2]	98.0	85.5	74.0	70.8	68.5	65.7	63.5	60.7
Clocks, lamps, and decorator items [2]	111.7	88.0	67.2	62.9	59.5	56.1	52.8	49.4
Nonelectric cookware and tableware [2]	98.4	91.3	97.1	96.6	97.9	97.7	97.2	93.3
Tools, hardware, outdoor equipment and supplies [2]	97.0	94.4	94.2	91.6	91.6	92.0	92.0	91.3

See footnotes at end of table.

Item	2000	2005	2009	2010	2011	2012	2013	2014
Tools, hardware, and supplies [2]	97.3	98.1	99.2	96.5	98.1	99.6	100.7	100.2
Outdoor equipment and supplies [2]	96.8	92.4	91.4	88.9	88.3	88.2	87.9	87.0
Housekeeping supplies	153.4	159.9	183.1	183.3	185.4	189.8	189.1	187.6
Household cleaning products [2]	105.1	107.9	121.4	120.6	121.4	123.0	121.3	119.1
Household paper products [2]	113.8	125.4	156.1	158.0	161.7	167.8	170.3	170.3
Miscellaneous household products [2]	104.3	106.4	116.8	116.9	117.9	120.8	120.1	119.8
Household operations [2]	110.5	130.3	150.3	150.3	151.8	155.2	157.6	161.6
Domestic services [2]	109.7	128.3	144.1	144.4	145.4	147.4	150.1	153.7
Gardening and lawncare services [2]	111.4	127.9	156.5	155.3	156.9	159.7	160.6	165.0
Apparel	**129.6**	**119.5**	**120.1**	**119.5**	**122.1**	**126.3**	**127.4**	**127.5**
Men's and boy's apparel	129.7	116.1	113.6	111.9	114.7	119.5	121.6	120.6
Men's apparel	133.1	121.4	118.6	117.5	119.8	124.3	126.7	125.0
Men's shirts and sweaters [2]	98.3	84.2	81.0	78.6	79.6	82.2	82.9	81.0
Boys' apparel	116.2	97.0	95.2	91.5	95.9	101.5	102.6	103.9
Women's and girl's apparel	121.5	110.8	108.1	107.1	109.2	113.0	113.3	114.4
Women's apparel	121.9	111.8	109.9	109.5	111.3	115.0	116.2	117.6
Women's suits and separates [2]	98.2	87.3	84.9	83.9	84.2	86.6	86.7	85.3
Women's underwear, nightwear, sportswear, and accessories [2]	101.8	95.4	93.1	96.0	98.6	101.7	103.2	106.3
Girls' apparel	119.7	105.3	99.0	95.4	98.5	103.2	99.6	99.0
Footwear	123.8	122.6	126.9	128.0	128.5	131.8	135.0	135.5
Men's footwear	129.5	121.3	126.4	127.6	129.2	133.4	136.8	138.0
Women's footwear	119.6	121.9	123.4	125.3	123.7	127.2	130.4	128.0
Jewelry and watches [4]	137.0	127.6	149.2	152.4	165.2	167.3	168.2	163.6
Jewelry [4]	141.2	131.3	157.0	161.2	176.6	178.2	177.6	170.6
Transportation	**153.3**	**173.9**	**179.3**	**193.4**	**212.4**	**217.3**	**217.4**	**215.9**
Private transportation	149.1	170.2	174.8	188.7	207.6	212.8	212.4	211.0
New and used motor vehicles [2]	100.8	95.6	93.5	97.1	99.8	100.6	100.9	100.8
New vehicles	142.8	137.9	135.6	138.0	141.9	144.2	145.8	146.3
Used cars and trucks	155.8	139.4	127.0	143.1	149.0	150.3	149.9	149.1
Leased cars and trucks [6]	(NA)	92.7	102.4	97.0	94.4	89.5	86.7	84.8
Motor fuel	129.3	195.7	202.0	239.2	302.6	312.7	303.9	292.4
Gasoline (all types)	128.6	194.7	201.6	238.6	301.7	311.5	302.6	290.9
Motor vehicle parts and equipment	101.5	111.9	134.1	137.0	143.9	148.6	146.4	144.8
Motor vehicle maintenance and repair	177.3	206.9	243.3	248.0	253.1	257.6	261.6	266.0
Motor vehicle insurance	256.7	329.9	357.0	375.2	388.7	402.5	419.4	437.2
Motor vehicle fees [2]	107.3	134.7	155.7	165.5	167.3	172.1	174.8	176.5
Public transportation	209.6	217.3	236.3	251.4	269.4	271.4	278.9	276.4
Airline fare	239.4	236.6	258.0	278.2	304.0	305.0	312.7	307.7
Medical care	**260.8**	**323.2**	**375.6**	**388.4**	**400.3**	**414.9**	**425.1**	**435.3**
Medical care commodities	238.1	276.0	305.1	314.7	324.1	333.6	335.1	343.4
Prescription drugs	285.4	349.0	391.1	407.8	425.0	440.1	442.6	458.3
Nonprescription drugs [4]	(NA)	(NA)	(NA)	100.0	98.6	99.3	99.4	98.5
Medical care services	266.0	336.7	397.3	411.2	423.8	440.3	454.0	464.8
Professional medical services	237.7	281.7	319.4	328.2	335.7	342.0	349.5	355.2
Physicians' services	244.7	287.5	320.8	331.3	340.3	347.3	354.2	359.1
Dental services	258.5	324.0	388.1	398.8	408.0	417.5	431.8	441.0
Eyeglasses and eye care [4]	149.7	163.2	175.5	176.7	178.3	179.9	180.8	183.9
Services by other medical professionals [4]	161.9	186.8	209.8	214.4	217.4	219.6	223.3	226.4
Hospital and related services	317.3	439.9	567.9	607.7	641.5	672.1	701.3	733.8
Hospital services [7]	115.9	161.6	210.7	227.2	241.2	253.6	265.4	278.8
Health insurance [9]	(NA)	(NA)	110.5	106.6	105.5	118.3	123.0	122.1
Recreation [2]	**103.3**	**109.4**	**114.3**	**113.3**	**113.4**	**114.7**	**115.3**	**115.5**
Video and audio [2]	101.0	104.2	101.3	99.1	98.4	99.4	99.7	99.8
Cable and satellite television and radio service [5]	266.8	331.9	367.6	372.4	379.0	395.6	406.5	416.1
Pets, pet products and services [2]	106.1	123.6	153.4	154.4	158.7	162.4	164.6	165.7
Sporting goods	119.0	115.5	119.9	118.8	118.5	118.7	118.1	116.5
Other recreational goods [2]	87.8	69.5	60.2	57.8	55.9	54.0	51.9	49.4
Other recreation services [2]	111.7	130.5	144.6	145.1	145.3	148.4	150.5	152.7
Club membership dues and fees for participant sports [2]	108.9	117.4	125.7	123.5	122.1	125.5	127.5	129.3
Admissions	230.5	282.3	317.8	322.8	325.0	332.1	336.2	341.9
Education and communication [2]	**102.5**	**113.7**	**127.4**	**129.9**	**131.5**	**133.8**	**135.9**	**137.5**
Education [2]	112.5	152.7	190.9	199.3	207.8	216.3	224.5	231.9
Tuition, other school fees, and childcare	324.0	440.9	549.0	573.2	597.2	621.0	643.7	664.8
College tuition and fees	331.9	475.1	606.7	638.2	670.3	702.8	732.4	759.5
Communication [2]	93.6	84.7	85.0	84.7	83.3	83.1	82.6	82.1
Information and information processing [2]	92.8	82.6	81.9	81.5	80.0	79.5	78.9	78.2
Telephone services [2]	98.5	94.9	102.4	102.4	101.2	101.7	101.6	101.1
Wireless telephone services [2]	76.0	65.0	64.3	62.4	60.1	59.7	58.6	57.4
Land-line telephone services [10]	(NA)	(NA)	(NA)	101.6	103.3	105.6	108.1	111.1
Information technology, hardware, and services [8]	25.9	13.6	9.7	9.4	9.0	8.7	8.5	8.4
Other goods and services	**271.1**	**313.4**	**368.6**	**381.3**	**387.2**	**394.4**	**401.0**	**408.1**
Tobacco and smoking products	394.9	502.8	730.3	807.3	834.8	853.5	876.8	903.3
Cigarettes [2]	159.9	203.5	297.4	329.0	340.0	347.5	357.1	368.4
Personal care	165.6	185.6	204.6	206.6	208.6	212.1	215.0	218.0
Personal care products	153.7	154.4	162.6	161.1	160.5	162.2	161.8	163.4
Hair, dental, shaving, and miscellaneous personal care products [2]	103.3	101.8	105.4	104.3	102.4	103.1	102.8	103.4
Cosmetics, perfume, bath, nail preparations and implements	166.8	171.3	183.6	182.2	184.3	186.7	186.4	189.3
Personal care services	178.1	203.9	227.6	229.6	230.8	234.2	238.8	242.0
Haircuts and other personal care services [2]	108.7	124.4	138.9	140.1	140.8	142.9	145.7	147.7
Miscellaneous personal services	252.3	303.0	344.5	354.1	362.9	372.7	381.9	389.7
Legal services [4]	189.3	241.8	278.1	288.1	297.4	303.5	311.8	318.5
Funeral expenses [4]	187.8	228.8	275.7	282.0	288.3	293.8	301.6	307.1

See footnotes at end of table.

Table 747. Consumer Price Indexes for All Urban Consumers (CPI-U) for Selected Items and Groups: 2000 to 2014-Continued.

See headnote on page 491.

Item	2000	2005	2009	2010	2011	2012	2013	2014
SPECIAL AGGREGATE INDEXES								
Commodities..	**149.2**	**160.2**	**169.7**	**174.6**	**183.9**	**187.6**	**187.7**	**187.9**
Commodities less food and beverages..................	137.7	142.5	144.4	150.4	159.9	162.7	161.5	159.6
Nondurables less food and beverages................	147.4	168.4	179.0	189.9	208.4	213.8	212.2	210.0
Nondurables less food, beverages, and apparel.......	162.5	202.6	219.6	238.1	267.0	273.2	269.8	266.2
Durables..	125.4	115.3	109.9	111.3	112.6	112.8	111.9	110.3
Services..	195.3	230.1	259.2	261.3	265.8	271.4	277.9	285.1
Rent of shelter [3]................................	201.3	233.7	259.9	258.8	262.2	267.8	274.0	281.8
Transportation services...........................	196.1	225.7	251.0	259.8	268.0	272.9	280.0	285.3
Other services..................................	229.9	268.4	304.0	309.6	314.4	322.3	328.7	334.4
All items less food..............................	173.0	196.0	214.0	217.8	224.5	229.0	232.3	235.8
All items less shelter............................	165.7	186.1	203.3	208.6	217.0	221.4	223.8	226.2
All items less medical care.......................	167.3	188.7	206.6	209.7	216.3	220.6	223.6	227.1
Commodities less food...........................	139.2	144.5	147.1	153.0	162.4	165.3	164.1	162.3
Nondurables less food...........................	149.1	170.1	181.5	191.9	209.6	215.0	213.6	211.7
Nondurables less food and apparel.................	162.9	201.2	218.7	235.6	262.1	268.2	265.4	262.3
Nondurables...................................	158.2	180.2	198.5	205.3	219.0	224.6	225.3	226.7
Apparel less footwear............................	126.2	114.4	114.2	113.3	116.2	120.4	121.1	121.1
Services less rent of shelter [3]....................	202.9	243.2	278.1	284.4	290.6	296.6	304.1	311.2
Services less medical care services................	188.9	221.2	248.1	249.6	253.6	258.5	264.5	271.5
Energy...	124.6	177.1	193.1	211.4	243.9	246.1	244.4	243.6
All items less energy............................	178.6	198.7	218.4	220.5	224.8	229.7	233.6	238.0
All items less food and energy....................	181.3	200.9	219.2	221.3	225.0	229.8	233.8	237.9
Commodities less food and energy commodities.......	144.9	140.3	142.0	143.6	145.5	147.3	147.3	146.8
Energy commodities.............................	129.5	197.4	205.3	242.6	306.4	316.0	307.4	296.9
Services less energy services.....................	202.1	236.6	265.9	268.3	273.1	279.7	286.4	293.5
Domestically produced farm food..................	170.1	195.0	220.4	221.6	232.5	238.7	241.4	247.9
Utilities and public transportation.................	152.6	176.6	200.3	203.1	206.5	207.5	212.1	216.7

NA Not available. [1] Special indexes based on a substantially smaller sample. [2] December 1997=100. [3] December 1982=100. [4] December 1986=100. [5] December 1983=100. [6] December 2001=100. [7] December 1996=100. [8] December 1988=100. [9] December 2005=100. [10] December 2009=100.

Source: U.S. Bureau of Labor Statistics, CPI Databases, "All Urban Consumers (Current Series)," <http://www.bls.gov/cpi/data.htm>, accessed May 2015.

Table 748. Single-Family Housing Price Indexes by State: 2000 to 2014

[Data are for the fourth quarter of the year shown. Index 1991, 1st quarter = 100. Purchase only indexes. Data are seasonally adjusted. The index reflects average price changes in repeat sales or refinancings on the same properties. The information is obtained by reviewing repeat mortgage transactions on single-family properties whose mortgages have been purchased or securitized by either Fannie Mae or Freddie Mac; for more information on methodology, see Appendix III]

State	2000	2005	2010	2013	2014	State	2000	2005	2010	2013	2014
U.S.........	**144.1**	**216.9**	**183.9**	**203.9**	**214.0**	MO.........	150.3	197.6	179.5	190.8	199.4
AL..........	142.9	183.0	176.1	186.6	197.1	MT.........	179.6	276.9	281.3	321.6	334.2
AK..........	136.9	207.8	219.4	233.5	241.3	NE.........	162.8	194.4	188.0	209.8	217.5
AZ..........	155.7	304.1	171.3	231.1	241.2	NV.........	128.3	271.0	125.2	162.2	176.8
AR..........	141.6	185.5	176.2	186.3	199.3	NH.........	146.7	238.3	195.6	198.7	206.7
CA..........	123.8	283.8	159.9	204.3	219.9	NJ.........	133.4	253.8	218.8	212.4	218.7
CO..........	217.3	271.0	261.0	307.5	331.6	NM.........	145.6	214.9	210.0	211.0	215.7
CT..........	118.0	195.3	168.1	165.5	166.7	NY.........	128.7	213.7	206.0	208.6	212.6
DE..........	121.5	208.9	188.7	182.3	183.5	NC.........	146.5	183.1	184.4	190.9	195.6
DC..........	134.4	324.1	324.8	410.2	461.6	ND.........	138.6	192.5	224.8	272.6	295.6
FL..........	139.9	300.0	173.8	209.5	225.8	OH.........	148.4	175.0	152.8	162.2	169.2
GA..........	151.7	191.3	153.8	177.8	190.8	OK.........	144.1	177.9	192.2	203.1	214.6
HI..........	92.6	203.6	176.3	204.9	215.3	OR.........	184.5	297.9	255.5	297.3	317.4
ID..........	154.9	229.6	191.3	222.6	233.8	PA.........	121.3	190.0	187.2	193.4	197.3
IL..........	145.8	203.9	175.7	177.6	184.2	RI.........	120.2	236.7	185.0	180.8	191.7
IN..........	142.4	165.8	157.0	167.8	172.5	SC.........	144.9	185.6	180.5	187.4	198.6
IA..........	157.6	191.2	194.4	207.7	213.5	SD.........	160.6	209.5	217.6	243.1	253.4
KS..........	153.9	187.9	188.9	196.2	204.2	TN.........	147.2	185.8	181.6	200.3	208.2
KY..........	150.7	184.5	188.2	194.5	202.1	TX.........	143.1	172.5	185.8	215.6	229.5
LA..........	157.0	212.9	226.0	242.4	249.4	UT.........	194.3	256.4	250.5	289.7	302.8
ME..........	133.1	220.4	202.9	205.0	208.4	VT.........	126.6	207.1	201.5	216.8	212.5
MD..........	122.3	255.1	208.6	223.5	222.0	VA.........	131.4	234.8	208.6	221.7	228.5
MA..........	157.0	252.8	216.1	230.5	238.9	WA.........	154.8	243.3	221.3	238.6	256.0
MI..........	173.8	201.6	144.8	168.3	181.5	WV.........	138.3	181.3	189.1	197.1	204.9
MN..........	172.6	253.5	207.7	226.6	235.4	WI.........	166.8	223.4	206.5	209.7	217.1
MS..........	142.6	177.8	172.2	179.4	183.9	WY.........	169.3	258.3	278.9	306.3	318.7

Source: Federal Housing Finance Agency, "House Price Index Datasets, Quarterly Data, Purchase-Only Indexes," <http://www.fhfa.gov/ DataTools/Downloads/Pages/House-Price-Index-Datasets.aspx#qpo>, accessed March 2015.

Table 749. Cost of Living Index for Selected Urban Areas, Annual Average: 2014

[Data are for a selected urban area within the larger metropolitan area shown. Measures relative price levels for consumer goods and services in participating areas appropriate for professional and executive households in the top income quintile. The nationwide average equals 100 and each index is read as a percent of the national average. The index does not measure inflation, but compares prices at a single point in time. Excludes taxes. Metropolitan areas as defined by the Office of Management and Budget. For definitions, urban areas, and components of MSAs, see source. Data are based on an annual average survey compiled from data submitted in the first 3 quarters of the year. To calculate the annual average index, actual and estimated prices are collected to calculate an annual average price for each item used to represent the various spending categories. The share of consumer spending devoted to the category determines that category's importance, or weight, in the Index. Weights are based on the Bureau of Labor Statistics' most recent Consumer Expenditure Survey]

Urban Area	Composite Index (100.0%)	Grocery items (13.96%)	Housing (27.80%)	Utilities (10.23%)	Trans-portation (12.12%)	Health care (4.41%)	Misc. goods and services (31.48%)
Abilene, TX.	93.1	92.2	89.7	83.7	100.9	90.1	97.0
Akron, OH.	101.1	110.8	107.9	92.3	110.0	88.5	92.1
Albany, GA.	92.5	110.5	77.3	91.5	96.9	98.4	95.8
Albany, NY.	106.9	98.0	117.4	88.4	109.7	103.4	107.0
Alexandria, LA.	97.4	99.8	93.0	85.6	93.4	99.9	105.2
Allentown, PA.	103.6	98.7	109.0	98.5	103.8	97.4	103.4
Amarillo, TX.	87.2	89.8	76.4	84.4	92.5	90.4	93.9
Ames, IA.	96.9	93.0	99.8	87.7	106.6	98.1	95.2
Anchorage, AK.	128.5	123.4	157.8	97.0	105.1	139.9	122.4
Anderson, SC.	89.6	105.3	73.0	94.7	89.6	99.6	94.3
Anniston-Calhoun County, AL.	88.6	93.5	73.2	103.0	90.2	83.2	95.6
Ardmore, OK.	88.4	101.1	73.6	82.2	97.3	92.0	93.9
Asheville, NC.	104.8	103.9	106.5	107.5	100.2	109.2	104.1
Ashland, OH.	84.0	98.6	63.3	84.4	96.6	93.7	89.6
Athens-Henderson County, TX.	89.2	95.8	70.3	101.3	93.1	91.1	97.3
Atlanta, GA.	99.6	104.6	97.0	90.7	102.1	101.3	101.5
Auburn-Opelika, AL.	98.1	105.1	82.8	95.2	93.3	92.6	112.2
Augusta-Aiken, GA-SC.	87.2	96.7	68.2	92.4	96.9	93.8	93.4
Austin, TX.	94.6	85.8	87.8	103.1	96.1	99.6	100.4
Bakersfield, CA.	106.3	109.8	104.6	112.6	115.1	106.8	100.9
Baltimore, MD.	109.5	108.6	143.6	92.6	100.4	89.6	91.6
Baton Rouge, LA.	94.6	105.0	89.6	84.4	97.5	102.7	95.4
Beaufort, SC.	97.3	110.3	85.1	107.9	93.3	98.9	100.2
Beaumont, TX.	98.7	89.3	98.7	96.6	96.9	91.1	105.4
Bellingham, WA.	109.8	103.2	129.5	74.3	110.1	110.8	106.6
Benton Harbor, MI.	92.5	101.4	82.9	92.1	96.8	95.1	95.1
Bergen-Passaic, NJ.	129.6	106.1	176.6	114.3	108.1	105.2	115.2
Bethesda-Gaithersburg-Frederick, MD.	128.3	109.2	200.2	108.6	105.2	92.0	93.5
Birmingham, AL.	91.5	101.6	75.8	95.8	90.6	84.4	100.7
Bismarck-Mandan, ND.	100.7	102.4	103.7	89.1	101.8	109.1	99.5
Blacksburg, VA.	97.6	92.5	90.8	108.0	96.9	102.6	102.2
Bloomington, IN.	91.0	94.4	82.3	88.6	100.0	94.9	93.9
Boise, ID.	94.7	93.6	86.5	88.6	106.1	103.9	98.8
Boston, MA.	137.7	113.9	175.0	135.6	107.1	120.6	130.1
Bowling Green, KY.	91.7	92.1	80.2	104.0	97.7	91.4	95.4
Bozeman, MT.	100.8	102.0	113.2	88.0	92.5	105.9	96.1
Brazoria County, TX.	93.1	84.5	88.5	97.5	92.8	100.5	98.6
Buffalo, NY.	98.2	94.7	108.9	102.5	102.5	87.8	88.8
Bullhead City, AZ.	93.8	98.3	85.9	77.7	101.5	103.1	99.6
Burlington, IA.	88.2	93.5	80.1	100.2	83.7	87.4	91.1
Burlington, NC.	94.5	101.7	78.9	95.7	96.9	98.6	103.3
Burlington-Chittenden County, VT.	119.0	106.4	143.4	122.9	109.2	107.5	107.2
Camden, SC.	92.7	103.8	80.4	96.7	88.2	90.1	99.5
Cedar City, UT.	89.0	98.7	76.1	86.5	96.6	88.3	94.1
Cedar Rapids, IA.	93.1	91.7	85.4	103.3	95.6	102.6	95.0
Champaign-Urbana, IL.	99.5	100.0	90.9	114.4	95.2	116.0	101.3
Charleston-N Charleston, SC.	100.8	109.0	94.7	112.6	96.0	105.2	100.0
Charlotte, NC.	95.0	100.0	85.5	106.6	96.7	101.3	95.8
Charlottesville, VA.	104.0	99.4	111.6	90.3	99.1	98.9	106.5
Chattanooga, TN.	94.2	96.7	87.1	94.7	100.4	98.6	96.2
Chicago, IL.	116.7	103.5	136.2	101.8	125.7	100.5	108.9
Cleveland, OH.	100.9	104.9	95.1	103.7	100.4	110.1	102.3
Cleveland, TN.	90.2	97.1	85.3	81.9	88.5	86.4	95.2
Colorado Springs, CO.	97.4	93.6	98.9	93.7	98.6	104.1	97.6
Columbia, MO.	94.7	96.1	88.1	97.0	91.0	101.8	99.5
Columbia, SC.	95.2	103.0	79.8	113.1	94.8	94.8	99.6
Columbus, OH.	90.2	92.9	79.4	95.9	99.3	95.7	92.4
Conroe, TX.	92.2	89.1	85.1	100.2	95.5	99.5	94.9
Cookeville, TN.	85.2	90.6	72.1	87.1	92.6	89.0	90.4
Corpus Christi, TX.	92.7	81.8	88.8	109.6	92.4	94.1	95.3
Covington, KY.	87.8	89.9	74.2	95.8	102.9	101.6	88.4
Dallas, TX.	95.8	101.5	75.4	102.8	100.2	100.0	106.6
Dalton, GA.	90.1	101.8	75.9	100.8	95.1	92.6	91.7
Danville City, VA.	95.2	98.8	84.4	112.4	95.1	94.0	97.7
Danville, IL.	90.1	94.7	70.5	109.1	108.2	93.5	91.9
Dare County, NC.	107.6	105.5	111.5	99.5	103.3	104.2	110.0
Davenport-Moline-Rock Island, IA-IL.	97.2	94.9	99.2	86.8	103.5	99.7	97.0
Dayton, OH.	92.5	95.3	77.8	101.6	99.8	91.1	98.6
Daytona Beach, FL.	92.9	103.8	83.4	92.0	100.5	95.2	93.5
Decatur, IL.	88.4	90.4	80.5	90.1	90.7	92.3	92.5
Decatur-Hartselle, AL.	88.9	98.3	70.5	108.4	92.9	88.7	93.2
Denton, TX.	93.0	93.0	88.2	85.8	101.3	95.4	95.9
Denver, CO.	107.5	98.5	124.0	97.7	101.5	103.8	102.5
Des Moines, IA.	92.0	93.4	84.4	93.4	99.0	96.9	94.1
Detroit, MI.	95.1	93.1	91.7	100.8	99.9	96.0	95.1
Dodge City, KS.	95.0	94.7	87.5	101.2	91.0	94.4	101.5
Dothan, AL.	88.1	102.1	81.1	87.0	91.8	83.1	87.6

See footnotes at end of table.

Table 749. Cost of Living Index for Selected Urban Areas, Annual Average: 2014-Continued.

See headnote on page 494.

Urban Area	Composite Index (100.0%)	Grocery items (13.96%)	Housing (27.80%)	Utilities (10.23%)	Trans-portation (12.12%)	Health care (4.41%)	Misc. goods and services (31.48%)
Dover, DE.	101.4	109.1	84.6	111.5	103.0	102.7	108.7
Dublin-Laurens County, GA.	89.1	96.0	76.2	97.4	94.3	85.6	93.2
Durham, NC.	91.9	98.5	77.1	88.5	100.6	98.8	98.8
Eau Claire, WI.	93.3	98.9	79.2	89.8	101.1	110.1	99.0
Edmond, OK.	95.9	88.6	94.7	100.8	98.8	94.9	97.5
El Paso, TX.	93.1	100.4	86.0	88.1	96.9	88.8	96.9
Enid, OK.	95.5	95.8	89.2	100.1	97.1	89.6	99.7
Erie, PA.	95.4	103.7	83.6	91.5	95.7	92.0	103.7
Evansville, IN.	93.9	93.4	84.3	106.1	95.2	94.5	97.9
Everett, WA.	107.4	102.8	126.0	88.2	106.5	122.8	97.5
Fairbanks, AK.	135.7	123.4	128.7	239.2	112.9	150.8	120.5
Fargo-Moorhead, ND-MN.	94.0	101.7	83.5	92.1	96.6	111.3	97.2
Fayetteville, AR.	89.8	93.6	80.2	102.7	86.0	91.0	93.8
Fayetteville-Fayette County, GA.	95.2	99.3	89.5	91.0	94.2	110.1	98.2
Findlay, OH.	97.2	101.6	80.2	101.6	101.3	95.5	107.5
Fitchburg-Leominster, MA.	109.2	95.4	106.8	116.5	122.3	116.7	108.9
Flagstaff, AZ.	117.9	112.7	154.7	95.1	107.5	104.5	100.9
Florence, AL.	91.4	96.6	81.7	101.1	93.8	86.8	94.3
Fond du Lac, WI.	94.6	101.8	79.4	98.0	100.5	108.2	99.7
Fort Lauderdale, FL.	115.1	108.3	144.6	97.9	110.5	97.3	102.0
Fort Wayne-Allen County, IN.	89.0	92.1	76.4	93.7	99.4	92.3	92.7
Fort Worth, TX.	99.7	95.5	93.6	96.5	99.5	101.6	107.8
Fresno, CA.	106.1	105.2	102.4	127.5	109.4	102.3	102.0
Gainesville, FL.	97.5	103.0	91.5	99.4	105.9	102.5	95.9
Glenwood Springs, CO.	115.5	99.5	140.4	94.8	110.3	117.5	109.2
Grand Junction, CO.	97.4	94.7	101.7	85.1	102.2	104.8	96.0
Grand Rapids, MI.	92.3	95.3	77.9	94.5	101.7	92.0	99.3
Green Bay, WI.	93.5	92.6	80.6	104.1	98.3	105.6	98.2
Greenville, SC.	94.6	100.6	78.5	96.1	95.3	108.4	103.4
Gunnison, CO.	104.9	101.5	120.2	82.1	99.4	99.8	103.0
Hammond, LA.	89.7	98.5	73.8	91.8	93.0	96.0	97.1
Hampton Roads-SE Virginia, VA.	100.7	96.0	92.9	107.6	97.4	107.9	107.6
Harlingen, TX.	81.4	86.1	69.9	96.4	87.7	97.8	80.0
Harrisburg, PA.	99.8	102.5	91.1	111.0	104.1	90.8	102.2
Harrisonburg, VA.	98.6	98.2	102.4	102.0	88.3	100.7	97.9
Hastings, NE.	97.1	101.1	94.0	101.7	92.9	100.0	97.7
Hattiesburg, MS.	85.9	95.8	71.4	93.0	94.5	88.3	88.3
Hilo, HI.	153.0	159.5	153.2	262.4	125.7	114.9	130.1
Hilton Head Island, SC.	106.1	112.1	108.0	102.5	96.6	104.7	106.9
Honolulu, HI.	174.9	154.7	267.4	214.3	125.9	112.1	116.9
Hot Springs, AR.	93.5	95.7	78.5	94.3	89.8	90.5	107.5
Houston, TX.	99.0	84.5	108.5	99.2	93.8	91.1	100.1
Huntsville, AL.	94.4	100.9	79.5	104.7	100.2	96.7	98.7
Hutchinson, KS.	90.8	90.4	81.0	95.2	95.0	100.0	95.3
Idaho Falls, ID.	84.2	94.9	61.6	79.7	95.5	102.6	93.8
Indianapolis, IN.	93.5	93.8	82.7	95.1	98.7	98.4	99.8
Indianapolis-Morgan County, IN.	90.1	97.7	75.0	97.5	96.4	97.5	94.3
Ithaca, NY.	106.2	100.4	114.9	90.8	111.0	108.2	103.9
Jackson, MS.	87.0	86.7	75.5	76.5	94.7	89.6	97.4
Jackson-Madison County, TN.	91.9	90.6	72.9	89.0	101.9	85.7	107.1
Jacksonville, FL.	98.3	102.6	85.8	107.1	103.9	89.7	103.5
Janesville, WI.	95.8	98.1	86.5	111.7	98.9	109.7	94.7
Jefferson City, MO.	91.9	98.7	78.4	98.8	92.6	96.1	97.6
Joliet-Will County, IL.	97.1	93.1	101.6	96.4	109.8	103.7	89.3
Jonesboro, AR.	87.0	93.0	78.3	84.8	87.8	85.1	92.6
Joplin, MO.	89.1	93.6	72.5	117.6	92.7	92.9	90.5
Juneau, AK.	132.4	129.3	158.8	145.5	108.7	150.2	112.8
Kalamazoo, MI.	87.2	86.9	70.0	97.6	99.5	96.2	93.1
Kansas City, MO-KS.	100.0	100.5	93.0	106.7	97.8	99.8	104.8
Kennewick-Richland-Pasco, WA.	95.2	95.4	101.1	89.0	97.1	106.9	89.6
Knoxville, TN.	87.3	89.5	79.5	92.4	85.1	91.1	91.9
Kodiak, AK.	136.1	140.4	152.6	156.7	125.0	140.3	116.7
Lafayette, IN.	90.1	95.4	73.7	100.6	106.9	98.2	91.3
Lafayette, LA.	95.9	94.5	94.0	92.7	100.9	86.8	98.7
Lake Charles, LA.	95.2	96.9	95.5	95.2	98.7	98.2	92.5
Lake Havasu City, AZ.	100.4	99.7	104.8	95.1	100.3	104.4	98.1
Laramie, WY.	93.6	98.1	95.1	99.0	90.6	98.7	88.9
Las Vegas, NV.	106.0	111.5	107.5	90.7	104.7	102.5	108.2
Lawton, OK.	94.2	94.9	91.0	87.6	101.3	102.1	95.1
Lexington, KY.	91.9	97.5	74.7	95.5	96.2	90.4	101.9
Lexington-Buena Vista-Rockbridge, VA.	92.5	94.9	92.3	101.3	93.1	87.0	89.3
Lima, OH.	95.7	99.4	79.7	109.1	101.2	105.8	100.2
Lincoln, NE.	90.6	96.6	76.0	93.9	96.9	96.2	96.6
Little Rock-North Little Rock, AR.	98.5	95.2	96.1	108.5	94.9	86.4	102.0
Longview, TX.	101.1	98.6	98.9	87.0	103.4	101.3	107.7
Los Angeles-Long Beach, CA.	135.1	104.8	205.1	112.2	112.1	112.2	106.3
Louisville, KY.	91.9	92.2	80.5	86.1	104.7	91.4	98.8
Lubbock, TX.	89.3	94.0	82.7	79.1	94.5	96.8	93.3
Lynchburg, VA.	92.6	93.4	85.1	108.8	85.7	95.1	96.0
Madison, WI.	107.0	103.2	114.7	100.6	106.2	115.5	103.1
Manchester, NH.	115.6	97.9	128.1	124.5	99.1	118.1	115.5
Manhattan, KS.	93.8	94.1	93.4	89.7	93.2	96.2	95.1
Mankato, MN.	95.3	104.2	81.7	88.6	101.2	103.3	102.3

See footnotes at end of table.

Table 749. Cost of Living Index for Selected Urban Areas, Annual Average: 2014-Continued.

See headnote on page 494.

Urban Area	Composite Index (100.0%)	Grocery items (13.96%)	Housing (27.80%)	Utilities (10.23%)	Transportation (12.12%)	Health care (4.41%)	Misc. goods and services (31.48%)
Marietta, GA.	96.8	103.4	92.1	90.1	99.0	100.2	98.8
Marshfield, WI.	96.4	95.7	88.0	93.3	106.6	108.9	99.5
Martinsburg-Berkeley County, WV.	90.6	94.1	76.3	92.2	105.2	95.3	94.9
Mason City, IA.	88.4	97.7	72.5	96.5	90.8	93.4	94.2
McAllen, TX.	84.3	83.7	77.0	92.2	94.8	82.8	84.5
Memphis, TN.	85.6	92.8	69.7	93.3	92.7	91.1	90.6
Miami-Dade County, FL.	111.4	108.6	125.6	97.7	111.2	103.4	105.6
Middlesex-Monmouth, NJ.	123.2	105.0	153.8	113.9	109.2	110.5	114.4
Midland, TX.	97.0	91.4	97.7	91.7	102.0	97.5	98.7
Milwaukee-Waukesha, WI.	102.1	101.8	104.0	112.7	98.8	116.0	96.4
Minneapolis, MN.	107.9	104.1	115.4	92.6	103.7	100.8	110.4
Minot, ND.	107.4	104.5	121.5	86.9	109.5	105.8	102.3
Mobile, AL.	92.6	104.1	78.9	107.4	93.1	87.2	95.5
Monroe, LA.	95.5	96.3	91.0	97.3	97.2	89.1	98.7
Montgomery, AL.	94.7	100.0	87.2	105.0	96.4	83.2	96.6
Morgantown, WV.	103.2	97.3	113.0	93.7	98.0	98.3	103.0
Morristown, TN.	89.8	92.6	74.9	97.4	93.8	92.2	97.5
Moses Lake, WA.	93.1	96.9	84.0	73.6	101.1	119.8	98.9
Muskogee, OK.	89.2	96.8	74.5	98.9	84.5	99.8	95.9
Myrtle Beach, SC.	94.2	104.3	71.4	118.8	95.9	97.2	100.9
Nacogdoches, TX.	95.9	91.5	88.3	102.0	100.6	93.1	101.3
Nashville-Murfreesboro, TN.	90.2	95.5	76.7	92.0	93.4	84.4	98.8
Nassau County, NY.	129.9	116.1	177.1	104.0	108.9	105.7	114.1
New Orleans, LA.	97.0	100.9	96.0	84.1	102.8	100.6	97.7
New York (Brooklyn), NY.	169.8	128.1	292.9	127.4	114.9	113.1	122.5
New York (Manhattan), NY.	222.6	135.2	439.5	136.6	125.3	112.4	150.8
Newark-Elizabeth, NJ.	127.2	107.9	164.8	114.8	107.7	104.1	117.4
Norman, OK.	83.7	86.9	69.4	86.5	88.1	91.6	91.1
Oakland, CA.	140.0	123.9	214.5	100.6	106.6	116.0	110.4
Odessa, TX.	99.2	89.5	104.0	97.1	97.1	105.3	100.0
Oklahoma City, OK.	90.1	91.0	82.6	92.7	94.2	95.8	93.2
Olympia, WA.	101.1	102.7	99.2	83.6	111.5	122.2	100.9
Omaha, NE.	88.3	93.2	77.9	95.0	96.7	102.0	87.9
Orange County, CA.	147.5	107.1	243.3	123.2	121.6	107.5	104.4
Orlando, FL.	100.0	101.6	93.5	108.4	99.2	93.3	103.7
Paducah, KY.	91.7	94.0	81.2	110.4	91.1	86.4	94.9
Palm Coast-Flagler County, FL.	94.4	106.8	80.0	89.5	99.1	95.9	101.1
Peoria, IL.	99.6	94.9	101.6	97.3	110.3	92.6	97.5
Philadelphia, PA.	119.5	114.3	135.4	121.8	106.6	98.7	114.8
Phoenix, AZ.	96.2	100.6	92.9	96.5	103.0	101.6	93.6
Pierre, SD.	102.3	111.3	113.5	89.9	91.0	95.0	97.7
Pittsburgh, PA.	96.4	99.0	87.4	101.0	107.9	98.8	97.2
Plano, TX.	99.1	100.4	90.2	101.9	101.3	105.3	103.7
Ponca City, OK.	91.9	92.0	79.3	99.1	91.1	100.4	99.9
Portland, ME.	110.1	96.9	122.1	89.5	109.8	119.0	110.8
Portland, OR.	125.1	114.4	160.9	90.8	111.7	114.3	116.2
Prescott-Prescott Valley, AZ.	97.9	96.6	105.2	88.2	93.1	94.7	97.4
Providence, RI.	122.4	106.7	135.3	124.8	104.5	118.9	124.6
Pryor Creek, OK.	88.7	96.2	72.7	94.3	90.0	90.6	97.0
Pueblo, CO.	84.8	95.5	70.6	91.1	98.5	95.8	83.8
Punta Gorda-Charlotte County, FL.	94.5	102.0	80.8	98.5	99.1	108.0	98.3
Quincy, IL.	93.8	97.4	93.8	91.7	97.4	101.8	90.5
Raleigh, NC.	93.3	101.9	77.8	101.2	100.4	103.6	96.4
Reno-Sparks, NV.	97.2	106.1	86.3	81.5	107.4	94.7	104.5
Richmond, IN.	85.1	86.8	77.1	88.7	96.0	88.1	85.7
Richmond, VA.	99.4	100.5	88.7	107.7	96.7	104.2	105.9
Rio Rancho, NM.	92.4	95.4	77.7	89.0	101.2	97.5	100.9
Riverside City, CA.	116.1	115.8	131.3	113.7	114.2	107.3	105.4
Roanoke, VA.	91.4	91.2	89.8	98.7	91.4	96.8	89.9
Rochester, NY.	99.2	96.2	91.4	93.1	111.6	100.1	104.5
Rockford, IL.	91.8	99.4	81.2	91.9	98.7	100.9	93.7
Round Rock, TX.	94.6	86.8	89.8	95.2	94.8	105.7	100.5
Sacramento, CA.	112.8	116.5	118.0	114.5	110.8	111.8	106.8
Salina, KS.	88.4	97.2	76.3	100.7	94.9	99.3	87.0
Salt Lake City, UT.	94.4	97.1	91.3	93.8	101.6	94.9	93.2
San Angelo, TX.	94.8	96.2	84.2	96.7	99.4	86.4	102.4
San Antonio, TX.	92.4	89.5	80.2	83.8	96.9	97.2	104.8
San Diego, CA.	135.4	105.6	204.2	111.3	117.0	112.9	105.9
San Francisco, CA.	167.5	123.9	303.8	101.5	110.5	119.0	116.5
San Marcos, TX.	86.0	82.0	77.5	88.1	95.9	92.9	89.7
Sarasota, FL.	101.2	102.3	101.1	99.0	102.1	109.3	99.9
Savannah, GA.	91.5	97.9	70.0	106.6	99.1	98.8	98.8
Seattle, WA.	126.9	111.7	165.6	98.3	118.1	116.6	113.5
Seguin, TX.	91.4	90.6	79.3	94.6	92.6	97.1	100.0
Sherman-Denison, TX.	86.4	94.8	76.1	86.6	95.0	85.3	88.5
Shreveport-Bossier City, LA.	91.1	93.5	85.1	97.0	92.1	89.1	93.4
Sierra Vista, AZ.	97.3	94.7	93.6	102.8	102.6	96.5	98.1
Slidell-St. Tammany Parish, LA.	98.5	98.1	93.6	111.5	100.0	93.2	99.1
South Bend, IN.	90.1	93.8	87.3	83.7	95.9	96.5	89.9
Spokane, WA.	95.6	91.9	87.9	78.9	103.3	111.8	104.3
Springfield, IL.	88.1	95.7	80.8	76.7	101.6	105.1	87.4
Springfield, MO.	90.4	96.4	73.3	101.9	93.7	98.6	96.6
St. Cloud, MN.	95.0	109.2	76.5	85.1	97.0	109.8	105.3

See footnotes at end of table.

Table 749. Cost of Living Index for Selected Urban Areas, Annual Average: 2014-Continued.

See headnote on page 494.

Urban Area	Composite Index (100.0%)	Grocery items (13.96%)	Housing (27.80%)	Utilities (10.23%)	Transportation (12.12%)	Health care (4.41%)	Misc. goods and services (31.48%)
St. George, UT..............................	93.1	97.3	90.9	87.5	95.2	91.4	94.3
St. Louis, MO-IL............................	93.7	105.2	73.2	115.3	98.6	102.6	96.7
St. Paul, MN................................	107.8	104.1	114.6	91.1	105.1	101.8	110.6
Stamford, CT................................	145.2	117.1	208.4	127.7	118.5	110.7	122.7
Statesboro-Bulloch County, GA............	92.1	100.9	76.8	91.2	98.4	84.1	100.7
Staunton-Augusta County, VA.............	93.4	94.7	90.3	101.3	91.0	94.6	93.7
Stillwater, OK...............................	92.9	96.6	83.8	95.2	93.9	100.6	97.0
Stockton, CA...............................	108.7	116.1	113.1	105.1	114.6	106.7	100.6
Sumter, SC.................................	91.6	102.4	77.2	104.5	91.6	91.9	95.4
Tacoma, WA................................	104.7	100.1	95.7	102.1	107.8	111.2	113.4
Tampa, FL..................................	92.4	98.8	76.3	103.7	102.3	91.3	96.3
Temple, TX.................................	86.3	84.5	77.6	80.8	88.4	94.7	94.6
Texarkana, TX-AR..........................	92.3	94.9	79.3	90.9	92.7	84.1	104.1
Thomasville-Lexington, NC.................	91.0	102.3	79.6	89.0	88.6	114.9	94.3
Topeka, KS.................................	92.9	94.6	84.0	89.0	92.6	96.2	100.9
Tracy, CA...................................	124.0	120.1	160.0	106.3	113.2	105.0	106.4
Truckee-Nevada County, CA...............	144.9	125.1	208.0	132.7	121.0	118.0	114.8
Tucson, AZ.................................	97.0	98.4	84.3	92.8	98.8	112.9	106.0
Tulsa, OK..................................	88.7	96.5	65.6	95.4	99.1	95.6	98.4
Tupelo, MS.................................	87.9	90.6	70.7	88.7	93.5	97.3	98.2
Twin Falls, ID..............................	91.8	90.8	79.0	91.5	110.1	93.2	96.4
Tyler, TX...................................	95.6	93.3	96.2	93.9	96.4	90.8	96.9
Valdosta, GA...............................	95.3	108.3	86.3	98.1	98.0	96.4	95.4
Vancouver, WA............................	102.9	96.9	97.6	92.6	108.7	108.5	110.5
Vero Beach-Indian River, FL...............	100.4	107.0	88.4	119.5	98.9	97.6	102.8
Waco, TX...................................	88.9	81.1	84.8	89.2	100.4	95.2	90.7
Washington-Arlington-Alexandria, DC-VA....	141.6	110.2	246.4	96.9	104.4	96.4	98.2
Waterloo-Cedar Falls, IA...................	92.2	93.9	93.1	84.1	91.9	98.4	92.5
Wichita, KS................................	91.3	95.9	73.0	110.5	96.4	96.7	96.6
Williamsport-Lycoming County, PA..........	99.4	102.6	91.6	122.1	101.4	98.1	96.9
Wilmington, DE.............................	108.2	107.2	109.6	114.4	104.3	100.0	108.2
Wilmington, NC.............................	99.5	106.0	89.3	103.7	103.5	111.8	101.0
Winchester, VA-WV.........................	101.9	100.4	98.5	103.1	90.0	102.4	109.7
Winston-Salem, NC.........................	91.1	102.7	67.1	105.7	96.6	106.5	98.0
Wooster, OH...............................	91.2	93.8	81.1	104.0	96.0	92.7	92.9
Yakima, WA................................	95.6	99.6	91.3	82.5	107.3	111.2	95.2
York County, PA............................	100.9	100.5	96.4	109.4	98.5	92.7	104.5
Yuma, AZ..................................	101.3	106.4	87.0	124.3	98.5	97.7	105.9

Source: C2ER, Arlington, VA, Cost of Living Index, Annual Average 2014 ©. See also <http://www.c2er.org>.

Table 750. Employment Cost Index for Total Compensation, Wages and Salaries, and Benefits: 2001 to 2014

[As of December (2005=100). Data are not seasonally adjusted. For data by industry, see Table 668]

Compensation type and occupation	2001	2005	2006	2007	2008	2009	2010	2011	2012	2013	2014
Total compensation:											
All civilian workers [1]...................	87.1	100.0	103.3	106.7	109.5	111.0	113.2	115.5	117.7	120.0	122.7
Private industry workers...............	87.3	100.0	103.2	106.3	108.9	110.2	112.5	115.0	117.1	119.4	122.2
State and local government workers..	86.2	100.0	104.1	108.4	111.6	114.2	116.2	117.7	119.9	122.2	124.7
Wages and salaries:											
All civilian workers [1]...................	89.9	100.0	103.2	106.7	109.6	111.2	113.0	114.6	116.5	118.7	121.2
Private industry workers...............	89.9	100.0	103.2	106.6	109.4	110.8	112.8	114.6	116.6	119.0	121.6
State and local government workers..	90.2	100.0	103.5	107.1	110.4	112.5	113.8	114.9	116.2	117.5	119.4
Benefits:											
All civilian workers [1]...................	80.6	100.0	103.6	106.8	109.1	110.7	113.9	117.5	120.3	123.0	126.2
Private industry workers...............	81.3	100.0	103.1	105.6	107.7	108.7	111.9	115.9	118.2	120.5	123.5
State and local government workers..	78.1	100.0	105.2	111.0	114.2	117.7	121.1	123.6	127.8	132.0	135.8

[1] Includes workers in the private nonfarm economy except those in private households and workers in the public sector except the federal government.

Source: U.S. Bureau of Labor Statistics, Employment Cost Trends, "Employment Cost Index," <http://www.bls.gov/ncs/ect/#data>, accessed August 2015.

Table 751. Average Prices of Selected Fuels and Electricity: 1990 to 2014

[Fuels in dollars per unit; electricity in cents per kWh. Represents price to end-users, except as noted]

Item	Unit	1990	2000	2005	2009	2010	2011	2012	2013	2014
Crude oil, composite [1]	Barrel	22.22	28.26	50.24	59.29	76.69	101.87	100.93	100.49	91.98
Motor gasoline: [2]										
Unleaded regular	Gallon	1.16	1.51	2.30	2.35	2.79	3.53	3.64	3.53	3.37
Unleaded premium	Gallon	1.35	1.69	2.49	2.61	3.05	3.79	3.92	3.84	3.71
No. 2 heating oil	Gallon	0.73	0.93	1.71	1.96	2.46	3.19	3.36	3.34	3.33
No. 2 diesel fuel	Gallon	0.73	0.94	1.79	1.83	2.31	3.12	3.20	3.12	2.92
Propane, consumer grade	Gallon	0.75	0.60	1.09	1.22	1.48	1.71	1.14	1.03	1.10
Residual fuel oil	Gallon	0.44	0.60	1.05	1.34	1.71	2.40	2.59	2.48	2.33
Natural gas, residential	1,000 cu/ft	5.80	7.76	12.70	12.14	11.39	11.03	10.65	10.32	10.97
Electricity, residential	kWh	7.83	8.24	9.45	11.51	11.54	11.72	11.88	12.12	12.50

[1] Refiner acquisition cost. [2] Average, all service.

Source: U.S. Energy Information Administration, *Monthly Energy Review*, April 2015. See also <http://www.eia.gov/totalenergy/data/monthly/>.

Table 752. Retail Gasoline Prices—Selected Areas: 2010 to 2014

[In dollars per gallon. Prices are annual averages]

Area	Regular				Midgrade				Premium			
	2010	2012	2013	2014	2010	2012	2013	2014	2010	2012	2013	2014
U.S. Total	**2.78**	**3.62**	**3.51**	**3.36**	**2.90**	**3.76**	**3.66**	**3.54**	**3.02**	**3.89**	**3.82**	**3.71**
Boston, MA	2.74	3.64	3.53	3.39	2.87	3.82	3.73	3.59	2.98	3.94	3.85	3.72
Chicago, IL	2.94	3.85	3.75	3.57	3.05	3.99	3.92	3.77	3.16	4.11	4.10	3.97
Cleveland, OH	2.75	3.58	3.49	3.35	2.86	3.70	3.61	3.50	2.96	3.81	3.74	3.65
Denver, CO	2.65	3.48	3.41	3.32	2.77	3.60	3.55	3.49	2.89	3.71	3.68	3.63
Houston, TX	2.59	3.42	3.29	3.13	2.74	3.60	3.50	3.37	2.87	3.74	3.66	3.56
Los Angeles, CA	3.11	4.09	3.95	3.78	3.21	4.19	4.05	3.89	3.31	4.29	4.15	3.99
Miami, FL	2.86	3.71	3.63	3.47	3.01	3.91	3.88	3.73	3.11	4.02	4.03	3.90
New York, NY	2.81	3.72	3.60	3.44	2.96	3.91	3.81	3.67	3.07	4.03	3.95	3.81
San Francisco, CA	3.12	4.04	3.90	3.78	3.23	4.15	4.01	3.90	3.34	4.25	4.11	4.00
Seattle, WA	3.00	3.85	3.68	3.60	3.12	3.98	3.82	3.73	3.23	4.09	3.93	3.84

Source: U.S. Energy Information Administration, "Weekly Retail Gasoline and Diesel Prices," <http://www.eia.gov/petroleum/data.cfm#prices>, accessed February 2015.

Table 753. Weekly Food Cost of a Nutritious Diet by Type of Family and Individual: 2010 and 2014

[In dollars. As of December. Assumes that food for all meals and snacks is purchased at the store and prepared at home. All four Food Plans are based on 2001-02 data and updated to current dollars by using the Consumer Price Index for specific food items. See source for details]

Family type	Thrifty plan		Low-cost plan		Moderate plan		Liberal plan	
	2010	2014	2010	2014	2010	2014	2010	2014
FAMILIES								
Family of two:								
19 to 50 years	81.10	90.20	103.40	115.60	128.40	144.00	160.80	180.30
51 to 70 years	76.90	85.40	99.20	110.40	122.60	137.70	148.00	166.20
Family of four:								
Couple, 19 to 50 years and children—								
2 to 3 and 4 to 5 years	118.10	131.40	150.20	167.90	185.50	207.60	229.90	257.50
6 to 8 and 9 to 11 years	135.60	151.10	176.60	198.90	221.00	247.70	268.50	300.80
INDIVIDUALS [1]								
Child:								
1 year	20.10	22.00	26.80	29.80	30.60	33.60	37.10	41.10
2 to 3 years	21.70	24.00	27.50	30.80	33.30	37.10	40.50	45.40
4 to 5 years	22.70	25.40	28.70	31.90	35.50	39.60	43.30	48.20
6 to 8 years	28.80	32.50	39.20	45.50	48.20	54.10	56.90	63.90
9 to 11 years	33.00	36.60	43.40	48.20	56.10	62.70	65.50	72.90
Male:								
12 to 13 years	35.10	39.10	49.50	55.50	61.70	69.70	72.70	81.70
14 to 18 years	36.20	40.10	50.80	56.10	63.80	71.80	73.40	82.80
19 to 50 years	39.00	43.50	50.30	56.30	62.90	70.50	77.10	86.90
51 to 70 years	35.60	39.60	47.60	53.00	58.60	66.10	71.10	79.80
71 years and over	35.80	39.90	47.00	52.70	58.50	65.20	71.90	80.70
Female:								
12 to 13 years	35.30	39.10	42.90	47.80	51.90	57.80	63.00	70.80
14 to 18 years	34.80	38.40	43.10	48.00	52.00	58.30	63.90	71.70
19 to 50 years	34.70	38.60	43.70	48.80	53.80	60.40	69.00	77.00
51 to 70 years	34.30	38.10	42.50	47.40	52.90	59.00	63.50	71.40
71 years and over	33.80	37.30	42.10	47.20	52.50	58.60	63.40	70.60

[1] The costs given are for individuals in 4-person families. For individuals in other size families, the following adjustments are suggested: 1-person, add 20 percent; 2-person, add 10 percent; 3-person, add 5 percent; 5- or 6-person, subtract 5 percent; and 7-or-more person, subtract 10 percent.

Source: U.S. Department of Agriculture, Center for Nutrition Policy and Promotion, *Official USDA Food Plans: Cost of Food at Home at Four Levels, U.S. Average, December 2014*, January 2015, and earlier reports. See also <http://www.cnpp.usda.gov/USDAFoodCost-Home.htm>.

Table 754. Food—Retail Prices of Selected Items: 1990 to 2014

[In dollars per pound, except as indicated. As of December. See Appendix III]

Food	1990	2000	2005	2010	2011	2012	2013	2014
Cereals and bakery products:								
Flour, white, all purpose	0.24	0.28	0.30	0.44	0.51	0.50	0.51	0.51
Rice, white, lg. grain, raw	0.49	(NA)	0.52	0.73	0.73	0.71	0.74	0.70
Spaghetti and macaroni	0.85	0.88	0.87	1.19	1.31	1.31	1.26	1.16
Bread, white, pan	0.70	0.99	1.05	1.39	1.42	1.44	1.39	1.47
Bread, whole wheat	(NA)	1.36	1.29	1.88	2.07	1.93	2.08	1.99
Beef:								
Ground beef, 100% beef	1.63	1.63	2.30	2.38	2.92	3.08	3.46	4.16
Ground chuck, 100% beef	2.02	1.98	2.61	2.93	3.27	3.46	3.59	4.22
Ground beef, lean and extra lean	(NA)	2.33	2.91	3.49	3.84	4.21	5.06	6.08
Beef roasts (all, uncooked)	(NA)	2.93	3.73	4.15	4.67	4.74	4.91	5.85
Beef steaks (all, uncooked)	(NA)	4.09	5.03	5.60	6.04	6.30	6.34	7.54
Round steak, USDA Choice	3.42	3.28	4.12	4.30	4.72	4.70	5.01	6.26
Sirloin steak, boneless	4.24	4.81	5.93	6.07	6.16	6.78	6.78	8.15
Pork:								
Bacon, sliced	2.28	3.03	3.33	4.16	4.55	4.64	5.54	5.53
Chops, center cut, bone-in	3.32	3.46	3.28	3.58	3.66	3.57	3.92	4.26
Ham, boneless, excluding canned	(NA)	2.75	3.09	3.47	3.66	3.74	4.06	4.35
Poultry and eggs:								
Chicken, fresh, whole	0.86	1.08	1.06	1.28	1.34	1.48	1.52	1.54
Chicken breast, boneless	(NA)	(NA)	(NA)	3.32	3.10	3.27	3.46	3.48
Chicken legs, bone-in	1.17	1.26	1.33	1.48	1.46	1.65	1.59	1.61
Turkey, frozen, whole	0.96	0.99	1.07	1.38	1.57	1.43	1.65	1.33
Eggs, Grade A, large, (dozen)	1.00	0.96	1.35	1.79	1.87	2.01	2.03	2.21
Dairy products:								
Milk, fresh, whole, fortified (per gal.)	(NA)	2.79	3.24	3.32	3.57	3.58	3.50	3.82
Butter, salted, grade AA, stick	1.92	2.80	2.98	3.42	3.32	(NA)	(NA)	(NA)
American processed cheese	(NA)	3.69	3.92	3.80	4.30	4.24	4.35	4.71
Cheddar cheese, natural	(NA)	3.76	4.43	4.93	5.43	5.87	5.39	5.44
Ice cream, prepack., bulk, reg. (1/2 gal.)	2.54	3.66	3.69	4.58	5.25	5.10	4.98	5.04
Fresh fruits and vegetables:								
Apples, Red Delicious	0.77	0.82	0.97	1.20	1.27	1.42	1.34	1.29
Bananas	0.43	0.49	0.48	0.59	0.60	0.61	0.59	0.59
Oranges, navel	0.56	0.62	0.89	1.02	0.98	1.04	1.13	1.25
Grapefruit	0.56	0.58	1.10	0.99	0.89	1.07	1.07	1.10
Grapes, Thompson seedless	(NA)	2.36	2.76	2.87	2.86	3.09	2.57	2.96
Lemons	0.97	1.11	1.51	1.60	1.54	1.53	1.63	1.97
Pears, Anjou	0.79	(NA)	1.00	1.42	1.33	(NA)	(NA)	(NA)
Strawberries	(NA)	(NA)	2.67	3.07	2.49	2.88	2.87	3.56
Lettuce, iceberg	0.58	0.85	0.85	0.99	0.95	0.87	0.99	1.11
Tomatoes, field grown	0.86	1.57	1.85	1.59	1.53	1.59	1.73	2.19
Peppers, sweet	(NA)	(NA)	(NA)	2.40	2.62	2.36	2.67	2.62
Potatoes, white	0.32	0.35	0.50	0.58	0.67	0.62	0.67	0.64
Sugar and fats and oils:								
Sugar, white, all sizes	0.43	0.41	0.45	0.64	0.70	0.68	0.59	0.61
Margarine, tubs, soft	(NA)	0.84	0.91	1.62	1.91	2.08	2.07	1.96
Peanut butter, creamy, all sizes	2.07	1.96	1.70	1.99	2.43	2.90	2.60	2.70
Nonalcoholic beverages:								
Coffee, 100% ground roast, all sizes	2.94	3.21	3.24	4.15	5.44	5.92	4.95	4.59

NA Not available.

Source: U.S. Bureau of Labor Statistics, *CPI Detailed Report*, December 2014; and CPI Databases, "Average Price Indexes," <http://www.bls.gov/cpi/data.htm>, accessed March 2015. See also <http://www.bls.gov/cpi/cpi_dr.htm>.

Table 755. Indexes of Spot Primary Market Prices: 1990 to 2014

[1967 = 100. Represents unweighted geometric average of price quotations of 23 commodities. Computed daily and therefore much more sensitive to changes in market conditions than a monthly producer price index]

Items and number	1990	1995	2000	2005	2007	2008	2009	2010	2011	2012	2013	2014
All commodities (23)	258.1	289.1	224.0	303.3	413.4	313.0	424.2	520.3	481.8	482.1	456.2	438.0
Foodstuffs (10)	206.4	236.4	184.7	241.7	335.9	294.2	344.7	440.3	435.5	423.9	364.7	369.4
Raw industrials (13)	301.2	332.2	255.8	354.7	477.0	326.5	489.4	583.8	516.5	526.8	532.4	492.6
Livestock and products (5)	292.7	307.4	265.5	326.6	402.6	310.8	407.6	528.0	575.4	599.7	547.8	556.2
Metals (5)	283.2	300.6	214.0	440.9	811.9	390.9	809.1	1,006.2	837.8	918.7	935.2	824.4
Textiles and fibers (4)	257.6	274.3	245.7	252.5	267.5	241.3	294.0	342.1	290.2	276.8	278.2	257.7
Fats and oils (4)	188.7	226.7	163.6	223.4	363.4	268.0	339.7	478.3	497.7	471.5	387.3	364.0

Source: Commodity Research Bureau, Chicago, IL, *CRB Commodity Index Report*, weekly ©. See also <http://www.crbtrader.com>.

Table 756. Producer Price Indexes—Intermediate and Final Demand: 2010 to 2014

[November 2009=100. Minus sign (-) indicates decrease. For information on producer prices, see Bureau of Labor Statistics, <http://www.bls.gov/opub/hom/homch14.htm>]

Commodity type	Index					Percent change [1]				
	2010	2011	2012	2013	2014	2010	2011	2012	2013	2014
FINAL DEMAND										
Total	**101.8**	**105.7**	**107.7**	**109.1**	**110.9**	**(NA)**	**3.8**	**1.9**	**1.3**	**1.6**
Final demand goods	102.8	109.9	111.7	112.6	114.0	(NA)	6.9	1.6	0.8	1.2
Final demand foods	103.7	112.5	115.9	117.8	121.6	(NA)	8.5	3.0	1.6	3.2
Final demand energy	107.2	126.2	126.3	125.3	124.2	(NA)	17.7	0.1	-0.8	-0.9
Other final demand goods	101.4	104.9	106.8	107.9	109.5	(NA)	3.5	1.8	1.0	1.5
Final demand services	101.3	103.4	105.4	107.1	109.0	(NA)	2.1	1.9	1.6	1.8
Final demand trade services	101.7	104.0	106.7	108.2	110.2	(NA)	2.3	2.6	1.4	1.8
Final demand transportation and warehousing services	103.2	110.0	114.2	115.3	117.7	(NA)	6.6	3.8	1.0	2.1
Other final demand services	100.9	102.5	103.9	105.8	107.5	(NA)	1.6	1.4	1.8	1.6
INTERMEDIATE DEMAND										
Processed goods for intermediate demand	183.4	199.9	200.7	200.8	201.9	6.3	9.0	0.4	(Z)	0.5
Processed foods and feeds	171.7	192.2	201.4	204.3	210.8	3.4	11.9	4.8	1.4	3.2
Processed energy goods	187.8	219.9	218.4	213.7	211.5	15.6	17.1	-0.7	-2.2	-1.0
Other processed materials	180.8	192.0	192.6	193.8	195.2	4.3	6.2	0.3	0.6	0.7
Unprocessed goods for intermediate demand	212.2	249.4	241.4	246.7	249.3	21.1	17.5	-3.2	2.2	1.1
Unprocessed foodstuffs and feedstuffs	152.4	188.4	196.4	200.2	210.1	13.3	23.6	4.2	1.9	4.9
Unprocessed energy materials	216.7	240.3	218.4	234.7	233.1	22.6	10.9	-9.1	7.5	-0.7
Unprocessed nonfood materials less energy	329.1	390.4	369.6	351.2	345.7	32.5	18.6	-5.3	-5.0	-1.6
Services for intermediate demand	101.1	103.2	105.3	107.2	108.9	(NA)	2.1	2.0	1.8	1.6
Trade services for intermediate demand	100.8	103.1	106.8	109.2	110.4	(NA)	2.3	3.6	2.2	1.1
Transportation and warehousing services for intermediate demand	103.3	109.3	113.3	116.1	119.4	(NA)	5.8	3.7	2.5	2.8
Other services for intermediate demand	100.7	102.1	103.4	105.0	106.5	(NA)	1.4	1.3	1.5	1.4

NA Not available. Z less than 0.05 percent. [1] Change from immediate prior year. 2010, change from 2009.

Source: U.S. Bureau of Labor Statistics, PPI Databases, "Commodity Data including "headline" FD-ID Indexes," <http://www.bls.gov/ppi/data.htm>, accessed August 2015.

Table 757. Producer Price Indexes—Intermediate and Final Demand by Commodity: 2000 to 2014

[1982=100, unless otherwise noted. For information on producer prices, see Bureau of Labor Statistics, <http://www.bls.gov/opub/hom/homch14.htm>]

Item	2000	2005	2010	2011	2012	2013	2014
Final demand (Nov. 2009=100)	(NA)	(NA)	**101.8**	**105.7**	**107.7**	**109.1**	**110.9**
Final demand goods (Nov. 2009=100)	(NA)	(NA)	**102.8**	**109.9**	**111.7**	**112.6**	**114.0**
Final demand foods (Nov. 2009=100)	(NA)	(NA)	**103.7**	**112.5**	**115.9**	**117.8**	**121.6**
Fresh fruits & melons	91.4	102.8	123.8	117.7	119.0	121.2	124.5
Fresh & dry vegetables	126.7	142.6	178.5	195.1	156.5	197.8	194.0
Grains	78.3	83.4	160.2	253.5	261.5	234.5	171.5
Eggs for fresh use (Dec. 1991=100)	84.9	79.6	123.4	138.4	138.7	147.7	169.6
Oilseeds	93.8	113.4	191.0	238.7	271.0	262.1	230.0
Bakery products	182.3	201.1	244.8	253.6	261.1	267.1	270.9
Milled rice	101.2	120.1	183.6	200.2	201.6	209.9	216.8
Pasta products (June 1985=100)	121.6	127.9	170.7	185.8	205.0	203.6	201.3
Beef & veal	113.7	147.4	157.1	180.7	198.8	198.8	236.7
Pork	113.4	131.9	142.6	160.4	153.8	159.3	190.5
Processed young chickens	110.4	136.2	149.0	143.5	166.6	172.8	178.3
Processed turkeys	98.7	105.1	132.1	148.7	146.4	149.1	170.7
Finfish & shellfish	198.1	222.6	272.4	287.6	287.5	299.4	322.4
Dairy products	133.7	154.5	174.0	195.9	192.8	199.7	221.7
Processed fruits & vegetables	128.6	140.4	176.6	183.2	192.2	193.3	193.7
Confectionery end products	170.6	205.1	236.4	249.3	259.4	267.1	275.5
Soft drinks	144.1	159.1	183.9	186.9	192.7	193.5	194.6
Roasted coffee	133.5	151.1	190.2	223.9	216.6	198.0	198.9
Shortening & cooking oils	132.4	176.7	233.6	301.1	294.2	276.3	256.1
Frozen specialty food	143.5	152.7	176.4	180.4	184.0	186.1	188.9
Final demand energy (Nov. 2009=100)	(NA)	(NA)	**107.2**	**126.2**	**126.3**	**125.3**	**124.2**
Liquefied petroleum gas	127.1	244.7	301.8	374.1	291.0	269.7	258.5
Residential electric power (Dec. 1990=100)	110.8	126.4	154.7	158.9	159.8	163.8	169.5
Residential natural gas (Dec. 1990=100)	135.5	216.8	201.7	199.1	179.8	193.0	210.4
Gasoline	94.6	168.6	225.3	295.7	303.1	292.6	276.2
Home heating oil & distillates	93.5	178.4	207.5	279.3	284.9	275.9	259.0
No. 2 diesel fuel	93.3	189.1	232.9	316.2	326.1	317.7	299.6
Other final demand goods (Nov. 2009=100)	(NA)	(NA)	**101.4**	**104.9**	**106.8**	**107.9**	**109.5**
Alcoholic beverages	140.6	158.5	175.1	180.8	186.9	190.2	191.7
Women's, girls', & infants' apparel (Dec. 2003=100)	(NA)	100.3	101.6	103.0	104.0	105.6	104.7
Men's & boys' apparel (Dec. 2003=100)	(NA)	98.7	101.5	106.6	113.3	114.2	114.5
Textile house furnishings	122.0	122.9	131.7	138.8	142.8	143.7	160.3
Footwear	144.9	148.1	162.4	168.0	176.5	185.1	191.1
Soaps & synthetic detergents	128.2	134.6	161.2	166.0	175.1	176.3	174.4
Cosmetics & other toilet preparations	137.4	143.0	149.9	152.1	153.8	155.3	160.3
Tires, tubes, & tread	93.0	108.1	138.1	154.0	159.1	156.3	152.5
Agricultural machinery & equipment	153.7	174.7	203.5	209.6	214.0	215.9	220.4
Construction machinery & equipment	148.6	168.3	191.4	197.4	205.4	210.7	214.3
Metal cutting machine tools	161.9	155.1	174.6	179.3	186.4	193.6	195.9
Pumps, compressors, & equipment	154.1	178.5	215.1	223.4	230.0	235.2	240.5
Industrial material handling equipment	134.7	150.6	183.1	187.7	194.4	197.9	202.4
Electronic computers (Dec. 2004=100)	261.6	85.5	30.3	26.8	24.8	22.5	21.3
Textile machinery	156.2	160.5	165.9	166.9	168.9	172.8	175.4
Paper industries machinery (June 1982=100)	164.7	178.1	197.2	200.7	204.7	208.6	213.0
Printing trades machinery	142.1	144.3	155.4	156.5	158.5	161.1	160.2
Transformers & power regulators	135.8	150.3	223.1	229.8	227.0	224.0	224.0
Oil field & gas field machinery	128.2	155.9	200.7	205.0	210.7	213.1	216.5
Mining machinery & equipment	146.1	175.9	221.5	233.7	245.3	253.0	256.1
Office & store machines & equipment	112.7	115.1	121.0	122.2	121.2	117.6	118.8
Household furniture	152.7	166.5	187.4	191.6	196.6	199.3	200.8
Household appliances	107.3	103.3	110.5	111.8	117.1	117.0	117.2
Home electronic equipment	71.8	62.6	52.9	52.4	52.4	51.0	51.2
Lawn & garden equipment, except tractors	132.0	134.5	141.7	140.5	142.6	142.7	143.5
Passenger cars	132.8	131.8	129.0	129.9	131.2	130.3	131.2
Light motor trucks	157.6	148.4	153.3	154.6	160.1	162.9	166.9
Heavy motor trucks	148.0	162.4	195.7	200.0	205.8	209.3	213.5
Truck trailers	139.4	157.1	181.5	190.0	195.8	195.2	197.0
Aircraft	184.2	223.5	263.0	269.9	278.4	283.0	287.7
Ships (Dec. 1985=100)	146.9	176.6	215.1	220.2	220.5	220.7	223.5
Railroad equipment	135.7	160.4	184.4	187.0	191.8	195.7	197.7
Final demand services (Nov. 2009=100)	(NA)	(NA)	**101.3**	**103.4**	**105.4**	**107.1**	**109.0**
Final demand trade services (Nov. 2009=100)	(NA)	(NA)	**101.7**	**104.0**	**106.7**	**108.2**	**110.2**
Machinery & equipment wholesaling (Mar. 2009=100)	(NA)	(NA)	101.2	102.3	107.2	110.3	112.0
Furnishings wholesaling (Mar. 2009=100)	(NA)	(NA)	78.5	73.5	77.6	82.1	90.4
Apparel wholesaling (Mar. 2009=100)	(NA)	(NA)	97.3	83.4	95.8	115.2	116.4
Food & alcohol wholesaling (June 2009=100)	(NA)	(NA)	105.7	109.7	108.2	98.5	99.9
Food & alcohol retailing (Mar. 2009=100)	(NA)	(NA)	98.9	107.5	112.6	115.1	120.1
Health, beauty, & optical goods retailing (Mar. 2009=100)	(NA)	(NA)	107.8	110.3	116.8	121.0	121.1
Apparel, jewelry, footwear, & accessories retailing (June 2009=100)	(NA)	(NA)	104.2	108.3	112.9	111.7	111.2
Automobiles & automobile parts retailing (June 2009=100)	(NA)	(NA)	105.9	110.4	106.8	102.7	103.4
Sporting goods, including boats, retailing (Mar. 2009=100)	(NA)	(NA)	96.6	96.8	100.6	104.1	109.6
Furniture retailing (Mar. 2009=100)	(NA)	(NA)	99.7	99.6	100.8	100.2	100.8
Major household appliances retailing (Mar. 2009=100)	(NA)	(NA)	97.3	87.1	94.2	88.4	80.4
Book retailing (Mar. 2009=100)	(NA)	(NA)	104.8	109.6	117.9	123.1	120.8
Final demand transportation & warehousing services (Nov. 2009=100)	(NA)	(NA)	**103.2**	**110.0**	**114.2**	**115.3**	**117.7**
Rail transportation of freight & mail (Dec. 2008=100)	(NA)	(NA)	101.6	110.5	115.5	118.8	121.1
Truck transportation of freight (June 2009=100)	(NA)	(NA)	102.0	108.0	111.8	113.3	115.5
Air transportation of freight (Dec. 2008=100)	(NA)	(NA)	100.1	111.3	116.1	114.9	115.8

See footnotes at end of table.

Table 757. Producer Price Indexes—Intermediate and Final Demand by Commodity: 2000 to 2014-Continued.

See headnote on page 501.

Item	2000	2005	2010	2011	2012	2013	2014
Courier, messenger, & U.S. postal services (June 2009=100)	(NA)	(NA)	105.5	112.1	117.5	122.8	128.8
Rail transportation of passengers (Dec. 2008=100)	(NA)	(NA)	100.7	105.1	109.1	112.5	113.3
Airline passenger services (Dec. 2008=100)	(NA)	(NA)	102.8	110.2	115.0	114.7	116.9
Other final demand services (Nov. 2009=100)	**(NA)**	**(NA)**	**100.9**	**102.5**	**103.9**	**105.8**	**107.5**
Sales of books	218.2	264.0	317.1	324.7	335.9	345.1	353.3
Cellphone & other wireless telecom services (Mar. 2009=100)	(NA)	(NA)	94.4	90.9	88.6	87.7	85.1
Cable & satellite subscriber services (Dec. 2008=100)	(NA)	(NA)	103.7	106.7	108.6	109.8	111.2
Internet access services (Mar. 2009=100)	(NA)	(NA)	98.3	97.7	97.8	97.7	97.9
Processed goods for intermediate demand	**129.2**	**154.0**	**183.4**	**199.9**	**200.7**	**200.8**	**201.9**
Processed materials less foods & feeds	**130.1**	**155.1**	**184.4**	**200.7**	**200.9**	**200.7**	**201.3**
Synthetic fibers	107.2	112.3	111.6	117.7	122.4	124.0	125.3
Processed yarns & threads	107.9	111.7	130.0	157.6	142.8	141.5	141.5
Finished fabrics	122.5	124.1	137.1	147.6	150.2	151.4	154.3
Commercial electric power	131.5	149.8	182.5	183.9	184.0	188.7	194.3
Industrial electric power	131.5	156.2	193.1	203.5	209.6	203.7	218.0
Commercial natural gas (Dec. 1990=100)	134.7	232.5	208.0	200.1	177.7	186.4	200.8
Industrial natural gas (Dec. 1990=100)	139.0	249.4	202.0	195.5	167.8	176.5	190.8
Natural gas to electric utilities (Dec. 1990=100)	120.7	204.0	174.8	166.1	153.5	164.4	180.1
Jet fuels	88.5	169.6	225.5	307.3	312.1	295.5	282.3
Prepared paint	160.8	187.9	237.1	248.1	270.3	273.7	276.3
Medicinal & botanical chemicals	146.2	136.0	175.2	175.7	178.0	176.0	176.8
Biological products, including diagnostics	172.2	195.1	223.7	231.4	236.8	245.5	252.5
Fats & oils, inedible	70.1	146.9	244.3	344.9	336.9	302.6	252.8
Plastic resins & materials	141.6	193.0	210.1	229.7	235.2	245.3	257.0
Synthetic rubber	119.1	151.3	215.5	269.9	262.2	231.6	224.8
Plastic construction products	135.8	158.8	190.9	199.0	207.1	208.1	211.1
Softwood lumber	178.6	203.6	160.8	160.5	171.7	199.8	205.6
Hardwood lumber	185.9	196.6	187.3	185.8	183.7	208.4	241.9
Millwork	176.4	197.2	207.0	210.1	216.5	225.8	232.3
Plywood	157.6	186.8	176.7	171.3	189.1	199.6	204.1
Paper	149.8	159.6	182.1	191.2	191.6	190.8	192.7
Paperboard	176.7	175.5	224.9	230.5	228.0	243.7	248.6
Paper boxes & containers	172.6	183.7	219.4	225.6	226.9	240.1	245.8
Foundry & forge shop products	136.5	156.2	191.2	201.7	207.9	208.7	210.4
Steel mill products	108.4	159.7	191.7	216.2	208.0	195.0	200.2
Primary nonferrous metals	113.6	158.2	210.3	238.9	215.8	200.3	192.0
Aluminum mill shapes	149.0	161.1	171.9	188.9	178.6	173.2	179.6
Copper & brass mill shapes	162.3	235.8	421.3	471.1	431.7	412.0	397.3
Nonferrous wire & cable	143.7	169.4	258.1	282.3	267.6	258.4	253.2
Hardware	151.2	168.0	194.0	199.3	202.7	204.6	207.6
Plumbing fixtures & brass fittings	180.4	197.6	231.4	237.0	241.5	245.7	252.6
Heating equipment	155.6	179.9	221.5	227.6	235.3	239.8	243.6
Fabricated structural metal products	144.9	175.1	201.1	211.2	214.1	213.2	215.6
Air conditioning & refrigeration equipment	135.3	146.2	163.8	168.3	171.1	174.4	177.7
Motors, generators, motor generator sets	146.2	157.8	190.6	202.1	206.5	208.5	211.6
Electronic components & accessories	97.1	87.0	73.5	71.0	69.3	69.0	68.6
Internal combustion engines	143.8	147.7	161.7	164.5	165.7	166.2	167.2
Machine shop products	138.0	151.0	174.7	179.3	182.4	183.3	183.6
Cement	150.1	176.4	193.5	187.8	190.6	199.3	208.1
Concrete products	147.8	177.2	210.6	210.8	215.0	221.0	230.3
Motor vehicle parts	113.6	113.1	121.8	123.9	125.2	125.7	125.8
Aircraft engines & engine parts (Dec. 1985=100)	141.0	165.9	197.4	204.0	211.5	215.7	220.2
Aircraft parts & auxiliary equipment (June 1985=100)	145.7	155.3	167.7	170.6	172.6	177.3	181.2
Medical/surgical/personal aid devices	146.0	159.2	169.0	171.6	173.0	174.7	174.7
Unprocessed goods for intermediate demand	**120.6**	**182.2**	**212.2**	**249.4**	**241.4**	**246.7**	**249.3**
Unprocessed foodstuffs & feedstuffs	**100.2**	**122.7**	**152.4**	**188.4**	**196.4**	**200.2**	**210.1**
Wheat	80.3	102.7	157.2	216.2	210.5	204.2	190.6
Corn	76.4	75.9	160.8	267.3	278.8	243.9	163.2
Slaughter cattle	104.1	131.5	139.8	170.7	185.3	187.9	230.7
Slaughter hogs	72.7	82.7	92.6	110.6	105.1	113.2	130.5
Slaughter chickens	127.6	181.0	221.3	210.0	235.4	280.9	298.2
Slaughter turkeys	120.7	131.1	173.0	200.6	208.0	193.6	213.0
Raw milk	92.0	113.5	121.9	150.6	138.4	149.6	179.2
Alfalfa hay	156.3	190.1	214.3	319.9	378.8	381.4	368.8
Raw cane sugar & byproducts	100.2	124.9	179.9	199.8	181.0	150.4	144.0
Unprocessed nonfood materials	**130.4**	**223.4**	**249.3**	**284.1**	**263.1**	**269.2**	**265.7**
Raw cotton	95.2	78.9	117.9	145.5	132.4	126.3	122.7
Hides & skins	174.0	189.9	224.9	272.7	272.2	305.7	326.6
Coal	87.9	116.8	189.5	207.1	211.4	208.1	199.9
Natural gas	155.5	335.4	185.8	171.4	117.9	153.9	182.4
Crude petroleum	85.2	150.1	218.6	275.5	273.6	281.2	259.2
Logs & timber	196.4	197.4	213.4	228.2	232.0	237.3	242.4
Wastepaper	282.5	230.9	421.5	482.5	370.7	363.6	342.0
Iron ore	94.8	116.9	147.1	165.4	180.8	127.0	135.4
Iron & steel scrap	142.1	289.8	541.1	646.8	566.0	526.7	543.1
Nonferrous metal ores (Dec. 1983=100)	68.0	150.0	298.6	373.2	359.7	330.6	313.8
Copper base scrap	123.7	258.6	548.2	638.2	605.7	582.3	532.3
Aluminum base scrap	177.0	210.1	241.6	268.2	236.9	226.1	242.5
Construction sand, gravel, & crushed stone	163.1	195.8	262.2	266.5	272.8	278.8	289.3

NA Not available.

Source: U.S. Bureau of Labor Statistics, PPI Databases, "Commodity Data including "headline" FD-ID Indexes," <http://www.bls.gov/ppi/data.htm>, accessed August 2015.

Table 758. Chain-Type Price Indexes for Personal Consumption Expenditures by Type of Expenditure: 1990 to 2014

[2009 = 100. For explanation of "chain-type," see text, Section 13. See also Table 697]

Type of Expenditure	1990	2000	2005	2010	2012	2013	2014
Personal consumption expenditures................	**67.4**	**83.1**	**92.3**	**101.7**	**106.1**	**107.6**	**109.1**
Household consumption expenditures [1].............	66.8	82.8	92.1	101.7	106.3	107.7	109.2
Food and beverages purchased for off-premises consumption..............	65.2	79.0	88.2	100.3	106.7	107.8	109.8
Food and nonalcoholic beverages purchased for off-premises consumption..........	65.1	78.3	87.8	100.3	107.5	108.5	110.8
Alcoholic beverages purchased for off-premises consumption.............	65.7	83.1	90.7	100.4	101.9	103.2	104.0
Food produced and consumed on farms............	101.9	85.4	104.6	113.1	134.8	140.9	154.9
Clothing, footwear, and related services............	114.4	107.9	100.5	99.5	104.7	105.7	106.1
Clothing...	117.4	110.2	101.4	99.2	104.8	105.5	106.0
Garments............	122.9	113.2	102.4	98.9	104.6	105.3	105.6
Women's and girls' clothing............	128.5	112.4	102.5	99.1	104.3	104.7	105.6
Men's and boys' clothing............	115.7	114.2	102.2	98.5	105.1	106.9	106.1
Children's and infants' clothing............	116.2	114.0	101.9	99.7	105.0	102.3	103.2
Footwear [2]............	100.6	97.3	96.6	100.9	104.0	106.5	106.8
Housing, utilities, and fuels............	56.6	74.5	88.5	100.5	104.0	106.6	109.7
Housing............	57.3	76.5	89.2	100.1	103.5	106.1	109.0
Rental of tenant-occupied nonfarm housing [3]............	56.2	74.4	87.5	100.1	104.5	107.4	110.6
Imputed rental of owner-occupied nonfarm housing [4]............	57.9	77.4	89.7	100.0	103.2	105.5	108.3
Household utilities and fuels............	52.9	65.6	85.4	102.5	106.1	109.1	113.4
Water supply and sanitation............	43.5	65.8	80.7	106.3	118.0	123.3	127.8
Electricity, gas, and other fuels............	55.7	65.6	86.9	101.3	102.5	104.8	108.9
Electricity............	61.0	66.7	78.3	100.2	101.8	104.0	107.7
Natural gas............	50.3	69.0	111.0	98.0	85.6	89.7	96.2
Fuel oil and other fuels............	40.9	54.1	88.6	117.0	150.7	149.0	148.9
Furnishings, household equipment, and routine household maintenance...	94.5	102.1	99.1	97.2	96.7	95.4	93.3
Furniture, furnishings, and floor coverings [5]............	106.5	113.4	105.2	95.5	93.1	90.6	87.7
Household textiles............	159.6	144.1	119.7	94.7	88.9	85.6	83.3
Household appliances [6]............	97.1	94.3	91.9	96.4	99.9	98.3	93.6
Glassware, tableware, and household utensils [7]............	116.0	116.1	103.7	97.4	91.7	90.5	86.9
Health............	52.1	75.7	89.1	102.6	106.9	108.2	109.8
Medical products, appliances, and equipment............	56.6	77.4	90.5	103.0	109.3	109.8	112.8
Pharmaceutical and other medical products [8]............	54.1	75.5	89.8	103.6	110.7	111.3	114.6
Pharmaceutical products............	53.9	75.3	89.7	103.7	110.9	111.4	114.8
Other medical products............	75.9	94.7	96.0	97.9	99.4	99.8	99.3
Therapeutic appliances and equipment............	70.8	89.2	94.4	99.4	101.0	101.5	102.2
Outpatient services............	56.9	80.7	90.6	102.2	104.9	105.8	106.8
Physician services [9]............	60.4	84.9	92.0	102.4	105.3	105.5	106.1
Dental services............	40.4	66.6	83.5	102.7	107.5	111.2	113.6
Paramedical services............	60.2	80.9	91.5	101.6	103.4	104.2	105.3
Hospital and nursing home services............	47.1	70.8	87.1	102.8	107.5	109.6	111.0
Hospitals [10]............	47.7	71.0	87.3	102.9	107.8	110.1	111.6
Nursing homes............	45.0	70.1	86.4	102.0	105.9	106.8	108.0
Transportation............	69.8	85.5	95.7	108.2	122.2	121.7	120.6
Motor vehicles............	87.8	109.6	105.4	106.5	110.6	111.4	111.5
New motor vehicles............	89.4	106.2	102.2	102.1	106.5	107.8	108.4
Net purchases of used motor vehicles............	83.5	116.7	113.0	114.5	117.5	116.9	115.7
Motor vehicle operation............	57.4	70.5	90.8	109.5	129.0	127.5	125.3
Motor vehicle parts and accessories............	80.0	78.4	84.9	101.9	108.3	108.5	108.2
Motor vehicle fuels, lubricants, and fluids............	49.7	63.4	95.8	118.2	154.7	150.4	144.7
Public transportation............	77.2	88.8	88.9	105.8	116.7	118.8	120.6
Ground transportation [11]............	55.4	70.5	85.9	104.3	112.8	117.3	117.9
Air transportation............	91.0	99.6	90.2	107.2	121.4	121.6	124.6
Water transportation............	127.9	142.4	113.0	101.1	97.5	97.0	96.3
Communication............	106.2	106.2	100.9	99.7	98.2	98.1	97.8
Telecommunication services............	103.4	100.0	95.1	99.3	97.7	97.2	96.4
Internet access............	180.6	125.8	125.1	100.7	99.3	100.3	101.4
Recreation............	115.0	111.4	104.4	97.5	94.7	93.7	92.8
Video and audio equipment, computers, and related services............	338.9	184.0	132.7	92.9	82.6	78.6	75.6
Video and audio equipment............	348.2	235.1	165.1	86.4	68.7	62.6	58.0
Sports and recreational goods and related services............	116.0	112.7	103.0	97.1	92.9	90.8	88.5
Sports and recreational vehicles............	81.4	94.2	96.3	100.4	104.4	104.9	104.6
Other sporting and recreational goods............	131.2	120.5	105.8	96.1	89.8	87.2	84.3
Magazines, newspapers, books, and stationery............	66.7	89.2	93.3	100.3	101.9	104.8	106.9
Education............	31.9	56.7	79.5	104.7	114.6	119.1	123.1
Higher education............	28.8	54.7	78.3	105.2	115.7	120.6	125.1
Net foreign travel and expenditures abroad by U.S. residents:							
Foreign travel by U.S. residents............	56.7	70.6	88.6	105.2	112.5	112.7	113.2
Less: Expenditures in the United States by nonresidents............	60.7	78.9	90.0	103.4	111.8	113.3	115.5

[1] Consists of household purchases of goods and services from business, government, nonprofit institutions, and the rest of the world. [2] Consists of shoes and other footwear, and of repair and hire of footwear. [3] Consists of rent for space (see footnote 4) and rent for appliances, furnishings, and furniture. [4] Consists of rent for space and for heating and plumbing facilities, water heaters, lighting fixtures, kitchen cabinets, linoleum, storm windows and doors, window screens, and screen doors, but excludes rent for appliances and furniture and purchases of fuel and electricity. [5] Includes clocks, lamps, lighting fixtures, and other household decorative items; also includes repair of furniture, furnishings, and floor coverings. [6] Consists of major household appliances, small electric household appliances, and repair of household appliances. [7] Consists of dishes, flatware, and non-electric cookware and tableware. [8] Excludes drug preparations and related products dispensed by physicians, hospitals, and other medical services. [9] Consists of offices of physicians, health maintenance organization medical centers, and freestanding ambulatory surgical and emergency centers. [10] Consists of nonprofit hospitals, proprietary hospitals, and government hospitals. Consists of primary sales of these hospitals for personal consumption. [11] Includes railway transportation, taxicab services, school and employee services, limousine services, and airport bus fares.

Source: U.S. Bureau of Economic Analysis, National Income and Product Accounts Tables, "Table 2.5.4. Price Indexes for Personal Consumption Expenditures by Function," <http://www.bea.gov/itable/>, accessed August 2015.

Table 759. Chain-Type Price Indexes for Gross Domestic Product: 1990 to 2014

[2009 = 100. For explanation of "chain-type," see text, Section 13]

Component	1990	2000	2005	2010	2011	2012	2013	2014
Gross domestic product	**66.8**	**81.9**	**92.0**	**101.2**	**103.3**	**105.2**	**106.9**	**108.7**
Personal consumption expenditures	**67.4**	**83.1**	**92.3**	**101.7**	**104.1**	**106.1**	**107.6**	**109.1**
Goods	87.2	94.8	97.0	101.6	105.4	106.7	106.2	105.8
Durable goods	126.3	120.3	107.7	98.6	97.7	96.4	94.7	92.5
Nondurable goods	70.5	82.7	91.6	103.1	109.2	111.8	112.0	112.7
Services	58.5	77.5	89.9	101.7	103.5	105.8	108.3	110.8
Gross private domestic investment	**80.1**	**85.6**	**94.5**	**99.1**	**100.5**	**101.9**	**103.4**	**105.3**
Fixed investment	79.3	85.5	94.5	99.2	100.5	102.1	103.7	105.7
Nonresidential	90.4	90.7	93.8	99.1	100.5	102.2	103.0	104.0
Structures	44.2	59.6	82.1	98.8	101.9	105.9	107.5	109.1
Equipment	124.6	105.4	98.6	98.0	98.9	99.9	100.3	101.0
Intellectual property products	86.5	96.1	96.0	100.5	101.9	103.0	103.7	104.6
Residential	57.1	76.1	98.1	99.6	100.4	101.3	106.5	112.9
Net exports of goods and services:								
Exports	87.5	87.2	94.7	104.3	111.0	112.0	112.1	112.3
Goods	94.7	88.4	95.5	105.0	113.0	113.5	112.9	112.1
Services	71.3	84.5	93.2	102.6	106.5	108.6	110.5	112.6
Imports	88.1	84.8	93.8	105.8	113.9	114.7	113.8	113.6
Goods	93.1	86.0	94.6	106.7	116.2	116.9	115.6	115.0
Services	68.6	80.0	91.1	101.8	104.1	104.8	105.9	107.2
Government consumption expenditures and gross investment	**55.7**	**73.4**	**88.2**	**102.7**	**105.7**	**107.4**	**109.1**	**111.1**
Federal	60.8	77.3	91.4	102.6	105.4	106.5	107.6	109.3
National defense	60.9	76.5	91.4	102.4	105.3	106.5	107.1	108.6
Nondefense	60.3	78.8	91.5	103.1	105.7	106.6	108.3	110.4
State and local	52.8	71.2	86.3	102.7	105.9	108.0	110.1	112.3

Source: U.S. Bureau of Economic Analysis, National Income and Product Accounts Tables, "Table 1.1.4. Price Indexes for Gross Domestic Product," <http://www.bea.gov/itable/>, accessed August 2015.

Table 760. Import and Export Price Indexes by End-Use Category: 1990 to 2015

[As of June. Import indexes are weighted by the 2000 Tariff Schedule of the United States Annotated, a scheme for describing and reporting product composition and value of U.S. imports. Import prices are based on U.S. dollar prices paid by importer. Export indexes are weighted by 2000 export values according to the Schedule B classification system of the U.S. Census Bureau. Prices used in these indexes were collected from a sample of U.S. manufacturers of exports and are factory transaction prices, except as noted. Minus sign (-) indicates decrease]

Year	Index (2000 = 100)						Percent change [1]					
	Imports			Exports			Imports			Exports		
	Total	Petro-leum imports	Non–petro-leum imports	Total	Agri-cultural exports	Non–agri-cultural exports	Total	Petro-leum imports	Non–petro-leum imports	Total	Agri-cultural exports	Non–agri-cultural exports
1990	90.8	55.4	96.4	95.1	107.7	93.5	-0.8	-13.4	0.5	-0.1	-4.0	0.5
1991	93.4	63.2	98.3	96.1	104.3	95.3	2.9	14.1	2.0	1.1	-3.2	1.9
1992	94.8	66.0	99.5	96.5	104.0	95.8	1.5	4.4	1.2	0.4	-0.3	0.5
1993	95.0	60.4	100.5	96.9	100.3	96.7	0.2	-8.5	1.0	0.4	-3.6	0.9
1994	96.3	57.6	102.6	98.5	109.3	97.5	1.4	-4.6	2.1	1.7	9.0	0.8
1995	101.4	62.9	107.6	104.5	117.0	103.3	5.3	9.2	4.9	6.1	7.0	5.9
1996	100.7	66.4	106.2	105.4	140.8	101.7	-0.7	5.6	-1.3	0.9	20.3	-1.5
1997	98.8	62.5	104.3	103.2	120.5	101.5	-1.9	-5.9	-1.8	-2.1	-14.4	-0.2
1998	93.1	44.3	100.5	99.9	110.8	98.8	-5.8	-29.1	-3.6	-3.2	-8.0	-2.7
1999	92.9	54.5	98.8	98.2	101.1	97.9	-0.2	23.0	-1.7	-1.7	-8.8	-0.9
2000	100.2	101.9	99.9	100.1	100.5	100.0	7.9	87.0	1.1	1.9	-0.6	2.1
2001	97.6	89.4	98.9	99.4	100.9	99.3	-2.6	-12.3	-1.0	-0.7	0.4	-0.7
2002	94.1	85.3	96.2	98.0	100.7	97.8	-3.6	-4.6	-2.7	-1.4	-0.2	-1.5
2003	96.2	96.4	97.3	99.5	110.0	98.7	2.2	13.0	1.1	1.5	9.2	0.9
2004	101.7	129.7	99.7	103.4	127.4	101.5	5.7	34.5	2.5	3.9	15.8	2.8
2005	109.2	181.5	102.0	106.7	123.9	105.4	7.4	39.9	2.3	3.2	-2.7	3.8
2006	117.3	242.6	104.2	111.2	124.1	110.3	7.4	33.7	2.2	4.2	0.2	4.6
2007	120.0	245.6	107.1	116.0	146.7	113.8	2.3	1.2	2.8	4.3	18.2	3.2
2008	145.5	450.3	114.9	126.1	195.2	121.2	21.3	83.3	7.3	8.7	33.1	6.5
2009	120.0	241.5	107.4	117.8	169.7	114.1	-17.5	-46.4	-6.5	-6.6	-13.1	-5.9
2010	125.2	267.4	110.7	122.2	165.3	119.1	4.3	10.7	3.1	3.7	-2.6	4.4
2011	142.2	397.8	116.4	134.5	217.2	128.6	13.6	48.8	5.1	10.1	31.4	8.0
2012	138.7	357.2	116.3	131.7	204.5	126.5	-2.5	-10.2	-0.1	-2.1	-5.8	-1.6
2013	138.8	364.9	115.7	132.8	224.2	126.2	0.1	2.2	-0.5	0.8	9.6	-0.2
2014	140.5	387.9	115.8	133.0	221.4	126.6	1.2	6.3	0.1	0.2	-1.2	0.3
2015	126.5	227.7	112.8	125.4	184.5	120.9	-10.0	-41.3	-2.6	-5.7	-16.7	-4.5

[1] Percent change from immediate prior year.

Source: U.S. Bureau of Labor Statistics, U.S. Import and Export Price Indexes, "History Tables: Complete Historical Index Information," <http://www.bls.gov/mxp/>, accessed July 2015.

Table 761. Export Price Indexes—Selected Commodities: 2000 to 2015

[2000 = 100. As of June. Indexes are weighted by 2000 export values according to the Schedule B commodity classification system of the U.S. Census Bureau. Prices used in these indexes were collected from a sample of U.S. manufacturers of exports and are factory transaction prices, see source]

Commodity	2000 [1]	2005	2010	2011	2012	2013	2014	2015
All commodities	**100.1**	**106.7**	**122.2**	**134.5**	**131.7**	**132.8**	**133.0**	**125.4**
Live animals and animal products	102.2	130.9	172.2	194.2	202.8	214.9	242.3	195.4
Fish	99.1	114.2	152.3	187.4	207.9	183.4	200.2	206.8
Vegetable products	100.0	130.3	177.5	256.3	241.3	271.7	252.6	206.9
Fruit and nuts	94.8	126.5	131.0	131.5	139.4	155.0	173.9	177.6
Cereals	100.0	118.1	171.4	319.1	264.3	307.0	246.5	194.4
Wheat and meslin	99.4	130.0	151.6	290.0	229.9	272.2	243.0	198.3
Corn (maize)	101.0	111.8	174.3	348.0	281.0	324.4	227.9	181.1
Oilseeds	102.8	136.2	196.2	268.0	267.6	299.5	293.9	204.7
Prepared foodstuffs, beverages, and tobacco	100.0	110.3	139.3	151.9	157.8	167.1	169.5	152.3
Mineral products	97.8	182.3	247.9	336.3	295.2	292.8	295.9	213.4
Fuels	97.4	172.8	239.2	333.4	290.7	289.7	292.7	206.9
Petroleum oils	97.4	184.8	231.5	346.3	317.7	326.6	333.6	230.7
Chemicals and related products	100.3	115.3	144.5	153.9	154.1	153.9	149.7	143.7
Plastics and rubber products	101.5	118.4	136.8	151.4	148.1	149.9	150.5	143.5
Hides, skins, and leather products	95.7	113.0	121.2	137.4	130.1	146.6	159.2	139.9
Woodpulp and paper products	101.6	101.9	117.6	127.2	117.8	122.7	123.8	123.7
Textiles	100.2	100.8	115.7	148.7	124.9	131.4	132.5	122.3
Stone and glass products	100.7	103.5	115.9	115.9	117.7	118.2	120.2	122.4
Gems and precious metals	98.1	106.5	211.0	278.0	277.6	253.9	245.7	233.8
Base metals	100.5	131.8	160.4	187.1	172.9	165.8	163.2	152.8
Iron and steel	101.7	164.0	194.3	244.5	209.3	186.7	191.8	165.5
Copper	98.7	143.1	217.0	278.2	242.4	236.9	225.0	190.8
Aluminum	98.4	113.2	117.8	139.1	124.9	122.5	119.8	115.5
Machinery	99.9	94.9	95.5	96.4	97.2	97.2	97.6	97.0
Nonelectrical machinery	100.0	100.5	106.8	108.7	110.6	111.5	112.9	113.5
Computer equipment	99.9	76.6	53.1	50.4	51.5	49.3	48.4	43.8
Electrical machinery	99.8	88.6	83.2	83.0	82.7	81.7	81.0	79.2
Transportation equipment	100.0	108.8	121.4	123.6	126.7	127.9	130.0	130.9
Motor vehicles and their parts	100.0	103.2	108.5	109.7	113.0	113.7	115.2	115.1
Instruments	100.0	101.3	106.2	105.3	106.0	107.1	107.7	107.6
Miscellaneous manufactured articles	100.4	100.6	108.1	110.0	110.4	110.5	110.5	111.3

[1] June 2000 may not equal 100 because indexes were reweighted to an "average" trade value in 2000.

Source: U.S. Bureau of Labor Statistics, U.S. Import and Export Price Indexes, "History Tables: Complete Historical Index Information," <http://www.bls.gov/mxp/>, accessed July 2015.

Table 762. Import Price Indexes—Selected Commodities: 2000 to 2015

[2000 = 100. As of June. Indexes are weighted by the 2000 Tariff Schedule of the United States Annotated, a scheme for describing and reporting product composition and value of U.S. imports. Import prices are based on U.S. dollar prices paid by importer]

Commodity	2000 [1]	2005	2010	2011	2012	2013	2014	2015
All commodities	**100.2**	**109.2**	**125.2**	**142.2**	**138.7**	**138.8**	**140.5**	**126.5**
Live animals and animal products	99.9	112.7	143.0	167.6	164.8	179.3	195.8	186.1
Meat	100.5	138.7	183.2	209.7	214.1	219.8	251.6	239.4
Fish	100.2	88.3	107.1	126.8	118.6	134.6	140.3	127.4
Vegetable products	97.1	116.9	169.5	210.6	221.0	204.2	196.4	201.9
Vegetables	93.9	136.8	326.2	299.8	322.1	347.5	354.0	459.9
Fruit and nuts	96.9	89.7	106.8	124.6	117.7	110.4	101.1	95.8
Prepared foodstuffs, beverages and tobacco	100.0	114.0	141.2	156.8	157.4	156.6	161.6	160.7
Mineral products	101.3	178.1	248.5	360.0	320.2	332.2	353.1	208.9
Fuels	101.3	177.5	244.9	356.1	316.4	329.0	350.3	206.2
Chemicals and related products	99.8	111.3	139.3	146.9	150.8	150.1	152.6	148.3
Organic chemicals	100.6	109.6	133.8	136.7	138.0	135.2	135.1	123.5
Pharmaceutical products	99.8	111.0	117.9	111.9	117.4	125.0	134.1	136.7
Plastics and rubber products	99.9	113.5	136.7	151.7	152.7	152.1	148.0	142.0
Hides, skins, and leather products	100.2	104.0	114.5	120.9	126.4	125.4	127.7	128.1
Wood products	100.5	124.2	134.3	129.6	140.7	150.6	146.4	138.5
Woodpulp and paper products	100.0	102.3	112.5	115.8	114.0	113.6	113.7	111.9
Textiles	99.7	100.4	103.1	112.9	115.3	114.1	114.1	114.6
Footwear	99.6	100.3	106.1	111.8	117.7	120.4	121.4	122.0
Stone and glass products	99.5	105.4	123.8	128.8	132.1	132.3	133.2	133.2
Gems and precious metals	99.3	98.3	161.5	198.0	199.1	186.2	180.2	171.3
Gold	98.3	150.7	430.5	539.4	566.3	504.8	446.7	424.4
Platinum	(NA)	125.7	292.6	336.5	260.2	272.7	283.8	249.7
Base metals	101.5	132.1	180.2	200.2	188.7	181.3	183.0	168.4
Iron and steel	104.1	170.6	238.8	263.5	241.7	215.6	222.4	181.6
Articles of iron and steel	100.6	122.7	149.9	160.1	160.8	155.4	154.0	148.5
Copper	97.2	142.7	313.8	392.5	349.4	339.8	327.2	303.3
Aluminum	97.9	113.2	132.8	156.9	137.7	137.6	140.8	131.5
Machinery	100.2	89.7	86.5	85.8	85.7	85.0	84.6	82.6
Nonelectrical machinery	99.8	90.1	87.9	88.6	89.8	89.7	89.7	87.8
Electrical machinery	100.5	89.4	85.2	83.1	81.8	80.6	79.8	77.7
Transportation equipment	100.0	104.4	109.7	114.7	115.8	116.2	116.1	114.6
Motor vehicles and their parts	100.1	103.8	108.8	113.9	114.8	115.0	114.9	113.2
Instruments	99.8	100.1	100.8	105.0	104.3	103.8	104.9	103.8
Miscellaneous manufactured articles	99.7	99.4	106.5	110.1	112.8	113.0	113.5	112.8
Furniture	99.5	103.4	109.4	113.5	116.5	116.8	117.7	117.3

NA Not available. [1] June 2000 may not equal 100 because indexes were reweighted to an "average" trade value in 2000.

Source: U.S. Bureau of Labor Statistics, U.S. Import and Export Price Indexes, "History Tables: Complete Historical Index Information," <http://www.bls.gov/mxp/>, accessed July 2015.

Section 15
Business Enterprise

This section relates to the place and behavior of the business firm and to business initiative in the American economy. It includes data on the number, type, and size of businesses; financial data of domestic and multinational U.S. corporations; business investments, expenditures, and profits; and sales and inventories.

The principal sources of these data are the *Survey of Current Business*, published online by the Bureau of Economic Analysis (BEA); the Web site of the Board of Governors of the Federal Reserve System at <http://www.federalreserve.gov/econresdata/statisticsdata.htm>; the annual *Statistics of Income (SOI)* reports of the Internal Revenue Service (IRS); and the U.S. Census Bureau's Economic Census, *County Business Patterns, Quarterly Financial Report for Manufacturing, Mining, and Trade Corporations (QFR), Survey of Business Owners*, and *Annual Capital Expenditures Survey*. See also BEA Interactive Tables <http://www.bea.gov/itable/index.cfm>.

Business firms—A firm is generally defined as a business organization or entity consisting of one or more domestic establishment locations under common ownership or control. The terms firm, business, company, and enterprise are used interchangeably throughout this section. A firm doing business in more than one industry is classified by industry according to the major activity of the firm as a whole.

The IRS concept of a business firm relates primarily to the legal entity used for tax reporting purposes. A sole proprietorship is an unincorporated business owned by one person and may include large enterprises with many employees and hired managers and part-time operators. A partnership is an unincorporated business owned by two or more persons, each of whom has a financial interest in the business. A corporation is a business that is legally incorporated under state laws. While many corporations file consolidated tax returns, most corporate tax returns represent individual corporations, some of which are affiliated through common ownership or control with other corporations filing separate returns.

Economic Census—The Economic Census is the major source of facts about the structure and functioning of the nation's economy. It provides essential information for government, business, industry, and the general public. It establishes benchmarks for economic indicators such as the gross domestic product estimates, production and price indexes, business sales, and other statistical series that measure short-term changes in economic conditions. The Census Bureau takes the Economic Census every 5 years, covering years ending in "2" and "7."

The Economic Census is collected on an establishment basis. A company operating at more than one location is required to file a separate report for each store, factory, shop, or other location. Companies engaged in distinctly different lines of activity at one location are requested to submit separate reports, if the business records permit such a separation, and if the activities are substantial in size. Each establishment is assigned a separate industry classification based on its primary activity and not that of its parent company. Establishments responding to the establishment survey are classified into industries on the basis of their principal product or activity (determined by self-reporting, annual sales volume, or products manufactured by a plant). The statistics issued by industry in the 2012 Economic Census are classified primarily on the 2012 North American Industry Classification System (NAICS).

Data from the 2012 Economic Census are released through the Census Bureau's American FactFinder® service on the Census Bureau Web site at <factfinder.census.gov>. More detailed information about the scope, coverage, methodology, classification system, data items, and publications for the Economic Censuses and related surveys is available at <http://www.census.gov/econ/census/>.

Survey of Business Owners—The Survey of Business Owners (SBO) provides statistics that describe the composition of U.S. businesses by gender, ethnicity, race and veteran status. Data from SBO are published in a series of releases: *American Indian- and Alaska Native-Owned Firms, Asian-Owned Firms, Black-Owned Firms, Hispanic-Owned Firms, Native Hawaiian- and Other Pacific Islander-Owned Firms, Women-Owned Firms, Veteran-Owned Firms, Characteristics of Business Owners*, and *Company Summary*. Data are presented by industry classifications, geographic area, and size of firm (employment and receipts). Each owner had the option of selecting more than one race and therefore is included in each race selected. For more information, see <http://www.census.gov/econ/sbo/>.

North American Industry Classification System (NAICS)—NAICS is the standard used by federal statistical agencies in classifying business establishments for the purpose of collecting, analyzing, and publishing statistical data related to the U.S. business economy. NAICS was developed under the auspices of the Office of Management and Budget (OMB), and adopted in 1997 to replace the Standard Industrial Classification (SIC) system. The official *2012 U.S. NAICS Manual* includes definitions for each industry, background information, tables showing changes between 2007 and 2012, and a comprehensive index. For more information, see <http://www.census.gov/eos/www/naics/>.

Noticeable changes were made to six of the twenty NAICS sectors during the 2012 revision of NAICS. Those sectors are 22 (utilities), 23 (construction), 31-33 (manufacturing), 42 (wholesale trade), 44-45 (retail trade) and 72 (accommodation and food services).

Quarterly Financial Report—The Quarterly Financial Report (QFR) program publishes quarterly aggregate statistics on the financial conditions of U.S. corporations. The QFR requests companies to report estimates from their statements of income and retained earnings, and balance sheets. The statistical data are classified and aggregated by type of industry and asset size. The QFR sample includes corporations that have a plurality of business activity in manufacturing industries with domestic assets of

$250,000 and above, and mining, wholesale, retail, and selected service industries with assets of $50 million and above. The data are available quarterly in the *Quarterly Financial Report for Manufacturing, Mining, and Trade Corporations* at <http://www.census.gov/econ/qfr/index.html>.

Multinational enterprises—BEA collects financial and operating data on U.S. multinational enterprises. These data provide a picture of the overall activities of foreign affiliates and U.S. parent enterprises, using a variety of indicators of their financial structure and operations. The data on foreign affiliates cover the entire operations of the affiliate, irrespective of the percentage of U.S. ownership. These data cover items such as sales, value added, employment and compensation of employees, capital expenditures, exports and imports, and research and development expenditures. Separate tabulations are available for all affiliates and for affiliates that are majority-owned by their U.S. parent(s). More information is available at <http://www.bea.gov/international/index.htm#omc>.

Statistical reliability—For a discussion of statistical collection, estimation, and sampling procedures and measures of reliability applicable to data from the Census Bureau and the Internal Revenue Service, see Appendix III.

Table 763. Number of Tax Returns, Receipts, and Net Income by Type of Business: 1990 to 2012

[14,783 represents 14,783,000. Covers active enterprises only. Nonfarm sole proprietorship and partnership data are for tax year shown which covers returns processed by the IRS during the following calendar year. Corporation data are for tax year shown which covers (a) corporate returns with accounting periods for the calendar year ending December of year shown and (b) those returns with accounting periods for the noncalendar year ending between July of year shown and June of the following year. Figures are estimates based on sample of unaudited tax returns; see Appendix III]

Item	Number of returns (1,000)			Business receipts [2] (bil. dol.)			Net income (less loss) [3] (bil. dol.)		
	Nonfarm proprietor-ships [1]	Partner-ships	Corpora-tions	Nonfarm proprietor-ships [1]	Partner-ships	Corpora-tions	Nonfarm proprietor-ships [1]	Partner-ships	Corpora-tions
1990...........	14,783	1,554	3,717	731	483	9,860	141	17	383
1991...........	15,181	1,515	3,803	713	483	9,966	142	21	361
1992...........	15,495	1,485	3,869	737	515	10,360	154	43	414
1993...........	15,848	1,468	3,965	757	561	10,866	156	67	510
1994...........	16,154	1,494	4,342	791	656	11,884	167	82	595
1995...........	16,424	1,581	4,474	807	761	12,786	169	107	736
1996...........	16,955	1,654	4,631	843	916	13,659	177	145	839
1997...........	17,176	1,759	4,710	870	1,142	14,461	187	168	957
1998...........	17,409	1,855	4,849	918	1,357	15,010	202	187	895
1999...........	17,576	1,937	4,936	969	1,616	16,314	208	228	985
2000...........	17,905	2,058	5,045	1,021	2,062	17,637	215	269	987
2001...........	18,338	2,132	5,136	1,017	2,278	17,504	217	276	649
2002...........	18,926	2,242	5,267	1,030	2,414	17,297	221	271	597
2003...........	19,710	2,375	5,401	1,050	2,546	18,264	230	301	822
2004...........	20,591	2,547	5,558	1,140	2,819	19,976	248	385	1,170
2005...........	21,468	2,764	5,671	1,223	3,280	21,800	270	546	2,027
2006...........	22,075	2,947	5,841	1,278	3,571	23,310	278	667	2,024
2007...........	23,123	3,096	5,869	1,324	3,847	24,217	281	683	1,950
2008...........	22,614	3,146	5,847	1,317	4,344	24,718	265	458	1,061
2009...........	22,660	3,169	5,825	1,178	3,562	21,585	245	410	971
2010...........	23,004	3,248	5,814	1,196	3,946	23,058	268	594	1,422
2011...........	23,427	3,285	5,823	1,266	4,455	25,198	283	581	1,406
2012...........	23,554	3,389	5,841	1,302	4,690	26,029	305	778	1,872

[1] Number of returns represents returns with nonfarm business net income or deficit. [2] Excludes investment income for S corporations; for definition, see footnote 1, Table 772. [3] Net income (less loss) is defined differently by form of organization, basically as follows: (a) Proprietorships: Total taxable receipts less total business deductions, including cost of sales and operations, depletion, and certain capital expensing, excluding charitable contributions and owners' salaries; (b) Partnerships: Total taxable receipts (including investment income except capital gains) less deductions, including cost of sales and operations and certain payments to partners, excluding charitable contributions, oil and gas depletion, and certain capital expensing; and (c) Corporations: Includes "Total net income (less deficit)" from S Corporations and is more comprehensive than what Statistics of Income generally publishes; net income is before income tax.

Source: U.S. Internal Revenue Service, "SOI Tax Stats - Integrated Business Data," <http://www.irs.gov/uac/SOI-Tax-Stats-Integrated-Business-Data>, accessed May 2015.

Table 764. Number of Business Tax Returns by Size of Receipts: 2000 to 2012

[In thousands (5,045 represents 5,045,000). Covers active enterprises only. Figures are estimates based on sample of unaudited tax returns; see Appendix III]

Size-class of receipts	2000	2004	2005	2006	2007	2008	2009	2010	2011	2012
Corporations, total...........	**5,045**	**5,558**	**5,671**	**5,841**	**5,869**	**5,847**	**5,825**	**5,814**	**5,823**	**5,841**
Under $25,000 [1]................	1,220	1,317	1,300	1,363	1,391	1,444	1,501	1,484	1,449	1,409
$25,000 to $49,999...............	305	334	340	341	356	368	399	385	379	396
$50,000 to $99,999...............	477	545	544	554	570	556	576	592	582	556
$100,000 to $499,999.............	1,515	1,703	1,755	1,780	1,766	1,734	1,714	1,731	1,743	1,761
$500,000 to $999,999.............	582	635	644	668	657	663	641	618	624	646
$1,000,000 or more...............	946	1,023	1,088	1,135	1,129	1,084	994	1,005	1,047	1,073
Partnerships, total.............	**2,058**	**2,547**	**2,764**	**2,947**	**3,096**	**3,146**	**3,169**	**3,248**	**3,285**	**3,389**
Under $25,000 [1]................	1,105	1,373	1,465	1,568	1,650	1,705	1,746	1,788	1,774	1,815
$25,000 to $49,999...............	183	193	218	240	233	230	241	238	254	272
$50,000 to $99,999...............	187	226	233	245	275	266	279	289	289	293
$100,000 to $499,999.............	353	436	489	498	530	537	511	531	556	565
$500,000 to $999,999.............	92	121	131	149	149	147	148	151	150	164
$1,000,000 or more...............	137	198	227	248	261	260	244	252	262	280
Nonfarm proprietorships, total.............	**17,905**	**20,591**	**21,468**	**22,075**	**23,123**	**22,614**	**22,660**	**23,004**	**23,427**	**23,554**
Under $25,000 [1]................	11,997	13,916	14,456	14,867	15,752	15,532	15,951	16,258	16,468	16,450
$25,000 to $49,999...............	2,247	2,536	2,587	2,721	2,796	2,729	2,722	2,652	2,740	2,838
$50,000 to $99,999...............	1,645	1,792	1,981	1,983	2,027	1,936	1,825	1,892	1,869	1,899
$100,000 to $499,999.............	1,733	2,020	2,091	2,139	2,173	2,051	1,834	1,869	2,002	1,999
$500,000 to $999,999.............	190	218	235	236	242	229	211	219	222	234
$1,000,000 or more...............	92	109	117	128	132	137	116	114	126	134

[1] Includes firms with no receipts.

Source: U.S. Internal Revenue Service, "Statistics of Income Bulletin, Historical Table 12," <http://www.irs.gov/uac/SOI-Tax-Stats-Historical-Table-12>, accessed July 2015.

Table 765. Number of Tax Returns, Receipts, and Net Income by Type of Business and Industry: 2012

[Tax returns in thousands (23,554 represents 23,554,000); receipts and income in billions of dollars (1,302 represents $1,302,000,000,000). Covers active enterprises only. Nonfarm sole proprietorship and partnership data are for tax year shown which covers returns processed by the IRS during 2013. Corporation data are for tax year shown which covers (a) corporate returns with accounting periods for the calendar year ending December 2012 and (b) those returns with accounting periods for the noncalendar year ending between July 2012 and June 2013. Figures are estimates based on sample of unaudited tax returns; see Appendix III. Based on the North American Industry Classification System (NAICS), 2012; see text, this section. Minus sign (-) indicates net loss]

Industry	2012 NAICS code	Number of returns (1,000)			Business receipts [1] (bil. dol.)			Net income (less loss) [2] (bil. dol.)		
		Non-farm propri-etor-ships	Part-ner-ships	Corpo-rations	Non-farm propri-etor-ships	Part-ner-ships	Corpo-rations	Non-farm propri-etor-ships	Part-ner-ships	Corpo-rations
Total..	(X)	23,554	3,389	5,841	1,302	4,690	26,029	305	778	1,774
Agriculture, forestry, fishing, and hunting [3]...........................	11	300	151	137	21	32	181	1	8	10
Mining..	21	111	32	39	14	163	456	1	59	18
Utilities......................................	22	15	3	6	1	160	506	(Z)	-5	-26
Construction...............................	23	2,649	161	687	189	209	1,195	34	9	36
Special trade contractors...............	238	2,088	66	431	131	59	546	26	3	23
Manufacturing.............................	31–33	364	67	247	27	1,086	7,983	3	62	514
Wholesale and retail trade [4].............	(X)	2,660	222	958	245	1,199	8,141	17	29	261
Wholesale trade........................	42	361	64	388	54	741	4,372	5	19	136
Retail trade [5]...........................	44–45	2,299	159	570	191	458	3,769	11	10	124
Motor vehicle and parts dealers........	441	128	17	82	38	147	778	1	3	15
Food and beverage stores..............	445	107	22	97	28	84	608	1	1	13
Gasoline stations......................	447	16	9	46	24	95	361	(Z)	1	3
Transportation and warehousing..........	48–49	1,133	42	211	93	183	818	13	7	30
Information [5]...............................	51	354	38	119	12	321	969	3	50	74
Broadcasting (except Internet)..........	515	95	4	6	4	59	101	1	8	10
Telecommunications...................	517	([6])	6	16	([6])	207	416	([6])	37	21
Finance and insurance...................	52	616	306	245	74	181	2,140	19	335	517
Real estate and rental and leasing.......	53	1,190	1,664	642	62	132	242	21	67	45
Professional, scientific, and technical services [5]......................	54	3,228	234	893	174	419	1,153	76	91	60
Legal services.........................	5411	354	34	125	40	146	107	17	54	13
Accounting, tax preparation, bookkeeping, and payroll services......	5412	383	34	85	15	73	52	7	17	6
Management, scientific, and technical consulting services......................	5416	872	60	226	47	78	213	26	11	18
Management of companies and enterprises...........................	55	(NA)	28	53	(NA)	15	181	(NA)	24	127
Administrative and support and waste management and remediation services....................	56	2,521	70	279	69	99	520	22	5	21
Educational services.....................	61	708	14	57	11	5	67	4	1	4
Health care and social assistance........	62	2,189	84	452	122	224	691	50	33	41
Arts, entertainment, and recreation.......	71	1,476	66	124	36	59	111	9	1	5
Accommodation and food services.......	72	442	124	303	52	174	468	3	1	28
Accommodation........................	721	60	32	33	6	68	87	(Z)	-1	9
Food services and drinking places......	722	382	92	270	46	106	381	2	2	19
Other services [5]...........................	81	3,116	82	388	95	28	208	27	2	9
Auto repair and maintenance............	8111	375	32	115	25	10	75	3	(Z)	2
Personal and laundry services..........	812	2,055	40	169	52	12	79	18	1	4
Religious, grantmaking, civic, professional, and similar organizations....................	813	264	[7] 2	46	4	[7] (Z)	9	2	[7] (Z)	(Z)
Unclassified...............................	(X)	483	(Z)	1	5	–	(Z)	2	–	(-Z)

– Represents zero. NA Not available. X Not applicable. Z Less than 500 or $500 million. [1] Excludes investment income for S corporations; for definition, see footnote 1, Table 772. [2] Net income (less loss) is defined differently by form of organization, basically as follows: (a) Proprietorships: Total taxable receipts less total business deductions, including cost of sales and operations, depletion, and certain capital expensing, excluding charitable contributions and owners' salaries; (b) Partnerships: Total taxable receipts (including investment income except capital gains) less deductions, including cost of sales and operations and certain payments to partners, excluding charitable contributions, oil and gas depletion, and certain capital expensing; and (c) Corporations: Total taxable receipts (including investment income, capital gains, and income from foreign subsidiaries deemed received for tax purposes, except for S corporations) less business deductions, including cost of sales and operations, depletion, certain capital expensing, and officers' compensation excluding S corporation charitable contributions and investment expenses; net income is before income tax. [3] For corporations, represents agricultural services only. [4] For corporations, includes trade business not identified as wholesale or retail. [5] Includes other industries, not shown separately. [6] Broadcasting includes telecommunications. [7] Estimate should be used with caution because of the small number of sample returns on which it is based.

Source: U.S. Internal Revenue Service, "SOI Tax Stats - Business Tax Statistics," <http://www.irs.gov/uac/SOI-Tax-Stats-Business-Tax-Statistics>, accessed May 2015.

Table 766. Nonfarm Sole Proprietorships—Selected Income and Deduction Items: 2000 to 2012

[In billions of dollars (1,021 represents $1,021,000,000,000), except as indicated. Data are for tax year shown which covers returns processed by the IRS during the following calendar year. All figures are estimates based on samples. Tax law changes have affected the comparability of the data over time; see Statistics of Income reports for a description. See Appendix III]

Item	2000	2005	2006	2007	2008	2009	2010	2011	2012
Number of returns (1,000)...........	17,905	21,468	22,075	23,123	22,614	22,660	23,004	23,427	23,554
Returns with net income (1,000)............	13,308	15,750	16,207	16,929	16,434	16,528	17,007	17,360	17,571
Business receipts............	1,021	1,223	1,278	1,324	1,317	1,178	1,196	1,266	1,302
Income from sales and operations............	1,008	1,205	1,259	1,304	1,296	1,159	1,176	1,246	1,281
Business deductions [1]............	806	953	1,001	1,044	1,054	935	929	984	998
Cost of sales and operations [1]............	387	397	410	423	435	366	367	394	390
Purchases............	269	253	260	264	281	239	240	256	251
Labor costs............	29	32	32	35	31	28	27	28	31
Materials and supplies............	43	56	60	62	57	45	45	49	50
Advertising............	10	14	15	16	15	14	13	13	14
Car and truck expenses............	46	71	75	82	85	75	73	83	86
Commissions............	12	15	16	15	13	12	12	13	14
Contract labor............	(NA)	28	35	37	35	32	34	38	42
Depreciation............	32	39	39	40	41	35	35	36	34
Insurance............	14	19	19	19	18	17	16	17	17
Interest paid [2]............	12	12	14	15	15	13	11	10	9
Legal and professional services............	7	10	10	11	11	10	10	11	11
Office expenses............	10	13	13	13	13	12	12	12	12
Rent paid [3]............	33	39	41	43	44	41	42	43	43
Repairs............	12	15	16	16	15	14	15	16	17
Salaries and wages (net)............	63	75	77	79	79	75	74	78	80
Supplies............	22	29	32	32	32	30	30	32	34
Taxes paid............	14	17	18	18	18	17	18	18	18
Travel............	8	11	12	13	13	11	12	13	13
Utilities............	19	23	24	25	25	24	24	27	28
Net income (less loss) [4]............	215	270	278	281	265	245	268	283	305
Net income [4]............	245	315	327	335	325	309	323	337	357
Constant (2005) Dollars [5]									
Business receipts............	1,152	1,223	1,238	1,246	1,213	1,075	1,077	1,117	1,128
Business deductions............	910	953	970	983	970	853	837	868	865
Net income (less loss)............	242	270	269	264	244	223	241	249	264
Net income............	277	315	317	315	299	282	291	297	310

NA Not available. [1] Includes other amounts not shown separately. [2] Interest paid includes "mortgage interest" and "other interest paid on business indebtedness." [3] Rent paid includes "Rent on machinery and equipment" and "Rent on other business property." [4] After adjustment for the passive loss carryover from prior years. Therefore, "business receipts" minus "total deductions" do not equal "net income." [5] Based on the overall implicit price deflator for gross domestic product.

Source: U.S. Internal Revenue Service, "SOI Tax Stats - Nonfarm Sole Proprietorship Statistics," <http://www.irs.gov/uac/SOI-Tax-Stats-Nonfarm-Sole-Proprietorship-Statistics>, accessed May 2015.

Table 767. Partnerships—Selected Income and Balance Sheet Items: 2000 to 2012

[In billions of dollars (6.694 represents $6.694,000,000,000), except as indicated. Covers active partnerships only. Data are for tax year shown which covers returns processed by the IRS during the following calendar year. All figures are estimates based on samples. See Appendix III]

Item	2000	2005	2006	2007	2008	2009	2010	2011	2012
Number of returns (1,000)............	2,058	2,764	2,947	3,096	3,146	3,169	3,248	3,285	3,389
Returns with net income (1,000)............	1,261	1,580	1,623	1,659	1,609	1,608	1,635	1,725	1,869
Number of partners (1,000)............	13,660	16,212	16,728	18,516	19,300	21,142	22,428	24,390	25,334
Assets [1, 2]............	6,694	13,734	17,146	20,386	19,260	18,798	19,820	20,574	22,015
Depreciable assets (net)............	1,487	2,176	2,490	2,865	3,254	3,181	3,263	3,337	3,570
Inventories, end of year............	150	315	446	339	431	277	277	285	304
Land............	359	607	731	820	885	892	913	922	957
Liabilities [1, 2]............	3,696	7,483	9,350	10,440	10,167	9,085	8,994	8,939	9,277
Accounts payable............	230	400	505	430	513	444	492	504	509
Short-term debt [3]............	252	373	456	565	582	432	481	394	326
Long-term debt [4]............	1,132	1,772	2,227	2,556	2,767	2,737	2,693	2,559	2,706
Nonrecourse loans............	639	914	1,103	1,210	1,283	1,282	1,225	1,213	1,212
Partners' capital accounts [2]............	2,999	6,251	7,796	9,946	9,092	9,713	10,826	11,636	12,738
Total receipts [1]............	2,405	3,863	4,301	4,727	5,169	4,265	4,721	5,212	5,557
Business receipts............	2,062	3,280	3,571	3,847	4,344	3,562	3,946	4,455	4,690
Deductions from a trade or business [1]............	2,136	3,317	3,634	4,043	4,711	3,749	4,026	4,532	4,689
Cost of goods sold/operations............	1,226	1,976	2,109	2,310	2,717	2,055	2,336	2,732	2,828
Salaries and wages............	201	293	332	373	403	390	405	436	463
Taxes paid............	31	47	53	56	63	62	63	69	73
Interest paid............	93	103	137	174	143	94	86	81	81
Depreciation............	59	71	79	86	130	125	130	172	137
Net income (less loss)............	269	546	667	683	458	410	594	581	778
Net income............	410	724	871	976	929	796	904	913	1,068

[1] Includes items not shown separately. [2] Assets, liabilities, and partners' capital accounts are understated because not all partnerships file complete balance sheets. [3] Mortgages, notes, and bonds payable in less than 1 year. [4] Mortgages, notes, and bonds payable in 1 year or more.

Source: U.S. Internal Revenue Service, "SOI Tax Stats - Partnership Statistics," <http://www.irs.gov/uac/SOI-Tax-Stats-Partnership-Statistics>, accessed May 2015.

Table 768. Partnerships—Selected Items by Industry: 2012

[In billions of dollars (22,015 represents $22,015,000,000,000), except as indicated. Covers active partnerships only. Data are for tax year shown which covers returns processed by the IRS during 2013. Figures are estimates based on samples. Based on the North American Industry Classification System (NAICS), 2012; see text, this section. Minus sign (-) indicates net loss]

Industry and year	2012 NAICS code	Number of partnerships (1,000) Total	Number of partnerships (1,000) With net income	Number of partnerships (1,000) With net loss	Total assets [1]	Business receipts	Total deduc- tions	Net income less loss	Net income	Net loss
Total [2].................................	(X)	**3,389**	**1,869**	**1,520**	**22,015**	**4,690**	**4,689**	**777.9**	**1,068.0**	**290.1**
Agriculture, forestry, fishing, and hunting..	11	151	74	77	206	32	40	8.3	15.2	6.9
Mining..	21	32	23	9	499	163	129	59.1	73.4	14.3
Utilities..	22	3	1	2	301	160	171	-4.7	7.8	12.5
Construction....................................	23	161	85	75	185	209	208	8.7	17.2	8.5
Manufacturing.................................	31–33	67	24	43	767	1,086	1,056	61.6	80.8	19.2
Wholesale trade.............................	42	64	37	27	230	741	734	18.9	25.4	6.6
Retail trade....................................	44–45	159	81	78	168	458	460	10.3	15.1	4.8
Transportation and warehousing........	48–49	42	19	23	436	183	188	7.3	16.6	9.3
Information.....................................	51	38	19	19	663	321	300	49.9	64.1	14.2
Finance and insurance....................	52	306	221	85	12,152	181	277	335.4	379.0	43.6
Real estate and rental and leasing.....	53	1,664	886	778	4,953	132	157	66.9	171.8	104.9
Professional, scientific, and technical services...........................	54	234	156	78	226	419	347	91.2	99.5	8.3
Management of companies and enterprises..................................	55	28	19	9	637	15	31	23.7	32.1	8.4
Administrative and support and waste management and remediation services..................	56	70	31	40	77	99	104	4.6	9.2	4.6
Educational services.......................	61	14	7	7	4	5	5	0.7	1.0	0.3
Health care and social assistance......	62	84	55	29	143	224	206	32.9	37.6	4.7
Arts, entertainment, and recreation.....	71	66	22	44	108	59	68	0.8	8.2	7.5
Accommodation and food services.....	72	124	57	66	239	174	178	0.9	11.3	10.4
Other services...............................	81	82	51	30	20	28	29	1.6	2.7	1.1

X Not applicable. [1] Total assets are understated because not all partnerships file complete balance sheets. [2] Includes businesses not allocable to individual industries.

Source: U.S. Internal Revenue Service, "SOI Tax Stats - Partnership Statistics," <http://www.irs.gov/uac/SOI-Tax-Stats-Partnership-Statistics-by-Sector-or-Industry>, accessed May 2015.

Table 769. Nonfinancial Noncorporate Business-Sector Balance Sheet: 2000 to 2014

[In billions of dollars (7,758 represents $7,758,000,000,000), except as noted. Represents year-end (4th quarter) outstandings]

Item	2000	2005	2008	2009	2010	2011	2012	2013	2014
Assets.................................	**7,758**	**12,593**	**13,273**	**11,975**	**12,550**	**13,278**	**14,267**	**15,433**	**16,109**
Nonfinancial assets.........................	6,286	9,996	9,579	8,398	8,822	9,364	10,051	11,139	11,581
Real estate [1]...............................	5,551	9,055	8,461	7,296	7,666	8,135	8,783	9,842	10,409
Residential.................................	3,290	5,817	4,749	4,273	4,411	4,600	4,976	5,542	5,822
Nonresidential.............................	2,261	3,239	3,712	3,023	3,255	3,535	3,807	4,301	4,587
Equipment [2]................................	453	574	700	696	709	741	763	785	743
Residential [3].............................	35	42	47	44	42	44	44	43	42
Nonresidential.............................	418	533	653	652	667	697	719	742	701
Intellectual property products [2].........	96	148	179	183	190	197	206	215	125
Inventories [2]...............................	185	218	240	223	257	291	298	297	304
Financial assets.............................	1,473	2,597	3,693	3,576	3,728	3,915	4,216	4,294	4,528
Checkable deposits and currency.......	181	374	519	534	532	553	612	615	649
Time and savings deposits................	248	324	358	353	356	362	372	383	410
Money market fund shares................	49	69	75	74	77	78	81	83	87
Credit market instruments [4].............	66	97	96	89	96	91	93	96	100
Treasury securities.......................	40	56	52	46	48	49	53	54	57
Mortgages..................................	23	36	39	38	42	36	34	35	37
Trade receivables...........................	342	431	523	496	533	594	599	616	648
Miscellaneous assets......................	587	1,302	2,122	2,029	2,134	2,237	2,459	2,501	2,634
Insurance receivables....................	77	99	112	102	132	120	136	109	116
Equity investment in GSEs [5]...........	3	4	6	6	7	7	7	8	9
Other...	506	1,198	2,004	1,921	1,996	2,110	2,316	2,385	2,509
Liabilities................................	**2,796**	**4,180**	**5,795**	**5,731**	**5,672**	**5,703**	**5,898**	**5,948**	**6,204**
Credit market instruments................	1,912	2,898	4,094	3,985	3,951	3,947	4,068	4,183	4,400
Depository institution loans n.e.c. [6]...	402	671	1,046	944	927	961	1,022	1,068	1,139
Other loans and advances................	129	135	177	172	171	171	181	187	196
Mortgages....................................	1,381	2,093	2,870	2,869	2,853	2,814	2,866	2,928	3,065
Trade payables..............................	267	335	381	398	428	483	496	513	538
Taxes payable...............................	65	87	106	100	99	100	107	111	117
Miscellaneous liabilities...................	549	858	1,211	1,243	1,189	1,168	1,220	1,134	1,141
Net worth................................	**4,962**	**8,412**	**7,477**	**6,244**	**6,878**	**7,575**	**8,369**	**9,485**	**9,905**
Debt/net worth (percent)...................	38.5	34.5	54.8	63.8	57.4	52.1	48.6	44.1	44.4

[1] At market value. [2] At replacement (current) cost. [3] Durable goods in rental properties. [4] Includes other items not shown separately. [5] GSEs = government-sponsored enterprises. Equity in the Farm Credit System. [6] Not elsewhere classified.

Source: Board of Governors of the Federal Reserve System, "Federal Reserve Statistical Release, Z.1, Financial Accounts of the United States," June 2015, <http://www.federalreserve.gov/releases/z1/>, accessed June 2015.

Table 770. Nonfinancial Corporate Business-Sector Balance Sheet: 2000 to 2014

[In billions of dollars (20,434 represents $20,434,000,000,000). Represents year-end (4th quarter) outstandings]

Item	2000	2005	2008	2009	2010	2011	2012	2013	2014
Assets	**20,434**	**26,068**	**29,515**	**27,184**	**28,958**	**30,545**	**31,979**	**34,917**	**37,028**
Nonfinancial assets	10,673	14,168	16,592	13,866	14,941	16,040	16,895	18,578	19,923
Real estate [1]	5,363	7,924	9,360	6,768	7,546	8,275	8,824	10,253	11,288
Equipment [2]	2,889	3,298	3,857	3,793	3,854	4,008	4,138	4,262	4,446
Intellectual property products [2]	1,081	1,322	1,564	1,601	1,669	1,747	1,839	1,917	1,997
Inventories [2]	1,340	1,624	1,810	1,705	1,873	2,010	2,094	2,147	2,192
Financial assets [3]	9,761	11,901	12,923	13,317	14,017	14,506	15,085	16,338	17,106
Checkable deposits and currency	226	268	84	155	234	264	218	304	369
Time and savings deposits	272	450	312	489	549	562	595	636	647
Money market fund shares	214	352	727	656	498	462	519	559	565
Credit market instruments	248	340	212	223	229	222	209	185	168
Mutual fund shares [1]	118	134	106	162	187	166	180	211	235
Trade receivables	1,939	2,108	2,086	2,055	2,157	2,241	2,293	2,570	2,679
U.S. direct investment abroad	1,352	2,206	3,011	3,245	3,403	3,759	4,081	4,370	4,594
Liabilities [3]	**9,632**	**11,182**	**13,224**	**12,904**	**13,227**	**13,878**	**14,695**	**15,471**	**16,177**
Credit market instruments	4,667	5,268	6,594	6,151	6,013	6,308	6,714	7,115	7,579
Commercial paper	278	90	131	58	83	116	130	145	182
Municipal securities [4]	154	227	415	452	485	494	509	518	518
Corporate bonds	2,275	2,670	2,981	3,197	3,376	3,538	3,862	4,142	4,406
Depository institution loans n.e.c. [5]	901	591	780	546	477	569	658	708	794
Other loans and advances	701	903	1,384	1,139	948	1,008	1,037	1,064	1,127
Mortgages	357	786	902	759	643	582	518	539	551
Trade payables	1,542	1,701	1,673	1,590	1,746	1,772	1,838	1,943	2,027
Foreign direct investment in U.S	1,180	1,549	2,050	1,986	2,129	2,231	2,409	2,610	2,712
Net worth (market value)	**10,802**	**14,887**	**16,291**	**14,280**	**15,731**	**16,667**	**17,284**	**19,445**	**20,851**
Debt/net worth (percent)	43.2	35.4	40.5	43.1	38.2	37.8	38.8	36.6	36.3

[1] At market value. [2] At replacement (current) cost. [3] Includes items not shown separately. [4] Industrial revenue bonds. Issued by state and local governments to finance private investment and secured in interest and principal by the industrial user of the funds. [5] Not elsewhere classified.

Source: Board of Governors of the Federal Reserve System, "Federal Reserve Statistical Release, Z.1, Financial Accounts of the United States," June 2015, <http://www.federalreserve.gov/releases/z1/>, accessed June 2015.

Table 771. Corporate Funds—Sources and Uses: 2000 to 2014

[In billions of dollars (451 represents $451,000,000,000)]

Item	2000	2005	2008	2009	2010	2011	2012	2013	2014
Profits before tax	451	1,005	880	752	1,039	1,009	1,245	1,299	1,515
− Taxes on corporate income	170	272	227	178	221	229	271	329	389
− Net dividends	251	171	474	351	375	441	521	537	559
+ Capital consumption allowance [1]	786	808	1,064	1,049	1,077	1,236	1,116	1,141	1,013
= U.S. internal funds, book	816	1,370	1,243	1,273	1,520	1,575	1,569	1,573	1,581
+ Foreign earnings retained abroad	103	−18	184	193	218	215	185	222	177
+ Inventory valuation adjustment (IVA)	−17	−32	−37	7	−41	−68	−9	3	(−Z)
− Net capital transfers	0	−16	−4	38	21	−6	−17	−6	−7
= Internal funds + IVA	902	1,335	1,393	1,434	1,677	1,729	1,761	1,805	1,764
Gross investment	1,108	1,171	412	1,569	1,381	931	999	1,595	1,438
Capital expenditures [2]	1,142	1,192	1,360	1,021	1,235	1,332	1,478	1,526	1,675
Fixed investment [3]	1,093	1,138	1,372	1,145	1,179	1,297	1,415	1,468	1,607
Inventory change + IVA	50	53	−30	−131	58	35	62	57	66
Net lending (+) or net borrowing (−)	−34	−21	−948	548	145	−401	−479	69	−236
Net acquisition of financial assets [2]	1,204	944	−609	300	633	493	506	1,071	677
Checkable deposits and currency	35	61	−59	71	80	30	−46	85	65
Time and savings deposits	35	50	−129	177	60	13	33	41	11
Credit market instruments [2]	26	42	−35	10	3	−7	−13	−24	−17
Municipal securities	7	(Z)	−3	1	−3	−2	1	−1	−9
Mutual fund shares	(Z)	1	−17	35	11	−13	−2	1	15
Trade receivables	282	278	−170	−31	106	84	52	277	109
U.S. direct investment abroad	138	25	263	270	303	404	316	317	330
Miscellaneous assets [2]	679	418	−615	−168	215	24	110	292	158
Insurance receivables	(Z)	21	11	−4	12	10	8	−7	8
Investment in finance company subsidiaries	65	64	−1	−9	27	8	3	15	14
Net increase in liabilities [2]	1,238	965	339	−249	488	894	985	1,001	913
Net funds raised in markets	240	−33	−53	−410	−322	−160	18	75	76
Net new equity issues	−118	−300	−316	−51	−251	−455	−345	−353	−388
Credit market instruments [2]	358	267	262	−359	−71	295	363	428	463
Commercial paper	48	−8	8	−73	25	33	14	14	38
Corporate bonds	151	−41	116	216	179	162	323	280	265
Depository institution loans n.e.c [4]	55	−27	64	−234	−87	92	108	50	86
Other loans and advances [5]	78	110	68	−161	−90	60	−34	54	63
Mortgages	25	191	−60	−144	−131	−61	−64	21	12
Trade payables	313	199	−225	−83	156	25	66	105	84
Foreign direct investment in U.S	249	99	190	105	157	193	170	207	80
Miscellaneous liabilities [2]	429	703	425	142	489	827	729	622	673
Claims of pension fund on sponsor	118	93	123	83	−21	−17	8	12	23

Z Less than $500 million. [1] Consumption of fixed capital plus capital consumption adjustment. [2] Includes other items not shown separately. [3] Nonresidential fixed investment plus residential fixed investment. [4] Not elsewhere classified. [5] Loans from rest of the world, U.S. government, and nonbank financial institutions.

Source: Board of Governors of the Federal Reserve System, "Federal Reserve Statistical Release, Z.1, Financial Accounts of the United States," June 2015, <http://www.federalreserve.gov/releases/z1/>, accessed June 2015.

Table 772. Corporations—Selected Financial Items: 2000 to 2012

[In billions of dollars (47,027 represents $47,027,000,000,000), except as noted. Covers active corporations only. Corporation data are for tax year shown which covers (a) corporate returns with accounting periods for the calendar year ending December of year shown and (b) those returns with accounting periods for the noncalendar year ending between July of year shown and June of the following year. All corporations are required to file returns except those specifically exempt. See source for changes in law affecting comparability of historical data. Based on samples; see Appendix III]

Item	2000	2005	2006	2007	2008	2009	2010	2011	2012
Number of returns (1,000)	5,045	5,671	5,841	5,869	5,847	5,825	5,814	5,823	5,841
Number with net income (1,000)	2,819	3,324	3,367	3,368	3,184	3,149	3,265	3,385	3,549
S Corporation returns [1](1,000)	2,860	3,684	3,873	3,990	4,050	4,095	4,128	4,159	4,205
Assets [2]	47,027	66,445	73,081	81,486	76,799	75,965	79,905	81,280	84,952
Cash	1,820	2,823	2,902	3,625	4,384	4,853	3,893	4,196	4,404
Notes and accounts receivable	8,754	11,962	13,611	15,315	13,855	12,544	12,718	13,089	13,016
Inventories	1,272	1,505	1,613	1,656	1,619	1,474	1,544	1,653	1,750
Investments in government obligations	1,236	1,613	1,714	1,785	2,193	2,501	2,730	2,859	3,002
Mortgage and real estate	2,822	4,777	5,232	5,177	5,450	4,847	7,914	7,615	7,579
Other investments	17,874	25,162	27,903	30,939	27,169	27,574	29,389	29,745	32,158
Depreciable assets	7,292	8,416	8,817	9,222	9,467	9,613	9,875	10,226	10,672
Depletable assets	191	310	382	497	587	629	661	757	855
Land	303	407	457	493	509	517	548	567	584
Liabilities [2]	47,027	66,445	73,081	81,486	76,799	75,965	79,905	81,280	84,952
Accounts payable	3,758	6,029	7,779	7,724	6,822	5,694	5,768	5,343	5,288
Short-term debt [3]	4,020	4,192	4,709	4,735	4,726	4,542	3,752	3,839	3,557
Long-term debt [4]	6,184	8,332	9,399	10,786	11,062	10,718	14,680	14,489	14,473
Net worth [5]	17,349	23,525	25,996	28,812	25,469	24,567	28,938	29,250	31,804
Capital stock	3,966	2,482	2,513	2,775	3,184	3,019	3,064	2,983	3,067
Paid-in or capital surplus	12,265	17,828	19,142	21,792	23,574	24,110	24,283	24,859	26,243
Retained earnings [6]	3,627	4,331	5,764	5,970	613	2,024	3,534	3,586	4,804
Receipts [2, 7]	20,606	25,505	27,402	28,763	28,590	24,773	26,199	28,336	29,404
Business receipts [7, 8]	17,637	21,800	23,310	24,217	24,718	21,585	23,058	25,198	26,029
Interest [9]	1,628	1,773	2,307	2,640	2,179	1,540	1,366	1,344	1,209
Rents and royalties	254	290	299	314	317	296	307	315	332
Deductions [2, 7]	19,692	23,613	25,502	26,974	27,687	23,944	24,944	27,093	27,713
Cost of goods sold [8]	11,135	13,816	14,800	15,513	16,080	13,286	14,502	16,180	16,579
Compensation of officers	401	445	474	479	467	428	435	454	479
Rent paid on business property	380	439	462	477	491	476	467	471	484
Taxes paid	390	473	497	509	469	473	493	519	546
Interest paid	1,272	1,287	1,787	2,085	1,659	1,070	888	860	814
Depreciation	614	531	564	599	759	712	728	874	709
Advertising	234	253	277	277	267	241	256	264	275
Net income (less loss) [7, 10]	928	1,949	1,933	1,837	984	919	1,356	1,323	1,774
Net income	1,337	2,235	2,240	2,253	1,807	1,615	1,836	1,829	2,175
Deficit	409	286	306	416	823	696	480	506	401
Income subject to tax	760	1,201	1,291	1,248	978	895	1,022	994	1,150
Income tax before credits [11]	266	419	453	437	342	313	358	349	403
Tax credits	62	107	100	106	114	108	135	128	135
Foreign tax credit	49	82	78	87	100	94	118	107	110
Income tax after credits [12]	204	312	353	331	229	205	223	221	268

[1] Represents certain small corporations with a limit on the number of shareholders, mostly individuals, electing to be taxed at the shareholder level. [2] Includes items not shown separately. [3] Payable in less than 1 year. [4] Payable in 1 year or more. [5] Net worth is the sum of "capital stock," "additional paid-in capital," "retained earnings, appropriated," "retained earnings, unappropriated," "adjustments to shareholders' equity," minus "cost of treasury stock." [6] Appropriated and unappropriated and "adjustments to shareholders' equity." [7] Receipts, deductions, and net income of S corporations are limited to those from trade or business. Those from investments are excluded. [8] Includes gross sales and cost of sales of securities, commodities, and real estate by exchanges, brokers, or dealers selling on their own accounts. Excludes investment income. [9] Includes tax-exempt interest in state and local government obligations. [10] Excludes regulated investment companies. [11] Consists of regular (and alternative tax) only. [12] Includes minimum tax, alternative minimum tax, adjustments for prior year credits, and other income-related taxes.

Source: U.S. Internal Revenue Service, "SOI Tax Stats - Corporation Complete Report," <http://www.irs.gov/uac/SOI-Tax-Stats-Corporation-Complete-Report>, accessed May 2015.

Table 773. Corporations by Receipt-Size Class and Industry: 2012

[Number of returns in thousands (5,841 represents 5,841,000); receipts and net income in billions of dollars (26,029 represents $26,029,000,000,000). Data are for tax year shown which covers (a) corporate returns with accounting periods for the calendar year ending December 2012 and (b) those returns with accounting periods for the noncalendar year ending between July 2012 and June 2013. Covers active enterprises only. Figures are estimates based on a sample of unaudited tax returns; see Appendix III. Numbers in parentheses represent North American Industry Classification System (NAICS) 2012 codes; see text, this section]

Industry	Total	Receipt-size class				
		Under $1 mil. [1]	$1 to $4.9 mil.	$5 to $9.9 mil.	$10 to $49.9 mil.	$50 mil. or more
Total: [2]						
Number of returns	**5,841**	**4,768**	**781**	**130**	**126**	**35**
Business receipts [3]	**26,029**	**949**	**1,667**	**882**	**2,434**	**20,097**
Net income (less loss)	**1,774**	**62**	**81**	**41**	**126**	**1,465**
Agriculture, forestry, fishing, and hunting (11):						
Returns	137	115	18	2	1	(Z)
Business receipts	181	19	39	16	28	78
Mining (21):						
Returns	39	30	6	2	1	(Z)
Business receipts	456	5	14	11	26	400
Utilities (22):						
Returns	6	5	1	(Z)	(Z)	(Z)
Business receipts	506	1	1	1	3	500
Construction (23):						
Returns	687	552	101	16	15	2
Business receipts	1,195	125	220	113	291	446
Manufacturing (31–33):						
Returns	247	149	56	16	19	7
Business receipts	7,983	37	130	111	399	7,307
Wholesale and retail trade (42, 44–45):						
Returns	958	646	208	44	47	13
Business receipts	8,141	168	476	311	972	6,214
Transportation and warehousing (48–49):						
Returns	211	167	31	7	6	1
Business receipts	818	34	65	48	100	571
Information (51):						
Returns	119	102	11	2	3	1
Business receipts	969	17	26	14	57	855
Finance and insurance (52):						
Returns	245	209	22	4	6	3
Business receipts [3]	2,140	34	33	16	46	2,012
Real estate and rental and leasing (53):						
Returns	642	619	20	1	1	(Z)
Business receipts	242	49	44	10	29	110
Professional, scientific, and technical services (54):						
Returns	893	778	91	11	10	2
Business receipts	1,153	136	192	78	195	552
Management of companies and enterprises (55):						
Returns	53	45	3	2	2	1
Business receipts [3]	181	(Z)	1	2	8	169
Administrative and support and waste management and remediation services (56):						
Returns	279	234	35	5	4	1
Business receipts	520	46	77	32	78	286
Educational services (61):						
Returns	57	51	4	1	(Z)	(Z)
Business receipts	67	8	10	5	8	36
Health care and social assistance (62):						
Returns	452	358	78	9	6	1
Business receipts	691	104	151	59	111	267
Arts, entertainment, and recreation (71):						
Returns	124	110	11	2	1	(Z)
Business receipts	111	18	23	15	13	41
Accommodation and food services (72):						
Returns	303	244	52	4	3	(Z)
Business receipts	468	78	101	24	48	217
Other services (81):						
Returns	388	352	33	2	1	(Z)
Business receipts	208	71	64	14	22	36

Z Less than 500 returns or $500 million in receipts. [1] Includes businesses without receipts. [2] Includes businesses not allocable to individual industries. [3] Size of total receipts was used instead of size of business receipts to classify data for "Finance and insurance" and "Management of companies and enterprises."

Source: U.S. Internal Revenue Service, "SOI Tax Stats - Corporation Complete Report," <http://www.irs.gov/uac/SOI-Tax-Stats-Corporation-Complete-Report>, accessed May 2015.

Table 774. Corporations by Asset-Size Class and Industry: 2012

[In billions of dollars (208 represents $208,000,000,000), except number of returns. Data are for tax year shown which covers (a)corporate returns with accounting periods for the calendar year ending December 2012 and (b) those returns with accounting periods for the noncalendar year ending between July 2012 and June 2013. Covers active corporations only. Excludes corporations not allocable by industry. Numbers in parentheses represent North American Industry Classification System (NAICS) 2012 codes; see text, this section]

Industry	Total	Asset-size class					
		Under $10 mil. [1]	$10 to $24.9 mil.	$25 to $49.9 mil.	$50 to $99.9 mil.	$100 to $249.9 mil.	$250 mil. and over
Agriculture, forestry, fishing, and hunting (11):							
Returns..........	137,299	135,894	852	298	135	75	44
Total receipts..........	208	127	17	10	10	15	29
Mining (21):							
Returns..........	38,915	36,989	853	376	220	182	295
Total receipts..........	505	48	11	9	10	16	411
Utilities (22):							
Returns..........	6,385	5,890	151	71	46	50	179
Total receipts..........	534	9	2	3	3	7	510
Construction (23):							
Returns..........	687,132	680,208	4,669	1,265	541	276	173
Total receipts..........	1,212	669	136	78	65	65	200
Manufacturing (31–33):							
Returns..........	247,231	231,387	7,546	3,139	1,839	1,424	1,896
Total receipts..........	8,513	567	224	182	196	299	7,044
Wholesale and retail trade (42, 44–45):							
Returns..........	958,094	937,446	12,780	3,913	1,846	1,098	1,011
Total receipts..........	8,306	1,964	654	412	358	427	4,491
Transportation and warehousing (48–49):							
Returns..........	211,276	208,953	1,256	446	242	179	201
Total receipts..........	844	239	41	28	28	36	472
Information (51):							
Returns..........	119,324	116,555	1,203	537	343	271	415
Total receipts..........	1,147	97	21	17	17	29	965
Finance and insurance (52):							
Returns..........	244,835	223,656	4,522	2,960	2,645	3,339	7,711
Total receipts..........	3,615	158	22	22	34	62	3,318
Real estate and rental and leasing (53):							
Returns..........	642,055	633,308	4,927	1,590	916	655	660
Total receipts..........	373	128	16	10	14	19	186
Professional, scientific, and technical services (54):							
Returns..........	892,576	887,203	2,981	990	607	410	387
Total receipts..........	1,195	580	74	47	47	59	387
Management of companies and enterprises (55):							
Returns..........	52,779	44,818	1,756	1,118	1,276	1,821	1,991
Total receipts..........	786	13	3	3	6	17	744
Administrative and support and waste management and remediation services (56):							
Returns..........	279,392	277,815	791	314	187	118	167
Total receipts..........	534	249	28	23	22	22	191
Educational services (61):							
Returns..........	56,523	56,199	159	65	38	38	25
Total receipts..........	68	30	3	3	3	6	23
Health care and social assistance (62):							
Returns..........	451,959	450,606	688	251	172	117	124
Total receipts..........	724	442	24	17	19	27	195
Arts, entertainment, and recreation (71):							
Returns..........	123,552	122,766	431	168	79	47	62
Total receipts..........	118	65	6	3	3	5	35
Accommodation and food services (72):							
Returns..........	302,724	301,144	957	263	128	105	128
Total receipts..........	505	241	18	12	11	23	200
Other services (81):							
Returns..........	388,264	387,625	414	112	54	28	32
Total receipts..........	216	170	9	6	4	4	22

[1] Includes returns with zero assets.

Source: U.S. Internal Revenue Service, "SOI Tax Stats - Corporation Complete Report," <http://www.irs.gov/uac/SOI-Tax-Stats-Corporation-Complete-Report>, accessed May 2015.

Table 775. Economic Census Summary (NAICS 2007 Basis): 2007 and 2012

[23 represents 23,000. Preliminary. Covers establishments with payroll. Data are based on the 2007 and 2012 Economic Censuses which are subject to nonsampling error. Data for the construction sector are also subject to sampling errors. For details on survey methodology and nonsampling and sampling errors, see Appendix III]

Kind of business	2007 NAICS code [1]	Establish- ments (1,000)		Sales, receipts, or shipments (bil. dol.)		Annual payroll (bil. dol.)		Paid employees [2] (1,000)	
		2007	2012	2007	2012	2007	2012	2007	2012
Mining, quarrying, and oil and gas extraction....	21	23	29	414	555	41	61	730	904
Oil & gas extraction.............	211	6	8	255	333	10	15	150	192
Mining (except oil & gas)............	212	6	6	86	93	12	14	211	208
Support activities for mining........	213	10	14	73	129	19	32	369	504
Utilities..........	22	17	18	584	522	52	59	637	655
Construction..........	23	729	(S)	1,732	(S)	331	(S)	7,316	(S)
Manufacturing..........	31–33	333	297	5,319	5,756	614	594	13,396	11,269
Wholesale trade..........	42	435	419	6,516	7,189	336	369	6,227	6,069
Merchant wholesalers, durable goods.........	423	255	244	2,898	2,964	207	222	3,619	3,483
Merchant wholesalers, nondurable goods......	424	135	131	2,991	3,601	116	132	2,320	2,285
Wholesale electronic markets and agents and brokers..........	425	45	45	627	625	13	15	289	300
Retail trade..........	44–45	1,128	1,063	3,918	4,228	363	371	15,515	14,738
Motor vehicle & parts dealers...........	441	127	116	891	871	73	70	1,914	1,709
Furniture & home furnishings stores...........	442	65	51	108	90	15	12	557	423
Electronics & appliance stores...........	443	51	48	109	105	11	10	486	428
Bldg. material & garden equipment & supplies dealers..........	444	91	78	318	279	38	34	1,331	1,145
Food & beverage stores...........	445	146	146	539	620	55	60	2,827	2,857
Health & personal care stores...........	446	88	92	234	275	28	32	1,068	1,013
Gasoline stations..........	447	119	115	450	556	15	16	891	862
Clothing & clothing accessories stores..........	448	156	147	216	233	27	28	1,644	1,659
Sporting goods, hobby, musical instrument, and book stores..........	451	57	48	81	79	9	9	619	531
General merchandise stores..........	452	46	49	577	641	54	58	2,763	2,777
Miscellaneous store retailers..........	453	122	106	104	98	14	14	792	715
Nonstore retailers..........	454	59	66	290	380	23	27	621	619
Transportation & warehousing [3]..........	48-49	220	213	640	744	173	182	4,454	4,307
Information..........	51	142	135	1,072	1,232	229	264	3,497	3,206
Publishing industries (except Internet)..........	511	31	27	282	259	81	80	1,093	865
Motion picture & sound recording industries....	512	24	25	95	95	18	16	336	306
Broadcasting (except Internet)..........	515	10	10	100	121	18	21	295	282
Telecommunications..........	517	52	49	491	563	75	74	1,251	1,095
Data processing, hosting, and related services..........	518	17	14	67	101	26	38	394	446
Other information services..........	519	7	10	37	92	10	34	128	212
Finance & insurance [4]..........	52	502	472	3,669	3,532	502	523	6,608	6,217
Real estate & rental & leasing [4]..........	53	384	349	485	491	85	88	2,188	1,980
Professional, scientific, & technical services.....	54	847	854	1,251	1,544	502	582	7,870	8,143
Management of companies & enterprises........	55	51	(S)	104	(S)	250	(S)	2,664	(S)
Admin/support waste management/remediation services..........	56	395	385	631	725	301	346	10,251	10,218
Administrative & support services..........	561	374	362	556	639	285	327	9,865	9,839
Waste management & remediation services....	562	22	24	75	86	17	18	386	379
Educational services..........	61	61	68	45	57	14	18	540	670
Health care and social assistance..........	62	785	831	1,668	2,051	663	804	16,792	18,587
Ambulatory health care services..........	621	548	583	668	843	275	344	5,703	6,574
Hospitals..........	622	7	7	703	860	265	316	5,529	5,772
Nursing & residential care facilities..........	623	76	80	169	205	75	86	3,071	3,375
Social assistance..........	624	154	161	128	143	48	58	2,489	2,866
Arts, entertainment, & recreation..........	71	125	124	189	201	58	64	2,061	2,092
Performing arts, spectator sports, & related industries..........	711	44	46	78	85	28	31	438	438
Museums, historical sites, & like institutions....	712	7	7	13	14	4	4	130	137
Amusement, gambling, & recreation industries..........	713	74	71	98	103	27	28	1,494	1,517
Accommodation & food services..........	72	634	661	614	710	171	197	11,601	12,028
Accommodation..........	721	63	64	180	196	46	51	1,971	1,954
Food services & drinking places..........	722	572	597	433	514	124	146	9,630	10,074
Other services (except public administration)....	81	540	528	405	432	99	108	3,479	3,456
Repair & maintenance..........	811	222	210	138	148	40	41	1,261	1,200
Personal and laundry services..........	812	210	212	82	88	27	29	1,338	1,354
Religious/grantmaking/prof/like organizations...	813	108	107	185	196	32	38	880	901

S Estimates did not meet publication standards. [1] Based on North American Industry Classification System, 2007; see text, this section. [2] For pay period including March 12. [3] For detailed industries, see Table 1075. [4] For detailed industries, see Table 1176.

Source: U.S. Census Bureau, "2012 Economic Census of the United States, Table EC1200CADV2 - All sectors: Core Business Statistics Series: Advance Comparative Statistics for the U.S. (2007 NAICS Basis): 2012 and 2007," <http://factfinder2.census.gov/faces/tableservices/ jsf/pages/productview.xhtml?pid=ECN_2012_US_00CADV2&prodType=table>, accessed April 2014.

Table 776. Nonemployer Establishments and Receipts by Industry: 2000 to 2013

[16,530 represents 16,530,000. Includes only firms subject to federal income tax. Nonemployers are businesses with no paid employees. Data originate chiefly from administrative records of the Internal Revenue Service; see Appendix III. Data for 2000 based on the North American Industry Classification System (NAICS), 1997. Data for 2010 based on NAICS 2007; data for 2013 based on NAICS 2012. See text, this section]

Kind of business	NAICS code	Establishments (1,000)			Receipts (mil. dol.)		
		2000	2010	2013	2000	2010	2013
All industries..........	(X)	16,530	22,111	23,006	709,379	950,814	1,052,025
Agriculture, forestry, fishing and hunting..........	11	223	237	240	9,196	10,115	10,937
Mining, quarrying, and oil and gas extraction..........	21	86	106	107	5,227	6,923	7,699
Utilities..........	22	14	17	19	504	698	879
Construction..........	23	2,014	2,424	2,368	107,538	120,151	132,282
Manufacturing..........	31–33	285	318	343	13,022	14,572	16,247
Wholesale trade..........	42	388	393	406	31,684	34,082	36,815
Retail trade..........	44–45	1,743	1,822	1,907	73,810	75,720	82,476
Transportation & warehousing..........	48–49	747	1,021	1,102	37,824	60,746	72,488
Information..........	51	238	311	327	7,620	10,739	11,945
Finance & insurance..........	52	692	717	706	49,058	50,626	51,506
Real estate & rental & leasing..........	53	1,696	2,343	2,448	133,398	209,549	237,172
Professional, scientific, & technical services..........	54	2,420	3,121	3,236	90,272	130,613	143,067
Admin/support waste mgt/remediation services..........	56	1,032	1,937	2,033	23,754	39,111	42,969
Educational services..........	61	283	567	617	3,736	7,703	8,687
Health care & social assistance..........	62	1,317	1,935	1,960	36,550	57,686	59,903
Arts, entertainment, & recreation..........	71	782	1,154	1,257	17,713	26,756	30,892
Accommodation & food services..........	72	218	329	346	13,418	14,355	15,306
Other services (except public administration)..........	81	2,350	3,358	3,584	55,056	80,669	90,754

X Not applicable.

Source: U.S. Census Bureau, Nonemployer Statistics, "Geographic Area Series: Nonemployer Statistics for the US, States, Metropolitan Areas, and Counties," <http://factfinder.census.gov>, accessed June 2015. See also <http://www.census.gov/econ/nonemployer/>.

Table 777. Establishments, Employees, and Payroll by Employment-Size Class: 1990 to 2013

[In units as noted (6,176 represents 6,176,000). Excludes most government employees, railroad employees, and self-employed persons. Employees are for the week including March 12. Covers establishments with payroll. An establishment is a single physical location where business is conducted or where services or industrial operations are performed. For statement on methodology, see Appendix III]

Employment-size class	Unit	1990	2000	2005	2009	2010	2011	2012	2013
Establishments, total..........	1,000	6,176	7,070	7,500	7,433	7,397	7,354	7,432	7,488
Under 20 employees..........	1,000	5,354	6,069	6,468	6,413	6,408	6,352	6,407	6,440
20 to 99 employees..........	1,000	684	826	856	852	824	835	854	873
100 to 499 employees..........	1,000	122	157	157	151	148	149	153	156
500 to 999 employees..........	1,000	10	12	12	11	11	11	11	12
1,000 or more employees..........	1,000	6	7	7	7	7	7	7	7
Employees, total..........	1,000	93,476	114,065	116,317	114,510	111,970	113,426	115,938	118,266
Under 20 employees..........	1,000	24,373	27,569	28,874	29,099	28,958	28,677	29,060	29,128
20 to 99 employees..........	1,000	27,414	33,147	34,302	33,895	32,730	33,275	33,995	34,799
100 to 499 employees..........	1,000	22,926	29,736	29,591	28,249	27,718	28,128	28,930	29,545
500 to 999 employees..........	1,000	6,551	8,291	8,053	7,770	7,331	7,608	7,847	8,063
1,000 or more employees..........	1,000	12,212	15,322	15,497	15,496	15,233	15,738	16,106	16,732
Annual payroll, total..........	Bil. dol.	2,104	3,879	4,483	4,856	4,941	5,165	5,414	5,622
Under 20 employees..........	Bil. dol.	485	818	970	1,037	1,057	1,081	1,121	1,142
20 to 99 employees..........	Bil. dol.	547	1,006	1,177	1,267	1,281	1,331	1,391	1,435
100 to 499 employees..........	Bil. dol.	518	1,031	1,176	1,253	1,280	1,341	1,409	1,469
500 to 999 employees..........	Bil. dol.	174	336	376	414	410	437	464	486
1,000 or more employees..........	Bil. dol.	381	690	784	885	913	976	1,029	1,090

Source: U.S. Census Bureau, County Business Patterns, "Geographic Area Series: County Business Patterns by Employment Size Class," <http://factfinder.census.gov>, accessed May 2015. See also <http://www.census.gov/econ/cbp/>.

Table 778. Establishments, Employees, and Payroll by Employment-Size Class and Industry: 2000 to 2013

[Establishments and employees in thousands (7,070.0 represents 7,070,000); payroll in billions of dollars (3,879,000,000,000). See headnote, Table 777. Data for 2000 based on the North American Industry Classification System (NAICS), 1997; 2010 data based on NAICS 2007; and 2013 data based on NAICS 2012. Svcs = services. See text, this section]

Industry	NAICS code	2000, total	2010, total	2013 Total	2013 Under 20 employees	2013 20 to 99 employees	2013 100 to 499 employees	2013 500 to 999 or employees	2013 1,000 more employees
Establishments, total [1]	(X)	7,070.0	7,396.6	7,488.4	6,439.9	873.3	156.3	11.8	7.1
Forestry, fishing & hunting, & agriculture support services	113–115	26.1	21.7	22.1	20.7	1.3	0.2	(Z)	(Z)
Mining, quarrying, and oil and gas extraction	21	23.7	27.1	28.7	22.7	4.7	1.2	0.1	0.1
Utilities	22	17.3	17.6	18.0	12.6	4.1	1.1	0.1	0.1
Construction	23	709.6	682.7	658.5	605.0	47.4	5.6	0.3	0.1
Manufacturing	31–33	354.5	300.0	292.1	203.8	64.3	21.3	2.0	0.8
Wholesale trade	42	446.2	414.6	419.6	358.4	52.9	7.7	0.5	0.2
Retail trade	44–45	1,113.6	1,068.0	1,063.6	912.4	123.9	27.0	0.3	(Z)
Transportation and warehousing	48–49	190.0	208.5	215.5	179.8	28.2	6.6	0.7	0.3
Information	51	133.6	135.4	135.6	109.0	20.8	5.0	0.6	0.2
Finance and insurance	52	423.7	473.5	472.2	432.7	31.7	6.3	0.9	0.6
Real estate and rental and leasing	53	300.2	347.3	357.5	342.5	13.4	1.5	0.1	(Z)
Professional, scientific, and technical services	54	722.7	851.5	869.4	803.6	55.2	9.4	0.7	0.5
Management of companies and enterprises	55	47.4	50.9	52.9	35.0	12.2	4.6	0.7	0.4
Admin/support waste mgt/remediation svcs	56	351.5	381.8	393.4	331.9	44.6	14.2	1.7	1.0
Educational services	61	68.0	90.1	98.1	75.3	18.2	3.7	0.5	0.4
Health care and social assistance	62	658.6	812.9	843.6	709.0	106.2	24.5	1.9	2.0
Arts, entertainment, and recreation	71	103.8	123.2	127.0	106.5	16.8	3.3	0.2	0.1
Accommodation and food services	72	542.4	644.0	673.8	479.7	184.1	9.4	0.4	0.2
Other services [2]	81	723.3	725.5	734.4	687.2	43.3	3.6	0.2	0.1
Unclassified establishments	99	99.0	20.5	12.1	12.1	(Z)	–	–	–
Employees, total [1]	(X)	114,065	111,970	118,266	29,128	34,799	29,545	8,063	16,732
Forestry, fishing & hunting, & agriculture support services	113–115	184	156	154	71	49	28	(NA)	6
Mining, quarrying, and oil and gas extraction	21	456	582	732	106	195	243	82	106
Utilities	22	655	638	639	68	179	219	92	79
Construction	23	6,573	5,389	5,470	2,152	1,821	1,029	191	277
Manufacturing	31–33	16,474	10,863	11,276	1,149	2,827	4,256	1,339	1,706
Wholesale trade	42	6,112	5,599	5,909	1,727	2,067	1,439	328	347
Retail trade	44–45	14,841	14,497	15,023	4,988	4,889	4,907	170	70
Transportation and warehousing	48–49	3,790	4,012	4,287	739	1,170	1,277	462	639
Information	51	3,546	3,124	3,266	493	867	996	409	501
Finance and insurance	52	5,963	5,929	6,064	1,844	1,224	1,296	627	1,073
Real estate and rental and leasing	53	1,942	1,946	1,972	1,084	505	275	54	54
Professional, scientific, and technical services	54	6,816	7,822	8,275	2,670	2,171	1,810	501	1,123
Management of companies and enterprises	55	2,874	2,833	3,099	(NA)	545	968	480	917
Admin/support waste mgt/remediation svcs	56	9,138	8,977	10,185	1,265	1,938	2,862	1,142	2,979
Educational services	61	2,532	3,274	3,513	366	774	694	318	1,360
Health care and social assistance	62	14,109	17,788	18,599	3,752	4,278	4,538	1,334	4,697
Arts, entertainment, and recreation	71	1,741	2,004	2,112	389	713	605	163	241
Accommodation and food services	72	9,881	11,312	12,395	3,191	7,009	1,491	264	439
Other services [2]	81	5,293	5,204	5,283	2,873	1,576	612	105	117
Unclassified establishments	99	144	(NA)	(NA)	(NA)	(Z)	–	–	–
Annual payroll, total [1]	(X)	3,879	4,941	5,622	1,142	1,435	1,469	486	1,090
Forestry, fishing & hunting, & agriculture support services	113–115	5	5	6	3	2	1	(D)	(Z)
Mining, quarrying, and oil and gas extraction	21	22	46	65	7	16	22	8	11
Utilities	22	41	55	60	5	15	21	10	9
Construction	23	240	261	294	94	104	67	12	17
Manufacturing	31–33	644	550	612	47	135	226	79	125
Wholesale trade	42	270	339	386	95	124	99	28	40
Retail trade	44–45	303	359	387	121	128	129	6	4
Transportation and warehousing	48–49	126	167	194	31	51	55	21	36
Information	51	209	224	273	32	57	86	38	60
Finance and insurance	52	347	472	538	112	119	129	59	120
Real estate and rental and leasing	53	59	80	92	45	26	15	3	3
Professional, scientific, and technical services	54	362	543	628	158	170	161	45	93
Management of companies and enterprises	55	211	282	326	20	51	103	50	102
Admin/support waste mgt/remediation svcs	56	210	304	366	51	72	90	33	120
Educational services	61	62	110	124	9	24	26	9	56
Health care and social assistance	62	431	753	832	168	168	162	64	269
Arts, entertainment, and recreation	71	43	62	68	16	16	21	8	6
Accommodation and food services	72	126	186	216	52	109	33	8	14
Other services [2]	81	110	140	153	74	47	23	4	5
Unclassified establishments	99	4	(Z)	(Z)	(Z)	(Z)	–	–	–

– Represents zero. D Data withheld to avoid disclosure. NA Not available. X Not applicable. Z Less than 50 establishments, 500 employees, or $500 million. [1] Totals for 2000 include auxiliaries. Beginning 2010, cases previously classified under NAICS code 95 (auxiliaries) are coded in the operating NAICS sector of the establishment. [2] Except public administration.

Source: U.S. Census Bureau, County Business Patterns, "Geographic Area Series: County Business Patterns by Employment Size Class," <http://factfinder.census.gov>, accessed May 2015. See also <http://www.census.gov/econ/cbp/>.

Table 779. Employer Firms, Employment, and Annual Payroll by Employment Size of Firm and Industry: 2011

[5,684 represents 5,684,000. A firm is an aggregation of all establishments owned by a parent company (within a geographic location and/or industry) with some annual payroll. A firm may be a single location or it can include multiple locations. Employment is measured in March and payroll is annual leading to some firms with zero employment. Numbers in parentheses represent North American Industry Classification System codes, 2007; see text, this section]

Industry and data type	Unit	Total	All industries—employment size of firm						
			0 to 4	5 to 9	10 to 19	20 to 99	100 to 499	Less than 500	500 or more
Total [1]:									
Firms..........	1,000	5,684	3,532	979	593	481	81	5,667	18
Employment..........	1,000	113,426	5,858	6,432	7,961	18,880	15,867	54,998	58,428
Annual payroll..........	Bil. dol	5,165	230	218	284	746	691	2,169	2,996
Construction (23):									
Firms..........	1,000	645	447	97	55	40	5	644	1
Employment..........	1,000	5,191	686	632	742	1,506	778	4,343	848
Annual payroll..........	Bil. dol	265	26	25	33	79	46	209	56
Manufacturing (31–33):									
Firms..........	1,000	255	107	47	39	47	12	251	4
Employment..........	1,000	10,984	199	315	526	1,904	2,028	4,973	6,011
Annual payroll..........	Bil. dol	575	8	11	21	85	97	222	353
Wholesale trade (42):									
Firms..........	1,000	309	178	52	36	33	7	306	3
Employment..........	1,000	5,626	302	344	477	1,233	977	3,333	2,293
Annual payroll..........	Bil. dol	357	15	17	25	67	57	181	176
Retail trade (44–45):									
Firms..........	1,000	654	395	133	70	47	7	652	2
Employment..........	1,000	14,699	738	875	928	1,739	1,063	5,344	9,355
Annual payroll..........	Bil. dol	371	18	20	24	56	36	155	216
Transportation & warehousing (48–49):									
Firms..........	1,000	165	106	24	16	14	3	163	2
Employment..........	1,000	4,106	159	155	208	521	470	1,512	2,594
Annual payroll..........	Bil. dol	176	6	5	7	20	19	58	118
Information (51):									
Firms..........	1,000	69	42	10	7	7	2	68	1
Employment..........	1,000	3,121	62	66	97	288	310	822	2,299
Annual payroll..........	Bil. dol	234	5	3	5	18	22	52	182
Finance & insurance (52):									
Firms..........	1,000	234	169	32	14	13	4	232	2
Employment..........	1,000	5,887	297	205	182	549	683	1,916	3,970
Annual payroll..........	Bil. dol	494	14	11	13	42	54	134	359
Professional, scientific and technical services (54):									
Firms..........	1,000	766	566	98	54	38	7	763	3
Employment..........	1,000	7,930	842	641	723	1,412	1,064	4,683	3,247
Annual payroll..........	Bil. dol	568	45	33	42	100	82	302	266
Management of companies and enterprises (55):									
Firms..........	1,000	27	3	1	1	6	9	20	7
Employment..........	1,000	2,922	4	4	7	71	289	374	2,548
Annual payroll..........	Bil. dol	299	1	(Z)	1	5	21	28	271
Admin/support waste mgt/ remediation services (56):									
Firms..........	1,000	321	208	47	29	26	8	318	3
Employment..........	1,000	9,390	312	307	386	1,059	1,356	3,421	5,969
Annual payroll..........	Bil. dol	326	12	10	13	37	41	113	213
Educational services (61):									
Firms..........	1,000	81	40	12	10	14	3	79	1
Employment..........	1,000	3,386	62	83	142	568	580	1,436	1,950
Annual payroll..........	Bil. dol	115	2	2	3	16	20	43	72
Health care and social assistance (62):									
Firms..........	1,000	634	323	145	83	62	17	629	4
Employment..........	1,000	18,059	600	958	1,098	2,470	3,275	8,402	9,657
Annual payroll..........	Bil. dol	780	31	39	46	98	109	323	457
Accommodation and food services (72):									
Firms..........	1,000	486	202	97	90	87	8	484	2
Employment..........	1,000	11,556	338	647	1,232	3,178	1,515	6,910	4,647
Annual payroll..........	Bil. dol	194	8	8	17	49	24	106	88
Other services (except public administration) (81):									
Firms..........	1,000	661	423	132	62	38	4	660	1
Employment..........	1,000	5,182	793	856	820	1,380	585	4,434	748
Annual payroll..........	Bil. dol	144	19	20	21	38	20	118	26

Z Less than $500 million. [1] Includes other industries, not shown separately.

Source: U.S. Small Business Administration, Office of Advocacy, Firm Size Data, "Statistics of U.S. Businesses," <http://www.sba.gov/advocacy/849/12162>, accessed May 2014.

Table 780. Employer Firms, Employment, and Payroll by Employment Size of Firm and State: 2010 and 2011

[5,735 represents 5,735,000. A firm is an aggregation of all establishments owned by a parent company (within a state) with some annual payroll. A firm may be a single location or it can include multiple locations. Employment is measured in March and payroll is annual leading to some firms with zero employment]

| State | Employer firms (1,000) | | | | | Employment, 2011 (1,000) | | | Annual payroll, 2011 (bil. dol.) | | |
| | 2010 | | 2011 | | | | | | | | |
	Total	Less than 20 employ-ees	Total	Less than 20 employ-ees	Less than 500 employ-ees	Total	Less than 20 employ-ees	Less than 500 employ-ees	Total	Less than 20 employ-ees	Less than 500 employ-ees
U.S.	5,735	5,160	5,684	5,104	5,667	113,426	20,251	54,998	5,164.9	732.8	2,169.4
AL	76	64	74	63	72	1,573	277	757	59.2	8.6	26.0
AK	16	14	16	14	16	255	56	134	13.4	2.6	6.3
AZ	102	88	101	87	98	2,109	331	928	86.5	11.5	33.4
AR	51	44	50	43	49	981	180	483	35.3	5.2	14.7
CA	690	616	690	615	684	12,698	2,386	6,332	663.6	99.4	280.9
CO	126	111	125	110	122	1,972	387	962	92.7	14.4	38.8
CT	73	62	72	61	69	1,443	257	710	82.1	11.4	34.2
DE	20	16	19	16	18	360	62	168	17.6	2.4	7.0
DC	17	12	17	12	16	478	56	224	32.9	3.7	13.9
FL	401	367	400	365	396	6,733	1,228	2,879	265.5	42.3	104.8
GA	170	149	168	146	164	3,328	555	1,479	141.5	18.9	54.1
HI	25	22	25	21	24	486	89	257	18.4	3.1	9.0
ID	37	32	36	31	35	483	117	272	16.9	3.4	8.2
IL	254	221	252	219	247	5,038	837	2,382	245.1	32.8	102.0
IN	111	95	109	93	106	2,441	398	1,157	94.7	12.3	39.6
IA	63	54	63	54	61	1,264	223	637	46.6	6.5	21.3
KS	59	50	58	49	56	1,113	203	589	43.7	6.4	20.3
KY	70	59	68	58	66	1,463	250	690	54.4	7.4	22.5
LA	81	69	81	68	78	1,617	301	876	65.8	10.0	31.8
ME	34	30	33	29	32	480	108	281	17.8	3.4	9.4
MD	108	93	107	91	104	2,104	375	1,079	101.3	14.9	47.1
MA	137	119	137	118	133	2,961	479	1,369	165.2	21.0	65.8
MI	174	153	172	150	169	3,379	620	1,724	145.8	21.7	66.1
MN	118	102	117	100	114	2,394	389	1,174	110.8	13.5	44.4
MS	46	39	45	38	43	888	168	432	29.6	4.7	13.0
MO	118	102	115	99	112	2,298	394	1,098	92.6	12.2	37.7
MT	31	28	31	28	30	336	102	226	11.3	2.9	7.0
NE	42	36	42	35	40	798	142	386	30.0	4.2	12.9
NV	47	40	47	39	45	1,001	150	411	38.7	5.8	15.4
NH	31	26	31	26	29	554	108	283	24.4	4.1	11.5
NJ	194	171	192	169	189	3,378	648	1,689	183.5	26.7	77.0
NM	36	30	35	29	34	598	123	328	22.0	3.8	10.8
NY	445	401	446	402	442	7,370	1,447	3,761	435.0	60.7	181.5
NC	169	147	166	144	162	3,285	582	1,531	131.6	18.4	51.8
ND	18	15	19	16	18	306	64	182	12.3	2.1	6.4
OH	190	163	188	160	184	4,433	706	2,075	182.1	23.2	74.2
OK	72	62	71	61	69	1,262	252	676	49.4	8.0	23.1
OR	88	77	87	76	85	1,342	303	750	56.1	9.4	26.2
PA	231	200	229	197	225	5,078	847	2,430	222.3	28.9	91.9
RI	25	21	24	20	23	406	81	222	17.3	3.0	8.5
SC	79	68	77	66	75	1,521	275	719	54.4	8.1	22.7
SD	22	19	21	18	21	327	75	198	11.2	2.2	6.1
TN	98	83	96	81	93	2,301	356	1,018	91.8	11.7	37.3
TX	394	343	396	343	390	8,988	1,442	4,120	414.1	54.1	164.0
UT	58	50	57	50	56	1,029	182	486	39.9	5.8	17.2
VT	19	16	18	16	18	264	62	157	9.6	2.0	5.6
VA	149	129	147	127	144	3,029	521	1,432	145.3	19.0	60.7
WA	144	128	142	125	139	2,355	488	1,222	118.6	17.3	49.4
WV	30	25	29	24	28	568	109	294	20.7	3.0	9.2
WI	110	94	109	92	106	2,354	400	1,200	95.5	12.8	42.0
WY	18	15	18	15	17	208	60	131	9.1	2.1	4.9

Source: U.S. Small Business Administration, Office of Advocacy, Research and Statistics, Firm Size Data, "Statistics of U.S. Businesses," <http://www.sba.gov/advocacy/849/12162>, accessed May 2014.

Table 781. Employer Firms, Establishments, Employment, and Annual Payroll by Firm Size: 1990 to 2011

[In thousands except as noted (5,074 represents 5,074,000). Firms are an aggregation of all establishments owned by a parent company with some annual payroll. Establishments are locations with active payroll in any quarter. This table illustrates the changing importance of enterprise sizes over time, not job growth, as enterprises can grow or decline and change enterprise size cells over time]

Item	Total	All industries—employment size of firm						
		0 to 4 [1]	5 to 9	10 to 19	20 to 99	100 to 499	Less than 500	500 or more
Firms:								
1990	5,074	3,021	952	563	454	70	5,060	14
2000	5,653	3,397	1,021	617	516	84	5,635	17
2005	5,984	3,678	1,050	630	521	87	5,966	17
2007	6,050	3,705	1,060	645	532	89	6,031	18
2008	5,930	3,618	1,044	633	526	90	5,912	18
2009	5,767	3,559	1,001	611	496	83	5,750	18
2010	5,735	3,575	968	617	475	82	5,717	17
2011	5,684	3,532	979	593	481	81	5,667	18
Establishments:								
1990	6,176	3,032	971	600	590	255	5,448	728
2000	7,070	3,406	1,035	652	674	312	6,080	990
2005	7,500	3,684	1,063	662	679	332	6,421	1,079
2007	7,705	3,711	1,074	682	723	356	6,546	1,159
2008	7,601	3,625	1,057	667	705	360	6,414	1,187
2009	7,433	3,565	1,015	646	673	354	6,253	1,180
2010	7,397	3,583	982	653	648	354	6,220	1,176
2011	7,354	3,540	993	627	652	350	6,162	1,192
Employment:								
1990	93,469	5,117	6,252	7,543	17,710	13,545	50,167	43,302
2000	114,065	5,593	6,709	8,286	20,277	16,260	57,124	56,941
2005	116,317	5,937	6,898	8,454	20,444	16,911	58,645	57,672
2007	120,604	6,139	6,975	8,656	20,923	17,174	59,867	60,737
2008	120,904	6,086	6,878	8,497	20,685	17,548	59,694	61,210
2009	114,510	5,966	6,581	8,191	19,390	16,153	56,282	58,228
2010	111,970	5,926	6,359	8,288	18,554	15,869	54,997	56,973
2011	113,426	5,858	6,432	7,961	18,880	15,867	54,998	58,428
Annual payroll (bil. dol.):								
1990	2,104	117	114	144	352	279	1,007	1,097
2000	3,879	186	174	231	608	528	1,727	2,152
2005	4,483	220	206	269	700	617	2,013	2,470
2007	5,027	235	222	292	769	687	2,205	2,822
2008	5,131	232	223	294	775	706	2,229	2,901
2009	4,856	220	213	278	719	655	2,085	2,771
2010	4,941	227	212	283	719	666	2,107	2,834
2011	5,165	230	218	284	746	691	2,169	2,996

[1] Employment is measured in March, thus some firms (start-ups after March, closures before March, and seasonal firms) will have zero employment and some annual payroll.

Source: U.S. Small Business Administration, Office of Advocacy, Research and Statistics, Firm Size Data, "Statistics of U.S. Businesses," <http://www.sba.gov/advocacy/849/12162>, accessed May 2014.

Table 782. Number of Active Establishments by Firm Age and Firm Size: 2012

[In thousands (2,842 represents 2,842,000). A firm may have one establishment (a single unit establishment) or many establishments (a multi-unit firm). Firms are defined at the enterprise level such that all establishments under the operational control of the enterprise are considered part of the firm. Data cover nonfarm private establishments with paid employees; major exclusions are self-employed individuals, employees of private households, railroad employees, agricultural production employees, and most government employees. Establishments are used in the tabulation of Business Dynamics Statistics (BDS) statistics. Although the BDS program is based on the same basic source data as the Census Bureau's County Business Patterns and Statistics of U.S. Business programs, differences in how the source data are processed lead to differences in published statistics. For more information about concepts and methodology, see <http://www.census.gov/ces/dataproducts/bds/>]

Firm age [1]	Firm size							Share of employment	Share of job creation	Share of job destruction
	1 to 4 employ- ees	5 to 9 employ- ees	10 to 19 employ- ees	20 to 99 employ- ees	100 to 499 employ- ees	Less than 500 employ- ees	500 or more employ- ees			
Total	2,842	1,032	632	664	349	5,519	1,155	1.00	1.00	1.00
Startups	358	32	14	8	1	413	(Z)	0.02	0.14	(X)
1 to 5 years	814	245	129	98	22	1,309	7	0.09	0.14	0.17
6 to 10 years	540	200	113	95	28	977	18	0.09	0.09	0.11
11 to 20 years	596	251	152	139	49	1,187	66	0.14	0.13	0.15
21 years and over	411	213	142	174	114	1,054	249	0.23	0.18	0.21
Born before 1976	122	91	81	149	136	580	815	0.43	0.32	0.35
Share of employment	0.05	0.06	0.07	0.17	0.14	0.49	0.51	(X)	(X)	(X)
Share of job creation	0.10	0.08	0.08	0.18	0.14	0.58	0.42	(X)	(X)	(X)

X Not applicable. Z Less than 500. [1] Establishment age is computed by taking the difference between the current year of operation and the birth year. Firm age is computed from the age of the establishments belonging to that particular firm.

Source: U.S. Census Bureau, Center for Economic Studies, "Business Dynamics Statistics," <http://www.census.gov/ces/dataproducts/bds/data_firm.html>, accessed June 2015.

Table 783. Firm Births and Deaths by Employment Size of Enterprise: 1990 to 2011

[In thousands (541.1 represents 541,100). Data represent activity from March of the beginning year to March of the ending year. Establishments with no employment in the first quarter of the beginning year were excluded. New firms represent new original establishments and deaths represent closed original establishments. Because of the methodology in determining new and closed original establishments, the U.S. Census Bureau considers these figures to be estimates]

Item	Births (initial locations)				Deaths (initial locations)			
	Total	Less than 20 employees	Less than 500 employees	500 employees or more	Total	Less than 20 employees	Less than 500 employees	500 employees or more
Firms:								
1990 to 1991......................	541.1	515.9	540.9	0.3	546.5	517.0	546.1	0.4
2000 to 2001......................	585.1	558.0	584.8	0.3	553.3	524.0	552.8	0.5
2005 to 2006......................	670.1	640.7	669.8	0.2	599.3	573.3	599.1	0.3
2006 to 2007......................	668.4	639.1	668.2	0.2	592.4	564.3	592.1	0.3
2007 to 2008......................	597.1	570.3	596.8	0.2	641.4	613.8	641.2	0.2
2008 to 2009 [1]..................	518.5	497.5	518.4	0.1	680.7	655.9	680.5	0.2
2009 to 2010 [1]..................	533.9	514.4	533.8	0.1	593.3	572.9	593.2	0.2
2010 to 2011 [1]..................	534.9	515.1	534.8	0.1	575.7	557.2	575.6	0.1
Employment:								
1990 to 1991......................	3,105	1,713	2,907	198	3,208	1,723	3,044	164
2000 to 2001......................	3,418	1,821	3,109	310	3,262	1,701	3,050	212
2005 to 2006......................	3,682	1,999	3,412	270	3,220	1,711	2,964	256
2006 to 2007......................	3,554	1,945	3,325	229	3,482	1,734	3,126	356
2007 to 2008......................	3,376	1,784	3,058	318	3,413	1,846	3,174	240
2008 to 2009 [1]..................	2,697	1,545	2,523	173	3,459	1,928	3,195	264
2009 to 2010 [1]..................	2,697	1,613	2,550	147	2,857	1,664	2,602	256
2010 to 2011 [1]..................	2,619	1,570	2,469	150	2,614	1,631	2,496	118

[1] Methodology from 2008 forward is defining firm births/deaths as establishment births/deaths for single location firms.

Source: U.S. Small Business Administration, Office of Advocacy, Research and Statistics, Firm Size Data, "Statistics of U.S. Businesses," <http://www.sba.gov/advocacy/firm-size-data>, accessed August 2014.

Table 784. Establishments and Employment Changes from Births, Deaths, Expansions, and Contractions by Employment Size of Enterprise: 2011 to 2012

[In thousands (6,596 represents 6,596,000), except percent. See headnote, Table 783. An establishment is a single physical location at which business is conducted or where services or industrial operations are performed. An enterprise is a business organization consisting of one or more domestic establishments under common ownership or control. Minus sign (-) indicates decrease]

Employment size of firm	Establishments			Employment		Percent change in employment due to—			
	Number in initial year	Births [1]	Deaths [2]	Number in initial year	Change in employment	Births [1]	Deaths [2]	Births and expansions [3]	Deaths and contractions [4]
Total...................	**6,596**	**746**	**651**	**113,408**	**2,505**	**4.9**	**-4.2**	**14.7**	**-12.5**
1 to 4.......................	2,821	451	403	5,854	870	13.8	-12.0	33.3	-18.4
5 to 9.......................	992	69	62	6,428	204	6.8	-5.9	18.8	-15.6
10 to 19....................	627	43	38	7,958	120	6.0	-5.3	16.5	-15.0
20 to 99....................	651	67	42	18,875	538	6.4	-4.5	16.3	-13.5
100 to 499.................	347	33	22	15,866	365	5.3	-3.7	15.2	-12.9
Less than 500............	5,438	662	568	54,981	2,097	6.9	-5.3	18.1	-14.3
500 or more..............	1,159	84	82	58,427	408	3.1	-3.1	11.5	-10.8

[1] Births are establishments that have zero employment in the first quarter of the initial year and positive employment in the first quarter of the subsequent year. [2] Deaths are establishments that have positive employment in the first quarter of the initial year and zero employment in the first quarter of the subsequent year. [3] Expansions are establishments that have positive first quarter employment in both the initial and subsequent years and increase employment during the time period between the first quarter of the initial year and the first quarter of the subsequent year. [4] Contractions are establishments that have positive first quarter employment in both the initial and subsequent years and decrease employment during the time period between the first quarter of the initial year and the first quarter of the subsequent year.

Source: U.S. Census Bureau, "Statistics of U.S. Businesses," <http://www.census.gov/econ/susb/>, accessed June 2015.

Table 785. Small Business Administration Loans to Minority-Owned Small Businesses: 2000 to 2014

[3,675 represents $3,675,000,000. For year ending September 30. A small business must be independently owned and operated, must not be dominant in its particular industry, and must meet standards set by the Small Business Administration as to its annual receipts or number of employees]

Minority group	Number of loans					Amount (mil. dol.)				
	2000	2010	2012	2013	2014	2000	2010	2012	2013	2014
Total minority loans [1]...................	**12,041**	**11,235**	**11,844**	**12,667**	**13,601**	**3,675**	**3,982**	**5,363**	**6,286**	**6,544**
Black.........................	2,183	1,707	1,226	1,242	1,618	415	345	300	386	388
Asian or Pacific Islander...................	5,827	5,942	6,497	7,200	7,330	2,390	2,743	3,943	4,713	4,793
Hispanic (incl. Puerto Rican)...............	3,491	3,192	3,700	3,862	4,268	767	806	1,037	1,083	1,257
American Indian............................	540	387	421	360	380	102	86	83	98	103

[1] Data for 2010, 2013 and 2014 include other minority loans not shown separately.

Source: U.S. Small Business Administration,"SBA Lending Statistics for Major Programs (as of 9/30/2014)," <https://www.sba.gov/offices/headquarters/ocpl/resources/1421811>, accessed July 2015.

Table 786. U.S. Firms—Ownership by Gender, Ethnicity, Race, and Veteran Status: 2012

[27,626 represents 27,626,000. Data are preliminary. Based on the 2012 Survey of Business Owners; see text, this section and Appendix III. Firm ownership type is determined by the group owning 51 percent or more of the equity, interest, or stock of the business. A minority-owned firm is one in which Blacks or African Americans, American Indians and Alaska Natives, Asians, Native Hawaiians and Other Pacific Islanders, and/or Hispanics own 51 percent or more of the interest or stock of the business. Detail categories will not sum to the total because the 'publicly held and other firms not classifiable by gender, ethnicity, race, and veteran status' category is not included in the preliminary tables. Moreover, each owner had the option of selecting more than one race and, therefore, is included in each race selected]

Firm ownership type	All firms [1]		Firms with paid employees			
	Firms (1,000)	Sales and receipts (bil. dol.)	Firms (1,000)	Sales and receipts (bil. dol.)	Employees (1,000)	Annual payroll (bil. dol.)
All firms.............	**27,626**	**33,537**	**5,424**	**32,478**	**115,249**	**5,236**
Female...........	9,932	1,616	1,053	1,383	8,983	290
Male...........	14,995	11,340	3,401	10,666	45,768	1,901
Equally male/female...........	2,496	1,360	779	1,235	7,094	214
Hispanic [2]...........	3,321	517	291	423	2,518	80
Equally Hispanic/non-Hispanic [2]...........	133	60	40	53	390	12
Non-Hispanic...........	23,970	13,740	4,902	12,808	58,936	2,313
Minority...........	7,996	1,566	923	1,344	7,722	248
Equally minority/nonminority...........	244	284	72	271	732	27
Nonminority...........	19,182	12,467	4,238	11,669	53,391	2,130
Veteran...........	2,541	1,470	451	1,375	5,513	221
Equally veteran/nonveteran...........	599	519	178	487	1,864	65
Nonveteran...........	24,283	12,328	4,605	11,422	54,467	2,119
White...........	21,748	12,986	4,524	12,110	55,902	2,212
Black or African American...........	2,593	188	111	141	1,045	31
American Indian and Alaska Native...........	274	42	27	35	221	8
Asian...........	1,937	794	489	720	3,839	125
Native Hawaiian and Other Pacific Islander...........	55	9	5	7	40	1
Some other race...........	1,179	122	80	89	655	19

[1] Both firms with paid employees and firms with no paid employees. [2] An Hispanic firm may be of any race and therefore may be included in more than one race group.

Source: U.S. Census Bureau, 2012 Economic Census, *Survey of Business Owners*, <http://www.census.gov/econ/sbo/>, accessed August 2015.

Table 787. Women-Owned Firms by Kind of Business: 2012

[9,932 represents 9,932,000. Data are preliminary. See headnote, Table 786]

Kind of business	2012 NAICS code [1]	All firms [2]		Firms with paid employees			
		Firms (1,000)	Sales and receipts (mil. dol.)	Firms (1,000)	Sales and receipts (mil. dol.)	Employees (1,000)	Annual payroll (mil. dol.)
Total [3]...........	(X)	**9,932**	**1,616,319**	**1,053**	**1,383,150**	**8,983**	**290,473**
Forestry, fishing and hunting, and agricultural support services...........	113–115	37	3,055	2	2,180	22	466
Mining, quarrying, and oil & gas extraction...........	21	23	33,210	2	32,117	46	3,119
Utilities...........	22	4	4,624	(Z)	4,551	5	273
Construction...........	23	267	98,383	55	90,486	450	21,143
Manufacturing...........	31–33	141	176,303	37	173,349	613	26,732
Wholesale trade...........	42	157	308,339	43	301,713	410	20,404
Retail trade...........	44–45	1,049	219,142	133	195,597	819	19,633
Transportation and warehousing [4]...........	48–49	159	47,198	22	41,636	270	9,888
Information...........	51	115	32,450	10	30,112	135	7,743
Finance and insurance [5]...........	52	222	64,048	35	55,937	202	11,051
Real estate and rental and leasing...........	53	726	79,465	60	37,822	209	7,710
Professional, scientific, and technical services...........	54	1,339	149,128	167	112,644	829	41,915
Management of companies and enterprises...........	55	2	5,743	2	5,742	59	4,570
Administrative and support and waste management and remediation services...........	56	1,084	86,033	69	70,699	1,219	32,658
Educational services...........	61	369	15,148	24	11,098	182	4,031
Health care and social assistance...........	62	1,610	139,977	174	109,790	1,677	46,929
Arts, entertainment, and recreation...........	71	473	21,826	20	13,859	152	4,891
Accommodation and food services...........	72	267	71,012	104	65,764	1,234	18,024
Other services (except public administration) [6]...........	81	1,891	60,966	94	27,825	446	9,247
Industries not classified...........	99	3	269	3	227	2	45

X Not applicable. Z Less than 500. [1] Based on the 2012 North American Industry Classification System (NAICS); see text, this section. [2] Both firms with paid employees and firms with no paid employees. [3] Firms with more than one establishment are counted in each industry in which they operate, but only once in the total. [4] Excludes rail transportation (NAICS 482), and the postal service (NAICS 491). [5] Excludes monetary authorities-central banks (NAICS 521) and funds, trusts, and other financial vehicles (NAICS 525). [6] Excludes religious, grantmaking, civic, professional, and similar organizations (NAICS 813) and private households (NAICS 814).

Source: U.S. Census Bureau, 2012 Economic Census, *Survey of Business Owners*, <http://www.census.gov/econ/sbo/>, accessed August 2015.

Table 788. Minority-Owned Firms by Kind of Business: 2012

[1,565,881 represents $1,565,881,000,000. Data are preliminary. See headnote, Table 786]

Kind of business	2012 NAICS code [1]	All firms [2] Firms	All firms [2] Sales and receipts (mil. dol.)	Firms with paid employees Firms	Firms with paid employees Sales and receipts (mil. dol.)	Firms with paid employees Employ-ees	Firms with paid employees Annual payroll (mil. dol.)
Total [3]............................	(X)	**7,996,226**	**1,565,881**	**923,140**	**1,344,170**	**7,721,623**	**247,900**
Forestry, fishing and hunting, and agricultural support services.........................	113–115	36,717	2,729	1,177	1,619	16,561	400
Mining, quarrying, and oil & gas extraction.................	21	8,639	4,898	1,245	4,178	19,605	1,046
Utilities..	22	5,514	2,466	222	2,360	2,208	149
Construction.................................	23	714,298	94,761	62,282	71,481	361,560	14,811
Manufacturing..............................	31–33	107,324	110,586	25,995	107,654	389,877	16,484
Wholesale trade...........................	42	162,683	351,941	56,469	341,753	435,539	20,424
Retail trade...................................	44–45	653,259	288,129	139,711	266,144	784,472	17,820
Transportation and warehousing [4]......	48–49	527,720	63,439	29,944	35,215	225,353	7,619
Information...................................	51	84,515	28,152	7,340	26,121	107,681	8,525
Finance and insurance [5].................	52	154,130	50,743	22,222	44,145	117,105	7,109
Real estate and rental and leasing......	53	393,279	43,796	27,008	18,837	91,852	3,264
Professional, scientific, and technical services..........	54	786,694	132,818	100,211	110,305	687,527	42,105
Management of companies and enterprises................	55	1,339	4,926	1,329	4,920	55,749	4,551
Administrative and support and waste management and remediation services...................	56	923,913	63,039	49,436	49,118	820,567	21,959
Educational services......................	61	168,350	7,443	9,792	5,675	85,305	2,044
Health care and social assistance........	62	1,054,396	127,365	137,623	107,624	1,206,345	41,671
Arts, entertainment, and recreation........	71	290,566	11,924	7,330	6,783	52,865	2,232
Accommodation and food services........	72	323,623	120,405	165,622	114,301	1,934,305	28,757
Other services (except public administration) [6]...........	81	1,600,344	56,160	79,524	25,832	325,885	6,910
Industries not classified.................	99	1,571	161	1,307	103	1,261	20

X Not applicable. [1] Based on the 2012 North American Industry Classification System (NAICS); see text, this section. [2] Both firms with paid employees and firms with no paid employees. [3] Firms with more than one establishment are counted in each industry in which they operate, but only once in the total. [4] Excludes rail transportation (NAICS 482), and the postal service (NAICS 491). [5] Excludes monetary authorities-central banks (NAICS 521) and funds, trusts, and other financial vehicles (NAICS 525). [6] Excludes religious, grantmaking, civic, professional, and similar organizations (NAICS 813) and private households (NAICS 814).

Source: U.S. Census Bureau, 2012 Economic Census, *Survey of Business Owners*, <http://www.census.gov/econ/sbo/>, accessed August 2015.

Table 789. Hispanic-Owned Firms by Kind of Business: 2012

[517,362 represents $517,362,000,000. Data are preliminary. See headnote, Table 786]

Kind of business	2012 NAICS code [1]	All firms [2] Firms	All firms [2] Sales and receipts (mil. dol.)	Firms with paid employees Firms	Firms with paid employees Sales and receipts (mil. dol.)	Firms with paid employees Employ-ees	Firms with paid employees Annual payroll (mil. dol.)
Total [3]............................	(X)	**3,320,563**	**517,362**	**291,335**	**423,005**	**2,518,045**	**79,733**
Forestry, fishing and hunting, and agricultural support services.........................	113-115	17,690	1,449	655	969	13,290	277
Mining, quarrying, and oil & gas extraction.............	21	4,887	2,719	726	2,200	12,673	641
Utilities..	22	3,211	1,466	149	1,395	1,721	65
Construction.................................	23	476,750	58,164	39,027	41,177	228,988	8,813
Manufacturing..............................	31-33	51,706	29,523	10,669	27,988	135,711	5,252
Wholesale trade...........................	42	64,658	101,846	17,381	98,065	131,556	5,683
Retail trade...................................	44-45	256,964	95,350	33,455	87,300	211,969	5,582
Transportation and warehousing [4]......	48-49	244,102	33,853	15,459	19,560	120,148	4,175
Information...................................	51	30,494	10,744	2,433	10,016	43,349	3,233
Finance and insurance [5].................	52	55,864	14,187	8,752	12,051	39,309	1,933
Real estate and rental and leasing......	53	145,597	14,065	10,298	6,167	32,583	1,165
Professional, scientific, and technical services.........	54	278,948	36,168	29,945	28,199	186,609	9,880
Management of companies and enterprises............	55	457	1,887	450	1,886	21,912	2,147
Administrative and support and waste management and remediation services................	56	529,212	29,232	25,626	20,816	381,279	9,278
Educational services......................	61	53,804	2,199	2,209	1,657	23,590	647
Health care and social assistance........	62	349,337	30,825	30,700	25,084	319,218	10,155
Arts, entertainment, and recreation........	71	101,979	4,091	2,412	2,293	18,969	766
Accommodation and food services........	72	100,701	29,161	38,232	27,157	499,531	7,582
Other services (except public administration) [6]........	81	554,732	20,387	23,385	8,999	95,361	2,454
Industries not classified.................	99	366	44	269	23	278	4

X Not applicable. [1] Based on the 2012 North American Industry Classification System (NAICS); see text, this section. [2] Both firms with paid employees and firms with no paid employees. [3] Firms with more than one establishment are counted in each industry in which they operate, but only once in the total. [4] Excludes rail transportation (NAICS 482), and the postal service (NAICS 491). [5] Excludes monetary authorities-central banks (NAICS 521) and funds, trusts, and other financial vehicles (NAICS 525). [6] Excludes religious, grantmaking, civic, professional, and similar organizations (NAICS 813) and private households (NAICS 814).

Source: U.S. Census Bureau, 2012 Economic Census, *Survey of Business Owners*, <http://www.census.gov/econ/sbo/>, accessed August 2015.

Table 790. Black-Owned Firms by Kind of Business: 2012

[187,638 represents $187,638,000,000. Data are preliminary. See headnote, Table 786]

Kind of business	2012 NAICS code [1]	All firms [2]		Firms with paid employees			
		Firms	Sales and receipts (mil. dol.)	Firms	Sales and receipts (mil. dol.)	Employees	Annual payroll (mil dol.)
Total [3]........	(X)	**2,593,168**	**187,638**	**110,786**	**140,542**	**1,045,120**	**31,400**
Forestry, fishing and hunting, and agricultural support services........	113–115	5,475	234	127	114	655	20
Mining........	21	1,038	175	42	148	490	19
Utilities........	22	1,657	30	5	7	14	1
Construction........	23	137,002	11,519	7,650	8,698	40,905	1,778
Manufacturing........	31–33	22,765	21,854	1,330	21,432	34,009	1,556
Wholesale trade........	42	24,658	28,396	2,380	27,459	21,400	1,141
Retail trade........	44–45	160,752	17,767	8,359	14,664	44,382	1,222
Transportation and warehousing [4]........	48–49	185,318	13,098	6,512	4,932	43,170	1,285
Information........	51	28,546	3,611	1,031	3,136	12,459	868
Finance and insurance [5]........	52	44,097	4,760	4,429	3,740	22,191	1,267
Real estate and rental and leasing........	53	79,013	5,013	3,009	2,308	12,590	425
Professional, scientific, and technical services........	54	207,356	16,947	13,921	12,501	88,823	5,041
Management of companies and enterprises........	55	216	641	215	641	8,901	454
Administrative and support and waste management and remediation services........	56	296,057	13,363	10,644	9,938	181,988	4,974
Educational services........	61	67,662	1,712	1,662	1,068	15,509	394
Health care and social assistance........	62	495,028	25,017	32,598	17,597	319,571	7,615
Arts, entertainment, and recreation........	71	124,524	3,915	1,929	1,900	9,508	582
Accommodation and food services........	72	60,445	8,589	6,957	7,707	156,220	2,089
Other services (except public administration) [6]........	81	651,356	10,952	7,854	2,522	31,868	664
Industries not classified........	99	611	48	540	30	467	6

X Not applicable. [1] Based on the 2012 North American Industry Classification System (NAICS); see text, this section. [2] Both firms with paid employees and firms with no paid employees. [3] Firms with more than one establishment are counted in each industry in which they operate, but only once in the total. [4] Excludes rail transportation (NAICS 482), and the postal service (NAICS 491). [5] Excludes monetary authorities-central banks (NAICS 521) and funds, trusts, and other financial vehicles (NAICS 525). [6] Excludes religious, grantmaking, civic, professional, and similar organizations (NAICS 813) and private households (NAICS 814).

Source: U.S. Census Bureau, 2012 Economic Census, *Survey of Business Owners*, <http://www.census.gov/econ/sbo/>, accessed August 2015.

Table 791. Asian–Owned Firms by Kind of Business: 2012

[793,552 represents $793,552,000,000. Data are preliminary. See headnote, Table 786]

Kind of business	2012 NAICS code [1]	All firms [2]		Firms with paid employees			
		Firms	Sales and receipts (mil. dol.)	Firms	Sales and receipts (mil. dol.)	Employees	Annual payroll (mil. dol.)
Total [3]........	(X)	**1,937,368**	**793,552**	**489,387**	**719,736**	**3,839,292**	**125,072**
Forestry, fishing and hunting, and agricultural support services........	113–115	6,425	524	138	201	814	32
Mining, quarrying, and oil & gas extraction........	21	1,231	1,229	144	1,155	3,152	205
Utilities........	22	544	779	35	768	279	71
Construction........	23	77,199	17,187	10,707	14,740	58,407	2,719
Manufacturing........	31–33	28,098	53,310	12,656	52,467	197,562	8,627
Wholesale trade........	42	68,476	206,752	35,322	201,598	265,598	12,658
Retail trade........	44–45	219,279	161,893	93,814	151,908	493,363	10,147
Transportation and warehousing [4]........	48–49	94,026	14,889	6,931	9,444	52,420	1,840
Information........	51	23,356	12,984	3,431	12,203	48,633	4,220
Finance and insurance [5]........	52	49,232	29,879	7,873	26,768	49,338	3,581
Real estate and rental and leasing........	53	155,357	23,331	12,532	9,977	42,933	1,507
Professional, scientific, and technical services........	54	278,550	75,006	51,992	65,808	382,932	25,918
Management of companies and enterprises........	55	572	2,070	570	2,064	21,440	1,661
Administrative and support and waste management and remediation services........	56	86,744	17,048	11,140	15,299	206,153	6,245
Educational services........	61	42,965	3,240	5,559	2,699	42,678	879
Health care and social assistance........	62	204,674	66,967	70,662	60,697	533,825	22,307
Arts, entertainment, and recreation........	71	55,138	3,123	2,530	1,976	20,606	596
Accommodation and food services........	72	158,517	80,070	117,624	76,963	1,235,151	18,481
Other services (except public administration) [6]........	81	387,623	23,204	46,458	12,951	183,531	3,370
Industries not classified........	99	549	66	455	48	480	9

X Not applicable. [1] Based on the 2012 North American Industry Classification System (NAICS); see text, this section. [2] Both firms with paid employees and firms with no paid employees. [3] Firms with more than one establishment are counted in each industry in which they operate, but only once in the total. [4] Excludes rail transportation (NAICS 482), and the postal service (NAICS 491). [5] Excludes monetary authorities-central banks (NAICS 521) and funds, trusts, and other financial vehicles (NAICS 525). [6] Excludes religious, grantmaking, civic, professional, and similar organizations (NAICS 813) and private households (NAICS 814).

Source: U.S. Census Bureau, 2012 Economic Census, *Survey of Business Owners*, <http://www.census.gov/econ/sbo/>, accessed August 2015.

Table 792. Native Hawaiian- and Other Pacific Islander-Owned Firms by Kind of Business: 2012

[8,586 represents $8,586,000,000. Data are preliminary. See headnote, Table 786]

Kind of business	2012 NAICS code[1]	All firms[2] Firms	Sales and receipts (mil. dol.)	Firms with paid employees Firms	Sales and receipts (mil. dol.)	Employees	Annual payroll (mil. dol.)
Total[3]	(X)	55,077	8,586	4,764	6,902	39,971	1,482
Forestry, fishing and hunting, and agricultural support services	113–115	632	17	1	(S)	(4)	(S)
Mining, quarrying, and oil & gas extraction	21	45	(S)	25	(S)	(5)	(S)
Utilities	22	23	(Z)	1	(S)	(4)	(S)
Construction	23	5,562	1,743	728	1,489	5,036	259
Manufacturing	31–33	966	594	253	576	2,912	113
Wholesale trade	42	1,291	1,081	159	1,024	1,704	81
Retail trade	44–45	4,752	925	504	807	3,130	82
Transportation and warehousing[6]	48–49	2,574	552	232	(S)	(7)	(S)
Information	51	626	107	54	91	328	17
Finance and insurance[8]	52	1,252	161	127	70	382	24
Real estate and rental and leasing	53	2,850	217	169	76	614	22
Professional, scientific, and technical services	54	6,332	934	607	766	3,690	256
Management of companies and enterprises	55	9	12	9	12	196	14
Administrative and support and waste management and remediation services	56	6,460	455	285	337	5,991	154
Educational services	61	1,316	38	89	(S)	(9)	(S)
Health care and social assistance	62	6,667	459	550	320	2,804	93
Arts, entertainment, and recreation	71	3,541	285	169	218	1,174	72
Accommodation and food services	72	1,465	352	454	308	5,370	80
Other services (except public administration)[10]	81	8,730	458	367	(S)	(7)	(S)
Industries not classified	99	11	1	11	1	13	(Z)

X Not applicable. S Withheld because estimate did not meet publication standards. Z Less than $500,000. [1] Based on the 2012 North American Industry Classification System (NAICS); see text, this section. [2] Both firms with paid employees and firms with no paid employees. [3] Firms with more than one establishment are counted in each industry in which they operate, but only once in the total. [4] 0 to 19 employees. [5] 1,000 to 2,499 employees. [6] Excludes rail transportation (NAICS 482), and the postal service (NAICS 491). [7] 2,500 to 4,999 employees. [8] Excludes monetary authorities-central banks (NAICS 521) and funds, trusts, and other financial vehicles (NAICS 525). [9] 100 to 249 employees. [10] Excludes religious, grantmaking, civic, professional, and similar organizations (NAICS 813) and private households (NAICS 814).

Source: U.S. Census Bureau, 2012 Economic Census, *Survey of Business Owners*, <http://www.census.gov/econ/sbo/>, accessed August 2015.

Table 793. American Indian- and Alaska Native-Owned Firms by Kind of Business: 2012

[42,216 represents $42,216,000,000. Data are preliminary. See headnote, Table 786]

Kind of business	2012 NAICS code[1]	All firms[2] Firms	Sales and receipts (mil. dol.)	Firms with paid employees Firms	Sales and receipts (mil. dol.)	Employees	Annual payroll (mil. dol.)
Total[3]	(X)	274,238	42,216	26,562	34,959	220,853	7,596
Forestry, fishing and hunting, and agricultural support services	113–115	7,006	419	252	248	1,661	55
Mining, quarrying, and oil & gas extraction	21	1,425	559	301	461	2,040	107
Utilities	22	296	195	14	187	154	8
Construction	23	36,095	7,663	4,905	6,385	30,417	1,372
Manufacturing	31–33	6,016	3,244	1,171	3,080	14,937	622
Wholesale trade	42	5,994	6,336	1,046	5,970	9,238	472
Retail trade	44–45	22,530	6,566	2,669	5,992	18,618	479
Transportation and warehousing[4]	48–49	11,428	1,492	944	902	5,740	191
Information	51	3,471	459	295	392	3,038	114
Finance and insurance[5]	52	6,229	1,382	1,245	1,093	5,247	238
Real estate and rental and leasing	53	11,171	1,081	917	572	3,160	152
Professional, scientific, and technical services	54	31,083	3,460	3,674	2,481	19,945	867
Management of companies and enterprises	55	64	274	64	274	1,584	155
Administrative and support and waste management and remediation services	56	29,201	2,880	2,041	2,443	41,392	1,166
Educational services	61	7,473	272	268	204	2,890	112
Health care and social assistance	62	29,280	2,285	3,093	1,797	29,699	716
Arts, entertainment, and recreation	71	16,023	733	296	483	2,548	221
Accommodation and food services	72	5,777	1,080	1,468	964	18,879	256
Other services (except public administration)[6]	81	43,750	1,834	1,976	1,028	9,637	293
Industries not classified	99	37	2	35	2	32	(Z)

X Not applicable. Z Less than $500,000. [1] Based on the 2012 North American Industry Classification System (NAICS); see text, this section. [2] Both firms with paid employees and firms with no paid employees. [3] Firms with more than one establishment are counted in each industry in which they operate, but only once in the total. [4] Excludes rail transportation (NAICS 482), and the postal service (NAICS 491). [5] Excludes monetary authorities-central banks (NAICS 521) and funds, trusts, and other financial vehicles (NAICS 525). [6] Excludes religious, grantmaking, civic, professional, and similar organizations (NAICS 813) and private households (NAICS 814).

Source: U.S. Census Bureau, 2012 Economic Census, *Survey of Business Owners*, <http://www.census.gov/econ/sbo/>, accessed August 2015.

Table 794. Bankruptcy Petitions Filed and Pending by Type and Chapter: 2000 to 2014

[For years ending June 30. Covers only bankruptcy cases filed under the Bankruptcy Reform Act of 1978. Bankruptcy: legal recognition that a company or individual is insolvent and must restructure or liquidate. Section 101 of the U.S. Bankruptcy Code defines consumer (nonbusiness) debt as that incurred by an individual primarily for a personal, family, or household purpose. If the debtor is a corporation or partnership, or if debt related to operation of a business predominates, the nature of the debt is business. Petitions "filed" means the commencement of a proceeding through the presentation of a petition to the clerk of the court; "pending" is a proceeding in which the administration has not been completed]

Item	2000	2005	2008	2009	2010	2011	2012	2013	2014
Total filed.............	1,276,922	1,637,254	967,831	1,306,315	1,572,597	1,529,560	1,311,602	1,137,978	1,000,083
Chapter 7 [1].................	885,447	1,196,212	615,748	907,603	1,133,320	1,083,671	914,015	778,845	669,976
Chapter 9 [2]..................	8	6	4	6	12	7	17	16	13
Chapter 11 [3].................	9,947	6,703	7,293	13,951	14,272	12,714	10,921	9,633	8,347
Chapter 12 [4].................	732	290	314	422	660	717	582	426	394
Chapter 13 [5]..................	380,770	433,945	344,421	384,187	424,242	432,333	385,949	348,994	321,278
Section 304 [6].................	18	98	(X)	(X)	(X)	(X)	(X)	(X)	(X)
Chapter 15 [7].................	(X)	(X)	51	146	91	118	118	64	74
Business [8].................	36,910	32,406	33,822	55,021	59,608	52,134	44,435	36,061	30,113
Nonbusiness [9].............	1,240,012	1,604,848	934,009	1,251,294	1,512,989	1,477,426	1,267,167	1,101,917	969,970
Chapter 7 [1].................	864,183	1,174,681	592,376	870,266	1,091,322	1,047,131	883,119	754,391	649,975
Chapter 11 [3]................	722	847	780	1,088	1,827	1,884	1,636	1,417	1,211
Chapter 13 [5]................	375,107	429,315	340,852	379,939	419,836	428,410	382,409	346,105	318,781
Total pending............	1,400,416	1,750,562	1,325,220	1,527,073	1,659,399	1,704,548	1,662,461	1,585,516	1,460,753

X Not applicable. [1] Chapter 7, liquidation of nonexempt assets of businesses or individuals. [2] Chapter 9, adjustment of debts of a municipality. [3] Chapter 11, individual or business reorganization. [4] Chapter 12, adjustment of debts of a family farmer with regular income, effective November 26, 1986. [5] Chapter 13, adjustment of debts of an individual with regular income. [6] Chapter 11, U.S.C., Section 304, cases ancillary to foreign proceedings. [7] Chapter 15 was added and Section 304 was terminated by changes in the Bankruptcy Laws effective October 17, 2005. [8] Business bankruptcies include those filed under Chapters 7, 9, 11, 12, 13, or 15. [9] Includes other petitions, not shown separately.

Source: Administrative Office of the United States Courts, "Bankruptcy Statistics," <http://www.uscourts.gov/Statistics/BankruptcyStatistics.aspx>, accessed June 2015.

Table 795. Bankruptcy Cases Filed by State: 2000 to 2014

[In thousands (1,276.9 represents 1,276,900). For years ending June 30. Covers only bankruptcy cases filed under the Bankruptcy Reform Act of 1978. Bankruptcy: legal recognition that a company or individual is insolvent and must restructure or liquidate. Petitions "filed" means the commencement of a proceeding through the presentation of a petition to the clerk of the court]

State	2000	2010	2013	2014	State	2000	2010	2013	2014
Total [1]..................	1,276.9	1,572.6	1,138.0	1,000.1	Missouri....................	26.3	32.9	27.1	22.3
Alabama.................	31.4	34.9	27.7	26.1	Montana..................	3.3	3.1	2.0	1.7
Alaska....................	1.4	1.1	0.7	0.5	Nebraska.................	5.6	7.9	5.6	4.9
Arizona..................	21.7	40.7	25.1	21.9	Nevada...................	14.3	31.0	15.7	12.3
Arkansas................	16.3	16.9	12.6	11.8	New Hampshire.........	3.9	5.7	3.6	2.9
California................	160.6	242.0	161.2	116.7	New Jersey..............	38.7	39.7	29.3	28.4
Colorado................	15.6	31.9	24.3	20.3	New Mexico.............	7.1	6.6	4.6	4.0
Connecticut.............	11.4	11.3	7.5	7.1	New York................	61.7	58.2	38.3	34.6
Delaware................	4.9	4.5	3.5	3.4	North Carolina...........	25.8	27.7	20.0	17.6
District of Columbia.....	2.6	1.3	0.8	0.8	North Dakota............	2.0	1.6	0.9	0.7
Florida...................	74.0	107.4	78.5	73.3	Ohio......................	53.6	72.9	49.8	43.6
Georgia..................	57.9	77.8	61.6	55.2	Oklahoma................	19.3	15.1	11.3	10.2
Hawaii...................	5.0	3.7	2.4	1.9	Oregon...................	18.1	20.1	14.0	13.1
Idaho....................	7.3	8.3	5.9	5.1	Pennsylvania.............	43.8	38.8	27.5	25.9
Illinois...................	62.3	80.8	69.1	62.9	Rhode Island.............	4.8	5.4	3.6	3.3
Indiana..................	37.5	49.3	35.1	31.2	South Carolina...........	11.7	9.7	7.7	7.6
Iowa.....................	8.2	10.4	5.9	5.5	South Dakota............	2.1	2.0	1.4	1.3
Kansas..................	11.4	11.4	8.7	8.0	Tennessee...............	47.1	52.5	43.3	40.7
Kentucky................	20.8	26.0	18.9	17.9	Texas....................	62.9	57.8	44.0	38.9
Louisiana................	23.1	19.5	15.9	15.6	Utah.....................	14.4	17.0	15.2	14.0
Maine....................	4.1	4.1	2.7	2.2	Vermont..................	1.6	1.7	0.9	0.8
Maryland................	31.1	29.1	23.2	21.9	Virginia..................	37.1	37.8	27.2	25.1
Massachusetts...........	16.7	22.9	14.0	11.4	Washington.............	31.2	33.5	26.5	22.9
Michigan................	36.4	71.0	45.4	38.6	West Virginia............	8.2	6.6	3.8	3.5
Minnesota...............	15.4	22.6	15.4	13.4	Wisconsin................	18.0	30.0	23.9	22.0
Mississippi..............	17.9	14.8	12.4	12.4	Wyoming.................	2.0	1.5	1.3	1.1

[1] Includes Island Areas, not shown separately.

Source: Administrative Office of the United States Courts, "Bankruptcy Statistics," <http://www.uscourts.gov/Statistics/BankruptcyStatistics.aspx>, accessed June 2015.

Table 796. Patents and Trademarks: 2000 to 2014

[In thousands (176.0 represents 176,000), unless otherwise noted. Calendar year data. Covers U.S. patents issued to citizens of the United States and residents of foreign countries. For data on foreign countries, see Table 1393]

Type	2000	2005	2008	2009	2010	2011	2012	2013	2014
Patents issued..............................	176.0	157.7	185.2	191.9	244.3	247.7	276.8	302.9	326.0
Inventions................................	157.5	143.8	157.8	167.3	219.6	224.5	253.2	277.8	300.7
Individuals.............................	22.4	14.7	12.6	12.6	16.6	15.6	17.2	18.7	19.3
Corporations:									
United States.......................	70.9	65.2	70.0	74.8	97.8	99.5	111.8	124.7	136.4
Foreign [1].........................	63.3	63.1	74.5	79.2	104.2	108.3	122.9	133.4	144.0
U.S. government.....................	0.9	0.7	0.7	0.7	0.9	0.9	1.0	1.0	1.0
Designs..................................	17.4	13.0	25.6	23.1	22.8	21.4	22.0	23.5	23.7
Botanical plants.........................	0.5	0.7	1.2	1.0	1.0	0.8	0.9	0.8	1.1
Reissues.................................	0.5	0.2	0.6	0.5	0.9	1.0	0.8	0.8	0.6
U.S. residents............................	96.9	82.6	92.0	95.0	121.2	121.3	134.2	147.7	158.7
Foreign country residents..............	79.1	75.2	93.2	96.9	123.2	126.5	142.6	155.3	167.3
Percent of total..........................	44.9	47.6	50.3	50.5	50.4	51.1	51.5	51.3	51.3
Trademarks:									
Applications filed........................	361.8	334.7	401.4	352.1	368.9	398.7	415.0	433.7	455.0

[1] Includes patents to foreign governments.

Source: U.S. Patent and Trademark Office, "Statistical Reports Available For Viewing, Calendar Year Patent Statistics," <http://www.uspto.gov/web/offices/ac/ido/oeip/taf/reports.htm> and "Data Visualization Center, Trademarks Dashboard," <http://www.uspto.gov /dashboards/trademarks/main.dashxml>, accessed June 2015; and unpublished sources.

Table 797. Patents by State and Island Areas: 2014

[Includes only U.S. patents granted to residents of the United States and territories]

State	Total	Inventions	Designs	Botanical plants	Reissues	State	Total	Inventions	Designs	Botanical plants	Reissues
Total...................	158,709	144,621	13,385	401	302	Missouri............	1,419	1,257	157	0	5
						Montana............	139	115	24	0	0
Alabama...............	557	500	49	7	1	Nebraska...........	397	364	32	0	1
Alaska.................	51	49	2	0	0	Nevada.............	969	834	135	0	0
Arizona................	2,671	2,517	146	3	5	New Hampshire. ..	952	889	60	0	3
Arkansas..............	259	204	52	2	1	New Jersey........	5,508	5,036	461	2	9
California..............	43,679	40,661	2,828	119	71	New Mexico........	445	423	22	0	0
Colorado..............	3,555	3,184	366	0	5	New York..........	9,769	8,904	844	7	14
Connecticut...........	2,502	2,309	187	0	6	North Carolina.....	3,707	3,411	286	2	8
Delaware..............	466	442	21	1	2	North Dakota.......	120	104	16	0	0
District of Columbia. . .	171	161	10	0	0	Ohio.................	4,384	3,755	621	5	3
Florida.................	5,022	4,210	775	28	9	Oklahoma..........	628	572	53	3	0
Georgia................	2,978	2,669	281	20	8	Oregon.............	2,919	2,391	448	73	7
Hawaii.................	160	136	21	3	0	Pennsylvania......	4,484	4,091	379	10	4
Idaho..................	1,045	1,012	33	0	0	Rhode Island.......	447	363	81	0	3
Illinois.................	5,924	5,106	785	20	13	South Carolina.....	999	907	81	10	1
Indiana................	2,265	2,049	213	1	2	South Dakota......	128	115	13	0	0
Iowa...................	1,057	1,000	55	0	2	Tennessee.........	1,181	1,060	116	1	4
Kansas................	1,036	960	75	0	1	Texas..............	10,691	10,022	638	4	27
Kentucky..............	714	646	63	2	3	Utah...............	1,526	1,374	148	0	4
Louisiana..............	487	434	43	10	0	Vermont............	610	578	32	0	0
Maine..................	222	212	7	0	3	Virginia.............	2,184	2,078	97	1	8
Maryland..............	2,005	1,851	143	0	11	Washington.........	7,148	6,448	669	16	15
Massachusetts........	7,079	6,725	337	2	15	West Virginia.......	137	134	1	2	0
Michigan...............	5,822	5,306	479	27	10	Wisconsin..........	2,651	2,107	526	12	6
Minnesota.............	5,082	4,626	442	3	11	Wyoming...........	131	122	8	0	1
Mississippi............	177	153	19	5	0	Island areas........	50	45	5	0	0

Source: U.S. Patent and Trademark Office, "Patent Counts By Origin and Type Calendar Year 2014," <http://www.uspto.gov/web/offices/ac/ ido/oeip/taf/st_co_14.htm>, accessed June 2015.

Table 798. Copyright Registration by Subject Matter: 2000 to 2013

[In thousands (497.6 represents 497,600). For years ending September 30. Comprises claims to copyrights registered for both U.S. and foreign works. Semiconductor chips and renewals are not considered copyright registration claims]

Subject matter	2000	2010	2012	2013	Subject matter	2000	2010	2012	2013
Total copyright claims....	497.6	636.0	508.7	496.2	Performing arts [2]..................	138.9	124.5	114.8	116.1
Monographs [1].................	169.7	245.8	198.5	180.6	Works of the visual arts [3]........	85.8	97.2	72.8	82.9
Serials.........................	69.0	90.5	48.2	44.2	Semiconductor chip products....	0.7	0.3	2.6	0.3
Sound recordings.............	34.2	77.9	74.3	72.4	Renewals......................	16.8	0.1	0.2	0.2

[1] Includes computer software and machine readable works. [2] Includes musical works, dramatic works, choreography, pantomimes, motion pictures, and filmstrips. [3] Two-dimensional works of fine and graphic art, including prints and art reproductions; sculptural works; technical drawings and models; photographs; commercial prints and labels; and works of applied arts, cartographic works, and multimedia works.

Source: The Library of Congress, *Annual Report of the Librarian of Congress, For the Fiscal Year Ending September 30, 2013*, 2014. See also <http://www.loc.gov/about/reports-and-budgets/annual-reports/>.

Table 799. Net Stock of Private Fixed Assets by Industry: 2000 to 2013

[In billions of dollars (21,398 represents $21,398,000,000,000). Estimates as of Dec. 31. Fixed assets are assets that are used repeatedly, or continuously, in processes of production for more than a year. Net stock estimates are presented in terms of current-cost, and cover equipment, structures, and intellectual property products. (pt) = part]

Industry	NAICS code [1]	2000	2010	2012	2013
Private fixed assets	(X)	**21,398**	**34,345**	**36,191**	**38,054**
Agriculture, forestry, fishing, and hunting	11	338	490	525	549
Farms [2]	111, 112	311	440	470	491
Forestry, fishing, and related activities	113-115	27	49	55	57
Mining	21	574	1,483	1,617	1,753
Oil and gas extraction	211	440	1,241	1,325	1,434
Mining, except oil and gas	212	90	136	166	183
Support activities for mining	213	44	105	126	136
Utilities	22	1,042	1,842	2,057	2,107
Construction	23	174	257	270	280
Manufacturing	31-33	2,268	3,130	3,345	3,448
Durable goods	(X)	1,267	1,614	1,710	1,759
Wood products	321	32	39	39	40
Nonmetallic mineral products	327	60	82	83	84
Primary metals	331	130	155	162	165
Fabricated metal products	332	123	156	164	168
Machinery	333	166	206	223	231
Computer and electronic products	334	345	456	483	495
Electrical equipment, appliances, and components	335	64	68	71	73
Motor vehicles, bodies and trailers, and parts	3361-3363	153	185	200	211
Other transportation equipment	3364, 3365, 3369	108	144	153	157
Furniture and related products	337	17	22	22	22
Miscellaneous manufacturing	339	68	101	109	112
Nondurable goods	(X)	1,001	1,516	1,635	1,689
Food and beverage and tobacco products	311, 312	197	288	311	323
Textile mills and textile product mills	313, 314	45	41	40	40
Apparel and leather and allied products	315, 316	18	18	17	17
Paper products	322	109	115	119	121
Printing and related support activities	323	44	51	51	51
Petroleum and coal products	324	107	175	180	181
Chemical products	325	406	735	820	855
Plastics and rubber products	326	77	93	97	99
Wholesale trade	42	347	502	554	583
Retail trade	44-45	655	1,126	1,187	1,216
Transportation and warehousing [3]	48-49	822	1,099	1,195	1,230
Air transportation	481	185	220	229	234
Railroad transportation	482	288	360	391	399
Water transportation	483	37	41	42	44
Truck transportation	484	71	108	123	131
Transit and ground passenger transportation	485	37	43	43	44
Pipeline transportation	486	74	165	194	203
Warehousing and storage	493	21	40	42	43
Information	51	1,187	1,792	1,898	1,956
Publishing industries (includes software)	511, 516 (pt)	112	180	188	191
Motion picture and sound recording industries	512	186	267	279	288
Broadcasting and telecommunications	515, 517	853	1,247	1,315	1,354
Information and data processing services	516 (pt), 518, 519	36	97	116	124
Finance and insurance	52	772	1,157	1,209	1,249
Federal Reserve banks	521	9	11	11	11
Credit intermediation and related activities	522	483	717	760	790
Securities, commodity contracts, and investments	523	90	152	151	152
Insurance carriers and related activities	524	173	238	244	250
Funds, trusts, and other financial vehicles	525	18	40	44	47
Real estate and rental and leasing	53	10,736	17,224	17,843	18,997
Real estate	531	10,510	16,885	17,462	18,588
Rental and leasing services and lessors of intangible assets [4]	532, 533	227	338	382	409
Professional, scientific, and technical services [3]	54	301	536	564	581
Legal services	5411	23	42	42	42
Computer systems design and related services	5415	54	75	73	73
Management of companies and enterprises [5]	55	269	371	391	403
Admin/support waste mgt	56	154	253	271	279
Administrative and support services	561	87	161	173	179
Waste management and remediation services	562	66	92	99	100
Educational services	61	218	474	517	540
Health care and social assistance	62	693	1,232	1,322	1,400
Ambulatory health care services	621	206	319	331	344
Hospitals	622	428	783	849	906
Nursing and residential care facilities	623	33	76	85	90
Social assistance	624	26	54	57	60
Arts, entertainment, and recreation	71	164	284	295	307
Performing arts, spectator sports, museums, and related activities	711, 712	83	141	148	153
Amusements, gambling, and recreation industries	713	80	143	147	155
Accommodation and food services	72	341	538	556	581
Accommodation	721	187	323	326	341
Food services and drinking places	722	154	215	230	239
Other services, except government	81	345	557	576	598

X Not applicable. [1] Based on North American Industry Classification System, 2007; see text this section. [2] NAICS crop and animal production. [3] Includes other activities, not shown separately. [4] Intangible assets include patents, trademarks, and franchise agreements, but not copyrights. [5] Consists of bank and other holding companies.

Source: U.S. Bureau of Economic Analysis, "Table 3.1ESI. Current-Cost Net Stock of Private Fixed Assets by Industry," <http://www.bea.gov/itable/>, accessed May 2015.

Table 800. Private Domestic Investment in Current and Chained (2009) Dollars: 2000 to 2013

[In billions of dollars (2,034 represents $2,034,000,000,000). Covers equipment, structures, and intellectual property products. Minus sign (-) indicates decrease. For explanation of chained dollars; see text, Section 13]

Item	2000	2005	2008	2009	2010	2011	2012	2013
CURRENT DOLLARS								
Gross private domestic investment...........	**2,034**	**2,527**	**2,425**	**1,878**	**2,101**	**2,240**	**2,479**	**2,648**
Less: Consumption of fixed capital...............	1,237	1,635	1,937	1,926	1,924	1,971	2,034	2,121
Equals: Net private domestic investment........	797	892	488	-48	177	269	445	527
Fixed investment..................................	1,979	2,468	2,457	2,026	2,039	2,198	2,414	2,574
Less: Consumption of fixed capital.............	1,237	1,635	1,937	1,926	1,924	1,971	2,034	2,121
Equals: Net fixed investment....................	743	832	520	100	116	227	380	453
Nonresidential..................................	1,494	1,612	1,941	1,633	1,658	1,812	1,972	2,054
Residential.....................................	485	856	516	392	381	386	442	520
Change in private inventories....................	55	60	-32	-148	62	42	65	74
CHAINED (2009) DOLLARS								
Gross private domestic investment...........	**2,376**	**2,673**	**2,396**	**1,878**	**2,120**	**2,230**	**2,436**	**2,556**
Less: Consumption of fixed capital...............	1,414	1,721	1,909	1,926	1,928	1,949	1,986	2,032
Equals: Net private domestic investment........	962	951	487	-48	192	281	450	524
Fixed investment..................................	2,316	2,611	2,433	2,026	2,056	2,187	2,368	2,479
Nonresidential..................................	1,648	1,717	1,934	1,633	1,674	1,802	1,932	1,991
Residential.....................................	638	873	498	392	382	385	437	488
Change in private inventories....................	66	64	-34	-148	58	38	57	64

Source: U.S. Bureau of Economic Analysis, "Table 5.2.5. Gross and Net Domestic Investment by Major Type" and "Table 5.2.6. Real Gross and Net Domestic Investment by Major Type, Chained Dollars," <http://www.bea.gov/itable/>, accessed May 2015.

Table 801. Information and Communications Technology (ICT) Equipment and Computer Software Expenditures: 2010 and 2013

[In millions of dollars (92,551 represents $92,551,000,000). Covers only companies with employees. The Information and Communication Technology Survey collects noncapitalized and capitalized data on information and communication technology equipment, including computer software. This survey is sent to a sample of approximately 46,500 private nonfarm employer businesses operating in the United States]

Type of expenditure and industry	NAICS code [1]	Noncapitalized expenditures [2]		Capitalized expenditures [3]	
		2010	2013	2010	2013
Total expenditures for ICT equipment and computer software...........	**(X)**	**92,551**	**117,980**	**169,647**	**212,900**
Total equipment expenditures..................	(X)	33,286	39,564	(X)	(X)
Purchases....................................	(X)	17,186	23,175	105,735	122,893
Computer and peripheral equipment...........	(X)	11,087	14,815	53,214	65,136
Information and communication technology equipment..............	(X)	5,797	7,963	47,343	52,842
Electromedical and electrotherapeutic apparatus.....................	(X)	302	396	5,178	4,914
Operating leases and rental payments........	(X)	16,100	16,389	(X)	(X)
Computer and peripheral equipment...........	(X)	10,286	10,498	(X)	(X)
Information and communication technology equipment..............	(X)	4,413	4,893	(X)	(X)
Electromedical and electrotherapeutic apparatus.....................	(X)	1,400	998	(X)	(X)
Total computer software expenditures..........	(X)	59,265	78,416	(X)	(X)
Purchases and payroll for developing software....	(X)	27,885	33,079	63,912	90,007
Software licensing and service/maintenance agreements..............	(X)	31,380	45,337	(X)	(X)
Forestry, fishing, and agricultural services....................	113–115	59	58	94	96
Mining...	21	1,204	1,628	1,044	2,046
Utilities...	22	1,694	2,258	4,300	5,743
Construction..	23	796	1,249	1,287	1,432
Manufacturing.....................................	31–33	15,716	16,558	15,125	20,531
Durable goods industries........................	321, 327, 33	10,173	10,417	8,774	12,849
Nondurable goods industries....................	31, 322-326	5,543	6,141	6,350	7,682
Wholesale trade....................................	42	2,895	4,040	6,014	7,765
Retail trade..	44–45	5,407	6,811	11,243	15,390
Transportation and warehousing................	48–49	1,800	2,316	3,102	3,897
Information..	51	13,370	16,253	57,917	69,459
Finance and insurance............................	52	22,026	28,589	26,123	31,610
Real estate and rental and leasing.............	53	1,206	1,211	1,750	2,366
Professional, scientific, and technical services....	54	10,620	14,644	12,079	15,129
Management of companies and enterprises....	55	1,154	1,452	1,994	3,028
Admin/support and waste management/remediation services...........	56	2,333	3,016	4,183	5,339
Educational services..............................	61	1,897	2,618	2,503	2,594
Health care and social assistance...............	62	7,839	10,150	15,121	18,093
Arts, entertainment, and recreation.............	71	502	912	1,041	1,350
Accommodation and food services..............	72	826	1,560	1,414	3,423
Other services (except public administration).............	81	1,427	1,841	2,403	2,210
Equipment expenditures serving multiple industry codes.................	(X)	816	817	807	1,402

X Not applicable. [1] Based on North American Industry Classification System, 2007; see text, this section. [2] Expenses for ICT equipment including computer software not charged to asset accounts for which depreciation or amortization accounts are ordinarily maintained. [3] Expenses for ICT equipment including computer software chargeable to asset accounts for which depreciation or amortization accounts are ordinarily maintained.

Source: U.S. Census Bureau, "2013 Information and Communication Technology Survey," March 2015 and earlier reports, <http://www.census.gov/econ/ict/index.html>.

Table 802. Capital Expenditures: 2000 to 2013

[In billions of dollars (1,161 represents $1,161,000,000,000). Based on a sample survey and subject to sampling error; see source for details]

Item	All companies				Companies with employees				Companies without employees			
	2000	2010	2012	2013	2000	2010	2012	2013	2000	2010	2012	2013
Capital expenditures, total	**1,161**	**1,106**	**1,424**	**1,488**	**1,090**	**1,036**	**1,334**	**1,398**	**71**	**70**	**89**	**90**
Structures	364	430	570	578	338	396	533	542	26	33	37	36
New	329	395	535	545	309	368	502	514	20	28	33	31
Used	35	34	35	33	29	29	31	28	6	6	4	5
Equipment	797	676	853	910	752	640	801	856	45	36	52	55
New	751	638	800	857	718	612	759	815	32	27	41	42
Used	46	38	53	54	34	28	42	41	12	10	11	13
Capitalized computer software [1]	(NA)	(NA)	(NA)	(NA)	(NA)	(NA)	87	90	(NA)	(NA)	(NA)	(NA)
Capital leases [1]	20	16	26	27	19	15	25	26	(Z)	1	1	1

NA Not available. Z Less than $500 million. [1]Included in structures and equipment data shown above.

Source: U.S. Census Bureau, "2013 Annual Capital Expenditures Survey," February 2015 and earlier reports, <http://www.census.gov/econ/aces/>, accessed May 2015.

Table 803. Capital Expenditures by Industry: 2010 and 2013

[In billions of dollars (1,036 represents $1,036,000,000,000). Covers only companies with employees. Data based on the North American Industry Classification System (NAICS), 2007; see text this section. Based on a sample survey and subject to sampling error; see source for details]

Industry	NAICS code	2010	2013	Industry	NAICS code	2010	2013
Total expenditures	**(X)**	**1,036**	**1,398**	Professional, scientific, and technical services	54	28	36
Forestry, fishing, and agricultural services	113–115	3	3	Management of companies and enterprises	55	5	6
Mining	21	116	198	Admin/support waste mgt/remediation services	56	17	22
Utilities	22	94	112	Educational services	61	23	23
Construction	23	18	28	Health care and social assistance	62	78	93
Manufacturing	31–33	161	220	Arts, entertainment, and recreation	71	12	15
Durable goods	321, 327, 33	87	121	Accommodation and food services	72	20	35
Nondurable goods	31, 322–326	74	99	Other services (except public administration)	81	21	19
Wholesale trade	42	31	38	Structure and equipment expenditures serving multiple industry categories	(X)	2	3
Retail trade	44–45	65	77				
Transportation and warehousing	48–49	59	93				
Information	51	97	123				
Finance and insurance	52	103	140				
Real estate and rental and leasing	53	81	114				

X Not applicable.

Source: U.S. Census Bureau, "2013 Annual Capital Expenditures Survey," February 2015 and earlier reports, <http://www.census.gov/econ/aces/>, accessed May 2015.

Table 804. Business Cycle Expansions and Contractions—Months of Duration: 1945 to 2009

[A trough is the low point of a business cycle; a peak is the high point. Contraction, or recession, is the period from peak to subsequent trough; expansion is the period from trough to subsequent peak. Business cycle reference dates are determined by the National Bureau of Economic Research, Inc]

Business cycle reference date				Contraction (Peak to trough)	Expansion (Previous trough to peak)	Length of cycle	
Peak		Trough				Trough from previous trough	Peak from previous peak
Month	Year	Month	Year				
February	1945	October	1945	8	[1]80	[1]88	[2]93
November	1948	October	1949	11	37	48	45
July	1953	May	1954	10	45	55	56
August	1957	April	1958	8	39	47	49
April	1960	February	1961	10	24	34	32
December	1969	November	1970	11	106	117	116
November	1973	March	1975	16	36	52	47
January	1980	July	1980	6	58	64	74
July	1981	November	1982	16	12	28	18
July	1990	March	1991	8	92	100	108
March	2001	November	2001	8	120	128	128
December	2007	June	2009	18	73	91	81
Average, all cycles: 1945 to 2009 (11 cycles)				11.1	59.4	69.5	68.5

[1] Previous trough: June 1938. [2] Previous peak: May 1937.

Source: National Bureau of Economic Research, Inc., Cambridge, MA, "US Business Cycle Expansions and Contractions," <http://www.nber.org/cycles.html>, accessed September 2015 ©.

Table 805. The Conference Board Leading, Coincident, and Lagging Economic Indexes®: 2000 to 2014

[299.4 represents 299,400]

Item	Unit	2000	2005	2010	2011	2012	2013	2014
The Conference Board Leading Economic Index® (LEI) for the U.S., composite	2010 = 100	109.4	122.3	100.0	105.3	107.6	111.1	117.5
Average weekly hours, manufacturing	Hours	41.2	40.6	41.1	41.4	41.6	41.8	42.0
Average weekly initial claims for unemployment insurance	1,000	299.4	330.6	458.5	408.2	374.9	342.8	308.4
Manufacturers' new orders, consumer goods and materials (1982 dollars)	Million dollars	152,061	150,517	121,931	124,769	128,926	131,640	134,768
Manufacturers' new orders, nondefense capital goods excl. aircraft (1982 dollars)	Million dollars	45,991	40,540	35,854	39,406	41,631	40,870	42,855
Building permits, new private housing units	1,000	1,598	2,160	604	624	829	987	1,052
Leading Credit Index™ (std. dev.)	Standard deviation above or below the mean	1.39	-0.65	-1.01	-0.59	-0.73	-1.17	-1.10
Interest rate spread, 10-year Treasury bonds less federal funds	Percent	-0.21	1.08	3.04	2.68	1.66	2.24	2.45
The Conference Board Coincident Economic Index® (CEI) for the U.S., composite	2010 = 100	98.3	102.6	100.0	102.5	105.2	107.1	109.8
Employees on nonagricultural payrolls	1,000	132,030	133,996	130,269	131,843	134,098	136,394	139,023
Index of industrial production	2012 = 100	95.9	99.6	94.4	97.2	100.0	101.9	105.7
Personal income less transfer payments (2009 dollars)	Billion dollars	9,081	9,860	9,987	10,460	10,877	10,949	11,227
Manufacturing and trade sales (2009 dollars)	Million dollars	971,916	1,087,146	1,035,075	1,069,068	1,100,769	1,139,237	1,179,224
Composite index of 7 lagging indicators	2010 = 100	90.7	95.0	100.0	102.2	105.4	109.4	113.6
Inventories to sales ratio, manufacturing and trade	Ratio	1.41	1.36	1.39	1.39	1.40	1.39	1.40
Average duration of unemployment	Weeks	12.7	18.4	33.1	39.4	39.5	36.6	33.7
Consumer installment credit to personal income ratio	Percent	18.8	21.2	20.4	20.5	20.5	21.3	21.8
Commercial and industrial loans outstanding (2009 dollars)	Million dollars	1,056,889	730,251	727,209	775,773	876,368	963,017	1,066,885
Change in labor cost per unit of output, manufacturing	Percent	2.4	-1.8	-1.9	-1.1	0.2	-0.9	0.4
Change in consumer price index for services	Percent	3.8	3.5	0.9	2.0	2.1	2.4	2.6
Average prime rate	Percent	9.2	6.2	3.3	3.3	3.3	3.3	3.3

Source: The Conference Board, New York, NY 10022-6601, *Business Cycle Indicators*, monthly. Reproduced with permission from The Conference Board, Inc. © 2015, The Conference Board, Inc. For more information, see <http://www.conference-board.org/data/>.

Table 806. Manufacturing and Trade—Sales and Inventories: 1992 to 2014

[In billions of dollars (540 represents $540,000,000,000), except ratios. Based on North American Industry Classification System (NAICS), 2007; see text, this section]

Year	Sales, average monthly [1]				Inventories [2]				Inventory-sales ratio [3]			
	Total	Manufac-turing	Retail trade	Mer-chant whole-salers	Total	Manufac-turing	Retail trade	Mer-chant whole-salers	Total	Manufac-turing	Retail trade	Mer-chant whole-salers
1992......	540	242	151	147	836	379	260	197	1.53	1.57	1.67	1.31
1993......	567	252	161	154	863	380	278	205	1.50	1.50	1.68	1.30
1994......	610	270	175	165	926	400	305	222	1.46	1.44	1.66	1.29
1995......	655	290	185	180	985	425	322	238	1.48	1.44	1.72	1.29
1996......	687	300	197	190	1,005	430	333	241	1.45	1.44	1.67	1.27
1997......	723	320	206	198	1,046	443	344	258	1.42	1.37	1.64	1.26
1998......	742	325	215	202	1,077	448	357	272	1.44	1.39	1.62	1.32
1999......	786	336	234	217	1,137	463	384	290	1.40	1.35	1.59	1.30
2000......	834	351	249	235	1,196	481	406	309	1.41	1.35	1.59	1.29
2001......	818	331	255	232	1,119	427	394	298	1.42	1.38	1.58	1.32
2002......	823	326	261	236	1,139	423	415	301	1.36	1.29	1.55	1.26
2003......	855	335	272	248	1,148	408	431	308	1.34	1.25	1.56	1.22
2004......	926	359	289	278	1,241	441	460	340	1.30	1.19	1.56	1.17
2005......	1,006	395	307	303	1,313	474	472	368	1.27	1.17	1.51	1.17
2006......	1,069	418	323	328	1,408	522	486	399	1.28	1.20	1.49	1.17
2007......	1,128	443	333	352	1,486	561	501	424	1.28	1.22	1.49	1.17
2008......	1,160	456	328	377	1,463	541	477	444	1.31	1.27	1.52	1.19
2009......	988	368	301	318	1,326	502	429	394	1.38	1.39	1.47	1.28
2010......	1,087	409	318	360	1,443	550	455	437	1.27	1.28	1.39	1.14
2011......	1,204	457	342	405	1,555	603	471	481	1.26	1.28	1.35	1.14
2012......	1,267	478	359	430	1,644	626	505	513	1.27	1.29	1.38	1.16
2013......	1,303	487	372	444	1,716	638	544	535	1.29	1.30	1.41	1.18
2014......	1,348	500	386	463	1,781	653	558	570	1.31	1.31	1.43	1.20

[1] Averages of monthly not-seasonally-adjusted figures. [2] Seasonally adjusted end-of-year data. [3] Averages of seasonally adjusted monthly ratios.

Source: U.S. Council of Economic Advisors, *Economic Indicators*, monthly. See also <http://www.gpo.gov/fdsys/browse/collection.action?collectionCode=ECONI>.

Table 807. Industrial Production Indexes by Industry: 2000 to 2014

[2007 = 100]

Industry	NAICS code [1]	2000	2005	2009	2010	2011	2012	2013	2014
Total index....................................	([2])	**92.2**	**95.5**	**85.7**	**90.6**	**93.6**	**97.1**	**99.9**	**104.1**
Manufacturing (SIC) [3].........................	([4])	**91.3**	**95.0**	**82.4**	**87.3**	**90.3**	**94.0**	**96.5**	**99.8**
Manufacturing (NAICS).......................	31–33	89.8	94.4	82.4	87.9	91.1	95.1	97.9	101.5
Durable goods...............................	([5])	84.8	91.2	78.6	87.2	93.2	100.0	104.4	109.8
Wood products............................	321	99.3	105.9	65.3	67.6	68.4	71.6	78.1	81.4
Nonmetallic mineral products..............	327	94.9	99.4	66.6	68.6	70.2	71.4	74.0	78.2
Primary metals...........................	331	100.3	95.2	74.0	91.1	97.4	99.6	100.8	105.2
Fabricated metal products..................	332	96.6	90.9	74.2	79.0	85.3	91.4	94.7	98.5
Machinery.................................	333	97.7	91.6	75.7	84.6	95.6	101.1	102.9	110.0
Computers and electronic products........	334	53.6	77.0	97.0	111.3	122.0	135.0	144.4	150.8
Electrical equipment, appliances, and components......................	335	113.9	95.3	75.6	78.6	83.4	86.0	88.4	91.4
Motor vehicles and parts....................	3361–3	97.4	102.3	58.6	77.8	84.8	97.4	105.0	113.2
Aerospace and other misc. transportation equipment..................	3364–9	76.0	80.2	92.8	94.0	94.3	102.2	105.4	109.7
Furniture and related products.............	337	103.6	105.5	65.5	64.7	66.5	68.4	70.6	75.6
Miscellaneous products.....................	339	86.8	99.5	94.2	97.5	98.4	102.8	109.8	114.8
Nondurable goods..........................	([6])	95.9	98.3	86.9	88.7	88.9	90.0	91.2	93.1
Food, beverage, and tobacco products.....	311, 2	95.3	99.8	96.5	96.7	96.8	100.2	101.4	103.2
Textile and product mills...................	313, 4	144.2	124.5	69.7	74.4	74.0	74.5	73.4	74.5
Apparel and leather.......................	315, 6	235.2	126.1	59.4	60.0	58.9	57.6	59.1	60.2
Paper.....................................	322	107.7	100.7	85.4	87.2	87.3	85.4	85.0	82.8
Printing and related support................	323	107.8	98.6	78.8	78.8	78.0	76.1	75.7	77.4
Petroleum and coal products...............	324	85.2	95.6	94.3	93.5	94.7	95.4	96.2	98.4
Chemical..................................	325	81.9	92.9	83.5	86.3	86.3	86.4	87.5	89.4
Plastics and rubber products...............	326	102.3	102.2	75.8	82.6	84.0	86.9	90.9	97.2
Other manufacturing (non-NAICS) [7]........	1133, 5111	121.9	107.4	80.7	76.4	74.3	72.8	68.9	65.9
Mining.......................................	21	**102.8**	**97.0**	**95.7**	**100.7**	**106.8**	**113.5**	**118.9**	**129.6**
Electric and gas utilities..................	2211, 2	**89.9**	**97.3**	**97.5**	**101.0**	**100.8**	**98.7**	**100.7**	**102.0**
Electric power generation, transmission, and distribution.................	2211	87.9	97.0	96.9	100.7	100.4	98.8	99.6	100.8
Natural gas distribution......................	2212	100.3	98.9	100.4	102.2	102.4	96.9	107.9	111.1

[1] Except as noted, based on North American Industry Classification System, 2007; see text, this section. [2] Includes NAICS codes 31–33, 1133, 5111, 21, 2211, and 2212. [3] Standard Industrial Classification (SIC); see text, this section. [4] Includes NAICS codes 31–33, 1133, and 5111. [5] Includes NAICS codes 321, 327, and 331–339. [6] Includes NAICS codes 311–316, and 322–326. [7] Those industries—logging and newspaper, periodical, book, and directory publishing—that have traditionally been considered to be manufacturing.

Source: Board of Governors of the Federal Reserve System, *Industrial Production and Capacity Utilization*, Statistical Release G.17, "Data Download Program," <http://www.federalreserve.gov/datadownload/default.htm>, accessed May 2015.

Table 808. Index of Industrial Capacity and Utilization Rate: 1990 to 2014

[2007 output = 100. Annual figures are averages of monthly data. The capacity index is an indicator of the maximum sustainable output a plant can maintain under realistic circumstances; capacity here is expressed as a proportion of 2007 actual output. Capacity utilization rate is a measure of output as a proportion of capacity; this is the output index divided by the capacity index]

| Year | Index of capacity | | Utilization rate | | | | |
| | Total industry | Manufacturing [1] | Total industry | Stage of process | | | Manufacturing [1] |
				Crude [2]	Primary and semifinished [3]	Finished [4]	
1990.........	75.4	71.9	82.5	87.7	82.7	80.7	81.7
1995.........	85.5	82.9	83.9	88.7	86.3	79.8	83.1
2000.........	113.3	114.6	81.4	88.6	84.0	76.6	79.6
2005.........	119.5	121.5	79.9	86.7	81.7	75.3	78.2
2006.........	121.7	124.2	80.2	88.2	81.1	76.0	78.4
2007.........	124.1	127.1	80.5	88.7	80.8	77.1	78.7
2008.........	124.5	127.8	77.6	87.0	76.8	74.1	74.6
2009.........	124.8	125.5	68.7	78.2	66.0	68.5	65.6
2010.........	122.7	122.9	73.8	83.9	71.9	72.2	71.1
2011.........	122.7	122.1	76.3	85.0	74.4	74.5	73.9
2012.........	125.7	124.5	77.3	85.3	75.0	76.3	75.5
2013.........	128.2	126.8	77.9	86.0	76.2	76.2	76.1
2014.........	131.6	129.4	79.1	86.9	77.6	77.1	77.2

[1] Manufacturing consists of those industries included in the North American Industry Classification System (NAICS) definition of manufacturing plus those industries–logging and newspaper, periodical, book, and directory publishing–that have traditionally been considered to be a part of manufacturing and are included in the industrial sector. [2] Crude processing covers a relatively small portion of total industrial capacity and consists of logging (NAICS 1133), much of mining (excluding stone, sand, and gravel mining, and oil and gas drilling, NAICS 21231, 21221–2, and 213111) and some basic manufacturing industries, including basic chemicals (NAICS 3251); fertilizers, pesticides, and other agricultural chemicals (NAICS 32531, 2); pulp, paper, and paperboard mills (NAICS 3221); and alumina, aluminum, and other nonferrous production and processing mills (NAICS 3313, 4). [3] Primary and semifinished processing loosely corresponds to the previously published aggregate, primary processing. Includes utilities and portions of several 2-digit SIC industries included in the former advanced processing group. These include printing and related support activities (NAICS 3231); paints and adhesives (NAICS 3255); and newspaper, periodical, book, and directory publishers (NAICS 5111). [4] Finished processing generally corresponds to the previously published aggregate, advanced processing. Includes oil and gas well drilling and carpet and rug mills.

Source: Board of Governors of the Federal Reserve System, *Industrial Production and Capacity Utilization*, Statistical Release G.17, "Data Download Program," <http://www.federalreserve.gov/datadownload/>, accessed May 2015.

Table 809. Corporate Profits, Taxes, and Dividends: 2000 to 2014

[In billions of dollars (781 represents $781,000,000,000). Covers corporations organized for profit and other entities treated as corporations. Represents profits to U.S. residents, without deduction of depletion charges and exclusive of capital gains and losses; intercorporate dividends from profits of domestic corporations are eliminated; and net receipts of dividends, reinvested earnings of incorporated foreign affiliates, and earnings of unincorporated foreign affiliates are added. Minus (-) sign indicates loss]

Item	2000	2005	2010	2011	2012	2013	2014
Corporate profits with IVA and CCA [1]...............	781	1,478	1,746	1,817	1,998	2,037	2,073
Taxes on corporate income...............	265	412	371	379	448	469	514
Profits after tax with IVA and CCA [1]...............	516	1,065	1,376	1,438	1,551	1,569	1,559
Net dividends...............	385	581	564	704	859	924	860
Undistributed profits with IVA and CCA [1]...............	131	485	812	734	691	645	699
Addenda for corporate cash flow:							
Net cash flow with IVA and CCA [1]...............	976	1,524	2,095	2,072	2,050	2,055	2,163
Undistributed profits with IVA and CCA [1]...............	131	485	812	734	691	645	699
Consumption of fixed capital...............	845	1,052	1,263	1,299	1,351	1,405	1,467
Less: Capital transfers paid (net)...............	–	12	-21	-39	-7	-6	3

– Represents or rounds to zero. [1] Inventory valuation adjustment (IVA) and capital consumption adjustment (CCA).

Source: U.S. Bureau of Economic Analysis, National Income and Product Accounts Tables, "Table 1.12. National Income by Type of Income," <http://www.bea.gov/itable/>, accessed July 2015.

Table 810. Corporate Profits With Inventory Valuation and Capital Consumption Adjustments—Financial and Nonfinancial Industries: 2000 to 2014

[In billions of dollars (781 represents $781,000,000,000). Based on the North American Industry Classification System, 2002; see text, this section. Minus sign (-) indicates loss. See headnote, Table 809]

Industry group	2000	2005	2010	2011	2012	2013	2014
Corporate profits with IVA/CCA [1]...............	**781**	**1,478**	**1,746**	**1,817**	**1,998**	**2,037**	**2,073**
Domestic industries...............	635	1,239	1,351	1,395	1,588	1,623	1,655
Rest of the world...............	146	239	395	422	410	415	418
Corporate profits with IVA [1]...............	**730**	**1,621**	**1,800**	**1,739**	**2,117**	**2,165**	**2,205**
Domestic industries...............	584	1,382	1,405	1,317	1,706	1,750	1,787
Financial [2]...............	150	410	406	376	479	424	423
Nonfinancial...............	434	972	998	941	1,227	1,326	1,363
Utilities...............	24	31	30	10	13	26	28
Manufacturing...............	176	278	288	298	396	426	440
Wholesale trade...............	60	96	102	94	135	146	148
Retail trade...............	51	122	119	114	154	159	158
Transportation and warehousing...............	10	28	45	30	54	53	65
Information...............	-12	91	95	84	101	129	127
Other nonfinancial [3]...............	126	327	320	310	375	386	398
Rest of the world...............	146	239	395	422	410	415	418

[1] Inventory valuation adjustment (IVA) and capital consumption adjustment (CCA). [2] Consists of finance and insurance and bank and other holding companies. [3] Consists of agriculture, forestry, fishing, and hunting; mining; construction; real estate and rental and leasing; professional, scientific, and technical services; administrative and waste management services; educational services; health care and social assistance; arts, entertainment, and recreation; accommodation and food services; and other services, except government.

Source: U.S. Bureau of Economic Analysis, National Income and Product Accounts Tables, "Table 6.16D. Corporate Profits by Industry," <http://www.bea.gov/itable/>, accessed June 2015.

Table 811. Corporate Profits Before Taxes by Industry: 2000 to 2014

[In billions of dollars (747 represents $747,000,000,000). Profits are without inventory valuation and capital consumption adjustments. Minus sign (-) indicates loss. See headnote, Table 809]

Industry	2002 NAICS code [1]	2000	2005	2010	2012	2013	2014
Corporate profits before tax.........................	(X)	**747**	**1,653**	**1,841**	**2,131**	**2,162**	**2,208**
Domestic industries................................	(X)	601	1,414	1,446	1,720	1,747	1,790
Agriculture, forestry, fishing, and hunting..........	11	1	5	8	13	12	11
Mining..................................	21	15	45	32	31	38	32
Utilities................................	221	25	32	30	12	27	28
Construction............................	23	36	82	27	44	53	61
Manufacturing............................	31-33	186	293	304	399	427	443
Wholesale trade............................	42	63	103	117	140	139	145
Retail trade............................	44-45	53	127	125	160	160	161
Transportation and warehousing..............	48-49	10	28	45	54	53	64
Information................................	51	-12	91	95	101	130	127
Finance and insurance....................	52	63	248	220	309	273	281
Real estate and rental and leasing.............	53	9	27	13	21	22	24
Professional, scientific, and technical services...	54	9	47	83	88	73	69
Management of companies and enterprises [2].....	551111, 2	87	162	186	170	150	142
Administrative and waste management services..............	56	9	24	28	31	31	33
Educational services........................	61	2	5	11	9	7	8
Health care and social assistance..............	62	23	54	78	85	87	94
Arts, entertainment, and recreation.............	71	3	8	8	11	13	14
Accommodation and food services.............	72	14	22	18	27	32	34
Other services, except public administration.........	81	6	11	15	17	18	18
Rest of the world [3]..............	(X)	146	239	395	410	415	418

X Not applicable. [1] Based on North American Industry Classification System, 2002; see text, this section. [2] Consists of bank and other holding companies. [3] Consists of receipts by all U.S. residents, including both corporations and persons, of dividends from foreign corporations, and, for U.S. corporations, their share of reinvested earnings of their incorporated foreign affiliates, and earnings of unincorporated foreign affiliates, net of corresponding payments.

Source: U.S. Bureau of Economic Analysis, National Income and Product Accounts Tables, "Table 6.17D. Corporate Profits Before Tax by Industry," <http://www.bea.gov/itable/>, accessed August 2015.

Table 812. Manufacturing, Mining, and Trade Corporations—Profits and Stockholders' Equity by Industry: 2013 and 2014

[Averages of quarterly figures at annual rates. Manufacturing data exclude estimates for corporations with less than $250,000 in assets at time of sample selection. Mining, wholesale and retail trade data excludes estimates for corporations with less than $50 million in assets at time of sample selection. Based on sample; see source for discussion of methodology. Based on North American Industry Classification System (NAICS), 2012; see text, this section]

Industry	2012 NAICS code	Ratio of profits after taxes to stockholders' equity (percent)		Profits after taxes per dollar of sales (cents)		Ratio of stockholders' equity to debt	
		2013	2014	2013	2014	2013	2014
Manufacturing........................	**31-33**	**15.7**	**15.2**	**8.9**	**8.8**	**1.8**	**1.7**
Nondurable manufacturing......................	(X)	16.3	14.8	8.6	8.3	1.5	1.5
Food..........................	311	14.5	11.2	5.4	4.5	1.3	1.3
Beverage and tobacco products..................	312	22.7	20.4	20.0	18.2	1.1	1.1
Textile mills and textile product mills..................	313, 314	10.7	14.4	4.6	5.7	2.1	1.9
Apparel and leather products..................	315, 316	20.7	19.4	9.4	8.8	2.5	2.4
Paper..........................	322	16.8	11.9	6.3	4.5	1.0	1.0
Printing and related support activities..................	323	25.3	17.6	4.6	3.6	0.5	0.6
Petroleum and coal products..................	324	13.3	12.8	5.4	5.8	2.7	2.8
Chemicals..........................	325	17.3	16.0	14.8	14.1	1.3	1.2
Plastics and rubber products..................	326	19.0	18.3	6.5	6.6	1.2	1.3
Durable manufacturing.........................	(X)	15.1	15.5	9.2	9.4	2.2	2.1
Wood products...........................	321	16.7	23.3	5.2	7.2	1.3	1.3
Nonmetallic mineral products..................	327	9.3	7.7	7.6	5.5	1.9	1.9
Primary metals..................	331	5.4	6.2	3.0	3.3	1.8	1.6
Fabricated metal products..................	332	18.6	18.9	7.2	7.5	1.5	1.5
Machinery..........................	333	17.1	16.3	8.9	8.7	2.0	1.9
Computer and electronic products..................	334	15.6	17.7	18.0	20.0	3.0	2.6
Electrical equipment, appliances, & components......	335	10.7	12.1	12.0	13.3	3.7	3.8
Transportation equipment..................	336	21.1	17.5	6.0	5.4	1.7	1.8
Furniture and related products..................	337	14.8	20.7	4.0	5.5	1.4	1.4
Miscellaneous manufacturing..................	339	12.6	12.9	11.7	11.6	1.9	1.8
All mining..........................	**21**	**5.7**	**2.5**	**9.4**	**3.7**	**1.8**	**1.8**
All wholesale trade..................	**42**	**11.9**	**12.1**	**1.7**	**1.7**	**1.3**	**1.3**
Durable goods..........................	423	10.9	10.5	2.2	2.1	1.6	1.5
Nondurable goods..........................	424, 425	13.7	14.7	1.3	1.4	1.0	1.0
All retail trade..................	**44-45**	**16.7**	**15.0**	**3.2**	**2.8**	**1.5**	**1.4**
Food and beverage stores..................	445	19.2	12.8	2.3	1.6	1.3	1.4
Clothing and general merchandise stores..............	448, 452	17.4	15.3	3.8	3.3	1.5	1.5
All other retail trade..........................	(X)	15.5	15.3	3.1	2.9	1.5	1.4

X Not applicable.

Source: U.S. Census Bureau, *Quarterly Financial Report for Manufacturing, Mining, and Trade Corporations*, <http://www.census.gov/econ/qfr/index.html>.

Table 813. U.S. Multinational Enterprises—Value Added, Employment, and Capital Expenditures: 1989 to 2012

[Value added and capital expenditures in billions of dollars (1,401 represents $1,401,000,000,000); employees in thousands. Data for 2012 are preliminary. For the years shown prior to 2009, the data items needed to calculate value added and capital expenditures for individual U.S. parents and foreign affiliates were collected for nonbank businesses only. The value added and capital expenditures statistics for bank parents and affiliates for those years are estimates. See headnote, Table 814. MNE = Multinational enterprise. MOFA = Majority-owned foreign affiliate]

Item	1989	1994	1999	2004	2009	2010	2011	2012
VALUE ADDED								
MNEs worldwide:								
Parents and MOFAs.....................	1,401	1,773	2,645	3,221	3,741	4,191	4,577	4,667
Parents.....................................	1,077	1,362	2,064	2,366	2,596	2,949	3,161	3,246
MOFAs......................................	324	411	580	854	1,145	1,242	1,416	1,421
EMPLOYEES								
MNEs worldwide:								
Parents and all affiliates..............	26,370	26,571	33,398	32,892	35,962	36,287	36,747	37,153
Parents and MOFAs...................	24,826	25,142	31,913	31,466	33,727	34,105	34,844	35,226
Parents...................................	19,617	19,330	23,985	22,446	22,933	22,791	22,994	23,110
Affiliates, total...........................	6,753	7,241	9,412	10,445	13,029	13,496	13,753	14,043
MOFAs...................................	5,209	5,812	7,928	9,020	10,794	11,313	11,850	12,116
Other......................................	1,544	1,429	1,484	1,426	2,235	2,182	1,902	1,928
CAPITAL EXPENDITURES								
MNEs worldwide:								
Parents and all affiliates..............	279	331	563	500	653	(NA)	(NA)	(NA)
Parents and MOFAs...................	263	306	531	476	599	607	717	804
Parents...................................	204	235	417	351	432	441	528	584
Affiliates, total...........................	75	96	146	149	221	(NA)	(NA)	(NA)
MOFAs...................................	59	72	115	125	167	166	189	220
Other......................................	16	25	31	24	54	(NA)	(NA)	(NA)

NA Not available.

Source: U.S. Bureau of Economic Analysis, *Survey of Current Business*, August 2014. See also <http://www.bea.gov/scb/date_guide.asp>.

Table 814. U.S. Multinational Enterprises—Selected Characteristics: 2012

[In billions of dollars (32,123 represents $32,123,000,000,000), except as indicated. Data for 2012 are preliminary. Consists of U.S. parent enterprises and their foreign affiliates. U.S. parent comprises the domestic operations of a multinational and is a U.S. person that owns or controls, directly or indirectly, 10 percent or more of the voting securities of an incorporated foreign business enterprise, or an equivalent interest in an unincorporated foreign business enterprise. A U.S. person can be an incorporated business enterprise. A majority-owned foreign affiliate (MOFA) is a foreign business enterprise in which a U.S. parent enterprise owns or controls more than 50 percent of the voting securities]

Industry	2007 NAICS code [1]	U.S. parents [2]				MOFAs [3]		
		Total assets	Capital expenditures	Value added	Employment (1,000)	Capital expenditures	Value added	Employment (1,000)
All industries.....................................	(X)	32,123	584	3,246	23,110	220	1,421	12,116
Mining [4]...	21	618	57	91	229	86	221	233
Oil and gas extraction............................	211	372	43	44	46	68	182	59
Manufacturing [4].................................	31-33	6,792	220	1,272	6,827	66	563	4,795
Food..	311	513	12	101	810	6	37	465
Beverages and tobacco products...............	312	272	4	54	141	3	62	258
Petroleum and coal products....................	324	1,070	64	167	282	3	57	28
Chemicals [4].......................................	325	1,385	26	206	761	12	126	616
Pharmaceuticals and medicines...............	3254	874	10	116	372	3	63	222
Machinery...	333	402	11	73	548	5	44	446
Computers and electronic products [4]..........	334	745	21	204	885	15	76	733
Computers and peripheral equipment........	3341	181	6	78	212	7	32	194
Transportation equipment [4]....................	336	1,369	56	232	1,570	11	59	950
Motor vehicles, bodies and trailers, and parts.	3361-3363	572	43	85	626	10	51	871
Wholesale trade.....................................	42	1,033	43	164	1,094	9	184	806
Retail trade [4]......................................	44, 45	640	32	270	4,319	9	76	1,335
General merchandise stores.....................	452	249	12	120	2,052	6	33	871
Information [4].......................................	51	1,783	67	378	1,753	9	65	471
Publishing industries..............................	511	280	5	82	368	1	29	147
Broadcasting (except Internet)..................	515	395	9	78	367	1	5	19
Telecommunications...............................	517	706	44	143	582	5	14	86
Finance and insurance [4]........................	52	18,697	45	394	2,588	6	93	659
Insurance carriers and related activities........	524	5,558	11	81	907	1	24	206
Professional, scientific, and technical services [4].	54	523	9	204	1,298	5	89	1,089
Computer systems design and related services.	5415	259	5	83	452	3	47	663
Other industries [4]................................	(X)	2,037	111	474	5,001	29	130	2,729
Transportation and warehousing................	48-49	449	25	122	1,015	3	21	317
Administration, support, and waste management.	56	189	5	82	1,145	1	30	873

X Not applicable. [1] Based on North American Industry Classification System, 2007; see text, this section. [2] Data are by industry of U.S. parent. [3] Data are by industry of foreign affiliate. [4] Includes other industries, not shown separately.

Source: U.S. Bureau of Economic Analysis, "Direct Investment and Multinational Enterprises," <http://www.bea.gov/iTable/index_MNC.cfm>, accessed June 2015.

Table 815. U.S. Multinational Enterprises—Value Added: 2010 and 2012

[In billions of dollars (4,191 represents $4,191,000,000,000). Data are based on the North American Industry Classification System (NAICS), 2007. See headnote, Table 814. Data are by industry of U.S. parent]

Industry	NAICS code	U.S. multinationals		U.S. parents		Majority-owned foreign affiliates	
		2010	2012	2010	2012	2010	2012
All industries.	(X)	4,191	4,667	2,949	3,246	1,242	1,421
Mining [1]	21	118	147	75	91	43	56
Oil and gas extraction.	211	58	75	41	44	18	30
Manufacturing [1]	31-33	1,900	2,088	1,147	1,272	753	816
Food.	311	145	149	96	101	49	48
Beverages and tobacco products.	312	67	78	49	54	18	23
Petroleum and coal products.	324	383	421	135	167	248	254
Chemicals [1]	325	337	362	197	206	140	156
Pharmaceuticals and medicines.	3254	187	208	113	116	74	93
Machinery.	333	104	119	69	73	35	45
Computers and electronic products [1]	334	235	299	155	204	80	95
Computers and peripheral equipment.	3341	68	116	38	78	31	38
Transportation equipment [1]	336	314	325	229	232	85	93
Motor vehicles, bodies and trailers, and parts.	3361-3363	133	139	83	85	49	54
Wholesale trade.	42	174	201	143	164	32	37
Retail trade [1]	44, 45	303	320	257	270	46	50
General merchandise stores.	452	(D)	(D)	122	120	(D)	(D)
Information [1]	51	392	450	333	378	58	72
Publishing industries.	511	100	115	72	82	27	32
Broadcasting (except Internet).	515	49	86	41	78	8	8
Telecommunications.	517	172	155	162	143	10	12
Finance and insurance [1]	52	480	559	357	394	123	165
Insurance carriers and related activities.	524	101	107	84	81	17	25
Professional, scientific, and technical services [1]	54	275	295	196	204	79	90
Computer systems design and related services.	5415	133	143	80	83	53	60
Other industries [1]	(X)	548	607	440	474	108	133
Transportation and warehousing.	48-49	132	139	116	122	17	18
Administration, support, and waste management.	56	99	110	73	82	26	28

D Data withheld to avoid disclosure. X Not applicable. [1] Includes other industries, not shown separately.

Source: U.S. Bureau of Economic Analysis, "Direct Investment and Multinational Enterprises," <http://www.bea.gov/iTable/index_MNC.cfm>, accessed June 2015.

Table 816. U.S. Majority-Owned Foreign Affiliates—Value Added by Industry of Affiliate and Country: 2012

[Preliminary. In millions of dollars (1,420,679 represents $1,420,679,000,000). See headnote, Table 814. Numbers in parentheses represent North American Industry Classification System 2007 codes; see text, this section]

Country	All industries [1]	Mining (21)	Manufacturing (31-33)		Wholesale trade (42)	Finance and insurance (52)	Professional, scientific, and technical services (54)
			Total [1]	Chemicals (325)			
All countries [2]	1,420,679	221,329	563,149	125,984	184,093	92,623	89,119
United Kingdom.	171,522	9,266	66,453	6,488	11,219	25,286	15,666
Canada.	140,073	11,698	56,563	9,284	17,120	5,657	8,478
Germany.	87,940	1,557	40,500	7,121	18,835	2,573	5,359
Ireland.	81,796	(D)	51,800	27,167	4,088	2,378	436
Australia.	60,073	13,306	17,390	2,239	7,545	5,655	6,292
Japan.	52,802	8	17,893	7,214	8,204	10,346	7,125
France.	52,211	88	26,905	6,198	8,745	2,870	3,753
China.	46,491	2,761	27,145	6,755	6,341	162	3,523
Brazil.	44,327	2,603	27,978	6,376	2,724	1,735	2,447
Mexico.	43,274	3,368	21,340	3,523	2,441	4,700	1,639
Singapore.	38,462	564	17,424	5,371	6,576	5,555	1,240
Switzerland.	37,550	(D)	10,903	4,167	16,862	804	1,820
Netherlands.	32,544	1,044	19,305	5,747	4,957	525	2,260
Norway.	30,906	21,438	5,655	204	1,165	508	595
Italy.	30,769	92	10,967	2,679	3,841	703	2,698

D Data withheld to avoid disclosure. [1] Includes other industries, not shown separately. [2] Includes other countries, not shown separately.

Source: U.S. Bureau of Economic Analysis, "Activities of U.S. Multinational Enterprises, Majority-owned Foreign Affiliates, Value Added by Country and Industry 2009-2012," <http://www.bea.gov/international/di1usdop.htm>, accessed June 2015.

Science and Technology

This section presents statistics on scientific, engineering, and technological resources, with emphasis on patterns of research and development (R&D) funding and on scientific, engineering, and technical personnel; education; and employment.

The National Science Foundation (NSF) gathers data chiefly through recurring surveys and report the data via detailed statistical tables; info briefs; and annual, biennial, and special reports; see <http://www.nsf.gov/statistics>. Areas of coverage include R&D expenditures; Federal R&D funding; scientific employment; graduate enrollment and support in academic science and engineering; characteristics of doctoral scientists and engineers and of recent graduates in the United States. Report titles include: *Science and Engineering Indicators; National Patterns of R&D Resources; Federal Funds for Research and Development; Federal R&D Funding by Budget Function; Federal S&E Support to Universities, Colleges, and Selected Nonprofit Institutions;* and *Research and Development in Industry.* Statistical surveys in these areas pose problems of concept and definition and the data should therefore be regarded as broad estimates rather than precise, quantitative statements. See sources for methodological and technical details.

The National Science Board's biennial *Science and Engineering Indicators* at <http://www.nsf.gov/statistics/seind/> contains data and analysis of international and domestic science and technology, including education and workforce statistics.

Research and development outlays—NSF defines research as "systematic study directed toward fuller scientific knowledge of the subject studied" and development as "the systematic use of scientific knowledge directed toward the production of useful materials, devices, systems, or methods, including design and development of prototypes and processes."

National coverage of R&D expenditures is developed primarily from periodic surveys in four principal economic sectors: (1) *government*, made up primarily of federal executive agencies; (2) *industry*, consisting of manufacturing and nonmanufacturing firms and the federally funded research and development centers (FFRDCs) they administer; (3) *universities and colleges*, composed of universities, colleges, and their affiliated institutions, agricultural experiment stations, and associated schools of agriculture and of medicine, and FFRDCs administered by educational institutions; and (4) *other nonprofit institutions*, consisting of such organizations as private philanthropic foundations, nonprofit research institutes, voluntary health agencies, and FFRDCs administered by nonprofit organizations.

The R&D funds reported consist of current operating costs, including planning and administration costs, except as otherwise noted. They exclude funds for routine testing, mapping and surveying, collection of general purpose data, dissemination of scientific information, and training of scientific personnel.

Scientists, engineers, and technicians—Scientists and engineers are defined as persons engaged in scientific and engineering work at a level requiring a knowledge of sciences equivalent at least to that acquired through completion of a 4-year college course. Technicians are defined as persons engaged in technical work at a level requiring knowledge acquired through a technical institute, junior college, or other type of training less extensive than 4-year college training. Craftsmen and skilled workers are excluded.

Table 817. Research and Development (R&D) Expenditures by Source of Funding: 1960 to 2012

[In millions of dollars (13,711 represents $13,711,000,000), except for percents]

Year	Total	Sources of funds					Percent of total				
		Federal govern-ment	Industry	Univer-sities/ colleges [1]	Non-profit	Non-federal govern-ment [2]	Federal govern-ment	Industry	Univer-sities/ colleges [1]	Non-profit	Non-federal govern-ment [2]
1960......	13,711	8,915	4,516	67	123	90	65.0	32.9	0.5	0.9	0.7
1970......	26,271	14,984	10,449	259	343	237	57.0	39.8	1.0	1.3	0.9
1980......	63,224	29,986	30,929	920	871	519	47.4	48.9	1.5	1.4	0.8
1983......	89,950	41,451	45,264	1,357	1,220	658	46.1	50.3	1.5	1.4	0.7
1984......	102,244	46,470	52,187	1,514	1,351	721	45.5	51.0	1.5	1.3	0.7
1985......	114,671	52,641	57,962	1,743	1,491	834	45.9	50.5	1.5	1.3	0.7
1986......	120,249	54,622	60,991	2,019	1,647	969	45.4	50.7	1.7	1.4	0.8
1987......	126,360	58,609	62,576	2,262	1,849	1,065	46.4	49.5	1.8	1.5	0.8
1988......	133,881	60,131	67,977	2,527	2,081	1,165	44.9	50.8	1.9	1.6	0.9
1989......	141,891	60,466	74,966	2,852	2,333	1,274	42.6	52.8	2.0	1.6	0.9
1990......	151,993	61,610	83,208	3,187	2,589	1,399	40.5	54.7	2.1	1.7	0.9
1991......	160,876	60,783	92,300	3,458	2,852	1,483	37.8	57.4	2.1	1.8	0.9
1992......	165,350	60,915	96,229	3,569	3,113	1,525	36.8	58.2	2.2	1.9	0.9
1993......	165,730	60,528	96,549	3,709	3,388	1,557	36.5	58.3	2.2	2.0	0.9
1994......	169,207	60,777	99,204	3,938	3,665	1,623	35.9	58.6	2.3	2.2	1.0
1995......	183,625	62,969	110,871	4,110	3,925	1,751	34.3	60.4	2.2	2.1	1.0
1996......	197,346	63,394	123,417	4,436	4,239	1,861	32.1	62.5	2.2	2.1	0.9
1997......	212,152	64,574	136,228	4,838	4,590	1,922	30.4	64.2	2.3	2.2	0.9
1998......	226,457	66,383	147,825	5,163	5,114	1,972	29.3	65.3	2.3	2.3	0.9
1999......	245,318	67,366	164,606	5,619	5,628	2,098	27.5	67.1	2.3	2.3	0.9
2000......	268,905	67,862	186,037	6,231	6,528	2,246	25.2	69.2	2.3	2.4	0.8
2001......	279,716	74,966	188,336	6,826	7,192	2,395	26.8	67.3	2.4	2.6	0.9
2002......	279,387	80,315	180,643	7,617	8,203	2,610	28.7	64.7	2.7	2.9	0.9
2003......	293,060	86,705	186,113	8,226	9,160	2,856	29.6	63.5	2.8	3.1	1.0
2004......	304,547	92,360	191,307	8,562	9,310	3,008	30.3	62.8	2.8	3.1	1.0
2005......	327,185	97,041	207,725	9,265	10,095	3,060	29.7	63.5	2.8	3.1	0.9
2006......	352,567	101,558	227,110	10,076	10,641	3,182	28.8	64.4	2.9	3.0	0.9
2007......	379,681	106,858	246,741	10,833	11,810	3,438	28.1	65.0	2.9	3.1	0.9
2008......	406,610	119,423	258,691	11,640	13,151	3,706	29.4	63.6	2.9	3.2	0.9
2009......	404,731	127,467	247,270	11,917	14,268	3,809	31.5	61.1	2.9	3.5	0.9
2010......	407,703	127,813	249,188	12,100	14,814	3,788	31.3	61.1	3.0	3.6	0.9
2011......	428,163	129,068	267,306	12,965	15,106	3,718	30.1	62.4	3.0	3.5	0.9
2012 [3]....	452,556	135,018	285,040	13,506	15,333	3,659	29.8	63.0	3.0	3.4	0.8

[1] Figures for university and college (U&C) R&D prior to 2003 cover only science and engineering (S&E) fields; in 2003 and later years, R&D in non-S&E fields is also included. Also, adjustments have been made to U&C R&D for 1998 and later years to eliminate double counting of funds passed through from one academic institution to another. [2] Nonfederal R&D expenditures to university and college performers. [3] Preliminary.

Source: U.S. National Science Foundation, *National Patterns of R&D Resources, 2011-2012 Data Update*, NSF 14-304, December 2013. See also <http://www.nsf.gov/statistics/natlpatterns/>.

Table 818. National Research and Development (R&D) Expenditures as a Percent of Gross Domestic Product by Country: 1990 to 2013

Year	United States	Japan [1]	Ger-many [2]	France	United Kingdom	Italy	Canada	South Korea	OECD total [3]	Russia	China
1990....	[4] 2.55	[7,8] 2.73	[9] 2.61	2.26	1.95	[10] 1.20	1.49	(NA)	[12] 2.18	[7] 2.03	(NA)
1995....	[4] 2.40	[7,8] 2.66	[9] 2.13	2.23	1.79	0.94	1.66	[11] 2.20	[5,12] 1.99	[7] 0.85	[7,13] 0.57
2000....	[4] 2.62	[7] 3.00	2.40	[5] 2.08	1.73	1.01	1.87	[11] 2.18	[12] 2.14	[7] 1.05	[5,7] 0.90
2003....	[4,5] 2.55	[7] 3.14	2.46	2.11	1.67	1.06	1.99	[11] 2.35	[12] 2.16	[7] 1.29	[7] 1.13
2004....	[4] 2.49	[7] 3.13	2.42	[5] 2.09	1.61	1.05	2.01	[11] 2.53	[12] 2.13	[7] 1.15	[7] 1.23
2005....	[4] 2.51	[7] 3.31	2.43	2.04	1.63	1.05	1.99	[11] 2.63	[12] 2.16	[7] 1.07	[7] 1.32
2006....	[4] 2.55	[7] 3.41	2.46	2.05	1.65	1.09	1.96	[11] 2.83	[12] 2.19	[7] 1.07	[7] 1.39
2007....	[4] 2.63	[7] 3.46	2.45	2.02	1.69	1.13	1.92	[5] 3.00	[12] 2.22	[7] 1.12	[7] 1.40
2008....	[4] 2.77	[5,7] 3.47	2.60	2.06	[9] 1.69	1.16	1.87	3.12	[12] 2.29	[7] 1.04	[7] 1.47
2009....	[4] 2.82	[7] 3.36	2.73	2.21	[9] 1.75	1.22	1.92	3.29	[12] 2.34	[7] 1.25	[5,7] 1.70
2010....	[4] 2.74	[7] 3.25	2.72	[5] 2.18	[9] 1.69	1.22	1.84	3.47	[12] 2.30	[7] 1.13	[7] 1.76
2011....	[4] 2.76	[7] 3.38	2.80	2.19	1.69	1.21	1.78	3.74	[12] 2.33	[7] 1.09	[7] 1.84
2012....	[4] 2.70	[7] 3.34	2.88	2.23	[9] 1.63	1.27	1.71	4.03	[12] 2.33	[7] 1.12	[7] 1.98
2013....	[4,6] 2.73	[7] 3.47	[6,9] 2.85	[6] 2.23	[6,9] 1.63	[6] 1.26	[6] 1.62	4.15	[12] 2.36	[7] 1.12	[7] 2.08

NA Not available. [1] Data on Japanese research and development after 1996 may not be consistent with data in earlier years because of changes in methodology. [2] Data for 1990 are for West Germany only. [3] Organization for Economic Cooperation and Development. [4] Excludes most or all capital expenditure. [5] Break in series with previous year for which data is available. [6] Provisional. [7] Compiled according to the System of National Accounts 1993. [8] National results adjusted by the Secretariat to meet OECD norms. [9] National estimate or projection. [10] Including extramural R&D expenditure. [11] Excluding R&D in the social sciences and humanities. [12] Secretariat estimate or projection based on national sources. [13] Underestimated or based on underestimated data.

Source: Organisation for Economic Co-operation and Development (OECD), 2015, "Main Science and Technology Indicators," OECD Science, Technology and R&D Statistics (database) ©, <http://dx.doi.org/10.1787/data-00182-en>, accessed July 2015.

Table 819. Research and Development (R&D) Expenditures By Performing Sector and Source of Funds: 1990 to 2012

[In millions of dollars (151,993 represents $151,993,000,000). For calendar year. FFRDCs are federally funded research and development centers]

Year	Total[1]	Federal government	Industry — Total	Industry — Funded by Federal government	Industry — Funded by Industry[2]	Industry FFRDCs	Univ. & colleges — Total	Univ. — Funded by Federal government	Univ. — Funded by Non-federal government[3]	Univ. — Funded by Industry	Univ. — Funded by Universities & colleges	Univ. — Funded by Non-profits	University & college FFRDCs[4]	Other nonprofit — Total	Other nonprofit — Funded by Federal government	Other nonprofit — Funded by Industry	Other nonprofit — Funded by Non-profits
RESEARCH AND DEVELOPMENT TOTAL																	
1990	151,993	15,671	107,404	25,802	81,602	2,323	16,939	9,939	1,399	1,166	3,187	1,249	4,894	4,126	2,346	440	1,340
2000	268,905	19,247	199,961	17,117	182,844	2,001	30,693	17,719	2,246	2,174	6,231	2,324	5,742	9,734	4,510	1,020	4,204
2006	352,567	28,240	247,669	24,304	223,365	3,122	48,951	29,600	3,182	2,563	10,076	3,530	7,306	14,336	6,044	1,182	7,111
2007	379,681	29,859	269,267	26,585	242,682	5,165	51,149	30,160	3,438	2,803	10,833	3,915	5,567	15,132	5,980	1,257	7,896
2008	406,610	29,839	290,681	36,360	254,321	6,346	53,917	31,178	3,706	3,069	11,640	4,324	4,766	16,363	6,236	1,301	8,827
2009	404,731	30,560	282,393	39,573	242,820	6,646	56,972	33,434	3,809	3,193	11,917	4,620	5,052	18,002	7,097	1,258	9,647
2010	407,703	31,970	278,977	34,199	244,778	7,214	60,369	36,565	3,788	3,145	12,100	4,771	5,315	18,401	7,093	1,265	10,043
2011[5]	428,163	35,775	294,093	31,309	262,784	6,956	62,457	37,714	3,718	3,189	12,965	4,872	5,246	18,120	6,553	1,333	10,234
2012[5]	452,556	37,574	316,700	36,300	280,400	6,808	62,723	37,393	3,659	3,242	13,506	4,923	5,174	18,113	6,305	1,398	10,410
BASIC RESEARCH																	
1990	23,029	2,319	4,629	869	3,760	499	11,126	6,889	847	705	1,929	756	2,470	1,922	947	245	730
2000	42,752	3,765	7,040	925	6,115	547	22,910	13,960	1,549	1,499	4,298	1,603	2,874	5,000	2,099	566	2,334
2006	62,996	4,716	8,384	1,444	6,940	652	37,205	23,312	2,285	1,840	7,233	2,535	3,344	7,454	2,849	656	3,948
2007	68,047	4,621	11,268	2,780	8,488	2,258	38,929	23,673	2,499	2,037	7,874	2,845	1,724	7,911	2,829	698	4,384
2008	72,105	4,957	12,368	1,475	10,893	2,423	40,582	24,149	2,679	2,218	8,412	3,124	1,672	8,697	3,073	722	4,901
2009	75,854	5,441	14,784	1,340	13,444	2,629	40,012	24,090	2,576	2,161	8,065	3,120	1,902	9,553	3,498	698	5,357
2010	77,386	5,111	16,371	1,406	14,965	2,848	39,588	24,526	2,397	1,990	7,656	3,051	2,203	9,693	3,414	702	5,576
2011[5]	74,161	4,911	13,020	677	12,343	2,673	40,281	24,786	2,329	1,997	8,117	3,051	2,213	9,489	3,066	740	5,683
2012[5]	74,849	5,086	13,955	785	13,170	2,446	40,045	24,295	2,275	2,016	8,398	3,061	2,160	9,624	3,067	776	5,780
APPLIED RESEARCH																	
1990	34,897	3,652	24,399	5,967	18,432	386	4,406	2,140	453	377	1,031	404	689	1,284	780	120	384
2000	56,681	6,105	39,176	2,682	36,494	269	6,494	3,194	571	553	1,585	591	1,291	3,155	1,831	258	1,066
2006	76,735	7,435	51,173	6,140	45,033	1,314	9,794	5,318	736	593	2,331	816	1,827	4,694	2,592	300	1,802
2007	83,551	7,222	57,570	8,945	48,625	1,168	10,249	5,548	770	628	2,426	877	1,354	4,902	2,583	318	2,001
2008	74,793	7,316	46,864	5,397	41,467	1,975	11,316	6,144	843	698	2,647	983	855	5,167	2,600	330	2,237
2009	72,891	7,874	41,055	7,797	33,258	2,010	13,444	7,708	928	778	2,903	1,127	1,282	5,813	3,049	319	2,445
2010	79,526	8,016	44,906	4,705	40,201	2,249	15,517	9,407	972	807	3,106	1,225	1,274	5,907	3,041	321	2,545
2011[5]	82,425	7,849	47,186	4,404	42,782	2,256	16,554	10,071	973	835	3,398	1,276	1,318	5,622	2,691	338	2,594
2012[5]	86,773	8,084	50,756	5,106	45,650	2,387	16,896	10,147	975	864	3,599	1,312	1,386	5,675	2,682	354	2,638
DEVELOPMENT																	
1990	94,067	9,700	78,376	18,966	59,410	1,438	1,407	910	99	83	226	89	1,735	920	619	75	226
2000	169,472	9,377	153,745	13,510	140,235	1,185	1,289	565	125	121	348	130	1,577	1,579	580	195	804
2006	212,836	16,089	188,112	16,720	171,392	1,156	1,952	970	162	130	512	179	2,136	2,189	603	226	1,360
2007	228,084	18,016	200,429	14,860	185,569	1,738	1,971	939	169	138	533	192	2,488	2,319	568	240	1,511
2008	259,713	17,566	231,449	29,488	201,961	1,948	2,020	885	185	153	581	216	2,239	2,500	562	249	1,689
2009	255,987	17,245	226,554	30,436	196,118	2,008	3,517	1,636	305	254	950	373	1,868	2,636	550	241	1,846
2010	250,791	18,844	217,700	28,088	189,612	2,118	5,265	2,633	419	348	1,338	528	1,838	2,801	638	242	1,921
2011[5]	271,577	23,015	233,887	26,228	207,659	2,027	5,623	2,856	416	357	1,450	545	1,715	3,010	797	255	1,958
2012[5]	290,935	24,404	251,989	30,409	221,580	1,975	5,783	2,951	409	362	1,510	550	1,628	2,814	555	267	1,992

[1] Total includes nonprofit FFRDCs, not shown separately. [2] Includes all nonfederal sources of industry R&D expenditures. [3] Includes all nonfederal sources. [4] Includes all R&D expenditures of FFRDCs administered by academic institutions and funded by the federal government. [5] Preliminary.

Source: National Science Foundation, National Center for Science and Engineering Statistics, *National Patterns of R&D Resources: 2011-12 Data Update*, NSF 14-304, December 2013. See also <http://www.nsf.gov/statistics/natlpatterns/>.

Table 820. Federal Obligations for Research in Current and Constant (2009) Dollars by Field of Science: 2010 to 2014

[In millions of dollars (63,728 represents $63,728,000,000). For years ending September 30. Excludes research and development (R&D) plant (facilities and fixed equipment)]

Field of science	Current dollars				Constant (2009) dollars [1]			
	2010	2012	2013	2014, prel.	2010	2012	2013	2014, prel.
Research, total	**63,728**	**61,947**	**59,200**	**62,663**	**62,959**	**58,877**	**55,364**	**57,655**
Basic	31,795	30,959	29,779	31,603	31,412	29,425	27,850	29,077
Applied	31,933	30,988	29,420	31,061	31,547	29,452	27,514	28,578
Life sciences	33,909	30,967	29,330	30,531	33,500	29,432	27,429	28,091
Psychology	2,156	2,087	1,935	1,986	2,130	1,983	1,810	1,827
Physical sciences	5,871	6,408	6,282	6,559	5,800	6,090	5,875	6,035
Environmental sciences	3,339	3,884	4,041	4,331	3,299	3,692	3,779	3,985
Mathematics and computer sciences	3,412	3,528	3,427	3,777	3,371	3,353	3,205	3,475
Engineering	11,081	11,403	10,948	11,496	10,948	10,838	10,239	10,577
Social sciences	1,197	1,125	1,237	1,431	1,183	1,069	1,157	1,316
Other sciences, n.e.c. [2]	2,763	2,546	1,999	2,554	2,730	2,420	1,870	2,350

[1] Based on gross domestic product implicit price deflator (updated July 2015). [2] Not elsewhere classified.

Source: U.S. National Science Foundation, *Federal Funds for Research and Development, Fiscal Years 2013-15*, NSF 15-324, June 2015, and earlier reports. See also <http://www.nsf.gov/statistics/fedfunds/>.

Table 821. Federal Budget Authority for Research and Development (R&D) in Current and Constant (2009) Dollars by Selected Budget Functions: 2011 to 2014

[In millions of dollars (142,457 represents $142,457,000,000). For year ending September 30. Excludes R&D plant. Represents budget authority. Functions shown are those for which $1 billion or more was authorized since 2001]

Function	Current dollars				Constant (2009) dollars [1]			
	2011	2012	2013	2014 [2]	2011	2012	2013	2014 [2]
Total [3]	**142,457**	**141,450**	**130,861**	**133,103**	**137,893**	**134,497**	**122,609**	**122,936**
National defense	82,972	79,559	70,620	70,338	80,314	75,648	66,167	64,965
Health	30,903	31,243	30,044	31,024	29,913	29,707	28,150	28,654
Space research and technology	8,398	10,661	10,476	10,847	8,129	10,137	9,815	10,018
Energy	2,233	2,197	2,269	2,379	2,161	2,089	2,126	2,197
General science	9,483	9,304	8,802	9,188	9,179	8,847	8,247	8,486
Natural resources and environment	2,171	2,147	2,020	2,205	2,101	2,041	1,893	2,037
Transportation	1,420	1,486	1,337	1,348	1,375	1,413	1,253	1,245
Agriculture	1,916	1,920	1,753	2,020	1,855	1,826	1,642	1,866

[1] Based on gross domestic product implicit price deflator. [2] Preliminary. [3] Includes other functions, not shown separately.

Source: U.S. National Science Foundation, *Federal R&D Funding by Budget Function*, NSF 15-306, November 2014, and earlier reports. See also <http://www.nsf.gov/statistics/fedbudget/>.

Table 822. Federal Research and Development (R&D) by Federal Agency: 2014 and 2015

[In millions of dollars (135,501 represents $135,501,000,000). For fiscal years ending September 30. R&D refers to actual research and development activities as well as R&D facilities. R&D facilities (also known as R&D plants) includes construction, repair, or alteration of physical plant used in the conduct of R&D. Based on Office of Management and Budget data]

Federal agency	2014 [1]	2015 [2]	Federal agency	2014 [1]	2015 [2]
Total research and development	**135,501**	**136,502**	Department of Homeland Security	1,032	876
Defense R&D	70,531	70,774	Department of Veterans Affairs	1,175	1,178
Nondefense R&D	64,970	65,728	Department of Interior	839	924
			U.S. Geological Survey	650	686
Department of Defense	66,086	65,690	Environmental Protection Agency	538	537
Science and technology	13,561	12,169	Department of Education	323	336
All other Department of Defense R&D	52,524	53,520	Smithsonian	232	252
Health and Human Services	30,823	31,053	International Assistance Programs	203	203
National Institutes of Health	29,252	29,524	Patient-Centered Outcomes Research		
All other Health and Human Services R&D	1,571	1,529	Trust Fund	464	528
Department of Energy	11,389	12,366	Department of Justice	89	89
Atomic Energy Defense	4,445	5,084	Nuclear Regulatory Commission	90	92
Office of Science	4,655	4,714	Department of State	77	77
Energy R&D	2,289	2,568	Dept. of Housing and Urban Development	61	85
NASA	11,491	11,556	Social Security Administration	47	88
National Science Foundation	5,552	5,566	Tennessee Valley Authority	17	16
Department of Agriculture	2,418	2,447	U.S. Postal Service	22	23
Department of Commerce	1,636	1,597	Army Corps of Engineers	11	11
NOAA [3]	666	689	Department of Treasury	8	8
NIST [4]	666	690	Department of Labor	4	4
Department of Transportation	873	897	Consumer Product Safety Commission	2	2

[1] Estimated. [2] Proposed budget outlays. [3] National Oceanic and Atmospheric Administration. [4] National Institute of Standards and Technology.

Source: American Association for the Advancement of Science (AAAS), *AAAS Report XXXIX: Research and Development FY2015* ©, 2015. See also <http://www.aaas.org/program/rd-budget-and-policy-program/>.

Table 823. Funds for Domestic Business Research and Development (R&D) Performed by Manufacturing and Nonmanufacturing Companies by Industry: 2011 to 2013

[Based on the Business R&D and Innovation Survey. For information about the survey, see <http://www.nsf.gov/statistics/srvyindustry>]

Industry	NAICS [1] code	Total R&D funds as a percent of net sales			Company R&D funds as a percent of net sales		
		2011	2012	2013	2011	2012	2013
All industries, total.	(X)	**3.2**	**3.3**	**3.3**	**2.6**	**2.7**	**2.7**
All manufacturing industries, total.	(X)	**3.9**	**3.8**	**3.8**	**3.2**	**3.1**	**3.1**
Chemicals.	325	4.8	4.3	4.5	4.3	3.8	4.0
Pharmaceuticals and medicines.	3254	11.8	12.7	10.3	10.6	11.2	9.0
Machinery.	333	3.8	3.7	3.4	3.5	3.4	3.3
Computer and electronic products.	334	9.9	9.8	10.6	8.5	8.6	9.0
Electrical equipment, appliances, and components.	335	3.3	2.8	2.9	3.2	2.6	2.6
Transportation equipment.	336	4.8	4.6	4.1	2.4	2.3	2.3
Motor vehicles, trailers, and parts.	3361-3363	(D)	(D)	2.4	2.1	2.2	2.0
Aerospace products and parts.	3364	11.3	10.1	7.6	3.3	2.9	2.8
All nonmanufacturing industries, total.	(X)	**2.3**	**2.5**	**2.7**	**1.9**	**2.1**	**2.2**
Information.	51	4.6	4.4	5.5	4.5	4.4	5.3
Software publishing.	5112	9.5	9.9	9.0	9.3	9.6	8.7
Finance and insurance.	52	0.4	0.4	0.7	0.4	0.4	0.7
Professional, scientific, and technical services.	54	8.6	10.0	8.4	5.3	5.9	4.2
Computer systems design and related services.	5415	7.8	9.3	8.4	6.9	7.6	7.3
Scientific research and development services.	5417	24.4	23.2	20.1	9.9	9.5	4.0

X Not applicable. D figure withheld to avoid disclosure of information pertaining to a specific organization or individual. [1] North American Industry Classification System (NAICS); see text, Section 15.

Source: U.S. National Science Foundation, National Center for Science and Engineering Statistics, *Business R&D Performance in the United States Increased in 2011*, InfoBrief NSF 13-335, September 2013; *Business R&D Performed in the United States Tops $300 Billion in 2012*, InfoBrief NSF 15-303, October 2014; and *Business R&D Performance in the United States Increases Over 6% to $323 Billion in 2013*, InfoBrief NSF 15-329, August 2015. See also <http://www.nsf.gov/statistics/industry/>.

Table 824. Domestic Business Research and Development (R&D) Funding in Current and Constant (2009) Dollars by Source and for Selected Industries: 2005 to 2013

[In millions of dollars (204,250 represents $204,250,000,000). For calendar years. Covers basic research, applied research, and development. Based on the Business R&D and Innovation Survey, sponsored by National Science Foundation; for information about the survey and methodology, see <http://www.nsf.gov/statistics/srvyindustry/>]

Industry	NAICS [1] code	2005	2010	2011	2012	2013
CURRENT DOLLARS						
Company and other funds.	(X)	204,250	244,778	262,784	271,629	293,166
Federal funds.	(X)	21,909	34,199	31,309	30,621	29,362
Total funds.	(X)	**226,159**	**278,977**	**294,093**	**302,250**	**322,528**
Chemicals and allied products.	325	42,995	58,038	55,324	57,225	61,664
Pharmaceuticals and medicines.	3254	34,839	49,415	45,949	48,146	52,426
Machinery.	333	8,531	9,955	14,709	14,254	12,650
Computer and electronic products.	334	(D)	59,875	62,704	65,068	67,205
Navigational, measuring, electromedical, and control instruments.	3345	15,204	(NA)	(NA)	(NA)	(NA)
Electrical equipment, appliances, and components.	335	2,424	3,321	3,595	3,087	4,136
Transportation equipment.	3361-3363	(D)	42,913	40,880	42,305	45,972
Aerospace products and parts.	3364	15,055	29,854	26,054	24,817	27,114
Information.	51	23,836	36,853	41,865	46,805	57,207
Software publishers.	5112	16,926	26,982	27,965	28,745	35,333
Professional, scientific, and technical services.	54	32,021	33,690	38,219	34,309	31,017
Computer systems design and related services.	5415	13,592	11,050	13,259	11,251	9,268
Scientific R&D services.	5417	12,299	12,140	15,301	16,544	14,201
CONSTANT (2009) DOLLARS [2]						
Company and other funds.	(X)	222,040	241,825	254,362	258,168	274,169
Federal funds.	(X)	23,817	33,786	30,306	29,104	27,459
Total funds.	(X)	**245,857**	**275,612**	**284,668**	**287,272**	**301,628**
Chemicals and allied products.	325	46,740	57,338	53,551	54,389	57,668
Pharmaceuticals and medicines.	3254	37,873	48,819	44,476	45,760	49,029
Machinery.	333	9,274	9,835	14,238	13,548	11,830
Computer and electronic products.	334	(D)	59,153	60,694	61,843	62,850
Navigational, measuring, electromedical, and control instruments.	3345	16,528	(NA)	(NA)	(NA)	(NA)
Electrical equipment, appliances, and components.	335	2,635	3,281	3,480	2,934	3,868
Transportation equipment.	3361-3363	(D)	42,395	39,570	40,209	42,993
Aerospace products and parts.	3364	16,366	29,494	25,219	23,587	25,357
Information.	51	25,912	36,408	40,523	44,486	53,500
Software publishers.	5112	18,400	26,657	27,069	27,321	33,043
Professional, scientific, and technical services.	54	34,810	33,284	36,994	32,609	29,007
Computer systems design and related services.	5415	14,776	10,917	12,834	10,693	8,667
Scientific R&D services.	5417	13,370	11,994	14,811	15,724	13,281

X Not applicable. NA Not available. D Figure withheld to avoid disclosure of information pertaining to a specific organization or individual. [1] North American Industry Classification System; see text, Section 15. [2] Based on gross domestic product implicit price deflator, update from August 27, 2015.

Source: U.S. National Science Foundation, National Center for Science and Engineering Statistics, *Research and Development in Industry*, annual; *Business R&D Performance Remained Virtually Unchanged in 2010*, InfoBrief NSF 13-324, June 2013; *Business R&D Performance in the United States Increased in 2011*, InfoBrief NSF 13-335, September 2013; *Business R&D Performed in the United States Tops $300 Billion in 2012*, InfoBrief NSF 15-303, October 2014; and *Business R&D Performance in the United States Increases Over 6% to $323 Billion in 2013*, InfoBrief NSF 15-329, August 2015. See also <http://www.nsf.gov/statistics/industry/>.

Table 825. Academic and Industrial Research and Development (R&D) Performed by State: 2011

[In millions of dollars (62,457 represents 62,457,000,000). Industry R&D data refer to calendar years; other R&D data refer to fiscal years but are used here as approximations to calendar year data. For definition of research and development see text this section]

State	Academic R&D[2] (mil. dol.)	Academic R&D per $1,000 of state GDP	Industry-performed R&D (mil. dol.)	Industry R&D per $1,000 of state GDP	State	Academic R&D[2] (mil. dol.)	Academic R&D per $1,000 of state GDP	Industry-performed R&D (mil. dol.)	Industry R&D per $1,000 of state GDP
U.S.[1]	62,457	4.14	294,093	19.51	MO	1,121	4.49	(D)	(D)
AL	901	5.05	1,879	10.52	MT	195	5.01	136	3.49
AK	196	3.83	84	1.64	NE	413	4.29	636	6.61
AZ	998	3.90	4,931	19.26	NV	165	1.27	638	4.93
AR	283	2.66	344	3.23	NH	360	5.68	2,069	32.67
CA	8,227	4.31	75,035	39.31	NJ	1,142	2.32	13,930	28.25
CO	1,291	4.88	4,310	16.28	NM	405	5.09	472	5.93
CT	946	4.20	7,504	33.29	NY	5,299	4.53	12,072	10.32
DE	189	2.94	2,097	32.57	NC	2,567	5.89	6,193	14.20
DC	493	4.60	415	3.87	ND	211	5.28	261	6.53
FL	2,126	2.85	5,988	8.02	OH	2,227	4.54	6,993	14.26
GA	1,717	4.11	3,839	9.20	OK	389	2.49	604	3.87
HI	364	5.20	252	3.60	OR	740	3.92	4,631	24.51
ID	142	2.49	1,171	20.51	PA	3,313	5.70	9,718	16.72
IL	2,353	3.51	12,038	17.96	RI	459	9.29	542	10.97
IN	1,270	4.47	6,158	21.66	SC	623	3.69	1,399	8.29
IA	725	4.96	2,314	15.84	SD	136	3.26	136	3.26
KS	526	3.90	1,509	11.20	TN	1,017	3.86	1,434	5.44
KY	596	3.55	1,278	7.61	TX	4,662	3.53	15,309	11.59
LA	729	3.07	459	1.93	UT	627	5.04	2,438	19.59
ME	140	2.67	295	5.62	VT	137	5.16	374	14.09
MD	3,417	11.20	5,101	16.71	VA	1,284	2.96	5,562	12.83
MA	2,949	7.59	15,722	40.46	WA	1,570	4.40	14,558	40.77
MI	2,160	5.61	13,660	35.47	WV	211	3.19	247	3.74
MN	899	3.21	6,174	22.05	WI	1,444	5.70	4,053	16.00
MS	470	4.82	235	2.41	WY	58	1.52	46	1.20

D Data withheld to avoid disclosing operations of individual companies. [1] U.S. totals will not equal state totals because the US totals include data for outlying areas (Puerto Rico, Guam, and Virgin Islands). R&D expenditures that can not be allocated to specific states, and double counting of U&C (universities and colleges) data (see footnote 2). [2] State level university R&D data have not been adjusted to eliminate double counting of funds passed through from one academic institution to another. See source for more information.

Source: National Science Foundation, *National Patterns of R&D Resources: 2011-12 Data Update*, NSF 14-304, December 2013. See also <http://www.nsf.gov/statistics/natlpatterns/>.

Table 826. Research and Development (R&D) Expenditures in Science and Engineering at Universities and Colleges in Current and Constant (2009) Dollars: 2005 to 2013

[In millions of dollars (45,774 represents $45,774,000,000). Totals may not add due to rounding. Reference period is the fiscal year of the surveyed institutions. Data are based the Higher Education R&D (HERD) Survey, which in 2010 succeeded the Survey of Research and Development Expenditures at Colleges and Universities; see source for details]

Characteristic	Current dollars				Constant (2009) dollars [1]			
	2005	2010	2012	2013	2005	2010	2012	2013
Expenditures, total................	**45,774**	**58,360**	**62,222**	**63,395**	**49,761**	**57,656**	**59,139**	**59,287**
Source of funds:								
Federal government......................	29,187	36,510	38,954	38,294	31,729	36,070	37,024	35,813
State and local government.............	2,940	3,605	3,432	3,398	3,196	3,562	3,262	3,178
Institutions' own funds...................	8,265	10,674	12,035	13,261	8,985	10,545	11,439	12,402
Industry................................	2,291	3,117	3,192	3,426	2,491	3,079	3,034	3,204
Other...................................	3,092	4,454	4,609	5,015	3,361	4,400	4,381	4,690
Field:								
Physical sciences.......................	3,703	4,622	4,724	4,646	4,025	4,566	4,490	4,345
Environmental sciences.................	2,554	2,992	3,179	3,199	2,777	2,956	3,022	2,992
Mathematical sciences..................	494	594	674	671	537	587	641	628
Computer sciences......................	1,404	1,638	1,820	2,068	1,526	1,618	1,730	1,934
Life sciences............................	27,604	34,949	37,187	37,585	30,008	34,528	35,344	35,150
Psychology.............................	825	1,078	1,188	1,152	897	1,065	1,130	1,077
Social sciences.........................	1,685	1,997	2,054	2,170	1,831	1,973	1,952	2,029
Other sciences.........................	761	1,161	1,102	1,175	827	1,147	1,048	1,099
Engineering............................	6,743	9,329	10,292	10,729	7,331	9,216	9,782	10,033

[1] Based on gross domestic product implicit price deflator (updated July 2015).

Source: U.S. National Science Foundation, "Higher Education Research and Development: Fiscal Year 2013, Data Tables," and earlier editions, <http://www.nsf.gov/statistics/herd/>, accessed August 2015.

Table 827. Federal Research and Development (R&D) Obligations to Selected Universities and Colleges: 1990 to 2012

[In millions of dollars (9,016.6 represents $9,016,600,000). For fiscal years ending September 30. For the top 40 institutions receiving federal R&D funds in 2012. Awards to the administrative offices of university systems are excluded from totals for individual institutions because that allocation of funds is unknown, but those awards are included in "total all institutions"]

Major institution ranked by total 2012 federal R&D obligations	1990	2000	2005	2010 [2]	2011	2012
Total, all institutions [1]......................	**9,016.6**	**17,289.8**	**24,662.0**	**30,630.1**	**27,937.5**	**27,384.8**
Johns Hopkins University......................	469.5	795.5	993.8	1,515.8	1,374.9	1,359.1
University of Washington—Seattle..............	217.2	396.1	593.8	736.6	643.1	668.8
University of Michigan, all campuses...........	176.4	346.7	473.6	686.6	647.5	623.3
University of California—San Diego.............	164.8	314.4	401.1	613.2	546.8	584.6
University of California—San Francisco.........	167.3	289.2	447.2	531.3	525.8	546.0
University of Pennsylvania.....................	142.5	348.5	519.4	609.0	515.7	497.0
Columbia University in the City of New York.....	154.1	284.6	423.4	497.6	464.1	479.0
University of Pittsburgh, all campuses..........	116.6	246.2	405.4	497.1	459.7	475.7
Stanford University............................	248.0	355.0	459.6	516.8	471.5	475.3
University of California—Los Angeles...........	176.7	372.4	497.5	548.8	493.1	475.0
Harvard University............................	148.1	299.9	405.5	527.5	458.7	465.5
Duke University...............................	116.1	232.2	431.4	496.8	436.8	431.7
University of North Carolina at Chapel Hill......	100.2	232.7	323.0	429.7	421.7	425.5
University of Wisconsin—Madison..............	155.2	263.4	374.5	461.9	420.7	420.4
Pennsylvania State University, all campuses....	136.4	230.1	261.0	413.1	476.5	414.7
Yale University................................	142.5	260.0	356.1	470.5	424.2	409.6
University of Colorado, all campuses...........	116.4	272.3	335.6	427.0	389.2	394.0
Washington University.........................	117.9	287.3	402.9	445.5	382.2	393.7
University of Minnesota, all campuses..........	137.5	276.8	329.3	420.3	489.9	388.9
Massachusetts Institute of Technology..........	218.3	248.9	342.4	340.2	320.8	360.8
Vanderbilt University..........................	70.6	138.4	279.2	399.1	352.6	359.3
Cornell University, all campuses...............	144.7	240.1	323.2	359.8	325.8	332.5
University of Southern California...............	122.7	203.9	307.0	378.9	308.9	306.8
Emory University..............................	49.6	145.6	223.5	303.1	312.1	303.3
Northwestern University.......................	61.1	151.5	215.1	282.0	285.9	302.7
University of California—Davis.................	68.9	148.5	217.2	313.2	284.3	282.1
University of California—Berkeley..............	121.7	196.2	245.5	306.0	275.5	276.8
Case Western Reserve University...............	71.3	179.4	287.7	287.0	276.6	272.4
University of Arizona..........................	92.8	162.7	201.0	230.6	238.9	265.1
Baylor College of Medicine....................	72.3	172.3	250.9	251.3	226.4	257.6
Georgia Institute of Technology, all campuses..	54.3	58.4	115.4	234.9	242.8	251.8
University of Rochester........................	102.5	153.2	248.5	293.8	249.9	251.6
New York University...........................	75.7	127.0	176.7	251.1	229.0	244.1
University of Texas at Austin...................	91.8	135.0	130.5	192.9	190.3	234.2
University of Chicago..........................	88.5	144.5	227.1	252.8	239.7	232.3
Ohio State University, all campuses............	80.1	140.7	216.6	311.6	230.9	231.8
University of Alabama at Birmingham...........	74.5	182.9	232.8	236.0	238.1	228.8
University of Maryland at College Park..........	64.7	120.7	124.9	179.9	156.9	221.4
Boston University.............................	59.4	139.4	200.4	226.0	227.3	216.3
University of Illinois at Urbana-Champaign......	99.7	156.1	188.3	230.3	326.5	210.5

[1] Includes other institutions, not shown separately. Total also includes a small amount of obligations to independent nonprofit institutions. [2] Includes American Recovery and Reinvestment Act of 2009 obligations.

Source: U.S. National Science Foundation, National Center for Science and Engineering Statistics, "Integrated Science and Engineering Resources Data System (WebCASPAR)," <https://webcaspar.nsf.gov/>, accessed July 2015. See also <http://www.nsf.gov/statistics/fedsupport/>.

Table 828. Graduate Science/Engineering Students in Doctorate-Granting Colleges by Characteristic and Field: 2000 to 2013

[In thousands (443.5 represents 443,500). As of Fall. Includes outlying areas. Based on the Survey of Graduate Students and Postdoctorates in Science; for information on methodology, see National Science Foundation (NSF) website <http://www.nsf.gov/statistics/publication.cfm>]

| Field of science or engineering | Total | | | Characteristic | | | | | | | | |
| | | | | Female | | | Foreign [1] | | | Part-time | | |
	2000	2010	2013	2000	2010	2013	2000	2010	2013	2000	2010	2013
Total, all surveyed fields.................	**443.5**	**575.8**	**574.0**	**201.8**	**265.0**	**257.9**	**123.3**	**165.9**	**187.7**	**123.6**	**142.5**	**134.05**
Science/engineering.........	374.8	508.1	518.9	150.3	215.3	217.9	118.0	158.3	180.4	99.3	121.7	118.7
Engineering, total............	98.8	141.8	146.8	19.7	32.9	35.0	46.3	64.2	75.1	28.2	35.4	35.1
Sciences, total [2].............	275.9	366.3	372.1	130.7	182.4	183.0	71.7	94.1	105.3	71.1	86.4	83.6
Physical sciences........	29.6	37.9	38.9	8.8	12.4	12.6	11.5	15.0	15.3	3.5	3.6	3.5
Environmental [3]..........	13.0	14.8	14.9	5.3	6.7	6.7	2.6	2.9	3.2	2.8	2.9	3.0
Math sciences.............	14.4	21.3	22.8	5.2	7.4	7.8	5.9	8.4	10.1	3.0	4.4	4.1
Computer sciences.......	40.3	45.9	49.7	11.7	11.2	12.7	19.7	22.6	28.4	16.7	15.8	14.4
Agricultural sciences......	11.3	14.6	15.4	4.8	7.2	7.8	2.4	3.2	3.6	2.4	4.1	4.4
Biological sciences........	53.1	69.5	71.2	27.8	39.3	40.2	11.6	16.9	17.0	7.6	9.5	10.3
Psychology [4]..............	40.3	45.2	43.3	29.0	33.8	32.1	2.1	2.9	2.8	10.8	11.7	11.1
Social sciences...........	73.9	95.9	92.9	38.1	51.0	49.1	15.8	18.8	20.8	24.3	28.1	26.8
Health fields, total [4].........	68.8	67.7	55.1	51.5	49.7	40.0	5.4	7.6	7.3	24.3	20.8	15.4

[1] Temporary residents. [2] Beginning in 2010, total includes newly eligible fields (communication, family and consumer science/human science, and multidisciplinary/interdisciplinary studies) and neuroscience, previously reported under health field "neurology," not shown separately. [3] Earth, atmospheric, and ocean sciences. [4] Beginning in 2010, the numbers for psychology and health reflect more rigorous follow-up with institutions regarding the exclusion of practitioner-oriented graduate degree programs and may not reflect changes in actual enrollments.

Source: U.S. National Science Foundation, National Center for Science and Engineering Statistics, "Integrated Science and Engineering Resources Data System (WebCASPAR)," <https://webcaspar.nsf.gov/>, accessed May 2015. See also <http://www.nsf.gov/statistics/gradpostdoc/>

Table 829. Temporary Visa Holders Awarded Doctorates in Science and Engineering by Country of Citizenship: 2000 to 2012

[Based on the Survey of Earned Doctorates; for information, see <http://www.nsf.gov/statistics/srvydoctorates/>]

Country of citizenship	2000	2004	2005	2006	2007	2008	2009	2010	2011	2012
All temporary visa holders.....	**7,949**	**9,496**	**10,777**	**11,956**	**12,802**	**13,045**	**12,556**	**11,664**	**12,164**	**12,705**
Science.............................	5,498	6,183	7,011	7,655	8,198	8,554	8,338	7,807	8,016	8,376
Engineering........................	2,451	3,313	3,766	4,301	4,604	4,491	4,218	3,857	4,148	4,329
COUNTRY										
Canada.............................	263	356	330	326	352	370	385	339	305	298
Mexico..............................	194	168	196	173	172	161	171	169	159	184
Brazil...............................	127	135	151	131	118	130	131	133	128	143
United Kingdom...................	68	75	72	84	85	87	76	73	69	61
France..............................	66	83	100	107	121	120	112	96	99	84
Germany...........................	172	154	145	130	128	140	170	155	158	155
China [1]............................	2,074	2,769	3,345	4,121	4,308	4,140	3,747	3,451	3,639	3,900
Japan...............................	177	170	187	194	210	209	190	172	177	178
South Korea........................	718	1,030	1,136	1,197	1,128	1,150	1,173	1,075	1,080	1,129
Taiwan..............................	649	395	443	452	477	462	542	501	570	579
Thailand............................	178	302	281	218	235	290	219	182	235	239
India................................	758	832	1,093	1,496	1,921	2,156	2,107	1,991	2,026	2,129
Iran.................................	41	46	113	125	130	132	139	144	193	275
Turkey..............................	248	324	321	321	409	466	445	404	422	351

[1] Includes Hong Kong.

Source: U.S. National Science Foundation, National Center for Science and Engineering Statistics, Survey of Earned Doctorates, special tabulation (2014).

Table 830. Science and Engineering (S&E) Degrees Awarded by Degree Level and Sex of Recipient: 1990 to 2012

[For a description of science and engineering degree categories, see source, Appendix B, <http://www.nsf.gov/statistics/nsf13327/>]

| Academic year ending | Bachelor's degree | | | | Master's degree | | | | Doctoral degree | | | |
	Total S&E	Men	Women	Percent women	Total S&E	Men	Women	Percent women	Total S&E [1]	Men	Women	Percent women [2]
1990...........	329,094	189,082	140,012	42.5	77,788	51,230	26,558	34.1	22,868	16,498	6,370	27.9
2000...........	398,602	197,650	200,952	50.4	96,230	54,560	41,670	43.3	25,966	16,518	9,394	36.3
2005...........	470,214	233,924	236,290	50.3	120,870	67,244	53,626	44.4	27,985	17,405	10,539	37.7
2006...........	478,858	238,029	240,829	50.3	120,999	66,249	54,750	45.2	29,873	18,375	11,479	38.5
2007...........	485,772	241,697	244,075	50.2	120,278	65,353	54,925	45.7	31,836	19,542	12,282	38.6
2008...........	496,168	246,719	249,449	50.3	126,404	68,810	57,594	45.6	32,837	19,857	12,973	39.5
2009...........	505,435	250,742	254,693	50.4	134,517	73,489	61,028	45.4	33,463	19,840	13,595	40.7
2010...........	525,374	261,091	264,283	50.3	139,926	76,266	63,660	45.5	33,120	19,570	13,540	40.9
2011...........	554,365	275,258	279,107	50.3	150,653	82,451	68,202	45.3	34,474	20,380	14,077	40.9
2012...........	589,330	291,791	297,539	50.5	161,371	87,810	73,561	45.6	35,809	21,233	14,534	40.6

[1] Total includes degree holders who did not report sex. [2] Percentages of women doctoral degree recipients are calculated based on the total of men plus women, not on the total number of degrees.

Source: U.S. National Science Foundation, Science and Engineering Degrees: 1966–2012, NSF-15-326, June 2015. See also <http://www.nsf.gov/statistics/degrees/>.

Table 831. Science and Engineering (S&E) Degrees as Share of Higher Education Degrees Conferred by State: 2011

[S&E degrees include physical, computer, agricultural, biological, earth, atmospheric, ocean, and social sciences; psychology; mathematics; and engineering]

State	S&E degrees conferred [1]	All higher education degrees [1]	S&E higher education degrees (percent)	State	S&E degrees conferred [1]	All higher education degrees [1]	S&E higher education degrees (percent)	State	S&E degrees conferred [1]	All higher education degrees [1]	S&E higher education degrees (percent)
U.S.........	733,609	2,506,134	29.3	KY.........	6,883	29,932	23.0	ND........	1,743	7,385	23.6
AL...........	9,933	39,751	25.0	LA........	7,562	29,072	26.0	OH........	23,094	88,516	26.1
AK...........	921	2,509	36.7	ME........	3,103	9,173	33.8	OK........	6,503	26,299	24.7
AZ...........	18,154	88,964	20.4	MD........	18,039	48,527	37.2	OR........	8,767	27,306	32.1
AR...........	4,121	18,344	22.5	MA........	28,989	90,422	32.1	PA........	37,253	127,084	29.3
CA...........	91,643	244,200	37.5	MI.........	23,488	79,340	29.6	RI........	4,077	13,718	29.7
CO...........	15,209	45,772	33.2	MN........	15,853	57,518	27.6	SC........	8,223	29,523	27.9
CT...........	9,790	29,759	32.9	MS........	4,278	18,366	23.3	SD........	2,153	6,729	32.0
DE...........	2,512	8,840	28.4	MO........	14,323	63,525	22.5	TN........	10,243	43,362	23.6
DC...........	7,743	19,033	40.7	MT........	2,313	6,814	33.9	TX........	42,413	153,270	27.7
FL...........	32,260	121,004	26.7	NE........	4,478	18,564	24.1	UT........	9,399	31,967	29.4
GA...........	17,367	64,301	27.0	NV........	2,814	10,532	26.7	VT........	3,343	8,535	39.2
HI...........	2,594	8,074	32.1	NH........	4,047	13,293	30.4	VA........	23,672	72,067	32.8
ID...........	2,942	11,076	26.6	NJ........	17,439	52,919	33.0	WA......	14,269	42,255	33.8
IL...........	30,855	117,325	26.3	NM........	3,339	11,725	28.5	WV......	5,050	19,040	26.5
IN...........	15,768	59,294	26.6	NY........	59,701	203,148	29.4	WI........	13,761	46,009	29.9
IA...........	13,296	47,054	28.3	NC........	20,896	66,530	31.4	WY......	981	2,407	40.8
KS...........	6,012	25,962	23.2								

[1] Includes bachelor's, master's, and doctorate degrees.

Source: National Science Foundation, *Science and Engineering Indicators, 2014*, February 2014. See also <http://www.nsf.gov/statistics/seind/>.

Table 832. Doctorates Conferred in Science and Engineering by Field, Sex, and Race/Ethnicity: 2013

[In percent, except as indicated. Based on the Survey of Earned Doctorates. For description of methodology, see <http://www.nsf.gov/statistics/srvydoctorates/>]

Characteristic	Total	Life sciences			Physical sciences			Social sciences			Engineering
		Total [1]	Biological sciences	Health sciences	Total [1]	Chemistry	Physics [2]	Total [1]	Psychology	Economics [3]	
Total conferred (number)...................	**38,959**	**12,305**	**8,471**	**2,505**	**9,290**	**2,491**	**2,205**	**8,401**	**3,600**	**1,185**	**8,963**
SEX											
Male..........................	57.5	44.7	47.0	32.3	70.9	60.3	79.4	40.7	27.8	64.7	77.1
Female.......................	42.4	55.3	53.0	67.7	29.0	39.6	20.6	59.3	72.2	35.3	22.9
RACE/ETHNICITY [4]											
Total conferred (number)...................	**23,345**	**8,438**	**5,851**	**1,849**	**4,869**	**1,447**	**1,200**	**6,300**	**3,070**	**477**	**3,738**
White [5]......................	72.5	71.6	71.5	69.0	77.1	76.4	81.1	72.5	72.9	75.1	68.9
Asian [5, 6]...................	9.8	10.5	11.7	9.3	9.6	8.3	7.8	6.1	5.1	12.2	15.1
Hispanic [7]..................	6.1	6.6	7.2	4.4	4.6	5.7	4.2	7.0	7.4	5.0	5.1
Black [5].....................	5.6	6.2	4.3	12.4	2.9	4.2	1.7	7.3	6.7	3.4	4.6
American Indian/Alaska Native [5]...................	0.3	0.4	0.3	0.5	0.1	0.1	0.1	0.4	0.5	0.0	0.1
Two or more races [5].........	2.6	2.5	2.9	2.0	2.5	2.7	2.6	3.0	2.9	1.9	2.3
Other/unknown [8].............	3.1	2.2	2.2	2.3	3.1	2.6	2.7	3.6	4.6	2.5	3.9

[1] Includes other fields, not shown separately. [2] Includes astronomy. [3] Includes econometrics. [4] Excludes those with temporary visas and those who did not report citizenship. [5] Non-Hispanic. [6] Excludes Native Hawaiians or Other Pacific Islanders. [7] Includes persons reporting Hispanic ethnicity, whether singly or in combination with one or more races. [8] Includes Native Hawaiians and other Pacific Islanders who are not Hispanic, recipients who are not Hispanic and did not indicate race, and recipients with unknown race and ethnicity.

Source: U.S. National Science Foundation, National Center for Science and Engineering Statistics, *Doctorate Recipients from U.S. Universities, 2013*, NSF 15-304, December 2014. See also <http://www.nsf.gov/statistics/srvydoctorates/>.

Table 833. Doctorates Awarded by Field of Study and Year of Doctorate: 2005 to 2012

[Based on the Survey of Earned Doctorates. For description of methodology, see <http://www.nsf.gov/statistics/srvydoctorates/>]

Field of study	2005	2007	2008	2009	2010	2011	2012
Total, all fields	43,384	48,133	48,778	49,553	48,032	48,908	51,008
Science and engineering, total	29,473	33,648	34,598	35,200	34,885	36,193	37,777
Engineering, total	6,427	7,749	7,864	7,643	7,548	7,985	8,427
Aeronautical/astronautical	219	267	266	297	252	261	307
Chemical	774	817	873	807	822	823	840
Civil	622	703	713	707	643	634	496
Electrical/electronics/communications	1,547	1,967	1,888	1,693	1,778	1,886	1,943
Industrial/manufacturing	221	279	280	251	215	258	227
Materials science	493	646	636	625	670	662	743
Mechanical	892	1,071	1,082	1,095	983	1,084	1,221
Other	1,659	1,999	2,126	2,168	2,185	2,377	2,650
Science, total	23,046	25,899	26,734	27,557	27,337	28,208	29,350
Life sciences	9,310	10,702	11,086	11,404	11,258	11,451	12,045
Agricultural sciences	1,160	1,321	1,198	1,283	1,100	1,208	1,256
Biological/biomedical sciences	6,367	7,238	7,797	8,025	8,046	8,140	8,440
Health sciences	1,783	2,143	2,091	2,096	2,112	2,103	2,349
Physical sciences, total	6,691	7,999	8,133	8,324	8,310	8,665	8,952
Chemistry	2,126	2,318	2,246	2,392	2,304	2,432	2,418
Computer and information sciences	1,129	1,655	1,787	1,610	1,664	1,713	1,845
Geosciences	714	875	865	877	862	852	841
Mathematics	1,205	1,388	1,400	1,553	1,590	1,606	1,702
Physics and astronomy	1,517	1,763	1,835	1,892	1,890	2,062	2,146
Social sciences, total	7,045	7,198	7,515	7,829	7,769	8,092	8,353
Anthropology	456	512	483	503	507	553	546
Economics	1,061	1,004	1,091	1,118	1,073	1,122	1,243
Political science	618	588	628	682	728	685	726
Psychology	3,322	3,276	3,358	3,472	3,422	3,578	3,614
Sociology	536	576	601	662	639	657	631
Other social sciences	1,052	1,242	1,354	1,392	1,400	1,497	1,593
Non-science and engineering, total	13,911	14,485	14,180	14,353	13,147	12,715	13,231
Education	6,227	6,448	6,561	6,528	5,288	4,670	4,802
Humanities	5,141	5,092	4,719	4,891	4,971	5,211	5,503
Professional/other/unknown	2,543	2,945	2,900	2,934	2,888	2,834	2,926

Source: U.S. National Science Foundation, National Center for Science and Engineering Statistics, Survey of Earned Doctorates, special tabulation (2014).

Table 834. Employed Scientists and Engineers by Sex, Race/Ethnicity, and Selected Characteristics: 2013

[In thousands (23,219 represents 23,219,000). Scientists and engineers are individuals who have a bachelor's or higher degree, and have an S&E (Science and Engineer) or S&E-related degree or occupation. Data is based on various National Science Foundation (NSF) and non-NSF surveys; see <http://www.nsf.gov/statistics/2015/nsf15311/technotes.cfm#datasources> for details]

Characteristic	Total [1]	Female	Male	Hispanic or Latino [2]	Asian [3]	Black or African American [3]	White [3]	More than one race [3]
All employed scientists and engineers	**23,219**	**10,699**	**12,520**	**1,757**	**2,646**	**1,450**	**16,866**	**358**
Age:								
Under 30 years	3,162	1,692	1,470	(S)	401	(S)	2,159	(S)
30-39 years	5,829	2,870	2,960	531	874	389	3,882	(S)
40-49 years	5,783	2,597	3,185	(S)	722	(S)	4,080	(S)
50-75 years	8,445	3,540	4,905	(S)	649	(S)	6,745	(S)
Employment status:								
Employed, full-time	19,320	8,059	11,261	1,473	2,289	1,268	13,900	280
Employed, part-time	3,872	2,630	1,243	283	346	181	2,952	78
Postdoctoral appointment	27	11	16	2	10	1	14	(S)
Highest degree attained:								
Bachelor's	13,230	6,055	7,175	1,109	1,317	838	9,657	210
Master's	6,787	3,455	3,332	439	825	480	4,918	92
Doctorate	1,142	409	733	51	236	46	788	17
Professional	2,060	780	1,280	158	268	86	1,503	39
By occupation:								
S&E occupations	5,642	1,639	4,003	341	966	268	3,961	83
Science occupations	4,104	1,411	2,693	240	748	212	2,826	64
Engineering occupations	1,538	228	1,310	101	219	56	1,135	20
S&E related occupations	7,339	4,134	3,206	561	881	450	5,266	124
Non-S&E related occupations	10,238	4,927	5,311	855	798	732	7,639	151
By employment sector:								
Business or industry	12,151	4,491	7,660	854	1,717	637	8,726	167
Federal government	1,011	350	661	105	86	109	682	24
Nonprofit	2,567	1,724	843	195	190	162	1,958	44
Self-employed	1,532	669	863	103	123	51	1,218	23
State or local government	1,547	764	782	157	127	184	1,034	29
Universities and 4-year colleges	1,830	989	841	126	293	121	1,247	35
Other educational institutions	2,581	1,712	869	217	109	186	2,001	37

S Figure does not meet publication standards. [1] Total includes other races, not shown separately. [2] Persons of Hispanic origin may be of any race. [3] Non-Hispanic.

Source: National Science Foundation, National Center for Science and Engineering Statistics, "Women, Minorities, and Persons with Disabilities in Science and Engineering - Data Tables," <http://www.nsf.gov/statistics/2015/nsf15311/tables.cfm>, accessed July 2015.

Table 835. Science and Engineering (S&E) Graduates by Occupation: 2010

[In thousands (16,658 represents 16,658,000). Data represents all employed college graduates who attained their highest degree in an S&E or S&E-related field]

Occupation	All employed S&E or S&E-related highest degree holders	Highest degree in S&E holders [1]						S&E related fields [5]
		Total	Computer and mathematical sciences	Biological, agricultural, and environmental life sciences [2]	Physical and related sciences [3]	Social and related sciences [4]	Engineering	
All occupations............................	**16,658**	**11,385**	**1,886**	**1,764**	**693**	**4,363**	**2,679**	**5,273**
S&E occupations............................	**4,325**	**4,000**	**1,013**	**529**	**353**	**559**	**1,546**	**325**
Computer & mathematical scientists........	1,710	1,579	960	52	49	164	354	131
Computer & information scientists [6]........	1,543	1,429	865	45	44	136	339	114
Computer engineers—software...........	367	348	202	2	10	13	121	19
Software developers....................	348	321	193	6	9	19	93	27
Computer system analysts..............	226	204	136	6	5	22	36	22
Computer support specialists............	137	125	78	6	3	19	18	12
Network/computer systems administrators..........................	117	106	68	4	5	14	16	11
Mathematical scientists.................	84	79	37	7	3	25	7	5
Biological, agricultural, & environmental life scientists [6]...............	538	468	3	396	35	22	12	70
Biological & medical scientists [6]...........	377	316	2	261	29	13	11	61
Biological scientists [7]................	122	114	(S)	104	3	5	2	8
Medical scientists (excluding practitioners)........................	128	88	1	68	10	5	4	40
Physical & related scientists [6]............	304	293	3	47	212	8	24	11
Chemists, except biochemists...........	98	96	(S)	17	72	S	6	2
Physicists & astronomers...............	34	33	(S)	(S)	26	S	5	1
Social & related scientists [6]...............	388	365	5	6	2	349	4	23
Psychologists, including clinical...........	153	149	(S)	2	(S)	146	(S)	4
Postsecondary teachers—social sciences...............................	109	105	1	1	(S)	103	(S)	4
Engineers [6]...............................	1,384	1,294	42	28	55	17	1,151	90
Electrical or computer hardware engineers............................	331	314	17	1	13	1	283	17
Mechanical engineers..................	270	250	3	(S)	3	2	242	20
Civil, architectural, or sanitary engineers..	218	208	1	1	4	4	199	10
S&E-related occupations...................	**5,419**	**1,584**	**304**	**461**	**104**	**330**	**384**	**3,835**
Health-related occupations [6].............	3,722	532	18	267	31	195	21	3,190
Diagnosing/treating practitioners [8]........	1,037	45	(S)	32	3	8	1	992
Registered nurses, pharmacists, dieticians, therapists, physician assistants, & nurse practitioners..........	1,826	133	(S)	63	4	60	4	1,693
S&E managers...........................	649	417	97	48	22	46	204	232
Medical & health services managers......	237	42	(S)	20	1	19	S	195
Engineering managers..................	228	206	11	4	6	(S)	176	22
Computer & information systems managers.............................	143	134	86	1	4	17	26	9
S&E precollege teachers [9]...............	381	196	54	61	20	50	11	185
S&E technicians & technologists [6]...........	486	405	114	85	29	37	141	81
Computer programmers.................	137	117	82	2	5	7	21	20
Electrical, electronic, industrial, & mechanical technicians..................	119	97	12	5	5	7	68	22
Other S&E-related occupations [6]..........	181	33	21	(S)	(S)	3	7	148
Architects.............................	141	15	4	(S)	(S)	(S)	7	126
Non-S&E occupations.......................	**6,914**	**5,802**	**568**	**775**	**237**	**3,473**	**749**	**1,112**
Non-S&E managers......................	1,187	988	112	116	55	451	254	199
Management-related occupations [6]........	1,270	1,109	148	123	45	651	142	161
Accountants, auditors, & other financial specialists......................	438	406	71	29	12	269	25	32
Personnel, training, & labor relations specialists...................	173	153	7	10	3	122	11	20
Non-S&E precollege teachers [6]............	444	300	22	25	11	231	11	144
Elementary............................	165	123	10	9	(S)	91	5	42
Secondary—other subjects..............	83	57	2	7	(S)	43	3	26
Special education—primary & secondary............................	93	56	2	3	(S)	49	(S)	37
Non-S&E postsecondary teachers.........	76	58	6	3	2	43	4	18
Social services & related occupations [6].....	469	400	4	10	2	378	6	69
Counselors [10].........................	248	203	(S)	6	(S)	192	2	45
Social workers........................	191	171	(S)	2	(S)	166	(S)	20
Sales & marketing occupations..........	1,155	995	87	163	38	599	109	160
Arts, humanities, & related occupations.....	247	194	26	23	7	130	9	53
Other non-S&E occupations [6]...............	2,067	1,759	164	311	77	992	215	308

S Data suppressed for reasons of confidentiality and/or reliability. [1] Includes bachelor's, master's, and doctorate degrees. [2] Biological sciences include biology, ecology, nutritional sciences, pharmacology, zoology and other related fields. [3] Physical sciences include chemistry; earth, atmospheric, and ocean sciences; physics and astronomy; and other related fields. [4] Social sciences include economics, political science, psychology, sociology and anthropology, linguistics, geography, history and philosophy of science, and other related fields. [5] S&E-related fields include health fields, science and math teacher education, technology and technical fields, architecture, and actuarial science. [6] Includes other occupations not shown separately. [7] Includes botanists, ecologists, zoologists, etc. [8] Includes dentists, optometrists, physicians, psychiatrists, podiatrists, surgeons, and veterinarians. [9] Secondary teachers in computer, mathematics, sciences, and social sciences. [10] Includes educational, vocational, mental health, substance abuse, etc.

Source: National Science Foundation, *Science and Engineering Indicators, 2014,* February 2014. See also <http://www.nsf.gov/statistics/seind/>.

Table 836. Civilian Employment of Scientists, Engineers, and Related Occupations by Occupation and Industry: 2012

[In thousands (332.7 represents 322,700). Standard Occupational Classification (SOC) system classifies workers into 840 detailed occupations. Industry classifications correspond to 2012 North American Industry Classification (NAICS) industrial groups. For definition of scientists and engineers, see text this section]

Occupation	Total employment, all workers	Wage and salary workers						Self employed [2]
		Mining (NAICS 21) [1]	Construction (NAICS 23)	Manufacturing (NAICS 31–33)	Information (NAICS 51)	Professional, scientific and technical services (NAICS 54)	Government	
Computer and information systems managers..........	332.7	0.7	0.6	30.7	35.0	91.8	22.6	10.4
Architectural and engineering managers.......	193.8	0.3	4.5	69.5	4.1	62.7	17.9	3.3
Natural science managers......................	51.6	0.3	(NA)	6.4	0.1	17.7	15.9	0.6
Computer and mathematical scientists [3].......	3,814.7	9.8	11.1	284.7	440.3	1,269.1	261.7	112.4
Computer occupations....................	3,682.3	9.7	11.1	277.4	435.4	1,238.4	241.0	110.2
Mathematical science occupations............	132.4	0.1	(NA)	7.3	4.9	30.7	20.7	2.1
Surveyors, cartographers, and photogrammetrists..............	54.5	1.3	3.5	0.4	0.2	35.6	9.1	1.4
Engineers [3].............................	1,589.6	40.7	42.7	545.6	34.5	492.3	197.6	29.9
Aerospace engineers..................	83.0	(NA)	(NA)	39.9	0.1	27.4	9.8	0.9
Civil engineers.......................	272.9	1.2	24.9	2.7	0.4	141.8	76.6	7.9
Computer hardware engineers............	83.3	(NA)	0.1	32.8	2.7	32.0	5.0	2.5
Electrical and electronics engineers..........	306.1	0.9	5.6	99.9	29.0	85.4	28.1	6.2
Industrial engineers [4]..................	247.4	4.1	6.5	159.8	1.0	32.9	5.5	1.6
Mechanical engineers..................	258.1	1.7	3.4	130.7	0.2	75.0	14.4	1.5
Drafters, engineering, and mapping technicians [3]	702.8	8.8	20.1	221.6	8.9	244.4	98.1	13.4
Engineering technicians, except drafters.....	449.1	7.7	4.2	166.5	7.3	115.1	83.3	1.1
Surveying and mapping technicians..........	54.0	0.8	1.1	0.1	0.2	30.7	10.7	6.1
Life, physical, and social science occupations....	1,249.1	24.3	0.5	111.8	1.8	328.7	317.8	67.8
Life scientists........................	294.5	(NA)	(NA)	29.6	(NA)	79.7	69.0	9.1
Physical scientists....................	297.4	13.7	0.2	37.5	1.1	105.4	78.2	9.1
Social scientists and related occupations....	290.4	0.3	(NA)	0.3	0.2	43.5	84.1	46.6
Life, physical, and social science technicians....	366.8	10.4	0.3	44.4	0.3	100.2	86.5	3.0

NA Not available. [1] Includes oil and gas extraction. [2] Includes unpaid family workers. [3] Includes other occupations not shown separately. [4] Includes health and safety engineers.

Source: U.S. Bureau of Labor Statistics, National Employment Matrix, "Employment Projections," <http://www.bls.gov/emp/tables.htm>, accessed February 2014.

Table 837. Top 20 Metropolitan Areas with the Largest Proportion of Workers in Science and Engineering Occupations: 2010 and 2012

[As of May. Ranked by top 20 metro areas in 2012. Data are from U.S. Bureau of Labor Statistics' Occupational Employment Statistics Survey. Excludes metropolitan statistical areas where S&E (science and engineering) proportions were suppressed. Differences among employment estimates may not be statistically significant, see source for details]

Metropolitan statistical area	2010		Percent of area workforce in S&E occupations	2012		Percent of area workforce in S&E occupations
	Workers employed			Workers employed		
	All occupations	S&E occupations		All occupations	S&E occupations	
U.S. total.............	127,097,160	5,549,980	4.4	130,287,700	5,968,240	4.6
San Jose-Sunnyvale-Santa Clara, CA..................	857,160	131,890	15.4	898,610	142,430	15.9
Boulder, CO..........	152,100	20,640	13.6	159,440	21,160	13.3
Huntsville, AL..........	202,410	27,780	13.7	203,400	26,590	13.1
Corvallis, OR..........	32,770	4,050	12.4	33,310	4,170	12.5
Framingham, MA NECTA [1]....	154,760	17,710	11.4	157,290	19,550	12.4
Durham-Chapel Hill, NC..........	266,990	31,590	11.8	272,250	32,690	12.0
Washington-Arlington-Alexandria, DC-VA-MD-WV.....	2,289,200	243,350	10.6	2,343,510	265,370	11.3
Lowell-Billerica-Chelmsford, MA-NH, NECTA [1].........	113,630	12,630	11.1	116,620	12,830	11.0
Seattle-Bellevue-Everett, WA..........	1,346,300	131,130	9.7	1,409,500	148,670	10.5
Bethesda-Rockville-Frederick, MD..........	551,550	54,820	9.9	560,000	54,380	9.7
Bloomington-Normal, IL..........	85,760	7,570	8.8	86,920	8,280	9.5
Kennewick-Pasco-Richland, WA..........	96,390	8,830	9.2	97,300	8,850	9.1
Boston-Cambridge-Quincy, MA, NECTA [1]..............	1,658,000	139,620	8.4	1,711,350	154,470	9.0
San Francisco-San Mateo-Redwood City, CA..........	(X)	(X)	(X)	1,000,430	89,480	8.9
Ann Arbor, MI..........	(X)	(X)	(X)	193,760	16,870	8.7
Fort Collins-Loveland, CO..........	125,100	10,070	8.0	132,630	11,060	8.3
Ames, IA..........	(X)	(X)	(X)	40,270	3,280	8.1
Olympia, WA..........	93,910	7,870	8.4	93,850	7,520	8.0
Austin-Round Rock-San Marcos, TX..........	759,910	60,600	8.0	812,600	64,780	8.0
College Station-Bryan, TX..........	92,510	8,110	8.8	92,990	7,370	7.9
Palm Bay-Melbourne-Titusville, FL..........	189,730	16,400	8.6	(X)	(X)	(X)
Kokomo, IN..........	37,790	3,160	8.4	(X)	(X)	(X)
Colorado Springs, CO..........	240,000	19,050	7.9	(X)	(X)	(X)

X Not applicable. [1] NECTA = New England City and Town Area.

Source: National Science Foundation, *Science and Engineering Indicators, 2014*, February 2014, and earlier reports. See also <http://www.nsf.gov/statistics/seind/>.

Table 838. High-Technology Establishments, Business Formations, and Employment by State: 2010

[Employment in thousands (111,957 represents 111,957,000). High-technology (high-tech) industries are those industries where employment in technology-oriented occupations accounts for a proportion of that industry's total employment that is at least twice the 4.9% average for all industries. Includes only private-sector businesses. For a complete list of included industries, see source]

State	All establishments		High technology establishments					
			Establishments		Net business formations		Employment	
	Total	Employment (1,000)	Total	Percent of all establish-ments	Total	Percent of all establish-ments	Total (1,000)	Percent of total employ-ment
United States.......	7,384,267	111,957	648,993	8.8	4,631	0.1	13,428	12.0
Alabama.............	99,097	1,568	6,786	6.9	-3	0.0	165	10.5
Alaska...............	19,922	255	1,698	8.5	49	0.3	37	14.5
Arizona..............	131,661	2,066	11,875	9.0	-213	-0.2	239	11.6
Arkansas............	65,069	965	4,852	7.5	120	0.2	96	10.0
California............	848,238	12,535	85,787	10.1	-8	0.0	1,715	13.7
Colorado............	151,765	1,956	18,306	12.1	97	0.1	304	15.5
Connecticut..........	89,078	1,437	7,472	8.4	-113	-0.1	196	13.6
Delaware............	24,263	359	3,256	13.4	-36	-0.2	45	12.4
District of Columbia...	21,478	463	3,507	16.3	134	0.6	68	14.7
Florida..............	490,492	6,624	44,577	9.1	616	0.1	585	8.8
Georgia.............	216,787	3,315	21,413	9.9	106	0.1	447	13.5
Hawaii..............	31,904	479	2,309	7.2	-32	-0.1	30	6.3
Idaho...............	43,365	488	3,071	7.1	-13	0.0	54	11.1
Illinois..............	313,654	4,979	28,886	9.2	92	0.0	606	12.2
Indiana.............	144,802	2,401	10,276	7.1	122	0.1	221	9.2
Iowa................	80,637	1,253	4,745	5.9	91	0.1	104	8.3
Kansas.............	74,163	1,127	6,144	8.3	31	0.0	157	13.9
Kentucky............	90,665	1,456	5,913	6.5	14	0.0	123	8.4
Louisiana............	103,234	1,600	7,850	7.6	117	0.1	141	8.8
Maine...............	40,506	480	2,652	6.6	-44	-0.1	38	7.9
Maryland............	134,417	2,075	15,589	11.6	342	0.3	331	16.0
Massachusetts........	169,475	2,928	17,148	10.1	-36	0.0	442	15.1
Michigan............	218,752	3,287	16,555	7.6	113	0.1	391	11.9
Minnesota...........	145,247	2,359	13,014	9.0	-54	0.0	309	13.1
Mississippi...........	59,196	881	3,496	5.9	25	0.0	63	7.2
Missouri.............	149,628	2,293	9,956	6.7	-262	-0.2	254	11.1
Montana.............	35,950	338	2,593	7.2	26	0.1	24	7.2
Nebraska............	51,803	769	3,361	6.5	32	0.1	64	8.3
Nevada..............	59,113	1,003	6,031	10.2	112	0.2	65	6.5
New Hampshire.......	37,385	562	3,539	9.5	-28	-0.1	75	13.4
New Jersey..........	228,577	3,366	23,686	10.4	31	0.0	519	15.4
New Mexico..........	44,134	600	3,611	8.2	-69	-0.2	70	11.7
New York............	518,527	7,264	38,636	7.5	530	0.1	745	10.3
North Carolina........	217,768	3,234	17,967	8.3	383	0.2	348	10.8
North Dakota.........	21,792	295	1,151	5.3	25	0.1	25	8.3
Ohio................	253,136	4,353	20,180	8.0	173	0.1	491	11.3
Oklahoma............	89,868	1,241	7,610	8.5	47	0.1	136	11.0
Oregon..............	107,181	1,351	8,587	8.0	198	0.2	164	12.2
Pennsylvania.........	296,514	4,976	23,956	8.1	198	0.1	556	11.2
Rhode Island.........	28,477	399	2,071	7.3	22	0.1	38	9.5
South Carolina.......	101,902	1,503	7,010	6.9	44	0.0	154	10.3
South Dakota.........	25,562	329	1,426	5.6	5	0.0	24	7.2
Tennessee...........	131,302	2,263	8,702	6.6	-156	-0.1	219	9.7
Texas...............	521,248	8,786	50,180	9.6	600	0.1	1,173	13.4
Utah................	68,725	1,022	7,139	10.4	156	0.2	121	11.8
Vermont.............	21,422	264	1,581	7.4	17	0.1	28	10.6
Virginia.............	192,780	2,999	23,623	12.3	567	0.3	530	17.7
Washington..........	175,486	2,326	15,335	8.7	185	0.1	388	16.7
West Virginia.........	38,599	560	2,490	6.5	99	0.3	47	8.4
Wisconsin...........	139,332	2,320	9,709	7.0	138	0.1	245	10.6
Wyoming.............	20,189	205	1,686	8.4	41	0.2	18	8.9

Source: National Science Foundation, *Science and Engineering Indicators, 2014*, February 2014. See <http://www.nsf.gov/statistics/seind/>.

Table 839. Employment and Median Salary of Worker With Highest Degree in Science and Engineering (S&E) Field, by Sex and Occupation: 2010

[Rounded to the nearest 1,000. Data are for full-time workers who typically work 35 or more hours weekly in their principal job. Data are from National Science Foundation's Scientists and Engineers Statistical Data System (SESTAT)]

Occupation	Total Number	Total Median salary (dollars)	Female Number	Female Percent	Female Median salary (dollars)	Male Number	Male Percent	Male Median salary (dollars)
All occupations.................	9,728,000	70,000	3,249,000	33.4	53,000	6,479,000	66.6	80,000
S&E...........................	3,610,000	80,000	840,000	23.3	69,000	2,770,000	76.7	85,000
Engineers..................	1,199,000	87,000	152,000	12.7	75,000	1,047,000	87.3	89,000
Computer and mathematical scientists..	1,485,000	85,000	309,000	20.8	77,000	1,176,000	79.2	87,000
Biological, agricultural, and other life scientists..............	416,000	60,000	178,000	42.8	52,000	237,000	57.0	65,000
Physical scientists...............	263,000	70,000	69,000	26.2	57,000	194,000	73.8	73,000
Social scientists.................	247,000	66,000	132,000	53.4	63,000	116,000	47.0	74,000
S&E related occupations...........	1,377,000	70,000	537,000	39.0	52,000	840,000	61.0	85,000
Health-related occupations........	381,000	49,000	254,000	66.7	46,000	126,000	33.1	56,000
Non-S&E related occupations..............	4,742,000	60,000	1,873,000	39.5	49,000	2,869,000	60.5	70,000

Source: National Science Foundation, National Center for Science and Engineering Statistics, *Science and Engineering Indicators 2014*, NSB 14-01, February 2014. See also <http://www.nsf.gov/statistics/seind/>.

Table 840. Federal Discretionary Outlays for General Science and Space and Other Technology: 1970 to 2014, and Projections for 2015 and 2016

[In millions of dollars (4.5 represents $4,500,000). For fiscal years ending in year shown; see text, Section 8]

Year	Current dollars Total	Current dollars General science and research	Current dollars Space/other technologies	Constant (2009) dollars Total	Constant (2009) dollars General science and research	Constant (2009) dollars Space/other technologies
1970.............	4.5	0.9	3.6	24.3	5.1	19.2
1980.............	5.8	1.4	4.5	15.8	3.7	12.1
1990.............	14.4	2.8	11.6	27.8	5.4	22.4
1995 [1]............	16.7	4.1	12.6	24.4	6.0	18.4
2000.............	18.6	6.2	12.4	24.6	8.2	16.5
2005.............	23.6	8.8	14.8	26.2	9.8	16.4
2006.............	23.5	9.0	14.5	25.2	9.7	15.5
2007.............	24.4	9.1	15.3	25.3	9.5	15.8
2008.............	26.7	9.5	17.2	27.0	9.6	17.4
2009.............	28.3	9.9	18.4	28.3	9.9	18.4
2010.............	30.0	11.6	18.4	29.7	11.5	18.2
2011.............	29.4	12.3	17.0	28.6	12.0	16.6
2012.............	28.9	12.3	16.6	27.8	11.9	16.0
2103.............	28.8	12.4	16.4	27.3	11.7	15.6
2014.............	28.5	11.9	16.6	26.5	11.1	15.4
2015, proj......	29.7	12.2	17.6	27.5	11.3	16.3
2016, proj......	30.8	12.7	18.1	28.1	11.6	16.5

[1] Due to the effects of the Credit Reform Act of 1990 on the measurement and classification of Federal credit activities, the discretionary outlays for years prior to 1992 are not strictly comparable to those for 1992 and beyond.

Source: U.S. Office of Management and Budget, *Fiscal Year 2016 Budget of the U.S. Government: Historical Tables*, February 2015. See also <http://www.whitehouse.gov/omb/budget>.

Table 841. Worldwide Space Launch Events: 2000 to 2014

[2,729 represents $2,729,000,000.) Data show all U.S. and international orbital launches. Launch data includes launch failures; launch failures happen when the payload does not reach a usable orbit or is destroyed as the result of a launch vehicle malfunction. In 2014 there were 3 launch failures: two government launches and one commercial launch]

Country/Region	Non-commercial launches 2000	2010	2013	2014	Commercial launches 2000	2010	2013	2014	Launch revenues for commercial launch events (mil. dol.) 2000	2010	2013	2014
Total.............	50	51	58	69	35	23	23	23	2,729	2,453	1,909	2,355
United States......	21	11	13	12	7	4	6	11	370	307	340	1,107
Russia.............	23	18	20	28	13	13	12	4	671	826	759	218
Europe.............	–	–	3	5	12	6	4	6	1,433	1,320	710	920
China..............	5	15	15	16	–	–	–	–	(X)	(X)	(X)	(X)
India...............	–	3	3	3	–	–	–	1	(X)	(X)	(X)	15
Japan..............	1	2	3	4	–	–	–	–	(X)	(X)	(X)	(X)
Israel..............	–	1	–	1	–	–	–	–	(X)	(X)	(X)	(X)
Iran................	–	–	–	–	–	–	–	–	(X)	(X)	(X)	(X)
Korea, North.......	–	–	–	–	–	–	–	–	(X)	(X)	(X)	(X)
Korea, South.......	–	1	1	–	–	–	–	–	(X)	(X)	(X)	(X)
Multinational.......	–	–	–	–	3	–	1	1	255	(X)	100	95

– Represents zero. X Not applicable.

Source: Federal Aviation Administration, *Commercial Space Transportation: 2014 Year in Review*, February 2015, and earlier editions. See also <http://www.faa.gov/about/office_org/headquarters_offices/ast/reports_studies/year_review>.

Agriculture

This section presents statistics on farms and farm operators; farm income, expenditures, and debt; farm output, productivity, and marketings; foreign trade in agricultural products; specific crops; livestock, poultry, and their products; and direct marketing to consumers and farm to school programs.

The principal sources are the data collected by the National Agricultural Statistics Service (NASS), the Economic Research Service (ERS), and the Foreign Agricultural Service (FAS) of the U.S. Department of Agriculture (USDA) and published in reports or databases. The ERS publishes data on farm assets, debt, and income on the Internet at <http://www.ers.usda.gov/topics/farm-economy/farm-sector-income-finances.aspx>. The ERS also provides data on commodity supply and disappearance via commodity outlook reports, yearbooks, and databases, available on the ERS site at <http://www.ers.usda.gov/data-products.aspx>. Sources of current data on agricultural exports and imports include the Global Agricultural Trade System database provided by the FAS at <http://www.fas.usda.gov/gats> and the "Foreign Agricultural Trade of the United States (FATUS)" data, published by the ERS, available on the ERS Internet site at <http://www.ers.usda.gov/data-products/foreign-agricultural-trade-of-the-united-states-(fatus).aspx>.

The field offices of the NASS collect data on crops, livestock and products, agricultural prices, farm employment, and other related subjects mainly through sample surveys. Information is obtained on crops and livestock items pertaining to agricultural production and marketing. State estimates and supporting information are sent to the Agricultural Statistics Board of NASS, which reviews the estimates and issues reports containing state and national data. Among these reports are annual summaries such as *Crop Production, Crop Values, Agricultural Prices,* and *Meat Animals Production, Disposition and Income*. The NASS also provides data through the QuickStats database at <http://quickstats.nass.usda.gov>.

The USDA conducts the Census of Agriculture every 5 years and collects information concerning all areas of farming and ranching operations, including production expenses, market value of products, and operator characteristics. The information from the 2012 Census of Agriculture is available in printed form in the Volume 1, Geographic Area Series; and on the Internet at <http://www.agcensus.usda.gov/Publications/2012/>. An evaluation of coverage has been conducted for each census of agriculture since 1945 to provide estimates of the completeness of census farm counts. Beginning with the 1997 Census of Agriculture, census farm counts and totals were statistically adjusted for coverage and reported at the county level. The size of the adjustments varies considerably by state. In general, farms not on the census mail list tended to be small in acreage, production, and sales of farm products. The response rate for the 2012 Census of Agriculture was 80.1 percent as compared with a response rate of 85.2 for the 2007 Census of Agriculture, 88.0 for the 2002 Census of Agriculture, and 86.2 percent for the 1997 Census of Agriculture.

For more explanation about census mail list compilation, collection methods, coverage measurement, and adjustments, see Appendix A, *2012 Census of Agriculture,* Volume 1 reports <http://www.agcensus.usda.gov/Publications/2012/>.

Farms and farmland—The definitions of a farm have varied through time. Since 1850, when minimum criteria defining a farm for census purposes first were established, the farm definition has changed nine times. The current definition, first used for the 1974 census, is any place from which $1,000 or more of agricultural products were produced and sold, or normally would have been sold, during the census year.

Acreage designated as "land in farms" consists primarily of agricultural land used for crops, pasture, or grazing. It also includes woodland and wasteland not actually under cultivation or used for pasture or grazing, provided it was part of the farm operator's total operation. Land in farms includes acres set aside under annual commodity acreage programs as well as acres idled by federal conservation programs for places meeting the farm definition. Land in farms is an operating unit concept and includes land owned and operated as well as land rented from others. All grazing land, except land used under government permits on a per-head basis, was included as "land in farms" provided it was part of a farm or ranch.

Farm income—The final agricultural sector output comprises cash receipts from farm marketings of crops and livestock, federal government payments made directly to farmers for farm-related activities, rental value of farm homes, value of farm products consumed in farm homes, and other farm-related income such as machine hire and custom work. Farm marketings represent quantities of agricultural products sold by farmers multiplied by prices received per unit of production at the local market. Information on prices received for farm products is generally obtained by the NASS Agricultural Statistics Board from surveys of firms (such as grain elevators, packers, and processors) purchasing agricultural commodities directly from producers. In some cases, the price information is obtained directly from the producers.

Crops—Estimates of crop acreage and production by the NASS are based on current sample survey data obtained from individual producers and objective yield counts, reports of carlot shipments, market records, personal field observations by field statisticians, and reports from other sources.

Prices received by farmers are marketing year average prices and do not include allowances for outstanding loans, government purchases, deficiency payments or disaster payments. These averages are based on monthly prices weighted by monthly sales during specific periods. All state marketing year average prices are based on individual state marketing years, while U.S. marketing year average prices are based on standard U.S. marketing years for each crop. For a description of how U.S. prices are computed as well as a listing of the crop marketing years, see *Crop Values Annual Summary*.

Value of production is computed by multiplying state prices by each state's production. The U.S. value of production is the sum of state values for all states. Value of production figures should not be confused with cash receipts from farm marketings which relate to sales during a calendar year, irrespective of the year of production.

Livestock—Annual inventory numbers of livestock and estimates of livestock, dairy, and poultry production prepared by the Department of Agriculture are based on information from farmers and ranchers obtained by probability survey sampling methods.

Statistical reliability—For a discussion of statistical collection and estimation, sampling procedures, and measures of statistical reliability pertaining to Department of Agriculture data, see Appendix III.

Table 842. Selected Characteristics of Farms by North American Industry Classification System (NAICS): 2012

[394,644,481 represents $394,644,481,000. See text this section and Appendix III]

Industry	2012 NAICS code [1]	Farms	Land in farms (acres)	Harvested cropland (acres)	Market value of agricultural products sold (1,000)		
					Total	Crops	Livestock [2]
Total	(X)	2,109,303	914,527,657	314,964,600	394,644,481	212,397,074	182,247,407
Crop production	111	1,054,987	454,064,220	262,297,534	209,421,055	200,168,398	9,252,657
Oilseed and grain farming	1111	369,332	289,765,872	213,227,680	127,712,682	120,552,373	7,160,309
Soybean farming	11111	89,946	39,465,959	32,408,918	16,070,358	15,835,107	235,251
Oilseed (except soybean) farming	11112	1,079	1,501,942	1,103,482	356,573	351,653	4,920
Dry pea and bean farming	11113	1,000	735,057	533,503	258,432	255,631	2,802
Wheat farming	11114	38,542	56,835,727	29,831,424	8,815,719	8,368,777	446,942
Corn farming	11115	167,043	107,075,030	88,821,359	65,231,965	63,396,809	1,835,157
Rice farming	11116	3,170	3,342,921	2,607,924	2,448,145	2,419,709	28,436
Other grain farming	11119	68,552	80,809,236	57,921,070	34,531,489	29,924,687	4,606,802
Vegetable and melon farming	11121	43,021	8,206,468	5,333,376	16,726,256	16,624,257	101,998
Potato farming	111211	2,529	2,630,696	1,999,092	4,010,500	3,995,512	14,989
Other vegetable (except potato) and melon farming	111219	40,492	5,575,772	3,334,284	12,715,756	12,628,746	87,010
Fruit and tree nut farming	1113	93,020	13,162,702	5,641,474	25,481,636	25,346,460	135,177
Orange groves	11131	6,141	1,268,406	672,041	1,981,134	1,955,556	25,579
Citrus (except orange) groves	11132	2,839	357,519	175,912	639,232	632,859	6,373
Noncitrus fruit and tree nut farming	11133	84,040	11,536,777	4,793,521	22,861,271	22,758,045	103,225
Apple orchards	111331	8,921	2,133,711	418,403	2,757,137	2,750,702	6,435
Grape vineyards	111332	17,580	2,683,393	1,205,918	6,836,734	6,816,072	20,661
Strawberry farming	111333	1,545	109,972	67,848	1,860,850	1,860,428	422
Berry (except strawberry) farming	111334	9,928	1,041,594	240,168	1,342,637	1,339,096	3,541
Tree nut farming	111335	23,414	3,841,338	2,101,087	6,990,605	6,942,604	48,001
Fruit and tree nut combination farming	111336	979	247,633	112,660	468,648	456,220	12,428
Other noncitrus fruit farming	111339	21,673	1,479,136	647,437	2,604,659	2,592,922	11,737
Greenhouse, nursery, and floriculture production	1114	52,777	4,502,514	1,483,765	14,736,375	14,694,443	41,932
Food crops grown under cover	11141	3,138	135,425	23,943	1,695,262	1,693,031	2,231
Nursery and floriculture production	11142	49,639	4,367,089	1,459,822	13,041,113	13,001,412	39,702
Nursery and tree production	111421	32,048	3,796,386	1,306,906	7,071,426	7,040,218	31,207
Floriculture production	111422	17,591	570,703	152,916	5,969,688	5,961,193	8,494
Other crop farming	1119	496,837	138,426,664	36,611,239	24,764,106	22,950,865	1,813,241
Tobacco farming	11191	5,132	1,574,110	803,519	1,262,097	1,210,614	51,482
Cotton farming	11192	8,915	11,157,031	7,232,673	4,661,521	4,610,462	51,059
Sugarcane farming	11193	526	1,326,957	934,255	1,361,015	1,356,475	4,540
Hay farming	11194	252,382	53,007,901	15,859,037	5,924,002	5,468,044	455,959
All other crop farming	11199	229,882	71,360,665	11,781,755	11,555,470	10,305,269	1,250,201
Animal production	112	1,054,316	460,463,437	52,667,066	185,223,427	12,228,676	172,994,750
Cattle ranching and farming	1121	678,911	367,223,798	44,311,752	112,182,806	8,365,288	103,817,518
Beef cattle ranching and farming including feedlots	11211	632,906	348,596,036	32,125,853	71,150,505	5,500,152	65,650,353
Beef cattle ranching and farming	112111	619,172	336,701,440	28,456,003	32,966,557	3,856,930	29,109,627
Cattle feedlots	112112	13,734	11,894,596	3,669,850	38,183,948	1,643,222	36,540,726
Dairy cattle and milk production	11212	46,005	18,627,762	12,185,899	41,032,301	2,865,136	38,167,165
Hog and pig farming	1122	21,687	5,207,594	3,617,583	22,645,102	2,239,182	20,405,920
Poultry and egg production	1123	52,849	6,352,747	1,951,105	43,703,626	943,395	42,760,231
Chicken egg production	11231	27,995	1,861,307	389,376	8,932,413	174,297	8,758,115
Broilers and other meat-type chicken production	11232	16,324	3,137,705	1,058,726	25,115,569	489,383	24,626,186
Turkey production	11233	2,521	779,300	380,638	5,732,622	218,157	5,514,465
Poultry hatcheries	11234	291	23,238	1,774	3,120,868	1,375	3,119,492
Other poultry production	11239	5,718	551,197	120,591	802,155	60,182	741,973
Sheep and goat farming	1124	73,272	11,729,223	344,163	766,044	47,781	718,263
Sheep farming	11241	31,316	7,911,730	240,007	572,472	39,717	532,755
Goat farming	11242	41,956	3,817,493	104,156	193,572	8,063	185,509
Animal aquaculture	1125	4,095	1,082,639	27,109	1,530,706	11,142	1,519,564
Other animal production	1129	223,502	68,867,436	2,415,354	4,395,143	621,890	3,773,253
Apiculture	11291	7,358	373,819	14,540	257,109	3,814	253,295
Horse and other equine production	11292	172,043	27,504,660	888,078	1,333,258	19,888	1,313,370
Fur-bearing animal and rabbit production	11293	633	22,524	2,286	13,491	199	13,292
All other animal production	11299	43,468	40,966,433	1,510,450	2,791,285	597,989	2,193,295

X Not applicable [1] Based on the North American Industry Classification System (NAICS) 2012; see text, Section 15. [2] Includes poultry, and their products sold.

Source: U.S. Department of Agriculture, National Agricultural Statistics Service, *2012 Census of Agriculture*, Vol. 1, May 2014. See also <http://www.agcensus.usda.gov/Publications/index.php>.

Table 843. Farms—Number and Acreage: 2000 to 2014

[As of June (2,167 represents 2,167,000). Based on 1974 census definition; for definition of farms and farmland, see text, this section. Data for census years have been adjusted for underenumeration]

Year	Unit	2000	2005	2008	2009	2010	2011	2012	2013	2014
Number of farms..........	1,000	2,167	2,099	2,185	2,170	2,150	2,131	2,110	2,102	2,084
Land in farms.............	Million acres	945	928	919	918	916	914	915	914	913
Average per farm........	Acres	436	442	421	423	426	429	433	435	438

Source: U.S. Department of Agriculture, National Agricultural Statistics Service, *Farm Numbers and Land in Farms, Final Estimates, 1998–2002*; *Farms and Land in Farms, Final Estimates, 2003-2007*; and *Farms and Land in Farms 2014 Summary*, February 2015. See also <http://www.nass.usda.gov/Publications/index.asp>.

Table 844. Farms—Number and Acreage by State: 2010 and 2014

[2,150 represents 2,150,000. As of June 1. See headnote, Table 843]

State	Farms (1,000) 2010	Farms (1,000) 2014	Land in farms (mil. acres) 2010	Land in farms (mil. acres) 2014	Acreage per farm 2010	Acreage per farm 2014	State	Farms (1,000) 2010	Farms (1,000) 2014	Land in farms (mil. acres) 2010	Land in farms (mil. acres) 2014	Acreage per farm 2010	Acreage per farm 2014
United States.....	2,150	2,084	916	913	426	438	Missouri............	103	98	29	28	279	290
Alabama...........	46	43	9	9	193	205	Montana............	29	28	61	60	2,082	2,147
Alaska............	1	1	1	1	1,181	1,092	Nebraska...........	50	49	45	45	917	921
Arizona............	18	20	25	26	1,378	1,327	Nevada.............	4	4	6	6	1,579	1,417
Arkansas...........	47	44	14	14	291	314	New Hampshire....	4	4	(Z)	(Z)	109	107
California..........	79	76	26	26	322	334	New Jersey........	10	9	1	1	74	79
Colorado...........	36	35	32	32	868	909	New Mexico........	22	25	43	43	1,973	1,749
Connecticut........	6	6	(Z)	(Z)	75	73	New York..........	36	36	7	7	197	202
Delaware...........	3	3	1	1	200	200	North Carolina.....	52	50	8	8	163	170
Florida.............	48	48	9	10	197	200	North Dakota.......	31	30	40	39	1,262	1,297
Georgia............	44	41	10	9	219	229	Ohio...............	75	75	14	14	184	188
Hawaii.............	7	7	1	1	153	160	Oklahoma..........	83	80	35	34	417	431
Idaho..............	25	24	12	12	453	484	Oregon............	37	35	16	16	439	474
Illinois.............	76	75	27	27	354	361	Pennsylvania.......	61	59	8	8	126	131
Indiana............	61	58	15	15	242	253	Rhode Island.......	1	1	(Z)	(Z)	56	56
Iowa..............	89	88	31	31	343	347	South Carolina.....	26	24	5	5	192	205
Kansas............	63	61	46	46	732	754	South Dakota.......	32	32	43	43	1,361	1,366
Kentucky...........	80	76	13	13	167	170	Tennessee.........	73	67	11	11	148	162
Louisiana...........	29	27	8	8	274	287	Texas..............	249	246	132	130	530	530
Maine.............	8	8	1	1	173	177	Utah..............	18	18	11	11	629	608
Maryland...........	13	12	2	2	164	165	Vermont............	7	7	1	1	172	171
Massachusetts.....	8	8	1	1	69	67	Virginia............	47	46	8	8	176	179
Michigan...........	53	52	10	10	187	193	Washington.........	38	37	15	15	382	401
Minnesota..........	77	74	26	26	342	350	West Virginia.......	22	21	4	4	161	169
Mississippi.........	40	37	11	11	275	294	Wisconsin...........	73	69	15	15	201	210
							Wyoming............	12	12	30	30	2,586	2,598

Z Less than 500,000 acres.

Source: U.S. Department of Agriculture, National Agricultural Statistics Service, *Farms and Land in Farms, 2014 Summary*, February 2015, and earlier reports. See also <http://www.nass.usda.gov/Publications/index.asp>.

Table 845. Farms by Size and Type of Organization: 1982 to 2012

[2,241 represents 2,241,000. For comments on adjustment, see text, this section]

Size and type of organization	Unit	Not adjusted for coverage 1982	Not adjusted for coverage 1987	Not adjusted for coverage 1992	Not adjusted for coverage 1997	Adjusted for coverage [1] 1997	Adjusted for coverage [1] 2002	Adjusted for coverage [1] 2007	Adjusted for coverage [1] 2012
Farms........................	1,000	2,241	2,088	1,925	1,912	2,216	2,129	2,205	2,109
Land in farms..................	Mil. acres	987	964	946	932	955	938	922	915
Average size of farm........................	Acres	440	462	491	487	431	441	418	434
Farms by size:									
1 to 9 acres............................	1,000	188	183	166	154	205	179	233	224
10 to 49 acres...........................	1,000	449	412	388	411	531	564	620	590
50 to 179 acres..........................	1,000	712	645	584	593	694	659	661	634
180 to 499 acres.........................	1,000	527	478	428	403	428	389	368	346
500 to 999 acres.........................	1,000	204	200	186	176	179	162	150	143
1,000 to 1,999 acres.....................	1,000	97	102	102	101	103	99	93	91
2,000 acres or more......................	1,000	65	67	71	75	74	78	80	82
Farms by type of organization:									
Family or individual......................	1,000	1,946	1,809	1,653	1,643	1,923	1,910	1,906	1,829
Partnership............................	1,000	223	200	187	169	186	130	174	138
Corporation............................	1,000	60	67	73	84	90	74	96	107
Other [2].................................	1,000	12	12	12	15	17	16	28	36

[1] Data have been adjusted for coverage; see text, this section. [2] Cooperative, estate or trust, institutional, etc.

Source: U.S. Department of Agriculture, National Agricultural Statistics Service, *2012 Census of Agriculture*, Vol. 1, May 2014, and earlier reports. See also <http://www.agcensus.usda.gov/Publications/index.php>.

Table 846. Farms—Number and Acreage by Size of Farm: 2007 and 2012

[2,205 represents 2,205,000. Data have been adjusted for coverage; see text, this section]

Size of farm	Number of farms (1,000)		Land in farms (mil. acres)		Cropland harvested (mil. acres)		Percent distribution, 2012		
	2007	2012	2007	2012	2007	2012	Number of farms	All land in farms	Cropland harvested
Total..........................	2,205	2,109	922.1	914.5	309.6	315.0	100.0	100.0	100.0
Under 10 acres.................	233	224	1.1	1.0	0.3	0.3	10.6	0.1	0.1
10 to 49 acres..................	620	590	15.9	15.1	4.3	4.1	27.9	1.7	1.3
50 to 69 acres..................	154	154	8.9	8.9	2.5	2.5	7.3	1.0	0.8
70 to 99 acres..................	192	185	15.8	15.2	4.5	4.4	8.8	1.7	1.4
100 to 139 acres...............	175	166	20.3	19.3	5.8	5.7	7.9	2.1	1.8
140 to 179 acres...............	139	129	22.0	20.3	6.6	6.3	6.1	2.2	2.0
180 to 219 acres...............	88	84	17.3	16.7	5.6	5.6	4.0	1.8	1.8
220 to 259 acres...............	68	64	16.3	15.1	5.7	5.5	3.0	1.7	1.8
260 to 499 acres...............	213	198	75.9	70.6	30.4	28.8	9.4	7.7	9.1
500 to 999 acres..............	150	143	104.1	99.0	51.6	49.5	6.8	10.8	15.7
1,000 to 1,999 acres...........	93	91	127.6	125.1	69.8	68.7	4.3	13.7	21.8
2,000 acres or more..........	80	82	496.9	508.2	122.5	133.6	3.9	55.6	42.4

Source: U.S. Department of Agriculture, National Agricultural Statistics Service, *2012 Census of Agriculture*, Vol. 1, May 2014. See also <http://www.agcensus.usda.gov/Publications/index.php>.

Table 847. Farms—Number, Acreage, and Value by Tenure of Principal Operator and Type of Organization: 2007 and 2012

[2,205 represents 2,205,000. Full owners own all the land they operate. Part owners own a part and rent from others the rest of the land they operate. A principal operator is the person primarily responsible for the on-site, day-to-day operation of the farm or ranch business. Data have been adjusted for coverage; see text, this section]

Item and year	Unit	Total [1]	Tenure of operator			Type of organization		
			Full owner	Part owner	Tenant	Family or individual	Partner- ship	Corpora- tion
NUMBER OF FARMS								
2007..................................	1,000	2,205	1,522	542	141	1,906	174	96
2012..................................	1,000	2,109	1,428	533	148	1,829	138	107
Under 50 acres....................	1,000	813	699	64	51	738	33	30
50 to 179 acres...................	1,000	634	465	130	39	568	34	21
180 to 499 acres..................	1,000	346	179	141	26	296	27	17
500 to 999 acres..................	1,000	143	46	83	14	113	15	12
1,000 acres or more..............	1,000	173	40	115	19	115	30	26
LAND IN FARMS								
2007..................................	Mil. acres	922	344	496	82	574	161	125
2012..................................	Mil. acres	915	336	491	87	562	156	131
Value of land and buildings, 2012..................	Bil. dol.	2,269	795	1,270	203	1,535	355	318
Value of farm products sold, 2012..................	Bil. dol.	395	141	210	43	197	86	105

[1] Includes other types, not shown separately.

Source: U.S. Department of Agriculture, National Agricultural Statistics Service, *2012 Census of Agriculture*, Vol. 1, May 2014, and earlier reports. See also <http://www.agcensus.usda.gov/Publications/index.php>.

Table 848. Corporate Farms—Characteristics by Type: 2012

[131.3 represents 131,300,000. Data have been adjusted for coverage; see text, this section and Appendix III]

Item	Unit	All corpora- tions	Family held corporations			Other corporations		
			Total	1 to 10 stock- holders	11 or more stock- holders	Total	1 to 10 stock- holders	11 or more stock- holders
Farms:								
2002..................................	Number	73,752	66,667	65,017	1,650	7,085	6,010	1,075
2007..................................	Number	96,074	85,837	83,796	2,041	10,237	9,330	907
2012								
Farms..................................	Number	106,716	95,142	92,834	2,308	11,574	10,438	1,136
Percent distribution.......................	Percent	100.0	89.2	87.0	2.2	10.8	9.8	1.1
Land in farms.............................	Mil. acres	131.3	118.8	110.8	8.0	12.5	8.8	3.7
Average per farm.........................	Acres	1,230	1,249	1,194	3,454	1,078	843	3,241
Value of—								
Land and buildings........................	Bil. dol.	318.3	283.9	269.0	15.0	34.4	24.4	10.0
Average per farm.........................	$1,000	2,983	2,984	2,897	6,487	2,969	2,334	8,807
Farm products sold........................	Bil. dol.	104.9	83.7	75.7	7.9	21.2	12.4	8.8
Average per farm.........................	$1,000	983	879	816	3,431	1,833	1,188	7,756

Source: U.S. Department of Agriculture, National Agricultural Statistics Service, *2012 Census of Agriculture*, Vol. 1, May 2014, and earlier reports. See also <http://www.agcensus.usda.gov/Publications/index.php>.

Table 849. Farms—Number, Acreage, and Value by State: 2007 and 2012

[2,205 represents 2,205,000. Data have been adjusted for coverage; see text, this section and Appendix III]

State	Number of farms (1,000)		Land in farms (mil. acres)		Average size of farm (acres)		Total value of land and buildings (bil. dol.)		Market value of agricultural products sold and government payments, 2012 (mil. dol.)	Total number of operators, 2012 (1,000)
	2007	2012	2007	2012	2007	2012	2007	2012		
U.S.	2,205	2,109	922.1	914.5	418	434	1,744.3	2,268.5	402,698	3,233
AL.	49	43	9.0	8.9	185	206	20.7	23.7	5,659	64
AK.	1	1	0.9	0.8	1,285	1,094	0.3	0.5	61	1
AZ.	16	20	26.1	26.2	1,670	1,312	19.5	16.9	3,763	34
AR.	49	45	13.9	13.8	281	306	32.5	36.4	10,039	70
CA.	81	78	25.4	25.6	313	328	162.5	160.5	42,774	126
CO.	37	36	31.6	31.9	853	881	33.1	40.8	7,946	59
CT.	5	6	0.4	0.4	83	73	5.1	4.8	555	10
DE.	3	2	0.5	0.5	200	208	5.3	4.2	1,284	4
FL.	47	48	9.2	9.5	195	200	52.1	49.7	7,742	75
GA.	48	42	10.2	9.6	212	228	31.6	29.7	9,397	62
HI.	8	7	1.1	1.1	149	161	8.6	10.2	667	11
ID.	25	25	11.5	11.8	454	474	22.7	26.1	7,901	41
IL.	77	75	26.8	26.9	348	359	101.5	169.8	17,740	109
IN.	61	59	14.8	14.7	242	251	52.9	78.8	11,478	90
IA.	93	89	30.7	30.6	331	345	104.2	195.6	31,604	132
KS.	66	62	46.3	46.1	707	747	42.2	75.3	18,903	93
KY.	85	77	14.0	13.0	164	169	37.5	39.5	5,237	114
LA.	30	28	8.1	7.9	269	281	16.7	20.2	3,948	42
ME.	8	8	1.3	1.5	166	178	3.0	3.4	773	13
MD.	13	12	2.1	2.0	160	166	14.4	14.1	2,307	19
MA.	8	8	0.5	0.5	67	68	6.4	5.5	500	13
MI.	56	52	10.0	9.9	179	191	34.2	40.0	8,834	80
MN.	81	75	26.9	26.0	332	349	69.2	109.9	21,748	111
MS.	42	38	11.5	10.9	273	287	21.4	24.8	6,622	56
MO.	108	99	29.0	28.3	269	285	63.2	78.9	9,489	153
MT.	30	28	61.4	59.8	2,079	2,134	47.6	46.9	4,440	45
NE.	48	50	45.5	45.3	953	907	52.7	107.9	23,461	76
NV.	3	4	5.9	5.9	1,873	1,429	3.6	5.5	767	7
NH.	4	4	0.5	0.5	113	108	2.3	2.0	194	7
NJ.	10	9	0.7	0.7	71	79	11.3	9.1	1,015	15
NM.	21	25	43.2	43.2	2,066	1,748	14.6	18.7	2,621	38
NY.	36	36	7.2	7.2	197	202	16.3	18.7	5,490	57
NC.	53	50	8.5	8.4	160	168	34.7	36.5	12,708	74
ND.	32	31	39.7	39.3	1,241	1,268	30.6	56.0	11,332	45
OH.	76	75	14.0	14.0	184	185	49.2	67.5	10,293	116
OK.	87	80	35.1	34.4	405	428	40.6	46.0	7,386	122
OR.	39	35	16.4	16.3	425	460	31.0	30.7	4,970	59
PA.	63	59	7.8	7.7	124	130	37.3	41.8	7,487	92
RI.	1	1	0.1	0.1	56	56	1.1	1.0	62	2
SC.	26	25	4.9	5.0	189	197	14.0	14.8	3,087	37
SD.	31	32	43.7	43.3	1,401	1,352	39.1	73.0	10,454	49
TN.	79	68	11.0	10.9	138	160	37.1	38.7	3,679	102
TX.	247	249	130.4	130.2	527	523	165.6	218.1	26,020	376
UT.	17	18	11.1	11.0	664	609	13.9	16.0	1,840	29
VT.	7	7	1.2	1.3	177	171	3.6	4.0	790	12
VA.	47	46	8.1	8.3	171	180	34.1	35.8	3,836	70
WA.	39	37	15.0	14.7	381	396	29.8	33.9	9,280	61
WV.	24	21	3.7	3.6	157	168	8.8	8.9	814	32
WI.	78	70	15.2	14.6	194	209	49.0	57.2	11,982	111
WY.	11	12	30.2	30.4	2,726	2,587	15.5	20.6	1,718	20

Source: U.S. Department of Agriculture, National Agricultural Statistics Service, *2012 Census of Agriculture*, Vol. 1, May 2014. See also <http://www.agcensus.usda.gov/Publications/index.php>.

Table 850. Farms—Number, Acreage, and Value of Sales by Size of Sales: 2007 and 2012

[2,205 represents 2,205,000. Data have been adjusted for coverage; see text, this section and Appendix III]

Market value of agricultural products sold	Farms (1,000)	Acreage Total (mil.)	Acreage Average per farm	Value of sales Total (mil. dol.)	Value of sales Average per farm (dol.)	Percent distribution Farms	Percent distribution Acreage	Percent distribution Value of sales
2007								
Total........................	2,205	922.1	418	297,220	134,807	100.0	100.0	100.0
Less than $2,500.................	900	121.5	135	435	483	40.8	13.2	0.1
$2,500 to $4,999.................	200	17.5	87	718	3,585	9.1	1.9	0.2
$5,000 to $9,999.................	219	27.6	126	1,553	7,104	9.9	3.0	0.5
$10,000 to $24,999..............	248	65.8	265	3,960	15,949	11.3	7.1	1.3
$25,000 to $49,999..............	155	59.8	386	5,480	35,419	7.0	6.5	1.8
$50,000 to $99,999..............	125	78.2	623	8,961	71,429	5.7	8.5	3.0
$100,000 to $249,999...........	148	147.6	1,000	24,213	164,156	6.7	16.0	8.1
$250,000 to $499,999...........	93	140.7	1,507	33,410	357,811	4.2	15.3	11.2
$500,000 to $999,999...........	61	119.4	1,965	42,691	702,417	2.8	13.0	14.4
$1,000,000 or more..............	56	144.0	2,593	175,800	3,167,050	2.5	15.6	59.1
2012								
Total........................	2,109	914.5	434	394,644	187,097	100.0	100.0	100.0
Less than $2,500.................	788	118.4	150	380	483	37.4	12.9	0.1
$2,500 to $4,999.................	191	19.6	102	688	3,592	9.1	2.1	0.2
$5,000 to $9,999.................	214	25.4	119	1,522	7,104	10.2	2.8	0.4
$10,000 to $24,999..............	245	59.4	243	3,908	15,954	11.6	6.5	1.0
$25,000 to $49,999..............	153	48.4	316	5,418	35,440	7.2	5.3	1.4
$50,000 to $99,999..............	129	64.0	495	9,251	71,507	6.1	7.0	2.3
$100,000 to $249,999...........	139	115.9	835	22,822	164,328	6.6	12.7	5.8
$250,000 to $499,999...........	94	121.1	1,288	33,964	361,045	4.5	13.2	8.6
$500,000 to $999,999...........	76	129.4	1,704	54,686	719,996	3.6	14.2	13.9
$1,000,000 or more..............	79	212.9	2,687	262,006	3,307,109	3.8	23.3	66.4

Source: U.S. Department of Agriculture, National Agricultural Statistics Service, *2012 Census of Agriculture*, Vol. 1, May 2014, and earlier reports. See also <http://www.agcensus.usda.gov/Publications/index.php>.

Table 851. Farms—Number, Value of Sales, and Government Payments by Economic Class of Farm: 2007 and 2012

[2,205 represents 2,205,000. Economic class of farm is a combination of market value of agricultural products sold and federal farm program payments. Data have been adjusted for coverage; see text, this section and Appendix III]

Economic class	Number of farms (1,000) 2007, total	Number of farms (1,000) 2012 Total	Number of farms (1,000) 2012 Receiving government payments	Market value of agricultural products sold and government payments (mil. dol.) 2007, total	Market value... 2012 Total	Market value... 2012 Agricultural products sold	Market value... 2012 Government payments
Total..........................	2,205	2,109	811	305,204	402,698	394,644	8,053
Less than $1,000.................	500	429	36	96	80	64	16
$1,000 to $2,499.................	271	237	72	448	393	291	101
$2,500 to $4,999.................	246	231	69	884	832	652	180
$5,000 to $9,999.................	255	249	78	1,811	1,769	1,459	310
$10,000 to $24,999..............	274	272	102	4,364	4,323	3,768	555
$25,000 to $49,999..............	164	162	80	5,795	5,736	5,225	510
$50,000 to $99,999..............	129	134	83	9,219	9,575	8,988	586
$100,000 to $249,999...........	149	142	102	24,401	23,196	22,221	975
$250,000 to $499,999...........	96	96	75	34,367	34,463	33,338	1,125
$500,000 to $999,999...........	64	78	60	44,578	55,663	54,256	1,408
$1,000,000 to $2,499,999........	42	58	42	62,751	90,534	89,003	1,531
$2,500,000 to $4,999,999........	10	15	10	33,190	50,511	50,002	509
$5 million or more.................	6	9	4	83,300	125,624	125,376	248

Source: U.S. Department of Agriculture, National Agricultural Statistics Service, *2012 Census of Agriculture*, Vol. 1, May 2014. See also <http://www.agcensus.usda.gov/Publications/index.php>.

Table 852. Family Farm Household Income and Wealth, 2009 to 2013, and by Farm Type, 2013

[In dollars, except for number of farms. Based on Agricultural Resource Management Survey (ARMS) Phase III. A family farm is defined as one in which the majority of the ownership of the farm business is held by related individuals. Nearly all farms (98 percent in 2013) are family farms. The farm operator is the person who runs the farm, making the day-to-day management decisions. The operator could be an owner, hired manager, cash tenant, share tenant, and/or a partner. If land is rented or worked on shares, the tenant or renter is the operator. For multiple-operator farms, a principal operator is identified as the individual making most of the day-to-day decisions about the operation. Over 35 percent of farms have more than one operator, but over three-quarters of these are operated by a husband-wife team. Therefore, both operators are considered part of the principal operator household. Minus sign (-) indicates loss]

Item	2009	2010	2011	2012	2013 Total	2013 ERS farm typology Rural residence farms [1]	2013 ERS farm typology Intermedi- ate farms [2]	2013 ERS farm typology Commer- cial farms [3]
Number of family farms	**2,131,007**	**2,143,063**	**2,114,668**	**2,043,483**	**2,045,352**	**1,160,514**	**696,780**	**188,058**
INCOME PER FAMILY FARM HOUSEHOLD								
Net earnings from farming activities	6,866	11,788	14,625	25,965	27,897	-1,375	2,485	302,694
Off-farm income of the household	70,302	72,671	72,665	86,482	90,476	111,146	58,514	81,344
Earned income	50,852	52,161	51,376	63,783	66,048	85,296	35,264	61,329
Unearned income	19,450	20,510	21,289	22,699	24,428	25,850	23,249	20,015
Total household income, mean [4]	77,169	84,459	87,290	112,447	118,373	109,771	60,998	384,038
WEALTH PER FAMILY FARM HOUSEHOLD								
Assets, mean [4]	1,030,993	1,082,120	1,131,522	1,464,358	1,463,649	1,093,076	1,305,357	4,336,955
Farm assets	761,887	799,316	856,589	950,818	948,758	529,135	919,281	3,647,480
Non-farm assets	269,106	282,804	274,933	513,540	514,891	563,941	386,076	689,475
Debt, mean [4]	115,980	123,640	120,213	174,488	152,024	99,002	110,663	632,474
Farm debt	66,148	67,404	69,387	77,098	79,577	23,672	56,430	510,330
Non-farm debt	49,832	56,235	50,827	97,390	72,447	75,330	54,232	122,144
Net worth, mean [4]	915,013	958,480	1,011,309	1,289,870	1,311,624	994,073	1,194,694	3,704,481
Farm net worth	695,745	731,911	787,203	(NA)	(NA)	(NA)	(NA)	(NA)
Non-farm net worth	219,274	226,568	224,106	(NA)	(NA)	(NA)	(NA)	(NA)

NA Not available. [1] Farms in which the principal operator is retired or has a major occupation other than farming. [2] Beginning in 2012, farms with farming as the operator's major occupation, but with less than $350,000 in gross sales. [3] Beginning in 2012, farms with more than $350,000 in gross sales. [4] For definition of mean see Guide to Tabular Presentation.

Source: U.S. Department of Agriculture, Economic Research Service, *Agricultural Income and Finance Situation and Outlook*, December 2011; and "Farm Household Income and Characteristics," <http://www.ers.usda.gov/data-products/farm-household-income-and-characteristics.aspx>, accessed March 2015.

Table 853. Farm Type, Acreage, and Production: 2000 to 2013

[2,166 represents 2,166,000. Based on Agricultural Resource Management Survey (ARMS). The farm typology used by the Economic Research Service was revised in 2013, and has been applied to data beginning in 2011. For more information, see <http://www.ers.usda.gov/publications/eib-economic-information-bulletin/eib110.aspx>]

Type of farm	Unit	2000	2005	2007	2008	2009	2010	2011	2012	2013
Total farms										
Number of farms	1,000	2,166	2,095	2,197	2,192	2,192	2,193	2,173	2,102	2,095
Total value of production	Mil. dol.	177,286	215,295	289,530	299,066	278,067	286,792	335,259	375,408	408,563
Total acres operated	Mil.	995	916	878	894	913	912	902	870	897
Acres operated per farm	Acres	459	437	400	408	417	416	415	414	428
Commercial farms [1]										
Number of farms	1,000	178	216	257	272	271	264	224	244	238
Total value of production	Mil. dol.	121,202	166,566	241,728	249,759	230,717	240,751	249,696	290,416	316,908
Total acres operated	Mil.	392	418	424	429	443	482	432	414	466
Acres operated per farm	Acres	2,205	1,939	1,650	1,580	1,635	1,829	1,931	1,698	1,955
Intermediate farms [2]										
Number of farms	1,000	668	550	546	583	577	618	685	706	697
Total value of production	Mil. dol.	41,813	33,872	30,933	32,718	30,830	30,325	63,250	64,740	65,718
Total acres operated	Mil.	392	307	237	253	270	242	279	276	259
Acres operated per farm	Acres	587	558	434	434	469	392	407	390	372
Residence farms [3]										
Number of farms	1,000	1,320	1,329	1,394	1,338	1,344	1,311	1,264	1,153	1,161
Total value of production	Mil. dol.	14,272	14,856	16,869	16,589	16,521	15,716	22,313	20,252	25,937
Total acres operated	Mil.	211	191	217	212	200	187	191	181	172
Acres operated per farm	Acres	160	144	156	158	149	143	151	157	148

[1] Data for 2010 and earlier include farms with sales of $250,000 or more. Beginning in 2011, data are for farms with $350,000 or more gross cash farm income and nonfamily farms. [2] Data for 2010 and earlier include small family farms whose operators report farming as their major occupation. Beginning in 2011, data are for farms with less than $350,000 in gross cash farm income and a principal operator whose primary occupation is farming. [3] Data for 2010 and earlier include retirement and residential farms. Beginning in 2011, data are for farms with less than $350,000 in gross cash farm income and where the principal operator is either retired or has a primary occupation other than farming.

Source: U.S. Department of Agriculture, Economic Research Service, "ARMS Farm Financial and Crop Production Practices," <http://www.ers.usda.gov/data-products/arms-farm-financial-and-crop-production-practices.aspx>, accessed April 2015.

Table 854. Farms with Renewable Energy Systems by Type of Farm: 2012

[Farms reporting renewable energy systems on their operation. Based on the 1974 definition of farms and farmland, see text, this section. Farm types are based on the USDA's Economic Research Service typology. Family farms, farms in which the majority of the business is owned by the operator and individuals related to the operator, are classified based on the gross cash farm income (GCFI). GCFI includes sales of crops and livestock, fees for delivering commodities under production contracts, government payments, and farm-related income]

| Energy system | All farms | Small family farms (GCFI less than $350,000) | | | | Mid-sized family farms (GCFI $350,000 to $999,999) | Large-scale family farms (GCFI greater than $1,000,000) | Non-family farms [3] |
		Total small family farms	Retirement or off-farm occupation [1]	Low sales (GCFI less than $150,000)	Moderate sales (GCFI $350,00 to $999,999)			
Number of farms, total.................	2,109,303	1,861,216	1,423,432	342,440	95,344	118,340	59,537	70,210
Number of farms with								
any renewable energy system......	**57,299**	**48,307**	**34,473**	**10,476**	**3,358**	**4,391**	**2,281**	**2,320**
Percent of all farms....................	2.7	2.6	2.4	3.1	3.5	3.7	3.8	3.3
By type of system:								
Solar panels...........................	36,331	32,217	23,005	7,464	1,748	1,742	802	1,570
Wind turbines.........................	9,054	6,646	4,460	1,485	701	1,253	713	442
Methane digesters......................	537	344	258	68	18	32	111	50
Geoexchange systems.................	9,403	7,809	6,122	1,107	580	906	446	242
Small hydro systems...................	1,323	1,168	843	275	50	51	21	83
Biodiesel..............................	4,099	3,061	1,958	734	369	547	283	208
Ethanol................................	2,364	1,623	1,021	338	264	443	211	87
Other..................................	1243	1121	755	305	61	47	9	66
Wind rights leased to others............	10,181	6,851	4,402	1,372	1,077	1,893	939	498

[1] Farms in which the principal operator is retired or has a major occupation other than farming. [2] Small family farms with farming as the operator's major occupation. [3] Any farm where the operator and persons related to the operator do not own a majority of the business.

Source: U.S. Department of Agriculture, National Agricultural Statistics Service, *2012 Census of Agriculture, Farm Typology*, Volume 2, January 2015. See also <http://www.agcensus.usda.gov/Publications/index.php>.

Table 855. Sales of Agricultural Products Direct to Consumers: 2002 to 2012

[812,204 represents $812,204,000. Farm operations who sell directly to consumers for human consumption at roadside stands, farmers' markets, pick-your-own, on-farm stores, and community support agricultural arrangements. Excludes non-edible products such as nursery crops, cut flowers, and wool, but includes livestock sales. Sales of agricultural products by vertically integrated operations through their own processing and marketing operations are also excluded]

| Size of farm | Number of farms | | | Value of direct sales ($1,000) | | |
	2002	2007	2012	2002	2007	2012
Total, all farms with direct sales.................	**116,733**	**136,817**	**144,530**	**812,204**	**1,211,270**	**1,309,827**
Percent of all farms.............................	5.5	6.2	6.9	0.4	0.4	0.3
BY VALUE OF SALES						
$1 to $499..	32,420	35,440	37,398	6,645	7,217	7,770
$500 to $999.....................................	19,145	20,547	20,170	13,124	14,013	13,685
$1,000 to $4,999.................................	42,660	49,957	52,750	93,611	113,960	121,750
$5,000 to $9,999.................................	9,598	13,060	14,452	64,517	88,174	97,308
$10,000 to $24,999..............................	7,256	10,032	11,045	108,766	151,063	164,774
$25,000 to $49,999..............................	2,831	3,903	4,244	96,322	133,328	143,722
$50,000 or more.................................	2,823	3,878	4,471	429,220	703,515	760,819
BY PRIMARY ACTIVITY OF FARM [1, 2]						
Oilseed and grains...............................	5,443	7,052	8,715	30,629	37,930	63,321
Vegetables and melons...........................	14,487	17,961	23,218	198,175	335,311	420,466
Fruit and tree nuts...............................	14,381	17,161	18,399	196,508	343,878	319,523
Greenhouse and nursery [3]......................	4,711	3,834	6,031	74,524	50,169	59,845
Beef cattle ranching and farming.................	27,133	35,984	35,980	76,955	141,427	147,315
Dairy cattle and milk production...................	3,180	3,221	2,982	41,602	52,594	43,546
Hog and pig farming..............................	4,745	5,227	3,897	16,085	18,970	15,970
Poultry and egg production........................	5,585	8,833	9,999	24,345	54,898	36,782
Sheep and goat farming..........................	7,653	9,127	10,198	10,993	16,613	19,647

[1] Based on the farms' North American Industry Classification (NAICS) codes, indicating main commodity type produced. [2] Includes other types, not shown separately. [3] Includes floriculture.

Source: U.S. Department of Agriculture, National Agricultural Statistics Service, *2012 Census of Agriculture*, Vol. 1, May 2014, and earlier reports. See also <http://www.agcensus.usda.gov/Publications/index.php>.

Table 856. Organic Agriculture—Number of Farms, Acreage, and Value of Sales, 2008 and 2014, and for Leading States, 2014

[3,164,995 represents $3,164,995,000. Includes all known organic producers that are either certified organic or exempt from certification in the United States (those grossing less than $5,000 annually from organic sales). Organic food must be produced without the use of conventional pesticides, petroleum-based or sewage sludge-based fertilizers, herbicides, pesticides, genetic engineering (biotechnology), antibiotics, growth hormones, or irradiation. Animals raised on an organic operation must be fed organic feed and given access to the outdoors. Land must have no prohibited substances applied to it for at least 3 years before the harvest of an organic crop]

Year and leading States	Organic farms (number)	Organic land (acres)	Value of sales ($1,000) [1]			
			Total product sales	Crops [2]	Livestock and poultry	Livestock and poultry products
2008......................	14,540	4,077,337	3,164,995	1,942,317	316,470	906,207
2014, total [3].........	**14,093**	**3,670,560**	**5,454,979**	**3,290,188**	**660,340**	**1,504,452**
California..............	2,805	687,168	2,231,241	1,659,305	271,354	300,582
Washington...........	716	73,841	514,897	386,701	(D)	(D)
Pennsylvania.........	679	97,617	313,456	91,362	112,467	109,627
Oregon.................	525	204,166	237,121	127,568	17,630	91,923
Wisconsin.............	1,228	228,605	200,800	48,513	24,908	127,379
Texas..................	234	126,639	199,094	78,169	17,680	103,245
New York..............	917	212,701	164,203	52,698	16,011	95,494
Colorado..............	157	115,116	146,799	52,198	(D)	(D)
Michigan...............	332	58,085	124,612	(D)	(D)	70,698
Iowa....................	612	97,448	102,626	50,741	(D)	(D)

D Data withheld to limit disclosure. [1] Value of sales of commodities; excludes value-added organic products. [2] Includes nursery and greenhouse. [3] Includes other states, not shown separately.

Source: U.S. Department of Agriculture, National Agricultural Statistics Service, *2012 Census of Agriculture: Organic Survey (2014)*, Vol. 3, Special Studies, Part 4, September 2015, and earlier reports. See also <http://www.agcensus.usda.gov/Publications/Organic_Survey/>.

Table 857. Adoption of Genetically Engineered Crops: 2000 to 2015

[As percent of all crops planted. As of June. Based on June Agricultural Survey conducted by National Agricultural Statistical Services (NASS). Excludes conventionally bred herbicide tolerant varieties. Insect resistant varieties include only those containing bacillus thuringiensis (Bt). The Bt varieties include those that contain more than one gene that can resist different types of insects. Stacked gene varieties include only those varieties containing biotech traits for both herbicide tolerance and insect resistance]

Genetically engineered crop	2000	2005	2007	2008	2009	2010	2011	2012	2013	2014	2015
Corn.............................	**25**	**52**	**73**	**80**	**85**	**86**	**88**	**88**	**90**	**93**	**92**
Insect resistant..................	18	26	21	17	17	16	16	15	5	4	4
Herbicide tolerant..............	6	17	24	23	22	23	23	21	14	13	12
Stacked gene....................	1	9	28	40	46	47	49	52	71	76	77
Cotton...........................	**61**	**79**	**87**	**86**	**88**	**93**	**90**	**94**	**90**	**96**	**94**
Insect resistant..................	15	18	17	18	17	15	17	14	8	5	5
Herbicide tolerant..............	26	27	28	23	23	20	15	17	15	12	10
Stacked gene....................	20	34	42	45	48	58	58	63	67	79	79
Soybean.........................	**54**	**87**	**91**	**92**	**91**	**93**	**94**	**93**	**93**	**94**	**94**
Insect resistant..................	(X)	(X)	(X)	(X)	(X)	(X)	(X)	(X)	(X)	(X)	(X)
Herbicide tolerant..............	54	87	91	92	91	93	94	93	93	94	94
Stacked gene....................	(X)	(X)	(X)	(X)	(X)	(X)	(X)	(X)	(X)	(X)	(X)

X Not applicable.

Source: U.S. Department of Agriculture, Economic Research Service, "Adoption of Genetically Engineered Crops in the U.S.," <http://www.ers.usda.gov/data-products/adoption-of-genetically-engineered-crops-in-the-us.aspx>, accessed July 2015.

Table 858. Farm Production Expenses: 2007 and 2012

[2,205 represents 2,205,000. Data have been adjusted for coverage; see text, this section and Appendix III]

Production expenses	2007			2012		
	Farms (1,000)	Expenses (mil. dol.)	Percent of total	Farms (1,000)	Expenses (mil. dol.)	Percent of total
Total...	**2,205**	**241,114**	**100.0**	**2,109**	**328,939**	**100.0**
Fertilizer..	1,148	18,107	7.5	1,012	28,533	8.7
Chemicals......................................	919	10,075	4.2	1,000	16,460	5.0
Seeds, plants, vines, and trees...................	776	11,741	4.9	829	19,493	5.9
Livestock and poultry...........................	491	38,004	15.8	545	41,586	12.6
Feed..	1,136	49,095	20.4	1,256	75,706	23.0
Gasoline and fuel...............................	2,149	12,912	5.4	1,988	16,573	5.0
Utilities...	1,103	5,918	2.5	1,353	8,262	2.5
Supplies, repairs, and maintenance...............	1,992	15,897	6.6	1,663	18,868	5.7
Farm labor [1]...................................	665	26,392	11.0	784	33,461	10.2
Customwork and custom hauling..................	362	4,091	1.7	462	6,611	2.0
Cash rent for land, buildings and grazing fees.....	490	13,275	5.5	560	21,001	6.4
Rent and lease for machinery, equipment, and farm share..	109	1,385	0.6	133	2,332	0.7
Interest expense................................	667	10,881	4.5	784	12,124	3.7
Property taxes..................................	1,996	6,223	2.6	1,980	7,429	2.3
Other production expenses.......................	1,116	17,119	7.1	1,135	20,501	6.2

[1] Includes hired and contract labor.

Source: U.S. Department of Agriculture, National Agricultural Statistics Service, *2012 Census of Agriculture*, Vol. 1, May 2014. See also <http://www.agcensus.usda.gov/Publications/index.php>.

Table 859. Participation in Farm to School Programs by State: 2012

[Percent of districts responding, except total. For school year ending in 2012. Farm to School programs include a variety of programs that connect schools with local producers and teaches children about farms and where their food comes from. Data are from the Farm to School Census, which collected data on farm to school activities. Includes charter schools if they are a part of a multi-site charter school district. Excludes private and all other charter schools, except as noted]

State	Total number of school districts	Percent of districts engaging in farm to school programs	Percent of districts that participate in any farm to school activity—Participation in specific activity						Spending on local food costs as a percent of total food costs [3]
			Served local foods [2]	Edible school garden or orchard activities	Served products from school based gardens or farms	Organized field trips to farms	Had farmers visit cafeteria or classroom	Integrated farm to school concepts into educational curriculum	
United States....	**13,133**	**39.4**	**83.0**	**30.8**	**23.2**	**29.9**	**16.6**	**12.3**	**12.8**
Alabama............	135	24.3	60.7	32.1	14.3	17.9	17.9	25.0	3.4
Alaska..............	49	43.2	73.7	31.6	21.1	–	–	15.8	7.0
Arizona............	250	26.7	79.5	38.6	9.1	29.5	11.4	18.2	20.0
Arkansas...........	239	12.2	40.9	40.9	27.3	45.5	18.2	4.5	7.3
California..........	860	50.6	81.0	44.9	29.4	33.5	19.6	18.7	18.7
Colorado...........	175	41.1	92.5	28.4	31.3	34.3	28.4	16.4	20.0
Connecticut........	156	67.5	92.9	28.2	11.8	25.9	12.9	3.5	10.5
Delaware...........	19	94.7	100.0	27.8	27.8	16.7	11.1	16.7	14.6
DC [1]...............	59	73.1	94.7	52.6	15.8	47.4	26.3	36.8	17.6
Florida.............	67	50.8	90.9	57.6	27.3	21.2	21.2	30.3	11.1
Georgia............	180	41.9	83.1	29.2	12.3	32.3	32.3	13.8	4.5
Hawaii..............	1	100.0	–	100.0	–	100.0	100.0	100.0	10.0
Idaho..............	115	43.8	87.0	26.1	34.8	23.9	10.9	8.7	15.4
Illinois.............	791	23.3	40.6	26.6	8.4	47.6	22.4	25.2	15.4
Indiana............	293	29.4	76.4	15.3	8.3	43.1	12.5	5.6	13.8
Iowa...............	348	29.3	73.2	35.4	32.9	40.2	17.1	14.6	6.0
Kansas [1]...........	424	30.7	61.7	31.2	21.5	55.9	21.5	19.4	6.0
Kentucky...........	174	38.0	88.9	25.9	24.1	31.5	25.9	11.1	3.2
Louisiana..........	71	26.9	28.6	64.3	14.3	50.0	14.3	14.3	14.7
Maine..............	179	78.0	97.2	54.9	63.4	54.9	31.0	29.6	5.6
Maryland...........	24	91.7	100.0	19.0	23.8	19.0	28.6	9.5	11.3
Massachusetts.....	320	71.3	93.7	29.5	27.3	18.3	7.4	10.9	15.9
Michigan...........	545	39.6	86.0	20.3	14.7	23.1	11.9	4.2	16.8
Minnesota..........	345	67.1	94.3	24.9	31.6	17.7	20.3	7.8	12.4
Mississippi.........	151	16.5	35.0	20.0	5.0	45.0	20.0	5.0	9.5
Missouri...........	523	25.9	82.9	11.1	8.5	26.5	12.8	3.4	14.6
Montana...........	226	33.5	87.9	27.1	18.6	44.8	15.5	20.7	12.8
Nebraska...........	249	21.9	81.8	11.4	9.1	18.2	9.1	–	10.2
Nevada............	19	13.3	100.0	100.0	–	–	–	–	(NA)
New Hampshire....	143	74.4	100.0	32.8	25.0	28.1	21.9	9.4	1.7
New Jersey........	500	50.0	89.0	22.0	16.5	14.7	9.2	11.0	16.7
New Mexico........	91	27.9	94.7	10.5	–	21.1	–	–	12.8
New York..........	639	57.6	90.0	33.0	27.5	26.6	13.4	12.4	16.7
North Carolina......	115	70.4	83.5	28.2	5.1	33.3	14.1	25.6	11.2
North Dakota.......	174	38.1	93.0	30.2	34.9	30.2	9.3	4.7	5.9
Ohio...............	615	28.2	81.2	21.1	12.8	27.8	9.0	3.0	10.4
Oklahoma..........	533	26.0	85.1	9.5	8.1	13.5	10.8	9.5	11.3
Oregon............	188	61.0	89.3	41.3	34.7	36.0	20.0	12.0	24.0
Pennsylvania.......	524	35.9	83.2	25.2	20.6	32.1	11.5	5.3	14.2
Rhode Island.......	37	97.1	100.0	3.0	–	15.2	33.3	–	10.8
South Carolina.....	81	52.3	85.3	47.1	17.6	61.8	35.3	29.4	13.0
South Dakota.......	171	24.2	75.9	3.4	10.3	20.7	6.9	3.4	5.0
Tennessee.........	140	43.5	85.2	33.3	18.5	40.7	16.7	9.3	6.1
Texas..............	1,013	18.9	58.4	26.3	6.9	11.3	4.4	5.0	12.3
Utah...............	42	31.6	100.0	8.3	8.3	16.7	8.3	–	23.3
Vermont............	201	85.1	93.8	81.4	82.5	52.6	25.8	33.0	16.2
Virginia............	132	61.6	85.7	36.4	22.1	28.6	24.7	6.5	10.5
Washington.........	283	45.0	91.3	26.0	24.0	23.1	20.2	8.7	22.5
West Virginia.......	55	42.6	75.0	45.0	50.0	45.0	50.0	20.0	10.6
Wisconsin..........	421	53.0	90.4	36.1	34.9	30.1	18.7	9.6	16.3
Wyoming...........	48	16.7	75.0	–	12.5	37.5	–	–	1.0

– Represents or rounds to zero. NA Not available. [1] Includes charter and private schools. [2] The definition of "local" is determined by individual districts. The Census questionnaire asked respondents how their district defines "local" as it relates to their food procurement. Respondents could choose from one of seven options or specify a different definition: (a) produced within a 50 mile radius, (b) produced within a 100 mile radius, (c) produced within a 200 mile radius, (d) produced within a day's drive, (e) produced within the state, (f) produced within the region, and (g) geographic along with other restrictions. [3] For districts participating in farm to school programs. Costs include milk.

Source: U.S. Department of Agriculture, Food and Nutrition Service, "The Farm to School Census," <http://www.fns.usda.gov/farmtoschool/census#/>, accessed July 2015. See also <http://www.fns.usda.gov/farmtoschool/>.

Table 860. Balance Sheet of the Farming Sector: 1990 to 2014

[In billions of dollars, except as indicated (841 represents $841,000,000,000). As of December 31. Balance sheet estimates exclude the personal portion of farm households' assets and debts]

Item	1990	2000	2006	2007	2008	2009	2010	2011	2012	2013	2014
Assets.....	**841**	**1,203**	**1,907**	**1,962**	**2,003**	**1,970**	**2,161**	**2,311**	**2,638**	**2,779**	**2,943**
Investments and other financial assets.....	38	57	75	59	84	72	135	107	139	87	111
Investment in cooperatives................	(NA)	(NA)	5	3	5	5	6	6	7	8	8
Financial assets and net accounts receivable....................	(NA)	(NA)	70	56	79	67	130	102	132	80	103
Inventories....................	97	110	140	160	164	152	168	185	182	192	209
Crops....................	23	28	41	54	59	53	57	62	65	60	61
Livestock and poultry....................	71	77	87	89	86	80	91	101	96	111	128
Purchased inputs [1]....................	3	5	12	16	19	19	20	21	22	21	20
Real estate [2]....................	619	946	1,537	1,549	1,567	1,554	1,651	1,795	2,073	2,253	2,377
Value of machinery and motor vehicles [3]...	86	90	155	195	189	191	207	223	244	247	245
Debt [4]....................	**131**	**164**	**216**	**241**	**261**	**268**	**279**	**294**	**297**	**315**	**348**
Real estate....................	68	85	113	132	148	146	154	167	173	184	199
Commercial banks [5]....................	15	30	37	41	46	44	51	53	64	69	74
Farm Credit System....................	23	30	50	58	63	69	72	75	80	85	89
Farm Service Agency....................	7	3	2	3	2	3	3	3	4	4	4
Farmer Mac [6]....................	(NA)	(NA)	1	3	2	2	4	4	4	4	4
Individuals and others [5]....................	14	11	10	16	20	14	10	18	9	10	15
Storage facility loans....................	–	(NA)	–	–	–	–	1	1	1	1	1
Life insurance companies....................	9	11	12	11	14	13	12	13	11	12	12
Nonreal estate....................	63	79	102	109	113	122	125	127	123	131	150
Commercial banks [5]....................	31	45	48	54	56	57	56	59	60	63	70
Farm Credit System....................	10	17	27	31	36	39	39	41	43	44	48
Farm Service Agency....................	10	4	3	3	3	3	4	4	3	3	4
Individuals and others [5]....................	12	13	24	20	18	23	26	23	17	21	28
Equity....................	**709**	**1,039**	**1,691**	**1,721**	**1,742**	**1,702**	**1,882**	**2,016**	**2,341**	**2,464**	**2,594**
FINANCIAL RATIOS (percent)											
Farm debt/asset ratio....................	15.6	13.6	11.3	12.3	13.0	13.6	12.9	12.7	11.3	11.3	11.8
Farm debt/equity ratio....................	18.5	15.8	12.8	14.0	15.0	15.8	14.8	14.6	12.7	12.8	13.4

– Represents or rounds to zero. NA Not available. [1] Purchased inputs represent value of prepaid expenses on supplies such as fertilizer and lime applied, seed, feed and other inputs purchases for next year's production. It also includes the seed, fertilizer, fuel, and other expenses already invested in crops. [2] Includes farmland, buildings and other service structures. Includes farm real estate assets leased from non-operator landlords. [3] Includes automobiles, trucks and farm machinery leased to farm operators. [4] Reflects outstanding agricultural sector debt where it is held rather than where it originated. Excludes debt on operator dwellings and for nonfarm purposes. Sector-level estimates of farm debt report aggregate data by lender type and therefore does not identify who owes the debt. [5] Beginning with 2012, farm sector debt held by savings associations is reported with the commercial bank lender group instead of the individuals and others grouping. [6] The Federal Agricultural Mortgage Corporation (known as Farmer Mac) operates as a federally sponsored enterprise providing a secondary market for agricultural real estate mortgage loans, rural housing mortgage loans, and rural utility cooperative loans.

Source: U.S. Department of Agriculture, Economic Research Service, "U.S. and State Farm Income and Wealth Statistics," <http://www.ers.usda.gov/data-products/farm-income-and-wealth-statistics.aspx>, accessed September 2015.

Table 861. Farm Sector Output and Value Added: 1990 to 2014

[In billions of dollars (179.9 represents $179,900,000,000). For definition of value added, see text, Section 13. Minus sign (-) indicates decrease]

Item	1990	2000	2005	2007	2008	2009	2010	2011	2012	2013	2014
CURRENT DOLLARS											
Farm output....................	**179.9**	**204.3**	**253.0**	**302.5**	**336.1**	**301.2**	**328.2**	**387.0**	**400.9**	**433.6**	**435.8**
Cash receipts from farm marketings....	171.9	197.6	241.4	290.0	318.9	289.8	322.2	369.1	404.7	403.6	410.0
Farm products consumed on farms.....	0.6	0.3	0.4	0.4	0.4	0.4	0.4	0.4	0.4	0.7	0.8
Other farm income....................	4.9	8.4	11.3	12.6	14.7	12.7	12.5	15.0	14.9	17.5	18.7
Change in farm finished goods inventories....................	2.4	-2.0	-0.1	-0.5	2.1	-1.7	-6.8	2.5	-19.1	11.7	6.4
Less: Intermediate goods and services consumed....................	102.1	128.3	148.5	189.0	209.8	191.4	198.5	220.7	249.4	243.6	258.6
Equals: Gross farm value added.......	**77.8**	**76.0**	**104.5**	**113.5**	**126.3**	**109.8**	**129.7**	**166.2**	**151.5**	**189.9**	**177.2**
Less: Consumption of fixed capital.......	17.9	22.8	27.8	31.0	32.9	34.2	35.0	35.1	37.8	41.1	44.3
Equals: Net farm value added..........	**59.8**	**53.2**	**76.7**	**82.6**	**93.5**	**75.6**	**94.7**	**131.2**	**113.7**	**148.8**	**132.9**
Compensation of employees..........	13.4	19.7	22.0	25.0	25.7	25.6	24.2	22.8	27.6	28.0	30.0
Taxes on production and imports........	3.8	4.6	5.3	6.7	6.7	6.7	6.9	7.3	7.5	7.7	7.9
Less: Subsidies to operators..............	7.6	20.0	20.9	10.6	10.3	10.4	10.5	8.8	8.9	9.1	8.9
Net operating surplus....................	50.3	48.8	70.2	61.4	71.4	53.7	74.2	109.9	87.5	122.3	103.9
CHAINED (2009) DOLLARS [1]											
Farm output, total....................	**(NA)**	**276.2**	**290.5**	**292.1**	**290.4**	**301.2**	**304.5**	**292.3**	**289.4**	**307.7**	**312.7**
Cash receipts from farm marketings....	(NA)	268.0	275.8	278.3	275.1	289.8	298.4	278.0	291.2	285.1	289.3
Farm products consumed on farms.....	(NA)	0.4	0.4	0.4	0.4	0.4	0.4	0.3	0.3	0.5	0.5
Other farm income....................	(NA)	12.5	15.2	13.7	13.2	12.7	12.3	12.3	11.4	13.7	17.0
Change in farm finished goods inventories....................	(NA)	-2.9	-0.1	-0.7	1.6	-1.7	-6.5	1.6	-12.2	7.0	4.0
Less: Intermediate goods and services consumed....................	(NA)	197.6	188.0	209.6	196.5	191.4	193.0	186.8	199.4	192.1	194.2
Equals: Gross farm value added.......	**(NA)**	**83.9**	**101.6**	**86.2**	**94.7**	**109.8**	**111.5**	**105.7**	**93.7**	**114.9**	**117.6**
Less: Consumption of fixed capital.......	(NA)	28.7	31.2	32.6	33.4	34.2	35.1	34.4	36.4	39.0	41.2
Equals: Net farm value added..........	**(NA)**	**56.1**	**70.5**	**54.8**	**61.8**	**75.6**	**76.4**	**71.7**	**60.3**	**77.0**	**78.0**

NA Not available. [1] For more information; see text, Section 13.

Source: U.S. Bureau of Economic Analysis, National Income and Product Accounts, "Table 7.3.5 Farm Sector Output, Gross Value Added, and Net Value Added," and "Table 7.3.6 Real Farm Sector Output, Real Gross Value Added, and Real Net Value Added, Chained Dollars," <http://www.bea.gov/itable/>, accessed August 2015.

Table 862. Value Added to Economy by Agricultural Sector: 1990 to 2014

[In billions of dollars (188.5 represents $188,500,000,000). Value of agricultural sector production is the gross value of the commodities and services produced within a year. Net value-added is the sector's contribution to the national economy and is the value of farm sector production minus the value of intermediate goods used. Net farm income is the farm operators' share of income from the sector's production activities. Minus sign (-) indicates decrease]

Item	1990	2000	2006	2007	2008	2009	2010	2011	2012	2013	2014
Value of agricultural production	**188.5**	**218.4**	**274.4**	**327.7**	**349.6**	**321.7**	**341.4**	**407.9**	**434.0**	**472.3**	**471.1**
Value of crop production	83.2	95.0	118.7	151.1	171.4	162.4	166.0	197.3	210.7	233.2	204.7
Cotton	5.5	2.9	5.5	6.5	5.3	4.3	7.5	7.3	8.2	6.5	7.4
Feed crops	18.7	20.5	29.4	42.3	58.4	51.1	55.1	71.7	82.1	70.8	64.9
Food grains	7.5	6.5	9.1	13.6	17.8	15.3	14.3	16.5	19.3	17.2	15.5
Fruits and tree nuts	9.4	12.3	17.3	18.7	18.6	19.2	21.6	24.2	28.1	29.9	29.8
Oil crops	12.3	13.5	18.5	24.6	28.3	36.3	36.5	35.3	46.9	47.3	43.3
Tobacco	2.7	2.3	1.2	1.3	1.4	1.5	1.2	1.1	1.5	1.5	1.8
Vegetables and melons	11.3	15.8	18.1	19.3	17.0	17.8	17.4	17.6	17.4	19.4	18.8
All other crops	12.9	18.6	23.1	23.9	24.7	24.0	24.4	25.2	25.9	27.7	26.4
Home consumption	0.1	0.2	0.1	0.1	0.1	0.1	0.1	0.1	0.1	0.2	0.2
Value of inventory adjustment [1]	2.8	2.2	-3.6	0.9	-0.3	-7.1	-12.3	-1.7	-18.9	12.7	-3.5
Value of livestock production	90.0	99.1	119.3	138.4	139.1	119.2	139.7	163.7	169.1	180.9	214.7
Milk	20.2	20.6	23.4	35.5	34.8	24.3	31.4	39.5	37.1	40.3	49.3
Meat animals	51.1	53.0	63.7	65.1	64.4	58.4	69.1	84.0	88.2	91.2	107.7
Miscellaneous livestock	2.5	4.1	4.8	4.9	4.9	5.3	5.1	5.9	6.2	6.7	6.9
Poultry and eggs	15.3	21.9	26.6	33.1	36.0	31.7	34.7	35.4	38.3	44.4	48.3
Home consumption	0.5	0.1	0.3	0.3	0.3	0.3	0.3	0.3	0.3	0.3	0.3
Value of inventory adjustment [1]	0.4	-0.6	0.5	-0.4	-1.3	-0.7	-0.9	-1.4	-1.0	-2.0	2.2
Farm-related income	15.3	24.4	36.4	38.1	39.1	40.2	35.8	46.9	54.2	58.2	51.7
Forest products sold	1.8	0.8	1.0	0.7	0.7	0.4	0.5	0.5	0.5	0.6	0.6
Gross imputed rental value of farm dwellings	7.2	12.7	19.5	20.6	16.3	16.6	15.8	16.2	15.0	17.2	16.3
Machine hire and custom work	1.8	2.2	2.6	2.7	3.0	4.0	3.8	4.0	3.9	4.4	4.4
Other farm income	4.5	8.7	13.2	14.2	19.1	19.1	15.7	26.3	34.8	36.0	30.3
Less: Intermediate product expenses [2]	90.7	119.1	150.7	179.9	198.5	186.9	189.1	215.6	237.4	239.9	255.1
Farm origin	39.5	47.9	61.1	73.4	80.9	78.4	82.2	96.2	106.3	109.9	116.6
Feed purchased	20.4	24.5	31.4	41.9	46.9	45.0	45.4	54.6	60.5	62.4	63.7
Livestock and poultry purchased	14.6	15.9	18.6	18.8	18.9	17.9	20.4	23.7	24.8	25.5	30.8
Seed purchased	4.5	7.5	11.0	12.6	15.1	15.5	16.3	17.8	20.9	21.9	22.1
Manufactured inputs	22.0	28.7	37.5	46.3	55.7	49.4	50.1	58.1	64.8	65.8	67.5
Electricity	2.6	3.0	3.8	4.3	4.6	4.6	4.6	4.9	5.4	5.5	5.9
Fertilizers, lime, and soil conditioners	8.2	10.0	13.3	17.7	22.5	20.1	21.0	25.1	28.9	28.3	28.1
Pesticides	5.4	8.5	9.0	10.5	11.7	11.5	10.7	11.8	14.0	14.6	15.8
Petroleum fuel and oils	5.8	7.2	11.3	13.8	16.9	13.2	13.8	16.2	16.5	17.3	17.7
Other intermediate expenses [2]	29.2	42.5	52.1	60.2	61.8	59.1	56.8	61.4	66.3	64.2	71.0
Machine hire and custom work	3.0	4.1	3.5	3.8	4.1	4.1	4.3	4.0	4.9	4.6	5.9
Marketing, storage, and transportation expenses	4.2	7.5	9.1	10.3	8.7	8.9	9.0	9.0	9.2	8.0	10.8
Repair and maintenance of capital items	8.6	10.9	12.5	14.3	14.6	14.5	14.6	15.3	16.5	17.2	17.8
Miscellaneous expenses [2]	13.4	19.9	27.1	31.7	34.5	31.6	28.9	33.1	35.6	34.4	36.5
Total insurance premiums [3]	3.4	4.8	6.2	7.1	9.6	8.0	7.5	9.6	10.4	10.6	10.6
Less: Contract labor	1.6	2.7	3.0	4.4	4.7	3.9	3.9	4.4	4.8	4.6	6.4
Plus: Net government transactions [4]	3.1	15.8	6.2	0.9	0.9	1.1	0.9	-1.6	-1.5	-1.4	-4.6
Direct government payments [5]	9.3	23.2	15.8	11.9	12.2	12.2	12.4	10.4	10.6	11.0	9.8
Property taxes [2]	6.2	7.4	9.6	11.0	11.3	11.1	11.5	12.0	12.2	12.4	14.3
Motor vehicle registration and licensing fees	0.4	0.5	0.6	0.6	0.6	0.6	0.6	0.7	0.7	0.7	0.7
Equals: Gross value added	**99.3**	**112.5**	**126.9**	**144.3**	**147.4**	**132.0**	**149.4**	**186.3**	**190.3**	**226.5**	**205.0**
Less: Capital consumption [2]	18.1	20.1	26.2	27.0	16.8	16.0	17.6	18.4	34.1	37.4	49.0
Equals: Net value added	**81.2**	**92.4**	**100.7**	**117.3**	**130.6**	**116.0**	**131.8**	**167.9**	**156.2**	**189.1**	**156.0**
Less: Factor payments to stakeholders [6]	35.0	41.7	43.2	47.3	55.1	56.3	57.4	56.0	64.8	65.3	64.9
Employee compensation [7]	12.4	17.9	21.2	24.5	25.2	25.2	23.6	22.6	27.4	27.7	28.1
Net rent paid to operator landlords	(NA)	(NA)	(NA)	(NA)	1.6	1.7	2.1	2.1	2.6	2.8	2.7
Net rent received by nonoperator landlords	9.0	9.2	7.6	7.6	11.4	11.9	14.8	15.3	18.0	19.9	18.4
Less: Real estate and nonreal estate interest	13.5	14.6	14.4	15.1	16.8	17.6	16.9	16.0	16.9	14.9	15.7
Equals: Net farm income	**46.3**	**50.7**	**57.4**	**70.0**	**75.5**	**59.6**	**74.4**	**111.9**	**91.4**	**123.7**	**91.1**

NA Not applicable. [1] A positive value of inventory change represents current-year production not sold by December 31. A negative value is an offset to production from prior years included in current-year sales. [2] Including expenses associated with operator dwellings. [3] Includes federal and private crop and livestock insurance premiums as well as casualty, hail, motor vehicle and all other insurance premiums. [4] Direct government payments minus motor vehicle registration and licensing fees and property taxes. [5] Government payments reflect payments made directly to all recipients in the farm sector, including landlords. The nonoperator landlords share is offset by its inclusion in rental expenses paid to these landlords and thus is not reflected in net farm income or net cash income. [6] Prior to 2008, factor payments to stakeholders only includes net rent paid to nonoperator landlords. [7] Includes hired labor and non-cash employee compensation.

Source: U.S. Department of Agriculture, Economic Research Service, "U.S. and State Farm Income and Wealth Statistics," <http://www.ers.usda.gov/data-products/farm-income-and-wealth-statistics.aspx>, accessed September 2015.

Table 863. Value of Agricultural Production, Income, and Government Payments by State: 2012 and 2013

[In millions of dollars (443,336 represents $443,336,000,000). Farm income data are after inventory adjustment and include income and expenses related to the farm operator's dwelling. Minus sign (-) indicates decrease]

State	Value of agricultural production		Net farm income		Govern-ment payments, 2013	State	Value of agricultural production		Net farm income		Govern-ment payments, 2013
	2012	2013	2012	2013			2012	2013	2012	2013	
U.S.	434,336	469,991	102,549	128,988	11,004	MO	11,562	12,554	2,548	3,415	428
AL	6,221	7,272	1,135	2,218	91	MT	4,607	5,365	1,157	1,767	250
AK	42	39	-8	-13	12	NE	25,281	27,148	5,249	8,366	600
AZ	4,340	4,641	1,073	1,245	47	NV	843	840	169	136	10
AR	10,637	11,427	2,416	2,913	347	NH	246	260	10	10	12
CA	46,841	48,834	13,174	12,113	249	NJ	1,246	1,277	259	235	10
CO	8,489	8,417	1,784	1,576	239	NM	3,766	4,068	1,053	1,318	116
CT	694	734	98	107	7	NY	6,065	6,443	1,409	1,579	75
DE	1,382	1,515	400	540	15	NC	13,630	14,327	3,641	3,306	411
FL	8,963	8,985	2,276	2,398	71	ND	11,767	10,804	3,827	2,579	601
GA	10,807	10,774	3,244	2,665	248	OH	11,201	12,726	2,176	3,648	258
HI	867	885	158	150	13	OK	7,552	7,924	1,715	1,686	357
ID	8,049	9,170	1,805	2,741	129	OR	5,043	5,368	743	818	116
IL	19,657	25,689	4,604	9,601	608	PA	8,486	8,934	1,963	2,258	94
IN	12,889	16,144	3,638	6,026	330	RI	84	86	8	5	2
IA	33,048	35,717	8,301	9,952	782	SC	3,406	3,552	720	931	106
KS	18,144	18,398	2,721	5,912	698	SD	11,065	13,394	2,899	4,683	304
KY	5,863	7,735	1,090	2,744	290	TN	4,687	5,117	1,141	1,404	148
LA	4,445	5,051	1,455	2,029	215	TX	25,357	26,228	4,172	4,121	1,125
ME	829	849	183	155	17	UT	1,990	2,113	327	376	39
MD	2,794	2,885	740	788	44	VT	862	975	173	253	16
MA	649	644	87	38	10	VA	4,431	4,965	804	1,232	111
MI	8,860	9,917	1,016	2,152	142	WA	10,467	10,732	2,357	2,764	191
MN	23,560	23,906	7,935	7,222	527	WV	919	1,036	101	205	17
MS	7,076	7,794	1,682	2,414	206	WI	12,647	14,316	2,609	3,918	222
						WY	1,981	2,014	310	288	46

Source: U.S. Department of Agriculture, Economic Research Service, "U.S. and State Farm Income and Wealth Statistics," <http://www.ers.usda.gov/data-products/farm-income-and-wealth-statistics.aspx>, accessed February 2015.

Table 864. Farm Income—Cash Receipts From Farm Marketings: 2010 to 2014

[In millions of dollars (318,430 represents $318,430,000,000). Represents gross receipts from commercial market sales as well as net Commodity Credit Corporation loans. The source estimates and publishes individual cash receipt values only for major commodities and major producing states. The U.S. receipts for individual commodities, computed as the sum of the reported states, may understate the value of sales for some commodities, with the balance included in the appropriate category labeled "other" or "miscellaneous." The degree of underestimation in some of the minor commodities can be substantial]

Commodities	2010	2012	2013	2014	Commodities	2010	2012	2013	2014
Total [1]	318,430	399,325	403,018	420,146	Broccoli	727	688	914	836
Animals and products	140,277	169,782	182,606	212,211	Carrots	647	662	736	709
Meat animals	69,144	88,182	91,219	107,671	Corn, sweet	952	1,112	1,164	1,022
Cattle and calves	51,246	66,090	67,457	81,251	Lettuce	2,213	1,988	2,568	2,410
Hogs	17,898	22,092	23,761	26,420	Lettuce, head	1,058	901	1,204	1,119
Dairy products, milk	31,372	37,065	40,277	49,349	Onions	1,050	942	969	934
Poultry/eggs [1]	34,690	38,288	44,368	48,292	Peppers, bell	592	514	600	618
Broilers	23,692	24,828	30,762	32,725	Tomatoes	2,281	1,885	2,316	2,460
Chicken eggs	6,553	7,929	8,679	10,166	Tomatoes, fresh	1,355	874	1,178	1,135
Turkeys	4,372	5,452	4,840	5,305	Cantaloupes	305	319	320	328
Miscellaneous animals [1]	5,071	6,247	6,743	6,898	Watermelons	499	477	514	431
Aquaculture	474	434	454	454	Fruits/nuts [1]	21,613	28,108	29,906	29,790
Honey	282	285	320	389	Grapefruit	291	279	257	232
Crops	178,153	229,544	220,412	207,935	Lemons	395	449	400	648
Food grains [1]	14,317	19,301	17,236	15,502	Oranges	1,997	2,622	2,073	1,960
Rice	3,263	2,722	3,165	3,546	Apples	2,311	3,315	3,133	2,856
Wheat	11,021	16,538	14,024	11,910	Cherries	756	894	876	874
Feed crops [1]	55,144	82,135	70,832	64,877	Grapes	4,024	5,661	6,136	5,819
Corn	47,540	72,018	59,951	53,679	Peaches	617	618	548	629
Hay	5,217	7,508	8,195	8,499	Pears	387	433	431	457
Sorghum grain	1,488	1,418	1,366	1,564	Blueberries	644	842	799	888
Cotton	7,465	8,230	6,516	7,439	Cranberries	299	386	287	254
Tobacco	1,233	1,544	1,548	1,802	Raspberries	259	290	343	526
Oil crops [1]	36,544	46,924	47,268	43,318	Strawberries	2,261	2,453	2,609	2,865
Peanuts	824	1,609	1,720	1,074	Almonds	2,903	4,817	6,385	5,892
Soybeans	34,665	44,099	44,469	41,284	Pistachios	1,159	1,438	1,636	1,593
Sunflower	507	610	522	441	Walnuts	1,028	1,506	1,825	1,841
Vegetables and melons [1]	17,407	17,409	19,417	18,780	All other crops [1]	24,430	25,891	27,689	26,426
Beans, dry	780	1,068	1,085	982	Sugarcane	1,075	1,363	1,248	953
Potatoes	3,338	3,780	3,812	3,742	Sugar beets	1,734	2,102	2,052	1,458
Sweet potatoes	472	462	597	699	Greenhouse/nursery	4,149	4,361	4,250	4,072
Beans, snap	434	470	506	393	Mushrooms	924	1,099	1,104	1,116

[1] Includes commodities not shown separately.

Source: U.S. Department of Agriculture, Economic Research Service, "U.S. and State Farm Income and Wealth Statistics," <http://www.ers.usda.gov/data-products/farm-income-and-wealth-statistics.aspx>, accessed September 2015.

Table 865. Cash Receipts for Selected Commodities—Leading States: 2014

[In millions of dollars (81,251 represents $81,251,000,000). See headnote Table 864]

State	Value	State	Value	State	Value	State	Value
Cattle and calves......	**81,251**	**Corn**...................	**53,679**	**Soybeans**............	**41,284**	**Milk**..................	**49,349**
Nebraska....................	12,854	Illinois..................	8,666	Illinois..................	5,811	California..............	9,358
Texas......................	11,011	Iowa....................	8,426	Iowa....................	5,289	Wisconsin.............	6,745
Kansas.....................	8,972	Nebraska.............	6,146	Indiana.................	3,442	New York.............	3,478
Iowa.......................	4,666	Minnesota.............	4,760	Minnesota.............	3,340	Idaho.................	3,198
Oklahoma.................	4,001	Indiana................	4,358	Nebraska..............	2,960	Pennsylvania..........	2,729

Source: U.S. Department of Agriculture, Economic Research Service, "U.S. and State Farm Income and Wealth Statistics," <http://www.ers.usda.gov/data-products/farm-income-and-wealth-statistics.aspx>, accessed September 2015.

Table 866. Farm Marketings, 2013 and 2014, and Principal Commodities, 2014, by State

[In millions of dollars (403,018 represents $403,018,000,000). See headnote Table 864]

State	2013			2014			2014
	Total	Animals and products	Crops	Total	Animals and products	Crops	State rank for total farm marketings and three principal commodities in order of marketing receipts
U.S.........	**403,018**	**182,606**	**220,412**	**420,146**	**212,211**	**207,935**	**Cattle and calves, corn, milk**
AL............	6,018	4,664	1,353	6,439	5,163	1,276	26—Broilers, cattle and calves, chicken eggs
AK............	30	5	25	32	6	26	50—Hay, mushrooms, cattle and calves
AZ............	4,228	1,853	2,375	4,402	2,385	2,017	29— Cattle and calves, milk, lettuce
AR............	10,293	5,232	5,062	10,396	5,747	4,649	12—Broilers, soybeans, rice
CA............	51,263	12,814	38,449	53,980	15,317	38,663	1—Milk, grapes, almonds
CO............	7,046	4,811	2,235	7,461	5,242	2,220	22—Cattle and calves, milk, corn
CT............	612	211	401	629	248	382	45—Milk, chicken eggs, cattle and calves
DE............	1,329	980	349	1,477	1,162	315	39—Broilers, corn, soybeans
FL............	8,413	1,966	6,447	8,215	2,382	5,832	13—Oranges, floriculture, cattle and calves
GA............	10,041	6,126	3,915	10,103	6,667	3,436	17—Broilers, cotton lint, chicken eggs
HI............	659	79	580	717	150	566	43—Cane for sugar, cattle and calves, coffee
ID............	8,097	4,656	3,441	8,663	5,471	3,192	20—Milk, cattle and calves, potatoes
IL............	17,011	2,729	14,282	18,608	3,205	15,403	6—Corn, soybeans, hogs
IN............	11,396	3,589	7,807	12,736	4,287	8,449	8—Corn, soybeans, hogs
IA............	30,592	14,103	16,490	30,911	16,875	14,036	2—Hogs, corn, soybeans
KS............	15,653	8,990	6,664	16,312	10,466	5,846	7—Cattle and calves, corn, wheat
KY............	6,174	3,357	2,817	6,548	3,665	2,883	28—Broilers, cattle and calves, soybeans
LA............	3,926	1,160	2,766	3,992	1,342	2,650	32—Soybeans, broilers, corn
ME............	793	354	439	838	405	433	42—Milk, potatoes, chicken eggs
MD............	2,427	1,392	1,035	2,417	1,469	948	36—Broilers, corn, milk
MA............	431	128	302	459	144	315	44—Cranberries, milk, turkeys
MI............	8,593	3,329	5,265	8,599	3,954	4,645	19—Milk, corn, soybeans
MN............	21,663	7,699	13,964	18,853	8,849	10,003	5—Corn, soybeans, hogs
MS............	6,525	3,529	2,996	6,656	3,785	2,871	25—Broilers, soybeans, corn
MO............	9,901	4,290	5,612	10,915	5,260	5,655	11—Soybeans, cattle and calves, corn
MT............	4,124	1,765	2,359	4,535	2,265	2,270	34—Cattle and calves, wheat, hay
NE............	23,087	11,706	11,381	24,718	14,531	10,186	4—Cattle and calves, corn, soybeans
NV............	694	463	230	867	603	264	46—Cattle and calves, hay, milk
NH............	221	119	103	250	144	106	48—Milk, turkeys, chicken eggs
NJ............	677	112	565	1,021	133	888	40—Floriculture, blueberries, corn
NM............	3,217	2,527	690	3,665	2,959	706	30—Milk, cattle and calves, hay
NY............	5,693	3,450	2,243	6,357	4,258	2,098	24—Milk, cattle and calves, corn
NC............	12,686	8,305	4,381	13,123	8,851	4,273	9—Broilers, hogs, tobacco
ND............	8,840	1,282	7,559	8,170	1,613	6,557	18—Soybeans, wheat, cattle and calves
OH............	10,788	3,514	7,274	10,275	4,105	6,170	15—Soybeans, corn, milk
OK............	7,014	5,450	1,564	7,567	6,227	1,339	23—Cattle and calves, hogs, broilers
OR............	4,948	1,554	3,394	5,204	1,903	3,301	27—Cattle and calves, milk, hay
PA............	7,477	4,778	2,699	8,289	5,691	2,598	21—Milk, cattle and calves, chicken eggs
RI............	72	23	49	75	26	49	49—Turkeys, chicken eggs, milk
SC............	2,921	1,690	1,231	2,717	1,594	1,122	35—Broilers, cattle and calves, corn
SD............	10,131	3,868	6,264	10,772	4,645	6,127	14—Cattle and calves, corn, soybeans
TN............	4,085	1,550	2,535	4,228	1,820	2,409	33—Cattle and calves, soybeans, broilers
TX............	22,291	15,377	6,914	24,865	17,030	7,835	3—Cattle and calves, milk, broilers
UT............	2,008	1,455	553	2,375	1,843	532	37—Cattle and calves, milk, hay
VT............	761	667	94	992	814	178	41—Milk, cattle and calves, maple products
VA............	3,839	2,422	1,418	4,168	2,830	1,339	31—Broilers, cattle and calves, milk
WA............	9,833	2,719	7,113	10,012	3,157	6,855	16—Apples, milk, cattle and calves
WV............	760	610	149	831	683	148	47—Cattle and calves, broilers, turkeys
WI............	12,009	7,883	4,125	12,884	9,406	3,477	10—Milk, cattle and calves, corn
WY............	1,728	1,271	458	1,826	1,434	393	38—Cattle and calves, hay, hogs

Source: U.S. Department of Agriculture, Economic Research Service, "U.S. and State Farm Income and Wealth Statistics," <http://www.ers.usda.gov/data-products/farm-income-and-wealth-statistics.aspx>, accessed September 2015.

Table 867. Indexes of Prices Received and Paid by Farmers: 2000 to 2014

[2011 = 100, except as noted]

Item	2000	2010	2013	2014	Item	2000	2010	2013	2014
Prices received, all products...	**59**	**82**	**107**	**108**	Livestock and poultry..........	71	86	108	154
Crops...................	55	79	105	92	Seed and plants...............	37	93	110	114
Food grains.....................	36	76	101	90	Fertilizer [2].....................	34	77	97	95
Feed grains....................	35	64	102	69	Agricultural chemicals..........	83	99	109	110
Cotton.........................	57	(NA)	(NA)	(NA)	Fuels...........................	36	78	98	98
Tobacco........................	99	(NA)	(NA)	(NA)	Supplies and repairs..........	72	96	104	106
Oil-bearing crops..............	40	79	112	99	Autos and trucks..............	103	97	103	104
Fruits and nuts................	59	87	115	133	Farm machinery...............	57	94	108	112
Commercial vegetables........	77	93	104	103	Building materials.............	71	97	105	107
Potatoes and dry beans.......	55	(NA)	(NA)	(NA)	Farm services................	72	98	106	109
Animals and products..........	64	86	109	129	Rent...........................	54	93	105	108
Livestock.....................	62	82	107	131					
Dairy products...............	61	81	100	119	Interest.........................	78	92	95	96
Poultry and eggs.............	71	101	123	133	Taxes..........................	55	96	103	105
Prices paid, total [1]..........	**59**	**90**	**106**	**111**	Wage rates....................	73	99	106	108
Production......................	54	88	107	114					
Feed...........................	45	80	118	115	Parity ratio (1910-14 = 100) [3]....	38	35	38	37

NA Not available. [1] Includes production items, interest, taxes, wage rates, and a family living component. The family living component is the Consumer Price Index for all urban consumers from the Bureau of Labor Statistics. See text, Section 14 and Table 744. [2] Includes lime and soil conditioners. [3] Ratio of prices received by farmers to prices paid.

Source: U.S. Department of Agriculture, National Agricultural Statistics Service, "Quick Stats," <http://quickstats.nass.usda.gov/>, accessed July 2015.

Table 868. Farm and Marketing Bill Share of the U.S. Food Dollar (Nominal) by Selected Characteristics: 1995 to 2013

[In percent. The food dollar series measures annual expenditures by U.S. consumers on domestically produced food; a food dollar represents the average $1 expenditure. Farm share is measured as the average payment from each food dollar expenditure that farmers receive for their raw food dollar commodities. The food marketing bill is measured as the average value added to the raw food dollar from each consumer food dollar expenditure. Based on input-output data from the Bureau of Labor Statistics and Bureau of Economic Analysis]

Item	1995	2000	2005	2008	2009	2010	2011	2012	2013
SHARE OF FOOD DOLLAR									
Food dollar, total									
Farm share..................	17.7	15.8	15.8	17.6	16.2	16.4	17.6	17.4	17.4
Marketing bill share......................	82.3	84.2	84.2	82.4	83.8	83.6	82.4	82.6	82.6
Food at home dollar									
Farm share..................	23.9	22.5	23.6	25.7	23.8	24.2	25.9	26.1	26.2
Marketing bill share...................	76.1	77.5	76.4	74.3	76.2	75.8	74.1	73.9	73.8
Food away from home dollar									
Farm share..................	9.2	6.2	5.1	6.0	5.5	5.5	6.0	5.9	6.0
Marketing bill share...................	90.8	93.8	94.9	94.0	94.5	94.5	94.0	94.1	94.0
Food and beverage dollar [1]									
Farm share..................	15.2	13.1	13.2	14.6	13.5	13.6	14.7	14.6	14.6
Marketing bill share...................	84.8	86.9	86.8	85.4	86.5	86.4	85.3	85.4	85.4
Home food and beverage dollar [1]									
Farm share..................	19.6	18.0	18.9	20.8	19.1	19.4	21.0	21.1	21.1
Marketing bill share...................	80.4	82.0	81.1	79.2	80.9	80.6	79.0	78.9	78.9
Away food and beverage dollar [1]									
Farm share..................	8.4	5.4	4.5	5.1	4.7	4.7	5.1	5.1	5.2
Marketing bill share...................	91.6	94.6	95.5	94.9	95.3	95.3	94.9	94.9	94.8
MARKETING BILL COST COMPONENTS									
Primary factors:									
Salary and benefits [2].....................	(NA)	52.9	50.4	49.7	49.7	49.0	48.8	48.9	48.6
Output taxes [3]....................	(NA)	7.3	8.0	8.9	9.3	9.3	9.0	8.8	8.8
Property income [4]...................	(NA)	34.6	35.6	34.0	35.9	35.9	35.5	35.8	36.7
Imports [5].........................	4.2	5.1	6.0	7.4	5.1	5.8	6.7	6.4	5.9
Industry groups: [6]									
Farm and agribusiness [7]...............	12.2	10.6	10.9	12.1	10.9	11.6	12.2	12.1	12.6
Food processing......................	19.0	18.2	15.8	14.9	17.4	16.7	15.8	15.8	15.5
Packaging..........................	4.2	4.2	3.6	3.3	2.9	2.8	2.8	2.7	2.6
Transportation.......................	3.9	3.8	3.6	3.6	3.4	3.3	3.4	3.3	3.3
Wholesale trade.....................	10.2	9.4	9.2	9.9	9.9	9.4	9.7	9.3	9.2
Retail trade.........................	12.6	13.0	13.7	13.7	14.0	13.9	13.3	13.0	13.1
Food services.......................	26.7	28.4	30.6	29.0	29.6	30.2	30.0	31.1	31.5
Energy.............................	3.5	4.7	5.5	6.8	4.4	5.0	5.6	5.6	5.2
Finance and insurance..............	3.6	3.8	3.3	2.9	3.7	3.4	3.3	3.3	3.2
Advertising.........................	2.7	2.5	2.5	2.4	2.3	2.4	2.5	2.5	2.5
Legal and accounting................	1.3	1.5	1.5	1.4	1.4	1.4	1.4	1.3	1.3

NA Not available. [1] Includes alcoholic beverages and soft drinks. [2] Pre-tax employee wages plus employer and employee costs for employee benefits. [3] Value of excise, sales, property, and severance taxes (less subsidies), customs duties, and other non-tax government fees levied on establishments. [4] Allocated compensation to various owners for services on behalf of a domestic establishment that directs sales to the U.S. food supply. Includes machinery, equipment, structures, natural resources, product inventory, and other tangible or intangible assets. [5] Food and non-food commodities imported from international sources and used by U.S. food supply chain industries producing for the U.S. market. [6] For each industry group the amount shown excludes value-added contributions to the food dollar that trace back to other supply chain industry groups. For example, the value of energy used by the transportation and packaging industries is deducted from those groups and included with the energy group. [7] Farm and agribusiness value-added contributions from non-farm supply chain industry groups, such as energy, transportation, and financial services, are deducted from the farm share and therefore the industry group series value for farms and agribusiness is smaller than the farm share value of the marketing bill series.

Source: U.S. Department of Agriculture, Economic Research Service, "Food Dollar Series," <http://www.ers.usda.gov/data-products/food-dollar-series/food-dollar-application.aspx>, accessed June 2015.

Table 869. Agricultural Exports and Imports—Volume by Principal Commodity: 2000 to 2014

[In thousands (1,436 represents 1,436,000). 1 Kiloliters equals 264.17 gallons. Includes Puerto Rico, U.S. territories, and shipments under foreign aid programs. Excludes fish, forest products, distilled liquors, manufactured tobacco, and products made from cotton; but includes raw tobacco, raw cotton, rubber, beer and wine, and processed agricultural products. Commodity and commodity grouping definitions used are Foreign Agricultural Trade of the United States (FATUS) groupings. See source for details]

Commodity	Unit	2000	2005	2010	2011	2012	2013	2014
EXPORTS								
Fruit juices and wine.	Kiloliters	1,436	1,398	1,498	1,708	1,492	1,531	1,450
Beef, pork, lamb, and poultry meats [1]	Metric tons	4,431	4,343	6,366	7,095	7,113	7,118	7,164
Wheat, unmilled.	Metric tons	27,568	27,040	27,608	32,802	25,765	32,913	25,405
Wheat products.	Metric tons	844	313	446	421	410	386	397
Rice, paddy, milled.	Metric tons	3,241	4,388	4,464	3,695	3,775	3,753	3,474
Feed grains.	Metric tons	54,946	50,865	54,504	49,241	33,285	26,144	57,109
Feed grain products.	Metric tons	657	3,442	1,081	1,038	996	850	917
Feeds and fodders [2]	Metric tons	13,065	11,422	19,024	18,164	17,747	20,350	26,622
Fresh fruits and nuts.	Metric tons	3,452	3,675	4,308	4,588	4,735	4,930	4,577
Fruit products.	Metric tons	387	394	570	617	596	578	612
Vegetables, fresh.	Metric tons	2,100	2,077	2,140	2,241	2,286	2,335	2,259
Vegetables, frozen and canned.	Metric tons	1,110	1,086	1,410	1,659	1,740	1,864	1,968
Oilcake and meal.	Metric tons	6,760	6,905	10,004	8,251	10,139	10,571	10,576
Oilseeds.	Metric tons	27,715	26,462	43,282	35,197	44,099	40,198	51,003
Vegetable oils.	Metric tons	2,043	1,937	3,544	2,876	3,072	2,668	2,612
Tobacco, unmanufactured.	Metric tons	180	154	179	184	160	159	150
Cotton, excluding linters.	Metric tons	1,485	3,405	2,956	2,760	2,752	2,790	2,166
IMPORTS								
Fruit juices.	Kiloliters	3,114	4,149	4,274	4,209	3,820	4,425	4,376
Wine.	Kiloliters	458	726	959	1,038	1,194	1,128	1,101
Malt beverages.	Kiloliters	2,346	2,995	3,161	3,201	3,249	3,225	3,450
Coffee, including products.	Metric tons	1,370	1,307	1,390	1,495	1,490	1,541	1,572
Rubber and allied gums, crude.	Metric tons	1,232	1,169	945	1,049	969	928	946
Beef, pork, lamb, and poultry meats [1]	Metric tons	1,564	1,778	1,351	1,249	1,316	1,379	1,696
Grains [3].	Metric tons	4,622	3,726	5,166	4,944	6,910	8,886	7,088
Biscuits, pasta, and noodles.	Metric tons	711	1,001	1,097	1,154	1,207	1,246	1,310
Feeds and fodders [2]	Metric tons	1,224	963	1,423	1,839	2,020	1,863	1,995
Fruits, nuts, and preparations [4]	Metric tons	8,357	9,570	10,934	11,236	11,918	12,752	13,077
Vegetables, fresh and frozen.	Metric tons	3,804	5,183	6,861	7,154	7,288	7,656	8,043
Tobacco, unmanufactured.	Metric tons	216	233	164	164	209	196	171
Oilseeds and oilnuts.	Metric tons	951	818	1,223	1,362	1,221	2,085	3,399
Vegetable oils and waxes.	Metric tons	1,846	2,386	3,730	4,350	4,182	4,534	4,662
Oilcake and meal.	Metric tons	1,254	1,541	1,504	2,489	3,079	3,348	3,713

[1] Includes variety meats. [2] Excluding oil meal. [3] Includes wheat, corn, oats, barley, and rice. [4] Includes bananas and plantains.

Source: U.S. Department of Agriculture, Foreign Agricultural Service, "Global Agricultural Trade System," <http://www.fas.usda.gov/gats/>, accessed July 2015.

Table 870. U.S. Exports and General Imports of Fertilizer and Agricultural Chemicals by Type: 2000 to 2014

[In thousands of metric tons (21,480 represents 21,480,000). Metric ton = 1.102 short tons or .984 long tons. Includes Puerto Rico, U.S. territories, and shipments under foreign aid programs. Commodity and commodity grouping definitions used are Foreign Agricultural Trade of the United States (FATUS) groupings. See source for details]

Commodity	2000	2005	2008	2009	2010	2011	2012	2013	2014
IMPORTS [1]									
Fertilizers, total.	**21,480**	**30,397**	**35,823**	**19,923**	**43,657**	**34,844**	**32,745**	**33,668**	**35,735**
Nitrogen.	10,552	17,901	16,786	12,655	17,171	17,722	18,054	17,374	17,861
Potassium.	9,324	10,215	10,798	4,628	10,230	10,650	8,415	9,690	10,647
Phosphate.	1,592	2,243	8,203	2,598	16,200	6,435	6,185	6,539	7,141
Mixed/organic fertilizer.	13	37	36	41	56	38	93	65	87
Agricultural chemicals, total.	**58**	**80**	**96**	**96**	**90**	**97**	**116**	**116**	**99**
Herbicides.	12	23	21	22	15	18	22	19	14
Fungicides.	17	21	26	28	25	25	26	26	28
Insecticides.	10	7	1	1	1	1	1	1	1
Other pesticides.	19	29	47	44	49	54	68	70	57
EXPORTS									
Fertilizers, total.	**21**	**32**	**10,780**	**11,324**	**10,310**	**10,885**	**10,673**	**11,162**	**10,847**
Nitrogen.	19	26	1,624	1,793	1,741	1,719	2,180	2,583	2,907
Potassium.	–	–	178	384	333	147	223	318	96
Phosphate.	2	6	8,552	8,689	7,820	8,634	7,761	7,580	7,123
Mixed/organic fertilizer.	–	–	426	458	416	386	509	681	721
Agricultural chemicals, total.	**154**	**127**	**140**	**123**	**146**	**151**	**160**	**170**	**158**
Herbicides.	60	56	74	69	83	84	91	95	84
Fungicides.	14	18	16	14	15	18	17	22	24
Insecticides.	62	23	26	21	27	27	29	27	27
Other pesticides.	19	29	24	18	22	23	23	25	23

– Represents or rounds to zero. [1] Total shipments arriving in the U.S., including both merchandise that enters consumption channels immediately and merchandise entered into bonded warehouses or Foreign Trade Zones under Customs custody.

Source: U.S. Department of Agriculture, Foreign Agricultural Service, "Global Agricultural Trade System," <http://www.fas.usda.gov/gats>, accessed April 2015.

Table 871. Agricultural Exports and Imports—Value: 1990 to 2014

[In billions of dollars, except percent (16.6 represents $16,600,000,000). Includes Puerto Rico, U.S. territories, and shipments under foreign aid programs. Excludes fish, forest products, distilled liquors, manufactured tobacco, and products made from cotton; but includes raw tobacco, raw cotton, rubber, beer and wine, and processed agricultural products]

Year	Trade balance	Exports, domestic products	Percent of all exports	Imports for consumption	Percent of all imports	Year	Trade balance	Exports, domestic products	Percent of all exports	Imports for consumption	Percent of all imports
1990.........	16.6	39.5	11	22.9	5	2008.........	34.3	114.8	10	80.5	4
1995.........	26.0	56.3	10	30.3	4	2009.........	26.8	98.5	10	71.7	5
2000.........	12.3	51.3	7	39.0	3	2010.........	34.0	115.8	10	81.9	4
2004.........	7.4	61.4	8	54.0	4	2011.........	37.5	136.4	11	99.0	5
2005.........	3.9	63.2	8	59.3	4	2012.........	38.5	141.4	10	102.9	5
2006.........	5.6	71.0	8	65.3	4	2013.........	40.2	144.4	11	104.2	5
2007.........	18.1	90.0	9	71.9	4	2014.........	38.7	150.5	11	111.7	5

Source: U.S. Department of Agriculture, Economic Research Service, "Foreign Agricultural Trade of the United States (FATUS)," <http://www.ers.usda.gov/data-products/foreign-agricultural-trade-of-the-united-states-(fatus).aspx>, accessed April 2015.

Table 872. Agricultural Imports—Value by Selected Commodity: 2000 to 2014

[In millions of dollars (38,974 represents $38,974,000,000). For calendar year. Includes Puerto Rico, U.S. territories, and shipments under foreign aid programs. Excludes fish, forest products, distilled liquors, manufactured tobacco, and products made from cotton; but includes raw tobacco, raw cotton, rubber, beer and wine, and processed agricultural products]

Commodity [1]	Value (mil. dol.)							Percent distribution		
	2000	2005	2010	2011	2012	2013	2014	2000	2010	2014
Total [2].....	38,974	59,291	81,863	98,959	102,919	104,228	111,732	100.0	100.0	100.0
Cattle, live..........	1,152	1,039	1,575	1,449	1,778	1,783	2,493	3.0	1.9	2.2
Beef and veal...............	2,399	3,651	2,830	3,161	3,674	3,755	5,617	6.2	3.5	5.0
Pork...............	997	1,281	1,185	1,288	1,284	1,428	1,754	2.6	1.4	1.6
Dairy products..........	1,671	2,686	2,619	2,944	3,177	3,193	3,522	4.3	3.2	3.2
Grains and feeds...........	3,075	4,527	7,788	8,934	10,132	11,317	11,051	7.9	9.5	9.9
Fruits and preparations.........	3,851	5,842	9,166	9,950	10,594	11,651	12,811	9.9	11.2	11.5
Vegetables and preparations [3]...........	3,958	6,410	9,318	10,290	10,474	11,369	11,604	10.2	11.4	10.4
Sugar and related products.............	1,555	2,494	4,047	5,144	4,783	4,274	4,471	4.0	4.9	4.0
Wine..........	2,207	3,762	4,279	4,857	5,108	5,295	5,383	5.7	5.2	4.8
Malt beverages..............	2,179	3,096	3,506	3,565	3,699	3,699	4,135	5.6	4.3	3.7
Oilseeds and products................	1,773	2,998	5,390	8,252	8,104	8,642	9,591	4.5	6.6	8.6
Coffee and products...............	2,700	2,976	4,943	8,097	7,019	5,809	6,324	6.9	6.0	5.7
Cocoa and products..............	1,404	2,751	4,295	4,681	4,096	4,159	4,731	3.6	5.2	4.2
Rubber, crude natural.............	842	1,552	2,820	4,773	3,382	2,559	1,954	2.2	3.4	1.7

[1] Commodity and commodity grouping definitions used are the Foreign Agricultural Trade of the United States (FATUS) commodity code groupings. See source for more details. [2] Includes other commodities, not shown separately. [3] Includes pulses.

Source: U.S. Department of Agriculture, Foreign Agricultural Service, "Global Agricultural Trade System (GATS)," <http://www.fas.usda.gov/gats>, accessed April 2015.

Table 873. Agricultural Imports—Value by Selected Country of Origin: 2000 to 2014

[In millions of dollars (38,974 represents $38,974,000,000). Totals include transshipments through Canada, but transshipments are not distributed by country after 1998. See headnote Table 871]

Country	Value (mil. dol.)							Percent distribution		
	2000	2005	2010	2011	2012	2013	2014	2000	2010	2014
Total..................	38,974	59,291	81,863	98,959	102,919	104,228	111,732	100.0	100.0	100.0
Canada..................	8,661	12,270	16,244	18,917	20,226	21,752	23,119	22.2	19.8	20.7
Mexico..................	5,077	8,331	13,578	15,837	16,395	17,679	19,271	13.0	16.6	17.2
European Union [1]..............	8,303	13,410	14,353	16,069	16,754	17,565	18,941	21.3	17.5	17.0
China..................	812	1,872	3,367	3,992	4,532	4,420	4,277	2.1	4.1	3.8
Australia [2]..................	1,592	2,421	2,307	2,362	2,677	2,751	3,897	4.1	2.8	3.5
Brazil..................	1,144	1,952	2,894	4,055	3,424	3,398	3,883	2.9	3.5	3.5
India..................	826	923	1,592	2,676	5,355	3,518	3,179	2.1	1.9	2.8
Indonesia..................	998	1,702	2,887	4,288	3,350	3,118	3,017	2.6	3.5	2.7
Chile..................	1,026	1,521	2,293	2,370	2,458	2,871	2,757	2.6	2.8	2.5
New Zealand [2]..................	1,132	1,712	1,666	1,976	2,237	2,179	2,610	2.9	2.0	2.3
Colombia..................	1,123	1,437	1,977	2,466	2,148	2,196	2,431	2.9	2.4	2.2
Thailand..................	779	1,094	2,034	2,626	2,414	2,235	2,229	2.0	2.5	2.0
Guatemala..................	710	920	1,387	1,888	2,009	1,815	1,893	1.8	1.7	1.7
Vietnam..................	200	422	970	1,284	1,365	1,476	1,775	0.5	1.2	1.6
Peru..................	196	448	974	1,320	1,241	1,270	1,625	0.5	1.2	1.5
Costa Rica..................	812	916	1,295	1,449	1,533	1,475	1,593	2.1	1.6	1.4
Argentina..................	672	831	1,159	1,629	1,696	1,781	1,513	1.7	1.4	1.4
Malaysia..................	353	666	1,729	2,424	1,914	1,597	1,491	0.9	2.1	1.3
Philippines..................	468	568	884	1,375	1,144	994	1,145	1.2	1.1	1.0
Ecuador..................	451	596	869	1,070	938	987	1,092	1.2	1.1	1.0
Rest of world..................	3,639	5,281	7,406	8,886	9,110	9,149	9,994	9.3	9.0	8.9

[1] For consistency, data for all years are shown on the basis of 27 countries in the European Union; see footnote 2, Table 1372. [2] Data is a summarization of component countries.

Source: U.S. Department of Agriculture, Foreign Agricultural Service, "Global Agricultural Trade System Online (GATS)," <http://www.fas.usda.gov/gats>, accessed April 2015.

Table 874. Selected Farm Products—U.S. and World Production and Exports: 2010 to 2014

[In millions of metric tons, except as indicated (58.9 represents 58,900,000). Metric ton = 1.102 short tons or .984 long tons]

Commodity	Unit	Amount United States 2010	2013	2014	Amount World 2010	2013	2014	United States as percent of world 2010	2013	2014
PRODUCTION [1]										
Wheat......................	Mil. metric tons	58.9	58.1	55.1	649.9	715.1	725.9	9.1	8.1	7.6
Corn for grain..............	Mil. metric tons	315.6	351.3	361.1	835.5	990.7	1,001.7	37.8	35.5	36.0
Soybeans..................	Mil. metric tons	90.7	91.4	108.0	264.3	283.2	318.6	34.3	32.3	33.9
Rice, milled................	Mil. metric tons	7.6	6.1	7.1	450.6	478.2	476.3	1.7	1.3	1.5
Cotton [2]....................	Million bales [3]	18.1	12.9	16.3	117.6	120.5	119.0	15.4	10.7	13.7
EXPORTS [4]										
Wheat [5]....................	Mil. metric tons	35.1	32.0	23.3	132.7	165.9	163.9	26.5	19.3	14.2
Corn.......................	Mil. metric tons	46.5	48.7	47.0	91.3	131.0	125.1	50.9	37.2	37.6
Soybeans..................	Mil. metric tons	41.0	44.8	49.7	91.7	112.9	119.5	44.7	39.7	41.6
Rice, milled basis..........	Mil. metric tons	3.5	3.0	3.3	35.1	41.7	43.0	10.0	7.2	7.6
Cotton [2]....................	Million bales [3]	14.4	10.5	11.0	35.2	40.1	34.6	40.8	26.3	31.8

[1] Production years vary by commodity. In most cases, includes harvests from July 1 of the year shown through June 30 of the following year. [2] For production and trade years ending in year shown. [3] Bales of 480 lb. net weight. [4] Trade years may vary by commodity. Wheat, corn, and soybean data are for trade year beginning in year shown. Rice data are for calendar year. [5] Includes wheat flour on a grain equivalent.

Source: U.S. Department of Agriculture, Foreign Agricultural Service, "Production, Supply and Distribution Online," <http://www.fas.usda.gov/psdonline/>, accessed July 2015.

Table 875. Percent of U.S. Agricultural Commodity Output Exported: 2000 to 2012

[In percent. All export shares are estimated from export and production volumes]

Commodity group	2000	2005	2007	2008	2009	2010	2011	2012
Total agriculture [1].....................	**19.0**	**19.2**	**21.2**	**19.4**	**19.4**	**21.4**	**20.1**	**18.5**
Livestock [2]............................	5.8	5.5	7.3	9.2	7.5	8.9	9.5	9.1
Red meat............................	8.1	7.4	9.4	13.2	12.2	13.3	16.2	15.8
Poultry..............................	10.3	9.9	11.0	12.4	12.4	12.1	12.5	13.2
Dairy...............................	1.1	1.6	3.0	4.7	2.3	4.5	4.8	4.4
Crops [3]...............................	21.3	21.6	23.7	21.3	21.5	23.6	22.1	20.4
Food grains...........................	45.9	47.1	60.2	40.3	41.5	58.0	52.2	45.6
Feed grains...........................	20.3	20.6	19.5	15.8	15.4	14.9	12.4	7.2
Oilseeds.............................	33.0	27.8	40.1	40.0	42.2	41.8	40.9	39.5
Fruit and nuts........................	17.4	20.3	21.2	21.2	20.9	23.8	25.8	24.3
Vegetables...........................	11.6	13.0	13.1	16.3	14.9	15.6	17.8	17.9
Sweeteners..........................	4.1	5.2	9.0	8.6	8.0	13.2	14.4	15.0
Wine and beer........................	6.6	8.0	10.2	11.3	8.6	9.3	9.9	9.3

[1] All export shares are computed from physical weights or weight equivalents. [2] Includes animal fats; excludes live farm animals and fish/shellfish. [3] Exports include vegetable oils and oilseed meal. Excludes nursery crops.

Source: U.S. Department of Agriculture, Economic Research Service, unpublished data.

Table 876. Top 10 U.S. Export Markets for Selected Commodities: 2014

[In thousands of metric tons (49,506 represents 49,506,000). Commodity and commodity grouping definitions used are the Foreign Agricultural Trade of the United States (FATUS) commodity code groupings. See source for details]

Corn Country	Amount	Wheat [1] Country	Amount	Soybeans Country	Amount	Poultry meat Country	Amount
World, total.........	**49,506**	**World, total...........**	**25,405**	**World, total............**	**50,107**	**World, total...........**	**3,809**
Japan.................	12,528	Japan.................	3,011	China.....................	31,342	Mexico..................	972
Mexico.................	10,337	Mexico.................	2,922	Mexico...................	3,546	Angola..................	234
Korea, South..........	4,625	Brazil..................	2,524	Indonesia................	1,987	Canada.................	186
Colombia..............	4,222	Philippines.............	2,361	Japan....................	1,811	China...................	161
Egypt.................	2,915	Nigeria................	2,199	Taiwan..................	1,462	Russia..................	144
Peru..................	2,355	Korea, South...........	1,414	Spain...................	1,123	Cuba...................	144
Taiwan................	1,704	Taiwan................	1,044	Germany................	1,083	Taiwan.................	119
Venezuela.............	1,195	Indonesia..............	925	Netherlands.............	1,015	Hong Kong..............	112
Saudi Arabia...........	1,141	Colombia..............	730	Turkey...................	767	Philippines..............	92
Canada...............	880	Venezuela.............	574	Korea, South............	692	Guatemala..............	88
Rest of world..........	7,606	Rest of world..........	7,701	Rest of world............	5,278	Rest of world............	1,557

[1] Unmilled.

Source: U.S. Department of Agriculture, Foreign Agricultural Service, "Global Agricultural Trade System Online (GATS)," <http://www.fas.usda.gov/gats/>, accessed July 2015.

Table 877. Agricultural Exports—Value by Principal Commodity: 2000 to 2014

[In millions of dollars (51,265 represents $51,265,000,000). Includes Puerto Rico, U.S. territories, and shipments under foreign aid programs. Excludes fish, forest products, distilled liquors, manufactured tobacco, and products made from cotton; but includes raw tobacco, raw cotton, rubber, beer and wine, and processed agricultural products. Commodity and commodity grouping definitions used are the Foreign Agricultural Trade of the United States (FATUS) commodity code groupings. See source for more details]

Commodity	Value (mil. dol.)							Percent distribution		
	2000	2005	2010	2011	2012	2013	2014	2000	2010	2014
Total agricultural exports......	51,265	63,182	115,820	136,444	141,406	144,379	150,466	100.0	100.0	100.0
Animals and animal products [1]....	11,600	12,227	22,340	27,861	29,010	31,237	32,890	22.6	19.3	21.9
Meat and meat products..........	5,276	4,299	9,336	12,087	12,393	12,810	14,370	10.3	8.1	9.6
Poultry and poultry products......	2,235	3,139	4,806	5,635	6,253	6,460	6,461	4.4	4.1	4.3
Grains and feeds [1]................	13,620	16,364	29,224	38,676	32,081	33,149	35,514	26.6	25.2	23.6
Wheat and products..............	3,578	4,520	7,061	11,465	8,495	10,779	8,012	7.0	6.1	5.3
Corn.............................	4,469	4,789	9,792	13,652	9,328	6,384	10,621	8.7	8.5	7.1
Fruits and preparations............	2,743	3,468	5,262	6,053	6,535	6,700	6,691	5.4	4.5	4.4
Nuts and preparations............	1,322	2,992	4,795	5,695	6,888	8,230	8,616	2.6	4.1	5.7
Vegetables and preparations [2].....	3,112	3,571	5,375	5,826	6,212	6,724	7,016	6.1	4.6	4.7
Oilseeds and products [1]...........	8,584	10,229	27,265	26,084	35,049	32,251	34,730	16.7	23.5	23.1
Soybeans.......................	5,258	6,274	18,611	17,591	24,607	21,562	24,201	10.3	16.1	16.1
Vegetable oils and waxes.........	1,259	1,656	3,903	4,020	4,166	3,547	3,236	2.5	3.4	2.2
Tobacco, unmanufactured.........	1,204	990	1,168	1,149	1,101	1,138	1,086	2.3	1.0	0.7
Cotton, excluding linters...........	1,873	3,921	5,734	8,386	6,225	5,591	4,395	3.7	5.0	2.9
Other............................	7,207	9,421	14,658	16,715	18,306	19,360	19,528	14.1	12.7	13.0

[1] Includes commodities not shown separately. [2] Includes pulses.

Source: U.S. Department of Agriculture, Foreign Agricultural Service, "Global Agricultural Trade System (GATS)," <http://www.fas.usda.gov/gats>, accessed July 2015.

Table 878. Agricultural Exports—Value by World Region and Selected Country of Destination: 2000 to 2014

[51,265 represents $51,265,000,000. Includes Puerto Rico, U.S. territories, and shipments under foreign aid programs. Excludes fish, forest products, distilled liquors, manufactured tobacco, and products made from cotton; but includes raw tobacco, raw cotton, rubber, beer and wine, and processed agricultural products]

Country	Value (mil. dol.)							Percent distribution		
	2000	2005	2010	2011	2012	2013	2014	2000	2010	2014
Total agricultural exports [1]......	51,265	63,182	115,820	136,444	141,406	144,379	150,466	100.0	100.0	100.0
Canada................................	7,643	10,619	16,897	19,041	20,627	21,374	21,892	14.9	14.6	14.5
Mexico................................	6,410	9,429	14,585	18,351	18,914	18,113	19,364	12.5	12.6	12.9
Caribbean..........................	1,408	1,913	3,172	3,419	3,530	3,535	3,665	2.7	2.7	2.4
Central America.....................	1,121	1,589	2,904	3,731	3,504	3,372	3,851	2.2	2.5	2.6
South America......................	1,704	1,943	4,240	5,284	5,449	7,437	8,097	3.3	3.7	5.4
Asia, excluding Middle East [2]........	19,877	22,543	49,766	58,316	63,130	62,322	65,491	38.8	43.0	43.5
Japan.............................	9,292	7,931	11,784	14,066	13,503	12,229	13,184	18.1	10.2	8.8
Korea, South......................	2,546	2,233	5,307	6,976	6,031	5,256	6,894	5.0	4.6	4.6
Taiwan............................	1,996	2,301	3,190	3,612	3,211	3,081	3,511	3.9	2.8	2.3
China [3]..........................	1,716	5,233	17,564	18,898	25,860	25,504	24,560	3.3	15.2	16.3
Indonesia.........................	668	958	2,246	2,814	2,497	2,823	2,920	1.3	1.9	1.9
Europe/Eurasia [2]...................	7,654	8,361	11,365	12,574	12,538	14,711	15,264	14.9	9.8	10.1
European Union [4]...................	6,516	7,059	8,925	9,678	10,114	11,902	12,581	12.7	7.7	8.4
Russia............................	580	972	1,132	1,241	1,655	1,208	908	1.1	1.0	0.6
Middle East..........................	2,323	2,844	5,993	7,673	5,992	6,473	6,565	4.5	5.2	4.4
Africa [2]............................	2,308	2,773	5,725	7,080	5,758	5,345	4,992	4.5	4.9	3.3
Egypt.............................	1,050	819	2,095	2,507	1,868	1,648	1,744	2.0	1.8	1.2
Oceania.............................	490	742	1,389	1,603	1,782	1,938	2,153	1.0	1.2	1.4

[1] Totals include transshipments through Canada, but transshipments are not distributed by country after 2000. [2] Includes areas not shown separately. [3] China includes Macao. However Hong Kong remains separate economically until 2050 and is not included. [4] For consistency, data for all years are shown on the basis of 28 countries in the European Union; see footnote 3, Table 1379.

Source: U.S. Department of Agriculture, Foreign Agricultural Service, "Global Agricultural Trade System (GATS)," <http://www.fas.usda.gov/gats>, accessed July 2015.

Table 879. Cropland Used for Crops and Acres Harvested: 1990 to 2014

[In millions of acres, except as indicated (341 represents 341,000,000)]

Item	1990	1995	2000	2005	2009	2010	2011	2012	2013	2014 [5]
Cropland used for crops.....................	341	332	345	336	333	335	328	340	336	340
Index (1977 = 100)......................	90	88	91	89	88	89	87	90	89	90
Cropland harvested [1]...........................	310	302	314	314	310	315	302	315	311	317
Crop failure................................	6	8	11	7	8	5	13	11	12	9
Cultivated summer fallow...................	25	22	20	16	15	14	14	13	13	14
Cropland idled by all federal programs [2, 3]...	62	55	31	35	34	31	31	30	27	25
Acres of crops harvested [4].................	322	314	325	321	319	322	311	324	321	326

[1] Land supporting one or more harvested crops. [2] Beginning in 2000, includes only the Conservation Reserve Program; all other federal acreage reduction programs were eliminated by the Federal Agricultural Improvement Act of 1996. [3] Data are for fiscal years. [4] Area in principal crops harvested plus acreages in fruits, vegetables for sale, tree nuts, and other minor crops. Acres are counted twice for land that is doublecropped. [5] Preliminary.

Source: U.S. Department of Agriculture, Economic Research Service, "Major Land Uses," <http://www.ers.usda.gov/data-products/major-land-uses.aspx>, accessed August 2015; Agricultural Resources and Environmental Indicators, 2006, and earlier reports; and Farm Service Agency, "CRP Enrollment and Rental Payments by State, 1986-2014," <http://www.fsa.usda.gov/programs-and-services/conservation-programs/reports-and-statistics/index>, accessed August 2015.

Table 880. Crops—Supply and Use: 2000 to 2014

[72 represents 72,000,000. Marketing year beginning January 1 for potatoes, May 1 for hay, June 1 for wheat, August 1 for cotton, September 1 for soybeans and corn. Acreage, production, and yield of all crops periodically revised on basis of census data]

Item	Unit	2000	2005	2010	2011	2012	2013	2014
CORN								
Acreage harvested...............	Million	72	75	81	84	87	87	83
Yield per acre....................	Bushel	137	148	153	147	123	158	171
Production........................	Mil. bu.	9,915	11,112	12,425	12,314	10,755	13,829	14,216
Imports...........................	Mil. bu.	7	9	28	29	160	36	27
Total supply [1].................	Mil. bu.	11,639	13,235	14,161	13,471	11,904	14,686	15,474
Ethanol..........................	Mil. bu.	630	1,603	5,019	5,000	4,641	5,134	5,200
Exports..........................	Mil. bu.	1,941	2,134	1,831	1,541	730	1,917	1,850
Total use [2]...................	Mil. bu.	9,740	11,268	13,033	12,482	11,083	13,454	13,696
Ending stocks...................	Mil. bu.	1,899	1,967	1,128	989	821	1,232	1,779
Price per unit [3]................	Dol./bu.	1.85	2.00	5.18	6.22	6.89	4.46	3.65
Value of production..............	Mil. dol.	18,499	22,194	64,530	76,651	74,155	61,928	52,372
SOYBEANS								
Acreage harvested...............	Million	72	71	77	74	76	76	83.1
Yield per acre....................	Bushel	38	43	44	42	40	44	47.8
Production........................	Mil. bu.	2,758	3,068	3,331	3,097	3,042	3,358	3,969
Imports...........................	Mil. bu.	4	3	14	16	41	72	[9] 25
Total supply [1].................	Mil. bu.	3,052	3,327	3,497	3,328	3,252	3,570	[9] 4,086
Crushings........................	Mil. bu.	1,640	1,739	1,648	1,703	1,689	1,734	[9] 1,795
Exports..........................	Mil. bu.	996	940	1,505	1,365	1,317	1,647	[9] 1,790
Total use [2]...................	Mil. bu.	2,804	2,878	3,282	3,159	3,111	3,478	[9] 3,701
Ending stocks...................	Mil. bu.	248	449	215	169	141	92	[9] 385
Price per unit [3]................	Dol./bu.	4.54	5.66	11.30	12.50	14.40	13.00	10.20
Value of production..............	Mil. dol.	12,467	17,297	37,571	38,542	43,723	43,583	40,289
WHEAT								
Acreage harvested...............	Million	53	50	47	46	49	45	46
Yield per acre....................	Bushel	42	42	46	44	46	47	44
Production........................	Mil. bu.	2,228	2,103	2,163	1,993	2,252	2,135	2,026
Imports [4].......................	Mil. bu.	90	81	97	112	123	169	144
Total supply [1].................	Mil. bu.	3,268	2,725	3,236	2,968	3,118	3,021	2,760
Exports..........................	Mil. bu.	1,062	1,003	1,291	1,051	1,012	1,176	855
Total use [2]...................	Mil. bu.	2,392	2,154	2,373	2,226	2,400	2,431	2,007
Ending stocks...................	Mil. bu.	876	571	863	743	718	590	753
Price per unit [3]................	Dol./bu.	2.62	3.42	5.70	7.24	7.77	6.87	5.99
Value of production..............	Mil. dol.	5,772	7,167	12,579	14,269	17,383	14,604	11,924
COTTON								
Acreage harvested...............	Million	13	14	11	9	9	8	9
Yield per acre....................	Pounds	632	831	812	790	892	821	838
Production........................	Mil. bales [5]	17	24	18	16	17	13	16
Imports...........................	Mil. bales [5]	–	–	–	–	–	–	–
Total supply [1].................	Mil. bales [5]	21	29	21	18	21	17	19
Exports..........................	Mil. bales [5]	7	18	14	12	13	11	10
Total use [2]...................	Mil. bales [5]	16	24	18	15	17	14	14
Ending stocks...................	Mil. bales [5]	6	6	3	3	4	2	5
Price per unit [3]................	Cents/lb.	51.6	49.7	84.6	93.5	75.7	83.8	65.7
Value of production..............	Mil. dol.	4,260	5,695	7,347	6,986	6,292	5,192	5,069
HAY								
Acreage harvested...............	Million	60	62	60	55	55	58	57
Yield per acre....................	Sh. tons	3	2	2	2	2	2	2
Production........................	Mil. sh. tons	154	150	145	130	117	135	140
Price per unit [6,7]..............	Dol./ton	84.60	98.20	114.00	178.00	191.00	176.00	180.00
Value of production..............	Mil. dol.	11,557	12,534	14,607	18,085	18,613	19,815	19,185
POTATOES								
Acreage harvested...............	Million	1	1	1	1	1	1	1
Yield per acre....................	Cwt. [8]	381	390	401	399	408	414	426
Production........................	Mil. cwt. [8]	514	424	405	430	465	435	447
Price per unit [3]................	Dol./cwt. [8]	5.08	7.04	9.20	9.41	8.63	9.71	8.62
Value of production..............	Mil. dol.	2,590	2,982	3,725	4,045	4,017	4,223	3,848

– Represents zero or rounds to less than half the unit of measurement shown. [1] Comprises production, imports, and beginning stocks. [2] Includes feed, residual, and other domestic uses not shown separately. [3] Marketing year average price. U.S. prices are computed by weighting U.S. monthly prices by estimated monthly marketings and do not include an allowance for outstanding loans and government purchases and payments. [4] Includes flour and selected other products expressed in grain-equivalent bushels. [5] Bales of 480 pounds, net weight. [6] Prices are for hay sold baled. [7] Season average prices received by farmers. U.S. prices are computed by weighting state prices by estimated sales. [8] Cwt = hundredweight (100 pounds). [9] Forecast.

Source: U.S. Department of Agriculture, National Agricultural Statistics Service, "Quick Stats", <http://quickstats.nass.usda.gov/>; and U.S. Department of Agriculture, Economic Research Service, "Feed Grains Database," "Oil Crops Yearbook," "Wheat Data," and "Cotton and Wool Yearbook," <http://www.ers.usda.gov/data-products.aspx>, accessed August 2015.

Table 881. Corn—Acreage, Production, and Value by Leading States: 2012 to 2014

[87,365 represents 87,365,000. One bushel of corn (bu.) = 56 pounds. State value of production is computed by multiplying the state price by its production; value for the United States is the sum of state values]

State	Acreage harvested (1,000 acres)			Yield per acre (bu.)			Production (mil. bu.)			Price per unit ($/bu.)			Value of production (mil. dol.)		
	2012	2013	2014	2012	2013	2014	2012	2013	2014	2012	2013	2014	2012	2013	2014
U.S. [1]....	87,365	87,451	83,136	123	158	171	10,755	13,829	14,216	6.89	4.46	3.65	74,155	61,928	52,372
IA.........	13,700	13,050	13,300	137	164	178	1,877	2,140	2,367	6.92	4.49	3.70	12,988	9,609	8,759
IL.........	12,250	11,800	11,750	105	178	200	1,286	2,100	2,350	6.87	4.52	3.65	8,837	9,494	8,578
NE........	9,100	9,550	8,950	142	169	179	1,292	1,614	1,602	6.85	4.47	3.75	8,852	7,214	6,008
MN.......	8,330	8,140	7,550	165	159	156	1,374	1,294	1,178	6.67	4.30	3.65	9,168	5,565	4,299
IN.........	6,030	5,830	5,770	99	177	188	597	1,032	1,085	7.23	4.47	3.60	4,316	4,613	3,905
SD........	5,300	5,860	5,320	101	137	148	535	803	787	6.72	4.05	3.25	3,597	3,251	2,559
KS........	3,950	4,000	3,800	95	126	149	375	504	566	7.04	4.49	3.75	2,642	2,263	2,123
OH.......	3,650	3,730	3,470	120	174	176	438	649	611	7.09	4.41	3.65	3,105	2,862	2,229
MO.......	3,300	3,200	3,380	75	136	186	248	435	629	7.34	4.57	3.40	1,817	1,989	2,138
WI.........	3,300	3,030	3,110	120	145	156	396	439	485	6.69	4.38	3.70	2,649	1,924	1,795
ND........	3,460	3,600	2,530	122	110	124	422	396	314	6.46	3.91	3.30	2,727	1,548	1,035
MI.........	2,380	2,230	2,210	132	155	161	314	346	356	6.69	4.18	3.65	2,102	1,445	1,299
TX........	1,550	1,950	1,990	129	136	148	200	265	295	7.12	5.14	4.45	1,424	1,363	1,311
KY........	1,530	1,430	1,430	68	170	158	104	243	226	6.96	4.67	3.75	724	1,135	847
PA........	1,000	1,090	1,030	131	146	154	131	159	159	7.21	4.47	3.75	945	711	595
CO........	1,010	980	1,010	133	131	146	134	128	147	6.86	4.61	4.10	922	592	605
TN........	960	810	840	85	156	168	82	126	141	7.28	4.87	3.75	594	615	529
NC........	820	860	780	117	142	132	96	122	103	7.48	4.96	4.05	718	606	417
NY........	680	690	680	134	137	148	91	95	101	6.78	4.52	3.90	618	427	392
AR........	695	870	530	178	186	187	124	162	99	6.81	5.12	4.05	842	829	401

[1] Includes other states, not shown separately.

Source: U.S. Department of Agriculture, National Agricultural Statistics Service, *Crop Production Annual Summary*, January 2015; and *Crop Values Annual Summary*, February 2015. See also <http://www.nass.usda.gov/index.asp>.

Table 882. Soybeans—Acreage, Production, and Value by Leading States: 2012 to 2014

[76,144 represents 76,144,000. One bushel of soybeans (bu.) = 60 pounds. State value of production is computed by multiplying the state price by its production; value for the United States is the sum of state values]

State	Acreage harvested (1,000 acres)			Yield per acre (bu.)			Production (mil. bu.)			Price per unit ($/bu.)			Value of production (mil. dol.)		
	2012	2013	2014	2012	2013	2014	2012	2013	2014	2012	2013	2014	2012	2013	2014
U.S. [1]...	76,144	76,253	83,061	40	44	48	3,042	3,358	3,969	14.40	13.00	10.20	43,723	43,583	40,289
IA........	9,310	9,250	9,820	45	46	52	419	421	506	14.40	13.10	10.10	6,033	5,513	5,108
IL........	8,930	9,480	9,780	43	50	56	384	474	548	14.60	13.20	10.30	5,606	6,257	5,641
MN......	7,000	6,620	7,270	44	42	42	305	278	305	14.30	12.90	10.20	4,354	3,587	3,114
ND......	4,730	4,630	5,870	35	31	35	163	141	203	14.00	12.40	9.60	2,285	1,751	1,944
MO......	5,270	5,610	5,600	30	36	47	158	202	260	14.50	13.10	10.00	2,292	2,646	2,604
IN........	5,120	5,190	5,490	44	52	56	225	267	307	14.70	13.20	10.30	3,312	3,528	3,167
NE.......	4,990	4,770	5,350	42	54	54	207	255	289	14.10	12.70	9.80	2,920	3,241	2,831
SD.......	4,720	4,580	5,110	31	41	45	144	185	230	14.20	12.50	9.40	2,044	2,319	2,162
OH.......	4,590	4,490	4,840	45	50	53	207	222	254	14.60	13.00	10.40	3,016	2,889	2,643
KS.......	3,820	3,540	3,960	23	37	36	88	131	143	14.30	12.80	9.70	1,256	1,677	1,383
AR.......	3,150	3,240	3,210	44	44	50	137	141	161	14.30	13.10	10.70	1,959	1,846	1,717
MS.......	1,950	1,990	2,200	45	46	52	88	92	114	14.50	13.10	11.10	1,272	1,208	1,270
MI........	1,990	1,920	2,140	43	45	43	86	85	92	14.00	12.90	10.10	1,198	1,102	929
WI.......	1,700	1,550	1,790	42	39	44	71	60	79	14.00	12.80	10.10	1,000	774	795

[1] Includes other states, not shown separately.

Source: U.S. Department of Agriculture, National Agricultural Statistics Service, *Crop Production Annual Summary*, January 2015; and *Crop Values Annual Summary*, February 2015. See also <http://www.nass.usda.gov/index.asp>.

Table 883. Wheat—Acreage, Production, and Value by Leading States: 2012 to 2014

[48,758 represents 48,758,000. One bushel of wheat (bu.) = 60 pounds. State value of production is computed by multiplying the price per unit by total production, for each state; value for the United States is the sum of production values for all states]

State	Acreage harvested (1,000 acres)			Yield per acre (bu.)			Production (mil. bu.)			Price per unit ($/bu.)			Value of production (mil. dol.)		
	2012	2013	2014	2012	2013	2014	2012	2013	2014	2012	2013	2014	2012	2013	2014
U.S. [1].....	48,758	45,332	46,381	46	47	44	2,252	2,135	2,026	7.77	6.87	6.00	17,375	14,616	11,960
KS.........	9,100	8,450	8,800	42	38	28	382	321	246	7.48	6.99	6.15	2,859	2,244	1,515
ND.........	7,765	6,025	7,490	44	45	46	340	273	347	8.07	6.62	5.75	2,745	1,810	1,996
MT.........	5,615	5,165	5,650	35	39	37	196	202	209	8.15	6.87	6.15	1,594	1,385	1,288
OK.........	4,300	3,400	2,800	36	31	17	155	105	48	7.45	6.99	6.45	1,153	737	307
SD.........	2,225	1,839	2,364	46	42	56	102	78	131	8.10	6.84	5.60	826	530	735
CO.........	2,212	1,639	2,358	31	25	38	69	41	90	7.75	6.97	5.95	537	289	534
TX.........	2,900	2,350	2,250	33	29	30	96	68	68	6.72	7.11	6.40	643	485	432
WA.........	2,165	2,175	2,250	67	67	48	144	146	108	8.07	6.95	6.60	1,163	1,011	716

[1] Includes other states, not shown separately.

Source: U.S. Department of Agriculture, National Agricultural Statistics Service, *Crop Production Annual Summary*, January 2015; and *Crop Values Annual Summary*, February 2015. See also <http://www.nass.usda.gov/index.asp>.

Table 884. Commercial Vegetable and Other Specified Crops—Area, Production, and Value: 2012 to 2014

[243 represents 243,000. Except as noted, relates to commercial production for fresh market and processing combined. Includes market garden areas but excludes minor producing acreage in minor producing states. Excludes production for home use in farm and nonfarm gardens. Value is for season or crop year and should not be confused with calendar-year income. Hundredweight (cwt.) is the unit used for fresh market yield and production and is equal to one hundred pounds]

Crop	Area harvested (1,000 acres)			Production (1,000 cwt.)			Value of production (mil. dol.) [1]		
	2012	2013	2014	2012	2013	2014	2012	2013	2014
Beans, snap....................	243	223	227	18,954	17,588	17,309	470	506	393
Fresh market..............	77	73	68	4,340	4,252	3,684	272	293	223
Processed..................	166	150	159	14,614	13,336	13,625	198	213	170
Beans, dry edible.............	1,690	1,316	1,666	31,925	24,576	29,206	1,235	982	1,015
Broccoli.....................	126	132	128	20,472	21,360	20,930	688	914	836
Cabbage [2]...................	57	59	63	19,752	21,750	22,359	359	429	455
Cantaloupes [2]..............	63	69	63	16,706	18,173	14,912	319	320	328
Carrots......................	84	85	86	30,294	31,294	31,815	662	736	709
Cauliflower..................	36	37	38	6,690	6,662	7,053	239	295	351
Celery.......................	29	29	29	19,752	18,003	18,393	359	458	307
Corn, sweet..................	578	543	527	87,097	79,598	76,702	1,112	1,164	1,022
Fresh market..............	217	228	215	27,910	28,561	25,346	735	806	732
Processed..................	360	315	312	59,187	51,037	51,356	377	358	290
Cucumbers...................	123	120	114	17,783	17,066	16,530	369	352	344
Garlic........................	26	24	24	4,319	3,867	3,868	227	232	259
Lettuce, head [2].............	142	129	122	50,976	45,150	44,438	901	1,204	1,119
Lettuce, leaf [2]...............	53	55	54	12,835	12,650	12,984	453	484	502
Lettuce, Romaine [2].........	89	91	85	28,256	26,620	24,679	633	880	789
Onions.......................	147	143	139	71,495	69,654	72,806	942	969	934
Peas, green [3]...............	195	178	188	8,145	7,121	7,257	177	152	133
Peppers, bell................	46	45	47	15,687	14,433	15,346	514	600	618
Spinach......................	42	44	47	6,866	7,393	7,725	237	254	271
Squash......................	42	40	39	7,369	6,149	5,745	234	229	192
Tomatoes....................	377	377	404	292,235	279,021	320,026	1,885	2,316	2,460
Fresh market..............	101	100	98	28,660	26,391	27,280	874	1,178	1,135
Processed..................	276	277	306	263,575	252,630	292,746	1,011	1,138	1,325
Watermelons [2]..............	116	114	109	36,153	36,102	31,952	477	514	431

[1] Fresh market vegetables valued at f.o.b. (free on board) shipping point. Processing vegetables are equivalent returns at packinghouse door. [2] Fresh market only. [3] Processed only.

Source: U.S. Department of Agriculture, National Agricultural Statistics Service, "Quick Stats," <http://quickstats.nass.usda.gov/>, accessed July 2015.

Table 885. Fruits and Nuts: Utilized Production and Value, 2010 to 2014; and Leading Producing States, 2014

[4,603 represents 4,603,000]

Fruits and nuts	Utilized production [1] (1,000 tons)				Value of utilized production (mil. dol.)				Leading states in order of production, 2014
	2010	2012	2013	2014	2010	2012	2013	2014	
FRUITS									
Apples [2].......................	4,603	4,463	5,170	5,594	2,311	3,315	3,133	2,856	WA, NY, MI
Avocados......................	174	(NA)	183	198	479	(NA)	361	351	CA, FL, HI
Blackberries, cultivated (OR)...	22	26	26	23	33	44	42	50	OR
Blueberries....................	247	274	305	334	644	842	799	888	ME, MI, WA
Cherries, sweet...............	308	418	296	359	716	843	772	767	WA, OR, MI
Cranberries...................	340	402	444	412	299	386	287	254	WI, MA, NJ
Dates (CA)....................	29	31	31	29	37	42	37	35	CA
Figs (fresh) (CA).............	41	35	33	32	22	20	20	18	CA
Grapefruit.....................	1,238	1,153	1,204	1,047	291	279	257	242	FL, TX, CA
Grapes (13 states)............	7,430	7,524	8,621	7,760	4,024	5,661	6,136	5,819	CA, WA, NY
Kiwifruit (CA).................	33	27	27	27	25	28	30	33	CA
Lemons.......................	882	850	912	824	395	449	400	641	CA, AZ
Nectarines....................	233	189	162	205	129	145	125	178	CA, WA
Olives (CA)...................	206	160	166	94	137	130	135	73	CA
Oranges......................	8,243	8,982	8,268	6,768	1,997	2,622	2,074	2,254	FL, CA, TX
Peaches......................	1,130	956	889	838	617	618	548	629	CA, SC, GA
Pears.........................	813	851	877	831	387	433	431	457	WA, OR, CA
Plums (CA)...................	142	115	93	113	79	80	62	103	CA
Prunes (dried basis) (CA).....	390	436	255	312	176	184	170	233	CA
Plums and prunes (fresh) [3].....	11	12	13	15	5	6	6	7	OR, WA, ID
Raspberries...................	75	84	92	113	259	290	343	526	CA, WA, OR
Strawberries..................	1,426	1,526	1,524	1,511	2,261	2,453	2,609	2,865	CA, FL, OR
Tangelos (FL).................	41	52	45	40	7	14	13	10	FL
Tangerines and mandarins.....	596	644	682	732	275	349	426	557	CA, FL, AZ
NUTS [4]									
Almonds (CA).................	1,414	1,655	1,733	1,546	2,903	4,817	6,385	5,892	CA
Hazelnuts (OR)...............	28	36	45	36	67	65	121	130	OR
Macadamia nuts (HI)...........	20	22	21	23	30	35	36	40	HI
Pecans (11 states).............	147	151	133	132	675	476	460	517	GA, NM, TX
Pistachios (CA)...............	261	276	235	257	1,159	1,438	1,636	1,593	CA
Walnuts (CA).................	504	497	492	570	1,028	1,506	1,825	1,841	CA

NA Not available. [1] Excludes quantities not harvested or not marketed. Utilized production is the amount sold plus the quantities used at home or held in storage. [2] Production in commercial orchards with 100 or more bearing-age trees. [3] Idaho, Michigan, Oregon and Washington. [4] In-shell equivalent.

Source: U.S. Department of Agriculture, National Agricultural Statistics Service, *Noncitrus Fruits and Nuts Final Estimates 2007-2012*, October 2014; *Citrus Fruits Final Estimates, 2008-2012*, August 2014; *Citrus Fruits 2015 Summary*, September 2015; and *Noncitrus Fruits and Nuts 2014 Summary*, July 2015. See also <http://www.nass.usda.gov/Publications/index.asp>.

Table 886. Nuts—Supply and Use: 2000 to 2013

[In thousands of pounds (shelled) (331,466 represents 331,466,000). Season begins in July for hazelnuts, August for almonds, September for pistachios, and October for pecans. For walnuts, season began in August through 2007; as of 2008, season begins September 1]

Year	Beginning stocks	Marketable production [1]	Imports	Supply, total	Consumption	Exports	Ending stocks
Total nuts: [2]							
2000	331,466	1,127,940	293,172	1,752,577	733,921	780,988	237,669
2010	422,217	2,482,242	487,969	3,392,428	1,199,062	1,786,058	407,308
2011	407,308	2,787,216	444,896	3,639,419	1,182,407	1,976,931	480,082
2012	480,082	2,762,569	512,250	3,754,901	1,313,353	1,979,483	462,065
2013, total [2, 3]	462,065	2,831,096	162,611	3,455,772	994,663	1,955,222	505,886
Almonds	317,226	1,971,002	35,277	2,323,505	636,355	1,336,586	350,564
Pecans	48,106	(NA)	86,704	265,578	109,293	78,190	78,095
Pistachios	55,102	237,582	550	293,235	56,760	197,495	38,980
Hazelnuts	882	36,673	14,602	52,158	16,204	32,031	3,922
Walnuts	40,749	436,444	11,834	489,028	148,092	306,611	34,325

NA Not available. [1] Utilized production minus inedibles and noncommercial usage. [2] Includes macadamia nuts, Brazil nuts, cashew nuts, pine nuts, chestnuts, and mixed nuts not shown separately. [3] Data are preliminary.

Source: U.S. Department of Agriculture, Economic Research Service, "Fruit and Tree Nut Yearbook Tables," <http://www.ers.usda.gov/data-products/fruit-and-tree-nut-data/yearbook-tables.aspx>, accessed September 2015. See also <http://www.ers.usda.gov/topics/crops/fruit-tree-nuts.aspx>.

Table 887. Honey—Number of Bee Colonies, Yield, and Production: 1990 to 2014

[3,220 represents 3,220,000. Includes only beekeepers with five or more colonies. Colonies were not included if honey was not harvested]

Year	Honey-producing colonies [1] (1,000)	Yield per colony (pounds)	Production (1,000 pounds)	Average price per pound (cents)	Value of production (1,000 dollars)
1990	3,220	61.7	198,674	54	106,688
1995	2,655	79.5	211,073	69	144,585
2000	2,622	84.0	220,286	60	132,865
2005	2,409	72.5	174,614	92	160,994
2010	2,692	65.6	176,462	162	285,692
2012	2,539	56.0	142,296	199	283,454
2013	2,640	56.6	149,499	214	320,077
2014	2,740	65.1	178,270	216	385,241

[1] Honey producing colonies are the maximum number of colonies from which honey was taken during the year. It is possible to take honey from colonies which did not survive the entire year.

Source: U.S. Department of Agriculture, National Agricultural Statistics Service, *Honey–Final Estimates 2008-2012*, September 2014, and earlier editions; and *Honey*, March 2015. See also <http://www.nass.usda.gov/Surveys/Guide_to_NASS_Surveys/Bee_and_Honey>.

Table 888. Vegetables and Dry Edible Beans—Supply and Utilization: 2000 to 2014

[40,556 represents 40,556,000,000. Data for calendar year except where noted. Vegetable data excludes melons]

Item	Unit	2000	2005	2010	2011	2012	2013	2014 [1]
VEGETABLES, FRESH MARKET								
Production	Mil. lbs.	40,556	40,332	37,918	37,543	38,200	36,905	36,862
Imports	Mil. lbs.	5,492	7,773	10,924	11,086	11,479	11,893	12,629
Total supply	Mil. lbs.	47,393	49,597	50,411	50,118	51,256	50,137	50,842
Exports	Mil. lbs.	3,709	3,712	3,382	3,435	3,538	3,484	3,350
Ending stocks	Mil. lbs.	1,266	1,280	1,488	1,578	1,338	1,351	1,625
Domestic consumption	Mil. lbs.	41,461	43,864	44,708	44,295	45,643	44,583	45,190
Per capita consumption	Lbs.	146.8	148.1	144.3	141.9	145.2	140.7	141.6
VEGETABLES, PROCESSED MARKET [2]								
Production	Mil. lbs.	35,369	33,265	36,559	35,358	37,886	35,801	39,887
Imports	Mil. lbs.	3,581	5,555	6,357	6,507	6,634	6,474	6,600
Total supply	Mil. lbs.	62,174	62,646	71,274	69,864	71,502	70,073	72,115
Exports	Mil. lbs.	4,479	4,889	6,627	8,140	8,121	9,733	10,661
Ending stocks	Mil. lbs.	23,291	20,838	27,999	26,982	27,798	25,629	25,928
Domestic consumption	Mil. lbs.	34,404	36,919	36,648	34,741	35,583	34,711	35,526
Per capita consumption	Lbs.	121.8	124.6	118.3	111.3	113.2	109.6	111.3
POTATOES, FRESH MARKET								
Utilized production [3]	Mil. lbs.	13,185	12,076	11,342	10,534	11,010	11,156	10,794
Imports	Mil. lbs.	806	788	916	1,084	778	861	1,028
Total supply	Mil. lbs.	13,990	12,863	12,258	11,618	11,788	12,018	11,822
Exports	Mil. lbs.	677	639	856	990	987	1,056	922
Domestic consumption	Mil. lbs.	13,314	12,224	11,402	10,628	10,802	10,962	10,900
Per capita consumption	Lbs.	47.2	41.3	36.8	34.1	34.4	34.8	34.4
DRY EDIBLE BEANS								
Production	Mil. lbs.	2,654	2,658	3,180	1,989	3,193	2,460	2,921
Imports	Mil. lbs.	128	228	287	319	306	260	286
Exports	Mil. lbs.	814	576	916	909	1,141	988	1,071
Domestic consumption	Mil. lbs.	2,143	1,795	2,171	1,769	1,977	1,828	2,024
Per capita consumption	Lbs.	7.6	6.1	7.0	5.7	6.3	5.8	6.3

[1] Preliminary. [2] Includes vegetables for canning and freezing. Excludes potatoes and mushrooms. [3] Crop year utilization for the past season and the current season distributed on a calendar year basis using National Agricultural Statistics Service potato marketing distributions.

Source: U.S. Department of Agriculture, Economic Research Service, *Vegetable and Pulses Yearbook*, March 2015. See also <http://www.ers.usda.gov/data-products/vegetables-and-pulses-data.aspx>.

Table 889. Horticultural Specialty Crop Operations, Value of Sales, and Total Land Area Used to Grow Horticultural Crops: 2009

[Horticultural specialty operation is defined as any place that produced and sold $10,000 or more of horticultural specialty products]

Item	Operations	Value of sales (1,000)	Total land area [1]			
			Green-houses (1,000 square feet)	Shade structures (1,000 square feet)	Natural shade (acres)	Area in open (acres)
Horticultural specialty crops, total [2]	**21,585**	**11,687,323**	**859,063**	**406,072**	**8,160**	**572,269**
Annual bedding/garden plants	7,989	2,305,913	258,823	13,858	140	6,815
Herbaceous perennial plants	6,416	843,788	27,101	4,330	314	3,981
Potted flowering plants for indoor or patio use	4,043	871,474	62,208	23,893	41	1,693
Foliage plants for indoor or patio use	2,728	509,873	39,583	76,645	144	2,314
Cut flowers	1,703	403,254	53,495	14,248	76	12,068
Cut cultivated greens	634	84,148	5,443	152,512	2,835	2,998
Nursery stock sold	8,441	3,850,363	217,482	87,228	4,184	323,539
Propagative material [3]	1,178	601,657	29,733	3,208	53	8,169
Sod, sprigs, or plugs	1,403	876,847	419	36	(D)	85,842
Dried bulbs, corms, rhizomes, and tubers	223	48,512	183	(D)	(D)	3,736
Food crops grown under protection	1,476	553,270	61,324	1,562	19	5,863
Transplants for commercial vegetable production [4]	502	330,647	32,095	467	4	7,250
Vegetable seeds	340	89,031	163	(D)	–	38,819
Flower seeds	141	30,825	289	308	2	5,695
Aquatic plants	375	26,000	1,373	134	1	1,320
Cut Christmas trees	2,699	249,821	1,010	95	84	45,091
Other	212	11,901	68,340	27,519	227	17,075

D Withheld to avoid disclosure. – Represents zero. [1] Total land area represents the land utilized on the operation as the area used for horticultural production. Includes volume of stacked benches and stacked pots and the area used to produce multiple crop types. [2] Excludes acres in production for Christmas trees or sod, sprigs, or plugs. [3] Includes cuttings, liners, tissue cultured plantlets, and prefinished plants. [4] Includes strawberries.

Source: U.S. Department of Agriculture, National Agricultural Statistics Service, *2009 Census of Horticultural Specialties*, Vol. 3, AC-07-SS-3. See also <http://www.agcensus.usda.gov/Publications/Census_of_Horticulture_Specialties/>.

Table 890. Meat Supply and Consumption: 2000 to 2014

[In millions of pounds (carcass weight equivalent) (82,372 represents 82,372,000,000). Carcass weight equivalent is the weight of the animal minus entrails, head, hide, and internal organs; includes fat and bone. Covers federal and state inspected, and farm slaughtered]

Year and type of meat	Production	Imports	Supply [1]	Exports	Consumption [2]	Ending stocks
RED MEAT AND POULTRY						
2000	82,372	4,144	88,460	9,343	77,073	2,044
2005	86,783	4,856	93,787	9,274	82,328	2,185
2010	91,769	3,459	97,222	13,961	81,147	2,113
2011	92,387	3,151	97,651	15,773	79,914	1,965
2012	92,598	3,312	97,876	16,004	79,663	2,208
2013	92,950	3,449	98,607	15,802	80,664	2,142
2014 [3]	91,855	4,297	98,294	15,656	80,572	2,066
RED MEATS, TOTAL						
2000	46,299	4,127	51,313	3,760	46,556	996
2005	45,849	4,803	51,805	3,373	47,367	1,066
2010	49,180	3,323	53,617	6,538	45,934	1,145
2011	49,346	3,022	53,513	8,000	44,351	1,162
2012	49,549	3,175	53,886	7,843	44,783	1,260
2013	49,273	3,302	53,835	7,589	45,016	1,230
2014 [3]	47,441	4,149	52,820	7,438	44,192	1,190
Beef:						
2000	26,888	3,032	30,332	2,468	27,338	525
2005	24,787	3,599	29,022	697	27,754	571
2010	26,412	2,298	29,275	2,300	26,390	585
2011	26,281	2,057	28,923	2,785	25,538	600
2012	25,995	2,220	28,815	2,452	25,755	608
2013	25,790	2,250	28,648	2,590	25,475	584
2014 [3]	24,320	2,947	27,850	2,573	24,686	591
Pork:						
2000	18,952	965	20,378	1,287	18,639	453
2005	20,705	1,024	22,239	2,666	19,093	480
2010	22,456	859	23,840	4,223	19,077	541
2011	22,775	803	24,120	5,196	18,382	542
2012	23,268	802	24,612	5,380	18,607	625
2013	23,204	880	24,709	4,992	19,099	618
2014 [3]	22,861	1,007	24,486	4,858	19,069	559
Veal:						
2000	225	(NA)	230	(NA)	225	5
2005	165	(NA)	169	(NA)	164	5
2010	145	(NA)	154	(NA)	150	4
2011	136	(NA)	140	(NA)	137	3
2012	125	(NA)	128	(NA)	123	5
2013	117	(NA)	123	(NA)	119	4
2014 [3]	100	(NA)	104	(NA)	98	6
Lamb and mutton:						
2000	234	130	372	5	354	13
2005	191	180	375	9	356	10
2010	168	166	348	16	317	15
2011	153	162	331	19	295	17
2012	161	154	331	11	299	21
2013	161	173	355	7	324	25
2014 [3]	161	195	380	7	340	34
POULTRY, TOTAL						
2000	36,073	16	37,147	5,583	30,516	1,048
2005	40,935	54	41,981	5,902	34,961	1,119
2010	42,589	136	43,605	7,423	35,214	968
2011	43,040	129	44,138	7,773	35,562	803
2012	43,049	137	43,989	8,161	34,879	949
2013	43,678	146	44,772	8,213	35,648	912
2014 [3]	44,414	148	45,474	8,218	36,379	876
Broilers:						
2000	30,209	13	31,017	4,918	25,302	798
2005	34,986	42	35,730	5,203	29,617	910
2010	36,515	107	37,238	6,762	29,703	773
2011	36,804	107	37,684	6,978	30,116	590
2012	36,643	111	37,345	7,274	29,420	651
2013	37,425	122	38,198	7,345	30,184	669
2014 [3]	38,137	117	38,923	7,304	30,939	680
Mature chicken:						
2000	531	2	541	220	312	9
2005	516	3	522	130	390	2
2010	504	4	510	79	427	4
2011	521	2	527	93	433	2
2012	517	2	521	90	430	1
2013	523	2	526	108	412	6
2014 [3]	521	2	529	110	416	3
Turkeys:						
2000	5,333	1	5,589	445	4,902	241
2005	5,432	9	5,730	570	4,954	206
2010	5,570	25	5,857	581	5,084	192
2011	5,715	21	5,927	703	5,013	211
2012	5,889	24	6,123	797	5,030	296
2013	5,729	22	6,048	759	5,051	237
2014 [3]	5,756	29	6,022	804	5,024	193

NA Not available. [1] Total supply equals production plus imports plus ending stocks of previous year. [2] Includes shipments to territories. [3] Preliminary data.

Source: U.S. Department of Agriculture, Economic Research Service, "Livestock and Meat Domestic Data," <http://www.ers.usda.gov/data-products/livestock-meat-domestic-data.aspx>, accessed June 2015.

Table 891. Livestock Inventory and Production: 1990 to 2014

[95.8 represents 95,800,000. Production in live weight; includes animals-for-slaughter market, younger animals shipped to other states for feeding or breeding purposes, farm slaughter and custom slaughter consumed on farms where produced, minus livestock shipped into States for feeding or breeding with an adjustment for changes in inventory]

Type of livestock	Unit	1990	1995	2000	2005	2009	2010	2011	2012	2013	2014
ALL CATTLE [1]											
Inventory (number on farms): [2]	Mil.	95.8	102.8	98.2	95.0	94.7	94.1	92.9	91.2	90.1	88.5
Total value	Bil. dol.	59.0	63.2	67.1	87.0	82.4	78.2	87.8	100.8	101.7	108.3
Value per head	Dol.	616	615	683	916	872	832	947	1,111	1,139	1,223
Production: Quantity	Bil. lb.	39.2	42.5	43.0	41.2	41.0	41.4	41.5	40.9	40.7	40.3
Cattle, price per 100 pounds [3]	Dol.	(NA)	(NA)	68.4	89.6	80.4	92.0	113.0	122.0	125.0	153.0
Calves, price per 100 pounds	Dol.	95.6	73.1	104.0	135.0	108.0	121.0	142.0	173.0	174.0	255.0
Value of production	Bil. dol.	29.3	24.7	28.5	36.3	31.9	36.9	45.1	48.1	48.5	60.8
HOGS AND PIGS											
Inventory (number on farms): [4]	Mil.	53.8	59.7	59.3	61.0	67.0	64.7	64.7	66.3	66.2	64.8
Total value	Bil. dol.	4.3	3.2	4.3	6.3	6.0	5.4	6.9	8.1	7.7	8.9
Value per head	Dol.	79	53	72	103	89	83	106	123	116	138
Production: Quantity	Bil. lb.	21.3	24.4	25.7	27.4	31.2	30.3	30.8	32.1	32.6	32.0
Price per 100 pounds	Dol.	53.7	40.5	42.3	49.6	42.0	55.1	66.5	64.2	67.2	77.1
Value of production	Bil. dol.	11.3	9.8	10.8	13.6	12.5	16.0	20.0	20.3	21.7	24.2
SHEEP AND LAMBS											
Inventory (number on farms): [2]	Mil.	11.4	9.0	7.0	6.1	5.7	5.6	5.5	5.4	5.3	5.2
Total value	Mil. dol.	901	671	670	798	765	761	931	1,185	946	984
Value per head	Dol.	79	93	95	130	133	135	170	221	177	188
Production: Quantity	Mil. lb.	781	602	512	472	422	405	(NA)	(NA)	(NA)	(NA)
Value of production	Mil. dol.	374	414	365	451	365	443	(NA)	(NA)	(NA)	(NA)

NA Not available. [1] Includes milk cows. [2] As of January 1. [3] Cattle weighing 500 pounds or more. [4] As of December 1 of preceding year.

Source: U.S. Department of Agriculture, National Agricultural Statistics Service, "Quick Stats," <http://quickstats.nass.usda.gov/>, accessed May 2015. See also <http://www.nass.usda.gov/Publications/index.asp>.

Table 892. Livestock Operations by Size of Herd: 2000 to 2012

[In thousands (1,076 represents 1,076,000). An operation is any place having one or more head on hand at any time during the year]

Size of herd	2000	2010	2011	2012	Size of herd	2000	2010	2011	2012
CATTLE [1]					**MILK COWS** [2]				
Total operations	1,076	935	922	913	Total operations	105	63	60	64
1 to 49 head	671	635	627	637	1 to 49 head	53	31	30	34
50 to 99 head	186	129	127	118	50 to 99 head	31	16	15	15
100 to 499 head	192	142	139	130	100 head or more	21	16	16	14
500 to 999 head	19	19	19	17					
1,000 head or more	10	11	11	11	**HOGS AND PIGS**				
					Total operations	87	69	69	63
BEEF COWS [2]					1 to 99 head	50	49	49	47
Total operations	831	742	734	728	100 to 499 head	17	5	5	4
1 to 49 head	655	588	583	594	500 to 999 head	8	3	2	2
50 to 99 head	100	82	81	71	1,000 to 1,999 head	6	4	3	3
100 to 499 head	71	66	64	57	2,000 to 4,999 head	5	5	6	5
500 head or more	6	6	6	6	5,000 head or more	2	3	3	3

[1] Includes calves. [2] Included in operations with cattle.

Source: U.S. Department of Agriculture, National Agricultural Statistics Service, *Livestock Operations Final Estimates 2003–2007*, March 2009; and *Farms, Land in Farms, and Livestock Operations 2012 Summary*, February 2013. Beginning with 2012 data, *2012 Census of Agriculture*, Vol. 1, May 2014. See also <http://www.agcensus.usda.gov/Publications/index.php>.

Table 893. Hogs and Pigs—Number, Production, and Slaughter by Leading States: 2012 to 2014

[66,224 represents 66,224,000. Production in live weight. See headnote Table 891]

State	Number on farms [1] (1,000)			Quantity produced (mil. lb.)			Value of production (mil. dol.)			Commercial slaughter [2] (mil. lb.)	
	2012	2013	2014	2012	2013	2014	2012	2013	2014	2013	2014
U.S. [3]	66,224	64,775	66,145	32,061	32,620	32,012	20,285	21,666	24,153	30,964	30,431
IA	20,600	20,200	20,900	10,345	11,170	11,549	6,174	6,891	8,018	8,185	8,197
NC	8,900	8,500	8,600	3,926	4,057	3,558	2,553	2,824	2,854	3,226	(D)
MN	7,650	7,800	7,900	3,939	3,912	3,785	2,410	2,523	2,784	2,787	2,671
IL	4,600	4,550	4,600	1,963	2,001	1,949	1,361	1,455	1,611	3,025	3,008
IN	3,800	3,650	3,600	1,753	1,644	1,640	1,081	1,057	1,199	2,299	2,301
NE	3,000	3,050	3,100	1,240	1,177	1,188	843	845	1,005	2,076	2,015
MO	2,750	2,750	2,750	1,314	1,309	1,482	905	960	1,201	2,386	2,450

D Data withheld to limit disclosure. [1] As of December 1. [2] Includes slaughter in federally inspected and other slaughter plants; excludes animals slaughtered on farms. [3] Includes other states, not shown separately.

Source: U.S. Department of Agriculture, National Agricultural Statistics Service, *Meat Animals Production, Disposition and Income Final Estimates 2008-2012*, October 2014; *Meat Animals Production, Disposition and Income 2014 Summary*, April 2015; and *Livestock Slaughter 2014 Summary*, April 2015. See also <http://www.nass.usda.gov/Publications/index.asp>.

Table 894. Cattle and Calves—Number, Production, and Value by Leading States: 2012 to 2015

[90,095 represents 90,095,000. Includes milk cows. See headnote, Table 891]

State	Number on farms [1] (1,000)			Production (mil. lb.)			Value of production (mil. dol.)			Commercial slaughter [2] (mil. lb.)	
	2013	2014	2015	2012	2013	2014	2012	2013	2014	2013	2014
U.S. [3]	90,095	88,526	89,800	40,920	40,695	40,280	48,060	48,479	60,770	42,559	40,045
TX	11,600	11,100	11,800	6,219	6,147	6,006	7,424	7,537	9,197	7,416	6,771
NE	6,400	6,250	6,300	5,079	5,050	5,124	5,820	5,861	7,414	9,390	9,300
KS	5,850	5,800	6,000	3,807	3,748	3,707	4,216	4,168	4,687	8,302	7,856
CA	5,300	5,250	5,150	2,113	2,039	1,895	2,319	2,275	2,630	2,249	1,771
OK	4,200	4,300	4,600	2,079	2,012	2,029	2,571	2,581	3,295	23	23
MO	3,700	3,850	4,000	1,170	1,125	1,170	1,593	1,569	2,120	61	63
IA	3,900	3,800	3,900	1,879	1,891	1,909	2,202	2,274	2,854	(D)	(D)
SD	3,850	3,700	3,700	1,531	1,480	1,524	1,953	1,938	2,539	(D)	(D)
WI	3,500	3,400	3,500	1,113	1,242	1,263	1,292	1,444	1,918	2,146	1,824
CO	2,650	2,550	2,600	1,763	1,746	1,583	2,140	2,162	2,410	3,457	3,343
MT	2,600	2,550	2,500	1,054	1,113	1,116	1,264	1,359	1,776	24	24

D Data withheld to limit disclosure. [1] As of January 1. [2] Data cover cattle only. Includes slaughter in federally inspected and other slaughter plants; excludes animals slaughtered on farms. [3] Includes other states, not shown separately.

Source: U.S. Department of Agriculture, National Agricultural Statistics Service, *Meat Animals Production, Disposition and Income Final Estimates 2008-2012*, October 2014; *Meat Animals Production, Disposition and Income 2014 Summary*, April 2015; and *Livestock Slaughter 2014 Summary*, April 2015. See also <http://www.nass.usda.gov/Publications/index.asp>.

Table 895. Milk Cows—Number, Production, and Value by Leading States: 2012 to 2014

[9,237 represents 9,237,000]

State	Number on farms [1] (1,000)			Milk produced on farms [2] (mil. lb.)			Milk produced per milk cow (pounds) [2]			Value of production [3] (mil. dol.)		
	2012	2013	2014	2012	2013	2014	2012	2013	2014	2012	2013	2014
U.S. [4]	9,237	9,224	9,257	200,642	201,231	206,046	21,722	21,816	22,258	37,248	40,477	49,585
CA	1,782	1,780	1,780	41,801	41,256	42,337	23,457	23,178	23,785	6,906	7,624	9,365
WI	1,270	1,271	1,271	27,224	27,572	27,795	21,436	21,693	21,869	5,281	5,597	6,810
NY	610	610	615	13,190	13,463	13,733	21,623	22,070	22,330	2,559	2,854	3,488
ID	580	573	575	13,558	13,431	13,873	23,376	23,440	24,127	2,427	2,579	3,205
PA	536	533	530	10,478	10,552	10,683	19,549	19,797	20,157	2,096	2,279	2,746
TX	436	437	463	9,596	9,610	10,310	22,009	21,991	22,268	1,794	1,960	2,536
MN	465	464	460	9,073	9,138	9,127	19,512	19,694	19,841	1,778	1,864	2,263
MI	375	380	390	8,991	9,164	9,609	23,976	24,116	24,638	1,699	1,879	2,316
NM	330	323	323	8,149	8,057	8,105	24,694	24,944	25,093	1,418	1,515	1,807

[1] Average number during year. Represents cows and heifers that have calved, kept for milk; excluding heifers not yet fresh. [2] Excludes milk sucked by calves. [3] Valued at average returns per 100 pounds of milk in combined marketings of milk and cream. Includes value of milk fed to calves. [4] Includes other states, not shown separately.

Source: U.S. Department of Agriculture, National Agricultural Statistics Service, *Milk Disposition and Income Final Estimates 2008-2012*, October 2014, and earlier reports; *Milk Cows and Production, Final Estimates 2008-2012*, September 2014, and earlier reports; and *Milk: Production, Disposition, and Income 2014 Summary*, April 2015, and earlier reports. See also <http://www.nass.usda.gov/Publications/index.asp>.

Table 896. Milk Production and Manufactured Dairy Products: 1990 to 2014

[193 represents 193,000]

Item	Unit	1990	2000	2005	2009	2010	2011	2012	2013	2014
Number of farms with milk cows	**1,000**	**193**	**105**	**78**	**65**	**63**	**60**	**58**	**(NA)**	**(NA)**
Cows and heifers that have calved, kept for milk	Mil. head	10.0	9.2	9.1	9.2	9.1	9.2	9.2	9.2	9.3
Milk produced on farms	Bil. lb.	148	167	177	189	193	196	201	201	206
Production per cow	1,000 lb.	14.8	18.2	19.6	20.6	21.1	21.3	21.7	21.8	22.3
Milk marketed by producers [1]	Bil. lb.	146	166	176	188	192	195	200	200	205
Value of milk produced	Bil. dol.	20.4	20.7	26.9	24.5	31.5	39.7	37.2	40.5	49.6
Cash receipts from marketing of milk and cream [1]	Bil. dol.	20.1	20.6	26.7	24.3	31.4	39.5	37.1	40.3	49.3
Number of dairy manufacturing plants	**Number**	**1,723**	**1,164**	**1,088**	**1,203**	**1,250**	**1,278**	**1,281**	**1,265**	**1,267**
Manufactured dairy products:										
Butter (including whey butter)	Mil. lb.	1,302	1,256	1,347	1,572	1,564	1,810	1,860	1,863	1,856
Cheese, total [2]	Mil. lb.	6,059	8,258	9,149	10,074	10,433	10,595	10,886	11,102	11,450
American (excl. full-skim American)	Mil. lb.	2,894	3,642	3,808	4,203	4,289	4,267	4,355	4,420	4,534
Cream and Neufchatel	Mil. lb.	431	687	715	767	745	715	808	842	852
All Italian varieties	Mil. lb.	2,207	3,289	3,803	4,181	4,416	4,585	4,633	4,735	4,950
Cottage cheese—creamed and lowfat	Mil. lb.	832	735	784	731	719	704	709	678	671
Nonfat dry milk [3]	Mil. lb.	902	1,457	1,210	1,512	1,563	1,499	1,764	1,478	1,765
Dry whey [4]	Mil. lb.	1,143	1,188	1,041	1,001	1,013	1,010	999	953	870
Yogurt, plain and fruit-flavored	Mil. lb.	(NA)	1,837	3,058	3,839	4,181	4,271	4,417	4,715	4,757
Ice cream, regular	Mil. gal.	824	980	960	918	929	888	1,052	897	872
Ice cream, lowfat [5]	Mil. gal.	352	373	360	400	415	415	669	401	412

NA Not available. [1] Comprises sales to plants and dealers, and retail sales by farmers direct to consumers. [2] Includes varieties not shown separately. [3] Includes dry skim milk for animal feed through 2000. [4] Includes animal but excludes modified whey production. [5] Includes freezer-made milkshake in most states.

Source: U.S. Department of Agriculture, National Agricultural Statistics Service, *Milk Disposition and Income Final Estimates 2008-2012*, October 2014, and earlier reports; *Dairy Products 2014 Summary*, April 2015, and earlier reports; *Milk Production, Disposition, and Income 2014 Summary*, April 2015, and earlier reports; and *Farms, Land in Farms, And Livestock Operations, 2012 Summary*, February 2013, and earlier reports. See also <http://www.nass.usda.gov/Publications/index.asp>.

Table 897. Milk Production and Commercial Use in All Products: 2000 to 2014

[In billions of pounds milkfat basis (167.4 represents 167,400,000,000) except as noted]

Year	Produc-tion	Farm use	Commercial Farm market-ings	Commercial Begin-ning stocks	Imports	Com-mercial supply, total	Commercial USDA net removals	Commercial Ending stocks[1]	Disap-pear-ance	Milk price per 100 pounds[2] (dollars)
2000......	167.4	1.3	166.1	6.1	4.5	176.7	0.8	6.8	169.0	12.40
2005......	176.9	1.1	175.8	7.1	7.4	190.3	–	7.9	182.5	15.19
2008......	190.0	1.1	188.9	10.3	5.3	204.5	–	10.0	194.5	18.45
2009......	189.3	1.0	188.3	10.0	5.6	203.9	0.9	11.2	191.7	12.93
2010......	192.9	1.0	191.9	11.2	4.1	207.2	0.3	10.8	196.1	16.26
2011......	196.3	1.0	195.3	10.8	3.5	209.6	–	10.9	198.7	20.14
2012......	200.6	1.0	199.7	10.9	4.1	214.7	–	12.2	202.5	18.50
2013......	201.2	1.0	200.3	12.2	3.7	216.2	–	11.2	205.0	18.50
2014......	206.0	1.0	205.1	11.2	4.3	220.6	–	11.2	209.3	18.50

– Represents or rounds to zero. [1] Includes commercial stocks of butter, cheese, nonfat dry milk, and dry whole milk. [2] Wholesale price received by farmers for all milk delivered to plants and dealers.

Source: U.S. Department of Agriculture, Economic Research Service, "Dairy Data," <http://www.ers.usda.gov/data-products/dairy-data.aspx>, accessed June 2015.

Table 898. Broiler Chicken, Turkey, and Egg Production: 1990 to 2014

[353 represents 353,000,000. For years ending November 30, except as noted]

Item	Unit	1990	1995	2000	2005	2009	2010	2011	2012	2013	2014
Chickens:[1]											
Number[2]...............	Million	353	388	437	456	455	457	454	467	475	479
Value per head[2]........	Dollars	2.29	2.41	2.44	2.52	3.32	3.58	3.79	4.04	4.15	4.10
Value, total[2]............	Mil. dol.	808	935	1,064	1,150	1,510	1,637	1,722	1,886	1,972	1,962
Number sold............	Million	208	180	218	194	176	173	182	179	186	188
Value of sales...........	Mil. dol.	94	60	64	65	65	73	81	79	88	97
PRODUCTION											
Broilers:[3]											
Number.................	Million	5,864	7,326	8,284	8,872	8,550	8,624	8,608	8,463	8,534	8,544
Weight.................	Bil. lb.	25.6	34.2	41.6	47.9	47.8	49.2	50.1	49.7	50.7	51.4
Production value........	Mil. dol.	8,366	11,762	13,989	20,878	21,823	23,692	22,988	24,828	30,762	32,725
Turkeys:[4]											
Number.................	Million	282	292	270	250	247	244	249	254	240	238
Weight.................	Bil. lb.	6.0	6.8	7.0	7.0	7.1	7.1	7.3	7.6	7.3	7.2
Production value........	Mil. dol.	2,393	2,769	2,828	3,108	3,573	4,372	4,988	5,452	4,840	5,305
Eggs:											
Average number of layers.................	Thousand	270,946	294,350	329,067	345,027	338,846	341,505	340,598	344,844	354,844	360,873
Eggs per layer..........	Number	251	254	257	262	268	269	271	274	275	277
Total production........	Billion	68.1	74.8	84.7	90.3	90.7	91.8	92.5	94.4	97.6	99.8
Production value........	Mil. dol.	4,021	3,893	4,359	4,067	6,191	6,553	7,356	7,929	8,679	10,166

[1] Excludes commercial broilers. [2] As of December 1. [3] Young chickens of the heavy breeds and other meat-type birds, to be marketed at 2-5 lbs. live weight and from which no pullets are kept for egg production. Not included in sales of chickens. [4] Data for turkeys are for year ending August 31.

Source: U.S. Department of Agriculture, National Agricultural Statistics Service, *Turkeys Final Estimates 1998–2002*, April 2004; *Poultry Production and Value Final Estimates 2008-2012*, October 2014, and earlier reports; *Chickens and Eggs Final Estimates 2008-2012*, September 2014, and earlier reports; *Poultry—Production and Value*, annual; and *Chickens and Eggs*, annual. See also <http://www.nass.usda.gov/Publications/index.asp>.

Table 899. Broiler Chickens and Turkey Production by Leading States: 2012 to 2014

[In millions of pounds, live weight production (49,656 represents 49,656,000,000)]

State	Broiler chickens 2012	2013	2014	Turkeys 2012	2013	2014	State	Broiler chickens 2012	2013	2014	Turkeys 2012	2013	2014
U.S.[1].....	49,656	50,678	51,373	7,562	7,278	7,217	MO......	1,304	1,332	1,385	583	544	1,178
AL..........	5,620	5,872	6,051	(NA)	(NA)	(NA)	NC......	5,677	5,900	6,044	1,192	1,139	544
AR..........	5,758	5,978	6,013	577	560	612	OH......	379	405	431	217	233	998
CA..........	(NA)	(NA)	(NA)	426	365	310	OK......	1,341	1,360	1,335	(NA)	(NA)	(NA)
DE..........	1,505	1,531	1,733	(NA)	(NA)	(NA)	PA.......	962	956	997	169	171	209
FL..........	357	393	387	(NA)	(NA)	(NA)	SC......	1,537	1,587	1,651	493	479	176
GA..........	7,626	7,607	7,548	(NA)	(NA)	(NA)	SD......	(NA)	(NA)	(NA)	193	176	189
IN..........	(NA)	(NA)	(NA)	614	663	754	TN......	872	949	939	(NA)	(NA)	(NA)
KY..........	1,733	1,671	1,725	(NA)	(NA)	(NA)	TX......	3,495	3,600	3,551	(NA)	(NA)	(NA)
MD........	1,605	1,618	1,554	(NA)	(NA)	(NA)	UT......	(NA)	(NA)	(NA)	106	109	97
MI..........	(NA)	(NA)	(NA)	(NA)	211	436	VA......	1,307	1,351	1,441	442	403	444
MN..........	271	284	281	1,168	1,126	206	WV......	376	385	372	89	81	82
MS..........	4,508	4,478	4,509	(NA)	(NA)	(NA)	WI.......	222	216	224	(NA)	(NA)	(NA)

NA Not available. [1] Includes other states, not shown separately.

Source: U.S. Department of Agriculture, National Agricultural Statistics Service, *Poultry—Production and Value Final Estimates 2008-2012*, October 2014, and earlier reports; and *Poultry—Production and Value*, April 2015, and earlier reports. See also <http://www.nass.usda.gov/Publications/index.asp>.

Forestry, Fishing, and Mining

This section presents data on the area, ownership, production, trade, reserves, and disposition of natural resources, defined here as including forestry, fisheries, and mining and mineral products.

Forestry—This section presents data on the area, ownership, and timber resource of commercial timberland; forestry statistics covering the National Forests and Forest Service cooperative programs; product data for lumber, pulpwood, woodpulp, paper and paperboard; and similar data.

The principal sources of data relating to forests and forest products are *Forest Resources of the United States, 2012; Timber Demand and Technology Assessment; U.S. Timber Production, Trade, Consumption, and Price Statistics, 1965 to 2011; Land Areas of the National Forest System*, issued annually by the Forest Service of the U.S. Department of Agriculture; *Agricultural Statistics* issued by the Department of Agriculture; and reports of the Annual Survey of Manufactures issued by the U.S. Census Bureau, see <http://www.census.gov/manufacturing/asm/>. Further sources used in this section and issued by the U.S. Census Bureau include the annual *County Business Patterns* reports, and the 2012 Economic Census. Additional information is published in the annual *Wood Pulp and Fiber Statistics* and *The Annual Statistics of Paper, Paperboard, and Wood Pulp* of the American Forest and Paper Association, Washington, DC.

The completeness and reliability of statistics on forests and forest products vary considerably. The data for forest land area and stand volumes are much more reliable for areas that have been recently surveyed than for those for which only estimates are available. In general, more data are available for lumber and other manufactured products such as particle board and softwood panels, etc., than for the primary forest products such as poles and piling and fuelwood.

Fisheries—The principal source of data relating to fisheries is data issued annually by the National Marine Fisheries Service (NMFS), National Oceanic and Atmospheric Administration (NOAA). The NMFS collects and disseminates data on commercial landings of fish and shellfish. Annual reports include quantity and value of commercial landings of fish and shellfish, disposition of landings, and number and kinds of fishing vessels and fishing gear. Reports for the fish-processing industry include annual output for wholesaling, and fish processing establishments and annual and seasonal employment. The principal source for these data is the annual *Fisheries of the United States*. Additional government sources include *Agricultural Statistics*, issued annually by the Department of Agriculture; and *Trout Production, Catfish Production*, and *Catfish Processing*, issued by the National Agricultural Statistics service of the U.S. Department of Agriculture.

Mining and mineral products—This section presents data relating to mineral industries and their products, summary measures of production and employment, and more detailed data on production, prices, imports and exports, consumption, and distribution for specific industries and products. Data on mining and mineral products may also be found in Sections 19, 21, 28, and 30 of this *Abstract*; data on mining employment may be found in Section 12.

Mining comprises the extraction of minerals occurring naturally (coal, ores, crude petroleum, natural gas) and quarrying, well operation, milling, refining and processing, and other preparation customarily done at the mine or well site or as a part of extraction activity. (Mineral preparation plants are usually operated together with mines or quarries.) Exploration for minerals is included as is the development of mineral properties.

The principal governmental sources of these data are the *Minerals Yearbook* and *Mineral Commodity Summaries*, published by the U.S. Geological Survey, U.S. Department of the Interior, and various monthly and annual publications of the Energy Information Administration, U.S. Department of Energy. See text, Section 19, for a list of Department of Energy publications.

Mineral statistics, with principal emphasis on commodity detail, have been collected by the U.S. Geological Survey and the former Bureau of Mines since 1880. Current data in U.S. Geological Survey publications include quantity and value of nonfuel minerals produced, sold, or used by producers, or shipped; quantity of minerals stocked; crude materials treated and prepared minerals recovered; and consumption of mineral raw materials.

The Economic Census, conducted by the Census Bureau at various intervals since 1840, collects data on mineral industries. Beginning with the 1967 census, legislation provides for a census to be conducted every 5 years for years ending in "2" and "7." Data for the 2012 Economic Census are currently being released on a continuing basis through 2016. Economic Census data are based on the North American Industry Classification System (NAICS). The Census provides, for the various types of mineral establishments, information on operating costs, capital expenditures, labor, equipment, and energy requirements in relation to their value of shipments and other receipts.

Table 900. Natural Resource–Related Industries—Establishments, Employees, and Annual Payroll by Industry: 2010 and 2013

[In units as indicated (1,453.0 represents 1,453,000; 83.03 represents $83,030,000,000). Excludes most government employees, railroad employees, and self-employed persons. See source for definitions and statement on reliability of data. An establishment is a single physical location where business is conducted or where services or industrial operations are performed. See Appendix III]

Industry	2012 NAICS Code [1]	Establishments (number)		Number of employees [2] (1,000)		Annual payroll (bil. dol.)	
		2010	2013	2010	2013	2010	2013
Natural resource–related industries, total.............	(X)	67,772	68,586	1,453.0	1,593.5	83.03	104.67
Forestry, fishing, hunting, and agriculture support...........	11	21,691	22,111	156.1	154.5	5.29	5.83
Forestry and logging...............	113	8,836	8,732	53.5	54.9	1.99	2.26
Timber tract operations.................	1131	382	451	2.1	3.1	0.10	0.19
Forest nurseries and gathering forest products..........	1132	168	174	1.5	1.7	0.05	0.05
Logging................	1133	8,286	8,107	50.0	50.1	1.84	2.02
Fishing, hunting and trapping................	114	2,403	2,575	7.7	7.5	0.33	0.36
Fishing...............	1141	2,110	2,259	6.1	6.0	0.29	0.31
Hunting and trapping................	1142	293	316	1.5	1.5	0.04	0.04
Agriculture and forestry support activities..................	115	10,452	10,804	94.9	92.2	2.97	3.21
Crop production support activities........................	1151	4,544	4,817	64.8	62.9	2.05	2.23
Animal production support activities................	1152	4,299	4,351	19.5	18.7	0.56	0.56
Forestry support activities.................	1153	1,609	1,636	10.5	10.6	0.36	0.42
Mining, quarrying and oil, and gas extraction................	21	27,092	28,720	581.6	732.2	46.14	64.78
Oil and gas extraction.................	211	7,859	8,037	109.2	131.8	12.63	16.99
Mining (except oil and gas)............................	212	6,665	6,436	192.4	203.3	12.83	14.65
Coal mining..........................	2121	1,048	984	81.4	84.0	5.88	6.46
Metal ore mining.........................	2122	329	374	32.1	41.3	2.62	3.64
Nonmetallic mineral mining and quarrying................	2123	5,288	5,078	78.9	78.0	4.33	4.54
Mining support activities.....................	213	12,568	14,247	280.0	397.1	20.68	33.14
Timber–related manufacturing.....................	(X)	18,989	17,755	715.4	706.8	31.60	34.07
Wood product manufacturing..................	321	14,387	13,363	350.3	352.1	11.99	13.44
Sawmills and wood preservation........................	3211	3,542	3,201	78.6	76.0	2.87	3.13
Veneer, plywood and engineered wood product manufacturing..................	3212	1,602	1,403	65.0	64.6	2.48	2.85
Other wood product manufacturing........................	3219	9,243	8,759	206.8	211.5	6.64	7.46
Paper manufacturing..................	322	4,602	4,392	365.1	354.7	19.62	20.63
Pulp, paper and paperboard mills........................	3221	474	446	111.6	107.3	7.69	8.01
Converted paper product manufacturing..................	3222	4,128	3,946	253.5	247.4	11.93	12.62

X Not applicable. [1] 2010 data based on 2007 North American Industry Classification System (NAICS). 2013 data based on 2012 NAICS. [2] Covers full- and part-time employees who are on the payroll in the pay period including March 12.

Source: U.S. Census Bureau, County Business Patterns, "Geography Area Series: County Business Patterns," <http://factfinder2.census.gov>, accessed April 2015. See also <http://www.census.gov/econ/cbp/index.htm>.

Table 901. Natural Resource–Related Industries—Establishments, Sales, Payroll, and Employees by Industry: 2007 and 2012

[414 represents $414,000,000,000. Includes only establishments with payroll. Data are based on the 2007 and 2012 economic censuses, which are subject to nonsampling error. For details on methodology and nonsampling and sampling errors, see Appendix III]

Industry	2007 NAICS code [1]	Establishments (number)		Value of shipments (bil. dol.)		Annual payroll (bil. dol.)		Paid employees [2] (1,000)	
		2007	2012	2007	2012	2007	2012	2007	2012
Mining.............	21	22,667	28,643	414	555	41	61	730	904
Oil & gas extraction.............	211	6,260	8,086	255	333	10	15	150	192
Mining (except oil & gas)...........	212	6,472	6,477	86	93	12	14	211	208
Mining support activities.................	213	9,935	14,080	73	129	19	32	369	504
Manufacturing [3].....................	31–33	332,536	296,605	5,319	5,756	614	594	13,396	11,269
Wood product manufacturing................	321	16,868	13,536	102	78	17	12	524	337
Paper manufacturing....................	322	4,988	4,480	177	182	21	20	418	352
Petroleum & coal products manufacturing...	324	2,283	2,189	615	844	9	9	106	101

[1] Data based on North American Industry Classification System (NAICS), 2007. [2] For pay period including March 12. [3] Includes other industries, not shown separately.

Source: U.S. Census Bureau, 2012 Economic Census, "EC1200CADV2: All sectors: Core Business Statistics Series: Advance Comparative Statistics for the U.S. (2007 NAICS Basis): 2012 and 2007," <http://factfinder2.census.gov>, accessed April 2014.

Table 902. Gross Domestic Product of Natural Resource-Related Industries in Current and Real (2009) Dollars by Industry: 2010 to 2014

[In billions of dollars (14,964.4 represents $14,964,400,000,000). Data are based on the 2007 North American Industry Classification System (NAICS); see text, Section 15. Data include nonfactor charges (capital consumption allowances, indirect business taxes, etc.) as well as factor charges against gross product; corporate profits and capital consumption allowances have been shifted from a company to an establishment basis]

Industry	Current dollars				Chained (2009) dollars			
	2010	2012	2013	2014	2010	2012	2013	2014
All industries, total [1]	**14,964.4**	**16,163.2**	**16,768.1**	**17,418.9**	**14,783.8**	**15,369.2**	**15,710.3**	**16,085.6**
Industries covered [2]	569.3	677.7	743.8	(NA)	487.8	522.7	547.6	(NA)
Percent of all industries	3.8	4.2	4.4	(NA)	3.3	3.4	3.5	(NA)
Private industries	12,826.5	13,972.0	14,556.4	15,175.3	12,650.2	13,185.8	13,482.8	13,829.7
Agriculture, forestry, fishing, and hunting	160.2	195.3	226.6	210.2	140.3	129.5	145.1	134.6
Farms	129.7	161.4	192.1	(NA)	111.5	99.7	113.9	(NA)
Forestry, fishing, and related activities	30.5	33.9	34.6	(NA)	28.8	31.2	31.5	(NA)
Mining	331.7	406.7	439.4	461.3	272.7	319.5	332.7	356.7
Oil and gas extraction	209.3	260.4	291.9	(NA)	158.6	193.4	204.4	(NA)
Mining, except oil and gas	77.3	80.8	78.8	(NA)	70.1	67.0	68.2	(NA)
Support activities for mining	45.1	65.6	68.7	(NA)	46.0	61.3	61.6	(NA)
Timber-related manufacturing	77.4	75.7	77.8	(NA)	74.8	73.7	69.8	(NA)
Wood products	22.1	23.9	25.9	(NA)	21.4	23.7	22.1	(NA)
Paper products	55.3	51.8	51.9	(NA)	53.4	50.0	47.7	(NA)

NA Not available. [1] Includes industries not shown separately. [2] Sum of agriculture/forestry/fishing/hunting, mining, and timber-related manufacturing.

Source: U.S. Bureau of Economic Analysis, Industry Economic Data, GDP-by-Industry, "Value Added by Industry" and "Real Value Added by Industry," <http://www.bea.gov/itable/>, accessed August 2015.

Table 903. Timber–Based Manufacturing Industries—Establishments, Shipments, Payroll, and Employees: 2007

[101,711,917 represents $101,711,917,000. Includes only establishments or firms with payroll. Data for industries with NAICS codes less than 6-digits were derived by summing values with the corresponding 6-digit NAICS codes. See Appendix III]

Industry	2007 NAICS code [1]	Establish-ments (number)	Value of shipments ($1,000)	Annual payroll ($1,000)	Paid employees [2]
Wood product manufacturing	321	16,868	101,711,917	17,426,832	523,899
Sawmills and wood preservation	3211	4,102	27,911,240	3,642,165	103,413
Sawmills	321113	3,589	22,075,666	3,144,796	90,044
Wood preservation	321114	513	5,835,574	497,369	13,369
Veneer, plywood, and engineered wood product manufacturing	3212	1,956	22,023,577	3,790,727	106,093
Other wood product manufacturing	3219	10,810	51,777,100	9,993,940	314,393
Millwork	32191	4,724	28,185,338	5,195,893	153,414
Wood container and pallet manufacturing	32192	2,918	7,232,718	1,530,952	58,762
All other wood product manufacturing	32199	3,168	16,359,044	3,267,095	102,217
Paper manufacturing	322	4,988	176,687,641	20,858,769	418,241
Pulp, paper, and paperboard mills	3221	486	80,550,214	7,925,398	125,483
Pulp mills	32211	39	5,027,052	504,435	7,268
Paper mills	32212	261	50,165,582	4,968,516	81,558
Paperboard mills	32213	186	25,357,580	2,452,447	36,657
Converted paper product manufacturing	3222	4,502	96,137,427	12,933,371	292,758
Paperboard container manufacturing	32221	2,409	50,934,721	7,384,792	165,978
Paper bag and coated and treated paper manufacturing	32222	888	21,685,546	2,800,595	60,366
Stationery product manufacturing	32223	545	8,129,269	1,179,779	31,130
Other converted paper product manufacturing	32229	660	15,387,891	1,568,205	35,284

[1] North American Industry Classification System, 2007. [2] For pay period including March 12.

Source: U.S. Census Bureau, 2007 Economic Census, "Economy–Wide Key Statistics," <http://www.census.gov/econ/census07/>, accessed September 2015.

Table 904. Timber-Based Manufacturing Industries—Employees, Payroll, and Shipments: 2013

[In thousands (11,082 represents 11,082,000). Based on the Annual Survey of Manufactures, see Appendix III]

Selected industry	2012 NAICS code [1]	All employees — Number (1,000)	All employees — Payroll Total (mil. dol.)	All employees — Payroll Per employee (dol.)	Production workers, total (1,000)	Value added by manufactures Total (mil. dol.)	Value added by manufactures Per production worker (dol.)	Value of shipments (mil. dol.)
Manufacturing, all industries [2]	31–33	11,082	602,878	54,400	7,747	2,398,392	309,570	5,846,768
Timber-based manufacturing, total	321–322	692	33,855	48,944	546	127,244	232,929	274,804
Percent of total manufacturing	(X)	6.24	5.62	(X)	7.05	5.31	(X)	4.70
Wood product manufacturing	321	346	13,378	38,681	278	36,979	133,186	88,561
Sawmills and wood preservation	3211	73	3,211	44,031	61	10,142	165,571	26,685
Veneer, plywood, and engineered wood product	3212	64	2,796	43,953	51	8,666	168,863	20,298
Other wood product	3219	209	7,371	35,215	165	18,172	110,079	41,578
Millwork	32191	98	3,784	38,507	79	9,700	123,404	22,358
Wood container and pallet	32192	49	1,476	30,298	40	3,313	82,355	7,216
All other wood products	32199	62	2,111	33,869	46	5,158	111,553	12,004
Manufactured (mobile) home	321991	24	734	30,423	17	1,522	91,416	3,830
Prefabricated wood building	321992	13	489	38,423	9	1,076	114,996	2,641
All other misc. wood product	321999	25	887	34,859	20	2,560	126,528	5,534
Paper manufacturing	322	346	20,477	59,207	269	90,265	336,021	186,243
Pulp, paper, and paperboard mills	3221	105	7,939	75,428	84	44,026	526,301	82,756
Pulp mills	32211	8	624	80,875	6	2,884	480,314	5,546
Paper mills	32212	64	4,678	72,872	52	25,025	485,517	48,012
Paperboard mills	32213	33	2,637	79,086	26	16,117	617,383	29,198
Converted paper product	3222	241	12,538	52,111	185	46,239	249,973	103,487
Paperboard container	32221	137	7,327	53,460	106	24,989	235,772	57,750
Paper bag and coated and treated paper	32222	49	2,579	52,976	37	9,418	255,391	21,414
Stationery product	32223	21	888	43,105	16	2,642	166,830	6,827
Other converted paper products	32229	34	1,744	50,901	26	9,190	349,764	17,495

X Not applicable. [1] North American Industry Classification System, 2012; see text, Section 15. [2] Includes other industries, not shown separately.

Source: U.S. Census Bureau, Annual Survey of Manufactures, "Statistics for Industry Groups and Industries: 2013," February 2015, <http://factfinder2.census.gov>.

Table 905. Forest Land and Timberland by Type of Owner and Region: 2012

[In thousands of acres (766,234 represents 766,234,000). As of January 1. Data are from the U.S. Forest Service's Forest Inventory and Analysis National Program. Forest land is land at least 10 percent stocked by forest trees of any size, including land that formerly had such tree cover and that will be naturally or artificially regenerated. The minimum area for classification of forest land is 1 acre or strips of timber with a crown width of at least 120 feet wide. Timberland is forest land that is producing or is capable of producing crops of industrial wood and that is not withdrawn from timber utilization by statute or administrative regulation]

Region	Forest land, total	Timberland Total	Federal Total	Federal National forest	Federal Bureau of Land Management lands	Federal Other	State, county, and municipal	Private [1]
Total	766,234	521,154	112,310	98,308	6,262	7,740	48,668	360,175
North	175,575	167,378	12,172	10,345	20	1,807	27,159	128,047
Northeast	84,846	79,822	3,122	2,443	0	679	10,453	66,246
North Central	90,730	87,556	9,049	7,902	20	1,128	16,706	61,802
South	244,716	210,048	18,067	12,696	6	5,365	9,350	182,631
Southeast	89,844	86,755	7,763	5,230	6	2,527	5,562	73,430
South Central	154,872	123,292	10,304	7,466	0	2,838	3,788	109,200
Rocky Mountains	131,338	71,023	48,062	44,941	2,863	258	3,138	19,823
Great Plains	6,724	6,179	1,272	1,071	16	185	232	4,675
Intermountain	124,614	64,844	46,790	43,870	2,847	73	2,906	15,148
Pacific Coast	214,604	72,705	34,010	30,326	3,374	310	9,021	29,675
Alaska	128,577	12,817	4,699	3,677	821	201	4,822	3,297
Pacific Northwest	52,222	42,197	19,860	17,512	2,248	100	3,699	18,638
Pacific Southwest [2]	33,805	17,690	9,451	9,137	305	8	499	7,740

[1] Includes Indian lands. [2] Includes Hawaii.

Source: U.S. Forest Service, National Assessment - Resources Planning Act (RPA), "2012 RPA Resource Tables," <http://www.fia.fs.fed.us/program-features/rpa/>, accessed August 2014.

Table 906. National Forest System Lands by State: 2014

[In thousands of acres (232,053 represents 232,053,000). As of September 30, 2014. Data do not include Delaware, District of Columbia, Hawaii, Iowa, Maryland, Massachusetts, New Jersey, or Rhode Island]

State	Total lands	National Forest System lands [1]	Other lands [2]	State	Total lands	National Forest System lands [1]	Other lands [2]
United States.......	**232,053**	**193,063**	**38,990**	Nevada...............	6,291	5,759	531
Alabama..............	1,290	671	620	New Hampshire......	847	748	98
Alaska................	23,482	22,238	1,244	New Mexico..........	10,336	9,312	1,025
Arizona...............	11,813	11,204	609	New York.............	17	16	–
Arkansas.............	3,549	2,593	956	North Carolina........	3,027	1,255	1,772
California.............	24,283	20,755	3,528	North Dakota.........	1,103	1,103	–
Colorado.............	15,960	14,482	1,478	Ohio.................	856	244	612
Connecticut..........	–	–	–	Oklahoma............	759	399	359
Florida...............	1,424	1,194	230	Oregon..............	17,659	15,701	1,958
Georgia..............	1,796	868	929	Pennsylvania........	741	514	227
Idaho................	21,714	20,444	1,270	South Carolina.......	1,381	632	749
Illinois...............	958	304	653	South Dakota........	2,431	2,006	424
Indiana...............	647	203	443	Tennessee...........	1,291	719	572
Kansas...............	109	109	–	Texas...............	2,002	757	1,245
Kentucky.............	2,205	819	1,386	Utah.................	9,211	8,190	1,021
Louisiana.............	1,032	609	424	Vermont.............	837	410	427
Maine................	94	54	41	Virginia..............	3,254	1,665	1,589
Michigan.............	4,887	2,874	2,013	Washington..........	11,989	9,326	2,663
Minnesota............	5,488	2,845	2,643	West Virginia.........	1,893	1,046	847
Mississippi...........	2,375	1,191	1,184	Wisconsin............	2,003	1,524	479
Missouri..............	3,091	1,506	1,586	Wyoming.............	9,726	9,215	511
Montana.............	19,189	17,179	2,009	Puerto Rico.........	56	29	27
Nebraska.............	562	351	211	Virgin Islands........	–	–	–

– Represents or rounds to zero. [1] National Forest System is a nationally significant system of federally owned units of forest, range, and related land consisting of national forests, purchase units, national grasslands, land utilization project areas, experimental forest areas, experimental range areas, designated experimental areas, and other land areas; water areas; and interests in lands that are administered by USDA Forest Service or designated for administration through the Forest Service. [2] Other lands are lands within the unit boundaries in private, state, county, and municipal ownership and the federal lands over which the Forest Service has no jurisdiction. Also includes lands offered to the United States and approved for acquisition and subsequent Forest Service administration, but to which title has not yet been accepted by the United States.

Source: U.S. Forest Service, *Land Areas of the National Forest System as of September 30, 2014*, November 2014. See also <http://www.fs.fed.us/land/staff/lar/LAR2014/lar2014index.html>.

Table 907. Timber Volume, Growth, and Removal on Timberland by Species Group and Region: 2011 and 2012

[In millions of cubic feet (1,101,544 represents 1,101,554,000,000). Data are from the U.S. Forest Service's Forest Inventory and Analysis National Program]

Region	2012 Net volume [1]						2011 Net growth and removals of growing stock					
	All timber [2]			Growing stock [3]			Timber growth [4]			Timber removals [5]		
	All species	Soft-woods	Hard-woods	All species	Soft-woods	Hard-woods	All species	Soft-woods	Hard-woods	All species	Soft-woods	Hard-woods
Total..............	**1,101,554**	**592,568**	**508,985**	**972,395**	**547,619**	**424,776**	**26,413**	**15,663**	**10,750**	**12,854**	**8,319**	**4,535**
North.................	308,459	65,956	242,503	267,803	58,761	209,043	6,516	1,512	5,004	2,360	640	1,720
Northeast..........	169,834	40,537	129,296	152,096	36,463	115,634	3,548	896	2,652	1,119	376	743
North Central.......	138,625	25,419	113,207	115,707	22,298	93,409	2,968	616	2,352	1,240	264	977
South................	358,567	136,280	222,288	306,623	128,956	177,667	13,809	8,808	5,002	8,048	5,335	2,714
Southeast..........	157,981	65,724	92,257	134,872	62,061	72,812	6,135	3,908	2,227	3,844	2,658	1,186
South Central.......	200,586	70,556	130,031	171,751	66,895	104,855	7,674	4,899	2,775	4,204	2,676	1,528
Rocky Mountains....	158,632	141,889	16,743	135,905	124,089	11,816	921	739	183	427	410	17
Great Plains........	8,285	2,548	5,737	4,760	2,021	2,739	103	21	82	36	28	8
Intermountain.......	150,347	139,341	11,006	131,145	122,068	9,077	818	717	101	391	382	9
Pacific Coast........	275,895	248,444	27,451	262,063	235,813	26,250	5,167	4,605	561	2,020	1,935	85
Alaska.............	37,458	33,967	3,491	35,762	32,453	3,309	254	133	121	66	59	7
Pacific Northwest...	166,312	153,099	13,213	158,206	145,473	12,732	3,331	3,040	291	1,599	1,521	78
Pacific Southwest [6].......	72,125	61,377	10,748	68,096	57,887	10,209	1,582	1,433	149	355	355	–

– Represents or rounds to zero. [1] As of January 1. [2] Includes growing stock, live cull and sound dead. [3] Live trees of commercial species meeting specified standards of quality or vigor. Cull trees are excluded. Includes only trees 5.0-inches in diameter or larger at 4 1/2 feet above ground. [4] The net increase in the volume of trees during a specified year. Components include the increment in net volume of trees at the beginning of the specific year surviving to its end, plus the net volume of trees reaching the minimum size class during the year, minus the volume of trees that died during the year, and minus the net volume of trees that became cull trees during the year. [5] The net volume of trees removed from the inventory during a specified year by harvesting, cultural operations such as timber stand improvement, or land clearing. [6] Includes Hawaii.

Source: U.S. Forest Service, National Assessment - Resources Planning Act (RPA), "2012 RPA Resource Tables," <http://www.fia.fs.fed.us/program-features/rpa/>, accessed August 2014.

Table 908. Timber Removals—Roundwood Product Output by Source and Species Group: 2011

[In million cubic feet (12,808 represents 12,808,000,000). Data are from U.S. Forest Service's Forest Inventory and Analysis National Program]

Source and species group	Total	Sawlogs	Pulpwood	Veneer logs	Other products [1]	Fuelwood [2]
Total	**12,808**	**4,988**	**5,033**	**700**	**283**	**1,804**
Softwoods	8,362	3,647	3,353	624	223	515
Hardwoods	4,446	1,341	1,680	76	60	1,289
Growing stock [3]	10,758	4,752	4,483	680	209	633
Softwoods	7,460	3,494	3,064	608	159	135
Hardwoods	3,298	1,257	1,419	73	50	498
Other sources [4]	2,050	236	550	19	74	1,170
Softwoods	902	152	289	16	64	379
Hardwoods	1,149	84	261	3	10	791

[1] Includes poles, pilings, posts, cooperage and miscellaneous products. [2] Downed and dead wood volume left on the ground after trees have been cut on timberland. [3] Includes live trees of commercial species meeting specified standards of quality or vigor. Cull trees are excluded. Includes only trees 5.0-inches in diameter or larger at 4.5 feet above the ground. [4] Includes salvable dead trees, rough and rotten trees, trees of noncommercial species, trees less than 5.0-inches in diameter at 4.5 feet above the ground, tops, and roundwood harvested from nonforest land (for example, fence rows).

Source: U.S. Forest Service, National Assessment - Resources Planning Act (RPA), "2012 RPA Resource Tables," <http://www.fia.fs.fed.us/program-features/rpa/>, accessed August 2014.

Table 909. Timber Products—Production, Foreign Trade, and Consumption by Type of Product: 1990 to 2011

[In millions of cubic feet, roundwood equivalent (15,459 represents 15,459,000,000)]

Type of Product	1990	1995	2000	2005	2006	2007	2008	2009	2010	2011
Industrial roundwood:										
Domestic production	15,459	15,265	15,199	14,750	14,356	13,560	11,549	10,478	10,660	11,094
Softwoods	10,850	9,978	9,998	10,362	10,008	9,396	8,304	7,173	7,448	7,750
Hardwoods	4,609	5,288	5,201	4,388	4,349	4,164	3,245	3,305	3,212	3,344
Imports	3,044	3,929	4,619	5,782	5,312	4,345	3,187	2,453	2,523	2,469
Exports	2,306	2,284	2,039	1,618	1,607	1,726	1,779	1,661	1,791	2,058
Consumption	16,197	16,910	17,779	18,913	18,061	16,180	12,957	11,270	11,392	11,505
Softwoods	11,618	11,767	12,501	14,018	13,336	11,805	9,694	7,973	8,123	8,218
Hardwoods	4,579	5,144	5,278	4,895	4,725	4,374	3,263	3,333	3,189	3,287
Lumber:										
Domestic production	7,317	6,857	7,384	7,680	7,505	6,921	5,395	4,576	4,569	4,950
Imports	1,905	2,545	2,943	3,744	3,415	2,743	1,894	1,347	1,422	1,403
Exports	589	462	435	362	390	359	345	288	234	387
Consumption	8,633	8,939	9,892	11,063	10,530	9,305	6,945	5,636	5,757	5,966
Plywood and veneer:										
Domestic production	1,423	1,303	1,187	1,068	989	898	745	616	655	653
Imports	97	107	154	373	339	264	184	146	161	163
Exports	109	89	51	37	35	40	45	34	55	52
Consumption	1,410	1,321	1,290	1,403	1,293	1,122	884	728	760	764
Pulp products:										
Domestic production	5,194	5,890	5,551	5,172	5,052	4,860	4,548	4,474	4,501	4,478
Imports	1,038	1,245	1,448	1,544	1,460	1,269	1,068	923	900	864
Exports	645	904	776	708	693	771	818	821	860	899
Consumption	5,587	6,231	6,223	6,008	5,820	5,358	4,798	4,575	4,541	4,442
Logs [1]:										
Imports	4	13	72	113	94	67	35	28	32	30
Exports	674	451	422	345	339	350	313	322	407	485
Pulpwood chips, exports	288	377	355	166	151	205	257	196	235	235
Fuelwood:										
Production and consumption	2,900	2,150	1,622	1,550	1,555	1,605	1,510	1,400	1,400	1,400

[1] Prior to 2010, pulpwood logs are not included in logs.

Source: U.S. Forest Service, *U.S. Timber Production, Trade, Consumption, and Price Statistics, 1965-2011*, June 2013. See also <http://www.treesearch.fs.fed.us/pubs/43952>.

Table 910. Selected Timber Products—Imports and Exports: 1990 to 2011

[In million board feet (13,107 represents 13,107,000,000), except as indicated]

Product	Unit	1990	1995	2000	2005	2007	2008	2009	2010	2011
IMPORTS										
Lumber, total.................	Mil. bd. ft.	13,107	17,556	20,243	25,753	18,906	13,042	9,236	9,769	9,633
From Canada..............	Mil. bd. ft.	11,918	16,990	18,616	21,841	16,775	11,653	8,393	6,151	8,946
Logs, total [1]..................	Mil. bd. ft. [2]	23	80.4	450	704	418	220	178	199	188
From Canada..............	Mil. bd. ft.	19	56	426	605	380	186	89	90	84
Paper and board [3]............	1,000 tons	12,195	14,238	17,356	17,958	16,321	14,675	11,218	11,144	10,670
Woodpulp....................	1,000 tons	4,893	5,969	7,227	6,762	6,793	6,272	5,044	6,163	6,117
Plywood.....................	Mil. sq. ft. [4]	1,687	1,951	2,902	6,964	4,972	3,462	2,751	3,042	3,081
EXPORTS										
Lumber, total.................	Mil. bd. ft.	10,890	6,980	6,372	5,171	5,176	5,068	4,210	3,631	4,378
To: Canada.................	Mil. bd. ft.	1,552	1535	1654	1532	1,414	1,347	1,075	1,465	1,351
Japan....................	Mil. bd. ft.	2,998	2309	768	188	200	271	301	422	462
European Union........	Mil. bd. ft.	1,619	1,212	1,195	816	841	547	412	494	463
Logs, total [1]..................	Mil. bd. ft. [2]	4,213	2,820	2,638	2,157	2,189	1,959	2,014	2,542	3,031
To: Canada.................	Mil. bd. ft. [2]	396	716	1,350	1,168	945	671	876	835	719
Japan....................	Mil. bd. ft. [2]	2,626	1,728	934	574	567	658	435	425	458
China....................	Mil. bd. ft. [2]	362	20	22	94	150	169	270	780	1,384
Paper and board [3]............	1,000 tons	5,163	7,621	8,701	7,125	8,066	8,654	7,750	8,781	9,331
Woodpulp....................	1,000 tons	5,905	8,261	6,409	6,413	6,831	7,790	7,519	8,265	9,068
Plywood.....................	Mil. sq. ft. [4]	1,766	1,517	916	686	732	824	619	1,004	949

[1] Prior to 2000, pulpwood logs are not included. [2] Log scale. [3] Includes paper and board products. Excludes hardboard. [4] 3/8 inch basis.

Source: U.S. Forest Service. *U.S. Timber Production, Trade, Consumption, and Price Statistics, 1965-2011*, June 2013. See also <http://www.treesearch.fs.fed.us/pubs/43952>.

Table 911. Lumber Production and Consumption by Species Group: 1990 to 2011

[In billion board feet (48.1 represents 48,100,000,000), except per capita in board feet. Per capita consumption based on estimated resident population as of July 1]

Item	1990	1995	2000	2005	2006	2007	2008	2009	2010	2011
Production, total............................	**48.1**	**44.9**	**48.6**	**50.9**	**49.7**	**45.8**	**36.0**	**30.2**	**30.5**	**33.0**
By species:										
Softwoods.....................................	35.8	32.2	36.0	39.8	38.7	35.2	29.2	23.2	24.8	26.8
Hardwoods....................................	12.3	12.6	12.6	11.2	11.0	10.6	6.8	7.0	5.7	6.2
Consumption, total........................	**57.4**	**59.5**	**66.1**	**74.5**	**70.9**	**62.5**	**46.9**	**37.7**	**38.7**	**40.8**
Per capita....................................	230	226	234	251	245	207	154	123	125	131
By species:										
Softwoods.....................................	45.7	47.6	54.0	63.6	60.6	52.6	40.7	31.1	32.9	34.4
Hardwoods....................................	11.7	11.9	12.1	10.9	10.3	9.9	6.2	6.6	5.8	6.4

Source: U.S. Forest Service, *U.S. Timber Production, Trade, Consumption, and Price Statistics, 1965-2011*, June 2013. See also <http://www.treesearch.fs.fed.us/pubs/43952>.

Table 912. Pulpwood Consumption, Woodpulp Production, and Paper and Board Production and Consumption: 1990 to 2011

[In thousands (99,361 represents 99,361,000) except where otherwise indicated]

Item	Unit	1990	1995	2000	2005	2007	2008	2009	2010	2011
Pulpwood consumption.........	1,000 cords [1]	99,361	97,052	95,904	96,804	88,733	81,289	79,167	80,059	73,502
Woodpulp production [2].........	1,000 tons	63,048	67,103	62,758	60,267	58,932	56,745	52,122	54,353	55,138
Paper and board: [3]										
Production.....................	1,000 tons	78,679	89,509	94,491	91,031	91,570	87,619	78,299	82,960	82,003
Consumption [4].................	1,000 tons	85,711	96,126	103,147	101,864	99,825	93,640	81,767	85,331	83,342
Per capita...................	Pounds	686	731	731	687	662	615	532	551	534

[1] One cord equals 128 cubic feet. [2] Includes dissolving and special alpha pulps; excludes defibrated/exploded pulps and screenings. [3] Excludes hardboard, wet machine board, and construction grades. [4] Production plus imports, minus exports.

Source: U.S. Forest Service. *U.S. Timber Production, Trade, Consumption, and Price Statistics, 1965-2011*, June 2013. See also <http://www.treesearch.fs.fed.us/pubs/43952>.

Table 913. Selected Timber Products—Producer Price Indexes: 1990 to 2014

[1982 = 100. For information about producer prices, see text, Section 14]

Product	1990	1995	2000	2005	2010	2011	2012	2013	2014
Lumber and wood products [1]	**129.7**	**178.1**	**178.2**	**196.5**	**192.7**	**194.7**	**201.6**	**214.9**	**224.2**
Lumber	124.6	173.4	178.8	198.6	167.3	166.6	172.5	198.7	214.9
Softwood lumber	123.8	178.5	178.6	203.6	160.8	160.5	171.7	199.8	205.6
Hardwood lumber	131.0	167.0	185.9	196.6	187.3	185.8	183.7	208.4	241.9
Millwork [1]	130.4	163.8	176.4	197.2	207.0	210.1	216.5	225.8	232.3
General millwork	132.0	165.4	178.0	196.1	211.2	214.2	220.0	225.8	232.3
Prefabricated structural members	122.3	163.5	175.1	206.9	185.6	189.4	198.5	224.5	231.7
Plywood	114.2	165.3	157.6	186.8	176.7	171.3	189.1	199.6	204.1
Softwood veneer and plywood	119.6	188.1	173.3	223.5	197.1	185.8	218.6	236.8	245.3
Hardwood veneer and plywood [2]	(NA)	(NA)	(NA)	(NA)	103.6	103.9	106.0	108.0	108.4
Other wood products [1]	114.7	143.7	130.5	139.2	142.5	144.1	146.6	151.3	159.8
Wood boxes	119.1	145.0	155.2	164.9	183.0	191.1	194.5	196.5	199.2
Pulp, paper, and allied products [1]	**141.2**	**172.2**	**183.7**	**202.6**	**236.9**	**245.1**	**244.2**	**248.8**	**250.5**
Pulp, paper, and prod., excl. bldg. paper [1]	132.9	163.4	161.4	169.8	206.8	216.0	213.6	218.2	220.9
Woodpulp	151.3	183.2	145.3	138.0	186.0	194.8	185.9	180.7	183.7
Wastepaper	138.9	371.1	282.5	230.9	421.5	482.5	370.7	363.6	342.0
Paper [1]	128.8	159.0	149.8	159.6	182.1	191.2	191.6	190.8	192.7
Writing and printing papers	129.1	158.4	146.6	156.1	179.5	185.8	184.9	182.7	183.9
Newsprint	119.6	161.8	127.5	138.5	125.6	137.2	(NA)	(NA)	(NA)
Paperboard	135.7	183.1	176.7	175.5	224.9	230.5	228.0	243.7	248.6
Converted paper and paperboard products [1]	135.2	157.0	162.7	176.1	209.0	216.6	218.6	224.7	228.4
Office supplies and accessories	121.4	134.9	133.8	143.1	159.9	164.7	167.7	171.1	174.1
Building paper & building board mill products	112.2	144.9	138.8	184.9	168.4	163.6	187.1	207.9	188.9

NA Not available. [1] Includes other products not shown separately. [2] December 2005 = 100.

Source: U.S. Bureau of Labor Statistics, "Producer Price Indexes," <http://www.bls.gov/ppi/>, accessed June 2015.

Table 914. Paper and Paperboard—Production and New Supply: 1990 to 2014

[In millions of short tons (80.55 represents 80,550,000). 1 short ton = 2,000 lbs]

Item	1990	1995	2000	2005	2010	2011	2012	2013	2014
Production, total	**80.55**	**91.21**	**96.05**	**92.61**	**83.70**	**82.73**	**81.83**	**81.33**	**80.58**
Paper, total	39.36	42.90	45.52	41.40	35.51	34.34	33.14	32.33	30.74
Paperboard, total	39.42	46.55	48.97	49.71	47.46	47.66	47.90	48.15	49.04
Unbleached kraft	20.36	22.73	21.80	22.58	21.36	21.62	21.84	22.00	22.22
Semichemical	5.64	5.67	5.95	6.41	5.44	5.43	5.41	5.31	4.87
Bleached kraft	4.26	5.16	5.30	5.58	5.62	5.52	5.48	5.40	5.47
Recycled	9.03	12.84	15.79	15.06	15.05	15.09	15.17	15.44	16.48
Wet machine board and construction grades	1.82	1.82	1.56	1.50	0.73	0.72	0.78	0.85	0.79
New supply, all grades, excluding products	**87.68**	**98.08**	**105.02**	**101.81**	**84.16**	**82.48**	**81.02**	**80.92**	**80.92**
Paper, total	49.49	52.77	57.13	53.69	40.34	38.50	37.03	36.54	35.85
Newsprint	13.41	12.76	12.92	10.12	5.00	4.57	4.41	3.92	4.00
Printing/writing papers	25.46	29.55	32.99	31.99	23.73	22.46	21.08	20.82	20.04
Packaging and industrial converting papers	4.72	4.24	4.27	4.05	4.18	4.00	4.07	4.13	4.21
Tissue	5.90	6.22	6.95	7.54	7.43	7.48	7.47	7.66	7.61
Paperboard, total	36.30	43.39	46.02	46.51	43.06	43.22	43.25	43.54	44.31

Source: American Forest and Paper Association, Washington, DC, *Annual Statistics of Paper, Paperboard and Wood Pulp ©*.

Table 915. Fishery Products—Domestic Catch, Imports, and Disposition: 1990 to 2013

[Live weight, in millions of pounds (16,349 represents 16,349,000,000). Data for 2013 are preliminary]

Item	1990	1995	2000	2005	2009	2010	2011	2012	2013
Total supply.................	**16,349**	**16,484**	**17,340**	**20,612**	**18,899**	**19,748**	**21,106**	**20,757**	**20,998**
For human food.................	12,662	13,584	14,738	18,147	16,637	17,560	18,732	18,065	18,582
For industrial use [2].............	3,687	2,900	2,599	2,382	2,262	2,188	2,374	2,692	2,416
Domestic catch..................	**9,404**	**9,788**	**9,069**	**9,707**	**8,031**	**8,231**	**9,858**	**9,634**	**9,880**
For human food..................	7,041	7,667	6,912	7,997	6,198	6,526	7,909	7,477	8,053
For industrial use [2].............	2,363	2,121	2,157	1,710	1,833	1,705	1,949	2,157	1,827
Imports [1]..........................	**6,945**	**6,696**	**8,271**	**10,905**	**10,868**	**11,517**	**11,248**	**11,123**	**11,118**
For human food..................	5,621	5,917	7,828	10,158	10,439	11,034	10,823	10,588	10,529
For industrial use [2].............	1,324	779	443	747	430	483	425	535	589
Exports [1]..........................	**4,627**	**5,166**	**5,758**	**8,420**	**5,738**	**6,129**	**7,695**	**8,259**	**8,915**
For human food..................	3,832	4,175	4,587	6,385	4,760	5,170	6,602	6,474	7,066
For industrial use [2].............	795	991	1,171	2,035	978	959	1,093	1,785	1,850
Disposition of domestic catch..................	**9,404**	**9,788**	**9,069**	**9,707**	**8,031**	**8,231**	**9,858**	**9,634**	**9,880**
Fresh and frozen [3]................	6,501	7,099	6,657	7,776	6,204	6,515	7,817	7,541	8,019
Canned [3]...........................	751	769	530	563	392	373	371	299	365
Cured................................	126	90	119	160	103	102	52	82	45
Reduced to meal, oil, etc........	2,026	1,830	1,763	1,208	1,332	1,241	1,618	1,712	1,451

[1] Excludes imports of edible fishery products consumed in Puerto Rico; includes landings of tuna caught by foreign vessels in American Samoa. [2] Processed into meal, oil, solubles, and shell products, or used as bait and animal food. [3] Includes for human food, and bait and animal food.

Source: U.S. National Oceanic and Atmospheric Administration, National Marine Fisheries Service, *Fisheries of the United States 2013*, September 2014, and earlier editions. See also <http://www.st.nmfs.noaa.gov/commercial-fisheries/index>.

Table 916. Fisheries—Quantity and Value of Domestic Catch: 1980 to 2013

[In millions of pounds (6,482 represents 6,482,000,000), except as noted. Data for 2013 are preliminary]

Year	Quantity (mil. lbs. [1]) Total	For human food	For industrial products [2]	Value (mil. dol.)	Average price per lb. (cents)	Year	Quantity (mil. lbs. [1]) Total	For human food	For industrial products [2]	Value (mil. dol.)	Average price per lb. (cents)
1980......	6,482	3,654	2,828	2,237	34.5	2006......	9,483	7,842	1,641	4,024	42.4
1985......	6,258	3,294	2,964	2,326	37.2	2007......	9,309	7,490	1,819	4,192	45.0
1990......	9,404	7,041	2,363	3,522	37.5	2008......	8,325	6,633	1,692	4,383	52.6
1995......	9,788	7,667	2,121	3,770	38.5	2009......	8,031	6,198	1,833	3,891	48.4
1999......	9,339	6,832	2,507	3,467	37.1	2010......	8,231	6,526	1,705	4,520	54.9
2000......	9,069	6,912	2,157	3,550	39.1	2011......	9,858	7,909	1,949	5,289	53.7
2004......	9,683	7,794	1,889	3,756	38.8	2012......	9,634	7,477	2,157	5,103	53.0
2005......	9,707	7,997	1,710	3,942	40.6	2013......	9,880	8,053	1,827	5,490	55.6

[1] Live weight. [2] Processed into meal, oil, solubles, and shell products, or used as bait and animal food.

Source: U.S. National Oceanic and Atmospheric Administration, National Marine Fisheries Service, *Fisheries of the United States 2013*, September 2014, and earlier editions. See also <http://www.st.nmfs.noaa.gov/commercial-fisheries/index>.

Table 917. Domestic Fish and Shellfish Catch and Value by Major Species Caught: 2000 to 2013

[In thousands (9,068,985 represents 9,068,985,000). Data for 2013 are preliminary]

Species	Quantity (1,000 lbs.) 2000	2010	2012	2013	Value ($1,000) 2000	2010	2012	2013
Total [1]......................	**9,068,985**	**8,230,587**	**9,634,464**	**9,878,552**	**3,549,481**	**4,519,510**	**5,102,578**	**5,490,498**
Fish, total [1]....................	**7,689,661**	**6,918,013**	**8,295,975**	**8,578,032**	**1,594,815**	**2,155,593**	**2,379,048**	**2,606,672**
Cod: Atlantic....................	25,060	17,714	10,507	4,990	26,384	28,119	22,192	10,466
Pacific......................	530,505	539,635	718,122	682,167	142,330	146,941	186,596	156,573
Flounder.........................	412,723	624,358	702,905	716,866	109,910	146,243	176,576	198,596
Halibut..........................	75,190	56,497	34,002	30,042	143,826	206,553	152,036	116,925
Herring, Atlantic...............	160,269	144,513	191,016	208,292	9,972	21,275	28,995	32,184
Herring, Pacific.................	74,835	108,868	78,892	90,084	12,043	23,308	19,905	17,007
Menhaden........................	1,760,498	1,471,803	1,770,508	1,466,970	112,403	107,193	127,727	129,313
Pollock, Alaska..................	2,606,802	1,947,580	2,872,187	3,003,144	160,525	282,399	343,311	406,437
Salmon...........................	628,638	787,740	635,805	1,069,070	270,213	554,816	489,125	756,576
Tuna.............................	50,779	48,047	59,517	55,569	95,176	108,453	163,885	146,410
Whiting (Atlantic, silver)........	26,855	17,564	16,292	13,718	11,370	10,862	10,325	8,751
Whiting (Pacific, hake).........	452,718	355,272	347,178	505,619	18,809	27,316	47,058	61,323
Shellfish, total [1].............	**1,379,324**	**1,276,366**	**1,300,610**	**1,257,187**	**1,954,666**	**2,341,902**	**2,701,071**	**2,857,917**
Clams............................	118,482	88,891	90,563	91,090	153,973	200,657	193,071	208,635
Crabs............................	299,006	349,604	367,212	332,495	405,006	572,797	680,654	713,914
Lobsters: American.............	83,180	115,433	149,550	149,323	301,300	396,757	429,280	460,131
Oysters..........................	41,146	28,080	33,087	44,817	90,667	117,590	155,112	217,500
Scallops, sea....................	32,747	57,454	57,301	40,952	164,609	455,088	559,196	467,323
Shrimp...........................	332,486	258,972	302,596	283,016	690,453	413,980	490,067	565,268
Squid, Pacific...................	259,508	286,403	213,969	230,173	27,077	70,706	63,580	73,725

[1] Includes other species not shown separately.

Source: U.S. National Oceanic and Atmospheric Administration, National Marine Fisheries Service, *Fisheries of the United States 2013*, September 2014, and earlier editions. See also <http://www.st.nmfs.noaa.gov/commercial-fisheries/index>.

Table 918. U.S. Private Aquaculture—Trout and Catfish Production and Value: 1990 to 2014

[67.8 represents 67,800,000. Data are for calendar year and foodsize fish (those over 12 inches long)]

Item	Unit	1990	1995	2000	2005	2010	2012	2013	2014
TROUT FOODSIZE									
Number sold....................	Mil.	67.8	60.2	58.4	55.6	38.7	41.7	41.2	48.2
Total weight....................	Mil. lb.	56.8	55.6	59.0	59.9	45.3	55.5	56.7	60.6
Total value of sales..............	Mil. dol.	64.6	60.8	63.3	63.5	63.2	86.0	91.2	95.1
Avg. price received by processors...................	Dol./lb.	1.14	1.09	1.07	1.06	1.40	1.55	1.61	1.57
Percent sold to processors...........	Percent	58	68	70	66	63	44	63	57
CATFISH FOODSIZE									
Number sold....................	Mil.	272.9	321.8	420.1	395.6	263.4	206.6	201.8	184.6
Total weight....................	Mil. lb.	392.4	481.5	633.8	605.5	478.9	340.2	337.1	307.5
Total value of sales..............	Mil. dol.	305.1	378.1	468.8	427.8	375.1	318.8	336.5	332.4
Avg. price received by processors....	Dol./lb.	0.78	0.79	0.74	0.71	0.78	0.94	1.00	1.08
Fish sold to processors..............	Mil. lb.	360.4	446.9	593.6	600.7	471.7	300.2	(NA)	(NA)
Avg. price paid by processors........	Cents/lb.	75.8	78.6	75.1	72.5	80.2	97.6	(NA)	(NA)
Processor sales.................	Mil. lb.	183.1	227.0	297.2	300.0	231.6	161.4	(NA)	(NA)
Avg. price received by processors...................	Dol./lb.	2.24	2.40	2.36	2.29	2.51	3.08	(NA)	(NA)
Inventory (Jan. 1)................	Mil. lb.	9.4	10.9	13.6	13.7	12.3	(NA)	(NA)	(NA)

NA Not available.

Source: U.S. Department of Agriculture, National Agricultural Statistics Service, *Trout Production*, March 2015, and *Catfish Production*, January 2015; see also <http://www.nass.usda.gov/Publications/index.asp>. U.S. Department of Agriculture, Economic Research Service, *Catfish: Grower and Processor Sales and Prices*, May 2013; see also <http://www.ers.usda.gov/data-products/aquaculture-data.aspx>.

Table 919. Supply of Selected Shellfish and Fish Products: 1990 to 2013

[In millions of pounds (734 represents 734,000,000). Totals available for U.S. consumption are supply minus exports plus imports. Round weight is the complete or full weight as caught. Data for 2013 are preliminary]

Species	Unit	1990	1995	2000	2005	2009	2010	2011	2012	2013
Shrimp........................	Heads-off weight	734	832	1,173	1,559	1,746	1,739	1,810	1,635	1,565
Tuna, canned..................	Canned weight	856	875	980	895	762	834	793	735	726
Snow crab....................	Round weight	37	42	122	171	224	197	177	202	229
Clams........................	Meat weight	152	144	133	120	116	105	107	109	111
Salmon, canned................	Canned weight	148	147	95	123	67	73	50	45	128
American lobster...............	Round weight	95	94	125	144	159	186	186	211	212
Spiny lobster..................	Round weight	89	89	99	83	57	60	54	51	31
Scallops......................	Meat weight	74	62	78	86	90	85	85	60	74
Sardines, canned..............	Canned weight	61	44	(NA)	(NA)	(NA)	(NA)	(NA)	(NA)	(NA)
Oysters......................	Meat weight	56	63	71	65	59	57	63	54	69
King crab....................	Round weight	19	21	41	78	62	44	35	63	54
Crab meat, canned............	Canned weight	9	12	29	59	59	66	63	67	61

NA Not available.

Source: U.S. National Oceanic and Atmospheric Administration, National Marine Fisheries Service, *Fisheries of the United States 2013*, September 2014, and earlier editions. See also <http://www.st.nmfs.noaa.gov/commercial-fisheries/index>.

Table 920. Canned, Fresh, and Frozen Fishery Products—Production and Value: 1990 to 2013

[Production in millions of pounds (1,178 represents 1,178,000,000); value in millions of dollars (1,562 represents $1,562,000,000). Fresh fishery products exclude Alaska and Hawaii. Canned fishery products data are for natural pack only. Data for 2013 are preliminary]

Product	Production (mil. lbs.)					Value (mil. dol.)				
	1990	2000	2010	2012	2013	1990	2000	2010	2012	2013
Canned, total..............	**1,178**	**1,747**	**956**	**881**	**961**	**1,562**	**1,626**	**1,414**	**1,615**	**1,775**
Tuna.........................	581	671	395	387	384	902	856	724	886	852
Salmon......................	196	171	146	120	203	366	288	356	410	572
Clam products................	110	127	110	72	73	76	120	98	66	90
Sardines, Maine..............	13	(Z)	[1] (D)	[1] (D)	[1] (D)	17	(Z)	[1] (D)	[1] (D)	[1] (D)
Shrimp......................	1	2	[1] (D)	[1] (D)	[1] (D)	3	11	[1] (D)	[1] (D)	[1] (D)
Crab [2].....................	1	(Z)	1	(Z)	(Z)	4	(Z)	8	2	(Z)
Oysters [3]..................	1	(Z)	[1] (D)	[1] (D)	[1] (D)	1	1	[1] (D)	[1] (D)	[1] (D)
Other.......................	275	776	303	301	302	193	350	228	250	261
Fish fillets and steaks [4].........	**441**	**368**	**585**	**692**	**753**	**843**	**823**	**1,486**	**1,844**	**2,074**
Cod.........................	65	56	49	64	69	132	167	131	216	232
Flounder....................	54	27	32	16	14	154	71	53	51	61
Haddock....................	7	6	23	11	11	24	24	89	54	56
Ocean perch, Atlantic.........	1	(Z)	1	1	1	1	1	3	4	5
Rockfish....................	33	11	2	2	2	53	25	6	8	5
Pollock, Atlantic.............	12	2	2	2	2	21	4	7	8	8
Pollock, Alaska..............	164	160	290	415	473	174	178	368	643	714
Other.......................	105	106	186	180	180	284	353	829	860	994

D Figure withheld to avoid disclosure pertaining to a specific organization or individual. Z Less than 500,000 pounds or $500,000. [1] Included with "other." [2] Includes crab meat specialties. [3] Includes oyster specialties. [4] Fresh and frozen.

Source: U.S. National Oceanic and Atmospheric Administration, National Marine Fisheries Service, *Fisheries of the United States 2013*, September 2014, and earlier editions. See also <http://www.st.nmfs.noaa.gov/commercial-fisheries/index>.

Table 921. Mineral and Mining Industries—Employment, Hours, and Earnings: 1990 to 2014

[In thousands (680 represents 680,000), except as noted. Industries based on North American Classification System (NAICS) 2012. Based on the Current Employment Statistics Program, see Appendix III]

Industry and item	Unit	1990	1995	2000	2005	2010	2012	2013	2014
All mining: [1]									
All employees............................	1,000	680	558	520	562	655	797	811	844
Production workers....................	1,000	469	391	383	419	483	598	592	614
Avg. weekly hours....................	Number	46.1	46.8	45.5	46.4	44.8	47.0	46.2	47.8
Avg. weekly earnings................	Dollars	630	711	770	884	1,086	1,229	1,258	1,301
Oil and gas extraction:									
All employees............................	1,000	190	152	125	126	159	187	194	198
Production workers....................	1,000	84	73	67	72	89	106	104	104
Avg. weekly hours....................	Number	44.4	43.6	41.3	44.3	39.0	46.6	45.3	45.9
Avg. weekly earnings................	Dollars	591	677	802	856	1,066	1,329	1,371	1,435
Coal mining:									
All employees............................	1,000	136	97	72	74	81	85	78	74
Production workers....................	1,000	110	78	59	61	70	74	67	63
Avg. weekly hours....................	Number	44.7	45.7	45.6	48.5	48.4	47.2	46.4	47.6
Avg. weekly earnings................	Dollars	822	929	945	1,071	1,366	1,349	1,361	1,442
Metal ore mining:									
All employees............................	1,000	53	48	38	29	37	45	44	44
Production workers....................	1,000	43	39	29	22	28	(NA)	(NA)	(NA)
Avg. weekly hours....................	Number	42.5	43.4	43.4	44.2	42.5	(NA)	(NA)	(NA)
Avg. weekly earnings................	Dollars	646	788	871	1,001	1,158	(NA)	(NA)	(NA)
Nonmetallic minerals mining, and quarrying:									
All employees............................	1,000	113	108	115	110	87	89	87	89
Production workers....................	1,000	85	81	87	84	65	(NA)	(NA)	(NA)
Avg. weekly hours....................	Number	45.0	46.3	46.1	45.9	43.8	(NA)	(NA)	(NA)
Avg. weekly earnings................	Dollars	532	632	722	830	848	(NA)	(NA)	(NA)

NA Not available. [1] Includes other industries not shown separately.

Source: U.S. Bureau of Labor Statistics, Current Employment Statistics, "Employment, Hours, and Earnings—National," <http://www.bls.gov/ces/home.htm>, accessed July 2015.

Table 922. Mine Safety: 2010 to 2014

[Reported injury rates per 200,000 employee hours]

Item	All Mines			Coal			Metal and non-metal		
	2010	2013	2014	2010	2013	2014	2010	2013	2014
Number of mines...........................	14,283	13,761	13,608	1,944	1,701	1,632	12,339	12,060	11,976
Number of miners..........................	361,176	374,522	366,584	135,500	123,259	116,010	225,676	251,263	250,574
Fatalities....................................	72	42	45	48	20	16	24	22	29
Fatal injury rate............................	0.02	0.01	0.01	0.04	0.02	0.02	0.01	0.01	0.01
All injury rate...............................	2.81	2.49	2.44	3.43	3.11	3.11	2.37	2.13	2.09
Total mining area inspection hours per mine..................................	63	59	58	259	248	252	23	22	23
Citations and orders [1]....................	170,065	118,203	121,474	96,352	63,217	62,684	73,713	54,986	58,790
S&S [2] citations and orders (percent).....	32	25	25	32	26	26	31	24	24
Amount assessed [3] (mil. dol.)............	163.5	94.3	94.5	110.7	64.9	61.2	52.9	29.4	33.3
Coal production (mil. tons)..............	(X)	(X)	(X)	1,086	984	1,000	(X)	(X)	(X)

X Not applicable. [1] Citations and orders are those not vacated. [2] A violation that "significantly and substantially" contributes to the cause and effect of a coal or other mine safety or health hazard. [3] Government penalties or fines.

Source: U.S. Mine Safety and Health Administration, Office of Program Education and Outreach Services, *Mine Safety and Health At a Glance,* July 2015, and earlier reports. See also <http://www.msha.gov/MSHAINFO/FactSheets/MSHAFCT10.HTM>.

Table 923. Mining and Primary Metal Production Indexes: 1990 to 2014

[Index 2012 = 100]

Industry group	NAICS [1] code	1990	1995	2000	2005	2010	2011	2012	2013	2014
Mining [2].................................	**21**	**93.0**	**90.9**	**89.9**	**84.8**	**88.1**	**93.1**	**100.0**	**106.5**	**118.0**
Oil and gas extraction [2]..............	211	88.7	86.0	83.5	76.3	85.7	89.7	100.0	110.8	126.3
Crude oil and natural gas............	211111	90.6	86.9	83.6	76.5	85.6	89.5	100.0	111.0	126.7
Coal mining............................	2121	108.4	106.7	109.4	113.1	106.9	108.3	100.0	97.0	97.8
Metal ore mining......................	2122	111.0	121.4	118.0	101.1	97.0	99.1	100.0	102.0	104.1
Iron ore..............................	21221	106.6	118.1	118.5	102.1	93.4	102.4	100.0	106.3	111.8
Gold ore and silver ore..............	21222	126.8	135.7	151.1	109.2	99.0	99.8	100.0	97.9	90.3
Copper, nickel, lead, and zinc.......	21223	122.7	140.6	122.8	99.1	96.3	96.4	100.0	106.4	115.6
Oil and gas drilling...................	213111	57.9	50.6	64.7	80.6	79.3	95.6	100.0	93.6	98.6
Primary metal manufacturing [2]......	**331**	**91.3**	**100.5**	**105.0**	**99.1**	**95.1**	**102.1**	**100.0**	**102.8**	**105.4**
Iron and steel..........................	3311, 3312	86.0	95.5	99.8	96.7	91.8	100.1	100.0	101.9	104.6
Aluminum..............................	3313	99.1	95.7	101.3	103.9	89.0	96.1	100.0	107.1	110.5
Nonferrous metals [2]..................	3314	88.6	100.7	90.5	80.4	108.3	111.7	100.0	104.5	103.9

[1] Based on the 2012 North American Industry Classification System (NAICS). [2] Includes other industries not shown separately.

Source: Board of Governors of the Federal Reserve System, "Industrial Production and Capacity Utilization, Statistical Release G.17," <http://www.federalreserve.gov/datadownload/default.htm>, accessed July 2015.

Table 924. Mineral Production: 1990 to 2013

[In units as indicated (1,029.1 represents 1,029,100,000). Data represent production as measured by mine shipments, mine sales, or marketable production; see Appendix IV]

Minerals and metals	Unit	1990	2000	2010	2012	2013
FUEL MINERALS						
Coal, total............................	Mil. sh. tons	1,029.1	1,073.6	1,084.4	1,016.5	984.8
Bituminous........................	Mil. sh. tons	693.2	574.3	489.5	485.4	471.2
Subbituminous....................	Mil. sh. tons	244.3	409.2	514.8	449.8	434.3
Lignite.............................	Mil. sh. tons	88.1	85.6	78.2	78.9	77.2
Anthracite........................	Mil. sh. tons	3.5	4.6	1.8	2.4	2.1
Natural gas (marketed production)............	Tril. cu. ft.	18.59	20.20	22.38	25.28	25.69
Petroleum (crude).........................	Mil. bbl. [1]	2,685	2,131	2,001	2,378	2,724
Uranium concentrate (recoverable content)........	Mil. lb.	8.9	4.0	4.2	4.1	4.7
NONFUEL MINERALS						
Asbestos (sales).........................	1,000 metric tons	(D)	5	–	–	–
Barite, primary, sold/used by producers [2]........	1,000 metric tons	430	392	662	666	700
Boron minerals, sold or used by producers........	1,000 metric tons	1,090	1,070	(D)	(D)	(D)
Bromine, sold or used by producers...........	1,000 metric tons	177	228	(D)	(D)	(D)
Cement (excludes Puerto Rico):.............	Mil. metric tons	(NA)	(NA)	66	74	77
Clays...................................	1,000 metric tons	42,900	40,800	25,600	25,900	24,000
Diatomite..............................	1,000 metric tons	631	677	595	735	782
Feldspar..............................	1,000 metric tons	630	790	500	560	550
Fluorspar, finished shipments............	1,000 metric tons	64	–	(NA)	(NA)	(NA)
Garnet (industrial).......................	1,000 metric tons	47	60	53	47	34
Gypsum, crude.........................	Mil. metric tons	15	20	10	16	16
Helium [3]............................	Mil. cu. meters	65	98	75	73	69
Lime, sold or used by producers............	Mil. metric tons	16	20	18	19	19
Mica, scrap/flake, sold or used by producers.......	1,000 metric tons	109	101	56	48	48
Peat, sales by producers.................	1,000 metric tons	721	847	628	488	465
Perlite, processed, sold or used............	1,000 metric tons	576	672	414	393	419
Phosphate rock, marketable...............	Mil. metric tons	46	39	26	30	31
Potash (K2O equivalent), marketable........	1,000 metric tons	1,710	1,300	930	900	960
Pumice & pumicite, sold and used..........	1,000 metric tons	443	1,050	241	338	269
Salt...................................	Mil. metric tons	37	46	43	37	40
Sand & gravel:[2]........................	Mil. metric tons	855	1,148	839	863	909
Construction [2]......................	Mil. metric tons	829	1,120	807	812	847
Industrial............................	Mil. metric tons	26	28	32	51	62
Soda ash (sodium carbonate).............	1,000 metric tons	9,100	10,200	10,600	11,100	11,500
Stone:.................................	Mil. metric tons	2,230	2,810	2,830	3,320	3,450
Crushed and broken..................	Mil. metric tons	1,110	1,560	1,160	1,170	1,180
Dimension [4]........................	1,000 metric tons	1,120	1,250	1,670	2,150	2,270
Sulfur: total shipments..................	1,000 metric tons	11,500	10,700	9,170	9,030	9,200
Talc and pyrophyllite, crude [5]...........	1,000 metric tons	1,270	851	604	515	542
Vermiculite concentrate.................	1,000 metric tons	209	150	100	100	100
METALS						
Aluminum..............................	1,000 metric tons	4,048	3,668	1,726	2,070	1,946
Copper (recoverable content).............	1,000 metric tons	1,590	1,450	1,110	1,170	1,250
Gold (recoverable content)...............	Metric tons	294	353	231	235	230
Iron ore, usable (gross weight)...........	Mil. metric tons	57	61	50	54	53
Lead (recoverable content)...............	1,000 metric tons	484	449	369	345	340
Magnesium metal.......................	1,000 metric tons	139	(D)	(D)	(D)	(D)
Molybdenum, mine......................	1,000 metric tons	62	41	59	62	61
Nickel ore, refinery byproduct.............	1,000 metric tons	330	(D)	(D)	(D)	(D)
Palladium metal........................	Kilograms	5,930	10,300	11,600	12,300	12,600
Platinum metal.........................	Kilograms	1,810	3,110	3,450	3,670	3,720
Silicon (Si content) [6]...................	1,000 metric tons	418	367	176	383	365
Silver (recoverable content)..............	Metric tons	2,120	1,860	1,280	1,060	1,040
Titanium concentrate, (TiO2 content).......	1,000 metric tons	(D)	300	200	300	200
Vanadium (recoverable content)..........	Metric tons	2,310	–	1,060	106	591
Zinc, ore and concentrate...............	1,000 metric tons	508	796	748	738	784

NA Not available. D Withheld to avoid disclosing individual company data. – Represents or rounds to zero. [1] 42-gal. bbl. [2] Data for 2013 are estimates. [3] Extracted from natural gas. Both grade A and crude helium. [4] Includes Puerto Rico. [5] After 1990, includes only talc. [6] For 2006-2010, ferrosilicon only; silicon metal withheld to avoid disclosing proprietary data. For 2011-2013, silicon alloys and metal.

Source: Nonfuels, through 1994, U.S. Bureau of Mines, thereafter; U.S. Geological Survey, *Mineral Commodity Summaries 2015,* January 2015, and earlier reports. Fuels, U.S. Energy Information Administration, *Annual Energy Review 2011,* September 2012, and earlier reports; *Annual Coal Report, 2013,* April 2015; and "Natural Gas Gross Withdrawals and Production," <http://www.eia.gov/naturalgas/data. cfm#production>, "Uranium & Nuclear Fuel Summary Production Statistics," <http://www.eia.gov/nuclear/data.cfm#biomass>, and "Crude Oil Production," <http://www.eia.gov/petroleum/data.cfm#crude>, accessed July 2015.

Table 925. Nonfuel Mineral Commodities—Summary: 2013

[1,946 represents 1,946,000. Average price in dollars per metric tons except as noted. < = less than]

Mineral	Unit	Mineral disposition				Average price per unit (dollars)	Employment (number)
		Production	Exports	Net import reliance [1,2] (percent)	Consumption, apparent		
Aluminum	1,000 metric tons	1,946	3,390	21	4,530	[4] 94.2	30,100
Antimony (contained)	Metric tons	–	3,980	82	25,100	[4] 4.63	24
Asbestos	Metric tons	–	27	100	772	[6] 1,508	(NA)
Barite	1,000 metric tons	700	200	74	2,740	[6] 116	624
Bauxite and alumina (metal equiv.)	1,000 metric tons	(NA)	2,321	100	2,380	[6,7] 27	(NA)
Beryllium (contained)	Metric tons	235	35	10	262	208	(NA)
Bismuth (contained)	Metric tons	–	816	92	1,060	[6] 8.71	(NA)
Boron (B2O3 content)	1,000 metric tons	(D)	[8] 232	([3])	(D)	[6,9] 615	1,180
Bromine (contained)	Metric tons	(D)	7,970	<25	(D)	(NA)	950
Cadmium (contained)	Metric tons	(D)	[12] 131	<25	(D)	[10,13] 1.92	(NA)
Cement	1,000 metric tons	[14] 76,804	1,670	7	81,700	[6] 95.00	10,300
Chromium	1,000 metric tons	[11] 150	235	63	400	[16] 310	(NA)
Clays	1,000 metric tons	[14,17] 24,000	4,140	([3])	20,400	(NA)	5,170
Cobalt (contained)	Metric tons	[15] 2,160	3,850	75	8,670	[4] 12.89	(NA)
Copper (mine, recoverable)	1,000 metric tons	1,250	348	[5] 34	1,770	[4] 3.34	12,100
Diamond, stones (industrial)	Million carats	63	–	3	65	[18] 15.50	(NA)
Diatomite	1,000 metric tons	782	92	([3])	691	[6] 293	660
Feldspar	1,000 metric tons	550	18	([3])	536	[6] 73	380
Fluorspar	1,000 metric tons	(NA)	16	100	548	[6] 350	6
Garnet (industrial)	Metric tons	33,900	14,400	80	167,000	(NA)	160
Gemstones	Million dollars	[36] 66.5	19,400	99	5,410	(NA)	1,100
Germanium (contained)	Kilograms	(D)	12,500	85	(NA)	[10] 1,900	(NA)
Gold (contained)	Metric tons	230	691	([3])	(NA)	[19] 1,415	12,958
Graphite (crude)	1,000 metric tons	–	9	100	52	[6,20] 1,330	(NA)
Gypsum (crude)	1,000 metric tons	16,300	142	10	32,200	[6] 8.83	4,500
Iodine	Metric tons	(D)	1,150	100	(D)	[10,21] 42.51	30
Iron ore (usable)	Million metric tons	[22] 53.0	11	([3])	47	[6] 104.90	5,644
Iron and steel scrap (metal)	Million metric tons	85	18	([3])	[37] 59	[6,23] 341	30,000
Iron and steel slag (metal)	1,000 metric tons	[24] 15.5	(Z)	8	16	[6] 17.00	1,700
Lead (contained)	1,000 metric tons	340	210	26	1,700	[4] 1.15	3,680
Lime	1,000 metric tons	19,200	270	1	19,300	[6,25] 117.80	5,100
Lithium	Metric tons	870	1,230	>50	(D)	[6] 6,800	70
Magnesium compounds	1,000 metric tons	297	21	41	506	(NA)	250
Magnesium metal	1,000 metric tons	(D)	16	27	120	[4] 2.13	420
Manganese (gross weight)	1,000 metric tons	–	9	100	794	[26] 4.61	(NA)
Mercury [38]	Metric tons	[15] (NA)	(Z)	(NA)	(NA)	[27] 1,850	(NA)
Mica, scrap and flake	1,000 metric tons	127	6	34	73	[6] 124	(NA)
Molybdenum (contained)	Metric tons	60,700	53,100	([3])	29,500	[10] 22.85	960
Nickel (contained) [28]	Metric tons	(D)	71,800	46	110,000	[29] 15,018	(NA)
Niobium (columbium)	Metric tons	–	435	100	8,140	[6] 43,415	(NA)
Nitrogen (fixed)-ammonia	1,000 metric tons	9,170	196	34	13,900	[6,30] 541	1,200
Peat	1,000 metric tons	465	41	66	1,380	[6] 25.37	560
Perlite	1,000 metric tons	419	51	25	555	[6] 55	117
Phosphate rock	1,000 metric tons	31,200	(NA)	1	(NA)	[6] 91.11	2,170
Platinum-group metals	Kilograms	[31] 16,320	39,640	[32] 84	[32] (NA)	[19,33] 1,490	1,770
Potash (K2O equivalent)	1,000 metric tons	960	289	82	(NA)	[6,34] 720	1,490
Pumice and pumicite	1,000 metric tons	269	12	18	329	[6] 34.60	140
Salt	1,000 metric tons	40,300	525	21	54,800	[6,35] 178.65	4,100
Silicon, metal [39]	1,000 metric tons	365	38	<30	(D)	[4] 1.22	(NA)
Silver (contained)	Metric tons	1,040	409	59	6,620	[19] 23.80	819
Soda ash (sodium carbonate)	1,000 metric tons	11,500	6,470	([3])	4,990	[40] 275	2,500
Stone (crushed)	Million metric tons	1,180	(Z)	1	1,230	[6] 9.99	65,900
Sulfur (all forms)	1,000 metric tons	9,210	1,804	19	11,400	[6,41] 68.83	2,600
Talc	1,000 metric tons	542	189	13	622	[6] 163	280
Thallium (contained)	Kilograms	–	22	100	(NA)	[10] 6,990	(NA)
Tin (contained)	Metric tons	[15] 13,800	5,870	72	39,900	[4] 10.41	(NA)
Titanium dioxide	1,000 metric tons	1,280	670	([3])	826	(NA)	3,400
Tungsten (contained)	Metric tons	[15] 8,610	7,730	41	14,700	[42] 358	(NA)
Vermiculite	1,000 metric tons	100	2	25	130	[6] 145-565	70
Zinc (contained)	1,000 metric tons	784	669	75	940	[4,43] .95	2,817
Zirconium (ZrO2)	Metric tons	(D)	20,740	([3])	(D)	[6,44] 1,050	(NA)

– Represents or rounds to zero. D Withheld to avoid disclosing company proprietary data. NA Not available. Z Less than .05 million metric tons or less than half a unit shown. [1] Data are rounded to no more than three significant digits; except prices. [2] Calculated as a percent of apparent consumption. [3] Net exporter. [4] Dollars per pound. [5] Refinery production. [6] Dollars per metric ton. [7] Bauxite, average value U.S. imports (f.a.s.). [8] Boric acid, gross weight. [9] Average value of mineral imports at port of exportation. [10] Dollars per kilogram. [11] Recycling production, based on reported stainless steel scrap receipts. [12] Unwrought cadmium and powders. [13] Average New York dealer price for 99.95% purity in 5-short-ton lots. Source: Platts Metals Week. [14] Excludes Puerto Rico. [15] Secondary production. [16] Unit value of imported chromite ore. Dollars per metric ton gross weight. [17] Excludes attapulgite. [18] Value of imports, dollars per carat. [19] Dollars per troy ounce. [20] Price of flake imports. Graphite lump/chip (Sri Lankan) price $1,720 per ton. [21] C.i.f. value, crude, per kilogram. [22] Shipments of usable ore. [23] Delivered, No. 1 Heavy Melting composite price. [24] Sales include imports and reprocessed slag from past years and decades, and only some from current production. [25] Quicklime only. [26] 46%-48% Mn metallurgical ore, per unit contained Mn, c.i.f. U.S. ports. [27] Dollars per 76-pound flask. [28] Primary and secondary materials. [29] London Metal Exchange cash price; dollars per metric ton. [30] F.o.b. Gulf Coast. [31] Platinum and palladium. [32] Platinum. [33] Dealer price of platinum. [34] Price of K2O, muriate. [35] Vacuum and open pan, bulk, pellets and packaged, f.o.b. mine and plant. [36] Natural gemstone production, $9.6 million; laboratory-created (synthetic) gemstone production, $56.9 million. [37] Iron and steel scrap reported consumption. [38] Mercury has not been produced as principal mineral commodity In U.S. since 1992. Mercury secondary production (recycled) not reported. [39] Silicon metal. Ferrosilicon statistics include: production (D), exports (10,000t), net import reliance (greater than 50%), and price 50% Si ($1.03 per pound). [40] Quoted year-end price, dense, bulk, f.o.b. Green River, WY, dollars per short ton. [41] Elemental sulfur, f.o.b. plant. [42] Dollars per metric ton unit WO3 (7.93 kilograms of contained tungsten per metric ton unit). [43] Platts Metals Week North American price for Special High Grade zinc. [44] Price for domestic zircon.

Source: U.S. Geological Survey, *Mineral Commodity Summaries, 2015*, January 2015. See also <http://minerals.er.usgs.gov/minerals/pubs/mcs/>.

Table 926. Selected Fuel and Nonfuel Mineral Products—Average Prices: 1990 to 2014

[Excludes Alaska and Hawaii, except as noted]

Year	Nonfuel minerals									Fuels		
	Copper, cath- ode (cents/ lb.)	Plati- num [1] (dol./troy oz.)	Gold (dol./troy oz.) [2]	Silver (dol./troy oz.) [2]	Lead [3] (cents/ lb.)	Nickel [4] (cents/ lb.)	Tin (New York) [4] (cents/ lb.)	Zinc [5] (cents/ lb.)	Sulfur, crude [6] (dol./ metric ton)	Bitumi- nous coal [7] (dol./ short ton)	Crude petrol- eum [7] (dol./ bbl.)	Natural gas [7] (dol./ 1,000 cu. ft.)
1990.........	123	467	385	4.82	46	402	386	75	80	27.43	20.03	1.71
1995.........	138	425	386	5.15	42	373	416	56	44	25.56	14.62	1.55
1999.........	76	379	280	5.25	44	273	366	53	38	23.92	15.56	2.19
2000.........	88	549	280	5.00	44	392	370	56	25	24.15	26.72	3.68
2001.........	77	533	272	4.39	44	270	315	44	10	25.36	21.84	4.00
2002.........	76	543	311	4.62	44	307	292	39	12	26.57	22.51	2.95
2003.........	85	694	365	4.91	44	437	340	41	29	26.57	27.56	4.88
2004.........	134	849	411	6.69	55	627	547	52	33	30.56	36.77	5.46
2005.........	174	900	446	7.34	61	669	483	67	31	36.80	50.28	7.33
2006.........	315	1,144	606	11.61	77	1,100	565	159	33	39.32	59.69	6.39
2007.........	328	1,308	699	13.43	124	1,688	899	154	36	40.80	66.52	6.25
2008.........	319	1,578	874	15.00	120	957	1,129	89	264	51.39	94.04	7.97
2009.........	241	1,208	975	14.69	87	665	837	78	2	55.44	56.35	3.67
2010.........	348	1,616	1,228	20.20	109	989	1,240	102	70	60.88	74.71	4.48
2011.........	406	1,725	1,572	35.26	122	1,038	1,575	106	160	68.50	95.73	3.95
2012.........	367	1,555	1,673	31.21	114	795	1,283	96	124	66.04	94.52	2.66
2013.........	340	1,490	1,415	23.80	115	681	1,352	96	69	60.61	95.99	(NA)
2014 [8].......	322	1,440	1,270	19.03	(NA)	765	(NA)	108	95	(NA)	87.39	(NA)

NA Not available. [1] Average annual dealer prices. [2] 99.95 percent purity. [3] North American delivered basis. [4] Composite price. [5] Platt's Metals Week price for North American Special High Grade zinc. Average prices for 1990 are for U.S. High Grade Zinc. [6] F.o.b. (Free on Board) works. [7] Average value at the point of production or domestic first purchase price. [8] Estimated.

Source: Nonfuels, through 1994, U.S. Bureau of Mines; thereafter, U.S. Geological Survey, *Mineral Commodity Summaries 2015*, January 2015 and earlier reports. Fuels, U.S. Energy Information Administration, *Monthly Energy Review*, June 2015 and earlier reports; and *Annual Coal Report, 2013*, April 2015 and earlier reports. See also <http://minerals.usgs.gov/minerals/pubs/mcs/> and <http://www.eia.gov/totalenergy/data/monthly/>.

Table 927. Value of Domestic Nonfuel Mineral Production by State: 2000 to 2013

[In millions of dollars (39,400 represents $39,400,000,000)]

State	2000	2010	2012	2013 [1]	State	2000	2010	2012	2013 [1]
United States [2]......	39,400	66,400	75,600	74,200					
Alabama..............	930	969	983	990	Montana.............	596	1,140	1,450	1,350
Alaska................	1,140	3,400	3,690	3,420	Nebraska............	[3] 84	234	317	307
Arizona...............	2,510	6,790	7,900	7,540	Nevada..............	2,980	7,700	11,000	9,040
Arkansas.............	484	709	806	1,020	New Hampshire......	[3] 57	[3] 94	[3] 88	102
California.............	3,270	2,890	3,250	3,110	New Jersey..........	[3] 291	[3] 258	[3] 270	[3] 462
Colorado.............	592	1,850	1,930	2,110	New Mexico.........	786	1,020	1,570	1,540
Connecticut..........	[3] 112	[3] 148	[3] 167	[3] 171	New York...........	1,020	1,310	1,250	1,210
Delaware.............	[3] 14	[3] 12	[3] 16	[3] 15	North Carolina......	744	880	909	1,030
Florida...............	1,820	2,680	3,820	3,840	North Dakota.......	35	[3] 70	[3] 219	[3] 244
Georgia..............	1,620	1,430	1,480	1,500	Ohio................	999	1,170	[3] 1,010	[3] 1,000
Hawaii...............	[3] 92	106	109	102	Oklahoma...........	473	702	746	755
Idaho................	358	1,180	813	991	Oregon.............	299	312	293	328
Illinois...............	913	924	1,220	1,220	Pennsylvania........	[3] 1,250	[3] 1,670	[3] 1,470	[3] 1,360
Indiana..............	695	782	801	821	Rhode Island........	[3] 20	[3] 33	[3] 45	[3] 30
Iowa.................	503	583	665	670	South Carolina......	[3] 551	[3] 468	[3] 508	[3] 538
Kansas...............	629	1,090	1,160	1,150	South Dakota.......	233	258	337	320
Kentucky.............	501	762	815	1,010	Tennessee...........	737	831	921	941
Louisiana............	325	549	[3] 400	[3] 395	Texas...............	1,950	2,780	3,460	3,740
Maine................	96	110	133	131	Utah................	1,430	4,380	3,330	3,310
Maryland.............	[3] 358	[3] 305	[3] 280	[3] 255	Vermont............	[3] 67	[3] 121	[3] 125	[3] 118
Massachusetts.........	[3] 200	[3] 233	[3] 251	[3] 232	Virginia............	710	1,040	1,180	1,110
Michigan.............	1,640	2,190	2,110	2,190	Washington.........	607	712	736	743
Minnesota............	1,460	[3] 4,180	[3] 4,450	[3] 4,650	West Virginia.......	172	272	313	313
Mississippi...........	149	198	183	161	Wisconsin...........	[3] 372	509	[3] 1,020	[3] 935
Missouri.............	1,370	2,010	2,270	2,440	Wyoming............	978	1,860	2,330	2,460

[1] Preliminary. [2] Includes undistributed not shown separately. [3] Partial data only; excludes values withheld to avoid disclosing individual company data.

Source: U.S. Geological Survey, *Minerals Yearbook, 2012*, July 2015, and earlier reports; and *Mineral Commodities Summaries 2014*, February 2014, and earlier reports. See also <http://minerals.er.usgs.gov/minerals/pubs/mcs/>.

Table 928. Principal Fuels, Nonmetals, and Metals—World Production and the U.S. Share: 2000 to 2012

[In units as indicated (5,138 represents 5,138,000,000), except as indicated; see Appendix IV]

Mineral	Unit	World production				U.S. share
		2000	2005	2010	2012	2012
FUELS [1]						
Coal	Mil. sh. tons	5,138	6,636	7,999	8,687	11.7
Petroleum (crude) [2]	Bil. bbl.	25.0	27.0	27.2	27.8	8.5
Natural gas (dry, marketable)	Tril. cu. ft.	87.1	98.3	112.6	119.5	20.1
Natural gas plant liquids	Bil. bbl.	2.3	2.9	3.2	3.4	25.5
NONMETALS						
Asbestos	1,000 metric tons	2,110	2,210	2,020	1,970	–
Barite	1,000 metric tons	6,470	7,870	7,950	[3] 9,200	7.2
Cement, hydraulic	Mil. metric tons	1,660	2,350	3,290	[3] 3,830	2.0
Feldspar	1,000 metric tons	9,580	16,800	20,800	[3] 18,300	2.8
Fluorspar	1,000 metric tons	4,470	5,360	7,000	[3] 7,070	–
Gypsum	Mil. metric tons	106	147	222	[3] 231	6.8
Mica (incl. scrap)	1,000 metric tons	328	354	1,110	[3] 1,100	4.3
Nitrogen (N content)	Mil. metric tons	108	122	127	136	6.4
Phosphate rock (gross wt.)	Mil. metric tons	132	152	184	[3] 215	14.0
Potash (K2O equivalent)	Mil. metric tons	27	34	34	33	2.7
Sulfur, elemental basis	Mil. metric tons	59	69	68	69	13.0
METALS, mine basis						
Bauxite	Mil. metric tons	136	178	238	[3] 258	(NA)
Copper	1,000 metric tons	13,300	15,000	16,200	17,000	6.9
Gold	Metric tons	2,570	2,470	2,580	2,690	8.7
Iron ore (gross wt.)	Mil. metric tons	1,079	1,550	2,590	2,930	1.8
Lead [4]	1,000 metric tons	3,170	3,470	4,150	[3] 5,170	6.7
Mercury	Metric tons	1,350	1,520	2,250	1,810	(NA)
Molybdenum	1,000 metric tons	133	186	247	259	23.3
Nickel [4]	1,000 metric tons	1,290	1,460	1,650	2,000	–
Silver	1,000 metric tons	18	21	24	26	4.1
Tantalum concentrates (Ta content)	Metric tons	1,040	1,380	6,790	[3] 7,160	–
Titanium mineral concentrates (titanium content) [5]	1,000 metric tons	(NA)	5,200	7,530	7,800	3.9
Tungsten [4]	1,000 metric tons	44	59	69	[3] 76	NA
Vanadium [4]	1,000 metric tons	56	56	72	74	0.4
Zinc [4]	1,000 metric tons	8,788	10,000	12,400	13,500	5.5
METALS, smelter basis						
Aluminum	1,000 metric tons	24,400	31,900	41,200	[3] 45,900	4.5
Cadmium	1,000 metric tons	20	20	23	[3] 21	(NA)
Copper	1,000 metric tons	11,000	13,500	15,600	16,100	3.0
Iron, pig	Mil. metric tons	573	802	1,030	1,110	2.9
Lead [5]	1,000 metric tons	6,580	7,660	9,530	[3] 10,200	12.0
Magnesium [6, 7]	1,000 metric tons	428	622	747	802	(NA)
Raw Steel	Mil. metric tons	850	1,140	1,430	1,550	5.7
Tin [8]	1,000 metric tons	278	296	335	[3] 321	3.5
Zinc	1,000 metric tons	9,137	10,300	12,800	12,800	2.0

– Represents zero. NA Not available. [1] Source: Energy Information Administration, "International Energy Statistics." [2] Crude oil including lease condensate. [3] Estimated. [4] Content of ore and concentrate. [5] Refinery production. [6] Primary production; no smelter processing necessary. [7] Starting 2005, excludes U.S. production. [8] Production from primary sources only.

Source: U.S. Energy Information Administration, "International Energy Statistics," <http://www.eia.gov/cfapps/ipdbproject/iedindex3.cfm>, accessed July 2015; and U.S. Geological Survey, *Minerals Yearbook 2012*, July 2015, and earlier reports.

Table 929. Petroleum Industry—Wells Drilled, Production, Foreign Trade, Reserves, and Refineries: 1990 to 2014

[602 represents 602,000. Includes all costs incurred for drilling and equipping wells to point of completion as productive wells or abandonment after drilling becomes unproductive. Based on sample of operators of different size drilling establishments]

Item	Unit	1990	1995	2000	2005	2010	2012	2013	2014
Crude oil producing wells, (Dec. 31)	1,000	602	574	534	498	520	(NA)	(NA)	(NA)
Daily output per well [1]	Bbl.	12.2	11.4	10.9	10.4	10.5	(NA)	(NA)	(NA)
Completed wells drilled, total	1,000	32.33	21.14	29.29	44.02	37.50	(NA)	(NA)	(NA)
Crude oil	1,000	12.84	8.25	8.09	10.78	16.25	(NA)	(NA)	(NA)
Natural gas	1,000	11.25	8.08	17.05	28.59	16.97	(NA)	(NA)	(NA)
Dry holes	1,000	8.25	4.81	4.15	4.65	4.28	(NA)	(NA)	(NA)
Average depth per well	Feet	4,827	5,542	4,932	5,459	7,183	(NA)	(NA)	(NA)
Average cost per well	$1,000	384	513	755	1,721	(NA)	(NA)	(NA)	(NA)
Average cost per foot	Dollars	76.07	87.22	142.16	306.50	(NA)	(NA)	(NA)	(NA)
Crude oil production, total [2]	Mil. bbl.	2,685	2,394	2,131	1,892	1,999	2,370	2,721	3,183
Value at wells [2, 3]	Bil. dol.	53.77	35.00	56.93	95.03	149.32	(NA)	(NA)	(NA)
Average price per barrel	Dollars	20.03	14.62	26.72	50.28	74.71	94.52	95.99	87.39
Lower 48 states [4]	Mil. bbl.	2,037	1,853	1,771	1,576	1,782	2,179	2,534	2,999
Alaska	Mil. bbl.	647	542	354	315	219	192	188	181
Onshore	Mil. bbl.	2,290	1,838	1,482	1,265	1,367	(NA)	(NA)	(NA)
Offshore	Mil. bbl.	395	556	649	625	632	(NA)	(NA)	(NA)
Imports: Crude oil [2, 5]	Mil. bbl.	2,151	2,639	3,320	3,696	3,363	3,121	2,821	2,681
Refined petroleum products	Mil. bbl.	775	586	874	1,310	942	758	777	692
Exports: Crude oil [2]	Mil. bbl.	40	35	18	12	15	25	49	128
Proved reserves	Bil. bbl.	26.3	22.4	22.0	21.8	23.3	30.5	33.4	(NA)
Operable refineries	Number	205	175	158	148	148	144	143	142
Daily capacity (Jan. 1)	1,000 bbl.	15,572	15,434	16,512	17,125	17,584	17,322	17,824	17,925
Refinery input, total	Mil. bbl.	5,325	5,555	5,964	6,136	6,345	6,407	6,577	6,779
Crude oil [2]	Mil. bbl.	4,894	5,100	5,514	5,555	5,374	5,490	5,589	5,785
Natural gas plant liquids	Mil. bbl.	171	172	139	161	161	186	181	187
Other liquids [6]	Mil. bbl.	260	283	311	420	810	731	807	808
Refinery output, total [7]	Mil. bbl.	5,574	5,838	6,311	6,497	6,735	6,794	6,974	7,174
Motor gasoline [8]	Mil. bbl.	2,540	2,722	2,910	3,036	3,306	3,267	3,370	3,493
Jet fuel (kerosene type)	Mil. bbl.	478	514	588	564	517	538	547	563
Distillate fuel oil	Mil. bbl.	1,067	1,152	1,310	1,443	1,542	1,665	1,727	1,794
Residual fuel oil	Mil. bbl.	347	288	255	229	213	183	170	159
Liquefied petroleum gases	Mil. bbl.	182	239	258	209	240	230	227	238
Utilization rate	Percent	87.1	92.0	92.6	90.6	86.4	88.7	88.3	90.4

NA Not available. [1] Based on number of wells producing at end of year. [2] Includes lease condensate. [3] Values based on domestic first purchase price. [4] Excluding Alaska and Hawaii. [5] Includes imports for the Strategic Petroleum Reserve. [6] Unfinished oils (net), other hydrocarbons, hydrogen, aviation and motor gasoline blending components (net). Beginning 1995, also includes oxygenates (net). [7] Includes other products not shown separately. [8] Finished motor gasoline. Beginning 1995, also includes ethanol blended into motor gasoline.

Source: U.S. Energy Information Administration, *Annual Energy Review 2011*, September 2012; and "Petroleum & Other Liquids Data," <http://www.eia.gov/naturalgas/data.cfm> and "Monthly Energy Review, Petroleum," <http://www.eia.gov/totalenergy/data/monthly/#petroleum>, accessed September 2015.

Table 930. Supply, Disposition, and Ending Stocks of Crude Oil and Petroleum Products: 2014

[In millions of barrels (3,183.0 represents 3,183,600,000). Minus sign (-) indicates decrease]

Commodity	Supply				Disposition				Ending stocks
	Field production [1]	Refinery and blender net production	Imports	Adjust-ments [2]	Stock change	Refinery and blender net inputs	Exports	Products supplied [3]	
Crude oil	3,183.0	(X)	2,677.9	79.5	31.1	5,783.2	126.2	–	1,084.7
Natural gas liquids and LRG [4]	1,081.9	240.3	51.8	(X)	48.3	186.4	257.9	874.3	175.4
Pentanes plus	141.2	(X)	5.2	(X)	6.3	55.9	63.1	14.0	20.6
Liquefied petroleum gases	940.7	240.3	46.6	(X)	42.0	130.5	194.9	860.3	154.8
Ethane/ethylene	391.0	2.0	0.1	(X)	4.5	(NA)	13.4	375.3	34.9
Propane/propylene	353.9	214.4	39.1	(X)	33.3	(NA)	154.4	419.8	77.9
Normal butane/butylene	98.7	27.3	4.6	(X)	3.2	56.8	27.1	43.5	33.2
Isobutane/isobutylene	97.1	-3.4	2.8	(X)	1.1	73.7	(NA)	21.7	8.7
Finished motor gasoline	(X)	3,513.3	18.0	-123.1	-9.1	(X)	161.3	3,256.7	30.6
Kerosene-type jet fuel	(X)	561.9	34.5	(X)	0.3	(X)	59.4	536.6	37.5
Distillate fuel oil [5]	(X)	1,790.2	70.6	18.5	8.8	(X)	406.8	1,463.7	136.1

–Represents or rounds to zero. NA Not available. X Not applicable. [1] Represents crude oil production on leases, natural gas liquids production at natural gas processing plants, new supply of other hydrocarbons/oxygenates and motor gasoline blending components, fuel ethanol, and distillate fuel oil. [2] Includes an adjustment for crude oil, previously referred to as "Unaccounted For Crude Oil." Also included is an adjustment for motor gasoline blending components, fuel ethanol, and distillate fuel oil. [3] Products supplied is equal to field production, plus refinery and blender net production, plus import, plus adjustments, minus stock change, minus refinery and blender net inputs, minus export. [4] Liquefied Refinery Gases (LRGs) are liquefied petroleum gases fractionated from refinery or still gases through compression and/or refrigeration. They are retained in the liquid state. Excludes still gas. [5] Distillate stocks located in the "Northeast Heating Oil Reserve" are not included.

Source: U.S. Energy Information Administration, "Petroleum Supply and Disposition," <http://www.eia.gov/petroleum/>, accessed July 2015.

Table 931. Crude Petroleum and Natural Gas—Production and Value for Major Producing States: 2010 to 2014

[In units as indicated (2,001 represents 2,001,000,000 barrels)]

State	Crude petroleum								Natural gas marketed production [1]			
	Quantity (mil. bbl.)				Value (mil. dol.) [4]				Quantity (bil. cu. ft.)			
	2010	2012	2013	2014	2010	2012	2013	2014	2010	2012	2013	2014
Total [2]...............	2,001	2,378	2,724	3,183	149,484	224,750	261,444	278,164	22,382	25,283	25,691	27,271
Alabama................	7	10	10	10	540	998	1,071	885	223	216	196	(NA)
Alaska [3]...............	219	192	188	181	15,833	18,987	18,004	15,677	374	351	338	342
Arkansas...............	6	7	7	7	407	584	617	583	927	1,146	1,140	(NA)
California..............	201	197	199	204	14,994	20,530	20,396	18,823	287	247	252	(NA)
Colorado..............	33	49	65	95	2,384	4,230	5,892	7,862	1,578	1,709	1,605	(NA)
Florida.................	2	2	2	2	(NA)	(NA)	(NA)	(NA)	12	1	–	(NA)
Illinois.................	9	9	9	10	664	790	882	836	2	2	3	(NA)
Indiana................	2	2	2	3	134	208	223	220	7	9	8	(NA)
Kansas.................	40	44	47	50	2,931	3,843	4,303	4,298	325	296	292	(NA)
Kentucky..............	3	3	3	3	178	278	264	292	135	106	95	(NA)
Louisiana.............	67	71	72	69	5,265	7,487	7,553	6,453	2,210	2,955	2,407	1,982
Michigan..............	7	7	8	7	520	675	744	648	131	129	124	(NA)
Mississippi...........	24	24	24	24	1,840	2,435	2,445	2,222	74	64	59	(NA)
Montana...............	25	26	29	29	1,779	2,199	2,599	2,364	88	67	63	(NA)
Nebraska..............	2	3	3	3	162	257	246	252	2	1	1	(NA)
New Mexico...........	65	85	101	124	4,945	7,500	9,339	10,315	1,292	1,216	1,195	1,228
New York..............	–	–	–	–	(NA)	(NA)	(NA)	(NA)	36	26	23	(NA)
North Dakota.........	113	244	314	397	7,944	20,496	28,321	32,887	82	172	236	(NA)
Ohio....................	5	5	12	19	350	476	1,102	1,595	78	84	186	(NA)
Oklahoma.............	69	93	114	124	5,181	8,366	10,708	11,090	1,827	2,023	2,144	2,310
Pennsylvania.........	4	4	5	6	255	380	471	516	573	2,257	3,259	(NA)
Texas..................	427	724	924	1,157	32,531	66,987	88,477	100,719	6,715	7,475	7,545	7,750
Utah....................	25	30	35	41	1,680	2,504	2,960	3,232	432	490	471	(NA)
West Virginia.........	2	3	8	10	130	224	690	814	265	540	718	(NA)
Wyoming..............	53	58	63	76	3,617	4,667	5,398	6,127	2,306	2,022	1,858	1,808
Federal offshore......	588	481	476	528	(NA)	(NA)	(NA)	(NA)	(NA)	(NA)	(NA)	(NA)
Lower 48 states........	1,782	2,185	2,536	3,002	133,718	205,672	243,428	262,489	22,008	24,932	25,353	26,929

– Represents or rounds to zero. NA Not available. [1] Excludes nonhydrocarbon gases. [2] Includes other states, not shown separately. State production includes state offshore production, as well as extractions from the Gulf not distributed to states. U.S. level totals shown in Table 929 and Table 936 may contain revisions not carried to state level. [3] Alaska crude oil production and value for North Slope only. [4] Crude petroleum production value calculated using production quantity and domestic crude oil first purchase price.

Source: U.S. Energy Information Administration, "Petroleum & Other Liquids Data," <http://www.eia.gov/petroleum/data.cfm>, and "Natural Gas Data," <http://www.eia.gov/naturalgas/data.cfm>; accessed July 2015.

Table 932. Crude Oil and Natural Gas—Reserves by State: 2010 to 2013

[23,267 mil. bbl. represents 23,267,000,000 barrels. As of December 31. Proved reserves are estimated quantities of the mineral, which geological and engineering data demonstrate with reasonable certainty, to be recoverable in future years from known reservoirs under existing economic and operating conditions. Based on a sample of operators of oil and gas wells]

Area	2010		2011		2012		2013	
	Crude oil proved reserves (mil. bbl.)	Natural gas (bil. cu. ft.)	Crude oil proved reserves (mil. bbl.)	Natural gas (bil. cu. ft.)	Crude oil proved reserves (mil. bbl.)	Natural gas (bil. cu. ft.)	Crude oil proved reserves (mil. bbl.)	Natural gas (bil. cu. ft.)
United States [1]........	23,267	304,625	26,544	334,067	30,529	308,036	33,371	338,264
Alabama.................	42	2,629	46	2,475	51	2,228	44	1,597
Alaska....................	3,722	8,838	3,816	9,424	3,336	9,579	2,898	7,316
Arkansas.................	40	14,178	38	16,370	53	11,035	40	13,518
California.................	2,938	2,647	3,005	2,934	2,974	1,999	2,876	1,887
Colorado.................	386	24,119	423	24,821	618	20,666	896	22,381
Florida...................	18	56	22	6	24	16	38	15
Illinois...................	64	(NA)	54	(NA)	51	(NA)	42	(NA)
Indiana..................	8	(NA)	7	(NA)	13	(NA)	8	(NA)
Kansas..................	295	3,673	343	3,486	375	3,308	372	3,592
Kentucky................	15	2,613	17	2,006	9	1,408	17	1,663
Louisiana...............	424	29,277	417	30,358	463	21,949	503	20,164
Michigan................	40	2,919	44	2,505	56	1,750	64	1,807
Mississippi..............	247	853	238	860	266	607	223	595
Montana.................	369	944	384	778	386	602	413	575
Nebraska................	10	(NA)	14	(NA)	13	(NA)	10	(NA)
New Mexico.............	823	15,412	866	15,005	965	13,586	1,171	13,576
New York................	(NA)	281	(NA)	253	(NA)	184	(NA)	144
North Dakota...........	1,814	1,667	2,649	2,381	3,761	3,569	5,677	5,420
Ohio.....................	42	832	41	758	39	1,233	42	3,161
Oklahoma...............	710	26,345	879	27,830	934	26,599	1,019	26,873
Pennsylvania...........	22	13,960	24	26,529	27	36,348	15	49,674
Texas....................	5,674	88,997	7,014	98,165	9,614	86,924	10,468	90,349
Utah.....................	449	6,981	504	7,857	613	7,548	613	6,829
Virginia..................	(NA)	3,215	(NA)	2,832	(NA)	2,579	(NA)	2,373
West Virginia...........	17	7,000	21	10,345	7	14,611	17	22,765
Wyoming................	567	35,074	660	35,290	706	30,094	723	33,618
Federal offshore........	4,496	11,765	4,976	10,420	5,131	9,392	5,137	8,193
Lower 48 states..........	19,545	295,787	22,728	324,643	27,193	298,457	30,473	330,948

NA Not available. [1] Includes other states, not shown separately.

Source: U.S. Energy Information Administration, "Petroleum & Other Liquids Data," <http://www.eia.gov/petroleum/data.cfm>; and "Natural Gas Data," <http://www.eia.gov/naturalgas/data.cfm>; accessed July 2015.

Table 933. Federal Offshore Leasing, Exploration, Production, and Revenue: 1990 to 2014

[In units, as indicated (56.79 represents 56,790,000). Data presented by fiscal year. See source for explanation of terms and for reliability statement]

Item	Unit	1990	1995	2000	2005	2010	2012	2013	2014
Tracts offered.............................	Number	10,459	10,995	7,992	11,447	6,958	11,307	11,163	11,843
Tracts leased..............................	Number	825	835	553	989	446	570	358	403
Acres offered.............................	Millions	56.79	59.70	42.89	61.08	36.96	60.06	59.29	62.44
Acres leased..............................	Millions	4.30	4.34	2.92	5.24	2.37	2.99	1.94	2.10
New wells being drilled:									
Active......................................	Number	120	237	236	135	48	(NA)	(NA)	(NA)
Suspended...............................	Number	266	155	139	59	76	(NA)	(NA)	(NA)
Cumulative wells (since 1953):									
Wells completed........................	Number	13,167	13,423	13,733	13,398	10,404	(NA)	(NA)	(NA)
Wells plugged and abandoned.......	Number	14,677	21,478	26,893	31,884	36,695	(NA)	(NA)	(NA)
Revenue, total [1].......................	Bil. dol.	3.4	2.7	5.2	6.3	5.3	6.9	9.1	7.4
Bonuses, oil and gas..................	Bil. dol.	0.8	0.4	0.4	0.6	1.0	0.7	0.3	1.0
Royalties, oil and gas.................	Bil. dol.	2.6	2.1	4.1	5.5	3.6	5.7	5.9	5.9
Rentals, oil and gas....................	Bil. dol.	0.1	0.1	0.2	0.2	0.2	0.2	0.3	0.2
Sales value [2]...........................	Bil. dol.	17.0	13.8	27.4	37.2	25.1	41.3	42.8	43.7
Oil..	Bil. dol.	7.0	6.3	11.5	15.4	21.3	37.8	39.3	40.0
Natural gas...............................	Bil. dol.	9.5	7.5	15.9	21.8	3.7	3.5	3.4	3.7
Sales volume: [3]									
Oil..	Mil. bbl.	324	409	566	332	261	347	373	396
Natural gas...............................	Bil. cu. ft.	5,093	4,692	4,723	3,504	1,043	1,127	964	852

NA Not available [1] Includes revenues from sources and commodities not shown separately, including oil condensate, salt, sulfur, and wind. [2] Sales value is value at time of sale, not current value. Excludes gas plant products. [3] Excludes sales volumes for gas lost, gas plant products, and sulfur.

Source: U.S. Department of the Interior, Bureau of Ocean Energy Management, Regulation and Enforcement, *Outer Continental Shelf Lease Sale Statistics*, December 2014; and Office of Natural Resources Revenue, "Annual Reported Royalty Revenue," <http://statistics.onrr.gov/ReportTool.aspx>, accessed July 2015. See also <http://www.boem.gov/Outer-Continental-Shelf-Lease-Sale-Statistics/>.

Table 934. Natural Gas Plant Liquids—Production and Value: 1990 to 2014

[Barrels of 42 gallons (569 represents 569,000,000)]

Item	Unit	1990	1995	2000	2005	2010	2011	2012	2013	2014
Field production [1]......................	Mil. bbl.	569	643	699	627	757	809	881	951	1,082
Pentanes plus...........................	Mil. bbl.	113	122	112	97	101	106	116	127	141
Liquefied petroleum gases............	Mil. bbl.	456	521	587	529	656	703	765	824	941
Natural gas processed.................	Tril. cu. ft.	15	17	17	15	16	17	18	18	(NA)

NA Not available. [1] Includes other finished petroleum products, not shown separately.

Source: U.S. Energy Information Administration, "Natural Gas Data," <http://www.eia.gov/naturalgas/index.cfm>, accessed July 2015.

Table 935. Net U.S. Imports of Selected Minerals and Metals as Percent of Apparent Consumption: 1980 to 2014

[In percent. Based on net imports which equal the difference between imports and exports plus or minus government stockpile and industry stock changes]

Minerals and metals	1980	1990	1995	2000	2005	2010	2012	2013	2014 [1]
Bauxite [2].............................	(NA)	98	99	100	100	100	100	100	100
Fluorspar..............................	87	91	92	100	100	100	100	100	100
Manganese...........................	98	100	100	100	100	100	100	100	100
Niobium................................	100	100	100	100	100	100	100	100	100
Strontium..............................	100	100	100	100	100	100	100	100	100
Tantalum...............................	90	86	80	80	100	100	100	100	100
Mica (sheet)...........................	100	100	100	100	100	100	100	100	100
Vanadium..............................	35	(D)	84	100	100	82	99	94	100
Titanium................................	(NA)	(NA)	70	79	71	65	78	86	91
Platinum................................	(NA)	(NA)	(NA)	78	93	91	90	84	85
Potash..................................	65	68	75	80	80	83	82	82	84
Zinc.....................................	60	64	71	72	67	73	71	75	81
Barite...................................	44	71	65	84	84	75	81	74	79
Cobalt..................................	93	84	79	78	83	81	77	75	76
Tin.......................................	79	71	84	88	78	73	74	72	74
Chromium.............................	67	80	75	77	68	63	69	63	72
Palladium..............................	(NA)	(NA)	(NA)	84	84	49	57	60	65
Silver....................................	7	(NA)	(NA)	43	72	65	54	59	63
Nickel...................................	76	64	60	54	48	41	49	46	54
Tungsten..............................	53	81	90	66	68	63	39	41	43
Aluminum..............................	([3])	([3])	23	33	41	14	11	21	33
Copper.................................	16	15	27	37	42	32	36	34	31
Iron and steel........................	13	13	21	18	15	6	11	12	17
Sulfur...................................	14	15	21	18	24	19	18	19	11
Gypsum................................	21	27	30	27	27	12	9	10	10

D Withheld to avoid disclosure. NA Not available. [1] Preliminary. [2] Includes alumina. [3] Net exporter.

Source: Through 1990, U.S. Bureau of Mines; thereafter, U.S. Geological Survey, *Mineral Commodity Summaries 2015*, January 2015, and earlier reports. See also <http://minerals.usgs.gov/minerals/pubs/mcs/>.

Table 936. Natural Gas—Supply, Consumption, Reserves, and Marketed Production: 1990 to 2014

[270 represents 270,000. Data are for dry natural gas, plus a small amount of supplemental gaseous fuels. Minus sign (-) indicates debit]

Item	Unit	1990	1995	2000	2005	2010	2011	2012	2013	2014 [8]
Producing wells (year-end).........	1,000	270	299	342	426	488	515	483	487	(NA)
Production value at wells............	Bil. dol.	31.8	30.3	74.3	138.8	100.3	(NA)	(NA)	(NA)	(NA)
Avg. per 1,000 cu. ft.................	Dollars	1.71	1.55	3.68	7.33	4.48	3.95	2.66	(NA)	(NA)
Proved reserves [1]...................	Tril. cu. ft.	169	165	177	204	305	349	323	354	(NA)
Marketed production [2]...........	**Bil. cu. ft.**	**18,594**	**19,506**	**20,198**	**18,927**	**22,382**	**24,036**	**25,283**	**25,691**	**27,271**
Minus: Extraction losses [3].........	Bil. cu. ft.	784	908	1,016	876	1,066	1,134	1,250	1,357	1,553
Equals: Dry production..............	Bil. cu. ft.	17,810	18,599	19,182	18,051	21,316	22,902	24,033	24,334	25,718
Plus: Supplemental gas supplies...	Bil. cu. ft.	123	110	90	64	65	60	61	55	56
Equals: Dry production with supplemental gas...................	Bil. cu. ft.	17,932	18,709	19,272	18,114	21,380	22,962	24,095	24,388	25,775
Plus: Withdrawals from storage [4]...	Bil. cu. ft.	1,934	2,974	3,498	3,057	3,274	3,074	2,818	3,702	3,586
Plus: Imports.......................	Bil. cu. ft.	1,532	2,841	3,782	4,341	3,741	3,469	3,138	2,883	2,695
Plus: Balancing item [5].............	Bil. cu. ft.	307	396	-306	236	115	-94	-66	-77	115
Equals: Total supply................	Bil. cu. ft.	21,706	24,920	26,246	25,748	28,511	29,411	29,984	30,896	32,171
Minus: Exports.....................	Bil. cu. ft.	86	154	244	729	1,137	1,506	1,619	1,572	1,514
Minus: Additions to storage [4].......	Bil. cu. ft.	2,433	2,566	2,684	3,002	3,291	3,422	2,825	3,156	3,838
Equals: Consumption, total.......	**Bil. cu. ft.**	**19,174**	**22,207**	**23,333**	**22,014**	**24,087**	**24,477**	**25,538**	**26,131**	**26,821**
Lease and plant fuel................	Bil. cu. ft.	1,236	1,220	1,151	1,112	1,286	1,323	1,396	1,475	1,566
Pipeline fuel [6].....................	Bil. cu. ft.	660	700	642	584	674	688	731	862	884
Residential........................	Bil. cu. ft.	4,391	4,850	4,996	4,827	4,782	4,714	4,150	4,914	5,073
Commercial [7].....................	Bil. cu. ft.	2,623	3,031	3,182	2,999	3,103	3,155	2,895	3,279	3,461
Industrial..........................	Bil. cu. ft.	(NA)	(NA)	8,142	6,601	6,826	6,994	7,226	7,414	7,655
Vehicle fuel........................	Bil. cu. ft.	(Z)	5	13	23	29	30	30	34	33
Electric power sector...............	Bil. cu. ft.	3,245	4,237	5,206	5,869	7,387	7,574	9,111	8,153	8,149
World production (dry)..............	Tril. cu. ft.	74	78	87	98	113	116	119	121	(NA)
U.S. production (dry)...............	Tril. cu. ft.	18	19	19	18	21	23	24	24	26
U.S. percent of world..............	Percent	24.2	23.8	22.0	18.4	18.9	19.7	20.1	20.1	(NA)

NA Not available. Z Less than 500 million cubic feet. [1] Estimated, end of year. [2] Marketed production includes gross withdrawals from reservoirs less quantities used for reservoir repressuring and quantities vented or flared. Excludes nonhydrocarbon gases subsequently removed. [3] Volumetric reduction in natural gas resulting from the removal of natural gas plant liquids, which are transferred to petroleum supply. [4] Underground storage. [5] Quantities lost and imbalances in data due to differences among data sources. Since 1980, excludes intransit shipments that cross U.S.-Canada border (i.e., natural gas delivered to its destination via the other country). [6] Natural gas consumed in the operation of pipelines and delivery to consumers. [7] Includes deliveries to municipalities and public authorities for institutional heating and other purposes. [8] Data for 2014 are preliminary.

Source: U.S. Energy Information Administration, "Natural Gas Data," <http://www.eia.gov/naturalgas/data.cfm>, "Monthly Energy Review, Natural Gas," <http://www.eia.gov/totalenergy/data/monthly/#naturalgas>, and "International Energy Statistics," <http://www.eia.gov/countries/data.cfm>, accessed September 2015.

Table 937. Unconventional Dry Natural Gas Production and Proved Reserves: 2012 and 2013

[In billions of cubic feet (1,655 represents 1,655,000,000,000). For states not shown, no production or reserves were reported]

State	Production				Proved reserves [1]			
	Coalbed methane [2]		Shale gas [3]		Coalbed methane [2]		Shale gas [3]	
	2012	2013	2012	2013	2012	2013	2012	2013
U.S...............	**1,655**	**1,466**	**10,371**	**11,415**	**13,591**	**12,392**	**129,396**	**159,115**
Alabama................	91	62	(NA)	(NA)	1,006	413	(NA)	(NA)
Alaska..................	–	–	–	–	–	–	–	–
Arkansas...............	2	2	1,027	1,026	10	13	9,779	12,231
California...............	–	–	90	89	–	–	777	756
Colorado...............	486	444	9	18	5,074	4,391	53	136
Florida.................	–	–	(NA)	(NA)	–	–	(NA)	(NA)
Kansas.................	34	30	1	3	183	189	2	3
Kentucky...............	–	–	4	4	–	–	34	46
Louisiana...............	–	–	2,204	1,510	–	–	13,523	11,483
Michigan...............	–	–	108	101	–	–	1,345	1,418
Mississippi.............	–	–	2	5	–	–	19	37
Montana................	3	1	16	19	11	16	216	229
New Mexico............	355	356	13	16	2,772	2,856	176	258
New York...............	–	–	(NA)	(NA)	–	–	(NA)	(NA)
North Dakota...........	–	–	203	268	–	–	3,147	5,059
Ohio...................	(NA)	(NA)	14	101	(NA)	(NA)	483	2,319
Oklahoma..............	68	65	637	698	439	440	12,572	12,675
Pennsylvania...........	15	13	2,036	3,076	106	161	32,681	44,325
Texas..................	11	8	3,649	3,876	81	57	44,778	49,055
Utah...................	55	50	(NA)	(NA)	518	523	(NA)	(NA)
Virginia................	99	93	3	3	1,535	1,387	135	126
West Virginia..........	9	8	345	498	107	113	9,408	18,078
Wyoming...............	426	331	7	102	1,736	1,810	216	856

– Represents or rounds to zero. NA Not available. [1] Proved reserves of natural gas as of December 31 of the report year are the estimated quantities which analysis of geological and engineering data demonstrate with reasonable certainty to be recoverable in future years from known reservoirs under existing economic and operating conditions. [2] Methane is generated during coal formation and is contained in the coal microstructure. Typical recovery entails pumping water out of the coal to allow the gas to escape. Methane is the principal component of natural gas. Coal bed methane can be added to natural gas pipelines without any special treatment. [3] Natural gas produced from low permeability shale formations.

Source: U.S. Energy Information Administration, "Natural Gas Data," <http://www.eia.gov/naturalgas/data.cfm>, accessed July 2015.

Table 938. Coal Supply, Disposition, and Prices: 2000 to 2014

[In millions of short tons (1,073.6 represents 1,073,600,000). 1 short ton = 2,000 lbs]

Item	2000	2005	2010	2011	2012	2013	2014
United States, total supply.................	**1,073.6**	**1,131.5**	**1,084.4**	**1,095.6**	**1,016.5**	**984.8**	**999.7**
Consumption by sector:							
Total..	1,084.1	1,126.0	1,048.5	1,002.9	889.2	924.4	916.9
Electric power............................	985.8	1,037.5	975.1	932.5	823.6	858.0	851.4
Coke plants..............................	28.9	23.4	21.1	21.4	20.8	21.5	20.4
Other industrial plants................	65.2	60.3	49.3	46.2	42.8	43.1	42.8
Combined heat and power (CHP)...	28.0	25.9	24.6	22.3	20.1	19.8	19.9
Noncombined heat and power......	37.2	34.5	24.7	23.9	22.8	23.3	22.9
Commercial..............................	3.7	4.3	3.1	2.8	2.0	2.0	2.2
Residential [1]...........................	0.5	0.4	(NA)	(NA)	(NA)	(NA)	(NA)
Year-end coal stocks:							
Total [2]...................................	140.0	144.3	231.7	232.0	238.9	200.3	203.2
Electric power............................	102.0	101.1	174.9	172.4	185.1	147.9	151.4
Coke plants..............................	1.5	2.6	1.9	2.6	2.5	2.2	1.9
Other industrial plants................	4.6	5.6	4.5	4.5	4.5	4.1	4.8
Producers/distributors................	31.9	35.0	49.8	51.9	46.2	45.7	44.8
U.S. coal trade:							
Net exports [3]...........................	46.0	19.5	62.4	94.2	116.6	108.8	86.0
Exports...................................	58.5	49.9	81.7	107.3	125.7	117.7	97.3
Steam coal............................	25.7	21.3	25.6	37.7	55.9	52.0	34.3
Metallurgical coal...................	32.8	28.7	56.1	69.5	69.9	65.7	63.0
Imports...................................	12.5	30.5	19.4	13.1	9.2	8.9	11.4
Average delivered price (dollars per short ton):							
Electric utilities.........................	24.28	31.22	44.27	46.24	45.77	45.03	(NA)
Independent power producers......	(NA)	30.39	41.49	(NA)	(NA)	(NA)	(NA)
Coke plants..............................	44.38	83.79	153.59	184.44	190.55	156.99	(NA)
Other industrial plants................	31.46	47.63	64.38	70.66	70.33	69.16	(NA)
Average free alongside ship (f.a.s.):							
Exports...................................	34.90	67.10	120.41	(NA)	(NA)	(NA)	(NA)
Steam coal............................	29.67	47.64	65.54	(NA)	(NA)	(NA)	(NA)
Metallurgical coal...................	38.99	81.56	145.44	(NA)	(NA)	(NA)	(NA)
Imports...................................	30.10	46.71	71.77	(NA)	(NA)	(NA)	(NA)

NA Not available. [1] Beginning in 2008, residential coal consumption data are not collected by Energy Information Administration. [2] Includes other stocks, not shown separately. [3] Exports minus imports.

Source: U.S. Energy Information Administration, *Annual Coal Report 2013*, April 2015, and earlier reports; and "Coal Data," <http://www.eia.gov/coal/data.cfm>, and "Monthly Energy Review, Coal," <http://www.eia.gov/totalenergy/data/monthly/#coal>, accessed September 2015.

Table 939. Coal and Coke—Summary: 1990 to 2013

[In millions of short tons (1,029 represents 1,029,000,000), except as indicated. Includes coal consumed at mines. Recoverability varies between 40 and 90 percent for individual deposits; 50 percent or more of overall U.S. coal reserve base is believed to be recoverable]

Item	Unit	1990	1995	2000	2005	2010	2011	2012	2013
COAL									
Production, total [1,2]..................	**Mil. sh. tons**	**1,029**	**1,033**	**1,074**	**1,131**	**1,084**	**1,096**	**1,016**	**985**
Value [3].................................	Bil. dol.	22.39	19.45	18.02	26.69	38.61	40.39	(NA)	(NA)
Anthracite production [2].............	Mil. sh. tons	3.5	4.7	4.6	1.7	1.7	2.2	2.4	2.1
Bituminous coal and lignite [4]......	Mil. sh. tons	1,026	1,028	1,069	1,130	1,083	1,093	1,014	983
Underground...........................	Mil. sh. tons	425	396	374	369	337	346	342	342
Surface [2]..............................	Mil. sh. tons	605	637	700	762	745	748	673	641
Exports.................................	Mil. sh. tons	106	89	58	50	82	107	126	118
Imports.................................	Mil. sh. tons	3	9	13	30	19	13	9	9
Consumption [5]........................	Mil. sh. tons	904	962	1,084	1,126	1,049	1,003	889	924
Electric power sector [6]..............	Mil. sh. tons	783	850	986	1,037	975	932	824	858
Industrial..............................	Mil. sh. tons	115	106	94	84	70	68	64	65
Number of mines......................	Number	3,243	2,104	1,453	1,415	1,285	1,325	1,229	1,061
Daily employment.....................	1,000	131	90	72	79	86	92	90	80
Production, by state:									
Alabama.................................	Mil. sh. tons	29	25	19	21	20	19	19	19
Illinois...................................	Mil. sh. tons	60	48	33	32	33	38	48	52
Indiana..................................	Mil. sh. tons	36	26	28	34	35	37	37	39
Kentucky................................	Mil. sh. tons	173	154	131	120	105	109	91	80
Montana.................................	Mil. sh. tons	38	39	38	40	45	42	37	42
Ohio......................................	Mil. sh. tons	35	26	22	25	27	28	26	25
Pennsylvania..........................	Mil. sh. tons	71	62	75	67	59	59	55	54
Virginia..................................	Mil. sh. tons	47	34	33	28	22	23	19	17
West Virginia..........................	Mil. sh. tons	169	163	158	154	135	135	120	113
Wyoming................................	Mil. sh. tons	184	264	339	404	443	439	401	388
Other states...........................	Mil. sh. tons	187	192	197	206	161	167	162	156
World production......................	Mil. sh. tons	5,294	4,963	5,126	6,617	8,010	8,480	8,660	8,990
Percent U.S. of world................	Percent	19.4	20.8	20.9	17.1	13.5	12.9	11.7	11.0
COKE									
Production...............................	Mil. sh. tons	27.6	20.0	20.8	16.7	15.0	15.4	15.2	15.3
Imports...................................	Mil. sh. tons	0.8	3.8	3.8	3.5	1.2	1.4	1.1	0.1
Exports...................................	Mil. sh. tons	0.6	1.4	1.1	1.7	1.5	1.0	1.0	0.8
Consumption [7]........................	Mil. sh. tons	27.8	25.8	23.2	18.2	14.8	15.8	15.5	14.4

[1] Includes bituminous coal, subbituminous coal, lignite, and anthracite. [2] Beginning 2005, includes a small amount of refuse recovery. [3] Coal values are based on free-on-board rail/barge prices, which are the free-on-board prices of coal at the point of first sale, excluding freight or shipping and insurance costs. [4] Includes subbituminous. [5] Includes some categories not shown separately. [6] Electricity-only and combined-heat-and-power (CHP) plants whose primary business is to sell electricity and/or heat to the public. [7] Consumption is calculated as the sum of production and imports minus exports and stock change.

Source: U.S. Energy Information Administration, *Annual Energy Review 2011*, September 2012; *Annual Coal Report 2013*, April 2015; *Quarterly Coal Report*, July 2015; and "International Energy Statistics," <http://www.eia.gov/countries/data.cfm>, accessed September 2015. See also <http://www.eia.gov/totalenergy> and <http://www.eia.gov/coal/annual/>.

Table 940. Demonstrated Coal Reserves by Major Producing State: 2012 and 2013

[Reserves in millions of short tons (481,385 represents 481,385,000,000). As of January 1 the following year. The demonstrated reserve base represents the sum of coal in both measured and indicated resource categories of reliability. Measured resources of coal are estimates that have a high degree of geologic assurance from sample analyses and measurements from closely spaced and geological well-known sample sites. Indicated resources are estimates based partly from sample and analyses and measurements and partly from reasonable geologic projections]

State	2012				2013			
		Reserves				Reserves		
			Method of mining				Method of mining	
	Number of mines	Total reserves	Under-ground	Surface	Number of mines	Total reserves	Under-ground	Surface
United States [1]	**1,229**	**481,385**	**329,814**	**151,571**	**1,061**	**479,914**	**329,125**	**150,789**
Alabama	46	3,974	844	3,130	39	3,940	817	3,124
Alaska	1	6,094	5,423	672	1	6,092	5,423	670
Arkansas	2	416	272	144	2	416	272	144
Colorado	12	15,832	11,073	4,759	10	15,787	11,029	4,758
Illinois	24	103,995	87,493	16,502	24	103,895	87,400	16,495
Indiana	29	9,100	8,556	544	27	9,039	8,522	516
Iowa	(NA)	2,189	1,732	457	(NA)	2,189	1,732	457
Kansas	1	971	(NA)	971	1	971	(NA)	971
Kentucky	357	28,713	16,130	12,583	270	28,571	16,021	12,551
Kentucky, Eastern	330	9,652	644	9,008	246	9,588	605	8,983
Kentucky, Western	27	19,061	15,486	3,574	24	18,983	15,416	3,567
Maryland	21	612	564	48	21	609	562	47
Missouri	2	5,986	1,479	4,507	1	5,985	1,479	4,506
Montana	6	118,851	70,925	47,927	6	118,792	70,907	47,885
New Mexico	4	11,892	6,073	5,819	4	11,860	6,061	5,799
North Dakota	4	8,797	(NA)	8,797	4	8,763	(NA)	8,763
Ohio	39	22,985	17,306	5,679	31	22,940	17,271	5,669
Oklahoma	7	1,540	1,225	315	9	1,539	1,224	314
Pennsylvania	235	26,677	22,522	4,155	228	26,582	22,438	4,144
Anthracite [2]	65	7,183	3,841	3,341	65	7,180	3,841	3,339
Bituminous	170	19,495	18,681	814	163	19,402	18,597	805
Tennessee	14	753	500	253	11	751	498	252
Texas	12	12,019	(NA)	12,019	11	11,966	(NA)	11,966
Utah	9	5,091	4,825	267	9	5,058	4,792	266
Virginia	96	1,408	920	488	82	1,378	896	482
Washington	(NA)	1,340	1,332	8	(NA)	1,340	1,332	8
West Virginia	264	31,281	28,010	3,271	219	31,074	27,846	3,228
Wyoming	18	59,951	42,456	17,495	17	59,463	42,447	17,015

NA Not available. [1] Includes other states not shown separately. [2] All of the anthracite mines in the United States are located in northeastern Pennsylvania.

Source: U.S. Energy Information Administration, *Annual Coal Report, 2013*, January 2015, and earlier reports. See also <http://www.eia.gov/coal/annual/>.

Table 941. Uranium Concentrate Industry—Summary: 1990 to 2014

[In units as indicated (1.7 represents 1,700,000). See also Section 19, Table 962]

Item	Unit	1990	1995	2000	2009	2010	2011	2012	2013	2014
Exploration and development, surface drilling	Mil. ft.	1.7	1.3	1.0	3.7	4.9	6.3	7.2	3.8	1.3
Expenditures	Mil. dol.	(NA)	2.6	5.6	35.4	44.6	53.6	66.6	49.9	28.2
Number of mines operated	Number	39	12	10	20	9	11	12	12	11
Underground	Number	27	–	1	14	4	5	6	3	2
Open pit	Number	2	–	–	–	–	–	–	–	–
In situ leaching	Number	7	5	4	4	4	5	5	7	8
Other sources [1]	Number	3	7	5	2	1	1	1	2	1
Mine production	1,000 pounds	5,876	3,528	3,123	4,145	4,237	4,114	4,335	4,577	4,912
Underground	1,000 pounds	(D)	–	(D)	(D)	(D)	(D)	(D)	(D)	(D)
Open pit	1,000 pounds	1,881	–	–	–	–	–	–	–	–
In situ leaching	1,000 pounds	(D)	3,372	2,995	(D)	(D)	(D)	(D)	(D)	(D)
Other sources [1]	1,000 pounds	3,995	156	128	(D)	(D)	(D)	(D)	(D)	(D)
Uranium concentrate production	1,000 pounds	8,886	6,043	3,958	3,708	4,228	3,991	4,146	4,659	4,891
Concentrate shipments from mills and plants	1,000 pounds	12,957	5,500	3,187	3,620	5,137	4,000	3,911	4,655	4,593
Employment	Person-years [2]	1,335	1,107	627	1,096	1,073	1,191	1,196	1,156	787

– Represents zero. D Data withheld to avoid disclosing figures for individual companies. NA Not available. [1] Includes mine water, mill site cleanup and mill tailings, and well field restoration as sources of uranium. [2] A person-year is defined as one whole year, or fraction thereof, worked by an employee, including contracted man power. 12 months worked is 1 person year.

Source: U.S. Energy Information Administration, through 2002, *Uranium Industry,* annual. Thereafter, *Domestic Uranium Production Report,* April 2015, and earlier reports. See also <http://www.eia.gov/uranium/production/annual/>.

Table 942. Crude Petroleum and Natural Gas Extraction Industry—Establishments, Employees, and Payroll by State: 2013

[15,669,403 represents $15,669,403,000. Excludes self-employed individuals, employees of private households, railroad employees, agricultural production employees, and most government employees. See source for definitions and statement on reliability of data. An establishment is a single physical location where business is conducted or where services or industrial operations are performed. See Appendix III]

State	Crude petroleum and natural gas extraction (NAICS 211111) [1]			State	Crude petroleum and natural gas extraction (NAICS 211111) [1]		
	Establish-ments	Number of employees [2]	Annual payroll ($1,000)		Establish-ments	Number of employees [2]	Annual payroll ($1,000)
United States	**7,676**	**120,071**	**15,669,403**	Mississippi	82	950	121,919
Alabama	33	478	45,435	Missouri	12	33	1,947
Alaska	23	(7)	(D)	Montana	92	968	127,042
Arizona	21	60	5,482	Nebraska	21	107	5,118
Arkansas	103	1,909	172,640	Nevada	21	76	5,345
California	214	7,397	1,037,842	New Hampshire	2	(3)	(D)
Colorado	411	6,309	1,031,307	New Mexico	158	2,838	281,324
Connecticut	5	(6)	(D)	New York	42	352	42,768
Delaware	3	(3)	(D)	North Carolina	6	(4)	3,740
District of Columbia	3	(3)	(D)	North Dakota	67	2,492	263,615
Florida	27	179	13,231	Ohio	197	1,653	101,945
Georgia	2	(4)	(D)	Oklahoma	1,186	17,804	2,137,471
Hawaii	1	(3)	(D)	Oregon	3	(3)	(D)
Idaho	3	2	151	Pennsylvania	195	5,525	682,231
Illinois	173	981	59,261	Rhode Island	1	(3)	(D)
Indiana	45	217	12,923	South Carolina	1	(3)	(D)
Iowa	1	(3)	(D)	South Dakota	6	(4)	(D)
Kansas	409	2,701	182,538	Tennessee	13	156	9,773
Kentucky	76	675	48,806	Texas	3,143	49,185	7,245,977
Louisiana	371	6,639	776,420	Utah	60	1,660	200,439
Maryland	3	(3)	(D)	Virginia	18	(5)	(D)
Massachusetts	4	(3)	1,680	Washington	6	(3)	(D)
Michigan	75	888	66,587	West Virginia	175	2,257	181,185
Minnesota	4	13	1,413	Wisconsin	4	(5)	(D)
				Wyoming	155	2,496	263,551

D Withheld to avoid disclosing data for individual companies; data are included in higher level totals. [1] North American Industry Classification System, 2012. [2] Covers full- and part-time employees who are on the payroll in the pay period including March 12. [3] 0 to 19 employees. [4] 20 to 99 employees. [5] 100 to 249 employees. [6] 250 to 499 employees. [7] 1,000 to 2,499 employees.

Source: U.S. Census Bureau, County Business Patterns, "Geography Area Series: County Business Patterns," <http://factfinder2.census.gov>, accessed April 2015. See also <http://www.census.gov/econ/cbp/>.

Table 943. Natural Gas Liquid Extraction Industry—Establishments, Employees, and Payroll by State: 2013

[1,322,362 represents $1,322,362,000. Excludes self-employed individuals, employees of private households, railroad employees, agricultural production employees, and most government employees. See source for definitions and statement on reliability of data. An establishment is a single physical location where business is conducted or where services or industrial operations are performed. See Appendix III]

State	Natural gas liquid extraction (NAICS 211112) [1]			State	Natural gas liquid extraction (NAICS 211112) [1]		
	Establish-ments	Number of employees [2]	Annual payroll ($1,000)		Establish-ments	Number of employees [2]	Annual payroll ($1,000)
United States	**361**	**11,718**	**1,322,362**	Michigan	11	126	12,068
Alabama	2	(4)	(D)	Mississippi	4	153	16,712
Alaska	2	(6)	(D)	Montana	2	(4)	(D)
Arizona	1	(3)	(D)	New Mexico	19	(6)	(D)
Arkansas	2	(4)	(D)	North Carolina	1	(3)	(D)
California	8	182	23,888	North Dakota	2	(5)	(D)
Colorado	22	1,508	219,208	Ohio	11	107	11,277
Florida	3	(3)	(D)	Oklahoma	39	1,218	92,055
Idaho	1	(3)	(D)	Pennsylvania	13	(8)	(D)
Illinois	2	(5)	(D)	Tennessee	1	(3)	(D)
Indiana	2	(4)	(D)	Texas	121	3,153	312,623
Kansas	12	(5)	(D)	Utah	3	(5)	(D)
Kentucky	4	(4)	(D)	Virginia	1	(3)	(D)
Louisiana	45	841	74,672	West Virginia	8	(7)	(D)
				Wyoming	19	(7)	(D)

D Withheld to avoid disclosing data for individual companies; data are included in higher level totals. [1] North American Industry Classification System, 2012. [2] Covers full- and part-time employees who are on the payroll in the pay period including March 12. [3] 0 to 19 employees. [4] 20 to 99 employees. [5] 100 to 249 employees. [6] 250 to 499 employees. [7] 500 to 999 employees. [8] 1,000 to 2,499 employees.

Source: U.S. Census Bureau, County Business Patterns, "Geography Area Series: County Business Patterns," <http://factfinder2.census.gov>, accessed April 2015. See also <http://www.census.gov/econ/cbp/>.

Energy and Utilities

This section presents statistics on fuel resources, energy production and consumption, electric energy, renewable energy, the electric and gas utility industries, sewage treatment facilities, and public drinking water systems. The principal sources are the U.S. Department of Energy's Energy Information Administration (EIA), the Edison Electric Institute, Washington, DC, and the American Gas Association, Arlington, VA. The Department of Energy was created in October 1977 and assumed and centralized the responsibilities of all or part of several agencies including the Federal Power Commission (FPC), the U.S. Bureau of Mines, the Federal Energy Administration, and the U.S. Energy Research and Development Administration. For additional data on transportation, see Section 23; on fuels, see Section 18; and on energy-related housing characteristics, see Section 20.

The EIA, in its *Annual Energy Review*, provides statistics and trend data on energy supply, demand, and prices. Information is included on petroleum and natural gas, coal, electricity, hydroelectric power, nuclear power, solar, wind, wood, and geothermal energy. Due to budget constraints, in 2013 the EIA suspended publication of the *Annual Energy Review*. In order to continue publishing similar data, the EIA expanded their coverage of data in their *Monthly Energy Review*, which presents current supply, disposition, and price data and monthly publications on petroleum, coal, natural gas, and electric power. Additional EIA reports include the *Electric Power Annual*; *Natural Gas Annual*; *Petroleum Supply Annual*; *U.S. Crude Oil, Natural Gas, and Natural Gas Liquids Reserves Annual Report*; *Electric Sales, Revenue, and Price*; *State Energy Consumption, Price, and Expenditure Data*; *Annual Energy Outlook*; *Uranium Marketing Annual Report; Domestic Uranium Production Report—Quarterly*; and *International Energy Statistics*. These various reports contain state, national, and international data on the production of electricity, net summer capability of generating plants, fuels used in energy production, energy sales and consumption, and hydroelectric power.

Data on residential energy consumption, expenditures, and conservation activities are available from EIA's Residential Energy Consumption Survey (RECS) and are published every 4 years. The Commercial Buildings Energy Consumption Survey (CBECS), conducted on a quadrennial basis, collects information on the stock of U.S. commercial buildings, their energy-related characteristics, and their energy consumption and expenditures. Data on manufacturing energy consumption, use, and expenditures are also collected every 4 years from EIA's Manufacturing Energy Consumption Survey (MECS). Due to the long gaps between the RECS, CBECS, and MECS, tables are rotated in and out of Section 19 in an effort to keep the data as current as possible. The results from these surveys are published at <http://www.eia.gov/consumption/>.

The Edison Electric Institute's annual *Statistical Year Book of the Electric Power Industry* contains data on the distribution of electric energy by public utilities. The American Gas Association, in its annual yearbook, *Gas Facts*, presents data on gas utilities and financial and operating statistics.

Btu conversion factors—Various energy sources are converted from original units to the thermal equivalent using British thermal units (Btu). A Btu is the amount of energy required to raise the temperature of 1 pound of water 1 degree Fahrenheit (F) at or near 39.2 degrees F. Factors are calculated annually from the latest final annual data available; some are revised as a result.

Electric power industry—In recent years, EIA has restructured the industry categories it once used to gather and report electricity statistics. The electric power industry, previously divided into electric utilities and non-utilities, now consists of the Electric Power Sector, the Commercial Sector, and the Industrial Sector.

The Electric Power Sector is composed of electricity-only and combined-heat-and-power plants (CHPs) whose primary business is to sell electricity, or electricity and heat, to the public.

Electricity-only plants are composed of traditional electric utilities, and nontraditional participants, including energy service providers, power marketers, independent power producers (IPPs), and the portion of CHPs that produce only electricity.

A utility is defined as a corporation, person, agency, authority, or other legal entity or instrumentality aligned with distribution facilities for delivery of electric energy for use primarily by the public. Electric utilities include investor-owned electric utilities, municipal and state utilities, federal electric utilities, and rural electric cooperatives.

An independent power producer is an entity defined as a corporation, person, agency, authority, or other legal entity or instrumentality that owns or operates facilities whose primary business is to produce electricity for use by the public. They are not generally aligned with distribution facilities and are not considered electric utilities.

Combined-heat-and-power producers are plants designed to produce both heat and electricity from a single heat source. These types of electricity producers can be independent power producers or industrial or commercial establishments. As some independent power producers are CHPs, their information is included in the data for the combined-heat-and-power sector.

The Commercial Sector consists of commercial CHPs and commercial electricity-only plants. Industrial CHPs and industrial electricity-only plants make up the Industrial Sector. For more information, please refer to the *Electric Power Annual 2013* Web site at <http://www.eia.gov/electricity/annual/>.

Table 944. Utilities—Establishments, Revenue, Payroll, and Employees by Kind of Business: 2012

[530,580 represents $530,580,000,000. Includes only establishments or firms with payroll. Data based on preliminary results from the 2012 Economic Census. See headnote, Table 774 and Appendix III]

Kind of business	2012 NAICS code [1]	Establish- ments (number)	Revenue Total (mil. dol.)	Revenue Per paid employee (dol.)	Annual payroll Total (mil. dol.)	Annual payroll Per paid employee (dol.)	Paid employees for pay period including March 12 (number)
Utilities.................................	**22**	**17,578**	**530,580**	**816,292**	**58,767**	**90,412**	**649,988**
Electric power generation, transmission, & distribution.................................	2211	10,290	429,053	823,751	49,804	95,619	520,853
Electric power generation.....................	22111	2,635	119,479	839,979	14,312	100,616	142,240
Hydroelectric power generation...........	221111	405	2,393	694,445	271	78,746	3,446
Fossil fuel electric power generation......	221112	1,389	79,685	1,053,085	7,228	95,519	75,668
Nuclear electric power generation.........	221113	144	29,946	566,015	5,897	111,468	52,906
Other electric power generation..........	221119	697	7,455	729,464	915	89,559	10,220
Electric power transmission, control & distribution.................................	22112	7,655	309,574	817,654	35,492	93,742	378,613
Electric bulk power transmission & control.................................	221121	271	10,887	793,229	1,511	110,071	13,725
Electric power distribution..................	221122	7,384	298,687	818,573	33,981	93,128	364,888
Natural gas distribution......................	2212	2,420	87,719	1,040,189	6,693	79,361	84,330
Water, sewage, & other systems.............	2213	4,872	12,301	272,108	2,298	50,832	45,205
Water supply & irrigation systems..........	22131	4,046	9,426	261,324	1,824	50,567	36,072
Sewage treatment facilities.................	22132	727	1,434	203,754	311	44,176	7,036
Steam & air-conditioning supply...........	22133	99	1,441	686,962	163	77,724	2,097

[1] North American Industry Classification System, 2012; see text, Section 15.

Source: U.S. Census Bureau, 2012 Economic Census, EC1222I2, "Utilities: Industry Series: Preliminary Comparative Statistics for the U.S. (2007 NAICS Basis): 2012 and 2007," <http://factfinder.census.gov/>, accessed January 2015.

Table 945. Utilities—Employees, Annual Payroll, and Establishments by Utility Type: 2013

[60,179 represents $60,179,000,000. Excludes most government employees, railroad employees, and self-employed persons. An establishment is a single physical location where business is conducted or where services or industrial operations are performed. See Appendix III]

Industry	2012 NAICS code [1]	Number of employ- ees [2]	Annual payroll (mil. dol.)	Average payroll per employ- ee (dol.)	Establishments by employment size-class Total	Under 20 employ- ees	20 to 99 employ- ees	100 to 499 employ- ees	500 employ- ees and over
Utilities, total.........................	**22**	**638,575**	**60,179**	**94,239**	**18,004**	**12,596**	**4,116**	**1,108**	**184**
Electric power generation, transmission and distribution.............	2211	512,381	50,745	99,037	10,602	6,428	3,130	871	173
Electric power generation....................	22111	135,415	14,535	107,334	2,737	1,805	659	214	59
Hydroelectric power generation........	221111	3,150	262	83,290	407	363	42	2	–
Fossil fuel electric power generation.................................	221112	72,760	7,568	104,019	1,417	739	474	197	7
Nuclear electric power generation.................................	221113	50,410	5,831	115,672	147	64	22	9	52
Solar electric power generation.................................	221114	890	95	107,203	102	88	14	–	–
Wind electric power generation.................................	221115	2,852	328	115,129	231	201	26	4	–
Geothermal electric power generation.................................	221116	1,186	112	94,230	41	29	10	2	–
Biomass electric power generation.................................	221117	1,239	98	79,006	106	82	24	–	–
Other electric power generation.................................	221118	2,928	239	81,745	286	239	47	–	–
Electric power transmission, control & distribution....................	22112	376,966	36,210	96,057	7,865	4,623	2,471	657	114
Electric bulk power transmission & control.................................	221121	13,621	1,569	115,176	267	155	73	32	7
Electric power distribution..............	221122	363,345	34,641	95,340	7,598	4,468	2,398	625	107
Natural gas distribution.....................	2212	84,165	7,035	83,584	2,533	1,725	601	196	11
Water, sewage, & other systems.........	2213	42,029	2,399	57,087	4,869	4,443	385	41	–
Water supply & irrigation systems.................................	22131	33,703	1,901	56,398	4,028	3,711	280	37	–
Sewage treatment facilities..............	22132	6,228	311	49,972	733	663	67	3	–
Steam & air-conditioning supply........	22133	2,098	187	89,278	108	69	38	1	–

– Represents zero. [1] North American Industry Classification System, 2012; see text, Section 15. [2] Covers full- and part-time employees who are on the payroll in the pay period including March 12.

Source: U.S. Census Bureau, County Business Patterns, "Geography Area Series: County Business Patterns by Employment Size Class," <http://factfinder2.census.gov>, accessed April 2015. See also <http://www.census.gov/econ/cbp/>.

Table 946. Energy Supply and Disposition by Type of Fuel: 1973 to 2014

[In quadrillion British thermal units (Btu) (63.56 represents 63,560,000,000,000,000). For definition of Btu, see source and text, this section]

Year	Production					Renewable energy [4]					Net imports, total [7]	Consumption					Renewable energy, [4] total
	Total [1]	Crude oil [2]	Dry natural gas	Coal [3]	Nuclear electric power	Total [1]	Hydroelectric power [5]	Biomass [6]	Solar/photovoltaic	Wind		Total [1,8]	Petroleum [9]	Dry natural gas [10]	Coal	Nuclear electric power	
1973	63.56	19.49	22.19	13.99	0.91	4.41	2.86	1.53	(NA)	(NA)	12.58	75.68	34.84	22.51	12.97	0.91	4.41
1975	61.32	17.73	19.64	14.99	1.90	4.69	3.15	1.50	(NA)	(NA)	11.71	71.96	32.73	19.95	12.66	1.90	4.69
1980	67.18	18.25	19.91	18.60	2.74	5.43	2.90	2.48	(NA)	(NA)	12.10	78.07	34.20	20.24	15.42	2.74	5.43
1985	67.70	18.99	16.98	19.33	4.08	6.08	2.97	3.02	(Z)	(Z)	7.58	76.39	30.92	17.70	17.48	4.08	6.08
1990	70.70	15.57	18.33	22.49	6.10	6.04	3.05	2.74	0.06	0.03	14.06	84.49	33.55	19.60	19.17	6.10	6.04
1995	71.17	13.89	19.08	22.13	7.08	6.56	3.21	3.10	0.07	0.03	17.68	91.03	34.44	22.67	20.09	7.08	6.56
1996	72.49	13.72	19.34	22.79	7.09	7.01	3.59	3.16	0.07	0.03	19.02	94.02	35.67	23.08	21.00	7.09	7.01
1997	72.47	13.66	19.39	23.31	6.60	7.02	3.64	3.11	0.07	0.03	20.63	94.60	36.16	23.22	21.45	6.60	7.02
1998	72.88	13.24	19.61	24.05	7.07	6.49	3.30	2.93	0.07	0.03	22.24	95.02	36.82	22.83	21.66	7.07	6.49
1999	71.74	12.45	19.34	23.30	7.61	6.52	3.27	2.97	0.07	0.05	23.48	96.65	37.84	22.91	21.62	7.61	6.52
2000	71.33	12.36	19.66	22.74	7.86	6.11	2.81	3.01	0.07	0.06	24.90	98.82	38.27	23.82	22.58	7.86	6.11
2001	71.73	12.28	20.17	23.55	8.03	5.16	2.24	2.62	0.06	0.07	26.32	96.17	38.19	22.77	21.91	8.03	5.16
2002	70.71	12.16	19.38	22.73	8.15	5.73	2.69	2.71	0.06	0.11	25.72	97.65	38.23	23.51	21.90	8.15	5.73
2003	69.94	11.96	19.63	22.09	7.96	5.95	2.79	2.80	0.06	0.11	26.99	97.92	38.79	22.83	22.32	7.96	5.95
2004	70.23	11.55	19.07	22.85	8.22	6.07	2.69	3.00	0.06	0.14	29.14	100.09	40.23	22.92	22.47	8.22	6.08
2005	69.43	10.97	18.56	23.19	8.16	6.23	2.70	3.10	0.06	0.18	30.20	100.19	40.30	22.57	22.80	8.16	6.24
2006	70.75	10.77	19.02	23.79	8.21	6.59	2.87	3.21	0.07	0.26	29.92	99.49	39.82	22.24	22.45	8.21	6.64
2007	71.41	10.75	19.79	23.49	8.46	6.52	2.45	3.47	0.08	0.34	29.34	101.03	39.49	23.66	22.75	8.46	6.53
2008	73.22	10.61	20.70	23.85	8.43	7.21	2.51	3.87	0.09	0.55	26.02	98.91	36.91	23.84	22.39	8.43	7.19
2009	72.66	11.33	21.14	21.62	8.36	7.64	2.67	3.95	0.10	0.72	22.77	94.14	34.96	23.42	19.69	8.36	7.62
2010	74.78	11.60	21.81	22.04	8.43	8.11	2.54	4.32	0.13	0.92	21.69	97.48	35.49	24.57	20.83	8.43	8.07
2011	77.97	11.95	23.41	22.22	8.27	9.16	3.10	4.50	0.17	1.17	18.38	96.90	34.82	24.95	19.66	8.27	9.06
2012	79.20	13.79	24.61	20.68	8.06	8.81	2.63	4.41	0.23	1.34	15.80	94.49	34.02	26.09	17.38	8.06	8.78
2013	81.89	15.80	24.99	20.00	8.24	9.33	2.56	4.65	0.31	1.60	12.84	97.25	34.61	26.82	18.04	8.24	9.36
2014	87.15	18.34	26.52	20.29	8.33	9.66	2.47	4.80	0.43	1.73	10.99	98.46	34.78	27.59	17.99	8.33	9.62

NA Not available. Z Less than 5 trillion. [1] Includes other types of fuel, not shown separately. [2] Includes lease condensate. [3] Beginning 1989, includes waste coal supplied. Beginning 2001, also includes a small amount of refuse recovery. [4] Electricity net generation from conventional hydroelectric power, geothermal, solar, and wind. Consumption of electricity from wood, waste, and alcohol fuels; geothermal heat pump and direct use energy; and solar thermal direct use energy. [5] Conventional hydroelectricity net generation. [6] Organic nonfossil material of biological origin constituting a renewable energy source. [7] Imports minus exports. [8] Includes coal coke net imports and electricity net imports, not shown separately. [9] Petroleum products supplied, including natural gas plant liquids and crude oil burned as fuel. Does not include biofuels that have been blended with petroleum. [10] Excludes supplemental gaseous fuels.

Source: U.S. Energy Information Administration, *Monthly Energy Review*, May 2015. See also <http://www.eia.gov/totalenergy/data/monthly/>.

Table 947. Energy Supply and Disposition by Type of Fuel—Estimates, 2012 and 2013, and Projections, 2015 to 2035

[Quadrillion Btu (79.63 represents 79,630,000,000,000,000) per year. Btu = British thermal unit. For definition of Btu, see source and text, this section. Projections are "reference" or mid-level forecasts. See report for methodology and assumptions used in generating projections]

Type of Fuel	2012	2013	Projections				
			2015	2020	2025	2030	2035
Production, total........................	**79.63**	**82.69**	**89.64**	**98.66**	**100.86**	**103.66**	**103.92**
Crude oil and lease condensate..........................	13.70	15.61	19.49	22.18	21.53	21.09	19.76
Natural gas plant liquids.................................	3.26	3.55	4.36	5.48	5.66	5.70	5.61
Natural gas, dry..	24.64	25.06	27.15	29.60	31.33	33.91	35.06
Coal [1]...	20.68	19.99	20.10	21.68	22.24	22.55	22.46
Nuclear power..	8.06	8.27	8.11	8.42	8.46	8.47	8.51
Renewable energy [2].................................	8.53	8.95	9.27	10.42	10.75	11.04	11.57
Other [3]...	0.75	1.26	1.16	0.87	0.89	0.91	0.94
Imports, total...........................	**26.42**	**24.54**	**21.98**	**20.25**	**21.25**	**21.73**	**23.58**
Crude oil [4]...	18.66	16.96	15.04	13.60	14.89	15.67	17.71
Petroleum products [5].................................	4.21	4.30	3.90	4.60	4.52	4.39	4.26
Natural gas...	3.22	2.94	2.65	1.91	1.70	1.57	1.55
Other imports [6].....................................	0.34	0.33	0.38	0.14	0.14	0.10	0.06
Exports, total...........................	**11.22**	**11.73**	**12.82**	**18.13**	**20.11**	**22.37**	**23.39**
Petroleum [7]...	6.50	7.25	8.86	11.20	12.03	12.64	13.28
Natural gas...	1.63	1.59	1.81	4.45	5.21	6.39	6.76
Coal...	3.09	2.89	2.15	2.48	2.88	3.33	3.36
Consumption, total......................	**94.40**	**97.14**	**97.83**	**100.84**	**101.97**	**102.87**	**103.85**
Petroleum products [8]................................	35.16	35.91	36.06	37.06	36.89	36.47	36.26
Natural gas...	26.14	26.86	27.27	26.85	27.60	28.83	29.59
Coal...	17.33	18.01	18.09	19.18	19.33	19.16	19.03
Nuclear power..	8.06	8.27	8.11	8.42	8.46	8.47	8.51
Renewable energy [9].................................	7.33	7.69	7.92	8.99	9.33	9.61	10.13
Other [10]..	0.39	0.40	0.37	0.34	0.35	0.33	0.32
Net imports of petroleum................	**16.37**	**14.01**	**10.09**	**7.00**	**7.38**	**7.43**	**8.69**
Prices (2013 dollars per unit):							
Crude oil spot prices (dol. per barrel)							
Brent Spot Price..................................	113.31	108.64	55.62	79.13	91.13	105.64	122.20
West Texas Intermediate Spot Price...............	95.53	97.91	52.72	72.96	85.02	99.48	116.25
Natural Gas at Henry Hub (dol. per mil. BTU).........	2.79	3.73	3.69	4.88	5.46	5.69	6.60
Coal minemouth price (dol. per ton) [11].............	40.54	37.24	34.07	37.89	40.33	43.69	46.66
Average Electric Price (cents per kWh)................	10.0	10.1	10.1	10.5	11.0	11.1	11.3

[1] Includes waste coal. [2] Includes grid-connected electricity from conventional hydroelectric; wood and wood waste; landfill gas; municipal solid waste; other biomass; wind; photovoltaic and solar thermal sources; nonelectric energy from renewable sources, such as active and passive solar systems, and wood. Excludes electricity imports using renewable sources and nonmarketed renewable energy. [3] Includes nonbiogenic municipal solid waste, liquid hydrogen, methanol, and some domestic inputs to refineries. [4] Includes imports of crude oil for the Strategic Petroleum Reserve. [5] Includes imports of finished petroleum products, imports of unfinished oils, alcohols, ethers, blending components, and renewable fuels such as ethanol. [6] Includes coal, coal coke (net), and electricity (net). [7] Includes crude oil and petroleum products. [8] Includes petroleum-derived fuels and non-petroleum-derived fuels, such as ethanol, biodiesel, and coal-based synthetic liquids. Petroleum coke, which is a solid, is included. Also included are natural gas plant liquids, crude oil consumed as a fuel, and liquid hydrogen. [9] Includes grid-connected electricity from wood and wood waste, non-electric energy from wood, and biofuels heat and coproducts used in the production of liquid fuels, but excludes the energy content of the liquid fuels. Also includes non-biogenic municipal solid waste and net electricity imports. [10] Includes non-biogenic municipal solid waste and net electricity imports. [11] Includes reported prices for both open market and captive mines.

Source: U.S. Energy Information Administration, *Annual Energy Outlook 2015*, April 2015. See also <http://www.eia.gov/forecasts/aeo/index.cfm>.

Table 948. Energy Consumption by End-Use Sector: 1973 to 2014

[Trillion Btu (14,897.4 represents 14,897,400,000,000,000). Btu=British thermal unit. For residential and commercial, industrial, and transportation sectors. Represents consumption of fossil fuels and renewable energy, plus electricity retail sales and electrical system energy losses. For definition of Btu, see source and text, this section. See Appendix III]

Year	Residential	Commercial [1]	Industrial [2]	Transportation	Year	Residential	Commercial [1]	Industrial [2]	Transportation
1973........	14,897.4	9,543.0	32,623.3	18,612.8	1994........	18,111.6	14,097.1	33,520.3	23,365.1
1974........	14,654.3	9,393.3	31,787.2	18,120.4	1995........	18,518.2	14,689.6	33,969.7	23,851.1
1975........	14,813.4	9,492.5	29,413.0	18,245.0	1996........	19,503.6	15,171.6	34,903.2	24,439.2
1976........	15,410.3	10,063.3	31,392.8	19,100.8	1997........	18,964.2	15,680.8	35,199.3	24,751.3
1977........	15,661.7	10,207.6	32,263.0	19,821.6	1998........	18,954.1	15,967.1	34,841.5	25,260.1
1978........	16,132.3	10,511.9	32,687.6	20,617.1	1999........	19,556.0	16,375.8	34,762.7	25,949.5
1979........	15,812.7	10,648.0	33,924.7	20,471.5	2000........	20,423.9	17,174.8	34,662.4	26,555.3
1980........	15,753.4	10,578.3	32,039.4	19,696.7	2001........	20,041.1	17,136.1	32,719.1	26,282.2
1981........	15,261.5	10,615.9	30,711.6	19,514.0	2002........	20,789.9	17,344.9	32,660.9	26,845.7
1982........	15,530.9	10,860.3	27,614.5	19,089.2	2003........	21,124.0	17,345.2	32,552.9	26,900.2
1983........	15,425.0	10,938.4	27,427.8	19,176.6	2004........	21,087.2	17,654.3	33,515.4	27,842.8
1984........	15,959.6	11,443.9	29,569.9	19,655.6	2005........	21,620.4	17,851.7	32,441.1	28,280.3
1985........	16,041.3	11,451.2	28,815.8	20,087.9	2006........	20,681.2	17,704.7	32,390.2	28,716.7
1986........	15,975.1	11,606.1	28,273.6	20,788.8	2007........	21,533.7	18,249.4	32,384.7	28,859.5
1987........	16,263.2	11,946.0	29,378.9	21,468.9	2008........	21,689.4	18,396.5	31,333.0	27,486.3
1988........	17,132.6	12,578.1	30,677.4	22,317.7	2009........	21,106.6	17,879.8	28,464.2	26,687.1
1989........	17,785.7	13,193.4	31,319.9	22,477.9	2010........	21,844.0	18,046.9	30,523.1	27,059.1
1990........	16,945.3	13,319.8	31,809.8	22,419.6	2011........	21,404.0	17,966.0	30,812.5	26,712.1
1991........	17,420.3	13,499.8	31,399.3	22,118.0	2012........	19,965.3	17,391.7	30,908.2	26,219.3
1992........	17,355.8	13,440.9	32,570.8	22,415.1	2013........	21,213.7	17,950.8	31,309.9	26,781.8
1993........	18,217.7	13,819.6	32,627.8	22,711.7	2014........	21,618.9	18,392.5	31,307.7	27,142.4

[1] Commercial sector fuel use, including that at commercial combined-heat-and-power (CHP) and commercial electricity-only plants. [2] Industrial sector fuel use, including that at industrial combined-heat-and-power (CHP) and industrial electricity-only plants.

Source: U.S. Energy Information Administration, *Monthly Energy Review*, May 2015. See also <http://www.eia.gov/totalenergy/data/monthly/>.

Table 949. Energy Consumption by Mode of Transportation: 2000 to 2012

[40 represents 40,000,000,000,000. Btu = British thermal unit. For conversion rates for each fuel type, see source]

Mode	Trillion Btu			Physical units			
	2000	2010	2012	Unit	2000	2010	2012
AIR [1]							
Aviation gasoline	40	27	25	Mil. gal.	333	221	206
Jet fuel	2,008	1,686	1,585	Mil. gal.	14,876	12,492	11,743
HIGHWAY							
Light duty vehicle, short wheel base and motorcycle [2]	9,159	10,902	11,068	Mil. gal.	73,275	87,215	88,541
Light duty vehicle, long wheel base [2]	6,617	4,531	4,387	Mil. gal.	52,939	36,251	35,093
Single-unit 2-axle 6-tire or more truck	1,195	1,887	1,786	Mil. gal.	9,563	15,097	14,287
Combination truck [3]	3,208	3,741	3,491	Mil. gal.	25,666	29,927	27,926
Bus	139	240	257	Mil. gal.	1,112	1,921	2,059
TRANSIT [4]							
Electricity	18	22	22	Mil. kWh	5,382	6,414	6,506
Diesel	82	88	85	Mil. gal.	591	633	613
Gasoline and other nondiesel fuels [5]	3	12	13	Mil. gal.	24	98	102
Compressed natural gas	6	18	17	Mil. gal.	44	126	124
RAIL [6]							
Distillate/diesel fuel	526	493	508	Mil. gal.	3,795	3,557	3,663
Electricity	2	2	2	Mil. kWh	470	559	549
WATER							
Residual fuel oil	960	770	721	Mil. gal.	6,410	5,143	4,820
Distillate/diesel fuel oil	314	278	245	Mil. gal.	2,261	2,003	1,768
Gasoline	141	146	137	Mil. gal.	1,124	1,167	1,093
PIPELINE							
Natural gas	662	695	751	Mil. cu. ft.	642,210	674,124	728,163

[1] Includes general aviation and certified carriers, domestic operations only. Also includes fuel used in air taxi operations, but not commuter operations. [2] Beginning in 2010, data were calculated using a new methodology developed by the Federal Highway Administration (FHWA). Data for these years are based on new categories and are not comparable to previous years. The new category "Light duty vehicle, short wheel base" includes passenger cars, light trucks, vans and sport utility vehicles with a wheelbase (WB) equal to or less than 121 inches. The new category "Light duty vehicle, long wheel base" includes large passenger cars, vans, pickup trucks, and sport/utility vehicles with wheelbases (WB) larger than 121 inches. [3] A power unit (truck tractor) and one or more trailing units (a semitrailer or trailer). [4] Includes light, heavy, and commuter rail; motor bus; trolley bus; van pools; automated guideway; and demand-responsive vehicles. [5] Gasoline and all other nondiesel fuels include gasoline, liquefied petroleum gas, liquefied natural gas, methane, ethanol, bunker fuel, kerosene, grain additive, and other fuel. [6] Includes Amtrak and freight service carriers that have an annual operating revenue of $250 million or more.

Source: U.S. Department of Transportation, Bureau of Transportation Statistics, "National Transportation Statistics," <http://www.bts.gov/publications/national_transportation_statistics/>, accessed November 2014.

Table 950. Renewable Energy Consumption Estimates by Source: 1990 to 2014

[In trillion Btu (6,040.7 represents 6,040,700,000,000,000). For definition of Btu, see source and text, this section. Renewable energy is obtained from sources that are essentially inexhaustible, unlike fossil fuels of which there is a finite supply]

Source and sector	1990	2000	2010	2011	2012	2013	2014
Consumption, total	**6,040.7**	**6,106.4**	**8,065.6**	**9,059.3**	**8,776.8**	**9,356.1**	**9,622.5**
Conventional hydroelectric power [1]	3,046.4	2,811.1	2,538.5	3,102.9	2,628.7	2,562.4	2,468.7
Geothermal energy [2]	170.7	164.4	208.0	212.3	211.6	214.0	222.2
Biomass [3]	2,735.1	3,008.2	4,269.7	4,405.5	4,369.1	4,673.2	4,770.5
Solar energy [4]	59.4	65.6	125.9	171.1	227.4	305.2	426.6
Wind energy [5]	29.0	57.1	923.4	1,167.6	1,340.1	1,601.4	1,734.5
Residential [6]	**641.1**	**489.2**	**590.9**	**643.0**	**645.8**	**838.6**	**871.4**
Wood [7]	580.0	420.0	440.0	450.0	420.0	580.0	580.0
Geothermal [2]	5.5	8.6	36.8	39.6	39.6	39.6	39.6
Solar [4]	55.6	60.6	114.1	153.4	186.2	219.0	251.8
Commercial [8]	**98.2**	**127.7**	**130.4**	**135.9**	**130.4**	**143.4**	**144.4**
Biomass [3]	94.0	119.1	110.9	114.6	108.5	119.9	119.2
Geothermal [2]	2.8	7.6	18.5	19.7	19.7	19.7	19.7
Hydroelectric [1]	1.4	1.0	0.8	0.8	0.2	0.3	0.4
Industrial [9]	**1,717.0**	**1,928.1**	**2,205.3**	**2,267.8**	**2,252.8**	**2,263.8**	**2,306.0**
Biomass [3]	1,684.2	1,881.5	2,184.8	2,246.0	2,225.9	2,226.0	2,275.5
Geothermal [2]	1.9	4.4	4.2	4.2	4.2	4.2	4.2
Hydroelectric [1]	30.9	42.2	16.3	17.5	22.4	33.0	25.7
Transportation	**60.4**	**134.9**	**1,074.7**	**1,158.1**	**1,162.1**	**1,277.6**	**1,289.2**
Fuel ethanol	60.4	134.9	1,041.4	1,045.0	1,044.6	1,071.5	1,092.4
Biodiesel [10]	(NA)	(NA)	33.2	113.1	114.7	182.3	178.9
Electric power [11]	**3,523.9**	**3,426.5**	**4,064.4**	**4,854.5**	**4,585.8**	**4,832.7**	**5,011.4**
Biomass [3]	316.5	452.8	459.4	436.7	452.6	469.6	506.6
Geothermal [2]	160.5	143.8	148.5	148.8	148.1	150.5	158.7
Hydroelectric [1]	3,014.0	2,767.9	2,521.5	3,085.1	2,606.0	2,528.9	2,442.6
Solar [4]	3.8	5.0	11.8	16.8	39.6	83.2	170.5
Wind [5]	29.0	57.1	923.3	1,167.1	1,339.4	1,600.4	1,733.1

NA Not available. [1] Power produced from the kinetic energy of falling water. [2] As used at electric power plants, hot water or steam extracted from geothermal reservoirs in the Earth's crust that is supplied to steam turbines at electric power plants that drive generators to produce electricity. [3] Wood and wood-derived fuels, municipal solid waste (from biogenic sources, landfill gas, sludge waste, agricultural byproducts, and other biomass), fuel ethanol, and biodiesel. [4] The radiant energy of the sun, which can be converted into other forms of energy, such as heat or electricity. Solar thermal and photovoltaic electricity net generation and solar thermal direct use energy. [5] Energy present in wind motion that can be converted to mechanical energy for driving pumps, mills, and electric power generators. Wind pushes against sails, vanes, or blades radiating from a central rotating shaft. [6] Living quarters for private households, excludes institutional living quarters. [7] Wood and wood-derived fuels. [8] Service-providing facilities and equipment of businesses, governments, and other private and public organizations. Includes institutional living quarters and sewage treatment facilities. Includes commercial combined-heat-and-power and commercial electricity-only plants. [9] All facilities and equipment used for producing, processing, or assembling goods. Includes industrial combined-heat-and-power and industrial electricity-only plants. [10] Any liquid biofuel suitable as a diesel fuel substitute, additive, or extender. [11] Electricity-only and combined-heat-and-power plants whose primary business is to sell electricity and/or heat to the public. Includes sources not shown separately.

Source: U.S. Energy Information Administration, *Monthly Energy Review*, May 2015. See also <http://www.eia.gov/totalenergy/data/monthly/>.

Table 951. Energy Consumption—End-Use Sector and Selected Source by State: 2013

[In trillions of British thermal units (97,145 represents 97,145,000,000,000,000 Btu), except as indicated. For definition of Btu, see source and text, this section. U.S. totals may not equal sum of states due to independent rounding and/or interstate flows of electricity that are not allocated to the states. For technical notes and documentation, see source <http://www.eia.gov/state/seds/seds-technical-notes-updates.cfm>]

State	Total [1,2]	Per capita [3] (mil. Btu)	End-use sector [4] Resi-dential	Com-mercial	Indus-trial [2]	Trans-portation	Source Petro-leum [5]	Natural gas (dry) [6]	Coal	Hydro-electric power [7]	Nuclear electric power
U.S.	97,145	307	21,182	17,894	31,379	26,689	35,820	26,858	18,039	2,562	8,244
AL.	1,931	400	359	257	847	470	530	629	565	123	426
AK.	609	826	49	63	324	173	243	333	15	14	–
AZ.	1,415	213	398	346	211	460	514	341	455	56	328
AR.	1,093	369	241	177	399	276	330	288	327	25	125
CA.	7,684	200	1,480	1,484	1,812	2,908	3,371	2,483	38	227	187
CO.	1,472	279	367	286	417	402	474	486	364	12	–
CT.	748	208	249	189	82	228	320	240	8	4	178
DE.	274	297	65	57	90	62	99	101	18	–	–
DC.	171	263	37	111	3	20	16	34	(Z)	–	–
FL.	4,078	208	1,168	968	475	1,466	1,593	1,245	505	2	277
GA.	2,795	280	688	531	753	823	918	635	426	35	344
HI.	277	197	36	39	61	141	236	3	15	1	–
ID.	530	328	127	88	180	135	164	107	8	81	–
IL.	4,011	311	1,012	804	1,245	950	1,234	1,074	1,027	1	1,015
IN.	2,900	441	570	385	1,326	620	785	683	1,199	4	–
IA.	1,516	490	254	216	747	300	427	336	402	7	56
KS.	1,163	402	236	210	430	287	414	289	327	(Z)	75
KY.	1,823	414	385	284	713	440	589	236	915	31	–
LA.	3,835	828	344	269	2,562	660	1,715	1,501	228	10	177
ME.	407	306	86	59	135	128	189	66	2	34	–
MD.	1,404	236	432	425	117	431	488	209	183	16	149
MA.	1,443	215	453	291	243	456	571	454	42	9	45
MI.	2,843	287	774	601	736	733	862	832	658	14	302
MN.	1,860	343	417	358	636	448	609	479	268	5	112
MS.	1,142	382	211	160	402	368	434	428	98	–	114
MO.	1,857	307	538	411	365	542	632	281	807	11	87
MT.	401	395	85	77	121	118	173	82	166	92	–
NE.	872	466	164	140	372	195	239	180	293	11	72
NV.	657	235	162	121	166	208	227	282	65	26	–
NH.	303	229	93	70	40	99	147	56	17	14	114
NJ.	2,315	260	599	601	267	847	1,003	713	26	(Z)	349
NM.	689	330	124	126	237	201	257	253	256	1	–
NY.	3,625	184	1,072	1,134	376	1,043	1,280	1,322	69	238	468
NC.	2,524	256	692	556	556	721	823	445	494	66	420
ND.	589	813	73	85	290	140	222	89	393	18	–
OH.	3,745	324	914	695	1,216	920	1,168	946	1,104	5	168
OK.	1,623	421	323	258	588	454	533	683	336	21	–
OR.	997	254	258	191	246	301	340	244	39	316	–
PA.	3,795	297	930	631	1,318	916	1,209	1,147	1,126	24	822
RI.	194	184	66	49	20	58	81	89	–	(Z)	–
SC.	1,591	333	352	260	527	453	504	237	257	30	567
SD.	390	462	73	65	156	95	117	85	34	39	–
TN.	2,136	329	532	428	580	596	689	286	400	119	298
TX.	12,944	488	1,686	1,610	6,575	3,073	6,260	4,137	1,597	5	400
UT.	831	286	175	164	242	250	290	259	355	5	–
VT.	134	213	43	26	16	49	78	10	–	12	51
VA.	2,411	291	627	612	439	733	817	434	291	12	306
WA.	2,039	292	495	383	569	593	731	328	75	746	88
WV.	738	398	174	112	281	170	191	151	771	17	–
WI.	1,804	314	445	369	578	412	526	450	455	19	122
WY.	535	918	49	63	309	114	162	156	521	7	–

– Represents zero. Z Less than 50 billion Btu. [1] Includes other sources, not shown separately. [2] U.S. total energy and U.S. industrial sector include net imports of coal coke that are not allocated to the states. [3] Based on estimated resident population as of July 1. [4] End-use sector data include electricity sales and associated electrical system energy losses. [5] Includes fuel ethanol blended into motor gasoline. [6] Includes supplemental gaseous fuels. [7] Conventional hydroelectric power. Does not include pumped-storage hydroelectricity.

Source: U.S. Energy Information Administration, "State Energy Data System," <http://www.eia.gov/state/seds/>, accessed September 2015.

Table 952. Energy Expenditures and Average Fuel Prices by Source and Sector: 1980 to 2013

[In millions of dollars (374,347 represents $374,347,000,000), except as indicated. Btu = British thermal units. For definition of Btu, see text, this section. End-use sector and electric utilities exclude expenditures and prices on energy sources such as hydropower, solar, wind, and geothermal. Also excludes expenditures for reported amounts of energy consumed by the energy industry for production, transportation, and processing operations]

Source and Sector	1980	1990	2000	2005	2009	2010	2011	2012	2013
EXPENDITURES (mil. dol.)									
Total [1,2,3]	374,347	474,831	687,824	1,045,910	1,063,889	1,208,443	1,388,618	1,351,513	1,375,306
Natural gas [4]	51,062	65,278	119,094	200,356	159,362	161,301	155,943	132,829	151,705
Petroleum products	237,676	237,672	359,396	596,286	580,867	711,441	891,849	879,736	878,116
Motor gasoline [5]	124,408	126,558	192,153	312,047	317,082	376,492	462,435	473,216	467,338
Coal	22,607	28,602	28,080	36,932	45,898	50,474	50,441	45,245	45,517
Retail electricity	98,095	176,691	231,578	295,787	350,435	365,913	368,009	360,863	372,081
Residential sector [6]	69,277	110,905	155,299	215,186	240,753	249,375	249,232	235,128	250,457
Commercial sector [2,3]	47,074	79,605	113,423	155,165	174,679	177,664	180,402	171,944	179,360
Industrial sector [2,3]	94,316	103,531	141,079	208,396	185,411	218,011	247,864	225,911	233,272
Transportation sector [2]	163,680	180,790	278,024	467,163	463,046	563,393	711,120	718,530	712,217
Motor gasoline [5]	121,809	123,845	189,836	304,875	311,613	369,433	453,895	464,635	458,633
Electric utilities [3]	38,027	40,627	60,053	95,928	84,825	94,789	92,725	82,171	89,069
AVERAGE FUEL PRICES (dol. per mil. Btu)									
All sectors [1]	6.89	8.29	10.31	15.55	17.18	18.86	21.81	21.78	21.41
Residential sector [6]	7.46	11.87	14.21	19.16	22.04	22.41	22.85	23.49	22.71
Commercial sector [3]	7.83	11.87	13.90	18.59	20.66	20.92	21.16	21.03	20.75
Industrial sector [3]	4.71	5.29	6.48	10.40	11.15	12.00	13.50	12.20	12.40
Transportation sector	8.61	8.33	10.75	16.91	17.87	21.43	27.48	28.34	27.66
Electric utilities [3]	1.77	1.48	1.71	2.61	2.45	2.63	2.65	2.41	2.62

[1] Includes other sources not shown separately. [2] There is a discontinuity in this time series between 1988 and 1989 due to the expanded coverage of the use of wood and biomass waste beginning in 1989. [3] There are no direct fuel costs for hydroelectric, geothermal, wind, photovoltaic, or solar thermal energy. [4] Natural gas as it is consumed; includes supplemental gaseous fuels that are commingled with natural gas. [5] Beginning 1995, includes fuel ethanol blended into motor gasoline. [6] There are no direct fuel costs for geothermal, photovoltaic, or solar thermal energy.

Source: U.S. Energy Information Administration, "State Energy Data System (SEDS)," <http://www.eia.gov/state/seds/>, accessed July 2015.

Table 953. Fuel Ethanol and Biodiesel—Summary: 2000 to 2014

[233.1 represents 233,100,000,000,000. Btu=British thermal units. For definition of Btu, see source and text, this section. Minus sign (-) indicates an excess of exports over imports, except where noted]

Fuel	2000	2005	2008	2009	2010	2011	2012	2013	2014 [1]
FUEL ETHANOL									
Feedstock [2] (tril. Btu)	233.1	549.5	1,286.3	1,503.2	1,823.5	1,904.2	1,800.7	1,805.1	1,941.4
Production:									
1,000 barrels	38,627	92,961	221,637	260,424	316,617	331,646	314,714	316,493	341,419
Tril. Btu	137.6	331.2	789.7	927.9	1,127.5	1,180.7	1,120.4	1,126.4	1,214.8
Net imports [3] (1,000 barrels)	116	3,234	12,610	4,720	-9,115	-24,365	-5,891	-5,761	-18,454
Stocks [4] (1,000 barrels)	3,400	5,563	14,226	16,594	17,941	18,238	20,350	16,424	18,739
Stock change [5,6] (1,000 barrels)	-624	-439	3,691	2,368	1,347	297	2,112	-3,926	2,320
Consumption:									
1,000 barrels	39,367	96,634	230,556	262,776	306,155	306,984	306,711	314,658	320,645
Tril. Btu	140.3	344.3	821.5	936.3	1,090.2	1,092.9	1,091.9	1,119.9	1,140.9
BIODIESEL									
Feedstock [7] (tril. Btu)	(NA)	11.7	87.7	66.7	44.4	125.2	128.2	175.9	160.4
Production:									
1,000 barrels	(NA)	2,162	16,145	12,281	8,177	23,035	23,588	32,368	29,523
Tril. Btu	(NA)	11.58	86.52	65.81	43.82	123.45	126.41	173.46	158.21
Net imports (1,000 barrels)	(NA)	1	-8,918	-4,640	-2,024	-908	-2,203	3,477	3,085
Stocks [4] (1,000 barrels)	(NA)	(NA)	(NA)	711	672	2,005	1,984	3,810	3,036
Stock change [5,6] (1,000 barrels)	(NA)	(NA)	(NA)	711	-39	1,028	-20	1,825	-778
Consumption:									
1,000 barrels	(NA)	2,163	7,228	7,663	6,192	21,099	21,406	34,020	33,385
Tril. Btu	(NA)	11.6	38.7	41.1	33.2	113.1	114.7	182.3	178.9

NA Not available. [1] Preliminary. [2] Feedstock data are estimates. Total corn and other biomass inputs to the production of fuel ethanol. [3] Through 2009, data are for fuel ethanol imports only; data for fuel ethanol exports are not available. Beginning in 2010, data are for fuel ethanol imports minus fuel ethanol exports. [4] Imports minus exports. Stocks are at end of year. [5] A negative number indicates a decrease in stocks. [6] Data for 2014 derived using the preliminary 2013 stock value, not the final 2013 value shown under "Stocks." [7] Feedstock data are estimates. Total vegetable oil and other biomass inputs to the production of biodiesel.

Source: U.S. Energy Information Administration, *Monthly Energy Review*, May 2015. See also <http://www.eia.gov/totalenergy/data/monthly/>.

Table 954. Energy Expenditures—End-Use Sector and Selected Source by State: 2013

[In millions of dollars (1,375,306 represents $1,375,306,000,000). End-use sector and electric utilities exclude expenditures on energy sources such as hydroelectric, photovoltaic, solar thermal, wind, and geothermal. Also excludes expenditures for reported amounts of energy consumed by the energy industry for production, transportation, and processing operations. For technical notes and documentation, see source, <http://www.eia.gov/state/seds/seds-technical-notes-complete.cfm>]

State	Total [1,2]	End-use sector				Source			
		Resi-dential	Com-mercial	Indus-trial [2]	Transpor-tation	Petroleum products [3]	Natural gas [4]	Coal	Electricity sales
U.S.	1,375,306	250,457	179,360	233,272	712,217	878,116	151,705	45,517	372,081
AL.	24,156	4,252	2,850	4,817	12,237	13,766	3,091	1,732	7,901
AK.	7,075	774	859	910	4,532	5,759	496	73	1,005
AZ.	22,785	4,595	3,446	2,257	12,488	14,086	2,037	947	7,670
AR.	14,002	2,319	1,413	2,851	7,419	8,803	1,679	789	3,687
CA.	136,936	20,351	20,418	14,093	82,074	88,293	14,821	130	37,033
CO.	19,701	3,663	2,571	2,669	10,798	12,423	2,355	703	5,258
CT.	15,335	4,835	2,714	1,038	6,748	9,418	1,922	32	4,669
DE.	3,854	904	607	594	1,749	2,109	702	58	1,216
DC.	2,193	444	1,233	24	492	475	403	–	1,314
FL.	66,153	13,352	9,939	4,142	38,720	41,601	6,852	1,737	22,678
GA.	40,021	8,213	5,353	5,029	21,427	23,666	4,411	1,372	12,648
HI.	7,538	1,051	1,286	1,189	4,012	5,702	118	32	3,154
ID.	6,963	1,197	684	1,335	3,747	4,518	621	22	1,833
IL.	49,297	9,357	6,169	8,229	25,542	30,306	7,261	2,128	11,519
IN.	33,372	5,367	3,214	8,128	16,663	19,091	4,405	3,569	9,112
IA.	17,265	2,756	1,965	4,396	8,149	11,314	2,046	737	3,775
KS.	15,253	2,493	1,854	3,465	7,441	9,985	1,568	581	3,790
KY.	22,423	3,470	2,229	4,620	12,104	14,445	1,417	2,200	6,471
LA.	39,558	3,380	2,507	18,503	15,168	29,379	4,729	667	6,350
ME.	7,449	1,735	1,006	973	3,735	5,360	591	8	1,406
MD.	22,972	5,385	4,202	1,320	12,064	13,861	1,913	621	7,216
MA.	27,837	7,613	3,994	3,240	12,991	16,350	4,367	180	8,020
MI.	40,647	9,108	5,817	5,818	19,905	23,104	6,049	1,902	11,521
MN.	24,690	4,568	3,249	4,372	12,501	15,509	2,838	567	6,379
MS.	15,762	2,416	1,720	2,487	9,138	10,337	1,811	387	4,373
MO.	26,722	5,403	3,478	3,088	14,752	16,735	2,426	1,553	7,538
MT.	5,533	861	679	765	3,229	3,917	473	307	1,158
NE.	10,294	1,578	1,091	2,228	5,398	6,601	995	423	2,683
NV.	10,178	1,946	1,123	1,419	5,691	6,270	1,493	181	3,180
NH.	6,083	1,699	1,006	474	2,904	4,159	566	71	1,579
NJ.	39,243	7,937	6,881	2,559	21,866	24,601	5,352	100	10,153
NM.	9,155	1,336	1,128	1,223	5,469	6,438	885	593	2,107
NY.	65,972	18,595	16,023	3,449	27,905	34,749	10,677	237	22,836
NC.	37,332	7,745	4,903	4,360	20,324	22,959	3,076	1,882	11,991
ND.	7,629	722	793	2,608	3,507	5,676	280	852	1,299
OH.	50,156	9,911	5,855	8,504	25,887	30,275	6,052	2,853	13,715
OK.	19,546	3,104	2,040	3,279	11,124	12,673	3,146	698	4,629
OR.	14,879	2,671	1,742	1,827	8,639	9,543	1,495	78	4,019
PA.	54,067	12,637	6,136	9,884	25,409	32,700	7,340	3,359	14,242
RI.	3,913	1,252	714	263	1,685	2,357	755	–	1,067
SC.	21,726	3,988	2,425	3,240	12,074	13,217	1,458	968	7,265
SD.	4,709	747	520	904	2,538	3,168	462	71	1,081
TN.	28,925	4,984	3,965	3,922	16,053	18,024	1,850	1,052	8,818
TX.	162,054	18,701	12,907	57,497	72,950	121,330	14,013	3,190	32,035
UT.	11,005	1,641	1,342	1,379	6,644	7,443	1,266	728	2,462
VT.	3,257	953	527	298	1,479	2,272	102	–	817
VA.	34,283	6,739	4,774	3,126	19,644	21,844	2,799	1,052	9,897
WA.	26,509	4,530	3,110	2,602	16,267	17,790	2,270	155	6,521
WV.	8,886	1,656	936	2,132	4,161	5,520	596	2,022	2,483
WI.	24,716	5,041	3,398	4,236	12,041	14,434	2,997	1,109	7,256
WY.	5,458	484	567	1,668	2,739	3,760	378	813	1,255

– Represents or rounds to zero. [1] There are no direct fuel costs for hydroelectric, geothermal, wind, photovoltaic, or solar thermal energy. The U.S. total includes $156 million for coal coke net imports, which are not allocated to the states. [2] Includes sources not shown separately, such as electricity imports and exports and coal coke net imports, which are not allocated to the states. [3] Includes fuel ethanol blended into motor gasoline. [4] Includes supplemental gaseous fuels.

Source: U.S. Energy Information Administration, "State Energy Data System," <http://www.eia.gov/state/seds/>, accessed September 2015.

Table 955. Energy Imports and Exports by Type of Fuel: 1980 to 2014

[In quadrillion Btu (12.10 represents 12,100,000,000,000,000 Btu). Btu=British thermal units; for definition, see text, this section]

Type of fuel	1980	1990	1995	2000	2005	2009	2010	2011	2012	2013	2014
Net imports, total [1]	**12.10**	**14.06**	**17.68**	**24.90**	**30.20**	**22.77**	**21.69**	**18.37**	**15.78**	**12.75**	**11.09**
Coal	-2.39	-2.70	-2.08	-1.21	-0.51	-0.95	-1.62	-2.42	-2.88	-2.69	-2.13
Natural gas (dry)	0.96	1.46	2.74	3.62	3.71	2.76	2.69	2.04	1.58	1.37	1.25
Petroleum [2]	13.50	15.29	16.82	22.31	26.85	20.87	20.58	18.70	16.94	13.93	11.87
Other [3]	0.04	0.01	0.20	0.18	0.14	0.08	0.04	0.05	0.13	0.14	0.10
Imports, total	15.80	18.82	22.18	28.87	34.66	29.69	29.87	28.75	27.06	24.60	23.31
Coal	0.03	0.07	0.24	0.31	0.76	0.57	0.48	0.33	0.21	0.21	0.26
Natural gas (dry)	1.01	1.55	2.90	3.87	4.45	3.85	3.83	3.56	3.22	2.96	2.76
Petroleum [2]	14.66	17.12	18.80	24.42	29.20	25.07	25.36	24.63	23.36	21.13	20.04
Other [3]	0.10	0.08	0.24	0.26	0.25	0.21	0.19	0.23	0.28	0.31	0.25
Exports, total	3.69	4.75	4.50	3.96	4.46	6.92	8.18	10.38	11.28	11.85	12.22
Coal	2.42	2.77	2.32	1.53	1.27	1.51	2.10	2.75	3.09	2.89	2.39
Natural gas (dry)	0.05	0.09	0.16	0.25	0.74	1.08	1.15	1.52	1.63	1.59	1.51
Petroleum	1.16	1.82	1.98	2.11	2.34	4.19	4.78	5.93	6.42	7.20	8.17
Other [3]	0.07	0.07	0.05	0.08	0.11	0.13	0.15	0.18	0.14	0.17	0.15

[1] Net imports equals imports minus exports. Minus sign (-) indicates exports are greater than imports. [2] Includes imports into the Strategic Petroleum Reserve. [3] Coal coke, small amounts of electricity transmitted across U.S. borders with Canada and Mexico, and small amounts of biodiesel.

Source: U.S. Energy Information Administration, *Monthly Energy Review*, March 2015. See also <http://www.eia.gov/totalenergy/>.

Table 956. U.S. Foreign Trade in Natural Gas, Crude Oil, Petroleum Products, and Coal: 1980 to 2014

[985 represents 985,000,000,000 cu. ft. Minus sign (-) indicates trade deficit]

Mineral fuel	Unit	1980	1990	1995	2000	2005	2010	2012	2013	2014 [1]
Natural gas:										
Imports	Bil. cu. ft.	985	1,532	2,841	3,782	4,341	3,741	3,138	2,883	2,695
Exports	Bil. cu. ft.	49	86	154	244	729	1,137	1,619	1,572	1,524
Net trade [2]	Bil. cu. ft.	-936	-1,447	-2,687	-3,538	-3,612	-2,604	-1,519	-1,311	-1,171
Crude oil: [3]										
Imports [4]	Mil. barrels	1,926	2,151	2,639	3,320	3,696	3,363	3,121	2,821	2,678
Exports	Mil. barrels	105	40	35	18	12	15	25	49	126
Net trade [2]	Mil. barrels	-1,821	-2,112	-2,604	-3,301	-3,684	-3,348	-3,096	-2,773	-2,552
Petroleum products:										
Imports	Mil. barrels	(NA)	(NA)	586	874	1,310	942	758	777	688
Exports	Mil. barrels	(NA)	273	312	362	414	843	1,148	1,273	1,399
Net trade [2]	Mil. barrels	(NA)	(NA)	-274	-512	-896	-98	390	496	712
Coal:										
Imports	Mil. sh. tons	1	3	9	13	30	19	9	9	11
Exports	Mil. sh. tons	92	106	89	58	50	82	126	118	97
Net trade [2]	Mil. sh. tons	91	103	79	46	19	62	117	109	86

NA Not available. [1] Preliminary. [2] Exports minus imports. [3] Includes lease condensate. [4] Includes Strategic Petroleum Reserve imports.

Source: U.S. Energy Information Administration, *Monthly Energy Review*, May 2015; and "Petroleum and Other Liquids, Imports/Exports & Movements," <http://www.eia.gov/petroleum/data.cfm#imports>, accessed May 2015.

Table 957. Crude Oil Imports Into the U.S. by Country of Origin: 1980 to 2014

[In millions of barrels (1,921 represents 1,921,000,000). A barrel contains 42 gallons. Crude oil imports are reported by the Petroleum Administration for Defense (PAD) District in which they are to be processed. A PAD District is a geographic aggregation of the 50 states and D.C. into 5 districts. Includes crude oil imported for storage in the Strategic Petroleum Reserve (SPR). Total Organization of Petroleum Exporting Countries (OPEC) excludes, and non-OPEC includes, petroleum imported into the United States indirectly from members of OPEC, primarily from Caribbean and West European areas, as petroleum products that were refined from crude oil produced by OPEC]

Country of origin	1980	1990	1995	2000	2005	2009	2010	2011	2012	2013	2014
Total imports	**1,921**	**2,151**	**2,639**	**3,311**	**3,670**	**3,307**	**3,344**	**3,256**	**3,108**	**2,817**	**2,678**
OPEC, total [1, 2, 3, 4]	**1,410**	**1,283**	**1,219**	**1,659**	**1,738**	**1,594**	**1,654**	**1,531**	**1,471**	**1,274**	**1,093**
Algeria	166	23	10	(Z)	83	101	119	65	44	10	2
Angola [2]	(NA)	86	131	108	164	164	139	122	81	74	50
Ecuador [3]	6	(NA)	35	46	101	64	71	69	64	83	77
Iraq	10	188	–	226	190	164	151	168	173	124	133
Kuwait [5]	10	29	78	96	79	68	71	70	112	119	113
Nigeria	307	286	227	319	387	281	360	280	148	87	22
Saudi Arabia [5]	456	436	460	556	525	361	394	433	496	484	423
Venezuela	57	243	420	446	449	352	333	317	332	275	268
Non-OPEC, total [2, 3, 4, 6]	**511**	**869**	**1,419**	**1,652**	**1,932**	**1,713**	**1,690**	**1,725**	**1,637**	**1,544**	**1,585**
Brazil	(NA)	–	–	2	34	107	93	84	68	40	53
Canada	73	235	380	492	600	707	720	806	881	938	1,053
Colombia	(NA)	51	76	116	57	93	124	141	147	134	107
Congo, Republic of the	(NA)	(NA)	(NA)	(NA)	9	24	26	21	11	7	1
Mexico	185	251	375	479	566	400	416	402	356	310	285
Russia	(NA)	(Z)	5	3	70	85	92	93	37	16	7
United Kingdom	63	57	124	106	80	38	44	13	7	8	3

– Represents zero. NA Not available. Z Represents less than 500,000 barrels. [1] OPEC includes the nations shown, as well as Iran, Libya, Qatar, and United Arab Emirates. [2] Angola joined OPEC at the beginning of 2007. Prior to 2007, it is included in the non-OPEC total. [3] Ecuador withdrew from OPEC on Dec. 31, 1992; therefore, it is included under OPEC prior to 1995. From 1995 through 2007, it is included in the Non-OPEC total. In Nov. 2007, Ecuador rejoined OPEC; imports for 2008 are included in the OPEC total. [4] Former OPEC members include Gabon, which withdrew from OPEC on Dec. 31, 1994, and Indonesia, which suspended its membership as of Jan. 2009. Prior to those dates, data are included in OPEC totals; thereafter, data are included in the Non-OPEC totals. [5] Imports from the Neutral Zone between Kuwait and Saudi Arabia are included in Saudi Arabia. [6] Non-OPEC total includes nations not shown.

Source: U.S. Energy Information Administration, *Petroleum Supply Monthly*, February 2015, and earlier reports. See also <http://www.eia.gov/petroleum/supply/monthly/>.

Table 958. Crude Oil and Refined Products—Summary: 1980 to 2014

[13,481 represents 13,481,000 bbl. Barrels (bbl.) contain 42 gallons. Data are averages]

Year	Crude oil [1] (1,000 bbl. per day)					Refined oil products (1,000 bbl. per day)			Total oil imports [5] (1,000 bbl. per day)	Crude oil stocks [1,2] (mil. bbl.)	
	Input to refineries	Domestic production	Imports		Exports	Domestic demand	Imports	Exports		Total [6]	Strategic reserve [7]
			Total [3]	Strategic reserve [4]							
1980....	13,481	8,597	5,263	44	287	17,056	1,646	258	6,909	466	108
1981....	12,470	8,572	4,396	256	228	16,058	1,599	367	5,996	594	230
1982....	11,774	8,649	3,488	165	236	15,296	1,625	579	5,113	644	294
1983....	11,685	8,688	3,329	234	164	15,231	1,722	575	5,051	723	379
1984....	12,044	8,879	3,426	197	181	15,726	2,011	541	5,437	796	451
1985....	12,002	8,971	3,201	118	204	15,726	1,866	577	5,067	814	493
1986....	12,716	8,680	4,178	48	154	16,281	2,045	631	6,224	843	512
1987....	12,854	8,349	4,674	73	151	16,665	2,004	613	6,678	890	541
1988....	13,246	8,140	5,107	51	155	17,283	2,295	661	7,402	890	560
1989....	13,401	7,613	5,843	56	142	17,325	2,217	717	8,061	921	580
1990....	13,409	7,355	5,894	27	109	16,988	2,123	748	8,018	908	586
1991....	13,301	7,417	5,782	(NA)	116	16,714	1,844	885	7,627	893	569
1992....	13,411	7,171	6,083	10	89	17,033	1,805	861	7,888	893	575
1993....	13,613	6,847	6,787	15	98	17,237	1,833	904	8,620	922	587
1994....	13,866	6,662	7,063	12	99	17,718	1,933	843	8,996	929	592
1995....	13,973	6,560	7,230	(NA)	95	17,725	1,605	855	8,835	895	592
1996....	14,195	6,465	7,508	(NA)	110	18,309	1,971	871	9,478	850	566
1997....	14,662	6,452	8,225	(NA)	108	18,620	1,936	896	10,162	868	563
1998....	14,889	6,252	8,706	(NA)	110	18,917	2,002	835	10,708	895	571
1999....	14,804	5,881	8,731	8	118	19,519	2,122	822	10,852	852	567
2000....	15,067	5,822	9,071	8	50	19,701	2,389	990	11,459	826	541
2001....	15,128	5,801	9,328	11	20	19,649	2,543	951	11,871	862	550
2002....	14,947	5,744	9,140	16	9	19,761	2,390	975	11,530	877	599
2003....	15,304	5,649	9,665	(NA)	12	20,034	2,599	1,014	12,264	907	638
2004....	15,475	5,441	10,088	77	27	20,731	3,057	1,021	13,145	961	676
2005....	15,220	5,181	10,126	52	32	20,802	3,588	1,133	13,714	1,008	685
2006....	15,242	5,088	10,118	8	25	20,687	3,589	1,292	13,707	1,001	689
2007....	15,156	5,077	10,031	7	27	20,680	3,437	1,405	13,468	983	697
2008....	14,648	5,000	9,783	19	29	19,498	3,132	1,773	12,915	1,028	702
2009....	14,336	5,350	9,013	56	44	18,771	2,678	1,980	11,691	1,052	727
2010....	14,724	5,482	9,213	(NA)	42	19,180	2,580	2,311	11,793	1,060	727
2011....	14,806	5,645	8,935	(NA)	47	18,882	2,501	2,939	11,436	1,027	696
2012....	14,999	6,497	8,527	(NA)	67	18,490	2,071	3,137	10,598	1,061	695
2013....	15,312	7,465	7,730	(NA)	134	18,961	2,129	3,487	9,859	1,053	696
2014....	15,844	8,711	7,337	(NA)	346	19,035	1,884	3,834	9,221	1,085	691

NA Not available. [1] Includes lease condensate. [2] Crude oil at end of period. Includes commercial and Strategic Petroleum Reserve stocks. [3] Includes Strategic Petroleum Reserve. [4] SPR is the Strategic Petroleum Reserve. Through 2000, includes imports by SPR only; beginning in 2004, includes imports by SPR, and imports into SPR by others. [5] Crude oil (including Strategic Petroleum Reserve imports) plus refined products. [6] Beginning in 1981, includes stocks of Alaskan crude oil in transit. [7] Crude oil stocks in the Strategic Petroleum Reserve include non-U.S. stocks held under foreign or commercial storage agreements.

Source: U.S. Energy Information Administration, *Monthly Energy Review*," June 2015, and earlier reports. See also <http://www.eia.gov/totalenergy/data/monthly/>.

Table 959. Petroleum and Coal Products Corporations—Sales, Net Profit, and Profit Per Dollar of Sales: 1990 to 2014

[318.5 represents $318,500,000,000. Through 2000, covers Standard Industrial Classification (SIC) group 29. Beginning 2001, covers North American Industry Classification System (NAICS) 324. Profit rates are averages of quarterly figures at annual rates]

Item	Unit	1990	1995	2000	2005	2009	2010	2011	2012	2013	2014
Sales..................................	Bil. dol.	318.5	283.1	455.2	956.0	846.0	1,077.1	1,411.3	1,377.4	1,342.5	1,277.6
Net profit:											
Before income taxes................	Bil. dol.	23.1	16.5	55.5	120.2	41.9	56.0	125.7	117.6	79.8	82.4
After income taxes.................	Bil. dol.	17.8	13.9	42.6	96.3	43.1	54.2	108.0	99.0	73.0	74.3
Depreciation [1].....................	Bil. dol.	18.7	16.7	15.5	18.6	28.0	30.8	29.4	29.1	29.2	32.4
Profits per dollar of sales:											
Before income taxes................	Cents	7.3	5.8	12.2	12.6	5.1	5.3	8.9	8.5	5.9	6.3
After income taxes.................	Cents	5.6	4.9	9.4	10.1	5.2	5.1	7.7	7.2	5.4	5.8
Profits on stockholders' equity:											
Before income taxes................	Percent	16.4	12.6	29.4	38.0	10.2	12.2	24.6	22.9	14.6	14.2
After income taxes.................	Percent	12.7	10.6	22.6	30.4	10.5	11.8	21.1	19.3	13.3	12.8

[1] Includes depletion and accelerated amortization of emergency facilities.

Source: U.S. Census Bureau, *Quarterly Financial Report for Manufacturing, Mining, Trade, and Selected Service Industries*. See also <http://www.census.gov/econ/qfr/>.

Table 960. Nuclear Power Plants—Number, Capacity, and Generation: 1980 to 2014

[51.8 represents 51,800,000 kilowatts (kW)]

Item	1980	1990	1995	2000	2005	2008	2009	2010	2011	2012	2013	2014 [5]
Operable generating units [1, 2]	71	112	109	104	104	104	104	104	104	104	100	99
Net summer capacity [2, 3] (mil. kW)	51.8	99.6	99.5	97.9	100.0	100.8	101.0	101.2	101.4	101.9	99.2	98.6
Net generation (bil. kWh)	251.1	576.9	673.4	753.9	782.0	806.2	798.9	807.0	790.2	769.3	789.0	797.1
Percent of total electricity net generation	11.0	19.0	20.1	19.8	19.3	19.6	20.2	19.6	19.3	19.0	19.4	19.5
Capacity factor [4] (percent)	56.3	66.0	77.4	88.1	89.3	91.1	90.3	91.1	89.1	86.1	89.9	91.7

[1] Total of nuclear generating units holding full-power licenses, or equivalent permission to operate, at the end of the year. For example, although Tennessee Valley Authority's Browns Ferry 1 was shut down in 1985, the unit remained fully licensed and thus continued to be counted as operable. It was eventually reopened in 2007. [2] As of year-end. [3] Net summer capacity is the peak steady hourly output that generating equipment is expected to supply to system load, exclusive of auxiliary and other power plant, as demonstrated by a test at the time of summer peak demand. [4] Weighted average of monthly capacity factors. Monthly factors are derived by dividing actual monthly generation by the maximum possible generation for the month (number of hours in the month multiplied by the net summer capacity at the end of the month). [5] Data for 2014 are preliminary.

Source: U.S. Energy Information Administration, *Monthly Energy Review*, April 2015. See also <http://www.eia.gov/totalenergy/data/monthly/>.

Table 961. Nuclear Power Plants—Number of Reactors, Net Generation, and Net Summer Capacity by State: 2013

[789,016 represents 789,016,000,000 kilowatt hours (kWh)]

State	Number of reactors [1]	Nuclear net generation Total (mil. kWh)	Nuclear net generation Percent of total [2]	Nuclear net summer capacity Total (mil. kWh)	Nuclear net summer capacity Percent of total [2]	State	Number of reactors [1]	Nuclear net generation Total (mil. kWh)	Nuclear net generation Percent of total [2]	Nuclear net summer capacity Total (mil. kWh)	Nuclear net summer capacity Percent of total [2]
U.S.	104	789,016	19.4	99.2	9.4	MS	1	10,865	20.6	1.4	9.1
AL	5	40,816	27.1	5.0	15.6	MO	1	8,367	9.1	1.2	5.5
AZ	3	31,431	27.7	3.9	14.1	NE	2	6,865	18.5	1.2	14.7
AR	2	11,945	19.8	1.8	12.3	NH	1	10,927	55.2	1.2	28.2
CA	4	17,912	9.0	2.2	3.0	NJ	4	33,380	51.6	4.1	21.6
CT	2	17,080	48.0	2.1	24.0	NY	6	44,756	32.9	5.4	13.6
FL	5	26,526	11.9	3.6	6.1	NC	5	40,242	32.0	5.1	16.9
GA	4	32,903	27.2	4.1	10.6	OH	2	16,121	11.7	2.1	6.6
IL	11	97,131	47.8	11.6	25.8	PA	9	78,714	34.7	9.7	22.6
IA	1	5,321	9.4	0.6	3.8	SC	7	54,252	57.0	6.6	28.5
KS	1	7,168	14.8	1.2	8.2	TN	3	28,494	35.8	3.4	15.9
LA	2	16,954	16.6	2.1	8.1	TX	4	38,315	8.8	5.0	4.5
MD	2	14,264	39.8	1.7	13.9	VT	1	4,846	70.4	0.6	49.4
MA	1	4,331	13.2	0.7	5.0	VA	4	29,326	38.1	3.6	14.4
MI	4	28,921	27.4	3.9	13.0	WA	1	8,461	7.4	1.1	3.7
MN	3	10,708	20.9	1.7	10.6	WI	3	11,675	17.7	1.2	6.9

[1] As of Jan. 1, 2013. During 2013, 4 reactors were taken out of service: the Crystal River plant in Florida with one reactor in February, the Kewaunee plant in Wisconsin with one reactor in April, and the San Onofre plant in California with two reactors in June. [2] For total electric power generation and capacity by source, see Table 967.

Source: U.S. Energy Information Administration, *Electric Power Annual*, "Detailed State Data," <http://www.eia.gov/electricity/data/state/>, accessed April 2015.

Table 962. Uranium Concentrate—Supply, Inventories, and Average Prices: 1990 to 2014

[8.89 represents 8,890,000 pounds (lbs.). Years ending December 31. For additional data on uranium, see Table 924 and Table 924]

Item	Unit	1990	1995	2000	2005	2010	2011	2012	2013	2014
Production [1]	Mil. lb.	8.89	6.04	3.98	2.69	4.23	3.99	4.15	4.66	4.89
Exports [2]	Mil. lb.	2.0	9.8	13.6	20.5	23.1	16.7	18.0	18.9	20.0
Imports [2]	Mil. lb.	23.7	41.3	44.9	65.5	55.3	54.4	56.2	57.3	58.6
Electric plant purchases from domestic suppliers	Mil. lb.	20.5	22.3	24.3	27.3	16.2	19.8	(NA)	(NA)	(NA)
Loaded into U.S. nuclear reactors [3]	Mil. lb.	(NA)	51.1	51.5	58.3	44.3	50.9	49.5	42.6	50.5
Inventories, total	Mil. lb.	129.1	72.5	111.3	93.8	111.3	112.1	120.9	134.4	134.6
At domestic suppliers	Mil. lb.	26.4	13.7	56.5	29.1	24.7	22.3	23.3	21.3	18.6
At electric plants	Mil. lb.	102.7	58.7	54.8	64.7	86.5	89.8	97.6	113.1	116.0
Average price per pound: Purchased imports [4]	Dollars	12.55	10.20	9.84	14.83	47.01	54.00	51.44	48.24	44.11
Domestic purchases	Dollars	15.70	11.11	11.45	13.98	44.88	53.41	(NA)	(NA)	(NA)

NA Not available. [1] Data are for uranium concentrate, a yellow or brown powder obtained by the milling of uranium ore, processing of in situ leach mining solutions, or as a by-product of phosphoric acid production. [2] Includes transactions by uranium buyers (consumers). Buyer imports and exports prior to 1990 are believed to be small. [3] Does not include any fuel rods removed from reactors and later reloaded into the reactor. [4] For purchases made by U.S. suppliers and by U.S. owners and operators of civilian nuclear power plants.

Source: U.S. Energy Information Administration, through 2010, *Annual Energy Review*; thereafter, *Uranium Marketing Annual Report*, May 2015, and *Domestic Uranium Production Report–Quarterly*, May 2015. See also <http://www.eia.gov/nuclear/>.

Table 963. Renewable Energy Generating Capacity and Generation Projections: 2013 to 2040

[In gigawatts, unless otherwise noted. Reference case projections are business-as-usual trend estimates, given known technology, as well as market, demographic, and technological trends. Based on results from EIA's National Energy Modeling System]

Net summer capacity and generation	Reference case								Annual growth 2013-2040 (percent)
	2013	2014	2015	2020	2025	2030	2035	2040	
Electric power sector [1]									
Net summer capacity:									
Conventional hydropower......................	78.26	78.38	78.64	79.25	79.57	79.70	79.77	80.11	0.1
Geothermal [2]..........	2.65	2.65	2.65	3.84	5.28	6.98	8.20	9.09	4.7
Municipal waste [3]...........	3.66	3.72	3.80	3.81	3.81	3.81	3.81	3.81	0.1
Wood and other biomass [4].....................	3.34	3.41	3.45	3.49	3.49	3.65	4.17	5.48	1.8
Solar thermal....................	1.29	1.66	1.77	1.77	1.77	1.77	1.77	1.77	1.2
Solar photovoltaic [5]................	5.20	8.27	10.41	14.41	14.66	15.71	17.85	22.17	5.5
Wind....................	60.30	65.09	75.79	81.97	83.03	86.34	95.55	108.18	2.2
Total electric power sector capacity.........	**154.70**	**163.19**	**176.52**	**188.57**	**191.63**	**197.99**	**211.16**	**230.64**	**1.5**
Generation (bil. kWh):									
Conventional hydropower......................	265.74	255.05	267.21	290.95	292.78	293.36	293.84	295.58	0.4
Geothermal [2]...........	16.52	16.57	16.88	26.78	38.47	52.36	62.30	69.56	5.5
Biogenic municipal waste [6].................	16.45	18.96	19.78	20.05	20.30	20.09	20.05	20.22	0.8
Wood and other biomass.................	12.23	11.32	11.61	24.68	36.19	40.45	47.11	58.78	6.0
Dedicated plants.....................	11.09	10.29	10.59	13.41	15.08	16.74	20.45	30.31	3.8
Cofiring........................	1.14	1.03	1.02	11.27	21.11	23.71	26.66	28.47	12.7
Solar thermal....................	0.94	2.29	2.88	3.62	3.63	3.63	3.62	3.63	5.1
Solar photovoltaic [5]................	7.98	15.19	19.68	29.71	30.28	32.62	37.55	47.14	6.8
Wind....................	167.57	178.04	192.26	230.55	233.80	243.30	276.12	317.14	2.4
Total electric power sector generation.......	**487.42**	**497.43**	**530.30**	**626.45**	**655.55**	**685.91**	**740.70**	**812.14**	**1.9**
End-use sectors [7]									
Net summer capacity:									
Conventional hydropower.....................	0.29	0.29	0.29	0.29	0.29	0.29	0.29	0.29	0.0
Geothermal......................	0.00	0.00	0.00	0.00	0.00	0.00	0.00	0.00	(X)
Municipal waste [3]............	0.47	0.47	0.47	0.47	0.47	0.47	0.47	0.47	0.0
Biomass.....................	5.00	5.03	5.18	5.40	5.44	5.44	5.46	5.64	0.4
Solar photovoltaic [5]................	6.17	7.31	8.66	11.39	15.51	21.52	28.69	36.67	6.8
Wind....................	0.21	0.30	0.48	0.66	0.73	0.89	1.11	1.52	7.7
Total end-use sector capacity...........	**12.13**	**13.40**	**15.07**	**18.20**	**22.43**	**28.61**	**36.01**	**44.58**	**4.9**
Generation (bil. kWh):									
Conventional hydropower......................	1.38	1.38	1.38	1.38	1.38	1.38	1.38	1.38	0.0
Geothermal......................	–	–	–	–	–	–	–	–	(X)
Municipal waste [3]............	3.65	3.65	3.65	3.63	3.63	3.63	3.63	3.63	0.0
Biomass.....................	27.16	27.32	28.17	29.10	29.32	29.35	29.42	30.47	0.4
Solar photovoltaic [5]................	9.62	11.39	13.47	17.92	24.77	34.66	46.34	59.33	7.0
Wind....................	0.26	0.39	0.64	0.88	0.98	1.22	1.54	2.11	8.0
Total End-Use Sector Generation.............	**42.08**	**44.13**	**47.31**	**52.91**	**60.08**	**70.24**	**82.31**	**96.93**	**3.1**
Total, all sectors									
Net summer capacity:									
Conventional hydropower......................	78.55	78.66	78.93	79.53	79.86	79.99	80.06	80.40	0.1
Geothermal......................	2.65	2.65	2.65	3.84	5.28	6.98	8.20	9.09	4.7
Municipal waste..................	4.13	4.19	4.27	4.28	4.28	4.28	4.28	4.28	0.1
Wood and other biomass [4].................	8.34	8.44	8.63	8.90	8.93	9.09	9.63	11.12	1.1
Solar [5]......................	12.66	17.25	20.84	27.57	31.94	39.00	48.31	60.61	6.0
Wind....................	60.50	65.39	76.27	82.66	83.78	87.26	96.69	109.72	2.2
Total capacity, all sectors....................	**166.83**	**176.58**	**191.59**	**206.77**	**214.06**	**226.60**	**247.18**	**275.22**	**1.9**
Generation (bil. kWh):									
Conventional hydropower......................	267.12	256.43	268.59	292.33	294.17	294.74	295.23	296.97	0.4
Geothermal......................	16.52	16.57	16.88	26.78	38.47	52.36	62.30	69.56	5.5
Municipal waste..................	20.10	22.61	23.43	23.68	23.93	23.71	23.68	23.85	0.6
Wood and other biomass..................	39.39	38.64	39.78	53.79	65.51	69.80	76.53	89.25	3.1
Solar [5]......................	18.54	28.87	36.03	51.26	58.68	70.91	87.52	110.10	6.8
Wind....................	167.83	178.43	192.90	231.53	234.88	244.62	277.76	319.35	2.4
Total generation, all sectors..................	**529.50**	**541.56**	**577.62**	**679.36**	**715.64**	**756.15**	**823.01**	**909.07**	**2.0**

– Represents zero. X Not applicable. [1] Includes electricity-only and combined heat and power plants that have a regulatory status. [2] Includes both hydrothermal resources and near-field enhanced geothermal systems (EGS). [3] Includes municipal waste, landfill gas, and municipal sewage sludge. [4] Facilities co-firing biomass and coal are classified as coal. [5] Does not include off-grid photovoltaics (PV). [6] Includes biogenic municipal waste, landfill gas, and municipal sludge. [7] Includes combined heat and power plants and electricity-only plants in the commercial and industrial sectors and small on-site generating systems in the residential, commercial, and industrial sectors used primarily for own-use generation, but which many also sell some power to the grid.

Source: U.S. Energy Information Administration, *Annual Energy Outlook 2015*, April 2015. See also <http://www.eia.gov/forecasts/aeo/>.

Table 964. Electricity Net Generation by Sector and Fuel Type: 1990 to 2014

[3,037.8 represents 3,037,800,000,000 kilowatt hours (kWh). Data are for fuels consumed to produce electricity. Also includes fuels consumed to produce useful thermal output at a small number of electric utility combined-heat-and-power (CHP) plants]

Source and sector	Unit	1990	1995	2000	2005	2010	2011	2012	2013	2014 [1]
Net generation, total	**Bil. kWh.**	**3,037.8**	**3,353.5**	**3,802.1**	**4,055.4**	**4,125.1**	**4,100.1**	**4,047.8**	**4,066.0**	**4,092.9**
Electric power sector, total	Bil. kWh.	2,901.3	3,194.2	3,637.5	3,902.2	3,972.4	3,948.2	3,890.4	3,903.7	3,936.0
Commercial sector [2]	Bil. kWh.	5.8	8.2	7.9	8.5	8.6	10.1	11.3	12.2	12.7
Industrial sector [3]	Bil. kWh.	130.8	151.0	156.7	144.7	144.1	141.9	146.1	150.0	144.3
Net generation by source, all sectors:										
Fossil fuels, total	Bil. kWh.	2,103.6	2,293.9	2,692.5	2,909.5	2,883.4	2,788.9	2,775.0	2,746.0	2,749.7
Coal [4]	Bil. kWh.	1,594.0	1,709.4	1,966.3	2,012.9	1,847.3	1,733.4	1,514.0	1,581.1	1,585.7
Petroleum [5]	Bil. kWh.	126.5	74.6	111.2	122.2	37.1	30.2	23.2	27.2	30.5
Natural gas [6]	Bil. kWh.	372.8	496.1	601.0	761.0	987.7	1,013.7	1,225.9	1,124.8	1,121.9
Other gases [7]	Bil. kWh.	10.4	13.9	14.0	13.5	11.3	11.6	11.9	12.9	11.6
Nuclear electric power	Bil. kWh.	576.9	673.4	753.9	782.0	807.0	790.2	769.3	789.0	797.1
Hydroelectric pumped storage [8]	Bil. kWh.	-3.5	-2.7	-5.5	-6.6	-5.5	-6.4	-5.0	-4.7	-6.2
Renewable energy, total	Bil. kWh.	357.2	384.8	356.5	357.7	427.4	513.3	494.6	522.1	539.8
Conventional hydroelectric power	Bil. kWh.	292.9	310.8	275.6	270.3	260.2	319.4	276.2	268.6	258.7
Biomass, total	Bil. kWh.	45.8	56.9	60.7	54.3	56.1	56.7	57.6	60.9	64.3
Wood [9]	Bil. kWh.	32.5	36.5	37.6	38.9	37.2	37.4	37.8	40.0	43.0
Waste [10]	Bil. kWh.	13.3	20.4	23.1	15.4	18.9	19.2	19.8	20.8	21.3
Geothermal	Bil. kWh.	15.4	13.4	14.1	14.7	15.2	15.3	15.6	15.8	16.6
Solar [11]	Bil. kWh.	0.4	0.5	0.5	0.6	1.2	1.8	4.3	9.0	18.3
Wind	Bil. kWh.	2.8	3.2	5.6	17.8	94.7	120.2	140.8	167.8	181.8
Other [12]	Bil. kWh.	3.6	4.1	4.8	12.8	12.9	14.2	13.8	13.6	12.6
Consumption of fuels for electricity generation:										
Coal [4]	Mil. short tons	792.5	860.6	994.9	1,041.4	979.7	934.9	825.7	860.7	854.4
Petroleum, total [13]	Mil. bbl.	218.8	132.6	195.2	206.8	65.1	52.4	41.0	47.5	53.7
Distillate fuel oil [13]	Mil. bbl.	18.1	19.6	31.7	20.7	14.1	11.2	9.3	9.8	14.6
Residual fuel oil [14]	Mil. bbl.	190.7	95.5	143.4	141.5	24.0	14.3	11.8	11.8	14.8
Other liquids [15]	Mil. bbl.	0.4	0.7	1.4	3.0	2.1	1.8	1.6	1.7	2.6
Petroleum coke.	Mil. short tons	1.9	3.4	3.7	8.3	5.0	5.0	3.7	4.9	4.3
Natural gas [6]	Bil. cu. ft.	3,691.6	4,737.9	5,691.5	6,036.4	7,680.2	7,883.9	9,484.7	8,596.3	8,503.0
Other gases [7]	Tril. Btu.	111.8	132.5	126.0	109.9	90.1	91.3	103.4	115.3	106.6
Biomass.	Tril. Btu.	653.5	795.6	825.9	585.3	630.3	626.2	680.7	695.8	723.4
Wood [9]	Tril. Btu.	442.3	479.9	495.8	355.3	349.5	347.6	390.3	397.9	430.1
Waste [10]	Tril. Btu.	211.2	315.7	330.1	230.1	280.8	278.6	290.4	297.9	293.3
Other [12]	Tril. Btu.	36.0	42.0	46.2	173.0	184.4	205.3	203.6	200.1	183.5

[1] Preliminary. [2] Commercial combined-heat-and-power (CHP) and commercial electricity-only plants. [3] Industrial CHP and industrial electricity-only plants. [4] Anthracite, bituminous coal, subbituminous coal, lignite, waste coal, and coal synfuel. [5] Distillate fuel oil, residual fuel oil, petroleum coke, jet fuel, kerosene, other petroleum, waste oil, and beginning in 2011, propane. [6] Includes a small amount of supplemental gaseous fuels that cannot be identified separately. [7] Blast furnace gas and other manufactured and waste gases derived from fossil fuels. Through 2010, also includes propane. [8] Pumped storage facility production minus energy used for pumping. [9] Wood and wood-derived fuels. [10] Municipal solid waste from biogenic sources, landfill gas, sludge waste, tires, agricultural byproducts, and other biomass. Through 2000, also includes nonrenewable waste (municipal solid waste from non-biogenic sources and tire-derived fuels). [11] Solar thermal and photovoltaic energy. [12] Batteries, chemicals, hydrogen, pitch, purchased steam, sulfur, miscellaneous technologies, and beginning 2001, nonrenewable waste (municipal solid waste from nonbiogenic sources, and tire-derived fuels). [13] Fuel oil numbers 1, 2, and 4. For 1990 through 2000, electric utility data also include small amounts of kerosene and jet fuel. [14] Fuel oil numbers 5 and 6. For 1990 through 2000, electric utility data also include a small amount of fuel oil number 4. [15] Jet fuel, kerosene, other petroleum liquids, waste oil, and beginning in 2011, propane.

Source: U.S. Energy Information Administration, *Monthly Energy Review*, June 2015. See also <http://www.eia.gov/totalenergy/data/monthly>.

Table 965. Total Electric Net Summer Capacity for All Sectors by Energy Source: 1990 to 2013

[In million kilowatts (734.1 represents 734,100,000). Data are at end of year. For plants that use multiple sources of energy, capacity is assigned to the predominant energy source]

Source	1990	1995	2000	2005	2009	2010	2011	2012	2013
Net summer capacity, total	**734.1**	**769.5**	**811.7**	**978.0**	**1,025.4**	**1,039.1**	**1,051.3**	**1,063.0**	**1,060.1**
Fossil fuels, total	527.8	554.2	598.9	757.1	774.3	782.2	786.2	781.2	774.3
Coal [1]	307.4	311.4	315.1	313.4	314.3	316.8	317.6	309.7	303.3
Petroleum [2]	77.9	66.6	61.8	58.5	56.8	55.6	51.5	47.2	43.5
Natural gas [3]	140.8	174.5	219.6	383.1	401.3	407.0	415.2	422.4	425.4
Other gases [4]	1.6	1.7	2.3	2.1	1.9	2.7	1.9	1.9	2.1
Nuclear electric power	99.6	99.5	97.9	100.0	101.0	101.2	101.4	101.9	99.2
Hydroelectric pumped storage	19.5	21.4	19.5	21.3	22.2	22.2	22.3	22.4	22.4
Renewable energy, total	86.8	93.9	94.9	98.7	127.1	132.6	139.9	155.9	161.8
Conventional hydroelectric power	73.9	78.6	79.4	77.5	78.5	78.8	78.7	78.7	79.2
Biomass, total	8.1	10.3	10.0	9.8	11.3	11.4	11.6	12.3	13.4
Wood [5]	5.5	6.7	6.1	6.2	6.9	7.0	7.1	7.5	8.4
Waste [6]	2.5	3.5	3.9	3.6	4.3	4.4	4.5	4.8	5.0
Geothermal	2.7	3.0	2.8	2.3	2.4	2.4	2.4	2.6	2.6
Solar [7]	0.3	0.3	0.4	0.4	0.6	0.9	1.5	3.2	6.6
Wind	1.8	1.7	2.4	8.7	34.3	39.1	45.7	59.1	60.0
Other [8]	0.5	0.5	0.5	0.9	0.9	0.9	1.4	1.7	2.3

[1] Anthracite, bituminous coal, subbituminous coal, lignite, waste coal, and coal synfuel. [2] Distillate fuel oil, residual fuel oil, petroleum coke, jet fuel, kerosene, other petroleum, and waste oil. [3] Includes a small amount of supplemental gaseous fuels that cannot be identified separately. [4] Blast furnace gas, propane gas, and other manufactured and waste gases derived from fossil fuels. [5] Wood and wood-derived fuels. [6] Municipal solid waste from biogenic sources, landfill gas, sludge waste, agricultural byproducts, and other biomass. Also includes nonrenewable waste (municipal solid waste from nonbiogenic sources, and tire-derived fuels). [7] Solar thermal and photovoltaic energy. [8] Batteries, chemicals, hydrogen, pitch, purchased steam, sulfur, and miscellaneous technologies.

Source: U.S. Energy Information Administration, *Electric Power Annual 2013*, March 2015, and earlier reports. See also <http://www.eia.gov/electricity/annual/>.

Table 966. Electricity—End Use and Average Retail Prices: 1990 to 2013

[Beginning 2003, the category "other" has been replaced by "transportation," and the categories "commercial" and "industrial" have been redefined. Data represent revenue from electricity retail sales divided by the amount of retail electricity sold (in kilowatt-hours). Prices include state and local taxes, energy or demand charges, customer service charges, environmental surcharges, franchise fees, fuel adjustments, and other miscellaneous charges applied to end-use customers during normal billing operations. Prices do not include deferred charges, credits, or other adjustments, such as fuel or revenue from purchased power, from previous reporting periods. Data are for a census of electric utilities. Beginning in 2000 data also include energy service providers selling to retail customers]

Item	1990	1995	2000	2005	2009	2010	2011	2012	2013
END USE (Billion kilowatt-hours)									
Total end use [1]	**2,837.1**	**3,164.0**	**3,592.4**	**3,811.0**	**3,723.7**	**3,886.8**	**3,882.6**	**3,832.3**	**3,868.6**
Direct use [2]	124.5	150.7	170.9	150.0	126.9	131.9	132.8	137.7	143.5
Retail sales, total [3]	**2,712.6**	**3,013.3**	**3,421.4**	**3,661.0**	**3,596.8**	**3,754.8**	**3,749.8**	**3,694.6**	**3,725.1**
Residential	924.0	1,042.5	1,192.4	1,359.2	1,364.8	1,445.7	1,422.8	1,374.5	1,394.9
Commercial [4]	838.3	953.1	1,159.3	1,275.1	1,306.9	1,330.2	1,328.1	1,327.1	1,344.2
Industrial [5]	945.5	1,012.7	1,064.2	1,019.2	917.4	971.2	991.3	985.7	978.4
Transportation [6]	4.8	5.0	5.4	7.5	7.8	7.7	7.7	7.3	7.6
AVERAGE RETAIL PRICES (Cents per kilowatt-hour)									
Total	**6.57**	**6.89**	**6.81**	**8.14**	**9.82**	**9.83**	**9.90**	**9.84**	**10.07**
Residential	7.83	8.40	8.24	9.45	11.51	11.54	11.72	11.88	12.12
Commercial [7]	7.34	7.69	7.43	8.67	10.16	10.19	10.24	10.09	10.28
Industrial [5]	4.74	4.66	4.64	5.73	6.83	6.77	6.82	6.67	6.84
Transportation [6]	(NA)	(NA)	(NA)	8.57	10.66	10.56	10.46	10.21	10.55
Other [8]	6.40	6.88	6.56	(NA)	(NA)	(NA)	(NA)	(NA)	(NA)

NA Not available. [1] The sum of "total retail sales" and "direct use." [2] Use of electricity that is 1) self-generated, 2) produced by either the same entity that consumes the power or an affiliate, and 3) used in direct support of a service or industrial process located within the same facility or group of facilities that house the generating equipment. Direct use is exclusive of station use. [3] Electricity retail sales to ultimate customers reported by electric utilities and, beginning in 2000, other energy service providers. [4] Includes public street and highway lighting, interdepartmental sales, and other sales to public authorities. [5] Beginning 2003, includes agriculture and irrigation. [6] Includes sales to railroads and railways. [7] Beginning 2003, includes public street and highway lighting, interdepartmental sales, and other sales to public authorities. [8] Public street and highway lighting, interdepartmental sales, other sales to public authorities, agriculture and irrigation, and transportation including railroads and railways.

Source: U.S. Energy Information Administration, *Electric Power Annual 2013*, March 2015, and earlier reports. See also <http://www.eia.gov/electricity/>.

Table 967. Electric Power Industry—Net Generation and Net Summer Capacity by State: 2000 to 2013

[3,802.1 represents 3,802,100,000,000. Capacity as of December 31. Covers utilities for public use]

State	Net generation (bil. kWh) 2000	2010	2012	2013 Total (bil. kWh)	2013 Percent from— Petro-leum	Natural gas	Hydro-electric	Nuclear	Coal	Net summer capacity (mil. kW) 2012	2013
U.S.....	3,802.1	4,125.1	4,047.8	4,066.0	0.7	27.7	6.6	19.4	38.9	1,063.0	1,060.1
AL.......	124.4	152.2	152.9	150.6	(Z)	30.9	8.6	27.1	31.2	32.5	32.4
AK.......	6.2	6.8	6.9	6.5	12.6	52.7	22.1	–	9.6	2.1	2.4
AZ.......	88.9	111.8	110.9	113.3	(Z)	26.2	5.2	27.7	38.4	27.6	27.9
AR.......	43.9	61.0	65.0	60.3	0.1	20.1	4.4	19.8	52.9	16.4	14.8
CA.......	208.1	204.1	199.5	200.1	(Z)	59.7	11.9	9.0	0.4	71.3	73.8
CO.......	44.2	50.7	52.6	52.9	(Z)	20.2	2.3	32.3	63.7	14.9	14.8
CT.......	33.0	33.3	36.1	35.6	0.9	44.3	1.1	–	1.9	9.1	8.8
DE.......	6.0	5.6	8.6	7.8	0.3	76.4	–	–	19.9	3.4	3.2
DC.......	0.1	0.2	0.1	0.1	–	100.0	–	–	–	(Z)	(Z)
FL.......	191.8	229.1	221.1	222.4	1.2	62.5	0.1	11.9	20.8	59.1	58.8
GA.......	123.9	137.6	122.3	121.0	0.2	33.3	3.1	27.2	33.3	38.5	38.2
HI.......	10.6	10.8	10.5	10.3	70.3	–	0.8	–	13.7	2.7	2.8
ID.......	11.9	12.0	15.5	15.2	(Z)	22.3	55.8	–	0.6	4.9	4.9
IL.......	178.5	201.4	197.6	203.0	(Z)	3.4	0.1	47.8	43.3	45.1	45.0
IN.......	127.8	125.2	114.7	110.4	1.4	8.2	0.4	–	83.9	26.8	27.2
IA.......	41.5	57.5	56.7	56.7	0.2	2.5	1.3	9.4	58.8	16.0	15.9
KS.......	44.8	47.9	44.4	48.5	0.1	4.1	(Z)	14.8	61.4	14.1	14.2
KY.......	93.0	98.2	89.9	89.7	1.6	1.6	3.6	–	92.8	21.1	21.0
LA.......	92.9	102.9	103.4	102.0	4.8	51.5	1.0	16.6	20.4	25.5	26.2
ME.......	14.0	17.0	14.4	14.0	1.7	34.7	25.4	–	0.4	4.5	4.5
MD.......	51.1	43.6	37.8	35.9	0.5	8.1	4.8	39.8	43.3	12.2	12.3
MA.......	38.7	42.8	36.2	32.9	1.2	64.6	3.0	13.2	12.0	14.3	13.7
MI.......	104.2	111.6	108.2	105.4	0.5	11.7	1.3	27.4	53.4	30.3	30.1
MN.......	51.4	53.7	52.2	51.3	0.1	12.3	1.0	20.9	45.8	15.4	15.8
MS.......	37.6	54.5	54.6	52.8	(Z)	60.2	–	20.6	16.5	15.4	15.6
MO.......	76.6	92.3	91.8	91.6	0.1	4.8	1.2	9.1	83.1	22.0	21.8
MT.......	26.5	29.8	27.8	27.7	1.7	2.2	34.8	–	53.7	6.3	6.3
NE.......	29.1	36.6	34.2	37.1	0.1	1.2	3.0	18.5	72.1	8.3	8.4
NV.......	35.5	35.1	35.2	36.4	0.1	68.0	7.4	–	14.4	10.5	10.7
NH.......	15.0	22.2	19.3	19.8	0.5	20.7	7.2	55.2	7.4	4.3	4.4
NJ.......	58.1	65.7	65.3	64.8	0.2	41.8	(Z)	51.6	3.1	18.9	19.0
NM.......	34.0	36.3	36.6	35.9	0.2	25.0	0.3	–	67.3	8.4	7.9
NY.......	138.1	137.0	135.8	136.1	0.7	39.9	18.3	32.9	3.5	39.5	39.9
NC.......	122.3	128.7	116.7	125.9	0.2	22.2	5.5	32.0	37.4	30.4	30.0
ND.......	31.3	34.7	36.1	35.0	0.1	0.2	5.3	–	78.5	6.5	6.6
OH.......	149.1	143.6	129.7	137.3	1.0	15.8	0.4	11.7	68.9	32.9	32.5
OK.......	55.6	72.3	77.9	73.7	(Z)	40.8	3.0	–	40.7	23.5	23.3
OR.......	51.8	55.1	60.9	59.9	(Z)	24.0	55.3	–	6.3	15.5	15.7
PA.......	201.7	229.8	223.4	226.8	0.2	22.0	1.1	34.7	39.0	45.4	43.0
RI.......	6.0	7.7	8.3	6.2	0.8	98.3	0.1	–	–	1.8	1.8
SC.......	93.3	104.2	96.8	95.2	0.1	12.4	3.3	57.0	25.6	23.1	23.0
SD.......	9.7	10.0	12.0	10.1	0.1	5.0	40.2	–	28.2	4.1	4.1
TN.......	95.8	82.3	77.7	79.7	0.2	6.3	15.6	35.8	40.8	21.3	21.3
TX.......	377.7	411.7	429.8	433.4	0.2	47.0	0.1	8.8	34.5	109.6	109.6
UT.......	36.6	42.2	39.4	42.5	0.1	15.5	1.2	–	80.6	7.6	7.7
VT.......	6.3	6.6	6.6	6.9	0.1	–	18.7	70.4	–	1.2	1.3
VA.......	77.2	73.0	70.7	76.9	0.4	29.5	1.6	38.1	27.5	24.8	24.8
WA.......	108.2	103.5	116.8	114.2	(Z)	10.0	68.5	7.4	5.9	30.9	30.7
WV.......	92.9	80.8	73.4	75.9	0.2	0.4	2.3	–	95.3	16.3	16.3
WI.......	59.6	64.3	63.7	66.0	0.5	12.3	3.0	17.7	61.6	18.0	17.3
WY.......	45.5	48.1	49.6	52.5	0.1	1.0	1.4	–	88.5	8.4	8.4

– Represents zero. Z Represents less than .05 percent of net electricity generation.

Source: U.S. Energy Information Administration, *Electric Power Annual*, "Data Tables" and "Detailed State Data," <http://www.eia.gov/electricity/annual/>, accessed April 2015.

Table 968. Electric Power Industry—Capability, Peak Load, and Capacity Margin: 1980 to 2014

[558,237 represents 558,237,000 kilowatts (kW). Excludes Alaska and Hawaii. Capability represents the maximum kilowatt output with all power sources available and with hydraulic equipment under actual water conditions, allowing for maintenance, emergency outages, and system operating requirements. Capacity margin is the difference between capability and peak load. Minus sign (-) indicates decrease]

Year	Capability at the time of— Summer peak load (1,000 kW) Amount	Change from prior year	Winter peak load (1,000 kW) Amount	Change from prior year	Noncoincident peak load Summer (1,000 kW)	Winter (1,000 kW)	Capacity margin Summer Amount (1,000 kW)	Percent of capability	Capacity margin Winter Amount (1,000 kW)	Percent of capability
1980	558,237	13,731	572,195	17,670	427,058	384,567	131,179	23.5	187,628	32.8
1985	621,597	17,357	636,475	14,350	460,503	423,660	161,094	25.9	212,815	33.4
1990	685,091	11,775	696,757	11,508	546,331	484,231	138,760	20.3	212,526	30.5
1991	690,915	5,824	703,212	6,455	551,418	485,761	139,497	20.2	217,451	30.9
1992	695,436	4,521	707,752	4,540	548,707	492,983	146,729	21.1	214,769	30.3
1993	694,250	-1,186	711,957	4,205	575,356	521,733	118,894	17.1	190,224	26.7
1994	702,985	8,735	715,090	3,133	585,320	518,253	117,665	16.7	196,837	27.5
1995	714,222	11,237	727,679	12,589	620,249	544,684	93,973	13.2	182,995	25.1
1996	730,376	16,154	737,637	9,958	616,790	554,081	113,586	15.6	183,556	24.9
1997	737,855	7,479	736,666	-971	637,677	529,874	100,178	13.6	206,792	28.1
1998	744,670	6,815	735,090	-1,576	660,293	567,558	84,377	11.3	167,532	22.8
1999	765,744	21,074	748,271	13,181	682,122	570,915	83,622	10.9	177,356	23.7
2000	808,054	42,310	767,505	19,234	678,413	588,426	129,641	16.0	179,079	23.3
2001	788,990	-19,064	806,598	39,093	687,812	576,312	101,178	12.8	230,286	28.6
2002	833,380	44,390	850,984	44,386	714,565	604,986	118,815	14.3	245,998	28.9
2003	856,131	22,751	882,120	31,136	709,375	593,874	146,756	17.1	288,246	32.7
2004	875,870	19,739	864,849	-17,271	704,459	618,701	171,411	19.6	246,148	28.5
2005	882,125	6,255	878,110	13,261	758,876	626,365	123,249	14.0	251,745	28.7
2006	891,226	9,101	899,551	21,441	789,475	640,981	101,751	11.4	258,570	28.7
2007	914,397	23,171	913,650	14,099	782,227	637,905	132,170	14.5	275,745	30.2
2008	909,504	-4,893	927,781	14,131	752,470	643,557	157,034	17.3	284,224	30.6
2009	916,449	6,945	920,002	-7,779	725,958	668,818	190,491	20.8	251,184	27.3
2010	923,559	7,110	935,262	15,260	767,948	651,418	155,611	16.8	283,844	30.3
2011	892,426	-31,133	893,206	-42,056	782,469	648,190	109,957	12.3	245,016	27.4
2012	927,060	34,634	941,660	48,454	767,762	621,387	159,298	17.2	320,273	34.0
2013	908,348	-18,712	921,966	-19,694	777,015	663,629	131,333	14.5	258,337	28.0
2014	933,830	25,482	953,453	31,487	784,017	674,231	149,813	16.0	279,222	29.3

Source: Edison Electric Institute, Washington, DC, *Statistical Yearbook of the Electric Power Industry*, annual ©. See also <http://www.eei.org>.

Table 969. Electric Energy Retail Sales by Class of Service and State: 2013

[In billions of kilowatt-hours (3,725.1 represents 3,725,100,000,000). Data include both bundled and unbundled consumers]

State	Total [1]	Residential	Commercial	Industrial	State	Total [1]	Residential	Commercial	Industrial
United States	**3,725.1**	**1,394.9**	**1,344.2**	**978.4**	Missouri	83.4	35.3	30.5	17.6
Alabama	87.9	31.4	22.6	33.9	Montana	14.0	4.9	4.9	4.2
Alaska	6.3	2.1	2.8	1.3	Nebraska	30.7	10.1	9.4	11.3
Arizona	75.7	33.1	30.0	12.5	Nevada	35.2	12.1	9.3	13.8
Arkansas	46.7	18.2	11.9	16.6	New Hampshire	11.0	4.6	4.5	2.0
California	261.5	89.3	124.0	47.4	New Jersey	74.6	28.5	38.2	7.6
Colorado	53.4	18.5	20.1	14.8	New Mexico	23.1	6.8	9.0	7.3
Connecticut	29.8	13.1	13.0	3.5	New York	147.9	50.8	76.3	17.9
Delaware	11.3	4.6	4.2	2.6	North Carolina	129.8	56.3	46.6	26.9
District of Columbia	11.1	2.0	8.5	0.2	North Dakota	16.0	5.0	5.7	5.3
Florida	221.9	113.3	92.1	16.4	Ohio	150.3	52.2	46.7	51.4
Georgia	130.5	53.5	45.4	31.4	Oklahoma	59.9	23.2	19.8	16.9
Hawaii	9.5	2.6	3.3	3.6	Oregon	47.6	19.3	16.1	12.2
Idaho	24.2	8.6	6.3	9.3	Pennsylvania	146.3	54.3	43.1	48.0
Illinois	141.8	46.4	50.5	44.4	Rhode Island	7.8	3.2	3.7	0.9
Indiana	105.5	33.4	24.3	47.8	South Carolina	78.6	28.8	21.1	28.7
Iowa	46.8	14.7	12.5	19.6	South Dakota	12.2	4.8	4.7	2.7
Kansas	39.8	13.6	15.2	11.0	Tennessee	96.9	40.9	33.6	22.5
Kentucky	84.8	26.8	21.0	37.0	Texas	378.8	140.3	136.5	102.0
Louisiana	85.8	30.7	24.3	30.8	Utah	30.5	9.4	11.0	10.0
Maine	11.9	4.7	4.0	3.2	Vermont	5.6	2.1	2.0	1.4
Maryland	61.9	27.4	30.0	3.9	Virginia	110.5	45.4	47.8	17.2
Massachusetts	55.3	20.7	17.7	16.5	Washington	92.9	36.0	29.7	27.2
Michigan	103.0	34.0	37.7	31.3	West Virginia	31.4	11.6	7.8	12.0
Minnesota	68.6	22.8	23.0	22.7	Wisconsin	69.1	22.1	23.7	23.4
Mississippi	48.8	18.5	14.2	16.1	Wyoming	17.1	2.8	4.1	10.2

[1] Includes transportation, not shown separately.

Source: U.S. Energy Information Administration, "Electric Sales, Revenue, and Average Price," <http://www.eia.gov/electricity/sales_revenue_price/index.cfm>, accessed March 2015.

Table 970. Electric Energy Average Retail Price by Class of Service and State: 2013

[In cents per kilowatt-hour (kWh). Data include both bundled and unbundled consumers]

State	Total [1]	Residential	Commercial	Industrial	State	Total [1]	Residential	Commercial	Industrial
United States	**10.07**	**12.12**	**10.28**	**6.84**	Missouri	9.04	10.60	8.80	6.29
Alabama	9.02	11.26	10.51	5.95	Montana	8.58	10.33	9.54	5.43
Alaska	16.49	18.12	15.58	15.83	Nebraska	8.74	10.31	8.60	7.44
Arizona	10.14	11.71	9.85	6.66	Nevada	9.03	11.89	9.01	6.52
Arkansas	7.93	9.59	8.05	6.04	New Hampshire	14.30	16.33	13.52	11.40
California	14.28	16.19	14.22	10.96	New Jersey	13.70	15.73	12.77	10.80
Colorado	9.88	11.93	9.86	7.34	New Mexico	9.25	11.68	9.74	6.36
Connecticut	15.66	17.55	14.63	12.61	New York	15.44	18.79	15.35	6.58
Delaware	10.90	12.95	10.20	8.43	North Carolina	9.24	10.97	8.76	6.45
District of Columbia	11.85	12.57	11.94	5.54	North Dakota	8.20	9.12	8.39	7.13
Florida	10.22	11.27	9.39	7.61	Ohio	9.20	12.01	9.35	6.22
Georgia	9.69	11.46	9.99	6.27	Oklahoma	7.86	9.67	7.77	5.49
Hawaii	33.26	36.98	34.05	29.87	Oregon	8.44	9.90	8.68	5.80
Idaho	7.58	9.32	7.37	6.10	Pennsylvania	9.81	12.79	9.25	6.97
Illinois	8.26	10.63	8.14	5.94	Rhode Island	13.72	15.20	12.92	11.82
Indiana	8.73	10.99	9.60	6.70	South Carolina	9.24	11.99	9.88	6.01
Iowa	8.07	11.05	8.44	5.62	South Dakota	8.86	10.26	8.51	6.97
Kansas	9.72	11.64	9.68	7.39	Tennessee	9.13	9.98	10.00	6.29
Kentucky	7.69	9.79	8.56	5.66	Texas	8.66	11.35	8.02	5.81
Louisiana	8.04	9.43	8.96	5.92	Utah	8.15	10.37	8.32	5.87
Maine	11.86	14.35	11.74	8.34	Vermont	14.62	17.14	14.66	10.84
Maryland	11.66	13.25	10.68	8.36	Virginia	8.96	10.84	8.00	6.63
Massachusetts	14.51	15.83	14.23	13.18	Washington	7.09	8.70	7.78	4.23
Michigan	11.21	14.59	11.06	7.72	West Virginia	7.91	9.52	8.17	6.20
Minnesota	9.41	11.81	9.42	6.98	Wisconsin	10.51	13.55	10.75	7.40
Mississippi	9.11	10.78	10.10	6.34	Wyoming	7.55	10.16	8.57	6.42

[1] Includes transportation, not shown separately.

Source: U.S. Energy Information Administration, "Electric Sales, Revenue, and Average Price," <http://www.eia.gov/electricity/sales_revenue_price/index.cfm>, accessed March 2015.

Table 971. Total Electric Power Industry—Generation, Sales, Revenue, and Customers: 1990 to 2014

[2,808 represents 2,808,000,000,000 Kilowatt hours (kWh). Sales and revenue are to and from ultimate customers. Commercial and Industrial are not wholly comparable on a year-to-year basis due to changes from one classification to another. For the 2005 period forward, the Energy Information Administration replaced the "Other" sector with the Transportation sector. The Transportation sector consists entirely of electrified rail and urban transit systems. Data previously reported in "Other" have been relocated to the Commercial sector, except for Agriculture (i.e., irrigation load), which have been relocated to the Industrial sector]

Class	Unit	1990	2000	2005	2009	2010	2011	2012	2013	2014 [1]
Generation [2]	**Bil. kWh**	**2,808**	**3,802**	**4,055**	**3,950**	**4,125**	**4,100**	**4,048**	**4,066**	**4,093**
Sales [3]	**Bil. kWh**	**2,713**	**3,421**	**3,661**	**3,597**	**3,755**	**3,750**	**3,695**	**3,725**	**3,724**
Residential or domestic	Bil. kWh	924	1,192	1,359	1,364	1,446	1,423	1,375	1,395	1,403
Percent of total	Percent	34.1	34.9	37.1	37.9	38.5	37.9	37.2	37.4	37.7
Commercial [4]	Bil. kWh	751	1,055	1,275	1,307	1,330	1,328	1,327	1,344	1,358
Industrial [5]	Bil. kWh	946	1,064	1,019	917	971	991	986	978	955
Revenue [3]	**Bil. dol.**	**178.2**	**233.2**	**298.0**	**353.3**	**368.9**	**371.0**	**363.7**	**376.9**	**389.1**
Residential or domestic	Bil. dol.	72.4	98.2	128.4	157.0	166.8	166.7	163.3	170.5	175.4
Percent of total	Percent	40.6	42.1	43.1	44.4	45.2	44.9	44.9	45.2	45.1
Commercial [4]	Bil. dol.	55.1	78.4	110.5	132.9	135.6	135.9	133.9	138.7	145.9
Industrial [5]	Bil. dol.	44.9	49.4	58.4	62.5	65.8	67.6	65.8	66.9	67.0
Ultimate customers [3]	**Million**	**110.6**	**127.6**	**138.4**	**143.5**	**144.1**	**144.5**	**145.3**	**146.4**	**147.3**
Residential or domestic	Million	97.1	111.7	120.8	125.2	125.7	126.1	126.8	127.9	128.7
Commercial [4]	Million	12.1	14.3	16.9	17.6	17.7	17.6	17.7	17.8	17.9
Industrial [5]	Million	0.5	0.5	0.7	0.8	0.7	0.7	0.7	0.7	0.7
Avg. kWh used per customer	**1,000**	**24.5**	**26.8**	**26.5**	**25.1**	**26.0**	**25.9**	**25.4**	**25.4**	**25.3**
Residential	1,000	9.5	10.7	11.3	10.9	11.5	11.3	10.8	10.9	10.9
Commercial [4]	1,000	62.2	73.5	75.6	74.4	75.3	75.3	74.9	75.6	75.9
Avg. annual bill per customer	**Dollar**	**1,612**	**1,828**	**2,154**	**2,462**	**2,559**	**2,568**	**2,503**	**2,574**	**2,642**
Residential	Dollar	745	879	1,063	1,254	1,327	1,322	1,287	1,333	1,363
Commercial [4]	Dollar	4,562	5,464	6,551	7,570	7,670	7,706	7,553	7,799	8,159
Avg. revenue per kWh sold	**Cents**	**6.57**	**6.81**	**8.14**	**9.8**	**9.8**	**9.9**	**9.8**	**10.1**	**10.4**
Residential	Cents	7.83	8.24	9.45	11.5	11.5	11.7	11.9	12.2	12.5
Commercial [4]	Cents	7.34	7.43	8.67	10.2	10.2	10.2	10.1	10.3	10.7
Industrial [5]	Cents	4.74	4.64	5.73	6.8	6.8	6.8	6.7	6.8	7.0

[1] Preliminary. [2] "Generation" includes batteries, chemicals, hydrogen, pitch, sulfur, purchased steam, and miscellaneous technologies, which are not separately displayed. [3] Includes other types, not shown separately. Data for 1990 are as of December 31; data for following years are average yearly customers. [4] Small light and power. [5] Large light and power.

Source: Edison Electric Institute, Washington, DC, *Statistical Yearbook of the Electric Power Industry*, annual ©. See also <http://www.eei.org>.

Table 972. Revenue and Expense Statistics for Major U.S. Investor-Owned Electric Utilities: 1995 to 2013

[In millions of nominal dollars (199,967 represents $199,967,000,000). Covers investor-owned electric utilities that during each of the last 3 years met any one or more of the following conditions: 1 million megawatt-hours of total sales, 100 megawatt-hours of annual sales for resale, 500 megawatt-hours of annual power exchange delivered, and 500 megawatt-hours of annual wheeling for others. Missing or erroneous respondent data may result in slight imbalances in some of the expense account subtotals]

Item	1995	2000	2005	2010	2011	2012	2013
Utility operating revenues	**199,967**	**233,915**	**265,652**	**285,512**	**280,520**	**270,912**	**281,901**
Electric utility	183,655	213,634	234,909	260,119	255,573	249,166	257,718
Other utility	16,312	20,281	30,743	25,393	24,946	21,745	24,183
Utility operating expenses	**165,321**	**210,250**	**236,786**	**253,022**	**247,118**	**235,694**	**244,316**
Electric utility	150,599	191,564	207,830	234,173	228,873	220,722	227,483
Operation	91,881	132,607	150,645	166,922	161,460	152,379	156,077
Production	68,983	107,554	120,586	128,831	122,520	111,714	115,046
Cost of fuel	29,122	32,407	36,106	44,138	42,779	38,998	41,127
Purchased power	29,981	62,608	77,902	67,284	61,447	54,570	55,529
Other	9,880	12,561	6,599	17,409	18,294	18,146	18,390
Transmission	1,425	2,713	5,664	6,948	6,876	7,183	7,881
Distribution	2,561	3,092	3,502	4,007	4,044	4,181	4,197
Customer accounts	3,613	4,239	4,229	5,091	5,180	5,086	5,107
Customer service	1,922	1,826	2,291	4,741	5,311	5,640	5,906
Sales	348	405	219	185	185	221	203
Administrative and general	13,028	12,768	14,130	17,120	17,343	18,353	17,738
Maintenance	11,767	12,064	12,033	14,957	15,772	15,489	15,505
Depreciation	19,885	20,636	17,123	20,951	22,555	23,677	24,723
Taxes and other	27,065	24,479	26,805	31,343	29,086	29,177	31,179
Other utility	14,722	18,686	28,956	18,849	18,245	14,972	16,833
Net utility operating income	**34,646**	**23,665**	**28,866**	**32,490**	**33,402**	**35,218**	**37,585**

Source: U.S. Energy Information Administration, *Electric Power Annual 2013*, March 2015, and earlier reports. See also <http://www.eia.gov/electricity/annual/>.

Table 973. Renewable Energy Net Generation of Electricity by Source and State: 2014

[In millions of kilowatt-hours (258,749 represents 258,749,000,000). Data based on results from the Energy Information Agency's annual survey form EIA-923. For more on net generation, see Table 967]

State	Hydro-electric	Other renewable [1] Total	Wind	Bio-mass [2]	Solar	State	Hydro-electric	Other renewable [1] Total	Wind	Bio-mass [2]	Solar
U.S.	**258,749**	**281,060**	**181,791**	**64,319**	**18,321**	MO	700	1,245	1,131	101	13
AL	9,684	3,295	(NA)	3,295	(NA)	MT	11,215	1,966	1,966	–	(NA)
AK	1,530	206	154	53	(NA)	NE	1,204	2,804	2,736	68	(NA)
AZ	6,163	3,813	472	239	3,101	NV	2,409	4,358	300	25	1,028
AR	2,525	1,607	(NA)	1,607	(NA)	NH	1,361	1,995	417	1,578	(NA)
CA	16,409	43,223	13,776	6,962	9,891	NJ	(S)	1,712	12	1,022	677
CO	1,740	7,706	7,351	87	268	NM	142	2,842	2,263	18	543
CT	357	802	(NA)	790	12	NY	25,547	6,483	3,971	2,437	76
DE	(NA)	122	(S)	59	59	NC	5,107	3,383	(NA)	2,460	922
DC	(NA)	(NA)	(NA)	(NA)	(NA)	ND	2,531	6,359	6,349	10	(NA)
FL	221	5,206	(NA)	4,964	241	OH	404	2,016	1,152	803	60
GA	3,301	4,310	(NA)	4,178	132	OK	1,546	12,185	11,862	323	(NA)
HI	82	1,236	585	349	48	OR	34,939	8,875	7,580	1,081	30
ID	9,170	3,416	2,778	589	(NA)	PA	2,725	6,098	3,584	2,434	80
IL	123	10,798	10,077	661	60	RI	(S)	231	(S)	208	16
IN	352	4,033	3,495	385	153	SC	2,806	2,231	(NA)	2,225	(S)
IA	719	16,454	16,295	158	(NA)	SD	5,500	2,916	2,916	–	(NA)
KS	(S)	10,902	10,844	59	(NA)	TN	9,589	1,104	51	1,021	31
KY	3,090	461	(NA)	461	(NA)	TX	566	41,548	39,371	1,873	304
LA	1,090	2,711	(NA)	2,711	(NA)	UT	633	1,260	665	71	(S)
ME	3,287	4,638	1,095	3,543	(NA)	VT	1,127	796	306	461	29
MD	1,623	1,024	324	588	113	VA	1,282	3,735	(NA)	3,735	(NA)
MA	969	1,830	224	1,187	419	WA	78,700	9,029	7,264	1,764	1
MI	1,458	6,692	3,875	2,817	(NA)	WV	1,345	1,455	1,451	4	(NA)
MN	519	10,768	9,060	1,704	(S)	WI	2,078	3,268	1,609	1,658	(NA)
MS	(NA)	1,494	(NA)	1,494	(NA)	WY	838	4,420	4,420	(NA)	(NA)

– Represents or rounds to zero. NA Not available. S Reporting Standards not met. [1] Summation of all renewable sources including wind, solar, biomass, geothermal and other renewable sources other than hydroelectric dams. Includes items not shown separately. [2] Includes landfill gas and municipal solid waste biogenic (paper and paper board, wood, food, leather, textiles, and yard trimmings). Also includes agriculture by-products/crops, sludge waste, and other biomass solids, liquids, gases, black liquor and wood/woodwaste solids and liquids.

Source: Energy Information Administration, "Electricity Data Browser," <http://www.eia.gov/electricity/data/browser/>, accessed August 2015.

Table 974. Major Power Outages by Type of Disturbance and Duration: 2014

[Data shown for power outages lasting longer than 48 hours]

Type of Disturbance	Month	Area Affected	Duration	Number of Customers Affected [1]
Fuel Supply Emergency - (Coal)..................	Feb.	Niagara County, New York	1,009 Hours, 0 Minutes	(NA)
Fuel Supply Emergency - (Coal)..................	July	Wisconsin	630 Hours, 34 Minutes	(NA)
Fuel Supply Emergency - (Coal)..................	Feb.	New York	432 Hours, 0 Minutes	(NA)
Fuel Supply Emergency - (Coal)..................	March	Weston, Wisconsin	312 Hours, 0 Minutes	(NA)
Fuel Supply Emergency - (Natural Gas)..........	Jan.	Illinois	262 Hours, 30 Minutes	(NA)
Fuel Supply Emergency - (Coal)..................	April	Wisconsin	141 Hours, 8 Minutes	(NA)
Severe Weather - Snow/Ice.......................	Feb.	Pennsylvania	115 Hours, 40 Minutes	144,000
Severe Weather - Snow/Ice.......................	Feb.	Maryland, West Virginia	114 Hours, 0 Minutes	101,580
Severe Weather - Thunderstorms................	Oct.	Texas	114 Hours, 0 Minutes	500,000
Severe Weather - Thunderstorms................	July	West Virginia	102 Hours, 0 Minutes	71,000
Severe Weather - Thunderstorms................	July	Maryland, West Virginia	101 Hours, 50 Minutes	96,000
Electrical System Separation (Islanding).........	Sept.	Estacada, Oregon	94 Hours, 50 Minutes	123
Severe Weather - Snow/Ice.......................	Feb.	North Carolina	75 Hours, 10 Minutes	200,000
Severe Weather - Thunderstorms................	July	Pennsylvania	74 Hours, 30 Minutes	260,000
Severe Weather - Wind...........................	Nov.	Michigan	73 Hours, 0 Minutes	186,154
Severe Weather - Thunderstorms................	July	Eastern Pennsylvania	71 Hours, 53 Minutes	69,000
Severe Weather...............................	April	Michigan	71 Hours, 30 Minutes	164,000
Severe Weather - Snow/Ice.......................	Feb.	South Carolina	69 Hours, 37 Minutes	120,124
Severe Weather - Wind...........................	Nov.	Washington	69 Hours, 0 Minutes	68,000
Severe Weather - Thunderstorms................	June	Shelby County, Tennessee	68 Hours, 45 Minutes	38,500
Severe Weather - Snow/Ice.......................	Feb.	Northern/Northeastern Georgia	68 Hours, 42 Minutes	373,835
Severe Weather - Thunderstorms................	July	Southeast Michigan	67 Hours, 30 Minutes	140,000
Severe Weather - Thunderstorms................	July	Pennsylvania	66 Hours, 0 Minutes	298,165
Electrical System Separation (Islanding).........	Sept.	Oregon	65 Hours, 18 Minutes	123
Severe Weather - Thunderstorms................	July	Upstate New York	59 Hours, 39 Minutes	65,000
Severe Weather - High Winds....................	Dec.	Northern California	51 Hours, 42 Minutes	84,500

NA Not available. [1] Number of customers affected are preliminary estimates.

Source: U.S. Energy Information Administration, *Electric Power Monthly*, March 2015. See also <http://www.eia.gov/electricity/monthly/>.

Table 975. Gas Utility Industry—Summary: 1990 to 2013

[54,261 represents 54,261,000. Covers natural, manufactured, mixed, and liquid petroleum gas. Based on a questionnaire mailed to all privately and municipally owned gas utilities in the United States, except those with annual revenues less than $25,000]

Item	Unit	1990	1995	2000	2005	2010	2011	2012	2013
End users [1]..........................	**1,000**	**54,261**	**58,728**	**61,262**	**64,395**	**64,960**	**65,088**	**64,669**	**64,406**
Residential......................	1,000	49,802	53,955	56,494	59,569	60,246	60,405	60,020	59,788
Commercial.......................	1,000	4,246	4,530	4,610	4,678	4,582	4,556	4,518	4,482
Industrial.........................	1,000	166	181	157	145	129	125	122	123
Other............................	1,000	48	61	2	2	3	3	8	12
Sales [2].............................	**Tril. Btu** [3]	**9,842**	**9,221**	**9,232**	**8,848**	**7,980**	**7,886**	**7,086**	**8,023**
Residential......................	Tril. Btu	4,468	4,803	4,741	4,516	4,371	4,287	3,673	4,337
Percent of total.................	Percent	45	52	51	51	55	54	52	54
Commercial.......................	Tril. Btu	2,192	2,281	2,077	2,056	1,842	1,813	1,574	1,820
Industrial.........................	Tril. Btu	3,010	1,919	1,698	1,654	1,209	1,184	1,193	1,263
Other............................	Tril. Btu	171	218	715	622	558	602	647	603
Revenues [2].........................	**Mil. dol.**	**45,153**	**46,436**	**59,243**	**96,909**	**72,886**	**69,296**	**57,020**	**65,887**
Residential......................	Mil. dol.	25,000	28,742	35,828	55,680	47,231	45,046	37,704	42,937
Percent of total.................	Percent	55	62	60	57	65	65	66	65
Commercial.......................	Mil. dol.	10,604	11,573	13,339	22,653	16,578	15,632	12,650	14,684
Industrial.........................	Mil. dol.	8,996	5,571	7,432	13,751	6,437	5,867	4,535	5,711
Other............................	Mil. dol.	553	549	2,645	4,825	2,640	2,751	2,130	2,556
Prices per mil. Btu [3]...............	**Dollars**	**4.59**	**5.05**	**6.42**	**10.95**	**9.13**	**8.79**	**8.05**	**8.21**
Residential......................	Dollars	5.60	6.00	7.56	12.33	10.81	10.51	10.27	9.90
Commercial.......................	Dollars	4.84	5.07	6.42	11.02	9.00	8.62	8.04	8.07
Industrial.........................	Dollars	2.99	2.98	4.38	8.31	5.32	4.95	3.80	4.52
Gas mains mileage................	**1,000**	**1,189**	**1,278**	**1,369**	**1,438**	**1,531**	**1,557**	**1,563**	**1,574**
Field and gathering.................	1,000	32	31	27	23	19	20	18	17
Transmission......................	1,000	292	297	297	297	308	305	299	303
Distribution........................	1,000	865	950	1,046	1,118	1,204	1,232	1,246	1,254
Construction expenditures [4]....	**Mil. dol.**	**7,899**	**10,760**	**8,624**	**10,089**	**11,042**	**17,099**	**15,112**	**17,382**
Transmission......................	Mil. dol.	2,886	3,380	1,590	3,368	3,524	7,416	5,291	6,580
Distribution........................	Mil. dol.	3,714	5,394	5,437	5,129	5,674	6,988	7,357	8,002
Production and storage...........	Mil. dol.	309	367	138	179	151	339	295	326
General...........................	Mil. dol.	770	1,441	1,273	1,070	1,185	1,653	1,552	1,904
Underground storage..............	Mil. dol.	219	177	185	343	509	703	616	570

[1] Annual average. [2] Excludes sales for resale. [3] For definition of Btu, see text, this section. [4] Includes general.

Source: American Gas Association, Washington, DC, *Gas Facts* ©, annual. See also <http://www.aga.org>.

Table 976. Gas Utility Industry—Customers, Sales, and Revenues by State: 2013

[64,406 represents 64,406,000. See headnote, Table 975. For definition of Btu, see text, this section]

State	Customers [1] (1,000) Total	Resi-dential	Sales [2] (tril. Btu) Total	Resi-dential	Revenues [2] (mil. dol.) Total	Resi-dential	State	Customers [1] (1,000) Total	Resi-dential	Sales [2] (tril. Btu) Total	Resi-dential	Revenues [2] (mil. dol.) Total	Resi-dential
U.S....	64,406	59,788	8,031	4,341	65,888	42,937	MO......	1,502	1,358	168	109	1,657	1,158
AL.......	837	766	100	36	993	542	MT.......	296	262	33	21	263	170
AK.......	138	124	45	20	345	170	NE......	503	460	64	37	461	303
AZ.......	1,229	1,172	78	41	851	552	NV......	836	794	95	43	673	393
AR.......	591	523	59	36	536	366	NH......	113	99	13	7	162	99
CA.......	10,895	10,472	664	476	5,973	4,593	NJ......	2,619	2,429	288	209	2,891	2,218
CO.......	1,823	1,672	215	139	1,555	1,058	NM......	619	572	55	37	439	321
CT.......	564	512	84	46	911	594	NY......	3,717	3,465	419	301	4,560	3,581
DE.......	168	156	17	10	205	139	NC......	1,281	1,161	130	72	1,306	824
DC.......	136	130	14	10	162	123	ND......	154	134	36	12	211	90
FL.......	720	679	50	15	566	277	OH......	674	637	83	61	707	542
GA.......	415	378	59	17	473	201	OK......	1,024	932	100	68	850	642
HI.......	29	26	3	1	118	29	OR......	781	700	88	48	812	502
ID.......	400	360	44	28	331	222	PA......	2,479	2,303	264	202	2,882	2,273
IL........	3,791	3,550	520	408	4,049	3,255	RI......	254	232	26	19	350	265
IN........	1,747	1,600	207	141	1,633	1,158	SC......	651	593	92	29	763	361
IA.......	994	895	134	75	994	652	SD......	200	176	27	14	194	115
KS.......	941	859	102	70	931	693	TN......	1,228	1,094	157	73	1,266	672
KY.......	817	735	105	54	860	510	TX......	4,742	4,424	1,379	212	7,035	2,170
LA.......	961	902	218	40	1,192	419	UT......	919	854	112	72	875	603
ME......	34	25	6	2	76	29	VT......	47	41	10	4	102	54
MD......	906	853	84	64	921	722	VA......	1,190	1,103	126	79	1,276	900
MA......	1,604	1,473	229	128	2,558	1,687	WA......	1,206	1,102	141	86	1,441	948
MI........	3,171	2,950	422	315	3,589	2,784	WV......	374	340	45	27	396	265
MN.......	1,596	1,459	279	144	1,976	1,146	WI......	1,864	1,693	269	147	1,953	1,236
MS......	493	443	56	26	428	225	WY......	132	118	19	10	138	83

[1] Averages for the year. [2] Excludes sales for resale.

Source: American Gas Association, Washington, DC, Gas Facts ©, annual. See also <http://www.aga.org>.

Table 977. Privately Owned Gas Utility Industry—Balance Sheet and Income Account: 1990 to 2013

[In millions of dollars (121,686 represents $121,686,000,000). The gas utility industry consists of pipeline and distribution companies. Excludes operations of companies distributing gas in bottles or tanks]

Item	1990	1995	2000	2005	2009	2010	2011	2012	2013
COMPOSITE BALANCE SHEET									
Assets, total........................	121,686	141,965	165,709	196,215	219,467	220,860	234,617	259,806	251,284
Total utility plant........................	112,863	143,636	162,206	207,976	235,426	239,718	248,580	269,676	268,750
Depreciation and amortization........	49,483	62,723	69,366	91,794	91,958	92,012	92,423	93,668	94,583
Utility plant (net)........................	63,380	80,912	92,839	116,183	143,468	147,707	156,157	176,009	174,167
Investment and fund accounts.......	23,872	26,489	10,846	16,331	9,649	7,132	10,606	13,408	13,137
Current and accrued assets..........	23,268	18,564	35,691	32,325	27,703	27,288	25,766	26,646	26,784
Deferred debits [1].....................	9,576	13,923	24,279	29,574	37,037	37,307	40,628	41,856	35,485
Liabilities, total.................	121,686	141,965	165,709	196,215	219,467	220,860	234,617	259,806	251,284
Capitalization, total....................	74,958	90,581	96,079	120,949	135,797	133,414	138,254	153,903	152,236
Capital stock.......................	43,810	54,402	47,051	62,470	74,517	74,157	77,657	87,463	87,781
Long-term debts....................	31,148	35,548	48,267	58,264	61,280	59,223	60,637	66,268	64,402
Current and accrued liabilities.......	29,550	28,272	42,312	34,936	28,711	28,564	29,864	32,133	32,506
Deferred income taxes [2]............	11,360	14,393	17,157	24,937	30,236	34,401	39,034	45,821	44,651
Other liabilities and credits...........	5,818	8,715	10,161	15,393	24,723	24,515	27,465	28,121	21,944
COMPOSITE INCOME ACCOUNT									
Operating revenues, total........	66,027	58,390	72,042	102,018	87,419	82,315	78,750	68,359	75,541
Minus: Operating expenses [3]........	60,137	50,760	64,988	89,385	76,240	71,761	69,747	59,258	64,767
Operation and maintenance.......	51,627	37,966	54,602	77,673	61,865	57,758	55,200	44,413	49,332
Federal, state, and local taxes......	4,957	6,182	6,163	7,513	7,889	7,569	7,988	8,303	8,543
Equals: Operating income...........	5,890	7,630	7,053	12,632	11,179	10,554	10,004	9,100	10,774
Utility operating income..............	6,077	7,848	7,166	12,812	11,428	11,045	10,463	9,972	11,342
Income before interest charges......	8,081	9,484	7,589	13,972	12,232	12,368	10,991	10,241	11,318
Net income.............................	4,410	5,139	4,245	9,777	8,458	8,619	7,308	7,096	7,739
Dividends..............................	3,191	4,037	3,239	2,419	2,162	2,080	2,061	1,799	1,454

[1] Includes capital stock discount and expense and reacquired securities. [2] Includes reserves for deferred income taxes. [3] Includes expenses not shown separately.

Source: American Gas Association, Washington, DC, Gas Facts ©, annual. See also <http://www.aga.org>.

Table 978. Sewage Treatment Facilities and Employees: 2010 and 2013

[2010 data based on the North American Industry Classification System (NAICS), 2007; 2013 data based on NAICS 2012; see text, Section 15]

State	Sewage treatment facilities (NAICS 22132) 2010 Number of establishments	2010 Paid employees	2013 Number of establishments	2013 Paid employees	State	Sewage treatment facilities (NAICS 22132) 2010 Number of establishments	2010 Paid employees	2013 Number of establishments	2013 Paid employees
U.S.........	686	6,627	733	6,228	MO.............	18	83	21	(2)
AL.............	14	206	16	225	MT.............	3	26	5	(2)
AK.............	1	(1)	3	(1)	NE.............	(NA)	(NA)	2	(2)
AZ.............	17	(2)	20	(2)	NV.............	(NA)	(NA)	1	(1)
AR.............	3	(1)	4	(1)	NH.............	10	(2)	9	(2)
CA.............	47	(4)	48	(4)	NJ.............	15	(4)	14	117
CO.............	7	64	10	62	NM.............	2	(1)	7	37
CT.............	12	(3)	12	173	NY.............	28	335	26	284
DE.............	3	(2)	4	58	NC.............	26	(3)	27	(3)
DC.............	(NA)	(NA)	(NA)	(NA)	ND.............	1	(1)	(NA)	(NA)
FL.............	63	464	65	562	OH.............	12	101	15	(3)
GA.............	8	(3)	14	(3)	OK.............	20	(3)	20	213
HI.............	14	(2)	14	(3)	OR.............	6	(2)	7	(2)
ID.............	8	(2)	8	(2)	PA.............	44	334	46	404
IL.............	30	243	33	259	RI.............	5	(2)	5	(2)
IN.............	35	424	38	441	SC.............	6	(2)	7	46
IA.............	4	(2)	6	(2)	SD.............	(NA)	(NA)	(NA)	(NA)
KS.............	2	(1)	2	(2)	TN.............	10	107	8	89
KY.............	10	(3)	10	(2)	TX.............	62	584	66	390
LA.............	29	336	26	343	UT.............	1	(1)	2	(1)
ME.............	2	(1)	1	(1)	VT.............	2	(1)	4	(1)
MD.............	7	42	7	61	VA.............	5	(2)	7	(2)
MA.............	20	(4)	21	(4)	WA.............	4	(2)	6	(2)
MI.............	22	(3)	23	156	WV.............	14	77	11	71
MN.............	6	(1)	9	(2)	WI.............	4	21	4	9
MS.............	21	538	18	214	WY.............	3	(1)	1	(1)

NA Not available. [1] 0 to 19 employees. [2] 20 to 99 employees. [3] 100 to 249 employees. [4] 250 to 499 employees.

Source: U.S. Census Bureau, County Business Patterns, "Geography Area Series, County Business Patterns," <http://factfinder2.census.gov/>, accessed April 2015. See also <http://www.census.gov/econ/cbp/>.

Table 979. Public Drinking Water Systems by Size of Community Served and Source of Water: 2014

[As of October. Covers systems that provide water for human consumption through pipes and other constructed conveyances to at least 15 service connections or serve an average of at least 25 persons for at least 180 days per year. Based on reported data in the Safe Drinking Water Information System maintained by the Environmental Protection Agency]

Type of system	Total [1]	Size of community served 500 or fewer persons	501 to 3,300 persons	3,301 to 10,000 persons	10,001 to 100,000 persons	100,001 persons or more	Water source Ground water	Surface water
Total systems..............................	153,138	124,720	18,891	5,192	3,902	433	137,978	14,980
COMMUNITY WATER SYSTEMS [2]								
Number of systems..........................	50,808	27,990	13,561	4,954	3,872	431	39,035	11,743
Percent of systems.........................	100	55	27	10	8	1	77	23
Population served (1,000)....................	303,355	4,696	19,460	28,857	110,134	140,208	87,067	216,284
Percent of population.......................	100	2	6	10	36	46	29	71
NONTRANSIENT NONCOMMUNITY WATER SYSTEM [3]								
Number of systems..........................	18,225	15,525	2,537	146	16	1	17,333	857
Percent of systems.........................	100	85	14	1	–	–	95	5
Population served (1,000)....................	6,340	2,155	2,703	821	458	203	5,261	1,075
Percent of population.......................	100	34	43	13	7	3	83	17
TRANSIENT NONCOMMUNITY WATER SYSTEM [4]								
Number of systems..........................	84,105	81,205	2,793	92	14	1	81,610	2,380
Percent of systems.........................	100	97	3	–	–	–	97	3
Population served (1,000)....................	12,756	7,280	2,647	496	333	2,000	10,200	2,542
Percent of population.......................	100	57	21	4	3	16	80	20

– Represents zero. [1] Includes a small number of systems for which the water source (ground vs. surface) is unknown. [2] A public water system that supplies water to the same population year-round. [3] A public water system that regularly supplies water to at least 25 of the same people at least 6 months per year, but not year-round. Some examples are schools, factories, and office buildings which have their own water systems. [4] A public water system that provides water in a place such as a gas station or campground where people do not remain for long periods of time and is open at least 60 day per year.

Source: U.S. Environmental Protection Agency, "SDWISFED Drinking Water Data," <http://water.epa.gov/scitech/datait/databases/drink/>, accessed July 2015.

Table 980. Public Drinking Water Systems—Number and Population Served by State: 2013

[316,983 represents 316,983,000. As of October. Covers systems supplying drinking water to at least 25 people or having 15 service connections for 180 or more days per year. Based on reported data in the Safe Drinking Water Information System maintained by the Environmental Protection Agency]

State	Number of systems	Population served (1,000)				State	Number of systems	Population served (1,000)			
		Total	Community[1]	Non-transient, non-community[2]	Transient, non-community[3]			Total	Community[1]	Non-transient, non-community[2]	Transient, non-community[3]
U.S.[4]	149,155	316,983	298,613	5,915	12,455	MO	2,716	5,552	5,362	78	111
AL	598	5,578	5,559	13	6	MT	2,152	1,023	711	127	184
AK	1,512	828	666	60	103	NE	1,313	1,674	1,584	55	35
AZ	1,534	6,495	6,256	122	117	NV	571	2,792	2,672	96	24
AR	1,071	2,751	2,719	12	20	NH	2,433	1,175	859	92	224
CA	7,717	38,782	37,548	387	847	NJ	3,776	9,791	9,020	351	420
CO	2,019	7,503	7,201	67	235	NM	1,141	1,957	1,834	49	75
CT	2,525	2,843	2,672	112	59	NY	8,671	21,443	18,333	297	2,814
DE	494	1,028	955	22	51	NC	5,938	8,251	7,826	115	310
DC	6	650	650	(Z)	–	ND	626	665	630	10	25
FL	5,404	19,666	19,186	233	246	OH	4,752	10,778	10,181	214	383
GA	2,421	8,706	8,563	66	77	OK	1,683	3,619	3,557	25	37
HI	133	1,477	1,463	12	2	OR	2,549	3,600	3,342	71	187
ID	1,942	1,393	1,244	51	98	PA	8,934	11,860	10,662	470	729
IL	5,556	12,420	11,930	142	349	RI	485	1,106	1,023	28	54
IN	4,150	5,459	4,890	195	374	SC	1,446	4,050	3,969	39	42
IA	1,873	2,885	2,761	48	75	SD	644	779	746	9	25
KS	1,012	2,706	2,681	21	4	TN	832	6,603	6,523	27	53
KY	453	4,555	4,541	10	4	TX	6,944	26,441	25,658	515	268
LA	1,378	4,907	4,798	59	50	UT	1,010	2,927	2,820	28	80
ME	1,890	913	664	65	184	VT	1,332	589	449	45	95
MD	3,399	5,710	5,256	156	299	VA	2,713	7,127	6,649	300	177
MA	1,744	9,538	9,319	74	145	WA	4,106	7,480	6,953	147	379
MI	11,035	8,897	7,594	304	999	WV	998	1,578	1,515	32	30
MN	6,967	4,889	4,287	69	532	WI	11,430	4,978	4,057	205	717
MS	1,234	3,205	3,130	64	11	WY	803	555	457	24	74

– Represents zero. Z Less than 500. [1] A public water system that supplies water to the same population year-round. [2] A public water system that regularly supplies water to at least 25 of the same people at least 6 months per year, but not year-round. Some examples are schools, factories, and office buildings which have their own water systems. [3] A public water system that provides water in a place such as a gas station or campground where people do not remain for long periods of time and is open at least 60 days per year. [4] Includes outlying areas, not shown separately.

Source: U.S. Environmental Protection Agency, "SDWISFED Drinking Water Data," <http://water.epa.gov/scitech/datait/databases/drink/>, accessed July 2015.

Construction and Housing

This section presents data on the construction industry and on various indicators of its activity and costs; on housing units and their characteristics and occupants; and on the characteristics and vacancy rates for commercial buildings.

The principal source of these data is the U.S. Census Bureau, which issues a variety of current publications, as well as data from the decennial census. Current construction statistics compiled by the Census Bureau appear in its *New Residential Construction* and *New Residential Sales* press releases and Web sites at <www.census.gov/construction/nrc/> and <www.census.gov/construction/nrs/>. *Construction Spending* presents data on all types of construction. Reports of the censuses of construction industries (see below) are also issued on various topics.

Other Census Bureau publications include the quarterly *Housing Vacancies and Homeownership*, the quarterly *Survey of Market Absorption*, the biennial *American Housing Survey* (formerly *Annual Housing Survey*), and other reports of the censuses of housing and of construction industries.

Other sources include Dodge Data & Analytics, New York, NY, which presents national and state data on construction contracts; the National Association of Home Builders with data on housing starts; the NATIONAL ASSOCIATION OF REALTORS®, which presents data on existing home sales; the Bureau of Economic Analysis, which presents data on residential fixed assets; the U.S. Energy Information Administration, which provides data on commercial buildings through its periodic sample surveys; and the Federal Financial Institutions Examination Council, which provide data on home loans and home improvement loans.

Censuses and surveys—Censuses of the construction industry were first conducted by the Census Bureau for 1929, 1935, and 1939; beginning in 1967, a census has been taken every 5 years (through 2012, for years ending in "2" and "7"). Data from the 2012 Economic Census are being released on a continuing basis through 2016. The construction sector of the Economic Census covers all employer establishments primarily engaged in (1) building construction by general contractors or operative builders; (2) heavy (nonbuilding) construction by general contractors; and (3) construction by special trade contractors. This sector includes construction management and land subdividers and developers. The 2007 census was conducted in accordance with the 2007 North American Industrial Classification System (NAICS). See text, Section 15, Business Enterprise.

The *American Housing Survey* (*Current Housing Reports* Series H-150 and H-170), which began in 1973, provided an annual and ongoing series of data on selected housing and demographic characteristics until 1983. In 1984, the name of the survey was changed from the *Annual Housing Survey*. Currently, national data are collected every other year, and data for selected metropolitan areas are collected on a rotating basis. Initially, the metropolitan area data were not combined with the national data and used for area-specific estimates. Beginning with the 2011 survey, a supplemental sample of housing units was selected for 29 metropolitan units and combined with the national sample in order to produce metropolitan estimates using the national survey. All samples represent a cross section of the housing stock in their respective areas. Estimates are subject to both sampling and nonsampling errors; caution should therefore be used in making comparisons between years.

Data on residential mortgages were collected continuously from 1890 to 1970, except 1930, as part of the decennial census by the Census Bureau. Since 1973, mortgage status data have been presented in the *American Housing Survey*. Data on mortgage activity are covered in Section 25, Banking and Finance.

Housing units—In general, a housing unit is a house, an apartment, a group of rooms or a single room occupied or intended for occupancy as separate living quarters; that is, the occupants live separately from any other individual in the building, and there is direct access from the outside or through a common hall. Transient accommodations, barracks for workers, and institutional-type quarters are not counted as housing units.

Statistical reliability—For a discussion of statistical collection and estimation, sampling procedures, and measures of statistical reliability applicable to Census Bureau data, see Appendix III.

Table 981. Construction—Establishments, Employees, and Payroll by Kind of Business (NAICS Basis): 2012 and 2013

[5,261 represents 5,261,000. Covers establishments with payroll. Excludes most government employees, railroad employees, and self-employed persons. For statement on methodology, see Appendix III]

Kind of business	NAICS code [1]	Establishments		Paid employees [2] (1,000)		Annual payroll (mil. dol.)	
		2012	2013	2012	2013	2012	2013
Construction.................................	**23**	**652,902**	**658,483**	**5,261**	**5,470**	**275,202**	**293,999**
Construction of buildings............................	236	192,052	196,559	1,040	1,120	54,626	61,762
Residential building construction....................	2361	151,034	155,497	519	558	22,342	25,593
New single-family housing construction (except for-sale builders).........................	236115	45,798	48,145	144	159	5,951	6,908
New multifamily housing construction (except for-sale builders).........................	236116	2,615	2,707	25	27	1,669	1,880
New housing for-sale builders....................	236117	13,576	13,686	81	89	4,906	6,002
Residential remodelers............................	236118	89,045	90,959	269	284	9,816	10,803
Nonresidential building construction..............	2362	41,018	41,062	521	562	32,284	36,170
Industrial building construction...................	23621	3,167	3,180	73	78	4,323	4,789
Commercial and institutional building construction....................................	23622	37,851	37,882	448	485	27,960	31,380
Heavy and civil engineering construction...........	237	39,133	39,065	850	877	55,934	57,607
Utility system construction........................	2371	18,686	19,155	466	518	29,842	33,112
Water and sewer line and related structures. ..	23711	11,453	11,159	153	149	8,769	8,613
Oil and gas pipeline and related structures.....	23712	2,046	2,093	143	163	10,480	11,824
Power and communication line and related structures................................	23713	5,187	5,903	170	207	10,592	12,675
Land subdivision.................................	2372	6,182	5,551	53	23	3,923	1,398
Highway, street, and bridge construction.........	2373	10,043	10,121	251	250	16,999	17,512
Other heavy and civil engineering construction..	2379	4,222	4,238	79	85	5,170	5,586
Specialty trade contractors.........................	238	421,717	422,859	3,371	3,473	164,642	174,630
Foundation, structure, and building exterior contractors...................................	2381	85,801	85,312	658	676	28,408	30,650
Poured concrete foundation and structures contractors...................................	23811	19,026	18,745	167	174	7,539	8,221
Structural steel and precast concrete contractors...................................	23812	3,327	3,282	60	60	3,006	3,224
Framing contractors..............................	23813	10,078	10,135	53	62	1,856	2,209
Masonry contractors.............................	23814	18,324	17,928	120	119	4,832	5,034
Glass and glazing contractors....................	23815	4,963	5,409	41	46	1,934	2,255
Roofing contractors..............................	23816	17,491	17,355	146	145	6,116	6,421
Siding contractors...............................	23817	7,437	7,277	31	28	1,128	1,099
Other foundation, structure, and building exterior contractors.............................	23819	5,155	5,181	40	42	1,998	2,187
Building equipment contractors...................	2382	170,002	170,887	1,630	1,680	88,043	92,473
Electrical contractors............................	23821	70,215	70,471	683	710	37,262	39,428
Plumbing, heating, and air-conditioning contractors...................................	23822	93,000	93,508	822	841	43,018	44,908
Other building equipment contractors............	23829	6,787	6,908	125	130	7,764	8,137
Building finishing contractors......................	2383	102,700	103,005	609	634	24,578	26,588
Drywall and insulation contractors...............	23831	17,138	17,053	184	193	7,934	8,680
Painting and wall covering contractors..........	23832	31,376	31,296	163	166	6,203	6,528
Flooring contractors..............................	23833	13,567	13,708	59	62	2,293	2,562
Tile and terrazzo contractors.....................	23834	8,543	8,660	42	44	1,591	1,786
Finish carpentry contractors.....................	23835	25,845	25,851	106	111	4,231	4,521
Other building finishing contractors..............	23839	6,231	6,437	55	58	2,327	2,512
Other specialty trade contractors..................	2389	63,214	63,655	475	482	23,612	24,920
Site preparation contractors......................	23891	34,142	33,867	281	286	14,490	15,202
All other specialty trade contractors..............	23899	29,072	29,788	194	197	9,123	9,718

[1] Data based on North American Industry Classification System (NAICS) 2012. See text, Section 15. [2] Employees on the payroll for the pay period including March 12.

Source: U.S. Census Bureau, County Business Patterns, "Geography Area Series, County Business Patterns," <http://factfinder2.census.gov/>, accessed April 2015. See also <http://www.census.gov/econ/cbp/>.

Table 982. Construction Materials—Producer Price Indexes: 2005 to 2014

[1982 = 100, except as noted. This index, more formally known as the special commodity grouping index for construction materials, covers materials incorporated as integral part of a building or normally installed during construction and not readily removable. Excludes consumer durables such as kitchen ranges, refrigerators, etc. For discussion of producer price indexes, see text, Section 14]

Commodity	2005	2008	2009	2010	2011	2012	2013	2014
Construction materials	**169.6**	**196.4**	**189.2**	**194.5**	**201.1**	**205.8**	**209.3**	**214.4**
Architectural coatings	203.3	249.0	269.7	264.1	276.3	309.5	308.4	309.4
Plastic construction products	158.8	185.6	186.2	190.9	199.0	207.1	208.1	211.1
Softwood cut stock and dimension	205.1	201.4	200.2	206.0	202.5	194.1	203.9	207.4
Softwood lumber, not edge worked [1]	115.0	81.3	72.8	85.8	85.6	92.8	110.4	113.4
Softwood lumber, made from purchased lumber [1]	111.2	121.5	109.1	111.5	112.2	115.3	121.2	126.4
Hardwood cut stock and dimension	198.4	193.6	186.0	186.2	189.2	189.1	221.7	275.8
Hardwood flooring [2]	168.0	154.2	153.2	161.2	163.4	163.2	184.8	199.6
Millwork	197.2	204.8	205.4	207.0	210.1	216.5	225.8	232.3
Softwood veneer and plywood	223.5	193.1	171.9	197.1	185.8	218.6	236.8	245.3
Hardwood veneer and plywood [3]	(NA)	103.8	103.1	103.6	103.9	106.0	108.0	108.4
Prefabricated wood buildings and components [4]	206.1	221.8	219.5	215.6	216.2	224.0	231.6	236.4
Building paper and building board mill products	184.9	163.9	156.5	168.4	163.6	187.1	207.9	188.9
Pressure and soil pipe and fittings, cast iron	240.8	333.4	335.0	348.4	373.5	394.0	389.9	390.6
Hot rolled steel sheet and strip, incl. tin mill products [5]	125.4	188.3	121.2	150.7	161.6	149.9	136.1	140.3
Hot rolled steel bars, plates, and structural shapes [5]	159.8	227.6	171.0	192.9	223.0	213.3	199.8	206.8
Aluminum extruded and drawn pipe and tube [6]	102.2	106.0	88.4	98.1	110.9	103.2	96.0	101.1
Builders' hardware [7]	179.2	215.1	217.1	219.4	230.6	234.2	235.0	242.2
Plumbing fixtures and fittings	197.6	226.7	228.9	231.4	237.0	241.5	245.7	252.6
Heating equipment	179.9	208.8	219.1	221.5	227.6	235.3	239.8	243.6
Metal doors, sash, and trim	184.9	205.6	209.2	208.1	219.0	225.9	226.3	228.1
Sheet metal products	169.4	192.5	186.8	191.0	201.6	200.4	196.3	198.6
Fabricated structural metal bar joists and concrete reinforcing bars	163.0	195.5	184.1	176.1	179.9	183.0	183.3	187.9
Fabricated metal pipe, tube, and fittings [8]	(NA)	(NA)	(NA)	(NA)	(NA)	100.6	101.0	101.9
Residential electric lighting fixtures, except portable [9]	106.9	117.0	121.3	121.1	124.0	125.6	127.2	128.1
Elevators, escalators, and other lifts	123.5	134.7	134.9	133.8	135.6	138.0	140.1	143.1
Air purification equipment/industrial and commercial fans and blowers	170.9	190.0	191.7	192.2	199.8	204.0	206.0	211.7
Plumbing and heating valves (low pressure) [10]	182.2	246.1	252.3	249.5	262.1	272.4	277.6	285.8
Electric switches [11]	101.9	120.7	122.1	124.4	131.6	145.0	147.8	152.4
Wire connectors for electrical circuitry [11]	106.9	123.7	127.9	132.1	133.7	135.7	139.1	141.8
Current-carrying wiring devices not elsewhere classified [12]	(NA)	103.8	104.4	105.2	108.4	110.0	111.1	112.1
Noncurrent-carrying electrical conduit and fittings [6, 13]	106.6	123.4	114.0	119.2	128.6	133.3	134.6	135.4
Other noncurrent-carrying wiring devices [6, 14]	102.3	123.2	126.2	124.6	130.3	131.9	133.3	135.1
Carpets and rugs	145.3	159.0	166.1	167.5	173.8	177.4	178.4	182.8
Hard surface floor coverings	169.0	192.5	198.0	203.2	216.5	227.9	(NA)	(NA)
Float, sheet, and plate glass	96.0	100.2	95.4	88.2	86.7	83.9	85.8	88.8
Construction sand, gravel, and crushed stone	195.8	247.7	259.1	262.2	266.5	272.8	278.8	289.3
Cement, hydraulic	176.4	209.7	206.8	193.5	187.8	190.6	199.3	208.1
Concrete products	177.2	210.6	214.0	210.6	210.8	215.0	221.0	230.3
Clay construction products excluding refractories	165.4	180.1	179.5	179.4	176.1	173.6	175.8	178.1
Prepared asphalt and tar roofing and siding products	125.0	176.7	218.1	218.9	226.0	221.2	229.7	224.5
Roofing asphalts, pitches, coatings, and cement	155.0	234.0	217.8	227.5	258.7	277.8	265.7	265.8
Gypsum products	229.6	213.2	213.8	206.6	201.9	230.3	268.7	290.6
Insulation materials	142.2	141.7	144.1	146.6	155.9	164.7	173.4	182.9
Paving mixtures and blocks	156.9	272.4	269.0	279.4	296.2	316.5	317.9	323.6
Cut stone and stone products [4]	145.1	149.3	147.9	147.8	147.8	147.9	148.8	152.3

NA Not available. [1] December 2003 = 100. [2] June 1984 = 100. [3] December 2005 = 100. [4] June 1984 = 100. [5] June 1982 = 100. [6] December 2004 = 100. [7] Includes lock units, key blanks, door and window hardware, cabinet hardware, etc. [8] December 2011 = 100. [9] June 1998 = 100. [10] December 1982 = 100. [11] December 1999 = 100. [12] June 2006 = 100. [13] Includes plastic conduit and fittings. [14] Includes boxes, covers, bar hangers, etc.

Source: U.S. Bureau of Labor Statistics, "Producer Price Indexes," <http://www.bls.gov/ppi/data.htm>, accessed May 2015.

Table 983. Value of New Construction Put in Place: 1980 to 2014

[In millions of dollars (273,936 represents $273,936,000,000). Represents value of construction put in place during year; differs from building permit and construction contract data in timing and coverage. Includes installed cost of normal building service equipment and selected types of industrial production equipment (largely site fabricated). Excludes cost of shipbuilding, land, and most types of machinery and equipment. For methodology, see Appendix III]

| Year | Total | Private | | | Public | | |
		Total	Residential buildings	Non-residential	Total	Federal	State and local
1980	273,936	210,290	100,381	109,909	63,646	9,642	54,004
1990	476,778	369,300	191,103	178,197	107,478	12,099	95,379
1996	599,693	453,018	257,495	195,523	146,675	15,325	131,350
1997	631,853	478,416	264,696	213,720	153,437	14,087	139,350
1998	688,515	533,737	296,343	237,394	154,778	14,318	140,460
1999	744,551	575,469	326,302	249,167	169,082	14,025	155,057
2000	802,756	621,431	346,138	275,293	181,325	14,168	167,157
2001	840,249	638,337	364,414	273,922	201,912	15,082	186,830
2002	847,874	634,435	396,696	237,739	213,438	16,578	196,860
2003	891,497	675,370	446,035	229,335	216,127	17,913	198,214
2004	991,356	771,173	532,900	238,273	220,183	18,342	201,841
2005	1,104,136	869,976	611,899	258,077	234,160	17,300	216,860
2006	1,167,222	911,837	613,731	298,105	255,385	17,555	237,831
2007	1,152,351	863,278	493,246	370,032	289,073	20,580	268,494
2008	1,068,436	759,698	350,257	409,440	308,738	23,731	285,007
2009	904,929	590,034	245,912	344,121	314,895	28,439	286,456
2010	806,040	502,074	238,819	263,255	303,966	31,133	272,833
2011	788,343	501,936	244,133	257,803	286,407	31,654	254,753
2012	861,245	581,935	280,574	301,360	279,311	26,933	252,378
2013	918,349	647,667	335,379	312,288	270,682	23,727	246,955
2014	962,057	686,359	338,693	347,666	275,698	22,735	252,963

Source: U.S. Census Bureau, "Construction Spending," <http://www.census.gov/construction/c30/c30index.html>, accessed July 2015.

Table 984. New Privately Owned Housing Units Authorized by State: 2013 and 2014

[990.8 represents 990,800. Based on about 20,000 places in United States having building permit systems in 2013 and 2014]

| State | Housing units (1,000) | | | Valuation (mil. dol.) | | | State | Housing units (1,000) | | | Valuation (mil. dol.) | | |
	2013	2014 Total	2014 1-unit [1]	2013	2014 Total	2014 1-unit [1]		2013	2014 Total	2014 1-unit [1]	2013	2014 Total	2014 1-unit [1]
U.S.	990.8	1,046.4	634.6	177,656	193,243	148,534	MO	13.7	16.0	9.1	2,234	2,683	2,034
AL	11.8	13.4	9.5	2,072	2,205	1,855	MT	4.9	3.9	2.0	793	647	467
AK	1.1	1.5	1.1	258	354	299	NE	7.5	7.6	4.7	1,150	1,206	944
AZ	25.2	27.0	16.8	5,444	5,666	4,441	NV	11.2	13.0	8.9	1,753	1,755	1,466
AR	7.5	7.7	5.3	1,206	1,250	1,065	NH	2.8	3.4	2.2	566	653	512
CA	80.7	83.6	39.2	18,263	18,742	11,739	NJ	24.2	28.2	11.0	3,211	4,070	2,339
CO	27.5	28.7	17.1	5,950	6,480	5,178	NM	5.2	4.8	4.1	832	882	821
CT	5.4	5.3	2.8	1,171	1,148	928	NY	32.6	36.3	10.4	4,752	5,582	3,044
DE	4.8	5.2	4.1	593	615	525	NC	51.3	49.9	35.1	8,261	8,620	7,373
DC	3.3	4.2	0.3	280	374	61	ND	10.5	12.2	4.5	1,357	1,636	891
FL	86.8	84.1	56.3	18,161	19,549	15,743	OH	19.9	19.9	12.5	3,346	3,754	3,065
GA	36.2	39.4	27.5	5,655	6,541	5,399	OK	13.6	14.2	10.2	2,321	2,457	2,124
HI	3.9	3.1	2.2	1,019	1,012	854	OR	14.8	16.6	8.6	2,688	3,243	2,219
ID	8.1	8.8	6.3	1,546	1,655	1,422	PA	21.7	25.1	16.4	3,750	4,714	3,491
IL	15.5	20.6	10.6	3,087	4,212	2,731	RI	0.9	1.0	0.8	180	195	182
IN	18.0	17.8	12.1	3,066	3,222	2,749	SC	24.7	27.5	21.5	4,882	5,424	4,954
IA	10.9	10.3	7.0	1,992	1,908	1,543	SD	5.5	4.7	2.8	734	689	520
KS	8.3	7.5	4.9	1,469	1,417	1,125	TN	23.8	27.6	17.9	3,871	4,550	3,742
KY	9.0	9.5	6.1	1,234	1,305	1,077	TX	147.5	167.0	99.7	22,356	26,296	20,816
LA	14.0	15.3	12.8	2,570	2,889	2,630	UT	15.8	17.5	11.3	3,269	3,361	2,728
ME	3.4	3.2	2.7	619	613	565	VT	1.5	1.5	1.0	263	281	229
MD	17.9	16.3	10.5	2,811	2,889	2,142	VA	31.9	28.7	18.8	4,862	4,656	3,824
MA	14.6	14.5	7.3	3,768	3,301	2,070	WA	33.0	33.9	17.9	6,684	7,017	5,000
MI	15.8	15.9	12.4	3,278	3,315	2,955	WV	2.6	2.7	1.9	366	395	341
MN	17.3	17.0	10.7	3,691	3,680	2,854	WI	13.9	14.6	8.6	2,478	2,599	2,037
MS	6.8	6.9	5.5	956	1,033	945	WY	2.3	1.9	1.6	536	503	478

[1] The 1-unit structure category is a single-family home. It includes fully detached, semi-detached (semi-attached, side-by-side), row houses, and townhouses.

Source: U.S. Census Bureau, Construction Reports, "Building Permits Survey," <http://www.census.gov/construction/bps/>, accessed August 2015.

Table 985. Value of Private Construction Put in Place: 2000 to 2014

[In millions of dollars (621,431 represents $621,431,000,000). Represents value of construction put in place during year; differs from building permit and construction contract data in timing and coverage. See Appendix III]

Type of construction	2000	2005	2008	2009	2010	2011	2012	2013	2014
Total construction [1]	**621,431**	**869,976**	**759,698**	**590,034**	**502,074**	**501,936**	**581,935**	**647,667**	**686,359**
Residential	346,138	611,899	350,257	245,912	238,819	244,133	280,574	335,379	338,693
New single family	236,788	433,510	185,776	105,336	112,569	108,178	132,015	170,768	193,600
New multifamily	28,259	47,297	44,338	28,538	14,686	15,037	22,510	31,500	41,806
Improvements [2]	81,091	131,092	120,144	112,038	111,564	120,918	126,050	133,111	103,287
Nonresidential	275,293	258,077	409,440	344,121	263,255	257,803	301,360	312,288	347,666
Lodging	16,304	12,666	35,364	25,388	11,201	8,395	10,197	13,028	15,698
Office [1]	52,407	37,276	55,502	37,282	24,368	23,738	27,448	30,133	38,403
General	49,637	32,962	50,137	33,346	22,203	21,231	25,111	28,419	36,500
Financial	2,689	4,285	5,054	3,720	2,122	2,284	1,945	1,597	1,863
Commercial	64,055	66,584	82,654	51,128	37,154	39,153	44,312	50,947	60,761
Automotive [1]	5,967	5,614	5,640	4,535	3,546	4,270	4,834	4,639	4,945
Sales	1,629	2,834	2,430	1,564	1,355	1,816	2,079	1,956	2,075
Service/parts	3,009	1,805	1,843	2,056	1,679	1,977	2,221	2,313	2,122
Parking	1,330	975	1,367	916	511	478	534	370	748
Food/beverage	8,786	7,795	8,029	4,868	4,605	5,268	5,845	6,594	7,426
Food	4,792	3,128	3,124	1,978	2,027	2,840	2,430	2,937	3,651
Dining/drinking	2,935	4,078	3,976	2,237	1,911	1,650	2,436	2,141	2,133
Fast food	1,058	590	930	653	667	779	979	1,516	1,642
Multiretail [1]	14,911	22,750	31,963	18,390	12,486	13,361	14,904	16,686	20,144
General merchandise	5,100	6,740	4,373	3,976	3,794	3,368	3,773	2,942	2,947
Shopping center	6,803	12,462	22,780	11,447	6,725	6,748	7,934	9,806	13,339
Shopping mall	2,523	2,631	4,045	2,171	1,332	2,356	2,288	2,938	2,884
Other commercial [1]	13,537	11,744	12,087	6,300	4,220	3,720	3,934	4,786	4,619
Drug store	1,682	1,315	1,967	1,882	1,077	721	765	893	981
Building supply store	2,592	2,416	2,539	1,118	772	611	493	506	527
Other stores	8,136	7,075	6,552	2,528	1,741	1,743	2,069	2,468	2,362
Warehouse [1]	14,822	12,827	16,707	9,730	5,661	6,543	7,047	8,766	13,793
General commercial	13,511	11,468	15,482	8,781	5,229	6,219	6,575	8,107	13,060
Ministorage	1,263	1,311	1,125	873	401	241	365	472	584
Farm	5,988	5,854	8,227	7,305	6,637	5,991	7,748	9,476	9,835
Health care	19,455	28,495	38,437	35,309	29,552	28,906	31,429	29,696	28,556
Hospital	10,183	18,250	25,571	24,723	21,528	20,483	21,223	19,199	17,700
Medical building	5,066	8,031	9,242	7,531	5,276	5,429	6,415	7,015	6,936
Special care	4,206	2,213	3,625	3,055	2,748	2,995	3,791	3,482	3,921
Educational [1]	11,683	12,788	18,624	16,851	13,418	14,081	16,625	16,919	16,699
Preschool	770	516	746	716	492	349	396	420	482
Primary/secondary	2,948	2,718	3,919	3,362	2,585	2,973	2,795	2,997	3,713
Higher education [1]	6,333	6,946	11,587	10,812	8,322	8,477	10,809	10,868	10,432
Instructional	3,058	3,556	5,463	6,211	4,993	4,658	5,786	4,928	4,893
Dormitory	1,356	1,537	3,791	2,496	1,654	2,165	2,902	3,924	3,589
Sports/recreation	645	821	841	832	790	660	709	981	962
Other educational [1]	1,318	2,294	1,965	1,643	1,687	1,869	2,206	2,226	1,737
Gallery/museum	920	1,745	1,708	1,395	1,522	1,468	1,407	1,486	1,293
Religious	8,030	7,715	7,197	6,177	5,237	4,205	3,819	3,565	3,242
House of worship	5,656	5,992	5,884	5,001	4,214	3,256	3,143	3,055	2,768
Other religious	2,347	1,723	1,313	1,176	1,023	950	675	510	474
Auxiliary building	1,280	1,251	1,122	1,031	795	651	521	419	348
Public safety	423	408	623	471	241	205	103	125	219
Amusement and recreation [1]	8,768	7,507	10,508	8,402	6,483	6,744	6,217	6,916	7,481
Theme/amusement park	747	200	324	280	353	472	512	670	820
Sports	1,068	807	2,280	2,023	1,596	1,096	1,043	1,336	1,853
Fitness	1,152	1,425	2,051	1,763	1,150	1,067	1,251	1,310	1,137
Performance/meeting center	732	1,072	1,102	796	565	510	517	673	569
Social center	2,368	1,626	1,552	1,134	914	662	614	789	790
Movie theater/studio	1,461	1,248	601	338	426	510	362	618	731
Transportation [1]	6,879	7,124	9,934	9,056	9,894	9,537	10,883	11,029	11,823
Air	1,804	748	776	512	259	535	1,044	921	658
Land	4,907	6,214	9,020	8,484	9,503	8,944	9,810	9,988	10,785
Railroad	4,263	5,816	8,378	8,042	8,973	8,546	9,279	9,272	10,025
Communication	18,799	18,846	26,343	19,712	17,689	17,536	15,952	17,619	16,919
Power	29,344	29,210	69,242	76,064	66,117	64,262	86,402	81,278	89,389
Electricity	23,374	22,678	52,799	60,394	48,972	50,291	68,967	54,411	62,236
Gas	4,891	5,239	10,560	10,849	8,297	10,357	10,317	10,897	11,506
Oil	1,003	1,293	5,883	4,821	8,848	3,614	7,118	15,970	15,647
Sewage and waste disposal	508	240	665	468	439	520	597	356	239
Water supply	714	326	466	319	717	635	373	591	559
Manufacturing	37,583	28,413	53,625	57,355	40,607	39,768	46,774	49,863	57,239
Food/beverage/tobacco	3,985	4,446	4,587	3,342	4,000	4,792	4,380	4,934	6,387
Textile/apparel/leather/furniture	561	487	333	274	591	301	171	377	804
Wood	483	933	357	397	438	369	335	732	636
Paper/printing/publishing	1,327	1,181	1,081	871	634	684	1,190	1,016	681
Petroleum/coal	1,255	734	14,993	23,892	11,612	5,453	4,777	4,036	5,606
Chemical	3,798	6,263	12,768	10,310	7,580	7,345	10,848	15,483	23,200
Plastic/rubber	1,645	834	1,052	583	728	947	1,686	1,537	2,305
Nonmetallic mineral	1,898	1,105	2,882	1,815	1,150	896	857	916	872
Primary metal	1,976	793	3,379	4,772	4,738	3,130	4,691	4,487	3,522
Fabricated metal	2,148	664	1,498	1,507	1,104	1,593	1,726	1,484	894
Machinery	864	872	933	1,075	1,030	1,373	1,631	1,442	1,136
Computer/electronic/electrical	6,392	4,039	2,166	3,711	4,614	8,815	9,592	7,312	5,014
Transportation equipment	6,318	3,518	4,612	3,590	1,962	3,260	3,869	5,132	5,074

[1] Includes other types of construction, not shown separately. [2] Private residential improvement does not include expenditures on rental, vacant, or seasonal properties.

Source: U.S. Census Bureau, "Construction Spending," <http://www.census.gov/construction/c30/c30index.html>, accessed July 2015.

Table 986. Value of State and Local Government Construction Put in Place: 2000 to 2014

[In millions of dollars (167,157 represents $167,157,000,000)]

Type of construction	2000	2005	2008	2009	2010	2011	2012	2013	2014
Total construction [1]	167,157	216,860	285,007	286,456	272,833	254,753	252,378	246,955	252,963
Residential	2,962	4,047	4,894	5,772	7,576	5,962	4,672	4,537	4,136
Multifamily	2,945	3,740	4,072	4,849	6,536	5,182	3,935	3,574	3,445
Nonresidential	164,196	212,813	280,113	280,684	265,256	248,791	247,705	242,418	248,827
Office	4,494	5,211	8,515	9,170	8,317	7,440	6,055	5,220	5,379
Commercial [1]	1,820	1,882	1,965	2,003	1,456	1,682	1,412	1,119	870
Automotive	1,233	1,490	1,425	1,141	769	840	942	696	498
Parking	1,143	1,357	1,252	1,031	675	680	799	621	440
Warehouse	330	218	312	440	286	319	171	133	178
Health care	2,829	5,059	7,010	6,837	6,193	7,009	7,040	6,928	6,249
Hospital	1,949	3,429	5,320	5,352	4,789	5,317	5,522	5,439	4,857
Medical building	490	1,168	909	876	747	906	982	970	961
Special care	390	463	782	609	657	785	536	520	431
Educational [1]	46,818	65,750	84,489	83,703	71,948	67,965	65,622	60,027	61,033
Primary/secondary [1]	33,764	44,184	57,770	54,650	44,559	40,760	39,389	36,050	35,548
Elementary	12,272	14,251	18,305	17,241	13,171	10,795	11,195	10,580	11,646
Middle/junior high	5,820	9,069	10,937	10,278	7,029	8,116	7,557	7,730	6,746
High	13,326	19,892	27,985	26,729	24,055	21,389	20,276	17,339	16,389
Higher education [1]	10,749	18,033	23,542	25,081	24,384	24,315	23,328	21,790	22,723
Instructional	6,317	9,275	13,251	14,734	14,138	13,373	11,931	11,755	11,916
Parking	514	1,013	732	596	593	717	532	398	436
Administration	294	387	290	382	357	433	430	409	534
Dormitory	1,078	2,918	3,043	3,183	3,371	3,965	4,435	3,845	3,486
Library	308	588	791	871	662	568	322	157	260
Student union/cafeteria	322	880	1,398	1,440	1,147	1,227	1,464	1,378	1,358
Sports/recreation	966	1,769	2,559	2,357	2,398	2,358	2,356	2,594	2,906
Infrastructure	835	1,138	1,241	1,291	1,381	1,461	1,735	1,065	1,697
Other educational [1]	1,645	2,735	2,485	3,077	2,223	1,831	2,054	1,500	2,027
Library/archive	976	2,098	1,557	1,865	1,386	1,159	1,385	1,016	1,076
Public safety [1]	5,854	6,013	9,666	9,432	7,586	7,245	7,641	6,592	6,224
Correctional	4,754	3,958	6,375	5,780	4,624	4,929	5,126	4,395	4,048
Detention	3,907	2,936	4,524	3,409	2,789	3,166	3,306	2,554	2,215
Police/sheriff	848	1,022	1,851	2,371	1,836	1,762	1,820	1,841	1,833
Other public safety	1,100	2,055	3,291	3,652	2,962	2,316	2,515	2,197	2,176
Fire/rescue	994	1,675	2,367	2,470	1,747	1,477	1,627	1,403	1,485
Amusement and recreation [1]	7,583	7,340	10,872	10,585	9,668	8,542	8,876	8,081	8,799
Sports	2,289	1,587	2,548	2,389	1,819	1,223	1,127	1,289	1,877
Performance/meeting center	2,075	1,921	1,631	1,704	1,841	1,805	1,804	1,474	1,801
Convention center	1,397	1,350	1,040	1,013	1,119	1,112	1,316	917	1,172
Social center	1,152	1,006	1,587	1,646	1,561	1,054	1,008	1,127	892
Neighborhood center	886	866	1,231	1,480	1,395	887	890	1,050	777
Park/camp	1,930	2,728	4,975	4,733	4,259	4,277	4,825	4,098	4,104
Transportation	13,000	16,256	23,230	25,461	26,493	23,340	24,797	25,871	27,795
Air [1]	6,700	8,993	11,579	12,562	11,897	9,867	9,799	9,768	10,821
Passenger terminal	2,930	3,310	6,164	6,916	6,503	5,681	4,992	5,310	4,876
Runway	3,196	4,861	4,551	4,839	4,710	3,760	4,313	3,780	5,004
Land [1]	5,165	5,936	9,969	11,327	12,954	11,811	13,047	13,984	15,142
Passenger terminal	1,253	907	2,053	2,789	3,380	3,223	2,978	2,946	3,746
Mass transit	1,484	3,208	4,371	5,223	6,447	5,846	7,033	7,189	7,118
Railroad	1,471	552	585	747	751	662	850	1,459	1,693
Water	1,136	1,327	1,682	1,572	1,642	1,661	1,952	2,118	1,833
Dock/marina	863	930	1,287	1,309	1,115	1,247	1,502	1,583	1,364
Dry dock/marine terminal	236	397	395	263	527	414	450	536	469
Power [1]	5,501	8,320	10,992	11,775	10,770	9,492	9,794	10,951	10,694
Electrical	5,257	7,091	10,192	9,387	9,972	7,886	7,136	8,334	9,021
Distribution	2,087	1,786	3,487	3,276	3,253	2,486	2,046	2,151	3,285
Highway and street	51,574	63,157	80,424	81,254	81,309	78,369	79,722	80,610	83,449
Pavement	37,929	45,177	52,837	55,186	51,433	47,954	47,566	46,282	50,345
Lighting	856	1,232	1,532	1,300	1,975	1,754	1,738	1,525	1,227
Retaining wall	1,099	675	888	959	1,250	1,033	845	895	872
Tunnel	894	373	264	302	810	873	1,359	1,477	1,039
Bridge	9,302	14,244	23,690	22,075	24,222	25,545	27,050	28,811	28,852
Toll/weigh	325	320	196	268	214	238	338	129	139
Maintenance building	293	96	102	128	275	237	187	373	271
Rest facility/streetscape	878	1,042	916	1,036	1,130	735	640	1,119	704
Sewage and waste disposal	14,000	18,336	24,102	23,455	24,555	21,196	20,946	21,037	22,028
Sewage/dry waste [1]	9,338	11,717	14,044	13,261	13,234	11,975	12,077	11,591	12,663
Plant	2,765	3,369	3,957	3,453	3,755	3,260	3,022	2,376	2,606
Line/pump station	6,326	8,243	9,823	9,494	9,375	8,619	8,956	9,072	9,919
Waste water	4,663	6,620	10,058	10,194	11,321	9,222	8,869	9,446	9,364
Plant	3,229	5,231	8,688	8,497	9,428	7,836	7,414	7,861	7,338
Line/drain	1,434	1,389	1,370	1,697	1,893	1,386	1,455	1,585	2,026
Water supply	9,528	13,483	16,017	14,838	14,420	13,393	12,746	12,919	12,700
Plant	3,067	4,943	6,500	6,327	5,683	5,391	4,833	4,358	4,228
Well	378	360	460	480	383	389	336	480	530
Line	4,644	6,234	6,191	5,398	6,246	5,867	5,631	5,777	5,754
Pump station	625	776	1,293	1,372	970	744	633	734	837
Reservoir	266	502	633	335	393	427	639	804	616
Tank/tower	548	668	940	926	744	574	674	765	735
Conservation and development [1]	933	1,752	2,251	2,016	2,035	2,289	2,225	2,500	3,019
Dam/levee	303	405	772	761	783	874	727	822	1,063
Breakwater/jetty	270	726	645	702	675	649	853	1,022	1,095
Dredging	140	211	179	248	173	198	184	214	241

[1] Includes other types of construction, not shown separately.

Source: U.S. Census Bureau, "Construction Spending," <http://www.census.gov/construction/c30/c30index.html>, accessed July 2015.

Table 987. Construction Contracts Started—Value of Construction and Floor Space of Buildings by Class of Construction: 1990 to 2014

[246.0 represents $246,000,000,000. Dollar value data includes new construction, additions, and alterations. Square footage data includes new construction and additions; alterations which create no net new square footage are not included]

Year	Total	Residential buildings	Nonresidential buildings									Non-building construction
			Total	Commercial [1]	Manufacturing	Education [2]	Health	Public	Religious	Social and recreational	Miscellaneous	
VALUE (bil. dol.)												
1990	246.0	100.9	95.4	44.8	8.4	16.6	9.2	5.7	2.2	5.3	3.1	49.7
1995	306.5	127.9	114.2	46.6	13.8	22.9	10.8	6.3	2.8	7.1	3.8	64.4
2000	472.9	208.3	173.3	80.9	8.9	40.9	12.4	7.5	4.6	13.8	4.4	91.3
2001	496.5	219.7	169.1	70.2	8.0	47.0	14.4	7.8	4.8	12.0	4.8	107.7
2002	504.0	248.7	155.1	59.6	5.5	45.3	16.1	7.3	5.1	11.5	4.7	100.2
2003	531.7	283.4	156.1	58.8	6.9	47.7	15.8	7.1	4.5	11.0	4.3	92.3
2004	593.2	333.1	164.4	67.3	8.0	44.0	17.6	7.2	4.5	11.6	4.4	95.6
2005	670.2	384.0	182.4	72.2	10.1	49.1	22.3	7.9	4.1	11.7	5.0	103.8
2006	689.5	342.1	217.3	92.9	13.7	53.8	24.3	8.2	4.1	14.3	5.9	130.1
2007	640.8	261.5	239.1	100.7	20.7	58.1	24.4	12.4	3.8	13.4	5.5	140.2
2008	558.2	160.5	243.0	81.4	31.0	63.7	30.0	13.4	3.6	13.5	6.5	154.7
2009	426.3	112.2	169.3	47.3	9.7	54.0	20.4	15.5	3.3	11.6	7.6	144.7
2010	435.3	122.1	163.9	42.2	9.5	53.4	24.8	10.6	2.4	11.2	9.8	149.4
2011	441.3	127.0	165.9	48.3	17.3	47.9	23.4	9.5	2.1	10.3	7.0	148.4
2012	492.3	166.4	159.9	55.0	13.1	43.3	22.9	8.7	1.9	8.6	6.4	166.0
2013	544.8	210.4	178.1	67.3	18.8	43.5	22.0	6.6	1.8	11.4	6.6	156.3
2014	592.7	231.4	218.9	80.8	34.9	50.0	22.8	7.6	1.7	13.6	7.5	142.4
FLOOR SPACE (mil. sq. ft.)												
1990	3,020	1,817	1,203	694	128	152	69	47	29	51	32	(X)
1995	3,454	2,172	1,281	700	163	186	70	40	33	56	33	(X)
2000	4,982	3,113	1,869	1,180	111	273	88	44	49	94	29	(X)
2001	4,828	3,159	1,669	988	93	295	92	44	50	81	27	(X)
2002	4,792	3,356	1,436	810	68	277	97	37	52	71	26	(X)
2003	5,093	3,689	1,404	794	75	270	92	35	45	67	26	(X)
2004	5,518	4,061	1,457	875	86	231	94	34	43	68	27	(X)
2005	5,872	4,345	1,528	927	79	246	108	33	37	67	29	(X)
2006	5,282	3,647	1,635	1,015	83	254	110	33	35	73	33	(X)
2007	4,312	2,645	1,667	1,051	91	247	104	51	31	66	27	(X)
2008	2,952	1,573	1,379	772	80	253	109	49	28	59	28	(X)
2009	1,888	1,112	776	332	36	199	68	48	25	42	26	(X)
2010	1,843	1,164	680	279	47	175	73	34	15	35	22	(X)
2011	1,863	1,159	704	325	55	157	76	27	14	33	18	(X)
2012	2,260	1,479	781	422	62	136	72	24	13	33	19	(X)
2013	2,709	1,835	874	533	54	131	73	16	11	36	19	(X)
2014	2,913	1,929	984	603	76	147	68	16	10	44	20	(X)

X Not applicable. [1] Includes nonindustrial warehouses. [2] Includes science facilities.

Source: Dodge Data & Analytics (copyright) 1-800-591-4462.

Table 988. Construction Contracts Started—Value by Region: 2010 to 2014

[In millions of dollars (435,326 represents $435,326,000,000). Includes new construction, additions and alterations]

Region	2010	2011	2012	2013	2014		
					Total [1]	Residential	Nonresidential
U.S.	**435,326**	**441,315**	**492,288**	**544,787**	**592,704**	**231,397**	**218,910**
New England	19,894	19,783	19,756	24,258	22,123	8,076	9,153
Middle Atlantic	54,197	49,001	53,945	63,765	69,004	25,522	27,166
East North Central	52,077	48,727	52,067	57,647	63,352	20,585	24,436
West North Central	32,189	31,498	38,685	44,879	43,087	14,071	15,333
South Atlantic	80,170	87,185	108,095	108,902	122,588	59,612	33,796
East South Central	25,657	28,058	24,996	26,399	27,858	11,326	9,829
West South Central	67,590	66,814	85,962	96,703	109,739	39,225	49,050
Mountain	39,257	39,215	40,744	45,015	51,976	22,406	18,806
Pacific	64,297	71,033	68,038	77,220	82,978	30,573	31,342

[1] Includes nonbuilding construction, not shown separately.

Source: Dodge Data & Analytics (copyright) 1-800-591-4462.

Table 989. Construction of New Privately Owned Housing Units Started: 1960 to 2014

[In thousands of units (1,252 represents 1,252,000). For composition of regions, see map inside front cover.]

Year	Total	1 unit structures	Northeast	Midwest	South	West
1960	1,252	995	221	292	429	309
1970	1,434	813	218	294	612	311
1980	1,292	852	125	218	643	306
1990	1,193	895	131	253	479	329
1995	1,354	1,076	118	290	615	331
1996	1,477	1,161	132	322	662	361
1997	1,474	1,134	137	304	670	363
1998	1,617	1,271	149	331	743	395
1999	1,641	1,302	156	347	746	392
2000	1,569	1,231	155	318	714	383
2001	1,603	1,273	149	330	732	391
2002	1,705	1,359	158	350	782	416
2003	1,848	1,499	163	374	839	472
2004	1,956	1,611	175	356	909	516
2005	2,068	1,716	190	357	996	525
2006	1,801	1,465	167	280	910	444
2007	1,355	1,046	143	210	681	321
2008	906	622	121	135	453	196
2009	554	445	62	97	278	117
2010	587	471	72	98	298	120
2011	609	431	68	101	308	133
2012	781	535	80	128	398	175
2013	925	618	97	150	464	215
2014	1,003	648	110	163	496	235

Source: U.S. Census Bureau, "New Residential Construction," <http://www.census.gov/construction/nrc/historical_data/>, accessed June 2015.

Table 990. Characteristics of New Privately Owned Single-Family Houses Completed: 2000 to 2014

[Percent distribution, except total houses (1,242 represents 1,242,000). Data are percent distribution of characteristics for all houses completed (includes new houses completed, houses built for sale completed, contractor-built and owner-built houses completed, and houses completed for rent). Percents exclude houses for which characteristics specified were not reported]

Characteristic	2000	2010	2013	2014	Characteristic	2000	2010	2013	2014
Total houses (1,000)	**1,242**	**496**	**569**	**620**	Bedrooms	100	100	100	100
					2 or less	11	13	10	10
Construction type	100	100	100	100	3	54	52	46	44
Site built	94	95	96	97	4 or more	35	35	44	46
Modular	3	2	2	2	Bathrooms	100	100	100	100
Other	3	2	2	1	1-1/2 or less	7	8	5	4
Exterior wall material	100	100	100	100	2	39	36	30	30
Brick	20	23	25	23	2-1/2 or more	34	32	32	30
Wood	14	8	5	5	3 baths or more	20	25	33	36
Stucco	17	17	22	23	Heating fuel	100	100	100	100
Vinyl siding	39	36	31	30	Gas	70	54	61	60
Aluminum siding	1	(NA)	(NA)	(NA)	Electricity	27	43	38	38
Fiber cement	(NA)	13	16	18	Oil	3	1	(Z)	(NA)
Other	8	2	2	2	Other	1	2	1	1
Floor area	100	100	100	100	Heating system	100	100	100	100
Under 1,400 sq. ft	14	13	8	8	Warm air furnace	71	56	58	57
1,400 to 1,799 sq. ft	22	19	16	14	Electric heat pump	23	38	38	39
1,800 to 2,399 sq. ft	29	27	27	26	Other	6	5	3	3
2,400 to 2,999 sq. ft	17	18	20	21	Central air-conditioning	100	100	100	100
3,000 to 3,999 sq. ft	13	15	19	20	With	85	88	91	91
4,000 or more	5	7	10	11	Without	15	12	9	9
Average (sq. ft.)	2,266	2,392	2,598	2,657					
Median (sq. ft.)	2,057	2,169	2,384	2,453	Fireplaces	100	100	100	100
Number of stories	100	100	100	100	No fireplace	40	51	49	49
1	47	47	41	42	1 or more	59	49	51	51
2 or more [1]	52	53	59	58					
Foundation	100	100	100	100	Parking facilities	100	100	100	100
Full or partial basement	37	30	29	28	Garage	89	85	91	91
Slab	46	52	55	57	Carport	1	1	1	1
Crawl space	17	18	16	15	No garage or carport	11	13	9	9

NA Not available. Z Less than 0.5 percent. [1] Includes houses with 1-1/2 and 2-1/2 stories, and split-level houses.

Source: U.S. Census Bureau and U.S. Department of Housing and Urban Development, "Characteristics of New Housing," <http://www.census.gov/construction/chars/>, accessed June 2015.

Table 991. Housing Starts and Average Length of Time From Start to Completion of New Privately Owned Single-Family Homes: 1980 to 2014

[852 represents 852,000. For buildings started in permit issue places]

Year	Total [1]	Purpose of construction			Region [2]			
		Built for sale	Contractor built	Owner built	North-east	Mid-west	South	West
STARTS (1,000)								
1980	852	526	149	164	87	142	428	196
1990	895	529	196	147	104	193	371	226
1993	1,126	716	225	162	116	251	498	261
1994	1,198	763	245	169	123	268	522	286
1995	1,076	712	199	133	102	234	485	256
1996	1,161	774	218	144	112	254	524	271
1997	1,134	784	189	131	111	238	507	278
1998	1,271	882	209	144	122	273	574	303
1999	1,302	912	208	142	126	289	580	308
2000	1,231	871	195	128	118	260	556	297
2001	1,273	919	186	129	111	269	590	303
2002	1,359	999	198	125	118	277	628	336
2003	1,499	1,120	205	127	116	309	686	388
2004	1,611	1,240	198	130	128	306	743	433
2005	1,716	1,358	197	129	138	306	831	441
2006	1,465	1,121	189	119	118	235	757	356
2007	1,046	760	151	104	93	171	540	242
2008	622	408	107	74	63	102	324	133
2009	445	297	83	51	44	76	232	93
2010	471	306	83	55	52	79	247	93
2011	431	287	74	47	41	74	229	86
2012	535	373	82	47	46	92	283	114
2013	618	457	91	45	55	102	326	134
2014	648	460	110	50	51	106	346	145
COMPLETION (months)								
1980	6.9	6.2	5.5	10.1	7.7	8.0	6.1	7.4
1990	6.4	5.9	5.3	10.3	9.3	5.6	5.7	6.9
1993	5.6	4.9	5.4	9.0	7.2	5.5	5.2	6.0
1994	5.6	4.9	5.3	9.1	7.1	5.7	5.3	5.6
1995	5.9	5.2	5.8	9.5	7.4	6.0	5.4	6.0
1996	6.0	5.2	5.8	9.9	8.2	6.1	5.6	5.6
1997	6.0	5.2	5.9	9.8	7.3	6.2	5.6	5.8
1998	6.0	5.4	6.0	9.5	7.1	6.2	5.5	6.1
1999	6.1	5.5	6.4	9.2	7.0	6.4	5.7	6.3
2000	6.2	5.6	6.5	9.2	7.5	6.4	5.9	6.0
2001	6.2	5.6	7.0	9.2	7.6	6.5	5.8	6.3
2002	6.1	5.5	6.6	9.6	7.3	6.4	5.6	6.2
2003	6.2	5.5	6.8	9.9	7.5	6.7	5.7	6.2
2004	6.2	5.7	7.0	9.1	7.3	6.7	5.8	6.3
2005	6.4	5.9	7.6	9.8	7.7	6.6	6.0	6.8
2006	6.9	6.3	7.8	10.7	8.3	7.1	6.3	7.4
2007	7.1	6.5	7.9	10.2	8.5	7.4	6.5	8.0
2008	7.7	6.8	8.5	11.1	8.9	8.2	6.7	9.0
2009	7.9	6.6	8.7	11.9	10.7	8.2	6.7	9.0
2010	6.9	5.8	7.6	11.0	10.1	7.3	5.9	7.3
2011	6.6	5.4	7.7	10.8	8.9	6.9	5.9	6.8
2012	6.0	4.9	7.3	10.5	8.5	6.5	5.2	6.1
2013	6.0	5.0	7.5	11.0	8.4	6.7	5.5	5.6
2014	6.2	5.4	7.5	10.8	8.6	6.9	5.7	6.2

[1] Includes units built for rent not shown separately. [2] For composition of regions, see map, inside front cover.

Source: U.S. Census Bureau, "New Residential Construction," <http://www.census.gov/construction/nrc/>, accessed June 2015.

Table 992. Price Indexes of New Single-Family Houses Sold by Region: 1970 to 2014

[2005 = 100. Based on kinds of homes sold in 2005. Includes value of the lot. For composition of regions, see map, inside front cover]

Year	Total	Northeast	Midwest	South	West
1970	14.9	13.4	17.9	18.2	10.2
1980	38.9	30.2	41.2	44.4	31.9
1990	55.7	58.0	58.6	60.6	46.2
2000	75.6	73.0	83.5	80.7	64.4
2002	81.4	80.2	86.1	86.3	71.5
2003	86.0	84.3	90.6	89.4	78.2
2004	92.8	91.6	96.7	94.4	88.2
2005	100.0	100.0	100.0	100.0	100.0
2006	104.7	102.6	102.9	105.4	105.2
2007	104.9	101.5	102.8	107.5	102.6
2008	99.5	100.8	98.9	103.7	92.7
2009	95.1	97.1	96.0	101.1	84.8
2010	95.0	101.1	96.9	99.5	85.4
2011	94.3	100.0	97.8	99.6	83.1
2012	97.6	102.1	101.5	102.7	86.3
2013	104.7	108.2	105.3	110.1	94.7
2014	112.3	120.0	113.1	117.2	102.6

Source: U.S. Census Bureau, "Construction Price Indexes," <http://www.census.gov/construction/cpi/>, accessed July 2015.

Table 993. New Privately Owned Single-Family Houses Sold by Region and Type of Financing, 1980 to 2014, and by Sales-Price Group, 2014

[In thousands (545 represents 545,000). Based on a national probability sample of monthly interviews with builders or owners of one-family houses for which building permits have been issued or, for nonpermit areas, on which construction has started. For details, see source and Appendix III. For composition of regions, see map inside front cover]

Year and sales-price group	Total sold	Region				Financing type			
		Northeast	Midwest	South	West	Conven-tional [1]	FHA and VA	Rural Housing Service [2]	Cash
1980.................	545	50	81	267	145	316	196	14	32
1985.................	688	112	82	323	171	414	208	11	64
1990.................	534	71	89	225	149	347	138	10	50
1995.................	667	55	125	300	187	499	129	9	39
2000.................	877	71	155	406	244	699	138	4	40
2005.................	1,283	81	205	638	358	1,151	79	1	52
2007.................	776	65	118	411	181	695	52	2	30
2008.................	485	35	70	266	114	358	104	(NA)	23
2009.................	375	31	54	202	87	234	124	(NA)	17
2010.................	323	31	45	173	74	189	116	(NA)	19
2011.................	306	21	45	168	72	190	96	(NA)	20
2012.................	368	29	47	195	97	234	110	(NA)	24
2013.................	429	31	61	233	105	296	103	(NA)	31
2014.................	**437**	**28**	**59**	**243**	**108**	**311**	**89**	**(NA)**	**37**
Under $200,000..........	100	2	16	73	9	64	28	(NA)	7
$200,000 to $299,999....	141	7	19	79	35	91	37	(NA)	12
$300,000 to $499,999....	135	8	17	66	44	104	20	(NA)	11
$500,000 and over........	62	10	7	25	20	53	1	(NA)	8

NA Not available. [1] Includes houses reporting other types of financing. [2] Prior to 2000, the Farmers Home Administration.

Source: U.S. Census Bureau and U.S. Department of Housing and Urban Development, "Characteristics of New Housing," <http://www.census.gov/construction/chars/>, accessed June 2015.

Table 994. Median Sales Price of New Privately Owned Single-Family Houses Sold by Region: 1980 to 2014

[In dollars. For definition of median, see Guide to Tabular Presentation. For composition of regions, see map inside front cover. Based on a national probability sample of monthly interviews with builders or owners of one-family houses selected from building permits and a canvassing of areas not requiring permits. For more details, see source]

Year	U.S.	North-east	Mid-west	South	West	Year	U.S.	North-east	Mid-west	South	West
1980........	64,600	69,500	63,400	59,600	72,300	2008........	232,100	343,600	198,900	203,700	294,800
1985........	84,300	103,300	80,300	75,000	92,600	2009........	216,700	302,500	189,200	194,800	263,700
1990........	122,900	159,000	107,900	99,000	147,500	2010........	221,800	329,900	197,700	196,800	259,300
1995........	133,900	180,000	134,000	124,500	141,000	2011........	227,200	322,800	203,300	211,400	256,000
2000........	169,000	227,400	169,700	148,000	196,400	2012........	245,200	368,800	230,600	227,000	270,000
2005........	240,900	343,800	216,900	197,300	332,600	2013........	268,900	371,200	255,300	246,600	310,500
2007........	247,900	320,200	208,600	217,700	330,900	2014........	282,800	402,800	269,700	257,700	333,900

Source: U.S. Census Bureau, ""New Residential Sales," <http://www.census.gov/construction/nrs/>, accessed June 2015.

Table 995. New Manufactured (Mobile) Homes Placed for Residential Use and Average Sales Price by Region: 1990 to 2014

[195.4 represents 195,400. A mobile home is a moveable dwelling, 8 feet or more wide and 40 feet or more long, designed to be towed on its own chassis, with transportation gear integral to the unit when it leaves the factory, and without need of permanent foundation. Excluded are travel trailers, motor homes, and modular housing. Data are based on a probability sample and subject to sampling variability; see source. For composition of regions, see map inside front cover]

Year	Units placed (1,000)					Average sales price (dollars)				
	Total	Northeast	Midwest	South	West	U.S.	Northeast	Midwest	South	West
1990............	195.4	18.8	37.7	108.4	30.6	27,800	30,000	27,000	24,500	39,300
1995............	319.4	15.0	57.5	203.2	43.7	35,300	35,800	35,700	33,300	44,100
2000............	280.9	14.9	48.7	178.7	38.6	46,400	47,000	47,900	44,300	54,100
2001............	196.2	12.2	37.6	116.4	30.0	48,900	50,000	49,100	46,500	58,000
2002............	174.3	11.8	34.2	101.0	27.2	51,300	53,200	51,700	48,000	62,600
2003............	139.8	11.2	25.2	77.2	26.1	54,900	57,300	55,100	50,500	67,700
2004............	124.4	11.0	20.6	67.4	25.5	58,200	60,200	58,800	52,300	73,200
2005............	122.9	9.2	17.1	68.1	28.5	62,600	67,000	60,600	55,700	79,900
2006............	112.4	7.9	14.5	66.1	23.9	64,300	65,300	59,100	58,900	83,400
2007............	94.8	7.0	10.8	59.4	17.7	65,400	66,100	64,900	59,900	85,500
2008............	80.5	5.0	8.2	54.0	13.3	64,700	68,400	65,700	59,600	84,900
2009............	54.5	3.5	5.3	37.8	7.9	63,100	61,600	65,400	59,300	81,500
2010............	50.7	3.8	5.8	34.6	6.6	62,800	65,200	60,700	60,000	79,000
2011............	47.6	3.3	6.3	31.5	6.5	60,500	62,700	60,800	58,400	70,600
2012............	52.8	3.9	7.9	34.4	6.6	62,200	63,400	60,900	60,100	75,300
2013............	56.3	4.0	7.5	37.4	7.5	64,000	66,500	62,900	61,200	79,100
2014 [1]............	44.1	3.0	6.8	27.5	6.8	65,300	67,900	60,600	63,000	80,700

[1] Data not comparable to prior years due to a change in methodology. See source for details.

Source: U.S. Census Bureau, "Manufactured Housing at a Glance," <http://www.census.gov/construction/mhs/mhsindex.html>, accessed September 2015.

Table 996. Existing Single-Family Homes Sold and Price by Region: 1990 to 2014

[2,914 represents 2,914,000. Includes existing detached single-family homes and townhomes; excludes condos and co-ops. Based on data (adjusted and aggregated to regional and national totals) reported by participating real estate multiple listing services. For definition of median, see Guide to Tabular Presentation. See Table 998 for data on condos and co-ops. For composition of regions, see map inside front cover]

Year	Homes sold (1,000)					Median sales price (dollars)				
	U.S.	Northeast	Midwest	South	West	U.S.	Northeast	Midwest	South	West
1990	2,914	513	804	1,008	589	97,300	146,200	76,700	86,300	141,200
1995	3,519	615	940	1,212	752	117,000	146,500	96,500	99,200	153,600
1996	3,797	656	986	1,283	872	122,600	147,800	102,800	105,000	160,200
1997	3,964	683	1,004	1,356	921	129,000	152,400	108,900	111,300	169,000
1998	4,495	745	1,129	1,592	1,029	136,000	157,100	116,300	118,000	179,500
1999	4,649	728	1,145	1,704	1,072	141,200	160,700	121,600	122,100	189,400
2000	4,603	715	1,116	1,707	1,065	147,300	161,200	125,600	130,300	199,200
2001	4,735	710	1,154	1,795	1,076	156,600	169,400	132,300	139,600	211,700
2002	4,974	730	1,217	1,872	1,155	167,600	190,100	138,300	149,700	234,300
2003	5,446	770	1,323	2,073	1,280	180,200	220,300	143,700	159,700	254,700
2004	5,958	821	1,389	2,310	1,438	195,200	254,400	151,500	171,800	289,100
2005	6,180	838	1,411	2,457	1,474	219,000	281,600	168,300	181,100	340,300
2006	5,677	787	1,314	2,352	1,224	221,900	280,300	164,800	183,700	350,500
2007	4,398	587	1,091	1,819	901	217,900	288,100	161,400	178,800	342,500
2008	3,665	471	882	1,439	873	196,600	271,500	150,500	169,400	276,100
2009	3,870	480	918	1,460	1,012	172,100	243,200	142,900	155,000	215,400
2010	3,708	465	859	1,426	958	173,100	243,900	140,800	153,700	220,700
2011	3,787	449	863	1,471	1,004	166,200	237,500	135,800	149,300	204,500
2012	4,128	492	1,002	1,605	1,029	177,200	237,200	143,700	158,400	234,300
2013	4,484	540	1,122	1,775	1,047	197,400	248,900	155,700	174,200	276,400
2014	4,344	533	1,060	1,789	962	208,900	252,200	164,200	182,900	294,400

Source: NATIONAL ASSOCIATION OF REALTORS ®. See also <http://www.realtor.org/research-and-statistics>.

Table 997. Median Sales Price of Existing Single-Family Homes by Selected Metropolitan Area: 2010 and 2014

[In thousands of dollars (173.1 represents $173,100). Includes existing detached single-family homes and townhouses. Areas are metropolitan statistical areas defined by Office of Management and Budget as of 2004]

Metropolitan area	2010	2014	Metropolitan area	2010	2014
United States, total	**173.1**	**208.9**	New Haven-Milford, CT	231.0	215.0
Allentown-Bethlehem-Easton, PA-NJ	224.0	180.0	New Orleans-Metairie-Kenner, LA	159.7	165.0
Anaheim-Santa Ana-Irvine, CA	546.4	687.9	New York-Northern New Jersey-		
Atlanta-Sandy Springs-Marietta, GA	114.8	159.5	Long Island, NY-NJ-PA	393.7	394.9
			New York-Wayne-White Plains, NY-NJ	450.0	468.2
Atlantic City, NJ	226.4	207.6	Oklahoma City, OK	145.7	150.3
Baltimore-Towson, MD	246.1	244.1	Omaha, NE-IA	137.3	149.0
Boston-Cambridge-Quincy, MA-NH	357.3	389.8	Orlando, FL	134.7	180.0
Boulder, CO	358.1	390.7	Philadelphia-Camden-		
Bridgeport-Stamford-Norwalk, CT	408.6	393.7	Wilmington, PA-NJ-DE-MD	214.9	220.7
Charleston-North Charleston, SC	200.5	228.2	Phoenix-Mesa-Scottsdale, AZ	139.2	198.5
Chicago-Naperville-Joliet, IL	191.4	205.9	Portland-South Portland-Biddeford, ME	218.0	227.7
Cincinnati-Middletown, OH-KY-IN	128.0	140.5	Portland-Vancouver-Beaverton, OR-WA	237.3	286.0
Cleveland-Elyria-Mentor, OH	114.5	122.6	Providence-New Bedford-Fall River, RI-MA	228.5	238.8
Colorado Springs, CO	195.5	222.3	Raleigh-Cary, NC	190.4	208.6
Dallas-Fort Worth-Arlington, TX	143.8	188.3	Reno-Sparks, NV	179.5	247.5
Deltona-Daytona Beach-Ormond Beach, FL	115.6	135.1	Richmond, VA	(NA)	220.2
Denver-Aurora, CO	232.4	310.2	Riverside-San Bernardino-Ontario, CA	179.3	273.9
Des Moines, IA	150.9	171.5	Sacramento-Arden-Arcade-Roseville, CA	184.2	268.7
Eugene-Springfield, OR	196.3	200.9	Saint Louis, MO-IL	131.1	141.7
Hartford-West Hartford-East Hartford, CT	235.8	224.9	Salem, OR	173.5	187.7
Honolulu, HI	607.6	682.8	Salt Lake City, UT	206.5	239.1
Houston-Baytown-Sugar Land, TX	155.0	198.4	San Diego-Carlsbad-San Marcos, CA	385.7	497.9
Indianapolis, IN	123.3	144.6	San Francisco-Oakland-Fremont, CA	525.6	737.6
Las Vegas-Paradise, NV	138.0	198.0	San Jose-Sunnyvale-Santa Clara, CA	595.0	860.0
Little Rock-N. Little Rock, AR	132.5	131.7	Seattle-Tacoma-Bellevue, WA	295.7	355.8
Los Angeles-Long Beach-Santa Ana, CA	323.3	449.5	Tampa-St. Petersburg-Clearwater, FL	134.2	151.5
Louisville, KY-IN	134.6	142.8	Trenton-Ewing, NJ	250.7	267.1
Madison, WI	217.7	228.2	Tucson, AZ	156.6	175.8
Memphis, TN-MS-AR	120.2	138.6	Virginia Beach-Norfolk-		
Miami-Fort Lauderdale-Miami Beach, FL	201.9	266.0	Newport News, VA-NC	205.0	196.0
Milwaukee-Waukesha-West Allis, WI	205.9	207.8	Washington-Arlington-		
Minneapolis-St. Paul-Bloomington, MN-WI	170.6	210.1	Alexandria, DC-VA-MD-WV	325.3	383.8

NA Not available.

Source: NATIONAL ASSOCIATION OF REALTORS ®. See also <http://www.realtor.org/research-and-statistics>.

Table 998. Existing Apartment Condos and Co-Ops—Units Sold and Median Sales Price by Region: 1990 to 2014

[272 represents 272,000. Data shown here reflect revisions from prior estimates. For definition of median, see Guide to Tabular Presentation. For composition of regions, see map inside front cover]

Year	Units sold (1,000)					Median sales price (dollars)				
	U.S.	Northeast	Midwest	South	West	U.S.	Northeast	Midwest	South	West
1990	272	73	55	80	64	86,900	107,500	70,200	64,200	114,600
1991	261	76	55	75	55	87,500	104,600	73,900	65,600	114,500
1992	282	88	61	77	56	87,700	100,600	79,000	66,600	117,400
1993	312	98	66	89	59	86,000	96,800	78,900	66,500	112,000
1994	343	108	68	101	66	88,800	97,100	86,200	66,700	118,600
1995	333	108	66	96	63	89,000	92,500	90,700	67,800	114,800
1996	370	120	72	105	73	92,600	95,100	95,200	70,600	119,800
1997	407	134	79	111	83	97,300	98,600	99,100	73,300	128,900
1998	470	157	92	126	95	102,500	100,900	106,400	76,800	137,700
1999	534	182	102	145	105	110,100	109,800	114,600	80,700	143,900
2000	571	197	106	160	108	114,000	108,500	121,700	84,200	149,100
2001	601	203	116	174	108	125,600	121,200	134,800	93,200	160,400
2002	657	221	129	193	114	144,900	143,500	148,600	109,900	187,000
2003	732	250	146	211	125	168,500	178,100	162,600	126,900	222,400
2004	820	292	161	230	137	197,100	214,100	181,000	156,600	258,000
2005	896	331	177	245	143	223,900	245,100	189,100	187,300	283,800
2006	801	299	169	211	122	221,900	249,700	190,900	184,000	264,700
2007	624	126	100	236	162	226,300	256,100	195,200	185,100	263,300
2008	459	103	71	164	121	209,800	252,500	188,200	166,800	218,500
2009	464	105	58	180	121	175,600	232,800	157,100	132,700	162,100
2010	474	95	53	202	124	171,700	242,200	150,500	118,500	154,700
2011	477	89	52	210	126	165,100	237,700	129,000	107,800	176,000
2012	528	104	66	229	129	173,700	240,100	127,800	123,900	196,700
2013	603	118	79	265	141	194,900	250,200	138,300	147,900	249,200
2014	591	112	76	262	141	204,300	254,900	149,300	154,700	273,300

Source: NATIONAL ASSOCIATION OF REALTORS ®. See also <http://www.realtor.org/research-and-statistics>.

Table 999. New Unfurnished Apartments Completed and Rented in 3 Months by Region: 1990 to 2013

[214.3 represents 214,300. Structures with five or more units, privately financed, nonsubsidized, unfurnished rental apartments. Based on sample and subject to sampling variability; see source for details. For composition of regions, see map, inside front cover]

Year and rent	Number (1,000)					Percent rented in 3 months				
	U.S.	Northeast	Midwest	South	West	U.S.	North-east	Midwest	South	West
1990	214.3	12.7	44.3	77.2	80.0	67	66	75	64	65
1995	155.0	7.1	31.7	78.5	37.7	73	74	75	72	73
2000	226.2	14.8	39.5	125.9	45.9	72	85	76	67	77
2001	193.1	16.5	31.6	97.4	47.6	64	83	67	60	64
2002	204.1	19.4	34.5	96.2	54.0	59	51	69	57	58
2003	166.5	19.8	35.5	72.0	39.2	61	72	62	56	63
2004	153.8	13.1	31.7	72.7	36.3	62	75	59	60	65
2005	113.0	4.7	20.5	57.8	30.0	64	75	64	62	64
2006	116.4	5.8	13.6	68.4	28.6	58	41	58	60	56
2007	104.8	5.6	9.5	61.8	28.0	55	66	58	52	58
2008	146.4	8.9	17.2	88.2	32.1	50	52	58	48	51
2009	163.0	10.0	17.2	93.3	42.4	51	56	74	49	44
2010	89.1	5.9	16.2	42.8	24.1	61	79	68	60	55
2011	74.7	10.9	18.6	38.8	6.4	59	67	53	60	54
2012	104.5	8.9	17.8	54.3	23.5	63	88	60	61	61
2013	**134.2**	**14.2**	**14.3**	**75.8**	**29.9**	**63**	**63**	**78**	**60**	**64**
Less than $950	27.3	1.0	4.2	19.4	2.7	67	48	86	63	72
$950 to $1,049	12.6	0.2	1.9	9.4	1.1	60	85	83	57	63
$1,050 to $1,149	11.7	0.2	1.6	8.4	1.5	66	83	75	65	64
$1,150 to $1,249	11.9	0.1	1.0	8.5	2.3	60	79	79	57	66
$1,250 to $1,349	10.0	0.7	0.6	6.3	2.2	62	73	69	58	68
$1,350 or more	60.9	11.9	5.0	23.8	20.1	62	63	75	59	62
Median asking rent	1,090	1,350	1,236	1,011	1,271	(X)	(X)	(X)	(X)	(X)

X Not applicable.

Source: U.S. Census Bureau, "Survey of Market Absorption of New Multifamily Units, Annual 2014 Absorptions (Completions in 2013)," and earlier releases, <http://www.census.gov/housing/soma/data/annual.html>, accessed May 2015.

Table 1000. Total Housing Inventory for the United States: 1990 to 2014

[In thousands (106,283 represents 106,283,000), except percent. Data for 2000-2012 have been revised based on vintage 2010 and 2012 housing controls. Based on the Current Population Survey and the Housing Vacancy Survey and subject to sampling error; see source and Appendix III for details]

Item	1990	1995	2000	2005	2009	2010	2011	2012	2013	2014
All housing units	**106,283**	**112,655**	**116,264**	**125,363**	**131,269**	**131,742**	**132,034**	**132,349**	**132,793**	**133,270**
Vacant	12,059	12,669	13,680	15,880	18,974	18,898	18,720	18,204	18,123	17,809
Year-round vacant	9,128	9,570	10,315	12,060	14,262	14,415	14,210	13,754	13,693	13,379
For rent	2,662	2,946	2,980	3,763	4,431	4,320	4,078	3,811	3,674	3,405
For sale only	1,064	1,022	1,088	1,468	2,035	1,999	1,899	1,551	1,530	1,441
Rented or sold	660	810	935	1,073	1,002	915	982	984	1,069	1,065
Held off market	4,742	4,793	5,313	5,755	6,794	7,181	7,250	7,408	7,420	7,468
Occasional use	1,485	1,667	1,901	1,909	2,087	2,263	2,263	2,277	2,378	2,229
Usual residence elsewhere	1,068	801	1,050	1,142	1,197	1,265	1,194	1,258	1,249	1,354
Other	2,189	2,325	2,363	2,703	3,510	3,653	3,793	3,873	3,791	3,885
Seasonal [1]	2,931	3,099	3,364	3,820	4,712	4,483	4,510	4,450	4,430	4,430
Total occupied	94,224	99,985	102,584	109,484	112,295	112,844	113,314	114,145	114,669	115,461
Owner	60,248	64,739	69,223	75,411	75,635	75,423	74,946	74,689	74,660	74,427
Renter	33,976	35,246	33,362	34,073	36,660	37,421	38,370	39,457	40,007	41,034
PERCENT DISTRIBUTION										
All housing units	100.0	100.0	100.0	100.0	100.0	100.0	100.0	100.0	100.0	100.0
Vacant	11.3	11.2	11.8	12.7	14.5	14.3	14.2	13.8	13.6	13.4
Total occupied	88.7	88.8	88.2	87.3	85.5	85.7	85.8	86.2	86.4	86.6
Owner	56.7	57.5	59.5	60.2	57.6	57.3	56.8	56.4	56.2	55.8
Renter	32.0	31.3	28.7	27.2	27.9	28.4	29.1	29.8	30.1	30.8

[1] Includes vacant seasonal mobile homes.

Source: U.S. Census Bureau, "Housing Vacancies and Home Ownership," <http://www.census.gov/housing/hvs/>, accessed February 2015.

Table 1001. Occupied Housing Inventory by Age of Householder: 1990 to 2014

[In thousands (94,224 represents 94,224,000). Data for 2000-2009 have been revised based on Vintage 2010 estimates; data from 2010 through 2014 are based on Vintage 2013 estimate. Based on the Current Population Survey and Housing Vacancy Survey; see source for details]

Age of householder	1990	1995	2000	2005	2009	2010	2011	2012	2013	2014
Total	**94,224**	**99,986**	**102,584**	**109,484**	**112,295**	**112,844**	**113,314**	**114,145**	**114,669**	**115,461**
Under 25 years old	5,143	5,502	5,966	6,614	6,157	6,113	6,067	6,053	6,126	6,111
25 to 29 years old	9,508	8,662	8,199	8,893	9,153	9,120	9,045	8,750	8,729	8,812
30 to 34 years old	11,213	11,206	9,941	9,696	9,412	9,564	9,937	9,937	9,963	10,044
35 to 39 years old	10,914	11,993	11,576	10,648	10,273	9,882	9,649	9,534	9,503	9,659
40 to 44 years old	9,893	11,151	12,016	11,858	10,797	10,618	10,495	10,634	10,351	10,121
45 to 49 years old	8,038	10,080	10,837	11,916	11,962	11,792	11,427	10,932	10,705	10,509
50 to 54 years old	6,532	7,882	9,416	10,716	11,704	11,823	11,762	11,807	11,836	11,674
55 to 59 years old	6,182	6,355	7,457	9,614	10,314	10,528	10,827	11,252	11,310	11,334
60 to 64 years old	6,446	5,860	6,013	7,422	8,996	9,427	9,822	9,917	9,966	10,141
65 to 69 years old	6,407	6,088	5,680	5,968	6,880	7,100	7,292	7,958	8,310	8,694
70 to 74 years old	5,397	5,693	5,421	5,073	5,333	5,496	5,546	5,794	6,171	6,429
75 years old and over	8,546	9,514	10,061	11,066	11,314	11,382	11,446	11,576	11,701	11,934

Source: U.S. Census Bureau, "Housing Vacancies and Home Ownership," <http://www.census.gov/housing/hvs/>, accessed May 2015.

Table 1002. Vacancy Rates for Housing Units—Characteristics: 2000 to 2014

[In percent. Rate is relationship between vacant housing for rent or for sale and the total rental and homeowner supply, which comprises occupied units, units rented or sold and awaiting occupancy, and vacant units available for rent or sale. Based on the Current Population/Housing Vacancy Survey; see source for details. For composition of regions, see map inside front cover]

Characteristic	Rental units					Homeowner units				
	2000	2010	2012	2013	2014	2000	2010	2012	2013	2014
Total units	**8.0**	**10.2**	**8.7**	**8.3**	**7.6**	**1.6**	**2.6**	**2.0**	**2.0**	**1.9**
Northeast	5.6	7.6	7.3	7.1	6.0	1.2	1.7	1.9	1.8	1.7
Midwest	8.8	10.8	9.3	9.1	8.0	1.3	2.6	2.0	2.1	1.8
South	10.5	12.7	10.8	10.0	9.5	1.9	2.8	2.2	2.2	2.2
West	5.8	8.2	6.4	6.2	5.6	1.5	2.7	1.9	1.6	1.6
Units in structure:										
1 unit	7.0	9.2	8.1	7.9	7.3	1.5	2.2	1.8	1.8	1.7
2 units or more	8.7	11.1	9.3	8.8	7.9	4.7	9.2	7.2	6.6	5.2
5 units or more	9.2	11.7	9.6	9.1	8.3	5.8	9.2	6.9	6.3	4.7
Units with—										
3 rooms or less	10.3	13.8	11.9	11.3	10.1	10.4	14.8	13.9	12.2	11.1
4 rooms	8.2	10.5	8.7	8.1	7.4	2.9	5.7	4.4	4.2	3.8
5 rooms	6.9	8.9	8.0	7.5	7.0	2.0	3.0	2.2	2.4	2.1
6 rooms or more	5.2	7.1	6.1	6.5	5.9	1.1	1.7	1.4	1.4	1.4

Source: U.S. Census Bureau, "Housing Vacancies and Home Ownership," <http://www.census.gov/housing/hvs/>, accessed February 2015.

Table 1003. Housing Units and Tenure—States: 2013

[132,808 represents 132,808,000. The American Community Survey universe includes the household population and the population living in institutions, college dormitories, and other group quarters. Based on a sample and subject to sampling variability; see Appendix III]

State	Housing units (1,000)		Vacant				Housing tenure			
							Owner-occupied units		Renter-occupied units	
	Total	Occu-pied	Total	For sea-sonal use [1]	For rent only	For sale only	Total (1,000)	Average house-hold size (persons)	Total (1,000)	Average house-hold size (persons)
United States.............	132,808	116,291	16,517	5,382	2,991	1,417	73,844	2.71	42,447	2.54
Alabama...................	2,190	1,822	368	84	60	37	1,240	2.62	582	2.52
Alaska.....................	307	246	61	32	8	3	156	2.97	90	2.72
Arizona....................	2,892	2,401	492	222	91	45	1,490	2.67	911	2.74
Arkansas..................	1,330	1,126	204	53	42	23	740	2.58	386	2.51
California..................	13,791	12,651	1,141	367	260	91	6,805	3.00	5,846	2.93
Colorado..................	2,247	2,003	244	116	40	18	1,292	2.62	711	2.49
Connecticut...............	1,488	1,340	148	29	32	17	888	2.71	451	2.37
Delaware..................	412	339	73	41	10	5	243	2.69	96	2.57
District of Columbia.......	303	272	31	4	11	2	111	2.31	161	2.18
Florida....................	9,048	7,212	1,836	917	263	123	4,672	2.62	2,539	2.70
Georgia...................	4,110	3,547	563	103	137	60	2,222	2.78	1,325	2.69
Hawaii....................	526	450	76	37	19	3	253	3.15	197	2.86
Idaho.....................	676	588	88	45	10	8	408	2.69	180	2.69
Illinois....................	5,290	4,783	506	51	108	60	3,154	2.73	1,629	2.43
Indiana...................	2,810	2,498	311	47	60	36	1,712	2.64	786	2.37
Iowa......................	1,350	1,236	113	21	23	13	875	2.52	361	2.18
Kansas...................	1,240	1,114	126	13	27	14	736	2.63	378	2.33
Kentucky..................	1,937	1,706	231	39	41	25	1,149	2.57	556	2.37
Louisiana.................	1,991	1,728	263	53	49	18	1,140	2.66	588	2.49
Maine.....................	723	548	175	120	13	8	384	2.46	163	2.12
Maryland..................	2,404	2,162	242	55	55	23	1,437	2.77	725	2.50
Massachusetts............	2,814	2,536	277	122	48	17	1,561	2.71	976	2.28
Michigan..................	4,525	3,832	693	284	74	54	2,704	2.60	1,129	2.35
Minnesota.................	2,369	2,120	249	128	25	22	1,517	2.60	603	2.21
Mississippi................	1,283	1,091	192	40	35	16	733	2.64	358	2.68
Missouri..................	2,719	2,363	356	89	58	35	1,582	2.58	780	2.29
Montana..................	486	406	79	39	8	7	272	2.48	135	2.33
Nebraska.................	807	731	76	15	15	6	482	2.62	248	2.23
Nevada...................	1,187	1,003	184	59	54	11	544	2.73	458	2.76
New Hampshire...........	616	519	97	64	9	5	364	2.58	155	2.22
New Jersey...............	3,578	3,176	402	134	76	35	2,034	2.85	1,142	2.55
New Mexico...............	905	754	152	55	24	16	512	2.75	242	2.62
New York..................	8,126	7,219	907	332	148	65	3,873	2.78	3,346	2.48
North Carolina............	4,395	3,757	637	218	110	57	2,415	2.59	1,343	2.49
North Dakota..............	339	298	41	13	7	3	193	2.52	105	1.99
Ohio......................	5,124	4,565	559	53	103	62	3,016	2.56	1,549	2.29
Oklahoma.................	1,682	1,447	235	38	45	23	949	2.63	499	2.51
Oregon...................	1,684	1,524	160	62	28	16	927	2.56	597	2.46
Pennsylvania..............	5,565	4,939	626	170	96	57	3,405	2.61	1,534	2.25
Rhode Island..............	462	406	55	21	12	5	245	2.61	161	2.30
South Carolina............	2,159	1,795	364	129	68	28	1,224	2.59	571	2.57
South Dakota.............	370	331	39	15	5	4	223	2.54	109	2.26
Tennessee................	2,841	2,490	351	74	73	36	1,653	2.59	837	2.47
Texas....................	10,256	9,111	1,145	237	301	92	5,634	2.96	3,477	2.64
Utah.....................	1,006	899	107	47	18	10	623	3.25	277	3.00
Vermont..................	324	253	71	52	4	3	180	2.47	73	2.14
Virginia...................	3,413	3,056	357	88	73	30	2,005	2.67	1,051	2.54
Washington...............	2,928	2,645	284	101	50	29	1,638	2.65	1,007	2.48
West Virginia..............	879	739	141	47	17	10	534	2.49	204	2.31
Wisconsin.................	2,633	2,289	344	188	42	28	1,538	2.56	751	2.22
Wyoming..................	265	224	41	17	6	2	155	2.59	69	2.42

[1] For seasonal, recreational, or occasional use.

Source: U.S. Census Bureau, 2013 American Community Survey, B25002, "Occupancy Status"; B25003, "Tenure"; B25004, "Vacancy Status"; and B25010, "Average Household Size of Units by Tenure"; <http://factfinder2.census.gov/>, accessed December 2014.

Table 1004. Homeownership and Rental Vacancy Rates by State: 2014

[From the Current Population Survey/Housing Vacancy Survey, and includes the civilian noninstitutionalized population, people in noninstitutional group quarters, and military households off post or with families on post (must include 1 household member who is a civilian adult). Based on a sample and subject to sampling variability, see Appendix III]

State	Homeowner vacancy rate	Rental vacancy rate	State	Homeowner vacancy rate	Rental vacancy rate	State	Homeowner vacancy rate	Rental vacancy rate
U.S.	1.9	7.6	Kansas	2.2	8.8	North Carolina	2.2	8.1
Alabama	2.5	14.0	Kentucky	2.4	6.5	North Dakota	0.9	8.6
Alaska	2.2	6.8	Louisiana	2.1	8.4	Ohio	1.6	7.4
Arizona	2.7	9.5	Maine	1.8	5.1	Oklahoma	1.9	11.4
Arkansas	3.3	14.7	Maryland	1.4	7.5	Oregon	1.8	4.1
California	1.1	4.5	Massachusetts	1.3	5.6	Pennsylvania	2.2	8.7
Colorado	1.2	4.9	Michigan	1.5	8.2	Rhode Island	1.5	6.7
Connecticut	1.4	5.8	Minnesota	1.4	5.6	South Carolina	2.7	12.0
Delaware	1.8	7.4	Mississippi	2.4	11.1	South Dakota	1.2	8.3
DC	1.6	6.5	Missouri	1.9	9.9	Tennessee	2.3	8.5
Florida	2.5	10.1	Montana	1.6	4.0	Texas	1.5	9.5
Georgia	2.8	9.7	Nebraska	1.3	5.5	Utah	1.5	8.6
Hawaii	1.6	8.3	Nevada	2.6	9.7	Vermont	1.9	5.0
Idaho	2.4	6.1	New Hampshire	1.8	5.6	Virginia	1.7	7.4
Illinois	2.3	9.2	New Jersey	1.6	6.2	Washington	1.6	4.9
Indiana	2.3	10.8	New Mexico	2.1	10.8	West Virginia	2.2	9.1
Iowa	2.0	5.7	New York	1.7	4.9	Wisconsin	1.7	4.6
						Wyoming	1.6	8.0

Source: U.S. Census Bureau, "Housing Vacancies and Home Ownership," <http://www.census.gov/housing/hvs/>, accessed February 2015.

Table 1005. Homeownership and Rental Vacancy Rates by Metropolitan Area: 2014

[Based on the Current Population Survey/Housing Vacancy Survey; see headnotes Table 1002 and Table 1004. Data are based on 2000 metropolitan/nonmetropolitan definitions; see source for explanation. Subject to sampling error; see source and Appendix III for details]

Metropolitan area	Homeowner vacancy rate	Rental vacancy rate	Metropolitan area	Homeowner vacancy rate	Rental vacancy rate
Inside metropolitan areas	1.8	7.4	Milwaukee-Waukesha-West Allis, WI	1.5	4.5
Akron, OH	0.8	6.3	Minneapolis-St. Paul-Bloomington, MN-WI	1.4	4.4
Albany-Schenectady-Troy, NY	1.4	4.2	Nashville-Davidson-Murfreesboro, TN	2.4	4.0
Albuquerque, NM	1.9	7.5	New Haven-Milford, CT	1.2	4.8
Allentown-Bethlehem-Easton, PA-NJ	1.7	5.7	New Orleans-Metairie-Kenner, LA	1.6	8.5
Atlanta-Sandy Springs-Marietta, GA	2.5	8.8	New York-Northern New Jersey-Long Island, NY	1.6	4.6
Austin-Round Rock, TX	0.8	10.9	Oklahoma City, OK	1.7	10.1
Bakersfield, CA	0.6	4.6	Omaha-Council Bluffs, NE-IA	1.8	5.5
Baltimore-Towson, MD	1.3	7.4	Orlando, FL	3.1	14.6
Baton Rouge, LA	1.8	7.2	Oxnard-Thousand Oaks-Ventura, CA	2.1	2.5
Birmingham-Hoover, AL	2.7	13.0	Philadelphia-Camden-Wilmington, PA	2.0	9.7
Boston-Cambridge-Quincy, MA-NH	0.8	4.9	Phoenix-Mesa-Scottsdale, AZ	2.9	9.7
Bridgeport-Stamford-Norwalk, CT	1.6	5.6	Pittsburgh, PA	1.2	6.1
Buffalo-Cheektowaga-Tonawanda, NY	2.1	8.0	Portland-Vancouver-Beaverton, OR-WA	1.3	3.6
Charlotte-Gastonia-Concord, NC-SC	1.7	6.0	Poughkeepsie-Newburg-Middletown, NJ	0.3	3.0
Chicago-Naperville-Joliet, IL	2.6	9.1	Providence-New Bedford-Fall River RI-MA	1.6	6.8
Cincinnati-Middletown, OH-KY-IN	2.2	7.9	Raleigh-Cary, NC	0.6	5.3
Cleveland-Elyria-Mentor, OH	1.5	7.0	Richmond, VA	1.9	12.0
Columbia, SC	1.5	9.5	Riverside-San Bernardino-Ontario, CA	2.0	6.5
Columbus, OH	1.7	7.0	Rochester, NY	1.1	6.6
Dallas-Ft. Worth-Arlington, TX	1.5	9.8	Sacramento-Arden-Arcade-Roseville, CA	1.0	6.5
Dayton, OH	0.4	8.9	St. Louis, MO-IL	2.4	10.3
Denver-Aurora, CO	0.8	3.3	Salt Lake City, UT	1.8	9.8
Detroit-Warren-Livonia, MI	1.2	9.5	San Antonio, TX	1.2	7.3
El Paso, TX	1.5	9.2	San Diego-Carlsbad-San Marcos, CA	1.3	4.8
Fresno, CA	0.1	4.6	San Francisco-Oakland-Freemont, CA	0.4	3.2
Grand Rapids-Wyoming, MI	1.6	3.7	San Jose-Sunnyvale-Santa Clara, CA	0.6	2.9
Greensboro-High Point, NC	2.0	8.6	Seattle-Bellevue-Everett, WA	1.2	4.4
Hartford-West Hartford-East Hartford, CT	1.3	6.0	Springfield, MA	1.5	4.9
Honolulu, HI	1.1	5.6	Syracuse, NY	2.7	8.1
Houston-Baytown-Sugar Land, TX	1.3	8.6	Tampa-St. Petersburg-Clearwater, FL	2.4	8.4
Indianapolis, IN	2.2	10.9	Toledo, OH	2.9	10.3
Jacksonville, FL	2.6	11.1	Tucson, AZ	2.1	9.0
Kansas City, MO-KS	1.5	9.5	Tulsa, OK	1.2	9.7
Las Vegas-Paradise, NV	2.9	10.1	Virginia Beach-Norfolk-Newport News, VA	2.0	6.6
Los Angeles-Long Beach-Santa Ana, CA	0.8	4.6	Washington-Arlington-Alexandria, DC-VA-MD-WV	1.4	6.7
Louisville, KY-IN	2.2	5.5	Worcester, MA	1.9	4.5
Memphis, TN-AR-MS	2.0	15.1			
Miami-Fort Lauderdale-Miami Beach, FL	1.8	7.0			

Source: U.S. Census Bureau, "Housing Vacancies and Home Ownership," <http://www.census.gov/housing/hvs/>, accessed February 2015.

Table 1006. Housing Units—Characteristics by Tenure and Region: 2013

[In thousands of units (132,832 represents 132,832,000), except as indicated. As of Fall. Based on the American Housing Survey; see Appendix III. For composition of regions, see map, inside front cover]

Characteristic	Total housing units	Sea-sonal units	Year-round units Occupied Total	Owner	Renter	North-east	Mid-west	South	West	Vacant units
Total units.................	**132,832**	**4,056**	**115,894**	**75,676**	**40,218**	**21,110**	**25,922**	**42,980**	**25,882**	**12,882**
Percent distribution.................	100.0	3.1	87.2	57.0	30.3	15.9	19.5	32.4	19.5	9.7
Units in structure:										
Single family detached.................	84,324	2,425	75,128	63,414	11,714	11,647	18,201	29,123	16,156	6,771
Single family attached.................	7,615	228	6,650	4,057	2,593	1,871	1,166	2,230	1,383	737
2 to 4 units.................	10,805	241	9,150	1,390	7,760	2,738	1,996	2,321	2,095	1,414
5 to 9 units.................	6,664	106	5,682	597	5,085	1,008	1,101	1,974	1,599	876
10 to 19 units.................	6,185	153	5,266	468	4,799	904	1015	2,061	1,286	766
20 or more units.................	9,861	360	8,101	1,173	6,928	2,441	1,468	2,130	2,063	1,401
Manufactured/mobile home [1].........	7,378	544	5,917	4,577	1,340	502	975	3,140	1,300	917
Year structure built:										
Median year (est.).................	1974	1975	1975	1976	1972	1959	1971	1979	1977	1972
1980 or later.................	50,952	1,604	44,930	31,695	13,234	4,801	8,487	20,481	11,161	4,417
1970 to 1979.................	25,165	824	21,930	13,105	8,825	2,897	4,834	8,881	5,318	2,411
1960 to 1969.................	15,400	459	13,484	8,608	4,876	2,464	3,038	4,898	3,084	1,457
1950 and earlier.................	41,315	1,167	35,550	22,268	13,282	10,947	9,562	8,721	6,319	4,598
Stories in structure: [2]										
1 story.................	43,538	1,684	37,446	26,495	10,950	1,176	4,253	20,992	11,025	4,408
2 stories.................	44,651	1,087	39,368	25,038	14,330	6,136	10,635	12,713	9,883	4,196
3 stories.................	28,212	477	25,479	16,675	8,805	9,208	8,647	4,851	2,774	2,255
4 or more stories.................	9,052	263	7,685	2,891	4,794	4,088	1,412	1,284	901	1,106
Foundation: [3]										
Full basement.................	29,259	389	26,886	23,422	3,464	9,252	11,529	4,037	2,068	1,984
Partial building.................	9,012	149	8,296	7,358	938	2,171	3,393	1,567	1,165	566
Crawlspace.................	20,540	869	17,738	14,140	3,598	799	2,394	9,363	5,181	1,934
Concrete slab.................	31,264	929	27,580	21,623	5,957	1,200	1,856	15,638	8,886	2,754
Equipment:										
With complete facilities [4].........	127,240	3,545	113,880	75,311	38,569	20,697	25,443	42,407	25,333	9,815
Lacking complete facilities [4].......	5,592	511	2,014	365	1,649	413	479	573	548	3,067
Kitchen sink.................	131,580	3,856	115,621	75,590	40,032	21,032	25,857	42,911	25,821	12,103
Refrigerator.................	129,465	3,664	115,593	75,546	40,047	21,046	25,835	42,884	25,827	10,209
Cooking stove or range.................	129,603	3,680	115,158	75,416	39,742	20,959	25,781	42,721	25,697	10,765
Dishwasher.................	86,957	2,140	78,286	57,697	20,588	12,601	16,389	30,436	18,861	6,532
Washing machine.................	104,369	2,339	96,455	73,367	23,088	15,663	21,900	37,810	21,082	5,575
Clothes dryer.................	101,823	2,302	94,067	72,217	21,850	14,991	21,671	36,740	20,666	5,453
Disposal in kitchen sink.................	67,224	1,498	60,430	41,076	19,353	5,717	13,529	21,820	19,363	5,297
Main heating equipment: [5]										
Warm-air furnace.................	84,525	2,011	74,676	51,669	23,007	9,304	21,293	26,708	17,371	7,838
Steam or hot water system.................	13,752	176	12,488	7,228	5,260	9,190	1,921	507	870	1,088
Electric heat pump.................	16,109	782	13,508	9,662	3,847	393	746	10,937	1,432	1,819
Built-in electric units.................	5,976	254	5,103	2,022	3,081	1,334	1,184	794	1,791	619
Floor, wall, or pipeless furnace........	5,228	145	4,588	1,740	2,847	370	341	1,049	2,828	495
Room heaters with flue.................	995	47	852	501	351	135	93	381	243	96
Room heaters without flue.................	1,227	57	1,034	636	398	25	59	882	68	136
Portable electric heaters.................	1,841	103	1,575	784	792	48	50	1051	426	163
Stoves.................	1,336	176	1,056	864	191	209	154	378	316	104
Fireplaces, with and without inserts...	329	52	247	216	31	28	46	66	109	30
None.................	864	174	389	175	214	2	3	45	339	301
Main cooling equipment:										
Central air conditioning.................	93,971	2,293	83,806	60,594	23,213	7,859	19,725	41,338	14,885	7,872
One or more room units.................	27,430	526	25,245	13,213	12,033	11,085	5,504	4,881	3,777	1,659
Source of water:										
Public system or private company....	(NA)	(NA)	102,450	63,950	38,500	17,807	21,891	38,468	24,284	(NA)
Well serving 1 to 5 units.................	(NA)	(NA)	13,093	11,471	1,622	3,210	3,986	4,356	1,541	(NA)
Means of sewage disposal:										
Public sewer.................	(NA)	(NA)	94,700	57,097	37,603	16,861	21,195	33,662	22,983	(NA)
Septic tank chemical toilet.................	(NA)	(NA)	21,163	18,559	2,603	4,246	4,720	9,298	2,899	(NA)

NA Not available. [1] Includes trailers. Includes width not reported, not shown separately. [2] Excludes mobile homes; includes basements and finished attics. [3] Excludes manufactured/mobile homes. [4] A complete kitchen includes sink, refrigerator, oven or burners. [5] Includes other items, not shown separately.

Source: U.S. Census Bureau, "American Housing Survey: National Summary Tables – AHS 2013," <http://www.census.gov/programs-surveys/ahs/data.html>, accessed December 2014.

Table 1007. Housing Units by Units in Structure and State: 2013

[In percent, except as indicated (132,808 represents 132,808,000). The American Community Survey universe includes the household population and the population living in institutions, college dormitories, and other group quarters. Based on a sample and subject to sampling variability; see Appendix III]

State	Total housing units (1,000)	1-unit detached	1-unit attached	2 units	3 or 4 units	5 or 9 units	10 or 19 units	20 or more units	Mobile homes	Boat, RV, van, etc.
U.S.	132,808	61.5	5.8	3.8	4.5	4.8	4.5	8.6	6.3	0.1
AL.	2,190	68.2	1.6	2.1	3.0	4.3	3.4	3.7	13.6	0.1
AK.	307	64.5	7.0	5.0	7.2	4.7	2.5	4.4	4.6	0.1
AZ.	2,892	63.7	4.6	1.4	3.5	4.3	5.3	6.4	10.6	0.3
AR.	1,330	69.3	1.6	3.2	3.3	3.1	3.5	3.0	12.9	0.1
CA.	13,791	58.1	6.8	2.5	5.7	6.3	5.3	11.5	3.7	0.1
CO.	2,247	63.1	7.0	1.7	3.3	4.7	5.7	10.2	4.1	0.1
CT.	1,488	58.8	5.5	8.1	9.2	5.4	3.6	8.4	0.9	(Z)
DE.	412	58.3	15.1	1.5	2.4	3.9	5.5	4.2	9.2	(Z)
DC.	303	11.8	25.1	3.5	8.0	7.0	10.5	34.1	(Z)	(Z)
FL.	9,048	54.0	6.3	2.2	3.9	5.1	6.1	13.2	9.1	0.1
GA.	4,110	66.3	3.5	2.3	3.0	5.5	4.8	5.4	9.1	0.1
HI.	526	54.0	7.8	2.1	4.3	6.7	5.4	19.6	0.2	(Z)
ID.	676	74.0	2.6	2.6	3.8	2.6	2.0	3.3	8.9	0.2
IL.	5,290	58.5	5.8	5.7	6.7	6.4	4.2	10.1	2.6	(Z)
IN.	2,810	72.4	3.9	2.5	3.6	4.6	4.0	4.0	5.1	(Z)
IA.	1,350	73.9	3.9	2.5	3.2	3.6	3.8	5.6	3.4	(Z)
KS.	1,240	72.3	4.7	2.3	3.2	3.8	3.8	4.8	5.1	(Z)
KY.	1,937	67.7	2.7	3.0	3.9	4.8	3.3	2.9	11.7	0.1
LA.	1,991	65.1	2.9	4.2	4.2	3.2	2.8	4.2	13.3	0.1
ME.	723	69.8	2.1	4.9	5.6	3.6	1.9	3.3	8.6	(Z)
MD.	2,404	51.3	21.5	1.6	2.2	4.9	8.6	8.3	1.6	(Z)
MA.	2,814	51.9	5.2	10.3	11.3	5.8	4.2	10.5	0.8	(Z)
MI.	4,525	71.9	4.8	2.5	2.5	4.2	3.7	5.0	5.4	(Z)
MN.	2,369	67.4	7.4	2.4	2.1	2.3	3.4	11.6	3.5	(Z)
MS.	1,283	69.2	1.4	2.3	3.3	4.7	2.5	2.1	14.4	0.1
MO.	2,719	70.0	3.3	3.5	4.7	3.8	3.6	4.5	6.6	0.1
MT.	486	69.1	2.7	3.7	4.8	2.8	2.2	3.8	10.7	0.1
NE.	807	72.8	3.7	1.9	2.5	4.1	4.7	6.7	3.7	(Z)
NV.	1,187	59.6	4.1	1.2	6.3	9.3	5.9	8.1	5.4	0.1
NH.	616	62.8	5.1	6.0	5.9	4.8	2.9	6.5	6.0	(Z)
NJ.	3,578	53.2	9.4	9.9	6.4	5.0	5.1	10.2	0.9	(Z)
NM.	905	64.7	4.1	1.9	3.4	2.6	2.7	3.8	16.6	0.1
NY.	8,126	41.8	5.0	10.5	7.5	5.2	4.1	23.4	2.4	(Z)
NC.	4,395	65.3	4.0	2.1	2.7	4.7	4.0	3.8	13.4	(Z)
ND.	339	60.2	5.7	2.3	4.3	3.5	5.3	10.7	7.9	(Z)
OH.	5,124	68.6	4.5	4.4	4.4	5.0	4.1	5.2	3.8	(Z)
OK.	1,682	72.3	2.0	2.4	2.6	3.6	3.7	3.6	9.7	0.1
OR.	1,684	63.6	4.3	2.9	4.6	4.2	3.6	8.0	8.4	0.3
PA.	5,565	57.0	18.5	4.7	4.2	3.4	2.5	5.7	4.1	(Z)
RI.	462	55.8	3.5	11.6	12.4	4.7	3.4	7.4	1.1	0.1
SC.	2,159	62.5	2.8	2.2	2.8	4.7	3.7	4.3	16.9	0.1
SD.	370	69.0	3.1	2.1	3.7	4.0	4.2	5.4	8.6	(Z)
TN.	2,841	68.9	3.1	3.0	3.4	4.6	3.7	3.9	9.3	0.1
TX.	10,256	65.0	2.7	2.0	3.3	5.0	6.4	8.2	7.3	0.2
UT.	1,006	69.3	5.9	3.2	4.6	2.9	4.7	5.7	3.6	(Z)
VT.	324	66.7	4.0	5.8	7.0	4.8	1.5	3.3	6.9	(Z)
VA.	3,413	61.5	11.2	1.8	2.8	4.7	5.9	7.1	5.0	(Z)
WA.	2,928	62.9	3.8	2.6	3.8	4.6	5.2	9.6	7.2	0.2
WV.	879	70.8	2.1	2.3	2.9	2.9	1.5	2.5	15.0	0.1
WI.	2,633	66.5	4.3	6.5	3.7	5.0	3.4	6.8	3.7	(Z)
WY.	265	66.8	3.6	1.9	4.8	3.5	2.4	3.3	13.7	0.1

Z Less than .05 percent.

Source: U.S. Census Bureau, 2013 American Community Survey, Table B25024, "Units in Structure," <http://factfinder2.census.gov/>, accessed December 2014.

Table 1008. Housing Units—Size of Units and Lot: 2013

[In thousands (132,832 represents 132,832,000), except as indicated. As of Fall. Based on the American Housing Survey; see Appendix III. For composition of regions, see map inside front cover]

Item	Total housing units	Sea-sonal units	Year-round units Occupied Total	Owner	Renter	North-east	Mid-west	South	West	Vacant units
Total units.............	**132,832**	**4,056**	**115,894**	**75,676**	**40,218**	**21,110**	**25,922**	**42,980**	**25,882**	**12,882**
Rooms:										
1 room..............................	375	43	221	8	213	68	46	40	66	112
2 rooms............................	1,333	135	931	77	854	283	125	181	343	267
3 rooms............................	11,104	539	9,065	941	8,124	2,289	1,830	2,522	2,425	1,500
4 rooms............................	22,454	1,288	17,752	5,360	12,392	3,243	3,915	6,269	4,326	3,414
5 rooms............................	28,770	991	24,473	15,036	9,437	3,678	5,497	9,926	5,372	3,306
6 rooms............................	28,325	625	25,321	19,800	5,521	4,570	5,417	10,158	5,176	2,380
7 rooms............................	18,973	227	17,651	15,459	2,192	3,237	4,228	6,585	3,602	1,095
8 or more rooms.................	21,498	209	20,480	18,995	1,485	3,743	4,865	7,299	4,573	809
Complete bathrooms:										
No bathrooms......................	1,517	343	372	139	233	105	74	114	79	802
1 bathroom.........................	46,324	1,650	38,989	14,346	24,643	9,474	9,487	11,986	8,043	5,685
1 and one-half bathrooms.....	17,163	377	15,504	11,295	4,210	3,936	4,880	4,126	2,562	1,282
2 or more bathrooms............	67,828	1,686	61,029	49,896	11,133	7,595	11,482	26,754	15,198	5,114
Square footage of unit: [1]										
Less than 500.....................	3,872	241	3,078	483	2,594	958	617	738	764	553
500 to 749.........................	10,173	515	8,176	1,497	6,679	1,750	1,613	2,672	2,141	1,483
750 to 999.........................	15,926	681	13,323	4,401	8,922	2,210	2,931	4,815	3,368	1,922
1,000 to 1,499....................	31,208	1,029	26,945	16,906	10,039	3,775	5,998	10,824	6,349	3,234
1,500 to 1,999....................	24,495	603	21,840	17,910	3,931	3,251	4,603	8,805	5,182	2,051
2,000 to 2,499....................	16,041	334	14,556	12,868	1,688	2,420	3,457	5,598	3,081	1,151
2,500 to 2,999....................	8,050	182	7,446	6,852	594	1,294	1,631	2,931	1,590	423
3,000 to 3,999....................	7,614	144	7,042	6,578	464	1,275	1,753	2,660	1,354	428
4,000 or more.....................	4,999	120	4,553	3,993	561	965	1,064	1,684	840	326
Not reported.......................	10,453	206	8,935	4,188	4,747	3,213	2,255	2,254	1,214	1,312
Median square footage.........	1,500	1,200	1,500	1,800	971	1,500	1,500	1,500	1,445	1,200
Lot size:										
Single detached and attached units and mobile homes [2]...........	95,906	2,976	84,827	69,844	14,983	13,493	19,678	33,584	18,072	8,104
Less than one-eighth acre......	16,081	605	13,762	9,851	3,912	2,427	3,066	4,348	3,920	1,715
One-eighth to one-quarter acre...	25,076	669	22,206	17,700	4,505	2,550	5,136	7,479	7,040	2,201
One-quarter to one-half acre......	16,921	418	15,279	13,191	2,087	2,309	3,817	6,192	2,961	1,224
One-half up to one acre..........	10,218	274	9,211	7,928	1,284	1,888	1,893	4,319	1,111	732
1 up to 5 acres....................	20,390	697	18,068	15,520	2,548	3,305	3,880	8,740	2,144	1,625
5 up to 10 acres..................	3,074	103	2,743	2,512	231	388	788	1,106	460	229
10 or more acres.................	4,147	210	3,558	3,142	416	626	1,098	1,399	436	378
Median acreage..................	0.25	0.28	0.26	0.31	0.18	0.34	0.27	0.34	0.18	0.25

[1] Figures differ from previously published data in that square footage data has been expanded to include all units. [2] Does not include cooperatives or condominiums.

Source: U.S. Census Bureau, "American Housing Survey: National Summary Tables – AHS 2013," <http://www.census.gov/programs-surveys/ahs/data.html>, accessed December 2014.

Table 1009. Occupied Housing Units—Tenure by Race of Householder: 1995 to 2013

[In thousands (97,693 represents 97,693,000), except percent. As of Fall. Based on the American Housing Survey; see Appendix III]

Race of householder and tenure	1995	2001	2003 [1]	2005	2007	2009	2011	2013
ALL RACES [2]								
Occupied units, total..............	**97,693**	**106,261**	**105,842**	**108,871**	**110,692**	**111,806**	**114,907**	**115,894**
Owner-occupied.......................	63,544	72,265	72,238	74,931	75,647	76,428	76,091	75,676
Percent of occupied...............	65.0	68.0	68.3	68.8	68.3	68.4	66.2	65.3
Renter-occupied......................	34,150	33,996	33,604	33,940	35,045	35,378	38,816	40,218
WHITE [3]								
Occupied units, total..............	**81,611**	**85,292**	**87,483**	**89,449**	**90,413**	**91,137**	**92,820**	**93,298**
Owner-occupied.......................	56,507	62,465	63,126	65,023	65,554	65,935	65,357	65,099
Percent of occupied...............	69.2	73.2	72.2	72.7	72.5	72.3	70.4	69.8
Renter-occupied......................	25,104	22,826	24,357	24,426	24,859	25,202	27,463	28,199
BLACK [3]								
Occupied units, total..............	**11,773**	**13,292**	**13,004**	**13,447**	**13,856**	**13,993**	**14,694**	**15,023**
Owner-occupied.......................	5,137	6,318	6,193	6,471	6,464	6,547	6,662	6,482
Percent of occupied...............	43.6	47.5	47.6	48.1	46.7	46.8	45.3	43.1
Renter-occupied......................	6,637	6,974	6,811	6,975	7,392	7,446	8,033	8,542
HISPANIC ORIGIN [4]								
Occupied units, total..............	**7,757**	**9,814**	**11,038**	**11,651**	**12,609**	**12,739**	**13,841**	**14,681**
Owner-occupied.......................	3,245	4,731	5,106	5,752	6,364	6,439	6,530	6,899
Percent of occupied...............	41.8	48.2	46.3	49.4	50.5	50.5	47.2	47.0
Renter-occupied......................	4,512	5,083	5,931	5,899	6,244	6,300	7,311	7,783

[1] Based on 2000 census controls. [2] Includes other races not shown separately. [3] The 2003 American Housing Survey (AHS) allowed respondents to choose more than one race. Beginning in 2003, data represent householders who selected this race group only and exclude householders reporting more than one race. The AHS in prior years only allowed respondents to report one race group. See also comments on race in the text for Section 1 and the below cited source. [4] Persons of Hispanic origin may be of any race.

Source: U.S. Census Bureau, "American Housing Survey: National Summary Tables – AHS 2013," <http://www.census.gov/programs-surveys/ahs/data.html>, accessed December 2014.

Table 1010. Homeownership Rates by Age of Householder and Household Type: 1990 to 2014

[In percent. Represents the proportion of owner households to the total number of occupied households. Based on the Current Population Survey/Housing Vacancy Survey; see headnote, Table 1004, source, and Appendix III for details]

Age of householder and household type	1990	1995	2000	2005	2009	2010	2011	2012	2013	2014
United States	**63.9**	**64.7**	**67.4**	**68.9**	**67.4**	**66.9**	**66.1**	**65.4**	**65.1**	**64.5**
AGE OF HOUSEHOLDER										
Less than 25 years old	15.7	15.9	21.7	25.7	23.3	22.8	22.6	21.7	22.2	21.7
25 to 29 years old	35.2	34.4	38.1	40.9	37.7	36.8	34.6	34.3	34.1	32.7
30 to 34 years old	51.8	53.1	54.6	56.8	52.5	51.6	49.8	47.9	48.1	47.1
35 to 39 years old	63.0	62.1	65.0	66.6	63.4	61.9	59.8	56.9	55.8	56.0
40 to 44 years old	69.8	68.6	70.6	71.7	68.7	67.9	66.9	65.5	65.0	63.2
45 to 49 years old	73.9	73.7	74.7	75.0	72.3	72.0	71.0	69.9	69.6	68.5
50 to 54 years old	76.8	77.0	78.5	78.3	76.5	75.0	74.4	73.4	72.6	72.6
55 to 59 years old	78.8	78.8	80.4	80.6	78.6	77.7	77.3	76.2	75.8	75.4
60 to 64 years old	79.8	80.3	80.3	81.9	80.6	80.4	79.8	78.6	77.6	77.2
65 to 69 years old	80.0	81.0	83.0	82.8	82.0	81.6	81.7	81.1	80.5	80.3
70 to 74 years old	78.4	80.9	82.6	82.9	81.9	82.4	83.3	83.5	82.8	81.6
75 years old and over	72.3	74.6	77.7	78.4	78.9	78.9	79.3	80.0	80.0	78.6
Less than 35 years old	38.5	38.6	40.8	43.0	39.7	39.1	37.7	36.7	36.8	35.8
35 to 44 years old	66.3	65.2	67.9	69.3	66.2	65.0	63.5	61.4	60.6	59.7
45 to 54 years old	75.2	75.2	76.5	76.6	74.4	73.5	72.7	71.7	71.2	70.7
55 to 64 years old	79.3	79.5	80.3	81.2	79.5	79.0	78.5	77.3	76.6	76.3
65 years and over	76.3	78.1	80.4	80.6	80.5	80.5	80.9	81.1	80.8	79.9
TYPE OF HOUSEHOLD										
Family households:										
Married-couple families	78.1	79.6	82.4	84.2	82.8	82.1	81.5	80.8	80.7	80.3
Male householder, no spouse present	55.2	55.3	57.5	59.1	56.9	56.9	55.6	55.9	55.3	54.5
Female householder, no spouse present	44.0	45.1	49.1	51.0	49.0	48.6	48.1	46.7	46.7	46.2
Nonfamily households:										
One-person	49.0	50.5	53.6	55.6	55.1	55.3	55.0	54.5	53.9	53.3
Male householder	42.4	43.8	47.4	50.3	50.9	51.3	50.6	49.8	49.8	49.1
Female householder	53.6	55.4	58.1	59.6	58.6	58.6	58.5	58.3	57.2	56.6
Other:										
Male householder	31.7	34.2	38.0	41.7	40.2	40.7	39.5	39.8	39.8	37.7
Female householder	32.5	33.0	40.6	44.7	42.5	41.9	43.1	41.0	41.9	41.4

Source: U.S. Census Bureau, "Housing Vacancies and Home Ownership," <http://www.census.gov/housing/hvs/>, accessed February 2015.

Table 1011. Homeownership Rates by State: 1990 to 2014

[In percent. Represents the proportion of owner households to the total number of occupied households. See headnote, Table 1004]

State	1990	2000	2005	2010	2013	2014	State	1990	2000	2005	2010	2013	2014
United States	**63.9**	**67.4**	**68.9**	**66.9**	**65.1**	**64.5**	Missouri	64.0	74.2	72.3	71.2	71.3	70.5
Alabama	68.4	73.2	76.6	73.2	72.7	72.1	Montana	69.1	70.2	70.4	68.1	67.4	66.9
Alaska	58.4	66.4	66.0	65.7	64.6	64.9	Nebraska	67.3	70.2	70.2	70.4	68.2	66.7
Arizona	64.5	68.0	71.1	66.6	65.1	63.5	Nevada	55.8	64.0	63.4	59.7	56.0	56.0
Arkansas	67.8	68.9	69.2	67.9	65.4	65.4	New Hampshire	65.0	69.2	74.0	74.9	74.1	72.2
California	53.8	57.1	59.7	56.1	54.3	54.2	New Jersey	65.0	66.2	70.1	66.5	64.9	65.2
Colorado	59.0	68.3	71.0	68.5	64.4	65.0	New Mexico	68.6	73.7	71.4	68.6	67.3	66.3
Connecticut	67.9	70.0	70.5	70.8	68.5	67.4	New York	53.3	53.4	55.9	54.5	53.0	52.9
Delaware	67.7	72.0	75.8	74.7	74.1	74.3	North Carolina	69.0	71.1	70.9	69.5	67.3	66.4
Dist. of Columbia	36.4	41.9	45.8	45.6	44.6	41.5	North Dakota	67.2	70.7	68.5	67.1	68.0	64.5
Florida	65.1	68.4	72.4	69.3	66.1	64.9	Ohio	68.7	71.3	73.3	69.7	67.9	67.3
Georgia	64.3	69.8	67.9	67.1	64.2	62.9	Oklahoma	70.3	72.7	72.9	69.2	69.9	69.3
Hawaii	55.5	55.2	59.8	56.1	57.3	58.4	Oregon	64.4	65.3	68.2	66.3	64.2	62.8
Idaho	69.4	70.5	74.2	72.4	71.5	69.6	Pennsylvania	73.8	74.7	73.3	72.2	71.5	69.7
Illinois	63.0	67.9	70.9	68.8	67.2	66.4	Rhode Island	58.5	61.5	63.1	62.8	61.5	61.8
Indiana	67.0	74.9	75.0	71.2	71.7	70.1	South Carolina	71.4	76.5	73.9	74.8	72.4	72.9
Iowa	70.7	75.2	73.9	71.1	69.8	69.4	South Dakota	66.2	71.2	68.4	70.6	67.8	69.2
Kansas	69.0	69.3	69.5	67.4	63.5	64.7	Tennessee	68.3	70.9	72.4	71.0	66.8	66.7
Kentucky	65.8	73.4	71.6	70.3	67.5	67.6	Texas	59.7	63.8	65.9	65.3	63.3	62.2
Louisiana	67.8	68.1	72.5	70.4	67.8	65.3	Utah	70.1	72.7	73.9	72.5	70.9	70.9
Maine	74.2	76.5	73.9	73.8	73.5	71.0	Vermont	72.6	68.7	74.2	73.6	73.0	73.5
Maryland	64.9	69.9	71.2	68.9	66.9	66.2	Virginia	69.8	73.9	71.2	68.7	68.1	68.7
Massachusetts	58.6	59.9	63.4	65.3	65.3	63.0	Washington	61.8	63.6	67.6	64.4	62.7	63.6
Michigan	72.3	77.2	76.4	74.5	73.9	73.8	West Virginia	72.0	75.9	81.3	79.0	76.8	75.6
Minnesota	68.0	76.1	76.5	72.6	73.4	71.4	Wisconsin	68.3	71.8	71.1	71.0	68.5	67.8
Mississippi	69.4	75.2	78.8	74.8	74.2	73.2	Wyoming	68.9	71.0	72.8	73.4	70.5	70.8

Source: U.S. Census Bureau, "Housing Vacancies and Home Ownership," <http://www.census.gov/housing/hvs/>, accessed February 2015.

Table 1012. Occupied Housing Units—Costs by Region: 2013

[75,676 represents 75,676,000. As of Fall. See headnote, Table 1013, for an explanation of housing costs. Based on the American Housing Survey; see Appendix III. For composition of regions, see map inside front cover]

Category	Number (1,000)					Percent distribution				
	Total units	North-east	Mid-west	South	West	Total units	North-east	Mid-west	South	West
OWNER-OCCUPIED UNITS Total	75,676	13,472	18,049	28,697	15,458	100.0	100.0	100.0	100.0	100.0
Monthly housing costs:										
Less than $200	2,558	199	456	1,428	476	3.4	1.5	2.5	5.0	3.1
$200 to $299	5,317	331	1,186	3,002	796	7.0	2.5	6.6	10.5	5.1
$300 to $399	6,283	610	1,762	2,830	1,080	8.3	4.5	9.8	9.9	7.0
$400 to $499	5,652	801	1,626	2,227	999	7.5	5.9	9.0	7.8	6.5
$500 to $699	8,845	1,656	2,423	3,385	1,380	11.7	12.3	13.4	11.8	8.9
$700 to $999	11,575	2,102	3,223	4,505	1,745	15.3	15.6	17.9	15.7	11.3
$1,000 to $1,499	15,197	2,685	4,057	5,444	3,011	20.1	19.9	22.5	19.0	19.5
$1,500 to $2,499	13,663	3,182	2,551	4,237	3,692	18.1	23.6	14.1	14.8	23.9
$2,500 or more	6,585	1,904	766	1,638	2,277	8.7	14.1	4.2	5.7	14.7
Median (dol.) [1]	934	1,159	836	797	1,199	(X)	(X)	(X)	(X)	(X)
RENTER-OCCUPIED UNITS Total	40,218	7,639	7,874	14,283	10,424	100.0	100.0	100.0	100.0	100.0
Monthly housing costs:										
Less than $200	1,122	187	236	440	260	2.8	2.4	3.0	3.1	2.5
$200 to $299	1,603	391	394	466	352	4.0	5.1	5.0	3.3	3.4
$300 to $399	1,446	335	350	490	272	3.6	4.4	4.4	3.4	2.6
$400 to $499	2,136	370	575	834	357	5.3	4.8	7.3	5.8	3.4
$500 to $699	6,924	987	1,904	2,731	1,301	17.2	12.9	24.2	19.1	12.5
$700 to $999	10,822	1,676	2,465	4,149	2,531	26.9	21.9	31.3	29.0	24.3
$1,000 to $1,499	9,108	2,025	1,181	3,053	2,850	22.6	26.5	15.0	21.4	27.3
$1,500 to $2,499	4,095	1,070	315	964	1,746	10.2	14.0	4.0	6.7	16.7
$2,500 or more	887	273	68	169	377	2.2	3.6	0.9	1.2	3.6
No cash rent	2,076	324	388	987	377	5.2	4.2	4.9	6.9	3.6
Median (dol.) [1]	850	945	729	810	995	(X)	(X)	(X)	(X)	(X)

X Not applicable. [1] For explanation of median, see Guide to Tabular Presentation.

Source: U.S. Census Bureau, "American Housing Survey: National Summary Tables – AHS 2013," <http://www.census.gov/programs-surveys/ahs/data.html>, accessed December 2014.

Table 1013. Occupied Housing Units—Financial Summary by Selected Characteristics of the Householder: 2013

[In thousands of units (115,894 represents 115,894,000), except as indicated. As of Fall. Housing costs include real estate taxes, property insurance, utilities, fuel, water, garbage collection, homeowner association fees, cooperative or condominium fees, mobile home fees, and mortgage. Based on the American Housing Survey; see Appendix III]

Characteristic	Total occupied units	Tenure		Black [1]		Hispanic origin [2]		Elderly [3]		Households below poverty level	
		Owner	Renter	Owner	Renter	Owner	Renter	Owner	Renter	Owner	Renter
Total units [4]	115,894	75,676	40,218	6,482	8,542	6,899	7,783	21,656	5,151	7,253	11,140
Monthly housing costs:											
$199 or less	3,681	2,558	1,122	310	381	246	209	1,297	216	819	819
$200 to $299	6,919	5,317	1,603	552	479	390	280	2,743	508	1,089	1,139
$300 to $399	7,729	6,283	1,446	561	413	544	186	3,136	412	900	690
$400 to $499	7,788	5,652	2,136	458	475	433	305	2,743	346	702	986
$500 to $699	15,768	8,845	6,924	732	1,558	734	1,240	3,680	843	1,079	2,228
$700 to $999	22,395	11,575	10,822	1,020	2,455	1,107	2,348	3,003	1,086	1,041	2,461
$1,000 to $1,499	24,305	15,197	9,108	1,360	1,784	1,490	2,074	2,478	721	849	1,447
$1,500 to $2,499	17,757	13,663	4,095	1,067	519	1,466	777	1,734	358	560	456
$2,500 or more	7,472	6,585	887	421	69	489	86	841	158	215	89
Median amount (dol.) [5]	896	934	850	888	791	998	895	540	699	515	634
Monthly housing costs as percent of income: [6]											
Less than 5 percent	3,462	3,184	278	156	32	199	47	831	35	11	21
5 to 9 percent	11,835	10,695	1,140	729	185	681	154	3,470	109	59	32
10 to 14 percent	14,629	12,317	2,312	924	402	918	332	3,661	183	121	79
15 to 19 percent	15,399	11,790	3,609	847	618	904	586	2,791	323	261	120
20 to 24 percent	13,673	9,354	4,319	773	814	802	719	2,254	363	282	298
25 to 29 percent	10,819	6,641	4,178	616	876	665	852	1,720	575	340	522
30 to 34 percent	7,889	4,565	3,324	451	765	578	634	1,188	418	360	470
35 to 39 percent	5,534	3,063	2,471	283	579	386	534	924	327	287	360
40 percent or more	27,788	12,870	14,918	1,535	3,384	1,618	3,345	4,574	2,242	4,398	7,027
Median amount (percent) [5,7]	23	19	33	22	36	24	37	19	39	77	74

[1] For persons who selected this race group only. See footnote 3, Table 1009. [2] Persons of Hispanic origin may be of any race. [3] Householders 65 years old and over. [4] Include units with no cash rents, not shown separately. [5] For explanation of median, see Guide to Tabular Presentation. [6] Money income before taxes. [7] Excludes households with zero or negative income and those with no cash rent.

Source: U.S. Census Bureau, "American Housing Survey: National Summary Tables – AHS 2013," <http://www.census.gov/programs-surveys/ahs/data.html>, accessed December 2014.

Table 1014. Owner-Occupied Housing Units—Value and Costs by State: 2013

[In percent, except as indicated (73,844 represents 73,844,000). The American Community Survey universe includes the household population and excludes the population living in institutions, college dormitories, and other group quarters. Based on a sample and subject to sampling variability; see Appendix III. For definition of median, see Guide to Tabular Presentation]

State	Total (1,000)	Percent of units with value of—			Median value (dol.)	Median selected monthly owner costs [1] (dol.)	Selected monthly owner costs as a percent income in the past 12 months			
		$99,999 or less	$100,000 to $199,999	$200,000 or more			Less than 15 percent	15.0 to 24.9 percent	25.0 to 29.9 percent	30.0 percent or more
U.S.	73,844	25.7	30.8	43.5	173,900	1,436	22.1	34.6	11.2	31.6
AL.	1,240	40.2	34.7	25.1	122,700	1,093	26.7	36.3	10.0	26.3
AK.	156	10.5	22.7	66.8	254,000	1,746	22.4	37.7	13.1	26.7
AZ.	1,490	25.9	34.6	39.5	166,000	1,277	22.2	34.5	10.8	31.4
AR.	740	45.8	35.0	19.2	109,500	979	30.1	35.3	9.1	24.7
CA.	6,805	9.5	13.4	77.1	373,100	2,059	15.4	29.8	12.5	41.6
CO.	1,292	11.5	26.3	62.2	240,500	1,516	21.6	36.8	11.1	30.0
CT.	888	6.9	24.5	68.5	267,000	1,986	18.0	33.9	12.5	35.1
DE.	243	14.0	27.2	58.7	226,200	1,504	23.9	34.1	10.8	30.6
DC.	111	5.0	5.5	89.5	470,500	2,236	27.1	32.2	11.6	28.4
FL.	4,672	31.5	32.7	35.8	153,300	1,368	18.5	31.0	11.0	38.6
GA.	2,222	34.0	35.0	31.0	141,600	1,288	23.8	34.5	10.4	30.5
HI.	253	3.8	5.8	90.4	500,000	2,220	15.1	28.0	13.0	43.5
ID.	408	22.5	43.8	33.7	159,000	1,142	22.3	35.4	11.8	29.9
IL.	3,154	25.7	33.1	41.1	169,600	1,565	20.7	35.2	11.1	32.6
IN.	1,712	38.0	40.5	21.5	122,200	1,062	29.0	38.0	9.3	23.3
IA.	875	36.6	40.1	23.4	126,900	1,118	29.7	39.7	9.4	20.9
KS.	736	38.4	36.3	25.3	129,700	1,241	26.3	39.5	11.6	22.1
KY.	1,149	40.3	36.9	22.9	120,900	1,074	27.0	37.4	9.6	25.5
LA.	1,140	35.6	35.4	29.0	140,300	1,166	30.2	33.5	8.7	27.2
ME.	384	23.4	35.8	40.8	172,800	1,268	21.2	35.5	11.3	31.5
MD.	1,437	9.0	20.0	71.0	280,200	1,867	21.2	34.8	12.1	31.6
MA.	1,561	5.5	14.6	79.9	327,200	1,976	19.4	34.3	12.3	33.7
MI.	2,704	42.3	34.6	23.1	117,500	1,207	24.8	36.6	10.6	27.5
MN.	1,517	18.1	38.9	43.0	180,100	1,438	23.5	38.8	11.8	25.6
MS.	733	51.1	30.2	18.7	97,500	1,021	26.2	33.0	9.8	30.3
MO.	1,582	35.0	38.6	26.4	133,200	1,162	25.8	37.3	10.0	26.4
MT.	272	21.9	31.3	46.9	190,100	1,259	23.0	35.7	12.1	28.9
NE.	482	32.6	43.3	24.1	132,700	1,226	25.9	39.6	10.8	23.2
NV.	544	24.2	36.8	39.0	165,300	1,361	20.0	32.7	10.9	35.7
NH.	364	11.0	26.7	62.3	233,300	1,778	16.5	36.4	13.1	33.7
NJ.	2,034	7.5	16.4	76.1	307,700	2,296	15.5	30.7	12.6	40.7
NM.	512	28.3	36.1	35.6	159,200	1,193	24.9	31.9	10.8	31.1
NY.	3,873	17.9	20.9	61.2	277,600	1,956	20.1	30.7	11.1	37.6
NC.	2,415	28.4	37.3	34.2	154,300	1,205	24.8	35.4	10.4	28.9
ND.	193	31.3	34.2	34.5	155,400	1,207	32.5	40.4	9.3	17.6
OH.	3,016	36.3	40.3	23.4	127,000	1,209	25.4	37.6	10.6	26.0
OK.	949	42.3	37.3	20.4	116,500	1,094	28.5	36.2	10.4	24.2
OR.	927	13.5	27.8	58.6	229,700	1,502	17.8	34.4	12.1	35.1
PA.	3,405	27.3	34.3	38.3	164,200	1,373	23.9	35.8	11.0	28.8
RI.	245	7.8	32.0	60.1	232,300	1,751	18.8	32.6	12.3	36.1
SC.	1,224	34.7	35.4	29.8	139,200	1,144	24.7	34.8	9.7	29.8
SD.	223	34.1	39.2	26.6	138,400	1,150	25.5	40.1	12.2	21.9
TN.	1,653	32.4	38.6	29.0	140,300	1,138	23.2	36.9	10.8	28.4
TX.	5,634	36.1	36.1	27.8	132,000	1,375	24.8	36.5	10.6	27.4
UT.	623	9.8	36.4	53.9	211,400	1,377	21.7	36.3	12.7	29.0
VT.	180	12.4	31.5	56.1	218,300	1,482	17.6	34.7	12.7	34.8
VA.	2,005	14.8	25.9	59.3	239,300	1,645	22.5	35.4	12.2	29.4
WA.	1,638	10.8	25.1	64.2	250,800	1,667	18.0	34.9	12.5	34.1
WV.	534	48.7	33.4	18.0	103,200	939	32.1	34.1	10.1	23.4
WI.	1,538	21.4	42.8	35.8	163,000	1,352	19.8	38.9	11.8	29.1
WY.	155	17.8	34.1	48.1	195,500	1,330	25.6	37.8	12.5	23.7

[1] For homes with a mortgage. Includes all forms of debt where the property is pledged as security for repayment of the debt, including deeds of trust, land contracts, home equity loans. Also includes cost of property insurance, utilities, real estate taxes, etc.

Source: U.S. Census Bureau, 2013 American Community Survey, B25075, "Value"; B25077, "Median Value"; B25088, "Median Selected Monthly Owner Costs by Mortgage Status"; and B25091, "Mortgage Status by Selected Monthly Owner Cost as a Percentage of Household Income in the Past 12 Months"; <http://factfinder2.census.gov>, accessed December 2014. See also <http://www.census.gov/acs/www/>.

Table 1015. Renter-Occupied Housing Units—Gross Rent by State: 2013

[In percent, except as indicated (42,447 represents 42,447,000). The American Community Survey universe includes the household population, and excludes the population living in institutions, college dormitories, and other group quarters. Based on a sample and subject to sampling variability; see Appendix III]

State	Total [1] (1,000)	Percent of units with gross rent of—					Median gross rent (dol.)	Gross rent as a percent of household income in the past 12 months [2]			
		$299 or less	$300 to $499	$500 to $749	$750 to $999	$1,000 or more		Less than 15.0 percent	15.0 to 24.9 percent	25.0 to 29.0 percent	30.0 percent or more
U.S.	42,447	4.6	7.3	20.7	23.0	39.2	905	11.2	22.9	10.6	47.6
AL.	582	6.7	14.3	30.6	22.2	15.7	694	13.4	20.4	9.8	43.6
AK.	90	1.5	5.1	10.4	19.6	55.7	1,117	14.9	24.9	12.5	39.8
AZ.	911	2.5	6.1	23.2	26.2	37.0	890	11.8	24.2	10.5	45.8
AR.	386	5.8	14.7	37.5	21.2	11.0	659	11.8	23.2	10.1	42.2
CA.	5,846	2.8	3.3	8.9	17.4	64.5	1,224	8.6	21.2	10.9	54.1
CO.	711	3.1	4.2	18.8	24.7	45.2	971	9.7	24.4	11.3	49.0
CT.	451	6.1	5.8	9.7	22.8	51.1	1,040	11.0	21.9	11.0	49.3
DE.	96	4.8	4.1	11.9	26.1	46.7	999	9.8	23.9	11.1	46.7
DC.	161	7.7	3.0	5.9	14.7	65.9	1,307	11.4	24.6	11.7	46.7
FL.	2,539	2.9	4.2	16.3	27.5	44.5	972	8.0	20.6	10.3	53.4
GA.	1,325	4.1	7.6	23.4	28.1	31.0	850	10.5	21.7	10.7	47.8
HI.	197	3.4	3.4	6.0	11.2	69.1	1,414	9.2	20.5	10.9	50.8
ID.	180	4.9	12.0	33.3	22.0	20.5	725	11.7	23.7	11.9	43.1
IL.	1,629	5.2	7.1	20.5	26.9	35.9	885	12.2	24.1	10.4	45.8
IN.	786	5.1	10.5	34.4	26.8	17.1	730	12.3	23.7	9.8	45.2
IA.	361	5.2	15.7	36.3	21.0	15.3	679	16.2	25.2	10.8	39.6
KS.	378	4.5	11.9	30.9	24.1	22.1	745	13.5	25.4	11.3	41.3
KY.	556	7.6	14.3	33.3	21.3	13.1	668	13.2	23.5	10.1	40.1
LA.	588	5.7	11.0	27.2	23.9	22.5	763	12.7	19.7	9.1	45.5
ME.	163	7.6	10.0	27.3	23.9	23.1	760	9.0	21.2	13.0	47.8
MD.	725	4.4	3.5	7.4	16.0	64.6	1,210	10.2	24.3	11.3	48.4
MA.	976	7.0	7.7	11.2	17.2	53.6	1,077	12.2	23.6	11.4	47.5
MI.	1,129	5.8	9.2	29.9	25.8	23.6	768	11.4	22.2	10.0	48.2
MN.	603	6.3	9.3	22.4	25.8	31.5	832	12.6	25.6	11.0	44.8
MS.	358	7.7	12.7	29.4	23.7	14.4	708	10.9	21.4	9.4	43.5
MO.	780	5.3	11.8	31.8	24.4	20.0	734	12.7	23.4	10.6	44.7
MT.	135	6.7	15.8	30.0	19.9	19.5	690	13.1	23.8	10.9	42.5
NE.	248	4.6	13.4	34.5	24.1	17.7	714	13.6	27.6	10.3	41.3
NV.	458	1.7	3.6	20.7	27.8	43.2	952	11.5	25.7	10.9	46.7
NH.	155	4.5	5.2	12.6	26.3	47.5	995	9.7	28.0	11.9	45.3
NJ.	1,142	4.8	3.4	6.6	18.1	63.8	1,171	10.6	22.7	10.7	51.1
NM.	242	5.4	11.1	26.8	23.7	24.9	772	10.9	22.4	10.2	46.0
NY.	3,346	5.3	6.3	13.1	16.3	55.5	1,109	12.0	21.4	10.3	50.8
NC.	1,343	4.5	8.7	29.6	26.8	23.0	778	11.0	23.9	10.4	45.1
ND.	105	6.3	13.4	32.9	20.6	18.9	690	18.5	25.3	8.2	38.6
OH.	1,549	6.3	12.1	34.6	25.1	16.6	709	13.5	23.6	10.6	44.6
OK.	499	5.8	11.8	34.0	23.4	16.6	705	14.6	24.6	10.0	40.4
OR.	597	3.4	6.0	20.7	29.9	36.1	887	10.4	23.5	10.3	50.2
PA.	1,534	5.8	8.8	24.0	25.0	30.2	828	12.1	22.6	10.8	46.1
RI.	161	8.9	6.8	15.0	29.4	36.8	918	11.4	23.0	10.7	49.3
SC.	571	5.2	9.7	28.2	25.7	21.2	766	10.8	21.9	9.1	45.2
SD.	109	10.4	17.1	33.3	19.1	12.6	637	15.7	28.1	11.6	36.4
TN.	837	5.5	10.8	29.6	24.7	20.8	748	11.1	22.7	10.5	44.6
TX.	3,477	3.4	6.4	24.8	27.6	32.5	857	12.7	25.1	10.7	44.2
UT.	277	3.1	5.7	21.7	27.7	36.2	881	12.4	25.6	11.2	43.6
VT.	73	7.7	5.7	20.4	27.7	32.7	865	8.0	23.2	11.8	50.3
VA.	1,051	4.1	5.5	13.5	18.7	52.9	1,086	10.9	24.4	11.8	45.6
WA.	1,007	4.0	4.6	15.9	24.5	46.9	989	10.3	24.6	11.2	48.0
WV.	204	7.3	17.1	33.2	16.3	9.6	620	14.4	19.1	9.2	38.4
WI.	751	4.9	9.3	32.3	28.9	20.0	758	12.3	25.4	11.8	44.3
WY.	69	5.1	10.5	26.4	25.6	23.9	780	16.5	25.1	10.7	37.4

[1] Includes units with no cash rent. [2] Percentage calculated from totals which include units "not computed"; therefore, rows will not total 100 percent.

Source: U.S. Census Bureau, 2013 American Community Survey, B25063, "Gross Rent"; B25064, "Median Gross Rent"; and B25070, "Gross Rent as a Percentage of Household Income in Past 12 Months"; <http://factfinder.census.gov>, accessed December 2014.

Table 1016. Mortgage Characteristics—Owner-Occupied Units: 2013

[In thousands (75,676 represents 75,676,000). As of Fall. Based on the American Housing Survey; see Appendix III]

Mortgage characteristic	Total owner occupied units	Housing unit characteristics		Household characteristics			
		New construc-tion [1]	Mobile homes	Black [2]	His-panic [3]	Elderly [4]	Below poverty level
ALL OWNERS							
Total.............	**75,676**	**1,816**	**4,577**	**6,482**	**6,899**	**21,656**	**7,253**
Mortgages currently on property: [5]							
None, owned free and clear.......	27,326	351	2,927	2,094	2,154	14,121	4,125
Regular and home equity mortgages [6]........	47,928	1,458	1,642	4,334	4,715	7,139	3,048
Regular mortgage..........	45,557	1,433	1,563	4,184	4,554	6,144	2,870
Home equity lump sum mortgage..........	2,041	20	57	190	143	456	129
Home equity line of credit..........	3,928	33	63	150	221	995	155
Number of regular and home equity mortgages:							
1 mortgage..........	42,959	1,414	1,583	3,975	4,337	6,532	2,878
2 mortgages..........	4,874	43	59	356	376	597	170
3 mortgages or more..........	96	–	–	2	3	10	–
Type of mortgage:							
Regular and home equity lump sum..........	1,133	10	22	88	67	125	33
With home equity line of credit..........	16	–	–	2	1	2	–
No home equity line of credit..........	1,118	10	22	86	67	123	33
Regular, no home equity lump sum..........	44,424	1,423	1,541	4,097	4,487	6,019	2,837
With home equity line of credit..........	2,413	18	18	98	133	326	70
No home equity line of credit..........	42,011	1,405	1,522	3,999	4,354	5,693	2,767
Home equity lump sum, no regular..........	907	10	35	102	76	332	96
With home equity line of credit..........	35	–	–	3	3	4	3
No home equity line of credit..........	872	10	35	99	73	328	93
No regular or home equity lump sum..........	29,211	373	2,980	2,195	2,268	15,181	4,287
With home equity line of credit..........	1,464	14	44	47	85	664	83
No home equity line of credit..........	27,748	359	2,935	2,148	2,183	14,517	4,204
OWNERS WITH ONE OR MORE REGULAR OR LUMP SUM HOME EQUITY MORTGAGES							
Total.............	**46,464**	**1,443**	**1,597**	**4,287**	**4,630**	**6,476**	**2,966**
Type of primary mortgage:							
FHA..........	9,200	311	157	1,433	1,272	828	520
VA..........	1,660	179	31	208	146	233	53
RHS/RD [7]..........	558	33	28	54	67	30	58
Other types..........	29,670	791	1,056	2,014	2,645	4,233	1,674
Mortgage origination:							
Placed new mortgage(s)..........	46,219	1,437	1,581	4,250	4,588	6,433	2,910
Primary obtained when property acquired........	26,490	1,249	1,306	2,836	3,189	2,934	2,116
Obtained later..........	19,729	188	275	1,415	1,399	3,499	794
Assumed..........	201	5	16	32	29	36	46
Wrap-around..........	25	1	–	4	7	6	6
Combination of the above..........	19	–	–	1	5	1	4
Payment plan of primary mortgage: [8]							
Fixed payment, self amortizing..........	37,325	1,233	1,205	3,279	3,624	4,794	1,980
Adjustable rate mortgage..........	1,225	13	12	119	116	182	90
Adjustable term mortgage..........	110	–	–	9	12	50	13
Graduated payment mortgage..........	133	1	2	9	16	1	10
Balloon..........	200	–	6	23	46	18	13
Combination of the above..........	108	3	8	6	12	27	6
Payment plan of secondary mortgage: [8]							
Units with two or more mortgages..........	2,478	25	40	256	241	264	98
Fixed payment, self amortizing..........	2,029	12	40	226	182	212	77
Adjustable rate mortgage..........	97	13	–	8	6	6	5
Adjustable term mortgage..........	41	–	–	2	5	7	3
Graduated payment mortgage..........	16	–	–	–	1	–	–
Balloon..........	19	–	–	2	4	7	–
Combination of the above..........	21	–	–	3	–	4	–
Reason primary refinanced:							
Units with a refinanced primary mortgage [6]........	16,835	175	211	1,175	1,181	2,410	514
To get a lower interest rate..........	13,659	156	131	778	837	1,863	343
To reduce monthly payment..........	5,496	52	55	441	436	741	162
To reduce payment period..........	2,521	9	11	138	132	259	28
To increase payment period..........	407	6	–	20	19	71	9
To receive cash..........	1,531	2	26	171	127	292	67
To suspend or temporarily reduce payments......	161	–	6	20	17	19	1
Other reason..........	1,353	12	45	151	107	210	87
Cash received in primary mortgage refinance:							
Units receiving refinance cash..........	1,531	2	26	171	127	292	67
Median amount received (dol.)..........	20,000	–	15,000	20,000	20,000	25,000	20,000

– Represents or rounds to zero. [1] Constructed in the past 4 years. [2] For persons who selected this race group only. See footnote 3, Table 1009. [3] Persons of Hispanic origin may be of any race. [4] 65 years old and over. [5] Regular mortgages include all mortgages not classified as home-equity or reverse. [6] Figures may not add to total because more than one category may apply to a unit. [7] Rural Housing Service/Rural Development mortgage. [8] Includes plans not reported or others not shown separately.

Source: U.S. Census Bureau, "American Housing Survey: National Summary Tables – AHS 2013," <http://www.census.gov/programs-surveys/ahs/data.html>, accessed December 2014.

Table 1017.
Table 1017. Home Purchase Loans by Race/Ethnicity and Sex: 2013

[Amount in millions of dollars (714,634 represents $714,634,000,000). Data is the final 2013 National Aggregate data]

Race and gender [1,2,3]	Applications received		Loans originated		Applications approved, not accepted		Applications denied		Applications withdrawn		Files closed for incompleteness	
	Number	Amount (million dollars)	Number	Amount (million dollars)	Number	Amount (million dollars)	Number	Amount (million dollars)	Number	Amount (million dollars)	Number	Amount (million dollars)
Total..........	3,086,463	714,634	2,102,721	511,454	190,541	37,718	448,217	78,618	278,253	69,358	66,731	17,486
White..........	2,323,377	511,101	1,633,902	374,677	135,318	25,402	308,282	52,337	201,051	47,506	44,824	11,179
Male..........	751,741	159,467	504,697	111,772	46,967	8,459	115,163	19,365	68,406	15,832	16,508	4,040
Female..........	477,363	80,989	324,316	58,162	27,866	3,845	73,640	9,528	42,198	7,730	9,343	1,724
Joint (male/female)..........	1,088,550	269,464	802,110	204,089	59,665	12,959	118,146	23,245	89,864	23,805	18,765	5,365
Black..........	111,429	15,970	49,573	8,836	11,170	1,093	39,221	4,018	8,827	1,561	2,638	461
Male..........	38,456	5,703	17,907	3,184	3,688	369	12,535	1,394	3,281	571	1,045	185
Female..........	46,943	5,780	20,019	3,083	4,382	382	17,844	1,604	3,635	550	1,063	161
Joint (male/female)..........	25,096	4,390	11,488	2,542	2,901	325	8,322	975	1,871	434	514	113
Hispanic or Latino..........	181,411	30,667	102,637	19,301	14,830	1,873	42,172	5,503	16,858	3,073	4,914	917
Male..........	81,755	13,795	45,654	8,565	6,995	877	19,166	2,524	7,690	1,405	2,250	423
Female..........	46,830	6,939	26,348	4,304	3,355	385	11,298	1,314	4,513	729	1,316	207
Joint (male/female)..........	51,991	9,818	30,374	6,381	4,330	598	11,356	1,629	4,610	928	1,321	283
Asian..........	234,462	73,720	161,226	51,094	13,591	4,443	29,968	8,781	22,831	7,189	6,846	2,214
Male..........	99,153	29,760	67,440	20,354	5,991	1,865	12,654	3,585	9,974	3,005	3,094	952
Female..........	50,886	13,373	34,459	9,136	2,825	776	7,370	1,829	4,793	1,246	1,439	385
Joint (male/female)..........	83,815	30,394	59,054	21,508	4,684	1,774	9,838	3,336	7,959	2,908	2,280	868
Native Hawaiian/Other Pacific Islander..........	7,210	1,649	4,464	1,074	403	90	1,359	254	775	180	209	51
Male..........	3,116	666	1,887	426	170	32	630	114	337	73	92	22
Female..........	1,994	395	1,218	255	109	23	395	61	213	44	59	13
Joint (male/female)..........	2,055	579	1,333	387	120	35	324	77	221	63	57	16
American Indian/Alaska Native..........	13,023	1,857	5,995	1,052	1,529	142	4,232	441	978	175	289	47
Male..........	5,386	814	2,548	463	588	60	1,716	190	422	83	112	18
Female..........	4,107	505	1,708	272	482	38	1,498	135	302	44	117	16
Joint (male/female)..........	2,863	470	1,305	273	411	41	902	104	187	40	58	13
Two or more minority races..........	1,462	347	849	222	90	20	319	51	157	43	47	11
Male..........	562	125	319	75	37	7	112	18	72	21	22	4
Female..........	478	97	273	62	23	4	119	17	49	11	14	3
Joint (male/female)..........	405	122	254	83	29	9	78	16	33	10	11	4
Joint [4]..........	47,637	14,226	33,358	10,519	2,915	756	6,382	1,376	3,978	1,251	1,004	324
Race not available [5]..........	347,863	95,765	213,354	63,981	25,525	5,771	58,454	11,359	39,656	11,453	10,874	3,200
Male..........	48,022	11,871	25,299	7,151	4,722	822	10,259	1,804	6,153	1,615	1,589	480
Female..........	27,751	5,393	14,645	3,288	2,341	322	6,434	875	3,484	732	847	176
Joint (male/female)..........	57,889	17,483	36,186	11,821	4,445	978	8,930	1,949	6,675	2,140	1,653	596

[1] Applicants are shown in only one race category. [2] Total includes those cases in which gender was reported and in those in which gender information was not available. [3] Applicants are shown in only one gender category. [4] "Joint" means with two applicants, one reported a single designation of "White" and the other applicant reported one or more minority racial designations. [5] "Not available" includes situations in which information was reported as not provided or not applicable.

Source: Federal Financial Institutions Examination Council, "Home Mortgage Disclosure Act National Aggregate Report," <http://www.ffiec.gov/Hmda/default.htm>, accessed June 2015.

Table 1018. Heating Equipment and Fuels for Occupied Units: 2005 to 2013

[108,871 represents 108,871,000. As of Fall. Data for 2005 to 2009 based on population controls from Census 2000. Data beginning 2011 based on Census 2010 controls. Based on American Housing Survey. See Appendix III]

Type of equipment or fuel	Number (1,000)					Percent distribution	
	2005	2007	2009	2011	2013	2011	2013
Occupied units, total.........................	108,871	110,692	111,806	114,907	115,894	100.0	100.0
Heating equipment:							
Warm air furnace.........................	68,275	69,582	71,141	73,687	74,676	64.1	64.4
Steam or hot water......................	12,880	12,760	12,506	12,624	12,488	11.0	10.8
Heat pumps..............................	12,484	12,996	13,264	13,523	13,508	11.8	11.7
Built-in electric units...................	4,699	4,802	4,761	4,865	5,103	4.2	4.4
Floor, wall, or pipeless furnace.........	5,102	4,994	4,802	4,505	4,588	3.9	4.0
Room heaters with flue.................	1,294	1,135	950	932	852	0.8	0.7
Room heaters without flue..............	1,327	1,188	1,109	1,094	1,034	1.0	0.9
Fireplaces, stoves, portable heaters or other....	2,411	2,756	2,887	3,208	3,256	2.8	2.8
None......................................	399	478	386	468	389	0.4	0.3
House main heating fuel:							
Electricity................................	34,263	36,079	37,851	40,385	41,849	35.1	36.1
Utility gas...............................	56,317	56,681	56,806	57,721	58,534	50.2	50.5
Bottled, tank, or liquid propane gas....	6,228	6,095	5,817	5,415	5,112	4.7	4.4
Fuel oil, kerosene, etc..................	9,929	9,317	8,813	8,599	7,625	7.5	6.6
Coal or coke............................	95	91	98	79	99	0.1	0.1
Wood and other fuel....................	1,640	1,487	2,035	2,240	2,286	1.9	2.0
None......................................	398	464	386	468	389	0.4	0.3
Cooking fuel:							
Electricity................................	65,297	66,276	67,078	68,879	69,319	59.9	59.8
Gas [1]...................................	43,316	44,194	44,477	45,759	46,349	39.8	40.0
Other fuel...............................	51	26	68	92	71	0.1	0.1
None......................................	206	17	183	177	154	0.2	0.1

[1] Includes utility, bottled, tank, and liquid propane gas.

Source: U.S. Census Bureau, "American Housing Survey: National Summary Tables – AHS 2013," <http://www.census.gov/programs-surveys/ahs/data.html>, accessed December 2014.

Table 1019. Occupied Housing Units—Housing Indicators by Selected Characteristics of the Householder: 2013

[In thousands of units (115,894 represents 115,894,000). As of Fall. Based on the American Housing Survey; see Appendix III]

Characteristic	Total occupied units	Tenure		Black [1]		Hispanic origin [2]		Elderly [3]		Households below poverty level	
		Owner	Renter	Owner	Renter	Owner	Renter	Owner	Renter	Owner	Renter
Total units..................	115,894	75,676	40,218	6,482	8,542	6,899	7,783	21,656	5,151	7,253	11,140
Amenities:											
Porch, deck, balcony or patio.........	98,521	69,581	28,941	5,671	5,738	6,145	5,222	19,836	3,319	6,355	7,608
Telephone available....................	113,307	74,377	38,930	6,329	8,188	6,827	7,539	21,400	4,999	7,102	10,757
Usable fireplace.......................	40,233	34,435	5,799	2,222	923	2,257	834	9,418	526	1,975	914
Separate dining room..................	62,176	48,453	13,723	4,417	3,060	4,257	2,689	13,824	1,536	4,022	3,369
With 2 or more living rooms or recreation rooms......................	37,086	33,377	3,709	2,444	586	2,013	406	9,505	386	1,854	498
Garage or carport with home.........	77,058	61,097	15,960	4,307	2,198	5,343	3,116	17,881	1,949	4,838	3,393
Cars and trucks available:											
No cars, trucks, or vans..............	9,444	2,074	7,370	385	2,503	153	1,425	1,216	1,897	713	3,690
1 car with or without trucks or vans...	53,616	33,978	19,638	3,007	4,121	2,845	3,504	12,082	2,425	3,900	4,939
2 cars...................................	31,183	23,785	7,397	1,852	1,075	2,184	1,481	5,194	426	1,263	1,106
3 or more cars..........................	9,865	8,376	1,489	667	176	901	344	1202	48	367	141
1 or more trucks or vans..............	48,478	36,948	11,529	2,774	1,711	3,829	2,750	8,764	902	2,886	2,522
Selected deficiencies:											
Signs of rats in last 12 months.......	1,034	572	461	75	132	73	141	148	50	84	176
Signs of mice in last 12 months......	10,498	7,160	3,338	552	820	413	689	1,984	383	705	1,113
Holes in floors.........................	1,045	465	580	50	162	63	142	75	45	113	245
Open cracks or holes..................	5,098	2,577	2,521	354	684	245	506	541	185	387	904
Paint (interior of unit).................	1,841	804	1,037	114	301	71	221	169	104	145	424
No electrical wiring.....................	190	111	79	5	16	16	37	32	14	24	41
Exposed wiring.........................	1,893	1078	815	88	192	85	189	307	111	145	318
Rooms without electric outlet.........	1,621	813	808	72	207	72	163	234	78	110	270
Water leakage from inside structure [4]........................	7,928	4,126	3,802	846	952	515	693	1,605	278	745	1,106
Water leakage from outside structure [4]......................	9,446	6,445	3,000	131	706	70	537	172	237	89	882

[1] For persons who selected this race group only. See footnote 3, Table 1009. [2] Persons of Hispanic origin may be of any race. [3] Householders 65 years old and over. [4] During the 12 months prior to the survey.

Source: U.S. Census Bureau, "American Housing Survey: National Summary Tables – AHS 2013," <http://www.census.gov/programs-surveys/ahs/data.html>, accessed December 2014.

Table 1020. Home Remodeling—Number of Households With Work Done by Amount Spent: 2014

[In thousands, except percent (1,360 represents 1,360,000). As of Fall 2014. For work done in the prior 12 months. Based on household survey and subject to sampling error; see source]

Remodeling project	Total households with work done [1] Number	Total households with work done [1] Percent of households	Households with work done by outside contractor	Number of households by amount spent Under $1,000	Number of households by amount spent $1,000 to $2,999	Number of households by amount spent Over $3,000
Conversion of garage/attic/basement into living space	1,360	1.10	284	238	271	248
Remodel bathroom	6,149	4.98	2,069	2,151	1,236	1,320
Remodel kitchen	3,782	3.06	1,443	1,079	664	1,330
Remodel bedroom	2,892	2.34	438	1,575	361	292
Add/extend garage	380	0.31	179	30	18	166
Aluminum windows	629	0.51	264	171	91	134
Vinyl windows	2,054	1.66	1,266	580	453	682
Clad-wood/wood windows	435	0.35	216	65	52	149
Ceramic tile floors	2,185	1.77	836	1,058	319	240
Skylights	435	0.35	134	95	104	42
Ceramic wall tile	856	0.69	290	379	151	71
Convert room to home office	1,122	0.91	78	637	134	28
Convert room to home theater	430	0.35	17	71	25	20
Remodel other rooms	2,513	2.03	477	1,187	435	365
Add bathroom	644	0.52	141	105	113	169
Add other rooms - exterior addition	428	0.35	177	33	34	194
Add deck/porch/patio	2,284	1.85	874	390	650	812
Roofing	3,771	3.05	2,481	512	515	1,811
Siding - vinyl/metal	1,221	0.99	591	207	293	413
Hardwood floors	2,279	1.85	952	468	668	655
Laminate flooring	2,195	1.78	735	958	636	237
Vinyl flooring	1,349	1.09	354	778	177	37
Carpeting	3,055	2.47	1,955	1,068	1,038	259
Kitchen cabinets	1,685	1.36	621	400	291	467
Kitchen counter tops	1,840	1.49	964	342	350	580
Exterior doors	2,233	1.81	922	1,151	353	167
Interior doors	1,656	1.34	431	936	135	85
Garage doors	1,186	0.96	710	547	284	59
Concrete or masonry work	1,685	1.36	777	614	310	370
Swimming pool - in ground	330	0.27	151	28	14	123

[1] Includes no response and amount unknown.

Source: GfK US, LLC, the GfK MRI Division ©, <http://www.gfkmri.com/>.

Table 1021. Home Improvement Loans by Race: 2013

[Applications in thousands (832.9 represents 832,900); values in millions of dollars (57,739.9 represents $57,739,900,000). Data is the final 2013 National Aggregate data]

Item	Unit	Total [1,2]	White, total	Black, total	Asian, total	Joint, total [3]	Hispanic or Latino [4]
Applications received							
Number	1,000	832.9	607.8	85.4	21.3	9.8	75.8
Amount	Mil. dol.	57,739.9	43,261.6	2,286.2	2,882.1	949.0	3,011.1
Loans originated							
Number	1,000	424.6	340.6	26.0	10.3	5.3	27.6
Amount	Mil. dol.	35,523.6	27,611.0	846.8	1,767.0	580.4	1,352.7
Applications approved but not accepted							
Number	1,000	37.9	27.6	2.8	1.1	0.4	3.3
Amount	Mil. dol.	2,428.9	1,806.1	89.9	143.0	40.9	135.6
Applications denied							
Number	1,000	316.1	200.5	53.3	8.0	3.4	41.1
Amount	Mil. dol.	13,298.2	9,198.6	1,098.9	622.0	221.0	1,151.1
Applications withdrawn							
Number	1,000	41.7	30.3	2.5	1.4	0.5	2.9
Amount	Mil. dol.	4,676.3	3,361.5	180.5	248.5	71.9	270.3
Files closed for incompleteness							
Number	1,000	12.6	8.9	0.8	0.5	0.2	0.9
Amount	Mil. dol.	1,812.9	1,284.5	70.2	101.5	34.8	101.5

[1] Applicants are shown in only one race category. Applicants are categorized by the race of the first person listed on the application unless the 'joint' designation applies. [2] Total includes other races, not shown separately. [3] Joint means one applicant on an application reports a single designation of "White" and the other applicant reports one or more minority racial designations. [4] Persons of Hispanic origin may be of any race.

Source: Federal Financial Institutions Examination Council, "Home Mortgage Disclosure Act National Aggregate Report," <http://www.ffiec.gov/Hmda/default.htm>, accessed June 2015.

Table 1022. Net Stock of Residential Fixed Assets: 1990 to 2013

[In billions of dollars (5,851 represents $5,851,000,000,000). End of year estimates]

Item	1990	1995	2000	2005	2009	2010	2011	2012	2013
Total residential fixed assets	**5,851**	**7,416**	**10,041**	**15,483**	**16,037**	**16,115**	**16,228**	**16,665**	**17,770**
By type of owner and legal form of organization:									
Private	5,702	7,228	9,810	15,148	15,709	15,783	15,891	16,317	17,400
Corporate	63	73	100	151	167	170	169	172	178
Noncorporate	5,639	7,154	9,710	14,997	15,542	15,613	15,722	16,145	17,222
Government	149	188	232	335	329	332	337	348	370
Federal	52	62	75	103	99	98	99	101	107
State and local	97	127	156	232	230	234	238	247	263
By tenure group: [1]									
Owner-occupied	4,184	5,485	7,596	12,052	12,479	12,527	12,642	13,021	13,968
Tenant-occupied	1,641	1,902	2,410	3,379	3,502	3,533	3,529	3,585	3,736

[1] Excludes stocks of other nonfarm residential assets, which consists primarily of dormitories and of fraternity and sorority houses.

Source: U.S. Bureau of Economic Analysis, Fixed Assets Accounts Tables, "Table 5.1 Current-Cost Net Stock of Residential Fixed Assets by Type of Owner, Legal Form of Organization, and Tenure Group," <http://www.bea.gov/iTable/index_FA.cfm>, accessed January 2015.

Table 1023. Commercial Buildings—Summary: 2012

[5,557 represents 5,557,000. Includes mall buildings. Building type based on predominant activity in which the occupants were engaged. Based on the Commercial Buildings Energy Consumption Survey (CBECS), a sample survey of building representatives conducted in 2012; subject to sampling variability]

Characteristic	All buildings (1,000)	Total floor-space (mil. sq. ft.)	Total workers in all buildings (1,000)	Mean square foot per building [1] (1,000)	Mean square foot per worker [1]	Mean operating hours per week [1]
All buildings	**5,557**	**87,043**	**88,182**	**15.7**	**987**	**62**
Building floorspace (sq. ft.):						
1,001 to 5,000	2,777	8,036	10,232	2.9	785	56
5,001 to 10,000	1,231	8,910	9,231	7.2	965	62
10,001 to 25,000	882	14,083	14,183	16.0	993	65
25,001 to 50,000	332	11,917	11,327	35.9	1,052	72
50,001 to 100,000	199	13,938	12,354	69.9	1,128	80
100,001 to 200,000	90	12,415	11,310	137.9	1,098	89
200,001 to 500,000	38	10,670	10,347	284.3	1,031	100
Over 500,000	8	7,074	9,196	885.0	769	117
Principal activity within building:						
Education	389	12,237	10,885	31.5	1,124	53
Food sales	177	1,252	1,172	7.1	1,067	121
Food service	380	1,819	3,431	4.8	530	82
Health care	157	4,155	7,613	26.5	546	60
Inpatient	10	2,374	4,281	247.8	555	168
Outpatient	147	1,781	3,333	12.1	535	53
Lodging	158	5,826	3,066	36.9	1,900	165
Mercantile	602	11,330	9,117	18.8	1,243	64
Retail (other than mall)	438	5,439	4,023	12.4	1,352	62
Enclosed and strip malls	164	5,890	5,094	35.9	1,156	69
Office	1,012	15,952	33,756	15.8	473	55
Public assembly	352	5,559	3,108	15.8	1,789	56
Public order and safety	84	1,440	1,854	17.2	776	113
Religious worship	412	4,557	1,940	11.1	2,350	31
Service	619	4,627	4,031	7.5	1,148	56
Warehouse and storage	796	13,032	6,362	16.4	2,048	67
Other	125	2,002	1,611	16.0	1,242	61
Vacant	296	3,256	236	11.0	13,811	8
Number of establishments:						
One	4,205	54,944	52,072	13.1	1,055	64
2 to 5	862	17,756	18,916	20.6	939	65
6 to 10	147	4,425	5,890	30.1	751	77
11 to 20	68	3,704	5,276	54.8	702	70
More than 20	27	3,821	6,028	140.9	634	84
Currently unoccupied	248	2,393	–	9.6	(X)	–
Year constructed:						
Before 1920	362	3,980	3,309	11.0	1,203	48
1920 to 1945	488	6,020	6,003	12.3	1,003	52
1946 to 1959	599	7,381	6,566	12.3	1,124	51
1960 to 1969	639	10,362	9,851	16.2	1,052	61
1970 to 1979	684	10,846	12,536	15.9	865	61
1980 to 1989	915	15,185	17,468	16.6	869	65
1990 to 1999	845	13,803	13,432	16.3	1,028	68
2000 to 2003	375	7,215	7,471	19.2	966	66
2004 to 2007	347	6,524	5,993	18.8	1,089	69
2008 to 2012	303	5,726	5,552	18.9	1,031	76

– Represents zero. X Not applicable. [1] For explanation of mean, see Guide to Tabular Presentation.

Source: U.S. Energy Information Administration, "2012 CBECS Survey Data," <http://www.eia.gov/consumption/commercial/data/2012/>, accessed March 2015.

Manufactures

This section presents summary data for manufacturing as a whole and more detailed information for major industry groups and selected products. The types of measures shown at the different levels include data for establishments, employment and payroll, value and quantity of production and shipments, value added by manufacture, inventories, and various indicators of financial status.

The principal sources of these data are U.S. Census Bureau reports of the censuses of manufactures conducted every 5 years, the *Annual Survey of Manufactures*. Reports on current activities of industries or current movements of individual commodities are compiled by such government agencies as the Bureau of Economic Analysis; Bureau of Labor Statistics; the Department of Commerce, International Trade Administration; and by private research or trade associations.

The *Quarterly Financial Report* publishes up-to-date aggregate statistics on the financial results and position of U.S. corporations. Based upon a sample survey, the QFR presents estimated statements of income and retained earnings, balance sheets, and related financial and operating ratios for manufacturing corporations with assets of $250,000 or over, and mining, wholesale trade and retail trade corporations with assets of $50 million and over or above industry-specific receipt cut-off values. These statistical data are classified by industry and by asset size.

Several private trade associations provide industry coverage for certain sections of the economy.

Censuses and annual surveys—The first census of manufactures covered the year 1809. Between 1809 and 1963, a census was conducted at periodic intervals. Since 1967, it has been taken every 5 years (for years ending in "2" and "7"). Results from the 2012 census are presented in this section utilizing the North American Industry Classification System (NAICS). Data from the 2012 Economic Census are being released on a continuing basis through 2016. For additional information see text, Section 15, Business Enterprise, and the Census Bureau Web site at <https://www.census.gov/econ/census/>. Census data, either directly reported or estimated from administrative records, are obtained for every manufacturing plant with one or more paid employees.

The *Annual Survey of Manufactures* (ASM), conducted for the first time in 1949, collects data for the years between censuses for the more general measure of manufacturing activity covered in detail by the censuses. The annual survey data are estimates derived from a scientifically selected sample of establishments. The *ASM* is a sample survey of approximately 50,000 establishments conducted annually, except for years ending in 2 and 7, at which time ASM statistics are included in the manufacturing sector of the Economic Census.

In 2012, there were approximately 297,000 active manufacturing establishments. For sample efficiency and cost considerations, the 2007 manufacturing population is partitioned into two groups: (1)

establishments eligible to be mailed a questionnaire, defined as the mail stratum, which is comprised of larger single-location manufacturing companies and all manufacturing establishments of multi-location companies, supplemental annually with large, and (2) establishments not eligible to be mailed a questionnaire, defined as the nonmail stratum, which includes small- and medium-sized single establishment companies.

Establishments and classification—Each of the establishments covered in the 2012 Economic Census—Manufacturing was classified in accordance with the industry definitions in the 2012 NAICS manual. In the NAICS system, an industry is generally defined as a group of establishments that have similar production processes. To the extent practical, the system uses supply-based or production-oriented concepts in defining industries. The resulting group of establishments must be significant in terms of number, value added by manufacture, value of shipments, and number of employees. Establishments frequently make products classified both in their industry (primary products) and other industries (secondary products). Industry statistics (employment, payroll, value added by manufacture, value of shipments, etc.) reflect the activities of the establishments, which may make both primary and secondary products. Product statistics, however, represent the output of all establishments without regard for the classification of the producing establishment. For this reason, when relating the industry statistics, especially the value of shipments, to the product statistics, the composition of the industry's output should be considered.

Establishment—An establishment is a single physical location where business is conducted or where services or industrial operations are performed. Data in this sector includes those establishments where manufacturing is performed. A separate report is required for each manufacturing establishment (plant) with one employee or more that is in operation at any time during the year. An establishment not in operation for any portion of the year is requested to return the report form with the proper notation in the "Operational Status" section of the form. In addition, the establishment is requested to report data on any employees, capital expenditures, inventories, or shipment from inventories during the year.

Durable goods—Items with a normal life expectancy of 3 years or more. Automobiles, furniture, household appliances, and mobile homes are common examples.

Nondurable goods—Items which generally last for only a short time (3 years or less). Food, beverages, clothing, shoes, and gasoline are common examples.

Statistical reliability—For a discussion of statistical collection and estimation, sampling procedures, and measures of statistical reliability applicable to Census Bureau data, see Appendix III.

Table 1024. Manufacturing—Contribution to Gross Domestic Product in Current and Real (2009) Dollars by Industry: 2000 to 2014

[In billions of dollars (10,284.8 represents $10,284,800,000,000). Value added GDP is the contribution of each industry's labor and capital to its gross output and to the overall gross domestic product (GDP) of the United States. Value added is equal to an industry's gross output (sales or receipts and other operating income, commodity taxes, and inventory change) minus its intermediate inputs (consumption of goods and services purchased from other industries or imported). Current-dollar value added is calculated as the sum of distributions by an industry to its labor and capital which are derived from the components of gross domestic income]

Industry	2007 NAICS code [1]	2000	2005	2010	2012	2013	2014
CURRENT DOLLARS							
Gross domestic product, total [2]	(X)	**10,284.8**	**13,093.7**	**14,964.4**	**16,163.2**	**16,768.1**	**17,418.9**
Private industries	(X)	8,956.0	11,366.3	12,826.5	13,972.0	14,556.4	15,175.3
Manufacturing	31–33	1,555.3	1,704.2	1,830.6	1,994.6	2,028.5	2,090.7
Durable goods	33, 321, 327	927.0	959.5	956.6	1,054.3	1,088.5	1,135.9
Wood products	321	28.3	34.9	22.1	23.9	25.9	(NA)
Nonmetallic mineral products	327	42.7	49.1	36.2	38.8	40.3	(NA)
Primary metals	331	47.0	56.6	48.4	63.0	63.6	(NA)
Fabricated metal products	332	121.7	122.9	120.3	137.6	139.9	(NA)
Machinery	333	113.3	114.9	122.1	143.6	144.6	(NA)
Computer and electronic products	334	225.9	211.0	249.0	252.6	255.1	(NA)
Electrical equipment, appliances, and components	335	45.8	43.2	50.0	49.1	50.6	(NA)
Motor vehicles, bodies and trailers, and parts	3361–63	138.1	136.9	92.9	126.3	138.0	(NA)
Other transportation equipment	3364–66, 69	71.2	89.9	112.2	117.0	123.2	(NA)
Furniture and related products	337	33.6	33.8	22.2	23.9	24.7	(NA)
Miscellaneous manufacturing	339	59.4	66.2	81.2	78.6	82.5	(NA)
Nondurable goods	31, 32 (except 321 and 327)	628.4	744.7	874.0	940.3	940.0	954.8
Food and beverage and tobacco products	311, 312	164.1	179.9	229.7	230.6	235.1	(NA)
Textile mills and textile product mills	313, 314	28.0	20.8	15.6	16.3	16.8	(NA)
Apparel and leather and allied products	315, 316	22.2	13.9	10.5	10.3	10.4	(NA)
Paper products	322	62.4	51.9	55.3	51.8	51.9	(NA)
Printing and related support activities	323	43.7	44.6	38.8	37.1	36.8	(NA)
Petroleum and coal products	324	53.1	142.7	130.0	181.7	169.7	(NA)
Chemical products	325	189.0	227.3	330.8	341.5	345.7	(NA)
Plastics and rubber products	326	65.9	63.5	63.3	71.1	73.4	(NA)
CHAINED (2009) DOLLARS							
Gross domestic product, total [2]	(X)	**12,559.7**	**14,234.2**	**14,783.8**	**15,369.2**	**15,710.3**	**16,085.6**
Private industries	(X)	10,826.2	12,311.1	12,650.2	13,185.8	13,482.8	13,829.7
Manufacturing	31–33	1,603.3	1,776.7	1,818.2	1,836.8	1,862.6	1,924.3
Durable goods	33, 321, 327	806.1	930.1	976.1	1,071.0	1,089.3	1,116.7
Wood products	321	25.1	26.1	21.4	23.7	22.1	(NA)
Nonmetallic mineral products	327	51.3	55.1	37.3	39.8	39.2	(NA)
Primary metals	331	46.9	44.3	38.4	49.7	56.8	(NA)
Fabricated metal products	332	162.1	152.0	129.3	141.1	139.5	(NA)
Machinery	333	130.2	129.9	127.8	145.3	140.5	(NA)
Computer and electronic products	334	91.8	153.8	255.8	272.1	273.3	(NA)
Electrical equipment, appliances, and components	335	53.6	51.9	51.3	48.1	48.7	(NA)
Motor vehicles, bodies and trailers, and parts	3361–63	106.9	129.6	99.8	138.7	149.8	(NA)
Other transportation equipment	3364–66, 69	92.3	98.6	112.3	113.4	116.4	(NA)
Furniture and related products	337	40.6	39.6	23.3	24.0	24.8	(NA)
Miscellaneous manufacturing	339	62.3	68.0	81.9	77.8	80.3	(NA)
Nondurable goods	31, 32 (except 321 and 327)	807.1	850.6	843.8	777.9	786.2	819.5
Food and beverage and tobacco products	311, 312	209.8	212.1	233.3	218.4	219.9	(NA)
Textile mills and textile product mills	313, 314	29.7	22.3	15.6	14.9	15.6	(NA)
Apparel and leather and allied products	315, 316	19.7	13.3	10.8	10.4	10.5	(NA)
Paper products	322	72.6	64.9	53.4	50.0	47.7	(NA)
Printing and related support activities	323	40.7	44.6	39.7	39.9	39.5	(NA)
Petroleum and coal products	324	75.9	127.5	98.5	84.2	90.1	(NA)
Chemical products	325	263.4	284.7	330.4	299.0	297.2	(NA)
Plastics and rubber products	326	78.5	75.9	65.3	67.4	67.8	(NA)

NA Not available. X Not applicable. [1] North American Industry Classification System, 2007; see text, Section 15. [2] Includes industries, not shown separately. For additional industries, see Table 690.

Source: U.S. Bureau of Economic Analysis, Industry Economic Accounts, Gross Domestic Product by Industry, "GDP by Industry/VA, GO, II," <http://www.bea.gov/industry/gdpbyind_data.htm>, accessed August 2015.

Table 1025. Manufacturing—Selected Industry Statistics by State: 2012

[11,214 represents 11,214,000. Based on the 2012 Economic Census and the 2012 Nonemployer Statistics. See Appendix III]

State	Employers				Nonemployers	
	Number of establishments	Number of employees (1,000)	Annual payroll (mil. dol.)	Sales, shipments, receipts or revenue (mil. dol.)	Number of establishments	Sales, shipments, receipts or revenue (mil. dol.)
United States........	**297,191**	**11,214**	**593,397**	**5,696,730**	**344,658**	**16,164**
Alabama.............	4,283	233	11,099	124,810	4,472	185
Alaska................	527	12	515	(D)	1,130	38
Arizona...............	4,269	132	8,193	51,243	6,897	302
Arkansas.............	2,688	154	6,291	62,713	2,733	118
California............	38,741	1,163	69,317	512,303	45,927	2,640
Colorado.............	4,898	115	6,230	50,447	7,324	293
Connecticut...........	4,350	164	10,546	55,160	3,646	230
Delaware.............	573	26	1,393	22,597	643	39
District of Columbia....	113	1	61	310	267	10
Florida...............	12,890	277	14,270	96,924	21,526	1,057
Georgia..............	7,456	334	15,317	155,837	10,179	453
Hawaii................	796	11	465	(D)	2,163	89
Idaho................	1,759	52	2,445	20,201	2,674	89
Illinois...............	13,868	542	28,414	281,038	10,978	493
Indiana...............	8,141	453	23,041	242,764	6,995	322
Iowa.................	3,598	204	10,021	116,669	3,053	115
Kansas...............	2,875	152	7,578	86,076	2,891	124
Kentucky.............	3,782	214	10,140	129,284	3,860	182
Louisiana.............	3,308	136	8,489	271,191	4,413	195
Maine................	1,650	49	2,424	16,045	2,608	91
Maryland.............	3,096	100	5,909	39,533	4,517	180
Massachusetts........	6,806	234	14,395	81,928	6,073	322
Michigan.............	12,444	514	27,611	238,892	12,399	582
Minnesota............	7,313	298	15,823	123,076	7,623	300
Mississippi...........	2,252	133	5,919	66,442	2,497	95
Missouri..............	6,097	243	11,921	111,535	6,237	283
Montana..............	1,237	16	715	11,535	2,108	71
Nebraska.............	1,844	92	4,003	57,499	1,620	54
Nevada...............	1,706	38	1,979	14,719	2,301	134
New Hampshire........	1,851	67	3,924	18,896	2,274	110
New Jersey...........	7,758	231	14,095	108,855	6,676	430
New Mexico...........	1,389	27	1,349	29,102	3,173	91
New York.............	16,475	427	22,073	148,880	18,373	876
North Carolina........	8,953	404	18,191	202,345	10,352	384
North Dakota..........	745	24	1,043	14,427	640	25
Ohio.................	14,482	627	33,135	313,630	13,302	677
Oklahoma.............	3,610	133	6,416	74,295	4,012	193
Oregon...............	5,289	152	8,122	51,350	7,193	269
Pennsylvania..........	13,988	544	28,058	231,396	14,067	744
Rhode Island..........	1,509	40	2,076	11,262	1,184	51
South Carolina........	3,854	207	10,082	99,161	4,152	180
South Dakota..........	1,025	42	1,765	16,883	968	31
Tennessee............	5,823	294	14,181	139,960	6,300	292
Texas................	19,782	767	42,530	702,603	32,514	1,557
Utah.................	3,163	108	5,763	50,046	4,024	160
Vermont..............	1,013	31	1,594	9,315	1,890	55
Virginia..............	5,101	228	11,586	96,390	5,610	212
Washington...........	6,992	248	14,462	131,531	8,816	338
West Virginia..........	1,245	49	2,604	24,553	1,295	44
Wisconsin............	8,995	437	21,879	177,729	7,127	330
Wyoming.............	553	10	631	10,784	962	33
Puerto Rico..........	1,653	84	2,875	76,575	(NA)	(NA)

NA Not available. D Withheld to avoid disclosing data on individual companies.

Source: U.S. Census Bureau, "2012 Economic Census, EC1200A1: All sectors: Geographic Area Series: Economy-Wide Key Statistics: 2012," <http://factfinder.census.gov/>, accessed September 2015. See also <http://www.census.gov/econ/census/>.

Table 1026. Manufacturing—Establishments, Employees, and Annual Payroll by Industry: 2012 and 2013

[115,938 represents 115,938,000. Excludes most government employees, railroad employees, and self-employed persons. See Appendix III]

Industry	NAICS code [1]	Establishments		Employees (1,000) [2]		Payroll (mil. dol.)	
		2012	2013	2012	2013	2012	2013
All industries, total........................	(X)	7,431,808	7,488,353	115,938	118,266	5,414,256	5,621,697
Manufacturing, total....................	31–33	297,221	292,094	11,192	11,276	598,562	611,832
Percent of all industries.................	(X)	4.0	3.9	9.7	9.5	11.1	10.9
Food..	311	25,798	25,267	1,414	1,414	54,840	56,409
Beverage and tobacco products...........	312	5,075	6,250	151	161	7,712	8,308
Textile mills..............................	313	2,358	2,591	107	105	4,116	4,139
Textile product mills......................	314	6,216	6,565	111	114	3,634	3,843
Apparel manufacturing....................	315	6,457	6,449	112	112	2,886	2,791
Leather and allied products................	316	1,143	1,131	27	26	917	853
Wood products............................	321	13,723	13,363	341	352	12,479	13,441
Paper......................................	322	4,465	4,392	356	355	20,275	20,629
Printing and related support activities......	323	27,526	26,718	472	463	19,775	19,741
Petroleum and coal products...............	324	2,183	2,155	98	97	9,292	9,784
Chemical..................................	325	13,309	12,969	739	741	54,841	55,867
Plastics and rubber products...............	326	12,688	12,468	698	707	31,151	31,962
Nonmetallic mineral products..............	327	15,242	14,870	345	350	16,424	17,220
Primary metal.............................	331	4,716	4,532	396	393	23,536	23,564
Fabricated metal products.................	332	55,377	54,948	1,379	1,400	68,023	69,214
Machinery.................................	333	24,157	23,877	1,044	1,058	60,447	61,117
Computer and electronic products.........	334	13,248	12,948	850	843	64,602	64,732
Electrical equipment, appliance and components.............................	335	5,800	5,704	337	332	18,108	18,333
Transportation equipment...................	336	11,832	11,756	1,315	1,369	82,905	87,363
Furniture and related products.............	337	16,294	15,699	341	341	13,003	13,205
Miscellaneous.............................	339	29,614	27,442	559	545	29,599	29,315

X Not applicable. [1] Data based on North American Industry Classification System (NAICS) 2012; see text, Section 15. [2] Covers full- and part-time employees who are on the payroll in the pay period including March 12.

Source: U.S. Census Bureau, County Business Patterns, "Geography Area Series, County Business Patterns," <http://factfinder2.census.gov/>, accessed April 2015. See also <http://www.census.gov/econ/cbp/>.

Table 1027. Manufacturing—Establishments, Employees, and Annual Payroll by State: 2013

[11,276 represents 11,276,000. Excludes most government employees, railroad employees, and self-employed persons. Data are for North American Industry Classification System (NAICS), 2012, codes 31–33. See Appendix III]

State	Establish- ments	Employees (1,000) [1]	Payroll (mil. dol.)	State	Establish- ments	Employees (1,000) [1]	Payroll (mil. dol.)
United States.....	292,094	11,276	611,832	Missouri..............	5,957	245	12,125
Alabama..............	4,199	242	11,597	Montana..............	1,231	17	770
Alaska................	527	12	523	Nebraska.............	1,780	91	3,993
Arizona...............	4224	137	8,342	Nevada...............	1,705	40	2,074
Arkansas.............	2,610	154	6,412	New Hampshire.....	1,804	68	4,226
California.............	38,154	1,147	71,552	New Jersey..........	7,587	221	13,694
Colorado.............	4,866	119	6,732	New Mexico..........	1,351	28	1,396
Connecticut..........	4,258	153	10,990	New York............	16,165	429	22,438
Delaware.............	567	26	1,461	North Carolina.......	8,787	408	18,916
District of Columbia...	102	1	50	North Dakota........	730	23	1,097
Florida................	12711	282	14,551	Ohio.................	14,237	633	33,839
Georgia...............	7285	341	16,068	Oklahoma............	3,541	133	6,591
Hawaii................	772	12	488	Oregon..............	5,222	152	7,844
Idaho.................	1,739	57	2,872	Pennsylvania........	13,710	540	28,541
Illinois................	13,608	547	30,683	Rhode Island........	1,442	37	2,033
Indiana...............	8046	463	24,101	South Carolina.......	3,812	215	10,626
Iowa..................	3,532	208	10,314	South Dakota........	1012	44	1,816
Kansas...............	2,836	160	8,366	Tennessee...........	5,650	300	14,809
Kentucky.............	3,716	219	10,663	Texas................	19,537	790	46,022
Louisiana.............	3,252	126	8,093	Utah.................	3,169	112	6,057
Maine.................	1,622	49	2,406	Vermont..............	985	30	1,528
Maryland.............	2,994	100	6,096	Virginia..............	4,976	233	12,252
Massachusetts.......	6,699	228	15,185	Washington..........	6,932	246	14,680
Michigan.............	12,428	526	28,795	West Virginia........	1,216	49	2,629
Minnesota............	7,237	300	16,536	Wisconsin............	8,830	434	22,173
Mississippi...........	2,180	138	6,169	Wyoming.............	562	10	615

[1] Covers full- and part-time employees who are on the payroll in the pay period including March 12.

Source: U.S. Census Bureau, County Business Patterns, "Geography Area Series: County Business Patterns," <http://factfinder2.census.gov>, accessed July 2015. See also <http://www.census.gov/econ/cbp>.

Table 1028. Manufactures—Summary by Selected Industry: 2013

[Employee data in thousands (11,082.2 represents 11,082,200); financial data in millions of dollars (602,878 represents $602,878,000,000), except as noted. Based on data from the 2013 Annual Survey of Manufactures]

| Industry based on shipments | 2012 NAICS code [1] | All employees | | | Produc-tion workers [2] (1,000) | Value added by manufac-tures [3] (mil. dol.) | Value of ship-ments [4] (mil. dol.) |
| | | Number [2] (1,000) | Payroll | | | | |
			Total (mil. dol.)	Per employee (dol.)			
Manufacturing, total..........................	31–33	**11,082.2**	**602,878**	**54,400**	**7,747.5**	**2,398,392**	**5,846,768**
Food [5]..	311	1,372.2	55,651	40,558	1,083.7	269,173	760,811
Grain and oil seed milling...................	3112	52.0	3,004	57,752	38.3	29,029	103,589
Sugar and confectionery products............	3113	68.5	3,057	44,642	50.3	14,839	33,337
Fruit and vegetable preserving and specialty food..........	3114	162.4	6,557	40,376	136.3	33,219	71,236
Dairy products.............................	3115	129.9	6,588	50,732	95.5	31,100	111,936
Animal slaughtering and processing...........	3116	475.5	15,765	33,156	416.8	55,742	205,803
Bakeries and tortilla.......................	3118	245.9	9,525	38,728	169.8	36,596	66,173
Beverage and tobacco products..............	312	149.2	8,076	54,122	86.9	87,741	147,591
Beverage.................................	3121	135.8	7,216	53,119	76.9	55,609	107,253
Textile mills..............................	313	102.9	4,098	39,839	83.5	12,791	31,284
Textile product mills......................	314	109.0	3,805	34,900	83.9	9,805	22,826
Apparel..................................	315	97.4	2,768	28,410	77.0	6,409	12,323
Cut and sew apparel......................	3152	77.7	2,175	27,987	61.2	4,702	9,133
Leather and allied products.................	316	25.2	844	33,421	19.6	2,233	5,295
Wood products [5]........................	321	345.8	13,378	38,681	277.6	36,979	88,561
Sawmills and wood preservation.............	3211	72.9	3,211	44,031	61.3	10,142	26,685
Paper....................................	322	345.9	20,477	59,207	268.6	90,265	186,243
Pulp, paper, and paperboard mills...........	3221	105.3	7,939	75,428	83.7	44,026	82,756
Converted paper products.................	3222	240.6	12,538	52,111	185.0	46,239	103,487
Printing and related support activities.........	323	432.4	19,869	45,952	301.8	49,005	82,663
Petroleum and coal products...............	324	101.5	9,694	95,532	67.4	133,253	865,691
Chemical [5].............................	325	718.2	52,442	73,021	434.1	375,910	797,828
Basic chemical...........................	3251	148.1	12,048	81,366	91.5	102,700	280,530
Pharmaceutical and medicine..............	3254	230.4	19,039	82,628	123.8	131,421	187,517
Soap, cleaning compound, and toilet preparation...........	3256	90.7	5,445	60,032	58.9	48,498	90,156
Plastics and rubber products.................	326	703.7	31,875	45,297	540.7	104,700	227,104
Plastics products.........................	3261	574.8	25,583	44,506	441.2	86,985	182,848
Rubber product..........................	3262	128.9	6,292	48,826	99.5	17,716	44,256
Nonmetallic mineral products...............	327	348.4	16,966	48,692	265.1	58,755	105,502
Glass and glass product...................	3272	82.7	4,166	50,401	65.4	13,460	23,719
Cement and concrete products.............	3273	149.6	7,114	47,558	114.4	22,908	44,005
Primary metal [5].........................	331	386.3	23,195	60,051	303.4	88,657	262,187
Iron and steel mills and ferroalloy...........	3311	100.7	7,744	76,889	79.8	33,865	107,612
Foundries...............................	3315	123.7	5,998	48,478	101.3	17,986	32,098
Fabricated metal products [5]...............	332	1,379.9	69,157	50,119	1,017.0	183,909	345,089
Forging and stamping.....................	3321	111.5	5,697	51,101	83.9	15,512	34,560
Architectural and structural metals...........	3323	322.2	15,461	47,981	232.2	38,151	77,474
Machine shops, turned product and screw, nut, and bolt........	3327	384.1	19,291	50,222	290.8	42,952	68,599
Coating, engraving, heat treating, and allied activities.........	3328	122.5	5,465	44,619	95.4	16,453	27,133
Machinery [5]............................	333	1,057.7	61,023	57,695	683.4	191,751	394,073
Agriculture, construction, and mining machinery...........	3331	213.9	11,938	55,818	147.3	51,532	113,620
Industrial machinery......................	3332	97.0	6,818	70,269	52.0	17,575	32,139
HVAC and commercial refrigeration equipment..............	3334	132.2	6,171	46,664	93.3	20,633	43,116
Metalworking machinery...................	3335	143.1	8,123	56,752	101.1	17,804	30,197
Computer and electronic products [5]........	334	811.6	60,800	74,913	382.9	197,972	325,808
Computer and peripheral equipment........	3341	48.3	3,487	72,149	16.5	15,044	29,416
Communications equipment...............	3342	107.1	9,486	88,591	48.2	23,198	44,317
Semiconductor and other electronic component..........	3344	254.1	16,036	63,100	156.4	66,485	103,758
Navigational, measuring, medical, and control instruments......	3345	377.0	30,515	80,934	147.3	89,853	142,677
Electrical equipment, appliance, and component..............	335	332.2	17,963	54,077	221.0	60,254	123,287
Electrical equipment......................	3353	115.1	6,474	56,227	72.4	19,356	39,081
Other electrical equipment and component....	3359	132.6	7,472	56,351	86.2	25,373	52,765
Transportation equipment [5]...............	336	1,383.5	88,273	63,803	968.7	302,139	836,967
Motor vehicle............................	3361	166.9	12,048	72,172	143.6	63,919	280,687
Motor vehicle parts......................	3363	482.5	24,831	51,465	372.7	75,042	226,605
Aerospace product and parts..............	3364	424.9	35,332	83,157	227.7	116,245	223,864
Ship and boat building....................	3366	132.1	7,490	56,690	89.7	20,289	33,561
Furniture and related products [5]...........	337	342.3	13,566	39,635	252.6	36,687	69,374
Miscellaneous [5].........................	339	537.0	28,957	53,921	328.5	100,003	156,262
Medical equipment and supplies............	3391	281.1	17,125	60,929	168.5	64,264	95,318

[1] North American Industrial Classification System, 2012; see text, Section 15. [2] Includes all full-time and part-time employees on payrolls of operating manufacturing establishments. All employees represents the average of production workers plus all other employees for the payroll period ended nearest the 12th of March. [3] Adjusted value added; takes into account (a) value added by merchandising operations (that is, difference between the sales value and cost of merchandise sold without further manufacture, processing, or assembly), plus (b) net change in finished goods and work-in-process inventories between beginning and end of year. [4] This item covers the received or receivable net selling values, "free on board" (FOB) plant (exclusive of freight and taxes), of all products shipped as well as all miscellaneous receipts. In the case of multiunit companies, the manufacturer was requested to report the value of products transferred to other establishments of the same company at full economic or commercial value. [5] Includes industries not shown separately.

Source: U.S. Census Bureau, Annual Survey of Manufactures, "Geographic Area Statistics: Statistics for All Manufacturing by State: 2013," February 2015, <http://factfinder2.census.gov/>, accessed April 2015. See also <http://www.census.gov/manufacturing/asm/>.

Table 1029. Manufactures—Summary by State: 2013

[Employment data in thousands (11,082.2 represents 11,082,200); financial data in millions of dollars (602,878 represents $602,878,000,000). Based on data from the 2013 Annual Survey of Manufactures. Data are for North American Industry Classification System (NAICS) 2012 codes 31–33. Sum of state totals may not add to U.S. total due to independent rounding. See Appendix III]

| State | All employees [1] | | | Production workers [1] | | Value added by manufactures [2] | | Value of shipments [3] (mil. dol.) |
| | Number (1,000) | Payroll | | Number (1,000) | Wages (mil. dol.) | | | |
		Total (mil. dol.)	Per employee (dol.)			Total (mil. dol.)	Per production worker (dol.)	
United States..............	11,082.2	602,878	54,400	7,747.5	340,635	2,398,392	309,570	5,846,768
Alabama.....................	233.3	11,426	48,967	175.8	7,420	47,357	269,405	128,280
Alaska........................	11.7	521	44,454	9.5	369	1,726	181,473	7,444
Arizona.......................	129.9	8,207	63,177	74.0	3,311	27,451	371,069	52,848
Arkansas.....................	150.5	6,380	42,381	122.3	4,526	25,152	205,643	62,128
California....................	1,137.9	70,111	61,617	723.8	32,522	245,765	339,535	524,494
Colorado.....................	111.7	6,351	56,876	74.1	3,267	23,683	319,722	52,196
Connecticut.................	163.4	10,761	65,862	97.7	4,823	34,068	348,523	58,164
Delaware....................	26.4	1,433	54,292	18.4	797	5,923	322,133	22,220
District of Columbia........	1.2	56	46,592	0.7	31	151	201,869	249
Florida.......................	271.3	14,455	53,276	180.2	7,387	51,285	284,524	101,260
Georgia......................	334.0	16,060	48,081	253.0	9,958	66,159	261,451	161,453
Hawaii........................	10.8	465	42,979	6.9	268	1,140	164,903	6,418
Idaho.........................	52.6	2,608	49,584	39.3	1,618	8,815	224,402	20,840
Illinois........................	545.0	29,949	54,949	382.0	16,531	112,179	293,660	284,863
Indiana.......................	454.4	23,876	52,543	342.2	15,402	100,326	293,216	245,119
Iowa..........................	203.4	10,197	50,133	148.0	6,171	45,848	309,831	119,366
Kansas.......................	159.2	8,346	52,417	114.0	5,196	28,874	253,380	89,324
Kentucky.....................	215.2	10,580	49,158	167.3	7,350	44,475	265,910	133,906
Louisiana....................	131.2	8,407	64,078	93.6	5,173	57,752	617,055	263,037
Maine.........................	48.0	2,464	51,336	35.5	1,618	7,942	223,587	16,507
Maryland.....................	98.0	5,954	60,759	59.7	2,706	22,098	369,852	40,516
Massachusetts..............	231.7	14,770	63,753	138.7	6,496	46,539	335,608	82,533
Michigan.....................	524.5	28,908	55,114	382.0	18,045	98,438	257,669	250,874
Minnesota...................	295.7	16,268	55,010	192.8	8,220	55,721	289,011	126,899
Mississippi..................	132.8	5,953	44,837	103.2	3,969	22,522	218,272	66,029
Missouri......................	235.7	12,053	51,136	174.3	7,594	46,364	266,050	109,517
Montana......................	15.8	787	49,751	11.0	477	3,592	326,644	12,443
Nebraska.....................	91.3	4,100	44,918	70.3	2,768	20,041	284,949	57,683
Nevada.......................	38.5	2,100	54,599	25.6	1,145	8,720	340,159	16,178
New Hampshire.............	65.6	3,938	60,075	40.1	1,746	10,628	264,906	19,381
New Jersey..................	222.9	13,730	61,586	143.4	6,606	43,341	302,239	103,300
New Mexico.................	24.9	1,299	52,262	16.8	752	13,790	820,342	25,169
New York.....................	414.1	22,013	53,160	277.4	11,756	72,861	262,624	144,754
North Carolina..............	400.0	18,612	46,529	298.3	11,455	106,757	357,920	212,569
North Dakota................	23.2	1,079	46,544	17.5	687	5,729	326,604	15,552
Ohio..........................	628.9	33,854	53,829	451.1	20,489	124,349	275,687	320,150
Oklahoma....................	128.4	6,563	51,109	94.2	4,150	24,257	257,604	74,969
Oregon.......................	146.6	7,699	52,528	103.4	4,379	37,145	359,361	63,488
Pennsylvania................	534.3	28,358	53,076	375.6	16,621	103,791	276,359	235,470
Rhode Island................	37.9	2,037	53,679	25.3	1,064	6,053	239,165	11,522
South Carolina..............	208.2	10,476	50,315	156.5	6,629	39,443	251,963	104,350
South Dakota...............	41.9	1,799	42,924	30.4	1,137	6,483	213,124	16,967
Tennessee...................	290.8	14,471	49,755	211.6	8,863	61,365	289,948	143,613
Texas.........................	759.9	43,747	57,572	524.2	24,916	239,012	455,948	731,708
Utah..........................	106.6	5,798	54,364	71.3	3,163	21,891	307,010	48,418
Vermont......................	29.3	1,509	51,495	19.2	792	3,885	202,364	9,209
Virginia.......................	224.5	11,991	53,418	158.4	6,920	57,435	362,515	99,971
Washington..................	248.8	15,012	60,345	164.0	8,328	62,637	381,999	139,165
West Virginia................	46.3	2,564	55,336	34.6	1,649	10,912	315,321	24,566
Wisconsin....................	434.3	22,175	51,055	310.8	12,938	83,725	269,422	179,294
Wyoming.....................	9.6	610	63,487	7.4	437	2,797	378,705	10,396

[1] Includes all full-time and part-time employees on the payrolls of operating manufacturing establishments during the pay period that included March 12. Included are employees on paid sick leave, paid holidays, and paid vacations; not included are proprietors and partners of unincorporated businesses. [2] Value added is derived by subtracting the cost of materials, supplies, containers, fuel, purchased electricity, and contract work from the value of shipments (products manufactured plus receipts for services rendered). The result of this calculation is adjusted by the addition of value added by merchandising operations (i.e., the difference between the sales value and the cost of merchandise sold without further manufacture, processing, or assembly) plus the net change in finished goods and work-in-process between the beginning and end of year inventories. [3] Includes extensive and unmeasurable duplication from shipments between establishments in the same industry classification.

Source: U.S. Census Bureau, Annual Survey of Manufactures, "Geographic Area Statistics for All Manufacturing by State: 2013," February 2015, <http://factfinder2.census.gov/>, accessed April 2015. See also <http://www.census.gov/manufacturing/asm/>.

Table 1030. Manufacturing Industries—Employees by Industry: 2000 to 2014

[Annual averages of monthly figures (132,019 represents 132,019,000). Covers all full- and part-time employees who worked during, or received pay for, any part of the pay period including the 12th of the month. Minus sign (-) indicates decrease. See also head note, Table 649]

Industry	2012 NAICS code [1]	All employees (1,000) 2000	2010	2012	2013	2014	Percent change 1990-2000	2000-2010	2010-2014
All industries....................	(X)	132,019	130,275	134,104	136,393	139,042	20.5	-1.3	6.7
Manufacturing....................	31–33	17,263	11,528	11,927	12,020	12,188	-2.4	-33.2	5.7
Percent of all industries..........................	(X)	13.1	8.8	8.9	8.8	8.8	(X)	(X)	(X)
Durable goods........................	(X)	10,877	7,064	7,470	7,548	7,685	1.3	-35.1	8.8
Wood products [2].....................	321	615	342	339	353	372	13.3	-44.4	8.7
Sawmills & wood preservation.............	3211	134	82	85	86	91	-9.6	-38.5	10.2
Nonmetallic mineral products [2].........	327	554	371	365	373	386	4.9	-33.1	4.0
Cement & concrete products.................	3273	234	170	164	168	174	20.1	-27.4	2.2
Primary metals [2].....................	331	622	362	402	395	401	-9.7	-41.7	10.5
Iron & steel mills & ferroalloy production.......	3311	135	87	93	91	91	-27.7	-35.9	5.7
Steel products from purchased steel........	3312	73	52	60	59	60	4.0	-28.7	15.3
Alumina & aluminum production.................	3313	101	54	59	58	60	-7.3	-46.3	10.7
Foundries....................	3315	217	112	128	125	127	1.4	-48.4	13.6
Fabricated metal products [2]...........	332	1,753	1,282	1,410	1,432	1,455	8.9	-26.9	13.5
Architectural & structural metals.............	3323	428	321	341	350	362	20.0	-25.0	12.6
Machine shops & threaded products.........	3327	365	313	364	368	371	18.4	-14.4	18.6
Coating, engraving, & heat treating metals....	3328	175	122	136	137	139	22.7	-30.0	13.3
Machinery [2]....................	333	1,457	996	1,099	1,105	1,129	3.3	-31.6	13.3
Agricultural, construction, & mining machinery.................	3331	222	208	247	250	255	-2.8	-6.4	22.6
HVAC & commercial refrigeration equipment.................	3334	194	125	128	127	128	17.7	-35.9	3.0
Metalworking machinery.................	3335	274	155	177	178	182	2.5	-43.3	17.4
Turbine & power transmission equipment......	3336	111	92	102	99	103	-2.4	-17.6	12.1
Other general purpose machinery.............	3339	344	226	252	256	265	2.4	-34.4	17.2
Computer & electronic products [2]...............	334	1,820	1,095	1,089	1,066	1,050	-4.3	-39.9	-4.1
Computer & peripheral equipment.............	3341	302	158	157	158	163	-17.8	-47.8	3.3
Communications equipment.................	3342	239	117	108	101	94	7.0	-50.8	-20.4
Semiconductors & electronic components.................	3344	676	369	383	375	368	17.8	-45.4	-0.4
Electronic instruments.................	3345	488	406	400	394	388	-23.2	-16.7	-4.5
Electrical equipment & appliances [2]...............	335	591	360	373	374	375	-6.7	-39.2	4.2
Electrical equipment.................	3353	210	136	144	144	144	-13.9	-35.1	5.7
Other electrical equipment & components.................	3359	191	119	128	126	125	-2.3	-37.8	5.3
Transportation equipment [2]..................	336	2,057	1,333	1,461	1,509	1,563	-3.6	-35.2	17.2
Motor vehicles.................	3361	291	153	168	182	199	7.4	-47.6	30.6
Motor vehicle bodies & trailers.................	3362	183	107	127	135	141	40.8	-41.4	31.5
Motor vehicle parts.................	3363	840	419	483	509	537	28.6	-50.1	28.1
Aerospace products & parts.................	3364	517	478	499	495	488	-38.5	-7.5	2.2
Ship & boat building.................	3366	154	125	129	132	139	-11.3	-19.1	11.2
Furniture & related products [2].................	337	680	357	351	360	373	13.0	-47.5	4.5
Household & institutional furniture.............	3371	441	223	218	224	235	10.7	-49.3	5.4
Miscellaneous manufacturing....................	339	728	567	580	581	583	6.2	-22.1	2.8
Medical equipment & supplies.............	3391	305	303	309	307	308	7.7	-0.7	1.6
Other miscellaneous manufacturing............	3399	423	264	271	274	275	5.1	-37.6	4.2
Nondurable goods.......................	(X)	6,386	4,464	4,457	4,472	4,503	-8.2	-30.1	0.9
Food manufacturing [2]................	311	1,553	1,451	1,469	1,474	1,481	3.0	-6.6	2.1
Fruit & vegetable preserving & specialty.......	3114	197	173	172	170	169	-9.5	-12.6	-2.1
Dairy products....................	3115	136	130	134	134	134	-5.9	-4.2	2.5
Animal slaughtering & processing...............	3116	507	489	484	482	480	18.6	-3.5	-1.9
Bakeries & tortilla manufacturing.............	3118	306	277	285	286	294	4.9	-9.7	6.3
Textile mills [2]................	313	378	119	119	117	118	-23.1	-68.5	-1.3
Fabric mills..................	3132	192	53	56	55	56	-29.0	-72.2	4.5
Textile product mills [2]................	314	230	119	116	114	115	-2.5	-48.2	-3.7
Textile furnishings mills.................	3141	129	57	52	52	52	1.3	-55.7	-9.1
Apparel [2]....................	315	484	157	148	145	140	-46.4	-67.6	-10.4
Cut & sew apparel....................	3152	380	124	122	120	115	-49.3	-67.4	-7.3
Paper & paper products....................	322	605	395	380	378	371	-6.6	-34.7	-5.9
Pulp, paper, & paperboard mills.................	3221	191	112	108	107	104	-19.7	-41.3	-7.2
Converted paper products.................	3222	413	282	272	271	267	1.1	-31.7	-5.4
Printing & related support activities.............	323	807	488	462	452	453	-0.2	-39.6	-7.2
Petroleum & coal products....................	324	123	114	112	110	111	-19.4	-7.5	-2.8
Chemicals [2]....................	325	980	787	783	793	804	-5.3	-19.8	2.2
Basic chemicals....................	3251	188	142	142	143	147	-24.4	-24.5	3.4
Pharmaceuticals & medicines.................	3254	274	277	270	276	280	32.4	0.9	1.0
Soaps, cleaning compounds, and toiletries....	3256	129	102	103	104	105	-2.4	-20.6	2.5
Plastics & rubber products [2].................	326	951	625	645	659	675	15.3	-34.3	8.0
Plastics products....................	3261	737	502	515	528	542	19.2	-31.9	8.0
Rubber products....................	3262	214	123	130	131	133	3.5	-42.5	8.1
Miscellaneous nondurable goods manufacturing.................	329	276	211	223	230	237	-21.4	-23.5	12.2
Beverages....................	3291	175	167	179	186	195	1.2	-4.5	16.9
Tobacco and Tobacco Products.................	3292	32	17	14	14	14	-28.4	-48.8	-17.6
Leather & allied products....................	3293	69	28	30	30	28	-48.3	-59.6	1.4

X Not applicable. [1] Based on the North American Industry Classification System, 2012 (NAICS); see text, this section and Section 15. [2] Includes other industries, not shown separately.

Source: U.S. Bureau of Labor Statistics, Current Employment Statistics, "Employment, Hours, and Earnings—National," <http://www.bls.gov/ces/data.htm>, accessed April 2015.

Table 1031. Manufacturing—Value of Imports and Exports by Commodity: 2012

[In thousands of dollars (19,341,586 represents 19,341,586,000. Values are based on manufacturing data from the 2012 Economic Census and administrative records from official U.S. import and export merchandise trade statistics]

Commodity description	Product code [1]	Value of product shipments [2]	Total export value of goods [3]	General import value of goods [4]
Food manufacturing:				
Dog and cat food	311111	19,341,586	1,312,913	710,893
Flour milling products	311211	15,008,593	711,995	799,170
Wet corn milling products	311221	15,219,347	3,154,041	622,077
Soybean and other oilseed products	311224	37,099,080	7,674,513	6,496,060
Fats and oils refining and blending products	311225	18,799,872	840,027	325,402
Frozen specialty food	311412	18,163,176	110,471	131,311
Fruit and vegetable canning products	311421	23,573,936	2,854,171	5,137,439
Fluid milk products	311511	33,606,180	242,042	50,466
Cheese products	311513	37,741,737	1,124,092	1,095,750
Dry, condensed, and evaporated dairy products	311514	19,493,558	3,692,772	1,281,652
Animal (except poultry) slaughtering products	311611	89,610,646	14,874,308	6,384,447
Poultry processing products	311615	57,020,635	5,475,458	331,674
Beverage and tobacco product manufacturing:				
Soft drinks	312111	36,781,817	879,840	2,004,341
Brewery products	312120	27,871,988	2,560,263	3,805,427
Distillery products	312140	15,098,207	1,773,145	5,745,644
Tobacco products	312230	38,718,754	526,755	871,451
Wood product manufacturing:				
Sawmill products	321113	17,554,812	2,883,337	4,168,099
Paper manufacturing:				
Paper (except newsprint) mill products	322121	42,085,288	3,165,017	3,713,321
Paperboard mill products	322130	27,998,964	4,891,473	1,525,199
Corrugated and solid fiber boxes	322211	31,502,772	1,344,634	327,820
Paper bags and coated and treated paper	322220	20,968,661	4,750,143	3,122,337
Printing and related support activities manufacturing:				
Commercial printing products (except screen and books)	323111	62,605,846	3,678,027	3,399,514
Petroleum and coal products manufacturing:				
Petroleum refinery products	324110	760,885,180	110,513,657	93,715,107
Chemical manufacturing:				
Petrochemicals	325110	80,874,237	1,767,806	3,037,381
Ethyl alcohol	325193	32,797,086	1,903,471	1,839,338
Plastics materials and resins	325211	85,987,380	30,075,495	11,594,166
Pharmaceutical preparations	325412	120,299,771	30,752,560	62,233,319
Biological products (except diagnostic)	325414	24,133,278	10,490,808	11,179,727
Paints and coatings	325510	23,391,205	2,527,778	884,941
Soaps and other detergents	325611	23,325,651	1,453,527	977,758
Toilet preparations	325620	32,105,253	7,946,455	6,448,849
Plastics and rubber products manufacturing:				
Unlaminated plastics film and sheet (except packaging)	326113	18,144,360	7,078,199	5,691,560
All other plastics products	326199	77,980,375	10,295,754	15,813,759
Tires (except retreading)	326211	18,262,546	6,136,178	14,569,709
Nonmetallic mineral product manufacturing:				
Ready-mix concrete	327320	19,723,903	4,778	97
Primary metal manufacturing:				
Iron and steel mill products and ferroalloys	331110	108,220,256	18,288,261	39,338,573
Copper rolled, drawn, extruded, and alloy products	331420	21,752,575	3,353,181	3,753,742
Fabricated metal product manufacturing:				
Fabricated structural metal products	332312	24,093,835	1,816,113	3,114,745
Sheet metal work products	332322	19,306,097	243,025	55,172
Machinery manufacturing:				
Farm machinery and equipment	333111	37,482,904	10,093,947	7,902,470
Construction machinery	333120	39,143,168	26,576,307	17,437,724
Oil and gas field machinery and equipment	333132	23,499,253	8,302,821	2,052,918
Air-conditioning and warm air heating equipment and commercial and industrial refrigeration equipment	333415	29,159,656	5,152,309	7,675,913
Turbines and turbine generator set units	333611	17,302,337	12,080,547	5,938,499
Computer and electronic product manufacturing:				
Radio and tv broadcasting and wireless communications equipment	334220	25,079,630	33,642,472	91,280,808
Semiconductors and related devices	334413	70,708,079	41,679,827	38,818,076
Electromedical and electrotherapeutic apparatus	334510	27,298,411	10,512,564	9,067,204
Search, detection, navigation, guidance, aeronautical, and nautical systems and instruments	334511	44,134,640	4,015,262	6,745,140
Transportation equipment manufacturing:				
Automobiles	336111	(D)	44,081,690	145,913,302
Light truck and utility vehicles	336112	124,757,328	8,374,651	10,841,499
Heavy duty trucks	336120	28,550,888	7,394,590	9,445,384
Motor vehicle gasoline engines and engine parts	336310	27,626,656	8,641,167	17,347,711
Motor vehicle electrical and electronic equipment	336320	18,074,631	5,993,369	15,817,789
Motor vehicle transmission and power train parts	336350	35,113,212	2,456,813	8,618,000
Motor vehicle seating and interior trim	336360	20,310,991	1,686,837	5,812,743
Motor vehicle metal stampings	336370	27,587,912	1,458,929	534,234
Ships and ship repair	336611	24,090,124	2,541,850	931,924
Miscellaneous manufacturing:				
Surgical and medical instruments	339112	36,856,180	14,718,609	10,227,598
Surgical appliances and supplies	339113	32,469,051	10,853,534	12,065,380

D Withheld to avoid disclosing data for individual companies; data are included in higher level totals where appropriate. [1] Based on North American Industry Classification (NAICS) product codes. [2] Includes total value of all products produced and shipped by all producers. For selected products, this can represent value of receipts, value of production, or value of work done. [3] Exports measure total physical movement of merchandise out of the U.S. to foreign countries whether such merchandise is exported from within the U.S. Customs territory, from a U.S. Customs bonded warehouse, or a U.S. Foreign Trade Zone. [4] Imports include commodities of foreign origin as well as goods of domestic origin returned to the U.S. with no change in condition or after having been processed and/or assembled in other countries.

Source: U.S. Census Bureau, *Manufacturing and International Trade Report: 2012*, June 2015. See also <https://www.census.gov/foreign-trade/index.html>.

Table 1032. Manufacturing Industries—Average Weekly Hours and Average Weekly Overtime Hours of Production Workers: 2000 to 2014

[Covers all full- and part-time employees who worked during, or received pay for, any part of the pay period including the 12th of the month]

Industry	2012 NAICS code [1]	Average weekly hours of production workers					Average weekly overtime hours for production workers				
		2000	2010	2012	2013	2014	2000	2010	2012	2013	2014
Total..........................	**31–33**	**41.3**	**41.1**	**41.7**	**41.8**	**42.0**	**4.7**	**3.8**	**4.2**	**4.3**	**4.5**
Durable goods.....................	**(X)**	**41.8**	**41.4**	**42.0**	**42.2**	**42.5**	**4.8**	**3.8**	**4.3**	**4.4**	**4.6**
Wood products.....................	321	41.0	39.1	41.1	42.7	42.0	4.1	3.0	3.9	4.6	4.3
Nonmetallic mineral products.....	327	41.6	41.7	42.2	42.5	43.3	6.1	4.7	5.1	5.4	5.8
Primary metals......................	331	44.2	43.7	43.8	43.8	44.2	6.5	5.7	6.2	6.5	7.1
Fabricated metal products........	332	41.9	41.4	42.0	42.3	42.6	4.9	3.8	4.3	4.4	4.8
Machinery..........................	333	42.3	42.1	42.8	42.9	43.0	5.1	3.9	4.5	4.6	4.8
Computer and electronic products.....................	334	41.4	40.9	40.4	40.5	40.8	4.6	2.9	2.7	2.8	3.0
Electrical equipment and appliances......................	335	41.6	41.1	41.6	41.8	41.7	3.7	3.6	4.2	4.2	4.5
Transportation equipment........	336	43.3	42.9	43.8	43.6	43.6	5.6	4.7	5.2	5.1	5.3
Furniture and related products....	337	39.2	38.5	40.0	40.3	40.9	3.5	2.3	3.3	3.3	3.6
Miscellaneous manufacturing.....	339	39.0	38.7	39.2	40.1	40.2	3.1	2.7	2.7	3.0	3.2
Nondurable goods.................	**(X)**	**40.3**	**40.8**	**41.1**	**41.2**	**41.3**	**4.5**	**3.8**	**4.1**	**4.3**	**4.3**
Food manufacturing...............	311	40.1	40.7	40.6	40.8	40.8	4.9	4.5	4.5	4.6	4.5
Textile mills........................	313	41.4	41.2	42.6	41.5	41.5	4.8	3.3	3.9	4.1	4.3
Textile product mills................	314	38.7	39.0	39.7	38.4	38.0	3.4	2.4	2.8	3.1	2.8
Apparel............................	315	35.7	36.6	37.1	38.1	38.5	2.1	1.1	2.2	2.2	2.0
Paper and paper products........	322	42.8	42.9	42.9	43.1	43.6	5.7	4.9	4.6	4.8	4.9
Printing and related support activities..........................	323	39.2	38.2	38.5	38.6	39.0	3.7	2.2	2.3	2.6	2.9
Petroleum and coal products......	324	42.7	43.0	47.1	46.4	46.1	6.5	6.4	8.0	7.9	7.3
Chemicals..........................	325	42.2	42.2	42.4	42.9	42.7	5.0	3.6	4.4	4.7	4.6
Plastics and rubber products......	326	40.8	41.9	41.8	41.8	42.3	3.9	4.0	3.8	4.1	4.5
Misc. nondurable manufacturing..	329	40.5	37.8	39.1	39.7	39.7	5.4	2.3	3.6	3.7	3.5

X Not applicable. [1] Based on the North American Industry Classification System (NAICS), 2012; see text, this section and Section 15.

Source: U.S. Bureau of Labor Statistics, Current Employment Statistics, "Employment, Hours, and Earnings - National," <http://www.bls.gov/ces/data.htm/>, accessed April 2015.

Table 1033. Indexes of Employment and Hours of All Persons in Manufacturing: 2000 to 2013

[2002 = 100. Based on Current Employment Statistics and supplemented with Current Population Survey. Employment and hours of all persons include those of paid employees, the self employed (partners and proprietors), and unpaid family workers. See text, Section 12]

Industry	2007 NAICS code [1]	Employment					Hours				
		2000	2010	2011	2012	2013	2000	2010	2011	2012	2013
Food manufacturing..............	311	101.5	94.8	95.9	97.2	97.7	103.1	97.3	97.2	99.7	99.7
Beverage and tobacco products......................	312	99.1	88.9	91.3	93.0	97.2	106.3	84.3	91.4	91.1	100.1
Textile mills........................	313	127.9	42.7	42.4	42.4	40.8	130.4	42.9	42.4	43.4	41.5
Textile product mills..............	314	109.7	58.8	57.6	57.8	58.5	109.5	60.4	57.7	58.3	56.1
Apparel manufacturing...........	315	135.3	48.1	45.7	45.6	43.2	131.1	49.3	46.7	45.8	43.8
Leather and allied products.....	316	124.8	52.5	55.7	57.5	55.8	126.2	54.1	60.7	65.9	61.5
Wood product manufacturing. ..	321	111.8	63.4	62.2	62.4	64.3	115.0	62.7	62.6	64.5	68.0
Paper manufacturing............	322	110.2	72.1	70.6	69.5	69.3	115.7	75.2	73.5	71.4	71.9
Printing and related support activities..........................	323	114.2	70.6	66.6	64.7	63.1	116.1	70.0	66.2	64.8	63.8
Petroleum and coal products....	324	103.7	95.6	94.2	94.7	93.4	102.4	94.7	94.7	104.7	101.7
Chemical manufacturing.........	325	106.2	85.5	84.9	85.7	85.6	104.6	85.5	84.7	85.1	86.5
Plastics and rubber products....	326	112.4	73.7	74.9	76.5	77.3	113.5	76.0	77.5	78.5	79.9
Nonmetallic mineral products. ..	327	107.2	72.9	72.0	73.4	73.5	107.1	73.8	72.8	73.8	74.0
Primary metal products..........	331	122.1	71.4	76.3	79.4	78.0	126.1	73.4	80.3	81.3	79.8
Fabricated metal products.......	332	112.7	83.4	87.0	90.7	92.6	116.1	84.2	89.1	93.7	95.9
Machinery manufacturing........	333	118.5	81.0	85.9	89.5	89.5	123.8	84.8	91.5	94.6	93.9
Computer and electronic products......................	334	121.6	73.0	73.5	72.5	70.9	126.8	75.9	75.4	74.5	72.8
Electrical equipment and appliances......................	335	118.9	72.5	73.9	75.1	75.6	122.3	73.5	73.8	76.8	78.6
Transportation equipment.......	336	112.3	72.9	75.7	79.6	81.8	113.9	73.6	77.3	82.5	84.3
Furniture and related products..	337	111.1	59.7	58.5	58.5	59.8	110.5	57.5	59.2	59.6	60.8
Miscellaneous manufacturing. ..	339	107.3	82.7	83.3	84.1	84.4	107.7	83.6	85.1	86.0	87.2

[1] North American Industry Classification System, 2007; see text, Section 15.

Source: U.S. Bureau of Labor Statistics, Labor Productivity and Costs, "Hours and Employment by Industry," May 2014, <http://www.bls.gov/lpc/tables.htm>.

Table 1034. Average Hourly Earnings of Production Workers in Manufacturing Industries by State: 2011 to 2014

[In dollars. Data are based on the North American Industry Classification System (NAICS), 2012. Based on the Current Employment Statistics Program. Covers full- and part-time employees who received pay for any part of the pay period including the 12th of the month. Excludes proprietors, self-employed, unpaid family or volunteer workers, farm workers, and domestic workers. See source, and Appendix III]

State	2011	2012	2013	2014	State	2011	2012	2013	2014
United States	**18.93**	**19.08**	**19.30**	**19.56**	Montana	18.34	17.88	17.19	17.29
Alabama	16.93	18.31	18.15	18.31	Nebraska	16.58	16.65	16.76	17.19
Alaska	19.60	18.02	17.43	20.38	Nevada	16.29	16.00	15.83	16.38
Arizona	17.60	18.16	18.69	18.49	New Hampshire	18.24	18.13	18.53	18.76
Arkansas	14.50	15.20	15.43	15.96	New Jersey	19.07	19.33	18.94	19.55
California	19.49	20.20	20.90	20.91	New Mexico	16.22	15.70	16.32	16.71
Colorado	23.64	25.09	24.65	25.05	New York	18.44	18.54	19.25	19.42
Connecticut	24.79	23.96	21.79	22.40	North Carolina	16.04	16.55	16.72	16.71
Delaware	15.94	15.73	15.96	16.63	North Dakota	17.04	18.05	18.70	19.17
Florida	18.81	19.65	20.34	20.09	Ohio	19.25	19.35	19.46	19.80
Georgia	17.69	17.90	18.08	18.09	Oklahoma	15.65	16.89	17.82	18.08
Hawaii	18.20	19.15	19.38	18.37	Oregon	17.96	18.66	18.73	19.31
Idaho	20.97	20.92	21.33	21.49	Pennsylvania	17.49	18.26	19.16	19.02
Illinois	18.01	19.17	19.45	19.49	Rhode Island	16.29	18.26	18.93	18.38
Indiana	18.02	18.47	18.42	18.77	South Carolina	16.72	17.01	17.92	18.65
Iowa	16.50	17.41	17.94	18.87	South Dakota	16.34	16.95	17.16	17.33
Kansas	19.49	18.44	18.11	18.51	Tennessee	16.63	16.64	17.21	17.50
Kentucky	18.90	18.43	18.87	19.73	Texas	16.42	18.56	19.91	21.09
Louisiana	21.15	20.43	21.99	22.04	Utah	18.03	17.99	18.07	18.39
Maine	20.21	20.50	20.86	20.55	Vermont	17.24	18.22	18.40	18.45
Maryland	18.60	16.64	18.02	19.34	Virginia	18.51	18.54	19.08	19.46
Massachusetts	20.47	20.90	21.53	21.40	Washington	23.98	24.14	24.34	25.16
Michigan	21.11	20.71	20.11	20.47	West Virginia	18.03	18.61	18.75	19.29
Minnesota	19.04	19.19	19.85	19.88	Wisconsin	17.71	18.05	18.56	18.95
Mississippi	15.12	15.90	17.45	17.83	Wyoming	22.19	22.69	21.58	20.99
Missouri	18.67	18.06	18.55	19.02	Puerto Rico	12.73	12.65	13.03	13.78

Source: U.S. Bureau of Labor Statistics, Current Employment Statistics, "Employment, Hours, and Earnings – National," <http://www.bls.gov/ces/data.htm>; and "Employment, Hours, and Earnings – State and Metro Area," <http://www.bls.gov/sae/data.htm>; accessed April 2015.

Table 1035. Manufacturing Full–Time Equivalent (FTE) Employees and Wages by Industry: 2000 to 2014

[123,384 represents 123,384,000. Based on National Income and Product Account tables. Full-time equivalent employees equals the number of employees on full-time schedules plus the number of employees for part-time schedules converted to full-time basis]

Industry	2002 NAICS code [1]	Full-time equivalent (FTE) employees (1,000)				Wage and salary accruals per FTE worker (dol.)			
		2000	2010	2013	2014	2000	2010	2013	2014
Domestic industries, total	(X)	**123,384**	**120,594**	**126,661**	**131,039**	**39,166**	**52,951**	**56,240**	**57,137**
Manufacturing	31–33	**16,948**	**11,231**	**11,747**	**11,928**	**43,957**	**60,018**	**63,575**	**65,466**
Percent of all industries	(X)	13.7	9.3	9.3	9.1	112.2	113.3	113.0	114.6
Durable goods	(X)	10,713	6,908	7,412	7,534	46,573	63,346	66,868	68,919
Wood products	321	602	334	343	357	30,351	38,152	41,240	43,516
Nonmetallic mineral products	327	549	357	365	376	39,021	50,623	53,654	55,308
Primary metals	331	611	353	393	392	45,836	61,058	64,331	66,870
Fabricated metal products	332	1,735	1,249	1,400	1,427	37,766	51,441	53,749	55,509
Machinery	333	1,427	976	1,086	1,103	46,612	62,655	66,636	69,013
Computer and electronic products	334	1,779	1,079	1,048	1,035	70,449	95,998	103,466	108,602
Electrical equipment, appliances, and components	335	583	351	366	372	40,241	59,422	65,323	66,041
Motor vehicles, bodies and trailers, and parts	3361–3363	1,301	673	819	866	48,754	58,384	59,327	61,200
Other transportation equipment	3364–3365	740	645	680	672	53,294	79,409	86,327	89,885
Furniture and related products	337	671	346	350	367	29,571	39,985	42,309	42,505
Miscellaneous manufacturing	339	715	547	561	569	38,744	56,906	61,474	62,380
Nondurable goods	(X)	6,235	4,322	4,335	4,393	39,464	54,700	57,946	59,545
Food and beverage and tobacco products	311–312	1,727	1,561	1,597	1,639	33,956	44,711	46,610	47,468
Textile mills and textile product mills	313–314	588	230	223	225	29,013	39,110	41,659	43,078
Apparel and leather and allied products	315	539	179	168	162	24,198	38,238	39,095	41,029
Paper products	322	598	382	367	356	45,834	61,583	65,372	68,431
Printing and related support activities	323	757	472	441	442	39,142	45,793	47,743	48,650
Petroleum and coal products	324	120	109	110	107	62,998	97,164	108,738	113,344
Chemical products	325	967	775	786	799	61,314	84,795	90,904	94,406
Plastics and rubber products	326	938	615	644	665	35,624	47,775	50,460	51,352

X Not applicable. [1] North American Industry Classification System, 2002; see text, Section 15.

Source: U.S. Bureau of Economic Analysis, National Income and Product Accounts Tables, "Table 6.5D. Full-Time Equivalent Employees by Industry," and "Table 6.6D. Wages and Salaries Per Full-Time Equivalent Employee by Industry," <http://www.bea.gov/itable/>, accessed August 2015.

Table 1036. Manufacturers' Shipments, Inventories, and New Orders: 1995 to 2014

[In billions of dollars (3,480 represents $3,480,000,000,000), except ratio. Based on the Manufacturers' Shipments, Inventories, and Orders (M3) survey. See source for details]

Year	Shipments	Inventories (December 31) [1]	Ratio of inventories to shipments [2]	New orders	Unfilled orders (December 31)
1995	3,480	415	1.41	3,427	443
1996	3,597	421	1.40	3,567	485
1997	3,835	433	1.36	3,780	508
1998	3,900	439	1.37	3,808	492
1999	4,032	453	1.34	3,957	501
2000	4,209	470	1.37	4,161	545
2001	3,970	417	1.33	3,869	506
2002	3,915	412	1.30	3,823	476
2003	4,015	398	1.20	3,976	503
2004	4,309	429	1.17	4,289	555
2005	4,742	461	1.14	4,764	652
2006	5,016	509	1.22	5,090	796
2007	5,319	547	1.22	5,397	947
2008	5,468	528	1.43	5,447	996
2009	4,420	490	1.29	4,191	825
2010	4,905	535	1.27	4,876	868
2011	5,481	587	1.29	5,481	949
2012	5,737	609	1.30	5,738	1,023
2013	5,847	619	1.29	5,852	1,090
2014	5,996	634	1.33	6,055	1,215

[1] Inventories are stated at current cost. [2] Ratio based on December seasonally adjusted inventory data.

Source: U.S. Census Bureau, Manufacturers' Shipments, Inventories, and Orders, "Historical Data," <http://www.census.gov/manufacturing/m3/historical_data/index.html>, accessed August 2015.

Table 1037. Ratios of Manufacturers' Inventories to Shipments and Unfilled Orders to Shipments by Industry Group: 2000 to 2014

[Based on the Manufacturers' Shipments, Inventories, and Orders (M3) survey. See source for details]

Industry	2007 NAICS code [1]	2000	2005	2010	2011	2012	2013	2014
INVENTORIES-TO-SHIPMENTS RATIO [2]								
All manufacturing industries	(X)	**1.37**	**1.14**	**1.27**	**1.29**	**1.30**	**1.29**	**1.33**
Durable goods	(X)	1.56	1.33	1.62	1.63	1.64	1.66	1.65
Wood products	321	1.41	1.17	1.39	1.37	1.31	1.35	1.36
Nonmetallic mineral products	327	1.27	1.03	1.47	1.39	1.41	1.42	1.32
Primary metals	331	1.77	1.45	1.55	1.50	1.62	1.63	1.68
Fabricated metals	332	1.56	1.44	1.60	1.53	1.60	1.62	1.59
Machinery	333	2.04	1.66	1.84	1.83	1.90	1.91	1.98
Computers and electronic products	334	1.46	1.38	1.54	1.65	1.64	1.56	1.60
Electrical equipment, appliances, and components	335	1.40	1.33	1.45	1.55	1.59	1.66	1.54
Transportation equipment	336	1.42	1.11	1.65	1.73	1.63	1.71	1.67
Furniture and related products	337	1.37	1.14	1.19	1.13	1.12	1.13	1.08
Miscellaneous products	339	1.83	1.66	1.73	1.65	1.69	1.61	1.62
Nondurable goods	(X)	1.13	0.94	0.98	0.99	1.00	0.99	1.03
Food products	311	0.86	0.75	0.78	0.79	0.81	0.80	0.78
Beverages and tobacco products	312	1.49	1.37	1.63	1.50	1.61	1.60	1.57
Textile mills	313	1.55	1.21	1.23	1.36	1.30	1.21	1.28
Textile product mills	314	1.88	1.19	1.73	1.57	1.63	1.59	1.55
Apparel	315	1.92	1.49	1.56	1.78	1.91	1.97	2.04
Leather and allied products	316	2.00	1.80	1.71	1.66	1.73	1.83	1.88
Paper products	322	1.11	1.07	0.96	1.02	1.02	1.00	1.00
Printing	323	0.79	0.80	0.80	0.75	0.75	0.81	0.81
Petroleum and coal products	324	0.68	0.66	0.73	0.74	0.72	0.70	0.78
Basic chemicals	325	1.36	1.14	1.23	1.24	1.28	1.26	1.29
Plastics and rubber products	326	1.24	1.10	1.19	1.24	1.28	1.31	1.26
UNFILLED ORDERS-TO-SHIPMENTS RATIO								
Durable goods	(X)	4.01	4.54	6.15	6.07	6.37	6.78	6.94
Primary metals	331	1.53	1.87	1.89	1.70	1.58	1.58	1.56
Fabricated metals	332	2.13	2.52	2.81	2.67	2.84	2.88	2.82
Machinery	333	2.65	2.80	3.80	3.94	3.77	3.82	3.79
Computers and electronic products	334	4.25	5.05	6.10	6.35	6.68	5.88	6.17
Electrical equipment, appliances, and components	335	1.83	2.05	1.96	2.00	2.11	2.24	2.35
Transportation equipment	336	8.07	9.22	14.15	14.22	13.84	15.54	15.47
Furniture and related products	337	1.29	1.30	1.40	1.34	1.25	1.39	1.39

X Not applicable. [1] Based on the North American Industry Classification System, 2007; see text, this section and Section 15. [2] Ratio based on December seasonally adjusted inventory data.

Source: U.S. Census Bureau, Manufacturers' Shipments, Inventories, and Orders, "Historical Data," <http://www.census.gov/manufacturing/m3/historical_data/index.html>, accessed August 2015.

Table 1038. Value of Manufacturers' Shipments, Inventories, and New Orders by Industry: 2000 to 2014

[In billions of dollars (4,209 represents $4,209,000,000,000). Based on the Manufacturers' Shipments, Inventories, and Orders (M3) survey. See source for details]

Industry	2007 NAICS code [1]	2000	2010	2011	2012	2013	2014
SHIPMENTS							
All manufacturing industries	(X)	**4,209**	**4,905**	**5,481**	**5,737**	**5,847**	**5,996**
Durable goods	(X)	2,374	2,291	2,493	2,658	2,707	2,838
Wood products	321	94	70	70	78	89	97
Nonmetallic mineral products	327	97	90	93	98	106	116
Primary metals	331	157	233	279	268	262	279
Fabricated metals	332	268	294	324	340	345	361
Machinery	333	292	318	365	407	394	408
Computers and electronic products	334	511	331	338	339	326	339
Electrical equipment, appliances, and components	335	125	110	119	124	123	126
Transportation equipment	336	640	637	692	788	837	874
Furniture and related products	337	75	59	62	67	69	72
Miscellaneous products	339	115	150	153	150	156	165
Nondurable goods	(X)	1,835	2,615	2,988	3,079	3,140	3,158
Food products	311	435	649	709	739	761	805
Beverages and tobacco products	312	112	131	135	142	148	148
Textile mills	313	52	29	31	30	31	31
Textile product mills	314	34	21	22	22	23	23
Apparel	315	60	13	13	13	12	13
Leather and allied products	316	10	5	6	5	5	6
Paper products	322	165	170	176	181	186	195
Printing	323	104	82	82	82	83	84
Petroleum and coal products	324	235	627	838	851	866	833
Basic chemicals	325	449	698	773	795	798	785
Plastics and rubber products	326	178	189	204	219	227	235
INVENTORIES (as of December 31)							
All manufacturing industries	(X)	**470**	**537**	**587**	**609**	**619**	**634**
Durable goods	(X)	298	314	344	357	365	388
Wood products	321	10	8	8	9	10	11
Nonmetallic mineral products	327	10	10	11	12	12	13
Primary metals	331	22	31	36	35	36	39
Fabricated metals	332	34	41	43	45	46	48
Machinery	333	49	52	59	62	62	64
Computers and electronic products	334	63	41	45	44	42	43
Electrical equipment, appliances, and components	335	15	14	15	16	16	16
Transportation equipment	336	69	90	100	108	113	124
Furniture and related products	337	8	6	6	6	6	7
Miscellaneous products	339	18	22	20	21	22	22
Nondurable goods	(X)	172	222	243	252	254	247
Food products	311	32	43	48	51	52	53
Beverages and tobacco products	312	14	18	18	19	19	20
Textile mills	313	6	3	3	3	3	3
Textile product mills	314	5	3	3	3	3	3
Apparel	315	9	2	2	2	2	2
Leather and allied products	316	2	1	1	1	1	1
Paper products	322	15	14	15	15	15	16
Printing	323	6	5	5	5	5	5
Petroleum and coal products	324	13	42	49	48	49	39
Basic chemicals	325	52	72	78	82	81	81
Plastics and rubber products	326	18	19	21	23	24	24
NEW ORDERS							
All manufacturing industries	(X)	**4,161**	**4,876**	**5,481**	**5,738**	**5,852**	**6,055**
Durable goods	(X)	2,327	2,261	2,493	2,660	2,712	2,897
Wood products	321	94	66	(NA)	(NA)	(NA)	(NA)
Nonmetallic mineral products	327	97	92	(NA)	(NA)	(NA)	(NA)
Primary metals	331	154	242	282	261	263	281
Fabricated metals	332	270	301	328	344	347	365
Machinery	333	295	334	383	404	391	417
Computers and electronic products	334	436	262	267	273	251	283
Electrical equipment, appliances, and components	335	126	111	120	125	124	129
Transportation equipment	336	663	643	736	861	917	971
Furniture and related products	337	75	59	62	67	70	73
Miscellaneous products	339	117	151	(NA)	(NA)	(NA)	(NA)
Nondurable goods	(X)	1,835	2,614	(NA)	(NA)	(NA)	(NA)

NA Not available. X Not applicable. [1] Based on the North American Industry Classification System, 2007; see text, this section and Section 15.

Source: U.S. Census Bureau, Manufacturers' Shipments, Inventories, and Orders, "Annual Benchmark Data and Benchmark Procedures," <http://www.census.gov/manufacturing/m3/index.html>; and "Historical Data," <http://www.census.gov /manufacturing/m3/historical_data/index.html>; accessed August 2015.

Table 1039. Value of Manufacturers' Shipments, Inventories, and New Orders by Market Grouping: 2000 to 2014

[In billions of dollars (4,209 represents $4,209,000,000,000). Based on the Manufacturers' Shipments, Inventories, and Orders (M3) survey. See source for details]

Market grouping	2000	2005	2010	2011	2012	2013	2014
SHIPMENTS							
All manufacturing industries	**4,209**	**4,742**	**4,905**	**5,481**	**5,737**	**5,847**	**5,996**
Consumer goods	1,501	1,895	2,055	2,367	2,443	2,509	2,512
Consumer durable goods	391	423	329	352	374	402	405
Consumer nondurable goods	1,109	1,473	1,726	2,016	2,069	2,107	2,107
Aircraft and parts	112	114	149	158	188	197	210
Defense aircraft and parts	25	38	64	56	59	59	57
Nondefense aircraft and parts	87	76	85	102	129	138	153
Construction materials and supplies	445	510	443	471	500	523	558
Motor vehicles and parts	471	501	401	446	507	542	563
Computers and related products	110	65	38	29	32	29	27
Information technology industries	400	295	260	261	274	271	279
Nondefense capital goods	808	730	721	795	892	891	935
Excluding aircraft	758	687	667	731	805	799	832
Defense capital goods	67	92	131	121	118	116	115
INVENTORIES (December 31)							
All manufacturing industries	**470**	**461**	**535**	**587**	**609**	**619**	**634**
Consumer goods	128	140	168	179	186	189	183
Consumer durable goods	26	27	22	22	24	26	27
Consumer nondurable goods	102	113	146	157	162	164	156
Aircraft and parts	36	33	56	62	67	70	77
Defense aircraft and parts	9	12	12	13	13	12	12
Nondefense aircraft and parts	27	22	43	49	54	58	64
Construction materials and supplies	49	53	52	56	58	61	64
Motor vehicles and parts	22	23	22	25	28	30	33
Computers and related products	8	4	4	4	4	4	4
Information technology industries	51	38	35	38	38	37	38
Nondefense capital goods	127	107	134	149	157	161	171
Excluding aircraft	107	90	99	110	114	114	117
Defense capital goods	17	16	21	21	21	20	21
NEW ORDERS							
All manufacturing industries	**4,161**	**4,764**	**4,876**	**5,481**	**5,738**	**5,852**	**6,055**
Consumer goods	1,502	1,894	2,055	2,368	2,443	2,510	2,512
Consumer durable goods	393	421	329	352	374	403	405
Consumer nondurable goods	1,109	1,473	1,726	2,016	2,069	2,107	2,107
Aircraft and parts	131	179	157	202	257	272	297
Defense aircraft and parts	31	36	64	59	71	52	56
Nondefense aircraft and parts	99	143	93	143	186	219	242
Construction materials and supplies	447	517	450	470	500	524	564
Motor vehicles and parts	468	503	402	447	509	543	567
Computers and related products	108	64	36	29	32	29	27
Information technology industries	410	300	262	272	281	257	290
Nondefense capital goods	831	814	740	851	947	972	1,037
Excluding aircraft	768	704	676	754	815	804	856
Defense capital goods	80	82	138	134	124	96	114

Source: U.S. Census Bureau, Manufacturers' Shipments, Inventories, and Orders, "Historical Data," <http://www.census.gov/manufacturing/m3/historical_data/>, accessed August 2015.

Table 1040. Finances and Profits of Manufacturing Corporations: 2001 to 2014

[In billions of dollars (4,295 represents $4,295,000,000,000). Data exclude estimates for corporations with less than $250,000 in assets at time of sample selection. Minus sign (-) indicates loss]

Item	2001 [1]	2005 [1]	2007 [1]	2008 [2]	2009 [2]	2010 [2]	2011 [2]	2012 [3]	2013 [3]	2014 [3]
Net sales	4,295	5,411	6,060	6,374	5,110	5,756	6,486	6,668	6,743	6,912
Net operating profit	186	359	416	358	289	420	479	508	497	540
Net profit:										
Before taxes	83	524	603	388	361	584	722	676	722	747
After taxes	36	401	443	266	286	478	594	564	601	612
Cash dividends	103	179	178	182	172	180	184	212	242	262
Net income retained in business	-66	222	265	84	115	298	410	353	359	350

[1] Based on the North American Industry Classification System, 2002. [2] Based on the North American Industry Classification System, 2007. [3] Based on the North American Industry Classification System, 2012; see text, Section 15.

Source: U.S. Census Bureau, Quarterly Financial Report for Manufacturing, Mining, Trade, and Selected Service Industries. See also <http://www.census.gov/econ/qfr>.

Table 1041. Manufacturing Corporations—Assets and Profits by Asset Size: 1990 to 2014

[In millions of dollars (2,629,458 represents $2,629,458,000,000). Corporations and assets as of end of 4th quarter; profits for entire year. Through 2000, based on Standard Industrial Classification code (SIC); beginning 2001, based on the North American Industry Classification System; see text, Section 15. For corporations above a certain asset value based on complete canvass. The asset value for complete canvass was raised in 1988 to $50 million and in 1995 to $250 million. Asset sizes less than these values are sampled, except as noted. For details regarding survey description, data analysis, and methodology, see source, 4th quarter report. Minus sign (-) indicates loss]

| Year | Total | Asset–size class | | | | | | |
		Under $10 million [1]	$10 to $25 million	$25 to $50 million	$50 to $100 million	$100 to $250 million	$250 million to $1 billion	$1 billion and over
Assets:								
1990	2,629,458	142,498	74,477	55,914	72,554	123,967	287,512	1,872,536
2000	4,852,106	171,666	85,482	72,122	90,866	149,714	389,537	3,892,720
2001 [2]	4,747,789	169,701	84,664	67,493	88,088	131,617	393,752	3,812,474
2002	4,823,219	166,191	82,369	62,654	81,667	134,821	407,423	3,888,095
2003	5,162,852	161,462	80,681	62,592	77,205	126,826	392,192	4,261,894
2004	5,538,113	163,072	80,085	71,674	81,741	126,950	414,144	4,600,447
2005	5,828,716	165,195	85,785	68,731	87,818	142,900	423,917	4,854,370
2006	6,179,142	168,537	93,786	72,494	91,877	146,651	418,501	5,187,295
2007	6,891,131	180,319	98,348	80,400	93,017	144,254	433,634	5,861,160
2008	6,819,681	180,025	99,430	80,757	98,478	137,907	420,104	5,802,981
2009	6,942,972	166,590	106,773	71,642	76,308	126,202	413,856	5,981,600
2010	7,432,384	165,598	105,661	74,081	82,713	130,428	405,113	6,468,791
2011	7,907,376	169,045	114,818	76,809	86,452	130,488	435,889	6,893,876
2012	8,331,651	173,043	112,237	81,304	90,724	130,768	440,070	7,303,505
2013	8,838,478	173,571	116,199	88,598	86,532	138,222	439,357	7,795,999
2014	9,112,941	177,597	124,729	98,344	86,287	133,790	451,678	8,040,517
Net profit: [3]								
1990	110,128	8,527	5,160	2,769	2,661	3,525	7,110	80,377
2000	275,313	16,578	6,820	3,403	2,742	3,510	15,121	227,136
2001 [2]	36,168	8,387	3,366	-408	403	-543	-6,782	31,746
2002	134,686	10,003	2,784	807	1,699	3,356	-1,227	117,262
2003	237,041	9,821	3,374	2,005	2,256	2,973	4,115	212,497
2004	348,151	14,970	5,745	3,858	3,080	5,140	12,787	302,571
2005	401,344	17,357	6,057	4,066	3,781	7,678	15,967	346,438
2006	470,282	22,301	8,685	5,260	4,601	8,901	21,405	399,131
2007	442,734	22,930	9,006	4,402	6,518	8,400	17,565	373,915
2008	266,346	18,182	7,472	5,820	3,739	3,403	2,239	225,492
2009	286,491	9,692	5,979	4,617	2,500	2,723	2,653	258,310
2010	477,884	16,637	7,670	4,181	5,880	5,390	19,494	417,121
2011	594,335	20,357	9,257	5,209	5,730	6,808	17,568	529,406
2012	564,191	23,042	11,500	6,452	6,727	5,820	19,727	490,924
2013	601,368	24,740	10,202	6,468	6,141	6,982	21,000	525,835
2014	611,963	27,002	12,354	5,674	6,031	6,929	19,515	534,455

[1] Excludes estimates for corporations with less than $250,000 in assets at time of sample selection. [2] Beginning 2001, data reported based on the North American Industry Classification System. [3] After taxes.

Source: U.S. Census Bureau, *Quarterly Financial Report for Manufacturing, Mining, Trade, and Selected Service Industries*. See also <http://www.census.gov/econ/qfr>.

Table 1042. Manufacturing Corporations—Selected Finances: 1990 to 2014

[In billions of dollars (2,811 represents $2,811,000,000,000). Data are not necessarily comparable from year to year due to changes in accounting procedures, industry classifications, sampling procedures, etc.; for details, see source. See headnote, Table 1040. Minus sign (-) indicates loss]

| Year | All manufacturing corporations | | | Durable goods | | | Nondurable goods | | |
| | | Profits [1] | | | Profits [1] | | | Profits [1] | |
	Sales	Before taxes	After taxes	Sales	Before taxes	After taxes	Sales	Before taxes	After taxes
1990	2,811	158	110	1,357	57	41	1,454	101	69
1995	3,528	275	198	1,808	131	94	1,721	144	104
2000	4,548	381	275	2,457	191	132	2,091	190	144
2001 [2]	4,295	83	36	2,321	-69	-76	1,974	152	112
2002	4,217	196	135	2,261	45	21	1,955	149	113
2003	4,397	306	237	2,283	118	88	2,114	188	149
2004	4,934	447	348	2,537	200	157	2,397	248	192
2005	5,411	524	401	2,731	211	161	2,681	313	240
2006	5,783	605	470	2,910	249	193	2,873	356	278
2007	6,060	603	443	3,016	247	159	3,044	356	283
2008	6,374	388	266	2,970	98	43	3,405	290	223
2009	5,110	361	286	2,427	84	55	2,683	276	232
2010	5,756	584	478	2,708	287	232	3,048	297	245
2011	6,486	722	594	2,927	335	284	3,558	387	310
2012	6,668	676	564	3,102	303	260	3,567	373	304
2013	6,743	722	601	3,178	358	294	3,566	365	308
2014	6,912	747	612	3,343	385	315	3,569	361	297

[1] Beginning 1998, profits before and after income taxes reflect inclusion of minority stockholders' interest in net income before and after income taxes. [2] Beginning 2001, data reported based on the North American Industry Classification System.

Source: U.S. Census Bureau, *Quarterly Financial Report for Manufacturing, Mining, Trade, and Selected Service Industries*. See also <http://www.census.gov/econ/qfr>.

Table 1043. Motor Vehicle Manufactures—Summary by Selected Industry: 2013

[42,055 represents $42,055,000,000. Based on the Annual Survey of Manufactures; see Appendix III]

Industry	2012 NAICS code [1]	All employees [2]			Production workers [2]	Value of product shipments [3] (mil. dol.)
		Number	Payroll			
			Total (mil. dol.)	Payroll per employee (dol.)		
Motor vehicle manufacturing, total.....................	3361-3363	766,327	42,055	54,878	610,217	542,005
Motor vehicle, total....................	3361	166,937	12,048	72,172	143,572	280,687
Automobile and light duty motor vehicle....................	33611	138,609	10,460	75,467	122,022	253,327
Automobile................................	336111	73,803	5,460	73,975	63,842	115,229
Light truck and utility vehicle....................	336112	64,806	5,001	77,167	58,180	138,098
Heavy duty truck..........................	33612	28,328	1,588	56,049	21,549	27,360
Motor vehicle body and trailer......................	3362	116,904	5,175	44,270	93,917	34,713
Motor vehicle body and trailer manufacturing..............	33621	116,904	5,175	44,270	93,917	34,713
Motor vehicle body.......................	336211	41,474	1,871	45,112	32,033	11,985
Truck trailer........................	336212	27,847	1,157	41,549	23,082	8,017
Motor home..........................	336213	7,828	381	48,609	6,106	3,031
Travel trailer and camper..................	336214	39,754	1,767	44,443	32,697	11,681
Motor vehicle parts.......................	3363	482,486	24,831	51,465	372,728	226,605
Motor vehicle gasoline engine and engine parts...........	33631	50,796	3,151	62,041	39,799	32,077
Motor vehicle electrical and electronic equipment.........	33632	53,807	2,661	49,457	40,108	21,027
Motor vehicle steering and suspension.................	33633	30,601	1,475	48,208	22,325	12,290
Motor vehicle brake system...................	33634	22,860	1,098	48,022	17,286	11,077
Motor vehicle transmission and power train parts.........	33635	62,159	3,853	61,986	48,559	35,852
Motor vehicle seating and interior trim....................	33636	53,398	2,272	42,556	39,496	25,435
Motor vehicle metal stamping....................	33637	87,292	4,625	52,988	70,440	31,160
Other motor vehicle parts.....................	33639	121,571	5,695	46,844	94,714	57,687

[1] North American Industry Classification System, 2012; see text, Section 15. [2] Includes all full-time and part-time employees on the payrolls of operating manufacturing establishments during any part of the pay period that included the 12th of the month specified on the report form. Included are employees on paid sick leave, paid holidays, and paid vacations; not included are proprietors and partners of unincorporated businesses. [3] Includes extensive and unmeasurable duplication from shipments between establishments in the same industry classification.

Source: U.S. Census Bureau, Annual Survey of Manufactures, "Statistics for Industry Groups and Industries: 2013," <http://factfinder2.census.gov/>, accessed September 2015.

Table 1044. Motor Vehicle Manufactures—Employees, Payroll, and Shipments by Major Producing State: 2013

[12,048,209 represents $12,048,209,000. Data are from the 2012 Annual Survey of Manufactures. Industry based on the 2012 North American Industry Classification System (NAICS); see text, Section 15. See footnote 3, Table 1043 for information regarding shipments. Based on the Annual Survey of Manufactures; see Appendix III]

State	Motor vehicle manufacturing (NAICS 3361)			Motor vehicle parts manufacturing (NAICS 3363)		
	Employees	Payroll ($1,000)	Value of shipments ($1,000)	Employees	Payroll ($1,000)	Value of shipments ($1,000)
United States [1].................	166,937	12,048,209	280,686,963	482,486	24,831,251	226,605,019
Alabama..........................	10,818	820,772	22,960,162	20,518	930,926	12,723,259
Arizona............................	58	4,853	(D)	2,492	128,069	(D)
Arkansas...........................	12	(D)	(D)	5,946	256,900	1,802,367
California...........................	4,174	373,718	3,276,243	14,401	689,309	5,265,671
Florida.............................	490	22,744	(D)	2,995	139,868	957,715
Georgia............................	(8)	(D)	(D)	12,286	582,662	8,158,824
Illinois.............................	10,576	635,984	14,101,093	27,196	1,215,895	8,765,626
Indiana............................	12,926	972,357	(D)	50,577	2,811,596	23,652,053
Iowa...............................	51	2,879	(D)	4,598	201,120	1,545,838
Kentucky..........................	16,982	1,299,871	(D)	27,966	1,300,672	14,524,928
Massachusetts....................	(3)	(D)	(D)	1,366	89,616	513,467
Michigan..........................	34,271	2,577,996	(D)	95,646	5,441,797	48,170,181
Minnesota.........................	1,294	54,098	(D)	2,388	116,948	646,488
Mississippi........................	(9)	(D)	(D)	5,095	220,930	2,172,086
Missouri...........................	6,559	487,674	(D)	10,197	454,145	4,037,752
Nebraska..........................	34	(D)	(D)	3,548	168,015	1,283,886
New Hampshire....................	(2)	(D)	(D)	1,449	50,848	239,423
New Jersey........................	47	2,716	59,106	818	39,477	315,339
New Mexico.......................	(2)	(D)	(D)	225	(D)	38,429
New York..........................	91	4,571	30,205	10,191	640,265	3,933,743
North Carolina....................	(8)	(D)	(D)	14,348	741,767	8,350,643
Ohio...............................	18,514	1,378,731	34,289,495	63,876	3,537,433	28,926,253
Oklahoma.........................	(6)	(D)	(D)	1,400	62,832	480,223
Oregon............................	(6)	(D)	(D)	1,344	60,164	363,119
Pennsylvania......................	(7)	(D)	(D)	8,358	374,281	2,887,492
South Carolina....................	(9)	(D)	(D)	16,346	833,933	8,870,689
Tennessee.........................	6,747	547,062	(D)	32,149	1,531,383	18,175,411
Texas..............................	7,615	610,856	21,860,872	12,322	592,949	5,752,269
Utah...............................	–	–	–	3,526	204,223	1,867,226
Virginia............................	(7)	(D)	(D)	4,263	207,423	1,229,610
Washington........................	(5)	(D)	(D)	2,367	105,837	768,219
West Virginia......................	(4)	(D)	(D)	2,091	122,287	2,386,910
Wisconsin.........................	(9)	(D)	(D)	9,978	442,287	4,174,822

– Represents zero. D Withheld to avoid disclosing data on individual companies. [1] Includes states not shown separately. [2] Employee class size of 0 to 19. [3] Employee class size of 20 to 99. [4] Employee class size of 100 to 249. [5] Employee class size of 250 to 499. [6] Employee class size of 500 to 999. [7] Employee class size of 1,000 to 2,499. [8] Employee class size of 2,500 to 4,999. [9] Employee class size of 5,000 to 9,999.

Source: U.S. Census Bureau, Annual Survey of Manufactures, "Geographic Area Statistics: Statistics for all Manufacturing by State: 2013," <http://factfinder.census.gov/>, accessed September 2015.

Table 1045. Net Orders for U.S. Civil Jet Transport Aircraft: 1990 to 2013

[1990 data are net new firm orders; beginning 2000, net announced orders. Minus sign (-) indicates net cancellations. In 1997, Boeing acquired McDonnell Douglas]

Type of aircraft and customer	1990	2000	2005	2009	2010	2011	2012	2013
Total number [1]	**670**	**585**	**1,004**	**142**	**530**	**805**	**1,203**	**1,355**
U.S. customers	259	412	220	24	232	596	443	304
Foreign customers	411	193	811	118	298	209	760	1,051
Boeing 737, total	189	378	571	178	486	551	1,124	1,046
U.S. customers	38	302	152	34	206	525	407	196
Foreign customers	151	86	439	144	280	26	717	850
Boeing 747, total	153	24	43	2	-1	-1	1	12
U.S. customers	24	1	13	-2	-2	-1	–	–
Foreign customers	129	18	30	4	1	–	1	12
Boeing 757, total [2]	66	43	(X)	(X)	(X)	(X)	(X)	(X)
U.S. customers	33	38	(X)	(X)	(X)	(X)	(X)	(X)
Foreign customers	33	14	(X)	(X)	(X)	(X)	(X)	(X)
Boeing 767, total	60	6	15	2	3	42	22	2
U.S. customers	23	-2	–	-1	–	31	19	2
Foreign customers	37	14	20	3	3	11	3	–
Boeing 777, total	34	113	154	19	46	200	68	113
U.S. customers	34	60	10	-7	3	37	4	11
Foreign customers	–	53	146	26	43	163	64	102
Boeing 787, total	–	–	235	-59	-4	13	-12	182
U.S. customers	–	–	45	–	25	4	13	95
Foreign customers	–	–	190	-59	-29	9	-25	87
McDonnell Douglas MD-11, total [3]	52	–	–	(X)	(X)	(X)	(X)	(X)
U.S. customers	16	–	–	(X)	(X)	(X)	(X)	(X)
Foreign customers	36	–	–	(X)	(X)	(X)	(X)	(X)
McDonnell Douglas MD-80/90, total [3]	116	–	–	(X)	(X)	(X)	(X)	(X)
U.S. customers	91	–	–	(X)	(X)	(X)	(X)	(X)
Foreign customers	25	–	–	(X)	(X)	(X)	(X)	(X)
McDonnell Douglas MD-95, total [3]	–	21	–	(X)	(X)	(X)	(X)	(X)
U.S. customers	–	13	–	(X)	(X)	(X)	(X)	(X)
Foreign customers	–	8	–	(X)	(X)	(X)	(X)	(X)

X Not applicable. – Represents zero. [1] Beginning 2000, includes unidentified customers. [2] Boeing 757 is no longer in production; the last delivery occurred in 2005. [3] McDonnell Douglas aircraft are no longer in production; last aircraft were delivered in 2006.

Source: © 2014 Aerospace Industries Association of America, Inc. See also <http://www.aia-aerospace.org/economics/aerospace_statistics/>.

Table 1046. Aerospace Industry Sales by Product Group and Customer: 2005 to 2014

[In billions of dollars (168.6 represents $168,600,000,000). Data for 2014 are preliminary]

Group	2005	2008	2009	2010	2011	2012	2013	2014
CURRENT DOLLARS								
Total sales	**168.6**	**211.1**	**210.7**	**209.4**	**214.9**	**222.5**	**219.4**	**228.4**
Product group:								
Aircraft, total	86.6	112.2	110.8	110.2	113.1	120.7	121.8	127.8
Civil [1]	37.2	48.2	51.3	48.2	53.2	62.2	69.7	75.3
Military	49.4	64.0	59.5	62.1	59.9	58.6	52.2	52.6
Missiles	20.8	24.6	24.7	23.5	22.7	21.8	20.7	19.9
Space	35.8	44.1	45.8	46.0	49.1	48.8	46.3	48.8
Related products and services [2]	25.4	30.2	29.4	29.7	30.0	31.1	30.6	31.9
Customer group:								
Aerospace products and services, total	143.2	180.9	181.2	179.7	184.9	191.4	188.8	196.5
DOD [3]	80.7	103.4	101.7	103.5	101.1	95.7	87.3	87.3
NASA [4]	16.1	18.1	19.3	19.4	19.9	19.5	19.1	19.8
Other customers [5]	46.4	59.4	60.3	56.8	63.9	76.2	82.5	89.5
Related products and services [2]	25.4	30.2	29.4	29.7	30.0	31.1	30.6	31.9
CONSTANT (2009) DOLLARS [6]								
Total sales	**175.7**	**212.4**	**210.7**	**209.6**	**214.0**	**219.5**	**215.2**	**222.9**
Product group:								
Aircraft, total	90.2	112.9	110.8	110.3	112.6	119.2	119.5	124.7
Civil [1]	38.7	48.5	51.3	48.2	52.9	61.4	68.4	73.4
Military	51.5	64.4	59.5	62.1	59.7	57.8	51.1	51.3
Missiles	21.7	24.7	24.7	23.5	22.7	21.5	20.3	19.4
Space	37.3	44.4	45.8	46.1	48.9	48.2	45.4	47.7
Related products and services [2]	26.4	30.4	29.4	29.7	29.9	30.7	30.1	31.1
Customer group:								
Aerospace products and services, total	149.2	182.0	181.2	179.9	184.1	188.9	185.2	191.8
DOD [3]	84.1	104.1	101.7	103.6	100.7	94.4	85.6	85.2
NASA [4]	16.8	18.2	19.3	19.4	19.9	19.3	18.7	19.3
Other customers [5]	48.4	59.8	60.7	56.9	63.6	75.2	80.9	87.3
Related products and services [2]	26.4	30.4	29.4	29.7	29.9	30.7	30.1	31.1

[1] All civil sales of aircraft (domestic and export sales of jet transports, commuters, business, and personal aircraft and helicopters). [2] Electronics, software, and ground support equipment, plus sales of non-aerospace products which are produced by aerospace-manufacturing use technology, processes, and materials derived from aerospace products. [3] Department of Defense. [4] National Aeronautics and Space Administration. [5] Includes civil aircraft sales (see footnote 1), commercial space sales, all exports of military aircraft and missiles and related propulsion and parts. [6] Based on Aerospace Industry Association's aerospace composite price deflator (2009=100).

Source: © 2014 Aerospace Industries Association of America, Inc., *2014 Year-end Review and Forecast*, December 2014. See also <http://www.aia-aerospace.org>.

Table 1047. General Aviation Airplane Shipments and Billings: 1990 to 2013

[2,008 represents 2,008,000,000. Data are for U.S. manufactured airplanes. Totals may not add up due to rounding]

Type of Airplane	1990	1995	2000	2005	2010	2011	2012	2013
Airplane units shipped (number)	**1,144**	**1,077**	**2,816**	**2,857**	**1,334**	**1,465**	**1,518**	**1,615**
Total piston	695	576	1,913	2,095	746	706	708	754
Single-engine	608	515	1,810	2,024	679	639	645	674
Multi-engine	87	61	103	71	67	67	63	80
Total turbine	449	501	903	762	588	759	810	861
Turboprop	281	255	315	240	224	395	463	527
Business jet	168	246	588	522	364	364	347	334
Factory net billings (mil. dol.)	**2,008**	**2,842**	**8,558**	**8,667**	**7,875**	**8,266**	**8,017**	**11,069**
Total Piston	92	123	446	712	368	368	374	456
Single-engine	68	(NA)	(NA)	(NA)	(NA)	(NA)	(NA)	(NA)
Multi-engine	24	(NA)	(NA)	(NA)	(NA)	(NA)	(NA)	(NA)
Total turbine	1,916	2,719	8,112	7,954	7,506	7,898	7,643	10,613
Turboprop	644	653	934	749	724	831	867	1,358
Business jet	1,272	2,066	7,178	7,205	6,782	7,068	6,776	9,255

NA Not available.

Source: General Aviation Manufacturers Association, *2013 General Aviation Statistical Databook & 2014 Industry Outlook* ©, 2014. See also <www.gama.aero>.

Table 1048. Semiconductors, Electronic Components, and Other Electronic Component Manufacturing Equipment—Value of Shipments: 2008 to 2013

[In millions of dollars (9,765 represents $9,765,000,000). Data are from the Annual Survey of Manufacturers (ASM) and are based on the North American Industry Classification System (NAICS). In years ending in 2 and 7, ASM statistics are included in the Economic Census]

Product description	Product code	2008	2009	2010	2011	2012	2013
Semiconductor machinery manufacturing	333242	(NA)	(NA)	(NA)	(NA)	9,765	9,032
Semiconductor machinery manufacturing	333295	9,257	5,554	9,210	11,870	(NA)	(NA)
Electron tube manufacturing	334411	1,195	1,057	1,157	1,174	(NA)	(NA)
Bare printed circuit board manufacturing	334412	5,586	3,997	4,589	4,445	4,773	4,491
Semiconductors and related device manufacturing	334413	67,707	55,932	71,847	79,456	47,211	59,986
Integrated circuit packages	3344131	52,057	40,503	53,636	62,297	(NA)	46,724
Transistors	3344134	1,004	647	658	676	(NA)	539
Diodes and rectifiers	3344137	606	322	417	379	(NA)	269
Other semiconductor devices (incl. chips, wafers, and heat sinks)	334413A	11,391	12,524	14,341	13,467	(NA)	10,463
Other semiconductor and related device	334413W	2,648	1,936	2,794	2,639	(NA)	1,991
Electronic capacitor manufacturing	334414	968	790	972	1,070	(NA)	(NA)
Electronic resistor manufacturing	334415	658	478	582	548	(NA)	(NA)
Capacitor, resistor, coil, transformer, and other inductor manufacturing	334416	1,783	1,502	1,744	2,120	3,522	3,464
Capacitors for electronic circuitry	3344161	(NA)	(NA)	(NA)	(NA)	(NA)	916
Resistors for electronic circuitry	3344162	(NA)	(NA)	(NA)	(NA)	(NA)	407
Electronic coils, transformers, and other inductors	3344163	(NA)	(NA)	(NA)	(NA)	(NA)	2,052
Other capacitor, resistor, coil, transformer, and other inductor	334416W	(NA)	(NA)	(NA)	(NA)	(NA)	90
Electronic connector manufacturing	334417	4,744	3,965	4,587	4,985	5,393	5,468
Printed circuit assembly, electronic assembly manufacturing	334418	21,959	16,631	18,197	18,151	16,383	16,882
External modems, consumer	3344184	515	443	716	705	(NA)	260
Printed circuit assemblies, loaded boards and modules	334418B	19,811	14,866	16,181	16,146	(NA)	15,677
Other printed circuit assembly, electronic assembly	334418W	1,632	1,321	1,301	1,300	(NA)	945
Other electronic component manufacturing	334419	10,786	8,322	8,664	9,331	10,717	11,082
Crystals, filters, piezoelectric, & other related electronic devices	3344191	1,285	919	878	998	(NA)	1,028
Electron tubes and parts, excluding glass blanks	3344192	(NA)	(NA)	(NA)	(NA)	(NA)	1,082
All other misc. transducers (incl. elect-electronic input/output)	3344194	1,425	1,174	1,200	1,266	(NA)	749
Switches, mechanical, for electronic circuitry	3344197	1,124	807	1,070	1,094	(NA)	961
Microwave components and devices (excl. antennae, tubes, etc.)	334419A	1,533	1,275	1,276	1,601	(NA)	1,693
All other miscellaneous electronic components	334419E	4,195	3,599	3,437	3,413	(NA)	4,648
Other electronic component manufacturing [2]	334419W	1,225	[1] 548	802	959	(NA)	921

NA Not available. [1] Sampling error exceeds 40 percent. [2] Not specified by kind.

Source: U.S. Census Bureau, Annual Survey of Manufactures, "Value of Products Shipments: Value of Shipments for Product Classes"; and Economic Census 2012, "Subject Series: Product Summary: Products or Services Statistics"; <http://factfinder.census.gov>, accessed September 2015.

Table 1049. Computers and Peripheral Equipment Manufacturing—Value of Shipments: 2008 to 2013

[In millions of dollars (38,023 represents $38,023,000,000). Data are from the Annual Survey of Manufacturers (ASM) and are based on the North American Industry Classification System (NAICS). ASM statistics are included in the Economic Census in years ending in 2 and 7]

Product description	Product code	2008	2009	2010	2011	2012	2013
Electronic computers manufacturing	334111	38,023	31,433	16,987	6,814	8,116	7,948
Host computers, multiusers (mainframes, servers, etc.)	3341111	10,363	(D)	12,008	3,911	(NA)	4,527
Single user computers, microprocessor-based	3341117	26,698	(D)	4,295	2,255	(NA)	2,549
Other computers (array, analog, hybrid, and special-use computers)	334111D	429	365	375	345	(NA)	530
Other electronic computer [2]	334111W	533	[1] 253	[1] 309	[1] 303	(NA)	342
Computer storage devices manufacturing	334112	9,152	6,406	7,942	8,545	8,619	9,072
Computer storage devices [3]	3341121	7,356	5,230	7,108	7,747	(NA)	7,092
Parts, attachments, and accessories for computer storage devices	3341124	1,586	902	652	603	(NA)	1,920
Other computer storage device mfg. [2]	334112W	210	275	182	196	(NA)	60
Computer terminal and other computer peripheral equipment manufacturing	334118	(NA)	(NA)	(NA)	(NA)	10,634	10,682
Computer terminals (excluding point-of-sale and funds-transfer devices, parts, attachments, and accessories)	3341181	(NA)	(NA)	(NA)	(NA)	(NA)	381
Parts, attachments, and accessories for computer terminals (excluding point-of-sale and funds-transfer devices)	3341182	(NA)	(NA)	(NA)	(NA)	(NA)	21
All other miscellaneous computer peripheral (input/output) equipment [3]	3341183	(NA)	(NA)	(NA)	(NA)	(NA)	7,253
Parts, subassemblies, and accessories for computer peripheral equipment (excluding digital cameras) [3]	3341184	(NA)	(NA)	(NA)	(NA)	(NA)	1,295
Point-of-sale terminals and fund-transfer devices	3341185	(NA)	(NA)	(NA)	(NA)	(NA)	957
Parts and attachments for point-of-sale terminals and fund-transfer devices	3341186	(NA)	(NA)	(NA)	(NA)	(NA)	135
Computer terminal and other computer peripheral equipment , total [2]	334118W	(NA)	(NA)	(NA)	(NA)	(NA)	639
Magnetic and optical recording media	334613	1,622	875	753	603	321	(S)
Software and other prerecorded compact disc, tape, and record reproducing	334614	(NA)	(NA)	(NA)	(NA)	2,670	2,546

NA Not available. D Withheld to avoid disclosing data on individual companies. [1] Sampling error exceeds 40 percent. [2] Not specified by kind. [3] Excluding parts, attachments, accessories, etc.

Source: U.S. Census Bureau, Annual Survey of Manufactures, "Value of Products Shipments: Value of Shipments for Product Classes"; and Economic Census 2012, "Manufacturing: Subject Series: Product Summary: Products or Services Statistics: 2012"; <http://factfinder.census.gov>, accessed September 2015.

Table 1050. Communications Equipment Manufacturing—Value of Shipments: 2007 to 2013

[In millions of dollars (19,145 represents $19,145,000,000). Data are from the Annual Survey of Manufacturers (ASM) and are based on the North American Industry Classification System (NAICS). In years ending in 2 and 7, ASM statistics are included in the Economic Census]

Product description	Product code	2007	2008	2009	2010	2011	2012	2013
Telephone apparatus manufacturing	334210	19,145	[1] 7,236	7,623	8,340	8,188	7,171	7,393
Telephone switching and switchboard equipment	3342101	2,535	2,302	1,693	1,719	1,562	(NA)	772
Carrier line equipment and non-consumer modems	3342104	3,290	2,679	2,208	2,406	2,647	(NA)	2,323
Wireline voice and data network equipment	3342107	12,348	(S)	3,036	3,453	3,197	(NA)	3,621
Other telephone apparatus manufacturing	334210W	971	657	687	762	782	(NA)	677
Radio and television broadcast and wireless communications equipment	334220	36,031	35,787	27,838	26,663	26,114	26,345	26,415
Broadcast, studio, and related electronic equipment	3342202	3,805	4,105	3,684	4,549	4,599	(NA)	2,166
Wireless networking equipment	3342203	6,148	4,982	1,950	1,528	1,088	(NA)	2,288
Radio station equipment	3342205	17,691	15,396	13,796	12,225	11,328	(NA)	9,936
Other communications systems and equipment	3342209	6,078	8,950	7,397	7,804	8,465	(NA)	10,434
Other radio and television broadcast and wireless communications equipment	334220W	2,309	2,354	[1] 1,011	(S)	(S)	(NA)	1,591
Other communications equipment manufacturing	334290	4,291	3,553	3,482	4,801	4,906	4,663	4,922
Alarm systems (incl. electric sirens and horns)	3342901	1,830	1,510	1,423	1,258	1,377	(NA)	2,195
Vehicular and pedestrian traffic control equipment	3342902	1,362	1,235	1,185	2,656	2,641	(NA)	1,700
Intercommunications systems (incl. inductive paging systems)	3342903	535	313	336	453	455	(NA)	552
Other communications equipment [2]	334290W	565	495	538	434	432	(NA)	475
External modems, consumer	3344184	414	515	443	716	705	(NA)	260

NA Not available. S Estimates do not meet publication standards. [1] Sampling error exceeds 40 percent. [2] Not specified by kind.

Source: U.S. Census Bureau, Annual Survey of Manufactures, "Value of Products Shipments: Value of Shipments for Product Classes"; and Economic Census 2012, "Manufacturing: Subject Series: Product Summary: Products or Services Statistics: 2012"; <http://factfinder.census.gov>, accessed September 2015.

Table 1051. Pharmaceutical Preparations—Value of Shipments: 2007 to 2013

[In millions of dollars (128,016 represents $128,016,000,000). Data are from the Annual Survey of Manufactures (ASM) and based on the North American Industry Classification System (NAICS). The ASM is not conducted in years ending in 2 and 7; data for those years are based on final results of the Economic Census]

Product description	Product code	2007	2008	2009	2010	2011	2012	2013
Pharmaceutical preparations, except biologicals............	325412	128,632	127,914	125,249	114,131	123,950	(NA)	122,350
Affecting neoplasms, endocrine system, and metabolic disease............	3254121	28,525	32,974	33,225	27,167	27,957	(NA)	25,460
Acting on the central nervous system and sense organs....	3254124	29,419	27,225	27,415	25,235	26,010	(NA)	25,377
Acting on the cardiovascular system...........................	3254127	12,021	11,888	12,038	10,441	11,076	(NA)	7,082
Acting on the respiratory system.............................	325412A	16,528	15,739	13,831	14,249	20,545	(NA)	21,561
Acting on the digestive system or genito-urinary system....	325412D	10,174	9,626	8,792	7,780	7,138	(NA)	4,728
Acting on the skin...	325412G	3,596	3,379	3,884	4,148	3,586	(NA)	3,075
Vitamin, nutrient, and hematinic preparations.................	325412L	8,234	8,768	8,898	8,980	10,244	(NA)	7,874
Affecting parasitic and infective diseases (excl. diagnostics)...	325412P	10,834	9,488	9,287	8,400	8,892	(NA)	14,205
Preparations for veterinary use (excl. diagnostics) [1]........	325412T	3,208	3,043	2,592	2,674	2,851	(NA)	2,278
In vivo diagnostic substances................................	325412V	2,648	2,376	1,917	1,660	1,904	(NA)	2,559
Other pharmaceutical preparation manufacturing [2]..........	325412W	3,446	3,408	3,370	3,397	3,747	(NA)	8,152

[1] Including medicinal premixes and medicated pet care products; excluding pet flea and tick products. [2] Not specified by kind.

Source: U.S. Census Bureau, Annual Survey of Manufactures, "Value of Products Shipments: Value of Shipments for Product Classes," <http://factfinder2.census.gov>, accessed April 2015.

Table 1052. Household Appliances Manufacturing—Value of Shipments: 2007 to 2013

[In millions of dollars (4,650 represents $4,650,000,000). Data are from the Annual Survey of Manufacturers (ASM) and are based on the North American Industry Classification System (NAICS). In years ending in 2 and 7, ASM statistics are included in the Economic Census]

Product description	Product code	2007	2008	2009	2010	2011	2012	2013
Household cooking appliance manufacturing....................	335221	4,650	4,033	3,674	3,719	3,781	4,369	5,044
Electric household ranges, ovens, and surface cooking units & equipment.....................................	3352211	2,584	2,198	1,980	1,895	1,908	(NA)	3,156
Gas household ranges, ovens, and surface cooking units & equipment.....................................	3352213	1,300	1,141	1,043	1,121	1,154	(NA)	1,121
Other household ranges and cooking equipment..............	3352215	754	680	648	690	707	(NA)	753
Other household cooking appliance manufacturing............	335221W	11	14	3	13	12	(NA)	14
Household refrigerator and home freezer manufacturing........	335222	5,510	4,416	3,538	3,481	3,512	3,497	3,350
Household refrigerators (incl. combination refrigerator-freezers)...	3352221	4,911	(D)	(D)	(D)	2,880	(NA)	2,919
Household laundry equipment manufacturing....................	335224	4,678	4,223	3,551	3,528	3,578	3,553	3,542
Other major household appliance manufacturing.................	335228	4,309	4,354	3,654	3,761	3,946	4,385	4,197
Household water heaters, electric, for permanent installation...	3352281	694	717	638	613	673	(NA)	842
Household water heaters, except electric......................	3352283	1,078	1,000	923	983	1,092	(NA)	1,075
All other misc. household appliances (including parts)........	3352285	2,503	2,586	2,065	2,151	2,168	(NA)	2,251
Other major household appliance manufacturing [1].............	335228W	34	51	28	14	13	(NA)	30

[1] Not specified by kind.

Source: U.S. Census Bureau, Annual Survey of Manufactures, "Value of Products Shipments: Value of Shipments for Product Classes"; and Economic Census 2012, "Manufacturing: Subject Series: Product Summary: Products or Services Statistics: 2012"; <http://factfinder.census.gov>, accessed September 2015.

Section 22
Wholesale and Retail Trade

This section presents statistics relating to the distributive trades, specifically wholesale trade and retail trade. Data shown for the trades are classified by kind of business and cover sales, establishments, employees, payrolls, and other items. The principal sources of these data are from the U.S. Census Bureau and include the *2007* and *2012 Economic Censuses*, annual and monthly surveys, and the *County Business Patterns* program. These data are supplemented by several tables from trade associations, such as the National Automobile Dealers Association.

Data on wholesale and retail trade also appear in several other sections. For instance, labor force employment and earnings data appear in Section 12, Labor Force, Employment, and Earnings; gross domestic product of the industry (Table 690) appears in Section 13, Income, Expenditures, Poverty, and Wealth; and financial data (several tables) from the quarterly *Statistics of Income Bulletin*, published by the Internal Revenue Service, appear in Section 15, Business Enterprise.

Censuses—Censuses of wholesale trade and retail trade have been taken at various intervals since 1929. Beginning with the 1967 census, legislation provides for a census of each area to be conducted every 5 years (for years ending in "2" and "7"). The industries covered in the censuses and surveys of business are defined in the North American Industry Classification System (NAICS). Retail trade refers to places of business primarily engaged in retailing merchandise to the general public; and wholesale trade, to establishments primarily engaged in selling goods to other businesses and normally operating from a warehouse or office that have little or no display of merchandise. Census Bureau tables in this section generally utilize either the 2007 or 2012 NAICS codes. NAICS codes are reviewed every 5 years to identify areas for revision, so that the classification system can keep pace with the changing economy. For information on this system and how it affects the comparability of wholesale and retail statistics historically, see text, Section 15, Business Enterprise, and especially the Census Bureau Web site at <http://www.census.gov/eos/www/naics>.

The *2007* and *2012 Economic Censuses* have three series of publications for these two sectors: 1) subject series with reports such as product lines and establishment and firm sizes, 2) geographic reports with individual reports for each state, and 3) industry series with individual reports for industry groups. Data for the *2012 Economic Census* are being released on a continuing basis through 2016. For information on these series, see the Census Bureau Web site at <http://www.census.gov/econ/census/>.

Current surveys—Current sample surveys conducted by the Census Bureau cover various aspects of wholesale and retail trade. Its *Monthly Retail Trade and Food Services* release at <http://www.census.gov/retail> contains monthly estimates of sales, inventories, and inventory/sales ratios for the United States, by kind of business. Annual figures on retail sales, year-end inventories, purchases, accounts receivable, and gross margins by kind of business are located on the Census Bureau Web site at <https://www.census.gov/retail/#arts>.

Statistics from the Census Bureau's monthly wholesale trade survey include national estimates of sales, inventories, and inventory/sales ratios for merchant wholesalers excluding manufacturers' sales branches and offices. Data are presented by major summary groups "durable and nondurable," and 4-digit NAICS industry groups. Merchant wholesalers excluding manufacturers' sales branches and offices are those wholesalers who take title to the goods they sell (e.g., jobbers, exporters, importers, industrial distributors). These data, based on reports submitted by a sample of firms, appear in the *Monthly Wholesale Trade Report*. This report, along with monthly sales, inventories, and inventories/sales ratios, also provides data on annual sales, inventories, and year-end inventories/sales ratios. The *Annual Wholesale Trade Survey* provides data on merchant wholesalers excluding manufacturer sales branches and offices as well as summary data for all merchant wholesalers. This report also provides separate data for manufacturer sales branches and offices, and electronic markets, agents, brokers, and commission merchants. Included in the *Annual Wholesale Trade Report* are data on annual sales, year-end inventories, inventories/sales ratios, operating expenses, purchases, and gross margins. Data are presented by major summary groups "durable and nondurable" and 4-digit NAICS industry groups. These reports are available on the Census Bureau Web site at <http://www.census.gov/wholesale/>.

E-commerce—Electronic commerce (or e-commerce) is the sale of goods and services over the Internet and extranet, electronic data interchange (EDI) network, electronic mail, or other online systems. Payment may or may not be made online. E-commerce data are collected in four separate Census Bureau surveys. These surveys use different measures of economic activity such as shipments for manufacturing, sales for wholesale and retail trade, and revenues for service industries. Data can be found at <http://www.census. gov/econ/estats>. Consequently, measures of total economic and e-commerce activity vary by economic sector, are conceptually and definitionally different, and therefore, are not additive. This edition has several tables on e-commerce sales, such as Tables 1056, 1066, and 1067 in this section; and Table 1286 in Section 27, Accommodation, Food Services, and Other Services.

Statistical reliability—For a discussion of statistical collection and estimation, sampling procedures, and measures of statistical reliability applicable to Census Bureau data, see Appendix III.

Table 1053. Wholesale and Retail Trade—Establishments, Sales, Payroll, and Employees: 2007 and 2012

[435.0 represents 435,000. Covers establishments with payroll. For statement on methodology, see Appendix III]

Kind of business	2007 NAICS code [1]	Establishments (1,000)		Sales (bil. dol.)		Annual payroll (bil. dol.)		Paid employees (1,000)	
		2007	2012	2007	2012	2007	2012	2007	2012
Wholesale trade.............	**42**	**435.0**	**418.8**	**6,516**	**7,189**	**336**	**369**	**6,227**	**6,069**
Wholesale trade, durable goods................	423	255.0	243.6	2,898	2,964	207	222	3,619	3,483
Wholesale trade, nondurable goods............	424	134.6	130.6	2,991	3,601	116	132	2,320	2,285
Wholesale electronic markets and agents and brokers.................	425	45.4	44.5	627	625	13	15	289	300
Retail trade................	**44–45**	**1,128.1**	**1,063.0**	**3,918**	**4,228**	**363**	**371**	**15,515**	**14,738**
Motor vehicle and parts dealers................	441	126.8	116.2	891	871	73	70	1,914	1,709
Furniture and home furnishings stores..............	442	65.1	51.4	108	90	15	12	557	423
Electronics and appliance stores................	443	50.8	47.7	109	105	11	10	486	428
Building material and garden equipment and supplies dealers................	444	91.1	77.9	318	279	38	34	1,331	1,145
Food and beverage stores................	445	146.1	145.9	539	620	55	60	2,827	2,857
Health and personal care stores................	446	88.5	92.3	234	275	28	32	1,068	1,013
Gasoline stations................	447	118.8	114.5	450	556	15	16	891	862
Clothing and clothing accessories stores................	448	156.5	147.3	216	233	27	28	1,644	1,659
Sporting goods, hobby, book, and music stores.....	451	57.4	48.1	81	79	9	9	619	531
General merchandise stores................	452	45.9	48.8	577	641	54	58	2,763	2,777
Miscellaneous store retailers................	453	121.9	106.4	104	98	14	14	792	715
Nonstore retailers................	454	59.4	66.3	290	380	23	27	621	619

NA Not available. [1] North American Industrial Classification System; see text, Section 15.

Source: U.S. Census Bureau, 2012 Economic Census, "EC1200CADV2: All sectors: Core Business Statistics Series: Advance Comparative Statistics for the U.S. (2007 NAICS Basis): 2012 and 2007," <http://factfinder2.census.gov>, accessed September 2015.

Table 1054. Wholesale Trade—Nonemployer Firms and Receipts by Industry Type: 2013

[36,814,965 represents $36,814,965,000. Includes only firms subject to federal income tax. Nonemployers are businesses with no paid employees. A firm is a single physical location where business is conducted or services or industrial operations are performed. Each distinct business income tax return filed by a nonemployer business is counted as a firm]

Industry type	2012 NAICS code [1]	Firms				Receipts ($1,000)
		Total	Corpora-tions [2]	Individual proprietor-ships [3]	Partner-ships [4]	
Wholesale trade, total.............	**42**	**406,469**	**67,826**	**311,780**	**26,863**	**36,814,965**
Durable goods merchant wholesalers.............	**423**	**202,671**	**37,000**	**151,745**	**13,926**	**19,123,612**
Motor vehicle and motor vehicle parts and supplies merchant wholesalers................	4231	17,377	3,434	12,873	1,070	2,445,347
Furniture and home furnishing merchant wholesalers..............	4232	12,735	2,025	9,960	750	1,036,313
Lumber and other construction materials merchant wholesalers................	4233	7,579	1,515	5,422	642	817,183
Professional and commercial equipment and supplies merchant wholesalers................	4234	11,212	2,111	8,198	903	1,130,304
Metal and mineral (except petroleum) merchant wholesalers................	4235	3,270	697	2,345	228	411,900
Household appliance and electrical and electronic goods merchant wholesalers................	4236	10,434	2,938	6,559	937	1,218,550
Hardware and plumbing and heating equipment and supplies merchant wholesalers................	4237	4,619	1,080	3,149	390	459,316
Machinery, equipment, and supplies merchant wholesalers................	4238	18,735	4,961	12,249	1,525	2,422,363
Miscellaneous durable goods merchant wholesalers..............	4239	116,710	18,239	90,990	7,481	9,182,336
Nondurable goods merchant wholesalers................	**424**	**149,646**	**24,035**	**115,244**	**10,367**	**13,666,774**
Paper and paper product merchant wholesalers................	4241	5,726	982	4,418	326	467,442
Drugs and druggists' sundries merchant wholesalers..............	4242	2,937	630	2,038	269	277,069
Apparel, piece goods, and notions merchant wholesalers................	4243	25,236	3,983	19,493	1,760	1,737,023
Grocery and related products merchant wholesalers..............	4244	29,056	5,140	21,911	2,005	4,105,769
Farm product raw material merchant wholesalers................	4245	5,733	564	4,904	265	602,777
Chemical and allied products merchant wholesalers..............	4246	3,556	1,009	2,175	372	448,190
Petroleum and petroleum products merchant wholesalers................	4247	2,169	392	1,577	200	304,785
Beer, wine, and distilled alcoholic beverage merchant wholesalers................	4248	5,413	858	3,710	845	490,474
Miscellaneous nondurable goods merchant wholesalers................	4249	69,820	10,477	55,018	4,325	5,233,245
Wholesale electronic markets and agents and brokers..........	**425**	**54,152**	**6,791**	**44,791**	**2,570**	**4,024,579**
Business to business electronics markets............	42511	9,086	1,097	7,497	492	728,187
Wholesale trade agents and brokers................	42512	45,066	5,694	37,294	2,078	3,296,392

[1] North American Industry Classification System, 2012; see text, Section 15. [2] A legally incorporated business under state laws. [3] Also referred to as "sole proprietorship," an unincorporated business with a sole owner. Includes self-employed persons. [4] An unincorporated business where two or more persons join to carry on a trade or business with each having a shared financial interest in the business.

Source: U.S. Census Bureau, Nonemployer Statistics, "Geographic Area Series: Nonemployer Statistics by Legal Form of Organization," <http://factfinder2.census.gov>, accessed May 2015. See also <http://www.census.gov/econ/nonemployer/>.

Table 1055. Wholesale Trade—Establishments, Employees, and Payroll: 2012 and 2013

[420.5 represents 420,500. Covers establishments with payroll. Excludes self-employed individuals, employees of private households, railroad employees, agricultural production employees, and most government employees. For statement on methodology, see Appendix III]

Kind of business	NAICS code [1]	Establishments (1,000)		Employees [2] (1,000)		Payroll (bil. dol.)	
		2012	2013	2012	2013	2012	2013
Wholesale trade, total..........................	**42**	**420.5**	**419.6**	**5,776**	**5,909**	**370.1**	**386.3**
Merchant wholesalers, durable goods........................	423	243.6	242.6	3,273	3,351	221.2	231.5
Motor vehicle/motor vehicle parts and supply merchant wholesalers...................	4231	25.0	24.8	367	373	18.1	19.0
Furniture and home furnishing merchant wholesalers..........	4232	13.1	12.5	142	144	7.7	8.0
Lumber and other construction materials merchant wholesalers...................	4233	16.7	16.5	189	195	9.8	10.5
Professional and commercial equipment and supplies merchant wholesalers...................	4234	35.3	35.9	641	661	54.5	56.5
Metal and mineral (except petroleum) merchant wholesalers...................	4235	10.9	10.6	154	154	9.3	9.3
Household appliances and electrical and electronic goods merchant wholesalers...................	4236	29.7	29.8	514	528	47.8	50.6
Hardware, plumbing and heating equipment and supplies merchant wholesalers...................	4237	19.5	19.4	225	228	13.2	13.8
Machinery, equipment, and supplies merchant wholesalers...................	4238	58.8	58.3	698	730	43.7	46.7
Miscellaneous durable goods merchant wholesalers..........	4239	34.6	34.8	344	338	17.1	17.2
Merchant wholesalers, nondurable goods....................	**424**	**130.7**	**130.0**	**2,209**	**2,259**	**133.6**	**139.1**
Paper and paper product merchant wholesalers..........	4241	10.7	10.3	149	148	8.2	8.1
Drugs and druggists' sundries merchant wholesalers..........	4242	10.0	9.9	277	295	28.6	32.1
Apparel, piece goods and notions merchant wholesalers.....	4243	16.2	16.1	192	199	11.0	11.4
Grocery and related product merchant wholesalers............	4244	34.0	34.4	756	781	38.4	39.8
Farm product raw material merchant wholesalers.............	4245	6.2	6.2	61	62	3.2	3.3
Chemical and allied products merchant wholesalers..........	4246	13.2	13.0	151	152	10.7	10.9
Petroleum and petroleum products merchant wholesalers.....	4247	6.9	6.7	103	102	7.1	7.0
Beer, wine, and distilled alcoholic beverages..................	4248	4.4	4.5	184	188	10.7	11.0
Miscellaneous nondurable goods merchant wholesalers......	4249	29.2	28.9	336	330	15.7	15.6
Wholesale electronic markets and agents and brokers.....	**425**	**46.2**	**47.1**	**295**	**300**	**15.3**	**15.7**

[1] Data based on 2012 North American Industry Classification System (NAICS). [2] Covers full- and part-time employees who are on the payroll in the pay period including March 12.

Source: U.S. Census Bureau, County Business Patterns, "Geography Area Series, County Business Patterns," <http://factfinder2.census.gov/>, accessed April 2015. See also <http://www.census.gov/econ/cbp/>.

Table 1056. Merchant Wholesale Trade Sales—Total and E-Commerce: 2013

[5,322,612 represents $5,322,612,000,000. Covers only businesses with paid employees. Excludes manufacturers' sales branches and offices. Based on the Annual Wholesale Trade Survey, see Appendix III]

Kind of business	2007 NAICS code [1]	Value of sales (mil. dol.)		E-commerce as percent of total sales	Percent distribution of E-commerce sales
		Total	E-commerce		
Total merchant wholesale trade.......................................	**42**	**5,322,612**	**1,102,982**	**20.7**	**100.0**
Durable goods..	**423**	**2,452,714**	**492,451**	**20.1**	**44.6**
Motor vehicles, parts and supplies..........................	4231	398,310	162,332	40.8	14.7
Furniture and home furnishings................................	4232	71,242	10,037	14.1	0.9
Lumber and other construction materials.......................	4233	103,531	6,092	5.9	0.6
Professional and commercial equipment and supplies................	4234	428,077	104,834	24.5	9.5
Computer equipment and supplies..........................	42343	223,806	59,083	26.4	5.4
Metals and minerals (except petroleum)........................	4235	168,878	9,229	5.5	0.8
Electrical goods..........................	4236	517,144	118,764	23.0	10.8
Hardware, plumbing and heating equipment...................	4237	116,225	13,485	11.6	1.2
Machinery, equipment and supplies.........................	4238	401,130	38,646	9.6	3.5
Miscellaneous durable goods..........................	4239	248,177	29,032	11.7	2.6
Nondurable goods..........................	**424**	**2,869,898**	**610,531**	**21.3**	**55.4**
Paper and paper products..........................	4241	88,325	24,346	27.6	2.2
Drugs, drug proprietaries and druggists' sundries....................	4242	482,837	(S)	(S)	(S)
Apparel, piece goods and notions..........................	4243	155,380	38,569	24.8	3.5
Groceries and related products..........................	4244	571,407	107,899	18.9	9.8
Farm product raw materials..........................	4245	260,275	10,510	4.0	1.0
Chemical and allied products..........................	4246	125,430	13,318	10.6	1.2
Petroleum and petroleum products..........................	4247	810,124	41,653	5.1	3.8
Beer, wine, and distilled alcoholic beverages..........................	4248	124,499	8,987	7.2	0.8
Miscellaneous nondurable goods..........................	4249	251,621	26,062	10.4	2.4

S Figure does not meet publication standards. [1] North American Industry Classification System, 2007. See text, Section 15.

Source: U.S. Census Bureau, "Annual Wholesale Trade Survey - 2013," <http://www.census.gov/wholesale/index.html>, and "E-Stats - Measuring the Electronic Economy," <http://www.census.gov/econ/estats>; accessed June 2015.

Table 1057. Merchant Wholesalers—Summary: 2000 to 2013

[In billions of dollars (2,814.6 represents $2,814,600,000,000), except ratios. Inventories and inventories/sales ratios, as of December, not seasonally adjusted. Excludes manufacturers' sales branches and offices. Data adjusted using preliminary results of the 2012 Economic Census. Based on data from the Annual Wholesale Trade Survey and the Monthly Wholesale Trade Survey; see Appendix III]

Kind of business	2007 NAICS code [1]	2000	2005	2009	2010	2011	2012	2013
SALES								
Merchant wholesalers.....................................	**42**	**2,814.6**	**3,638.5**	**3,816.8**	**4,318.4**	**4,862.6**	**5,165.2**	**5,322.6**
Durable goods...	**423**	**1,486.7**	**1,830.3**	**1,739.7**	**1,990.9**	**2,220.6**	**2,379.1**	**2,452.7**
Motor vehicles, parts, and supplies..........................	4231	222.2	303.8	254.3	299.2	332.9	389.3	398.3
Furniture and home furnishings.............................	4232	52.7	63.0	54.5	57.5	61.2	66.9	71.2
Lumber and other construction materials...................	4233	87.2	139.0	85.4	85.3	87.1	92.5	103.5
Professional, commercial equipment and supplies.........	4234	282.2	332.8	354.2	399.0	414.5	416.6	428.1
Computer, peripheral equipment and software............	42343	174.8	179.0	182.0	219.9	222.9	219.2	223.8
Metal and mineral (except petroleum)......................	4235	93.8	136.1	109.9	133.8	167.1	174.3	168.9
Electrical and electronic goods.............................	4236	260.0	284.4	341.6	395.1	433.7	481.7	517.1
Hardware, plumbing, heating equipment and supplies.....	4237	72.1	95.0	90.1	95.7	103.2	111.0	116.2
Machinery, equipment, and supplies........................	4238	256.1	287.7	275.1	303.3	353.7	391.1	401.1
Miscellaneous durable goods...............................	4239	160.3	188.5	174.5	222.2	267.2	255.6	248.2
Nondurable goods..	**424**	**1,327.9**	**1,808.2**	**2,077.1**	**2,327.5**	**2,642.0**	**2,786.1**	**2,869.9**
Paper and paper products..................................	4241	77.8	87.2	81.7	84.0	85.8	86.6	88.3
Drugs and druggists' sundries..............................	4242	176.0	322.4	390.8	413.8	440.4	457.1	482.8
Apparel, piece goods, and notions..........................	4243	96.5	121.2	126.5	137.2	144.2	149.1	155.4
Grocery and related products...............................	4244	374.7	422.2	476.6	494.4	524.0	549.4	571.4
Farm product raw materials.................................	4245	102.7	106.0	165.3	183.9	228.0	246.5	260.3
Chemical and allied products...............................	4246	62.3	90.9	89.4	103.0	116.8	122.0	125.4
Petroleum and petroleum products.........................	4247	195.8	379.1	433.4	587.1	756.4	806.5	810.1
Beer, wine, and distilled alcoholic beverages..............	4248	71.3	92.2	108.3	110.6	115.6	121.2	124.5
Miscellaneous nondurable goods...........................	4249	170.9	187.1	205.0	213.3	230.7	247.6	251.6
INVENTORIES								
Merchant wholesalers..................................	**42**	**309.7**	**369.4**	**396.0**	**439.7**	**482.6**	**514.6**	**535.9**
Durable goods...	**423**	**198.5**	**233.0**	**231.2**	**253.4**	**281.6**	**305.2**	**321.0**
Motor vehicles, parts, and supplies..........................	4231	28.8	38.0	37.1	40.7	47.6	49.4	51.1
Furniture and home furnishings.............................	4232	6.4	8.0	7.3	8.2	8.6	9.1	9.8
Lumber and other construction materials...................	4233	8.3	13.9	9.9	10.4	10.5	11.2	12.6
Professional, commercial equipment and supplies.........	4234	27.3	27.7	28.8	31.4	32.7	34.9	36.5
Computer, peripheral equipment and software............	42343	12.1	11.2	11.2	12.7	12.7	13.4	14.2
Metal and mineral (except petroleum)......................	4235	13.6	20.9	18.9	22.2	26.4	28.5	28.5
Electrical and electronic goods.............................	4236	31.3	30.0	30.9	34.7	38.3	41.8	43.6
Hardware, plumbing, heating equipment and supplies....	4237	11.5	15.4	15.6	16.6	18.1	18.6	19.0
Machinery, equipment, and supplies........................	4238	51.1	55.9	60.6	65.0	73.3	84.7	92.2
Miscellaneous durable goods...............................	4239	20.2	23.1	22.1	24.2	26.2	27.0	27.6
Nondurable goods..	**424**	**111.2**	**136.4**	**164.8**	**186.3**	**201.1**	**209.4**	**214.9**
Paper and paper products..................................	4241	6.7	7.1	6.7	7.1	7.2	7.2	7.6
Drugs and druggists' sundries..............................	4242	23.9	30.4	35.4	38.3	41.0	41.8	47.3
Apparel, piece goods, and notions..........................	4243	14.2	17.5	17.0	20.4	22.8	23.1	24.4
Grocery and related products...............................	4244	20.5	22.2	24.9	26.8	30.0	30.9	31.4
Farm product raw materials.................................	4245	11.5	11.3	20.8	29.1	27.4	30.7	28.4
Chemical and allied products...............................	4246	6.0	8.2	8.7	9.9	11.2	12.1	12.5
Petroleum and petroleum products.........................	4247	5.2	12.7	20.4	22.1	25.2	25.3	24.0
Beer, wine, and distilled alcoholic beverages..............	4248	6.5	8.3	10.4	10.8	11.6	12.5	13.2
Miscellaneous nondurable goods...........................	4249	16.6	18.5	20.5	21.9	24.6	25.7	26.2
INVENTORIES/SALES RATIO								
Merchant wholesalers..................................	**42**	**1.10**	**1.02**	**1.04**	**1.02**	**0.99**	**1.00**	**1.01**
Durable goods...	**423**	**1.34**	**1.27**	**1.33**	**1.27**	**1.27**	**1.28**	**1.31**
Motor vehicles, parts, and supplies..........................	4231	1.30	1.25	1.46	1.36	1.43	1.27	1.28
Furniture and home furnishings.............................	4232	1.22	1.27	1.34	1.43	1.40	1.36	1.38
Lumber and other construction materials...................	4233	0.96	1.00	1.16	1.22	1.20	1.21	1.21
Professional, commercial equipment and supplies.........	4234	0.97	0.83	0.81	0.79	0.79	0.84	0.85
Computer, peripheral equipment and software............	42343	0.69	0.63	0.62	0.58	0.57	0.61	0.63
Metal and mineral (except petroleum)......................	4235	1.45	1.54	1.72	1.66	1.58	1.64	1.69
Electrical and electronic goods.............................	4236	1.20	1.06	0.90	0.88	0.88	0.87	0.84
Hardware, plumbing, heating equipment and supplies.....	4237	1.60	1.62	1.73	1.74	1.75	1.67	1.63
Machinery, equipment, and supplies........................	4238	1.99	1.94	2.20	2.14	2.07	2.17	2.30
Miscellaneous durable goods...............................	4239	1.26	1.23	1.27	1.09	0.98	1.06	1.11
Nondurable goods..	**424**	**0.84**	**0.75**	**0.79**	**0.80**	**0.76**	**0.75**	**0.75**
Paper and paper products..................................	4241	0.87	0.81	0.82	0.84	0.84	0.84	0.86
Drugs and druggists' sundries..............................	4242	1.36	0.94	0.91	0.92	0.93	0.91	0.98
Apparel, piece goods, and notions..........................	4243	1.47	1.45	1.34	1.49	1.58	1.55	1.57
Grocery and related products...............................	4244	0.55	0.53	0.52	0.54	0.57	0.56	0.55
Farm product raw materials.................................	4245	1.12	1.07	1.26	1.58	1.20	1.25	1.09
Chemical and allied products...............................	4246	0.97	0.91	0.97	0.96	0.96	0.99	0.99
Petroleum and petroleum products.........................	4247	0.27	0.33	0.47	0.38	0.33	0.31	0.30
Beer, wine, and distilled alcoholic beverages..............	4248	0.91	0.90	0.96	0.97	1.00	1.03	1.06
Miscellaneous nondurable goods...........................	4249	0.97	0.99	1.00	1.03	1.07	1.04	1.04

[1] North American Industry Classification System, 2007. See text, Section 15.

Source: U.S. Census Bureau, "2012 Annual Wholesale Trade Report," <http://www.census.gov/wholesale/>, accessed March 2015.

Table 1058. Wholesale and Retail Trade—Establishments, Employees, and Payroll by State: 2012 and 2013

[5,776 represents 5,776,000. Covers establishments with payroll. Excludes self-employed individuals, employees of private households, railroad employees, agricultural production employees, and most government employees. Data based on 2012 North American Industry Classification System (NAICS). See text, Section 15. For statement on methodology, see Appendix III]

State	Wholesale trade (NAICS 42)						Retail trade (NAICS 44, 45)					
	Establishments		Employees [1] (1,000)		Annual payroll (mil. dol.)		Establishments		Employees [1] (1,000)		Annual payroll (mil. dol.)	
	2012	2013	2012	2013	2012	2013	2012	2013	2012	2013	2012	2013
U.S.........	420,501	419,648	5,776	5,909	370,089	386,347	1,063,842	1,063,616	14,808	15,023	377,039	387,295
AL............	5,422	5,423	71	72	3,649	3,757	18,230	18,034	223	222	5,277	5,342
AK............	746	758	9	9	511	557	2,503	2,503	33	33	987	1,004
AZ............	6,669	6,623	92	96	5,716	5,912	17,554	17,803	287	296	7,517	7,908
AR............	3,483	3,488	43	43	2,217	2,219	10,940	10,915	137	138	3,148	3,219
CA............	59,372	59,269	807	834	60,531	63,888	106,425	106,820	1,540	1,596	43,490	45,109
CO............	7,257	7,244	91	96	6,167	6,671	18,488	18,593	245	255	6,634	6,967
CT............	4,374	4,355	72	72	5,261	5,282	12,623	12,573	184	184	5,140	5,226
DE............	1,034	1,064	16	15	1,278	1,226	3,620	3,615	52	53	1,302	1,331
DC............	436	465	4	4	357	331	1,744	1,719	20	20	621	585
FL............	31,730	31,735	289	299	15,640	16,386	71,292	72,347	966	986	24,517	25,705
GA............	13,163	13,081	188	194	11,505	12,033	33,473	33,438	437	440	10,465	10,836
HI............	1,743	1,728	18	19	841	886	4,631	4,682	68	70	1,846	1,911
ID............	2,033	2,030	26	27	1,234	1,338	5,823	5,789	73	75	1,837	1,917
IL............	19,293	19,182	308	311	20,655	21,626	40,031	39,701	597	593	14,911	14,811
IN............	7,814	7,764	112	114	5,996	6,162	21,679	21,522	310	309	7,191	7,293
IA............	4,954	4,931	67	67	3,293	3,363	12,109	11,977	176	179	3,969	4,065
KS............	4,563	4,501	62	63	3,340	3,461	10,585	10,433	147	147	3,410	3,484
KY............	4,352	4,344	69	70	3,897	3,939	15,251	15,210	203	202	4,716	4,759
LA............	5,637	5,583	76	77	4,078	4,260	16,774	16,556	224	227	5,461	5,637
ME............	1,552	1,603	17	18	845	895	6,359	6,350	81	81	1,946	1,993
MD............	5,759	5,754	84	88	5,536	5,827	18,186	18,248	284	287	7,320	7,478
MA............	8,050	8,083	130	138	10,202	11,269	24,434	24,203	357	352	9,630	9,516
MI............	11,523	11,427	160	168	9,923	10,489	34,901	34,820	442	449	10,674	10,981
MN............	8,276	8,235	129	132	9,237	9,649	19,252	19,157	291	293	7,023	7,211
MS............	2,850	2,850	35	35	1,607	1,651	11,586	11,529	137	137	3,028	3,103
MO............	8,044	7,855	120	121	6,234	6,210	21,396	21,321	305	305	7,415	7,456
MT............	1,540	1,573	14	15	667	705	4,825	4,799	56	56	1,375	1,411
NE............	3,180	3,185	41	43	2,163	2,344	7,295	7,240	107	108	2,563	2,610
NV............	2,977	2,958	34	34	1,923	1,939	8,145	8,289	132	135	3,573	3,695
NH............	1,875	1,857	24	24	1,615	1,632	6,160	6,088	97	97	2,435	2,528
NJ............	14,713	14,555	254	258	21,313	22,324	31,774	31,711	437	445	12,991	13,038
NM............	1,954	1,907	22	25	1,043	1,469	6,595	6,571	93	93	2,268	2,301
NY............	32,764	32,675	360	366	24,182	24,903	77,611	78,052	905	921	24,132	25,375
NC............	11,878	11,850	170	178	10,621	11,557	34,270	34,198	452	458	10,688	11,046
ND............	1,624	1,704	22	23	1,249	1,336	3,191	3,203	47	49	1,227	1,291
OH............	14,275	14,239	223	224	12,581	12,967	36,664	36,408	563	553	13,841	13,570
OK............	4,666	4,698	59	61	3,260	3,346	13,059	13,161	171	175	4,181	4,354
OR............	5,415	5,412	76	78	4,955	5,133	13,940	13,915	187	191	4,860	4,993
PA............	15,097	14,968	247	247	15,702	16,119	44,046	43,900	649	656	15,674	15,929
RI............	1,382	1,350	19	21	1,159	1,421	3,788	3,761	47	47	1,212	1,261
SC............	5,051	5,012	63	67	3,302	3,493	17,594	17,677	222	224	5,024	5,250
SD............	1,489	1,514	18	18	836	887	3,881	3,889	51	51	1,183	1,227
TN............	6,926	6,918	112	110	6,434	6,318	22,595	22,349	308	311	7,593	7,819
TX............	32,722	33,143	484	501	31,975	33,465	78,433	79,084	1,164	1,207	29,620	30,907
UT............	3,656	3,693	55	53	3,029	3,158	9,053	9,151	134	138	3,429	3,558
VT............	826	814	11	11	590	583	3,535	3,424	39	38	992	996
VA............	7,412	7,393	103	104	6,085	6,307	27,469	27,169	415	416	10,235	10,437
WA............	9,384	9,388	125	125	7,726	7,642	21,590	21,564	305	312	8,823	9,005
WV............	1,570	1,575	21	22	952	1,029	6,400	6,270	86	86	1,939	1,947
WI............	7,163	7,033	114	113	6,474	6,461	19,357	19,245	295	298	6,884	7,072
WY............	833	859	8	9	504	523	2,683	2,640	30	30	818	827

[1] Covers full- and part-time employees who are on the payroll in the pay period including March 12.

Source: U.S. Census Bureau, County Business Patterns, "Geography Area Series, County Business Patterns," <http://factfinder2.census.gov/>, accessed April 2015. See also <http://www.census.gov/econ/cbp/index.html>.

Table 1059. Retail Trade—Establishments, Employees, and Payroll: 2012 and 2013

[1,063.8 represents 1,063,800. Covers establishments with payroll. Excludes self-employed individuals, employees of private households, railroad employees, agricultural production employees, and most government employees. For statement on methodology, see Appendix III]

Kind of business	NAICS code [1]	Establishments (1,000)		Employees (1,000) [2]		Payroll (bil. dol.)	
		2012	2013	2012	2013	2012	2013
Retail trade, total..............	**44–45**	**1,063.8**	**1,063.6**	**14,808**	**15,023**	**377.0**	**387.3**
Motor vehicle and parts dealers..............	441	116.4	117.0	1,719	1,763	71.6	75.5
Automobile dealers..............	4411	45.0	46.0	1,099	1,141	53.0	56.6
New car dealers..............	44111	21.3	21.4	975	1,010	48.5	51.7
Used car dealers..............	44112	23.7	24.6	124	131	4.5	4.9
Other motor vehicle dealers..............	4412	14.2	14.0	125	127	4.8	5.1
Recreational vehicle dealers..............	44121	2.6	2.6	33	34	1.4	1.6
Motorcycle and boat and other motor vehicle dealers.........	44122	11.6	11.4	92	94	3.4	3.5
Motorcycle, ATV, and all other motor vehicle dealers.........	441228	6.9	6.8	62	64	2.2	2.3
Automotive parts, accessories, and tire stores..............	4413	57.2	57.0	494	494	13.8	13.9
Automotive parts, accessories and tire stores..............	44131	37.0	36.7	322	322	7.9	7.9
Tire dealers..............	44132	20.2	20.3	172	173	5.9	5.9
Furniture and home furnishing stores..............	442	51.6	51.1	423	427	11.7	12.3
Furniture stores..............	4421	23.7	23.5	195	197	6.5	6.7
Home furnishings stores..............	4422	27.9	27.6	228	230	5.2	5.5
Floor covering stores..............	44221	11.4	11.2	61	60	2.2	2.3
Other home furnishings stores..............	44229	16.5	16.4	167	170	3.0	3.2
Window treatment stores..............	442291	1.8	1.8	6	6	0.2	0.2
Electronics and appliance stores..............	443	49.7	48.0	428	408	10.5	10.9
Household appliance stores..............	443141	8.4	9.1	60	63	1.8	2.0
Electronics stores..............	443142	41.3	38.9	368	345	8.7	8.8
Building material & garden equip. & supplies dealers..............	444	78.3	77.3	1,170	1,237	35.2	36.7
Building material & supplies dealers [3]..............	4441	60.4	59.4	1,027	1,091	31.2	32.4
Home centers..............	44411	6.6	6.5	([5])	([5])	(D)	(D)
Hardware stores..............	44413	15.5	15.3	138	133	3.2	3.2
Lawn & garden equip. & supplies stores [3]..............	4442	17.9	17.9	143	145	4.0	4.3
Nursery, garden center, and farm supply stores..............	44422	13.9	14.0	119	122	3.2	3.5
Food & beverage stores..............	445	145.6	149.3	2,872	2,912	60.9	61.9
Grocery stores..............	4451	91.5	93.6	2,582	2,606	55.2	56.0
Supermarkets & grocery (except convenience) stores.........	44511	66.0	66.3	2,471	2,483	53.4	53.9
Convenience stores..............	44512	25.5	27.3	111	124	1.8	2.1
Specialty food stores..............	4452	21.8	22.9	139	149	2.5	2.7
Beer, wine, & liquor stores [4]..............	4453	32.3	32.8	151	157	3.1	3.3
Health & personal care stores [3]..............	446	92.4	93.7	1,010	1,016	32.6	33.1
Pharmacies & drug stores..............	44611	43.3	43.5	717	700	24.8	25.2
Cosmetics, beauty supplies, & perfume stores..............	44612	15.3	16.3	108	125	2.0	2.2
Optical goods stores..............	44613	12.9	12.7	78	82	2.1	2.1
Gasoline stations..............	447	114.0	112.5	863	884	15.9	16.4
Gasoline stations with convenience stores..............	44711	97.9	96.9	721	740	12.7	13.1
Other gasoline stations..............	44719	16.1	15.6	142	144	3.2	3.3
Clothing & clothing accessories stores..............	448	147.4	146.4	1,631	1,710	28.3	29.2
Clothing stores [3]..............	4481	97.6	97.2	1,299	1,371	20.7	21.4
Men's clothing stores..............	44811	7.9	7.2	59	54	1.6	1.4
Women's clothing stores..............	44812	38.7	36.0	399	364	5.9	5.6
Children's & infants' clothing stores..............	44813	6.9	7.0	82	85	1.0	1.0
Family clothing stores..............	44814	25.4	27.3	606	695	9.4	10.4
Shoe stores..............	4482	25.5	25.1	202	207	3.5	3.7
Jewelry, luggage, & leather goods stores..............	4483	24.4	24.1	129	132	4.1	4.1
Jewelry stores..............	44831	23.4	23.1	124	126	3.9	3.9
Sporting goods, hobby, book, & music stores..............	451	46.3	46.6	512	539	9.1	9.8
Sporting goods/hobby/musical instrument stores [3]..............	4511	37.9	38.4	418	445	7.7	8.2
Sporting goods stores..............	45111	20.9	21.6	225	246	4.6	5.0
Hobby, toy, and game stores..............	45112	8.3	8.2	123	128	1.9	2.0
Book, periodical, & music stores [3]..............	4512	8.4	8.2	94	93	1.5	1.5
Book stores..............	451211	7.2	7.1	([6])	84	1.3	1.3
General merchandise stores..............	452	48.9	50.1	2,872	2,801	60.1	59.6
Department stores..............	4521	8.2	8.1	1,085	1,037	20.1	19.5
Other general merchandise stores..............	4529	40.7	42.0	1,787	1,764	40.0	40.1
Warehouse clubs & superstores..............	45291	5.2	5.2	([5])	1,420	34.7	34.5
All other general merchandise stores..............	45299	35.5	36.8	322	344	5.4	5.6
Miscellaneous store retailers [3]..............	453	107.0	107.3	713	733	14.5	14.9
Florists..............	4531	14.3	14.2	62	62	1.0	1.0
Office supplies, stationery, and gift stores..............	4532	32.6	31.3	246	243	4.4	4.3
Office supplies and stationery stores..............	45321	7.4	7.0	94	86	1.9	1.8
Gift, novelty, and souvenir stores..............	45322	25.1	24.3	152	157	2.5	2.5
Used merchandise stores..............	4533	19.8	20.2	171	185	3.0	3.3
Other miscellaneous store retailers [3]..............	4539	40.3	41.7	233	242	6.0	6.2
Pet and pet supplies stores..............	45391	8.8	8.9	101	104	2.0	2.1
Nonstore retailers [3]..............	454	66.1	64.4	596	593	26.7	27.0
Electronic shopping & mail-order houses..............	4541	30.2	31.1	366	383	18.6	18.9
Direct selling establishments..............	4543	31.7	29.3	188	172	6.8	6.9
Fuel dealers..............	45431	9.2	8.8	77	71	3.1	3.1

D Figure withheld to avoid disclosure. [1] Data based on North American Industry Classification System (NAICS), 2012. See text, Section 15. [2] Covers full- and part-time employees who are on the payroll in the pay period including March. [3] Includes other kinds of business, not shown separately. [4] Includes government employees. [5] 100,000 or more employees. [6] 50,000 to 99,999 employees.

Source: U.S. Census Bureau, County Business Patterns, "Geography Area Series: County Business Patterns," <http://factfinder2.census.gov>, accessed April 2015. See also <http://www.census.gov/econ/cbp/>.

Table 1060. Retail Trade—Nonemployer Firms and Receipts by Industry Type: 2013

[82,476,313 represents $82,476,313,000. See headnote, Table 1054]

Industry type	2012 NAICS code [1]	Firms Total	Firms Corporations [2]	Firms Individual proprietorships [3]	Firms Partnerships [4]	Receipts ($1,000)
Retail trade, total..........................	44–45	1,906,597	112,584	1,723,170	70,843	82,476,313
Motor vehicle & parts dealers........................	441	161,941	15,459	139,792	6,690	17,349,353
Furniture & home furnishings stores.....................	442	39,694	5,205	31,751	2,738	2,464,571
Electronics and appliance stores.....................	443	26,085	3,107	21,765	1,213	1,279,996
Building material & garden equip. & supplies dealers...........	444	37,388	3,692	31,932	1,764	2,353,973
Building material & supplies dealers................	4441	25,792	2,930	21,576	1,286	1,796,228
Food & beverage stores.....................	445	105,461	11,610	86,793	7,058	7,951,061
Grocery stores......................	4451	41,686	4,922	34,511	2,253	3,689,359
Specialty food stores.....................	4452	52,023	4,808	43,614	3,601	2,596,660
Health & personal care stores.....................	446	149,273	6,443	139,655	3,175	3,624,770
Gasoline stations.....................	447	8,589	1,652	6,304	633	1,136,185
Clothing & clothing accessories stores.....................	448	159,153	9,285	142,841	7,027	5,671,563
Clothing stores.....................	4481	107,634	6,487	95,564	5,583	3,796,158
Jewelry, luggage, and leather goods stores.....................	4483	46,381	2,332	42,860	1,189	1,598,918
Sporting goods, hobby, musical instrument, & book stores......	451	78,110	5,244	68,339	4,527	3,527,561
Book stores and news dealer.....................	4512	16,979	781	15,572	626	565,680
General merchandise stores.....................	452	36,670	3,013	31,636	2,021	1,697,756
Miscellaneous store retailers.....................	453	275,264	20,760	239,376	15,128	12,367,863
Office supplies, stationery, and gift stores.....................	4532	52,145	3,815	45,465	2,865	1,870,845
Nonstore retailers.....................	454	828,832	27,114	782,849	18,869	23,049,501
Electronic shopping & mail-order houses.....................	4541	121,675	7,697	108,275	5,703	6,201,203
Direct selling establishments.....................	4543	685,866	17,529	656,728	11,609	16,119,389

[1] North American Industry Classification System, 2012; see text, Section 15. [2] A legally incorporated business under state laws. [3] Also referred to as "sole proprietorship," an unincorporated business with a sole owner. Includes self-employed persons. [4] An unincorporated business where two or more persons join to carry on a trade or business with each having a shared financial interest in the business.

Source: U.S. Census Bureau, Nonemployer Statistics, "Geographic Area Series: Nonemployer Statistics by Legal Form of Organization," <http://factfinder2.census.gov>, accessed May 2015. See also <http://www.census.gov/econ/nonemployer/>.

Table 1061. Retail Industries—Employees, Average Weekly Hours, and Average Hourly Earnings: 2000 to 2014

[Annual averages of monthly figures (15,280 represents 15,280,000). Covers all full- and part-time employees who worked during, or received pay for, any part of the pay period including the 12th of the month]

Industry	2012 NAICS code [1]	Employees (1,000) 2000	Employees (1,000) 2010	Employees (1,000) 2014	Average weekly hours [2] 2000	Average weekly hours [2] 2010	Average weekly hours [2] 2014	Average hourly earnings [2] (dol.) 2000	Average hourly earnings [2] (dol.) 2010	Average hourly earnings [2] (dol.) 2014
Retail trade, total [3].....................	44,45	15,280	14,440	15,364	30.7	30.2	30.0	10.87	13.25	14.39
Motor vehicle and parts dealers [3].....................	441	1,847	1,629	1,861	35.9	36.5	37.2	14.94	17.06	18.69
Automobile dealers.....................	4411	1,217	1,012	1,185	35.1	36.7	37.2	16.95	18.22	20.30
Auto parts, accessories, and tire stores...........	4413	499	489	537	38.2	36.9	37.9	11.04	14.54	15.33
Furniture and home furnishings stores...........	442	544	438	455	31.2	29.1	29.8	12.33	15.25	16.29
Electronics and appliance stores [3].....................	443	647	522	491	30.6	31.6	36.9	13.16	16.83	21.50
Electronics stores.....................	443142	560	465	432	30.0	31.3	37.1	13.41	17.02	22.26
Building material and garden supply stores [3]......	444	1,142	1,132	1,235	35.6	33.9	31.7	11.25	14.11	14.85
Building material and supplies dealers...........	4441	982	1,005	1,083	36.2	34.2	31.5	11.30	14.13	14.89
Lawn and garden equipment and supplies stores.....................	4442	160	127	152	32.5	31.6	33.6	10.89	13.98	14.53
Food and beverage stores [3].....................	445	2,993	2,808	2,994	31.7	29.0	29.0	9.76	12.03	12.46
Grocery stores.....................	4451	2,582	2,461	2,621	31.9	29.0	29.2	9.71	12.12	12.52
Supermarkets and other grocery stores..........	44511	2,438	2,323	2,464	31.9	28.9	29.2	9.84	12.27	12.67
Convenience stores.....................	44512	145	138	157	31.0	31.3	30.6	7.45	9.43	10.24
Specialty food stores.....................	4452	270	211	227	31.6	29.7	27.6	9.97	11.13	12.05
Beer, wine, and liquor stores.....................	4453	141	136	146	28.6	27.2	26.9	10.40	11.89	11.75
Health and personal care stores [3].....................	446	928	981	1,021	29.8	29.4	29.1	11.68	16.99	17.40
Pharmacies and drug stores.....................	44611	677	715	711	29.7	29.3	29.1	11.89	17.59	18.01
Gasoline stations [3].....................	447	936	819	881	31.6	30.7	30.7	8.05	10.25	10.62
Gasoline stations with convenience stores.......	44711	787	719	776	31.3	30.4	30.5	7.87	9.99	10.43
Clothing and clothing accessories stores [3].........	448	1,322	1,353	1,379	24.9	21.2	21.5	9.96	11.59	12.55
Clothing stores.....................	4481	954	1,040	1,041	24.4	20.1	20.1	9.88	10.91	12.01
Shoe stores.....................	4482	193	182	200	24.9	23.3	23.5	8.96	11.80	12.83
Jewelry, luggage, and leather goods stores.......	4483	175	131	137	27.7	28.1	29.6	11.48	15.56	15.26
Sporting goods, hobby, book, and music stores [3]...	451	603	579	613	26.6	23.4	23.6	9.38	11.69	12.77
Sporting goods and musical instrument stores....	4511	437	459	523	27.0	23.8	23.6	9.55	11.82	12.99
Book stores and news dealers.....................	4512	166	120	90	25.4	22.0	23.5	8.91	11.10	11.57
General merchandise stores.....................	452	2,820	2,998	3,114	27.8	31.7	29.3	9.22	10.98	11.51
Miscellaneous store retailers [3].....................	453	1,007	762	818	29.1	28.0	28.9	10.20	12.50	13.89
Florists.....................	4531	130	69	64	29.6	22.4	27.0	8.95	11.05	11.58
Office supplies, stationary, and gift stores........	4532	471	303	293	29.7	27.1	28.6	10.46	13.06	14.91
Used merchandise stores.....................	4533	107	125	164	26.7	29.5	28.6	8.07	10.72	10.85
Other miscellaneous store retailers...............	4539	300	264	297	28.9	29.8	29.8	11.09	13.07	15.08
Pet and pet supplies stores.....................	45391	72	99	114	27.0	27.4	27.8	9.78	12.83	13.81
Nonstore retailers [3].....................	454	492	421	504	35.4	36.3	36.8	13.22	17.73	20.13
Electronic shopping and mail-order houses.......	4541	257	247	329	36.2	35.9	36.6	13.38	18.22	21.38

[1] Based on the North American Industry Classification System (NAICS), 2012; see text, this section and Section 15. [2] Data shown for production and nonsupervisory employees. [3] Includes other kind of businesses, not shown separately.

Source: U.S. Bureau of Labor Statistics, Current Employment Statistics, "Employment, Hours, and Earnings—National," <http://www.bls.gov/ces/data.htm>, accessed April 2015.

Table 1062. Retail Trade and Food Services—Sales by Kind of Business: 2000 to 2013

[In billions of dollars (3,287.5 represents $3,287,500,000,000). Data have been adjusted using preliminary results of the 2012 Economic Census]

Kind of business	2007 NAICS code [1]	2000	2005	2009	2010	2011	2012	2013
Retail sales and food services, total..........	44, 45, 722	**3,287.5**	**4,085.7**	**4,066.8**	**4,288.3**	**4,601.8**	**4,831.1**	**5,011.7**
Retail sales, total...................................	44, 45	**2,983.3**	**3,689.3**	**3,614.5**	**3,820.9**	**4,106.0**	**4,306.2**	**4,469.0**
GAFO, total [2]...................................	(X)	862.7	1,059.6	1,088.4	1,114.6	1,155.9	1,192.2	1,213.5
Motor vehicle and parts dealers.....................	441	796.2	888.3	671.9	743.2	814.6	888.0	962.0
Automobile dealers................................	4411	687.8	753.1	552.2	621.5	686.3	754.6	822.1
New car dealers..............................	44111	630.1	681.9	486.9	550.0	610.7	674.5	737.6
Other motor vehicle dealers......................	4412	45.0	65.2	45.3	43.5	45.1	49.1	54.8
Auto parts, accessories, and tire stores..........	4413	63.4	70.1	74.4	78.2	83.2	84.3	85.1
Furniture and home furnishings stores............	442	91.2	109.1	84.9	85.4	87.7	91.6	94.9
Furniture stores...............................	4421	50.6	58.7	45.8	46.6	47.6	49.7	50.5
Home furnishings stores......................	4422	40.6	50.4	39.1	38.8	40.1	41.9	44.4
Electronics and appliance stores [3]..............	443	82.2	100.5	95.5	97.6	100.3	102.6	103.7
Appliances, televisions, and other electronics stores.....................	44311	58.2	77.4	72.9	71.6	72.3	73.1	73.4
Building materials, garden equipment, and supply stores [3]................................	444	229.0	320.8	261.8	260.7	269.7	281.9	302.2
Hardware stores..............................	44413	16.2	18.9	18.7	18.7	20.1	20.8	21.1
Food and beverage stores [3].....................	445	444.8	508.5	569.1	581.5	610.3	629.9	643.5
Grocery stores................................	4451	402.5	457.7	510.4	521.3	548.3	564.9	576.4
Supermarkets and other grocery (except convenience) stores.....................	44511	381.4	435.5	489.5	498.7	524.4	540.4	550.4
Beer, wine and liquor stores..................	4453	28.5	33.6	40.4	41.7	42.8	44.9	46.6
Health and personal care stores.....................	446	155.2	210.1	253.3	261.2	272.7	275.8	283.8
Pharmacies and drug stores..................	44611	130.9	179.2	217.3	222.3	231.3	230.4	236.2
Gasoline stations................................	447	249.8	378.9	391.5	448.7	532.4	555.4	551.6
Clothing and clothing accessory, stores [3]..........	448	167.7	201.0	204.2	212.8	228.0	238.8	244.5
Clothing stores [3].............................	4481	118.1	145.6	151.2	157.9	167.6	175.3	178.5
Women's clothing stores....................	44812	31.4	37.1	36.9	38.9	41.7	43.9	43.9
Shoe stores.................................	4482	22.9	25.3	25.7	27.3	29.4	31.2	33.0
Jewelry stores...............................	44831	24.8	28.4	25.6	25.7	28.8	29.8	30.3
Sporting goods, hobby, book & music stores [3]....	451	75.8	80.9	80.1	80.2	80.5	82.8	84.4
Sporting goods stores........................	45111	25.3	30.7	36.5	37.3	39.0	42.1	44.4
Hobby, toy, and game stores.................	45112	16.9	16.3	15.5	15.7	16.0	16.5	16.8
General merchandise stores [3]....................	452	404.2	528.4	589.2	604.2	625.4	643.0	653.1
Department stores (excluding leased depts.)....	4521	232.5	215.3	186.8	185.1	183.8	177.8	171.7
Discount department stores...............	452112	136.2	130.5	123.2	119.8	117.6	114.3	110.6
Department stores (including leased depts.) [4]....	4521	239.9	220.7	190.0	188.1	187.0	181.0	175.1
Discount department stores...............	452112	139.6	133.2	124.9	121.4	119.2	115.9	112.1
Warehouse clubs and superstores..............	45291	139.6	271.9	354.6	368.1	386.4	406.4	419.6
Miscellaneous store retailers [3]....................	453	106.7	107.3	101.8	104.3	108.4	110.1	112.6
Office supplies, stationery, and gift stores........	4532	41.7	39.8	34.5	34.3	34.0	33.4	32.9
Office supplies and stationery stores..........	45321	22.7	22.2	19.4	18.8	18.1	17.4	16.5
Used merchandise stores....................	4533	9.8	9.3	10.9	11.9	13.2	14.8	15.9
Nonstore retailers [3]................................	454	180.5	255.6	311.2	340.9	376.1	406.4	432.8
Electronic shopping and mail-order houses......	4541	113.8	175.9	235.4	262.9	293.6	325.8	348.1
Fuel dealers.................................	45431	26.7	34.3	33.6	35.8	39.9	36.4	38.2
Food services and drinking places [5]...........	722	**304.3**	**396.5**	**452.4**	**467.5**	**495.8**	**524.9**	**542.7**

X Not applicable. [1] North American Industry Classification System, 2007; see text, Section 15. [2] GAFO (General Merchandise, Apparel, Furniture, and Office Supplies) represents stores classified in the following NAICS codes: 442, 443, 448, 451, 452, and 4532. [3] Includes other kinds of businesses, not shown separately. [4] Includes data for leased departments operated within department stores. Data are not included in aggregate kind-of-business totals. [5] See also Table 1289.

Source: U.S. Census Bureau, "2013 Annual Retail Trade Report," <http://www.census.gov/retail/index.html>, accessed March 2015.

Table 1063. Retail Trade Corporations—Sales, Net Profit, and Profit Per Dollar of Sales: 2013 and 2014

[$2,525 represents $2,525,000,000,000. Represents 2012 North American Industry Classification System (NAICS) groups 44 and 45. Profit rates are averages of quarterly figures at annual rates. Covers corporations with assets of $50,000,000 or more]

Item	Unit	Total retail trade		Food and beverage stores (NAICS 445)		Clothing and general merchandise stores (NAICS 448, 452)		All other retail stores	
		2013	2014	2013	2014	2013	2014	2013	2014
Sales.................................	Bil. dol.	2,525	2,635	447	462	858	886	1,220	1,287
Net profit:									
Before income taxes........................	Bil. dol.	118.9	116.2	12.7	11.4	50.6	47.1	55.6	58.0
After income taxes.........................	Bil. dol.	80.6	74.6	10.3	7.3	32.4	29.8	37.9	37.6
Profits per dollar of sales:									
Before income taxes........................	Cents	4.7	4.4	2.8	2.4	5.9	5.3	4.6	4.5
After income taxes.........................	Cents	3.2	2.8	2.3	1.6	3.8	3.3	3.1	2.9
Profits on stockholders' equity:									
Before income taxes........................	Percent	24.7	23.4	23.7	19.7	27.1	24.2	22.9	23.6
After income taxes.........................	Percent	16.7	15.0	19.2	12.8	17.4	15.3	15.6	15.3

Source: U.S. Census Bureau, *Quarterly Financial Report for Manufacturing, Mining, Trade, and Selected Service Industries.* See also <http://www.census.gov/econ/qfr/>.

Table 1064. Retail Trade and Food Services—Estimated Per Capita Sales by Selected Kind of Business: 2000 to 2013

[Estimates are shown in dollars and are based on data from the Annual Retail Trade Survey and the Census Bureau's Population Estimates Program. Based on estimated resident population estimates as of July 1. Data have been adjusted using preliminary results of the 2012 Economic Census. For additional information, see <http://www.census.gov/popest/>. For statement on methodology, see Appendix III]

Kind of business	2007 NAICS code [1]	2000	2005	2009	2010	2011	2012	2013
Retail and food service sales	44–45, 722	11,651	13,826	13,257	13,862	14,763	15,380	15,835
Retail sales, total	44–45	10,573	12,484	11,782	12,351	13,172	13,709	14,120
Total (excluding motor vehicle and parts dealers)	44–45, ex 441	7,751	9,478	9,592	9,949	10,559	10,882	11,081
Motor vehicle and parts dealers	441	2,822	3,006	2,190	2,402	2,613	2,827	3,039
Furniture and home furnishings stores	442	323	369	277	276	281	291	300
Electronics and appliance stores	443	291	340	311	316	322	327	328
Building material and garden equipment and supplies dealers	444	812	1,086	853	843	865	897	955
Food and beverage stores	445	1,576	1,721	1,855	1,880	1,958	2,005	2,033
Health and personal care stores	446	550	711	826	844	875	878	897
Gasoline stations	447	885	1,282	1,276	1,450	1,708	1,768	1,743
Clothing and clothing accessories stores	448	594	680	666	688	731	760	773
Sporting goods, hobby, book, and music stores	451	269	274	261	259	258	264	267
General merchandise stores	452	1,433	1,788	1,921	1,953	2,006	2,047	2,063
Miscellaneous store retailers	453	378	363	332	337	348	350	356
Nonstore retailers	454	640	865	1,015	1,102	1,206	1,294	1,367
Food services and drinking places, total	722	1,078	1,342	1,475	1,511	1,591	1,671	1,715

[1] North American Industry Classification System, 2007; see text, Section 15.

Source: U.S. Census Bureau, "2013 Annual Retail Trade Survey," <http://www.census.gov/retail/>, accessed March 2015.

Table 1065. Retail Trade—Merchandise Inventories and Inventory/Sales Ratios by Kind of Business: 2011 to 2014

[Inventories in billions of dollars (471.0 represents $471,000,000,000). As of Dec. 31. Estimates exclude food services. Includes warehouses. Adjusted for seasonal variations. Sales data also adjusted for holiday and trading-day differences. Based on data from the Monthly Retail Trade Survey, Annual Retail Trade Survey, and administrative records; see Appendix III. Data have been adjusted using results of the 2007 Economic Census]

Kind of business	2007 NAICS code [1]	Inventories				Inventory/sales ratio			
		2011	2012	2013	2014	2011	2012	2013	2014
Retail Inventories, total [2]	44–45	471.0	505.2	543.5	558.3	1.35	1.38	1.44	1.44
Total excluding motor vehicle and parts dealers	44–45 ex 441	338.5	348.5	365.9	373.9	1.22	1.21	1.24	1.25
Motor vehicle and parts dealers	441	132.5	156.6	177.6	184.5	1.85	2.02	2.17	2.07
Furniture, home furnishings, electronics, and appliance stores	442, 443	26.3	27.3	27.1	27.3	1.66	1.64	1.65	1.58
Building material and garden equipment and supplies dealers	444	43.6	45.0	48.1	49.9	1.85	1.85	1.90	1.84
Food and beverage stores	445	40.2	41.2	42.8	44.4	0.79	0.78	0.78	0.79
Clothing and clothing accessories stores	448	44.4	46.6	49.7	51.1	2.28	2.31	2.42	2.44
General merchandise stores	452	76.6	77.7	80.6	81.0	1.46	1.45	1.48	1.45
Department stores	4521	31.3	29.8	30.0	28.7	2.07	2.06	2.12	2.04

[1] North American Industry Classification System, 2007; see text, Section 15. [2] Includes other kind of businesses, not shown separately.

Source: U.S. Census Bureau, Monthly Retail Trade Report, "Retail Inventories and Inventories/Sales Ratios," March 2015, <http://www.census.gov/retail/index.html>, accessed May 2015.

Table 1066. Retail Trade Sales—Total and E-Commerce by Kind of Business: 2013

[4,469,022 represents $4,469,022,000,000. Covers retailers with and without payroll. Based on the Annual Retail Trade Survey; see Appendix III]

Kind of business	2007 NAICS code [1]	Value of sales (mil. dol.)		E-commerce as percent of total sales	Percent distribution of E-commerce sales
		Total	E-commerce		
Retail trade, total [2]	44-45	4,469,022	260,669	5.8	100.0
Motor vehicle and parts dealers	441	961,981	27,525	2.9	10.6
Furniture and home furnishings stores	442	94,879	574	0.6	0.2
Electronics and appliance stores	443	103,744	1,250	1.2	0.5
Building material and garden equipment and supplies stores	444	302,150	1,164	0.4	0.4
Food and beverage stores	445	643,520	941	0.1	0.4
Health and personal care stores	446	283,761	690	0.2	0.3
Clothing and clothing accessories stores	448	244,548	3,396	1.4	1.3
Sporting goods, hobby, book, and music stores	451	84,393	2,176	2.6	0.8
General merchandise stores	452	653,093	88	–	–
Miscellaneous store retailers	453	112,618	2,474	2.2	0.9
Nonstore retailers	454	432,759	220,391	50.9	84.5
Electronic shopping and mail-order houses	45411	348,126	219,417	63.0	84.2

– Represents or rounds to zero. [1] North American Industry Classification System, 2007; see text, Section 15. [2] Includes other kinds of businesses, not shown separately.

Source: U.S. Census Bureau, "E-Stats - Measuring the Electronic Economy," <http://www.census.gov/econ/estats>, accessed June 2015.

Table 1067. Electronic Shopping and Mail-Order Houses—Total and E-Commerce Sales by Merchandise Line: 2012 and 2013

[325,817 represents $325,817,000,000. Represents 2007 North American Industry Classification System code 45411 which comprises establishments primarily engaged in retailing all types of merchandise using nonstore means, including catalogs, toll-free telephone numbers, or electronic media, such as interactive television or computer. Covers businesses with and without paid employees. Based on the Annual Retail Survey; see Appendix III]

Merchandise lines	2012 Value of sales (million dollars)		2012 E-commerce as percent of total sales	2013 Value of sales (million dollars)		2013 E-commerce as percent of total sales
	Total	E-commerce		Total	E-commerce	
Total.........	325,817	193,583	59.4	348,126	219,417	63.0
Books and magazines.........	10,883	9,651	88.7	11,381	10,210	89.7
Clothing and clothing accessories (includes footwear).........	40,044	33,248	83.0	46,545	40,032	86.0
Computer hardware.........	25,569	14,226	55.6	26,299	14,731	56.0
Computer software.........	8,021	5,365	66.9	8,291	5,410	65.3
Drugs, health aids, beauty aids.........	90,277	14,540	16.1	90,742	17,026	18.8
Electronics and appliances.........	26,310	22,067	83.9	26,546	22,753	85.7
Food, beer, and wine.........	7,002	4,876	69.6	7,365	5,153	70.0
Furniture and home furnishings.........	19,325	15,984	82.7	23,158	20,030	86.5
Music and videos.........	9,954	8,984	90.3	11,185	10,253	91.7
Office equipment and supplies.........	8,502	6,794	79.9	8,067	(S)	(S)
Sporting goods.........	8,373	6,245	74.6	9,749	7,844	80.5
Toys, hobby goods, and games.........	7,547	5,923	78.5	8,704	(S)	(S)
Other merchandise [1].........	43,874	29,755	67.8	47,798	33,981	71.1
Nonmerchandise receipts [2].........	20,136	15,925	79.1	22,296	18,354	82.3

S Figure does not meet publication standards. [1] Includes jewelry, collectibles, souvenirs, auto parts and accessories, hardware, and lawn and garden equipment and supplies. [2] Includes auction commissions, shipping and handling, customer training, customer support, and advertising.

Source: U.S. Census Bureau, "E-Stats - Measuring the Electronic Economy," <http://www.census.gov/econ/estats/>, accessed June 2015.

Table 1068. Franchised New Car Dealerships—Summary: 2000 to 2014

[In units as indicated (650 represents $650,000,000,000)]

Item	Unit	2000	2005	2007	2008	2009	2010	2011	2012	2013	2014
Dealerships [1].........	Number	20,490	19,898	19,226	18,495	16,918	16,181	16,049	16,125	16,170	16,396
Sales.........	Bil. dol.	650	699	693	571	492	553	609	676	730	806
New light duty vehicle sales [2].....	Millions	(NA)	16.9	16.1	13.2	10.4	11.6	12.7	14.4	15.5	16.4
New cars sold.........	Millions	8.8	7.7	7.6	6.8	5.5	5.6	6.1	7.2	7.6	7.7
New light trucks sold.........	Millions	(NA)	9.3	8.5	6.4	4.9	5.9	6.6	7.2	7.9	8.7
Used vehicles sold.........	Millions	20.5	19.7	18.5	15.0	14.9	15.3	15.6	17.1	17.4	(NA)
Employment.........	1,000	1,114	1,138	1,115	1,057	913	892	934	963	1,009	1,056
Annual payroll.........	Bil. dol.	46.1	51.5	53.9	53.2	43.5	42.4	45.8	51.6	53.7	58.1
Advertising expenses.........	Bil. dol.	6.4	7.7	7.9	6.8	5.4	5.9	6.4	7.2	7.6	(NA)
Dealer pretax profits as a percentage of sales.........	Percent	1.6	1.6	1.5	1.0	1.5	2.1	2.3	2.2	2.2	2.2
Inventory: [3] Domestic: [4]											
Total.........	1,000	3,183	2,991	2,712	2,478	1,697	1,687	(NA)	(NA)	(NA)	(NA)
Days' supply.........	Days	68	70	67	80	72	60	57	62	66	(NA)
Imported: [4]											
Total.........	1,000	468	566	619	687	519	494	(NA)	(NA)	(NA)	(NA)
Days' supply.........	Days	50	52	51	65	61	55	46	52	58	(NA)

NA Not available. [1] Light vehicle dealerships, as of December 31. [2] Data provided by Ward's Automotive Reports. [3] Annual average. [4] Classification based on where automobiles are produced (i.e., automobiles manufactured by foreign companies but produced in the U.S., Canada, and Mexico are classified as domestic).

Source: National Automobile Dealers Association, <www.nada.org>. *NADA Data 2014: Annual Financial Profile of America's Franchised New-Car Dealerships*, annual ©.

Table 1069. Retail Sales and Leases of New and Used Vehicles: 1990 to 2010

[In thousands, except as noted (52,484 represents 52,484,000)]

Item	1990	2000	2004	2005	2006	2007	2008	2009	2010
Vehicle sales and leases, total (number of vehicles)......	**52,484**	**64,320**	**62,839**	**64,626**	**62,744**	**61,562**	**52,845**	**48,545**	**51,434**
New vehicle sales and leases.........	14,954	22,700	20,294	20,488	20,178	20,143	16,315	13,053	14,550
New vehicle sales.........	13,890	17,410	16,850	16,990	16,460	16,230	13,300	10,550	11,580
New vehicle leases.........	1,064	5,290	3,444	3,498	3,718	3,913	3,015	2,503	2,970
Used vehicle sales [1].........	37,530	41,620	42,545	44,138	42,566	41,419	36,530	35,492	36,884
Vehicle sales, total value (bil. dol.) [2]......	**447**	**736**	**765**	**776**	**786**	**774**	**643**	**575**	**635**
New vehicle sales (bil. dol.).........	227	380	407	421	445	435	351	274	311
Used vehicle sales (bil. dol.).........	220	356	358	355	341	339	292	301	324
Average price (current dol.): [2]									
New vehicle sales.........	16,350	21,850	24,082	24,796	26,854	26,950	26,477	26,245	26,850
Used vehicle sales.........	5,857	8,547	8,410	8,036	8,009	8,186	7,986	8,483	8,786

[1] Used car sales include sales from franchised dealers, independent dealers, and casual sales. [2] Includes leased vehicles.

Source: U.S. Bureau of Transportation Statistics, "National Transportation Statistics," <http://www.bts.gov/publications/national_transportation_statistics>, September 2015.

Table 1070. New Motor Vehicle Sales and Car Production: 1990 to 2014

[In thousands (14,137 represents 14,137,000). Data are primarily from "Ward's Automotive Reports" published by Ward's Communications, Southfield, MI]

Type of vehicle	1990	2000	2009	2010	2011	2012	2013	2014
New motor vehicle sales	**14,137**	**17,812**	**10,602**	**11,772**	**13,041**	**14,789**	**15,883**	**16,842**
New-car sales	9,300	8,778	5,402	5,636	6,090	7,244	7,585	7,688
Domestic	6,897	6,762	3,558	3,792	4,143	5,119	5,433	5,589
Import	2,403	2,016	1,843	1,844	1,947	2,125	2,153	2,098
New-truck sales	4,837	9,034	5,201	6,137	6,951	7,544	8,298	9,154
Light	4,560	8,572	5,001	5,919	6,645	7,198	7,946	8,748
Domestic	3,957	7,720	4,117	5,020	5,663	6,138	6,707	7,388
Import	603	852	884	899	983	1,061	1,239	1,360
Heavy	278	462	200	218	306	346	352	407
Domestic-car production	6,231	5,471	2,196	2,731	2,977	4,109	4,369	4,253
Average expenditure per new car [1] (dol.)	14,371	21,041	23,276	24,296	(NA)	(NA)	(NA)	(NA)
Domestic (dol.)	13,936	19,586	22,148	23,095	(NA)	(NA)	(NA)	(NA)
Import (dol.)	15,510	25,965	25,499	26,808	(NA)	(NA)	(NA)	(NA)

NA Not available. [1] Estimate based on the manufacturer's suggested retail price.

Source: U.S. Bureau of Economic Analysis, National Economic Accounts, "Supplemental Estimates: Motor Vehicles," <http://www.bea.gov/national/index.htm#supp>, accessed March 2015.

Table 1071. Food and Alcoholic Beverage Expenditures by Sales Outlet: 1990 to 2013

[In billions of dollars (569.6 represents $569,600,000,000)]

Sales outlet	1990	2000	2005	2008	2009	2010	2011	2012	2013
Food sales, total [1]	**569.6**	**835.8**	**1,057.6**	**1,213.5**	**1,208.2**	**1,243.7**	**1,310.9**	**1,372.3**	**1,423.9**
Food at home	324.6	443.1	547.9	623.8	621.9	638.9	672.2	697.5	717.9
Food stores [2]	256.4	302.8	338.9	378.3	377.9	385.6	405.5	418.5	430.1
Other stores [3]	25.6	74.8	133.8	160.0	160.3	167.1	176.3	185.3	188.3
Home-delivered, mail order	5.3	18.7	18.5	19.6	18.5	19.2	20.1	21.4	25.1
Farmers, manufacturers, wholesalers	25.6	32.4	38.9	45.3	44.5	45.9	48.2	49.7	51.0
Home production and donations	11.7	14.4	17.8	20.7	20.6	21.3	22.2	22.6	23.4
Food away from home [4]	245.0	392.6	509.6	589.7	586.3	604.8	638.7	674.8	705.9
Alcoholic beverage sales, total	**69.4**	**107.1**	**129.1**	**148.9**	**147.2**	**152.9**	**161.3**	**168.6**	**174.3**
Packaged alcoholic beverages	34.9	48.2	63.5	79.1	78.0	80.9	85.0	89.0	90.8
Liquor stores	18.6	24.4	32.1	38.1	38.9	40.0	41.0	43.0	45.7
Food stores	10.8	15.8	18.6	20.3	20.3	20.7	21.8	22.5	23.0
All other	5.4	8.0	12.8	20.6	18.8	20.2	22.2	23.5	22.1
Alcoholic drinks away from home	34.5	58.9	65.6	69.8	69.3	72.0	76.3	79.6	83.5
Eating and drinking places [5]	26.5	41.5	51.2	54.7	53.8	54.9	58.1	61.3	64.6
Hotels and motels [5]	3.2	6.4	4.7	4.8	4.7	4.7	4.8	4.9	4.9
All other	4.8	11.0	9.7	10.3	10.8	12.4	13.5	13.5	14.1

[1] Includes taxes and tips. [2] Excludes sales to restaurants and institutions. [3] Includes eating and drinking establishments, trailer parks, commissary stores, and military exchanges. [4] Includes food supplied and donated. [5] Includes tips.

Source: U.S. Department of Agriculture, Economic Research Service, "Food Expenditures," <http://www.ers.usda.gov/data-products/food-expenditures.aspx>, accessed March 2015.

Section 23
Transportation

This section presents data on civil air transportation, both passenger and cargo, and on water transportation, including inland waterways, oceanborne commerce, the merchant marine, cargo, and vessel tonnages.

This section also presents statistics on revenues, passenger and freight traffic volume, and employment in various revenue-producing modes of the transportation industry, including motor vehicles, trains, and pipelines. Data are also presented on highway mileage and finances, motor vehicle travel, accidents, and registrations; and characteristics of public transit, railroads, and pipelines.

The principal source of transportation data is the annual *National Transportation Statistics* publication of the U.S. Bureau of Transportation Statistics. Principal sources of air and water transportation data are the *Annual Report* issued by Airlines for America, Washington, DC and the annual *Waterborne Commerce of the United States* issued by the Corps of Engineers of the Department of Army. In addition, the U.S. Census Bureau in its Commodity Flow Survey (part of the Census of Transportation, taken every 5 years through 2012, for years ending in "2" and "7") provides data on the type, weight, and value of commodities shipped by manufacturing establishments in the United States, by means of transportation, origin, and destination. Data from the 2012 Economic Census are being released on a continuing basis through 2016. This census was conducted in accordance with the 2012 North American Industry Classification System (NAICS). See text, Section 15, Business Enterprise, for a discussion of the Economic Census and NAICS.

The Bureau of Transportation Statistics (BTS) was established within the U.S. Department of Transportation (DOT) in 1992 to collect, report, and analyze transportation data. Today, BTS is a component of the DOT Research and Innovative Technology Administration (RITA). BTS products include reports to Congress, the Secretary of Transportation, and stakeholders in the nation's transportation community. These stakeholders include: federal agencies, state and local governments, metropolitan planning organizations, universities, the private sector and general public. Congress requires, by congressional mandate, laid out in 49 U.S.C. 111 (1), the BTS to report on transportation statistics to the President and Congress. *The Transportation Statistics Annual Report* (TSAR), provides a data overview of U.S. transportation issues. As required by Congress, each TSAR has two essential components: a review of the state of transportation statistics with recommendations for improvements and a presentation of the data. The BTS publication *National Transportation Statistics* (NTS), a companion report to the TSAR, has more comprehensive and longer time-series data. NTS presents information on the U.S. transportation system, including its physical components, safety record, economic performance, energy use, and environmental impacts. The BTS publication *State Transportation Statistics* presents a statistical profile of transportation in the 50 states and the District of Columbia. This profile includes infrastructure, freight movement and passenger travel, system safety, vehicles, transportation-related economy and finance, energy usage and the environment.

The principal compiler of data on public roads and on operation of motor vehicles is the U.S. Department of Transportation's (DOT) Federal Highway Administration (FHWA). These data appear in FHWA's annual *Highway Statistics* and other publications.

The U.S. National Highway Traffic Safety Administration (NHTSA), through its *Traffic Safety Facts FARS/GES Annual Report*, presents descriptive statistics about traffic crashes of all severities, from those that result in property damage to those that result in the loss of human life. The data for this report is a compilation of motor vehicle crash data from the Fatality Analysis Reporting System (FARS) and the General Estimates System (GES). Other publications and reports can be found at the National Center for Statistics and Analysis (NCSA), Publications and Data Request, located on the Internet at <http://www-nrd.nhtsa.dot.gov/CATS/>. DOT's Federal Railroad Administration (FRA), Office of Safety Analysis presents railroad safety information including accidents and incidents, inspections and highway-rail crossing data in its annual report *Railroad Safety Statistics*. The Web site is located at <http://safetydata.fra.dot.gov/officeofsafety>.

Civil aviation—Federal promotion and regulation of civil aviation have been carried out by the Federal Aviation Administration (FAA) and the Civil Aeronautics Board (CAB). The CAB promoted and regulated the civil air transportation industry within the United States and between the United States and foreign countries. The Board granted licenses to provide air transportation service, approved or disapproved proposed rates and fares, and approved or disapproved proposed agreements and corporate relationships involving air carriers. In December 1984, the CAB ceased to exist as an agency. Some of its functions were transferred to the DOT, as outlined below. The responsibility for investigation of aviation accidents resides with the National Transportation Safety Board.

The Office of the Secretary, DOT aviation activities include: negotiation of international air transportation rights, selection of U.S. air carriers to serve capacity controlled international markets, oversight of international rates and fares, maintenance of essential air service to small communities, and consumer affairs. DOT's Bureau of Transportation Statistics (BTS) handles aviation information functions formerly assigned to CAB. Prior to BTS, the Research and Special Programs Administration handled these functions.

The principal activities of the FAA include: the promotion of air safety; controlling the use of navigable airspace; prescribing regulations dealing with the competency of airmen, airworthiness of aircraft and air traffic control; operation of air route traffic control centers, airport traffic control towers, and flight service stations; the design, construction, maintenance, and inspection of navigation, traffic control, and communications equipment; and the development of general aviation.

The CAB published monthly and quarterly financial and traffic statistical data for the certificated route air carriers. BTS continues these publications, including both certificated and noncertificated (commuter) air carriers. The FAA annually publishes data on the use of airway facilities; data related to the location of airmen, aircraft, and airports; the volume of activity in the field of nonair carrier (general aviation) flying; and aircraft production and registration.

General aviation comprises all civil flying (including such commercial operations as small demand air taxis, agriculture application, powerline patrol, etc.) but excludes certificated route air carriers, supplemental operators, large-aircraft commercial operators, and commuter airlines.

Air carriers and service—The CAB previously issued "certificates of public convenience and necessity" under Section 401 of the Federal Aviation Act of 1958 for scheduled and nonscheduled (charter) passenger services and cargo services. It also issued certificates under Section 418 of the Act to cargo air carriers for domestic all-cargo service only. The DOT Office of the Secretary now issues the certificates under a "fit, willing, and able" test of air carrier operations. Carriers operating only a 60-seat-or-less aircraft are given exemption authority to carry passengers, cargo, and mail in scheduled and nonscheduled service under Part 298 of the DOT (formerly CAB) regulations. Exemption authority carriers who offer scheduled passenger service to an essential air service point must meet the "fit, willing, and able" test.

Vessel shipments, entrances, and clearances—Shipments by dry cargo vessels comprise shipments on all types of watercraft, except tanker vessels; shipments by tanker vessels comprise all types of cargo, liquid and dry, carried by tanker vessels. A vessel is reported as entered only at the first port which it enters in the United States, whether or not cargo is unloaded at that port.

A vessel is reported as cleared only at the last port at which clearance is made to a foreign port, whether or not it takes on cargo. Army and Navy vessels entering or clearing without commercial cargo are not included in the figures.

Units of measurement—Cargo (or freight) tonnage and shipping weight both represent the gross weight of the cargo including the weight of containers, wrappings, crates, etc. However, shipping weight excludes lift and cargo vans and similar substantial outer containers. Other tonnage figures generally refer to stowing capacity of vessels, 100 cubic feet being called 1 ton. Gross tonnage comprises the space within the frames and the ceiling of the hull, together with those closed-in spaces above deck available for cargo, stores, passengers, or crew, with certain minor exceptions. Net or registered tonnage is the gross tonnage less the spaces occupied by the propelling machinery, fuel, crew quarters, master's cabin, and navigation spaces. Substantially, it represents space available for cargo and passengers. The net tonnage capacity of a ship may bear little relation to weight of cargo. Deadweight tonnage is the weight in long tons required to depress a vessel from light water line (that is, with only the machinery and equipment on board) to load line. It is, therefore, the weight of the cargo, fuel, etc., which a vessel is designed to carry with safety.

Federal-aid highway systems—The Intermodal Surface Transportation Efficiency Act (ISTEA) of 1991 eliminated the historical Federal-Aid Highway Systems and created the National Highway System (NHS) and other federal-aid highway categories. The final NHS was approved by Congress in December of 1995 under the National Highway System Designation Act.

Functional systems—Roads and streets are assigned to groups according to the character of service intended. The functional systems are (1) arterial highways that generally handle the long trips, (2) collector facilities that collect and disperse traffic between the arterials and the lower systems, and (3) local roads and streets that primarily serve direct access to residential areas, farms, and other local areas.

Regulatory bodies—The Federal Energy Regulatory Commission (FERC) is an independent agency that regulates the interstate transmission of electricity, natural gas, and oil. FERC also reviews proposals to build liquefied natural gas (LNG) terminals and interstate natural gas pipelines as well as licensing hydropower projects. The Energy Policy Act of 2005 gave FERC additional responsibilities such as regulating the transmission and wholesale sales of electricity in interstate commerce.

Railroads—The Surface Transportation Board (STB) was created in the Interstate Commerce Commission Termination Act of 1995, Pub. L. No.104-88, 109 Stat. 803 (1995) (ICCTA), and is the successor agency to the Interstate Commerce Commission. The STB is an economic regulatory agency that Congress charged with the fundamental missions of resolving railroad rate and service disputes and reviewing proposed railroad mergers. The STB is decisionally independent, although it is administratively affiliated with the Department of Transportation.

The STB serves as both an adjudicatory and a regulatory body. The agency has jurisdiction over railroad rate and service issues and rail restructuring transactions (mergers, line sales, line construction, and line abandonment); certain trucking company, moving van, and noncontiguous ocean shipping company rate matters; certain intercity passenger bus company structure, financial, and operational matters; and rates and services of certain pipelines not regulated by the Federal Energy Regulatory Commission. Other ICC regulatory functions were either eliminated or transferred to the Federal Highway Administration or the Bureau of Transportation Statistics within DOT.

Class I Railroads are regulated by the STB and subject to the Uniform System of Accounts and required to file annual and periodic reports. Railroads are classified based on their annual operating revenues. The class to which a carrier belongs is determined by comparing its adjusted operating revenues for 3 consecutive years to the following scale: Class I, $250 million or more; Class II, $20 million to $250 million; and Class III, $0 to $20 million. Operating revenue dollar ranges are indexed for inflation.

Postal Service—The U.S. Postal Service provides mail processing and delivery services within the United States. The Postal Accountability and Enhancement Act of 2006 was the first major legislative change to the Postal Service since 1971 when the Postal Reorganization Act of 1970 created the Postal Service as an independent establishment of the Federal Executive Branch. The Act of 2006 changed the way the U.S. Postal Service operates and conducts business. Now annual rate increases for market dominant products are linked to the Consumer Price Index and the Postal Service has more flexibility for pricing competitive products, enabling it to respond to dynamic market conditions and changing customer needs.

Revenue and cost analysis describes the Postal Service's system of attributing revenues and costs to classes of mail and service. This system draws primarily upon probability sampling techniques to develop estimates of revenues, volumes, and weights, as well as costs by class of mail and special service. The costs attributed to classes of mail and special services are primarily incremental costs which vary in response to changes in volume; they account for roughly 60 percent of the total costs of the Postal Service. The balance represents "institutional costs." Statistics on revenues, volume of mail, and distribution of expenditures are presented in the Postal Service's annual report, *Cost and Revenue Analysis*, and its *Annual Report of the Postmaster General,* and its annual *Comprehensive Statement on Postal Operations.*

Statistical reliability—For a discussion of statistical collection and estimation, sampling procedures, and measures of statistical reliability applicable to Census Bureau data, see Appendix III.

Table 1072. Transportation-Related Components of U.S. Gross Domestic Product: 2000 to 2013

[In billions of dollars (1,048.0 represents $1,048,000,000,000), except percent. For explanation of chained dollars, see Section 13 text. Minus sign (-) indicates a decrease]

Item	2000	2005	2010	2011	2012	2013
CURRENT DOLLARS						
Total transportation-related final demand [1]	**1,048.0**	**1,251.1**	**1,307.9**	**1,465.8**	**1,536.1**	**1,580.1**
Total gross domestic product (GDP)	10,284.8	13,093.7	14,964.4	15,517.9	16,163.2	16,768.1
Transportation as a percent of GDP	10.2	9.6	8.7	9.4	9.5	9.4
Personal consumption of transportation	795.3	960.8	942.2	1,052.0	1,103.6	1,132.1
Motor vehicles and parts	363.2	410.0	342.0	363.5	395.1	417.7
Motor vehicle fuels, lubricants, and fluids	168.6	261.4	307.3	380.4	388.6	381.8
Transportation services	263.5	289.4	292.9	308.1	319.9	332.6
Gross private domestic investment	177.6	186.7	137.4	183.4	222.3	239.2
Transportation structures	6.8	7.1	9.9	9.5	10.9	11.0
Transportation equipment	170.8	179.6	127.5	173.9	211.4	228.2
Net exports of transportation-related goods and service [2]	-104.7	-133.2	-75.9	-78.9	-99.5	-102.4
Exports (+)	174.3	206.9	255.6	293.2	324.1	344.9
Civilian aircraft, engines, and parts	48.1	55.9	71.9	80.4	94.3	105.0
Automotive vehicles, engines, and parts	80.4	98.4	112.0	133.0	146.2	152.6
Other transportation	45.8	52.6	71.7	79.8	83.6	87.3
Imports (-)	279.0	340.1	331.5	372.1	423.6	447
Civilian aircraft, engines, and parts	26.4	25.8	31.3	35.5	40.1	46.9
Automotive vehicles, engines, and parts	195.0	238.7	225.6	255.2	298.5	309.6
Other transportation	57.6	75.6	74.6	81.4	85.0	90.8
Government transportation-related purchases	179.8	236.8	304.2	309.3	309.7	311.2
Federal purchases [3]	19.0	29.8	38.9	40.9	41.6	39.3
State and local purchases [3]	151.8	191.1	240.6	243.8	248.6	256.2
Defense-related purchases [4]	9.0	15.9	24.7	24.6	19.5	15.7
CHAINED (2009) DOLLARS						
Total transportation-related final demand [1]	**1,336.2**	**1,377.2**	**1,239.5**	**1,287.6**	**1,322.5**	**1,356.7**
Total gross domestic product (GDP)	12,559.7	14,234.2	14,783.8	15,020.6	15,369.2	15,710.3
Transportation as a percent of GDP	10.6	9.7	8.4	8.6	8.6	8.6
Personal consumption of transportation	945.0	1,007.7	870.4	882.6	908.8	937.4
Motor vehicles and parts	346.4	400.0	323.4	333.8	357.9	376.0
Motor vehicle fuels, lubricants, and fluids	265.8	273.0	259.9	254.7	251.3	253.8
Transportation services	332.8	334.7	287.1	294.1	299.6	307.6
Gross private domestic investment	212.9	205.8	146.7	192.3	228.0	241.5
Transportation structures	8.8	7.9	9.8	9.3	10.4	10.4
Transportation equipment	204.1	197.9	136.9	183.0	217.6	231.1
Net exports of transportation-related goods and service [2]	-104.7	-132.8	-75.5	-76.3	-94.1	-98.2
Exports (+)	217.0	226.0	247.5	273.3	295.5	312.3
Civilian aircraft, engines, and parts	69.9	66.9	70.1	75.5	86.2	94.2
Automotive vehicles, engines, and parts	86.8	102.5	111.5	130.1	140.5	145.8
Other transportation	60.3	56.6	65.9	67.7	68.8	72.3
Imports (-)	321.7	358.8	323.0	349.6	389.6	410.5
Civilian aircraft, engines, and parts	37.7	31.6	30.5	33.3	35.7	41.0
Automotive vehicles, engines, and parts	211.9	250.1	224.2	245.8	281.4	292.7
Other transportation	72.1	77.1	68.3	70.5	72.5	76.8
Government transportation-related purchases	283.0	296.5	297.9	289.0	279.8	276.0
Federal purchases [3]	25.3	33.3	37.8	38.6	38.8	36.1
State and local purchases [3]	245.5	245.5	236.0	228.1	223.4	226.0
Defense-related purchases [4]	12.2	17.7	24.1	22.3	17.6	13.9

[1] Sum of total personal consumption of transportation, total gross private domestic investment, net exports of transportation-related goods and services, and total government transportation-related purchases. [2] Exports minus imports. [3] Federal purchases and state and local purchases are the sum of consumption expenditures and gross investment. [4] Defense-related purchases are the sum of transportation of material and travel.

Source: U.S. Bureau of Transportation Statistics, "National Transportation Statistics," <http://www.bts.gov/publications/national_transportation_statistics/>, accessed April 2015.

Table 1073. Employment in Transportation and Warehousing: 2000 to 2014

[In thousands (4,410 represents 4,410,000). Annual average of monthly figures. Based on Current Employment Statistics program; see Appendix III]

Industry	NAICS code [1]	2000	2005	2010	2011	2012	2013	2014
Transportation and warehousing	**48–49**	**4,410**	**4,361**	**4,191**	**4,302**	**4,416**	**4,498**	**4,640**
Air transportation	481	614	501	458	457	459	444	442
Rail transportation	482	232	228	216	228	231	231	235
Water transportation	483	56	61	62	61	64	65	67
Truck transportation	484	1,406	1,398	1,250	1,301	1,349	1,382	1,416
Transit and ground passenger	485	372	389	430	440	440	449	465
Pipeline transportation	486	46	38	42	43	44	45	47
Scenic and sightseeing	487	28	29	27	28	28	29	31
Support activities	488	537	552	543	562	580	598	625
Couriers and messengers	492	605	571	528	529	534	544	574
Warehousing and storage	493	514	595	633	653	687	711	738

[1] North American Industry Classification System 2012, see text, Sections 12 and 15.

Source: U.S. Bureau of Labor Statistics, Current Employment Statistics, "Employment, Hours, and Earnings—National," <http://www.bls.gov/ces/data.htm/>, accessed April 2015.

Table 1074. Transportation and Warehousing—Establishments, Employees, and Payroll, by Kind of Business: 2012 and 2013

[Employment in thousands (4,223.4 represents 4,233,400); payroll in millions ($184,933.2 represents $184,933,200,000). Covers establishments with payroll. Excludes self-employed individuals, railroad employees, and most government employees. For statement on methodology, see Appendix III. County Business Patterns excludes rail transportation (NAICS 482) and the National Postal Service (NAICS 491)]

Industry	NAICS code [1]	Establishments 2012	Establishments 2013	Paid employees (1,000) 2012	Paid employees (1,000) 2013	Annual payroll (mil. dol.) 2012	Annual payroll (mil. dol.) 2013
Transportation & warehousing......	**48–49**	**214,492**	**215,547**	**4,233.4**	**4,287.2**	**184,933.2**	**193,656.7**
Air transportation......	481	4,978	4,864	428.1	418.9	25,225.6	26,921.1
Scheduled air transportation......	4811	2,626	2,497	391.8	382.0	22,581.3	24,136.0
Scheduled passenger air transportation......	481111	2,250	2,057	382.0	371.2	21,824.0	23,375.6
Scheduled freight air transportation......	481112	376	440	9.8	10.8	757.3	760.4
Nonscheduled air transportation......	4812	2,352	2,367	36.3	37.0	2,644.3	2,785.1
Water transportation......	483	1,795	1,556	69.1	66.7	4,893.5	4,737.9
Deep sea, coastal, & Great Lakes water transportation......	4831	1,089	988	49.5	46.0	3,592.2	3,315.9
Inland water transportation......	4832	706	568	19.6	20.7	1,301.3	1,421.9
Inland water freight transportation......	483211	345	355	16.9	18.7	1,188.6	1,317.9
Inland water passenger transportation......	483212	361	213	2.7	2.0	112.7	104.0
Truck transportation......	484	111,763	112,849	1,344.4	1,366.6	57,988.7	60,555.1
General freight trucking......	4841	64,586	65,997	913.6	904.0	39,344.6	39,783.8
General freight trucking, local......	48411	28,308	26,891	237.0	182.1	9,852.2	7,208.4
General freight trucking, long distance......	48412	36,278	39,106	676.7	722.0	29,492.4	32,575.5
Specialized freight trucking......	4842	47,177	46,852	430.8	462.6	18,644.1	20,771.2
Used household & office goods moving......	48421	7,715	7,752	85.5	92.3	2,914.0	3,162.8
Specialized freight (except used goods) trucking, local......	48422	30,480	29,230	218.1	205.5	9,572.8	9,380.9
Specialized freight (except used goods) trucking, long-distance......	48423	8,982	9,870	127.2	164.8	6,157.2	8,227.5
Transit & ground passenger transportation......	485	18,955	19,198	461.8	473.4	11,209.5	11,587.0
Urban transit systems......	4851	1,048	917	50.6	52.0	1,972.2	2,147.5
Mixed mode systems......	485111	99	33	2.8	(²)	90.7	(D)
Commuter rail......	485112	13	9	(³)	2.6	(D)	217.4
Bus and other motor vehicle mode systems......	485113	857	839	44.4	47.2	1,672.5	1,809.9
Other......	485119	79	36	0.7	1.5	26.1	93.7
Interurban & rural bus transportation......	4852	578	533	17.4	15.8	546.6	422.9
Taxi & limousine service......	4853	7,505	7,963	72.5	73.8	1,789.4	1,844.4
Taxi service......	48531	3,047	3,190	32.7	32.4	731.0	729.1
Limousine service......	48532	4,458	4,773	39.8	41.4	1,058.4	1,115.4
School & employee bus transportation......	4854	4,293	4,189	210.9	216.9	4,150.2	4,287.8
Charter bus industry......	4855	1,385	1,356	31.3	34.0	850.7	926.8
Other transit & ground passenger transportation......	4859	4,146	4,240	79.1	80.9	1,900.4	1,957.5
Special needs transportation......	485991	2,906	2,878	64.0	63.4	1,554.0	1,545.9
Pipeline transportation......	486	3,627	3,791	49.0	52.0	5,479.8	6,070.4
Pipeline transportation of crude oil......	4861	651	726	10.4	12.1	1,346.1	1,496.5
Pipeline transportation of natural gas......	4862	2,364	2,427	33.3	33.3	3,574.0	3,852.3
Other pipeline transportation......	4869	612	638	5.3	6.7	559.7	721.6
Scenic & sightseeing transportation......	487	2,461	2,618	22.6	24.6	774.2	836.6
Scenic & sightseeing transportation, land......	4871	584	606	8.1	9.4	236.3	280.6
Scenic & sightseeing transportation, water......	4872	1,654	1,783	12.0	12.5	426.2	444.3
Scenic & sightseeing transportation, other......	4879	223	229	2.5	2.6	111.7	111.7
Support activities for transportation......	488	43,212	42,679	638.7	640.7	29,917.7	30,715.7
Support activities for air transportation......	4881	5,952	5,855	168.0	174.2	7,033.1	7,128.2
Airport operations......	48811	2,270	2,099	84.7	87.0	2,515.6	2,468.7
Air traffic control......	488111	251	185	1.6	(³)	101.8	(D)
Other support activities for air transportation......	48819	2,019	3,756	83.2	87.1	2,413.8	4,659.5
Support activities for rail transportation......	4882	1,210	1,391	27.3	34.4	1,270.6	1,681.3
Support activities for water transportation......	4883	2,437	2,530	91.5	98.5	5,337.0	6,225.3
Port and harbor operations......	48831	525	383	25.4	7.0	1,345.9	420.7
Marine cargo handling......	48832	343	458	43.8	66.3	2,601.1	4,086.2
Navigational services to shipping......	48833	850	847	12.5	12.5	839.0	929.4
Other support activities for water transportation......	48839	719	842	9.8	12.7	551.0	789.0
Support activities for road transportation......	4884	11,257	11,228	91.1	86.1	2,852.1	2,754.5
Motor vehicle towing......	48841	8,528	8,610	55.1	53.7	1,697.0	1,719.4
Freight transportation arrangement......	4885	20,852	20,194	243.3	231.9	12,860.2	12,418.3
Other support activities for transportation......	4889	1,504	1,481	17.5	15.7	564.8	508.2
Couriers & messengers......	492	13,613	13,633	527.9	522.6	21,609.3	22,403.8
Couriers......	4921	9,143	9,073	497.9	489.0	20,758.2	21,436.6
Local messengers & local delivery......	4922	4,470	4,560	30.0	33.6	851.1	967.2
Warehousing & storage......	493	14,088	14,359	691.7	721.7	27,835.0	29,829.2

D Data withheld to avoid disclosure. [1] Data based on North American Industry Classification System (NAICS) 2012. See text, Section 15. [2] 500 to 999 employees. [3] 1,000 to 2,499 employees.

Source: U.S. Census Bureau, County Business Patterns, "Geography Area Series, County Business Patterns," <http://factfinder2.census.gov/>, accessed April 2015. See also <http://www.census.gov/econ/cbp/>.

Table 1075. Transportation and Warehousing—Establishments, Revenue, Payroll, and Employees by Industry: 2007 and 2012

[639,916 represents $639,916,000,000. For establishments with payroll. Based on the 2007 and 2012 Economic Censuses. Paid employees for pay period including March 12. See Appendix III]

Industry type	NAICS code [1]	Number of establishments	Revenue (mil. dol.)	Annual payroll (mil. dol.)	Paid employees (1,000)
Transportation and warehousing total, 2007	**48–49**	**219,706**	**639,916**	**173,183**	**4,454.4**
Air transportation	481	5,661	146,612	26,120	478.2
Water transportation	483	1,721	34,447	4,544	76.0
Truck transportation	484	120,390	217,833	58,266	1,507.9
Transit and ground passenger transportation	485	17,791	26,465	9,844	444.9
Pipeline transportation	486	2,529	25,718	3,219	37.0
Scenic and sightseeing transportation	487	2,542	2,448	653	24.4
Support activities for transportation	488	42,130	86,596	24,579	608.4
Couriers and messengers	492	13,004	77,877	20,431	557.2
Warehousing and storage	493	13,938	21,921	25,526	720.5
Transportation and warehousing total, 2012 prelim.	**48–49**	**213,131**	**743,621**	**181,995**	**4,307.0**
Air transportation	481	4,979	188,872	26,206	447.3
Water transportation	483	1,794	38,364	4,960	70.0
Truck transportation	484	111,238	238,911	57,624	1,377.2
Transit and ground passenger transportation	485	18,873	28,659	11,195	496.7
Pipeline transportation	486	3,444	38,014	5,119	48.6
Scenic and sightseeing transportation	487	2,411	3,014	776	25.8
Support activities for transportation	488	42,923	106,708	27,620	619.8
Couriers and messengers	492	13,530	70,555	21,037	532.3
Warehousing and storage	493	13,939	30,524	27,458	689.4

[1] Data based on the 2007 North American Industry Classification System (NAICS); see text, Section 15. [2] Excludes large certificated passenger carriers that do not report to the Office of Airline Information, U.S. Department of Transportation.

Source: U.S. Census Bureau, EC1200CADV2, "Advance Comparative Statistics for the U.S. (2007 NAICS Basis): 2012 and 2007," <http://factfinder.census.gov/>, accessed April 2014.

Table 1076. Transportation and Warehousing—Nonemployer Establishments and Receipts by Kind of Business: 2010 to 2013

[1,021.2 represents 1,021,200. Includes only firms subject to federal income tax. Nonemployers are businesses with no paid employees. Data originate chiefly from administrative records of the Internal Revenue Service; see Appendix III]

Kind of business	NAICS code [1]	Establishments (1,000)			Receipts (mil. dol.)		
		2010	2012	2013	2010	2012	2013
Transportation and warehousing	**48–49**	**1,021.2**	**1,059.0**	**1,102.3**	**60,746**	**69,902**	**72,488**
Air transportation	481	19.1	18.7	18.6	1,219	1,276	1,237
Water transportation	483	6.6	6.6	6.6	490	500	505
Truck transportation	484	490.3	502.1	512.7	42,485	49,463	50,883
General freight trucking	4841	445.1	457.4	467.7	39,277	46,034	47,455
General freight trucking, local	48411	168.7	167.5	169.5	12,144	13,657	14,090
General freight trucking, long-distance	48412	276.4	289.9	298.2	27,133	32,377	33,366
Specialized freight trucking	4842	45.2	44.8	45.0	3,207	3,429	3,428
Transit and ground passenger transportation	485	218.4	247.9	271.7	7,463	9,017	9,917
Urban transit system	4851	1.1	1.4	1.5	39	51	52
Interurban and rural bus transportation	4852	1.5	1.5	1.6	67	69	68
Taxi and limousine service	4853	176.4	202.3	223.8	6,107	7,481	8,352
School and employee bus transportation	4854	6.9	6.8	6.7	191	196	195
Charter bus industry	4855	3.8	4.0	4.0	172	190	184
Other transit and ground passenger transportation	4859	28.7	31.9	34.0	887	1,030	1,066
Pipeline transportation	486	0.9	1.1	1.1	76	84	90
Scenic and sightseeing transportation	487	4.9	5.5	5.3	163	180	187
Support activities for transportation	488	105.2	108.9	115.3	4,624	5,121	5,335
Couriers and messengers	492	166.6	158.1	160.7	3,772	3,777	3,836
Warehousing and storage	493	9.2	10.2	10.3	455	485	499

[1] 2010 data based on the 2007 North American Industry Classification System (NAICS); beginning 2012, data based on 2012 NAICS.

Source: U.S. Census Bureau, Nonemployer Statistics, "Geographic Area Series: Nonemployer Statistics by Legal Form of Organization," <http://factfinder.census.gov/>, accessed June 2015. See also <http://www.census.gov/econ/nonemployer/index.html>.

Table 1077. Transportation System Mileage Within the United States: 1980 to 2012

[3,860 represents 3,860,000. Numbers, except where indicated]

System	Unit	1980	1985	1990	1995	2000	2005	2010	2011	2012
Highway [1]	1,000	3,860	3,864	3,867	3,912	3,936	3,996	4,067	4,078	4,093
Class 1 rail [2]	Number	164,822	145,764	119,758	108,264	99,250	95,664	95,573	95,387	(NA)
Amtrak [2]	Number	24,000	24,000	24,000	24,000	23,000	22,007	21,178	21,225	(NA)
Transit: [3]										
Commuter rail [4]	Number	(NA)	3,574	4,132	4,160	5,209	7,118	7,630	7,576	7,722
Heavy rail [5]	Number	(NA)	1,293	1,351	1,458	1,558	1,622	1,617	1,617	1,622
Light rail [6]	Number	(NA)	384	483	568	834	1,188	1,497	1,740	1,724
Navigable channels [7]	Number	26,000	26,000	26,000	26,000	26,000	26,000	25,320	25,000	25,000
Oil pipeline [8]	Number	(NA)	(NA)	(NA)	(NA)	(NA)	162,919	183,203	183,370	185,569
Gas pipeline [9]	1,000	1,052	1,111	1,270	1,332	1,377	1,489	1,549	1,564	1,566

NA Not available. [1] All public road and street mileage in the 50 states and the District of Columbia. Beginning in 1998, approximately 43,000 miles of Bureau of Land Management Roads are excluded. [2] Data represent miles of road owned (aggregate length of road, excluding yard tracks, sidings, and parallel lines). Portions of Class I freight railroads, Amtrak, and Commuter rail networks share common trackage. Amtrak data represent miles of road operated. [3] Transit system length is measured in directional route-miles; see source. [4] Also called metropolitan rail or regional rail. [5] Also called metro, subway, rapid transit, or rapid rail. [6] Also called streetcar, tramway, or trolley. [7] Estimated sums of domestic waterways which include rivers, bays, channels, and the inner route of the Southeast Alaskan Islands, but does not include the Great Lakes or deep ocean traffic. Beginning in 2007, includes waterways connecting the Great Lakes and the St. Lawrence Seaway inside the U.S. [8] Includes trunk and gathering lines for crude-oil pipeline. Oil pipeline data has been discontinued for years prior to 2001. [9] Excludes service pipelines.

Source: U.S. Bureau of Transportation Statistics, "National Transportation Statistics," <http://www.bts.gov/publications/national_transportation_statistics>, accessed April 2015.

Table 1078. U.S. Aircraft, Vehicles, and Other Conveyances: 2000 to 2012

[Number, or in thousands (133,621 represents 133,621,000), as indicated]

Mode	2000	2005	2006	2007	2008	2009	2010	2011	2012
Air:									
Air carrier [1]	8,055	8,225	8,089	8,044	7,856	7,771	7,431	7,028	7,422
General aviation [2] (active fleet)	217,533	224,352	221,943	231,607	228,663	223,877	223,370	222,250	209,034
Highway, registered vehicles (1,000):									
Light duty vehicle, short wheel base [3]	(NA)	(NA)	(NA)	196,491	196,763	193,980	190,203	183,523	183,172
Passenger cars [3]	133,621	136,568	135,400	(NA)	(NA)	(NA)	(NA)	(NA)	(NA)
Motorcycle	4,346	6,227	6,679	7,138	7,753	7,930	8,010	8,438	8,455
Light duty vehicle, long wheel base [4]	(NA)	(NA)	(NA)	39,187	39,685	40,488	40,242	50,319	50,589
Other 2-axle 4-tire vehicles [4]	79,085	95,337	99,125	(NA)	(NA)	(NA)	(NA)	(NA)	(NA)
Trucks [5]	5,926	6,395	6,649	8,117	8,288	8,356	8,217	7,819	8,190
Truck, combination	2,097	2,087	2,170	2,635	2,585	2,617	2,553	2,452	2,469
Bus	746	807	822	834	843	842	846	666	765
Transit:									
Motor bus	58,578	62,284	64,025	63,359	63,151	63,343	63,108	61,127	61,245
Light rail cars [6]	1,306	1,645	1,801	1,802	1,948	2,059	2,096	2,284	2,348
Heavy rail cars [7]	10,311	11,110	11,052	11,222	11,377	11,461	11,510	14,942	10,469
Trolley bus	652	615	609	559	590	531	571	479	570
Commuter rail cars and locomotives	5,497	6,290	6,300	6,279	6,494	6,722	6,768	6,971	6,938
Demand response	22,087	28,346	29,406	29,433	30,773	34,235	33,555	31,846	31,929
Other [8]	7,705	11,622	12,454	12,953	14,953	17,766	18,066	18,965	16,996
Rail:									
Class I, freight cars	560,154	474,839	475,415	460,172	450,297	416,180	397,730	380,699	380,641
Class I, locomotive	20,028	22,779	23,732	24,143	24,003	24,045	23,893	24,250	24,707
Nonclass I freight cars	132,448	120,195	120,688	120,463	109,487	108,233	101,755	95,972	92,742
Car companies' and shippers' freight cars	688,194	717,211	750,404	805,074	833,188	839,020	809,544	806,554	842,802
Amtrak, passenger train car	1,894	1,186	1,191	1,164	1,177	1,214	1,274	1,301	2,090
Amtrak, locomotive	378	258	319	270	278	274	282	287	485
Water:									
Non-self-propelled vessels [9]	31,360	33,152	32,211	31,654	31,238	31,008	31,412	31,498	31,550
Self-propelled vessels [10]	8,202	8,976	8,898	9,041	9,063	9,101	9,100	9,023	8,980
Ocean-going self-propelled vessels (1,000 gross tons and over) [11]	282	231	229	220	225	217	221	214	198
Recreational boats (1,000)	12,782	12,942	12,746	12,876	12,693	12,722	12,439	12,174	12,102

NA Not available. [1] Air carrier aircraft are those carrying passengers or cargo for hire under 14 CFR 121 and 14 CFR 135. [2] Includes air taxi aircraft. [3] Data for 2000-06 are for passenger cars. Beginning 2007, data are for Light Duty Vehicles Short Wheel Base—passenger cars, light trucks, vans and sport utility vehicles with a wheelbase of 121 inches or less. [4] Data for 2000-06 are for 2-axle, 4-tire vehicles other than passenger cars, motorcycles, and buses. Beginning 2007, data are for Light Duty Vehicles Long Wheel Base—large passenger cars, vans, pickup trucks, and sport/utility vehicles with wheelbases larger than 121 inches. [5] Includes trucks on a single frame with at least 2 axles and 6 tires. [6] Fixed rail streetcar or trolley, for example. [7] Metro, subway, or rapid transit, for example. [8] Includes Alaska railroad, automated guideway transit, cable car, ferry boat, inclined plane, monorail, and vanpool. [9] Includes dry-cargo barges, tank barges, and railroad-car floats. [10] Includes dry-cargo and/or passenger, offshore supply vessels, railroad-car ferries, tankers, and towboats. [11] 2000-06 data include private and government owned vessels of 1,000 gross tons or more. Beginning 2007, data are reported only for privately owned vessels of 1,000 gross tons or more. 2009 data include privately owned vessels of 10,000 deadweight tons or more, not including the Great Lakes vessels.

Source: U.S. Bureau of Transportation Statistics, "National Transportation Statistics," <http://www.bts.gov/publications/national_transportation_statistics>, accessed April 2015.

Table 1079. Shipment Characteristics by Mode of Transportation: 2007 and 2012

[11,684,872 represents $11,684,872,000,000, unless otherwise noted. For business establishments in mining, manufacturing, wholesale trade, and selected retail and services industries. 2012 industries classified by the 2007 North American Industry Classification System (NAICS). 2007 industries classified by 2002 NAICS. Selected auxiliary establishments are also included. Based on the 2012 Economic Census; see Appendix III]

Mode of transportation	Value (mil. dol.)		Tons (1,000)		Ton-miles (mil.)		Average miles per shipment	
	2007	2012	2007	2012	2007	2012	2007	2012
All modes	11,684,872	13,852,143	12,543,425	11,299,409	3,344,658	2,969,506	619	630
Single modes	9,539,037	11,900,364	11,698,128	10,905,518	2,894,251	2,697,418	234	262
Truck [1]	8,335,789	10,132,229	8,778,713	8,060,166	1,342,104	1,247,717	206	227
For-hire truck	4,955,700	6,504,636	4,075,136	4,298,693	1,055,646	1,050,942	599	508
Private truck	3,380,090	3,627,592	4,703,576	3,761,472	286,457	196,775	57	58
Rail	436,420	473,070	1,861,307	1,628,537	1,344,040	1,211,481	728	805
Water	114,905	301,554	403,639	575,996	157,314	192,866	520	908
Great Lakes	(S)	424	17,792	31,403	6,887	10,959	657	347
Inland water	91,004	218,927	343,307	424,542	117,473	118,742	144	275
Deep sea	23,058	59,878	42,540	72,987	32,954	22,130	923	1,157
Air (includes truck and air)	252,276	450,575	3,611	4,845	4,510	5,810	1,304	1,295
Pipeline [2]	399,646	542,936	650,859	635,975	(S)	(S)	(S)	(S)
Multiple modes	1,866,723	1,950,753	573,729	357,047	416,642	271,832	975	922
Parcel, U.S. Postal Service or courier	1,561,874	1,688,242	33,900	28,490	27,961	22,716	975	922
Truck and rail	187,248	224,833	225,589	213,814	196,772	169,524	1,007	988
Truck and water	58,389	29,035	145,521	56,720	98,396	48,568	1,429	1,562
Rail and water	13,892	7,976	54,878	55,570	47,111	29,170	1,928	1,073
Other multiple modes	45,320	668	113,841	2,452	46,402	1,853	1,182	(S)
Other and unknown modes	279,113	1,026	271,567	36,844	33,764	256	116	(S)

S Data do not meet publication standards due to high sampling variability or other reasons. [1] Truck as a single mode includes shipments that went by private truck only, for-hire truck only, or a combination of private truck and for-hire truck. [2] Commodity Flow Survey data exclude shipments of crude oil.

Source: U.S. Department of Transportation, Bureau of Transportation Statistics, and U.S. Census Bureau, Commodity Flow Survey, "Shipment Characteristics by Origin Geography by Mode: 2012 and 2007," <http://factfinder2.census.gov>, accessed July 2015. See also <http://www.census.gov/econ/cfs/>.

Table 1080. Hazardous Shipments—Value, Tons, and Ton-Miles: 2007 and 2012

[1,448,218 represents $1,448,218,000,000. For business establishments in mining, manufacturing, wholesale trade, and selected retail industries. 2012 data cover industries classified by the 2007 North American Industry Classification System (NAICS). 2007 data cover industries classified by 2002 NAICS. Also includes auxiliary establishments of multi-establishment companies. Based on the Commodity Flow Survey, conducted as part of the Economic Census; see Appendix III]

Mode of transportation and class of material	Value (mil. dol.)		Tons (1,000)		Ton-miles (mil.)		Average miles per shipment	
	2007	2012	2007	2012	2007	2012	2007	2012
All modes	1,448,218	2,334,425	2,231,133	2,580,153	323,457	307,524	96	114
Single modes	1,370,615	2,304,743	2,111,622	2,552,868	279,105	275,628	65	68
Truck [1]	837,074	1,466,021	1,202,825	1,531,405	103,997	96,559	59	56
For-hire truck	358,792	870,893	495,077	882,288	63,288	62,018	214	150
Private truck	478,282	595,128	707,748	649,117	40,709	34,541	32	33
Rail	69,213	79,222	129,743	110,988	92,169	84,850	578	808
Water	69,186	217,816	149,794	283,561	37,064	54,902	383	212
Air (includes truck and air)	1,735	4,380	(S)	261	(S)	271	1,095	1,120
Pipeline [2]	393,408	537,304	628,905	626,652	(S)	(S)	(S)	(S)
Multiple modes [3]	71,069	29,682	111,022	27,285	42,886	31,896	834	654
Parcel, U.S. Postal Service or courier	7,675	10,294	236	305	151	178	836	650
Other and unknown modes	6,534	(NA)	8,489	(NA)	1,466	(NA)	58	(NA)
Class of Material	1,448,218	2,334,425	2,231,133	2,580,153	323,457	307,524	96	114
Class 1, Explosives	11,754	18,397	3,047	4,045	911	1,012	738	840
Class 2, Gases	131,810	125,054	250,506	164,794	55,260	33,157	51	57
Class 3, Flammable and combustible liquid	1,170,455	2,016,681	1,752,814	2,203,490	181,615	204,573	91	93
Class 4, Flammable solid; spontaneously combustible material; dangerous when wet material	4,067	5,415	20,408	11,321	5,547	5,804	309	565
Class 5, Oxidizers and organic peroxides	6,695	7,562	14,959	12,025	7,024	5,479	361	437
Class 6, Toxic materials and infectious substances	21,198	15,196	11,270	7,612	5,667	3,607	467	513
Class 7, Radioactive materials	20,633	12,288	515	(S)	37	39	(S)	34
Class 8, Corrosive materials	51,475	75,850	114,441	125,287	44,395	37,784	208	264
Class 9, Miscellaneous hazardous material	30,131	57,981	63,173	51,006	23,002	16,068	484	530

NA Not available. S Data do not meet publication standards. [1] Truck as a single mode includes shipments that went by private truck only, for-hire truck only, or a combination of private truck and for-hire truck. [2] Commodity Flow Survey Data exclude shipments of crude oil. [3] Includes other modes not shown. Multimode data for 2012 and 2007 are not comparable due to methodological changes; see source.

Source: U.S. Department of Transportation, Bureau of Transportation Statistics, and U.S. Census Bureau, *United States: 2012, Hazardous Materials*, February 2015; and 2012 Commodity Flow Survey, CF1200H01, "Hazardous Materials Series: HazMat Shipment Characteristics by Mode," and CF1200H02, "Hazardous Materials Series: HazMat Shipment Characteristics by Hazardous Class," <http://factfinder2.census. gov>, accessed February 2015. See also <http://www.census.gov/econ/cfs/>.

Table 1081. Transportation Accidents, Deaths, and Injuries: 2000 to 2013

[Number, except in thousands (6,394 represents 6,394,000) as indicated]

Mode	Accidents					Deaths					Injuries				
	2000	2005	2010	2012	2013	2000	2005	2010	2012	2013	2000	2005	2010	2012	2013
Air:															
Air carrier [1]	1,985	1,782	1,505	1,539	(NA)	764	603	476	449	429	359	305	278	274	250
Air carrier [1]	56	40	29	27	(NA)	92	22	–	–	9	31	14	17	18	9
Commuter [2]	12	6	6	4	(NA)	5	–	–	–	6	7	–	2	–	9
On-demand [3]	80	65	30	37	(NA)	71	18	17	9	27	12	20	3	–	16
General aviation	1,837	1,671	1,440	1,471	(NA)	596	563	457	440	387	309	271	256	247	216
Land:															
Highway crashes (1,000) [4]	6,394	6,159	5,419	5,615	(NA)	41.9	43.5	33.0	33.8	32.7	3,189	2,699	2,239	2,362	2,313
Passenger car occupants	4,926	4,499	(NA)	(NA)	(NA)	20.7	18.5	12.5	12.4	12.0	2,052	1,573	1,253	1,328	1,296
Motorcyclists	69	101	(NA)	(NA)	(NA)	2.9	4.6	4.5	5.0	4.7	58	87	82	93	88
Light truck occupants	3,208	3,382	(NA)	(NA)	(NA)	11.5	13.0	9.8	9.4	9.2	887	872	733	762	750
Large truck occupants	438	423	(NA)	(NA)	(NA)	0.8	0.8	0.5	0.7	0.7	31	27	20	25	24
Bus occupants	56	50	(NA)	(NA)	(NA)	–	0.1	–	–	–	18	11	17	12	23
Pedestrians	(NA)	(NA)	(NA)	(NA)	(NA)	4.8	4.9	4.3	4.8	4.7	78	64	70	76	66
Pedalcyclists	(NA)	(NA)	(NA)	(NA)	(NA)	0.7	0.8	0.6	0.7	0.7	51	45	52	49	48
Other	(NA)	(NA)	(NA)	(NA)	(NA)	0.6	0.8	0.7	0.7	0.7	15	18	13	16	16
Railroad [5]	14,024	11,816	10,031	9,457	(NA)	937	884	734	677	706	11,643	9,550	8,377	8,425	8,704
Highway-rail grade crossing [6]	607	571	453	446	(NA)	425	359	261	230	231	1,219	1,053	888	972	972
Transit [7]	24,261	8,151	3,492	3,539	(NA)	295	149	221	264	266	56,697	19,028	25,222	23,325	24,622
Waterborne	13,143	9,946	9,889	9,813	(NA)	888	829	821	765	642	5,112	4,125	3,770	3,327	2,768
Waterborne (vessel related) [8]	5,403	4,977	5,285	5,298	(NA)	53	(NA)	(NA)	(NA)	(NA)	150	(NA)	(NA)	(NA)	(NA)
Recreational boating [9]	7,740	4,969	4,604	4,515	(NA)	701	697	672	651	560	4,355	3,451	3,153	3,000	2,620
Pipeline	380	720	590	570	(NA)	38	16	19	10	9	81	48	109	58	44
Hazard liquid	146	369	350	364	(NA)	1	2	1	3	1	4	4	4	4	5
Gas	234	351	240	206	(NA)	37	14	18	7	8	77	46	105	54	39

– Represents or rounds to zero. NA Not available. [1] See footnote 1, Table 1088. Injuries classified as serious. [2] See footnote 2, Table 1088. Injuries classified as serious. [3] See footnote 3, Table 1088. Injuries classified as serious. [4] Highway crashes often involve more than one motor vehicle, and hence "total highway crashes" is smaller than the sum of the components. Data on deaths are from U.S. National Highway Traffic Safety Administration and are based on deaths within 30 days of the accident. Includes only police reported crashes. For more details, see Table 1119. [5] Accidents and incidents resulting from freight and passenger rail operations including commuter rail. Grade crossing accidents are also included when classified as a train accident. Deaths and injuries exclude those in highway-rail grade crossing accidents involving motor vehicles. Injury figures also include occupational illness. [6] Accidents and incidents occurring at highway-rail crossings resulting from freight and passenger rail operations including commuter rail. Public highway-rail grade crossing incidents, fatalities, and injuries involving motor vehicles are excluded and counted under Highway. Highway-rail grade crossing injuries, except train occupants, are also counted under Highway. [7] Includes motor bus, commuter rail, heavy rail, light rail, demand response, van pool, and automated guideway. Starting with 2002, only injuries requiring immediate medical treatment away from the scene now qualify as reportable. [8] Vessel-related deaths and injuries include those involving damage to vessels, such as collisions or groundings. Totals include deaths and injuries not related to vessel casualties, not shown separately. [9] Covers occurrences involving a vessel or its equipment that results in 1) a death; 2) an injury that requires medical treatment beyond first aid; 3) damage to a vessel and other property, totaling to more than $500 or complete loss of a vessel; or 4) the disappearance of the vessel under circumstances that indicate death or injury. Federal regulations (33 CFR 173-4) require the operator of any vessel that is numbered or used for recreational purposes to submit an accident report.

Source: U.S. Bureau of Transportation Statistics, "National Transportation Statistics," <http://www.bts.gov/publications/national_transportation_statistics>, accessed September 2015.

Table 1082. U.S. Scheduled Airline Industry—Summary: 2007 to 2014

[In units as indicated (769.6 represents $769,600,000). For calendar years or as of December 31. For domestic and international operations. Covers carriers certificated under Section 401 of the Federal Aviation Act. Minus sign (-) indicates loss]

Item	Unit	2007	2008	2009	2010	2011	2012	2013	2014
SCHEDULED SERVICE									
Revenue passengers enplaned......	Mil.	769.6	743.3	703.9	720.5	730.8	736.7	743.2	762.1
Revenue passenger miles...........	Bil.	829.4	812.4	769.5	798.0	814.4	823.2	840.4	862.1
Available seat miles..................	Bil.	1,037.7	1,021.3	957.2	972.6	992.7	994.5	1,011.2	1,033.8
Revenue passenger load factor......	Percent	79.9	79.5	80.4	82.1	82.0	82.8	83.1	83.4
Mean passenger trip length [1]........	Miles	1,078	1,093	1,093	1,108	1,114	1,117	1,131	1,131
Cargo ton miles......................	Mil.	29,571	28,119	24,970	27,885	28,123	27,790	26,441	27,236
Aircraft departures..................	1,000	11,399	10,897	10,145	10,095	10,058	9,864	9,745	9,536
FINANCES									
Total operating revenue [2].........	**Mil. dol.**	**174,696**	**186,087**	**155,051**	**174,677**	**193,041**	**196,105**	**200,245**	**207,708**
Passenger revenue...................	Mil. dol.	107,678	111,511	91,443	103,978	114,299	115,975	120,642	126,706
Cargo revenue.......................	Mil. dol.	24,002	29,192	23,014	17,622	1,589	889	1,023	1,140
Charter revenue.....................	Mil. dol.	5,544	4,338	3,841	3,254	604	976	877	930
Other revenue.......................	Mil. dol.	37,472	41,047	36,753	49,824	76,548	78,265	77,703	78,932
Total operating expense..............	Mil. dol.	165,353	189,437	152,716	164,160	186,005	188,592	187,726	191,029
Operating profit (or loss).............	Mil. dol.	9,344	-3,350	2,335	10,517	7,036	7,513	12,519	16,678
Interest income (or expense)........	Mil. dol.	-3,915	-3,743	-4,214	-4,215	-3,970	-3,740	-3,334	-3,005
Net profit (or loss)....................	Mil. dol.	7,691.4	-23,749.8	-2,610.3	3,666.0	1,392.2	363.7	12,710.6	8,514.3
Passenger revenue per passenger mile...................................	Cents	13.0	13.7	11.9	13.0	14.0	14.1	14.4	14.7
Operating profit margin...............	Percent	5.3	-1.8	1.5	6.0	3.6	3.8	6.3	8.0
Net profit margin.....................	Percent	4.4	-12.8	-1.7	2.1	0.7	0.2	6.3	4.1
EMPLOYEES									
Average full-time equivalents......	**1,000**	**613.9**	**608.9**	**573.9**	**564.4**	**577.3**	**584.5**	**584.0**	**589.1**

[1] For definition of mean, see Guide to Tabular Presentation. [2] Includes other types of revenues, not shown separately.

Source: Airlines for America, ©; and Bureau of Transportation Statistics, <http://www.transtats.bts.gov/>, accessed June 2015.

Table 1083. Passenger Airline Cost Indexes: 1980 to 2014

[2000 = 100. To be included in the cost index, carriers must have met the following criteria on an annual basis: 1) must report both passenger revenue and revenue passenger miles (RPMs), and 2) passenger revenue must be greater than or equal to 25 percent of total operating revenue]

Index	1980	1990	2000	2005	2006	2007	2008	2009	2010	2011	2012	2013	2014
Composite index [1]......	**77.4**	**101.1**	**100.0**	**136.1**	**149.7**	**153.0**	**203.6**	**145.7**	**158.0**	**190.6**	**195.3**	**187.6**	**190.7**
Labor costs...................	52.0	73.1	100.0	117.3	119.0	119.1	119.7	127.4	135.3	136.9	145.6	148.9	157.5
Fuel.........................	113.7	98.1	100.0	206.6	242.8	258.0	379.4	233.9	268.8	349.7	356.4	331.1	336.4
Aircraft ownership [2].........	33.5	71.1	100.0	98.9	98.7	94.0	91.1	92.8	92.9	91.8	90.9	93.9	94.2
Nonaircraft ownership.......	40.4	88.1	100.0	106.1	104.2	106.6	118.8	115.2	111.4	111.5	106.7	108.5	106.2
Professional services.......	27.0	67.5	100.0	105.5	111.2	115.8	125.3	118.5	118.5	121.4	115.7	118.6	122.0
Food and beverage..........	88.5	125.5	100.0	61.3	57.9	57.8	60.0	59.7	59.5	61.7	60.6	61.9	62.0
Landing fees................	49.2	81.0	100.0	130.7	135.6	136.7	148.5	158.9	169.8	166.5	165.4	165.4	169.6
Maintenance material.......	73.3	119.2	100.0	59.1	62.2	69.9	76.8	83.5	82.9	92.2	101.1	102.9	109.1
Aircraft insurance............	246.1	161.0	100.0	157.1	181.0	152.3	124.0	150.7	164.9	163.8	158.0	132.0	96.9
Nonaircraft insurance.......	73.3	68.2	100.0	319.9	259.3	222.1	195.3	184.4	188.2	168.2	167.1	142.9	114.9
Passenger commissions....	121.5	227.0	100.0	31.6	29.2	28.3	27.0	26.7	26.4	25.6	22.4	23.3	21.9
Communication..............	50.3	85.7	100.0	73.3	68.5	71.2	79.2	77.2	75.3	80.0	75.0	74.4	71.2
Advertising and promotion.........	112.9	165.0	100.0	75.5	80.9	67.3	59.0	61.7	61.0	65.3	63.2	65.0	56.8
Utilities and office supplies...............	67.9	97.7	100.0	87.6	94.3	102.2	108.9	99.8	118.4	119.2	110.8	122.5	125.2
Transportation-related expenses..............	46.0	55.0	100.0	159.8	171.3	168.6	196.2	158.9	157.7	185.0	184.0	191.0	191.8
Employee business expenses..............	40.9	70.5	100.0	101.0	107.4	118.6	123.3	116.8	120.7	128.0	135.5	146.1	163.0
Other operating expenses...	56.0	87.4	100.0	122.2	121.5	129.7	173.8	140.0	138.4	159.2	162.6	161.0	158.9
Interest [3]...................	160.7	182.0	100.0	120.6	133.5	120.3	105.6	116.2	121.8	118.6	117.7	105.8	92.5

[1] Weighted average of all components, including interest. [2] Includes lease, aircraft and engine rentals, depreciation, and amortization. [3] Interest on long-term debt and capital and other interest expense.

Source: Airlines for America, Washington, DC, *U.S. Passenger Airline Cost Index* ©. See also <http://www.airlines.org/>.

Table 1084. Airline Fuel Consumption and Fuel Costs: 2003 to 2014

[18,301 represents 18,301,000,000. Data are shown for scheduled and unscheduled service on U.S. carriers with over $20 million in revenue per year]

Year	Total fuel consumption (million gallons)	Total fuel cost (million dollars)	Cost per gallon (dollars)	Domestic service			International service		
				Consumption (million gallons)	Cost (million dollars)	Cost per gallon (dollars)	Consumption (million gallons)	Cost (million dollars)	Cost per gallon (dollars)
2003	18,301	15,487	0.85	13,082	10,915	0.83	5,219	4,572	0.88
2004	19,683	22,758	1.16	14,091	16,027	1.14	5,592	6,732	1.20
2005	19,950	33,175	1.66	13,976	22,951	1.64	5,975	10,224	1.71
2006	19,712	38,772	1.97	13,694	26,480	1.93	6,018	12,292	2.04
2007	19,886	41,862	2.11	13,682	28,411	2.08	6,205	13,451	2.17
2008	18,872	57,888	3.07	12,686	37,876	2.99	6,187	20,013	3.23
2009	17,061	32,331	1.90	11,339	21,544	1.90	5,721	10,787	1.89
2010	17,298	39,350	2.27	11,257	25,571	2.27	6,042	13,779	2.28
2011	17,558	53,515	3.05	11,035	33,730	3.06	6,523	19,785	3.03
2012	16,946	53,415	3.15	10,440	33,189	3.18	6,506	20,227	3.11
2013	16,824	50,629	3.01	10,337	31,513	3.05	6,487	19,117	2.95
2014	16,807	48,124	2.86	10,485	30,201	2.88	6,321	17,923	2.84

Source: U.S. Bureau of Transportation Statistics, "Airline Fuel Cost and Consumption," <http://www.transtats.bts.gov/fuel.asp>, accessed June 2015.

Table 1085. Top 40 Airports in 2013—Passengers Enplaned: 2003 and 2013

[In thousands (656,710 represents 656,710,000), except rank. For calendar year. Intl = international. Airports ranked by total passengers enplaned on U.S. carrier scheduled domestic and international service and foreign carrier scheduled international service from the United States]

Airport	2003 Rank	2003 Total	2013 Rank	2013 Total	Airport	2003 Rank	2003 Total	2013 Rank	2013 Total
All airports	(X)	656,710	(X)	696,931	Baltimore, MD (BWI Intl)	23	9,548	21	11,041
					Fort Lauderdale, FL (Hollywood Intl)	26	8,277	22	10,694
Total, top 40 [1]	(X)	508,751	(X)	579,904	Washington, DC (Dulles Intl)	32	6,733	23	9,748
Atlanta, GA (Hartsfield Intl)	1	38,256	1	44,675	Chicago, IL (Midway)	25	8,681	24	9,727
Chicago O'Hare Intl, IL	2	30,835	2	29,992	Salt Lake City Intl, UT	24	8,933	25	9,667
Dallas/Fort Worth Intl, TX	3	24,725	3	28,491	Washington, DC (Ronald Reagan Washington Natl)	31	6,957	26	8,740
Los Angeles Intl, CA	4	20,939	4	25,860	San Diego, CA (San Diego Intl)	29	7,467	27	8,662
Denver Intl, CO	6	17,745	5	25,185	Honolulu Intl, HI	27	7,659	28	8,138
Charlotte-Douglas Intl, NC	16	11,414	6	21,242	Tampa, FL (Tampa Intl)	28	7,476	29	8,037
Phoenix Sky Harbor Intl, AZ	5	18,031	7	19,157	Portland Intl, OR	34	5,963	30	7,401
San Francisco Intl, CA	14	12,232	8	18,853	St. Louis, MO (Lambert-St Louis Intl)	21	9,932	31	6,194
Las Vegas, NV (McCarran Intl)	7	16,899	9	18,480	Houston, TX (William P. Hobby)	45	3,704	32	5,372
Houston, Intercontinental, TX	9	15,693	10	17,946	Nashville Intl, TN	43	3,927	33	5,023
New York, NY (JFK Intl)	19	10,821	11	17,039	Austin-Bergstrom Intl, TX	47	3,166	34	4,899
Minneapolis-St. Paul Intl, MN	8	16,047	12	16,201	Kansas City Intl, MO	38	4,825	35	4,821
Seattle-Tacoma Intl, WA	12	12,799	13	15,979	Oakland Intl, CA	33	6,520	36	4,693
Newark, NJ (Liberty Intl)	11	13,155	14	15,879	New Orleans Intl, LA	40	4,589	37	4,554
Detroit, MI (Wayne Co)	10	15,604	15	15,508	Raleigh/Durham Intl, NC (Raleigh-Durham International)	44	3,886	38	4,448
Miami Intl, FL	17	11,289	16	15,442	Santa Ana, CA (John Wayne Airport)	42	4,266	39	4,425
Orlando Intl, FL	13	12,579	17	15,279	Cleveland, OH (Cleveland-Hopkins Intl)	37	4,989	40	4,356
Philadelphia Intl, PA	15	11,511	18	14,509					
Boston, MA (Logan Intl)	22	9,898	19	13,257					
New York, NY (La Guardia)	18	11,049	20	12,821					

X Not applicable. [1] The 2003 total for the top 40 airports will not sum from the individual airports because some top 40 airports in 2013 were not in the top 40 in 2003.

Source: U.S. Bureau of Transportation Statistics, "National Transportation Statistics," <http://www.bts.gov/publications/national_transportation_statistics>, accessed July 2015.

Table 1086. Top 25 Domestic Airline Markets—Average Daily Passengers: 2014

[For calendar year. Data are for the top 25 markets and include all commercial airports in each metro area. Data represent traffic each way between origin and final destinations]

Market	Passengers	Market	Passengers
New York - Los Angeles	3,531	New York - Miami	1,593
Los Angeles - San Francisco	2,757	Boston - Washington	1,547
New York - Chicago	2,654	Honolulu - Los Angeles	1,546
New York - San Francisco	2,569	Seattle - San Francisco	1,514
Atlanta - New York	2,072	Boston - Chicago	1,496
Honolulu - Kahului	1,913	Las Vegas - Los Angeles	1,493
Ft. Lauderdale - New York	1,832	Las Vegas - San Francisco	1,485
Los Angeles - Seattle	1,811	Denver - Las Vegas	1,479
Los Angeles - Chicago	1,793	New York - Orlando	1,476
Denver - Phoenix	1,774	Denver - Los Angeles	1,447
Boston - San Francisco	1,684	Boston - Los Angeles	1,445
Chicago - San Francisco	1,617	Dallas - Chicago	1,398
		Orlando - Philadelphia	1,395

Source: Airlines for America, Washington, DC, ©. See also <http://www.airlines.org>.

Table 1087. Commuter/Regional Airline Operations Summary: 2005 to 2013

[In units as indicated (152.6 represents 152,600,000). Calendar year data. Commuter/regional airlines primarily operate aircraft of 75 passengers or less and 18,000 pounds of payload capacity serving short haul and small community markets. Represents operations within all North America by U.S. regional carriers. Averages are means. For definition of mean, see Guide to Tabular Presentation]

Item	Unit	2005	2009	2010	2011	2012	2013
Passenger carriers operating............................	Number	75	61	61	60	54	52
Passengers enplaned.....................................	Millions	152.6	163.5	163.5	160.7	161.7	157.0
Average passengers enplaned per carrier............	1,000	2,034.0	2,680.3	2,680.3	2,678.3	2,994.4	3,018.7
Revenue passenger miles (RPM)......................	Billions	67.4	75.8	75.8	76.6	75.9	75.3
Average RPMs per carrier...............................	Millions	898.8	1,243.0	1,243.0	1,276.6	1,405.9	1,448.3
Available seat miles......................................	Billions	95.6	99.2	99.2	100.5	97.5	96.3
Average load factor......................................	Percent	70.5	76.5	76.5	76.2	77.9	78.2
Departures completed....................................	Millions	5.43	4.75	4.75	4.60	4.53	4.38
Airports served..	Number	666	673	673	681	623	614
Average trip length.......................................	Miles	442	464	464	476	469	474
Average seating capacity (seats).....................	Number	50	56	56	56	56	56
Fleet flying hours...	1,000	5,714	5,211	5,211	5,165	4,925	4,824

Source: Regional Airline Association, *2014 Annual Report* ©, and previous releases. See also <http://www.raa.org/>.

Table 1088. U.S. Air Carrier Aircraft Accidents: 2000 to 2014

[For years ending December 31]

Item	Unit	2000	2005	2010	2011	2012	2013	2014, prelim.
Air carrier accidents, all services [1]........	**Number**	**56**	**40**	**30**	**31**	**27**	**23**	**28**
Fatal accidents...............................	Number	3	3	1	–	–	2	–
Fatalities......................................	Number	92	22	2	–	–	9	–
Aboard...	Number	92	20	2	–	–	9	–
Rates per 100,000 flight hours:								
Accidents......................................	Rate	0.31	0.21	0.16	0.17	0.15	0.13	0.16
Fatal accidents...............................	Rate	0.02	0.02	0.01	0.00	0.00	0.01	0.00
Commuter air carrier accidents [2]............	Number	12	6	6	4	4	7	4
Fatal accidents...............................	Number	1	–	–	–	–	2	–
Fatalities......................................	Number	5	–	–	–	–	5	–
Aboard...	Number	5	–	–	–	–	5	–
Rates per 100,000 flight hours:								
Accidents......................................	Rate	3.25	2.00	1.91	1.23	1.25	2.18	1.14
Fatal accidents...............................	Rate	0.27	–	–	–	–	0.62	0.00
On-demand air taxi accidents [3].............	Number	80	65	30	50	36	44	35
Fatal accidents...............................	Number	22	11	6	16	8	10	8
Fatalities......................................	Number	71	18	17	41	12	25	20
Aboard...	Number	68	16	17	41	12	25	20
Rates per 100,000 flight hours:								
Accidents......................................	Rate	2.04	1.70	0.96	(NA)	1.02	1.30	1.02
Fatal accidents...............................	Rate	0.56	0.29	0.19	(NA)	0.23	0.30	0.23
General aviation accidents [4].................	Number	1,837	1,671	1,440	1,470	1,470	1,224	1,221
Fatal accidents...............................	Number	345	321	271	269	272	222	253
Fatalities......................................	Number	596	563	458	452	437	391	419
Aboard...	Number	585	558	455	441	437	386	410
Rates per 100,000 flight hours:								
Accidents......................................	Rate	6.57	7.20	6.63	(NA)	7.04	6.26	6.74
Fatal accidents...............................	Rate	1.21	1.38	1.24	(NA)	1.30	1.12	1.40

– Represents zero. NA Not available. [1] U.S. air carriers operating under 14 CFR 121. Beginning 2000, includes aircraft with 10 or more seats, previously operating under 14 CFR 135. [2] All scheduled service of U.S. air carriers operating under 14 CFR 135. Beginning 2000, only aircraft with fewer than 10 seats. [3] All nonscheduled service of U.S. air carriers operating under 14 CFR 135. [4] U.S. civil registered aircraft not operated under 14 CFR 121 or 135.

Source: U.S. National Transportation Safety Board, Investigations Data and Stats, "Review of Accident Data—2014 Preliminary Aviation Statistics," <http://www.ntsb.gov/investigations/>, accessed September 2015.

Table 1089. U.S. Airline Carrier Delays, Cancellations, and Diversions: 2000 to 2013

[In thousands (5,683.0 represents 5,683,000). For calendar year. See headnote, Table 1090]

Item	2000	2005	2006	2007	2008	2009	2010	2011	2012	2013
Total operations.......	**5,683.0**	**7,140.6**	**7,141.9**	**7,455.5**	**7,009.7**	**6,450.3**	**6,450.1**	**6,085.3**	**6,096.8**	**6,369.5**
Delays:										
Late departures [1]........	1,131.7	1,279.4	1,424.8	1,573.0	1,327.2	1,084.3	1,111.9	1,042.4	991.8	1,229.3
Late arrivals [2]............	1,356.0	1,466.1	1,615.5	1,804.0	1,524.7	1,218.3	1,174.9	1,109.9	1,015.2	1,269.3
Cancellations [3]............	187.5	133.7	121.9	160.8	137.4	89.4	113.3	116.0	78.9	96.0
Diversions [4]................	14.3	14.0	16.2	17.2	17.3	15.5	15.5	14.4	12.5	14.2

[1] Late departures comprise flights departing 15 minutes or more after the scheduled departure time. [2] Late arrivals comprise flights arriving 15 minutes or more after the scheduled arrival time. [3] A cancelled flight is one that was not operated, but was listed in a carrier's computer reservation system within seven days of the scheduled departure. [4] A diverted flight is one that left from the scheduled departure airport but flew to a destination point other than the scheduled destination point.

Source: U.S. Bureau of Transportation Statistics, "National Transportation Statistics," <http://www.bts.gov/publications/national_transportation_statistics>, accessed April 2015.

Table 1090. On-Time Flight Arrivals and Departures at Major U.S. Airports: 2014

[In percent. Quarterly, based on gate arrival and departure times for domestic scheduled operations of U.S. major airlines. All U.S. airlines with 1 percent or more of total U.S. domestic scheduled airline passenger revenues are required to report on-time data. A flight is considered on time if it operated less than 15 minutes after the scheduled time shown in the carrier's computerized reservation system. See source for data on individual airlines]

Airport	On-time arrivals				On-time departures			
	1st quarter	2nd quarter	3rd quarter	4th quarter	1st quarter	2nd quarter	3rd quarter	4th quarter
Total, all airports	**72.2**	**76.1**	**78.0**	**78.6**	**72.9**	**76.9**	**79.3**	**80.0**
Total, major airports	72.8	77.1	78.7	79.6	72.5	77.1	79.1	80.4
Atlanta, Hartsfield	74.1	81.6	82.6	86.5	71.0	78.8	81.0	84.9
Boston, Logan International	74.2	78.7	78.5	78.7	76.3	82.3	82.2	83.6
Baltimore/Washington International	71.4	76.7	78.3	83.1	62.7	70.1	72.9	77.9
Charlotte, Douglas	76.7	81.9	82.2	84.7	77.3	79.2	81.2	85.8
Washington, Reagan National	72.5	77.7	78.8	82.5	75.8	81.3	83.7	85.8
Denver International	70.9	76.5	79.0	79.2	66.3	72.3	75.9	74.8
Dallas-Fort Worth International	77.0	76.0	76.5	72.1	74.6	74.6	75.3	71.5
Detroit, Metro Wayne County	75.7	83.4	84.6	84.5	74.1	82.1	84.6	84.3
Newark International	67.1	64.6	73.9	75.5	64.2	68.7	75.5	76.7
Fort Lauderdale-Hollywood International	64.6	77.0	74.6	81.3	66.9	75.9	75.4	82.9
Washington/Dulles	70.0	75.1	78.0	79.5	64.7	73.5	75.7	78.9
Houston, George Bush	73.1	74.8	79.3	79.9	70.6	73.5	78.7	80.4
New York, JFK International	71.3	74.8	75.1	79.0	71.1	80.1	79.7	83.2
Las Vegas, McCarran International	74.0	77.0	80.2	80.0	72.0	73.2	76.4	77.5
Los Angeles International	74.5	76.6	79.7	77.6	77.0	78.2	80.1	78.3
New York, La Guardia	67.0	69.8	75.1	73.3	69.7	76.2	79.9	78.7
Orlando International	71.3	78.0	76.8	81.1	70.8	76.0	75.8	82.6
Chicago, Midway	66.8	73.8	76.4	79.8	57.6	62.6	68.0	73.9
Miami International	79.5	82.2	79.8	82.5	80.1	81.8	81.1	82.8
Minneapolis-St. Paul International	77.2	81.0	84.2	82.6	78.0	81.8	85.1	84.8
Chicago, O'Hare	63.8	65.5	69.2	71.6	60.5	67.1	70.0	70.8
Portland International	75.9	81.0	82.3	78.8	82.6	85.4	86.0	84.2
Philadelphia International	71.3	77.7	78.1	77.6	72.5	79.8	81.4	81.8
Phoenix, Sky Harbor International	79.9	80.2	80.3	82.8	78.1	76.2	78.4	81.9
San Diego International, Lindbergh Field	72.9	76.2	79.7	79.1	75.5	77.1	80.6	79.4
Seattle-Tacoma International	79.7	83.0	82.7	81.5	83.4	85.5	84.4	84.0
San Francisco International	67.6	71.3	71.5	66.1	73.5	75.4	76.3	71.2
Salt Lake City International	82.1	86.6	87.5	85.8	84.4	87.2	87.9	87.2
Tampa, Tampa International	70.4	77.6	78.2	81.4	72.5	78.6	80.6	83.1

Source: U.S. Department of Transportation, Bureau of Transportation Statistics, "TranStats," <http://www.transtats.bts.gov/>, accessed June 2015.

Table 1091. Consumer Complaints Filed Against U.S. Airlines: 1990 to 2014

[Calendar year data. Represents complaints filed by consumers to the U.S. Department of Transportation (DOT), Aviation Consumer Protection Division, regarding service problems with air carrier personnel. See source for data on individual airlines]

Complaint category	1990	2000	2005	2009	2010	2011	2012	2013	2014
Total	**7,703**	**20,564**	**6,900**	**8,821**	**10,988**	**11,546**	**15,338**	**13,176**	**15,532**
Flight problems [1]	3,034	8,698	1,942	2,041	3,337	3,656	4,249	3,980	4,973
Baggage	1,329	2,753	1,586	1,607	1,938	1,852	2,182	2,134	2,667
Ticketing/boarding [2]	624	1,405	679	1,583	1,510	1,448	2,456	1,900	2,258
Customer service [3]	758	4,074	800	1,103	1,345	1,287	1,988	1,836	1,708
Refunds	701	803	530	669	730	985	1,185	920	1,157
Fares [4]	312	708	219	436	465	634	1,010	503	916
Disability [5]	(NA)	612	430	519	572	628	741	683	774
Oversales [6]	399	759	284	370	544	508	503	426	515
Discrimination [7]	(NA)	(NA)	100	131	143	128	99	80	68
Advertising	96	42	45	53	77	82	202	96	130
Tours [8]	29	25	(X)	(X)	(X)	(X)	(X)	(X)	(X)
Animals	(NA)	1	3	5	8	9	5	6	2
Smoking [9]	74	(X)	(X)	(X)	(X)	(X)	(X)	(X)	(X)
Credit [9]	5	(X)	(X)	(X)	(X)	(X)	(X)	(X)	(X)
Other [10]	342	684	282	304	319	329	717	612	364

NA Not available. X Not applicable. [1] Cancellations, delays, and other deviations from schedule. [2] Errors in reservations and ticketing; problems in making reservations and obtaining tickets. Includes disability complaints prior to 1998. [3] Unhelpful employees, inadequate meals or cabin service, treatment of delayed passengers. [4] Incorrect or incomplete information about fares, discount fare conditions, and availability, etc. [5] Prior to 2000, included in ticketing/boarding. [6] All bumping problems, whether or not airline complied with DOT regulations. [7] Allegations of discrimination by airlines due to factors other than disability, such as race, religion, national origin or sex. [8] Included in "Other" beginning 2002. [9] Included in "Other" beginning 2000. [10] Frequent flyer, smoking, tours credit, cargo problems, security, airport facilities, claims for bodily injury, and others not classified above.

Source: U.S. Department of Transportation, Aviation Consumer Protection Division, *Air Travel Consumer Report*, February 2015, and earlier reports. See also <http://www.dot.gov/airconsumer>.

Table 1092. Airports, Aircraft, and Airmen: 1980 to 2013

[As of December 31 or for years ending December 31]

Item	1980	1990	2000	2009	2010	2011	2012	2013
Airports, total [1]	**15,161**	**17,490**	**19,281**	**19,750**	**19,802**	**19,782**	**19,711**	**19,453**
Public [1]	4,814	5,589	5,317	5,178	5,175	5,172	5,171	5,155
Percent—with lighted runways	66.2	71.4	75.9	(NA)	(NA)	(NA)	(NA)	(NA)
With paved runways	72.3	70.7	74.3	(NA)	(NA)	(NA)	(NA)	(NA)
Private	10,347	11,901	13,964	14,298	14,353	14,339	14,269	14,009
Percent—with lighted runways	15.2	7.0	7.2	(NA)	(NA)	(NA)	(NA)	(NA)
With paved runways	13.3	31.5	32.0	(NA)	(NA)	(NA)	(NA)	(NA)
Military	(NA)	(NA)	(NA)	274	274	271	271	289
Certificated [2]	730	680	651	559	551	547	542	542
Civil	(X)	(X)	563	(X)	(X)	(X)	(NA)	(NA)
Civil military	(X)	(X)	88	(X)	(X)	(X)	(NA)	(NA)
General aviation	14,431	16,810	18,630	19,191	19,251	19,235	19,169	18,911
Active air carrier fleet [3]	**3,805**	**6,083**	**8,049**	**(NA)**	**(NA)**	**(NA)**	**(NA)**	**(NA)**
Fixed wing	3,803	6,072	8,010	(NA)	(NA)	(NA)	(NA)	(NA)
Helicopter [4]	2	11	39	(NA)	(NA)	(NA)	(NA)	(NA)
General aviation fleet [5]	**211,043**	**198,000**	**217,533**	**223,877**	**223,370**	**(NA)**	**209,034**	**199,927**
Fixed-wing	200,094	184,500	183,276	177,446	176,272	(NA)	165,257	158,911
Turbojet	2,992	4,100	7,001	11,268	11,484	(NA)	11,793	11,637
Turboprop	4,089	5,300	5,762	9,055	9,369	(NA)	10,304	9,619
Piston	193,013	175,200	170,513	157,123	155,419	(NA)	143,160	137,655
Rotorcraft	6,001	6,900	7,150	9,984	10,102	(NA)	10,055	9,765
Other	4,945	6,600	6,700	5,480	5,684	(NA)	5,006	4,277
Gliders	(X)	(X)	2,041	1,808	1,899	(NA)	1,820	1,594
Lighter than air	(X)	(X)	4,660	3,672	3,785	(NA)	3,186	2,684
Experimental	(X)	(X)	20,407	29,497	29,662	(NA)	26,715	24,918
Airman certificates held:								
Pilot, total	**827,071**	**702,659**	**625,581**	**594,285**	**627,588**	**617,128**	**610,576**	**599,086**
Women	52,902	40,515	35,607	36,808	42,218	41,316	40,621	39,621
Student [6]	199,833	128,663	93,064	72,280	119,119	118,657	119,946	120,285
Recreational	(X)	87	340	234	212	227	218	238
Sport	(X)	(X)	(X)	3,248	3,682	4,066	4,493	4,824
Airplane:								
Private	357,479	299,111	251,561	211,619	202,020	194,441	188,001	180,214
Commercial	183,442	149,666	121,858	125,738	123,705	120,865	116,400	108,206
Air transport	69,569	107,732	141,596	144,600	142,198	142,511	145,590	149,824
Rotorcraft only [7]	6,030	9,567	7,775	15,298	15,377	15,220	15,126	15,114
Glider only	7,039	7,833	9,387	21,268	21,275	21,141	20,802	20,381
Flight instructor certificates	60,440	63,775	80,931	94,863	96,473	97,409	98,328	98,842
Instrument ratings	260,462	297,073	311,944	323,495	318,001	314,122	311,952	307,120
Nonpilot [8]	**368,356**	**492,237**	**547,453**	**682,315**	**686,717**	**695,515**	**701,291**	**707,155**
Mechanic	250,157	344,282	344,434	329,027	331,989	335,431	337,775	338,844
Repairmen	(X)	(X)	38,208	41,389	41,267	40,802	40,444	39,952
Parachute rigger	9,547	10,094	10,477	8,362	8,407	8,491	8,474	8,491
Ground instructor	61,550	66,882	72,326	75,461	75,205	74,586	73,599	72,493
Dispatcher	6,799	11,002	16,340	20,132	20,691	21,363	21,862	22,401
Flight navigator	1,936	1,290	570	181	174	146	141	126
Flight attendant	(X)	(X)	(X)	156,741	159,946	167,037	172,357	179,531
Flight engineer	38,367	58,687	65,098	51,022	49,038	47,659	46,639	45,317

NA Not available. X Not applicable. [1] Includes civil and joint-use civil-military airports, heliports, STOL (short takeoff and landing) ports, and seaplane bases in the U.S. and its territories. Sole-use military airports are included beginning in 2007. Public airports are under public agency control; private airports are owned by a private individual or corporation. [2] Certificated airports serve air-carriers with aircraft seating more than 9 passengers. As of 2005, the Federal Aviation Administration (FAA) no longer certificates military airports. [3] Air-carrier aircraft carry passengers or cargo for hire under 14 CFR 121 (large aircraft—more than 30 seats) and 14 CFR 135 (small aircraft—30 seats or fewer). Beginning in 1990, the number of aircraft is the monthly average reported in use for the last three months of the year. Prior to 1990, it was the number of aircraft reported in use during December of a given year. [4] 2000 change in helicopters due to estimating methods. [5] Beginning 1995 excludes commuters. [6] Beginning 2010, duration of validity for student pilot certificates for pilots under age 40 increased from 36 to 60 months. [7] Data for 1980 are for helicopters only. [8] All certificates on record. No medical examination required.

Source: U.S. Bureau of Transportation Statistics, "National Transportation Statistics," <http://www.bts.gov/publications/national_transportation_statistics>, accessed February 2015. U.S. Federal Aviation Administration, "U.S. Civil Airmen Statistics," and "General Aviation and Air Tax (Part 135) Activity Surveys," <http://www.faa.gov/data_research/aviation_data_statistics/>, accessed February 2015. Prior to 2000: FAA Statistical Handbook of Aviation, annual.

Table 1093. Worldwide Airline Accidents and Fatalities by World Region: 2014

[Number, except departures in thousands (33,000 represents 33,000,000)]

Region	Departures (1,000)	Accidents	Accident rates [1]	Fatalities	Fatal accidents
World	**33,000**	**98**	**3**	**904**	**7**
Africa (AFI)	700	6	8.6	118	1
Asia and Pacific (APAC)	10,200	18	1.8	449	3
Europe (EUR) [2]	8,900	26	2.9	298	1
Middle East (MID)	3,000	7	2.3	39	2
Americas (PA)	9,900	41	4.1	–	–

– Represents zero. [1] Number of accidents per million departures of scheduled commercial operations that involve the transportation of passengers, cargo and mail for remuneration or hire. [2] Europe region includes Algeria, Morocco, and Tunisia.

Source: International Civil Aviation Organization, Montreal, Canada, Safety Report, 2015 ©. See also <http://www.icao.int/safety/Pages/Safety-Report.aspx>.

Table 1094. Freight Carried on Major U.S. Waterways: 1990 to 2013

[In millions of short tons (4.2 represents 4,200,000). One short ton equals 2,000 pounds]

Waterway	1990	2000	2005	2009	2010	2011	2012	2013
Atlantic Intracoastal Waterway...........	4.2	3.1	2.7	2.5	2.9	2.9	2.7	2.9
Great Lakes.................................	167.1	187.5	169.4	108.7	129.5	134.7	126.8	127.6
Gulf Intracoastal Waterway..............	115.4	113.8	116.1	108.1	116.2	112.6	113.8	115.4
Mississippi River system [1].............	659.1	715.5	678.0	622.1	663.2	672.5	683.5	670.0
Mississippi River main stem............	475.3	515.6	464.6	447.7	483.2	499.0	508.6	493.7
Ohio River system [2].....................	260.0	274.4	280.1	229.5	245.2	239.6	239.1	239.4
Columbia River...........................	51.4	55.2	51.5	46.0	54.7	54.2	56.8	55.3
Snake River...............................	4.8	6.7	5.3	4.4	3.4	2.7	3.3	3.7

[1] Main channels and all tributaries of the Mississippi, Illinois, Missouri, and Ohio Rivers. [2] Main channels and all navigable tributaries and embayments of the Ohio, Tennessee, and Cumberland Rivers.

Source: U.S. Army Corps of Engineers, *Waterborne Commerce of the United States, 2013*, 2015, and earlier reports. See also <http://www.navigationdatacenter.us/wcsc/wcsc.htm>.

Table 1095. Waterborne Commerce by Type of Commodity: 2000 to 2013

[In millions of short tons (2,424.6 represents 2,424,600,000). One short ton equals 2,000 pounds. Domestic trade includes all commercial movements between United States ports and on inland rivers, Great Lakes, canals, and connecting channels of the United States and its territories and possessions. Foreign commerce is waterborne import, export and in-transit traffic between the United States, Puerto Rico and the Virgin Islands and any foreign country; these statistics do not include traffic between any foreign country and selected U.S. territories and possessions (American Samoa, Guam, North Mariana Islands and U.S. Outlying Islands)]

Commodity	2000	2005	2010	2013 Total	2013 Domestic	2013 Foreign imports	2013 Foreign exports
Total............................	2,424.6	2,527.6	2,334.4	2,274.8	891.2	758.7	624.9
Coal.............................	297.0	316.6	309.6	312.3	193.2	8.6	110.5
Petroleum and petroleum products.....................	1,044.0	1,111.4	1,018.8	927.5	328.1	429.8	169.6
Crude petroleum.........................	571.4	602.7	508.5	418.9	102.3	313.3	3.2
Petroleum products [1]...................	472.4	508.8	510.4	508.6	225.8	116.5	166.4
Gasoline...............................	125.2	156.1	137.8	124.6	65.6	30.8	28.2
Distillate fuel oil......................	91.7	141.1	185.4	198.7	60.3	64.2	74.3
Residual fuel oil.......................	131.6	96.1	81.1	65.3	51.5	7.6	6.2
Chemicals and related products......................	172.4	174.9	180.1	180.5	70.8	48.5	61.2
Fertilizers..............................	35.1	34.5	35.8	39.9	17.2	13.3	9.3
Other chemicals and related products................	137.3	140.4	144.3	140.6	53.5	35.2	51.9
Crude material, inedible................	380.3	386.0	307.0	331.4	169.0	82.1	80.3
Forest products, wood and chips.........	33.1	29.4	20.8	28.9	5.6	4.6	18.7
Pulp and waste paper...................	13.6	18.7	21.4	24.0	0.1	2.3	21.7
Soil, sand, gravel, rock, and stone [1].....	165.0	177.9	120.3	126.2	91.6	30.5	4.1
Limestone.............................	67.4	73.5	61.3	59.9	42.4	14.1	3.4
Phosphate rock........................	3.4	6.0	4.6	5.8	3.4	2.4	0.0
Sand & gravel.........................	79.0	80.2	46.3	51.8	42.3	9.0	0.5
Iron ore and scrap........................	97.9	85.7	82.0	85.4	54.2	6.3	24.9
Marine shells............................	0.3	–	0.1	0.1	0.1	–	–
Nonferrous ores and scrap................	29.2	29.2	23.9	29.5	5.9	17.9	5.7
Sulphur, clay, and salt...................	11.3	8.7	6.3	7.6	1.3	1.6	4.7
Slag....................................	4.0	6.0	4.3	5.0	2.0	2.9	–
Other nonmetal minerals.................	25.9	30.4	27.8	24.6	8.2	16.0	0.4
Primary manufactured goods............	153.0	166.4	103.7	117.1	32.1	66.1	18.9
Papers products........................	12.1	13.7	13.7	13.1	0.2	5.3	7.5
Lime, cement, and glass.................	55.9	62.4	27.6	29.8	14.7	13.5	1.7
Primary iron and steel products..........	57.1	52.1	33.5	49.7	15.5	31.7	2.5
Primary nonferrous metal products..................	25.5	33.5	26.7	22.3	1.6	13.8	6.9
Primary wood products.................	2.5	4.8	2.2	2.1	0.1	1.8	0.2
Food and farm products................	283.3	251.3	300.1	270.1	75.7	43.4	150.9
Fish....................................	2.4	3.0	3.1	3.2	0.1	1.9	1.2
Grain [1]................................	145.2	124.0	131.8	100.6	37.5	3.7	59.4
Wheat.................................	43.4	36.4	38.4	49.7	15.5	0.5	33.8
Corn..................................	88.2	75.2	81.8	41.7	18.9	2.0	20.8
Oilseeds [1].............................	57.6	47.2	76.9	73.2	26.5	1.1	45.5
Soybeans.............................	47.3	40.8	67.4	62.5	22.7	0.7	39.0
Vegetables products....................	8.9	8.3	12.9	13.1	1.4	5.9	5.8
Processed grain and animal feed..................	23.1	18.4	20.6	22.1	4.7	0.9	16.5
Other agricultural products.............	46.1	50.5	54.9	57.8	5.4	29.9	22.5
All manufactured equip, machinery and products.....	83.6	110.3	104.1	121.0	20.9	74.6	25.5
Waste and scrap, n.e.c. [2]...............	4.3	2.0	1.3	1.3	1.3	–	–
Unknown or n.e.c. [2]...................	6.8	8.7	9.6	13.7	0.1	5.6	8.1

– Represents or rounds to zero. [1] Includes commodities not shown separately. [2] Not elsewhere classified.

Source: U.S. Army Corps of Engineers, *Waterborne Commerce of the United States, 2013*, 2015, and earlier editions. See also <http://www.navigationdatacenter.us/wcsc/wcsc.htm>.

Table 1096. Top 30 U.S. Ports by Tons of Traffic: 2013

[In thousands of short tons (36,579 represents 36,579,000), except rank. One short ton equals 2,000 lbs. For calendar year. Represents tons of cargo shipped from or received by the specified port. Excludes cargo carried on general ferries; coal and petroleum products loaded from shore facilities directly onto bunkers of vessels for fuel; and amounts of less than 100 tons of government-owned equipment in support of Corps of Engineers projects]

Port name	Rank	Total	Domestic	Foreign Total	Inbound	Outbound
Baltimore, MD...........................	16	36,579	6,586	29,993	10,645	19,347
Baton Rouge, LA.........................	8	63,875	38,732	25,143	14,430	10,713
Beaumont, TX............................	4	94,404	33,371	61,032	48,544	12,488
Corpus Christi, TX......................	7	76,158	31,911	44,247	28,470	15,777
Duluth-Superior, MN and WI............	17	36,477	28,729	7,748	660	7,088
Houston, TX.............................	2	229,247	69,696	159,551	76,449	83,102
Huntington - Tristate [1]................	15	46,831	46,831	–	–	–
Lake Charles, LA........................	11	56,577	25,493	31,085	22,125	8,960
Long Beach, CA.........................	5	84,493	10,821	73,672	46,020	27,653
Los Angeles, CA........................	9	57,929	5,923	52,005	31,506	20,499
Mobile, AL..............................	12	53,993	23,321	30,671	12,493	18,178
New Orleans, LA........................	6	77,159	43,156	34,003	15,414	18,589
New York, NY and NJ...................	3	123,323	46,716	76,606	56,145	20,461
Newport News, VA......................	24	29,771	765	29,006	309	28,697
Norfolk Harbor, VA......................	14	48,894	6,554	42,340	9,362	32,977
Pascagoula, MS.........................	21	32,428	8,323	24,105	16,445	7,660
Philadelphia, PA........................	26	26,046	11,188	14,858	13,970	888
Pittsburgh, PA..........................	20	32,746	32,746	–	–	–
Plaquemines, LA, Port of..............	10	56,876	33,786	23,090	1,502	21,588
Port Arthur, TX.........................	18	34,699	9,539	25,160	9,653	15,507
Port Everglades, FL....................	30	21,703	9,853	11,850	8,330	3,520
Portland, OR............................	28	23,427	8,391	15,036	3,545	11,491
Richmond, CA...........................	27	23,544	9,439	14,106	11,240	2,866
Savannah, GA...........................	23	31,990	1,756	30,234	13,341	16,893
South Louisiana, LA, Port of...........	1	238,586	126,851	111,734	38,247	73,487
St. Louis, MO and IL...................	19	33,575	33,575	–	–	–
Tacoma, WA.............................	29	22,906	4,512	18,394	7,272	11,122
Tampa, FL...............................	22	32,407	21,702	10,705	5,765	4,940
Texas City, TX..........................	13	49,674	19,282	30,392	18,977	11,415
Valdez, AK..............................	25	28,166	28,163	3	3	–

– Represents or rounds to zero. [1] The Port of Huntington is the largest inland shipping port in the United States. Port operations occur in Ashland, KY; Ironton, OH; and Huntington, WV.

Source: U.S. Army Corps of Engineers, *Waterborne Commerce of the United States, 2013*, 2015. See also <http://www.navigationdatacenter.us/wcsc/wcsc.htm>.

Table 1097. Top 30 U.S. Ports/Waterways Ranked by Container Traffic: 2013

[In thousands of twenty-foot equivalent units (TEUs) (34,484.7 represents 34,484,700). For calendar year. For the 30 leading ports/waterways in total TEUs. A TEU is a measure of containerized cargo capacity equal to one standard 20-foot length by 8-foot width by 8-foot, 6 inch height container. Does not include empty containers]

Port/waterway name	Rank	Total loaded	Domestic loaded Total [1]	Inbound	Outbound	Foreign loaded Total	Inbound
Total U.S. [2]......................	(X)	34,484.7	5,628.3	2,209.7	2,210.1	30,064.9	17,988.5
Anchorage, AK.........................	19	259.9	289.4	202.5	57.4	–	–
Baltimore, MD..........................	16	555.4	28.0	11.4	9.8	534.2	331.9
Boston, MA.............................	24	161.1	–	–	–	161.1	96.5
Camden-Gloucester, NJ..............	29	91.0	66.3	20.1	41.0	29.8	24.6
Charleston, SC.........................	9	1,289.1	–	–	–	1,289.1	668.0
Chester, SC............................	30	87.7	–	–	–	87.7	54.3
Gulfport, MS............................	22	168.5	–	–	–	168.5	95.2
Honolulu, HI............................	11	867.1	1,124.8	520.6	320.2	26.3	19.1
Houston, TX............................	8	1,563.1	26.2	12.7	13.5	1,536.8	646.2
Jacksonville, FL........................	12	752.4	470.4	84.3	359.9	308.1	152.9
Juneau, AK.............................	28	103.1	150.5	75.1	28.0	–	–
Ketchikan, AK..........................	27	133.5	199.5	47.1	86.4	(Z)	(Z)
Long Beach, CA........................	2	5,297.6	406.6	64.1	292.0	4,941.5	3,456.6
Los Angeles, CA.......................	1	5,556.2	–	–	–	5,556.2	3,859.9
Miami, FL...............................	14	709.5	–	–	–	709.5	350.6
Mobile, AL..............................	23	165.3	–	–	–	165.3	68.4
New Orleans, LA.......................	17	301.7	–	–	–	301.7	82.9
New York (NY and NJ).................	3	4,208.7	119.8	44.6	51.8	4,112.3	2,757.3
Norfolk Harbor, VA.....................	5	1,872.5	75.5	30.9	23.6	1,817.9	891.9
Oakland, CA............................	6	1,762.2	230.9	26.6	136.3	1,599.3	776.3
Palm Beach, FL........................	26	144.0	–	–	–	144.0	36.5
Philadelphia, PA........................	18	264.2	71.2	13.5	48.4	202.2	148.8
Port Everglades, FL....................	15	698.7	26.8	2.0	24.8	671.9	306.5
Portland, OR............................	25	148.4	11.8	5.9	0.1	142.5	71.6
San Juan, PR...........................	13	752.3	604.9	463.5	110.1	178.7	157.4
Savannah, GA...........................	4	2,349.2	–	–	–	2,349.2	1,139.8
Seattle, WA.............................	10	1,236.7	483.9	101.6	188.3	946.8	516.6
Tacoma, WA.............................	7	1,574.0	280.3	64.3	197.2	1,312.5	763.1
Wilmington, NC.........................	20	222.9	–	–	–	222.9	106.0
Wilmington, DE.........................	21	193.3	–	–	–	193.3	168.7

– Represents zero. X Not applicable. Z Less than 50 TEUs. [1] Includes empty TEUs. [2] Includes other ports/waterways not shown separately.

Source: U.S. Army Corps of Engineers, Navigation Data Center, Waterborne Commerce Statistics Center, "2013 Waterborne Container Traffic for U.S. Ports," <http://www.navigationdatacenter.us/wcsc/wcsc.htm>, accessed April 2015.

Table 1098. Highway Mileage—Urban and Rural by Ownership: 1990 to 2013

[In thousands (3,880 represents 3,880,000). As of December 31. Includes Puerto Rico beginning 2000]

Type and control of roadways	1990	1995	2000	2008	2009	2010	2011	2012	2013
Total mileage [1]	**3,880**	**3,912**	**3,951**	**4,059**	**4,063**	**4,084**	**4,094**	**4,109**	**4,132**
Urban mileage [2]	757	819	859	1,079	1,086	1,103	1,108	1,127	1,192
Under state control	96	112	112	152	152	(NA)	153	154	160
Under local control [1]	661	706	746	920	926	(NA)	945	960	1,021
Rural mileage	3,123	3,093	3,092	2,980	2,977	2,980	2,985	2,983	2,941
Under state control	703	691	664	633	632	(NA)	631	631	625
Under local control [1]	2,242	2,231	2,311	2,223	2,221	(NA)	2,227	2,224	2,174
Under federal control [2]	178	170	117	124	124	(NA)	127	128	141

NA Not available. [1] Includes state park, state toll, other state agency, other local agency and other roadways not identified by ownership. [2] Includes roadways in federal parks, forest, and reservations that are not part of the state and local highway system.

Source: U.S. Federal Highway Administration, "Highway Statistics 2013," and earlier reports, <http://www.fhwa.dot.gov/policyinformation/statistics.cfm>, accessed April 2015.

Table 1099. Highway Mileage by State—Functional Systems and Urban/Rural Status: 2013

[As of December 31. Excludes Puerto Rico. For definition of functional systems, see text, this section]

State	Total	Functional systems					Urban	Rural
		Interstate	Other freeways and expressways	Arterial	Collector	Local		
United States	**4,115,462**	**47,575**	**16,445**	**400,787**	**803,807**	**2,846,848**	**1,177,986**	**2,937,476**
Alabama	101,837	1,002	42	9,673	22,386	68,733	25,153	76,685
Alaska	15,680	1,081	–	1,571	3,300	9,727	2,432	13,248
Arizona	66,441	1,168	226	5,796	8,072	51,178	26,311	40,129
Arkansas	101,656	656	238	7,203	21,061	72,499	16,413	85,243
California	174,989	2,451	1,532	28,470	32,223	110,313	94,187	80,801
Colorado	88,565	952	352	8,906	16,245	62,109	19,692	68,873
Connecticut	21,474	346	279	2,725	3,206	14,918	15,213	6,261
Delaware	6,393	41	30	650	1,039	4,633	3,034	3,359
District of Columbia	1,501	12	16	270	157	1,047	1,501	–
Florida	122,088	1,495	752	12,838	14,560	92,442	81,647	40,441
Georgia	128,620	1,247	149	14,180	23,037	90,006	51,387	77,233
Hawaii	4,430	55	34	790	752	2,800	2,566	1,864
Idaho	48,082	612	–	4,249	10,611	32,611	5,548	42,534
Illinois	145,708	2,185	135	14,636	22,169	106,583	47,614	98,094
Indiana	97,553	1,188	294	8,464	22,523	65,084	28,088	69,465
Iowa	114,429	782	–	9,778	31,629	72,240	12,654	101,775
Kansas	140,687	874	595	9,093	33,698	96,427	13,639	127,048
Kentucky	79,598	801	604	5,565	16,562	56,066	12,643	66,955
Louisiana	61,427	926	53	5,632	9,972	44,844	17,409	44,018
Maine	22,882	367	18	2,181	5,914	14,401	3,009	19,873
Maryland	32,422	481	304	3,806	5,059	22,772	18,970	13,452
Massachusetts	36,370	575	345	6,422	4,550	24,478	30,205	6,165
Michigan	122,141	1,244	705	14,303	24,458	81,431	37,886	84,255
Minnesota	138,767	914	166	13,520	30,408	93,759	22,208	116,560
Mississippi	75,116	700	77	7,663	15,892	50,784	11,978	63,138
Missouri	131,900	1,379	1,379	9,108	25,109	94,925	24,367	107,532
Montana	74,933	1,192	–	6,088	16,245	51,408	4,146	70,787
Nebraska	93,770	482	442	7,702	20,772	64,371	6,486	87,284
Nevada	40,139	596	55	3,417	5,612	30,460	8,297	31,842
New Hampshire	16,098	225	84	1,662	2,642	11,485	5,032	11,065
New Jersey	39,293	431	488	5,903	4,437	28,034	33,406	5,887
New Mexico	70,772	1,000	–	4,963	9,188	55,620	37,131	33,640
New York	114,728	1,724	936	13,665	20,737	77,666	48,522	66,206
North Carolina	106,202	1,255	466	9,552	17,351	77,579	37,475	68,727
North Dakota	87,078	571	–	5,941	11,929	68,637	2,153	84,925
Ohio	123,297	1,574	867	10,386	22,869	87,602	47,522	75,775
Oklahoma	112,940	933	191	8,226	25,490	78,100	17,728	95,213
Oregon	71,228	730	57	7,054	18,589	44,798	12,926	58,302
Pennsylvania	119,936	1,857	858	12,905	19,847	84,470	46,066	73,870
Rhode Island	6,106	70	77	837	887	4,235	4,742	1,364
South Carolina	66,232	851	81	7,152	15,089	43,059	16,626	49,606
South Dakota	82,558	679	14	6,415	19,004	56,446	3,246	79,312
Tennessee	95,536	1,104	155	9,150	17,994	67,132	25,521	70,015
Texas	313,228	3,415	1,414	31,866	65,154	211,378	100,310	212,918
Utah	46,254	937	13	3,759	8,162	33,384	11,235	35,020
Vermont	14,266	320	18	1,303	3,119	9,506	1,452	12,813
Virginia	74,748	1,119	290	8,474	14,394	50,472	24,469	50,279
Washington	82,448	764	1,026	7,386	17,292	55,980	25,542	56,906
West Virginia	38,750	555	13	3,485	8,635	26,063	5,701	33,049
Wisconsin	115,145	743	572	12,338	23,501	77,990	23,578	91,567
Wyoming	29,024	914	3	3,668	10,279	14,161	2,920	26,104

– Represents zero.

Source: U.S. Federal Highway Administration, "Highway Statistics 2013," <http://www.fhwa.dot.gov/policyinformation/statistics.cfm>, accessed February 2015.

Table 1100. Bridge Inventory—Total Deficient and Obsolete: 2000 to 2014, and by State, 2014

[Based on the National Bridge Inventory program; for details, see source]

State and year	Number of bridges	Deficient and obsolete					
		Total number	Percent	Structurally deficient [1]		Functionally obsolete [2]	
				Number	Percent	Number	Percent
2000........................	587,735	180,642	30.7	89,460	15.2	91,182	15.5
2001........................	590,153	177,501	30.1	86,144	14.6	91,357	15.5
2002........................	591,243	174,854	29.6	84,031	14.2	90,823	15.4
2003........................	592,337	172,629	29.1	82,283	13.9	90,346	15.3
2004........................	594,100	170,047	28.6	79,971	13.5	90,076	15.2
2005........................	595,668	167,873	28.2	77,863	13.1	90,010	15.1
2006........................	597,561	165,013	27.6	75,422	12.6	89,591	15.0
2007........................	599,880	163,146	27.2	74,066	12.3	89,080	14.8
2008........................	601,506	162,072	26.9	72,883	12.1	89,189	14.8
2009........................	603,310	159,862	26.5	72,402	12.0	87,460	14.5
2010........................	604,493	156,289	25.9	70,431	11.7	85,858	14.2
2011........................	605,103	153,591	25.4	68,759	11.4	84,832	14.0
2012........................	607,380	151,497	24.9	66,749	11.0	84,748	14.0
2013........................	607,751	147,870	24.3	63,522	10.5	84,348	13.9
U.S. total, 2014..........	**610,749**	**145,890**	**23.9**	**61,365**	**10.0**	**84,525**	**13.8**
Alabama......................	16,088	3,532	22.0	1,388	8.6	2,144	13.3
Alaska.......................	1,544	351	22.7	153	9.9	198	12.8
Arizona......................	8,035	940	11.7	256	3.2	684	8.5
Arkansas.....................	12,806	2,855	22.3	861	6.7	1,994	15.6
California....................	25,406	6,807	26.8	2,501	9.8	4,306	16.9
Colorado.....................	8,668	1,388	16.0	529	6.1	859	9.9
Connecticut..................	4,218	1,457	34.5	378	9.0	1,079	25.6
Delaware.....................	865	171	19.8	48	5.5	123	14.2
District of Columbia........	253	178	70.4	14	5.5	164	64.8
Florida......................	12,137	2,003	16.5	243	2.0	1,760	14.5
Georgia......................	14,795	2,408	16.3	785	5.3	1,623	11.0
Hawaii.......................	1,137	483	42.5	61	5.4	422	37.1
Idaho........................	4,431	877	19.8	406	9.2	471	10.6
Illinois.....................	26,588	4,187	15.7	2,216	8.3	1,971	7.4
Indiana......................	19,019	4,103	21.6	1,902	10.0	2,201	11.6
Iowa.........................	24,300	6,205	25.5	5,022	20.7	1,183	4.9
Kansas.......................	25,085	4,229	16.9	2,416	9.6	1,813	7.2
Kentucky.....................	14,194	4,444	31.3	1,191	8.4	3,253	22.9
Louisiana....................	12,982	3,781	29.1	1,837	14.2	1,944	15.0
Maine........................	2,419	796	32.9	364	15.0	432	17.9
Maryland.....................	5,305	1,421	26.8	317	6.0	1,104	20.8
Massachusetts................	5,141	2,683	52.2	459	8.9	2,224	43.3
Michigan.....................	11,072	3,049	27.5	1,295	11.7	1,754	15.8
Minnesota....................	12,961	1,193	9.2	830	6.4	363	2.8
Mississippi..................	17,091	3,565	20.9	2,275	13.3	1,290	7.5
Missouri.....................	24,385	6,455	26.5	3,310	13.6	3,145	12.9
Montana......................	5,251	914	17.4	400	7.6	514	9.8
Nebraska.....................	15,374	3,640	23.7	2,654	17.3	986	6.4
Nevada.......................	1,898	249	13.1	34	1.8	215	11.3
New Hampshire................	2,467	775	31.4	324	13.1	451	18.3
New Jersey...................	6,609	2,343	35.5	621	9.4	1,722	26.1
New Mexico...................	3,951	643	16.3	284	7.2	359	9.1
New York.....................	17,456	6,745	38.6	2,012	11.5	4,733	27.1
North Carolina...............	18,117	5,334	29.4	2,199	12.1	3,135	17.3
North Dakota.................	4,429	944	21.3	701	15.8	243	5.5
Ohio.........................	26,986	6,532	24.2	2,080	7.7	4,452	16.5
Oklahoma.....................	23,147	5,791	25.0	4,216	18.2	1,575	6.8
Oregon.......................	8,052	1,858	23.1	439	5.5	1,419	17.6
Pennsylvania.................	22,691	9,438	41.6	5,050	22.3	4,388	19.3
Rhode Island.................	766	429	56.0	174	22.7	255	33.3
South Carolina...............	9,338	1,922	20.6	1,031	11.0	891	9.5
South Dakota.................	5,872	1,412	24.0	1,174	20.0	238	4.1
Tennessee....................	20,077	3,946	19.7	1,083	5.4	2,863	14.3
Texas........................	52,937	9,999	18.9	1,127	2.1	8,872	16.8
Utah.........................	3,014	419	13.9	102	3.4	317	10.5
Vermont......................	2,745	882	32.1	206	7.5	676	24.6
Virginia.....................	13,800	3,574	25.9	1,120	8.1	2,454	17.8
Washington...................	8,120	2,093	25.8	382	4.7	1,711	21.1
West Virginia................	7,187	2,501	34.8	960	13.4	1,541	21.4
Wisconsin....................	14,109	1,971	14.0	1,212	8.6	759	5.4
Wyoming......................	3,127	706	22.6	422	13.5	284	9.1
Puerto Rico..................	2,304	1,269	55.1	301	13.1	968	42.0

[1] Bridges are structurally deficient if they have been restricted to light vehicles, require immediate rehabilitation to remain open, or are closed. [2] Bridges are functionally obsolete if they have deck geometry, load carrying capacity, clearance or approach roadway alignment that no longer meet the criteria for the system of which the bridge is carrying a part.

Source: U.S. Federal Highway Administration, Office of Bridges and Structures, "Deficient Bridges by State and Highway System 2014," <http://www.fhwa.dot.gov/bridge/nbi.cfm>, accessed May 2015.

Table 1101. Funding for Highways and Disposition of Highway–User Revenue: 1990 to 2012

[In millions of dollars (75,444 represents $75,444,000,000). Data compiled from reports of state and local authorities]

Type	1990	1995	2000	2007	2008	2009	2010	2011	2012
Total receipts	**75,444**	**96,269**	**131,115**	**193,876**	**192,718**	**195,680**	**220,977**	**204,939**	**216,561**
Current income	69,880	87,620	119,815	168,219	172,785	169,453	187,960	177,861	195,307
Highway-user revenues	44,346	59,331	81,335	98,210	94,152	93,563	93,830	95,138	105,153
Other taxes and fees	19,827	21,732	31,137	54,189	61,163	61,562	80,220	66,968	69,273
Investment income, other receipts	5,707	6,557	7,342	15,820	17,471	14,328	13,910	15,754	20,881
Bond issue proceeds [1]	5,564	8,649	11,301	25,657	19,933	26,227	33,017	27,078	21,254
Funds drawn from or placed in reserves [2]	-36	-2,791	-8,418	-12,815	-10,660	-102	-15,664	1,501	4,758
Total funds available	75,408	93,478	122,697	181,061	182,058	195,578	205,313	206,440	221,319
Total disbursements	**75,408**	**93,478**	**122,697**	**181,061**	**182,058**	**195,578**	**205,313**	**206,440**	**221,319**
Current disbursements	72,457	88,994	117,592	173,095	173,869	185,843	193,034	192,727	198,670
Capital outlay	35,151	44,228	61,323	90,911	91,144	94,525	100,175	101,612	105,199
Maintenance and traffic services	20,365	24,319	30,636	44,715	44,972	49,432	48,773	46,311	47,990
Administration and research	6,501	8,419	10,020	14,428	14,711	15,599	16,165	16,590	16,023
Highway law enforcement and safety	7,235	8,218	11,031	14,723	14,565	17,421	18,080	17,374	17,847
Interest on debt	3,205	3,810	4,583	8,318	8,477	8,867	9,842	10,840	11,611
Bond retirement [1]	2,951	4,484	5,105	7,966	8,189	9,734	12,279	13,713	22,649

[1] Proceeds and redemptions of short-term notes and refunding issues are excluded. [2] Negative numbers indicate that funds were placed in reserves.

Source: U.S. Federal Highway Administration, "Highway Statistics 2012," and earlier reports, <http://www.fhwa.dot.gov/policyinformation/statistics.cfm>, accessed April 2014.

Table 1102. State Motor Fuel Tax and Related Receipts, 2010 to 2013; and Gasoline Tax Rates, 2013

[648 represents $648,000,000. Federal tax rate is 18.4 cents a gallon. This table includes revenues from State taxes on all motor-vehicle fuels and related receipts due to motor-fuel taxation and administration. In many States, however, the tax on special fuels (fuels other than gasoline and gasohol) is applicable only to the amount used on the highways. For the States that apply the tax to all fuel sold, the revenue and refunds covering the nonhighway portion of these special fuels have been excluded]

State	Net receipts (mil. dol.) 2010	2011	2012	2013	Tax rate, [1] 2013	State	Net receipts (mil. dol.) 2010	2011	2012	2013	Tax rate, [1] 2013
AL	648	650	643	635	18.00	MO	684	686	705	666	17.00
AK	25	30	32	32	8.00	MT	187	192	197	203	27.75
AZ	629	637	611	634	18.00	NE	319	333	320	314	26.30
AR	482	444	508	478	21.50	NV	457	459	481	486	24.00
CA	3,014	5,252	5,383	5,238	39.50	NH	144	146	144	143	19.63
CO	557	556	556	566	22.00	NJ	556	556	529	527	10.50
CT	632	629	700	681	25.00	NM	270	275	270	280	18.88
DE	113	114	113	113	23.00	NY	1,589	1,611	1,642	1,658	26.65
DC	21	30	23	22	23.50	NC	1,541	1,652	1,851	1,882	37.75
FL	2,184	2,187	2,189	2,276	16.90	ND	146	169	201	209	23.00
GA	474	456	448	459	7.50	OH	1,771	1,800	1,817	1,764	28.00
HI	78	87	84	84	17.00	OK	431	440	462	433	17.00
ID	227	223	224	228	25.00	OR	610	432	479	571	30.00
IL	1,248	1,248	1,214	1,183	19.00	PA	3,341	2,100	2,115	2,089	31.20
IN	817	837	810	807	18.00	RI	139	138	137	136	32.00
IA	429	437	441	437	21.00	SC	509	515	538	537	16.00
KS	436	425	423	425	24.00	SD	134	130	141	135	22.00
KY	655	731	789	837	30.90	TN	825	845	842	836	20.00
LA	593	613	583	585	20.00	TX	3,061	3,085	3,174	3,209	20.00
ME	247	244	244	258	30.00	UT	338	355	357	353	24.50
MD	721	674	725	745	23.50	VT	96	99	103	104	19.20
MA	654	660	660	651	24.00	VA	871	902	889	899	11.10
MI	945	941	930	935	19.00	WA	1,180	1,194	1,160	1,177	37.50
MN	831	842	851	866	28.50	WV	349	355	346	373	34.70
MS	378	400	402	396	18.40	WI	952	968	964	964	30.90
						WY	94	96	93	108	24.00

[1] State gasoline tax rates in cents per gallon. In effect December 31.

Source: U.S. Federal Highway Administration, "Highway Statistics 2013," and earlier reports, <http://www.fhwa.dot.gov/policyinformation/statistics.cfm>, accessed January 2015.

Table 1103. Public Obligations for Highways—Changes in Indebtedness During the Year: 2000 to 2013

[In millions of dollars (56,264 represents $56,264,000,000). Table summarizes state indebtedness from all state bond issues, including the toll facility issues and the state issues for local roads. This table is compiled from reports of state authorities. Table also summarizes the change in status of the highway obligations of local governments including toll authorities]

Item	2000	2005	2008	2009	2010	2011	2012	2013
STATE GOVERNMENT								
Obligations outstanding, beginning of year.........	56,264	82,476	102,039	111,600	138,798	157,728	166,402	181,075
Obligations issued....................................	9,067	19,784	20,769	22,372	26,895	23,240	18,789	27,163
Obligations retired....................................	3,897	14,072	12,183	8,326	11,143	12,617	15,283	15,783
Obligations outstanding, end of year...............	61,434	88,187	110,625	125,646	154,550	168,351	169,908	192,455
LOCAL GOVERNMENT [1, 2]								
Obligations outstanding, beginning of year.........	34,904	44,406	52,478	55,514	65,679	(NA)	75,668	(NA)
Bonds outstanding, beginning of year.............	34,229	43,403	51,103	53,894	63,891	(NA)	73,547	(NA)
Bonds outstanding, end of year..................	34,949	46,168	53,895	56,334	67,707	(NA)	79,244	(NA)
Obligations outstanding, end of year...............	35,557	47,170	55,414	58,123	69,794	(NA)	81,552	(NA)

NA Not available. [1] Short-term notes data not shown. The data are included in beginning and ending year obligations. [2] The number of local government data estimated varied year to year.

Source: U.S. Federal Highway Administration, "Highway Statistics 2013," and earlier reports, <http://www.fhwa.dot.gov/policyinformation/statistics.cfm>, accessed September 2015.

Table 1104. State Disbursements for Highways by State: 2000 to 2013

[In millions of dollars (89,832 represents $89,832,000,000). Comprise disbursements from current revenues or loans for construction, maintenance, interest and principal payments on highway bonds, transfers to local units, and miscellaneous. Includes transactions by state toll authorities. Data exclude amounts allocated for collection expenses and nonhighway purposes, and mass transit]

State	2000	2005	2008	2009	2010	2011	2012	2013
United States............	**89,832**	**116,517**	**139,584**	**143,767**	**145,944**	**149,959**	**156,715**	**152,179**
Alabama.....................	1,246	1,519	1,916	1,969	1,781	1,840	1,987	1,988
Alaska.......................	501	643	730	935	756	806	819	991
Arizona......................	2,040	2,458	2,806	2,988	2,663	2,723	3,112	3,125
Arkansas....................	817	1,078	1,051	1,072	1,376	1,341	1,374	1,783
California....................	6,750	8,308	14,697	21,808	19,961	16,585	17,155	12,337
Colorado.....................	1,392	1,652	1,695	1,906	2,249	2,577	2,485	2,580
Connecticut.................	1,304	1,434	1,370	2,175	1,761	1,733	1,939	1,982
Delaware....................	595	1,104	683	711	1,353	1,191	1,888	1,368
District of Columbia.........	244	327	335	469	582	413	478	432
Florida......................	4,208	7,369	8,698	7,194	7,867	6,966	7,486	9,547
Georgia.....................	1,567	2,070	3,817	3,506	2,926	3,123	3,033	2,679
Hawaii......................	272	506	444	504	460	414	465	463
Idaho.......................	492	608	802	890	959	877	775	791
Illinois......................	3,447	4,201	6,299	5,385	[1] 5,385	4,928	6,211	5,711
Indiana......................	1,932	2,235	3,280	3,280	2,839	3,023	2,709	2,825
Iowa........................	1,494	1,392	1,505	1,721	1,888	1,698	1,980	1,837
Kansas......................	1,206	1,394	1,487	1,464	1,571	1,478	2,049	1,419
Kentucky....................	1,651	1,723	2,404	2,522	2,528	2,073	2,314	2,537
Louisiana...................	1,301	1,387	2,488	3,480	2,457	2,283	2,798	2,079
Maine.......................	488	616	739	652	684	705	[1] 705	[1] 705
Maryland....................	1,599	2,049	2,747	2,800	2,255	2,519	2,813	2,483
Massachusetts..............	3,524	3,196	2,898	2,810	2,923	[1] 2,923	[1] 2,923	[1] 2,923
Michigan....................	2,748	3,561	3,269	3,178	3,484	3,015	3,014	3,022
Minnesota...................	1,692	2,131	2,352	2,365	2,625	3,336	2,585	2,840
Mississippi..................	1,039	1,081	1,346	1,301	1,345	1,262	1,305	1,414
Missouri.....................	1,818	2,069	2,545	2,846	2,814	3,007	2,707	2,408
Montana.....................	474	664	651	708	778	754	891	723
Nebraska....................	745	876	1,352	1,398	1,409	1,443	1,423	1,508
Nevada......................	651	865	906	1,221	1,007	968	1,253	1,064
New Hampshire.............	387	389	681	641	793	[1] 792	[1] 792	[1] 792
New Jersey..................	4,503	7,119	3,921	4,222	5,201	6,453	6,954	7,492
New Mexico.................	1,162	911	860	1,272	1,163	1,632	934	1,296
New York....................	5,307	9,638	7,537	6,977	7,711	8,516	[1] 8,515	[1] 8,515
North Carolina..............	2,621	3,698	3,584	3,659	3,646	4,312	4,346	4,505
North Dakota...............	385	456	471	478	559	618	854	1,022
Ohio........................	3,351	4,040	4,631	4,852	4,520	4,754	4,950	4,835
Oklahoma...................	1,417	1,163	1,634	1,765	2,040	3,383	2,469	1,818
Oregon......................	1,010	1,628	1,364	1,395	1,522	1,382	1,937	1,263
Pennsylvania...............	4,517	4,567	5,956	6,979	8,835	9,220	7,320	7,134
Rhode Island...............	256	407	419	389	540	480	616	511
South Carolina..............	970	1,360	1,470	1,353	1,899	1,609	1,686	1,523
South Dakota...............	466	466	451	500	532	547	592	677
Tennessee..................	1,440	1,718	1,771	1,936	2,076	2,094	2,160	2,187
Texas.......................	5,665	8,918	15,948	9,883	9,365	11,693	13,411	15,024
Utah........................	1,072	986	1,229	1,855	2,303	2,248	2,225	1,608
Vermont.....................	287	310	395	400	436	556	719	518
Virginia.....................	2,678	3,384	3,875	3,572	3,334	3,882	4,465	4,487
Washington.................	1,871	2,625	3,901	3,807	4,149	4,937	5,768	6,491
West Virginia...............	1,170	1,425	1,208	1,410	1,327	1,388	1,395	1,275
Wisconsin...................	1,663	2,363	2,392	2,549	2,702	2,892	3,312	3,071
Wyoming....................	396	429	574	611	605	564	614	568

[1] Amount shown represents data reported for 1 or 2 years previous.

Source: U.S. Federal Highway Administration, "Highway Statistics 2013," and earlier reports, <http://www.fhwa.dot.gov/policyinformation/statistics.cfm>, accessed June 2015.

Table 1105. State Motor Vehicle Registrations: 1990 to 2013

[In thousands (188,798 represents 188,798,000). Compiled principally from information obtained from state authorities, see source for details. Excludes motorcycles; see Table 1107]

Type	1990	2000	2005	2010	2011	2012	2013
All motor vehicles	**188,798**	**221,475**	**241,194**	**242,061**	**244,778**	**253,639**	**255,877**
Private and commercial	185,541	217,567	237,140	237,784	241,068	249,887	251,863
Publicly owned	3,257	3,908	4,054	4,277	3,710	3,753	4,014
Automobiles [1]	133,700	133,621	136,568	130,892	125,657	111,290	113,676
Private and commercial	132,164	132,247	135,192	129,434	124,136	109,834	112,128
Publicly owned	1,536	1,374	1,376	1,458	1,520	1,456	1,548
Buses	627	746	807	846	666	765	865
Private and commercial	275	314	331	347	312	301	361
Publicly owned	351	432	476	499	354	464	503
Trucks [1]	54,470	87,108	103,819	110,322	118,456	133,130	132,931
Private and commercial	53,101	85,005	101,616	108,003	116,620	131,322	130,998
Publicly owned	1,369	2,103	2,203	2,319	1,836	1,808	1,934

[1] Trucks include pickups, panels, and delivery vans. Beginning 1995 personal passenger vans, passenger minivans, and utility-type vehicles are no longer included in automobiles but are included in trucks.

Source: U.S. Federal Highway Administration, "Highway Statistics," January 2015, and earlier reports, <http://www.fhwa.dot.gov/policyinformation/statistics.cfm>, accessed May 2015.

Table 1106. Alternative Fueled Vehicles and Estimated Consumption of Vehicle Fuels by Fuel Type: 2005 to 2011

[In thousands, (420,778 represents 420,778,000). Vehicles in use do not include concept and demonstration vehicles that are not ready for delivery to end users. Vehicles in use represent accumulated acquisitions, less retirements, as of the end of each calendar year. (g-e-g = gasoline equivalent gallons)]

Vehicles and fuel consumption	Unit	2005	2009	2010	2011
ALTERNATIVE FUELED VEHICLES IN USE					
Total	**Number**	**592,125**	**826,318**	**938,643**	**1,191,786**
Compressed Natural Gas (CNG)	Number	117,699	114,270	115,863	118,214
Electric [1]	Number	51,398	57,185	57,462	67,295
Ethanol, 85 percent (E85) [2, 3]	Number	246,363	504,297	618,506	862,837
Hydrogen	Number	119	357	421	527
Liquefied Natural Gas (LNG)	Number	2,748	3,176	3,354	3,436
Liquefied Petroleum Gas (LPG)	Number	173,795	147,030	143,037	139,477
Other fuels [4]	Number	3	3	–	–
FUEL CONSUMPTION					
Alternative fuels:	1,000 gal. (g-e-g)	420,778	431,107	457,755	515,920
Compressed Natural Gas (CNG)	1,000 gal. (g-e-g)	166,878	199,513	210,007	220,247
Electric [1]	1,000 gal. (g-e-g)	5,219	4,956	4,847	7,635
Ethanol, 85 percent (E85) [2]	1,000 gal. (g-e-g)	38,074	71,213	90,323	137,165
Hydrogen	1,000 gal. (g-e-g)	25	140	152	174
Liquefied Natural Gas (LNG)	1,000 gal. (g-e-g)	22,409	25,652	26,072	26,242
Liquefied Petroleum Gas (LPG)	1,000 gal. (g-e-g)	188,171	129,631	126,354	124,457
Other fuels [4]	1,000 gal. (g-e-g)	2	2	–	–
Biodiesel	1,000 gal. (g-e-g)	93,281	334,809	270,107	910,968
Oxygenates:					
Methyl Tertiary Butyl Ether (MTBE)	1,000 gal. (g-e-g)	1,654,500	(X)	(X)	(X)
Ethanol in Gasohol	1,000 gal. (g-e-g)	2,756,663	7,343,133	8,527,431	8,563,841
Total alternative and replacement fuels	**1,000 gal. (g-e-g)**	**4,925,222**	**7,677,942**	**8,797,538**	**9,474,809**
FUEL CONSUMPTION IN NATIVE UNITS					
Alternative fuels:					
Compressed Natural Gas (CNG)	million cubic feet	20,106	24,038	25,302	26,536
Electric [1]	1,000 kwh	173,967	165,200	161,567	254,500
Ethanol, 85 percent (E85) [2]	1,000 gallons	52,881	98,907	125,449	190,507
Hydrogen	1,000 kilograms	23	128	138	158
Liquefied Natural Gas (LNG)	1,000 gallons	33,953	38,867	39,503	39,761
Liquefied Petroleum Gas (LPG)	1,000 gallons	254,285	175,177	170,749	168,185
Biodiesel	1,000 gallons	90,827	326,000	263,000	887,000
Oxygenates:					
Methyl Tertiary Butyl Ether (MTBE)	1,000 gallons	2,035,320	(X)	(X)	(X)
Ethanol in Gasohol	1,000 gallons	4,013,679	10,753,990	12,495,404	12,548,757

– Represents zero. X Not applicable. [1] Excludes gasoline-electric and diesel-electric hybrids because the input fuel is gasoline or diesel rather than an alternative transportation fuel. [2] The remaining portion of E85 percent ethanol is gasoline. Consumption data include the gasoline portion of the fuel. [3] For 2010, the EIA estimates that the number of E85 vehicles that are capable of operating on E85, gasoline, or both, is about 8.6 million. Many of these alternative-fueled vehicles (AFVs) are sold and used as traditional gasoline-powered vehicles. In this table, AFVs in use include only those E85 vehicles believed to be used as AFVs. These are primarily fleet-operated vehicles. [4] May include P-Series fuel or any other fuel designated by the Secretary of Energy as an alternative fuel in accordance with the Energy Policy Act of 1995.

Source: U.S. Energy Information Administration, "Alternatives to Traditional Transportation Fuels," <http://www.eia.gov/renewable/data.cfm>, accessed September 2013.

Table 1107. State Motor Vehicle Registrations, 1990 to 2013; and Motorcycle Registrations and Licensed Drivers, 2013

[In thousands (188,798 represents 188,798,000). Motor vehicle registrations cover publicly, privately, and commercially owned vehicles. Some states did not provide complete current registration data. Table displays estimates by FHWA, transaction data, or previous year data shown, see source and earlier editions for more information. For uniformity, data have been adjusted to a calendar-year basis as registration years in states differ; figures represent net numbers where possible, excluding reregistrations and nonresident registrations. See also Table 1105. Data for farm trucks, which are registered at a nominal fee and restricted to use in the vicinity of the owner's farm, is not included for some States. See source for details]

State	Motor vehicle registrations [1]						2013		Motor-cycle registra-tions [2], in 2013	Licensed drivers in 2013
	1990	2000	2005	2010	2011	2012	Total	Auto-mobile (incl. taxis)		
U.S..........	188,798	221,475	241,194	242,061	253,216	253,639	255,877	113,676	8,405	212,160
AL.............	3,744	3,960	4,545	4,654	4,812	4,845	4,787	2,075	118	3,859
AK.............	477	594	673	710	758	775	786	201	32	529
AZ.............	2,825	3,795	3,972	4,320	5,109	5,163	5,381	2,257	188	4,791
AR.............	1,448	1,840	1,940	2,073	2,448	2,480	2,418	865	74	2,097
CA.............	21,926	27,698	32,487	31,014	29,177	27,702	28,075	13,823	800	24,390
CO............	3,155	3,626	1,808	4,180	4,332	4,562	4,683	1,820	185	3,837
CT.............	2,623	2,853	3,059	3,082	2,829	2,706	2,856	1,475	91	2,534
DE.............	526	630	737	799	929	944	947	448	30	724
DC.............	262	242	237	212	316	322	333	219	4	406
FL.............	10,950	11,781	15,691	14,373	15,469	15,666	15,132	7,425	545	13,670
GA............	5,489	7,155	8,063	7,702	7,534	7,647	7,780	3,435	200	6,607
HI.............	771	738	948	904	1,148	1,232	1,335	568	41	915
ID.............	1,054	1,178	1,374	1,325	1,625	1,644	1,692	599	65	1,111
IL.............	7,873	8,973	9,458	10,079	10,445	10,132	10,193	4,797	352	8,262
IN.............	4,366	5,571	4,955	5,698	6,133	6,004	5,574	2,265	219	4,500
IA.............	2,632	3,106	3,398	3,313	3,497	3,511	3,541	1,366	183	2,144
KS.............	2,012	2,296	2,368	2,436	2,446	2,449	2,628	1,031	99	2,018
KY.............	2,909	2,826	3,428	3,589	3,763	3,671	4,032	1,715	110	3,019
LA.............	2,995	3,557	3,819	4,086	4,053	3,889	3,957	1,507	114	3,278
ME.............	977	1,024	1,075	1,054	1,171	1,180	1,199	488	63	1,011
MD............	3,607	3,848	4,322	4,557	3,906	3,983	3,834	1,919	100	4,140
MA............	3,726	5,265	5,420	5,334	5,695	4,950	4,985	2,511	125	4,766
MI.............	7,209	8,436	8,247	9,286	9,183	7,798	8,192	3,594	267	6,987
MN............	3,508	4,630	4,647	4,848	4,910	5,099	5,219	2,212	237	3,331
MS............	1,875	2,289	1,978	2,016	2,037	2,052	2,074	872	28	1,969
MO............	3,905	4,580	4,589	5,153	5,170	5,685	5,821	2,485	185	4,280
MT.............	783	1,026	1,009	926	1,219	1,489	1,540	445	171	767
NE.............	1,384	1,619	1,703	1,802	1,887	1,888	1,891	733	56	1,375
NV.............	853	1,220	1,349	1,362	2,152	2,130	2,203	978	71	1,756
NH.............	946	1,052	1,174	1,203	1,278	1,302	1,409	625	74	1,061
NJ.............	5,652	6,390	6,262	6,628	7,940	7,911	7,061	3,645	152	6,081
NM............	1,301	1,529	1,548	1,612	1,772	1,806	1,882	716	65	1,457
NY.............	10,196	10,235	11,863	10,255	10,431	10,449	10,674	5,203	345	[3] 11,211
NC.............	5,162	6,223	6,148	5,743	6,250	7,793	7,814	3,496	195	6,823
ND.............	630	694	695	736	786	810	845	255	36	514
OH............	8,410	10,467	10,634	9,801	10,217	10,116	10,360	4,863	402	8,030
OK.............	2,649	3,014	3,725	3,357	3,429	3,440	3,460	1,376	127	2,418
OR.............	2,445	3,022	2,897	3,050	3,128	3,527	3,604	1,521	90	2,773
PA.............	7,971	9,260	9,864	9,991	10,303	10,471	10,461	4,810	401	8,897
RI.............	672	760	812	782	919	854	853	459	32	749
SC.............	2,521	3,095	3,339	3,661	3,827	3,897	3,987	1,751	113	3,536
SD.............	704	793	854	926	995	1,004	1,015	332	87	604
TN.............	4,444	4,820	4,980	5,114	5,302	5,393	5,452	2,284	164	4,605
TX.............	12,800	14,070	17,470	17,194	19,617	20,238	20,171	7,955	444	15,447
UT.............	1,206	1,628	2,210	2,655	1,883	1,981	2,061	876	65	1,661
VT.............	462	515	508	567	605	607	612	259	29	543
VA.............	4,938	6,046	6,591	6,149	6,998	7,117	7,051	3,296	190	5,603
WA............	4,257	5,116	5,598	4,683	5,881	5,850	6,393	2,800	227	5,302
WV............	1,225	1,442	1,352	1,436	1,458	1,459	1,453	542	58	1,177
WI.............	3,815	4,366	4,725	4,968	5,244	5,215	5,339	2,257	323	4,171
WY............	528	586	646	663	798	799	831	229	31	421

[1] Automobiles, trucks, and buses (excludes motorcycles). Excludes vehicles owned by military services. [2] Private and commercial. [3] New York did not provide 2013 data on licensed drivers; table shows 2012 data.

Source: U.S. Federal Highway Administration, "Highway Statistics 2013," and earlier reports, <http://www.fhwa.dot.gov/policyinformation/statistics.cfm>, accessed April 2015.

Table 1108. Motor Vehicle Distance Traveled by Type of Vehicle: 1970 to 2013

[1,110 represents 1,110,000,000,000. The travel data by vehicle type and stratification of trucks are estimated by the Federal Highway Administration (FHWA)]

Year	Vehicle—miles of travel (bil.)[1]					Average miles traveled per vehicle (1,000)[1]				
	Total[2]	Light duty vehicle short WB[3]	Buses[4]	Light duty vehicle long WB[3]	Trucks[5,6]	Total[2]	Light duty vehicle short WB[3]	Buses[4]	Light duty vehicle long WB[3]	Trucks[5,6]
1970	1,110	920	4.5	123	62	10.0	10.0	12.0	8.7	13.6
1980	1,527	1,122	6.1	291	108	9.5	8.8	11.5	10.4	18.7
1990	2,144	1,418	5.7	575	146	11.1	10.3	9.1	11.9	23.6
1995	2,423	1,438	6.4	790	178	11.8	11.2	9.4	12.0	26.5
1996	2,486	1,470	6.6	817	183	11.8	11.3	9.4	11.8	26.1
1997	2,562	1,503	6.8	851	191	12.1	11.6	9.8	12.1	27.0
1998	2,632	1,550	7.0	868	196	12.2	11.8	9.8	12.2	25.4
1999	2,691	1,569	7.7	901	203	12.2	11.9	10.5	12.0	26.0
2000	2,747	1,967	14.8	491	262	12.2	11.0	19.8	14.6	29.1
2001	2,796	1,987	13.0	512	272	11.9	10.7	17.3	14.7	28.9
2002	2,856	2,036	13.3	520	276	12.2	11.1	17.5	14.3	29.4
2003	2,890	2,051	13.4	528	286	12.2	11.1	17.2	14.8	30.3
2004	2,965	2,083	13.5	569	284	12.2	11.0	17.0	15.2	29.7
2005	2,989	2,096	13.2	581	285	12.1	11.0	16.3	14.8	28.8
2006	3,014	2,048	14.0	633	301	12.0	10.5	17.1	16.3	29.1
2007	3,031	2,104	14.5	587	304	11.9	10.7	17.4	15.0	28.3
2008	2,977	2,025	14.8	605	311	11.6	10.3	17.6	15.3	28.6
2009	2,957	2,016	14.4	617	288	11.6	10.4	17.1	15.2	26.3
2010	2,967	2,026	13.8	623	287	11.9	10.7	16.3	15.5	26.6
2011	2,950	2,046	13.8	604	268	11.7	11.2	20.7	12.0	26.1
2012	2,969	2,063	14.8	601	269	11.7	11.3	19.3	11.9	25.3
2013	2,988	2,074	15.2	603	275	11.7	11.2	17.5	11.7	26.0

[1] FHWA updated table VM-1 from 2000 to 2013 using an enhanced methodology implemented in March 2011. Prior to 2000, "Light Duty Vehicles Short WB" were categorized as "Cars"; and "Light Duty Vehicles Long WB" were categorized as "Vans, pickups, sport utility vehicles." [2] Motorcycles included with "Cars" through 1994; thereafter in total, not shown separately. [3] Light Duty Vehicles Short WB—passenger cars, light trucks, vans and sport utility vehicles with a wheelbase (WB) equal to or less than 121 inches. Light Duty Vehicles Long WB—large passenger cars, vans, pickup trucks, and sport/utility vehicles with WB larger than 121 inches. [4] Includes school buses. [5] Includes combination trucks. [6] 2000 to 2013: Single-Unit—single frame trucks that have 2-axles and at least 6 tires or a gross vehicle weight rating exceeding 10,000 lbs.

Source: U.S. Federal Highway Administration, "Highway Statistics 2013," and earlier reports, <http://www.fhwa.dot.gov/policyinformation/statistics.cfm>, accessed April 2015.

Table 1109. Domestic Motor Fuel Consumption by Type of Vehicle: 1970 to 2013

[Consumption in billions (92.3 represents 92,300,000,000 gallons). See Table 1108. Comprises all fuel types used for propulsion of vehicles under state motor fuels laws. Excludes federal purchases for military use. Minus sign (-) indicates decrease]

Year	Annual fuel consumption (bil. gal.)[1]						Average miles per gallon[1]				
	All vehicles[2]	Annual percent change[3]	Light duty vehicle short WB[2,4]	Buses[5]	Light duty vehicle long WB[4]	Trucks[6,7]	All vehicles[2]	Light duty vehicle short WB[2,4]	Buses[5]	Light duty vehicle long WB[4]	Trucks[6,7]
1970	92.3	4.8	67.8	0.8	12.3	11.3	12.0	13.5	5.5	10.0	5.5
1980	115.0	-5.9	70.2	1.0	23.8	20.0	13.3	16.0	6.0	12.2	5.4
1990	130.8	-0.8	69.8	0.9	35.6	24.5	16.4	20.3	6.4	16.1	6.0
1995	143.8	2.1	68.1	1.0	45.6	29.0	16.8	21.1	6.6	17.3	6.1
1996	147.4	2.5	69.2	1.0	47.4	29.6	16.9	21.2	6.6	17.2	6.2
1997	150.4	2.0	69.9	1.0	49.4	29.9	17.0	21.5	6.7	17.2	6.4
1998	155.4	3.3	71.7	1.1	50.5	32.0	16.9	21.6	6.7	17.2	6.1
1999	161.4	3.9	73.2	1.1	52.8	33.9	16.7	21.4	6.7	17.0	6.0
2000	162.5	0.7	88.9	2.2	28.9	42.0	16.9	22.1	6.7	17.0	6.2
2001	163.5	0.6	87.8	1.9	30.1	43.0	17.1	22.6	6.8	17.0	6.3
2002	168.7	3.2	91.5	1.9	30.8	43.3	17.0	22.3	6.9	16.9	6.4
2003	170.0	0.8	91.6	1.9	31.3	44.8	17.0	22.4	7.1	16.9	6.4
2004	173.5	2.1	93.4	1.9	33.8	44.4	17.1	22.3	7.1	16.9	6.4
2005	174.8	0.7	93.2	1.9	34.4	44.5	17.2	22.5	7.1	16.9	6.4
2006	175.0	0.1	88.6	2.0	37.0	46.4	17.2	23.1	7.1	17.1	6.5
2007	176.2	0.7	89.6	2.0	36.9	47.2	17.2	22.9	7.2	17.1	6.4
2008	170.8	-3.1	85.6	2.1	34.9	47.7	17.4	23.7	7.2	17.3	6.5
2009	168.1	-1.6	85.7	2.0	35.7	44.3	17.6	23.5	7.2	17.3	6.5
2010	170.4	1.4	86.8	1.9	36.3	45.0	17.4	23.3	7.2	17.2	6.4
2011	168.5	-1.1	88.4	1.9	35.3	42.4	17.5	23.2	7.1	17.1	6.3
2012	168.6	0.1	88.6	2.1	35.1	42.4	17.6	23.3	7.2	17.1	6.4
2013	169.7	0.6	88.6	2.1	35.2	43.3	17.6	23.4	7.2	17.2	6.4

[1] See footnote 1, Table 1108. [2] Motorcycles included with "Cars" through 1994; thereafter in total, not shown separately. [3] Change from immediate prior year. [4] Light Duty Vehicles Short WB—passenger cars, light trucks, vans and sport utility vehicles with a wheelbase (WB) equal to or less than 121 inches. Light Duty Vehicles Long WB—large passenger cars, vans, pickup trucks, and sport/utility vehicles with (WB) larger than 121 inches. [5] Includes school buses. [6] Includes combination trucks. [7] Beginning 2000: Single-Unit—single frame trucks that have 2-axles and at least 6 tires or a gross vehicle weight rating over 10,000 lbs.

Source: U.S. Federal Highway Administration, "Highway Statistics 2013," and earlier reports, <http://www.fhwa.dot.gov/policyinformation/statistics.cfm>, accessed April 2015.

Table 1110. Traffic Fatalities—Number and Rate by State: 2000 to 2013

[For deaths within 30 days of the accident]

State	2000	2010	2012	2013	Fatality rate [1] 2010	Fatality rate [1] 2013	State	2000	2010	2012	2013	Fatality rate [1] 2010	Fatality rate [1] 2013
U.S.	41,945	32,999	33,561	32,719	1.11	1.09	MO	1,157	821	826	757	1.16	1.09
AL	996	862	865	852	1.34	1.31	MT	237	189	205	229	1.69	1.90
AK	106	56	59	51	1.17	1.05	NE	276	190	212	211	0.98	1.09
AZ	1,036	759	825	849	1.27	1.40	NV	323	257	258	262	1.16	1.06
AR	652	571	552	483	1.70	1.44	NH	126	128	108	135	0.98	1.05
CA	3,753	2,720	2,857	3,000	0.84	0.91	NJ	731	556	589	542	0.76	0.73
CO	681	450	472	481	0.96	1.02	NM	432	349	365	310	1.38	1.24
CT	341	320	236	276	1.02	0.89	NY	1,460	1,201	1,168	1,199	0.92	0.92
DE	123	101	114	99	1.13	1.06	NC	1,557	1,320	1,292	1,289	1.29	1.23
DC	48	24	15	20	0.67	0.57	ND	86	105	170	148	1.27	1.47
FL	2,999	2,444	2,424	2,407	1.25	1.25	OH	1,366	1,080	1,123	989	0.97	0.88
GA	1,541	1,247	1,192	1,179	1.12	1.08	OK	650	668	708	678	1.40	1.41
HI	132	113	126	102	1.13	1.01	OR	451	317	336	313	0.94	0.93
ID	276	209	184	214	1.32	1.34	PA	1,520	1,324	1,310	1,208	1.32	1.22
IL	1,418	927	956	991	0.88	0.94	RI	80	67	64	65	0.81	0.84
IN	886	754	779	783	1.00	1.00	SC	1,065	809	863	767	1.65	1.57
IA	445	390	365	317	1.24	1.00	SD	173	140	133	135	1.58	1.48
KS	461	431	405	350	1.44	1.16	TN	1,307	1,032	1,014	995	1.47	1.40
KY	820	760	746	638	1.58	1.36	TX	3,779	3,023	3,398	3,382	1.29	1.38
LA	938	721	722	703	1.59	1.47	UT	373	253	217	220	0.95	0.81
ME	169	161	164	145	1.11	1.03	VT	76	71	77	69	0.98	0.97
MD	588	496	505	465	0.88	0.82	VA	929	740	777	740	0.90	0.92
MA	433	347	349	326	0.64	0.58	WA	631	460	444	436	0.80	0.76
MI	1,382	942	938	947	0.97	1.00	WV	411	315	339	332	1.64	1.73
MN	625	411	395	387	0.73	0.68	WI	799	572	615	543	0.96	0.91
MS	949	641	582	613	1.61	1.58	WY	152	155	123	87	1.66	0.93

[1] Deaths per 100 million vehicle miles traveled.

Source: U.S. National Highway Traffic Safety Administration, *Traffic Safety Facts 2013*, DOT-HS-812-139, 2015. See also <http://www.nhtsa.gov/NCSA>.

Table 1111. Motor Vehicle Occupants and Nonoccupants Killed and Injured: 1990 to 2013

[Injuries in thousands (3,231 represents 3,231,000). For deaths within 30 days of the accident]

Year	Total	Occupants Total	Passenger cars	Light trucks [1]	Large trucks [1]	Buses	Other/unknown [2]	Motorcycle occupants [3]	Nonoccupants Total	Pedestrian	Pedal-cyclist	Other/unknown [2]
KILLED												
1990	44,599	33,890	24,092	8,601	705	32	460	3,244	7,465	6,482	859	124
2000	41,945	33,451	20,699	11,526	754	22	450	2,897	5,597	4,763	693	141
2001	42,196	33,243	20,320	11,723	708	34	458	3,197	5,756	4,901	732	123
2002	43,005	34,105	20,569	12,274	689	45	528	3,270	5,630	4,851	665	114
2003	42,884	33,627	19,725	12,546	726	41	589	3,714	5,543	4,774	629	140
2004	42,836	33,276	19,192	12,674	766	42	602	4,028	5,532	4,675	727	130
2005	43,510	33,070	18,512	13,037	804	58	659	4,576	5,864	4,892	786	186
2006	42,708	32,119	17,925	12,761	805	27	601	4,837	5,752	4,795	772	185
2007	41,259	30,527	16,614	12,458	805	36	614	5,174	5,558	4,699	701	158
2008	37,423	26,791	14,646	10,816	682	67	580	5,312	5,320	4,414	718	188
2009	33,883	24,526	13,135	10,312	499	26	554	4,469	4,888	4,109	628	151
2010	32,999	23,371	12,491	9,782	530	44	524	4,518	5,110	4,302	623	185
2011	32,479	22,510	12,014	9,302	640	55	499	4,630	5,339	4,457	682	200
2012	33,782	23,017	12,361	9,418	697	39	502	4,986	5,779	4,818	734	227
2013	32,719	22,383	11,977	9,155	691	48	512	4,668	5,668	4,735	743	190
INJURED (1,000)												
1990	3,231	2,960	2,376	505	42	33	4	84	187	105	75	7
2000	3,189	2,997	2,052	887	31	18	10	58	134	78	51	5
2001	3,033	2,841	1,927	861	29	15	9	60	131	78	45	8
2002	2,926	2,735	1,805	879	26	19	6	65	126	71	48	7
2003	2,889	2,697	1,756	889	27	18	7	67	124	70	46	8
2004	2,788	2,594	1,643	900	27	16	7	76	118	68	41	9
2005	2,699	2,494	1,573	872	27	11	10	87	118	64	45	8
2006	2,575	2,375	1,475	857	23	10	11	88	112	61	44	7
2007	2,491	2,264	1,379	841	23	12	8	103	124	70	43	10
2008	2,346	2,120	1,304	768	23	15	9	96	130	69	52	9
2009	2,217	2,011	1,216	759	17	12	7	90	116	59	51	7
2010	2,239	2,027	1,253	733	20	17	5	82	130	70	52	8
2011	2,217	2,010	1,240	728	23	13	6	81	126	69	48	9
2012	2,362	2,134	1,328	762	25	12	6	93	136	76	49	10
2013	2,313	2,099	1,296	750	24	23	5	88	125	66	48	11

[1] See footnotes 2 and 3, Table 1113. [2] Includes combination trucks. [3] Includes mopeds, three wheel motorcycles, off-road motorcycles, etc.

Source: U.S. National Highway Traffic Safety Administration, *Traffic Safety Facts 2013*, DOT-HS-812-139, 2015. See also <http://www.nhtsa.gov/NCSA>.

Table 1112. Fatal Motor Vehicle Accidents—National Summary: 2000 to 2013

[Based on data from the Fatality Analysis Reporting System (FARS). FARS gathers data on accidents that result in loss of human life. FARS is operated and maintained by National Highway Traffic Safety Administration's (NHTSA), National Center for Statistics and Analysis (NCSA). FARS data are gathered on motor vehicle accidents that occurred on a roadway customarily open to the public, resulting in the death of a person within 30 days of the accident. Collection of these data depend on the use of police, hospital, medical examiner/coroner, and Emergency Medical Services reports; state vehicle registration, driver licensing, and highway department files; and vital statistics documents and death certificates. See source for further detail]

Item	2000	2005	2008	2009	2010	2011	2012	2013
Fatal crashes, total..................................	**37,526**	**39,252**	**34,172**	**30,862**	**30,296**	**29,867**	**31,006**	**30,057**
One vehicle involved................................	21,117	22,678	20,644	18,745	18,156	17,991	18,705	18,074
Two or more vehicles involved..................	16,409	16,574	13,528	12,052	12,040	11,766	12,095	11,983
Persons killed in fatal crashes [1]...............	**41,945**	**43,510**	**37,423**	**33,883**	**32,999**	**32,479**	**33,782**	**32,719**
Occupants..	33,451	33,070	26,791	24,526	23,371	22,510	23,017	22,383
Drivers..	22,914	23,237	19,279	17,670	16,864	16,474	16,838	16,472
Passengers.......................................	10,451	9,750	7,441	6,793	6,451	5,972	6,106	5,844
Other..	86	83	71	63	56	64	73	67
Motorcyclists.....................................	2,897	4,576	5,312	4,469	4,518	4,630	4,986	4,668
Nonoccupants......................................	5,597	5,864	5,320	4,888	5,110	5,339	5,779	5,668
Pedestrians.......................................	4,763	4,892	4,414	4,109	4,302	4,457	4,818	4,735
Pedalcyclists.....................................	693	786	718	628	623	682	734	743
Other..	141	186	188	151	185	200	227	190
Occupants killed by vehicle type:								
Passenger cars...................................	20,699	18,512	14,646	13,135	12,491	12,014	12,361	11,977
Mini-compact (95 inches)......................	1,113	452	270	212	171	185	188	159
Subcompact (95 to 99 inches)................	3,660	2,536	1,667	1,333	1,252	1,166	1,156	1,047
Compact (100 to 104 inches).................	7,022	6,288	4,780	4,128	3,954	3,789	3,834	3,610
Intermediate (105 to 109) inches............	5,204	5,571	4,763	4,393	4,227	4,050	4,050	4,083
Full-size (110 to 114) inches.................	2,287	2,491	2,210	2,175	1,982	1,958	2,098	2,108
Largest (115 inches and over)...............	897	796	755	674	681	669	751	722
Unknown..	516	378	201	180	168	164	194	248
Motorcycles and other motorized cycles......	2,897	4,576	5,312	4,469	4,518	4,630	4,957	4,668
Motorcycles......................................	2,783	4,418	5,060	4,222	4,266	4,343	4,623	4,336
Other motorized cycles........................	114	158	252	240	236	269	334	332
Light trucks [2]......................................	11,526	13,037	10,816	10,312	9,782	9,302	9,418	9,155
Pickup..	6,003	6,067	5,097	4,801	4,486	4,270	4,343	4,171
Utility...	3,358	4,831	4,214	4,104	3,942	3,884	3,885	3,811
Van..	2,129	2,112	1,492	1,396	1,346	1,128	1,167	1,136
Other..	36	27	13	11	8	20	23	37
Large trucks [3].....................................	754	804	682	499	530	635	697	691
Medium trucks..................................	106	118	91	81	79	96	121	48
Heavy trucks....................................	648	686	592	422	447	539	576	520
Buses..	22	58	67	26	44	54	39	48
Other vehicles....................................	401	492	523	481	451	427	431	456
Unknown..	49	167	57	82	92	79	78	56
Persons involved in fatal crashes............	**100,716**	**101,262**	**84,510**	**76,309**	**(NA)**	**(NA)**	**(NA)**	**(NA)**
Occupants..	94,325	94,614	78,500	70,845	68,927	67,143	69,531	67,514
Drivers..	57,280	59,220	50,416	45,337	44,599	43,840	45,664	44,574
Passengers.......................................	36,889	35,231	27,924	25,470	(NA)	(NA)	(NA)	(NA)
Other..	156	163	160	145	(NA)	(NA)	(NA)	(NA)
Nonoccupants......................................	6,391	6,648	6,010	5,464	(NA)	(NA)	(NA)	(NA)
Vehicle miles traveled (VMT) (bil.) [4]............	2,747	2,989	2,977	2,957	2,967	2,950	2,970	2,988
Licensed drivers (1,000).........................	190,625	200,549	208,321	209,618	210,115	211,875	211,815	212,160
Registered vehicles (1,000) [5]..................	217,993	247,031	259,360	258,958	257,312	265,043	265,647	269,294
Percent distribution of fatal accidents by the highest driver BAC in accident: [6]								
0.00 percent.....................................	62.7	63.3	63.1	62.3	64.0	64.0	64.0	63.0
0.01 to 0.07 percent............................	5.6	5.4	5.6	5.6	5.0	5.0	5.0	6.0
0.08 percent and over..........................	31.4	31.1	31.1	31.9	31.0	30.0	31.0	31.0
Percent distribution of fatal accidents by the highest BAC in accident: [6]								
0.00 percent.....................................	58.7	59.5	58.6	58.0	(NA)	(NA)	(NA)	(NA)
0.01 to 0.07 percent............................	5.9	5.6	5.8	5.7	(NA)	(NA)	(NA)	(NA)
0.08 percent and over..........................	35.4	34.9	35.5	36.3	(NA)	(NA)	(NA)	(NA)
Fatalities per 100,000 resident population								
Under 5 years old...............................	3.70	2.94	1.95	2.02	1.99	1.79	2.03	1.99
5 to 9 years old.................................	3.55	3.00	1.95	1.84	1.73	1.69	1.68	1.66
10 to 15 years old...............................	5.65	4.67	3.41	3.02	2.70	2.56	2.47	2.35
16 to 20 years old...............................	29.38	27.48	20.78	18.08	15.45	15.44	14.82	13.79
21 to 24 years old...............................	27.02	27.73	23.25	19.11	19.43	18.69	19.05	18.06
25 to 34 years old...............................	17.29	17.82	15.66	13.69	13.43	13.15	13.95	13.39
35 to 44 years old...............................	15.08	15.08	12.88	11.62	11.07	10.64	11.19	10.82
45 to 54 years old...............................	13.79	14.59	13.07	12.10	11.28	11.35	11.71	11.31
55 to 64 years old...............................	13.61	13.88	12.03	10.87	10.90	10.45	11.14	11.03
65 to 74 years old...............................	15.29	15.16	12.26	11.42	10.89	11.26	11.22	10.87
75 years old and over...........................	23.29	20.47	16.56	15.52	16.70	15.18	14.97	15.04
Fatalities per 100 million VMT [4]................	1.53	1.46	1.26	1.15	1.11	1.10	1.14	1.09
Fatalities per 100,000 licensed drivers..........	22.00	21.70	17.96	16.16	15.71	15.33	15.95	15.42
VMT per registered vehicle [4].....................	12,657	12,169	11,478	11,419	11,531	11,130	11,176	11,096
Fatalities per 100,000 registered vehicles.......	19.33	17.71	14.43	13.08	12.82	12.25	12.72	12.15
Fatal crashes per 100 million VMT [4]............	1.37	1.31	1.15	1.04	1.02	1.01	1.04	1.01
Fatalities per 100,000 resident population.......	14.87	14.72	12.31	11.05	10.67	10.42	10.76	10.35

NA Not available. [1] Deaths within 30 days of the accident. Starting with 1995, total does not include motorcyclist data. [2] Trucks with a gross vehicle weight rating of 10,000 pounds or less, including pickups, vans, truck-based station wagons, and utility vehicles. [3] Trucks with a gross vehicle weight rating of over 10,000 pounds. [4] VMT = vehicle miles of travel. [5] Data on motor vehicle registrations for 2011 and beyond are not strictly comparable to data for prior years due to methodology changes. See source for details. [6] BAC = blood alcohol concentration.

Source: National Highway Traffic Safety Administration, *Traffic Safety Facts, 2013*, and earlier reports; and "Fatality Analysis Reporting System," <http://www.nhtsa.gov/FARS>, accessed July 2015.

Table 1113. Vehicles Involved in Crashes by Vehicle Type, Rollover Occurrence, and Crash Severity: 2013

[Excludes motorcycles]

Crash severity by vehicle type	Total Number	Rollover occurrence			
		Yes		No	
		Number	Percent	Number	Percent
Vehicles involved in all crashes [1]..................	**9,958,000**	**201,000**	**2.0**	**9,757,000**	**98.0**
Passenger cars.........................	5,669,000	75,000	1.3	5,594,000	98.7
Light trucks: [2]					
Pickup..................................	1,374,000	42,000	3.1	1,331,000	96.9
Utility....................................	1,883,000	60,000	3.2	1,823,000	96.8
Van......................................	604,000	8,000	1.3	596,000	98.7
Other....................................	7,000	(Z)	5.8	7,000	94.2
Large truck [3].........................	342,000	12,000	3.5	330,000	96.5
Bus......................................	67,000	(Z)	0.2	66,000	99.8
Other/unknown.......................	11,000	3,000	23.3	9,000	76.7
Fatal crashes.............................	**40,094**	**7,667**	**19.1**	**32,427**	**80.9**
Passenger cars.........................	17,834	2,644	14.8	15,190	85.2
Light trucks: [2]					
Pickup..................................	7,843	1,997	25.5	5,846	74.5
Utility....................................	6,795	1,930	28.4	4,865	71.6
Van......................................	2,121	311	14.7	1,810	85.3
Other....................................	98	13	13.3	85	86.7
Large truck [3].........................	3,906	517	13.2	3,389	86.8
Bus......................................	280	13	4.6	267	95.4
Other/unknown.......................	1,217	242	19.9	975	80.1

Z less than 500 or 0.05 percent. [1] Includes injury and property-only crashes, not shown separately. [2] Trucks of 10,000 pounds gross vehicle weight rating or less, including pickups, vans, truck-based station wagons and utility vehicles. [3] Trucks over 10,000 pounds gross vehicle weight rating.

Source: U.S. National Highway Traffic Safety Administration, *Traffic Safety Facts 2013*, DOT-HS-812-139, 2015. See also <http://www.nhtsa.gov/NCSA>.

Table 1114. Distracted Drivers—Crashes, Road Fatalities, and Injuries: 2005 to 2013

["Distraction" is defined as a specific type of inattention that occurs when drivers divert their attention from the driving task to focus on some other activity instead. "Distraction" is a subset of "inattention" (which also includes fatigue, and physical and emotional conditions of the driver). For more information, including revision in coding of "distracted driving," see appendix in source report]

Description	2005	2008	2009	2010	2011	2012	2013
FATAL CRASHES [1]							
Total..................................	**39,252**	**34,172**	**30,797**	**30,196**	**29,757**	**30,800**	**30,057**
Drivers involved................................	59,220	50,416	45,230	44,440	43,668	45,337	44,574
Fatalities..	43,510	37,423	33,808	32,885	32,367	33,561	32,719
Crashes involving driver distraction: [2]........	4,026	5,307	4,898	2,843	3,020	3,050	2,910
Percent........................	10	16	16	9	10	10	10
Drivers involved.............................	4,217	5,477	5,084	2,912	3,085	3,119	2,959
Percent........................	7	11	11	7	7	7	7
Fatalities..	4,472	5,838	5,474	3,092	3,331	3,328	3,154
Percent........................	10	16	16	9	10	10	10
PEOPLE INJURED IN CRASHES: [3]							
Total..................................	**2,699,000**	**2,346,000**	**2,217,000**	**2,239,000**	**2,217,000**	**2,362,000**	**2,313,000**
Involving driver distraction:							
Estimate.......................................	604,000	466,000	448,000	416,000	387,000	421,000	424,000
Percent of total...........................	22	20	20	19	17	18	18

[1] Source: NHTSA's Fatality Analysis Reporting System (FARS). [2] For multi-vehicle crashes, the crash was reported as a distracted-driving crash if at least one driver was reported as distracted. In some of these multi-vehicle crashes, multiple drivers were reported as distracted. [3] Source: National Automotive Sampling System (NASS) General Estimates System (GES).

Source: U.S. National Highway Traffic Safety Administration, *Distracted Driving 2013*, April 2015, and earlier reports. See also <http://www-nrd.nhtsa.dot.gov/CATS/index.aspx> and <www.distraction.gov>.

Table 1115. Traffic Fatalities by State and Highest Driver Blood Alcohol Concentration (BAC) in the Crash: 2013

[See headnote, Table 1117. A positive blood alcohol concentration (BAC level .01 g/dL and higher) indicates that alcohol was consumed by the person tested, and the incident is alcohol related or alcohol involved; a BAC level of .08 g/dL or more indicates that the person was alcohol impaired]

State	Traffic fatalities, total [1]	(BAC=.00)		Alcohol involved driving fatalities (BAC=.01–.07)		Alcohol impaired driving fatalities (BAC=.08 or more)		Total fatalities involving alcohol (BAC=.01 or more)	
		Number	Percent	Number	Percent	Number	Percent	Number	Percent
United States......	**32,719**	**20,713**	**63**	**1,820**	**6**	**10,076**	**31**	**11,896**	**36**
Alabama...............	852	543	64	48	6	260	31	308	36
Alaska.................	51	34	66	1	3	15	30	16	32
Arizona...............	849	574	68	43	5	219	26	262	31
Arkansas.............	483	324	67	34	7	123	25	156	32
California.............	3,000	1,963	65	158	5	867	29	1,025	34
Colorado..............	481	309	64	28	6	142	30	170	35
Connecticut...........	276	145	52	17	6	114	41	132	48
Delaware..............	99	57	57	4	4	38	39	43	43
District of Columbia...	20	13	67	0	2	6	31	7	33
Florida.................	2,407	1,607	67	115	5	676	28	790	33
Georgia...............	1,179	824	70	52	4	297	25	349	30
Hawaii.................	102	57	56	12	12	33	33	45	44
Idaho..................	214	138	64	15	7	58	27	73	34
Illinois.................	991	601	61	67	7	322	32	389	39
Indiana................	783	541	69	43	6	198	25	241	31
Iowa...................	317	204	64	10	3	103	32	113	36
Kansas................	350	230	66	18	5	102	29	119	34
Kentucky..............	638	444	70	26	4	167	26	193	30
Louisiana.............	703	427	61	39	5	234	33	272	39
Maine..................	145	91	63	12	8	42	29	54	37
Maryland..............	465	289	62	34	7	141	30	175	38
Massachusetts........	326	179	55	24	7	118	36	142	44
Michigan..............	947	638	67	54	6	255	27	309	33
Minnesota............	387	272	70	20	5	95	25	115	30
Mississippi............	613	372	61	30	5	210	34	240	39
Missouri...............	757	468	62	39	5	248	33	287	38
Montana...............	229	125	55	12	5	92	40	104	45
Nebraska..............	211	136	65	10	5	60	28	70	33
Nevada................	262	168	64	15	6	79	30	94	36
New Hampshire.......	135	83	61	7	5	46	34	52	39
New Jersey...........	542	358	66	38	7	146	27	184	34
New Mexico...........	310	192	62	25	8	93	30	118	38
New York..............	1,199	756	63	78	6	364	30	442	37
North Carolina........	1,289	858	67	57	4	371	29	428	33
North Dakota.........	148	73	49	12	8	62	42	73	49
Ohio...................	989	664	67	51	5	271	27	322	33
Oklahoma.............	678	472	70	37	5	170	25	206	30
Oregon................	313	189	61	17	5	105	33	122	39
Pennsylvania.........	1,208	774	64	64	5	368	30	431	36
Rhode Island.........	65	37	57	4	6	24	38	28	43
South Carolina.......	767	379	49	49	6	335	44	384	50
South Dakota.........	135	85	63	7	5	41	31	48	36
Tennessee............	995	666	67	51	5	277	28	327	33
Texas.................	3,382	1,829	54	213	6	1,337	40	1,550	46
Utah...................	220	175	79	6	3	38	17	44	20
Vermont...............	69	45	66	5	8	18	27	24	34
Virginia................	740	435	59	48	6	254	34	302	41
Washington...........	436	267	61	20	4	149	34	169	39
West Virginia.........	332	220	66	21	6	91	27	112	34
Wisconsin.............	543	329	61	32	6	178	33	210	39
Wyoming..............	87	58	67	4	5	25	29	29	33
Puerto Rico...........	344	185	54	31	9	127	37	158	46

[1] Total fatalities include those in which there was no driver or motorcycle rider present.

Source: U.S. National Highway Traffic Safety Administration, *Traffic Safety Facts 2013*, DOT-HS-812-139, 2015. See also <http://www.nhtsa.gov/NCSA>.

Table 1116. Alcohol Involvement for Drivers in Fatal Crashes: 2000 to 2013

[BAC = blood alcohol concentration. NHTSA estimates alcohol involvement when alcohol test results are unknown, see source for more information]

Age, sex, and vehicle type	2000 Total drivers in fatal crashes	2000 Percent with .08% BAC or greater	2010 Total drivers in fatal crashes	2010 Percent with .08% BAC or greater	2011 Total drivers in fatal crashes	2011 Percent with .08% BAC or greater	2012 Total drivers in fatal crashes	2012 Percent with .08% BAC or greater	2013 Total drivers in fatal crashes	2013 Percent with .08% BAC or greater
Total drivers involved in fatal crashes [1]	**57,280**	**21**	**44,599**	**22**	**43,840**	**21**	**45,664**	**21**	**44,574**	**21**
Drivers by age group:										
Under 16 years old	320	10	159	6	115	8	121	8	139	8
16 to 20 years old	8,024	18	4,505	18	4,307	20	4,241	18	3,883	17
21 to 24 years old	5,950	32	4,608	34	4,488	32	4,765	32	4,609	33
25 to 34 years old	11,739	28	8,567	30	8,549	30	9,019	29	8,762	29
35 to 44 years old	11,132	26	7,333	25	7,084	24	7,365	24	7,183	24
45 to 54 years old	8,234	18	7,517	21	7,513	21	7,660	21	7,343	20
55 to 64 years old	4,766	12	5,577	14	5,572	14	5,930	13	5,911	14
65 to 74 years old	3,134	8	2,902	8	2,960	8	3,239	8	3,357	8
75 years old and over	3,147	4	2,688	4	2,528	5	2,554	5	2,567	5
Drivers by sex:										
Male	41,795	24	32,079	24	31,918	24	33,351	24	32,442	23
Female	14,790	13	11,859	15	11,265	14	11,604	14	11,364	15
Drivers by vehicle type:										
Passenger cars	27,661	24	17,710	24	17,401	24	18,171	23	17,731	23
Light trucks [2]	20,393	22	17,385	22	16,706	21	17,230	21	16,738	21
Large trucks [3]	4,948	1	3,456	1	3,594	1	3,774	2	3,858	2
Motorcycles	2,971	32	4,647	28	4,761	29	5,108	28	4,769	27

[1] Includes age and sex unknown, and other and unknown types of vehicles. [2] See footnote 2, Table 1113. [3] See footnote 3, Table 1113.

Source: U.S. National Highway Traffic Safety Administration, *Traffic Safety Facts 2013*, DOT-HS-812-139, 2015, and earlier reports. See also <http://www.nhtsa.gov/NCSA>.

Table 1117. Fatalities by Highest Driver Blood Alcohol Concentration (BAC) in the Crash: 1990 to 2013

[A motor vehicle crash is alcohol impaired if at least one driver involved in the crash is determined to have a BAC of .08 gram per deciliter (g/dl) or higher. Thus, any fatality that occurs in an alcohol impaired crash is considered an alcohol impaired driving fatality. A person is considered to be legally impaired with a BAC of .08 g/dl or more. See source for more information]

Item	1990	2000	2005	2009	2010	2011	2012	2013
Total fatalities [1]	**44,599**	**41,945**	**43,510**	**33,883**	**32,999**	**32,479**	**33,782**	**32,719**
BAC=.00								
Number	23,823	26,082	27,423	21,051	21,005	20,848	21,563	20,713
Percent	53.4	62.2	63.0	62.1	63.7	64.2	63.8	63.3
BAC=.01–.07								
Number	2,901	2,422	2,404	1,972	1,771	1,662	1,782	1,820
Percent	6.5	5.8	5.5	5.8	5.4	5.1	5.3	5.6
Alcohol impaired driving fatalities: BAC=.08 or more								
Number	17,705	13,324	13,582	10,759	10,136	9,865	10,336	10,076
Percent	39.7	31.8	31.2	31.8	30.7	30.4	30.6	30.8

[1] Total fatalities include those in which there was no driver or motorcycle rider present.

Source: U.S. National Highway Traffic Safety Administration, *Traffic Safety Facts 2013*, DOT-HS-812-139, 2015. See also <http://www.nhtsa.gov/NCSA>.

Table 1118. Crashes by Crash Severity: 2000 to 2013

[6,394 represents 6,394,000. A crash is a police-reported event that produces injury and/or property damage, involves a vehicle in transport and occurs on a trafficway or while the vehicle is in motion after running off the trafficway. A fatal crash involves at least 1 person dying within 30 days of the crash]

Item	2000	2005	2007	2008	2009	2010	2011	2012	2013
Crashes (1,000)	**6,394**	**6,159**	**6,024**	**5,811**	**5,505**	**5,419**	**5,338**	**5,615**	**5,687**
Fatal	37.5	39.3	37.4	34.2	30.8	30.3	29.9	31.0	30.1
Nonfatal injury	2,070	1,816	1,711	1,630	1,517	1,542	1,530	1,634	1,591
Property damage only	4,286	4,304	4,275	4,146	3,957	3,847	3,778	3,950	4,066
Percent of total crashes:									
Fatal	0.6	0.6	0.6	0.6	0.6	0.6	0.6	0.6	0.5
Nonfatal injury	32.4	29.5	28.4	28.1	27.6	28.5	28.7	29.1	28.0
Property damage only	67.0	69.9	71.0	71.4	71.9	71.0	70.8	70.3	71.5

Source: U.S. National Highway Traffic Safety Administration, *Traffic Safety Facts 2013*, DOT-HS-812-139, 2015. See also <http://www.nhtsa.gov/NCSA>.

Table 1119. Motor Vehicle Crashes—Number and Deaths: 2000 to 2013

[6,394 represents 6,394,000]

Item	Unit	2000	2005	2008	2009	2010	2011	2012	2013
CRASHES									
Total [1]	**1,000**	**6,394**	**6,159**	**5,811**	**5,505**	**5,419**	**5,338**	**5,615**	**5,687**
Fatal	1,000	38	39	34	31	30	30	31	30
Injury	1,000	2,070	1,816	1,630	1,517	1,542	1,530	1,634	1,591
Property Damage Only	1,000	4,286	4,304	4,146	3,957	3,847	3,778	3,950	4,066
DEATHS									
Deaths within 30 days of crash	**1,000**	**41.9**	**43.5**	**37.4**	**33.9**	**33.0**	**32.5**	**33.8**	**32.7**
Occupants	1,000	33.5	33.1	26.8	24.5	23.4	22.5	23.0	22.4
Passenger cars	1,000	20.7	18.5	14.6	13.1	12.5	12.0	12.4	12.0
Light trucks [2]	1,000	11.5	13.0	10.8	10.3	9.8	9.3	9.4	9.2
Large trucks [2]	1,000	0.8	0.8	0.7	0.5	0.5	0.6	0.7	0.7
Buses	1,000	(Z)	0.1	0.1	(Z)	(Z)	0.1	(Z)	(Z)
Other/unknown	1,000	0.5	0.7	0.6	0.6	0.5	0.5	0.5	0.5
Motorcycle riders [3]	1,000	2.9	4.6	5.3	4.5	4.5	4.6	5.0	4.7
Nonoccupants	1,000	5.6	5.9	5.3	4.9	5.1	5.3	5.8	5.7
Pedestrians	1,000	4.8	4.9	4.4	4.1	4.3	4.5	4.8	4.7
Pedalcyclist	1,000	0.7	0.8	0.7	0.6	0.6	0.7	0.7	0.7
Other/unknown	1,000	0.1	0.2	0.2	0.2	0.2	0.2	0.2	0.2
TRAFFIC DEATH RATES [4]									
Per 100 million vehicle miles	Rate	1.5	1.5	1.3	1.2	1.1	1.1	1.1	1.1
Per 100,000 licensed drivers	Rate	22.0	21.7	18.0	16.2	15.7	15.3	16.0	15.4
Per 100,000 registered vehicles	Rate	19.3	17.7	14.4	13.1	12.8	12.3	12.7	12.2
Per 100,000 resident population	Rate	14.9	14.7	12.3	11.1	10.7	10.4	10.8	10.4

(Z) Represents less than 50 deaths. [1] Covers police-reported accidents in which at least one person dies within 30 days of the crash; or no one dies but at least one person is injured; or no one is injured but property damage has occurred. [2] See footnotes 2 and 3 in Table 1113. [3] Includes motor scooters, minibikes, and mopeds. [4] Based on 30-day definition of traffic deaths.

Source: U.S. National Highway Traffic Safety Administration, *Traffic Safety Facts, 2013*, DOT-HS-812-139, 2015. See also <http://www.nhtsa.gov/NCSA>.

Table 1120. Licensed Drivers and Number in Fatal Accidents by Age and Sex: 2013

[105,008 represents 105,008,000]

Age group	Licensed drivers (1,000)			Drivers in fatal accidents			Accident rates per number of drivers [2]	
	Male	Female	Both sexes	Male	Female	Both sexes [1]	Male	Female
Total	**105,008**	**107,152**	**212,160**	**32,442**	**11,364**	**44,574**	**30.9**	**10.6**
19 years old and under	4,598	4,384	8,982	2,014	879	2,895	43.8	20.1
Under 16 years old	31	31	62	102	37	139	323.9	119.9
16 years old	584	584	1,169	221	123	345	37.8	21.1
17 years old	1,024	987	2,010	376	172	549	36.7	17.4
18 years old	1,381	1,299	2,680	613	264	877	44.4	20.3
19 years old	1,578	1,484	3,061	702	283	985	44.5	19.1
20 to 24 years old	8,945	8,723	17,668	4,263	1,472	5,736	47.7	16.9
20 years old	1,690	1,605	3,294	837	290	1,127	49.5	18.1
21 years old	1,747	1,687	3,435	909	275	1,184	52.0	16.3
22 years old	1,807	1,769	3,576	855	320	1,175	47.3	18.1
23 years old	1,858	1,831	3,689	861	306	1,168	46.3	16.7
24 years old	1,843	1,832	3,675	801	281	1,082	43.5	15.3
25 to 29 years old	9,129	9,213	18,341	3,485	1,203	4,691	38.2	13.1
30 to 34 years old	9,083	9,273	18,357	3,033	1,037	4,071	33.4	11.2
35 to 39 years old	8,567	8,707	17,274	2,619	908	3,527	30.6	10.4
40 to 44 years old	9,333	9,412	18,745	2,741	915	3,656	29.4	9.7
45 to 49 years old	9,621	9,678	19,299	2,745	920	3,665	28.5	9.5
50 to 54 years old	10,207	10,401	20,608	2,824	853	3,678	27.7	8.2
55 to 59 years old	9,564	9,835	19,399	2,594	807	3,401	27.1	8.2
60 to 64 years old	8,179	8,478	16,657	1,896	613	2,510	23.2	7.2
65 to 69 years old	6,494	6,733	13,227	1,473	500	1,973	22.7	7.4
70 to 74 years old	4,533	4,775	9,307	971	413	1,384	21.4	8.6
75 to 79 years old	3,091	3,329	6,420	689	313	1,002	22.3	9.4
80 to 84 years old	2,076	2,323	4,399	578	302	880	27.8	13.0
85 and over	1,588	1,888	3,477	467	218	685	29.4	11.5

[1] Total includes 790 unknown/unreported instances. [2] Per 100,000 male/female licensed drivers. Rates for drivers 19 years old and under are likely overstated because of a higher proportion of unlicensed drivers.

Source: U.S. Federal Highway Administration, "Highway Statistics 2013," <http://www.fhwa.dot.gov/policy/ohpi/hss/index.cfm>; and National Highway Traffic Safety Administration, "Fatality Analysis Reporting System," <http://www.nhtsa.gov/FARS>; accessed September 2015.

Table 1121. Speeding-Related Traffic Fatalities by Road Type and State: 2013

[Speeding consists of exceeding the posted speed limit or driving too fast for the road conditions or any speed-related violation charged (racing, driving above speed limit, speed greater than reasonable, exceeding special speed limit)]

State	Traffic fatalities, total	Speeding-related fatalities by roadway function class							
		Total[2]	Interstate		Non-Interstate				
			Rural	Urban	Freeway and express-way	Other principal arterial	Minor arterial	Collector	Local
United States [1]	**32,719**	**9,613**	**548**	**690**	**316**	**1,982**	**1,709**	**1,937**	**2,370**
Alabama	852	253	12	8	3	43	61	80	43
Alaska	51	22	6	–	3	3	2	4	4
Arizona	849	290	45	20	14	58	44	68	41
Arkansas	483	72	4	5	–	9	8	21	25
California	3,000	961	40	102	104	320	198	123	74
Colorado	481	150	8	19	2	56	31	19	15
Connecticut	276	64	3	2	1	14	14	5	25
Delaware	99	37	–	2	1	11	3	13	6
District of Columbia	20	9	–	3	–	–	–	–	6
Florida	2,407	344	22	21	–	87	15	1	197
Georgia	1,179	197	14	19	2	34	44	35	46
Hawaii	102	44	1	3	6	11	8	7	8
Idaho	214	50	10	–	–	8	7	17	4
Illinois	991	421	27	37	–	98	88	99	72
Indiana	783	217	17	9	–	–	27	39	125
Iowa	317	51	3	4	–	9	8	12	15
Kansas	350	111	4	5	–	30	17	23	32
Kentucky	638	125	7	8	–	18	10	50	32
Louisiana	703	193	5	11	3	27	43	65	38
Maine	145	50	2	1	–	6	7	1	33
Maryland	465	148	–	18	6	35	29	36	23
Massachusetts	326	88	2	9	5	6	27	5	33
Michigan	947	255	9	27	10	53	47	54	54
Minnesota	387	84	5	4	2	20	20	18	15
Mississippi	613	113	13	–	–	20	9	28	43
Missouri	757	308	3	22	12	46	57	86	82
Montana	229	76	15	–	–	15	10	19	16
Nebraska	211	39	2	–	–	12	4	3	17
Nevada	262	87	9	3	2	30	25	5	11
New Hampshire	135	66	–	6	–	8	1	17	34
New Jersey	542	118	2	11	12	25	22	21	25
New Mexico	310	122	13	3	–	54	11	20	19
New York	1,199	358	19	5	6	97	26	13	192
North Carolina	1,289	413	12	13	8	61	137	60	121
North Dakota	148	59	5	–	–	16	11	8	19
Ohio	989	273	11	24	4	41	37	78	78
Oklahoma	678	174	10	10	3	29	31	53	38
Oregon	313	95	3	1	1	24	21	37	8
Pennsylvania	1,208	550	36	20	15	108	124	134	113
Rhode Island	65	17	–	–	–	6	5	–	5
South Carolina	767	306	15	13	–	50	69	105	25
South Dakota	135	38	1	–	–	7	7	10	13
Tennessee	995	236	13	27	1	33	46	73	43
Texas	3,382	1,175	70	137	72	189	142	197	368
Utah	220	75	10	11	–	16	11	–	27
Vermont	69	18	1	2	–	1	2	8	4
Virginia	740	132	9	17	3	22	34	29	14
Washington	436	181	4	12	7	41	37	50	26
West Virginia	332	130	15	5	0	21	32	37	20
Wisconsin	543	178	5	10	8	43	36	37	39
Wyoming	87	40	6	1	–	11	4	14	4
Puerto Rico	344	149	11	4	3	29	55	33	14

– Represents zero. [1] US totals do not include Puerto Rico. [2] Includes fatalities that occurred on roads for which the type was unknown.

Source: U.S. National Highway Traffic Safety Administration, *Traffic Safety Facts 2013*, DOT-HS-812-139, 2015. See also <http://www.nhtsa.gov/NCSA>.

Table 1122. Roadway Traffic Congestion by Urbanized Area: 2014

[15,142 represents 15,142,000. Various federal, state, and local information sources were used to develop the database with the primary source being the Federal Highway Administration's Highway Performance Monitoring System]

Urbanized area	Daily vehicle miles of travel (1,000)		Annual person hours of delay		Annual congestion cost [1]		
	Freeway	Arterial streets	Total hours (1,000)	Per auto commuter [2]	Delay and fuel cost (million dollars)	Per person (dollars) [2]	Fuel wasted (gal. per person) [2]
U.S., average....................	**15,142**	**14,786**	**59,767**	**52**	**1,371**	**1,189**	**23**
Akron, OH..........................	5,847	4,493	12,283	27	284	634	15
Albany-Schenectady, NY.................	7,273	5,623	20,409	42	479	991	21
Albuquerque, NM.....................	4,736	7,834	20,452	36	501	886	19
Allentown, PA-NJ....................	5,427	5,231	17,114	30	393	694	15
Atlanta, GA.........................	51,003	46,002	148,666	52	3,214	1,130	20
Austin, TX..........................	13,273	11,237	51,116	52	1,140	1,159	22
Baltimore, MD.......................	28,412	19,258	87,620	47	2,075	1,115	21
Birmingham, AL......................	10,059	7,473	19,385	34	501	891	16
Boston, MA-NH-RI....................	41,097	36,127	153,994	64	3,363	1,388	30
Bridgeport-Stamford, CT-NY..............	10,030	5,649	37,119	49	898	1,174	22
Buffalo, NY.........................	6,709	9,164	26,851	40	620	918	21
Charleston-North, Charleston, SC.........	3,971	6,141	18,422	41	470	1,047	20
Charlotte, NC-SC....................	12,776	10,348	34,153	43	770	963	17
Chicago, IL-IN......................	57,279	79,284	302,609	61	7,222	1,445	29
Cincinnati, OH-KY-IN.................	18,088	15,593	48,485	41	1,159	989	21
Cleveland, OH......................	18,297	13,364	45,051	38	1,046	887	22
Colorado Springs, CO................	4,652	5,366	16,058	35	356	772	17
Columbus OH.......................	16,360	11,421	40,025	41	921	933	20
Dallas-Fort, Worth-Arlington, TX..........	64,411	41,713	186,535	53	4,202	1,185	22
Dayton, OH.........................	7,006	5,280	14,604	25	346	590	13
Denver-Aurora, CO..................	21,709	21,048	91,479	49	2,061	1,101	24
Detroit, MI.........................	33,441	44,627	155,358	52	3,514	1,183	25
El Paso, TX-NM.....................	5,777	5,633	19,127	33	439	760	16
Fresno, CA.........................	3,160	7,289	11,823	23	251	495	11
Grand Rapids, MI...................	5,617	7,539	21,536	39	470	854	19
Hartford, CT........................	11,022	7,073	28,296	45	656	1,038	21
Honolulu, HI........................	6,066	3,252	27,672	50	616	1,125	26
Houston, TX........................	51,673	39,211	203,173	61	4,924	1,490	29
Indianapolis, IN....................	12,735	16,382	46,435	43	1,142	1,060	23
Jackson, MS........................	4,602	6,208	12,287	38	282	878	15
Jacksonville, FL....................	11,801	9,189	29,680	38	659	842	15
Kansas City, MO-KS.................	22,986	12,479	45,570	39	1,085	933	18
Las Vegas -Henderson, NV.............	11,297	14,267	63,693	46	1,375	984	21
Los Angeles-Long Beach-Anaheim, CA....	121,603	119,049	622,509	80	13,318	1,711	25
Louisville-Jefferson Co., KY-IN..........	12,020	9,178	35,622	43	860	1,048	22
Memphis, TN-MS-AR.................	9,339	13,122	37,824	43	939	1,080	21
Miami, FL..........................	40,928	49,525	195,946	52	4,444	1,169	24
Milwaukee, WI......................	11,170	14,241	37,659	38	984	987	22
Minneapolis-St Paul, MN-WI.............	30,259	26,451	99,710	47	2,196	1,035	18
Nashville-Davidson, TN................	16,339	11,781	38,977	45	1,013	1,168	22
New Haven, CT......................	7,820	3,929	16,430	40	384	932	19
New Orleans, LA....................	5,422	8,239	39,159	45	1,014	1,161	22
New York-Newark, NY-NJ-CT............	122,655	110,098	628,241	74	14,712	1,739	35
Oklahoma City, OK...................	11,088	13,287	45,652	49	1,030	1,110	23
Omaha, NE-IA......................	5,369	5,978	18,224	32	407	707	17
Orlando, FL.........................	12,928	17,251	52,723	46	1,207	1,044	21
Oxnard, CA.........................	2,093	3,255	6,282	23	134	494	8
Philadelphia, PA-NJ-DE-MD.............	36,224	45,884	157,183	48	3,669	1,112	23
Phoenix-Mesa, AZ...................	29,548	39,686	155,730	51	3,641	1,201	25
Pittsburgh, PA......................	9,093	14,740	44,758	39	1,030	889	21
Portland, OR-WA....................	13,874	13,882	72,341	52	1,763	1,273	29
Providence, RI-MA...................	11,302	10,286	37,809	43	846	951	21
Raleigh, NC........................	8,588	10,138	23,128	34	504	734	13
Richmond, VA.......................	11,719	9,492	26,104	34	558	729	14
Riverside-San Bernardino, CA...........	32,679	17,079	99,058	59	2,201	1,316	18
Sacramento, CA....................	16,200	17,371	60,220	43	1,334	958	19
Salt Lake City-West Valley City, UT........	8,600	8,400	26,925	37	779	1,059	22
San Antonio, TX....................	21,270	12,956	64,328	44	1,462	1,002	20
San Diego, CA......................	39,817	22,543	79,412	42	1,658	887	11
San Francisco-Oakland, CA.............	28,137	24,086	146,013	78	3,143	1,675	33
San Jose, CA.......................	27,553	17,794	104,559	67	2,230	1,422	28
Seattle, WA.........................	28,010	27,708	139,842	63	3,294	1,491	28
St Louis, MO-IL.....................	31,260	19,537	69,350	43	1,637	1,020	21
Tampa-St Petersburg, FL..............	14,418	27,894	71,628	41	1,589	907	18
Toledo, OH-MI......................	4,332	4,729	15,905	38	381	920	20
Tucson, AZ.........................	3,826	11,760	35,993	47	856	1,128	23
Tulsa, OK..........................	8,036	9,129	30,341	44	682	984	20
Virginia Beach, VA..................	13,003	15,875	48,274	45	1,020	953	19
Washington, DC-VA-MD................	39,071	45,433	204,375	82	4,560	1,834	35
Worcester, MA......................	6,107	5,243	13,143	38	302	865	18

[1] Value of extra time (delay) and the extra fuel consumed by vehicles traveling at slower speeds. Fuel cost per gallon is the average price for each state. [2] Per auto commuter data are based on estimated commuters in the urban area.

Source: Texas A&M Transportation Institute, College Station, Texas, *2015 Urban Mobility Report*, August 2015 ©. See also <http://mobility.tamu.edu/ums/>.

Table 1123. Commuting to Work by Transportation Method and State: 2013

[In percent, except as indicated. Workers in thousands (142,962 represents 142,962,000). For workers 16 years old and over. The American Community Survey universe includes the household population and the population living in institutions, college dormitories, and other group quarters. Based on a sample and subject to sampling variability; see Appendix III]

State	Total workers (1,000)	Percent of workers who commuted to work by—						Mean travel time to work (min.)
		Car, truck, or van		Public transpor-tation [1]	Walking	Taxi, motorcycle, bicycle or other means	Working at home	
		Drove alone	Car-pooled					
U.S.	142,962	76.4	9.4	5.2	2.8	1.3	4.4	25.8
AL.	1,984	86.4	8.5	0.5	1.0	1.0	2.5	24.2
AK.	358	66.7	13.0	1.8	8.8	4.4	4.3	19.2
AZ.	2,754	76.3	11.0	2.4	2.1	1.8	5.5	24.8
AR.	1,223	83.4	10.1	0.5	1.7	1.3	2.8	21.4
CA.	16,746	73.2	10.9	5.3	2.7	1.5	5.2	27.9
CO.	2,577	74.7	9.7	3.3	2.9	1.2	6.9	24.6
CT.	1,736	77.9	8.3	5.1	3.1	0.9	4.3	25.5
DE.	424	80.3	9.1	3.5	2.1	0.8	3.7	25.4
DC.	330	32.3	5.3	38.5	13.6	1.3	4.4	29.9
FL.	8,353	79.6	9.4	2.1	1.5	1.5	5.1	26.1
GA.	4,291	79.6	10.3	2.1	1.5	1.4	4.9	27.0
HI.	672	67.6	13.5	6.1	4.2	2.9	4.4	26.8
ID.	697	78.8	9.6	0.7	3.1	1.4	5.5	20.1
IL.	5,973	73.6	8.3	9.1	3.1	1.0	4.2	28.0
IN.	2,975	83.0	8.8	1.2	2.0	1.2	3.3	23.2
IA.	1,548	80.9	8.6	1.1	3.7	1.0	4.2	18.9
KS.	1,389	82.4	9.1	0.5	2.5	1.1	4.0	19.1
KY.	1,867	82.8	9.6	1.1	2.3	0.9	3.2	22.6
LA.	1,984	82.6	9.6	1.3	1.7	1.7	2.4	25.2
ME.	629	77.4	10.6	0.7	3.9	1.2	5.7	23.3
MD.	2,947	74.0	9.0	9.1	2.4	0.9	4.2	32.5
MA.	3,326	71.8	7.4	9.9	4.8	0.9	4.4	28.6
MI.	4,275	82.4	8.8	1.5	2.2	0.8	3.8	24.0
MN.	2,774	78.4	8.6	3.6	2.9	0.9	4.9	23.0
MS.	1,181	84.0	10.3	0.4	1.5	1.6	1.9	23.6
MO.	2,774	81.7	9.2	1.6	2.0	1.1	4.1	23.2
MT.	475	75.1	10.1	0.7	5.3	1.3	6.0	18.0
NE.	954	81.5	9.3	0.8	2.7	0.8	4.4	18.1
NV.	1,247	78.4	10.5	3.4	2.2	1.5	3.6	23.7
NH.	678	81.2	8.1	1.0	3.1	0.9	5.4	26.8
NJ.	4,166	72.0	8.0	11.1	2.9	1.6	4.0	30.9
NM.	865	79.2	10.5	1.1	2.3	1.6	4.4	21.5
NY.	9,025	52.8	6.9	27.9	6.4	1.3	4.0	32.1
NC.	4,349	81.1	10.0	1.1	1.9	1.1	4.5	23.9
ND.	388	79.0	10.1	0.4	4.5	1.1	4.4	17.9
OH.	5,242	83.6	7.8	1.7	2.2	0.8	3.5	23.2
OK.	1,704	83.4	9.7	0.5	1.7	1.1	3.4	21.3
OR.	1,746	71.6	10.3	4.3	4.0	1.1	6.3	22.8
PA.	5,868	76.8	8.3	5.6	3.9	0.9	3.9	26.0
RI.	505	80.3	8.0	2.7	4.1	1.3	3.1	24.0
SC.	2,065	82.9	9.0	0.7	2.5	1.3	3.3	23.7
SD.	427	79.7	9.2	0.3	4.2	1.0	5.2	17.0
TN.	2,837	83.9	9.2	0.7	1.4	1.1	3.5	24.5
TX.	11,939	80.2	10.7	1.6	1.6	1.5	4.1	25.5
UT.	1,307	76.0	11.8	2.3	2.6	1.3	5.1	21.2
VT.	315	75.4	9.7	1.2	5.3	0.7	6.8	22.5
VA.	4,018	77.4	9.4	4.4	2.5	1.3	4.5	27.7
WA.	3,205	72.7	10.1	6.3	3.5	1.3	5.3	26.0
WV.	739	81.5	10.8	0.7	2.8	1.1	3.1	25.8
WI.	2,822	80.5	8.2	2.0	3.5	0.9	4.1	22.1
WY.	291	77.1	10.8	1.5	4.6	1.5	3.7	17.5
PR.	1,026	81.4	8.8	2.5	3.2	1.6	2.2	30.2

[1] Excluding taxicabs.

Source: U.S. Census Bureau, 2013 American Community Survey, B08006, "Sex of Worker by Means of Transportation to Work" and R0801, "Mean Travel Time to Work of Workers 16 Years Old and Over Who Did Not Work At Home (Minutes)," <http://factfinder2.census.gov>, accessed December 2014.

Table 1124. Passenger Transit Industry—Summary: 1990 to 2013

[16,053 represents $16,053,000,000. Includes Puerto Rico. Includes aggregate information for all transit systems in the United States. Excludes nontransit services such as taxicab, school bus, unregulated jitney (a small bus or automobile that transports passengers on a route for a small fare), sightseeing bus, intercity bus, and special application mass transportation systems (e.g., amusement parks, airports, island, and urban park ferries). Includes active vehicles only]

Item	Unit	1990	2000	2005	2010	2011	2012	2013
Operating systems...................	Number	5,078	6,000	6,429	7,300	7,100	7,200	6,804
Motor bus systems..............	Number	2,688	2,262	1,500	1,206	1,175	1,365	1,268
Revenue vehicles, active...........	Number	93,553	131,918	150,827	174,425	175,258	176,729	178,613
Motor bus.......................	Number	58,714	75,013	82,027	66,239	69,175	70,187	71,139
Commuter rail..................	Number	5,007	5,498	6,392	6,927	7,237	7,103	7,369
Demand response [1]...............	Number	16,471	33,080	41,958	68,621	65,336	68,632	38,559
Heavy rail.......................	Number	10,419	10,591	11,110	11,510	11,342	10,469	10,380
Light rail........................	Number	913	1,577	1,645	2,104	2,257	2,310	2,387
Trolley bus.....................	Number	832	951	615	571	479	570	560
Other............................	Number	1,197	5,208	7,080	18,453	19,432	17,458	18,218
Operating funding, total.............	Mil. dol.	16,053	24,243	31,708	39,117	41,310	43,577	46,048
Agency funds...................	Mil. dol.	6,786	11,004	12,559	14,675	15,602	16,205	16,734
Passenger funding.............	Mil. dol.	5,891	8,746	10,269	12,556	13,558	14,180	14,984
Other.........................	Mil. dol.	895	2,258	2,290	2,119	2,044	2,025	1,749
Government funds [2]...............	Mil. dol.	9,267	13,239	19,149	24,442	25,708	27,372	29,314
Directly generated [3].............	Mil. dol.	([4])	1,959	2,694	2,549	2,563	2,825	2,936
Local.........................	Mil. dol.	5,327	5,319	6,658	8,458	9,069	9,546	10,228
State.........................	Mil. dol.	2,970	4,967	7,495	9,761	10,048	11,139	12,038
Federal.......................	Mil. dol.	970	994	2,303	3,675	4,028	3,862	4,112
Operating expense.................	Mil. dol.	15,742	22,646	30,295	37,755	38,362	39,701	42,188
Vehicle operations...............	Mil. dol.	6,654	10,111	13,793	17,009	17,590	17,988	18,625
Maintenance....................	Mil. dol.	4,631	6,445	8,259	9,797	10,015	10,433	11,137
General administration...........	Mil. dol.	3,450	3,329	4,075	5,731	5,674	5,786	6,637
Purchased transportation.........	Mil. dol.	1,008	2,761	4,168	5,218	5,083	5,494	5,789
Capital expenditures.................	Mil. dol.	(NA)	9,587	12,383	17,824	17,057	18,168	18,229
Vehicle-miles operated.............	Million	3,242	4,081	4,601	5,455	5,378	5,392	5,392
Motor bus.......................	Million	2,130	2,315	2,485	2,413	2,414	2,405	2,414
Trolley bus.....................	Million	14	14	13	12	12	12	12
Heavy rail.......................	Million	537	595	646	666	655	656	674
Light rail........................	Million	24	53	69	94	94	99	107
Commuter rail..................	Million	213	271	303	345	347	349	362
Demand response [1]...............	Million	306	759	978	1,694	1,612	1,618	1,565
Other............................	Million	18	74	107	232	244	253	259
Trips taken.......................	Million	8,799	9,363	9,815	10,218	10,319	10,584	10,650
Motor bus.......................	Million	5,677	5,678	5,855	5,256	5,234	5,367	5,330
Trolley bus.....................	Million	126	122	107	99	98	99	96
Heavy rail.......................	Million	2,346	2,632	2,808	3,550	3,647	3,743	3,817
Light rail........................	Million	175	320	381	457	479	498	510
Commuter rail..................	Million	328	413	423	464	472	477	487
Demand response [1]...............	Million	68	105	125	190	191	211	223
Other............................	Million	79	93	117	203	197	189	186
Avg. fare per trip..................	Cents	67	93	102	123	131	134	142
Employees, number (avg.) [5]........	1,000	273	360	367	394	398	401	399
Payroll, employee..................	Mil. dol.	7,226	10,400	12,177	14,286	14,331	14,369	14,546
Fringe benefits, employee...........	Mil. dol.	3,986	5,413	8,093	10,342	10,597	11,048	11,066

NA Not available. [1] This operation (also called paratransit or dial-a-ride) is comprised of passenger cars, vans or small buses operating in response to calls from passengers or their agents to the transit operator, who then dispatches a vehicle to pick up the passengers and transport them to their destinations. [2] Represents the sum of federal, state, and local assistance, and that portion of directly generated funds that accrue from tax collections, toll transfers from other sectors of operations, and bond proceeds. [3] These are any funds generated from taxes controlled by the transit agency. [4] Funds data are included in local government data through 1993. [5] Through 1990, represents employee equivalents of 2,080 hours = one employee; beginning 1995, equals actual employees.

Source: American Public Transportation Association, Washington, DC, *Public Transportation Fact Book*, annual ©. See also <http://www.apta.com/resources/statistics/Pages/default.aspx>.

Table 1125. Top Twenty Cities—Public Transit Savings: 2015

[Individuals who ride public transportation can save on average $9,472 annually based on the August 18, 2015 national average gas price and the national unreserved monthly parking rate. On a per month basis, transit riders can save on average $789 per month versus driving. See source report and other monthly "Transit Savings" releases for information and methodology on how savings are calculated. The cities with the highest transit ridership are ranked in order of their transit savings based on the purchase of a monthly public transit pass and factoring in local gas prices and the local monthly unreserved parking rate]

City	Savings (dollars)		City	Savings (dollars)	
	Monthly	Annual		Monthly	Annual
New York........................	1,343	16,114	Minneapolis.....................	994	11,932
San Francisco..................	1,219	14,630	Denver	982	11,784
Boston..........................	1,181	14,169	Baltimore.......................	959	11,510
Chicago.........................	1,129	13,547	Washington, DC.................	943	11,316
Philadelphia....................	1,102	13,218	Cleveland.......................	934	11,213
Seattle..........................	1,101	13,215	Pittsburgh.......................	926	11,114
Los Angeles....................	1,083	12,993	Las Vegas......................	903	10,838
Honolulu........................	1,062	12,749	Atlanta..........................	891	10,695
San Diego.......................	1,033	12,399	Miami...........................	890	10,684
Portland.........................	997	11,966	Dallas...........................	877	10,524

Source: American Public Transportation Association, Media Center, Press Releases ©. See also <http://www.apta.com/mediacenter/pressreleases/2015/Pages/20150820_Transit-Savings.aspx>.

Table 1126. Characteristics of Rail Transit by Transit Authority: 2013

[8,194.7 represents $8,194,700,000]

Mode and transit agency	Metro area served	Directional route–miles [1,2]	Number of high-way-rail cross-ings [1]	Number of stations	Fare revenues earned (mil. dol.)	Total operating expenses (mil. dol.)	Unlinked passenger trips (million)
Total [3]............	(X)	12,149.5	7,148	3,227	8,194.7	15,333.9	4,809.1
Heavy rail............	(X)	1,622.0	27	1,044	4,943.6	8,173.1	3,816.8
Chicago Transit Authority............	Chicago	207.8	25	145	278.2	513.6	229.1
Greater Cleveland Regional Transit Authority........	Cleveland	38.1	–	18	6.7	28.1	6.4
Los Angeles County Metropolitan Transportation Authority, Metro........	Los Angeles	31.9	–	16	34.8	117.0	49.5
Maryland Transit Administration............	Baltimore	29.4	–	14	12.9	51.7	15.2
Massachusetts Bay Transportation Authority........	Boston	76.3	–	53	191.9	315.5	168.7
Metropolitan Atlanta Rapid Transit Authority.........	Atlanta	96.1	–	38	75.6	208.2	69.6
Miami-Dade Transit............	Miami	49.8	–	23	22.8	77.7	21.2
MTA New York City Transit............	New York	487.5	–	468	3,030.7	4,763.5	2,656.5
Port Authority Trans-Hudson Corporation........	New York	28.6	2	13	141.3	330.5	70.5
Port Authority Transit Corporation............	Philadelphia	31.5	–	13	26.0	46.8	10.5
San Francisco Bay Area Rapid Transit District.......	San Francisco	209.0	–	44	406.1	525.0	126.5
Southeastern Pennsylvania Transportation Authority........	Philadelphia	74.9	–	75	95.7	186.7	101.0
Staten Island Rapid Transit Operating Authority, MTA Staten Island Railway........	New York	28.6	–	22	7.3	42.8	7.0
Washington Metropolitan Area Transit Authority.....	Washington	211.8	–	86	605.5	909.5	273.8
Alternativa de Transporte Integrado ATI.............	San Juan, PR	20.6	–	16	8.0	56.7	11.0
Commuter rail [4]........	(X)	8,691.3	3,406	1,242	2,698.6	5,326.2	475.7
Alaska Railroad Corporation............	Anchorage	959.9	133	10	15.5	35.6	0.2
Altamont Corridor Express........	San Jose	172.0	127	10	5.8	14.9	0.9
Central Puget Sound Regional Transit Authority.....	Seattle	163.8	66	12	9.5	38.6	3.0
Connecticut Department of Transportation..........	Hartford	101.2	3	9	2.2	26.8	0.9
Dallas Area Rapid Transit............	Dallas	72.3	44	10	8.8	27.0	2.1
Delaware Transit Corporation............	Delaware	(NA)	(NA)	(NA)	4.1	5.2	–
Maryland Transit Administration............	Baltimore	400.4	40	42	42.9	121.6	9.0
Massachusetts Bay Transportation Authority........	Boston	776.1	258	137	169.0	351.4	35.2
Metro Transit............	Minneapolis	77.9	36	7	2.6	17.8	0.8
Metro-North Commuter Railroad Company, MTA Metro-North Railroad............	New York	545.7	157	112	618.8	1,071.6	83.3
MTA Long Island Rail Road............	New York	638.2	343	124	632.2	1,219.0	99.3
New Jersey Transit Corporation............	New York	1,001.8	330	164	491.4	917.1	80.1
North County Transit District............	San Diego	82.2	34	8	7.2	18.8	1.6
Northeast Illinois Regional Commuter Railroad Corporation,............	Chicago	975.4	571	241	309.4	664.1	73.6
Northern Indiana Commuter Transportation District............	Chicago	179.8	117	20	19.3	39.5	3.6
Northern New England Passenger Rail Authority....	Boston	287.6	103	12	8.1	14.6	0.6
Peninsula Corridor Joint Powers Board dba: Caltrain............	San Francisco	153.7	55	32	62.4	102.0	16.4
Pennsylvania Department of Transportation.........	Philadelphia	144.4	4	12	10.4	18.7	0.6
Regional Transportation Authority............	Nashville	62.8	35	6	0.8	4.2	0.3
Rio Metro Regional Transit District............	Albuquerque	193.1	86	13	3.0	27.1	1.1
South Florida Regional Transportation Authority.....	Miami	142.2	73	18	12.0	58.1	4.2
Southeastern Pennsylvania Transportation Authority............	Philadelphia	446.9	283	154	137.4	246.8	37.2
Southern California Regional Rail Authority............	Los Angeles	777.8	423	55	84.4	189.3	13.4
Utah Transit Authority............	Salt Lake City	174.5	65	16	6.6	35.7	3.8
Virginia Railway Express............	Washington	161.5	20	18	34.7	60.7	4.6

– Represents zero. X Not applicable. NA Not available. [1] Vehicles operated in maximum services (VOMS) include directly operated (DO) and Purchase Transportation (PT) by mode. [2] The mileage in each direction over which public transportation vehicles travel while in revenue service. The mileage is computed without regard to the number of traffic lanes or rail tracks existing in the right-of-way. [3] Includes light rail, not shown separately. [4] Excludes commuter-type services operated independently by Amtrak.

Source: U.S. Department of Transportation, Federal Transit Administration, National Transit Database, "Table 21: Passenger Stations," "Table 23: Transit Way Mileage - Rail Modes," and "Table 26: Fare per Passenger and Recovery Ratio," <http://www.ntdprogram.gov/ntdprogram/data.htm>, accessed September 2015.

Table 1127. Transit Ridership in Selected Urbanized Areas: 2012

[Passenger trips in thousands (10,214,018 represents 10,214,018,000)]

Urbanized areas	2010 Population Total	Annual unlinked passenger trips [1] (1,000)	Unlinked passenger trips per capita	Percent distribution Motor bus	Heavy rail [2]	Light rail [3]	Commuter rail [4]	Other [5]
U.S. urbanized areas....................	209,569,050	10,214,018	48.7	50.7	36.5	5.0	4.6	3.2
Atlanta, GA...............................	4,515,419	139,959	31.0	48.3	50.4	–	–	1.3
Baltimore, MD............................	2,203,663	107,991	49.0	67.6	14.3	8.2	8.1	1.9
Boston, MA-NH-RI.....................	4,181,019	408,893	97.8	30.3	40.7	18.3	8.8	1.9
Chicago, IL-IN...........................	8,608,208	664,108	77.1	52.4	34.8	–	11.7	1.1
Cincinnati, OH-KY-IN..................	1,624,827	21,445	13.2	98.2	–	–	–	1.8
Cleveland, OH...........................	1,780,673	49,115	27.6	79.5	12.7	5.8	–	2.0
Dallas-Fort Worth-Arlington, TX.........	5,121,892	80,607	15.7	57.6	–	35.4	2.7	4.2
Denver-Aurora, CO.....................	2,374,203	98,716	41.6	77.7	–	20.9	–	1.4
Detroit, MI................................	3,734,090	46,479	12.4	90.5	–	–	–	9.5
Houston, TX..............................	4,944,332	82,223	16.6	80.9	–	13.8	–	5.2
Indianapolis, IN.........................	1,487,483	10,243	6.9	97.4	–	–	–	2.6
Kansas City, MO-KS....................	1,519,417	17,189	11.3	96.3	–	–	–	3.7
Las Vegas-Henderson, NV.............	1,886,011	65,867	34.9	91.7	–	–	–	8.3
Los Angeles-Long Beach-Anaheim, CA.........	12,150,996	679,932	56.0	80.1	7.2	8.9	2.1	1.8
Miami, FL.................................	5,502,379	168,182	30.6	78.3	11.4	–	2.4	7.8
Milwaukee, WI...........................	1,376,476	47,497	34.5	98.4	–	–	0.0	1.6
Minneapolis-St. Paul, MN-WI..........	2,650,890	94,674	35.7	85.8	–	11.1	0.7	2.4
New York-Newark, NY-NJ-CT...........	18,351,295	4,178,127	227.7	28.8	63.6	0.5	6.2	0.9
Orlando, FL..............................	1,510,516	29,531	19.6	96.5	–	–	–	3.5
Philadelphia, PA-NJ-DE-MD............	5,441,567	371,544	68.3	50.2	29.7	7.8	9.9	2.4
Phoenix-Mesa, AZ.......................	3,629,114	75,431	20.8	78.6	–	18.6	–	2.8
Pittsburgh, PA...........................	1,733,853	67,410	38.9	83.5	–	11.5	–	5.0
Portland, OR-WA........................	1,849,898	113,365	61.3	59.1	–	39.7	–	1.2
Riverside-San Bernardino, CA.........	1,932,666	25,566	13.2	95.9	–	–	–	4.1
Sacramento, CA.........................	1,723,634	31,087	18.0	54.7	–	43.7	–	1.6
San Antonio, TX.........................	1,758,210	47,508	27.0	96.9	–	–	–	3.1
San Diego, CA...........................	2,956,746	102,031	34.5	62.6	–	33.0	1.6	2.8
San Francisco-Oakland, CA............	3,281,212	440,217	134.2	39.0	28.0	11.8	3.1	18.1
San Jose, CA............................	1,664,496	43,741	26.3	74.3	–	24.0	–	1.7
Seattle, WA..............................	3,059,393	196,621	64.3	67.3	–	5.3	1.4	25.9
St. Louis, MO-IL.........................	2,150,706	50,287	23.4	64.1	–	34.1	–	1.9
Tampa-St. Petersburg, FL..............	2,441,770	30,511	12.5	96.6	–	1.0	–	2.4
Virginia Beach, VA......................	1,439,666	18,839	13.1	86.5	–	8.8	–	4.7
Washington, DC-VA-MD.................	4,586,770	479,674	104.6	40.3	58.2	–	1.0	0.5

– Represents zero. [1] The number of times passengers board public transportation vehicles. A passenger is counted each time he or she boards a vehicle even if the boarding is part of the same journey from origin to destination. [2] Also called metro, subway, rapid transit, or rapid rail. [3] Also called hybrid rail, streetcar, tramway, or trolley. [4] Also called metropolitan rail or regional rail. [5] Other includes automated guideway, cable car, demand response, ferry boat, inclined plane, monorail, trolley bus, and van pool (see footnote 1, Table 1124).

Source: U.S. Bureau of Transportation Statistics, "State Transportation Statistics," <http://www.rita.dot.gov/bts/sites/rita.dot.gov.bts/files/publications/state_transportation_statistics/index.html>, accessed July 2015.

Table 1128. Federal Transit Administration Funding (FTA) by State: 2010 and 2011

[In millions of dollars (10,290.7 represents $10,290,700,000). For fiscal years ending September 30]

State	2010	2011	State	2010	2011	State	2010	2011	State	2010	2011
Total [1]...	10,290.7	9,991.6	ID.........	17.4	19.0	MO........	104.6	91.5	PA........	424.4	445.4
AL........	46.6	45.6	IL.........	571.0	535.4	MT........	16.2	15.0	RI.........	28.1	28.4
AK........	72.0	64.4	IN.........	85.5	75.1	NE........	28.9	23.3	SC........	43.8	44.1
AZ........	169.3	115.4	IA.........	50.7	52.5	NV........	49.4	46.9	SD........	11.4	14.3
AR........	26.4	26.4	KS........	28.8	27.1	NH........	11.9	12.5	TN........	79.8	78.1
CA........	1,299.0	1,339.7	KY........	70.9	50.0	NJ........	685.7	475.9	TX........	642.6	680.1
CO........	260.5	253.9	LA........	67.3	60.2	NM........	35.5	31.3	UT........	264.8	245.3
CT........	143.9	184.8	ME........	16.0	17.2	NY........	1,730.9	1,838.9	VT........	18.8	13.6
DE........	24.2	19.6	MD........	191.2	184.4	NC........	116.2	101.8	VA........	117.9	206.7
DC........	283.7	212.2	MA........	395.4	337.6	ND........	13.7	12.0	WA........	365.5	377.3
FL........	386.2	383.5	MI........	146.2	169.6	OH........	192.2	180.1	WV........	23.4	25.1
GA........	184.2	188.9	MN........	116.6	149.4	OK........	42.8	40.8	WI........	84.7	90.1
HI........	77.2	120.0	MS........	25.4	23.3	OR........	166.6	91.6	WY........	8.1	12.7

[1] Includes data for Island Areas of the U.S. and unallocated funds, not shown separately.

Source: U.S. Department of Transportation, Federal Transit Administration, "FTA Allocations for Formula and Discretionary Programs by State FY1998-2014," http://www.fta.dot.gov/12853_88.html>, accessed August 2014.

Table 1129. Commuting Time to Work for Top Metropolitan Statistical Areas: 2013

[136,733 represents 136,733,000, except percent. For workers 16 years and over who did not work at home. Covers any mode of travel. Based on a sample, subject to sampling variability]

Metropolitan Statistical Area	Total commuters	Percent over 35 minutes	Commuting time (in minutes)								
			Less than 10 minutes	10 to 14 minutes	15 to 19 minutes	20 to 24 minutes	25 to 29 minutes	30 to 34 minutes	35 to 44 minutes	45 to 59 minutes	60 or more minutes
United States.................	**136,733**	**23**	**17,963**	**19,101**	**21,259**	**20,180**	**8,559**	**18,583**	**8,968**	**10,696**	**11,424**
Atlanta-Sandy Springs-Roswell, GA.........	2,370	32	186	255	313	361	135	367	194	288	271
Baltimore-Columbia-Towson, MD..........	1,311	32	101	133	178	184	89	205	117	142	163
Boston-Cambridge-Newton, MA-NH.........	2,298	33	227	256	281	288	145	349	208	260	284
Charlotte-Concord-Gastonia, NC-SC........	1,030	23	107	142	165	158	72	154	82	84	66
Chicago-Naperville-Elgin, IL-IN-WI..........	4,280	34	384	448	515	547	259	653	403	511	558
Dallas-Ft. Worth-Arlington, TX............	3,112	26	300	376	446	445	211	526	241	317	250
Denver-Aurora-Lakewood, CO..............	1,267	25	112	141	186	206	94	212	110	115	90
Detroit-Warren-Dearborn, MI...............	1,799	24	184	217	270	278	142	272	159	160	118
Houston-The Woodlands-Sugar Land, TX. ..	2,834	29	237	306	393	404	167	492	216	315	304
Los Angeles-Long Beach-Anaheim, CA.....	5,664	28	446	661	810	840	320	979	419	527	660
Miami-Ft. Lauderdale-West Palm Beach, FL...	2,509	25	187	277	351	409	169	479	207	229	202
Minneapolis-St. Paul-Bloomington, MN-WI...	1,723	22	187	219	264	282	145	254	138	141	95
New York-Newark-Jersey City, NY-NJ-PA....	8,888	41	672	815	931	1,012	453	1,319	784	1,101	1,802
Orlando-Kissimmee-Sanford, FL.............	991	24	68	123	150	156	74	184	84	89	62
Philadelphia-Camden-Wilmington, PA-NJ-DE-MD.............................	2,685	29	266	310	368	383	168	405	225	278	281
Phoenix-Mesa-Scottsdale, AZ.................	1,788	23	179	225	261	288	137	290	138	160	111
Pittsburgh, PA.............................	1,077	25	133	141	156	158	72	151	87	98	80
Portland-Vancouver-Hillsboro, OR-WA.......	1,022	22	117	134	164	162	74	145	72	84	72
Riverside-San Bernardino-Ontario, CA......	1,617	31	168	199	233	211	89	211	104	143	260
St. Louis, MO-IL...........................	1,276	22	133	167	194	208	99	196	105	106	67
San Diego-Carlsbad, CA....................	1,383	19	122	186	247	248	114	208	87	92	79
San Francisco-Oakland-Hayward, CA.......	2,049	34	148	227	270	273	116	325	174	232	283
Seattle-Tacoma-Bellevue, WA................	1,683	29	144	180	235	258	118	264	148	173	162
Tampa-St. Petersburg-Clearwater, FL........	1,200	24	134	148	179	197	80	177	90	110	86
Washington-Arlington-Alexandria, DC-VA-MD-WV.............................	2,963	40	181	247	340	358	177	472	293	405	490

Source: U.S. Census Bureau, 2013 American Community Survey, B08134, "Means of Transportation to Work by Travel Time to Work," <http://www.census.gov/acs/www/>, accessed November 2014.

Table 1130. Commuters Who Ride Bicycles or Walk to Work by Sex—Selected Cities: 2011

[Covers cities with the highest percent of commuters who walk or bike to work, based on the National Household Travel Survey and the American Community Survey. Data are weighted 3-year averages for 2009-2011]

Leading cities	Walking			Leading cities	Bicycling		
	Percent of commuters who walk to work	Percent male	Percent female		Percent of commuters who bike to work	Percent male	Percent female
Boston, MA.................	15.0	51	49	Portland, OR......................	6.1	63	37
Washington, DC............	11.8	52	48	Minneapolis, MN..................	3.6	65	35
New York City, NY.........	10.3	47	53	Seattle, WA.......................	3.4	70	30
San Francisco, CA.........	9.9	49	51	San Francisco, CA................	3.3	68	32
Honolulu, HI...............	9.7	45	55	Washington, DC..................	2.9	64	36
Philadelphia, PA...........	8.8	45	55	Oakland, CA......................	2.5	66	34
Seattle, WA...............	8.6	54	46	Tucson, AZ.......................	2.5	70	30
Baltimore, MD..............	6.8	46	54	New Orleans, LA..................	2.3	63	37
Chicago, IL................	6.3	48	52	Sacramento, CA...................	2.3	65	35
Minneapolis, MN...........	6.3	58	42	Denver, CO.......................	2.2	68	32
New Orleans, LA...........	5.6	53	47	Philadelphia, PA..................	1.9	60	40
Portland, OR...............	5.3	53	47	Boston, MA.......................	1.7	68	32
Milwaukee, WI.............	5.2	55	45	Honolulu, HI......................	1.6	77	23
Atlanta, GA................	4.5	60	40	Albuquerque, NM.................	1.4	69	31
Cleveland, OH.............	4.4	49	51	Austin, TX........................	1.3	75	25
Oakland, CA...............	4.2	55	45	Chicago, IL.......................	1.3	74	26
Denver, CO................	4.1	54	46	Long Beach, CA...................	1.2	78	22
Miami, FL..................	3.9	56	44	Atlanta, GA.......................	1.1	77	23
Los Angeles, CA...........	3.7	51	49	Los Angeles, CA..................	1.0	78	22
Tucson, AZ................	3.7	48	52	Mesa, AZ.........................	1.0	80	20
Detroit, MI.................	3.2	61	39	San Diego, CA....................	0.9	71	29
Colorado Springs, CO.....	3.0	56	44	San Jose, CA.....................	0.9	82	18
Sacramento, CA...........	3.0	48	52	Baltimore, MD....................	0.8	77	23
San Diego, CA............	3.0	57	43	Fresno, CA.......................	0.8	59	41
Columbus, OH.............	2.9	55	45	Colorado Springs, CO............	0.7	72	28

Source: Alliance for Biking and Walking, *Biking and Walking in the United States: 2014 Benchmarking Report* ©. See also <http://www.peoplepoweredmovement.org/>.

Table 1131. Truck Transportation, Couriers and Messengers, and Warehousing and Storage—Estimated Revenue: 2009 to 2013

[In millions of dollars (180,460 represents $180,460,000,000). For taxable employer firms. Estimates have been adjusted to the results of the 2007 Economic Census]

Kind of business	NAICS code [1]	2009	2010	2011	2012	2013
Truck transportation..................	**484**	**180,460**	**194,616**	**216,440**	**231,869**	**238,958**
General freight trucking, local........................	48411	17,750	19,336	21,109	22,338	23,250
General freight trucking, long-distance, truckload.....	484121	70,587	77,526	87,100	92,320	94,331
General freight trucking, long-distance, less than truckload.....	484122	29,484	32,019	35,913	38,017	39,384
Used household and office goods moving..................	48421	11,891	11,940	12,433	12,940	13,603
Specialized freight (except used goods) trucking, local.........	48422	26,046	27,643	31,017	34,627	35,935
Specialized freight (except used goods) trucking, long-distance..................	48423	24,702	26,152	28,868	31,627	32,455
Couriers and messengers................	**492**	**69,849**	**71,622**	**78,502**	**82,735**	**85,365**
Couriers and express delivery services..................	4921	67,145	68,799	75,434	79,375	81,846
Local messengers and local delivery..................	4922	2,704	2,823	3,068	3,360	3,519
Warehousing and storage................	**493**	**22,538**	**24,245**	**25,601**	**26,922**	**27,848**
General warehousing and storage..................	49311	15,704	16,770	17,973	19,077	19,788
Refrigerated warehousing and storage..................	49312	3,467	4,034	3,906	4,012	4,011
Farm product warehousing and storage..................	49313	801	743	832	811	829
Other warehousing and storage..................	49319	2,566	2,698	2,890	3,022	3,220

[1] Data are based on 2007 North American Industry Classification System (NAICS); see text, this section and Section 15.

Source: U.S. Census Bureau, Annual & Quarterly Services, "2013 Annual Services," <http://www.census.gov/services/index.html>, accessed January 2015.

Table 1132. Truck Transportation—Revenue and Equipment Inventory: 2010 to 2013

[In millions of dollars (194,616 represents $194,616,000,000), except where noted. For all employer firms regardless of tax status. Covers NAICS 484. Estimates have been adjusted to the results of the 2007 Economic Census. Data are based on the 2007 North American Industry Classification System (NAICS); see text, this section and Section 15]

Item	2010	2011	2012	2013
Total operating revenue..................	**194,616**	**216,440**	**231,869**	**238,958**
Total motor carrier revenue..................	179,661	200,189	214,513	221,461
Revenue by commodities handled:				
Agricultural and fish products..................	18,642	20,566	22,773	22,800
Grains, alcohol, and tobacco products..................	9,200	9,901	10,442	10,754
Stone, nonmetallic minerals, and metallic ores..................	11,873	13,129	14,226	14,095
Coal and petroleum products..................	9,886	11,467	12,576	13,241
Pharmaceutical and chemical products..................	9,075	9,794	10,882	11,595
Wood products, textiles, and leathers..................	15,524	17,076	17,994	18,504
Base metal and machinery..................	19,489	21,567	23,112	23,017
Electronic, motorized vehicles, and precision instruments..................	10,677	11,267	12,209	12,610
Used household and office goods..................	9,894	10,556	10,686	11,487
New furniture and miscellaneous manufactured products..................	15,581	17,102	18,334	18,840
Other goods..................	49,820	57,764	61,279	64,518
Hazardous materials..................	10,782	12,629	14,946	15,305
Inventory of revenue-generating equipment (1,000):				
Trucks..................	159	165	195	214
Owned and/or leased with drivers..................	144	149	176	192
Leased without drivers..................	15	16	19	(S)
Truck-tractors..................	664	673	710	742
Owned and/or leased with drivers..................	578	584	618	650
Leased without drivers..................	86	89	92	92
Trailers..................	1,568	1,595	1,654	1,739
Owned and/or leased with drivers..................	1,375	1,399	1,451	1,548
Leased without drivers..................	193	196	203	191

S Estimate does not meet publication standards.

Source: U.S. Census Bureau, Annual & Quarterly Services, "2013 Annual Services," <http://www.census.gov/services/index.html>, accessed January 2015.

Table 1133. Petroleum Pipeline Companies—Characteristics: 1980 to 2014

[173 represents 173,000. Covers pipeline companies operating in interstate commerce and subject to the jurisdiction of the Federal Energy Regulatory Commission]

Item	Unit	1980	1990	2000	2005	2010	2011	2012	2013	2014
Miles of pipeline, total..........	1,000	173	168	152	131	148	150	152	152	161
Gathering lines.................	1,000	36	32	18	14	10	13	14	15	15
Trunk lines......................	1,000	136	136	134	118	138	137	138	137	146
Total deliveries..................	Mil. Bbl.	10,600	11,378	14,450	12,732	13,518	13,568	14,136	14,594	16,170
Crude oil........................	Mil. Bbl.	6,405	6,563	6,923	6,675	7,204	7,032	7,471	8,122	9,289
Products........................	Mil. Bbl.	4,195	4,816	7,527	6,057	6,314	6,537	6,665	6,471	6,881
Total trunk line traffic...........	Bil. Bbl. miles	3,405	3,500	3,508	3,485	3,565	3,608	3,770	3,800	4,193
Crude oil........................	Bil. Bbl. miles	1,948	1,891	1,602	1,571	1,634	1,653	1,760	1,760	2,059
Products........................	Bil. Bbl. miles	1,458	1,609	1,906	1,914	1,931	1,955	2,009	2,053	2,134
Carrier property value..........	Mil. dol.	19,752	25,828	29,648	29,526	45,380	49,157	54,071	67,890	84,910
Operating revenues............	Mil. dol.	6,356	7,149	7,483	7,917	11,219	12,562	14,007	15,734	19,281
Net income.....................	Mil. dol.	1,912	2,340	2,705	3,076	4,582	6,109	6,423	6,981	9,573

Source: PennWell Publishing Co., Houston, TX, *Oil & Gas Journal*, annual ©. See also <http://www.ogj.com/>.

Table 1134. U.S. Postal Service—Summary: 1990 to 2014

[166,301 represents 166,301,000,000 except as indicated. For years ending September 30. Includes Puerto Rico and all Island Areas]

Item	1990	2000	2005	2010	2012	2013	2014
Offices, stations, and branches............	**40,067**	**38,060**	**37,142**	**36,222**	**35,369**	**35,434**	**35,641**
Number of post offices......................	28,959	27,876	27,385	27,077	26,755	26,670	26,669
Number of stations and branches..............	11,108	10,184	9,757	9,145	8,614	8,764	8,972
Delivery points (mil.)..................	**(NA)**	**135.9**	**144.3**	**150.9**	**152.1**	**152.9**	**153.9**
Residential..............................	(NA)	123.9	131.3	137.5	139.2	140.0	141.0
City....................................	(NA)	76.1	78.5	80.5	81.0	81.3	81.7
P.O. Box................................	(NA)	15.9	15.6	15.7	16.0	15.9	15.9
Rural/highway contract..................	(NA)	31.9	37.2	41.2	42.1	42.8	43.5
Business.................................	(NA)	12.1	13.0	13.3	13.0	12.9	12.9
Pieces of mail handled (mil.)...............	**166,301**	**207,882**	**211,743**	**170,859**	**159,835**	**158,222**	**155,375**
Domestic................................	165,503	206,782	210,891	167,208	155,408	153,771	150,461
First-class mail [1,2].................	89,270	103,526	98,071	77,592	68,674	65,754	63,603
Priority mail [2,3,4]..................	518	1,223	888	779	824	871	920
Express mail [2,3,5]..................	59	71	56	43	40	39	36
Periodicals (formerly 2nd class).........	10,680	10,365	9,070	7,269	6,741	6,359	6,045
Standard Mail (formerly Standard A) [2]......	63,725	90,057	100,942	81,841	79,496	80,806	80,311
Package Services (formerly Standard B).....	663	1,128	1,166	657	646	571	550
U.S. Postal Service.....................	538	363	621	438	440	631	454
Free for the blind......................	35	47	76	68	57	55	48
Shipping Services Volume [2,3,6]......	(X)	(X)	(X)	3,057	3,501	3,715	4,015
International economy mail (surface) [3]........	166	79	23	([3])	([3])	([3])	([3])
International, airmail or total [3,7]......	632	1,021	829	594	926	902	899
Employees, total (1,000)...................	**843**	**901**	**803**	**672**	**629**	**618**	**618**
Career.....................................	**761**	**788**	**705**	**584**	**528**	**491**	**488**
Headquarters..........................	2	2	3	3	3	3	3
Headquarters support..................	6	6	4	5	4	4	4
Inspection Service.....................	4	4	3	2	2	2	2
Inspector General......................	(X)	1	1	1	1	1	1
Field Career..........................	749	775	693	573	518	481	478
Postmasters.........................	27	26	25	23	17	18	17
Supervisors/managers.................	43	39	33	28	24	23	23
Professional, administrative, and technical..........................	10	10	9	6	5	4	4
Clerks..............................	290	282	222	157	140	119	119
Mail handlers.......................	51	61	56	49	42	40	39
City carriers........................	236	241	228	192	177	167	165
Motor vehicle operators..............	7	9	9	7	7	7	7
Rural carriers.......................	42	57	64	67	67	66	66
Special delivery messengers.........	2	(X)	(X)	(X)	(X)	(X)	(X)
Building and equipment maintenance.......	33	42	40	37	35	31	33
Vehicle maintenance.................	5	6	5	5	5	5	5
Other [8]...........................	1	2	2	(X)	(X)	(X)	(X)
Non-career.................................	**83**	**114**	**98**	**88**	**101**	**127**	**130**
Casuals...............................	27	30	19	7	6	2	2
Transitional...........................	(X)	13	8	16	14	–	–
Rural part-time........................	43	58	57	52	48	47	48
Relief/Leave replacements..............	12	12	12	11	9	13	13
Non-bargaining temporary..............	(Z)	1	1	2	4	(Z)	(Z)
Compensation and employee benefits (mil. dol.)...............................	34,214	49,532	53,932	48,909	47,689	46,708	46,000
Avg. salary per employee (dol.) [9].......	37,570	50,103	62,635	72,099	(NA)	(NA)	(NA)
Pieces of mail per employee (1,000).........	197	231	264	254	254	256	251
Total revenue (mil. dol.) [10]................	**40,074**	**64,540**	**69,993**	**67,077**	**65,247**	**67,341**	**67,854**
Operating postal revenue.....................	39,201	64,476	69,798	67,052	65,223	67,318	67,830
Mail revenue............................	**37,892**	**62,284**	**66,649**	**53,106**	**49,975**	**51,056**	**50,478**
First-class mail [1,2].................	24,023	35,516	36,062	32,111	28,856	28,110	28,335
Priority mail [2,3,4]..................	1,555	4,837	4,634	5,455	5,937	6,375	6,884
Express mail [2,3,5]..................	630	996	872	829	802	794	760
Periodicals (formerly 2nd class).............	1,509	2,171	2,161	1,879	1,731	1,658	1,625
Standard Mail (formerly Standard A) [2]......	8,082	15,193	18,954	16,728	16,428	16,915	17,428
Package Services (formerly Standard B)...	919	1,912	2,201	1,531	1,610	1,136	837
Shipping Services [2,3,6]..............	(X)	(X)	(X)	10,156	11,592	12,597	13,743
International economy mail (surface) [3]......	222	180	134	([3])	([3])	([3])	([3])
International, airmail or total [3,7].............	941	1,477	1,631	2,388	2,816	3,016	3,024
Service revenue............................	**1,310**	**2,191**	**3,150**	**3,790**	**3,656**	**3,583**	**3,609**
Registry [11]........................	174	98	77	48	39	35	35
Certified [11].......................	310	385	601	791	663	715	687
Insurance [11]......................	47	109	132	128	109	108	92
Collect-on-delivery....................	26	22	9	7	6	4	4
Money orders........................	155	235	208	182	165	155	164
Other [11]..........................	592	1,342	2,122	2,635	2,674	2,565	2,627
Operating expenses (million dollars) [12].....	**40,490**	**62,992**	**68,283**	**75,426**	**80,964**	**72,128**	**73,178**

– Represents zero. NA Not available. X Not applicable. Z Fewer than 500. [1] Items mailed at 1st class rates and weighing 11 ounces or less. [2] Beginning 2010, Express Mail, Priority Mail, First-Class Parcels, and Standard Parcels are not included in Mail categories but reclassified under Shipping and Package Services. [3] "Volume" and "Mailing & Shipping Revenue" restructured for the "Postal Accountability and Enhancement Act (PAEA) of 2006." Some categories eliminated. [4] Provides 2 to 3 day delivery service. [5] Overnight delivery of packages weighing up to 70 pounds. [6] Beginning 2010, also includes Package Services. [7] Airmail only, for 2005 and earlier. Beginning 2010, total international, including all international revenues and pieces formerly included in First-Class Mail, Standard Mail, and Package Services. [8] Includes discontinued operations, area offices, and nurses. Beginning 2010, nurses are included with clerks, and not "other" employment is reported. [9] For career bargaining unit employees. Includes fringe benefits. [10] Net revenues after refunds of postage. Includes operating reimbursements, stamped envelope purchases, indemnity claims, and miscellaneous revenue and expenditure offsets. Shown in year which gave rise to the earnings. [11] Beginning 2000, return receipt revenue broken out from registry, certified, and insurance and included in "other." [12] Shown in year in which obligation was incurred.

Source: U.S. Postal Service, *2014 Annual Report to Congress*, 2014; *Revenue, Pieces & Weight, FY2014*; and earlier reports and unpublished data. See also <http://about.usps.com/who-we-are/financials/welcome.htm>.

Table 1135. U.S. Postal Service Rates for Letters and Postcards: 1991 to 2015

[In dollars. International rates exclude Canada and Mexico]

| Domestic mail date of rate change | Letters | | Post-cards | Express mail— first 1/2 pound [1] | International air mail date of rate change | Letters | Post-cards |
	First ounce	Each added ounce					
1991 (Feb. 3).................	0.29	0.23	0.19	9.95	**First 1/2 ounce**		
1995 (Jan. 1).................	0.32	0.23	0.20	10.75	1991 (Feb. 3).............	0.50	0.40
1999 (Jan. 10)...............	0.33	0.22	0.20	11.75	1995 (July 9).............	0.60	0.40
2001 (Jan. 7).................	0.34	0.21	0.20	12.25	1999 (Jan. 10)............	0.60	0.50
2001 (July 1).................	0.34	0.23	0.21	12.45	**First ounce [2]**		
2002 (June 30)...............	0.37	0.23	0.23	13.65	2001 (Jan. 7).............	0.80	0.70
2006 (Jan. 8).................	0.39	0.24	0.24	14.40	2006 (Jan. 8).............	0.84	0.75
2007 (May 14)...............	0.41	0.17	0.26	16.25	2007 (May 14)............	0.90	0.90
2008 (May 12)...............	0.42	0.17	0.27	[3] 12.60	2008 (May 12)............	0.94	0.94
2009 (May 11)...............	0.44	0.17	0.28	[4] 13.05	2009 (May 11)............	0.98	0.98
2010 (Jan. 4).................	0.44	0.17	0.28	[5] 13.65	2010 (no change).......	0.98	0.98
2011 (Apr. 17)...............	0.44	0.20	0.29	[6] 13.25	2011 (no change)........	0.98	0.98
2012 (Jan. 22)...............	0.45	0.20	0.32	[7] 12.95	2012 (Jan. 22)...........	1.05	1.05
2013 (Jan. 27)...............	0.46	0.20	0.33	[8] 14.10	2013 (Jan. 27)...........	1.10	1.10
2014 (Jan. 26)...............	0.49	0.21	0.34	[9] 16.95	2014 (Jan. 26)...........	1.15	1.15
2015 (May 31)...............	0.49	0.22	0.35	[9] 16.95	2015 (May 31)...........	1.20	1.20

[1] On May 12, 2008, the Postal Service initiated a zoned pricing structure for Express Mail. [2] International letter prices after the first ounce vary according to the price group that is applicable to each destination country. [3] Prices increased on May 12, 2008. Prices range from $12.60 to zones 1 and 2 to $19.50 to zone 8. [4] Prices increased on January 18, 2009. Prices range from $13.05 to zones 1 and 2 to $21.20 to zone 8. [5] Prices range from $13.65 to zones 1 and 2 to $22.20 to zone 8. [6] Prices changed on January 2, 2011. Prices range from $13.25 to zones 1 and 2 to $26.65 to zone 8. [7] Prices range from $12.95 to zones 1 and 2 to $28.00 to zone 8. [8] Prices range from $14.10 to zones 1 and 2 to $30.60 to zone 8. [9] Beginning January 2014, the Postal Service implemented a Zone 9. Prices range from $16.95 to zones 1 and 2 to $38.05 to zone 9.

Source: U.S. Postal Service, *Domestic Rate History*, July 2009; and "Price List Notice 123," <http://pe.usps.com/text/dmm300/Notice123.htm>, accessed June 2015.

Information and Communications

This section presents statistics on the various information and communications media: publishing, including newspapers, periodicals, books, and software; motion pictures, sound recordings, broadcasting, and telecommunications; and information services, such as libraries. Statistics on computer use and Internet access are also included.

Information industry—The U.S. Census Bureau's *Service Annual Survey, Information Services Sector*, provides estimates of revenues and expenses of firms in the information sector of the economy. Data are based on the North American Industry Classification System (NAICS). The information sector is a recently created economic sector. It comprises establishments engaged in the following processes: (1) producing and distributing information and cultural products, (2) providing the means to transmit or distribute these products as well as data or communications, and 3) processing data. It includes establishments previously classified in the Standard Industrial Classification (SIC) in manufacturing (publishing); transportation, communications, and utilities (telecommunications and broadcasting); and services (software publishing, motion picture production, data processing, online information services, and libraries).

The main components of the information sector include the publishing industries, including software publishing, and both traditional publishing and publishing exclusively on the Internet; the motion picture and sound recording industries; the broadcasting industries, including traditional broadcasting and broadcasting exclusively over the Internet; the telecommunications industries; and Web search portals, data processing industries, and information services.

Several industries in the information sectors have been consolidated. Telecommunications now encompasses wired (including broadband Internet service providers), wireless (including mobile), and satellite telecommunications. Broadcasting covers radio, television, and cable and other subscription programming. Internet publishing, and broadcasting, and web search portals are now grouped together.

Data from 1998 to 2003 are based on the 1997 NAICS; 2004 to 2010 data are based variously based on 2002 and 2007 NAICS; beginning in 2011, data are all based on 2007 NAICS, with data for various previous years revised to accommodate the new NAICS codes. Major revisions in many communications industries affect the comparability of these data. The following URL contains detailed information about NAICS, see <http://www.census.gov/eos/www/naics/>. See also the text in Section 15, Business Enterprise.

The 1997 Economic Census was the first economic census to cover the new information sector of the economy. The census, conducted every 5 years, for the years ending "2" and "7," provides information on the number of establishments, receipts, payroll, and paid employees for the United States and various geographic levels. The most recent reports are from the 2007 Economic Census. This census was conducted in accordance with the 2007 NAICS. Data

from the 2012 Economic Census are being released on a continuing basis through 2016.

The Federal Communications Commission (FCC), established in 1934, regulates wire and radio communications. Only the largest carriers and holding companies file annual financial reports which are publically available. The FCC has jurisdiction over interstate and foreign communication services but not over intrastate or local services. Also, the gross operating revenues of the telephone carriers reporting publically available data annually to the FCC are estimated to cover about 90 percent of the revenues of all U.S. telephone companies. Data are not comparable with Census Bureau's *Service Annual Survey* because of coverage and different accounting practices for those telephone companies which report to the FCC.

Reports filed by the broadcasting industry cover all radio and television stations operating in the United States. The private radio services represent the largest and most diverse group of licensees regulated by the FCC. These services provide voice, data communications, point-to-point, and point-to-multipoint radio communications for fixed and mobile communicators. Major users of these services are small businesses, the aviation industry, the maritime trades, the land transportation industry, the manufacturing industry, state and local public safety and governmental authorities, emergency medical service providers, amateur radio operators, and personal radio operations (CB and the General Mobile Radio Service). The FCC also licenses entities as private and common carriers. Private and common carriers provide fixed and land mobile communications service on a for-profit basis.

Statistics on publishing are available from the Census Bureau, as well as from various private agencies. Editor & Publisher Co., Irvin, CA, presents annual data on the number and circulation of daily and Sunday newspapers in its *Data Book*. The Association of American Publishers and Book Industry Study Group, New York, NY, provides data on book shipments. Data on public libraries are from the Institute of Museums and Library Services. Data on media use among the general public, including recent trends in use of the Internet and social media, and mobile electronic devices are collected by the Pew Research Center's Internet and American Life Project, Washington, DC. Gfk Mediamark Research and Intelligence also collects data on Internet use, as well as use of other traditional media.

Statistical reliability—For a discussion of statistical collection and estimation, sampling procedures, and measures of statistical reliability applicable to Census Bureau data, see Appendix III.

Table 1136. Information Industries—Type of Establishment, Employees, and Payroll: 2013

[Employees in thousands (3,266.1 represents 3,266,100); payroll in millions of dollars (273,297 represents $273,297,000,000). Excludes self-employed individuals, employees of private households, railroad employees, agricultural production employees, and most government employees. For more information see source and Appendix III]

| Industry | 2012 NAICS code [1] | Establishments | | | | Employ-ees [6] (1,000) | Annual payroll (mil. dol.) |
		Total [2]	Corpora-tions [3]	Sole proprietor-ships [4]	Non-profits [5]		
Information industries........................	**51**	**135,627**	**75,402**	**4,212**	**5,078**	**3,266.1**	**273,297**
Publishing industries (except Internet)...............	511	27,090	13,200	1,226	743	865.4	83,486
Newspaper, periodical, book, and directory........	5111	18,178	7,489	1,076	734	437.4	24,608
Newspaper publishers............................	51111	7,480	3,589	525	165	218.7	9,219
Periodical publishers............................	51112	6,160	2,276	312	314	102.8	7,692
Book publishers............................	51113	2,619	927	139	215	67.4	5,008
Directory and mailing list publishers...............	51114	1,079	491	42	16	26.6	1,818
Other publishers............................	51119	840	206	58	24	21.8	871
Greeting card publishers........................	511191	102	33	9	0	15.1	544
All other publishers........................	511199	738	173	49	24	6.7	328
Software publishers............................	5112	8,912	5,711	150	9	428.0	58,878
Motion picture and sound recording industries.......	512	25,239	7,044	1,189	568	344.4	16,936
Motion picture and video industries.................	5121	21,482	6,124	951	484	321.5	15,005
Motion picture and video production..............	51211	13,891	3,358	541	259	164.0	11,085
Motion picture and video distribution..............	51212	381	140	16	13	3.3	371
Motion picture and video exhibition..............	51213	4,690	2,038	287	198	127.2	1,515
Motion picture theaters (except drive-ins)........	512131	4,471	1,999	234	197	126.2	1,498
Drive-in motion picture theaters..................	512132	219	39	53	1	1.0	17
Post production and other motion picture and video industries........................	51219	2,520	588	107	14	27.0	2,033
Teleproduction and other postproduction services..................	512191	2,306	527	92	7	24.9	1,884
Other motion picture and video industries........	512199	214	61	15	7	2.1	150
Sound recording industries...........................	5122	3,757	920	238	84	23.0	1,932
Record production............................	51221	361	86	20	4	1.0	70
Integrated record production/distribution..........	51222	402	147	15	8	7.2	934
Music publishers............................	51223	772	219	56	6	5.3	434
Sound recording studios..........................	51224	1,698	356	126	10	5.8	316
Other sound recording industries..................	51229	524	112	21	56	3.6	177
Broadcasting (except Internet).........................	515	9,624	4,852	264	1,164	278.6	21,688
Radio and television broadcasting....................	5151	8,866	4,493	230	1,002	217.8	14,454
Radio broadcasting............................	51511	6,703	3,255	192	725	94.2	5,020
Radio networks........................	515111	797	275	30	181	11.4	822
Radio stations........................	515112	5,906	2,980	162	544	82.9	4,198
Television broadcasting............................	51512	2,163	1,238	38	277	123.6	9,434
Cable and other subscription programming........	5152	758	359	34	162	60.9	7,234
Telecommunications...................................	517	48,180	38,576	460	257	1,067.0	74,910
Wired telecommunications carriers...................	5171	31,260	28,709	186	229	746.4	52,491
Wireless telecommunications carriers (except satellite)............................	5172	11,590	8,126	33	8	256.7	17,015
Satellite telecommunications...........................	5174	552	204	17	3	8.2	894
Other telecommunications............................	5179	4,778	1,537	224	17	55.6	4,510
Telecommunications resellers....................	517911	2,352	680	88	4	26.4	1,631
All other telecommunications....................	517919	2,426	857	136	13	29.2	2,879
Data processing, hosting, and related services..................	518	14,276	7,771	439	141	488.9	43,020
Other information services............................	519	11,218	3,959	634	2,205	221.8	33,257
News syndicates............................	51911	505	353	11	17	7.8	655
Libraries and archives............................	51912	2,277	111	75	2,006	27.7	888
Internet publishing and broadcasting and Web search portals..................	51913	7,238	3,238	288	155	176.3	30,986
All other information services......................	51919	1,198	257	260	27	10.0	729

[1] 2012 North American Industry Classification System; see text, this section and Section 15. [2] Includes other types of establishments, not shown separately. [3] An incorporated business that is granted a charter recognizing it as a separate legal entity having its own privileges, and liabilities distinct from those of its members. [4] An unincorporated business with a sole owner. [5] An organization that does not distribute surplus funds to its owners or shareholders, but instead uses surplus funds to help pursue its goals. Most non-profit organizations are exempt from income taxes. [6] For employees on the payroll for the pay period including March 12.

Source: U.S. Census Bureau, County Business Patterns, "CB1300A12: Geography Area Series: County Business Patterns by Legal Form of Organization," <http://factfinder2.census.gov>, accessed April 2015.

Table 1137. Information Sector Services—Estimated Revenue and Expenses: 2011 to 2013

[In millions of dollars (1,160,546 represents $1,160,546,000,000). For all employer firms regardless of tax status. Estimates have been adjusted to the results of the 2007 Economic Census. Beginning with 2011, data are based on the 2007 NAICS; data for 2010 have been restated to reflect comparable data on the 2007 NAICS basis. Based on the Service Annual Survey; see Appendix III]

Industry	2007 NAICS [1] code	Operating revenue			Operating expenses		
		2011	2012	2013	2011	2012	2013
Information industries..............................	**51**	**1,160,546**	**1,209,206**	**1,250,526**	**893,093**	**931,017**	**954,794**
Publishing industries (except Internet)...............	511	275,854	277,882	287,234	190,864	195,370	199,393
Newspaper publishers................................	51111	33,168	32,248	30,853	31,082	30,365	29,096
Periodical publishers................................	51112	38,906	39,287	39,088	31,128	31,936	31,698
Book publishers.....................................	51113	28,006	27,441	29,049	16,779	16,576	17,940
Directory and mailing list publishers................	51114	13,042	12,183	10,795	10,542	9,139	8,574
Greeting card publishers..........................	511191	3,822	3,720	3,620	2,594	2,559	2,448
All other publishers..............................	511199	1,693	1,724	1,526	1,229	1,236	1,055
Software publishers..................................	5112	157,217	161,279	172,303	97,510	103,559	108,582
Motion picture and sound recording industries.......	512	95,751	99,977	103,511	77,021	78,360	82,039
Motion picture and video production and distribution [2]...	5121x	63,840	67,082	70,015	53,257	54,367	56,929
Motion picture and video exhibition................	51213	13,309	14,545	15,285	10,657	11,085	12,086
Teleproduction and other postproduction services..	512191	5,083	4,976	5,087	4,700	4,551	4,662
Other motion picture and video industries........	512199	527	479	351	439	402	273
Record production..................................	51221	490	481	672	345	364	473
Integrated record production/distribution...........	51222	7,324	7,214	6,713	5,055	5,018	5,003
Music publishers....................................	51223	3,868	3,887	4,010	1,421	1,464	1,476
Sound recording studios...........................	51224	873	898	930	752	787	801
Other sound recording industries..................	51229	437	415	448	395	322	336
Broadcasting (except Internet).......................	515	112,995	120,996	125,311	80,907	83,944	86,611
Radio networks....................................	515111	5,131	5,638	6,234	4,221	4,501	4,786
Radio stations.....................................	515112	12,255	12,539	12,227	9,439	9,748	9,631
Television broadcasting............................	51512	35,291	38,651	38,492	30,132	30,688	30,788
Cable and other subscription programming.......	5152	60,318	64,168	68,358	37,115	39,007	41,406
Telecommunications..................................	517	539,611	556,587	569,174	432,021	445,995	448,186
Wired telecommunications carriers [3]..............	5171	302,007	307,329	310,168	253,575	256,137	255,209
Wireless telecommunications carriers [4] (except satellite).....................................	5172	209,116	218,513	226,003	157,800	167,607	169,392
Satellite telecommunications.......................	5174	5,434	5,671	5,767	3,953	4,107	4,006
Telecommunications resellers [5]...................	517911	10,119	10,920	12,082	7,069	7,839	8,739
All other telecommunications [6]...................	517919	12,935	14,154	15,154	9,624	10,305	10,840
Data processing, hosting, and related services......	518	81,965	89,755	95,476	71,062	78,642	84,382
Other information services...........................	519	54,370	64,009	69,820	41,218	48,706	54,183
News syndicates..................................	51911	2,177	2,322	2,294	1,844	1,965	1,951
Libraries and archives..............................	51912	2,139	1,924	2,124	1,764	1,867	1,906
Internet publishing and broadcasting, and Web search portals [7]...............................	51913	47,391	56,677	62,501	35,193	42,154	47,860
Other information services.........................	51919	2,663	3,086	2,901	2,417	2,720	2,466

[1] North American Industry Classification System (NAICS), 2007; see text, Section 15. [2] Includes 2007 NAICS 51211 (Motion Picture and Video Production) and 2007 NAICS 51212 (Motion Picture and Video Distribution). [3] Includes 2002 NAICS 5171 (Wired Telecommunications Carriers), 2002 NAICS 5175 (Cable and Other Program Distribution), and a portion of 2002 NAICS 518111 (Internet Service Providers). [4] Includes 2002 NAICS 517211 (Paging), 2002 NAICS 517212 (Cellular and Other Wireless Telecommunications) and a portion of 2002 NAICS 518111 (Internet Service Providers). [5] Includes 2002 NAICS 5173 (Telecommunications Resellers). [6] Includes 2002 NAICS 517910 (Other Telecommunications) and a portion of 2002 NAICS 518111 (Internet Service Providers). [7] Includes 2002 NAICS 516 (Internet Publishing and Broadcasting) and 2002 NAICS 518112 (Web Search Portals).

Source: U.S. Census Bureau, Annual & Quarterly Services, "2013 Annual Services," <http://www.census.gov/services/index.html>, accessed December 2014.

Table 1138. Information Industries—Establishments, Revenue, Payroll, and Employees by Kind of Business: 2012

[1,231,919 represents $1,231,919,000,000. For establishments with payroll. Based on the 2012 Economic Census; see Appendix III. Data for 2012 are preliminary]

Kind of business	2012 NAICS code [1]	Establish-ments	Receipts (mil. dol.)	Annual payroll (mil. dol.)	Paid employees (1,000)
Information industries...................................	**51**	**134,652**	**1,231,919**	**263,505**	**3,206**
Publishing industries (except Internet).............................	511	26,886	259,228	79,884	865
Newspaper, periodical, book, & directory publishers...............	5111	18,818	100,266,363	24,854,946	461,382
Software publishers...	5112	8,676	169,772	57,137	419
Motion picture & sound recording industries.........................	512	24,816	95,389	16,480	306
Motion picture & video industries...............................	5121	21,229	80,993	14,353	281
Sound recording industries..................................	5122	3,748	11,028	1,959	25
Broadcasting (except Internet).................................	515	9,527	124,460	20,169	279
Cable & other subscription programming...........................	5152	772	61,094	6,028	54
Telecommunications...	517	50,576	546,922	76,033	1,142
Wired telecommunications carriers..............................	5171	32,609	285,080	54,142	787
Wireless telecommunications carriers (except satellite)............	5172	13,428	226,010	17,066	293
Satellite telecommunications..................................	5174	535	6,638	862	10
Other telecommunications....................................	5179	4,004	29,194	3,963	52
Data processing, hosting, and related services.....................	518	14,319	104,154	40,705	486
Other information services....................................	519	10,497	93,106	34,858	229

[1] North American Industry Classification System, 2012; see text, this section and Section 15.

Source: U.S. Census Bureau, 2012 Economic Census, "Table EC1200A1: All Sectors: Geographic Area Series: Economy-Wide Key Statistics: 2012," <http://factfinder2.census.gov/>, accessed April 2015.

Table 1139. Information Industries—Establishments, Employees, and Payroll by State: 2013

[Annual payroll in millions of dollars (273,296.8 represents $273,296,800,000). Based on Census Bureau's County Business Patterns and Nonemployer Statistics programs. Data are for North American Industry Classification System (NAICS) 2012 code 51]

State	Establish-ments	Annual payroll (mil. dol.)	Paid employ-ees [1]	Non-employer establish-ments	State	Establish-ments	Annual payroll (mil. dol.)	Paid employ-ees [1]	Non-employer establish-ments
U.S.........	**135,627**	**273,296.8**	**3,266,084**	**326,526**	MO.........	2,360	3,487.1	55,531	4,568
AL...........	1,466	1,764.7	34,447	2,930	MT.........	642	419.7	9,043	955
AK...........	394	405.6	6,561	514	NE.........	909	1,279.6	21,085	1,326
AZ...........	2,057	2,804.2	47,817	5,840	NV.........	1,190	931.8	16,542	3,215
AR...........	971	1,411.5	25,784	1,673	NH.........	769	1,095.9	13,984	1,482
CA...........	21,536	69,917.3	582,259	59,681	NJ.........	3,757	8,950.7	94,715	10,385
CO...........	3,031	6,368.6	81,292	7,295	NM.........	751	517.6	11,644	1,601
CT...........	1,656	2,996.2	39,120	3,913	NY.........	11,286	27,423.7	272,164	29,773
DE...........	446	334.3	6,372	878	NC.........	3,388	5,170.9	79,105	8,288
DC...........	703	2,298.6	20,854	1,524	ND.........	348	389.9	6,651	447
FL...........	7,940	10,716.2	155,169	23,066	OH.........	3,609	5,327.1	86,491	8,952
GA...........	4,001	9,846.9	127,080	10,560	OK.........	1,438	1,381.8	28,119	2,687
HI...........	506	490.5	8,244	1,130	OR.........	1,950	2,273.2	37,062	4,677
ID...........	633	542.4	11,996	1,468	PA.........	5,098	8,943.9	116,681	10,205
IL...........	5,300	8,979.6	123,824	11,772	RI.........	455	438.2	7,259	945
IN...........	2,078	2,141.0	42,217	4,675	SC.........	1,326	1,834.9	34,328	3,283
IA...........	1,517	1,442.7	30,432	2,149	SD.........	447	285.7	6,676	574
KS...........	1,337	2,805.0	38,725	2,186	TN.........	2,388	2,623.3	49,615	6,568
KY...........	1,458	1,292.4	32,838	2,680	TX.........	8,945	16,356.2	226,590	23,072
LA...........	1,382	1,263.1	25,217	3,191	UT.........	1,367	2,392.6	37,863	3,927
ME...........	806	564.1	11,683	1,291	VT.........	496	410.9	6,777	839
MD...........	2,467	4,123.5	53,899	6,797	VA.........	3,894	7,852.6	92,779	7,857
MA...........	3,713	10,848.0	110,581	7,927	WA.........	3,268	16,625.5	123,018	7,123
MI...........	3,448	4,786.2	71,069	8,166	WV.........	656	524.0	11,225	863
MN...........	2,572	4,401.6	62,114	5,439	WI.........	2,217	3,089.5	54,393	4,103
MS...........	898	541.8	13,011	1,502	WY.........	357	184.5	4,139	564

[1] Number of paid employees for pay period including March 12.

Source: U.S. Census Bureau, County Business Patterns, "CB1300A11. Geography Area Series: County Business Patterns, 2013"; and Nonemployer Statistics, "NS1300A2. Geographic Area Series: Nonemployer Statistics for the U.S."; <http://factfinder2.census.gov/>, accessed May 2015. See also <http://www.census.gov/econ/cbp/> and <http://www.census.gov/econ/nonemployer/>.

Table 1140. Utilization and Number of Selected Media: 2000 to 2013

[100.2 represents 100,200,000]

Media	Unit	2000	2005	2006	2007	2008	2009	2010	2011	2012	2013
Households with—											
Telephones [1]	Millions	100.2	107.0	108.8	112.2	112.7	114.0	114.0	114.4	116.9	118.4
Telephone service [1]	Percent	94.1	92.9	93.4	94.9	95.0	95.7	95.5	95.6	95.8	95.7
Landline households with											
wireless telephone [2]	Percent	(X)	42.4	45.6	58.9	58.5	59.4	58.1	55.0	52.5	49.5
Wireless-only [2]	Percent	(X)	7.3	10.5	13.6	17.5	22.7	26.6	31.6	35.8	39.4
Total broadcast stations [3, 4]	Number	(NA)	27,354	27,807	29,593	29,832	30,503	30,630	30,411	30,470	30,432
Radio stations	Number	(NA)	13,660	13,837	13,977	14,253	14,420	14,619	14,952	15,196	15,358
AM stations	Number	4,685	4,757	4,754	4,776	4,786	4,790	4,782	4,766	4,738	4,727
FM commercial	Number	5,892	6,231	6,266	6,309	6,427	6,479	6,526	6,542	6,598	6,612
FM educational	Number	(NA)	2,672	2,817	2,892	3,040	3,151	3,311	3,644	3,860	4,019
Television stations [3]	Number	1,663	1,750	1,756	1,759	1,759	1,782	1,781	1,783	1,781	1,784
Commercial	Number	1,288	1,370	1,376	1,379	1,378	1,392	1,390	1,387	1,386	1,388
VHF TV band	Number	567	588	587	583	582	373	368	360	358	358
UHF TV band	Number	721	782	789	796	796	1,019	1,022	1,027	1,028	1,030
Educational	Number	(NA)	380	380	380	381	390	391	396	395	396
VHF TV band	Number	(NA)	126	128	128	129	107	107	107	107	107
UHF TV band	Number	(NA)	254	252	252	252	283	284	289	288	289
Broadband subscribers: [5]											
Total fixed broadband [6]	Millions	6.8	47.8	60.2	70.2	75.7	80.0	84.5	88.3	92.5	96.0
Mobile wireless [7]	Millions	(NA)	(NA)	(NA)	(NA)	26.5	56.3	97.5	141.9	170.1	197.4

NA Not available. X Not applicable. [1] As of November. Based on Current Population Survey. Source: Federal Communications Commission, prior to 2012, *Telephone Subscribership in the United States,* December 2011, and earlier reports. Beginning 2012, *Universal Service Monitoring Report, 2014,* and earlier reports. See also <http://transition.fcc.gov/wcb/iatd/lec.html> and <http://transition.fcc.gov/wcb/iatd/monitor.html>. [2] For January to June. Based on National Health Interview Survey. For families living in the same housing unit. Source: U.S. National Center for Health Statistics, *Wireless Substitution: Early Release of Estimates From the National Health Interview Survey, January–June 2014,* December 2014, and earlier reports. See also <http://www.cdc.gov/nchs/nhis/releases.htm#wireless>. [3] As of December, 31. Source: Federal Communications Commission Encyclopedia, "Broadcast Station Totals," <https://www.fcc.gov/encyclopedia/broadcast-radio-am-and-fm-application-status-lists>, accessed June 2015. [4] Includes Class A, Low Power TV, UHF and VHF Translators; FM Translators and Boosters; and Low Power FM stations. [5] As of December. Internet access over 200 kilobits per second in at least one direction. Based on FCC Form 477. Source: Federal Communications Commission, Wireline Competition Bureau, *Internet Access Services: Status as of December 31, 2013,* October 2014. [6] Includes aDSL, sDSL, cable modem, fiber-to-the-premises, satellite, fixed wireless, power line, and other. [7] Data prior to 2008 not shown due to reporting instruction changes on FCC Form 477 between June 2008 and December 2008; see source for details.

Source: Compiled from sources mentioned in footnotes.

Table 1141. Multimedia Audiences—Summary: 2014

[In percent, except total population (238,128 represents 238,128,000). As of Fall 2014. For persons age 18 and over. Represents the percent of persons using each media type during an average week, except as noted. Based on a sample and subject to sampling error]

Item	Total pop. (1,000)	TV viewing	TV prime time viewing	Cable TV viewing [1]	Radio listening	Newspaper reading [2]	Accessed Internet
Total	**238,128**	**90.26**	**80.70**	**79.74**	**82.84**	**52.14**	**78.84**
18 to 24 years old	30,176	82.44	68.22	74.30	85.59	42.73	94.93
25 to 34 years old	41,977	84.72	73.85	72.61	87.51	41.46	92.95
35 to 44 years old	40,106	89.00	78.84	78.36	89.87	46.26	88.42
45 to 54 years old	43,690	92.51	83.30	83.36	87.31	53.87	80.22
55 to 64 years old	38,665	94.36	87.54	83.35	82.01	58.22	73.60
65 years old and over	43,514	96.28	89.00	84.83	66.22	67.26	48.52
Male	114,733	89.80	79.98	79.02	84.26	50.91	78.17
Female	123,395	90.69	81.37	80.41	81.53	53.29	79.47
White only	176,371	89.91	81.10	80.87	82.63	53.65	80.45
Black only	28,772	94.38	85.16	81.15	84.11	56.65	72.64
Other races/multiple classifications	32,985	88.55	74.66	72.48	82.88	40.14	75.68
Employed:							
Full time	114,439	89.61	80.01	80.81	89.54	50.45	89.05
Part time	29,041	87.08	74.00	77.10	85.44	49.94	88.23
Not employed	94,648	92.03	83.60	79.26	73.94	54.86	63.63
Household income:							
Less than $50,000	98,080	89.36	79.87	71.96	76.77	50.38	63.74
$50,000 to $74,999	43,795	90.82	80.27	82.19	83.62	52.82	83.40
$75,000 to $149,999	67,939	91.03	82.09	85.38	88.25	53.78	90.56
$150,000 or more	28,314	90.65	80.93	89.35	89.69	53.28	96.01

[1] In the past 7 days. [2] One or more issues over a 28-day period.

Source: GfK Mediamark Research & Intelligence, LLC, New York, NY, Fall 2014 ©. See also <http://www.mri.gfk.com/en/gfk-mri.html>.

Table 1142. Book Publishers' Net Shipments: 2010 to 2013

[Represents net publishers' shipments after returns. Covers print and digital formats. Includes all titles released by publishers in the United States and imports which appear under the imprints of American publishers. Multivolume sets, such as encyclopedias, are counted as one unit. Due to changes in methodology and scope, these data are not comparable to those previously published]

Type of publication	2010, estimated	2011, estimated	2012, estimated	2013, estimated
Total	**2,527,032,135**	**2,395,736,824**	**2,621,564,255**	**2,586,957,173**
Trade [1]	2,267,410,578	2,091,763,263	2,355,490,342	2,316,950,660
Higher education	53,138,459	56,502,508	56,299,516	57,018,956
Elementary and high school	79,690,484	118,829,228	97,602,285	103,988,793
Professional	120,486,010	120,203,654	105,920,577	102,046,421
Scholarly	4,199,561	7,566,782	5,745,576	6,239,391

[1] Includes adult, juvenile, and religious.

Source: The Association of American Publishers and Book Industry Study Group, Inc., New York, NY, *BookStats, Volume Four ©,* 2014. See also <http://www.bisg.org/>.

Table 1143. Books Published by Subject: 2005 to 2013

[Data shown are print ISBN (International Standard Book Number) counts, by year of publication. Data are compiled in June of the following year. Includes ISBNs that have not been assigned a subject, books that do not have prices, and books with alternative book bindings (such as stapled and laminated)]

Subject	2005	2007	2008	2009	2010	2011	2012	2013 [1]
Total............................	282,500	407,646	561,580	1,335,475	4,152,906	1,608,751	2,352,797	1,413,095
Agriculture...........................	1,483	1,259	1,556	1,363	1,833	1,773	2,194	1,470
Arts................................	8,762	9,291	10,304	9,860	10,910	10,701	11,320	11,083
Biography...........................	8,904	11,414	11,375	13,795	12,291	12,163	11,333	10,842
Business...........................	7,885	7,722	8,873	9,351	10,194	10,109	13,989	11,116
Computers..........................	6,092	6,069	5,638	5,276	7,553	6,986	7,028	6,959
Cooking............................	3,062	2,836	3,164	2,643	3,057	2,963	3,168	3,181
Education..........................	6,951	7,162	9,640	9,578	10,839	11,820	11,122	10,669
Fiction............................	34,927	53,590	53,058	48,738	46,641	43,016	49,853	50,498
General works......................	2,017	2,211	2,400	2,562	3,004	2,708	2,507	2,446
History............................	12,686	14,406	13,477	15,480	14,659	12,270	11,959	12,471
Home economics.....................	1,634	1,775	1,644	1,656	1,699	1,579	1,664	1,508
Juveniles..........................	32,112	31,009	29,825	33,028	31,371	30,836	33,239	32,902
Language...........................	5,669	4,879	6,181	5,426	4,929	4,358	4,537	4,475
Law...............................	5,468	5,195	5,533	5,915	5,908	5,795	5,531	6,072
Literature..........................	6,297	9,974	10,843	11,456	9,315	7,054	7,004	8,591
Medicine...........................	11,688	10,777	11,022	11,093	12,869	13,690	15,077	13,400
Music..............................	4,076	3,540	4,131	4,570	3,927	3,948	4,273	5,294
Personal finance....................	542	582	598	699	595	636	591	538
Philosophy and psychology..........	10,556	13,098	12,605	13,949	14,277	14,011	15,018	15,479
Poetry and drama...................	9,414	11,610	11,700	13,474	11,723	9,653	10,038	10,156
Religion............................	16,785	19,540	18,296	20,527	18,937	18,518	19,854	18,653
Science............................	12,626	12,714	14,100	15,608	20,706	19,010	18,852	18,684
Sociology and economics............	23,750	24,546	24,737	26,904	28,581	28,356	28,442	29,399
Sports and recreation...............	6,438	6,362	6,262	5,971	6,639	6,198	6,197	5,807
Technology.........................	7,138	7,131	7,666	8,688	11,599	10,131	11,564	9,769
Travel..............................	4,941	5,678	5,101	4,800	4,572	3,755	3,603	3,450
Nontraditional/not classified [2].....	30,597	123,276	271,851	1,033,065	3,844,278	1,316,714	2,042,840	1,108,183

[1] Projected. [2] Consists of reprints (often public domain), other titles printed on-demand, and wiki-based material. Also includes records not yet classified or not classifiable.

Source: © ProQuest LLC, Bowker®, a ProQuest affiliate, "ISBN Annual Output Reports," <http://www.bowker.com/tools-resources/Bowker-Data.html>, accessed June 2015.

Table 1144. Publishing Industries—Estimated Revenue by Source and Media Type: 2010 to 2013

[In millions of dollars (265,718 represents $265,718,000,000). For all employer firms regardless of tax status. Data are based on the 2007 North American Industry Classification System (NAICS), and cover 2007 NAICS 51111, 51112, 51113, and 51114. Estimates have been adjusted to the results of the 2007 Economic Census. See text, this section and Section 15, and Appendix III]

Source of revenue and media type	2010	2011	2012	2013
Publishing industries (except Internet) [1]......................................	**265,718**	**275,854**	**277,882**	**287,234**
Newspaper publishers...	**34,695**	**33,168**	**32,248**	**30,853**
Subscription and sales..	8,831	8,644	8,525	8,587
Advertising space...	21,193	19,862	18,670	17,346
Classified advertising..	5,285	4,840	(S)	3,916
All other advertising...	15,908	15,022	(S)	13,430
Other operating revenue...	4,671	4,662	5,053	4,920
Printing services...	1,263	1,318	1,435	1,559
Distribution services...	1,319	1,239	1,237	1,272
All other...	2,089	2,105	2,381	2,089
Print newspapers..	28,052	26,339	24,320	23,107
Online newspapers..	1,679	1,905	2,623	2,433
Other media newspapers...	293	262	252	393
Periodical publishers..	**38,395**	**38,906**	**39,287**	**39,088**
Subscription and sales..	12,965	13,146	14,555	14,459
Advertising space...	16,788	16,881	16,495	16,746
Other operating revenue...	8,642	8,879	8,237	7,883
Printing services for others.......................................	1,495	1,463	1,235	1,251
Licensing of rights to content.....................................	523	533	550	578
All other...	6,624	6,883	6,452	6,054
Print periodicals..	24,796	24,947	24,679	24,732
Online periodicals..	4,098	4,134	5,285	5,418
Other media periodicals...	859	946	1,086	1,055
Book publishers...	**28,121**	**28,006**	**27,441**	**29,049**
Textbooks..	8,716	8,766	8,351	10,251
Children's books..	3,233	3,210	3,510	3,299
General reference books...	646	681	574	561
Professional, technical, and scholarly books.......................	5,203	5,151	5,195	4,678
Adult trade books...	6,718	6,634	6,263	6,460
All other operating revenue..	3,605	3,564	3,548	3,800
Print books...	20,167	19,642	18,834	19,369
Online books...	3,343	3,826	4,312	5,089
Other media books..	1,006	974	747	791
Directory and mailing list publishers............................	**13,475**	**13,042**	**12,183**	**10,795**
Subscription and sales..	2,335	2,311	(S)	4,074
Advertising space...	10,402	10,069	7,351	6,263
Print directories, databases, and other collections of information....	8,302	8,230	7,285	6,498
Online directories, databases, and other collections of information...	3,955	3,708	3,971	3,529
Other media directories, databases, and other collections of information......	480	442	(S)	310

S Figure does not meet publication standards. [1] Includes other industries not shown separately.

Source: U.S. Census Bureau, Annual & Quarterly Services, "2013 Annual Services," <http://www.census.gov/services/index.html>, accessed December 2014.

Table 1145. Daily and Sunday Newspapers—Number and Circulation: 1970 to 2014

[Circulation in millions (62.1 represents 62,100,000). Number of newspapers as of February 1 the following year, except as noted. Circulation figures as of 6-month period ended primarily September 30 of year shown. For English language newspapers only]

Type	1970	1980	1990	2000	2005	2008	2009	2010	2011	2012	2013[3]	2014[3]
NUMBER												
Total daily newspapers [1]	**1,748**	**1,745**	**1,611**	**1,480**	**1,452**	**1,408**	**1,397**	**(NA)**	**1,381**	**1,425**	**1,395**	**1,331**
Morning	334	387	559	766	817	872	869	(NA)	930	983	980	953
Evening	1,429	1,388	1,084	727	645	546	528	(NA)	451	442	444	402
Sunday newspapers	586	736	863	917	914	902	919	(NA)	899	980	934	923
NET PAID CIRCULATION (mil.)												
Total daily newspapers [1]	62.1	62.2	62.3	55.8	53.3	48.6	46.3	(NA)	44.2	43.2	40.7	40.4
Morning	25.9	29.4	41.3	46.8	46.1	42.8	40.8	(NA)	40.1	38.4	37.0	36.8
Evening	36.2	32.8	21.0	9.0	7.2	5.8	5.5	(NA)	4.1	4.7	3.7	3.7
Sunday newspapers	49.2	54.7	62.6	59.4	55.3	49.1	46.8	(NA)	48.3	44.6	43.3	42.8
PER CAPITA CIRCULATION [2]												
Total daily newspapers [1]	0.30	0.27	0.25	0.20	0.18	0.16	0.15	(NA)	0.14	0.14	0.13	0.13
Morning	0.13	0.13	0.17	0.17	0.16	0.14	0.13	(NA)	0.13	0.12	0.12	0.12
Evening	0.18	0.14	0.08	0.03	0.02	0.02	0.02	(NA)	0.01	0.02	0.01	0.01
Sunday newspapers	0.24	0.24	0.25	0.21	0.19	0.16	0.15	(NA)	0.16	0.14	0.14	0.13

NA Not available. [1] All-day newspapers are counted in both morning and evening rows but only once in total. Circulation is divided equally between morning and evening. [2] Based on U.S. Census Bureau estimated resident population as of July 1 as of year shown. [3] Number of newspapers as of January 1 of following year.

Source: Editor & Publisher, 17782 Cowan Ste C, Irvin, CA 92614, *Editor & Publisher Newspaper DataBook* ©, annual. See also <http://www.editorandpublisher.com/>.

Table 1146. Daily and Sunday Newspapers—Number and Circulation: Total, 1995 to 2014, and by State, 2014

[Circulation in thousands (58,193 represents 58,193,000). Number of newspapers as of February 1 the following year, except as noted. Circulation as of 6-month period ended primarily September 30 of year shown. For English language newspapers only]

State	Daily Number	Daily Circulation [1] Net paid (1,000)	Daily Circulation [1] Per capita [2]	Sunday Number	Sunday Net paid circulation [1] (1,000s)	State	Daily Number	Daily Circulation [1] Net paid (1,000)	Daily Circulation [1] Per capita [2]	Sunday Number	Sunday Net paid circulation [1] (1,000s)
Total, 1995	1,533	58,193	0.22	888	61,529	IA	36	411	0.13	14	417
Total, 1996	1,520	56,983	0.21	890	60,798	KS	28	266	0.09	13	226
Total, 1997	1,509	56,728	0.21	903	60,484	KY	22	375	0.08	14	413
Total, 1998	1,489	56,182	0.20	898	60,066	LA	21	398	0.09	15	500
Total, 1999	1,483	55,979	0.20	905	59,894	ME	7	148	0.11	6	171
Total, 2000	1,480	55,773	0.20	917	59,421	MD	9	160	0.03	8	441
Total, 2001	1,468	55,578	0.19	913	59,090	MA	33	882	0.13	19	954
Total, 2002	1,457	55,186	0.19	913	58,780	MI	47	957	0.10	25	1,096
Total, 2003	1,456	55,185	0.19	917	58,495	MN	22	740	0.14	14	946
Total, 2004	1,457	54,626	0.19	915	57,753	MS	19	226	0.08	18	238
Total, 2005	1,452	53,345	0.18	914	55,270	MO	36	586	0.10	20	724
Total, 2006	1,437	52,329	0.18	907	53,175	MT	11	144	0.14	8	146
Total, 2007	1,422	50,742	0.17	907	51,246	NE	16	260	0.14	7	236
Total, 2008	1,408	48,598	0.16	902	49,115	NV	6	400	0.14	6	382
Total, 2009	1,397	46,278	0.15	919	46,895	NH	11	150	0.11	8	145
Total, 2010	(NA)	(NA)	(NA)	(NA)	(NA)	NJ	17	1,041	0.12	15	1,147
Total, 2011	1,381	44,243	0.14	899	48,301	NM	17	677	0.32	14	650
Total, 2012	1,425	43,154	0.14	980	44,612	NY	56	6,832	0.35	39	5,234
Total, 2013[3]	1,395	40,712	0.13	934	43,292	ND	45	828	0.08	40	955
						ND	10	119	0.16	7	119
Total, 2014 [3]	**1,331**	**40,420**	**0.13**	**923**	**42,751**	OH	81	1,535	0.13	48	1,829
AL	21	230	0.05	16	231	OK	33	366	0.09	26	436
AK	7	85	0.12	4	66	OR	15	460	0.12	12	463
AZ	12	421	0.06	11	726	PA	74	1,869	0.15	50	2,218
AR	27	410	0.14	16	466	RI	5	100	0.10	2	106
CA	79	3,679	0.09	64	4,122	SC	16	392	0.08	14	465
CO	27	726	0.14	17	827	SD	11	112	0.13	5	99
CT	18	399	0.11	15	527	TN	26	595	0.09	19	716
DE	2	105	0.11	2	100	TX	74	1,838	0.07	72	2,607
DC	3	502	0.76	2	665	UT	6	368	0.12	6	505
FL	36	2,338	0.12	33	2,463	VT	8	77	0.12	4	57
GA	33	635	0.06	28	741	VA	20	3,134	0.38	17	1,924
HI	6	258	0.18	5	269	WA	19	680	0.10	16	882
ID	12	153	0.09	10	247	WV	19	257	0.14	13	252
IL	61	1,509	0.12	30	1,800	WI	33	633	0.11	18	731
IN	69	885	0.13	32	1,004	WY	9	72	0.12	6	65

NA Not available. [1] Circulation figures based on the principal community served by a newspaper which is not necessarily the same location as the publisher's office. [2] Per capita based on estimated resident population as of July 1 of year shown. [3] Number of newspapers as of January 1 of following year.

Source: Editor & Publisher, 17782 Cowan Ste C, Irvin, CA 92614, *Editor & Publisher Newspaper DataBook* ©, annual. See also <http://www.editorandpublisher.com/>.

Table 1147. Software Publishers—Estimated Revenue by Type: 2010 to 2013

[In millions of dollars (145,425 represents $145,425,000,000). For all employer firms regardless of tax status. Covers NAICS 5112. Estimates have been adjusted to the results of the 2007 Economic Census. Data are based on the 2007 NAICS. See text, this section, and Section 15, See also Appendix III]

Item	2010	2011	2012	2013
Operating revenue	**145,425**	**157,217**	**161,279**	**172,303**
Source of revenue:				
System software publishing [1]	48,913	49,143	50,398	56,887
Operating system software	17,811	16,835	16,237	18,967
Network software	14,369	15,098	16,064	17,749
Database management software	9,502	9,774	10,342	11,613
Development tools and programming languages software	3,637	3,754	3,537	4,034
Application software publishing [1]	54,981	59,584	59,924	62,573
General business productivity and home use applications	24,902	27,011	27,386	29,404
Cross-industry application software	13,178	14,815	14,881	17,148
Vertical market application software	9,030	9,627	9,650	8,531
Utilities application software	2,561	3,186	2,865	2,882
Other services [1]	(NA)	48,490	50,957	(NA)
Custom application design and development	4,401	4,977	5,140	(S)
Information technology technical consulting services	4,467	5,062	5,362	5,777
Resale of computer hardware and software	4,311	5,901	5,672	6,614
Information technology-related training services	1,637	1,692	2,032	1,932
Breakdown of revenue by software sales type:				
System software	48,913	49,143	50,398	56,887
Personal computer software	17,022	(D)	14,698	15,481
Enterprise or network software	18,789	19,930	21,197	24,365
Mainframe computer software	9,454	9,250	10,207	11,781
Other system software	3,648	(D)	4,296	5,260
Application software	54,981	59,584	59,924	62,573
Personal computer software	16,380	17,788	18,161	18,226
Enterprise or network software	27,661	30,536	30,191	32,205
Mainframe computer software	1,910	1,764	1,584	1,528
Other application software	9,030	9,496	9,988	10,614

NA Not available. S Data do not meet publication standards. D Figure withheld to avoid disclosure of data of individual companies; data are included in higher level totals where available. [1] Includes other sources of revenue, not shown separately.

Source: U.S. Census Bureau, Annual & Quarterly Services, "2013 Annual Services," <http://www.census.gov/services/index.html>, accessed December 2014.

Table 1148. Internet Publishing and Broadcasting, and Web Search Portals—Estimated Revenue and Expenses: 2010 to 2013

[In millions of dollars (41,725 represents $41,725,000,000). For all employer firms regardless of tax status. Beginning with 2010, data are based on the 2007 North American Industry Classification System (NAICS), and cover NAICS 51913. 2007 NAICS 51913 includes 2002 NAICS 516 (Internet Publishing and Broadcasting) and 2002 NAICS 518112 (Web Search Portals). Estimates have been adjusted to the results of the 2007 Economic Census. See text, Section 15, and Appendix III]

Item	2010	2011	2012	2013
Operating revenue	**41,725**	**47,391**	**56,677**	**62,501**
Source of revenue:				
Publishing and broadcasting of content on the Internet	14,613	15,849	18,700	19,837
Online advertising space	20,797	23,942	28,408	32,109
Licensing of rights to use intellectual property	998	1,542	2,197	2,439
All other operating revenue	(S)	(S)	7,372	8,116
Revenue by type of customer:				
Household consumers and individual users	(S)	(S)	14,904	16,215
Business firms, not-for-profit organizations, and government	(S)	(S)	41,773	46,286
Operating expenses	**30,735**	**35,193**	**42,154**	**47,860**

S Data do not meet publication standards.

Source: U.S. Census Bureau, Annual & Quarterly Services, "2013 Annual Services," <http://www.census.gov/services/index.html>, accessed December 2014.

Table 1149. Motion Picture and Sound Recording Industries—Estimated Revenue and Sources of Revenue: 2009 to 2013

[In millions of dollars (90,398 represents $90,398,000,000). For all employer firms regardless of tax status. Estimates have been adjusted to the results of the 2007 Economic Census. Data for 2009 and prior are based on the 2002 North American Industry Classification System (NAICS). Beginning with 2010, data are based on the 2007 NAICS. See text Section 15 and Appendix III]

Kind of business	2009	2010	2011	2012	2013
Operating revenue	**90,398**	**94,221**	**94,824**	**99,081**	**102,391**
Motion picture and video industries	**75,979**	**81,331**	**82,759**	**87,082**	**90,738**
Motion picture and video production and distribution [1,2]	57,910	62,567	63,840	67,082	70,015
Domestic licensing of rights to motion picture films	10,633	13,787	13,509	14,106	14,385
Domestic licensing of rights to television programs	9,968	11,365	12,355	13,369	14,215
International licensing of rights to motion picture films	6,710	9,100	8,100	8,113	8,939
International licensing of rights to television programs	3,317	3,174	3,543	3,997	4,537
Sale of audiovisual works for wholesale, retail, and rental markets	12,511	11,121	11,364	9,438	8,739
Motion picture and video exhibition [1]	13,293	13,454	13,309	14,545	15,285
Feature film exhibition revenue	8,959	9,101	8,859	9,537	9,926
Food and beverage sales	3,825	3,789	3,858	4,217	4,483
Postproduction services and other motion picture and video industries [1]	4,776	5,310	5,610	5,455	5,438
Audiovisual postproduction services	2,601	3,167	3,489	3,480	3,612
Motion picture film laboratory services	366	418	320	(S)	145
Duplication and copying services	1,124	1,185	1,229	1,122	1,091
Sound recording industries	**14,419**	**12,890**	**12,065**	**11,999**	**11,653**
Integrated record production and distribution [1]	8,665	8,258	7,324	7,214	6,713
Licensing revenue	1,392	(NA)	(NA)	(NA)	517
Sales of recordings	6,493	6,467	5,591	5,546	5,313
Music publishers [1]	4,155	3,793	3,868	3,887	4,010
Licensing of rights to use musical compositions	2,861	3,068	3,100	3,215	3,275
Print music	(S)	268	272	231	224
Sound recording studios [1]	749	839	873	898	930
Studio recording	441	620	646	644	626

NA Not available. S Data do not meet publication standards. [1] Includes other sources of revenue not shown separately. [2] Beginning 2010, includes NAICS 51211 (Motion Picture and Video Production) and NAICS 51212 (Motion Picture and Video Distribution).

Source: U.S. Census Bureau, Annual & Quarterly Services, "2013 Annual Services," <http://www.census.gov/services/index.html>, accessed December 2014.

Table 1150. Recording Media—Manufacturers' Shipments and Value: 2000 to 2014

[1,079.2 represents 1,079,200,000. Data are net after returns. Formats with no retail value equivalent included at wholesale value. Based on reports of Recording Industry Association of America member companies who distribute about 85 percent of the music sold in the U.S. Data are supplemented by other sources]

Medium	2000	2005	2008	2009	2010	2011	2012	2013	2014
UNIT SHIPMENTS (mil.)									
Total	**1,079.2**	**1,303.2**	**1,921.2**	**1,829.7**	**1,741.0**	**1,826.8**	**1,806.8**	**1,690.8**	**1,523.8**
Physical [1]	**1,079.2**	**748.8**	**385.8**	**313.1**	**267.7**	**255.8**	**212.7**	**187.2**	**163.0**
Compact disk [2]	942.5	705.4	368.4	296.6	253.0	240.8	198.2	172.2	144.1
Music video [3]	18.2	33.8	13.2	11.6	9.1	7.7	6.0	4.7	4.1
LP/EP (long play/extended play)	2.2	1.0	2.9	3.5	4.2	5.5	6.9	9.4	13.2
Single [4]	40.3	5.1	1.1	1.2	1.3	1.7	1.5	0.9	1.5
Other recordings [5]	76.0	3.5	0.2	0.2	0.1	0.1	0.1	(-Z)	0.1
Digital	**(X)**	**554.4**	**1,535.4**	**1,516.6**	**1,473.3**	**1,571.0**	**1,594.1**	**1,503.6**	**1,360.8**
Download single	(X)	366.9	1,042.7	1,124.4	1,177.4	1,332.3	1,392.2	1,327.9	1,200.4
Download album	(X)	13.6	63.6	74.5	85.8	103.9	116.7	118.0	117.6
Kiosk [6]	(X)	0.7	1.6	1.7	1.7	1.3	2.0	3.7	1.6
Music video	(X)	1.9	20.8	20.5	18.4	16.3	10.5	8.4	6.8
Mobile [7]	(X)	170.0	405.1	294.3	188.5	115.4	69.3	39.4	26.7
Paid subscription [8]	(X)	1.3	1.6	1.2	1.5	1.8	3.4	6.2	7.7
VALUE (mil. dol.)									
Total	**14,323.7**	**12,289.9**	**8,776.8**	**7,629.8**	**6,825.1**	**6,939.1**	**6,824.9**	**6,815.0**	**6,782.5**
Physical [1]	**14,323.7**	**11,195.0**	**5,766.9**	**4,601.8**	**3,663.7**	**3,381.0**	**2,772.3**	**2,444.8**	**2,272.1**
Compact disk [2]	13,214.5	10,520.2	5,471.3	4,318.8	3,389.4	3,100.7	2,485.6	2,123.5	1,854.1
Music video [3]	281.9	602.2	227.3	209.6	177.6	151.0	116.6	104.7	90.5
LP/EP (long play/extended play)	27.7	14.2	56.7	63.8	88.9	119.4	160.7	210.7	314.9
Single [4]	173.6	24.1	6.4	5.6	5.2	8.1	7.9	5.4	9.7
Other recordings [5]	626.0	34.3	5.2	4.0	2.6	1.8	1.5	0.5	2.9
Digital	**(X)**	**1,094.9**	**3,009.9**	**3,028.0**	**3,161.4**	**3,558.1**	**4,052.6**	**4,370.2**	**4,510.4**
Download single	(X)	363.3	1,032.2	1,172.0	1,336.4	1,522.4	1,623.6	1,567.6	1,409.6
Download album	(X)	135.7	635.3	744.3	872.0	1,070.8	1,204.8	1,232.1	1,150.8
Kiosk [6]	(X)	1.0	2.6	6.3	6.4	2.7	3.7	6.2	2.6
Music video	(X)	3.7	41.3	40.9	36.6	32.4	20.8	16.7	13.6
Mobile [7]	(X)	421.6	977.1	702.8	448.0	276.2	166.9	98.0	66.5
SoundExchange distributions	(X)	20.4	100.0	155.5	249.2	292.0	462.0	590.4	773.4
Paid subscription [8]	(X)	149.2	221.4	206.2	212.4	247.8	399.9	639.2	799.1
On-demand streaming [9]	(X)	(X)	(X)	(X)	(X)	113.8	170.9	220.0	294.8

Z less than 50,000. X Not applicable [1] Includes items not shown separately. [2] Prior to 2006, includes DualDisc. [3] Includes DVD video. [4] CD, cassette, and vinyl singles. [5] DVD audio, super audio CD (SACD), and prior to 2009, cassette. [6] Singles and albums. [7] Master ringtones, ringbacks, music videos, full length downloads and other mobile. Beginning 2013, master ringtones and ringbacks only. [8] Streaming, tethered, and other paid subscription services not operating under statutory licenses. Volume is annual average number of subscribers for subscription services. [9] Advertising supported audio and music video services not operating under statutory licenses.

Source: Recording Industry Association of America, Washington, DC, *News and Notes on 2014 RIAA Music Industry Shipment and Revenue Statistics* ©; and "RIAA Shipment Database," <https://www.riaa.com/keystatistics.php?content_selector=research-shipment-database-overview>, accessed September 2015.

Table 1151. Radio and Television Broadcasting—Estimated Revenue and Expenses: 2010 to 2013

[6,234 represents $6,234,000,000. For all employer firms regardless of tax status. Estimates have been adjusted to the results of the 2007 Economic Census. Data based on the 2007 North American Industry Classification System (NAICS). See text, Section 15 and Appendix III]

Item	2010	2011	2012	2013
RADIO NETWORKS (NAICS 51511)				
Total operating revenue	**6,234**	**5,638**	**5,131**	**4,883**
National/regional/local air time	1,050	928	818	790
Public and non-commercial programming services	460	472	461	443
All other operating revenue	4,724	4,238	3,852	3,650
RADIO STATIONS (NAICS 515112)				
Total operating revenue	**12,227**	**12,539**	**12,255**	**12,135**
National/regional/local air time	10,306	10,390	10,354	10,369
Public and non-commercial programming services	674	610	629	590
All other operating revenue	1,247	1,539	1,272	1,176
TELEVISION BROADCASTING (NAICS 51512)				
Total operating revenue	**38,492**	**38,651**	**35,291**	**35,334**
National/regional/local air time	29,435	30,526	27,757	27,961
Public and non-commercial programming services	1,817	1,613	1,509	1,682
All other operating revenue	7,240	6,512	6,025	5,691
RADIO AND TELEVISION BROADCASTING (NAICS 5151)				
Operating expenses, total	**44,223**	**43,792**	**44,937**	**45,205**
Personnel costs	13,598	13,773	14,739	15,143
Gross annual payroll	11,253	11,395	12,216	12,504
Employer's cost for fringe benefits	1,740	1,770	1,990	2,204
Temporary staff and leased employee expense	605	608	533	435
Expensed equipment	175	179	123	102
Expensed purchases of other materials, parts, and supplies	217	209	187	217
Expensed purchases of software	191	204	178	178
Purchased electricity and fuels (except motor fuel)	357	361	363	368
Lease and rental payments	868	867	859	901
Purchased repair and maintenance	260	268	287	305
Purchased advertising and promotional services	1,244	1,295	1,429	1,546
Broadcast rights and music license fees	12,155	11,096	12,947	12,909
Network compensation fees (networks only)	496	448	434	529
Depreciation and amortization charges	2,550	2,457	2,611	2,559
Governmental taxes and license fees	258	244	282	339
Other operating expenses	11,854	12,391	10,498	10,109
Data processing and other purchased computer services	(NA)	(NA)	162	208
Purchased communication services	(NA)	(NA)	341	384
Water, sewer, refuse removal, and other utility payments	(NA)	(NA)	29	30
Purchased professional and technical services	(NA)	(NA)	950	953
All other operating expenses	(NA)	(NA)	9,016	8,534

NA Not available.

Source: U.S. Census Bureau, Annual & Quarterly Services, "2013 Annual Services," <http://www.census.gov/services/index.html>, accessed December 2014.

Table 1152. Cable and Premium TV—Summary: 1990 to 2014

[In units as indicated (50,520 represents 50,520,000). Cable TV for calendar year. Premium TV as of December 31 of year shown]

	Cable TV				Premium TV					
			Revenue [1]		Units [2]			Monthly rate [4]		
Year	Average basic sub-scribers (1,000)	Average monthly basic rate (dol.)	Total (mil. dol.)	Basic (mil. dol.)	Total premium [3] (1,000)	Premium cable (1,000)	Non-cable delivered premium (1,000)	All premium weighted average [5] (dollars)	Premium cable (dollars)	Non-cable delivered premium (dollars)
1990	50,520	16.78	17,405	10,174	39,902	(NA)	(NA)	10.35	(NA)	(NA)
1995	60,550	23.07	23,669	16,763	60,098	51,173	8,925	8.32	8.54	6.99
1998	64,650	27.81	30,568	21,574	83,886	58,562	25,325	8.60	8.74	8.22
1999	65,500	28.92	33,392	22,732	89,655	60,205	29,450	8.75	8.85	8.50
2000	66,302	30.37	35,963	24,161	103,440	66,768	36,672	8.72	8.81	8.48
2001	66,884	32.87	41,374	26,384	115,525	75,633	39,892	8.97	9.10	8.66
2002	66,729	34.71	47,573	27,797	125,662	81,128	44,534	9.19	9.29	9.00
2003	66,374	36.59	52,123	29,142	127,377	83,421	43,956	9.38	9.45	9.23
2004	66,102	38.14	57,105	30,252	140,060	90,843	49,217	9.91	9.92	9.88
2005	65,764	39.63	62,515	31,278	149,067	96,910	52,157	9.95	9.97	9.93
2006	65,787	41.17	68,743	32,505	158,069	101,464	56,605	10.01	10.02	9.98
2007	65,655	42.72	75,218	33,657	171,043	109,960	61,083	10.05	10.06	10.02
2008	64,821	44.28	81,023	34,442	149,749	92,540	57,209	10.08	10.10	10.06
2009	63,432	46.13	84,425	35,113	150,651	85,975	64,676	10.12	10.13	10.09
2010	61,516	47.89	88,025	35,352	166,241	88,359	77,882	10.15	10.17	10.13
2011	59,489	49.90	91,458	35,623	175,322	90,425	84,896	10.19	10.21	10.17
2012	57,796	51.68	94,647	35,845	183,459	91,363	92,095	10.23	10.25	10.21
2013	56,041	53.28	96,312	35,833	186,785	91,124	95,660	10.24	10.26	10.23
2014	54,384	54.92	99,328	35,840	189,812	92,907	96,904	10.24	10.25	10.22

NA Not available. [1] Includes total video, residential telephony and high-speed access revenue. [2] Individual program services sold to subscribers with more than one unit often sold to an individual household. [3] Includes multipoint distribution service (MDS), satellite TV (STV), multipoint multichannel distribution service (MMDS), satellite master antenna TV (SMATV), C-band satellite, DBS satellite, and telecommunications video for full- and mini- premium services. [4] Weighted average representing 8 months of unregulated basic rate and 4 months of FCC rolled-back rate. [5] Includes average premium unit price based on data for major premium services.

Source: SNL Kagan, a division of SNL Financial, LC. From the *Broadband Cable Financial Databook* ©, annual; the *Cable Program Investor* and *Cable TV Investor: Deals & Finance* ©, monthly newsletters; and various other SNL Kagan publications ©. See also <http://www.snl.com/Sectors/Media/Default.aspx>.

Table 1153. Cable and Other Subscription Programming—Estimated Revenue and Expenses: 2010 to 2013

[In millions of dollars (55,168 represents $55,168,000,000). For all employer firms regardless of tax status. Based on the 2007 North American Industry Classification System. Covers NAICS 5152. Estimates have been adjusted to the results of the 2007 Economic Census. See text, this section and Section 15, and Appendix III]

Item	2010	2011	2012	2013
Operating revenue, total.................................	**55,168**	**60,318**	**64,168**	**68,358**
Source of revenue:				
Advertising and program revenue [1].................................	31,354	33,821	36,764	38,964
Air time.................................	21,269	23,586	23,304	24,949
All other operating services revenue.................................	2,545	2,911	4,100	4,445
Operating expenses, total.................................	**34,319**	**37,115**	**39,007**	**41,406**
Personnel costs.................................	6,754	6,945	7,199	7,502
Gross annual payroll.................................	5,435	5,588	5,751	6,052
Employer's cost for fringe benefits.................................	993	1,061	1,164	1,220
Temporary staff and leased employee expense.................................	326	296	284	230
Expensed equipment.................................	83	80	78	82
Expensed purchases of other materials, parts, and supplies.................................	74	73	67	64
Expensed purchases of software.................................	80	84	101	111
Purchased electricity and fuels (except motor fuels).................................	68	70	65	66
Lease and rental payments.................................	615	610	653	684
Purchased repairs and maintenance.................................	90	100	133	132
Purchased advertising and promotional services.................................	2,640	2,825	2,758	2,683
Program and production costs.................................	16,551	18,126	19,539	21,135
Depreciation and amortization charges.................................	4,122	4,550	4,335	4,545
Governmental taxes and license fees.................................	66	64	101	93
Other operating expenses.................................	3,176	3,588	3,978	4,309
Data processing and other purchased computer services.................................	(NA)	(NA)	50	54
Purchased communication services.................................	(NA)	(NA)	99	98
Water, sewer, refuse removal, and other utility payments.................................	(NA)	(NA)	11	11
Purchased professional and technical services.................................	(NA)	(NA)	528	604
All other operating expenses.................................	(NA)	(NA)	3,290	3,542

NA Not available. [1] Licensing of rights to broadcast specialty programming protected by copyright.

Source: U.S. Census Bureau, Annual & Quarterly Services, "2013 Annual Services," <http://www.census.gov/services/index.html>, accessed December 2014.

Table 1154. Telecommunications Industry Revenue by Service Type: 2010 to 2013

[Revenue in millions of dollars (446,386.1 represents $446,386,100,000). Data are based on carrier Form 499-A filings to the Federal Communications Commission, and are the basis for establishing Universal Service Fund (USF) program collections]

Category	Revenue (mil. dol.)			
	2010	2011	2012	2013
Total reported revenue.................................	446,386.1	475,576.2	479,729.0	494,980.6
Total telecommunications revenue.................................	**273,157.9**	**261,037.8**	**255,241.6**	**243,088.0**
Non-telecommunications revenue.................................	173,228.2	214,538.4	224,487.4	251,892.1
Local service and payphone revenue.................................	**102,846.8**	**98,312.6**	**95,422.3**	**93,104.8**
Local exchange and Federal/State USF support.................................	56,992.5	52,717.8	50,598.3	49,015.8
Pay telephone.................................	196.8	136.3	361.5	359.2
Local private line.................................	26,808.5	28,242.5	29,101.2	29,631.7
Other local.................................	3,031.6	3,145.1	2,408.0	1,746.0
Subscriber line charges.................................	7,481.3	6,703.2	6,194.6	5,968.4
Access.................................	8,336.0	7,367.7	6,758.6	6,383.6
Mobile service revenue.................................	**111,643.0**	**107,392.5**	**105,183.4**	**98,160.3**
Toll service revenue.................................	**50,006.3**	**46,347.1**	**44,623.6**	**42,837.1**
Operator.................................	3,585.0	3,161.8	3,092.0	3,064.0
Non-operator switched toll.................................	27,132.0	27,556.7	25,340.1	23,345.0
Long distance private line.................................	14,343.7	11,442.7	12,262.2	12,542.4
Other long distance.................................	4,945.5	4,185.9	3,929.3	3,885.7

Source: U.S. Federal Communications Commission, *Universal Service Monitoring Report, 2014.* See also <https://www.fcc.gov/encyclopedia/federal-state-joint-board-monitoring-reports>.

Table 1155. Wired and Wireless Telecommunications Carriers—Estimated Revenue: 2010 to 2013

[In millions of dollars (293,929 represents $293,929,000,000). For all employer firms regardless of tax status. Data are based on 2007 North American Industry Classification System (NAICS) and cover NAICS 5171 Wired Telecommunications Carriers and NAICS 5172 Wireless Telecommunications Carriers (except satellite). Estimates have been adjusted to the results of the 2007 Economic Census. See text, this section and Section 15, and Appendix III]

Item	2010	2011	2012	2013
Wired telecommunications carriers operating revenue [1]	**293,929**	**302,007**	**307,329**	**310,168**
Fixed local telephony	45,754	41,934	38,720	33,579
Fixed long-distance telephony	20,872	21,372	19,438	17,700
Fixed all distance	2,760	2,745	2,038	1,345
Carrier services	19,010	19,874	19,003	17,636
Private network services	22,027	22,207	22,051	21,448
Subscriber line charges	3,438	4,345	4,291	3,826
Internet access services	53,933	60,662	67,852	75,490
Internet telephony	10,323	12,315	13,480	13,963
Telecommunications network installation services	526	425	429	493
Reselling services for telecommunications equipment, retail	1,773	1,736	1,370	1,404
Rental of telecommunications equipment	718	569	508	522
Repair and maintenance services for telecommunications equipment	390	(S)	686	609
Basic programming package	55,027	56,433	59,810	63,026
Premium programming package	21,293	23,373	23,402	22,792
Pay-per-view	3,453	3,355	3,443	(S)
Air time (advertising and program content)	5,063	5,142	(S)	(S)
Rental and reselling services for program distribution equipment	8,196	9,410	11,519	12,439
Installation services for connections to program distribution networks	1,130	1,141	1,339	1,463
Website hosting services	304	292	151	144
All other operating revenue	17,939	14,102	12,972	13,947
Wireless telecommunications carrier operating revenue [2]	**195,526**	**209,116**	**218,513**	**226,003**
Messaging (paging) services	904	886	537	(S)
Mobile telephony	57,154	55,664	53,045	59,987
Mobile long distance	3,324	3,228	(D)	(D)
Mobile all distance	(S)	61,065	63,491	57,978
Internet access services	(S)	(S)	60,958	64,249
Telecommunication network installation services	(S)	(S)	167	190
Reselling services for telecommunications equipment, retail	18,405	20,526	22,959	23,936
Rental of telecommunications equipment	327	353	332	420
Repair and maintenance services for telecommunications equipment	1,196	1,340	(D)	(D)
All other operating revenue	11,278	12,822	12,306	13,304

S Data do not meet publication standards. D Estimate in table is withheld to avoid disclosing data of individual companies; data are included in higher level totals. [1] Includes 2002 NAICS 5171 (Wired Telecommunications Carriers), 2002 NAICS 5175 (Cable and Other Program Distribution), and a portion of 2002 NAICS 518111 (Internet Service Providers). [2] Includes 2002 NAICS 517211 (Paging), 2002 NAICS 517212 (Cellular and Other Wireless Telecommunications), and a portion of 2002 NAICS 518111 (Internet Service Providers). Excludes satellite telecommunications.

Source: U.S. Census Bureau, Annual & Quarterly Services, "2013 Annual Services," <http://www.census.gov/services/index.html>, accessed December 2014.

Table 1156. Average Annual Telephone Service Expenditures by All Consumer Units: 2001 to 2013

[In dollars except percent distribution. Based on the Consumer Expenditure Survey. Expenditures reported are direct out-of-pocket expenditures. A consumer unit is defined as members of a household related by blood, marriage, adoption, or some other legal arrangement; a single person living alone or sharing a household with others, but who is financially independent; or two or more persons living together who share responsibility for at least two out of the three major types of expenses: food, housing, and other expenses]

Year	Average annual telephone service (dollars)				Percent distribution			
	Total telephone services	Residential and other telephone services [1]	Cellular phone service	Other services [2]	Total telephone services	Residential and other telephone services [1]	Cellular phone service	Other services [2]
2001	914	686	210	19	100.0	75.1	23.0	2.1
2002	957	641	294	22	100.0	67.0	30.7	2.3
2003	956	620	316	20	100.0	64.9	33.1	2.1
2004	990	592	378	20	100.0	59.8	38.2	2.0
2005	1,048	570	455	23	100.0	54.4	43.4	2.2
2006	1,087	542	524	21	100.0	49.9	48.2	1.9
2007	1,110	482	608	20	100.0	43.4	54.8	1.8
2008	1,127	467	643	17	100.0	41.4	57.0	1.5
2009	1,162	434	712	17	100.0	37.3	61.2	1.4
2010	1,178	401	760	17	100.0	34.1	64.5	1.4
2011	1,226	381	826	20	100.0	31.1	67.3	1.6
2012	1,239	359	862	19	100.0	28.9	69.6	1.5
2013	1,271	358	913	(NA)	100.0	28.2	71.8	(NA)

NA Not available. [1] Beginning 2013, data are shown for residential telephone, phone cards, VoIP, and pay phone services combined. Prior to 2013, data are shown for residential and pay telephone services. [2] Phone cards, pager services, and beginning in 2007, Voice over Internet Protocol, known as VoIP.

Source: U.S. Bureau of Labor Statistics, Consumer Expenditure Survey, unpublished data; and "Annual Calendar Year Tables, 2013," <http://www.bls.gov/cex/home.htm>, accessed April 2015.

Table 1157. Cellular Telecommunications Industry: 2000 to 2014

[In units as indicated (109.5 represents 109,500,000). Calendar year data, except as noted. Based on a survey sent to facilities-based commercial mobile radio service providers, including cellular, personal communications services, advanced wireless service, mobile WiMAX, and enhanced special mobile radio (ESMR) systems. The number of operational systems beginning 2000 differs from that reported for previous periods as a result of the consolidated operation of ESMR systems in a broader service area instead of by a city-to-city basis]

Item	Unit	2000	2005	2009	2010	2011	2012	2013	2014
Wireless subscriber connections [1]	Millions	109.5	207.9	285.6	296.3	316.0	326.5	335.7	355.4
Wireless penetration	Percent	38	69	93	94	100	102	104	110
Cell sites [2]	Number	104,288	183,689	247,081	253,086	283,385	301,779	304,360	298,055
Employees	Number	184,449	233,067	249,247	250,393	238,071	230,101	230,409	232,169
Service revenue	Mil. dol.	52,466	113,538	152,552	159,930	169,767	185,014	189,193	187,848
Capital investment [3]	Mil. dol.	89,624	199,025	285,122	310,015	335,332	365,426	398,568	430,624
Average monthly bill [4]	Dollars	45.27	49.98	48.16	47.21	47.00	(NA)	(NA)	(NA)
Average length of call [4]	Minutes	2.6	3.0	1.8	1.8	1.8	1.8	(NA)	(NA)
Voice minutes, annual reported	Billions	258.9	1,495.5	2,275.3	2,241.3	2,295.5	2,299.9	2,618.2	2,454.9
Voice minutes, monthly [5]	Minutes	248.0	716.0	726.0	683.0	650.0	633.0	690.0	610.0
Wireless data usage (megabytes), annual	Billions	(NA)	(NA)	(NA)	388.0	866.8	1,468.0	3,229.8	4,060.7
Number of text messages [6]	Billions	(Z)	9.8	152.7	187.7	193.1	171.3	153.1	169.3
Number of MMS [6, 7]	Billions	(NA)	0.2	5.1	4.3	5.0	7.0	10.1	15.4

NA Not available. Z Entry less than half the unit of measurement shown. [1] Number of active wireless devices. Does not represent individual subscribers. [2] The basic geographic unit for wireless telecommunications coverage. [3] Beginning 2005, cumulative capital investment figure reached by summing the incremental capital investment in year shown with cumulative capital investment of prior year. [4] As of December 31. [5] Derived, based on minutes divided by reported devices. [6] Number of messages in final month of survey (December). [7] Multimedia Messaging Service.

Source: CTIA-The Wireless Association, Washington, DC, *Annual Wireless Industry Survey* ©.

Table 1158. Landline and Wireless Telephone Status of Households and Adults: 2010 to 2014

[In percent. Data cover 6-month period from January to June. Based on in-person interviews of a sample of the civilian noninstitutionalized population, conducted for the National Health Interview Survey]

Telephone status and characteristics	2010	2011	2012	2013	2014
HOUSEHOLDS					
Landline with wireless	58.1	55.0	52.5	49.5	44.7
Landline without wireless	12.9	11.2	9.4	8.5	8.5
Wireless only	26.6	31.6	35.8	39.4	44.0
Without any telephone	2.0	2.0	2.1	2.3	2.6
Other [1]	0.3	0.3	0.2	0.1	0.1
ADULTS					
Landline with wireless	62.2	58.8	56.1	52.8	47.3
Wireless mostly [2]	17.7	18.2	17.6	17.7	16.6
Landline without wireless	10.9	9.0	7.8	6.9	7.0
Wireless only	24.9	30.2	34.0	38.0	43.1
Without any telephone	1.7	1.8	1.9	2.2	2.4
Other [1]	0.3	0.2	0.2	0.1	0.2
ADULTS IN WIRELESS ONLY HOUSEHOLDS					
Sex:					
Male	26.2	31.4	35.2	39.7	44.3
Female	23.7	29.1	32.9	36.5	41.9
Age:					
18 to 24 years	39.9	46.8	49.5	54.3	57.8
25 to 29 years	51.3	58.1	60.1	65.6	69.3
30 to 34 years	40.4	46.2	55.1	59.9	64.9
35 to 44 years	27.0	34.3	39.1	44.5	52.5
45 to 64 years	16.9	21.6	25.8	29.8	35.7
65 and over years	5.4	7.9	10.5	12.6	15.7
Race/ethnicity:					
White only, non-Hispanic	22.7	27.6	30.4	35.1	39.6
Black only, non-Hispanic	28.5	32.5	37.7	39.4	44.9
Asian only, non-Hispanic	18.8	27.7	33.4	35.2	41.3
Hispanic or Latino, any race	34.7	40.8	46.5	49.9	56.1
Education:					
Some high school or less	28.6	32.1	36.4	41.7	46.6
High school graduate or GED [3]	23.6	30.8	33.9	37.2	43.3
Some post-high school, no degree	26.5	31.8	36.7	40.6	45.6
4-year college degree or higher	22.7	26.9	30.1	34.5	39.0
Household poverty status: [4]					
Poor	39.3	46.8	51.8	54.7	59.1
Near poor	32.9	38.1	42.3	47.5	50.8
Not poor	21.7	27.7	30.7	35.3	40.8
Home ownership status:					
Owned or home being bought	15.5	20.6	23.2	27.2	32.9
Renting	47.1	52.5	58.2	61.5	64.6
Other arrangement	34.9	38.4	37.7	42.6	52.2

[1] Other includes landline and non-landline, with unknown wireless telephone. [2] Wireless mostly is for adults living in households with both landline and cellular telephones but in which all families receive all or almost all calls on cell phones. [3] GED is General Educational Development (high school equivalency diploma). [4] Based on household income and household size using the U.S. Census Bureau's poverty thresholds. "Poor" persons are defined as those below the poverty threshold. "Near poor" persons have incomes of 100% to less than 200% of the poverty threshold. "Not poor" persons have incomes of 200% of the poverty threshold or greater.

Source: U.S. National Center for Health Statistics, *Wireless Substitution: Early Release of Estimates From the National Health Interview Survey, January–June 2014*, December 2014, and earlier reports. See also <http://www.cdc.gov/nchs/nhis/releases.htm#wireless>.

Table 1159. Mobile Electronic Device Ownership by Device Type and Owner Characteristics: 2014

[In percent. Cell phone data based on January 2014 surveys; tablet and e-book reader data based on January 2-5, 2014 survey; and smartphone data based on December 4-7 and December 18-21, 2014 surveys. Surveys are generally conducted among approximately 1,000 persons age 18 and older, in English and Spanish, on landline and cellular telephones]

Owner characteristic	Tablet computer	E-book reader [1]	Cellular telephone	Smart-phone
Total	**42**	**32**	**90**	**64**
SEX				
Men	42	29	93	66
Women	43	33	88	63
RACE/ETHNICITY				
White	41	35	90	61
Black	34	24	90	70
Hispanic	45	18	92	71
AGE				
18 to 29 years	48	28	98	85
30 to 49 years	52	40	97	79
50 to 64 years	37	32	88	54
65 years and older	25	22	74	27
EDUCATION				
High school graduate or less	29	22	87	52
Some college	45	33	93	69
College or higher	59	44	93	78
HOUSEHOLD INCOME				
Less than $30,000	26	14	84	50
$30,000 to $49,999	45	36	90	71
$50,000 to $74,999	47	42	99	72
$75,000 and over	65	53	98	84
METRO STATUS				
Urban	43	32	88	68
Suburban	43	32	92	66
Rural	38	29	88	52

[1] Handheld electronic device for reading books in electronic format.

Source: Pew Research Center ©. Cell phone data, <http://www.pewinternet.org/data-trend/mobile/cell-phone-and-smartphone-ownership-demographics/>, accessed May 2015; tablet and e-book reader data, *E-Reading Rises as Device Ownership Jumps,* January 16, 2014; and smartphone data, *U.S. Smartphone Use in 2015,* April 1, 2015. See also <http://www.pewinternet.org/category/publications/report/>.

Table 1160. Data Processing, Hosting, and Related Services—Estimated Revenue and Expenses: 2010 to 2013

[In millions of dollars (76,156 represents $76,156,000,000). For all employer firms regardless of tax status. Data are based on the 2007 North American Industry Classification System (NAICS), and cover NAICS 518. Estimates have been adjusted to the results of the 2007 Economic Census. See text, Section 15, and Appendix III]

Item	2010	2011	2012	2013
Total operating revenue	**76,156**	**81,965**	**89,755**	**95,476**
Data processing, information technology infrastructure provisioning, and hosting services	54,571	58,545	65,091	69,664
Information technology design and development services	2,199	2,456	2,949	2,704
Information technology technical support services	(S)	2,532	2,675	2,778
Information technology technical consulting services	3,707	3,949	3,969	4,367
Information and document transformation services	2,159	2,445	2,561	2,533
Software publishing	(S)	1,948	(S)	(S)
Reselling services for computer hardware and software, retail	712	631	(S)	(S)
All other operating revenue	8,331	9,459	(S)	11,047
Total operating expenses	**66,013**	**71,062**	**78,642**	**84,382**
Gross annual payroll	26,410	28,186	31,281	33,206
Employer's cost for fringe benefits	4,126	4,524	5,349	5,621
Temporary staff and leased employee expense	2,071	2,347	2,416	2,643
Expensed equipment	979	998	767	751
Expensed purchases of other materials, parts, and supplies	3,691	3,725	2,663	2,398
Expensed purchases of software	1,801	1,930	1,922	2,215
Purchased electricity and fuels (except motor fuels)	680	736	561	548
Lease and rental payments	2,526	2,788	2,573	2,831
Purchased repair and maintenance	910	1,018	897	977
Purchased advertising and promotional services	(S)	1,771	1,843	1,827
Depreciation and amortization charges	5,820	6,495	6,861	7,435
Governmental taxes and license fees	(S)	(S)	(S)	546
All other operating expenses	14,851	15,917	20,984	23,384

S Data do not meet publication standards.

Source: U.S. Census Bureau, Annual & Quarterly Services, "2013 Annual Services," <http://www.census.gov/services/index.html>, accessed December 2014.

Table 1161. Cellular Telephone Activities and Applications Among Adults by Cell Phone User Characteristics: 2015

[In percent. Based on a survey conducted from June 10 to July 12, 2015 among 2,001 adults age 18 or older, including 1,300 cell phone interviews]

Characteristic	Activities conducted on cell phone					
	Location-based services [1]	Listen to online radio or music service	Video call or chat	Buy a product online	Get sports scores or analysis	Watch movies or TV shows via paid subscription service
Total	**71**	**54**	**35**	**48**	**36**	**27**
SEX						
Male	72	53	36	48	47	23
Female	71	56	34	47	25	30
RACE/ETHNICITY						
White, non-Hispanic	68	47	33	46	33	23
Black, non-Hispanic	75	70	34	50	45	30
Hispanic	78	68	40	46	40	33
AGE						
18 to 29 years old	90	80	61	67	47	47
30 to 49 years old	87	71	42	58	45	33
50 to 64 years old	57	36	19	33	29	14
65 years old and over	37	14	9	22	13	3
EDUCATION						
High school graduate or less	60	51	26	33	32	27
Some college	75	56	39	54	33	28
College or higher	82	57	43	59	45	24
HOUSEHOLD INCOME						
Less than $30,000	60	50	28	30	28	27
$30,000 to $49,999	78	57	38	55	37	31
$50,000 to $74,999	71	54	35	50	38	22
$75,000 and over	88	64	48	66	48	30
METRO STATUS						
Urban	75	61	40	51	40	29
Suburban	73	53	36	48	37	27
Rural	59	42	22	40	25	20

[1] Get directions, recommendations, or other information from cell phone based on location.

Source: Pew Research Center, Princeton Survey Research Associates International, July 2015 data ©. See also <http://www.pewinternet.org/>.

Table 1162. Social Media—Use of Social Networking Sites Among Adult Internet Users: 2014

[As percent of all Internet users. Based on responses from 1,597 Internet users participating in public opinion surveys of 2,003 adults age 18 and older, conducted September 11-21, 2014 in English and Spanish on landline and cellular telephones. Margin of error for results based on all Internet users is plus or minus 2.9 percentage points]

Characteristic	Social networking site				
	Facebook	Twitter	Instagram	Pinterest	LinkedIn
Total	**71**	**23**	**26**	**28**	**28**
SEX					
Male	66	24	22	13	28
Female	77	21	29	42	27
RACE ETHNICITY					
White, non-Hispanic	71	21	21	32	29
Black, non-Hispanic	67	27	38	12	28
Hispanic	73	25	34	21	18
AGE					
18 to 29 years old	87	37	53	34	23
30 to 49 years old	73	25	25	28	31
50 to 64 years old	63	12	11	27	30
65 years old and over	56	10	6	17	21
EDUCATION					
High school graduate or less	70	16	23	22	12
Some college	71	24	31	30	22
College graduate or higher	74	30	24	32	50
INCOME					
Under $30,000	77	20	28	22	15
$30,000 to $49,999	69	21	23	28	21
$50,000 to $74,999	74	27	26	30	31
$75,000 and over	72	27	26	34	44
METRO STATUS					
Urban	71	25	28	25	32
Suburban	72	23	26	29	29
Rural	69	17	19	30	14
EMPLOYMENT STATUS					
Employed	(NA)	(NA)	(NA)	(NA)	32
Not employed	(NA)	(NA)	(NA)	(NA)	21

NA Not available.

Source: Pew Research Center, *Social Media Update 2014*, January 2015 ©. See also <http://www.pewinternet.org/2015/01/09/social-media-update-2014/>.

Table 1163. Household Computer and Internet Use by Selected Characteristics: 2013

[In percent, except as noted. Handheld computers include smartphones (mobile wireless), and other handheld wireless computers. Based on the American Community Survey. Please note that although the ACS includes people living in group quarters, computer and Internet use data were not collected from group quarters]

Household characteristics	Total households (1,000)	Households with a computer			Households with Internet use [1]	
		Total	Desktop or laptop computer	Handheld computer	With some Internet service subscription	With high-speed Internet connection [2]
Total households................................	**116,291**	**83.8**	**78.5**	**63.6**	**74.4**	**73.4**
Age of householder:						
15 to 34 years................................	22,331	92.1	82.1	83.3	77.7	77.4
35 to 44 years................................	20,745	92.5	86.4	80.7	82.5	81.9
45 to 64 years................................	46,015	86.8	82.7	65.2	78.7	77.6
65 years and older............................	27,201	65.1	62.3	31.8	58.3	56.3
Race/ethnicity of householder:						
White alone, non-Hispanic....................	80,699	85.4	81.4	63.4	77.4	76.2
Black alone, non-Hispanic....................	13,816	75.8	66.3	58.9	61.3	60.6
Asian alone, non-Hispanic....................	4,941	92.5	90.0	78.6	86.6	86.0
Hispanic (of any race)........................	14,209	79.7	70.0	63.7	66.7	65.9
Limited English-speaking household:						
No..	111,084	84.7	79.6	64.6	75.5	74.4
Yes..	5,207	63.9	54.9	43.7	51.4	50.6
Metro status:						
Metro area.....................................	98,607	85.1	79.9	65.9	76.1	75.2
Non-metro area...............................	17,684	76.5	70.6	51.1	64.8	63.1
Household income:						
Less than $25,000............................	27,605	62.4	53.9	39.6	48.4	47.2
$25,000 to $49,999..........................	27,805	81.1	74.0	55.2	69.0	67.6
$50,000 to $99,999..........................	34,644	92.6	88.4	71.9	84.9	83.8
$100,000 to $149,999........................	14,750	97.1	95.1	84.5	92.7	92.1
$150,000 and more...........................	11,487	98.1	96.8	90.2	94.9	94.5
Education of householder: [3]						
Less than high school graduate.............	12,855	56.0	47.2	36.5	43.8	42.7
High school graduate [4].....................	28,277	73.9	66.9	48.5	62.9	61.4
Some college or associate's degree..........	34,218	89.0	83.9	67.0	79.2	78.0
Bachelor's degree or higher..................	36,349	95.5	93.5	79.3	90.1	89.4

[1] About 4.2 percent of all households reported household Internet use without a paid subscription. These households are not included in this table. [2] Covers any Internet service type except dial-up. [3] Householders age 25 and older. [4] Includes high school equivalency.

Source: U.S. Census Bureau, *Computer and Internet Use in the United States: 2013,* November 2014. See also <http://www.census.gov/hhes/computer/>.

Table 1164. Percent of Households with a Computer and Paid Internet Subscription by State: 2013

[In percent. Survey respondents could select more than one type of computer and more than one type of Internet subscription. Household computer can include desktop, laptop, netbook or notebook computer, and handheld computer including smartphone, tablet, and other devices. Based on the American Community Survey. Please note that although the ACS includes people living in group quarters, computer and Internet use data were not collected from group quarters]

State	Total	Type of Internet Subscription			State	Total	Type of Internet Subscription		
		Dial-up Internet service	Broadband Internet service [1]	No paid Internet service [2]			Dial-up Internet service	Broadband Internet service [1]	No paid Internet service [2]
U.S.......	**83.8**	**1.0**	**72.9**	**9.9**	MO........	82.3	1.2	69.4	11.7
AL.........	77.0	1.2	62.9	12.9	MT........	83.7	1.7	71.5	10.5
AK.........	90.0	0.9	78.7	10.5	NE........	83.2	1.2	72.3	9.7
AZ.........	84.4	0.9	73.6	10.0	NV........	86.3	0.8	75.2	10.3
AR.........	77.8	1.4	60.4	16.0	NH........	89.0	0.8	80.5	7.6
CA.........	86.8	0.9	77.4	8.5	NJ........	86.3	0.7	78.5	7.1
CO.........	89.3	1.1	79.1	9.1	NM........	77.0	1.2	63.9	11.8
CT.........	85.1	0.6	77.1	7.4	NY........	83.8	0.7	74.6	8.5
DE.........	85.2	0.9	74.2	10.1	NC........	81.4	1.0	70.2	10.2
DC.........	84.6	0.6	73.0	11.0	ND........	83.7	1.1	72.1	10.5
FL.........	84.4	0.9	73.8	9.6	OH........	82.1	1.2	70.7	10.3
GA.........	83.5	0.8	71.8	10.9	OK........	81.2	1.1	66.3	13.9
HI.........	86.4	0.9	78.2	7.3	OR........	87.7	1.2	77.1	9.4
ID.........	87.0	1.6	72.9	12.5	PA........	81.4	1.2	71.9	8.2
IL.........	83.4	1.0	73.5	8.9	RI........	83.5	0.4	76.0	7.1
IN.........	81.8	1.4	69.2	11.2	SC........	79.8	1.0	66.1	12.7
IA.........	83.1	1.3	71.8	9.9	SD........	82.4	1.4	70.6	10.3
KS.........	84.0	1.0	72.5	10.5	TN........	79.2	1.0	66.5	11.6
KY.........	79.2	1.0	68.0	10.2	TX........	83.8	0.9	71.4	11.5
LA.........	77.4	0.9	64.3	12.2	UT........	91.3	1.0	79.3	11.0
ME.........	83.6	1.3	72.4	10.0	VT........	85.5	1.6	75.0	8.9
MD.........	87.4	0.9	78.5	8.0	VA........	85.4	1.2	75.4	8.8
MA.........	86.3	0.7	79.1	6.5	WA........	88.3	1.1	78.5	8.7
MI.........	83.3	1.3	70.2	11.8	WV........	75.4	1.2	64.4	9.8
MN.........	86.5	1.3	76.1	9.0	WI........	83.1	1.4	72.7	9.1
MS.........	73.8	1.2	56.9	15.6	WY........	87.9	1.1	75.0	11.8

[1] Broadband (high-speed) Internet service includes DSL, cable, fiber optic, mobile broadband, satellite, or fixed wireless subscription. [2] Includes households accessing the Internet without a subscription and also households with no Internet access.

Source: U.S. Census Bureau, 2013 American Community Survey, "B28003. Presence of a Computer and Type of Internet Subscription in Household," <http://factfinder.census.gov>, accessed May 2015. See also <http://www.census.gov/hhes/computer/>.

Table 1165. Internet Access by Selected User Characteristics: 2014

[In percent, except as noted (238,128 represents 238,128,000). For persons aged 18 and over. As of Fall 2014. Based on sample and subject to sampling error]

Characteristic	Total adults	Accessed the Internet					
		At home	At work	At school or a library	At another place	Using a cellphone or smart-phone	Using WiFi or wireless connection outside of home
Total adults (1,000) [1]	**238,128**	**188,137**	**97,273**	**30,584**	**76,276**	**151,056**	**68,876**
PERCENT DISTRIBUTION							
Total	100.00	100.00	100.00	100.00	100.00	100.00	100.00
Age:							
18 to 34 years old	30.30	34.61	35.84	54.64	41.93	41.86	41.31
35 to 54 years old	35.19	37.46	45.36	31.97	39.53	40.14	39.94
55 years old and over	34.51	27.93	18.81	13.39	18.54	18.00	18.75
Sex:							
Male	48.18	47.94	50.89	44.37	48.88	48.12	48.97
Female	51.82	52.06	49.11	55.63	51.12	51.88	51.03
Census region: [2]							
Northeast	18.16	18.86	19.34	19.07	20.50	18.41	20.68
Midwest	37.52	35.93	36.41	33.76	34.66	36.76	36.10
South	21.51	21.55	20.91	21.31	18.85	20.59	18.51
West	22.81	23.66	23.34	25.85	25.98	24.23	24.70
Household size:							
1 to 2 persons	45.50	41.36	38.90	33.61	36.96	35.64	37.22
3 to 4 persons	37.15	40.16	43.89	44.74	42.71	43.48	43.17
5 or more persons	17.36	18.48	17.22	21.65	20.33	20.87	19.61
Any child in household	39.46	43.32	46.97	46.72	47.23	48.93	46.42
Marital status:							
Single [3]	27.68	28.99	27.42	48.95	33.89	33.37	34.12
Married	53.19	55.63	59.24	39.50	53.01	53.31	53.29
Other [4]	22.59	19.08	17.14	17.26	17.63	17.74	16.75
Education:							
Graduated college plus	28.93	34.70	45.41	38.77	38.94	35.31	42.75
Attended college	28.96	31.88	32.38	37.81	32.34	33.48	33.28
Did not attend college	42.11	33.42	22.21	23.43	28.72	31.22	23.97
Employment status:							
Employed full-time	48.06	53.41	83.91	42.31	57.49	58.75	59.41
Employed part-time	12.20	13.51	15.27	22.02	14.92	14.27	15.53
Occupation of employed:							
Professional	13.53	16.59	28.71	24.73	19.02	17.82	21.68
Management/business/financial	9.74	11.77	21.17	7.69	14.01	13.30	15.12
Sales/office	13.66	15.75	25.00	14.50	16.63	17.29	18.28
Natural resources/construction/maintenance	5.63	5.34	5.80	1.92	5.33	5.68	4.33
Other	17.69	17.47	18.49	15.49	17.41	18.94	15.53
Sector of employment:							
Business	31.43	34.45	49.49	24.60	37.28	38.23	37.24
Government	9.45	11.09	18.56	19.13	12.50	11.69	12.25
Other	14.57	15.75	21.61	13.39	16.67	17.08	18.73
Household income:							
Less than $50,000	41.19	32.83	20.22	37.84	28.24	30.30	25.90
$50,000 to $74,999	18.39	19.59	18.29	16.83	17.22	18.44	16.72
$75,000 to $149,999	28.53	33.01	41.14	30.88	35.58	34.70	36.91
$150,000 or more	11.89	14.57	20.35	14.46	18.97	16.56	20.47

[1] Includes other labor force status not shown separately. [2] For composition of regions, see map inside front cover. [3] Never married. [4] Includes separated, divorced, and widowed, and also persons engaged to be married.

Source: GfK Mediamark Research & Intelligence, LLC, New York, NY, Fall 2014 ©. See also <http://www.mri.gfk.com/en/gfk-mri.html>.

Table 1166. Internet Activities of Adults by Geographic Community Type: 2010 to 2015

[In percent. For Internet users age 18 and over who have ever performed the activity. Based on telephone surveys of persons with landline and cellular telephones. In September 2010, 3,001 persons were interviewed, including 1,000 cell phone users. Landline sample response rate was 13.6 percent; cellular sample response rate was 17 percent. In November 2010, 2,257 persons were interviewed, including 755 cell phone users. Landline sample response rate was 13.7 percent; cellular sample response rate was 15 percent. In May 2011, 2,277 persons were interviewed, including 755 cell phone users. Landline sample response rate was 13.6 percent; cellular sample response rate was 11.5 percent. In February 2012, 2,253 persons were interviewed, including 901 cell phone users. Landline sample response rate was 11 percent; cellular sample response rate was 11 percent. In December 2012, 2,261 persons were interviewed, including 908 cell phone users. Landline sample response rate was 11 percent; cellular sample response rate was 13 percent. In May 2013, 2,252 persons were interviewed, including 1,127 cell phone users. Landline sample response rate was 10 percent; cellular sample response rate was 13 percent. In July 2013, 1,003 persons were interviewed, including 502 cell phone users. In April 2015 1,907 persons were interviewed, including 1,235 cell phone users. In July 2015, 2,001 persons were interviewed, including 1,300 cell phone users. Beginning in Feb 2012, interviews were conducted in English and Spanish]

Activity	Survey date (month, year)	Total adults	Internet users performing activity			
			Total	Urban	Suburban	Rural
Buy a product online.	May 2011	55	71	73	72	70
Buy or make a reservation for travel.	May 2011	51	65	66	66	60
Categorize or tag online content like a photo, news story or blog post.	Sept. 2010	24	33	37	32	25
Create or work on your own online journal or blog.	May 2011	11	14	16	13	11
Do any banking online.	May 2013	51	61	62	66	42
Get news online.	Dec. 2012	60	74	76	74	67
Look for health or medical information online.	May 2011	55	71	72	69	81
Look for news or information about politics.	Dec. 2012	50	61	63	61	57
Look online for info about a job.	July 2015	54	62	66	62	55
Look for information on Wikipedia.	Feb. 2012	47	58	65	57	50
Make a donation to a charity online.	May 2011	19	25	31	26	15
Make a phone call online, using a service such as Skype or Vonage.	Dec. 2012	24	30	33	29	26
Pay bills online.	Sept. 2010	42	57	55	62	45
Pay to access or download digital content online, such as music video, or newspaper articles.	Sept. 2010	32	43	47	43	35
Play online games.	Sept. 2010	27	36	36	38	34
Post a comment or review online about a product you bought or a service you received.	Sept. 2010	24	32	34	35	24
Rate a product, service, or person.	May 2011	29	37	40	38	26
Research a product or service online.	Sept. 2010	58	78	79	79	77
Search online for a map or driving directions.	Sept. 2010	60	82	84	83	79
Send instant messages.	Nov. 2010	34	46	49	47	42
Send or read e-mail.	Nov. 2010	68	92	93	93	90
Take part in chat rooms or online discussions with other people.	Sept. 2010	17	22	25	21	20
Use a search engine to find information.	Feb. 2012	73	91	90	93	90
Use a social networking site like Facebook, LinkedIn or Google Plus.	July 2015	65	76	76	76	77
Use Twitter.	April 2015	20	23	30	21	14
Visit a local, state, or federal government web site.	Dec. 2012	43	53	51	55	53
Watch a video on a video-sharing site.	July 2013	58	72	75	72	66

Source: Pew Research Center, Internet Project ©. See also <http://www.pewinternet.org/>.

Table 1167. Percent of Adults Who Own Electronic Devices by Type and Age: 2015

[In percent. Data are based on a survey of 1,907 adults age 18 and over, conducted March 17-April 12, 2015 (margin of error 2.6 percentage points). Interviews were conducted over landline and cellular telephones, in English and Spanish]

Device	Total adults	Age 18 to 29	Age 30 to 49	Age 50 to 64	Age 65 and over
Cell phone.	92	98	96	90	78
Smartphone.	67	89	82	56	29
E-reader, such as Kindle or Nook.	19	18	19	19	19
Tablet computer, such as iPad.	45	50	57	37	32
Desktop or laptop computer.	73	78	81	70	55

Source: Pew Research Center, Internet Project ©, <http://www.pewinternet.org/>.

Table 1168. Typical Daily Internet Activities of Adult Internet Users: 2010 to 2012

[In percent. For Internet users age 18 and over who have ever performed the activity. Based on telephone surveys of persons with land-line telephones and cell phones. In September 2010, 3,001 persons were interviewed, including 1,000 cell phone users. Landline sample response rate was 13.6 percent; cellular sample response rate was 17 percent. In November 2010, 2,257 persons were interviewed, including 755 cell phone users. Landline sample response rate was 13.7 percent; cellular sample response rate was 15 percent. In May 2011, 2,277 persons were interviewed, including 755 cell phone users. Landline sample response rate was 13.6 percent; cellular sample response rate was 11.5 percent. In February 2012, 2,253 persons were interviewed, including 901 cell phone users. Landline sample response rate was 11 percent; cellular sample response rate was 11 percent. Beginning in 2011, surveys were conducted in English and Spanish]

Activity	Survey date (month, year)	Total Internet users	Age 18 to 29 years old	Age 30 to 49 years old	Age 50 to 64 years old	Age 65 years old and over	Sex Male	Sex Female
Buy a product online	May 2011	6	7	5	7	7	7	5
Buy or make a reservation for travel	May 2011	4	4	4	3	1	4	3
Categorize or tag online content like a photo, news story or blog post	Sept. 2010	11	18	12	5	4	12	10
Create or work on your own online journal or blog	May 2011	4	4	6	3	2	6	3
Do any banking online	May 2011	24	19	28	27	15	24	23
Get news online	May 2011	45	43	51	44	32	52	39
Look for health or medical information online	May 2011	10	8	9	11	10	8	11
Look for news or information about politics	May 2011	30	27	34	34	19	36	26
Look online for info about a job	May 2011	11	15	12	9	1	11	11
Look for information on Wikipedia	Feb. 2012	16	19	15	15	11	18	13
Make a donation to a charity online	May 2011	1	1	1	2	1	1	1
Make a phone call online, using a service, such as Skype or Vonage	May 2011	5	6	5	5	2	6	4
Pay bills online	Sept. 2010	15	14	19	11	11	15	15
Pay to access or download digital content online, such as music video, or newspaper articles	Sept. 2010	10	13	9	12	3	13	8
Play online games	Sept. 2010	13	16	15	10	9	13	13
Post a comment or review online about a product you bought or a service you received	Sept. 2010	4	6	5	2	3	5	4
Rate a product, service, or person	May 2011	4	4	4	2	2	5	4
Research a product or service online	Sept. 2010	28	27	32	26	16	31	24
Search online for a map or driving directions	Sept. 2010	14	15	17	12	7	16	12
Send instant messages	Nov. 2010	18	29	17	13	4	18	18
Send or read e-mail	Nov. 2010	61	64	63	61	46	59	64
Take part in chat rooms or online discussions	Sept. 2010	7	9	9	5	2	8	6
Use a search engine to find information	Feb. 2012	59	66	65	52	38	59	60
Use a social networking site, like Facebook, LinkedIn or Google Plus	Feb. 2012	48	70	52	31	18	42	54
Use Twitter	Feb. 2012	8	17	7	4	1	8	8
Visit a local, state, or federal government Web site	May 2011	13	11	15	13	6	14	12
Watch a video on a video-sharing site	May 2011	28	47	27	20	11	32	25

Source: Pew Research Center, Internet & American Life Project Surveys ©. See also <http://www.pewinternet.org>.

Table 1169. Online News Consumption by Selected Characteristics: 2000 to 2012

[In percent. Covers Internet users age 18 and over who report getting news online "ever" or "yesterday." Based on telephone surveys of persons with land-line telephones, except as noted. In May 2010, 2,252 persons were interviewed, including 744 cell phone users. Landline sample response rate was 21.8 percent; cellular sample response rate was 19.3 percent. In May 2011, 2,277 persons were interviewed, including 755 cell phone users. Landline sample response rate was 13.6 percent; cellular sample response rate was 11.5 percent. In August 2012, 2,253 persons were interviewed, including 900 cell phone users. Landline sample response rate was 12 percent; cellular sample response rate was 11 percent. Beginning in 2011, surveys were conducted in English and Spanish.]

Characteristic	"Ever" get news online 2000	2010	2011 [1]	2012 [1]	Got news online "yesterday" 2000	2010	2011 [1]	2012 [1]
Total adult Internet users	**60**	**75**	**76**	**78**	**22**	**43**	**45**	**(NA)**
Age:								
18 to 29 years old	56	75	72	84	16	44	43	(NA)
30 to 49 years old	63	78	83	83	25	45	51	(NA)
50 to 64 years old	57	76	77	71	25	42	44	(NA)
65 years old and over	53	62	60	66	28	34	32	(NA)
Sex:								
Male	66	77	77	76	29	48	52	(NA)
Female	53	74	76	80	16	38	39	(NA)
Race/ethnicity:								
White, non-Hispanic	60	75	76	79	23	43	46	(NA)
Black, non-Hispanic	63	72	77	74	13	42	34	(NA)
English-speaking Hispanic	57	73	72	73	23	35	40	(NA)
Annual household income:								
Less than $30,000	55	64	65	69	21	28	31	(NA)
$30,000 to $49,999	57	74	79	80	20	35	44	(NA)
$50,000 to $74,999	63	78	82	81	22	47	52	(NA)
$75,000 or more	69	84	88	89	31	60	62	(NA)
Frequency of Internet use:								
Daily	66	82	(NA)	(NA)	33	54	(NA)	(NA)
Several times per week	59	64	(NA)	(NA)	17	14	(NA)	(NA)
Less often	51	38	(NA)	(NA)	12	5	(NA)	(NA)

NA Not available. [1] Includes interviews conducted in English and Spanish.

Source: Pew Research Center, Internet & American Life Project Surveys from March 2000, May 2010, May 2011, and August 2012 ©. See also <http://www.pewinternet.org>.

Table 1170. Adult Computer and Internet Users by Selected Characteristics: 2000 to 2015

[In percent. Covers persons age 18 and over who use a computer or the Internet at a workplace, school, home, or anywhere else, on at least an occasional basis. Based on telephone surveys of persons with landline telephones unless otherwise noted. Beginning 2011, surveys include interviews conducted in English and Spanish. Data for 2015 are from July 2015 interviews with 2,001 persons, including 1,300 cell phone users. Data for 2014 (except broadband vs. dial-up statistics) are from interviews with 1,006 persons, including 504 cellular telephone users. Data for 2010 are from interviews with 2,252 persons, including 744 cell phone users. 2010 landline sample had 21.8 percent response rate; cellular sample had 19.3 percent response rate. For 2000, Internet users include persons who ever go online to access the Internet or World Wide Web or to send and receive e-mail. For 2005, Internet users include those who at least occasionally use the Internet or send and receive e-mail]

Characteristic	Adult computer users					Adult Internet users				
	2000	2005	2010	2014	2015	2000	2005	2010	2014	2015
Total adults	**65**	**71**	**77**	**81**	**(NA)**	**53**	**69**	**79**	**87**	**87**
Age:										
18 to 29 years old	82	83	89	89	(NA)	72	82	95	97	97
30 to 49 years old	76	81	86	86	(NA)	62	80	87	93	97
50 to 64 years old	61	72	78	84	(NA)	48	68	78	88	80
65 years old and over	21	31	42	56	(NA)	15	28	42	57	65
Sex:										
Male	66	72	78	80	(NA)	56	70	79	87	87
Female	64	70	76	81	(NA)	51	67	79	86	87
Race/ethnicity:										
White, non-Hispanic	66	72	79	(NA)	(NA)	55	70	80	85	87
Black, non-Hispanic	59	60	72	(NA)	(NA)	42	54	71	81	84
Hispanic	64	75	74	(NA)	(NA)	48	73	82	(NA)	84
Education:										
Less than high school	28	36	43	[2]([2])	(NA)	19	35	52	[2]([2])	68
High school graduate [1]	56	63	67	[2]66	(NA)	41	59	67	[2]76	77
Some college	80	81	88	89	(NA)	69	80	90	91	93
College graduate or higher	88	90	96	94	(NA)	79	88	96	97	97
Annual household income:										
Less than $30,000	48	52	58	65	(NA)	35	50	63	77	78
$30,000 to $49,999	74	76	82	84	(NA)	61	74	84	85	87
$50,000 to $74,999	85	88	89	92	(NA)	74	86	89	93	94
$75,000 or more	90	92	96	96	(NA)	81	91	95	99	97

NA Not available. [1] Includes those with a GED certificate. [2] Data are combined for respondents who completed and did not complete high school.

Source: Pew Research Center, Pew Internet & American Life Project Surveys conducted September-December 2000, September and December of 2005, May 2010, May 2013, January 2014, and July 2015 ©. See also <http://www.pewinternet.org>.

Table 1171. Number of Public Libraries and Library Services by State: 2012

[1,497,098 represents 1,497,098,000. Data are generally for the fiscal year ending in June; see source for reporting periods. Based on a census of all public libraries that meet the definition of a Federal State Cooperative System (FSCS) Public Library, which can have one or more outlets (central, branch, bookmobile) that provide direct service to the public]

State	Number of public libraries [1]	Library visits (1,000s)	Per capita visits [2]	Per capita circulation of materials [2]	Average number of public use Internet computers [3]	State	Number of public libraries [1]	Library visits (1,000s)	Per capita visits [2]	Per capita circulation of materials [2]	Average number of public use Internet computers [3]
U.S.	**9,082**	**1,497,098**	**4.9**	**8.0**	**16.4**	MO	147	30,346	5.6	10.0	13.7
AL	219	16,791	3.6	4.5	17.9	MT	82	4,679	4.7	7.6	10.9
AK	77	3,316	5.1	7.1	8.1	NE	265	8,760	6.0	9.4	9.8
AZ	91	28,111	4.3	7.8	24.2	NV	22	11,128	4.1	7.4	18.8
AR	56	10,801	4.1	5.4	10.3	NH	218	7,553	7.7	11.6	6.3
CA	183	163,570	4.3	6.1	18.4	NJ	297	48,062	5.5	7.1	17.8
CO	115	32,774	6.5	13.1	23.4	NM	85	7,454	4.5	5.7	17.0
CT	183	23,287	6.9	9.7	18.2	NY	756	115,248	5.9	8.2	16.8
DE	21	4,562	5.1	7.0	18.0	NC	77	40,644	4.2	5.7	18.9
DC	1	2,547	4.0	5.3	36.0	ND	75	2,377	3.8	6.7	8.1
FL	79	82,460	4.3	6.6	29.9	OH	251	87,376	7.6	16.4	16.8
GA	61	33,351	3.2	4.2	19.1	OK	118	14,379	4.7	7.1	14.1
HI	1	5,347	3.9	5.0	9.1	OR	128	23,253	6.3	17.2	13.8
ID	101	9,440	6.8	10.9	11.6	PA	456	46,879	3.8	5.6	12.5
IL	622	77,437	6.6	10.3	17.8	RI	48	6,092	5.8	7.1	20.7
IN	237	38,664	6.3	12.7	19.3	SC	42	18,301	3.9	5.6	20.0
IA	533	19,499	6.5	9.7	8.0	SD	112	3,998	5.3	8.9	6.7
KS	321	14,726	6.0	10.7	9.9	TN	185	20,895	3.4	4.2	17.1
KY	119	19,870	4.5	6.8	22.2	TX	551	75,153	3.2	5.5	22.3
LA	68	16,830	3.7	4.5	15.0	UT	72	19,142	6.8	13.5	15.8
ME	229	7,036	6.2	8.4	7.6	VT	163	3,880	6.5	7.8	6.4
MD	24	29,209	5.1	10.0	24.2	VA	91	39,646	5.0	9.7	16.0
MA	359	42,617	6.5	9.9	13.4	WA	61	43,096	6.4	12.1	20.3
MI	389	55,512	5.7	8.9	18.7	WV	97	5,831	3.2	3.6	8.0
MN	138	26,211	4.9	10.5	15.9	WI	382	35,648	6.3	11.1	13.4
MS	51	9,669	3.2	2.8	11.4	WY	23	3,640	6.4	8.8	10.7

[1] Of the 9,082 public libraries, there are 8,895 central libraries and 7,641 branch libraries; 1,540 libraries have library branches; and 567 libraries have bookmobiles. [2] Per capita rate based on total unduplicated population of legal service area given by the state library agency of each state. [3] See footnote 5 in Table 1174.

Source: Institute of Museum and Library Services, *Public Libraries in the United States Survey: Fiscal Year 2012*, December 2014; and "Supplementary Tables," <http://www.imls.gov/research/publications.aspx>, accessed April 2015.

Table 1172. Public Library Holdings by Type, by State: 2012

[In thousands (783,882 represents 783,882,000). Data are generally for the fiscal year ending in June; see source for reporting periods. Based on a census of all public libraries, conducted by Institute of Museum and Library Services. Covers only libraries that meet the definition of a Federal State Cooperative System (FSCS) public library. Previous editions of this table showed data for all libraries, including non-FSCS libraries. State data comparisons should be made with caution because of differences in reporting periods and adherence to survey definitions. Data are not subject to sampling error; census results may contain nonsampling error]

| State | Type of Holding | | | | | | | |
| | Print materials [1] | Current print serial subscrip-tions | Electronic books | Databases | Audio | | Video | |
					Physical units	Down-loadable titles	Physical units	Down-loadable titles
Total.....................	783,882	1,509	87,179.3	470.6	47,499	28,319.2	57,108	1,463.0
Alabama.................	9,671	10	877.9	16.2	457	131.4	583	0.3
Alaska....................	2,354	6	305.1	4.2	117	221.3	243	(Z)
Arizona...................	8,399	16	2,125.5	3.9	658	350.0	946	26.1
Arkansas.................	6,501	8	157.4	5.0	238	63.7	493	1.1
California.................	68,912	101	1,355.0	4.2	3,671	445.3	4,925	8.6
Colorado.................	11,367	25	622.8	1.9	935	322.3	1,249	21.6
Connecticut.............	14,522	23	712.5	6.3	812	895.0	1,039	3.6
Delaware.................	1,697	7	320.9	0.8	122	104.5	168	–
District of Columbia......	1,334	2	19.5	0.1	84	11.4	132	2.5
Florida....................	32,481	53	1,394.1	5.4	2,129	870.0	3,395	38.2
Georgia..................	16,637	20	273.7	11.7	652	272.0	972	9.0
Hawaii...................	3,394	3	11.7	0.1	266	5.3	149	–
Idaho.....................	4,350	7	45.2	5.3	233	39.3	289	0.1
Illinois...................	43,846	98	2,382.3	21.0	3,302	992.6	3,094	448.3
Indiana..................	24,321	49	1,248.1	16.5	1,548	387.1	2,004	2.3
Iowa.....................	12,105	33	2,017.2	10.2	662	1,109.3	844	0.4
Kansas..................	9,473	20	47.9	16.7	467	14.5	757	1.3
Kentucky................	8,803	40	3,239.8	4.8	495	713.8	665	73.4
Louisiana................	11,934	38	325.0	5.7	423	146.2	870	20.9
Maine....................	5,964	10	770.5	14.4	232	305.3	322	(Z)
Maryland.................	13,022	27	588.5	0.8	1,209	644.7	1,010	0.8
Massachusetts...........	32,668	48	2,485.9	19.0	1,446	936.9	1,782	32.5
Michigan.................	33,728	65	1,236.2	15.0	1,925	591.4	2,252	4.2
Minnesota...............	15,164	31	2,750.8	6.9	901	376.7	937	18.2
Mississippi...............	5,734	8	47.0	2.7	218	5.4	318	0.9
Missouri.................	17,220	43	417.8	3.2	987	103.9	1,028	1.8
Montana.................	2,700	5	801.2	2.7	113	399.0	170	22.8
Nebraska................	5,949	15	962.8	6.1	255	408.5	325	0.2
Nevada..................	4,441	6	120.1	1.0	419	46.8	524	1.9
New Hampshire..........	5,874	12	2,031.4	5.7	276	1,171.2	378	–
New Jersey..............	29,075	52	1,729.0	12.5	2,036	–	1,934	–
New Mexico.............	4,271	7	54.3	4.7	228	55.6	245	1.2
New York................	70,074	160	5,040.2	18.6	4,062	1,888.7	4,636	108.7
North Carolina...........	16,519	23	2,791.8	5.3	722	368.3	730	9.3
North Dakota.............	2,294	4	233.8	3.5	95	84.1	117	8.9
Ohio......................	44,120	123	17,711.2	103.9	3,706	5,417.0	4,771	172.5
Oklahoma................	7,441	9	243.9	4.6	443	44.6	383	0.9
Oregon..................	9,926	19	2,567.0	4.2	780	1,143.0	884	140.6
Pennsylvania.............	26,694	49	2,786.2	11.9	2,083	720.6	1,690	99.3
Rhode Island.............	4,428	6	431.5	2.5	146	293.4	224	3.1
South Carolina...........	9,343	16	181.3	1.9	431	62.5	644	8.8
South Dakota.............	2,988	5	35.7	6.1	122	8.5	165	2.1
Tennessee...............	11,525	13	80.1	12.9	570	20.8	660	0.8
Texas....................	40,707	53	1,144.3	27.9	1,966	525.4	2,459	25.6
Utah.....................	6,964	11	334.5	3.7	625	608.2	637	10.2
Vermont..................	2,881	6	90.3	3.1	129	46.6	177	(Z)
Virginia..................	18,332	25	1,058.4	1.1	1,035	205.0	1,118	0.5
Washington..............	14,842	45	734.3	1.5	1,276	315.6	1,508	9.0
West Virginia.............	5,140	6	3.4	1.7	207	4.8	271	0.1
Wisconsin................	19,265	45	20,230.4	19.3	1,427	4,328.8	1,821	120.5
Wyoming.................	2,488	5	4.1	1.9	158	93.1	167	–

– Represents zero. Z Less than 50. [1] Includes books, and non-serial government documents.

Source: Institute of Museum and Library Services, *Public Libraries in the United States Survey, Fiscal Year 2012*, December 2014; and "Supplementary Tables," <http://www.imls.gov/research/pls_publications.aspx>, accessed May 2015.

Table 1173. Public Library Technology Services and Resources Available for Patrons: 2013

[In percent, except as indicated. Based on sample survey of public libraries at the branch/outlet level; survey excludes bookmobiles. The survey collected responses from 3,392 libraries (70.1% response rate), September through November 2013. See source for details]

Item	Total	Metropolitan status			
		City	Suburb	Town	Rural
Average number of public access Internet workstations (number).............	19.8	40.2	24.8	17.6	9.4
Public library outlets offering public wireless Internet access (percent).............	97.5	99.2	99.3	98.3	95.3
Technology services and resources available (percent):					
Licensed databases.........................	100.0	100.0	100.0	100.0	100.0
Online homework assistance...................	96.5	100.0	97.6	95.3	95.0
Online job/employment resources..............	95.6	98.7	94.4	96.3	94.6
Digital/virtual reference.....................	91.5	96.7	95.8	90.1	87.8
E-books....................................	89.5	95.7	96.7	90.5	82.2
Online language learning.....................	55.1	82.4	69.8	47.9	39.1
Work space(s) for mobile workers.............	53.3	46.0	58.3	54.2	52.9
Digitized special collections..................	44.0	69.7	46.0	40.7	34.0
Mobile apps to access library services and resources.........	42.6	64.7	52.8	37.5	30.2
Mobile device-enabled website................	40.0	58.3	55.7	34.5	26.3
Scanned codes.............................	24.5	41.4	34.4	18.5	15.0
Free video conferencing services.............	22.2	22.4	17.9	22.1	24.6
Subscribed video conferencing services........	7.6	8.0	5.2	6.8	9.3
Collaborative and group work software.........	3.6	7.1	2.9	1.9	3.4
Print on Demand (POD)......................	1.8	4.0	1.1	1.6	1.3

Source: Information Policy and Access Center, University of Maryland, College Park, MD, *2013 Digital Inclusion Survey: Survey Findings and Results*, by John Carlo Bertot, et al., July 2014 ©. See also <http://ipac.umd.edu/>.

Table 1174. Public Libraries—Selected Characteristics: 2012

[Total operating income in millions of dollars (11,494.3 represents $11,494,300,000). Data are generally for the fiscal year ending in June; see source for reporting periods. Based on a census of all public libraries in the 50 states and the District of Columbia. See source for details]

Population of service area	Number of—		Operating income			Paid staff [3]		Avg. number of public use Internet computers per stationary outlet [5]
	Public libraries	Stationary outlets [1]	Total [2] (mil. dol.)	Source (percentage)		Total	Librarians with ALA-MLS [4]	
				State government	Local government			
Total...................	9,082	16,536	11,494.3	6.9	84.4	136,851	31,601	16.4
Fewer than 1,000......	987	991	33.4	7.5	74.2	703	29	4.5
1,000 to 2,499.........	1,475	1,489	105.2	4.9	78.3	2,015	144	6.0
2,500 to 4,999.........	1,257	1,295	183.7	5.9	79.1	3,117	383	7.9
5,000 to 9,999.........	1,501	1,646	436.2	6.6	82.4	6,677	1,136	10.5
10,000 to 24,999......	1,750	2,231	1,205.4	5.8	86.5	16,036	3,698	14.7
25,000 to 49,999......	990	1,728	1,435.2	6.4	87.0	17,830	4,358	17.9
50,000 to 99,999......	563	1,598	1,450.1	7.9	85.7	17,447	4,236	19.3
100,000 to 249,999....	364	2,033	1,847.0	7.4	86.0	22,565	4,943	20.5
250,000 to 499,999....	111	1,216	1,364.9	7.4	86.1	16,027	3,894	23.2
500,000 to 999,000....	56	1,132	1,782.6	7.0	80.9	18,465	4,381	27.8
1,000,000 or more.....	28	1,177	1,650.7	6.2	81.6	15,969	4,400	29.4

[1] The sum of central and branch libraries. The total number of central libraries is 8,895; the total of branch libraries is 7,641. [2] Includes income from the federal government (0.5%) and other sources (8.5%), not shown separately. [3] Full-time equivalents. [4] Librarians with master's degrees from a graduate library education program accredited by the American Library Association (ALA). Total librarians, including those without ALA-MLS, is 46,808. [5] The average per stationary outlet was calculated by dividing the total number of public use Internet computers in central and branch outlets by the total number of such outlets.

Source: Institute of Museum and Library Services, *Public Libraries in the United States Survey: Fiscal Year 2012*, December 2014; and "Supplementary Tables," <http://www.imls.gov/research/pls_publications.aspx>, accessed April 2015.

Section 25
Banking, Finance, and Insurance

This section presents data on the nation's finances, various types of financial institutions, money and credit, securities, insurance, and real estate. The primary sources of these data are publications of several departments of the federal government, especially the U.S. Treasury Department, and independent agencies such as the Federal Deposit Insurance Corporation, the Board of Governors of the Federal Reserve System, and the Securities and Exchange Commission. National data on insurance are available primarily from private organizations, such as the American Council of Life Insurers and the National Association of Insurance Commissioners.

Financial Accounts of the United States—The Federal Reserve Board brings together statistics on all of the major forms of financial instruments to present an economy-wide view of asset and liability relationships in the Financial Accounts of the United States. The accounts relate borrowing and lending to one another and to the nonfinancial activities that generate income and production. Each claim outstanding is included simultaneously as an asset of the lender and as a liability of the debtor. The accounts also indicate the balance between asset totals and liability totals over the economy as a whole. Several publications of the Federal Reserve Board contain information on these financial accounts: Summary data on flows and outstandings in the statistical release *Financial Accounts of the United States* (quarterly); and concepts and organization of the accounts in *Financial Accounts Guide* <http://www.federalreserve.gov/apps/fof/>. Data are also available on the Federal Reserve Board's Web site at <http://www.federalreserve.gov/releases/z1/>.

Survey of Consumer Finances (SCF)—The Federal Reserve Board, in cooperation with the Treasury Department, sponsors this survey, which is conducted every 3 years to provide detailed information on the finances of U.S. families. Among the topics covered are the balance sheet, pension, income, and other demographic characteristics of U.S. families. The survey also gathers information on the use of financial institutions. Since 1992, data for the SCF have been collected by the National Organization for Research at the University of Chicago. Data and information on the survey are available on the Federal Reserve Board's Web site at <http://www.federalreserve.gov/econresdata/scf/scfindex.htm>.

Banking system—Banks in this country are organized under the laws of both the states and the federal government and are regulated by several bank supervisory agencies. National banks are supervised by the Comptroller of the Currency. *Reports of Condition and Income*, commonly known as call reports, have been collected from national banks since 1863. Summaries of these reports are published in the Comptroller's *Annual Report*, which also presents data on the structure of the national banking system.

The Federal Reserve System was established in 1913 to exercise central banking functions, some of which are shared with the U.S. Treasury. It includes national banks and such state banks that voluntarily join the system. Statements of state bank members are consolidated by the Federal Reserve Board with data for national banks collected by the Comptroller of the Currency into totals for all member banks of the system. Balance sheet data for member banks and other commercial banks are available on the Federal Reserve Board's Web site at <http://www. federalreserve.gov/econresdata/statisticsdata.htm>.

The Federal Deposit Insurance Corporation (FDIC), established in 1933, insures each depositor up to $250,000. Major item balance sheet and income data for all insured financial institutions are published in the *FDIC Quarterly Banking Profile*. This publication is also available on the Internet at the following address: <http://www5.fdic.gov/qbp/>. Quarterly financial information for individual institutions is available through the FDIC and Federal Financial Institutions Examination Council Web sites at <http://www.fdic. gov> and <http://www.ffiec.gov>.

Credit unions—Federally chartered credit unions are under the supervision of the National Credit Union Administration. State-chartered credit unions are supervised by the respective state supervisory authorities. The administration publishes comprehensive program and statistical information on all federal and federally insured state credit unions in the *Annual Report of the National Credit Union Administration*.

Other credit agencies—Insurance companies, finance companies dealing primarily in installment sales financing, and personal loan companies represent important sources of funds for the credit market. Statistics on loans, investments, cash, etc., of life insurance companies are published principally by the American Council of Life Insurers in its *Life Insurers Fact Book*. Consumer credit data are available on the Federal Reserve Board's Web site at <http://www.federalreserve.gov/econresdata/ statisticsdata.htm>. Government corporations and credit agencies make available credit of specified types or to specified groups of private borrowers, either by lending directly or by insuring or guaranteeing loans made by private lending institutions. Data on operations of government credit agencies, along with other government corporations, are available in reports of individual agencies.

Securities—The Securities and Exchange Commission (SEC) was established in 1934 to protect the interests of the public and investors against malpractices in the securities and financial markets and to provide the fullest possible disclosure of information regarding securities to the investing public.

Data on the securities industry and securities transactions are also available from a number of private sources. The Securities Industry and Financial Markets Association (SIFMA), New York, NY, <http://www.sifma.org/>, publishes the *SIFMA Fact Book*. The Investment Company Institute, Washington, DC, <http://www.ici.org/>, publishes a reference book, research newsletters, and a variety of research reports that examine the industry, its shareholders, or industry issues. The annual *Investment Company Fact Book* is a guide to trends and statistics observed in the investment company industry. Institute research reports provide a detailed examination of shareholder demographics and other aspects of fund ownership.

Among the many sources of data on stock and bond prices and sales are the New York Stock Exchange, New York, NY, <http://www.nyse.com/>; NASDAQ, Washington, DC, <http://www.nasdaq.com/>; Global Financial Data, Los Angeles, CA, <http://www.globalfinancialdata.com/>; and S&P Dow Jones Indices LLC, a part of McGraw Hill Financial, <http://us.spindices.com/>.

Insurance—Insuring companies, which are regulated by the various states or the District of Columbia, are classified as either life or property. Both life and property insurance companies may underwrite health insurance. Insuring companies, other than those classified as life, are permitted to underwrite one or more property lines provided they are so licensed and have the necessary capital or surplus. There are a number of published sources for statistics on the various classes of insurance—life, health, fire, marine, and casualty. Organizations representing certain classes of insurers publish reports for these classes. The American Council of Life Insurers publishes statistics on life insurance purchases, ownership, benefit payments, and assets in its *Life Insurers Fact Book*.

Statistical reliability—For a discussion of statistical collection, estimation, and sampling procedures and measures of reliability applicable to data from the Census Bureau and the Federal Reserve Board's Survey of Consumer Finances, see Appendix III.

Table 1175. Gross Domestic Product in Finance, Insurance, Real Estate, Rental and Leasing Industries in Current and Chained (2009) Dollars: 2000 to 2014

[In billions of dollars, except percent (750 represents $750,000,000,000.) Represents value added by industry. Data based on the 2007 North American Industry Classification System (NAICS). See text, Section 15. For definition of gross domestic product and explanation of chained dollars, see text, Section 13, Income]

Industry	NAICS code	Current Dollars				Chained (2009) dollars			
		2000	2010	2013	2014	2000	2010	2013	2014
Finance & insurance, total...............	52	**750**	**1,006**	**1,207**	**1,261**	**783**	**969**	**1,067**	**1,085**
Percent of gross domestic product......	(X)	7.3	6.7	7.2	7.2	6.2	6.6	6.8	6.7
Federal Reserve banks, credit inter-mediation, and related activities..........	521, 522	328	410	519	(NA)	311	388	442	(NA)
Securities, commodity contracts, & investments...................	523	131	200	224	(NA)	146	192	206	(NA)
Insurance carriers & related activities......	524	276	365	421	(NA)	321	360	389	(NA)
Funds, trusts, & other financial vehicles. ..	525	16	31	42	(NA)	13	29	30	(NA)
Real estate & rental & leasing, total. ...	53	**1,242**	**1,946**	**2,175**	**2,266**	**1,540**	**1,957**	**2,080**	**2,112**
Percent of gross domestic product......	(X)	12.1	13.0	13.0	13.0	12.3	13.2	13.2	13.1
Real estate...................	531	1,105	1,784	1,989	(NA)	1,372	1,795	1,898	(NA)
Rental & leasing services and lessors of intangible assets....................	532, 533	137	162	186	(NA)	169	162	181	(NA)

NA Not available. X Not applicable.

Source: U.S. Bureau of Economic Analysis, "Value Added by Industry" and "Real Value Added by Industry," <http://www.bea.gov/iTable/index_industry_gdpIndy.cfm>, accessed May 2015.

Table 1176. Finance and Insurance/Real Estate and Rental and Leasing – Establishments, Revenue, Payroll, and Employees by Kind of Business: 2007 and 2012

[3,669 represents $3,669,000,000,000. Data are preliminary. For establishments with payroll. Based on the 2007 and 2012 Economic Censuses; see Appendix III]

Kind of business	2007 NAICS code [1]	Establishments (number)		Revenue (bil. dol.)		Annual payroll (bil. dol.)		Paid employees (1,000)	
		2007	2012	2007	2012	2007	2012	2007	2012
Finance & insurance [2]....................	52	**501,713**	**471,754**	**3,669**	**3,532**	**502.4**	**522.7**	**6,608**	**6,217**
Monetary authorities—central bank.............	521	47	56	45	101	1.3	1.7	19	18
Credit intermediation & related activities........	522	231,439	197,877	1,343	1,161	180.9	186.8	3,280	2,923
Security, commodity contracts, & like activity...	523	85,475	97,798	612	517	166.3	167.2	885	937
Insurance carriers & related activities...........	524	184,752	176,023	1,669	1,754	153.9	167.0	2,423	2,339
Real estate & rental & leasing................	53	**384,297**	**348,565**	**485**	**491**	**84.8**	**88.1**	**2,188**	**1,980**
Real estate.........................	531	316,730	291,916	330	332	61.3	63.4	1,529	1,443
Rental & leasing services....................	532	65,120	54,063	122	129	21.1	21.5	630	500
Lessors of other nonfinancial intangible assets....................	533	2,447	2,586	33	29	2.3	3.2	29	37

[1] Based on the North American Industry Classification System (NAICS); see text, Section 15. [2] Total does not include NAICS 525, Funds, trusts, and other financial vehicles.

Source: U.S. Census Bureau, EC1200CADV2, "Advance Comparative Statistics for the U.S. (2007 NAICS Basis): 2012 and 2007," <http://factfinder.census.gov/>, accessed April 2014.

Table 1177. Finance and Insurance—Nonemployer Establishments and Receipts by Kind of Business: 2010 to 2013

[716.8 represents 716,800. Includes only firms subject to federal income tax. Nonemployers are businesses with no paid employees. Data originate chiefly from administrative records of the Internal Revenue Service; see Appendix III]

Kind of business	NAICS code [1]	Establishments (1,000)			Receipts (mil. dol.)		
		2010	2012	2013	2010	2012	2013
Finance and insurance....................	52	**716.8**	**720.6**	**706.4**	**50,626**	**52,046**	**51,506**
Credit intermediation & related activities....................	522	53.3	48.0	45.3	2,790	2,987	2,878
Depository credit intermediation...................	5221	6.2	6.0	5.9	181	188	188
Nondepository credit intermediation...................	5222	21.8	21.4	20.6	1,554	1,697	1,677
Activities related to credit intermediation...................	5223	25.3	20.5	18.9	1,056	1,102	1,012
Security, commodity contracts, & like activity..................	523	273.4	274.6	269.9	29,202	29,162	28,593
Securities & commodity contracts interm & brokerage.......	5231	29.8	29.4	27.7	4,969	4,551	4,648
Investment banking and securities dealing...................	52311	7.2	7.3	7.0	1,748	1,473	1,218
Securities brokerage....................	52312	18.6	18.1	17.2	2,589	2,461	2,848
Commodity contracts dealing...................	52313	1.1	1.2	1.1	236	209	223
Commodity contracts brokerage...................	52314	2.9	2.7	2.4	397	408	360
Securities & commodity exchanges....................	5232	1.9	1.9	1.8	660	544	348
Other financial investment activities....................	5239	241.7	243.3	240.3	23,573	24,068	23,597
Insurance carriers & related activities....................	524	390.1	398.1	391.2	18,634	19,897	20,035
Insurance carriers....................	5241	2.7	1.7	1.8	185	150	158
Agencies & other insurance-related activities.................	5242	387.4	396.4	389.4	18,449	19,747	19,877
Insurance agencies & brokerages....................	52421	270.5	276.2	272.3	13,854	14,701	14,796
Other insurance related activities....................	52429	116.9	120.2	117.1	4,595	5,045	5,081

[1] Data for 2010 are based on 2007 North American Industry Classification System (NAICS); data for 2012 and 2013 based on 2012 NAICS. For more information, see text, Section 15.

Source: U.S. Census Bureau, "Nonemployer Statistics," <http://www.census.gov/econ/nonemployer/index.html>, accessed June 2015.

Table 1178. Finance and Insurance—Establishments, Employees, and Payroll: 2010 and 2013

[473.5 represents 473,500. Covers establishments with payroll. Employees are for the week including March 12. Excludes most government employees, railroad employees, and self-employed persons. For statement on methodology, see Appendix III]

Kind of business	NAICS code [1]	Establishments (1,000)		Employees (1,000)		Payroll (bil. dol.)	
		2010	2013	2010	2013	2010	2013
Finance & insurance, total [2]	**52**	**473.5**	**472.2**	**5,929**	**6,064**	**472.4**	**537.7**
Monetary authorities—central bank	521	(Z)	0.1	18	19	1.6	1.9
Credit intermediation & related activities	522	199.1	195.0	2,757	2,839	160.2	193.3
Depository credit intermediation [2]	5221	124.4	124.0	1,982	2,010	111.6	131.7
Commercial banking	52211	92.7	96.1	1,528	1,616	91.2	111.5
Savings institutions	52212	13.8	9.4	199	133	9.8	8.1
Credit unions	52213	17.8	18.5	251	258	10.3	11.9
Nondepository credit intermediation [2]	5222	41.6	41.7	521	577	34.9	45.4
Real estate credit	522292	14.3	12.8	216	251	14.2	21.4
Activities related to credit intermediation	5223	33.1	29.2	254	251	13.7	16.2
Security, commodity contracts & like activity [2]	523	96.4	101.5	874	882	156.4	167.4
Security & commodity contracts intermediation & brokerage [2]	5231	45.4	49.3	435	412	82.0	79.8
Securities brokerage	52312	38.3	42.5	309	291	45.7	44.8
Other financial investment activities [2]	5239	50.9	52.2	434	465	73.6	86.5
Portfolio management	52392	19.1	23.0	232	263	51.0	62.7
Insurance carriers & related activities	524	176.9	174.7	2,273	2,319	153.1	174.1
Insurance carriers [2]	5241	33.3	31.2	1,421	1,443	104.7	121.0
Direct life insurance carriers	524113	8.9	9.1	360	344	28.6	33.5
Direct health & medical insurance carriers	524114	4.8	4.6	459	504	31.0	38.6
Direct property & casualty insurance carriers	524126	14.4	13.8	529	516	39.3	42.1
Agencies & other insurance-related activities [2]	5242	143.6	143.5	852	875	48.4	53.1
Insurance agencies & brokerages	52421	131.4	132.2	646	656	36.3	39.4

Z Less than 50. [1] 2010 data based on 2007 North American Industry Classification System (NAICS); 2013 data based on 2012 NAICS. For more information, see text, Section 15. [2] Includes businesses not shown separately.

Source: U.S. Census Bureau, County Business Patterns, "Geography Area Series: County Business Patterns," <http://factfinder.census.gov/>, accessed May 2015. See also <http://www.census.gov/econ/cbp/>.

Table 1179. Revenues of Finance and Insurance Industries: 2005 to 2013

[In billions of dollars (295.8 represents $295,800,000,000). Covers taxable employer firms only. Based on Service Annual Survey. Estimates have been adjusted to the results of the 2007 Economic Census. See Appendix III]

Kind of business	NAICS code [1]	2005	2009	2010	2011	2012	2013
Finance & insurance, total	**52**	**(NA)**	**3,354.9**	**3,325.2**	**3,377.3**	**3,506.9**	**3,586.1**
Monetary authorities--central bank	521	(NA)	62.6	88.5	88.0	100.5	90.5
Credit intermediation & related activities [2]	522	(NA)	1,211.5	1,119.3	1,089.9	1,071.0	1,067.5
Commercial banking	52211	(NA)	360.0	347.5	341.4	337.6	335.5
Savings institutions	52212	(NA)	49.2	46.6	42.7	38.4	36.0
Credit unions	52213	(NA)	54.5	52.0	51.8	52.8	52.5
Nondepository credit intermediation	5222	(NA)	(NA)	613.8	595.3	574.7	570.7
Credit card issuing	52221	(NA)	95.5	94.5	106.1	105.2	110.7
Sales financing	52222	(NA)	99.4	92.8	85.9	85.6	93.8
Other nondepository credit intermediation	52229	(NA)	(S)	426.5	403.4	383.9	366.2
Activities related to credit intermediation [2]	5223	(NA)	52.4	57.2	56.5	65.1	70.6
Financial transactions processing, reserve, and clearinghouse activities	52232	(NA)	37.1	40.3	38.8	42.5	47.6
Securities, commodity contracts, and other financial investment activities [2]	523	(NA)	526.0	532.9	544.2	547.7	581.0
Securities and commodity contracts intermediation and brokerage [2]	5231	295.8	(NA)	(NA)	(NA)	(NA)	(NA)
Investment banking and securities dealing	52311	155.5	167.6	155.9	142.3	138.4	139.2
Securities brokerage	52312	131.8	115.6	114.5	118.3	119.2	126.3
Other financial investment activities [2]	5239	132.6	(NA)	(NA)	(NA)	(NA)	(NA)
Portfolio management	52392	113.6	154.7	167.1	178.8	186.0	206.0
Insurance carriers & related activities [2]	524	(NA)	1,554.9	1,584.4	1,655.2	1,787.7	1,847.0
Insurance carriers [2]	5241	(NA)	1,412.1	1,440.5	1,501.8	1,615.9	1,662.9
Direct life, health, medical insurance carriers	52411	(NA)	993.4	1,015.5	1,066.9	1,163.0	1,190.2
Other direct insurance carriers	52412	(NA)	388.2	393.3	403.2	418.8	436.2
Insurance agencies & brokerages	52421	(NA)	104.8	104.0	108.2	112.4	120.7

NA Not available. S Estimate does not meet publication standards. [1] Data is based on 2007 NAICS; see text, this section and Section 15. [2] Includes other kinds of business, not shown separately.

Source: U.S. Census Bureau, Annual and Quarterly Services, "2013 Annual Services," <http://www.census.gov/services/index.html>, accessed May 2015.

Table 1180. Financial Accounts of the United States—Financial Assets of Financial and Nonfinancial Institutions by Holder Sector: 2000 to 2014

[In billions of dollars (92,387 represents $92,387,000,000,000). As of Dec. 31]

Sector	2000	2005	2007	2008	2009	2010	2011	2012	2013	2014
All sectors	92,387	129,710	156,370	147,560	152,310	160,574	165,237	176,214	192,763	202,778
Households [1]	34,264	45,475	52,967	45,997	48,618	52,888	54,071	58,418	65,352	68,315
Nonfinancial business	11,233	14,497	17,349	16,617	16,894	17,745	18,420	19,301	20,632	21,634
Nonfinancial corporations	9,761	11,901	13,753	12,923	13,317	14,017	14,506	15,085	16,338	17,106
Nonfinancial noncorporate	1,473	2,597	3,596	3,693	3,576	3,728	3,915	4,216	4,294	4,528
Federal government	570	644	704	1,292	1,387	1,612	1,411	1,517	1,719	1,901
State and local government	1,661	2,317	2,788	2,623	2,672	2,773	2,741	2,844	2,881	3,058
Monetary authority	636	879	951	2,271	2,266	2,452	2,945	2,955	4,074	4,555
Private depository institutions	7,504	11,084	13,145	14,462	13,554	13,697	14,580	14,986	15,920	16,898
U.S.-chartered depository institutions	6,333	9,446	11,028	12,150	11,441	11,473	11,839	12,218	12,795	13,647
Foreign banking offices in U.S.	704	904	1,313	1,469	1,218	1,268	1,736	1,721	2,037	2,093
Banks in U.S.-affiliated areas	62	106	105	102	95	80	76	76	85	92
Credit unions	406	628	699	740	801	876	929	971	1,003	1,066
Property-casualty insurance companies	858	1,246	1,386	1,306	1,380	1,360	1,380	1,442	1,540	1,587
Life insurance companies	3,136	4,351	4,950	4,514	4,824	5,168	5,340	5,615	5,977	6,227
Private pension funds	4,286	5,398	6,155	5,297	5,965	6,614	6,717	7,241	8,112	8,542
Defined benefit plans	1,785	2,251	2,495	2,573	2,626	2,836	2,947	3,018	3,068	3,099
Defined contribution plans	2,500	3,147	3,660	2,724	3,339	3,778	3,770	4,224	5,043	5,443
Federal government retirement funds	2,003	2,495	2,714	2,758	2,922	3,159	3,266	3,385	3,543	3,683
State and local government employee retirement funds	2,272	3,483	3,958	4,050	4,282	4,778	4,934	5,099	5,234	5,453
Money market mutual funds	1,812	1,993	3,033	3,757	3,259	2,755	2,643	2,650	2,679	2,688
Mutual funds	4,433	6,046	7,823	5,388	6,921	7,873	7,871	9,326	11,544	12,604
Closed-end funds	142	270	316	203	229	243	241	257	284	285
Exchange-traded funds	66	301	608	531	773	987	1,043	1,324	1,671	1,969
Government-sponsored enterprises (GSE)	1,965	2,822	3,176	3,409	3,048	6,722	6,480	6,275	6,361	6,400
Agency- and GSE-backed mortgage pools	2,493	3,548	4,464	4,961	5,377	1,139	1,305	1,437	1,569	1,645
Asset-backed securities issuers	1,497	3,390	4,513	4,102	3,290	2,236	1,989	1,769	1,482	1,386
Finance companies	1,213	1,857	1,911	1,852	1,662	1,589	1,569	1,494	1,473	1,501
Real estate investment trusts	65	306	318	251	263	302	433	594	644	726
Security brokers and dealers	2,020	3,569	4,686	3,506	3,269	3,504	3,533	3,706	3,408	3,255
Holding companies	899	1,651	2,141	2,430	3,317	3,313	3,357	4,284	4,244	4,335
Funding corporations	1,156	1,409	1,741	2,285	1,774	1,610	1,454	1,343	1,306	1,322
Rest of the world	6,204	10,678	14,572	13,699	14,362	16,054	17,513	18,951	21,114	22,809

[1] Includes nonprofit organizations.

Source: Board of Governors of the Federal Reserve System, "Federal Reserve Statistical Release, Z.1, Financial Accounts of the United States," <http://www.federalreserve.gov/releases/z1/>, accessed August 2015.

Table 1181. Financial Accounts of the United States—Credit Market Debt Outstanding: 2000 to 2014

[In billions of dollars (27,158 represents $27,158,000,000,000). As of December 31. Excludes corporate equities and mutual fund shares. Represents credit market debt owed by sectors shown]

Item	2000	2005	2007	2008	2009	2010	2011	2012	2013	2014
Credit market debt.....................	**27,158**	**41,488**	**50,106**	**52,464**	**52,191**	**52,332**	**53,272**	**55,041**	**56,677**	**58,784**
Domestic nonfinancial.............................	18,121	27,180	31,903	33,755	34,470	35,618	36,751	38,411	39,762	41,439
Household sector [1]..........................	6,960	11,721	13,831	13,851	13,560	13,231	13,058	13,055	13,170	13,512
Nonfinancial corporate business................	4,667	5,268	6,337	6,594	6,151	6,013	6,308	6,714	7,115	7,579
Nonfinancial noncorporate business............	1,912	2,898	3,775	4,094	3,985	3,951	3,947	4,068	4,183	4,400
Federal government............................	3,385	4,702	5,122	6,362	7,805	9,386	10,454	11,594	12,353	13,020
State and local governments....................	1,198	2,590	2,837	2,855	2,968	3,038	2,985	2,980	2,941	2,927
Financial sectors.................................	8,168	12,958	16,207	17,105	15,716	14,456	14,036	13,802	13,949	14,202
U.S.-chartered depository institutions...........	531	728	991	990	718	883	832	720	687	722
Foreign banking offices in U.S...................	2	1	1	–	–	–	–	–	–	–
Credit unions...................................	3	15	32	41	27	26	24	25	27	35
Life insurance companies.......................	2	11	29	55	48	45	47	52	59	72
Government-sponsored enterprises (GSE).....	1,826	2,592	2,910	3,182	2,707	6,435	6,247	6,093	6,200	6,276
Agency- and GSE-backed mortgage pools.....	2,493	3,548	4,464	4,961	5,377	1,139	1,305	1,437	1,569	1,645
Asset-backed securities issuers................	1,504	3,395	4,517	4,105	3,292	2,236	1,989	1,769	1,482	1,386
Finance companies.............................	807	1,109	1,280	1,200	1,044	1,281	1,262	1,205	1,209	1,238
Real estate investment trusts...................	168	395	421	367	340	340	365	401	579	663
Brokers and dealers............................	41	62	65	143	93	130	92	90	112	124
Holding companies.............................	288	482	711	808	1,254	1,237	1,221	1,416	1,403	1,394
Funding corporations...........................	503	620	786	1,253	817	704	652	594	621	647
Rest of the world....................................	868	1,351	1,997	1,604	2,006	2,258	2,485	2,827	2,966	3,143

– Represents zero. [1] Includes nonprofit organizations.

Source: Board of Governors of the Federal Reserve System, "Federal Reserve Statistical Release, Z.1, Financial Accounts of the United States," June 2015, <http://www.federalreserve.gov/releases/z1/>, accessed June 2015.

Table 1182. Financial Accounts of the United States—Financial Assets and Liabilities of Foreign Sector: 2000 to 2014

[In billions of dollars (6,204 represents $6,204,000,000,000). As of December 31. Minus sign (-) indicates loss]

Type of instrument	2000	2005	2007	2008	2009	2010	2011	2012	2013	2014
Total financial assets.....................	**6,204**	**10,678**	**14,572**	**13,699**	**14,362**	**16,054**	**17,513**	**18,951**	**21,114**	**22,809**
Special Drawing Rights allocations.............	6	7	8	8	55	54	54	54	54	51
Net interbank assets.............................	82	37	-68	288	86	24	238	102	414	381
U.S. checkable deposits and currency.........	236	300	306	370	361	390	472	540	591	671
U.S. time deposits..............................	226	223	299	372	299	308	356	393	445	492
Money market fund shares......................	11	23	46	70	77	70	74	97	108	111
Security repurchase agreements...............	91	705	1,098	563	489	582	678	672	734	857
Credit market instruments.......................	2,452	5,143	7,271	7,482	7,662	8,414	8,945	9,509	9,732	10,328
Open market paper............................	114	157	226	165	117	102	103	103	102	108
Treasury securities............................	1,021	1,984	2,376	3,253	3,671	4,459	5,004	5,571	5,795	6,156
Treasury bills...............................	178	265	303	758	750	710	648	662	686	672
Other Treasury securities....................	844	1,720	2,074	2,495	2,920	3,749	4,357	4,910	5,109	5,485
Agency- and GSE-backed securities [1]........	348	1,006	1,577	1,402	1,150	1,096	1,078	1,001	885	903
Municipal securities...........................	8	29	45	51	59	72	72	72	76	80
U.S. corporate bonds.........................	843	1,804	2,775	2,384	2,484	2,523	2,491	2,618	2,734	2,911
Loans to U.S. corporate business.............	117	163	271	226	182	162	196	144	140	170
U.S. corporate equities..........................	1,483	2,118	2,956	1,925	2,658	3,216	3,397	3,953	5,161	5,835
Mutual fund shares.............................	149	163	230	138	182	260	370	495	552	624
Trade receivables..............................	46	53	80	86	93	112	129	140	144	161
Foreign direct investment in U.S. [2].............	1,421	1,906	2,346	2,397	2,398	2,624	2,799	2,994	3,177	3,297
Total liabilities..........................	**3,328**	**5,710**	**8,159**	**7,876**	**8,149**	**8,862**	**9,431**	**9,907**	**10,266**	**10,615**
U.S. official reserve assets [3]...................	57	54	59	66	119	121	137	139	133	119
U.S. private deposits...........................	803	1,165	1,636	1,303	1,258	1,304	1,066	923	955	856
Security repurchase agreements...............	0	381	681	402	455	664	765	805	722	756
Credit market instruments.......................	868	1,351	1,997	1,604	2,006	2,258	2,485	2,827	2,966	3,143
Commercial paper.............................	121	384	413	342	401	399	345	373	407	384
Bonds.......................................	582	825	1,426	1,091	1,448	1,678	1,914	2,187	2,250	2,419
Depository institution loans n.e.c. [4]..........	115	110	137	152	138	162	205	238	277	305
Other loans and advances....................	50	31	21	19	19	20	21	30	32	34
Trade payables.................................	37	34	48	44	45	51	55	56	45	46
U.S. direct investment abroad [2]................	1,532	2,652	3,553	3,749	4,077	4,274	4,599	4,973	5,284	5,536
Miscellaneous liabilities.........................	31	74	185	707	188	191	324	184	161	159
U.S. equity in IBRD, etc. [5].....................	36	44	47	49	50	53	55	58	60	62
Nonofficial foreign currencies..................	3	3	27	556	13	3	102	12	3	4
Investment by holding companies.............	-7	27	111	102	125	136	166	115	98	92

[1] GSE = Government-sponsored enterprises. [2] Direct investment is valued on a current-cost basis. [3] Excludes monetary gold. [4] NEC = not elsewhere classified. [5] IBRD = International Bank for Reconstruction and Development.

Source: Board of Governors of the Federal Reserve System, "Federal Reserve Statistical Release, Z.1, Financial Accounts of the United States," June 2015, <http://www.federalreserve.gov/releases/z1/>, accessed June 2015.

Table 1183. Financial Accounts of the United States—Assets of Households and Nonprofit Organizations: 2000 to 2014

[34,264 represents $34,264,000,000,000. As of December 31. See also Table 742]

Type of instrument	Total (billion dollars)							Percent distribution		
	2000	2005	2010	2011	2012	2013	2014	2000	2010	2014
Total financial assets...................	34,264	45,475	52,888	54,071	58,418	65,352	68,315	100.0	100.0	100.0
Deposits...............................	4,462	6,257	8,071	8,716	9,239	9,600	10,144	13.0	15.3	14.8
Foreign deposits...................	48	64	67	57	50	52	47	0.1	0.1	0.1
Checkable deposits and currency........	405	286	424	729	892	1,014	1,128	1.2	0.8	1.7
Time and savings deposits...............	3,072	4,965	6,451	6,820	7,187	7,398	7,867	9.0	12.2	11.5
Money market fund shares.............	937	943	1,129	1,110	1,110	1,136	1,102	2.7	2.1	1.6
Credit market instruments [1].................	2,466	3,461	4,915	4,395	4,209	3,857	3,314	7.2	9.3	4.9
Treasury securities......................	578	426	1,123	717	943	957	697	1.7	2.1	1.0
Agency and GSE-backed securities [2]....	588	587	334	299	177	141	41	1.7	0.6	0.1
Municipal securities....................	532	1,601	1,871	1,806	1,661	1,606	1,540	1.6	3.5	2.3
Corporate and foreign bonds.............	565	599	1,361	1,355	1,235	977	875	1.6	2.6	1.3
Other loans and advances [3]..............	2	9	26	23	21	26	24	(Z)	(Z)	(Z)
Mortgages.............................	104	141	100	101	87	76	69	0.3	0.2	0.1
Consumer credit (student loans).........	(NA)	(NA)	78	74	66	59	54	(NA)	0.1	0.1
Corporate equities [4]......................	8,097	8,026	8,696	8,498	9,676	12,502	13,361	23.6	16.4	19.6
Mutual fund shares.....................	2,585	3,521	4,605	4,622	5,630	7,023	7,695	7.5	8.7	11.3
Security credit..........................	461	623	725	726	757	815	869	1.3	1.4	1.3
Life insurance reserves....................	819	1,083	1,137	1,199	1,186	1,233	1,283	2.4	2.2	1.9
Pension entitlements [5]...................	10,020	13,471	17,036	17,448	18,461	19,894	20,784	29.2	32.2	30.4
Equity in noncorporate business...........	4,974	8,424	6,894	7,587	8,386	9,503	9,925	14.5	13.0	14.5
Miscellaneous assets....................	379	609	808	879	873	925	940	1.1	1.5	1.4

NA Not available. Z Less than .05 percent. [1] Includes other instruments not shown separately. [2] GSE = government-sponsored enterprises. [3] Syndicated loans to nonfinancial corporate business by nonprofits and domestic hedge funds. [4] Only those directly held and those in closed-end and exchange-traded funds. Other equities are included in mutual funds, life insurance reserves, and pension entitlements. [5] See also Table 1224.

Source: Board of Governors of the Federal Reserve System, "Federal Reserve Statistical Release, Z.1, Financial Accounts of the United States," June 2015, <http://www.federalreserve.gov/releases/z1/>, accessed June 2015.

Table 1184. Financial Assets Held by Families by Type of Asset: 2010 and 2013

[Median value in thousands of constant 2013 dollars (23.0 represents $23,000). All dollar figures are adjusted to 2013 dollars using the "current methods" version of the consumer price index for all urban consumers published by U.S. Bureau of Labor Statistics. Families include one-person units; for definition of family, see text, Section 1. Based on Survey of Consumer Finances; see Appendix III]

Age of family head and family income	Any financial asset [1]	Trans-action accounts [2]	Certifi-cates of deposit	Savings bonds	Stocks [3]	Pooled invest-ment funds [4]	Retire-ment accounts [5]	Life insur-ance [6]	Other man-aged [7]
PERCENT OF FAMILIES OWNING ASSET									
2010, total...............	94.1	92.5	12.2	12.0	15.1	8.7	50.4	19.7	5.7
2013, total...............	**94.5**	**93.2**	**7.8**	**10.0**	**13.8**	**8.2**	**49.2**	**19.2**	**5.2**
Under 35 years old........	92.6	90.2	5.2	9.0	7.2	4.2	39.3	9.2	1.3
35 to 44 years old.........	93.1	91.8	4.4	12.5	14.3	6.3	55.4	13.3	2.0
45 to 54 years old........	93.3	91.8	6.7	10.4	14.7	8.2	56.5	17.1	3.9
55 to 64 years old........	95.7	94.6	5.8	10.8	15.5	10.6	59.3	24.4	7.1
65 to 74 years old........	97.4	97.1	11.7	9.4	18.4	11.8	48.0	29.4	11.9
75 years old and over..	97.2	96.7	18.8	6.8	15.3	10.3	29.0	30.4	9.2
Percentiles of income: [8]									
Less than 20.............	81.8	78.9	4.8	4.0	4.2	2.2	8.8	10.9	1.5
20 to 39.9...............	92.9	90.8	6.3	5.1	5.5	2.7	27.9	16.0	3.2
40 to 59.9...............	98.2	97.2	7.6	8.0	9.3	6.0	50.8	19.3	4.4
60 to 79.9...............	99.8	99.1	9.2	14.7	14.4	8.5	70.4	23.8	6.3
80 to 89.9...............	99.8	99.8	9.6	18.5	25.4	12.3	83.7	23.1	8.6
90 to 100...............	100.0	100.0	11.9	18.2	45.3	30.8	92.7	28.7	12.9
MEDIAN VALUE [9]									
2010, total...............	23.0	3.8	21.4	1.1	21.4	85.7	47.2	7.8	75.0
2013, total...............	**21.3**	**4.1**	**16.0**	**1.0**	**27.0**	**80.0**	**59.0**	**8.0**	**100.0**
Under 35 years old........	5.8	2.2	4.0	0.7	6.6	11.0	12.0	2.5	13.0
35 to 44 years old........	20.4	3.8	6.3	0.7	20.0	48.0	42.7	7.0	40.0
45 to 54 years old........	31.8	4.0	10.0	1.0	16.0	53.0	87.0	8.0	70.0
55 to 64 years old........	52.7	5.0	25.0	1.2	30.0	143.0	104.0	9.8	100.0
65 to 74 years old........	72.0	7.0	31.0	3.0	50.0	155.0	149.0	9.0	125.0
75 years old and over....	28.7	7.0	22.0	3.0	76.0	145.0	69.0	8.0	110.0

[1] Includes other types of financial assets, not shown separately. [2] Checking, savings, and money market deposit accounts, money market mutual funds, and call accounts at brokerages. [3] Covers only those stocks that are directly held by families outside mutual funds, retirement accounts, and other managed assets. [4] Excludes money market mutual funds and indirectly held mutual funds and includes all other types of directly held pooled investment funds, such as traditional open-ended and closed-end mutual funds, real estate investment trusts, and hedge funds. [5] The tax-deferred retirement accounts consist of IRAs, Keogh accounts, and certain employer-sponsored accounts. Employer-sponsored accounts include 401(k), 403(b), and thrift saving accounts from current or past jobs; other current job plans from which loans or withdrawals can be made; and accounts from past jobs from which the family expects to receive the account balance in the future. [6] The value of such policies according to their current cash value, not their death benefit. [7] Includes personal annuities and trusts with an equity interest and managed investment accounts. [8] Percentiles of income distribution in 2013 dollars: 20th: $23,300; 40th: $40,500; 60th: $63,100; 80th: $104,500; 90th: $154,600. Percentile: A value on a scale of zero to 100 that indicates the percent of a distribution that is equal to or below it. [9] Median value of financial asset for families holding such assets.

Source: Board of Governors of the Federal Reserve System, 2013 Survey of Consumer Finances, *Changes in U.S. Family Finances From 2010 to 2013: Evidence from the Survey of Consumer Finances*, Federal Reserve Bulletin, Vol. 100, No. 4, September 2014. See also <http://www.federalreserve.gov/econresdata/scf/scfindex.htm>.

Table 1185. Financial Accounts of the United States—Liabilities of Households and Nonprofit Organizations: 2000 to 2014

[7,349 represents $7,349,000,000,000. As of December 31. Minus sign (-) indicates decrease. See also Table 742]

Type of instrument	Total (billlion dollars)							Percent distribution		
	2000	2005	2010	2011	2012	2013	2014	2000	2010	2014
Total liabilities..........................	**7,349**	**12,162**	**13,782**	**13,571**	**13,638**	**13,792**	**14,169**	**100.0**	**100.0**	**100.0**
Credit market instruments...........................	6,960	11,721	13,231	13,058	13,055	13,170	13,512	94.7	96.0	95.4
Home mortgages [1]...................................	4,814	8,913	9,916	9,696	9,490	9,406	9,403	65.5	71.9	66.4
Consumer credit..	1,741	2,321	2,647	2,755	2,923	3,099	3,317	23.7	19.2	23.4
Municipal securities..................................	138	213	263	255	241	228	223	1.9	1.9	1.6
Depository institution loans, not elsewhere classified [2]...........................	15	-17	61	12	63	93	213	0.2	0.4	1.5
Other loans and advances.........................	119	119	136	138	139	141	144	1.6	1.0	1.0
Commercial mortgages..............................	133	173	208	201	199	204	212	1.8	1.5	1.5
Security credit..	235	232	278	239	304	339	370	3.2	2.0	2.6
Trade payables...	135	186	249	250	254	255	258	1.8	1.8	1.8
Unpaid life insurance premiums [3]...........	20	22	25	24	25	28	29	0.3	0.2	0.2

[1] Includes loans made under home equity lines of credit and home equity loans secured by junior liens. [2] Includes loans extended by the Federal Reserve to financial institutions such as domestic hedge funds through the Term Asset-Backed Securities Loan Facility (TALF). [3] Includes deferred premiums.

Source: Board of Governors of the Federal Reserve System, "Federal Reserve Statistical Release, Z.1, Financial Accounts of the United States," June 2015, <http://www.federalreserve.gov/releases/z1/>, accessed June 2015.

Table 1186. Financial Debt Held by Families by Type of Debt: 2010 and 2013

[Median debt in thousands of constant 2013 dollars (75.7 represents $75,700). See headnote, Table 1184]

Age and race of family head and family income	Any debt	Secured by residential property		Installment loans	Credit card balances [2]	Lines of credit not secured by residential property	Other [3]
		Primary residence [1]	Other				
PERCENT OF FAMILIES HOLDING DEBT							
2010, total............................	74.9	47.0	5.4	46.4	39.4	2.1	6.4
2013, total............................	**74.5**	**42.9**	**5.3**	**47.2**	**38.1**	**1.9**	**6.6**
Under 35 years old....................	77.1	28.6	2.4	63.5	36.8	2.1	5.7
35 to 44 years old.....................	84.8	53.5	5.0	58.2	41.7	2.6	7.7
45 to 54 years old.....................	82.3	56.1	7.9	52.8	44.3	1.7	9.7
55 to 64 years old.....................	78.7	48.9	7.8	43.3	43.4	1.7	7.7
65 to 74 years old.....................	66.4	42.2	4.8	29.3	32.8	2.2	4.2
75 years old and over................	41.4	19.9	2.7	15.7	21.1	0.7	2.0
White non-Hispanic....................	75.3	48.4	6.1	46.3	38.5	2.0	6.5
Nonwhite or Hispanic.................	72.9	31.6	3.5	49.0	37.4	1.6	6.8
Percentiles of income: [4]							
Less than 20............................	52.2	13.6	0.7	32.4	19.5	0.7	4.2
20 to 39.9...............................	66.7	25.8	2.1	41.3	34.2	1.5	5.3
40 to 59.9...............................	80.7	40.1	3.9	52.7	46.8	1.6	5.3
60 to 79.9...............................	87.0	62.9	5.6	56.4	49.8	2.3	9.1
80 to 89.9...............................	87.5	71.9	9.5	61.2	48.7	3.6	10.5
90 to 100...............................	84.5	72.6	18.7	45.0	32.2	3.2	7.9
MEDIAN DEBT [5]							
2010, total............................	75.7	116.8	104.0	13.6	2.8	6.4	4.8
2013, total............................	**60.4**	**115.0**	**90.0**	**14.9**	**2.3**	**4.4**	**4.0**
Under 35 years old....................	31.0	120.0	83.0	18.0	1.5	1.2	2.0
35 to 44 years old.....................	96.5	140.0	100.0	16.3	2.5	4.0	4.0
45 to 54 years old.....................	100.0	121.0	90.0	14.4	2.6	10.0	4.9
55 to 64 years old.....................	63.4	102.0	85.0	13.0	3.0	12.0	5.0
65 to 74 years old.....................	44.0	81.0	55.0	10.2	2.3	17.0	5.6
75 years old and over................	20.0	54.0	60.0	10.1	1.9	50.0	2.3
White non-Hispanic....................	82.2	118.0	99.0	15.1	2.7	8.5	5.0
Nonwhite or Hispanic.................	29.0	114.0	65.0	13.0	1.7	1.2	2.4

[1] Debt secured by residential property consists of first-lien and junior-lien mortgages and home equity lines of credit secured by the primary residence. [2] Families that had an outstanding balance on any of their credit cards after paying their most recent bills. [3] Includes loans on insurance policies, loans against pension accounts, borrowing on margin accounts, and unclassified loans. [4] See footnote 8, Table 1184. [5] Median amount of financial debt for families holding such debts.

Source: Board of Governors of the Federal Reserve System, 2013 Survey of Consumer Finances, *Changes in U.S. Family Finances From 2010 to 2013: Evidence from the Survey of Consumer Finances*, Federal Reserve Bulletin, Vol. 100, No. 4, September 2014. See also <http://www.federalreserve.gov/econresdata/scf/scfindex.htm>.

Table 1187. Amount of Debt Held by Families—Percent Distribution by Type and Purpose of Debt: 2007 to 2013

[See headnote, Table 1184]

Type and purpose of debt	2007	2010	2013	Type and purpose of debt	2007	2010	2013
TYPE OF DEBT				**PURPOSE OF DEBT**			
Total	**100.0**	**100.0**	**100.0**	**Total**	**100.0**	**100.0**	**100.0**
Secured by residential property:				Primary residence:			
Primary residence	74.6	74.2	73.8	Purchase	79.8	79.5	79.6
Other	10.1	9.8	9.0	Improvement	2.3	1.9	1.7
Lines of credit not secured				Other residential property	0.5	0.4	0.5
by residential property	0.4	1.0	0.7	Investments, excluding			
Installment loans	10.2	11.1	13.1	real estate	2.2	2.5	2.1
Credit card balances	3.5	2.9	2.4	Vehicles	5.5	4.7	5.1
Other	1.1	1.0	1.1	Goods and services	5.8	5.2	4.0
				Education	4.0	5.8	7.1

Source: Board of Governors of the Federal Reserve System, 2013 Survey of Consumer Finances, *Changes in U.S. Family Finances From 2010 to 2013: Evidence from the Survey of Consumer Finances*, Federal Reserve Bulletin, Vol. 100, No. 4, September 2014, and previous reports. See also <http://www.federalreserve.gov/econresdata/scf/scfindex.htm>.

Table 1188. Ratios of Debt Payments to Family Income: 2007 to 2013

[In percent. All dollar figures are adjusted to 2013 dollars using the "current methods" version of the consumer price index for all urban consumers published by the U.S. Bureau of Labor Statistics. Families include one-person units; for definition of family, see text, Section 1. Based on Survey of Consumer Finances, see Appendix III. For definition of median, see Guide to Tabular Presentation]

Age of family head and family income (constant [2013] dollars)	Ratio of debt payments to family income						Percent of debtors with—					
	Aggregate			Median for debtors			Ratios above 40 percent			Any payment 60 days or more past due		
	2007	2010	2013	2007	2010	2013	2007	2010	2013	2007	2010	2013
All families	14.6	14.7	12.1	18.6	18.2	15.9	14.7	13.9	11.0	7.1	10.8	9.3
Under 35 years old	19.7	17.0	14.9	17.6	16.3	13.7	15.0	11.7	8.0	9.4	10.4	11.6
35 to 44 years old	18.6	18.4	13.6	20.3	20.8	16.1	12.7	16.5	9.8	8.6	15.8	11.4
45 to 54 years old	15.1	16.2	13.9	19.6	19.2	18.7	16.3	15.4	11.8	7.3	12.6	12.0
55 to 64 years old	12.7	12.6	11.2	17.6	17.7	16.4	14.8	13.1	14.0	4.9	8.4	6.4
65 to 74 years old	9.7	11.3	8.9	18.4	17.0	14.3	15.3	12.0	12.3	4.4	6.1	4.7
75 years old and over	4.4	6.8	6.0	13.2	14.1	10.7	13.9	11.9	10.0	1.0	3.2	2.7
Percentiles of income: [1]												
Less than 20	17.6	23.5	15.7	18.8	16.0	13.1	26.7	26.2	23.4	15.1	21.1	16.4
20 to 39.9	17.2	16.8	14.7	16.7	17.5	15.2	19.7	18.6	18.1	11.3	15.2	14.1
40 to 59.9	19.9	19.5	16.2	20.4	20.1	16.4	14.5	15.3	11.2	8.3	10.4	10.0
60 to 79.9	21.8	19.4	16.6	21.9	20.4	17.7	12.8	11.1	5.9	4.3	8.8	7.3
80 to 89.9	19.7	18.1	16.6	19.1	19.3	18.5	8.1	5.3	4.1	1.9	5.3	4.3
90 to 100	8.5	9.4	7.4	12.6	13.1	11.8	3.8	2.9	1.6	0.2	2.1	1.0
Percentiles of net worth: [1]												
Less than 25	14.9	19.3	16.7	12.0	13.9	12.2	10.6	15.0	12.4	16.8	22.2	21.0
25 to 49.9	22.5	19.3	16.9	23.4	21.1	18.1	19.5	15.2	13.6	7.6	13.4	10.4
50 to 74.9	20.4	19.2	16.8	21.7	20.6	17.8	15.6	14.2	10.1	4.2	6.7	5.0
75 to 89.9	17.0	15.9	14.0	18.2	16.6	15.4	13.0	11.0	7.7	1.2	2.1	1.8
90 to 100	8.1	8.8	6.5	12.7	13.5	11.3	11.1	10.9	7.8	0.7	1.2	1.0
Owner occupied	15.7	16.2	13.2	22.9	22.2	19.7	18.1	17.1	13.8	4.8	8.7	6.5
Renter occupied or other	7.9	7.0	6.6	8.4	6.8	6.8	5.4	5.0	4.3	13.5	16.6	15.9

[1] See footnote 8, table 1184. Percentiles of distribution of net worth in 2013 dollars: 25th: $8,800; 50th: $81,200; 75th: $317,300; and 90th: $941,700.

Source: Board of Governors of the Federal Reserve System, 2013 Survey of Consumer Finances, *Changes in U.S. Family Finances from 2010 to 2013: Evidence from the Survey of Consumer Finances*, Federal Reserve Bulletin, Vol. 100, No. 4, September 2014. See also <http://www.federalreserve.gov/econresdata/scf/scfindex.htm>.

Table 1189. Household Debt-Service Payments and Financial Obligations as a Percentage of Disposable Personal Income: 2000 to 2014

[As of end of year, seasonally adjusted. Mortgage debt service ratio (DSR) is defined as the total quarterly required mortgage payments divided by total quarterly disposable personal income. The consumer DSR is defined as the total quarterly required consumer debt payments divided by total quarterly disposable personal income. The financial obligations ratio adds automobile lease payments, rental payments on tenant-occupied property, homeowners' insurance, and property tax payments to the debt service ratio]

Year	Financial obligations ratio	Household debt service ratio			Year	Financial obligations ratio	Household debt service ratio		
		Total	Mortgage	Consumer			Total	Mortgage	Consumer
2000	17.1	12.1	5.7	6.4	2010	16.1	11.0	6.0	5.0
2005	17.3	12.6	6.5	6.1	2011	15.7	10.4	5.4	5.0
2007	18.1	13.2	7.2	6.0	2012	15.0	9.8	4.9	4.9
2008	17.8	12.7	6.9	5.8	2013	15.4	10.0	4.8	5.2
2009	17.0	11.9	6.5	5.4	2014	15.3	9.9	4.6	5.3

Source: Board of Governors of the Federal Reserve System, "Household Debt Service and Financial Obligations Ratios," <http://www.federalreserve.gov/releases/housedebt>, accessed May 2015.

Table 1190. FDIC-Insured Financial Institutions—Number and Assets by State and Island Areas: 2014

[In billions of dollars, except as indicated (15,553.8 represents $15,553,800,000,000). As of December 31. Information is obtained primarily from the Federal Financial Institutions Examination Council (FFIEC) Call Reports and the Office of Thrift Supervision's Thrift Financial Reports. Data are based on the location of each reporting institution's main office. Reported data may include assets located outside of the reporting institution's home state]

State or Island Area	Number of institutions	Total	Assets by asset size of bank — Less than $100 mil.	Assets by asset size of bank — $100 mil. to $1 bil.	Assets by asset size of bank — Greater than $1 bil.
Total.......	6,509	15,553.8	109.8	1,232.0	14,211.9
AL..........	133	240.6	3.0	23.2	214.4
AK..........	5	5.9	–	1.1	4.8
AZ..........	22	19.8	0.6	4.0	15.2
AR..........	109	65.5	1.8	22.9	40.7
CA..........	210	606.5	1.2	50.1	555.2
CO..........	97	48.3	1.9	16.3	30.1
CT..........	44	92.9	0.2	13.9	78.7
DE..........	21	907.4	0.1	2.4	904.9
DC..........	4	2.1	–	1.0	1.1
FL..........	179	160.4	1.8	42.5	116.1
GA..........	210	284.4	4.0	32.2	248.2
HI..........	9	46.4	–	1.4	45.0
ID..........	12	5.0	0.3	3.5	1.2
IL..........	521	420.2	10.8	84.8	324.7
IN..........	124	73.8	1.5	25.6	46.6
IA..........	320	76.0	6.8	47.1	22.0
KS..........	281	66.0	7.8	33.9	24.2
KY..........	181	56.7	2.3	35.4	19.0
LA..........	138	64.0	2.0	31.6	30.4
ME..........	28	38.1	0.4	10.7	27.0
MD..........	68	34.0	0.6	18.1	15.3
MA..........	147	396.0	1.2	40.5	354.3
MI..........	118	59.1	2.0	23.2	33.9
MN..........	338	69.0	9.4	38.1	21.6
MS..........	83	78.0	1.2	20.3	56.6
MO..........	302	161.2	6.3	47.3	107.6
MT..........	61	28.5	1.8	6.8	19.9

State or Island Area	Number of institutions	Total	Assets by asset size of bank — Less than $100 mil.	Assets by asset size of bank — $100 mil. to $1 bil.	Assets by asset size of bank — Greater than $1 bil.
NE..........	201	69.1	5.2	24.3	39.6
NV..........	18	132.8	0.3	3.3	129.2
NH..........	19	10.7	–	6.6	4.2
NJ..........	98	156.9	0.4	27.0	129.5
NM..........	43	17.1	0.3	8.5	8.3
NY..........	159	903.4	0.8	40.8	861.8
NC..........	68	1,824.7	0.8	15.4	1,808.5
ND..........	84	24.7	2.3	11.6	10.8
OH..........	212	2,883.4	3.9	36.9	2,842.5
OK..........	221	95.6	5.1	33.3	57.2
OR..........	28	31.8	0.4	5.0	26.5
PA..........	189	233.4	1.5	52.9	179.1
RI..........	10	111.8	(Z)	1.9	109.8
SC..........	65	36.9	0.9	15.0	21.0
SD..........	73	2,938.1	1.7	10.7	2,925.6
TN..........	174	90.0	1.8	42.5	45.7
TX..........	507	445.8	7.5	100.3	338.1
UT..........	53	526.0	0.5	10.7	514.7
VT..........	12	6.1	(Z)	4.3	1.7
VA..........	97	641.4	0.5	22.9	618.0
WA..........	59	63.1	0.7	14.4	48.0
WV..........	60	29.5	0.8	11.0	17.7
WI..........	250	102.6	4.7	47.0	50.9
WY..........	32	7.3	0.4	7.0	–
GU..........	3	1.9	–	0.5	1.5
FM..........	1	0.1	–	0.1	–
PR..........	6	63.5	–	–	63.5
VI..........	2	0.2	–	0.2	–

– Represents zero. Z Less than $50 million. GU—Guam, FM—Federated States of Micronesia, PR—Puerto Rico, VI—Virgin Islands.

Source: U.S. Federal Deposit Insurance Corporation, "Statistics on Banking," <http://www2.fdic.gov/sdi/sob/>, accessed June 2015.

Table 1191. FDIC-Insured Financial Institutions—Income and Selected Measures of Financial Condition: 2000 to 2014

[In billions of dollars, except as indicated (511.9 represents $511,900,000,000). Includes Island Areas. Includes foreign branches of U.S. banks. Minus sign (-) indicates decrease]

Item	2000	2005	2008	2009	2010	2011	2012	2013	2014
Interest income..........................	511.9	522.2	603.2	541.2	536.9	507.4	486.7	470.4	469.8
Interest expense.........................	276.6	205.1	245.5	143.5	106.9	84.8	65.9	53.3	47.1
Net interest income.................	235.3	317.0	357.7	397.7	430.0	422.6	420.8	417.1	422.7
Provisions for loan losses...............	32.1	29.8	176.2	249.7	158.0	77.5	57.8	32.5	29.7
Noninterest income......................	165.6	223.4	207.7	260.5	235.7	230.1	248.7	252.2	246.7
Noninterest expense.....................	242.3	317.4	368.3	406.1	391.8	411.7	421.2	416.8	421.9
Income taxes.............................	43.6	64.6	6.3	6.1	38.4	50.7	58.3	69.7	67.5
Net income attributable to bank........	81.5	133.8	4.5	-10.0	85.5	118.4	141.1	154.4	152.7
PERFORMANCE RATIOS									
Return on assets [1] (percent).........	1.14	1.28	0.03	-0.08	0.65	0.88	1.00	1.07	1.01
Return on equity [2] (percent).........	13.53	12.43	0.35	-0.73	5.85	7.79	8.91	9.54	9.03
Net interest margin [3] (percent)......	3.77	3.47	3.16	3.49	3.76	3.60	3.42	3.26	3.14
Net charge-offs [4].....................	26.3	31.6	100.4	188.9	187.6	113.3	82.2	53.6	39.5
Net charge-offs to loans and leases, total (percent)........................	0.59	0.49	1.29	2.52	2.55	1.55	1.10	0.69	0.49
Net charge-off rate, credit card loans (percent).............................	4.36	4.74	5.44	9.26	10.08	5.45	3.95	3.35	3.12
CONDITION RATIOS									
Equity capital to assets (percent)................	8.49	10.28	9.33	10.88	11.15	11.16	11.17	11.16	11.15
Noncurrent assets plus other real estate owned to assets [5] (percent)....	0.71	0.50	1.91	3.37	3.11	2.61	2.20	1.63	1.20

[1] Net income (including securities transactions and nonrecurring items) as a percentage of average total assets. [2] Net income as a percentage of average total equity capital. [3] Interest income less interest expense as a percentage of average earning assets (i.e. the profit margin a bank earns on its loans and investments). [4] Total loans and leases charged off (removed from balance sheet because of uncollectibility), less amounts recovered on loans and leases previously charged off. [5] Noncurrent assets: the sum of loans, leases, debt securities and other assets that are 90 days or more past due, or in nonaccrual status. Other real estate owned, primarily foreclosed property.

Source: U.S. Federal Deposit Insurance Corporation, *Quarterly Banking Profile*, Fourth Quarter 2014, and earlier reports. See also <http://www2.fdic.gov/qbp/>.

Table 1192. FDIC-Insured Financial Institutions—Number, Assets, and Liabilities: 2000 to 2014

[In billions of dollars, except as indicated (7,463 represents $7,463,000,000,000). As of December 31. Includes Island Areas. Except as noted, excludes insured branches of foreign banks. Includes foreign branches of U.S. banks]

Item	2000	2005	2008	2009	2010	2011	2012	2013	2014
Commercial bank offices, total [1]	73,218	81,062	90,034	89,950	89,150	89,494	89,760	88,737	88,256
Number of main offices	8,315	7,526	7,088	6,841	6,531	6,292	6,097	5,877	5,643
Number of branches	64,903	73,536	82,946	83,109	82,619	83,202	83,663	82,860	82,613
Savings institutions, total	1,589	1,307	1,218	1,171	1,127	1,065	986	935	866
COMMERCIAL BANKS AND SAVINGS INSTITUTIONS									
Number of financial institutions reporting	**9,904**	**8,833**	**8,305**	**8,012**	**7,658**	**7,357**	**7,083**	**6,812**	**6,509**
Assets, total [2]	**7,463**	**10,879**	**13,841**	**13,087**	**13,319**	**13,891**	**14,451**	**14,731**	**15,554**
Net loans and leases [2]	4,572	6,641	7,700	7,053	7,144	7,283	7,534	7,757	8,187
Real estate loans [2]	2,396	4,140	4,705	4,462	4,267	4,134	4,092	4,066	4,171
1-4 family residential mortgages	1,340	2,042	2,045	1,916	1,900	1,883	1,894	1,830	1,842
Nonfarm nonresidential	525	826	1,066	1,091	1,071	1,061	1,073	1,109	1,150
Construction and development	197	450	591	451	321	240	203	210	239
Home equity loans [3]	151	534	668	662	637	604	554	510	492
Multifamily residential real estate	117	188	206	213	213	219	233	263	297
Commercial and industrial loans	1,086	1,086	1,494	1,214	1,184	1,346	1,494	1,567	1,715
Loans to individuals [2]	672	949	1,089	1,058	1,316	1,308	1,324	1,353	1,418
Credit cards and related plans	266	396	445	421	702	688	696	691	718
Other loans to individuals	406	512	583	575	556	562	570	602	635
Auto loans	(NA)	(NA)	(NA)	(NA)	(NA)	300	320	353	386
Loans to depository institutions	118	162	112	112	109	119	103	113	101
Lease financing receivables	167	139	121	109	102	100	105	111	115
Less: Reserve for losses	71	77	174	229	231	191	162	136	123
Securities	1,361	1,893	2,035	2,500	2,668	2,850	3,010	3,002	3,219
Domestic office assets	6,702	9,825	12,321	11,650	11,693	12,097	12,572	12,949	13,866
Foreign office assets	760	1,054	1,520	1,437	1,626	1,794	1,878	1,782	1,688
Liabilities and capital, total [2]	**7,463**	**10,879**	**13,841**	**13,087**	**13,319**	**13,891**	**14,451**	**14,731**	**15,554**
Deposits	4,915	7,141	9,036	9,227	9,423	10,186	10,817	11,192	11,764
Foreign office deposits	707	921	1,539	1,530	1,550	1,428	1,370	1,401	1,396
Domestic office deposits	4,208	6,221	7,496	7,697	7,873	8,758	9,447	9,791	10,368
Interest-bearing deposits	3,437	5,004	6,073	6,144	6,184	6,493	6,906	7,178	7,514
Noninterest-bearing deposits	771	1,217	1,423	1,553	1,689	2,265	2,541	2,613	2,854
Equity capital	633	1,119	1,291	1,445	1,511	1,569	1,629	1,655	1,742

NA Not available. [1] Includes insured branches of foreign banks that file a Call Report. [2] Includes other items not shown separately. [3] For one- to four-family residential properties.

Source: U.S. Federal Deposit Insurance Corporation, "FDIC Quarterly Banking Profile," <www2.fdic.gov/qbp/>; and "Historical Statistics on Banking," <http://www2.fdic.gov/hsob/index.asp>; accessed June 2015.

Table 1193. FDIC-Insured Financial Institutions by Asset Size: 2014

[14,484.2 represents $14,484,200,000,000. See headnote, Table 1191]

Item	Unit	Total	Less than $100 mil.	$100 mil. to $1 bil.	$1 bil. to $10 bil.	Greater than $10 bil.
COMMERCIAL BANKS						
Institutions reporting	Number	5,642	1,645	3,439	467	91
Assets, total	Bil. dol.	14,484.2	96.8	1,045.3	1,288.1	12,054.1
Deposits	Bil. dol.	10,945.5	82.3	876.8	1,013.0	8,973.5
Net income attributable to bank	Bil. dol.	140.7	0.8	10.4	14.2	115.3
Return on assets	Percent	1.00	0.79	1.02	1.14	0.99
Return on equity	Percent	8.97	6.80	9.48	9.70	8.86
Equity capital to assets	Percent	11.11	11.78	10.93	11.78	11.05
Noncurrent assets plus other real estate owned to assets	Percent	1.17	1.44	1.39	1.28	1.14
Net charge-offs to loans and leases	Percent	0.49	0.23	0.24	0.30	0.54
Percentage of banks losing money	Percent	5.10	9.91	3.31	2.14	1.10
SAVINGS INSTITUTIONS						
Institutions reporting	Number	867	227	517	107	16
Assets, total	Bil. dol.	1,069.4	13.1	186.7	288.3	581.3
Deposits	Bil. dol.	818.4	10.2	147.5	214.9	445.8
Net income attributable to bank	Bil. dol.	12.0	0.1	1.7	2.3	7.9
Return on assets	Percent	1.16	0.83	0.91	0.84	1.41
Return on equity	Percent	9.87	5.19	7.18	6.72	12.82
Equity capital to assets	Percent	11.77	16.13	12.77	12.49	10.99
Noncurrent assets plus other real estate owned to assets	Percent	1.49	1.59	1.34	2.00	1.29
Net charge-offs to loans and leases	Percent	0.55	0.19	0.17	0.15	0.94
Percentage of banks losing money	Percent	12.80	22.03	11.22	2.80	(NA)

NA Not available.

Source: U.S. Federal Deposit Insurance Corporation, *Quarterly Banking Profile*, Fourth Quarter 2014; and "Statistics on Depository Institutions," <http://www2.fdic.gov/sdi/index.asp>, accessed May 2015. See also <http://www2.fdic.gov/qbp/>.

Table 1194. FDIC-Insured Financial Institutions—Deposit Insurance Fund (DIF) Indicators: 2000 to 2014

[In billions of dollars, except as indicated (7,472 represents $7,472,000,000,000). As of December 31. Includes Island Areas. Except as noted, includes insured branches of foreign banks. Minus sign (-) indicates decrease]

Item	2000	2005	2008	2009	2010	2011	2012	2013	2014
Number of institutions reporting.................	9,920	8,845	8,314	8,021	7,667	7,366	7,092	6,821	6,518
Assets, total [1]..	7,472	10,895	13,894	13,112	13,319	13,892	14,451	14,723	15,554
Domestic deposits, total [2].......................	4,212	6,230	7,505	7,705	7,888	8,782	9,475	9,825	10,408
Estimated insured deposits [3].................	3,055	3,891	4,751	5,408	6,302	6,973	7,405	6,011	6,204
DIF balance (BIF/SAIF prior to 2006)..........	42	49	17	-21	-7	12	33	47	63
Reserve ratio [4]......................................	1.36	1.25	0.36	-0.39	-0.12	0.17	0.45	0.79	1.01
Number of problem institutions.................	94	52	252	702	884	813	651	467	291
Assets of problem institutions..................	23.8	6.6	159.4	402.8	390.0	319.4	232.7	152.7	86.7
Number of assisted institutions................	–	–	5	8	–	–	–	–	–
Assets of assisted institutions.................	–	–	1,306.0	1,917.5	–	–	–	–	–
Number of failed institutions...................	7	–	25	140	157	92	51	24	18
Assets of assisted institutions.................	0.4	–	371.9	169.7	92.1	34.9	11.6	6.0	2.9

– Represents zero. [1] Covers only insured commercial banks and savings institutions. Excludes U.S. branches of foreign banks. [2] Excludes foreign office deposits, which are uninsured. [3] In general, insured deposits are total domestic deposits minus estimated uninsured deposits. Prior to September 30, 2009 insured deposits included deposits in accounts of $100,000 or less; beginning September 30, 2009, insured deposits include deposits in accounts of $250,000 or less. The Dodd-Frank Wall Street Reform and Consumer Protection Act (Dodd-Frank) temporarily provided unlimited coverage for noninterest bearing transaction accounts for two years beginning December 31, 2010, and ending December 31, 2012. [4] DIF balance as percent of DIF-insured deposits.

Source: U.S. Federal Deposit Insurance Corporation, *Quarterly Banking Profile*, Fourth Quarter 2014, and earlier reports. See also <http://www2.fdic.gov/qbp/>.

Table 1195. FDIC-Insured Financial Institutions—Number of Offices and Deposits by State: 2014

[10,113 represents $10,113,000,000,000. As of June 30. Includes insured U.S. branches of foreign banks. The term "offices" includes both main offices and branches. "Banking office" is defined to include all offices and facilities that actually hold deposits, and does not include loan production offices, computer centers, and other nondeposit installations, such as automated teller machines (ATMs). Several institutions have designated home offices that do not accept deposits; these have been included to provide a more complete listing of all offices. The figures for each geographical area only include deposits of offices located within that area. Based on the Summary of Deposits survey]

State	Number of offices	Total deposits (bil. dol.)	State	Number of offices	Total deposits (bil. dol.)	State	Number of offices	Total deposits (bil. dol.)
Total [1].....	94,725	10,113	IA...............	1,583	76	NC...............	2,571	340
			KS...............	1,491	67	ND...............	429	25
U.S...........	94,263	10,052	KY...............	1,724	71	OH...............	3,879	272
AL.............	1,553	89	LA...............	1,593	96	OK...............	1,381	79
AK.............	130	11	ME...............	499	38	OR...............	1,065	62
AZ.............	1,314	97	MD...............	1,669	124	PA...............	4,477	318
AR.............	1,388	54	MA...............	2,227	346	RI...............	261	27
CA.............	7,267	1,086	MI...............	2,846	177	SC...............	1,358	70
CO.............	1,572	109	MN...............	1,752	255	SD...............	462	418
CT.............	1,259	113	MS...............	1,177	48	TN...............	2,221	122
DE.............	278	416	MO...............	2,373	158	TX...............	6,808	720
DC.............	235	41	MT...............	399	21	UT...............	575	449
FL.............	5,450	462	NE...............	1,090	58	VT...............	251	12
GA.............	2,526	197	NV...............	527	149	VA...............	2,537	240
HI.............	282	37	NH...............	431	29	WA...............	1,832	123
ID.............	520	21	NJ...............	3,171	286	WV...............	661	31
IL.............	4,697	435	NM...............	510	28	WI...............	2,203	137
IN.............	2,221	108	NY...............	5,308	1,293	WY...............	230	14

[1] Includes outlying areas not shown separately.

Source: U.S. Federal Deposit Insurance Corporation, "Summary of Deposits," <http://www2.fdic.gov/sod/>, accessed June 2015.

Table 1196. U.S. Banking Offices of Foreign Banks—Summary: 2000 to 2014

[In billions of dollars, except as indicated (1,358 represents $1,358,000,000,000). As of December. Covers the U.S. offices of foreign banking organizations that are located in the 50 states and the District of Columbia. Offices located in Puerto Rico, American Samoa, Guam, the Virgin Islands and other U.S.-affiliated insular areas are excluded. Foreign-owned institutions are those owned by a bank located outside of the United States and its affiliated insular areas. The U.S. offices of foreign banking organizations consist of U.S. branches and agencies of foreign banks and bank subsidiaries of foreign banking organizations. The latter are U.S. commercial banks of which more than 25 percent are owned by a foreign banking organization or where the relationship is reported as being a controlling relationship by the filer of the FR Y-10 (Report of Changes in Organizational Structure) report form]

Item	2000	2005	2009	2010	2011	2012	2013	2014	Share [1]		
									2000	2010	2014
Assets.......................	1,358	2,123	2,872	2,838	3,159	3,274	3,539	3,735	18.9	20.4	22.0
Loans, total.................	557	802	1,019	960	1,064	1,117	1,198	1,335	13.5	13.7	16.3
Business loans............	308	276	381	326	371	415	445	512	25.0	25.1	26.4
Deposits.....................	770	1,162	1,802	1,752	1,718	1,866	2,017	2,149	16.5	18.3	17.7

[1] Foreign owned banks plus U.S. branches and offices of foreign banks as percent of all banks in the United States.

Source: Board of Governors of the Federal Reserve System, "Share Data for U.S. Offices of Foreign Banks," December 2014, <http://www.federalreserve.gov/Releases/iba/fboshr.htm>, accessed June 2015.

Table 1197. Federal and State-Chartered Credit Unions—Summary: 2000 to 2014

[43,883 represents 43,883,000. As of December 31, except as noted. Federal data include District of Columbia, Puerto Rico, Guam, and Virgin Islands. Excludes state-insured, privately insured, and noninsured state-chartered credit unions and corporate central credit unions, which have mainly other credit unions as members]

Year	Operating credit unions		Number of failed institutions [1]	Members (1,000)		Assets (mil. dol.)		Loans outstanding (mil. dol.)		Savings (mil. dol.)	
	Federal	State		Federal	State	Federal	State	Federal	State	Federal	State
2000......	6,336	3,980	29	43,883	33,705	242,881	195,363	163,851	137,485	210,188	169,053
2005......	5,393	3,302	27	47,914	36,896	377,827	300,868	249,521	208,731	321,831	255,588
2007......	5,036	3,065	12	48,474	38,363	417,578	335,885	289,169	237,755	349,101	283,298
2008......	4,847	2,959	19	49,130	39,453	447,124	364,132	309,277	256,720	373,366	307,762
2009......	4,714	2,840	31	49,604	40,333	482,684	402,069	311,154	261,285	408,832	343,835
2010......	4,589	2,750	29	50,081	40,447	500,075	414,395	306,276	258,555	427,603	358,877
2011......	4,447	2,647	16	50,743	41,093	525,633	436,121	308,845	262,640	449,316	378,093
2012......	4,272	2,547	22	51,797	42,043	557,119	464,612	322,675	275,066	474,903	402,948
2013......	4,105	2,449	17	52,499	43,762	571,326	490,588	343,780	301,440	485,500	424,587
2014......	3,927	2,346	15	53,396	45,888	596,140	526,042	373,397	338,874	499,681	451,106

[1] For calendar year. A failed institution is defined as a credit union which has ceased operation because it was involuntarily liquidated or merged with assistance from the National Credit Union Share Insurance Fund.

Source: National Credit Union Administration, *National Credit Union Administration 2014 Annual Report,* June 2015, and earlier reports. See also <http://www.ncua.gov/Legal/Documents/Reports/AR2014.pdf> and <http://www.ncua.gov/Legal/Documents/Reports/2014-Historic-Stats.pdf>.

Table 1198. Noncash Payments by Method of Payment, and ATM Cash Withdrawals: 2009 and 2012

[108.1 represents 108,100,000,000. Estimates are based on survey data gathered from depository and financial institutions, payment networks, processors, and issuers by the Federal Reserve. The 2013 Study combines information gathered in three related survey efforts. Some estimates are based on data collected in the 2013 Depository and Financial Institutions Payments Survey (DFIPS), which was sent to a nationally representative, stratified random sample of depository and financial institutions. Other estimates are based on 2012 data collected in the 2013 Networks, Processors, and Issuers Payments Surveys (NPIPS) through a set of 15 census-style surveys of payment networks, processors, and card issuers. Finally, some estimates are from data collected in the 2013 Check Sample Survey (CSS), which are based on the information from a random sample of checks processed by a selected number of large commercial banks during 2012]

Method of payment	Transactions (billions)		Value (trillion dollars)		Average value per transaction (dollars)	
	2009	2012	2009	2012	2009	2012
Noncash payments, total.............	**108.1**	**122.4**	**(NA)**	**174.4**	**(NA)**	**1,425**
Checks (paid)............................	24.5	18.3	31.6	25.9	1,291	1,410
Commercial banks......................	20.7	15.8	29.2	24.0	1,412	1,518
Credit unions...........................	2.1	1.5	0.7	0.7	352	428
Savings institutions....................	1.3	0.8	1.3	1.0	973	1,264
U.S. Treasury checks...................	0.2	0.1	0.3	(NA)	1,545	(NA)
Postal money orders....................	0.1	0.1	(Z)	(NA)	183	(NA)
Electronic payments:						
Automated Clearing House (ACH)......	19.1	21.7	(NA)	144.1	(NA)	6,638
Debit cards.............................	37.5	47.0	1.4	1.8	37	39
Credit cards [1]........................	21.0	26.2	1.9	2.5	89	94
Prepaid [2].............................	5.9	9.2	0.1	0.2	23	24
Memo:						
ATM cash withdrawals................	**6.0**	**5.8**	**0.6**	**0.7**	**108**	**118**
Checks (written) [3]....................	27.8	21.1	32.4	26.5	1,165	1,257
Checks converted to ACH..............	3.3	2.7	0.8	0.6	227	227

NA Not available. Z Less than $50 billion. [1] Credit cards include both general purpose and private-label cards. [2] Includes general purpose and private label prepaid cards, which use funds from a nontraditional prefunded transaction account. [3] Includes the use of checks as source documents to initiate electronic payments.

Source: Board of Governors of the Federal Reserve System *The 2013 Federal Reserve Payments Study, Recent and Long-Term Payment Trends in the United States: 2003 – 2012, Summary Report and Detailed Report,* July 2014. See also <http://www.frbservices.org/communications/payment_system_research.html>.

Table 1199. Debit Cards: Holders, Number, Transactions, and Volume: 2000 and 2010, and Projections, 2014

[160 represents 160,000,000]

Type of debit card	Cardholders (mil.)			Number of cards (mil.)			Number of point-of-sale transactions (mil.)			Purchase volume (bil. dol.)		
	2000	2010	2014, proj.	2000	2010	2014, proj.	2000	2010	2014, proj.	2000	2010	2014, proj.
Total [1]........................	**160**	**185**	**197**	**235**	**4,008**	**5,099**	**9,571**	**49,281**	**66,049**	**342**	**1,825**	**2,517**
Bank [2]..........................	137	164	175	137	516	647	5,290	36,879	47,455	210	1,387	1,809
EFT networks [3]..................	159	184	194	223	281	302	2,979	7,239	12,131	100	262	470
Private label prepaid [4]..........	(NA)	(NA)	(NA)	(NA)	3,447	4,552	1,280	5,125	6,299	31	172	227
ACH network [5]...................	11	13	25	11	13	25	22	39	164	1	3	11

NA Not available. [1] Cardholders may hold more than one type of card. Bank cards and EFT cards are the same pieces of plastic that carry multiple brands. The total card figure shown does not include any duplication. [2] Visa and MasterCard debit cards, including prepaid cards. Beginning 2010, includes Interlink & MasterCard PIN debit. [3] Cards issued by financial institution members of regional and national switches such as Star, Interlink (for 2000), Pulse, Nyce, etc. EFT = Electronic funds transfer. [4] Prepaid cards without the Visa, MasterCard, American Express, or Discover logos. [5] ACH = Automated clearing house. Retail cards such as those issued by Target, Nordstrom, etc.

Source: The Nilson Report, Carpinteria, CA, twice-monthly newsletter. © Used by permission.

Table 1200. Credit Cards: Holders, Number, Purchase Volume, and Debt: 2000 and 2010, and Projections, 2014

[159 represents 159,000,000]

Type of credit card	Cardholders (mil.)			Number of cards (mil.)			Credit card purchase volume (bil. dol.)			Credit card debt outstanding (bil. dol.)		
	2000	2010	2014, proj.	2000	2010	2014, proj.	2000	2010	2014, proj.	2000	2010	2014, proj.
Total [1]	159	152	172	1,425	993	1,058	1,242	2,061	2,886	680	812	882
Visa	93	100	113	255	240	281	487	809	1,213	268	332	347
MasterCard	86	75	83	200	171	191	281	479	607	212	240	258
Store	114	95	103	597	318	344	120	138	184	92	92	108
Oil company	76	38	28	98	35	33	45	47	65	5	6	7
Discover	36	41	43	50	55	52	69	106	127	48	50	56
American Express	23	34	38	33	49	55	221	476	684	50	90	103
The rest [2]	7	6	14	192	124	102	18	5	6	5	2	2

[1] Cardholders may hold more than one type of card. [2] Includes Universal Air Travel Plan (UATP), phone cards, automobile rental, and miscellaneous cards; credit card purchase volume and cardholders excludes phone cards.

Source: The Nilson Report, Carpinteria, CA, twice-monthly newsletter. © Used by permission.

Table 1201. Consumer Credit Outstanding and Finance Rates: 2000 to 2014

[In billions of dollars (1,717 represents $1,717,000,000,000), except percent. Covers most short- and intermediate-term credit extended to individuals, excluding loans secured by real estate. Estimated amounts of seasonally adjusted credit outstanding as of end of year; finance rates, annual averages]

Type of credit	2000	2005	2007	2008	2009	2010	2011	2012	2013	2014
Total	1,717	2,291	2,615	2,650	2,552	2,647	2,755	2,923	3,099	3,318
Revolving	683	830	1,002	1,004	916	839	841	846	858	890
Nonrevolving [1]	1,034	1,461	1,613	1,646	1,636	1,807	1,914	2,077	2,241	2,428
FINANCE RATES (percent)										
Commercial banks:										
New automobiles (48 months)	9.34	7.07	7.77	7.02	6.72	6.21	5.73	4.91	4.43	4.24
Other consumer goods (24 months)	13.90	12.06	12.38	11.37	11.10	10.87	10.88	10.71	10.20	10.22
Credit card plans, all accounts	15.78	12.51	13.30	12.08	13.40	13.78	12.74	12.06	11.91	11.87
Credit card plans, accounts assessed interest	14.92	14.55	14.68	13.57	14.31	14.26	13.09	12.96	12.95	13.19
Finance companies:										
New automobiles [2]	(NA)	(NA)	(NA)	5.89	5.19	4.70	4.45	4.63	4.67	4.88

NA Not available. [1] Comprises automobile loans and all other loans not included in revolving credit, such as loans for mobile homes, education, boats, trailers, or vacations. These loans may be secured or unsecured. [2] Covers most of the captive and non-captive finance companies. Amount of finance weighted.

Source: Board of Governors of the Federal Reserve System, Data Releases, Household Finances, "Consumer Credit-G.19" and "Finance Companies-G.20," <http://www.federalreserve.gov/econresdata/statisticsdata.htm>, accessed May 2015.

Table 1202. Consumer Credit by Type of Holder: 2000 to 2014

[In billions of dollars (1,741 represents $1,741,000,000,000). As of December 31. Not seasonally adjusted]

Type of holder	2000	2005	2007	2008	2009	2010	2011	2012	2013	2014
Total	1,741	2,321	2,615	2,650	2,552	2,647	2,755	2,923	3,099	3,317
Households (nonprofit organizations) [1]	(NA)	(NA)	88	95	89	78	74	66	59	54
Nonfinancial corporate business	81	60	56	55	53	45	47	48	44	43
Federal government [2]	60	90	116	135	223	356	485	617	730	841
U.S.-chartered depository institutions	616	816	895	965	906	1,186	1,193	1,219	1,272	1,343
Credit unions	184	229	237	236	237	226	223	244	266	303
Government-sponsored enterprises	37	–	–	–	–	–	–	–	–	–
Asset-backed securities issuers	528	610	653	610	572	50	46	50	49	50
Finance companies	234	517	572	554	472	705	688	680	679	684
Memo:										
Credit card loans [3]	702	857	1,002	1,004	916	839	841	846	858	890
Auto loans	581	823	801	777	719	713	751	809	879	958
Student loans [4]	(NA)	(NA)	637	731	832	912	1,012	1,131	1,223	1,325
Other consumer credit [5]	458	641	175	138	85	181	151	136	139	144

– Represents or rounds to zero. NA Not available. [1] Student loans originated under the Federal Family Education Loan Program. [2] Includes loans originated by the Department of Education under the Federal Direct Loan Program and Perkins Loans, as well as Federal Family Education Loan Program loans that the government purchased from depository institutions, finance companies, and nonprofit and educational institutions, and loans in default. [3] Revolving credit that also includes overdraft plans on checking accounts and other loans without a fixed repayment schedule. [4] Includes student loans held by nonprofit organizations, the federal government, depository institutions, and finance companies. Data begin in 2006. [5] Prior to 2006, includes student loans.

Source: Board of Governors of the Federal Reserve System, "Federal Reserve Statistical Release, Z.1, Financial Accounts of the United States," June 2015, <http://www.federalreserve.gov/releases/z1>, accessed June 2015.

Table 1203. Mortgage Debt Outstanding by Type of Property and Holder: 2000 to 2014

[In billions of dollars (6,769 represents $6,769,000,000,000). As of December 31]

Type of property and holder	2000	2005	2007	2008	2009	2010	2011	2012	2013	2014
MORTGAGES BY TYPE										
Total [1]	**6,769**	**12,110**	**14,624**	**14,717**	**14,427**	**13,795**	**13,483**	**13,267**	**13,279**	**13,454**
Home [2]	5,122	9,421	11,241	11,154	10,939	10,447	10,201	9,976	9,885	9,887
Multifamily residential	402	669	797	848	855	852	856	889	926	999
Commercial	1,160	1,916	2,474	2,580	2,487	2,342	2,259	2,229	2,290	2,386
Farm	85	105	113	135	146	154	167	173	178	183
Household sector	104	141	111	112	111	100	101	87	76	69
Federal government	76	77	82	96	108	107	110	111	115	117
State and local governments	131	159	194	188	193	205	202	206	206	219
U.S.-chartered depository institutions	2,350	4,055	4,659	4,615	4,372	4,195	4,050	4,029	3,983	4,091
Foreign banking offices in U.S.	17	21	39	44	38	35	33	31	30	38
Credit unions	120	226	280	312	317	317	321	328	346	372
Life insurance companies	236	285	326	342	326	317	332	344	363	385
Government-sponsored enterprises (GSE)	264	589	643	705	708	5,021	4,924	4,824	4,878	4,870
Agency- and GSE-backed mortgage pools	2,493	3,548	4,464	4,961	5,377	1,139	1,305	1,437	1,569	1,645
Asset-backed securities issuers	604	2,156	2,972	2,620	2,250	1,922	1,703	1,493	1,222	1,120
Finance companies	238	541	550	483	430	244	211	179	157	148
Real estate investment trusts	18	147	123	76	46	45	56	64	199	245
HOME MORTGAGES [2]										
Total [1]	**5,122**	**9,421**	**11,241**	**11,154**	**10,939**	**10,447**	**10,201**	**9,976**	**9,885**	**9,887**
Household sector	87	118	91	91	83	75	67	59	51	43
Federal government	16	13	14	16	22	24	24	25	26	27
State and local governments	67	82	100	97	100	105	104	106	106	113
U.S.-chartered depository institutions	1,556	2,730	3,069	2,884	2,693	2,616	2,538	2,509	2,394	2,402
Credit unions	120	226	280	312	317	317	321	328	346	372
Government-sponsored enterprises (GSE)	210	454	448	457	433	4,691	4,588	4,476	4,545	4,538
Agency- and GSE-backed mortgage pools	2,426	3,446	4,372	4,864	5,267	1,069	1,217	1,322	1,421	1,472
Asset-backed securities issuers	385	1,649	2,214	1,903	1,579	1,303	1,109	928	792	701
Finance companies	187	490	494	416	366	170	150	133	115	105
Real estate investment trusts	8	128	81	34	9	9	20	26	23	41
Memo:										
Home equity loans included above [1,3]	408	917	1,133	1,116	1,033	928	854	770	703	673
U.S.-chartered depository institutions	308	701	873	895	841	783	723	653	596	568
Credit unions	41	76	94	99	95	88	82	76	72	74

[1] Includes other holders not shown separately. [2] Mortgages on one- to four-family properties including mortgages on farm houses. [3] Loans made under home equity lines of credit and home equity loans secured by junior liens. Excludes home equity loans held by individuals.

Source: Board of Governors of the Federal Reserve System, "Federal Reserve Statistical Release, Z.1, Financial Accounts of the United States," June 2015, <http://www.federalreserve.gov/releases/z1/>, accessed June 2015.

Table 1204. Characteristics of Conventional First Mortgage Loans for Purchase of Single-Family Homes: 2000 to 2012

[In percent, except as indicated (for purchase price, 234.9 represents $234,900). Annual averages. Covers fully amortized conventional mortgage loans used to purchase single-family nonfarm homes. Excludes refinancing loans, nonamortized and balloon loans, loans insured by the Federal Housing Administration, and loans guaranteed by the Veterans Administration. Based on a sample of mortgage lenders, including savings and loans associations, savings banks, commercial banks, and mortgage companies. Data for 2012 are unweighted]

Loan characteristics	New homes						Previously occupied homes					
	2000	2005	2009	2010	2011	2012	2000	2005	2009	2010	2011	2012
Contract interest rate, all loans [1]	7.4	5.9	5.0	4.7	4.5	3.6	7.9	5.8	5.1	4.8	4.6	3.7
Fixed-rate loans	8.0	6.1	5.0	4.7	4.5	3.7	8.2	6.0	5.1	4.9	4.7	3.8
Adjustable-rate loans [2]	6.5	5.3	([5])	4.3	(NA)	(NA)	7.2	5.6	([5])	4.2	(NA)	(NA)
Initial fees, charges [3]	0.69	0.54	1.00	0.82	0.73	1.14	0.66	0.33	0.55	0.71	0.89	0.99
Effective interest rate, all loans [4]	7.5	5.9	5.1	4.8	4.6	3.7	8.1	5.9	5.1	4.9	4.7	3.8
Fixed-rate loans	8.2	6.2	5.2	4.8	4.6	3.8	8.3	6.0	5.2	5.0	4.8	3.9
Adjustable-rate loans [2]	6.5	5.3	([5])	4.4	(NA)	(NA)	7.2	5.6	([5])	4.3	(NA)	(NA)
Term to maturity (years)	29.2	29.2	28.8	28.5	28.5	28.5	28.6	28.3	28.1	27.5	28.0	27.4
Purchase price ($1,000)	234.9	328.5	332.3	335.3	326.5	376.0	191.8	291.3	303.6	297.7	290.3	354.0
Loan-to-price ratio	77.4	75.2	73.9	73.4	77.2	76.9	77.9	74.6	74.6	74.2	76.2	75.5
Percent of loans with adjustable rates	40	29	([5])	3	6	9	21	30	([5])	5	13	12

NA Not available. [1] Initial interest rate paid by the borrower as specified in the loan contract. [2] Loans with a contractual provision for periodic adjustments in the contract interest rate. [3] Includes all fees, commissions, discounts, and "points" paid by the borrower, or seller, in order to obtain the loan. Excludes those charges for mortgage, credit, life, or property insurance; for property transfer; and for title search and insurance. [4] Contract interest rate plus fees and charges amortized over a ten year period. [5] Insufficient data to report meaningful numbers.

Source: U.S. Federal Housing Finance Agency, Research and Analysis, "Monthly Interest Rate Survey Data, Historical Summary Tables," <http://www.fhfa.gov/Default.aspx?Page=252>, accessed August 2013.

Table 1205. Mortgage Originations and Delinquency and Foreclosure Rates: 2000 to 2014

[In percent, except as indicated (1,139 represents $1,139,000,000,000). Covers one- to four-family residential nonfarm mortgage loans. Mortgage origination is the making of a new mortgage, including all steps taken by a lender to attract and qualify a borrower, process the mortgage loan, and place it on the lender's books. Based on the National Delinquency Survey which covers 45 million loans on one- to four-unit properties, representing between 80 to 85 percent of all 'first-lien' residential mortgage loans outstanding. Loans surveyed were reported by approximately 120 lenders, including mortgage bankers, commercial banks, and thrifts]

Item	2000	2005	2008	2009	2010	2011	2012	2013	2014
MORTGAGE ORIGINATIONS									
Total (bil. dol.)	**1,139**	**2,908**	**1,509**	**1,995**	**1,572**	**1,262**	**1,750**	**2,003**	**1,122**
Purchase (bil. dol.)	905	1,512	731	664	473	404	503	571	638
Refinance (bil. dol.)	234	1,397	777	1,331	1,099	858	1,247	1,432	484
DELINQUENCY RATES [1]									
Total	**4.4**	**4.5**	**6.9**	**9.4**	**9.3**	**8.0**	**7.4**	**6.7**	**5.9**
Prime conventional loans	2.3	2.3	4.3	6.5	6.5	5.3	4.6	3.9	3.4
Subprime conventional loans	11.9	10.8	19.9	25.5	25.9	23.0	20.6	21.0	19.1
Federal Housing Administration loans	9.1	12.5	13.0	14.0	12.8	12.3	11.6	10.6	9.7
Veterans Administration loans	6.8	7.0	7.2	7.9	7.5	6.8	6.4	5.8	5.2
FORECLOSURE RATES									
Total loans in foreclosure process [2]	**1.2**	**1.0**	**3.3**	**4.3**	**4.6**	**4.4**	**4.1**	**3.2**	**2.5**
Prime conventional loans	0.4	0.4	1.9	3.0	3.5	3.4	3.0	2.2	1.5
Subprime conventional loans	9.4	3.3	13.7	15.1	14.5	14.7	13.0	11.1	9.8
Federal Housing Administration loans	1.7	2.3	2.4	3.2	3.5	3.4	4.0	3.6	2.8
Veterans Administration loans	1.2	1.1	1.7	2.2	2.4	2.3	2.3	5.8	1.5
Loans entering foreclosure process [3]	**1.5**	**1.6**	**4.2**	**5.4**	**5.0**	**4.1**	**3.5**	**2.5**	**1.8**
Prime conventional loans	0.6	0.7	2.4	4.0	4.0	3.3	2.6	1.6	1.1
Subprime conventional loans	9.2	5.6	16.5	16.2	12.9	12.1	9.5	8.2	6.1
Federal Housing Administration loans	2.3	3.4	3.8	4.8	4.7	3.3	4.5	3.3	2.5
Veterans Administration loans	1.5	1.5	2.3	3.1	3.3	2.4	2.2	1.9	1.4

[1] Number of loans delinquent 30 days or more as percentage of mortgage loans serviced in survey. Annual average of quarterly figures. Delinquency rate does not include loans in the process of foreclosure. [2] Percentage of loans in the foreclosure process at year-end, not seasonally adjusted. [3] Percentage of loans entering foreclosure process at year-end, not seasonally adjusted.

Source: Mortgage Bankers Association of America, Washington, DC, "MBA Mortgage Originations Estimates," National Delinquency Survey, quarterly, <http://www.mortgagebankers.org/>; and unpublished data ©.

Table 1206. Delinquency Rates and Charge-Off Rates on Loans at Insured Commercial Banks: 2000 to 2014

[In percent. Annual averages of quarterly figures, not seasonally adjusted. Delinquent loans are those past due 30 days or more and still accruing interest as well as those in nonaccrual status. They are measured as a percentage of end-of-period loans. Charge-offs, which are the value of loans removed from the books and charged against loss reserves, are measured net of recoveries as a percentage of average loans and annualized. Includes only U.S.-chartered commercial banks]

Type of loan	2000	2005	2008	2009	2010	2011	2012	2013	2014
DELINQUENCY RATES									
Total loans	**2.18**	**1.57**	**3.67**	**6.56**	**6.96**	**5.83**	**5.02**	**3.96**	**3.00**
Real estate	1.89	1.37	4.67	8.46	9.69	8.81	8.01	6.44	4.83
Residential [1,2]	2.11	1.55	5.01	9.14	10.81	10.40	10.37	8.96	7.20
Commercial [2,3]	1.49	1.07	4.43	7.90	8.53	6.87	4.81	3.06	1.88
Consumer	3.55	2.81	3.76	4.70	4.15	3.23	2.80	2.45	2.22
Credit cards	4.50	3.70	5.02	6.52	4.90	3.55	2.88	2.50	2.23
Other	2.98	2.23	3.01	3.57	3.32	2.89	2.71	2.41	2.21
Leases	1.60	1.28	1.59	2.30	1.89	1.04	0.80	0.87	0.75
Business	2.22	1.51	1.88	3.91	3.46	2.01	1.34	1.00	0.80
Agricultural production	2.54	1.30	1.19	2.37	3.04	2.11	1.56	1.15	0.91
Farmland [2]	2.20	1.59	1.75	2.88	3.57	3.50	2.88	2.24	1.71
CHARGE-OFF RATES									
Total loans	**0.66**	**0.54**	**1.44**	**2.65**	**2.66**	**1.63**	**1.12**	**0.69**	**0.48**
Real estate	0.10	0.06	1.23	2.27	2.15	1.46	1.07	0.48	0.20
Residential [1,2]	0.12	0.08	1.33	2.33	2.12	1.58	1.36	0.65	0.29
Commercial [2,3]	0.06	0.05	1.19	2.35	2.32	1.39	0.71	0.26	0.07
Consumer	2.36	2.74	3.53	5.49	5.90	3.62	2.54	2.17	1.92
Credit cards	4.47	4.83	5.52	9.42	9.43	5.68	3.99	3.48	3.16
Other	1.14	1.38	2.35	3.05	2.05	1.40	1.03	0.86	0.77
Leases	0.31	0.59	0.53	1.29	0.72	0.20	0.21	0.15	0.08
Business	0.76	0.26	0.98	2.30	1.70	0.85	0.48	0.30	0.22
Agricultural production	0.25	0.07	0.18	0.50	0.79	0.25	0.26	0.05	0.04
Farmland [2]	0.04	0.04	0.10	0.34	0.43	0.35	0.27	0.08	0.04

[1] Residential real estate loans include loans secured by one- to four-family properties, including home equity lines of credit. [2] Booked in domestic offices only. [3] Commercial real estate loans include construction and land development loans, loans secured by multifamily residences, and loans secured by nonfarm, nonresidential real estate, only.

Source: Board of Governors of the Federal Reserve, Data Releases, Bank Assets and Liabilities, "Charge-Off and Delinquency Rates on Loans and Leases at Commercial Banks," <http://www.federalreserve.gov/releases/chargeoff/>, accessed May 2015.

Table 1207. Money Stock: 2000 to 2014

[In billions of dollars (1,088 represents $1,088,000,000,000). As of December. Seasonally adjusted averages of daily figures]

Item	2000	2005	2007	2008	2009	2010	2011	2012	2013	2014
M1, total	**1,088**	**1,375**	**1,377**	**1,607**	**1,698**	**1,842**	**2,168**	**2,458**	**2,655**	**2,910**
Currency [1]	531	725	761	816	864	919	1,002	1,091	1,160	1,252
Travelers' checks [2]	8	7	6	6	5	5	4	4	4	3
Demand deposits [3]	310	324	303	473	448	519	752	921	1,022	1,166
Other checkable deposits [4]	239	319	306	312	381	399	411	443	469	489
M2, total	**4,904**	**6,654**	**7,452**	**8,177**	**8,482**	**8,783**	**9,636**	**10,424**	**10,985**	**11,630**
M1	1,088	1,375	1,377	1,607	1,698	1,842	2,168	2,458	2,655	2,910
Non-M1 components of M2	3,816	5,279	6,076	6,570	6,784	6,941	7,468	7,966	8,330	8,720
Retail money funds	889	682	930	1,021	781	675	663	643	639	626
Savings deposits (including money market deposit accounts)	1,881	3,603	3,870	4,091	4,816	5,334	6,033	6,686	7,132	7,584
Commercial banks	1,426	2,775	3,042	3,322	3,979	4,410	5,034	5,727	6,108	6,503
Thrift institutions	455	829	828	769	836	924	999	959	1,024	1,082
Small time deposits [5]	1,046	994	1,276	1,458	1,188	933	771	637	559	510
Commercial banks	701	647	859	1,079	868	662	543	460	415	378
Thrift institutions	345	347	417	379	320	271	229	177	144	132

[1] Currency outside U.S. Treasury, Federal Reserve Banks and the vaults of depository institutions. [2] Outstanding amount of U.S. dollar-denominated travelers' checks of nonbank issuers. Travelers' checks issued by depository institutions are included in demand deposits. [3] Demand deposits at domestically chartered commercial banks, U.S. branches and agencies of foreign banks, and Edge Act corporations (excluding those amounts held by depository institutions, the U.S. government, and foreign banks and official institutions) less cash items in the process of collection and Federal Reserve float. [4] Negotiable order of withdrawal (NOW) and automatic transfer service (ATS) balances at domestically chartered commercial banks, U.S. branches and agencies of foreign banks, Edge Act corporations, and thrift institutions, credit union share draft balances, and demand deposits at thrift institutions. [5] Small-denomination time deposits are those issued in amounts of less than $100,000. All Individual Retirement Account (IRA) and Keogh account balances at commercial banks and thrift institutions are subtracted from small time deposits.

Source: Board of Governors of the Federal Reserve System, Data Releases, Money Stock and Reserve Balances, "Money Stock Measures – H.6," <http://www.federalreserve.gov/releases/h6/>, accessed May 2015.

Table 1208. Volume of Debt Markets by Type of Security: 2000 to 2014

[In billions of dollars (2,507 represents $2,507,000,000,000). Covers debt markets as represented by the source]

Type of Security	2000	2005	2009	2010	2011	2012	2013	2014
NEW ISSUE VOLUME [1]								
Total	**2,507**	**5,522**	**6,728**	**7,088**	**6,073**	**7,131**	**6,585**	**5,936**
U.S. Treasury securities [2]	312	746	2,075	2,304	2,103	2,305	2,140	2,215
Federal agency debt [3]	447	635	1,087	1,204	838	721	420	377
Municipal	198	407	410	433	295	382	335	338
Mortgage-backed securities [4]	772	2,691	2,103	1,978	1,700	2,157	2,088	1,346
Asset-backed securities [5]	190	289	152	107	124	201	189	225
Corporate debt [6]	588	753	902	1,063	1,012	1,365	1,414	1,435
AVERAGE DAILY TRADING VOLUME								
Total	**357.6**	**918.6**	**817.8**	**893.7**	**852.6**	**842.9**	**810.6**	**725.2**
U.S. Treasury securities [2,7]	206.5	554.5	407.9	528.2	567.8	518.9	545.4	505.4
Federal agency debt [7]	72.8	78.8	77.7	11.2	9.6	9.7	6.5	5.3
Municipal [8]	8.8	16.9	12.5	13.3	11.3	11.3	11.2	9.9
Mortgage-backed securities [4,7]	69.5	251.8	299.9	320.6	243.3	280.4	222.8	177.9
Corporate [6]	(NA)	16.6	19.9	20.5	20.6	22.6	24.7	26.7
VOLUME OF SECURITIES OUTSTANDING								
Total	**17,322**	**26,423**	**33,863**	**35,386**	**35,686**	**36,587**	**37,727**	**39,000**
U.S. Treasury securities [2]	2,952	4,166	7,261	8,853	9,928	11,046	11,854	12,505
Federal agency debt	1,854	2,616	2,727	2,539	2,327	2,096	2,057	2,029
Municipal	1,481	3,019	3,672	3,772	3,719	3,714	3,671	3,652
Mortgage-backed securities [4]	4,119	7,206	9,342	9,221	9,044	8,815	8,720	8,728
Asset-backed securities [5]	700	1,275	1,682	1,476	1,330	1,254	1,252	1,336
Money market instruments [9]	2,816	3,537	3,244	2,981	2,719	2,612	2,714	2,903
Corporate debt [6]	3,401	4,604	5,935	6,543	6,618	7,050	7,459	7,846

NA Not available. [1] Covers only long-term issuance. [2] Marketable public debt. [3] Includes overnight discount notes. Beginning 2004, excludes Sallie Mae. [4] Includes only Government National Mortgage Association (GNMA), Federal National Mortgage Association (FNMA), Federal Home Loan Mortgage Corporation (FHLMC) mortgage-backed securities (MBS), and collateralized mortgage obligations (CMOs), and CMBS, and private-label MBS/CMOs. [5] Excludes mortgage-backed assets. Includes auto, credit card, home equity loans, manufacturing, student loan and other. Collaterized debt obligations are included. [6] Includes nonconvertible corporate debt, Yankee bonds, and MTNs (Medium-Term Notes), but excludes all issues with maturities of one year or less, agency debt, and all certificates of deposit. [7] Primary dealer trading volume through 2009. Starting in 2010, the data is no longer sourced from primary dealers. [8] Includes customer-to-dealer and dealer-to-dealer transactions. [9] Commercial paper, bankers acceptances, and large time deposits.

Source: The Securities Industry and Financial Markets Association, New York, NY. © Based on data supplied by Board of Governors of the Federal Reserve System, U.S. Dept. of Treasury, Thomson Reuters, FHLMC, FNMA, GNMA, Federal Home Loan Banks, Student Loan Marketing Association, Federal Farm Credit Banks, Tennessee Valley Authority, Bloomberg, Loan Performance, Dealogic, and Municipal Securities Rulemaking Board. For more information: <http://www.sifma.org/>.

Table 1209. Bond Yields: 2000 to 2014

[Percent per year. Annual averages of daily figures]

Type	2000	2005	2007	2008	2009	2010	2011	2012	2013	2014
U.S. Treasury, constant maturities: [1]										
1-year	6.11	3.62	4.53	1.83	0.47	0.32	0.18	0.17	0.13	0.12
2-year	6.26	3.85	4.36	2.01	0.96	0.70	0.45	0.28	0.31	0.46
3-year	6.22	3.93	4.35	2.24	1.43	1.11	0.75	0.38	0.54	0.90
5-year	6.16	4.05	4.43	2.80	2.20	1.93	1.52	0.76	1.17	1.64
7-year	6.20	4.15	4.51	3.17	2.82	2.62	2.16	1.22	1.74	2.14
10-year	6.03	4.29	4.63	3.66	3.26	3.22	2.78	1.80	2.35	2.54
20-year	6.23	4.64	4.91	4.36	4.11	4.03	3.62	2.54	3.12	3.07
Municipal (Bond Buyer, 20 bonds)	5.71	4.40	4.40	4.85	4.62	4.29	4.51	3.73	4.27	4.23
High-grade municipal bonds (Standard & Poor's) [2]	5.77	4.29	4.42	4.80	4.64	4.16	4.29	3.14	3.96	3.78

[1] Yields on actively traded non-inflation-indexed issues adjusted to constant maturities. Yields are based on closing indicative prices quoted by secondary market participants. Data from U.S. Treasury. [2] Source: U.S. Council of Economic Advisors, Economic Indicators, monthly.

Source: Except as noted, Board of Governors of the Federal Reserve System, "H15, Selected Interest Rates," <http://www.federalreserve.gov/releases/h15/data.htm>, accessed May 2015.

Table 1210. Securities Industry—Financial Summary: 2000 to 2013

[In billions of dollars, except as indicated (349.5 represents $349,500,000,000). Minus sign (-) indicates loss]

Type	2000	2005	2007	2008	2009	2010	2011	2012	2013
Number of firms	7,258	6,016	5,561	5,261	5,132	4,907	4,708	4,761	4,555
Revenues, total	**349.5**	**332.5**	**495.1**	**303.2**	**287.0**	**262.0**	**245.8**	**264.4**	**272.5**
Commissions	54.1	46.8	54.3	56.3	49.0	47.0	47.7	40.6	40.1
Trading/investment gains	70.8	30.7	4.1	-60.0	45.3	31.2	10.2	26.9	21.2
Underwriting profits	18.7	19.9	26.5	18.7	22.6	24.4	22.9	27.9	32.0
Margin interest	24.5	13.3	32.3	18.4	4.5	5.0	6.2	7.2	7.1
Mutual fund sales	19.4	20.7	26.2	22.3	17.2	18.8	19.4	20.1	21.6
Other	161.9	201.2	351.6	247.6	148.4	135.5	139.3	141.7	150.4
Expenses, total	**310.4**	**311.3**	**490.4**	**328.7**	**211.6**	**224.0**	**228.9**	**229.9**	**243.8**
Interest expense	131.9	140.2	282.2	128.0	21.9	22.4	20.3	20.6	16.6
Compensation	95.2	88.8	105.7	96.1	95.4	102.1	102.4	104.7	110.0
Commissions/clearance paid	15.5	18.6	25.9	26.5	23.3	24.0	25.4	24.2	25.1
Other	67.8	63.6	76.6	78.1	71.0	75.5	80.8	80.4	92.2
Net income, pretax	**39.1**	**21.2**	**4.7**	**-25.5**	**75.4**	**38.0**	**16.8**	**34.6**	**28.6**
Pre-tax profit margin (percent)	11.2	6.4	0.9	-8.4	26.3	14.5	6.9	13.1	10.5
Pre-tax return on equity (percent)	31.1	13.1	2.5	-13.9	38.2	17.1	7.5	14.7	12.0
Assets	2,866	5,215	6,772	4,436	4,340	4,757	4,662	4,892	4,591
Liabilities	2,728	5,051	6,586	4,255	4,125	4,526	4,444	4,658	4,348
Ownership equity	138	164	186	181	214	231	218	234	243

Source: U.S. Securities and Exchange Commission, "Select SEC and Market Data Fiscal 2014," and earlier reports, <http://www.sec.gov/about.shtml>, accessed June 2015.

Table 1211. Total Returns of Stocks, Bonds, and Treasury Bills: 1980 to 2014

[Average annual percent change. Stock return data are based on the Standard & Poor's 500 index. Minus sign (-) indicates loss]

| Period | Stocks | | | | Treasury bills, total return | Bonds (10-year), total return |
	Total return before inflation	Capital gains	Dividends and reinvestment	Total return after inflation		
1980 to 1989	17.55	12.59	4.40	11.85	9.13	13.01
1990 to 1999	18.21	15.31	2.51	14.85	4.95	8.02
2000 to 2009	-0.45	-2.73	2.27	-3.39	2.74	6.63
2001	-11.89	-13.04	1.32	-13.68	3.32	5.53
2002	-22.10	-23.37	1.65	-23.91	1.61	15.37
2003	28.68	26.38	1.82	26.31	1.03	0.46
2004	10.88	8.99	1.73	7.38	1.43	4.61
2005	4.91	3.00	1.85	1.45	3.30	3.09
2006	15.80	13.62	1.91	11.97	4.97	2.21
2007	5.49	3.53	1.89	1.35	4.52	10.54
2008	-37.00	-38.49	1.88	-37.10	1.24	20.23
2009	26.25	23.45	2.44	23.11	0.15	-9.50
2010	15.06	12.78	2.02	13.36	0.03	7.26
2011	2.96	0.00	2.96	0.83	0.06	16.89
2012	16.00	13.41	2.29	14.02	0.08	2.77
2013	32.39	29.60	2.15	30.43	0.05	-8.56
2014	13.69	11.39	2.06	12.83	0.03	10.74

Source: Global Financial Data, Los Angeles, CA, "GFD Guide to Total Returns," <http://www.globalfinancialdata.com>, and unpublished data ©.

Table 1212. New Security Issues of Corporations by Type of Offering: 2000 to 2014

[In billions of dollars (1,075 represents $1,075,000,000,000). Represents gross proceed of issues maturing in more than one year. Figures are the principal amount or the number of units multiplied by the offering price. Excludes secondary offerings, employee stock plans, investment companies other than closed-end, intracorporate transactions, Yankee bonds, and private placements listed. Stock data include ownership securities issued by limited partnerships]

Type of Offering	2000	2010	2013	2014	Type of Offering	2000	2010	2013	2014
Total......................	1,075	1,025	1,529	(NA)	Nonfinancial...........	360	498	715	727
					Financial..............	679	396	623	759
Bonds, total.....................	940	894	1,338	1,486	Stocks, total.............	135	131	192	175
Sold in the U.S..............	827	880	1,297	1,423	Nonfinancial...........	118	61	102	92
Sold abroad..................	112	14	41	63	Financial..............	17	70	90	83

NA Not available.

Source: Board of Governors of the Federal Reserve System, "New Security Issues, U.S. Corporations," <http://www.federalreserve.gov/econresdata/releases/corpsecure/current.htm>, accessed August 2015.

Table 1213. Equities, Corporate Bonds, and Municipal and Treasury Securities—Holdings and Net Purchases by Type of Investor: 2000 to 2014

[In billions of dollars (17,575 represents $17,575,000,000,000). Holdings as of December 31. Minus sign (-) indicates net sales]

Type of investor	Holdings					Net purchases				
	2000	2010	2012	2013	2014	2000	2010	2012	2013	2014
EQUITIES [1]										
Total [2]...................	**17,575**	**23,552**	**26,205**	**33,629**	**36,256**	**5.6**	**19.9**	**-73.3**	**84.8**	**269.2**
Household sector [3]................	8,097	8,696	9,676	12,502	13,361	-640.3	-183.9	-194.7	-30.7	28.5
State and local governments.............	93	127	138	164	178	6.1	0.3	1.6	0.2	5.5
Property-casualty insurance companies....................	191	215	252	310	325	0.3	-20.9	4.6	3.7	2.6
Life insurance companies................	892	1,372	1,503	1,743	1,798	111.5	12.7	16.1	13.7	28.1
Private pension funds.................	1,891	1,849	1,974	2,408	2,587	63.7	22.7	-18.5	4.2	-6.8
Federal government retirement funds. ..	57	141	148	206	235	5.2	5.4	-4.1	9.1	4.2
State and local government retirement funds...............................	1,421	1,930	2,019	2,433	2,420	13.5	-78.6	-77.4	-166.6	-175.1
Mutual funds....................	3,227	4,763	5,109	6,852	7,392	193.1	44.3	-38.1	162.5	75.3
Exchange-traded funds.................	66	854	1,093	1,427	1,675	42.4	88.3	132.9	166.8	188.2
Brokers and dealers..................	77	117	127	172	188	9.6	-18.5	9.7	18.6	8.7
Rest of the world [4].................	1,483	3,216	3,953	5,161	5,835	199.7	127.8	126.8	-76.6	118.0
CORPORATE & FOREIGN BONDS										
Total [2]...................	**4,841**	**10,337**	**10,919**	**11,111**	**11,587**	**345.9**	**-239.6**	**222.9**	**390.1**	**480.8**
Household sector [3]................	565	1,361	1,235	977	875	76.2	-422.2	-178.3	-227.8	-131.9
U.S.-chartered depository institutions....	311	551	544	559	522	47.2	-98.2	-9.0	15.2	-37.4
Foreign banking offices in U.S............	53	238	231	196	197	7.7	-9.4	-6.2	-34.1	0.9
Property-casualty insurance companies....................	188	323	383	411	428	6.4	24.3	19.6	28.1	17.0
Life insurance companies................	1,215	2,030	2,162	2,223	2,292	47.9	102.9	45.0	60.8	69.3
Private pension funds.................	264	438	567	572	585	-76.6	82.1	83.8	5.5	13.0
State and local government retirement funds...............................	317	397	367	425	454	4.8	5.9	-16.9	57.7	29.5
Mutual funds....................	338	1,243	1,719	1,999	2,318	-10.5	122.3	306.0	279.3	318.9
Exchange-traded funds.................	–	74	155	175	210	–	18.7	47.6	19.5	34.8
Rest of the world [4].................	843	2,523	2,618	2,734	2,911	168.3	-36.8	-19.7	205.2	211.9
MUNICIPAL SECURITIES [5]										
Total [2]...................	**1,481**	**3,772**	**3,714**	**3,671**	**3,652**	**23.6**	**99.7**	**-4.9**	**-43.2**	**-18.8**
Household sector [3]................	532	1,871	1,661	1,606	1,540	6.2	43.6	-144.6	-55.2	-66.0
U.S.-chartered depository institutions....	117	255	365	419	452	3.4	30.3	67.8	53.8	32.7
Property-casualty insurance companies....................	184	348	328	326	322	-14.9	-21.0	-2.9	-1.7	-4.7
Money market mutual funds.............	242	387	337	308	282	32.6	-53.4	-20.6	-28.3	-26.7
Mutual funds....................	230	525	627	614	658	-9.0	46.7	86.2	-13.5	43.8
TREASURY SECURITIES										
Total [2]...................	**3,358**	**9,361**	**11,569**	**12,328**	**12,996**	**-294.9**	**1,579.6**	**1,140.6**	**759.5**	**667.2**
Household sector [3]................	578	1,123	943	957	697	-210.7	317.2	215.4	-194.3	-174.7
State and local governments.............	310	596	606	592	661	5.5	9.4	45.3	-13.8	68.6
Monetary authority.................	512	1,021	1,666	2,209	2,461	33.7	244.9	2.7	542.6	252.6
U.S.-chartered depository institutions....	97	218	243	217	420	-36.4	93.0	69.3	-26.1	203.3
Life insurance companies.................	58	157	181	169	183	-4.6	23.2	5.5	-12.2	14.3
Private pension funds.................	111	207	278	315	334	-9.6	31.2	44.4	36.4	19.6
Federal government retirement funds. ..	34	130	166	178	196	2.0	10.1	12.1	12.4	18.0
State and local governments retirement funds..................	180	173	195	207	216	-20.2	10.7	12.9	12.6	8.8
Money market mutual funds.............	92	335	458	488	413	-12.5	-71.0	14.5	30.2	-75.3
Mutual funds....................	127	381	568	623	742	10.2	123.0	120.8	55.0	119.5
Rest of the world [4].................	1,021	4,459	5,571	5,795	6,156	-75.2	740.4	589.7	431.3	276.1

– Represents zero. [1] Excludes mutual fund shares; see Table 1219. [2] Includes other types, not shown separately. [3] Includes nonprofit organizations. [4] Holdings and net purchases of U.S. issues by foreign residents. [5] Includes loans.

Source: Board of Governors of the Federal Reserve System, "Federal Reserve Statistical Release, Z.1, Financial Accounts of the United States," June 2015, <http://www.federalreserve.gov/releases/z1/>, accessed June 2015.

Table 1214. Foreign Securities Held by U.S. Residents: 2010 to 2013

[In billions of dollars (6,763 represents $6,763,000,000,000). Estimates for end of calendar year. See also Table 1295]

Country	Total 2010	Total 2012	Total 2013	Corporate stocks 2010	Corporate stocks 2012	Corporate stocks 2013	Long-term and short-term debt 2010	Long-term and short-term debt 2012	Long-term and short-term debt 2013
Total holdings [1].........................	**6,763**	**7,941**	**9,130**	**4,647**	**5,312**	**6,473**	**2,116**	**2,630**	**2,658**
Australia..........................	323	351	338	150	147	144	174	204	194
Belgium...........................	35	46	65	29	39	48	7	7	17
Bermuda...........................	160	178	211	134	150	179	25	29	32
Brazil.............................	235	216	180	194	150	129	41	66	51
Canada............................	695	808	826	409	376	405	287	432	421
Cayman Islands....................	366	797	901	166	574	677	200	223	224
China [2]..........................	102	120	103	101	119	101	2	1	3
Curacao [3]........................	(NA)	(NA)	86	(NA)	(NA)	83	(NA)	(NA)	4
France............................	366	375	466	244	257	343	122	118	123
Germany...........................	299	330	391	207	228	302	92	101	89
Hong Kong.........................	135	145	140	133	139	135	2	5	5
India.............................	91	79	86	86	76	82	5	3	3
Ireland...........................	132	181	281	101	134	228	31	47	53
Israel............................	64	57	63	45	37	46	19	19	16
Italy.............................	66	110	124	51	54	75	14	55	48
Japan.............................	519	521	686	450	427	604	69	93	82
Jersey............................	42	49	75	21	39	65	21	10	10
Korea, South......................	148	175	183	122	141	147	26	34	36
Luxembourg........................	100	105	125	33	31	46	68	73	79
Mexico............................	109	157	154	77	77	71	32	80	83
Netherlands.......................	233	286	386	120	146	230	112	141	156
Norway............................	56	73	77	23	24	29	33	49	48
Russia............................	62	67	71	56	55	57	7	12	14
Singapore.........................	64	73	89	56	59	62	8	13	27
South Africa......................	78	86	77	70	71	65	8	15	12
Spain.............................	87	99	133	66	63	92	22	36	41
Sweden............................	122	122	165	63	66	88	59	55	77
Switzerland.......................	327	333	443	319	322	430	8	11	13
Taiwan............................	95	88	98	94	87	98	(Z)	(Z)	(Z)
United Kingdom....................	1,001	1,129	1,344	626	758	978	375	370	366

NA Not available. Z Less than $500 million. [1] Includes other countries, not shown separately. [2] Excludes Hong Kong, Macau, and Taiwan. [3] Separate reporting for Curacao began with the 2013 survey. In previous years, data were reported as part of Netherlands Antilles.

Source: U.S. Department of Treasury, "Securities (c): Annual Cross-U.S. Border Portfolio Holdings, PART B: U.S. Residents' Portfolio Holdings of Foreign Securities," <http://www.treasury.gov/resource-center/data-chart-center/tic/Pages/fpis.aspx#usclaims>, accessed August 2015.

Table 1215. U.S. Securities Held by Foreign Residents: 2010 and 2014

[In billions of dollars (10,691 represents $10,691,000,000,000). Estimates as of June. Long-term securities include all forms of equity and all debt securities with an original term-to-maturity of over one year.]

Region and country	U.S. securities, total [1] 2010	U.S. securities, total [1] 2014	U.S Treasury long-term securities 2010	U.S Treasury long-term securities 2014	Long-term corporate debt 2010	Long-term corporate debt 2014	U.S. corporate stocks 2010	U.S. corporate stocks 2014
Total [2].........................	**10,691**	**16,417**	**3,343**	**5,382**	**2,493**	**2,972**	**2,814**	**6,356**
Australia..........................	118	238	14	23	22	30	74	170
Belgium...........................	408	713	31	353	342	307	19	34
Bermuda...........................	249	355	42	98	91	109	44	93
Brazil............................	169	263	132	228	2	1	2	7
British Virgin Islands............	85	176	4	12	22	19	42	128
Canada............................	424	988	29	48	80	143	298	769
Cayman Islands....................	743	1,409	36	100	303	364	290	838
China [3].........................	1,611	1,817	1,108	1,261	11	24	127	320
Denmark...........................	49	98	5	15	14	29	26	53
France............................	194	269	15	52	52	42	115	157
Germany...........................	195	320	46	64	65	109	57	137
Hong Kong.........................	293	263	60	107	16	12	33	74
India.............................	41	75	21	69	3	(Z)	1	2
Ireland...........................	356	675	27	77	130	229	77	204
Israel............................	37	67	8	21	3	4	13	35
Italy.............................	41	70	21	31	3	11	13	27
Japan.............................	1,393	1,917	737	1,160	130	167	224	361
Korea, South......................	122	180	34	47	9	15	13	59
Luxembourg........................	622	1,198	49	111	302	482	172	502
Mexico............................	84	144	31	52	12	3	17	42
Netherlands.......................	247	303	22	32	57	60	152	195
Norway............................	136	297	14	86	25	33	90	176
Russia............................	170	115	121	114	(Z)	1	(Z)	(Z)
Singapore.........................	176	307	47	95	28	55	91	142
Sweden............................	81	157	14	30	11	9	49	113
Switzerland.......................	397	634	87	154	110	109	162	331
Taiwan............................	228	397	149	178	18	40	12	31
United Kingdom....................	798	1,289	72	132	369	369	324	741
International & regional organizations.............	78	110	43	77	15	13	5	5

Z Less than $500 million. [1] Includes short-term debt and other long-term debt. [2] Includes other countries not shown separately. [3] Excludes Hong Kong, Macau, and Taiwan.

Source: U.S. Department of Treasury, "Securities (c): Annual Cross-U.S. Border Portfolio Holdings, PART A: Foreign Residents' Portfolio Holdings of U.S. Securities," <http://www.treasury.gov/resource-center/data-chart-center/tic/Pages/fpis.aspx>, accessed August 2015.

Table 1216. Stock Prices and Yields: 2000 to 2014

[Closing values as of end of December, except as noted]

Index	2000	2005	2010	2011	2012	2013	2014
STOCK PRICES							
Standard & Poor's indices: [1]							
S&P 500 composite (1941–43 = 10)	1,320	1,248	1,257	1,258	1,426	1,848	2,059
S&P 400 MidCap Index (1982 = 100)	517	738	907	879	1,020	1,343	1,452
S&P 600 SmallCap Index (Dec. 31, 1993 = 100)	220	351	416	415	477	666	695
S&P 500 Citigroup Value Index (Dec. 31, 1974 = 35)	636	648	590	573	657	847	928
S&P 500 Citigroup Growth Index (Dec. 31, 1974 = 35)	688	597	659	678	761	992	1,122
Russell indices: [2]							
Russell 1000 (Dec. 31, 1986 = 130)	700	679	697	693	790	1,030	1,144
Russell 2000 (Dec. 31, 1986 = 135)	484	673	784	741	849	1,164	1,205
Russell 3000 (Dec. 31, 1986 = 140)	726	723	749	743	846	1,108	1,224
N.Y. Stock Exchange common stock index:							
Composite (Dec. 31, 2002 = 5000)	6,946	7,754	7,964	7,477	8,444	10,400	10,839
Yearly high	7,165	7,868	7,983	8,718	8,519	10,407	11,335
Yearly low	6,095	6,903	6,356	6,415	7,223	8,571	9,732
American Stock Exchange Composite Index							
(Dec. 29, 1995 = 550)	898	1,759	2,208	2,278	2,356	2,426	2,444
NASDAQ Composite Index (Feb. 5, 1971 = 100)	2,471	2,205	2,653	2,605	3,020	4,177	4,736
Nasdaq-100 (Jan. 31, 1985 = 125)	2,342	1,645	2,218	2,278	2,661	3,592	4,236
Industrial (Feb. 5, 1971 = 100)	1,483	1,860	2,184	2,168	2,595	3,715	3,789
Banks (Feb. 5, 1971 = 100)	1,939	3,078	1,847	1,618	1,873	2,602	2,676
Computers (Oct. 29, 1993 = 200)	1,295	992	1,372	1,379	1,551	2,046	2,453
Transportation (Feb. 5, 1971 = 100)	1,160	2,438	2,562	2,173	2,281	2,965	3,955
Telecommunications (Oct. 29, 1993 = 200)	463	184	226	197	201	249	271
Biotech (Oct. 29, 1993 = 200)	1,085	790	970	1,085	1,431	2,370	3,178
Dow-Jones and Co., Inc.:							
Composite (65 stocks)	3,317	3,638	4,033	4,232	4,442	5,642	6,474
Industrial (30 stocks)	10,787	10,718	11,578	12,218	13,104	16,577	17,823
Transportation (20 stocks)	2,947	4,196	5,107	5,020	5,307	7,401	9,140
Utility (15 stocks)	412	405	405	465	453	491	618
COMMON STOCK YIELDS (percent)							
Standard & Poor's Composite Index (500 stocks): [3]							
Dividend-price ratio [4]	1.15	1.83	1.98	2.05	2.24	2.14	2.04
Earnings-price ratio [5]	3.63	5.36	6.04	6.77	6.20	5.57	5.25

[1] Standard & Poor's Indices are market-value weighted and are chosen for market size, liquidity, and industry group representation. The S&P 500 index represents 500 large publicly-traded companies. The S&P MidCap Index tracks mid-cap companies. The S&P SmallCap Index consists of 600 domestic small-cap stocks. [2] The Russell 1000 and 3000 indices show respectively the 1000 and 3000 largest capitalization stocks in the United States. The Russell 2000 index shows the 2000 largest capitalization stocks in the United States after the first 1000. [3] Source: U.S. Council of Economic Advisors, *Economic Indicators*, monthly. [4] Aggregate cash dividends (based on latest known annual rate) divided by aggregate market value based on Wednesday closing prices. Averages of monthly figures. [5] Averages of quarterly ratios which are ratio of earnings (after taxes) for 4 quarters ending with particular quarter- to-price index for last day of that quarter.

Source: Except as noted, Global Financial Data, Los Angeles, CA ©, <http://www.globalfinancialdata.com/>.

Table 1217. Stock Ownership by Age of Head of Family and Family Income: 2007 to 2013

[Median value in thousands of constant (2013) dollars (38.2 represents $38,200). All dollar figures are adjusted to 2013 dollars using the "current methods" version of the consumer price index for all urban consumers published by U.S. Bureau of Labor Statistics. Families include one-person units; for definition of family, see text, Section 1. Based on Survey of Consumer Finance; see Appendix III. For definition of median, see Guide to Tabular Presentation]

Age of family head and family income (constant (2013) dollars)	Families having direct or indirect stock holdings [1] (percent)			Median value among families with holdings			Stock holdings share of group's financial assets (percent)		
	2007	2010	2013	2007	2010	2013	2007	2010	2013
All families	**53.2**	**49.8**	**48.8**	**38.2**	**31.1**	**35.8**	**53.6**	**46.8**	**51.3**
Under 35 years old	41.6	39.8	38.6	7.3	7.5	7.1	45.6	39.2	46.5
35 to 44 years old	55.9	50.0	53.9	28.1	21.2	23.5	54.7	50.5	53.6
45 to 54 years old	63.1	57.9	54.9	50.5	40.3	44.0	53.4	48.4	55.9
55 to 64 years old	60.8	59.7	57.2	87.6	60.8	60.0	55.4	48.2	51.5
65 to 74 years old	53.1	45.5	49.2	62.9	81.4	117.4	55.5	44.1	49.0
75 years old and over	40.2	41.9	34.5	50.5	58.5	81.4	47.8	43.9	48.3
Percentiles of income: [2]									
Less than 20	14.2	12.3	11.4	6.7	5.4	6.6	39.0	40.9	31.8
20 to 39.9	36.4	31.0	26.7	9.1	7.8	10.0	34.6	30.9	33.6
40 to 59.9	53.0	51.4	49.3	20.2	12.9	14.0	39.9	37.3	41.4
60 to 79.9	73.3	68.2	69.4	37.1	22.8	28.0	53.1	41.6	43.5
80 to 89.9	86.2	82.3	81.8	72.1	62.6	68.8	49.6	44.7	49.6
90 to 100	91.6	90.4	93.0	248.1	285.6	281.9	57.7	50.6	55.7

[1] Indirect holdings are those in pooled investment trusts, retirement accounts and other managed assets. [2] See footnote 8, Table 1184.

Source: Board of Governors of the Federal Reserve System, 2013 Survey of Consumer Finances, *Changes in U.S. Family Finances From 2010 to 2013: Evidence from the Survey of Consumer Finances,* Federal Reserve Bulletin, Vol. 100, No. 4, September 2014. See also <http://www.federalreserve.gov/econresdata/scf/scfindex.htm>.

Table 1218. Transaction Activity in Equities, Options, and Security Futures, 2000 to 2013, and by Exchange, 2013

[In billions of dollars (36,275 represents $36,275,000,000,000). Market value of all sales of equities and options listed on an exchange or subject to last-sale reporting. Also reported are the value of such options that were exercised and the value of single-stock futures that were delivered. Excludes options and futures on indexes]

Year and exchange	Market value of sales			
	Total	Equity trading	Option trading	Option exercises and futures deliveries
2000	36,275	35,557	485	233
2004	27,876	27,158	223	495
2005	34,568	33,223	350	995
2006	43,941	41,798	531	1,611
2007	66,136	63,064	861	2,211
2008	82,012	78,653	1,096	2,264
2009	59,850	57,565	710	1,574
2010	64,008	61,146	725	2,137
2011	70,100	66,683	923	2,494
2012	59,371	55,620	938	2,813
2013, total	62,899	59,515	752	2,633
BATS (Better Alternative Trading System) Exchange, Inc.	5,397	5,257	30	110
BATS Y-Exchange, Inc.	1,150	1,150	–	–
BOX Options Exchange LLC	70	–	16	55
C2 Options Exchange, Inc.	44	–	10	34
Chicago Board Options Exchange, Inc.	738	215	118	404
The Chicago Stock Exchange, Inc.	364	364	–	–
EDGA Exchange, Inc.	1,594	1,594	–	–
EDGX Exchange, Inc.	4,434	4,434	–	–
FINRA, Inc. [1]	19,606	19,606	–	–
International Securities Exchange, LLC	504	–	111	393
Miami International Securities Exchange, LLC	26	–	7	19
NASDAQ OMX BX	1,533	1,508	6	20
NASDAQ OMX PHLX	1,437	412	226	799
The Nasdaq Stock Market LLC	10,721	10,420	69	233
National Stock Exchange	198	198	–	–
New York Stock Exchange, Inc.	6,729	6,729	–	–
NYSE Amex LLC	441	63	85	294
NYSE Arca, Inc.	7,870	7,565	67	238
OneChicago, LLC	14	–	–	14
Topaz Exchange LLC	29	–	8	21

– Represents zero. [1] Financial Industry Regulatory Authority.

Source: U.S. Securities and Exchange Commission, "Select SEC and Market Data 2014," <http://www.sec.gov/about.shtml>, accessed June 2015.

Table 1219. Mutual Fund Shares—Holdings and Net Purchases by Type of Investor: 2000 to 2014

[In billions of dollars (4,433.1 represents $4,433,100,000,000). Holdings as of Dec. 31. For definition of mutual fund, see headnote, Table 1222. Excludes money market mutual funds, exchange-traded funds, and funding vehicles for variable annuities. Minus sign (-) indicates net sales]

Type of investor	Holdings					Net purchases				
	2000	2010	2012	2013	2014	2000	2010	2012	2013	2014
Total	**4,433.1**	**7,873.0**	**9,326.1**	**11,544.4**	**12,603.6**	**237.6**	**370.1**	**624.9**	**638.4**	**594.2**
Households, nonprofit organizations	2,585.4	4,605.0	5,630.4	7,023.0	7,695.3	79.4	247.9	581.1	611.0	520.0
Nonfinancial corporate business	118.0	186.8	179.6	211.0	234.9	0.3	11.1	-1.7	1.0	15.3
State and local governments	30.8	58.7	66.2	79.1	86.7	1.2	3.1	0.8	0.1	2.8
U.S.-chartered depository institutions	15.0	45.0	45.8	57.9	59.7	2.5	-5.8	-1.1	1.6	-0.7
Credit unions	2.2	1.5	2.3	2.2	2.1	-0.3	0.2	0.4	-0.1	-0.1
Property-casualty insurance companies	2.9	10.2	11.8	14.8	16.8	0.4	-0.1	1.8	1.0	1.4
Life insurance companies	97.0	186.7	201.7	235.8	246.4	5.5	33.9	0.4	1.1	1.3
Private pension funds	1,175.6	2,148.9	2,385.6	2,974.8	3,231.7	107.1	35.0	-26.2	31.9	21.0
State and local government retirement funds	257.0	370.1	307.3	393.7	406.1	50.7	-13.4	-20.4	10.8	-16.1
Rest of the world	149.0	260.0	495.4	552.0	623.9	-9.2	58.2	89.7	-20.0	49.3

Source: Board of Governors of the Federal Reserve System, "Federal Reserve Statistical Release, Z.1, Financial Accounts of the United States," June 2015, <http://www.federalreserve.gov/releases/z1/>, accessed June 2015.

Table 1220. Households Owning Mutual Funds by Age and Income: 2004 and 2014

[In percent. Ownership includes money market, stock, bond, and hybrid mutual funds, variable annuities, and mutual funds owned through Individual Retirement Accounts (IRAs), Keoghs, and employer-sponsored retirement plans. In 2014, an estimated 53,200,000 households own mutual funds. A mutual fund is an open-end investment company that continuously issues and redeems shares that represent an interest in a pool of financial assets]

Age of household head [1]	Percent distribution, 2014 [3]	As a percent of all households		Household income [2]	Percent distribution, 2014 [3]	As a percent of all households	
		2004	2014 [3]			2004	2014 [3]
Total...................	100	45	43	Less than $25,000.......	4	12	7
Less than 35 years old...	17	37	34	$25,000 to $34,999......	5	26	21
35 to 44 years old........	19	55	49	$35,000 to $49,999......	11	43	36
45 to 54 years old........	24	53	53	$50,000 to $74,999......	21	62	52
55 to 64 years old........	22	50	50	$75,000 to $99,999......	19	74	67
65 years old and over....	18	30	34	$100,000 to $199,999. ..	31	84	77
				$200,000 and over.......	9	75	78

[1] Age is based on the sole or co-decision maker for household saving and investing. [2] Total reported is household income before taxes in prior year. [3] In 2014, the survey was revised to include a dual frame random digit dial (RDD) sample design. See source for details.

Source: Burham, Kimberly, Michael Bogdan, and Daniel Schrass, Investment Company Institute, Washington, DC, *ICI Research Perspective*, "Ownership of Mutual Funds, Shareholder Sentiment, and Use of the Internet, 2014"; Vol. 20, No. 8, November 2014, <www.ici.org/pdf/per20-08.pdf> ©.

Table 1221. Characteristics of Mutual Fund Owners: 2014

[In percent, except as indicated. Mutual fund ownership includes holdings of money market, stock, bond, and hybrid mutual funds; and funds owned through variable annuities, Individual Retirement Accounts (IRAs), Keoghs, and employer-sponsored retirement plans. 2014 data based on a national probability sample of 2,599 primary financial decision-makers in households with mutual fund investments. For definition of mutual fund, see headnote, Table 1222. For definition of median, see Guide to Tabular Presentation]

Characteristic	Total	Age [1]				Household income [2]			
		Under 35 years old	35 to 54 years old	55 to 64 years old	65 years old and over	Less than $50,000	$50,000 to $99,000	$100,000 to $149,000	$150,000 or more
Median age [1] (years)............................	51	30	46	60	71	54	51	50	50
Median household income [2] (dol.)............	85,000	75,000	95,000	88,400	64,000	36,000	71,800	118,000	190,000
Median household financial assets [3] (dollars).................................	200,000	50,000	200,000	350,000	375,000	50,000	150,000	300,000	500,000
Own an IRA..	62	59	59	63	71	52	60	65	75
Household with defined contribution retirement plan(s) [4]..........................	85	88	92	86	63	71	85	93	90
401(k) plan......................................	73	80	83	71	46	55	72	85	82
403(b), state, local, or federal government plan.................................	35	32	34	40	34	29	36	37	39
Median mutual fund assets (dol.)..............	103,000	30,000	100,000	200,000	200,000	35,000	90,000	150,000	375,000
Own:									
Equity funds.....................................	86	83	88	86	82	74	84	91	93
Bond funds......................................	45	30	46	51	50	31	44	50	56

[1] See Table 1220, footnote 1. [2] See Table 1220, footnote 2. [3] Includes assets in employer-sponsored retirement plans but excludes value of primary residence. [4] For definition of defined contribution plan, see headnote, Table 569.

Source: Burham, Kimberly, Michael Bogdan, and Daniel Schrass, Investment Company Institute, Washington, DC, *ICI Research Perspective*, "Characteristics of Mutual Fund Investors, 2014," Vol. 20, No. 9, November 2014, <www.ici.org/pdf/per20-09.pdf> ©.

Table 1222. Mutual Funds—Summary: 2000 to 2014

[Number of funds and assets as of December 31 (6,965 represents $6,965,000,000,000). A mutual fund is an open-end investment company that continuously issues and redeems shares that represent an interest in a pool of financial assets. Excludes data for funds that invest in other mutual funds. Minus sign (-) indicates net redemptions]

Type of fund	Unit	2000	2005	2008	2009	2010	2011	2012	2013	2014
Number of funds, total.....................	**Number**	**8,155**	**7,977**	**8,039**	**7,666**	**7,554**	**7,587**	**7,588**	**7,713**	**7,923**
Equity funds.....................................	Number	4,370	4,571	4,794	4,591	4,515	4,525	4,496	4,539	4,646
Hybrid funds....................................	Number	508	481	511	481	494	519	562	602	661
Bond funds.......................................	Number	2,238	2,055	1,951	1,890	1,893	1,911	1,950	2,017	2,088
Money market funds, taxable [1]...........	Number	704	593	534	476	442	431	400	382	365
Money market funds, tax-exempt [2]...........	Number	335	277	249	228	210	201	180	173	163
Assets, total................................	**Bil. dol.**	**6,965**	**8,891**	**9,603**	**11,113**	**11,833**	**11,632**	**13,052**	**15,035**	**15,852**
Equity funds.....................................	Bil. dol.	3,934	4,885	3,637	4,873	5,597	5,213	5,939	7,763	8,314
Hybrid funds....................................	Bil. dol.	361	621	562	718	841	883	1,029	1,267	1,352
Bond funds.......................................	Bil. dol.	824	1,358	1,571	2,207	2,591	2,844	3,391	3,286	3,461
Money market funds, taxable [1]...........	Bil. dol.	1,611	1,690	3,339	2,917	2,474	2,400	2,406	2,448	2,464
Money market funds, tax-exempt [2]...........	Bil. dol.	234	336	494	399	330	292	287	271	261
Net new cash flow:										
Equity funds.....................................	Bil. dol.	316	124	-229	-2	-24	-129	-153	160	25
Hybrid funds....................................	Bil. dol.	-37	43	-26	20	35	40	45	71	27
Bond funds.......................................	Bil. dol.	-50	25	30	371	232	118	306	-71	44
Money market funds...........................	Bil. dol.	159	62	637	-539	-525	-124	–	15	6

– Represents zero. [1] Funds invest in short-term, high-grade securities sold in the money market. [2] Funds invest in municipal securities with relatively short maturities.

Source: Investment Company Institute, Washington, DC, *Investment Company Fact Book*, annual ©. For more information, see <http://www.ici.org/>.

Table 1223. Retirement Assets by Type of Asset: 2000 to 2014

[In billions of dollars, except as indicated (11,607 represents $11,607,000,000,000). As of December 31]

Institution	2000	2005	2009	2010	2011	2012	2013	2014
Retirement assets, total............................	**11,607**	**14,608**	**16,411**	**18,206**	**18,400**	**20,096**	**23,258**	**24,553**
IRA assets [1].............................	2,629	3,425	4,488	5,029	5,241	5,907	6,966	7,443
Bank and thrift deposits [2]............	250	278	431	461	482	508	507	505
Life insurance companies [3]...........	201	300	283	302	304	319	343	357
Mutual funds...........................	1,270	1,790	2,136	2,444	2,430	2,775	3,343	3,546
Other assets [1,4]......................	907	1,056	1,638	1,823	2,025	2,304	2,773	3,034
Traditional [1].........................	2,407	3,034	3,941	4,340	4,531	5,109	6,019	6,421
Roth [1]...............................	78	156	239	355	365	420	505	550
SEP and SAR-SEP [1,5]...............	134	193	247	265	275	300	350	373
SIMPLE [1,6]..........................	10	42	61	69	70	78	92	99
Defined contribution plans.................	2,962	3,743	4,210	4,768	4,745	5,253	6,187	6,684
401(k) plans..........................	1,739	2,399	2,746	3,148	3,141	3,526	4,190	4,565
Other private-sector defined contribution plans [7]...........	500	413	402	449	420	441	525	560
403(b) plans..........................	521	624	664	718	706	759	847	871
Thrift Savings Plan [8]................	92	164	230	264	285	315	381	427
457 plans.............................	110	143	169	189	193	212	245	261
Private-sector defined benefit plans..........	2,020	2,262	2,228	2,481	2,525	2,709	3,051	3,200
State and local government defined benefit plans...........	2,340	2,827	2,843	3,065	2,943	3,113	3,670	3,708
Federal defined benefit plans [9]...............	705	908	1,095	1,161	1,230	1,270	1,370	1,438
Annuities [10]........................	951	1,443	1,546	1,701	1,716	1,845	2,014	2,081
Memo:								
Mutual fund retirement assets.........	2,558	3,670	4,339	4,963	4,913	5,634	6,832	7,271
Percent of total retirement assets........	22	25	26	27	27	28	29	30
Percent of all mutual funds..............	37	41	39	42	42	43	45	46

[1] Data for 2011 through 2014 are estimated or preliminary. [2] Includes Keogh deposits. [3] Annuities held by IRAs, excluding variable annuity mutual fund IRA assets. [4] Excludes mutual fund assets held through brokerage accounts, which are included in mutual funds. [5] Simplified Employee Pension (SEP) IRAs and salary reduction (SAR) IRAs. [6] Savings Incentive Match Plan for Employees (SIMPLE) IRAs. [7] Includes Keoghs and other defined contribution plans (profit-sharing, thrift-savings, stock bonus, and money purchase) without 401(k) features. [8] Federal Employees Retirement System (FERS) Thrift Savings Plan (TSP) as reported by the Federal Reserve Board. [9] Federal pension plans include U.S. Treasury security holdings of the civil service retirement and disability fund, the military retirement fund, the judicial retirement funds, the Railroad Retirement Board, and the foreign service retirement and disability fund. These plans also include securities held in the National Railroad Retirement Investment Trust. [10] Annuities include all fixed and variable annuity reserves at life insurance companies less annuities held by IRAs, 403(b) plans, 457 plans, and private pension funds. Some of these annuity reserves represent assets of individuals held outside retirement plan arrangements and IRAs; however, information to separate out such reserves is not available.

Source: Investment Company Institute, "The U.S. Retirement Market, First Quarter 2015" (June), <http://www.ici.org/info/ret_15_q1_data.xls.>.

Table 1224. Pension Funds—Summary: 2000 to 2014

[In billions of dollars (8,561 represents $8,561,000,000,000). As of end of year. Covers private pension funds, state and local government employee retirement funds, and federal government retirement funds defined benefit plans and defined contribution plans (including 401(k) type plans). Excludes social security trust funds; see Table 563]

Type of pension fund	2000	2005	2008	2009	2010	2011	2012	2013	2014
Total financial assets [1].................	**8,561**	**11,376**	**12,105**	**13,170**	**14,551**	**14,917**	**15,726**	**16,889**	**17,679**
Money market fund shares..............	94	123	201	188	180	197	176	181	183
Credit market instruments [1].............	1,405	1,503	1,745	1,679	1,833	1,940	2,105	2,244	2,330
Treasury securities.................	325	340	392	457	509	569	638	700	746
Agency- and GSE (government-sponsored enterprises)-backed securities...........	378	444	362	351	359	375	411	431	425
Corporate and foreign bonds............	581	631	870	753	841	874	943	1,005	1,046
Corporate equities......................	3,369	4,228	2,780	3,436	3,920	3,729	4,141	5,047	5,242
Mutual fund shares......................	1,433	2,051	1,698	2,230	2,519	2,416	2,693	3,369	3,638
Miscellaneous assets [1].................	2,074	3,347	5,600	5,555	6,010	6,537	6,521	5,956	6,190
Unallocated insurance contracts [2]........	463	533	448	589	621	625	639	668	700
Nonmarketable Treasury securities [3]........	705	883	1,015	1,077	1,143	1,214	1,254	1,352	1,421
Claims of pension fund on sponsor [4]........	678	1,707	3,468	3,212	3,524	3,929	3,839	3,116	3,196
Pension entitlements (liabilities) [5]................	**8,649**	**11,469**	**12,235**	**13,311**	**14,694**	**15,065**	**15,885**	**17,062**	**17,858**
Memo:									
Defined benefit plan funded status:									
Pension entitlements, total................	**5,743**	**7,762**	**8,976**	**9,315**	**10,176**	**10,569**	**10,887**	**11,130**	**11,458**
Funded by assets [6].......................	5,065	6,056	5,508	6,103	6,652	6,640	7,048	8,013	8,262
Unfunded...............................	678	1,707	3,468	3,212	3,524	3,929	3,839	3,116	3,196
Household retirement assets, total [7]................	**12,316**	**16,422**	**17,444**	**19,397**	**21,482**	**22,091**	**23,724**	**26,161**	**27,491**
Defined benefit plans.......................	5,655	7,669	8,847	9,174	10,033	10,421	10,727	10,956	11,278
Defined contribution plans................	2,905	3,706	3,259	3,996	4,519	4,496	4,999	5,933	6,400
Individual retirement assets (IRAs) [8]......	2,629	3,425	3,681	4,488	5,029	5,241	5,907	6,966	7,443
Annuities at life insurance companies [9]...............	1,126	1,622	1,658	1,739	1,901	1,933	2,091	2,306	2,369

[1] Includes other types of assets not shown separately. [2] Assets of pension plans held at life insurance companies. [3] Nonmarketable government securities held by the civil service retirement and disability fund, Railroad Retirement Board, judicial retirement fund, military retirement fund, and foreign service retirement and disability fund. [4] Unfunded defined benefit pension entitlements. [5] Actuarial value of accrued pension entitlements in defined benefit plans and assets of defined contribution plans. These liabilities are assets of the household sector. [6] Total defined benefit financial assets plus nonfinancial assets less claims of pension fund on sponsor. [7] Households' retirement assets in tax-deferred accounts, including employer sponsored pension plans, IRAs, Roth IRAs, and annuities. [8] IRA assets are not included in above assets or entitlements. Includes annuities held in IRAs at life insurance companies. [9] Excludes annuities held in IRAs at life insurance companies.

Source: Board of Governors of the Federal Reserve System, "Federal Reserve Statistical Release, Z.1, Financial Accounts of the United States," June 2015, <http://www.federalreserve.gov/releases/z1/>, accessed June 2015.

Table 1225. Private Pension Funds by Type of Asset/Liability: 2000 to 2014

[In billions of dollars (4,286 represents $4,286,000,000,000). As of December 31. Covers private defined benefit plans and defined contribution plans (including 401(k) type plans). Minus sign (-) indicates overfunding]

Type of instrument	2000	2005	2008	2009	2010	2011	2012	2013	2014
Total financial assets [1]	**4,286**	**5,398**	**5,297**	**5,965**	**6,614**	**6,717**	**7,241**	**8,112**	**8,542**
Money market fund shares	81	87	156	147	136	153	136	138	137
Credit market instruments [1]	614	686	766	775	896	970	1,116	1,167	1,200
Treasury securities	111	114	143	176	207	234	278	315	334
Agency and GSE-backed securities [2]	195	248	184	177	184	188	210	226	225
Corporate and foreign bonds	264	288	372	356	438	483	567	572	585
Corporate equities	1,891	2,359	1,324	1,568	1,849	1,751	1,974	2,408	2,587
Mutual fund shares	1,176	1,651	1,418	1,888	2,149	2,121	2,386	2,975	3,232
Miscellaneous assets [1]	389	521	1,588	1,542	1,537	1,669	1,582	1,377	1,336
Unallocated insurance contracts [3]	364	408	339	454	469	485	504	537	563
Pension entitlements (liabilities) [4]	**4,327**	**5,437**	**5,333**	**6,002**	**6,650**	**6,753**	**7,278**	**8,148**	**8,578**
Funded status of defined benefit plans:									
Pension entitlements	1,826	2,290	2,608	2,663	2,872	2,984	3,054	3,105	3,136
Funded by assets [5]	2,020	2,321	1,931	2,165	2,426	2,466	2,665	2,974	3,116
Unfunded	-193	-30	677	498	447	517	390	131	19
Defined benefit plan assets	1,785	2,251	2,573	2,626	2,836	2,947	3,018	3,068	3,099
Defined contribution plan assets	2,500	3,147	2,724	3,339	3,778	3,770	4,224	5,043	5,443

[1] Includes other types of assets not shown separately. [2] GSE=Government-sponsored enterprises. [3] Assets of private pension plans held at life insurance companies (e.g., GICs, variable annuities). [4] Actuarial value of accrued pension entitlements in defined benefit plans and assets of defined contribution plans. [5] Total defined benefit financial assets plus nonfinancial assets less claims of pension fund on sponsor.

Source: Board of Governors of the Federal Reserve System, "Federal Reserve Statistical Release, Z.1, Financial Accounts of the United States," June 2015, <http://www.federalreserve.gov/releases/z1/>, accessed June 2015.

Table 1226. Public Employee Retirement Systems—Assets and Liabilities: 2000 to 2014

[In billions of dollars (2.272 represents $2,272,000,000,000). As of December 31. Minus sign (-) indicates overfunding]

Type of instrument	2000	2005	2008	2009	2010	2011	2012	2013	2014
STATE AND LOCAL GOVERNMENT EMPLOYEE DEFINED BENEFIT PLANS									
Total financial assets [1]	**2,272**	**3,483**	**4,050**	**4,282**	**4,778**	**4,934**	**5,099**	**5,234**	**5,453**
Credit market instruments [1]	755	738	856	773	795	803	806	886	921
Treasury securities	180	159	137	162	173	182	195	207	216
Agency and GSE-backed securities [2]	182	190	173	169	170	181	192	199	194
Corporate and foreign bonds	317	339	492	391	397	384	367	425	454
Corporate equities	1,421	1,758	1,372	1,751	1,930	1,843	2,019	2,433	2,420
Mutual fund shares	257	400	280	342	370	295	307	394	406
Miscellaneous assets [1]	-226	521	1,461	1,338	1,596	1,904	1,884	1,435	1,615
Claims of pension fund on sponsor [3]	-334	314	1,255	1,117	1,343	1,661	1,649	1,193	1,359
Pension entitlements (liabilities) [4]	**2,319**	**3,537**	**4,144**	**4,387**	**4,885**	**5,045**	**5,223**	**5,371**	**5,597**
Funded status of defined benefit plans:									
Pension entitlements	2,006	3,141	3,799	3,960	4,409	4,604	4,762	4,863	5,066
Funded by assets [5]	2,340	2,827	2,544	2,843	3,065	2,943	3,113	3,670	3,708
Unfunded	-334	314	1,255	1,117	1,343	1,661	1,649	1,193	1,359
Defined benefit plan assets	1,959	3,087	3,705	3,855	4,302	4,493	4,639	4,726	4,923
Defined contribution plan assets	313	396	345	427	476	441	460	509	530
FEDERAL GOVERNMENT EMPLOYEE RETIREMENT FUNDS									
Total financial assets [1]	**2,003**	**2,495**	**2,758**	**2,922**	**3,159**	**3,266**	**3,385**	**3,543**	**3,683**
Credit market instruments [1]	35	78	123	131	142	167	183	192	209
Treasury securities	34	68	113	120	130	153	166	178	196
Corporate equities	57	111	84	117	141	134	148	206	235
Miscellaneous assets	1,911	2,306	2,551	2,675	2,877	2,964	3,054	3,144	3,239
Nonmarketable Treasury securities	705	883	1,015	1,077	1,143	1,214	1,254	1,352	1,421
Claims of pension fund on sponsor [6]	1,206	1,423	1,536	1,598	1,734	1,751	1,800	1,792	1,818
Pension entitlements (liabilities) [7]	**2,003**	**2,495**	**2,758**	**2,922**	**3,159**	**3,266**	**3,385**	**3,543**	**3,683**
Funded status of defined benefit plans:									
Pension entitlements	1,911	2,331	2,569	2,693	2,895	2,981	3,070	3,162	3,256
Funded by assets [8]	705	908	1,033	1,095	1,161	1,230	1,270	1,370	1,438
Unfunded [6]	1,206	1,423	1,536	1,598	1,734	1,751	1,800	1,792	1,818
Defined benefit plan assets	1,911	2,331	2,569	2,693	2,895	2,981	3,070	3,162	3,256
Defined contribution plan assets	92	164	189	230	264	285	315	381	427

[1] Includes other types of instruments not shown separately. [2] GSE=Government sponsored enterprises. [3] Unfunded defined benefit pension entitlements. [4] Actuarial value of accrued defined benefit pension entitlements. [5] Total defined benefit financial assets plus nonfinancial assets less claims of pension fund on sponsor. [6] Unfunded defined benefit pension entitlements and suspended investments in the Thrift Savings Plan G Fund by the Treasury. [7] Actuarial value of accrued pension entitlements in defined benefit plans and assets of defined contribution plans, including suspended investments in the Thrift Savings Plan G Fund. [8] Total defined benefit financial assets less defined benefit claims of pension fund on sponsor.

Source: Board of Governors of the Federal Reserve System, "Federal Reserve Statistical Release, Z.1, Financial Accounts of the United States," June 2015, <http://www.federalreserve.gov/releases/z1/>, accessed June 2015.

Table 1227. Life Insurance in Force and Purchases in the United States—Summary: 1990 to 2014

[389 represents 389,000,000. As of December 31 or calendar year, as applicable. Covers life insurance with life insurance companies only. Data represents all life insurance in force on lives of U.S. residents whether issued by U.S. or foreign companies]

Year	Number of policies, total (millions)	Life insurance in force Value (bil. dol.)			Life insurance purchases [1] Number (1,000)			Amount (bil. dol.)		
		Total [2]	Individual	Group	Total	Individual	Group	Total	Individual	Group
1990.......	389	9,393	5,391	3,754	28,791	14,199	14,592	1,529	1,070	459
2000.......	369	15,953	9,376	6,376	34,882	13,345	21,537	2,515	1,594	921
2005.......	373	18,399	9,970	8,263	34,519	11,407	23,112	2,836	1,796	1,040
2008.......	335	19,120	10,254	8,717	28,599	10,207	18,392	2,943	1,870	1,073
2009.......	291	18,138	10,324	7,688	29,190	10,139	19,051	2,900	1,744	1,156
2010.......	284	18,426	10,484	7,831	28,621	10,123	18,498	2,809	1,673	1,135
2011.......	286	19,219	10,994	8,120	27,177	10,309	16,867	2,832	1,673	1,160
2012.......	272	19,321	11,215	8,012	27,063	10,306	16,757	2,800	1,679	1,121
2013.......	275	19,662	11,365	8,215	25,264	9,929	15,336	2,779	1,640	1,139
2014.......	278	20,115	11,826	8,209	27,147	9,440	17,707	2,759	1,590	1,168

[1] Excludes revivals, increases, dividend additions, and reinsurance acquired. Includes long-term credit insurance (life insurance on loans of more than 10 years' duration). [2] Includes other types of policies not shown separately such as credit.

Source: American Council of Life Insurers, Washington, DC, *Life Insurers Fact Book*, annual ©.

Table 1228. U.S. Life Insurance Companies—Summary: 2000 to 2014

[811.5 represents $811,500,000,000. As of December 31 or calendar year, as applicable. Covers domestic and foreign business of U.S. companies. Includes annual statement data for companies that primarily are health insurance companies. Beginning in 2005, includes fraternal benefit societies]

Item	Unit	2000	2005	2008	2009	2010	2011	2012	2013	2014
U.S. companies [1]...........	Number	1,269	1,119	976	946	917	895	868	850	830
Income [2]...........	Bil. dol.	811.5	779.0	940.6	781.4	862.6	915.3	952.4	906.7	999.4
Life insurance premiums..........	Bil. dol.	130.6	142.3	147.2	124.6	104.6	127.5	135.4	130.6	138.3
Annuity considerations [3].........	Bil. dol.	306.7	277.1	328.1	231.6	293.6	334.9	348.1	287.7	361.6
Health insurance premiums..........	Bil. dol.	105.6	118.3	165.0	166.2	172.7	171.6	172.3	175.1	158.4
Investment and other..........	Bil. dol.	268.5	241.4	300.3	259.1	291.6	281.3	296.6	313.4	341.1
Payments under life insurance and annuity contracts..........	Bil. dol.	375.2	365.7	445.1	374.9	365.6	393.2	402.2	411.6	443.8
Payments to life insurance beneficiaries..........	Bil. dol.	44.1	53.0	59.9	59.5	58.4	62.1	63.3	64.3	67.9
Surrender values under life insurance [4]..........	Bil. dol.	27.2	39.2	58.6	48.1	35.8	33.5	31.5	28.7	27.8
Surrender values under. annuity contracts [4,5]..........	Bil. dol.	214.0	190.3	236.7	182.7	184.1	206.2	216.8	222.8	256.7
Policyholder dividends..........	Bil. dol.	20.0	17.9	19.1	16.2	15.9	15.5	15.5	16.0	16.7
Annuity payments [5]..........	Bil. dol.	68.7	63.9	69.6	67.1	70.1	74.5	74.0	78.8	73.8
Matured endowments..........	Bil. dol.	0.6	0.6	0.6	0.6	0.6	0.6	0.4	0.4	0.4
Other payments..........	Bil. dol.	0.6	0.7	0.6	0.8	0.7	0.7	0.6	0.7	0.7
Health insurance benefit payments..........	Bil. dol.	78.8	79.6	118.9	122.0	122.5	120.6	123.8	127.5	113.6
BALANCE SHEET										
Assets..........	Bil. dol.	3,182	4,482	4,648	4,959	5,311	5,493	5,777	6,150	6,406
Mortgage-backed securities..........	Bil. dol.	(NA)	(NA)	633	658	631	607	583	562	567
Government bonds..........	Bil. dol.	364	590	331	413	463	463	459	464	479
Corporate securities..........	Bil. dol.	2,238	3,136	2,671	2,979	3,271	3,353	3,619	3,978	4,133
Bonds..........	Bil. dol.	1,241	1,850	1,535	1,593	1,700	1,807	1,894	1,974	2,061
Stocks..........	Bil. dol.	997	1,285	1,136	1,386	1,570	1,546	1,725	2,006	2,072
Mortgages..........	Bil. dol.	237	295	353	336	327	343	354	374	395
Real estate..........	Bil. dol.	36	33	32	28	28	29	31	31	32
Policy loans..........	Bil. dol.	102	110	122	123	127	129	131	132	133
Other..........	Bil. dol.	204	319	576	504	515	568	601	610	666
Interest earned on assets [6]..........	Percent	7.05	4.90	5.70	4.60	4.33	4.35	4.25	4.20	4.61
Obligations and surplus funds [7]..........	Bil. dol.	3,182	4,482	4,648	4,959	5,311	5,493	5,777	6,150	6,406
Policy reserves..........	Bil. dol.	2,712	3,360	3,471	3,812	4,098	4,244	4,449	4,780	4,956
Annuities [8]..........	Bil. dol.	1,875	2,189	2,150	2,438	2,660	2,729	2,920	3,186	3,299
Group..........	Bil. dol.	960	758	716	798	863	871	958	1,029	1,050
Individual..........	Bil. dol.	881	1,415	1,422	1,624	1,780	1,840	1,943	2,137	2,228
Supplementary contracts [9]..........	Bil. dol.	34	16	13	16	17	18	19	20	22
Life insurance..........	Bil. dol.	742	1,029	1,134	1,178	1,224	1,286	1,302	1,365	1,423
Health insurance..........	Bil. dol.	96	141	186	196	214	229	228	228	234
Liabilities for deposit-type contracts [10]..........	Bil. dol.	21	456	454	416	420	413	431	450	468
Capital and surplus..........	Bil. dol.	188	256	263	301	319	321	340	348	368

NA Not available. [1] Includes life insurance companies that sell accident and health insurance. [2] Premiums are net of reinsurance business and fluctuate with reinsurance activities as well as sale changes. [3] Beginning 2005, excludes certain deposit-type funds from income due to codification. [4] "Surrender values" include annuity withdrawals of funds. [5] Beginning 2005, excludes payments under deposit-type contracts. [6] Net rate. [7] Includes other obligations not shown separately. [8] Beginning 2005, excludes reserves for guaranteed interest contracts (GICs). [9] Data for 2000 include reserves for contracts with and without life contingencies; beginning 2005, includes only reserves for contracts with life contingencies. [10] Policyholder dividend accumulations for all years. Beginning 2005, also includes liabilities for guaranteed interest contracts, supplementary contracts without life contingencies, and premium and other deposits.

Source: American Council of Life Insurers, Washington, DC, *Life Insurers Fact Book*, annual ©.

Table 1229. Property and Casualty Insurance—Summary: 2000 to 2014

[In billions of dollars (305.1 represents $305,100,000,000). Minus sign (-) indicates loss]

Item	2000	2005	2010	2011	2012	2013	2014
Premiums, net written [1]	305.1	427.6	423.8	438.0	456.7	477.0	502.6
Automobile, private [2]	120.0	159.6	160.3	163.3	168.0	174.9	183.4
Automobile, commercial [2]	19.8	26.8	21.1	21.0	22.1	23.9	25.7
Fire	(NA)	7.9	10.2	10.3	10.8	11.2	11.5
Homeowners' multiple peril	32.7	53.0	61.3	64.1	67.8	72.8	77.9
Commercial multiple peril	(NA)	29.7	28.9	30.0	31.5	33.2	34.4
Marine, inland and ocean	8.3	11.2	11.2	11.5	12.3	13.0	13.9
Workers' compensation	26.2	39.7	31.5	35.7	38.7	40.9	43.6
Other liability [3]	(NA)	39.4	35.7	36.5	38.3	42.1	44.2
Reinsurance	(NA)	6.6	12.3	13.2	14.7	12.5	11.5
Losses and expenses	321.3	421.4	430.4	468.8	462.1	449.6	472.8
Underwriting gain/loss	-27.3	-5.6	-10.5	-36.2	-15.4	15.2	12.3
Investment income earned	42.0	49.7	47.6	49.2	48.0	47.3	46.2
Net income after taxes	4.4	44.2	35.2	19.5	35.1	63.4	55.5

NA Not available. [1] Excludes state funds, after reinsurance transactions. Includes other lines of insurance not shown separately. [2] Includes premiums for automobile liability and physical damage. [3] Coverages protecting against legal liability resulting from negligence, carelessness, or failure to act.

Source: Insurance Information Institute, New York, NY, "Facts and Statistics," <http://www.iii.org/insurance-topics/features/facts-and-statistics> ©, accessed August 2015. See also <http://www.iii.org>.

Table 1230. Automobile Insurance—Average Expenditures Per Insured Vehicle by State: 2010 and 2011

[In dollars. Average expenditure equals total premiums written divided by liability car-years. A car-year is equal to 365 days of insured coverage for a single vehicle. The average expenditures for automobile insurance in a state are affected by a number of factors, including the underlying rate structure, the coverages purchased, the deductibles and limits selected, the types of vehicles insured, and the distribution of driver characteristics. The National Association of Insurance Commissioners does not rank state average expenditures and does not endorse any conclusions drawn from this data]

State	2010	2011	State	2010	2011	State	2010	2011	State	2010	2011
U.S.	792	797	ID	548	535	MO	678	675	PA	812	815
AL	651	654	IL	733	727	MT	657	655	RI	985	1,004
AK	890	873	IN	624	622	NE	593	603	SC	738	750
AZ	805	777	IA	547	553	NV	931	905	SD	525	540
AR	662	666	KS	625	626	NH	706	706	TN	641	650
CA	746	737	KY	723	745	NJ	1,157	1,184	TX	848	843
CO	730	724	LA	1,121	1,111	NM	704	692	UT	717	713
CT	965	970	ME	582	577	NY	1,079	1,109	VT	630	634
DE	1,031	1,052	MD	948	956	NC	600	600	VA	674	680
DC	1,134	1,138	MA	891	942	ND	529	550	WA	815	806
FL	1,037	1,091	MI	945	984	OH	619	620	WV	830	834
GA	749	755	MN	693	696	OK	702	716	WI	613	601
HI	766	748	MS	745	741	OR	724	724	WY	621	620

Source: National Association of Insurance Commissioners (NAIC), Kansas City, MO, *Auto Insurance Database Report*, annual ©. Reprinted with permission of the NAIC. Further reprint or distribution strictly prohibited without prior written permission of the NAIC.

Table 1231. Renters and Homeowners Insurance—Average Premiums by State: 2011

[In dollars. Average premium equals premiums divided by exposure per house-years. A house-year is equal to 365 days of insured coverage for a single dwelling and is the standard measurement for homeowners insurance. The National Association of Insurance Commissioners does not rank state average expenditures and does not endorse any conclusions drawn from these data]

State	Renters [1]	Home-owners [2]	State	Renters [1]	Home-owners [2]	State	Renters [1]	Home-owners [2]
U.S.	187	978	KY	175	839	OH	183	644
AL	230	1,163	LA	238	1,672	OK	235	1,366
AK	171	924	ME	150	714	OR	170	559
AZ	200	675	MD	161	800	PA	154	764
AR	220	1,029	MA	213	1,072	RI	183	1,139
CA	208	967	MI	208	774	SC	199	1,091
CO	175	961	MN	150	1,056	SD	117	721
CT	196	1,096	MS	252	1,409	TN	213	915
DE	159	664	MO	182	1,022	TX [3]	225	1,578
DC	167	1,083	MT	147	818	UT	147	563
FL	210	1,933	NE	151	958	VT	155	748
GA	228	906	NV	199	689	VA	155	782
HI	176	907	NH	152	811	WA	174	626
ID	160	518	NJ	168	915	WV	178	743
IL	172	822	NM	189	793	WI	133	592
IN	179	779	NY	210	1,097	WY	156	770
IA	149	713	NC	132	869			
KS	177	1,103	ND	117	969			

[1] Based on the HO-4 renters insurance policy for tenants. Includes broad named-peril coverage for the personal property of tenants. [2] Based on the HO-3 homeowner package policy for owner-occupied dwellings, 1–4 family units. Provides "all risks" coverage (except those specifically excluded in the policy) on buildings, broad named-peril coverage on personal property, and is the most common package written. [3] The Texas Insurance Commissioner promulgates residential policy forms which are similar but not identical to the standard forms.

Source: National Association of Insurance Commissioners (NAIC), Kansas City, MO, *Dwelling Fire, Homeowners Owner-Occupied, and Homeowners Tenant and Condominium/Cooperative Unit Owners Insurance* ©. Reprinted with permission of the NAIC. Further reprint or distribution strictly prohibited without prior written permission of the NAIC.

Table 1232. Real Estate and Rental and Leasing—Nonemployer Establishments and Receipts by Kind of Business: 2010 to 2013

[2,343.1 represents 2,343,100. Includes only firms subject to federal income tax. Nonemployers are businesses with no paid employees. Data originate chiefly from administrative records of the Internal Revenue Service; see Appendix III]

Kind of business	NAICS code [1]	Establishments (1,000)			Receipts (mil. dol.)		
		2010	2012	2013	2010	2012	2013
Real estate & rental & leasing, total............	**53**	**2,343.1**	**2,389.9**	**2,448.3**	**209,549**	**227,428**	**237,172**
Real estate..........	531	2,262.2	2,308.1	2,367.7	203,065	220,591	230,343
Lessors of real estate............	5311	989.3	1,057.8	1,090.1	135,015	143,842	148,344
Offices of real estate agents & brokers............	5312	641.6	611.9	624.6	25,502	29,782	33,205
Activities related to real estate..........	5313	631.3	638.5	653.0	42,549	46,966	48,794
Rental & leasing services..........	532	78.9	79.6	78.3	6,288	6,608	6,583
Automotive equipment rental & leasing............	5321	18.3	18.2	17.7	990	1,031	1,043
Consumer goods rental............	5322	18.3	19.1	18.8	779	842	834
General rental centers............	5323	4.8	5.3	5.6	409	450	450
Commercial/industrial equipment rental & leasing............	5324	37.5	37.0	36.2	4,109	4,285	4,256
Lessors of other nonfinancial intangible assets............	533	2.0	2.2	2.3	197	229	246

[1] Data for 2010 based on 2007 North American Industry Classification System (NAICS); beginning in 2012, data based on 2012 NAICS. For more information, see text, Section 15.

Source: U.S. Census Bureau, Nonemployer Statistics, "Geographic Area Series: Nonemployer Statistics for the US, States, Metropolitan Areas, and Counties," <http://factfinder.census.gov>, accessed June 2015. See also <http://www.census.gov/econ/nonemployer/>.

Table 1233. Real Estate and Rental and Leasing—Establishments, Employees, and Payroll: 2010 and 2013

[347.3 represents 347,300. Covers establishments with payroll. Data for 2010 based on the North American Industry Classification System (NAICS), 2007; 2013 data based on NAICS 2012; see text, section 15, Business Enterprise. Employees are for the week including March 12. Most government employees are excluded. For statement on methodology, see Appendix III]

Kind of business	NAICS code	Establishments (1,000)		Employees (1,000)		Payroll (bil. dol.)	
		2010	2013	2010	2013	2010	2013
Real estate & rental & leasing, total............	**53**	**347.3**	**357.5**	**1,946.4**	**1,972.1**	**80.5**	**92.3**
Real estate..........	531	287.8	302.4	1,407.9	1,439.4	58.7	66.7
Lessors of real estate............	5311	114.4	123.0	513.3	547.2	18.7	22.2
Offices of real estate agents & brokers............	5312	89.2	91.9	278.0	259.2	12.7	15.2
Activities related to real estate [1]............	5313	84.2	87.5	616.6	633.0	27.4	29.4
Residential property managers............	531311	39.2	42.2	380.5	404.8	13.6	15.5
Rental & leasing services..........	532	57.2	52.7	509.4	496.2	19.3	22.2
Automotive equipment rental & leasing............	5321	11.1	14.3	149.2	158.2	5.5	6.3
Passenger car rental & leasing............	53211	5.6	9.0	([2])	([2])	3.5	4.1
Truck, utility trailer & RV rental & leasing............	53212	5.6	5.3	46.0	46.3	2.0	2.2
Consumer goods rental [1]............	5322	27.9	21.2	193.0	148.2	5.1	4.8
Video tape & disc rental............	53223	10.9	3.2	79.9	25.1	1.2	0.5
Home health equipment rental............	532291	3.8	3.5	36.6	35.1	1.6	1.4
General rental centers............	5323	4.2	2.9	25.3	17.9	0.9	0.7
Commercial/industrial equipment rental & leasing [1]............	5324	13.9	14.3	141.8	171.9	7.9	10.4
Construction, transportation, mining equipment rental and leasing............	53241	5.5	5.3	55.4	65.0	3.4	4.6
Lessors of other nonfinancial intangible assets............	533	2.4	2.5	29.2	36.5	2.4	3.4

[1] Includes industries not shown separately. [2] Over 100,000 employees.

Source: U.S. Census Bureau, County Business Patterns, "Geography Area Series: County Business Patterns," <http://factfinder.census.gov>, accessed May 2015. See also <http://www.census.gov/econ/cbp/index.html>.

Table 1234. Real Estate and Rental and Leasing Services—Revenue by Kind of Business: 2005 to 2013

[In millions of dollars (107,559 represents $107,559,000,000). Covers taxable employer firms. Data are based on the 2007 North American Industry Classification System (NAICS); see text, this section and Section 15. Estimates have been adjusted using the results of the 2007 Economic Census. Based on Service Annual Survey; see Appendix III]

Kind of business	NAICS code	2005	2009	2010	2011	2012	2013
Real estate and rental and leasing, total............	**53**	**(NA)**	**(NA)**	**412,889**	**433,803**	**464,576**	**497,066**
Real estate..........	531	(NA)	(NA)	274,356	287,397	308,980	332,513
Lessors of real estate [1]............	5311	(NA)	(NA)	166,353	177,219	188,567	199,136
Lessors of residential buildings and dwellings............	53111	(NA)	(NA)	67,296	73,435	79,295	84,221
Lessors of nonresidential buildings (exc miniwarehouses)............	53112	(NA)	(NA)	85,365	89,611	94,401	99,428
Offices of real estate agents and brokers............	5312	(NA)	52,358	53,598	54,840	62,512	72,008
Activities related to real estate [1]............	5313	(NA)	54,295	54,405	55,338	57,901	61,369
Real estate property managers............	53131	(NA)	37,887	38,446	39,539	40,884	43,364
Rental and leasing services [1]............	532	107,559	110,223	111,250	117,765	126,455	132,415
Automotive equipment rental and leasing [1]............	5321	42,324	41,987	42,385	45,583	48,061	49,740
Passenger car rental and leasing............	53211	26,305	28,537	28,922	31,305	33,215	34,556
Consumer goods rental............	5322	22,840	(NA)	21,914	21,259	21,428	21,143
Commercial/industrial equip. rental & leasing [1]............	5324	38,842	42,409	43,054	46,972	52,913	57,493
Construction/transportation/mining equipment rental and leasing............	53241	21,123	22,187	21,802	24,282	27,950	30,202
Lessors of other nonfinancial intangible assets............	533	(NA)	23,992	27,283	28,641	29,141	32,138

NA Not available. [1] Includes other kinds of business, not shown separately.

Source: U.S. Census Bureau, Annual and Quarterly Services, "2013 Annual Services," <http://www.census.gov/services/index.html>, accessed May 2015.

Section 26
Arts, Recreation, and Travel

This section presents data on the arts, entertainment, and recreation economic sector of the economy, and personal recreational activities, the arts and humanities, and domestic and foreign travel.

Arts, entertainment, and recreation industry—The U.S. Census Bureau surveys—County Business Patterns, Economic Census, Nonemployer Statistics, and Service Annual Survey—provide data on the arts, entertainment, and recreation sector. The *County Business Patterns* ' annual data includes number of establishments, number of employees, first quarter and annual payrolls, and number of establishments by employment size class. The *Economic Census*, conducted every five years for the years ending '2' and '7', provides information on the number of establishments, receipts, payroll, and paid employees for the United States and various geographic levels. Data for the 2012 Economic Census are being released on a continuing basis through 2016. Nonemployer statistics are an annual tabulation of economic data by industry for active businesses without paid employees that are subject to federal income tax. The *Service Annual Survey* provides estimates of operation revenue of taxable firms and revenues and expenses of firms exempt from federal taxes for industries in this sector of the economy. See Appendix III for more details.

Recreation and leisure activities—Data on the participation in various recreation and leisure time activities are based on several sample surveys. Data on the public's involvement with arts events and activities are published by the National Endowment for Arts (NEA). The NEA's *Survey of Public Participation in the Arts* remains the largest periodic study of arts participation in the United States. The most recent data are from the 2012 survey. Data on participation in fishing, hunting, and other forms of wildlife associated recreation are published periodically by the U.S. Department of Interior, Fish and Wildlife Service. The most recent data are from the 2011 survey. Data on participation in various sports recreation activities are published by the National Sporting Goods Association. GfK Mediamark Research and Intelligence, LLC also conducts periodic surveys on sports and leisure activities, as well as other topics.

Parks and recreation—The Department of the Interior has responsibility for administering the national parks. The National Park Service publishes information on visits to national park areas in its annual report, *National Park Statistical Abstract.* Additional data regarding acreage and visits for each area administered by the service, plus certain "related" areas can be found at: <https://irma.nps.gov/Stats/>. Statistics for state parks are compiled by the National Association of State Park Directors in its annual *Statistical Report of State Park Operations.*

Travel—Statistics on arrivals and departures to the United States, cities and states visited by overseas travelers, and tourism sales and employment are reported by the International Trade Administration (ITA), Office of Travel & Tourism Industries (OTTI). Data on domestic travel and travel expenditures are published by the research department of the U.S. Travel Association. Other data on household transportation characteristics are in Section 23, Transportation.

Statistical reliability—For a discussion of statistical collection and estimation, sampling procedures, and measures of statistical reliability applicable to Census Bureau data, see Appendix III.

Table 1235. Arts, Entertainment, and Recreation Services—Estimated Revenue: 2005 to 2013

[In millions of dollars (166,912 represents $166,912,000,000). For taxable and tax-exempt employer firms. Data are based on the 2007 North American Industry Classification System (NAICS). Selected estimates have been adjusted using the results of the 2007 Economic Census. Based on the Service Annual Survey, see Appendix III]

Industry	NAICS Code	2005	2009	2010	2011	2012	2013
Arts, entertainment, and recreation	71	**166,912**	**188,158**	**191,982**	**202,194**	**212,170**	**222,202**
Performing arts, spectator sports, and related industries	711	65,405	79,940	81,581	84,932	88,637	91,807
Performing arts companies	7111	13,144	14,321	14,822	15,946	15,745	15,366
Spectator sports	7112	24,842	31,590	32,379	33,726	34,216	35,760
Sports teams and clubs	711211	14,564	20,691	21,504	22,342	22,667	24,079
Racetracks	711212	7,358	7,069	7,216	7,532	7,892	7,737
Other spectator sports	711219	2,920	3,830	3,659	3,852	3,657	3,944
Promoters of performing arts, sports, and similar events	7113	12,374	16,167	16,327	16,611	18,469	19,696
Agents and managers for artists, athletes, entertainers and other public figures	7114	4,176	5,025	4,968	5,309	5,502	5,801
Independent artists, writers, and performers	7115	10,869	12,837	13,085	13,340	14,705	15,184
Museums, historical sites, and similar institutions	712	12,471	11,588	11,736	11,810	12,492	13,902
Amusement, gambling, and recreation industries	713	89,036	96,630	98,665	105,452	111,041	116,493
Amusement parks and arcades	7131	11,926	13,330	13,991	17,263	18,466	19,626
Amusement and theme parks	71311	10,491	11,589	12,197	15,377	16,462	17,682
Amusement arcades	71312	1,435	1,741	1,794	1,886	2,004	1,944
Gambling industries	7132	24,040	25,100	25,729	27,372	28,870	30,363
Casinos (except casino hotels)	71321	15,753	16,410	16,619	17,434	18,320	19,367
Other gambling industries	71329	8,287	8,690	9,110	9,938	10,550	10,996
Other amusement and recreation industries	7139	53,070	58,200	58,945	60,817	63,705	66,504
Golf courses and country clubs	71391	19,356	20,342	19,980	20,073	21,071	21,090
Skiing facilities	71392	1,989	2,440	2,514	2,597	2,641	2,901
Marinas	71393	3,561	3,303	3,461	3,555	3,642	3,751
Fitness and recreational sports centers	71394	18,286	21,966	22,503	23,470	24,413	26,073
Bowling centers	71395	3,232	3,123	3,103	3,200	3,228	3,422
All other amusement and recreation industries	71399	6,646	7,026	7,384	7,922	8,710	9,267

Source: U.S. Census Bureau, Annual & Quarterly Services, "2013 Annual Services," <http://www.census.gov/services.index.html>, accessed January 2015.

Table 1236. Arts, Entertainment, and Recreation—Establishments, Revenue, Payroll, and Employees by Kind of Business: 2002 and 2007

[141,904 represents $141,904,000,000. For establishments with payroll only. Definition of paid employees varies among NAICS sectors. Data are based on the 2002 and 2007 economic censuses which are subject to nonsampling error. For details on survey methodology, sampling and nonsampling errors, see Appendix III]

Kind of business	2002 NAICS code [1]	Number of establishments		Revenue (mil. dol.)		Annual payroll (mil. dol.)		Paid employees (1,000)	
		2002	2007	2002	2007	2002	2007	2002	2007
Arts, entertainment, and recreation, total	71	**110,313**	**124,620**	**141,904**	**189,417**	**45,169**	**58,359**	**1,849**	**2,061**
Performing arts, spectator sports, and related industries [2]	711	37,735	43,868	58,286	77,773	21,231	27,839	423	438
Performing arts companies	7111	9,303	8,838	10,864	13,574	3,267	3,980	138	128
Spectator sports	7112	4,072	4,237	22,313	30,403	10,206	14,136	108	121
Promoters of performing arts, sports and similar events	7113	5,236	6,647	12,169	16,122	2,184	2,957	102	121
Agents and managers for artists, athletes, entertainers and others	7114	3,262	3,534	3,602	4,919	1,251	1,694	17	19
Museums, historical sites, and similar institutions [2]	712	6,663	7,125	8,608	13,285	2,935	3,662	123	130
Amusement, gambling, and recreation industries [2]	713	65,915	73,627	75,010	98,359	21,002	26,859	1,303	1,494
Amusement parks and arcades	7131	3,015	3,145	9,443	13,544	2,069	2,802	122	134
Gambling industries	7132	2,072	2,327	18,893	25,135	3,596	4,566	158	170
Other amusement and recreation services	7139	60,828	68,155	46,674	59,680	15,337	19,490	1,023	1,190

[1] Based on 2002 North American Industry Classification System (NAICS); see text, this section and section 15. [2] Includes other industries not shown separately.

Source: U.S. Census Bureau, 2007 Economic Census, Core Business Statistics, "Comparative Statistics 2007 and 2002, Arts, Entertainment and Recreation," <http://www.census.gov/econ/census07/>, accessed September 2014.

Table 1237. Arts, Entertainment, and Recreation—Nonemployer Establishments and Receipts by Kind of Business (NAICS Basis): 2010 to 2013

[Firms in thousands (1,154 represents 1,154,000); receipts in millions of dollars (26,756 represents $26,756,000,000). Includes only firms subject to federal income tax. Nonemployers are businesses with no paid employees but with annual receipts of $1,000 or more]

Kind of business	NAICS code [1]	Firms (1,000)			Receipts (mil. dol.)		
		2010	2012	2013	2010	2012	2013
Arts, entertainment, and recreation.............................	**71**	**1,154**	**1,237**	**1,257**	**26,756**	**30,281**	**30,892**
Performing arts, spectator sports, and related industries.........	711	1,005	1,075	1,098	21,053	24,131	24,621
Performing arts companies...............................	7111	61	68	79	1,249	1,476	1,556
Spectator sports...	7112	152	167	163	2,515	2,871	2,927
Promoters of performing arts, sports, and similar events.........	7113	45	52	53	1,699	2,081	2,186
Agents/managers for artists, athletes, and other public figures...	7114	36	38	38	1,300	1,517	1,486
Independent artists, writers, and performers...............	7115	710	749	766	14,290	16,186	16,465
Museums, historical sites, and similar institutions..............	712	6	6	6	95	111	113
Amusement, gambling, and recreation industries.................	713	143	156	153	5,607	6,039	6,158
Amusement parks and arcades............................	7131	5	5	4	251	245	245
Gambling industries....................................	7132	10	10	10	1,185	1,130	1,184
Other amusement and recreation services..............	7139	128	141	138	4,171	4,664	4,729

[1] Data for 2010 are based on 2007 North American Industry Classification System; beginning in 2012, data based on 2012 NAICS. see text, Section 15.

Source: U.S. Census Bureau, Nonemployer Statistics, "Geographic Area Series: Nonemployer Statistics for the US, States, Metropolitan Areas, and Counties," <http://factfinder2.census.gov>, accessed June 2015. See also <http://www.census.gov/econ/nonemployer/>.

Table 1238. Arts, Entertainment, and Recreation—Establishments, Employees, and Payroll by Kind of Business (NAICS Basis): 2010 and 2013

[Employees in thousands (2,003.6 represents 2,003,600); payroll in millions of dollars (62,319 represents $62,319,000,000). Covers establishments with paid employees. Excludes self-employed individuals, employees of private households, railroad employees, agricultural production employees, and most government employees. For statement on methodology, see Appendix III]

Kind of business	2012 NAICS code [1]	Establishments		Employees [2] (1,000)		Payroll (mil. dol.)	
		2010	2013	2010	2013	2010	2013
Arts, entertainment, & recreation..................	**71**	**123,151**	**126,952**	**2,003.6**	**2,112.0**	**62,319**	**67,982**
Performing arts, spectator sports......................	711	44,325	46,928	424.8	455.1	30,747	33,158
Performing arts companies...........................	7111	8,649	8,725	117.5	117.9	3,970	4,132
Theater companies & dinner theaters..............	71111	3,266	3,283	62.2	67.4	1,972	2,033
Dance companies...............................	71112	682	675	9.0	8.9	231	250
Musical groups & artists.........................	71113	4,306	4,440	36.4	35.9	1,441	1,643
Other performing arts companies....................	71119	395	327	9.9	5.8	326	206
Spectator sports..................................	7112	4,351	4,243	118.5	127.7	15,528	17,281
Sports teams & clubs..........................	711211	841	971	55.1	63.6	13,298	14,941
Racetracks..................................	711212	681	695	45.2	47.5	1,278	1,448
Other spectator sports.......................	711219	2,829	2,577	18.1	16.6	953	892
Promoters of performing arts, sports, & similar events......	7113	6,608	7,071	127.1	149.0	3,256	3,587
Promoters of performing arts, sports, & similar events with facilities.....	71131	2,764	2,879	102.7	120.7	2,240	2,355
Promoters of performing arts, sports, & similar events without facilities...	71132	3,844	4,192	24.5	28.4	1,015	1,231
Agents/managers for artists, athletes, and other public figures...........	7114	3,547	3,868	17.7	17.6	1,934	1,992
Independent artists, writers, & performers...........	7115	21,170	23,021	44.1	42.9	6,058	6,167
Museums, historical sites, & similar institutions.......	712	7,327	7,448	125.9	139.9	3,763	4,358
Museums..	71211	4,795	5,058	80.0	87.3	2,419	2,793
Historical sites.................................	71212	1,213	1,135	9.6	12.0	224	317
Zoos & botanical gardens.........................	71213	587	613	30.2	34.5	930	1,044
Nature parks & other similar institutions.............	71219	732	642	6.1	6.1	191	203
Amusement, gambling, & recreation industries.......	713	71,499	72,576	1,452.9	1,517.0	27,810	30,466
Amusement parks & arcades.........................	7131	3,053	3,264	146.1	172.6	2,813	3,619
Amusement & theme parks.....................	71311	551	485	115.9	133.8	2,428	3,138
Amusement arcades...........................	71312	2,502	2,779	30.2	38.8	386	482
Gambling industries...............................	7132	2,672	2,893	173.7	164.3	5,110	5,066
Casinos (except casino hotels).....................	71321	368	329	119.6	108.6	3,654	3,460
Other gambling industries.........................	71329	2,304	2,564	54.2	55.6	1,456	1,606
Other amusement & recreation services..............	7139	65,774	66,419	1,133.1	1,180.1	19,886	21,780
Golf courses & country clubs.....................	71391	11,890	11,597	296.0	295.5	8,044	8,427
Skiing facilities.................................	71392	382	379	81.5	78.6	724	775
Marinas..	71393	3,937	3,844	26.7	26.4	927	951
Fitness & recreational sports centers...............	71394	29,913	30,393	560.6	601.0	7,292	8,313
Bowling centers.................................	71395	4,297	3,976	74.9	70.6	963	980
All other amusement & recreation industries........	71399	15,355	16,230	93.4	108.1	1,936	2,334

[1] 2010 data based on 2007 North American Industry Classification System (NAICS); 2013 data based on 2012 NAICS; see text, this section and Section 15. [2] For employees on the payroll for the period including March 12.

Source: U.S. Census Bureau, County Business Patterns, "Geography Area Series, County Business Patterns," <http://factfinder2.census.gov/>, accessed April 2015. See also <http://www.census.gov/econ/cbp/>.

Table 1239. Expenditures Per Consumer Unit for Entertainment and Reading: 1985 to 2013

[Data are annual averages. In dollars, except as indicated. Based on the Consumer Expenditure Survey (CES). For description of survey, see text, Section 13; also see headnote, Table 706. For composition of regions, see map, inside front cover]

| Year and characteristic | Entertainment and reading | | Entertainment | | | | Reading |
	Total	Percent of total expenditures	Total	Fees and admissions	Audio and visual equipment and services	Other entertainment, supplies, and equipment services [1]	
1985.	1,311	5.6	1,170	320	371	479	141
1990.	1,575	5.6	1,422	371	454	597	153
1995.	1,775	5.5	1,612	433	542	637	163
1998.	1,907	5.4	1,746	449	535	762	161
1999.	2,050	5.5	1,891	459	608	824	159
2000.	2,009	5.3	1,863	515	622	727	146
2001.	2,094	5.3	1,953	526	660	767	141
2002.	2,218	5.5	2,079	542	692	845	139
2003.	2,187	5.4	2,060	494	730	835	127
2004.	2,348	5.4	2,218	528	788	903	130
2005.	2,514	5.4	2,388	588	888	912	126
2006.	2,493	5.2	2,376	606	906	863	117
2007.	2,816	5.7	2,698	658	987	1,053	118
2008.	2,951	5.8	2,835	616	1,036	1,183	116
2009.	2,803	5.7	2,693	628	975	1,090	110
2010.	2,604	5.4	2,504	581	954	970	100
2011.	2,687	5.4	2,572	594	977	1,001	115
2012.	2,714	5.3	2,605	614	979	1,011	109
2013, total.	**2,584**	**5.1**	**2,482**	**569**	**964**	**949**	**102**
Age of reference person:							
Under 25 years old.	1,289	4.2	1,243	245	576	422	46
25 to 34 years old.	2,274	4.7	2,214	498	899	817	60
35 to 44 years old.	3,063	5.2	2,958	736	1,139	1,084	105
45 to 54 years old.	3,158	5.2	3,070	747	1,064	1,259	88
55 to 64 years old.	2,783	5.0	2,651	551	1,021	1,079	132
65 years old and older.	2,165	5.2	2,027	449	858	720	138
65 to 74 years old.	2,634	5.6	2,488	579	961	949	146
75 years old and over.	1,549	4.5	1,422	276	723	423	127
Hispanic or Latino origin of reference person:							
Hispanic.	1,673	4.0	1,635	287	770	578	38
Non-Hispanic.	2,721	5.2	2,609	611	993	1,005	112
Race of reference person: [2]							
White, and all other races [2].	2,772	5.3	2,661	615	978	1,068	111
Asian.	2,410	4.0	2,321	789	990	542	89
Black.	1,394	3.8	1,344	190	866	288	50
Region of residence:							
Northeast.	2,732	4.8	2,615	753	1,011	851	117
Midwest.	2,573	5.1	2,460	546	941	973	113
South.	2,244	4.9	2,165	401	946	818	79
West.	3,047	5.5	2,928	724	981	1,223	119
Size of consumer unit:							
One person.	1,621	5.2	1,547	288	703	557	74
Two or more persons.	2,993	5.0	2,878	689	1,076	1,113	115
Two persons.	2,812	5.2	2,676	585	1,016	1,074	136
Three persons.	2,687	4.6	2,604	576	1,059	968	83
Four persons.	3,553	5.2	3,452	958	1,225	1,268	101
Five persons or more.	3,351	5.1	3,238	858	1,103	1,277	113
Income before taxes:							
Quintiles of income:							
Lowest 20 percent.	1,039	4.6	1,002	112	548	341	37
Second 20 percent.	1,484	4.6	1,416	198	750	468	68
Third 20 percent.	2,081	4.9	1,997	349	885	763	84
Fourth 20 percent.	2,983	5.1	2,866	563	1,149	1,154	117
Highest 20 percent.	5,340	5.4	5,133	1,625	1,489	2,018	207
Education:							
Less than a high school graduate.	1,095	4.2	1,065	61	560	444	30
High school graduate.	1,584	4.6	1,530	168	821	541	54
High school graduate with some college.	2,037	4.9	1,965	305	850	809	72
Associate's degree.	2,720	5.3	2,636	419	1,037	1,180	84
Bachelor's degree.	3,218	5.1	3,089	802	1,106	1,181	129
Master's, professional, doctoral degree.	4,377	5.4	4,158	1,472	1,251	1,435	219

[1] Other equipment and services include pets, toys, hobbies, and playground equipment; and other entertainment supplies, equipment, and services. [2] All other races includes Native Hawaiian or other Pacific Islander, American Indian or Alaska Native, and approximately 1 percent reporting more than one race.

Source: U.S. Bureau of Labor Statistics, Consumer Expenditure Survey, "Consumer Expenditures in 2013," <http://www.bls.gov/cex/home. htm#tables>, accessed January 2015.

Table 1240. Arts and Culture Production—Value Added and Employment by Industry: 2007 to 2012

[In millions of dollars (623,271 represents $623,271,000,000); employment in thousands (5,200 represents 5,200,000)]

Industry	2007	2008	2009	2010	2011	2012
VALUE ADDED						
Total	623,271	642,171	618,818	656,784	672,881	698,695
Core arts and cultural production	117,841	125,454	115,447	120,056	125,909	129,011
Performing arts	10,600	11,586	12,336	16,149	16,968	16,116
Independent artists, writers, and performers	15,786	16,641	17,317	17,587	18,300	19,297
Agents/managers for artists	1,801	1,880	1,912	1,757	2,063	2,113
Promoters of performing arts and similar events	8,500	9,193	7,682	5,914	6,169	7,553
Museums	4,783	4,354	4,865	3,982	4,230	5,075
Advertising	22,535	24,642	23,271	24,620	25,781	29,289
Architectural services	17,492	18,041	14,938	14,139	14,539	13,910
Landscape architectural services	3,083	3,157	2,663	2,554	2,475	2,305
Interior design services	8,412	8,865	6,048	7,019	7,621	6,308
Industrial design services	1,372	1,412	1,116	1,422	1,747	1,512
Graphic design services	7,367	7,861	6,013	7,355	7,480	6,573
All other design services	650	610	467	562	647	639
Computer systems design	1,822	1,961	1,965	2,151	2,405	2,696
Photography and photofinishing services	7,572	8,316	7,726	7,428	7,818	8,045
Fine arts education	2,080	2,798	2,743	3,084	3,161	2,855
Education services	3,986	4,137	4,385	4,333	4,506	4,726
Supporting arts and cultural production	482,033	492,959	479,992	514,818	524,768	547,003
Rental and leasing	8,427	7,352	6,821	5,389	4,731	5,288
Other support services	376	392	368	395	412	439
Publishing	80,862	78,263	72,008	74,327	75,181	77,850
Motion pictures	61,744	68,341	73,975	89,792	92,711	95,868
Sound recording	11,427	11,664	13,248	13,834	14,401	16,303
Broadcasting	107,124	109,898	103,924	109,575	113,467	121,091
Other information services	20,791	23,907	22,326	24,598	26,680	31,961
Printed goods manufacturing	10,896	10,078	8,726	8,458	8,512	8,066
Jewelry and silverware manufacturing	2,920	2,809	3,222	3,307	2,900	3,884
Musical instruments manufacturing	651	756	779	1000	996	893
Custom architectural woodwork and metalwork manufacturing	2,516	2,396	2,014	1,930	1,886	1,902
Camera and motion picture equipment manufacturing	322	334	277	314	359	316
Other goods manufacturing	2,110	2,033	1,833	1,964	1,923	1,951
Grant-making and giving services	559	433	507	499	502	519
Unions	872	1,013	1,066	1,042	1,098	1,147
Government	88,286	91,945	93,089	94,988	95,536	96,109
Construction	13,364	12,065	11,548	16,078	12,920	10,356
Wholesale and transportation industries	26,520	27,208	22,955	25,538	27,471	29,000
Retail industries	42,265	42,073	41,306	41,790	43,081	44,059
All other industries [1]	23,397	23,759	23,380	21,910	22,205	22,681
EMPLOYMENT						
Total	5,200	5,162	4,833	4,698	4,682	4,676
Core arts and cultural production	1,062	1,065	973	930	944	956
Performing arts	109	109	102	100	101	100
Independent artists, writers, and performers	39	38	35	35	36	37
Agents/managers for artists	21	22	21	21	21	22
Promoters of performing arts and similar events	72	74	76	73	76	79
Museums	117	120	117	116	118	122
Advertising	140	142	129	124	129	134
Architectural services	145	144	118	104	103	102
Landscape architectural services	33	31	25	22	22	21
Interior design services	27	26	21	18	19	19
Industrial design services	27	28	24	24	25	25
Graphic design services	75	73	65	61	62	61
All other design services	2	3	2	2	2	2
Computer systems design	15	16	16	16	17	18
Photography and photofinishing services	110	106	93	85	82	78
Fine arts education	36	39	37	39	41	43
Education services	95	95	93	90	92	93
Supporting arts and cultural production	3,921	3,881	3,653	3,583	3,554	3,537
Rental and leasing	85	78	68	54	45	42
Other support services	4	4	4	4	4	4
Publishing	420	408	367	348	347	345
Motion pictures	364	368	348	357	359	367
Sound recording	16	14	14	13	13	13
Broadcasting	430	430	405	397	395	401
Other information services	38	40	39	40	43	48
Printed goods manufacturing	143	133	116	106	103	99
Jewelry and silverware manufacturing	36	33	28	27	26	26
Musical instruments manufacturing	10	9	8	8	8	8
Custom architectural woodwork and metalwork manufacturing	39	38	31	29	29	29
Camera and motion picture equipment manufacturing	3	2	2	2	2	2
Other goods manufacturing	27	25	20	19	19	19
Grant-making and giving services	5	5	5	4	5	5
Unions	16	18	19	17	18	16
Government	1,179	1,189	1,178	1,150	1,130	1,114
Construction	139	117	103	124	106	92
Wholesale and transportation industries	209	208	175	180	189	193
Retail industries	759	762	725	703	715	714
All other industries [1]	217	216	207	186	184	183

[1] Consists of the industries with secondary production that is designated as artistic and cultural production.

Source: U.S. Bureau of Economic Analysis, Arts and Cultural Production Satellite Accounts, *Spending on Arts and Cultural Production Continues to Increase*, January 2015. See also <http://www.bea.gov/industry/index.htm#supplemental>.

Table 1241. Personal Consumption Expenditures for Recreation: 1990 to 2014

[In billions of dollars (314.7 represents $314,700,000,000), except percent. Represents market value of purchases of goods and services by individuals and nonprofit institutions]

Type of product or service	1990	2000	2005	2010	2012	2013	2014
Total recreation expenditures	**314.7**	**633.7**	**804.6**	**888.3**	**968.2**	**1,001.4**	**1,040.7**
Percent of total personal consumption [1]	8.2	9.3	9.1	8.7	8.8	8.8	8.8
Video and audio equipment, computers, and related services	81.1	181.2	239.0	276.4	295.7	301.7	306.6
Video and audio equipment	43.7	79.9	101.4	99.5	102.7	103.1	103.6
Information processing equipment	9.6	44.1	67.0	90.3	98.6	101.2	102.6
Services related to video and audio goods and computers	27.8	57.2	70.6	86.6	94.4	97.3	100.3
Sports and recreational goods and related services	74.2	146.0	184.1	174.2	192.5	202.5	213.2
Sports and recreational vehicles	16.6	34.9	49.1	35.6	40.3	44.1	47.4
Other sporting and recreational goods	55.4	106.8	130.0	134.2	147.5	153.6	160.8
Maintenance and repair of recreational vehicles and sports equipment	2.1	4.2	4.9	4.4	4.7	4.9	5.0
Membership clubs, sports centers, parks, theaters, and museums	49.7	91.9	117.9	141.8	154.9	160.5	168.8
Membership clubs and participant sports centers	14.3	26.4	34.3	39.5	42.4	44.1	45.9
Amusements parks, campgrounds, and related recreational services	19.2	31.1	33.6	38.8	44.6	47.0	50.3
Admissions to specified spectator amusements	14.4	30.6	43.7	57.3	61.5	62.5	65.4
Motion picture theaters	5.1	8.6	9.7	11.8	12.4	12.9	12.9
Live entertainment, excluding sports	4.5	10.4	18.3	26.3	28.5	28.0	30.0
Spectator sports	4.8	11.6	15.7	19.2	20.6	21.6	22.4
Museums and libraries	1.9	3.8	6.4	6.1	6.4	6.9	7.2
Magazines, newspapers, books, and stationery	47.3	81.0	85.0	89.9	100.1	103.6	107.6
Gambling	23.7	67.6	96.5	105.6	114.3	118.1	123.3
Pets, pet products, and related services	18.8	39.7	57.2	75.9	84.1	88.1	92.8
Photographic goods and services	16.7	19.7	17.7	15.4	16.6	16.8	16.9
Package tours [2]	3.2	6.7	7.2	9.1	9.9	10.2	11.5

[1] See Table 697. [2] Consists of tour operators' and travel agents' margins. Purchases of travel and accommodations included in tours are accounted for separately in other personal consumption expenditures categories.

Source: U.S. Bureau of Economic Analysis, National Income and Product Accounts, "Table 2.5.5. Personal Consumption Expenditures by Function," <http://www.bea.gov/iTable/index_nipa.cfm>, accessed August 2015.

Table 1242. Performing Arts—Selected Data: 1990 to 2014

[Sales, receipts, and expenditures in millions of dollars (282 represents $282,000,000). For season ending in year shown, except as indicated]

Item	1990	1995	2000	2005	2009	2010	2011	2012	2013	2014
Legitimate theater: [1]										
Broadway shows:										
New productions	40	33	37	39	43	39	42	41	46	42
Attendance (mil.)	8.0	9.0	11.4	11.5	12.1	11.9	12.5	12.3	11.6	12.2
Playing weeks [2,3]	1,070	1,120	1,464	1,494	1,548	1,464	1,588	1,522	1,430	1,496
Gross ticket sales	282	406	603	769	943	1,020	1,081	1,139	1,139	1,269
Broadway road tours: [4]										
Attendance (mil.)	11.1	9.9	11.4	12.9	14.3	15.9	13.1	12.7	13.8	13.9
Playing weeks	944	882	854	1,027	1,112	1,250	1,003	947	983	992
Gross ticket sales	367	547	553	706	881	947	803	811	877	933
Nonprofit professional theatres: [5]										
Companies reporting [6]	185	215	262	1,490	1,825	1,807	1,876	1,782	1,773	1,770
Gross income	308	444	791	1,647	1,779	1,913	2,040	2,026	2,127	2,240
Earned income	188	281	466	845	811	964	1,038	1,058	1,136	1,190
Contributed income	119	163	325	802	968	948	1,002	968	991	1,050
Gross expenses	306	445	708	1,530	1,892	1,870	1,936	1,986	2,051	2,150
Productions	2,265	2,646	3,241	12,000	17,000	16,000	14,600	18,500	21,600	22,000
Performances	46,131	56,608	66,123	169,000	187,000	163,000	177,000	211,000	215,800	216,000
Total attendance (mil.)	15.2	18.6	22.0	32.5	30.0	31.0	34.0	36.7	34.9	32.8
OPERA America professional member companies: [7]										
Number of companies reporting [8]	98	88	98	93	84	97	83	(NA)	(NA)	(NA)
Expenses [8]	321	435	637	742	816	883	688	(NA)	(NA)	(NA)
Performances [8]	2,336	2,120	1,768	1,893	1744	1,677	1,407	(NA)	(NA)	(NA)
Total attendance (mil.) [8,9]	7.5	4.1	6.2	5	4.3	6.8	6.6	(NA)	(NA)	(NA)
Main season attendance (mil.) [8,10]	4.1	3.9	3.8	3.3	2.9	2.2	1.8	(NA)	(NA)	(NA)
Symphony orchestras: [11]										
Concerts	18,931	29,328	33,154	37,196	32,813	35,348	35,968	40,522	(NA)	(NA)
Attendance (mil.)	24.7	30.9	31.7	26.5	25.4	26	26.4	25.6	(NA)	(NA)
Gross revenue	378	536	734	812	969	1,030	1,038	1,006	(NA)	(NA)
Operating expenses	622	859	1,126	1,513	1,864	1,849	1,822	1,923	(NA)	(NA)
Support	258	351	521	626	726	695	820	921	(NA)	(NA)

NA Not available [1] Source: The Broadway League, New York, NY. For season ending in year shown. [2] All shows (new productions and holdovers from previous seasons). [3] Eight performances constitute one playing week. [4] North American Tours include U.S. and Canadian companies. [5] Source: Theatre Communications Group, New York, NY. For years ending on or prior to August 31. [6] Beginning in 2002, nonprofit theatre data is based on survey responses and extrapolated data from IRS Form 990. [7] Source: OPERA America, © 2004, 2005, 2011 Cultural Data Project. © 2001, 2009 OPERA America. For years ending on or prior to August 31. [8] U.S. and Canadian companies for 2009-10; U.S. companies only for all other years. [9] Includes educational performances, outreach, etc. [10] For paid performances. Data for the Metropolitan Opera are not included. [11] Source: League of American Orchestras, New York, NY. For years ending August 31. Prior to 1995, represents 254 U.S. orchestras; beginning 1995, data based on 1,200 orchestras and represents all U.S. orchestras, excluding college/university and youth orchestras.

Source: Compiled from sources listed in footnotes. See also <http://www.livebroadway.com/>; <http://www.tcg.org/>; <http://www.operaamerica.org/>; and <http://www.americanorchestras.org/>.

Table 1243. Arts and Humanities—Selected Federal Aid Programs: 1990 to 2013

[In millions of dollars (170.8 represents $170,800,000), except as indicated. For fiscal year ending September 30. FY2009 and FY2010 include funds from the American Recovery and Reinvestment Act]

Type of fund and program	1990	1995	2000	2005	2009	2010	2011	2012	2013
National Endowment for the Arts:									
Funds available [1]	170.8	152.1	85.2	108.8	186.8	153.1	142.4	125.5	119.6
Program appropriation [2]	152.3	138.1	79.6	99.5	178.1	138.7	125.4	115.2	109.1
Grants awarded (number) [3]	4,252	3,534	1,906	2,161	3,075	2,731	2,425	2,194	2,143
Funds obligated [4,5]	157.6	147.9	83.5	104.4	176.2	141.1	134.2	117.8	113.9
National Endowment for the Humanities:									
Funds available [1]	140.6	152.3	102.6	119.8	134.5	146.6	163.9	155.5	146.1
Program appropriation	114.2	125.7	82.7	99.9	114.7	125.7	113.2	107.8	102.2
Matching funds [6]	26.3	25.7	15.1	15.9	14.3	14.3	14.3	10.7	10.2

[1] Includes other program funds not shown separately. Excludes administrative funds. [2] FY1990–FY1996 include Regular Program Funds, Treasury Funds, Challenge Grant Funds, and Policy, Planning, and Research Funds. FY1997 includes Regular Program Funds, Matching Grant Funds, and Policy, Research and Technology Funds. FY1998–FY 2000 includes Regular Program Funds and Matching Grant Funds. [3] Excludes cooperative agreements and interagency agreements. [4] Includes obligations for new grants, supplemental awards on previous years' grants, cooperative agreements, and interagency agreements. Excludes obligations funded with administrative funds. [5] Beginning with 1997 data, the grantmaking structure changed from discipline-based categories to thematic ones. [6] Represents federal funds obligated only upon receipt or certification by endowment of matching nonfederal gifts. Funds for matching grants are not allocated by program area because they are awarded on a grant-by-grant basis.

Source: U.S. National Endowment for the Arts, unpublished data; and U.S. National Endowment for the Humanities, unpublished data.

Table 1244. Total State Arts Agency Legislative Appropriations: 2014 to 2015

[In thousands of dollars (306,498 represents 306,498,000). For fiscal year ending June 30 in most states. The National Assembly of State Arts Agencies (NASAA) is the membership organization of the nations' state and jurisdictional arts agencies. Legislative appropriations include funds designated to the state arts agency by state legislatures. These include line items, which are not controlled by the agency but passed through to designated entities. State arts agencies also receive monies from other sources including other state funds, the federal government (primarily the National Endowment for the Arts), private funds, and legislative earmarks. Minus sign (-) indicates decrease in spending]

State	Legislative appropriations including line items		Percent change, 2014 to 2015	State	Legislative appropriations including line items		Percent change, 2014 to 2015	State	Legislative appropriations including line items		Percent change, 2014 to 2015
	2014, revised	2015, enacted			2014, revised	2015, enacted			2014, revised	2015, enacted	
U.S. [1]	306,498	353,011	15.2	KS [7]	200	200	–	NC	7,163	7,266	1.4
AL	3,641	3,984	9.4	KY	2,798	2,767	-1.1	ND	755	761	0.8
AK	801	803	0.2	LA	2,085	2,236	7.2	OH	11,349	11,349	–
AZ [2]	1,000	1,000	(NA)	ME	737	766	4.0	OK	4,010	3,790	-5.5
AR [3]	2,041	3,869	89.5	MD	15,440	16,209	5.0	OR	2,188	2,309	5.6
CA [4]	5,925	9,205	55.4	MA	11,082	12,000	8.3	PA	9,065	9,530	5.1
CO	2,000	2,100	5.0	MI	7,000	9,000	28.6	RI	1,647	2,116	28.5
CT	6,318	7,095	12.3	MN	34,189	34,189	–	SC	2,966	3,032	2.2
DE	3,303	3,340	1.1	MS	1,787	1,830	2.4	SD	745	772	3.7
DC [5]	11,754	15,803	34.5	MO	7,468	7,189	-3.7	TN	6,992	7,000	0.1
FL	10,575	47,060	345.0	MT	522	557	6.6	TX	5,582	5,824	4.3
GA	586	597	1.7	NE	1,454	1,507	3.7	UT	4,781	2,576	-46.1
HI [6]	5,161	5,826	12.9	NV	1,280	1,269	-0.9	VT	642	645	0.6
ID	691	702	1.7	NH	347	394	13.4	VA	3,795	3,599	-5.2
IL	10,142	10,109	-0.3	NJ	17,396	16,396	-5.7	WA	1,125	1,093	-2.8
IN	2,832	2,832	–	NM	1,441	1,490	3.4	WV	1,069	911	-14.7
IA	1,234	1,234	–	NY	39,974	39,974	–	WI	780	780	–
								WY	1,169	1,223	4.5

– Represents zero. NA Not available. [1] Includes U.S. territories. [2] Arizona: The agency's FY2014 and FY2015 legislative appropriation is nonrecurring and is drawn from interest on the state's rainy-day fund. [3] Arkansas: $2.225 million of the FY2015 appropriation is in general improvement funds, which may be released at the governor's discretion. The governor released $150,000 in general improvement funds in FY2014. [4] California: $5 million of the agency's FY2015 appropriation are one-time funds from the state's general fund. [5] District of Columbia: The increase is due to a change in how public art funds are allocated to the agency. The agency's public art program was funded through the D.C. capital budget in FY2014. These funds are under local control in FY2015. [6] Hawaii: The agency's FY2015 general fund appropriation is subject to a 5% to 10% restriction. The amount of that restriction will not be finalized until later in the fiscal year. [7] Kansas: The FY2014 and FY2015 amounts reflect new funds appropriated in each year. However, not all appropriated funds were expended by the agency in FY2013. The agency will use $166,477 of FY2013 funds in FY2015.

Source: National Assembly of State Arts Agencies, *State Arts Agency Revenues, Fiscal Year 2015,* February 2015. See also <http://www.nasaa-arts.org/>.

Table 1245. Personal Participation in Various Arts or Creative Activities by Selected Characteristics: 2012

[In percent, except as indicated (235.0 represents 235,000,000). For persons 18 years old and over. Represents creating or performing at least once in the prior 12 months]

Item	Adult population (millions)	Music	Dance	Films/ videos	Photos	Visual Arts	Pottery/ jewelry	Weaving/ sewing[1]	Creative writing
Total............................	**235.0**	**5.0**	**1.3**	**2.8**	**12.4**	**5.7**	**4.5**	**13.2**	**5.9**
Sex:									
Male............................	113.1	5.6	0.9	3.6	11.5	4.7	2.1	2.4	5.6
Female..........................	121.9	4.5	1.6	2.1	13.2	6.7	6.8	23.2	6.2
Race and ethnicity:									
White alone....................	155.7	5.3	1.1	2.9	14.3	6.4	5.1	14.8	6.7
African American alone......	26.8	4.3	1.7	3.0	8.0	3.4	4.2	9.5	4.3
Hispanic........................	35.0	4.1	1.5	2.2	7.9	3.7	2.5	9.4	4.1
Other alone....................	17.5	5.5	1.2	3.2	10.9	6.9	4.5	11.9	5.2
Age:									
18 to 24 years old............	30.4	8.6	2.7	4.5	13.4	9.3	7.1	9.8	10.2
25 to 34 years old............	41.0	5.0	1.0	3.6	15.4	6.0	4.2	10.6	6.4
35 to 44 years old............	39.6	4.2	1.4	4.2	14.0	5.6	4.4	10.8	6.4
45 to 54 years old............	43.7	5.3	1.0	2.5	12.4	5.0	4.6	13.5	4.3
55 to 64 years old............	38.3	4.4	0.9	2.0	11.9	5.7	4.6	15.5	5.3
65 to 74 years old............	23.8	3.0	1.2	1.2	10.0	4.0	3.6	19.0	4.1
75 years old and older.......	18.1	3.8	0.5	0.5	5.3	3.3	2.3	16.5	4.6

[1] Includes weaving, crocheting, knitting, quilting, needlepoint, and sewing.

Source: U.S. National Endowment for the Arts, *A Decade of Arts Engagement: Findings From the Survey of Public Participation in the Arts, 2002–2012*, January 2015. See also <http://arts.gov/publications/decade-arts-engagement-findings-survey-public-participation-arts-2002-2012>.

Table 1246. Attendance/Participation Rates for Various Arts Activities by Selected Characteristics: 2012

[In percent, except as indicated (235.0 represents 235,000,000). For persons 18 years old and over. Represents attendance at least once in the prior twelve months. Excludes elementary and high school performances]

Item	Adult population (million)	Jazz concert	Classical music concert	Musicals	Non- musical plays	Art muse- ums/ galleries	Craft/ visual art festivals	Parks/ historic build- ings[1]	Live book reading or story- telling[2]
Total............................	**235.0**	**8.1**	**8.8**	**15.2**	**8.3**	**21.0**	**22.4**	**23.9**	**4.1**
Sex:									
Male............................	113.1	7.9	8.0	12.9	7.3	18.7	18.2	23.1	3.0
Female..........................	121.9	8.3	9.5	17.3	9.2	23.1	26.4	24.6	5.1
Race and ethnicity:									
White alone....................	155.7	8.4	11.0	18.4	10.1	24.1	26.2	28.3	4.2
African American alone......	26.8	11.2	4.0	9.3	6.2	11.9	12.0	13.1	5.2
Hispanic........................	35.0	5.0	3.3	7.3	3.6	14.3	16.8	13.8	2.5
Other alone....................	17.5	7.4	7.3	11.2	4.9	21.2	16.3	21.2	4.7
Age:									
18 to 24 years old............	30.4	9.2	6.7	13.0	6.4	18.3	18.3	20.5	4.6
25 to 34 years old............	41.0	8.0	7.3	13.6	7.5	22.0	21.6	25.1	5.2
35 to 44 years old............	39.6	7.8	6.4	12.9	7.3	21.2	22.0	23.3	4.8
45 to 54 years old............	43.7	7.9	8.2	16.9	9.5	22.0	24.6	26.2	3.3
55 to 64 years old............	38.3	10.0	11.0	19.0	9.0	22.5	25.8	26.5	4.0
65 to 74 years old............	23.8	7.9	13.9	17.7	10.6	22.4	26.1	25.5	3.6
75 years old and older.......	18.1	3.9	10.9	11.9	7.8	15.5	15.0	15.0	2.2
Education:									
Grade school..................	9.9	0.9	0.9	1.6	0.3	3.6	5.9	3.9	1.2
Some high school.............	19.0	1.3	1.6	2.9	1.8	4.3	8.0	5.9	1.5
High school graduate........	70.9	4.5	3.1	8.3	3.9	9.9	16.3	13.3	1.8
Some college..................	68.7	8.2	7.3	14.6	7.8	19.7	23.6	25.0	4.2
College graduate.............	43.0	13.1	15.9	26.7	14.6	37.2	32.9	38.4	6.6
Graduate school..............	23.5	17.9	26.0	32.1	20.0	49.3	36.9	48.8	9.2
Income:									
Less than $20,000............	40.9	4.8	3.9	6.2	3.8	10.2	12.3	12.1	3.0
$20,000 to $50,000...........	76.0	5.3	5.6	9.6	5.8	14.0	17.9	16.2	3.5
$50,000 to $75,000...........	43.9	8.2	9.2	16.8	7.9	22.1	24.5	25.1	4.4
$75,000 to $100,000..........	27.6	10.2	10.3	20.1	11.6	26.5	28.9	30.1	5.4
$100,000 to $150,000........	27.1	12.6	15.1	24.6	13.5	33.8	30.5	38.8	4.7
$150,000 and over............	19.6	16.3	19.4	32.4	16.6	43.2	36.4	46.6	5.5

[1] Visiting historic parks or monuments or touring buildings or neighborhoods for the historic or design value. [2] Examples include author readings, poetry, or storytelling events.

Source: U.S. National Endowment for the Arts, *A Decade of Arts Engagement: Findings From the Survey of Public Participation in the Arts, 2002–2012*, January 2015. See also <http://arts.gov/publications/decade-arts-engagement-findings-survey-public-participation-arts-2002-2012>.

Table 1247. Attendance at/Participation in Various Leisure Activities Including Reading by Selected Characteristics: 2012

[In percent, except as indicated (235.0 represents 235,000,000). See headnote, Table 1245]

Item	Adult popu-lation (mil.)	Attendance at—			Participation in—		Reading—		
		Movies	Sports events [1]	Film festival	Exercise/ playing sports	Book club/ reading group	Fiction books	Non-fiction books	Litera-ture [2]
Total............................	235.0	59.4	30.3	2.4	45.7	3.5	44.4	42.7	47.0
Sex:									
Male..........................	113.1	58.2	34.7	2.4	47.5	1.9	33.3	36.8	37.0
Female........................	121.9	60.4	26.4	2.5	44.0	5.1	54.5	48.2	56.1
Race and ethnicity:									
White alone..................	155.7	61.6	34.0	2.6	49.3	3.8	59.2	47.0	52.3
African American alone.....	26.8	53.3	21.9	1.6	37.7	5.0	36.8	38.0	40.2
Hispanic......................	35.0	54.8	24.3	2.2	38.5	1.4	26.9	29.0	31.0
Other alone..................	17.5	57.5	21.4	3.1	40.8	2.9	37.9	38.6	41.7
Age:									
18 to 24 years old...........	30.4	75.7	40.7	3.0	58.5	2.8	45.3	39.2	47.9
25 to 34 years old...........	41.0	68.5	36.2	3.0	52.8	3.0	45.0	41.3	47.9
35 to 44 years old...........	39.6	68.3	35.2	2.2	49.3	3.7	42.6	41.3	45.1
45 to 54 years old...........	43.7	59.9	32.2	2.6	44.9	4.0	43.0	41.9	44.7
55 to 64 years old...........	38.3	50.6	24.5	2.4	40.8	3.8	45.4	45.4	48.2
65 to 74 years old...........	23.8	44.1	20.8	2.0	37.2	4.6	48.8	48.6	51.9
75 years old and older.......	18.1	30.6	11.2	1.2	24.1	3.0	40.4	42.6	43.8
Education:									
Grade school.................	9.9	21.6	7.8	1.0	12.2	1.7	12.1	19.2	16.9
Some high school............	19.0	36.7	13.6	0.4	24.1	0.4	21.5	21.2	22.9
High school graduate........	70.9	48.6	22.0	0.9	35.0	2.2	33.1	31.0	36.9
Some college................	68.7	64.9	33.1	2.6	49.2	2.8	49.1	45.7	50.3
College graduate............	43.0	75.3	44.4	3.9	62.6	5.6	60.5	57.3	63.0
Graduate school.............	23.5	76.8	42.2	6.0	68.8	9.2	65.8	68.8	69.5
Income:									
Less than $20,000...........	40.9	39.4	14.5	1.7	31.3	2.3	34.3	35.3	36.5
$20,000 to $50,000..........	76.0	50.3	32.9	1.8	35.4	2.4	37.6	36.7	42.2
$50,000 to $75,000..........	43.9	65.3	33.0	3.1	48.9	4.2	46.6	44.8	47.7
$75,000 to $100,000.........	27.6	74.8	42.4	3.1	56.1	3.9	41.9	39.7	52.8
$100,000 to $150,000........	27.1	73.0	43.9	2.4	63.3	5.3	56.8	51.2	57.0
$150,000 and over...........	19.6	77.9	49.9	3.7	69.4	6.1	61.3	58.6	63.3

[1] Includes amateur or professional sports events. [2] Includes plays, poetry, novels, or short stories.

Source: U.S. National Endowment for the Arts, *A Decade of Arts Engagement: Findings From the Survey of Public Participation in the Arts, 2002–2012*, January 2015. See also <http://arts.gov/publications/decade-arts-engagement-findings-survey-public-participation-arts-2002-2012>.

Table 1248. Household Pet Ownership: 2011

[In percent, except as indicated (69.9 represents 69,900,000). Based on a sample survey of 50,347 households in 2012]

Item	Unit	Dogs	Cats	Birds	Horses
2011: Total companion pet population [1]............................	**Million**	**69.9**	**74.1**	**8.3**	**4.9**
Number of households owning pets............................	Million	43.3	36.1	3.7	1.8
Percent of households owning companion pets [1]......................	Percent	36.5	30.4	3.1	1.5
Average number owned per household........................	Number	1.6	2.1	2.3	2.7
PERCENT OF HOUSEHOLDS OWNING PETS					
Annual household income:					
Under $20,000................................	Percent	34.5	34.1	4.3	1.4
$20,000 to $34,999...........................	Percent	40.0	36.8	4.0	2.1
$35,000 to $54,999...........................	Percent	42.4	35.6	3.9	1.9
$55,000 to $84,999...........................	Percent	43.8	34.0	3.3	1.9
$85,000 and over............................	Percent	43.9	31.7	3.1	1.9
Household size: [1]					
One person..................................	Percent	26.8	29.8	2.6	1.3
Two persons.................................	Percent	40.1	34.6	3.2	1.8
Three persons...............................	Percent	50.0	38.3	4.2	2.2
Four persons................................	Percent	53.7	34.9	4.3	2.0
Five or more persons.........................	Percent	54.2	38.1	6.8	2.6
VETERINARY CARE AND EXPENDITURES					
Households obtaining veterinary care [2]................................	Percent	81.3	55.1	12.4	53.8
Average visits per household per year....................	Number	2.6	1.6	0.3	1.9
Expenditures per household per year (mean).........................	Dollars	378	191	33	373
Expenditures per animal (mean)............................	Dollars	227	90	14	133

[1] As of December 31, 2011. [2] During the year.

Source: American Veterinary Medical Association, Schaumburg, IL, *U.S. Pet Ownership and Demographics Sourcebook, 2012*, ©. See also <http://www.avma.org/reference/marketstats/sourcebook.asp>.

Table 1249. Adult Participation in Selected Leisure Activities by Frequency: 2014

[In thousands (18,336 represents 18,336,000), except percent. For Fall 2014. Percent is based on total projected population of 238,128,000. Based on sample and subject to sampling error; see source]

| Activity | Participated in the last 12 months [1] | | Frequency of participation | | | | | | | |
| | | | Two or more times a week | | Once a week | | Two to three times a month | | Once a month | |
	Number (1,000)	Percent	Number (1,000)	Percent	Number (1,000)	Percent	Number (1,000)	Percent	Number (1,000)	Percent
Adult education courses	18,336	7.70	4,306	1.81	1,850	0.78	908	0.38	1,534	0.64
Aquarium attendance	12,020	5.05	88	(Z)	116	0.05	180	0.08	508	0.21
Attend auto shows	13,512	5.67	198	0.08	234	0.10	397	0.17	833	0.35
Attend art galleries or shows	16,640	6.99	152	0.06	153	0.06	783	0.33	1,621	0.68
Attend classical music/opera performances	9,232	3.88	133	0.06	48	(Z)	327	0.14	1,011	0.42
Attend country music performances	14,617	6.14	162	0.07	91	(Z)	311	0.13	714	0.30
Attend dance performances	9,347	3.93	69	(Z)	201	0.08	348	0.15	533	0.22
Attend horse races	5,827	2.45	146	0.06	135	0.06	149	0.06	385	0.16
Attend other music performances [2]	23,955	10.06	282	0.12	378	0.16	1,000	0.42	2,427	1.02
Attend rock music performances	20,308	8.53	149	0.06	105	(Z)	687	0.29	1,392	0.58
Baking	56,750	23.83	8,523	3.58	8,976	3.77	11,593	4.87	9,159	3.85
Barbecuing	68,793	28.89	8,818	3.70	11,356	4.77	14,905	6.26	9,621	4.04
Billiards/pool	17,653	7.41	1,348	0.57	893	0.38	1,696	0.71	1,838	0.77
Bird watching	10,580	4.44	4,585	1.93	682	0.29	633	0.27	627	0.26
Board games	32,573	13.68	2,061	0.87	3,091	1.30	6,290	2.64	5,608	2.36
Book clubs	6,800	2.86	222	0.09	470	0.20	383	0.16	2,495	1.05
Chess	7,209	3.03	537	0.23	431	0.18	708	0.30	907	0.38
Concerts on radio	5,766	2.42	806	0.34	577	0.24	601	0.25	402	0.17
Cooking for fun	54,503	22.89	20,662	8.68	8,200	3.44	7,751	3.25	3,625	1.52
Crossword puzzles	24,479	10.28	9,970	4.19	2,940	1.23	2,367	0.99	1,633	0.69
Dance/go dancing	18,370	7.71	2,269	0.95	1,107	0.46	1,863	0.78	2,719	1.14
Dining out	107,943	45.33	19,910	8.36	23,391	9.82	26,524	11.14	13,895	5.84
Entertain friends or relatives at home	86,114	36.16	7,033	2.95	9,907	4.16	17,726	7.44	18,694	7.85
Fantasy sports league	10,310	4.33	2,985	1.25	1,759	0.74	562	0.24	667	0.28
Furniture refinishing	8,115	3.41	216	0.09	168	0.07	377	0.16	812	0.34
Go to bars/night clubs	40,708	17.10	2,816	1.18	3,817	1.60	6,516	2.74	6,905	2.90
Go to beach	61,473	25.82	2,412	1.01	2,233	0.94	5,595	2.35	6,135	2.58
Go to live theater	31,004	13.02	407	0.17	562	0.24	1,506	0.63	3,488	1.46
Go to museums	29,091	12.22	104	(Z)	368	0.15	837	0.35	2,514	1.06
Home decoration and furnishing	21,992	9.24	1,169	0.49	924	0.39	2,026	0.85	3,978	1.67
Karaoke	7,964	3.34	433	0.18	303	0.13	486	0.20	867	0.36
Painting, drawing	14,337	6.02	2,522	1.06	1,575	0.66	1,533	0.64	1,180	0.50
PC/computer games (play online with software)	17,384	7.30	8,867	3.72	1,444	0.61	992	0.42	627	0.26
PC/computer games (play online without software)	22,535	9.46	12,969	5.45	1,861	0.78	1,437	0.60	558	0.23
PC/computer games (play offline with software)	15,672	6.58	7,434	3.12	1,655	0.69	1,389	0.58	597	0.25
Photo album/scrap book	12,375	5.20	665	0.28	565	0.24	1,124	0.47	1,995	0.84
Photography	23,369	9.81	4,685	1.97	2,409	1.01	3,818	1.60	3,210	1.35
Picnic	24,824	10.42	524	0.22	793	0.33	1,413	0.59	2,899	1.22
Play bingo	9,061	3.81	665	0.28	567	0.24	654	0.27	1,089	0.46
Play cards	36,501	15.33	4,271	1.79	4,018	1.69	5,045	2.12	5,369	2.25
Play musical instrument	15,631	6.56	5,517	2.32	1,678	0.70	1,377	0.58	1,275	0.54
Reading books	80,795	33.93	44,397	18.64	6,924	2.91	6,702	2.81	5,572	2.34
Reading comic books	6,733	2.83	1,407	0.59	592	0.25	674	0.28	620	0.26
Sudoku puzzles	22,650	9.51	7,404	3.11	2,647	1.11	2,149	0.90	1,971	0.83
Trivia games	11,734	4.93	2,362	0.99	1,116	0.47	1,015	0.43	1,284	0.54
Video/electronic games (console)	23,885	10.03	9,327	3.92	2,866	1.20	2,433	1.02	1,537	0.65
Video/electronic games (portable)	10,859	4.56	4,762	2.00	670	0.28	847	0.36	471	0.20
Woodworking	9,358	3.93	1,371	0.58	861	0.36	1,172	0.49	1,159	0.49
Word games	23,382	9.82	9,663	4.06	1,942	0.82	2,556	1.07	1,584	0.67
Zoo attendance	27,377	11.50	151	0.06	175	0.07	640	0.27	1,269	0.53

Z Represents less than 0.05. [1] Includes those participating less than once a month not shown separately. [2] Excluding country and rock.

Source: GfK US, LLC, the GfK MRI Division ©. See also <http://www.gfkmri.com/>.

Table 1250. Selected Recreational Activities: 1990 to 2014

[18,719 represents 18,719,000]

Activity	Unit	1990	2000	2005	2010	2011	2012	2013	2014
Golf facilities [1]	Number	12,846	15,489	16,052	15,890	15,753	15,619	15,516	15,372
Tennis players: [2]	1,000	(NA)	(NA)	(NA)	18,719	17,772	17,020	17,678	17,904
Skiing: [3]									
Skier visits [4]	Million	50.0	52.2	56.9	59.8	60.5	51.0	56.9	56.5
Operating resorts	Number	591	503	492	471	486	475	478	470
Boating: [5]									
People participating in recreational boating [6]	Million	67.4	67.5	57.9	75.0	82.7	87.8	88.5	87.3
Retail expenditures on boating [7]	Mil. dol.	13,731	27,065	37,317	30,434	32,271	35,591	36,736	(NA)
Recreational boats in use by boat type [8]	Million	16.0	16.8	17.7	16.5	16.0	16.0	15.8	15.8
Outboard	Million	(NA)	8.3	8.5	8.1	8.0	7.9	7.9	7.9
Inboard	Million	(NA)	1.0	1.1	1.1	1.0	1.1	1.1	1.0
Sterndrive	Million	(NA)	1.6	1.7	1.5	1.5	1.4	1.4	1.4
Personal watercraft	Million	(NA)	1.2	1.2	1.3	1.3	1.3	1.3	1.2
Sailboat	Million	(NA)	1.6	1.6	1.6	1.6	1.6	1.5	1.6
Other	Million	(NA)	3.1	3.6	3.0	2.6	2.7	2.7	2.8

NA Not available. [1] Source: National Golf Foundation, Jupiter, FL. [2] Source: Tennis Industry Association, Hilton Head, SC. Based on a nationwide telephone survey of households, in which all household members ages 6 and up are enumerated with data on tennis participation collected for each person. Data prior to 2007 is not available due to new methodology being implemented after 2007. [3] Source: National Ski Areas Association, Lakewood, CO. ©. [4] Represents one person visiting a ski area for all or any part of a day or night, and includes full-and half-day, night, complimentary, adult, child, season, and other types of tickets. Data are estimated and are for the season ending in the year shown. [5] Source: National Marine Manufacturers Association, Chicago, IL. ©. [6] People participating is now measured as adults 18 years and older. [7] Represents estimated expenditures for new and used boats, motors and engines, accessories, safety equipment, fuel, insurance, docking, maintenance, launching, storage, repairs, and other expenses. [8] 2011 data are estimated.

Source: Compiled from sources listed in footnotes.

Table 1251. Amusement Park Attendance at Top 15 U.S. Facilities: 2010 to 2014

[In thousands (109,321 represents 109,321,000). Covers gated commercial theme parks, amusement parks, and water parks with annual attendance of one million or more]

Park name	Location	Attendance				
		2010	2011	2012	2013	2014
Total Top 15	(X)	**109,321**	**112,509**	**116,420**	**119,951**	**123,039**
Magic Kingdom, Walt Disney World	Lake Buena Vista, FL	16,972	17,142	17,536	18,588	19,332
Disneyland	Anaheim, CA	15,980	16,140	15,963	16,202	16,769
EPCOT, Walt Disney World	Lake Buena Vista, FL	10,825	10,825	11,063	11,229	11,454
Disney's Animal Kingdom	Lake Buena Vista, FL	9,886	9,783	9,998	10,198	10,402
Disney's Hollywood Studios	Lake Buena Vista, FL	9,603	9,699	9,912	10,110	10,312
Disney's California Adventure	Anaheim, CA	6,278	6,341	7,775	8,514	8,769
Universal Studios Florida	Orlando, FL	5,925	6,044	6,195	7,062	8,263
Universal's Islands of Adventure	Orlando, FL	5,949	7,674	7,981	8,141	8,141
Universal Studios Hollywood	Universal City, CA	5,040	5,141	5,912	6,148	6,824
SeaWorld Florida	Orlando, FL	5,100	5,202	5,358	5,090	4,683
Busch Gardens	Tampa, FL	4,200	4,284	4,348	4,087	4,128
SeaWorld California	San Diego, CA	3,800	4,294	4,444	4,311	3,794
Knotts Berry Farm	Buena Park, CA	3,600	3,654	3,508	3,683	3,683
Cedar Point	Sandusky, OH	3,051	3,143	3,221	3,382	3,247
Kings Island	Kings Island, OH	3,112	3,143	3,206	3,206	3,238

X Not applicable.

Source: Themed Entertainment Association and AECOM, *2014 Theme Index: Global Attractions Attendance Report* ©, and previous reports. See also <http://www.teaconnect.org/> and <http://www.aecom.com/What+We+Do/Economics>.

Table 1252. Reading in Print, Electronic, and Audio Formats Among Adults: 2013

[In percent. Data shown for adults aged 18 years and older who read at least one book in the formats shown during 2013. Based on a telephone survey conducted January 2-5, 2014 among a nationally representative sample of 1,005 adults]

Characteristic	Total	Print	E-book	Audio-book	Characteristic	Total	Print	E-book	Audio-book
Total	**76**	**69**	**28**	**14**	EDUCATION				
					High school graduate or less	64	57	14	10
SEX					Some college	83	78	32	15
Men	69	64	23	14	College graduate	88	78	45	21
Women	82	74	33	15					
					HOUSEHOLD INCOME				
RACE/ETHNICITY					Less than $30,000	68	63	14	12
White	76	71	29	14	$30,000 to $49,999	75	70	28	16
Black	81	75	30	19	$50,000 to $74,999	85	78	42	19
Hispanic	67	56	16	14	$75,000 and higher	83	74	46	14
AGE					METRO STATUS				
18 to 29 years	79	73	37	15	Urban	77	71	29	15
30 to 49 years	75	66	32	16	Suburban	75	67	31	14
50 to 64 years	77	71	27	16	Rural	76	72	18	14
65 years and older	70	66	12	10					

Source: Pew Research Center, *E-Reading Rises as Device Ownership Jumps*, January 2014 ©. See also <http://pewinternet.org/Reports/2014/E-Reading-Update.aspx>.

Table 1253. Leisure Time Use on Weekends and Holidays by Type of Activity and Selected Demographic Characteristics: 2014

[Data are based on interviews of approximately 11,600 individuals 15 years old and over who reported their activities for one 24-hour period. Respondents engaging in more than one activity at a time reported only their primary activity; except for child care, secondary activities were not reported]

Selected Characteristics	Average hours per day spent on all leisure and sports activities			Percent distribution of leisure time on weekends and holidays						
	All days (hours)	Week-days (hours)	Weekends and holidays (hours)	Sports, exercise, recreation	Socializing, communicating	Watching TV	Reading	Relaxing, thinking	Playing games, using computers for leisure	Other[1]
Total, 15 years old and over	**5.30**	**4.79**	**6.50**	**5.1**	**15.7**	**51.5**	**5.4**	**4.8**	**8.0**	**9.5**
Sex:										
Men	5.71	5.11	7.10	6.2	14.1	52.5	4.1	4.6	9.6	8.9
Women	4.93	4.50	5.93	3.9	17.5	50.4	6.9	4.7	6.4	10.3
Age:										
15 to 19 years	5.74	5.26	6.85	9.3	13.1	42.9	2.0	2.6	18.1	11.8
20 to 24 years	5.45	5.07	6.38	7.4	19.4	43.4	2.7	2.0	14.4	10.7
25 to 34 years	4.34	3.70	5.83	6.7	19.7	45.1	2.1	4.8	9.3	12.3
35 to 44 years	4.10	3.50	5.52	6.3	19.2	50.7	3.4	4.0	5.4	10.7
45 to 54 years	4.75	4.13	6.19	4.5	16.8	53.8	4.5	5.2	6.5	8.7
55 to 64 years	5.45	4.93	6.70	3.4	13.0	57.5	6.9	4.8	5.8	8.7
65 to 74 years	6.94	6.60	7.72	3.1	12.4	56.7	9.3	5.1	5.4	8.0
75 years and over	8.02	7.89	8.31	1.7	10.7	57.3	12.3	8.3	4.8	5.1
Race/ethnicity:										
White	5.27	4.76	6.47	5.3	15.6	51.0	5.9	4.3	8.0	9.7
Black	5.90	5.45	6.96	3.3	15.4	56.8	1.9	7.0	7.0	8.6
Asian	4.38	3.70	5.70	6.1	18.6	45.3	7.0	5.4	8.6	8.8
Hispanic origin	4.63	4.10	5.93	4.9	20.7	51.1	1.7	5.1	6.1	10.3
Employment status:										
Employed	4.26	3.62	5.79	6.2	17.4	48.5	4.3	4.7	7.4	11.4
Full-time workers	4.05	3.32	5.80	6.2	17.9	48.1	4.3	4.8	6.7	11.7
Part-time workers	5.03	4.71	5.75	6.1	15.7	49.9	4.7	3.8	9.9	9.9
Not employed	6.93	6.64	7.60	3.8	13.6	55.1	6.6	4.9	8.8	7.4
Weekly earnings:[2]										
$0 - $560	4.49	3.88	5.84	3.6	19.3	49.0	2.1	5.1	8.2	12.5
$561 - $850	4.18	3.35	6.13	6.2	17.0	49.8	4.2	4.6	8.2	10.1
$851 - $1,345	4.00	3.25	6.01	6.7	17.8	49.3	4.5	5.3	4.3	12.3
$1,346 and higher	3.96	3.10	5.95	8.4	17.3	46.9	5.4	3.7	6.4	11.8
Presence and age of children:										
No household children under 18	5.90	5.43	7.00	4.6	13.9	53.0	6.3	4.9	8.7	8.7
Household children under 18	4.29	3.72	5.64	6.2	19.7	48.4	3.4	4.3	6.7	11.2
Children 13 to 17 years, none younger	4.94	4.36	6.32	5.9	16.1	51.9	4.3	3.8	6.8	11.2
Children 6 to 12 years, none younger	4.27	3.60	5.84	6.5	20.2	46.1	3.8	4.1	7.7	11.6
Youngest child under 6 years	3.96	3.47	5.12	6.3	21.3	48.4	2.5	4.9	5.9	10.9
Educational attainment, 25 years and over:										
Less than a high school diploma	6.25	5.85	7.12	3.9	13.5	60.5	2.4	10.5	2.8	6.3
High school graduates, no college	5.73	5.31	6.76	2.8	13.5	58.4	5.6	5.2	5.9	8.7
Some college or associate degree	5.16	4.59	6.43	4.0	15.9	53.5	5.3	4.2	7.9	8.9
Bachelor's degree and higher	4.56	3.93	6.05	6.6	18.2	45.3	8.3	4.0	6.6	10.9

[1] Includes other leisure and sports activities, not elsewhere classified, and travel related to leisure and sports activities. [2] These values are based on usual weekly earnings. The earnings data are limited to wage and salary workers (both incorporated and unincorporated self-employed workers are excluded). Each earnings range represents approximately 25 percent of full-time wage and salary workers who held only one job.

Source: U.S. Bureau of Labor Statistics, *American Time Use Survey, 2014*, Bulletin USDL-15-1236, June 2015. See also <http://www.bls.gov/tus/>.

Table 1254. Characteristics of Selected Spectator Sports: 1990 to 2014

[54,824 represents 54,824,000]

Sport	Unit	1990	1995	2000	2005	2010	2011	2012	2013	2014
Baseball, major leagues: [1]										
Regular season attendance........	1,000	54,824	50,469	72,749	74,926	73,054	73,416	74,859	74,028	73,730
National League..................	1,000	24,492	25,110	39,851	41,644	40,890	40,741	41,475	39,437	39,246
American League...............	1,000	30,332	25,359	32,898	33,282	32,164	32,675	33,384	34,591	34,484
Playoffs attendance [2]............	1,000	479	533	1,314	1,191	1,210	1,745	1,476	1,424	1,127
World Series attendance..........	1,000	209	286	277	168	244	343	170	258	291
Players' salaries: [3]										
Average...................	$1,000	598	1,111	1,896	2,476	3,015	3,095	(NA)	(NA)	(NA)
Basketball: [4,5]										
NCAA—Men's college:										
Teams......................	Number	768	866	937	984	1,027	1,030	1,040	1,050	(NA)
Attendance....................	1,000	28,741	28,225	28,949	30,940	32,632	32,781	32,869	32,510	(NA)
NCAA—Women's college:										
Teams......................	Number	782	864	958	1,018	1,048	1,055	1,055	1,069	(NA)
Attendance [6]...................	1000	2,777	4,962	8,825	9,903	11,160	11,211	11,339	11,182	(NA)
NCAA—Men's college: [5] football:										
Teams......................	Number	534	600	624	618	644	638	644	657	655
Attendance....................	1000	35,330	35,638	39,059	43,487	49,671	49,699	48,959	50,291	49,073
National Hockey League: [7]										
Regular season attendance........	1,000	12,580	9,234	18,800	(NA)	20,996	20,928	12,793	21,759	21,533
Playoffs attendance.............	1,000	1,356	1,329	1,525	(NA)	1,702	1,592	1,632	1,776	1,701
Professional rodeo: [8]										
Rodeos.....................	Number	754	739	688	662	570	572	591	611	607
Performances.................	Number	2,159	2,217	2,081	1,940	1,671	1,669	1,663	1,686	1,652
Members....................	Number	5,693	6,894	6,255	6,127	5,323	5,137	5,138	5,071	4,898
Permit-holders...............	Number	3,290	3,835	3,249	2,701	1,881	1,883	1,939	1,912	1,793
Total prize money..................	Mil. dol.	18.2	24.5	32.3	36.6	39.9	38.8	39.3	39.6	41.1

NA Not available. [1] Source: Major League Baseball (previously, The National League of Professional Baseball Clubs), New York, NY, ©. National League Green Book ©, and The American League of Professional Baseball Clubs, New York, NY, American League Red Book ©. [2] Beginning 1995, two rounds of playoffs were played. Prior years had one round. [3] Source: Major League Baseball Players Association, New York, NY. ©. [4] Season beginning in year shown. [5] Source: National Collegiate Athletic Association, Indianapolis, IN ©. [6] Attendance for women's basketball includes doubleheaders with men's teams beginning with the 1997 season, if attendance was taken by halftime of the women's game. [7] For season ending in year shown. Source: National Hockey League, Montreal, Quebec. ©. In September 2004, franchise owners locked out their players upon the expiration of the collective bargaining agreement. The entire season was cancelled in February 2005. [8] Source: Professional Rodeo Cowboys Association, Colorado Springs, CO, Official Professional Rodeo Media Guide, annual ©.

Source: Compiled from sources listed in footnotes

Table 1255. Adult Attendance at Sports Events by Frequency: 2014

[In thousands (189 represents 189,000), except percent. For Fall 2014. Percent is based on total projected population of 238,128,000. Data not comparable to previous years. Based on a survey and subject to sampling error; see source]

Event	Attend regularly		Attend on occasion		Event	Attend regularly		Attend on occasion	
	Num-ber (1,000)	Per-cent	Num-ber (1,000)	Per-cent		Num-ber (1,000)	Per-cent	Num-ber (1,000)	Per-cent
Alpine skiing and ski jumping...	189	0.08	548	0.23	Greyhound racing.............	79	0.03	390	0.16
Auto racing – NASCAR........	257	0.11	3,181	1.34	Gymnastics..................	258	0.11	639	0.27
Auto racing – other.............	433	0.18	1,981	0.83	High school sports.............	5,426	2.28	10,540	4.43
Baseball:					Ice hockey:				
College.....................	433	0.18	2,091	0.88	NHL regular season..........	737	0.31	4,706	1.98
Professional (MLB)...........	1,776	0.75	17,088	7.18	NHL playoffs and Stanley Cup finals..........	250	0.10	1,163	0.49
Basketball:					Lacrosse (MLL)...............	119	0.05	343	0.14
College.....................	1,117	0.47	4,963	2.08	Marathon, triathlon & other				
Professional (NBA, WNBA)...	661	0.28	4,217	1.77	endurance events............	334	0.14	1,333	0.56
Beach volleyball –					Mixed martial arts (MMA).....	110	0.05	748	0.31
professional...................	128	0.05	327	0.14	Motorcycle racing...........	325	0.14	1,016	0.43
Bicycle racing.................	225	0.09	674	0.28	Olympics – Summer..........	176	0.07	536	0.22
Bowling.....................	426	0.18	1,025	0.43	Olympics – Winter...........	144	0.06	413	0.17
Boxing......................	179	0.08	698	0.29	Poker........................	34	0.01	115	0.05
Bull riding – professional.......	181	0.08	770	0.32	Rodeo.......................	203	0.09	1,433	0.60
Equestrian events.............	206	0.09	851	0.36	Soccer:				
Extreme sports – Summer.....	144	0.06	324	0.14	MLS......................	228	0.10	1,192	0.50
Extreme sports – Winter........	107	0.04	327	0.14	World Cup.................	216	0.09	567	0.24
Figure skating................	71	0.03	286	0.12	Tennis:				
Fishing......................	475	0.20	1,303	0.55	Men's....................	159	0.07	699	0.29
Football:					Women's..................	174	0.07	594	0.25
College.....................	2,452	1.03	9,929	4.17	Track & field.................	303	0.13	1,167	0.49
Professional (NFL) Monday					Truck and tractor				
or Thursday night games....	853	0.36	4,304	1.81	pull/ mud racing...........	229	0.10	926	0.39
NFL weekend games.........	982	0.41	7,177	3.01	Weightlifting.................	120	0.05	303	0.13
NFL playoffs/Super Bowl......	444	0.19	2,360	0.99	Wrestling:				
Golf:					WWE.....................	186	0.08	1,186	0.50
PGA........................	179	0.08	1,608	0.68	Other professional...........	116	0.05	447	0.19
LPGA.......................	72	0.03	519	0.22					
Other........................	169	0.07	509	0.21					

Source: GfK US, LLC, the GfK MRI Division ©. See also <http://www.gfkmri.com>.

Table 1256. Participation in NCAA Sports by Sex: 2013/14

[For the academic year]

Sport	Males			Females		
	Teams	Athletes	Average squad	Teams	Athletes	Average squad
Total.	**9,012**	**271,055**	**(X)**	**10,322**	**207,814**	**(X)**
Archery [1]	(X)	(X)	(X)	(X)	(X)	(X)
Badminton [1]	(X)	(X)	(X)	(X)	(X)	(X)
Baseball	943	33,431	35.5	(X)	(X)	(X)
Basketball	1,081	18,320	16.9	1,101	16,319	14.8
Bowling	(X)	(X)	(X)	61	575	9.4
Cross country [2]	982	14,218	14.5	1,061	15,922	15.0
Equestrian [1,2]	9	21	2.3	49	1,538	31.4
Fencing [2]	34	644	18.9	42	673	16.0
Field hockey	(X)	(X)	(X)	270	5,902	21.9
Football	664	71,291	107.4	(X)	(X)	(X)
Golf [2]	824	8,654	10.5	631	5,076	8.0
Gymnastics	17	370	21.8	82	1,513	18.5
Ice hockey	138	3,976	28.8	90	2,140	23.8
Lacrosse	339	12,682	37.4	443	10,330	23.3
Rifle [2]	27	203	7.5	34	194	5.7
Rowing	58	2,423	41.8	145	7,688	53.0
Rugby [1,2]	1	49	49.0	6	204	34
Sailing [1,2]	24	465	19.4	(X)	(X)	(X)
Sand volleyball [1]	(X)	(X)	(X)	39	611	15.7
Skiing [2]	32	450	14.1	34	447	13.1
Soccer	818	23,602	28.9	1,022	26,358	25.8
Softball	(X)	(X)	(X)	997	19,047	19.1
Squash [1]	31	493	15.9	29	399	13.8
Swimming/diving [2]	421	9,630	22.9	539	12,333	22.9
Synchronized swimming [1]	(X)	(X)	(X)	2	41	20.5
Tennis	766	8,081	10.5	931	9,028	9.7
Track, indoor [2]	670	24,785	37.0	754	25,876	34.3
Track, outdoor [2]	754	27,514	36.5	835	27,752	33.2
Volleyball	109	1,720	15.8	1,064	16,647	15.6
Water polo	44	1,051	23.9	61	1,201	19.7
Wrestling	226	6,982	30.9	(X)	(X)	(X)

X Not applicable. [1] Sport recognized by the NCAA but does not have an NCAA championship. [2] Co-ed sport.

Source: The National Collegiate Athletic Association (NCAA), Indianapolis, IN, *NCAA Sports Sponsorship and Participation Rates Report* ©. See also <http://www.ncaapublications.com/>.

Table 1257. Participation in High School Athletic Programs by Sex: 1980 to 2015

[For academic years. Data based on number of state associations reporting and may underrepresent the number of schools with and participants in athletic programs]

Year	Participants [1]		Sex and sport	Most popular sports, 2014–2015 [2]	
	Males	Females		Schools	Participants
1980–81	3,503,124	1,853,789	**MALE**		
1985–86	3,344,275	1,807,121	Football (11-player)	14,154	1,083,617
1990–91	3,406,355	1,892,316	Track & field (outdoor)	16,358	578,632
1991–92	3,429,853	1,940,801	Basketball	18,072	541,479
1992–93	3,416,389	1,997,489	Baseball	15,899	486,567
1993–94	3,472,967	2,130,315	Soccer	11,838	432,569
1994–95	3,536,359	2,240,461	Wrestling	10,597	258,208
1995–96	3,634,052	2,367,936	Cross country	14,635	250,981
1996–97	3,706,225	2,474,043	Tennis	9,725	157,240
1997–98	3,763,120	2,570,333	Golf	13,528	148,823
1998–99	3,832,352	2,652,726	Swimming & diving	7,156	137,087
1999–00	3,861,749	2,675,874			
2000–01	3,921,069	2,784,154			
2001–02	3,960,517	2,806,998			
2002–03	3,988,738	2,856,358	**FEMALE**		
2003–04	4,038,253	2,865,299	Track & field (outdoor)	16,309	478,726
2004–05	4,110,319	2,908,390	Volleyball	15,534	432,176
2005–06	4,206,549	2,953,355	Basketball	17,653	429,504
2006–07	4,321,103	3,021,807	Soccer	11,502	375,681
2007–08	4,372,115	3,057,266	Softball (fast pitch)	15,115	364,103
2008–09	4,422,662	3,114,091	Cross country	14,287	221,616
2009–10	4,455,740	3,172,637	Tennis	10,099	182,876
2010–11	4,494,406	3,173,549	Swimming & diving	7,526	166,838
2011–12	4,484,987	3,207,533	Competitive spirit squads	5,358	125,763
2012–13	4,490,854	3,222,723	Lacrosse	2,446	84,785
2013–14	4,527,994	3,267,664			
2014–15	4,519,312	3,287,735			

[1] A participant is counted in each sport participated in. [2] Ten most popular sports for each gender, ranked by number of participants.

Source: National Federation of State High School Associations, Indianapolis, IN, *The 2014–2015 High School Athletics Participation Survey* ©. Reprinted with permission of the National Federation of State High School Associations. See also <http://www.nfhs.org/>.

Table 1258. Participants in Selected Sports Activities: 2013

[In thousands (288,012 represents 288,012,000). Data are based on an online survey of 40,000 individuals. The questionnaire asked the heads of households and up to three other household members who were at least seven years of age to indicate their age, the sports in which they participated in 2013, and the number of days of participation in 2013. A participant is defined as an individual seven years of age or older who participates in a sport more than once a year; selected fitness activities required participation of 6 or more days during 2013. See source for methodology]

Activity	Total (Number)	Sex		Age (years)								Household income (dollars)						
		Male	Female	7-17	18-24	25-34	35-44	45-54	55-64	65-74	75 and over	Under 25,000	25,000-34,999	35,000-49,999	50,000-74,999	75,000-99,999	100,000-149,999	150,000 and over
Total persons age 7 and older	288,012	141,210	146,802	45,868	31,616	42,654	40,847	44,630	38,901	24,181	19,316	67,021	37,026	39,757	50,661	33,064	34,360	26,123
Aerobic exercising [1]	44,096	12,431	31,665	3,788	5,482	9,534	8,503	6,487	5,185	3,092	2,024	6,773	4,514	4,904	7,568	5,815	7,783	6,739
Archery, target	8,251	5,038	3,213	2,506	1,509	1,190	1,266	1,006	531	220	22	1,279	981	1,110	1,553	1,592	917	819
Backpacking [2]	12,249	6,724	5,526	2,301	1,664	2,594	2,897	1,430	931	379	54	1,787	1,073	1,456	2,497	1,803	2,246	1,389
Baseball	11,675	8,581	3,094	5,276	1,454	1,856	1,535	948	481	125	–	1,982	852	1,662	1,974	1,572	1,972	1,661
Basketball	25,545	17,732	7,814	10,332	4,513	4,397	3,458	1,916	779	151	–	5,275	2,869	3,347	4,369	2,895	4,118	2,674
Bicycle riding [1]	35,619	18,390	17,229	10,097	3,260	4,808	5,587	4,743	4,173	2,146	806	6,653	3,258	3,940	6,215	4,406	5,887	5,260
Billiards/Pool	19,540	11,139	8,401	1,849	3,548	4,708	3,708	3,147	1,679	640	263	3,956	2,345	2,666	3,879	2,167	2,474	2,052
Boating, motor/power	13,111	7,615	5,496	1,731	1,314	2,345	1,839	2,462	1,978	948	494	1,396	1,037	1,463	2,482	1,826	2,720	2,188
Bowling	35,200	17,458	17,742	8,355	5,414	7,091	5,638	4,142	2,724	1,151	685	6,312	3,736	4,646	6,623	4,733	6,019	3,130
Camping [3]	39,285	19,810	19,475	8,062	4,141	6,481	7,028	5,983	4,161	2,159	1,271	7,010	5,100	5,119	7,659	5,860	5,437	3,101
Cheerleading	3,539	577	2,963	2,371	486	314	271	97	–	–	–	376	345	497	730	540	597	454
Dart throwing	9,760	5,360	4,400	1,140	1,319	2,529	2,041	1,562	866	229	73	2,285	1,029	1,278	1,909	1,237	1,133	888
Exercise walking [1]	96,254	35,505	60,748	6,785	7,771	14,173	14,928	17,696	16,550	11,291	7,059	19,062	11,898	11,987	16,813	11,691	13,674	11,129
Exercise with equipment [1]	53,102	23,000	30,099	2,727	7,758	10,256	8,857	8,182	7,229	4,748	3,294	8,510	6,066	6,239	9,041	7,036	8,561	7,649
Fishing, fresh water	27,021	16,770	10,251	4,953	2,472	4,673	4,550	4,355	3,354	1,973	692	4,367	4,011	3,606	5,409	3,551	3,498	2,579
Fishing, salt water	9,511	6,304	3,208	1,464	1,039	1,473	1,408	1,704	1,325	734	364	1,373	1,245	1,251	2,036	1,203	1,058	1,344
Football, tackle	7,514	6,757	757	4,871	998	910	450	214	72	–	–	1,526	936	1,199	1,292	996	866	699
Golf	18,920	13,503	5,418	2,073	1,889	3,122	2,951	3,047	2,911	2,010	916	1,477	1,521	2,025	3,333	2,819	4,131	3,613
Gymnastics	5,119	1,539	3,580	3,136	370	699	431	246	187	45	4	496	437	908	1,001	611	1,057	609
Hiking	39,370	18,314	21,056	4,953	4,160	7,442	7,142	6,645	5,026	2,917	1,085	5,867	4,317	4,831	7,498	5,250	6,853	4,754
Hockey, ice	3,471	2,537	935	1,105	721	698	403	454	89	–	–	311	192	378	736	448	518	888
Hunting with bow & arrow	5,671	4,536	1,139	669	749	1,254	995	1,146	644	190	25	588	738	737	1,274	994	809	531
Hunting with firearms	16,312	13,173	3,139	2,081	1,676	2,607	2,433	3,145	2,530	1,285	555	2,253	2,377	2,586	3,586	2,293	2,206	1,011
In-line roller skating	5,705	2,268	3,437	2,490	594	1,188	875	372	110	52	24	995	604	685	1,270	919	717	514
Kayaking	8,119	4,167	3,952	1,263	1,023	1,939	1,190	1,014	971	536	183	937	708	976	1,631	951	1,551	1,364
Lacrosse	2,786	1,515	1,271	1,333	413	496	313	183	36	11	–	327	249	334	546	303	555	473
Mountain biking, off road	5,239	3,398	1,841	1,154	639	1,112	1,134	799	295	100	6	868	652	595	870	599	917	738
Muzzleloading	3,164	2,424	740	454	292	640	641	524	365	201	48	338	431	574	658	424	463	275
Paintball games	4,803	3,316	1,487	1,747	1,094	941	590	260	138	27	6	872	545	753	1,061	791	378	403
Running/jogging [1]	41,996	20,242	21,754	8,809	8,091	10,082	7,943	3,907	2,233	716	216	6,525	4,570	4,531	7,321	5,527	7,549	5,975
Skateboarding	4,998	3,332	1,666	2,595	1,114	710	344	175	59	–	–	1,028	447	735	1,036	705	712	335
Skiing, alpine	6,056	3,467	2,588	1,640	805	1,007	1,084	924	414	150	31	269	209	645	861	697	1,229	2,146
Skiing, cross country	2,525	1,344	1,181	445	349	469	423	381	309	133	17	257	79	427	638	317	470	337
Snowboarding	4,530	2,774	1,756	1,187	1,184	1,200	624	257	78	–	–	472	285	616	887	537	847	885
Soccer	12,850	7,503	5,347	6,921	1,787	2,129	1,210	606	145	27	24	1,885	1,221	1,307	2,803	1,569	2,582	1,483
Softball	9,974	4,985	4,989	3,167	1,431	1,964	1,753	914	504	183	62	1,397	1,024	1,440	1,867	1,364	1,657	1,227
Target shooting, live ammunition	19,041	13,684	5,357	2,154	2,395	4,240	2,941	3,516	2,197	1,249	348	2,835	2,304	2,847	3,992	2,531	2,895	1,636
Target shooting, airgun	4,801	3,484	1,317	1,409	564	836	793	687	253	145	112	822	559	951	1,025	737	378	328
Tennis	12,571	5,833	6,738	2,749	2,067	2,338	2,169	1,505	962	537	243	1,259	816	1,404	2,663	1,675	2,672	2,082
Volleyball	10,121	4,122	5,999	3,669	1,785	2,110	1,247	833	320	83	77	1,708	1,262	1,140	1,743	1,404	1,466	1,400
Water skiing	3,639	2,107	1,532	691	788	968	346	525	265	30	26	280	228	522	771	373	719	746
Weightlifting [1]	31,323	19,440	11,883	2,899	5,794	6,534	5,606	4,945	3,110	1,552	883	5,072	3,133	3,327	5,030	4,767	5,417	4,576
Workout at club [1]	34,118	14,635	19,482	1,421	5,363	6,112	6,015	5,038	4,575	3,084	2,510	4,380	3,369	3,678	5,364	4,951	6,144	6,231
Wrestling	3,113	2,503	610	1,575	600	490	302	134	14	–	–	641	464	460	334	405	469	340
Yoga	25,856	4,531	21,325	1,321	3,986	6,846	4,485	4,092	3,079	1,384	664	4,595	2,803	2,812	4,694	3,232	4,111	3,609

– Represents zero. [1] Participant engaged in activity at least six times in the year. [2] Includes wilderness camping. [3] Vacation/overnight.

Source: National Sporting Goods Association, Mt. Prospect, IL, *Sports Participation in the United States, 2014 Edition* ©. See also <http://www.nsga.org/research>.

Table 1259. Consumer Purchases of Sporting Goods by Consumer Characteristics: 2013

[Shown as percent of dollar purchases. Data are based on an online survey of over 19,000 households. Because surveys prior to 2010 were conducted by mail, current data may not be fully comparable to past years]

| Characteristic | Total | Footwear | | | | | Equipment | | | | |
		Aerobic shoes	Cross-train/ fitness shoes	Gym shoes/ sneakers	Jog-ging/ running shoes	Walking shoes	Multi pur-pose home gyms	Rod/ reel combi-nation	Golf club sets	Rifles	Soccer balls
Total.............................	100.0	100.0	100.0	100.0	100.0	100.0	100.0	100.0	100.0	100.0	100.0
Age of user:											
Under 14 years old..............	18.0	9.0	4.0	18.8	6.0	4.3	–	6.6	4.0	6.0	58.7
14 to 17 years old................	5.3	2.7	4.4	11.9	5.7	2.1	–	3.3	7.3	–	13.1
18 to 24 years old................	9.9	5.4	8.7	8.9	8.2	3.2	9.6	3.4	1.9	3.9	5.5
25 to 34 years old................	13.6	21.5	15.2	12.3	18.3	8.6	22.3	20.4	7.1	22.9	7.2
35 to 44 years old................	12.8	26.8	18.0	13.7	25.0	11.4	29.1	10.9	11.9	14.0	5.0
45 to 64 years old................	26.3	26.6	39.3	24.6	30.1	42.2	37.7	41.9	45.9	34.8	7.7
65 years old and over...........	14.1	8.0	10.4	9.8	6.7	28.2	1.3	13.5	21.9	18.4	2.8
Sex of user:											
Male................................	49.2	16.1	36.8	39.7	38.9	34.7	50.2	80.0	70.6	87.4	63.5
Female..............................	50.8	83.9	63.2	60.3	61.1	65.3	49.8	20.0	29.4	12.6	36.5
Annual household income:											
Under $15,000....................	10.5	4.0	3.8	5.0	3.8	6.1	–	5.7	–	0.7	3.3
$15,000 to $24,999.............	12.9	6.6	5.5	10.6	5.2	10.5	0.1	8.5	0.3	8.0	3.6
$25,000 to $34,999.............	12.8	7.8	6.4	8.8	7.0	11.8	3.2	11.3	3.1	7.9	6.0
$35,000 to $49,999.............	13.8	7.0	9.0	10.3	7.8	10.6	10.0	9.0	8.6	12.1	6.8
$50,000 to $74,999.............	17.6	16.0	16.2	17.0	16.7	18.1	19.7	19.4	16.5	25.2	16.8
$75,000 to $99,999.............	11.5	18.2	16.8	13.7	17.1	13.1	14.9	14.2	10.8	22.2	15.6
$100,000 to $149,999..........	11.9	19.5	21.3	18.6	21.9	16.0	41.9	15.5	29.0	11.8	25.6
$150,000 and over..............	9.0	20.9	21.0	16.0	20.5	13.8	10.2	16.4	31.7	12.1	22.3
Education of household head:											
Less than high school...........	11.4	0.6	0.5	1.8	0.9	1.5	–	2.7	–	0.2	3.3
High school........................	29.5	7.8	9.1	12.4	8.7	14.6	5.4	17.8	11.2	15.8	10.0
Some college......................	28.7	32.0	31.6	35.6	27.4	36.0	34.4	36.2	25.5	39.5	26.7
College graduate.................	30.4	59.6	58.8	50.2	63.0	47.9	60.2	43.3	63.3	44.5	60.0

– Represents or rounds to zero.

Source: National Sporting Goods Association, Mt. Prospect, IL, *The Sporting Goods Market in 2014* ©. See also <http://www.nsga.org/research>.

Table 1260. National Park System—Summary: 1990 to 2014

[In units as indicated (986 represents $986,000,000). For year ending September 30, except as noted. Includes data for five areas in Puerto Rico and Virgin Islands, one area in American Samoa, and one area in Guam]

Item	1990	1995	2000	2005	2010	2012	2013	2014
FINANCES (mil. dol.): [1]								
Expenditures reported.........................	986	1,445	1,833	2,451	3,239	3,079	2,812	2,737
Salaries and wages........................	459	633	799	984	1,237	1,229	1,194	1,174
Improvements, maintenance..............	160	234	299	361	531	537	471	507
Construction..................................	109	192	215	381	443	288	262	152
Other..	259	386	520	725	1,028	1,025	885	904
Funds available.................................	1,506	2,225	3,316	4,218	5,402	4,626	4,533	4,532
Appropriations..............................	1,053	1,325	1,881	2,425	2,848	2,783	2,960	2,804
Other [2]......................................	453	900	1,435	1,793	2,554	1,843	1,573	1,728
Revenue from operations................. [3]	79	106	234	286	387	402	390	473
RECREATION VISITS (millions): [3]								
All areas...	258.7	269.6	285.9	273.5	281.3	282.8	273.6	292.8
National parks [4]...........................	57.7	64.8	66.1	63.5	64.6	64.9	63.5	68.9
National monuments.......................	23.9	23.5	23.8	20.9	23.0	21.8	18.7	24.5
National historical, commemorative, archaeological [5].......................	57.5	56.9	72.2	74.9	80.0	87.0	85.1	87.1
National parkways..........................	29.1	31.3	34.0	31.7	28.6	29.4	27.5	28.5
National recreation areas [4].............	47.2	53.7	50.0	46.8	49.0	44.7	44.0	45.2
National seashores and lakeshores.......	23.3	22.5	22.5	21.7	22.2	23.1	22.4	22.3
National Capital Parks.....................	7.5	5.5	5.4	4.3	3.0	1.8	2.8	3.3
Recreation overnight stays (millions).......	17.6	16.8	15.4	13.5	14.4	14.3	13.5	14.1
In commercial lodgings...................	3.9	3.8	3.7	3.4	3.5	4.6	4.3	4.7
In Park Service campgrounds............	7.9	7.1	5.9	5.2	5.5	5.3	5.0	5.3
In backcountry..............................	1.7	2.2	1.9	1.7	1.8	1.8	2.2	1.9
Other..	4.2	3.7	3.8	3.2	3.8	2.6	2.0	2.3
LAND (1,000 acres): [6]								
Total...	76,362	77,355	78,153	79,048	80,527	80,390	80,473	80,469
Parks..	46,089	49,307	49,785	49,910	50,662	50,640	50,741	50,727
Recreation areas..............................	3,344	3,353	3,388	3,391	3,418	3,420	3,420	3,420
Other..	26,929	24,695	24,980	25,747	26,447	26,330	26,312	26,322
Acquisition, net...............................	21	27	186	17	23	9	10	8

[1] Financial data are those associated with the National Park System. Certain other functions of the National Park Service (principally the activities absorbed from the former Heritage Conservation and Recreation Service in 1981) are excluded. [2] Includes funds carried over from prior years. [3] For calendar year. Includes other areas, not shown separately. [4] For 1990, combined data for North Cascades National Park and two adjacent National Recreation Areas are included in National Parks total. [5] Includes military areas. [6] Federal land only, as of December 31. Federal land acreages, in addition to National Park Service administered lands, also include lands within national park system area boundaries but under the administration of other agencies. Year-to-year changes in the federal lands figures includes changes in the acreages of these other lands and hence often differ from "net acquisition."

Source: U.S. National Park Service, *National Park Statistical Abstract 2014*, March 2015, and earlier reports; and unpublished data. See also <https://irma.nps.gov/Stats/>.

Table 1261. National Park Service (NPS) Visits and Acreage by State: 2014

| State | Recreation visits [1] | Gross area acres | Federal land | | | Nonfederal land | |
			NPS fee acres [2]	NPS less than fee acres [3]	Other federal fee acres [4]	Other public acres [5]	Private acres
Total [6]	292,800,082	84,479,064	79,672,759	356,991	439,620	1,378,465	2,631,228
Alabama	753,178	22,737	17,405	202	13	3,288	1,827
Alaska	2,684,693	54,654,154	52,425,769	105,469	8	372,996	1,749,913
Arizona	10,747,219	2,947,312	2,649,269	115	76,800	56,824	164,304
Arkansas	3,132,898	104,977	98,307	3,428	20	2,742	479
California	37,363,392	8,144,518	7,582,045	22,437	11,048	350,586	178,403
Colorado	6,031,874	737,812	661,506	6,756	42,451	862	26,237
Connecticut	34,082	7,782	5,846	1,055	–	874	6
Delaware	–	900	890	3	–	1	6
District of Columbia	37,701,216	7,131	6,975	12	6	134	4
Florida	10,667,459	2,638,658	2,468,328	1,330	44,493	99,997	24,510
Georgia	7,491,109	63,338	39,781	167	1,461	16,855	5,074
Hawaii	5,213,817	369,166	357,814	1	22	11,228	100
Idaho	553,739	518,224	511,600	1,226	173	901	4,324
Illinois	218,132	115	12	–	–	17	86
Indiana	1,778,385	15,540	10,753	500	–	3,390	897
Iowa	216,898	2,713	2,708	–	–	5	1
Kansas	98,591	11,636	462	281	–	39	10,854
Kentucky	1,828,192	95,942	94,103	137	–	838	864
Louisiana	510,522	23,545	16,799	–	1,063	2,572	3,111
Maine	2,574,717	91,826	67,003	12,673	22	10,648	1,480
Maryland	6,815,195	73,893	41,041	5,938	480	23,791	2,643
Massachusetts	9,850,586	57,962	32,961	1,029	44	21,919	2,009
Michigan	1,993,139	718,148	631,852	767	42	58,515	26,972
Minnesota	811,616	301,330	139,632	3,193	142	98,790	59,573
Mississippi	6,557,120	118,587	103,998	5,228	–	70	9,291
Missouri	3,385,772	83,476	54,385	9,262	–	14,070	5,760
Montana	4,590,398	1,274,364	1,214,307	1,866	6,137	1,464	50,591
Nebraska	254,198	45,735	5,896	484	845	435	38,075
Nevada	5,314,681	778,512	774,833	–	2,508	81	1,091
New Hampshire	37,785	21,015	13,211	1,556	5,772	162	315
New Jersey	4,389,637	99,313	35,539	140	3,208	59,036	1,390
New Mexico	1,602,114	391,078	376,890	5	2,524	4,629	7,030
New York	16,141,397	72,992	33,715	3,903	164	19,904	15,307
North Carolina	16,710,759	407,225	363,483	12,272	20,782	3,289	7,399
North Dakota	581,851	72,568	71,258	256	151	55	847
Ohio	2,470,177	34,544	20,284	1,355	84	8,505	4,315
Oklahoma	1,165,269	10,241	10,008	9	189	8	27
Oregon	1,033,254	199,319	192,127	1,404	4,976	295	517
Pennsylvania	9,005,244	138,683	51,587	2,597	387	20,061	64,051
Rhode Island	51,523	5	5	–	–	–	–
South Carolina	1,519,746	32,348	31,972	61	5	51	259
South Dakota	3,861,090	302,998	147,059	122,324	–	78	33,537
Tennessee	8,470,460	384,978	358,140	1,714	9,608	3,263	12,253
Texas	4,680,387	1,247,918	1,205,059	85	1,013	5,074	36,687
Utah	10,551,040	2,117,683	2,097,786	833	1,142	12,808	5,115
Vermont	39,086	23,265	9,836	3,874	8,809	544	202
Virginia	22,870,531	364,371	305,164	7,056	25,050	7,101	19,999
Washington	7,652,073	1,967,532	1,834,584	2,144	100,194	12,814	17,796
West Virginia	1,541,805	92,721	65,170	370	386	6,894	19,902
Wisconsin	625,850	133,755	61,779	11,449	802	47,628	12,097
Wyoming	6,387,455	2,396,424	2,344,972	21	48,462	1,293	1,675

– Represents or rounds to zero. [1] See footnote 1, Table 1262. [2] See footnote 2, Table 1262. [3] See footnote 3, Table 1262. [4] See footnote 4, Table 1262. [5] See footnote 5, Table 1262. [6] Includes Island Areas of the U.S., not shown separately.

Source: U.S. National Park Service, Land Resources Division, unpublished data. See also <https://irma.nps.gov/Stats/>.

Table 1262. National Park Service (NPS) Visits and Acreage by Type of Area: 2014

| Type of area | Recreation visits [1] | Gross area acres | Federal land | | | Non-federal land | |
			NPS fee acres [2]	NPS less than fee acres [3]	Other federal fee acres [4]	Other public acres [5]	Private acres
Total [6]	292,800,082	84,479,064	79,672,759	356,991	439,620	1,378,465	2,631,228
National historic sites	9,928,346	34,655	21,819	855	58	960	10,963
National historical parks	30,465,360	185,140	133,254	4,179	1,499	28,839	17,370
National memorials	36,030,173	10,734	9,743	9	25	76	881
National monuments	24,454,576	2,002,795	1,832,634	14,744	27,251	8,249	119,915
National parks	68,928,098	52,202,066	50,453,087	228,010	46,246	568,222	906,501
National recreation areas	45,218,953	3,703,665	3,153,547	23,795	242,902	112,077	171,344
National seashores	18,546,676	596,905	404,611	14,947	61,226	106,820	9,301
National parkways	28,525,215	179,222	158,761	9,108	213	403	10,738

[1] Recreation visit represents the entry of a person onto lands or waters administered by the NPS for recreational purposes excluding government personnel, through traffic, tradespeople, and persons residing within park boundaries. [2] Complete Federal ownership of all rights in the land. [3] Federal ownership of some rights in the land. [4] Tracts under the administration of another federal agency (e.g., U.S. Forest Service, Department of the Army, etc). Bureau of Land Management tracts are also identified as Other Fee (Federal) until they are withdrawn for NPS use; then status changes to Fee (Federal). [5] Non-federal tracts owned by the state, county, and/or other municipalities, including quasi-public entities. [6] Includes other areas, not shown separately.

Source: U.S. National Park Service, Land Resources Division, unpublished data. See also <https://irma.nps.gov/Stats/>.

Table 1263. State Parks and Recreation Areas by State: 2014

[In units as indicated (18,207 represents 18,207,000). For year ending June 30. Data are shown as reported by state park directors. In some states, park agency has forests, fish and wildlife areas, and/or other areas under its control. In other states, park agency is responsible for state parks only]

State	Acreage (1,000)	Visitors (1,000) [1]	Total revenue generated ($1,000)	Operating expenditures ($1,000)	Revenue share of operating expenditures
United States..........	**18,207**	**739,616**	**1,101,235**	**2,451,906**	**44.9**
Alabama...............	48	4,619	31,176	38,297	81.4
Alaska.................	3,387	4,639	3,083	11,220	27.5
Arizona................	64	2,311	13,030	20,303	64.2
Arkansas..............	54	8,084	24,282	57,834	42.0
California.............	1,624	75,557	123,122	443,891	27.7
Colorado..............	1,238	11,948	28,371	53,305	53.2
Connecticut...........	207	8,285	6,733	17,491	38.5
Delaware..............	26	5,037	15,071	22,753	66.2
Florida................	758	27,172	58,190	82,307	70.7
Georgia...............	93	7,498	24,393	40,793	59.8
Hawaii.................	34	14,032	4,522	9,360	48.3
Idaho..................	59	5,008	9,360	15,718	59.6
Illinois................	481	40,165	7,784	71,163	10.9
Indiana................	172	16,796	48,738	58,602	83.2
Iowa...................	71	17,190	4,394	16,883	26.0
Kansas................	164	6,657	7,461	11,413	65.4
Kentucky..............	45	6,887	47,678	79,397	60.1
Louisiana.............	44	1,747	9,899	30,409	32.6
Maine.................	98	2,558	6,473	8,176	79.2
Maryland..............	135	10,327	17,182	33,323	51.6
Massachusetts........	354	30,019	11,233	68,495	16.4
Michigan..............	294	23,325	47,771	58,883	81.1
Minnesota............	287	8,858	14,170	72,278	19.6
Mississippi...........	25	1,129	8,055	13,256	60.8
Missouri..............	207	18,537	9,685	49,909	19.4
Montana..............	46	2,127	2,481	8,852	28.0
Nebraska.............	135	12,605	20,326	22,841	89.0
Nevada...............	146	3,217	3,776	12,115	31.2
New Hampshire........	231	1,128	20,073	20,073	100.0
New Jersey...........	444	15,521	11,731	36,238	32.4
New Mexico...........	197	3,848	5,071	19,857	25.5
New York..............	4,264	60,847	91,774	224,338	40.9
North Carolina........	222	14,772	7,495	36,923	20.3
North Dakota..........	35	1,148	3,171	5,193	61.1
Ohio..................	174	42,867	27,448	62,860	43.7
Oklahoma.............	70	8,783	32,648	28,929	112.9
Oregon...............	108	46,286	20,844	57,139	36.5
Pennsylvania.........	297	38,000	22,608	90,075	25.1
Rhode Island.........	10	1,234	6,374	9,346	68.2
South Carolina........	90	7,731	24,039	27,728	86.7
South Dakota.........	102	7,808	20,438	18,018	113.4
Tennessee............	169	32,063	34,354	82,154	41.8
Texas.................	629	6,763	46,060	107,610	42.8
Utah [2]...............	151	3,537	15,130	15,624	96.8
Vermont...............	71	962	8,246	9,018	91.4
Virginia...............	72	9,038	18,395	36,265	50.7
Washington...........	122	33,797	38,553	58,963	65.4
West Virginia..........	177	7,704	20,062	43,236	46.4
Wisconsin.............	157	15,526	16,241	23,849	68.1
Wyoming..............	120	3,918	2,036	9,205	22.1

[1] Includes overnight visitors. [2] Data for Utah are for reporting year ended June 30, 2013.

Source: National Association of State Park Directors, Raleigh NC, *Statistical Report of State Park Operations: 2013-2014, Annual Information Exchange for the Period July 1, 2013 through June 30, 2014* ©, May 2015. See also <http://www.naspd.org/>.

Table 1264. Participants in Wildlife-Related Recreation Activities: 2011

[In thousands (37,397 represents 37,397,000). For persons 16 years old and over engaging in activity at least once in 2011. Based on survey and subject to sampling error; see source for details]

Participant	Number	Days of participation	Trips	Participant	Number	Days of participation
Total sportspersons [1]	**37,397**	**835,725**	**711,645**	**Wildlife watchers** [1]	**71,776**	**(X)**
Total anglers	33,112	553,841	455,005	Away from home [2]	22,496	335,625
Freshwater	27,547	455,862	368,805	Observe wildlife	19,808	268,798
Excluding Great Lakes	27,060	443,223	353,620	Photograph wildlife	12,354	110,459
Great Lakes	1,665	19,661	15,185	Feed wildlife	5,399	59,255
Saltwater	8,889	99,474	86,200			
				Around the home [3]	68,598	(X)
Total hunters	13,674	281,884	256,640	Observe wildlife	45,046	(X)
Big game	11,570	212,116	167,320	Photograph wildlife	25,370	(X)
Small game	4,506	50,884	43,135	Feed wildlife	52,817	(X)
Migratory birds	2,583	23,263	21,315	Visit public parks	12,311	(X)
Other animals	2,168	34,434	24,869	Maintain plantings or natural areas	13,399	(X)

X Not applicable. [1] Detail does not add to total due to multiple responses and nonresponse. [2] Persons taking a trip of at least 1 mile from home for activity. [3] Activity within 1 mile of home.

Source: U.S. Fish and Wildlife Service, *2011 National Survey of Fishing, Hunting, and Wildlife Associated Recreation*, December 2012. See also <http://www.census.gov/prod/www/fishing.html>.

Table 1265. Expenditures for Wildlife-Related Recreation Activities: 2011

[41,789 represents $41,789,000,000. For persons 16 years old and over. Based on survey and subject to sampling error; see source for details]

Expenditure item	Fishing Expenditures (mil. dol.)	Fishing Spenders Number (1,000)	Fishing Spenders Percent	Hunting Expenditures (mil. dol.)	Hunting Spenders Number (1,000)	Hunting Spenders Percent	Wildlife watching Expenditures [1] (mil. dol.)	Wildlife watching Spenders Number (1,000)	Wildlife watching Spenders Percent [2]
Total, all items [3]	**41,789**	**30,289**	**91**	**33,702**	**13,364**	**98**	**54,890**	**55,980**	**78**
Total trip-related	21,789	29,309	89	10,421	11,914	87	17,275	19,905	88
Food and lodging	7,711	25,158	76	3,881	10,289	75	9,349	17,017	76
Food	5,435	24,891	75	3,218	10,253	75	5,465	16,740	74
Lodging	2,276	5,983	18	663	1,881	14	3,884	6,851	30
Transportation	6,262	25,293	76	4,768	10,990	80	6,007	18,647	83
Public	804	2,222	7	304	648	5	2,521	3,029	13
Private	5,458	24,504	74	4,464	10,885	80	6,486	17,768	79
Other trip costs	7,817	25,143	76	1,772	4,581	34	1,918	9,359	42
Equipment expenditures									
Equipment [4]	6,142	21,527	65	7,738	10,400	76	11,323	47,951	67
Auxiliary equipment	1,107	4,420	13	1,845	5,101	37	1,555	6,445	9
Special equipment [5]	8,258	2,296	7	4,389	613	4	14,272	2,219	3
Other expenditures									
Magazines and books	108	2,483	8	107	1,934	14	420	8,480	12
Land leasing and ownership	3,434	924	3	7,129	2,279	17	5,677	1,233	2
Membership dues/contributions	322	1,728	5	383	1,885	14	2,164	10,756	15
Plantings	(X)	(X)	(X)	703	1,273	9	2,204	8,818	12
Licenses, stamps, tags, and permits	629	17,166	52	986	10,214	75	(X)	(X)	(X)

X Not applicable. [1] Information on trip-related expenditures for wildlife watching was collected for away-from-home participants only. Equipment and other expenditures for wildlife watching are base on information collected from both away-fro-home and around-the-home participants. [2] Percent of wildlife-watching participants column is base on away-from-home participants for trip-related expenditures. For equipment and other expenditures the percent of wildlife-watching participants is based on total participants. [3] Total not adjusted for multiple responses or nonresponse. [4] Includes fishing, hunting, and wild-life watching. [5] Special equipment includes boats, campers, cabins, trail bikes, etc.

Source: U.S. Fish and Wildlife Service, *2011 National Survey of Fishing, Hunting, and Wildlife Associated Recreation*, December 2012. See also <http://www.census.gov/prod/2012pubs/fwh11-nat.pdf>.

Table 1266. Tribal Gaming Revenues: 2009 to 2014

[Revenue in millions of dollars (26,482 represents $26,482,000,000). For year ending September 30]

Region	2009 Number of operations	2009 Revenue	2010 Number of operations	2010 Revenue	2011 Number of operations	2011 Revenue	2012 Number of operations	2012 Revenue	2013 Number of operations	2013 Revenue	2014 Number of operations	2014 Revenue
Total [1]	**419**	**26,482**	**422**	**26,503**	**421**	**27,154**	**425**	**27,900**	**449**	**28,032**	**449**	**28,459**
Region I	49	2,521	50	2,655	49	2,764	49	2,874	51	2,903	51	2,927
Region II	62	6,970	62	6,794	63	6,903	64	6,957	66	6,993	68	7,298
Region III	47	2,600	48	2,539	48	2,614	48	2,717	48	2,739	48	2,708
Region IV	120	4,384	119	4,452	119	4,565	120	4,798	128	4,745	130	4,675
Region V	113	3,225	116	3,352	115	3,592	117	3,816	128	3,900	132	4,078
Region VI	28	6,783	27	6,711	27	6,716	27	6,739	28	6,752	30	6,773

[1] Portland (Region I): Alaska, Idaho, Oregon, and Washington. Sacramento (Region II): California, and Northern Nevada. Phoenix (Region III): Arizona, Colorado, New Mexico, and Southern Nevada. St. Paul (Region IV): Iowa, Michigan, Minnesota, Montana, North Dakota, Nebraska, South Dakota, Wisconsin, and Wyoming. Oklahoma City/Tulsa (Region V): Oklahoma, Texas, Kansas. Washington (Region VI): Alabama, Connecticut, Florida, Louisiana, Mississippi, North Carolina, and New York.

Source: National Indian Gaming Commission, *Gaming Revenue Reports 2010-2014*, July 2015, and earlier reports; and *Gaming Revenues by Region 2013 and 2014*, and earlier reports. See also <http://www.nigc.gov/Gaming_Revenue_Reports.aspx>.

Table 1267. Real Tourism Output: 2005 to 2014

[In millions of dollars (681,024 represents $681,024,000,000)]

Commodity	Direct output (current dollars)			Real output (chained 2009 dollars)		
	2005	2010	2014	2005	2010	2014
Total............	**681,024**	**701,356**	**913,128**	**752,607**	**678,716**	**799,439**
Traveler accommodations............	121,924	129,651	168,704	133,129	130,757	152,714
Food services and drinking places............	101,965	105,700	130,712	118,378	104,448	119,412
Domestic passenger air transportation services............	79,398	80,094	98,550	87,937	74,679	81,188
International passenger air transportation services............	30,371	43,096	51,202	30,477	38,785	41,100
Passenger rail transportation services............	1,460	1,862	2,256	1,726	1,847	2,039
Passenger water transportation services............	9,883	10,976	12,761	8,746	10,852	13,410
Interurban bus transportation............	1,636	1,370	1,472	1,953	1,310	1,287
Interurban charter bus transportation............	1,764	1,625	1,885	2,107	1,550	1,649
Urban transit systems and other transportation services......	4,298	4,227	4,462	4,965	4,060	3,881
Taxi service............	3,983	4,090	4,398	4,573	3,934	3,838
Scenic and sightseeing transportation services............	2,496	2,467	3,098	2,767	2,459	2,972
Automotive rental............	26,940	28,007	34,338	34,863	28,234	31,980
Other vehicle rental............	762	763	928	853	747	822
Automotive repair services............	13,913	12,390	11,824	16,362	12,156	10,996
Parking lots and garages............	2,168	2,322	2,307	2,649	2,248	1,954
Highway tolls............	679	702	767	837	664	666
Travel arrangement and reservation services............	31,665	36,771	47,370	33,766	36,765	46,601
Motion pictures and performing arts............	14,736	14,040	26,325	16,700	13,855	24,695
Spectator sports............	6,732	5,179	5,546	7,910	5,071	5,109
Participant sports............	12,183	10,073	12,043	13,045	10,171	11,918
Gambling............	37,721	41,286	46,400	41,452	40,614	42,553
All other recreation and entertainment............	13,955	12,110	11,546	15,749	12,004	11,018
Gasoline............	54,926	61,592	101,373	56,865	51,958	65,909
Nondurable PCE [1] commodities other than gasoline............	105,467	90,962	132,858	116,065	89,976	122,550

[1] Personal consumption expenditures.

Source: U.S. Bureau of Economic Analysis, "Industry Economic Accounts, U.S. Travel and Tourism Satellite Accounts for 1998-2014," <http://www.bea.gov/industry/tourism_data.htm>, accessed July 2015.

Table 1268. Travel Forecast Summary: 2013 to 2020

[In billions of dollars (16,768.1 represents $16,768,100,000,000)]

Indicator	Unit	2013	2014	2015 [1]	2016 [1]	2017 [1]	2018 [1]	2019 [1]	2020 [1]
Real GDP............	Billions	16,768.1	17,418.9	18,100.7	19,035.1	19,941.0	20,860.9	21,822.2	22,813.8
Unemployment rate............	Percent	7.4	6.2	5.4	5.0	5.0	5.1	5.0	5.0
Consumer price index (CPI) [2]......	Percent	233.0	236.7	237.6	243.2	248.5	253.9	262.8	268.7
Travel price index (TPI) [2]............	Percent	275.6	279.6	275.5	285.7	295.3	305.3	327.2	334.7
Total travel expenditures in U.S.....	Billions	886.3	927.9	940.6	978.2	1,019.60	1,063.0	1,114.0	1,233.80
U.S. residents............	Billions	750.7	790.9	802.0	832.7	864.7	898.1	938.4	1,025.80
International visitors [3]............	Billions	135.6	137.0	138.6	145.5	154.9	164.9	175.4	208.0
Total international visitors to the United States............	Millions	70.0	74.8	77.6	80.8	84.5	88.3	92.2	96.4
Overseas arrivals to the United States............	Millions	32.0	34.4	35.6	37.5	39.5	41.6	43.8	46.4
Total domestic person trips [4]........	Millions	2,059.6	2,109.3	2,151.1	2,189.1	2,223.9	2,258.5	2,292.6	2,326.6
Business............	Millions	444.6	450.4	458.3	465.0	470.2	476.0	482.3	488.8
Leisure............	Millions	1,615.1	1,658.9	1,692.8	1,724.1	1,753.7	1,782.5	1,810.3	1,837.8

[1] Projected. [2] 1982 through 1984 = 100. [3] Excludes international visitors' spending on traveling to the U.S. on U.S. flag carriers, and other miscellaneous transportation. [4] One person on one trip 50 miles or more, one way, away from home or including one or more nights away from home.

Source: U.S. Travel Association, *Travel Industry Forecasts,* July 2015. See also <http://www.ustravel.org/research/travel-industry-forecasts>.

Table 1269. Chain–Type Price Indexes for Direct Tourism Output: 2000 to 2014

[Index numbers, 2009=100. For explanation of chain-type price indexes, see text, Section 13]

Tourism goods and services group	2000	2005	2007	2008	2009	2010	2011	2012	2013	2014
All tourism goods and services.......	**79.0**	**90.4**	**97.7**	**103.3**	**100.0**	**103.3**	**108.5**	**111.5**	**112.1**	**114.3**
Traveler accommodations..................	80.1	91.6	99.5	102.9	100.0	99.2	100.9	103.9	105.1	109.5
Transportation.............................	77.6	91.5	100.9	109.7	100.0	107.6	117.3	120.7	120.0	121.4
Passenger air transportation.............	79.3	93.1	100.7	110.1	100.0	108.6	116.6	122.0	121.3	124.2
All other transportation-related commodities...............................	76.3	90.3	101.0	109.4	100.0	106.9	117.8	119.8	119.2	119.5
Food services and drinking places........	74.8	86.1	92.1	96.4	100.0	101.2	103.6	106.8	109.1	111.7
Recreation, entertainment, and shopping.................................	82.5	90.5	95.2	98.7	100.0	101.1	103.6	105.9	106.9	108.3
Recreation and entertainment.............	78.5	90.1	96.0	99.4	100.0	101.2	102.9	105.1	106.3	107.6
Shopping....................................	85.7	90.9	94.4	98.1	100.0	101.1	104.2	106.6	107.4	108.9

Source: U.S. Bureau of Economic Analysis, Travel and Tourism Satellite Accounts, *Travel and Tourism Spending Accelerated In The Fourth Quarter of 2014*, March 2015. See also <http://bea.gov/industry/tourism_data.htm>.

Table 1270. Tourism Sales and Employment by Industry Segment: 2005 to 2014

[Sales in billions of dollars (692.1 represents $692,100,000,000); employment in thousands (5,697 represents 5,697,000). Direct tourism-related sales comprise all output purchased directly by visitors (e.g., traveler accommodations, passenger air transportation, souvenirs). Direct tourism-related employment comprises all jobs where the workers are engaged in the production of direct tourism-related sales (output), such as hotel staff, airline pilots, and souvenir sellers]

Tourism commodity group	Direct tourism sales (bil. dol.)				Tourism industry group	Direct tourism employment (1,000)			
	2005	2010	2013	2014		2005	2010	2013	2014
All goods and services.......	**692.1**	**706.7**	**855.9**	**894.0**	**All tourism industries**......	**5,697**	**4,946**	**5,366**	**5,492**
Traveler accommodations........	124.9	133.7	159.0	172.1	Traveler accommodations......	1,334	1,278	1,375	1,398
Transportation....................	266.7	292.3	373.2	385.5	Transportation...................	1,155	995	1,051	1,072
Passenger air transportation....	109.8	123.2	149.8	156.7	Air transportation services....	474	424	441	444
All other transportation-related commodities...................	156.9	169.1	223.4	228.8	All other transportation-related industries.................	681	571	610	628
Food services and drinking places...........................	106.3	105.9	129.4	136.9	Food services and drinking places...........................	1,760	1,554	1,771	1,830
Recreation, entertainment, and shopping...................	194.2	174.9	194.3	199.5	Recreation, entertainment, and shopping...................	1,218	939	965	983
Recreation/entertainment........	86.6	83.9	90.6	92.1	Recreation/entertainment.....	631	511	534	544
Shopping.........................	107.6	91.0	103.7	107.5	Shopping........................	587	428	432	439
					All other industries..............	229	180	204	208

Source: U.S. Bureau of Economic Analysis, Travel and Tourism Satellite Accounts, *Travel and Tourism Spending Accelerated In The Fourth Quarter of 2014*, March 2015. See also <http://www.bea.gov/industry/index.htm#satellite>.

Table 1271. Top States and Cities Visited by Overseas Travelers: 2000 to 2014

[25,975 represents 25,975,000. Includes travelers for business and pleasure, international travelers in transit through the United States, and students. Excludes travel by international personnel and international businessmen employed in the United States. Starting with the 2006 data, the statistical policy for visitation estimates of international visitation requires a minimum sample of 400 respondents. States and cities are ranked by the latest overseas visitors data]

State and other area	Overseas visitors [1] (1,000)				City	Overseas visitors [1] (1,000)			
	2000	2005	2013	2014		2000	2005	2013	2014
Total overseas travelers [2,3]..................	**25,975**	**21,679**	**32,038**	**34,419**	New York, NY [4]....................	5,714	5,810	9,579	9,741
New York........................	5,922	6,092	9,804	9,982	Miami, FL........................	2,935	2,081	4,005	4,853
Florida..........................	6,026	4,379	7,209	8,501	Los Angeles-Long Beach, CA..	3,533	2,580	3,781	4,406
California........................	6,364	4,791	6,472	7,159	Orlando, FL......................	3,013	2,016	3,716	4,130
Hawaiian Islands.................	2,727	2,255	3,172	3,063	San Francisco, CA..............	2,831	2,124	3,044	3,132
Nevada..........................	2,364	1,821	2,916	3,063	Las Vegas, NV..................	2,260	1,778	2,851	2,994
Texas............................	1,169	954	1,570	1,549	Oahu/Honolulu, HI..............	2,234	1,821	2,563	2,478
Massachusetts...................	1,429	867	1,378	1,514	Washington, DC.................	1,481	1,106	1,698	1,927
Illinois...........................	1,377	1,149	1,442	1,377	Boston, MA.....................	1,325	802	1,282	1,411
Guam............................	1,325	1,127	1,474	1,342	Chicago, IL......................	1,351	1,084	1,378	1,308
Pennsylvania.....................	649	629	993	964	San Diego, CA..................	701	499	833	1033
New Jersey......................	909	997	929	964	Houston, TX.....................	442	(B)	801	860
Arizona..........................	883	564	833	929	Atlanta, GA......................	701	564	577	723
Georgia..........................	805	650	705	860	Philadelphia, PA.................	390	434	673	620
Washington......................	468	369	513	620	Flagstaff, AZ [5].................	(B)	(B)	545	620
Utah.............................	(B)	(B)	481	551	Anaheim-Santa Ana, CA........	494	390	481	585
Colorado.........................	519	(B)	384	447	Seattle, WA......................	416	347	481	585
North Carolina...................	416	(B)	384	447	Dallas-Plano-Irving, TX.........	494	(B)	449	413
Virginia..........................	364	(B)	352	413	San Jose, CA...................	494	347	416	413

B Figure too small to meet statistical standards for reliability of a derived figure. [1] Excludes visitors from Canada and Mexico. [2] A person is counted in each area visited, but only once in the total. [3] Includes other states and cities, not shown separately. [4] Data include New York City-White Plains-Wayne, NY-NJ grouped together. [5] Data include Flagstaff, Grand Canyon, and Sedona grouped together.

Source: U.S. Department of Commerce, International Trade Administration, Office of Travel and Tourism, *Overseas Visitation Estimates for U.S.: States, Cities, and Census Regions: 2014*, June 2015, and earlier reports. See also <http://travel.trade.gov/outreachpages/inbound.general_information.inbound_overview.html>.

Table 1272. Domestic and International Travel Expenditures by State: 2013

[In millions of dollars (887,855 represents $887,855,000,000). Shows aggregate spending by foreign visitors and by U.S. residents on domestic overnight trips and day trips of 50 miles or more, one way, away from home]

State	Total (mil. dol.)	Percent distribution	Rank	State	Total (mil. dol.)	Percent distribution	Rank	State	Total (mil. dol.)	Percent distribution	Rank
U.S. total...	887,855	100.0	(X)	KS	7,009	0.8	35	ND	3,095	0.3	44
				KY	8,267	0.9	31	OH	17,735	2.0	14
AL	8,529	1.0	30	LA	10,576	1.2	24	OK	7,508	0.8	34
AK	2,408	0.3	48	ME	3,424	0.4	43	OR	9,721	1.1	29
AZ	16,593	1.9	18	MD	15,116	1.7	19	PA	23,563	2.7	8
AR	6,327	0.7	37	MA	18,482	2.1	13	RI	1,875	0.2	50
CA	116,054	13.1	1	MI	17,265	1.9	15	SC	12,253	1.4	23
CO	16,666	1.9	17	MN	12,544	1.4	22	SD	2,692	0.3	47
CT	10,013	1.1	27	MS	6,068	0.7	38	TN	16,715	1.9	16
DE	1,792	0.2	51	MO	12,857	1.4	21	TX	61,173	6.9	4
DC	9,752	1.1	28	MT	4,017	0.5	41	UT	7,530	0.8	33
FL	78,648	8.9	2	NE	4,504	0.5	39	VT	2,225	0.3	49
GA	24,970	2.8	7	NV	31,973	3.6	6	VA	21,979	2.5	9
HI	19,932	2.2	12	NH	3,791	0.4	42	WA	14,503	1.6	20
ID	4,160	0.5	40	NJ	20,096	2.3	11	WV	2,895	0.3	46
IL	34,581	3.9	5	NM	6,632	0.7	36	WI	10,174	1.1	25
IN	10,081	1.1	26	NY	62,184	7.0	3	WY	2,993	0.3	45
IA	7,959	0.9	32	NC	20,963	2.4	10	Other [1]	34,997	3.9	(X)

X Not applicable. [1] This category includes foreign visitor spending in U.S. territories, and Canadian and Mexican visitor spending in the U.S. Those dollars are not represented in state totals.

Source: U.S. Travel Association, Washington, DC, *Impact of Travel on State Economies 2014* ©, 2014. See also <http://www.ustravel.org/research>.

Table 1273. Average Cost of Airfare for Domestic Routes: 1995 to 2014

[In dollars, except percent. Fares based on domestic itinerary fares. Itinerary fares consist of round-trip fares unless the customer does not purchase a return trip. In that case, the one-way fare is included. Fares are based on the total ticket value which consists of the price charged by the airlines plus any additional taxes and fees levied by an outside entity at the time of purchase. Fares include only the price paid at the time of the ticket purchase and do not include other fees paid at the airport or onboard the aircraft. Averages do not include frequent-flyer or "zero fares" or a few abnormally high reported fares]

Year	Current Dollars			Constant (2014) dollars [1]		
		Percent change			Percent change	
	Average fare	From previous year	Cumulative from 1995	Average fare	From previous year	Cumulative from 1995
1995	292	(NA)	(NA)	454	(NA)	(NA)
1996	277	-5.3	-5.3	418	-7.9	-7.9
1997	287	3.8	-1.7	424	1.4	-6.7
1998	309	7.6	5.8	450	6.2	-0.9
1999	324	4.7	10.8	461	2.4	1.5
2000	339	4.7	16.0	467	1.3	2.9
2001	321	-5.4	9.7	429	-8.2	-5.6
2002	312	-2.6	6.9	411	-4.1	-9.4
2003	315	1.0	7.9	406	-1.3	-10.6
2004	305	-3.2	4.5	383	-5.7	-15.7
2005	307	0.6	5.2	373	-2.7	-17.9
2006	329	6.9	12.4	386	3.6	-15.0
2007	325	-1.0	11.3	372	-3.6	-18.1
2008	346	6.5	18.5	381	2.4	-16.1
2009	310	-10.4	6.2	343	-10.1	-24.5
2010	336	8.3	15.0	365	6.5	-19.6
2011	364	8.3	24.5	383	4.9	-15.6
2012	375	3.0	28.3	387	0.9	-14.9
2013	382	1.9	30.7	389	0.6	-14.3
2014	392	2.5	34.1	391	0.6	-13.8

NA Not available. [1] Rate calculated using Bureau of Labor Statistics Consumer Price Index.

Source: U.S. Department of Transportation, Bureau of Transportation Statistics, "Annual U.S Domestic Average Itinerary Fare in Current and Constant Dollars," <http://www.rita.dot.gov/bts/airfares/programs/economics_and_finance/air_travel_price_index/html/AnnualFares.html>, accessed April 2015.

Table 1274. International Travel: 1990 to 2014

[In thousands (44,619 represents 44,619,000). U.S. travelers cover residents of the United States, its territories and possessions. International travelers to the U.S. include travelers for business and pleasure, excludes travel by international personnel and international businessmen employed in the United States. Some traveler data revised since originally issued]

Item and area	1990	1995	2000	2005	2010	2011	2012	2013	2014
U.S. TRAVELERS TO FOREIGN COUNTRIES BY WORLD REGION OF DESTINATION [1]									
Total.............	44,619	51,285	61,327	63,502	61,060	59,210	60,697	61,344	68,176
Canada..............	12,252	13,005	15,189	14,390	11,871	11,597	11,887	11,478	11,515
Mexico..............	16,377	18,771	19,285	20,325	20,682	20,590	20,308	20,851	25,882
Total overseas..............	15,990	19,059	26,853	28,787	28,507	27,023	28,502	29,015	30,780
Europe..............	8,043	8,596	13,373	11,976	9,806	9,674	10,204	10,039	10,804
INTERNATIONAL TRAVELERS TO U.S. BY VISITOR REGION OF RESIDENCE									
Total.............	39,363	43,318	51,238	49,206	60,010	62,821	66,657	69,995	74,757
Canada..............	17,263	14,663	14,667	14,862	20,176	21,337	22,697	23,407	23,003
Mexico..............	7,041	8,016	10,596	12,665	13,472	13,601	14,199	14,547	17,334
Total overseas [2]	15,059	20,639	25,975	21,679	26,363	27,883	29,761	32,041	34,419
Europe..............	6,659	8,793	11,597	10,313	11,985	12,660	12,478	12,894	13,732
Asia..............	4,360	6,616	7,554	6,198	7,020	7,247	8,311	9,085	9,641
South America..............	1,328	2,449	2,941	1,820	3,250	3,757	4,416	5,142	5,481
Caribbean..............	1,137	1,044	1,331	1,135	1,201	1,091	1,131	1,156	1,339
Oceania..............	662	588	731	737	1,095	1,243	1,322	1,433	1,555
Central America..............	412	509	822	696	760	747	803	834	933
Middle East..............	365	454	702	527	736	811	925	1,058	1,225
Africa..............	137	186	295	252	316	327	373	439	513

[1] A person is counted in each area visited but only once in the total. [2] "Overseas" excludes Canada and Mexico.

Source: U.S. Department of Commerce, International Trade Administration, Office of Travel and Tourism, *2014 United States Resident Travel Abroad,* July 2015; and *International Visitation to the United States: A Statistical Summary of U.S. Visitation (2014),* June 2015. See also <http://www.tinet.ita.doc.gov/outreachpages/outbound.general_information.outbound_overview.html> and <http://www.tinet.ita.doc.gov/outreachpages/inbound.general_information.inbound_overview.html>.

Table 1275. International Travelers and Payments: 2000 to 2014

[In units as indicated (86,184 represents $86,184,000,000). See headnote, Table 1274]

Year	Travel and passenger fare (mil. dol.)				U.S. net travel and passenger receipts (mil. dol.)	U.S. travelers to international countries (1,000)	International travelers to the U.S. (1,000) [3]
	Payments by U.S. travelers		Receipts from international visitors				
	Total [1]	Travel payments [2]	Total [1]	Travel receipts [2]			
2000............	86,184	65,787	120,384	100,187	34,200	61,327	44,681
2005............	101,419	79,988	122,079	101,470	20,660	63,502	49,206
2006............	106,848	84,206	126,778	105,140	19,930	63,663	50,977
2007............	112,788	89,235	144,224	119,037	31,436	64,049	56,135
2008............	119,837	92,545	164,718	133,761	44,881	63,653	58,007
2009............	102,953	81,421	146,005	119,902	43,052	62,171	55,103
2010............	110,049	86,623	167,997	137,010	57,948	61,060	60,010
2011............	116,447	89,700	187,630	150,867	71,183	59,210	62,821
2012............	129,882	100,317	200,613	161,249	70,731	60,697	66,657
2013............	136,706	104,677	214,773	173,131	78,067	61,570	69,995
2014............	145,678	110,788	220,756	177,240	75,078	68,303	74,757

[1] Includes passenger fares, not shown separately. [2] Travel payments and receipts cover purchases of goods and services by U.S. persons traveling abroad, and by foreign travelers in the U.S. Goods and services include food, lodging, recreation, gifts, entertainment, local transportation, and other items. [3] Beginning in 2014, prior years are not comparable due to a change in methodology for counting U.S. overseas arrivals.

Source: U.S. Department of Commerce, International Trade Administration, Office of Travel and Tourism Industries, *International Visitation to the United States: A Statistical Summary of U.S. Visitation (2014),* June 2015; and "U.S. Travel and Tourism Statistics," <http://tinet.ita.doc.gov/outreachpages/inbound.general_information.inbound_overview.html>, accessed June 2015.

Table 1276. Top 20 U.S. Gateway Airports for Nonstop International Air Travel Passengers: 2014

[190,450 represents 190,450,000. International passengers are residents of any country traveling nonstop to and from the United States on U.S. and foreign carriers. The data cover all passengers arriving and departing from U.S. airports on nonstop commercial international flights with 60 seats or more]

Gateway airport	Airport code	2014	Gateway airport	Airport code	2014
Total passengers....................	(X)	**190,450**	Washington (Dulles), DC................	IAD	6,994
Total, top 20.............................	(X)	**171,428**	Dallas-Ft. Worth, TX....................	DFW	6,903
Top 20, percentage of total...............	(X)	90.0	Honolulu, HI............................	HNL	4,927
			Fort Lauderdale, FL.....................	FLL	4,504
New York (JFK), NY.......................	JFK	27,515	Boston, MA.............................	BOS	4,454
Miami, FL................................	MIA	20,019	Orlando, FL............................	MCO	4,269
Los Angeles, CA.........................	LAX	18,680	Philadelphia, PA........................	PHL	3,960
Newark, NJ..............................	EWR	11,493	Seattle-Tacoma, WA.....................	SEA	3,678
Chicago (O'Hare), IL.....................	ORD	11,293	Detroit, MI.............................	DTW	3,363
Atlanta, GA..............................	ATL	10,583	Las Vegas, NV..........................	LAS	3,284
San Francisco, CA.......................	SFO	10,066	Charlotte, NC...........................	CLT	3,136
Houston (G. Bush), TX...................	IAH	9,601	Guam Island, GU.......................	GUM	2,707

X Not applicable.

Source: U.S. Department of Transportation, Research and Innovative Technology Administration, Bureau of Transportation Statistics, Office of Airline Information, "T-100 International Segment data," <http://www.transtats.bts.gov/Fields.asp?Table_ID=261>, accessed September 2015.

Table 1277. Crossings for Top 5 U.S.-Canadian and U.S.-Mexican Border Land Passenger Gateways: 2014

[31,980 represents 31,980,000]

Item and gateway	Entering the U.S. (1,000)	Item and gateway	Entering the U.S. (1,000)
All U.S.-Canadian land gateways [1]		**All U.S.-Mexican land gateways** [1]	
Personal vehicles	31,980	Personal vehicles	69,624
Personal vehicle passengers	59,664	Personal vehicle passengers	129,244
Buses	104	Buses	214
Bus passengers	2,244	Bus passengers	2,783
Train passengers	283	Train passengers	12
Pedestrians	424	Pedestrians	41,223
Top five gateways		**Top five gateways**	
Personal vehicles:		Personal vehicles:	
Buffalo-Niagara Falls, NY	5,447	San Ysidro, CA	11,946
Blaine, WA	4,874	El Paso, TX	11,595
Detroit, MI	4,027	Otay Mesa, CA	6,910
Port Huron, MI	1,976	Laredo, TX	5,251
Point Roberts, WA	1,190	Hidalgo, TX	4,565
Personal vehicle passengers:		Personal vehicle passengers:	
Buffalo-Niagara Falls, NY	11,617	San Ysidro, CA	21,116
Blaine, WA	9,711	El Paso, TX	19,135
Detroit, MI	7,050	Otay Mesa, CA	12,040
Port Huron, MI	3,864	Laredo, TX	10,335
Champlain-Rouses Pt., NY	2,561	Hidalgo, TX	9,252
Pedestrians:		Pedestrians:	
Buffalo-Niagara Falls, NY	275	San Ysidro, CA	7,925
Sumas, WA	59	El Paso, TX	6,572
Point Roberts, WA	20	Calexico, CA	4,567
Calais, ME	19	Laredo, TX	3,447
International Falls, MN	16	Otay Mesa, CA	3,416

[1] Data reflect all personal vehicles and buses, passengers, and pedestrians entering the U.S.-Canadian border and U.S.-Mexican border, regardless of nationality.

Source: U.S. Department of Transportation, Bureau of Transportation Statistics, "Border Crossing / Entry Data," <www.transtats.bts.gov/bordercrossing.aspx>, accessed July 2015.

Table 1278. Foreign Visitors for Pleasure Admitted by Country of Citizenship: 2000 to 2013

[In thousands (30,511 represents 30,511,000). For years ending September 30. Represents non-U.S. citizens admitted to the country for a temporary period of time, for pleasure (tourists). Includes nonimmigrant admission classes B2 (temporary visitors for pleasure), GMT (Commonwealth of the Northern Marianas Islands visa waiver program–temporary visitors for pleasure to Guam or Northern Mariana Islands), and WT (visa waiver program–temporary visitors for pleasure)]

Country and region	2000 [1]	2005	2010	2013	Country and region	2000 [1]	2005	2010	2013
All countries [2]	**30,511**	**23,815**	**35,131**	**48,346**	Thailand	76	37	48	62
					Turkey	93	57	74	116
Europe [3]	**11,806**	**10,016**	**11,741**	**12,799**	United Arab Emirates	36	3	8	17
Austria	182	116	166	188	**Africa** [3]	**327**	**212**	**274**	**421**
Belgium	254	154	227	240	Egypt	44	19	34	64
Czech Republic	44	26	58	77	Nigeria	27	40	62	114
Denmark	150	153	244	250	South Africa	114	64	63	87
Finland	95	76	106	124	**Oceania** [3]	**748**	**723**	**1,046**	**1,498**
France	1,113	1,007	1,371	1,595	Australia	535	527	843	1,234
Germany	1,925	1,248	1,599	1,823	New Zealand	170	184	191	248
Greece	60	40	54	55	**North America** [3, 4]	**6,501**	**5,546**	**12,754**	**20,148**
Hungary	58	30	49	60	Canada	277	23	87	2,518
Iceland	27	34	35	47	Mexico	3,972	4,070	11,010	15,855
Ireland	325	398	406	387	**Caribbean**	**1,404**	**876**	**999**	**1,016**
Italy	626	636	924	975	Bahamas, The	24	257	250	225
Netherlands	559	483	598	601	Dominican Republic	195	189	219	239
Norway	144	117	197	259	Haiti	72	65	90	97
Poland	116	119	103	113	Jamaica	240	152	180	183
Portugal	86	81	120	142	Trinidad and Tobago	133	106	129	137
Russia	74	53	134	265	**Central America**	**792**	**578**	**657**	**759**
Spain	370	402	692	760	Costa Rica	172	109	143	169
Sweden	321	249	330	441	El Salvador	175	147	105	98
Switzerland	400	207	315	404	Guatemala	177	135	159	178
United Kingdom	4,671	4,232	3,768	3,681	Honduras	87	75	101	130
Asia [3]	**7,853**	**5,688**	**6,255**	**8,636**	Nicaragua	47	33	38	46
China [5]	656	221	482	1,278	Panama	106	64	94	118
India	253	247	490	759	**South America** [3]	**2,867**	**1,498**	**2,785**	**4,738**
Indonesia	62	42	44	72	Argentina	515	145	375	649
Israel	319	220	253	274	Bolivia	48	18	31	40
Japan	4,946	3,758	3,252	3,667	Brazil	706	385	976	1,871
Korea, South	606	528	896	1,270	Chile	194	82	119	194
Malaysia	64	32	37	58	Colombia	411	282	455	699
Pakistan	47	34	39	54	Ecuador	122	119	169	235
Philippines	163	144	179	217	Peru	190	142	162	212
Saudi Arabia	67	10	36	100	Uruguay	66	24	35	59
Singapore	131	57	72	104	Venezuela	570	270	423	713
Taiwan	(NA)	201	183	314					

NA Not available. [1] Due to the temporary expiration of the Visa Waiver Program from May through October 2000, data for business and pleasure not available separately for 2000. [2] Total includes visitors of unknown country of citizenship. [3] Total includes other countries, not shown separately. [4] The majority of short-term admissions from Canada and Mexico are excluded. [5] Prior to 2005, data for China includes Taiwan. Beginning in 2005, data for China includes Hong Kong and Macau.

Source: U.S. Dept. of Homeland Security, Office of Immigration Statistics, *2013 Yearbook of Immigration Statistics: Supplemental Tables*, August 2014, and earlier reports. See also <http://www.dhs.gov/yearbook-immigration-statistics>.

Accommodation, Food Services, and Other Services

This section presents statistics relating to services other than those covered in the previous sections on wholesale and retail trade, transportation, communications, financial services, and recreation services. Data shown for services are classified by kind of business and cover sales or receipts, establishments, employees, payrolls, and other items.

The principal sources of these data are from the U.S. Census Bureau and include the 2007 and 2012 Economic Census, annual surveys, and the County Business Patterns program. These data are supplemented by data from several sources including the National Restaurant Association on food and drink sales (Table 1287) and the American Hotel & Lodging Association on lodging (Table 1285).

Data on these services also appear in several other sections. For instance, labor force employment and earnings data appear in Section 12, Labor Force, Employment, and Earnings; gross domestic product of the industry (Table 690) appears in Section 13, Income, Expenditures, Poverty, and Wealth; and financial data (several tables) from the quarterly *Statistics of Income Bulletin*, published by the Internal Revenue Service, appear in Section 15, Business Enterprise.

Censuses—Limited coverage of the service industries started in 1933. Beginning with the 1967 census, legislation provides for a census of each area to be conducted every 5 years (for years ending in "2" and "7"). For more information on the most current census, see the Census Bureau's Economic Census Web site at <http://www.census.gov/econ/census/>. The industries covered in the censuses and surveys of business are defined in the North American Industry Classification System (NAICS). For information on

NAICS, see the Census Web site at <http://www.census.gov/eos/www/naics/>.

In general, the 2007 and 2012 Economic Censuses have three series of publications for these sectors: 1) subject series with reports such as product lines, and establishment and firm sizes, 2) geographic reports with individual reports for each state, and 3) industry series with individual reports for industry groups.

Data from the 2012 Economic Census are being released on a continuing basis through 2016.

Current surveys—The Service Annual Survey provides annual estimates of nationwide receipts for selected personal, business, leasing and repair, amusement and entertainment, social and health, and other professional service industries in the United States. For selected social, health, and other professional service industries, separate estimates are developed for receipts of taxable firms and revenue and expenses for firms and organizations exempt from federal income taxes. Several service sectors from this survey are covered in other sections of this publication. The estimates for tax exempt firms in these industries are derived from a sample of employer firms only. Estimates obtained from annual and monthly surveys are based on sample data and are not expected to agree exactly with results that would be obtained from a complete census of all establishments. Data include estimates for sampling units not reporting. Data are released in the *Quarterly Services Report* and the *Annual Services Report* at <http://www.census.gov/services/>.

Statistical reliability—For a discussion of statistical collection and estimation, sampling procedures, and measures of statistical reliability applicable to Census Bureau data, see Appendix III.

Table 1279. Selected Service-Related Industries—Establishments, Sales, Payroll, and Employees by Kind of Business: 2012

[1,543,690,388 represents $1,543,690,388,000. Covers only establishments with payroll. For statement on methodology, see Appendix III]

Kind of business	2012 NAICS code [1]	Establish- ments, (number)	Sales or receipts ($1,000)	Annual payroll (1,000)	Paid employ- ees [2] (1,000)
Professional, scientific, and technical services..................	**54**	**854,274**	**1,543,690,338**	**582,443,020**	**8,143**
Professional, scientific, and technical services..................	541	854,274	1,543,690,338	582,443,020	8,143
Management of companies and enterprises..................	**55**	**52,380**	**83,838,395**	**307,488,960**	**3,066**
Administrative and support and waste management and remediation services..................	**56**	**385,314**	**724,942,308**	**345,629,713**	**10,218**
Administrative and support services..................	561	361,733	639,082,259	327,315,512	9,839
Waste management and remediation services..................	562	23,237	79,619,380	17,909,688	374
Accommodation and food services..................	**72**	**662,487**	**708,358,763**	**196,151,056**	**12,006**
Accommodation..................	721	63,896	195,445,123	50,155,220	1,952
Food services and drinking places..................	722	598,585	513,013,940	146,066,545	10,057
Other services (except public administration)..................	**81**	**528,371**	**432,235,441**	**108,380,040**	**3,456**
Repair and maintenance..................	811	210,248	146,730,092	41,606,048	1,199
Personal and laundry services..................	812	212,468	86,549,714	28,633,007	1,346
Religious, grantmaking, civic, professional, and similar organizations..................	813	106,911	197,715,365	38,049,034	886

[1] North American Industrial Classification System, 2012; see text, Section 15. [2] For employees on the payroll during the pay period including March 12.

Source: U.S. Census Bureau, 2012 Economic Census, "EC1200A1: All sectors: Geographic Area Series: Economy-Wide Key Statistics: 2012," <http://factfinder2.census.gov>, accessed September 2015.

Table 1280. Selected Service-Related Industries—Nonemployer Establishments and Receipts by Kind of Business: 2011 to 2013

[3,164 represents 3,164,000. Includes only firms subject to federal income tax. Nonemployers are businesses with no paid employees. Data originate chiefly from administrative records of the Internal Revenue Service; see Appendix III]

Kind of business	NAICS code [1]	Firms (1,000)			Receipts (mil. dol.)		
		2011	2012	2013	2011	2012	2013
Professional, scientific, and technical services..................	**54**	**3,164**	**3,212**	**3,236**	**136,702**	**142,975**	**143,067**
Professional, scientific, and technical services [2]..................	541	3,164	3,212	3,236	136,702	142,975	143,067
Legal services..................	5411	276	281	278	17,699	18,486	18,009
Accounting, tax preparation, bookkeeping, and payroll services..................	5412	361	362	359	8,983	9,284	9,143
Architectural, engineering [3]..................	5413	230	230	229	10,431	10,888	10,999
Management, scientific and technical consulting..................	5416	654	661	668	30,900	32,432	31,973
Scientific research and development services..................	5417	33	36	35	1,210	1,266	1,269
Administrative and support and waste management and remediation services..................	**56**	**1,985**	**2,006**	**2,033**	**40,887**	**42,443**	**42,969**
Administrative and support services [2]..................	561	1,965	1,983	2,012	39,427	40,917	41,489
Office administrative services..................	5611	210	219	223	3,340	3,652	3,723
Business support services..................	5614	222	227	222	5,882	6,107	5,938
Services to buildings and dwellings..................	5617	1,233	1,223	1,254	22,165	22,708	23,389
Waste management and remediation services..................	562	21	23	20	1,460	1,526	1,480
Accommodation and food services..................	**72**	**341**	**341**	**346**	**14,863**	**15,021**	**15,306**
Accommodation..................	721	56	58	58	3,018	3,140	3,191
Food services and drinking places..................	722	285	283	288	11,845	11,881	12,115
Full-service restaurants [4]..................	7221	46	(X)	(X)	3,090	(X)	(X)
Limited-service eating places [4]..................	7222	49	(X)	(X)	3,042	(X)	(X)
Special food services..................	7223	160	165	169	4,045	4,362	4,504
Drinking places (alcoholic beverages)..................	7224	30	30	28	1,668	1,695	1,641
Restaurants and other eating places..................	7225	(X)	88	92	(X)	5,824	5,969
Full-service restaurants..................	722511	(X)	41	42	(X)	2,889	2,918
Limited-service eating places..................	722513	(X)	37	36	(X)	2,660	2,695
Other services (except public administration)..................	**81**	**3,517**	**3,523**	**3,584**	**85,693**	**88,545**	**90,754**
Repair and maintenance [2]..................	811	755	750	752	26,297	26,805	27,248
Automotive repair and maintenance..................	8111	327	325	325	13,706	13,797	13,918
Personal and household goods repair [5]..................	8114	325	321	325	8,480	8,767	9,044
Personal and laundry services..................	812	2,556	2,560	2,622	56,247	58,484	60,246
Personal care services..................	8121	1,235	1,246	1,301	25,738	26,832	27,931
Death care services..................	8122	16	17	17	830	839	849
Drycleaning and laundry services..................	8123	34	34	32	1,805	1,778	1,749
Other personal services..................	8129	1,271	1,263	1,272	27,874	29,035	29,717
Religious, grantmaking, civic, professional, and similar organizations..................	813	205	213	209	3,149	3,256	3,260

X Not applicable. [1] North American Industry Classification System, see text, Section 15. Data for 2011 based on NAICS 2007. Beginning 2012, data based on NAICS 2012. [2] Includes other kinds of business not shown separately. [3] Includes related services. [4] Beginning 2012, see under NAICS 7225. [5] Includes maintenance.

Source: U.S. Census Bureau, Nonemployer Statistics, "Geographic Area Series: Nonemployer Statistics by Legal Form of Organization," <http://factfinder2.census.gov>, accessed May 2015. See also <http://www.census.gov/econ/nonemployer/>.

Table 1281. Selected Service-Related Industries—Establishments, Employees, and Payroll by Industry: 2012 and 2013

[859 represents 859,000, except payroll. Covers establishments with paid employees. Excludes self-employed individuals, employees of private households, railroad employees, agricultural production employees, and most government employees; see source for NAICS and other exclusions. For statement on methodology, see Appendix III]

Industry	2012 NAICS code [1]	Establishments (1,000)		Employees [2] (1,000)		Annual payroll (bil. dol.)	
		2012	2013	2012	2013	2012	2013
Professional, scientific, & technical services...............	**54**	**859**	**869**	**8,016**	**8,275**	**595.0**	**628.0**
Professional, scientific, & technical services...................	541	859	869	8,016	8,275	595.0	628.0
Legal services..........................	5411	188	187	1,152	1,167	94.9	96.1
Offices of lawyers..................	54111	173	173	1,059	1,069	90.4	91.1
Accounting, tax preparation, bookkeeping, and payroll services...........	5412	128	128	1,297	1,280	62.5	63.6
Tax preparation services.............	541213	27	28	201	187	2.1	2.0
Architectural, engineering, & related services [3]...........	5413	108	108	1,319	1,412	103.5	112.8
Architectural services................	54131	21	21	146	150	10.5	11.0
Engineering services.................	54133	5	5	23	23	1.2	1.3
Specialized design services [3]...................	5414	30	30	114	110	6.7	6.3
Graphic design services..............	54143	15	15	50	50	2.6	2.7
Computer systems design & related services [3]...........	5415	130	132	1,464	1,586	128.1	143.9
Custom computer programming services...............	541511	65	65	634	707	54.3	61.0
Computer systems design services..................	541512	47	48	533	619	48.1	59.4
Management, scientific, technical consulting services [3]....	5416	152	159	1,024	1,070	81.5	84.3
Management consulting services..............	54161	121	126	842	883	68.3	70.6
Environmental consulting services...............	54162	10	10	76	76	4.8	4.9
Scientific research & development services..............	5417	17	18	627	608	66.0	66.9
Research & development in the physical engineering & life sciences.............	54171	16	16	591	569	63.7	64.4
Advertising & related services [3].................	5418	38	38	448	464	29.1	30.4
Advertising agencies...............	54181	13	13	173	186	14.4	15.3
Public relations agencies............	54182	8	8	51	52	4.5	4.8
Other professional, scientific, & tech services............	5419	68	70	572	579	22.6	23.7
Veterinary services..................	54194	30	30	310	317	10.3	10.8
Management of companies and enterprises..............	**55**	**52**	**53**	**3,037**	**3,099**	**316.0**	**325.8**
Administrative and support and waste management and remediation services..............	**56**	**387**	**393**	**9,866**	**10,185**	**350.4**	**366.0**
Administrative & support services [3]..........................	561	364	370	9,499	9,811	331.3	346.7
Employment services..................	5613	47	49	4,971	5,276	178.1	194.4
Temporary help services..	56132	31	33	2,792	2,957	79.0	84.1
Business support services [3]...............	5614	33	33	772	758	25.2	24.9
Telephone call centers.............	56142	5	5	435	423	11.2	10.7
Collection agencies................	56144	5	5	130	128	4.7	4.8
Credit bureaus.....................	56145	1	1	19	20	2.1	2.2
Travel arrangement & reservation services...............	5615	20	23	224	224	12.1	12.2
Travel agencies...................	56151	13	16	97	100	5.6	5.5
Investigation & security services..................	5616	26	26	836	868	23.3	24.2
Investigation, guard, & armored car services...............	56161	16	16	720	743	18.3	18.4
Security systems services...........	56162	10	11	115	125	5.0	5.8
Services to buildings & dwellings.......	5617	180	182	1,705	1,710	42.9	44.0
Waste management & remediation services..................	562	24	24	368	374	19.1	19.3
Waste collection....................	5621	11	11	182	193	8.9	9.6
Waste treatment & disposal..........	5622	3	2	59	52	3.7	3.2
Remediation & other waste management services........	5629	10	10	126	129	6.5	6.5
Accommodation & food services................	**72**	**663**	**674**	**11,985**	**12,395**	**203.6**	**216.3**
Accommodation........................	721	64	65	1,937	1,963	50.8	52.7
Traveler accommodation...............	7211	55	55	1,884	1,910	49.3	51.2
Hotels (except casino hotels) & motels............	72111	50	50	1,454	1,489	35.8	37.6
RV (recreational vehicle) parks & recreational camps......	7212	7	7	40	42	1.2	1.3
Rooming & boarding houses............	7213	2	2	12	11	0.2	0.2
Food services & drinking places............	722	599	609	10,049	10,432	152.8	163.6
Drinking places (alcoholic beverages)................	7224	42	42	350	357	5.1	5.4
Restaurants and other eating places...........	7225	517	526	9,025	9,369	134.2	143.5
Full-service restaurants............	722511	232	236	4,774	4,896	78.5	84.0
Limited-service restaurants.........	722513	225	227	3,588	3,771	46.5	49.3
Cafeterias, grill buffets, and buffets...............	722514	6	6	122	123	1.6	1.7
Snack and nonalcoholic beverage bars........	722515	54	56	540	579	7.6	8.5
Other services (except public administration)..............	**81**	**731**	**734**	**5,256**	**5,283**	**149.6**	**153.3**
Repair & maintenance [3]...........................	811	211	211	1,180	1,196	42.7	44.4
Automotive repair & maintenance..........	8111	157	158	813	826	25.7	26.8
Personal & household goods repair & maintenance........	8114	20	20	68	67	2.0	2.0
Personal & laundry services [3]................	812	213	216	1,327	1,346	29.4	30.0
Personal care services...............	8121	118	120	640	656	12.0	12.3
Death care services.................	8122	21	21	137	136	4.5	4.6
Drycleaning & laundry services........	8123	36	36	291	292	7.2	7.4
Religious/grantmaking/civic/professional [4]...................	813	307	307	2,749	2,741	77.5	78.9
Religious organizations...............	8131	183	184	1,686	1,685	33.0	33.5
Grantmaking & giving services.............	8132	19	19	175	175	9.4	9.5
Social advocacy organizations........	8133	17	17	149	151	6.3	6.5
Civic & social organizations.........	8134	27	26	241	239	4.7	4.7
Business/professional/labor/political [4]........	8139	61	61	498	491	24.1	24.7
Labor unions [4].......................	81393	15	15	155	152	5.2	5.3

NA Not available. [1] North American Industry Classification System (NAICS), 2012. See text, section 15. [2] Includes employees on the payroll for the pay period including March 12. [3] Includes other kinds of business, not shown separately. [4] Also includes other similar organizations.

Source: U.S. Census Bureau, County Business Patterns, "Geography Area Series, County Business Patterns," <http://factfinder2.census.gov/>, accessed April 2015. See also <http://www.census.gov/econ/cbp/>.

Table 1282. Employed Persons in Service Industries—Sex, Race, and Hispanic or Latino Origin by Industry: 2014

[17,004 represents 17,004,000. Civilian noninstitutionalized population 16 years and older. Based on the Current Population Survey (CPS); see text, Section 1, and Appendix III. For information on employees in other sectors, see Table 633 and Table 651]

Industry	2012 NAICS code [1]	Total employed (1,000)	Percent of total			
			Female	Black [2]	Asian [2]	Hispanic or Latino [3]
Professional and business services..........................	(X)	17,004	41.2	9.5	7.5	16.0
Professional and technical services.........................	54	10,327	42.6	6.5	10.1	8.2
Legal services.........................	5411	1,656	54.1	6.9	4.4	10.4
Accounting, tax preparation, bookkeeping, and payroll services.........................	5412	1,075	62.3	7.8	7.0	7.7
Architectural, engineering, and related services................	5413	1,466	24.8	4.1	6.7	7.3
Specialized design services.........................	5414	419	58.3	5.4	6.2	10.8
Computer systems design and related services..............	5415	2,344	25.4	7.8	21.3	5.3
Management, scientific, and technical consulting services.........................	5416	1,522	40.4	6.8	9.0	8.3
Scientific research and development services................	5417	547	48.8	6.2	15.7	7.8
Advertising, public relations, and related services.............	5418	582	46.4	6.6	5.7	10.5
Other professional, scientific, and technical services [4].........................	5419	396	54.7	6.4	4.4	12.0
Veterinary services.........................	54194	320	81.0	2.4	0.4	10.3
Management, administrative, and waste services...........	55-56	6,677	39.2	14.0	3.4	28.2
Management of companies and enterprises....................	55	206	50.7	4.5	8.0	8.5
Employment services.........................	5613	983	54.7	21.5	4.4	21.1
Business support services....................	5614	793	63.6	18.1	3.7	14.5
Travel arrangement and reservation services....................	5615	284	60.2	7.4	12.8	13.0
Investigations and security services....................	5616	759	23.9	24.0	4.3	16.4
Services to buildings and dwellings [5]....................	5617	1,475	53.9	13.0	2.0	41.0
Landscaping services.........................	56173	1,390	8.4	7.0	1.3	43.1
Other administrative and support services....................	5611,2,9	246	45.2	6.5	5.8	17.7
Waste management and remediation services..................	562	543	17.7	12.1	1.2	24.9
Accommodation and food services..........................	72	10,407	52.8	12.4	7.1	25.2
Accommodation.........................	721	1,511	57.8	14.8	10.5	27.2
Traveler accommodation.........................	7211	1,420	58.7	15.4	11.0	28.1
Recreational vehicle parks and camps, and rooming and board houses....................	7212,3	91	44.2	4.7	2.5	12.9
Food services and drinking places....................	722	8,896	51.9	12.0	6.6	24.9
Restaurants and other food services [6]....................	722, excl. 7224	8,635	51.9	12.1	6.7	25.2
Drinking places, alcoholic beverages..........................	7224	261	54.3	6.3	1.6	16.1
Other services...........................	81	7,169	52.8	10.2	7.0	19.0
Other services (except private households).....................	81	6,349	47.7	10.4	7.3	16.7
Repair and maintenance.........................	811	2,064	12.2	7.0	3.3	23.2
Automotive repair and maintenance [7].........................	8111	1,225	9.4	6.7	3.2	24.2
Car washes.........................	811192	173	14.3	15.0	2.0	39.2
Electronic and precision equipment repair and maintenance....................	8112	151	16.5	7.5	5.1	12.9
Commercial and industrial machinery and equipment repair and maintenance.....................	8113	311	8.6	4.3	1.4	23.1
Personal and household goods repair and maintenance [8].....................	8114	199	29.9	5.4	6.4	10.9
Footwear and leather goods repair.........................	81143	4	(Z)	(Z)	(Z)	(Z)
Personal and laundry services.........................	812	2,368	72.5	11.7	13.2	16.7
Barber shops.........................	812111	128	24.1	34.6	4.6	24.8
Beauty salons.........................	812112	930	93.8	11.7	6.1	16.2
Nail salons and other personal care services..................	812113, 81219	493	77.2	5.7	38.8	7.2
Drycleaning and laundry services.....................	8123	285	57.4	11.8	14.3	32.5
Funeral homes, cemeteries, and crematories....................	8122	146	36.5	9.7	0.9	14.4
Other personal services.........................	8129	387	55.9	12.6	4.3	16.7
Membership associations and organizations.....................	813	1,917	55.3	12.4	4.2	9.9
Religious organizations.........................	8131	1,047	48.1	10.1	4.1	7.9
Civic, social, advocacy organizations, grantmaking and giving services....................	8132,3,4	671	66.1	15.7	4.3	13.3
Business, professional, political, and similar organizations [9]....................	8139	136	63.8	11.0	4.5	9.5
Labor unions.........................	81393	63	41.5	16.6	6.4	7.1
Private households.........................	814	820	92.2	8.9	5.1	36.5

X Not applicable. Z Base less than 50,000. [1] Based on the North American Industry Classification System, 2012; see Section 15. [2] The Current Population Survey (CPS) allows respondents to choose more than one race. Data represent persons who selected this race group only and exclude persons reporting more than one race. See also comments on race in text for Section 1. [3] Persons of Hispanic or Latino ethnicity may be of any race. [4] Excludes NAICS 54194 (veterinary services). [5] Excludes NAICS 56173 (landscaping services). [6] Excludes NAICS 7224 (drinking places, alcoholic beverages). [7] Excludes NAICS 811192 (car washes). [8] Excludes NAICS 81143 (footwear and leather goods repair). [9] Excludes NAICS 81393 (labor unions).

Source: U.S. Bureau of Labor Statistics, "Labor Force Statistics from the Current Population Survey," <http://www.bls.gov/cps/tables.htm#annual>, accessed March 2015.

Table 1283. Selected Service-Related Industries—Establishments, Employees, and Annual Payroll by State: 2013

[Employees in thousands (8,275 represents 8,275,000); payroll in millions of dollars (628,015 represents $628,015,000,000). Covers establishments with paid employees. Excludes most government employees, railroad employees, and self-employed persons. Data are from Census Bureau's County Business Patterns program. For statement on methodology, see Appendix III]

State	Professional, scientific, and technical services (NAICS 54) [1]			Administrative and support and waste management and remediation services (NAICS 56) [1]			Accommodation and food services (NAICS 72) [1]		
	Establish-ments	Employ-ees [2] (1,000)	Annual payroll (mil. dol.)	Establish-ments	Employ-ees [2] (1,000)	Annual payroll (mil. dol.)	Establish-ments	Employ-ees [2] (1,000)	Annual payroll (mil. dol.)
United States........	869,445	8,275	628,015	393,354	10,185	365,965	673,810	12,395	216,339
Alabama.................	9,241	93	6,085	4,200	134	3,561	8,383	161	2,234
Alaska...................	1,929	19	1,303	1,151	19	860	2,135	28	715
Arizona..................	16,473	129	7,895	8,150	233	7,861	11,892	259	4,486
Arkansas...............	5,756	34	1,702	2,625	57	1,665	5,441	96	1,262
California...............	117,282	1,149	99,592	42,454	1,262	50,907	80,054	1,465	28,218
Colorado................	24,316	183	14,237	8,534	227	9,913	12,966	250	4,579
Connecticut............	9,266	105	9,246	5,300	87	3,571	8,425	137	2,750
Delaware...............	2,649	31	2,797	1,401	31	797	2,035	37	644
District of Columbia.....	5,278	98	11,527	1,095	33	1,378	2,435	63	1,690
Florida..................	72,363	445	28,241	33,799	1,308	52,088	37,809	832	15,353
Georgia.................	28,241	230	16,107	11,924	326	10,885	19,124	385	5,858
Hawaii..................	3,261	22	1,404	1,805	50	1,535	3,568	101	2,742
Idaho...................	4,218	32	1,763	2,202	34	896	3,551	55	790
Illinois..................	38,766	393	31,277	16,861	475	14,967	27,695	483	8,536
Indiana.................	12,780	106	6,406	7,174	188	5,326	13,146	261	3,700
Iowa....................	6,260	50	2,692	3,573	75	2,161	7,098	115	1,560
Kansas..................	7,129	60	3,778	3,489	72	2,214	6,061	108	1,476
Kentucky................	8,164	68	3,182	3,982	97	2,515	7,809	162	2,235
Louisiana...............	11,982	96	5,674	4,666	104	3,485	9,231	198	3,364
Maine...................	3,488	23	1,275	2,014	22	658	4,082	49	952
Maryland................	20,115	267	21,828	8,032	179	6,577	11,554	211	3,778
Massachusetts..........	21,474	262	25,923	10,235	185	8,286	17,196	279	5,573
Michigan................	21,533	243	16,724	11,574	311	9,585	19,645	354	5,311
Minnesota..............	16,516	137	9,736	7,310	161	5,598	11,373	227	3,572
Mississippi.............	4,762	31	1,529	2,196	51	1,278	5,238	118	1,895
Missouri................	13,393	161	10,243	7,379	154	4,931	12,455	243	3,698
Montana................	3,642	18	848	1,714	19	551	3,465	48	728
Nebraska...............	4,519	88	4,304	2,603	59	1,891	4,367	71	945
Nevada.................	8,343	54	3,308	4,209	99	2,939	6,001	297	8,712
New Hampshire.........	3,805	31	1,830	2,257	45	1,921	3,620	54	951
New Jersey.............	29,651	307	26,327	13,981	304	10,788	20,462	297	5,756
New Mexico.............	4,713	45	2,785	1,842	32	942	4,184	82	1,328
New York...............	60,406	603	52,208	26,236	545	27,269	50,978	709	15,618
North Carolina..........	23,155	202	13,552	12,065	272	8,182	19,823	369	5,577
North Dakota...........	1,772	14	868	1020	14	477	1,981	36	567
Ohio....................	23,987	234	14,948	13,236	369	11,011	23,675	453	6,280
Oklahoma...............	9,605	69	4,066	4,455	95	3,032	7,501	142	2,048
Oregon.................	11,800	84	5,786	5,430	88	2,650	10,787	155	2,673
Pennsylvania............	29,431	320	23,291	15,281	307	10,245	28,451	444	7,058
Rhode Island...........	2,997	22	1,330	1,699	22	731	3,013	45	790
South Carolina..........	9,906	82	5,064	5,492	163	4,803	9,916	191	2,908
South Dakota...........	1,911	11	499	1,074	10	309	2,372	39	571
Tennessee..............	10,908	101	6,243	6,721	227	6,784	12,166	251	3,889
Texas...................	63,980	647	51,259	26,726	945	33,272	50,094	1,022	16,447
Utah....................	9,406	87	4,386	4,148	119	3,800	5,226	100	1,483
Vermont................	2,111	22	1,095	1,084	7	224	1,957	31	541
Virginia.................	29,831	438	38,373	10,559	245	9,463	17,136	323	5,342
Washington.............	20,367	194	15,797	9,152	139	5,862	16,502	241	4,699
West Virginia...........	2,970	25	1,191	1,473	33	913	3,654	66	938
Wisconsin...............	11,388	101	5,983	6,783	146	4,201	14,277	223	3,016
Wyoming................	2,206	9	512	989	6	207	1,801	28	503

[1] North American Industry Classification System, 2012. See text, section 15. [2] For employees on the payroll for the pay period including March 12.

Source: U.S. Census Bureau, County Business Patterns, "Geography Area Series, County Business Patterns," <http://factfinder2.census.gov/>, accessed April 2015. See also <http://www.census.gov/econ/cbp/>.

Table 1284. Professional, Scientific, and Technical Services—Estimated Revenue by Kind of Business: 2008 to 2013

[In millions of dollars (1,286,720 represents $1,286,720,000,000). For taxable employer firms. Estimates have been adjusted to the results of the 2007 Economic Census. Based on the Service Annual Survey and administrative data; see Appendix III]

Kind of business	2007 NAICS code [1]	2008	2009	2010	2011	2012	2013
Professional, scientific, and technical services (except notaries) [2, 3]	**54**	**1,286,720**	**1,220,642**	**1,264,267**	**1,333,393**	**1,387,710**	**1,414,930**
Offices of lawyers	54111	229,893	223,087	226,057	233,951	236,150	232,151
Other legal services	54119	11,741	11,167	11,231	10,999	12,694	14,180
Offices of certified public accountants	541211	69,233	68,915	66,509	67,826	72,983	75,928
Tax preparation services	541213	5,526	5,665	5,664	5,746	5,719	6,097
Payroll services	541214	31,050	28,932	29,073	32,133	35,773	37,878
Other accounting services	541219	14,251	14,519	14,896	15,726	16,624	17,548
Architectural services	54131	37,759	29,802	26,050	26,958	26,847	27,393
Landscape architectural services	54132	4,365	3,385	3,058	2,974	2,827	3,057
Engineering services	54133	199,943	178,375	172,403	180,005	173,853	168,769
Testing laboratories	54138	13,469	12,701	13,631	14,615	14,340	15,027
Other related services [4]	5413x	12,379	10,697	11,057	12,183	13,664	14,337
Interior design services	54141	9,290	6,814	6,394	6,846	7,251	7,620
Graphic design services	54143	8,286	7,133	7,478	7,686	7,666	7,629
All other design services [5]	5414y	2,387	2,233	2,237	2,710	2,913	2,920
Computer systems design and related services	5415	265,719	260,466	283,790	305,445	326,505	332,768
Management consulting services [6]	54161	121,001	109,654	118,096	125,025	131,359	139,029
Environmental consulting services	54162	11,125	10,856	11,095	11,248	10,980	10,933
Other scientific and technical consulting services	54169	14,870	15,215	17,148	18,565	20,343	22,212
Research and development in physical, engineering and life sciences	54171	73,069	75,812	84,243	93,948	100,122	104,995
Research and development in social sciences and humanities	54172	1,698	1,734	1,843	1,895	1,898	2,132
Advertising agencies	54181	32,058	30,887	33,476	34,900	39,665	41,133
Public relations agencies	54182	9,247	8,855	10,004	10,249	10,890	11,509
Media buying agencies	54183	4,955	4,321	4,375	4,823	5,519	5,693
Media representatives	54184	3,691	3,407	3,559	3,774	3,878	4,146
Display advertising	54185	9,142	7,595	7,799	7,987	8,371	8,373
Direct mail advertising	54186	11,486	10,048	10,745	11,059	11,207	11,118
All other advertising [7]	5418y	18,621	17,405	18,886	19,629	20,675	21,733
Marketing research and public opinion polling	54191	16,322	15,501	16,738	17,391	16,728	16,839
Photography studios, portrait	541921	5,139	4,956	4,808	4,689	4,667	4,655
Commercial photography	541922	1,878	1,560	1,539	1,531	1,698	1,839
Translation and interpretation services	54193	2,122	3,069	3,276	3,196	3,201	2,911
Veterinary services	54194	25,794	25,658	26,634	27,168	28,851	30,120
All other professional, scientific, and technical services	54199	9,211	10,218	10,475	10,513	11,849	12,258

[1] Based on the North American Industry Classification System, 2007; see Section 15. [2] Data prior to 2011 have been restated to reflect comparable data on the 2007 NAICS basis for more detailed levels within this aggregate. [3] Excludes NAICS 54112 (Offices of Notaries). [4] Includes NAICS 54134 (Drafting Services), NAICS 54135 (Building Inspection Services), NAICS 54136 (Geophysical Surveying and Mapping Services), and NAICS 54137 (Surveying and Mapping Services, except Geophysical Services). [5] Includes NAICS 54142 (Industrial Design Services) and NAICS 54149 (Other Specialized Design Services). [6] A portion of NAICS 54161 (Management Consulting Services) moved to NAICS 56131 (Employment Placement Agencies and Executive Search Services) with the 2007 NAICS update. Data prior to 2011 have been restated to reflect comparable data on the 2007 NAICS basis. [7] Includes NAICS 54187 (Advertising Material Distribution Services) and NAICS 54189 (Other Services Related to Advertising).

Source: U.S. Census Bureau, Annual & Quarterly Services, "2013 Annual Services," <http://www.census.gov/services/index.html>, accessed February 2015.

Table 1285. Lodging Industry Summary: 1990 to 2013

Year	Average occupancy rate (percent)	Average room rate (dollars)	2013 Item	2013 Establish-ments [1]	2013 Rooms	2013 Item	2013 Business traveler	2013 Leisure traveler
1990	63.3	57.96	Total	52,887	4,926,543	Typical night:		
2000	63.7	85.89				Made reservations		
2005	63.1	91.04	By Size:			(percent)	96	94
2008	60.4	107.40	Under 75 rooms	29,264	1,252,647	Amount paid (dol.)	$143.00	$123.00
2009	54.7	98.07	75–149 rooms	17,536	1,839,031	Length of stay		
2010	57.6	98.06	150–299 rooms	4,408	882,146	(percent):		
2011	60.0	101.70	300–500 rooms	1,142	424,887	One night	40	50
2012	61.4	106.15	Over 500 rooms	537	527,832	Two nights	23	26
2013	62.2	110.35				Three or more	37	24

[1] Based on properties with 15 or more rooms.

Source: American Hotel & Lodging Association, Washington, DC, "Lodging Industry Profile ©," <http://www.ahla.com/content.aspx?id=36332>, accessed July 2014.

Table 1286. Selected Service Industries—E-Commerce Revenue: 2012 and 2013

[407,799 represents $407,799,000,000. Includes data only for businesses with paid employees, except for accommodation and food services, which also includes businesses with and without paid employees. Except as noted, based on the Service Annual Survey. E-commerce is defined as the value of goods and services sold online. The term "online" includes the use of the internet, intranet, extranet, as well as proprietary networks that run systems such as Electronic Data Interchange (EDI)]

Kind of business	2007 NAICS code [1]	E-commerce revenue (mil. dol.)		E-commerce as percent of total revenue, 2013	E-commerce revenue, percent distribution, 2013
		2012	2013		
Selected service industries, total [2]...........	(X)	**407,799**	**442,608**	**3.5**	**100.0**
Selected transportation and warehousing [3]...............	4849y	89,166	98,228	12.0	22.2
Air transportation.........	481	55,351	60,709	30.1	13.7
Water transportation.........	483	4,828	5,308	12.6	1.2
Truck transportation.........	484	16,537	17,433	7.3	3.9
Information.........	51	102,287	111,563	8.9	25.2
Publishing industries (except Internet)...............	511	59,634	66,812	23.3	15.1
Telecommunications...............	517	9,629	7,667	1.3	1.7
Data processing, hosting, and related services............	518	9,705	10,945	11.5	2.5
Finance and insurance [4].............	52	79,739	86,670	2.4	19.6
Securities and commodity contracts intermediation and brokerage............	5231	16,101	16,900	6.0	3.8
Real estate and rental and leasing............	53	25,108	27,739	5.6	6.3
Selected professional, scientific, and technical services [5].........	54	24,146	25,066	1.7	5.7
Computer systems design and related services............	5415	7,646	7,830	2.4	1.8
Administrative and support and waste management and remediation services............	56	23,601	23,672	3.2	5.3
Travel arrangement and reservation services............	5615	12,573	13,747	32.3	3.1
Educational services [6].........	61	4,269	4,479	7.9	1.0
Health care and social assistance............	62	965	1,083	0.1	0.2
Arts, entertainment, and recreation............	71	7,167	7,874	3.5	1.8
Accommodation and food services [7]............	72	40,598	(S)	(S)	(S)
Other services (except public administration) [8]............	81	10,499	11,695	2.6	2.6
Repair and maintenance.........	811	1,275	1,250	0.8	0.3
Personal and laundry services.........	812	2,737	3,049	3.2	0.7
Religious, grantmaking, civic, professional, and similar organizations............	813	6,487	7,396	3.6	1.7

X Not applicable. S Data do not meet publication standards. [1] North American Industry Classification System (NAICS), 2007; see text Section 15. [2] Includes other kinds of business, not shown separately. [3] Excludes NAICS 482 (Rail Transportation) and NAICS 491 (Postal Service). [4] Excludes NAICS 525 (Funds, Trusts, and Other Financial Vehicles). [5] Excludes NAICS 54112 (Offices of Notaries). [6] Excludes NAICS 6111 (Elementary and Secondary Schools), NAICS 6112 (Junior Colleges), and NAICS 6113 (Colleges, Universities, and Professional Schools). [7] Estimates are based on data from the 2013 Annual Retail Trade Survey. [8] Excludes NAICS 81311 (Religious Organizations), NAICS 81393 (Labor Unions and Similar Labor Organizations), NAICS 81394 (Political Organizations), and NAICS814 (Private Households).

Source: U.S. Census Bureau, "E-Stats - Measuring the Electronic Economy," <http://www.census.gov/econ/estats/>, accessed June 2015.

Table 1287. Commercial and Noncommercial Services—Food and Drink Sales: 2011 to 2015

[In millions of dollars (611,080 represents $611,080,000,000). Data refer to sales to consumers of food and alcoholic beverages. Sales are estimated. For details, see source]

Type of place or service	Sales (mil. dol.)				
	2011	2012	2013	2014	2015 [1]
Total [2].............	**611,080**	**638,997**	**659,552**	**683,095**	**709,238**
Commercial restaurant services [2].............	557,572	583,672	602,671	624,070	648,050
Eating and drinking places [2].............	427,163	446,813	459,853	474,564	491,637
Tableservice restaurants.............	196,166	202,836	207,704	213,498	219,690
Quickservice and fast-casual restaurants.............	170,215	180,343	186,114	192,836	201,128
Cafeterias, grill-buffets and buffets.............	8,234	8423.07	8,583	8,429	8,336
Snack and nonalcoholic beverage bars.............	26,704	28,269	29,763	31,221	32,845
Bars and taverns [3].............	18,324	19,038	19,438	19,943	20,562
Noncommercial restaurant services.............	51,166	52,905	54,404	56,463	58,536
Military restaurant services [4].............	2,343	2,420	2,476	2,561	2,652

[1] Projection. [2] Includes other groupings, not shown separately. [3] For establishments serving food. [4] Continental U.S. only.

Source: National Restaurant Association, Washington, DC, *National Restaurant Association 2015 Restaurant Industry Forecast*, annual ©.

Table 1288. Administrative and Support and Waste Management and Remediation Services—Estimated Revenue by Kind of Business: 2008 to 2013

[In millions of dollars (647,973 represents $647,973,000,000). For taxable and tax-exempt employer firms. Estimates have been adjusted to results of the 2007 Economic Census. Based on the Service Annual Survey and administrative data; see Appendix III]

Kind of business	2007 NAICS code [1]	2008	2009	2010	2011	2012	2013
Administrative and support and waste management and remediation services [2]	**56**	**647,973**	**601,867**	**642,681**	**682,707**	**716,877**	**745,195**
Administrative and support services [2]	561	569,121	529,065	560,747	598,845	632,542	659,116
Office administrative services	5611	40,970	42,558	45,520	50,148	55,321	57,793
Facilities support services	5612	28,994	29,280	29,946	33,688	33,198	31,970
Employment placement agencies and executive search services [3]	56131	19,582	16,710	17,079	19,953	20,986	21,490
Temporary help services	56132	103,792	86,111	100,689	113,668	120,849	127,342
Professional employer organizations	56133	88,657	87,609	95,099	100,531	109,951	116,659
Document preparation services	56141	3,286	2,891	2,825	2,694	2,891	2,859
Telephone answering services	561421	2,327	2,260	2,287	2,328	2,113	2,069
Telemarketing bureaus and other contact centers	561422	14,829	14,501	13,348	13,601	14,239	14,663
Private mail centers	561431	2,146	1,947	1,953	1,974	2,064	2,065
Other business service centers (including copy shops)	561439	8,177	7,220	7,071	6,479	6,445	6,594
Collection agencies	56144	11,986	11,120	11,742	12,024	12,570	12,519
Credit bureaus	56145	7,860	7,760	7,794	7,987	9,128	9,621
Repossession services	561491	810	862	764	673	561	642
Court reporting and stenotype services	561492	2,207	2,205	2,233	2,220	2,083	2,061
All other business support services	561499	9,169	8,860	9,227	9,353	8,989	9,052
Travel agencies	56151	17,093	14,792	16,449	17,605	17,869	17,484
Tour operators	56152	5,279	4,887	5,283	5,389	5,784	6,107
Convention and visitors bureaus	561591	1,559	1,437	1,414	1,490	1,638	1,740
All other travel arrangement and reservation services	561599	14,075	12,747	13,851	14,789	15,630	17,230
Investigation services	561611	3,820	3,889	4,085	4,200	4,302	4,580
Security guards and patrol services	561612	19,619	19,129	18,082	17,896	18,292	18,728
Armored car services	561613	2,365	2,385	2,394	2,514	2,512	2,503
Security systems services (except locksmiths)	561621	15,624	15,312	15,822	17,506	18,637	19,619
Locksmiths	561622	1,637	1,464	1,488	1,507	1,546	1,580
Exterminating and pest control services	56171	8,936	9,135	9,543	9,743	10,486	11,163
Janitorial services	56172	34,887	32,591	33,565	34,561	34,959	36,032
Landscaping services	56173	53,200	47,929	49,307	51,833	54,718	58,649
Carpet and upholstery cleaning services	56174	3,097	2,870	2,629	2,799	2,855	3,010
Other services to buildings and dwellings	56179	5,233	5,091	4,876	5,061	5,693	6,216
Packaging and labeling services	56191	5,188	4,874	5,309	5,526	5,772	6,287
Convention and trade show organizers	56192	11,998	9,618	10,128	11,241	12,226	12,216
All other support services	56199	20,719	19,021	18,945	17,864	18,235	18,573
Waste management and remediation services	562	78,852	72,802	81,934	83,862	84,335	86,079
Solid waste collection	562111	39,495	36,797	37,962	39,247	39,195	39,694
Hazardous waste collection	562112	1,986	1,824	1,994	1,905	1,977	2,322
Other waste collection	562119	1,795	1,428	1,417	1,540	1,680	1,524
Hazardous waste treatment and disposal	562211	5,972	5,945	6,605	7,106	7,425	7,845
Solid waste landfill	562212	5,695	4,983	5,091	5,306	5,576	6,032
Solid waste combustors and incinerators	562213	2,123	1,729	(S)	1,938	1,916	1,933
Other nonhazardous waste treatment and disposal	562219	706	554	504	497	542	559
Remediation services	56291	12,544	12,256	17,860	16,603	16,599	16,502
Materials recovery facilities	56292	4,636	3,679	4,854	5,752	5,246	5,156
Septic tank and related services	562991	2,573	2,403	2,504	2,618	2,897	3,126
All other miscellaneous waste management services	562998	1,327	1,204	1,246	1,350	1,282	1,386

S Figure does not meet publication standards. [1] North American Industry Classification System, 2007; see text, Section 15. [2] Data prior to 2011 have been restated to reflect comparable data on the 2007 NAICS basis for more detailed levels within this aggregate. [3] Includes 2002 NAICS 561310 (Employment Placement Agencies) and a portion of 2002 NAICS 541612 (Human Resources and Executive Search Consulting Services).

Source: U.S. Census Bureau, Annual & Quarterly Services, "2013 Annual Services," <http://www.census.gov/services/index.html>, accessed February 2015.

Table 1289. Estimated Accommodation and Food Service Sales by Kind of Business: 2000 to 2013

[In millions of dollars (441,944 represents $441,944,000,000). Estimates are based on data from the Annual Retail Trade Survey and administrative records and have been adjusted to preliminary results of the 2012 Economic Census]

Kind of business	2007 NAICS code [1]	2000	2005	2009	2010	2011	2012	2013
Accommodation and food services, total	**72**	**441,944**	**558,465**	**622,747**	**642,783**	**683,045**	**723,479**	**751,258**
Accommodation	721	137,683	162,002	170,377	175,307	187,247	198,585	208,540
Traveler accommodation	7211	133,118	156,856	164,344	169,173	180,929	191,672	201,555
RV parks and recreational camps	7212	3,588	4,108	4,779	4,832	4,903	5,192	5,225
Rooming and boarding houses	7213	977	1,038	1,254	1,302	1,415	1,721	1,760
Food services and drinking places [2]	722	304,261	396,463	452,370	467,476	495,798	524,894	542,718
Full service restaurants	7221	133,579	174,119	193,985	198,908	214,081	227,559	234,778
Limited service eating places	7222	127,519	169,034	195,022	203,477	214,323	226,107	235,855
Drinking places	7224	15,330	18,053	19,990	20,236	20,623	21,466	21,507

[1] North American Industry Classification System, 2007; see text, Section 15. [2] Includes other kinds of business not shown separately.

Source: U.S. Census Bureau, "Annual Accommodation and Food Services—2013," <http://www.census.gov/retail/>, accessed March 2015.

Table 1290. Other Services—Estimated Revenue for Employer Firms by Kind of Business: 2009 to 2013

[In millions of dollars (363,920 represents $363,920,000,000). For taxable and tax exempt employer firms. Estimates have been adjusted to the results of the 2007 Economic Census. Based on the Service Annual Survey; see Appendix III]

Kind of business	2007 NAICS code [1]	2009	2010	2011	2012	2013
Other services (except public administration) [2,3]	**81**	**363,920**	**384,313**	**399,778**	**422,722**	**448,249**
Repair and maintenance	811	128,212	131,468	140,629	146,298	149,670
General automotive repair	811111	34,864	36,559	38,620	40,269	41,581
Automotive transmission repair	811113	2,422	2,199	2,345	2,335	2,273
Other automotive mechanical and electrical repair and maintenance	811118	2,197	2,298	2,403	2,401	2,449
Automotive body, paint, interior repair and maintenance	811121	24,390	25,500	28,203	29,273	30,019
Automotive glass replacement shops	811122	3,265	3,031	3,117	2,977	3,002
Automotive oil change and lubrication shops	811191	4,902	4,969	4,885	4,872	4,811
Car washes	811192	5,661	5,801	5,887	6,388	6,750
All other automotive repair and maintenance	811198	1,221	1,359	1,478	1,625	1,838
Consumer electronics repair and maintenance	811211	1,709	1,503	1,027	952	935
Computer and office machine repair and maintenance	811212	6,999	7,123	7,034	6,832	6,992
Communication equipment repair and maintenance	811213	2,992	3,024	3,184	3,162	3,136
Other electronic and precision equipment repair and maintenance	811219	7,276	7,500	7,917	8,047	7,871
Commercial and industrial machinery and equipment (except automotive and electronic) repair and maintenance	8113	23,510	24,030	27,888	29,955	30,234
Home and garden equipment and appliance repair and maintenance	81141	2,464	2,388	2,329	2,664	2,839
Reupholstery and furniture repair	81142	948	914	923	964	1,056
Other personal and household goods repair and maintenance	81149	2,453	2,319	2,435	2,568	2,826
Personal and laundry services	812	81,391	82,776	86,065	90,067	94,352
Beauty shops	812112	18,913	19,507	19,018	19,535	20,283
Diet and weight reducing centers	812191	1,606	1,323	1,428	1,495	1,322
Other personal care services	812199	4,018	4,238	4,750	5,549	6,142
Funeral homes and funeral services	81221	12,181	12,566	12,845	13,045	13,628
Cemeteries and crematories	81222	2,999	2,971	3,076	3,148	3,252
Coin-operated laundries and drycleaners	81231	3,299	3,546	3,569	3,680	3,764
Dry-cleaning and laundry services (except coin-operated)	81232	7,664	7,538	7,871	7,843	7,942
Linen supply	812331	4,593	4,667	4,803	5,173	5,282
Industrial launders	812332	6,412	6,216	6,537	6,765	6,991
Pet care (except veterinary) services	81291	2,544	2,772	2,996	3,357	3,706
Photofinishing	81292	1,913	1,907	2,200	2,516	2,682
Parking lots and garages	81293	8,330	8,388	8,881	8,971	9,343
All other personal services	81299	4,673	4,673	5,237	5,541	6,081
Religious, grantmaking, civic, professional, and similar organizations [4]	813	154,317	170,069	173,084	186,357	204,227
Grantmaking and giving services	8132	59,944	71,998	72,740	82,296	96,377
Social advocacy organizations	8133	21,221	22,676	23,833	23,965	24,275
Civic and social organizations	8134	14,750	15,042	15,053	15,573	16,429
Business, professional, labor, political, and similar organizations [5]	8139	58,402	60,353	61,458	64,523	67,146

[1] Based on the North American Industry Classification System, 2007; see Section 15. [2] Data prior to 2011 have been restated to reflect comparable data on the 2007 NAICS basis. [3] Excludes NAICS 8131 (Religious Organizations), NAICS 81393 (Labor Unions and Similar Labor Organizations), NAICS 81394 (Political Organizations), and NAICS 814 (Private Households). [4] Excludes NAICS 8131 (Religious Organizations), NAICS 81393 (Labor Unions and Similar Labor Organizations), and NAICS 81394 (Political Organizations). [5] Excludes NAICS 81393 (Labor Unions and Similar Labor Organizations) and NAICS 81394 (Political Organizations).

Source: U.S. Census Bureau, Annual & Quarterly Services, "2013 Annual Services," <http://www.census.gov/services/index.html>, accessed February 2015.

Table 1291. National Nonprofit Associations—Number by Type: 1980 to 2015

[Data compiled during last few months of year previous to year shown and the beginning months of year shown]

Type	1980	1990	2000	2005	2010 [1]	2011	2012	2013	2014	2015
Total	**14,726**	**22,289**	**21,840**	**22,720**	**23,983**	**24,168**	**23,809**	**25,252**	**24,851**	**23,891**
Trade, business, commercial	3,118	3,918	3,880	3,789	3,761	3,792	3,715	3,835	3,673	3,487
Agriculture and environment	677	940	1,103	1,170	1,442	1,449	1,463	1,505	1,461	1,421
Legal, governmental, public admin., military	529	792	790	868	913	915	893	926	917	894
Scientific, engineering, technical	1,039	1,417	1,302	1,354	1,563	1,569	1,561	1,606	1,570	1,507
Educational	[2] 2,376	1,291	1,297	1,318	1,444	1,446	1,444	1,497	1,408	1,344
Cultural	([2])	1,886	1,786	1,733	1,717	1,721	1,677	1,730	1,674	1,610
Social welfare	994	1,705	1,829	2,072	2,673	2,727	2,805	3,149	3,254	3,166
Health, medical	1,413	2,227	2,495	2,982	3,481	3,511	3,569	3,907	4,099	4,069
Public affairs	1,068	2,249	1,776	1,854	1,734	1,749	1,697	1,805	1,740	1,601
Fraternal, nationality, ethnic	435	573	525	550	461	465	347	470	431	398
Religious	797	1,172	1,123	1,147	1,056	1,058	1,023	1,043	994	964
Veteran, hereditary, patriotic	208	462	835	774	585	587	565	600	583	545
Hobby, avocational	910	1,475	1,330	1,433	1,374	1,385	1,330	1,404	1,356	1,287
Athletic sports	504	840	717	762	946	955	931	959	940	899
Labor unions	235	253	232	208	188	190	182	188	173	162
Chambers of Commerce [3]	105	168	143	135	142	144	135	142	136	125
Greek and non-Greek letter societies	318	340	296	349	305	305	299	306	299	294
Fan clubs	(NA)	581	381	314	198	200	173	180	143	118

NA Not available. [1] Beginning in 2007, there was an increase in the number of associations due to an increase in newly discovered and established associations. [2] Data for cultural associations included with educational associations. [3] National and binational. Includes trade and tourism organizations.

Source: Gale, Cengage Learning, Farmington Hills, MI, compiled from Encyclopedia of Associations ©, annual.

Section 28
Foreign Commerce and Aid

This section presents data on the flow of goods, services, and capital between the United States and other countries; changes in official reserve assets of the United States; international investments; and foreign assistance programs.

The Bureau of Economic Analysis publishes current figures on U.S. international transactions and the U.S. international investment position in its monthly *Survey of Current Business* and in an interactive database on the Internet at <http://www.bea.gov/itable/index.cfm>. Statistics for the foreign aid programs are presented by the Agency for International Development (USAID) in its annual *U.S. Overseas Loans and Grants*.

The principal source of merchandise import and export data is the U.S. Census Bureau. Current data are presented monthly in *U.S. International Trade in Goods and Services Report* Series FT 900. The *Guide to Foreign Trade Statistics*, found on the Census Bureau Web site at <http://www.census.gov/foreign-trade/guide/index.html>, lists the Census Bureau's monthly and annual products and services in this field. In addition, the International Trade Administration and the Bureau of Economic Analysis present summary as well as selected commodity and country data for U.S. foreign trade on their Web sites: <http://www.trade.gov/mas/ian/tradestatistics/> and <http://www.bea.gov/international/index.htm>, respectively. The merchandise trade data published by the Bureau of Economic Analysis in the *Survey of Current Business* and on the Web include balance of payments adjustments to the Census Bureau data. The U.S. Treasury Department's *Monthly Treasury Statement of Receipts and Outlays of the United States Government* contains information on import duties. The International Trade Commission, U.S. Department of Agriculture (agricultural products), U.S. Department of Energy (mineral fuels, like petroleum and coal), and the U.S. Geological Survey (minerals) release various reports and specialized products on U.S. trade.

International accounts—The international transactions tables (Tables 1292, 1293, and 1296) show, for given time periods, the transfer of goods, services, grants, and financial assets and liabilities between the United States and the rest of the world. The international investment position table (Table 1295) presents, for specific dates, the value of U.S. investments abroad and of foreign investments in the United States. The movement of foreign and U.S. capital as presented in the balance of payments is not the only factor affecting the total value of foreign investments. Among the other factors are changes in the valuation of assets or liabilities, including changes in prices of securities, defaults, expropriations, and write-offs.

Direct investment abroad means the ownership or control, directly or indirectly, by one person of 10 percent or more of the voting securities of an incorporated business enterprise or an equivalent interest in an unincorporated business enterprise. Direct investment position is the value of U.S. parents' claims on the equity of and receivables due from foreign affiliates, less foreign affiliates' receivables due from their U.S. parents. Income consists of parents' shares in the earnings of their affiliates plus net interest received by parents on intercompany accounts, less withholding taxes on dividends and interest.

Foreign aid—Foreign assistance is divided into three major categories—grants (military supplies and services and other grants), credits, and other assistance (through net accumulation of foreign currency claims from the sale of agricultural commodities). *Grants* are transfers for which no payment is expected (other than a limited percentage of the foreign currency "counterpart" funds generated by the grant), or which at most involve an obligation on the part of the receiver to extend aid to the United States or other countries to achieve a common objective. *Credits* are loan disbursements or transfers under other agreements which give rise to specific obligations to repay, over a period of years, usually with interest. All known returns to the U.S. government stemming from grants and credits (reverse grants, returns of grants, and payments of principal) are taken into account in net grants and net credits, but no allowance is made for interest or commissions. *Other assistance* represents the transfer of U.S. farm products in exchange for foreign currencies (plus, since enactment of Public Law 87-128, currency claims from principal and interest collected on credits extended under the farm products program), less the government's disbursements of the currencies as grants, credits, or for purchases. The net acquisition of currencies represents net transfers of resources to foreign countries under the agricultural programs, in addition to those classified as grants or credits.

Exports—Export statistics consist of goods valued at more than $2,500 per commodity shipped by individuals and organizations (including exporters, freight forwarders, and carriers) from the U.S. to other countries. The Census Bureau compiles export data primarily from three sources: Shipper's Export Declaration documents filed with Customs and Border Protection and sent to the Census Bureau (3 percent of all transactions), data in electronic form submitted directly by exporters and their agents (63 percent); and special computer tapes from Canada for U.S. exports to Canada (34 percent). Estimates are made for low-value exports by country of destination, and based on bilateral trade patterns. They include U.S. exports under mutual security programs and exclude shipments to U.S. Armed Forces for their own use.

The value reported in the export statistics is generally equivalent to a free alongside ship (f.a.s.) value at the U.S. port of export, based on the transaction price, including inland freight, insurance, and other charges incurred in placing the merchandise alongside the carrier at the U.S. port of exportation. This value, as defined, excludes the cost of loading merchandise aboard the exporting carrier and also excludes freight, insurance, and any other charges or transportation and other costs beyond the U.S. port of exportation. The country of destination is defined as the country of ultimate destination or country where the merchandise is to be consumed, further processed, or manufactured, as known to the shipper at the time of exportation. When ultimate destination is not known, the shipment is statistically credited to the last country to which the shipper knows the merchandise will be shipped in the same form as exported.

Statistics for U.S. exports to Canada are based on import documents filed with Canadian agencies and forwarded to the U.S. Census Bureau under a 1987 data exchange agreement. Under this agreement, each country eliminated most cross-border export documents; maintains detailed statistics on cross-border imports; exchanges monthly files of cross-border import statistics; and publishes exchanged statistics in place of previously compiled export statistics.

Prior to 1989, exports were based on Schedule B, Statistical Classification of Domestic and Foreign Commodities Exported from the United States. Beginning in 1989, Schedule B classifications are based on the Harmonized System and coincide with the Standard International Trade Classification, Revision 3. This revision will affect the comparability of most export series beginning with the 1989 data for commodities.

Imports—Import statistics consist of goods valued at more than $2,000 per commodity shipped by individuals and organizations (including importers and customs brokers) into the U.S. from other countries. The Census Bureau compiles import data from records filed with Customs and Border Protection, usually within 10 days after the merchandise enters the United States. Estimates are made for low-value shipments by country of origin, based on previous bilateral trade patterns and periodically updated. Country of origin is defined as country where the merchandise was grown, mined, or manufactured. If country of origin is unknown, country of shipment is reported. Statistics for over 95 percent of all commodity transactions are compiled from records filed electronically with Customs and forwarded as computer tape files to the U.S. Census Bureau. Statistics for other transactions are compiled from

hard-copy documents filed with Customs and forwarded on a flow basis for U.S. Census Bureau processing.

Data on import values are presented on two valuations bases in this section: the c.i.f. (cost, insurance, and freight) and the customs import value (as appraised by the U.S. Customs Service in accordance with legal requirements of the Tariff Act of 1930, as amended). This latter valuation, primarily used for collection of import duties, frequently does not reflect the actual transaction value.

Imports are classified either as "General imports" or "Imports for consumption." *General imports* are a combination of entries for immediate consumption, entries into customs bonded warehouses, and entries into U.S. Foreign Trade Zones, thus generally reflecting total arrivals of merchandise. *Imports for consumption* are a combination of entries for immediate consumption, withdrawals from warehouses for consumption, and entries of merchandise into U.S. customs territory from U.S. Foreign Trade Zones, thus generally reflecting the total of the commodities entered into U.S. consumption channels.

Beginning in 1989, import statistics are based on the Harmonized Tariff Schedule of the United States, which coincides with import Standard International Trade Classification, Revision 3. This revision will affect the comparability of most import series beginning with the 1989 data.

Area coverage—Except as noted, the geographic area covered by the export and import trade statistics is the United States Customs area (includes the 50 states, the District of Columbia, and Puerto Rico), the U.S. Virgin Islands (effective January 1981), and U.S. Foreign Trade Zones (effective July 1982).

Statistical reliability—For a discussion of statistical collection and estimation, sampling procedures, and measures of statistical reliability applicable to Census Bureau data, see Appendix III.

Table 1292. U.S. International Transactions by Type of Transaction: 2000 to 2014

[In millions of dollars (1,471,532 represents $1,471,532,000,000). Minus sign (-) indicates debits. N.i.e. is not indicated elsewhere]

Type of transaction	2000	2005	2007	2008	2009	2010	2011	2012	2013	2014
Exports of goods and services and income receipts	**1,471,532**	**1,895,983**	**2,569,492**	**2,751,949**	**2,285,922**	**2,630,799**	**2,987,571**	**3,098,059**	**3,201,282**	**3,306,574**
Exports of goods and services	1,075,321	1,286,022	1,653,548	1,841,612	1,583,053	1,853,606	2,127,021	2,218,989	2,279,937	2,343,205
Goods	784,940	913,016	1,165,151	1,308,795	1,070,331	1,290,273	1,499,240	1,562,578	1,592,043	1,632,639
General merchandise	778,718	906,104	1,150,198	1,288,516	1,055,433	1,271,966	1,463,990	1,524,738	1,557,698	1,609,715
Foods, feeds, and beverages	47,871	58,955	84,264	108,349	93,908	107,719	126,247	133,049	136,160	143,751
Industrial supplies and materials	171,108	236,812	316,284	386,917	293,540	388,561	485,258	483,232	492,296	500,007
Capital goods except automotive	357,000	358,426	433,019	457,655	391,498	447,839	494,202	527,459	534,524	551,321
Automotive vehicles, parts, and engines	80,356	98,406	121,264	121,451	81,715	112,008	133,036	146,158	152,670	159,690
Consumer goods except food and automotive	89,305	115,228	145,863	161,157	149,287	164,909	174,719	180,994	188,370	198,300
Other general merchandise	33,078	38,276	49,505	52,987	45,486	50,931	50,529	53,846	53,678	56,646
Net exports of goods under merchanting	159	1,330	1,547	1,465	797	411	511	552	462	296
Nonmonetary gold	6,063	5,582	13,406	18,813	14,101	17,896	34,739	37,289	33,883	22,628
Services	290,381	373,006	488,396	532,817	512,722	563,333	627,781	656,411	687,894	710,565
Maintenance and repair services n.i.e.	5,011	7,624	10,020	10,586	12,863	14,549	16,436	17,186	18,648	22,389
Transport[1]	45,758	52,622	65,824	74,973	62,189	71,656	79,830	83,944	87,415	90,031
Travel (for all purposes including education)[2]	100,187	101,470	119,037	133,761	119,902	137,010	150,867	161,632	172,901	177,241
Insurance services	3,631	7,566	10,841	13,403	14,586	15,114	15,114	16,692	17,058	17,417
Financial services	22,117	39,878	61,376	63,027	64,437	72,348	78,271	76,692	84,091	87,290
Charges for the use of intellectual property n.i.e.	51,808	74,448	97,803	102,125	98,406	107,521	123,333	124,440	127,927	130,362
Telecommunications, computer, and information services	12,215	15,515	20,192	23,119	23,816	25,038	29,171	32,510	35,035	35,885
Other business services	40,497	58,302	82,382	92,738	95,984	101,029	112,568	120,382	121,873	129,514
Government goods and services n.i.e.[3,4]	9,156	15,582	20,921	19,084	20,538	19,784	22,191	22,835	22,946	20,438
Primary income receipts	358,822	543,982	844,033	823,707	614,379	684,915	759,727	769,479	794,763	823,353
Investment income	354,427	539,186	838,814	818,342	608,639	678,984	753,622	763,177	788,007	816,445
Compensation of employees	4,395	4,796	5,219	5,364	5,740	5,931	6,105	6,302	6,756	6,909
Secondary income (current transfer) receipts[5]	37,390	65,980	71,912	86,630	88,491	92,278	100,822	109,590	126,582	140,016
Imports of goods and services and income payments	**1,882,288**	**2,641,418**	**3,288,135**	**3,438,590**	**2,666,714**	**3,072,759**	**3,447,924**	**3,547,729**	**3,578,042**	**3,696,100**
Imports of goods and services	1,447,837	2,000,267	2,358,922	2,550,339	1,966,827	2,348,263	2,675,646	2,755,762	2,758,331	2,851,529
Goods	1,231,722	1,691,820	1,986,347	2,141,287	1,580,025	1,938,950	2,239,886	2,303,749	2,294,630	2,374,101
General merchandise	1,225,780	1,691,201	1,977,283	2,127,790	1,569,630	1,924,446	2,221,911	2,284,535	2,276,882	2,358,653
Foods, feeds, and beverages	46,489	69,072	82,974	90,439	82,861	92,492	108,257	111,127	116,004	126,683
Industrial supplies and materials	303,768	533,686	648,412	798,796	469,641	610,268	765,553	734,803	686,692	672,611
Capital goods except automotive	347,706	382,833	449,117	458,698	374,054	450,406	513,430	551,777	557,893	595,732
Automotive vehicles, parts, and engines	194,954	238,715	258,497	233,204	159,186	225,641	255,226	298,498	309,572	328,499
Consumer goods except food and automotive	284,634	412,734	479,758	485,679	429,853	485,121	515,868	518,821	533,957	559,392
Other general merchandise	48,229	54,161	58,524	60,974	54,034	60,519	63,578	69,508	72,764	75,736
Nonmonetary gold	5,942	4,618	9,064	13,497	10,395	14,504	17,975	19,214	17,748	15,448
Services	216,115	304,448	372,575	409,052	386,801	409,313	435,761	452,013	463,700	477,428
Maintenance and repair services n.i.e.	2,569	3,015	5,209	5,742	5,938	6,909	8,236	8,015	7,486	7,468
Transport[1]	57,606	75,643	79,326	83,988	64,133	74,628	81,377	84,985	90,634	94,219
Travel (for all purposes including education)[2]	65,787	79,988	89,235	92,545	81,421	86,623	89,700	100,338	104,107	110,787
Insurance services	11,284	28,710	47,517	58,913	63,801	61,478	55,654	55,513	53,420	50,096
Financial services	10,936	12,126	19,197	17,218	14,415	15,502	17,368	16,703	18,519	19,503
Charges for the use of intellectual property n.i.e.	16,606	25,577	26,479	29,623	31,297	32,551	36,087	32,661	38,999	42,124
Telecommunications, computer, and information services	12,397	15,975	22,384	24,655	25,784	29,015	32,756	32,779	33,812	33,314
Other business services	24,414	35,960	54,968	67,488	68,553	70,646	83,289	87,157	91,389	95,752
Government goods and services n.i.e.[3,6]	14,516	27,454	28,260	28,880	31,460	31,960	31,293	27,861	25,334	24,163
Primary income payments	339,643	476,349	743,429	677,561	490,794	507,254	538,766	557,301	570,220	585,369
Investment income	328,688	460,441	727,707	660,500	476,376	493,292	524,582	542,356	554,392	569,031
Compensation of employees	10,955	15,909	15,722	17,061	14,418	13,962	14,184	14,946	15,828	16,339
Secondary income (current transfer) payments[5]	94,808	164,801	185,784	210,691	209,093	217,242	233,512	234,665	249,492	259,202
Capital transfer receipts and other credits	**35**	**15,462**	**494**	**6,170**	**140**	**157**	**1,186**	**7,668**	**412**	**–**
Capital transfer payments and other debits	**36**	**2,346**	**110**	**159**	**–**	**–**	**–**	**764**	**–**	**45**
Net U.S. acquisition of financial assets[7]	**589,315**	**572,317**	**1,572,509**	**-309,468**	**132,204**	**963,449**	**496,320**	**167,398**	**643,915**	**792,145**
Direct investment assets	188,004	61,925	532,939	351,724	313,726	354,575	440,405	377,899	399,203	357,190
Equity	171,644	51,621	431,378	360,130	262,058	343,040	401,533	322,558	336,930	355,622

See footnotes at end of table.

Table 1292. U.S. International Transactions by Type of Transaction: 2000 to 2014—Continued.

Type of transaction	2000	2005	2007	2008	2009	2010	2011	2012	2013	2014
Debt instruments	16,360	10,304	101,561	-8,406	51,669	11,535	38,872	55,341	62,273	1,568
Portfolio investment assets	159,713	267,290	380,807	-284,269	375,883	199,620	85,365	238,763	476,237	538,058
Equity and investment fund shares	106,714	186,684	147,782	-38,550	63,696	79,150	6,950	95,755	284,303	436,526
Debt securities [8]	52,999	80,606	233,025	-245,720	312,186	120,469	78,415	143,008	191,935	101,531
Other investment assets [8]	241,308	257,196	658,641	-381,770	-609,662	407,420	-45,327	-453,724	-228,426	-99,520
Currency and deposits	(NA)	82,879	375,146	123,493	-394,461	150,249	-89,161	-519,346	-121,540	-147,354
Loans	(NA)	173,031	272,812	-501,550	-215,735	251,128	39,821	64,933	-116,691	54,595
Insurance technical reserves	(NA)	(NA)	(NA)	(NA)	(NA)	(NA)	(NA)	(NA)	(NA)	(NA)
Trade credit and advances	680	1,286	10,683	-3,712	535	6,043	4,013	689	9,805	-6,761
Reserve assets	290	-14,094	122	4,848	52,256	1,835	15,877	4,460	-3,099	-3,583
Special drawing rights	722	-4,511	154	106	48,230	31	-1,752	37	22	23
Reserve position in the International Monetary Fund	-2,308	-10,200	-1,021	3,473	3,357	1,293	18,079	4,032	-3,438	-3,849
Other reserve assets	1,876	617	989	1,269	669	511	-450	391	317	243
Currency and deposits	(NA)	224	517	587	138	55	110	24	3	5
Securities	(NA)	309	288	443	480	439	-598	365	313	234
Other claims	(NA)	84	184	239	51	17	39	3		4
Net U.S. incurrence of liabilities [7]	**1,067,016**	**1,273,038**	**2,183,538**	**454,051**	**318,350**	**1,386,345**	**977,073**	**615,711**	**1,041,959**	**977,421**
Direct investment liabilities	350,066	138,328	340,066	332,734	153,787	259,345	257,411	232,001	287,163	131,831
Equity	259,380	112,459	190,418	294,861	148,465	203,148	185,051	193,797	211,762	68,854
Debt instruments	90,686	25,869	149,648	37,874	5,322	56,197	72,361	38,204	75,401	62,977
Portfolio investment liabilities	441,966	832,037	1,156,612	523,683	357,352	820,434	311,626	746,988	501,975	705,030
Equity and investment fund shares	193,600	89,258	275,617	126,804	219,302	178,952	123,357	239,065	-67,486	155,077
Debt securities [8]	248,366	742,779	880,995	396,879	138,050	641,481	188,269	507,923	569,461	549,953
Other investment liabilities	274,984	302,673	686,860	-402,367	-192,789	306,566	408,036	-363,278	252,821	140,559
Currency and deposits	(NA)	-124,782	239,302	74,441	-74,225	115,678	475,678	-245,669	201,981	51,031
Loans	(NA)	415,824	426,981	-483,554	-172,464	172,256	-84,789	-129,242	38,503	75,265
Insurance technical reserves	(NA)	(NA)	(NA)	(NA)	(NA)	(NA)	(NA)	(NA)	(NA)	(NA)
Trade credit and advances	10,375	11,632	20,576	6,746	6,301	18,632	17,147	11,633	12,337	14,263
Special drawing rights allocations					47,598					—
Financial derivatives, net [9]	(NA)	(NA)	-6,222	32,947	-44,816	-14,076	-35,006	7,064	2,213	-54,372
Statistical discrepancy [10]	-66,944	31,597	101,008	-49,941	149,970	5,146	-54,219	1,516	-18,658	149,923
Balance on current account (exports less imports)	-410,756	-745,434	-718,643	-686,641	-380,792	-441,961	-460,354	-449,670	-376,760	-389,526
Balance on goods and services	-372,517	-714,245	-705,375	-708,726	-383,774	-494,658	-548,625	-536,773	-478,394	-508,324
Balance on goods	-446,783	-782,804	-821,196	-832,492	-509,694	-648,678	-740,646	-741,171	-702,587	-741,462
Balance on services	74,266	68,558	115,821	123,765	125,920	154,020	192,020	204,398	224,193	233,138
Balance on primary income	19,178	67,632	100,604	146,146	123,584	177,661	220,961	212,178	224,543	237,984
Balance on secondary income	-57,418	-98,822	-113,872	-124,061	-120,602	-124,964	-132,690	-125,075	-122,910	-119,185
Balance on capital account	**-1**	**13,116**	**384**	**6,010**	**-140**	**-157**	**-1,186**	**6,904**	**-412**	**-45**
Net lending/borrowing from current- and capital-account transactions [11, 12]	-410,757	-732,319	-718,260	-680,631	-380,932	-442,118	-461,540	-442,765	-377,172	-389,571
Net lending/borrowing from financial-account transactions [11, 12]	-477,701	-700,721	-617,251	-730,572	-230,962	-436,972	-515,759	-441,249	-395,831	-239,648

—Represents zero. NA Not available. [1] Includes passenger fares. [2] All travel purposes include 1) business travel, including expenditures by border, seasonal, and other short-term workers and 2) personal travel, including health-related and education-related travel. [3] Includes goods and services supplied by and to embassies, consulates, and military bases; goods and services acquired from the host economy by diplomatic and military personnel; and services supplied by and to governments that are not included in other service categories. [4] Includes transfers under U.S. military sales contracts. [5] Secondary income (current transfer) receipts and payments include U.S. government grants and pensions, fines and penalties, withholding taxes, personal transfers (remittances), insurance-related transfers, and other current transfers. [6] Includes direct defense expenditures. [7] Excluding financial derivatives. [8] Includes transactions in U.S. Treasury and other U.S. securities. [9] Transactions for financial derivatives are only available as a net value equal to transactions for assets less transactions for liabilities. A positive value represents net U.S. cash payments arising from derivatives contracts, and a negative value represents net U.S. cash receipts. [10] The statistical discrepancy is the difference between total debits and total credits recorded in the current, capital, and financial accounts. In the current and capital accounts, credits and debits are labeled in the table. In the financial account, an acquisition of an asset or a repayment of a liability is a debit, and an incurrence of a liability or a disposal of an asset is a credit. [11] Net lending means that U.S. residents are net suppliers of funds to foreign residents, and net borrowing means the opposite. Net lending or net borrowing can be computed from current- and capital-account transactions or from financial-account transactions. The two amounts differ by the statistical discrepancy. [12] Net lending or net borrowing from financial-account transactions is the net U.S. acquisition of financial assets excluding financial derivatives less net U.S. incurrence of liabilities excluding financial derivatives plus financial derivatives other than reserves.

Source: Bureau of Economic Analysis, International Economic Accounts, "Table 1.2. U.S. International Transactions, Expanded Detail," <http://www.bea.gov/international/index.htm>, accessed August 2015.

Table 1293. U.S. Balances on International Transactions by Area and Selected Country: 2013 and 2014

[In millions of dollars (–376,760 represents -$376,760,000,000). Country data are based on information available from U.S. reporting sources. In some instances, the statistics may not necessarily reflect the ultimate foreign transactor. Minus sign (-) indicates debits]

Area or Country	2013, balance on—				2014, balance on—			
	Current account	Goods	Services	Primary income [1]	Current account	Goods	Services	Primary income [1]
All areas	**-376,760**	**-702,587**	**224,193**	**224,543**	**-389,526**	**-741,462**	**233,138**	**237,984**
Europe	3,495	-135,049	56,210	85,232	10,657	-158,869	64,474	103,302
European Union	-6,727	-127,032	43,368	72,782	7,651	-143,453	50,550	92,106
Euro Area [2]	-14,337	-106,341	25,088	63,405	-10,699	-123,255	30,976	73,682
Germany	-76,565	-67,608	-5,555	-7,830	-81,423	-74,537	-4,626	-3,935
Italy	-24,300	-22,213	-1,832	178	-26,180	-25,328	-2,296	1,776
Netherlands	85,795	22,781	6,402	56,077	87,546	21,833	6,971	58,161
United Kingdom	19,008	-5,487	13,052	9,298	32,009	-892	13,834	17,775
Canada	19,862	-36,192	32,082	24,413	13,311	-40,843	31,279	23,128
Latin America, other Western Hemisphere	54,668	-34,335	38,274	69,795	57,277	-27,475	36,527	67,583
Brazil	43,951	16,830	19,109	8,287	38,476	12,311	19,809	6,956
Mexico	-60,053	-59,965	12,504	827	-62,203	-60,682	10,514	1,334
Asia and Pacific	-414,833	-446,604	78,497	-14,402	-448,792	-486,446	81,596	-15,196
Australia	46,655	16,769	12,611	16,862	40,311	15,762	12,648	11,930
China	-324,863	-318,794	23,190	-26,906	-343,438	-343,193	28,077	-25,108
Hong Kong	43,502	37,266	1,847	4,709	42,835	35,652	2,393	4,901
India	-30,292	-19,784	-5,825	2,889	-32,868	-22,889	-5,592	3,380
Japan	-89,576	-74,773	16,412	-31,430	-81,203	-68,665	15,461	-30,985
Korea, South	-9,421	-19,521	10,161	88	-13,188	-23,732	10,231	331
Singapore	35,808	12,779	6,019	17,029	37,963	13,607	5,977	18,536
Taiwan	-15,400	-12,121	4,575	-7,625	-16,446	-13,565	5,306	-7,822
Middle East	-29,368	-36,586	11,402	6,044	-25,257	-30,916	11,940	4,382
Africa	-19,997	-14,283	5,149	8,469	-2,844	2,791	5,867	7,140
International organizations and unallocated	9,411	462	2,579	44,993	6,122	296	1,455	47,644

[1] Primary income consists of investment income and compensation of employees. [2] See footnote 3, Table 1358.

Source: U.S. Bureau of Economic Analysis, International Economic Accounts, "Table 1.1. U.S. International Transactions" and "Table 1.3. U.S. International Transactions, Expanded Detail by Area and Country," <http://www.bea.gov/international/index.htm>, accessed August 2015.

Table 1294. U.S. Government Reserve Assets: 1990 to 2013

[In billions of dollars (83.3 represents $83,300,000,000). As of end of year]

Type	1990	2000	2005	2006	2007	2008	2009	2010	2011	2012	2013
Total.	83.3	67.6	65.1	65.9	70.6	77.6	130.8	132.4	148.0	150.2	144.6
Gold stock.	11.1	11.0	11.0	11.0	11.0	11.0	11.0	11.0	11.0	11.0	11.0
Special drawing rights.	11.0	10.5	8.2	8.9	9.5	9.3	57.8	56.8	55.0	55.1	55.2
Reserve position in IMF [1].	52.2	14.8	8.0	5.0	4.2	7.7	11.4	12.5	30.1	34.2	30.8
Foreign currencies.	9.1	31.2	37.8	40.9	45.8	49.6	50.5	52.1	51.9	49.9	47.6

[1] International Monetary Fund.

Source: Data prior to 2005, U.S. Department of the Treasury, *Treasury Bulletin*. Beginning in 2005, Board of Governors of the Federal Reserve System, "International Summary Statistics," January 2015 and earlier releases, <http://www.federalreserve.gov/econresdata/statisticsdata.htm>.

Table 1295. U.S. International Investment Position by Type of Investment: 2008 to 2014

[In billions of dollars (-3,995 represents -$3,995,000,000,000). Estimates as of end of 4th quarter. Minus sign (-) indicates loss or deficit]

Type of investment	2008	2009	2010	2011	2012	2013	2014
U.S. net international investment position	**-3,995**	**-2,628**	**-2,512**	**-4,455**	**-4,518**	**-5,328**	**-7,020**
Net international investment position excluding financial derivatives	-4,155	-2,754	-2,622	-4,541	-4,576	-5,405	-7,094
Financial derivatives other than reserves, net	160	126	110	86	58	77	74
U.S. assets	**19,423**	**19,426**	**21,768**	**22,209**	**22,562**	**24,159**	**24,596**
Assets excluding financial derivatives	13,296	15,937	18,116	17,492	18,942	21,139	21,371
Financial derivatives other than reserves, gross positive fair value	6,127	3,490	3,652	4,717	3,620	3,020	3,225
By functional category:							
Direct investment at market value	3,707	4,945	5,486	5,215	5,968	7,117	7,124
Equity	2,928	4,097	4,621	4,320	4,984	6,052	6,052
Debt instruments	779	848	866	895	985	1,065	1,072
Portfolio investment	4,321	6,059	7,160	6,872	7,984	9,207	9,573
Equity and investment fund shares	2,748	3,995	4,900	4,501	5,322	6,473	6,720
Debt securities	1,572	2,063	2,260	2,370	2,662	2,734	2,853
Financial derivatives other than reserves, gross positive fair value	6,127	3,490	3,652	4,717	3,620	3,020	3,225
Over-the-counter contracts	6,065	3,461	3,622	4,669	3,586	2,983	3,157
Exchange-traded contracts	62	29	31	48	34	37	68
Other investment	4,974	4,529	4,980	4,869	4,417	4,367	4,240
Currency and deposits	2,813	2,540	2,767	2,582	2,062	1,992	1,785
Loans	2,117	1,944	2,162	2,232	2,300	2,322	2,409
Trade credit and advances	44	45	51	55	56	53	46
Reserve assets	294	404	489	537	572	448	434
Monetary gold	227	284	368	400	433	315	315
Special drawing rights	9	58	57	55	55	55	52
Reserve position in the International Monetary Fund	8	11	12	30	34	31	25
Other reserve assets	49	50	52	52	50	47	42
U.S. liabilities	**23,419**	**22,054**	**24,280**	**26,664**	**27,080**	**29,487**	**31,615**
Liabilities excluding financial derivatives	17,451	18,691	20,738	22,033	23,518	26,544	28,465
Financial derivatives other than reserves, gross negative fair value	5,968	3,363	3,542	4,631	3,562	2,942	3,151
By functional category:							
Direct investment at market value	3,091	3,619	4,099	4,199	4,661	5,781	6,229
Equity	2,001	2,514	2,928	2,968	3,407	4,441	4,839
Debt instruments	1,091	1,105	1,171	1,231	1,254	1,340	1,389
Portfolio investment	9,476	10,463	11,869	12,647	13,979	15,542	16,917
Equity and investment fund shares	2,132	2,918	3,546	3,842	4,545	5,865	6,665
Debt securities	7,343	7,546	8,323	8,805	9,434	9,678	10,252
Financial derivatives other than reserves, gross negative fair value	5,968	3,363	3,542	4,631	3,562	2,942	3,151
Over-the-counter contracts	5,905	3,334	3,512	4,581	3,528	2,906	3,086
Exchange-traded contracts	63	30	30	49	34	37	64
Other investment	4,884	4,609	4,769	5,187	4,878	5,221	5,319
Currency and deposits	2,332	2,248	2,365	2,839	2,602	2,800	2,838
Loans	2,458	2,212	2,238	2,165	2,081	2,218	2,267
Trade credit and advances	86	93	112	129	141	149	163
Special drawing rights allocations	8	55	54	54	54	54	51

Source: U.S. Bureau of Economic Analysis, International Economic Accounts, International Investment Position "Table 1.2 U.S. Net International Investment Position at the End of the Period, Expanded Detail," <http://www.bea.gov/international/index.htm>, accessed August 2015.

Table 1296. International Service Transactions by Selected Type of Service and Selected Country: 2000 to 2014

[In millions of dollars (290,381 represents $290,381,000,000). Country data are based on information available from U.S. reporting sources. In some instances, the statistics may not necessarily reflect the ultimate foreign transactor. N.i.e. is not elsewhere indicated]

Type of service and country	Exports				Imports			
	2000	2010	2013	2014	2000	2010	2013	2014
Services, total........................	**290,381**	**563,333**	**687,894**	**710,565**	**216,115**	**409,313**	**463,700**	**477,428**
TYPE OF SERVICE								
Maintenance and repair services n.i.e. [1]..........	5,011	14,549	18,648	22,389	2,569	6,909	7,486	7,468
Transport..................................	45,758	71,656	87,415	90,031	57,606	74,628	90,634	94,219
Sea transport.............................	11,554	15,905	17,322	18,152	21,787	29,496	36,264	36,254
Air transport [2]..........................	31,267	51,579	65,523	67,498	32,678	41,377	50,104	53,697
Passenger............................	20,197	30,987	41,642	43,516	20,397	23,426	32,029	34,890
Other modes of transport [3].............	2,938	4,172	4,570	4,381	3,141	3,755	4,266	4,268
Travel.....................................	100,187	137,010	172,901	177,241	65,787	86,623	104,107	110,787
Business...............................	42,664	39,523	39,411	40,358	22,640	21,274	21,116	18,264
Expenditures by border, seasonal, and other short-term workers.............................	5,975	6,344	7,164	7,255	366	1,065	1,209	1,261
Other business travel..................	36,689	33,179	32,247	33,103	22,274	20,209	19,907	17,003
Personal...............................	57,523	97,487	133,490	136,883	43,147	65,349	82,990	92,523
Health related........................	1,501	2,876	3,312	3,468	155	1,019	1,443	1,624
Education related.....................	10,348	20,937	27,410	30,795	2,032	5,468	6,489	6,824
Other personal travel.................	45,674	73,674	102,768	102,620	40,960	58,862	75,058	84,075
Insurance services........................	3,631	14,397	17,058	17,417	11,284	61,478	53,420	50,096
Direct insurance........................	628	4,029	3,987	4,272	1,683	4,374	4,737	4,935
Reinsurance.............................	3,002	8,981	11,283	11,304	9,601	55,660	47,380	43,656
Auxiliary insurance services [4]...........	(NA)	1,387	1,787	1,841	(NA)	1,444	1,303	1,504
Financial services [2]......................	22,117	72,348	84,091	87,290	10,936	15,502	18,519	19,503
Financial management, financial advisory, and custody services......................	(NA)	27,319	33,357	33,162	(NA)	4,105	5,190	5,755
Credit card and other credit-related services.....	(NA)	10,460	17,439	19,309	(NA)	3,702	6,160	6,482
Charges for the use of intellectual property n.i.e. [2].................................	51,808	107,521	127,927	130,362	16,606	32,551	38,999	42,124
Industrial processes......................	(NA)	36,333	44,904	48,723	(NA)	18,847	22,508	23,783
Computer software [5]....................	(NA)	36,008	42,464	39,514	(NA)	5,228	6,481	6,773
Trademarks and franchise fees...........	(NA)	19,131	22,041	22,618	(NA)	4,635	4,629	3,811
Telecommunications, computer, and information services..................	12,215	25,038	35,035	35,885	12,397	29,015	33,812	33,314
Telecommunications services............	5,266	10,911	14,471	13,550	6,167	7,986	7,348	6,656
Computer services......................	4,358	8,991	13,779	15,310	5,934	19,407	24,438	24,386
Information services....................	2,591	5,137	6,784	7,025	295	1,622	2,026	2,272
Other business services..................	40,497	101,029	121,873	129,514	24,414	70,646	91,389	95,752
Research and development services............	7,116	22,446	29,258	33,192	3,346	22,170	30,978	33,048
Professional and management consulting services.................................	17,621	46,749	55,649	59,487	10,648	27,690	34,462	38,163
Technical, trade-related, and other business services [6].....................	15,760	31,834	36,965	36,834	10,420	20,786	25,949	24,542
Government goods and services n.i.e. [7]..........	9,156	19,784	22,946	20,438	14,516	31,960	25,334	24,163
AREA AND COUNTRY								
Europe......................................	107,416	214,164	252,552	267,497	97,718	172,108	196,341	203,023
European Union...........................	93,485	179,237	205,863	219,266	84,215	143,615	162,496	168,716
Euro Area [8]............................	56,433	110,572	128,748	139,763	52,511	90,824	103,660	108,787
France.................................	10,351	16,761	19,153	19,643	10,842	15,820	15,177	16,594
Germany...............................	15,848	24,896	27,451	28,186	15,822	28,397	33,006	32,812
Italy...................................	5,706	8,452	8,942	8,625	6,824	9,552	10,773	10,921
Netherlands...........................	7,052	12,990	15,729	16,711	5,978	8,061	9,328	9,740
United Kingdom........................	31,706	53,568	60,779	63,597	27,238	42,307	47,727	49,764
Canada....................................	24,808	53,126	62,773	61,353	18,239	27,351	30,692	30,074
Latin America, other Western Hemisphere.........	54,194	106,293	131,339	131,554	38,752	87,596	93,065	95,027
Brazil....................................	6,494	18,405	26,725	28,249	1,530	5,143	7,616	8,440
Mexico...................................	15,780	24,614	29,788	30,000	11,200	13,966	17,284	19,487
Asia and Pacific............................	83,301	154,029	197,399	205,216	48,509	95,203	118,903	123,621
Australia.................................	5,719	15,690	19,465	19,394	2,637	5,269	6,854	6,747
China....................................	5,099	22,500	37,313	42,460	3,202	10,609	14,123	14,383
Hong Kong...............................	3,652	5,775	9,019	10,015	4,017	6,419	7,173	7,622
India.....................................	2,789	10,322	13,546	15,200	1,909	14,711	19,371	20,792
Japan....................................	36,862	43,259	46,444	46,698	16,326	24,589	30,032	31,237
Korea, South.............................	6,661	15,451	20,999	20,675	5,699	9,334	10,838	10,444
Singapore................................	6,358	10,380	11,564	11,941	1,995	4,279	5,545	5,964
Taiwan...................................	5,380	9,742	11,781	12,763	3,693	5,865	7,206	7,456
Middle East................................	9,101	21,148	26,805	27,764	5,234	18,049	15,403	15,823
Africa......................................	6,184	11,997	14,191	14,475	3,710	7,934	9,042	8,608
International organizations and unallocated........	5,377	2,576	2,835	2,706	3,954	1,071	256	1,251

NA Not available. [1] Covers maintenance and repair services by residents of country on goods owned by residents of another country. Excludes maintenance and repair of transportation equipment, construction maintenance and repair, and computer maintenance and repair. [2] Includes other types not shown separately. [3] Includes freight services performed by truck, rail, pipeline, in space, and port services for rail and water transport. [4] Includes agents' commissions, brokerage services, insurance consulting services, actuarial services, and other insurance services. [5] Includes receipts and payments for rights to reproduce and distribute. Excludes licenses for use; these licenses are included under computer services. [6] Includes construction, architectural and engineering services, waste treatment, operational leasing, trade-related, and other business services. [7] See footnote 3, Table 1292. Exports include transfers under U.S. military sales contracts; imports include direct defense expenditures. [8] See footnote 3, Table 1358.

Source: U.S. Bureau of Economic Analysis, International Economic Accounts, "Table 3.1. U.S. International Trade in Services," and "Table 3.3. U.S. International Trade in Services by Area and Country, Not Seasonally Adjusted Detail," <http://www.bea.gov/international/index.htm>, accessed August 2015.

Table 1297. Foreign Direct Investment Position in the United States on a Historical-Cost Basis: by Selected Country, 2000 to 2014, and by Industry, 2014

[In millions of dollars (1,256,867 represents $1,256,867,000,000). Foreign direct investment is defined as the ownership or control, directly or indirectly, by one foreign entity (as used here, "entity" is synonymous with "person" as the term is used in a broad legal sense including any individual, branch, partnership, association, trust, corporation, or government) of 10 percent or more of the voting interest of a U.S. business enterprise. Data are based on surveys of U.S. affiliates of foreign companies]

| Country | All industries total | | | | 2014 | | | |
	2000	2010	2012	2013	Total [1]	Manufac-turing	Wholesale trade	Finance and insurance [2]
All countries	1,256,867	2,280,044	2,604,033	2,754,704	2,901,059	1,045,522	345,609	355,171
Canada	114,309	192,463	219,822	235,247	261,247	57,145	7,408	53,338
Europe [3]	887,014	1,659,774	1,830,192	1,894,777	1,977,215	813,484	168,801	236,156
Austria	3,007	4,532	5,341	6,012	6,887	3,232	(D)	1
Belgium	14,787	69,565	103,169	92,197	89,097	49,391	21,951	(D)
Denmark	4,025	7,772	7,964	10,084	12,912	3,576	5,283	2
Finland	8,875	4,943	6,012	7,251	9,100	2,108	5,250	(Z)
France	125,740	189,763	218,091	208,793	223,164	94,133	21,278	27,483
Germany	122,412	203,077	196,934	207,131	224,114	72,962	21,647	14,041
Ireland	25,523	24,097	17,867	17,067	16,195	-2,159	696	4,155
Italy	6,576	20,142	21,890	24,843	21,824	5,998	2,207	(D)
Luxembourg	58,930	170,309	204,814	221,999	242,862	109,352	9,805	29,454
Netherlands	138,894	234,408	265,882	261,358	304,848	147,243	11,061	54,910
Norway	2,665	10,478	18,654	17,940	17,565	978	14,443	(D)
Spain	5,068	43,095	47,072	48,438	58,138	5,690	(D)	2,609
Sweden	21,991	38,780	41,598	39,038	41,909	28,993	5,128	135
Switzerland	64,719	180,642	187,268	202,703	224,021	100,890	18,067	45,775
United Kingdom	277,613	400,435	463,664	501,241	448,548	167,135	30,498	53,914
Latin America and other Western Hemisphere	53,691	62,130	95,212	116,031	127,032	22,820	6,566	4,737
South and Central America [3]	13,384	17,943	24,125	25,108	27,123	9,240	1,017	1,111
Brazil	882	1,357	3,410	1,104	616	-444	-992	848
Mexico	7,462	10,970	13,618	17,036	17,710	4,852	1,449	258
Venezuela	792	3,122	4,379	3,871	5,127	(D)	25	1
Other Western Hemisphere [3]	40,307	44,187	71,087	90,923	99,909	13,580	5,549	3,626
Curacao	(X)	(X)	5,207	5,162	2,779	509	26	32
Netherlands Antilles	3,807	2,819	(X)	(X)	(X)	(X)	(X)	(X)
U.K. Islands, Caribbean	15,191	38,477	75,009	93,635	100,000	14,936	12,904	19,501
Africa	2,700	2,265	3,726	2,317	2,321	-9	660	-6
Middle East [3]	6,506	16,808	20,785	22,073	20,338	5,814	5,079	2,563
Israel	3,012	8,714	9,547	10,052	8,982	5,896	(D)	(D)
Asia and Pacific [3]	192,647	346,605	434,296	484,259	512,906	146,269	157,095	58,383
Australia	18,775	35,632	49,630	47,616	47,340	9,324	3,558	4,881
China	277	3,300	6,927	8,451	9,465	1,049	-116	(D)
Hong Kong	1,493	4,440	10,151	7,135	7,604	1,044	1,965	(Z)
India	96	4,102	5,896	7,757	7,823	717	185	(D)
Japan	159,690	255,012	307,665	350,295	372,800	115,427	118,331	46,178
Korea, South	3,110	15,746	25,194	31,800	36,056	4,996	26,740	140
Singapore	5,087	21,517	19,958	19,283	20,609	10,110	4,577	(D)
Taiwan	3,174	4,642	5,465	6,563	5,676	2,761	803	-29

D Suppressed to avoid disclosure of data of individual companies. X Not applicable. Z Between -$500,000 and +$500,000. [1] Includes other industries, not shown separately. [2] Excludes depository institutions. [3] Includes other countries, not shown separately.

Source: U.S. Bureau of Economic Analysis, International Economic Accounts, "Direct Investment and Multinational Enterprises," <http://www.bea.gov/iTable/index_MNC.cfm>, accessed August 2015.

Table 1298. U.S. Majority-Owned Affiliates of Foreign Companies—Selected Financial and Operating Data by Industry of Affiliate: 2012

[In billions of dollars (12,662 represents $12,662,000,000,000), except as indicated. Data are preliminary. A majority-owned U.S. affiliate is a U.S. business enterprise in which a foreign entity ("entity" is used here in a broad legal sense including any individual, branch, partnership, association, trust, corporation, or government) has a direct or indirect voting interest greater than 50 percent]

Industry	NAICS code [2]	Total assets	Sales	Employ-ment (1,000)	Employee compen-sation	Gross property, plant, and equipment	Mer-chandise exports	Mer-chandise imports
All industries	(X)	12,662	3,690	5,771	456	1,801	334	666
Manufacturing [1]	31-33	1,990	1,570	2,174	187	805	208	308
Petroleum and coal products	324	319	359	55	11	223	31	91
Chemicals	325	501	307	320	39	146	43	54
Machinery	333	141	102	222	20	27	19	17
Transportation equipment	336	309	296	506	35	138	57	87
Wholesale trade	42	704	1,027	570	52	234	112	331
Retail trade	44-45	86	159	518	17	55	1	13
Information	51	250	122	239	23	62	1	(D)
Finance and insurance	52	8,372	355	390	67	90	–	–
Real estate and rental and leasing	53	134	25	50	3	109	(D)	(D)
Professional, scientific, and technical services	54	152	100	295	31	17	1	–
Other industries	(X)	974	333	1,535	77	429	(D)	(D)

– Represents or rounds to zero. D Suppressed to avoid disclosure of data of individual companies. X Not applicable. [1] Includes other industries not shown separately. [2] Based on the North American Industry Classification System (NAICS); see text, Section 15.

Source: U.S. Bureau of Economic Analysis, "Foreign Direct Investment in the United States," <http://www.bea.gov/international/di1fdiop.htm>, accessed April 2015.

Table 1299. Employment of Majority-Owned U.S. Affiliates of Foreign Companies by State: 2007 to 2012

[In thousands (5,588.2 represents 5,588,200). A U.S. majority-owned affiliate is a U.S. business enterprise in which a foreign entity (as used here, "entity" is synonymous with "person" as the term is used in a broad legal sense, including any individual, branch, partnership, association, trust, corporation, or government) has a direct or indirect voting interest greater than 50 percent]

State and other area	2007	2008	2009	2010	2011	2012
Total	5,588.2	5,636.2	5,290.3	5,435.4	5,699.4	5,771.2
Alabama	81.1	80.5	77.7	81.9	85.5	86.4
Alaska	11.4	14.2	13.0	14.1	14.3	14.4
Arizona	73.2	76.3	74.3	77.0	80.8	83.0
Arkansas	36.6	35.5	32.8	35.9	39.2	41.5
California	602.9	600.5	562.7	584.0	595.3	602.8
Colorado	83.5	85.1	81.6	80.9	82.7	83.6
Connecticut	103.3	106.6	101.5	100.9	101.6	100.2
Delaware	28.7	31.6	29.1	26.7	29.2	26.5
District of Columbia	16.3	15.6	19.6	22.4	22.6	23.4
Florida	248.2	255.6	235.2	232.9	242.6	245.8
Georgia	180.6	179.6	170.1	189.5	196.6	196.3
Hawaii	31.0	27.6	26.7	26.8	29.8	32.1
Idaho	14.4	18.0	13.9	13.4	13.7	13.9
Illinois	280.5	273.1	251.8	252.7	270.3	272.8
Indiana	149.1	140.4	132.1	136.0	146.4	152.7
Iowa	45.5	48.8	45.4	44.9	48.1	51.2
Kansas	58.9	55.6	55.5	54.5	58.0	58.4
Kentucky	92.9	94.9	86.0	89.2	94.4	95.4
Louisiana	49.1	50.6	49.1	56.1	57.4	58.3
Maine	29.6	30.3	29.9	30.3	30.7	32.5
Maryland	103.6	108.6	103.5	101.6	104.0	106.1
Massachusetts	183.7	184.8	182.9	187.3	192.3	193.2
Michigan	152.6	150.2	138.9	145.4	179.2	187.6
Minnesota	98.2	97.0	92.8	90.7	94.8	97.9
Mississippi	26.5	28.1	26.9	26.8	27.8	34.1
Missouri	82.4	92.7	84.0	81.7	88.3	89.6
Montana	8.1	8.0	6.8	6.3	6.1	7.2
Nebraska	23.4	26.4	24.8	23.9	25.6	27.0
Nevada	33.8	38.0	34.1	39.0	39.9	40.0
New Hampshire	38.9	40.4	39.3	39.3	39.4	38.6
New Jersey	227.4	239.0	227.2	222.9	227.6	225.1
New Mexico	17.0	17.6	15.8	15.3	19.1	20.2
New York	429.3	410.6	390.4	398.9	414.9	405.4
North Carolina	211.0	202.4	185.6	194.7	203.3	203.4
North Dakota	7.5	12.0	11.1	11.5	14.8	15.3
Ohio	238.2	229.4	212.5	210.2	220.9	224.0
Oklahoma	35.4	37.9	34.9	38.6	41.8	48.2
Oregon	45.8	47.6	42.9	43.0	46.3	46.3
Pennsylvania	264.4	272.8	253.6	261.3	269.2	275.3
Rhode Island	25.7	22.0	24.2	26.1	26.5	27.3
South Carolina	111.3	112.3	101.5	108.4	115.7	115.9
South Dakota	6.8	8.0	7.3	7.2	8.9	9.6
Tennessee	139.2	129.7	119.8	117.2	125.3	125.7
Texas	422.6	444.8	413.3	451.4	474.0	476.4
Utah	33.2	33.4	28.9	31.4	32.8	35.6
Vermont	10.1	10.6	10.7	11.1	11.4	11.9
Virginia	158.1	163.4	151.3	147.8	155.9	154.4
Washington	90.5	93.9	93.5	94.4	96.4	97.9
West Virginia	21.1	22.2	22.4	28.7	26.8	29.3
Wisconsin	82.0	82.0	72.7	77.5	86.0	85.6
Wyoming	8.9	10.8	8.8	7.8	7.9	9.0
Puerto Rico	20.9	20.4	19.4	21.9	20.5	18.2
Other U.S. areas	12.6	17.0	15.0	13.9	15.0	17.2
Foreign	1.0	1.8	5.4	2.3	1.6	1.5

Source: U.S. Bureau of Economic Analysis, International Economic Accounts, "Direct Investment and Multination Companies (MNCs)," <http:bea.gov/iTable/index_MNC.cfm>, accessed April 2015.

Table 1300. U.S. Direct Investment Position Abroad, Capital Outflows, and Income by Industry of Foreign Affiliates: 2000 to 2014

[In millions of dollars (1,316,247 represents $1,316,247,000,000). See headnote, Table 1301]

Industry	2000	2005	2010	2011	2012	2013	2014
DIRECT INVESTMENT POSITION ON A HISTORICAL-COST BASIS							
All industries, total [1]	**1,316,247**	**2,241,656**	**3,741,910**	**4,050,026**	**4,410,015**	**4,693,348**	**4,920,653**
Mining	72,111	109,280	172,819	198,805	208,897	214,870	223,878
Manufacturing [1]	343,899	430,737	518,321	536,656	582,583	630,505	662,640
Food	23,497	27,638	47,704	52,388	56,580	64,638	65,702
Chemicals	75,807	106,975	111,327	127,350	131,626	136,554	147,623
Primary and fabricated metals	21,644	23,013	18,674	20,818	25,142	26,784	26,725
Machinery	22,229	26,433	41,285	46,224	51,925	50,673	52,916
Computer and electronic products	59,909	50,773	72,935	75,170	84,125	88,712	99,149
Electrical equipment, appliances, and components	10,005	15,449	19,941	9,404	11,261	12,990	12,785
Transportation equipment	49,887	50,739	49,636	46,091	43,857	53,162	56,035
Other manufacturing	(NA)	129,716	156,819	159,210	178,067	196,992	201,704
Wholesale trade	93,936	132,915	168,722	182,011	208,539	234,452	255,111
Information	52,345	102,848	126,063	133,658	141,793	147,229	161,330
Depository institutions (banking)	40,152	66,707	118,585	101,240	112,199	127,122	125,169
Finance and insurance	217,086	463,981	734,859	733,469	775,772	737,805	708,949
Professional, scientific, and technical services	32,868	57,164	81,874	81,503	91,488	98,183	108,204
Holding companies (nonbank)	(NA)	710,386	1,584,903	1,808,505	2,002,880	2,205,498	2,357,609
Other industries	441,886	167,640	235,764	274,178	285,864	297,683	317,763
FINANCIAL OUTFLOWS [INFLOWS(-)] WITHOUT CURRENT-COST ADJUSTMENT							
All industries, total [1]	**142,627**	**15,369**	**277,779**	**396,569**	**318,196**	**307,927**	**316,549**
Mining	2,174	12,015	11,884	30,154	25,651	9,502	13,288
Manufacturing [1]	43,002	28,121	33,320	58,522	55,689	58,838	60,615
Food	2,014	1,171	5,341	5,067	5,506	4,597	5,152
Chemicals	3,812	3,911	7,614	20,211	5,301	11,764	15,034
Primary and fabricated metals	1,233	-703	546	2,568	3,080	1,120	982
Machinery	2,659	2,077	4,229	7,257	7,247	4,916	5,218
Computer and electronic products	17,303	3,607	6,772	6,779	9,798	5,075	13,723
Electrical equipment, appliances, and components	2,100	1,662	1,743	-1,028	1,617	1,711	452
Transportation equipment	7,814	-250	-380	5,805	4,460	7,606	6,498
Other manufacturing	(NA)	16,645	7,456	11,863	18,680	22,049	13,556
Wholesale trade	11,938	12,517	15,487	22,133	23,224	18,770	25,805
Information	16,531	2,831	8,777	9,455	8,866	16,671	17,468
Depository institutions	-1,274	-4,751	-4,811	-5,928	2,335	-9,162	-871
Finance and insurance	21,659	13,079	21,887	25,145	21,766	24,309	8,718
Professional, scientific, and technical services	5,441	-2,055	2,774	9,325	10,583	11,080	13,060
Holding companies (nonbank)	(NA)	-66,351	169,743	211,268	142,346	159,700	151,557
Other industries	40,690	19,964	18,718	36,495	27,737	18,220	26,910
INCOME WITHOUT CURRENT-COST ADJUSTMENT [2]							
All industries, total [1]	**133,692**	**271,877**	**417,605**	**448,235**	**438,089**	**450,619**	**448,942**
Mining	13,164	24,559	29,138	38,620	29,005	26,525	22,650
Manufacturing [1]	42,230	46,896	61,240	66,666	60,903	64,281	68,221
Food	2,681	3,558	4,322	5,604	4,957	4,876	4,993
Chemicals	11,552	13,056	14,088	15,622	15,172	16,657	18,396
Primary and fabricated metals	1,536	1,815	1,349	1,617	1,531	1,595	958
Machinery	2,257	2,253	4,465	5,129	5,538	5,582	4,104
Computer and electronic products	8,860	7,714	11,440	9,915	6,677	9,145	13,484
Electrical equipment, appliances, and components	1,079	1,703	1,653	1,076	1,299	1,382	1,482
Transportation equipment	4,107	1,936	6,471	8,825	6,455	7,843	8,572
Other manufacturing	(NA)	14,862	17,452	18,880	19,274	17,200	16,233
Wholesale trade	14,198	24,494	24,538	27,854	25,789	24,836	27,264
Information	-964	10,832	12,229	14,103	15,483	15,963	15,968
Depository institutions	2,191	164	1,328	7,818	10,385	7,853	5,375
Finance and insurance	15,210	27,911	35,143	33,636	38,081	39,632	39,020
Professional, scientific, and technical services	3,548	9,272	8,856	10,304	9,750	10,721	10,653
Holding companies (nonbank)	(NA)	109,566	220,101	223,612	217,706	228,858	224,467
Other industries	42,504	18,184	25,033	25,621	30,987	31,952	35,325

NA Not available. [1] Includes other industries, not shown separately. [2] Prior to 2006, income is shown net of withholding taxes. Beginning 2006, income is shown gross of withholding taxes.

Source: U.S. Bureau of Economic Analysis, International Economic Accounts, "Direct Investment and Multinational Enterprises," <http://www.bea.gov/iTable/index_MNC.cfm>, accessed August 2015.

Table 1301. U.S. Direct Investment Position Abroad on a Historical-Cost Basis by Selected Country: 2000 to 2014

[In millions of dollars (1,316,247 represents $1,316,247,000,000). U.S. investment abroad is the ownership or control by one U.S. person of 10 percent or more of the voting securities of an incorporated foreign business enterprise or an equivalent interest in an unincorporated foreign business enterprise. Negative position can occur when a U.S. parent company's liabilities to the foreign affiliate are greater than its equity in and loans to the foreign affiliate]

Country	2000	2005	2009	2010	2011	2012	2013	2014
All countries.................	1,316,247	2,241,656	3,565,020	3,741,910	4,050,026	4,410,015	4,693,348	4,920,653
Canada.............................	132,472	231,836	274,807	295,206	330,041	366,709	390,172	386,121
Europe [1].............................	687,320	1,210,679	1,991,191	2,034,559	2,246,394	2,445,652	2,650,757	2,781,666
Austria..............................	2,872	11,236	10,954	11,485	12,556	14,327	15,641	15,787
Belgium.............................	17,973	49,306	46,610	43,975	50,984	49,144	51,702	48,128
Czech Republic...............	1,228	2,729	5,372	5,268	5,840	6,016	6,990	7,247
Denmark...........................	5,270	6,914	13,053	11,802	14,942	14,306	13,605	14,108
Finland.............................	1,342	1,950	1,659	1,597	2,123	2,007	1,919	1,784
France..............................	42,628	60,526	90,879	78,320	76,283	75,185	77,690	76,823
Germany...........................	55,508	100,473	110,149	103,319	119,648	121,072	123,322	115,533
Greece..............................	795	1,884	1,919	1,775	1,440	1,065	-583	-447
Hungary............................	1,920	2,795	4,090	4,237	6,305	7,500	6,189	5,879
Ireland..............................	35,903	55,173	129,829	158,851	184,804	212,411	247,755	310,598
Italy..................................	23,484	24,528	29,944	27,137	26,896	27,317	28,018	26,733
Luxembourg......................	27,849	79,937	219,082	272,206	357,898	408,205	445,498	465,160
Netherlands......................	115,429	240,205	497,471	514,689	595,658	647,365	717,035	753,224
Norway..............................	4,379	8,533	24,238	28,541	32,727	43,326	41,842	39,522
Poland..............................	3,884	5,575	13,412	13,152	12,744	13,137	12,540	11,516
Portugal............................	2,664	2,138	2,803	2,612	2,421	2,061	1,978	2,053
Russia..............................	1,147	9,363	20,763	10,040	11,285	13,389	13,140	9,263
Spain................................	21,236	50,197	58,341	52,390	45,351	27,978	34,146	36,363
Sweden.............................	25,959	30,153	36,702	23,275	33,422	33,635	35,968	28,842
Switzerland.......................	55,377	100,692	131,707	119,891	107,341	122,417	126,652	152,879
Turkey..............................	1,826	2,563	3,675	4,155	4,027	4,945	4,366	4,384
United Kingdom................	230,762	351,513	495,382	501,247	485,029	537,041	576,516	587,943
Latin America and other Western Hemisphere............	266,576	379,582	718,478	752,788	788,987	828,721	849,777	897,679
South America [1]...............	84,220	73,311	119,765	136,598	149,562	147,490	140,508	139,421
Argentina......................	17,488	10,103	12,610	11,747	13,885	13,393	13,447	13,418
Brazil...........................	36,717	30,882	55,380	66,963	74,840	76,821	69,335	70,457
Chile............................	10,052	11,127	25,404	30,747	33,265	27,537	28,617	27,560
Colombia.......................	3,693	4,292	6,050	6,181	6,236	7,251	7,373	7,085
Ecuador........................	832	941	1,339	1,283	793	571	581	650
Peru.............................	3,130	5,542	6,435	7,196	6,216	6,651	5,364	6,486
Venezuela.....................	10,531	8,934	10,248	10,255	12,086	12,781	13,365	11,169
Central America [1].............	73,841	82,496	97,127	97,752	98,226	114,848	113,033	118,424
Costa Rica.....................	1,716	1,598	2,155	1,827	1,849	1,034	998	955
Honduras.......................	399	821	852	936	799	722	772	754
Mexico..........................	39,352	73,687	84,047	85,751	85,599	104,388	102,418	107,825
Panama.........................	30,758	4,826	6,060	5,156	5,849	4,709	4,636	4,687
Other Western Hemisphere [1]...	108,515	223,775	501,586	518,438	541,200	566,384	596,235	639,834
Barbados.......................	2,141	3,881	5,804	7,524	11,738	11,242	12,552	14,682
Bermuda........................	60,114	113,222	287,933	265,524	277,313	279,555	256,137	273,792
Dominican Republic.........	1,143	815	1,193	1,432	1,216	1,088	1,183	1,224
U.K. Islands, Caribbean........	33,451	83,164	160,627	191,680	193,688	218,648	263,096	287,546
Africa [1].............................	11,891	22,756	43,941	54,816	56,996	55,849	59,569	64,233
Egypt................................	1,998	5,475	10,257	12,599	15,428	17,341	18,795	21,320
Nigeria..............................	470	1,105	4,938	5,058	5,307	5,369	5,029	5,173
South Africa......................	3,562	3,969	5,447	6,017	5,870	5,471	6,377	6,181
Middle East [1]......................	10,863	21,115	33,776	34,431	35,951	40,306	46,626	52,168
Israel................................	3,735	7,978	9,018	9,464	9,008	8,977	9,758	10,801
Saudi Arabia.....................	3,661	3,830	7,530	7,436	8,132	9,500	10,084	10,064
United Arab Emirates..............	683	2,285	4,118	4,935	6,603	8,481	11,717	15,035
Asia and Pacific [1]..................	207,125	375,689	502,826	570,111	591,657	672,777	696,447	738,786
Australia...........................	34,838	75,669	106,212	125,421	133,000	165,106	169,917	180,315
China................................	11,140	19,016	54,069	58,996	53,661	54,514	59,886	65,767
Hong Kong........................	27,447	36,415	50,720	41,264	46,713	56,086	60,001	66,240
India................................	2,379	7,162	21,752	24,666	19,000	25,413	25,036	27,963
Indonesia..........................	8,904	8,603	9,743	10,558	12,046	11,441	11,250	13,536
Japan...............................	57,091	81,175	91,196	113,523	120,482	125,283	120,508	108,068
Korea, South.....................	8,968	19,760	23,930	26,233	28,172	32,202	33,036	34,896
Malaysia...........................	7,910	11,097	9,740	11,791	11,627	10,898	12,959	14,357
New Zealand.....................	4,271	5,191	6,141	6,724	7,930	8,476	7,646	7,760
Philippines........................	3,638	6,522	4,602	5,399	4,897	3,988	4,180	5,071
Singapore.........................	24,133	76,390	87,909	102,778	119,395	145,236	159,759	179,764
Taiwan..............................	7,836	14,356	19,894	22,188	16,073	17,546	16,809	17,073
Thailand............................	5,824	10,252	9,457	12,999	11,840	10,773	9,825	11,729

[1] Includes other countries, not shown separately.

Source: U.S. Bureau of Economic Analysis, International Economic Accounts, "Direct Investment and Multinational Enterprises," <http://www.bea.gov/iTable/index_MNC.cfm>, accessed August 2015.

Table 1302. U.S. Foreign Economic and Military Aid by Major Recipient Country: 2000 to 2013

[In millions of dollars (17,117 represents $17,117,000,000). For years ending September 30. Annual figures are for obligations. Total aid may not add due to rounding]

Region/Country	2000	2005	2010	2012	2013 Total	2013 Economic aid	2013 Military aid
Total [1]	17,117	35,155	49,619	50,617	39,930	31,902	8,027
Middle East & North Africa [1]	6,799	13,371	8,840	9,216	8,953	4,162	4,790
Egypt	2,076	1,527	1,617	1,447	1,552	316	1,236
Iraq	1	7,766	2,082	1,943	426	364	62
Israel	3,863	2,714	2,838	3,112	2,961	18	2,943
Jordan	448	683	766	1,160	1,204	872	332
Lebanon	35	25	159	225	374	284	90
Morocco	51	61	56	54	51	42	10
West Bank/Gaza [2]	122	347	687	457	991	991	–
Yemen	57	29	122	190	243	224	20
Sub-Saharan Africa [1]	2,031	5,113	8,612	9,409	8,268	7,915	352
Angola	105	68	100	69	52	51	1
Botswana	1	42	51	64	71	70	1
Burkina Faso	18	33	37	59	52	51	1
Chad	4	63	186	163	77	76	1
Congo, Democratic Republic of	33	119	369	383	330	317	13
Ethiopia	278	684	868	832	635	634	1
Ghana	67	72	110	143	133	131	2
Kenya	94	258	573	989	823	785	38
Lesotho	2	4	33	33	39	39	–
Liberia	22	149	184	214	197	190	7
Madagascar	27	156	60	72	35	35	–
Malawi	44	81	181	176	554	554	–
Mali	44	52	127	278	180	167	13
Mozambique	88	105	302	338	279	279	–
Namibia	16	49	89	109	63	63	–
Nigeria	113	151	409	528	505	495	9
Rwanda	39	83	173	169	144	144	–
Senegal	37	48	657	138	102	100	2
Somalia	14	45	156	479	326	147	179
South Africa	57	185	467	496	474	472	2
South Sudan [3]	–	–	–	627	490	470	20
Sudan	51	1,041	923	359	266	266	–
Tanzania	45	136	422	436	417	415	3
Uganda	76	290	430	394	524	521	4
Zambia	35	143	269	350	303	302	1
Zimbabwe	21	60	253	164	166	166	–
Latin America & Caribbean [1]	2,301	2,602	4,414	2,479	2,134	1,895	240
Bolivia	241	162	92	35	1	1	–
Colombia	1,169	824	795	688	238	148	91
El Salvador	35	58	62	52	71	61	9
Guatemala	72	65	165	136	105	95	10
Haiti	85	224	1,400	473	362	360	2
Honduras	42	288	40	63	101	93	8
Mexico	44	103	718	210	416	345	71
Peru	204	178	204	97	124	116	7
Asia [1]	1,163	4,720	15,245	16,026	7,403	5,411	1,992
Afghanistan	54	2,214	10,877	12,920	4,347	2,468	1,880
Bangladesh	78	84	195	309	214	210	4
Cambodia	28	70	72	108	91	82	9
India	188	202	117	125	79	78	1
Indonesia	242	543	309	272	759	744	15
Mongolia	26	19	38	23	28	24	4
Nepal	23	71	67	72	112	108	3
Pakistan	24	757	2,680	1,207	741	728	13
Philippines	82	156	201	194	214	169	45
Sri Lanka	11	160	82	33	43	42	1
Oceania [1]	165	162	210	201	202	201	1
Micronesia, Federated States of	81	94	90	97	92	92	–
Eurasia [1]	1,462	2,341	2,155	1,578	1,339	1,102	237
Armenia	104	78	55	-5	53	34	19
Georgia	112	110	229	208	152	95	56
Kazakhstan	53	68	331	173	154	92	61
Kyrgyzstan	47	51	128	105	54	40	14
Moldova	49	32	294	43	30	28	2
Russia	709	1,574	506	442	462	441	20
Ukraine	200	157	315	273	244	203	41
Eastern Europe [1]	1,045	718	713	393	377	283	94
Kosovo	–	–	163	29	60	56	4
Poland	85	96	221	49	54	33	21
Western Europe	24	133	79	39	98	89	9

– Represents zero or less than $50,000. [1] Includes other countries, not shown separately. [2] See footnote 6, Table 1342. [3] South Sudan seceded from Sudan in July 2011.

Source: U.S. Agency for International Development, *U.S. Overseas Loans and Grants: Obligations and Loan Authorizations, July 1, 1945–September 30, 2013*, and earlier reports. See also <https://explorer.usaid.gov/reports-greenbook.html>.

Table 1303. U.S. Foreign Economic and Military Aid Programs: 1980 to 2013

[In millions of dollars (9,682 represents $9,682,000,000). For years ending September 30. Total foreign aid programs are the sum of economic and military assistance. Major components in recent years include U.S. Agency for International Development (USAID), U.S. Department of Agriculture (USDA), State Department, and voluntary contributions to international financial institutions. Annual figures are in obligations]

Year and world region	Total foreign assistance	Military assistance	Economic assistance, by funding agency					
			Total	USAID	USDA	State Department	Other U.S. agencies	Multilateral organizations
1980	9,682	2,110	7,572	4,062	1,437	459	137	1,478
1985	18,107	5,780	12,327	8,132	2,052	431	164	1,548
1990	16,003	4,959	11,044	6,964	1,643	590	377	1,469
1995	15,673	4,122	11,551	7,281	1,401	132	956	1,781
2000	17,117	4,935	12,182	5,907	1,941	2,278	945	1,110
2005	35,155	7,810	27,345	9,760	2,250	4,985	8,597	1,753
2006	37,827	12,614	25,213	8,433	1,988	5,280	8,019	1,492
2007	41,202	13,747	27,454	11,085	1,792	5,611	7,233	1,734
2008	48,143	16,133	32,010	9,673	2,833	9,707	7,909	1,889
2009	48,545	14,456	34,089	12,917	2,619	11,407	4,903	2,243
2010	49,619	14,840	34,780	11,771	3,800	11,150	5,155	2,903
2011	49,385	18,310	31,075	10,111	2,748	10,233	5,329	2,653
2012	50,617	17,443	33,174	11,324	2,969	12,263	3,475	3,144
2013, total	**39,930**	**8,027**	**31,902**	**11,775**	**1,659**	**10,819**	**4,611**	**3,038**
Asia	7,403	1,992	5,411	2,832	146	1,066	1,192	175
Eurasia	1,339	237	1,102	298	1	98	704	–
Eastern Europe	377	94	283	157	–	13	113	–
Latin America and Caribbean	2,134	240	1,895	757	70	674	244	149
Middle East and North Africa	8,953	4,790	4,162	2,849	99	1,180	34	–
Oceania	202	1	201	16	–	7	178	–
Sub-Saharan Africa	8,268	352	7,915	1,963	721	4,357	680	194
Western Europe	98	9	89	7	–	71	10	–
Canada	21	–	21	–	–	–	21	–
World, not specified	11,136	312	10,824	2,895	622	3,352	1,435	2,520

– Represents or rounds to zero.

Source: U.S. Agency for International Development, *U.S. Overseas Loans and Grants: Obligations and Loan Authorizations, July 1, 1945–September 30, 2013*, and earlier reports. See also <https://explorer.usaid.gov/reports-greenbook.html>.

Table 1304. U.S. International Trade in Goods by Related Parties: 2000 to 2014

[In millions of dollars (1,205,339 represents $1,205,339,000,000). "Related party trade" is trade by U.S. companies with their subsidiaries abroad as well as trade by U.S. subsidiaries of foreign companies with their parent companies]

Country and commodity	NAICS code [2]	2000	2010	2012	2013	2014
IMPORTS FOR CONSUMPTION						
Total imports	(X)	1,205,339	1,898,610	2,251,035	2,239,750	2,313,960
Related party trade, total [1]	**(X)**	**563,084**	**922,202**	**1,131,902**	**1,122,570**	**1,178,746**
Mexico	(X)	89,068	135,984	173,059	180,295	196,974
Canada	(X)	100,689	138,222	173,937	173,699	182,359
China	(X)	18,061	107,038	121,813	124,490	135,856
Japan	(X)	108,290	93,892	113,391	107,362	102,348
Germany	(X)	37,781	53,951	72,754	77,661	84,785
Korea, South	(X)	22,056	29,298	33,835	36,891	43,482
Transportation equipment	336	161,150	179,516	239,222	248,952	260,984
Computer & electronic products	334	166,279	203,900	214,767	214,911	224,037
Chemicals	325	45,452	134,065	150,167	148,615	153,632
Oil & gas	211	13,241	80,071	104,770	95,341	97,469
Machinery, except electrical	333	39,918	53,747	79,537	75,128	84,405
Petroleum & coal products	324	12,655	54,618	77,932	71,336	66,802
EXPORTS						
Total exports	(X)	780,418	1,277,504	1,546,455	1,578,851	1,623,443
Related party trade, domestic exports, total [1]	**(X)**	**196,596**	**314,489**	**381,695**	**390,896**	**488,540**
Canada	(X)	64,133	88,689	101,002	104,172	108,750
Mexico	(X)	34,249	49,313	65,352	72,919	77,808
China	(X)	1,552	13,436	16,556	19,763	21,986
Japan	(X)	20,313	16,718	19,327	17,996	18,827
Netherlands	(X)	6,845	15,070	16,297	16,909	17,712
Belgium	(X)	4,184	9,777	12,303	13,000	15,663
Transportation equipment	336	46,288	55,400	69,036	75,432	83,642
Chemicals	325	26,376	64,548	77,735	77,535	81,371
Petroleum & coal products	324	1,253	23,101	41,942	41,842	38,402
Machinery, except electrical	333	19,831	32,301	39,779	38,516	37,787
Computer & electronic products	334	51,210	42,689	39,498	39,104	37,391
Miscellaneous manufactured commodities	339	4,628	13,668	15,359	16,517	16,998

X Not applicable. [1] Includes other countries and other commodities, not shown separately. [2] Based on the North American Industry Classification System (NAICS); see text, Section 15.

Source: U.S. Census Bureau, *U.S. Goods Trade: Imports and Exports by Related-Parties 2014*, May 2015, and earlier reports. See also <http://www.census.gov/foreign-trade/index.html>.

Table 1305. U.S. International Trade in Goods and Services: 2000 to 2014

[In millions of dollars (-372,517 represents -$372,517,000,000). Data are presented on a balance of payments basis and will not agree with the following merchandise trade tables in this section. Minus sign (-) indicates deficit]

Category	2000	2005	2010	2011	2012	2013	2014
TRADE BALANCE							
Total...........................	**-372,517**	**-714,245**	**-494,658**	**-548,625**	**-536,773**	**-478,394**	**-508,324**
Goods...........................	-446,783	-782,804	-648,678	-740,646	-741,171	-702,587	-741,462
Services........................	74,266	68,558	154,020	192,020	204,398	224,193	233,138
Maintenance and repair services, n.i.e. [1]	2,442	4,609	7,640	8,200	9,171	11,162	14,921
Transport [2]	-11,848	-23,021	-2,972	-1,547	-1,041	-3,219	-4,188
Travel for all purposes [3]	34,400	21,482	50,387	61,167	61,294	68,794	66,454
Insurance services............	-7,653	-21,144	-47,081	-40,540	-38,723	-36,362	-32,679
Financial services.............	11,181	27,752	56,846	60,903	59,989	65,572	67,787
Charges for the use of intellectual property, n.i.e. [1,4]	35,202	48,871	74,970	87,246	85,779	88,928	88,238
Telecommunications, computer, and information services...	-182	-460	-3,977	-3,585	-269	1,223	2,571
Other business services [5]	16,083	22,342	30,383	29,279	33,225	30,484	33,762
Government goods and services, n.i.e. [1,6]	-5,360	-11,872	-12,176	-9,102	-5,026	-2,388	-3,725
EXPORTS							
Total...........................	**1,075,321**	**1,286,022**	**1,853,606**	**2,127,021**	**2,218,989**	**2,279,937**	**2,343,205**
Goods...........................	784,940	913,016	1,290,273	1,499,240	1,562,578	1,592,043	1,632,639
Services........................	290,381	373,006	563,333	627,781	656,411	687,894	710,565
Maintenance and repair services, n.i.e. [1]	5,011	7,624	14,549	16,436	17,186	18,648	22,389
Transport [2]	45,758	52,622	71,656	79,830	83,944	87,415	90,031
Travel for all purposes [3]	100,187	101,470	137,010	150,867	161,632	172,901	177,241
Insurance services............	3,631	7,566	14,397	15,114	16,790	17,058	17,417
Financial services.............	22,117	39,878	72,348	78,271	76,692	84,091	87,290
Charges for the use of intellectual property, n.i.e. [1,4]	51,808	74,448	107,521	123,333	124,440	127,927	130,362
Telecommunications, computer, and information services...	12,215	15,515	25,038	29,171	32,510	35,035	35,885
Other business services [5]	40,497	58,302	101,029	112,568	120,382	121,873	129,514
Government goods and services, n.i.e. [1,6]	9,156	15,582	19,784	22,191	22,835	22,946	20,438
IMPORTS							
Total...........................	**1,447,837**	**2,000,267**	**2,348,263**	**2,675,646**	**2,755,762**	**2,758,331**	**2,851,529**
Goods...........................	1,231,722	1,695,820	1,938,950	2,239,886	2,303,749	2,294,630	2,374,101
Services........................	216,115	304,448	409,313	435,761	452,013	463,700	477,428
Maintenance and repair services, n.i.e. [1]	2,569	3,015	6,909	8,236	8,015	7,486	7,468
Transport [2]	57,606	75,643	74,628	81,377	84,985	90,634	94,219
Travel for all purposes [3]	65,787	79,988	86,623	89,700	100,338	104,107	110,787
Insurance services............	11,284	28,710	61,478	55,654	55,513	53,420	50,096
Financial services.............	10,936	12,126	15,502	17,368	16,703	18,519	19,503
Charges for the use of intellectual property, n.i.e. [1,4]	16,606	25,577	32,551	36,087	38,661	38,999	42,124
Telecommunications, computer, and information services...	12,397	15,975	29,015	32,756	32,779	33,812	33,314
Other business services [5]	24,414	35,960	70,646	83,289	87,157	91,389	95,752
Government goods and services, n.i.e. [1,6]	14,516	27,454	31,960	31,293	27,861	25,334	24,163

[1] N.i.e. means not included elsewhere. [2] Includes passenger fares. [3] All travel purposes include 1) business travel, including expenditures by border, seasonal, and other short-term workers and 2) personal travel, including health-related and education-related travel. [4] Includes charges for the use of proprietary rights, such as patents, trademarks, and copyrights, and charges for licenses to use, reproduce, distribute, and sell or purchase intellectual property. [5] Includes three categories: "other business services" (including research and development, management, advertising, and so on); "construction"; and "personal, cultural and recreational services" (including fees related to the production of motion pictures, radio, and television programs, downloaded recording and manuscripts, telemedicine, online education, and receipts or payments for cultural, sporting, and performing arts activities, and so on). [6] Includes goods and services supplied by and to embassies, consulates, and military bases; goods and services acquired by diplomatic and military personnel in the host economy; and services supplied by and to governments not included in other categories of services.

Source: U.S. Bureau of Economic Analysis, "International Economic Accounts: Trade in Goods and Services," <http://www.bea.gov/international/index.htm#trade>, accessed June 2015.

Table 1306. U.S. Freight Gateways—Value of Shipments: 2014

[In billions of dollars (3,968.6 represents $3,968,600,000,000), except as indicated. For the top 50 gateways ranked by value of shipments]

Port	Mode	Rank	Total trade	Exports	Imports	Exports as a percent of total
Total U.S. merchandise trade........................	(X)	(X)	**3,968.6**	**1,623.4**	**2,345.2**	**40.9**
Top 50 gateways..............................	(X)	(X)	3,251.0	1,321.0	1,930.0	40.6
As a percent of total..................................	(X)	(X)	81.9	81.4	82.3	(X)
Los Angeles, CA............................	Water	1	291.3	40.0	251.3	13.7
Laredo, TX....................................	Land	2	199.1	91.8	107.4	46.1
JFK International Airport, NY........................	Air	3	194.3	96.1	98.3	49.4
Chicago, IL..................................	Air/Land	4	176.4	44.1	132.3	25.0
Newark, NJ..................................	Water	5	171.6	16.1	155.5	9.4
Houston, TX.................................	Water	6	167.2	92.1	75.1	55.1
Detroit, MI..................................	Land	7	149.8	79.8	69.9	53.3
New Orleans, LA...........................	Air/Water	8	129.7	64.1	65.6	49.4
Long Beach, CA............................	Water	9	104.5	37.3	67.2	35.7
Port Huron, MI.............................	Land	10	96.9	48.4	48.5	50.0
Los Angeles International Airport, CA...................	Air	11	96.3	49.1	47.2	51.0
Buffalo-Niagara Falls, NY.............................	Land	12	92.3	49.2	43.2	53.3
Charleston, SC.............................	Water	13	75.5	30.4	45.1	40.3
Norfolk-Newport News, VA.............	Water	14	71.6	30.6	41.0	42.7
El Paso, TX.................................	Land	15	67.9	31.0	36.9	45.7
Miami International Airport, FL.....................	Air	16	62.8	38.3	24.5	61.0
Anchorage, AK..............................	Air	17	55.9	17.2	38.7	30.8
Dallas-Fort Worth, TX.....................	Air	18	55.1	19.6	35.5	35.6
San Francisco International Airport, CA................	Air	19	53.3	27.5	25.9	51.5
Baltimore, MD..............................	Water	20	52.5	18.6	33.9	35.5
Savannah, GA..............................	Water	21	52.3	–	52.3	–
New York, NY...............................	Water	22	51.3	39.7	11.6	77.4
Oakland, CA................................	Water	23	50.2	21.1	29.1	42.0
Cleveland, OH..............................	Air	24	48.3	26.0	22.3	53.9
Tacoma, WA................................	Water	25	43.5	2.6	41.0	5.9
Otay Mesa Station, CA..................	Land	26	40.4	14.4	26.1	35.5
Atlanta, GA.................................	Air	27	34.5	14.0	20.4	40.7
Port Arthur, TX............................	Water	28	33.1	9.4	23.7	28.4
Sault Ste Marie, MI.......................	Water	29	31.5	29.7	1.8	94.3
Hildago, TX.................................	Land	30	30.6	11.4	19.2	37.2
Blaine, WA..................................	Land	31	28.6	17.3	11.2	60.7
Pembina, ND...............................	Land	32	28.4	17.7	10.7	62.4
Seattle, WA.................................	Water	33	27.6	13.2	14.4	47.8
Everett, WA.................................	Water	34	27.3	25.7	1.6	94.1
Port Everglades, FL.......................	Water	35	27.1	13.6	13.5	50.2
Nogales, AZ................................	Land	36	26.9	10.6	16.3	39.4
Champlain-Rouses Point, NY..........	Land	37	26.6	10.5	16.1	39.4
Corpus Christi, TX........................	Water	38	25.5	12.6	12.9	49.3
Philadelphia, PA...........................	Water	39	24.6	5.3	19.3	21.7
Eagle Pass, TX............................	Land	40	24.6	7.8	16.8	31.6
Miami, FL....................................	Water	41	24.0	10.7	13.2	44.8
Gramercy, LA...............................	Water	42	23.5	17.7	5.8	75.5
Jacksonville, FL............................	Water	43	23.4	10.9	12.5	46.6
Portal, ND...................................	Land	44	21.6	13.7	7.8	63.6
Brunswick, GA.............................	Water	45	21.1	5.5	15.6	26.2
San Juan International Airport, PR....	Land	46	18.9	11.1	7.9	58.5
Houston Intercontinental Airport. TX....................	Air	47	18.8	10.1	8.7	53.8
Morgan City, LA...........................	Water	48	18.3	1.7	16.6	9.5
Brownsville, TX............................	Land	49	18.1	10.1	8.0	55.7
Lake Charles, LA..........................	Water	50	16.5	5.5	10.9	33.7

X Not applicable. – Represents or rounds to zero.

Source: U.S. Census Bureau, Foreign Trade Division, "USA Trade Online," <https://usatrade.census.gov/>, accessed April 2015.

Table 1307. U.S. Exports and General Imports of Merchandise by Customs District: 2005 to 2014

[In billions of dollars (901.1 represents $901,100,000,000). Exports are f.a.s. (free alongside ship) value basis; imports are on customs-value basis. These data may differ from those in Table 1304, Table 1310, and Table 1311. For methodology, see Foreign Trade Statistics in Appendix III]

Customs district	Exports					General imports				
	2005	2010	2012	2013	2014	2005	2010	2012	2013	2014
Total [1]	901.1	1,278.5	1,545.7	1,579.6	1,623.4	1,673.5	1,913.9	2,276.3	2,268.3	2,345.2
Anchorage, AK	12.1	14.5	16.0	15.3	17.9	10.4	16.2	15.0	9.8	14.6
Baltimore, MD	9.0	14.7	22.0	21.3	18.8	29.6	28.8	33.6	33.0	35.4
Boston, MA	10.4	8.2	7.1	6.9	7.6	21.7	19.2	20.9	22.2	23.1
Buffalo, NY	35.0	40.6	48.1	45.5	49.2	42.6	39.2	42.3	42.4	44.2
Charleston, SC	16.2	19.5	24.8	25.9	30.5	31.9	29.4	39.7	40.2	44.2
Chicago, IL	29.9	35.8	38.0	40.1	44.1	78.7	125.6	149.5	152.5	166.4
Cleveland, OH	20.8	25.4	31.5	33.3	33.5	49.0	69.2	87.0	89.2	98.0
Columbia-Snake, OR	6.3	12.3	15.8	14.7	15.2	14.2	12.2	13.6	13.3	13.4
Dallas/Fort Worth, TX	17.8	18.1	19.2	18.8	20.6	31.8	38.4	48.8	53.7	56.8
Detroit, MI	106.9	113.2	128.6	122.5	131.8	123.1	106.0	124.6	122.5	128.6
Duluth, MN	1.9	2.6	4.6	6.4	5.5	9.3	6.8	8.4	9.7	10.1
El Paso, TX	19.9	29.3	38.3	39.6	41.3	28.0	44.1	52.0	51.7	49.9
Great Falls, MT	9.8	17.4	21.7	23.7	18.4	27.1	26.9	28.0	28.5	29.5
Honolulu, HI	2.4	7.4	9.8	11.4	12.6	3.7	4.6	6.5	5.6	5.0
Houston/Galveston, TX	47.0	94.5	126.8	128.9	131.5	89.4	116.9	147.1	122.9	121.8
Laredo, TX	60.5	81.4	105.3	112.4	123.4	78.7	104.2	133.9	140.8	156.6
Los Angeles, CA	78.4	105.1	121.1	126.8	128.2	215.5	242.7	282.8	287.9	289.8
Miami, FL	34.1	58.9	73.2	67.9	65.5	31.8	36.6	51.4	52.7	50.4
Milwaukee, WI	0.1	0.1	0.3	0.1	0.2	1.3	0.9	0.9	1.1	1.2
Minneapolis, MN	2.3	2.6	2.8	2.8	2.8	6.9	13.6	16.8	16.9	17.1
Mobile, AL	5.0	8.7	12.8	12.8	12.1	14.3	20.8	26.6	24.8	24.9
New Orleans, LA	32.6	69.1	92.9	94.3	100.5	97.8	125.3	150.7	140.7	134.1
New York, NY	90.9	136.3	158.3	155.1	153.6	176.7	190.6	223.6	224.1	233.4
Nogales, AZ	6.9	8.9	12.0	13.9	13.8	13.0	17.4	19.0	22.0	20.8
Norfolk, VA	16.8	21.1	27.7	29.8	30.7	23.5	23.9	28.8	29.3	32.9
Ogdensburg, NY	13.3	16.2	17.8	18.0	18.2	28.2	27.8	27.7	28.8	29.3
Pembina, ND	13.6	21.3	28.3	31.0	32.6	12.8	14.7	18.0	19.5	20.1
Philadelphia, PA	10.2	14.3	16.9	17.7	18.0	47.8	56.9	61.3	59.0	55.0
Port Arthur, TX	2.1	6.5	10.3	14.5	16.0	20.9	26.4	35.4	36.5	29.7
Portland, ME	2.8	4.4	4.9	5.0	5.2	11.2	9.8	12.0	13.6	15.6
Providence, RI	0.1	0.3	0.4	0.3	0.5	4.4	5.8	8.0	8.8	8.3
San Diego, CA	15.0	16.2	19.9	20.6	22.2	28.4	32.4	36.6	38.3	42.0
San Francisco, CA	36.6	47.1	50.5	54.1	54.9	62.4	60.6	68.7	69.8	74.7
San Juan, PR	9.7	19.7	16.3	17.4	17.8	19.5	19.4	26.0	24.1	23.7
Savannah, GA	24.7	41.0	51.7	47.5	49.3	47.9	68.0	80.6	81.9	92.6
Seattle, WA	44.1	58.5	75.9	89.9	85.4	51.7	52.6	62.8	62.8	67.0
St. Albans, VT	4.3	3.3	3.2	3.1	2.7	12.6	6.9	9.5	10.3	10.0
St. Louis, MO	1.3	1.0	0.9	0.5	1.0	9.7	11.5	22.0	23.9	21.6
Tampa, FL	10.1	14.4	17.0	17.6	16.2	19.3	16.4	20.4	20.4	21.1
Virgin Islands, U.S.	0.5	1.9	0.9	1.0	1.4	9.1	10.5	1.2	0.5	0.7
Washington, DC	3.7	6.0	5.4	5.1	5.4	3.7	8.2	6.8	5.6	6.6
Wilmington, NC	2.2	5.3	5.8	5.4	5.3	15.4	12.8	14.6	13.4	13.3

[1] Totals include the following special districts, not shown separately: vessels under their own power or afloat, low valued imports and exports, and mail shipments. Totals may also include data for two or more Customs Districts that have been combined and published under an arbitrary designation, as a solution to disclosure situations.

Source: U.S. Census Bureau, U.S. Foreign Trade Division, "USA Trade Online," <https://usatrade.census.gov/>, accessed April 2015.

Table 1308. U.S. Exports of Goods by State of Origin: 2010 to 2014

[In millions of dollars (1,278,263 represents $1,278,263,000,000), except as indicated. Exports are on a f.a.s. (free alongside ship) value basis. Exports are based on origin of movement]

State and other areas	2010	2013	2014 Total	2014 Rank	State and other areas	2010	2013	2014 Total	2014 Rank
Total	**1,278,263**	**1,578,893**	**1,623,273**	(X)	Nebraska	5,820	7,389	7,863	33
United States	**1,207,883**	**1,506,577**	**1,548,715**	(X)	Nevada	5,912	8,763	7,701	34
Alabama	15,502	19,299	19,518	23	New Hampshire	4,367	4,276	4,424	42
Alaska	4,155	4,565	5,153	40	New Jersey	32,154	36,494	36,836	12
Arizona	15,636	19,396	21,124	21	New Mexico	1,541	2,720	3,789	43
Arkansas	5,219	7,155	6,857	36	New York	69,696	83,995	86,007	4
California	143,192	168,128	174,129	2	North Carolina	24,905	29,304	31,291	15
Colorado	6,727	8,689	8,368	32	North Dakota	2,536	3,715	5,290	39
Connecticut	16,056	16,476	15,941	25	Ohio	41,494	50,549	52,130	9
Delaware	4,966	5,403	5,293	38	Oklahoma	5,353	6,914	6,300	37
District of Columbia	1,501	2,708	936	(X)	Oregon	17,671	18,626	20,920	22
Florida	55,365	60,461	58,637	7	Pennsylvania	34,928	40,928	40,227	10
Georgia	28,950	37,578	39,365	11	Rhode Island	1,949	2,160	2,394	46
Hawaii	684	598	1,452	50	South Carolina	20,329	26,110	29,704	16
Idaho	5,157	5,784	5,136	41	South Dakota	1,259	1,574	1,590	48
Illinois	50,058	65,849	68,182	5	Tennessee	25,943	32,390	32,957	14
Indiana	28,745	34,152	35,453	13	Texas	206,961	279,695	289,023	1
Iowa	10,880	13,867	15,101	26	Utah	13,809	16,065	12,266	28
Kansas	9,905	12,452	12,004	30	Vermont	4,277	4,017	3,643	44
Kentucky	19,343	25,286	27,541	17	Virginia	17,163	17,941	19,194	24
Louisiana	41,356	63,079	65,085	6	Washington	53,353	81,939	90,646	3
Maine	3,164	2,681	2,752	45	West Virginia	6,449	8,474	7,496	35
Maryland	10,163	11,752	12,241	29	Wisconsin	19,790	23,075	23,433	19
Massachusetts	26,304	26,798	27,364	18	Wyoming	983	1,337	1,757	47
Michigan	44,768	58,456	55,751	8	Puerto Rico	22,784	19,918	20,323	(X)
Minnesota	18,904	20,720	21,372	20	Virgin Islands	1,899	996	1,453	(X)
Mississippi	8,229	12,368	11,414	31	Other [1]	45,698	51,463	52,859	(X)
Missouri	12,926	12,931	14,141	27	Timing adjustments	(NA)	-61	-77	(X)
Montana	1,389	1,499	1,529	49					

X Not applicable. NA Not available. [1] Includes unreported, not specified, special category, estimated shipments, and re-exports.

Source: U.S. Census Bureau, *U.S. International Trade in Goods and Services*, Series FT-900, December 2014, and earlier reports. See also <http://www.census.gov/foreign-trade/data/index.html>.

Table 1309. U.S. Agricultural Exports by State: 2000 to 2013

[In millions of dollars (51,265 represents $51,265,000,000). Calendar year. Export estimates based on U.S. farm cash receipts]

State	2000	2005	2010	2012	2013	State	2000	2005	2010	2012	2013
U.S.	**51,265**	**63,182**	**115,820**	**141,406**	**144,379**	MO	1,438	1,704	3,542	3,933	4,043
AL	517	719	1,070	1,392	1,524	MT	494	629	1,104	1,286	1,635
AK	20	10	12	14	16	NE	2,341	2,571	5,689	6,730	6,729
AZ	457	623	1,034	1,249	1,415	NV	65	63	108	157	173
AR	1,324	1,947	3,114	4,100	4,040	NH	33	38	69	74	83
CA	6,645	9,412	13,838	17,768	20,062	NJ	250	299	432	531	566
CO	870	806	1,521	1,748	1,724	NM	293	335	641	687	791
CT	131	151	240	280	311	NY	507	594	1,292	1,559	1,723
DE	133	145	240	319	301	NC	1,786	2,043	3,296	4,241	4,184
FL	1,924	2,154	3,199	3,796	4,036	ND	1,065	1,496	3,406	4,347	4,074
GA	1,021	1,236	2,201	2,663	2,987	OH	1,547	1,718	3,566	4,478	4,385
HI	142	179	359	419	452	OK	787	976	1,536	1,823	1,902
ID	707	812	1,504	2,054	2,445	OR	792	1,009	1,393	1,832	2,111
IL	3,309	3,797	7,905	8,704	8,011	PA	708	858	1,767	2,221	2,386
IN	1,827	2,042	4,352	5,068	4,817	RI	12	20	30	32	34
IA	3,638	4,613	9,613	11,631	10,422	SC	393	454	764	947	929
KS	1,943	2,204	4,522	4,431	4,980	SD	1,230	1,394	2,970	3,733	3,807
KY	1,322	1,326	1,478	1,920	2,278	TN	563	792	1,271	1,610	1,903
LA	609	789	1,635	2,036	2,223	TX	2,535	3,470	5,821	6,504	5,609
ME	146	133	236	288	300	UT	162	199	342	464	502
MD	347	323	601	802	768	VT	49	60	152	185	231
MA	108	126	215	242	239	VA	517	562	885	1,219	1,233
MI	947	1,188	2,558	3,152	3,409	WA	1,379	1,759	3,025	4,050	4,491
MN	2,311	2,866	6,589	8,412	7,988	WV	60	61	117	160	166
MS	751	1,117	1,777	2,529	2,336	WI	967	1,248	2,530	3,231	3,218
						WY	144	111	259	353	389

Source: U.S. Department of Agriculture, Economic Research Service, "State Export Data," <http://www.ers.usda.gov/data-products/state-export-data.aspx>, accessed August 2015.

Table 1310. U.S. Exports, Imports, and Trade Balance by Country: 2005 to 2014

[In millions of dollars (901,082 represents $901,082,000,000). Data reflect trade between foreign countries and the U.S., Puerto Rico, the U.S. Virgin Islands, and U.S. Foreign Trade Zones. Data are shown on a Census Basis. Country totals include exports of special category commodities, if any. For methodology, see Foreign Trade Statistics in Appendix III. Minus sign (-) denotes an excess of imports over exports]

Country	Exports, domestic and foreign 2005	2010	2012	2013	2014	General imports 2005	2010	2012	2013	2014	Merchandise trade balance 2005	2010	2012	2013	2014
Total [1]	**901,082**	**1,278,495**	**1,545,821**	**1,578,439**	**1,620,532**	**1,673,455**	**1,913,857**	**2,276,267**	**2,268,371**	**2,347,685**	**-772,373**	**-635,362**	**-730,446**	**-689,931**	**-727,153**
Afghanistan	262	2,151	1,522	1,410	792	67	85	37	46	72	195	2,066	1,485	1,364	720
Algeria	1,106	1,194	1,363	1,849	2,617	10,446	14,518	9,993	4,831	4,629	-9,340	-13,324	-8,630	-2,982	-2,012
Angola	929	1,294	1,491	1,443	2,039	8,484	11,940	9,824	8,743	5,720	-7,555	-10,646	-8,333	-7,300	-3,681
Antigua and Barbuda	190	158	205	145	217	4	6	10	10	8	186	153	195	136	209
Argentina	4,122	7,392	10,258	10,348	10,826	4,584	3,803	4,350	4,642	4,243	-462	3,589	5,908	5,706	6,583
Armenia	65	114	64	91	61	46	76	89	101	96	19	38	-24	-10	-36
Aruba	559	541	710	1,100	1,358	2,920	20	827	42	60	-2,361	521	-117	1,058	1,298
Australia	15,589	21,805	31,161	26,123	26,582	7,342	8,583	9,567	9,273	10,672	8,246	13,222	21,595	16,850	15,910
Austria	2,544	2,429	3,420	3,520	3,825	6,103	6,835	9,449	9,780	10,769	-3,558	-4,407	-6,030	-6,261	-6,944
Azerbaijan	132	253	493	381	950	45	1,989	1,095	1,136	1,012	87	-1,736	-602	-755	-62
Bahamas, The	1,787	3,178	3,479	3,450	3,324	700	815	563	599	532	1,087	2,363	2,916	2,851	2,793
Bahrain	351	1,235	1,177	1,018	1,060	432	420	701	636	965	-81	815	476	382	94
Bangladesh	320	576	508	709	1,113	2,693	4,294	4,916	5,353	5,278	-2,373	-3,718	-4,407	-4,645	-4,164
Barbados	395	397	459	452	540	32	43	54	55	51	363	355	404	397	489
Belarus	35	133	102	95	93	345	175	153	105	131	-310	-41	-51	-10	-38
Belgium	18,691	25,458	29,438	31,928	34,790	13,023	15,552	17,368	19,012	20,885	5,668	9,906	12,071	12,916	13,904
Belize	218	289	266	241	237	98	120	162	127	97	119	169	104	114	140
Benin	72	463	573	605	781	1	(Z)	3	3	5	72	462	570	602	776
Bermuda	490	637	622	537	646	87	23	84	61	37	403	614	539	477	610
Bolivia	219	508	763	1,051	1,010	293	680	1,682	1,252	1,935	-74	-172	-919	-201	-925
Botswana	67	49	48	82	53	178	170	221	278	318	-111	-121	-173	-196	-265
Brazil	15,372	35,418	43,771	44,093	42,429	24,436	23,958	32,123	27,631	30,537	-9,064	11,460	11,648	16,462	11,893
British Virgin Islands	125	146	172	313	387	34	19	14	6	11	91	127	158	306	376
Brunei	50	124	158	558	549	563	12	86	17	32	-513	112	71	541	517
Bulgaria	268	171	249	307	359	454	260	509	514	604	-186	-89	-261	-206	-246
Cambodia	70	154	226	241	328	1,767	2,301	2,692	2,771	2,847	-1,697	-2,147	-2,465	-2,530	-2,519
Cameroon	117	132	253	336	301	158	297	308	367	186	-41	-165	-55	-31	115
Canada	211,899	249,257	292,651	300,755	312,421	290,384	277,637	324,263	332,558	347,798	-78,486	-28,380	-31,613	-31,803	-35,377
Chad	54	90	37	42	67	1,498	2,044	2,660	2,459	2,329	-1,444	-1,954	-2,624	-2,418	-2,262
Chile	5,134	10,907	18,773	17,518	16,515	6,664	7,018	9,367	10,385	9,476	-1,531	3,889	9,407	7,133	7,039
China	41,192	91,911	110,517	121,721	123,676	243,470	364,953	425,619	440,434	466,755	-202,278	-273,042	-315,103	-318,713	-343,079
Colombia	5,462	12,068	16,357	18,369	20,107	8,849	15,659	24,622	21,626	18,300	-3,387	-3,592	-8,265	-3,257	1,807
Congo, Rep. of	104	254	237	222	322	1,623	3,316	1,489	1,167	424	-1,519	-3,062	-1,251	-944	-103
Congo, Democratic Rep. of	65	94	200	170	182	264	528	41	76	154	-199	-434	159	94	27
Costa Rica	3,599	5,178	7,237	7,223	6,964	3,415	8,697	12,046	11,914	9,500	183	-3,519	-4,810	-4,691	-2,536
Cote d'Ivoire	124	163	188	168	239	1,198	1,177	1,100	1,013	1,193	-1,074	-1,014	-911	-846	-953
Croatia	159	312	310	309	340	364	(X)	444	425	463	-206	(X)	-134	-116	-123
Curacao [2]	(X)	(X)	692	688	612	(X)	(X)	850	402	369	(X)	(X)	-158	286	243
Cyprus	84	134	167	143	152	31	11	29	44	64	54	123	138	100	88
Czech Republic	1,054	1,411	1,832	1,943	2,302	2,193	2,450	3,931	3,923	4,345	-1,139	-1,039	-2,098	-1,980	-2,042
Denmark	1,918	2,132	2,225	2,231	2,361	5,144	6,012	6,777	6,494	7,504	-3,226	-3,880	-4,553	-4,263	-5,143
Djibouti	48	123	119	165	111	3	3	12	4	12	46	120	107	161	99
Dominican Republic	4,719	6,579	6,967	7,156	7,922	4,604	3,672	4,370	4,261	4,520	115	2,908	2,597	2,895	3,403
Ecuador	1,964	5,409	6,693	7,666	8,164	5,759	7,451	9,484	11,491	10,856	-3,795	-2,042	-2,792	-3,826	-2,692
Egypt	3,159	6,833	5,498	5,175	6,473	2,091	2,238	3,000	1,615	1,410	1,068	4,594	2,498	3,561	5,062
El Salvador	1,854	2,434	3,096	3,274	3,304	1,989	2,206	2,588	2,437	2,396	-134	228	508	837	909
Equatorial Guinea	281	272	233	756	575	1,561	2,214	1,700	898	255	-1,280	-1,942	-1,467	-142	320
Ethiopia	456	773	1,275	689	1,669	62	128	183	194	207	394	645	1,092	495	1,462
Fiji	28	44	56	67	80	169	179	189	174	184	-141	-135	-133	-107	-104
Finland	2,254	2,180	2,566	2,349	2,150	4,342	3,884	5,110	4,668	5,016	-2,088	-1,704	-2,544	-2,319	-2,866
France	22,259	26,970	30,813	31,735	31,301	33,842	38,356	41,646	45,706	46,874	-11,583	-11,386	-10,833	-13,971	-15,573
French Polynesia	112	122	130	126	130	60	53	59	37	40	52	69	70	90	90
Gabon	99	243	319	308	417	2,816	2,212	1,886	1,112	798	-2,716	-1,969	-1,567	-804	-381

See footnotes at end of table.

Table 1310. U.S. Exports, Imports, and Trade Balance by Country: 2005 to 2014—Continued

See headnote on page 828.

Country	Exports, domestic and foreign					General imports					Merchandise trade balance				
	2005	2010	2012	2013	2014	2005	2010	2012	2013	2014	2005	2010	2012	2013	2014
Georgia	214	301	541	601	628	194	198	226	175	392	20	103	315	426	236
Germany	34,184	48,155	48,803	47,362	49,363	84,751	82,450	109,226	114,349	123,260	-50,567	-34,295	-60,423	-66,987	-73,896
Ghana	337	989	1,323	982	1,186	158	273	291	366	272	179	716	1,031	617	915
Gibraltar	163	1,494	5,109	3,576	2,531	5	1	(Z)	(Z)	(Z)	159	1,494	5,109	3,576	2,531
Greece	1,192	1,107	804	739	773	884	798	987	954	1,048	309	309	-183	-215	-275
Grenada	82	71	72	95	84	6	8	8	10	10	77	64	64	86	74
Guatemala	2,835	4,477	5,749	5,553	5,964	3,137	3,523	4,491	4,172	4,217	-302	954	1,258	1,381	1,747
Guyana	177	291	360	318	370	120	299	523	466	501	57	-8	-163	-148	-131
Haiti	710	1,209	1,050	1,227	1,277	447	551	775	847	908	262	658	276	380	369
Honduras	3,254	4,606	5,715	5,373	5,961	3,749	3,933	4,648	4,543	4,643	-495	674	1,067	830	1,317
Hong Kong	16,351	26,571	37,472	42,340	40,858	8,892	4,296	5,456	5,689	5,869	7,459	22,274	32,016	36,651	34,989
Hungary	1,023	1,290	1,566	1,727	1,843	2,561	2,491	3,201	3,768	5,284	-1,538	-1,201	-1,635	-2,041	-3,441
Iceland	512	325	371	513	365	269	201	284	291	298	243	124	87	222	66
India	7,919	19,249	22,106	21,811	21,608	18,804	29,533	40,513	41,809	45,244	-10,886	-10,284	-18,407	-19,997	-23,637
Indonesia	3,054	6,948	7,998	9,097	8,284	12,014	16,478	18,002	18,874	19,361	-8,960	-9,531	-10,004	-9,777	-11,077
Iran	96	211	251	308	187	174	95	2	2	(Z)	-79	117	249	306	187
Iraq	1,374	1,643	2,054	2,022	2,106	9,054	12,143	19,265	13,306	13,827	-7,680	-10,500	-17,212	-11,284	-11,721
Ireland	8,447	7,276	7,393	6,632	7,806	28,733	33,848	33,372	31,496	33,956	-20,286	-26,572	-25,980	-24,864	-26,149
Israel	9,737	11,295	14,274	13,742	15,083	16,830	20,985	22,131	22,783	22,962	-7,093	-9,690	-7,858	-9,041	-7,879
Italy	11,524	14,220	16,097	16,754	16,968	31,009	28,514	36,965	38,709	42,115	-19,485	-14,294	-20,868	-21,955	-25,147
Jamaica	1,701	1,661	1,989	1,980	2,182	376	328	507	415	285	1,325	1,334	1,482	1,565	1,897
Japan	54,681	60,472	69,976	65,216	66,827	138,004	120,552	146,432	138,574	134,004	-83,323	-60,080	-76,456	-73,358	-67,176
Jordan	644	1,172	1,766	2,084	2,050	1,267	974	1,156	1,197	1,401	-623	198	611	887	650
Kazakhstan	538	730	884	1,150	1,009	1,101	1,872	1,565	1,421	1,411	-563	-1,142	-681	-271	-402
Kenya	573	375	569	636	1,641	348	311	390	452	591	225	64	179	183	1,050
Korea, South	27,572	38,821	42,283	41,687	44,471	43,781	48,875	58,899	62,433	69,518	-16,210	-10,055	-16,616	-20,747	-25,047
Kuwait	1,975	2,775	2,682	2,598	3,649	4,335	5,382	13,021	12,637	11,437	-2,360	-2,607	-10,339	-10,039	-7,788
Kyrgyzstan	31	79	146	106	72	5	2	9	4	2	27	76	136	103	69
Laos	10	13	34	24	29	4	59	25	31	33	6	-47	9	-6	-4
Latvia	178	345	515	495	428	362	193	246	273	275	-185	152	269	222	154
Lebanon	466	2,009	1,040	1,034	1,269	86	84	81	92	72	379	1,925	959	943	1,196
Liberia	69	191	241	173	184	91	180	144	97	83	-22	11	97	77	101
Libya	84	666	549	865	532	1,590	2,117	2,493	2,558	225	-1,506	-1,451	-1,944	-1,694	307
Liechtenstein	20	29	22	22	31	296	213	310	297	293	-276	-183	-288	-275	-262
Lithuania	390	628	757	854	681	634	637	1,176	1,554	1,094	-244	-9	-419	-700	-413
Luxembourg	711	1,440	1,903	1,849	1,516	389	451	553	641	755	323	989	1,350	1,208	761
Macau	102	225	346	351	433	1,249	141	95	95	74	-1,147	84	251	257	359
Macedonia	32	33	21	55	34	48	37	87	62	167	-17	-4	-66	-7	-133
Madagascar	28	116	64	64	47	324	108	110	180	216	-295	8	-46	-116	-169
Malawi	28	37	64	55	51	116	72	66	73	67	-87	-35	-2	-19	-16
Malaysia	10,461	14,080	12,818	13,007	13,068	33,685	25,901	25,935	27,289	30,420	-23,224	-11,822	-13,117	-14,283	-17,352
Malta	194	457	391	564	918	283	262	255	212	173	-89	196	136	352	744
Marshall Islands	75	91	142	66	95	17	12	19	17	15	58	79	123	49	80
Martinique	35	297	371	382	291	22	23	26	43	82	13	274	344	339	208
Mauritania	86	84	292	246	149	1	53	1	131	101	85	32	291	115	48
Mexico	120,248	163,665	215,875	226,070	240,249	170,109	229,986	277,594	280,555	294,074	-49,861	-66,321	-61,719	-54,485	-53,825
Mongolia	22	116	665	280	168	144	12	42	20	15	-122	104	623	260	153
Morocco	481	1,948	2,170	2,484	2,102	446	686	932	976	992	35	1,262	1,238	1,508	1,110
Mozambique	63	224	352	303	375	12	65	39	76	100	51	159	313	227	275
Namibia	112	110	185	235	343	130	195	231	262	256	-17	-85	-47	-27	87
Nepal	25	28	37	33	36	111	61	84	78	87	-87	-32	-47	-45	-50
Netherlands	26,468	34,740	40,618	42,507	43,075	14,862	19,056	22,260	19,235	20,818	11,606	15,685	18,359	23,273	22,257
Netherlands Antilles [2]	1,138	2,943	(X)	(X)	(X)	922	1,026	(X)	(X)	(X)	215	1,917	(X)	(X)	(X)
New Zealand	2,592	2,820	3,229	3,226	4,258	3,155	2,764	3,437	3,487	3,979	-563	57	-208	-261	279
Nicaragua	625	981	1,128	1,060	1,009	1,181	2,008	2,748	2,806	3,104	-555	-1,026	-1,620	-1,747	-2,095
Niger	79	49	37	46	59	66	27	82	2	5	13	22	-44	44	54
Nigeria	1,620	4,061	5,029	6,389	5,968	24,239	30,516	19,014	11,724	3,839	-22,620	-26,455	-13,985	-5,335	2,129

See footnotes at end of table.

Table 1310. U.S. Exports, Imports, and Trade Balance by Country: 2005 to 2014-Continued.

See headnote on page 828.

Country	Exports, domestic and foreign					General imports					Merchandise trade balance				
	2005	2010	2012	2013	2014	2005	2010	2012	2013	2014	2005	2010	2012	2013	2014
Norway	1,942	3,100	3,501	4,617	4,422	6,776	6,950	6,566	5,511	5,358	-4,834	-3,850	-3,065	-894	-936
Oman	571	1,105	1,747	1,571	2,016	555	773	1,354	1,023	976	16	332	393	549	1,040
Pakistan	1,252	1,901	1,530	1,646	1,512	3,253	3,509	3,628	3,688	3,672	-2,002	-1,608	-2,098	-2,043	-2,160
Panama	2,162	6,066	9,829	10,565	10,467	327	381	540	449	431	1,835	5,685	9,288	10,116	10,037
Papua New Guinea	55	186	391	167	143	58	97	118	129	100	-3	89	273	38	43
Paraguay	896	1,810	1,743	1,933	2,116	52	62	197	277	197	844	1,748	1,546	1,656	1,919
Peru	2,309	6,750	9,349	10,119	10,054	5,119	5,243	6,418	8,127	6,077	-2,810	1,506	2,930	1,992	3,977
Philippines	6,895	7,377	8,087	8,404	8,453	9,250	7,982	9,581	9,269	10,144	-2,355	-605	-1,493	-865	-1,691
Poland	1,268	2,983	3,346	3,778	3,660	1,949	2,964	4,621	4,885	5,152	-681	19	-1,275	-1,107	-1,492
Portugal	1,132	1,058	1,097	844	1,136	2,329	2,142	2,610	2,831	3,209	-1,197	-1,084	-1,513	-1,987	-2,073
Qatar	987	3,160	3,578	4,958	5,173	448	466	1,012	1,301	1,742	539	2,693	2,566	3,658	3,431
Romania	609	730	833	747	978	1,208	1,008	1,620	1,716	2,103	-599	-278	-788	-970	-1,126
Russia	3,962	5,994	10,695	11,145	10,753	15,307	25,691	29,365	27,086	23,658	-11,344	-19,697	-18,670	-15,941	-12,905
Rwanda	11	31	31	25	21	6	22	33	24	41	4	9	-3	1	-19
Saudi Arabia	6,805	11,506	17,961	18,960	18,705	27,193	31,413	55,667	51,807	47,041	-20,387	-19,907	-37,706	-32,847	-28,336
Senegal	141	219	149	229	173	4	5	17	17	25	138	214	132	212	147
Serbia	—	105	128	142	135	—	164	146	524	279	—	-60	-18	-382	-144
Sierra Leone	38	61	101	82	88	9	29	18	42	29	29	32	83	41	59
Singapore	20,466	29,009	30,523	30,667	30,237	15,110	17,428	20,232	17,843	16,426	5,356	11,581	10,291	12,824	13,811
Sint Maarten [2]	(X)	(X)	702	833	782	(X)	(X)	55	60	50	(X)	(X)	648	773	733
Slovakia	150	256	336	296	445	961	1,073	1,780	1,764	2,100	-811	-817	-1,444	-1,468	-1,655
Slovenia	234	328	308	270	301	413	465	562	575	699	-179	-137	-254	-305	-398
South Africa	3,907	5,632	7,553	7,293	6,370	5,886	8,220	8,672	8,465	8,318	-1,979	-2,589	-1,120	-1,172	-1,948
Spain	6,839	10,355	9,552	10,244	10,200	8,615	8,554	11,768	11,668	14,416	-1,776	1,802	-2,216	-1,424	-4,216
Sri Lanka	198	179	224	312	350	2,083	1,748	2,257	2,451	2,676	-1,885	-1,569	-2,033	-2,139	-2,326
St. Kitts and Nevis	94	131	106	143	185	50	51	57	54	56	44	80	49	89	129
St. Lucia	135	402	377	594	694	32	18	15	17	18	103	384	362	578	676
Suriname	246	362	499	450	519	165	191	289	303	453	80	171	211	147	66
Sweden	3,715	4,740	5,248	4,318	4,340	13,821	10,497	10,222	9,174	10,266	-10,106	-5,758	-4,974	-4,856	-5,926
Switzerland	10,718	20,704	26,406	26,559	22,176	13,000	19,137	25,673	28,275	31,191	-2,282	1,567	734	-1,716	-9,015
Syria	155	503	20	22	7	324	429	20	19	12	-169	74	(Z)	2	-6
Taiwan	21,614	26,050	24,337	25,470	26,670	34,826	35,847	38,861	37,939	40,582	-13,211	-9,797	-14,524	-12,469	-13,911
Tajikistan	29	57	54	52	25	241	2	27	1	4	-212	56	27	51	21
Tanzania	96	164	245	412	302	34	43	115	70	86	63	121	131	342	216
Thailand	7,257	8,976	10,888	11,797	11,810	19,890	22,694	26,067	26,169	27,123	-12,633	-13,717	-15,179	-14,372	-15,313
Togo	28	158	371	1,008	1,025	6	9	52	8	9	21	149	319	1,000	1,016
Trinidad and Tobago	1,417	1,925	2,478	2,404	2,411	7,891	6,613	8,158	6,494	5,995	-6,474	-4,688	-5,681	-4,090	-3,584
Tunisia	261	573	615	870	831	264	406	738	749	521	-3	167	-123	121	311
Turkey	4,239	10,539	12,475	12,073	11,645	5,182	4,207	6,294	6,669	7,357	-943	6,331	6,181	5,404	4,289
Turkmenistan	215	40	92	262	456	135	48	90	31	20	80	-8	2	231	435
Turks and Caicos Islands	238	189	210	226	282	9	12	10	11	8	228	178	200	215	274
Uganda	63	94	100	123	78	26	58	35	47	46	37	36	66	76	32
Ukraine	533	1,349	1,936	1,925	1,240	1,098	1,078	1,350	1,036	934	-565	271	587	889	306
United Arab Emirates	8,120	11,663	22,559	24,453	22,069	1,468	1,145	2,253	2,293	2,814	6,651	10,517	20,306	22,159	19,255
United Kingdom	38,568	48,410	54,861	47,348	53,823	51,033	49,805	55,006	52,850	54,392	-12,465	-1,395	-145	-5,502	-569
Uruguay	357	975	1,360	1,755	1,606	732	235	358	423	456	-376	740	1,002	1,332	1,150
Uzbekistan	74	101	285	356	213	96	68	26	27	14	-22	33	259	330	199
Venezuela	6,421	10,645	17,517	13,201	11,138	33,978	32,707	38,724	31,997	30,219	-27,557	-22,063	-21,207	-18,796	-19,082
Vietnam	1,193	3,706	4,623	5,036	5,734	6,631	14,868	20,268	24,654	30,589	-5,438	-11,162	-15,645	-19,618	-24,854
Yemen	219	398	470	518	369	279	181	87	66	41	-60	216	382	453	328
Zambia	29	56	147	141	114	32	30	63	38	56	-7	27	84	103	59
Zimbabwe	46	68	54	61	49	94	59	53	14	65	-15	9	1	47	-16

— Zero or rounds to zero. X Not applicable. Z Entry would amount to less than half the unit of measurement shown. [1] Includes timing adjustment and unidentified and unidentified countries, not shown separately. [2] The Netherlands Antilles dissolved on October 10, 2010. Curacao and Sint Maarten became autonomous territories of the Kingdom of the Netherlands.

Source: U.S. Census Bureau, *U.S. International Trade in Goods and Services, Annual Revision for 2014*, Series FT-900, June 2015, and earlier reports. See also <http://www.census.gov/foreign-trade/Press-Release/ft900_index.html>.

Table 1311. U.S. Exports and General Imports by Selected Commodity Groups: 2012 to 2014

[In millions of dollars (1,545,821 represents $1,545,821,000,000). All data are presented on a Census basis. For methodology, see Foreign Trade Statistics in Appendix III]

Selected commodity	Exports			General imports		
	2012	2013	2014	2012	2013	2014
Total [1]	**1,545,821**	**1,578,439**	**1,620,532**	**2,276,267**	**2,268,370**	**2,347,685**
Manufactured goods [2]	1,157,124	1,176,883	1,192,583	1,809,135	1,834,001	1,927,026
Agricultural commodities [2]	141,532	144,343	150,006	103,239	104,380	111,855
Food and live animals [3]	96,931	103,201	108,494	84,580	88,210	97,055
Live animals other than fish	1,174	969	927	2,611	2,639	3,542
Meat and preparations	17,480	17,911	19,332	6,226	6,507	8,914
Cereals and preparations	24,454	24,265	26,892	8,461	9,691	9,235
Vegetables and fruits	19,905	21,686	22,245	24,600	26,415	28,193
Coffee, tea, cocoa, and spices	2,991	3,096	3,147	12,831	11,798	13,021
Feeding stuff for animals	11,217	13,158	13,172	2,655	2,883	3,101
Crude materials except fuels [3]	90,461	85,187	85,535	36,599	34,856	36,504
Hides, skins, and furskins, raw	2,785	3,137	2,927	228	288	307
Oil seeds and oleaginous fruits	26,996	24,101	26,121	1,101	1,645	2,199
Crude rubber	3,977	3,257	3,148	5,458	4,248	3,772
Cork and wood	5,504	6,520	7,273	5,172	6,402	7,188
Pulp and waste paper	8,953	8,659	8,689	3,354	3,619	3,588
Textile fibers including waste	8,688	8,228	6,916	1,402	1,294	1,419
Crude fertilizers	2,584	2,479	2,813	2,839	2,598	2,934
Metalliferous ores and metal scrap	28,053	25,806	24,485	9,105	8,291	8,835
Mineral fuels and lubricants [3]	136,054	147,539	153,697	423,860	379,758	347,477
Coal, coke, and briquettes	15,076	11,459	8,718	1,508	1,019	1,196
Petroleum products and preparations	111,949	123,217	126,928	408,509	363,141	326,715
Gas, natural and manufactured	8,795	12,507	17,487	11,929	13,169	16,896
Animal and vegetable oils [3]	4,010	3,178	2,793	5,856	5,667	5,776
Animal oil and fat	892	765	725	241	260	244
Fixed vegetable fats and oil, crude	2,594	1,986	1,682	5,447	5,254	5,379
Chemicals and related products [3]	198,063	198,800	203,076	196,187	195,471	207,714
Organic chemicals	42,372	42,481	39,574	52,252	52,312	52,169
Inorganic chemicals	12,293	11,206	11,431	15,500	14,194	13,137
Dyeing, tanning, and coloring materials	7,884	7,551	7,697	3,757	3,813	3,967
Medicinal and pharmaceutical products	42,558	41,366	46,264	68,887	66,799	76,166
Fertilizers	4,497	4,099	3,725	8,744	7,959	8,104
Plastics in primary forms	33,770	34,549	35,137	13,283	13,997	15,754
Plastics in nonprimary forms	11,657	12,090	12,808	8,436	8,942	9,629
Manufactured goods by material	117,137	115,817	117,755	234,768	234,788	254,193
Leather and leather manufactures	1,109	1,347	1,437	1,232	1,279	1,398
Rubber manufactures	10,265	9,947	10,177	21,018	21,072	21,821
Cork and wood manufactures	2,127	2,182	2,216	7,962	9,045	9,569
Paper and paperboard	15,854	16,139	16,034	15,621	15,978	16,698
Textile yarn, fabric	12,527	12,857	13,261	24,743	25,813	26,996
Nonmetallic mineral manufactures	13,367	12,540	13,050	37,555	41,912	45,121
Iron and steel	19,283	18,443	18,427	42,776	36,624	46,828
Nonferrous metals	16,795	15,724	15,548	39,418	38,270	38,538
Manufactures of metals	25,809	26,639	27,606	44,444	44,794	47,223
Machinery and transport equipment	507,042	513,981	534,213	869,887	886,879	939,287
Power generating machinery	39,629	38,415	40,186	62,864	60,711	66,378
Specialized industrial machinery	53,731	49,202	48,744	45,010	42,281	47,298
Metalworking machinery	6,251	6,046	5,813	10,325	9,923	9,932
General industrial machinery	64,468	66,628	70,252	81,670	83,472	92,447
Office machinery	22,608	21,549	21,849	118,866	117,472	117,903
Telecommunications equipment	23,081	23,631	23,715	143,883	146,207	152,582
Electrical machinery	77,783	78,498	80,905	144,323	149,914	158,714
Road vehicles	116,903	118,739	121,548	235,323	244,463	256,882
Transport equipment	102,588	111,274	121,200	27,622	32,436	37,151
Miscellaneous manufactured articles [3]	119,478	121,697	122,935	318,987	333,225	348,643
Prefabricated buildings	3,010	3,139	3,245	9,309	10,404	11,483
Furniture	5,755	6,130	6,476	35,612	38,005	41,462
Travel goods	541	586	568	9,998	10,586	10,995
Apparel and clothing accessories	3,454	3,425	3,424	84,917	87,918	90,157
Footwear	824	789	826	23,887	24,811	26,014
Scientific and controlling equipment	50,212	50,119	50,006	45,874	47,425	50,480
Photographic equipment	6,837	6,559	6,462	13,098	13,512	14,331
Miscellaneous commodities [4]	77,082	75,219	64,409	85,885	88,705	89,444
Re-exports	**193,610**	**207,370**	**221,163**	**(X)**	**(X)**	**(X)**

X Not applicable. [1] Total exports including re-exports (exports of foreign merchandise). [2] Manufactured Goods is based on the North American Industry Classification System (NAICS) and Agricultural Commodities is based on the Harmonized System commodities specified by the U.S. Department of Agriculture definition. All other commodity detail is based on Standard International Trade Classification (SITC). [3] Includes other commodities, not shown separately. [4] Includes special transactions, coin, nonmonetary gold, and the low value estimate.

Source: U.S. Census Bureau, *U.S. International Trade in Goods and Services, Annual Revision for 2014*, Series FT-900, June 2015. See also <http://www.census.gov/foreign-trade/Press-Release/ft900_index.html>.

Table 1312. U.S. Total and Aerospace Foreign Trade: 1990 to 2014

[In millions of dollars (-101,718 represents -$101,718,000,000), except percent. Data are reported as exports of domestic merchandise, including Department of Defense shipments and undocumented exports to Canada, f.a.s. (free alongside ship) basis, and imports for consumption, customs value basis. Minus sign (-) indicates deficit]

Year	U.S. merchandise trade			Aerospace trade					
						Exports			
	Trade balance [1]	Imports	Exports	Trade balance [1]	Imports	Total	Percent of U.S. exports	Civil	Military
1990........	-101,718	495,311	393,592	27,282	11,801	39,083	9.9	31,517	7,566
1995........	-158,801	743,543	584,742	21,562	11,509	33,071	5.7	25,079	7,991
2000.......	-436,104	1,218,022	781,918	26,735	27,944	54,679	7.0	45,566	9,113
2001.......	-411,899	1,140,999	729,100	26,035	32,473	58,508	8.0	49,371	9,137
2002.......	-468,263	1,161,366	693,103	29,533	27,242	56,775	8.2	47,348	9,427
2003.......	-532,350	1,257,121	724,771	27,111	25,393	52,504	7.2	44,366	8,138
2004.......	-654,830	1,469,704	814,875	31,002	25,815	56,817	7.0	47,772	9,045
2005.......	-772,373	1,673,455	901,082	39,783	27,649	67,433	7.5	57,587	9,845
2006.......	-827,971	1,853,938	1,025,967	54,809	30,453	85,262	8.3	71,857	13,404
2007.......	-808,763	1,956,962	1,148,199	60,614	36,610	97,224	8.5	83,977	13,247
2008.......	-816,199	2,103,641	1,287,442	57,389	37,694	95,082	7.4	82,264	12,819
2009.......	-503,582	1,559,625	1,056,043	56,034	25,132	81,166	7.7	70,500	10,666
2010.......	-635,362	1,913,857	1,278,495	43,188	34,569	77,757	6.1	66,936	10,821
2011.......	-725,447	2,207,954	1,482,508	46,750	38,879	85,630	5.8	75,065	10,565
2012.......	-730,446	2,276,267	1,545,821	55,754	43,940	99,694	6.4	86,610	13,083
2013.......	-689,931	2,268,371	1,578,439	61,027	49,806	110,833	7.0	97,331	13,502
2014.......	-727,153	2,347,685	1,620,532	61,185	57,708	118,893	7.3	104,145	14,748

[1] Exports minus imports.

Source: © 2014 Aerospace Industries Association of America, Inc., *2014 Year-End Review and Forecast*, <http://www.aia-aerospace.org/research_reports/aerospace_statistics/>; and U.S. Census Bureau, *U.S. International Trade in Goods and Services, Annual Revision for 2014*, Series FT-900, June 2015, and earlier reports, <http://www.census.gov/foreign-trade/Press-Release/ft900_index.html>.

Table 1313. U.S. High Technology Exports by Industry and Selected Major Country: 2011 to 2013

[In billions of dollars (198.0 represents $198,000,000,000)]

Selected industry	2011	2012	2013	Selected country	2011	2012	2013
Total exports..........	**198.0**	**203.2**	**204.7**	Canada..................	27.8	28.7	28.0
Computers and office equipment.....	48.6	49.4	48.3	China..................	13.6	13.9	16.0
Consumer electronics..................	10.8	10.5	9.7	Japan..................	8.2	9.3	8.6
Communications equipment..........	33.3	35.3	37.6	Korea, South.............	6.7	7.0	6.6
Semiconductors and				Malaysia..................	7.3	6.3	6.0
electronic components...............	55.2	52.3	53.2	Mexico..................	35.2	36.6	38.6
Industrial electronics..................	48.6	51.1	51.5	Singapore...............	6.6	5.9	6.0
Magnetic and optical media...........	1.5	4.6	4.4	European Union 27 [1]. ...	32.8	31.6	30.9

[1] See footnote 2, Table 1372.

Source: TechAmerica Foundation, Washington, DC, unpublished data ©. See also <http://www.techamericafoundation.org/>.

Table 1314. U.S. Exporting and Importing Companies by Employment-Size Class: 2010 and 2013

[Value in millions of dollars (1,140,406 represents $1,140,406,000,000). Data include all companies that can be linked to import and/or export transactions. Trade values are taken from the transactions used to compile the official U.S. Trade statistics; company information is taken from the Business Register. For information on data limitations, see Technical Documentation in source]

Employment-size class and company type	Number		Known value [1] (mil. dol.)		Percent of—			
					Number		Known value	
	2010	2013	2010	2013	2010	2013	2010	2013
EXPORTERS								
All companies, total..........	**293,988**	**304,223**	**1,140,406**	**1,400,955**	**100.0**	**100.0**	**100.0**	**100.0**
By employment-size:								
1 to 19 employees...............	112,572	112,882	82,739	95,626	38.3	37.1	7.3	6.8
20 to 49 employees...............	30,984	31,727	45,037	49,895	10.5	10.4	3.9	3.6
50 to 99 employees...............	15,179	16,089	43,710	45,678	5.2	5.3	3.8	3.3
100 to 249 employees...........	11,581	12,260	59,349	84,870	3.9	4.0	5.2	6.1
250 to 499 employees...........	4,336	4,717	46,254	72,438	1.5	1.6	4.1	5.2
500 or more employees.........	6,490	6,880	755,466	929,886	2.2	2.3	66.2	66.4
Unknown [2]......................	112,846	119,668	107,851	122,562	38.4	39.3	9.5	8.7
IMPORTERS								
All companies, total..........	**181,648**	**184,208**	**1,679,522**	**1,986,142**	**100.0**	**100.0**	**100.0**	**100.0**
By employment-size:								
1 to 19 employees...............	77,796	78,448	112,664	128,915	42.8	42.6	6.7	6.5
20 to 49 employees...............	18,487	19,415	71,093	80,683	10.2	10.5	4.2	4.1
50 to 99 employees...............	9,472	10,258	58,075	64,267	5.2	5.6	3.5	3.2
100 to 249 employees...........	7,820	8,305	96,080	113,834	4.3	4.5	5.7	5.7
250 to 499 employees...........	3,174	3,498	69,812	94,763	1.7	1.9	4.2	4.8
500 or more employees.........	5,013	5,369	1,148,183	1,367,772	2.8	2.9	68.4	68.9
Unknown [2]......................	59,886	58,915	123,616	135,906	33.0	32.0	7.4	6.8

[1] Known value is defined as the portion of U.S. total exports and general imports that could be matched to specific companies. Export values are on f.a.s. or "free alongside ship basis." [2] Includes missing employment data, nonemployers, and companies that reported annual payroll but did not report any employees on their payroll.

Source: U.S. Census Bureau, *Profile of U.S. Importing and Exporting Companies 2012-2013*, April 2015, and earlier reports. See also <http://www.census.gov/foreign-trade/statistics/press-release/>.

Table 1315. Domestic Exports and Imports for Consumption of Merchandise by Selected NAICS Product Category: 2000 to 2014

[In millions of dollars (712,285 represents $712,285,000,000). Includes nonmonetary gold. For methodology, see Foreign Trade Statistics in Appendix III. NAICS = North American Industry Classification System; see text, Section 15]

Product category	2000	2005	2010	2012	2013	2014
Domestic exports, total.............................	**712,285**	**798,997**	**1,122,416**	**1,353,897**	**1,372,039**	**1,402,273**
Agricultural, forestry, and fishery products...............	29,153	37,109	65,737	78,269	76,488	80,677
Agricultural products, total.............................	23,596	30,683	58,009	68,710	66,246	70,308
Livestock and livestock products......................	1,255	1,118	1,540	2,339	2,363	2,201
Forestry products, not elsewhere specified.............	1,644	1,686	2,178	2,299	2,761	2,843
Fish, fresh or chilled, and other marine products.......	2,658	3,622	4,010	4,922	5,117	5,326
Mining, total..	6,187	12,629	26,234	34,760	37,619	48,011
Oil and gas...	1,706	4,547	9,090	10,933	17,324	29,097
Minerals and ores.....................................	4,481	8,082	17,144	23,827	20,296	18,913
Manufacturing, total....................................	644,440	708,205	952,409	1,163,293	1,182,567	1,193,380
Food and kindred products............................	24,966	28,937	50,910	63,404	67,285	69,422
Beverages and tobacco products......................	5,568	3,423	5,341	6,846	8,130	8,202
Textiles and fabrics...................................	7,010	8,483	7,832	8,574	8,926	9,379
Textile mill products..................................	2,236	2,344	2,582	2,855	2,934	2,852
Apparel and accessories..............................	8,104	4,075	3,071	3,289	3,253	3,169
Leather and allied products...........................	2,322	2,300	2,420	2,833	3,227	3,357
Wood products.......................................	4,854	4,463	5,073	5,905	6,492	7,229
Paper products.......................................	15,539	16,640	22,962	24,434	24,840	23,993
Printed, publishing, & similar products.................	4,869	5,526	6,020	5,978	5,810	5,539
Petroleum and coal products..........................	8,862	17,979	61,003	110,725	118,224	117,376
Chemicals..	77,649	114,821	171,443	188,564	189,333	191,565
Plastics and rubber products [1].......................	16,970	18,784	24,255	28,560	28,947	31,079
Nonmetallic mineral products [1]......................	7,830	6,663	9,223	10,128	10,345	11,054
Primary metal products...............................	20,126	27,455	49,708	73,769	69,561	59,095
Fabricated metal products.............................	21,737	23,370	32,667	40,114	42,912	43,566
Machinery, except electrical...........................	85,038	97,001	126,040	150,509	141,871	136,448
Computers and electronic products [1].................	161,449	122,744	121,111	123,456	122,654	122,975
Electrical equipment, appliances, and components [1]...	25,401	26,457	30,998	36,914	38,318	47,532
Transportation equipment [1]...........................	121,701	144,985	176,397	226,200	240,347	249,392
Furniture and fixtures.................................	2,882	2,844	3,980	4,902	4,948	5,149
Miscellaneous manufactured commodities..............	19,327	28,909	39,373	44,653	44,211	45,009
Special classification provisions........................	32,505	41,055	77,186	77,574	75,364	80,205
Waste & scrap..	4,948	10,389	29,411	27,731	23,683	20,983
Used or second-hand merchandise.....................	1,950	2,570	4,712	4,961	5,455	–
Goods returned or reimported.........................	333	65	29	26	24	33
Special classification provision, not elsewhere specified............................	25,274	28,030	43,034	44,856	46,203	45,138
Imports for consumption, total......................	**1,205,339**	**1,664,497**	**1,899,886**	**2,251,035**	**2,239,750**	**2,313,960**
Agricultural, forestry, and fishery products...............	24,378	30,761	42,683	50,560	53,951	58,456
Agricultural products, total.............................	11,771	15,818	24,014	29,245	31,740	33,667
Livestock and livestock products......................	3,085	3,277	4,115	4,683	5,212	6,383
Forestry products, not elsewhere specified.............	1,409	2,250	3,356	4,117	3,389	2,758
Fish, fresh or chilled, and other marine products.......	8,113	9,416	11,198	12,515	13,610	15,647
Mining, total..	79,841	192,115	235,394	264,567	230,398	205,362
Oil and gas...	76,166	185,621	228,066	255,678	222,265	196,517
Minerals and ores.....................................	3,675	6,494	7,328	8,889	8,132	8,845
Manufacturing, total....................................	1,040,329	1,372,004	1,549,521	1,849,273	1,862,313	1,956,646
Food and kindred products............................	18,944	29,779	41,037	54,170	52,837	57,094
Beverages and tobacco products......................	8,350	12,849	15,514	18,190	19,053	20,016
Textiles and fabrics...................................	7,042	7,450	6,524	7,608	7,845	8,415
Textile mill products..................................	7,347	13,508	15,824	17,233	18,112	19,602
Apparel and accessories..............................	62,928	74,478	75,407	81,186	83,997	86,271
Leather and allied products...........................	21,463	26,559	30,857	36,167	37,433	38,552
Wood products.......................................	15,388	23,654	11,363	13,009	15,335	16,614
Paper products.......................................	19,080	22,094	21,029	21,283	22,009	20,855
Printed, publishing, & similar products.................	4,197	5,599	5,323	5,266	5,182	5,270
Petroleum and coal products..........................	40,156	81,359	102,161	135,872	124,317	113,155
Chemicals..	76,606	131,936	187,631	209,868	206,539	214,541
Plastics and rubber products..........................	17,362	28,072	34,363	43,349	44,591	49,303
Nonmetallic mineral products.........................	14,740	18,445	16,078	18,524	19,427	20,889
Primary metal products...............................	43,833	64,666	79,025	100,974	92,378	101,556
Fabricated metal products.............................	27,974	41,026	46,691	59,927	61,007	65,106
Machinery, except electrical...........................	79,366	109,619	104,797	146,947	142,026	159,052
Computers and electronic products....................	250,694	269,921	324,372	354,092	354,725	364,658
Electrical equipment, appliances, and components....	39,567	55,179	68,462	81,132	85,647	97,534
Transportation equipment.............................	213,110	251,386	239,809	313,891	331,631	353,648
Furniture and fixtures.................................	15,607	25,096	25,702	28,565	30,476	33,271
Miscellaneous manufactured commodities..............	56,577	79,329	97,552	102,022	107,747	111,245
Special classification provisions........................	60,791	69,617	72,253	86,636	93,089	93,496
Waste & scrap..	1,875	3,207	5,260	7,300	6,460	6,761
Used or second-hand merchandise.....................	6,345	6,026	6,403	8,070	9,289	–
Goods returned or reimported.........................	33,851	37,024	40,985	51,870	56,453	61,127
Special classification provision, not elsewhere specified............................	18,720	23,359	19,605	19,396	20,887	15,368

– Represents zero or rounds to less than half the unit of measurement shown. [1] Due to non-disclosure requirements, certain 10-digit Schedule B commodity classifications for 2011, 2012, and 2013 are subject to suppression and require a change in aggregation.

Source: U.S. Census Bureau, *U.S. International Trade in Goods and Services*, series FT-900, December 2014, and earlier reports. See also <http://www.census.gov/foreign-trade/data/index.html>.

Table 1316. Export and Import Unit Value Indexes—Selected Countries: 2009 to 2013

[Indexes in U.S. dollars, 2000 = 100. A unit value is an implicit price derived from value and quantity data]

Country	Export unit value					Import unit value				
	2009	2010	2011	2012	2013	2009	2010	2011	2012	2013
United States	**135.1**	**163.5**	**189.3**	**197.7**	**201.9**	**127.5**	**156.4**	**179.9**	**185.5**	**185.1**
Australia	241.6	332.9	423.3	401.5	395.7	231.3	281.9	340.7	364.8	338.5
Belgium	197.0	217.0	253.4	237.3	249.5	199.6	220.9	263.5	248.0	254.3
Canada	114.3	140.1	163.2	164.6	165.6	134.8	164.5	189.4	194.0	193.8
France	148.3	160.3	182.5	174.0	177.4	165.9	180.7	213.0	199.5	201.3
Germany	203.5	228.7	267.8	255.3	263.9	186.8	212.7	253.0	234.5	239.4
Greece	174.6	238.5	289.2	302.7	311.3	207.9	200.4	201.8	189.2	186.1
Ireland	150.1	150.9	162.8	151.2	147.9	123.2	118.4	130.8	123.3	127.9
Italy	169.2	186.0	217.6	208.4	215.2	173.9	204.0	234.0	204.6	199.9
Japan	121.2	160.6	171.7	166.6	149.2	145.4	182.9	225.4	233.4	219.5
Korea, South	211.0	270.7	322.3	318.0	324.9	201.3	265.0	326.8	323.8	321.3
Netherlands	214.1	246.9	286.9	281.2	285.3	203.5	237.2	275.1	271.1	271.1
Norway	194.4	217.6	267.1	268.1	255.2	200.5	224.9	264.0	253.9	261.9
Spain	197.7	221.3	266.6	256.8	274.4	188.3	210.0	241.8	216.6	217.5
Sweden	150.5	182.4	215.1	198.5	192.7	164.9	204.9	243.5	223.6	217.8
Switzerland	214.3	243.0	291.7	280.7	284.6	188.3	213.6	252.3	239.7	242.9
United Kingdom	124.6	146.1	177.9	166.1	190.1	149.5	170.2	195.0	198.9	188.5

Source: World Bank, "World Development Indicators" database ©, <http://data.worldbank.org/>, accessed August 2015.

Table 1317. U.S. Trade with China, Leading Commodity Imports and Exports: 2010 to 2014

[In billions of dollars (365.0 represents $365,000,000,000), except as noted]

Commodity	NAICS code [1]	2010	2011	2012	2013	2014	2013-2014 percent change
IMPORTS FROM CHINA							
Total imports [2]	(X)	**365.0**	**399.4**	**425.6**	**440.4**	**466.8**	**6.0**
Computer equipment	3341	59.8	68.3	68.8	68.1	67.0	-1.6
Communications equipment	3342	33.5	39.8	51.8	58.8	64.2	9.0
Misc. manufactured commodities	3399	34.2	32.7	32.6	32.4	33.5	3.4
Apparel	3152	26.6	27.6	26.9	27.4	27.1	-1.0
Semiconductors and other electronic components	3344	18.3	19.8	19.0	19.4	22.4	15.8
Footwear	3162	15.7	16.5	16.9	16.8	16.8	0.4
Audio and video equipment	3343	19.5	15.9	15.9	13.8	14.6	5.9
Furniture and kitchen cabinets	3371	11.1	11.4	12.2	13.2	14.0	5.9
Household appliances and misc. machines	3352	9.1	9.6	10.3	11.7	12.2	4.5
Motor vehicle parts	3363	7.0	8.3	9.4	10.5	12.1	16.1
EXPORTS TO CHINA							
Total exports [2]	(X)	**85.8**	**97.1**	**103.4**	**114.0**	**170.2**	**49.3**
Oilseeds and grains	1111	11.3	11.6	16.5	15.7	22.2	40.9
Aerospace products and parts	3364	5.7	6.3	7.9	12.1	19.0	57.7
Motor vehicles	3361	3.2	5.0	5.5	8.3	16.6	98.7
Waste and scrap	9100	8.5	11.5	9.5	8.7	10.5	20.7
Navigational, measuring, electromedical, and control instruments	3345	3.5	3.9	4.8	5.3	7.3	36.2
Semiconductors and other electronic components	3344	6.1	4.3	3.4	4.4	7.3	65.6
Basic chemicals	3251	4.1	4.7	4.7	5.1	6.7	32.3
Resin, synthetic rubber, artificial and synthetic fibers and filaments	3252	4.3	4.5	4.2	4.2	6.5	54.0
Other general purpose machinery	3339	2.4	3.0	2.9	3.1	4.8	56.6
Meat products and meat packaging products	3116	1.3	2.0	2.4	2.8	3.6	30.3

X Not applicable. [1] Based on the North American Industry Classification System (NAICS); see text, Section 15. [2] Includes items not shown separately.

Source: U.S. International Trade Commission, "Interactive Tariff and Trade DataWeb," <http://dataweb.usitc.gov/>, accessed August 2015.

Table 1318. U.S. Trade in Processed Foods By Commodity: 2000 to 2014

[Includes Puerto Rico, U.S. territories, and shipments under foreign aid programs. Metric ton = 1.102 short tons or .984 long tons]

Product category	Units	2000	2010	2012	2013	2014
Processed foods imports, total [1,2]	**Metric tons**	**11,054,749**	**16,834,276**	**18,388,765**	**19,059,434**	**19,859,603**
Beer and wine	Kiloliters	2,771,174	4,078,532	4,393,973	4,300,367	4,500,529
Beer	Kiloliters	2,331,185	3,146,395	3,233,328	3,210,926	3,434,325
Wine	Kiloliters	439,989	932,137	1,160,646	1,089,441	1,066,204
Distilled spirits and other alcoholic beverages	Kiloliters	47,708	36,640	49,852	62,417	64,250
Chocolate and confectionery [2]	Metric tons	858,136	1,362,569	1,373,049	1,410,457	1,462,366
Chocolate	Metric tons	525,437	820,017	827,520	854,006	857,504
Sugar confectionery	Metric tons	293,105	499,236	507,867	518,409	566,828
Condiments and sauces	Metric tons	351,000	569,652	596,901	610,290	630,370
Fats and oils [2]	Metric tons	1,698,793	3,518,341	3,925,577	4,230,738	4,309,493
Olive oil	Metric tons	203,960	275,435	321,421	287,683	310,684
Soybean oil	1,000 kilograms	35,949	53,697	64,567	84,448	69,424
Vegetable oils (excl. soybean)	Metric tons	1,427,711	3,075,082	3,387,343	3,680,780	3,774,759
Food preparations [2]	Metric tons	1,111,342	2,052,605	2,301,534	2,351,864	2,585,828
Baking inputs, mixes, and types of dough [3]	Metric tons	682,340	1,097,081	1,189,215	1,262,516	1,290,445
Non-alcoholic beverages [2]	Kiloliters	3,689,991	5,552,744	5,370,080	6,019,255	6,020,581
Bottled drinks [4]	Kiloliters	555,954	1,222,531	1,534,621	1,569,820	1,628,912
Juices	Kiloliters	3,134,037	4,330,213	3,835,459	4,449,434	4,391,669
Pasta and processed cereals [2]	Metric tons	517,471	881,572	953,498	995,623	1,094,001
Breakfast cereals and other breakfast products	Metric tons	113,024	277,763	292,369	311,209	338,256
Pasta	Metric tons	316,886	367,974	409,111	412,854	437,486
Prepared/preserved meats	Metric tons	197,083	143,248	138,997	147,909	148,524
Prepared/preserved seafood	Metric tons	876,402	1,283,775	1,230,347	1,220,785	1,287,616
Processed fruit	Metric tons	865,350	1,422,793	1,682,482	1,800,763	1,806,471
Processed vegetables and pulses [2]	Metric tons	1,695,961	2,455,785	2,636,166	2,622,569	2,631,324
Frozen potato products [5]	Metric tons	527,642	725,033	804,226	828,916	810,363
Processed/prepared dairy products [2]	Metric tons	245,530	230,269	265,448	254,370	281,157
Cheese	Metric tons	188,707	138,539	153,964	147,196	164,777
Cream & powdered/condensed milk	Metric tons	18,897	33,250	40,285	36,407	39,446
Ice cream	Metric tons	9,151	30,263	32,684	24,417	23,920
Yogurt and dairy drinks	Liters	23,060	11,197	731,328	784,892	401,208
Snack foods	Metric tons	627,030	1,126,307	1,155,587	1,172,747	1,219,009
Baked snack foods [6]	Metric tons	480,515	899,781	980,176	1,018,946	1,058,552
Mixes of nuts and fruit [7]	Metric tons	92,782	156,182	63,711	70,011	80,068
Potato chips	Metric tons	23,758	40,569	48,484	45,871	42,179
Prepared peanuts and peanut butter	Metric tons	29,976	29,774	63,217	37,920	38,211
Spices	Metric tons	192,577	300,902	326,871	338,430	337,912
Syrups and sweeteners [2]	Metric tons	1,106,543	866,613	1,036,084	1,043,780	1,136,725
Fructose and fructose syrup	Metric tons	66,513	92,496	91,914	96,042	118,773
Glucose and glucose syrup	Metric tons	113,647	217,058	216,017	213,153	245,576
Processed foods exports, total [2]	**Metric tons**	**10,908,071**	**17,719,580**	**20,591,646**	**20,131,880**	**20,520,574**
Beer and wine	Kiloliters	526,828	703,995	826,568	902,766	927,464
Beer	Kiloliters	262,305	320,694	444,888	495,882	529,547
Wine	Kiloliters	264,523	383,301	381,680	406,884	397,918
Distilled spirits and other alcoholic beverages	Kiloliters	23,884	23,969	23,164	28,891	44,776
Chocolate and confectionery [2]	Metric tons	302,600	420,212	507,739	513,670	541,164
Chocolate	Metric tons	192,742	303,757	378,192	373,648	393,289
Sugar confectionery	Metric tons	98,043	108,527	121,313	133,663	140,165
Condiments and sauces	Metric tons	363,963	638,943	725,520	795,134	919,423
Fats and oils [2]	Metric tons	1,998,801	3,356,665	2,832,107	2,440,627	2,368,261
Soybean oil	1,000 kilograms	586,786	1,656,926	950,942	815,554	891,322
Vegetable oils (excl. soybean)	Metric tons	1,044,199	1,066,611	1,160,202	954,498	831,359
Food preparations [2]	Metric tons	2,492,061	3,397,278	5,389,031	5,027,216	4,914,650
Baking inputs, mixes, and types of dough [3]	Metric tons	1,904,460	2,280,017	4,150,891	3,767,720	3,616,594
Non-alcoholic beverages [2]	Kiloliters	1,661,547	1,617,263	1,707,340	1,736,521	1,658,545
Bottled drinks [4]	Kiloliters	487,448	636,964	676,157	691,765	688,816
Juices	Kiloliters	1,174,098	980,299	1,031,184	1,044,756	969,728
Pasta and processed cereals [2]	Metric tons	683,017	983,674	864,467	794,069	829,288
Breakfast cereals and other breakfast products	Metric tons	265,399	568,666	484,345	436,806	448,614
Pasta	Metric tons	102,295	181,765	201,106	197,008	206,624
Prepared/preserved meats	Metric tons	313,841	643,614	624,426	742,547	808,305
Prepared/preserved seafood	Metric tons	434,173	457,886	528,174	518,153	550,388
Processed fruit	Metric tons	388,844	571,165	631,629	621,840	669,575
Processed vegetables and pulses [2]	Metric tons	1,272,076	1,679,157	2,109,043	2,269,261	2,406,792
Frozen potato products [5]	Metric tons	568,709	790,607	1,009,615	1,013,923	1,048,799
Processed/prepared dairy products [2]	Metric tons	398,655	1,179,545	1,310,619	1,597,060	1,615,978
Cheese	Metric tons	47,760	173,327	259,962	316,185	368,384
Cream & powdered/condensed milk	Metric tons	114,847	466,853	489,525	637,873	625,935
Ice cream	Metric tons	41,652	35,680	49,604	64,019	68,189
Snack foods	Metric tons	490,079	784,168	908,128	983,266	1,012,180
Baked snack foods [6]	Metric tons	274,577	476,137	595,306	638,505	663,301
Mixes of nuts and fruit [7]	Metric tons	72,748	160,303	145,703	150,899	170,121
Potato chips	Metric tons	106,040	86,510	88,936	82,050	83,913
Prepared peanuts and peanut butter	Metric tons	36,713	61,218	78,183	111,813	94,844
Soups	1,000 kilograms	97,212	140,420	165,623	174,435	171,919
Syrups and sweeteners [2]	Metric tons	726,427	2,525,583	2,921,430	2,545,014	2,524,108
Fructose and fructose syrup	Metric tons	322,904	1,395,278	1,664,799	1,372,462	1,405,747
Glucose and glucose syrup	Metric tons	209,686	738,966	800,559	680,877	618,102
Molasses	Kiloliters	199,070	203,841	168,049	109,968	78,785

[1] Imports for consumption. Excludes merchandise entered into bonded warehouses of Foreign Trade Zones under Customs custody; see source for details. [2] Includes commodities not shown separately. [3] Includes pudding. [4] Includes soda, juice mixes, beer, milk-based drinks, etc. [5] Includes French fries. [6] Pastries, pretzels, corn chips, etc. [7] Includes packaged and microwaveable popcorn.

Source: U.S. Department of Agriculture, Foreign Agricultural Service, "Global Agricultural Trade System," <http://www.fas.usda.gov/gats>, accessed August 2015.

Section 29
Puerto Rico and the Island Areas

This section presents summary economic and social statistics for Puerto Rico, the U.S. Virgin Islands, Guam, American Samoa, and the Northern Mariana Islands. Primary sources include the decennial censuses of population and housing and the annual Puerto Rico Community Survey conducted by the U.S. Census Bureau; County Business Patterns and other Census Bureau publications and databases; other U.S. government publications, such as the *National Vital Statistics Reports* (NSVR) series, issued by the National Center for Health Statistics; and the annual *Economic Report for the Governor and Legislative Assembly* of the Puerto Rico Planning Board.

Jurisdiction—The United States gained jurisdiction over these areas as follows: the islands of Puerto Rico and Guam, surrendered by Spain in December 1898, were ceded to the United States by the Treaty of Paris, ratified in 1899. Puerto Rico became a commonwealth on July 25, 1952, thereby achieving a high degree of local autonomy under its own constitution. The U.S. Virgin Islands, comprising approximately 50 islands and cays, was purchased by the United States from Denmark in 1917. American Samoa, a group of seven islands, was acquired in accordance with a convention among the United States, Great Britain, and Germany, ratified in 1900 (Swains Island was annexed in 1925). By an agreement approved by the United Nations Security Council and the United States, the Northern Mariana Islands, previously under Japanese mandate, was administered by the United States between 1947 and 1986 under the United Nations trusteeship system. The Northern Mariana Islands became a U.S. commonwealth in 1986.

Censuses—Because characteristics of Puerto Rico and the island areas differ, the presentation of census data for them is not uniform. The 1960 Census of Population covered all the territories listed above except the Northern Mariana Islands (their census was conducted in April 1958 by the Office of the High Commissioner of the Trust Territory of the Pacific Islands), while the 1960 Census of Housing excluded American Samoa. The 1970, 1980, 1990, 2000, and 2010 censuses of population and housing covered all five areas. Beginning in 1967, Congress authorized the Economic Censuses, to be taken at 5-year intervals, for years ending in "2" and "7." Prior economic censuses were conducted in Puerto Rico for 1949, 1954, 1958, and 1963 and in Guam and the U.S. Virgin Islands for 1958 and 1963. In 1967, the census of construction industries was added for the first time in Puerto Rico; in 1972, the U.S. Virgin Islands and Guam were covered; and in 1982, the Economic Census was taken for the first time for the Northern Mariana Islands. Agricultural censuses have been conducted with increasing regularity in Puerto Rico since 1910, in the U.S. Virgin Islands since 1917, and in Guam and American Samoa since 1920; the first agricultural census in the Northern Mariana Islands was conducted in 1970.

Puerto Rico Community Survey—The Puerto Rico Community Survey (PRCS) began in 2005 and was an important element in the Census Bureau's re-engineered 2010 census plan. The American Community Survey (ACS) is the equivalent of the PRCS for the United States (50 states and District of Columbia). The PRCS collects and produces population and housing information every year instead of every 10 years. About 36,000 households are surveyed each year from across every municipio in Puerto Rico.

Information in other sections—In addition to the statistics presented in this section, other data on Puerto Rico and the island areas are included in many tables showing distribution by states in various sections of the *Abstract*. See "Puerto Rico" and "Island Areas of the U.S." in the Index.

Selected Island Areas of the United States

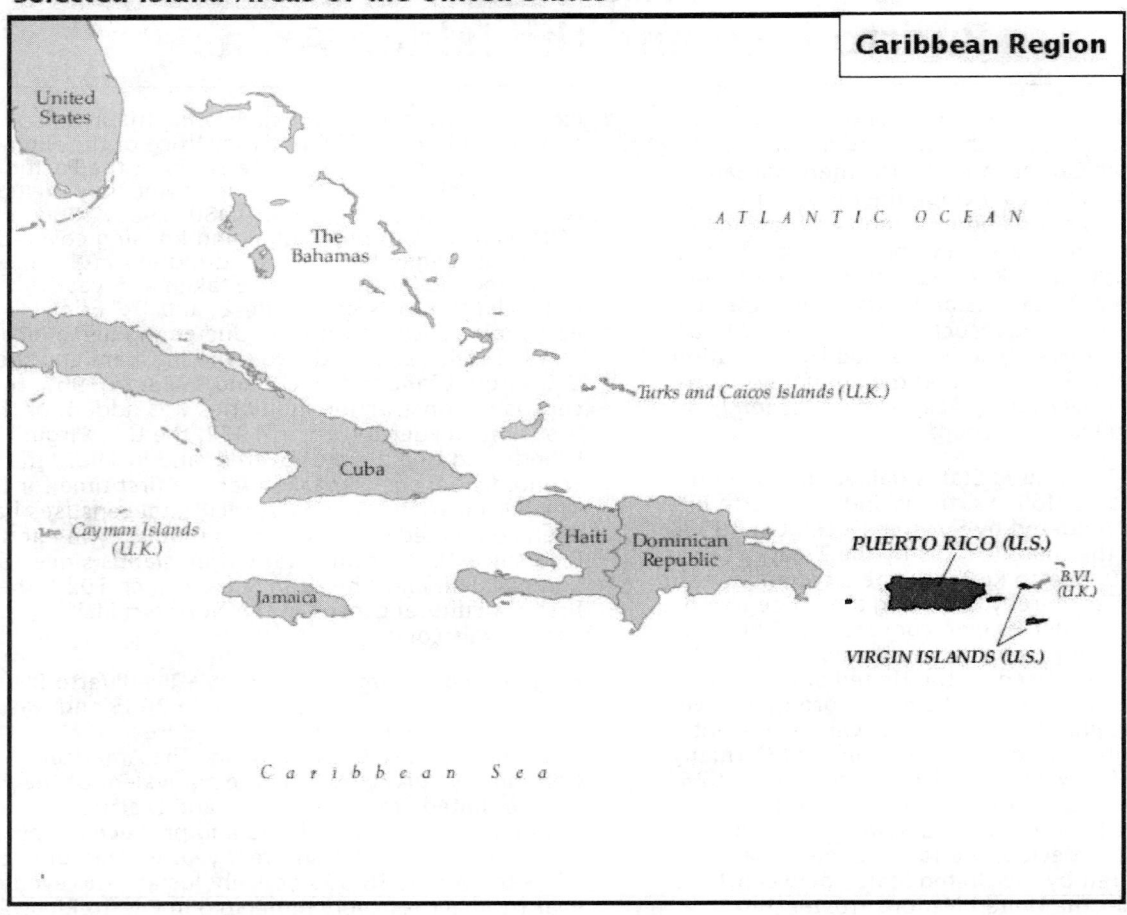

Caribbean Region

United States

A T L A N T I C   O C E A N

The Bahamas

Turks and Caicos Islands (U.K.)

Cuba

Cayman Islands (U.K.)

Haiti Dominican Republic

PUERTO RICO (U.S.)

B.V.I. (U.K.)

Jamaica

VIRGIN ISLANDS (U.S.)

C a r i b b e a n   S e a

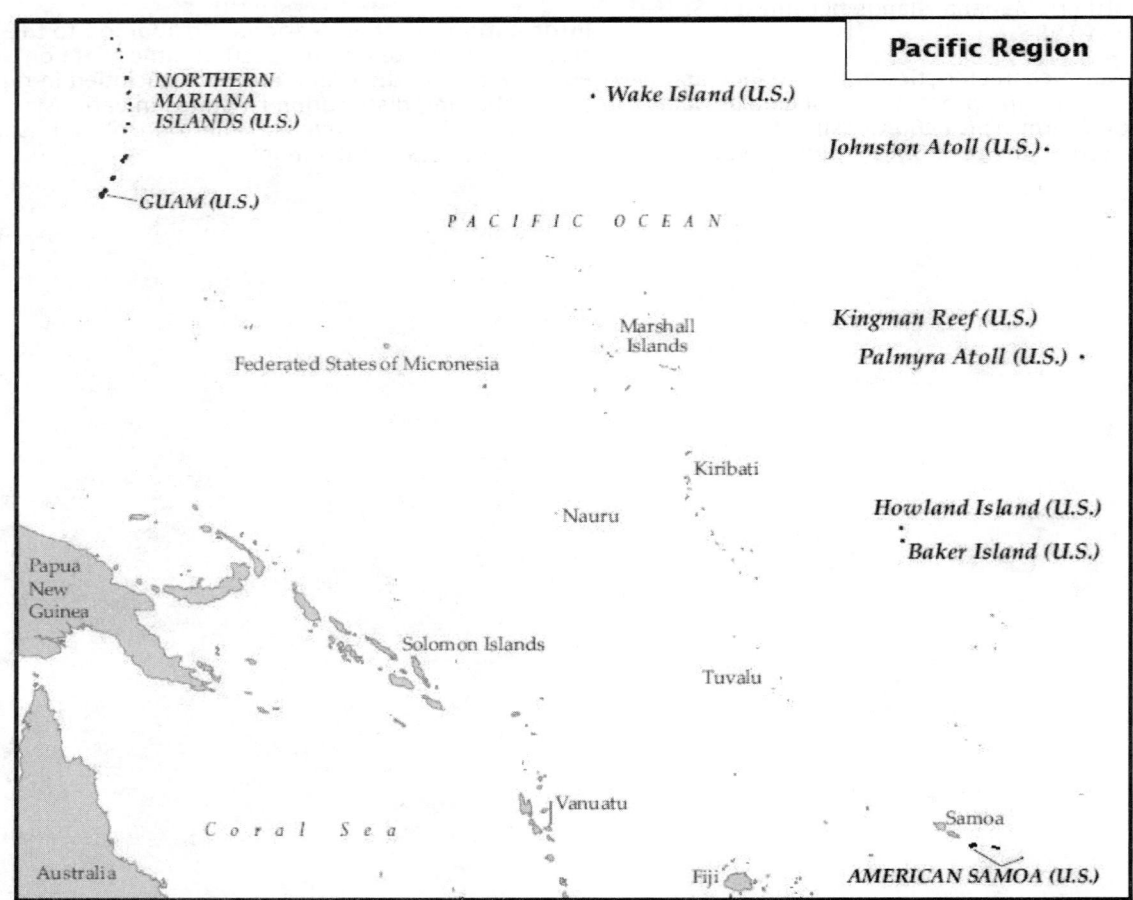

Pacific Region

NORTHERN MARIANA ISLANDS (U.S.)

• *Wake Island (U.S.)*

Johnston Atoll (U.S.) •

—*GUAM (U.S.)*

P A C I F I C   O C E A N

Marshall Islands

Kingman Reef (U.S.)

Palmyra Atoll (U.S.) •

Federated States of Micronesia

Kiribati

Howland Island (U.S.)

Nauru

• *Baker Island (U.S.)*

Papua New Guinea

Solomon Islands

Tuvalu

Vanuatu

Samoa

C o r a l   S e a

Australia

Fiji

AMERICAN SAMOA (U.S.)

Table 1319. Estimated and Projected Resident Population of Puerto Rico and Island Areas: 2000 to 2030

[In thousands (58 represents 58,000). Population as of July 1. Population data generally are de facto figures for the present territory. Data are adjusted to the 2010 Census of Population. See text, Section 30, for general comments regarding the data. For details of methodology, coverage, and reliability, see source]

Area	2000	2005	2010	2011	2012	2013	2014	Projected		
								2020	2025	2030
American Samoa...............	58	57	55	55	55	55	55	54	53	52
Guam..........................	155	158	159	160	160	160	161	168	177	184
Northern Mariana Islands......	70	71	54	52	51	51	51	58	62	66
Puerto Rico...................	3,811	3,821	3,721	3,700	3,673	3,646	3,621	3,520	3,476	3,414
Virgin Islands.................	109	108	106	106	105	105	104	100	96	91

Source: U.S. Census Bureau, "International Data Base (IDB)," <http://www.census.gov/population/international/data/idb/informationGateway.php>, accessed July 2015.

Table 1320. Births, Deaths, and Infant Deaths for Puerto Rico and the Island Areas: 2000 to 2013

[Births, deaths, and infant deaths by place of residence. Rates for 2000 based on population enumerated as of April 1; for other years, on population estimated as of July 1]

Area and year	Births		Deaths		Infant deaths	
	Number	Rate [1]	Number	Rate [1]	Number	Rate [2]
Puerto Rico:						
2000..........................	59,333	15.6	28,365	7.4	574	9.7
2010..........................	42,153	11.3	29,153	7.8	341	8.1
2011..........................	41,080	11.1	29,758	8.0	345	8.4
2012..........................	38,900	10.6	29,665	8.1	361	9.3
2013..........................	36,486	10.1	29,009	8.0	261	7.2
Guam:						
2000..........................	3,766	24.2	648	4.2	22	5.8
2010..........................	3,416	21.4	857	5.4	48	14.1
2011..........................	3,294	20.6	825	5.2	42	12.8
2012..........................	3,590	22.4	883	5.5	43	11.7
2013..........................	3,285	20.5	873	5.4	31	9.4
Virgin Islands:						
2000..........................	1,564	14.4	641	5.9	21	13.4
2010..........................	1,600	15.1	715	6.7	13	(B)
2011..........................	1,491	14.1	711	6.7	13	(B)
2012..........................	1,415	13.4	723	6.9	13	(B)
2013..........................	(NA)	(NA)	(NA)	(NA)	(NA)	(NA)
American Samoa:						
2000..........................	1,731	30.0	219	3.8	11	(B)
2010..........................	1,234	22.2	224	4.0	14	(B)
2011..........................	1,256	22.8	276	5.0	7	(B)
2012..........................	1,163	21.2	276	5.0	6	(B)
2013..........................	1,077	19.7	262	4.8	10	(B)
Northern Marianas:						
2000..........................	1,431	20.5	136	2.0	11	(B)
2010..........................	1,072	20.0	174	3.3	4	(B)
2011..........................	1,033	19.8	165	3.2	2	(B)
2012..........................	853	16.6	163	3.2	6	(B)
2013..........................	686	13.4	185	3.6	8	(B)

B Base figure too small to meet statistical standards of reliability. NA Not available. [1] Per 1,000 population. [2] Rates are infant deaths (under 1 year) per 1,000 live births.

Source: U.S. National Center for Health Statistics, National Vital Statistics Reports (NVSR), *Births: Final Data for 2013*, Vol. 64, No. 1, January 2015, and earlier reports; and *Deaths: Final Data for 2013*, Vol. 64, No. 2, and earlier reports. See also <http://www.cdc.gov/nchs/nvss.htm>.

Table 1321. Public Elementary and Secondary Schools by Island Area: 2012

[Enrollment and staff are for Fall of year shown. Revenues and expenditures are for school year ending in year shown]

Item	Puerto Rico	Guam	U.S. Virgin Islands	American Samoa	Northern Marianas
Enrollment (Fall)........................	434,609	31,186	15,192	[1] 16,400	10,646
Elementary (pre-kindergarten to grade 8 and elementary ungraded)................	305,048	21,166	10,302	[1] 11,763	7,396
Secondary (grades 9 to 12)...............	129,561	10,020	4,890	[1] 4,637	3,250
Total staff (Fall).........................	54,381	3,923	2,208	[1] 1,869	891
School district staff....................	3,993	397	113	[1] 186	93
School staff............................	36,359	3,328	1,682	[1] 1,364	695
Teachers............................	30,986	2,291	1,129	[1] 971	409
Student support staff.................	4,865	36	68	[1] 218	24
Other support services staff...........	9,164	162	345	[1] 101	79
Revenues, total [2] ($1,000)...............	3,374,611	307,591	221,673	99,334	65,214
Current expenditures [3] ($1,000)...........	3,351,423	290,575	183,333	80,105	68,775
Per pupil [3] (dollars)...................	7,403	9,300	11,669	[1] 3,481	6,246

[1] 2006 data. [2] Includes federal, territorial, local, and private revenues. [3] Includes current expenditures only, and excludes capital expenditures, interest on school debt, community services, private school programs, adult education, and other expenditures not directly allocable to public school operations.

Source: U.S. National Center for Education Statistics, *Digest of Education Statistics*, "Advance Release of Selected 2014 Digest Tables," <http://www.nces.ed.gov/programs/digest/>, accessed May 2015.

Table 1322. Occupational Employment and Average Annual Wages in Guam, Puerto Rico, and Virgin Islands: 2014

[The Occupational Employment Survey (OES) program conducts a semiannual mail survey designed to produce estimates of employment and wages for specific occupations. For more details on the survey, see <http://www.bls.gov/oes/oes_emp.htm#scope>]

Selected occupation	SOC code [1]	Guam		Puerto Rico		Virgin Islands	
		Employment	Average annual wages [2]	Employment	Average annual wages [2]	Employment	Average annual wages [2]
Total, all occupations [3, 4]...............	(X)	**59,900**	**33,280**	**902,930**	**27,510**	**38,060**	**34,960**
Management occupations..............................	11	5,150	63,560	37,010	70,500	2,580	68,840
Business and financial operations....................	13	2,380	47,460	39,510	38,110	1,430	50,280
Computer and mathematical occupations...........	15	570	47,690	9,170	42,880	370	51,450
Architecture and engineering.........................	17	840	57,530	13,580	53,820	150	56,230
Life, physical, and social sciences...................	19	350	49,610	7,380	44,550	880	29,170
Community and social services......................	21	670	40,860	15,730	28,050	350	39,460
Legal occupations......................................	23	310	65,400	4,530	63,240	440	88,180
Education, training, and library occupations.........	25	4,450	38,390	67,050	35,160	2,720	39,340
Arts, design, entertainment, sports, and media.....	27	660	30,260	6,820	35,190	170	42,210
Healthcare practitioner and technical occupations.................................	29	1,800	60,650	49,930	35,490	1,080	56,300
Healthcare support.....................................	31	590	23,620	11,060	19,630	430	26,000
Protective service occupations.......................	33	2,650	33,010	58,250	20,120	2,610	33,240
Food preparation and serving related occupations.................................	35	6,220	18,270	72,640	18,020	4,010	22,320
Buildings and grounds cleaning and maintenance...............................	37	2,990	18,740	43,580	18,580	2,160	23,080
Personal care and service occupations.............	39	1,450	22,290	15,980	18,660	960	22,000
Sales and related occupations.......................	41	4,560	21,740	110,610	22,060	4,000	26,650
Office and administrative support....................	43	10,500	27,240	166,720	23,570	8,040	31,350
Farming, fishing, and forestry........................	45	50	30,410	1,640	22,390	50	25,320
Construction and extraction...........................	47	5,260	30,230	31,130	21,240	1,190	37,450
Installation, maintenance, and repair................	49	3,350	31,620	29,070	27,780	1,610	35,630
Production occupations................................	51	1,740	28,230	63,340	22,740	680	28,660
Transportation and material moving.................	53	3,370	32,090	48,200	21,690	2,160	28,030

X Not applicable. [1] Office of Management and Budget's Standard Occupational Classification (SOC) is used to define occupations. SOC categorizes workers into 1 about 800 detailed occupations and aggregates; and the detailed occupations into 23 major occupational groups. [2] Annual wages have been calculated by multiplying the hourly mean wage by a "year-round, full-time" hours figure of 2,080 hours; for those occupations where there is not an hourly mean wage published, the annual wage has been directly calculated from the reported survey data. [3] Estimates do not sum to the total because the total may include data for occupations for which separate employment estimates could not be published. See source for more information. [4] Estimates do not include self-employed workers.

Source: U.S. Bureau of Labor Statistics, "Occupational Employment Statistics," <http://www.bls.gov/oes/current/oessrcst.htm>, accessed April 2015.

Table 1323. Prisoners in Custody of Correctional Authorities in U.S. Territories and Commonwealths: 2011 and 2012

[As of December 31]

Jurisdiction	Total inmates			Sentenced to more than 1 year			
	2011	2012	Percent change 2011-2012	2011	2012	Percent change 2011-2012	Incarceration rate, 2012 [1]
Total [2].........................	**13,010**	**13,810**	**6.1**	**9,940**	**10,550**	**6.1**	**260**
American Samoa.................	167	192	15.0	117	(NA)	(NA)	(NA)
Guam.............................	632	(NA)	(NA)	240	(NA)	(NA)	(NA)
Northern Mariana Islands........	162	168	3.7	91	109	19.8	212
Puerto Rico......................	11,470	12,244	6.7	9,210	9,781	6.2	265
U.S. Virgin Islands..............	(NA)	577	(NA)	(NA)	281	(NA)	267

NA Not available. [1] The number of prisoners with a sentence of more than 1 year per 100,000 persons in the resident population on July 1, 2012. [2] Includes population counts for the U.S. Virgin Islands in 2011 and Guam and American Samoa in 2012 that were imputed because of nonresponse. See source for more information.

Source: U.S. Bureau of Justice Statistics, *Correctional Populations in the United States, 2012*, NCJ 243936, December 2013. See also <http://www.bjs.gov/index.cfm?ty=pbdetail&iid=4843>.

Table 1324. Selected Social, Demographic, and Housing Characteristics in Puerto Rico: 2010 and 2013

[The Puerto Rico Community Survey universe includes the household population and the population living in institutions, college dormitories, and other group quarters. Based on a sample and subject to sampling variability; see text, this section and Appendix III]

Characteristic	2010		2013	
	Number	Percent	Number	Percent
Total population.................	**3,722,133**	**100.0**	**3,615,086**	**100.0**
SEX				
Male...............................	1,785,266	48.0	1,729,120	47.8
Female.............................	1,936,867	52.0	1,885,966	52.2
AGE				
Under 5 years......................	223,247	6.0	199,347	5.5
5 to 9 years.......................	236,531	6.4	211,587	5.9
10 to 14 years.....................	268,378	7.2	248,980	6.9
15 to 19 years.....................	284,254	7.6	268,619	7.4
20 to 24 years.....................	264,790	0.1	269,135	7.4
25 to 34 years.....................	482,756	13.0	439,708	12.2
35 to 44 years.....................	487,539	13.1	473,876	13.1
45 to 54 years.....................	486,273	13.1	469,242	13.0
55 to 59 years.....................	219,460	5.9	221,081	6.1
60 to 64 years.....................	223,184	6.0	213,848	5.9
65 to 74 years.....................	313,604	8.4	345,893	9.6
75 to 84 years.....................	170,712	4.6	181,961	5.0
85 years and over..................	61,405	1.6	71,809	2.0
MARITAL STATUS				
Males 15 years and over.........	**1,410,023**	**100.0**	**1,387,905**	**100.0**
Never married......................	566,489	40.2	588,088	42.4
Now married, except separated......	610,584	43.3	566,341	40.8
Separated..........................	39,169	2.8	34,731	2.5
Widowed............................	39,752	2.8	43,106	3.1
Divorced...........................	154,029	10.9	155,639	11.2
Females 15 years and over.......	**1,583,954**	**100.0**	**1,567,267**	**100.0**
Never married......................	523,558	33.1	548,626	35.0
Now married, except separated......	601,632	38.0	560,206	35.7
Separated..........................	50,458	3.2	51,836	3.3
Widowed............................	171,416	10.8	171,070	10.9
Divorced...........................	236,890	15.0	235,529	15.0
HOUSEHOLDS				
Total households................	**1,319,448**	**100.0**	**1,253,690**	**100.0**
Family households (families).......	966,123	73.2	895,080	71.4
With own children under 18 years..	405,933	30.8	357,106	28.5
Married-couple families............	557,851	42.3	508,856	40.6
With own children under 18 years..	200,406	15.2	173,177	13.8
Male householder, no wife present..	82,129	6.2	79,221	6.3
With own children under 18 years..	39,285	3.0	33,675	2.7
Female householder, no husband present..	326,143	24.7	307,003	24.5
With own children under 18 years..	166,242	12.6	150,254	12.0
Nonfamily households...............	353,325	26.8	358,610	28.6
Householder living alone...........	306,036	23.2	312,506	24.9
65 years and over................	125,754	9.5	138,513	11.0
Average household size.............	2.79	(X)	2.85	(X)
Average family size................	3.28	(X)	3.43	(X)
DISABILITY STATUS				
Total civilian noninstitutionalized population..	**3,695,636**	**100.0**	**3,588,641**	**100.0**
With a disability..................	726,334	19.7	754,974	21.0

X Not applicable.

Source: U.S. Census Bureau, 2013 Puerto Rico Community Survey, DP02PR, "Selected Social Characteristics in Puerto Rico," and DP05, "Demographic and Housing Estimates," <http://factfinder2.census.gov>, accessed May 2015. See also <http://www.census.gov/acs/www/about_the_survey/puerto_rico_community_survey/>.

Table 1325. Owner and Renter Occupied Housing by Household Type in Puerto Rico: 2013

[The Puerto Rico Community Survey universe includes the household population and the population living in institutions, college dormitories, and other group quarters. Based on a sample and subject to sampling variability; see text, this section and Appendix III]

Household type	Owner occupied	Renter occupied	Household type	Owner occupied	Renter occupied
Total households..................	**865,343**	**388,347**			
Family households.................	**645,736**	**249,344**	Householder 15 to 34 years.........	14,383	52,686
Married-couple family..............	419,531	89,325	Householder 35 to 64 years.........	108,296	67,887
Householder 15 to 34 years.........	25,976	26,178	Householder 65 years and over....	52,694	11,057
Householder 35 to 64 years.........	261,466	48,927	**Nonfamily households**.................	**219,607**	**139,003**
Householder 65 years and over.....	132,089	14,220	Householder living alone..............	194,301	118,205
Other family.......................	226,205	160,019	Householder 15 to 34 years.........	7,446	17,622
Male householder, no wife present..	50,832	28,389	Householder 35 to 64 years.........	86,491	62,434
Householder 15 to 34 years........	6,260	11,262	Householder 65 years and over....	100,364	38,149
Householder 35 to 64 years........	30,869	14,845	Householder not living alone..........	25,306	20,798
Householder 65 years and over....	13,703	2,282	Householder 15 to 34 years.........	3,375	8,008
Female householder,			Householder 35 to 64 years.........	15,543	11,117
no husband present.................	175,373	131,630	Householder 65 years and over....	6,388	1,673

Source: U.S. Census Bureau, 2013 Puerto Rico Community Survey, B25011, "Tenure by Household Type and Age of Householder," <http://factfinder2.census.gov>, accessed May 2015. See also <http://www.census.gov/acs/www/about_the_survey/puerto_rico_community_survey/>.

Table 1326. Puerto Rico—Socioeconomic Summary: 1990 to 2014

[3,512 represents 3,512,000, except as indicated]

Item	Unit	1990	2000	2005	2010	2011	2012	2013	2014
POPULATION									
Total [1]	1,000	3,512	3,808	3,824	3,731	3,708	3,681	3,641	3,594
Persons per family	Number	3.7	3.4	3.3	3.2	3.1	3.1	3.1	3.0
LABOR FORCE [2]									
Total [3]	1,000	1,124	1,303	1,357	1,285	1,246	1,212	1,182	1,162
Employed [4]	1,000	963	1,159	1,213	1,075	1,044	1,027	1,014	996
Agriculture [5]	1,000	36	24	25	18	19	20	17	17
Manufacturing	1,000	168	159	135	101	97	95	95	86
Trade	1,000	185	239	256	238	234	228	226	231
Government	1,000	222	249	268	256	230	224	213	205
Unemployed	1,000	161	143	144	209	202	184	165	167
Unemployment rate [6]	Rate	14.0	11.0	10.6	16.3	16.2	15.2	14.0	14.4
Compensation of employees	Mil. dol.	13,639	23,504	29,372	29,870	29,290	29,671	29,879	29,777
Average compensation	Dollar	14,854	20,280	24,214	27,786	28,056	28,891	29,466	29,897
Salary and wages	Mil. dol.	13,639	23,504	25,393	25,793	25,269	25,522	25,710	25,625
INCOME [7]									
Personal income:									
Current dollars	Mil. dol.	21,105	38,856	49,929	59,983	61,179	62,227	64,258	63,779
Constant (1954) dollars	Mil. dol.	5,551	8,491	10,030	9,958	10,068	10,016	10,367	10,026
Disposable personal income:									
Current dollars	Mil. dol.	19,914	36,239	46,597	57,111	58,717	59,865	61,964	61,444
Constant (1954) dollars	Mil. dol.	5,238	7,919	9,173	9,481	9,663	9,635	9,997	9,659
Average family income:									
Current dollars	Dollar	22,232	34,693	43,086	51,449	51,152	52,411	54,709	53,244
Constant (1954) dollars	Dollar	5,847	7,581	8,655	8,541	8,418	8,436	8,826	8,370
TOURISM [7]									
Number of visitors	1,000	3,426	4,566	5,073	4,379	4,214	4,197	4,238	4,455
Visitor expenditures	Mil. dol.	1,366	2,388	3,239	3,211	3,143	3,193	3,334	3,438
Average per visitor	Dollar	399	523	638	733	746	761	787	772
Net income from tourism	Mil. dol.	383	615	771	(NA)	(NA)	(NA)	(NA)	(NA)

NA Not available. [1] 1990 and 2000 enumerated as of April 1; for all other years the population is the average of population estimates at the beginning and the end of the fiscal year. [2] Annual average of monthly figures. For fiscal years. [3] For population 16 years old and over. [4] Includes other employment not shown separately. [5] Includes forestry and fisheries. [6] Percent unemployed of the labor force. [7] For fiscal years.

Source: Puerto Rico Planning Board, San Juan, PR, *Economic Report for the Governor and Legislative Assembly, 2014*, and earlier reports. See also <http://www.gdb-pur.com/economy/statistical-appendix.html>.

Table 1327. Puerto Rico—Business Summary by Industry: 2013

[Payroll in thousands of dollars (17,161,875 represents $17,161,875,000). Covers establishments with payroll. Excludes self-employed individuals, employees of private households, railroad employees, agricultural production employees, and most government employees. For statement on methodology, see Appendix III]

Industry	2012 NAICS code [1]	Establishments	Employees [2]	Annual payroll ($1,000)
Total, all industries	(X)	**44,585**	**687,836**	**17,161,875**
Agriculture, forestry, fishing and hunting	11	8	165	1,188
Mining, quarrying, and oil and gas extraction	21	47	687	13,059
Utilities	22	25	385	24,037
Construction	23	1,958	29,601	571,987
Manufacturing	31–33	1,779	75,672	2,918,241
Wholesale trade	42	2,177	32,429	1,177,600
Retail trade	44–45	10,112	130,650	2,352,597
Transportation and warehousing	48–49	1,023	15,066	421,494
Information	51	571	17,679	673,150
Finance and insurance	52	1,889	34,609	1,609,210
Real estate and rental and leasing	53	1,636	11,541	258,076
Professional, scientific, and technical services	54	4,354	29,995	1,037,736
Management of companies and enterprises	55	103	4,887	275,442
Administrative, support, and waste mgt/remediation services	56	1,816	80,041	1,484,079
Educational services	61	946	39,279	837,725
Health care and social assistance	62	7,612	84,307	2,002,311
Arts, entertainment, and recreation	71	432	3,460	69,738
Accommodation and food services	72	4,386	77,269	1,060,445
Other services (except public administration)	81	3,408	19,810	369,100
Industries not classified	99	303	304	4,660

X Not applicable. [1] Based on the 2012 North American Industry Classification System. See text, Section 15. [2] Covers full- and part-time employees who are on the payroll in the pay period including March 12.

Source: U.S. Census Bureau, County Business Patterns, "Geography Area Series: County Business Patterns for Puerto Rico and the Island Areas," <http://factfinder2.census.gov/>, accessed April 2015. See also <http://www.census.gov/econ/cbp/>.

Table 1328. Puerto Rico—Gross Product and Net Income: 1990 to 2014

[In millions of dollars (21,619 represents $21,619,000,000). For fiscal years ending June 30. Data for 2014 are preliminary. Minus sign (-) indicates decrease]

Item	1990	2000	2010	2011	2012	2013	2014
Gross product.	**21,619**	**41,419**	**64,295**	**65,721**	**68,086**	**68,768**	**69,202**
Agriculture.	434	407	822	795	816	836	858
Manufacturing.	12,126	24,489	46,577	46,760	46,971	47,736	49,332
Contract construction and mining [1].	720	2,157	1,518	1,332	1,369	1,317	1,188
Transportation, warehousing, and utilities.	2,468	2,579	2,923	2,765	3,021	2,672	2,985
Trade (wholesale and retail).	4,728	6,093	7,466	7,696	7,628	7,746	7,940
Finance, insurance, and real estate.	3,896	10,511	19,026	19,980	20,559	20,793	20,405
Services [2].	3,015	9,987	11,993	12,248	12,345	12,657	12,971
Government.	3,337	5,478	8,350	8,216	8,278	8,238	7,830
Commonwealth.	2,884	4,601	6,862	6,703	6,740	6,665	6,286
Municipalities.	453	877	1,488	1,513	1,537	1,573	1,544
Rest of the world.	-8,985	-20,283	-34,087	-34,631	-33,479	-33,758	-34,474
Statistical discrepancy.	-121	585	-294	559	577	531	167
Net income.	**17,941**	**32,610**	**50,246**	**51,038**	**54,207**	**54,783**	**55,758**
Agriculture.	486	385	824	798	819	837	862
Manufacturing.	11,277	22,627	43,292	43,357	43,575	44,306	45,874
Mining [1].	26	34	21	14	23	23	20
Contract construction.	679	1,764	1,206	1,029	1,096	1,045	924
Transportation, warehousing, and utilities.	1,778	1,961	2,128	1,870	2,146	1,849	2,089
Trade (wholesale and retail).	3,420	4,995	6,155	6,388	6,368	6,472	6,634
Finance, insurance, and real estate.	3,280	8,175	13,099	14,524	15,741	15,841	15,804
Services [2].	2,643	7,475	9,257	9,473	9,641	9,931	10,195
Government.	3,337	5,478	8,350	8,216	8,278	8,238	7,830
Rest of the world.	-8,985	-20,283	-34,087	-34,631	-33,479	-33,758	-34,474

[1] Mining includes only quarries. [2] Includes all other services not elsewhere classified.

Source: Puerto Rico Planning Board, San Juan, PR, *Economic Report for the Governor and Legislative Assembly, 2014*, and earlier reports. See also <http://www.gdb-pur.com/economy/statistical-appendix.html>.

Table 1329. Puerto Rico—Transfer Payments: 2000 to 2014

[In millions of dollars (8,659 represents $8,659,000,000). Data represent transfer payments between federal and state governments and other nonresidents. Data for 2014 are preliminary]

Item	2000	2005	2010	2011	2012	2013	2014
Total receipts.	**8,659**	**10,551**	**16,504**	**17,050**	**16,900**	**16,963**	**18,393**
Federal government.	7,966	9,673	15,585	15,987	15,919	15,824	17,282
Transfers to individuals [1].	7,868	9,547	15,352	15,754	15,674	15,609	17,068
Veterans benefits.	491	491	733	837	764	875	957
Medicare.	1,196	1,825	2,529	2,603	2,757	3,341	3,968
Old age, disability, survivors (social security).	3,863	5,118	7,074	7,320	7,551	7,327	7,925
Nutritional assistance.	1,193	1,306	1,605	1,767	1,897	1,868	1,869
Industry subsidies.	98	127	233	233	244	215	214
U.S. state governments.	15	15	29	24	20	29	30
Other nonresidents.	679	863	890	1,040	961	1,109	1,081
Total payments.	**2,763**	**3,583**	**3,804**	**3,710**	**3,416**	**3,634**	**3,739**
Federal government.	2,693	3,516	3,586	3,376	3,305	3,542	3,632
Transfers from individuals [1].	1,326	1,792	1,862	1,657	1,556	1,767	1,878
Contribution to Medicare.	191	303	392	401	416	439	415
Employee contribution for social security.	1,133	1,483	1,467	1,253	1,138	1,324	1,458
Transfers from industries.	51	74	92	105	105	104	95
Unemployment insurance.	234	221	207	211	212	214	217
Employer contribution for social security.	1,081	1,429	1,424	1,404	1,433	1,458	1,441
Other nonresidents [2].	70	67	218	333	110	92	107
Net balance.	**5,897**	**6,968**	**12,700**	**13,341**	**13,484**	**13,329**	**14,654**
Federal government.	5,273	6,157	11,999	12,610	12,613	12,282	13,650
U.S. state governments.	10	10	26	20	16	26	27
Other nonresidents.	614	801	675	710	855	1,021	977

[1] Includes other receipts and payments not shown separately. [2] Includes U.S. state governments.

Source: Puerto Rico Planning Board, San Juan, PR, *Economic Report to the Governor and Legislative Assembly, 2014*, and earlier reports. See also <http://www.gdb-pur.com/economy/statistical-appendix.html>.

Table 1330. Puerto Rico—Merchandise Imports and Exports: 1980 to 2014

[In millions of dollars (9,018 represents $9,018,000,000). Data shown is trade for the San Juan, Puerto Rico Customs District. Imports are imports for consumption; see text, Section 28]

Item	1980	1990	2000	2005	2007	2008	2009	2010	2011	2012	2013	2014
Imports.	9,018	16,200	27,006	40,499	43,482	41,560	38,780	39,766	44,736	45,407	43,811	42,741
From U.S.	5,345	10,792	15,172	20,994	22,402	19,777	20,038	20,641	20,346	19,808	20,314	20,848
From other.	3,673	5,408	11,834	19,505	21,080	21,783	18,742	19,125	24,391	25,599	23,497	21,892
Exports.	6,576	20,402	43,191	56,836	62,401	63,659	59,594	67,347	56,767	58,646	61,630	67,019
To U.S.	5,643	17,915	38,335	47,121	47,507	46,439	40,779	47,630	40,942	42,308	44,229	49,194
To other.	933	2,487	4,856	9,715	14,894	17,219	18,815	19,717	15,825	16,338	17,401	17,824

Source: U.S. Census Bureau, Foreign Trade Division, *U.S. Trade with Puerto Rico and U.S. Possessions* (FT 895), 2014 and earlier reports; *U.S. Merchandise Trade: Selected Highlights* (FT 920), December 2011 and earlier reports; and "USA Trade Online," <https://usatrade.census.gov/>, accessed April 2015.

Table 1331. Puerto Rico—Agricultural Summary: 2007 and 2012

[1 cuerda = 0.97 acre]

All farms	Unit	2007	2012	All farms	Unit	2007	2012
Farms.........................	Number	15,745	13,159	Tenants...................	Number	2,425	2,728
Farm land..................	Cuerdas	557,530	584,988	Farms by type of			
Average size of farm.....	Cuerdas	35.4	44.5	organization:			
Approximate land area....	Cuerdas	2,254,365	2,254,365	Individual or family......	Number	13,958	11,938
Proportion in farms.......	Percent	24.7	25.9	Partnership.............	Number	49	117
Farms by size:				Corporation.............	Number	575	738
Less than 10 cuerdas....	Number	7,502	5,129	Other....................	Number	1,163	366
10 to 19 cuerdas.........	Number	3,545	2,859	Farms by value of sales:			
20 to 49 cuerdas.........	Number	2,680	2,872	Less than $1,000.........	Number	4,442	1,837
50 to 99 cuerdas.........	Number	865	940	$1,000 to $2,499.........	Number	2,771	2,015
100 to 174 cuerdas.......	Number	524	563	$2,500 to $4,499.........	Number	2,428	1,986
175 to 259 cuerdas.......	Number	207	401	$5,000 to $7,499.........	Number	1,206	1,209
260 cuerdas or more.....	Number	422	395	$7,500 to $9,999.........	Number	882	771
Tenure of operator:				$10,000 to $19,999......	Number	1,497	1,521
Operators................	Number	15,745	13,159	$20,000 to $39,999......	Number	1,030	968
Full owners..............	Number	11,402	9,362	$40,000 to $59,999......	Number	281	394
Part owners.............	Number	1,918	1,069	$60,000 or more.........	Number	1,208	1,322

Source: U.S. Department of Agriculture, National Agricultural Statistics Service (NASS), *2012 Census of Agriculture: Puerto Rico, Island and Municipio Data*, Geographic Area Series, Volume 1: Part 52, June 2014. See also <http://www.agcensus.usda.gov/Publications>.

Table 1332. Puerto Rico—Farms and Market Value of Agricultural Products Sold: 2012

[For market value, 547,629 represents $547,629,000]

Type of product	Number of farms	Market value ($1,000)	Average value per farm (dol.)	Type of product	Number of farms	Market value ($1,000)	Average value per farm (dol.)
Total.........................	**13,159**	**547,629**	**41,616**	Horticultural specialties.........	657	37,534	57,129
Crops........................	9,367	271,320	(NA)	Grasses and other crops.......	532	14,589	27,422
Coffee......................	4,478	29,273	6,537	Livestock, poultry, and their			
Pineapples..................	42	1,906	45,375	products........................	4,119	276,309	67,081
Plantains...................	3,628	80,505	22,190	Cattle and calves...............	2,911	33,606	11,544
Bananas....................	1,474	12,106	8,213	Poultry and poultry products. ..	706	40,376	57,189
Grains......................	781	8,539	10,934	Dairy products..................	318	189,425	595,677
Root crops or tubers.........	1,242	8,192	6,596	Hogs and pigs..................	532	8,019	15,074
Fruits and coconuts..........	1,926	31,541	16,377	Aquaculture....................	51	688	13,490
Vegetables and melons [1].......	1,528	47,135	30,848	Other............................	630	4,195	6,659

NA Not available. [1] Includes hydroponic crops.

Source: U.S. Department of Agriculture, National Agricultural Statistics Service (NASS), *2012 Census of Agriculture: Puerto Rico, Island and Municipio Data*, Geographic Area Series, Volume 1: Part 52, June 2014. See also <http://www.agcensus.usda.gov/Publications>.

Table 1333. Guam, Virgin Islands, Northern Mariana Islands, and American Samoa—Economic Summary by Sector: 2012

[Sales and payroll in millions of dollars (7,737 represents $7,737,000,000). Data for establishments with annual payroll. Based on the 2012 Economic Census of Island Areas; see Appendix III]

Selected kinds of business	Guam	Virgin Islands	Northern Mariana Islands	American Samoa	Selected kinds of business	Guam	Virgin Islands	Northern Mariana Islands	American Samoa
Total:					Paid employees [2].....	2,505	686	716	253
Establishments [1]......	3,099	2,414	1,339	377	Retail trade:				
Sales....................	7,737	6,831	1,324	1,154	Establishments........	630	560	284	136
Annual payroll.........	1,287	1,129	208	114	Sales...................	1,980	1,318	314	210
Paid employees [2].....	53,579	32,465	14,215	7,070	Annual payroll.........	184	142	31	17
Construction:					Paid employees [2].....	8,879	6,596	2,463	1,435
Establishments........	320	161	62	20	Professional, scientific,				
Sales....................	750	238	37	31	& technical services:				
Annual payroll.........	167	58	8	5	Establishments........	241	232	105	22
Paid employees [2].....	6,722	1,729	821	432	Sales....................	294	307	29	20
Manufacturing:					Annual payroll.........	105	95	10	5
Establishments........	54	57	39	25	Paid employees [2]....	2,737	2,108	602	254
Sales....................	123	1,963	21	(D)	Accommodation &				
Annual payroll.........	28	168	7	(D)	food services:				
Paid employees [2].....	1,282	1,984	592	([3])	Establishments........	450	279	142	36
Wholesale trade:					Sales...................	790	539	180	29
Establishments........	177	64	74	16	Annual payroll.........	189	161	38	6
Sales....................	982	221	247	275	Paid employees [2]....	12,575	6,864	3,195	574
Annual payroll.........	66	25	11	5					

D Withheld to avoid disclosing data for individual companies; data are included in higher level totals. [1] Includes other industries, not shown separately. [2] For pay period including March 12. [3] 1,000 to 2,499 employees.

Source: U.S. Census Bureau, 2012 Economic Census of the Island Areas, Geographic Area Series, "General Statistics by Kind of Business," <http://factfinder2.census.gov/>, accessed July 2014. See also <http://www.census.gov/econ/islandareas/>.

Table 1334. Puerto Rico—School Enrollment and Educational Attainment by Level: 2005 to 2013

[The Puerto Rico Community Survey universe includes the household population and the population living in institutions, college dormitories, and other group quarters. Based on a sample and subject to sampling variability; see text, this section and Appendix III]

Characteristic	2005	2008	2009	2010	2011	2012	2013
EDUCATIONAL ENROLLMENT							
Population 3 years and over enrolled in school.....	1,138,768	1,104,134	1,096,131	995,743	991,812	983,155	942,530
Nursery school, preschool...........................	69,731	53,882	57,136	55,298	56,486	58,639	55,475
Kindergarten..	52,261	47,085	46,834	45,366	45,657	44,606	42,217
Elementary school (grades 1-8)....................	486,546	469,220	454,396	414,233	400,439	394,200	376,924
High school (grades 9-12)...........................	242,548	240,730	239,894	213,581	212,136	207,820	199,044
College or graduate school.........................	287,682	293,217	297,871	267,265	277,094	277,890	268,870
EDUCATIONAL ATTAINMENT							
Population 25 years and over.......................	2,431,653	2,571,234	2,595,507	2,444,933	2,443,515	2,432,137	2,417,418
Less than 9th grade..................................	547,055	573,136	546,525	484,138	461,611	440,807	419,215
9th to 12th grade, no diploma......................	269,039	275,535	271,320	262,682	243,839	225,826	234,868
High school graduate (includes equivalency)......	588,130	622,098	659,863	623,709	648,204	650,650	653,505
Some college, no degree............................	290,283	339,512	338,465	317,797	304,832	306,603	291,031
Associate's degree...................................	231,848	217,084	222,600	212,186	215,478	219,146	233,730
Bachelor's degree....................................	377,437	398,934	419,040	389,954	416,008	428,778	416,877
Graduate or professional degree...................	127,861	144,935	137,694	154,467	153,543	160,327	168,192
Percent high school graduate or higher.............	66.4	67.0	68.5	69.5	71.1	72.6	72.9
Percent bachelor's degree or higher................	20.8	21.2	21.4	22.3	23.3	24.2	24.2

Source: U.S. Census Bureau, 2013 Puerto Rico Community Survey, DP02PR, "Selected Social Characteristics in Puerto Rico," <http://factfinder2.census.gov>, accessed May 2015. See also <http://www.census.gov/acs/www/about_the_survey/puerto_rico_community_survey/>.

Table 1335. Virgin Islands—Business Summary by Industry: 2013

[Payroll in thousands of dollars (967,432 represents $967,432 ,000). Covers establishments with payroll. Excludes self-employed individuals, employees of private households, railroad employees, agricultural production employees, and most government employees. For statement on methodology, see Appendix III]

Industry	2012 NAICS code [1]	Establishments	Employees [2]	Annual payroll ($1,000)
Total, all industries......................................	(X)	**2,619**	**29,977**	**967,432**
Agriculture, forestry, fishing and hunting................................	11	1	([3])	(D)
Mining, quarrying, and oil and gas extraction........................	21	2	([3])	(D)
Utilities..	22	7	([5])	(D)
Construction..	23	177	1,552	53,987
Manufacturing..	31-33	55	692	30,164
Wholesale trade...	42	70	1,030	57,395
Retail trade..	44-45	558	6,363	137,372
Transportation and warehousing..............................	48-49	111	1,553	52,440
Information..	51	41	([6])	(D)
Finance and insurance..	52	117	1,252	67,516
Real estate and rental and leasing...........................	53	195	1,187	39,223
Professional, scientific, and technical services..............	54	238	986	50,129
Management of companies and enterprises..................	55	6	([5])	(D)
Administrative, support, and waste mgt/remediation services...........	56	152	1,838	60,404
Educational services..	61	40	739	20,050
Health care and social assistance...........................	62	264	2,938	124,367
Arts, entertainment, and recreation..........................	71	59	652	14,621
Accommodation and food services...........................	72	293	6,671	160,180
Other services (except public administration)...............	81	221	1,360	37,349
Industries not classified.......................................	99	12	([4])	228

X Not applicable. D Withheld to avoid disclosing data for individual companies; data are included in total. [1] Based on the 2012 North American Industry Classification System. See text, Section 15. [2] Covers full- and part-time employees who are on the payroll in the pay period including March 12. [3] 0 to 19 employees. [4] 20 to 99 employees. [5] 100 to 249 employees. [6] 500 to 999 employees.

Source: U.S. Census Bureau, County Business Patterns, "Geography Area Series: County Business Patterns for Puerto Rico and the Island Areas," <http://factfinder2.census.gov/>, accessed April 2015. See also <http://www.census.gov/econ/cbp/>.

Table 1336. Guam—Business Summary by Industry: 2013

[Payroll in thousands of dollars (1,354,347 represents $1,354,347,000). Covers establishments with payroll. Excludes self-employed individuals, employees of private households, railroad employees, agricultural production employees, and most government employees. For statement on methodology, see Appendix III]

Industry	2012 NAICS code [1]	Establishments	Employees [2]	Annual payroll ($1,000)
Total, all industries.	(X)	3,415	54,269	1,354,347
Agriculture, forestry, fishing and hunting.	11	2	([3])	(D)
Mining, quarrying, and oil and gas extraction.	21	1	([3])	(D)
Utilities.	22	5	([4])	3,702
Construction.	23	349	5,435	145,142
Manufacturing.	31-33	58	1,513	44,684
Wholesale trade.	42	217	2,874	78,853
Retail trade.	44-45	684	8,728	191,627
Transportation and warehousing.	48-49	99	2,708	97,888
Information.	51	55	1,329	46,880
Finance and insurance.	52	134	2,130	86,528
Real estate and rental and leasing.	53	260	1,960	41,644
Professional, scientific, and technical services.	54	249	2,900	116,347
Management of companies and enterprises.	55	10	80	2,518
Administrative, support, and waste mgt/remediation services.	56	166	3,931	82,394
Educational services.	61	57	1,081	22,588
Health care and social assistance.	62	197	3,221	117,598
Arts, entertainment, and recreation.	71	74	1,274	23,209
Accommodation and food services.	72	482	12,495	196,616
Other services (except public administration).	81	284	2,510	54,918
Industries not classified.	99	32	([4])	877

X Not applicable. D Withheld to avoid disclosing data for individual companies; data are included in total. [1] Based on the 2012 North American Industry Classification System. See text, Section 15. [2] Covers full- and part-time employees who are on the payroll in the pay period including March 12. [3] 0 to 19 employees. [4] 20 to 99 employees.

Source: U.S. Census Bureau, County Business Patterns, "Geography Area Series: County Business Patterns for Puerto Rico and the Island Areas," <http://factfinder2.census.gov/>, accessed April 2015. See also <http://www.census.gov/econ/cbp/>.

Table 1337. Northern Marianas—Business Summary by Industry: 2013

[Payroll in thousands of dollars (188,129 represents $188,129,000). Covers establishments with payroll. Excludes self-employed individuals, employees of private households, railroad employees, agricultural production employees, and most government employees. For statement on methodology, see Appendix III]

Industry	2012 NAICS code [1]	Establishments	Employees [2]	Annual payroll ($1,000)
Total, all industries.	(X)	1,401	11,436	188,129
Agriculture, forestry, fishing and hunting.	11	3	([3])	(D)
Mining, quarrying, and oil and gas extraction.	21	1	([3])	(D)
Utilities.	22	6	([5])	(D)
Construction.	23	57	247	2,254
Manufacturing.	31-33	36	391	4,376
Wholesale trade.	42	78	607	8,369
Retail trade.	44-45	303	1,961	29,041
Transportation and warehousing.	48-49	43	921	15,295
Information.	51	22	329	9,487
Finance and insurance.	52	50	257	7,125
Real estate and rental and leasing.	53	120	406	5,184
Professional, scientific, and technical services.	54	91	329	8,316
Management of companies and enterprises.	55	5	([3])	509
Administrative, support, and waste mgt/remediation services.	56	120	1,040	15,946
Educational services.	61	54	240	3,990
Health care and social assistance.	62	35	500	16,978
Arts, entertainment, and recreation.	71	45	444	5,987
Accommodation and food services.	72	162	2,813	35,490
Other services (except public administration).	81	131	463	6,513
Industries not classified.	99	39	([4])	713

X Not applicable. D Withheld to avoid disclosing data for individual companies; data are included in total. [1] Based on the 2012 North American Industry Classification System. See text, Section 15. [2] Covers full- and part-time employees who are on the payroll in the pay period including March 12. [3] 0 to 19 employees. [4] 20 to 99 employees. [5] 250 to 499 employees.

Source: U.S. Census Bureau, County Business Patterns, "Geography Area Series: County Business Patterns for Puerto Rico and the Island Areas," <http://factfinder2.census.gov/>, accessed April 2015. See also <http://www.census.gov/econ/cbp/>.

Table 1338. American Samoa—Business Summary by Industry: 2013

[Payroll in thousands of dollars (116,596 represents $116,596,000). Covers establishments with payroll. Excludes self-employed individuals, employees of private households, railroad employees, agricultural production employees, and most government employees. For statement on methodology, see Appendix III]

Industry	2012 NAICS code [1]	Establishments	Employees [2]	Annual payroll ($1,000)
Total, all industries..	(X)	**464**	**6,988**	**116,596**
Agriculture, forestry, fishing and hunting..	11	2	([3])	(D)
Construction...	23	25	307	4,758
Manufacturing..	31-33	34	([6])	(D)
Wholesale trade...	42	22	232	4,037
Retail trade..	44-45	157	1,279	17,534
Transportation and warehousing...	48-49	30	313	4,443
Information...	51	10	146	3,329
Finance and insurance..	52	10	([4])	(D)
Real estate and rental and leasing..	53	20	93	1,342
Professional, scientific, and technical services............................	54	22	([4])	(D)
Management of companies and enterprises..................................	55	3	6	167
Administrative, support, and waste mgt/remediation services.............	56	18	79	1,629
Educational services..	61	5	122	1,543
Health care and social assistance...	62	14	([5])	(D)
Arts, entertainment, and recreation...	71	3	([3])	135
Accommodation and food services..	72	34	502	5,354
Other services (except public administration)..............................	81	48	405	4,859
Industries not classified..	99	7	([3])	182

X Not applicable. D Withheld to avoid disclosing data for individual companies; data are included in total. [1] Based on the 2012 North American Industry Classification System. See text, Section 15. [2] Covers full- and part-time employees who are on the payroll in the pay period including March 12. [3] 0 to 19 employees. [4] 100 to 249 employees. [5] 500 to 999 employees. [6] 1,000 to 2,499 employees.

Source: U.S. Census Bureau, County Business Patterns, "Geography Area Series: County Business Patterns for Puerto Rico and the Island Areas," <http://factfinder2.census.gov/>, accessed April 2015. See also <http://www.census.gov/econ/cbp/>.

This section presents statistics for the world as a whole and for many countries on a comparative basis with the United States. Data are shown for population, births and deaths, social and economic indicators, finances, agriculture, energy, climate, science and technology, communications, and military affairs.

Statistics for individual countries may be found primarily in official national publications, generally in the form of yearbooks, issued by most countries in their own national languages and expressed in their own customary units of measure. For a listing of selected publications, see Appendix I, Guide to Foreign Statistical Abstracts.

For international comparisons, the United Nations Statistics Division compiles data as submitted by member countries and issues a number of summary publications, generally in English and French. Among these are the annual *Statistical Yearbook; Demographic Yearbook; Population and Vital Statistics Report; International Trade Statistics Yearbook; Energy Statistics Yearbook; Industrial Commodity Statistics Yearbook; National Accounts Statistics;* and the *Monthly Bulletin of Statistics.* Specialized agencies of the United Nations also issue international summary publications on various topics, including agricultural, labor, health, and trade statistics. Among these are *Food Outlook* and the *Statistical Pocketbook* issued by the Food and Agriculture Organization (FAO); *World Employment and Social Outlook* issued by the International Labor Organization (ILO); *World Health Statistics* issued by the World Health Organization (WHO); and the *Handbook of Statistics* issued by the Conference on Trade and Development (UNCTAD).

The U.S. Census Bureau publishes estimates and projections of key demographic measures for countries and regions of the world in its International Data Base at <http://www.census.gov/population/international/>.

The International Monetary Fund (IMF), the World Bank, and the Organisation for Economic Co-operation and Development (OECD) also compile international statistics. The IMF publishes a series of reports related to financial data. These include *World Economic Outlook, International Financial Statistics*, and *Balance of Payments Statistics Yearbook.* The World Bank publishes many reports on a wide range of topics related to international development. Three of their flagship statistical publications are *World Development Report, World Development Indicators*, and *Global Economic Prospects.* The OECD also produces numerous statistical publications in fields including economics, health, and education. Among these are the *OECD Factbook; Economic Outlook; National Accounts of OECD Countries; Science, Technology and Industry Outlook; International Migration Outlook; Employment Outlook*; and *Education at a Glance.*

Statistical coverage and country classifications— Problems of space and availability of data limit the number of countries and the extent of statistical coverage shown. The lists of countries and territories included in individual tables are generally based on source publications and databases, as cited.

In the last quarter-century, several important changes took place in the status of the world's nations. In 1991, the Soviet Union broke up into 15 independent countries: Armenia, Azerbaijan, Belarus, Estonia, Georgia, Kazakhstan, Kyrgyzstan, Latvia, Lithuania, Moldova, Russia, Tajikistan, Turkmenistan, Ukraine, and Uzbekistan.

Germany was reunified in 1990, when the German Democratic Republic (former East Germany) joined the Federal Republic of Germany (former West Germany) to form a single country. On January 1, 1993, Czechoslovakia was succeeded by two independent countries: the Czech Republic and Slovakia.

Following the breakup of the Socialist Federal Republic of Yugoslavia in 1992, the United States recognized Bosnia and Herzegovina, Croatia, Slovenia, and Macedonia as independent countries. Serbia and Montenegro, both former republics of Yugoslavia, became independent of one another on May 31, 2006. This separation is reflected in the population estimates of Table 1342, but some tables may still show both countries as combined. On February 17, 2008, Kosovo declared its independence from Serbia.

The Treaty of Maastricht created the European Union (EU) in 1992 with 12 member countries. The EU is not a state intended to replace existing states, but it is more than just an international organization. Its member states have set up common institutions to which they delegate some of their sovereignty so that decisions on specific matters of joint interest can be made democratically at a European level. This pooling of sovereignty is also called "European integration." The EU has grown in size with successive waves of accessions in 1995, 2004, 2007, and 2013. The 28 current members of the EU are: Austria, Belgium, Bulgaria, Croatia, Cyprus, Czech Republic, Denmark, Estonia, Finland, France, Germany, Greece, Hungary, Ireland, Italy, Latvia, Lithuania, Luxembourg, Malta, the Netherlands, Poland, Portugal, Romania, Slovakia, Slovenia, Spain, Sweden, and the United Kingdom.

In 1992, the EU decided to establish an economic and monetary union (EMU), with the introduction of a single European currency managed by a European Central Bank. The single currency—the euro—became a reality on January 1, 2002, when euro notes and coins replaced national currencies in 12 of the then 15 countries of the European Union (Belgium, Germany, Greece, Spain, France, Ireland, Italy, Luxembourg, the Netherlands, Austria, Portugal, and Finland). Since then, 13 additional countries have acceded to EU membership, but Cyprus, Estonia, Latvia, Lithuania, Malta, Slovakia, and Slovenia have been the only new members of the EU to adopt the euro as the national currency.

Elsewhere in the world, Eritrea announced its independence from Ethiopia in April 1993 and was subsequently recognized as an independent nation by the United States. In the South Pacific, the Marshall Islands, Micronesia, and Palau gained independence from the United States in 1991. In May of 2002, Timor-Leste won independence from Indonesia. The Netherlands Antilles dissolved on October 10, 2010. As a result, Curaçao and Sint Maarten became autonomous territories of the Netherlands. Most recently, Sudan and South Sudan became separate countries as of July 2011.

The population estimates and projections used in Tables 1339 through 1342, 1344, and 1345 were prepared by the U.S. Census Bureau. For each country, available data on population by age and sex, fertility, mortality, and international migration were evaluated and, where necessary, adjusted for inconsistencies and errors in the data. Comprehensive population projections were made by the cohort-component method based on an assessment of probable future trends.

Economic associations—The Organisation for European Economic Co-operation (OEEC) was originally a regional grouping of Western European countries established in 1948 for the purpose of harmonizing national economic policies and conditions. It was succeeded on September 30, 1961 by the Organisation for Economic Co-operation and Development (OECD). The current member nations of the OECD are Australia, Austria, Belgium, Canada, Chile, Czech Republic, Denmark, Estonia, Finland, France, Germany, Greece, Hungary, Iceland, Ireland, Israel, Italy, Japan, Luxembourg, Mexico, the Netherlands, New Zealand, Norway, Poland, Portugal, Slovak Republic, Slovenia, South Korea, Spain, Sweden, Switzerland, Turkey, the United Kingdom, and the United States.

Quality and comparability of the data—The quality and comparability of the data presented here are affected by a number of factors:

1 The year for which data are presented may not be the same for all subjects for a particular country or for a given subject for different countries, though the data shown are the most recent available. All such variations have been noted. The data shown are for calendar years except as otherwise specified.

2 The statistical bases, methods of estimating, methods of data collection, extent of coverage, precision of definition, scope of territory, and margins of error may vary for different items within a particular country, and for like items for different countries. Footnotes and headnotes to the tables describe some of the major coverage qualifications attached to the figures; considerably more detail is presented in the source publications. Many of the measures shown are merely rough indicators of magnitude.

3 Figures shown in this section for the United States may not always agree with figures shown in the preceding sections. Discrepancies may be attributable to the use of differing original sources, differences in the definition of geographic limits (the 50 states, continental U.S. only, or the U.S. including certain outlying areas and possessions), or to possible adjustments made to the U.S. figures

in order to make them more comparable with figures from other countries.

International comparisons of national accounts data—To compare national accounts data for different countries, it is necessary to convert each country's data into a common unit of currency, usually the U.S. dollar. The market exchange rates, which often are used in converting national currencies, do not necessarily reflect the relative purchasing power in the various countries. It is necessary that the goods and services produced in different countries be valued consistently if the differences observed are meant to reflect real differences in the volumes of goods and services produced. The use of purchasing power parities (see Tables 1353, 1354, and 1360) instead of exchange rates is intended to achieve this objective.

The method used to present the data shown in Table 1360 is to construct volume measures directly by revaluing the goods and services sold in different countries at a common set of international prices. By dividing the ratio of the gross domestic products of two countries expressed in their own national currencies by the corresponding ratio calculated at constant international prices, it is possible to derive the implied purchasing power parity (PPP) between the two currencies concerned. PPPs show how many units of currency are needed in one country to buy the same amount of goods and services that one unit of currency will buy in the other country. For further information, see *National Accounts of OECD Countries, Volume I, Main Aggregates*, issued annually by the Organisation for Economic Co-operation and Development (OECD), Paris, France.

International Standard Industrial Classification—The original version of the International Standard Industrial Classification of All Economic Activities (ISIC) was adopted in 1948. A number of countries have utilized ISIC as the basis for devising their industrial classification schemes. Substantial comparability has been attained among the industrial classification schemes of many countries, including the United States, by ensuring that national classification categories correspond to ISIC categories. The United Nations, the International Labour Organization, the Food and Agriculture Organization, and other international bodies use ISIC in publishing and analyzing statistical data. Revisions of ISIC were issued in 1958, 1968, 1989, 2002, and 2008.

International Maps—A series of regional world maps is provided within this section. References are included in Table 1342 for easy location of individual countries on the maps. Map projection will be distorted due to being portrayed on a flat surface. For additional information and maps see the Central Intelligence Agency's *The World Factbook*, at <https://www.cia.gov/library/publications/the-world-factbook/>.

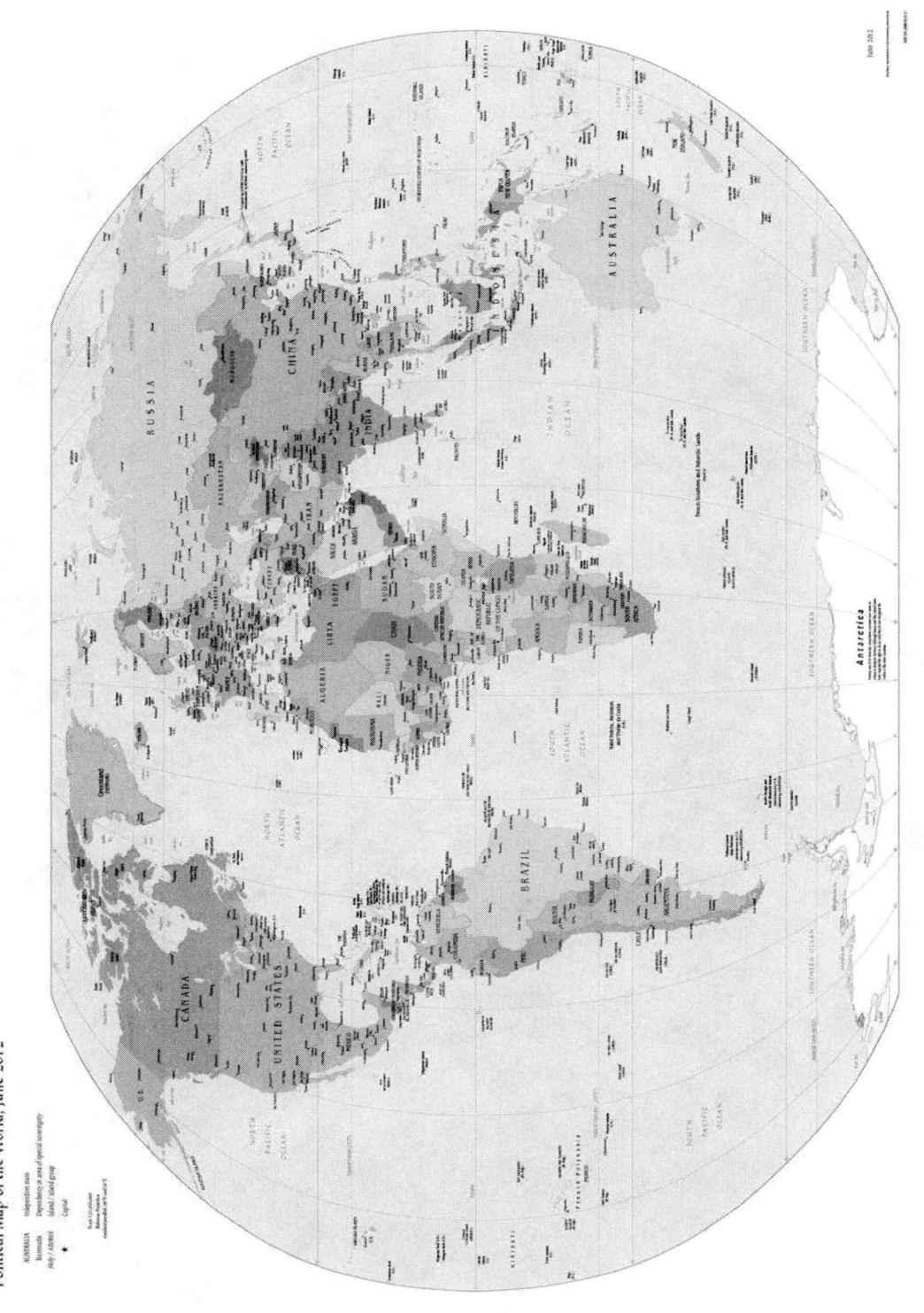

50
Political Map of the World, June 2012

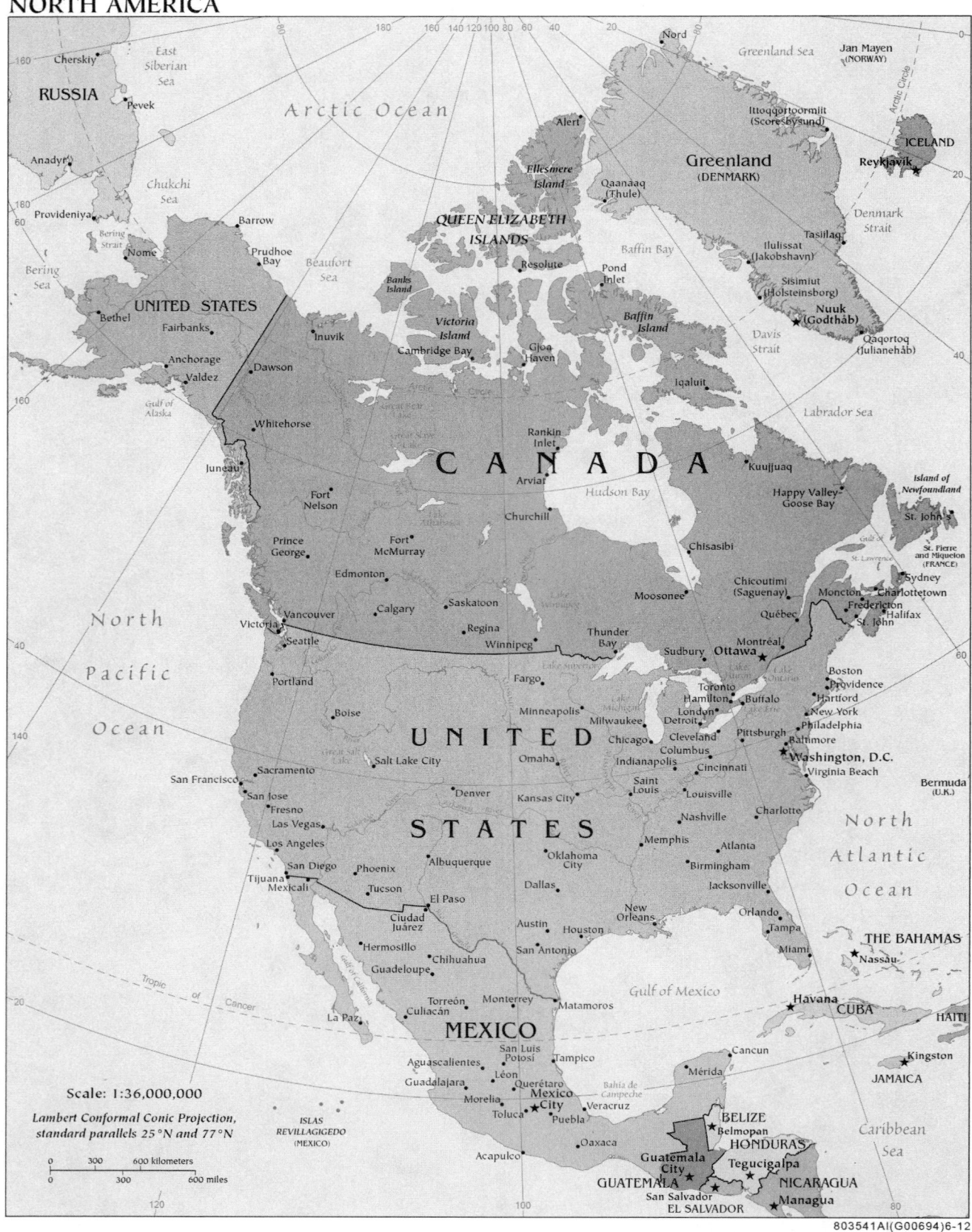

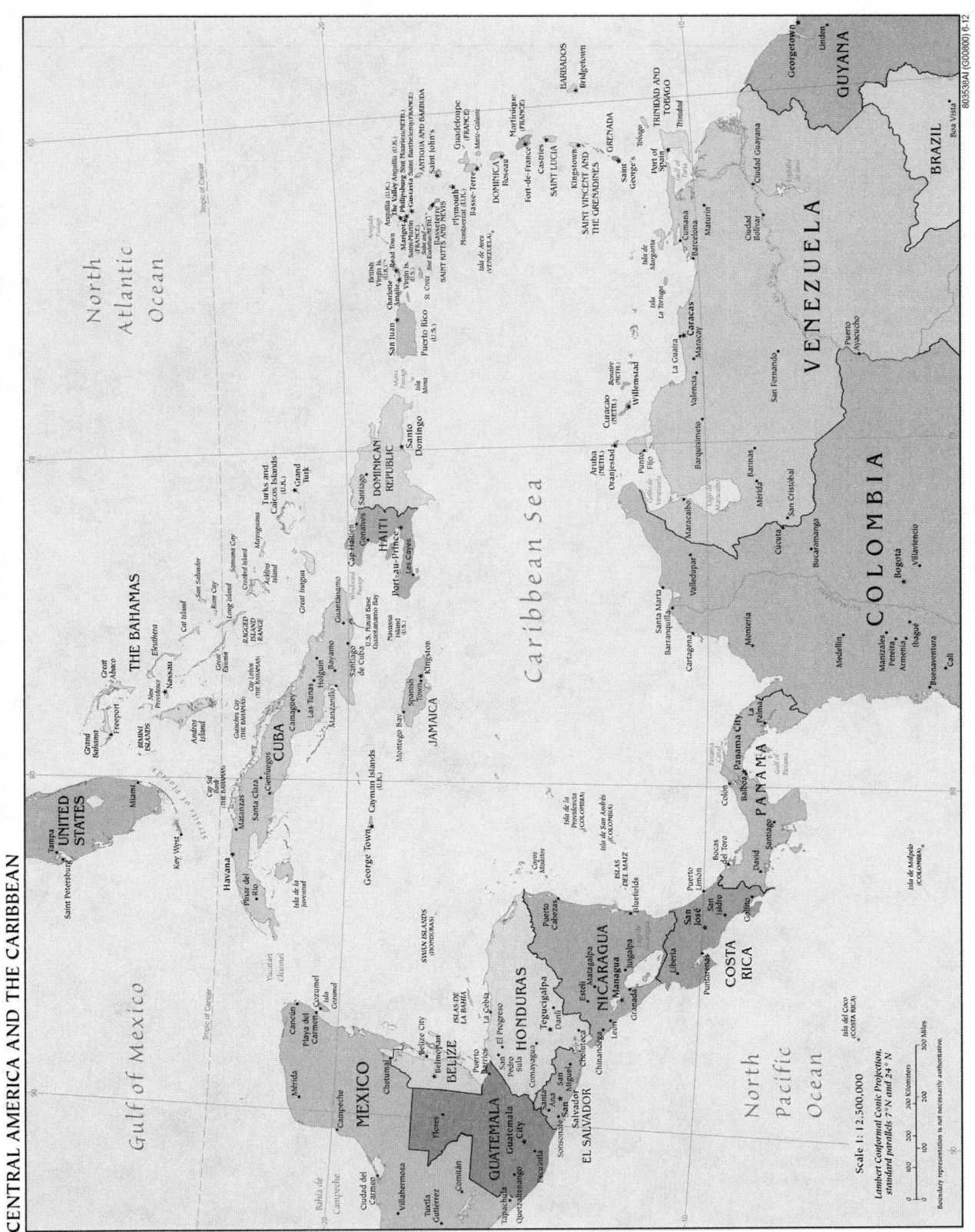

CENTRAL AMERICA AND THE CARIBBEAN

North Atlantic Ocean

Gulf of Mexico

Caribbean Sea

North Pacific Ocean

UNITED STATES

THE BAHAMAS

CUBA

MEXICO

BELIZE

GUATEMALA

EL SALVADOR

HONDURAS

NICARAGUA

COSTA RICA

PANAMA

JAMAICA

HAITI

DOMINICAN REPUBLIC

COLOMBIA

VENEZUELA

GUYANA

BRAZIL

Scale 1: 12,500,000

Lambert Conformal Conic Projection,
standard parallels 7°N and 24°N

0   100   200   300 Kilometers
0   100   200   300 Miles

Boundary representation is not necessarily authoritative

803530A1 (G00800) 6-12

Scale 1:19,300,000
Lambert Conformal Conic Projection,
standard parallels 40°N and 68°N

803539AI (G00772) 6-12

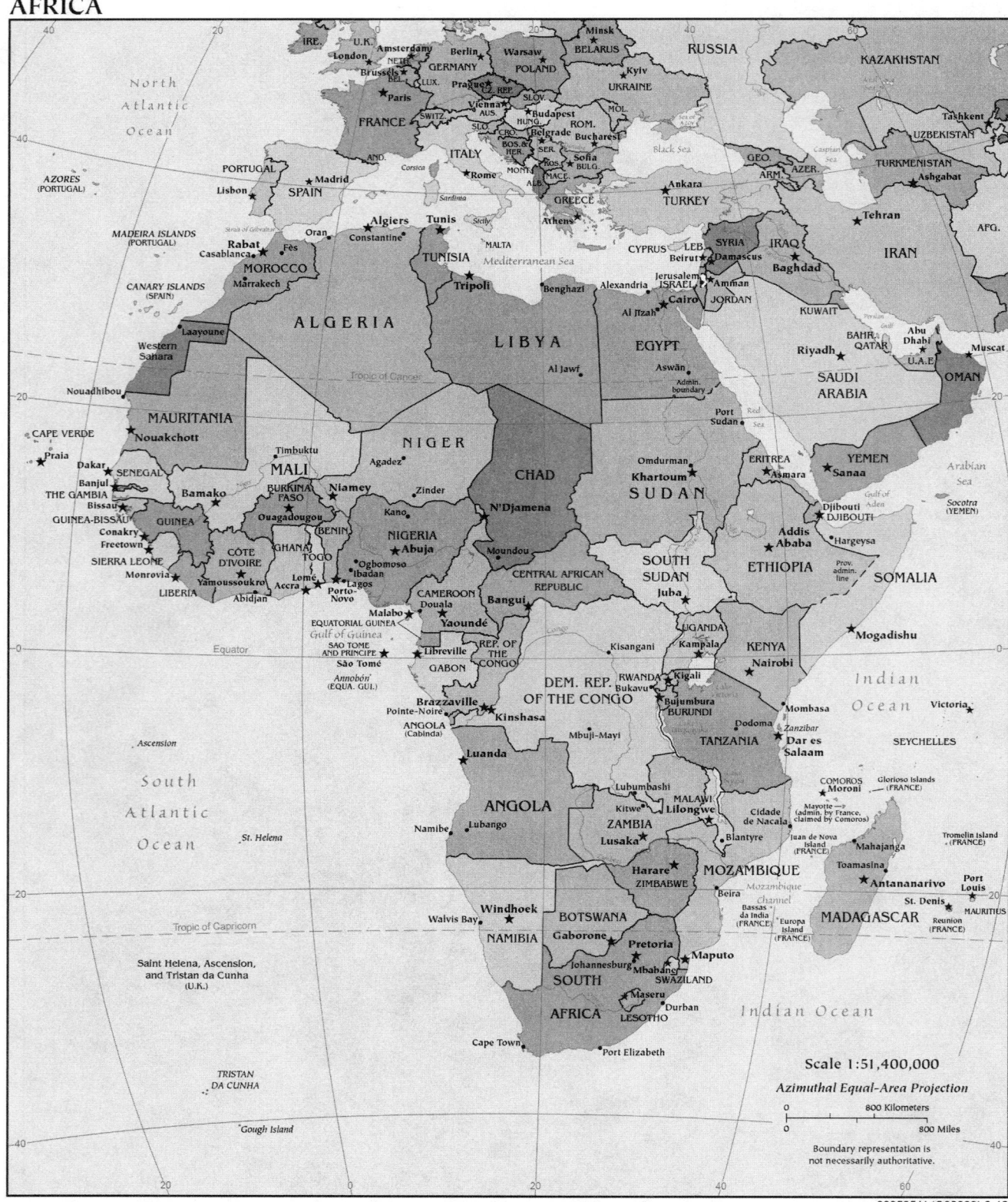

Scale 1:51,400,000

Azimuthal Equal-Area Projection

0   800 Kilometers
0   800 Miles

Boundary representation is
not necessarily authoritative.

803535AI (G00392) 6-12

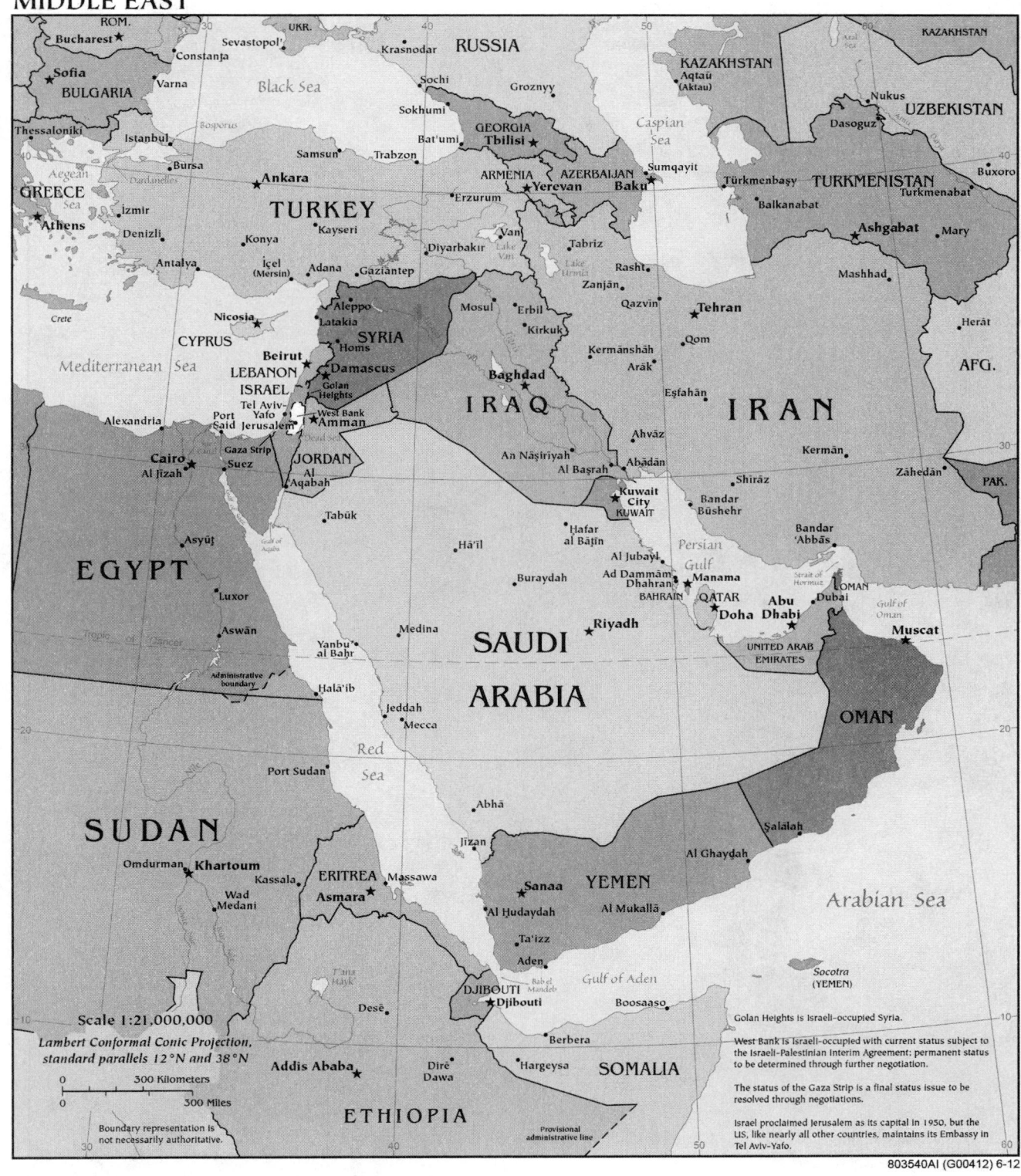

Golan Heights is Israeli-occupied Syria.

West Bank is Israeli-occupied with current status subject to the Israeli-Palestinian Interim Agreement; permanent status to be determined through further negotiation.

The status of the Gaza Strip is a final status issue to be resolved through negotiations.

Israel proclaimed Jerusalem as its capital in 1950, but the US, like nearly all other countries, maintains its Embassy in Tel Aviv-Yafo.

Scale 1:21,000,000

Lambert Conformal Conic Projection, standard parallels 12°N and 38°N

0   300 Kilometers
0   300 Miles

Boundary representation is not necessarily authoritative.

803540AI (G00412) 6-12

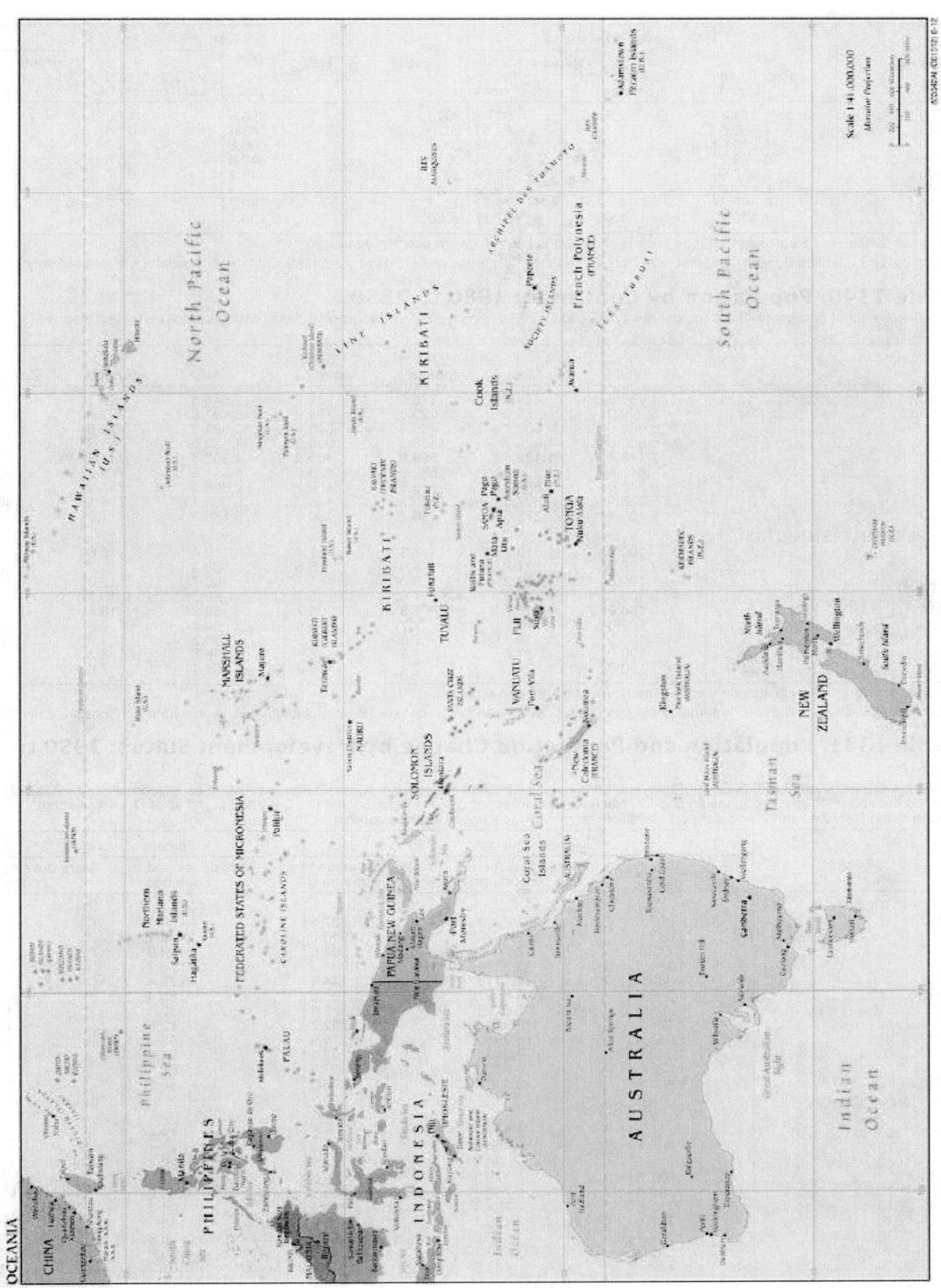

Scale 1:41,000,000

Miller Projection

Table 1339. Total World Population: 1980 to 2050

[4,451.4 represents 4,451,400,000. As of midyear]

Year	Population (mil.)	Average annual [1] Growth rate (percent)	Average annual [1] Population change (mil.)	Year	Population (mil.)	Average annual [1] Growth rate (percent)	Average annual [1] Population change (mil.)
1980............	4,451.4	1.87	83.05	2015............	7,256.5	1.08	78.28
1985............	4,856.5	1.73	84.11	2020............	7,643.4	0.98	74.85
1990............	5,289.0	1.56	82.63	2025............	8,006.6	0.86	69.14
1995............	5,699.2	1.41	80.24	2030............	8,340.6	0.76	63.27
2000............	6,088.6	1.26	76.65	2035............	8,646.3	0.67	57.93
2005............	6,473.0	1.21	78.22	2040............	8,925.9	0.59	52.87
2010............	6,866.3	1.13	77.72	2045............	9,180.2	0.52	47.71
2014............	**7,178.7**	**1.08**	**77.77**	2050............	9,408.1	(NA)	(NA)

NA Not available. [1] Represents change from year shown to immediate succeeding year.

Source: U.S. Census Bureau, "International Data Base (IDB)," <http://www.census.gov/population/international/data/>, accessed July 2015.

Table 1340. Population by Continent: 1980 to 2050

[In millions, except percent (4,451.4 represents 4,451,400,000). As of midyear. For geographic classification of individual countries, see source]

Year	World	Africa	North America [1]	South America	Asia	Europe	Oceania
1980..............	4,451.4	478.5	370.8	239.7	2,644.5	695.2	22.5
1990..............	5,289.0	630.0	423.3	294.9	3,191.8	722.6	26.4
2000..............	6,088.6	802.7	485.6	345.6	3,693.8	730.5	30.4
2010..............	6,866.3	1,025.7	538.9	390.0	4,136.5	740.3	34.9
2014..............	**7,178.7**	**1,129.4**	**559.0**	**405.9**	**4,302.8**	**744.8**	**36.7**
2020..............	7,643.4	1,295.2	589.6	428.0	4,541.5	749.8	39.3
2030..............	8,340.6	1,597.0	635.5	459.2	4,858.5	747.3	43.1
2040..............	8,925.9	1,927.6	670.8	480.2	5,065.1	736.1	46.1
2050..............	9,408.1	2,275.6	696.7	490.0	5,180.3	717.0	48.5
PERCENT DISTRIBUTION							
1980..............	100.0	10.8	8.3	5.4	59.4	15.6	0.5
1990..............	100.0	11.9	8.0	5.6	60.3	13.7	0.5
2000..............	100.0	13.2	8.0	5.7	60.7	12.0	0.5
2010..............	100.0	14.9	7.8	5.7	60.2	10.8	0.5
2014..............	**100.0**	**15.7**	**7.8**	**5.7**	**59.9**	**10.4**	**0.5**
2020..............	100.0	16.9	7.7	5.6	59.4	9.8	0.5
2030..............	100.0	19.1	7.6	5.5	58.3	9.0	0.5
2040..............	100.0	21.6	7.5	5.4	56.7	8.2	0.5
2050..............	100.0	24.2	7.4	5.2	55.1	7.6	0.5

[1] Data for North America include Central America and Caribbean area.

Source: U.S. Census Bureau, "International Data Base (IDB)," <http://www.census.gov/population/international/data/>, accessed July 2015.

Table 1341. Population and Population Change by Development Status: 1950 to 2050

[2,557.6 represents 2,557,600,000. As of midyear. Minus sign (-) indicates decrease. "Less developed" countries include all of Africa, all of Asia except Japan, the Transcaucasian and Central Asian republics, all of Latin America and the Caribbean, and all of Oceania except Australia and New Zealand. For details on classification of individual countries, see source]

Year	Number (millions) World	Number (millions) Less developed countries	Number (millions) More developed countries	Percent of world Less developed countries	Percent of world More developed countries
POPULATION					
1950..................	2,557.6	1,750.6	807.1	68.4	31.6
1960..................	3,043.0	2,132.2	910.8	70.1	29.9
1970..................	3,712.7	2,709.1	1,003.6	73.0	27.0
1980..................	4,451.4	3,369.6	1,081.7	75.7	24.3
1990..................	5,289.0	4,144.9	1,144.1	78.4	21.6
2000..................	6,088.6	4,895.0	1,193.5	80.4	19.6
2010..................	6,866.3	5,629.5	1,236.9	82.0	18.0
2014..................	**7,178.7**	**5,926.0**	**1,252.7**	**82.6**	**17.4**
2020..................	7,643.4	6,368.5	1,274.9	83.3	16.7
2030..................	8,340.6	7,043.5	1,297.1	84.4	15.6
2040..................	8,925.9	7,622.2	1,303.8	85.4	14.6
2050..................	9,408.1	8,110.1	1,298.0	86.2	13.8
POPULATION CHANGE					
1950–1960..............	485.4	381.7	103.7	78.6	21.4
1960–1970..............	669.7	576.8	92.9	86.1	13.9
1970–1980..............	738.7	660.5	78.1	89.4	10.6
1980–1990..............	837.6	775.3	62.3	92.6	7.4
1990–2000..............	799.6	750.1	49.5	93.8	6.2
2000–2010..............	777.8	734.4	43.3	94.4	5.6
2010–2020..............	777.1	739.1	38.0	95.1	4.9
2020–2030..............	697.2	675.0	22.2	96.8	3.2
2030–2040..............	585.3	578.7	6.6	98.9	1.1
2040–2050..............	482.2	487.9	-5.7	101.2	-1.2

Source: U.S. Census Bureau, "International Data Base (IDB)," <http://www.census.gov/population/international/data>, accessed July 2015.

Table 1342. Population and Land Area by Country or Territory: 2000 to 2020

[6,088,571 represents 6,088,571,000. Covers countries or territories with populations of 5,000 or more in 2014. Population estimates were derived from information available as of July 2015. See text of this section for general comments concerning the data. For details of methodology, coverage, and reliability, see source. Minus sign (-) indicates decrease]

Country or territory	Map refer- ence [1]	Mid-year population (1,000)				Popula- tion rank, 2014	Annual growth rate [2], 2010 to 2020	Popula- tion per sq. mile, 2014	Land area [3], (sq. mile)
		2000	2010	2014	2020, proj.				
World................	S0	**6,088,571**	**6,866,332**	**7,178,723**	**7,643,402**	(X)	**1.07**	141	50,895,243
Afghanistan.................	S7	22,461	29,121	31,823	36,644	40	2.30	126	251,827
Albania.................	S4	3,158	2,987	3,020	3,075	136	0.29	285	10,578
Algeria.................	S5	30,638	35,950	38,814	42,973	33	1.78	42	919,595
Andorra.................	S4	65	85	85	86	200	0.13	473	181
Angola.................	S5	12,683	17,043	19,088	22,484	58	2.77	40	481,354
Antigua and Barbuda.................	S2	75	87	91	98	198	1.24	534	171
Argentina.................	S3	37,336	41,343	43,024	45,379	32	0.93	41	1,056,642
Armenia.................	S6	3,100	3,072	3,061	3,021	135	-0.17	281	10,889
Australia.................	S8	19,053	21,516	22,508	23,939	55	1.07	8	2,966,153
Austria.................	S4	8,113	8,448	8,616	8,859	93	0.48	271	31,832
Azerbaijan.................	S6	8,463	9,302	9,686	10,206	91	0.93	304	31,903
Bahamas, The.................	S2	283	310	322	338	179	0.84	83	3,865
Bahrain.................	S6	655	1,180	1,314	1,505	156	2.43	4,478	293
Bangladesh.................	S7	132,151	156,118	166,281	183,109	8	1.59	3,308	50,258
Barbados.................	S2	274	286	290	295	180	0.31	1,745	166
Belarus.................	S4	10,033	9,680	9,608	9,478	92	-0.21	123	78,340
Belgium.................	S4	10,264	10,866	11,237	11,721	77	0.76	961	11,690
Belize.................	S2	248	315	341	380	177	1.88	39	8,805
Benin.................	S5	6,619	9,056	10,161	11,956	87	2.78	238	42,711
Bhutan.................	S7	606	700	734	782	165	1.11	49	14,824
Bolivia.................	S3	8,195	9,947	10,631	11,640	82	1.57	25	418,265
Bosnia and Herzegovina.................	S4	3,806	3,885	3,872	3,836	128	-0.13	196	19,763
Botswana.................	S5	1,680	2,029	2,156	2,312	143	1.30	10	218,816
Brazil.................	S3	174,315	195,834	202,657	211,716	5	0.78	62	3,266,199
Brunei.................	S8	325	395	423	464	174	1.62	208	2,033
Bulgaria.................	S4	7,909	7,391	7,228	6,967	100	-0.59	172	41,888
Burkina Faso.................	S5	11,588	16,242	18,365	21,978	59	3.02	174	105,715
Burma.................	S7	47,439	53,414	55,746	59,126	24	1.02	221	252,321
Burundi.................	S5	6,716	9,121	10,396	12,632	85	3.26	1,048	9,915
Cambodia.................	S7	12,351	14,454	15,458	16,927	68	1.58	227	68,153
Cameroon.................	S5	15,818	20,822	23,131	26,969	53	2.59	127	182,514
Canada.................	S1	31,100	33,760	34,835	36,387	38	0.75	10	3,511,023
Cape Verde.................	S5	430	509	539	583	173	1.37	346	1,557
Central African Republic.................	S5	3,980	4,845	5,278	5,991	118	2.12	22	240,535
Chad.................	S5	7,943	10,543	11,412	12,756	76	1.90	24	486,180
Chile.................	S3	15,175	16,760	17,364	18,187	64	0.82	60	287,187
China.................	S7	1,268,302	1,336,681	1,361,344	1,394,016	1	0.42	378	3,600,947
Colombia.................	S3	38,910	44,205	46,245	49,085	29	1.05	115	401,044
Comoros.................	S5	545	706	767	846	163	1.81	889	863
Congo, Republic of.................	S5	2,939	4,238	4,662	5,293	124	2.22	35	131,854
Congo, Democratic Republic........	S5	52,445	69,851	77,434	89,250	19	2.45	89	875,312
Costa Rica.................	S2	3,883	4,516	4,755	5,098	123	1.21	241	19,714
Cote d'Ivoire.................	S5	16,885	21,059	22,849	25,504	54	1.92	186	122,782
Croatia.................	S4	4,411	4,487	4,471	4,427	125	-0.13	207	21,612
Cuba.................	S2	11,072	11,098	11,047	10,932	78	-0.15	261	42,402
Cyprus.................	S6	920	1,103	1,172	1,267	160	1.39	329	3,568
Czech Republic.................	S4	10,269	10,551	10,627	10,702	83	0.14	356	29,825
Denmark.................	S4	5,337	5,516	5,569	5,642	114	0.23	340	16,384
Djibouti.................	S5	669	741	810	922	162	2.19	91	8,950
Dominica.................	S2	71	73	73	74	201	0.19	253	290
Dominican Republic.................	S2	8,469	9,824	10,350	11,109	86	1.23	555	18,656
Ecuador.................	S3	12,446	14,791	15,654	16,905	67	1.34	146	106,889
Egypt.................	S5	65,159	80,472	86,895	96,260	15	1.79	226	384,345
El Salvador.................	S2	5,850	6,052	6,126	6,217	108	0.27	766	8,000
Equatorial Guinea.................	S5	491	651	722	836	166	2.51	67	10,831
Eritrea.................	S5	4,197	5,793	6,381	7,260	106	2.26	164	38,996
Estonia.................	S4	1,380	1,303	1,272	1,229	157	-0.59	78	16,366
Ethiopia.................	S5	64,365	86,043	96,633	114,640	13	2.87	250	386,102
Fiji.................	S8	805	876	903	936	161	0.66	128	7,056
Finland.................	S4	5,169	5,355	5,454	5,572	116	0.40	47	117,304
France.................	S4	61,255	64,941	66,259	67,848	21	0.44	268	247,270
Gabon.................	S5	1,236	1,545	1,673	1,877	153	1.94	17	99,486
Gambia, The.................	S5	1,357	1,755	1,926	2,174	149	2.14	499	3,861
Georgia.................	S6	4,819	4,903	4,936	4,930	121	0.06	183	26,911
Germany.................	S4	82,184	81,644	80,997	80,160	16	-0.18	602	134,623
Ghana.................	S5	18,981	23,571	25,758	29,340	48	2.19	293	87,851
Greece.................	S4	10,559	10,750	10,776	10,742	81	-0.01	214	50,443
Grenada.................	S2	102	108	110	113	190	0.48	829	133
Guatemala.................	S2	11,085	13,550	14,647	16,264	69	1.83	354	41,374
Guinea.................	S5	8,350	10,324	11,474	13,420	75	2.62	121	94,872
Guinea-Bissau.................	S5	1,279	1,565	1,693	1,893	152	1.90	156	10,857
Guyana.................	S3	785	746	736	750	164	0.06	10	76,004
Haiti.................	S2	8,413	9,649	9,997	10,693	88	1.03	939	10,641
Honduras.................	S2	6,359	7,989	8,599	9,465	94	1.69	199	43,201
Hungary.................	S4	10,147	9,992	9,919	9,772	89	-0.22	287	34,598
Iceland.................	S1	281	318	328	351	178	0.98	9	38,707
India.................	S7	1,006,300	1,173,108	1,236,345	1,326,093	2	1.23	1,077	1,147,956
Indonesia.................	S8	214,091	243,423	253,610	267,020	4	0.93	363	699,451
Iran.................	S6	68,632	76,923	80,841	86,543	17	1.18	137	591,352
Iraq.................	S6	23,128	30,526	35,975	42,213	35	3.24	213	168,868

See footnotes at end of table.

Country or territory	Map reference [1]	Mid-year population (1,000)				Population rank, 2014	Annual growth rate [2], 2010 to 2020	Population per sq. mile, 2014	Land area [3], (sq. mile)
		2000	2010	2014	2020, proj.				
Ireland	S4	3,822	4,623	4,833	5,177	122	1.13	182	26,596
Israel	S6	6,097	7,368	7,921	8,675	98	1.63	1,009	7,849
Italy	S4	57,784	60,749	61,680	62,403	23	0.27	543	113,568
Jamaica	S2	2,616	2,847	2,930	3,051	138	0.69	701	4,182
Japan	S7	126,776	127,579	127,103	125,507	10	-0.16	903	140,728
Jordan	S6	4,785	6,501	7,930	7,690	97	1.68	231	34,287
Kazakhstan	S7	15,687	17,085	17,949	19,092	61	1.11	17	1,042,360
Kenya	S5	30,606	40,843	45,010	49,858	30	1.99	205	219,746
Kiribati	S8	85	99	104	112	193	1.17	334	313
Korea, North	S7	22,785	24,326	24,852	25,643	49	0.53	535	46,490
Korea, South	S7	46,839	48,636	49,040	49,362	27	0.15	1,311	37,421
Kosovo	S4	1,700	1,815	1,859	1,933	150	0.63	442	4,203
Kuwait	S6	1,972	2,543	2,743	2,994	140	1.63	399	6,880
Kyrgyzstan	S6	4,937	5,410	5,604	5,965	113	0.98	76	74,055
Laos	S7	5,397	6,368	6,804	7,447	103	1.57	76	89,112
Latvia	S4	2,368	2,115	2,008	1,881	146	-1.17	84	24,034
Lebanon	S6	3,834	4,492	5,883	5,470	109	1.97	1,489	3,950
Lesotho	S5	1,916	1,920	1,942	1,969	148	0.26	166	11,720
Liberia	S5	2,601	3,685	4,092	4,727	127	2.49	110	37,189
Libya	S5	5,025	6,110	6,244	6,943	107	1.28	9	679,362
Liechtenstein	S4	33	36	37	39	213	0.80	604	62
Lithuania	S4	3,489	3,089	2,914	2,731	139	-1.23	120	24,201
Luxembourg	S4	438	509	558	628	171	2.10	559	998
Macedonia	S4	2,015	2,072	2,092	2,113	145	0.19	213	9,820
Madagascar	S5	15,712	20,847	23,202	26,956	52	2.57	103	224,534
Malawi	S5	11,129	15,183	17,377	21,197	63	3.34	478	36,324
Malaysia	S8	23,151	28,275	30,073	32,652	43	1.44	237	126,895
Maldives	S7	300	396	394	392	176	-0.10	3,421	115
Mali	S5	10,788	14,583	16,456	19,623	66	2.97	35	471,118
Malta	S4	390	407	413	419	175	0.30	3,382	122
Marshall Islands	S8	53	66	71	78	202	1.68	1,016	70
Mauritania	S5	2,501	3,205	3,517	4,005	132	2.23	9	397,955
Mauritius	S5	1,186	1,294	1,331	1,379	155	0.64	1,698	784
Mexico	S1	99,775	114,061	120,287	128,650	11	1.20	160	750,561
Micronesia, Federated States of	S8	108	107	106	102	192	-0.45	390	271
Moldova	S4	4,180	3,732	3,583	3,364	131	-1.04	282	12,699
Monaco	S4	32	31	31	31	217	0.12	39,508	1
Mongolia	S7	2,461	2,783	2,953	3,168	137	1.29	5	599,831
Montenegro	S4	732	667	650	639	167	-0.42	125	5,194
Morocco	S5	28,113	31,627	32,987	34,956	39	1.00	191	172,317
Mozambique	S5	17,997	22,417	24,692	28,603	50	2.44	81	303,623
Namibia	S5	1,893	2,128	2,198	2,263	142	0.61	7	317,874
Nauru	S8	10	9	9	10	224	0.54	1,170	8
Nepal	S7	24,818	28,952	30,987	34,209	41	1.67	560	55,348
Netherlands	S4	15,930	16,574	16,877	17,280	65	0.42	1,290	13,086
New Zealand	S8	3,802	4,252	4,402	4,615	126	0.82	42	103,363
Nicaragua	S2	4,866	5,604	5,849	6,203	110	1.02	126	46,328
Niger	S5	10,725	15,270	17,466	21,151	62	3.26	36	489,076
Nigeria	S5	123,945	160,341	177,156	204,909	7	2.45	504	351,649
Norway	S4	4,492	4,891	5,148	5,467	120	1.11	44	117,484
Oman	S6	2,432	2,968	3,220	3,635	134	2.03	27	119,499
Pakistan	S6	152,429	184,405	196,174	213,719	6	1.48	659	297,637
Palau	S8	19	21	21	22	219	0.38	120	177
Panama	S2	2,900	3,411	3,608	3,894	130	1.33	126	28,703
Papua New Guinea	S8	4,813	6,065	6,553	7,259	105	1.80	38	174,850
Paraguay	S3	5,418	6,376	6,704	7,192	104	1.20	44	153,399
Peru	S3	25,797	28,948	30,148	31,915	42	0.98	61	494,209
Philippines	S7	76,452	93,137	99,378	109,181	12	1.59	863	115,124
Poland	S4	38,654	38,616	38,594	38,282	34	-0.09	328	117,474
Portugal	S4	10,336	10,736	10,814	10,842	80	0.10	306	35,317
Qatar	S6	640	1,719	2,123	2,444	144	3.52	475	4,473
Romania	S4	22,447	21,959	21,730	21,303	57	-0.30	245	88,761
Russia	S7	147,054	142,527	142,470	141,722	9	-0.06	23	6,323,482
Rwanda	S5	8,398	11,056	12,337	14,327	73	2.59	1,295	9,524
Saint Kitts and Nevis	S2	46	50	52	54	208	0.76	512	101
Saint Lucia	S2	153	161	163	166	186	0.34	698	234
Saint Vincent and the Grenadines	S2	108	104	103	101	195	-0.28	685	150
Samoa	S8	176	192	197	204	184	0.60	181	1,089
San Marino	S4	27	31	33	34	214	0.84	1,390	24
Sao Tome and Principe	S5	141	176	190	211	185	1.83	512	372
Saudi Arabia	S6	21,312	25,732	27,346	29,819	46	1.47	33	830,000
Senegal	S5	9,469	12,323	13,636	15,736	72	2.44	183	74,336
Serbia	S4	7,604	7,345	7,210	7,012	101	-0.46	241	29,913
Seychelles	S5	79	88	92	96	197	0.83	522	176
Sierra Leone	S5	3,809	5,246	5,744	6,625	111	2.33	208	27,653
Singapore	S8	4,063	5,140	5,567	6,210	115	1.89	20,989	265
Slovakia	S4	5,400	5,426	5,444	5,441	117	0.03	293	18,573
Slovenia	S4	2,011	2,003	1,988	1,951	147	-0.26	256	7,780
Solomon Islands	S8	434	559	610	685	168	2.03	56	10,805
Somalia	S5	7,501	9,768	10,428	11,757	84	1.85	43	242,216
South Africa	S5	44,913	51,123	53,007	56,464	25	0.99	113	468,909
South Sudan [4]	S5	6,296	9,584	11,563	14,558	74	4.18	46	248,777

See footnotes at end of table.

Country or territory	Map refer- ence [1]	Mid-year population (1,000)				Popula- tion rank, 2014	Annual growth rate [2], 2010 to 2020	Popula- tion per sq. mile, 2014	Land area [3], (sq. mile)
		2000	2010	2014	2020, proj.				
Spain	S4	40,589	46,506	47,738	50,016	28	0.73	248	192,657
Sri Lanka	S7	19,041	21,084	21,866	22,889	56	0.82	876	24,954
Sudan [4]	S5	27,067	32,997	35,482	39,161	37	1.71	49	718,723
Suriname	S3	464	546	573	610	170	1.10	10	60,232
Swaziland	S5	1,144	1,354	1,420	1,513	154	1.11	214	6,643
Sweden	S4	8,924	9,432	9,724	10,202	90	0.78	61	158,431
Switzerland	S4	7,277	7,770	8,062	8,404	95	0.78	522	15,443
Syria	S6	16,514	21,766	17,952	22,346	60	0.26	253	70,900
Taiwan	S7	22,185	23,127	23,360	23,603	51	0.20	1,875	12,456
Tajikistan	S7	6,230	7,487	8,052	8,874	96	1.70	147	54,637
Tanzania	S5	33,193	44,288	49,639	58,553	26	2.79	145	342,009
Thailand	S7	62,902	66,720	67,741	68,977	20	0.33	343	197,256
Timor-Leste	S8	767	1,088	1,202	1,384	159	2.41	209	5,743
Togo	S5	4,992	6,587	7,351	8,608	99	2.68	350	20,998
Tonga	S8	100	106	106	106	191	0.04	385	277
Trinidad and Tobago	S2	1,252	1,229	1,224	1,209	158	-0.16	618	1,980
Tunisia	S5	9,508	10,525	10,938	11,494	79	0.88	182	59,985
Turkey	S6	65,970	74,687	78,402	82,018	18	0.94	264	297,157
Turkmenistan	S6	4,385	4,941	5,172	5,529	119	1.12	28	181,441
Tuvalu	S8	10	10	11	11	222	0.80	1,074	10
Uganda	S5	22,916	31,507	35,919	43,518	36	3.23	472	76,101
Ukraine	S4	49,014	45,768	44,944	43,923	31	-0.41	201	223,681
United Arab Emirates	S6	3,219	4,976	5,629	6,495	112	2.67	174	32,278
United Kingdom	S4	59,140	62,348	63,743	65,761	22	0.53	682	93,410
United States	**S1**	**282,162**	**309,347**	**318,857**	**334,503**	**3**	**0.78**	**90**	**3,531,905**
Uruguay	S3	3,220	3,301	3,333	3,388	133	0.26	49	67,574
Uzbekistan	S6	25,042	27,866	28,930	30,565	44	0.92	176	164,248
Vanuatu	S8	191	245	267	298	183	1.96	57	4,706
Venezuela	S3	23,493	27,223	28,868	31,276	45	1.39	85	340,561
Vietnam	S7	79,178	89,571	93,422	98,721	14	0.97	780	119,719
Yemen	S6	17,236	23,210	26,053	29,884	47	2.53	128	203,850
Zambia	S5	9,984	13,042	14,639	17,427	70	2.90	51	287,028
Zimbabwe	S5	11,820	11,652	13,772	15,832	71	3.07	92	149,362
TERRITORIES AND DEPENDENCIES									
American Samoa	S8	58	55	55	54	207	-0.31	710	77
Anguilla	S1	11	15	16	18	220	2.03	458	35
Aruba	S1	90	105	111	119	189	1.33	1,592	69
Bermuda	S1	63	68	70	72	203	0.50	3,350	21
Cayman Islands	S1	38	50	55	62	206	2.10	539	102
Cook Islands	S8	16	11	10	9	223	-2.93	111	91
Curacao [5]	S2	134	143	148	151	188	0.54	861	171
Faroe Islands	S4	46	49	50	52	210	0.51	93	538
French Polynesia	S8	236	269	280	295	181	0.93	190	1,478
Gaza Strip [6]	S6	1,130	1,604	1,816	2,121	151	2.79	13,068	139
Gibraltar	S4	27	29	29	30	218	0.24	11,629	3
Greenland	S1	57	58	58	58	205	(Z)	(Z)	836,330
Guam	S8	155	159	161	168	187	0.54	767	210
Guernsey	S4	62	65	66	67	204	0.35	2,186	30
Hong Kong	S7	6,656	7,029	7,113	7,250	102	0.31	17,169	414
Isle of Man	S4	76	84	87	90	199	0.76	393	221
Jersey	S4	87	93	97	101	196	0.79	2,155	45
Macau	S7	432	568	588	614	169	0.79	53,996	11
Montserrat	S2	4	5	5	5	228	0.49	132	39
New Caledonia	S8	211	252	268	290	182	1.39	38	7,056
Northern Mariana Islands	S8	70	54	51	58	209	0.75	287	179
Puerto Rico	S2	3,811	3,721	3,621	3,520	129	-0.56	1,057	3,424
Saint Barthelemy	S2	7	7	7	7	226	-0.39	896	8
Saint Helena	S5	7	8	8	8	225	0.25	65	119
Saint Martin	S2	28	30	32	33	216	0.74	1,501	21
Saint Pierre and Miquelon	S1	6	6	6	5	227	-1.06	61	93
Sint Maarten [5]	S2	31	38	40	44	212	1.46	3,069	13
Turks and Caicos Islands	S2	19	43	49	56	211	2.58	134	366
Virgin Islands, British	S2	23	30	33	37	215	2.32	560	58
Virgin Islands, U.S.	S2	109	106	104	100	194	-0.59	780	134
Wallis and Futuna	S8	15	15	16	16	221	0.33	284	55
West Bank [6]	S6	1,980	2,515	2,731	3,058	141	1.96	1,254	2,178
Western Sahara	S5	336	492	555	652	172	2.83	5	102,703

X Not applicable. Z Less than 0.05 percent or less than 1 person per square mile. [1] See maps for geographic locations, as indicated. [2] Computed by the exponential method. For explanation of average annual percent change, see Guide to Tabular Presentation. [3] Data converted from square kilometers to square miles. [4] Sudan and South Sudan became separate countries in July 2011. [5] The Netherlands Antilles dissolved on October 10, 2010. Curacao and Sint Maarten became autonomous territories of the Kingdom of the Netherlands. [6] The Gaza Strip and West Bank are Israeli occupied with interim status subject to Israeli/Palestinian negotiations. The final status is yet to be determined.

Source: U.S. Census Bureau, "International Data Base (IDB)," <http://www.census.gov/population/international/data/>, accessed July 2015.

Table 1343. Foreign or Foreign-Born Population, Labor Force, and Net Migration in Selected OECD Countries: Selected Years 2000 to 2012

[30,273 represents 30,273,000. In Australia and the United States, the data refer to residents who are foreign born. In the European countries and Japan, they represent the legal nationality or citizenship status of residents. Data are based on censuses, population registers, residence permits, and/or labor force surveys. For details about data methodology for individual countries, see source]

Country	Foreign population					Foreign labor force				Average net migration 2009-2012 (per 1,000 population)[1]
	Number (1,000)			Percent of total population		Number (1,000)				
	2000	2010	2012	2000	2010	2000	2005	2008	2009	
United States......	**30,273**	**39,917**	**40,738**	**11.0**	**12.9**	**18,029**	**22,422**	**25,086**	**24,815**	**2.3**
Australia..............	4,412	5,862	6,190	23.0	26.5	2,373	2,618	3,000	3,144	9.7
Austria..............	702	913	1,004	8.8	11.1	320	374	474	479	3.3
Belgium..............	862	1,119	1,195	8.4	10.3	388	440	469	498	6.6
Denmark............	259	346	(NA)	4.8	6.2	101	115	145	(NA)	4.0
France..............	(NA)	3,825	4,036	(NA)	6.0	1,578	1,406	1,558	1,540	0.7
Germany............	7,297	6,754	7,214	8.9	8.3	3,546	3,823	3,893	(NA)	1.6
Italy................	1,380	4,570	4,388	2.4	7.6	838	1,419	1,387	(NA)	3.1
Japan...............	1,686	2,133	2,034	1.3	1.7	155	180	212	213	-0.4
Luxembourg.........	165	221	239	37.3	43.9	153	196	233	231	17.1
Netherlands.........	668	760	796	4.2	4.6	300	287	(NA)	(NA)	2.0
Spain...............	1,371	5,751	5,520	(NA)	12.5	455	1,689	1,882	(NA)	-1.1
Sweden.............	472	633	667	5.4	6.8	222	177	(NA)	(NA)	5.6
Switzerland.........	1,384	1,720	1,825	19.3	22.0	717	830	927	974	7.5
United Kingdom.....	2,342	4,524	4,788	4.0	7.4	1,107	1,504	2,278	2,280	(NA)

NA Not available. [1] Or latest period available.

Source: Organisation for Economic Co-operation and Development (OECD), 2015, "International Migration Database," OECD International Migration Statistics (database) ©, <http://dx.doi.org/10.1787/data-00342-en>; and "Labour Force Statistics: Population and vital statistics," OECD Employment and Labour Market Statistics (database) ©, <http://dx.doi.org/10.1787/data-00287-en>; accessed July 2015.

Table 1344. Youth and Elderly Population Distribution by Country: 2014 and 2020

[Percent of total population, as of mid-year. Covers countries with 11 million or more population in 2014]

Country	2014		2020, proj.		Country	2014		2020, proj.	
	Under 15 years old	65 years old and over	Under 15 years old	65 years old and over		Under 15 years old	65 years old and over	Under 15 years old	65 years old and over
World...............	**25.8**	**8.3**	**24.8**	**9.5**	Malawi.............	46.9	2.7	45.9	2.7
Afghanistan..........	42.0	2.5	40.6	2.7	Malaysia...........	28.8	5.5	26.8	6.9
Algeria..............	28.4	5.2	29.6	6.2	Mali................	47.6	3.0	46.3	2.9
Angola..............	43.2	2.9	42.1	3.1	Mexico.............	27.9	6.6	26.0	7.7
Argentina............	24.9	11.4	23.7	12.4	Morocco............	26.7	6.3	24.9	7.5
Australia.............	18.0	15.1	17.6	17.0	Mozambique........	45.3	2.9	44.1	2.9
Bangladesh..........	32.3	5.0	28.3	5.8	Nepal..............	31.6	4.5	27.6	5.1
Belgium.............	17.0	18.1	17.2	19.2	Netherlands.........	16.9	17.6	16.1	19.8
Brazil...............	23.8	7.6	21.1	9.2	Niger..............	49.8	2.6	47.9	2.7
Burkina Faso........	45.4	2.5	44.3	2.4	Nigeria............	43.2	3.1	41.7	3.2
Burma..............	26.4	5.3	24.7	6.2	Pakistan...........	33.3	4.3	29.7	4.8
Cambodia...........	31.6	4.0	30.2	4.6	Peru...............	27.3	6.9	25.4	8.0
Cameroon...........	42.9	3.1	41.6	3.3	Philippines.........	34.3	4.2	32.4	4.9
Canada.............	15.5	17.3	15.4	20.1	Poland.............	14.7	15.1	14.8	18.7
Chad...............	44.7	3.0	41.4	3.1	Romania...........	14.6	15.4	14.1	17.6
Chile...............	20.7	9.9	19.8	11.8	Russia.............	16.4	13.3	17.2	15.5
China...............	17.1	9.6	17.3	12.3	Rwanda............	42.1	2.5	40.0	2.9
Colombia............	25.3	6.7	23.3	8.4	Saudi Arabia........	27.6	3.2	25.0	3.8
Congo, Dem. Rep....	43.1	2.6	40.3	2.7	Senegal............	42.5	2.9	40.4	3.1
Cote d'Ivoire.........	38.4	3.3	35.6	3.7	South Africa........	28.5	5.4	27.9	6.1
Cuba...............	16.3	12.6	14.9	14.5	South Sudan [1]......	45.8	2.1	42.8	2.2
Ecuador.............	28.5	6.9	25.8	8.1	Spain..............	15.4	17.6	15.0	18.5
Egypt...............	32.1	5.0	30.3	6.0	Sri Lanka...........	24.7	8.7	23.1	10.6
Ethiopia.............	44.2	2.8	42.7	3.0	Sudan [1]............	40.8	3.3	36.5	3.4
France..............	18.7	18.3	18.4	20.5	Syria..............	33.1	3.9	30.8	4.5
Germany............	13.0	21.1	12.9	23.0	Taiwan.............	14.0	12.0	12.4	15.7
Ghana..............	38.6	4.1	37.4	4.4	Tanzania...........	44.6	2.9	42.7	3.1
Guatemala...........	36.2	4.2	33.0	4.9	Thailand...........	17.6	9.5	16.4	11.8
Guinea..............	42.0	3.6	41.0	3.8	Tunisia............	23.0	7.9	22.8	9.2
India...............	28.5	5.8	26.3	6.7	Turkey.............	25.8	6.9	23.4	8.4
Indonesia............	26.2	6.5	23.9	7.8	Uganda............	48.7	2.1	47.4	1.9
Iran................	23.7	5.2	23.3	6.1	Ukraine............	14.9	15.5	16.2	17.0
Iraq................	40.6	3.3	38.1	3.8	United Kingdom.....	17.3	17.5	17.6	18.5
Italy................	13.8	21.0	13.4	22.1	**United States**......	**19.2**	**14.5**	**18.4**	**16.9**
Japan...............	13.2	25.8	12.5	29.2	Uzbekistan..........	24.9	4.8	23.2	5.9
Kazakhstan..........	25.1	7.0	26.1	8.4	Venezuela..........	28.2	5.9	26.1	7.4
Kenya..............	42.1	2.8	36.8	3.3	Vietnam............	24.3	5.7	22.6	6.9
Korea, North.........	21.5	9.7	20.5	9.7	Yemen.............	41.7	2.6	37.7	2.9
Korea, South.........	14.1	12.7	12.6	15.6	Zambia............	46.2	2.4	45.7	2.3
Madagascar.........	40.7	3.2	38.9	3.5	Zimbabwe..........	38.4	3.5	37.5	3.6

[1] Data for Sudan exclude South Sudan, which became an independent country in July 2011.

Source: U.S. Census Bureau, "International Data Base (IDB)," <http://www.census.gov/population/international/data/>, accessed July 2015

Table 1345. Births, Deaths, and Life Expectancy by Country or Territory: 2014 and 2020

[Covers countries with 12 million or more population in 2014]

Country or territory	Crude birth rate [1] 2014	Crude birth rate [1] 2020, proj.	Crude death rate [2] 2014	Crude death rate [2] 2020, proj.	Expectation of life at birth (years) 2014	Expectation of life at birth (years) 2020, proj.	Infant mortality rate [3] 2014	Infant mortality rate [3] 2020, proj.	Total fertility rate per woman [4] 2014	Total fertility rate per woman [4] 2020, proj.
World	**18.7**	**17.6**	**7.8**	**7.9**	**68.4**	**69.8**	**36.4**	**31.6**	**2.43**	**2.36**
Afghanistan	38.8	36.7	14.1	12.7	50.5	52.8	117.2	104.3	5.43	4.82
Algeria	24.0	20.0	4.3	4.4	76.4	77.5	21.8	17.6	2.78	2.59
Angola	39.0	37.5	11.7	10.5	55.3	57.5	80.0	69.9	5.43	5.07
Argentina	16.9	15.6	7.3	7.3	77.5	78.5	10.0	8.5	2.25	2.15
Australia	12.2	11.9	7.1	7.5	82.1	82.5	4.4	4.1	1.77	1.76
Bangladesh	21.6	19.5	5.6	5.6	70.7	72.4	45.7	36.8	2.45	2.24
Brazil	14.7	13.6	6.5	6.9	73.3	74.7	19.2	15.9	1.79	1.73
Burkina Faso	42.4	39.9	12.0	10.6	54.8	56.9	76.8	67.8	5.93	5.49
Burma	18.7	17.3	8.0	7.9	65.9	68.0	44.9	37.2	2.18	2.09
Cambodia	24.4	21.3	7.8	7.3	63.8	65.9	51.4	43.7	2.66	2.39
Cameroon	36.6	34.2	10.4	9.0	57.4	60.3	55.1	47.6	4.82	4.46
Canada	10.3	10.1	8.3	9.0	81.7	82.2	4.7	4.4	1.59	1.61
Chile	14.0	13.1	5.9	6.5	78.4	79.4	7.0	6.2	1.84	1.77
China	12.3	11.6	7.4	8.2	75.3	76.1	12.7	11.4	1.57	1.60
Colombia	16.7	15.4	5.4	5.6	75.3	76.6	15.0	12.3	2.07	1.94
Congo, Dem. Rep	35.6	31.3	10.3	9.1	56.5	58.8	73.2	63.6	4.80	3.99
Cote d'Ivoire	29.3	26.1	9.7	9.1	58.0	59.9	60.2	51.6	3.63	3.15
Ecuador	18.9	17.0	5.0	5.2	76.4	77.5	17.9	15.0	2.29	2.09
Egypt	23.4	20.8	4.8	4.8	73.5	74.9	22.4	17.9	2.87	2.67
Ethiopia	37.7	35.2	8.5	7.2	60.8	63.7	55.8	45.6	5.23	4.75
France	12.5	11.9	9.1	9.6	81.7	82.2	3.3	3.2	2.08	2.06
Germany	8.4	8.6	11.3	12.1	80.4	81.1	3.5	3.3	1.43	1.47
Ghana	31.4	29.6	7.4	6.6	65.8	68.2	38.5	32.1	4.09	3.90
Guatemala	25.5	22.7	4.8	4.6	71.7	73.4	23.5	19.2	2.99	2.57
India	19.9	18.2	7.4	7.3	67.8	69.7	43.2	35.4	2.51	2.35
Indonesia	17.0	15.4	6.3	6.6	72.2	73.7	25.2	20.4	2.18	2.04
Iran	18.2	16.2	5.9	6.0	70.9	72.4	39.0	33.6	1.85	1.81
Iraq	32.0	29.1	3.8	3.8	74.9	74.9	37.5	37.5	4.18	3.82
Italy	8.8	8.4	10.1	10.7	82.0	82.5	3.3	3.2	1.42	1.47
Japan	8.1	7.3	9.4	10.2	84.5	86.0	2.1	1.9	1.40	1.43
Kazakhstan	19.6	16.4	8.3	8.2	70.2	72.0	21.6	17.9	2.34	2.16
Kenya	28.3	20.8	7.0	6.6	63.5	65.1	40.7	34.0	3.54	2.57
Korea, North	14.5	14.5	9.2	9.4	69.8	71.6	24.5	20.0	1.98	1.92
Korea, South	8.3	8.2	6.6	7.6	79.8	81.1	3.9	3.6	1.25	1.29
Madagascar	33.1	29.9	7.0	6.2	65.2	67.3	44.9	37.8	4.28	3.78
Malawi	41.8	40.1	8.7	7.2	60.0	63.2	48.0	39.5	5.66	5.31
Malaysia	20.1	18.3	5.0	5.3	74.5	75.9	13.7	11.4	2.58	2.43
Mali	45.5	41.8	13.2	11.3	55.0	57.3	104.3	91.6	6.16	5.51
Mexico	19.0	17.6	5.2	5.4	75.4	76.7	12.6	10.7	2.29	2.19
Morocco	18.5	16.9	4.8	5.0	76.5	77.7	24.5	19.5	2.15	2.07
Mozambique	38.8	37.2	12.3	10.9	52.6	54.8	72.4	60.5	5.27	4.90
Nepal	21.1	19.7	6.6	6.4	67.2	69.2	40.4	33.2	2.30	2.11
Netherlands	10.8	11.0	8.6	9.2	81.1	81.7	3.7	3.5	1.78	1.77
Niger	46.1	42.5	12.7	11.0	54.7	57.1	86.3	76.1	6.89	6.08
Nigeria	38.0	35.9	13.2	11.7	52.6	55.0	74.1	65.6	5.25	4.88
Pakistan	23.2	20.7	6.6	6.2	67.1	69.0	57.5	47.2	2.86	2.42
Peru	18.6	17.0	6.0	6.2	73.2	74.7	20.2	16.7	2.22	2.04
Philippines	24.6	22.9	6.2	6.0	68.7	70.0	22.9	20.0	3.13	2.92
Poland	9.9	8.9	10.1	10.6	77.2	78.3	4.6	4.3	1.32	1.38
Romania	9.3	8.5	11.9	12.0	74.7	76.0	10.2	8.7	1.32	1.38
Russia	11.9	10.0	13.8	13.4	70.2	71.9	7.1	6.5	1.61	1.60
Rwanda	34.6	31.0	9.2	8.0	59.3	61.7	59.6	51.3	4.62	4.17
Saudi Arabia	18.8	17.8	3.3	3.4	74.8	76.1	14.6	12.0	2.17	2.04
Senegal	35.1	31.8	8.7	7.6	61.0	63.2	52.7	45.7	4.52	4.04
South Africa	20.9	19.2	10.2	9.3	61.5	64.8	34.0	27.8	2.34	2.22
Spain	9.9	8.7	9.0	9.3	81.5	82.0	3.3	3.2	1.48	1.51
Sri Lanka	16.2	14.2	6.1	6.5	76.4	77.5	9.0	7.8	2.13	2.01
Sudan [5]	30.0	26.0	7.9	6.9	63.3	65.5	52.9	45.0	3.92	3.24
Syria	22.8	19.7	6.5	4.0	68.4	75.6	15.8	13.7	2.68	2.34
Taiwan	8.6	8.0	7.0	7.9	79.8	80.6	4.5	4.2	1.11	1.14
Tanzania	36.8	34.6	8.2	7.1	61.2	63.9	43.7	36.4	4.95	4.59
Thailand	11.3	10.7	7.7	8.3	74.2	75.6	9.9	8.6	1.50	1.54
Turkey	16.7	14.8	5.9	6.1	74.3	75.7	19.6	15.8	2.08	1.96
Uganda	44.2	41.4	11.0	9.4	54.5	57.2	60.8	51.8	5.97	5.44
Ukraine	10.9	9.6	14.5	14.0	71.3	72.9	8.3	7.4	1.53	1.56
United Kingdom	12.2	11.9	9.3	9.5	80.4	81.1	4.4	4.1	1.90	1.86
United States	12.5	12.4	8.1	8.3	79.5	80.4	5.9	5.6	1.87	1.87
Uzbekistan	17.0	16.1	5.3	5.4	73.3	74.8	19.8	16.3	1.80	1.74
Venezuela	19.4	18.1	5.3	5.6	74.4	75.3	19.3	17.0	2.35	2.22
Vietnam	16.3	14.5	5.9	6.0	72.9	74.4	19.0	15.7	1.85	1.77
Yemen	31.0	25.8	6.5	5.6	64.8	66.9	50.4	41.9	4.09	3.20
Zambia	42.5	40.4	12.9	11.6	51.8	53.6	66.6	56.0	5.76	5.49
Zimbabwe	32.5	29.9	10.6	9.8	55.7	59.3	26.6	25.3	3.56	3.40

[1] Number of births during 1 year per 1,000 persons (based on midyear population). [2] Number of deaths during 1 year per 1,000 persons (based on midyear population). [3] Number of deaths of children under 1 year of age per 1,000 live births in a calendar year. [4] Average number of children that would be born if all women lived to the end of childbearing age, based on birth rates for each specified year. [5] Data exclude South Sudan, which became a separate country in July 2011.

Source: U.S. Census Bureau, "International Data Base (IDB)," <http://www.census.gov/population/international/data/>, accessed July 2015.

Table 1346. Life Expectancy at Birth and at Age 65 by Sex—Selected Countries: 2010 and 2013

Country	Life expectancy at birth (years)				Life expectancy at age 65 (years)			
	Females		Males		Females		Males	
	2010	2013	2010	2013	2010	2013	2010	2013
United States............	**81.0**	**81.2**	**76.2**	**76.4**	**20.3**	**20.5**	**17.7**	**17.9**
Australia..................	84.0	84.3	79.5	80.1	21.8	22.1	18.9	19.2
Austria...................	83.5	83.8	77.8	78.6	21.4	21.5	17.9	18.2
Belgium...................	83.0	83.2	77.5	78.1	21.3	21.4	17.6	17.8
Brazil....................	77.6	78.6	70.2	71.3	19.2	19.5	16.4	16.4
Canada....................	83.4	(NA)	79.0	(NA)	21.6	(NA)	18.6	(NA)
Czech Republic...........	80.9	81.3	74.5	75.2	19.0	19.3	15.5	15.7
Denmark...................	81.4	82.4	77.2	78.3	19.7	20.4	17.0	17.7
Finland...................	83.5	84.1	76.9	78.0	21.5	21.8	17.5	18.0
France....................	85.3	85.6	78.2	79.0	23.4	23.6	18.9	19.3
Germany...................	83.0	83.2	78.0	78.6	20.9	21.1	17.8	18.2
Greece....................	83.3	84.0	78.0	78.7	20.9	21.6	18.2	18.7
Hungary...................	78.6	[1] 79.1	70.7	[1] 72.2	18.2	[1] 18.4	14.1	[1] 14.5
Iceland...................	84.1	83.7	79.8	80.5	21.5	21.2	18.3	18.8
Ireland...................	83.1	83.1	78.5	79.0	20.8	20.8	17.7	18.1
Israel [3]................	83.6	83.9	79.7	80.3	21.2	21.3	18.9	19.2
Italy.....................	84.7	85.2	79.5	80.3	22.1	22.6	18.3	18.9
Japan.....................	86.3	86.6	79.6	80.2	23.8	24.0	18.7	19.1
Korea, South.............	84.1	85.1	77.2	78.5	21.6	22.4	17.2	18.0
Mexico....................	77.0	77.4	71.1	71.7	18.5	18.6	16.6	16.7
Netherlands..............	83.0	83.2	78.9	79.5	21.0	21.2	17.7	18.2
New Zealand..............	82.7	[2] 83.2	78.9	[2] 79.5	21.0	[2] 21.3	18.5	[2] 18.9
Norway....................	83.3	83.8	79.0	79.8	21.2	21.4	18.0	18.5
Poland....................	80.7	81.2	72.2	73.0	19.5	19.9	15.1	15.5
Portugal.................	83.2	84.0	76.8	77.6	21.0	21.6	17.2	17.8
Russia....................	74.9	76.3	63.1	65.1	16.5	17.4	12.1	13.1
South Africa.............	56.1	58.8	52.7	54.7	(NA)	(NA)	(NA)	(NA)
Spain.....................	85.5	86.1	79.2	80.2	22.9	23.4	18.6	19.2
Sweden....................	83.6	83.8	79.6	80.2	21.2	21.3	18.3	18.8
Switzerland..............	84.9	85.0	80.3	80.7	22.5	22.4	19.0	19.4
Turkey....................	76.8	[2] 79.4	71.8	[2] 73.7	16.0	[2] 18.5	14.0	[2] 14.9
United Kingdom...........	82.6	82.9	78.6	79.2	20.8	20.9	18.2	18.6

NA Not available. [1] Break in series. [2] Estimated. [3] The statistical data for Israel are supplied by and under the responsibility of the relevant Israeli authorities. The use of such data by the OECD is without prejudice to the status of the Golan Heights, East Jerusalem and Israeli settlements in the West Bank under the terms of international law.

Source: Organisation for Economic Co-operation and Development (OECD), 2015, "OECD Health Data: Non-medical Determinants of Health," OECD Health Statistics (database) ©, <http://dx.doi.org/10.1787/data-00546-en>, accessed July 2015.

Table 1347. Percentage of the Adult Population Considered to Be Obese: 2005 to 2013

[Obesity rates are defined as the percentage of the population with a Body Mass Index (BMI) over 30 kg/m^2. The BMI is a single number that evaluates an individual's weight status in relation to height (weight/height^2). Obesity estimates derived from health examinations are generally higher and more reliable than those coming from self-reports because they preclude any misreporting of people's height and weight. However, health examinations are only conducted regularly in a few countries. For more information on methods, see source]

Country	2005	2007	2008	2009	2010	2011	2012	2013
Obese population, measured								
United States................	**(NA)**	**(NA)**	**34.3**	**(NA)**	**36.1**	**(NA)**	**35.3**	**(NA)**
Australia.........................	(NA)	24.6	(NA)	(NA)	(NA)	28.3	(NA)	(NA)
Canada............................	23.7	(NA)	24.2	(NA)	25.4	(NA)	(NA)	25.8
Czech Republic...................	17.0	(NA)	22.0	(NA)	21.0	(NA)	(NA)	(NA)
Japan.............................	3.9	3.3	3.4	3.9	3.5	4.1	3.6	3.7
Korea, South.....................	3.5	3.9	3.7	3.8	4.1	4.3	4.6	4.7
Luxembourg........................	18.6	20.0	20.3	[1] 22.1	22.5	23.5	23.0	22.7
Mexico............................	30.2	(NA)	(NA)	(NA)	(NA)	(NA)	[2] 32.4	(NA)
New Zealand......................	(NA)	26.5	(NA)	27.8	(NA)	(NA)	[2] 28.4	30.6
Slovak Republic..................	17.6	(NA)	16.9	(NA)	(NA)	(NA)	(NA)	(NA)
United Kingdom...................	23.2	24.0	24.5	23.0	26.1	24.8	24.7	24.9
Obese population, self-reported								
United States................	**25.1**	**26.4**	**27.6**	**27.7**	**28.1**	**28.5**	**28.6**	**28.7**
Canada............................	15.2	16.2	16.6	17.2	17.5	17.7	17.7	18.2
Chile.............................	(NA)	(NA)	(NA)	12.1	(NA)	(NA)	(NA)	(NA)
Denmark...........................	11.4	(NA)	(NA)	(NA)	13.4	(NA)	(NA)	14.2
Estonia...........................	(NA)	(NA)	18.0	(NA)	16.9	(NA)	19.0	(NA)
Finland...........................	14.1	14.9	15.7	14.9	15.6	16.6	15.8	15.7
France............................	(NA)	(NA)	11.2	(NA)	12.9	(NA)	14.5	(NA)
Germany...........................	13.6	(NA)	(NA)	14.7	(NA)	(NA)	(NA)	15.7
Greece............................	(NA)	(NA)	18.1	(NA)	19.6	(NA)	(NA)	(NA)
Iceland...........................	(NA)	20.1	(NA)	(NA)	21.0	(NA)	22.2	(NA)
Israel [3]........................	(NA)	(NA)	13.8	(NA)	15.7	(NA)	(NA)	15.7
Italy.............................	9.9	9.9	9.9	10.3	10.3	10.0	10.4	10.3
Korea, South.....................	(NA)	(NA)	1.8	2.0	2.0	2.1	2.2	2.4
Netherlands......................	10.7	11.2	11.1	11.8	11.4	11.4	12.0	11.8
Norway............................	9.0	(NA)	10.0	(NA)	(NA)	(NA)	10.0	(NA)
Spain.............................	(NA)	(NA)	(NA)	16.0	(NA)	16.6	(NA)	(NA)
Sweden............................	10.9	10.6	10.3	10.9	11.3	11.0	11.8	11.7
Turkey............................	(NA)	(NA)	15.2	(NA)	16.9	(NA)	17.2	(NA)

NA Not available. [1] Break in series. [2] Estimated. [3] See footnote 3, Table 1346.

Source: Organisation for Economic Co-operation and Development (OECD), 2015, "OECD Health Data: Non-medical Determinants of Health," OECD Health Statistics (database) ©, <http://dx.doi.org/10.1787/data-00546-en>, accessed August 2015.

Table 1348. Daily Tobacco Consumption by Country and Sex: 2000 to 2013

[Daily smokers as percent of population aged over 15. Includes tobacco forms consumed by smoking only]

Country	Total				Females				Males			
	2000	2010	2012	2013	2000	2010	2012	2013	2000	2010	2012	2013
United States.........	**19.1**	**15.1**	**14.2**	**13.7**	**17.3**	**13.6**	**12.5**	**11.9**	**21.2**	**16.7**	**15.9**	**15.6**
Brazil..................	(NA)	14.1	12.1	11.3	(NA)	11.7	9.2	8.6	(NA)	16.8	15.5	14.4
Canada.................	(NA)	16.3	16.1	14.9	(NA)	13.7	13.5	12.9	(NA)	19.0	18.7	16.9
Czech Republic........	(NA)	22.8	22.9	22.2	(NA)	16.5	19.6	17.4	(NA)	29.3	26.3	27.2
Estonia.................	30.3	26.2	26.0	(NA)	20.0	18.7	18.3	(NA)	45.0	36.8	36.2	(NA)
Finland.................	23.4	19.0	17.0	15.8	20.3	15.7	14.0	13.2	27.3	23.2	20.9	19.1
France..................	27.0	23.3	24.1	(NA)	21.0	20.7	20.2	(NA)	33.0	26.4	28.7	(NA)
Iceland.................	22.4	14.2	13.8	11.4	22.0	13.9	12.8	12.1	22.8	14.5	14.9	10.7
Israel [2]...............	24.1	[1] 18.5	(NA)	16.2	15.4	12.6	(NA)	10.8	34.0	[1] 24.8	(NA)	21.9
Italy...................	24.4	23.1	22.1	21.1	17.4	17.1	16.5	15.9	31.9	29.6	28.1	26.7
Japan..................	27.0	19.5	20.7	19.3	11.5	8.4	9.0	8.2	47.4	32.2	34.1	32.2
Korea..................	(NA)	22.9	21.6	19.9	(NA)	5.2	5.8	4.3	(NA)	40.8	37.6	36.2
Luxembourg............	(NA)	18.3	16.8	15.7	(NA)	15.7	15.2	13.9	(NA)	20.9	18.4	17.6
Netherlands............	32.0	20.9	18.4	18.5	29.0	18.8	16.3	16.3	35.0	23.1	20.6	20.9
New Zealand...........	25.0	(NA)	16.5	15.5	25.0	(NA)	15.8	14.9	25.0	(NA)	17.2	16.2
Norway................	32.0	19.0	16.0	15.0	32.0	19.0	16.0	14.0	31.0	19.0	16.0	15.0
Sweden................	18.9	13.6	12.8	10.7	21.0	12.5	13.1	11.7	16.8	14.7	12.4	9.8
United Kingdom.......	27.0	20.0	20.0	(NA)	26.0	20.0	19.0	(NA)	28.0	21.0	22.0	(NA)

NA Not available. [1] Break in series. [2] See footnote 3, Table 1346.

Source: Organisation for Economic Co-operation and Development (OECD), 2015, "OECD Health Data: Non-medical Determinants of Health," OECD Health Statistics (database) ©, <http://dx.doi.org/10.1787/data-00546-en>, accessed July 2015.

Table 1349. Road Traffic Fatalities by Country: 2000 to 2013

[Fatalities include any person killed immediately or dying within 30 days as a result of an injury accident. For countries that do not apply the threshold of 30 days, conversion coefficients are estimated so that comparisons on the basis of the 30 day-definition can be made]

Country	2000	2005	2010	2012	2013	Country	2000	2005	2010	2012	2013
United States.....	**41,945**	**43,510**	**32,999**	**33,561**	**(NA)**	Japan...............	10,410	7,990	5,806	5,237	5,152
Australia..........	1,817	1,627	1,353	1,299	1,192	Korea, South......	10,236	6,376	5,505	5,392	5,092
Austria............	976	768	552	[1] 531	455	Latvia..............	588	442	218	177	179
Azerbaijan........	596	1,065	925	1,168	1,164	Lithuania...........	641	773	299	302	256
Belgium...........	1,470	1,089	841	[2] 770	724	Mexico.............	5,224	4,710	5,032	4,539	(NA)
Bulgaria...........	1,012	957	776	601	601	Moldova...........	406	391	452	442	295
Canada............	2,903	2,898	2,237	2,104	2,150	Netherlands.......	1,166	817	640	650	570
China.............	(NA)	98,738	65,225	(NA)	(NA)	New Zealand......	462	405	375	308	254
Croatia............	655	597	426	393	368	Norway...........	341	224	208	145	187
Czech Republic. ..	1,486	1,286	802	742	654	Poland............	6,294	5,444	3,907	[2] 3,577	3,357
Denmark..........	498	331	255	167	191	Portugal...........	1,857	1,247	937	718	(NA)
Estonia...........	204	170	78	87	81	Romania...........	2,499	2,641	2,377	2,042	1,861
Finland............	396	379	272	255	258	Russia.............	29,594	33,957	26,567	27,991	27,025
France............	8,079	5,318	3,992	3,653	3,268	Serbia.............	1,048	841	656	684	646
Germany..........	7,503	5,361	3,648	3,600	3,339	Slovak Republic. ..	648	600	353	352	251
Greece...........	2,037	1,658	1,258	[2] 988	874	Slovenia...........	313	258	138	130	125
Hungary..........	1,200	1,278	740	605	591	Spain.............	5,776	3,857	2,478	1,903	1,680
Iceland............	32	19	8	9	15	Sweden...........	591	440	266	285	260
India..............	78,911	94,968	134,513	138,258	137,572	Switzerland.......	592	409	327	339	269
Ireland............	415	396	212	162	189	Turkey.............	5,510	4,505	4,045	3,750	3,685
Italy..............	7,061	5,818	4,090	[2] 3,653	(NA)	United Kingdom. ..	3,580	3,336	1,905	1,802	1,766

NA Not available. [1] Break in series. [2] Estimated or provisional.

Source: International Transport Forum (ITF) / Organisation for Economic Co-operation and Development (OECD), 2015, "Road injury accidents," Transport Statistics ©. See also <http://www.internationaltransportforum.org/>.

Table 1350. Suicide Rates by Sex and Country: 2012

[Deaths due to intentional self-harm per 100,000 persons]

Country	Total	Men	Women	Country	Total	Men	Women
United States [1].........	**12.5**	**20.5**	**5.2**	Italy......................	6.3	10.5	2.6
Australia [2]...............	10.1	15.6	4.8	Japan....................	19.1	27.8	10.8
Austria...................	13.7	23.1	5.7	Korea, South............	29.1	43.2	17.8
Belgium..................	17.4	26.7	9.0	Luxembourg.............	9.4	14.8	4.3
Brazil....................	5.8	9.5	2.4	Mexico..................	5.0	8.6	1.7
Canada [2]................	10.5	15.9	5.3	Netherlands.............	10.0	14.0	6.3
Chile....................	11.0	19.0	3.7	New Zealand [2]..........	11.3	17.7	5.2
Czech Republic..........	14.7	26.0	4.7	Norway..................	10.2	14.7	5.8
Denmark.................	11.3	17.5	5.4	Poland..................	15.7	28.7	3.8
Estonia..................	16.6	30.7	5.3	Portugal.................	9.0	16.0	3.2
Finland..................	15.6	24.2	7.6	Russia [2]................	21.0	39.0	6.9
France [2]................	15.8	25.4	7.5	Slovak Republic [1]........	11.3	20.7	3.2
Germany.................	10.5	16.4	5.2	South Africa.............	1.1	1.8	0.5
Greece..................	4.2	7.1	1.5	Spain....................	6.9	11.2	3.1
Hungary.................	22.0	38.0	9.1	Sweden..................	11.6	16.8	6.8
Ireland [1]................	11.0	17.4	4.6	Switzerland..............	12.0	18.4	6.4
Israel [3]..................	6.4	10.9	2.3	United Kingdom..........	7.0	11.3	2.9

[1] 2010 data. [2] 2011 data. [3] See footnote 3, Table 1346.

Source: Organisation for Economic Co-operation and Development (OECD), 2015, "Health Status," OECD Health Statistics database ©, <http://dx.doi.org/10.1787/data-00540-en>, accessed July 2015.

Table 1351. Health Expenditures by Country: 1990 to 2013

[In percent. GDP = gross domestic product]

Country	Total expenditures on health (percent of GDP)					Public expenditures on health (percent of total)				
	1990	2000	2010	2012	2013	1990	2000	2010	2012	2013
United States.............	**11.3**	**12.5**	**16.4**	**16.4**	**16.4**	**40.1**	**44.0**	**48.4**	**48.0**	**48.2**
Australia....................	6.5	7.6	8.5	8.8	(NA)	66.2	68.4	68.0	67.6	(NA)
Austria.....................	7.7	9.2	10.1	10.1	10.1	74.4	75.5	76.1	76.4	76.2
Belgium....................	7.1	8.0	9.9	10.2	10.2	(NA)	74.6	77.7	77.7	77.8
Canada....................	8.4	8.3	10.6	10.2	10.2	74.3	70.0	69.9	70.5	70.6
Czech Republic...........	3.8	5.7	6.9	7.1	7.1	97.1	89.8	83.3	83.7	84.1
Denmark...................	8.0	8.1	10.4	10.4	10.4	82.4	83.1	84.6	85.2	84.3
Finland....................	7.2	6.7	8.2	8.5	8.6	80.0	71.0	74.1	75.3	75.0
France....................	8.0	9.5	10.8	10.8	10.9	76.0	78.9	78.0	78.5	78.7
Germany [1]...............	8.0	9.8	11.0	10.8	11.0	75.4	78.6	75.7	75.6	76.3
Greece....................	6.0	7.2	9.2	9.1	9.2	54.1	61.6	67.7	67.9	65.5
Hungary...................	(NA)	6.8	7.7	7.5	7.4	(NA)	69.6	64.3	62.9	64.6
Iceland....................	7.4	9.0	8.8	8.7	8.7	86.2	80.6	80.4	80.6	80.7
Ireland....................	5.6	5.6	8.5	8.1	(NA)	73.2	75.4	69.2	68.5	(NA)
Italy......................	7.0	7.6	8.9	8.8	8.8	81.3	72.6	78.5	77.0	77.4
Japan.....................	5.8	7.4	9.5	10.1	10.2	77.6	80.4	81.9	82.6	83.2
Korea, South.............	3.7	4.0	6.5	6.7	6.9	39.0	50.5	58.0	56.3	55.9
Luxembourg...............	(NA)	5.9	7.2	6.6	(NA)	(NA)	82.0	84.9	82.5	(NA)
Mexico....................	4.3	4.9	6.2	6.1	6.2	40.4	45.2	47.1	50.1	51.1
Netherlands...............	7.1	7.0	10.4	11.0	11.1	71.2	66.4	87.0	87.0	87.6
New Zealand..............	6.7	7.5	9.7	9.8	9.5	82.4	78.0	80.6	80.1	79.8
Norway....................	7.1	7.7	8.9	8.8	8.9	82.8	81.7	84.7	84.8	85.0
Poland....................	4.3	5.3	6.5	6.3	6.4	(NA)	68.9	71.7	70.0	70.6
Portugal..................	5.5	8.3	9.8	9.3	9.0	64.9	71.2	70.0	65.4	66.0
Slovak Republic...........	(NA)	5.3	7.8	7.7	7.6	(NA)	89.2	71.9	72.2	74.2
Spain.....................	6.1	6.8	9.1	8.9	(NA)	78.4	71.4	74.0	71.7	(NA)
Sweden...................	7.3	7.4	8.5	10.8	11.0	79.6	85.5	81.9	84.5	84.1
Switzerland...............	7.4	9.3	10.5	11.0	11.1	51.0	55.4	64.1	64.7	66.1
Turkey....................	2.5	4.7	5.3	5.0	5.1	59.9	61.7	78.0	79.2	78.4
United Kingdom...........	5.1	6.3	8.6	8.5	8.5	84.3	84.5	88.5	86.5	86.6

NA Not available. [1] Data prior to 1991 are for former West Germany.

Source: Organisation for Economic Co-operation and Development (OECD), 2015, "Health expenditure and financing: Health expenditure indicators," OECD Health Statistics (database) ©, <http://dx.doi.org/10.1787/data-00349-en>, accessed July 2015.

Table 1352. Physicians and Inpatient Hospital Care—Selected Countries: 2000 to 2013

Country	Practicing physicians per 1,000 population				Acute inpatient hospital care							
					Beds per 1,000 population				Average length of stay (days)			
	2000	2010	2012	2013	2000	2010	2012	2013	2000	2010	2012	2013
United States........	**2.3**	**2.4**	**2.5**	**2.6**	**3.0**	**2.6**	**2.5**	**(NA)**	**5.8**	**5.4**	**(NA)**	**(NA)**
Australia...............	2.5	(NA)	[1] 3.3	3.4	3.6	3.4	3.4	(NA)	6.1	5.0	4.8	(NA)
Austria................	3.9	4.8	4.9	5.0	6.3	5.6	5.5	5.4	7.6	6.6	6.5	6.5
Belgium...............	2.8	2.9	2.9	3.0	4.7	4.1	4.0	4.0	7.7	7.2	7.0	6.6
Canada...............	(NA)	(NA)	[1] 2.5	(NA)	3.2	1.7	1.7	(NA)	7.2	7.7	7.6	(NA)
Czech Republic.......	3.4	3.6	3.7	3.7	5.7	4.9	4.6	4.4	7.9	7.0	6.6	6.6
Denmark..............	2.9	3.6	3.6	(NA)	3.5	2.9	(NA)	2.5	3.8	(NA)	(NA)	(NA)
Estonia...............	3.1	3.2	3.3	3.3	5.4	3.5	3.6	3.4	7.3	5.5	5.6	5.5
Finland................	2.5	3.0	3.0	3.0	3.5	3.0	2.9	2.8	6.9	7.0	6.9	6.8
France................	(NA)	(NA)	3.1	3.1	4.1	3.5	3.4	3.4	5.6	5.8	5.7	(NA)
Germany..............	3.3	3.7	4.0	4.1	6.1	5.3	5.4	5.3	10.1	8.1	7.8	7.7
Hungary..............	2.7	2.9	3.1	3.2	[1] 5.8	4.1	4.0	4.0	7.1	5.4	5.2	(NA)
Ireland...............	(NA)	(NA)	[1] 2.7	2.7	2.8	2.2	2.1	2.1	6.4	6.0	5.9	5.7
Israel [2].............	3.5	3.3	3.3	3.4	2.3	1.9	1.9	1.9	4.6	4.3	4.3	4.3
Italy..................	(NA)	(NA)	3.9	3.9	4.1	2.9	2.8	(NA)	7.0	6.7	6.8	6.8
Japan................	1.9	2.2	2.3	(NA)	9.6	8.0	7.9	7.9	24.8	18.2	17.5	17.2
Korea, South.........	1.3	2.0	2.1	2.2	3.9	5.5	6.1	6.2	11.0	10.0	9.2	8.9
Mexico...............	1.6	2.0	2.1	2.2	1.7	1.6	1.5	1.6	(NA)	(NA)	(NA)	(NA)
Netherlands..........	(NA)	(NA)	(NA)	(NA)	3.1	3.3	3.3	(NA)	9.0	5.6	6.4	(NA)
New Zealand.........	2.2	2.6	2.7	2.8	(NA)	2.5	2.6	2.6	4.3	6.0	5.8	5.3
Norway...............	3.4	4.1	4.2	4.3	3.1	2.5	2.3	2.3	6.0	6.3	5.8	5.5
Poland................	2.2	2.2	2.2	2.2	5.2	4.4	4.3	4.3	(NA)	7.3	6.8	6.7
Portugal..............	(NA)	(NA)	(NA)	(NA)	3.0	2.8	[1] 2.9	2.8	7.8	7.0	[1] 7.5	7.2
Russia................	4.6	5.0	4.9	4.9	(NA)	(NA)	(NA)	(NA)	13.5	(NA)	10.2	(NA)
Slovak Republic......	3.2	(NA)	(NA)	(NA)	5.7	4.8	4.4	4.2	8.4	6.6	6.2	6.2
Slovenia..............	2.2	2.4	2.5	2.6	4.5	3.7	3.6	3.6	7.1	5.5	6.9	6.3
Spain.................	3.2	3.8	3.8	3.8	2.8	2.4	2.3	2.3	7.1	6.3	6.1	6.0
Sweden..............	3.1	3.9	4.0	(NA)	2.5	2.0	2.0	1.9	6.8	5.9	5.6	(NA)
Switzerland...........	(NA)	3.8	3.9	4.0	4.1	3.1	3.0	2.9	9.3	6.6	6.1	5.9
Turkey................	(NA)	(NA)	(NA)	(NA)	1.9	2.4	2.6	2.6	5.6	3.9	3.9	3.8
United Kingdom.......	2.0	2.7	2.8	2.8	3.2	2.4	2.3	2.3	(NA)	5.9	5.9	5.9

NA Not available. [1] Estimated. [2] The statistical data for Israel are supplied by and under the responsibility of the relevant Israeli authorities. The use of such data by the OECD is without prejudice to the status of the Golan Heights, East Jerusalem and Israeli settlements in the West Bank under the terms of international law.

Source: Organisation for Economic Co-Operation and Development (OECD), 2015, "Health care resources," OECD Health Statistics (database) ©, <http://dx.doi.org/10.1787/data-00541-en>; and "Health care utilisation," OECD Health Statistics (database) ©, <http://dx.doi.org/10.1787/data-00542-en>; accessed July 2015.

Table 1353. Gross National Income (GNI) by Country: 2010 and 2014

[For total GNI, 64,589,179 represents $64,589,179,000,000. GNI is the sum of value added by all resident producers, plus any product taxes (less subsidies) not included in the valuation of output, plus net receipts of primary income from abroad]

Country	Gross national income [1]				GNI on purchasing power parity basis [2]			
	Total (mil. dol.)		Per capita (dol.)		Total (mil. dol.)		Per capita (dol.)	
	2010	2014	2010	2014	2010	2014	2010	2014
World [3]	64,589,179	78,259,778	9,382	10,858	87,935,599	108,347,740	12,773	15,032
United States	15,143,104	17,601,119	48,950	55,200	15,121,100	17,812,700	48,880	55,860
Afghanistan	14,430	21,131	510	680	45,732	61,853	1,610	1,980
Algeria	161,207	213,374	4,350	5,340	453,105	540,564	12,230	13,540
Angola	75,262	117,412	3,850	5,300	121,025	158,392	6,190	7,150
Australia	1,024,242	1,519,375	46,490	64,680	827,666	1,007,361	37,570	42,880
Azerbaijan	48,657	72,425	5,370	7,590	132,225	161,328	14,600	16,910
Bangladesh	118,314	171,595	780	1,080	393,638	530,134	2,600	3,340
Belarus	56,862	69,525	5,990	7,340	142,934	166,766	15,060	17,610
Belgium	515,402	527,971	47,200	47,030	436,175	483,009	39,940	43,030
Brazil	1,914,233	2,375,298	9,810	11,760	2,757,357	3,212,750	14,130	15,900
Cambodia	10,672	15,614	740	1,010	33,658	47,487	2,340	3,080
Canada	1,511,465	1,836,937	44,450	51,690	1,335,670	1,542,427	39,280	43,400
Chile	183,808	264,761	10,720	14,900	289,737	383,370	16,890	21,570
China	5,752,321	10,069,180	4,300	7,380	12,305,377	17,918,963	9,200	13,130
Colombia	254,311	380,813	5,480	7,780	471,222	616,645	10,150	12,600
Congo, Dem. Rep	19,715	28,684	320	410	36,816	48,813	590	700
Costa Rica	32,262	48,140	6,910	9,750	55,218	68,627	11,820	13,900
Cote d'Ivoire	24,421	32,286	1,290	1,550	51,803	69,691	2,730	3,350
Czech Republic	201,170	(NA)	19,210	(NA)	262,030	(NA)	25,020	(NA)
Denmark	337,384	345,772	60,820	61,310	235,751	260,306	42,500	46,160
Dominican Republic	51,234	62,696	5,110	5,950	105,235	131,083	10,510	12,450
Ecuador	65,929	96,607	4,390	6,040	134,801	177,658	8,990	11,120
Egypt	196,206	273,120	2,510	3,280	795,796	919,249	10,190	11,020
Ethiopia	33,248	53,189	380	550	91,939	144,439	1,060	1,500
France	2,847,703	2,851,748	43,800	43,080	2,379,920	2,629,541	36,600	39,720
Germany	3,661,915	3,853,487	44,780	47,640	3,302,563	3,789,008	40,390	46,840
Ghana	30,412	42,928	1,250	1,620	72,257	104,694	2,980	3,960
Greece	307,655	242,002	27,580	22,090	315,733	286,303	28,310	26,130
Guatemala	39,475	54,565	2,750	3,440	93,422	115,193	6,510	7,260
Hong Kong	236,168	291,997	33,620	40,320	338,090	409,651	48,130	56,570
India	1,555,615	2,035,887	1,290	1,610	5,314,157	7,302,457	4,410	5,760
Indonesia	611,760	923,738	2,540	3,650	1,949,021	2,592,314	8,100	10,250
Iraq	136,353	219,883	4,400	6,410	378,333	502,774	12,220	14,670
Ireland	201,108	205,984	44,100	44,660	165,782	188,276	36,350	40,820
Israel	224,740	287,462	29,480	34,990	214,437	267,394	28,130	32,550
Italy	2,234,511	2,102,846	37,700	34,280	2,052,605	2,128,949	34,630	34,710
Japan	5,376,601	5,339,076	41,980	42,000	4,437,372	4,821,128	34,650	37,920
Kazakhstan	121,371	201,806	7,440	11,670	272,437	373,130	16,690	21,580
Kenya	40,444	58,086	990	1,280	99,935	131,824	2,440	2,890
Kiribati	194	237	1,980	2,280	233	268	2,390	2,580
Korea, South	1,053,302	1,365,796	21,320	27,090	1,506,812	1,745,785	30,500	34,620
Lebanon	36,653	44,547	8,440	9,880	68,245	78,143	15,720	17,330
Malaysia	230,463	321,700	8,150	10,660	546,449	720,019	19,330	23,850
Mexico	1,034,763	1,235,721	8,780	9,980	1,724,716	2,068,292	14,630	16,710
Morocco	92,298	102,804	2,870	3,020	198,178	244,656	6,160	7,180
Netherlands	885,970	863,031	53,320	51,210	748,122	803,216	45,030	47,660
Nigeria	232,964	526,467	1,460	2,950	757,525	1,013,734	4,740	5,680
Norway	432,367	529,301	88,430	103,050	290,422	338,848	59,400	65,970
Pakistan	184,123	260,332	1,060	1,410	743,098	944,874	4,290	5,100
Peru	128,542	197,216	4,390	6,410	262,828	354,275	8,980	11,510
Philippines	256,027	344,006	2,740	3,440	684,793	830,634	7,330	8,300
Poland	480,659	521,847	12,630	13,730	760,746	915,206	20,000	24,090
Portugal	242,471	221,692	22,930	21,320	274,801	291,229	25,990	28,000
Romania	170,581	186,639	8,430	9,370	323,990	378,908	16,000	19,030
Russia	1,424,980	1,930,436	9,980	13,210	2,837,390	3,609,666	19,860	24,710
Saudi Arabia	518,894	(NA)	19,040	(NA)	1,234,062	(NA)	45,270	(NA)
Serbia	42,656	41,505	5,850	5,820	84,132	86,590	11,540	12,150
Singapore	227,378	301,639	44,790	55,150	356,367	439,044	70,200	80,270
South Africa	317,112	367,019	6,240	6,800	588,671	685,677	11,590	12,700
Spain	1,496,363	(NA)	32,130	(NA)	1,485,661	(NA)	31,900	(NA)
Sri Lanka	46,760	70,166	2,260	3,400	151,313	211,947	7,330	10,270
Sudan [4]	55,350	67,278	1,210	1,740	135,153	154,396	2,960	3,980
Sweden	504,642	596,878	53,810	61,600	402,104	452,580	42,880	46,710
Thailand	286,740	363,356	4,320	5,410	798,260	937,630	12,020	13,950
Turkey	719,574	823,117	9,980	10,850	1,156,631	1,443,937	16,030	19,040
Turkmenistan	20,530	42,544	4,070	8,020	45,318	77,069	8,990	14,520
Uganda	17,417	25,570	510	660	49,567	65,663	1,460	1,690
Ukraine	137,235	152,065	2,990	3,560	347,351	366,152	7,570	8,560
United Kingdom	2,540,102	2,754,110	40,470	42,690	2,279,410	2,475,105	36,320	38,370
Uruguay	35,060	55,914	10,400	16,360	54,371	69,138	16,120	20,220
Uzbekistan	37,230	64,266	1,300	2,090	120,571	179,386	4,220	5,840
Venezuela	334,452	395,597	11,520	12,820	463,020	528,766	15,940	17,140
Vietnam	110,302	171,905	1,270	1,890	367,548	485,179	4,230	5,350
Zambia	18,278	26,396	1,380	1,760	41,681	57,938	3,150	3,860

NA Not available. [1] Gross national income calculated using the World Bank Atlas conversion factor; for details, see source. [2] For explanation of purchasing power parity (PPP), see headnote, Table 1354. [3] Includes other countries not shown separately. [4] Sudan and South Sudan became separate countries in July 2011. Data for 2014 exclude South Sudan.

Source: The World Bank, Washington, DC, "World Development Indicators" database ©, <http://data.worldbank.org/data-catalog/world-development-indicators>, accessed August 2015.

Table 1354. Real Gross Domestic Product (GDP) Per Capita and Per Employed Persons by Country: 1990 to 2013

[U.S. figures based on the System of National Income and Product Accounts (NIPA) from the Bureau of Economic Analysis. Data for all other countries are based on the 1993 or 2008 United Nations System of National Accounts (SNA). Per capita data based on total resident population. Real GDP is a macroeconomic measure of the size of an economy adjusted for price changes and inflation. Employment data include people serving in the armed forces. Real dollars are calculated based on 2013 Purchasing Power Parities (PPPs). PPPs are currency conversion rates used to convert GDP expressed in different currencies to a common value (U.S. dollars in this case). A PPP for a given country is the number of national currency units needed to buy the specific basket of goods and services that one dollar will buy in the United States. See text, this section]

Country	Real GDP per capita (2013 U.S. dollars)							Real GDP per employed person (2013 U.S. dollars)						
	1990	2000	2005	2010	2011	2012	2013	1990	2000	2005	2010	2011	2012	2013
United States..........	37,956	47,166	51,022	50,605	51,166	52,210	52,716	78,374	96,299	105,447	111,512	112,965	113,996	114,867
Canada.................	32,427	38,639	42,070	42,855	43,589	43,985	44,527	67,662	80,457	83,525	83,900	84,712	85,172	85,803
Australia..............	30,666	38,170	42,419	45,814	46,380	47,538	48,165	66,990	80,645	85,068	87,309	88,404	90,690	91,723
Japan..................	31,463	34,289	36,121	36,765	36,582	37,323	37,927	59,914	65,996	70,449	72,739	72,455	74,089	74,839
Korea, South..........	12,545	21,620	26,301	31,319	32,393	32,984	33,898	29,737	47,910	55,240	63,924	65,142	65,298	66,419
Singapore.............	28,731	42,961	47,851	58,831	60,609	60,184	61,279	59,498	83,057	98,133	99,238	100,962	98,389	100,237
Austria................	30,963	38,417	41,389	44,021	45,252	45,632	45,767	67,514	83,424	87,949	88,727	89,727	89,359	89,109
Belgium...............	30,053	36,366	38,979	41,118	41,813	41,729	41,787	77,922	90,726	94,746	95,604	95,947	95,627	95,794
Czech Republic.......	18,372	19,432	23,811	27,287	27,815	27,566	27,347	37,920	41,120	49,611	55,028	56,046	55,255	54,778
Denmark...............	30,759	38,283	40,034	39,299	39,617	39,378	39,450	59,784	74,033	78,598	77,914	78,918	78,891	79,320
Finland................	27,513	32,545	36,668	38,007	39,012	38,662	38,106	55,308	73,345	80,166	80,470	81,431	80,754	79,856
France.................	29,238	33,786	35,539	35,606	36,130	35,951	35,852	71,562	80,760	84,926	86,157	87,355	87,400	87,573
Germany[1]............	30,007	35,117	36,065	38,892	40,274	40,634	40,889	64,067	73,518	76,526	78,486	79,988	79,657	79,937
Ireland................	19,706	36,915	42,638	38,869	39,303	38,939	38,369	58,795	83,203	91,242	95,442	99,267	100,013	99,576
Italy...................	28,775	33,115	34,037	32,664	32,676	31,721	31,021	72,218	83,497	82,414	80,509	80,634	78,840	77,935
Netherlands...........	31,217	40,053	41,799	43,977	44,180	43,428	42,880	69,707	78,546	82,487	84,305	84,502	83,608	83,673
Norway................	38,183	51,875	56,569	57,706	58,215	59,818	60,008	78,665	100,449	110,563	104,190	104,052	104,989	104,392
Spain..................	23,180	29,637	32,315	31,669	31,517	30,810	30,222	66,095	73,297	73,047	77,855	79,381	81,526	83,027
Sweden................	29,967	35,524	40,215	43,236	44,432	44,782	45,437	56,379	73,710	83,244	87,229	87,756	87,966	89,264
United Kingdom.......	27,017	35,432	40,093	39,545	39,763	39,593	40,061	57,805	76,354	84,417	85,086	85,604	84,683	85,711

1 Prior to 1991, data are for the former West Germany.

Source: The Conference Board, Inc., "Total Economy Database™", September 2014 update. Reproduced with permission from The Conference Board, Inc. © 2015 The Conference Board, Inc.

Table 1355. Sectoral Contributions to Gross Value Added: 2010 and 2014

[In percent. According to the 2008 System of National Accounts (SNA) and the International Standard Industrial Classification (ISIC), Revision 4 (2008), with some exceptions, value added is estimated at basic prices and includes financial intermediation services indirectly measured (FISIM). Value added represents an industry's contribution to national GDP and is calculated as the difference between production and intermediate inputs. Value added comprises labor costs, consumption of fixed capital, indirect taxes less subsidies, and net operating surplus and mixed income]

Country	Agriculture [1] 2010	Agriculture [1] 2014	Industry [2] Total 2010	Industry [2] Total 2014	Industry [2] Manufacturing 2010	Industry [2] Manufacturing 2014	Services 2010	Services 2014
United States [3]	1.2	[4] 1.4	16.5	[4] 16.6	12.5	[4] 12.4	78.5	[4] 78.1
Australia	2.5	[4] 2.5	20.5	[4] 18.6	7.9	[4] 6.8	69.1	[4] 70.4
Austria	1.4	1.3	22.1	22.1	18.6	18.7	70.0	70.3
Belgium	0.9	0.7	18.1	16.8	15.1	14.0	75.5	76.8
Chile	3.5	3.3	32.2	27.2	11.8	12.4	57.0	61.5
China	10.1	[4] 10.0	40.0	[4] 37.0	(NA)	(NA)	43.2	[4] 46.1
Czech Republic	1.7	2.6	29.9	32.6	23.4	[4] 24.9	61.5	59.5
Denmark	1.4	1.3	18.3	18.1	12.6	13.9	75.8	76.2
Estonia	3.2	3.7	22.1	21.1	15.7	16.0	68.8	68.2
Finland	2.7	2.8	23.5	19.8	19.5	16.2	67.3	71.2
France	1.8	1.7	13.5	13.8	11.3	11.2	78.6	78.9
Germany	0.7	0.8	25.7	25.9	22.0	22.3	69.3	68.6
Greece	3.3	3.8	10.9	11.6	7.7	8.5	81.5	82.8
Hungary	3.6	4.4	26.3	26.4	21.9	23.3	66.0	64.8
Indonesia	14.3	13.7	34.6	32.8	22.6	21.6	41.8	43.3
Italy	2.0	2.2	18.7	18.5	15.8	15.5	73.7	74.4
Japan [5]	1.2	[4] 1.2	22.1	[4] 20.4	19.7	[4] 18.5	71.3	[4] 72.6
Korea	2.5	2.3	33.1	33.3	30.7	30.3	59.3	59.4
Mexico	3.3	[4] 3.3	27.1	[4] 27.1	17.4	[4] 17.7	61.5	[4] 62.2
Netherlands	1.9	2.0	16.8	16.9	11.8	12.4	76.0	76.6
Norway	1.8	1.7	33.7	32.6	8.1	7.8	59.2	59.9
Poland	3.0	3.3	24.7	25.9	17.5	19.2	64.1	63.3
Portugal	2.2	2.3	16.8	17.0	13.2	13.2	75.2	76.5
Slovak Republic	2.8	3.7	26.5	24.7	20.9	20.4	61.7	63.3
Slovenia	2.0	2.2	24.2	27.1	20.2	22.8	67.4	65.0
Spain	2.6	2.5	17.2	17.5	13.3	13.2	71.4	74.4
Sweden	1.6	1.4	23.0	19.7	18.6	16.0	69.4	73.0
Switzerland	0.7	[4] 0.7	21.2	[4] 20.6	19.2	[4] 18.7	73.0	[4] 73.6
Turkey	9.5	8.0	21.7	22.0	17.4	17.8	64.2	64.9
United Kingdom	0.7	0.6	14.7	13.5	10.2	9.4	78.7	79.6

NA Not available. [1] Includes forestry, fishing, and hunting sectors. [2] Includes energy. [3] Value added is estimated at factor cost for U.S. [4] Data is for 2013. [5] Value added is estimated approximately at market prices for Japan.

Source: Organisation for Economic Co-operation and Development (OECD), 2015, "National Accounts at a Glance," OECD National Accounts Statistics (database) ©, <http://dx.doi.org/10.1787/data-00369-en>, accessed July 2015.

Table 1356. Index of Industrial Production by Country: 2000 to 2014

[Annual averages of monthly data. Industrial production indexes generally measure output in the manufacturing, mining, electric, gas, and water utilities sectors. Minus sign (-) indicates decrease]

Country	Index (2010 = 100) 2000	2005	2009	2010	2011	2012	2013	2014	Annual percent change 2009 to 2010	2010 to 2011	2011 to 2012	2012 to 2013	2013 to 2014
United States	101.8	105.4	94.6	100.0	103.3	107.2	110.3	114.9	5.7	3.3	3.8	2.9	4.1
Australia	83.8	89.5	95.7	100.0	101.1	104.6	106.7	111.4	4.5	1.1	3.5	2.0	4.4
Austria	77.4	90.7	93.5	100.0	106.2	107.4	108.2	108.1	6.9	6.1	1.2	0.7	-0.1
Belgium	70.9	85.4	90.1	100.0	104.0	101.9	102.8	103.8	10.9	4.0	-2.1	0.9	0.9
Brazil	74.7	87.1	90.7	100.0	100.4	98.1	100.1	97.0	10.2	0.4	-2.3	2.1	-3.2
Canada	110.6	111.9	95.4	100.0	104.0	105.6	107.1	111.4	4.8	4.0	1.6	1.4	4.0
Chile	79.2	99.0	99.5	100.0	105.4	113.3	113.5	112.5	0.5	5.4	7.5	0.2	-0.9
Czech Republic	70.0	90.6	92.1	100.0	105.9	105.0	104.9	110.1	8.6	5.9	-0.8	-0.1	5.0
Denmark	110.7	116.3	98.1	100.0	101.8	101.9	102.4	103.2	2.0	1.8	0.2	0.4	0.8
Finland	91.2	100.0	94.7	100.0	101.7	99.6	96.5	94.6	5.7	1.7	-2.1	-3.1	-1.9
France	111.7	111.5	95.0	100.0	102.2	99.6	98.8	97.6	5.2	2.2	-2.6	-0.8	-1.2
Germany	89.4	95.3	89.6	100.0	108.7	108.1	108.4	110.5	11.6	8.7	-0.6	0.3	1.9
Greece	116.9	116.3	104.6	100.0	94.3	92.4	89.5	87.5	-4.4	-5.7	-2.0	-3.2	-2.2
Hungary	70.5	92.7	90.5	100.0	105.6	103.7	104.9	112.7	10.5	5.6	-1.8	1.1	7.5
India	48.8	65.8	91.1	100.0	104.8	105.5	106.2	108.1	9.7	4.8	0.7	0.6	1.8
Ireland	68.2	91.1	92.3	100.0	99.6	98.1	95.9	117.9	8.3	-0.4	-1.5	-2.2	22.9
Italy	118.0	113.0	93.5	100.0	101.3	95.0	92.1	91.6	6.9	1.3	-6.2	-3.1	-0.5
Japan	104.3	106.1	87.0	100.0	97.1	97.7	96.9	98.7	15.0	-2.9	0.7	-0.9	1.9
Korea, South	53.4	71.9	86.0	100.0	106.0	107.4	108.2	108.2	16.3	6.0	1.4	0.7	0.1
Mexico [1]	90.8	96.8	95.6	100.0	103.5	106.3	105.8	107.7	4.6	3.5	2.8	-0.5	1.8
Netherlands	89.6	93.7	93.0	100.0	99.5	99.0	99.5	96.7	7.6	-0.5	-0.5	0.5	-2.8
New Zealand	91.0	102.8	96.5	100.0	97.6	97.6	98.5	101.1	3.7	-2.4	0.0	0.9	2.6
Norway	118.6	113.5	105.9	100.0	95.0	96.7	94.1	96.1	-5.6	-5.0	1.8	-2.7	2.1
Poland	56.9	74.3	90.0	100.0	106.8	108.1	110.6	114.4	11.1	6.8	1.2	2.3	3.4
Russia	69.1	91.4	93.2	100.0	105.0	108.5	109.0	110.8	7.3	5.0	3.3	0.5	1.7
Spain	116.6	119.4	99.2	100.0	98.6	92.2	90.7	91.9	0.8	-1.4	-6.6	-1.6	1.2
Sweden	98.7	107.3	91.4	100.0	102.7	100.5	95.8	94.0	9.4	2.7	-2.2	-4.7	-1.8
Switzerland	82.4	83.7	96.0	100.0	103.6	106.3	107.1	108.6	4.1	3.6	2.6	0.8	1.4
Turkey	68.5	86.1	88.6	100.0	110.1	112.8	116.3	120.5	12.8	10.1	2.5	3.1	3.6
United Kingdom	112.6	108.2	97.0	100.0	99.2	96.5	96.0	97.6	3.1	-0.8	-2.7	-0.5	1.6

[1] Including construction.

Source: Organisation for Economic Co-operation and Development (OECD), 2015, "Key short-term indicators," Main Economic Indicators (database) ©, <http://dx.doi.org/10.1787/data-00039-en>, accessed July 2015.

Table 1357. Selected Indexes of Manufacturing Productivity, Unit Labor Costs, Employment, and Hours Worked by Country: 2000 to 2014

[2002 = 100. Data refer to all employed persons (including employees, self-employed, and unpaid family workers). Minus sign (-) indicates decrease]

Index	United States	Australia	Canada	France	Germany	Italy	Japan[1]	Netherlands	South Korea	Sweden	United Kingdom
Output per hour worked:[2]											
2000	89.6	95.5	99.5	94.2	97.7	100.1	98.0	98.3	89.7	93.5	93.5
2010	151.2	114.4	109.2	127.2	124.4	110.5	144.7	128.4	181.3	150.8	133.5
2012	146.3	116.7	112.7	135.6	129.8	113.8	145.8	133.7	187.9	150.7	134.9
2013	147.3	117.7	113.3	136.4	129.5	115.0	150.5	135.5	193.3	154.7	133.6
2014	149.4	117.5	117.8	138.8	130.3	113.3	153.3	139.8	193.7	155.2	136.3
Average annual percent change:											
2000-2009	5.6	1.5	1.3	3.2	1.7	0.3	3.1	3.1	7.4	3.8	3.7
2010-2014	0.8	1.3	2.3	2.9	4.0	2.7	4.2	3.0	2.8	4.4	1.4
2013-2014	1.4	-0.2	4.0	1.8	0.6	-1.5	1.9	3.2	0.2	0.3	2.1
Hourly labor cost, national currency basis:[3, 4]											
2000	94.0	92.1	93.6	91.7	96.4	93.8	99.6	93.0	85.9	90.5	90.7
2010	129.8	141.3	126.5	129.1	117.7	130.6	97.0	124.4	193.9	127.5	147.1
2012	134.4	153.1	135.3	136.7	122.9	137.6	99.0	130.1	208.6	139.1	156.6
2013	135.2	156.5	138.1	139.1	126.5	140.7	100.2	134.9	214.9	142.2	161.4
2014	137.8	163.8	141.8	141.8	128.7	143.0	102.7	139.6	215.4	144.9	166.2
Average annual percent change:											
2000-2009	3.9	4.3	3.6	3.6	2.4	3.3	-0.2	4.1	8.5	4.1	5.2
2010-2014	1.5	3.2	2.2	2.7	1.9	2.5	0.9	1.4	3.2	2.2	3.0
2013-2014	1.9	4.6	2.7	1.9	1.7	1.6	2.5	3.4	0.2	1.9	3.0
Real hourly compensation, CPI deflated, national currency basis:											
2000	98.2	98.9	98.1	95.1	99.7	98.8	97.9	100.1	92.4	94.7	93.9
2010	107.1	112.9	108.0	112.1	104.3	111.0	97.9	109.6	154.9	117.7	115.9
2012	105.3	116.2	110.5	113.8	104.6	110.4	100.2	109.4	156.3	124.1	113.7
2013	104.4	115.7	111.8	114.3	106.0	111.5	101.2	110.6	158.5	127.2	113.7
2014	104.7	118.1	112.6	116.0	106.9	113.2	100.9	113.3	156.6	129.9	114.4
Average annual percent change:											
2000-2009	1.3	1.1	1.4	1.7	0.8	1.0	0.1	2.0	5.4	3.0	2.6
2010-2014	-0.5	0.6	0.4	1.2	0.4	0.7	0.5	-0.5	0.8	1.4	-0.6
2013-2014	0.3	2.1	0.7	1.4	0.9	1.5	-0.3	2.4	-1.3	2.1	0.6
Unit labor costs, national currency basis:[3]											
2000	104.9	96.5	94.0	97.4	98.7	93.7	101.5	94.6	95.8	96.8	97.1
2010	85.9	123.5	115.9	101.5	94.6	118.3	67.0	96.9	106.9	84.5	110.2
2012	91.9	131.2	120.0	100.9	94.7	120.8	67.9	97.3	111.0	92.3	116.1
2013	91.8	133.0	121.9	102.0	97.7	122.3	66.6	99.6	111.2	91.9	120.8
2014	92.2	139.4	120.4	102.2	98.8	126.2	67.0	99.8	111.2	93.3	121.9
Average annual percent change:											
2000-2009	-1.6	2.7	2.3	0.4	0.7	2.9	-3.2	1.0	1.0	0.3	1.4
2010-2014	0.7	1.9	0.0	-0.2	-2.0	-0.2	-3.2	-1.6	0.5	-2.1	1.6
2013-2014	0.5	4.8	-1.2	0.2	1.1	3.1	0.6	0.3	0.0	1.6	0.9
Output per employed person:[2]											
2000	91.3	95.4	99.9	97.9	98.9	101.2	98.6	99.0	92.0	95.8	94.5
2010	154.0	111.8	106.1	127.5	121.3	103.3	143.4	127.5	169.6	154.2	134.2
2012	150.6	113.9	110.3	135.7	126.5	104.5	145.7	133.8	170.1	151.0	135.3
2013	152.0	114.5	110.8	136.6	126.6	105.9	149.4	135.3	174.1	154.2	136.6
2014	154.8	111.8	115.1	138.8	128.8	105.5	153.0	139.8	174.9	154.5	138.8
Average annual percent change:											
2000-2009	5.2	1.1	0.7	2.4	0.7	-0.6	2.6	2.6	6.1	3.5	3.4
2010-2014	1.7	1.0	2.6	3.1	5.1	2.9	5.4	3.5	2.3	4.6	2.2
2013-2014	1.9	-2.3	3.8	1.7	1.8	-0.4	2.4	3.3	0.5	0.2	1.7
All employed persons:											
2000	113.0	100.6	103.5	101.2	101.8	99.6	106.9	102.5	96.3	100.8	110.4
2010	76.0	92.7	80.6	81.1	92.9	90.7	88.7	86.3	98.5	82.9	71.6
2012	78.5	89.8	81.5	79.8	96.6	88.3	87.0	84.6	107.1	82.4	71.3
2013	78.9	87.3	80.8	78.6	96.8	85.4	85.0	83.3	108.1	80.2	70.6
2014	80.0	87.7	80.0	77.5	97.2	85.4	84.7	82.2	111.8	79.0	71.1
Average annual percent change:											
2000-2009	-3.6	-0.2	-2.1	-1.7	-0.6	-0.6	-1.9	-1.4	0.7	-1.7	-4.3
2010-2014	0.5	-1.5	-0.2	-1.8	0.5	-2.0	-1.3	-1.5	3.5	-1.3	-0.7
2013-2014	1.4	0.4	-0.9	-1.4	0.4	0.0	-0.4	-1.3	3.5	-1.5	0.6
Hours worked of all employed persons:											
2000	115.1	100.5	103.9	105.2	103.1	100.7	107.5	103.3	98.8	103.3	111.5
2010	77.4	90.6	78.4	81.3	90.6	84.9	87.9	85.7	92.1	84.8	72.0
2012	80.8	87.6	79.7	79.9	94.1	81.1	87.0	84.6	96.9	82.5	71.6
2013	81.4	84.9	79.0	78.8	94.6	78.6	84.4	83.2	97.3	79.9	72.2
2014	82.9	83.5	78.2	77.6	96.1	79.4	84.5	82.1	101.0	78.6	72.4
Average annual percent change:											
2000-2009	-4.0	-0.7	-2.6	-2.5	-1.5	-1.6	-2.3	-1.9	-0.5	-2.0	-4.6
2010-2014	1.4	-1.7	0.2	-1.5	1.6	-1.8	-0.2	-1.1	3.0	-1.2	0.0
2013-2014	1.9	-1.7	-1.1	-1.5	1.6	1.1	0.1	-1.2	3.7	-1.7	0.2

[1] Data for all countries (except Japan) are prepared according to the System of National Accounts (SNA) 2008 or its European counterpart, the European System of Accounts 2010 (ESA 2010). Data for Japan are based on SNA 1993. [2] Output is defined as value added. [3] "Compensation" data are used as a proxy for "Labor Cost" when payroll tax and subsidies data are not available to adjust worker compensation to an employer labor cost basis. [4] To clarify the concepts that are represented in the data series, "Hourly compensation" was renamed to "Hourly labor cost." The underlying calculation methodology and adjustments to the series for comparability have not changed.

Source: The Conference Board, Inc., International Labor Comparisons program, "International Comparisons of Manufacturing Productivity and Unit Labor Cost Trends 2014, Summary and Time Series Tables," May 2015, <https://www.conference-board.org/ilcprogram>. Reproduced with permission from The Conference Board, Inc. © 2015 The Conference Board, Inc.

Table 1358. Indexes of Hourly Compensation Costs for Employees in Manufacturing by Country: 2000 to 2013

[United States = 100. Compensation costs include pay for time worked (base wages and salaries, overtime pay, bonuses and premiums paid each pay period, and cost of living adjustments), directly-paid benefits (pay for leave time, irregular bonuses, and pay in kind), employer social insurance expenditures (legally required, private, and contractual social benefit costs), and labor-related taxes (minus subsidies). Data are adjusted for exchange rates. Regional averages are trade-weighted to account for differences in countries' relative importance to U.S. trade in manufactured goods. See source for detail]

Area or country	2000	2010	2011	2012	2013	Area or country	2000	2010	2011	2012	2013
United States.........	**100**	**100**	**100**	**100**	**100**	Hungary...............	12	24	26	25	26
Total [1]................	**63**	**78**	**83**	**81**	**80**	Ireland.[1]............	66	117	120	114	116
OECD [2]................	66	83	87	86	85	Israel.................	49	55	60	57	61
Europe................	85	113	119	115	118	Italy..................	67	97	103	97	102
Euro Area [3]...........	86	117	123	117	122	Japan [6].............	100	91	100	99	80
Eastern Europe [4]......	13	27	29	28	29	Mexico................	19	18	18	18	19
East Asia ex-Japan [5]..	35	41	45	47	48	Netherlands...........	84	114	118	111	116
Argentina [6]............	33	37	45	53	55	New Zealand.........	36	59	66	70	71
Australia...............	66	114	131	134	130	Norway...............	98	165	182	177	181
Austria.................	88	115	122	118	122	Philippines............	4	5	6	6	6
Belgium................	105	146	155	146	151	Poland................	14	24	26	24	25
Brazil..................	17	29	33	30	29	Portugal...............	24	35	37	35	35
Canada................	73	99	102	103	100	Singapore.............	47	56	65	68	66
Czech Republic........	14	33	36	33	33	Slovakia...............	10	31	33	32	34
Denmark...............	89	140	148	138	141	South Korea..........	39	51	54	57	60
Estonia................	10	27	29	29	32	Spain.................	50	77	80	75	77
Finland................	79	116	124	118	123	Sweden..............	94	123	135	135	141
France.................	85	112	120	114	118	Switzerland...........	108	147	170	172	174
Germany...............	102	127	134	129	135	Taiwan [6]............	29	24	26	26	26
Greece................	40	64	64	54	52	United Kingdom......	83	83	86	87	85

[1] Trade-weighted average for all 33 foreign economies listed. [2] Organisation for Economic Co-operation and Development; see text, this section. [3] Euro Area includes Austria, Belgium, Estonia, Finland, France, Germany, Greece, Ireland, Italy, the Netherlands, Portugal, Slovakia and Spain. [4] Czech Republic, Estonia, Hungary, Poland, and Slovakia. [5] South Korea, Philippines, Singapore, and Taiwan. Excludes Japan. [6] Except for Argentina, Japan and Taiwan, data relate to manufacturing as defined by the International Standard Industrial Classification of All Economic Activities (ISIC) Revision 4.

Source: The Conference Board, Inc., International Labor Comparisons program, "International Comparisons of Hourly Compensation Costs in Manufacturing, 2013," December 2014, <https://www.conference-board.org/ilcprogram/compensation>. Reproduced with permission from The Conference Board, Inc. © 2015 The Conference Board, Inc.

Table 1359. Annual Percent Change in Labor Productivity and Hours Worked by Country: 1996 to 2014

[Annual percent change for period shown. Labor productivity growth refers to the growth in gross domestic product (GDP) per hour worked. Data are derived from The Conference Board Total Economy Database. Regional labor productivity growth rates are aggregated using shares in nominal PPP converted GDP; regional hours growth is weighted using total hours shares. Growth rates are the averages of yearly growth rates. Minus sign (-) indicates decrease]

Country	Labor productivity		Total hours worked		Country	Labor productivity		Total hours worked	
	1996-2005	2006-2014	1996-2005	2006-2014		1996-2005	2006-2014	1996-2005	2006-2014
Advanced economies [1].......	2.2	1.1	0.5	0.2	Czech Republic.......	3.5	3.4	-0.6	-0.7
United States.......	**2.5**	**2.5**	**0.9**	**0.9**	Estonia.................	6.7	6.5	0.2	0.5
Japan...............	1.9	1.9	-0.9	-1.0	Hungary...............	3.3	3.6	0.3	0.4
					Latvia.................	5.5	5.6	1.1	1.4
European Union (EU-15, old) [2]......	1.5	0.6	0.8	-(Z)	Lithuania..............	5.8	5.9	0.4	0.4
Austria................	1.7	1.9	0.7	0.5	Malta.................	3.5	3.6	0.1	-0.1
Belgium..............	1.5	1.3	0.9	1.1	Poland................	4.3	4.3	-0.1	-0.3
Denmark.............	1.3	1.2	0.8	0.9	Romania..............	4.9	4.9	-2.1	-2.2
Finland...............	2.6	2.7	1.2	1.1	Slovakia...............	4.7	4.5	-0.5	-0.6
France...............	1.8	1.9	0.5	0.4	Slovenia..............	4.2	3.9	-0.3	0.1
Germany..............	1.7	1.7	-0.4	-0.4	European Union (EU-28, enlarged) [5]...	1.8	0.8	0.5	-(Z)
Greece..............	2.5	2.4	1.2	1.5	Addenda:				
Ireland...............	3.8	3.7	3.3	3.2	Other advanced economies [1]..........	2.9	2.1	0.8	0.8
Italy.................	0.6	0.6	0.9	0.9	Australia...............	2.2	2.1	1.5	1.5
Luxembourg.........	1.6	1.7	3.0	3.2	Canada...............	1.5	1.7	1.7	1.7
Netherlands........	1.6	1.7	1.1	0.8	Hong Kong............	1.7	2.2	1.7	1.1
Portugal..............	1.4	1.3	1.1	1.0	Iceland................	3.6	3.7	1.2	1.2
Spain................	0.2	0.1	3.6	3.8	Israel..................	1.5	1.5	2.2	1.9
Sweden.............	2.8	2.9	0.3	0.3	New Zealand.........	1.2	1.2	2.3	2.2
United Kingdom....	2.2	2.3	0.8	0.8	Norway...............	2.3	2.1	0.6	0.5
European Union (EU-13, new) [3]....	3.9	2.4	-0.5	(Z)	Singapore.............	3.4	3.5	1.8	1.5
Bulgaria.............	2.2	3.9	-0.4	-0.7	South Korea..........	5.0	5.0	-(Z)	-0.2
Croatia [4]...........	3.9	3.7	0.1	0.1	Switzerland...........	1.5	1.4	0.4	0.6
Cyprus...............	1.8	1.9	1.9	2.0	Taiwan................	4.1	3.9	0.3	0.3

Z Less than 0.05 percent. [1] "Advanced" includes the U.S., EU-15, Japan, and "other advanced" economies. [2] Referring to membership of the European Union until 30 April 2004. [3] Referring to membership of the European Union as of 1 January 2007. [4] Referring to labor productivity based on persons engaged, not hours worked. [5] Referring to all 28 current members of the European Union.

Source: The Conference Board, Inc., "Total Economy Database™," May 2015. Reproduced with permission from The Conference Board, Inc. © 2015 The Conference Board, Inc.

Table 1360. Comparative Price Levels—Selected OECD Countries: May 2015

[Purchasing power parities (PPPs) are rates of currency conversion that eliminate the differences in price levels between countries. Comparative price levels are defined as the ratios of PPPs to exchange rates. The PPPs are given in national currency units per U.S. dollar. Each column shows the number of specified monetary units needed in each of the countries listed to buy the same representative basket of consumer goods and services. In each case the representative basket costs a hundred units in the country whose currency is specified. For example, in May 2015, an item that costs $1.00 in the United States would cost $0.95 (U.S. dollars) in Japan]

Country	United States (USD)	Australia (AUD)	Canada (CAD)	Chile (Chilean peso)	France (EUR)	Germany (EUR)	Italy (EUR)	Japan (JPY)	Korea (KRW)	Mexico (MXN)	Spain (EUR)	Turkey (TRY)	United Kingdom (GBP)
United States	100	81	93	145	102	109	109	106	119	157	121	173	82
Australia [1]	123	100	115	179	125	134	134	130	147	194	149	214	102
Austria	98	79	91	142	99	106	106	103	117	153	118	169	81
Belgium	99	80	92	144	101	108	108	105	118	156	119	171	82
Canada	107	87	100	156	109	117	117	114	128	169	130	186	89
Chile	69	56	64	100	70	75	75	73	82	108	83	119	57
Czech Republic	58	47	54	85	59	64	64	62	70	92	70	101	48
Denmark	125	101	116	182	127	136	136	132	149	196	151	216	103
Estonia	69	56	65	101	71	76	76	73	83	109	84	120	57
Finland	110	89	102	160	112	120	120	116	131	173	133	191	91
France	98	80	91	143	100	107	107	104	117	154	118	170	81
Germany	92	74	85	134	93	100	100	97	110	144	111	159	76
Greece	77	62	71	112	78	84	84	81	92	121	93	133	63
Hungary	52	42	48	75	52	56	56	55	62	81	62	89	43
Iceland	111	90	104	162	113	121	121	118	133	175	134	193	92
Ireland	107	86	99	155	108	116	116	113	127	168	128	185	88
Israel [2]	110	89	102	160	112	120	120	116	132	173	133	191	91
Italy	92	74	85	133	93	100	100	97	110	144	111	159	76
Japan	95	77	88	138	96	103	103	100	113	149	114	164	78
Korea, South	84	68	78	122	85	91	91	89	100	132	101	145	69
Luxembourg	109	89	102	159	111	119	119	115	130	172	132	189	90
Mexico	64	52	59	93	65	69	69	67	76	100	77	110	52
Netherlands	101	82	94	146	102	110	110	106	120	158	121	174	83
New Zealand [1]	114	93	106	166	116	125	125	121	137	180	138	198	94
Norway	134	109	125	196	137	146	146	142	160	211	162	233	111
Poland	51	41	47	74	52	55	55	54	61	80	61	88	42
Portugal	73	59	68	106	74	79	79	77	87	114	88	126	60
Slovak Republic	62	50	57	90	63	67	67	65	73	97	74	107	51
Slovenia	74	60	69	108	75	81	81	78	88	116	89	128	61
Spain	83	67	77	121	84	90	90	88	99	130	100	144	68
Sweden	108	88	101	158	110	118	118	115	130	170	131	188	89
Switzerland	161	130	150	234	164	175	175	170	192	253	194	279	133
Turkey	58	47	54	84	59	63	63	61	69	91	70	100	48
United Kingdom	121	98	113	176	123	132	132	128	145	191	146	210	100

[1] Estimates based on quarterly consumer prices. [2] The statistical data for Israel are supplied by and under the responsibility of the relevant Israeli authorities. The use of such data by the OECD is without prejudice to the status of the Golan Heights, East Jerusalem and Israeli settlements in the West Bank under the terms of international law.

Source: Organisation for Economic Co-operation and Development (OECD), 2015 "Prices: Comparative Price Levels," Main Economic Indicators (database) ©, <http://dx.doi.org/10.1787/data-00536-en>, accessed June 2015.

Table 1361. Indexes of Living Costs Abroad: 2015

[As of January 2015. Washington, DC=100. Indexes compare the costs in dollars of representative goods and services (excluding housing and education) purchased at the foreign location and the cost of comparable goods and services in the Washington, DC area. The indexes are place-to-place comparisons at specific times and currency exchange rates. They cannot be used for measuring cost changes over time at a foreign location. Since the indexes reflect only the expenditure pattern and living costs of American families, they are not comparable to the living costs of foreign nationals living in their own country. Survey dates show month/day/year]

Country/Territory	City	Survey date	Local index [1]	Country/Territory	City	Survey date	Local index [1]
Algeria	Algiers	3/16/2013	112	Kyrgyzstan	Bishkek	7/30/2013	133
Angola	Luanda	6/29/2013	206	Laos	Vientiane	6/6/2013	132
Argentina	Buenos Aires	1/16/2013	152	Latvia	Riga	5/8/2013	130
Armenia	Yerevan	3/14/2010	113	Lebanon	Beirut	6/24/2012	119
Australia	Canberra	5/9/2013	182	Liberia	Monrovia	8/8/2012	143
Austria	Vienna	12/3/2013	176	Libya	Tripoli	1/5/2007	116
Azerbaijan	Baku	3/31/2013	155	Lithuania	Vilnius	7/22/2012	129
Bahrain	(X)	12/8/2013	132	Luxembourg	(X)	1/24/2011	164
Bangladesh	Dhaka	2/4/2013	78	Macedonia	Skopje	4/11/2010	125
Belarus	Minsk	9/26/2013	111	Madagascar	Antananarivo	6/26/2013	153
Belgium	Brussels	3/18/2011	173	Malawi	Lilongwe	3/12/2014	132
Bermuda	(X)	5/16/2012	176	Malaysia	Kuala Lumpur	11/21/2010	133
Bolivia	La Paz	7/21/2011	120	Mali	Bamako	2/12/2014	154
Bosnia-Herzegovina	Sarajevo	4/4/2012	125	Mauritania	Nouakchott	10/17/2012	137
Botswana	Gaborone	3/11/2012	145	Mexico	Mexico City	9/27/2012	122
Brazil	Sao Paulo	6/5/2014	155	Moldova	Chisinau	5/1/2012	122
Bulgaria	Sofia	6/4/2012	126	Mongolia	Ulaanbaatar	6/2/2011	139
Burma	Rangoon	10/9/2013	112	Montenegro	Podgorica	8/7/2012	123
Burundi	Bujumbura	5/20/2012	146	Morocco	Casablanca	2/11/2014	151
Cambodia	Phnom Penh	3/4/2013	128	Mozambique	Maputo	1/26/2012	155
Cameroon	Yaounde	7/31/2012	154	Nepal	Kathmandu	9/22/2009	103
Canada	Ottawa	10/19/2012	158	Netherlands	The Hague	11/28/2011	155
Chad	Ndjamena	1/30/2012	163	New Zealand	Wellington	9/27/2010	159
Chile	Santiago	4/5/2013	158	Nicaragua	Managua	8/11/2014	115
China	Beijing	3/20/2013	156	Niger	Niamey	11/28/2012	135
Colombia	Bogota	7/31/2012	149	Nigeria	Abuja	10/6/2013	163
Costa Rica	San Jose	6/3/2013	149	Norway	Oslo	12/3/2012	190
Cote d'Ivoire	Abidjan	3/11/2013	151	Oman	Muscat	5/17/2010	131
Croatia	Zagreb	4/16/2014	133	Pakistan	Islamabad	12/10/2004	102
Cuba	Havana	4/22/2012	131	Panama	Panama City	6/11/2013	122
Cyprus	Nicosia	1/30/2012	155	Papua New Guinea	Port Moresby	12/5/2013	145
Czech Republic	Prague	7/12/2012	140	Paraguay	Asuncion	5/6/2013	120
Dem. Rep. of Congo	Kinshasa	2/16/2012	194	Peru	Lima	3/8/2012	150
Denmark	Copenhagen	12/10/2012	187	Philippines	Manila	9/16/2012	120
Djibouti	Djibouti City	2/11/2014	155	Poland	Warsaw	7/31/2012	131
Dominican Republic	Santo Domingo	11/5/2012	125	Portugal	Lisbon	2/13/2011	154
Ecuador	Quito	12/3/2013	148	Qatar	Doha	12/8/2012	132
Egypt	Cairo	3/13/2006	96	Romania	Bucharest	6/14/2012	116
El Salvador	San Salvador	4/21/2014	137	Russia	Moscow	5/8/2011	206
Equatorial Guinea	Malabo	2/18/2010	177	Rwanda	Kigali	2/26/2013	155
Estonia	Tallinn	1/9/2012	137	Saudi Arabia	Riyadh	4/9/2010	122
Ethiopia	Addis Ababa	4/2/2013	122	Senegal	Dakar	4/18/2012	150
Fiji	Suva	6/16/2010	125	Serbia	Belgrade	10/27/2013	120
Finland	Helsinki	4/14/2009	171	Sierra Leone	Freetown	5/14/2014	155
France	Paris	4/29/2012	174	Singapore	(X)	12/11/2013	152
Gabon	Libreville	8/7/2011	165	Slovakia	Bratislava	6/17/2012	135
Georgia	Tbilisi	4/14/2009	140	South Africa	Johannesburg	9/30/2010	143
Germany	Berlin	12/6/2012	171	Spain	Madrid	4/23/2012	147
Ghana	Accra	5/16/2012	163	Sri Lanka	Colombo	3/30/2012	136
Greece	Athens	10/22/2013	150	Sudan	Khartoum	12/14/2013	168
Guatemala	Guatemala City	2/10/2014	125	Sweden	Stockholm	5/13/2010	185
Guyana	Georgetown	4/13/2012	155	Switzerland	Geneva	11/15/2010	217
Haiti	Port-au-Prince	9/24/2012	145	Syria	Damascus	10/13/2010	116
Honduras	Tegucigalpa	7/18/2012	114	Taiwan	Taipei	9/2/2013	140
Hong Kong	(X)	6/8/2014	147	Tajikistan	Dushanbe	10/28/2012	111
Hungary	Budapest	6/10/2012	126	Tanzania	Dar es Salaam	5/8/2012	130
Iceland	Reykjavik	6/27/2012	150	Thailand	Bangkok	10/31/2012	128
India	New Delhi	12/11/2012	122	Tunisia	Tunis	1/9/2014	121
Indonesia	Jakarta	9/16/2013	122	Turkey	Istanbul	4/11/2011	135
Iraq	Baghdad	7/21/2004	74	Uganda	Kampala	9/23/2012	137
Ireland	Dublin	7/7/2010	164	Ukraine	Kyiv	3/11/2013	127
Israel	Tel Aviv	6/8/2010	146	United Arab Emirates	Dubai	3/2/2014	130
Italy	Rome	2/5/2012	171	United Kingdom	London	3/19/2012	208
Jamaica	Kingston	10/8/2014	129	Uruguay	Montevideo	1/29/2014	157
Japan	Tokyo City	5/12/2011	213	Uzbekistan	Tashkent	7/4/2012	135
Jordan	Amman	3/12/2013	140	Venezuela	Caracas	12/11/2011	175
Kazakhstan	Astana	5/9/2014	146	Vietnam	Hanoi	5/27/2014	117
Kenya	Nairobi	8/15/2011	155	Yemen	Sanaa	4/25/2009	92
Korea, South	Seoul	11/18/2013	210	Zambia	Lusaka	6/15/2014	143
Kuwait	Kuwait City	5/22/2012	116	Zimbabwe	Harare	6/2/2010	156

X Not applicable. [1] The local index measures living costs for private American citizens and excludes special price advantages available only to U.S. government employees. The local index is a comparison of prices at the foreign post and in Washington, DC, with the price ratios weighted by the expenditure pattern of American employees living at the foreign post. This is the index most appropriate for use by business firms and other private organizations to establish cost-of-living allowances for their American employees stationed abroad.

Source: U.S. Department of State, Bureau of Administration, "Indexes of Living Costs Abroad, Quarters Allowances, and Hardship Differentials," January 2015, <http://aoprals.state.gov/content.asp?content_id=186&menu_id=81>.

Table 1362. Consumer Expenditures Spent on Food, Alcohol, and Tobacco Consumed at Home by Selected Country: 2013

Country/Territory	Food [1]	Alcoholic beverages and tobacco	Country/Territory	Food [1]	Alcoholic beverages and tobacco	Country/Territory	Food [1]	Alcoholic beverages and tobacco
United States	6.7	2.1	Georgia	33.2	5.2	Peru	36.5	6.0
Algeria	42.6	2.2	Germany	12.0	3.2	Philippines	42.4	1.2
Argentina	20.7	4.5	Greece	16.6	4.4	Poland	17.7	6.0
Australia	10.0	3.5	Guatemala	40.1	1.7	Portugal	18.6	3.1
Austria	9.9	3.5	Hong Kong	14.3	1.9	Qatar	12.0	0.3
Azerbaijan	45.3	1.6	Hungary	16.8	7.4	Romania	28.3	3.5
Bahrain	13.7	0.4	India	29.6	2.8	Russia	30.5	8.3
Belarus	37.3	7.7	Indonesia	33.2	5.4	Saudi Arabia	25.5	0.6
Belgium	13.8	3.5	Iran	25.0	0.4	Serbia	27.4	5.9
Bolivia	28.7	1.9	Ireland	10.4	5.9	Singapore	6.7	2.0
Bosnia-Herzegovina	31.3	6.3	Israel	15.2	2.5	Slovakia	17.8	5.0
Brazil	15.7	2.3	Italy	14.1	2.8	Slovenia	15.2	5.2
Bulgaria	17.6	6.2	Japan	13.6	2.6	South Africa	19.2	6.0
Cameroon	45.8	2.1	Jordan	37.5	6.2	South Korea	13.4	2.1
Canada	9.5	3.5	Kazakhstan	43.5	1.3	Spain	13.8	3.0
Chile	15.6	3.0	Kenya	46.9	3.5	Sweden	12.2	3.6
China	26.1	3.6	Kuwait	18.5	0.5	Switzerland	8.9	3.7
Colombia	17.9	3.0	Latvia	18.8	8.1	Taiwan	13.6	2.1
Costa Rica	20.2	0.9	Lithuania	23.7	7.4	Thailand	28.0	3.5
Croatia	31.1	3.7	Macedonia	34.2	3.4	Tunisia	22.7	3.3
Czech Republic	16.1	9.9	Malaysia	20.7	1.8	Turkey	22.0	4.9
Denmark	11.2	3.6	Mexico	25.1	2.2	Turkmenistan	38.8	2.2
Dominican Republic	24.1	4.2	Montenegro	20.5	3.6	Ukraine	38.6	7.8
Ecuador	23.1	0.8	Morocco	35.8	3.8	United Arab Emirates	14.1	0.2
Egypt	37.4	4.0	Netherlands	11.8	3.1	United Kingdom	9.3	3.5
Estonia	19.6	9.0	New Zealand	15.4	5.5	Uruguay	18.4	1.2
Finland	12.5	4.8	Nigeria	56.7	1.4	Uzbekistan	30.8	2.5
France	13.8	3.3	Norway	13.0	4.3	Venezuela	19.9	3.6
			Pakistan	48.1	0.9	Vietnam	35.5	2.8

[1] Includes nonalcoholic beverages.

Source: U.S. Department of Agriculture, Economic Research Service, Food Expenditure Series, "Expenditures on food and alcoholic beverages that were consumed at home by selected countries," <http://www.ers.usda.gov/data-products/food-expenditures.aspx>, accessed March 2015.

Table 1363. Gross Public Debt, Expenditures, and Receipts as Percent of GDP by Country: 2000 to 2016

[Percent of nominal gross domestic product. Gross debt, expenditures, and receipts refer to the general government sector, which is a consolidation of accounts for the central, state, and local governments plus social security. Expenditures, or total outlays, are defined as current outlays plus capital outlays. Receipts cover current receipts, but exclude capital receipts. Nontax receipts consist of property income (including dividends and other transfers from public enterprises), fees, charges, sales, fines, and capital transfers received by the general government, etc.]

Country	Gross debt 2000	Gross debt 2010	Gross debt 2016 [1]	Expenditures 2000	Expenditures 2010	Expenditures 2016 [1]	Receipts 2000	Receipts 2010	Receipts 2016 [1]
United States [2]	48.1	101.8	111.1	33.9	42.8	37.2	34.6	30.7	33.7
Australia	27.2	30.0	46.8	34.6	36.7	35.7	36.1	32.0	34.2
Austria	70.4	90.8	97.8	50.3	52.9	51.2	48.2	48.4	49.1
Belgium	120.6	107.4	128.9	48.7	52.3	52.1	48.6	48.4	50.5
Canada	84.2	89.5	95.5	40.5	43.3	39.1	43.4	38.3	38.0
Czech Republic	24.0	46.3	55.0	40.3	43.0	41.4	36.8	38.6	40.1
Denmark	60.5	53.8	55.0	52.7	57.1	56.9	54.6	54.3	54.3
Estonia	6.8	11.9	11.4	36.4	40.5	38.3	36.3	40.7	38.8
Finland	50.9	55.9	76.2	48.0	54.8	59.1	54.9	52.1	56.1
France	72.0	97.1	122.8	51.1	56.5	56.0	49.8	49.7	52.8
Germany	59.7	84.2	74.9	44.7	47.3	43.2	45.7	43.2	44.3
Greece	111.1	128.7	187.6	45.6	52.0	49.0	41.8	41.0	46.2
Hungary	61.3	86.6	98.3	47.1	49.5	48.3	44.1	45.0	46.0
Iceland	40.4	90.8	79.0	40.7	48.8	41.3	42.3	39.3	41.8
Ireland	38.5	83.7	111.4	31.1	66.2	35.9	36.0	33.6	34.0
Israel [3]	80.1	71.1	63.7	48.0	41.3	39.8	44.7	37.3	37.3
Italy	118.8	126.0	158.4	45.4	49.9	49.6	44.1	45.6	47.6
Japan	136.1	193.2	231.7	38.7	40.7	40.7	31.2	32.4	34.9
Korea	(NA)	31.8	35.5	24.7	31.0	32.1	29.1	32.0	33.1
Luxembourg	8.8	26.4	34.7	36.4	44.0	43.8	42.1	43.5	44.2
Netherlands	60.1	67.7	81.2	41.7	48.3	44.3	43.6	43.2	43.1
New Zealand	36.2	37.3	34.7	37.5	47.8	39.0	39.2	41.1	41.3
Norway	32.2	48.4	35.4	42.0	45.0	48.0	57.1	56.0	54.3
Poland	45.2	61.0	66.7	(NA)	45.9	41.1	(NA)	38.2	38.8
Portugal	62.0	104.1	144.5	42.6	51.8	47.7	39.4	40.6	45.0
Slovak Republic	57.9	46.9	59.9	51.8	42.0	41.0	39.7	34.5	38.7
Slovenia	(NA)	46.6	101.8	46.1	49.3	46.9	42.5	43.7	44.4
Spain	65.2	66.7	117.2	39.1	45.6	40.6	38.1	36.2	37.6
Sweden	56.9	44.4	51.2	53.6	52.1	51.8	56.8	52.1	51.3
Switzerland	52.7	44.9	44.7	34.2	32.9	33.5	33.7	33.3	33.7
United Kingdom	49.5	87.3	113.1	33.6	48.3	41.8	39.1	38.6	39.3

NA Not available. [1] Projection. [2] Receipts exclude the operating surpluses of public enterprises, while expenditures include them. [3] See footnote 2, Table 1360.

Source: Organisation for Economic Co-operation and Development (OECD), 2015, "OECD Economic Outlook No. 97 (Edition 2015/1)," OECD Economic Outlook: Statistics and Projections (database) ©, <http://dx.doi.org/10.1787/data-00759-en>, accessed July 2015.

Table 1364. Percent Distribution of Tax Receipts by Country and Tax Type: 2010 to 2013

Country	Total [1]	Income and profits taxes [2]			Social security contributions			Taxes on goods and services [5]		
		Total [3]	Individual	Corporate	Total [4]	Employees	Employers	Total [3]	General consumption taxes [6]	Taxes on specific goods, services [7]
United States:										
2010.............	100.0	42.9	33.2	9.8	25.9	11.5	13.0	18.2	8.3	7.0
2013 [8].............	100.0	47.6	38.6	9.0	24.2	10.7	12.3	17.1	7.7	6.7
Australia:										
2010.............	100.0	56.8	38.5	18.3	0.0	0.0	0.0	28.7	13.7	11.9
2012.............	100.0	58.1	39.2	18.9	0.0	0.0	0.0	28.1	12.4	11.0
Canada:										
2010.............	100.0	46.6	34.9	10.6	15.3	6.1	8.7	24.4	14.0	8.8
2013 [8].............	100.0	47.1	36.8	9.0	15.9	6.4	9.0	24.3	14.5	8.2
Chile:										
2010.............	100.0	38.4	(NA)	(NA)	6.9	6.6	0.3	51.3	38.7	9.8
2013 [8].............	100.0	35.8	(NA)	(NA)	7.1	6.9	0.2	53.1	40.2	9.7
Czech Republic:										
2010.............	100.0	20.2	10.2	10.0	44.8	9.1	28.2	33.2	20.5	10.8
2013 [8].............	100.0	20.6	10.7	9.9	43.3	8.9	27.5	34.3	21.8	10.8
France:										
2010.............	100.0	21.9	16.9	5.0	38.7	9.4	26.3	25.1	16.9	7.5
2013 [8].............	100.0	24.2	18.5	5.7	37.2	9.2	25.1	24.1	15.7	7.7
Germany:										
2010.............	100.0	28.6	24.2	4.3	39.2	17.2	18.5	29.4	20.0	8.4
2013 [8].............	100.0	31.0	26.0	5.0	38.1	16.9	17.9	27.9	19.2	7.8
Greece:										
2010.............	100.0	22.1	14.1	7.7	35.2	13.1	16.3	39.0	24.3	11.9
2012.............	100.0	24.3	20.6	3.3	32.0	13.5	14.2	37.8	22.2	12.0
Italy:										
2010.............	100.0	32.9	27.2	6.6	31.4	5.6	21.6	25.9	14.6	8.5
2013 [8].............	100.0	33.4	27.1	6.9	30.4	5.4	20.9	25.0	13.6	8.6
Japan:										
2010.............	100.0	30.2	18.6	11.6	41.1	17.8	18.6	18.7	9.6	7.2
2012.............	100.0	31.1	18.6	12.5	41.6	19.3	18.8	18.0	9.2	6.9
Korea, South:										
2010.............	100.0	28.2	14.3	13.9	22.8	9.5	9.9	33.9	17.6	15.2
2013 [8].............	100.0	29.3	15.4	14.0	26.3	11.0	11.9	30.7	17.0	11.8
Turkey:										
2010.............	100.0	21.3	14.0	7.3	24.9	9.4	13.7	47.7	21.7	24.1
2013 [8].............	100.0	20.2	13.9	6.3	27.4	10.9	15.5	46.1	22.0	22.4
United Kingdom:										
2010.............	100.0	37.5	28.8	8.8	19.0	7.5	11.0	30.8	18.8	10.7
2013 [8].............	100.0	35.6	27.9	7.7	18.9	7.4	11.0	33.0	21.0	10.7

NA Not available. [1] Includes property taxes, employer payroll taxes other than social security contributions, and miscellaneous taxes not shown separately. [2] Includes taxes on capital gains. [3] Includes other taxes, not shown separately. [4] Includes contributions of self-employed persons, not shown separately. [5] Taxes on the production, sales, transfer, leasing, and delivery of goods and services and rendering of services. [6] Primarily value-added and sales taxes. [7] For example, excise taxes on alcohol, tobacco, and gasoline. [8] Data are provisional/estimates.

Source: Organisation for Economic Co-operation and Development (OECD), 2015, "Revenue Statistics: Comparative tables," OECD Tax Statistics (database) ©, <http://dx.doi.org/10.1787/data-00262-en>, accessed June 2015.

Table 1365. Household Tax Burden by Country: 2014

[Percent of gross wage earnings of the average worker. The tax burden reflects income tax plus employee social security contributions less cash benefits]

Country	Single person without children	One-earner family with two children	Country	Single person without children	One-earner family with two children
OECD average [1].............	25.54	20.13	Israel [3]...................	16.50	16.50
			Italy......................	31.61	24.67
United States.................	**24.84**	**12.84**	Japan.....................	21.74	20.27
Australia........................	23.39	23.39	Korea, South.............	13.38	10.68
Austria..........................	34.60	32.58	Luxembourg.............	29.89	18.40
Belgium.........................	42.33	31.05	Mexico....................	10.04	10.04
Canada..........................	23.27	16.34	Netherlands..............	31.38	28.80
Chile.............................	7.00	7.00	New Zealand.............	17.25	17.25
Czech Republic.................	23.14	6.59	Norway....................	28.83	27.68
Denmark........................	38.40	34.37	Poland....................	24.79	18.23
Estonia..........................	19.66	13.83	Portugal..................	27.26	17.18
Finland..........................	30.66	30.66	Slovak Republic.........	22.87	10.91
France [2].......................	28.70	21.91	Slovenia..................	33.20	24.86
Germany........................	39.54	21.07	Spain.....................	22.98	15.41
Greece..........................	24.91	28.72	Sweden...................	24.38	24.38
Hungary.........................	34.50	26.53	Switzerland..............	17.39	10.82
Iceland..........................	28.48	19.64	Turkey....................	27.42	25.72
Ireland..........................	20.46	12.31	United Kingdom.........	23.71	23.71

[1] The Organisation for Economic Co-operation and Development (OECD) is comprised of the 34 member countries shown above. See text, this section. [2] Figures correspond to tax calculations that are based on the tax legislation relating to the income earned in the selected year. [3] See footnote 2, Table 1360.

Source: Organisation for Economic Co-operation and Development (OECD), 2015, "Taxing Wages: Comparative tables," OECD Tax Statistics (database) ©, <http://dx.doi.org/10.1787/data-00265-en>, accessed June 2015.

Table 1366. Household Net Saving Rates by Country: 2000 to 2013

[As a percentage of household disposable income. Household savings are estimated by subtracting household consumption expenditure from household disposable income, plus the change in net equity of households in pension funds. Households include households plus nonprofit institutions serving households. Net saving rates are measured after deducting consumption of fixed capital (depreciation), with respect to assets used in enterprises operated by households, as well as owner-occupied dwellings. The household saving rate is calculated as the ratio of household savings to household disposable income (plus the change in net equity of households in pension funds). Minus sign (-) indicates an excess of expenditures over income]

Country	2000	2005	2006	2008	2009	2010	2011	2012	2013
United States..............	4.3	2.6	3.4	5.1	6.4	5.8	6.2	7.5	5.0
EU-28 [1].................	7.1	5.7	5.0	5.0	7.0	5.7	5.1	4.8	4.7
Australia [2]...............	2.3	1.1	1.8	10.0	9.1	10.2	11.2	10.3	9.7
Austria...................	10.5	10.7	11.3	11.9	11.3	9.4	7.8	9.0	7.3
Belgium..................	11.7	9.9	10.6	11.2	12.8	10.1	8.5	7.5	6.9
Canada..................	3.8	1.5	3.5	3.9	5.1	4.3	4.3	5.0	4.9
Chile....................	(NA)	(NA)	(NA)	7.0	12.3	8.8	8.6	9.9	9.7
Czech Republic...........	6.0	6.1	7.8	6.3	8.5	7.6	6.0	6.2	4.3
Denmark.................	-6.0	-4.6	-1.7	-4.2	0.8	2.1	0.9	–	-0.4
France...................	10.0	9.4	9.4	9.5	10.8	10.4	10.0	9.6	9.5
Germany.................	8.9	10.0	10.0	10.5	10.0	9.9	9.6	9.4	9.1
Greece..................	(NA)	(NA)	-3.4	-5.6	-4.5	-9.0	-8.2	-8.3	-16.4
Hungary.................	6.1	7.2	7.9	3.5	5.5	6.1	6.8	4.8	5.4
Ireland..................	-3.5	1.9	-0.6	6.3	12.2	9.6	7.3	8.5	8.1
Italy....................	7.3	8.9	8.3	7.6	6.8	4.0	3.5	2.0	3.8
Japan...................	7.0	1.6	1.3	0.6	2.3	2.1	2.6	1.4	–
Korea, South.............	(NA)	(NA)	(NA)	(NA)	(NA)	4.7	3.9	3.9	5.1
Mexico..................	(NA)	8.2	9.1	8.1	8.4	8.8	6.9	6.1	5.4
Netherlands..............	6.9	6.7	5.0	5.4	8.7	5.1	6.0	6.5	7.8
New Zealand [2]...........	-2.6	-5.9	-3.3	-1.1	1.1	3.0	1.7	2.2	(NA)
Poland..................	11.0	3.0	2.7	0.8	3.2	3.0	-0.5	-0.5	(NA)
Russia..................	(NA)	11.0	12.4	10.1	13.1	15.5	13.8	13.5	(NA)
Slovenia................	6.7	9.5	11.3	9.7	7.9	6.2	5.8	3.5	6.8
South Africa.............	1.0	0.1	-0.8	-1.2	-0.7	-0.6	-0.3	–	–
Spain...................	6.4	4.1	2.3	2.6	9.5	4.6	6.0	3.5	4.9
Sweden.................	4.0	5.4	6.9	12.7	12.2	10.9	12.6	15.2	15.6
Switzerland..............	15.3	14.0	15.8	16.7	17.1	17.0	17.8	17.5	(NA)
United Kingdom..........	5.3	0.6	-0.6	-0.8	3.5	5.5	2.9	2.3	0.3

– Represents or rounds to zero. NA Not available. [1] See footnote 4, Table 1379 for list of EU-28 countries. [2] Data refer to fiscal year.

Source: Organisation for Economic Co-operation and Development (OECD), 2015, "National Accounts at a Glance," OECD National Accounts Statistics (database) ©, <http://dx.doi.org/10.1787/data-00369-en>, accessed July 2015.

Table 1367. Insurance and Pensions by Country: 2013

[4,976,749 reresents 4,976,749,000,000]

Country	Insurance						Pensions [2]		
	Investment assets (mil. U.S. dollars) [1]	Direct gross premiums (percent of GDP)	Total gross premiums (mil. U.S. dollars)		Gross claims payments (mil. U.S. dollars)		Investment assets (mil. U.S. dollars)	Contri-butions (percent of GDP) [3]	Benefits paid (percent of GDP)
			Life	Non-life	Life	Non-life			
United States........	4,976,749	10.7	881,541	1,408,380	335,840	799,206	23,078,507	(NA)	(NA)
Australia..............	83,658	5.2	48,122	39,467	43,657	24,410	1,500,180	7.6	4.9
Belgium..............	308,035	7.1	21,639	15,769	24,258	10,708	27,213	0.3	0.2
Canada..............	626,369	4.9	32,379	66,134	4,727	34,346	2,427,293	3.0	3.0
Chile.................	46,275	4.2	7,830	3,946	7,500	1,810	162,988	3.9	1.0
Czech Republic.......	(NA)	4.0	3,659	4,343	2,627	2,517	14,951	1.1	0.3
Denmark.............	327,012	10.3	(NA)	10,442	19,780	7,752	661,173	0.6	0.8
Estonia..............	1,225	3.2	227	547	134	263	2,587	1.4	(Z)
Finland..............	79,196	5.0	7,419	5,635	5,213	3,794	159,314	1.1	1.4
France..............	2,445,233	9.1	172,106	103,514	151,709	71,742	271,357	0.1	(Z)
Germany.............	1,775,453	6.9	120,236	213,319	91,951	101,341	235,474	0.3	0.2
Greece..............	14,596	2.2	2,237	3,167	2,311	1,063	136	(Z)	(Z)
Hong Kong...........	(NA)	13.2	32,425	5,431	(NA)	1,810	103,045	3.4	(NA)
Hungary.............	5,098	2.7	1,952	1,632	1,712	920	5,506	0.3	0.1
Iceland..............	903	2.8	33	385	11	257	24,336	6.5	5.0
Israel [4].............	41,049	4.8	7,378	6,570	3,503	3,869	153,613	2.6	1.7
Italy................	642,863	7.6	115,093	45,992	90,945	32,757	163,359	0.6	0.3
Korea, South........	590,085	13.3	100,255	68,920	47,812	21,993	292,753	2.5	1.7
Luxembourg..........	55,086	40.5	22,701	1,992	17,345	1,613	1,323	0.3	0.1
Mexico..............	55,340	2.1	12,525	14,664	6,437	6,357	194,770	1.0	0.4
Netherlands..........	(NA)	5.9	22,485	25,307	29,964	17,188	1,335,092	5.7	4.4
Norway..............	177,291	5.0	13,835	11,694	7,800	7,404	40,908	0.4	0.2
Poland..............	32,947	3.5	9,893	8,417	7,305	4,339	102,911	0.7	(Z)
Portugal.............	47,168	7.5	11,979	5,016	11,397	3,724	22,268	0.4	0.3
Slovak Republic......	6,721	3.1	1,641	1,317	994	664	9,926	0.4	(Z)
Slovenia.............	5,616	5.3	628	2,178	439	1,314	3,209	0.4	0.1
Spain...............	325,412	5.2	34,381	42,759	31,377	26,196	199,630	0.4	0.3
Sweden.............	376,908	4.6	14,192	13,015	9,927	10,610	399,517	(NA)	(NA)
Switzerland..........	438,177	9.8	35,786	38,468	30,129	22,149	807,893	9.0	5.0
Turkey...............	5,527	1.6	2,071	11,135	1,236	4,962	35,543	(NA)	(NA)
United Kingdom.......	1,331,284	12.2	246,444	93,898	291,023	52,535	2,810,564	2.9	3.3

NA Not available or not applicable. Z Less than 0.05 percent. [1] Includes total investment assets of direct insurance companies (excludes re-insurance). [2] Includes private, autonomous pension funds of all types (occupational and personal, mandatory and voluntary). [3] Pension contributions include employee and employer contributions combined. [4] See footnote 2, Table 1360.

Source: Organisation for Economic Co-operation and Development (OECD), Insurance Statistics (database) ©, <http://www.oecd.org/daf/fin/insurance/oecdinsurancestatistics.htm>; and Global Pension Statistics (database) ©, <http://www.oecd.org/daf/fin/private-pensions/globalpensionstatistics.htm>; accessed June 2015.

Table 1368. Annual Percent Changes in Consumer Prices by Country: 2010 to 2014

[Percent change from previous year. Inflation as measured by the consumer price index reflects the annual percentage change in the cost to the average consumer of acquiring a basket of goods and services that may be fixed or adjusted at specified intervals, such as yearly. For general comments concerning the data, see text, this section. For additional qualifications of the data for individual countries, see source. Minus sign (-) indicates decrease]

Country	2010	2011	2012	2013	2014	Country	2010	2011	2012	2013	2014
World [1]	3.5	5.0	3.7	2.6	2.5	Kazakhstan	7.1	8.3	5.1	5.8	6.7
United States	1.6	3.2	2.1	1.5	1.6	Kenya	4.0	14.0	9.4	5.7	6.9
Afghanistan	0.9	10.2	7.2	7.7	4.6	Korea, South	3.0	4.0	2.2	1.3	1.3
Australia	2.8	3.3	1.8	2.4	2.5	Malaysia	1.7	3.2	1.7	2.1	3.1
Austria	1.8	3.3	2.5	2.0	1.6	Mexico	4.2	3.4	4.1	3.8	4.0
Bangladesh	8.1	10.7	6.2	7.5	7.0	Mongolia	10.1	9.5	15.0	8.6	13.0
Belarus	7.7	53.2	59.2	18.3	18.1	Myanmar	7.7	5.0	1.5	5.5	5.5
Brazil	5.0	6.6	5.4	6.2	6.3	Netherlands	1.3	2.3	2.5	2.5	1.0
Cambodia	4.0	5.5	2.9	2.9	3.9	New Zealand	2.3	4.4	0.9	1.3	0.8
China	3.3	5.4	2.7	2.6	2.0	Nigeria	13.7	10.8	12.2	8.5	8.1
Colombia	2.3	3.4	3.2	2.0	2.9	Norway	2.4	1.3	0.7	2.1	2.0
Croatia	1.0	2.3	3.4	2.2	-0.2	Pakistan	13.9	11.9	9.7	7.7	7.2
Czech Republic	1.4	1.9	3.3	1.4	0.3	Philippines	3.8	4.6	3.2	3.0	4.1
Denmark	2.3	2.8	2.4	0.8	0.6	Poland	2.7	4.3	3.6	1.0	0.1
Egypt	11.3	10.1	7.1	9.4	10.1	Romania	6.1	5.8	3.3	4.0	1.1
Ethiopia	8.1	33.2	22.8	8.1	7.4	Russia	6.9	8.4	5.1	6.8	7.8
France	1.5	2.1	2.0	0.9	0.5	Saudi Arabia	5.3	5.8	2.9	3.5	2.7
Germany	1.1	2.1	2.0	1.5	0.9	Singapore	2.8	5.3	4.5	2.4	1.0
Ghana	10.7	8.7	9.2	11.6	15.5	South Africa	4.3	5.0	5.7	5.4	6.4
Greece	4.7	3.3	1.5	-0.9	-1.3	Spain	1.8	3.2	2.4	1.4	-0.1
Haiti	5.7	8.4	6.3	5.9	4.6	Sri Lanka	6.2	6.7	7.5	6.9	3.3
Honduras	4.7	6.8	5.2	5.2	6.1	Sudan	13.2	22.1	37.4	30.0	36.9
India	12.0	8.9	9.3	10.9	6.4	Sweden	1.2	3.0	0.9	(-Z)	-0.2
Indonesia	5.1	5.4	4.3	6.4	6.4	Switzerland	0.7	0.2	-0.7	-0.2	(-Z)
Iran	10.1	20.6	27.4	39.3	17.2	Thailand	3.3	3.8	3.0	2.2	1.9
Ireland	-0.9	2.6	1.7	0.5	0.2	Turkey	8.6	6.5	8.9	7.5	8.9
Israel	2.7	3.5	1.7	1.5	0.5	Ukraine	9.4	8.0	0.6	-0.3	12.2
Italy	1.5	2.7	3.0	1.2	0.2	United Kingdom	3.3	4.5	2.8	2.6	1.5
Japan	-0.7	-0.3	(-Z)	0.4	2.7	Venezuela	28.2	26.1	21.1	40.6	62.2
Jordan	5.0	4.4	4.8	5.5	2.8	Vietnam	8.9	18.7	9.1	6.6	4.1

NA Not available. Z Less than 0.05 percent. [1] Includes other countries not shown separately.

Source: The World Bank, Washington, DC, World Development Indicators database, "Inflation, consumer prices (annual %)" ©, <http://data.worldbank.org/data-catalog/world-development-indicators>, accessed August 2015.

Table 1369. Unemployment Rates by Country: 1990 to 2014

[Annual averages. The standardized unemployment rates shown here are calculated as the number of unemployed persons as a percentage of the civilian labor force. The unemployed are persons of working age who, in the reference period, are without work, are available for work, and have taken specific steps to find work]

Country	1990	2000	2005	2007	2008	2009	2010	2011	2012	2013	2014
OECD, total [1]	(NA)	6.1	6.6	5.6	5.9	8.1	8.3	7.9	(NA)	(NA)	(NA)
EU-27 [2]	(NA)	9.2	8.9	7.1	7.0	8.9	9.6	9.6	10.4	10.7	(NA)
United States	5.6	4.0	5.1	4.6	5.8	9.3	9.6	9.0	8.1	7.4	6.2
Australia	6.9	6.3	5.0	4.4	4.2	5.6	5.2	5.1	5.2	5.7	6.1
Austria	3.2	3.6	5.2	4.4	3.8	4.8	4.4	4.2	4.3	4.9	(NA)
Belgium	8.9	7.0	8.4	7.5	7.0	7.9	8.3	7.1	7.6	8.4	(NA)
Canada	8.1	6.8	6.8	6.0	6.1	8.3	8.1	7.5	7.3	7.1	6.9
Chile	(NA)	9.2	8.0	7.1	7.8	9.7	8.1	7.2	(NA)	(NA)	(NA)
Czech Republic	0.8	8.9	8.0	5.3	4.4	6.7	7.3	6.8	7.0	7.0	6.1
Denmark	8.3	4.5	4.8	3.8	3.4	6.0	7.5	7.6	7.5	7.0	(NA)
Estonia	0.7	14.6	8.1	4.6	5.5	13.6	16.8	12.4	10.1	8.7	(NA)
Finland	3.2	9.8	8.4	6.9	6.4	8.3	8.4	7.8	7.7	8.2	(NA)
France	7.6	8.0	8.3	7.5	7.0	8.7	8.8	8.6	9.2	9.7	(NA)
Germany	4.8	7.8	11.2	8.7	7.6	7.8	7.1	6.0	5.5	5.3	(NA)
Greece	7.0	11.3	9.8	8.2	7.3	9.0	12.0	16.5	23.8	27.3	26.6
Hungary	(NA)	6.5	7.3	7.5	7.9	10.1	11.2	11.1	11.1	10.2	7.8
Iceland	1.8	2.3	2.6	2.3	3.0	7.2	7.6	7.1	6.0	5.4	(NA)
Ireland	13.0	4.6	4.8	4.8	5.8	12.3	13.9	14.6	15.0	13.9	(NA)
Israel [3]	(NA)	8.8	9.0	7.3	6.8	7.5	6.6	5.6	6.9	6.2	(NA)
Italy	11.5	10.7	7.8	6.2	6.8	7.9	8.5	8.5	10.8	12.3	(NA)
Japan	2.1	4.7	4.4	3.9	4.0	5.1	5.0	4.6	4.4	4.0	(NA)
Korea, South	2.5	4.4	3.7	3.2	3.2	3.6	3.7	3.4	3.2	3.1	(NA)
Luxembourg	1.1	2.4	4.1	4.2	4.2	5.5	5.8	5.7	6.1	6.9	7.1
Mexico	2.7	2.6	3.5	3.4	3.5	5.2	5.2	5.2	4.8	5.0	(NA)
Netherlands	7.7	2.7	4.7	3.2	2.8	3.4	4.5	4.4	5.3	6.7	(NA)
New Zealand	8.0	6.2	3.8	3.7	4.2	6.2	6.5	6.5	6.9	6.2	(NA)
Norway	5.3	3.5	4.6	2.5	2.6	3.2	3.6	3.3	3.2	3.5	3.5
Poland	6.5	16.1	17.7	9.6	7.1	8.2	9.6	9.6	10.1	10.3	9.0
Portugal	4.6	4.0	7.7	8.0	7.6	9.5	10.9	12.8	15.7	16.3	(NA)
Slovak Republic	(NA)	18.8	16.2	11.0	9.6	12.1	14.4	13.6	14.0	14.2	(NA)
Spain	16.3	13.9	9.2	8.3	11.3	17.9	20.0	21.5	24.9	26.2	(NA)
Sweden	1.8	5.9	7.8	6.2	6.2	8.3	8.6	7.8	8.0	8.0	(NA)
Switzerland	0.5	2.5	4.2	3.4	3.2	4.1	4.2	3.8	3.9	4.1	(NA)
Turkey	8.0	6.5	10.6	10.3	11.0	14.0	11.9	9.8	9.2	9.7	(NA)
United Kingdom	6.9	5.5	4.7	5.3	5.3	7.7	7.8	7.9	7.9	7.7	(NA)

NA Not available. [1] For complete OECD membership listing, see Section 30 introduction. [2] See footnote 2, Table 1372. [3] See footnote 2, Table 1360.

Source: Organisation for Economic Co-operation and Development (OECD), 2015, "Labour Force Statistics: Summary tables," OECD Employment and Labour Market Statistics (database) ©, <http://dx.doi.org/10.1787/data-00286-en>, accessed July 2015.

Table 1370. Civilian Labor Force, Employment, and Unemployment by Country: 1970 to 2013

[Labor force and employment in thousands (82,771 represents 82,771,000). Data are based on U.S. labor force definitions (see source) except that age limits of the working-age population vary as follows: Data for the United States, Canada, Spain, and the United Kingdom refer to persons aged 16 years and over. Data for Australia, France, Germany, Japan, Netherlands, and South Korea refer to persons aged 15 years and over. Data may not be comparable to prior years due to breaks in series resulting from changes in methodology. For specific methodological information for individual countries, see source]

Year	United States	Canada	Australia	Japan	South Korea	France	Germany[1]	Netherlands	Spain	United Kingdom
Civilian labor force (1,000):										
1970	82,771	8,395	5,478	50,957	10,094	21,428	26,247	(NA)	(NA)	(NA)
1980	106,940	11,725	6,693	55,895	14,485	23,499	27,256	5,769	13,279	26,762
1990	125,840	14,047	8,444	62,986	18,572	24,581	29,412	6,650	15,154	28,777
2000	142,583	15,632	9,498	66,710	22,135	25,969	39,343	7,906	17,482	28,962
2005	149,321	17,056	10,404	65,386	23,743	27,028	40,786	8,308	20,735	30,148
2010	153,889	18,263	11,628	65,521	24,749	28,018	41,639	8,723	22,941	31,405
2011	153,616	18,434	11,815	65,067	25,099	28,056	42,100	8,720	22,971	31,642
2012	154,975	18,616	11,972	64,642	25,501	28,313	42,189	8,859	22,924	31,992
2013	155,389	18,823	12,152	64,765	25,873	28,468	42,534	8,936	22,634	32,291
Labor force participation rate:[2]										
1970	60.4	57.8	62.1	64.8	57.8	57.9	56.9	(NA)	(NA)	(NA)
1980	63.8	65.0	62.1	62.7	59.2	57.9	54.7	54.5	50.4	62.8
1990	66.5	67.4	64.7	62.6	60.1	55.7	55.0	56.0	50.2	64.4
2000	67.1	66.0	64.2	61.7	61.2	55.4	56.8	62.2	52.3	62.8
2005	66.0	67.3	65.4	59.5	62.0	55.3	57.6	63.5	57.1	63.1
2010	64.7	67.0	66.3	59.1	61.0	55.7	58.8	65.0	59.8	63.2
2011	64.1	66.8	66.4	58.7	61.1	55.5	59.3	64.6	59.8	63.2
2012	63.7	66.7	66.1	58.4	61.3	55.8	59.2	65.1	59.8	63.4
2013	63.2	66.5	65.9	58.5	61.5	55.8	59.5	65.1	59.4	63.5
Civilian employment (1,000):										
1970	78,678	7,919	5,388	50,146	9,617	20,898	26,107	(NA)	(NA)	(NA)
1980	99,303	10,872	6,284	54,598	13,683	22,223	26,486	5,418	11,778	24,929
1990	118,793	12,964	7,859	61,706	18,085	22,605	27,952	6,134	12,857	26,724
2000	136,891	14,677	8,902	63,790	21,156	23,730	36,211	7,660	15,387	27,375
2005	141,730	16,032	9,881	62,910	22,856	24,596	36,202	7,867	18,822	28,681
2010	139,064	16,969	11,022	62,421	23,829	25,383	38,688	8,333	18,309	28,929
2011	139,869	17,238	11,215	62,332	24,244	25,452	39,596	8,331	17,972	29,078
2012	142,469	17,445	11,347	62,152	24,681	25,502	39,873	8,390	17,155	29,444
2013	143,929	17,669	11,465	62,565	25,066	25,501	40,264	8,336	16,638	29,831
Employment-population ratio:[3]										
1970	57.4	54.5	61.1	63.8	55.1	56.5	56.6	(NA)	(NA)	(NA)
1980	59.2	60.3	58.3	61.3	55.9	54.7	53.1	51.1	44.7	58.5
1990	62.8	62.2	60.2	61.3	58.6	51.2	52.3	51.7	42.6	59.8
2000	64.4	62.0	60.2	59.0	58.5	50.6	52.3	60.3	46.0	59.4
2005	62.7	63.3	62.1	57.3	59.7	50.3	51.2	60.1	51.8	60.0
2010	58.5	62.3	62.9	56.3	58.7	50.5	54.6	62.1	47.7	58.2
2011	58.4	62.5	63.0	56.2	59.1	50.4	55.8	61.8	46.8	58.0
2012	58.6	62.5	62.7	56.1	59.4	50.2	56.0	61.7	44.8	58.3
2013	58.6	62.5	62.2	56.5	59.5	50.0	56.3	60.7	43.7	58.7
Unemployment rate:										
1970	4.9	5.7	1.7	1.6	4.7	2.5	0.5	(NA)	(NA)	(NA)
1980	7.1	7.3	6.1	2.3	5.5	5.4	2.8	6.1	11.3	6.8
1990	5.6	7.7	6.9	2.0	2.6	8.0	5.0	7.8	15.2	7.1
2000	4.0	6.1	6.3	4.4	4.4	8.6	8.0	3.1	12.0	5.5
2005	5.1	6.0	5.0	3.8	3.7	9.0	11.2	5.3	9.2	4.9
2010	9.6	7.1	5.2	4.7	3.7	9.4	7.1	4.5	20.2	7.9
2011	8.9	6.5	5.1	4.2	3.4	9.3	5.9	4.5	21.8	8.1
2012	8.1	6.3	5.2	3.9	3.2	9.9	5.5	5.3	25.2	8.0
2013	7.4	6.1	5.6	3.4	3.1	10.4	5.3	6.7	26.5	7.6
Men	7.6	6.6	5.7	3.2	3.3	10.4	5.7	7.1	26.0	8.1
Women	7.1	5.6	5.6	3.6	2.9	10.4	4.9	6.3	27.1	7.1
Total population	7.4	6.1	5.6	3.4	3.1	10.4	5.3	6.7	26.5	7.6
Under 25 years old	15.5	12.4	12.2	6.3	9.4	24.4	8.0	11.1	56.2	20.8
Teenagers[4]	22.9	18.0	16.3	5.9	10.4	32.1	8.5	14.0	75.0	29.8
20 to 24 years old	12.8	9.5	9.6	6.4	9.2	22.5	7.8	8.9	52.3	17.0
25 years old and over	6.1	5.1	4.3	3.1	2.7	8.9	5.0	5.9	24.1	5.5

NA Not available. [1] Unified Germany for 1991 onward. Prior to 1991, data relate to the former West Germany. [2] Civilian labor force as a percent of the civilian working-age population. Germany includes the institutionalized population as part of the working-age population. [3] Civilian employment as a percent of the civilian working-age population. Germany includes the institutionalized population as part of the working-age population. [4] 16 to 19-year-olds in the United States, Canada, Spain, and the United Kingdom; 15 to 19-year-olds in Australia, Japan, South Korea, France, Germany, and Netherlands.

Source: The Conference Board, Inc., International Labor Comparisons program, "International Comparisons of Annual Labor Force Statistics, 2013," August 2014, <https://www.conference-board.org/ilcprogram/laborforceannual>. Reproduced with permission from The Conference Board, Inc. © 2015 The Conference Board, Inc.

Table 1371. Youth Educational Enrollment and Employment Status by Country: 2012

[Percent of total youth population for selected age groups]

Country	15 to 19 years old			20 to 24 years old			25 to 29 years old		
	In education	Not in education		In education	Not in education		In education	Not in education	
	Total	Employed	Not employed	Total	Employed	Not employed	Total	Employed	Not employed
United States.....	**85.5**	**6.8**	**7.7**	**40.2**	**42.1**	**17.7**	**14.0**	**65.8**	**20.2**
Australia...........	81.1	11.6	7.2	41.7	46.1	12.2	17.3	67.6	15.1
Brazil..............	68.3	16.5	15.2	23.0	53.3	23.7	11.1	67.6	21.3
Canada.............	81.6	11.1	7.3	42.1	43.0	14.8	13.5	69.7	16.8
Czech Republic....	93.4	2.7	4.0	50.1	36.5	13.4	12.2	67.4	20.4
France.............	90.6	2.5	6.9	43.3	36.6	20.1	5.3	72.3	22.4
Germany..........	94.1	2.9	3.0	51.0	37.8	11.2	18.9	66.5	14.6
Greece.............	93.7	1.0	5.3	73.3	11.4	15.4	55.0	26.4	18.5
Ireland.............	87.1	3.3	9.6	41.8	32.5	25.7	11.8	61.7	26.5
Italy...............	85.1	3.0	12.0	38.9	29.5	31.5	15.6	55.4	29.0
Korea, South.......	89.0	2.5	8.5	42.4	35.1	22.5	8.8	66.4	24.7
Mexico.............	61.6	21.5	17.0	28.5	48.0	23.6	7.8	65.1	27.1
Netherlands.......	93.4	4.2	2.4	58.3	34.5	7.1	22.2	67.3	10.6
Norway............	82.4	14.6	3.0	40.6	48.8	10.7	14.6	74.0	11.4
Poland.............	94.5	1.6	3.9	52.0	29.1	18.9	11.4	66.2	22.4
Spain..............	86.0	2.6	11.4	43.9	25.2	30.9	13.2	54.3	32.5
Sweden............	90.3	5.6	4.1	45.0	41.5	13.5	24.1	64.8	11.1
Switzerland........	88.6	6.7	4.7	43.7	44.2	12.1	17.4	71.3	11.3
Turkey.............	64.4	12.8	22.8	38.4	30.6	30.9	17.1	48.8	34.1
United Kingdom. ..	82.3	8.2	9.5	33.6	46.1	20.2	14.0	67.7	18.3

Source: Organisation for Economic Co-operation and Development (OECD), 2014, "Indicator C5: Transition from school to work: Where are the 15-29 year-olds?," Education at a Glance 2014: OECD Indicators, OECD Publishing ©, <http://dx.doi.org/10.1787/888933118903>, accessed September 2014.

Table 1372. Female Labor Force Participation Rates by Country: 1990 to 2013

[In percent. Female labor force of all ages divided by female population 15-64 years old]

Country	1990	2000	2010	2012	2013	Country	1990	2000	2010	2012	2013
OECD, total [1]........	**(NA)**	**60.4**	**63.0**	**(NA)**	**(NA)**	Ireland...............	43.3	57.0	63.2	63.0	64.2
EU–27 [2]...............	(NA)	60.3	64.6	66.0	(NA)	Italy.................	46.1	47.1	51.3	55.1	54.1
United States........	**68.6**	**70.8**	**68.9**	**69.1**	**68.9**	Japan.................	60.3	64.0	68.6	69.5	71.5
Australia..............	62.2	65.9	71.4	72.2	72.3	Korea.................	51.2	54.9	58.3	59.4	60.2
Austria................	55.7	62.8	70.3	71.4	71.9	Luxembourg.........	50.5	69.4	[4] 96.3	(NA)	(NA)
Belgium...............	52.4	56.6	62.0	61.4	62.5	Mexico...............	23.4	43.3	48.6	50.2	50.0
Canada...............	67.5	69.8	74.3	74.7	75.3	Netherlands..........	52.4	65.5	72.8	74.6	(NA)
Chile.................	(NA)	38.5	52.1	(NA)	(NA)	New Zealand.........	65.4	68.0	74.1	75.5	76.2
Czech Republic.......	69.1	64.2	62.3	64.4	66.2	Norway...............	71.2	76.2	77.1	77.8	77.9
Denmark..............	78.3	75.7	76.7	76.7	(NA)	Poland...............	(NA)	60.5	55.7	56.8	57.2
Estonia...............	74.9	68.2	73.6	74.5	75.0	Portugal.............	62.4	67.1	73.8	73.0	71.2
Finland...............	73.8	72.2	73.3	74.5	74.6	Slovak Republic......	(NA)	63.1	62.3	62.0	63.0
France [3]...............	59.1	64.5	67.0	67.9	68.5	Spain.................	41.5	52.0	66.4	68.6	68.9
Germany [3]..........	56.7	63.6	71.5	72.6	73.3	Sweden...............	80.9	75.0	77.5	79.8	(NA)
Greece................	43.3	49.5	58.0	58.5	(NA)	Switzerland..........	65.7	76.8	82.1	83.5	(NA)
Hungary..............	(NA)	52.1	55.8	57.8	58.3	Turkey...............	36.3	30.3	30.4	32.6	34.1
Iceland...............	(NA)	82.8	82.1	81.7	83.1	United Kingdom.....	66.4	67.8	70.5	70.1	72.3

NA Not available. [1] For complete OECD membership listing, see Section 30 introduction. [2] European Union-27: Austria, Belgium, Bulgaria, Cyprus, Czech Republic, Denmark, Estonia, Finland, France, Germany, Greece, Hungary, Ireland, Italy, Latvia, Lithuania, Luxembourg, Malta, Netherlands, Poland, Portugal, Romania, Slovak Republic, Slovenia, Spain, Sweden, and United Kingdom. [3] Prior to 1991, data are for former West Germany. [4] Estimated.

Source: Organisation for Economic Co-operation and Development (OECD), 2015, "Labour Force Statistics: Summary tables," OECD Employment and Labour Market Statistics (database) ©, <http://dx.doi.org/10.1787/data-00286-en>, accessed July 2015.

Table 1373. Civilian Employment-Population Ratio: 1990 to 2013

[Civilian employment as a percent of the civilian working-age population. Data may not be comparable to prior years due to breaks in series resulting from changes in methodology; for information for individual countries, see source. See headnote, Table 1370]

Country	Women					Men				
	1990	2000	2005	2010	2013	1990	2000	2005	2010	2013
United States..................	**54.3**	**57.5**	**56.2**	**53.6**	**53.2**	**72.0**	**71.9**	**69.6**	**63.7**	**64.4**
Canada..........................	54.1	56.0	58.1	58.5	58.6	70.6	68.2	68.6	66.2	66.5
Australia........................	49.4	52.3	55.0	56.5	56.4	71.3	68.2	69.4	69.4	68.2
Japan...........................	48.0	46.4	45.7	45.7	46.5	75.4	72.5	69.7	67.7	67.3
South Korea.....................	46.2	47.0	48.4	47.8	48.8	71.8	70.7	71.6	70.1	70.8
France..........................	42.0	44.0	45.0	46.0	46.0	61.5	57.9	56.3	55.4	54.4
Germany [1, 2]....................	40.5	44.0	44.7	48.9	51.0	65.6	61.2	58.1	60.6	61.9
Italy............................	29.2	32.7	34.1	34.5	34.4	60.0	57.0	56.8	54.4	51.7
Netherlands.....................	38.5	50.6	52.5	56.2	55.6	65.4	70.2	68.0	68.2	66.0
Sweden.........................	61.8	56.1	56.0	55.3	56.9	70.7	64.2	63.8	63.3	63.7
United Kingdom.................	50.3	52.5	53.7	52.9	53.4	70.0	66.9	66.8	63.8	64.1

[1] Unified Germany for 1991 onward. Prior to 1991, data relate to the former West Germany. [2] Germany includes institutionalized population as part of the working-age population.

Source: The Conference Board, Inc., International Labor Comparisons program, "International Comparisons of Annual Labor Force Statistics, 2013," August 2014, <https://www.conference-board.org/ilcprogram/laborforceannual>. Reproduced with permission from The Conference Board, Inc. © 2015 The Conference Board, Inc.

Table 1374. Civilian Employment by Sector and Country: 2010 and 2013

[139,064 represents 139,064,000. Civilian employment approximating U.S. concepts. Data based on U.S. labor force definitions except that age limits of the working-age population vary as follows: Data for the United States, Canada, and the United Kingdom refer to persons aged 16 years and over. Data for Australia, France, Germany, Italy, Japan, and South Korea refer to persons aged 15 years and over. Data may not be comparable to prior years due to breaks in series resulting from changes in methodology. For specific methodological information for individual countries, see source. Sectors are based on International Standard Industrial Classification (ISIC), unless otherwise indicated]

Sector and Year	United States [1]	Canada [1]	Australia	Japan [2]	South Korea	France	Germany	Italy	United Kingdom
TOTAL EMPLOYMENT (1,000)									
2010, total............	139,064	16,969	11,022	62,421	23,829	25,383	38,688	22,597	28,929
Agriculture, forestry, fishing [3]........	2,206	369	367	2,420	1,566	750	632	856	351
Industry [4]............	23,889	3,216	2,172	15,620	5,802	5,313	10,415	6,175	5,173
Manufacturing....................	14,081	1,743	981	10,580	4,028	3,383	7,737	4,214	2,849
Services [5]............	112,969	13,384	8,484	44,381	16,461	19,321	27,641	15,566	23,404
2013, total............	143,929	17,669	11,465	62,565	25,066	25,501	40,264	22,167	29,831
Agriculture, forestry, fishing [3]........	2,130	378	314	2,200	1,520	790	578	804	314
Industry [4]............	25,205	3,356	2,207	15,360	5,954	4,964	10,630	5,693	5,208
Manufacturing....................	14,869	1,733	925	10,370	4,184	3,168	7,804	4,082	2,918
Services [5]............	116,594	13,936	8,945	45,005	17,592	19,747	29,056	15,669	24,310
PERCENT DISTRIBUTION [6]									
2010, total............	100.0	100.0	100.0	100.0	100.0	100.0	100.0	100.0	100.0
Agriculture, forestry, fishing [3]........	1.6	2.2	3.3	3.9	6.6	3.0	1.6	3.8	1.2
Industry [4]............	17.2	19.0	19.7	25.0	24.3	20.9	26.9	27.3	17.9
Manufacturing....................	10.1	10.3	8.9	16.9	16.9	13.3	20.0	18.6	9.8
Services [5]............	81.2	78.9	77.0	71.1	69.1	76.1	71.4	68.9	80.9
2013, total............	100.0	100.0	100.0	100.0	100.0	100.0	100.0	100.0	100.0
Agriculture, forestry, fishing [3]........	1.5	2.1	2.7	3.5	6.1	3.1	1.4	3.6	1.1
Industry [4]............	17.5	19.0	19.2	24.6	23.8	19.5	26.4	25.7	17.5
Manufacturing....................	10.3	9.8	8.1	16.6	16.7	12.4	19.4	18.4	9.8
Services [5]............	81.0	78.9	78.0	71.9	70.2	77.4	72.2	70.7	81.5

[1] Data for the United States and Canada are based on the North American Industry Classification System (NAICS). [2] Data for Japan are based on the Japanese Standard Industrial Classification System (JSIC). [3] Includes hunting. [4] Includes manufacturing, mining, and construction. [5] Transportation, communication, public utilities, trade, finance, public administration, private household services, and miscellaneous services. [6] Percent of total civilian employment.

Source: The Conference Board, Inc., International Labor Comparisons program, "International Comparisons of Annual Labor Force Statistics, 2013," August 2014, <https://www.conference-board.org/ilcprogram/laborforceannual>. Reproduced with permission from The Conference Board, Inc. © 2015 The Conference Board, Inc.

Table 1375. Educational Performance and Attainment by Country: 2012 and 2013

Country	Student mean scores in reading, science, and mathematics proficiency, 2012 [1]			Educational attainment of adult population (25 to 64 years old), 2013 (percent)		
	Reading scale	Mathematics scale	Science scale	Below upper secondary	Upper secondary and vocational	Tertiary and higher [2]
United States.....................	497.6	481.4	497.4	10.4	45.7	43.9
Australia..........................	511.8	504.2	521.5	24.3	36.2	39.5
Austria...........................	489.6	505.5	505.8	16.9	62.4	20.7
Brazil............................	410.1	391.5	404.7	53.6	32.7	13.7
Canada...........................	523.1	518.1	525.4	10.4	36.4	53.2
Chile.............................	441.4	422.6	444.9	(NA)	(NA)	(NA)
Czech Republic...................	492.9	499.0	508.3	7.2	72.4	20.5
Denmark..........................	496.1	500.0	498.5	21.7	42.8	35.4
France............................	505.5	495.0	499.0	24.9	43.0	32.1
Germany..........................	507.7	513.5	524.1	13.7	57.8	28.5
Greece............................	477.2	453.0	466.7	30.0	42.6	27.4
Ireland............................	523.2	501.5	522.0	23.3	35.3	41.5
Israel [3].........................	485.8	466.5	470.1	15.0	37.6	47.4
Italy..............................	489.8	485.3	493.5	41.8	41.9	16.3
Japan............................	538.1	536.4	546.7	(NA)	52.7	47.3
Korea............................	535.8	553.8	537.8	16.3	40.6	43.1
Mexico...........................	423.6	413.3	414.9	61.6	19.7	18.7
Netherlands.......................	511.2	523.0	522.1	24.2	41.9	33.9
New Zealand......................	512.2	499.7	515.6	28.6	36.8	34.6
Norway...........................	503.9	489.4	494.5	17.6	42.6	39.8
Poland............................	518.2	517.5	525.8	9.9	64.4	25.8
Russia............................	475.1	482.2	486.3	(NA)	(NA)	(NA)
Spain.............................	487.9	484.3	496.4	44.3	21.9	33.7
Sweden...........................	483.3	478.3	484.8	11.8	51.1	37.0
Switzerland.......................	509.0	530.9	515.3	12.8	48.2	38.9
Turkey............................	475.5	448.0	463.4	65.2	18.9	15.9
United Kingdom...................	499.3	493.9	514.1	20.8	37.3	41.9

NA Not available. [1] Proficiency scores are based on the Program for International Student Assessment (PISA), an international standardized test which takes place in three-year cycles. PISA tests are administered to a nationally representative sample of fifteen-year-old students in each country. [2] Tertiary education entails completion of an advanced course of study or research program leading to an associate's, bachelor's, master's, or doctorate degree, usually 2 years or longer in duration. [3] See footnote 2, Table 1360.

Source: Organisation for Economic Co-operation and Development (OECD), "Annex B1.1 Results (tables)" in *PISA 2012 Results: What Students Know and Can Do: Student Performance in Mathematics, Reading and Science, PISA, Vol. 1*, Revised Edition, February 2014, OECD Publishing, <http://dx.doi.org/10.1787/9789264208780-en>; and "Education at a glance: Education and learning outputs and outcomes," OECD Education Statistics (database) ©, <http://dx.doi.org/10.1787/data-00749-en>, accessed July 2015.

Table 1376. World Supply and Utilization of Major Crops and Livestock: 2005 to 2015

[In millions of units (215.8 represents 215,800,000). For major crops, data are for marketing or trade year ending in year shown, unless otherwise indicated. For livestock and dairy, data are for calendar year]

Commodity	2005	2009	2010	2011	2012	2013	2014	2015 [1]
Wheat:								
Area (hectares)	215.8	224.2	225.6	216.8	220.8	216.4	221.2	223.4
Production (metric tons)	626.8	683.6	687.0	649.9	696.1	658.5	716.8	726.3
Exports (metric tons)	113.2	143.1	135.3	134.1	153.8	147.1	162.4	161.5
Consumption (metric tons)	606.1	643.3	652.9	654.0	697.5	679.2	703.8	715.9
Ending stocks (metric tons)	156.3	169.1	203.2	199.1	197.6	176.9	190.0	200.4
Corn:								
Area (hectares)	145.4	158.7	158.4	164.6	172.0	177.4	181.4	178.1
Production (metric tons)	716.9	799.8	824.8	835.5	888.2	869.1	990.6	999.4
Exports (metric tons)	76.0	83.6	92.7	91.7	103.7	100.5	130.2	121.0
Consumption (metric tons)	688.8	782.7	819.3	853.3	866.7	869.1	945.8	970.8
Ending stocks (metric tons)	131.1	145.4	144.1	127.7	132.4	137.0	174.5	197.0
Rice, milled:								
Area (hectares)	151.8	158.1	155.6	158.4	160.5	158.6	161.5	160.3
Production (metric tons)	400.8	449.3	440.6	450.6	467.7	472.7	478.2	476.1
Exports (metric tons)	28.9	29.4	31.8	36.5	39.9	39.5	43.1	43.2
Consumption (metric tons)	406.2	436.1	435.2	443.3	456.4	466.2	478.1	482.1
Ending stocks (metric tons)	74.0	92.6	94.9	100.1	106.9	110.6	107.3	98.7
Coarse grains: [2]								
Area (hectares)	298.3	314.7	307.5	306.0	317.4	316.6	322.6	322.2
Production (metric tons)	1,016.1	1,108.5	1,117.4	1,099.2	1,155.9	1,137.4	1,281.7	1,288.5
Exports (metric tons)	101.2	110.4	118.8	116.0	133.4	132.2	164.8	161.3
Consumption (metric tons)	979.8	1,079.3	1,113.7	1,129.6	1,154.9	1,135.7	1,238.1	1,267.7
Ending stocks (metric tons)	179.3	192.3	196.0	165.6	166.6	168.2	211.8	232.6
Oilseeds:								
Area (hectares)	219.0	230.5	236.1	245.0	248.9	256.3	260.2	264.1
Production (metric tons)	383.9	399.7	447.4	461.1	447.9	476.0	505.8	535.6
Exports (metric tons)	74.4	94.6	106.9	108.4	111.3	118.1	133.7	137.4
Consumption (metric tons)	368.9	404.3	424.7	446.0	467.1	470.3	494.1	511.5
Ending stocks (metric tons)	59.6	58.0	75.5	85.9	67.3	68.2	77.6	97.2
Coffee, green:								
Production (60 kg bags)	121.6	136.2	128.6	140.4	143.9	154.9	154.3	146.3
Exports (60 kg bags)	94.9	102.9	104.8	115.3	116.5	119.1	123.4	122.2
Consumption (60 kg bags)	116.8	125.5	138.3	134.5	142.4	142.5	142.8	146.0
Ending stocks (60 kg bags)	41.0	39.6	28.8	28.6	25.6	35.2	39.7	33.5
Sugar, centrifugal:								
Production (metric tons)	140.7	143.8	153.2	162.2	172.4	177.6	175.6	174.3
Exports (metric tons)	47.0	45.0	48.3	53.8	54.9	55.1	57.5	54.2
Consumption (metric tons)	141.6	153.8	154.1	155.4	159.4	164.9	166.7	170.6
Ending stocks (metric tons)	34.7	29.8	28.0	29.5	35.3	42.6	44.0	44.3
Cotton:								
Area (hectares)	35.7	30.6	30.2	33.5	36.0	34.4	32.7	33.8
Production (480 lb. bales)	121.5	108.3	103.4	117.6	127.5	123.6	120.4	118.9
Exports (480 lb. bales)	34.9	30.2	35.7	35.2	46.1	46.6	40.1	34.2
Consumption (480 lb. bales)	108.0	108.9	119.6	115.6	103.6	106.8	108.4	111.4
Ending stocks (480 lb. bales)	60.9	62.2	47.2	50.7	73.9	90.5	102.5	110.0
Beef:								
Beef cow beginning stocks (head)	217.3	213.0	203.0	199.1	204.8	207.3	205.1	198.9
Production (metric tons) [3]	56.0	58.1	58.5	58.1	58.5	59.5	59.7	59.0
Exports (metric tons) [3]	7.4	7.4	7.8	8.1	8.1	9.1	10.0	10.2
Consumption (metric tons) [3]	55.5	57.2	57.4	56.5	57.0	57.8	57.6	56.7
Ending stocks (metric tons) [3]	0.5	0.7	0.6	0.6	0.7	0.7	0.7	0.5
Pork:								
Sow beginning stocks (head)	82.3	79.3	79.4	77.4	78.9	79.6	78.8	74.9
Production (metric tons) [3]	93.8	100.4	103.0	103.6	107.0	108.9	110.5	110.9
Exports (metric tons) [3]	5.0	5.6	6.0	7.0	7.3	7.0	6.9	6.8
Consumption (metric tons) [3]	93.5	100.3	102.9	103.3	106.5	108.5	110.0	110.3
Ending stocks (metric tons) [3]	0.8	0.8	0.8	0.8	1.0	1.0	1.0	0.8
Chicken (broilers):								
Beginning stocks (metric tons)	0.6	0.6	0.5	0.5	0.5	0.6	0.6	0.6
Production (metric tons)	64.4	73.9	78.4	81.3	83.4	84.6	86.3	87.3
Exports (metric tons)	6.9	8.5	8.9	9.6	10.1	10.3	10.5	10.4
Consumption (metric tons)	63.7	72.9	77.2	80.0	81.8	83.1	84.7	85.5
Ending stocks (metric tons)	0.6	0.5	0.5	0.5	0.6	0.6	0.6	0.6
Dairy:								
Dairy cows beginning stocks (head)	228.0	228.2	229.0	232.1	234.5	236.7	241.4	242.6
Milk production (metric tons) [4]	491.0	504.5	514.4	529.7	544.7	551.7	570.4	582.5
Milk exports (metric tons) [4]	0.4	0.5	0.5	0.6	0.7	0.7	0.8	0.9
Milk consumption (metric tons) [4]	490.9	504.4	514.2	529.6	544.6	551.7	570.5	582.7

[1] Preliminary. [2] Coarse grains include corn, barley, sorghum, oats, rye, millet, and mixed grains. [3] Carcass weight equivalent (CWE). [4] Includes milk from cows as well as other bovines.

Source: U.S. Department of Agriculture, Foreign Agricultural Service, "Production, Supply and Distribution (PS&D) Online database," <http://www.fas.usda.gov/psdonline/>, accessed June 2015.

Table 1377. World Crop Production Summary: 2013 to 2015

[In millions of metric tons (716.8 represents 716,800,000)]

Country	Wheat 2013–2014	Wheat 2014–2015 prel.	Coarse grains[1] 2013–2014	Coarse grains[1] 2014–2015 prel.	Rice (milled) 2013–2014	Rice (milled) 2014–2015 prel.	Oilseeds[2] 2013–2014	Oilseeds[2] 2014–2015 prel.	Cotton 2013–2014	Cotton 2014–2015 prel.
World	**716.8**	**726.3**	**1,281.7**	**1,288.5**	**478.2**	**476.1**	**505.8**	**535.6**	**120.4**	**118.9**
Total foreign	658.7	671.2	914.6	911.4	472.1	469.1	406.8	418.4	107.5	102.5
United States	**58.1**	**55.1**	**367.1**	**377.1**	**6.1**	**7.1**	**99.0**	**117.2**	**12.9**	**16.3**
Canada	37.5	29.3	28.7	21.9	(3)	(3)	23.4	21.7	(3)	(3)
Mexico	3.4	3.7	32.0	31.9	0.1	0.2	0.9	1.2	0.9	1.4
Russia	52.1	59.1	35.7	40.4	0.6	0.7	13.6	13.0	(3)	(3)
Ukraine	22.3	24.8	39.9	39.3	0.1	0.0	16.7	16.3	(3)	(3)
China	121.9	126.2	225.1	222.2	142.5	144.5	58.9	57.6	32.8	30.0
India	93.5	95.9	43.2	40.4	106.5	102.5	36.8	35.4	31.0	29.5
Indonesia	(3)	(3)	9.1	9.4	36.3	36.3	11.5	12.1	(3)	(3)
Pakistan	24.0	25.5	5.6	5.6	6.7	6.9	5.1	5.5	9.5	10.6
Thailand	(3)	(3)	5.0	4.9	20.5	18.8	0.6	0.6	(3)	(3)
Argentina	10.5	12.5	35.7	32.2	1.0	1.0	57.0	63.8	1.2	1.1
Brazil	5.3	6.0	82.6	83.6	8.3	8.4	90.2	97.6	8.0	7.0
Australia	26.9	24.0	12.4	11.5	0.6	0.5	5.8	4.2	4.1	2.2
South Africa	1.9	1.8	15.6	11.8	(3)	(3)	1.9	1.6	(3)	0.1
Turkey	18.8	15.3	13.1	9.5	0.5	0.5	2.4	2.5	2.3	3.2
All others	240.7	247.4	330.8	346.7	148.3	148.9	82.0	85.4	17.6	17.4

[1] Includes corn, barley, sorghum, oats, rye, millet, and mixed grains. [2] Includes soybean, cottonseed, peanut (in shell), sunflower seed, rapeseed for individual countries. Copra and palm kernel are added to world totals. [3] Indicates no reported or insignificant production.

Source: U.S. Department of Agriculture, Foreign Agricultural Service, *World Agricultural Production*, June 2015. See also <http://www.fas.usda.gov/data/world-agricultural-production>.

Table 1378. Meat Production by Type and Country: 2010 and 2014

[In thousands of metric tons (58,485 represents 58,485,000). Carcass weight equivalent basis for beef, veal, and pork. Chicken (16-week-old broiler) weight based on ready-to-cook equivalent]

Country	Beef and veal[1] 2010	Beef and veal[1] 2014	Country	Pork 2010	Pork 2014	Country	Chicken[2] 2010	Chicken[2] 2014
World	**58,485**	**59,690**	**World**	**103,033**	**110,476**	**World**	**78,357**	**86,348**
United States	**12,046**	**11,078**	China	50,712	56,710	**United States**	**16,563**	**17,299**
Brazil	9,115	9,723	EU-28[3]	22,627	22,400	China	12,550	13,080
EU-28[3]	8,101	7,410	**United States**	**10,186**	**10,368**	Brazil	12,312	12,692
China	6,531	6,890	Brazil	3,195	3,313	EU-28[3]	9,202	10,095
India	3,125	4,125	Russia	1,981	2,510	India	2,650	3,725
Argentina	2,620	2,700	Vietnam	2,217	2,425	Russia	2,310	3,250
Australia	2,129	2,595	Canada	1,779	1,815	Mexico	2,822	2,980
Mexico	1,745	1,827	Philippines	1,260	1,353	Argentina	1,680	2,050
Pakistan	1,485	1,675	Mexico	1,175	1,290	Turkey	1,420	1,956
Russia	1,435	1,370	Japan	1,292	1,264	Thailand	1,280	1,570
Other countries	10,153	10,297	Other	6,609	7,028	Other	15,568	17,651

[1] May include meat of other bovines. [2] Excludes chicken paws. [3] See footnote 3, Table 1379.

Source: U.S. Department of Agriculture, Foreign Agricultural Service, "Production, Supply and Distribution Online," <http://apps.fas.usda.gov/psdonline>, accessed June 2015.

Table 1379. Meat Consumption by Type and Country: 2010 and 2014

[In thousands of metric tons (57,391 represents 57,391,000). Carcass weight equivalent basis for beef, veal, and pork. Chicken (16-week-old broiler) weight based on ready-to-cook equivalent]

Country	Beef and veal[1] 2010	Beef and veal[1] 2014	Country	Pork 2010	Pork 2014	Country	Chicken[2] 2010	Chicken[2] 2014
World	**57,391**	**57,629**	**World**	**102,899**	**109,954**	**World**	**77,182**	**84,668**
United States	**12,038**	**11,244**	China	50,799	57,169	**United States**	**13,473**	**14,034**
Brazil	7,592	7,896	EU-28[3]	20,951	20,237	China	12,457	12,910
EU-28[3]	8,202	7,480	**United States**	**8,654**	**8,647**	EU-28[3]	8,955	9,667
China	6,520	7,297	Brazil	2,577	2,759	Brazil	9,041	9,137
Argentina	2,346	2,503	Russia	2,896	3,024	India	2,648	3,716
Russia	2,488	2,279	Japan	2,488	2,543	Mexico	3,361	3,693
India	2,208	2,043	Vietnam	2,199	2,389	Russia	2,957	3,658
Mexico	1,938	1,839	Mexico	1,784	1,991	Japan	2,080	2,218
Pakistan	1,451	1,616	Korea, South	1,539	1,737	Argentina	1,475	1,773
Japan	1,225	1,226	Philippines	1,418	1,552	South Africa	1,491	1,727
Other countries	11,383	12,206	Other countries	7,594	7,906	Other countries	19,244	22,135

[1] May include meat of other bovines. [2] Excludes chicken paws. [3] European Union-28: Austria, Belgium, Bulgaria, Croatia, Cyprus, Czech Republic, Denmark, Estonia, Finland, France, Germany, Greece, Hungary, Ireland, Italy, Latvia, Lithuania, Luxembourg, Malta, Netherlands, Poland, Portugal, Romania, Slovakia, Slovenia, Spain, Sweden, and United Kingdom.

Source: U.S. Department of Agriculture, Foreign Agricultural Service, "Production, Supply and Distribution Online," <http://apps.fas.usda.gov/psdonline>, accessed June 2015.

Table 1380. Wheat, Rice, and Corn—Exports and Imports of Leading Countries: 2010 to 2015

[In thousands of metric tons (22,279 represents 22,279,000). Wheat data represent trade years ending in June of year shown; corn data represent trade years ending in September of year shown; rice data represent trade years ending in December of year shown. Countries listed are the ten leading exporters or importers in 2015]

Leading country	Exports			Leading country	Imports		
	2010	2014	2015 [1]		2010	2014	2015 [1]
WHEAT				**WHEAT**			
EU-28 [2]	22,279	32,033	34,500	Egypt	10,500	10,170	11,400
United States	24,143	31,497	23,000	Indonesia	5,364	7,392	7,700
Russia	18,556	18,568	22,200	Algeria	5,167	7,484	7,100
Canada	18,992	22,157	24,000	Brazil	6,691	7,061	6,000
Australia	13,764	18,339	17,500	Japan	5,502	6,123	5,800
Ukraine	9,337	9,755	11,500	Iran	3,650	6,600	5,800
Argentina	5,255	1,675	4,000	EU-28 [2]	5,358	3,974	6,000
Kazakhstan	7,871	8,000	6,000	Nigeria	3,990	4,550	4,600
Turkey	4,363	4,293	4,000	Philippines	3,197	3,482	4,600
Uruguay	1,039	1,345	1,200	Mexico	3,196	4,636	4,600
RICE				**RICE**			
Thailand	9,047	10,969	11,000	China	366	4,168	4,500
India	2,228	10,907	9,800	Nigeria	2,000	3,200	4,000
Vietnam	6,734	6,325	6,700	Iran	1,520	1,650	1,700
Pakistan	4,000	3,300	3,900	Saudi Arabia	1,069	1,410	1,460
United States	3,868	3,042	3,450	EU-28 [2]	1,235	1,556	1,550
Burma	700	1,688	1,850	Philippines	2,400	1,800	1,800
Cambodia	750	1,000	1,100	Iraq	1,188	1,080	1,250
Uruguay	808	957	950	South Africa	733	910	1,100
Brazil	430	850	800	Senegal	685	1,200	1,100
Argentina	468	494	560	Indonesia	1,150	1,225	1,250
CORN				**CORN**			
United States	49,696	50,707	46,000	Japan	15,971	15,121	15,000
Brazil	8,623	22,041	21,500	EU-28 [2]	2,758	15,919	8,000
Ukraine	5,072	20,004	18,000	Mexico	8,298	10,954	10,000
Argentina	16,973	12,846	17,000	Korea, South	8,461	10,406	9,600
Russia	427	4,192	2,800	Egypt	5,832	8,726	7,500
Serbia	1,343	1,736	2,900	Saudi Arabia	1,872	2,684	3,500
EU-28 [2]	1,569	2,401	3,000	Colombia	3,651	4,334	4,400
Paraguay	1,359	2,714	2,000	Taiwan	4,521	4,189	4,200
India	1,917	3,889	1,500	Algeria	2,569	4,156	4,000
South Africa	1,586	2,104	1,000	Iran	4,300	5,500	6,000

[1] Preliminary. [2] See footnote 3, Table 1379.

Source: U.S. Department of Agriculture, Foreign Agricultural Service (FAS), "Production, Supply and Distribution Online," <http://www.fas.usda.gov/psdonline>, accessed June 2015.

Table 1381. World Production of Major Mineral Commodities: 2010 to 2014

[Units are as noted. Th. represents thousand, mil. represents million, and bil. represents billion]

Commodity	Unit	2010	2012	2013	2014, prel.	Leading producers, 2013
MINERAL FUELS						
Coal	mil. short tons	7,999	8,687	(NA)	(NA)	China, United States, India [5]
Dry natural gas	bil. cubic feet	112,574	119,454	121,283	(NA)	United States, Russia, Iran
Natural gas plant liquids	mil. barrels [1]	3,234	3,446	3,495	3,672	United States, Saudi Arabia, Russia
Petroleum, crude	mil. barrels [1]	27,249	27,798	27,830	28,409	Russia, Saudi Arabia, United States
NONMETALLIC MINERALS						
Cement, hydraulic	mil. metric tons	3,290	3,830	4,080	4,180	China, India, United States
Diamond, gem and industrial	mil. carats	128	128	(NA)	(NA)	Russia, Congo (Dem. Rep.), Botswana [5]
Nitrogen in ammonia	mil. metric tons	127.0	136	143	144	China, India, Russia
Phosphate rock, marketable	mil. metric tons	184	215	225	220	China, United States, Morocco/Western Sahara
Potash, marketable	mil. metric tons	34.1	33.1	34.5	35.0	Canada, Russia, Belarus
Salt	mil. metric tons	269	261	262	269	China, United States, India
Sulfur, elemental basis	mil. metric tons	68.4	69.1	70.4	72.4	China, United States, Russia
METALS						
Aluminum [2]	mil. metric tons	41.2	45.9	47.6	49.3	China, Russia, Canada
Bauxite, gross weight	mil. metric tons	238	258	283	234	Australia, Indonesia, China
Chromium, gross weight	th. metric tons	24,400	25,600	28,800	29,000	South Africa, Kazakhstan, Turkey
Copper, metal content [3]	th. metric tons	16,200	17,000	18,300	18,700	Chile, China, Peru
Gold, metal content	metric tons	2,580	2,690	2,800	2,860	China, Australia, United States, Russia
Iron ore, gross weight [4]	mil. metric tons	2,590	2,930	3,110	3,220	China, Australia, Brazil
Lead, metal content [3]	th. metric tons	4,150	5,170	5,490	5,460	China, Australia, United States
Manganese ore, metal content	th. metric tons	14,800	15,500	16,900	18,000	South Africa, China, Australia
Nickel, metal content [3]	th. metric tons	1,650	2,000	2,630	2,400	Philippines, Indonesia, Russia
Steel, crude	mil. metric tons	1,430	1,550	1,620	1,650	China, Japan, United States
Tin, metal content [3]	th. metric tons	255	243	294	296	China, Indonesia, Peru
Zinc, metal content	th. metric tons	12,400	13,500	13,400	13,300	China, Australia, Peru

NA Not available. [1] 42-gallon barrels. [2] Unalloyed ingot metal. [3] Mine output. [4] Includes iron ore concentrates and iron ore agglomerates. [5] Leading producers in 2012.

Source: Mineral fuels, U.S. Energy Information Administration, "International Energy Statistics," <http://www.eia.gov/cfapps/ipdbproject/iedindex3.cfm>, accessed September 2015. Nonmetallic minerals and metals, U.S. Bureau of Mines, *Nonmetallic Minerals and Metals* through 1990; thereafter, U.S. Geological Survey, *Minerals Yearbook*, annual, and *Mineral Commodity Summaries 2015*, January 2015 and earlier editions.

Table 1382. Net Electricity Generation by Energy Source and Country: 2012

[21,531.7 represents 21,531,700,000,000. kWh = kilowatt hours. Ranked for top 40 countries]

Country	Total [1] (bil. kWh)	Amount				Percent distribution			
		Fossil fuels [2]	Hydro	Nuclear	Non-hydro renew-ables [3]	Fossil fuels [2]	Hydro	Nuclear	Non-hydro renew-ables [3]
World, total [4]	21,531.7	14,497.7	3,646.1	2,344.8	1,068.8	67.3	16.9	10.9	5.0
China	4,768.3	3,675.0	856.4	92.7	147.2	77.1	18.0	1.9	3.1
United States	4,047.8	2,775.0	276.2	769.3	232.1	68.6	6.8	19.0	5.7
India	1,052.5	862.9	124.6	29.7	35.4	82.0	11.8	2.8	3.4
Russia	1,012.5	679.0	164.4	166.3	3.5	67.1	16.2	16.4	0.3
Japan	966.4	828.8	74.7	17.2	47.6	85.8	7.7	1.8	4.9
Canada	616.2	129.9	376.7	89.1	20.6	21.1	61.1	14.5	3.3
Germany	585.2	349.9	21.0	94.1	121.7	59.8	3.6	16.1	20.8
Brazil	537.6	71.0	411.2	15.2	40.3	13.2	76.5	2.8	7.5
France	533.3	44.9	58.1	407.4	24.6	8.4	10.9	76.4	4.6
Korea, South	499.7	350.1	3.9	143.6	3.2	70.1	0.8	28.7	0.6
United Kingdom	335.7	232.5	5.2	64.0	35.0	69.3	1.6	19.1	10.4
Italy	281.0	189.9	41.5	–	50.3	67.6	14.8	–	17.9
Spain	280.0	135.9	20.3	58.7	66.4	48.6	7.3	21.0	23.7
Mexico	278.7	226.5	31.5	8.4	12.3	81.2	11.3	3.0	4.4
Saudi Arabia	255.4	255.4	–	–	–	100.0	–	–	–
Iran	239.2	225.4	12.3	1.3	0.2	94.2	5.2	0.6	0.1
South Africa	239.0	225.2	2.0	12.4	0.4	94.2	0.8	5.2	0.2
Australia	235.2	211.4	13.9	–	9.9	89.9	5.9	–	4.2
Taiwan	233.7	184.5	5.6	38.7	5.1	79.0	2.4	16.6	2.2
Turkey	228.3	163.7	57.3	–	7.4	71.7	25.1	–	3.2
Ukraine	187.1	91.2	10.4	84.9	0.8	48.7	5.5	45.4	0.4
Indonesia	185.3	163.1	12.7	–	9.6	88.0	6.8	–	5.2
Sweden	161.0	2.7	78.1	61.5	18.8	1.7	48.5	38.2	11.7
Thailand	156.4	142.7	8.7	–	5.0	91.2	5.5	–	3.2
Egypt	155.3	140.5	13.2	–	1.5	90.5	8.5	–	1.0
Poland	152.7	136.1	2.0	–	14.9	89.1	1.3	–	9.7
Norway	144.6	2.7	140.5	–	1.9	1.8	97.1	–	1.3
Argentina	127.9	90.6	29.0	5.9	2.8	70.8	22.7	4.6	2.1
Malaysia	126.8	117.0	9.0	–	0.9	92.2	7.1	–	0.7
Venezuela	123.0	41.8	81.2	–	–	34.0	66.0	–	–
Vietnam	118.2	65.2	52.9	–	0.1	55.1	44.7	–	0.1
United Arab Emirates	100.5	100.5	–	–	–	100.0	–	–	–
Netherlands	94.9	79.1	0.1	3.7	12.0	83.4	0.1	3.9	12.6
Pakistan	92.9	58.0	29.6	5.3	–	62.5	31.8	5.7	–
Kazakhstan	86.1	78.6	7.6	–	–	91.2	8.8	–	–
Czech Republic	81.9	45.5	2.1	28.6	5.9	55.6	2.6	34.9	7.2
Belgium	76.1	27.6	0.4	38.5	10.1	36.2	0.5	50.6	13.3
Philippines	69.7	49.0	10.1	–	10.5	70.4	14.6	–	15.1
Finland	67.5	17.2	16.7	22.1	11.5	25.5	24.7	32.7	17.1
Chile	66.9	41.7	20.0	–	5.3	62.3	29.8	–	7.9

– Represents or rounds to zero. [1] Electricity generated from fossil fuels, hydro, nuclear, geothermal, solar, wind, tidal, biomass, and waste resources. [2] Electricity generated from coal, oil, and gas resources. [3] Electricity generated from geothermal, solar, wind, tidal and wave, biomass, and waste resources. [4] Includes countries not shown separately.

Source: U.S. Energy Information Administration, "International Energy Statistics Database," <http://www.eia.gov/countries/data.cfm>, accessed March 2015.

Table 1383. World Primary Energy Production by Region and Type: 1980 to 2012

[In quadrillion Btu (287.3 represents 287,300,000,000,000,000). Btu = British thermal unit. For Btu conversion factors, see source]

Region and type	1980	1990	1995	2000	2005	2009	2010	2011	2012
World total	287.3	349.5	363.0	395.9	452.8	480.9	505.4	518.5	537.3
REGION									
North America	83.2	91.8	96.1	98.8	98.3	99.6	102.0	105.7	107.1
United States [1]	67.2	70.7	71.2	71.3	69.4	72.7	74.8	78.0	79.2
Central and South America	12.1	16.7	21.1	26.0	28.0	29.5	30.3	31.7	31.8
Europe	40.1	46.9	49.0	50.6	48.6	44.8	45.5	43.7	44.0
Eurasia [2]	56.5	72.1	51.8	54.0	66.2	66.3	70.6	72.7	73.7
Middle East	42.3	41.0	48.3	57.5	65.6	67.1	71.7	76.4	77.7
Africa	17.4	21.7	24.0	27.7	34.3	36.0	37.1	33.9	36.0
Asia and Oceania	35.8	59.4	72.6	81.3	111.8	137.5	148.3	154.5	167.0
TYPE OF FUEL									
Petroleum [3]	133.1	136.2	141.8	156.4	169.9	168.8	173.0	173.6	177.6
Dry natural gas	54.8	76.0	80.4	89.6	101.6	108.7	116.5	120.4	123.4
Coal	71.2	90.9	87.8	92.5	119.2	136.8	144.8	152.5	164.2
Hydroelectric power	17.9	22.3	25.3	26.8	29.1	31.6	33.4	33.9	34.7
Nuclear electric power	7.6	20.4	23.3	25.7	27.3	26.6	27.4	26.2	24.5
Non-hydroelectric renewables [4]	0.3	1.6	2.1	2.7	4.0	6.4	7.6	9.2	10.4

[1] Includes biomass, geothermal, and solar energy produced in the United States and not used for generating electricity. [2] Prior to 1992, data were for the former U.S.S.R. [3] Includes crude oil, lease condensate, and natural gas plant liquids. [4] Including geothermal, solar, wind, tidal and wave, biomass, and waste resources.

Source: U.S. Energy Information Administration, "International Energy Statistics Database," <http://www.eia.gov/cfapps/ipdbproject/IEDIndex3.cfm>, accessed June 2015.

Table 1384. World Primary Energy Consumption by Region and Type: 1980 to 2012

[In quadrillion Btu (283.1 represents 283,100,000,000,000,000). Btu = British thermal unit. For Btu conversion factors, see source]

Region and type	1980	1990	2000	2005	2007	2008	2009	2010	2011	2012
World, total [1]	**283.1**	**347.0**	**398.3**	**455.1**	**478.7**	**485.7**	**480.0**	**508.1**	**520.3**	**524.1**
REGION										
North America	91.6	100.1	118.2	120.8	122.2	120.1	114.6	117.8	118.6	116.2
United States [2]	**78.1**	**84.5**	**98.8**	**100.3**	**101.3**	**99.3**	**94.6**	**97.5**	**97.5**	**95.1**
Central and South America	11.5	14.5	20.8	23.4	24.8	25.7	25.6	27.1	28.0	28.7
Europe	71.7	76.3	81.2	85.4	85.5	85.6	80.9	84.1	82.1	81.4
Eurasia [3]	46.7	60.9	39.1	42.7	44.2	44.7	39.4	43.4	44.7	46.1
Middle East	5.8	11.2	17.3	23.2	25.2	27.1	28.3	29.7	30.9	32.2
Africa	6.8	9.5	12.0	14.5	15.0	16.3	16.2	16.7	16.7	17.3
Asia and Oceania	48.9	74.4	109.5	145.1	161.8	166.3	175.0	189.2	199.3	202.1
TYPE OF FUEL										
Petroleum [4]	131.9	136.2	155.5	171.0	174.8	173.8	170.5	176.8	177.8	179.9
Dry natural gas	53.9	75.3	89.8	102.6	109.0	112.5	108.7	117.6	120.7	124.0
Coal	69.9	89.1	95.5	118.4	129.7	132.1	132.8	142.1	148.5	146.8
Renewable electric power [5]	18.2	23.9	29.5	33.1	35.2	37.0	38.0	41.0	43.1	45.1

[1] Includes nuclear electric power, not shown separately. [2] Includes biomass, geothermal, and solar energy consumed in the United States and not used for generating electricity. [3] Prior to 1992, data were for the former U.S.S.R. [4] Includes all refined petroleum products. [5] Includes geothermal, solar, wind, tidal, biomass, waste, and hydroelectric power.

Source: U.S. Energy Information Administration, "International Energy Statistics Database," <www.eia.gov/countries/data.cfm>, accessed March 2015.

Table 1385. World Daily Crude Oil Production by Major Producing Country: 1980 to 2014

[In thousands of barrels per day (59,558 barrels represents 59,558,000 barrels). Includes lease condensate. Ranked for top 30 countries, as of current year]

Country	1980	1990	2000	2005	2010	2011	2012	2013	2014
World, total [1]	**59,558**	**60,497**	**68,527**	**73,771**	**72,609**	**74,386**	**74,504**	**75,887**	**76,054**
Russia	(X)	(X)	6,479	9,043	9,694	9,774	9,922	10,054	10,107
Saudi Arabia	9,900	6,410	8,404	9,550	8,900	9,458	9,832	9,693	9,735
United States	**8,597**	**7,355**	**5,822**	**5,182**	**5,482**	**5,645**	**6,497**	**7,441**	**8,653**
China	2,114	2,774	3,249	3,609	4,078	4,059	4,085	4,164	4,189
Canada	1,435	1,553	1,977	2,369	2,741	2,901	3,138	3,325	3,603
Iraq	2,514	2,040	2,571	1,878	2,399	2,626	2,983	3,054	3,368
Iran	1,662	3,088	3,696	4,139	4,080	4,054	3,387	3,113	3,236
United Arab Emirates	1,709	2,117	2,368	2,535	2,415	2,679	2,804	2,820	2,820
Kuwait	1,656	1,175	2,079	2,529	2,300	2,530	2,635	2,650	2,619
Venezuela	2,168	2,137	3,155	2,565	2,410	2,500	2,500	2,500	2,500
Mexico	1,936	2,553	3,104	3,423	2,621	2,600	2,593	2,562	2,459
Nigeria	2,055	1,810	2,165	2,627	2,455	2,550	2,520	2,367	2,423
Brazil	182	631	1,269	1,634	2,055	2,105	2,061	2,024	2,255
Angola	150	475	746	1,239	1,899	1,746	1,777	1,831	1,742
Kazakhstan	(X)	(X)	718	1,288	1,525	1,553	1,514	1,573	1,632
Norway	486	1,630	3,222	2,698	1,869	1,752	1,607	1,530	1,568
Qatar	472	406	742	978	1,459	1,571	1,551	1,553	1,540
Algeria	1,106	1,180	1,214	1,692	1,540	1,540	1,532	1,462	1,420
Colombia	126	440	691	526	786	914	944	1,003	990
Oman	282	685	970	774	865	886	919	940	943
Azerbaijan	(X)	(X)	280	433	1,035	983	922	871	846
Indonesia	1,577	1,462	1,428	1,067	953	918	875	828	790
India	182	660	646	665	751	782	777	772	768
Malaysia	283	619	690	726	638	570	586	570	597
Ecuador	204	285	395	532	486	500	504	526	556
Argentina	491	483	761	704	626	581	551	540	532
Egypt	595	873	768	623	568	551	539	514	478
Libya	1,787	1,375	1,410	1,633	1,650	465	1,367	918	470
Australia	380	575	722	446	484	414	406	338	354
Vietnam	–	50	316	374	318	309	347	337	298

X Not applicable. – Represents zero. [1] Includes countries not shown separately.

Source: U.S. Energy Information Administration, "International Energy Statistics Database," <http://www.eia.gov/cfapps/ipdbproject/IEDIndex3.cfm>, accessed June 2015.

Table 1386. Energy Consumption by Country: 2010 to 2012

[For total consumption, 508.1 represents 508,100,000,000,000,000. For per capita consumption, 74.0 represents 74,000,000. Btu = British thermal units. Total primary energy consumption includes the consumption of petroleum, dry natural gas, coal, and net nuclear, hydroelectric, and non-hydroelectric renewable electricity. See text of this section for general comments about the data. For data qualifications for countries and Btu conversion factors, see source]

Country	Total (quad. Btu) 2010	Total (quad. Btu) 2012	Per capita (mil. Btu) 2010	Per capita (mil. Btu) 2011 [1]	Country	Total (quad. Btu) 2010	Total (quad. Btu) 2012	Per capita (mil. Btu) 2010	Per capita (mil. Btu) 2011 [1]
World, total	508.1	524.1	74.0	74.9	Japan	21.8	20.3	170.8	164.1
United States	97.5	95.1	315.2	312.8	Jordan	0.3	0.3	50.4	42.4
Algeria	1.9	2.2	52.1	55.0	Kazakhstan	2.3	2.8	137.0	149.5
Argentina	3.5	3.7	85.6	88.0	Korea, North	0.8	0.8	33.7	33.8
Australia	5.9	6.0	276.3	282.6	Korea, South	10.8	11.5	222.6	232.0
Austria	1.5	1.5	185.8	179.1	Kuwait	1.3	1.6	526.1	577.3
Bahrain	0.6	0.6	468.0	451.2	Libya	0.9	0.7	153.4	98.5
Bangladesh	1.0	1.1	6.1	6.4	Malaysia	3.0	3.1	107.5	108.8
Belarus	1.1	1.2	116.7	123.1	Mexico	7.3	7.8	64.8	68.3
Belgium	2.8	2.6	272.5	257.5	Morocco	0.7	0.6	23.1	21.6
Brazil	11.5	12.1	58.5	60.2	Netherlands	4.3	4.0	257.6	244.8
Bulgaria	0.7	0.8	103.5	109.4	New Zealand	0.9	0.9	203.3	202.4
Burma	0.2	0.3	4.5	5.0	Nigeria	0.8	0.9	5.0	5.0
Canada	13.0	13.4	384.6	393.7	Norway	1.8	1.9	394.0	386.8
Chile	1.3	1.4	78.9	82.9	Pakistan	2.6	2.6	14.2	13.5
China	94.9	105.9	71.4	77.5	Peru	0.9	1.1	30.4	29.6
Colombia	1.4	1.5	31.1	33.7	Philippines	1.2	1.3	12.2	12.4
Congo, Dem. Rep.	0.1	0.1	1.7	1.5	Poland	4.0	3.9	105.3	105.7
Cuba	0.4	0.4	36.0	36.9	Portugal	1.1	1.0	104.1	99.2
Czech Republic	1.6	1.6	157.0	155.0	Romania	1.4	1.5	64.5	69.0
Denmark	0.8	0.7	150.2	142.9	Russia	30.0	31.5	210.7	213.4
Ecuador	0.6	0.6	40.2	39.8	Saudi Arabia	8.3	9.3	323.3	339.0
Egypt	3.2	3.5	40.4	41.6	Serbia	0.7	0.7	96.6	99.5
Finland	1.3	1.2	246.9	233.8	South Africa	5.7	5.7	115.5	115.4
France	11.0	10.7	169.8	165.9	Spain	6.2	6.0	134.3	130.8
Germany	14.0	13.5	171.7	165.4	Sweden	2.2	2.2	242.6	235.8
Greece	1.3	1.2	125.5	121.5	Switzerland	1.3	1.3	169.5	157.5
Guatemala	0.2	0.2	15.7	17.5	Syria	1.0	0.9	45.7	41.7
Haiti	(Z)	(Z)	3.2	3.1	Taiwan	4.9	4.8	212.4	209.9
Hong Kong	1.4	1.2	192.7	180.7	Tanzania	0.1	0.1	2.7	2.7
Hungary	1.1	1.0	105.4	102.7	Thailand	4.5	5.2	67.6	74.0
Iceland	0.2	0.2	688.7	688.3	Trinidad and Tobago	0.9	0.9	768.2	757.5
India	22.9	23.9	19.5	19.7	Tunisia	0.3	0.3	29.4	30.7
Indonesia	6.3	6.4	25.8	25.7	Turkey	4.5	5.1	57.7	61.4
Iran	9.2	9.6	119.9	122.1	Ukraine	5.0	5.0	111.2	118.8
Iraq	1.5	1.6	51.5	49.9	United Arab Emirates	3.6	3.8	719.1	728.4
Ireland	0.6	0.6	137.5	126.6	United Kingdom	8.9	8.6	143.1	134.5
Israel	1.0	1.0	129.7	133.5	Venezuela	3.2	3.4	118.6	117.2
Italy	7.7	7.2	126.1	123.0	Vietnam	2.0	2.3	22.6	24.6

Z Represents less than 0.05 quadrillion Btu. [1] 2012 per capita data not available as of publication date.

Source: U.S. Energy Information Administration, "International Energy Statistics Database," <http://www.eia.gov/cfapps/ipdbproject/IEDIndex3.cfm>, accessed September 2015.

Table 1387. World Energy Consumption by Region and Energy Source, 2005 to 2010, and Projections, 2020 to 2040

[In quadrillion Btu (471.1 represents 471,100,000,000,000,000). Btu = British thermal units. For Btu conversion factors, see source. Energy totals include net imports of coal coke and electricity generated from biomass in the United States. The electricity portion of the national consumption values consists of generation for domestic use plus an adjustment for electricity trade based on a fuel's share of total generation in the exporting country. OECD = Organization for Economic Co-operation and Development; see text, this section]

Region and energy source	2005	2009	2010	Projections 2020	Projections 2030	Projections 2040	Average annual percent change 2010-2040
World, total	471.1	498.4	523.9	629.8	729.2	819.6	1.50
OECD Americas	122.8	117.0	120.2	126.1	132.9	143.6	0.60
United States	100.5	94.9	97.9	100.5	102.3	107.2	0.30
OECD Europe	82.2	80.0	82.5	85.5	90.9	94.6	0.46
OECD Asia	38.8	37.7	39.6	43.0	45.4	46.4	0.53
Non-OECD Europe and Eurasia	49.5	43.7	47.2	53.3	60.8	67.1	1.18
Non-OECD Asia	113.3	148.1	159.0	230.3	290.4	337.5	2.54
Middle East	22.9	26.6	27.8	36.6	42.5	48.8	1.90
Africa	17.0	18.4	18.9	21.9	27.4	35.0	2.07
Central and South America	24.5	26.9	28.7	33.2	38.8	46.6	1.63
Liquids	170.8	171.3	176.1	194.7	210.9	232.6	0.93
Natural gas	105.0	108.7	116.8	136.0	162.6	191.3	1.66
Coal	122.3	139.1	147.4	180.3	207.9	219.5	1.34
Nuclear	27.5	26.7	27.3	37.9	49.5	57.2	2.50
Other	45.4	52.6	56.2	81.0	98.3	119.1	2.53

Source: U.S. Energy Information Administration, *International Energy Outlook 2013*, July 2013, and earlier reports. See also <http://www.eia.gov/oiaf/ieo/ieorefcase.html>.

Table 1388. World Dry Natural Gas Production by Major Producing Country: 1980 to 2013

[In billion cubic feet (53,375 represents 53,375,000,000,000). Ranked for top 30 countries, as of current year]

Country	Natural gas production								
	1980	1990	2000	2005	2009	2010	2011	2012	2013
World, total [1]................	53,375	73,694	87,100	98,302	105,179	112,574	116,255	119,454	121,283
United States..................	19,403	17,810	19,182	18,051	20,624	21,316	22,902	24,033	24,334
Russia...........................	(X)	(X)	19,335	21,224	19,303	21,536	22,213	21,764	22,139
Iran..............................	250	837	2,127	3,655	4,986	5,161	5,361	5,640	5,696
Qatar............................	184	276	1,028	1,617	3,154	4,166	5,198	5,546	5,598
Canada..........................	2,759	3,849	6,470	6,561	5,634	5,390	5,218	5,070	5,129
China............................	505	508	962	1,763	2,975	3,334	3,629	3,666	3,986
Norway..........................	917	976	1,867	3,072	3,664	3,756	3,580	4,052	3,840
Saudi Arabia...................	334	1,077	1,759	2,516	2,770	3,096	3,258	3,508	3,526
Netherlands....................	3,398	2,693	2,559	2,773	2,786	3,131	2,851	2,843	3,052
Turkmenistan..................	(X)	(X)	1,642	2,225	1,347	1,600	2,338	2,437	2,995
Algeria..........................	411	1,787	2,940	3,151	2,876	2,988	2,923	3,053	2,813
Indonesia.......................	654	1,602	2,237	2,001	2,557	2,841	2,693	2,619	2,486
Malaysia.........................	56	654	1,600	1,967	2,133	2,171	2,180	2,190	2,260
Australia........................	313	723	1,159	1,266	1,492	1,708	1,810	1,977	2,179
Uzbekistan.....................	(X)	(X)	1,992	2,108	2,169	2,123	2,226	2,222	2,106
Egypt............................	30	286	646	1,501	2,214	2,166	2,163	2,140	2,034
United Arab Emirates.........	200	780	1,355	1,659	1,724	1,811	1,847	1,918	1,928
Mexico...........................	900	903	1,314	1,349	1,722	1,799	1,744	1,671	1,640
Trinidad and Tobago..........	81	177	493	1,069	1,437	1,499	1,434	1,508	1,511
Thailand.........................	–	208	658	837	1,091	1,281	1,306	1,182	1,476
Pakistan.........................	286	482	856	1,088	1,367	1,400	1,383	1,457	1,412
United Kingdom................	1,323	1,754	3,826	3,118	2,087	1,988	1,546	1,452	1,359
Nigeria..........................	38	131	440	791	912	1,024	1,107	1,503	1,356
Argentina.......................	280	630	1,321	1,611	1,461	1,416	1,369	1,329	1,303
India.............................	51	399	795	1,056	1,437	1,848	1,682	1,448	1,218
Oman............................	28	99	322	699	875	957	937	1,115	1,127
Bangladesh.....................	50	162	343	494	692	703	710	778	807
Venezuela.......................	517	761	961	828	651	697	733	803	771
Ukraine..........................	(X)	(X)	636	685	715	684	699	699	745
Brazil............................	42	97	257	345	363	445	515	598	744

X Not applicable. – Represents zero. [1] Includes countries not shown separately.

Source: U.S. Energy Information Administration, "International Energy Statistics Database," <http://www.eia.gov/cfapps/ipdbproject/IEDIndex3.cfm>, accessed June 2015.

Table 1389. World Coal Production by Major Producing Country: 1980 to 2012

[In millions of short tons (4,179.6 represents 4,179,600,000). Coal includes anthracite, subanthracite, bituminous, subbituminous, lignite, and brown coal. Ranked for top 30 countries, as of current year]

Country	Coal production								
	1980	1990	2000	2005	2008	2009	2010	2011	2012
World, total [1]................	4,179.6	5,345.0	5,137.7	6,636.3	7,471.0	7,601.6	7,999.5	8,443.8	8,687.3
China............................	683.6	1,189.7	1,525.1	2,588.1	3,099.1	3,301.8	3,560.6	3,878.0	4,017.9
United States..................	829.7	1,029.1	1,073.6	1,131.5	1,171.8	1,074.9	1,084.4	1,095.6	1,016.5
India.............................	125.8	247.6	370.0	473.3	570.0	614.9	619.8	633.8	649.6
Indonesia.......................	0.6	11.6	84.5	188.0	274.2	321.0	358.3	397.2	488.1
Australia........................	115.2	225.5	338.1	408.5	432.4	449.6	467.8	443.4	463.8
Russia...........................	(X)	(X)	264.9	311.8	336.2	304.2	354.6	354.9	390.2
South Africa....................	131.9	193.2	248.9	270.1	278.0	275.0	280.6	278.6	285.8
Germany........................	(X)	(X)	226.0	227.0	214.3	202.4	201.0	207.9	217.1
Poland...........................	253.5	237.1	179.2	175.0	158.0	148.4	146.3	152.7	158.2
Kazakhstan.....................	(X)	(X)	85.4	96.1	122.4	111.2	122.3	128.4	138.9
Colombia........................	4.5	22.6	42.0	65.1	81.0	80.3	82.0	94.6	98.6
Turkey...........................	20.8	52.3	69.7	64.3	87.5	87.6	80.9	83.9	76.6
Canada..........................	40.4	75.3	76.2	72.0	74.7	69.4	74.8	74.0	73.3
Ukraine..........................	(X)	(X)	68.8	66.5	65.5	60.6	60.6	69.1	71.2
Greece...........................	25.6	57.2	70.4	76.5	72.4	71.5	62.3	64.7	68.1
Czech Republic................	(X)	(X)	71.8	68.4	66.4	62.2	60.9	63.8	60.6
Vietnam.........................	5.7	5.1	12.8	37.6	43.8	48.6	49.4	49.0	46.4
Korea, North...................	48.6	51.0	32.8	38.2	35.6	34.8	35.3	43.1	43.2
Serbia...........................	(X)	(X)	(X)	(X)	42.7	42.4	41.9	45.3	41.9
Romania.........................	38.8	42.1	32.3	34.3	39.5	37.4	34.3	39.1	37.5
Mongolia........................	5.3	7.9	5.7	8.3	11.3	16.0	27.9	35.2	37.0
Bulgaria.........................	33.3	34.9	29.2	27.2	31.7	30.0	32.4	40.9	35.8
Thailand.........................	1.6	13.7	19.6	23.0	20.2	19.6	20.2	23.5	20.2
United Kingdom................	143.8	104.1	33.7	22.1	19.4	19.2	19.6	19.7	18.0
Mexico...........................	4.0	8.6	12.5	11.9	12.6	11.6	14.1	17.4	16.7
Bosnia and Herzegovina.......	(X)	(X)	8.2	10.1	12.4	12.6	12.1	13.9	13.9
Hungary.........................	28.7	19.7	15.5	10.5	10.4	9.9	10.0	10.5	10.2
Kosovo..........................	(X)	(X)	(X)	(X)	8.5	9.5	9.5	9.1	9.6
Philippines......................	0.4	1.4	1.5	3.2	4.0	5.2	7.3	7.6	8.8
Macedonia......................	(X)	(X)	8.3	7.6	8.4	8.2	7.4	9.0	8.2

X Not applicable. [1] Includes countries not shown separately.

Source: U.S. Energy Information Administration, "International Energy Statistics Database," <http://www.eia.gov/cfapps/ipdbproject/IEDIndex3.cfm>, accessed September 2015.

Table 1390. Carbon Dioxide Emissions From Consumption of Fossil Fuels by Country: 1980 to 2012

[In million metric tons of carbon dioxide (18,434.7 represents 18,434,700,000). Ranked for top 25 countries, as of current year. Includes carbon dioxide emissions from the consumption of petroleum, natural gas, coal, and the flaring of natural gas]

Region/Country	1980	1990	2000	2005	2008	2009	2010	2011	2012
World, total [1].........	18,434.7	21,610.4	24,041.0	27,876.4	29,644.6	29,435.6	31,154.8	32,155.0	32,310.3
China............	1,448.5	2,268.9	3,165.3	5,116.3	6,166.6	6,816.1	7,388.5	8,126.7	8,106.4
United States...........	4,775.6	5,040.8	5,863.8	5,999.1	5,840.5	5,429.8	5,580.0	5,483.2	5,270.4
India............	291.2	578.6	991.0	1,181.4	1,449.0	1,642.9	1,714.9	1,752.7	1,830.9
Russia............	(X)	(X)	1,498.8	1,587.5	1,629.1	1,479.0	1,685.1	1,710.0	1,781.7
Japan............	947.0	1,047.0	1,201.4	1,241.3	1,216.3	1,104.9	1,177.3	1,200.3	1,259.1
Germany............	(X)	(X)	854.7	833.6	812.6	758.2	797.0	784.4	788.3
Korea, South...........	131.7	242.1	438.8	493.8	521.8	524.4	584.0	650.5	657.1
Iran............	116.8	202.1	321.5	451.1	512.0	562.6	566.6	594.5	603.6
Saudi Arabia...........	176.9	208.0	290.5	401.9	421.6	437.7	506.6	551.4	582.7
Canada............	457.4	470.6	573.3	609.6	574.2	544.9	547.9	551.6	550.8
Brazil............	185.7	237.3	344.4	370.8	427.4	407.0	461.4	476.6	500.2
United Kingdom...........	613.6	601.8	560.3	583.1	563.9	516.2	529.5	488.3	498.9
South Africa...........	235.0	298.0	386.0	432.4	490.0	477.6	478.8	471.5	473.2
Indonesia...........	85.8	156.0	267.6	326.1	370.2	405.7	431.1	450.1	456.2
Mexico............	240.3	302.2	382.9	397.8	452.8	421.1	434.0	446.2	453.8
Australia............	198.8	267.6	356.3	409.2	429.6	434.8	431.1	426.5	420.6
Italy............	371.8	415.4	447.7	471.9	449.7	407.6	419.8	411.6	385.8
France............	488.9	367.7	401.7	414.0	421.6	386.4	385.6	374.3	364.5
Spain............	195.0	224.1	315.6	382.9	354.7	327.8	312.6	318.2	312.4
Taiwan............	70.6	118.3	256.1	288.8	290.4	259.6	292.9	311.3	307.1
Turkey............	68.6	129.5	201.9	230.9	272.9	269.1	268.5	294.9	296.9
Thailand............	33.6	83.9	161.8	241.8	255.1	267.9	287.3	293.4	290.7
Ukraine............	(X)	(X)	324.9	351.1	342.4	245.5	277.7	298.1	290.4
Poland............	428.9	333.8	292.6	287.6	294.7	286.5	304.6	308.1	289.5
Netherlands............	201.1	211.1	246.4	251.0	229.5	222.9	234.3	239.7	239.6

X Not applicable. [1] Includes other countries not shown separately.

Source: U.S. Energy Information Administration, "International Energy Statistics Database," <http://www.eia.gov/countries/data.cfm>, accessed March 2015.

Table 1391. Average Temperatures and Precipitation—Selected International Cities

[In degrees Fahrenheit, except as noted. Data are generally based on a standard 30-year period; for details, see source. Minus sign (-) indicates degrees below zero]

City	January Average high	January Average low	January Warm-est	January Coldest	January Average pre-cipitation (inches)	July Average high	July Average low	July Warm-est	July Coldest	July Average pre-cipitation (inches)
Amsterdam, Netherlands. ...	41	34	57	3	3.1	69	55	90	39	2.9
Athens, Greece.............	55	44	70	28	1.9	89	73	108	61	0.2
Baghdad, Iraq...............	58	38	75	25	1.1	110	78	122	61	–
Bangkok, Thailand..........	89	71	95	54	0.4	90	78	99	72	6.2
Beijing, China.............	34	17	54	1	0.2	86	72	104	63	8.8
Berlin, Germany.............	35	26	58	-11	(NA)	73	56	95	41	(NA)
Bogota, Colombia...........	66	43	84	27	1.9	64	47	82	32	1.8
Brasilia, Brazil.............	81	64	95	54	(NA)	79	52	97	37	(NA)
Buenos Aires, Argentina. ...	85	64	104	44	4.2	58	41	88	23	2.3
Cairo, Egypt.................	65	49	86	32	0.2	93	72	108	63	–
Frankfurt, Germany..........	38	30	56	-4	1.8	75	57	97	38	2.4
Geneva, Switzerland........	39	29	57	-2	2.2	77	56	96	41	2.8
Hong Kong, China..........	67	58	79	43	1.1	89	81	97	70	14.3
Istanbul, Turkey.............	46	37	64	16	3.7	82	66	100	50	0.7
Jakarta, Indonesia..........	83	75	92	72	(NA)	88	74	92	67	(NA)
Karachi, Pakistan...........	76	55	93	39	0.3	89	83	109	68	3.5
Lagos, Nigeria.............	82	79	93	64	(NA)	79	76	88	70	(NA)
London, England............	45	36	61	15	2.4	72	56	93	45	1.8
Madrid, Spain.............	51	32	68	14	1.8	90	61	104	46	0.4
Manila, Philippines..........	86	71	95	61	0.8	88	76	99	70	15.9
Mexico City, Mexico........	70	45	86	26	0.3	74	56	86	37	5.1
Montreal, Canada............	21	7	52	-31	2.8	79	61	93	43	3.4
Moscow, Russia............	21	11	46	-33	1.4	71	55	95	41	3.2
Nairobi, Kenya.............	77	58	88	45	1.8	71	54	85	43	0.5
New Delhi, India............	68	48	85	32	0.9	93	81	111	70	7.9
Paris, France.............	43	34	59	1	(NA)	75	58	95	41	(NA)
Rio De Janeiro, Brazil.......	91	74	109	64	5.3	81	64	102	52	1.8
Rome, Italy.............	55	39	64	19	3.2	83	66	100	55	0.6
Seoul, Korea.............	33	21	55	-1	(NA)	82	71	97	55	(NA)
Singapore, Singapore.......	85	73	100	66	9.4	86	76	99	70	5.9
Sydney, Australia...........	79	65	109	49	4.0	62	44	80	32	2.5
Tel Aviv, Israel.............	62	46	84	32	(NA)	87	69	100	50	(NA)
Tokyo, Japan.............	48	35	66	25	2.0	82	71	95	55	5.3
Toronto, Canada.............	28	15	59	-24	1.9	79	60	99	45	2.8

– Represents zero. NA Not available.

Source: U.S. National Oceanic and Atmospheric Administration, *Climates of the World*. See also <http://www.ncdc.noaa.gov/oa/oldpubs/>.

Table 1392. Telephones, Cellular Phones, and Internet Use by Country: 2014

[Rates per 100 inhabitants. For data qualifications for individual countries, see source]

Country	Telephone lines [1]	Cell phone subscribers [2]	Internet users [3]	Country	Telephone lines [1]	Cell phone subscribers [2]	Internet users [3]
United States	**40.12**	**98.41**	**87.36**	Jordan	5.00	147.80	44.00
Afghanistan	0.33	74.88	6.39	Kenya	0.40	73.84	43.40
Argentina	22.58	158.74	64.70	Korea, South	59.54	115.54	84.33
Australia	38.89	131.23	84.56	Malaysia	14.61	148.83	67.50
Azerbaijan	18.87	110.91	61.00	Mexico	17.04	82.54	44.39
Bangladesh	0.69	75.92	9.60	Morocco	7.43	131.71	56.80
Brazil	21.84	138.95	57.60	Myanmar	0.98	49.47	2.10
Canada	46.65	82.98	87.12	Netherlands	42.41	116.42	93.17
China	17.90	92.27	49.30	Nigeria	0.10	77.84	42.68
Colombia	14.68	113.08	52.57	Norway	22.72	116.51	96.30
Croatia	36.72	104.43	68.57	Pakistan	2.65	73.33	13.80
Cuba	11.23	22.48	30.00	Panama	14.99	158.05	44.92
Egypt	7.57	114.31	31.70	Poland	13.18	156.45	66.60
Ethiopia	0.85	31.59	2.90	Romania	21.26	105.91	54.08
France	60.03	100.36	83.75	Russia	27.67	155.14	70.52
Germany	56.89	120.42	86.19	Saudi Arabia	13.36	179.56	63.70
Greece	46.90	114.96	63.21	South Africa	8.10	149.68	49.00
Haiti	0.39	64.71	11.40	Spain	40.56	107.85	76.19
Honduras	6.45	93.52	19.08	Sweden	39.67	127.84	92.52
Hong Kong	61.09	239.30	74.56	Switzerland	53.63	140.54	87.00
India	2.13	74.48	18.00	Syria	18.13	70.95	28.09
Indonesia	11.72	126.18	17.14	Thailand	8.46	144.44	34.89
Iran	38.98	87.79	39.35	Turkey	16.52	94.79	51.04
Iraq	5.60	94.91	11.30	Ukraine	24.64	144.08	43.40
Israel	37.07	121.45	71.45	United Kingdom	52.35	123.58	91.61
Italy	33.68	154.25	61.96	Venezuela	25.31	98.95	57.00
Japan	50.09	120.23	90.58	Vietnam	6.01	147.11	48.31

[1] Telephone lines are fixed telephone lines that connect a subscriber's terminal equipment to the public switched telephone network and have a port on a telephone exchange. Integrated services digital network channels and fixed wireless subscribers are included. [2] Mobile cellular telephone subscriptions are subscriptions to a public mobile telephone service using cellular technology, which provide access to the public switched telephone network. Post-paid and prepaid subscriptions are included. [3] Internet users are individuals who have used the Internet (from any location) in the last 12 months. Internet can be used via a computer, mobile phone, personal digital assistant, games machine, digital TV, etc.

Source: The World Bank, Washington, DC, "World Development Indicators" database ©, <http://data.worldbank.org/data-catalog/world-development-indicators>, accessed August 2015.

Table 1393. Patents by Country: 2014

[Includes only U.S. patents granted to residents of areas outside of the United States and its territories. For information on types of patents, see <http://www.uspto.gov/web/offices/ac/ido/oeip/taf/patdesc.htm>. Countries are in rank order. See also Table 796 and Table 797]

Country	Total [1]	Utility (inventions)	Designs	Country	Total [1]	Utility (inventions)	Designs
Total	**167,324**	**156,057**	**10,272**	Switzerland	2,601	2,398	199
Japan	56,006	53,849	1,975	Australia	2,019	1,693	273
Korea, South	18,161	16,469	1,630	Finland	1,465	1,338	116
Germany	17,594	16,550	930	Belgium	1,305	1,220	72
Taiwan	12,254	11,332	908	Austria	1,281	1,180	96
China	7,921	7,236	676	Denmark	1,263	1,051	151
Canada	7,693	7,043	617	Singapore	1,010	946	60
United Kingdom	7,156	6,487	603	Spain	857	789	62
France	7,103	6,691	395	Hong Kong	818	606	211
Israel	3,617	3,471	122	Norway	601	547	54
India	3,044	2,987	57	Ireland	491	467	23
Italy	3,033	2,628	393	Russia	448	445	3
Sweden	2,946	2,767	177				
Netherlands	2,842	2,505	98	Other countries	3,795	3,362	371

[1] Includes patents for botanical plants and reissues, not shown separately.

Source: U.S. Patent and Trademark Office, "General Patent Statistics Reports Available for Viewing," <http://www.uspto.gov/web/offices/ac/ido/oeip/taf/reports_stco.htm>, accessed March 2015.

Table 1394. Global Telecommunications Indicators: 2000 to 2014

[In millions (975 represents 975,000,000), except as indicated]

Indicators	2000	2005	2010	2011	2012	2013	2014
NUMBER (million)							
Fixed telephone lines [1]	975	1,243	1,229	1,202	1,179	1,138	1,099
Mobile cellular subscribers [1]	738	2,205	5,298	5,893	6,265	6,666	6,965
Fixed broadband Internet subscribers [2]	(NA)	220	533	605	661	710	750
Secure internet servers [3]	(NA)	0.40	1.06	1.27	1.27	1.14	1.37
PER 100 INHABITANTS							
Fixed telephone lines [1]	15.95	19.44	17.76	17.18	16.67	15.91	15.18
Mobile cellular subscriptions [1]	12.08	33.91	76.57	84.28	88.56	93.14	96.27
Internet users [1]	6.77	15.80	29.20	31.82	35.15	37.99	40.69
Fixed broadband Internet subscribers [2]	(NA)	3.68	8.19	9.03	10.14	10.03	9.60

NA Not available. [1] See footnotes, Table 1392. [2] Includes broadband subscribers using a digital subscriber line, cable modem, or other high-speed technology. [3] Includes servers using encryption technology in Internet transactions.

Source: The World Bank, Washington, DC, "World Development Indicators" database ©, <http://data.worldbank.org/data-catalog/world-development-indicators>, accessed August 2015.

Table 1395. Foreign Stock Market Activity—MSCI Indexes: 2010 to 2014

[Index figures shown are as of December 31. January 1, 1970 = 100, except as noted. Minus sign (-) indicates decrease. Based on share prices denominated in U.S. dollars]

Index and country	Index 2010	Index 2013	Index 2014	Percent change[1] 2013	Percent change[1] 2014	Index and country	Index 2010	Index 2013	Index 2014	Percent change[1] 2013	Percent change[1] 2014
ALL COUNTRY (AC) INDEXES						Hong Kong	8,724	9,577	9,771	8.1	2.0
AC World Index[2]	331	409	417	20.3	2.1	Japan	2,496	2,763	2,606	24.9	-5.7
AC World Index[2] except USA[2]	263	281	263	12.3	-6.3	Singapore	4,212	4,133	4,110	-1.8	-0.6
AC Asia Pacific[2]	138	141	138	9.3	-2.5						
AC Europe[2]	407	482	436	20.1	-9.6	**EMERGING MARKETS (EM)**					
European Union[2]	365	433	392	21.3	-9.5	EM Far East index[2]	405	401	402	0.4	0.4
						China[4]	66	63	66	0.4	4.7
DEVELOPED MARKETS						India[4]	559	407	496	-5.3	21.9
World index	1,280	1,661	1,710	24.1	2.9	Indonesia	833	665	826	-25.0	24.1
EAFE index[3]	1,658	1,916	1,775	19.4	-7.3	Korea, South	410	443	387	3.1	-12.6
Europe index	1,457	1,759	1,608	21.7	-8.6	Malaysia	453	507	439	4.2	-13.4
Pacific index	2,269	2,430	2,304	15.2	-5.2	Pakistan[4, 5]	98	(NA)	(NA)	(NA)	(NA)
Far East index	2,710	2,973	2,839	20.8	-4.5	Philippines	351	467	578	-4.3	23.7
						Sri Lanka[4, 5]	288	(NA)	(NA)	0.0	(NA)
United States	**1,201**	**1,768**	**1,965**	**29.9**	**11.1**	Taiwan	313	290	310	6.6	6.9
Canada	1,861	1,756	1,746	3.3	-0.6	Thailand	340	350	396	-16.9	13.3
						EM Latin America index	4,614	3,201	2,728	-15.7	-14.8
Australia	884	874	808	-0.3	-7.5	Argentina[5]	3,573	(NA)	(NA)	(NA)	(NA)
New Zealand[2]	99	131	135	6.2	2.6	Brazil	3,761	2,218	1,832	-18.7	-17.4
						Chile	2,910	1,843	1,575	-23.0	-14.5
Austria	1,509	1,277	882	10.9	-30.9	Colombia[4]	1,113	1,038	807	-23.7	-22.3
Belgium	1,051	1,557	1,587	24.6	1.9	Mexico	6,473	6,977	6,263	-2.0	-10.2
Denmark	5,494	7,310	7,648	23.4	4.6	Peru[4]	1,817	1,102	1,203	-31.0	9.2
Finland[2]	493	505	484	41.6	-4.1						
France	1,492	1,747	1,540	23.3	-11.9	EM Europe, Middle East, and Africa index[6]	392	328	271	-8.0	-17.6
Germany	1,711	2,230	1,959	28.2	-12.2	Czech Republic[7]	504	369	339	-14.9	-7.9
Ireland[2]	106	171	172	38.9	1.0	Egypt[7]	860	676	853	6.2	26.2
Italy	316	298	264	16.9	-11.4	Greece[2, 8]	224	118	71	46.2	-40.0
Netherlands	1,998	2,576	2,448	28.5	-5.0	Hungary[7]	663	467	329	-9.0	-29.6
Norway	2,965	3,095	2,314	5.3	-25.2	Jordan[5]	132	(NA)	(NA)	(NA)	(NA)
Portugal[2]	125	99	60	7.5	-39.8	Morocco[5, 7]	461	(NA)	(NA)	(NA)	(NA)
Spain	502	515	485	27.7	-5.8	Poland[4]	1,016	888	739	-1.7	-16.8
Sweden	6,888	8,161	7,358	21.4	-9.8	Russia[7]	932	787	405	-2.6	-48.5
Switzerland	3,915	5,172	5,051	23.8	-2.3	South Africa[4]	612	529	543	-8.8	2.5
United Kingdom	1,138	1,375	1,255	16.2	-8.7	Turkey	625	456	532	-28.1	16.7
Israel	282	199	239	8.0	20.1						

NA Not available. [1] Percent change during calendar year (e.g., Jan. 1 through December 31). Adjusted for foreign exchange fluctuations relative to U.S. dollar. [2] January 1, 1988 = 100. [3] Europe, Australasia, Far East Index. Comprised of all European and Far East countries classified as developed markets plus Australia, New Zealand, and Israel (reclassified May 2010). [4] January 1, 1993 = 100. [5] Reclassified as a Frontier Market. [6] January 1, 2001 = 100. [7] January 1, 1995 = 100. [8] Reclassified as an Emerging Market in November 2013.

Source: MSCI <http://www.msci.com/products/indices/> ©. The MSCI data contained herein is the property of MSCI Inc. (MSCI). MSCI, its affiliates and information providers make no warranties with respect to any such data. The MSCI data contained herein is used under license and may not be further used, distributed, or disseminated without the express written consent of MSCI.

Table 1396. Foreign Stock Market Indices: 1980 to 2014

[As of year end. The DAX-30 index is a total return index which includes dividends, whereas the other foreign indices are price indices which exclude dividends]

Year	London FTSE 100	Tokyo Nikkei 225	Hong Kong Hang Seng	Germany DAX-30	Paris CAC-40	Dow Jones Europe STOXX 50
1980	647	7,116	1,477	481	(X)	(X)
1985	1,413	13,113	1,752	1,366	(X)	(X)
1990	2,144	23,849	3,025	1,398	1,518	835
1995	3,689	19,868	10,073	2,254	1,872	1,538
2000	6,223	13,786	15,096	6,434	5,926	4,557
2001	5,217	10,543	11,397	5,160	4,625	3,707
2002	3,940	8,579	9,321	2,893	3,064	2,408
2003	4,477	10,677	12,576	3,965	3,558	2,660
2004	4,814	11,489	14,230	4,256	3,821	2,775
2005	5,619	16,111	14,876	5,408	4,715	3,349
2006	6,221	17,226	19,965	6,597	5,542	3,697
2007	6,457	15,308	27,813	8,067	5,614	3,684
2008	4,434	8,860	14,388	4,810	3,218	2,065
2009	5,413	10,546	21,873	5,957	3,936	2,579
2010	5,900	10,229	23,035	6,914	3,805	2,586
2011	5,572	8,455	18,434	5,898	3,160	2,370
2012	5,898	10,395	22,657	7,612	3,641	2,578
2013	6,749	16,291	23,306	9,552	4,296	2,919
2014	6,566	17,451	23,605	9,806	4,273	3,004

X Not applicable.

Source: Global Financial Data, Los Angeles, CA ©, <http://www.globalfinancialdata.com>.

Table 1397. Foreign Exchange Rates by Country and Currency: 2014

[Foreign currency units per U.S. dollar. Rates shown are annual averages, including market and official exchange rates]

Country	Currency	2014 [1]	Country	Currency	2014 [1]
Afghanistan	Afghani	(NA)	Kuwait	Kuwaiti dinar	0.29
Albania	Lek	105.48	Kyrgyzstan	Som	52.66
Algeria	Algerian dinar	79.60	Laos	Kip	8,052.00
Angola	Kwanza	98.15	Latvia	Lat	0.75
Argentina	Argentine peso	8.22	Lebanon	Lebanese pound	1,507.50
Armenia	Dram	415.90	Lesotho	Loti	10.60
Australia	Australian dollar	1.10	Liberia	Liberian dollar	86.65
Austria	Euro	0.75	Libya	Libyan dinar	1.28
Azerbaijan	Manat	0.78	Lithuania	Lita	2.56
Bahrain	Bahrain dinar	0.38	Macedonia	Denar	50.56
Bangladesh	Taka	77.57	Madagascar	Malagasy ariary	2,393.50
Belarus	Belarusian ruble	10,685.00	Malawi	Kwacha	412.10
Belgium	Euro	0.75	Malaysia	Ringgit	3.24
Benin	CFA franc	491.20	Mali	CFA franc	491.20
Bhutan	Ngultrum	60.42	Mauritania	Ouguiya	299.50
Bolivia	Boliviano	6.96	Mauritius	Mauritian rupee	30.43
Bosnia/Herzegovina	Konvertibilna marka	1.47	Mexico	Peso	13.14
Botswana	Pula	9.19	Moldova	Leu	13.97
Brazil	Real	2.36	Mongolia	Togrog	1,817.40
Brunei	Brunei dollar	1.24	Morocco	Dirham	8.24
Bulgaria	Leva	1.47	Mozambique	Metical	31.20
Burkina Faso	CFA franc	491.20	Namibia	Namibia dollar	9.65
Burma	Kyat	975.50	Nepal	Nepalese rupee	97.40
Burundi	Burundi franc	1,548.50	Netherlands	Euro	0.75
Cambodia	Riel	4,075.00	New Zealand	New Zealand dollar	1.21
Cameroon	CFA franc	491.20	Nicaragua	Cordoba	26.01
Canada	Canadian dollar	1.10	Niger	CFA franc	491.20
Central African Rep	CFA franc	491.20	Nigeria	Naira	157.30
Chad	CFA franc	491.20	Norway	Krone	6.16
Chile	Chilean peso	568.00	Oman	Omani rial	0.38
China	Renminbi yuan	6.14	Pakistan	Pakistan rupee	102.89
Colombia	Colombian peso	1,992.00	Panama	Balboa	1.00
Congo, Dem. Rep.	Congolese franc	926.80	Papua New Guinea	Kina	2.44
Congo, Republic of	CFA franc	491.20	Paraguay	Guarani	4,451.70
Costa Rica	Colon	539.30	Peru	Nuevo sol	2.84
Cote d'Ivoire	CFA franc	491.20	Philippines	Philippine peso	44.40
Croatia	Kuna	5.75	Poland	Zloty	3.14
Cuba	Peso	22.57	Portugal	Euro	0.75
Czech Republic	Koruna	20.63	Qatar	Riyal	3.64
Denmark	Krone	5.59	Romania	Leu	3.35
Djibouti	Djibouti franc	177.70	Russia	Ruble	67.70
Dominican Republic	Dominican peso	43.50	Rwanda	Rwandan franc	684.30
Ecuador	U.S. dollar	1.00	Saint Lucia	East Caribbean dollar	2.70
Egypt	Egyptian pound	7.10	Saudi Arabia	Riyal	3.75
El Salvador	U.S. dollar	1.00	Senegal	CFA franc	494.40
Eritrea	Nakfa	15.38	Serbia	Serbian dinar	87.71
Estonia	Euro	0.75	Sierra Leone	Leone	4,376.10
Ethiopia	Birr	21.13	Singapore	Singapore dollar	1.27
Fiji	Fijian dollar	1.99	Slovakia	Euro	0.75
Finland	Euro	0.75	Slovenia	Euro	0.75
France	Euro	0.75	Somalia	Somali shilling	(NA)
Gabon	CFA franc	491.20	South Africa	Rand	10.79
Gambia, The	Dalasi	39.98	Spain	Euro	0.75
Georgia	Lari	1.76	Sri Lanka	Sri Lankan rupee	130.40
Germany	Euro	0.75	Sudan	Sudanese dinar	5.79
Ghana	Cedi	2.88	Suriname	Suriname dollar	3.30
Greece	Euro	0.75	Swaziland	Emalangeni	10.60
Guatemala	Quetzal	7.83	Sweden	Krona	6.76
Guinea	Guinean franc	7,025.00	Switzerland	Swiss franc	0.91
Guyana	Guyana dollar	206.90	Syria	Syrian pound	152.90
Haiti	Gourde	45.25	Taiwan	New Taiwan dollar	31.72
Honduras	Lempira	21.10	Tajikistan	Tajik somoni	4.92
Hong Kong	Hong Kong dollar	7.75	Tanzania	Tanzania shilling	1,647.80
Hungary	Forint	231.70	Thailand	Baht	32.48
Iceland	Krona	116.10	Trinidad and Tobago	Tr. and Tob. dollar	6.40
India	Rupee	60.30	Tunisia	Tunisian dinar	1.70
Indonesia	Rupiah	12,388.00	Turkey	Lira	2.19
Iran	Rial	25,780.20	Turkmenistan	Manat	2.85
Iraq	Dinar	1,166.00	Uganda	Uganda shilling	2,600.30
Ireland	Euro	0.75	Ukraine	Hryvnia	11.58
Israel	Shekel	3.91	United Arab Emirates	Dirham	3.67
Italy	Euro	0.75	United Kingdom	Pound sterling	0.60
Jamaica	Jamaican dollar	111.00	Uruguay	Uruguayan peso	23.18
Japan	Yen	105.80	Uzbekistan	Soum	2,313.60
Jordan	Jordanian dinar	0.71	Venezuela	Bolivar	6.28
Kazakhstan	Tenge	179.30	Vietnam	Dong	21,149.00
Kenya	Kenyan shilling	87.63	West Bank and Gaza	Israeli shekel	3.91
Korea, North	North Korean won	(NA)	Yemen	Yemeni rial	214.90
Korea, South	Won	1,053.00	Zambia	Zambian kwacha	6.10

NA Not available. [1] End-of-year values were used if annual averages were unavailable. Some values were estimated using partial year data.

Source: Central Intelligence Agency, "The World Factbook," <https://www.cia.gov/library/publications/the-world-factbook/>, accessed September 2015.

Table 1398. Research and Development (R&D) Expenditures by Sector and Country: 2013

[Total and per capita expenditures in millions of dollars (1,128,468 represents $1,128,468,000,000). Gross domestic expenditure on R&D (GERD) may include financing from abroad. Selected data are preliminary or estimated. For methodological information for individual countries, see source. GDP = gross domestic product]

Country	Gross domestic expenditure on R&D (GERD)			Percent of GERD performed by:			
	Total (million current PPP U.S. dollars) [1]	Per capita (million current PPP U.S. dollars) [1]	Percent of GDP	Government sector	Business enterprise sector	Higher education sector	Private non-profit sector
OECD total [2]..........	1,128,468	895	2.4	11.3	68.1	18.2	2.4
EU-28 [2]................	342,431	673	1.9	12.8	62.7	23.5	1.0
EU-15 [3]................	317,928	789	2.1	12.1	63.6	23.3	1.1
**United States [4].......	456,977	1,444	2.7	11.2	70.6	14.2	4.1**
Argentina...............	5,438	131	0.6	47.0	20.7	30.5	1.7
Australia [5]............	20,956	932	2.1	11.2	57.9	28.1	3.0
Austria.................	11,282	1,331	3.0	5.1	68.8	25.6	0.5
Belgium................	10,603	955	2.3	8.8	69.1	21.7	0.4
Canada................	24,565	699	1.6	9.2	50.5	39.8	0.5
Chile..................	1,494	85	0.4	4.7	35.5	38.8	21.0
China.................	336,495	247	2.1	16.2	76.6	7.2	(NA)
Czech Republic........	5,813	553	1.9	18.3	54.1	27.2	0.3
Denmark..............	7,513	1,339	3.1	2.4	65.4	31.8	0.4
Estonia...............	592	449	1.7	8.9	47.7	42.3	1.1
Finland...............	7,176	1,319	3.3	8.9	68.9	21.5	0.7
France................	55,218	838	2.2	13.1	64.8	20.7	1.3
Germany..............	100,991	1,230	2.9	15.1	66.9	18.0	(NA)
Greece...............	2,274	206	0.8	28.0	33.3	37.4	1.2
Hungary..............	3,250	328	1.4	14.9	69.4	14.4	(NA)
Iceland...............	271	836	2.0	12.7	53.4	32.6	1.3
Ireland [6]............	3,271	713	1.6	4.8	72.0	23.1	(NA)
Israel [7].............	11,033	1,370	4.2	2.1	82.7	14.1	1.0
Italy..................	26,520	437	1.3	14.9	54.0	28.2	2.9
Japan.................	160,247	1,258	3.5	9.2	76.1	13.5	1.3
Korea, South..........	68,937	1,373	4.1	10.9	78.5	9.2	1.3
Luxembourg...........	571	1,048	1.2	23.3	61.4	15.3	(NA)
Mexico...............	10,020	85	0.5	(NA)	(NA)	(NA)	(NA)
Netherlands...........	15,377	915	2.0	12.2	55.7	32.1	(NA)
New Zealand..........	1,828	410	1.2	23.2	46.4	30.4	(NA)
Norway...............	5,514	1,085	1.7	16.0	52.5	31.5	(NA)
Poland................	7,918	206	0.9	26.8	43.6	29.3	0.3
Portugal..............	3,943	377	1.4	5.8	47.6	37.8	8.8
Romania..............	1,453	73	0.4	49.2	30.7	19.7	0.4
Russia................	40,695	285	1.1	30.3	60.6	9.0	0.1
Singapore [6]..........	8,177	1,539	2.0	10.0	60.9	29.0	(NA)
Slovak Republic.......	1,191	220	0.8	20.5	46.3	33.1	0.2
Slovenia..............	1,538	747	2.6	13.0	76.5	10.4	0.0
South Africa [6]........	4,871	95	0.7	22.9	44.3	30.7	2.1
Spain.................	19,133	411	1.2	18.7	53.1	28.0	0.2
Sweden...............	14,151	1,474	3.3	3.7	68.9	27.1	0.2
Switzerland [6]..........	13,251	1,657	3.0	0.8	69.3	28.1	1.8
Taiwan................	30,511	1,305	3.0	13.4	75.5	10.8	0.3
Turkey................	13,315	176	0.9	10.4	47.5	42.1	(NA)
United Kingdom.......	39,859	622	1.6	7.3	64.5	26.3	1.9

NA Not available or not applicable. [1] Purchasing power parities (PPPs) are currency conversion rates used to convert different currencies to a common value (U.S. dollars in this case). See introductory text, this section. [2] For full membership listing of the Organisation for Economic Co-operation and Development (OECD) and the European Union-28, see introductory text, this section. [3] European Union-15: Austria, Belgium, Denmark, Finland, France, Germany, Greece, Ireland, Italy, Luxembourg, Netherlands, Portugal, Spain, Sweden, and United Kingdom. [4] Excludes all or most capital expenditures. [5] 2011 data. [6] 2012 data. [7] Excludes defense expenditures. The statistical data for Israel are supplied by and under the responsibility of the relevant Israeli authorities. The use of such data by the OECD is without prejudice to the status of the Golan Heights, East Jerusalem and Israeli settlements in the West Bank under the terms of international law.

Source: Organisation for Economic Co-cooperation and Development (OECD), 2015, "Main Science and Technology Indicators," OECD Science, Technology and R&D Statistics (database) ©, <http://dx.doi.org/10.1787/data-00182-en>, accessed July 2015.

Table 1399. Development Assistance Outlays by Donor Country: 2013

[135,072 represents $135,072,000, except percent. Official development assistance (ODA) includes concessional loans and grants made by donor governments to developing countries and to multilateral institutions such as the United Nations or the World Bank]

Country	Official development assistance (ODA)			Multilateral ODA (mil. current U.S. dol.)	Net private grants (mil. current U.S. dol.)
	Net disbursements (mil. current U.S. dollars)	Percent of GNI [1]	Percent of total DAC [2] ODA		
DAC countries, total [2]...........	135,072	0.30	100.0	41,519	29,727
United States.....................	**31,497**	**0.18**	**23.3**	**5,113**	**22,579**
Australia........................	4,846	0.33	3.6	696	(NA)
Austria.........................	1,171	0.27	0.9	628	-1
Belgium.........................	2,300	0.45	1.7	992	664
Canada..........................	4,947	0.28	3.7	1,436	1,922
Czech Republic..................	211	0.11	0.2	154	(NA)
Denmark.........................	2,927	0.85	2.2	793	85
Finland.........................	1,435	0.54	1.1	613	16
France..........................	11,339	0.41	8.4	4,538	(NA)
Germany.........................	14,228	0.38	10.5	4,777	1,416
Greece..........................	239	0.10	0.2	195	(NA)
Iceland.........................	35	0.25	–	6	(NA)
Ireland.........................	846	0.46	0.6	300	87
Italy...........................	3,430	0.17	2.5	2,563	58
Japan...........................	11,582	0.23	8.6	2,970	458
Korea, South....................	1,755	0.13	1.3	446	331
Luxembourg......................	429	1.00	0.3	131	(NA)
Netherlands.....................	5,435	0.67	4.0	1,789	1,514
New Zealand.....................	457	0.26	0.3	107	76
Norway..........................	5,581	1.07	4.1	1,266	(NA)
Poland..........................	472	0.10	0.3	351	(NA)
Portugal........................	488	0.23	0.4	186	7
Slovak Republic.................	86	0.09	0.1	70	(NA)
Slovenia........................	62	0.13	–	41	(NA)
Spain...........................	2,375	0.18	1.8	1,430	–
Sweden..........................	5,827	1.01	4.3	1,909	11
Switzerland.....................	3,200	0.45	2.4	695	503
United Kingdom..................	17,871	0.71	13.2	7,326	–

– Represents or rounds to zero. NA Not available. [1] Gross national income. See headnote, Table 1353. [2] Development Assistance Committee (DAC) of the Organisation for Economic Co-operation and Development (OECD), comprised of 28 developed countries, as shown above, and European Union Institutions, not shown separately.

Source: Organisation for Economic Co-operation and Development (OECD), 2015, "Detailed aid statistics: Official and private flows," OECD International Development Statistics (database) ©, <http://dx.doi.org/10.1787/data-00072-en>, accessed July 2015.

Table 1400. Net Flow of Financial Resources to Developing Countries and Multilateral Organizations by Donor Country: 2000 to 2013

[134,228 represents $134,228,000,000. Net flow covers official and private loans, grants, development assistance, and technical assistance, minus amortization on loans. Military flows are excluded. GNI = gross national income. For explanation of GNI, see headnote, Table 1353]

Country	Amount (million dollars)				Percent of GNI			
	2000	2010	2012	2013	2000	2010	2012	2013
DAC countries total [1]..............	**134,228**	**510,106**	**473,965**	**445,037**	**0.54**	**1.25**	**1.06**	**0.98**
United States.........................	**25,252**	**214,378**	**162,440**	**148,801**	**0.25**	**1.47**	**0.98**	**0.87**
Australia........................	1,891	14,531	21,906	23,170	0.51	1.23	1.46	1.58
Austria.........................	1,135	6,372	4,797	866	0.61	1.70	1.22	0.20
Belgium.........................	2,281	7,896	2,703	10,218	1.00	1.68	0.55	2.01
Canada..........................	6,483	22,642	18,515	11,109	0.95	1.46	1.03	0.62
Czech Republic..................	16	228	220	211	0.03	0.13	0.12	0.11
Denmark.........................	2,176	4,794	2,400	4,371	1.39	1.52	0.74	1.27
Finland.........................	1,087	4,312	1,527	996	0.91	1.78	0.62	0.37
France..........................	5,557	35,198	29,578	10,523	0.41	1.35	1.11	0.38
Germany.........................	12,331	41,637	34,717	51,219	0.66	1.24	1.00	1.37
Greece..........................	229	761	907	869	0.20	0.26	0.36	0.36
Iceland.........................	9	29	26	35	0.10	0.29	0.22	0.25
Ireland.........................	740	2,695	956	1,933	0.93	1.57	0.56	1.06
Italy...........................	10,846	9,608	11,186	16,703	1.01	0.48	0.56	0.81
Japan...........................	11,423	48,249	48,977	58,459	0.24	0.86	0.80	1.15
Korea...........................	44	11,834	12,415	15,038	0.01	1.17	1.09	1.14
Luxembourg......................	129	411	399	429	0.73	1.07	1.00	1.00
Netherlands.....................	6,947	13,013	19,943	19,428	1.85	1.67	2.56	2.39
New Zealand.....................	142	426	629	581	0.32	0.32	0.39	0.33
Norway..........................	1,437	5,876	4,752	5,580	0.87	1.41	0.93	1.07
Poland..........................	29	378	421	472	0.02	0.08	0.09	0.10
Portugal........................	4,622	162	475	2,275	4.45	0.07	0.23	1.06
Slovak Republic.................	6	74	80	86	0.03	0.09	0.09	0.09
Slovenia........................	(NA)	59	58	62	(NA)	0.13	0.13	0.13
Spain...........................	23,471	10,340	1,977	8,013	4.25	0.75	0.15	0.59
Sweden..........................	3,952	5,127	14,156	10,447	1.76	1.10	2.63	1.82
Switzerland.....................	1,765	23,444	14,342	13,293	0.64	4.01	2.20	1.85
United Kingdom..................	10,230	25,632	63,461	29,849	0.72	1.12	2.57	1.18

NA Not available. [1] The OECD Development Assistance Committee (DAC) is comprised of the above-listed member countries plus the European Union.

Source: Organisation for Economic Co-operation and Development (OECD), 2015, "Detailed aid statistics: Official and private flows," OECD International Development Statistics (database) ©, <http://dx.doi.org/10.1787/data-00072-en>, accessed July 2015.

Table 1401. External Debt by Developing Country: 2000 to 2013

[In millions of U.S. dollars (9,763 represents $9,763,000,000). Total external debt is debt owed to nonresidents repayable in foreign currency, goods, or services. Total external debt is the sum of public, publicly guaranteed, and private nonguaranteed long-term debt, use of International Monetary Fund (IMF) credit, and short-term debt. Short-term debt includes all debt having an original maturity of one year or less and interest in arrears on long-term debt]

Country	2000	2010	2012	2013	Country	2000	2010	2012	2013
Angola	9,763	16,949	20,106	24,004	Lebanon	10,250	24,591	28,951	30,947
Argentina	147,029	120,791	133,042	136,272	Malaysia	41,946	135,800	195,064	213,129
Bangladesh	15,596	25,752	26,188	27,804	Mauritius	967	2,734	10,221	10,919
Belarus	2,604	28,397	33,756	39,108	Mexico	152,260	262,022	375,830	443,012
Bosnia and Herzegovina	2,800	9,935	10,577	11,078	Mongolia	960	5,928	15,385	18,921
Brazil	242,512	352,364	440,507	482,470	Morocco	20,790	27,250	33,815	39,261
Bulgaria	12,009	50,318	50,656	52,995	Nigeria	31,582	7,207	10,059	13,792
China	145,648	559,772	750,746	874,463	Pakistan	32,954	61,960	60,938	56,461
Colombia	33,159	63,815	79,871	91,978	Panama	6,606	11,382	13,247	16,471
Costa Rica	4,738	8,547	14,510	17,443	Papua New Guinea	2,305	5,965	23,128	21,733
Cote d'Ivoire	12,187	10,665	9,168	11,288	Paraguay	3,135	12,652	12,880	13,430
Dominican Republic	4,652	13,497	22,100	23,831	Peru	28,813	42,154	54,150	56,661
Ecuador	13,338	14,963	16,931	20,280	Philippines	58,456	60,775	61,390	60,609
Egypt	29,178	36,542	39,998	44,430	Romania	11,252	124,136	130,419	133,996
El Salvador	4,535	11,059	13,189	13,372	Serbia [1]	11,573	32,935	34,444	36,397
Ethiopia	5,509	7,347	10,462	12,557	South Africa	25,435	107,131	144,871	139,845
Georgia	1,826	9,519	13,149	13,694	Sri Lanka	9,173	19,898	23,520	25,168
Ghana	6,254	9,300	12,568	15,832	Sudan [2]	16,085	22,233	21,793	22,416
Guatemala	3,948	15,039	14,053	16,823	Tanzania	7,183	8,987	11,581	13,024
Hungary	30,754	215,935	201,380	196,739	Thailand	79,830	106,323	134,222	135,379
India	101,130	291,651	395,071	427,562	Tunisia	11,355	22,472	25,261	25,827
Indonesia	143,655	198,268	245,821	259,069	Turkey	116,787	299,183	337,096	388,243
Jamaica	4,716	14,099	14,219	13,790	Ukraine	13,890	125,173	135,872	147,712
Jordan	11,063	17,215	18,846	23,970	Uzbekistan	4,980	7,782	8,871	10,605
Kazakhstan	12,890	119,145	135,502	148,456	Venezuela	42,753	97,081	118,927	118,758
Kenya	6,189	8,801	11,569	13,471	Vietnam	12,859	44,923	59,119	65,461

[1] Data from 2000 to 2005 are for Serbia and Montenegro. In June 2006, Serbia and Montenegro became separate countries, so starting 2006, data exclude Montenegro. Data from 2008 onward exclude Kosovo, which declared independence that year. [2] Data for Sudan include South Sudan, which became an independent state in July 2011.

Source: The World Bank, Washington, DC, "External debt stocks, total," World Development Indicators (database) ©, <http://data.worldbank.org/data-catalog/world-development-indicators>, accessed June 2015.

Table 1402. Foreign Direct Investment Flows in Selected Countries: 2010 to 2014

[In billions of dollars (205.9 represents $205,900,000,000). Data are converted to U.S. dollars using the yearly average exchange rate]

Country	Inflows					Outflows				
	2010	2011	2012	2013	2014	2010	2011	2012	2013	2014
United States	**205.9**	**236.1**	**175.2**	**236.3**	**97.8**	**301.1**	**419.1**	**333.0**	**349.5**	**358.0**
Argentina	11.3	10.8	15.3	11.4	6.0	1.0	1.5	1.1	1.1	1.9
Australia	36.4	57.0	55.8	54.2	51.9	19.8	1.7	5.6	-3.1	-0.4
Austria	-21.7	17.2	7.5	10.7	3.8	-14.2	32.5	20.7	16.4	8.0
Brazil	48.5	66.7	65.3	64.0	62.5	11.6	-1.0	-2.8	-3.5	-3.5
Canada	28.4	39.7	39.3	70.5	53.9	34.7	52.1	53.9	50.5	52.7
Chile	16.8	16.9	25.0	16.6	22.9	10.5	13.7	17.1	7.6	13.0
China	243.7	280.1	241.2	290.9	289.1	58.0	48.4	65.0	73.0	80.4
Czech Republic	6.1	2.3	8.0	3.6	5.9	1.2	-0.3	1.8	4.0	-0.5
Estonia	1.0	1.0	1.6	0.6	1.7	0.2	-1.5	1.0	0.4	0.2
France	13.9	33.6	15.8	16.8	(NA)	48.2	53.0	33.9	10.0	(NA)
Germany	(NA)	(NA)	(NA)	20.3	-2.2	(NA)	(NA)	(NA)	32.2	108.2
Greece	0.3	1.1	1.7	2.8	2.2	1.6	1.8	0.7	-0.8	0.9
Hungary	-37.3	23.6	15.0	-3.0	6.8	-41.1	21.4	12.3	-2.8	6.2
Indonesia	13.8	19.2	19.1	18.9	22.3	2.7	7.7	5.4	6.7	7.0
Ireland	(NA)	(NA)	45.2	37.0	7.7	(NA)	(NA)	15.3	24.0	31.8
Israel [1]	5.5	9.1	8.1	11.8	1.8	8.0	9.2	3.3	4.7	1.1
Italy	(NA)	(NA)	(NA)	24.3	(NA)	(NA)	(NA)	(NA)	29.1	(NA)
Japan	-1.3	-1.8	1.7	2.3	2.1	56.3	107.6	122.5	135.7	113.7
Korea, South	(NA)	(NA)	(NA)	6.1	(NA)	(NA)	(NA)	(NA)	31.5	(NA)
Netherlands	135.8	349.9	256.9	568.3	20.0	210.6	388.4	256.8	613.4	33.8
New Zealand	1.0	4.0	3.4	1.6	3.4	0.7	2.5	-0.5	0.5	(-Z)
Poland	14.3	20.7	6.1	2.9	(NA)	7.5	8.2	0.8	-1.4	(NA)
Portugal	2.4	7.4	8.2	2.2	8.9	-9.8	16.5	-9.2	-0.1	6.7
Russia	31.7	36.9	30.2	53.4	27.9	41.1	48.6	28.4	70.7	63.4
Slovenia	0.1	1.1	0.3	-0.1	1.6	(-Z)	0.2	-0.3	-0.2	(-Z)
Spain	(NA)	(NA)	(NA)	30.5	(NA)	(NA)	(NA)	(NA)	14.6	(NA)
Sweden	0.1	12.9	16.4	3.6	10.0	20.4	29.9	29.0	28.9	12.2
Turkey	9.1	16.1	13.3	12.4	12.1	1.5	2.3	4.1	3.5	6.7
United Kingdom	58.9	41.8	59.6	47.7	72.3	46.6	107.8	29.0	-15.0	-59.7

NA Not available. Z Less than 50 million. [1] See footnote 2, Table 1360.

Source: Organisation for Economic Co-operation and Development (OECD), 2015, "Benchmark definition, 4th edition (BMD4): Foreign direct investment: financial flows, main aggregates," OECD International Direct Investment Statistics (database) ©, <http://dx.doi.org/10.1787/data-00741-en>, accessed June 2015.

Table 1403. International Transaction Balances, Reserve Assets, and Trade in Relation to Gross Domestic Product (GDP) by Country: 2010 and 2013

[In millions of U.S. dollars (-443,932 represents -$443,932,000,000), except as noted. Minus sign (-) indicates deficit]

Country	Current account balance		Reserve assets [1]		Goods and services trade balance		Exports as percent of GDP (%)		Imports as percent of GDP (%)	
	2010	2013	2010	2013	2010	2013	2010	2013	2010	2013
United States	**-443,932**	**-400,253**	**121,392**	**133,534**	**-512,660**	**-508,190**	**12.4**	**13.5**	**15.8**	**16.5**
Algeria	12,308	869	162,614	194,712	11,321	6,018	38.4	33.1	31.4	30.3
Angola	7,506	8,348	19,749	32,780	15,207	18,699	61.4	55.8	42.9	40.7
Argentina	1,360	-4,696	49,734	28,143	11,677	-447	17.4	14.3	14.8	14.4
Australia	-44,714	-50,227	38,659	49,745	-11,098	-19,199	19.5	19.9	20.4	21.1
Austria	11,478	4,439	9,589	12,474	12,276	15,209	50.7	53.5	47.5	49.9
Azerbaijan	15,040	12,232	6,409	14,401	17,788	16,076	54.3	48.7	20.7	26.9
Bangladesh	1,168	2,366	10,564	17,564	-6,634	-10,830	16.0	19.5	21.8	26.8
Belgium	8,468	919	16,499	18,139	8,572	7,042	76.2	82.8	74.5	81.4
Brazil	-47,273	-81,108	287,056	356,214	-22,995	-55,894	10.7	12.0	11.8	14.4
Bulgaria	-796	963	15,421	18,335	-1,360	-316	55.1	68.4	57.9	69.0
Canada	-56,626	-54,665	56,998	71,821	-30,682	-29,344	29.1	30.2	31.0	31.8
Chile	3,581	-10,125	27,816	41,084	13,902	-1,816	38.1	32.4	31.7	33.1
China	237,810	182,807	2,866,079	3,839,548	182,024	259,756	26.2	23.3	23.2	20.6
Colombia	-8,663	-12,330	27,766	42,758	-5,249	-9,903	15.9	17.6	17.8	20.2
Czech Republic	-7,351	-1,106	41,909	55,798	6,415	12,124	66.2	77.2	63.1	71.4
Denmark	18,183	24,023	73,503	86,099	19,554	19,281	49.7	54.3	43.6	48.5
Dominican Republic	-4,006	-2,467	3,849	4,679	-5,821	-3,513	21.9	25.4	32.9	31.2
Ecuador	-1,607	-1,290	1,435	3,328	-3,139	-2,315	27.9	29.2	32.4	31.6
Egypt	-4,504	(NA)	33,612	13,608	-11,465	-18,289	21.3	18.1	26.6	24.8
Finland	5,944	-2,466	7,327	9,369	3,136	-2,310	38.7	38.4	37.4	39.3
France	-22,034	-40,213	55,800	50,849	-49,816	-52,235	26.0	28.5	27.9	30.4
Georgia	-1,196	-927	2,264	2,823	-2,073	-2,090	35.0	44.7	52.8	57.6
Germany	193,326	242,325	62,295	67,365	176,889	216,754	42.3	45.6	37.1	39.8
Ghana	-2,747	-5,685	4,763	5,249	-5,285	-6,292	29.5	33.4	45.9	46.3
Greece	-30,275	1,409	1,309	1,420	-25,696	-7,181	22.1	30.2	30.7	33.2
Honduras	-682	-1,655	2,671	2,982	-2,839	-3,778	45.8	47.9	63.7	68.4
Hong Kong	16,012	4,153	268,649	311,129	13,432	1,616	219.4	227.9	213.5	227.3
India	-54,516	-49,226	275,277	276,493	-74,621	-55,081	22.0	25.2	26.3	28.1
Indonesia	5,144	-29,102	92,908	96,364	14,323	-7,212	24.3	24.0	22.4	24.8
Iraq	6,488	(NA)	50,357	76,112	7,391	10,300	39.4	40.8	34.1	36.3
Ireland	2,319	14,438	1,843	1,403	38,130	48,279	95.7	105.3	78.2	84.5
Israel	7,855	6,893	70,907	81,786	4,801	3,992	35.0	32.9	33.0	31.6
Italy	-74,304	20,122	47,684	50,775	-41,849	49,573	25.2	28.8	27.1	26.5
Jamaica	-934	-1,320	2,501	1,818	-2,413	-3,283	31.3	29.8	49.5	52.6
Japan	217,550	34,068	1,061,490	1,237,218	65,656	-139,699	15.2	16.2	14.0	19.0
Jordan	-1,882	-3,359	13,057	13,224	-5,497	-9,903	48.2	42.5	69.0	72.0
Kazakhstan	1,411	-118	25,223	19,127	21,245	26,790	44.2	38.2	29.9	26.7
Kenya	-2,369	(NA)	4,320	6,598	-5,165	-8,511	20.7	17.9	33.6	33.4
Korea, South	28,850	81,148	291,491	341,650	34,859	65,011	49.4	53.9	46.2	48.9
Kuwait	36,727	69,783	21,237	29,353	41,918	79,146	66.7	71.6	30.4	26.5
Lebanon	-7,552	-10,983	31,514	36,748	-9,729	-6,339	36.3	56.9	61.9	71.2
Malaysia	26,998	11,732	104,884	133,444	42,006	29,051	93.3	81.7	76.3	72.4
Mexico	-4,934	-29,682	120,265	175,432	-12,648	-11,242	29.9	31.7	31.1	32.6
Mongolia	-886	-3,192	2,197	2,096	-718	-2,561	46.7	40.0	56.7	60.4
Morocco	-3,925	-7,844	22,613	18,404	-8,924	-13,731	33.2	33.6	43.1	46.9
Netherlands	57,760	87,089	18,471	22,591	69,951	88,175	72.0	82.9	63.6	72.6
New Zealand	-3,433	-5,932	16,723	16,318	3,364	3,238	30.5	29.2	28.2	27.5
Nigeria	14,459	(NA)	34,919	45,427	29,070	26,041	25.3	18.0	17.4	13.0
Norway	50,258	50,962	52,798	58,283	48,123	53,192	39.8	38.8	28.6	28.6
Pakistan	-1,354	-4,416	14,346	5,156	-10,354	-15,581	13.5	13.2	19.4	19.9
Panama	-3,076	-4,920	2,714	2,848	424	(NA)	70.6	(NA)	69.1	(NA)
Peru	-3,782	-9,126	42,648	64,423	4,615	-1,542	26.6	23.9	23.5	24.6
Philippines	7,179	11,384	55,363	75,689	-3,618	-11,065	34.8	27.9	36.6	32.0
Poland	-26,863	-6,988	88,822	102,236	-8,654	9,922	40.5	46.1	42.3	44.2
Portugal	-24,215	1,160	3,652	2,778	-18,013	1,992	29.9	39.6	37.4	38.7
Romania	-7,258	-1,780	43,361	44,811	-9,442	-1,064	35.4	42.0	41.2	42.5
Russia	67,452	34,801	443,586	469,603	123,146	123,205	29.2	28.6	21.1	22.7
Saudi Arabia	66,751	135,478	444,722	725,292	87,628	157,743	49.7	52.1	33.1	30.9
Serbia	-2,550	-2,790	12,715	14,803	-5,915	-4,875	32.9	41.2	47.9	51.9
Singapore	55,943	54,084	225,503	272,864	62,459	70,180	199.3	191.6	172.8	168.3
South Africa	-5,492	-21,194	38,175	44,864	4,660	-8,319	28.6	31.0	27.4	33.2
Spain	-62,498	10,668	19,146	35,430	-18,683	47,476	25.5	31.6	26.8	28.1
Sri Lanka	-1,075	-2,627	6,710	6,611	-4,118	-6,404	22.4	22.5	30.7	32.0
Sudan	-1,725	-4,481	1,036	193	1,648	-4,358	19.7	9.6	17.2	16.1
Sweden	29,402	42,090	42,565	60,495	26,702	29,182	46.2	44.0	40.7	38.9
Switzerland	81,490	73,153	223,481	495,958	62,343	83,034	64.2	72.1	53.5	60.0
Tanzania	-1,960	-4,703	3,905	4,674	-3,230	-5,949	18.7	17.7	29.1	31.1
Thailand	9,946	-3,781	167,530	161,328	23,695	12,724	71.3	73.6	63.9	70.3
Tunisia	-2,104	-3,879	9,459	7,287	-2,115	-4,309	50.1	47.0	54.8	56.2
Turkey	-45,312	-64,658	80,713	110,927	-40,584	-53,866	21.2	25.6	26.8	32.2
Ukraine	-3,016	-16,518	33,327	18,776	-3,844	-16,778	50.7	43.0	53.6	52.1
United Kingdom	-63,006	-120,215	68,345	92,404	-57,259	-52,736	28.7	30.1	31.1	32.1
Venezuela	8,812	5,327	13,137	6,038	43,019	-17,630	28.5	24.8	17.6	29.5
Vietnam	-4,276	9,471	12,467	25,893	-9,521	3,695	72.0	83.6	80.2	81.5

NA Not available. [1] Reserve assets are comprised of special drawing rights and reserve position in International Monetary Fund (IMF), and foreign exchange holdings. Gold holdings are excluded.

Source: The World Bank, Washington, DC, "World Development Indicators" database ©, <http://data.worldbank.org/data-catalog/world-development-indicators>, accessed August 2015.

Table 1404. International Tourism Arrivals, Expenditures, and Receipts—Leading Countries: 2000 to 2013

[Arrivals at national borders in thousands of non-resident tourists (706,484 represents 706,484,000). Expenditures and receipts in millions of current U.S. dollars (451,422 represents $451,422,000,000). Receipts are money spent by foreign tourists while traveling inside the country shown and include prepayment for goods or services in destination country. Expenditures are money spent by tourists from a given country of origin while traveling outside their home country. Data exclude receipts and expenditures for international transport. Ranked for top 50 countries in tourist arrivals as of 2013. Sources and collection methods differ, thus caution should be used in comparing data across countries]

Country	Arrivals (1,000)					Expenditures (mil. dol.)					Receipts (mil. dol.)				
	2000	2005	2010	2012	2013	2000	2005	2010	2012	2013	2000	2005	2010	2012	2013
World [1]	706,484	837,160	979,887	1,071,612	1,123,200	451,422	662,502	863,095	1,001,620	1,086,439	493,893	707,212	959,847	1,108,046	1,188,292
France	77,190	74,988	77,648	83,051	84,726	22,533	31,727	38,608	39,829	42,870	32,855	43,954	46,471	53,408	56,557
United States	51,238	49,206	60,010	66,657	69,768	67,860	79,990	86,623	100,316	104,678	100,716	101,469	137,010	161,250	173,130
Spain	46,403	55,914	52,677	57,464	60,661	5,922	15,046	16,764	15,274	16,287	29,802	47,789	52,187	55,988	60,384
China	31,229	46,809	55,664	57,725	55,686	13,114	21,759	54,880	101,977	128,576	16,231	29,296	45,814	50,028	51,664
Italy	41,181	36,513	43,626	46,360	47,704	15,685	22,370	26,907	26,249	26,947	27,493	35,319	38,438	40,960	43,835
Turkey	9,586	20,273	31,364	35,698	37,795	1,713	3,104	5,194	4,094	4,817	7,636	19,191	22,585	25,345	27,997
Germany	18,983	21,500	26,875	30,411	31,545	52,824	74,189	77,578	80,867	91,320	18,611	29,121	34,564	38,068	41,217
United Kingdom	23,212	28,039	28,295	29,282	31,169	38,262	59,532	49,972	51,341	52,490	21,769	30,573	32,399	36,244	40,589
Russia	21,169	22,201	22,281	28,177	30,792	8,848	16,972	26,693	42,798	53,453	3,429	5,870	8,830	10,759	11,988
Thailand	9,579	11,567	15,936	22,354	26,547	2,772	3,800	5,623	6,219	6,650	7,483	9,577	20,116	33,827	42,082
Malaysia	10,222	16,431	24,577	25,033	25,715	2,075	3,711	8,324	11,545	11,950	5,011	8,846	18,152	20,251	21,026
Hong Kong	8,814	14,773	20,085	23,770	25,661	12,502	13,305	17,357	20,077	21,215	5,868	10,179	21,689	31,205	36,109
Austria	17,982	19,952	22,004	24,151	24,813	6,232	9,316	10,125	9,992	10,253	9,899	16,243	18,758	18,938	20,090
Ukraine	6,431	17,631	21,203	23,013	24,671	470	2,805	3,742	5,104	5,763	394	3,125	3,788	4,842	5,083
Mexico	20,641	21,915	23,290	23,403	24,151	5,499	7,600	7,255	8,449	9,122	8,294	11,803	11,992	12,739	13,949
Greece	13,096	14,765	15,007	15,518	17,920	4,558	3,039	2,854	2,365	2,435	9,219	13,334	12,479	13,217	16,087
Canada	19,627	18,771	16,219	16,344	16,590	12,438	18,021	29,727	35,038	35,170	10,778	13,651	15,829	17,407	17,656
Poland	17,400	15,200	12,470	14,840	15,800	3,315	5,548	8,570	8,758	9,111	5,677	6,274	9,526	10,938	11,407
Macao	5,197	9,014	11,926	13,577	14,268	(NA)	552	1,154	1,603	1,738	(NA)	7,933	27,802	43,860	51,796
Saudi Arabia	6,585	8,037	10,850	14,276	13,380	(NA)	9,087	21,135	17,023	17,660	(NA)	4,626	6,712	7,432	7,651
Netherlands	10,003	10,012	10,883	11,680	12,783	12,191	16,140	19,489	20,077	20,471	7,197	10,450	12,861	13,735	15,591
Korea, South	5,322	6,023	8,798	11,140	12,176	7,132	15,406	18,766	20,645	21,676	6,834	5,806	10,328	13,429	14,272
Singapore	6,062	7,079	9,161	11,098	11,899	4,535	10,070	18,700	23,644	24,578	5,142	6,209	14,178	18,934	19,057
Croatia	5,831	7,743	9,111	10,369	10,955	568	754	833	926	903	2,758	7,370	8,051	8,637	9,518
Hungary	(NA)	9,979	9,510	10,353	10,675	1,651	2,277	2,404	1,968	1,906	3,733	4,120	5,587	5,114	5,268
Japan	4,757	6,728	8,611	8,358	10,364	31,884	37,565	27,950	27,906	21,861	3,373	12,430	13,224	14,581	15,093
Morocco	4,278	5,843	9,288	9,375	10,046	425	612	1,203	1,253	1,318	2,039	4,610	6,702	6,697	6,851
South Africa	5,872	7,369	8,074	9,188	9,537	2,085	3,374	5,595	4,069	3,429	2,677	7,516	9,085	9,996	9,245
Egypt	5,116	8,244	14,051	11,196	9,174	1,072	1,629	2,240	2,618	3,014	4,345	6,851	12,528	9,940	6,044
Bahrain	3,869	6,313	11,952	8,062	9,163	224	414	506	729	713	573	920	1,362	1,051	1,165
Czech Republic	(NA)	9,404	8,185	8,908	9,004	1,276	2,405	4,064	4,295	4,594	2,973	4,813	7,121	7,039	7,048
Switzerland	7,821	7,229	8,628	8,566	8,967	5,419	8,782	11,176	13,761	14,907	6,652	10,041	14,731	15,965	16,535
Indonesia	5,064	5,002	7,003	8,044	8,802	3,197	3,584	6,395	6,771	7,675	4,975	4,522	6,958	8,324	9,119
Denmark	3,535	9,178	8,744	8,443	8,557	4,669	6,850	9,082	9,600	10,131	3,671	5,704	6,135	6,396	6,396
Ireland	6,646	7,333	7,134	7,550	8,260	2,525	6,074	7,071	5,897	6,112	2,615	4,782	4,086	3,867	4,426
Portugal	5,599	5,769	6,756	7,503	8,097	2,228	3,050	3,905	3,784	4,142	5,243	7,676	10,007	11,000	12,281
Romania	5,264	5,839	7,498	7,937	8,019	425	925	1,636	1,833	1,997	359	1,052	1,136	1,463	1,446
Belgium	6,457	6,747	7,186	7,560	7,684	9,429	14,948	18,822	20,111	21,635	6,592	9,845	12,113	13,001	13,524
Vietnam	2,140	3,477	5,050	6,848	7,572	(NA)	(NA)	(NA)	(NA)	(NA)	(NA)	(NA)	(NA)	(NA)	(NA)
India	2,649	3,919	5,776	6,578	6,968	2,690	6,187	10,490	12,342	11,571	3,460	7,493	14,490	17,972	18,397
Bulgaria	2,785	4,837	6,047	6,541	6,898	538	1,309	1,232	1,301	1,525	1,074	2,412	3,571	3,689	4,051
Australia	4,931	5,499	5,790	6,032	6,382	6,387	11,749	22,558	27,974	28,376	9,289	16,750	28,472	31,743	31,104
Tunisia	5,058	6,378	6,903	5,950	6,269	263	374	547	593	675	1,682	2,143	2,645	2,227	2,191
Brazil	5,313	5,358	5,161	5,677	5,813	3,894	4,720	16,420	22,233	25,103	1,810	3,861	5,702	6,645	6,711
Argentina	2,909	3,823	5,325	5,587	5,571	4,425	2,790	4,878	5,905	5,569	2,904	2,729	4,942	4,887	4,313
Georgia	387	560	2,032	4,428	5,392	110	169	199	256	294	97	241	659	1,411	1,720
Sweden	3,828	4,883	5,183	5,146	5,229	8,048	10,306	13,065	15,776	17,564	4,064	6,665	8,653	10,763	11,476
Kazakhstan	1,471	3,143	3,196	4,807	4,926	408	753	1,273	1,685	1,729	356	701	1,005	1,347	1,460
Iran	1,342	1,889	2,938	3,834	4,769	668	3,724	9,655	6,550	(NA)	467	791	2,438	1,114	(NA)
Dominican Republic	2,978	3,691	4,125	4,563	4,690	309	352	395	399	378	2,860	3,518	4,163	4,687	5,065

NA Not available.   [1] Includes other countries not shown separately.

Source: The World Bank, Washington, DC, "World Development Indicators" database ©, <http://data.worldbank.org/data-catalog/world-development-indicators>, accessed August 2015.

Table 1405. Military Expenditures as a Percent of GDP, Selected Years 2006 to 2015, and Manpower, 2010, by Country

[For manpower, 120,022 represents 120,022,000. Manpower covers males and females deemed fit for military service, ages 16–49, who are not otherwise disqualified for health reasons]

Country	Expenditures Data as of year	Expenditures Percent of GDP [1]	Manpower in 2010 (1,000)	Country	Expenditures Data as of year	Expenditures Percent of GDP [1]	Manpower in 2010 (1,000)
United States............	2012	4.4	120,022	Kenya..................	2012	2.0	12,468
Afghanistan..............	2011	4.7	7,847	Korea, South.............	2012	2.8	21,033
Albania...................	2015	0.9	1,283	Kuwait....................	2011	3.4	1,364
Algeria...................	2012	4.5	17,249	Lebanon..................	2012	4.0	1,863
Angola...................	2012	3.6	3,039	Libya.....................	2012	3.1	2,970
Argentina................	2012	0.9	16,873	Macedonia................	2015	1.1	870
Armenia..................	2013	4.1	1,362	Malaysia.................	2014	1.5	12,423
Australia.................	2012	1.7	8,652	Mexico...................	2012	0.6	48,882
Austria...................	2014	0.6	3,134	Montenegro...............	2014	1.7	281
Azerbaijan...............	2013	4.7	3,738	Morocco..................	2012	3.6	14,403
Bahrain..................	2014	4.2	669	Nepal....................	2011	1.4	11,208
Bangladesh..............	2013	1.2	66,102	Netherlands..............	2013	1.2	6,324
Brazil....................	2012	1.5	83,836	Nigeria...................	2012	0.9	40,708
Bulgaria..................	2013	1.6	2,659	Oman....................	2012	8.6	1,480
Burma....................	2012	4.8	21,633	Pakistan.................	2013	3.5	75,327
Canada...................	2013	1.0	13,023	Peru.....................	2012	1.3	12,354
Chile.....................	2012	2.0	7,183	Philippines...............	2012	1.2	41,571
China....................	2012	2.0	618,589	Poland...................	2014	2.0	15,584
Colombia.................	2012	3.3	19,012	Romania.................	2013	1.3	9,058
Congo, Dem. Rep.......	2012	1.7	20,500	Russia...................	2014	3.5	46,813
Czech Republic..........	2015	1.0	4,061	Saudi Arabia.............	2012	8.0	13,043
Ecuador..................	2012	2.8	6,104	South Africa.............	2014	1.2	14,093
Egypt....................	2013	1.7	35,305	Spain....................	2012	0.9	18,721
France...................	2014	1.8	23,747	Sri Lanka................	2012	2.4	8,752
Georgia..................	2013	2.7	1,825	Sudan...................	2012	4.2	13,316
Germany.................	2012	1.4	29,538	Syria....................	2011	3.6	9,940
Ghana...................	2014	0.6	8,357	Taiwan...................	2012	2.2	10,025
Greece...................	2012	1.7	4,049	Thailand.................	2013	1.5	27,491
India....................	2013	2.4	489,571	Turkey...................	2014	2.4	35,005
Indonesia................	2012	0.8	107,539	Uganda..................	2013	2.2	8,514
Iran.....................	2006	2.5	39,566	Ukraine..................	2012	2.8	15,686
Iraq.....................	2014	8.7	13,013	United Arab Emirates....	2011	5.5	3,072
Ireland..................	2014	0.5	1,944	United Kingdom..........	2012	2.5	24,035
Israel...................	2012	5.7	2,964	Venezuela................	2013	2.6	11,690
Italy.....................	2012	1.7	22,596	Vietnam..................	2012	2.4	41,504
Japan....................	2012	1.0	43,931	Yemen...................	2012	4.0	8,174
Jordan...................	2012	4.7	2,824	Zimbabwe................	2014	2.8	3,174

[1] Spending on defense programs as percent of Gross Domestic Product (GDP), calculated on an exchange rate basis. For countries with no military forces, this figure can include expenditures on public security and police. Some data include estimates.

Source: Central Intelligence Agency, *The World Factbook*, <https://www.cia.gov/library/publications/the-world-factbook/index.html>, accessed September 2015.

Table 1406. Terrorism Attacks, Fatalities, Injuries, and Hostages Taken for Top 5 Countries and Perpetrator Groups: 2013 and 2014

[Data shown for top 5 countries and perpetrator groups of attacks in 2014. Based on data collected by the National Consortium for the Study of Terrorism and Responses to Terrorism (START) and maintained in the Global Terrorism Database. Any assessments and descriptions, including those regarding the nature of the incidents or the factual circumstances thereof, are offered only as part of the analytic work product of the National Consortium START and may not reflect the views of the U.S. Government]

Country and perpetrator group	2013 Attacks	2013 Fatalities	2013 Injuries	2013 Hostages taken	2014 Attacks	2014 Fatalities	2014 Injuries	2014 Hostages taken
Worldwide total..........................	9,964	18,066	32,880	3,137	13,463	32,727	34,791	9,428
By country:								
Iraq....................................	2,501	6,387	14,976	267	3,370	9,929	15,137	2,658
Pakistan..............................	1,941	2,351	5,075	417	1,821	1,757	2,837	869
Afghanistan...........................	1,149	3,111	3,724	273	1,591	4,505	4,699	719
India..................................	632	409	717	190	763	426	643	302
Nigeria................................	309	1,842	472	89	662	7,512	2,246	1,298
Syria..................................	222	1,084	1,776	214	232	1,698	1,473	872
By perpetrator:								
Islamic State of Iraq and the Levant (ISIL).................................	429	1,752	4,529	114	1,083	6,286	5,808	3,158
Taliban...............................	648	2,356	2,249	229	894	3,492	3,312	649
Al-Shabaab...........................	196	517	761	132	497	1,022	850	579
Boko Haram..........................	217	1,595	370	38	453	6,644	1,742	1,217
Maoists/Communist Party of India-Maoist............................	203	192	126	83	305	188	165	160

Source: U.S. State Department, Bureau of Counterterrorism, *Annex of Statistical Information: Country Reports on Terrorism 2014*, June 2015. See also <http://www.state.gov/j/ct/rls/crt/index.htm>.

Guide to Sources of Statistics, State Statistical Abstracts, and Foreign Statistical Abstracts

Alphabetically arranged, this guide contains references to important primary sources of statistical information for the United States and other countries. Secondary sources have been included if the information contained in them is presented in a particularly convenient form or if primary sources are not readily available. Nonrecurrent publications presenting compilations or estimates for years later than 2005, or types of data not available in regular series, are also included. Data are also available in press releases.

Valuable information may also be found in state reports and foreign statistical abstracts, which are included at the end of this appendix, and in reports for particular commodities, industries, or similar segments of our economic and social structures, many of which are not included here.

Publications listed under each subject are divided into two main groups: "U.S. Government" and "Nongovernment." The location of the publisher of each report is given except for federal agencies located in Washington, DC. Most federal publications may be purchased from the Superintendent of Documents, U.S. Government Printing Office, Washington, DC, tel. 202-512-1800, or at <http://bookstore.gpo.gov>. In some cases, federal publications may be obtained from the issuing agency.

Appendix I Table: Sources of Statistics, State Statistical Abstracts, and Foreign Statistical Abstracts

Title	Frequency	Paper	Internet PDF	Internet Other Formats
U.S. GOVERNMENT				
Administrative Office of the United States Courts				
http://www.uscourts.gov				
Calendar Year Reports on Authorized Wiretaps (state and federal)	Annual		X	
Federal Court Management Statistics	Quarterly		X	X
Federal Judicial Caseload Statistics	Annual		X	
Judicial Business of the United States Courts	Annual		X	
Statistical Tables for the Federal Judiciary	Semiannual		X	
Agency for International Development				
http://www.usaid.gov				
U.S. Overseas Loans and Grants: Obligations and Loan Authorizations	Annual		X	X
Army Corps of Engineers				
http://www.usace.army.mil				
Waterborne Commerce of the United States (in five parts)	Annual		X	X
Board of Governors of the Federal Reserve System				
http://www.federalreserve.gov				
Assets and Liabilities of Commercial Banks in the United States H.8	Weekly		X	X
Consumer Credit G.19	Monthly	X	X	X
Federal Reserve Bulletin	Periodic	X	X	X
Financial Accounts of the United States Z.1	Quarterly	X	X	X
Foreign Exchange Rates H.10	Weekly		X	X
Industrial Production and Capacity Utilization G.17	Monthly	X	X	X
Money Stock Measures H.6	Weekly		X	X
Bureau of Economic Analysis				
http://www.bea.gov				
Arts and Cultural Production Satellite Accounts	Ongoing		X	X
Health Care Satellite Account	Ongoing		X	X
International Economic Accounts	Ongoing		X	X
Survey of Current Business	Monthly	X	X	X
Bureau of Justice Statistics				
http://bjs.ojp.usdoj.gov				
Background Checks for Firearm Transfers	Annual		X	X
Capital Punishment	Annual		X	X
Census of Publicly Funded Forensic Crime Laboratories, 2009, August 2012	Periodic		X	X
Census of State and Federal Correctional Facilities, 2005, October 2008	Periodic		X	X
Civil Rights Complaints in U.S. District Courts, 1990-2006, August 2008	Periodic	X	X	X
Civil Trial Cases and Verdicts in Large Counties, 2005, September 2009	Periodic	X	X	X
Compendium of Federal Justice Statistics, 2009, December 2011	Periodic	X	X	X
Contacts Between Police and Public: Findings from the 2008 National Survey, October 2011	Periodic		X	X
Crimes Against the Elderly, 2003-2013	Periodic		X	X
Criminal Victimization	Annual		X	X
Family Violence Statistics	Periodic	X	X	X
Federal Law Enforcement Officers, 2008, June 2012	Periodic		X	X
Felony Defendants in Large Urban Counties, 2009, December 2013	Biennial		X	X
Felony Sentences in State Courts, 2006, December 2009	Biennial		X	X
HIV in Prisons, 2001-2010, September 2012	Periodic		X	X
Homicide Trends in the United States, 1980-2008	Periodic		X	X
Identity Theft Reported by Households, 2005-10, November 2011	Periodic		X	X
Immigration Offenders in the Federal Criminal Justice System, 2010, July 2012	Periodic		X	X
Indicators of School Crime and Safety	Annual		X	X
Intimate Partner Violence, 1993-2011, November 2013	Periodic	X	X	X

See footnotes at end of table.

Title	Frequency	Paper	Internet	
			PDF	Other *Formats*
Jail Inmates at Midyear, 2014, June 2015	Annual		X	X
Jails in Indian Country, 2013, July 2014	Annual		X	X
Justice Expenditure and Employment Extract Series, 2012, February 2015	Annual			X
Local Police Departments, 2013: Personnel, Policies, and Practices, May 2015	Periodic		X	X
Prisoners in 2014, September 2015	Annual		X	X
Probation and Parole in the United States, 2013, October 2014	Annual		X	X
Prosecutors in State Courts, 2007, December 2011	Biennial		X	X
Rape and Sexual Assault Victimization Among College-Age Females, 1995-2013	Periodic		X	X
Sheriffs' Offices, 2007, December 2012	Periodic	X	X	X
Sourcebook of Criminal Justice Statistics	Periodic		X	X
State Court Sentencing of Convicted Felons, 2004, July 2007	Periodic			X
Survey of State Criminal History Information Systems, 2012, January 2014	Biennial	X	X	X
Survey of State Procedures Related to Firearm Sales, 2005, November 2006	Periodic	X	X	X
Tort Trials and Verdicts in Large Counties, November 2004	Periodic	X	X	X
Tribal Crime Data Collection Activities, 2015, July 2015	Annual		X	X
Victims of Identity Theft, 2014, September 2015	Periodic		X	X
Bureau of Labor Statistics				
http://www.bls.gov				
100 Years of U.S. Consumer Spending: Data for the Nation, New York City, and Boston, Report 991	Periodic	X	X	
College Enrollment and Work Activity of High School Graduates	Annual		X	
Compensation and Working Conditions	Periodic		X	X
Consumer Expenditure Survey, Integrated Diary and Interview Survey data	Annual		X	X
Consumer Price Index (CPI) Detailed Report	Monthly		X	X
Consumer Prices	Monthly		X	X
Employer Costs for Employee Compensation	Quarterly		X	X
Employment and Earnings	Monthly		X	X
Employment and Wages	Annual		X	X
Employment Characteristics of Families	Annual		X	X
Employment Cost Index	Quarterly		X	X
The Employment Situation	Monthly		X	X
Geographic Profile of Employment and Unemployment	Annual		X	X
Metropolitan Area Employment and Unemployment	Monthly		X	X
Monthly Labor Review	Monthly		X	X
National Compensation Survey	Annual		X	X
Occupational Employment and Wages	Annual		X	X
Occupational Injuries and Illnesses in the United States by Industry	Annual		X	X
Occupational Projections and Training Data	Biennial		X	X
Producer Price Index (PPI) Detailed Report	Monthly		X	X
Productivity and Costs by Industry	Periodic		X	X
Real Earnings	Monthly		X	X
Regional and State Employment and Unemployment	Monthly		X	X
Relative Importance of Components in the Consumer Price Indexes	Annual		X	X
U.S. Import and Export Price Indexes	Monthly		X	X
Union Membership	Annual		X	X
Usual Weekly Earnings of Wage and Salary Workers	Quarterly		X	X
Work Experience of the Population	Annual		X	X
Bureau of Land Management				
http://www.blm.gov				
Public Land Statistics	Annual		X	
Census Bureau				
http://www.census.gov				
2012 Economic Census, Bridge Between North American Industry Classification System (NAICS) and Standard Industrial Classification (SIC)	Quinquennial			X
2012 Economic Census, Company Statistics Series, Survey of Business Owners	Quinquennial			X
2012 Economic Census, Company Statistics Series, Survey of Business Owners: American Indian- and Alaska Native-Owned Firms	Quinquennial			X
2012 Economic Census, Company Statistics Series, Survey of Business Owners: Asian-Owned Firms	Quinquennial			X
2012 Economic Census, Company Statistics Series, Survey of Business Owners: Black-Owned Firms	Quinquennial			X
2012 Economic Census, Company Statistics Series, Survey of Business Owners: Hispanic-Owned Firms	Quinquennial			X
2012 Economic Census, Company Statistics Series, Survey of Business Owners: Native Hawaiian- and other Pacific Islander-Owned Firms	Quinquennial			X
2012 Economic Census, Comparative Statistics	Quinquennial			X
2012 Economic Census, Industry/Geography	Quinquennial			X
American Community Survey, Annual Earnings and Poverty Report, 2013	Annual		X	
Annual Revision of Monthly Retail and Food Services: Sales and Inventories	Annual		X	
Annual Revision of Monthly Wholesale Distributors: Sales and Inventories	Annual		X	X
Annual Survey of Manufactures	Annual		X	
Census of Governments	Quinquennial		X	
Census of Housing Decennial (2010, most recent)	Decennial	X	X	X
Census of Population Decennial (2010, most recent)	Decennial	X	X	X
Computer and Internet Use in the United States: 2013	Annual		X	X
Consumer Income and Poverty, Income, Poverty, and Health Insurance Coverage in the United States	Annual	X	X	X
Consumer Income and Poverty, P60, and Household Economic Studies, P70	Periodic	X	X	
County Business Patterns	Annual		X	X
Current Construction Reports: New Residential Construction and New Residential Sales	Monthly		X	
Current Construction Reports: Value of Construction Put in Place, C30	Monthly		X	

Appendix I Table: Sources of Statistics, State Statistical Abstracts, and Foreign Statistical Abstracts-Continued.

See headnote on page 901.

Title	Frequency	Paper	Internet PDF	Internet Other Formats
Current Housing Reports, American Housing Survey for Selected Metropolitan Areas, H170	Biennial		X	X
Current Housing Reports, American Housing Survey for the United States, H150	Biennial	X	X	X
Current Housing Reports, Characteristics of Apartments Completed, H131	Annual		X	X
Current Housing Reports, Housing Vacancies, H111	Quarterly		X	X
Current Housing Reports, Survey of Market Absorption of Apartments (SOMA)	Quarterly		X	X
Current Housing Reports, Who Can Afford to Buy a Home in 2009, H121	Occasional	X	X	X
Current Population Reports (Series P20 and P23)	Periodic		X	X
Economic Census of Island Areas	Quinquennial			
International Data Base	Annual			X
International Population Reports (Series P95)	Periodic		X	
Manufacturing and International Trade Report: 2012	Annual		X	X
Manufacturer's Shipments, Inventories, and Orders	Monthly		X	X
Manufacturer's Shipments, Inventories, and Orders: 1992-2012	Annual			X
New York City Housing and Vacancy Survey, 2014	Every 3 years			X
Nonemployer Statistics	Annual			X
Population Estimates and Projections	Annual			X
Quarterly Financial Report for Manufacturing, Mining, and Trade Corporations	Quarterly		X	X
Service Annual Survey Report	Annual			X
Survey of Plant Capacity Utilization	Quarterly			X
U.S. International Trade in Goods and Services (FT900)	Annual		X	X
U.S. Trade with Puerto Rico and U.S. Possessions (FT 895)	Monthly		X	
Centers for Disease Control and Prevention, Atlanta, Georgia http://www.cdc.gov				
Morbidity and Mortality Weekly Report	Weekly	X	X	X
National Immunization Survey (NIS) – Children (19-35 months)	Annual		X	X
Centers for Medicare and Medicaid Services (CMS) http://www.cms.gov				
CMS Statistics	Annual		X	X
Data Compendium	Annual		X	X
Medicare and Medicaid Research Review (discontinued)	Irregular		X	
Medicare and Medicaid Statistical Supplement	Annual	X	X	X
Trustees Report	Annual	X	X	X
Wallet Card	Annual	X	X	X
Central Intelligence Agency, Langley, Virginia http://www.cia.gov				
World Factbook	Annual	X	X	X
Coast Guard (See Department of Homeland Security)				
Council of Economic Advisers http://www.whitehouse.gov/administration/eop/cea				
Economic Indicators	Monthly	X	X	X
Economic Report of the President	Annual	X	X	X
Department of Agriculture, Economic Research Service http://www.ers.usda.gov				
Agricultural Income and Finance	Annual	X	X	X
Amber Waves	Periodic		X	
America's Diverse Family Farms	Annual	X	X	
Cotton and Wool Yearbook	Annual			X
Feed Grains Yearbook	Annual		X	X
Food Expenditures	Annual			X
Fruit and Tree Nut Yearbook	Annual		X	X
Household Food Security in the United States in 2013: Statistical Supplement, No. 066	Annual		X	
Oil Crops Yearbook	Annual			X
Rice Yearbook	Annual			X
Situation and Outlook Reports. Issued for: agricultural exports, feed, fruit and tree nuts, livestock and poultry, oil crops, rice, sugar and sweeteners, vegetables, wheat, and world agriculture	Periodic	X	X	
Structure and Finances of U.S. Farms: Family Farm Report	Annual	X	X	
Sugar and Sweeteners Yearbook	Annual			X
Vegetable and Pulses Yearbook	Annual		X	X
World Agricultural Supply and Demand Estimates	Monthly	X	X	X
Department of Agriculture, Food and Nutrition Service http://www.fns.usda.gov/fns/				
Characteristics of Supplemental Nutrition Assistance Program Households	Annual	X	X	
WIC Participant and Program Characteristics	Biennial	X	X	
Department of Agriculture, Foreign Agricultural Service http://www.fas.usda.gov				
Livestock and Poultry World Markets and Trade	Semiannual	X	X	
Department of Agriculture, National Agricultural Statistics Service http://www.nass.usda.gov				
Agricultural Chemical Usage	Periodic			X
Agricultural Statistics	Annual	X	X	
Catfish Production	Semiannual	X	X	X
Cattle	Semiannual	X	X	X
Census of Agriculture	Quinquennial	X	X	X
Census of Agriculture: Organic Survey 2014	Periodic		X	X
Cherry Production	Annual	X	X	X
Chickens and Eggs	Monthly/ Annual	X	X	X
Citrus Fruits	Annual	X	X	X

See footnotes at end of table.

Title	Frequency	Paper	Internet PDF	Internet Other Formats
Cranberries	Annual	X	X	X
Crop Production	Monthly	X	X	X
Crop Progress	Weekly	X	X	X
Crop Values	Annual	X	X	X
Dairy Products	Monthly/ Annual	X	X	X
Farm Labor	Semiannual	X	X	X
Farms, Land in Farms, and Livestock Operations	Annual	X	X	X
Floriculture Crops	Annual	X	X	X
Agricultural Land Value and Cash Rents	Annual	X	X	X
Livestock Slaughter	Monthly	X	X	X
Meat Animals Production, Disposition, and Income	Annual	X	X	X
Milk Production	Monthly	X	X	X
Milk Production, Disposition, and Income	Annual	X	X	X
Noncitrus Fruits and Nuts	Semiannual	X	X	X
Poultry: Production and Value Summary	Annual	X	X	X
Stock Reports. Stocks of grain, peanuts, potatoes, and rice	Periodic	X	X	X
Trout Production	Annual	X	X	X
Turkey Hatchery	Monthly	X	X	X
Turkeys Raised	Annual	X	X	X
Usual Planting and Harvesting Dates	Periodic	X	X	X
Vegetables	Periodic	X	X	X
Weekly Weather and Crop Bulletin	Weekly	X	X	X
Winter Wheat and Rye Seedlings	Annual	X	X	X

Department of Agriculture, Natural Resources and Conservation Service
http://www.nrcs.usda.gov

National Resources Inventory	Periodic	X	X	

Department of Defense
http://www.defense.gov/News/Publications

Foreign Military Sales, Foreign Military Construction Sales, and Other Security Cooperation Historical Facts	Annual	X	X	
Personnel Statistics	Periodic		X	X

Department of Education
http://www.ed.gov

Annual Report for Federal Student Aid	Annual		X	
Annual Report on Teacher Quality	Annual		X	
Federal Campus-Based Programs Data Book	Annual			X
Federal Pell Grant Program, End of Year Report	Annual		X	X

Department of Health and Human Services
http://www.hhs.gov

Health Care Fraud and Abuse Control Program Annual Report	Annual	X	X	
Profile of Older Americans	Annual	X	X	X

Department of Homeland Security
http://www.dhs.gov/index.shtm

Budget in Brief	Annual	X	X	

Department of Homeland Security, Coast Guard
http://www.uscg.mil/default.asp

Coast Guard Snapshot	Periodic	X	X	X

Department of Homeland Security, Office of Immigration Statistics
http://www.dhs.gov/immigration-statistics

Yearbook of Immigration Statistics	Annual	X	X	X

Department of Housing and Urban Development
http://www.hud.gov

U.S. Housing Market Conditions	Quarterly		X	

Department of Justice, Bureau of Alcohol, Tobacco, Firearms and Explosives
http://www.atf.gov/

Firearms Commerce in the US [Annual Firearms Manufacturing and Export Report]	Annual		X	
Firearms Trace Data (by State)	Annual		X	

Department of Labor
http://www.dol.gov

Agency Financial Report	Annual	X	X	
Annual Performance Report	Annual	X	X	
Health Insurance Coverage Bulletin and March Current Population Survey Auxiliary Data	Annual		X	X

Department of State
http://www.state.gov

Country Reports on Terrorism 2014	Annual		X	
United States Contributions to International Organizations	Annual		X	X
Annex of Statistical Information: Country Reports on Terrorism 2014	Annual		X	X

Department of Transportation
http://www.dot.gov

Air Travel Consumer Report	Monthly	X	X	
Airport Activity Statistics of Certified Route Air Carriers	Annual	X	X	
Annual U.S Domestic Average Itinerary Fare in Current and Constant Dollars	Annual			X
National Transportation Statistics	Quarterly		X	X
U.S. International Air Travel Statistics	Quarterly, Annual	X	X	X
Wage Statistics of Class I Railroads in the United States	Annual	X	X	X

See footnotes at end of table.

See headnote on page 901.

Title	Frequency	Paper	Internet PDF	Internet Other Formats
Department of the Treasury, Alcohol and Tobacco Tax and Trade Bureau				
http://www.ttb.gov				
Tobacco Products Monthly Statistical Releases	Monthly	X	X	
Department of the Treasury, Bureau of the Fiscal Service				
https://www.fiscal.treasury.gov/				
Combined Statement of Receipts, Outlays, and Balances	Annual	X	X	X
Financial Report of the United States Government	Annual	X	X	X
Monthly Statement of the Public Debt of the United States	Monthly	X	X	X
Monthly Treasury Statement of Receipts and Outlays of the United States Government	Monthly	X	X	X
Treasury Bulletin	Quarterly	X	X	X
Department of Veterans Affairs				
http://www.va.gov				
Annual Benefits Report	Annual		X	
Compensation and Pension Data by County	Annual			X
Performance and Accountability Report	Annual	X	X	
Employment and Training Administration				
http://www.doleta.gov				
Unemployment Insurance Claims	Weekly			X
Energy Information Administration				
http://www.eia.gov				
Annual Coal Report	Annual		X	X
Annual Energy Outlook	Annual	X	X	X
Annual Energy Review (suspended for 2013)	Annual	X	X	X
Electric Power Annual	Annual		X	X
Electric Power Monthly	Monthly		X	X
Electric Sales, Revenue and Average Price	Annual		X	X
International Energy Outlook	Annual	X	X	X
International Energy Statistics portal	Ongoing		X	X
Monthly Energy Review	Monthly		X	X
Petroleum Marketing Annual	Monthly		X	X
Petroleum Marketing Monthly	Monthly		X	X
Petroleum Supply Annual	Annual		X	X
Petroleum Supply Monthly	Monthly		X	X
Quarterly Coal Report	Quarterly		X	X
Residential Energy Consumption Survey	Quadrennial		X	X
State Electricity Profiles	Annual		X	X
State Energy Data System Reports	Annual		X	X
U.S. Crude Oil, Natural Gas, and Natural Gas Liquids Reserves	Annual		X	X
Weekly Coal Production	Weekly			X
Environmental Protection Agency				
http://www.epa.gov				
Air Quality Data	Annual		X	X
Clean Watersheds Needs Survey	Quadrennial		X	
Drinking Water Infrastructure Needs Survey	Periodic		X	
National Water Quality Inventory Report to Congress	Biennial			X
Toxics Release Inventory National Analysis	Annual		X	X
Export-Import Bank of the United States				
http://www.exim.gov				
Annual Report	Annual	X	X	
Report to the U.S. Congress on Export Credit Competition and the Export-Import Bank of the United States	Annual	X	X	
Farm Credit Administration				
http://www.fca.gov/index.html				
Annual Report on the Farm Credit System	Annual	X	X	
Federal Bureau of Investigation				
http://www.fbi.gov/ucr/ucr.htm				
Crime in the United States	Annual		X	X
Hate Crime Statistics	Annual		X	X
Law Enforcement Officers Killed and Assaulted	Annual		X	X
Federal Communications Commission				
http://www.fcc.gov				
Annual Assessment of the Status of Competition in the Market for the Delivery of Video Programming	Annual		X	X
International Telecommunications Data	Annual	X	X	X
Internet Access Services	Semi-Annual		X	X
Local Telephone Competition	Semi-Annual		X	X
Quarterly Report on Informal Consumer Inquiries and Complaints	Quarterly		X	X
Report on Cable Industry Prices	Annual		X	X
Telecommunications Industry Revenues	Annual		X	X
Trends in Telephone Service	Annual	X	X	
Federal Deposit Insurance Corporation				
http://www.fdic.gov				
Annual Report	Annual	X	X	X
FDIC Quarterly	Quarterly	X	X	X
Historical Statistics on Banking	Annual			X
Quarterly Banking Profile	Quarterly		X	X
Statistics on Banking	Quarterly			X
Summary of Deposits	Annual			X
Federal Highway Administration				

See footnotes at end of table.

Title	Frequency	Paper	Internet	
			PDF	Other *Formats*
http://www.fhwa.dot.gov				
Highway Statistics	Annual	X	X	X
Federal Railroad Administration				
http://safetydata.fra.dot.gov/OfficeofSafety/default.aspx				
Railroad Safety Statistics	Annual	X	X	
Fish and Wildlife Service				
http://www.fws.gov				
National Survey of Fishing, Hunting, and Wildlife Associated Recreation	Quinquennial	X	X	
Forest Service				
http://www.fs.fed.us				
An Analysis of the Timber Situation in the United States 1952-2050	Periodic	X	X	
Land Areas of the National Forest System	Annual	X	X	X
RPA Assessment Tables	Periodic	X	X	X
U.S. Timber Production, Trade, Consumption, and Price Statistics 1965-2011	Biennial	X	X	
General Services Administration				
http://www.gsa.gov				
Federal Real Property Profile	Annual		X	X
Geological Survey				
http://www.usgs.gov/				
Estimated Use of Water in the United States	Quinquennial	X	X	X
Mineral Commodity Summaries	Annual	X	X	
Mineral Industry Surveys	Monthly/ Quarterly		X	X
Minerals Yearbook	Annual	X	X	X
Internal Revenue Service				
http://www.irs.gov/uac/Tax-Stats-2				
Corporation Income Tax Returns	Annual	X	X	X
Individual Income Tax Returns	Annual	X	X	X
IRS Data Book	Annual	X	X	X
Statistics of Income Bulletin	Quarterly	X	X	X
International Trade Administration, Office of Travel and Tourism Industries				
http://www.tinet.ita.doc.gov				
U.S. Travel and Tourism Statistics	Annual		X	X
International Trade Commission				
http://www.usitc.gov				
Recent Trends in U.S. Services Trade	Annual	X	X	
Library of Congress				
http://www.loc.gov				
Annual Report	Annual	X	X	
Maritime Administration				
http://www.marad.dot.gov				
Annual Report	Annual	X	X	
Fleet Statistics 1,000 Gross Tons or Greater	Annual			X
U.S. Waterborne Foreign Trade	Annual			X
Vessel Calls	Annual		X	X
Mine Safety and Health Administration				
http://www.msha.gov				
Informational Reports by Mining Industry: Coal, Metallic Minerals, Nonmetallic Minerals (except stone and coal), Sand and Gravel, and Stone	Annual		X	X
Mine Injuries and Worktime	Quarterly	X	X	X
National Aeronautics and Space Administration				
http://www.nasa.gov				
Annual Procurement Report	Annual	X	X	
National Center for Education Statistics				
http://nces.ed.gov				
Academic Libraries	Biennial		X	X
Characteristics of Private Schools in the United States	Annual	X	X	X
Characteristics of Schools, Districts, Teachers, Principals, and School Libraries in the United States	Annual	X	X	X
The Condition of Education	Annual	X	X	X
Digest of Education Statistics	Annual	X	X	X
Enrollment in Postsecondary Institutions, Graduation Rates, and Financial Statistics	Annual		X	
Indicators of School Crime and Safety	Annual	X	X	X
The Nation's Report Card: Civics 2014	Periodic	X	X	
The Nation's Report Card: Economics 2012	Periodic	X	X	
The Nation's Report Card: Geography 2014	Periodic	X	X	
The Nation's Report Card: U.S. History 2014	Periodic	X	X	
The Nation's Report Card: Mathematics 2013	Periodic	X	X	
The Nation's Report Card: Reading 2013	Periodic	X	X	
The Nation's Report Card: Science 2011	Periodic	X	X	
The Nation's Report Card: Writing 2011	Periodic	X	X	
Projections of Education Statistics	Annual	X	X	X
Status and Trends in the Education of Racial and Ethnic Groups	Irregular	X	X	X
Trends in High School Dropout and Completion Rates in the United States	Annual		X	X
National Center for Health Statistics				
http://www.cdc.gov/nchs/				
Health: United States	Annual	X	X	X

See footnotes at end of table.

Title	Frequency	Paper	Internet PDF	Internet Other Formats
National Health Statistics Reports	Periodic	X	X	
National Vital Statistics Reports	Periodic	X	X	
Vital and Health Statistics:				
Series 3: Analytical and Epidemiological Studies	Irregular	X	X	
Series 10: Data from the National Health Interview Survey	Irregular	X	X	
Series 11: Health and Nutrition Examination Survey Statistics	Irregular	X	X	
Series 13: Data on Health Resources Utilization	Irregular	X	X	
Series 20: Data on Mortality	Irregular	X	X	
Series 21: Data on Natality, Marriage, and Divorce	Irregular	X	X	
Series 23: Data from the National Survey of Family Growth	Irregular	X	X	
National Credit Union Administration				
http://www.ncua.gov				
Annual Report	Annual	X	X	
Yearend Statistics for Federally Insured Credit Unions	Annual	X	X	
National Endowment for the Arts				
http://www.nea.gov				
Annual Report	Annual		X	
Appropriations Request	Annual		X	
National Endowment for the Humanities				
http://www.neh.gov				
Annual Report	Annual		X	
Appropriations Request	Annual		X	
National Guard Bureau				
http://www.nationalguard.mil/				
Posture Statement	Annual		X	
National Highway Traffic Safety Administration				
http://www.nhtsa.gov				
Traffic Safety Facts	Annual	X	X	
National Oceanic and Atmospheric Administration				
http://www.noaa.gov				
Climatic Data for the World	Monthly		X	
Comparative Climatic Data	Annual	X	X	X
Daily Normals of Temperature, Precipitation, Heating Degree Days (HDD), and Cooling Degree Days (CDD)	Periodic			X
Fisheries of the United States	Annual	X	X	
Hourly Precipitation Data. Monthly with annual summary; for each state	Monthly		X	X
Local Climatological Data. Monthly with annual summary; for major cities	Monthly		X	X
Monthly Normals of Temperature, Precipitation, Heating Degree Days (HDD), and Cooling Degree Days (CDD)	Periodic			X
Our Living Oceans	Periodic	X	X	
Storm Data	Monthly		X	
Tornado Summaries	Monthly/ Annual			X
U.S. Climate Normals	Annual	X	X	X
National Park Service				
http://www.nps.gov				
National Park Statistical Abstract	Annual	X	X	
National Science Foundation				
http://www.nsf.gov/statistics				
Academic Institutional Profiles	Annual			X
Academic Research and Development Expenditures	Annual		X	X
Characteristics of Doctoral Scientists and Engineers in the United States	Biennial		X	X
Characteristics of Recent Science/Engineering Graduates	Biennial		X	X
Doctorate Recipients from U.S. Universities	Annual		X	X
Federal Funds for Research and Development	Annual		X	X
Federal Research and Development Funding by Budget Function	Annual		X	X
Federal Science and Engineering Support to Universities, Colleges, and Nonprofit Institutions	Annual		X	X
Graduate Students and Postdoctorates in Science and Engineering	Annual		X	X
National Patterns of Research and Development Resources	Annual		X	X
Research and Development in Industry	Annual		X	X
Science and Engineering Degrees	Biennial		X	X
Science and Engineering Degrees, by Race/Ethnicity of Recipients	Biennial		X	X
Science and Engineering Doctorate Awards	Annual		X	X
Science and Engineering Indicators	Biennial	X	X	X
Science and Engineering State Profiles	Annual			X
Science Resources Statistics Info Briefs (various topics)	Frequent	X	X	X
Scientific and Engineering Research Facilities at Universities and Colleges	Biennial		X	X
Women, Minorities, and Persons with Disabilities in Science and Engineering	Biennial		X	X
National Transportation Safety Board				
http://www.ntsb.gov				
Review of U.S. Civil Aviation Accidents	Annual		X	X
Office of Juvenile Justice and Delinquency Prevention				
http://ojjdp.gov				
Highlights of the National Youth Gang Survey	Annual	X	X	X
Juvenile Arrests	Annual	X	X	X
Juvenile Offenders and Victims	Periodic	X	X	X
Office of Management and Budget				
http://www.whitehouse.gov/omb				

See footnotes at end of table.

Appendix I Table: Sources of Statistics, State Statistical Abstracts, and Foreign Statistical Abstracts-Continued.

See headnote on page 901.

Title	Frequency	Paper	Internet PDF	Internet Other Formats
The Budget of the United States Government	Annual	X	X	
Office of Personnel Management http://www.opm.gov				
Demographic Profile of the Federal Workforce	Biennial		X	
Employment and Trends	Bimonthly		X	X
The Fact Book	Annual		X	X
Statistical Abstract for the Federal Employee Benefit Programs	Annual			X
Office of the Clerk, U.S. House of Representatives http://clerk.house.gov				
Statistics of the Presidential and Congressional Election	Biennial		X	
Patent and Trademark Office http://www.uspto.gov				
All Technologies (Utility Patents)	Annual	X	X	X
Patent Counts by Country/State and Year	Annual	X	X	X
Patenting Trends in the United States	Annual	X		X
Railroad Retirement Board http://www.rrb.gov/default.asp				
Annual Report	Annual	X	X	
Quarterly Benefit Statistics	Quarterly	X	X	
Securities and Exchange Commission http://www.sec.gov/about.shtml				
Select SEC and Market Data	Annual		X	
Small Business Administration http://www.sba.gov				
Loan Program Performance Reports	Annual		X	
Quarterly Bulletin	Quarterly		X	X
Small Business Lending in the United States	Annual	X	X	X
Small Business Economy	Annual		X	X
Small Business Profiles for States and Territories	Annual		X	X
Social Security Administration http://www.ssa.gov				
Annual Statistical Report on the Social Security Disability Insurance Program	Annual	X	X	X
Annual Statistical Supplement to the Social Security Bulletin	Annual	X	X	X
Congressional Statistics	Annual	X	X	X
Fast Facts & Figures about Social Security	Annual	X	X	X
Income of the Population 55 and over	Biennially	X	X	X
OASDI Beneficiaries by State and County	Annual	X	X	X
Social Security Bulletin	Quarterly	X	X	X
SSI Annual Statistical Report	Annual	X	X	X
SSI Recipients by State and County	Annual	X	X	X
Substance Abuse and Mental Health Services Administration http://www.samhsa.gov				
Behavioral Health, United States	Annual	X	X	
National Survey on Drug Use and Health (NSDUH)	Annual	X	X	X
National Survey on Substance Abuse Treatment Services (N-SSATS)	Annual	X	X	X
U.S. Copyright Office http://www.copyright.gov/				
Annual Report	Annual	X	X	
NONGOVERNMENT				
Aerospace Industries Association, Arlington, VA http://www.aia-aerospace.org				
Aerospace Foreign Trade: Export Activity	Annual		X	
Aerospace Foreign Trade: Import Activity	Annual		X	
Aerospace Industries Report 2012: Facts, Figures & Outlook for the Aviation and Aerospace Manufacturing Industry (Final Edition)	Annual	X	X	
Aerospace Industry Year-End Review and Forecast	Annual		X	
Manufacturing Production, Capacity, and Utilization in Aerospace and Aircraft and Parts	Quarterly		X	
Orders, Shipments, and Backlog for Large Civil Jet Transport Aircraft	Periodic		X	
Total and Production Workers Employment in the Aerospace Industry	Annual		X	
Airlines for America, Washington, DC http://www.airlines.org				
Airlines for America Economic Report 2011	Annual		X	
American Bureau of Metal Statistics, Inc., Chatham, NJ http://www.abms.com				
Non-Ferrous Metal Yearbook	Annual	X		X
American Council of Life Insurers, Washington, DC http://www.acli.com				
Life Insurers Fact Book	Annual		X	
American Dental Association, Chicago, IL http://www.ada.org				
Distribution of Dentists in the United States by Region and State 2009 (Final Edition)	Annual	X	X	
Survey of Dental Practice	Annual			X
American Forest and Paper Association, Washington, DC http://www.afandpa.org				
Monthly Exports/Imports Report	Monthly		X	
Monthly Statistics of Paper, Paperboard and Wood Pulp	Monthly		X	X
Paper Industry Annual Capacity and Fiber Consumption	Annual		X	

See footnotes at end of table.

Appendix I Table: Sources of Statistics, State Statistical Abstracts, and Foreign Statistical Abstracts-Continued.

See headnote on page 901.

Title	Frequency	Paper	Internet	
			PDF	Other Formats
Paper Industry Annual Statistical Summary	Annual		X	
American Gas Association, Washington, DC http://www.aga.org				
Gas Facts	Annual	X	X	
American Iron and Steel Institute, Washington, DC http://www.steel.org				
Annual Statistical Report	Annual	X	X	
American Medical Association, Chicago, IL http://www.ama-assn.org				
Physician Characteristics and Distribution in the U.S.	Annual	X		X
State Medical Licensure Statistics and License Requirements	Annual	X		X
American Osteopathic Association, Chicago, IL http://www.osteopathic.org/				
Osteopathic Medical Profession Report	Annual		X	
American Petroleum Institute, Washington, DC http://www.api.org				
Basic Petroleum Data Book	Semiannual	X	X	
Joint Association Survey on Drilling Costs	Annual	X	X	
Quarterly Well Completion Report	Quarterly	X	X	
American Public Transportation Association, Washington, DC http://www.apta.com				
Public Transportation Fact Book	Annual		X	X
Association for Manufacturing Technology, McLean, VA http://www.amtonline.org				
2010-11 Economic Handbook of the Machine Tool Industry (Final Edition)	Annual		X	X
Machine Tool Industry Data Base	Ongoing			X
Association of American Railroads, Washington, DC http://www.aar.org				
Analysis of Class I Railroads	Annual	X	X	X
Freight Commodity Statistics	Annual	X	X	X
Railroad Facts	Annual	X	X	
Association of Racing Commissioners International, Inc., Lexington, KY http://www.arci.com				
Pari-Mutuel Racing	Annual	X		
Berman Jewish Data Bank, Storrs, CT http://www.jewishdatabank.org				
Jewish Population in the United States	Annual		X	X
Bloomberg BNA, Washington, DC http://www.bna.com				
Basic Patterns in Union Contracts	Annual	X		
BNA's Employment Outlook Report	Quarterly	X		
BNA's Job Absence and Turnover Report	Quarterly	X		
Directory of U.S. Labor Organizations	Annual	X		
National Labor Relations Board Election Statistics	Semiannual	X	x	x
Source Book on Collective Bargaining	Annual	X		
Union Membership and Earnings Data Book	Annual	X		
Book Industry Study Group and Association of American Publishers, New York, NY http://www.bisg.org				
BookStats	Annual	X	X	X
Boy Scouts of America, Irving, TX http://www.scouting.org				
Scouting Annual Report	Annual		X	
Bowker, Ann Arbor, MI http://www.bowker.com				
ISBN Annual Output Reports	Annual		X	
Brookings Institution, Washington, DC				
Vital Statistics on Congress	Biennial		X	X
Chronicle of Higher Education, Inc., Washington, DC http://chronicle.com				
Almanac of Higher Education	Annual	X		X
College Board, New York, NY http://www.collegeboard.com				
College-Bound Seniors Total Group Profile Report	Annual		X	
Commodity Research Bureau, Chicago, IL http://www.crbtrader.com				
CRB Commodity Index Report	Weekly		X	X
CRB Commodity Yearbook	Annual	X		X
CRB Futures Perspective	Weekly in digital only/Monthly	X	X	
CRB Infotech CD	Monthly			X
Final Markets End-of-Day Data	Daily			X
Fundamental Market Service	Weekly		X	X
Trends In Futures	Daily		X	X

See footnotes at end of table.

Title	Frequency	Paper	Internet PDF	Internet Other Formats
Conference Board, New York, NY http://www.conference-board.org				
Business Cycle Indicators	Monthly		X	X
Corporate Contributions Report	Annual		X	
International Comparisons of Annual Labor Force Statistics	Annual		X	X
International Comparisons of Hourly Compensation Costs for Production Workers in Manufacturing	Annual		X	X
International Comparisons of Manufacturing Productivity and Unit Labor Cost Trends	Annual		X	X
Performance: Productivity, Employment, and Growth in the World's Economies	Irregular		X	
Congressional Quarterly (CQ) Press, Washington, DC http://www.cqpress.com				
America Votes	Biennial	X		
Consumer Electronics Association, Arlington, VA http://www.ce.org				
U.S. Consumer Electronics Sales and Forecasts	Semiannual		X	
Council of State Governments, Lexington, KY http://www.csg.org				
Book of the States	Annual	X	X	
Directory I: Elective Officials	Annual	X		
Directory II: Legislative Leadership, Committees, and Staff	Annual	X		
Directory III: Administrative Officials	Annual	X		
Credit Union National Association, Madison, WI http://www.cuna.org				
Operating Ratios and Spreads	Quarterly	X	X	
Dodge Data & Analytics, New York, NY http://construction.com/dodge/dodge-reports-print.asp				
Dodge Construction Potential Bulletin	Monthly		X	
Dow Jones and Company, New York, NY http://www.dj.com				
Wall Street Journal	Daily	X		X
Duncan McIntosh Company, Inc., Irvine, CA http://www.editorandpublisher.com				
Editor and Publisher	Monthly	X		X
Market Guide 2010 (Final Edition)	Periodic	X		
Newspaper Databook	Annual	X		X
Edison Electric Institute, Washington, DC http://www.eei.org				
Statistical Yearbook of the Electric Power Industry	Annual	X	X	X
Euromonitor International, London, England http://www.euromonitor.com				
Consumer Americas	Annual	X	X	
Consumer Asia Pacific and Australasia	Annual	X	X	
Consumer Europe	Annual	X	X	
Consumer Middle East and North Africa	Annual	X	X	
European Marketing Data and Statistics	Annual	X	X	
International Marketing Data and Statistics	Annual	X	X	
Retail Trade International	Annual	X	X	
World Consumer Income and Expenditure Patterns	Annual	X	X	
World Consumer Lifestyles Databook	Annual	X	X	
World Economic Factbook	Annual	X	X	
World Environmental Databook	Periodic	X	X	
World Health Databook	Periodic	X	X	
World Retail Data and Statistics	Annual	X	X	
Federal National Mortgage Association, Washington, DC http://www.fanniemae.com				
Annual Report on Form 10-K	Annual		X	
Food and Agriculture Organization of the United Nations, Rome, Italy http://www.fao.org				
World Fertilizer Trends and Outlook	Annual		X	
FAO Statistical Yearbook: World Food and Agriculture	Annual	X	X	
FAO Yearbook: Fishery and Aquaculture Statistics	Periodic	X	X	
Yearbook of Forest Products	Annual	X	X	
Foundation Center, New York, NY http://www.foundationcenter.org				
Foundation Yearbook 2011 (Final Edition)	Annual	X		
FC Stats	Annual			X
General Aviation Manufacturers Association, Washington, DC http://www.gama.aero/home.php				
General Aviation Aircraft Shipment Report	Quarterly		X	
General Aviation Statistical Databook & Industry Outlook	Annual		X	
Girl Scouts of the USA, New York, NY http://www.girlscouts.org				
Annual Report	Annual		X	
Giving USA Foundation, Chicago, IL http://www.givingusa.org/				
Giving USA	Annual	X	X	X

See footnotes at end of table.

Appendix I Table: Sources of Statistics, State Statistical Abstracts, and Foreign Statistical Abstracts-Continued.

See headnote on page 901.

Title	Frequency	Paper	Internet PDF	Internet Other Formats
Guttmacher Institute, New York, NY http://www.guttmacher.org				
Perspectives on Sexual and Reproductive Health	Quarterly	X	X	
Health Forum, an American Hospital Association Company, Chicago, IL http://www.ahadataviewer.com/				
AHA Annual Survey Data Base	Annual			X
AHA Hospital Statistics	Annual	X		X
IHS Global, Inc., Englewood, CO http://www.janes.com				
IHS Jane's All the World's Aircraft: Development & Production	Annual	X		X
IHS Jane's Defence: C4ISR & Mission Systems	Annual	X		X
IHS Jane's Fighting Ships	Annual	X		X
IHS Jane's Flight Avionics	Annual	X		X
IHS Jane's Land Warfare Platforms: Armoured Fighting Vehicles	Annual	X		X
IHS Jane's Land Warfare Platforms: Logistics, Support & Unmanned	Annual	X		X
IHS Jane's Merchant Ships	Annual	X		X
IHS Jane's Simulation & Training Systems	Annual	X		X
IHS Jane's Space Systems & Industry	Annual	X		X
IHS Jane's Weapons: Air-Launched	Annual	X		X
IHS Jane's Weapons: Infantry	Annual	X		X
Independent Petroleum Association of America, Washington, DC http://www.ipaa.org				
IPAA Oil & Gas Producing Industry in Your State	Annual	X	X	
U.S. Petroleum Statistics	Annual	X	X	
Infobase Publishing, New York, NY http://www.worldalmanac.com				
The World Almanac and Book of Facts	Annual	X		
Information Today, Inc., Medford, NJ http://www.infotoday.com				
American Library Directory	Annual	X		
Library and Book Trade Almanac (formerly The Bowker Annual)	Annual	X		
Institute for Criminal Justice Ethics, New York, NY http://johnjayresearch.org/cje/				
Criminal Justice Ethics	Three Issues per Year	X	X	
Insurance Information Institute, New York, NY http://www.iii.org				
The Financial Services Fact Book (published jointly with the Financial Services Roundtable)	Annual	X		X
The I.I.I. Insurance Fact Book	Annual	X	X	X
Inter-American Development Bank, Washington, DC http://www.iadb.org				
Annual Report	Annual	X	X	
Development in the Americas	Periodic	X		
International Air Transport Association, Montreal, Canada and Geneva, Switzerland http://www.iata.org				
World Air Transport Statistics	Annual	X	X	X
International City Management Association, Washington, DC http://www.icma.org				
ICMA Chief Administrative Officers Salary & Compensation Survey	Annual		X	
Municipal Year Book	Annual	X	X	
International Labour Organization, Geneva, Switzerland http://www.ilo.org				
Yearbook of Labour Statistics	Annual	X		X
International Monetary Fund, Washington, DC http://www.imf.org				
Annual Report	Annual	X	X	X
Balance of Payments Statistics	Monthly	X	X	X
Direction of Trade Statistics	Monthly	X	X	X
Government Finance Statistics Yearbook	Annual	X	X	X
International Financial Statistics	Monthly	X	X	X
International Telecommunication Union, Geneva, Switzerland http://www.itu.int/home/index.html				
ITU Yearbook of Statistics	Annual	X	X	
World Telecommunication/ICT Indicators	Annual	X	X	X
Investment Company Institute, Washington, DC http://www.ici.org				
Investment Company Fact Book	Annual		X	X
Joint Center for Housing Studies of Harvard University, Cambridge, MA http://www.jchs.harvard.edu/				
The State of the Nation's Housing	Annual		X	
Media Source, Inc., New York, NY http://www.mediasourceinc.net/				
Library Journal	Semimonthly	X		X
School Library Journal	Monthly	X		X

See footnotes at end of table.

Appendix I Table: Sources of Statistics, State Statistical Abstracts, and Foreign Statistical Abstracts-Continued.

See headnote on page 901.

Title	Frequency	Paper	Internet PDF	Internet Other Formats
National Academy of Social Insurance, Washington, DC				
http://www.nasi.org/				
Workers Compensation: Benefits, Coverage, and Costs	Annual	X	X	
National Association of Home Builders, Washington, DC				
http://www.nahb.org				
HousingEconomics.com (online subscription)	Ongoing			X
National Association of Latino Elected and Appointed Officials, Los Angeles, CA				
http://www.naleo.org				
National Directory of Latino Elected Officials	Annual		X	X
National Association of Realtors, Chicago, IL				
http://www.realtor.org				
Economist's Outlook	Daily			X
Investment and Vacation Home Buyers Survey	Annual	X	X	
NAR Member Profile	Annual	X	X	
NAR Profile of Home Buyer and Sellers	Annual	X	X	
National Association of State Budget Officers, Washington, DC				
http://www.nasbo.org				
Fiscal Survey of the States	Semiannual	X	X	
State Expenditure Report	Annual	X	X	
National Association of State Park Directors, Raleigh, NC				
http://www.naspd.org				
Statistical Report of State Park Operations: Annual Information Exchange	Annual	X	X	
National Catholic Educational Association, Arlington, VA				
http://www.ncea.org				
Dollars & Sense: A Report for the National Catholic Educational Association Secondary Schools Department	Biennial	X	X	
Financing the Mission: A Profile of Catholic Elementary Schools in the U.S.	Biennial	X	X	
Ganley's Catholic Schools in America	Annual	X	X	
U.S. Catholic Elementary and Secondary Schools: The Annual Statistical Report on Schools, Enrollment and Staffing	Annual	X	X	
National Council of the Churches of Christ in the USA, Washington, DC				
http://www.ncccusa.org				
Yearbook of American and Canadian Churches	Annual	X		X
National Education Association, Washington, DC				
http://www.nea.org				
Rankings & Estimates: Rankings of the States and Estimates of School Statistics	Annual	X	X	
National Fire Protection Association, Quincy, MA				
http://www.nfpa.org				
National Fire Protection Association (NFPA) Journal	Bimonthly	X		X
National Golf Foundation, Jupiter, FL				
http://www.ngf.org				
Golf Facilities in the U.S.	Annual	X	X	
National Marine Manufacturers Association, Chicago, IL				
http://www.nmma.org				
Recreational Boating Statistical Abstract	Annual		X	X
U.S. Recreational Boat Registration Statistics	Annual		X	
National Restaurant Association, Washington, DC				
http://www.restaurant.org				
Restaurant Industry 2020	Recurring		X	
Restaurant Industry Forecast	Annual		X	
Restaurant Industry Operations Report	Recurring	X	X	
Restaurant Industry Pocket Factbook	Annual	X	X	
Restaurant Performance Index	Monthly		X	
Restaurant Trendmapper (online subscription)	Ongoing			X
National Safety Council, Itasca, IL				
http://www.nsc.org				
Injury Facts	Annual	X	X	
National Sporting Goods Association, Mount Prospect, IL				
http://www.nsga.org				
Sporting Goods Market	Annual	X	X	
Sports Participation	Annual	X	X	
NYSE Euronext, New York, NY				
http://www.nyse.com				
NYSE Facts & Figures (formerly the online NYSE Fact Book)	Ongoing			X
Organisation for Economic Cooperation and Development, Paris, France				
http://www.oecd-ilibrary.org/				
www.data.oecd.org				
CO2 Emissions From Fuel Combustion	Annual	X	X	X
Coal Information	Annual	X	X	X
Digital Economy Outlook	Biennial	X	X	X
Education at a Glance: OECD Indicators	Annual	X	X	X
Electricity Information	Annual	X	X	X
Energy Balances of Non-OECD Countries	Annual	X	X	X
Energy Balances of OECD Countries	Annual	X	X	X
Energy Prices and Taxes	Quarterly	X	X	
Energy Statistics of Non-OECD Countries	Annual	X	X	
Energy Statistics of OECD Countries	Annual	X	X	

See footnotes at end of table.

Title	Frequency	Paper	Internet	
			PDF	Other *Formats*
Environmental Outlook	Periodic	X	X	X
Financial Accounts	Annual	X	X	X
Financial Balance Sheets	Annual	X	X	X
General Government Accounts	Annual	X	X	X
Geographical Distribution of Financial Flows to Developing Countries	Annual	X	X	X
International Migration Outlook	Annual	X	X	X
International Trade by Commodity Statistics	Ongoing	X	X	X
Issue 1: Main Aggregates	Annual	X	X	X
Issue 2: Detailed Tables	Annual	X	X	X
ITF Transport Outlook	Annual	X	X	X
Main Economic Indicators	Monthly	X	X	X
Main Science and Technology Indicators	Semiannual	X	X	X
National Accounts at a Glance	Annual	X	X	X
National Accounts of OECD Countries	Annual	X	X	X
Natural Gas Information	Annual	X	X	
Nuclear Energy Data	Annual	X	X	X
OECD Central Government Debt Statistics	Annual	X	X	X
OECD Communications Outlook	Biennial	X	X	X
OECD Economic Outlook	Semiannual	X	X	X
OECD Economic Surveys	Periodic	X	X	X
OECD Employment Outlook	Annual	X	X	X
OECD Factbook	Annual	X	X	X
OECD-FAO Agricultural Outlook	Annual	X		X
OECD Health Statistics	Annual			X
OECD Insurance Statistics	Annual	X	X	X
OECD International Development Statistics	Annual			X
OECD Journal: Economic Studies	Periodic	X	X	
OECD Journal: Financial Market Trends	Periodic	X	X	X
OECD Quarterly International Trade Statistics	Quarterly	X	X	X
OECD Review of Fisheries: Policies and Summary Statistics	Biennial	X	X	X
OECD Science, Technology, and Industry Outlook	Biennial	X	X	
OECD Science, Technology and R&D Statistics	Ongoing			X
OECD Society at a Glance	Biennial	X	X	X
OECD Territorial Reviews	Periodic	X	X	X
Oil Information	Annual	X	X	
Oil, Gas, Coal, and Electricity Quarterly Statistics	Quarterly	X	X	X
Pensions at a Glance	Biennial	X	X	X
PISA (OECD Programme for International Student Assessment)	Periodic	X	X	X
Quarterly National Accounts	Quarterly	X	X	X
Revenue Statistics	Annual	X	X	X
Taxing Wages	Annual	X	X	X
Uranium: Resources Production and Demand	Biennial	X	X	X
World Energy Outlook	Annual	X	X	
Penguin Group (USA), Inc., New York, NY				
http://www.penguin.com/				
The New York Times Almanac 2011 (Final Edition)	Annual	X		
PennWell Corporation, Tulsa, OK				
http://www.pennwell.com				
Offshore	Monthly	X	X	X
Oil and Gas Journal	Weekly	X	X	X
Pew Research Center				
http://www.pewinternet.org				
Social Media Update	Periodic		X	X
Puerto Rico Planning Board, San Juan, PR				
http://www.jp.gobierno.pr				
Construction Industry	Periodic	X		
Economic Report to the Governor	Annual	X	X	X
External Trade Statistics, 2007	Periodic	X	X	X
Income and Product	Annual	X	X	
Statistical Appendix-Economic Report to the Governor	Annual	X	X	X
PWxyz, LLC, New York, NY				
http://www.publishersweekly.com				
Publishers Weekly	Weekly	X		X
Radio Advertising Bureau, Dallas, TX				
http://www.rab.com				
Media Facts	Ongoing			X
Why Radio: Fact Sheets	Ongoing			X
Regional Airline Association, Washington, DC				
http://www.raa.org				
Regional Airlines Association Annual Report	Annual		X	X
Securities Industry and Financial Markets Association, New York, NY				
http://www.sifma.org				
SIFMA Fact Book	Annual	X		X
U.S. Foreign Activity Report	Quarterly		X	X
Standard and Poor's Financial Services LLC, New York, NY				
http://www.standardandpoors.com				
Analyst's Handbook	Monthly	X		X
Corporation Records: Corporate Description	Monthly	X	X	X
Corporation Records: Daily News	Daily	X	X	X
Daily Stock Price Records	Quarterly			X

See footnotes at end of table.

Title	Frequency	Paper	Internet PDF	Internet Other Formats
United Nations Conference on Trade and Development, Geneva, Switzerland				
http://www.unctad.org				
Development and Globalization: Facts and Figures	Periodic	X	X	X
Handbook of Statistics	Annual	X	X	X
United Nations Statistics Division, New York, NY				
http://unstats.un.org/unsd/default.htm				
Demographic Yearbook (Series R)	Annual	X	X	
Energy Balances and Electricity Profiles (Series W)	Annual	X	X	
Energy Statistics Yearbook (Series J)	Annual	X	X	
Industrial Commodity Statistics Yearbook: Production Statistics	Annual	X	X	
International Trade Statistics Yearbook (Series G)	Annual	X	X	
Main Aggregates and Detailed Tables	Annual	X	X	X
Monthly Bulletin of Statistics (Series Q)	Monthly	X	X	
National Accounts Statistics: Analysis of Main Aggregates	Annual	X		
National Accounts Statistics (Series X)	Annual	X	X	
Population and Vital Statistics Report (Series A)	Quarterly	X	X	
Statistical Yearbook	Annual	X	X	
World Statistics Pocketbook (Series V)	Annual	X	X	
World's Women: Progress in Statistics	Quinquennial	X	X	
University of Michigan, Institute for Social Research, Inter-University Consortium for Political and Social Research, Ann Arbor, MI				
http://www.icpsr.umich.edu/icpsrweb/ICPSR/studies/8475				
American National Election Studies Cumulative Data File	Biennial			X
Warren Communications News, Washington, DC				
http://www.warren-news.com				
Cable and TV Station Coverage Atlas	Annual			X
Television and Cable Factbook	Ongoing			X
World Bank Group, Washington, DC				
http://www.worldbank.org				
Atlas of Global Development	Periodic	X	X	
Global Development Finance	Annual	X	X	
The Little Data Book	Annual	X	X	
World Development Indicators	Annual	X		X
World Health Organization, Geneva, Switzerland				
http://www.who.int/en/				
AIDS Epidemic Update	Periodic	X	X	
World Health Statistics Report	Annual	X	X	
World Trade Organization, Geneva, Switzerland				
http://www.wto.org				
International Trade Statistics	Annual	X	X	X
STATE STATISTICAL ABSTRACTS FROM UNIVERSITIES				
Pennsylvania State University, Pennsylvania State Data Center, Middletown, PA				
http://pasdc.hbg.psu.edu/				
Pennsylvania Abstract: A Statistical Fact Book	Annual	X	X	X
State University of New York: Nelson A. Rockefeller Institute of Government, Albany, NY				
http://www.rockinst.org/				
New York State Statistical Yearbook	Annual	X	X	X
University of Florida: Bureau of Economic and Business Research, Gainesville, FL				
http://www.bebr.ufl.edu/				
Florida Statistical Abstract Online	Ongoing			X
University of Georgia: Selig Center for Economic Growth, Athens, GA				
http://www.terry.uga.edu/selig/				
Georgia Statistical Abstract	Biennial	X	X	X
University of Kansas: Institute for Policy and Social Research, Lawrence, KS				
http://www.ipsr.ku.edu/ksdata/ksah/				
Kansas Statistical Abstract	Annual		X	X
University of Missouri-Columbia: Economic and Policy Analysis Research Center, Columbia, MO				
http://eparc.missouri.edu/				
Missouri Statistical Data Archive (online)	Ongoing		X	
University of Oklahoma: Center for Economic and Management Research, Norman, OK				
http://www.ou.edu/content/price/centersresearch/cemr/cemr_publications.html				
Oklahoma Statistical Abstract	Periodic	X		
STATE STATISTICAL ABSTRACT FROM AN ASSOCIATION				
Texas State Historical Association, Austin, TX				
https://www.tshaonline.org/publications/books/31961				
Texas Almanac	Biennial	X	X	X
STATE STATISTICAL ABSTRACTS FROM STATE AGENCIES				
California Department of Finance, Economic Research Unit, Sacramento, CA				
http://www.dof.ca.gov/HTML/FS_DATA/STAT-ABS/Statistical_Abstract.php				
California Statistical Abstract	Periodic		X	

See footnotes at end of table.

See headnote on page 901.

Title	Frequency	Paper	Internet PDF	Internet Other Formats
Hawaii State Department of Business, Economic Development & Tourism, Honolulu, HI http://dbedt.hawaii.gov/economic/databook/ State of Hawaii Data Book	Annual		X	
Maryland State Data Center, Maryland Department of Planning, Baltimore, MD http://www.mdp.state.md.us/msdc/ Maryland Statistical Handbook	Periodic		X	
South Carolina, Budget and Control Board, Office of Research and Statistics, Columbia, SC http://abstract.sc.gov/ South Carolina Statistical Abstract	Ongoing			X
INTERNATIONAL STATISTICAL ABSTRACTS FROM A FOREIGN AGENCY				
Australia **Australian Bureau of Statistics, Canberra** http://www.abs.gov.au/ Year Book Australia, 2012	Annual	X	X	X
Austria **Statistik Austria, Wien** http://www.statistik.at/web_en/ Statistisches Jahrbuch Österreichs, 2015	Annual	X	X	X
Belgium **Statistics Belgium, Brussels** http://statbel.fgov.be/en Key Figures: Statistical Overview of Belgium, 2012	Annual	X	X	
Canada **Statistics Canada, Ottawa** http://www12.statcan.gc.ca/census-recensement/index-eng.cfm Canada Year Book, 2012 (Discontinued)	Annual		X	X
Czech Republic **Czech Statistical Office, Praha** http://www.czso.cz Statistical Yearbook of the Czech Republic, 2014	Annual	X	X	X
Denmark **Statistics Denmark, Copenhagen** http://www.dst.dk/en Statistical Yearbook, 2015	Annual		X	
Finland **Statistics Finland, Helsinki** http://www.stat.fi/index_en.html Statistical Yearbook of Finland, 2015	Annual	X		
France **National Institute of Statistics and Economic Studies, Paris** http://www.insee.fr/en/ Tableaux de l'Economie Francaise, 2015	Annual		X	X
Germany **Statistisches Bundesamt, Wiesbaden** https://www.destatis.de/EN/Homepage.html Statistisches Jahrbuch: Deutschland und Internationales, 2014	Annual		X	
Greece **Hellenic Statistical Authority, Pireus** http://www.statistics.gr/portal/page/portal/ESYE Statistical Yearbook of Greece, 2009/2010	Annual	X	X	
Hungary **Hungarian Central Statistical Office, Budapest** http://www.ksh.hu/?lang=en Statistical Yearbook of Hungary, 2014	Annual	X	X	X
Iceland **Statistics Iceland, Reykjavik** http://www.statice.is/ Statistical Yearbook of Iceland, 2014	Annual	X	X	X
Ireland **Central Statistics Office, Cork** http://www.cso.ie/en/ Statistical Yearbook of Ireland, 2014	Annual			X
Italy **Italian National Institute of Statistics, Rome** http://www.istat.it/en/ Annuario Statistico Italiano, 2014 Italian Statistical Abstract, 2012	Annual Annual	X X	X X	X
Japan **Statistics Bureau, Ministry of Internal Affairs and Communications, Tokyo** http://www.stat.go.jp/english/data/index.htm Japan Statistical Yearbook, 2015	Annual	X	X	X
Korea, South **Statistics Korea, Daejeon**				

See footnotes at end of table.

Title	Frequency	Paper	Internet	
			PDF	Other *Formats*
http://kostat.go.kr/portal/english/index.action Korea Statistical Yearbook	Annual	X		
Luxembourg **Service Central de la Statistique et des Etudes Economiques, Luxembourg** http://www.statistiques.public.lu/fr/acteurs/statec/index.html Annuaire statistique du Luxembourg, 2012	Annual	X	X	
Mexico **Instituto Nacional de Estadistica y Geografia, Aguascalientes** http://www.inegi.org.mx/ Anuario Estadistico de los Estados Unidos Mexicanos, 2014	Annual		X	X
Netherlands **Statistics Netherlands, The Hague** http://www.cbs.nl/en Statistical Yearbook of the Netherlands, 2013	Annual		X	X
New Zealand **Statistics New Zealand, Wellington** http://www.stats.govt.nz/ New Zealand Official Yearbook, 2012	Biennial		X	X
Norway **Statistics Norway, Oslo** Statistical Yearbook of Norway, 2013 (Discontinued)	Annual		X	
Poland **Central Statistical Office of Poland, Warsaw** http://stat.gov.pl/en/intrastat Concise Statistical Yearbook of Poland, 2015 Statistical Yearbook of the Republic of Poland, 2014	Annual Annual	X X	X X	
Portugal **Statistics Portugal, Lisbon** https://www.ine.pt/ Statistical Yearbook of Portugal, 2013	Annual	X	X	X
Russia **Russian Federation Federal State Statistics Service, Moscow** http://www.gks.ru/ Russia in Figures	Ongoing			X
Slovakia **Statistical Office of the Slovak Republic, Bratislava** http://slovak.statistics.sk/ Statisticka Rocenka Slovenskej Republiky, 2014	Annual	X	X	X
Spain **Instituto Nacional de Estadistica, Madrid** http://www.ine.es/en/welcome_en.htm Anuario Estadistico de Espana, 2015	Annual	X	X	
Sweden **Statistics Sweden, Stockholm** http://www.scb.se/en_/ Statistical Yearbook of Sweden, 2014 (Discontinued)	Annual	X	X	
Switzerland **Federal Statistical Office, Neuchâtel** http://www.bfs.admin.ch/bfs/portal/en/index.html Statistisches Jahrbuch der Schweiz, 2015	Annual	X		
Turkey **Turkish Statistical Institute, Ankara** http://www.turkstat.gov.tr Turkey's Statistical Yearbook, 2013 Turkey in Statistics, 2014	Annual Annual	X X	X X	X X
United Kingdom **Office for National Statistics, London** http://www.ons.gov.uk Annual Abstract of Statistics, 2011	Annual		X	

Source: ProQuest research.

Guide to State Statistical Abstracts

This bibliography includes the most recent statistical abstracts for states published since 2000, plus those that will be issued in 2015. For some states, a near equivalent has been listed in substitution for, or in addition to, a statistical abstract. All sources contain statistical tables on a variety of subjects for the state as a whole, its component parts, or both. Internet sites also contain statistical data.

Alabama

University of Alabama, Center for Business and Economic Research, Box 870221, Tuscaloosa, AL 35487-0221. 205-348-6191. Fax: 205-348-2951. Internet site <http://cber.cba.ua.edu/>.
Alabama Economic Outlook, 2015. Annual. Print.

Alaska

Department of Commerce, Community and Economic Development, P.O. Box 110804, Juneau, AK 99811. 907-465-2510. Fax: 907-465-3767. Internet site <http://www.commerce.state.ak.us/dnn/ded/Home.aspx>.
The Alaska Economic Performance Report, 2013. Online.

Arizona

University of Arizona, Economic and Business Research Center, Eller College of Management, 1130 East Helen Street, McClelland Hall, Rm. 103, P.O. Box 210108, Tucson, AZ 85721-0108. 520-621-2155. Internet site <http://ebr.eller.arizona.edu/>.
Arizona's Economy. Quarterly. Online.

Arkansas

University of Arkansas at Little Rock, Institute for Economic Advancement, Economic Research, 2801 South University Avenue, Little Rock, AR 72204-1099. 501-569-8519. Fax: 501-569-8538. Internet site <http://iea.ualr.edu/resourceslinks-101/library/publications.html>.
Arkansas State and Country Economic Data, 2013. Annual. Print and Online.
Arkansas Personal Income Handbook, 2013. Annual. Print and Online.

California

Department of Finance, 915 L Street, Sacramento, CA 95814. 916-445-3878. Internet site <http://www.dof.ca.gov/HTML/FS_DATA/STAT-ABS/Statistical_Abstract.php>.
California Statistical Abstract, 2008. Online.

Colorado

Colorado Department of Local Affairs, Division of Local Government, State Demography Office, 1313 Sherman Street, Room 521, Denver, CO 80203. 303-864-7720. Fax: 303-864-7759. Internet site <http://dola.colorado.gov/demog-cms/content/region-profiles>.
2012 and 2014 Region Profiles and Reports. Online.

Connecticut

Connecticut Department of Economic and Community Development, 505 Hudson Street, Hartford, CT 06106-7106. 860-270-8000. Internet site <http://www.ct.gov/ecd/site/default.asp>.
Connecticut Town Profiles, 2014. Recurring. Online.

Delaware

Delaware Economic Development Office, 99 Kings Highway, Dover, DE 19901-7305. 302-739-4271. Fax: 302-739-5749. Internet site <http://dedo.delaware.gov>.
Delaware Data Book, 2013. Online.

District of Columbia

Office of the City Administrator, John A. Wilson Building, 1350 Pennsylvania Avenue, NW, Suite 521, Washington, DC 20004. 202-478-9200. Fax: 202-727-9878. Internet site <http://opendata.dc.gov/>.
Open Data Catalog. Online.

Florida

University of Florida, Bureau of Economic and Business Research, P.O. Box 117148, 221 Matherly Hall, Gainesville, FL 32611-7145. 352-392-0171. Fax: 352-392-4739. Internet site <http://www.bebr.ufl.edu/data>.
Florida Statistical Abstract . Online.

Georgia

University of Georgia, Terry College of Business, Selig Center for Economic Growth, Brooks Hall, 310 Herty Drive, Athens, GA 30602-6269. 706-542-8100. Fax: 706-542-3835 Internet site <http://www.terry.uga.edu/selig>.
Georgia Statistical Abstract, 2014-15. Biennial. Print and Online.

University of Georgia, Carl Vinson Institute of Government, 201 N. Milledge Ave., Athens, GA 30602. 706-542-2736. Fax: 706-542-9301. Internet site <http://www.countyguide.uga.edu/>.
The Georgia County Guide, 2015. Annual. Print.

Hawaii

Hawaii State Department of Business, Economic Development & Tourism, Research and Economic Analysis Division, Statistics and Data Support Branch, P.O. Box 2359, Honolulu, HI 96804. 808-586-2355. Internet site <http://dbedt.hawaii.gov/economic/databook/>.
2014 State of Hawaii Data Book. Annual. Online.

Idaho

University of Idaho Extension , 875 Perimeter Drive. MS 2338, Moscow, ID 83844-2338. 208-885-5883. Internet site <http://indicatorsidaho.org/>.
Indicators Idaho. Online.

Illinois

University of Illinois, Institute of Government and Public Affairs, 1007 W. Nevada Street, Urbana, IL 61801, MC-037. 217-333-3340. Fax: 217-244-4817. Internet site <http://www.igpa.uillinois.edu/>.

Indiana

Indiana University, Kelley School of Business, Indiana Business Research Center, 100 S. College Avenue, Suite 240, Bloomington, IN 47404. 812-855-5507. Internet site <http://www.stats.indiana.edu/>.
STATS Indiana. Online.

Iowa

Iowa State University of Science and Technology: Community Indicators Program, 17 East Hall, Ames, IA 50010. 515-294-9903. Fax: 515-294-0592. Internet site <http://www.icip.iastate.edu/>.
Community Indicators. Online.

State Library of Iowa, State Data Center, Ola Babcock Miller Building, 1112 East Grand, Des Moines, IA 50319-0233. 800-248-4483. Fax: 515-242-6543. Internet site <http://www.iowadatacenter.org>.

Kansas

University of Kansas, Institute for Policy and Social Research, 1541 Lilac Lane, 607 Blake Hall, Lawrence, KS 66045-3129. 785-864-3701. Fax: 785-864-3683. Internet site <http://www.ipsr.ku.edu/ksdata/ksah/>.
Kansas Statistical Abstract, 2014. Online.

Kentucky

Kentucky Cabinet for Economic Development, Old Capitol Annex, 300 West Broadway, Frankfort, KY 40601. 800-626-2930. Internet site <http://www.thinkkentucky.com/>.

Louisiana

Louisiana State Census Data Center, Office of Electronic Services, 1201 N. Third Street, Suite 7-210, Baton Rouge, LA, 70802. 225-342-7000. Internet site <http://www.louisiana.gov/Explore/Demographics_and_Geography/>.

Maine

Department of Administrative and Financial Services, 78 State House Station, 19 Union Street, Augusta, ME 04333. 207-624-7800. Fax: 207-624-7804. Internet site <http://www.maine.gov/portal/about_me/statistics.html >.

Maryland

Maryland Department of Planning, 301 W. Preston St. Suite 702, Baltimore, MD 21201. 410-767-4500. Internet site <http://www.mdp.state.md.us/msdc/>.
2014 Maryland Statistical Handbook. Annual. Online.

Massachusetts

MassCHIP, Massachusetts Department of Public Health, 250 Washington Street, Boston, MA 02108-4619. 617-624-6000. Internet site <http://mass.gov/dph/masschip>. Instant Topics. Online.

Michigan

Michigan Economic Development Corporation, 300 N. Washington Square, Lansing, MI 48913. 1-888-522-0103. Internet site <http://www.michiganbusiness.org>.

Minnesota

Minnesota Department of Employment and Economic Development, 1st National Bank Building, 332 Minnesota Street, Ste. E200, Saint Paul, MN 55101-1351. 800-657-3858. Internet site <http://mn.gov/deed/data/>.
Compare Minnesota: Profiles of Minnesota's Economy & Population. Online.

Minnesota State Demographic Center, 658 Cedar Street Room 300, Saint Paul, MN 55155, 651-296-2557. Internet site <http://www.demography.state.mn.us/>.

Mississippi

Mississippi State University, University Libraries, P.O. Box 5408, Mississippi State, MS 39762. 662-325-7668. Internet site <http://guides.library.msstate.edu/>
Mississippi Statistical Abstract, 2007. Discontinued.

Missouri

University of Missouri—Columbia, Economic and Policy Analysis Research Center, 10 Professional Building, Columbia, MO 65211. 573-882-4805. Fax: 573-882-5563. Internet site <http://eparc.missouri.edu/>.
Missouri Statistical Data Archive. Online.

Montana

Montana Department of Commerce, Census and Economic Information Center, 301 S. Park Ave., P.O. Box 200505, Helena, MT 59620-0505, 406-841-2740. Fax: 406-841-2731. Internet site <http://ceic.mt.gov/>.

Nebraska

Nebraska Department of Economic Development, P. O. Box 94666, 301 Centennial Mall South, Lincoln, NE 68509-4666. 800-426-6505. Fax: 402-471-3778. Internet site <http://info.neded.org/>.

Nevada

Nevada Department of Administration, Budget Division, 209 East Musser Street, Room 200, Carson City, NV 89701-4298. 775-684-0222. Fax: 775-684-0260. Internet site <http://www.budget.nv.us/>.

New Hampshire

New Hampshire Office of Energy and Planning, 107 Pleasant Street, Concord, NH 03301-8501. 603-271-2155. Fax: 603-271-2615. Internet site <http://www.nh.gov/oep/index.htm>.

New Jersey

State of New Jersey Department of Labor and Workforce Development,1 John Fitch Plaza, P.O. Box 110 Trenton, NJ 08625-0110. 609-292-7376. Fax: 609-633-9240. Internet site <http://lwd.dol.state.nj.us/labor/lpa/LMI_index.html>.
Labor Market Information. Online.

New Mexico

University of New Mexico, Bureau of Business and Economic Research, MSC06 3510, 1 University of New Mexico, Albuquerque, NM 87131. 505-277-6626. Fax: 505-277-2773. Internet site <http://bber.unm.edu/>.
New Mexico Business, Current Economic Report . Print and Online. FOR-UNM Bulletin. Quarterly. Online.

New York

Nelson A. Rockefeller Institute of Government, 411 State Street, Albany, NY 12203-1003. 518-443-5522. Fax: 518-443-5788. Internet site <http://www.rockinst.org/>.
New York State Statistical Yearbook, 2014. Annual. Print and Online.

North Carolina

Office of State Budget and Management, 116 West Jones Street, Raleigh, NC 27603-8005. 919-807-4700. Internet site <http://www.osbm.state.nc.us>.
State Comparisons. Online.

North Dakota

University of North Dakota, College of Business and Public Administration, 293 Centennial Dr., Stop 8098, Grand Forks, ND 58202-8098. 701-777-2135. Fax: 701-777-2019. Internet site <http://business.und.edu/>.

Ohio

Office of Research, Ohio Development Services Agency, 77 South High Street, Columbus, OH 43215-1001. 614-466-2116. Internet site <http://www.odod.state.oh.us/research>.
Research Products and Services. Updated continuously.
Ohio County Trends. Online.

Oklahoma

University of Oklahoma, Center for Economic and Management Research, Michael F. Price College of Business, 307 West Brooks, Suite 4, Norman, OK 73019-4004. 405-325-2931. Fax: 405-325-7688. Internet site <http://www.ou.edu/price/centersresearch/cemr.html>.
Statistical Abstract of Oklahoma, Annual. Print and Online.

Oregon

Secretary of State, Archives Division, Archives Bldg., 800 Summer Street, NE, Salem, OR 97310. 503-378-4991 ext.1. Fax: 503-378-4188. Internet site <http://arcweb.sos.state.or.us/>.
Oregon Blue Book. 2015-2016 . Biennial. Online.

Pennsylvania

Pennsylvania State Data Center, Institute of State and Regional Affairs, Penn State Harrisburg, 777 West Harrisburg Pike, Middletown, PA 17057-4898. 717-948-6336. Fax: 717-948-6754. Internet site <http://pasdc.hbg.psu.edu>.
Pennsylvania Statistical Abstract, 2015. Print and electronic.

Rhode Island

Rhode Island Economic Development Corporation, 315 Iron Horse Way, Suite 101, Providence, RI 02908. 401-278-9100. Fax: 401-273-8270. Internet site <http://www.commerceri.com/>.
State and Community Profiles. Online.

South Carolina

South Carolina Revenue and Fiscal Affairs Offices, Health and Demographics Section, 1000 Assembly Street, Columbia, SC 29201. 803-898-9940. Internet site <http://abstract.sc.gov>.
South Carolina Statistical Abstract. Ongoing. Online.

South Dakota

South Dakota State University, Rural Life and Census Data Center, Box 504, Brookings, SD 57007. 605-688-4132. Fax: 605-677-5427. Internet site <http://www.sdstate.edu/soc/rlcdc/index.cfm>.
Preliminary Population Projections 2010-2035. Online.
South Dakota State and Demographic Profiles 2008. Online.

Tennessee

Tennessee State Data Center, 916 Volunteer Blvd., 716 Stokely Management Center, Knoxville, TN 37996-0570. 865-974-6070. Fax: 865-974-3100. Internet site <http://tndata.utk.edu/>.

Texas

Texas State Historical Association, 3001 Lake Austin Blvd. Suite 3.116, Austin, TX 78703. 512-471-2600. Fax: 512-473-8691. Internet site <http://www.tshaonline.org/publications/books/3196>.
Texas Almanac, 2014-2015. Biennial. Print and Online.

Texas State Data Center and Office of the State Demographer, Institute for Demographic and Socioeconomic Research (IDSER), 501 W. César E. Chavez Blvd., San Antonio, TX 78207-4415. 210-458-6543. Fax: 210-458-6541. Internet site <http://txsdc.utsa.edu/>.

Utah

Governor's Office of Management and Budget, Demographic & Economic Analysis, Suite 150, P.O. Box 132210, Salt Lake City, UT 84114-2210. 801-538-1027. Fax: 801-538-1547. Internet site <http://www.governor.utah.gov/dea>.
2015 Economic Report to the Governor. Annual. Online.
Utah Data Guide Newsletter, 2013. Quarterly. Online.

Vermont

Department of Labor, Labor Market Information, 3 Green Mountain Drive, P.O. Box 488, Montpelier, VT 05601-0488. 802-828-4202. Fax: 802-828-4050. Internet site <http://www.vtlmi.info/>.
Vermont Economic-Demographic Profile, 2015. Annual. Online.

Virginia

University of Virginia, Weldon Cooper Center for Public Service, 2400 Old Ivy Road P.O. Box 400206, Charlottesville, VA 22904-4206. 434-982-5522. Internet site <http://www.coopercenter.org/publications>.
Stat Chat. Online.
Numbers Count. Online.

Washington

Washington State Office of Financial Management, Forecasting Division, P.O. Box 43113, Olympia, WA 98504-3113. 360-902-0555. Internet site <http://www.ofm.wa.gov/>.
Washington State Data Book, 2013. Biennial. Online.

West Virginia

West Virginia University, College of Business and Economics, Bureau of Business and Economic Research, 1601 University Ave, P.O. Box 6025, Morgantown, WV 26506-6025. 304-293-7831. Internet site <http://be.wvu.edu/bber/index.htm >.
West Virginia Data Profile 2014. Annual. Online.
West Virginia Economic Outlook, 2015. Annual. Online.

Wisconsin

Wisconsin Legislative Reference Bureau, One East Main Street, Suite 200, Madison, WI 53703. 608-266-0341. Internet site <http://legis.wisconsin.gov/lrb/>.
2015-2016 Wisconsin Blue Book. Biennial. Online.

Wyoming

Department of Administration and Information, Economic Analysis Division, 2800 Central Avenue, Cheyenne, WY 82002-0060. 307-777-7504. Fax: 307-632-1819. Internet site <http://eadiv.state.wy.us/>.
The Equality State Almanac, 2010. Annual. Online.

Metropolitan and Micropolitan Statistical Areas: Concepts, Components, and Population

The United States Office of Management and Budget (OMB) defines metropolitan and micropolitan statistical areas according to published standards that are applied to U.S. Census Bureau data. The general concept of a metropolitan or micropolitan statistical area is that of a core area containing a substantial population nucleus, together with adjacent communities having a high degree of economic and social integration with that core. Currently defined metropolitan and micropolitan statistical areas are based on application of 2010 standards (which appeared in the Federal Register on June 28, 2010) to 2010 decennial census data. Current metropolitan and micropolitan statistical area definitions were announced by OMB effective February 2013.

Standard definitions of metropolitan areas were first issued in 1949 by the then Bureau of the Budget (predecessor of OMB), under the designation "standard metropolitan area" (SMA). The term was changed to "standard metropolitan statistical area" (SMSA) in 1959 and to "metropolitan statistical area" (MSA) in 1983. The term "metropolitan area" (MA) was adopted in 1990 and referred collectively to metropolitan statistical areas (MSAs), consolidated metropolitan statistical areas (cMSAs), and primary metropolitan statistical areas (PMSAs). The term "core-based statistical area" (CBSA) became effective in 2000 and refers collectively to metropolitan and micropolitan statistical areas.

OMB has been responsible for the official metropolitan areas since they were first defined, except for the period 1977 to 1981, when they were the responsibility of the Office of Federal Statistical Policy and Standards, U.S. Department of Commerce. The standards for defining metropolitan areas were modified in 1958, 1971, 1975, 1980, 1990, 2000, and 2010.

Defining Metropolitan and Micropolitan Statistical Areas—The 2010 standards provide that each CBSA must contain at least one urban area of 10,000 or more population. Each metropolitan statistical area must have at least one urbanized area of 50,000 or more inhabitants. Each micropolitan statistical area must have at least one urban cluster of at least 10,000 but less than 50,000 population.

Under the standards, the county (or counties) in which at least 50 percent of the population resides within urban areas of 10,000 or more population, or that contain at least 5,000 people residing within a single urban area of 10,000 or more population, is identified as a "central county" (counties). Additional "outlying counties" are included in the CBSA if they meet specified requirements of commuting to or from the central counties. Counties or equivalent entities form the geographic "building blocks" for metropolitan and micropolitan statistical areas throughout the United States and Puerto Rico.

If specified criteria are met, a metropolitan statistical area containing a single core with a population of 2.5 million or more may be subdivided to form smaller groupings of counties referred to as "metropolitan divisions."

As of February 2013, there are 381 metropolitan statistical areas and 536 micropolitan statistical areas in the United States. In addition, there are 7 metropolitan statistical areas and 5 micropolitan statistical areas in Puerto Rico.

Principal Cities and Metropolitan and Micropolitan Statistical Area Titles—The largest city in each metropolitan or micropolitan statistical area is designated a "principal city." Additional cities qualify if specified requirements are met concerning population size and employment. The title of each metropolitan or micropolitan statistical area consists of the names of up to three of its principal cities in order of descending population size and the name of each state into which the metropolitan or micropolitan statistical area extends. Titles of metropolitan divisions also typically are based on principal city names, but in certain cases consist of county names.

Defining New England City and Town Areas—Cities and towns are the primary units of local government in the six New England states, where counties, unlike elsewhere, have little or no official governmental functions. The 2010 standards provide for a set of geographic areas that are defined using cities and towns in the New England states. The New England city and town areas (NECTAs) are defined using the same criteria as metropolitan and micropolitan statistical areas and are identified as either metropolitan or micropolitan, based, respectively, on the presence of either an urbanized area of 50,000 or more population or an urban cluster of at least 10,000 but less than 50,000 population. If the specified criteria are met, a NECTA containing a single core with a population of at least 2.5 million may be subdivided to form smaller groupings of cities and towns referred to as New England city and town area divisions.

Changes in Definitions Over Time—Changes in the definitions of these statistical areas since the 1950 census have consisted chiefly of (1) the recognition of new areas as they reached the minimum required city or urbanized area population and (2) the addition of counties (or cities and towns in New England) to existing areas as new decennial census data showed them to qualify.

In some instances, formerly separate areas have been merged, components of an area have been transferred from one area to another, or components have been dropped from an area. The large majority of changes have taken place on the basis of decennial census data. However, Census Bureau data serve as the basis for intercensal updates in specified circumstances.

Because of these historical changes in geographic definitions, users must be cautious in comparing data for these statistical areas from different dates. For some purposes, comparisons of data for areas as defined at given dates may be appropriate; for other purposes, it may be preferable to maintain consistent area definitions. Historical metropolitan area definitions are available for 1999, 1993, 1990, 1983, 1981, 1973, 1970, 1963, 1960, and 1950.

Excluding Tables 21 through 23 in the Population section; Table 613 in the Labor Force section; Table 703 in the Income section, and the tables that follow in this appendix, the tables presenting data for metropolitan areas in this edition of the Statistical Abstract may be based on earlier metropolitan area definitions. See the Census Bureau website at <http://www.census.gov/population/metro/data/pastmetro.html> for information on historical delineations and component counties.

Table A. Metropolitan Statistical Areas and Components—Population: 2014

[In thousands (169 represents 169,000). Population as of July 2014. Metropolitan Statistical Areas defined by the U.S. Office of Management and Budget as of February 2013. All Metropolitan Statistical Areas are arranged alphabetically]

Metropolitan Statistical Area ~~Metropolitan Division ~~~~Component county	Population, 2014 (1,000)
Abilene, TX	**169**
Callahan County, TX	14
Jones County, TX	20
Taylor County, TX	135
Akron, OH	**704**
Portage County, OH	162
Summit County, OH	542
Albany, GA	**155**
Baker County, GA	3
Dougherty County, GA	92
Lee County, GA	29
Terrell County, GA	9
Worth County, GA	21
Albany, OR	**119**
Linn County, OR	119
Albany-Schenectady-Troy, NY	**880**
Albany County, NY	308
Rensselaer County, NY	160
Saratoga County, NY	225
Schenectady County, NY	156
Schoharie County, NY	32
Albuquerque, NM	**905**
Bernalillo County, NM	676
Sandoval County, NM	138
Torrance County, NM	16
Valencia County, NM	76
Alexandria, LA	**155**
Grant Parish, LA	22
Rapides Parish, LA	132
Allentown-Bethlehem-Easton, PA-NJ	**830**
Warren County, NJ	107
Carbon County, PA	64
Lehigh County, PA	358
Northampton County, PA	301
Altoona, PA	**126**
Blair County, PA	126
Amarillo, TX	**260**
Armstrong County, TX	2
Carson County, TX	6
Oldham County, TX	2
Potter County, TX	122
Randall County, TX	128
Ames, IA	**94**
Story County, IA	94
Anchorage, AK	**399**
Anchorage Municipality, AK	301
Matanuska-Susitna Borough, AK	98
Ann Arbor, MI	**357**
Washtenaw County, MI	357
Anniston-Oxford-Jacksonville, AL	**116**
Calhoun County, AL	116
Appleton, WI	**231**
Calumet County, WI	49
Outagamie County, WI	182
Asheville, NC	**442**
Buncombe County, NC	251
Haywood County, NC	59
Henderson County, NC	111
Madison County, NC	21
Athens-Clarke County, GA	**199**
Clarke County, GA	121
Madison County, GA	28
Oconee County, GA	35
Oglethorpe County, GA	15
Atlanta-Sandy Springs-Roswell, GA	**5,614**
Barrow County, GA	73
Bartow County, GA	102
Butts County, GA	23
Carroll County, GA	114
Cherokee County, GA	231
Clayton County, GA	268
Cobb County, GA	731
Coweta County, GA	136
Dawson County, GA	23
DeKalb County, GA	722
Douglas County, GA	139

Metropolitan Statistical Area ~~Metropolitan Division ~~~~Component county	Population, 2014 (1,000)
Fayette County, GA	110
Forsyth County, GA	204
Fulton County, GA	996
Gwinnett County, GA	878
Haralson County, GA	29
Heard County, GA	12
Henry County, GA	214
Jasper County, GA	13
Lamar County, GA	18
Meriwether County, GA	21
Morgan County, GA	18
Newton County, GA	104
Paulding County, GA	149
Pickens County, GA	30
Pike County, GA	18
Rockdale County, GA	88
Spalding County, GA	64
Walton County, GA	88
Atlantic City-Hammonton, NJ	**275**
Atlantic County, NJ	275
Auburn-Opelika, AL	**154**
Lee County, AL	154
Augusta-Richmond County, GA-SC	**584**
Burke County, GA	23
Columbia County, GA	139
Lincoln County, GA	8
McDuffie County, GA	21
Richmond County, GA	201
Aiken County, SC	165
Edgefield County, SC	27
Austin-Round Rock, TX	**1,943**
Bastrop County, TX	78
Caldwell County, TX	40
Hays County, TX	185
Travis County, TX	1,151
Williamson County, TX	489
Bakersfield, CA	**875**
Kern County, CA	875
Baltimore-Colombia-Towson, MD	**2,786**
Anne Arundel County, MD	560
Baltimore County, MD	827
Carroll County, MD	168
Harford County, MD	250
Howard County, MD	309
Queen Anne's County, MD	49
Baltimore city, MD	623
Bangor, ME	**153**
Penobscot County, ME	153
Barnstable Town, MA	**215**
Barnstable County, MA	215
Baton Rouge, LA	**825**
Ascension Parish, LA	117
East Baton Rouge Parish, LA	446
East Feliciana Parish, LA	20
Iberville Parish, LA	33
Livingston Parish, LA	136
Pointe Coupee Parish, LA	22
St. Helena Parish, LA	11
West Baton Rouge Parish, LA	25
West Feliciana Parish, LA	15
Battle Creek, MI	**135**
Calhoun County, MI	135
Bay City, MI	**106**
Bay County, MI	106
Beaumont-Port Arthur, TX	**405**
Hardin County, TX	56
Jefferson County, TX	252
Newton County, TX	14
Orange County, TX	83
Beckley, WV	**123**
Fayette County, WV	45
Raleigh County, WV	78
Bellingham, WA	**208**
Whatcom County, WA	208
Bend-Redmond, OR	**170**
Deschutes County, OR	170
Billings, MT	**167**
Carbon County, MT	10

Metropolitan Statistical Area ~~Metropolitan Division ~~~~Component county	Population, 2014 (1,000)
Golden Valley County, MT	1
Yellowstone County, MT	156
Binghamton, NY	**247**
Broome County, NY	197
Tioga County, NY	50
Birmingham-Hoover, AL	**1,144**
Bibb County, AL	23
Blount County, AL	58
Chilton County, AL	44
Jefferson County, AL	661
St. Clair County, AL	87
Shelby County, AL	207
Walker County, AL	65
Bismarck, ND	**127**
Burleigh County, ND	91
Morton County, ND	30
Oliver County, ND	2
Sioux County, ND	4
Blacksburg-Christiansburg-Radford, VA	**182**
Floyd County, VA	16
Giles County, VA	17
Montgomery County, VA	97
Pulaski County, VA	34
Radford city, VA	18
Bloomington, IL	**190**
De Witt County, IL	16
McLean County, IL	174
Bloomington, IN	**164**
Monroe County, IN	143
Owen County, IN	21
Bloomsburg-Berwick, PA	**86**
Columbia County, PA	67
Montour County, PA	19
Boise City, ID	**664**
Ada County, ID	426
Boise County, ID	7
Canyon County, ID	203
Gem County, ID	17
Owyhee County, ID	11
Boston-Cambridge-Newton, MA-NH	**4,732**
Boston, MA	**1,967**
Norfolk County, MA	692
Plymouth County, MA	507
Suffolk County, MA	767
Cambridge-Newton-Framingham, MA	**2,339**
Essex County, MA	769
Middlesex County, MA	1,570
Rockingham County-Strafford County, NH	**426**
Rockingham County, NH	301
Strafford County, NH	126
Boulder, CO	**313**
Boulder County, CO	313
Bowling Green, KY	**166**
Allen County, KY	20
Butler County, KY	13
Edmonson County, KY	12
Warren County, KY	120
Bremerton-Silverdale, WA	**254**
Kitsap County, WA	254
Bridgeport-Stamford-Norwalk, CT	**945**
Fairfield County, CT	945
Brownsville-Harlingen, TX	**420**
Cameron County, TX	420
Brunswick, GA	**115**
Brantley County, GA	18
Glynn County, GA	82
McIntosh County, GA	14
Buffalo-Cheektowaga-Niagara Falls, NY	**1,136**
Erie County, NY	923
Niagara County, NY	214
Burlington, NC	**156**
Alamance County, NC	156
Burlington-South Burlington, VT	**216**

See footnotes at end of table.

Table A. Metropolitan Statistical Areas and Components—Population: 2014-Continued.

See headnote on page 923.

Metropolitan Statistical Area ~~Metropolitan Division ~~~~Component county	Popu- lation, 2014 (1,000)
Chittenden County, VT	161
Franklin County, VT	49
Grand Isle County, VT	7
California-Lexington Park, MD	**110**
St. Mary's County, MD	110
Canton-Massillon, OH	**404**
Carroll County, OH	28
Stark County, OH	376
Cape Coral-Fort Myers, FL	**680**
Lee County, FL	680
Cape Girardeau, MO-IL	**98**
Alexander County, IL	7
Bollinger County, MO	12
Cape Girardeau County, MO	78
Carbondale-Marion, IL	**127**
Jackson County, IL	60
Williamson County, IL	67
Carson City, NV	**55**
Carson City, NV	55
Casper, WY	**82**
Natrona County, WY	82
Cedar Rapids, IA	**264**
Benton County, IA	26
Jones County, IA	20
Linn County, IA	218
Chambersburg-Waynesboro, PA	**153**
Franklin County, PA	153
Champaign-Urbana, IL	**237**
Champaign County, IL	207
Ford County, IL	14
Piatt County, IL	16
Charleston, WV	**223**
Boone County, WV	24
Clay County, WV	9
Kanawha County, WV	190
Charleston-North Charleston, SC	**728**
Berkeley County, SC	198
Charleston County, SC	381
Dorchester County, SC	148
Charlotte-Concord-Gastonia, NC-SC	**2,380**
Cabarrus County, NC	192
Gaston County, NC	211
Iredell County, NC	167
Lincoln County, NC	80
Mecklenburg County, NC	1,013
Rowan County, NC	139
Union County, NC	219
Chester County, SC	32
Lancaster County, SC	83
York County, SC	245
Charlottesville, VA	**227**
Albemarle County, VA	104
Buckingham County, VA	17
Fluvanna County, VA	26
Greene County, VA	19
Nelson County, VA	15
Charlottesville city, VA	46
Chattanooga, TN-GA	**545**
Catoosa County, GA	66
Dade County, GA	16
Walker County, GA	68
Hamilton County, TN	351
Marion County, TN	28
Sequatchie County, TN	15
Cheyenne, WY	**96**
Laramie County, WY	96
Chicago-Naperville-Elgin, IL-IN-WI	**9,555**
Chicago-Naperville-Arlington Heights, IL	**7,344**
Cook County, IL	5,246
DuPage County, IL	933
Grundy County, IL	50
Kendall County, IL	121
McHenry County, IL	307
Will County, IL	685
Elgin, IL	**633**
DeKalb County, IL	105
Kane County, IL	527
Gary, IN	**705**

Metropolitan Statistical Area ~~Metropolitan Division ~~~~Component county	Popu- lation, 2014 (1,000)
Jasper County, IN	33
Lake County, IN	490
Newton County, IN	14
Porter County, IN	167
Lake County-Kenosha County, IL-WI	**873**
Lake County, IL	705
Kenosha County, WI	168
Chico, CA	**224**
Butte County, CA	224
Cincinnati, OH-KY-IN	**2,149**
Dearborn County, IN	50
Ohio County, IN	6
Union County, IN	7
Boone County, KY	126
Bracken County, KY	8
Campbell County, KY	92
Gallatin County, KY	9
Grant County, KY	25
Kenton County, KY	164
Pendleton County, KY	14
Brown County, OH	44
Butler County, OH	374
Clermont County, OH	202
Hamilton County, OH	807
Warren County, OH	222
Clarksville, TN-KY	**278**
Christian County, KY	74
Trigg County, KY	14
Montgomery County, TN	190
Cleveland, TN	**120**
Bradley County, TN	103
Polk County, TN	17
Cleveland-Elyria, OH	**2,064**
Cuyahoga County, OH	1,260
Geauga County, OH	94
Lake County, OH	229
Lorain County, OH	304
Medina County, OH	176
Coeur d'Alene, ID	**147**
Kootenai County, ID	147
College Station-Bryan, TX	**243**
Brazos County, TX	209
Burleson County, TX	17
Robertson County, TX	17
Colorado Springs, CO	**687**
El Paso County, CO	664
Teller County, CO	23
Columbia, MO	**173**
Boone County, MO	173
Columbia, SC	**800**
Calhoun County, SC	15
Fairfield County, SC	23
Kershaw County, SC	63
Lexington County, SC	278
Richland County, SC	402
Saluda County, SC	20
Columbus, GA-AL	**314**
Russell County, AL	60
Chattahoochee County, GA	12
Harris County, GA	33
Marion County, GA	9
Muscogee County, GA	201
Columbus, IN	**80**
Bartholomew County, IN	80
Columbus, OH	**1,995**
Delaware County, OH	189
Fairfield County, OH	150
Franklin County, OH	1,231
Hocking County, OH	29
Licking County, OH	169
Madison County, OH	44
Morrow County, OH	35
Perry County, OH	36
Pickaway County, OH	57
Union County, OH	54
Corpus Christi, TX	**448**
Aransas County, TX	25
Nueces County, TX	356
San Patricio County, TX	67
Corvallis, OR	**86**
Benton County, OR	86

Metropolitan Statistical Area ~~Metropolitan Division ~~~~Component county	Popu- lation, 2014 (1,000)
Crestview-Fort Walton Beach-Destin, FL	**258**
Okaloosa County, FL	197
Walton County, FL	62
Cumberland, MD-WV	**101**
Allegany County, MD	73
Mineral County, WV	28
Dallas-Fort Worth-Arlington, TX	**6,954**
Dallas-Plano-Irving, TX	**4,604**
Collin County, TX	885
Dallas County, TX	2,519
Denton County, TX	753
Ellis County, TX	159
Hunt County, TX	88
Kaufman County, TX	111
Rockwall County, TX	88
Fort Worth-Arlington, TX	**2,350**
Hood County, TX	54
Johnson County, TX	157
Parker County, TX	123
Somervell County, TX	9
Tarrant County, TX	1,945
Wise County, TX	62
Dalton, GA	**143**
Murray County, GA	39
Whitfield County, GA	104
Danville, IL	**80**
Vermilion County, IL	80
Daphne-Fairhope-Foley, AL	**200**
Baldwin County, AL	200
Davenport-Moline-Rock Island, IA-IL	**383**
Henry County, IL	50
Mercer County, IL	16
Rock Island County, IL	146
Scott County, IA	171
Dayton, OH	**801**
Greene County, OH	164
Miami County, OH	104
Montgomery County, OH	533
Decatur, AL	**153**
Lawrence County, AL	33
Morgan County, AL	120
Decatur, IL	**108**
Macon County, IL	108
Deltona-Daytona Beach-Ormond Beach, FL	**610**
Flagler County, FL	102
Volusia County, FL	508
Denver-Aurora-Lakewood, CO	**2,754**
Adams County, CO	481
Arapahoe County, CO	619
Broomfield County, CO	62
Clear Creek County, CO	9
Denver County, CO	664
Douglas County, CO	315
Elbert County, CO	24
Gilpin County, CO	6
Jefferson County, CO	559
Park County, CO	16
Des Moines-West Des Moines, IA	**612**
Dallas County, IA	77
Guthrie County, IA	11
Madison County, IA	16
Polk County, IA	460
Warren County, IA	48
Detroit-Warren-Dearborn, MI	**4,297**
Detroit-Dearborn-Livonia, MI	**1,765**
Wayne County, MI	1,765
Warren-Troy-Farmington Hills, MI	**2,532**
Lapeer County, MI	88
Livingston County, MI	186
Macomb County, MI	860
Oakland County, MI	1,238
St. Clair County, MI	160
Dothan, AL	**148**
Geneva County, AL	27
Henry County, AL	17

See footnotes at end of table.

Table A. Metropolitan Statistical Areas and Components—Population: 2014-Continued.

See headnote on page 923.

Metropolitan Statistical Area ~~Metropolitan Division ~~~~Component county	Popu-lation, 2014 (1,000)
Houston County, AL	104
Dover, DE	**172**
Kent County, DE	172
Dubuque, IA	**96**
Dubuque County, IA	96
Duluth, MN-WI	**280**
Carlton County, MN	36
St. Louis County, MN	201
Douglas County, WI	44
Durham-Chapel Hill, NC	**543**
Chatham County, NC	69
Durham County, NC	294
Orange County, NC	140
Person County, NC	39
East Stroudsburg, PA	**166**
Monroe County, PA	166
Eau Claire, WI	**165**
Chippewa County, WI	63
Eau Claire County, WI	102
El Centro, CA	**179**
Imperial County, CA	179
Elizabethtown-Fort Knox, KY	**152**
Hardin County, KY	108
Larue County, KY	14
Meade County, KY	29
Elkhart-Goshen, IN	**202**
Elkhart County, IN	202
Elmira, NY	**88**
Chemung County, NY	88
El Paso, TX	**837**
El Paso County, TX	833
Hudspeth County, TX	3
Erie, PA	**278**
Erie County, PA	278
Eugene, OR	**358**
Lane County, OR	358
Evansville, IN-KY	**315**
Posey County, IN	26
Vanderburgh County, IN	182
Warrick County, IN	61
Henderson County, KY	46
Fairbanks, AK	**99**
Fairbanks North Star Borough, AK	99
Fargo, ND-MN	**228**
Clay County, MN	61
Cass County, ND	167
Farmington, NM	**124**
San Juan County, NM	124
Fayetteville, NC	**378**
Cumberland County, NC	326
Hoke County, NC	52
Fayetteville-Springdale-Rogers, AR-MO	**502**
Benton County, AR	242
Madison County, AR	16
Washington County, AR	221
McDonald County, MO	23
Flagstaff, AZ	**138**
Coconino County, AZ	138
Flint, MI	**413**
Genesee County, MI	413
Florence, SC	**207**
Darlington County, SC	68
Florence County, SC	139
Florence-Muscle Shoals, AL	**148**
Colbert County, AL	55
Lauderdale County, AL	93
Fond du Lac, WI	**102**
Fond du Lac County, WI	102
Fort Collins, CO	**324**
Larimer County, CO	324
Fort Smith, AR-OK	**280**
Crawford County, AR	62
Sebastian County, AR	127
Le Flore County, OK	50
Sequoyah County, OK	41
Fort Wayne, IN	**427**
Allen County, IN	366
Wells County, IN	28

Metropolitan Statistical Area ~~Metropolitan Division ~~~~Component county	Popu-lation, 2014 (1,000)
Whitley County, IN	33
Fresno, CA	**966**
Fresno County, CA	966
Gadsden, AL	**104**
Etowah County, AL	104
Gainesville, FL	**273**
Alachua County, FL	256
Gilchrist County, FL	17
Gainesville, GA	**191**
Hall County, GA	191
Gettysburg, PA	**102**
Adams County, PA	102
Glens Falls, NY	**127**
Warren County, NY	65
Washington County, NY	62
Goldsboro, NC	**124**
Wayne County, NC	124
Grand Forks, ND-MN	**102**
Polk County, MN	32
Grand Forks County, ND	70
Grand Island, NE	**85**
Hall County, NE	61
Hamilton County, NE	9
Howard County, NE	6
Merrick County, NE	8
Grand Junction, CO	**148**
Mesa County, CO	148
Grand Rapids-Wyoming, MI	**1,028**
Barry County, MI	59
Kent County, MI	629
Montcalm County, MI	63
Ottawa County, MI	276
Grants Pass, OR	**84**
Josephine County, OR	84
Great Falls, MT	**82**
Cascade County, MT	82
Greeley, CO	**278**
Weld County, CO	278
Green Bay, WI	**315**
Brown County, WI	257
Kewaunee County, WI	20
Oconto County, WI	37
Greensboro-High Point, NC	**747**
Guilford County, NC	512
Randolph County, NC	143
Rockingham County, NC	92
Greenville, NC	**175**
Pitt County, NC	175
Greenville-Anderson-Mauldin, SC	**862**
Anderson County, SC	193
Greenville County, SC	483
Laurens County, SC	67
Pickens County, SC	120
Gulfport-Biloxi-Pascagoula, MS	**386**
Hancock County, MS	46
Harrison County, MS	199
Jackson County, MS	141
Hagerstown-Martinsburg, MD-WV	**260**
Washington County, MD	150
Berkeley County, WV	110
Hammond, LA	**127**
Tangipahoa Parish, LA	127
Hanford-Corcoran, CA	**150**
Kings County, CA	150
Harrisburg-Carlisle, PA	**561**
Cumberland County, PA	244
Dauphin County, PA	271
Perry County, PA	46
Harrisonburg, VA	**131**
Rockingham County, VA	78
Harrisonburg city, VA	52
Hartford-West Hartford-East Hartford, CT	**1,214**
Hartford County, CT	898
Middlesex County, CT	165
Tolland County, CT	151
Hattiesburg, MS	**149**

Metropolitan Statistical Area ~~Metropolitan Division ~~~~Component county	Popu-lation, 2014 (1,000)
Forrest County, MS	76
Lamar County, MS	60
Perry County, MS	12
Hickory-Lenoir-Morganton, NC	**363**
Alexander County, NC	37
Burke County, NC	89
Caldwell County, NC	81
Catawba County, NC	155
Hilton Head Island-Bluffton-Beaufort, SC	**203**
Beaufort County, SC	176
Jasper County, SC	27
Hinesville, GA	**82**
Liberty County, GA	65
Long County, GA	17
Homosassa Springs, FL	**139**
Citrus County, FL	139
Honolulu, HI	**992**
Honolulu County, HI	992
Hot Springs, AR	**97**
Garland County, AR	97
Houma-Thibodaux, LA	**211**
Lafourche Parish, LA	98
Terrebonne Parish, LA	113
Houston-The Woodlands-Sugar Land, TX	**6,490**
Austin County, TX	29
Brazoria County, TX	338
Chambers County, TX	38
Fort Bend County, TX	685
Galveston County, TX	314
Harris County, TX	4,441
Liberty County, TX	78
Montgomery County, TX	519
Waller County, TX	47
Huntington-Ashland, WV-KY-OH	**363**
Boyd County, KY	49
Greenup County, KY	36
Lawrence County, OH	62
Cabell County, WV	97
Lincoln County, WV	22
Putnam County, WV	57
Wayne County, WV	41
Huntsville, AL	**441**
Limestone County, AL	91
Madison County, AL	350
Idaho Falls, ID	**138**
Bonneville County, ID	109
Butte County, ID	3
Jefferson County, ID	27
Indianapolis-Carmel-Anderson, IN	**1,971**
Boone County, IN	62
Brown County, IN	15
Hamilton County, IN	303
Hancock County, IN	72
Hendricks County, IN	156
Johnson County, IN	148
Madison County, IN	130
Marion County, IN	934
Morgan County, IN	70
Putnam County, IN	38
Shelby County, IN	45
Iowa City, IA	**164**
Johnson County, IA	142
Washington County, IA	22
Ithaca, NY	**105**
Tompkins County, NY	105
Jackson, MI	**160**
Jackson County, MI	160
Jackson, MS	**578**
Copiah County, MS	29
Hinds County, MS	244
Madison County, MS	102
Rankin County, MS	148
Simpson County, MS	27

See footnotes at end of table.

Table A. Metropolitan Statistical Areas and Components—Population: 2014-Continued.

See headnote on page 923.

Metropolitan Statistical Area ~~Metropolitan Division ~~~~Component county	Population, 2014 (1,000)
Yazoo County, MS	28
Jackson, TN	**130**
Chester County, TN	17
Crockett County, TN	15
Madison County, TN	98
Jacksonville, FL	**1,419**
Baker County, FL	27
Clay County, FL	200
Duval County, FL	898
Nassau County, FL	77
St. Johns County, FL	218
Jacksonville, NC	**188**
Onslow County, NC	188
Janesville-Beloit, WI	**161**
Rock County, WI	161
Jefferson City, MO	**151**
Callaway County, MO	45
Cole County, MO	77
Moniteau County, MO	16
Osage County, MO	14
Johnson City, TN	**201**
Carter County, TN	57
Unicoi County, TN	18
Washington County, TN	126
Johnstown, PA	**138**
Cambria County, PA	138
Jonesboro, AR	**127**
Craighead County, AR	103
Poinsett County, AR	24
Joplin, MO	**176**
Jasper County, MO	118
Newton County, MO	59
Kahului-Wailuku-Lahaina, HI	**163**
Kalawao County, HI	(Z)
Maui County, HI	163
Kalamazoo-Portage, MI	**334**
Kalamazoo County, MI	259
Van Buren County, MI	75
Kankakee, IL	**111**
Kankakee County, IL	111
Kansas City, MO-KS	**2,071**
Johnson County, KS	574
Leavenworth County, KS	79
Linn County, KS	10
Miami County, KS	33
Wyandotte County, KS	162
Bates County, MO	17
Caldwell County, MO	9
Cass County, MO	101
Clay County, MO	234
Clinton County, MO	20
Jackson County, MO	683
Lafayette County, MO	33
Platte County, MO	95
Ray County, MO	23
Kennewick-Richland, WA	**274**
Benton County, WA	186
Franklin County, WA	88
Killeen-Temple, TX	**425**
Bell County, TX	329
Coryell County, TX	76
Lampasas County, TX	20
Kingsport-Bristol-Bristol, TN-VA	**308**
Hawkins County, TN	57
Sullivan County, TN	157
Scott County, VA	22
Washington County, VA	55
Bristol city, VA	17
Kingston, NY	**180**
Ulster County, NY	180
Knoxville, TN	**858**
Anderson County, TN	76
Blount County, TN	126
Campbell County, TN	40
Grainger County, TN	23
Knox County, TN	449
Loudon County, TN	51
Morgan County, TN	22
Roane County, TN	53
Union County, TN	19
Kokomo, IN	**83**
Howard County, IN	83

Metropolitan Statistical Area ~~Metropolitan Division ~~~~Component county	Population, 2014 (1,000)
La Crosse-Onalaska, WI-MN	**137**
Houston County, MN	19
La Crosse County, WI	118
Lafayette, LA	**485**
Acadia Parish, LA	62
Iberia Parish, LA	74
Lafayette Parish, LA	236
St. Martin Parish, LA	53
Vermilion Parish, LA	60
Lafayette-West Lafayette, IN	**212**
Benton County, IN	9
Carroll County, IN	20
Tippecanoe County, IN	183
Lake Charles, LA	**204**
Calcasieu Parish, LA	197
Cameron Parish, LA	7
Lake Havasu City-Kingman, AZ	**203**
Mohave County, AZ	203
Lakeland-Winter Haven, FL	**635**
Polk County, FL	635
Lancaster, PA	**533**
Lancaster County, PA	533
Lansing-East Lansing, MI	**470**
Clinton County, MI	77
Eaton County, MI	109
Ingham County, MI	285
Laredo, TX	**267**
Webb County, TX	267
Las Cruces, NM	**214**
Doña Ana County, NM	214
Las Vegas-Henderson-Paradise, NV	**2,070**
Clark County, NV	2,070
Lawrence, KS	**117**
Douglas County, KS	117
Lawton, OK	**131**
Comanche County, OK	125
Cotton County, OK	6
Lebanon, PA	**136**
Lebanon County, PA	136
Lewiston, ID-WA	**62**
Nez Perce County, ID	40
Asotin County, WA	22
Lewiston-Auburn, ME	**107**
Androscoggin County, ME	107
Lexington-Fayette, KY	**494**
Bourbon County, KY	20
Clark County, KY	36
Fayette County, KY	311
Jessamine County, KY	51
Scott County, KY	51
Woodford County, KY	26
Lima, OH	**105**
Allen County, OH	105
Lincoln, NE	**319**
Lancaster County, NE	302
Seward County, NE	17
Little Rock-North Little Rock-Conway, AR	**729**
Faulkner County, AR	121
Grant County, AR	18
Lonoke County, AR	72
Perry County, AR	10
Pulaski County, AR	393
Saline County, AR	116
Logan, UT-ID	**131**
Franklin County, ID	13
Cache County, UT	118
Longview, TX	**217**
Gregg County, TX	123
Rusk County, TX	54
Upshur County, TX	40
Longview, WA	**102**
Cowlitz County, WA	102
Los Angeles-Long Beach-Anaheim, CA	**13,262**
Anaheim-Santa Ana-Irvine, CA	**3,146**
Orange County, CA	3,146

Metropolitan Statistical Area ~~Metropolitan Division ~~~~Component county	Population, 2014 (1,000)
Los Angeles-Long Beach-Glendale, CA	**10,117**
Los Angeles County, CA	10,117
Louisville/Jefferson County, KY-IN	**1,270**
Clark County, IN	114
Floyd County, IN	76
Harrison County, IN	39
Scott County, IN	24
Washington County, IN	28
Bullitt County, KY	78
Henry County, KY	16
Jefferson County, KY	760
Oldham County, KY	63
Shelby County, KY	45
Spencer County, KY	18
Trimble County, KY	9
Lubbock, TX	**306**
Crosby County, TX	6
Lubbock County, TX	294
Lynn County, TX	6
Lynchburg, VA	**258**
Amherst County, VA	32
Appomattox County, VA	15
Bedford County, VA	77
Campbell County, VA	55
Lynchburg city, VA	79
Macon, GA	**230**
Bibb County, GA	154
Crawford County, GA	12
Jones County, GA	29
Monroe County, GA	27
Twiggs County, GA	8
Madera, CA	**155**
Madera County, CA	155
Madison, WI	**634**
Columbia County, WI	57
Dane County, WI	516
Green County, WI	37
Iowa County, WI	24
Manchester-Nashua, NH	**405**
Hillsborough County, NH	405
Manhattan, KS	**98**
Pottawatomie County, KS	23
Riley County, KS	75
Mankato-North Mankato, MN	**98**
Blue Earth County, MN	65
Nicollet County, MN	33
Mansfield, OH	**122**
Richland County, OH	122
McAllen-Edinburg-Mission, TX	**831**
Hidalgo County, TX	831
Medford, OR	**210**
Jackson County, OR	210
Memphis, TN-MS-AR	**1,343**
Crittenden County, AR	50
Benton County, MS	8
DeSoto County, MS	171
Marshall County, MS	36
Tate County, MS	28
Tunica County, MS	11
Fayette County, TN	39
Shelby County, TN	939
Tipton County, TN	62
Merced, CA	**266**
Merced County, CA	266
Miami-Fort Lauderdale-West Palm Beach, FL	**5,930**
Fort Lauderdale-Pompano Beach-Deerfield Beach, FL	**1,869**
Broward County, FL	1,869
Miami-Miami Beach-Kendall, FL	**2,663**
Miami-Dade County, FL	2,663
West Palm Beach-Boca Raton-Delray Beach, FL	**1,398**
Palm Beach County, FL	1,398
Michigan City-La Porte, IN	**111**

See footnotes at end of table.

Metropolitan Statistical Area ~~Metropolitan Division ~~~~Component county	Population, 2014 (1,000)
LaPorte County, IN	111
Midland, MI	**83**
Midland County, MI	83
Midland, TX	**161**
Martin County, TX	5
Midland County, TX	156
Milwaukee-Waukesha-West Allis, WI	**1,572**
Milwaukee County, WI	956
Ozaukee County, WI	87
Washington County, WI	133
Waukesha County, WI	395
Minneapolis-St. Paul-Bloomington, MN-WI	**3,495**
Anoka County, MN	342
Carver County, MN	97
Chisago County, MN	54
Dakota County, MN	413
Hennepin County, MN	1,212
Isanti County, MN	38
Le Sueur County, MN	28
Mille Lacs County, MN	26
Ramsey County, MN	533
Scott County, MN	140
Sherburne County, MN	91
Sibley County, MN	15
Washington County, MN	249
Wright County, MN	130
Pierce County, WI	41
St. Croix County, WI	87
Missoula, MT	**113**
Missoula County, MT	113
Mobile, AL	**415**
Mobile County, AL	415
Modesto, CA	**532**
Stanislaus County, CA	532
Monroe, LA	**179**
Ouachita Parish, LA	156
Union Parish, LA	23
Monroe, MI	**150**
Monroe County, MI	150
Montgomery, AL	**373**
Autauga County, AL	55
Elmore County, AL	81
Lowndes County, AL	11
Montgomery County, AL	226
Morgantown, WV	**137**
Monongalia County, WV	103
Preston County, WV	34
Morristown, TN	**116**
Hamblen County, TN	63
Jefferson County, TN	53
Mount Vernon-Anacortes, WA	**120**
Skagit County, WA	120
Muncie, IN	**117**
Delaware County, IN	117
Muskegon, MI	**172**
Muskegon County, MI	172
Myrtle Beach-Conway-North Myrtle Beach, SC-NC	**418**
Brunswick County, NC	119
Horry County, SC	299
Napa, CA	**142**
Napa County, CA	142
Naples-Immokalee-Marco Island, FL	**349**
Collier County, FL	349
Nashville-Davidson-Murfreesboro-Franklin, TN	**1,793**
Cannon County, TN	14
Cheatham County, TN	40
Davidson County, TN	668
Dickson County, TN	51
Hickman County, TN	24
Macon County, TN	23
Maury County, TN	86
Robertson County, TN	68
Rutherford County, TN	289
Smith County, TN	19
Sumner County, TN	173
Trousdale County, TN	8

Metropolitan Statistical Area ~~Metropolitan Division ~~~~Component county	Population, 2014 (1,000)
Williamson County, TN	205
Wilson County, TN	125
New Bern, NC	**128**
Craven County, NC	105
Jones County, NC	10
Pamlico County, NC	13
New Haven-Milford, CT	**861**
New Haven County, CT	861
New Orleans-Metairie, LA	**1,252**
Jefferson Parish, LA	436
Orleans Parish, LA	384
Plaquemines Parish, LA	23
St. Bernard Parish, LA	44
St. Charles Parish, LA	53
St. James Parish, LA	22
St. John the Baptist Parish, LA	44
St. Tammany Parish, LA	246
New York-Newark-Jersey City, NY-NJ-PA	**20,093**
Dutchess County-Putnam County, NY	**396**
Dutchess County, NY	297
Putnam County, NY	99
Nassau County-Suffolk County, NY	**2,862**
Nassau County, NY	1,359
Suffolk County, NY	1,503
Newark, NJ-PA	**2,508**
Essex County, NJ	796
Hunterdon County, NJ	126
Morris County, NJ	500
Somerset County, NJ	333
Sussex County, NJ	145
Union County, NJ	553
Pike County, PA	56
New York-Jersey City-White Plains, NY-NJ	**14,327**
Bergen County, NJ	934
Hudson County, NJ	669
Middlesex County, NJ	836
Monmouth County, NJ	629
Ocean County, NJ	586
Passaic County, NJ	509
Bronx County, NY	1,438
Kings County, NY	2,622
New York County, NY	1,636
Orange County, NY	376
Queens County, NY	2,322
Richmond County, NY	473
Rockland County, NY	324
Westchester County, NY	973
Niles-Benton Harbor, MI	**155**
Berrien County, MI	155
North Port-Sarasota-Bradenton, FL	**749**
Manatee County, FL	352
Sarasota County, FL	397
Norwich-New London, CT	**274**
New London County, CT	274
Ocala, FL	**339**
Marion County, FL	339
Ocean City, NJ	**95**
Cape May County, NJ	95
Odessa, TX	**154**
Ector County, TX	154
Ogden-Clearfield, UT	**632**
Box Elder County, UT	52
Davis County, UT	330
Morgan County, UT	11
Weber County, UT	240
Oklahoma City, OK	**1,337**
Canadian County, OK	130
Cleveland County, OK	270
Grady County, OK	54
Lincoln County, OK	35
Logan County, OK	45
McClain County, OK	37
Oklahoma County, OK	766
Olympia-Tumwater, WA	**266**
Thurston County, WA	266
Omaha-Council Bluffs, NE-IA	**904**

Metropolitan Statistical Area ~~Metropolitan Division ~~~~Component county	Population, 2014 (1,000)
Harrison County, IA	14
Mills County, IA	15
Pottawattamie County, IA	93
Cass County, NE	26
Douglas County, NE	543
Sarpy County, NE	172
Saunders County, NE	21
Washington County, NE	20
Orlando-Kissimmee-Sanford, FL	**2,321**
Lake County, FL	316
Orange County, FL	1,253
Osceola County, FL	310
Seminole County, FL	443
Oshkosh-Neenah, WI	**170**
Winnebago County, WI	170
Owensboro, KY	**117**
Daviess County, KY	98
Hancock County, KY	9
McLean County, KY	9
Oxnard-Thousand Oaks-Ventura, CA	**846**
Ventura County, CA	846
Palm Bay-Melbourne-Titusville, FL	**557**
Brevard County, FL	557
Panama City, FL	**195**
Bay County, FL	179
Gulf County, FL	16
Parkersburg-Vienna, WV	**92**
Wirt County, WV	6
Wood County, WV	86
Pensacola-Ferry Pass-Brent, FL	**474**
Escambia County, FL	311
Santa Rosa County, FL	163
Peoria, IL	**380**
Marshall County, IL	12
Peoria County, IL	187
Stark County, IL	6
Tazewell County, IL	136
Woodford County, IL	39
Philadelphia-Camden-Wilmington, PA-NJ-DE-MD	**6,051**
Camden, NJ	**1,252**
Burlington County, NJ	450
Camden County, NJ	511
Gloucester County, NJ	291
Montgomery-Bucks-Chester, PA	**1,956**
Bucks County, PA	627
Chester County, PA	513
Montgomery County, PA	817
Philadelphia, PA	**2,123**
Delaware County, PA	563
Philadelphia County, PA	1,560
Wilmington, DE-MD-NJ	**720**
New Castle County, DE	553
Cecil County, MD	102
Salem County, NJ	65
Phoenix-Mesa-Scottsdale, AZ	**4,489**
Maricopa County, AZ	4,087
Pinal County, AZ	402
Pine Bluff, AR	**95**
Cleveland County, AR	8
Jefferson County, AR	72
Lincoln County, AR	14
Pittsburgh, PA	**2,356**
Allegheny County, PA	1,231
Armstrong County, PA	68
Beaver County, PA	169
Butler County, PA	186
Fayette County, PA	134
Washington County, PA	208
Westmoreland County, PA	359
Pittsfield, MA	**129**
Berkshire County, MA	129
Pocatello, ID	**83**
Bannock County, ID	83
Portland-South Portland, ME	**524**

See footnotes at end of table.

Table A. Metropolitan Statistical Areas and Components—Population: 2014-Continued.

See headnote on page 923.

Metropolitan Statistical Area ~~Metropolitan Division ~~~~Component county	Population, 2014 (1,000)
Cumberland County, ME	288
Sagadahoc County, ME	35
York County, ME	201
Portland-Vancouver-Hillsboro, OR-WA	**2,348**
Clackamas County, OR	395
Columbia County, OR	49
Multnomah County, OR	777
Washington County, OR	563
Yamhill County, OR	102
Clark County, WA	451
Skamania County, WA	11
Port St. Lucie, FL	**444**
Martin County, FL	153
St. Lucie County, FL	291
Prescott, AZ	**219**
Yavapai County, AZ	219
Providence-Warwick, RI-MA	**1,609**
Bristol County, MA	554
Bristol County, RI	49
Kent County, RI	165
Newport County, RI	82
Providence County, RI	632
Washington County, RI	127
Provo-Orem, UT	**571**
Juab County, UT	10
Utah County, UT	561
Pueblo, CO	**162**
Pueblo County, CO	162
Punta Gorda, FL	**168**
Charlotte County, FL	168
Racine, WI	**195**
Racine County, WI	195
Raleigh, NC	**1,243**
Franklin County, NC	63
Johnston County, NC	181
Wake County, NC	999
Rapid City, SD	**144**
Custer County, SD	8
Meade County, SD	27
Pennington County, SD	108
Reading, PA	**414**
Berks County, PA	414
Redding, CA	**180**
Shasta County, CA	180
Reno, NV	**444**
Storey County, NV	4
Washoe County, NV	440
Richmond, VA	**1,260**
Amelia County, VA	13
Caroline County, VA	30
Charles City County, VA	7
Chesterfield County, VA	332
Dinwiddie County, VA	28
Goochland County, VA	22
Hanover County, VA	102
Henrico County, VA	322
King William County, VA	16
New Kent County, VA	20
Powhatan County, VA	28
Prince George County, VA	37
Sussex County, VA	12
Colonial Heights city, VA	18
Hopewell city, VA	22
Petersburg city, VA	33
Richmond city, VA	218
Riverside-San Bernardino-Ontario, CA	**4,442**
Riverside County, CA	2,329
San Bernardino County, CA	2,113
Roanoke, VA	**313**
Botetourt County, VA	33
Craig County, VA	5
Franklin County, VA	56
Roanoke County, VA	94
Roanoke city, VA	99
Salem city, VA	25
Rochester, MN	**213**
Dodge County, MN	20
Fillmore County, MN	21
Olmsted County, MN	150
Wabasha County, MN	21
Rochester, NY	**1,083**

Metropolitan Statistical Area ~~Metropolitan Division ~~~~Component county	Population, 2014 (1,000)
Livingston County, NY	65
Monroe County, NY	750
Ontario County, NY	110
Orleans County, NY	42
Wayne County, NY	92
Yates County, NY	25
Rockford, IL	**342**
Boone County, IL	54
Winnebago County, IL	289
Rocky Mount, NC	**149**
Edgecombe County, NC	55
Nash County, NC	94
Rome, GA	**96**
Floyd County, GA	96
Sacramento-Roseville-Arden-Arcade, CA	**2,244**
El Dorado County, CA	183
Placer County, CA	372
Sacramento County, CA	1,482
Yolo County, CA	208
Saginaw, MI	**195**
Saginaw County, MI	195
St. Cloud, MN	**192**
Benton County, MN	40
Stearns County, MN	153
St. George, UT	**152**
Washington County, UT	152
St. Joseph, MO-KS	**127**
Doniphan County, KS	8
Andrew County, MO	17
Buchanan County, MO	89
DeKalb County, MO	13
St. Louis, MO-IL [1]	**2,806**
Bond County, IL	17
Calhoun County, IL	5
Clinton County, IL	38
Jersey County, IL	23
Macoupin County, IL	46
Madison County, IL	267
Monroe County, IL	34
St. Clair County, IL	266
Franklin County, MO	102
Jefferson County, MO	223
Lincoln County, MO	54
St. Charles County, MO	379
St. Louis County, MO	1,002
Warren County, MO	33
St. Louis city, MO	317
Salem, OR	**404**
Marion County, OR	326
Polk County, OR	78
Salinas, CA	**431**
Monterey County, CA	431
Salisbury, MD-DE	**390**
Sussex County, DE	211
Somerset County, MD	26
Wicomico County, MD	102
Worcester County, MD	52
Salt Lake City, UT	**1,153**
Salt Lake County, UT	1,092
Tooele County, UT	62
San Angelo, TX	**118**
Irion County, TX	2
Tom Green County, TX	117
San Antonio-New Braunfels, TX	**2,329**
Atascosa County, TX	48
Bandera County, TX	21
Bexar County, TX	1,856
Comal County, TX	124
Guadalupe County, TX	147
Kendall County, TX	39
Medina County, TX	48
Wilson County, TX	46
San Diego-Carlsbad, CA	**3,263**
San Diego County, CA	3,263
San Francisco-Oakland-Hayward, CA	**4,594**
Oakland-Hayward-Berkeley, CA	**2,722**
Alameda County, CA	1,611

Metropolitan Statistical Area ~~Metropolitan Division ~~~~Component county	Population, 2014 (1,000)
Contra Costa County, CA	1,111
San Francisco-Redwood City-South San Francisco, CA	**1,611**
San Francisco County, CA	852
San Mateo County, CA	759
San Rafael, CA	**261**
Marin County, CA	261
San Jose-Sunnyvale-Santa Clara, CA	**1,953**
San Benito County, CA	58
Santa Clara County, CA	1,895
San Luis Obispo-Paso Robles-Arroyo Grande, CA	**279**
San Luis Obispo County, CA	279
Santa Cruz-Watsonville, CA	**272**
Santa Cruz County, CA	272
Santa Fe, NM	**148**
Santa Fe County, NM	148
Santa Maria-Santa Barbara, CA	**441**
Santa Barbara County, CA	441
Santa Rosa, CA	**500**
Sonoma County, CA	500
Savannah, GA	**373**
Bryan County, GA	34
Chatham County, GA	283
Effingham County, GA	55
Scranton-Wilkes-Barre-Hazleton, PA	**560**
Lackawanna County, PA	213
Luzerne County, PA	319
Wyoming County, PA	28
Seattle-Tacoma-Bellevue, WA	**3,671**
Seattle-Bellevue-Everett, WA	**2,840**
King County, WA	2,080
Snohomish County, WA	760
Tacoma-Lakewood, WA	**832**
Pierce County, WA	832
Sebastian-Vero Beach, FL	**145**
Indian River County, FL	145
Sebring, FL	**98**
Highlands County, FL	98
Sheboygan, WI	**115**
Sheboygan County, WI	115
Sherman-Denison, TX	**124**
Grayson County, TX	124
Shreveport-Bossier City, LA	**445**
Bossier Parish, LA	125
Caddo Parish, LA	253
De Soto Parish, LA	27
Webster Parish, LA	40
Sierra Vista-Douglas, AZ	**127**
Cochise County, AZ	127
Sioux City, IA-NE-SD	**169**
Plymouth County, IA	25
Woodbury County, IA	102
Dakota County, NE	21
Dixon County, NE	6
Union County, SD	15
Sioux Falls, SD	**248**
Lincoln County, SD	52
McCook County, SD	6
Minnehaha County, SD	183
Turner County, SD	8
South Bend-Mishawaka, IN-MI	**319**
St. Joseph County, IN	268
Cass County, MI	52
Spartanburg, SC	**321**
Spartanburg County, SC	294
Union County, SC	28
Spokane-Spokane Valley, WA	**541**
Pend Oreille County, WA	13
Spokane County, WA	484
Stevens County, WA	44
Springfield, IL	**212**
Menard County, IL	13
Sangamon County, IL	199
Springfield, MA	**629**
Hampden County, MA	468

See footnotes at end of table.

Table A. Metropolitan Statistical Areas and Components—Population: 2014-Continued.

See headnote on page 923.

Metropolitan Statistical Area ~~Metropolitan Division ~~~~Component county	Population, 2014 (1,000)
Hampshire County, MA.	161
Springfield, MO.	**452**
Christian County, MO.	82
Dallas County, MO.	16
Greene County, MO.	286
Polk County, MO.	31
Webster County, MO.	37
Springfield, OH.	**137**
Clark County, OH.	137
State College, PA.	**159**
Centre County, PA.	159
Staunton-Waynesboro, VA.	**120**
Augusta County, VA.	74
Staunton city, VA.	25
Waynesboro city, VA.	21
Stockton-Lodi, CA.	**716**
San Joaquin County, CA.	716
Sumter, SC.	**108**
Sumter County, SC.	108
Syracuse, NY.	**661**
Madison County, NY.	72
Onondaga County, NY.	468
Oswego County, NY.	121
Tallahassee, FL.	**376**
Gadsden County, FL.	46
Jefferson County, FL.	14
Leon County, FL.	284
Wakulla County, FL.	31
Tampa-St. Petersburg-Clearwater, FL.	**2,916**
Hernando County, FL.	176
Hillsborough County, FL.	1,316
Pasco County, FL.	485
Pinellas County, FL.	938
Terre Haute, IN.	**171**
Clay County, IN.	27
Sullivan County, IN.	21
Vermillion County, IN.	16
Vigo County, IN.	108
Texarkana, TX-AR.	**149**
Little River County, AR.	13
Miller County, AR.	43
Bowie County, TX.	93
The Villages, FL.	**114**
Sumter County, FL.	114
Toledo, OH.	**607**
Fulton County, OH.	43
Lucas County, OH.	435
Wood County, OH.	130
Topeka, KS.	**234**
Jackson County, KS.	14
Jefferson County, KS.	19
Osage County, KS.	16
Shawnee County, KS.	178
Wabaunsee County, KS.	7
Trenton, NJ.	**372**
Mercer County, NJ.	372
Tucson, AZ.	**1,005**
Pima County, AZ.	1,005
Tulsa, OK.	**969**
Creek County, OK.	71
Okmulgee County, OK.	39
Osage County, OK.	48
Pawnee County, OK.	16
Rogers County, OK.	90
Tulsa County, OK.	630
Wagoner County, OK.	76
Tuscaloosa, AL.	**238**
Hale County, AL.	15
Pickens County, AL.	20

Metropolitan Statistical Area ~~Metropolitan Division ~~~~Component county	Population, 2014 (1,000)
Tuscaloosa County, AL.	202
Tyler, TX.	**219**
Smith County, TX.	219
Utica-Rome, NY.	**297**
Herkimer County, NY.	64
Oneida County, NY.	233
Valdosta, GA.	**143**
Brooks County, GA.	15
Echols County, GA.	4
Lanier County, GA.	10
Lowndes County, GA.	114
Vallejo-Fairfield, CA.	**431**
Solano County, CA.	431
Victoria, TX.	**99**
Goliad County, TX.	8
Victoria County, TX.	91
Vineland-Bridgeton, NJ.	**157**
Cumberland County, NJ.	157
Virginia Beach-Norfolk-Newport News, VA-NC.	**1,717**
Currituck County, NC.	25
Gates County, NC.	12
Gloucester County, VA.	37
Isle of Wight County, VA.	36
James City County, VA.	73
Mathews County, VA.	9
York County, VA.	66
Chesapeake city, VA.	233
Hampton city, VA.	137
Newport News city, VA.	183
Norfolk city, VA.	245
Poquoson city, VA.	12
Portsmouth city, VA.	96
Suffolk city, VA.	87
Virginia Beach city, VA.	451
Williamsburg city, VA.	15
Visalia-Porterville, CA.	**458**
Tulare County, CA.	458
Waco, TX.	**260**
Falls County, TX.	17
McLennan County, TX.	243
Walla Walla, WA.	**64**
Columbia County, WA.	4
Walla Walla County, WA.	60
Warner Robins, GA.	**188**
Houston County, GA.	149
Peach County, GA.	27
Pulaski County, GA.	11
Washington-Arlington-Alexandria, DC-VA-MD-WV.	**6,034**
Silver Spring-Frederick-Rockville, MD.	**1,274**
Frederick County, MD.	244
Montgomery County, MD.	1,030
Washington-Arlington-Alexandria, DC-VA-MD-WV.	**4,760**
District of Columbia, DC.	659
Calvert County, MD.	91
Charles County, MD.	155
Prince George's County, MD.	904
Arlington County, VA.	227
Clarke County, VA.	14
Culpeper County, VA.	49
Fairfax County, VA.	1,138
Fauquier County, VA.	68
Loudoun County, VA.	363
Prince William County, VA.	446
Rappahannock County, VA.	7
Spotsylvania County, VA.	129
Stafford County, VA.	140

Metropolitan Statistical Area ~~Metropolitan Division ~~~~Component county	Population, 2014 (1,000)
Warren County, VA.	39
Alexandria city, VA.	151
Fairfax city, VA.	24
Falls Church city, VA.	14
Fredericksburg city, VA.	28
Manassas city, VA.	42
Manassas Park city, VA.	15
Jefferson County, WV.	56
Waterloo-Cedar Falls, IA.	**170**
Black Hawk County, IA.	133
Bremer County, IA.	25
Grundy County, IA.	12
Watertown-Fort Drum, NY.	**119**
Jefferson County, NY.	119
Wausau, WI.	**136**
Marathon County, WI.	136
Weirton-Steubenville, WV-OH.	**121**
Jefferson County, OH.	68
Brooke County, WV.	24
Hancock County, WV.	30
Wenatchee, WA.	**114**
Chelan County, WA.	75
Douglas County, WA.	40
Wheeling, WV-OH.	**145**
Belmont County, OH.	69
Marshall County, WV.	32
Ohio County, WV.	43
Wichita, KS.	**641**
Butler County, KS.	66
Harvey County, KS.	35
Kingman County, KS.	8
Sedgwick County, KS.	509
Sumner County, KS.	24
Wichita Falls, TX.	**152**
Archer County, TX.	9
Clay County, TX.	10
Wichita County, TX.	132
Williamsport, PA.	**117**
Lycoming County, PA.	117
Wilmington, NC.	**273**
New Hanover County, NC.	216
Pender County, NC.	56
Winchester, VA-WV.	**133**
Frederick County, VA.	82
Winchester city, VA.	28
Hampshire County, WV.	23
Winston-Salem, NC.	**655**
Davidson County, NC.	164
Davie County, NC.	41
Forsyth County, NC.	365
Stokes County, NC.	46
Yadkin County, NC.	38
Worcester, MA.	**930**
Windham County, CT.	117
Worcester County, MA.	813
Yakima, WA.	**248**
Yakima County, WA.	248
York-Hanover, PA.	**441**
York County, PA.	441
Youngstown-Warren-Boardman, OH-PA.	**553**
Mahoning County, OH.	233
Trumbull County, OH.	205
Mercer County, PA.	115
Yuba City, CA.	**170**
Sutter County, CA.	96
Yuba County, CA.	74
Yuma, AZ.	**203**
Yuma County, AZ.	203

Z represents less than 500. [1] The portion of Sullivan city in Crawford County, Missouri, is legally part of the St. Louis, MO-IL Metropolitan Statistical Area. The estimate shown here for the St. Louis, MO-IL Metropolitan Statistical Area does not include this area.

Source: U.S. Census Bureau, 2014 Population Estimates, <http://www.census.gov/popest/data/metro/totals/2014/>.

Table B. Microplitan Statistical Areas and Components—Population: 2014

[In thousands (42 represents 42,000). Population as of July 2014. Micropolitan Statistical Areas defined by the U.S. Office of Management and Budget as of February 2013. All Micropolitan Statistical Areas are arranged alphabetically]

Micropolitan Statistical Area ~~Component county	Population, 2014 (1,000)	Micropolitan Statistical Area ~~Component county	Population, 2014 (1,000)	Micropolitan Statistical Area ~~Component county	Population, 2014 (1,000)
Aberdeen, SD	**42**	Independence County, AR	37	Wexford County, MI	33
Brown County, SD	38	**Bay City, TX**	**37**	**Calhoun, GA**	**56**
Edmunds County, SD	4	Matagorda County, TX	37	Gordon County, GA	56
Aberdeen, WA	**71**	**Beatrice, NE**	**22**	**Cambridge, MD**	**33**
Grays Harbor County, WA	71	Gage County, NE	22	Dorchester County, MD	33
Ada, OK	**38**	**Beaver Dam, WI**	**89**	**Cambridge, OH**	**40**
Pontotoc County, OK	38	Dodge County, WI	89	Guernsey County, OH	40
Adrian, MI	**99**	**Bedford, IN**	**46**	**Camden, AR**	**30**
Lenawee County, MI	99	Lawrence County, IN	46	Calhoun County, AR	5
Alamogordo, NM	**65**	**Beeville, TX**	**33**	Ouachita County, AR	25
Otero County, NM	65	Bee County, TX	33	**Campbellsville, KY**	**25**
Albemarle, NC	**61**	**Bellefontaine, OH**	**46**	Taylor County, KY	25
Stanly County, NC	61	Logan County, OH	46	**Cañon City, CO**	**47**
Albert Lea, MN	**31**	**Bemidji, MN**	**46**	Fremont County, CO	47
Freeborn County, MN	31	Beltrami County, MN	46	**Canton, IL**	**36**
Albertville, AL	**95**	**Bennettsville, SC**	**28**	Fulton County, IL	36
Marshall County, AL	95	Marlboro County, SC	28	**Carlsbad-Artesia, NM**	**56**
Alexandria, MN	**37**	**Bennington, VT**	**36**	Eddy County, NM	56
Douglas County, MN	37	Bennington County, VT	36	**Cedar City, UT**	**47**
Alice, TX	**41**	**Berlin, NH-VT**	**38**	Iron County, UT	47
Jim Wells County, TX	41	Coos County, NH	32	**Cedartown, GA**	**41**
Alma, MI	**42**	Essex County, VT	6	Polk County, GA	41
Gratiot County, MI	42	**Big Rapids, MI**	**43**	**Celina, OH**	**41**
Alpena, MI	**29**	Mecosta County, MI	43	Mercer County, OH	41
Alpena County, MI	29	**Big Spring, TX**	**38**	**Centralia, IL**	**39**
Altus, OK	**26**	Glasscock County, TX	1	Marion County, IL	39
Jackson County, OK	26	Howard County, TX	37	**Centralia, WA**	**75**
Americus, GA	**36**	**Big Stone Gap, VA**	**59**	Lewis County, WA	75
Schley County, GA	5	Dickenson County, VA	15	**Charleston-Mattoon, IL**	**64**
Sumter County, GA	31	Wise County, VA	40	Coles County, IL	53
Amsterdam, NY	**50**	Norton city, VA	4	Cumberland County, IL	11
Montgomery County, NY	50	**Blackfoot, ID**	**45**	**Chillicothe, OH**	**77**
Andrews, TX	**17**	Bingham County, ID	45	Ross County, OH	77
Andrews County, TX	17	**Bluefield, WV-VA**	**105**	**Claremont-Lebanon, NH-VT**	**218**
Angola, IN	**34**	Tazewell County, VA	43	Grafton County, NH	90
Steuben County, IN	34	Mercer County, WV	62	Sullivan County, NH	43
Arcadia, FL	**35**	**Blytheville, AR**	**44**	Orange County, VT	29
DeSoto County, FL	35	Mississippi County, AR	44	Windsor County, VT	56
Ardmore, OK	**49**	**Bogalusa, LA**	**46**	**Clarksburg, WV**	**94**
Carter County, OK	49	Washington Parish, LA	46	Doddridge County, WV	8
Arkadelphia, AR	**23**	**Boone, IA**	**26**	Harrison County, WV	69
Clark County, AR	23	Boone County, IA	26	Taylor County, WV	17
Arkansas City-Winfield, KS	**36**	**Boone, NC**	**53**	**Clarksdale, MS**	**25**
Cowley County, KS	36	Watauga County, NC	53	Coahoma County, MS	25
Ashland, OH	**53**	**Borger, TX**	**22**	**Clearlake, CA**	**64**
Ashland County, OH	53	Hutchinson County, TX	22	Lake County, CA	64
Ashtabula, OH	**99**	**Bozeman, MT**	**97**	**Cleveland, MS**	**34**
Ashtabula County, OH	99	Gallatin County, MT	97	Bolivar County, MS	34
Astoria, OR	**37**	**Bradford, PA**	**43**	**Clewiston, FL**	**39**
Clatsop County, OR	37	McKean County, PA	43	Hendry County, FL	39
Atchison, KS	**17**	**Brainerd, MN**	**92**	**Clinton, IA**	**48**
Atchison County, KS	17	Cass County, MN	29	Clinton County, IA	48
Athens, OH	**65**	Crow Wing County, MN	63	**Clovis, NM**	**51**
Athens County, OH	65	**Branson, MO**	**85**	Curry County, NM	51
Athens, TN	**53**	Stone County, MO	31	**Coffeyville, KS**	**34**
McMinn County, TN	53	Taney County, MO	54	Montgomery County, KS	34
Athens, TX	**79**	**Breckenridge, CO**	**29**	**Coldwater, MI**	**44**
Henderson County, TX	79	Summit County, CO	29	Branch County, MI	44
Auburn, IN	**42**	**Brenham, TX**	**34**	**Columbus, MS**	**60**
DeKalb County, IN	42	Washington County, TX	34	Lowndes County, MS	60
Auburn, NY	**79**	**Brevard, NC**	**33**	**Columbus, NE**	**33**
Cayuga County, NY	79	Transylvania County, NC	33	Platte County, NE	33
Augusta-Waterville, ME	**121**	**Brookhaven, MS**	**35**	**Concord, NH**	**147**
Kennebec County, ME	121	Lincoln County, MS	35	Merrimack County, NH	147
Austin, MN	**39**	**Brookings, OR**	**22**	**Connersville, IN**	**23**
Mower County, MN	39	Curry County, OR	22	Fayette County, IN	23
Bainbridge, GA	**27**	**Brookings, SD**	**33**	**Cookeville, TN**	**108**
Decatur County, GA	27	Brookings County, SD	33	Jackson County, TN	12
Baraboo, WI	**63**	**Brownwood, TX**	**38**	Overton County, TN	22
Sauk County, WI	63	Brown County, TX	38	Putnam County, TN	74
Bardstown, KY	**45**	**Bucyrus, OH**	**42**	**Coos Bay, OR**	**62**
Nelson County, KY	45	Crawford County, OH	42	Coos County, OR	62
Barre, VT	**59**	**Burley, ID**	**44**	**Cordele, GA**	**23**
Washington County, VT	59	Cassia County, ID	24	Crisp County, GA	23
Bartlesville, OK	**52**	Minidoka County, ID	20	**Corinth, MS**	**37**
Washington County, OK	52	**Burlington, IA-IL**	**47**	Alcorn County, MS	37
Bastrop, LA	**27**	Henderson County, IL	7	**Cornelia, GA**	**44**
Morehouse Parish, LA	27	Des Moines County, IA	40	Habersham County, GA	44
Batavia, NY	**59**	**Butte-Silver Bow, MT**	**35**	**Corning, NY**	**98**
Genesee County, NY	59	Silver Bow County, MT	35	Steuben County, NY	98
Batesville, AR	**37**	**Cadillac, MI**	**48**	**Corsicana, TX**	**48**
		Missaukee County, MI	15	Navarro County, TX	48

Table B. Micropolitan Statistical Areas and Components—Population: 2014-Continued.

See headnote on page 930.

Micropolitan Statistical Area ~~Component county	Population, 2014 (1,000)
Cortland, NY	**49**
Cortland County, NY	49
Coshocton, OH	**37**
Coshocton County, OH	37
Craig, CO	**13**
Moffat County, CO	13
Crawfordsville, IN	**38**
Montgomery County, IN	38
Crescent City, CA	**27**
Del Norte County, CA	27
Crossville, TN	**58**
Cumberland County, TN	58
Cullman, AL	**81**
Cullman County, AL	81
Cullowhee, NC	**41**
Jackson County, NC	41
Danville, KY	**54**
Boyle County, KY	30
Lincoln County, KY	24
Danville, VA	**105**
Pittsylvania County, VA	62
Danville city, VA	42
Dayton, TN	**33**
Rhea County, TN	33
Decatur, IN	**35**
Adams County, IN	35
Defiance, OH	**39**
Defiance County, OH	39
Del Rio, TX	**49**
Val Verde County, TX	49
Deming, NM	**25**
Luna County, NM	25
DeRidder, LA	**36**
Beauregard Parish, LA	36
Dickinson, ND	**30**
Stark County, ND	30
Dixon, IL	**35**
Lee County, IL	35
Dodge City, KS	**35**
Ford County, KS	35
Douglas, GA	**43**
Coffee County, GA	43
Dublin, GA	**58**
Johnson County, GA	10
Laurens County, GA	48
DuBois, PA	**81**
Clearfield County, PA	81
Dumas, TX	**22**
Moore County, TX	22
Duncan, OK	**44**
Stephens County, OK	44
Dunn, NC	**127**
Harnett County, NC	127
Durango, CO	**54**
La Plata County, CO	54
Durant, OK	**44**
Bryan County, OK	44
Dyersburg, TN	**38**
Dyer County, TN	38
Eagle Pass, TX	**57**
Maverick County, TX	57
Easton, MD	**38**
Talbot County, MD	38
Edwards, CO	**53**
Eagle County, CO	53
Effingham, IL	**34**
Effingham County, IL	34
El Campo, TX	**41**
Wharton County, TX	41
El Dorado, AR	**40**
Union County, AR	40
Elizabeth City, NC	**64**
Camden County, NC	10
Pasquotank County, NC	40
Perquimans County, NC	13
Elk City, OK	**24**
Beckham County, OK	24
Elkins, WV	**29**
Randolph County, WV	29
Elko, NV	**55**
Elko County, NV	53
Eureka County, NV	2

Micropolitan Statistical Area ~~Component county	Population, 2014 (1,000)
Ellensburg, WA	**43**
Kittitas County, WA	43
Emporia, KS	**33**
Lyon County, KS	33
Enid, OK	**63**
Garfield County, OK	63
Enterprise, AL	**51**
Coffee County, AL	51
Escanaba, MI	**37**
Delta County, MI	37
Espanola, NM	**40**
Rio Arriba County, NM	40
Eureka-Arcata-Fortuna, CA	**135**
Humboldt County, CA	135
Evanston, WY	**21**
Uinta County, WY	21
Fairfield, IA	**17**
Jefferson County, IA	17
Fairmont, WV	**57**
Marion County, WV	57
Fallon, NV	**24**
Churchill County, NV	24
Faribault-Northfield, MN	**65**
Rice County, MN	65
Farmington, MO	**66**
St. Francois County, MO	66
Fergus Falls, MN	**58**
Otter Tail County, MN	58
Fernley, NV	**52**
Lyon County, NV	52
Findlay, OH	**75**
Hancock County, OH	75
Fitzgerald, GA	**17**
Ben Hill County, GA	17
Forest City, NC	**67**
Rutherford County, NC	67
Forrest City, AR	**27**
St. Francis County, AR	27
Fort Dodge, IA	**37**
Webster County, IA	37
Fort Leonard Wood, MO	**53**
Pulaski County, MO	53
Fort Madison-Keokuk, IA-IL-MO	**61**
Hancock County, IL	19
Lee County, IA	35
Clark County, MO	7
Fort Morgan, CO	**28**
Morgan County, CO	28
Fort Polk South, LA	**52**
Vernon Parish, LA	52
Frankfort, IN	**33**
Clinton County, IN	33
Frankfort, KY	**72**
Anderson County, KY	22
Franklin County, KY	50
Fredericksburg, TX	**26**
Gillespie County, TX	26
Freeport, IL	**46**
Stephenson County, IL	46
Fremont, NE	**37**
Dodge County, NE	37
Fremont, OH	**60**
Sandusky County, OH	60
Gaffney, SC	**56**
Cherokee County, SC	56
Gainesville, TX	**39**
Cooke County, TX	39
Galesburg, IL	**52**
Knox County, IL	52
Gallup, NM	**74**
McKinley County, NM	74
Garden City, KS	**41**
Finney County, KS	37
Kearny County, KS	4
Gardnerville Ranchos, NV	**48**
Douglas County, NV	48
Georgetown, SC	**61**
Georgetown County, SC	61
Gillette, WY	**48**
Campbell County, WY	48
Glasgow, KY	**53**

Micropolitan Statistical Area ~~Component county	Population, 2014 (1,000)
Barren County, KY	43
Metcalfe County, KY	10
Glenwood Springs, CO	**75**
Garfield County, CO	57
Pitkin County, CO	18
Gloversville, NY	**54**
Fulton County, NY	54
Grants, NM	**27**
Cibola County, NM	27
Great Bend, KS	**27**
Barton County, KS	27
Greeneville, TN	**68**
Greene County, TN	68
Greenfield Town, MA	**71**
Franklin County, MA	71
Greensburg, IN	**27**
Decatur County, IN	27
Greenville, MS	**49**
Washington County, MS	49
Greenville, OH	**52**
Darke County, OH	52
Greenwood, MS	**42**
Carroll County, MS	10
Leflore County, MS	31
Greenwood, SC	**94**
Abbeville County, SC	25
Greenwood County, SC	70
Grenada, MS	**22**
Grenada County, MS	22
Guymon, OK	**22**
Texas County, OK	22
Hailey, ID	**28**
Blaine County, ID	21
Camas County, ID	1
Lincoln County, ID	5
Hannibal, MO	**39**
Marion County, MO	29
Ralls County, MO	10
Harrison, AR	**45**
Boone County, AR	37
Newton County, AR	8
Hastings, NE	**31**
Adams County, NE	31
Hays, KS	**29**
Ellis County, KS	29
Heber, UT	**28**
Wasatch County, UT	28
Helena, MT	**77**
Jefferson County, MT	12
Lewis and Clark County, MT	66
Helena-West Helena, AR	**20**
Phillips County, AR	20
Henderson, NC	**45**
Vance County, NC	45
Hereford, TX	**19**
Deaf Smith County, TX	19
Hermiston-Pendleton, OR	**88**
Morrow County, OR	11
Umatilla County, OR	77
Hillsdale, MI	**46**
Hillsdale County, MI	46
Hilo, HI	**194**
Hawaii County, HI	194
Hobbs, NM	**70**
Lea County, NM	70
Holland, MI	**114**
Allegan County, MI	114
Hood River, OR	**23**
Hood River County, OR	23
Houghton, MI	**39**
Houghton County, MI	36
Keweenaw County, MI	2
Hudson, NY	**62**
Columbia County, NY	62
Huntingdon, PA	**46**
Huntingdon County, PA	46
Huntington, IN	**37**
Huntington County, IN	37
Huntsville, TX	**84**
Trinity County, TX	14
Walker County, TX	70
Huron, SD	**18**

See footnotes at end of table.

Micropolitan Statistical Area ~~Component county	Population, 2014 (1,000)
Beadle County, SD	18
Hutchinson, KS	**64**
Reno County, KS	64
Hutchinson, MN	**36**
McLeod County, MN	36
Indiana, PA	**88**
Indiana County, PA	88
Indianola, MS	**27**
Sunflower County, MS	27
Ionia, MI	**64**
Ionia County, MI	64
Iron Mountain, MI-WI	**30**
Dickinson County, MI	26
Florence County, WI	4
Jackson, OH	**33**
Jackson County, OH	33
Jackson, WY-ID	**33**
Teton County, ID	10
Teton County, WY	23
Jacksonville, IL	**40**
Morgan County, IL	35
Scott County, IL	5
Jacksonville, TX	**51**
Cherokee County, TX	51
Jamestown, ND	**21**
Stutsman County, ND	21
Jamestown-Dunkirk-Fredonia, NY	**132**
Chautauqua County, NY	132
Jasper, IN	**55**
Dubois County, IN	42
Pike County, IN	13
Jefferson, GA	**62**
Jackson County, GA	62
Jesup, GA	**30**
Wayne County, GA	30
Junction City, KS	**37**
Geary County, KS	37
Juneau, AK	**32**
Juneau City and Borough, AK	32
Kalispell, MT	**95**
Flathead County, MT	95
Kapaa, HI	**70**
Kauai County, HI	70
Kearney, NE	**55**
Buffalo County, NE	48
Kearney County, NE	7
Keene, NH	**76**
Cheshire County, NH	76
Kendallville, IN	**48**
Noble County, IN	48
Kennett, MO	**31**
Dunklin County, MO	31
Kerrville, TX	**51**
Kerr County, TX	51
Ketchikan, AK	**14**
Ketchikan Gateway Borough, AK	14
Key West, FL	**77**
Monroe County, FL	77
Kill Devil Hills, NC	**39**
Dare County, NC	35
Tyrrell County, NC	4
Kingsville, TX	**33**
Kenedy County, TX	(Z)
Kleberg County, TX	32
Kinston, NC	**58**
Lenoir County, NC	58
Kirksville, MO	**30**
Adair County, MO	26
Schuyler County, MO	4
Klamath Falls, OR	**65**
Klamath County, OR	65
Laconia, NH	**60**
Belknap County, NH	60
La Grande, OR	**26**
Union County, OR	26
LaGrange, GA	**69**
Troup County, GA	69
Lake City, FL	**68**
Columbia County, FL	68
Lamesa, TX	**13**
Dawson County, TX	13

Micropolitan Statistical Area ~~Component county	Population, 2014 (1,000)
Laramie, WY	**38**
Albany County, WY	38
Las Vegas, NM	**28**
San Miguel County, NM	28
Laurel, MS	**85**
Jasper County, MS	17
Jones County, MS	68
Laurinburg, NC	**36**
Scotland County, NC	36
Lawrenceburg, TN	**42**
Lawrence County, TN	42
Lebanon, MO	**35**
Laclede County, MO	35
Levelland, TX	**24**
Hockley County, TX	24
Lewisburg, PA	**45**
Union County, PA	45
Lewisburg, TN	**31**
Marshall County, TN	31
Lewistown, PA	**47**
Mifflin County, PA	47
Lexington, NE	**26**
Dawson County, NE	24
Gosper County, NE	2
Liberal, KS	**23**
Seward County, KS	23
Lincoln, IL	**30**
Logan County, IL	30
Lock Haven, PA	**40**
Clinton County, PA	40
Logan, WV	**35**
Logan County, WV	35
Logansport, IN	**38**
Cass County, IN	38
London, KY	**127**
Knox County, KY	32
Laurel County, KY	60
Whitley County, KY	36
Los Alamos, NM	**18**
Los Alamos County, NM	18
Ludington, MI	**29**
Mason County, MI	29
Lufkin, TX	**88**
Angelina County, TX	88
Lumberton, NC	**135**
Robeson County, NC	135
Macomb, IL	**32**
McDonough County, IL	32
Madison, IN	**32**
Jefferson County, IN	32
Madisonville, KY	**46**
Hopkins County, KY	46
Magnolia, AR	**24**
Columbia County, AR	24
Malone, NY	**51**
Franklin County, NY	51
Malvern, AR	**33**
Hot Spring County, AR	33
Manitowoc, WI	**80**
Manitowoc County, WI	80
Marietta, OH	**61**
Washington County, OH	61
Marinette, WI-MI	**65**
Menominee County, MI	24
Marinette County, WI	41
Marion, IN	**69**
Grant County, IN	69
Marion, NC	**45**
McDowell County, NC	45
Marion, OH	**66**
Marion County, OH	66
Marquette, MI	**68**
Marquette County, MI	68
Marshall, MN	**26**
Lyon County, MN	26
Marshall, MO	**23**
Saline County, MO	23
Marshall, TX	**67**
Harrison County, TX	67
Marshalltown, IA	**41**
Marshall County, IA	41
Martin, TN	**34**

Micropolitan Statistical Area ~~Component county	Population, 2014 (1,000)
Weakley County, TN	34
Martinsville, VA	**66**
Henry County, VA	52
Martinsville city, VA	14
Maryville, MO	**23**
Nodaway County, MO	23
Mason City, IA	**51**
Cerro Gordo County, IA	43
Worth County, IA	8
Mayfield, KY	**38**
Graves County, KY	38
Maysville, KY	**17**
Mason County, KY	17
McAlester, OK	**45**
Pittsburg County, OK	45
McComb, MS	**53**
Amite County, MS	13
Pike County, MS	40
McMinnville, TN	**40**
Warren County, TN	40
McPherson, KS	**29**
McPherson County, KS	29
Meadville, PA	**87**
Crawford County, PA	87
Menomonie, WI	**44**
Dunn County, WI	44
Meridian, MS	**106**
Clarke County, MS	16
Kemper County, MS	10
Lauderdale County, MS	80
Merrill, WI	**28**
Lincoln County, WI	28
Mexico, MO	**26**
Audrain County, MO	26
Miami, OK	**32**
Ottawa County, OK	32
Middlesborough, KY	**28**
Bell County, KY	28
Milledgeville, GA	**54**
Baldwin County, GA	46
Hancock County, GA	9
Mineral Wells, TX	**28**
Palo Pinto County, TX	28
Minot, ND	**78**
McHenry County, ND	6
Renville County, ND	3
Ward County, ND	69
Mitchell, SD	**23**
Davison County, SD	20
Hanson County, SD	3
Moberly, MO	**25**
Randolph County, MO	25
Montrose, CO	**41**
Montrose County, CO	41
Morehead City, NC	**69**
Carteret County, NC	69
Morgan City, LA	**53**
St. Mary Parish, LA	53
Moscow, ID	**38**
Latah County, ID	38
Moses Lake, WA	**93**
Grant County, WA	93
Moultrie, GA	**46**
Colquitt County, GA	46
Mountain Home, AR	**41**
Baxter County, AR	41
Mountain Home, ID	**26**
Elmore County, ID	26
Mount Airy, NC	**73**
Surry County, NC	73
Mount Pleasant, MI	**71**
Isabella County, MI	71
Mount Pleasant, TX	**33**
Titus County, TX	33
Mount Sterling, KY	**46**
Bath County, KY	12
Menifee County, KY	6
Montgomery County, KY	27
Mount Vernon, IL	**39**
Jefferson County, IL	39
Mount Vernon, OH	**61**
Knox County, OH	61

See footnotes at end of table.

Micropolitan Statistical Area ~~Component county	Population, 2014 (1,000)
Murray, KY	**38**
Calloway County, KY	38
Muscatine, IA	**43**
Muscatine County, IA	43
Muskogee, OK	**70**
Muskogee County, OK	70
Nacogdoches, TX	**65**
Nacogdoches County, TX	65
Natchez, MS-LA	**52**
Concordia Parish, LA	20
Adams County, MS	32
Natchitoches, LA	**39**
Natchitoches Parish, LA	39
Newberry, SC	**38**
Newberry County, SC	38
New Castle, IN	**49**
Henry County, IN	49
New Castle, PA	**89**
Lawrence County, PA	89
New Philadelphia-Dover, OH	**93**
Tuscarawas County, OH	93
Newport, OR	**46**
Lincoln County, OR	46
Newport, TN	**35**
Cocke County, TN	35
Newton, IA	**37**
Jasper County, IA	37
New Ulm, MN	**25**
Brown County, MN	25
Nogales, AZ	**47**
Santa Cruz County, AZ	47
Norfolk, NE	**48**
Madison County, NE	35
Pierce County, NE	7
Stanton County, NE	6
North Platte, NE	**37**
Lincoln County, NE	36
Logan County, NE	1
McPherson County, NE	(Z)
North Vernon, IN	**28**
Jennings County, IN	28
North Wilkesboro, NC	**69**
Wilkes County, NC	69
Norwalk, OH	**59**
Huron County, OH	59
Oak Harbor, WA	**79**
Island County, WA	79
Ogdensburg-Massena, NY	**111**
St. Lawrence County, NY	111
Oil City, PA	**54**
Venango County, PA	54
Okeechobee, FL	**39**
Okeechobee County, FL	39
Olean, NY	**79**
Cattaraugus County, NY	79
Oneonta, NY	**61**
Otsego County, NY	61
Ontario, OR-ID	**53**
Payette County, ID	23
Malheur County, OR	30
Opelousas, LA	**84**
St. Landry Parish, LA	84
Orangeburg, SC	**90**
Orangeburg County, SC	90
Oskaloosa, IA	**22**
Mahaska County, IA	22
Othello, WA	**19**
Adams County, WA	19
Ottawa, KS	**26**
Franklin County, KS	26
Ottawa-Peru, IL	**151**
Bureau County, IL	34
LaSalle County, IL	111
Putnam County, IL	6
Ottumwa, IA	**44**
Davis County, IA	9
Wapello County, IA	35
Owatonna, MN	**37**
Steele County, MN	37
Owosso, MI	**69**
Shiawassee County, MI	69
Oxford, MS	**53**

Micropolitan Statistical Area ~~Component county	Population, 2014 (1,000)
Lafayette County, MS	53
Oxford, NC	**59**
Granville County, NC	59
Ozark, AL	**49**
Dale County, AL	49
Paducah, KY-IL	**98**
Massac County, IL	15
Ballard County, KY	8
Livingston County, KY	9
McCracken County, KY	65
Pahrump, NV	**42**
Nye County, NV	42
Palatka, FL	**72**
Putnam County, FL	72
Palestine, TX	**58**
Anderson County, TX	58
Pampa, TX	**23**
Gray County, TX	23
Paragould, AR	**44**
Greene County, AR	44
Paris, TN	**32**
Henry County, TN	32
Paris, TX	**50**
Lamar County, TX	50
Parsons, KS	**21**
Labette County, KS	21
Payson, AZ	**53**
Gila County, AZ	53
Pecos, TX	**14**
Reeves County, TX	14
Peru, IN	**36**
Miami County, IN	36
Picayune, MS	**55**
Pearl River County, MS	55
Pierre, SD	**22**
Hughes County, SD	18
Stanley County, SD	3
Sully County, SD	1
Pinehurst-Southern Pines, NC	**93**
Moore County, NC	93
Pittsburg, KS	**39**
Crawford County, KS	39
Plainview, TX	**35**
Hale County, TX	35
Platteville, WI	**52**
Grant County, WI	52
Plattsburgh, NY	**82**
Clinton County, NY	82
Plymouth, IN	**47**
Marshall County, IN	47
Point Pleasant, WV-OH	**57**
Gallia County, OH	30
Mason County, WV	27
Ponca City, OK	**45**
Kay County, OK	45
Pontiac, IL	**38**
Livingston County, IL	38
Poplar Bluff, MO	**43**
Butler County, MO	43
Portales, NM	**20**
Roosevelt County, NM	20
Port Angeles, WA	**73**
Clallam County, WA	73
Port Clinton, OH	**41**
Ottawa County, OH	41
Port Lavaca, TX	**22**
Calhoun County, TX	22
Portsmouth, OH	**77**
Scioto County, OH	77
Pottsville, PA	**146**
Schuylkill County, PA	146
Price, UT	**21**
Carbon County, UT	21
Prineville, OR	**21**
Crook County, OR	21
Pullman, WA	**47**
Whitman County, WA	47
Quincy, IL-MO	**77**
Adams County, IL	67
Lewis County, MO	10
Raymondville, TX	**22**

Micropolitan Statistical Area ~~Component county	Population, 2014 (1,000)
Willacy County, TX	22
Red Bluff, CA	**63**
Tehama County, CA	63
Red Wing, MN	**46**
Goodhue County, MN	46
Rexburg, ID	**51**
Fremont County, ID	13
Madison County, ID	38
Richmond, IN	**68**
Wayne County, IN	68
Richmond-Berea, KY	**104**
Madison County, KY	87
Rockcastle County, KY	17
Rio Grande City, TX	**63**
Starr County, TX	63
Riverton, WY	**41**
Fremont County, WY	41
Roanoke Rapids, NC	**73**
Halifax County, NC	53
Northampton County, NC	20
Rochelle, IL	**52**
Ogle County, IL	52
Rockingham, NC	**46**
Richmond County, NC	46
Rock Springs, WY	**45**
Sweetwater County, WY	45
Rolla, MO	**45**
Phelps County, MO	45
Roseburg, OR	**107**
Douglas County, OR	107
Roswell, NM	**66**
Chaves County, NM	66
Russellville, AR	**85**
Pope County, AR	63
Yell County, AR	22
Ruston, LA	**48**
Lincoln Parish, LA	48
Rutland, VT	**60**
Rutland County, VT	60
Safford, AZ	**38**
Graham County, AZ	38
St. Marys, GA	**52**
Camden County, GA	52
Salem, OH	**106**
Columbiana County, OH	106
Salina, KS	**62**
Ottawa County, KS	6
Saline County, KS	56
Sandpoint, ID	**42**
Bonner County, ID	42
Sandusky, OH	**76**
Erie County, OH	76
Sanford, NC	**60**
Lee County, NC	60
Sault Ste. Marie, MI	**38**
Chippewa County, MI	38
Sayre, PA	**62**
Bradford County, PA	62
Scottsbluff, NE	**39**
Banner County, NE	1
Scotts Bluff County, NE	36
Sioux County, NE	1
Scottsboro, AL	**53**
Jackson County, AL	53
Searcy, AR	**79**
White County, AR	79
Sedalia, MO	**42**
Pettis County, MO	42
Selinsgrove, PA	**40**
Snyder County, PA	40
Selma, AL	**42**
Dallas County, AL	42
Seneca, SC	**75**
Oconee County, SC	75
Seneca Falls, NY	**35**
Seneca County, NY	35
Sevierville, TN	**95**
Sevier County, TN	95
Seymour, IN	**44**
Jackson County, IN	44
Shawano, WI	**46**
Menominee County, WI	5

See footnotes at end of table.

Table B. Microplitan Statistical Areas and Components—Population: 2014-Continued.

See headnote on page 930.

Micropolitan Statistical Area ~~Component county	Population, 2014 (1,000)
Shawano County, WI............	42
Shawnee, OK...........................	**72**
Pottawatomie County, OK......	72
Shelby, NC........................	**97**
Cleveland County, NC...........	97
Shelbyville, TN..................	**47**
Bedford County, TN...............	47
Shelton, WA......................	**61**
Mason County, WA................	61
Sheridan, WY.....................	**30**
Sheridan County, WY............	30
Show Low, AZ.....................	**108**
Navajo County, AZ................	108
Sidney, OH........................	**49**
Shelby County, OH................	49
Sikeston, MO......................	**39**
Scott County, MO..................	39
Silver City, NM...................	**29**
Grant County, NM.................	29
Snyder, TX.........................	**17**
Scurry County, TX.................	17
Somerset, KY......................	**64**
Pulaski County, KY................	64
Somerset, PA......................	**76**
Somerset County, PA............	76
Sonora, CA........................	**54**
Tuolumne County, CA...........	54
Spearfish, SD......................	**25**
Lawrence County, SD............	25
Spencer, IA........................	**17**
Clay County, IA.....................	17
Spirit Lake, IA....................	**17**
Dickinson County, IA............	17
Starkville, MS.....................	**49**
Oktibbeha County, MS..........	49
Statesboro, GA...................	**72**
Bulloch County, GA..............	72
Steamboat Springs, CO.......	**24**
Routt County, CO.................	24
Stephenville, TX.................	**40**
Erath County, TX..................	40
Sterling, CO.......................	**23**
Logan County, CO................	23
Sterling, IL........................	**57**
Whiteside County, IL............	57
Stevens Point, WI................	**70**
Portage County, WI..............	70
Stillwater, OK.....................	**80**
Payne County, OK................	80
Storm Lake, IA...................	**21**
Buena Vista County, IA.........	21
Sturgis, MI........................	**61**
St. Joseph County, MI...........	61
Sulphur Springs, TX............	**36**
Hopkins County, TX..............	36
Summerville, GA.................	**25**
Chattooga County, GA..........	25
Summit Park, UT.................	**39**
Summit County, UT..............	39
Sunbury, PA......................	**94**
Northumberland County, PA....	94
Susanville, CA....................	**32**
Lassen County, CA...............	32
Sweetwater, TX..................	**15**
Nolan County, TX.................	15
Tahlequah, OK...................	**48**
Cherokee County, OK...........	48
Talladega-Sylacauga, AL.......	**92**
Coosa County, AL.................	11
Talladega County, AL............	81
Taos, NM..........................	**33**
Taos County, NM..................	33
Taylorville, IL.....................	**34**
Christian County, IL..............	34
The Dalles, OR...................	**26**
Wasco County, OR................	26
Thomaston, GA..................	**26**
Upson County, GA................	26
Thomasville, GA.................	**45**
Thomas County, GA..............	45
Tiffin, OH..........................	**56**
Seneca County, OH...............	56
Tifton, GA.........................	**41**

Micropolitan Statistical Area ~~Component county	Population, 2014 (1,000)
Tift County, GA....................	41
Toccoa, GA........................	**25**
Stephens County, GA............	25
Torrington, CT...................	**185**
Litchfield County, CT............	185
Traverse City, MI................	**148**
Benzie County, MI................	18
Grand Traverse County, MI.....	91
Kalkaska County, MI.............	17
Leelanau County, MI.............	22
Troy, AL...........................	**33**
Pike County, AL....................	33
Truckee-Grass Valley, CA......	**99**
Nevada County, CA...............	99
Tullahoma-Manchester, TN....	**101**
Coffee County, TN................	54
Franklin County, TN..............	41
Moore County, TN................	6
Tupelo, MS........................	**140**
Itawamba County, MS...........	24
Lee County, MS....................	85
Pontotoc County, MS............	31
Twin Falls, ID....................	**104**
Jerome County, ID................	23
Twin Falls County, ID............	81
Ukiah, CA.........................	**88**
Mendocino County, CA..........	88
Union City, TN-KY..............	**37**
Fulton County, KY................	6
Obion County, TN................	31
Urbana, OH.......................	**39**
Champaign County, OH.........	39
Uvalde, TX........................	**27**
Uvalde County, TX................	27
Valley, AL.........................	**34**
Chambers County, AL............	34
Van Wert, OH....................	**28**
Van Wert County, OH...........	28
Vermillion, SD...................	**14**
Clay County, SD...................	14
Vernal, UT........................	**37**
Uintah County, UT................	37
Vernon, TX........................	**13**
Wilbarger County, TX............	13
Vicksburg, MS....................	**57**
Claiborne County, MS...........	9
Warren County, MS...............	48
Vidalia, GA.......................	**36**
Montgomery County, GA........	9
Toombs County, GA..............	27
Vincennes, IN....................	**38**
Knox County, IN...................	38
Vineyard Haven, MA............	**17**
Dukes County, MA................	17
Wabash, IN.......................	**32**
Wabash County, IN...............	32
Wahpeton, ND-MN.............	**23**
Wilkin County, MN................	6
Richland County, ND............	16

Z Less than 500

Source: U.S. Census Bureau, 2014 Population Estimates, <http://www.census.gov/popest/data/metro/totals/2014/>.

Micropolitan Statistical Area ~~Component county	Population, 2014 (1,000)
Wapakoneta, OH................	**46**
Auglaize County, OH.............	46
Warren, PA........................	**41**
Warren County, PA................	41
Warrensburg, MO...............	**54**
Johnson County, MO............	54
Warsaw, IN........................	**79**
Kosciusko County, IN............	79
Washington, IN..................	**33**
Daviess County, IN...............	33
Washington, NC.................	**48**
Beaufort County, NC.............	48
Washington Court House, OH..................................	**29**
Fayette County, OH..............	29
Watertown, SD...................	**28**
Codington County, SD..........	28
Watertown-Fort Atkinson, WI..	**84**
Jefferson County, WI.............	84
Wauchula, FL.....................	**27**
Hardee County, FL................	27
Waycross, GA.....................	**55**
Pierce County, GA................	19
Ware County, GA..................	36
Weatherford, OK................	**30**
Custer County, OK................	30
West Plains, MO.................	**40**
Howell County, MO...............	40
Whitewater-Elkhorn, WI........	**104**
Walworth County, WI............	104
Williston, ND.....................	**32**
Williams County, ND.............	32
Willmar, MN......................	**42**
Kandiyohi County, MN...........	42
Wilmington, OH.................	**42**
Clinton County, OH..............	42
Wilson, NC........................	**81**
Wilson County, NC...............	81
Winnemucca, NV................	**17**
Humboldt County, NV...........	17
Winona, MN......................	**51**
Winona County, MN..............	51
Wisconsin Rapids-Marshfield, WI..................................	**74**
Wood County, WI.................	74
Woodward, OK...................	**22**
Woodward County, OK..........	22
Wooster, OH......................	**116**
Wayne County, OH...............	116
Worthington, MN...............	**22**
Nobles County, MN..............	22
Yankton, SD......................	**23**
Yankton County, SD..............	23
Zanesville, OH...................	**86**
Muskingum County, OH.........	86
Zapata, TX........................	**14**
Zapata County, TX................	14

Limitations of the Data

Introduction—The data presented in this *Statistical Abstract* come from many sources. The sources include not only federal statistical bureaus and other organizations that collect and issue statistics as their principal activity, but also governmental administrative and regulatory agencies, private research bodies, trade associations, insurance companies, health associations, private organizations, and philanthropic foundations. Consequently, the data vary considerably as to reference periods, definitions of terms and, for ongoing series, the number and frequency of time periods for which data are available.

The statistics presented were obtained and tabulated by various methods. Some statistics are based on complete enumerations or censuses while others are based on samples. Some information is extracted from records kept for administrative or regulatory purposes (school enrollment, hospital records, securities registration, financial accounts, social security records, income tax returns, etc.), while other information is obtained explicitly for statistical purposes through surveys. The estimation procedures vary from highly sophisticated scientific techniques, to crude "informed guesses."

Each set of data relates to a group of individuals or units of interest referred to as the *target universe,* or *target population*, or simply as the *universe* or *population*.

Prior to data collection, the target universe should be clearly defined. For example, if data are to be collected for the universe of households in the United States, it is necessary to define a "household." The target universe may not be completely tractable. Cost and other considerations may restrict data collection to a *survey universe* based on an available list. This list is called a *survey frame, sampling frame, or survey sample.*

The data in many tables are based on data obtained for all population units, *a census*, or on data obtained for only a portion, or *sample*, of the population units. When the data presented are based on a sample, the sample is usually a scientifically selected *probability sample*. This is a sample selected from a list or sampling frame in such a way that every possible sample has a known chance of selection and usually each unit selected can be assigned a number, greater than zero and less than or equal to one, representing its likelihood or probability of selection.

For large-scale sample surveys, the probability sample of units is often selected as a multistage sample. The first stage of a multistage sample is the selection of a probability sample of large groups of population members, referred to as primary sampling units (PSUs). For example, in a national multistage household sample, PSUs are often counties or groups of counties. The second stage of a multistage sample is the selection, within each PSU selected at the first stage, of smaller groups of population units, referred to as secondary sampling units. In subsequent stages of selection, smaller and smaller nested groups are chosen until the ultimate sample of population units is obtained. To qualify a multistage sample as a probability sample, all stages of sampling must be carried out using probability sampling methods.

Prior to selection at each stage of a multistage (or a single stage) sample, a list of the sampling units or sampling frame for that stage must be obtained. For example, for the first stage of selection of a national household sample, a list of the counties and county groups that form the PSUs must be compiled. For the final stage of selection, lists of households, and sometimes persons within the households, have to be compiled in the field. For surveys of economic entities and for the economic censuses, the U.S. Census Bureau generally uses a frame constructed from the Bureau's Business Register. The Business Register contains all establishments with payroll in the United States including small single establishment firms as well as large multi-establishment firms.

Wherever the quantities in a table refer to an entire universe, but are constructed from data collected in a sample survey, the table quantities are referred to as *sample estimates*. In constructing a sample estimate, an attempt is made to come as close as is feasible to the corresponding universe quantity that would be obtained from a complete census of the universe. Estimates based on a sample will, however, generally differ from the hypothetical census figures. Two classifications of errors are associated with estimates based on sample surveys:

1 *Sampling error*—the error arising from the use of a sample, rather than a census, to estimate population quantities and

2 *Nonsampling error*—those errors arising from nonsampling sources. Nonsampling errors can include mistakes made in data collection or data processing, misunderstandings of the interviewer or the respondent, and data entry errors. As discussed below, the magnitude of the sampling error for an estimate can usually be estimated from the sample data. However, the magnitude of the nonsampling error for an estimate can rarely be estimated. Consequently, actual error in an estimate exceeds the error that can be estimated.

The particular sample used in a survey is only one of a large number of possible samples of the same size which could have been selected using the same sampling procedure. Estimates derived from the different samples would, in general, differ from each other. The *standard error* (SE) is a measure of the variation among the estimates derived from all possible samples. The standard error is the most commonly used measure of the sampling error of an estimate. Valid estimates of the standard errors of survey estimates can usually be calculated from the data collected in a probability sample. For convenience, the standard error is sometimes expressed as a percent of the estimate and is called the relative standard error or *coefficient of variation* (CV). For example, an estimate of 200 units with an estimated standard error of 10 units has an estimated CV of 5 percent.

A sample estimate and an estimate of its standard error or CV can be used to construct interval estimates that have a prescribed confidence that the interval includes the average of the estimates derived from all possible samples with a known probability. To illustrate, if all possible samples were selected under essentially the same general conditions, and using the same sample design, and if an estimate and its estimated standard error were calculated from each sample, then: 1) approximately 68 percent of the intervals from one standard error below the estimate to one standard error above the estimate would include the average estimate derived from all possible samples; 2) approximately 90 percent of the intervals from 1.6 standard errors below the estimate to 1.6 standard errors above the estimate would include the average estimate derived from all possible samples; and 3) approximately 95 percent of the intervals from two standard errors below the estimate to two standard errors above the estimate would include the average estimate derived from all possible samples.

Thus, for a particular sample, one can say with the appropriate level of confidence (e.g., 90 percent or 95 percent) that the average of all possible samples is included in the constructed interval. Example of a confidence interval: An estimate is 200 units with a standard error of 10 units. An approximately 90 percent confidence interval (plus or minus 1.6 standard errors) is from 184 to 216.

All surveys and censuses are subject to nonsampling errors. Nonsampling errors are of two kinds—*random* and *nonrandom*. Random nonsampling errors arise because of the varying interpretation of questions (by respondents or interviewers) and varying actions of coders, keyers, and other processors. Some randomness is also introduced when respondents must estimate. Nonrandom nonsampling errors result from total nonresponse (no usable data obtained for a sampled unit), partial or item nonresponse (only a portion of a response may be usable), inability or unwillingness on the part of respondents to provide correct information, difficulty interpreting questions, mistakes in recording or keying data, errors of collection or processing, and coverage problems (overcoverage and undercoverage of the target universe). Random nonresponse errors usually, but not always, result in an understatement of sampling errors and thus an overstatement of the precision of survey estimates. Estimating the magnitude of nonsampling errors would require special experiments or access to independent data and, consequently, the magnitudes are seldom available.

Nearly all types of nonsampling errors that affect surveys also occur in complete censuses. Since surveys can be conducted on a smaller scale than censuses, nonsampling errors can presumably be controlled more tightly. Relatively more funds and effort can perhaps be expended toward eliciting responses, detecting and correcting response error, and reducing processing errors. As a result, survey results can sometimes be more accurate than census results.

To compensate for suspected nonrandom errors, adjustments of the sample estimates are often made. For example, adjustments are frequently made for nonresponse, both total and partial. Adjustments made for either type of nonresponse are often referred to as *imputations*. Imputation for total nonresponse is usually made by substituting for the questionnaire responses of the nonrespondents the "average" questionnaire responses of the respondents. These imputations usually are made separately within various groups of sample members, formed by attempting to place respondents and nonrespondents together that have "similar" design or ancillary characteristics. Imputation for item nonresponse is usually made by substituting for a missing item the response to that item of a respondent having characteristics that are "similar" to those of the nonrespondent.

For an estimate calculated from a sample survey, the *total error* in the estimate is composed of the sampling error, which can usually be estimated from the sample, and the nonsampling error, which usually cannot be estimated from the sample. The total error present in a population quantity obtained from a complete census is composed of only nonsampling errors. Ideally, estimates of the total error associated with data given in the *Statistical Abstract* tables should be given. However, due to the unavailability of estimates of nonsampling errors, only estimates of the levels of sampling errors, in terms of estimated standard errors or coefficients of variation, are available. To obtain estimates of the estimated standard errors from the sample of interest, see the source cited at the end of each table.

Source of Additional Material: The Federal Committee on Statistical Methodology (FCSM) is an interagency committee dedicated to improving the quality of federal statistics, online at <http://fcsm.sites.usa.gov>.

Principal data bases—Beginning below are brief descriptions of over 30 of the sample surveys and censuses that provide a substantial portion of the data contained in this *Abstract*.

U.S. DEPARTMENT OF AGRICULTURE, National Agriculture Statistics Service

Census of Agriculture

Universes, Frequency, and Types of Data: Complete count of U.S. farms and ranches conducted once every 5 years with data at the national, state, and county level. Data published on farm numbers and related items/characteristics. Covers any place from which $1,000 or more of agricultural products were produced and sold, or normally would have been sold during the census year.

Type of Data Collection Operation: Complete census for number of farms; land in farms; farm income; agriculture products sold; farms by type of organization; total cropland; irrigated land; farm operator characteristics; livestock and poultry inventory and sales; and selected crops harvested. Market value of land, buildings, and products sold, total farm production expenses, machinery and equipment, and fertilizer and chemicals.

Data Collection and Imputation Procedures: Data collection is by mailing questionnaires to all farmers and ranchers. Producers can return their forms by mail or online. Nonrespondents are contacted by telephone and correspondence follow-ups. Collection is supplemented by electronic data reporting on the Internet, and personal enumeration for special classes of records in census operations. Imputations were made for all nonresponse item/characteristics and coverage adjustments were made to account for missed farms and ranches. The response rate for the 2012 Census was 80.1 percent.

Estimates of Sampling Error: Weight adjustments were made to account for the undercoverage and whole-unit nonresponse of farms on the Census Mail List (CML), and misclassification as to whether a farm or not a farm. These were treated as sampling errors.

Nonsampling Errors: Nonsampling errors are due to incompleteness of the census mailing list, duplications on the list, respondent reporting errors, errors in editing reported data, and in imputation for missing data. Evaluation studies are conducted to measure certain nonsampling errors such as list coverage and classification error. It is a reasonable assumption that the net effect of non-measurable errors is zero (the positive errors cancel the negative errors).

Sources of Additional Material: U.S. Department of Agriculture (NASS), 2012 Census of Agriculture, Appendix A Census of Agriculture Methodology, Appendix B General Explanation and Census of Agriculture Report Form, at <http://www.agcensus.usda.gov/Publications/2012/>.

Basic Area Frame Sample

Universe, Frequency, and Types of Data: The June Agricultural Survey collects data annually from the 48 contiguous states and Hawaii on crop acreage, grain stocks, cattle inventory, hog inventory, sheep inventory, poultry inventory, land values, cash rents, farm numbers, and sales. The survey also serves to measure list incompleteness and is subsampled for multiple frame surveys.

Type of Data Collection Operation: Stratified probability sample of about 11,000 land area units of about 1 sq. mile (range from 0.1 sq. mile in cities to several sq. miles in open grazing areas). All farm operators within the boundaries of selected segments are interviewed. Sample represents 42,000 operating arrangements; over 35,000 interviews are conducted. About 20 percent of the sample replaced annually.

Data Collection and Imputation Procedures: Data collection is via face-to-face interviews. Imputation is based on enumerator observation or data reported by respondents having similar agricultural characteristics.

Estimates of Sampling Error: Estimated CVs range from 1 percent to 2 percent for regional estimates to 3 percent to 6 percent for state estimates of major crop acres and livestock inventories.

Nonsampling Errors: These are minimized through rigid quality controls on the collection process and careful review of all reported data.

Sources of Additional Material: U.S. Department of Agriculture, National Agricultural Statistics Service, *The Fact Finders for Agriculture: The NASS at Work*, March 2007.

Multiple Frame Surveys

Universe, Frequency, and Types of Data: Surveys of U.S. farm operators to obtain data on major livestock inventories, selected crop acreage and production, grain stocks, and farm labor characteristics, farm economic data, and chemical use data. Estimates are made quarterly, semi-annually, or annually depending on the data series.

Type of Data Collection Operation: Primary frame is obtained from general or special purpose lists, supplemented by a probability sample of land areas used to estimate for list incompleteness.

Data Collection and Imputation Procedures: Mail, telephone, or personal interviews used for initial data collection. Mail nonrespondent follow-up by phone and personal interviews. Imputation based on average of respondents.

Estimates of Sampling Error: Estimated CVs range from 1 percent to 2 percent at the U.S. level for crop and livestock data series and 3 to 5 percent for economic data. Regional CVs range from 3 to 6 percent, while state estimate CVs run 5 to 10 percent.

Nonsampling Errors: In addition to above, replicated sampling procedures used to monitor effects of changes in survey procedures.

Sources of Additional Material: U.S. Department of Agriculture, National Agricultural Statistics Service), *The Fact Finders for Agriculture: The NASS at Work*, March 2007.

Objective Yield Surveys

Universe, Frequency, and Types of Data: Monthly forecasts and end-of-season estimates of planted and harvested acres, yield, and production of winter wheat, corn for grain, soybeans, fall potatoes, and upland cotton. All acres for harvest as grain in the leading producing states are eligible for this survey. Survey samples are selected from participants in the March Crops/Stocks Survey or the June Agricultural Survey.

Type of Data Collection Operation: Random location of plots in probability sample. Field work begins April 25 for winter wheat and July 25 for all the other crops. Sample units are visited at the end of each month during the growing season.

Data Collection and Imputation Procedures: Enumerators count and measure plant characteristics in sample fields. Production is measured from plots at harvest. Harvest loss is measured from post harvest gleanings.

Estimates of Sampling Error: CVs for national estimates of production are about 2 to 3 percent.

Nonsampling Errors: In addition to above, replicated sampling procedures are used to monitor effects of changes in survey procedures.

Sources of Additional Material: U.S. Department of Agriculture, National Agricultural Statistics Service, Statistical Methods Branch, *The Yield Forecasting Program of NASS*, May 2012.

U.S. BUREAU OF JUSTICE STATISTICS (BJS)

National Crime Victimization Survey (NCVS)

Universe, Frequency, and Types of Data: Annual survey of U.S. household members age 12 and older to obtain data on criminal victimization for compilation of annual estimates; approximately 160,000 persons in 90,000 households are interviewed. Survey includes nonfatal crimes and household property crimes reported and not reported to the police. The Survey does not include homicide, arson, and commercial crimes.

Type of Data Collection Operation: Data collection conducted by the Census Bureau for the Bureau of Justice Statistics. Persons interviewed are asked about the number and characteristics of victimization experiences during the prior 6 months.

Data Collection and Imputation Procedures: For the 2013 NCVS, 160,040 persons age 12 and older in 90,630 households were interviewed; response rate was 88% for eligible persons and 84% for households. Eligible household members are interviewed every 6 months for a total of 7 interviews. Households stay in the sample for about 3 years. New households rotate into the sample on an ongoing basis. Personal interviews are used in the first interview; the intervening interviews are conducted by telephone whenever possible. Being a sample survey, the NCVS uses weights to inflate sample point estimates to known population totals and to compensate for survey nonresponse and other aspects of the sample design.

Estimates of Sampling Error: Standard of errors for 2013 victimization rates per 1,000 persons age 12 and older or 1,000 households, are: 1.6 for all violent crimes; 0.2 for rape/sexual assault; 0.3 for robbery; 1.4 for assault; 0.6 for domestic violence; 0.7 for all serious violent crimes; 0.2 for firearm violence; 2.9 for all property crimes; 1.1 for household burglary; 2.5 for theft; and 0.4 for motor vehicle theft.

Nonsampling Errors: Respondent recall errors may include reporting incidents for other than the reference period; interviewer coding and processing errors; and possible mistaken reporting or classifying of events.

Sources of Additional Material: U.S. Bureau of Justice Statistics, *Criminal Victimization in the United States, 2013,* September 2014.

U.S. BUREAU OF LABOR STATISTICS

Consumer Expenditure Survey (CES)

Universe, Frequency and Types of Data: Consists of two continuous components: a quarterly interview survey and a weekly diary survey. These nationwide surveys collect data on consumer expenditures, income, characteristics, and assets and liabilities. Samples are national probability samples of households that are representative of the civilian noninstitutional population. The surveys have been ongoing since 1980.

Type of Data Collection Operation: The Interview Survey is a panel rotation survey. Each panel is interviewed for five quarters and then dropped from the survey. About 7,000 consumer units provide usable interviews each quarter. The Diary Survey sample is new each year and consists of about 7,000 consumer units. Data are collected on an ongoing basis in 91 PSUs.

Data Collection and Imputation Procedures: For the Interview Survey, data are collected by personal interview with each consumer unit interviewed once per quarter for five consecutive quarters. The Interview Survey is designed to collect information that respondents can recall for 3 months or longer, such as large or recurring expenditures. For the Diary Survey, respondents record all their expenditures in a self-reporting diary for two consecutive 1-week periods. The Diary Survey is designed to pick up small, frequently purchased items which can be difficult to recall over a long period of time. These items include food, beverages, and household and personal care products and services. Missing or invalid attributes, expenditures, or incomes are imputed. Assets and liabilities are not imputed. The U.S. Census Bureau collects the data for the Bureau of Labor Statistics.

Estimates of Sampling Error: Beginning with the release of 2012 data, separate standard error tables are no longer issued; standard errors are included in the combined expenditure, share, and standard error tables.

Nonsampling Errors: Includes differences in the interpretation of questions, inability or unwillingness of respondents to provide correct information, and data processing errors. They occur regardless of whether data are collected from a sample or from the entire population.

Sources of Additional Material: Bureau of Labor Statistics, <http://www.bls.gov/cex>; and "BLS Handbook of Methods," Chapter 16, <http://www.bls.gov/opub/hom/pdf/homch16.pdf>.

Consumer Price Index (CPI)

Universe, Frequency, and Types of Data: A monthly survey of price changes of all types of consumer goods and services purchased by urban wage earners and clerical workers prior to 1978, and urban consumers thereafter. Both indexes continue to be published. The BLS calculates CPI indexes for 38 geographic areas across the U.S., and for 211 item categories called item strata, which cover all consumer purchases.

Type of Data Collection Operation: Prior to 1978, and since 1998, sample of various consumer items in 87 urban areas; from 1978-1997, in 85 PSUs, except from January 1987 through March 1988, when 91 areas were sampled.

Data Collection and Imputation Procedures: For 2014, the BLS collected monthly prices for a sample of approximately 80,900 commodities and services in approximately 23,700 outlets. The BLS also collected approximately 6,100 rents each month. Prices of food, fuel, and a few other items are obtained monthly; prices of most other commodities and services are collected every month in the three largest geographic areas and every other month in others. Imputation is a procedure for handling missing information. The CPI uses imputation for a number of cases, including refusals, inability to collect data for some other reason (the item may be out of season), and the inability to make a satisfactory estimate of the quality change. For noncomparable substitutions, an estimate of constant-quality price change is made by imputation.

Estimates of Sampling Error: BLS annually calculates and publishes variance estimates of the 1-month, 2-month, 6-month and 12-month percent changes in the CPI-U. The standard error is the square root of the variance. The CPI may contain sampling error due to the fact that the CPI is estimated from a sample of consumer purchases; it is not a complete measure of price change. For the latest data, including information on how to use the estimates of standard error, see "Variance Estimates for Price Changes in the Consumer Price Index, January-December 2014." Information is available online through the CPI home page at <http://www.bls.gov/cpi>, or <http://www.bls.gov/cpi/cpivar2014.pdf>.

Nonsampling Errors: Errors result from omitting part of a target population or including units outside of the target population, inaccurate or incomplete reporting, difficulties in defining concepts and their operational implementation, and introduction of product quality changes and new products.

Sources of Additional Material: U.S. Bureau of Labor Statistics, <http://www.bls.gov/cpi/home.htm>; and "BLS Handbook of Methods," Chapter 17, <http://www.bls.gov/opub/hom/pdf/homch17.pdf>.

Current Employment Statistics (CES) Program

Universe, Frequency, and Types of Data: Monthly survey of approximately 143,000 businesses and government agencies representing approximately 588,000 worksites throughout the U.S., clustered by unemployment insurance account number. Sample is updated annually. A semiannual update is performed each summer to select units from the population of business openings and other units not previously eligible for the selection. The CES collects data on employment, hours, and earnings at detailed industry levels. The CES series are estimates of nonfarm wage and salary jobs, not of employed persons; an individual with 2 jobs is counted twice by the payroll survey. The CES excludes employees in agriculture and private households, and the self-employed.

Type of Data Collection Operation: The BLS uses various collection techniques. Data collection centers (DCCs) perform initial enrollment of each firm via telephone, collect the data for several months via Computer Assisted Telephone Interviewing (CATI), and, where possible, transfer respondents to a self-reporting mode such as touch-tone data entry (TDE), Fax, or Internet collection. Very large, multi-establishment firms are often enrolled via personal visit, and ongoing reporting is established via electronic data interchange (EDI). These firms provide electronic files to BLS that include data from all their worksites. All firms with 1,000 or more employees are asked to participate in the survey, as is a sample of firms across all employment sizes. When firms are rotated into the sample, they are retained for 2 years or more. When a respondent is rotated out of the sample, BLS will not ask the firm to participate for at least 3 years. Approximately 60 percent of the CES sample for the private industries overlaps from the previous sample to the current year sample.

Data Collection and Imputation Procedures: Each month, respondents extract the employment, hours, and earnings data from their payroll records and submit it to the BLS. Data are collected for the pay period that includes the 12th of each month.

BLS staff prepare national estimates of employment, hours, and earnings. State agencies cooperate with the BLS to develop state and metropolitan area estimates.

Estimates of Sampling Errors: The magnitude of sampling error, or variance, is directly related to the size of the sample and the percentage of universe coverage achieved by the sample. The establishment survey sample covers over one-third of total universe employment; this yields a relatively small variance on the total nonfarm estimates.

Nonsampling Errors: Estimates of employment adjusted annually to reflect complete universe. Average adjustment is 0.3 percent over the last decade, with an absolute range from than 0.1 percent to 0.7 percent.

Sources of Additional Material: U.S. Bureau of Labor Statistics, "BLS Handbook of Methods," Chapter 2, <http://www.bls.gov/opub/hom/homch2.htm>; and Current Employment Statistics, "Technical Notes," <http://www.bls.gov/web/empsit/cestn.htm>.

National Compensation Survey (NCS)

Universe, Frequency, and Types of Data: NCS collects data on occupational earnings, employment costs trends, and prevalence of employee benefits, with an emphasis on health insurance and retirement benefits. The NCS includes establishments in private industry and in state and local government; major exclusions are workers in federal and quasi-federal agencies, military personnel, agricultural workers, workers in private households, the self-employed, and unpaid workers. The NCS produces information on workers' earnings and benefits in a variety of occupations at different work levels. NCS is responsible for two quarterly releases: the Employment Cost Index (ECI), which measures percent changes in the cost of employment, and the Employer Costs for Employee Compensation (ECEC), which measures costs per hour worked for individual benefits. The survey provides data by industry, occupational group, bargaining status, metropolitan area status, census region, and census division. ECEC also provides data by establishment-size class. Incidence and detailed provisions of employee benefit plans in private establishments are issued for broad occupational groups and selected industries, by establishment employment size, census division, and selected worker characteristics.

Type of Data Collection Operation: The sample of establishments is drawn by dividing the sample by industry and ownership. Number of establishments and occupations covered are reported monthly in NCS news releases. Each sample establishment is selected using a method of sampling called probability proportional to employment size. A probability sample of occupations within a sampled establishment is performed using a method called probability selection of occupations. The methodology and procedures used to estimate vary by product line. NCS replaces its sample on a continual basis. Private industry establishments are in the survey for approximately 5 years, with one fifth of the sample rotating out and replaced by a new panel each year.

Data Collection and Imputation Procedures: A personal visit to the establishment is the initial source for collecting data. Communication via mail, fax, and telephone provide quarterly updates. Imputation is done for individual benefits. To address the problems of nonresponse and missing data, the NCS adjusts the weights of the remaining establishments and imputes missing values; missing values for an initially responding establishment are replaced by values from the original interview; missing values for an item are replaced by values derived from establishments with similar characteristics.

Estimates of Sampling Error: NCS uses standard errors to evaluate published series. These standard errors are available at <http://www.bls.gov/ncs/ect/home.htm>.

Nonsampling Errors: Nonsampling errors have a number of potential sources. The primary sources are (1) survey nonresponse and (2) data collection and processing errors. Nonsampling errors are not measured. Quality assurance programs reduces the potential for nonsampling errors. These programs include the use of reinterviews, interview observations, validating data, and the systematic professional review of data. The programs also serve as a training device that provides feedback on errors for field economists (or data collectors). Quality assurance programs also provide information on sources of error. This information is used to improve procedures that result in fewer errors.

Sources of Additional Material: Bureau of Labor Statistics, "BLS Handbook of Methods," Chapter 8, see <http://www.bls.gov/opub/hom//pdf/homch8.pdf>.

Producer Price Index (PPI)

Universe, Frequency, and Types of Data: Monthly survey of producing companies to determine price changes of all commodities and services produced in the United States for sale in commercial transactions. Price changes are from the perspective of the seller. Data on agriculture, forestry, fishing, manufacturing, mining, natural gas, electricity, construction, public utilities, wholesale trade, retail trade, transportation, healthcare, and other services. Domestic production of goods for the military is included, as are goods shipped between establishments owned by the same company. The PPI program covers approximately 72 percent of the service sector's output as measured by revenue reported in the 2007 Economic Census. The BLS releases each month about 10,000 PPIs for individual products and groups of products.

Type of Data Collection Operation: PPIs are based on selling prices reported by establishments of all sizes selected by probability sampling, with the probability of selection proportionate to size. Individual items and transaction terms from these firms also are chosen by probability proportionate to size. BLS periodically updates the PPI sample of survey respondents to better reflect current conditions when the structure, membership, technology, or product mix of an industry shifts significantly and to spread reporting burden among smaller firms. Results of these resampling efforts are incorporated into the PPI with the release of data for January and July. More than 100,000 price quotations per month are organized into three sets of PPIs: (1) Final demand-Intermediate demand (FD-ID) indexes, (2) commodity indexes, and (3)

indexes for the net output of industries and their products. The FD-ID structure organizes products by class of buyer and degree of fabrication, as well as by stage of production. The commodity structure organizes products by similarity of end use or product type. The entire output of various industries is sampled to derive price indexes for the net output of industries and their products.

Data Collection and Imputation Procedures: BLS strongly encourages cooperating companies to supply actual transaction prices at the time of shipment to minimize the use of list prices. Prices submitted by survey respondents are effective on the Tuesday of the week containing the 13th day of the month. This survey is conducted via mail, facsimile, and the Internet. Each month approximately 100,000 prices are collected from 25,000 reporters. Missing prices are estimated by those received for similar products or services. The current standard base period for most commodity-oriented PPI series is 1982, but many indexes that began after 1982 are based on the month of their introduction. The FD-ID indexes typically have a reference base of November 2009 = 100. All unadjusted PPIs are routinely subject to revision only once, 4 months after their original publication, to reflect late reports and corrections by company respondents. Once revised, indexes are considered final.

Estimates of Sampling Error: Not applicable.

Nonsampling Errors: Not available at present.

Sources of Additional Material: U.S. Bureau of Labor Statistics, PPI methodology, <http://www.bls.gov/ppi/methodology.htm>; and "BLS Handbook of Methods," Chapter 14, <http://stats.bls.gov/opub/hom/homch14.htm>.

BOARD OF GOVERNORS OF THE FEDERAL RESERVE SYSTEM

Survey of Consumer Finances

Universe, Frequency, and Types of Data: Triennial sample survey of families. In this survey a given household is divided into a primary economic unit and other economic units. The primary economic unit, which may be a single individual, is generally chosen as the person or couple who either holds the title to the home or is listed on the lease, along with all other people in the household who are financially interdependent with that person or couple. The primary economic unit is used as the reference family. The survey collects detailed data on the composition of family balance sheets, pensions, income, the terms of loans, and relationships with financial institutions. It also gathers information on the employment history and pension rights of the survey respondent and the spouse or partner of the respondent.

Type of Data Collection Operation: The survey employs a two-part strategy for sampling families. Some families are selected by standard multistage area probability sampling methods applied to all 50 states. The remaining families in the survey are selected using statistical records derived from tax returns, under the strict rules governing confidentiality and the rights of potential respondents to refuse participation; this sample is designed to oversample wealthy households. For the 2013 Survey of Consumer Finances, 6,026 interviews were completed: 4,568 from the area probability sample, and 1,458 from the list sample. Response rates for the area-probability sample was about 70 percent and for the list sample about 33 percent.

Data Collection and Imputation Procedures: National Opinion Research Center (NORC) at the University of Chicago has collected data for the survey since 1992. The majority of interviews for SCF 2013 were conducted in person. Since 1995, interviews are conducted via telephone if more convenient for respondents. Interviews were computer-assisted. Adjustments for nonresponse are made through multiple imputation of unanswered questions and through weighting adjustments based on data used in the sample design for families that refused participation.

Estimates of Sampling Error: The SCF attempts to reduce sampling error by designing the sample to reduce important sources of variability. Sampling error is estimated using replication methods. Replication methods draw samples, called replicates, from the set of actual respondents, and compute weights for all cases in each of the replicates.

Nonsampling Errors: Proper training and monitoring of interviewers, careful design of questionnaires, and systematic editing of the resulting data were used to control inaccurate survey responses.

Sources of Additional Material: Board of Governors of the Federal Reserve System, "Changes in U.S. Family Finances from 2010 to 2013: Evidence from the Survey of Consumer Finances," *Federal Reserve Bulletin*, September 2014, <http://www.federalreserve.gov/Pubs/Bulletin>.

U.S. CENSUS BUREAU

2012 Economic Census

Universe, Frequency, and Types of Data: Conducted every 5 years to obtain data on number of establishments, number of employees, payroll, total sales/receipts/revenue, and other industry-specific statistics. The universe is all establishments with paid employees excluding agriculture, forestry, fishing and hunting, and government. (Non-employer Statistics, discussed separately, covers those establishments without paid employees.) For the 2012 Economic Census, 3.9 million businesses received economic census forms. See also <http://www.census.gov/econ/census/about/history.html>

The 2007 Economic Census used a cutoff of 5,000 or more population or jobs to identify the economic places valid for publication. The 2012 Economic Census reduced the cutoff to 2,500 resulting in nearly 5,000 new places to be published in the Census.

Type of Data Collection Operation: For most economic census sectors and programs, all large- and medium-size firms and all multi-establishment firms were sent report forms to be completed for each of their establishments. For most sectors and programs, report forms were also mailed to a sample of small employers (those with paid employees). This sample consists of single-establishment firms with payroll below a specified cut off. The cut off and sampling rate varies by economic census sector, industry, and

geography. Data for firms with no paid employees were obtained from administrative records of other federal agencies.

Data Collection and Imputation Procedures: Mail questionnaires were used with both mail and telephone follow-ups for nonrespondents. Businesses also had the option to respond electronically. Data for nonrespondents and for small employer firms not mailed a questionnaire were obtained from administrative records of other federal agencies, or imputed.

Estimates of Sampling Error: No measures of sampling variability are provided for sample-based estimates derived from the economic census, except for the construction sector. For additional information about sampling errors, see the methodology text for the sector of interest. Estimates of sampling error for construction industries are included with the data as published on the Census Bureau Web site.

Nonsampling Errors: Nonsampling errors may be attributed to an inability to identify all cases in the actual universe; definition and classification difficulties; differences in interpretation of questions; errors in recording or coding data; and other errors of collection, response, coverage, processing, and estimation for missing or misreported data.

Sources of Additional Material: U.S. Census Bureau, see <http://www.census.gov/econ/census>.

American Community Survey (ACS)

Universe, Frequency, and Types of Data: Nationwide survey of approximately 3.54 million households per year, to obtain data about demographic, social, economic, and housing characteristics of housing units and the people residing in them. It covers the household population and, beginning in 2006, also includes the group quarter population living in correctional facilities, skilled-nursing homes, military barracks, college residence halls, and other group quarters.

Type of Data Collection Operation: Housing unit address sampling is performed twice a year in both August and January. First-phase of sampling defines the universe for the second stage of sampling through two steps. First, all addresses that were eligible for the second-phase sampling within the past four years are excluded from eligibility.

This ensures that no address is in sample more than once in any 5-year period. The second step is to select a 20 percent systematic sample of "new" units, i.e. those units that have never appeared on a previous Master Address File (MAF) extract. All new addresses are systematically assigned to either the current year or to one of four back-samples. This procedure maintains five equal partitions of the universe. The second-phase sampling is done on the current year's partition and results in approximately 3,540,000 housing unit addresses in the U.S. and 36,000 in Puerto Rico (PR). **Group quarter sampling** is performed separately from the housing unit sampling. The sampling begins with separating the small (15 persons or fewer) and the large (more than 15 persons) group quarters. The target sampling rate for both groups is a 2.5% sample of the group quarters population. It results in approximately 195,000 group quarter residents being selected.

Data Collection and Imputation Procedures: The American Community Survey is conducted every month on independent samples. The data collection operation for housing units (HUs) consists of four modes: Internet, mail, telephone, and personal visit. For most housing units, the first phase includes a mailed request to respond by Internet, followed later by an option to complete a paper questionnaire and return it by mail. If no response is received by mail or Internet, the Census Bureau follows up with computer-assisted telephone interviewing (CATI) when a telephone number is available. If the Census Bureau is unable to reach an occupant using CATI, or if the household refuses to participate, the address may be selected for computer-assisted personal interviewing (CAPI). Mailable addresses with neither a response to the mailout nor a telephone interview are sampled at a rate of 1 in 2, 2 in 5, or 1 in 3 based on the expected rate of completed interviews at the tract level. Unmailable addresses are sampled at a rate of 2 in 3. Those addresses selected through this process are assigned to Field Representatives (FRs), who visit the addresses, verify their existence, determine their occupancy status, and conduct interviews. **Collection of group quarters** data is conducted primarily through FR interviews. Their methods include completing the questionnaire while speaking to the resident in person or over the telephone, or leaving paper questionnaires for residents to complete for themselves and then pick them up later. This last option is used for data collection in federal prisons. If needed, a personal interview can be conducted with a proxy, such as a relative or guardian. After data collection is completed, any remaining incomplete or inconsistent information on the questionnaire are imputed during the final automated edit of the collected data.

Estimates of Sampling Error: The data in the ACS products are estimates and can vary from the actual values that would have been obtained by conducting a census of the entire population. The estimates from the chosen sample addresses can also vary from those that would have been obtained from a different set of addresses. This variation causes uncertainty, which can be measured using statistics such as standard error, margin of error, and confidence interval. All ACS estimates are accompanied by margin of errors to assist users.

Nonsampling Errors: Other types of errors may occur during any of the various complex operations used to select, collect and process survey data. An important goal of the ACS is to minimize the amount of nonsampling error introduced through coverage issues in the sample list, nonresponse from sample housing units, and transcribing or editing data. One way of accomplishing this is by finding additional sources of addresses, following up on nonrespondents and maintaining quality control systems.

Sources of Additional Material: U.S. Census Bureau, American Community Survey, <http://www.census. gov/programs-surveys/acs/>; U.S. Census Bureau, American Community Survey Accuracy of the Data documents available on the Internet, <http://www.census.gov/programs-surveys/acs/ methodology.html>.

American Housing Survey

Universe, Frequency, and Types of Data: Conducted biennially in odd numbered years, to obtain data on occupied or vacant housing units in the United States (group quarters are excluded). Data include characteristics of occupied housing units, vacant units, new housing and mobile home units, financial characteristics, recent mover households, housing and neighborhood quality indicators, and energy characteristics. The AHS 2013 sample includes approximately 84,400 housing units, which includes a separate metropolitan area sample covering 25 metro areas, and an additional 5,300 subsidized housing units. The total includes 2,715 ineligible units and about 10,000 units that did not produce interviews. Overall response rate is 86 percent, and the weighted overall response rate is 85 percent. The sample covered 394 primary sampling units (878 counties and cities in all States and DC).

Type of Data Collection Operation: Census Bureau interviewers visit or telephone the household occupying each housing unit in the sample. For unoccupied units, they obtain information from landlords, rental agents, or neighbors.

Data Collection and Imputation Procedures: Housing units participating in the AHS are scientifically selected to represent a cross section of all housing in the nation. The same basic sample of housing units is interviewed every two years until a new sample is selected. The U.S. Census Bureau updates the sample by adding newly constructed housing units and units discovered through coverage improvement efforts. Each housing unit in the AHS national sample is weighted and represents about 2,000 housing units in the United States. The 2013 AHS basic weight is 2,148.

Estimates of Sampling Error: Most numbers from the AHS are counts of housing units (for example, units with basements or units with an elderly person). These counts have error from sampling. As with the other types of errors, readers should be wary of numbers with large errors from sampling. For the national sample, illustrations of the Standard Error (SE) of the estimates are provided in the Appendix D of the 2013 report.

Nonsampling Errors: These may result from incorrect or incomplete responses, errors in coding and recording, and processing errors. Appendix D of the 2013 report has a complete discussion of the errors.

Sources of Additional Material: U.S. Census Bureau, *American Housing Survey, Methodology and other Technical Documentation,* <http://www.census.gov /programs-surveys/ahs/>.

Annual Survey of Public Employment and Payroll, and Census of Governments

Universe, Frequency, and Types of Data: The survey is conducted annually except in years ending in '2' and '7', when a census of all state and local governments is done. Covers the civilian employees of all the Federal Government agencies (except the Central Intelligence Agency, the National Security Agency, and the Defense Intelligence Agency), all agencies of the 50 state governments, and about 90,690 local governments (i.e., counties, municipalities, townships, special districts, and school districts) including the District of Columbia. The survey measures the number of state, local and federal civilian government employees and their gross payrolls for the pay period including March 12. The survey provides state and local government data on full-time and part-time employment, part-time hours worked, full-time equivalent employment, and payroll statistics by governmental function. The survey provides Federal Government data on total employees, full-time employees, and total March payroll by governmental function. Overall response rate for the 2013 Census of Governments was 81.4 percent. All 50 state governments responded to the survey.

Type of Data Collection Operations: Census Bureau staff compiled Federal Government data from records of the U.S. Office of Personnel Management. Forty-six of the state governments provided data from central payroll records for all or most of their agencies/institutions. Data for agencies and institutions for the remaining state governments were obtained by mail canvass questionnaires. Local governments were also canvassed using a mail questionnaire. However, elementary and secondary school system data in Delaware, Florida, and North Dakota were supplied by special arrangements with the state education agency in each of these states. All respondents receiving the mail questionnaire had the option of completing the survey using a web-based survey instrument developed for reporting the data. The online survey instrument was completed by 24.2% of the state-level responding units and 72.9% of the local government respondents.

Editing and Imputation Procedures: Editing is a process that ensures survey data are accurate, complete, and consistent. Efforts are made at all phases of collection, processing, and tabulation to minimize errors. Although some edits are built into the Internet data collection instrument and the data entry programs, the majority of the edits are performed after the case has been loaded into the Census Bureau's database. Edits consist primarily of two types: consistency and a ratio of the current years reported value to the prior year's value. The consistency edits check the logical relationships of data items reported on the form. For example, if part-time employees and payroll are reported then part-time hours must be reported. The current year/prior year edits compare data for the number of employees, the function reported for the employees, and the average salary between reporting years. If data fall outside of acceptable tolerance levels, the item is flagged for review. Some additional checks are made comparing data from the Annual Finance Survey to data reported on the Annual Survey of Public Employment and Payroll to verify that employees reported on the Annual Survey of Public Employment and Payroll at a particular function have a corresponding expenditure on the Finance Survey. For both types of edits, the edit results are reviewed by analysts and adjusted when needed. When the analyst is unable to resolve or accept the edit failure, contact is made with the respondent to verify or correct the reported data.

Imputation: For general purpose governments and for schools, imputations were based on recent historical data from either a prior year annual survey or the most recent Census of Governments, as available. These data were adjusted by a growth rate that was determined by the growth of units that were similar (in size, geography, and type of government) to the nonrespondent. If no recent historical data were available, imputations were based on the data from a randomly selected donor

that was similar to the nonrespondent. This donor's data were adjusted by dividing each data item by the population (or enrollment) of the donor and multiplying the result by the nonrespondent's population (or enrollment). For special districts, if prior year data are available, the data are brought forward with a national level growth rate applied. Otherwise, the data are imputed to be zero. In cases where good secondary data sources exist, the data from those sources were used.

Estimates of Sampling Error: For intercensal surveys, estimated coefficients of variation for all variables are given in tabulations on the Web site. For U.S. and state-and-local government-level estimates of total full-time equivalents and total payroll, most relative standard errors are generally less than 1 percent, but vary considerably for detailed characteristics.

Nonsampling Errors: Sample data are subject to nonsampling errors such as inability to obtain data for every variable from all units in the sample, inaccuracies in classification, response errors, misinterpretation of questions, mistakes in keying and coding, and coverage errors. These same errors may be evident in census collections and may affect the Census of Governments data used to adjust the sample during the estimation phase and used in the imputation process.

Sources of Additional Material: Census Bureau, Government Employment and Payroll, <http://www.census.gov/govs/apes/about_the_survey.html> and <http://www.census.gov/govs/apes/how_data_collected.html>.

Annual Survey of State and Local Government Finances

Universe, Frequency, and Types of Data: In the years ending in "2" and "7," the Census Bureau conducts a census of the entire universe of all 50 state governments and 89,004 local governments (counties, municipalities, townships, special districts, and school districts). In intervening years, the Bureau conducts and an annual survey of a sample of state and local governments. The survey collects data on government revenue (including taxes, charges, interest, and other earnings), expenditures by function and accounting category, debt, and financial assets by type.

Type of Data Collection Operations: Data for the annual survey were collected via mail canvass, Internet, and central collection from State sources. In 28 states, all or part of the general purpose finance data for local governments were obtained from cooperative arrangements between the Census Bureau and a state government agency. These usually involved a data collection effort carried out to meet the needs of both agencies: the state agency for purposes of audit, oversight, or information, and the Census Bureau for statistical purposes. Data for the balance of local governments in this annual survey were obtained via mail questionnaires sent to county, municipal, township, special district, and school district governments. School district data were collected via cooperative arrangements with state education agencies. Data for state governments were compiled by analysts of the Census Bureau, usually with the cooperation and assistance of state officials. The data were compiled from state government audits, budgets, and other financial reports, either in printed or electronic format. The compilation generally involved recasting the state financial records into the classification categories used for reporting by the Census Bureau.

Data Collection and Imputation Procedures: Survey is conducted by mail with mail follow-ups of nonrespondents. All governments had the option of submitting responses via the Internet. Imputation for all nonresponse items is based on previous year reports or, for governments without historical data, data from a randomly selected similar unit are adjusted by the ratio of the populations of the nonresponding and the randomly selected donor governments. The overall unit response rate of the 2013 Annual Survey of Local Government Finances was 91.1 percent. The overall unit response rate of the 2013 Annual Survey of State Government Finances was 100.0 percent.

Estimates of Sampling Error: The local government statistics in the intercensal survey years are developed from a sample survey. Therefore, the local totals, as well as aggregates of state and local government data, are considered estimated amounts subject to sampling error. State government finance data are not subject to sampling. Consequently, state-local aggregates shown here have a relative standard error less than or equal to the local government estimates they include. Estimates of major United States totals for local governments are subject to a computed sampling variability of less than one-half of 1 percent. State and local government totals are generally subject to sampling variability of less than 3 percent. The coefficient of variations are available from the source tables, and can be used to derive the standard error of the estimates.

Nonsampling Errors: The estimates are also subject to inaccuracies in classification, response, and processing. Efforts were made at all phases of collection, processing, and tabulation to minimize errors. Data are also subject to errors from imputations for missing data, errors from misreported data, errors from miscoding, and difficulties in identifying every unit that should be included in the report. Every effort was made to keep such errors to a minimum through examining, editing, and tabulating the data reported by government officials. For more information, see <http://www.census.gov/govs/local/data_processing_2013.html>.

Sources of Additional Material: Census Bureau, State and Local Government Finances, <http://www.census.gov/govs/local/how_data_collected.html>.

Annual Survey of Manufactures (ASM)

Universe, Frequency, and Types of Data: The Annual Survey of Manufactures is a sample survey conducted annually, except for years ending in '2' and '7,' for all manufacturing establishments having one or more paid employees. Survey includes approximately 50,000 establishments selected from a universe of approximately 297,000 manufacturing establishments within North American Industry Classification System (NAICS) codes 31-33 with records in the 2012 Economic Census. The unit response rate for the current ASM cycle is about 72 percent. The purpose of the ASM is to provide key intercensal measures of manufacturing activity, products, and location for

the public and private sectors. The ASM provides statistics on employment, payroll, worker hours, payroll supplements, cost of materials, value added by manufacturing, capital expenditures, inventories, and energy consumption. It also provides estimates of value of shipments for 1,384 seven-digit NAICS product classes.

Type of Data Collection Operation: The ASM surveys approximately 50,000 establishments; about 15,600 establishments are selected with certainty, and the remaining establishments are selected with probability proportional to a composite measure of establishment size. The sample universe is updated from two sources: Internal Revenue Service administrative records are used to include new single-unit manufacturers and the Company Organization Survey identifies new establishments of multiunit forms.

Data Collection and Imputation Procedures: Survey is conducted by mail with telephone and mail follow-ups of nonrespondents. Imputation (for all nonresponse items) is based on previous year reports, or for new establishments in survey, on industry averages.

Estimates of Sampling Error: Statistics for the industry groups and industries, and product shipments include estimated relative standard errors. Relative standard errors vary by industry and product category.

Nonsampling Errors: Includes errors due to collection, reporting, and transcription errors, many of which are corrected through computer and clerical checks.

Sources of Additional Material: Census Bureau, Annual Survey of Manufactures, "How the Data are Collected," <http://www.census.gov/manufacturing/asm/index.html>.

Census of Population and Housing

Universe, Frequency, and Types of Data: Complete count of U.S. population conducted every 10 years since 1790. Data obtained on number and characteristics of people in the United States, U.S. outlying territories and Federally affiliated Americans overseas.

Type of Data Collection Operation: In the 1990, 2000, and 2010 censuses the 100 percent items included: age, date of birth, sex, race, Hispanic origin, and relationship to householder. In 1980, approximately 19 percent of the housing units were included in the sample; in 1990 and 2000, approximately 17 percent.

Data Collection and Imputation Procedures: In 1980, 1990, 2000, and 2010 mail questionnaires were used extensively with personal interviews in the remainder. Extensive telephone and personal follow-up for nonrespondents was done in the censuses. Imputations were made by using reported data for a person or housing unit with similar characteristics.

Estimates of Sampling Error: Sampling errors for data are estimated for all items collected by sample and vary by characteristic and geographic area. The coefficients of variation (CVs) for national and state estimates are generally very small.

Nonsampling Errors: Since 1950, evaluation programs have been conducted to provide information on the magnitude of some sources of nonsampling errors such as response bias and undercoverage in each census. Results from the evaluation program for the 1990 census indicated that the estimated net undercoverage amounted to about 1.61 percent of the total resident population. Census 2000 had a national overcount of 0.49 percent (0.20 percent standard error) for the household population. For the 2010 Census, the Census Coverage Measurement Program found a net overcount of 0.01 percent (0.14 percent standard error) of the resident population.

Sources of Additional Material: U.S. Census Bureau, The Coverage of Population in the 1980 Census, PHC80-E4; *Content Reinterview Study: Accuracy of Data for Selected Population and Housing Characteristics as Measured by Reinterview*, PHC80-E2; *1980 Census of Population*, Vol. 1, (PC80-1), Appendixes B, C, and D. *Content Reinterview Survey: Accuracy of Data for Selected Population and Housing Characteristics as Measured by Reinterview*, 1990, CPH-E-1; *Effectiveness of Quality Assurance, CPH-E-2; Programs to Improve Coverage in the 1990 Census*, 1990, CPH-E-3. Documentation regarding the 2010 Census is available at <http://www.census.gov/2010census/news/press-kits/ccm/ccm.html>.

County Business Patterns

Universe, Frequency, and Types of Data: County Business Patterns is an annual tabulation of basic data items extracted from the Business Register, a file of all known single- and multi-location employer companies maintained and updated by the U.S. Census Bureau. Data include number of establishments, number of employees, first quarter and annual payrolls, and number of establishments by employment size class. Data are excluded for self-employed individuals, private households, railroad employees, agricultural production workers, and most government employees.

Type of Data Collection Operation: The annual Company Organization Survey and the Economic Census provide individual establishment data for multilocation companies. Data for single establishment companies are obtained from various Census Bureau programs, such as the Annual Survey of Manufactures and Current Business Surveys, as well as from administrative records of the Internal Revenue Service, the Social Security Administration, and the Bureau of Labor Statistics.

Estimates of Sampling Error: Payroll and employment data are not subject to sampling error.

Nonsampling Errors: The data are subject to nonsampling errors, such as inability to identify all cases in the universe; definition and classification difficulties; differences in interpretation of questions; errors in recording or coding the data obtained; and estimation of employers who reported too late to be included in the tabulations and for records with missing or misreported data. Employment data are missing from approximately 12 percent of incoming administrative payroll records. For these records, employment is imputed as the average employment of the two adjacent quarters, using average wage data for the prior year, or, based on average wage for the industry and geographic area. Payroll data is imputed for less than 1 percent of all incoming administrative records. Other missing data are also imputed through various methods.

Sources of Additional Material: U. S. Census Bureau, County Business Patterns, <http://www.census.gov/econ/cbp/index.html> and <http://www.census.gov/econ/cbp/methodology.htm>.

Current Population Survey (CPS)

Universe, Frequency, and Types of Data: Nationwide monthly sample designed primarily to produce national and state estimates of labor force and other characteristics of the civilian noninstitutionalized population 16 years of age and older, including sex, age, race, marital status, educational attainment, and family structure. In addition to the monthly survey, each March the CPS produces the Annual Social and Economic (ASEC) Supplement, which contains the basic monthly demographic and labor force data covered by the CPS, plus additional data on work experience, income, health insurance coverage, poverty, receipt of noncash benefits, and migration.

Type of Data Collection Operation: Multistage probability sample that currently includes 60,000 households from 824 sample areas. Sample size increased in some states to improve data reliability for those areas on an annual average basis. A continual sample rotation system is used. Households are in sample 4 months, out for 8 months, and in for 4 more. Month-to-month overlap is 75 percent; year-to-year overlap is 50 percent. The CPS questionnaire is a completely computerized document that is administered by Census Bureau field representatives across the country through both personal and telephone interviews. Questions refer to respondent activities during the prior week.

Data Collection and Imputation Procedures: For first and fifth months that a household is in sample, personal interviews; other months, approximately 85 percent of the data collected by phone. The CPS makes imputations for missing and inconsistent data items. The CPS uses 3 imputation methods for item nonresponse: relational imputation, which infers the missing value from other characteristics on the person's record or within the household; longitudinal edits for most of the labor force edits, as appropriate; and "hot deck" allocation, a method of assigning a missing value from a record with similar characteristics, which is the hot deck. Hot decks are defined by variables such as age, race, and sex.

Estimates of Sampling Error: Sufficient sample is allocated to maintain, at most, a 1.9 percent coefficient of variation on national monthly estimates of unemployment, assuming a 6 percent unemployment rate. This translates into a change of 0.2 percentage point in the unemployment rate being significant at a 90 percent confidence level. For each of the 50 States and for the District of Columbia, the design maintains a coefficient of variation of at most 8 percent on the annual average estimate of unemployment, assuming a 6 percent unemployment rate.

Nonsampling Errors: Estimates of response bias on unemployment are available. Estimates of unemployment rate from reinterviews range from -2.4 percent to 1.0 percent of the basic CPS unemployment rate (over a 30-month span from January 2004 through June 2006). Eligible CPS households are approximately 82 percent of the assigned households, with a corresponding response rate of 92 percent.

Sources of Additional Material: U.S. Census Bureau and Bureau of Labor Statistics, *Current Population Survey: Design and Methodology*, (Technical Paper 66), available on the Internet <http://www.census.gov/prod/2006pubs/tp-66.pdf> and the Bureau of Labor Statistics, <http://www.bls.gov/cps/>; "BLS Handbook of Methods," Chapter 1, available on the Internet at <http://www.bls.gov/opub/hom/homch1_a.htm>; and <http://www.census.gov/cps/methodology/>.

Foreign Trade—Export Statistics

Universe, Frequency, and Types of Data: The export statistics consist of goods valued at more than $2,500 per commodity shipped by individuals and organizations (including exporters, freight forwarders, and carriers) from the U.S. to other countries. Data are compiled in terms of commodity classification, quantities, values, shipping weights, method of transportation (air or vessel), state of (movement) origin, customs district, customs port, country of destination, and whether contents are domestic goods or reexports. Data are continuously compiled and processed. Documents are collected as shipments depart, and processed on a flow basis. Reports summarize shipments made during calendar months, quarters, and years. Statistics are reported monthly approximately 40 to 45 days after the end of the calendar month and on a year-to-date basis.

Type of Data Collection Operation: Statistics for exported goods transactions are compiled from three sources: Shipper's Export Declaration documents filed with Customs and Border Protection (CBP) and sent to the U.S. Census Bureau (3 percent of all transactions), comparable data in electronic form submitted directly by exporters and their agents (63 percent), and special computer tapes from Canada for U.S. exports to Canada (34 percent). Estimates are made for low-value exports by country of destination, and based on bilateral trade patterns. Statistics for U.S. exports to Canada are based on import documents filed with Canadian agencies and forwarded to the U.S. Census Bureau under a 1987 data exchange agreement. Under this agreement, each country eliminated most cross-border export documents; maintains detailed statistics on cross-border imports; exchanges monthly files of cross-border import statistics; and publishes exchanged statistics in place of previously compiled export statistics.

Estimates of Sampling Error: Not applicable.

Nonsampling Errors: The goods data are a complete enumeration of EEI reported in AES and are not subject to sampling errors; but they are subject to several types of nonsampling errors. Quality assurance procedures are performed at every stage of collection, processing and tabulation; however the data are still subject to several types of nonsampling errors. The most significant of these include reporting errors, undocumented shipments, timeliness, data capture errors, and errors in the estimation of low-valued transactions.

Sources of Additional Material: Foreign Trade Statistics Overview, <http://www.census.gov/foreign-trade/about/index.html>.

Foreign Trade—Import Statistics

Universe, Frequency, and Types of Data: The import statistics consist of goods valued at more than $2,000 per commodity shipped by individuals and organizations (including importers and customs brokers) into the U.S. from other countries. Data are compiled in terms of commodity classification, quantities, values, shipping weights, methods of transportation (air or vessel), duties collected, unit prices, and market share, country of origin, customs district, customs port, import charges and duties. Data are continuously compiled and processed. Documents are collected as shipments arrive and processed on a flow basis. Reports summarize shipments made during calendar months and years. Statistics are reported monthly approximately 40 to 45 days after the end of the calendar month and on a year-to-date basis.

Type of Data Collection Operation: A full compilation (i.e., a census) is taken of import shipments, plus U.S. Census Bureau estimates of low-valued imports and BEA estimates of trade in services. Statistics for imported goods shipments are compiled from the records filed with Customs and Border Protection (CBP), usually within 10 days after the merchandise enters the United States. Estimates are made for low-value shipments by country of origin, based on previous bilateral trade patterns and periodically updated. Statistics for over 95 percent of all commodity transactions are compiled from records filed electronically with CBP and forwarded as computer tape files to the U.S. Census Bureau. Statistics for other transactions are compiled from hard-copy documents filed with CBP and forwarded on a flow basis for U.S. Census Bureau processing.

Estimates of Sampling Error: Not applicable.

Nonsampling Errors: The goods data are a complete enumeration of documents collected by the U.S. Customs and Border Protection and are not subject to sampling errors; but they are subject to several types of nonsampling errors. Quality assurance procedures are performed at every stage of collection, processing, and tabulation; however the data are still subject to several types of nonsampling errors. The most significant of these include reporting errors, undocumented shipments, timeliness, data capture errors, and errors in the estimation of low-valued transactions.

Sources of Additional Material: Foreign Trade Statistics Overview, <http://www.census.gov/foreign-trade/about/index.html>.

Monthly and Annual Retail Trade Survey

Universe, Frequency, and Types of Data: The size of the Monthly Retail Trade Survey (MRTS) sample is approximately 12,000 employer firms. Statistics are available at the national level only. The MRTS covers Retail Trade North American Industry Classification System (NAICS) sectors 44-45, including store and nonstore retailers; and Food Services NAICS subsector 722, including establishments preparing food and beverages for immediate on- and off-premises consumption. The Annual Retail Trade Survey (ARTS) covers employer businesses in the retail trade sector and the accommodation and food services sector, and requests data on sales, inventories, purchases, operating expenses, and other financial items.

Type of Data Collection Operation: Probability sample of all firms from a list frame. The list frame is the Bureau's Business Register updated quarterly for recent birth Employer Identification Numbers (EINs) issued by the Internal Revenue Service and assigned an industry classification by the Social Security

Administration. The largest firms are included monthly; a sample of others is included every month also. New samples were introduced with the 2011 Annual Retail Trade Survey (ARTS) and the April 2013 Monthly Retail Trade Survey (MRTS). These samples are designed to produce estimates based on the 2007 North American Industry Classification System (NAICS). The information used to create these sampling units was extracted from data collected as part of the 2007 Economic Census and from establishment records contained on the Census Bureau's Business Register as updated to December 2010.

Data Collection and Imputation Procedures: Data are collected by mail questionnaire with telephone follow-ups and fax reminders for nonrespondents. Imputation is made for each nonresponse item and each item failing edit checks. For both unit and item nonresponse, a missing value is replaced by a predicted value obtained from an appropriate model for nonresponse. This imputation uses survey data and administrative data as input. In any given month, imputed data amount to about 24.7 percent of the total monthly retail and food services sales estimate and about 30 percent of the total retail end-of-month inventory estimate. For the annual survey, imputed data amount to about 7.6 percent of the total retail sales and food services estimate and about 7.2 percent of the total retail end-of-year inventory estimate.

Estimates of Sampling Error: Estimated CVs and standard errors are included in monthly reports available on the Internet; see <http://www.census.gov/retail/index.html#mrts>.

Nonsampling Errors: Nonsampling errors are difficult to measure and can be attributed to many sources: the inclusion of erroneous units in the survey (overcoverage), the exclusion of eligible units from the survey (undercoverage), nonresponse, misreporting, mistakes in recording and coding responses, misinterpretation of questions, and other errors of collection, response, coverage, or processing. Although nonsampling error is not measured directly, the Census Bureau employs quality control procedures throughout the process to minimize this type of error.

Sources of Additional Material: Census Bureau, Monthly and Annual Retail Trade, <http://www.census.gov/retail/index.html> and <http://www.census.gov/retail/how_surveys_are_collected.html>.

Monthly Survey of Construction

Universe, Frequency, and Types of Data: Collects data for Census Bureau's New Residential Construction, New Residential Sales, and Characteristics of New Housing programs. Covers new, privately-owned residential buildings currently authorized by a building permit or started in areas not requiring a building permit. Data collected include start and completion dates, sales date, sales price (single-family houses only), and the physical characteristics of housing units. Survey data are available monthly and annually for housing starts since 1959, for new home sales since 1963, and for completions since 1968. Reported data are for building or sales activity taking place during the applicable reference period. Monthly data collection begins the first day after the reference month and continues through the 7th working day.

Type of Data Collection Operation: A multistage probability sample of approximately 900 of the 20,000 permit-issuing jurisdictions in the U.S. was selected. Each month in each of these permit offices, field representatives list and select a sample of permits for which to collect data. To obtain data in areas where building permits are not required, a multistage probability sample of over 70 land areas (census tracts or subsections of census tracts) was selected. All roads in these areas are canvassed and data are collected on all new residential construction found. Sampled buildings are followed up until they are completed (and sold, if for sale), or abandoned. Permits for one-to-four-unit buildings are sampled at an overall rate of 1 in 50. All permits authorizing buildings with 5 or more housing units in the sampled permit offices are selected.

Data Collection and Imputation Procedures: Data are obtained by telephone inquiry and/or field visit. Nonresponse/undercoverage adjustment factors are used to account for late reported data. Each month, housing starts, completions, and sales estimates derived from this survey are adjusted by the total numbers of authorized housing units (obtained from the Building Permits Survey) to develop national and regional estimates. Estimates are adjusted to reflect variations by region and type of construction, and to account for late reports and houses started or sold before a permit has been issued. Reported data are seasonally adjusted.

Estimates of Sampling Error: Data are subject to sampling errors. Estimates of the standard errors have been computed from the sample data for selected statistics. They are presented in the source tables in the form of average relative standard errors (RSEs). The relative standard error equals the standard error divided by the estimated value to which it refers.

Nonsampling Errors: Nonsampling errors are attributed to definitional problems, differences in interpretation of questions, incorrect reporting, inability to obtain information about all cases in the sample, and processing errors.

Sources of Additional Material: All data are available on the Internet at <http://www.census.gov/construction/nrc/>, and <http://www.census.gov/construction/nrs/>. Further documentation of the survey is also available at those sites.

Nonemployer Statistics

Universe, Frequency, and Types of Data: Nonemployer statistics are an annual tabulation of economic data by industry for active businesses without paid employees or payroll, that are subject to federal income taxes, and that have receipts of $1,000 or more ($1 or more for the construction sector). Excluded are corporations and partnerships with over $1 million in receipts (except for service-type industries, maximum is $2 million). Maximum receipts for sole proprietorships depends on industry classification. Data showing the number of firms and receipts by industry are available for the U.S., states, counties, and metropolitan areas. Most types of businesses covered by the Census Bureau's economic statistics programs are included in the nonemployer statistics. Tax-exempt and agricultural-production businesses are excluded from nonemployer statistics.

Type of Data Collection Operation: The universe of nonemployer firms is created annually as a byproduct of the Census Bureau's Business Register processing for employer establishments. If a business is active but without paid employees, then it becomes part of the potential nonemployer universe. Industry classification and receipts are available for each potential nonemployer business. These data are obtained primarily from the annual business income tax returns of the Internal Revenue Service (IRS). The potential nonemployer universe undergoes a series of complex processing, editing, and analytical review procedures at the Census Bureau to distinguish nonemployers from employers, and to correct and complete data items used in creating the data tables.

Estimates of Sampling Error: Data are tabulated from administrative records, and are not subject to sampling error.

Nonsampling Errors: The data are subject to nonsampling errors, such as inability to identify all cases that should be included, difficulties with definitions and classification, errors in recording or coding data, and other coverage and processing errors. The improper inclusion of possible employer establishments in the nonemployer universe is a primary source of nonsampling error. The Census Bureau takes several steps to identify and remove these establishments from the nonemployer universe.

Sources of Additional Material: U. S. Census Bureau, Nonemployer Statistics, <http://www.census.gov/econ/nonemployer/index.html>.

Service Annual Survey

Universe, Frequency, and Types of Data: The U.S. Census Bureau conducts the Service Annual Survey (SAS) to provide nationwide estimates of revenues and expenses for selected service industries. Estimates are summarized by industry classification based on the 2007 North American Industry Classification System (NAICS). The SAS was expanded in 2009. Selected service industries covered by the Service Annual Survey include all or part of the following NAICS sectors: Utilities (NAICS 22), Transportation and Warehousing (NAICS 48-49); Information (NAICS 51); Finance and Insurance (NAICS 52); Real Estate and Rental and Leasing (NAICS 53); Professional, Scientific, and Technical Services (NAICS 54); Administrative and Support and Waste Management and Remediation Services (NAICS 56); Educational Services (NAICS 61); Health Care and Social Assistance (NAICS 62); Arts, Entertainment, and Recreation (NAICS 71); and Other Services, except Public Administration (NAICS 81). Covers taxable firms and firms exempt from Federal income taxes. Questionnaires are mailed in January and request annual data for the prior year. Estimates are published approximately 12 months after the initial survey mailing.

Type of Data Collection Operation: The Service Annual Survey estimates are developed from a probability sample of employer firms and administrative records for nonemployers. Service Annual Survey questionnaires are mailed to a probability sample that is periodically reselected from a universe of firms located in the United States and having paid employees. The sample includes firms of all sizes and covers both taxable firms and firms exempt from federal income taxes. Updates to the sample

are made on a quarterly basis to account for new businesses. Firms without paid employees, or nonemployers, are included in the estimates through imputation and/or administrative records data provided by other federal agencies. Links to additional information about confidentiality protection, sampling error, nonsampling error, sample design, definitions, and copies of the questionnaires may be found at <http://www.census.gov/services/index.html>.

Estimates of Sampling Error: Estimates are based on a sample and subject to sampling error. The most recent Service Annual Survey results, including coefficients of variations (CVs), can be found on the Internet at <http://www.census.gov/services/index.html>. Additional information regarding sampling error may be found on the Internet at <http://www.census.gov/services/sas/sastechdoc.html>.

Nonsampling Errors: For both unit and item nonresponse, a missing value is replaced by a predicted value obtained from an appropriate model for nonresponse. The imputation uses survey data and administrative data as input.

Sources of Additional Material: U.S. Census Bureau, Current Business Reports, *Service Annual Survey*, Census Bureau Web site: <http://www.census.gov/services/index.html>.

Survey of Business Owners (SBO)

Universe, Frequency, and Types of Data: The Survey of Business Owners (SBO), conducted every 5 years since 1972 in the years ending in "2" and "7," provides statistics that describe the composition of U.S. businesses by owner characteristics. Data are presented for nonfarm businesses by sex, detailed ethnic and Hispanic group, and veteran status of the owner with 51 percent or more of stock or equity in the business. All U.S. firms operating during 2012 with receipts of $1,000 or more, with and without paid employees, which are classified by the North American Industry Classification System (NAICS) codes 11 through 99, are represented, except for the following: NAICS 111, 112, 482, 491, 521, 525, 813, 814, and 92. The published data include the number of firms, sales and receipts, number of paid employees, and annual payroll. Data are presented by industry classifications, geographic area (states, metropolitan and micropolitan statistical areas, counties, and corporate municipalities [places] including cities, towns, townships, villages, and boroughs), and size of firm (employment and receipts). Please note that businesses can be tabulated in more than one racial group if the owners report more than one race; Hispanic firms may be of any race.

Type of Data Collection Operation: The 2012 Survey of Business Owners (SBO) sent letters to a random sample of businesses asking recipients to respond to the survey electronically. The list of all firms (or universe) was compiled from a combination of business tax returns and data collected on other economic census reports. The Survey of Business Owners (SBO) is conducted on a company or firm basis rather than an establishment basis. Several methodology changes were made for the 2012 SBO, in comparison to the previous 2007 SBO. The Census Bureau expanded the use of direct data substitution from existing sources, such as the American Community Survey and the decennial

Census, to reduce the 2012 SBO sample size to 1.75 million firms from 2.3 million in 2007. The small sample size yielded sufficient quality, reduced overall respondent burden, and reduced costs associated with conducting a mail survey. Approximately half of the 2012 SBO sample was asked to respond to the survey electronically.

Data Collection and Imputation Procedures: The Census Bureau conducted follow-up mailings to nonrespondents, including sending letters to prompt electronic responses and paper forms. Responses came from approximately 66.2 percent of the 1.75 million businesses included in the SBO. For 2012 nonrespondents, 2007 data were substituted if available. For other nonrespondents, the Bureau used administrative data, and also imputed gender, ethnicity, race, and veteran status from donor respondents in the same sampling frame with similar characteristics. Imputed data account for approximately 24 percent of the firm count estimates by gender, ethnicity, race, and veteran status, and approximately 21 percent for the estimates of sales.

Estimates of Sampling Error: Sampling error is present in these estimates because they are based on the results of a sample survey and not on an enumeration of the entire universe. Since these estimates are based on a probability sample, it is possible to estimate the sampling variability of the survey estimates. The standard error (SE) provides a measure of the variation. The relative standard error (RSE) or coefficient of variation (CV) provides a measure of the magnitude of the variation relative to the estimate and is calculated as 100 multiplied by the ratio of the estimate to the SE. Relative standard errors for select data items are included in the data tables.

Nonsampling Errors: These stem from many sources: inability to obtain information for all cases in the universe, adjustments to the weights of respondents to compensate for nonrespondents, imputation for missing data, data errors and biases, mistakes in recording or keying data, errors in collection or processing, and coverage problems. Explicit measures of the effects of these nonsampling errors are not available. The Census Bureau detects and corrects most operational and data errors through an automated data edit designed to review the data for reasonableness and consistency. Quality control techniques were used to verify that operating procedures were carried out as specified.

Sources of Additional Materials: U.S. Census Bureau, Survey of Business Owners, <http://www.census.gov/econ/sbo/index.html>.

U.S. DEPARTMENT OF EDUCATION, National Center for Education Statistics

Integrated Postsecondary Education Data Survey (IPEDS), Completions

Universe, Frequency, and Types of Data: Annual survey of all Title IV (federal financial aid) eligible postsecondary institutions to obtain data on enrollments; faculty and staff finances; institutional prices; financial aid; and earned degrees and other formal awards, conferred by field of study, level of degree, sex, and by racial/ ethnic characteristics

(every other year prior to 1989, then annually). More than 7,500 institutions complete IPEDS surveys each year. The IPEDS universe is established during the fall collection period.

Type of Data Collection Operation: Complete census. The completion of all IPEDS surveys is mandatory for institutions that participate in or are applicants for participation in any federal student financial aid program (such as Pell grants and federal student loans) authorized by Title IV of the Higher Education Act of 1965. As respondents enter data online, the data collection system automatically calculates totals, averages, and percentages, and compares the responses with the previous year's submission for the same institution to ensure the data are reasonable. The system also compares data with other related values to ensure consistency of reporting within each survey component and across the data collection program. If data are still missing, analysts conduct imputations to complete the database.

Data Collection and Imputation Procedures: IPEDS consists of nine interrelated components that are collected over three collection periods (fall, winter, and spring) each year. Missing data are imputed by using data of similar institutions. With the exception of the Institutional Characteristics component, all items collected in each component were eligible for imputation. Within the Institutional Characteristics component, only cost of attendance and other institutional charges data were eligible for imputation. IPEDS applies a single imputation method for both unit and item nonresponse. The Nearest Neighbor procedure identifies data related to the key statistics of interest for each component (the distance measure), then uses those data to identify a responding institution similar to the nonresponding institution and uses the respondent's data as a substitute for the nonrespondent's missing items.

Estimates of Sampling Error: Not applicable.

Nonsampling Errors: Nonsampling errors may arise when respondents or interviewers interpret questions differently; when respondents must estimate values, or when coders, keyers, and other processors handle answers differently; when people who should be included in the universe are not; or when people fail to respond (completely or partially). Nonsampling errors usually, but not always, result in an underestimate of total survey error and thus an overestimate of the precision of survey estimates. Since estimating the magnitude of nonsampling errors often would require special experiments or access to independent data, these nonsampling errors are seldom measured. For universe surveys, an adjustment made for either type of nonresponse, total or partial, is often referred to as an imputation, which is often a substitution of the "average" questionnaire response for the nonresponse. For universe surveys, imputations are usually made separately within various groups of sample members that have similar survey characteristics.

Sources of Additional Material: U.S. Department of Education, National Center for Education Statistics, IPEDS Technical/Methodological reports, <http://nces.ed.gov/pubsearch/getpubcats. asp?sid=010>.

National Household Education Surveys (NHES) Program

Universe, Frequency, and Types of Data: The National Household Education Surveys Program is a system of surveys of the noninstitutionalized civilian population of the United States. NHES surveys have been conducted various years 1991 to 2012 and have varying universes of interest depending on the particular survey. Some surveys are recurring, others are fielded as 1-time surveys. Specific topics covered by each survey are at the NHES Web site <http://nces.ed.gov/nhes>. A list of the surveys fielded as part of NHES, each universe, and the years they were fielded is provided below.

1 Adult Education—Interviews were conducted with a representative sample of civilian, noninstitutionalized persons aged 16 and older who were not enrolled in grade 12 or below (1991, 1995, 1999, 2001, 2003, 2005).

2 Before- and After-School Programs and Activities—Interviews were conducted with parents of a representative sample of students in grades K through 8 (1999, 2001, 2005).

3 Civic Involvement—Interviews were conducted with representative samples of parents, youth, and adults (1996, 1999).

4 Early Childhood Program Participation—Interviews were conducted with parents of a representative sample of children from birth through grade 3, with the specific age groups varying by survey year (1991, 1995, 1999, 2001, 2005).

5 Household and Library Use—Interviews were conducted with a representative sample of U.S. households (1996).

6 Parent and Family Involvement in Education—Interviews were conducted with parents of a representative sample of children age three through grade 12 or in grades K through 12 depending on the survey year (1996, 1999, 2003, 2007, and 2012).

7 School Readiness—Interviews were conducted with parents of a representative sample of 3-7 year-old children (1993 and 1999) and of 3-5 year old children, not yet in kindergarten (2007).

8 School Safety and Discipline—Interviews were conducted with a representative sample of students in grades 6-12, their parents, and the parents of a representative sample of students in grades 3-12 (1993).

Type of Data Collection Operation: Through 2007, the NHES used telephone interviews to collect data. In 2012, the NHES was redesigned. The 2012 NHES switched to a mail survey, and samples were developed using household address information for all 50 states and the District of Columbia. The NHES 2012 sample was selected using a 2-stage address-based sampling frame. Black and Hispanic American households were sampled at a higher rate than other households. Data were collected using printed questionnaires mailed to sampled respondents.

Data Collection and Imputation Procedures: For telephone surveys, telephone numbers are selected using random digit dialing (RDD) techniques. Approximately 45,000 to 64,000 households are contacted in order to identify persons eligible for the surveys. Data are collected using computer-assisted telephone interviewing (CATI) procedures. Missing data are imputed using hot-deck imputation procedures. For the 2012 NHES, 159,994 addresses were sampled, with 99,426 screenings completed, and 32,086 screened households with eligible children. NHES nonrespondents received shortened versions of the survey, as a follow-up strategy to increase

participation. The 2012 NHES used 3 imputation methods for missing data items: unweighted sequential hot deck imputation, for the majority of the missing data; weighted random imputation, for a small number of variables; and manual imputation, in a very small number of cases for most variables. The 2012 Parent and Family Involvement in Education survey received 17,563 completed questionnaires; overall response rate was 57.6 percent.

Estimates of Sampling Error: Reports presenting NHES data include tables on standard errors.

Nonsampling Errors: For each NHES survey, efforts were made to prevent nonsampling errors and errors from bias from occurring and to compensate for them, where possible. For instance, during the survey design phase, cognitive interviews are conducted to assess respondents' knowledge of the survey topics, their comprehension of questions and terms, and the sensitivity of items. Data from the 2012 NHES went through a series of processing procedures; these procedures include data capture and imaging; the reformatting of keyed data; a preliminary interview status classification; and a series of computer edits; and other editing procedures.

Sources of Additional Material: Please see the NHES Web site at <http://nces.ed.gov/nhes>; technical notes in "Parent and Family Involvement in Education, from the National Household Education Surveys Program of 2012," NCES 2013-028.REV, May 2015, <http://nces.ed.gov/pubs2013/2013028rev.pdf>; and *National Household Education Surveys Program of 2012, Data File User's Manual*, May 2015, <https://nces.ed.gov/nhes/pdf/userman/NHES_2012_UsersManual.pdf>.

Schools and Staffing Survey (SASS)

Universe, Frequency and Types of Data: NCES designed the SASS survey system to emphasize teacher demand and shortage, teacher and administrator characteristics, school programs, and general conditions in schools. SASS also collects data on many other topics, including principals' and teachers' perceptions of school climate and problems in their schools; teacher compensation; district hiring practices; basic characteristics of the student population; and instructional time and teacher and school performance. The SASS has four core components: the School Questionnaire, the Teacher Questionnaire, the Principal Questionnaire, and the School District Questionnaire. For the 2003-04, 2007-08, and 2011-12 SASS, public charter schools were included in the sample. Surveys have been conducted every 3 to 4 years depending on budgetary constraints. The SASS includes data from public, private, and Bureau of Indian Education (BIE) school sectors.

Type of Data Collection Operation and Imputation Procedures: The 2007-08 SASS consisted of 5 questionnaires: district, principal, school, teacher, and school library media center questionnaires. The 2007-08 SASS was a mail-based survey, with telephone and field follow-up. The U.S. Census Bureau performs the data collection and begins by sending advance letters to the sampled Local Education Agencies (LEAs) and schools in August and September of collection years. Beginning in October, questionnaires are delivered by U.S. Census Bureau field representatives. The sampling frame for the public school sample is the most recent Common Core of Data (CCD) school file. CCD is a universe file that includes all elementary and secondary schools in the United States. Schools operated by the Department of Defense or those that offered only kindergarten or pre-kindergarten or adult education were excluded from the SASS sample. The list frame used for the private school sample is the most recent Private School Universe Survey (PSS) list, updated with association lists. An area frame supplement is based on the canvassing of private schools within specific geographical areas. A separate universe of schools funded by the Bureau of Indian Education (BIE) is drawn from the Program Education Directory maintained by the BIE. To avoid duplicates in the BIE files, BIE schools in the CCD school file are treated as public schools. SASS used four methods to impute values for questionnaire items that respondents did not answer. These were: (1) using data from other items on the questionnaire; (2) extracting data from a related component of SASS; (3) extracting data from the sampling frame (CCD or PSS); and (4) extracting data from the record of a sampled case with similar characteristics (commonly known as the "hot deck" method for imputing item response).

Estimates of Sampling Error: Sample errors can be calculated using replicate weights and Balanced Repeated Replication complex survey design methodology. Errors depend on cell sizes and range from less than 1 percent to over 5 percent (for reasonable cell sizes).

Nonsampling Errors: Because of unit nonresponse, bias may exist in some sample cells. However, bias has been adjusted for in the weighting process. Analysis of bias has been studied and no significant bias has been detected.

Sources of Additional Material: Please see the SASS Web site at <http://nces.ed.gov/surveys/sass/>.

U.S. DEPARTMENT OF JUSTICE, FEDERAL BUREAU OF INVESTIGATION

Uniform Crime Reporting (UCR) Program

Universe, Frequency, and Types of Data: Monthly reports on the number of criminal offenses that become known to law enforcement agencies. In 2013, a total of 18,415 city, university and college, county, state, tribal, and federal law enforcement agencies contributed data to the FBI. In 2013, law enforcement agencies active in the UCR Program represented more than 316 million U.S. inhabitants. The UCR Program collects information regarding the violent crimes of murder and nonnegligent manslaughter, rape, robbery, and aggravated assault as well as the property crimes of burglary, larceny-theft, motor vehicle theft, and arson. (Although the FBI classifies arson as a property crime, it does not estimate arson data because of variations in the level of participation by the reporting agencies. Consequently, arson is not included in the property crime estimate.) The program also collects arrest data for the offenses listed above plus 20 offenses that include all other crimes except traffic violations.

Type of Data Collection Operation: Crime statistics are based on reports of crime data submitted either directly to the FBI by contributing law enforcement

agencies or through cooperating state UCR Programs. UCR program participation is voluntary. Beginning with the 2013 data collections, all data must be submitted electronically, and after July 2013, the UCR Program will no longer accept paper submissions or the electronic submission of documents (i.e., Portable Document Format files).

Data Collection and Imputation Procedures: States with UCR programs collect data directly from individual law enforcement agencies and forward reports, prepared in accordance with UCR standards, to the FBI. Accuracy and consistency edits are performed by the FBI.

Estimates of Sampling Error: Not applicable.

Nonsampling Errors: Due to computer problems, changes in records management systems, personnel shortages, or a number of other reasons, some agencies cannot provide data for publication.

Sources of Additional Material: U.S. Department of Justice, Federal Bureau of Investigation, <https://www.fbi.gov/about-us/cjis/ucr/crime-in-the-u.s/2013/crime-in-the-u.s.-2013>; and *Crime in the United States*, annual, *Hate Crime Statistics*, annual, and *Law Enforcement Officers Killed and Assaulted*, annual, <http://www.fbi.gov/about-us/cjis/ucr/ucr>.

U.S. INTERNAL REVENUE SERVICE, TAX STATISTICS

Corporation Income Tax Returns

Universe, Frequency, and Types of Data: Annual study of unaudited corporation income tax returns, Forms 1120, 1120-F, 1120-L, 1120-PC, 1120-REIT, 1120-RIC, and 1120S, filed by corporations or businesses legally defined as corporations. The IRS Statistics of Income (SOI) Division collects data on corporations by size, industry, total assets, business receipts, deductions, liabilities, net income, income tax liability, tax credits, and other financial data. SOI aggregates these data for C corporations and passthrough entities, such as S corporations. The target population consists of all returns of active corporations organized for profit that are required to file one of the 1120 forms that are part of the SOI study.

Type of Data Collection Operation: Stratified probability sample of 116,000 returns for Tax Year 2012 (including inactive and non-eligible corporations), allocated to sample classes which are based on type of return, and either size of total assets alone or both size of total assets and a measure of income. Sampling rates for sample classes varied from 0.25 percent to 100 percent. The total realized sample for 2012, including inactive and noneligible corporations, is 116,532 returns.

Data Collection and Imputation Procedures: Computer selection of sample of tax return records. Data adjusted during editing for incorrect, missing, or inconsistent entries to ensure consistency with other entries on return and to comply with statistical definitions. If the missing data items are from the balance sheet, then imputation procedures are used. If data for a whole return are missing because the return is unavailable to SOI during the data capture process, imputation procedures are also used in certain cases. Beginning with the Tax

Year 2012 sample, the criteria for imputing balance sheets for returns with incomplete balance sheets changed significantly. Now, only the largest returns with incomplete balance sheets are subject to a balance sheet imputation procedure. As a result, the number of returns with imputed balance sheets will be negligible, and the IRS's Statistics of Income (SOI) division will perform imputation on an ad hoc basis only

Estimates of Sampling Error: Statistics of Income reports do not directly present the standard error. Instead, the ratio of the standard error to the estimate itself is presented in percentage form. This ratio is called the coefficient of variation (CV). The user of SOI data may multiply an estimate by its CV to recreate the standard error and to construct confidence intervals. Estimated CVs for Tax Year 2012 are published in the Statistics of Income, *Corporation Complete Report*, for 2012 in "Section 3: Description of the Sample and Limitation of the Data."

Nonsampling Errors: These may include coverage errors, processing errors, and response errors.

Sources of Additional Material: U.S. Internal Revenue Service, Statistics of Income, *Corporation Income Tax Returns*, <http://www.irs.gov/uac/SOI-Tax-Stats-Corporation-Tax-Statistics>.

Individual Income Tax Returns

Universe, Frequency, and Types of Data: Annual study of unaudited individual income tax returns, Forms 1040, 1040A, and 1040EZ, filed by U.S. citizens and residents. Data provided on various financial characteristics by size of adjusted gross income, marital status, and by taxable and nontaxable returns. Data by state, based on the population of returns filed, also include returns from 1040NR, filed by nonresident aliens plus certain self employment tax returns.

Type of Data Collection Operation: Stratified probability sample of 332,040 returns for tax year 2013. The sample is classified into sample strata based on the larger of total income or total loss amounts, the size of business plus farm receipts, and other criteria such as the potential usefulness of the return for tax policy modeling. Sampling rates for sample strata varied from 0.10 percent to 100 percent.

Data Collection and Imputation Procedures: Computer selection of sample of tax return records. Data adjusted during editing for incorrect, missing, or inconsistent entries to ensure consistency with other entries on return.

Estimates of Sampling Error: Coefficients of variation are available from source tables. Briefly, estimated CVs for tax year 2013 are: adjusted gross income less deficit, 0.09 percent; salaries and wages, 0.16 percent; and total income before tax credits, 0.14 percent. (State data not subject to sampling error.)

Nonsampling Errors: Processing errors and errors arising from the use of tolerance checks for the data.

Sources of Additional Material: U.S. Internal Revenue Service, *Statistics of Income, Individual Income Tax Returns* (Publication 1304), annual, <http://www.irs.gov/uac/SOI-Tax-Stats-Individual-Income-Tax-Return-Form-1040-Statistics>.

Partnership Income Tax Returns

Universe, Frequency, and Types of Data: Annual study of preaudited income tax returns of active partnerships related to financial and tax-related

activity during tax year 2012 and reported on Forms 1065 and 1065B to the IRS. Data are provided by industry, based on the NAICS industry coding used by IRS.

Type of Data Collection Operation: Tax Year 2012 statistics are estimates based on a stratified probability sample of 41,277 returns selected from a population of 3,588,156 partnerships. However, 487 returns were "out of scope," yielding a final sample of 40,790 returns and an estimated overall active population of 3,388,561 partnerships. Statistics of Income (SOI) stratified the population into classes based on industry, type of return, size of total assets, and size of certain receipt or income amounts from both ordinary business income (loss) and portfolio income (loss). From these classes, SOI selected returns at various probabilities (from 0.04 percent to 100 percent) and weighted them to represent the total population.

Data Collection and Imputation Procedures: The sample of tax return records are selected via computer after data are transcribed by IRS and placed on an administrative file. Data are manually adjusted during editing for incorrect, missing, or inconsistent entries to ensure consistency with other entries on return. Data not available due to regulations are handled with weighting adjustments.

Estimates of Sampling Error: Some of the estimated coefficients of variation (the estimated standard error of the total divided by the estimated total) for tax year 2012: number of partnerships, 0.58 percent; number of partners, 1.81 percent; total assets, 0.13 percent; total income, 0.20 percent; and business receipts, 0.17 percent.

Nonsampling Errors: The potential exists for coverage error due to unavailable returns; processing errors; and taxpayer reporting errors, since data are preaudit.

Sources of Additional Material: U.S. Internal Revenue Service, *Statistics of Income, Partnership Returns, 2012,* Winter 2015, <http://www.irs.gov/uac/SOI-Tax-Stats-SOI-Bulletin-Articles-Index-by-Topic>.

Sole Proprietorship Income Tax Returns

Universe, Frequency, and Types of Data: Annual study of unaudited income tax returns of nonfarm sole proprietorships, Form 1040 with business schedules. Data provided on various financial characteristics by industry.

Type of Data Collection Operation: Stratified probability sample of 89,775 returns from sole proprietorships for tax year 2012. The sample is classified based on presence or absence of certain business schedules; the larger of total income or loss; size of business plus farm receipts, and other criteria such as the potential usefulness of the return for tax policy modeling. Sampling rates vary from 0.1 percent to 100 percent.

Data Collection and Imputation Procedures: Computer selection of sample of tax return records. Data adjusted during editing for incorrect, missing, or inconsistent entries to ensure consistency with other entries on return.

Estimates of Sampling Error: Coefficients of Variation for tax year 2012 are available in source documentation. In brief, CVs for sole proprietorships, all nonfarm industries are: total business receipts, 0.56 percent; depreciation, 1.46 percent; and net income, 0.73 percent.

Nonsampling Errors: Processing errors and errors arising from the use of tolerance checks for the data.

Sources of Additional Material: U.S. Internal Revenue Service, *Statistics of Income, Sole Proprietorship Returns, 2012*, Winter 2015, <http://www.irs.gov/uac/SOI-Tax-Stats-SOI-Bulletin-Articles-Index-by-Topic>.

U.S. NATIONAL CENTER FOR HEALTH STATISTICS (NCHS)

National Health Interview Survey (NHIS)

Universe, Frequency, and Types of Data: Continuous data collection covering the civilian noninstitutional population to obtain information on demographic characteristics, conditions, injuries, impairments, use of health services, health behaviors, and other health topics.

Type of Data Collection Operation: Trained interviewers from the U.S. Census Bureau visit each selected household and administer NHIS in person. Current NHIS sample design oversamples black, Hispanic, and Asian Americans. The annual NHIS questionnaire (also called the Core) consists of four main components: Household Composition, Family Core, Sample Adult Core, and Sample Child Core. The Census Bureau collects data using a computer assisted personal interviewing mode. Multistage probability sample of 49,000 households (in 198 PSUs) from 1985 to 1994; 36,000 to 40,000 households (358 design PSUs or 449 effective PSUs when divided by state boundaries) from 1995 to 2005; an estimated completed 35,000 households (428 effective PSUs) beginning in 2006. Sample size for the 2012 NHIS was 42,366 households, with 108,131 persons in 43,345 families. The total family response rate was 77.6 percent.

Data Collection and Imputation Procedures: Some missing data items (e.g., race, ethnicity) are imputed using a hot deck imputation value. Sequential regression models are used to create multiple imputation files for family income. Unit nonresponse is compensated for by an adjustment to the survey weights. Since 2004, imputation has been performed for injury and poisoning episodes for which the respondent did not provide sufficient information to determine a month, day, and year of occurrence. (Note: the NHIS questionnaire was redesigned in 1997, and a new sample design was instituted in 2006.)

Estimates of Sampling Error: Because NHIS data are based on a sample of the population, they are subject to sampling error. Standard errors are reported to indicate the reliability of the estimates. Estimates and standard errors were calculated using SUDAAN software (21), which takes into account the complex sampling design of NHIS. The Taylor series linearization method was used for variance estimation in SUDAAN. Standard errors are shown in source tables.

Nonsampling Errors: Documentation on NHIS methods is available at <http://www.cdc.gov/nchs/nhis/methods.htm>.

Sources of Additional Material: National Center for Health Statistics, Summary Health Statistics for the U.S. Population: National Health Interview Survey, 2012, Vital and Health Statistics, Series 10, No. 259; Additional information is available on the Internet at <http://www.cdc.gov/nchs/nhis/about_nhis.htm>; Series 10 reports are available at <http://www.cdc.gov/nchs/products/series/series10.htm>.

National Survey of Family Growth (NSFG)

Universe, Frequency, and Types of Data: Periodic survey of men and women 15-44 years of age in the household population of the United States. Interview topics covered include births and pregnancies, marriage, divorce, and cohabitation, sexual activity, contraceptive use, medical care, and attitudes about childbearing and parenthood. The most sensitive data—on sexual behavior related to HIV and sexually transmitted disease risk—were collected in a self-administered form in which the data are entered into a computer. Cycle 6 of the 2002 NSFG in-person interviews were completed with 12,571 respondents 15-44 years of age—7,643 females and 4,928 males. Response rate was 79 percent overall—80 percent for females and 78 percent for males. For the 2006-2010 NSFG, the NSFG interviewed a national sample of 22,682 men (75 percent response rate) and women (78 percent response rate) 15-44 years of age. Population targets included 45 percent male, 55 percent female, 20 percent Hispanic, 20 percent black, and 20 percent teenage respondents. The 2006-10 sample was drawn from 110 primary sampling units.

Type of Data Collection Operation: The 2002 and 2006-10 NSFG were conducted in conjunction with Institute for Social Research at University of Michigan. Professional female interviewers conducted in-person, face-to-face interviews using laptop computers. In the 2002 (Cycle 6) NSFG, the sample was a multistage area probability sample of men and women 15-44 years of age in the household population of the United States. Only one person 15-44 was selected from households with one or more persons 15-44. In the self-administered portion, the respondent entered his or her own answers into the computer. Hispanic and Black persons, as well as those 15-19 years of age, were sampled at higher rates than White adults. All percentages and other statistics shown for the NSFG are weighted to make national estimates. The weights adjust for the different rates of sampling for each group, and for nonresponse. The 2006–2010 NSFG used a responsive design approach to manage the field work of the survey, to control costs, to oversample teenage and minority groups, and to reduce bias in the resulting sample. This approach represented a significant change in the design, methodology, and procedures of the survey. Interviews were conducted in English and Spanish. Monetary incentives were used to promote survey participation. Signed parental consent was required for survey participants aged 15–17.

Data Collection and Imputation Procedures: For about 650 key variables, referred to as "recodes," item missing values have been replaced in the NGSF data file by predicted or imputed values. The imputed values are identified through a companion variable or "imputation flag" to indicate whether the value for a particular case was imputed or reported. The imputation rates for most of these recodes are very low—usually less than 1.0%. The highest imputation rate was for income, with 10.8% imputed. Detailed discussion of data collection and imputation procedures is available in "Responsive Design, Weighting, and Variance Estimation in the 2006-2010 National Survey of Family Growth," *Vital and Health Statistics*, Series 2, No. 158, June 2013.

Estimates of Sampling Error: Estimates are subject to error, a difference between the true population value and the value estimated from the sample. This difference may be due to systematic or fixed sources of error, such as nonresponse or noncoverage bias or due to variable sources of error, including the use of a sample to represent the population. Detailed discussion of variance estimation is available in "Responsive Design, Weighting, and Variance Estimation in the 2006-2010 National Survey of Family Growth," *Vital and Health Statistics*, Series 2, No. 158, June 2013.

Nonsampling Errors: Detailed discussion of variance estimation is available in "Responsive Design, Weighting, and Variance Estimation in the 2006-2010 National Survey of Family Growth," *Vital and Health Statistics*, Series 2, No. 158, June 2013.

Sources of Additional Material: The following references can be found at <http://www.cdc.gov/nchs/nsfg.htm>. "National Survey of Family Growth, Cycle 6: Sample Design, Weighting, and Variance Estimation," *Vital and Health Statistics*, Series 2, Number 142, July 2006. "Plan and Operation of Cycle 6 of the National Survey of Family Growth," *Vital and Health Statistics*, Series 1, No. 42, August 2005. "Sexual Behavior and Selected Health Measures: Men and Women 15-44 Years of Age, United States, 2002," *Advance Data from Vital and Health Statistics*, No. 362, Sept 15, 2005. "Responsive Design, Weighting, and Variance Estimation in the 2006-2010 National Survey of Family Growth," *Vital and Health Statistics*, Series 2, No. 158, June 2013.

National Vital Statistics System

Universe, Frequency, and Types of Data: Annual data on births, deaths, marriages, divorces, and fetal deaths in the United States. Legal authority for the registration of these events resides individually with the 50 States, 2 cities (Washington, DC, and New York City), and 5 territories (Puerto Rico, the Virgin Islands, Guam, American Samoa, and the Commonwealth of the Northern Mariana Islands). These jurisdictions are responsible for maintaining registries of vital events and for issuing copies of birth, marriage, divorce, and death certificates.

Type of Data Collection Operation: Mortality data based on complete file of death records, except 1972, based on 50 percent sample. Natality statistics 1951-1971, based on 50 percent sample of birth certificates, except a 20 percent to 50 percent sample in 1967, received by NCHS.

Data Collection and Imputation Procedures: Reports based on records from registration offices of the jurisdictions listed above. Data pertaining to causes of death are classified and coded according to the International Classification of Diseases (ICD).

Estimates of Sampling Error: For recent years, there is no sampling for these files; the files are based on 100 percent of certificates registered.

Nonsampling Errors: Generally more than 99 percent of the births and deaths occurring in this country are registered.

Sources of Additional Material: U.S. National Center for Health Statistics, *Vital Statistics of the United States*, Vol. I and Vol. II, annual, and the *National Vital Statistics Reports*. See the NCHS Web site at <http://www.cdc.gov/nchs/nvss.htm>.

National Highway Traffic Safety Administration (NHTSA)

Fatality Analysis Reporting System (FARS)

Universe, Frequency, and Types of Data: FARS is a census of all fatal motor vehicle traffic crashes that occur throughout the United States including the District of Columbia and Puerto Rico on roadways customarily open to the public. The crash must be reported to the state/jurisdiction, and is classified as fatal if a directly related fatality occurs within thirty days of the crash.

Type of Data Collection Operation: One or more analysts, in each state, extract data from the official documents and enter the data into a standardized electronic database.

Data Collection and Imputation Procedures: Data are from various state documents, including police accident reports, death certificates, state vehicle registration files, coroner/medical examiner reports, vital statistics, and other records. Computerized edit checks monitor the accuracy and completeness of the data. The FARS incorporates a sophisticated mathematical multiple imputation procedure to develop a probability distribution of missing blood alcohol concentration (BAC) levels in the database for drivers, pedestrians, and cyclists.

Estimates of Sampling Error: Since this is census data, there are no sampling errors.

Nonsampling Errors: FARS represents a census of all police-reported crashes and captures all data reported at the state level. FARS data undergo a rigorous quality control process to prevent inaccurate reporting. However, these data are highly dependent on the accuracy of the police accident reports. Errors or omissions within police accident reports may not be detected.

Sources of Additional Material: Fatality Analysis Reporting System (FARS) Analytical User's Manual 1975-2013, <http://www.nhtsa.gov/FARS>.

Weights and Measures

U.S. Customary/Metric Conversion Table

[Conversions provided in the table are approximate]

Symbol	When you know U.S. customary	Multiply by	To find metric	Symbol
in	inches	2.54	centimeters	cm
ft	feet	30.48	centimeters	cm
yd	yards	0.091	meters	m
mi	miles	1.61	kilometers	km
in^2	square inches	6.45	square centimeters	cm^2
ft^2	square feet	0.09	square centimeters	cm^2
yd^2	square yards	0.84	square meters	m^2
mi^2	square miles	2.59	square kilometers	km^2
	acre	0.41	hectare	ha
oz	ounces	28.35	grams	g
lb	pounds	0.45	kilograms	kg
oz (troy)	troy ounces	31.1	grams	g
	short tons (2,000 lb)	0.91	metric tons	t
	long tons (2,240 lb)	1.02	metric tons	t
fl oz	fluid ounces	29.57	mililiters	mL
c	cups	0.24	liters	L
pt	pints	0.47	liters	L
qt	quarts	0.95	liters	L
gal	gallons	3.78	liters	L
ft^3	cubic feet	0.03	cubic meters	m^3
yd^3	cubic yards	0.76	cubic meters	m^3
°F	degrees Fahrenheit (subtract 32)	0.55	degrees Celsius	°C

Symbol	When you know metric	Multiply by	To find U.S. customary	Symbol
cm	centimeters	0.39	inches	in
cm	centimeters	0.03	feet	ft
m	meters	1.09	yards	yd
km	kilometers	0.62	miles	mi
cm^2	square centimeters	0.015	square inches	in^2
cm^2	square centimeters	10.76	square feet	ft^2
m^2	square meters	1.2	square yards	yd^2
km^2	square kilometers	0.39	square miles	mi^2
ha	hectare	2.47	acre	
g	grams	0.04	ounces	oz
kg	kilograms	2.21	pounds	lb
g	grams	0.04	troy ounces	oz (troy)
t	metric tons	1.1	short tons (2,000 lb)	
t	metric tons	0.98	long tons (2,240 lb)	
mL	mililiters	0.03	fluid ounces	fl oz
L	liters	4.23	cups	c
L	liters	2.13	pints	pt
L	liters	1.05	quarts	qt
L	liters	0.026	gallons	gal
m^3	cubic meters	35.32	cubic feet	ft^3
m^3	cubic meters	1.32	cubic yards	yd^3
°C	degrees Celsius (after multiplying, add 32)	1.8	degrees Fahrenheit	°F

Source: National Institute of Standards and Technology (NIST), Weights and Measures Division. See <http://www.nist.gov/pml/wmd/metric/unit-conversion.cfm>

Index

Note: Index citations refer to **table** numbers, not **page** numbers

Equipment and software expenditures, 801
Establishments, 775, 776, 778, 1236, 1237, 1238
Finances, 765, 768, 1235, 1237
Gaming, 1266
Gross domestic product, 690
Hires and separations, 656, 657
Hours, 649,
Nonemployers, 776, 1237
Occupational safety, 678
Payroll, 1238
Productivity, 658
Profits, 811
Receipts, revenue, 765, 768, 773, 774, 775, 776, 787, 788, 789, 790, 791, 792, 793, 1235, 1237
Value added, 1240
Asbestos, 924, 925, 928
Asia. (See Foreign countries.)
Asian and Pacific Islander population (See also Asian population):
Births, 88, 90, 91, 92, 93, 94
Business owners, 786, 791, 792
Consumer expenditures, 708
Criminal victimizations, 335, 338, 343
Deaths, death rates, 119, 120, 121, 128, 134, 137, 138, 140, 335
Degrees conferred, 312
Doctorates, 312, 832
Educational attainment, 253, 254
Health insurance coverage, 169
Heart disease, deaths, 134
Hospital visits, 196
HIV disease, 138
Income, 712, 713, 718, 719, 726, 727
Jail inmates, 375
Language, 258
Poverty, 731, 732, 735
Science doctorates, 832
Suicides, deaths, 128, 137, 530
Asian population, 5, 7, 9, 10, 11, 13, 20, 34, 40
Adoption, 80, 591
AIDS, 206
Births, 5, 100, 101, 102
Bullying, 326
Child care, 592, 587
Business owners, 786, 791, 792
Children, 9, 10, 11, 69, 80
College costs, 300, 302
College enrollment, 291, 293, 295, 317
Deaths, 5
Disabled students, 297
Educational attainment, 34, 253, 254, 255, 256
Elderly, 9, 10, 11
Family type, 67
Food stamp participants, 558, 559, 586
Foster care, 591
Grandparents living with grandchildren, 67, 70
Health care visits to professionals, 184
Health insurance coverage, 160, 167, 169
Households, 59, 64, 66, 75
Housing tenure, 34, 75
Immunization of children, 235
Income, 34, 712, 713, 715, 717, 718, 719, 723, 726, 727
Internet usage, 1163

Labor force, 605, 606, 607, 611, 614, 618, 626, 633, 665, 670, 685
Class of worker, 623
Displaced workers, 630
Earnings, 256, 665, 670
Industry, 640
Job search, 642
Multiple job holders, 626
Occupation, 34, 633, 639
Public assistance, 586, 593
Unemployment, 641, 642, 646
Leisure time use, 1253
Marital status, 56, 75
Migration, 5
Occupation, 34
Physical activity, 226
Poverty, 34, 731, 732, 733, 735, 736
Public assistance, 558, 559
School enrollment, 269, 291, 293, 295
States, 20
Veterans, 539
Voter registration and turnout, 430, 432
Weapons in schools, 324
Asparagus, 241
Assaults, 128, 129, 329, 330, 331, 332, 337, 338, 340, 341, 357
Asset-backed securities, 771, 1180, 1181, 1202, 1208
Assets, personal, 737, 740, 741, 742, 1184
Assisted reproduction, 113, 114
Assistance, public. (See Public aid, assistance.)
Associations, national, nonprofit, 599, 600, 601, 602, 1291
Asthma, 130, 186, 197, 209, 236
Astronomy, 833
Athletic goods. (See Sporting and athletic goods.)
ATMs (automated teller machines), 1198,
Attention deficit hyperactivity disorder (ADHD), 230
Audio and video equipment, 758, 1241
Auditing. (See Accounting, tax preparation, bookkeeping, and payroll services.)
Audits, 502
Australia. (See Foreign countries.)
Austria. (See Foreign countries.)
Authors, 633
Autism, 229, 231
Automobile dealers:
Earnings, 651
Employees, 651, 1059, 1068
Establishments, 1059, 1068
Inventories, 1065
Productivity, 658
Sales, 1062, 1068
Automobile Insurance, 1230
Automobile loans, 1201
Automobile rentals and leasing. (See Automotive equipment rental and leasing and Rental and leasing services.)
Automobiles (see also Motor vehicles):
Alternative fueled vehicles, 1106
Consumer expenditures, 697, 706, 707, 708, 709, 710
Energy consumption, 949
Expenditure per new car, 1070
Foreign trade, 1311
Imports, 1070

Note: Index citations refer to **table** numbers, not **page** numbers

---

Note: Index citations refer to **table** numbers, not **page** numbers

Delivery procedures, 95, 189
Education, 100, 103, 104
First births, 102
Foreign countries, 1345
Hispanic population, 5, 87, 89, 90, 91, 92, 93, 94,
95, 99, 100, 101, 102
Induction of labor, 98
Island areas of the U.S., 90, 96, 1320
Life expectancy, 115, 116, 117, 1346
Native Hawaiian, Other Pacific Islander, 5, 100
Poverty, 100, 104
Premature, 99
Race, 5, 87, 88, 89, 90, 91, 92, 93, 94, 95, 99,
100, 101, 102
States, 16, 90, 96
Twin and multiple, 89
Births, businesses, 783, 784
Birth control, 107, 108
Birth weights, 96
Black, African American population, 5, 7, 9, 10
11, 13, 20, 34, 38
Abortions, 109, 110
Adoption, 80, 591
Age and/or sex, 7, 9, 10, 11
AIDS, 206
Birth and birth rates, 5, 87, 88, 90, 94, 100
Births to teenage mothers, 92, 94, 98
Births to unmarried women, 93, 94, 102
Body weight, 224, 225
Breastfeeding, 112
Bullying, 326
Business owners, 786, 790
Cancer, 200, 202
Child care, 587, 592
Children, 9, 10, 11, 69, 80
Obesity, 237
Poverty, 732, 733
Cigarette smoking, 217
Congress, members of, 452
Consumer expenditures, 708
Contraceptive use, 107, 108
Criminal victimizations, 338, 343
Deaths and death rates, 5, 119, 120, 121, 125,
126, 128, 134, 137, 138
Degrees conferred, 312, 832
Disabled persons, 297
Educational attainment, 34, 253, 254, 255, 256
Elderly, 9, 10, 11, 733
Families, characteristics, 34, 64, 66, 67
Fertility, 91
Food stamp participants, 558, 559, 586
Foster care, children in, 591
Grandparents living with grandchildren, 67, 70
Hate crimes, 346
Health care, visits to professionals, 184, 187
Health insurance coverage, 160, 167, 169
Heart disease, deaths, 134
High school graduates and dropouts, 284, 285,
286
HIV disease, 138, 206
Homeschooled, 262
Homicides, 334, 335, 336
Hospital use, 187, 196
Households, characteristics, 62, 64, 66, 75
Housing, 34, 1009, 1013, 1016, 1019

Immunization of children, 235
Income, 34, 557, 712, 713, 715, 717, 718,
719, 723, 726, 727
Infant deaths, 125, 126
Internet access/use, 1162, 1163, 1170
Jail inmates, 375
Job search, 642
Labor force, 605, 606, 607, 611, 618, 665
Class of worker, 623
Displaced workers, 630
Earnings, 256, 487, 665, 670
Employed, 487, 606, 626, 627, 633, 639, 640
Educational attainment, 611, 614, 627, 646
Multiple job holders, 626
Unemployed, 606, 641, 642, 646
Leisure time use, 1253
Life expectancy, 115, 116, 117, 118
Living arrangements, 69
Marital status, 56, 75
Migration, 5
Minimum wage workers, 670
Nurses, 633
Occupations, 34, 633, 639
Physical activity, 226
Poverty, 34, 731, 732, 733, 735, 736
Property owners, 1013, 1016, 1019
Public assistance, 558, 559, 586, 593
Recreation activities, 1246, 1247
Schools and education:
American College Testing Program (ACT), 281
College costs, 300, 302
College enrollment, 288, 291, 292, 293, 317
Degrees conferred, 832
Enrollment, 250, 259, 269, 286, 291, 292, 293, 295
High school dropouts, 284, 285, 286
High school graduates, 286, 288
Parent participation, 268
Scholastic Assessment Test (SAT), 280
Teachers, 275, 279, 273, 274, 633
Weapons in school, 324
Sexual activity, 105
States, 20
Suicides, 128, 137, 530
Union membership, 685
Veterans, 539
Voter registration and turnout, 430, 432
Black lung benefit program, 575, 576
Blackberries, 885
Blast furnace and basic steel products. (See Iron and
steel products.)
Blind persons, 164, 231, 577
Blood alcohol concentration, 1112, 1115, 1116,
1117
Blood poisoning (See Septicemia.)
Blueberries, 241, 885
Boats and boating (See also Ships.), 1078, 1081,
1250
Body Mass Index (BMI), 225
Bolivia. (See Foreign countries.)
Bolts, nuts, etc. (See Iron and steel products.)
Bonds:
Foreign, 1214
Holdings by sector, 742, 1182, 1183, 1213, 1214,
1215
Life insurance companies, 1213, 1228

Note: Index citations refer to **table** numbers, not **page** numbers

ProQuest Statistical Abstract of the United States: 2016

Note: Index citations refer to **table** numbers, not **page** numbers

C

Cabbage, 241, 884
Cable and other pay television services, 747, 1152
Cable and other subscription programming:
Earnings, 651, 1136
Employees, 651, 1136
Establishments, 1136
Finances, 1137, 1153
Revenue, 1137, 1152, 1153
Cadmium, 925, 928
Cafeterias. (See Food services and drinking places.)
California. (See State data.)
Calves, 864, 890, 891, 894
Cambodia. (See Foreign countries.)
Cameroon. (See Foreign countries.)
Campaigns, fundraising, 453, 454, 455, 456, 457, 458
Camping, 1258
Canada, (See also Foreign countries.), 389, 392
Cancer (malignancies), 197, 200, 201, 202
Deaths, 127, 128, 129, 130, 131, 132, 133, 136, 201
Candy, 747
Cantaloupes, 884
Capacity utilization, index, 808
Cape Verde. (See Foreign countries.)
Capital (see also individual industries):
Banking, 1191, 1192
Expenditures, 800, 801, 802, 803, 813, 1028
New security issues, 1212
Residential, 1022
Stocks, 799, 1036
Utilities, 972, 977
Capital equipment, producer price indexes, 757
Capital gains, 505, 506
Capital punishment, 377, 378, 379
Carbon dioxide emissions, 404, 405, 1390
Cardiovascular disease. (See Heart disease.)
Carpal tunnel syndrome, 681
Carrots, 241, 884
Cars. (See Automobiles.)
Casualty insurance, 1229
Catalog and mail order sales, 1060, 1062, 1066, 1067
Catfish, 918
Catholic population. (See Religion.)
Cat ownership, 1248
CAT scans, 189
Cattle:
Dairy cows, 892, 895, 896
Farm marketings, sales, 864, 865
Imports, 872
Number on farms, 891, 892, 894
Prices, 757, 891
Production, 891, 894
Slaughter, 894
Value on farms, 891
Cauliflower, 241, 884
Celery, 241, 884
Cellular and other wireless telecommunications, 1136, 1137, 1154, 1155, 1157, 1158, 1161
Cellular telephones (see also Telephone carriers.), 1156, 1157, 1158, 1159, 1161, 1167, 1392, 1394
Cement (see also Nonmetallic mineral product

manufacturing), 924, 925, 928
Earnings, 651
Employment, 651, 925
Prices, 757, 925
Productivity, 658
World production, 1381
Central African Republic. (See Foreign countries.)
Central America. (See Foreign countries.)
Central and South American population (see also Hispanic or Latino origin population), 35, 87, 94
Cereal and bakery products:
Expenditures, prices, 706, 708, 709, 747
Per capita consumption, 242
Cerebrovascular diseases, deaths, 127, 128, 129, 130, 131, 132, 133, 135, 197
Certificates of deposit, 1184
Cesarean section deliveries, 95, 189
Chad. (See Foreign countries.)
Charitable contributions (see also Philanthropy), 510, 512, 599, 600, 602, 603
Charter schools, 276, 277
Checks, payments made, 1198
Cheerleading, 1258
Cheese (see also Dairy products), 242, 754, 896
Chemical engineering, degrees conferred, 833
Chemical products:
Foreign trade, 870, 1304, 1311, 1315
Price indexes, 757, 761, 762
Production, 807
Chemicals manufacturing (see also individual chemicals):
Capital, 799
Earnings, 651, 1028, 1035
Employees, 651, 1026, 1028, 1030, 1035
Establishments, 1026
Finances, 812
Foreign trade, 761, 762, 1031, 1315
Gross domestic product, 690, 1024
Industrial production index, 807
Inventories, 1037, 1038
Multinational companies, 814, 815, 816
Productivity, 658
Profits, 812
Research and development, 823, 824
Shipments, 1028, 1037, 1038
Toxic chemical releases, 410, 411
Waterborne commerce, 1095
Chemistry (see also Physical sciences):
Degrees conferred, 832, 833
Employment, 633
Salary offers, 310
Cherries, 241, 885
Chicken pox, 203
Chickens. (See Poultry.)
Child abuse, 372, 373
Child care, 587, 590, 592, 633, 637, 747
Expenditures for, 590, 592, 711
Tax credit, 513
Child day care services, 172, 595, 633, 651
Child support, 557, 588, 589, 590
Children (see also Births, Deaths, Marriages, Divorces, and Population):
Adopted, 79, 80, 81, 591
Age and/or sex, 6, 8, 9, 10, 11, 17, 79, 80
Aid, social welfare programs, 555, 557, 561, 579, 580, 582, 583, 585, 586, 588, 589, 593, 595

Note: Index citations refer to **table** numbers, not **page** numbers

AIDS, 206
Allergies, 239
American Indian, Alaska Native population, 9, 10, 11, 80
Asian population, 9, 10, 11, 69, 80
Asthma, 236
Attention Deficit Disorder, 230
Autism, 229, 231
Black, African American population, 9, 10, 11, 69, 80
Child abuse, 372, 373
Child day care, 587, 747
Child support, 557, 588, 589, 590
Cigarette smoking, 220
Cost of raising, 711
Crime, arrests, 355
Deaths and death rates, 120, 122, 124, 125, 126, 131, 132, 134, 135, 136, 137
Dependency ratios, 18
Developmental delay, 229
Disability status, 80, 207, 229, 230, 231, 232
Families with, 64, 65, 66, 67, 68, 76
Food cost, 753
Food insecurity, 215, 581
Food stamp program, 558, 585, 586
Foreign-born population, 38, 39
Foreign country, 1344, 1375
Foster care, 591
Grandparents living with grandchildren, 70
Head Start program, 593
Health insurance coverage, 157, 160, 167, 168, 169
High school dropouts, 284, 285
High school graduates, 283, 288
Hispanic origin population, 9, 10, 11, 69
Homeschooled, 262
Homicides, school-related, 327
Hospital use, 188, 196, 197
Hunger, 215
Immigrants, 48, 80
Immunization against diseases, 234, 235
Income, families with children, 722
Injuries, 213
Juvenile delinquency institutions, 370
Labor force (16 to 19 years old), 605
   Employed, 620, 623, 626, 628
   Employment status, 614
   Minimum wage workers, 670
   Multiple job holders, 626
   Participation rates, 615
   Sex, 605, 610
   Unemployed, 641, 642, 647
Language proficiency, 258
Learning disability, 229
Literacy, comparative, 1375
Living arrangements, 69, 78, 81
Mobility status, 29
Mothers in the labor force, 618, 625
Murders, 334
Native Hawaiian, Other Pacific Islander population, 9, 10, 11, 80
Obesity, 237
Physical activity, 238
Physician visits, 184

Pneumonia, 197
Poverty, 732, 733
Projections, 8, 11, 12
Races, two or more, 9, 10, 11
Respiratory infection, acute, 188
School enrollment, 246, 247, 248, 249, 250, 251, 252, 259, 264, 265, 267
Social security beneficiaries and payments, 561
Special education, 232
Stay-at-home parents, 68
Stepchildren, 79, 80, 81
Suicides, 131, 137, 139, 327
Chile. (See Foreign countries.)
China. (See Foreign countries.)
Chiropractors, 172
Chlamydia, 203, 204
Chocolate. (See Cocoa.)
Christian population. (See Religion.)
Chromium, 925, 935
Churches (see also Religion):
   Clergy, 633
   Construction value, 987
   Grants, foundations, 599
   Membership, 85
   Volunteers, 598
Cigar smoking, 220
Cigarettes (see also Tobacco):
   Consumption, 1348
   Smokers and use, 217, 218, 220, 221
Circuit boards, 1048
Circulation of media, 1140, 1145, 1146
Circulatory diseases, 211
Cirrhosis of liver, deaths, 128, 129, 130, 131, 132
Cities (see also Metropolitan statistical areas):
   Climate, 421, 422, 423, 424, 1391
   Commuting, 1122, 1125, 1127, 1130
   Crime, 330, 332
   Employees, earnings, payrolls, 490
   Foreign born, 37
   Income, 728
   Language spoken at home, 55
   Population, 24, 25, 37
   Poverty, 728
   Property tax rates, 474
   Roadway congestion, 1122
   Taxes, 473
   Travel, 1271
Citizenship, 40, 47
Citrus fruits, 241, 885
Civil aviation. (See Air transportation.)
Civil cases, U.S. Courts, 364, 365, 366, 367
Civil service employees. (See Government: Employees.)
Clams, 917, 919, 920
Classical music, 1246
Clay, 924, 925
Cleaning supplies, 708, 709
Clergy, 633
Climate, selected cities:
   Precipitation, 423, 1391
   Temperature, 420, 421, 422, 1391
Clocks and watches, 747
Clothing. (See Apparel goods.)

Note: Index citations refer to **table** numbers, not **page** numbers

---

Note: Index citations refer to **table** numbers, not **page** numbers

Computerized axial tomography (CAT scans), 189
Computers and electronic product manufacturing:
  Capital, 799
  Earnings, 651, 1028, 1035
  Employees, 651, 1026, 1028, 1030, 1035
  Establishments, 1026
  Finances, 812
  Foreign trade, 1315
  Gross domestic product, 690, 1024
  Industrial production index, 807
  Inventories, 1037, 1038, 1039
  Multinational companies, 814, 815
  Productivity, 658
  Prices, 761
  Profits, 812
  Research and development, 824
  Shipments, 1028, 1037, 1038, 1039, 1048, 1049
Concerts, symphony orchestras, 1242
Condensed and evaporated milk, 242
Congestion, on roads, 1122
Congo (Brazzaville). (See Foreign countries.)
Congo (Kinshasa). (See Foreign countries.)
Congress, U.S.:
  Apportionment of, 438
  Asians, 452
  Bills, acts, resolutions, 443, 444
  Blacks, 452
  Campaign finances, 457, 458
  Composition of, 441, 442, 451
  Congressional districts, 440
  Hispanics, 452
  Seniority, 451
  Time, in sessions, 443
  Women, 452
  Votes cast, 429, 437, 439, 440
Connecticut. (See State data.)
Construction industry (see also Building construction, and Highways):
  Building permits, 984
  Capital, 799, 801, 803
  Construction contracts, 987, 988
  Earnings, 649, 651, 661, 662, 775, 787, 788, 789, 790, 791, 792, 793, 1333
  Employees, 640, 649, 650, 651, 775, 778, 779, 787, 788, 789, 790, 791, 792, 793, 836, 981, 1333
  Equipment and software expenditures, 801
  Establishments, 775, 776, 778, 779, 981, 1333
  Finances, 765, 768, 1328
  Gross domestic product, 690, 1328
  Hires and separations, 656, 657
  Hours, 649
  Nonemployers, 776
  Occupational safety, 678, 680
  Profits, 811
  Residential, 984, 985, 986, 989, 990, 991
  Shipments, receipts, 765, 768, 773, 774, 775, 776, 787, 788, 789, 790, 791, 792, 793
  Unions, 685
  Value, of, 983, 985, 986, 987
Construction machinery, manufacturing:
  Earnings, 651, 1028
  Employees, 651, 1028
  Productivity, 658

Shipments, 1028
Construction materials. (See Building materials.)
Consumers:
  Consumer complaints, 342, 1091
  Consumer goods, 214, 757, 1159, 1167
  Credit, 769, 770, 1183, 1186, 1189, 1200, 1201, 1202, 1206
  Expenditures:
    Entertainment, 697, 706, 708, 709, 1239, 1241
    Education, 697, 706, 708, 709
    Food, 697, 706, 707, 708, 709, 710, 758, 868
    Health insurance, 155
    Housing, 697, 706, 707, 708, 709, 710, 758
    Medical care, 149, 150, 151, 152, 155, 156, 697, 706, 707, 708, 709, 710, 758
    Metropolitan areas, 707
    Pets, 1241
    Reading material, 706, 708, 709, 1239, 1241, 1252
    Sporting goods, 1241
    Transportation, 697, 706, 708, 709, 758
Consumer price indexes, 744, 745, 746, 747
  Foreign countries, 1361, 1368
  Medical care, 154, 745, 747
  Purchasing power of the dollar, 744
Consumption. (See individual commodities, and Personal consumption expenditures.)
Contraception, use of, 108
Convenience stores. (See Food and Beverage Stores.)
Copper:
  Consumption, 925, 935
  Foreign trade, 925, 935
  Prices, 757, 761, 762, 925, 926
  Production and value, 924, 925, 928, 1381
Copyrights, registration, 798
Corn:
  Acreage, 880, 881
  Consumption, 241, 242, 1376
  Ethanol, 880
  Farm marketings, sales, 864, 865
  Foreign trade, 874, 876, 877, 880, 1311, 1376, 1380
  Genetically engineered, 857
  Prices, 757, 761, 880, 881
  Production, 874, 880, 881, 884, 1376
  Supply and disappearance, 880
Corporations:
  Bonds, 1208
  Capital, 772
  Dividend payments, 809
  Finances, 763, 764, 765, 766, 767, 768, 770, 771, 772, 773, 774, 1063, 1180, 1181, 1219
  Manufacturing, 1040, 1041, 1042
  Nonfinancial, 770
  Philanthropy, 599
  Profits, 763, 809, 810, 811, 812, 1040, 1041, 1063
  Receipts, 763
  Sales, 768, 773, 774, 1040
  Taxes:
    Corporate income tax, 464, 465, 478, 479, 481, 809
    Returns, 763, 764, 765, 772, 773, 774

Note: Index citations refer to **table** numbers, not **page** numbers

---

Note: Index citations refer to **table** numbers, not **page** numbers

Public assistance recipients and/or payments, 577
Social security recipients, 561, 562
Students with disabilities, 230, 231, 232, 297
Supplemental security income recipients and payments, 577
Veterans receiving compensation, 536
Disability Insurance Trust Fund (Social Security), 499, 563
Disasters, natural, 416, 417, 419, 426
Diseases (see also specific Diseases, and Deaths and Death rates), 197, 203, 210, 681
Deaths from, 127, 128, 129, 130, 131, 132, 133
Expenditures for, 156
Dishwashers, in housing units, 1006
Disposable personal income (see also Income, and National income), 698, 699, 702, 1189
District Courts, U.S., 364, 365, 368
District of Columbia. (See State data.)
Dividends:
Corporation, 809
Individual income tax returns, 504, 505
National and/or personal income components, 698
Persons receiving income, 557
Divorces, (see also Marriages and Marital status), 86, 142, 143, 144
Djibouti. (See Foreign countries.)
Doctorates:
Conferred, 311, 312, 829, 830, 832
Field, 315, 832, 833
Non U.S. citizen, 829
Sex, 311, 830, 832
Doctors, M.D.s. (See Physicians.)
Dog ownership, 1248
Dominica. (See Foreign countries.)
Dominican Republic. (See Foreign countries.)
Dow-Jones stock index, 1216, 1396
Dress codes, 325
Drinking places. (See Food services and drinking places.)
Drinking water, 979, 980
Driving (see also Motor vehicles, and Transportation):
Crashes, 1113, 1114, 1118
Distracted driving, 1114
Fatal accidents, 1081, 1110, 1112, 1114, 1115, 1118, 1119, 1120
Intoxicated, 1115, 1116, 1117
Licensed drivers, 1107, 1120
Drought, 425
Drowning, 130, 139, 333
Drug stores and proprietary stores. (See Pharmacies and drug stores.)
Drugs, illegal:
Deaths/overdoses, 130, 141
Enforcement activities, 354, 361
Juveniles, 370, 371
Seizures, 354
Testing, schools, 325
Treatment, 219
Usage, 220, 221
Drugs and medicines (see also Pharmaceutical and medicine manufacturing):
Consumer price indexes, 154, 747
Expenditures for, 146, 148, 149, 150, 153, 155, 156
Foreign trade, 1311

Medicaid payments, 164
Price indexes, 154, 747, 758
Retail sales, 1067
Shipments, 1051
Use, 222
Dry-cleaning and laundry services:
Earnings, 651
Employees, 651, 1281
Establishments, 1280, 1281
Productivity, 658
Receipts, 1280, 1290
Dwellings. (See Housing and housing units, and Households or families.)

E

Earnings, (see also individual industries), 663, 664
Airlines, 1082
American Indian and Alaska Native-owned businesses, 786, 793
Asian-owned businesses, 786, 791
Black-owned businesses, 786, 790
College faculty, 307
College graduates, salaries, 310
Educational attainment, 256, 666, 725
Employment covered by social insurance, 560, 573, 574, 575
Family type, 720, 721
Foreign-born population, 38
Government employees:
Federal, 484, 485, 515, 516, 661, 663
State and local, 484, 485, 486, 487, 489, 661, 663
Hispanic or Latino origin-owned businesses, 789
Income tax returns (reported totals), 502, 503, 504, 505
Manufacturing, 901, 1026, 1028, 1034
Mineral industries, 921
Minimum wage workers, 669, 670
Minority-owned businesses, 788
Municipal employees, 490
Native Hawaiian and Other Pacific Islander-owned businesses, 792
Occupations, 635, 665, 667, 668, 672, 673
Personal income, 698, 700, 701, 702, 703
Private employer firms, 663
Public school systems, 278
Retail industries, 1061
School teachers, 264, 272, 273, 274, 275
States, 664
Union members, 685
Women, 665, 666, 672, 673, 787
Earthquakes, 417
Earth sciences, degrees conferred, 833
Eating and drinking places. (See Food services and drinking places.)
E-commerce. (See Electronic commerce.)
Economic aid, foreign, 1302, 1303
Ecuador. (See Foreign countries.)
Education:
American College Testing (ACT) Program, 281
Attainment, 32, 34, 253, 254, 255, 257, 268, 1375
American Indian, Alaska Native population, 34
Asian population, 34, 255

Note: Index citations refer to **table** numbers, not **page** numbers

---

Note: Index citations refer to **table** numbers, not **page** numbers

Note: Index citations refer to **table** numbers, not **page** numbers

---

Note: Index citations refer to **table** numbers, not **page** numbers

Research and development, 820, 826
    Salary, 310, 839
English, ability to speak, 53, 54, 55, 258, 268
Entertainment:
    Consumer expenditures, 697, 706, 708, 709,
        1239
    Consumer price indexes, 747
    Gaming, 1266
    Personal expenditures, 697, 708, 709, 1241
Environment (see also Pollution):
    Charitable contributions, 599
    Environmental industries, 409
    Volunteers, 598
    Wetlands, 397, 399
Environmental science, 820, 826, 828
Equatorial Guinea. (See Foreign countries.)
Eritrea. (See Foreign countries.)
Eskimo population. (See American Indian, Alaska
        Native population.)
Establishments. (See Business enterprise, and
        individual industries.)
Estate and gift taxes, 501
Estonia. (See Foreign countries.)
Ethane, 930
Ethanol, 880, 953
Ethiopia. (See Foreign countries.)
Ethnicities. (See Hispanic or Latino origin
        population.)
Ethylene, 930
Europe. (See Foreign countries.)
European Union. (See Foreign countries.)
Exchange-traded funds, 1180, 1213
Excise taxes, 498, 501
Executions of prisoners, 378, 379
Executive Office of the President (federal), 518
Exercise program, 1247
Exercise equipment, 214, 1259
Expectation of life (average lifetime), 116, 115, 117,
        118
    Foreign countries, 1345
    Projections, 115
Expenditures. (See individual subjects).
Expenditures of state and local government. (See
        individual governmental units.)
Expenditures of U.S. government, 462, 463,
        496, 696, 1302, 1303
    Aid to the arts and humanities, 1243
    Aid to state and local government, 462, 463
    Budget outlays, 492, 494, 495, 496, 497
    Education. (See Federal aid to education.)
    Food programs, federal, 583, 584
    Health, 146, 147, 148, 149, 150, 463
    Homeland security, 463, 542, 543, 544, 545, 546
    Hospitals, 190
    National defense, 522, 523, 759
    Outlays, 492, 494, 495, 496, 497
    Payrolls, 484, 485, 515, 516, 517
    Price indexes, 759
    Public debt, 493
    Research and development, 817, 818, 819, 821,
        822
    Schools, 244
    Science/space, 840
    Veterans benefits. (See Veterans Affairs.)

Exports. (See Foreign trade.)
Express mail, 1134, 1135

F

Fabricated metal product manufacturing:
    Capital, 799, 1300
    Earnings, 651, 1028, 1035
    Employees, 651, 1026, 1028, 1030, 1035
    Establishments, 1026
    Finance, 812
    Foreign trade, 1031, 1315
    Gross domestic product, 690, 1024
    Industrial production index, 807
    Occupational safety, 678
    Productivity, 658
    Profits, 812
    Shipments, 1028, 1037, 1038
    Toxic chemical releases, 411
Fabrics. (See Textile mill products.)
Falls, accidental deaths, 130, 131
Families. (See Households.)
Family and consumer sciences, degrees conferred,
        313, 314, 315
Family farms, 852, 853
Farm mortgage loans, 1203
Farms:
    Acreage, 843, 844, 845, 846, 847, 848, 853, 850,
        856
        Cropland, 396, 398, 842, 846, 879
        Crops harvested (see also individual crops), 879,
            880, 881, 882, 883, 884, 1376
        Farm type, 853
    Agrichemicals, 862, 867, 870
    Agricultural products:
        Exports, 1380
        Foreign countries, production, 1377, 1378
        Market value, 842
        Prices. (See Prices received by farmers.)
        Waterborne commerce, 1095
        World production, 1376, 1377, 1378
    Assets and liabilities, 860, 1180
    Corporate, 845, 848, 853
    Crops (see also individual crops):
        Acreage, 879, 880, 1331
        Fruits and nuts, 885, 886, 1332
        Income, 864, 866, 1331
        Production, 874, 879, 880, 1376, 1377
        Vegetables, 884, 888
    Debt, 860, 1203
    Expenses, 858, 862
    Family or individual, 845, 847, 852, 1331
    Farm land and buildings value, 847, 848, 849, 860
    Farm operators, 849
    Farm products sold, marketing receipts, 847, 848,
        849, 850, 851, 855, 861, 862, 864, 865, 866
        Fertilizers:
            Farm expenditures for, 862
            Foreign trade, 870, 1311
            Prices, 757, 867
    Farm to school programs, 859
    Government payments to farmers, 849, 851, 861,
        862, 863

Note: Index citations refer to **table** numbers, not **page** numbers

---

Note: Index citations refer to **table** numbers, not **page** numbers

Note: Index citations refer to **table** numbers, not **page** numbers

---

Note: Index citations refer to **table** numbers, not **page** numbers

Note: Index citations refer to **table** numbers, not **page** numbers

---

Note: Index citations refer to **table** numbers, not **page** numbers

---

Note: Index citations refer to **table** numbers, not **page** numbers

Note: Index citations refer to **table** numbers, not **page** numbers

Note: Index citations refer to **table** numbers, not **page** numbers

---

Note: Index citations refer to **table** numbers, not **page** numbers

Immigrants (see also Foreign-born population):
  Class of admission, 43, 48, 49
  Country of birth, 46, 49, 50, 51
  Deported, 547, 549, 550
  Doctorates, 829
  Foreign countries, 1343
  Interdiction, 551
  Orphans, adoption of, 46
  Refugees, 44, 48, 49, 51
  Unauthorized, 45
Immunization of children, 234, 235
Imports. (See Foreign trade.)
Income (see also Consumer expenditures, Earnings, and Poverty):
  Aggregate income, 716
  American Indian, Alaska Native population, 34
  Asian and Pacific Islander population, 713, 718, 719
  Asian population, 34, 712, 715, 717, 718, 719, 723, 726, 727
  Black, African American population, 34, 557, 712, 713, 715, 717, 718, 719, 723, 726, 727
  City, 728
  Consumer expenditures, 710
  Corporate, 763, 765, 772, 773
  Disposable personal, 698, 699, 702
  Distribution, 712, 714, 718, 720, 724
  Families, 34, 35, 705, 717, 718, 719, 720, 721, 722, 728, 1326
  Farms, 861, 863, 864, 866
  Foreign born, 38, 39
  Hispanic or Latino origin population, 34, 35, 557, 712, 713, 715, 717, 718, 719, 723, 726, 727
  Households:
    Age, 714
    Asian population, 712, 715
    Black, African American population, 712, 713, 715
    Computer use, 1165
    Educational attainment, 714
    Elderly, 714
    Hispanic origin population, 712, 713, 715
    Homeschooling, 262
    Internet access/use, 1163, 1170
    Mobility status, 30
    Recreation activities, physical activity, 226, 1259, 1265
    State data, 704
    Stock, mutual fund ownership, 1184, 1217, 1220, 1221
    Student loan debt, 318
    Taxes, 1365
    Tenure, 714
  Individuals, 557, 737, 738, 739
  Leisure time use, 1253
  Millionaires, 737, 738, 739
  National income, 687, 688, 689, 693, 699
  Native Hawaiian, Other Pacific Islander population, 34
  Participation in arts and leisure, 1246, 1247
  Per capita, 699, 701, 726
  Personal, 698, 700, 701, 702, 703
  Persons, 38, 723, 726, 727
    Educational attainment, 724, 725
    Source of income, 557

Savings, 694, 695
Sports participation, goods, 1258, 1259
State data:
  Gross domestic product, 691, 692
  Family, 705
  Household, 704
  Personal income, 700, 701, 702
  Wealth, 739
Veterans, 538
Income tax (see also Tax receipts):
  Alternative minimum tax, 507
  Average tax by income level, 509
  Capital gains, 505, 506
  Corporation, 501, 772
  Deductions, 510, 511, 512
  Foreign countries, 1364
  Individual, 502, 503, 505, 506, 507, 508, 509, 510, 511, 512, 514,
  Tax credits, 513
Index numbers. (See individual subjects.)
India. (See Foreign countries.)
Indian, American population. (See American Indian, Alaska Native population.)
Indian, Asian population. (See Asian Indian population.)
Indiana. (See State data.)
Individual retirement accounts (IRAs), 505, 511, 512, 565, 570, 571, 1221, 1223
Indo-European languages, 258
Indonesia. (See Foreign countries.)
Industrial energy, 948, 950, 951, 952, 954, 966, 969, 970, 971, 975
Industrial minerals, 924, 925
Industrial production indexes, 807, 1356
Industry. (See Corporations, and individual industries.)
Infant deaths (see also Deaths and death rates), 86, 124, 125, 126, 1320, 1345
Inflation. (See Consumer price indexes, and Prices.)
Information and communications technology equipment, 801, 1039, 1050
Information industry:
  Capital, 799, 801, 803
  Earnings, 649, 651, 661, 662, 775, 787, 788, 789, 790, 791, 792, 793, 1136, 1138, 1139
  Electronic commerce, 1286
  Employees, 640, 649, 650, 651, 775, 778, 779, 787, 788, 789, 790, 791, 792, 793, 836, 1136, 1138, 1139
  Equipment and software expenditures, 801
  Establishments, 775, 776, 778, 779, 1136, 1138, 1139
  Finances, 765, 768, 1137, 1300
  Gross domestic product, 690, 692
  Hires and separations, 656, 657
  Hours, 649
  Multinational companies, 814, 815
  Nonemployers, 776, 1139
  Occupational safety, 678, 680
  Productivity, 658
  Profits, 765, 810, 811
  Research and development, 823, 824
  Shipments, revenue, 765, 768, 773, 774, 775, 776, 788, 789, 790, 791, 792, 793, 1137, 1138

Note: Index citations refer to **table** numbers, not **page** numbers

ProQuest Statistical Abstract of the United States: 2016

Note: Index citations refer to **table** numbers, not **page** numbers

---

Note: Index citations refer to **table** numbers, not **page** numbers

Employment cost index, 668, 750, 1357, 1358
Employment taxes and contributions, 498
Environmentally sustainable jobs, 634
Females, 487, 606, 610, 611, 612, 614, 615, 616,
    617, 618, 632, 633, 640, 641, 642, 643, 644,
    646, 647, 652, 665, 667, 670, 672
Firm sizes, 782
Flexible schedules, 625
Foreign countries, 1359, 1369, 1370, 1372, 1373,
    1374
Foreign-owned firms, 1298, 1299
Government. (See Government: Employees.)
High technology, 838
Hires and separations, 656, 657
Hours, 649, 660, 1357, 1359
Indexes of compensation, 659, 1358
Internet access, 1141, 1165
Job creation, 782
Job gains/losses, 654, 655, 656, 657
Labor strikes, 683
Mass layoffs, 653
Metropolitan areas, 613
Minimum wage workers, 670
Mobility status, 29
Occupational groups. (See Occupations, and
    individual occupations.)
Occupational safety, 677, 678, 679, 680, 681
Part-time work, 629, 660, 675, 676
Poverty status, 734
Production workers, 1028, 1029, 1032, 1034,
    1043
Productivity, 658, 659, 1357, 1359
Projections, 605, 637, 638
Self-employed, 623, 624, 836
Social insurance coverage, 560
State data, 612, 636, 648, 664
Telecommuting, 676
Tenure with employer, 628
Unemployed workers:
    Age, 607, 641, 642
    Asian and Pacific Islander population, 606, 641,
        646
    Asian population, 606, 607, 614, 641, 642, 646
    Black, African American population, 606, 607,
        614, 641, 642, 646
    Educational attainment, 255, 646
    Foreign-born population, 607
    Foreign countries, 1369, 1370
    Hispanic origin population, 35, 606, 607, 614,
        641, 642, 646
    Industry, 644
    Job search activities, 642
    Occupation, 645
    Race, 606, 607, 614, 641, 642, 646
    Reason, 622, 631, 643, 647
    Sex, 606, 607, 612, 614, 615, 617, 641, 642,
        643, 644, 645, 646, 647
    States, 612, 648
Union membership, 684, 685, 686
Veterans, 519, 608
Work stoppages, 683
Workplace deaths/injuries, 677, 678, 679, 680,
    681
Workplace violence, 682

Labor organizations or unions: Membership, 684,
    685, 686
    Political action committees (PAC), 453, 454
Labor strikes, 683
Lacrosse, 1255, 1256, 1257, 1258
Lakes, 387, 388, 389, 390, 399
Lamb and mutton (see also Meat and meat
    products), 242, 890
Lambs. (See Sheep and lambs.)
Land (see also Farms, and Public lands):
    Area:
        Border lengths, 392
        Coastal, 27, 393
        Foreign countries, 1342
        Horticultural specialty crops, 889
        Island areas, 387
        Land cover/use, 396, 397, 398
        National parks, 1260, 1261, 1262
        States, 387
        United States, 1, 387
    Farmland, 396, 398, 843, 844, 845, 846, 847,
        856
    Federal land, 396, 905
    Foreign investors, 1298, 1299
    Forest, area and ownership, 396, 397, 398, 905
    Parks, 1260, 1261, 1262, 1263
    Shoreline, 393
    Use, 396, 397, 398
    Wetlands, 397, 399
Landfills (see also Solid waste), 406, 973
Languages spoken at home, 53, 54, 55, 258, 268
Laos. (See Foreign countries.)
Larceny, larceny-theft, 329, 330, 331, 332, 337,
    344, 345
Lard, 242
Latex. (See Rubber.)
Latvia. (See Foreign countries.)
Laundry, cleaning, and garment services. (See Dry-
    cleaning and laundry services.)
Law degrees conferred, 313, 314, 315, 316
Law enforcement (see also Courts, Correctional
    institutions, and Crime):
    Arrests, 328, 355, 356, 361
    Drug enforcement, 354, 361
    Employees, 352, 485
    Expenditures, 464, 465, 478, 480
    Handgun checks, 353
    Police officers, 352, 357, 485, 633
Lawn care, 747, 757
Lawyers (see also Legal services), 633
Lead, 401, 924, 925, 926, 928, 1381
Learning disabilities, 230
Leasing. (See Real estate, Rental and leasing
    industry.)
Leather and allied product, manufacturing (see also
    Footwear):
    Capital, 799
    Earnings, 651, 1028, 1035
    Employees, 651, 1026, 1028, 1030, 1035
    Establishments, 1026
    Foreign trade, 1315
    Gross domestic product, 690, 1024
    Industrial production index, 807
    Prices, 757
    Shipments, 1037, 1038
    Toxic chemical releases, 411

Note: Index citations refer to **table** numbers, not **page** numbers

Note: Index citations refer to **table** numbers, not **page** numbers

Lung disease. (See Pulmonary or respiratory disease.)
Luxembourg. (See Foreign countries.)
Lyme disease, 203, 204

M

Macadamia nuts, 885
Macedonia. (See Foreign countries.)
Machine tools, 747, 757
Machinery manufacturing:
  Capital, 799
  Earnings, 651, 1026, 1028, 1035
  Employees, 651, 1026, 1028, 1030, 1035
  Establishments, 1026
  Finances, 812
  Foreign trade, 761, 762, 1031, 1311
  Gross domestic product, 690, 1024
  Industrial production index, 807
  Inventories, 1038
  Price indexes, 761, 762
  Productivity, 658
  Profits, 812
  Research and development, 823, 824
  Shipments, 1028, 1037, 1038
  Toxic chemical releases, 411
Madagascar. (See Foreign countries.)
Magnesium, 925, 928
Mail, 1134, 1135
Mail order houses (including electronic shopping):
  Earnings, 651, 1061
  Employees, 651, 1059, 1061
  Establishments, 1059, 1060
  Productivity, 658
  Sales, 1060, 1062, 1066, 1067
Maine. (See State data.)
Malaria, 203
Malawi. (See Foreign countries.)
Malaysia. (See Foreign countries.)
Maldives. (See Foreign countries.)
Male householders. (See Households or families.)
Mali. (See Foreign countries.)
Malignant neoplasms. (See Cancer.)
Malt beverages (see also Beverages), 747, 869, 872
Malta. (See Foreign countries.)
Mammography testing, 216
Managed care health plans, 165
Management of companies and enterprises:
  Capital, 799, 801, 803
  Earnings, 651, 661
  Employees, 633, 651, 775, 778, 779, 1279, 1281
  Establishments, 775, 778, 779, 1279, 1280, 1281
  Equipment and software expenditures, 801
  Finances, 765, 768, 773, 774
  Gross domestic product, 690
  Profits, 775, 811
  Receipts, 765, 768, 773, 774, 1279, 1280
Managers. (See Proprietors.)
Manganese, 925, 935
Manganiferous ore, 924
Manufacturing industry (see also individual industries):
  Capital, 799, 801, 803
  Construction value, 985

Earnings, 649, 651, 661, 662, 775, 787, 788, 789, 790, 791, 792, 793, 1028, 1034, 1035, 1333
Economic indicators, 805
Employees, 640, 649, 650, 651, 775, 778, 779, 787, 788, 789, 790, 791, 792, 793, 836, 1025, 1027, 1029, 1030, 1033, 1035, 1333
Equipment and software expenditures, 801
Establishments, 775, 776, 778, 779, 1025, 1027, 1028, 1333
Finances, 765, 768, 812, 1040, 1041, 1042, 1300, 1328
Foreign countries, 1357, 1358
Foreign investments in U.S., 1297
Foreign trade, 1031
Form of organization, 1028
Gross domestic product, 690, 692, 1024, 1328
Hires and separations, 656, 657
Hours, 649, 1032, 1033
Industrial production index, 807, 1033
Inventories, 806, 1037, 1038, 1039
Investment abroad, 1300
Island areas of the United States, 1327, 1333
Multinational companies, 814, 815, 816
Nonemployers, 776, 1025
Occupational safety, 678, 680
Productivity, 658, 659, 808, 1033, 1357
Profits, 810, 811, 812, 1040, 1041, 1042
Sales, shipments, receipts, 765, 768, 773, 774, 775, 776, 787, 788, 789, 790, 791, 792, 793, 806, 1028, 1029, 1031, 1036, 1037, 1038, 1039, 1042, 1048, 1049, 1050, 1051, 1052
State data, 1027, 1029, 1034
Toxic chemical releases, 411
Union membership, 685
Margarine, 242, 738, 754
Marijuana (see also Drugs, illegal), 220, 221, 354, 361
Marine Corps, 525
Marital status:
  Asian population, 56, 75
  Black, African American population, 56, 75
  Computer use, 1165
  Contraceptive use, 107
  Couples with or without own household, 59
  Elderly, 32, 57, 75
  Employed persons, 616, 617, 619
  Foreign-born population, 38
  Hispanic origin population, 56
  Householder status, 66
  Internet access, 1165
  Labor force participation rates, 615, 616, 617, 618
  Male householder, 66
  Nonfamily householder, 71
  Same-sex couple households, 74, 75
  Sexual activity, 105
  Unmarried partners, 75, 76, 77
  Women in the labor force, 616, 617
Marriages (see also Marital status), 86, 142, 143, 144, 145
Married couples. (See Households or families.)

Note: Index citations refer to **table** numbers, not **page** numbers

Married persons. (See Marital status.)
Marshall Islands. (See Foreign countries.)
Maryland. (See State data.)
Massachusetts. (See State data.)
Maternal and child health services, expenditures for, 147
Mathematics:
    Degrees conferred, 313, 314, 315, 833
    Employment, 836, 839
    Literacy, 1375
    Research & development, 820, 826
    Salary, 310, 839
Mauritania. (See Foreign countries.)
Mauritius. (See Foreign countries.)
Measles, 203, 235
Meat and meat products (see also Food
        manufacturing, and individual meats):
    Consumer expenditures, 708, 709
    Consumption, 242, 890, 1376, 1379
    Farm marketings, 862, 864
    Foreign trade, 869, 875, 877, 890, 1311, 1376
    Price indexes, 747, 754, 755, 762
    Production, 890, 1376, 1378
    Supply, 890
Mechanical engineering, 833
Media (see also individual medium), 1140, 1141
Medicaid:
    Coverage, recipients, 160, 163, 164, 165, 167,
        558, 559
    Expenditures, 151, 153, 163, 164
    Federal payments, 497
    Nursing homes, 164
    State data, 163, 165
Medical care (see also Health services):
    Expenditures for, 146, 147, 148, 149, 150, 151,
        152, 153, 155, 156, 554, 555, 556, 706, 707,
        708, 709, 1351
    Insurance benefits, 147, 148, 151
    Price indexes, consumer, 154, 745, 746, 747, 758
Medical equipment and products:
    Expenditures for, 156
Medical equipment and supplies manufacturing,
        651, 658, 1028
Medical malpractice insurance, 1229
Medical records, security breaches, 178
Medical research, 147, 148
Medical schools, 176, 316
Medical sciences, employment, 174, 633
Medical services. (See Health services.)
Medicare:
    Ambulatory care visits, 187
    Benefit payments, expenditures, 147, 148, 151,
        152, 153, 161, 162, 166, 555
    Contributions, 161
    Enrollees, 158, 159, 167
    Federal payments, 161, 166, 496, 497
    Hospices, 180, 181
    Hospital visits, 187
    State data, 159
    Trust funds, 161, 499
Medicines (see Drugs and medicines, and
        Pharmaceutical and medicine manufacturing):
Melons, 241, 884

Membership organizations:
    Earnings, 651
    Employees, 651, 1282
    Establishments, 1281
    Revenue, 1290
Menhaden, 917
Meningitis, 203
Mental disorders and illness, 197, 228, 229, 231,
    233, 360, 681
Mental hospitals, 190, 193
Mercury, 925, 928
Metal detectors, in public schools, 325
Metal ore mining industry, 921, 922, 923
Metals, 921, 924, 925, 926, 928, 935
    Foreign trade, 935, 1311, 1315
    Prices, 757, 761, 762
    Production and value, 923, 924, 925
    Recycling, 406, 407, 408
    Spot market price indexes, 755
    World production, 928, 1381
Metalworking manufacturing, 651, 658, 1028,
Methamphetamine, (See also Drugs, illegal), 220,
    354, 361
Methane emissions, 404
Metropolitan statistical areas:
    Airline markets, 1085, 1086
    Civilian labor force, 613
    Commuting, 1129
    Components of change, 22
    Consumer expenditures, 707
    Consumer price index, 746, 749
    Crime, 330
    Housing prices, 997
    Income, 703
    Migration, 22
    Population, 21, 22
    Religious adherents, 84
    Science and engineering employment, 837
    States, 23
    Vacancy rates, housing, 1005
Mexican-origin population, 35
    Births and birth rates, 87, 94
    Educational attainment, 35, 253
    Labor force, 35, 606
Mexico. (See Foreign countries.)
Mica:
    Foreign trade (sheet), 935
    Production and value, 924, 925
    World production, 928
Michigan. (See State data.)
Microcomputers (See Computers.)
Micronesia, Federated States of. (See Foreign
    countries.)
Migraines, 212
Migration, 3, 4, 5, 16, 22, 29, 30, 31, 1343
Military assistance, 532, 533, 534, 1302, 1303
Military manpower, 524, 526, 529, 1405
Military outlays, 522, 523
Military sciences, degrees conferred, 314, 315
Military services:
    Casualties, 528
    Pay grades, 526
    Personnel, 524, 525, 526, 529

Note: Index citations refer to **table** numbers, not **page** numbers

---

Note: Index citations refer to **table** numbers, not **page** numbers

Note: Index citations refer to **table** numbers, not **page** numbers

Oil and gas extraction, 942, 943
Payroll and earnings, 651, 900, 901
Petroleum industry, 929
Sales and revenue, 901
Timber-related industry, 903, 904
Naturalized citizens, 38, 47, 432
Nauru. (See Foreign countries.)
Navy, personnel, 525
Nebraska. (See State data.)
Nectarines, 241, 885
Neonatal deaths (see also Deaths and death rates), 125
Nepal. (See Foreign countries.)
Nephritis, nephrotic syndrome, and nephrosis (See Kidney disease), 128, 129, 130, 131, 132
Netherlands. (See Foreign countries.)
Neurologists, 176
Nevada. (See State data.)
New Hampshire. (See State data.)
New Jersey. (See State data.)
New Mexico. (See State data.)
New York. (See State data.)
New York Stock Exchange, 1216, 1218
New Zealand. (See Foreign countries.)
Newspaper, book, and directory publishers:
    Earnings, 651, 1136
    Employees, 651, 1136, 1138
    Establishments, 1136, 1138
    Finances, 1137, 1144
    Productivity, 658
    Revenue, 1137, 1138, 1144
Newspapers (See also Publishing industry):
    Number and circulation, 1145, 1146
    Online-news, 1169
    Reading, 1141
    Recycling, 408
Newsprint, 913, 914
Nicaragua. (See Foreign countries.)
Nickel:
    Consumption, 925
    Employment, 925
    Foreign trade, 925, 935
    Prices, 925, 926
    Production and value, 924, 925, 928
    World production, 928, 1381
Niger. (See Foreign countries.)
Nigeria. (See Foreign countries.)
Niobium, 925, 935
Nitrogen in ammonia, 925, 928, 1381
Nonalcoholic beverages, 708, 709
Nonemployer establishments, 594, 776, 1025, 1054, 1060, 1076, 1177, 1232, 1237, 1280
Nonmetallic mineral mining and quarrying, except fuels, 799, 900, 921
Nonmetallic mineral product manufacturing (see also Metals and metal products):
    Earnings, 651, 1026, 1028, 1035
    Employees, 651, 1026, 1028, 1030, 1035
    Establishments, 1026
    Foreign trade, 1031, 1311, 1315
    Gross domestic product, 690, 1024
    Productivity, 658, 807
    Profits, 812
    Sales, shipments, receipts, 1028, 1037, 1038
Toxic chemical releases, 411

Nonprofit organizations, 599, 600, 601, 602, 651, 1290, 1291
North Carolina. (See State data.)
North Dakota. (See State data.)
North Korea. (See Foreign countries.)
Northern Mariana Islands. (See Island areas of the U.S.)
Norway. (See Foreign countries.)
Notifiable diseases, 203
Nuclear power, 960, 961, 962
    Capacity, 960, 961
    Consumption, 946, 947, 951, 1387
    Production, 946, 947, 960, 961, 964, 967, 1383
    Reactors, 960, 961
    State data, 961, 967
Nursing and residential care facilities:
    Capital, 799
    Earnings, 651, 775
    Employees, 174, 651, 775
    Establishments, 179, 775
    Expenditures, 146, 148, 149, 150, 153, 156
    Population, 72, 179
    Receipts, 172, 173, 775
Nursing personnel, 177, 633, 637
Nutrients and nutritional intake, 243
Nutritional deficiencies, deaths, 130
Nuts, 242, 875, 877, 886

O

Obesity, 225, 237, 1347
Obstetricians (see also Physicians), 176
Occupational safety, 677, 678, 680, 922
Occupations (see also individual occupations):
    American Indian, Alaska Native population, 34
    Asian population, 34, 633, 639
    Black, African American population, 34, 633, 639
    Earnings, 635, 665, 667, 672
    Employment, 34, 633, 635, 636, 639, 640, 667
    Employment cost index, 668, 750
    Hispanic origin population, 34, 633, 639
    Island areas, 1322
    Mobility status, 29
    Native Hawaiian, Other Pacific Islander population, 34
    Pension plan/health plan coverage, 675
    Self-employed, 624
    Science and engineering, 834, 835, 836, 839
    Women, 633
Office buildings. (See Commercial buildings.)
Office equipment. (See Computer and office equipment.)
Office supplies, stationery, and gift stores, 651, 658, 1059, 1062
Offshore leases, 933
Ohio. (See State data.)
Oil. (See Petroleum and products.)
Oil and gas extraction industry:
    Capital, 799
    Earnings, 651, 775, 900, 901, 921
    Employees, 651, 775, 900, 901, 921, 942, 943
    Establishments, 775, 900, 901, 942, 943

Note: Index citations refer to **table** numbers, not **page** numbers

---

Note: Index citations refer to **table** numbers, **not page** numbers

Note: Index citations refer to **table** numbers, not **page** numbers

Note: Index citations refer to **table** numbers, not **page** numbers

Employees, 649, 651, 775, 778, 779, 787, 788, 789, 790, 791, 792, 793, 836, 1279, 1280, 1281, 1282, 1283
Equipment and software expenditures, 801
Establishments, 775, 776, 778, 779, 1279, 1280, 1283
Finances, 765, 768, 1300
Gross domestic product, 690, 692
Hours, 649
Multinational companies, 814, 815, 816
Nonemployers, 776, 1280
Occupational safety, 678
Profits, 811
Research and development, 823, 824
Sales, receipts, 765, 768, 773, 774, 775, 776, 787, 788, 789, 790, 791, 792, 793, 1279, 1280, 1284
Profits, 772, 1068, 1191, 1193, 1210, 1229
Corporations, 694, 763, 809, 811, 812, 1040
Partnerships and proprietorships, 763, 766, 767
Projections:
Births, 1345
College enrollment, 246, 247
Deaths, 1345
Degrees conferred, 247
Employment, 637, 638
Energy, 947, 963
Health expenditures, 148
High school graduates, 247
Island areas, 1319
Labor force, 605, 637, 638
Life expectancy, 115, 1345
Population, 3, 8, 11, 12, 13, 1319, 1339, 1340, 1341, 1342
School enrollment, 246, 247
Teachers, 247
Propane, 751
Property and casualty insurance, 426, 1213, 1219, 1229
Fire losses, 382, 383, 385
Property crime, 329, 330, 331, 332, 344, 345, 355, 356
Property tax, 465
Rates, selected cities, 474
State and local government, 461, 464, 465
Proprietors' income, 698
Proprietorships, 763, 765, 766
Propylene, 930
Protective service workers. (See Public safety.)
Protein, available for consumption, 243
Protestants. (See Religions.)
Psychiatric care and institutions. (See Mental hospitals.)
Psychology:
Degrees conferred, 313, 314, 315, 832, 833
Employment, 633
Enrollment, 828
Research, U.S. government obligations for, 820, 826
Psychotherapeutic drugs, nonmedical use, 220
Public administration. (See Government.)
Public aid, assistance:
Benefits paid, 577, 578
Federal aid to state and local governments, 463

Federal expenditures, 147, 148, 150, 163, 164, 580, 582
Homeless, 596, 597
Island Areas of U.S., 1329
Program participation of household, 559
Recipients, 557, 577, 578, 579, 580
Public domain. (See Public lands.)
Public housing, 594
Public lands (see also Forests):
Area, 396, 398, 905, 1261, 1262
Leases, permits, licenses, 933
National forests, 905, 906
National park system, 1260, 1261, 1262
Ownership, 905
Recreation, 1260, 1261, 1262
States, 906, 1263
Public officials, prosecutions, 369
Public roads. (See Highways.)
Public safety (see also Law enforcement):
Employment, 633
Fire protection, 384, 485, 488
Police protection and correction, 485, 488
Expenditures:
Construction, value, 985, 986
State and local government, 359, 464, 472
State government, 478, 480
Volunteers, 598
Public schools. (See Education.)
Public transportation, 708, 709, 747
Public utilities, 945, 975, 976, 978, 979, 980
Publishing. (see also Books, and Newspapers.):
Books, 757, 1136, 1137, 1142, 1143, 1144
Directory and mailing list, 1136, 1137, 1144
Newspapers, 1136, 1137, 1144, 1145, 1146
Periodicals, 1136, 1137, 1144
Publishing industry:
Capital, 799
Earnings, 651, 775, 1028, 1035, 1136, 1138
Employees, 651, 775, 1026, 1028, 1035, 1136, 1138
Establishments, 775, 1026, 1136, 1138
Finances, 812, 1137
Gross domestic product, 690, 1024
Industrial production index, 807
Profit, 812
Receipts, revenue, 775, 1137, 1138
Puerto Rican population (see also Hispanic origin population):
Agriculture, 1331, 1332
Births, 87, 94
Deaths, 126, 133
Educational attainment, 253, 1334
Households, 1324, 1325
Labor force, 606
Population, 35, 1319, 1320
Summary, 1324, 1326
Tenure, 1325
Puerto Rico. (See Island areas of the U.S.)
Pulmonary diseases (see also Respiratory diseases), 127, 128, 129, 130, 131, 132, 133, 197, 203, 209
Pulp manufacturing, 900, 903, 904
Pulpwood, 908, 909, 910, 912

Note: Index citations refer to **table** numbers, not **page** numbers

Pumice and pumicite, 924, 925
Purchasing power of the dollar, 744

Q

Qatar. (See Foreign countries.)
Quarries. (See Mining industries.)
Quicksilver (mercury), 924, 925

R

Rabies, 203
Race (See individual race categories.)
Radio broadcasting industry (see also Broadcasting,
    and Telecommunications):
    Earnings, 651, 1136, 1138
    Employees, 651, 1136, 1138
    Establishments, 1136, 1138
    Finances, 1137, 1151
    Productivity, 658
    Revenue, 1137, 1138, 1151
    Stations, 1140
Radiologists, 176
Radios, 1140, 1141
Rail transportation industry (see also Railroads):
    Capital, 799
    Earnings, 651,
    Employees, 651, 1073, 1074,
    Establishments, 1074
    Gross domestic product, 690
    Shipments, 1079
Railroad employees' retirement funds, 555
Railroads:
    AMTRAK, 1077, 1078
    Energy consumption, 949
    Mileage owned and operated, 1077
    Occupational safety, 1081
    Passenger traffic and revenue, 1126, 1277
    Shipments, 1079
    Vehicles, 1078
Rainfall, selected cities, 1391
Rankings:
    Airport traffic, 1085, 1276
    Amusement parks, 1251
    Cities:
        Commuting, 1130
        Population, 24, 37
        Residential property tax, 474
        Science and engineering employment, 837
    Countries:
        Agricultural exports and imports, 1380
        Consumption of beef, pork, poultry, 1379
        Population, 1342
    Federal R&D obligations to higher education, 827
    Port traffic, 1096, 1097
    State:
        Domestic travel expenditures, 1272
        Exports, 1308
        Farm marketings, 866
        Foreign trade, 1308
        Freight, 1306

Government finances, 483
Personal income per capita, 701
Population, 15, 21
Public elementary/secondary school finances,
    261
Rape, 328, 329, 330, 331, 332, 337, 338, 340,
    531
Raspberries, 864, 885
Raw materials. (See Crude materials.)
Reading (see also Books, and Libraries), 706, 708,
    709, 1239, 1247, 1252, 1253
    E-book reader ownership, 1159, 1167, 1252
    Literacy, 1375
Real estate (see also Housing), 738
Real estate and rental and leasing industry:
    Capital, 799, 801, 803
    Earnings, 649, 651, 661, 775, 787, 788, 789, 790,
        791, 792, 793, 1176, 1233
    Employees, 633, 640, 649, 651, 775, 778, 787,
        788, 789, 790, 791, 792, 793, 1176, 1233
    Equipment and software expenditures, 801
    Establishments, 775, 776, 778, 1176, 1232, 1233
    Finances, 765, 768
    Gross domestic product, 690, 692, 1175
    Hires and separations, 656, 657
    Hours, 649
    Nonemployers, 776, 1232
    Productivity, 658
    Receipts, 765, 768, 773, 774, 775, 776, 787, 788,
        789, 790, 791, 792, 793, 1176, 1232, 1234
Real estate investment trust (REITs), 1180, 1181,
    1203
Receipts (see also Tax receipts, and individual
    industries):
    American Indian and Alaska Native-owned
        businesses, 793
    Asian-owned businesses, 791
    Black-owned businesses, 790
    Corporations, partnerships, and proprietorships,
        763, 764, 765, 766, 767, 768, 772, 773, 774,
        1054
    Hispanic- or Latino-owned businesses, 789
    International transportation, 1292
    Minority-owned businesses, 788
    Native Hawaiian and Other Pacific Islander-owned
        businesses, 786, 787
Revenue:
    Local governments, 465, 481
    State and local governments combined, 461, 464,
        465, 470, 471
    State governments, 465, 478, 483
    Tax collections, 479
        United States government, 464, 465, 492, 498,
        501
    Women-owned businesses, 787
Recreation (see also Arts, recreation, and travel,
    and Sports):
    Activities, 226, 1242, 1246, 1247, 1249,
        1250, 1258, 1260, 1263
    Art, 1245, 1246
    Building construction, value, 987
    Consumer expenditures, 697, 1239, 1259
    Consumer price indexes, 747, 758
    Employment and expenditures, government, 496
        All governments, 485, 488

Note: Index citations refer to **table** numbers, not **page** numbers

Note: Index citations refer to **table** numbers, not **page** numbers

Rural population, 26
Russell, stock index, 1216
Russia. (See Foreign countries.)
Rwanda. (See Foreign countries)

S

Safety and security measures, 325, 922
Saint Kitts and Nevis. (See Foreign countries.)
Saint Lucia. (See Foreign countries.)
Saint Vincent and the Grenadines. (See Foreign
    countries.)
Salad and cooking oils, consumption, 242
Salaries and wages. (See Earnings.)
Sales. (See individual commodities and industries.)
Salesworkers, 633, 645
Salmon, 917, 919, 920
Salmonellosis, 203
Salt (common), production/value, 924, 925, 1381
Samoa. (See Foreign countries.)
Samoa, American. (See Island areas of the U.S.)
Samoan population, 1319
San Marino. (See Foreign countries.)
Sand and gravel industry (see also Mining industry),
    757, 924
Sanitation. (See Refuse collection, and Sewage
    treatment.)
Sao Tome and Principe. (See Foreign countries.)
Sardines, 919, 920
Saudi Arabia. (See Foreign countries.)
Savings:
    Credit unions, 1197
    Deposits, 695, 1183
    Gross savings, sources and uses, 694
    Personal, 694, 698
    Rates, 1366
Savings banks. (See Savings institutions.)
Savings bonds, 1184
Savings institutions:
    Consumer credit, 1202
    Debt held by families, 1187
    Earnings, 1178
    Employees, 1178
    Establishments, 1178, 1192
    Finances, 1180, 1181, 1193, 1194, 1203, 1207
    Individual Retirement Accounts (IRAs), 1223
Saw logs, 909, 910
Saw mills, 900, 903, 904
Scallops, 917, 919
Scenic and sightseeing transportation industry, 651,
    1073, 1074, 1075
Scholastic Assessment Test (SAT), 280
Schools (see also Education):
    Boards, elected officials, 450
    Bullying, 326
    Districts, 459, 460
    Dress code, 325
    Farm to school programs, 859
    Fundraising, 268
    Homeschooling, 262
    Lunch programs, 583
    Number, 263, 271, 272, 276, 277, 290, 292
    Parent participation, 268
    Parent Teacher Association (PTA), 268
    Parent Teacher Organization (PTO), 268

Safety and security, 325
Special education, 232
States, 277
Types, 263, 276, 277
Volunteers, 268
Weapons, 324
Science, literacy, 1375
Scientific instruments. (See Instruments.)
Scientific research. (See Research and development.)
Scientists and engineers (see also individual fields):
    Characteristics, 828, 834
    Degrees conferred, 313, 314, 315, 829, 830, 831,
        832, 833
    Earnings, 839
    Employment, 633, 836, 837, 839
    Non U.S. citizens, 829
    Occupation, 836
Scrap metal. (See individual commodities.)
Seafood, 917, 919, 920
Securities (see also individual types of securities):
    Foreign holdings, 1182, 1215, 1292, 1295
    Foreign purchases and sales, 1395
    Government, 469, 769, 770, 1182, 1208, 1215
    Held by life insurance, 1228
    Holdings of banks, 769, 770, 1192
    Holdings of individuals and businesses, 1183
    New issues, 1208, 1212
    Prices, indexes, yields, and issues, 1209, 1216,
        1395
    Sales, stocks and bonds, 1208, 1395
    Savings of individuals, 695
    State and local government, 461, 469, 769, 770,
        1208
Securities, commodity contracts, and investments
    (industry):
    Capital, 799
    Earnings, 651, 1176, 1178
    Electronic commerce, 1286
    Employees, 651, 1176, 1178
    Establishments, 1176, 1177, 1178
    Finances, 1179, 1180, 1210
    Gross domestic product, 1175
    Nonemployers, 1177
    Profits, 1210
    Receipts, 1176, 1177
Sedatives, persons using, 220
Seeds, 862
Selenium, dietary, 243
Self-employed, 623, 624, 836
Semiconductors (see also Computer and electronic
    product components), 1048, 1313
Senators, U.S., 437, 441
Senegal. (See Foreign countries.)
Septicemia, 128, 129, 130, 131, 132
Serbia. (See Foreign countries.)
Service industries (see also specific sectors):
    Capital, 799, 801
    Earnings, 651, 661, 662, 787, 788, 789, 790, 791,
        792, 793, 1279, 1333
    Electronic commerce, 1286
    Employees, 174, 640, 650, 651, 775, 778, 787,
        788, 789, 790, 791, 792, 793, 1279, 1281,
        1327, 1333
    Equipment and software expenditures, 801

Note: Index citations refer to **table** numbers, not **page** numbers

Note: Index citations refer to **table** numbers, not **page** numbers

---

Note: Index citations refer to **table** numbers, not **page** numbers

Note: Index citations refer to **table** numbers, not **page** numbers

Note: Index citations refer to **table** numbers, not **page** numbers

Swaziland. (See Foreign countries.)
Sweden. (See Foreign countries.)
Sweet potatoes, 241
Swimming, 1256, 1257, 1258
Swine. (See Hogs.)
Switzerland. (See Foreign countries.)
Symphony orchestras, 1242
Synagogues. (See Religion.)
Syphilis, 203
Syria. (See Foreign countries.)

T

Taiwan. (See Foreign countries.)
Tajikistan. (See Foreign countries.)
Talc, pyrophyllite, and soapstone, 924, 925
Tangerines, 885
Tantalum, 928, 935
Tanzania. (See Foreign countries.)
Target shooting, 1258
Tariff. (See Customs receipts.)
Taxes:
    Corporate, 471, 479, 498, 501, 765, 772, 809
    Deductions, 510, 511, 512, 766, 767
    Employment taxes, 498, 501, 502
    Estate and gift taxes, 479, 501
    Excise taxes, 471, 478, 479, 483, 498, 501
    Individual income, 465, 471, 478, 479, 483, 498,
        501, 502, 503, 504, 505, 506, 507, 508, 509,
        510, 511, 512, 513, 514
Tax receipts:
    Foreign countries, 1363, 1364
    Governmental revenue, by type of tax, 465
    Motor-fuel taxes and motor-vehicle fees, 1102
    Federal budget receipts, 498
    Property taxes:
        Rates, selected cities, 474
        State and local government, 464, 465, 471, 479
    State and local government:
        City government, 474
        Households, 473
        Local government, 481
        State government, 478, 480, 483
        Type of tax, 464, 465, 471
Tea, 240, 242, 747
Teachers:
    Catholic schools, 271
    Conferences, 268
    Degrees conferred, 313, 314, 315
    Employment, 264, 270, 273, 274, 275, 279,
        290, 309, 633
    Projections, 247, 637
    Higher education institutions, 290
    Private schools, 270, 271, 274, 275
    Public schools, 247, 264, 272, 273, 275
        Salaries, 264, 272, 273
    States, 272
Technicians, 836
Teenagers:
    Abortions, 110
    AIDS, 206
    Alcohol use, 220
    American Indian, Alaska Native population, 9, 10,
        11

Asian population, 9, 10, 11
Births/birth rates, 88, 92, 93, 94, 96, 98
Black, African American population, 9, 10, 11
Bullying, in school, 326
Child abuse, 373
Cigarette smoking, 220
Contraception use, 107, 108
Cost of raising, 711
Crimes, arrests, 355
Depression, 233
Disabled, 297
Drug use, 220
Education:
    College costs, 300, 302
    College freshmen, characteristics, 298
    Enrollment, 246, 247, 248, 249, 250, 251, 252,
        264, 265, 267, 269, 271, 288, 289, 295,
        1371
    High school dropouts, 284, 285
    High school graduates, 264, 283, 288
    Test scores, 280, 281, 1375
Health insurance coverage, 167
Hispanic or Latino origin population, 9, 10, 11
Juvenile delinquency, 367, 370, 371
Labor force:
    Employed, 614, 620, 623, 626, 628, 1371
    Minimum wage workers, 670
    Multiple job holders, 626
    Participation rates, 615
    School enrollment status, 614, 1371
    Sex, 605, 610
    Unemployed, 614, 641, 642, 647, 1371
Marital status, 57
Missing persons, 362
Mobility status, 29
Murders, 334
Native Hawaiian, Other Pacific Islander
    population, 9, 10, 11
Physical activity, 238
Population, 6, 8, 9, 10, 11
Sexual activity, 105, 106
Sports activity participation, 1257, 1258
Sporting goods purchasers, 1259
Suicides, 131, 137, 139
Victimization, 324, 338
Telecommunications industry (See also
    Broadcasting):
    Broadcast stations, 1140
    Earnings, 651, 1136, 1138
    Employees, 651, 1136, 1138
    Establishments, 1136, 1138
    Finances, 765, 1137, 1138, 1154, 1155
    Productivity, 658
    Receipts, 765, 1137, 1155
Telecommuting, 676, 1123
Telemarketers, 633
Telephone carriers, 1154
    Cellular, 1157
Telephone communication:
    Earnings, 651, 1154
    Employees, 651, 1157
    Finances, 1157
    Price indexes, 747
    Shipments, 1050

Note: Index citations refer to **table** numbers, **not page** numbers

---

Note: Index citations refer to **table** numbers, not **page** numbers

Note: Index citations refer to **table** numbers, not **page** numbers

Turkmenistan. (See Foreign countries.)
Turks and Caicos Islands. (See Foreign countries.)
Tuvalu. (See Foreign countries.)
Typhoid fever, 203

U

Uganda (See Foreign countries.)
Ukraine (See Foreign countries.)
Ulcers, 210
Ultrasound, diagnostic, 189
Unemployment. (See Labor force, unemployed workers.)
Unemployment insurance:
  Beneficiaries, 557, 573, 574, 648
  Coverage, workers and earnings, 573, 574
  Governmental finances, 464, 478, 498
  Payments, 554, 555, 556, 573, 574
Union membership, 684, 685, 686
United Arab Emirates. (See Foreign countries.)
United Kingdom. (See Foreign countries.)
United States securities (see also Debt), 1183, 1192, 1208, 1209, 1213, 1215
Universities. (See Education, higher education institutions.)
Unpaid work, 620, 671
Uranium (see also Nuclear power), 924, 941, 962
Urban population, 26, 84
Urban transit systems, 1074, 1077, 1127
Uruguay. (See Foreign countries.)
Utah. (See State data.)
Utilities (see also Electric light power industry, and Gas utility industry.):
  Capital, 799, 801, 803, 975, 976
  Consumer expenditures, 697
  Cost of living, 749
  Customers and bills, 971, 975, 976
  Earnings, 649, 651, 661, 775, 787, 788, 789, 790, 791, 792, 793, 944, 945
  Electric, 968
  Employees, 640, 649, 651, 775, 778, 787, 788, 789, 790, 791, 792, 793, 944, 945
  Equipment and software expenditures, 801
  Establishments, 775, 776, 778, 945
  Expense, 972
  Finances, 765, 768
  Gross domestic product, 690
  Gas, 975, 976, 977
  Hours, 649
  Income, 972
  Industrial production index, 807
  Industry, 775, 944, 945, 968
  Investor owned, 972
  Net generation, 968, 971
  Net summer capacity, 963, 968
  Nonemployers, 776
  Occupational safety, 678, 680
  Price indexes, 746
  Productivity, 658
  Profits, 810, 811
  Revenue, 971, 972, 975, 976
  Sales, 765, 768, 773, 774, 775, 776, 787, 788, 789, 790, 791, 792, 793, 976
  Sewage treatment, 945, 978

State and local government expenditures, 464, 465, 472
States, 969, 970
Water, 945, 979, 980
Uzbekistan. (See Foreign countries.)

V

Vacancy rates, housing, 1000, 1002, 1003, 1004, 1005
Vaccination, 234, 235
Vanadium, 924, 928, 935
Vanuatu. (See Foreign countries.)
Veal (see also Beef, Meat, and meat products), 242, 757, 890, 1379
Vegetable oils. (See Oils.)
Vegetables (see also individual commodities):
  Acreage, 884
  Consumer expenditures, 708, 709
  Consumption, 241, 888
  Farm marketings, sales, 862, 855, 864
  Foreign trade, 869, 872, 875, 877, 888, 1311
  Prices, 747, 757, 761, 762
  Production, 884, 888
Vehicles. (See Motor vehicles.)
Veneer, wood products, 900, 903, 904
Venereal diseases (see also AIDS), 203
Venezuela. (See Foreign countries.)
Vermiculite, 924, 925
Vermont. (See State data.)
Vessels. (See Ships.)
Veterans:
  Business owners, 786
  Characteristics, 537, 538, 539
  Employment, 519, 608
  Number, 535, 537, 540
  Pensions and other benefits:
    Service-connected compensation, 536, 540
    Disbursements, 522, 540, 555
    Federal aid to state and local governments, 463
    Federal payments, 496, 497
    Veterans or dependents receiving, 536, 557
Veterans Affairs, Dept. of:
  Expenditures, 147, 150, 536, 540, 541, 554, 555, 556
  Home loans, 1205
Vetoed bills, Congressional, 444
Victimizations, criminal, 337, 338, 339, 341, 343, 344, 345, 346, 347, 349, 350
Vietnam. (See Foreign countries.)
Violent crime, (see also Crime), 329, 330, 331, 332, 333, 334, 335, 336, 349, 350, 355, 356
Virgin Islands. (See Island areas of the U.S.)
Virginia. (See State data.)
Visa holders, doctorates, 829
Vital statistics. (See Births and birth rates, Deaths and death rates, Divorces, and Marriages.)
Vitamins, 243
Vocational rehabilitation, 147, 595
Volleyball, 1255, 1256, 1257, 1258
Volunteer activities, 268, 598
Votes:
  Congressional, 429, 437, 439, 440
  Gubernatorial, 446

Note: Index citations refer to **table** numbers, not **page** numbers

---

Note: Index citations refer to **table** numbers, not **page** numbers

---

Note: Index citations refer to **table** numbers, not **page** numbers

Note: Index citations refer to **table** numbers, not **page** numbers